W9-CUZ-642

Textbook Internet resources are just a click away!

STEP 1 → Go to **glencoe.com**

STEP 2 → Connect to resources by entering codes.

GLA9879u1T   Enter this code with appropriate unit numbers.

STEP 3 → Access your **Online Student Edition**, teaching resources, and more:

Literature and Reading Resources

- Author Search
- Literature Classics
- Big Idea Web Quests
- Interactive Timelines and Being There Online
- Literary and Text Elements eFlashcards and Games
- Interactive Reading Practice

Selection Resources

- Audio Summaries
- Selection Quizzes
- Selection Vocabulary eFlashcards and Games
- Reading-Writing Connection Activities

Vocabulary Resources

- Academic and Selection Vocabulary eFlashcards and Games
- Multi-Language Glossaries

Writing, Grammar, and Research Resources

- Interactive Writing Models
- Writing and Research Handbook
- Graphic Organizers
- Sentence-Combining Activities
- Publishing Options

Media Literacy, Speaking, Listening, and Viewing Resources

- Media Analysis Guides
- Project Ideas and Templates
- Presentation Tips and Strategies

Assessment Resources

- End-of-Unit Assessment
- ACT/SAT Vocabulary eFlashcards and Games
- Test-Taking Tips and Strategies

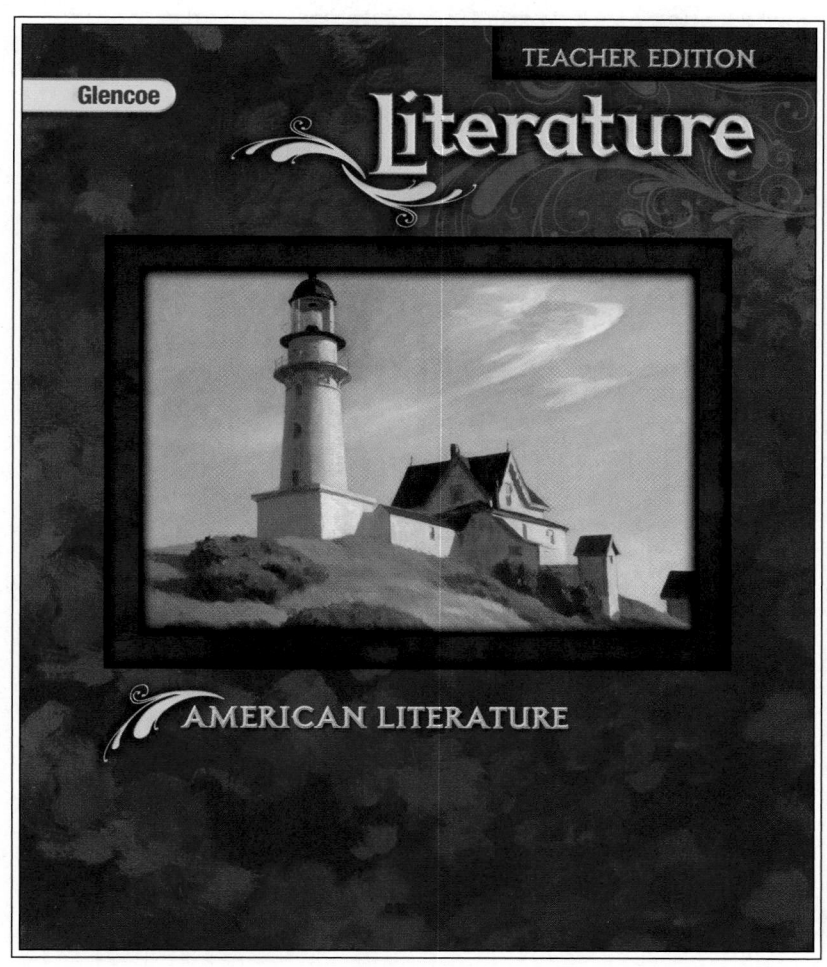

TEACHER EDITION

Program Consultants

Jeffrey D. Wilhelm, Ph.D.

Douglas Fisher, Ph.D.

Beverly Ann Chin, Ph.D.

Jacqueline Jones Royster, DA

Acknowledgments

Grateful acknowledgment is given authors, publishers, photographers, museums, and agents for permission to reprint the following copyrighted material. Every effort has been made to determine copyright owners. In case of any omissions, the Publisher will be pleased to make suitable acknowledgments in future editions.

Acknowledgments continued on page R110.

 Glencoe

The *McGraw·Hill* Companies

Send all inquiries to:
Glencoe/McGraw-Hill
8787 Orion Place
Columbus, OH 43240-4027

ISBN: (student edition) 978-0-07-877980-0
MHID: (student edition) 0-07-877980-4
ISBN: (teacher edition) 978-0-07-877987-9
MHID: (teacher edition) 0-07-877987-1

Printed in the United States of America.

1 2 3 4 5 6 7 8 9 10 027/043 13 12 11 10 09 08

Consultants

Senior Program Consultants

Jeffrey D. Wilhelm, PhD, a former middle and secondary school English and reading teacher, is currently Professor of Education at Boise State University. He is the author or coauthor of numerous articles and several books on the teaching of reading and literacy, including award-winning titles such as *You Gotta BE the Book* and *Reading Don't Fix No Chevys*. He also works with local schools as part of the Adolescent Literacy Project and recently helped establish the National Writing Project site at Boise State University.

Douglas Fisher, PhD, is Professor of Language and Literacy Education and Director of Professional Development at San Diego State University, where he teaches English language development and literacy. He also serves as Director of City Heights Educational Pilot, which won the Christa McAuliffe Award from the American Association of State Colleges and Universities. He has published numerous articles on reading and literacy, differentiated instruction, and curriculum design. He is coauthor of the book *Improving Adolescent Literacies: Strategies That Work* and coeditor of the book *Inclusive Urban Schools*.

Program Consultants

Beverly Ann Chin, PhD, is Professor of English, Director of the English Teaching Program, former Director of the Montana Writing Project, and former Director of Composition at the University of Montana in Missoula. She currently serves as a Member at Large of the Conference of English Leadership. Dr. Chin is a nationally recognized leader in English language arts standards, curriculum, and assessment. Formerly a high school teacher and an adult education reading teacher, Dr. Chin has taught in English language arts education at several universities and has received awards for her teaching and service.

Jacqueline Jones Royster, DA, is Professor of English and Senior Vice Provost and Executive Dean of the Colleges of Arts and Sciences at The Ohio State University. She is currently on the Writing Advisory Committee of the National Commission on Writing and serves as chair for both the Columbus Literacy Council and the Ohioana Library Association. In addition to the teaching of writing, Dr. Royster's professional interests include the rhetorical history of African American women and the social and cultural implications of literate practices. She has contributed to and helped to edit numerous books, anthologies, and journals.

Advisory Board

Special Consultants

Donald R. Bear, PhD
Professor, Department of Curriculum and Instruction. Director, E. L. Cord Foundation Center for Learning and Literacy at the University of Nevada, Reno. Author of *Words Their Way* and *Words Their Way with English Learners*.

Jana Echevarria, PhD
Professor, Educational Psychology, California State University, Long Beach. Author of *Making Content Comprehensible for English Learners: the SIOP Model*.

FOLDABLES **Study Organizer** **Dinah Zike, MEd,** was a classroom teacher and a consultant for many years before she began to develop Foldables®—a variety of easily created graphic organizers. Zike has written and developed more than 150 supplemental books and materials used in classrooms worldwide. Her *Big Book of Books and Activities* won the Teachers' Choice Award.

Glencoe National Reading and Language Arts Advisory Council

Mary A. Avalos, PhD
Assistant Department Chair, Department of Teaching and Learning
Research Assistant Professor, Department of Teaching and Learning
University of Miami
Coral Gables, Florida

Wanda J. Blanchett, PhD
Associate Dean for Academic Affairs and Associate Professor of Exceptional Education
School of Education
University of Wisconsin–Milwaukee
Milwaukee, Wisconsin

William G. Brozo, PhD
Professor of Literacy
Graduate School of Education
College of Education and Human Development
George Mason University
Fairfax, Virginia

Nancy Drew, EdD
LaPointe Educational Consultants
Corpus Christi, Texas

Susan Florio-Ruane, EdD
Professor
College of Education
Michigan State University
East Lansing, Michigan

Sharon Fontenot O'Neal, PhD
Associate Professor
Texas State University
San Marcos, Texas

Nancy Frey, PhD
Associate Professor of Literacy in Teacher Education
School of Teacher Education
San Diego State University
San Diego, California

Victoria Ridgeway Gillis, PhD
Associate Professor
Reading Education
Clemson University
Clemson, South Carolina

Kimberly Lawless, PhD
Associate Professor
Curriculum, Instruction and Evaluation
College of Education
University of Illinois at Chicago
Chicago, Illinois

William Ray, MA
Lincoln-Sudbury Regional High School
Sudbury, Massachusetts

Janet Saito-Furukawa, MEd
English Language Arts Specialist
District 4
Los Angeles, California

Bonnie Valdes, MEd
Independent Reading Consultant
CRISS Master Trainer
Largo, Florida

Teacher Reviewers

The following teachers contributed to the review of *Glencoe Literature*.

Bridget M. Agnew
St. Michael School
Chicago, Illinois

Monica Anzaldua Araiza
Dr. Juliet V. Garcia Middle School
Brownsville, Texas

Katherine R. Baer
Howard County Public Schools
Ellicott City, Maryland

Tanya Baxter
Roald Amundsen High School
Chicago, Illinois

Danielle R. Brain
Thomas R. Proctor Senior High
    School
Utica, New York

Yolanda Conder
Owasso Mid-High School
Owasso, Oklahoma

Gwenn de Mauriac
The Wiscasset Schools
Wiscasset, Maine

Courtney Doan
Bloomington High School
Bloomington, Illinois

Susan M. Griffin
Edison Preparatory School
Tulsa, Oklahoma

Cindi Davis Harris
Helix Charter High School
La Mesa, California

Joseph F. Hutchinson
Toledo Public Schools
Toledo, Ohio

Ginger Jordan
Florien High School
Florien, Louisiana

Dianne Konkel
Cypress Lake Middle School
Fort Myers, Florida

Melanie A. LaFleur
Many High School
Many, Louisiana

Patricia Lee
Radnor Middle School
Wayne, Pennsylvania

Linda Copley Lemons
Cleveland High School
Cleveland, Tennessee

Heather S. Lewis
Waverly Middle School
Lansing, Michigan

Sandra C. Lott
Aiken Optional School
Alexandria, Louisiana

Connie M. Malacarne
O'Fallon Township High School
O'Fallon, Illinois

Lori Howton Means
Edward A. Fulton Junior High
    School
O'Fallon, Illinois

Claire C. Meitl
Howard County Public Schools
Ellicott City, Maryland

Patricia P. Mitcham
Mohawk High School (Retired)
New Castle, Pennsylvania

Lisa Morefield
South-Western Career Academy
Grove City, Ohio

Kevin M. Morrison
Hazelwood East High School
St. Louis, Missouri

Jenine M. Pokorak
School Without Walls Senior
    High School
Washington, DC

Susan Winslow Putnam
Butler High School
Matthews, North Carolina

Paul C. Putnoki
Torrington Middle School
Torrington, Connecticut

Jane Thompson Rae
Cab Calloway High School of
    the Arts
Wilmington, Delaware

Stephanie L. Robin
N. P. Moss Middle School
Lafayette, Louisiana

Ann C. Ryan
Lindenwold High School
Lindenwold, New Jersey

Pamela Schoen
Hopkins High School
Minnetonka, Minnesota

Megan Schumacher
Friends' Central School
Wynnewood, Pennsylvania

Fareeda J. Shabazz
Paul Revere Elementary School
Chicago, Illinois

Molly Steinlage
Brookpark Middle School
Grove City, Ohio

Barry Stevenson
Garnet Valley Middle School
Glen Mills, Pennsylvania

Paul Stevenson
Edison Preparatory School
Tulsa, Oklahoma

Kathy Thompson
Owasso Mid-High School
Owasso, Oklahoma

Table of Contents for the Student Edition
and Teacher Edition T10

Correlations by Standard T44

Correlations by Selection T48

How to Use *Glencoe Literature* T52

American Literature Scope and Sequence T56

Essential Course of Study T60

Teacher Edition Walk-Through T64

Guide to Readability T72

The Headless Horseman Pursuing Ichabod Crane, 1858. John Quidor. Oil on canvas. Smithsonian American Art Museum, Washington, DC.

African American Vernacular English T73

Language Transfers T76

Classroom Resources

Print Resources T88

Technology Resources T91

Library Resources T95

Book Overview

How to Use *Glencoe Literature* T44

Be Cyber Safe and Smart.. 3

UNIT ONE

Early America **Beginnings–1800**.. 5
Part 1: The Sacred Earth and the Power of Storytelling.................................... 19
Part 2: Life in the New World 55
Part 3: The Road to Independence... 103

UNIT TWO

American Romanticism **1800–1860**... 173
Part 1: Individualism and Nature... 187
Part 2: The Dark Side of Romanticism.. 237

UNIT THREE

The Civil War Era **1850–1880**... 329
Part 1: Resistance to Slavery... 343
Part 2: The Civil War: A Nation Divided.. 373
Part 3: A Poetic Revolution... 407

UNIT FOUR

Regionalism and Realism **1880–1910**... 481
Part 1: Regionalism and Local Color... 495
Part 2: Realism and Naturalism 535

The Jolly Flatboatmen, 1877–78. George Caleb Bingham. Oil on canvas, 26¹/₁₆ x 36³/₈ in. Daniel J. Terra Acquisition Endowment Fund, 1992. Terra Foundation for American Art, Chicago, IL.

Room in New York, 1932.
Edward Hopper. Oil on
Canvas, 28½ x 35½ in.
F.M. Hall Collection.

UNIT FIVE

Beginnings of the Modern Age 1910–1930s 645
Part 1: Modern Poetry 659
Part 2: Modern Fiction 739
Part 3: The Harlem Renaissance 785

UNIT SIX

From Depression to Cold War 1930s–1960s 851
Part 1: The New Regionalism and the City 865
Part 2: The United States and the World 969

UNIT SEVEN

Into the 21st Century 1960s–Present 1137
Part 1: An Era of Protest 1151
Part 2: Nature and Technology 1213
Part 3: Extending and Remaking Traditions 1263

Reference Section
Literary Terms Handbook R1
Foldables® R22
Functional Documents R24
Writing Handbook R30
Reading Handbook R40
Language Handbook R42
Logic and Persuasion Handbook R62
Glossary/Glosario R66
Academic Word List R89
Index of Skills R92
Index of Authors and Titles R107
Acknowledgments R110

Contents

UNIT ONE

Skills and Standards

Early America
BEGINNINGS–1800

Timeline 6

By the Numbers 8

Being There 9

Historical, Social, and Cultural Forces 10

Big Ideas 11

ANONYMOUS I Have Killed the Deer .... Song 13

WILLIAM BRADFORD
from **Of Plymouth Plantation** .... Memoir 15

BENJAMIN FRANKLIN
from **The Autobiography** .... Autobiography 17

Wrap-Up 18

Part 1

THE SACRED EARTH AND THE
POWER OF STORYTELLING

Literary History Native American Mythology 20

Archetype, Identify Sequence   **JAMES MOONEY How the World Was Made** .... Myth 22

> *"There is another*
> *world under this,*
> *and it is like ours*
> *in everything . . ."*
>
> —Cherokee Myth

Tlingit Raven Rattle, ca. 1850. Native American. The Lowe Art Museum,
The University of Miami.

Cultural Perspective
N. SCOTT MOMADAY
from **The Way to Rainy Mountain** .... Memoir 27

Comparing Literature Across Time and Place 33

Oral Tradition, Question

JOSEPH BRUCHAC **The Sky Tree** .... Myth 34

CHINUA ACHEBE AND JOHN IROAGANACHI
How the Leopard Got His Claws .... Myth 38

LESLIE MARMON SILKO
Prayer to the Pacific .... Poem 44

*Author's Purpose,
Draw Conclusions
About Culture*

DEKANAWIDA
from **The Iroquois Constitution** .... Public Document 47

Vocabulary Workshop Academic Vocabulary 53

Part 2

LIFE IN THE NEW WORLD

Point of View, Recognize Bias

ÁLVAR NÚÑEZ CABEZA DE VACA
from **La Relación** .... Memoir 56

*Diction,
Monitor Comprehension*

WILLIAM BRADFORD
from **Of Plymouth Plantation** .... Memoir 62

The Slave Narrative, Respond

OLAUDAH EQUIANO
from **The Life of Olaudah Equiano** .... Autobiography 69

*"I had never seen among any people
such instances of brutal cruelty . . ."*
—Olaudah Equiano

*Allusion,
Analyze Historical Context*

MARY ROWLANDSON
from **A Narrative of the Captivity
and Restoration of Mrs. Mary Rowlandson** .... Memoir 80

Grammar Workshop Sentence Combining 87

Metaphor,
Draw Conclusions About
Author's Beliefs

ANNE BRADSTREET
Upon the Burning of Our House.............................Poem 89
To My Dear and Loving Husband...........................Poem 92

Imagery, Examine Connotation

JONATHAN EDWARDS
from **Sinners in the Hands of an Angry God**.......... Speech 95
Vocabulary Workshop Dictionary Usage.................................. 102

Part 3

THE ROAD TO INDEPENDENCE

Autobiography, Analyze Voice

BENJAMIN FRANKLIN
from **The Autobiography**
of Benjamin Franklin....................................Autobiography 104

Aphormism, Connect

from **Poor Richard's Almanac**................................ Proverb 110
Literary History The Rhetoric of Revolution 112

Rhetorical Question,
Analyze Figures of Speech

PATRICK HENRY
Speech to the Second Virginia Convention............ Speech 114

Text Structure,
Evaluate Argument

THOMAS JEFFERSON
The Declaration of Independence...........Public Document 120

WALTER ISAACSON
TIME How They Chose These Words.............................. 128

Vocabulary Workshop Word Origins:
Understanding Political and Historical Terms 131

Tone, Summarize

THOMAS PAINE
from **The Crisis, No. 1**...............................Public Document 132

Washington Crossing the Delaware, 1851. Emanuel Gottlieb Leutze.
Oil on canvas, 12²/₅ x 21¹/₄ in. Metropolitan Museum of Art, NY.

" . . . the harder the conflict, the
more glorious the triumph."
                                    —Thomas Paine

Contents

Couplet, Analyze Structure

PHILLIS WHEATLEY
To His Excellency, General Washington .... Poem 139

Description, Recognize Author's Purpose

ABIGAIL ADAMS Letter to John Adams .... Letter 144

Grammar Workshop Commas: Missing Commas with
Nonessential Elements 149

Historical Perspective
DAVID MCCULLOUGH
from John Adams .... Biography 150

Writing Workshop Writing a Persuasive Speech 154

Professional Model
BECKY CAIN
from Proposals for Electoral College Reform .... Speech 155

Speaking, Listening, and Viewing Workshop Delivering a
Persuasive Speech 162

Independent Reading 164

Assessment 166

BENJAMIN FRANKLIN
from The Whistle .... Essay 166

UNIT TWO

AMERICAN ROMANTICISM 1800-1860

Timeline 174

By the Numbers 176

Being There 177

Historical, Social, and Cultural Forces 178

Big Ideas 179

RALPH WALDO EMERSON
from Self-Reliance .... Essay 181

HENRY DAVID THOREAU
from **The Journal** ....Journal 183

EDGAR ALLAN POE
from **The Fall of the House of Usher** .... Short Story 185

Wrap-Up 186

PART 1

Individualism and Nature

Theme,
Recognize Author's Purpose
Figurative Language,
Draw Conclusions

RALPH WALDO EMERSON
from **Nature** .... Essay 188

from **Self-Reliance** .... Essay 194

MICHAEL D. LEMONICK
TIME **The Biology of Joy** ....Science Article 198

Thesis, Summarize

MARGARET FULLER
from **Woman in the Nineteenth Century** .... Essay 203

> "All men are
> privately
> influenced by
> women."
>
> —Margaret Fuller

The Morning Bell (a.k.a. The Old Mill), 1871. Winslow Homer. Oil on canvas, 24 x 38⅛ x 1 in. Yale University Art Gallery.

Literary History The Fireside Poets 210

Metaphor and Connect   HENRY DAVID THOREAU *from* **Walden** .... Memoir 212

Contents

Comparing Literature Across Time and Place................................220

Argument, Evaluate Evidence

HENRY DAVID THOREAU
from **Civil Disobedience**...Essay 221

MOHANDAS K. GANDHI
On the Eve of Historic Dandi March....................Speech 229

NELSON MANDELA
from **Long Walk to Freedom** ....Autobiography 231

PART 2   The Dark Side of Romanticism

Literary History American Short Stories.....................................238

Characterization,
Make and Verify Predictions

WASHINGTON IRVING
The Devil and Tom Walker.............................Short Story 240

Narrative Poem,
Analyze Sound Devices

EDGAR ALLAN POE   **The Raven** ....Poem 254

Suspense, Identify Sequence

The Pit and the Pendulum ....Short Story 262

Vocabulary Workshop Context Clues..277

Symbol, Make Inferences

NATHANIEL HAWTHORNE
The Minister's Black Veil.................................Short Story 278

Grammar Workshop
Misplaced and Dangling Modifiers...293

Motivation,
Monitor Comprehension

HERMAN MELVILLE *from* **Moby-Dick**...................Novel 294

"He looked not unlike the weather horizon when a storm is coming up . . ."
—Herman Melville

Historical Perspective

NATHANIEL PHILBRICK

from **In the Heart of the Sea** .... Essay 306

Writing Workshop Writing a Reflective Essay 310

Professional Model

ANNIE DILLARD

from **An American Childhood** .... Memoir 311

Speaking, Listening, and Viewing Workshop Delivering
a Reflective Essay 318

Independent Reading 320

Assessment 322

RALPH WALDO EMERSON *from* **Self-Reliance** ..... Essay 322

UNIT THREE

The Civil War Era

1850 – 1880

Timeline 330

By the Numbers 332

Being There 333

Historical, Social, and Cultural Forces 334

Big Ideas 335

FREDERICK DOUGLASS *from* **The Meaning
of July Fourth for the Negro** .... Speech 337

ABRAHAM LINCOLN *from* **Second Inaugural
Address, March 4, 1865** .... Speech 339

WALT WHITMAN **Cavalry Crossing a Ford** .... Poem 341

EMILY DICKINSON **The Lightening is
a Yellow Fork** .... Poem 341

Wrap-Up 342

PART 1 — Resistance to Slavery

Refrain,
Analyze Historical Context

ANONYMOUS **Swing Low, Sweet Chariot** .... Song 344

Go Down, Moses .... Song 347

Keep Your Hand on the Plow .... Song 348

"Oppressed so hard they could not stand, Let my people go."

—from "Go Down, Moses"

Going to Church, 1940–1941. William H. Johnson. Oil on burlap, 38⅛ x 45½ in. Smithsonian American Art Museum, Washington, DC.

Comparing Literature Across Time and Place 350

Autobiography,
Analyze Cause and Effect

FREDERICK DOUGLASS *from* **My Bondage and My Freedom** .... Autobiography 351

ROBERT HAYDEN **Frederick Douglass** .... Poem 359

QUINCY TROUPE **In Texas Grass** .... Poem 360

Literary History Slave Narratives and Civil War Memoirs, Letters, and Diaries 362

RICHARD LACAYO
TIME **Slavery Under Glass** 364

Oratory, Evaluate Argument

SOJOURNER TRUTH **And Ain't I a Woman?** ..... Speech 368

Vocabulary Workshop Denotation and Connotation 372

PART 2   *The Civil War: A Nation Divided*

Journal,
Distinguish Fact and Opinion

MARY CHESNUT *from* **Mary Chesnut's**
Civil War .... Memoir 374

Grammar Workshop **Using Transitional Expressions** 381

Diction, Determine Main Idea
and Supporting Details

ROBERT E. LEE *from* **Letter to His Family** .... Letter 382

Point of View,
Make and Verify Predictions

AMBROSE BIERCE
An Occurrence at Owl Creek Bridge .... Short Story 387

Parallelism, Analyze Style

ABRAHAM LINCOLN
The Gettysburg Address .... Speech 400

Political Perspective
GARY WILLS *from* **Lincoln at Gettysburg** .... Essay 404

PART 3   *A Poetic Revolution*

Free Verse, Paraphrase

WALT WHITMAN   **I Hear America Singing** .... Poem 408

When I Heard the Learn'd Astronomer .... Poem 411

Free Verse, Paraphrase

A Sight in Camp in the Daybreak Gray and Dim ..... Poem 413

Beat! Beat! Drums! .... Poem 414

Historical Narrative

from **Specimen Days** .... Memoir 416

Voice, Draw Conclusions

from **Song of Myself** .... Poem 421

"I am old and young, of the foolish
as much as the wise . . ."

—Walt Whitman

Literary Perspective
JUSTIN KAPLAN
from **Walt Whitman: A Life** .... Biography 430

EMILY DICKINSON **If you were coming
in the Fall**..Poem 437

My life closed twice before its close..........................Poem 440

The Soul selects her own Society ....Poem 441

Much Madness is divinest Sense................................Poem 442

Success is counted sweetest.....................................Poem 443

I heard a Fly buzz when I died ....Poem 445

The Bustle in a House...Poem 446

Because I could not stop for Death ....Poem 448

There's a certain Slant of light.................................Poem 450

This is my letter to the World...................................Poem 451

Literary Perspective
BILLY COLLINS
from **Emily Dickinson: An Introduction** .... Essay 455

Writing Workshop Historical Research Paper............................. 458

Multimedia Presentation Workshop Delivering a
Multimedia Report on a Historical Investigation......................... 468

Independent Reading 472

Assessment.. 474

FREDERICK DOUGLASS
from **My Bondage and My Freedom**............. Autobiography 474

Rhyme, Analyze Sound Devices

Personification, Clarify Meaning

UNIT FOUR

Regionalism and Realism
1880–1910

Timeline 482

By the Numbers... 484

Being There... 485

Historical, Social, and Cultural Forces 486

Big Ideas 487

WILLA CATHER *from* **O Pioneers!** .... Novel 489

KATE CHOPIN *from* **The Awakening** .... Novel 491

STEPHEN CRANE
from **The Red Badge of Courage** .... Novel 493

Wrap-Up 494

PART 1

Regionalism and Local Color

Dialect, Analyze Comic Devices

MARK TWAIN **The Celebrated Jumping Frog
of Calaveras County** .... Short Story 496

*Analogy, Compare and
Contrast Language*

Two Views of the River .... Memoir 504

NANCY GIBBS
TIME Life Along the Mississippi 508

*Dramatic Monologue,
Draw Conclusions About
Characters*

EDGAR LEE MASTERS
Lucinda Matlock .... Poem 514

Fiddler Jones .... Poem 517

*Point of View,
Identify Sequence*

WILLA CATHER **A Wagner Matinée** .... Short Story 519

Grammar Workshop Appositives 530

Tone, Evaluate Style

CHIEF JOSEPH
I Will Fight No More Forever .... Speech 531

PART 2

Realism and Naturalism

Literary History Urban America's Two Faces 536

*Flashback,
Make and Verify Predictions*

EDITH WHARTON **April Showers** .... Short Story 538

Vocabulary Workshop Thesaurus Use 549

Contents

Comparing Literature Across Time and Place......550

Conflict, Apply Background Knowledge

KATE CHOPIN **The Story of an Hour**.........Short Story....551

ANTON CHEKHOV **The Darling**.................Short Story....557

GABRIELA MISTRAL **Richness**.............................Poem....566

Rhyme Scheme, Clarify Meaning

PAUL LAURENCE DUNBAR **Douglass**.................Poem....568

We Wear the Mask...Poem....571

Irony, Make Inferences About Characters

EDWIN ARLINGTON ROBINSON
Richard Cory..Poem....573

Miniver Cheevy...Poem....576

Author's Purpose, Summarize

STEPHEN CRANE **The Open Boat**...............Short Story....578

"White waves paced to and fro in the moonlight."

—Stephen Crane

Moonlit Shipwreck at Sea, 1901. Thomas Moran.
Oil on canvas, 30 x 40¼ in. Private collection.

Setting, Analyze Cause-and-Effect Relationships

JACK LONDON **To Build a Fire**.....................Short Story....601

Geographic Perspective
BARRY LOPEZ *from* **Arctic Dreams: Imagination
and Desire in a Northern Landscape**.........................Essay....617

Writing Workshop Literary Analysis 624

Professional Model
BETTINA L. KNAPP
from **Stephen Crane: Tales of Adventure**.................Essay....625

Speaking, Listening, and Viewing Workshop
Oral Response to Literature...634

Independent Reading 636

Assessment 638

UPTON SINCLAIR *from* **The Jungle** .... Novel 638

UNIT FIVE

BEGINNINGS OF THE MODERN AGE
1910–1930s

Timeline 646

By the Numbers 648

Being There 649

Historical, Social, and Cultural Forces 650

Big Ideas 651

E. E. CUMMINGS *from* **I: Six Nonlectures** .... Speech 653

ERNEST HEMINGWAY
from **The Sun Also Rises** .... Novel 655

LANGSTON HUGHES *from* **The Negro Artist
and the Racial Mountain** .... Essay 657

Wrap-Up 658

PART 1

MODERN POETRY

Literary History Symbolist and Imagist Poetry 660

EZRA POUND **A Pact** .... Poem 662

In a Station of the Metro .... Poem 662

T. S. ELIOT
The Love Song of J. Alfred Prufrock .... Poem 666

WILLIAM CARLOS WILLIAMS
The Red Wheelbarrow .... Poem 676

This Is Just to Say .... Poem 679

Imagery, Question

*Allusion,
Connect to Cultural Context*

*Form,
Recognize Author's Purpose*

"*Forgive me*
They were delicious
So sweet
And so cold"

—William Carlos Williams

Plums and Pears. Paul Cezanne. Oil on canvas, 7¾ x 14 in.
The Barnes Foundation Collection, Merion Station, PA.

Vocabulary Workshop

Compound Words 681

Structure, Interpret Imagery   AMY LOWELL   **Summer Rain** .... Poem 682

Fireworks .... Poem 685

Comparing Literature Across Time and Place 687

Theme, Analyze Style   ARCHIBALD MACLEISH   **Ars Poetica** .... Poem 688

RAINER MARIA RILKE
from **Letters to a Young Poet** .... Letter 692

MARK STRAND   **Eating Poetry** .... Poem 694

ISHMAEL REED   **beware : do not read this poem** .... Poem 696

Tone,
Recognize Author's Purpose   WALLACE STEVENS   **Study of Two Pears** .... Poem 699

from **The Man with the Blue Guitar** .... Poem 702

Rhythm, Analyze Style   E. E. CUMMINGS   **somewhere I have never travelled,gladly beyond** .... Poem 704

anyone lived in a pretty how town .... Poem 707

Apostrophe,
Make Inferences About Theme   CARL SANDBURG   **Chicago** .... Poem 709

Grass .... Poem 712

Blank Verse, Compare and
Contrast Speakers   ROBERT FROST   **Mending Wall** .... Poem 714

Birches .... Poem 718

Stopping by Woods on a Snowy Evening .... Poem 721

Rhyme Scheme, Compare and
Contrast Speakers

Acquainted with the Night .... Poem 723

The Death of the Hired Man .... Poem 725

Political Perspective
JOHN F. KENNEDY
In Praise of Robert Frost .... Speech 735

MODERN FICTION

Literary History The Modern American Short Story 740

ERNEST HEMINGWAY
In Another Country .... Short Story 742

Grammar Workshop Sentence Structure: Using
Coordinating Conjunctions 751

Style,
Recognize Author's Purpose

Motivation,
Evaluate Sensory Details

F. SCOTT FITZGERALD Winter Dreams ...... Short Story 752

Stream of Consciousness,
Draw Conclusions About
the Protagonist

KATHERINE ANNE PORTER The Jilting
of Granny Weatherall .... Short Story 773

THE HARLEM RENAISSANCE

Sonnet, Interpret Imagery

JAMES WELDON JOHNSON My City .... Poem 786

Voice, Analyze Language

ZORA NEALE HURSTON
from Dust Tracks on a Road .... Autobiography 790

Vocabulary Workshop Distinct Meanings:
Understanding Homonyms 800

Meter, Analyze Tone

CLAUDE MCKAY If We Must Die .... Poem 801

The Tropics in New York .... Poem 804

ROBERT HUGHES
TIME Stanzas from a Black Epic 806

Repetition,
Make Predictions About Theme

LANGSTON HUGHES I, Too .... Poem 810

The Negro Speaks of Rivers .... Poem 813

Juxtaposition,
Analyze Concrete Details

When the Negro Was in Vogue .... Autobiography 817

Metaphor, Connect to Personal Experience

ARNA BONTEMPS
A black man talks of reaping......................................Poem 824

Stanza, Connect to Contemporary Issues

COUNTEE CULLEN **Any Human to Another** ....Poem 828

"Your grief and mine must intertwine Like sea and river."

—Countee Cullen

Rondout, New York, c. 1907. Leon Dabo. Oil on canvas. Indianapolis Museum of Art, IN.

Writing Workshop Writing a Literary Analysis: Poetry 832

Professional Model
LAWRENCE RAAB
from **Robert Frost's "Mending Wall"** .... Essay 833

Speaking, Listening, and Viewing Workshop Presenting
an Oral Interpretation of a Poem 840

Independent Reading 842

Assessment 844

LANGSTON HUGHES **Early Autumn**........... Short Story 844

UNIT SIX

FROM DEPRESSION TO COLD WAR
1930s–1960s

Timeline 852

By the Numbers.. 854

Being There.. 855

Historical, Social, and Cultural Forces 856

Big Ideas 857

JOHN STEINBECK
from **The Grapes of Wrath**......................................Novel.... 859

GWENDOLYN BROOKS kitchenette building
from **A Street in Bronzeville**.................................Poem.... 861

FRANKLIN D. ROOSEVELT
from **The Four Freedoms**..............................Speech.... 863

Wrap-Up 864

The New Regionalism and the City

JOHN STEINBECK **Breakfast** ....Short Story.... 866

Vocabulary Workshop Word Parts: Understanding
Roots, Prefixes, and Suffixes 873

WILLIAM FAULKNER **A Rose for Emily** ......Short Story.... 874

**Address upon Receiving the
Nobel Prize for Literature**.......................Speech.... 884

EUDORA WELTY **A Worn Path**....................Short Story.... 888

RICHARD WRIGHT *from* **Black Boy**.........Autobiography.... 898

Historical Perspective
ERSKINE CALDWELL AND MARGARET BOURKE-WHITE
You Have Seen Their Faces ....Photo Essay.... 909

FLANNERY O'CONNOR
The Life You Save May Be Your Own ....Short Story.... 913

Grammar Workshop Sentence Structure:
Introductory Phrases and Clauses..................................927

E. B. WHITE
The Second Tree from the Corner..................Short Story.... 928

GWENDOLYN BROOKS **To Don at Salaam** ....Poem.... 937

The Bean Eaters...Poem.... 940

BERNARD MALAMUD **The Magic Barrel** .... Short Story.... 942

JAMES BALDWIN **The Rockpile**...................Short Story.... 959

PART 1

*Implied Theme, Connect to
Personal Experience*

*Foreshadowing,
Identify Sequence*

Description, Visualize

*Flashforward, Compare and
Contrast Characters*

*Dialogue,
Apply Background Knowledge*

Plot, Analyze Text Structure

*Rhyme Scheme,
Evaluate Diction*

*Dialect,
Analyze Characterization*

*Foil, Make Generalizations
About Characters*

PART 2

The United States and The World

Author's Purpose,
Distinguish Fact and Opinion

FRANKLIN D. ROOSEVELT
War Message to Congress .... Public Document 970

Vocabulary Workshop
Word Origins: Math and Science 975

Imagery, Visualize

RANDALL JARRELL
The Death of the Ball Turret Gunner .... Poem 976

Comparing Literature Across Time and Place 980

Narrator,
Activate Prior Knowledge

ELIE WIESEL
from **All Rivers Run to the Sea** .... Memoir 981

GARRETT HONGO *from* **Kubota** .... Memoir 993

ART SPIEGELMAN
from **Maus: A Survivor's Tale** .... Graphic Novel 998

Point of View,
Draw Conclusions

JOHN HERSEY *from* **Hiroshima** .... Essay .. 1002

Idiom, Respond to Plot
and Characters

TOMÁS RIVERA **The Portrait** .... Short Story .. 1017

Literary History Cultural Rebels:
Writers of the Beat Generation 1024

Dialogue, Draw Conclusions
About Characters

ARTHUR MILLER **The Crucible** .... Drama .. 1026

"The rumor of witchcraft is all about . . ."

—Arthur Miller

Literary History Modern American Drama 1116

Writing Workshop Writing an Autobiographical Narrative 1118

Professional Model
EUDORA WELTY
from **One Writer's Beginnings** ....Autobiography .. 1119

Speaking, Listening, and Viewing Workshop
Presenting an Art or Photo Essay 1126

Independent Reading 1128

Assessment 1130

MARGARET BOURKE-WHITE
from **Dust Changes America**...................................... Essay .. 1130

UNIT SEVEN

Into the 21st Century
1960s–Present

Timeline 1138

By the Numbers.. 1140

Being There.. 1141

Historical, Social, and Cultural Forces 1142

Big Ideas 1143

MARTIN LUTHER KING, JR.
from **Letter from a Birmingham Jail** ....Letter .. 1145

DAVID WAGONER *from* **Lost**....................................Poem .. 1147

JUDITH ORTIZ COFER
from **The Latin Deli: An Ars Poetica** ....Poem .. 1149

Wrap-Up 1150

PART 1

An Era of Protest

RITA DOVE
TIME **The Torchbearer** .... Profile .. 1152

Structure, Paraphrase

MARTIN LUTHER KING JR.
from **Stride Toward Freedom** .... Memoir .. 1155

Anecdote, Activate Prior Knowledge

ALICE WALKER **Choice: A Tribute to Dr. Martin Luther King Jr.** .... Essay .. 1161

Vocabulary Workshop
Loaded Words 1166

Oral History, Analyze Cause-and-Effect Relationships

STUDS TERKEL *from* **Working: Roberto Acuna, Farm Worker** .... Oral History .. 1167

Grammar Workshop
Avoid Run-On Sentences 1179

Comparing Literature Across Time and Place 1180

Mood, Analyze Concrete Details

TIM O'BRIEN **Ambush** .... Short Story .. 1181

TRAN MONG TU **The Gift in Wartime** .... Poem .. 1186

PIN YATHAY *from* **Stay Alive, My Son** .... Memoir .. 1187

YUSEF KOMUNYAKAA
Camouflaging the Chimera .... Poem .. 1190

Figurative Language, Clarify Meaning

W. S. MERWIN **The Asians Dying** .... Poem .. 1192

Separation .... Poem .. 1195

When You Go Away .... Poem .. 1195

Artistic Perspective
MAYA LIN
Proposal for the Vietnam Veterans Memorial .... Public Document .. 1198

Rhythm, Analyze Rhetorical Devices

BOB DYLAN **A Hard Rain's A-Gonna Fall** .... Song .. 1202

"I saw ten thousand talkers whose tongues were all broken . . ."

—Bob Dylan

Verse Paragraph, Examine Connotation and Denotation

ANNE SEXTON **Courage** ....Poem .. 1208

PART 2   # Nature and Technology

Tone, Evaluate Sensory Details

ELIZABETH BISHOP **The Fish** ....Poem .. 1214

Filling Station ....Poem .. 1218

Simile, Interpret Imagery

THEODORE ROETHKE **Root Cellar** ....Poem .. 1222

Mood, Analyze Voice

SYLVIA PLATH **Sleep in the Mojave Desert** ....Poem .. 1226

Crossing the Water ....Poem .. 1229

Personification, Evaluate Figures of Speech

STANLEY KUNITZ **The War Against the Trees** ......Poem .. 1232

Scientific Perspective
RACHEL CARSON
from **Silent Spring** ....Essay .. 1236

Satire, Identify Genre

URSULA K. LE GUIN **SQ** ....Short Story .. 1239

Indirect Characterization, Connect to Contemporary Issues

JULIA ALVAREZ **Snow** ....Short Story .. 1253

Free Verse, Make Inferences About Theme

LOUISE GLÜCK **Cottonmouth Country** ....Poem .. 1257

Daisies ....Poem .. 1260

PART 3

Extending and Remaking Traditions

Exposition, Make Inferences About Characters

MAXINE HONG KINGSTON

from **The Woman Warrior** .... Memoir .. 1264

> "Finally Brave Orchid's children quit wandering and drooped on a railing."
>
> —Maxine Hong Kingston

A Sunny Day with Gentle Breeze, 1993. Zifen Qian. Oil on canvas, 42 x 56 in. Private collection.

Frame Story, Question

RAYMOND CARVER

Everything Stuck to Him .... Short Story .. 1274

Point of View, Examine Connotations

JUDITH ORTIZ COFER

El Olvido (Según las Madres) .... Poem .. 1282

Symbol, Summarize

NAOMI SHIHAB NYE

My Father and the Figtree .... Poem .. 1286

Personification, Connect to Personal Experience

BILLY COLLINS I Chop Some Parsley While Listening to Art Blakey's Version of "Three Blind Mice"...................................Poem .. 1291

Catalog, Distiguishing Fact and Opinion

LOUISE ERDRICH The Names of Women .... Essay .. 1296

Imagery, Analyze Sound Devices

SANDRA CISNEROS Salvador Late or Early .... Short Story .. 1304

Essay, Determine Main Idea and Supporting Details

TONI MORRISON Thoughts on the African-American Novel .... Essay .. 1308

Vocabulary Workshop Word Parts: Suffixes That Form Nouns... 1315

Literary History From Comic Strips to Graphic Novels.............. 1316

Magical Realism, Visualize

EDWIDGE DANTICAT Nineteen Thirty-Seven.................................... Short Story .. 1318

Narrative Poetry, Connect to Cultural Context

AI The Man With the Saxophone ....Poem .. 1331

Motif, Make Generalizations

ROSARIO MORALES AND AURORA LEVINS MORALES Ending Poem ....Poem .. 1336

Writing Workshop Editorial...1342

Professional Model
JEREMY BLACHMAN Job Posting: *The New York Times*........................Editorial .. 1343

Media Literacy Workshop Campaign Commercials.................. 1352

Speaking, Listening, and Viewing Workshop Conducting a Debate...1350

Independent Reading 1358

Assessment.. 1360

ANNIE DILLARD *from* "Transfiguration".. Essay .. 1360

WILLIAM STAFFORD Traveling Through the Dark .... Poem .. 1361

Reference Section

Literary Terms Handbook R1

Foldables® R22

Functional Documents R24

Writing Handbook R30

Using the Traits of Strong Writing R30

Research Paper Writing R33

Reading Handbook R40

Language Handbook R42

Grammar Glossary R42

Troubleshooter R49

Mechanics R55

Spelling R59

Logic and Persuasion Handbook R62

Glossary/Glosario R66

Academic Word List R89

Index of Skills R92

Index of Authors and Titles R107

Acknowledgments R110

Family in Interior. Poisson.
Haitian Folk Art.

Selections by Genre

Short Story

from **The Fall of the House of Usher** 185
Edgar Allan Poe

The Devil and Tom Walker 242
Washington Irving

The Pit and the Pendulum 263
Edgar Allan Poe

The Minister's Black Veil...........................280
Nathaniel Hawthorne

An Occurrence at Owl Creek Bridge 389
Ambrose Bierce

**The Celebrated Jumping Frog
of Calaveras County**.................................498
Mark Twain

A Wagner Matinee 521
Willa Cather

April Showers...540
Edith Wharton

Story of an Hour.......................................553
Kate Chopin

The Darling..557
Anton Chekhov

The Open Boat 580
Stephen Crane

To Build a Fire...603
Jack London

In Another Country 744
Ernest Hemingway

Winter Dreams 754
F. Scott Fitzgerald

The Jilting of Granny Weatherall 775
Katherine Anne Porter

Early Autumn...844
Langston Hughes

Breakfast...868
John Steinbeck

A Rose for Emily 876
William Faulkner

A Worn Path...890
Eudora Welty

The Life You Save May Be Your Own 915
Flannery O'Conner

The Second Tree from the Corner................930
E. B. White

The Magic Barrel 944
Bernard Malamud

The Rockpile...961
James Baldwin

The Portrait 1019
Tomas Rivera

Ambush 1183
Tim O'Brien

SQ..1241
Ursula K. Le Guin

Snow 1255
Julia Alvarez

Everything Stuck to Him 1276
Raymond Carver

Salvador Late or Early 1306
Sandra Cisneros

Nineteen Thirty-Seven 1320
Edwidge Danticat

Drama

The Crucible 1028
Arthur Miller

Graphic Novel

from **Maus: A Survivor's Tale**.......................998
Art Spiegelman

Myth

How the World Was Made 24
James Mooney

The Sky Tree..35
Joseph Bruchac

How the Leopard Got His Claws 38
Chinua Achebe and John Iroaganachi

Novel

from **Moby Dick** 296
Herman Melville

from **O Pioneers!** 489
Willa Cather

from **The Awakening**.....................................491
Kate Chopin

from **The Red Badge of Courage** 493
Stephen Crane

from **The Jungle** 638
Upton Sinclair

from **The Sun Also Rises**...........................655
Ernest Hemingway

from **The Grapes of Wrath**...........................859
John Steinbeck

Poetry

Prayer to the Pacific 44
Leslie Marmon Silko

Upon the Burning of Our House 91
Anne Bradstreet

To My Dear and Loving Husband...................92
Anne Bradstreet

To His Excellency, General Washington.........141
Phillis Wheatley

The Raven 256
Edgar Allan Poe

The Lightning is a Yellow Fork 341
Emily Dickinson

Cavalry Crossing a Ford..............................341
Walt Whitman

Frederick Douglass 359
Robert Hayden

In Texas Grass..360
Quincy Troupe

I Hear America Singing 410
Walt Whitman

When I Heard the Learn'd Astronomer 411
Walt Whitman

**A Sight in Camp in the
Daybreak Gray and Dim**...........................413
Walt Whitman

Beat! Beat! Drums! 414
Walt Whitman

from **Song of Myself**.....................................421
Walt Whitman

If you were coming in the Fall 436
Emily Dickinson

My life closed twice before its close 440
Emily Dickinson

The Soul selects her own Society 441
Emily Dickinson

Much Madness is divinest Sense...................442
Emily Dickinson

Success is counted sweetest 443
Emily Dickinson

I heard a Fly buzz when I died 445
Emily Dickinson

The Bustle in a House 446
Emily Dickinson

Because I could not stop for Death...............448
Emily Dickinson

There's a certain Slant of light 450
Emily Dickinson

This is my letter to the World.......................451
Emily Dickinson

Lucinda Matlock 516
Edgar Lee Masters

Fiddler Jones...517
Edgar Lee Masters

Richness 566
Gabriela Mistral

Douglass 570
Paul Lawrence Dunbar

We Wear the Mask......................................571
Paul Lawrence Dunbar

Richard Cory...575
Edwin Arlington Robinson

Miniver Cheevy 576
Edwin Arlington Robinson

In a Station of the Metro..............................664
Ezra Pound

A Pact 664
Ezra Pound

The Love Song of J. Alfred Prufrock............668
   T. S. Eliot

The Red Wheelbarrow.......................678
   William Carlos Williams

This Is Just To Say.........................679
   William Carlos Williams

Summer Rain...............................684
   Amy Lowell

Fireworks.................................685
   Amy Lowell

Ars Poetica...............................690
   Archibald MacLeish

Eating Poetry.............................694
   Mark Strand

beware : do not read this poem.............696
   Ishmael Reed

Study of Two Pears 701
   Wallace Stevens

from The Man with the Blue Guitar 702
   Wallace Stevens

somewhere i have never
   traveled,gladly beyond 706
   E. E. Cummings

anyone lived in a pretty how town.........707
   E. E. Cummings

Chicago...................................711
   Carl Sandburg

Grass 712
   Carl Sandburg

Mending Wall 716
   Robert Frost

Birches 718
   Robert Frost

Stopping by Woods on a Snowy Evening 721
   Robert Frost

Acquainted with the Night 723
   Robert Frost

The Death of the Hired Man 725
   Robert Frost

My City 788
   James Weldon Johnson

If We Must Die............................803
   Claude McKay

The Tropics in New York...................804
   Claude McKay

I, Too 812
   Langston Hughes

The Negro Speaks of Rivers 813
   Langston Hughes

A black man talks of reaping 826
   Arna Bontemps

Any Human to Another.....................830
   Countee Cullen

kitchenette building 861
   Gwendolyn Brooks

To Don at Salaam.........................939
   Gwendolyn Brooks

The Bean Eaters..........................940
   Gwendolyn Brooks

The Death of the Ball Turret Gunner.......978
   Randall Jarrell

from Lost 1147
   David Wagoner

from The Latin Deli: An Ars Poetica..........1149
   Judith Ortiz Cofer

The Gift in Wartime 1186
   Tran Mong Tu

Camouflaging the Chimera 1190
   Yusef Komunyakaa

The Asians Dying 1194
   W. S. Merwin

Separation 1195
   W. S. Merwin

When You Go Away.........................1195
   W. S. Merwin

Courage 1210
   Anne Sexton

The Fish 1216
   Elizabeth Bishop

Filling Station 1218
   Elizabeth Bishop

Root Cellar...............................1224
   Theodore Roethke

Sleep in the Mojave Desert................1228
   Sylvia Plath

Crossing the Water.................................1229
Sylvia Plath

The War Against the Trees........................1234
Stanley Kunitz

Daisies..1259
Louise Glück

Cottonmouth Country 1260
Louise Glück

El Olvido (Según las Madres)....................1284
Judith Ortiz Cofer

My Father and the Figtree 1288
Naomi Shahib Nye

I Chop Some Parsley While
Listening to Art Blakey's Version
of "Three Blind Mice" 1293
Billy Collins

The Man With the Saxophone 1333
Ai

Ending Poem 1338
Rosario Morales and Aurora Levins Morales

Traveling Through the Dark......................1361
William Stafford

Proverb
from Poor Richard's Almanac......................110
Benjamin Franklin

Song
I Have Killed the Deer................................13
Anonymous

Swing Low, Sweet Chariot..........................346
Anonymous

Go Down, Moses.....................................347
Anonymous

Keep Your Hand on the Plow 348
Anonymous

A Hard Rain's A-Gonna Fall 1204
Bob Dylan

Biography, Autobiography, and Memoir

from The Way to Rainy Mountain 27
N. Scott Momaday

from La Relación 58
Álvar Núñez Cabeza de Vaca

from Of Plymouth Plantation 64
William Bradford

from The Life of Olaudah Equiano..................71
Olaudah Equiano

from A Narrative of the Captivity
and Restoration of Mrs. Mary 82
Mary Rowlandson

from The Autobiography of
Benjamin Franklin 106
Benjamin Franklin

from John Adams.......................................150
David McCullough

from Walden...214
Henry David Thoreau

from Long Walk to Freedom.........................231
Nelson Mandela

from An American Childhood 311
Annie Dillard

from My Bondage and My Freedom...............353
Frederick Douglass

from Mary Chesnut's Civil War 376
Mary Chesnut

from Specimen Days....................................416
Walt Whitman

from Walt Whitman: A Life.........................430
Justin Kaplan

Two Views of the River 504
Mark Twain

from Dust Tracks on a Road 792
Zora Neale Hurston

When the Negro Was in Vogue....................817
Langston Hughes

from Black Boy..901
Richard Wright

from **All Rivers Run to the Sea** 983
Elie Wiesel

from **Kubota** 993
Garrett Hongo

from **One Writer's Beginnings** 1119
Eudora Welty

from **Stride Toward Freedom** 1157
Martin Luther King, Jr.

from **Stay Alive, My Son** 1187
Pin Yathay

from **The Woman Warrior** 1266
Maxine Hong Kingston

Essay

from **The Whistle** 166
Benjamin Franklin

from **Nature** 190
Ralph Waldo Emerson

from **Self-Reliance** 194
Ralph Waldo Emerson

from **Woman in the Nineteenth Century** 205
Margaret Fuller

from **Civil Disobedience** 222
Henry David Thoreau

from **In the Heart of the Sea** 306
Nathaniel Philbrick

from **Self-Reliance** 322
Ralph Waldo Emerson

from **Lincoln at Gettysburg** 404
Gary Wills

from **Emily Dickinson: An Introduction** 455
Billy Collins

from **Arctic Dreams: Imagination and
Desire in a Northern Landscape** 617
Barry Lopez

from **Stephen Crane: Tales of Adventure** 625
Bettina L. Knapp

from **How the Other Half Lives** 639
Jacob Riis

from **The Negro Artist and
the Racial Mountain** 657
Langston Hughes

from **Robert Frost's "Mending Wall"** 833
Lawrence Raab

from **Hiroshima** 1001
John Hersey

from **Dust Changes America** 1130
Margaret Bourke-White

**Choice: A Tribute to
Dr. Martin Luther King, Jr.** 1163
Alice Walker

Fable of Tomorrow from Silent Spring 1236
Rachel Carson

The Names of Women 1298
Louise Erdrich

Thoughts on the African-American Novel ...1310
Toni Morrison

from **"Transfiguration"** 1360
Annie Dillard

Letter, Journal, or Diary

Letter to John Adams 146
Abigail Adams

from **The Journal** 183
Henry David Thoreau

from **Letter to His Family** 384
Robert E. Lee

from **Letters to a Young Poet** 692
Rainer Maria Rilke

from **Letter from a Birmingham Jail** 1145
Martin Luther King, Jr.

Oral History

from **Working: Roberto Acuna,
Farm Worker** 1169
Studs Terkel

Photo Essay

You Have Seen Their Faces 909
Erskine Caldwell and Margaret Bourke-White

Public Document

from **The Iroquois Constitution** 49
Dekanawida

The Declaration of Independence 122
  Thomas Jefferson

from The Crisis, No. 1 134
  Thomas Paine

Speech

from Sinners in the Hands of
  an Angry God 97
  Jonathan Edwards

Speech to the Second Virginia Convention 116
  Patrick Henry

from Proposals for Electoral College Reform ...155
  Becky Cain

On the Eve of Historic Dandi March 229
  Mohandas k. Gandhi

from The Meaning of July Fourth
  for the Negro 337
  Frederick Douglass

from Second Inaugural Address,
  March 4, 1865 339
  Abraham Lincoln

And Ain't I a Woman? 370
  Sojourner Truth

The Gettysburg Address 402
  Abraham Lincoln

I Will Fight No More Forever 533
  Chief Joseph

from I: Six Nonlectures 653
  E. E. Cummings

In Praise of Robert Frost 735
  John F. Kennedy

from The Four Freedoms 863
  Franklin D. Roosevelt

Address upon Receiving
  the Nobel Prize for Literature 884
  William Faulkner

Contemplating Life, 1903. Richard Pfeiffer.

Features

Perspectives

Award-winning nonfiction book excerpts and primary source documents

Cultural Perspective *from* The Way
to Rainy Mountain 27
  N. Scott Momaday

Historical Perspective *from* John Adams 150
  David McCullough

Historical Perspective *from* In the Heart
of the Sea..306
  Nathaniel Philbrick

Political Perspective *from* Lincoln
at Gettysburg...404
  Gary Wills

Literary Perspective *from* Walt Whitman:
A Life...430
  Justin Kaplan

Literary Perspective *from* Emily Dickinson:
An Introduction..455
  Billy Collins

Geographic Perspective
from Arctic Dreams: Imagination and
Desire in a Northern Landscape...................617
  Barry Lopez

Political Perspective *"In* Praise of
Robert Frost"..735
  John F. Kennedy

Historical Perspective *You* Have Seen
Their Faces 909
  Erskine Caldwell and Margaret Bourke-White

Artistic Perspective *Proposal* for the
Vietnam Memorial...1198
  Maya Lin

Scientific Perspective *Fable* of Tomorrow
from Silent Spring..1236
  Rachel Carson

TIME

High-interest, informative magazine articles

How They Chose These Words...................128
  Walter Isaacson

The Biology of Joy.......................................198
  Michael D. Lemonick

Slavery Under Glass...................................364
  Richard Lacayo

Life Along the Mississippi.........................508
  Nancy Gibbs

Stanzas from a Black Epic.........................806
  Robert Hughes

The Torchbearer...1152
  Rita Dove

Comparing Literature

Across Time and Place

UNIT ONE

The Sky Tree
Joseph Bruchac..34

How the Leopard Got His Claws
Chinua Achebe and John Iroaganachi............38

Prayer to the Pacific
Leslie Marmon Silko 44

UNIT TWO

from **Civil Disobedience**
Henry David Thoreau...................................221

On the Eve of Historic Dandi March
Mohandas k. Gandhi....................................229

from **Long Walk to Freedom**
Nelson Mandela 231

UNIT THREE

from **My Bondage and My Freedom**
Frederick Douglass 351

Frederick Douglass
Robert Hayden..359

In Texas Grass
Quincy Troupe 360

UNIT FOUR

Story of an Hour
Kate Chopin..551

The Darling
Anton Chekhov...557

Richness
Gabriela Mistral 566

UNIT FIVE

Ars Poetica
Archibald MacLeish......................................688

from **Letters to a Young Poet**
Rainer Maria Rilke 692

Eating Poetry
Mark Strand 694

beware: do not read this poem
Ishmael Reed 696

UNIT SIX

from **All Rivers Run to the Sea**
Elie Wiesel 981

from **Kubota**
Garrett Hongo 993

from **Maus: A Survivor's Tale**
Art Spiegelman 998

UNIT SEVEN

Ambush
Tim O'Brien 1181

The Gift in Wartime
Tran Mong Tu...1186

from **Stay Alive, My Son**
Pin Yathay...1187

Camouflaging the Chimera
Yusef Komunyakaa 1190

Literary History

Native American Mythology..........................20

The Rhetoric of Revolution........................112

The Fireside Poets.................................210

The First American Short Stories.................238

Slave Narratives and Civil War Memoirs,
    Letters, and Diaries.............................362

The Two Faces of Urban America................536

Imagist and Symbolist Poetry......................660

The Modern American Short Story 740

Cultural Rebels: Writers of the
    Beat Generation 1024

Modern American Drama........................1116

From Comic Strips to Graphic Novels 1316

Independent Reading

Unit 1 164
Unit 2 320
Unit 3 472
Unit 4 636
Unit 5 842
Unit 6 1128
Unit 7 1358

ASSESSMENT

Unit 1 166
Unit 2 322
Unit 3 474
Unit 4 638
Unit 5 844
Unit 6 1130
Unit 7 1360

Skills Workshops

Writing Workshops

Persuasive Speech.................................... 154
PROFESSIONAL MODEL: *from* **Proposals for Electoral College Reform** by Becky Cain

Reflective Essay.. 310
PROFESSIONAL MODEL: *from* **An American Childhood** by Annie Dillard

Research Report....................................... 458

Literary Analysis...................................... 624
PROFESSIONAL MODEL: *from* **Stephen Crane: Tales of Adventure** by Bettina L. Knapp

Literary Analysis...................................... 832
PROFESSIONAL MODEL: *from* **Robert Frost's "Mending Wall"** by Lawrence Raab

Creative Nonfiction 1118
PROFESSIONAL MODEL: *from* **One Writer's Beginnings** by Eudora Welty

Editorial 1342
PROFESSIONAL MODEL: **Job Posting:** *The New York Times* by Jeremy Blachman

Speaking, Listening, and Viewing Workshops

Persuasive Speech 162
Reflective Presentation 318
Multimedia Presentation 468
Oral Response to Literature 634
Oral Interpretation of a Poem...................... 840
Photo Essay 1126
Debate... 1350

Media Workshop

Analyze Media Messages 1352

Grammar Workshops

Sentence Combining...................................... 87
Clauses as Modifiers.................................... 149
Misplaced and Dangling Modifiers 293
Transitional Expressions 381
Appositives 530
Coordinating Conjunctions 751
Introductory Phrases and Clauses 927
Avoid Run-On Sentences........................... 1179

Vocabulary Workshops

Academic Vocabulary 53
Dictionary Use 102
Word Origins: Political Science 131
Context Clues 277
Denotation and Connotation 372
Thesaurus Use 549
Compound Words 681
Homonyms 800
Roots, Prefixes, and Suffixes 873
Word Origins: Math and Science.................. 975
Loaded Words... 1166
Noun Suffixes 1315

How to Use *Glencoe Literature*

Why do I need this book?

Glencoe Literature is more than just a collection of stories, poems, nonfiction articles, and other literary works. Every part is built around **Big Ideas,** concepts that you will want to think about, talk about, and maybe even argue about. Big Ideas help you become part of an important conversation. You can join in lively discussions about who we are, where we have been, and where we are going.

Organization

The literature you will read is organized chronologically into seven units spanning early America to the present.

Each unit contains the following:

A **UNIT INTRODUCTION** provides you with the background information to help make your reading experience more meaningful.

- The **TIMELINE** helps you keep track of major literary and historical events.

- **BY THE NUMBERS** shows you figures and key data at a glance.
- **BEING THERE** gives you a glimpse of the geography related to the literary period.
- **HISTORICAL, CULTURAL, AND SOCIAL FORCES** explains the influences that shape a specific literary period.
- **BIG IDEAS** target three concepts that you can trace as you read the literature.

LITERARY SELECTIONS follow each Part Introduction. The selections are organized as follows.

Reading and Thinking

The main literary works in your textbook are arranged in three parts.

- Start with **BEFORE YOU READ**. Learn valuable background information about the literature and preview the skills and strategies that will guide your reading.

  MEET THE AUTHOR presents a detailed biography of the writer whose work you will read and analyze.

  LITERATURE AND READING PREVIEW lists the basic tools you will use to read and analyze the literary work.

- Next, read the **LITERATURE SELECTION**. As you flip through the literature, you will notice that parts of the text are highlighted in different colors. At the bottom of the page are color-coded questions that relate to the highlighted text. Yellow represents a *Big Idea*, magenta represents a *Literary Element*, and blue represents a *Reading Strategy*. These questions will help you gain a better understanding of the text.

- Wrap up the literature with **AFTER YOU READ**. Explore what you have learned through a wide range of reading, thinking, vocabulary, and writing activities.

Vocabulary

VOCABULARY WORDS that may be new or difficult are chosen from most selections. They are introduced on the **BEFORE YOU READ** page. Each word is accompanied by its pronunciation, its part of speech, its definition, and the page number on which it appears. The vocabulary word is also used in a sample sentence. Vocabulary words are highlighted in the literary work.

VOCABULARY PRACTICE On the **AFTER YOU READ** pages, you will be able to practice using the vocabulary words in an exercise. This exercise will show you how to apply a vocabulary strategy to understand new or difficult words.

ACADEMIC VOCABULARY Many of the **AFTER YOU READ** pages will also introduce you to a word that is frequently used in academic work. You will be prompted to complete an activity based on that word.

After You Read

Respond and Think Critically

Respond and Interpret

1. Which Bradstreet poem did you find more poignant? Explain.
2. (a)How did the speaker in "Upon the Burning of Our House" feel about her possessions before the fire? How does she feel afterward? (b)What do you think brought about the change in her perspective?
3. (a)In the final line, where does the speaker say her "hope and treasure" are? (b)What does this suggest about the speaker's home and possessions?
4. (a)In "To My Dear and Loving Husband," what does the speaker prize "more than whole mines of gold"? (b)Why do you think she compares the way she feels to mines of gold?

Analyze and Evaluate

5. In "Upon the Burning of Our House," how effective are Bradstreet's frequent references to her faith in conveying the poem's meaning? Explain.
6. How effective is the repetition in the opening lines of "To My Dear and Loving Husband"? Explain.

Connect

7. **Big Idea** Life in the New World How do Bradstreet's Puritan beliefs affect her perception of the world as represented by these poems?
8. **Connect to the Author** After reading *The Tenth Muse*, Bradstreet's poetic style changed (see page 89). What evidence of that do you see in these poems?

Literary Element Metaphor

SAT Skills Practice

1. The author uses the extended metaphor in lines 43–50 of "Upon the Burning of Our House" to describe
   (A) the specifications for rebuilding her house
   (B) her heavenly home built by God
   (C) her hope for recovering her lost money and furnishings
   (D) God's motivation for burning her house
   (E) her confusion at being homeless while God lives in glory
2. In line 7 of "To My Dear and Loving Husband" ("My love . . . cannot quench") the author is suggesting that her love is like a
   (A) boundless ocean
   (B) cascading waterfall
   (C) thirsty traveler
   (D) blazing fire
   (E) fertile breeding ground

Review: Author's Purpose

As you learned on page 48, an **author's purpose** is his or her intent in writing a literary work. Authors typically write for one or more of the following purposes: to persuade, to inform, to explain, to entertain, or to describe.

Partner Activity Meet with a classmate and discuss Bradstreet's purpose. Work with your partner to infer what Bradstreet's purpose was for writing each poem. Include details from the poem that you think reveal information about her purpose.

Literature Online
Selection Resources For Selection Quizzes, eFlashcards, and Reading-Writing Connection activities, go to glencoe.com and enter QuickPass code GLA9800u1.

ANNE BRADSTREET 93

Reading Strategy Draw Conclusions About Author's Beliefs

Authors often incorporate their own beliefs into their writing. Sometimes they state these beliefs explicitly. Other times it might be possible to infer the author's beliefs only by examining their word choice, use of figurative language, or rhetorical techniques. Review the chart you made on page 90. Then answer the following questions.

1. How does Bradstreet feel about worldly things?
2. List three pieces of evidence to support your opinion.

Vocabulary Practice

Practice with Synonyms With a partner, match each boldfaced vocabulary word below with its synonym on the right. Use a thesaurus or dictionary to check your answers.

1. bereft   a. payment
2. chide   b. aggravated
3. recompense   c. scold
                   d. revenge
                   e. stripped

Academic Vocabulary

Passing the **site** of her former home, Bradstreet reminisces about her life there.

Site is an academic word. In more casual usage, you might say workers are erecting a skyscraper at a building **site**. Using context clues, try to figure out the meaning of the word in the sentence about Bradstreet above. Check your definition in a dictionary.

For more on academic vocabulary, see pages 53–54.

Write with Style

Apply Extended Metaphor

Assignment Writers often use metaphors to explain ideas and convey feelings. Review the extended metaphor in "Upon the Burning of Our House" (lines 43–50). Then write one of your own to explain an idea and how you feel about it.

Get Ideas Think of a comparison between what you want to talk about and some other thing it is like. For example, you might sometimes think your school is like a zoo. Then brainstorm some ways the two things could be compared. For example, you might compare students to zoo animals. Finally, think of some examples for each comparison. Use a word web to keep track of your ideas.

EXAMPLE:
My School
Some animals just sit all day looking beautiful, and some do tricks to show how smart they are or act scary so people leave them alone. Others try to blend in with the rocks or leaves so it looks as though no one is home.

Give It Structure Choose your line breaks carefully to give your images maximum impact.

Look at Language Be careful not to take an extended metaphor too far. A few comparisons go a long way.

94 UNIT 1 EARLY AMERICA

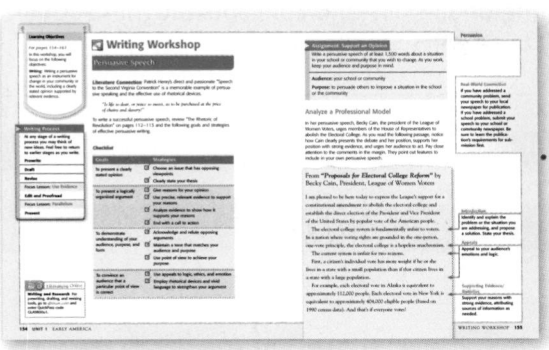

Writing Workshops

Each unit in **Glencoe Literature** includes a Writing Workshop. The workshop walks you through the writing process as you work on an extended piece of writing related to the unit.

- You will create writing goals and apply strategies to meet them.

- You will pick up tips and polish your critical skills as you analyze professional and workshop models.

- You will focus on mastering specific aspects of writing, including organization, grammar, and vocabulary.

- You will use a checklist to evaluate your own writing.

Assessment

At the end of each unit, you will be tested on the literature, reading, and vocabulary skills you have just learned. Designed to simulate standardized tests, this test will give you the practice you need to succeed while providing an assessment of how you have met the unit objectives.

Organizing Information

Graphic organizers—such as Foldables®, diagrams, and charts—help you keep your information and ideas organized.

This chart provides an overview of the scope and sequence for *Glencoe American Literature*. For a detailed scope and sequence of skills, see the chart at the beginning of each unit in the Teacher Edition. Refer also to the Index of Skills in the Reference Section in the back of the book for a comprehensive listing of all skills and concepts taught in *American Literature*.

✔ = Introduced   ✔ = Reviewed

	UNIT ONE	UNIT TWO	UNIT THREE	UNIT FOUR	UNIT FIVE	UNIT SIX	UNIT SEVEN
Literary Periods and Movements							
Pre-colonial Period	✔						
Colonial and Revolutionary Period	✔	✔					
Romanticism		✔	✔	✔		✔	
Transcendentalism		✔	✔				
Regionalism				✔	✔	✔	
Realism			✔	✔	✔	✔	
Naturalism				✔	✔		✔
Modernism					✔	✔	✔
Harlem Renaissance					✔		
New Regionalism						✔	
Contemporary Period							✔
Literary Criticism							
Analyzing Literature in Context							
Political	✔	✔	✔			✔	✔
Historical	✔	✔	✔	✔	✔	✔	✔
Social	✔	✔	✔	✔		✔	✔
Cultural	✔			✔	✔	✔	✔
Biographical	✔		✔		✔		✔
Philosophical	✔	✔		✔		✔	
Literary Genres							
Oral Tradition Forms							
Song	✔	✔	✔				✔
Myth, Folklore, and Legend	✔						
Fiction							
Short Story		✔	✔	✔	✔	✔	✔
Novel Excerpt		✔					
Graphic Novel						✔	

	UNIT ONE	UNIT TWO	UNIT THREE	UNIT FOUR	UNIT FIVE	UNIT SIX	UNIT SEVEN
Nonfiction							
Autobiography or Memoir	✔	✔	✔	✔	✔	✔	✔
Biography	✔		✔		✔		✔
Magazine Article	✔	✔	✔	✔	✔		✔
Newspaper Article							✔
Speech	✔	✔	✔	✔	✔	✔	✔
Informational Text	✔	✔	✔	✔	✔	✔	✔
Public Document	✔	✔	✔	✔	✔	✔	✔
Journal or Diary	✔	✔	✔		✔		
Letter	✔		✔		✔		
Poetry							
Narrative Poem	✔	✔	✔		✔		✔
Sonnet			✔	✔	✔		
Free Verse	✔	✔	✔	✔	✔	✔	✔
Drama						✔	

Literary Elements

	UNIT ONE	UNIT TWO	UNIT THREE	UNIT FOUR	UNIT FIVE	UNIT SIX	UNIT SEVEN
Literary Structure							
Plot		✔		✔	✔	✔	✔
Setting	✔	✔		✔	✔	✔	✔
Characters	✔	✔	✔	✔	✔	✔	✔
Point of View	✔	✔	✔	✔	✔	✔	✔
Theme		✔	✔	✔	✔	✔	✔
Voice and Tone	✔	✔	✔	✔	✔	✔	✔
Author's Purpose	✔	✔	✔	✔	✔	✔	✔
Literary Language							
Imagery	✔	✔	✔	✔	✔	✔	✔
Symbolism		✔			✔	✔	✔
Figures of Speech	✔	✔	✔	✔	✔	✔	✔
Sound Devices		✔	✔		✔		
Diction	✔		✔	✔	✔	✔	
Rhetorical Strategies	✔	✔	✔	✔	✔	✔	✔

✔ = Introduced ✔ = Reviewed

	UNIT ONE	UNIT TWO	UNIT THREE	UNIT FOUR	UNIT FIVE	UNIT SIX	UNIT SEVEN
Reading Skills							
Strategies							
Analyzing	✔	✔	✔	✔	✔	✔	✔
Clarifying	✔	✔	✔	✔			✔
Drawing Conclusions	✔	✔	✔	✔	✔	✔	
Making Inferences		✔	✔	✔	✔	✔	✔
Making Predictions		✔	✔	✔		✔	
Monitoring Comprehension	✔	✔					
Paraphrasing	✔		✔	✔			✔
Previewing	✔	✔	✔	✔	✔	✔	✔
Questioning	✔	✔	✔		✔		✔
Recognizing Bias	✔						✔
Summarizing	✔	✔	✔	✔	✔	✔	✔
Sythesizing	✔	✔	✔	✔	✔	✔	✔
Text Structures							
Cause and Effect	✔	✔	✔	✔	✔	✔	✔
Chronological Order	✔	✔		✔		✔	✔
Compare and Contrast	✔	✔	✔	✔	✔	✔	✔
Problem and Solution	✔						
Vocabulary Development							
Academic Vocabulary	✔	✔	✔	✔	✔	✔	✔
Analogies	✔	✔	✔	✔	✔	✔	✔
Antonyms	✔	✔		✔	✔	✔	✔
Context Clues							
Denotation and Connotation	✔	✔	✔	✔	✔	✔	✔
Multiple-Meaning Words	✔		✔	✔	✔	✔	✔
Word Parts: Roots, Prefixes, and Suffixes	✔		✔	✔	✔	✔	✔
Words Origins	✔					✔	
Synonyms	✔	✔	✔	✔	✔		✔
Word Usage	✔	✔	✔	✔	✔	✔	✔

	UNIT ONE	UNIT TWO	UNIT THREE	UNIT FOUR	UNIT FIVE	UNIT SIX	UNIT SEVEN
Writing and Grammar							
Types of Writing							
Creative Nonfiction		✔	✔		✔	✔	✔
Creative Writing: Fiction					✔		✔
Editorial							✔
Literary Analysis	✔	✔	✔	✔	✔	✔	✔
Persuasive	✔	✔		✔	✔	✔	
Research		✔	✔			✔	
Writing Process							
Prewriting, Drafting, Revising, Editing and Proofreading, Presenting	✔	✔	✔	✔	✔	✔	✔
Traits of Strong Writing	✔	✔	✔	✔	✔	✔	✔
Grammar, Usage, and Mechanics							
Parts of Speech	✔	✔	✔		✔	✔	✔
Capitalization and Punctuation	✔	✔		✔			✔
Sentence Structure/Sentence Combining/Transitional Expressions	✔	✔	✔	✔			✔
Speaking, Listening, and Viewing							
Debate	✔					✔	✔
Oral Interpretation of a Poem	✔	✔			✔		✔
Reflective Presentation		✔					
Oral Report		✔	✔	✔			
Oral Response to Literature	✔	✔	✔	✔	✔	✔	✔
Persuasive Speech	✔	✔	✔				
Photo Essay			✔			✔	✔
Media Literacy							
Multimedia Presentation			✔				
Multimedia Literacy Workshop							✔

Teaching the Standards: Grade 11

The following abbreviated curriculum is a suggestion for addressing those objectives that students commonly encounter on standardized tests. You may use it as a guide for prioritizing instruction in preparation for the tests.

Unit 1

Selections/Lessons	Pacing/Days	Genre	Where to Find Instruction	Commonly Tested Objectives
Comparing Literature: The Sky Tree AND How the Leopard Got His Claws AND Prayer to the Pacific	3–7	Myths AND Poetry	SE, p. 34 RW, RW-APP, pp. 1–16 RW-EL, pp. 1–16, 306	**Literary Study:** Analyzing oral tradition. **Reading:** Questioning. **Reading:** Comparing works across time and place.
Upon the Burning of Our House AND To My Dear and Loving Husband	1–4	Poetry	SE, p. 89 RW, RW-APP, pp. 17–24, 306 RW-EL, pp. 17–24, 307–308	**Literary Study:** Analyzing metaphor. **Reading:** Drawing conclusions about author's beliefs. **Reading:** Understanding synonyms.
TIME: How They Chose These Words	2–6	Historical Essay	SE, p. 128 RW, RW-APP, pp. 25–36, 307 RW-EL, pp. 25–36, 309–310	**Reading:** Determining the main idea and supporting details.
Letter to John Adams	1–4	Letter	SE, p. XX RW, RW-APP, pp. 37–44, 308 RW-EL, pp. 37–44, 311–312	**Literary Study:** Analyzing description. **Reading:** Recognizing author's purpose. **Reading:** Understanding analogies.

Unit 2

Selections/Lessons	Pacing/Days	Genre	Where to Find Instruction	Commonly Tested Objectives
Comparing Literature: *from* Civil Disobedience AND On the Eve of Historic Dandi March AND from *Long Walk to Freedom*	4–17	Essay AND Speech AND Autobiography	SE, p. 144 RW, RW-APP, pp. 45–78, 309–310 RW-EL, pp. 45–78, 313–315	**Literary Study:** Analyzing argument. **Literary Study:** Analyzing political assumptions. **Literary Study:** Comparing persuasive messages. **Reading:** Evaluating evidence **Reading:** Understanding antonyms
The Pit and the Pendulum	3–9	Short Story	SE, p. 263 RW, RW-APP, pp. 79–98 RW-EL, pp. 79–98, 316	**Literary Study:** Analyzing suspense. **Reading:** Identifying sequence. **Reading:** Understanding word origins.

[Note: **SE**= Student Edition; **RW**= *Read and Write*; **RW-APP**= Approaching Level; **RW-EL**= English Learner]

Unit 3

Selections/Lessons	Pacing/Days	Genre	Where to Find Instruction	Commonly Tested Objectives
Comparing Literature: *from* **My Bondage and My Freedom AND Frederick Douglass AND In Texas Grass**	2–7	Autobiography AND Poetry	SE, p. 351 RW, RW-APP, pp. 99–114 RW-EL, pp. 99–114, 317	**Literary Study:** Analyzing autobiography. **Reading:** Analyzing cause and effect. **Reading:** Comparing literature. **Reading:** Understanding denotation and connotation.
And Ain't I a Woman	1–4	Speech	SE, p. 368 RW, RW-APP, pp. 115–122 RW-EL, pp. 115–122, 318	**Literary Study:** Analyzing oratory. **Reading:** Evaluating argument. **Reading:** Understanding word usage.
from **Mary Chestnut's Civil War**	2–5	Memoir	SE, p. 374 RW, RW-APP, pp. 123–132 RW-EL, pp. 123–132, 319	**Literary Study:** Analyzing journal. **Reading:** Distinguishing fact and opinion. **Reading:** Understanding context clues.
I Hear America Singing AND When I Heard the Learn'd Astronomer	1–3	Poetry	SE, p. 408 RW, RW-APP, pp. 133–138, 311 RW-EL, pp. 133–138, 320–321	**Literary Study:** Analyzing free verse. **Reading:** Paraphrasing.
If you were coming in the Fall AND My Life closed twice AND The Soul selects	1–4	Poetry	SE, p. 437 RW, RW-APP, pp. 139–146, 312 RW-EL, pp. 139–146, 322–323	**Literary Study:** Analyzing rhyme. **Reading:** Analyzing sound devices.

Unit 4

Selections/Lessons	Pacing/Days	Genre	Where to Find Instruction	Commonly Tested Objectives
The Celebrated Jumping Frog of Calaveras County	3–7	Short Story	SE, p. 496 RW, RW-APP, pp. 147–158 RW-EL, pp. 147–158, 324	**Literary Study:** Analyzing dialect. **Reading:** Analyzing comic devices. **Reading:** Understanding word origins.
A Wagner Matinee	2–6	Short Story	SE, p. 519 RW, RW-APP, pp. 159–170, 313 RW-EL, pp. 159–170, 325–326	**Literary Study:** Analyzing point of view. **Reading:** Identifying sequence. **Reading:** Understanding analogies.
Douglass AND We Wear the Masks	1–4	Poetry	SE, p. 568 RW, RW-APP, pp. 171–178 RW-EL, pp. 171–178, 327	**Literary Study:** Analyzing rhyme scheme. **Reading:** Clarifying meaning. **Reading:** Understanding denotation and connotation.

Unit 5

Selections/Lessons	Pacing/Days	Genre	Where to Find Instruction	Commonly Tested Objectives
The Love Song of J. Alfred Prufrock	2–5	Poetry	SE, p. 666 RW, RW-APP, pp. 179–188, 314 RW-EL, pp. 179–188, 328–329	**Literary Study:** Analyzing allusion. **Reading:** Connecting to cultural context. **Reading:** Understanding antonyms.
The Jilting of Granny Weatherall	2–7	Short Story	SE, p. 773 RW, RW-APP, pp. 189–202, 315 RW-EL, pp. 189–202, 330–331	**Literary Study:** Analyzing stream of consciousness. **Reading:** Drawing conclusions about the protagonist. **Reading:** Understanding context clues.
When the Negro Was in Vogue	2–5	Autobiography	SE, p. 817 RW, RW-APP, pp. 203–212, 316 RW-EL, pp. 203–212, 332–333	**Literary Study:** Analyzing juxtaposition. **Reading:** Analyzing concrete details. **Reading:** Understanding synonyms.

Unit 6

Selections/Lessons	Pacing/Days	Genre	Where to Find Instruction	Commonly Tested Objectives
The Rockpile	2–7	Short Story	SE, p. 959 RW, RW-APP, pp. 213–226, 317 RW-EL, pp. 213–226, 334–335	**Literary Study:** Analyzing foil. **Reading:** Making generalizations about characters. **Reading:** Understanding analogies.
The Crucible, Act I	4–13	Drama	SE, p. 1026 RW, RW-APP, pp. 227–254, 318 RW-EL, pp. 227–254, 336–337	**Literary Study:** Analyzing dialogue. **Reading:** Drawing conclusions about characters. **Reading:** Understanding word parts.

[Note: **SE=** Student Edition; **RW=** *Read and Write;* **RW-APP=** Approaching Level; **RW-EL=** English Learner]

Unit 7

Selections/Lessons	Pacing/Days	Genre	Where to Find Instruction	Commonly Tested Objectives
Comparing Literature: Ambush AND The Gift in Wartime AND from *Stay Alive, My Son*	3–7	Short Story AND Poetry AND Memoir	SE, p. 1181 RW, RW-APP, pp. 255–268, 319 RW-EL, pp. 255–268, 338–339	**Literary Study:** Analyzing mood. **Reading:** Analyzing concrete details. Comparing literature. **Reading:** Understanding word origins.
Snow	1–4	Short Story	SE, p. 1253 RW, RW-APP, pp. 269–276 RW-EL, pp. 269–276, 340	**Literary Study:** Analyzing indirect characterization. **Reading:** Connecting to contemporary issues. **Reading:** Understanding word parts.
Salvador Late or Early	1–3	Short Story	SE, p. 1304 RW, RW-APP, pp. 277–282, 320 RW-EL, pp. 277–282, 341–342	**Literary Study:** Analyzing imagery. **Reading:** Analyzing sound devices.
Thoughts on the African-American Novel	2–6	Essay	SE, p. 1308 RW, RW-APP, pp. 283–294 RW-EL, pp. 283–294, 343	**Literary Study:** Analyzing an essay. **Reading:** Determining main idea and supporting details. **Reading:** Identifying and understanding word parts.

Reference Section

Selections/Lessons	Pacing/Days	Genre	Where to Find Instruction	Commonly Tested Objectives
Functional Documents	2–6	Functional Documents	SE, p. R24 RW, RW-APP, pp. 295–305, 321 RW-EL, pp. 295–305, 344–346	**Reading:** Analyzing expository texts.
	Total: 48–150 days			

To Teachers

Welcome to the Teacher Edition of *Glencoe Literature*. We have created this teacher edition based on the standards developed by experienced teachers and educational consultants. Teaching suggestions, additional resources, and leveled activities for differentiated instruction are all labeled and wrapped around the student text for your convenience.

Unit Scope and Sequence

Every unit of *Glencoe Literature* is organized around a carefully researched scope and sequence that includes the reading skills and strategies, literary elements, writing skills, and listening, speaking and viewing skills that students need in order to successfully progress through the program.

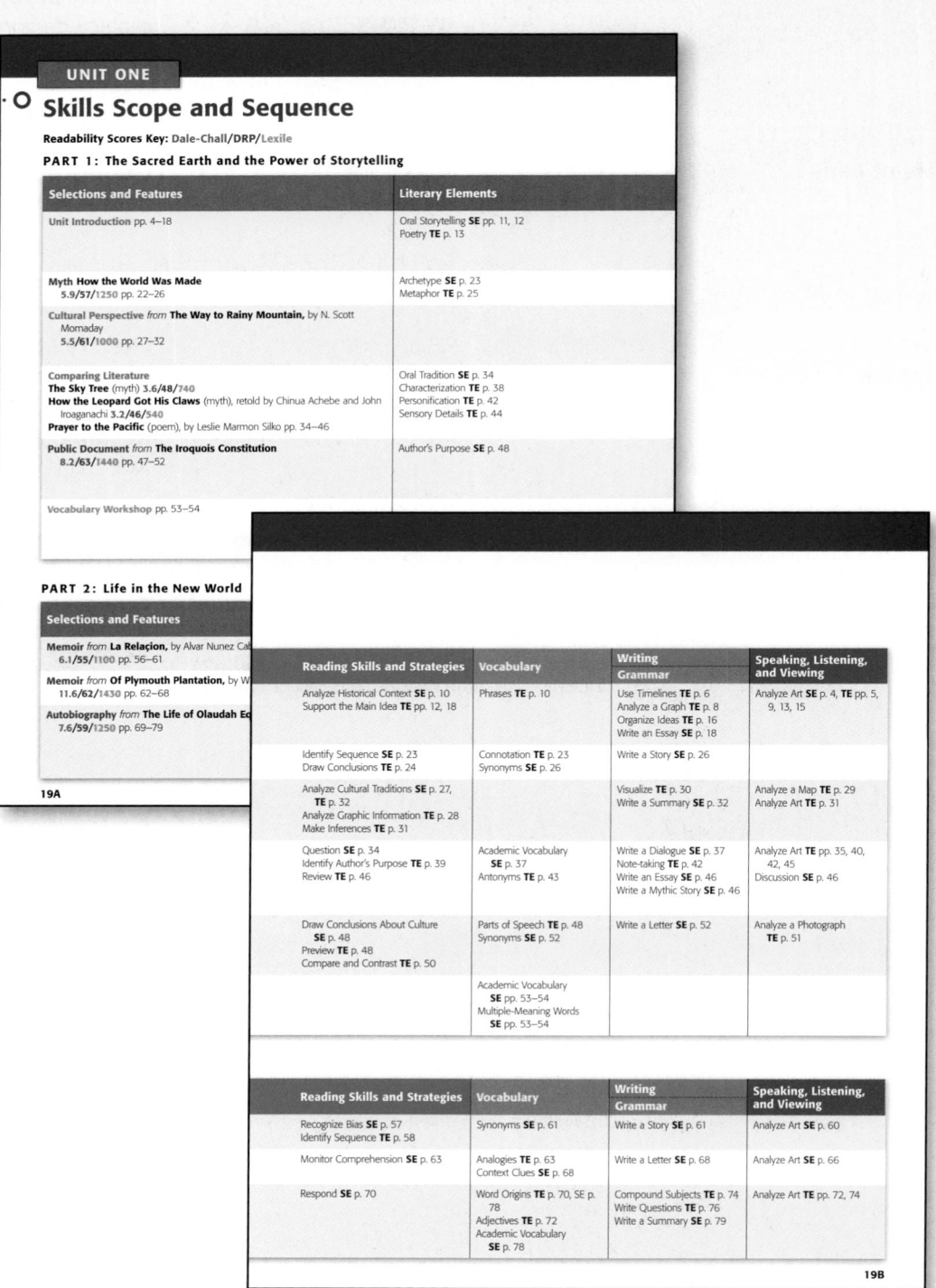

UNIT ONE

Skills Scope and Sequence

Readability Scores Key: Dale-Chall/DRP/Lexile

PART 1: The Sacred Earth and the Power of Storytelling

Selections and Features	Literary Elements
Unit Introduction pp. 4–18	Oral Storytelling **SE** pp. 11, 12 Poetry **TE** p. 13
Myth **How the World Was Made** 5.9/57/1250 pp. 22–26	Archetype **SE** p. 23 Metaphor **TE** p. 25
Cultural Perspective *from* **The Way to Rainy Mountain**, by N. Scott Momaday 5.5/61/1000 pp. 27–32	
Comparing Literature **The Sky Tree** (myth) 3.6/48/740 **How the Leopard Got His Claws** (myth), retold by Chinua Achebe and John Iroaganachi 3.2/46/540 **Prayer to the Pacific** (poem), by Leslie Marmon Silko pp. 34–46	Oral Tradition **SE** p. 34 Characterization **TE** p. 38 Personification **TE** p. 42 Sensory Details **TE** p. 44
Public Document *from* **The Iroquois Constitution** 8.2/63/1440 pp. 47–52	Author's Purpose **SE** p. 48
Vocabulary Workshop pp. 53–54	

PART 2: Life in the New World

Selections and Features
Memoir *from* **La Relaçion**, by Alvar Nunez Cab... 6.1/55/1100 pp. 56–61
Memoir *from* **Of Plymouth Plantation**, by W... 11.6/62/1430 pp. 62–68
Autobiography *from* **The Life of Olaudah Eq...** 7.6/59/1250 pp. 69–79

19A

Reading Skills and Strategies	Vocabulary	Writing Grammar	Speaking, Listening, and Viewing
Analyze Historical Context **SE** p. 10 Support the Main Idea **TE** pp. 12, 18	Phrases **TE** p. 10	Use Timelines **TE** p. 6 Analyze a Graph **TE** p. 8 Organize Ideas **TE** p. 16 Write an Essay **SE** p. 18	Analyze Art **SE** p. 4, **TE** pp. 5, 9, 13, 15
Identify Sequence **SE** p. 23 Draw Conclusions **TE** p. 24	Connotation **TE** p. 23 Synonyms **SE** p. 26	Write a Story **SE** p. 26	
Analyze Cultural Traditions **SE** p. 27, **TE** p. 32 Analyze Graphic Information **TE** p. 28 Make Inferences **TE** p. 31		Visualize **TE** p. 30 Write a Summary **SE** p. 32	Analyze a Map **TE** p. 29 Analyze Art **TE** p. 31
Question **SE** p. 34 Identify Author's Purpose **TE** p. 39 Review **TE** p. 46	Academic Vocabulary **SE** p. 37 Antonyms **TE** p. 43	Write a Dialogue **SE** p. 37 Note-taking **TE** p. 42 Write an Essay **SE** p. 46 Write a Mythic Story **SE** p. 46	Analyze Art **TE** pp. 35, 40, 42, 45 Discussion **SE** p. 46
Draw Conclusions About Culture **SE** p. 48 Preview **TE** p. 48 Compare and Contrast **TE** p. 50	Parts of Speech **TE** p. 48 Synonyms **SE** p. 52	Write a Letter **SE** p. 52	Analyze a Photograph **TE** p. 51
	Academic Vocabulary **SE** pp. 53–54 Multiple-Meaning Words **SE** pp. 53–54		

Reading Skills and Strategies	Vocabulary	Writing Grammar	Speaking, Listening, and Viewing
Recognize Bias **SE** p. 57 Identify Sequence **TE** p. 58	Synonyms **SE** p. 61	Write a Story **SE** p. 61	Analyze Art **SE** p. 60
Monitor Comprehension **SE** p. 63	Analogies **TE** p. 63 Context Clues **SE** p. 68	Write a Letter **SE** p. 68	Analyze Art **SE** p. 66
Respond **SE** p. 70	Word Origins **TE** p. 70, **SE** p. 78 Adjectives **TE** p. 72 Academic Vocabulary **SE** p. 78	Compound Subjects **TE** p. 74 Write Questions **TE** p. 76 Write a Summary **SE** p. 79	Analyze Art **TE** pp. 72, 74

19B

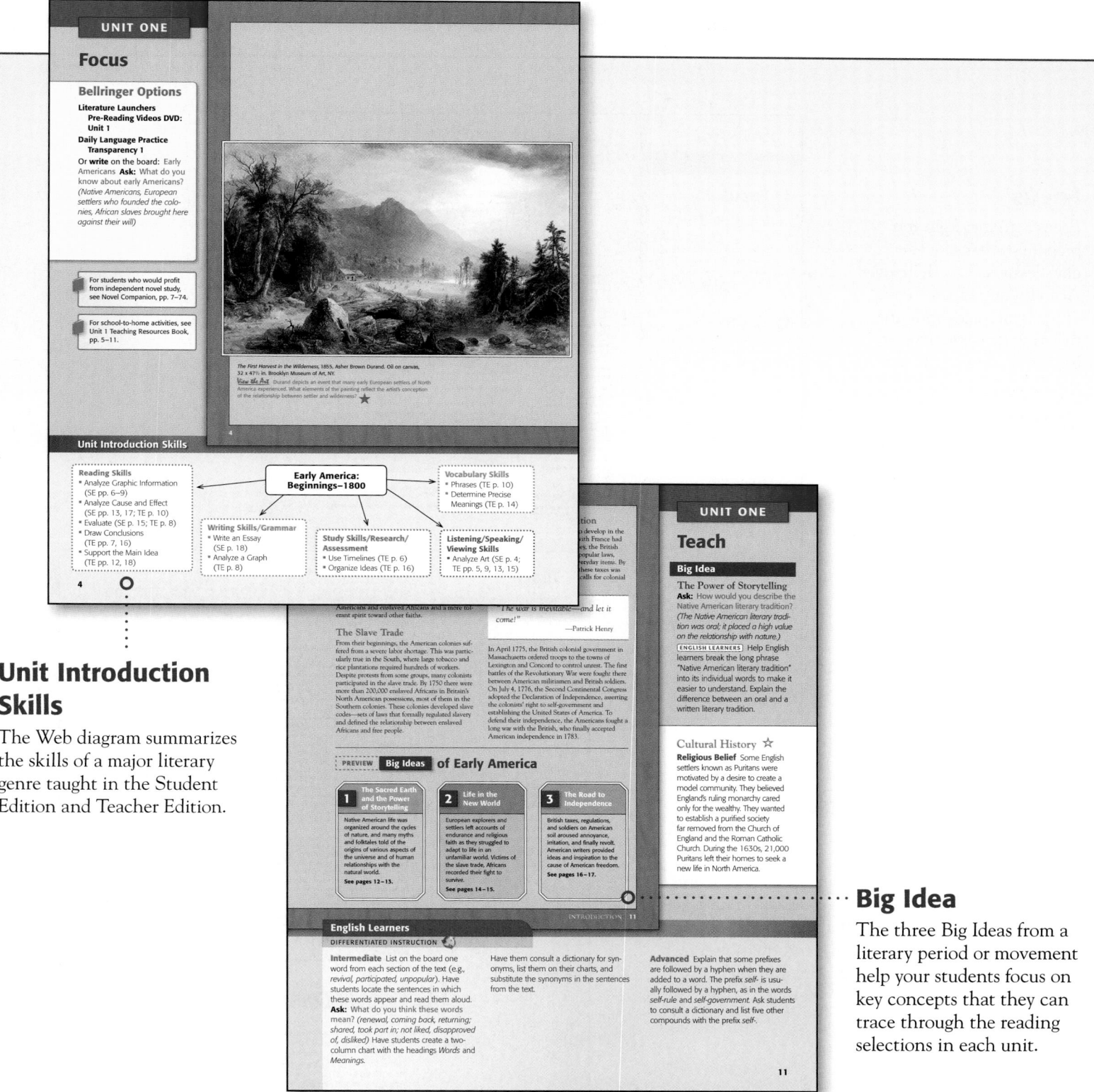

Unit Introduction Skills

The Web diagram summarizes the skills of a major literary genre taught in the Student Edition and Teacher Edition.

Big Idea

The three Big Ideas from a literary period or movement help your students focus on key concepts that they can trace through the reading selections in each unit.

Three Part Lesson Plan

The Teacher Edition of *Glencoe Literature* is organized in a three-part structure: **Focus, Teach,** and **Assess.**

Focus

Focus activities help you prepare students for the day's lessons. The **Bellringer Activity** provides a choice of transparencies and other teaching strategies that engage students and focus their attention.

Teach

In these sections, you will find leveled activities that correspond to and extend instruction in the Student Edition. Here you will also find information that enriches students' appreciation of art, photos, culture, or history as they apply to the selections being taught.

Brackets and Numbers

When students are asked to think about the text, you will see brackets that are color-coded and numbered so that the corresponding teacher information is readily identifiable.

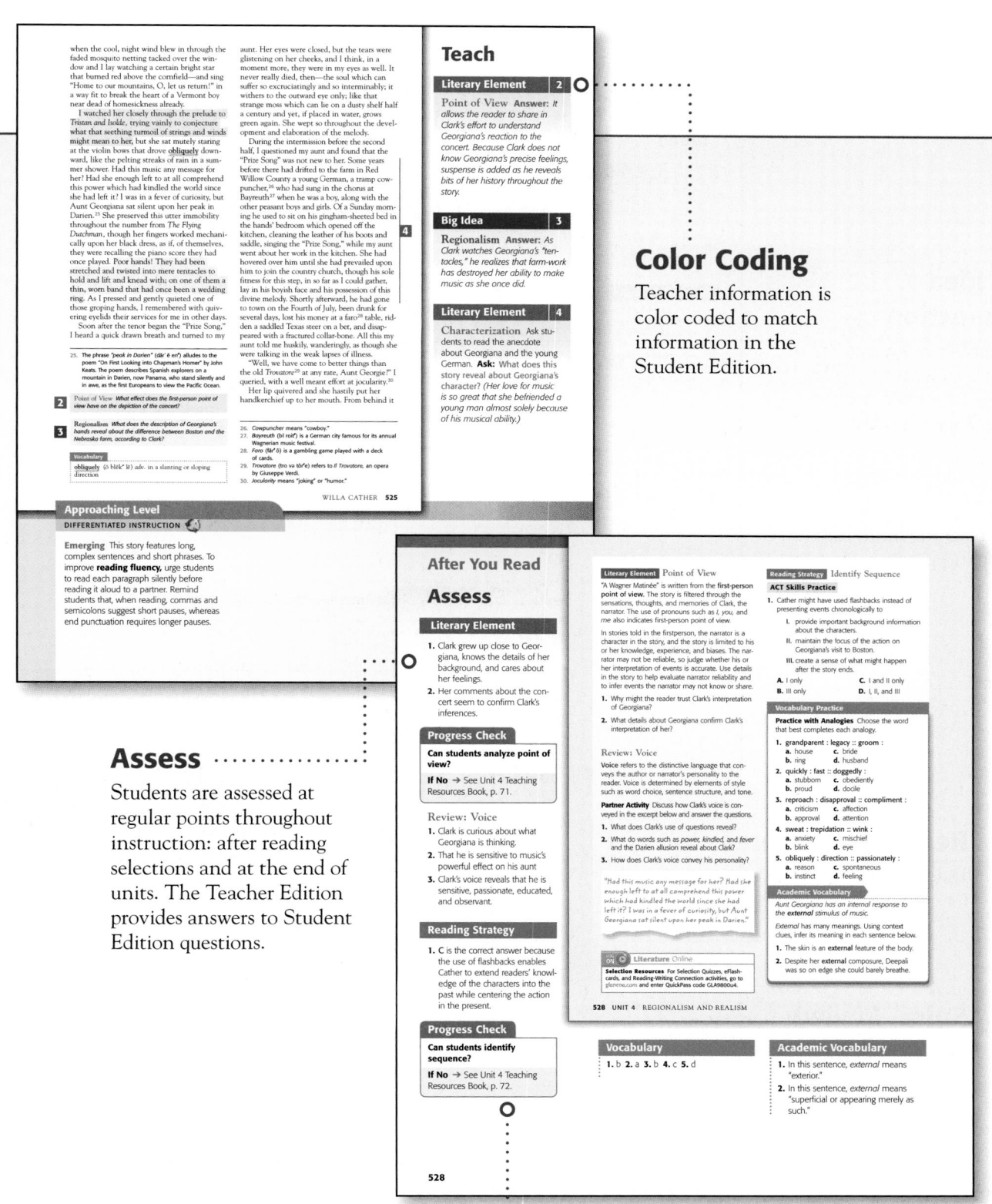

when the cool, night wind blew in through the faded mosquito netting tacked over the window and I lay watching a certain bright star that burned red above the cornfield—and sing "Home to our mountains, O, let us return!" in a way fit to break the heart of a Vermont boy near dead of homesickness already.

I watched her closely through the prelude to *Tristan and Isolde*, trying vainly to conjecture what that seething turmoil of strings and winds might mean to her, but she sat mutely staring at the violin bows that drove **obliquely** downward, like the pelting streaks of rain in a summer shower. Had this music any message for her? Had she enough left to at all comprehend this power which had kindled the world since she had left it? I was in a fever of curiosity, but Aunt Georgiana sat silent upon her peak in Darien.[25] She preserved this utter immobility throughout the number from *The Flying Dutchman*, though her fingers worked mechanically upon her black dress, as if, of themselves, they were recalling the piano score they had once played. Poor hands! They had been stretched and twisted into mere tentacles to hold and lift and knead with; on one of them a thin, worn band that had once been a wedding ring. As I pressed and gently quieted one of those groping hands, I remembered with quivering eyelids their services for me in other days.

Soon the tenor began the "Prize Song," I heard a quick drawn breath and turned to my aunt. Her eyes were closed, but the tears were glistening on her cheeks, and I think, in a moment more, they were in my eyes as well. It never really died, then—the soul which can suffer so excruciatingly and so interminably; it withers to the outward eye only; like that strange moss which can lie on a dusty shelf half a century and yet, if placed in water, grows green again. She wept so throughout the development and elaboration of the melody.

During the intermission before the second half, I questioned my aunt and found that the "Prize Song" was not new to her. Some years before there had drifted to the farm in Red Willow County a young German, a tramp cow-puncher,[26] who had sung in the chorus at Bayreuth[27] when he was a boy, along with the other peasant boys and girls. Of a Sunday morning he used to sit on his gingham-sheeted bed in the hands' bedroom which opened off the kitchen, cleaning the leather of his boots and saddle, singing the "Prize Song," while my aunt went about her work in the kitchen. She had hovered over him until she had prevailed upon him to join the country church, though his sole fitness for this step, in so far as I could gather, lay in his boyish face and his possession of this divine melody. Shortly afterward, he had gone to town on the Fourth of July, had been drunk for several days, lost his money at a faro[28] table, ridden a saddled Texas steer on a bet, and disappeared with a fractured collar-bone. All this my aunt told me huskily, wanderingly, as though she were talking in the weak lapses of illness.

"Well, we have come to better things than the old *Trovatore*[29] at any rate, Aunt Georgie?" I queried, with a well meant effort at jocularity.[30]

Her lip quivered and she hastily put her handkerchief up to her mouth. From behind it

25. The phrase *"peak in Darien"* (dâr´ē en´) alludes to the poem "On First Looking into Chapman's Homer" by John Keats. The poem describes Spanish explorers on a mountain in Darien, now Panama, who stand silently in awe, as the first Europeans to view the Pacific Ocean.

2 Point of View *What effect does the first-person point of view have on the depiction of the concert?*

3 Regionalism *What does the description of Georgiana's hands reveal about the difference between Boston and the Nebraska farm, according to Clark?*

Vocabulary
obliquely (ō blēk´ lē) *adv.* in a slanting or sloping direction

26. *Cowpuncher* means "cowboy."
27. *Bayreuth* (bī roit´) is a German city famous for its annual Wagnerian music festival.
28. *Faro* (fâr´ō) is a gambling game played with a deck of cards.
29. *Trovatore* (trō və tôr´e) refers to *Il Trovatore*, an opera by Giuseppe Verdi.
30. *Jocularity* means "joking" or "humor."

WILLA CATHER **525**

Teach

Literary Element | **2**

Point of View **Answer:** *It allows the reader to share in Clark's effort to understand Georgiana's reaction to the concert. Because Clark does not know Georgiana's precise feelings, suspense is added as he reveals bits of her history throughout the story.*

Big Idea | **3**

Regionalism **Answer:** *As Clark watches Georgiana's "tentacles," he realizes that farm-work has destroyed her ability to make music as she once did.*

Literary Element | **4**

Characterization Ask students to read the anecdote about Georgiana and the young German. **Ask:** What does this story reveal about Georgiana's character? *(Her love for music is so great that she befriended a young man almost solely because of his musical ability.)*

Color Coding

Teacher information is color coded to match information in the Student Edition.

Approaching Level

DIFFERENTIATED INSTRUCTION

Emerging This story features long, complex sentences and short phrases. To improve **reading fluency,** urge students to read each paragraph silently before reading it aloud to a partner. Remind students that, when reading, commas and semicolons suggest short pauses, whereas end punctuation requires longer pauses.

After You Read

Assess

Literary Element

1. Clark grew up close to Georgiana, knows the details of her background, and cares about her feelings.

2. Her comments about the concert seem to confirm Clark's inferences.

Progress Check

Can students analyze point of view?

If No → See Unit 4 Teaching Resources Book, p. 71.

Review: Voice

1. Clark is curious about what Georgiana is thinking.

2. That he is sensitive to music's powerful effect on his aunt

3. Clark's voice reveals that he is sensitive, passionate, educated, and observant.

Reading Strategy

1. C is the correct answer because the use of flashbacks enables Cather to extend readers' knowledge of the characters into the past while centering the action in the present.

Progress Check

Can students identify sequence?

If No → See Unit 4 Teaching Resources Book, p. 72.

528

Literary Element Point of View

"A Wagner Matinée" is written from the **first-person point of view**. The story is filtered through the sensations, thoughts, and memories of Clark, the narrator. The use of pronouns such as *I, you,* and *me* also indicates first-person point of view.

In stories told in the firstperson, the narrator is a character in the story, and the story is limited to his or her knowledge, experience, and biases. The narrator may not be reliable, so judge whether his or her interpretation of events is accurate. Use details in the story to help evaluate narrator reliability and to infer events the narrator may not know or share.

1. Why might the reader trust Clark's interpretation of Georgiana?

2. What details about Georgiana confirm Clark's interpretation of her?

Review: Voice

Voice refers to the distinctive language that conveys the author or narrator's personality to the reader. Voice is determined by elements of style such as word choice, sentence structure, and tone.

Partner Activity Discuss how Clark's voice is conveyed in the excerpt below and answer the questions.

1. What does Clark's use of questions reveal?

2. What do words such as *power, kindled,* and *fever* and the Darien allusion reveal about Clark?

3. How does Clark's voice convey his personality?

"Had this music any message for her? Had she enough left to at all comprehend this power which had kindled the world since she had left it? I was in a fever of curiosity, but Aunt Georgiana sat silent upon her peak in Darien."

Literature Online

Selection Resources For Selection Quizzes, eflashcards, and Reading-Writing Connection activities, go to glencoe.com and enter QuickPass code GLA9800u4.

528 UNIT 4 REGIONALISM AND REALISM

Reading Strategy Identify Sequence

ACT Skills Practice

1. Cather might have used flashbacks instead of presenting events chronologically to

    I. provide important background information about the characters.

    II. maintain the focus of the action on Georgiana's visit to Boston.

    III. create a sense of what might happen after the story ends.

    A. I only   **C.** I and II only
    B. III only   **D.** I, II, and III

Vocabulary Practice

Practice with Analogies Choose the word that best completes each analogy.

1. grandparent : legacy :: groom :
    a. house   **c.** bride
    b. ring   **d.** husband

2. quickly : fast :: doggedly :
    a. stubborn   **c.** obediently
    b. proud   **d.** docile

3. reproach : disapproval :: compliment :
    a. criticism   **c.** affection
    b. approval   **d.** attention

4. sweat : trepidation :: wink :
    a. anxiety   **c.** mischief
    b. blink   **d.** eye

5. obliquely : direction :: passionately :
    a. reason   **c.** spontaneous
    b. instinct   **d.** feeling

Academic Vocabulary

Aunt Georgiana has an internal response to the **external** stimulus of music.

External has many meanings. Using context clues, infer its meaning in each sentence below.

1. The skin is an **external** feature of the body.

2. Despite her **external** composure, Deepali was so on edge she could barely breathe.

Vocabulary

1. b 2. a 3. b 4. c 5. d

Academic Vocabulary

1. In this sentence, *external* means "exterior."

2. In this sentence, *external* means "superficial or appearing merely as such."

Assess

Students are assessed at regular points throughout instruction: after reading selections and at the end of units. The Teacher Edition provides answers to Student Edition questions.

Progress Check

IF a student needs help (based on a quick and informal assessment), THEN we provide a suggestion for reteaching.

Teaching Support

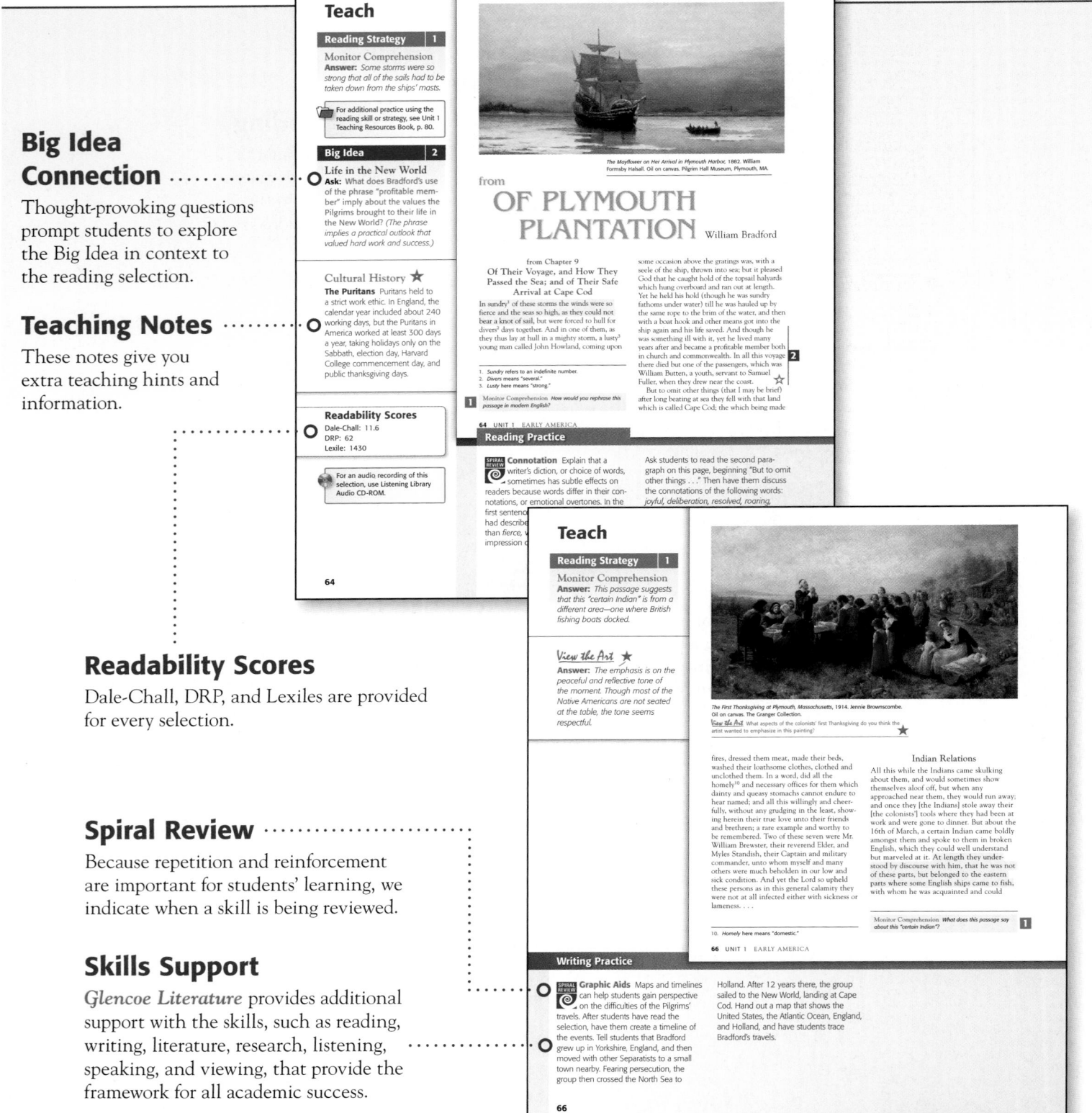

Big Idea Connection

Thought-provoking questions prompt students to explore the Big Idea in context to the reading selection.

Teaching Notes

These notes give you extra teaching hints and information.

Readability Scores

Dale-Chall, DRP, and Lexiles are provided for every selection.

Spiral Review

Because repetition and reinforcement are important for students' learning, we indicate when a skill is being reviewed.

Skills Support

Glencoe Literature provides additional support with the skills, such as reading, writing, literature, research, listening, speaking, and viewing, that provide the framework for all academic success.

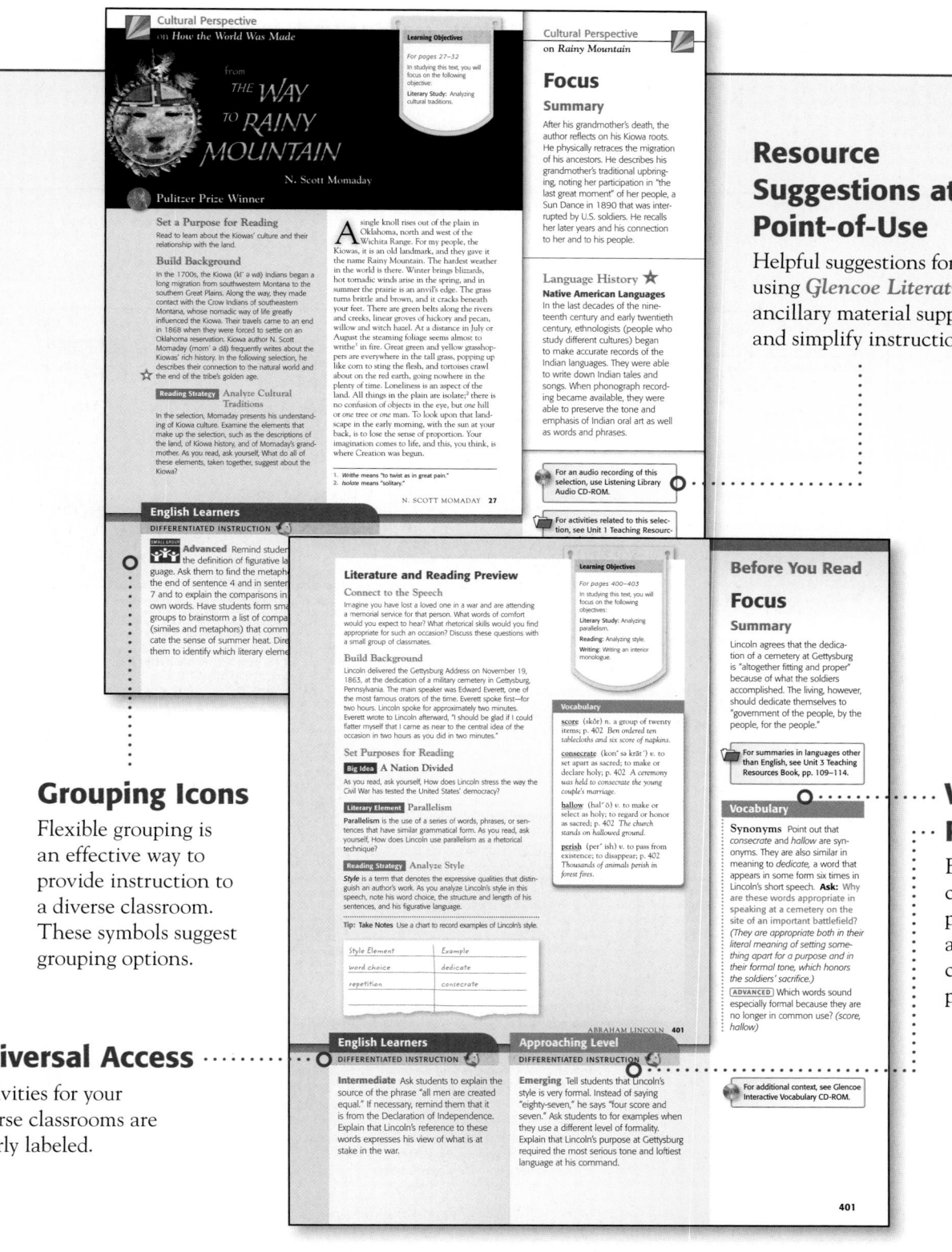

Grouping Icons

Flexible grouping is an effective way to provide instruction to a diverse classroom. These symbols suggest grouping options.

Universal Access

Activities for your diverse classrooms are clearly labeled.

Resource Suggestions at Point-of-Use

Helpful suggestions for using *Glencoe Literature* ancillary material support and simplify instruction.

Vocabulary Preteaching

Because vocabulary is a key component of reading success, we provide for the struggling students and English Learners in your classroom additional vocabulary preteaching activities.

Informational Text

The wide range of informational text in *Glencoe Literature* broadens the students' reading to include more than just poetry, short stories, and plays.

Perspectives

Award-winning book excerpts provide students with the in-depth information they need to explore the cultural, political, historical, and literary contexts of a reading selection.

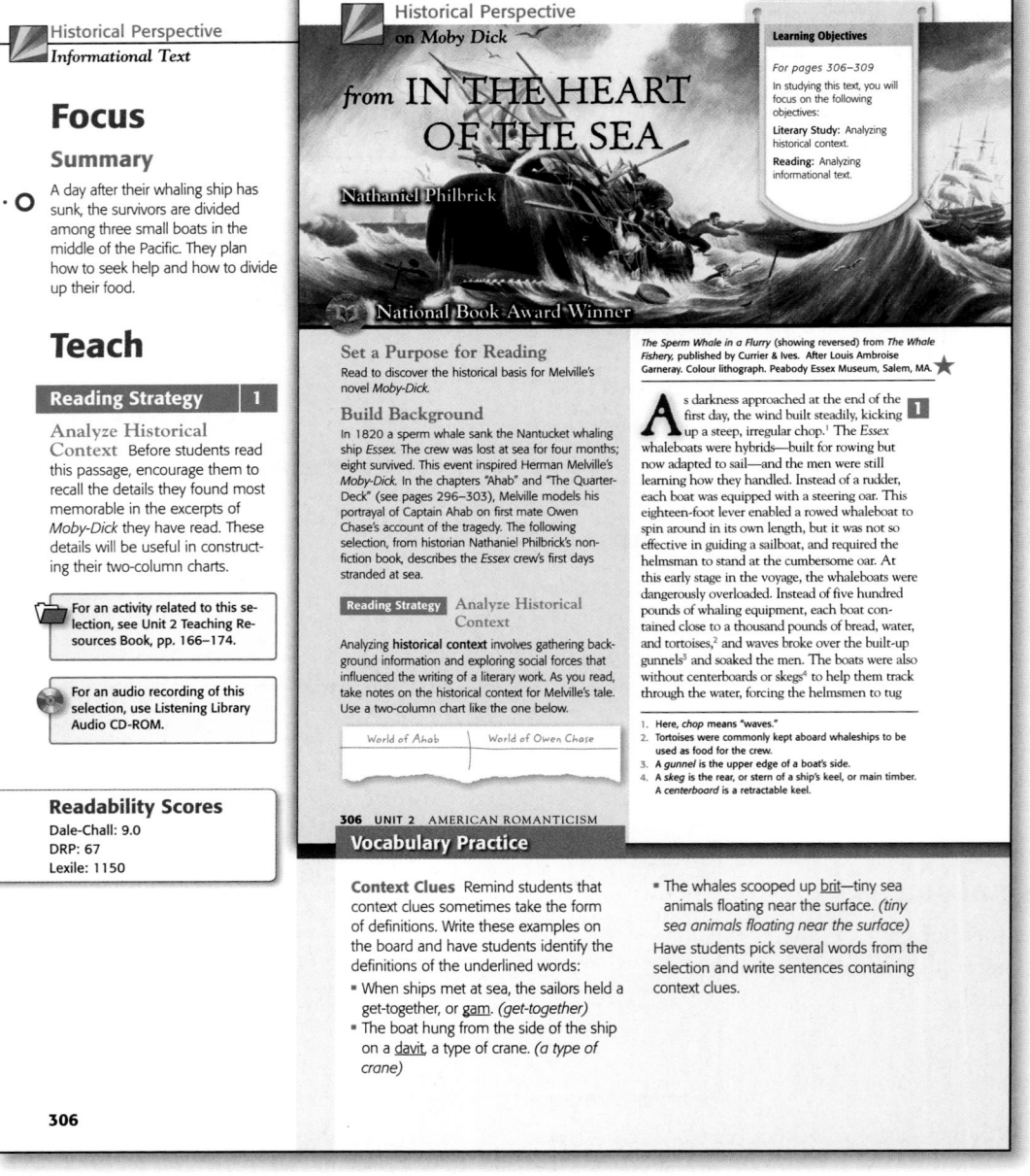

Historical Perspective
Informational Text

Focus

Summary

A day after their whaling ship has sunk, the survivors are divided among three small boats in the middle of the Pacific. They plan how to seek help and how to divide up their food.

Teach

Reading Strategy   1

Analyze Historical Context Before students read this passage, encourage them to recall the details they found most memorable in the excerpts of *Moby-Dick* they have read. These details will be useful in constructing their two-column charts.

📁 For an activity related to this selection, see Unit 2 Teaching Resources Book, pp. 166–174.

💿 For an audio recording of this selection, use Listening Library Audio CD-ROM.

Readability Scores
Dale-Chall: 9.0
DRP: 67
Lexile: 1150

Historical Perspective
on *Moby Dick*

from IN THE HEART OF THE SEA

Nathaniel Philbrick

⚓ National Book Award Winner

Learning Objectives

For pages 306–309
In studying this text, you will focus on the following objectives:

Literary Study: Analyzing historical context.

Reading: Analyzing informational text.

Set a Purpose for Reading
Read to discover the historical basis for Melville's novel *Moby-Dick.*

Build Background
In 1820 a sperm whale sank the Nantucket whaling ship *Essex.* The crew was lost at sea for four months; eight survived. This event inspired Herman Melville's *Moby-Dick.* In the chapters "Ahab" and "The Quarter-Deck" (see pages 296–303), Melville models his portrayal of Captain Ahab on first mate Owen Chase's account of the tragedy. The following selection, from historian Nathaniel Philbrick's non-fiction book, describes the *Essex* crew's first days stranded at sea.

Reading Strategy   Analyze Historical Context

Analyzing **historical context** involves gathering background information and exploring social forces that influenced the writing of a literary work. As you read, take notes on the historical context for Melville's tale. Use a two-column chart like the one below.

World of Ahab	World of Owen Chase

306   UNIT 2   AMERICAN ROMANTICISM

The Sperm Whale in a Flurry (showing reversed) from *The Whale Fishery,* published by Currier & Ives. After Louis Ambroise Garneray. Colour lithograph. Peabody Essex Museum, Salem, MA.

As darkness approached at the end of the first day, the wind built steadily, kicking up a steep, irregular chop.[1] The *Essex* whaleboats were hybrids—built for rowing but now adapted to sail—and the men were still learning how they handled. Instead of a rudder, each boat was equipped with a steering oar. This eighteen-foot lever enabled a rowed whaleboat to spin around in its own length, but it was not so effective in guiding a sailboat, and required the helmsman to stand at the cumbersome oar. At this early stage in the voyage, the whaleboats were dangerously overloaded. Instead of five hundred pounds of whaling equipment, each boat contained close to a thousand pounds of bread, water, and tortoises,[2] and waves broke over the built-up gunnels[3] and soaked the men. The boats were also without centerboards or skegs[4] to help them track through the water, forcing the helmsmen to tug

---

1. Here, *chop* means "waves."
2. Tortoises were commonly kept aboard whaleships to be used as food for the crew.
3. A *gunnel* is the upper edge of a boat's side.
4. A *skeg* is the rear, or stern of a ship's keel, or main timber. A *centerboard* is a retractable keel.

Vocabulary Practice

Context Clues Remind students that context clues sometimes take the form of definitions. Write these examples on the board and have students identify the definitions of the underlined words:

- When ships met at sea, the sailors held a get-together, or <u>gam</u>. *(get-together)*
- The boat hung from the side of the ship on a <u>davit</u>, a type of crane. *(a type of crane)*

- The whales scooped up <u>brit</u>—tiny sea animals floating near the surface. *(tiny sea animals floating near the surface)*

Have students pick several words from the selection and write sentences containing context clues.

306

TIME Articles

Linked to the Big Idea, an author, or a reading selection, these articles deliver the facts on topical issues.

TIME

Focus

Summary

The article begins with Dr. Richard Davidson studying the brain waves of a monk. Davidson is interested in learning if there are any changes in the monk's brain activity when he meditates. Research performed by Davidson and other scientists shows a connection between happiness and health.

Teach

Reading Strategy	**1**

Analyze Cause-and-Effect Relationships Point out that writers use different ways of organizing cause-and-effect arguments. A writer may first present an effect and then provide its causes; or a writer may present causes and conclude with their effect.

(APPROACHING) **Ask:** According to the first page of this article, what effect does happiness seem to have on health? *(Happiness seems to help people stay healthier.)*

Readability Scores
Dale-Chall: 11.9
DRP: 68
Lexile: 1110

198

Set a Purpose for Reading
Read to discover the biological roots of positive emotion and to connect these ideas with the optimism of Emerson and Thoreau.

Preview the Article
1. Analyze the photos of the monk on page 199 and the babies on page 200. What might these tell you about the article?
2. Skim the first paragraph. What connection do you think the writer is going to make between biology and joy?

Reading Strategy	Analyze

Cause-and-Effect Relationships

Cause and effect describes the relationship between an action and its consequence. The cause, or action, directly results in the effect, or consequence. As you read, ask yourself, What cause-and-effect relationships are discussed in this article and why are they important?

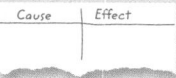

198 UNIT 2 AMERICAN ROMANTICISM

TIME

Scientists know plenty about depression. Now they are starting to understand the roots of positive emotion.

The Biology of JOY

By MICHAEL D. LEMONICK

IT ALL BEGAN WITH RICHARD DAVIDSON, A PROFESSOR OF psychology and psychiatry at the University of Wisconsin. Davidson was in a lab observing a Buddhist monk sink deep into blissful meditation when he noticed something that sent his own pulse racing. Davidson checked the data streaming to his computer from electrodes attached to the monk's skull. Electrical activity in the left prefrontal lobe of the monk's brain was shooting up at a tremendous rate. "It was exciting," Davidson recalls. "We didn't expect to see anything that dramatic."

When Davidson made his discovery, he had been studying the link between prefrontal-lobe activity and the bliss deep meditators experience. But even for someone with his experience, watching the brain crackle with activity as a person entered a trancelike state was something never seen before. It made clear, says Davidson, that happiness isn't just a vague feeling. Instead it's a physical state of the brain—one that you can bring on deliberately.

That's not all. As researchers have gained an understanding of the physical characteristics of a happy brain, they have come to see that those traits have a powerful influence on the rest of the body. Scientists have discovered that happiness or feelings of hopefulness, optimism, and contentment appear to lessen the risk or limit the severity of cardiovascular disease, lung disease, diabetes, high blood pressure, and colds. According to a Dutch study of elderly patients, those upbeat mental states reduced an individual's risk of death 50%.

Doctors have known for years that clinical depression—the

2

Writing Practice

Achieve Unity Explain to students that a paragraph is unified when all of its sentences support the main idea of the paragraph, usually expressed in the topic sentence. Ask students to state the main idea of paragraph three on this page that begins "That's not all...." *(Sentence two in paragraph three is the main idea)* Then ask them to point out the details that support the main idea. *(Lessen risk of diseases, colds, and death)* Finally, ask students to write a paragraph about what makes them optimistic. Remind them that the paragraph should have a clearly stated main idea that is supported by relevant details.

Guide to Readability

Throughout the teacher materials in your Teacher Edition, you will encounter DRP readability measures assigned to the reading selections in *Glencoe Literature*. You will also find readability scores based on the Lexile Framework® for Reading and the Dale-Chall Readability Formula. You can use these scores to select reading materials that are suitable for your entire class or for individual students.

Degrees of Reading Power® (DRP)

DRP values indicate the readability of prose text. The higher the value, the more difficult the text. The scale ranges from 1 to 100; commonly encountered English text tends to fall somewhere between 25 and 85. Although middle school texts have an average difficulty of 56, and high school texts have an average difficulty of 62, no single readability level is appropriate for each grade level. Rather, a typical classroom has materials with a range of readability levels available for use—some intended for less proficient readers, some for average readers, and some for stronger readers. The following chart shows the average DRP readability range for materials widely available for use at each grade. Some materials you might use, however, will certainly fall outside of the range for your particular grade.

Grade	DRP Readability Ranges
6	51–61
7	52–62
8	53–64
9	53–65
10	51–68
11	56–67
12	57–68

The Lexile® Framework

A Lexile measure assigned to a text is the specific number that describes the reading demands of the text. The typical Lexile Scale ranges from 200 to 1700 Lexiles. As with the DRP measures, there is not a direct translation from a specific Lexile measure to a specific grade level. Within any classroom, there will be a range of readers and a range of materials to be read. The levels shown on the following chart indicate the approximate range of Lexile scores for 50 percent of the materials found in a typical grade-level classroom. For example, the middle half of the instructional materials typically found in a sixth-grade classroom ranges in difficulty from about 850L to 1050L.

Grade	Text Measures (from Lexile Framework Map)
6	850L to 1050L
7	950L to 1075L
8	1000L to 1100L
9	1050L to 1150L
10	1100L to 1200L
11 and 12	1100L to 1300L

Dale-Chall Readability Formula

The Dale-Chall Formula is based on the average sentence length and the number of unfamiliar words in a passage. The idea behind this formula is that readers typically find it easier to read, process, and recall a passage if the words and sentences are familiar and grade appropriate. The Dale-Chall Formula assesses the difficulty of a passage by computing two different values from the text. The first measure is the average number of words per sentence. The second measure is the percentage of words in the passage not found on the grade appropriate Dale Word List. The following chart shows the average Dale-Chall readability scores for grades 5 thru 12.

Grade	Dale-Chall Readability Score
5-6th Grade	5.0 to 5.9
7-8th Grade	6.0 to 6.9
9-10th Grade	7.0 to 7.9
11-12th Grade	8.0 to 8.9

African American Vernacular English (AAVE)

Some of your students will be speakers of African American Vernacular English (AAVE). AAVE is a language system with well-formed rules for sounds, grammar, and meanings. Throughout the year you will help these students learn standard academic English by focusing on those places where AAVE differs from the standard and on those patterns that will have the most immediate impact on the students' reading and writing development.

These students will need help in understanding that what is appropriate in one setting is not appropriate in another, so they can shift easily and competently between varieties in different social contexts. Instruction will be more effective if it identifies nonstandard varieties of English as different, rather than inferior. All students should be taught standard English in a way that respects their home language.

Use the charts that follow to identify AAVE linguistic differences and instructional modifications that can help students as they learn to successfully and fluently speak, read, and write standard English. The modifications focus on the following:

- Providing students with clear enunciation examples during phonics and phonemic awareness lessons targeting difficult sounds. Then additional pronunciation practice is provided during small group phonics lessons.

- Using contrastive analysis during whole group and small group time in which students code switch between AAVE and standard English. The difference in each grammatical structure is highlighted and students are provided ample opportunities to practice standard English in speaking and writing. They are also taught the proper context for each usage.

- Using Discrimination Drills in which two sentences are read aloud or written on the board. One is standard English, the other reflects common AAVE structures. Students must determine which is standard English.

- Using Translation Drills in which students change an AAVE sentence into standard English.

Phonics Differences

English/Language Arts Skill	Linguistic Differences and Instructional Modifications
Digraph *th* as in bathroom	For many speakers of African American Vernacular English, the initial /th/ sound in function words such as *this* and *then* is often produced as a /d/ sound. In some words, such as *thing* and *through,* the /th/ sound is produced as a /t/ sound. At the ends of words and syllables, such as *bathroom* and *death,* the /th/ sound is replaced by the /f/ sound. This will affect students' spelling and speaking. Students will need additional articulation support prior to spelling these words.
Final Consonant *r*	Many speakers of African American Vernacular English drop the /r/ sound in words. For example, these students will say *sto'* for *store* or *do'* for *door.* Clearly pronounce these words, emphasizing the /r/ sound. Have students repeat several times, exaggerating the sound before spelling these words.
***r*-Blends**	Many speakers of African American Vernacular English drop the /r/ in words with *r*-Blends. For example, these students will say *th'ow* for *throw.* Clearly pronounce these words in the lesson, emphasizing the sounds of the *r*-Blend. Have students repeat several times, exaggerating the sound.

Final Consonant /l/ and Final l-Blends	Many speakers of African American Vernacular English drop the /l/ sound in words, particularly in words with -ool and -oal spelling patterns, such as cool and coal, and when the letter l precedes the consonants p, t, or k as in help, belt, and milk. These students will drop the l when spelling these words, as well. Provide additional articulation support prior to reading and spelling these words.
Final Consonant Blends	Many speakers of African American Vernacular English drop the final letter in a consonant blend (e.g., mp, nt, nk, lo, lt, lk). For example, they will say des' for desk. Clearly pronounce the final sound in these words and have students repeat several times, exaggerating the sound.
Plurals	When the letter -s is added to a word ending in a consonant blend, such as test (tests), many speakers of African American Vernacular English will drop the final sounds. Therefore they will say tes' or tesses. These students will need additional articulation support.
Contractions	Many speakers of African American Vernacular English drop the /t/ sound when pronouncing the common words it's, that's, and what's. These words sound more like i's, tha's, and wha's. These students will need additional articulation support in order to pronounce and spell these words.
Short Vowels i and e	When the /i/ and /e/ sounds appear before the consonants m or n in words, such as pen/pin and him/hem, many speakers of African American Vernacular English won't pronounce or hear the difference. Focus on articulation, such as mouth position for each vowel sound, during the lesson.
Inflectional Ending -ing	Many speakers of African American Vernacular English will pronounce words with -ing as /ang/. For example, they will say thang for thing. Emphasize the /i/ sound in these words to help students correctly spell and pronounce them.

Grammar, Usage, Mechanics Differences

English/Language Arts Skill	Linguistic Differences and Instructional Modifications
Subject-Verb Agreement (he is , he goes)	To acquire standard academic English speech and writing, speakers of African American Vernacular English need to learn to use -s with a verb and the third person and only there, as in he is and he goes. Many speakers of AAVE will leave out the -s or place it elsewhere, as in he go or we goes. Write a sentence from students' speech or writing. Then provide contrastive analysis work. Write the standard English form above that sentence. Discuss the key differences.
Subject-Verb Agreement (do/does, have/has, was/were)	Many speakers of African American Vernacular English have difficulties with subject-verb agreement when the verbs do/does, have/has, and was/were are used. Additional grammar instruction and practice will be needed. Write a sentence from students' speech or writing. Then provide contrastive analysis work. Write the standard English form above that sentence. Discuss the key differences.
Past Tense (-ed)	Many speakers of African American Vernacular English understand the use of -ed to form the past tense but leave it out or add sounds when pronouncing the word, as in pick or pickted for picked. Students will need additional work during small group time with -ed in order to know when and where to use it in writing.

Past Tense (simple past tense vs. past perfect tense)	Many speakers of African American Vernacular English will add *had* to the simple past tense, saying *We had picked* for *We picked.* The use of *had* indicates the past perfect tense in standard academic English. Other common nonstandard forms of irregular past-tense verbs include *He seen that* and *He had ran over there.*
The Verb "to be" (pronunciation)	In the first person present tense, many speakers of African American Vernacular English will properly use *I am* or *I'm*, but say it more like *"uhm."* Focus on pronunciation.
The Verb "to be" (writing)	To learn standard academic English, many speakers of African American Vernacular English will need to learn not to delete *is* and *are* when speaking and writing. For example, students might say *He my brother* or *She goin' over there.* Additional grammar instruction and practice will be needed. Use Discrimination and Translation Drills.
The Verb "to be" (speaking)	Many speakers of African American Vernacular English will use *was* in the singular and plural forms, as in *He was* and *They was.* Additional grammar instruction and practice will be needed.
The Verb "to be"	To learn standard academic English, many speakers of African American Vernacular English will need to learn to avoid using nonstandard forms, such as *He always be doing this,* in favor of *am, are,* and *is.* Also, additional instruction and practice will be needed to show the proper placement of the adverbs *always, never,* and *others.* For example, *He is always doing this* rather than *He always is doing this.* Write a sentence from students' speech or writing. Then provide contrastive analysis work. Write the standard English form above that sentence. Discuss the key differences.
Possessives ('s)	In standard academic English, *'s* is added to a noun to show possession. For many speakers of African American Vernacular English, the *'s* is absent. However, the *'s* is regularly added to mine, as in *This is mines.*
Possessive (whose)	The possessive pronoun whose is often not used by many speakers of African American Vernacular English. For example, students will say *I don't know who book this was.* Students will need additional instruction and practice to acquire this skill.
There is/There are	Many speakers of African American Vernacular English will need help in pronouncing *its* in standard academic English and in properly using the patterns *there is* and *there are.* In AAVE it is common to replace the word there with *it,* as in *It's a man at the door* rather than *There's a man at the door.* Use Discrimination and Translation Drills.
Plurals (nouns of measure)	Most speakers of African American Vernacular English correctly use the plural, except when it involves "nouns of measure," as in *It cost five dollars* or *She owe me five dollars.* However, the plural /s/ is often absent in writing, and students will need additional instruction and practice during small group time.
Negatives	Many speakers of African American Vernacular English will use several negatives in a sentence when only one is required, as in *Nobody never said nothing.* To master standard academic English, speakers of AAVE will need considerable practice to gain control of any, ever, and either after a negative word. Write a sentence from students' speech or writing. Then provide contrastive analysis work. Write the standard English form above that sentence. Discuss the key differences. In addition, use Discrimination and Translation Drills.

The Interaction Between English and Students' Primary Languages

By Jana Echevarria, PhD
California State University, Long Beach

Donald Bear, PhD
University of Nevada, Reno

It is important for teachers to understand why English Learners (ELs) use alternative pronunciations for some English words. Many English sounds do not exist or transfer to other languages, so English Learners may lack the auditory acuity to "hear" these English sounds and have difficulty pronouncing them. These students are not accustomed to positioning their mouth in a way the sound requires. The charts that appear on the following pages show that there is variation among languages, with some languages having more sounds in common and thus greater transfer to English than others.

For example, an English speaker may be able to pronounce the /r/ in the Spanish word pero ("but"), but not the /rr/ trill in perro ("dog"). The English speaker may also lack the auditory acuity to detect and the ability to replicate the tonal sounds of some Chinese words. Similarly, a Vietnamese speaker may have difficulty pronouncing /th/ in words such as thin or thanks.

Further, English Learners make grammatical errors due to interference from their native languages. In Spanish, the adjective follows the noun, so often English Learners say "the girl pretty" instead of "the pretty girl." While English changes the verb form with a change of subject (I walk. She walks.), some Asian languages keep the verb form constant across subjects. Adding /s/ to the third person may be difficult for some English Learners. Students may know the grammatical rule, but applying it consistently may be difficult, especially in spoken English.

When working with English Learners, you should also be aware of sociocultural factors that affect pronunciation. Students may retain an accent because it marks their social identity. Speakers of other languages may feel at a social distance from members of the dominant English-speaking culture.

English Learners improve their pronunciation in a nonthreatening atmosphere in which participation is encouraged. Opportunities to interact with native English speakers provide easy access to language models and give English Learners practice using English. However, students should not be forced to participate. Pressure to perform—or to perform in a certain way—can inhibit participation. In any classroom, teacher sensitivity to pronunciation differences contributes to a more productive learning environment.

Phonics, word recognition, and spelling are influenced by what students know about the sounds, word structure, and spelling in their primary languages. For example, beginning readers who speak Spanish and are familiar with its spelling will often spell short o with an a, a letter that in Spanish makes the short o sound. Similarly, English Learners who are unaccustomed to English consonant digraphs and blends (e.g., /ch/ and s-blends) spell /ch/ as sh because /sh/ is the sound they know that is closest to /ch/. Students learn about the way pronunciation influences their reading and spelling, beginning with large contrasts among sounds, then they study the finer discriminations. As vocabulary advances, the meaning of words leads students to the sound contrasts. For example, shoe and chew may sound alike initially, but meaning indicates otherwise. Students' reading and discussions of what they read advances their word knowledge as well as their knowledge in all language and literacy systems, including phonics, pronunciation, grammar, and vocabulary.

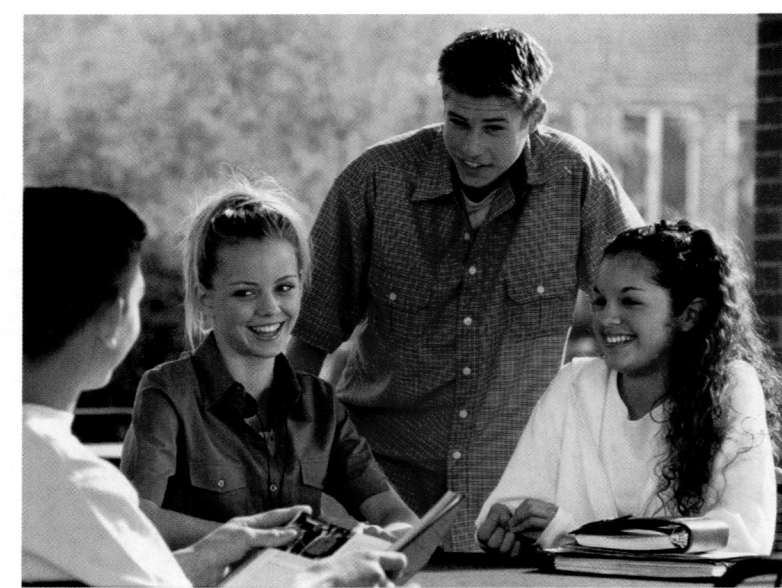

Phonics Transfers: Sound Transfers

This chart indicates areas where a positive transfer of sounds and symbols occurs for English Learners from their native languages into English. This symbol (✔) identifies a positive transfer. "Approximate" indicates that the sound is similar.

Consonants

Sound Transfers	Spanish	Cantonese	Vietnamese	Hmong	Korean	Khmer
/b/ as in bat	✔	approximate	approximate	approximate	approximate	✔
/k/ as in cake, kitten, peck	✔	✔	✔	✔	✔	✔
/d/ as in dog	✔	approximate	approximate	✔	approximate	✔
/f/ as in farm	✔	✔	✔	✔		
/g/ as in girl	✔	approximate	✔	approximate	approximate	
/h/ as in ham	✔	✔	✔	✔	✔	approximate
/j/ as in jet, page, ledge		approximate	approximate		approximate	
/l/ as in lion	✔	✔	✔	✔	✔	
/m/ as in mat	✔	✔	✔	✔	✔	✔
/n/ as in night	✔	✔	✔	✔	✔	✔
/p/ as in pen	✔	✔	✔	approximate	✔	✔
/kw/ as in queen	✔	approximate	✔		✔	✔
/r/ as in rope	approximate					✔
/s/ as in sink, city	✔	✔	✔	✔	✔	approximate
/t/ as in ton	✔	✔	approximate	approximate	✔	✔
/v/ as in vine	✔		✔	✔		
/w/ as in wind	✔	✔			✔	✔
/ks/ as in six	✔				✔	✔
/y/ as in yak	✔	✔		✔	✔	✔
/z/ as in zebra			✔			

Digraphs

/ch/ as in cheek, patch	✔	approximate		✔	✔	✔
/sh/ as in shadow			✔	✔	✔	
/hw/ as in whistle					✔	✔
/th/ as in path	approximate		approximate			
/TH/ as in that	approximate					

Digraphs (continued)

Sound Transfers	Spanish	Cantonese	Vietnamese	Hmong	Korean	Khmer
/ng/ as in sting	✔	✔	✔	✔	✔	approximate

Short Vowels

Sound Transfers	Spanish	Cantonese	Vietnamese	Hmong	Korean	Khmer
/a/ as in cat	approximate		approximate	✔	✔	
/e/ as in net	✔	approximate	approximate		✔	
/i/ as in kid	approximate	approximate			✔	
/o/ as in spot	approximate	approximate	approximate	approximate	approximate	✔
/u/ as in cup	approximate	approximate	✔		✔	✔

Long Vowels

Sound Transfers	Spanish	Cantonese	Vietnamese	Hmong	Korean	Khmer
/ā/ as in lake, nail, bay	✔	approximate	approximate	approximate	✔	✔
/ē/ as in bee, meat, cranky	✔	approximate	✔	✔	✔	✔
/ī/ as in kite, tie, light, dry	✔	approximate	✔	✔	✔	✔
/ō/ as in home, road, row	✔	approximate	approximate		✔	
/ū/ as in dune, fruit, blue	✔	approximate	✔	✔	✔	✔
/yü/ as in mule, cue	✔	approximate			✔	

r-Controlled Vowels

Sound Transfers	Spanish	Cantonese	Vietnamese	Hmong	Korean	Khmer
/är/ as in far	approximate	approximate				
/ôr/ as in corn	approximate	approximate				
/ûr/ as in stern, bird, suburb	approximate	approximate				
/âr/ as in air, bear						
/îr/ as in deer, ear						

Variant Vowels

Sound Transfers	Spanish	Cantonese	Vietnamese	Hmong	Korean	Khmer
/oi/ as in boil, toy	✔	approximate	approximate		✔	✔
/ou/ as in loud, down	✔	approximate	✔	approximate	✔	✔
/ô/ as in law	approximate	✔	✔	approximate	approximate	✔
/ô/ as in laundry	approximate	approximate	✔	approximate	approximate	✔
/ôl/ as in salt, call	approximate	approximate			approximate	✔
/o͞o/ as in moon, drew	✔	approximate	approximate	✔	✔	✔
/oo/ as in look		approximate	approximate		approximate	✔
/ə/ as in askew			approximate		✔	

Phonics Transfers: Sound Symbol Match

Consonants						
Sound Transfers	**Spanish**	**Cantonese**	**Vietnamese**	**Hmong**	**Korean**	**Khmer**
/b/ as in bat	✔		✔			
/k/ as in cake	✔		✔			
/k/ as in kitten	✔		✔	✔		
/k/ as in peck						
/d/ as in dog	✔		✔	✔		
/f/ as in farm	✔			✔		
/g/ as in girl	✔		✔			
/h/ as in ham			✔	✔		
/j/ as in jet, page, ledge						
/l/ as in lion	✔		✔	✔		
/m/ as in mat	✔		✔	✔		
/n/ as in night	✔		✔	✔		
/p/ as in pen	✔		✔	✔		
/kw/ as in queen			✔			
/r/ as in rope	approximate					
/s/ as in sink, city	✔		✔			
/t/ as in ton	✔		✔	✔		
/v/ as in vine	✔		✔	✔		
/w/ as in wind	✔					
/ks/ as in six	✔					
/y/ as in yak	✔			✔		
/z/ as in zebra						

Digraphs

Sound Transfers	Spanish	Cantonese	Vietnamese	Hmong	Korean	Khmer
/ch/ as in cheek, patch	✔					
/sh/ as in shadow						
/hw/ as in whistle						
/th/ as in path			✔			
/TH/ as in that						
/ng/ as in sting	✔		✔			

Short Vowels

Sound Transfers	Spanish	Cantonese	Vietnamese	Hmong	Korean	Khmer
/a/ as in cat			✔	✔		
/e/ as in net	✔		✔			
/i/ as in kid						
/o/ as in spot			✔	✔		
/u/ as in cup						

Long Vowels

Sound Transfers	Spanish	Cantonese	Vietnamese	Hmong	Korean	Khmer
/ā/ as in lake						
/ā/ as in nail						
/ā/ as in bay						
/ē/ as in bee						
/ē/ as in meat						
/ē/ as in cranky						
/ī/ as in kite, tie, light, dry						
/ō/ as in home, road, row						
/ū/ as in dune			✔	✔		
/ū/ as in fruit, blue						
/yü/ as in mule, cue						

r-Controlled Vowels

Sound Transfers	Spanish	Cantonese	Vietnamese	Hmong	Korean	Khmer
/är/ as in far	✔					
/ôr/ as in corn	✔					
/ûr/ as in stern	✔					
/ûr/ as in bird, suburb						
/âr/ as in air, bear						
/îr/ as in deer, ear						

Variant Vowels

Sound Transfers	Spanish	Cantonese	Vietnamese	Hmong	Korean	Khmer
/oi/ as in boil	✔		✔			
/oi/ as in toy	✔					
/ou/ as in loud						
/ou/ as in down						
/ô/ as in law						
/ô/ as in laundry						
/ôl/ as in salt	✔					
/ôl/ as in call						
/o͞o/ as in moon, drew						
/oo/ as in look						
/ə/ as in askew						

Grammar Transfers: Grammatical Form

This chart can be used to address common mistakes that some English Learners make when they transfer grammatical forms from their native languages into English.

Nouns

Grammatical Form	Transfer Mistakes in English	Native Language	Cause of Difficulty
Plural Marker -s	**Forgets plural marker *-s*** *I have 3 sister.*	Cantonese, Haitian Creole, Hmong, Korean, Vietnamese, Khmer	Native language does not use a plural marker.
Countable and Uncountable Nouns	**Confuses countable and uncountable nouns** *the homeworks* or *the informations*	Haitian Creole, Spanish	Countable and uncountable nouns are different in English and native language.
Possessives	**Uses prepositions to describe possessives** *the book of my brother* as opposed to *my brother's book*	Haitian Creole, Hmong, Spanish, Vietnamese	Possession is often described using a prepositional phrase.
	Avoids using *'s* *dog my father* as opposed to *my father's dog*	Haitian Creole, Vietnamese, Khmer	A noun follows the object in the native language.

Articles

	Consistently omits articles *He has book. They want dog not cat.*	Cantonese, Haitian Creole, Hmong, Korean, Vietnamese, Khmer	There is no article in the native language or no difference between the and a.
	Overuses articles *The English is difficult. The soccer is popular in the Europe.*	Haitian Creole, Hmong, Spanish	Some languages use articles that are omitted in English.
a/an	**Mistakes *one* for *a/an*** *She is one nurse.*	Haitian Creole, Hmong, Vietnamese	The native language either does not use articles or uses articles differently.

Pronouns

Gender-Specific Pronouns	Transfer Mistakes	Native Language	Cause of Difficulty
Gender-Specific Pronouns	**Uses pronouns with the inappropriate gender** *He is my sister.*	Cantonese, Haitian Creole, Hmong, Korean, Spanish, Khmer	The third person pronoun in the native language is gender free, or the personal pronoun is omitted.
	Uses inappropriate gender, particularly with neutral nouns *The day is sunny. She is beautiful.*	Spanish	Nouns have feminine or masculine gender in the native language, and the gender may be carried over into English.

Pronouns

Grammatical Form	Transfer Mistakes in English	Native Language	Cause of Difficulty
Object Pronouns	**Confuses subject and object pronouns** *Her talks to me.*	Cantonese, Hmong, Khmer	The same pronoun form is used for subject and object in the native language.
	Omits object pronouns *That girl is very rude, so nobody likes.*	Korean, Vietnamese	The native language does not use direct objects.
Pronoun and Number Agreement	**Uses the wrong number for pronouns** *I saw many red birds. It was pretty.*	Cantonese, Korean	The native language does not require number agreement.
Subject Pronouns	**Omits subject pronouns** *Mom isn't home. Is at work.*	Korean, Spanish	Subject pronouns may be dropped because in the native language the verb ending gives information about the number and/or gender.
Pronouns in Clauses	**Omits pronouns in clauses** *If don't do homework, they will not learn.*	Cantonese, Vietnamese	The native language does not need a subject in the subordinate clause.
Pronouns and Nouns	**Overuses pronouns with nouns** *This school, it very good.*	Hmong, Vietnamese	This is popular in speech in some languages. The speaker mentions a topic, then makes a comment about it.
	Avoids pronouns and repeats nouns *Carla visits her sister every Sunday, and Carla makes a meal.*	Korean, Vietnamese	In the native language, the speaker repeats nouns and does not use pronouns.
Pronoun one	**Omits the pronoun one** *I saw two dogs, and I like the small.*	Spanish	Adjectives can stand alone in the native language, but English requires a *noun* or *one.*
Possessive Forms	**Confuses possessive forms** *The book is my.*	Cantonese, Hmong, Vietnamese	Cantonese and Hmong speakers tend to omit the final *n* sound, which may create confusion between my and mine.

Verbs

Grammatical Form	Transfer Mistakes in English	Native Language	Cause of Difficulty
Present Tense	**Omits -s in present tense, third person agreement** *He like pizza.*	Cantonese, Haitian Creole, Hmong, Korean, Vietnamese, Khmer	Subject-verb agreement is not used in the native language.
Irregular Verbs	**Has problems with irregular subject-verb agreement** *Tom and Sue has a new car.*	Cantonese, Hmong, Korean, Khmer	Verbs' forms do not change to show the number of the subject in the native language.
Inflectional Endings	**Omits tense markers** *I study English yesterday.*	Cantonese, Haitian Creole, Hmong, Korean, Vietnamese, Khmer	The native language does not use inflectional endings to change verb tense.
Present and Future Tenses	**Incorrectly uses the present tense for the future tense** *I go next week.*	Cantonese, Korean	The native language may use the present tense to imply the future tense.
Negative Statements	**Omits helping verbs in negative statements** *Sue no coming to school.*	Cantonese, Korean, Spanish	The native language does not use helping verbs in negative statements.
Present-Perfect Tense	**Avoids the present-perfect tense** *Marcos live here for three months.*	Haitian Creole, Vietnamese	The native language does not use the present-perfect verb form.
Past-Continuous Tense	**Uses the past-continuous tense for recurring action in the past** *When I was young, I was talking a lot.*	Korean, Spanish	In the native language, the past-continuous tense is used but in English the expression used to or the simple past tense is used.
Main Verb	**Omits the main verb** *Talk in class not good.*	Cantonese	Cantonese does not require an infinitive marker when using a verb as a noun. Speakers may confuse the infinitive for the main verb.
Main Verbs in Clauses	**Uses two or more main verbs in one clause without any connectors** *I took a book went studied at the library.*	Hmong	In Hmong, verbs can be used consecutively without conjunctions or punctuation.
Linking Verbs	**Omits the linking verb** *He hungry.*	Cantonese, Haitian Creole, Hmong, Vietnamese, Khmer	In some languages, be is implied in the adjective form. In other languages, the concept is expressed with a verb.
Helping Verb in Passive Voice	**Omits the helping verb in the passive voice** *The homework done.*	Cantonese, Vietnamese	In Cantonese and Vietnamese, the passive voice does not require a helping verb.

Verbs

Grammatical Form	Transfer Mistakes in English	Native Language	Cause of Difficulty
Passive Voice	**Avoids the passive voice** *They speak English here.* *One speaks English here.* **English is spoken here.**	Haitian Creole	The passive voice does not exist in the native language.
Transitive Verbs	**Confuses transitive and intransitive verbs** *The child broke. The child broke <u>the plate</u>.*	Cantonese, Korean, Spanish	Verbs that require a direct object differ between English and the native language.
Phrasal Verbs	**Confuses related phrasal verbs** *I ate at the apple.* *I ate up the apple.*	Korean, Spanish	Phrasal verbs are not used in the native language, and there is often confusion over their meaning.
Have **and** *be*	**Uses have instead of be** *I have thirst. He has right.*	Spanish	Spanish and English have different uses for **have** and **be**.

Adjectives

Grammatical Form	Transfer Mistakes in English	Native Language	Cause of Difficulty
Word Order	**Places adjectives after nouns** *I saw a car red.*	Haitian Creole, Hmong, Spanish, Vietnamese, Khmer	Nouns often precede adjectives in the native language.
	Consistently places adjectives after nouns **This is a lesson new.**	Cantonese, Korean	Adjectives always follow nouns in the native language.
-er **and** *-est* **Endings**	**Avoids *-er* and *-est* endings** *I am more old than you.*	Hmong, Korean, Spanish, Khmer	The native language shows comparative and superlative forms with separate words.
-ing **and** *ed* **Endings**	**Confuses -ing and -ed forms** *Math is bored.*	Cantonese, Korean, Spanish, Khmer	Adjectives in the native language do not have active and passive meanings.

Adverbs

Grammatical Form	Transfer Mistakes in English	Native Language	Cause of Difficulty
Adjectives and Adverbs	**Uses an adjective where an adverb is needed** *Talk quiet.*	Haitian Creole, Hmong, Khmer	Adjectives and adverb forms are interchangeable in the native language.
Word Order	**Places adverbs before verbs** *He quickly ran.* *He ran quickly.*	Cantonese, Korean	Adverbs usually come before verbs in the native language, and this tendency is carried over into English.

Prepositions

Grammatical Form	Transfer Mistakes in English	Native Language	Cause of Difficulty
	Omits prepositions *I like come school.*	Cantonese	Cantonese does not use prepositions the way that English does.

How to Use the Grammar Transfer Charts

The grammar of many languages differs widely from English. For example, a student's primary language may use a different word order than English, may not use parts of speech in the same way, or may use different verb tenses. The Grammar Transfer Charts are designed to help you anticipate and understand possible student errors in speaking and writing standard English. With all grammar exercises, the emphasis is on oral communication, both as a speaker and listener.

1. Highlight Transferrable Skills

If the grammar skill transfers from the student's primary language to English, state that during the lesson. In many lessons an English Learner feature will indicate which skills do and do not transfer.

2. Preteach Non-Transferrable Skills

Prior to teaching a grammar lesson, check the chart to determine if the skill transfers from the student's primary language into English. If it does not, preteach the skill. Provide sentence frames and ample structured opportunities to use the skill in spoken English. Students need to talk, talk, and talk some more to master these skills.

3. Provide Additional Practice and Time

If the skill does NOT transfer from the student's primary language into English, the student will require more time and practice mastering it. Continue to review the skill using additional resources, such as the grammar lessons in the **Grammar and Language Workbook** in upcoming weeks.

4. Use Contrastive Analysis

Tell students when a skill does not transfer and include contrastive analysis work to make the student aware of how to correct their speaking and writing for standard English. For example, when a student uses an incorrect grammatical form, write the student sentence, then write the correct English form underneath. Explain the difference between the student's primary language and English. Have the student correct several other sentences using this skill.

5. Increase Writing and Speaking Opportunities

Increase the amount of structured writing and speaking opportunities for students needing work on specific grammatical forms. Sentence starters and paragraph frames, such as those found in the lessons, are ideal for both written and oral exercises.

6. Focus on Meaning

Always focus on the meanings of sentences in all exercises. As they improve and fine-tune their English speaking and writing skills, work with students on basic comprehension of spoken and written English.

To help students move to the next level of language acquisition and master English grammatical forms, recast their responses during classroom discussions or provide additional language for them to use as they respond further. Provide leveled-language sentence frames orally or in writing for students to use as they respond to questions and prompts. Below are samples.

English Learner Response Chart

Beginning (will respond by pointing or saying one word answers)	**Sample Frames** (simple, short sentences) *I see a _____.* *This is a _____.* *I like the _____.*
Early Intermediate (will respond with phrases or simple sentences)	**Sample Frames** (simple sentences with adjectives and adverbs added, and compound subjects or predicates) *I see a _____ _____.* *The _____ animal is _____.* *There are _____ and _____.*
Intermediate (will respond with simple sentences and limited academic language)	**Sample Frames** (harder sentences with simple phrases in consistent patterns; some academic language included) *The animal's prey is _____ because _____.* *The main idea is _____ because _____.* *He roamed the park so that _____.*
Early Advanced (will begin to use more sophisticated sentences and some academic language)	**Sample Frames** (complex sentences with increased academic language, beginning phrases and clauses, and multiple-meaning words) *When the violent storm hit, _____.* *As a result of the revolution, the army_____.* *Since most endangered animals are _____, they _____.*
Advanced (will have mastered some more complex sentence structures and is increasing the amount of academic language used)	Use the questions and prompts provided in the lessons for the whole group. Provide additional support learning and using academic language. These words are boldfaced throughout the lessons and sentence starters are often provided.

Classroom Resources: Print

Blackline Masters

Unit Teaching Resources

These blackline master booklets provide all the teaching materials you need to reinforce the content in each unit of *Glencoe Literature*. Worksheets include the following:

Unit Introduction
Big Idea Foldable
Big Idea School-to-Home Connection
- English
- Spanish
- Vietnamese
- Tagalog
- Cantonese
- Haitian Creole
- Hmong
Challenge Planner
Academic Vocabulary Development
Part Opener
Literary Focus
English Language Coach
Literary History
Comparing Literature Graphic Organizer
Grammar Workshop Practice
Media Workshop Practice
Selection Summaries
- English
- Spanish
- Vietnamese
- Tagalog
- Cantonese
- Haitian Creole
- Hmong
Literary Element
Reading Strategy
Selection Vocabulary Practice
Grammar Practice
Vocabulary Strategy
Selection Quick Check
- English
- Spanish
Spelling Practice
Writing Workshop Graphic Organizer
Writing Workshop Rubric
Speaking, Listening, and Viewing Activities
Speaking, Listening, and Viewing Workshop Rubric

Practice Books

Read and Write

INTERACTIVE These leveled consumable worktexts provide structured instruction and practice with selected readings from the anthology.

- On-Level provides fast-track instruction for on-level students.

- Approaching provides scaffolding for struggling or reluctant readers.

- English Learners helps students whose primary language is not English read and comprehend selection.

The Novel Companion

This worktext provides accelerated instruction for advanced students through novel study. With the tools for a detailed analysis of a novel and related reading for every unit of the anthology, students explore in more depth the Big Ideas around which the anthology is organized.

Spelling Power Workbook

Provides additional support for practice and mastery of spelling.

Writing

Glencoe Language Arts Writing Resources

This writing resource contains the following transparencies:

Writing Process Strategies Transparencies provide graphic organizers to help you guide your students through the various stages of the writing process.

Writing Practice Transparencies provide opportunities for students to practice writing in modes that are appropriate for their grade level including Narrative, Expository, and Persuasive Writing and Responding to Literary Texts.

Process of Revision Transparencies use base transparencies and corresponding overlays to show and explain actual revisions and edits. The set of revision transparencies guides students through the process of improving a sample essay. A blank Student Revision transparency is included so student volunteers can make their own revisions to improve the quality of an essay.

Writing Constructed Responses

This sourcebook with blackline masters helps students respond effectively to short essay questions.

Success in Writing: Research and Reports

These blackline masters reinforce and extend the coverage of research presented in the student edition.

Grammar and Language Workbook

This workbook provides full coverage of grammar, usage, and mechanics rules, examples, and practice exercises.

Grammar and Composition Handbook

This handbook is a handy desk reference tool providing full coverage of the writing process as well as rules and practice exercises for grammar, usage, and mechanics.

Grammar and Writing Transparencies

Help reinforce the skills taught in the grammar links and writing workshops.

Classroom Resources: Print

Assessment

Assessment Resources

This assessment tool provides three types of tests:

- Diagnostic assessment by learning objectives
- Formative tests and answer keys for selections
- Summative unit tests and answer keys

Standardized Test Prep and Practice

These materials feature exercises and activities that get students ready for standardized exams.

ACT/SAT Preparation and Practice Workbook

Fluency Practice and Assessment

English Language Development

English Language Coach

These worksheets provide extra support for English Learners.

Independent Reading

Ethnic Anthologies

The following anthologies offer students introductions to the richness and variety of literature written by African, Asian, Hispanic, and Native Americans. A Teacher's Guide for each anthology suggests answers to questions accompanying each selection to help further student discussion.

- *Glencoe African American Literature*
- *Glencoe Asian American Literature*
- *Glencoe Hispanic American Literature*
- *Glencoe Native American Literature*

InTIME Magazines

This lively collection of articles drawn from TIME helps students develop skills for reading informational text.

Transparencies

Bellringer Transparencies

include warm-up exercises to engage students and to provide a quick review of previously taught skills.

Fine Art Transparencies

enhance visual literacy and provide a strong humanities approach to literature.

Literary Elements Transparencies

help reinforce literary elements that are the focus of each lesson.

Read Aloud, Think Aloud Transparencies

model active reading

Classroom Resources: Technology

Classroom Planning, Management, and Instruction

TeacherWorks Plus CD-ROM

- Plan and manage daily lessons and activities
- Access all program resources
- Edit lesson plans and worksheets
- Track the standards taught in your classroom

Classroom Presentation Toolkit CD-ROM or DVD-ROM

- Present customizable lessons via PowerPoint
- Launch transparencies, audio, video, and software at point-of-use during instruction

Digital Learning

Online Student Edition and StudentWorks Plus CD-ROM or DVD-ROM

- Full-text synced-audio selection read support
- Audio summaries in multiple languages
- Search, highlighting, and notes tools
- Multimedia links to video, activities, animations, and graphic graphic organizers
- Access student workbooks, Student Media Toolkit, and Student Presentation Builder
- Daily Assignments and Grade Log

Assessment and Progress Monitoring

ExamView Assessment Suite CD-ROM

- Administer ready-made diagnostic, formative, and summative assessments in English or Spanish

- Edit assessment items or create new items as needed
- Monitor student progress through a variety of reporting options
- Provides real assessment-driven remediation options

Progress Reporter Online Assessment

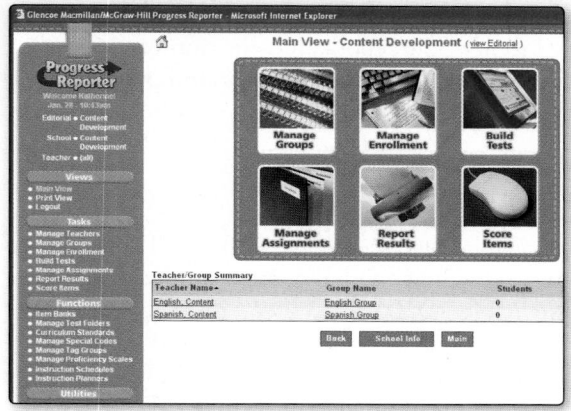

- Administer ready-made diagnostic, formative, and summative assessments online in English or Spanish
- Edit assessment items or create new items as needed
- Assessments administered online are scored automatically
- Essay questions are scored automatically
- Ready-made exams provide students with item rationales, explaining why each answer choice is correct or incorrect
- Automatically assigns reteaching and remediation based on student performance
- Monitor student progress by standard or by standard strand or through a variety of other reporting options

Literature Online: Assessment Resources

- End-of-Unit Assessment
- Test-taking Tips and Strategies

Literature and Reading

Literature Classics

- Choose from over 1,100 additional classic literature selections
- Search selections by author, title, date, genre, country, course/ grade level, and Big Question or Big Idea
- Reinforce instruction with Genre Focus Lesson Plans and blackline masters
- Available on CD-ROM and access via glencoe.com

Classroom Resources: Technology

Listening Library CD

- Help students improve overall comprehension and reading fluency with engaging recordings of the selections in *Glencoe Literature*
- Assist English Learners with audio selection summaries in their native language
- Use the Listening Library CDs in conjunction with the Listening Library Sourcebook, a collection of standards-based strategies and activities, found on your TeacherWorks™ Plus CD-ROM

Literature Launchers: Pre-Reading Videos DVD

- Each of the engaging video segments on this DVD brings the literature to life, providing a visual context for every Unit and key selections
- Use this DVD in conjunction with the Literature Launchers Teacher Guide, found on your TeacherWorks™ Plus CD-ROM, which provides teaching strategies and video-specific blackline masters.
- English and Spanish subtitles

Literature Library Teacher Resources CD-ROM

- Access all Glencoe Literature Library Study Guides
- Develop vocabulary with Vocabulary Puzzlemaker
- Assess with ExamView Assessment Suite

BookLink K-12 CD-ROM

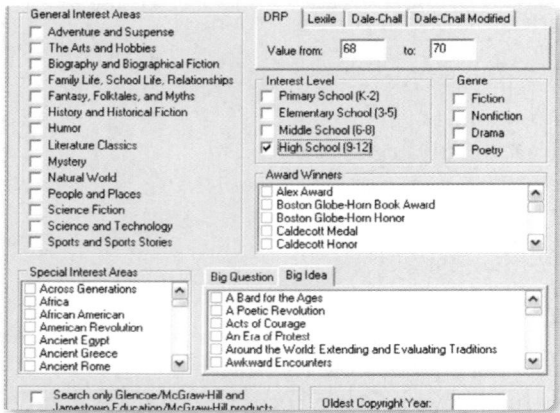

- Create customized reading lists for your students from a database of over 30,000 titles

- Search for award-winning titles and for books on state recommended reading lists
- Organize reading lists by students' reading level, author, genre, theme, or area of interest
- Find Degrees of Reading Power™ (DRP), Lexile™, and Dale-Chall scores for all selections in the Glencoe Literature program

Skill Level Up! A Skills-Based Language Arts Game CD-ROM

- Offers an innovative approach to Language Arts and Reading skills practice, assessment and remediation
- Skill Level Up!'s networkable game environment provides a context and purpose for learning by immersing students in an engaging adventure
- Features two access modes: the immersive story mode, which covers all the skills in the context of the adventure game play, or the skill-based assignment mode, which allows teachers to assign discrete activities according to their curriculum plan
- Adapts to each student's performance by offering remediation when necessary or enrichment activities when applicable
- Manage and track student performance using convenient assignment, tracking, and reporting functions featured in the program's management system
- Covers the following Reading Skills and Literary Elements:
  - Connecting
  - Questioning
  - Predicting
  - Point of View
  - Visualizing

- Rhyme
- Dialog
- Main Idea and Supporting Details/Paraphrasing and Summarizing
- Plot
- Conflict
- Interpreting
- Drawing Conclusions
- Setting
- Fact and Opinion
- Theme
- Author's Purpose and Perspective
- Voice, Style, Tone, Narrator
- Description, Imagery, Sensory Details
- Symbolism
- Inferring
- Figurative Language
- Analyzing Text Structure
- Meter and Rhythm
- Character and Characterization
- Sound Devices
- Genre
- Synthesizing

Literature Online: Literature, Reading, and Selection Resources (glencoe.com)

- Author and Artist Search
- Web Quest
- Selection Quizzes
- Selection Vocabulary eFlashcards
- Selection Reading-Writing Connection activities
- Reading Skills Review
- Interactive Reading Practice
- Literary Elements eFlashcards
- Fluency Practice
- Games

Vocabulary Development

Glencoe Interactive Vocabulary CD-ROM

- Generate flashcard sets from a visual glossary of selection, academic, content area, and social vocabulary terms
- Includes audio support in multiple languages for all terms
- Provides instructional modules and practice via an engaging game environment:

- signal words
- cognates/false cognates
- multiple meaning words
- synonyms and antonyms
- idioms
- analogies
- figures of speech
- context clues
- etymology
- troublesome words
- text features
- compound words
- homonyms

Vocabulary PuzzleMaker

- Create crossword puzzles, word search puzzles, and jumble puzzles in an instant
- Choose from selection and academic vocabulary (in both English and Spanish) and literary terms
- Available on CD-ROM and for download via glencoe.com

Skill Level Up! A Skills-Based Language Arts Game CD-ROM

- Using Context Clues
- Multiple Meaning Words
- Examining Words Origins
- Words with Special Meanings
- Denotation and Connotation
- Using Analogies
- Synonyms
- Antonyms
- Homonyms
- Word Parts/Structural Analysis: Base Words
- Word Parts/Structural Analysis: Prefixes
- Word Parts/Structural Analysis: Suffixes

Classroom Resources: Technology

Literature Online: Vocabulary and Spelling Resources (glencoe.com)
- Multi-Language Glossary
- Selection Vocabulary eFlashcards
- Academic Vocabulary eFlashcards
- Vocabulary Games
- Spelling Lessons
- Spelling Games

Writing

Glencoe Online Essay Grader powered by Bookette SkillWriter™ (glencoewriting.com)

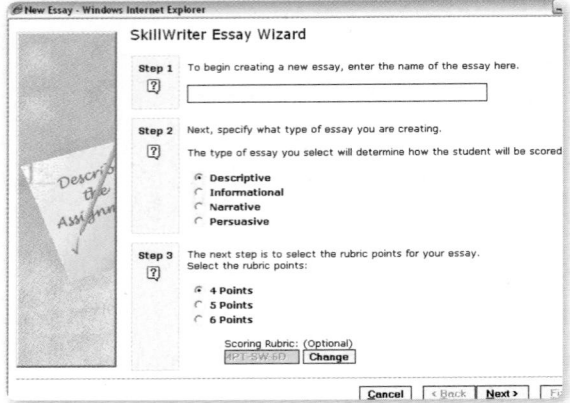

- Score student writing assignments and provide individualized feedback to each student automatically
- Assign prompts from Glencoe Literature Writing Workshops or create your own prompts!
- Manage demographic data, assign tests and run a variety of progress monitoring reports using the program's management system.

Literature Online: Writing and Research Resources (glencoe.com)
- Annotated Writing Models
- Interactive Writing Models
- Writing and Research Handbook
- Research Tips and Strategies
- Graphic Organizers
- Transition Bank
- Grammar Troubleshooter
- Sentence-Combining Practice

- Editing and Proofreading Marks
- Publishing Options

Speaking, Listening and Viewing

Skill Level Up! A Skills-Based Language Arts Game CD-ROM
- Analyzing Persuasive Techniques
- Listening Critically
- Examining Visuals in Literature and Media: Maps, Charts, Graphs
- Examining Visuals in Literature and Media: Visual Techniques

Student Presentation Builder
- Assign additional Unit-based multimedia presentation projects
- Includes a PowerPoint™ tutorial, a PowerPoint™ presentation template, and an image bank
- Available on StudentWorks Plus or via the Online Student Edition
- Teacher Guide is available on TeacherWorks Plus

Literature Online: Speaking, Listening, and Viewing Resources (glencoe.com)
- Project Ideas and Templates
- Presentation Tips and Strategies

Media Literacy

Glencoe Media Workshop DVD
- Engage students in the study and critical review of media from film footage of important events in history to analysis of commercials
- English and Spanish subtitles

Student Media Toolkit
- Provides additional interactive media analysis activities
- Includes media generator tools

Literature Online: Media Literacy Resources (glencoe.com)
- Media Analysis Guides
- Project Ideas

Library Resources

Glencoe Literature Library

Each *Glencoe Literature* Library volume consists of at least one complete extended-length reading accompanied by several related readings from a broad range of genres. A separate Study Guide for each book provides teaching notes and reproducible activity pages for students. Students may also find these activity pages at glencoe.com.

The Adventures of Huckleberry Finn by Mark Twain **DRP 54***

All Quiet on the Western Front by Erich Maria Remarque **DRP 52**

. . . And the Earth Did Not Devour Him by Tomas Rivera **DRP 52**

Animal Farm by George Orwell **DRP 60**

The Autobiography of Benjamin Franklin by Benjamin Franklin **DRP 64**

The Autobiography of Miss Jane Pittman by Ernest J. Gaines **DRP 49**

The Awakening by Kate Chopin **DRP 58**

Beowulf

Billy Budd by Herman Melville **DRP 68**

The Bridge of San Luis Rey by Thornton Wilder **DRP 55**

The Brothers Karamazov by Fyodor Dostoevsky **DRP 55**

The Canterbury Tales by Geoffrey Chaucer **DRP 59**

The Chosen by Chaim Potok **DRP 56**

A Country Doctor by Sarah Orne Jewett **DRP 59**

Cyrano de Bergerac by Edmond Rostand **DRP**

Ethan Frome by Edith Wharton **DRP 59**

Fallen Angels by Walter Dean Myers **DRP 47**

Frankenstein by Mary Shelley **DRP 64**

Great Expectations by Charles Dickens **DRP 60**

Gulliver's Travels by Jonathan Swift **DRP 67**

Hamlet by William Shakespeare

Heart of Darkness and The Secret Sharer by Joseph Conrad **DRP 58**

A House for Mr Biswas by V. S. Naipaul **DRP 58**

The House of the Seven Gables by Nathaniel Hawthorne **DRP 65**

The Importance of Being Earnest by Oscar Wilde **DRP**

Invisible Man by Ralph Ellison **DRP 57**

Jane Eyre by Charlotte Brontë **DRP 61**

Julius Caesar by William Shakespeare

The Jungle by Upton Sinclair **DRP 59**

The Mayor of Casterbridge by Thomas Hardy **DRP 60**

The Metamorphosis by Franz Kafka **DRP 57**

A Midsummer Night's Dream by William Shakespeare

My Ántonia by Willa Cather **DRP 57**

Narrative of the Life of Frederick Douglass by Frederick Douglass **DRP 62**

Nectar in a Sieve by Kamala Markandaya **DRP 56**

Night by Elie Wiesel **DRP 51**

One Day in the Life of Ivan Denisovich by Aleksandr Solzhenitsyn **DRP 56**

Our Town by Thornton Wilder

Picture Bride by Yoshiko Uchida **DRP 55**

Pride and Prejudice by Jane Austen **DRP 61**

A Raisin in the Sun by Lorraine Hansberry

The Red Badge of Courage by Stephen Crane **DRP 60**

The Return of the Native by Thomas Hardy **DRP 61**

The Scarlet Letter by Nathaniel Hawthorne **DRP 67**

Sense and Sensibility by Jane Austen **DRP 63**

A Separate Peace by John Knowles **DRP 59**

Silas Marner by George Eliot **DRP 55**

The Souls of Black Folk by W. E. B. Du Bois **DRP 66**

The Story of My Life by Helen Keller **DRP 59**

The Strange Case of Dr Jekyll and Mr Hyde by Robert Louis Stevenson **DRP 63**

A Tale of Two Cities by Charles Dickens **DRP 62**

The Tempest by William Shakespeare

Things Fall Apart by Chinua Achebe **DRP 56**

The Time Machine and The War of the Worlds by H. G. Wells **DRP 59**

To Kill a Mockingbird by Harper Lee **DRP 51**

Walden by Henry David Thoreau **DRP 62**

The Way to Rainy Mountain by N. Scott Momaday **DRP 55**

Wuthering Heights by Emily Brontë **DRP 61**

The Yearling by Marjorie Kinnan Rawlings **DRP 53**

*Degrees of Reading Power® DRP values indicate the readability of prose text. The higher the value, the more difficult the text. Though the scale ranges from 0 to 100, texts widely available for use at grades nine through twelve typically range from 53 to 68. Some materials, however, may certainly fall outside of this range.

Literary Map of the United States

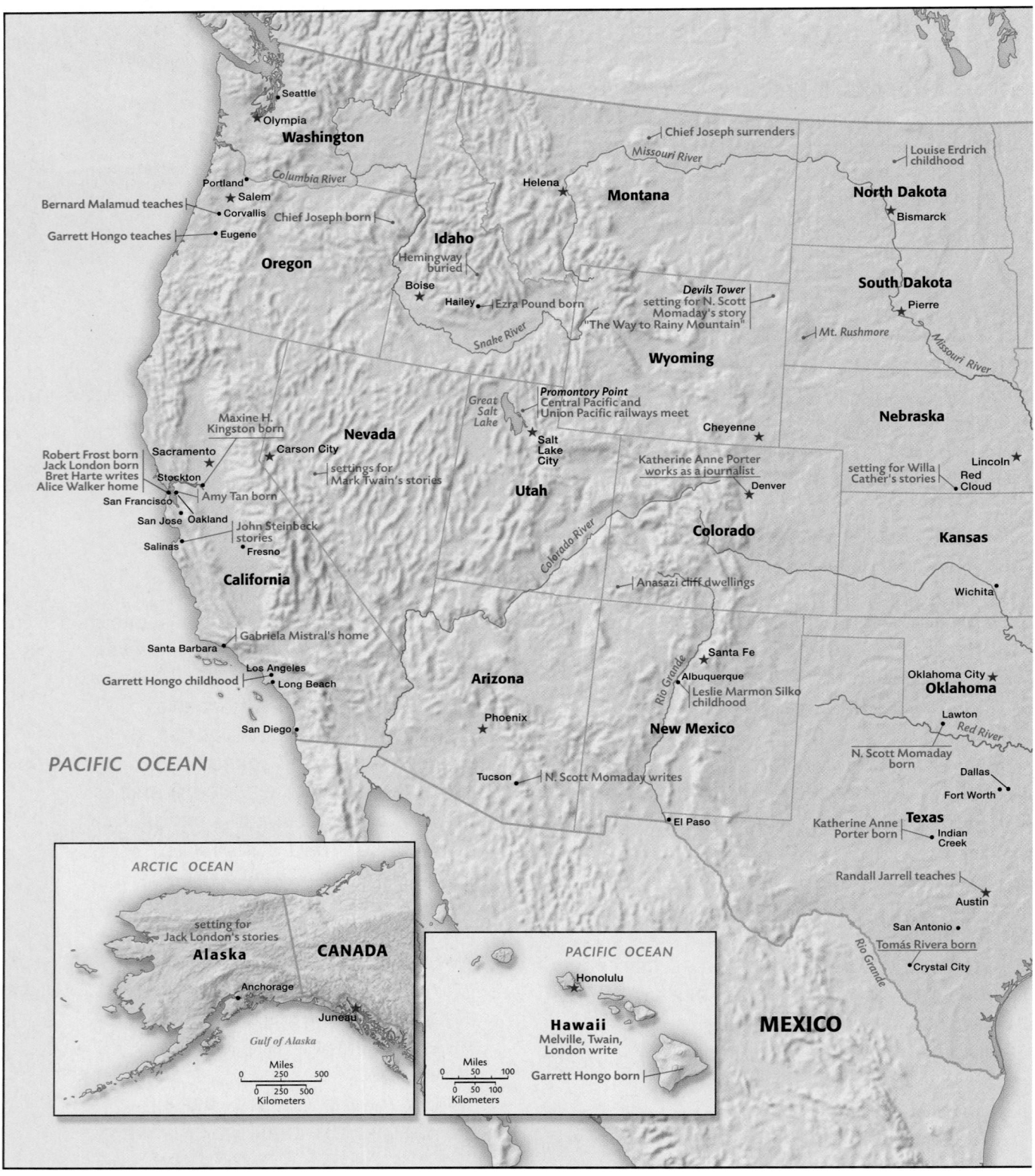

Seattle
★ Olympia
Washington

Chief Joseph surrenders
Missouri River

Louise Erdrich childhood

Portland
★ Salem
Bernard Malamud teaches
• Corvallis
Chief Joseph born
Garrett Hongo teaches • Eugene
Oregon

Helena ★
Montana

North Dakota
★ Bismarck

Columbia River

Hemingway buried
Idaho
Boise ★
Hailey • Ezra Pound born

Snake River

Devils Tower setting for N. Scott Momaday's story "The Way to Rainy Mountain"

South Dakota
★ Pierre

Mt. Rushmore

Missouri River

Wyoming

Promontory Point Central Pacific and Union Pacific railways meet

Great Salt Lake
Salt Lake City ★

Cheyenne ★

Nebraska

Maxine H. Kingston born
Nevada

Robert Frost born
Jack London born
Bret Harte writes
Alice Walker home
Sacramento ★
Carson City ★

settings for Mark Twain's stories

Utah

Katherine Anne Porter works as a journalist

setting for Willa Cather's stories
Lincoln ★
Red • Cloud

Stockton
San Francisco
San Jose • Oakland
Amy Tan born
John Steinbeck stories
Salinas • Fresno
California

Denver ★

Colorado

Kansas

Wichita •

Gabriela Mistral's home

Santa Barbara •

Anasazi cliff dwellings

Garrett Hongo childhood
Los Angeles • Long Beach

Arizona

Santa Fe •
Albuquerque •
Leslie Marmon Silko childhood
Rio Grande

Oklahoma City ★
Oklahoma

San Diego •

Phoenix ★

New Mexico

Lawton •
Red River

N. Scott Momaday born

Dallas •
Fort Worth •

PACIFIC OCEAN

Tucson • N. Scott Momaday writes

El Paso •

Katherine Anne Porter born
Texas
Indian Creek

Randall Jarrell teaches
★ Austin

San Antonio •
Rio Grande
Tomás Rivera born
• Crystal City

Alaska inset
ARCTIC OCEAN
setting for Jack London's stories
Alaska
CANADA
Anchorage •
Juneau ★
Gulf of Alaska

Miles
0   250   500
0   250   500
Kilometers

Hawaii inset
PACIFIC OCEAN
Honolulu •
Hawaii
Melville, Twain, London write
Garrett Hongo born

Miles
0   50   100
0   50   100
Kilometers

MEXICO
Rio Grande

CANADA

Bob Dylan born
Hibbing

Louise Erdrich born
Little Falls

F. Scott Fitzgerald childhood
St. Paul
Minneapolis
Minnesota

Tim O'Brien born
Austin

Lake Superior

Wisconsin
Eudora Welty studies
Madison
Milwaukee

Lake Michigan

Michigan
Lansing
Battle Creek
Detroit
Toledo

Lake Huron

Lake Ontario
Buffalo

Lake Erie
Cleveland
Lorain
Akron

Maine
Augusta
Gardiner

Vermont
Montpelier

New Hampshire

Concord
Massachusetts

Albany
New York
Boston

Providence
Hartford
Rhode Island

New York
Connecticut

Robert Hayden writes

Pennsylvania
Harrisburg
Trenton
New Jersey

Pittsburgh
Philadelphia

Archibald MacLeish born
Glencoe
Chicago
Oak Park
Ambrose Bierce childhood
Warsaw

Iowa
Des Moines
Sandra Cisneros childhood
Iowa City
Hemingway born
Omaha
Iowa Writers' Workshop
Galesburg

Illinois
Carl Sandburg born
Edgar Lee Masters childhood

Indiana
Indianapolis
Dayton

Toni Morrison born
Ohio
Columbus

Paul Laurence Dunbar born

Cincinnati

Ohio R.

West Virginia
Charleston

Baltimore
Annapolis
Dover
Delaware
Washington, D.C.
Maryland

1851 Women's Rights Convention

Mark Twain childhood
Lewistown
New Salem
Springfield
Gwendolyn Brooks born
Hannibal
Abraham Lincoln studies

Kansas City
Topeka
Jefferson City
St. Louis
Garnett
T. S. Eliot, Kate Chopin born

Edgar Lee Masters born
Missouri

Frankfort
Louisville
Paul Laurence Dunbar childhood

Kentucky

Lexington
Richmond

Virginia

Greensboro
Randall Jarrell teaches

see detailed map on next page

Langston Hughes born
Joplin

Robert Penn Warren born
Guthrie

Great Smoky Mtns.
Cherokee myths

Flat Rock
Raleigh
North Carolina
Charlotte

Tulsa

Randall Jarrell born
Robert Hayden teaches
Nashville
Tennessee

Carl Sandburg's last home

Arkansas
Memphis

Arkansas R.
Little Rock

setting for William Faulkner's stories

Oxford
Alabama

Martin Luther King Jr. born
Atlanta

Columbia
South Carolina

M. L. King Jr. jailed
Birmingham

Eatonton
Alice Walker born
Charleston
Ft. Sumter
First Civil War battle

Mississippi
Zora Neale Hurston born
Notasulga
Montgomery
Georgia

Mary Chesnut lives

Savannah
Flannery O'Connor born

Eudora Welty home
Jackson

Louisiana
Arna Bontemps born
Roxie
Richard Wright born

Tallahassee

Jacksonville
setting for Stephen Crane's story "The Open Boat"

Alexandria
Baton Rouge

James Weldon Johnson born

Zora Neale Hurston childhood

Toni Morrison teaches

Houston
New Orleans

setting for Kate Chopin's stories

William Faulkner meets Sherwood Anderson

Cabeza de Vaca lands

Florida
Lake Okeechobee

Eatonville

Gulf of Mexico

Miami

ATLANTIC OCEAN

Puerto Rico
Aurora Levins Morales childhood
Judith Ortiz Cofer born

Miles
0   25
Kilometers
0   25

N
W   E
S

Miles
0   50   100   150   200
0   100   200
Kilometers

Elizabeth Bishop writes
Hemingway writes

Key West

Map of the Eastern U.S.

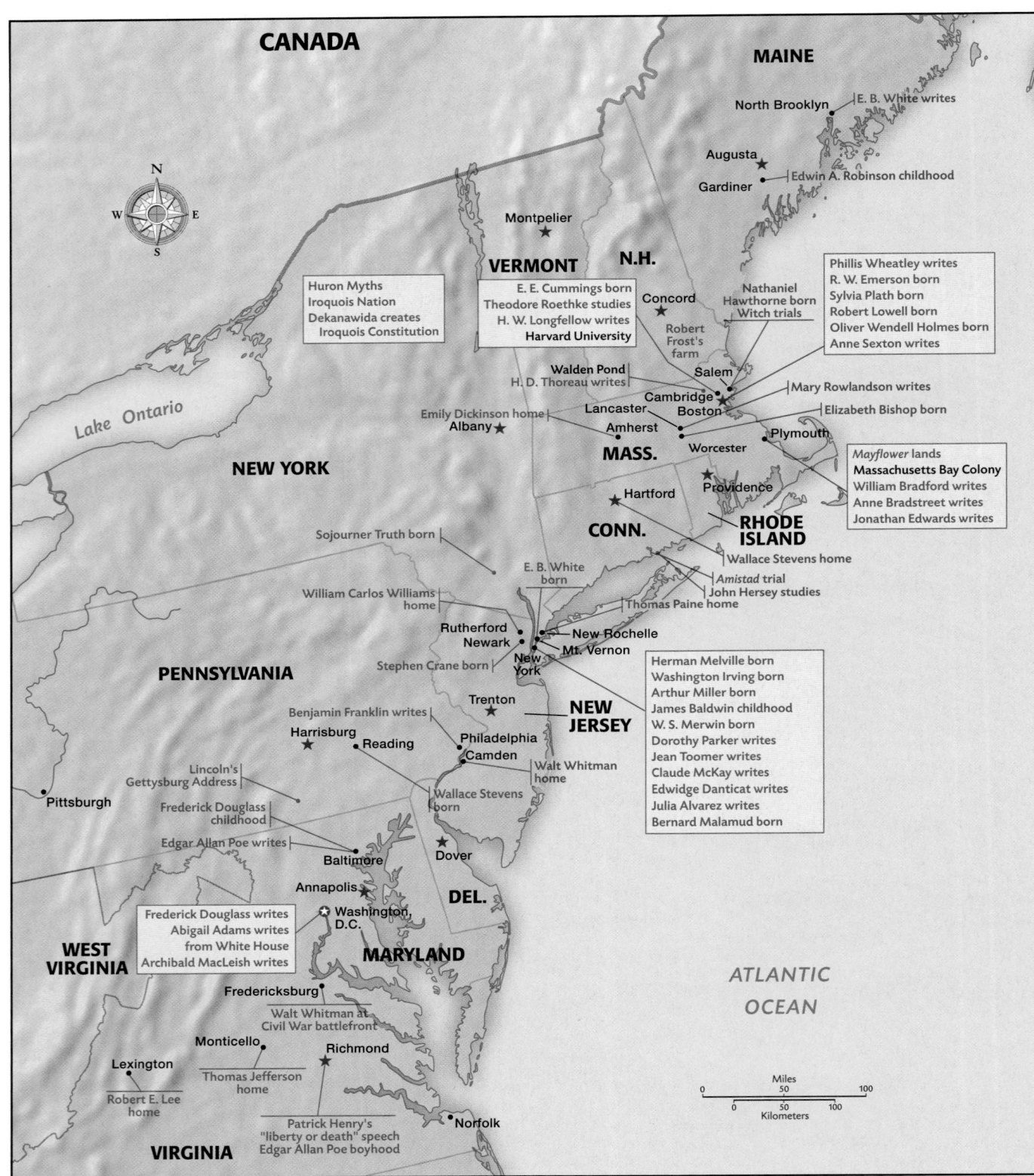

CANADA

MAINE

North Brooklyn · — E. B. White writes

Augusta ★

Gardiner · — Edwin A. Robinson childhood

Montpelier ★

VERMONT   N.H.

Concord ★

Phillis Wheatley writes
R. W. Emerson born
Sylvia Plath born
Robert Lowell born
Oliver Wendell Holmes born
Anne Sexton writes

Huron Myths
Iroquois Nation
Dekanawida creates
    Iroquois Constitution

E. E. Cummings born
Theodore Roethke studies
H. W. Longfellow writes
Harvard University

Nathaniel
Hawthorne born
Witch trials

Robert
Frost's
farm

Walden Pond
H. D. Thoreau writes

Salem

Mary Rowlandson writes

Cambridge
Boston

Lake Ontario

Emily Dickinson home
Albany ★

Lancaster
Amherst

Elizabeth Bishop born

NEW YORK

Worcester

Plymouth

MASS.

Hartford ★

Providence

Mayflower lands
Massachusetts Bay Colony
William Bradford writes
Anne Bradstreet writes
Jonathan Edwards writes

CONN.

RHODE
ISLAND

Sojourner Truth born

Wallace Stevens home

Amistad trial
John Hersey studies

E. B. White
born

William Carlos Williams
home

Thomas Paine home

Rutherford
Newark

New Rochelle

Mt. Vernon

PENNSYLVANIA

Stephen Crane born

New
York

Herman Melville born
Washington Irving born
Arthur Miller born
James Baldwin childhood
W. S. Merwin born
Dorothy Parker writes
Jean Toomer writes
Claude McKay writes
Edwidge Danticat writes
Julia Alvarez writes
Bernard Malamud born

Trenton ★

NEW
JERSEY

Benjamin Franklin writes

Harrisburg ★

Reading

Philadelphia

Camden

Lincoln's
Gettysburg Address

Walt Whitman
home

Pittsburgh

Frederick Douglass
childhood

Wallace Stevens
born

Edgar Allan Poe writes

Dover ★

Baltimore

DEL.

Annapolis ★

Frederick Douglass writes
Abigail Adams writes
    from White House
Archibald MacLeish writes

⊙ Washington,
   D.C.

WEST
VIRGINIA

MARYLAND

ATLANTIC
OCEAN

Fredericksburg

Walt Whitman at
Civil War battlefront

Monticello

Richmond ★

Lexington

Thomas Jefferson
home

Robert E. Lee
home

Norfolk

Patrick Henry's
"liberty or death" speech
Edgar Allan Poe boyhood

VIRGINIA

Miles
0   50   100
0   50   100
Kilometers

Be Cyber Safe and Smart

Cyber Safety

As you explore the *Glencoe Literature* program, you will have many opportunities to go online. When you use the Internet at school or home, you enter a kind of community—the cyber world. In this online world, you need to follow safety rules and protect yourself. Here are some tips to keep in mind:

▶ **Words to Know**

cyber world the world of computers and high-tech communications

cyber safety actions that protect Internet users from harm

cyber ethics responsible code of conduct for using the Internet

cyber bully a person who uses technology to frighten, bother, or harm someone else

cyber citizen a person who uses the Internet to communicate

☑ Be a responsible cyber citizen. Use the Internet to share knowledge that makes people's lives better. Respect other people's feelings and do not break any laws.

☑ Beware of cyber bullying. People can be hurt and embarrassed by comments that have been made public. You should immediately tell your teacher or counselor if you feel threatened by another student's computer postings.

☑ Do not give out personal information, such as your address and telephone number, without your parents' or guardians' permission.

☑ Tell your teacher, parent, or guardian right away if you find or read any information that makes you feel uneasy or afraid.

☑ Do not email your picture to anyone.

☑ Do not open email or text messages from strangers.

☑ Do not tell anyone your Internet password.

☑ Do not make illegal copies of computer games and programs, and software CDs.

LOG ON ▶ **Literature** Online

For more about internet safety and responsibility, go to glencoe.com

Skills Scope and Sequence

Readability Scores Key: Dale-Chall/DRP/Lexile

PART 1: The Sacred Earth and the Power of Storytelling

Selections and Features	Literary Elements
Unit Introduction pp. 4–18	Oral Storytelling **SE** pp. 11, 12 Poetry **TE** p. 13
LiteraryHistory: Native American Mythology pp. 20–21	Myth **SE** p. 20
Myth How the World Was Made by James Mooney 5.9/57/1250 pp. 22–26	Archetype **SE** p. 23 Metaphor **TE** p. 25
Cultural Perspective *from* **The Way to Rainy Mountain,** by N. Scott Momaday 5.5/61/1000 pp. 27–32	
Comparing Literature **The Sky Tree** (myth), retold by Joseph Bruchac 3.6/48/740 **How the Leopard Got His Claws** (myth), retold by Chinua Achebe and John Iroaganachi 3.2/46/540 **Prayer to the Pacific** (poem), by Leslie Marmon Silko pp. 34–46	Oral Tradition **SE** p. 34 Characterization **TE** p. 38 Personification **TE** p. 42 Sensory Details **TE** p. 44
Public Document *from* **The Iroquois Constitution** 8.2/63/1440 pp. 47–52	Author's Purpose **SE** p. 48
Vocabulary Workshop pp. 53–54	

PART 2: Life in the New World

Selections and Features	Literary Elements
Memoir *from* **La Relación,** by Alvar Núñez Cabeza de Vaca 6.1/55/1100 pp. 56–61	Point of View **SE** p. 57
Memoir *from* **Of Plymouth Plantation,** by William Bradford 11.6/62/1430 pp. 62–68	Diction **SE** p. 63 Point of View **TE** p. 65

Reading Skills and Strategies	Vocabulary	Writing Grammar	Speaking, Listening, and Viewing
Analyze Historical Context **SE** p. 10 Support the Main Idea **TE** pp. 12, 18	Phrases **TE** p. 10	Use Timelines **TE** p. 6 Analyze a Graph **TE** p. 8 Organize Ideas **TE** p. 16 Write an Essay **SE** p. 18	Analyze Art **SE** p. 4, **TE** pp. 5, 9, 13, 15
Analyze Literary Genres **SE** pp. 20–21		Respond to Literature **SE** p. 21	
Identify Sequence **SE** p. 23 Draw Conclusions **TE** p. 24	Connotation **TE** p. 23 Synonyms **SE** p. 26	Write a Story **SE** p. 26	
Analyze Cultural Traditions **SE** p. 27, **TE** p. 32 Analyze Graphic Information **TE** p. 28 Make Inferences **TE** p. 31		Visualize **TE** p. 30 Write a Summary **SE** p. 32	Analyze a Map **TE** p. 29 Analyze Art **TE** p. 31
Question **SE** p. 34 Identify Author's Purpose **TE** p. 39 Review **TE** p. 46	Academic Vocabulary **SE** p. 37 Antonyms **TE** p. 43	Write a Dialogue **SE** p. 37 Note-taking **TE** p. 42 Write an Essay **SE** p. 46 Write a Mythic Story **SE** p. 46	Analyze Art **TE** pp. 35, 40, 42, 45 Discussion **SE** p. 46
Draw Conclusions About Culture **SE** p. 48 Preview **TE** p. 48 Compare and Contrast **TE** p. 50	Parts of Speech **TE** p. 48 Synonyms **SE** p. 52	Write a Letter **SE** p. 52	Analyze a Photograph **TE** p. 51
	Academic Vocabulary **SE** pp. 53–54 Multiple-Meaning Words **SE** pp. 53–54		

Reading Skills and Strategies	Vocabulary	Writing Grammar	Speaking, Listening, and Viewing
Recognize Bias **SE** p. 57 Identify Sequence **TE** p. 58	Synonyms **SE** p. 61	Write a Story **SE** p. 61	Analyze Art **SE** p. 60
Monitor Comprehension **SE** p. 63	Analogies **TE** p. 63 Context Clues **SE** p. 68	Write a Letter **SE** p. 68	Analyze Art **SE** p. 66

Readability Scores Key: Dale-Chall/DRP/Lexile

PART 2: Life in the New World *(continued)*

Selections and Features	Literary Elements
Autobiography *from* **The Life of Olaudah Equiano,** by Olaudah Equiano **7.6/59/1250** pp. 69–79	Slave Narrative **SE** p. 70 Characterization **TE** p. 74 Point of View **SE** p. 78
Memoir *from* **A Narrative of the Captivity and Restoration of Mrs. Mary Rowlandson,** by Mary Rowlandson **7.9/57/1030** pp. 80–86	Allusion **SE** p. 81 Characterization **TE** p. 84
Grammar Workshop pp. 87–88	
Poems Upon the Burning of Our House and **To My Dear and Loving Husband,** by Anne Bradstreet, pp. 89–94	Metaphor **SE** p. 90 Speaker **TE** p. 91
Speech *from* **Sinners in the Hands of an Angry God,** by Jonathan Edwards **7.3/61/1280** pp. 95–101	Imagery **SE** p. 96 Calvinism **TE** p. 97 Archetype **SE** p. 100
Vocabulary Workshop p. 102	

PART 3: The Road to Independence

Selections and Features	Literary Elements
Autobiography *from* **The Autobiography of Benjamin Franklin,** by Benjamin Franklin **7.0/59/1170** pp.104–109	Autobiography **SE** p. 105
Proverbs *from* **Poor Richard's Almanack,** by Benjamin Franklin pp. 110–111	Aphorism **SE** p. 110
Literary History The Rhetoric of Revolution pp. 112–113	Rhetorical Devices **SE** p. 112
Speech Speech to the Second Virginia Convention, by Patrick Henry **8.4/60/930** pp. 114–119	Rhetorical Question **SE** p. 115

Reading Skills and Strategies	Vocabulary	Writing / Grammar	Speaking, Listening, and Viewing
Respond **SE** p. 70	Word Origins **TE** p. 70, SE p. 78 Adjectives **TE** p. 72 Academic Vocabulary **SE** p. 78	Compound Subjects **TE** p. 74 Write Questions **TE** p. 76 Write a Summary **SE** p. 79	Analyze Art **TE** pp. 72, 74
Analyze Historical Context **SE** p. 81	Parts of Speech **TE** p. 81 Word Usage **SE** p. 86	Interjections **TE** p. 82 Write a Character Analysis **TE** p. 84 Write a List **SE** p. 86	
		Sentence Combining **SE** pp. 87–88 Conjunctions **TE** p. 88	
Draw Conclusions About Author's Beliefs **SE** p. 90	Adjectives **TE** p. 90 Synonyms **SE** p. 94 Academic Vocabulary **SE** p. 94	Inverted Syntax **TE** p. 92 Apply Extended Metaphor **SE** p. 94	Analyze Art **TE** p. 92
Examine Connotation **SE** p. 96	Persuasive Words **TE** p. 96 Word Origins **SE** p. 101 Academic Vocabulary **SE** p. 101	Write Research Notes **TE** p. 98 Apply Diction **SE** p. 101	Analyze Art **SE** p. 98
	Dictionary Use **SE** p. 102 Homonyms **TE** p. 102		

Reading Skills and Strategies	Vocabulary	Writing / Grammar	Speaking, Listening, and Viewing
Analyze Voice **SE** p. 105 Question **TE** p. 106	Nouns **TE** p. 105 Word Parts **SE** p. 109	Conjunctions **TE** p. 108	Analyze Art **SE** p. 107
Connect **SE** p. 110	Academic Vocabulary **SE** p. 111	Write an Article **SE** p. 111	
Analyze American Literature **SE** p. 112 Analyze Political Cartoons **SE** p. 113			Analyze Art **SE** p. 112
Analyze Figures of Speech **SE** p. 115 Predict **TE** p. 116	Antonyms **SE** p. 119	Write a Speech **SE** p. 119	

Readability Scores Key: Dale-Chall/DRP/Lexile

PART 3: The Road to Independence *(continued)*

Selections and Features	Literary Elements
Public Document The Declaration of Independence, by Thomas Jefferson **12.6/71/1360** pp. 120–127	Text Structure **SE** p. 121 Tone **TE** p. 123 Author's Purpose **SE** p. 126
Historical Essay TIME: How They Chose These Words, by Walter Isaacson **7.9/68/1200** pp. 128–130	
Vocabulary Workshop p. 131	
Public Document *from* **The Crisis, No. 1,** by Thomas Paine **8.8/62/1050** pp. 132–138	Tone **SE** p. 133 Diction **SE** p. 137
Poem To His Excellency, General Washington, by Phillis Wheatley pp. 139–143	Couplet **SE** p. 140
Letter Letter to John Adams, by Abigail Adams **8.8/62/1350** pp. 144–148	Description **SE** p. 145
Grammar Workshop p. 149	
Historical Perspective *from* **John Adams,** by David McCullough **9.9/64/1270** pp. 150–153	Description **TE** p. 150
Writing Workshop pp. 154–161	
Speaking, Listening, and Viewing Workshop pp. 162–163	Rhetorical Devices **SE** p. 162
Independent Reading pp. 164–165	
Assessment pp. 166–171	

Reading Skills and Strategies	Vocabulary	Writing Grammar	Speaking, Listening, and Viewing

Evaluate Argument **SE** p. 121
Predict **TE** p. 122
	Word Parts **TE** p. 121
	Context Clues **SE** p. 126
	Academic Vocabulary
	    SE p. 126
		Parentheses **SE** p. 127
		Write a Persuasive Essay
		    SE p. 127
			Analyze Art **SE** p. 123
			Discussion **SE** p. 125

Determine Main Idea and Supporting Details **SE** p. 128 Preview **TE** p. 128		Draft and Revise **TE** p. 128	
	Word Origins **SE** p. 131		

Summarize **SE** p. 133
Analyze Arguments **TE** p. 134
	Denotation and Connotation
	    SE p. 138
	Academic Vocabulary
	    SE p. 138
		Apply Tone **SE** p. 138	Analyze Art **SE** p. 136
			Presentation **TE** p. 136

Analyze Structure **SE** p. 140 Paraphrase **TE** p. 140 Visualize **TE** p. 142	Academic Vocabulary **SE** p. 143	Write a Poem **SE** p. 143	
Recognize Author's Purpose **SE** p. 145 Preview and Make Inferences **TE** p. 146	Analogies **SE** p. 148	Write a Letter **SE** p. 148	
		Clauses as Modifiers **SE** p. 149	
Analyze Biographical Narrative **SE** p. 150 Compare and Contrast **TE** p. 150		Summarize **TE** p. 152 Block Quotations **TE** p. 152	
		Write a Persuasive Speech **SE** pp. 154–161 Transitions **TE** p. 158 Parallelism **SE** p. 161	Presentation **SE** p. 161
Reread **TE** p. 162		Write Appeals **SE** p. 162	Speech **SE** p. 163
		Write a Review **SE** p. 165	Book Review **TE** p. 164
Determine Main Idea and Supporting Details **TE** p. 168		Paraphrase **TE** p. 166 Organization **TE** p. 170 Write an Essay **SE** p. 171	

Focus

Bellringer Options

**Literature Launchers
Pre-Reading Videos DVD:
Unit 1**

**Daily Language Practice
Transparency 1**

Or **write** on the board: Early
Americans **Ask:** What do you
know about early Americans?
*(Native Americans, European
settlers who founded the colonies, African slaves brought here
against their will)*

 For students who would profit
from independent novel study,
see Novel Companion, pp. 7–74.

 For school-to-home activities, see
Unit 1 Teaching Resources Book,
pp. 5–11.

The First Harvest in the Wilderness, 1855, Asher Brown Durand. Oil on canvas,
32 x 47½ in. Brooklyn Museum of Art, NY.

View the Art Durand depicts an event that many early European settlers of North
America experienced. What elements of the painting reflect the artist's conception
of the relationship between settler and wilderness? ★

4

Unit Introduction Skills

**Early America:
Beginnings–1800**

Reading Skills
- Analyze Graphic Information
  (SE pp. 6–9)
- Analyze Cause and Effect
  (SE pp. 13, 17; TE p. 10)
- Evaluate (SE p. 15; TE p. 8)
- Draw Conclusions
  (TE pp. 7, 16)
- Support the Main Idea
  (TE pp. 12, 18)

Writing Skills/Grammar
- Write an Essay
  (SE p. 18)
- Analyze a Graph
  (TE p. 8)

**Study Skills/Research/
Assessment**
- Use Timelines (TE p. 6)
- Organize Ideas (TE p. 16)

Vocabulary Skills
- Phrases (TE p. 10)
- Determine Precise
  Meanings (TE p. 14)

**Listening/Speaking/
Viewing Skills**
- Analyze Art (SE p. 4;
  TE pp. 5, 9, 13, 15)

Early America

BEGINNINGS–1800

Looking Ahead

The roots of American literature display a rich, complex mixture of cultures and eras. Through oral tradition, the Native American peoples preserved their myths, tales, songs, and other lore from long ago. When Europeans reached the Americas, their writings recorded their experiences of exploration and settlement. Africans who were brought to the Americas by force wrote of the conditions of slavery. American literature developed further as writers played an important role in the colonial struggle for independence from Great Britain.

Keep the following questions in mind as you read:

>>> How did Native Americans view their relationship to the world around them?

>>> What were the major cultural features that the Puritans brought with them to New England?

>>> How did the development of society in colonial America lead to the Revolution?

5

Focus

Summary

This introduction gives an overview of historical, social, and cultural forces before 1800 in the land that is now the United States. It discusses Native American peoples who lived here first, Europeans who explored and settled during the 1500s and 1600s, and Africans who came against their will in the 1600s and the 1700s. Also covered are the role of religion in the colonial period and the discontent with Britain that led to the American Revolution.

View the Art ★

Answer: *Durand shows the wilderness surrounding and dwarfing the settlers' farmland and home, suggesting that the wilderness is greater and more powerful. He also shows the farm and the wilderness existing together in harmony, suggesting that the wilderness is welcoming and bountiful.*

The American painter Asher Durand (1796–1886) was an engraver before he became a painter. His skill as an engraver can be seen in his paintings, which are made with fine lines.

Unit Resources

Print Materials
- Unit 1 Teaching Resources, pp. 1–279
- Interactive Read and Write (On Level, Approaching, EL), pp. 1–44
- Novel Companion, pp. 7–74
- Bellringer Option Transparencies: Selection Focus 1–15; Daily Language Practice 1–18
- Assessment Resources, Selection Assessment, pp. 59–96

Technology
- TeacherWorks Plus CD
- StudentWorks Plus CD
- Literature Launchers: Pre-Reading Videos DVD, Unit 1
- Literature Online
- Interactive Vocabulary CD-ROM
- Listening Library CD-ROM
- ExamView CD-ROM
- Skill Level Up! CD-ROM

 For diagnostic and end-of-unit assessment, see Assessment Resources, pp. 1–8, 331–332.

Teach

Analyze Graphic Information Help students read the timeline and relate key events in American literature to U.S. and world history. Explain that this unit covers the era before 1800 in what is now the United States. Have students discuss one U.S. and one world event that they know of from this period.

ENGLISH LEARNERS Explain to English learners that the entries in the timeline are not full sentences. Have them read some of the entries aloud and add words that would complete the sentences.

Cultural History ☆

Early American Newspapers
The first colonial newspaper was the *Boston News-Letter,* published in 1704. It had a small circulation of about 300. Most colonial newspapers avoided controversy. Publishers could not challenge or criticize the government. This changed with the passage of the First Amendment in 1791.

Timeline 1500–1800

American flag, c. 1781

AMERICAN LITERATURE 1

1500

1542
La Relación by Álvar Núñez Cabeza de Vaca is published

1570
Dekanawida creates the Iroquois Constitution for the Iroquois Confederacy

1600

1630
William Bradford begins *Of Plymouth Plantation* ▼

1640
Bay Psalm Book is published

1650
Anne Bradstreet's poems are published in London

1682
Captivity narrative of Mrs. Mary Rowlandson is published

Pilgrims Going to Church, 1867. George Henry Boughton. Oil on canvas, 29 x 52 in. New York Historical Society, NY.

UNITED STATES EVENTS

1500

1492
Columbus makes his first voyage to the Americas

1521
Cortés conquers the Aztec empire

Aztec calendar stone ▶

1528–1536
Cabeza de Vaca wanders the American Southwest

1600

1607
Colony of Jamestown is founded in Virginia

1619
First Africans arrive in Virginia

1620
Pilgrims arrive at Cape Cod on *Mayflower*

1630
Massachusetts Bay Colony is founded

1637
Anne Hutchinson is banished for dissent

1675–1676
King Philip, Wampanoag chief, wages war

1681
William Penn founds the Pennsylvania colony

1692
Witchcraft trials begin in Salem, Massachusetts

WORLD EVENTS

1500

Martin ▶ Luther

1517
Reformation begins

1522
Magellan circumnavigates the globe

1558
Elizabeth I becomes queen of England

1600

1632
Shah Jahan begins Taj Mahal as tomb for his wife

1642
English Civil War begins

1649
English King Charles I executed; Puritan rule begins

1660
End of Puritan Commonwealth; English monarchy restored under Charles II

Taj Mahal ▶

LOG ON ▶ **Literature** Online

Literature and Reading To explore the Interactive Timeline, go to glencoe.com and enter QuickPass code GLA9800u1.

Study Skills Practice

Use Timelines Explain that a timeline is a chart that shows a sequence of events. Point out that there are three timelines in this chart. Explain how events are organized in columns in each timeline. Then ask students to read the label of each timeline and to explain the types of events in that timeline in a sentence.

Have students locate and record information from the timelines about exploration and discovery, the founding of American colonies, titles and authors of literary works, and other topics.

Benjamin Franklin ▶

1700

1704
First colonial newspaper is published ☆

1732
Benjamin Franklin's first *Poor Richard's Almanack* is published

1771
Benjamin Franklin begins his *Autobiography*

1773
Phillis Wheatley's poems are published in London

1776
Thomas Paine's *Common Sense* is published

1776
Thomas Paine begins *The Crisis* series

1782
Letters from an American Farmer by Michel Guillaume Jean de Crèvecoeur is published

1783 ▲
Noah Webster's *American Speller* is published

1787
Thomas Jefferson's *Notes on the State of Virginia* is published

1789
Interesting Narrative of the Life of Olaudah Equiano is published in London

2

1700

1735
John Peter Zenger trial helps establish freedom of the press

1736
Great Awakening religious revival begins

1739
Africans attack slaveholders in the Stono Rebellion

1754–1763
French and Indian War

1765 ▲
Stamp Act triggers protest throughout colonies

1770
British troops fire on colonists in Boston Massacre

1775
Battles of Lexington and Concord are fought

1776
Declaration of Independence is signed

1781
British surrender at Yorktown, ending the Revolutionary War

1783
Treaty of Paris is signed, confirming independence of United States

1788
U.S. Constitution is ratified

1789
George Washington becomes first president

1700

1726
Jonathan Swift's *Gulliver's Travels* is published

1760
George III becomes king of Great Britain

1778
James Cook lands on Hawaii

1789
French Revolution begins in Paris

1793
French rulers Louis XVI and Marie Antoinette are executed

◀ Revolutionary War drum

Reading Check

Analyze Graphic Information What was the history of the English monarchy between 1642 and 1660?

UNIT ONE

Teach

Reading Check

Answer: *A civil war began in 1642. In 1649, King Charles I was executed and the Puritan Commonwealth was established. In 1660, the monarchy was restored under Charles II.*

Reading Strategy | 2

Draw Conclusions **Ask:** What conclusions can you draw about the development of American literature in the colonial period? Which works may have been created as responses to the political and social issues of the era? *(Early literature was chiefly about exploration and early settlements. Later literature addressed broader political and social issues. Paine's* Common Sense *and* The Crisis, *for example, were responses to the political situation in the colonies. Jefferson's book was a social history of Virginia.)*

Approaching Level

DIFFERENTIATED INSTRUCTION

Emerging Explain to students that the style of a timeline differs from that of ordinary prose. For example, there is no terminal punctuation. Ask students to find several complete sentences in the timeline and to note that a period would normally be added. Then ask students to look for ways that shortcuts are taken in the entries. Have them identify the words that are left out in typical entries. *(The words* the *and* a *are usually omitted.)*

Established On the board copy one entry from the timeline. *(Example: Stamp Act triggers protest throughout colonies)* Ask students what they would add to this entry to make it a standard English sentence. *(appropriate articles and a period)* Have them rewrite several entries, adding the words and the punctuation that would normally appear in English usage. Direct them to check their work with a partner.

7

Teach

Evaluate Evidence Tell students to examine the religion graph.

Ask: Which religious group had the most churches? *(Congregational)*

Ask: Which groups are Protestant? *(all except Roman Catholic)*

Cultural History ☆

Slavery While the Southern plantation economy depended on slavery, the Northern economy never relied heavily on slave labor. In fact, slaves rarely made up more than 5 percent of the total population in the North. Two likely reasons for this phenomenon are (1) the Southern economy relied more heavily on large farms and (2) the antislavery sentiment among many Northerners discouraged an increased use of slaves.

By the Numbers

The Columbian Exchange

Following the arrival of European explorers and settlers in the Western Hemisphere, many plants and animals were carried between the Americas and Europe, Africa, and Asia. This complex interaction, called the Columbian Exchange, permanently altered Earth's ecosystems and changed many cultures around the world.

The results of the Columbian Exchange were mixed. The introduction to Europe of staple crops from the Americas, such as the potato, contributed to a European population explosion. However, Europeans unintentionally brought with them many diseases to which Native Americans had no immunity.

Devastating epidemics resulted, with some Native American groups suffering a 90 percent population loss in the first century after European contact.

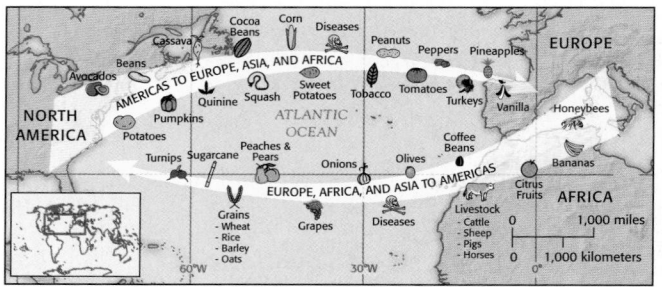

RELIGION IN THE COLONIES 1700s 1

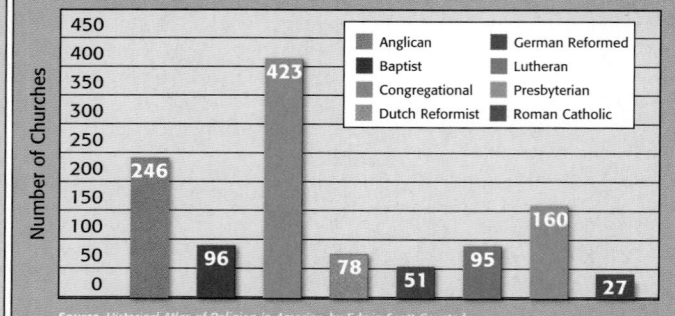

Source *Historical Atlas of Religion in America*, by Edwin Scott Gaustad

REVOLUTIONARY WAR CASUALTIES

American

- 7,200 battlefield deaths
- 8,200 battlefield wounded
- 1,400 missing in action
- 10,000 deaths from disease and other causes
- 8,500 deaths in British prisons

British

- 10,000 dead from all causes

SLAVERY

From 8 to 10 million enslaved Africans were taken to colonies in the Americas. Of these, only about 5% were taken to North America. At right is shown the distribution of enslaved Africans by colonial nartionality.

Slaves in the Colonies ☆ (in millions)

British (North America)	0.5
British, French, Dutch (Caribbean)	4
Portuguese (Brazil)	3.5
Spanish	1.5

NATIVE AMERICAN DIVERSITY

Native American cultures were extraordinarily diverse. Experts estimate that at least 300 distinct languages were spoken in North America when Columbus arrived.

Writing Practice

Analyze a Graph Tell students that when they read a list of facts, reorganizing the material will help them analyze the information. Have students take the items under the heading "Slavery" and represent them visually. Below their graphs, have students write a paragraph explaining conclusions they drew from viewing the graphed information. For example, students might create a bar graph like the one shown, using the following data:

Location of Colonies in Americas	Number of Enslaved People Taken There
Brazil	3.5 million
Spanish colonies	1.5 million
Caribbean colonies	4 million
North American colonies	500,000

Being There

The Cherokee, Iroquois, and Huron peoples lived in what is now the eastern United States. Great Britain's American colonies extended from present-day Maine to Georgia.

A *Town of Secota,* 16th century, Theodore de Bry. Engraving. Musée de la Marine, Paris.

2

B *Residence of David Twining,* 1845–1847, Edward Hicks. Oil on canvas. Private collection.

C *Tontine Coffee House,* c. 1797, Francis Guy. Oil on linen. New York Historical Society, NY.

LOG ON ▶ **Literature** Online

Literature and Reading For more about the history and literature of this period, go to glencoe.com and enter the QuickPass code GLA9800u1.

Reading Check

Analyze Graphic Information:
1. What animals were introduced into the Americas from Europe? What animal was taken from the Americas to Europe?

2. How do American Revolutionary War casualties compare with those of the British?

3. Where were most of colonial America's large cities located?

Teach

Reading Check

Answers:
1. *Cattle, sheep, pigs, horses, and honeybees moved from Europe to the Americas. The turkey was brought from the Americas to Europe.*
2. *There were 15,700 more American deaths than British deaths.*
3. *In the east, near oceans and other bodies of water*

Reading Strategy   **2**

Interpret Maps Point out to students that the uppercase letters below each work of art correspond to the letters on the map.

View the Art ★

A. Theodore de Bry made this engraving of a Native American town in the 1500s.

B. Edward Hicks (1780–1849) was a Quaker minister. As a child he lived with the Twining family in Pennsylvania.

C. Francis Guy's painting gives an idea of life in New York City in the late 1700s.

 SMALL GROUP

Emerging Have students select one of the three paintings and have them list the main objects that indicate the painting's time and place. Have them work in groups to create a list of vocabulary words to help them describe what they see. Ask each group of students to write a brief description of the painting they selected.

Established Ask students to write a diary entry from the point of view of someone who lives in the community depicted in the painting. Explain that a diary entry tells a brief story or explains some daily activity using the first person pronouns I, me, and mine. Remind students to make specific references to the period and location so that readers will know which painting is being referred to.

Teach

Analyze Cause and Effect

Read the text on page 10.

Ask: Why did European exploration have an enormous effect on world history? *(European exploration led to the founding of new countries that influenced historical events and caused many deaths in Native American civilizations.)*

ENGLISH LEARNERS Preview some of the vocabulary with English learners. Discuss the differences between *historical, social,* and *cultural* forces, and the meanings of such phrases as *social organization, complex societies,* and *cultural contact.*

Learning Objectives

In studying this text, you will focus on the following objectives:

Literary Studies: Analyzing literary periods, analyzing literary genres, evaluating historical influences.

Early America

BEGINNINGS–1800

Historical, Social, and Cultural Forces

Pulling Down the Statue of George III, 1857. William Walcutt. Oil on canvas. Lafayette College Art Collection, Easton, PA.

The Native Americans

When Europeans arrived in the Western Hemisphere in the 1490s, it was already home to hundreds of Native American peoples with different languages, cultures, and social values. The ancestors of these Native Americans had come to the Western Hemisphere from Asia thousands of years before.

The descendants of these early travelers developed different types of social organization, often based on the local environment. Some peoples, such as the Aztecs of Mexico and Central America, created complex societies with great cities, large-scale farming, and elaborate record keeping based on systems of writing. Others, such as the Plains Indians, who hunted buffalo, lived in portable dwellings and passed on their knowledge through oral tradition.

European Contact

Beginning about 1400, a number of forces prompted Europeans to start exploring the rest of the world. These forces included the growth of trade between Europe and Asia and advances in navigation and shipbuilding. European explorers brought many parts of the world into meaningful contact with one another for the first time in history. One of these explorers was Christopher Columbus, an Italian who commanded a Spanish fleet. In 1492 he made the first of four voyages from Spain to the Americas, opening the era of cultural contact between Europe and the Western Hemisphere.

The European exploration, conquest, and settlement of the Americas led to the founding of many new nations, including the United States. For the Native Americans, however, it was the beginning of an immense tragedy during which many of their societies were destroyed by war and disease.

1

Vocabulary Practice

Phrases After students read the section titled "European Contact," ask them to supply synonyms for the noun *contact.* *(communication, association, connection)* Then have students extend the meaning of the word *contact* to the phrase "cultural contact."

Ask: What does this phrase mean to you? What were some results of the cultural contact described in the passage? *(Students may reply that American Indians and the Europeans had different beliefs, which led to conflict.)* **Ask:** What are some of the costs and benefits of cultural contact? *(Costs include conflicts over land or beliefs; benefits include increased opportunities for trade and education.)*

Religious Belief

Religion was a major factor in American colonial culture. Groups of Protestants from England, such as the Pilgrims and Puritans, began founding settlements in New England in 1620. Other groups seeking religious freedom followed, including the Quakers, who settled in Pennsylvania in 1670. In the 1730s and 1740s, a religious revival called the Great Awakening spread throughout the American colonies. Two results of this movement were increased feelings of responsibility for Native Americans and enslaved Africans and a more tolerant spirit toward other faiths.

The Slave Trade

From their beginnings, the American colonies suffered from a severe labor shortage. This was particularly true in the South, where large tobacco and rice plantations required hundreds of workers. Despite protests from some groups, many colonists participated in the slave trade. By 1750 there were more than 200,000 enslaved Africans in Britain's North American possessions, most of them in the Southern colonies. These colonies developed slave codes—sets of laws that formally regulated slavery and defined the relationship between enslaved Africans and free people.

The American Revolution

In the mid-1760s, unrest began to develop in the American colonies. A long war with France had left Britain in debt. To raise money, the British government passed a series of unpopular laws, including taxes on a variety of everyday items. By the mid-1770s, resentment over these taxes was leading to political violence and calls for colonial self-rule.

> *"The war is inevitable—and let it come!"*
>
> —Patrick Henry

In April 1775, the British colonial government in Massachusetts ordered troops to the towns of Lexington and Concord to control unrest. The first battles of the Revolutionary War were fought there between American militiamen and British soldiers. On July 4, 1776, the Second Continental Congress adopted the Declaration of Independence, asserting the colonists' right to self-government and establishing the United States of America. To defend their independence, the Americans fought a long war with the British, who finally accepted American independence in 1783.

PREVIEW Big Ideas of Early America

1 The Sacred Earth and the Power of Storytelling	**2** Life in the New World	**3** The Road to Independence
Native American life was organized around the cycles of nature, and many myths and folktales told of the origins of various aspects of the universe and of human relationships with the natural world. **See pages 12–13.**	European explorers and settlers left accounts of endurance and religious faith as they struggled to adapt to life in an unfamiliar world. Victims of the slave trade, Africans recorded their fight to survive. **See pages 14–15.**	British taxes, regulations, and soldiers on American soil aroused annoyance, irritation, and finally revolt. American writers provided ideas and inspiration to the cause of American freedom. **See pages 16–17.**

2

Teach

Big Idea

The Power of Storytelling

Ask: How would you describe the Native American literary tradition? *(The Native American literary tradition was oral; it placed a high value on the relationship with nature.)*

ENGLISH LEARNERS Help English learners break the long phrase "Native American literary tradition" into its individual words to make it easier to understand. Explain the difference between an oral and a written literary tradition.

Cultural History ☆

Religious Belief Some English settlers known as Puritans were motivated by a desire to create a model community. They believed England's ruling monarchy cared only for the wealthy. They wanted to establish a purified society far removed from the Church of England and the Roman Catholic Church. During the 1630s, 21,000 Puritans left their homes to seek a new life in North America.

English Learners

DIFFERENTIATED INSTRUCTION

Intermediate List on the board one word from each section of the text (e.g., *revival, participated, unpopular*). Have students locate the sentences in which these words appear and read them aloud. **Ask:** What do you think these words mean? *(renewal, coming back, returning; shared, took part in; not liked, disapproved of, disliked)* Have students create a two-column chart with the headings *Words* and *Meanings*.

Have them consult a dictionary for synonyms, list them on their charts, and substitute the synonyms in the sentences from the text.

Advanced Explain that some prefixes are followed by a hyphen when they are added to a word. The prefix *self-* is usually followed by a hyphen, as in the words *self-rule* and *self-government.* Ask students to consult a dictionary and list five other compounds with the prefix *self-*.

Teach

The Sacred Earth and the Power of Storytelling

Reading Strategy 1

Connect Ask: What is your view of the Native American belief system that held the natural world to be sacred? *(Answers will vary.)*

Cultural History ☆

N. Scott Momaday Navarre Scott Momaday is a Native American writer whose work appears in Part 1 of this unit. He was born on a Kiowa reservation in Oklahoma in 1934. His parents were educators, and as a result the family lived on a number of different reservations during his childhood before eventually settling in New Mexico. His novel *House Made of Dawn* won the Pulitzer Prize for fiction in 1969. This success helped lead to the widespread acceptance of Native American literature into mainstream curricula.

Ask: What works of literature is Momaday referring to in the quotation? *(the Native American oral tradition, which is described in the section A Legacy of Stories, following the quotation.)*

We often have a strong feeling for the land where we live—its shapes and colors, its sounds and smells. In many Native American cultures, the entire earth and all of the living things that inhabited it were sacred. This reverence for the earth and its creatures was passed down orally from generation to generation. Speakers and storytellers were valued members of Native American communities.

The Cycle of Life 1

Native Americans saw animals, plants, and the forces of nature as part of a great sacred cycle of life that humans must treat with deep respect. Religious ceremonies were organized around the events of this natural cycle. Through dreams and visions, Native Americans sought contact with the spirits they believed to inhabit all living things. Through their tales and songs, Native Americans expressed their view of the sacredness of the natural world.

> *"Sell a country! Why not sell the air, the great sea, as well as the earth? Did not the Great Spirit make them all for the use of his children?"*
>
> —Tecumseh, Shawnee leader

Owning the Land

Native Americans' belief that the natural world is sacred affected their attitude toward land ownership. In their view, no one person could own land, which instead belonged in common to all people—and other living things—that inhabited it.

This concept of common ownership contrasted sharply with that of the Europeans, who began settling North America in the early 1600s. These settlers had a fierce desire to own their own land. Violent conflicts often resulted when Native American leaders signed treaties—which they usually did not understand—that opened lands to white settlement.

> *"American literature begins with the first human perception of the American landscape expressed and preserved in language."*
>
> —N. Scott Momaday ☆

A Legacy of Stories

The Native American oral tradition began approximately forty thousand years ago when the first humans crossed from Asia to Alaska via a land bridge now covered by the Bering Strait. As populations migrated south, unique cultures and languages developed in response to different environments. When European explorers first arrived in the New World, thousands of languages, some as unlike each other as English and Chinese, were spoken in the Americas. Each of these cultures developed its own stories and mythology.

It is likely that many early stories dramatized the struggle of the first Americans to survive. Stone Age hunters may have related tales of the hunt to groups sitting around campfires. Sacred stories were often at the heart of religious ceremonies, and in societies where myth and reality merged, rituals were thought to link the spirits of hunters and animals. Versions of the earliest stories have evolved through hundreds of generations and are still a living part of Native American traditions.

Reading Practice

Support the Main Idea Remind students that a paragraph often contains one main idea and details that support it. **Ask:** How can you find the main idea of a paragraph? *(Look for a sentence that states or sums up what the paragraph is about.)* Have students locate and write down the main idea of each paragraph on page 12. Then direct them to compare their answers.

Ask: How is the main idea developed in a paragraph? *(A main idea is supported by details.)* Have students record the main idea and supporting details in one paragraph. Here is an example for paragraph 2:

Main idea:
The religious beliefs of Native Americans were shaped by their attitude toward the natural world.

Supporting details:
- respect for animals, plants, nature
- religious ceremonies for seasons
- spirits believed to inhabit all of life
- sacredness of natural world expressed in tales and songs

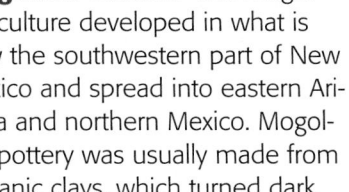

Mimbres style pottery bowl painted with the guardians of the four seasons, Mogollon culture, A.D. 10th century. Maxwell Museum of Anthropology, Albuquerque, NM. ★

I Have Killed the Deer Taos Pueblo Song

I have killed the deer.
I have crushed the grasshopper
And the plants he feeds upon.
I have cut through the heart
Of trees growing old and straight.
I have taken fish from water
And birds from the sky.
In my life I have needed death
So that my life can be.

When I die I must give life
To what has nourished me.
The earth receives my body
And gives it to the plants
And to the caterpillars
To the birds
And to the coyotes
Each in its own turn so that
The circle of life is never broken. **2**

Reading Check

Answer: *The Native American view that the natural world belongs to all people clashed with the Europeans' strong desire to own land.*

Literary Element | 2

Poetry Ask: Could the song "I Have Killed the Deer" be considered a poem? **Say:** Find examples of poetic devices, such as imagery, personification, and repetition. **Ask:** What are some similarities between songs and poetry? *(They may share such similar characteristics as rhythm, imagery, and literary devices.)*

View the Art ★

Mogollon Culture The Mogollon culture developed in what is now the southwestern part of New Mexico and spread into eastern Arizona and northern Mexico. Mogollon pottery was usually made from volcanic clays, which turned dark brown when the pots were fired. The Mimbres phase took place from about A.D. 1025 to 1300.

Reading Check

Analyze Cause and Effect How did Native Americans' religious views lead to conflict with Europeans?

English Learners

DIFFERENTIATED INSTRUCTION

Advanced Have students read the poem and look up any unfamiliar words. Have them ask questions about unclear phrases and lines. Then have partners read the poem aloud. **Ask:** How are the two stanzas of the poem related? *(In the first stanza the speaker tells how nature has nourished his life. In the second stanza he tells how he will become part of the eternal cycle when his body returns to the earth.)*

Have students read aloud the lines in which the speaker identifies the living things that have sustained him. *(deer, grasshopper, plants, trees, fish, bird)*
Ask: What do you think the circle in the last line refers to? *(the interdependence among all living things)*

Make Inferences Have students read the introductory paragraph. **Ask:** What is meant by the phrase "subdue a wilderness"? *(create human settlements by clearing brush, making paths, and building homes in the wilderness [The illustration on page 4 shows one example of this.])*

Literary History

John Winthrop The founding governor of Massachusetts Bay Colony, John Winthrop, wrote a sermon entitled "A Model of Christian Charity" while traveling to the New World. In this sermon Winthrop created his famous description of a "city upon a hill." He derived this description from a verse in the gospel of Matthew: "A city set on a hill cannot be hid." Winthrop wanted to inspire a sense of duty in his people by indicating that their community would serve as an example for others.

Big Idea 2

Life in the New World

For the Europeans who explored and settled North America, daily life was frequently a struggle to subdue a wilderness and to endure fierce conflicts with Native Americans. For Africans seized from their homes and enslaved in the Americas, life was a battle first to survive and then to hold on to their cultural identity.

A Collision of Cultures

Europeans began to explore North America in the early 1500s. Many explorers wrote grim reports of hardships encountered in the wilderness. The first arrivals were followed by other Europeans, settlers who built towns and started farms. As European settlement spread, conflict developed between the newcomers and Native Americans that often led to brutal wars. Their superior weapons enabled the Europeans to overcome their enemies. Even more destructive to the Native Americans were the diseases the newcomers brought with them. As a result of war and disease, few Native Americans survived beyond the end of the 1600s.

Puritan Style

The Puritans greatly influenced early American literature. They began to establish communities in New England in the 1620s after leaving England to escape what they saw as signs of corruption in the Church of England. These included elaborate rituals, a richly dressed clergy, and fine churches. In opposition to this, Puritans dressed plainly and held simple religious services in undecorated meetinghouses. They also believed that they had a God-given responsibility to establish an ideal way of life in America.

The Puritans' plainness and piety showed in their writing, which employed straightforward language and often focused on their faith. William Bradford (see pages 62–68) was a member of the Puritan group known as the Pilgrims, who settled Plymouth Colony in 1620. Bradford viewed writing primarily as a practical tool. At the beginning of his history of the Plymouth Colony, he said that he intended to produce a record of events in "a plain style, with singular regard unto the simple truth in all things."

> *"For we must consider that we shall be as a city upon a hill. The eyes of all people are upon us."*
>
> —John Winthrop

In 1734 Jonathan Edwards (see pages 95–101), a Congregational minister and a great spokesman for Puritanism, began a series of religious revivals in his community of Northampton, Massachusetts. Edwards' powerful sermons helped start the "Great Awakening," a movement that spread throughout the American colonies. Edwards maintained that a person had to repent and convert in order to be "born again." This idea of having a personal emotional experience that brings one to God was a central idea of the Great Awakening.

Surviving Slavery

The first enslaved Africans were brought to Virginia in 1619. By the 1700s, slave ships arrived regularly in the American colonies. Most of these people, like Olaudah Equiano (see pages 69–78), had been taken from their homes in West Africa by slave traders. After enduring the horrors of the "Middle Passage," the long sea voyage across the Atlantic, they reached the slave markets of the Americas. Despite brutal living conditions, these Africans struggled to preserve parts of their heritage—the social values and cultural traditions of their homelands—but usually without success.

Determine Precise Meanings Explain to students that they can determine the meaning of new words by using what they already know. Point out that they have seen that the word *subdue* in "subdue a wilderness" means "to conquer or tame." **Ask:** Using this knowledge, infer the meaning of the word *subdued* in each of these phrases:

- subdued lighting *(low intensity)*
- subdued voices *(soft)*
- subdued temper *(repressed)*

Have students determine the meanings of the word *elaborate* in these phrases.

- elaborate rituals
- elaborate precautions
- elaborate on a theory

Direct students to check their answers in a standard dictionary.

Pilgrims Going to Church, 1867. George Henry Boughton. Oil on canvas. Collection of the New York Historical Society.

from *Of Plymouth Plantation* by William Bradford

September 6. These troubles being blown over, and now all being compact together in one ship [the *Mayflower*], they put to sea again with a prosperous wind, which continued divers days together, which was some encouragement unto them; yet, according to the usual manner, many were afflicted with sea sickness. And I may not omit here a special work of God's providence. There was a proud and very profane young man, one of the seamen, of a lusty, able body, which made him the more haughty; he would always be condemning the poor people in their sickness, and cursing them daily with grievous execrations, and did not let to tell them that he hoped to help to cast half of them overboard before they came to their journey's end, and to make merry with what they had; and if he were by any gently reproved, he would curse and swear most bitterly. But it pleased God before they came half seas over, to smite this young man with a grievous disease, of which he died in a desperate manner, and so was himself the first that was thrown overboard. Thus his curses light on his own head, and it was an astonishment to all his fellows, for they noted it to be the just hand of God upon him. **2**

Reading Check

Evaluate Why did the Puritans adopt a plain style in their writing?

Teach

Reading Check

Answer: *The Puritan writing style was plain because it reflected the Puritan philosophy of simple, faith-based ideals.*

Reading Strategy 2

Clarify Help students understand the unfamiliar language and constructions in Bradford's journal entry. Point out unusual phrasing and words. Encourage students to decode meanings by using context clues and a dictionary.

View the Art ★

George Henry Boughton (1833–1905) was born in England and moved with his family to New York when he was a child. He studied art in Paris while in his late 20s and spent most of the rest of his life in London. While working as an illustrator, he created art for an edition of *The Scarlet Letter*.
Ask: Why might the artist show these churchgoers carrying guns? *(The artist may have been reflecting the attitude that Puritans were concerned about being attacked by Native Americans.)*

Approaching Level

DIFFERENTIATED INSTRUCTION

SMALL GROUP
Emerging Tell students to list questions they might have about William Bradford's writings. Have them work together to paraphrase the passage line by line. Have pairs share their paraphrases with the class. Then, discuss questions still remaining about the meaning of the passage.

Established Ask students to write a short summary of Bradford's journal. Have them include Bradford's beliefs and his details about the journey. Direct them to write three to five sentences summarizing and responding to the passage. Then, have students read their paragraphs aloud to the class to improve reading fluency.

Teach

Draw Conclusions **Ask:**
How did Benjamin Franklin's success reflect the values of the newly emerging American society? *(Because Franklin began his life in a poor family and ended up as highly successful in many fields, he embodied the new American society, in which individuals rose as a result of education, effort, and ability.)*

Political History ☆

The Declaration of Independence In addition to announcing the separation of the thirteen colonies from Great Britain, the Declaration of Independence identified the basic principles that would form the foundation of the new country. The most important principle was that ordinary citizens would play major roles in running their government.

Big Idea 3
The Road to Independence

A s human beings grow, they experience the challenges and rewards of becoming independent. Separated by a long, dangerous sea voyage from Britain, the American colonists became used to managing their own affairs. As colonial society developed, many Americans came to believe that this growth in responsibility should be matched with an increase in political and economic rights. In time, this belief would lead to revolution—resulting in a break with Britain, a long war, and full independence.

A "Natural Aristocracy"
The culture of the American colonies was shaped by the practical, self-reliant, pioneer spirit of settlers who had left their homelands to seek a better life. As the French-born American Michel Guillaume Jean de Crèvecoeur observed, "*He* is an American who, leaving behind him all his ancient prejudices and manners, receives new ones from the mode of life he has embraced, the new government he obeys, and the new rank he holds." The career of Benjamin Franklin (see pages 104–111) reflected the American colonists' ability to rise in the world. He began life as one of seventeen children in a poor family. He ended as a businessman, an influential politician, and a famous writer and scientist.

> "*Sloth, like rust, consumes faster than labor wears, while the used key is always bright.*"
>
> —Benjamin Franklin

Another important factor in the maturing of American colonial society was an emphasis on self-improvement through education. New England's Puritans, for example, established a system of public schools, believing that learning was a defense against evil. The effect of a bold, enterprising spirit coupled with education was the emergence in the American colonies of an outstanding political leadership, which one of these leaders, Thomas Jefferson (see pages 120–126), called a "natural aristocracy" of virtue and talent.

Political Rights
During the 1700s, America came under the influence of the European cultural movement known as the Enlightenment. Enlightenment thinkers believed that natural laws applied to social, political, and economic relationships. Among these was the concept that human beings possessed certain natural, or "inalienable" rights, basic rights that could never be taken away. Thomas Jefferson believed that the colonists had a natural right to be free. He also believed that they had a right—indeed a duty—to end what he saw as Britain's tyrannical rule of the colonies by establishing their own independent government. In the Declaration of Independence, Jefferson eloquently expressed the fundamental ideas behind the ☆ American Revolution.

Women's Lives
In colonial America, law and custom gave men greater authority and importance than women in politics and in the home. A married woman had few legal rights and was almost completely under her husband's control. Despite legal limitations, many colonial women worked outside the home, running farms and businesses. Women also played a vital role in the independence movement by organizing boycotts of British goods. During the Revolutionary War, women made important contributions on the home front and on the battlefront. However, the political rights they helped win would be denied them for another 140 years.

Study Skills Practice

Organize Ideas To help students better understand the concepts on this page, have them make a word web for each section.

Midnight Ride of Paul Revere, 1815. Artist Unknown.

Teach

Reading Check

Answer: *An effective group of leaders emerged as a result of American beliefs in education and the creation of a better life.*

Reading Strategy   2

Connect **Ask:** Do you think Franklin's recommendations still apply today? Why or why not? *(Answers will vary.)*

Literary History ☆

Paul Revere's Ride The American poet Henry Wadsworth Longfellow wrote a famous poem called "Paul Revere's Ride," in which he described events that took place on the night of April 18, 1775. On that night American colonists learned that British soldiers were advancing to the town of Lexington, Massachusetts, to arrest Samuel Adams and John Hancock. The warning was carried by a man on horseback, a silversmith called Paul Revere.

---

from *The Autobiography* by Benjamin Franklin

1. **Temperance.** Eat not to dullness; drink not to elevation.
2. **Silence.** Speak not but what may benefit others or yourself; avoid trifling conversation.
3. **Order.** Let all your things have their places; let each part of your business have its time.
4. **Resolution.** Resolve to perform what you ought; perform without fail what you resolve.
5. **Frugality.** Make no expense but to do good to others or yourself; i.e., waste nothing.
6. **Industry.** Lose no time; be always employed in something useful; cut off all unnecessary actions.
7. **Sincerity.** Use no hurtful deceit; think innocently and justly, and, if you speak, speak accordingly.
8. **Justice.** Wrong none by doing injuries or omitting the benefits that are your duty.
9. **Moderation.** Avoid extremes; forbear resenting injuries so much as you think they deserve.
10. **Cleanliness.** Tolerate no uncleanliness in body, clothes, or habitation.
11. **Tranquility.** Be not disturbed at trifles or at accidents common or unavoidable.
12. **Chastity.** Rarely use venery but for health or offspring, never to dullness, weakness, or the injury of your own or another's peace or reputation.
13. **Humility.** Imitate Jesus and Socrates. **2**

Reading Check

Analyze Cause and Effect How did the American colonies come to have an effective group of leaders at the time of the Revolution?

INTRODUCTION   **17**

English Learners

DIFFERENTIATED INSTRUCTION

PARTNERS **Intermediate** Have students work with a partner to read each of the thirteen items carefully to identify unfamiliar words. Then have them use dictionaries to choose a definition that fits the context of each word as it appears in Franklin's text.

Advanced Remind students that many words in English have multiple meanings and sometimes can be used as different parts of speech. Ask students to think of two ways in which the word *elevation* can be used (one meaning is "height"; another meaning is "dignity"). Ask how Franklin uses the word in his first rule *(drunkenness* or *intoxication).*

Have students identify three words with multiple meanings and determine how the words are used in Franklin's text. *(Examples: temperance, resolution, business)*

Assess

Legacy of the Period

Ask: Do Americans still display a willingness to criticize established authority? *(Students may say many people voice strong opinions about politics, especially controversial issues.)*

Cultural and Literary Links

As students read the unit, invite them to think about other literature that reflects values similar to those expressed by the writers.

 Activities

1. **Follow Up** Students should show an understanding of both Native American and Puritan characteristics.

2. **Build Visual Literacy** Encourage students to research Native American art to incorporate into their designs.

3. **Write** Ask students to consider whether virtue and talent are still highly prized.

Foldables: Study Organizer
Have students make and label the bound book. Then have them use it to keep track of literary elements.

Wrap-Up

Legacy of the Period

American literature began with the oral tradition of the Native Americans. This ancient legacy of stories, songs, prayers, history, and other lore enabled the Native Americans to preserve the outlines of a world that largely vanished. Disease and war followed the arrival of Europeans in the Western Hemisphere. In recent years, new generations of Native American writers have reinterpreted, in modern terms, the literary themes and forms of this tradition, as part of a continuing effort to explore Native American cultural identity.

The writings of the Puritans are part of a cultural tradition stretching back to the time of Martin Luther and the beginnings of the Protestant Reformation. Some of the most important features of this tradition, as interpreted by the Puritans, became central to the American cultural tradition. One example is the belief in a God-given mission to offer an example to the world of an ideal community. Another is the Puritan emphasis on simplicity and practicality.

Puritanism inspired the religious revival of the Great Awakening, which in turn inspired a desire for democracy and equality in its followers. To many Americans, this sense of equality applied not only to religion but to society as well. It encouraged in them a willingness to criticize established authority—including the authority of the British government.

Cultural and Literary Links

 Native American literature has flourished since the 1960s. Contributors to this renaissance include N. Scott Momaday, Louise Erdrich, Leslie Marmon Silko, and Sherman Alexie.

 The writings of Benjamin Franklin have inspired Americans and people around the world to undertake self-improvement. One well-known example is Frederick Douglass.

 In 1848, at the first U.S. women's rights convention, Elizabeth Cady Stanton modeled her "Declaration of Rights and Sentiments" on Jefferson's Declaration of Independence.

LOG ON ▶ **Literature** Online

Unit Resources For additional skills practice, go to glencoe.com and enter QuickPass code GLA9800u1.

Activities ⟫⟫

Choose one of the following activities to explore and develop as you read this unit.

1. Follow Up Go back to the Looking Ahead on page 5 and answer the questions.

2. Build Visual Literacy Alone or with other students, create a design expressing the Native American concept of the unending cycle of life.

3. Write Write a brief essay exploring how Jefferson's "natural aristocracy" of virtue and talent that formed the leadership of the American Revolution would regard those governing the United States today.

4. Take Notes Use this study organizer to keep track of the three big ideas in this unit.

FOLDABLES Study Organizer **BOUND BOOK**

Early America

Reading Practice

Support the Main Idea Explain that an outline can show the organization of ideas that appear in expository writing. Ask students to reread one of the "Big Idea" sections. Have them use the heads and subheads to analyze the organization of ideas. Then instruct them to use the heads as a framework for their outlines.

As they reread each section, direct students to list the ideas under each subhead.

THE SACRED EARTH AND THE POWER OF STORYTELLING

Crossing the Ford, Platte River, Colorado, 1867–1870. Thomas Worthington Whittredge. Oil on canvas. Century Association, NY.

 View the Art In this painting, the artist has chosen to make the people very small in relation to the landscape. Why do you think he might have done this? ★

"Let us tell the old stories,
Let us sing the sacred songs." **1**

—N. Scott Momaday, "Carriers of the Dream Wheel"

19

Analyze and Extend

Reading Strategy   1

Make Inferences Invite a student to read aloud the quotation. The speaker is a modern-day member of the Kiowa tribe, whose work is included in this section.

Say: Explain what Momaday means by "old stories" and "sacred songs." *(He refers to the history and beliefs of Native American culture transmitted through the oral tradition of folk tales, myths, and poetry.)*

 View the Art ★

Answer: *To show that the American wilderness was vast and powerful; to show that Native Americans lived in harmony with nature*

The artist Thomas Worthington Whittredge (1820–1910) went to the Great Plains between 1866 and 1871. Later he wrote, "Whoever crossed the plains at that period . . . could hardly fail to be impressed with its vastness and silence and the appearance everywhere of an innocent . . . existence."

English Learners

DIFFERENTIATED INSTRUCTION

SMALL GROUP
Beginning Ask: What adjectives describe the scene you see? *(serene, vast, awe-inspiring)* Have students work in small groups to suggest appropriate modifiers.

Intermediate Ask: What is the main characteristic of a plain? *(flat or level)* Have students consult a dictionary and read the meaning of the words "Great Plains" aloud.

 For additional support for English Learners, see Unit 1 Teaching Resources Book, p. 21.

Focus

Bellringer Options

Daily Language Practice Transparency 2

Or have students imagine they had no scientific explanation for why the moon seems to change shape throughout the month. Brainstorm ideas for a story that provides a creative explanation.

Say: Early Native Americans created stories to help them understand themselves and their world, and they used their oral tradition to pass their understanding from one generation to the next. Momaday's quotation shows one myth of creation from the Kiowas. **Ask:** What myths do you know that tell about the beginnings of the world? *(Answers will vary.)*

Teach

Archetypes Invite students to recall heroes and villains in movie series such as *Star Wars, Lord of the Rings,* and *Harry Potter.* These classic character roles represent archetypes.

Ask: How does each series represent this battle? Are the characters clear-cut, or a mix of good and evil impulses? *(Some characters go through changes and conflicts.)*

20

Learning Objectives

For pages 20–21

In studying this text, you will focus on the following objectives:

Literary Study:
Analyzing literary periods.
Analyzing literary genres.

Native American Mythology

CENTURIES BEFORE THE FIRST Europeans arrived on the shores of North America, Native Americans had established hundreds of thriving nations, each with a unique culture and heritage. Each nation had its own tradition of **oral literature**—stories that were passed down from one generation to the next as they were told and retold in the privacy of households and in tribal ceremonies. These stories embodied the tribe's past and told of its close relationship with the natural world. The result is a literature that is timeless, a literature created by no one author but by the people as a whole.

> *"You know, everything had to begin, and this is how it was: the Kiowas came one by one into this world through a hollow log."*
> —N. Scott Momaday
> from *The Way to Rainy Mountain*

Totem Pole at Saxman Totem Park, Ketchikan. Tlingit. Wood sculpture. Ketchikan, Alaska, USA.

Creation Myths

A **myth** is an anonymous, traditional story that explains a natural phenomenon, an aspect of human behavior, or a mystery of the universe. **Creation myths** tell how the world and human beings came to exist. **Origin myths** explain how natural phenomena, such as the stars, moon, and mountains, came to be or why a society has certain beliefs and customs. Elements of both creation myths and origin myths appear in one story, as in this myth of the Taos Pueblo people:

> *"When earth was still young and giants still roamed the land, a great sickness came upon them. All of them died except for one small boy. One day while he was playing, a snake bit him. The boy cried and cried. The blood came out, and finally he died. With his tears our lakes became. With his blood the red clay became. With his body our mountains became, and that was how earth became."*

20 UNIT 1 EARLY AMERICA

Reading Practice

SPIRAL REVIEW **Analyze Archetypes** Introduce another archetypal character: the fool. Point out that he or she is often linked to the trickster character in archetypal story patterns such as the following:

- The trickster wants something from the fool and proceeds to use trickery to get it.
- The fool goes on the offensive, trying in vain to outwit the wily trickster.
- The overconfident trickster gets tricked.

Challenge students to come up with examples of fools versus tricksters—from folktales, cartoons, movies, and modern fiction.

Archetypes

The myths told by peoples around the world share common elements known as archetypes. An **archetype** (är´ kə tīp´) is a symbol, story pattern, or character type that is found in the literature of many cultures. An example of an archetype is children with opposite qualities who are born of the same parent. In Iroquois myth, Sky Woman gives birth to twins, one good and one evil. This event explains the eternal struggle between light and dark and between order and chaos.

Tricksters

Another archetype found in Native American mythology is the **trickster.** This character type, frequently an animal—such as a coyote, a raven, or a mink—that speaks and displays other human traits, has two sides to its personality. Tricksters are rebels who defy authority and frequently cause trouble, but they are also clever and creative figures who can unexpectedly reveal wisdom. For example, in one Native American myth, the coyote brought death into the world when he realized that the earth would become too crowded if people were to live forever. In a Navajo myth, the Holy People were gathered to place the stars in the sky. This process was taking so long that Coyote grew impatient, snatched the bag of stars, and hurled it into the heavens, forming the Milky Way. A Kiowa myth explains how a trickster stole the sun from those living on the other side of the earth so that all people could share day and night equally.

The Function of Myths

Native American myths told by various tribes have several things in common. Many emphasize a strong

Tlingit Raven Rattle, ca. 1850. Native American. The Lowe Art Museum, The University of Miami.

 View the Art Native Americans used rattles to help maintain a rhythm during ceremonial dances. What features of this rattle reflect Native American beliefs? ★

spiritual bond between the Creator, humanity, and the entire natural world. They emphasize that it is the duty of human beings to maintain a balance within the natural world.

In many Native American cultures, each family group, or clan, believed it descended from a particular animal or other natural object, called the **totem.** Members of the bear clan, for example, honored the bear as their clan ancestor. The bear in turn served as the clan's guardian spirit, helping and protecting its members. The bear clan was responsible for preserving the myths of the bear.

Myths and rituals continue to play a central role in traditional Native American cultures. They are used to give people a sense of order and identity, to heal the sick, to ensure a plentiful supply of food, to teach moral lessons, and to initiate young people into adulthood and the wisdom of the tribal past.

LOG ON ▶ **Literature** Online

Literature and Reading For more about Native American mythology, go to glencoe.com and enter QuickPass code GLA9800u1.

Respond and Think Critically

1. In your opinion, what is the most vital role of mythology in a culture?

2. How do Native American myths express a dual view of reality?

3. What archetype do the myths of many cultures throughout the world have in common?

 ## English Learners

DIFFERENTIATED INSTRUCTION

Advanced Select several folk tales that revolve around a trickster character such as Raven or Coyote. For greater variety, include an African figure such as Anansi the Spider. Assign students to read and analyze the trickster character in one tale, and to prepare a presentation.

 ## Approaching Level

DIFFERENTIATED INSTRUCTION

Established Have students use the Internet to find images of Native American totems and totem poles and write descriptive labels. Have them present the images and their descriptions to the class.

Literary History

Teach

Big Idea 2

The Sacred Earth and the Power of Storytelling Native American oral literature reflects a respect for Earth. **Ask:** How would you characterize people's attitudes toward Earth today? *(Some people, nations, and political movements respect Earth; others have a total disregard for it, polluting and wiping out natural resources.)*

View the Art

Answer: *The artifact might represent a totem or a creation myth, since it bears the image of an animal's face.*

Assess

1. *Mythology helps people understand the world, strengthens cultural identity, and transmits values to succeeding generations.*

2. *Good and evil twins and the creative tricksters express this.*

3. *Heroes, magicians, monsters, tricksters, quests, cosmic disasters*

 For an activity related to this selection, see Unit 1 Teaching Resources Book, pp. 19–20.

 For an audio recording of this selection, use Listening Library Audio CD-ROM.

Before You Read

Focus

Bellringer Options

Daily Language Practice Transparency 3

Or tell students they will read a creation myth explaining how the world of the Cherokee came to be. **Ask:** If you were to write a creation myth, what major landmarks, plants, and animals would you include?

Political History ☆

The Indian Removal Act President Andrew Jackson forced all tribes to lands west of the Mississippi. Most tribes were pressured to sign treaties, and the lands they received in the West were inferior to those surrendered. A few tribes resisted. In 1831 the Cherokees took their case to the Supreme Court. The Court ruled in favor of the Cherokees, but officials ignored the decision and Jackson refused to enforce it.

Before You Read

How the World Was Made

Meet the Cherokee

Hundreds of years ago, the Cherokee were the largest Native American nation in what is now the southeastern United States. Like most other Native American peoples, the Cherokee possessed a vibrant oral culture. Myths helped the Cherokee understand the world around them, live in harmony with nature, and pass on their beliefs and values to their descendants.

In the mid-1500s, the Cherokee used stone tools and hunted bears, elk, and deer. They lived in log cabins with bark roofs, no windows, and a smoke hole in the roof, in towns of about 200 people. At any given time, the Cherokee were in either peace mode or war mode. Because they lived in an alternating state, the Cherokee government was made up of two sets of officials: a white chief, who ruled during peacetime, and a red chief, who ruled during wartime.

Treaty of Augusta The Cherokee had been friendly trading partners with the British throughout the 1700s but had fallen into debt. In the Treaty of Augusta in 1773, the Cherokee and Creek were forced to cede vast swaths of their tribal lands in Georgia to repay these debts to the British. Hoping to regain their traditional hunting grounds, the Cherokee pledged their support for the British at the beginning of the American Revolution. In the 1770s and 1780s, the Cherokee engaged in a flurry of skirmishes with the American army. They lost each time and were forced to surrender more lands.

Assimilation In the 1800s, the Cherokee learned to adapt by assimilating elements of white culture. They learned new farming, weaving, and construction methods. In 1821, Sequoyah, a half-Cherokee who had served in the U.S. Army, developed a system of writing the Cherokee language called a syllabary, a set of written characters in which each character represents a syllable. When Sequoyah pitched the syllabary to the tribal council, the chiefs

marveled at its prospects and immediately accepted the new technology. Within a few years, almost the entire Cherokee nation was literate. In 1828, the Cherokee used their syllabary to publish *The Cherokee Phoenix*, the first Native American newspaper. But adopting white cultural practices did nothing to disarm the westward expansion. In 1830, the Cherokee were forcibly removed from their land under the Indian Removal Act. Some 15,000 Cherokee were placed in internment camps. Meanwhile, settlers pillaged and burned Cherokee homes.

Trail of Tears In 1838–1839, the Cherokee were exiled from their ancestral home and forced to march 1,000 miles to present-day Oklahoma, then known as Indian Territory. As many as 4,000 Cherokee died during the grueling 116-day journey. The soldiers refused to slow down for the sick and exhausted. Today, most Cherokee still live in Oklahoma, while several thousand, the descendants of those who escaped the Trail of Tears, still live in North Carolina.

 Literature Online

Author Search For more about the Cherokee, go to glencoe.com and enter QuickPass code GLA9800u1.

Selection Skills

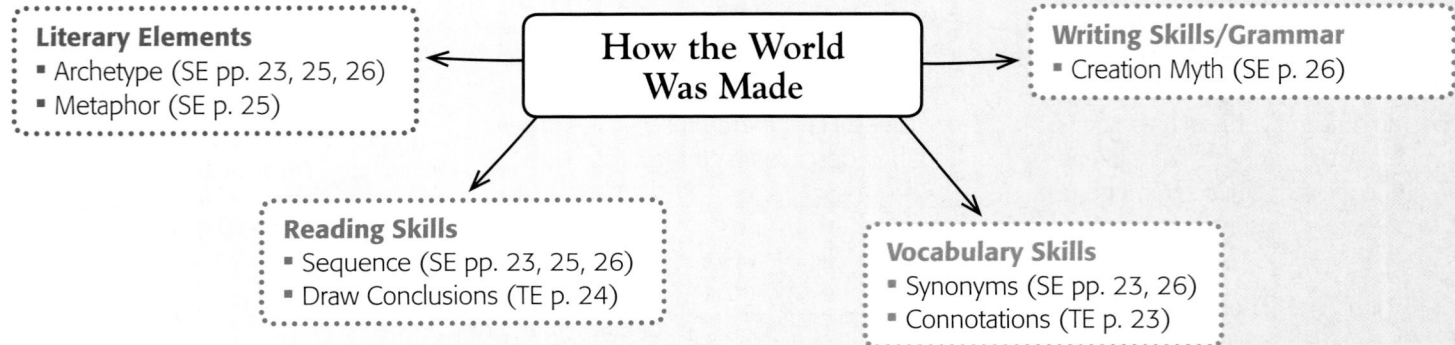

Literary Elements
- Archetype (SE pp. 23, 25, 26)
- Metaphor (SE p. 25)

How the World Was Made

Writing Skills/Grammar
- Creation Myth (SE p. 26)

Reading Skills
- Sequence (SE pp. 23, 25, 26)
- Draw Conclusions (TE p. 24)

Vocabulary Skills
- Synonyms (SE pp. 23, 26)
- Connotations (TE p. 23)

Literature and Reading Preview

Connect to the Myth

People often talk about where they come from—both geographically and in terms of their family, culture, and traditions. Why do people consider this information important? Write a journal entry in which you explain your origins, and what this information means to you.

Build Background

Myths usually come from ancient oral traditions. Early civilizations did not make the clear distinction between history and mythology that we do today. They took their myths very seriously as explanations of how the world came to be as it is.

Set Purposes for Reading

Big Idea The Sacred Earth and the Power of Storytelling

As you read "How the World Was Made," ask yourself, What does this story reveal about the Cherokees' relationship with nature?

Literary Element Archetype

An **archetype** is a character type, a descriptive detail, an image, or a story pattern that recurs frequently in the literature from many cultures and evokes strong emotional responses. As you read "How the World Was Made," ask yourself, What archetypal elements are present in this story?

Reading Strategy Identify Sequence

Identifying sequence is finding the logical order of ideas or events. Common forms of sequencing include time order, spatial order, and order of importance. Often, two or more types of sequencing are used in one literary work. In fact, all three are employed in this Cherokee genesis myth.

Tip: Take Notes Use a chart to record an example of each type of sequencing.

Detail	Type of Sequencing	Why
p. 25 "Men came after the animals and plants"	Order of Importance (also time order)	Animals and plants were created first so men would have food to survive

Learning Objectives

For pages 22–26
In studying this text, you will focus on the following objectives:

Literary Study: Analyzing archetype.

Reading: Analyzing sequence.

Writing: Writing a story.

Vocabulary

vault (vôlt) *n.* an arched structure forming a roof or ceiling; p. 24 *The church's vault arched high over our heads.*

alight (ə līt´) *v.* to descend and come to rest; p. 24 *The cat watched the pigeon alight on the roof.*

conjurer (kon´ jər ər) *n.* one who performs magic; sorcerer; p. 25 *The conjurer amused the audience with his tricks.*

Tip: Synonyms Synonyms are words that have the same or similar meanings. Sometimes you can determine the meaning of a word by using clues in the text to identify a synonym. In the third paragraph, we learn the birds had to return because they "found no place to *alight*." In the context of the story, this must mean that the earth was still wet, leaving the birds no place to land. *Land* and *alight* are synonyms.

Before You Read

Focus

Summary

The world is created when the animals in Gălûñ´lătĭ, a place in the sky, need more room. Waterbeetle goes below the water that is beneath the sky and stirs up mud to form land. Man and woman are created and soon rule the land.

 For summaries in languages other than English, see Unit 1 Teaching Resources Book, pp. 22–27.

Vocabulary

Connotations Have students look up *ceiling* and *sorcerer* in a standard dictionary. **Ask:** How are the connotations of the word *vault* different from those of *ceiling*? (*Ceiling is the covering of a room;* vault *is associated with large spaces.*) **Ask:** How are the connotations of *conjurer* different from those of *sorcerer*? (sorcerer *is associated with evil forces;* a conjurer *is good at tricks.*)

English Learners

DIFFERENTIATED INSTRUCTION

Intermediate Explain that writers use **transitional expressions** to connect ideas and make the sequence of ideas and events logical. Provide a list for students to keep as reference:

Time Order: *before, eventually, finally, later, next, then*
Space Order: *above, across, below, here, inside, there*
Order of Importance: *first, mainly, more important, to begin with, to sum up*

Demonstrate how students can create their own charts to identify connecting words and learn how they are used. Direct students to fill in the chart as they read selections in this unit.

Type of Sequencing	Transitional Words	Examples
time order	then	"then it dived to the bottom" (p. 24)
space order	beyond	"beyond the arch" (p. 24)
order of importance	at first	"At first the earth was flat" (p.24)

Teach

The Sacred Earth and the Power of Storytelling

Answer: *Water-beetle's crucial role in the creation of Earth reveals the importance of animals in the Cherokee culture. According to this myth, without animals, the world in which the Cherokee live would not exist.*

[APPROACHING] Ask students having difficulty to locate the sentence that tells where the animals lived before the world was made and why they were unhappy. Then ask them to find the sentence that explains why the animals were unable to descend to the land at first. *(first sentence of second paragraph; first few sentences of third paragraph)*

 For an audio recording of this selection, use Listening Library Audio CD-ROM.

Readability Scores

Dale-Chall: 5.9
DRP: 57
Lexile: 1250

How the World Was Made

(Cherokee–Great Smoky Mountains)
Retold by James Mooney

The earth is a great island floating in a sea of water, and suspended at each of the four cardinal points[1] by a cord hanging down from the sky **vault,** which is of solid rock. When the world grows old and worn out, the people will die and the cords will break and let the earth sink down into the ocean, and all will be water again. The Indians are afraid of this.

When all was water, the animals were above in Gălûñ´lătĭ (go lun(g) lot´ i), beyond the arch; but it was very much crowded, and they were wanting more room. They wondered what was below the water, and at last Dâyuni´sĭ (dô yun ē´ si), "Beaver's Grandchild," the little Water-beetle, offered to go and see if it could learn. It darted in every direction over the surface of the water, but could find no firm place to rest. Then it dived to the bottom and came up with some soft mud, which began to grow and spread on every side until it became the island which we call the earth. It was afterward fastened to the sky with four cords, but no one remembers who did this.

At first the earth was flat and very soft and wet. The animals were anxious to get down, and sent out different birds to see if it was yet dry, but they found no place to **alight** and came back again to Gălûñ´lătĭ. At last it seemed to be time, and they sent out the Buzzard and told him to go and make ready for them. This was the Great Buzzard, the father of all the buzzards we see now. He flew all over the earth, low down near the ground, and it was still soft. When he reached the Cherokee country, he was very tired, and his wings began to flap and strike the ground, and wherever they struck the earth there was a valley, and where they turned up again there was a mountain. When the animals above saw this, they were afraid that the whole world would be mountains, so they called him back, but the Cherokee country remains full of mountains to this day.

When the earth was dry and the animals came down, it was still dark, so they got the

---

1. The *four cardinal points* are the four main directions on a compass (north, south, east, and west).

1 **The Sacred Earth and the Power of Storytelling**
What does Water-beetle's role in the story reveal about the Cherokees' relationship with animals?

Vocabulary

vault (vôlt) *n.* an arched structure forming a ceiling

Vocabulary

alight (ə līt´) *v.* to descend and come to rest

24 UNIT 1　EARLY AMERICA

Reading Practice

 SPIRAL REVIEW **Draw Conclusions** Remind students that creation myths are a culture's attempt to make sense of the world. Thus, the crawfish's meat is spoiled in "How the World Was Made" to reflect the Cherokee aversion to eating crawfish.

Have students select details from this myth and draw conclusions about what these details suggest about Cherokee culture. *(For example, students may mention how animals are given the gift of seeing and go about in the dark to explain what the Cherokee observed about nocturnal animals.)*

sun and set it in a track to go every day across the island from east to west, just overhead. It was too hot this way, and Tsiska′gĭlĭ′ (chēs kä′ gi li′) the Red Crawfish, had his shell scorched a bright red, so that his meat was spoiled; and the Cherokee do not eat it. The **conjurers** put the sun another hand-breadth[2] higher in the air, but it was still too hot. They raised it another time, and another, until it was seven handbreadths high and just under the sky arch. Then it was right, and they left it so. This is why the conjurers call the highest place Gûlkwâ′gine Di′gălûñlătiyûñ′ (gul kwô′ gē nā dē′ gol un(g) lot ē yun(g′)), "the seventh height," because it is seven hand-breadths above the earth. Every day the sun goes along under this arch, and returns at night on the upper side to the starting place.

There is another world under this, and it is like ours in everything—animals, plants, and people—save that the seasons are different. The streams that come down from the mountains are the trails by which we reach this underworld, and the springs at their heads are the doorways by which we enter it, but to do this one must fast and go to water and have one of the underground people for a guide. We know that the seasons in the underworld are different from ours, because the water in the springs is always warmer in winter and cooler in summer than the outer air.

When the animals and plants were first made—we do not know by whom—they were told to watch and keep awake for seven nights, just as young men now fast and keep awake

---

2. A *hand-breadth* is a unit of measurement based on the width of a hand. It varies from 2½ to 4 inches.

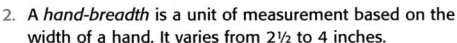

2 Archetype *What other stories have you read that include an underworld?*

3 Identify Sequence *When do the following events take place in relation to those you have already read about?*

Vocabulary

conjurer (kon′ jər ər) *n.* one who performs magic

Cherokee drinking vessel in the shape of an owl.

---

when they pray to their medicine.[3] They tried to do this, and nearly all were awake through the first night, but the next night several dropped off to sleep, and the third night others were asleep, and then others, until, on the seventh night, of all the animals only the owl, the panther, and one or two more were still awake. To these were given the power to see and to go about in the dark, and to make prey of the birds and animals which must sleep at night. Of the trees only the cedar, the pine, the spruce, the holly, and the laurel were awake to the end, and to them it was given to be always green and to be greatest for medicine, but to the others it was said: "Because you have not endured to the end you shall lose your hair every winter."

Men came after the animals and plants. At first there were only a brother and sister until he struck her with a fish and told her to multiply, and so it was. In seven days a child was born to her, and thereafter every seven days another, and they increased very fast until there was danger that the world could not keep them. Then it was made that a woman should have only one child in a year, and it has been so ever since. ✎

---

3. Many Native American cultures believe that each living thing has its own *medicine*, or spirit, that gives it power.

CHEROKEE MYTH **25**

Teach

Literary Element **2**

Metaphor **Answer:** *Students may say Greek mythology: Demeter and Persephone, Hercules.*

Reading Strategy **3**

Identify Sequence
Answer: *Before the part of the story already read*

ENGLISH LEARNERS Have students locate text connectors that clarify organization.

Literary Element **4**

Metaphor Direct students to the end of the next to last paragraph—"you [trees] shall lose your hair every winter"—to help them decode the meaning. *(The myth refers to the trees' foliage as hair.)*

ENGLISH LEARNERS Ask English learners to explain the similarities between the leaves on trees and hair on a head.

Cultural History ☆

Evergreens Explain that the cedar, pine, spruce, holly, and laurel are not the only trees in Cherokee country that do not "lose their hair." Three other trees that are always green are the juniper, fir, and cypress.

Approaching Level

DIFFERENTIATED INSTRUCTION 🐟

Emerging This story is three tales in one. Ask students to create three graphic organizers: a flow chart of paragraphs 1–4, a web of details for paragraph 5, and a flow chart of paragraphs 6–7. Have students use one visual to practice storytelling.

Example:

All was water.

↓

Water-beetle dives and brings up mud.

↓

Mud spreads out to form Earth.

To check students' understanding of the selection, see Unit 1 Teaching Resources Book, p. 31.

After You Read

Assess

1. The Water-beetle's dive into the sea, the Buzzard's sculpting wings, or the conjurers shifting the sun

2. (a) He brings up soft mud that grows into Earth. (b) Every creature has worth.

3. (a) They move the sun up. (b) Magicians who control nature

4. (a) The owl, panther, other animals; the cedar, pine, spruce, holly and laurel. (b) Vigilance and perseverance are rewarded.

5. (a) "No one remembers" or "we do not know" (b) It adds to the mystery.

6. Equal; they believe animals had a major role in creating Earth.

7. (a) Narratives are memorable. (b) They feel close to nature; it is part of a meaningful order.

8. Answers will vary.

 For additional assessment, see Assessment Resources, pp. 59–60.

 To create custom assessments using software, use ExamView Assessment Suite.

Literary Element

1. The seven-night vigil

2. Such tests as the sword in the stone from the Arthurian legend or Hercules' tasks

Progress Check

Can students identify the sequence of a story?

If No → See Unit 1 Teaching Resources Book, p. 29.

After You Read

Respond and Think Critically

Respond and Interpret

1. Which events in this myth do you find most memorable and why?

2. (a)What is the little Water-beetle's role in the creation of Earth? (b)What does this tell you about Cherokee reverence for all creatures?

3. (a)What do the "conjurers" do? (b)Who do you think the conjurers are? Explain.

4. (a)Which animals and plants are able to keep awake for seven nights? (b)What moral lesson might this episode teach?

Analyze and Evaluate

5. (a)What does the narrator say when Cherokee tradition has no answer or explanation for an occurrence? (b)How does the narrator's phrasing enhance the myth? Explain.

6. For the Cherokee, are humans more important than plants or animals or equal to them? Support your view with examples from the myth.

Connect

7. **Big Idea** The Sacred Earth and the Power of Storytelling (a)Why do the Cherokee people explain natural phenomena, such as mountains, underground springs, nocturnal predators, or evergreen trees, in story terms? (b)What do these explanations suggest about the Cherokee relationship with nature?

8. **Connect to the Author** (a)Why do you think Mooney chose to live with the Cherokee for three years? (b)How might this story have been affected if Mooney had chosen to merely visit them?

Literary Element Archetype

One example of an archetype found in myths and folktales from many cultures is a daunting challenge or test that only heroic characters can overcome.

1. How does this archetype appear in "How the World Was Made"?

2. What examples of this archetype can you recall from other myths and folktales?

Reading Strategy Identify Sequence

In a myth, such as "How the World Was Made," events usually occur in chronological, or time order.

1. Using the chart you made on p. 23, list the sequence of events in the myth.

2. Which detail is an exception to the time order?

 Literature Online

Selection Resources For Selection Quizzes, eFlash-cards, and Reading-Writing Connection activities, go to glencoe.com and enter QuickPass code GLA9800u1.

Vocabulary Practice

Practice with Synonyms A synonym is a word that has the same or nearly the same meaning as another word. With a partner, match each boldfaced vocabulary word below with one synonym from the right column. You will not use all the answer choices. Use a thesaurus or dictionary to check your answers.

1. vault   a. unburden
2. alight   b. dome
3. conjurer   c. land
            d. magician
            e. fly

Writing

Write a Story In three or four paragraphs, write your own creation myth. You may write about the Earth or an imaginary world. Include a character who plays the archetypal "hero" role and overcomes a test or challenge.

Reading Strategy

1. Creation of Earth, creation of mountains and valleys, placement of sun, creation and testing of animals and plants, creation of humans.

2. The description of the underworld introduces a spatial element into the overall chronological sequence.

Vocabulary

1. b 2. c 3. d

Writing

Students' creation myths should follow a clear narrative structure and use proper grammar and sentence structure.

from

THE WAY TO RAINY MOUNTAIN

N. Scott Momaday

Pulitzer Prize Winner

Learning Objectives

For pages 27–32

In studying this text, you will focus on the following objective:

Literary Study: Analyzing cultural traditions.

Set a Purpose for Reading

Read to learn about the Kiowas' culture and their relationship with the land.

Build Background

In the 1700s, the Kiowa (kī' ə wä) Indians began a long migration from southwestern Montana to the southern Great Plains. Along the way, they made contact with the Crow Indians of southeastern Montana, whose nomadic way of life greatly influenced the Kiowa. Their travels came to an end in 1868 when they were forced to settle on an Oklahoma reservation. Kiowa author N. Scott Momaday (mom' ə dä) frequently writes about the Kiowas' rich history. In the following selection, he describes their connection to the natural world and the end of the tribe's golden age.

Reading Strategy Analyze Cultural Traditions

In the selection, Momaday presents his understanding of Kiowa culture. Examine the elements that make up the selection, such as the descriptions of the land, of Kiowa history, and of Momaday's grandmother. As you read, ask yourself, What do all of these elements, taken together, suggest about the Kiowa?

A single knoll rises out of the plain in Oklahoma, north and west of the Wichita Range. For my people, the Kiowas, it is an old landmark, and they gave it the name Rainy Mountain. The hardest weather in the world is there. Winter brings blizzards, hot tornadic winds arise in the spring, and in summer the prairie is an anvil's edge. The grass turns brittle and brown, and it cracks beneath your feet. There are green belts along the rivers and creeks, linear groves of hickory and pecan, willow and witch hazel. At a distance in July or August the steaming foliage seems almost to writhe[1] in fire. Great green and yellow grasshoppers are everywhere in the tall grass, popping up like corn to sting the flesh, and tortoises crawl about on the red earth, going nowhere in the plenty of time. Loneliness is an aspect of the land. All things in the plain are isolate;[2] there is no confusion of objects in the eye, but *one* hill or *one* tree or *one* man. To look upon that landscape in the early morning, with the sun at your back, is to lose the sense of proportion. Your imagination comes to life, and this, you think, is where Creation was begun.

---

1. *Writhe* means "to twist as in great pain."
2. *Isolate* means "solitary."

English Learners

DIFFERENTIATED INSTRUCTION

SMALL GROUP

Advanced Remind students of the definition of figurative language. Ask them to find the metaphors at the end of sentence 4 and in sentence 7 and to explain the comparisons in their own words. Have students form small groups to brainstorm a list of comparisons (similes and metaphors) that communicate the sense of summer heat. Direct them to identify which literary elements they are using. *(For example: "The prairie was a sizzling griddle"= metaphor; "The leaves danced like pasta shells in boiling water" = simile.)*

Focus

Summary

After his grandmother's death, the author reflects on his Kiowa roots. He physically retraces the migration of his ancestors. He describes his grandmother's traditional upbringing, noting her participation in "the last great moment" of her people, a Sun Dance in 1890 that was interrupted by U.S. soldiers. He recalls her later years and his connection to her and to his people.

Language History

Native American Languages

In the last decades of the nineteenth century and early twentieth century, ethnologists (people who study different cultures) began to make accurate records of the Indian languages. They were able to write down Indian tales and songs. When phonograph recording became available, they were able to preserve the tone and emphasis of Indian oral art as well as words and phrases.

 For an audio recording of this selection, use Listening Library Audio CD-ROM.

 For activities related to this selection, see Unit 1 Teaching Resources Book, pp. 22–32.

Readability Scores

Dale-Chall: 5.5
DRP: 61
Lexile: 1000

Teach

Reading Strategy | 1

Fact and Opinion Say:
Momaday's memoir combines facts about the Kiowas with his opinions about his people's history. Ask students to find an example of each on this page and to explain how they know which is a fact and which is an opinion. *(A fact is an event in the Kiowas' surrender or the Kiowa name of Momaday's grandmother. An opinion is the description of the Kiowa as "among the finest horsemen the world has ever known.")*

Cultural History ☆

Names English-language names for Native American peoples tend to be different from the names in Native American languages. For example, the English-language name *Kiowa* comes from the Spanish word *Caygua,* which is based on *kygu,* the Kiowas' name for themselves in their own language. Have students research the origins of other English-language names for Native American peoples and what these people call themselves in their own languages.

I returned to Rainy Mountain in July. My grandmother had died in the spring, and I wanted to be at her grave. She had lived to be very old and at last infirm.[3] Her only living daughter was with her when she died, and I was told that in death her face was that of a child.

I like to think of her as a child. When she was born, the Kiowas were living the last great moment of their history. For more than a hundred years they had controlled the open range from the Smoky Hill River to the Red, from the headwaters of the Canadian to the fork of the Arkansas and Cimarron. In alliance with the Comanches, they had ruled the whole of the southern Plains. War was their sacred business, and they were among the finest horsemen the world has ever known. But warfare for the Kiowas was preeminently[4] a matter of disposition rather than of survival, and they never understood the grim, unrelenting advance of the U.S. Cavalry. When at last, divided and ill-provisioned, they were driven onto the Staked Plains in the cold rains of autumn, they fell into panic. In Palo Duro Canyon they abandoned their crucial stores to pillage[5] and had nothing then but their lives. In order to save themselves, they surrendered to the soldiers at Fort Sill and were imprisoned in the old stone corral that now stands as a military museum. My grandmother was spared the humiliation of those high gray walls by eight or ten years, but she must have known from birth the affliction of defeat, the dark brooding of old warriors.

Her name was Aho, and she belonged to the last culture to evolve in North America. Her forebears came down from the high country in western Montana nearly three centuries ago. They were a mountain people, a mysterious tribe of hunters whose language has never been positively classified in any major group. In the late seventeenth century they began a long migration to the south and east. It was a journey toward the dawn, and it led to a golden age. Along the way
☆ the Kiowas were befriended by the Crows, who

gave them the culture and religion of the Plains. They acquired horses, and their ancient nomadic spirit was suddenly free of the ground. They acquired Tai-me,[6] the sacred Sun Dance doll, from that moment the object and symbol of their worship, and so shared in the divinity of the sun. Not least, they acquired the sense of destiny, therefore courage and pride. When they entered upon the southern Plains they had been transformed. No longer were they slaves to the simple necessity of survival; they were a lordly and dangerous society of fighters and thieves, hunters and priests of the sun. According to their origin myth, they entered the world through a hollow log. From one point of view, their migration was the fruit of an old prophecy, for indeed they emerged from a sunless world.

Although my grandmother lived out her long life in the shadow of Rainy Mountain, the immense landscape of the continental interior lay like memory in her blood. She could tell of the Crows, whom she had never seen, and of the Black Hills, where she had never been. I wanted to see in reality what she had seen more perfectly in the mind's eye, and traveled fifteen hundred miles to begin my pilgrimage.

Yellowstone, it seemed to me, was the top of the world, a region of deep lakes and dark timber, canyons and waterfalls. But, beautiful as it is, one might have the sense of confinement there. The skyline in all directions is close at hand, the high wall of the woods and deep cleavages of shade. There is a perfect freedom in the mountains, but it belongs to the eagle and the elk, the badger and the bear. The Kiowas reckoned their stature by the distance they could see, and they were bent and blind in the wilderness.

Descending eastward, the highland meadows are a stairway to the plain. In July the inland slope of the Rockies is luxuriant[7] with flax and buckwheat, stonecrop and larkspur.[8] The earth **1**

---

3. *Infirm* means "physically weak" or "feeble."
4. *Preeminently* means "primarily."
5. *Pillage* means "to loot" or "to plunder."

6. *Tai-me* (tī′ mā), the Sun Dance doll, wears a robe of white feathers.
7. *Luxuriant* means "marked by rich or plentiful growth."
8. *Flax* is a flowering plant whose fibers are spun to make cloth. *Buckwheat* is a plant whose seeds are used as a cereal grain. *Stonecrop* is a flowering plant found on rocks and walls. *Larkspur* is known for its showy flower stalks.

Reading Practice

Graphic Aids Direct students to the map of migration routes, and have them identify the features on the map. **Ask:** What features make this a political map? *(state boundaries, names of states)* **Ask:** What features make this a physical map? *(mountain ranges, rivers)* Explain that when two species are crossed, such as two plants, the result is a *hybrid.*

Ask: What makes this a hybrid map? Why was a hybrid map used for the migration routes? *(It mixes features of political and physical maps. A political map shows the states through which the Kiowa traveled. A physical map shows mountains that help explain why this route was taken.)*

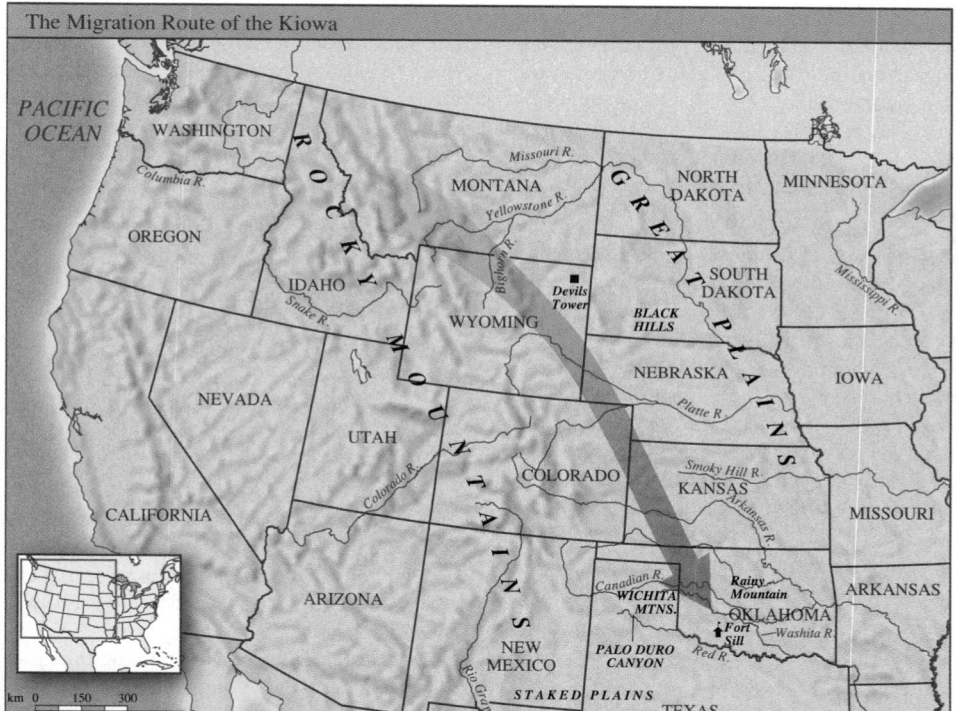

The Migration Route of the Kiowa

View the Map The Kiowa gradually migrated south and east over some 200 years. Why do you think it was so important for N. Scott Momaday to physically retrace his ancestors' long journey?

unfolds and the limit of the land recedes. Clusters of trees, and animals grazing far in the distance, cause the vision to reach away and wonder to build upon the mind. The sun follows a longer

2 course in the day, and the sky is immense beyond all comparison. The great billowing clouds that sail upon it are shadows that move upon the grain like water, dividing light. Farther down, in the land of the Crows and Blackfeet, the plain is yellow. Sweet clover takes hold of the hills and bends upon itself to cover and seal the soil. There the Kiowas paused on their way; they had come to the place where they must change their lives. The sun is at home on the plains. Precisely there does it have the certain character of a god. When the Kiowas came to the land of the Crows, they could see the dark lees[9] of the hills at dawn across

the Bighorn River, the profusion of light on the grain shelves, the oldest deity ranging after the solstices.[10] Not yet would they veer southward to the caldron of the land that lay below; they must wean their blood[11] from the northern winter and hold the mountains a while longer in their view. They bore Tai-me in procession to the east.

A dark mist lay over the Black Hills, and the land was like iron. At the top of a ridge I caught sight of Devils Tower[12] upthrust against the gray sky as if in the birth of time the core

9. *Lees* are the sides of hills that are away from the wind.

10. *Solstices:* In the Northern Hemisphere, the summer and winter solstices are the longest and shortest days of the year.
11. *Wean their blood* means "to become acclimated by removing themselves gradually."
12. *Devils Tower,* an 865-foot-high column of volcanic rock in Wyoming, became a national monument in 1906.

N. SCOTT MOMADAY **29**

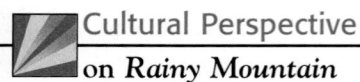

Cultural Perspective
on *Rainy Mountain*

Teach

Reading Strategy | 1

Compare and Contrast

Ask: How was the Sun Dance a central part of Kiowa religious beliefs? *(The Kiowa revered the Sun. Tai-me was the Sun Dance doll, an object they worshipped.)* Have students use Momaday's description to reconstruct what the original Sun Dance might have been like. Direct them to compare and contrast the original ritual with the 1887 and 1890 rituals.
Ask: How do these events reflect what happened to the Kiowa and other Native Americans in the nineteenth century? *(Native American traditions were eroded and eliminated.)*

Cultural History ☆

Myth Ask: What does the myth included here explain? *(It explains how the Big Dipper was formed.)* **Say:** This myth also exemplifies the close connection between animals and people, a common theme in Native American folklore.

---

of the earth had broken through its crust and the motion of the world was begun. There are things in nature that engender[13] an awful quiet in the heart of man; Devils Tower is one of them. Two centuries ago, because they could not do otherwise, the Kiowas made a legend at the base of the rock. My grandmother said:

Eight children were there at play, seven sisters and their brother. Suddenly the boy was struck dumb; he trembled and began to run upon his hands and feet. His fingers became claws, and his body was covered with fur. Directly there was a bear where the boy had been. The sisters were terrified; they ran, and the bear after them. They came to the stump of a great tree, and the tree spoke to them. It bade them climb upon it, and as they did so it began to rise into the air. The bear came to kill them, but they were just beyond its reach. It reared against the tree and scored the bark all around with its claws. The seven sisters were borne into the sky, and they became the stars of the Big Dipper.[14]

☆

From that moment, and so long as the legend lives, the Kiowas have kinsmen in the night sky. Whatever they were in the mountains, they could be no more. However tenuous their well-being, however much they had suffered and would suffer again, they had found a way out of the wilderness.

My grandmother had a reverence for the sun, a holy regard that now is all but gone out of mankind. There was a wariness in her, and an ancient awe. She was a Christian in her later years, but she had come a long way about, and she never forgot her birthright. As a child she had been to the Sun Dances; she had taken part in those annual rites, and by them she had learned the restoration of her people in the presence of Tai-me. She was about seven when the last Kiowa Sun Dance was held in 1887 on the Washita River above Rainy Mountain Creek. The buffalo were gone. In order to consummate[15] the ancient sacrifice—to impale the

1

---

13. *Engender* means "to give rise to" or "to produce."
14. The *Big Dipper* is part of a larger constellation called Ursa Major, the Great Bear.
15. *Consummate* means "to bring to completion."

---

head of a buffalo bull upon the medicine tree—a delegation of old men journeyed into Texas, there to beg and barter for an animal from the Goodnight herd. She was ten when the Kiowas came together for the last time as a living Sun Dance culture. They could find no buffalo; they had to hang an old hide from the sacred tree. Before the dance could begin, a company of soldiers rode out from Fort Sill under orders to disperse the tribe. Forbidden without cause the essential act of their faith, having seen the wild herds slaughtered and left to rot upon the ground, the Kiowas backed away forever from the medicine tree. That was July 20, 1890, at the great bend of the Washita. My grandmother was there. Without bitterness, and for as long as she lived, she bore a vision of deicide.[16]

1

Now that I can have her only in memory, I see my grandmother in the several postures that were peculiar to her: standing at the wood stove on a winter morning and turning meat in a great iron skillet; sitting at the south window, bent above her beadwork, and afterwards, when her vision failed, looking down for a long time into the fold of her hands; going out upon a cane, very slowly as she did when the weight of age came upon her; praying. I remember her most often at prayer. She made long, rambling prayers out of suffering and hope, having seen many things. I was never sure that I had the right to hear, so exclusive were they of all mere custom and company. The last time I saw her she prayed standing by the side of her bed at night, naked to the waist, the light of a kerosene lamp moving upon her dark skin. Her long, black hair, always drawn and braided in the day, lay upon her shoulders and against her breasts like a shawl. I do not speak Kiowa, and I never understood her prayers, but there was something inherently sad in the sound, some merest hesitation upon the syllables of sorrow. She began in a high and descending pitch, exhausting her breath to silence; then again and again—and always the same intensity of effort, of something that is, and is not, like urgency in the human voice.

---

16. *Deicide* is the killing of a god.

Writing Practice

⚡ **Visualize** Have students read descriptive passages aloud (such as the grandmother's various "postures," the house, her visitors) while listeners close their eyes and visualize the scene. Direct them to imagine concrete sensory details that appeal to different senses: sight, hearing, smell, taste, and touch. They can add details describing the characters' actions and feelings. Have them create webs for each passage, showing details derived from the text and details they added. Direct students to write a descriptive paragraph using words from their webs.

Teach

Big Idea | **2**

The Sacred Earth and the Power of Storytelling Ask: How does this selection (1) capture the Kiowas' reverence for nature and (2) exemplify the power of storytelling? *(1. The sun is central to their spiritual life. 2. The myth in the memoir; the poetic storytelling style)*

Reading Strategy | **3**

**Make Inferences Have students cite evidence from the second paragraph for inferences about gender roles in Kiowa culture and Kiowas' attitude toward intertribal wars. *(Men were warriors, and women were homemakers; the men relished warfare.)*

 View the Art The author says on p. 30 that the Kiowa created a legend around Devils Tower "because they could not do otherwise." Looking at this photograph, what do you think Momaday meant? ★

Transported so in the dancing light among the shadows of her room, she seemed beyond the reach of time. But that was illusion; I think I knew then that I should not see her again.

Houses are like sentinels in the plain, old keepers of the weather watch. There, in a very little while, wood takes on the appearance of great age. All colors wear soon away in the wind and rain, and then the wood is burned gray and **2** the grain appears and the nails turn red with rust. The windowpanes are black and opaque;[17] you imagine there is nothing within, and indeed there are many ghosts, bones given up to the land. They stand here and there against the sky, and you approach them for a longer time than you expect. They belong in the distance; it is their domain.[18]

Once there was a lot of sound in my grand- mother's house, a lot of coming and going, **3** feasting and talk. The summers there were full of excitement and reunion. The Kiowas are a summer people; they abide the cold and keep to themselves, but when the season turns and the land becomes warm and vital they cannot hold still; an old love of going returns upon them. The aged visitors who came to my grandmother's house when I was a child were made of lean and leather, and they bore them- selves upright. They wore great black hats and bright ample shirts that shook in the wind. They rubbed fat upon their hair and wound their braids with strips of colored cloth. Some of them painted their faces and carried the scars of old and cherished enmities.[19] They **3** were an old council of warlords, come to remind and be reminded of who they were. Their wives and daughters served them well. The women might indulge themselves; gossip was at once the mark and compensation of their servitude. They made loud and elaborate talk among themselves, full of jest and gesture, fright and false alarm. They went abroad[20] in fringed and flowered shawls, bright beadwork and German silver.[21] They were at home in

---

17. *Opaque* means "unable to let light through."
18. A *domain* is "a territory over which control is exercised."

19. *Enmities* means "deep-seated hatreds."
20. Here, *abroad* means "away from one's home."
21. *German silver* is an alloy that resembles real silver.

N. SCOTT MOMADAY **31**

View the Art ★

Answer: *Students may say that Native American people often created stories around important aspects of nature, such as animals, plants, and the landscape. Devils Tower is a very imposing rock formation in an otherwise flat terrain, which makes it a prime candidate for such a myth. It also resembles the base of a tree trunk, as mentioned in the myth.*

Devils Tower was the central image in the movie *Close Encounters of the Third Kind* (1977).

Teach

Reading Strategy

Analyze Cultural Traditions

Say: On this page, Momaday weaves frogs, a cricket, grasshoppers, and birds into his narrative. **Ask:** What memories, events, or ideas does he associate with each animal? *(frogs: his childhood, when his people celebrated freely; cricket: a life that is made whole at Rainy Mountain; grasshoppers: his culture's connection to the plains; scissortail: life, perhaps his grandmother's spirit, continuing)*

Assess

1. Student summaries should describe the migration of the ancestors, his grandmother's upbringing, the Sun Dance, and the author's reflections on his grandmother and his connection to her and to his people.

2. Students may be shocked or saddened.

3. (a) It is a special landmark for the Kiowas. (b) Students may say it is the starkness or beauty of the landscape; or that Momaday is writing metaphorically about the creation of his tribal history.

4. (a) She told Kiowa legends, revered the sun, and had been to the Sun Dance. (b) They are stoic and resilient survivors.

5. (a) She knew Kiowas who were forced onto the reservation. She spoke the Kiowa language, prayed in the old way, and retained the old beliefs. (b) Students must support their answers with textual evidence.

---

the kitchen, and they prepared meals that were banquets.

There were frequent prayer meetings, and great nocturnal feasts. When I was a child I played with my cousins outside, where the lamplight fell upon the ground and the singing of the old people rose up around us and carried away into the darkness. There were a lot of good things to eat, a lot of laughter and surprise. And afterwards, when the quiet returned, I lay down with my grandmother and could hear the frogs away by the river and feel the motion of the air.

Now there is a funeral silence in the rooms, the endless wake of some final word. The walls have closed in upon my grandmother's house. When I returned to it in mourning, I saw for the first time in my life how small it was. It was late at night, and there was a white moon, nearly full. I sat for a long time on the stone steps by the kitchen door. From there I could see out across the land; I could see the long row of trees by the creek, the low light upon the rolling plains, and the stars of the Big Dipper. Once I looked at the moon and caught sight of a strange thing. A cricket had perched upon the handrail, only a few inches away from me. My line of vision was such that the creature filled the moon like a fossil. It had gone there, I thought, to live and die, for there, of all places, was its small definition made whole and eternal. A warm wind rose up and purled[22] like the longing within me.

The next morning I awoke at dawn and went out on the dirt road to Rainy Mountain. It was already hot, and the grasshoppers began to fill the air. Still, it was early in the morning, and the birds sang out of the shadows. The long yellow grass on the mountain shone in the bright light, and a scissor-tail hied[23] above the land. There, where it ought to be, at the end of a long and legendary way, was my grandmother's grave. Here and there on the dark stones were ancestral names. Looking back once, I saw the mountain and came away. ᴏᴡ

Visual Vocabulary
A *scissortail,* a type of flycatcher, is a small gray and pink bird with a forked tail.

---

22. *Purled* means "rippled with a murmuring sound."
23. *Hied* means "went quickly."

Respond and Think Critically

Respond and Interpret

1. Write a brief summary of the main ideas in this excerpt before you answer the following questions. For help on writing a summary, see page 79.

2. How did you react to the description of the end of the Kiowas' old way of life?

3. (a) What is the importance of Rainy Mountain? (b) Why, do you think, does Momaday feel that Rainy Mountain is "where Creation was begun"?

4. (a) What Kiowa traditional beliefs were part of the grandmother's life? (b) What do you learn about the Kiowa people from the way that they respond to the end of their traditional lifestyle?

Analyze and Evaluate

5. (a) Explain why Momaday considers his grandmother a living embodiment of Kiowa history. (b) Did you find this description convincing? Why or why not?

6. Momaday watches a cricket that he says came to Rainy Mountain to die, "for there, of all places, was its small definition made whole and eternal." He also describes his grandmother's grave. Which of these works best for you as a symbol? Explain.

Connect

7. Momaday once said, "I don't see any validity in the separation of man and landscape." He has also called human alienation from nature "one of the great afflictions of our time." How are these ideas embodied in the selection?

6. Students must support their answers with textual evidence.

7. He expresses these ideas through descriptions of the Kiowa attachment to the landscape and worship of the sun. Momaday describes people who remain close to nature.

📁 **For additional assessment, see Assessment Resources, pp. 61–62.**

Comparing Literature

Across Time and Place

Compare Literature About the Power of Storytelling

Oral cultures use storytelling to pass on ancient traditions. The three literary works compared here—a Huron myth, a West African folktale, and a Native American poem—reflect this tradition of storytelling in different ways.

The Sky Tree by the Eastern Woodland Huron .... myth 34

How the Leopard Got His Claws by Chinua Achebe and John Iroaganachi............................ myth 38
WEST AFRICA, 1972

Prayer to the Pacific by Leslie Marmon Silko ....poem 44

COMPARE THE [Big Idea] The Sacred Earth and the Power of Storytelling

Storytellers played a vital role in oral cultures. They preserved ancient myths and traditions and made them live for new generations. As you read, ask yourself, How do these selections reveal the power of storytelling?

COMPARE Mythic Elements

A **myth** is a traditional story that explains a belief, a custom, or a force of nature. Certain mythic elements, such as creation or journeys, are used by storytellers in many different cultures. As you read, ask yourself, What elements of myths are found in these selections?

COMPARE Cultures

The writers featured here each reflect their times and places, as well as transmit the heritage and belief systems of their cultures. As you read, ask yourself, What does each selection suggest about its culture of origin?

LOG ON ▶ **Literature** Online

Author Search For more about the Eastern Woodland Huron, Chinua Achebe and John Iroaganachi, and Leslie Marmon Silko, go to glencoe.com and enter QuickPass code GLA9800u1.

Learning Objectives

For pages 34–46

In studying these texts, you will focus on the following objective:

Literary Study: Comparing cultural context.

Comparing Literature

Across Time and Place

Focus

Bellringer Options

Literature Launchers:
   Pre-Reading Videos DVD,
   Selection Launcher
Selection Focus
   Transparency 2
Daily Language Practice
   Transparency 4

Or **draw** attention to the text under the head Compare Cultures. Have students brainstorm a list of images and writings they would include in a time capsule to reflect their time, place, customs, and beliefs. **Ask:** Why do you feel these images and writings are important in our culture? *(Students may identify the theme or topic of each work and explain how it offers insight into contemporary life.)*

Selection Skills

Literary Elements
- Oral Tradition (SE pp. 34, 37)
- Characterization (TE p. 38)
- Archetypes (TE p. 39)
- Personification (TE p. 42)
- Sensory Details (TE p. 44)

Vocabulary Skills
- Academic Vocabulary (SE p. 37)
- Antonyms (TE p. 43)

Comparing Literature

Reading Skills
- Question (SE pp. 34, 36, 37)
- Author's Purpose (TE p. 39)
- Critical Thinking (TE p. 41)
- Review (TE p. 46)

Study Skills/ Research/ Assessment
- Notetaking (TE p. 42)

Listening/Speaking/Viewing Skills
- Analyze Art (SE pp. 35, 40, 42; TE p. 45)
- Repetition (TE p. 40)

Writing Skills/Grammar
- Write a Dialogue (SE p. 37)
- Quickwrite (SE p. 43)
- Write an Essay (SE p. 46)
- Write a Report (TE p. 34)
- Punctuate Dialogue (TE p. 36)

Focus

Connect

Ask: What have you learned about Cherokee and Kiowa traditions and beliefs? *(Students may draw on the previous selections, including the myth about the Big Dipper.)* How do you think these selections may be similar or different from those you have just read? *(Answers will vary.)*

Literary History ☆

The World Tree In the Norse creation myth, there is a huge ash tree, called the World Tree (Yggdrasil), which supports the nine worlds of the Norse cosmos. Its roots and branches spread throughout all the worlds.

Summary

To save her sick husband, Aataentsic dives out of Sky Land toward the water below. The animals build a mud island on Turtle's back, where she lands and where the tree takes root.

> **Interactive Read and Write**
> Other options for teaching this selection can be found in
> - Interactive Read and Write for EL Students, pp. 1–16
> - Interactive Read and Write for Approaching-Level Students, pp. 1–16
> - Interactive Read and Write for On-Level Students, pp. 1–16

34

Before You Read

The Sky Tree

Meet the **Huron**

The Huron people believed that Earth was an island resting on the back of the Great Turtle that swam in the primal waters. So their name for themselves, *Wendat*, in their own language means "islanders." The name *Huron*, meaning "boar's head" or "rough hair," was given to them by the French explorers with whom they traded furs. In the 1600s, the Huron were members of a confederacy of tribes living northeast of the Great Lakes in what is now southern Canada. Even before the French arrived, the Huron were great traders. In the mid-1600s, their long conflict with the Iroquois nations (see page 47) reached a climax when the Iroquois seized control of the fur trade and forced the Huron to flee their homelands.

Connect to the Myth

What would you risk to save the person you love most? Discuss this question with a partner.

Build Background

☆ "The Sky Tree" is an example of a type of creation story known as an earth-diver myth. In this type of myth a being dives into the primal waters to retrieve mud. This mud is spread on the back of the Great Turtle, eventually growing to form an island that becomes Earth.

Set Purposes for Reading

Big Idea The Sacred Earth and the Power of Storytelling

As you read "The Sky Tree," ask yourself, What beliefs about people's relationship with the natural world does this myth reveal?

Literary Element Oral Tradition

Oral tradition is literature that passes by word of mouth from one generation to the next. As you read "The Sky Tree," ask yourself, Why did the Huron create and preserve this story?

Reading Strategy Question

Questioning is asking yourself at regular intervals whether you have understood what you have read.

Tip: Take Notes As you read "The Sky Tree," write down questions that puzzle you in the left-hand column of a double-entry journal. See the example below.

Question	Answer
What is the meaning of Aataentsic's act in cutting down the Sky Tree?	

Writing Practice

SMALL GROUP

Research Mythology Have students work in small groups to investigate one of the stories involving trees in different mythologies. Suggest the following topics:

- The World Tree in Norse mythology
- The oak tree in European mythologies
- Druid worship of trees
- Trees in Mesoamerican mythologies (Mayan, Aztec, etc.)

Direct students to use a minimum of three sources, including library books and online articles. Instruct them to identify their sources in their reports. Ask each group to share the report with the class.

The Sky Tree

Huron—Eastern Woodland
Retold by Joseph Bruchac

In the beginning, Earth was covered with water. In Sky Land, there were people living as they do now on Earth. In the middle of that land was the great Sky Tree. All of the food which the people in that Sky Land ate came from the great tree. The old chief of that land lived with his wife, whose name was Aataentsic,[1] meaning "Ancient Woman," in their longhouse[2] near the great tree. It came to be that the old chief became sick and nothing could cure him. He grew weaker and weaker until it seemed he would die. Then a dream came to him and he called Aataentsic to him.

"I have dreamed," he said, "and in my dream I saw how I can be healed. I must be given the fruit which grows at the very top of Sky Tree. You must cut it down and bring that fruit to me."

Aataentsic took her husband's stone ax and went to the great tree. As soon as she struck it, it split in half and toppled over. As it fell a hole opened in Sky Land and the tree fell through the hole. Aataentsic returned to the place where the old chief waited.

"My husband," she said, "when I cut the tree it split in half and then fell through a great hole. Without the tree, there can be no life. I must follow it."

Then, leaving her husband she went back to the hole in Sky Land and threw herself after the great tree.

As Aataentsic fell, Turtle looked up and saw her. Immediately Turtle called together all the water animals and told them what she had seen.

"What should be done?" Turtle said.

Beaver answered her. "You are the one who saw this happen. Tell us what to do."

"All of you must dive down," Turtle said. "Bring up soil from the bottom, and place it on my back."

Immediately all of the water animals began to dive down and bring up soil. Beaver, Mink, Muskrat, and Otter each brought up pawfuls of wet soil and placed the soil on the Turtle's back until they had made an island of great size. When they were through, Aataentsic settled down gently on the new Earth and the pieces of the great tree fell beside her and took root.

---

1. *Aataentsic* was the Earth-mother in Huron mythology. The Huron believed themselves to be the children of Aataentsic.
2. A *longhouse* was a bark-covered Native American communal dwelling that could have space for multiple families as well as rooms for tribal ceremonies.

1 Question *Why is the old chief's dream important to the story?*

The Sacred Earth and the Power of Storytelling
How does this part of the story reflect a Native American attitude toward the natural world? **2**

THE HURON **35**

Comparing Literature
Across Time and Place

Teach

Reading Strategy   1

Question
Answer: *The dream inspires the actions that led to Earth's creation. If the old chief had not told his dream, his wife may never have cut down the Sky Tree.*

Ask volunteers to share any questions they noted in their journals. As a group, attempt to resolve them.

For additional practice using the reading skill or strategy, see Unit 1 Teaching Resources Book, p. 41.

Big Idea   2

The Sacred Earth and the Power of Storytelling
Answer: *Animals are responsible for the creation of the world and thus deserve respect.*

Ask: How does this myth reflect the Huron beliefs about the roles of husbands and wives? *(The Hurons pay tribute here to a devoted wife.)*

Readability Scores
Dale-Chall: 3.6
DRP: 48
Lexile: 740

Comparing Literature

Across Time and Place

View the Art ★

Ernest Smith (1907–1975), a member of the Seneca tribe, spent most of his life in California. He painted *Sky Woman* while working for the Works Progress Administration during the Great Depression.

Ask: Why did the artist choose this moment in the story to depict in his painting? *(The artist may have chosen this scene because it is the climactic moment when Aataentsic sacrifices herself so that there can be life. This event causes Turtle and the other animals to create Earth.)*

Sky Woman, 1936. Ernest Smith. Oil on canvas, 24¼ x 18⅛ in. Rochester Museum & Science Center, Rochester, NY.

★

Grammar Practice

SMALL GROUP SPIRAL REVIEW Punctuate Dialogue Have students look at the dialogue in the selection.

Ask: What do you notice about the way dialogue is punctuated? *(indentation, commas inside quotation marks, no capitalization after interruption)* Point out to students that when writing dialogue they should keep the following rules in mind:

- Capitalize the first word in dialogue.

- Do not capitalize the first word after interruption in the dialogue.
- Enclose end punctuation within quotation marks.
- Indent each new line of dialogue.

Example:

   "Why are you so late?" asked Jay's mother.
   "I came home earlier," he explained, "but you were not here."

Have students work together in small groups to create dialogue in which they demonstrate each of these rules. Write their dialogue on the board to demonstrate the rules.

36

After You Read

Respond and Think Critically

Respond and Interpret

1. Would you describe Aataentsic's actions as heroic? Why or why not?
2. (a)What is the Sky Tree? (b)Why is it important to the people in Sky Land?
3. (a)Why does Aataentsic cut down the Sky Tree? (b)What does this action reveal about her relationship with her husband?
4. (a)Which animal observes Aataentsic's fall? (b)What role does this animal assume?

Analyze and Evaluate

5. (a)What is the function of the old chief's dream in "The Sky Tree"? (b)What does this myth sug-

gest about the importance that Native Americans attribute to knowledge gained from dreams?

6. (a)What motivates Aataentsic to follow the Sky Tree into the hole? (b)How do you view her actions?

Connect

7. **Big Idea** The Sacred Earth and the Power of Storytelling What does the role of the water animals in the creation of Earth suggest about Native American attitudes toward other living creatures?

8. **Connect to Today** How does the role of animals in our culture compare with the role depicted in this myth?

Literary Element Oral Tradition

Oral tradition is a way of recording the past, glorifying leaders, and teaching moral values.

1. Why do you think the Huron preserved and perpetuated a myth such as "The Sky Tree"?
2. How might this myth have been used by the Huron to teach a moral lesson?

Reading Strategy Question

Review the questions that you wrote in your double-entry journal (see page 34) and try to answer them now.

Academic Vocabulary

*Storytelling serves an important **function** in Native American culture.*

Function is an academic word that can have different meanings in different subject areas. Using context clues, try to figure out the meaning of *function* in each sentence below.

1. The **function** of the heart is to pump blood.
2. The virus deleted some **functions**, without which the application can't work.

For more on academic vocabulary, see pages 53–54.

Literature Online

Selection Resources For Selection Quizzes, eFlashcards, and Reading-Writing Connection activities, go to glencoe.com and enter QuickPass code GLA9800u1.

Writing

Write a Dialogue Imagine that this story continues and Aataentsic returns to the Sky Land to cure her husband. What would they say to each other? Write a short dialogue between these two characters, keeping in mind the values represented in this story and how the characters might express them.

THE HURON **37**

Assess

1. Some may say she was heroic to try to save her husband's life. Others may question her wisdom in cutting down the only source of food in Sky Land.
2. (a) A great tree in the middle of Sky Land (b) It is the source of food.
3. (a) In an attempt to save her husband's life (b) She would do anything to save his life.
4. (a) Turtle (b) He assumes leadership of the animals.
5. (a) It prompts Aataentsic to cut down the Tree. (b) Native Americans value knowledge from dreams.
6. (a) She tries to protect life. (b) As heroic because she risks harm to protect life
7. Native Americans attach great importance to other living creatures.
8. Students may say that animals were wise and treated as equals in the myth. Today people feel they are superior to all animals.

Progress Check

Do students understand oral tradition?

If No → See Unit 1 Teaching Resources Book, p. 40.

Literary Element

1. They may have wanted to preserve their religious beliefs, to celebrate their ancestor Aataentsic, and to offer an example of unselfish devotion and courage.
2. They might have taught the danger of hasty actions, the value of sacrifice, and the importance of working together for a common goal.

Reading Strategy

Questions and answers should relate to key details, such as the placement of the turtle and the moral lesson of the selection.

Writing

Students' dialogues should reflect an understanding of the values of the characters and events in the story and should be punctuated correctly.

Academic Vocabulary

1. In biology, an organ's function is the purpose it serves for the body.
2. In computer science, a function is a procedure within an application that performs a specific task.

37

Focus

Summary

Wise King Leopard rules the animals, who live together in peace. One day the dog, the only animal with teeth and claws, attacks the other animals and drives out the leopard. The animals declare the dog to be their new leader. The leopard has teeth and claws made for him by a blacksmith, acquires sound from Thunder, and returns to maul the dog. The outcast dog becomes a slave of the hunter, and from then on, the animals live as enemies.

Literary History ☆

African Proverbs Proverbs are an important part of the African oral tradition. Like folktales, proverbs express some wisdom about human experience. Chinua Achebe frequently uses proverbs in his writing. Some African proverbs resemble familiar American sayings. The African proverb "You do not teach the paths of the forest to an old gorilla" has its counterpart in the American saying "You can't teach an old dog new tricks."

Build Background

West African writer Chinua Achebe's myth is an adaptation of a children's story by teacher and writer John Iroaganachi. Achebe's version is full of dark undertones that suggest an allegorical link to the British colonial era and the Nigerian Civil War, which lasted from 1967 to 1970. Various military regimes, representing hostile ethnic groups, have periodically seized power in Nigeria since it declared its independence from Britain in 1960.

How the Leopard Got His Claws

Retold by Chinua Achebe
and John Iroaganachi

☆ *If you look at the world in terms of storytelling, you have, first of all, the man who agitates, the man who drums up the people—I call him the drummer. Then you have the warrior, who goes forward and fights. But you also have the story-teller who recounts the event, and this is the one who survives, who outlives all the others. It is the storyteller who makes us what we are, who creates history. The storyteller creates the memory that the survivors must have; otherwise, their surviving would have no meaning.*

—Chinua Achebe

In the beginning . . . all the animals in the forest lived as friends. Their king was the leopard. He was strong, but gentle and wise. He ruled the animals well, and they all liked him.

At that time the animals did not fight one another. Most of them had no sharp teeth or claws. They did not need them. Even King Leopard had only small teeth. He had no claws at all.

Only the dog had big, sharp teeth. The other animals said he was ugly, and they laughed at him.

"It is foolish to carry sharp things in the mouth," said the tortoise.

"I think so, too," said the goat.

The monkey jumped in and began to tease the dog.

"Don't worry, my dear friend," said the monkey. "You need your teeth to clear your farm."

The animals laughed at the monkey's joke.

Reading Practice

SPIRAL REVIEW ☉ **Characterization** Explain that in African myths and folktales, the chief characters are animals. Some characters, such as Anansi the Spider and Tortoise, are popular and appear in many stories. The animals behave like human beings but retain their animal natures. Have students choose one of the following characters: leopard, dog, goat, tortoise. Direct them to take notes on their charac-ters while reading the story. Tell them to focus on the character's attitudes and behavior toward the other animals.

Ask: What human characteristics do these animals possess? (examples: humor, fear, wisdom, anger, cowardice) Have students indicate whether their character's attitude changes during the course of the story.

When the farming season came round, King Leopard led the animals to their farmland. They all worked hard to prepare their plots. At the end of the day they returned home tired. They sat on log benches in the village square. As they rested they told stories and drank palm wine.[1]

But soon it would be the rainy season, and the animals would have no shelter from the rain.

The deer took this problem to King Leopard. They talked about it for a long time. King Leopard decided to call the animals together to discuss it.

One bright morning . . . King Leopard beat his royal drum. When the animals heard the drum, they gathered at the village square. The tortoise was there. The goat was there, too. The sheep, the grass-cutter,[2] the monkey, the hedgehog,[3] the baboon, the dog and many others were there.

King Leopard greeted them and said, "I have called you together to plan how we can make ourselves a common shelter."

"This is a good idea," said the giraffe.

"Yes, a very good idea," said many other animals.

"But why do we need a common house?" said the dog. He had never liked King Leopard.

1 "The dog has asked a good question," said the duck. "Why do we need a common shelter?"

"We do need somewhere to rest when we return from our farms," replied King Leopard.

"And besides," said the goat, "we need a shelter from the rain."

"I don't mind being wet," said the duck. "In fact, I like it. I know that the goat does not like water on his body. Let him go and build a shelter."

---

1. *Palm wine* is created from the sap of a palm tree.
2. The *grass-cutter* is a type of rodent.
3. A *hedgehog* is a small, hairy mammal; some varieties have quills.

"We need a shelter," said the monkey, jumping up and down in excitement.

"Perhaps we need one, perhaps we don't," said the lazy baboon sitting on the low fence of the square.

The dog spoke again. "We are wasting our time. Those who need a shelter should build it. I live in a cave, and it is enough for me." Then he walked away. The duck followed him out. **1**

"Does anyone else want to leave?" asked King Leopard. No one answered or made a move to go.

"Very well," said King Leopard. "Let the rest of us build the village hall."

The animals soon scattered about to find building materials. The tortoise copied the pattern on his back and made the plan of the roof. The giant rat and mouse dug the foundations. Some animals brought sticks, some ropes, others made roof-mats.

As they built the house, they sang many happy songs. They also told many jokes. Although they worked very hard, everyone was merry.

After many weeks they finished the building.

It was a fine building. The animals were pleased with it. They agreed to open it with a very special meeting.

On the opening day the animals, their wives and children gathered in the hall. King Leopard then made a short speech. He said: "This hall is yours to enjoy. You worked very hard together to build it. I am proud of you."

The animals clapped their hands and gave three cheers to their king.

From that day they rested in their new hall whenever they returned from their farm.

But the dog and the duck kept away from the hall.

One morning the animals went to their farms as usual. King Leopard went to visit a chief in another village.

At first the sun was shining. Then strong winds began to blow. Dark clouds hid the sun.

CHINUA ACHEBE AND JOHN IROAGANACHI   **39**

Comparing Literature
Across Time and Place

Teach

Literary Element   **1**

Archetypes Have students recall what an archetype is. *(It is a symbol, character, or story pattern found in many cultures. Refer students to p. 23 or Literary Handbook, p. R2.)* **Say:** Identify the hero and villain that Achebe presents as this tale opens. Provide support for your choices. *(Students should agree that the wise and gentle King Leopard is the hero, while the disagreeable dog is the villain.)*

Reading Strategy

Author's Purpose
Ask: What purposes might an author have for writing a piece of literature? *(An author may write to inform, describe, entertain, or persuade.)*

Point out that this selection is as much a fable—a brief story with a moral message—as it is a myth. The author wants to entertain but also to persuade readers that one form of governing is admirable, while another is contemptible.

Approaching Level

DIFFERENTIATED INSTRUCTION

SMALL GROUP **Established** To help students further distinguish between each character, plan a choral reading of the story with different students assigned to read the dialogue of each character and a narrator to read the descriptive paragraphs. Encourage students reading character parts to create a distinct voice fitting the personality of the animal. Assign a small group of students to read the songs on the following pages with rhythm and percussive accompaniment. Allow students time to practice and rehearse before the full class reading of the selection.

Readability Scores
Dale-Chall: 3.2
DRP: 46
Lexile: 540

Comparing Literature

Across Time and Place

Teach

Big Idea   1

The Sacred Earth and the Power of Storytelling In West Africa, the storytelling tradition is kept alive by storytellers called griots (grē-ōz′). Originally, such people were the keepers of history as well as entertainers, traveling about and telling or singing their stories. Today, they usually are entertainers who may record their performances on CDs and give live performances on television or on the radio.

Say: There is a close connection between storytelling and music in West African culture. **Ask:** How does Achebe capture this in his retelling? (*He includes highly rhythmic songs.*)

View the Art ★

Answer: *While there is a baboon in the story, the fierce facial expression of the sculpture also might bring the dog to mind.*

The first rain was coming. The songbirds stopped their singing. The humming insects became quiet. Lightning flashed across the dark clouds. Claps of thunder sounded. The rain poured and poured.

The animals in their farms saw the rain coming and began to hurry to the village hall.

The dog also saw the rain coming and returned to his cave. But it was a very, very heavy rain. Water began to enter the cave. Soon it was flooded.

Baboon, 1978. Felipe Benito Archuleta. Carved and painted cottonwood and pine with glue and sawdust. Smithsonian American Art Museum, Washington, DC.

View the Art Felipe Benito Archuleta often carves animals with fierce teeth and snouts to accentuate their ferocity. Does this baboon resemble any of the animals in the story? Explain. ★

The dog ran from one end of his cave to the other. But the water followed him everywhere. At last he ran out of the cave altogether and made straight for the hall of the animals.

The deer was already there. He was surprised to see the dog enter the hall.

"What do you want here?" said the deer to the dog.

"It is none of your business," replied the dog.

"It is my business," said the deer. "Please go out, this hall is for those who built it."

Then the dog attacked the deer and bit him with his big, sharp teeth. The deer cried with pain. The dog seized him by the neck and threw him out into the rain.

The other animals came in one after the other.

The dog barked and threw each of them out. They stood together shivering and crying in the rain. The dog kept barking and showing his teeth.

Then the deer cried out:

> O Leopard our noble king,
> Where are you?
> Spotted king of the forest,
> Where are you?
> Even if you are far away
> Come, hurry home:
> The worst has happened to us
> The worst has happened to us . . .
> The house the animals built
> The cruel dog keeps us from it,
> The common shelter we built
> The cruel dog keeps us from it,
> The worst has happened to us
> The worst has happened to us . . .   **1**

The cry of the deer rang out loud and clear. It was carried by the wind. King Leopard heard it on his way back from his journey and began to run toward the village hall.

As he got near, he saw the animals, wet and sheltering under a tree. They were all crying.

Listening and Speaking Practice

SPIRAL REVIEW **Repetition** Have students search for examples of repetition in the selection. (*"Nobody has a right."*) **Ask:** What effect does repetition have on the reader? (*Students might respond that it adds to the storytelling quality or emphasizes key points.*) Point out that repetition is an effective device often used in speeches.

Say: Write and deliver a brief speech for one of the characters using repetition. For example, write a speech the leopard might give when the animals seek him out or that the animals might give to persuade him to return.

As he got nearer still, he could see the dog walking up and down inside the hall.

King Leopard was very angry. "Come out of the hall at once," he said to the dog. The dog barked and rushed at him. They began to fight. The dog bit the leopard and tore his skin with his claws. King Leopard was covered with blood. The dog went back to the hall. He stood at the door barking and barking. "Who is next? Who! Who!" he barked.

King Leopard turned to the animals and said: "Let us go in together and drive out the enemy. He is strong, but he is alone. We are many. Together we can drive him out of our house."

But the goat said: "We cannot face him. Look at his strong teeth! He will only tear us to pieces!"

"The goat is right," said the animals. "He is too strong for us."

The tortoise stood up and said: "I am sure we are all sorry about what has happened to the leopard. But he was foolish to talk to the dog the way he did. It is foolish to annoy such a powerful person as the dog. Let us make peace with him. I don't know what you others think. But I think he should have been our king all along. He is strong; he is handsome. Let us go on our knees and salute him."

"Hear! Hear!" said all the animals. "Hail the dog!"

Tears began to roll down the face of the leopard. His heart was heavy. He loved the animals greatly. But they had turned their backs on him. Now he knew they were cowards. So he turned his back on them and went away. Because of his many wounds he was weak and tired. So he lay down after a while to rest under a tree, far from the village.

The animals saw him go. But they did not care. They were too busy praising their new

"Look at his strong teeth! He will only tear us to pieces!"

king, the dog. The tortoise carved a new staff for him. The toad made a new song in his praise:

> The dog is great
> The dog is good
> The dog gives us our daily food.
> We love his head, we love his jaws
> We love his feet and all his claws.

The dog looked round the circle of animals and asked, "Where is the leopard?"

"We think he has gone away, O King," said the goat.

"Why? He has no right to go away," said the dog. "Nobody has a right to leave our village and its beautiful hall. We must all stay together."

"Indeed," shouted the animals. "We must stay together! The leopard must return to the village! Our wise king has spoken! It is good to have a wise king!"

The dog then called out the names of six strong animals and said to them: "Go at once and bring back the leopard. If he should refuse to follow you, you must drag him along. If we let him go, others may soon follow his wicked example until there is no one left in our village. That would be a very bad thing indeed. It is my duty as your king to make sure that we all live together. The leopard is a wicked animal. That is why he wants to go away and live by himself. It is our duty to stop him. Nobody has a right to go away from our village and our beautiful hall."

"Nobody has a right to go away from the village," sang all the animals as the six messengers went to look for the leopard.

They found him resting under the tree beyond the village. Although he was wounded and weak he still looked like a king. So the six

CHINUA ACHEBE AND JOHN IROAGANACHI **41**

Teach

Reading Strategy 2

Critical Thinking

Ask: Which of the dog's statements contradicts something he said on page 39, when the animals were discussing building a shelter? *(Earlier the dog had objected to the animals' living in a common shelter. Now he says that the animals must all live together.)*

Ask: What does this contradiction add to your knowledge of the dog's character? *(The dog will shift his principles to suit his purposes.)*

English Learners

DIFFERENTIATED INSTRUCTION

Beginning Students may have trouble with the words *leopard* and *tortoise* because the vowel pairs in each have atypical sound associations. Reinforce the more common associations for the vowel pairs *eo* and *oi* (for example, *people, geography, choice*) as you note the proper pronunciation for these words and have students repeat them.

Intermediate Ask students to recall the events of the story before King Leopard hears the cry of the deer. Direct them to list the major events of the story to this point and to compare their lists with those of other students. Have them present a summary of events orally, in detailed sentences that distinguish the characteristics of the animals.

Comparing Literature

Across Time and Place

Teach

Literary Element   1

Personification Say: One form of personification gives human traits to animals. Find examples of personification on pages 42–43. *(animals talking, living in a village they have built, throwing stones, dancing, or beating a drum)*

View the Art ★

Answer: *The leopard is viewed by many cultures as a symbol of power. Using such a strong symbol to honor one's ancestors might have been a declaration of their power, a sign of respect for one's ancestors, or an expression of the family's dominance.*

This brass water jug was made by a West African craftworker in the 1700s. Aquamaniles, common to the religious traditions of several continents, were used for the washing of hands during rituals.

---

messengers stood at a little distance and spoke to him.

"Our new king, the dog, has ordered you to return to the village," they said.

"He says that no one has a right to leave the village," said the pig.

"Yes, no one has a right to leave our village and its beautiful hall," said the others.

The leopard looked at them with contempt. Then he got up slowly. The six animals fell back. But the leopard did not go toward them. He turned his back on them and began to go away—slowly and painfully. One of the animals picked up a stone and threw it at him. Then all the others immediately picked up stones and began to throw. As they threw they chanted: "No one has a right to leave our village! No one has a right to leave our village!"

Although some of the stones hit the leopard and hurt him, he did not turn round even once. He continued walking until he no longer heard the noise of the animals.

The leopard traveled seven days and seven nights. Then he came to the house of the blacksmith. The old man was sitting at his forge. The leopard said to him: "I want the strongest teeth you can make from iron. And I want the most deadly claws you can make from bronze."

The blacksmith said: "Why do you need such terrible things?" The leopard told his story. Then the blacksmith said: "I do not blame you."

The blacksmith worked a whole day on the teeth, and another full day on the claws. The leopard was pleased with them. He put them on and thanked the blacksmith. Then he left and went to the house of Thunder.

The leopard knocked at the door and Thunder roared across the sky.

"I want some of your sound in my voice," said the leopard. "Even a little bit."

"Why do you want my sound in your voice?" asked Thunder. "And why have you got those terrible teeth and claws?"

The leopard told his story. "I do not blame you," said Thunder. He gave the sound to the

leopard. "Thank you for the gift," said the leopard. And he began his journey home.

The leopard journeyed for seven days and seven nights and returned to the village of the animals. There he found the animals dancing in a circle round the dog. He stood for a while watching them with contempt and great anger. They were too busy to notice his presence. He made a deep, terrifying roar. At the same time he sprang into the center of the circle. The animals stopped their song. The dog dropped his staff. The leopard seized him and bit and clawed him without mercy. Then he threw him out of the circle.

All the animals *trembled.*

But they were too afraid to run. The leopard turned to them and said:

"You miserable worms. You shameless cowards. I was a kind and gentle king, but you turned against me. From today I shall rule the forest with terror. The life of our village is ended."

"What about our hall?" asked the tortoise with a trembling voice.

"Let everyone take from the hall what he put into it," said the leopard.

The animals began to weep as they had wept long ago in the rain. "Please forgive us, O Leopard," they cried.

"Let everyone take from the hall what he put into it," repeated the leopard. "And hurry up!" he thundered.

So the animals pulled their hall apart. Some carried away the wood, and some took the roof-mats. Others took away doors and windows. The toad brought his talking drum and began to beat it to the leopard and to sing:

> Alive or dead the leopard is king.
> Beware my friend, don't twist his tail.

But the leopard roared like thunder and the toad dropped his drum and the animals scattered in the forest.

The dog had already run a long way when the leopard roared. Now he ran faster and

---

Study Skills Practice

Note-taking To help students keep track of the many characters in the story, have them create a graphic organizer to distinguish between each character. Assist students in selecting dialogue from each character that reveals something about its personality. In the second row, ask students to draw conclusions about each character based on what the character says and other clues from the story.

Character:	Dog	Leopard	Goat	Thunder
What character says:				
What I think about character:				

Aquamanile (Water Jug) in the Shape of a Leopard, Benin. British Museum, London.
View the Art This leopard-shaped vessel was used by Nigerian kings to honor their ancestors during a hand washing ceremony. From what you read in this story, why do you think the symbol of the leopard was chosen for this task? ⭐

Comparing Literature
Across Time and Place

Teach

Vocabulary | 2

Antonyms Say: Find antonym pairs in the final paragraph in the story. *(Students should note friends/enemies; strong/weak.)* Then scan pages 42 and 43 for words you can use to generate an antonym. *(Examples include, with story word listed first, contempt/respect, terrifying/calming, kind/cruel, gentle/rough, weep/laugh, and slave/master.)*

Quickwrite

Answer: *Students may say that Achebe's myth shows that violence breeds more violence and hostility. They might also note that the relationship between the dog and the hunter hurts the animal kingdom.*

faster. His body was covered with blood, and he was very, very weak. He wanted to stop and rest a little. But the fear of the leopard was greater than his weakness. So he staggered and fell and got up and staggered on and on and on. . . .

After many days the dog came to the house of the hunter.

"Please protect me from the leopard," he cried.

"What will you do for me in return?" asked the hunter.

"I will be your slave," said the dog. "Any day you are hungry for meat I shall show you

the way to the forest. There we can hunt together and kill my fellow animals."

"All right, come in," said the hunter.

Today the animals are no longer friends, but enemies. The strong among them attack and kill the weak. The leopard, full of anger, eats up anyone he can lay his hands on. The hunter, led by the dog, goes to the forest from time to time and shoots any animals he can find. Perhaps the animals will make peace among themselves someday and live together again. Then they can keep away the hunter who is their common enemy. ✍ | 2

Quickwrite

The animal leaders in Achebe's myth use violence to seize and wield power. What lessons do you think Achebe suggests through his depiction of the animals and their encounters with the hunter? Write a paragraph explaining your views.

CHINUA ACHEBE AND JOHN IROAGANACHI **43**

Approaching Level
DIFFERENTIATED INSTRUCTION

Emerging Prepare students for the Quickwrite activity by brainstorming a list of ideas. Break down parts of the writing prompt and instruct students to respond to each section individually. For example, the first sentence of the Quickwrite is "The animal leaders in Achebe's myth use violence to seize and wield power." Have students list examples of violence and power in the story before having them freewrite.

Next, read the question, "What lessons do you think Achebe suggests through his depiction of animales and their encounters with the hunter?" Discuss and clarify the question and have students list ideas and reactions before freewriting. Finally, ask students to review their writing from the first sentence and the question and draft a paragraph that combines their responses.

Focus

Summary

The speaker reverently and gratefully addresses the Pacific Ocean as the giver of rain, based on the Native American belief that Indians came from China, riding across the ocean on giant turtles.

View the Art ★

Julie Lankford Olds (1962–) is a member of the Native American tribe known as the Miami. In her paintings, she illustrates important Native American beliefs, such as the close ties between people and nature.

Ask: What part of the poem does the art illustrate? *(Lines 18–19: "Indians came riding across the ocean / carried by giant sea turtles.")*

Build Background

Leslie Marmon Silko grew up hearing traditional Native American stories and myths at the Laguna Pueblo Reservation near Albuquerque, New Mexico.

Silko's poem uses myth to draw a comparison between the west-to-east movement of rain clouds and the migration of early peoples to America. Historians have theorized that tens of thousands of years ago these migrants arrived in America from Asia. They most likely traveled across a land bridge where the Bering Strait now separates Asia and North America.

Prayer to the Pacific

Leslie Marmon Silko

Our Life on His Back, 1993. Julie Lankford Olds. Oil on canvas, 12 x 16 in. Historic Prophetstown, Battleground, IN. ★

Reading Practice

Sensory Details Say: Poetry is often filled with images that appeal to the reader's senses of sight, sound, smell, taste, and touch. Find details in this selection that appeal to your senses. Create a chart that notes these details.

Ask: Which three senses are well-represented? *(sight, touch, and taste)* Have students brainstorm possible smells and sounds that the poet might have included.

Prayer to the Pacific

Sight   Taste   Touch

I traveled to the ocean
　　　　　distant
　　　　　　　　from my southwest land of sandrock
　　　　　　　　to the moving blue water
5　　　　　　Big as the myth of origin.

Pale
pale water in the yellow-white light of
　　　　　　sun　floating west
　　　　　　　　　to China
10　　　　　　　　where ocean herself was born.
Clouds that blow across the sand are wet.

Squat in the wet sand and speak to the Ocean:
　　　　　I return to you　turquoise　the red coral you sent us,
　　　　　sister spirit of Earth.
15　Four round stones in my pocket　I carry back the ocean
　　　　　　to suck and to taste.

Thirty thousand years ago
　　　　　　Indians came riding across the ocean
　　　　　　carried by giant sea turtles.
20　Waves were high that day
　　　　　great sea turtles waded　slowly out
　　　　　　　　　from the gray sundown sea.
Grandfather Turtle rolled in the sand　four times
　　　　　and disappeared
25　　　　　　　　swimming into the sun.

And so　from that time
　　　　　immemorial,[1]
　　　　　　　as the old people say,
rain clouds drift from the west
30　　　　　　　gift from the ocean.

Green leaves in the wind
Wet earth on my feet
　　　　　swallowing raindrops
　　　　　　　clear from China.

---

1. *Immemorial* means "extending back beyond memory or record."

💬 **Discussion Starter**

What attitude toward nature does the speaker's explanation of the origin of rain illustrate? Use specific details from the poem to support your opinions.

LESLIE MARMON SILKO　**45**

Comparing Literature
Across Time and Place

Teach

Discussion Starter

Answer: *Students may point out that the speaker observes the ocean flowing west and rain clouds moving east, as her ancestors did. They might relate this cyclical movement to the importance that Native Americans place on the seasons.*

Cultural History ☆

Turtle as Trickster In some Native American tales, Turtle is a trickster figure with a reputation for deception and trickery. In one story, Terrapin the Turtle enters a race with Rabbit. He gets his family of turtles to impersonate him and appear at points along the route. Thus he fools Rabbit into thinking he is in the lead.

English Learners

DIFFERENTIATED INSTRUCTION

Intermediate Have students paraphrase the poem. Direct them to include details such as the Indians' origins and mode of travel, the time of the poem's events, Grandfather Turtle's actions, and the source of the rains. Have them write an opening sentence that identifies the poem by title and author and states the poet's purpose.

Beginning Review word parts: *prefix, suffix,* and *root.* Have students break down the word *immemorial* (line 27) into prefix *(im-)* + root *(memor)* + suffix *(-al).*
Ask: How does the spelling of *memory* change when the suffix is added? *(The letter* y *changes to* i.) Explain that the Latin root *memor* means "mindful."

Have students brainstorm other words with this root, such as *commemorate, memorable, memorandum.*

Assess

 Writing Activity

Students' essays should be well-organized and should use supporting evidence from the text. The essays should also reflect an understanding of oral tradition and the function of creation myths.

Group Activity

1. The Huron myth tells how land emerged from water; Achebe's tale explains relationships among animals; Silko's poem tells why clouds move from west to east.

2. The Huron tale is a traditional "earth-diver myth"; Achebe's tale retells a West African folktale; Silko's poem comes from the Pueblo culture.

3. It reveals that the story is mythic and may have a moral lesson or explain the origin of human life.

4. Student responses should connect their life experiences to the myths.

Speaking and Listening

Evaluate student performances using the following criteria:

▪ Does a student's performance show a grasp of the culture represented?

▪ Does the story feature elements of creation myths?

▪ How well does the student use techniques of public speaking, such as eye contact, facial expressions, and clear pronunciation?

Wrap-Up: Comparing Literature

Across Time and Place

• ***The Sky Tree*** by the Eastern Woodland Huron

• ***How the Leopard Got His Claws*** by Chinua Achebe and John Iroaganachi

• ***Prayer to the Pacific*** by Leslie Marmon Silko

COMPARE THE **Big Idea** The Sacred Earth and the Power of Storytelling

Writing Activity In what ways do these selections reveal the power of storytelling and reflect the tradition of the creation myth in oral cultures? Write a brief essay in which you answer this question. State your thesis in an introductory paragraph, cite evidence from the selections in the body paragraphs, and reinforce your thesis in the concluding paragraph.

COMPARE Mythic Elements

Group Activity Personification, supernatural occurrences, and stories about the origin of the universe are features of myths in a variety of cultures. The Huron myth, Achebe's myth, and Silko's poem use these elements for a variety of purposes. In a small group, discuss the following questions. Cite evidence from the selections to support your points.

1. How does each writer describe different aspects of the origin of the universe?

2. What is the importance of the writer's cultural background in each of these selections?

3. How does personification of animals contribute to each selection?

4. What insight about life offered by the writer do you find most compelling?

COMPARE Cultures

Speaking and Listening Before the writers in various cultures recorded their stories in books, storytellers recounted tales orally. Research one of the cultures represented by the selections: Huron (also called Wyandot), Nigerian, or Pueblo. Compare and contrast the belief systems of these cultures. Then compose a mythic story that describes the origin of some aspect of life. If possible, tell your story to the class.

46 UNIT 1 EARLY AMERICA

Reading Practice

Review Remind students that the oral tradition is discussed in the Unit Introduction on page 12. Creation myths are discussed in the Literary Periods section, pages 20–21. Have students review these pages. Then ask students to reread the quote from Chinua Achebe on page 38. **Ask:** Why are storytellers powerful? *(Students should offer a variety of reasons: they can create or alter history; they can dramatize an event and influence their audience; they pass traditions from one generation to the next; they explain natural phenomena; they have "the last word.")*

Before You Read

from *The Iroquois Constitution*

☆ Meet **Dekanawida**
(1550–1600)

When Iroquois tribes in present-day New York State were torn apart by fighting, one man stepped in to instill peace. Dekanawida (dək uhn ä wē′ dä) believed from an early age that he was predestined to unite the Iroquois nation. "It is my business to stop the shedding of blood among human beings," he said.

Traditional accounts of his life vary. He was thought to be a Huron born around 1550 near what is now Kingston, Ontario. In one account, Dekanawida was the son of a virgin mother who, in the months leading up to his birth, observed omens that told he would be a source of evil and destruction for the Huron. To save her tribe, Dekanawida's mother tried three times to drown her infant son in an icy river, but to her disbelief, woke up each following morning with the child in her arms. His mother interpreted this as a sign that he was fated to live and began to rear the boy.

> "The Word I bring is that all peoples shall love one another and live together in peace."
>
> —Dekanawida

A Quest for Peace As a young man, Dekanawida trekked southward on a spiritual quest to perform his destined work. He forged a strong friendship with Hiawatha, an Onandaga tribal leader. Both men agreed that continual warring was making the tribes vulnerable to outside attack. Legend has it that Dekanawida was the laconic mastermind of the Iroquois Constitution. Because Dekanawida may have had a speech impediment, Hiawatha, a charismatic leader and great orator, was his

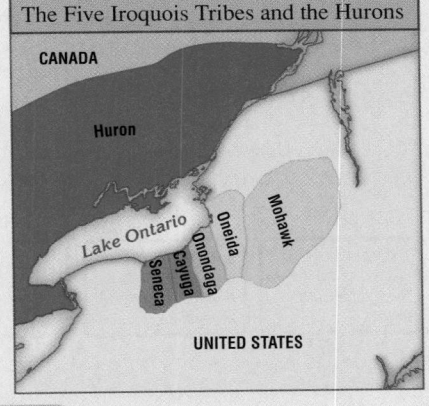

spokesman and interlocutor. Dekanawida was highly esteemed by the Iroquois. In fact, he was the first "pine tree chief," or chief chosen on the basis of merit rather than heredity.

In 1570, the two leaders established an alliance among the five nations of the Iroquois—the Seneca, Cayuga, Oneida, Onondaga, and Mohawk. Dekanawida created the alliance's constitution, which established rules for decision making and debate. Around 1600, after he had completed his work, he mysteriously vanished. But thanks to the peaceful government he had helped create, the confederacy was able to resist outside pressures for almost two hundred years.

The Five Iroquois Tribes and the Hurons

CANADA

Huron

Lake Ontario

Seneca
Cayuga
Onondaga
Oneida
Mohawk

UNITED STATES

LOG ON ▶ **Literature** Online

Author Search For more about Dekanawida, go to glencoe.com and enter QuickPass code GLA9800u1.

Before You Read

Focus

Bellringer Options

Selection Focus Transparency 3
Daily Language Practice Transparency 5

Or read the Preamble to the U.S. Constitution aloud. Have students restate it in their own words. *(We the people of the United States have created a constitution to establish peace and freedom for ourselves and our descendants and to ensure that our government is fair, helps its citizens live a decent life, and guarantees them basic rights.)* Have students think of the U.S. Constitution as they read.

Literary History ☆

Culture Heroes Dekanawida and Hiawatha are Native American culture heroes. A culture hero is a leader celebrated for his or her achievements. Dekanawida and Hiawatha are associated with establishing the Iroquois Confederacy.

Skills Practice

Literary Elements
- Author's Purpose (SE pp. 48, 49, 51, 52)

from The Iroquois Constitution

Listening/Speaking/Viewing Skills
- Analyze Art (TE p. 51)

Reading Skills
- Draw Conclusions (SE pp. 48, 49, 50, 52)
- Preview (TE p. 48)
- Compare and Contrast (TE p. 50)

Vocabulary Skills
- Synonyms (SE p. 52)

Writing Skills/Grammar
- Write a Letter (SE p. 52)

Before You Read

Focus

Summary

Dekanawida explains how five nations are to unite and conduct their relations on a site he determines in Onondaga territory. He establishes a council that has final authority in decision-making. The constitution details the arrangement of the matriarchal society, how leaders should conduct themselves, what festivals to observe, and what symbols represent the Confederacy.

 For summaries in languages other than English, see Unit 1 Teaching Resources Book, pp. 45–50.

Vocabulary

Recognize Parts of Speech
Point out that the word *temper* on the vocabulary list is a verb. **Say:** Name the part of speech of the word *temper* in the following sentence: *She was afraid of losing her temper.* (noun) Explain that in English a word can often perform many jobs. Direct students to write sentences illustrating *temper* used as a verb and as a noun.

 For additional context, see Glencoe Interactive Vocabulary CD-ROM.

Literature and Reading Preview

Connect to the Text
What is the best way to come to an agreement during a conflict? Freewrite for a few minutes on this topic.

Build Background
Founded around 1570, the Iroquois Confederacy brought nearly 200 years of peace and prosperity to the five Iroquois nations. Benjamin Franklin considered Dekanawida's system so effective that he urged the colonists to view it as a model.

Set Purposes for Reading

Big Idea **The Sacred Earth and the Power of Storytelling**

As you read this selection from the Iroquois Constitution, ask yourself, How does Dekanawida's language reflect the Native Americans' reverence for the natural world?

Literary Element **Author's Purpose**

The **author's purpose** is the author's intent in creating a work. As you read the Constitution, ask yourself, How do its provisions support Dekanawida's goals?

Reading Strategy **Draw Conclusions About Culture**

When you **draw a conclusion,** you use a number of pieces of information to make a general statement about people, places, events, or ideas. As you read, ask yourself, What conclusions about Iroquois society can I draw based on the values expressed in this constitution?

....

Tip: Conclusions Diagram Use a diagram to record details from the selection as well as your conclusions about the Iroquois.

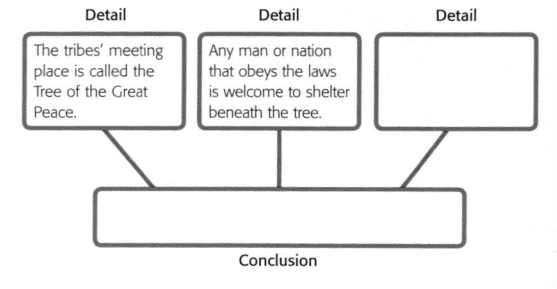

Detail — The tribes' meeting place is called the Tree of the Great Peace.

Detail — Any man or nation that obeys the laws is welcome to shelter beneath the tree.

Detail —

Conclusion

Learning Objectives

For pages 47–52
In studying this text, you will focus on the following objectives:

Literary Study: Analyzing author's purpose.

Reading: Drawing conclusions about culture.

Writing: Writing a summary.

Vocabulary

disposition (dis´ pə zish´ ən) *n.* one's general way of thinking or feeling; p. 49 *Julia had a cheerful disposition.*

convene (kən vēn´) *v.* to come together; assemble; p. 50 *Congress will convene to hear the president's speech tonight.*

posterity (pos ter´ ə tē) *n.* generations of the future; all of one's descendants; p. 50 *Mr. Norris requires students to create a record of their thoughts for posterity.*

temper (tem´ pər) *v.* to modify or moderate; soften; p. 51 *Alvaro tempers his anger by counting to ten.*

deliberation (di lib´ ə rā´ shən) *n.* careful consideration; p. 51 *After long deliberation, the city council voted to build a new library.*

Reading Practice

 SMALL GROUP

Preview Before reading the excerpt from the Iroquois Constitution, students may benefit from previewing the selection. Have students work in small groups to examine all the subheads in the selection and discuss what they think each section of the Constitution is about. Then ask students to make up questions based on the subheads, such as "What is the significance of the Tree of Great Peace?" or "What does the Tree of Great Peace look like?" Have students come up with at least one question for each subhead. Tell students to find answers to their questions when they read the selection.

from The Iroquois Constitution

Dekanawida

The Tree of the Great Peace

I am Dekanawida and with the Five Nations' Confederate Lords I plant the Tree of the Great Peace. I plant it in your territory, Adodarho,[1] and the Onondaga Nation, in the territory of you who are Firekeepers.[2]

I name the tree the Tree of the Great Long Leaves. Under the shade of this Tree of the Great Peace we spread the soft white feathery down of the globe thistle[3] as seats for you, Adodarho, and your cousin Lords.

We place you upon those seats, spread soft with the feathery down of the globe thistle, there beneath the shade of the spreading branches of the Tree of Peace. There shall you sit and watch the Council Fire of the Confederacy of the Five Nations, and all the affairs of the Five Nations shall be transacted at this place.

Roots have spread out from the Tree of the Great Peace, one to the north, one to the east, one to the south, and one to the west. The name of these roots is the Great White Roots and their nature is Peace and Strength.

If any man or any nation outside the Five Nations shall obey the laws of the Great Peace and make known their **disposition** to the Lords of the Confederacy, they may trace the Roots to the Tree and if their minds are clean and they are obedient and promise to obey the wishes of the Confederate Council, they shall be welcomed to take shelter beneath the Tree of the Long Leaves.

We place at the top of the Tree of the Long Leaves an Eagle who is able to see afar. If he sees in the distance any evil approaching or any danger threatening, he will at once warn the people of the Confederacy.

The Care of the Fire

The Smoke of the Confederate Council Fire shall ever ascend and pierce the sky so that other nations who may be allies may see the Council Fire of the Great Peace.

You, Adodarho, and your thirteen cousin Lords shall faithfully keep the space about the Council Fire clean and you shall allow neither dust nor dirt to accumulate. I lay a Long Wing before you as a broom. As a weapon against a crawling creature I lay a staff with you so that you may thrust it away from the Council Fire.

The Laws of the Council

Whenever the Confederate Lords shall assemble for the purpose of holding a council, the Onondaga Lords shall open it by expressing their gratitude to their cousin Lords and greeting them, and they shall make an address and offer thanks to the earth where men dwell, to the streams of

---

1. *Adodarho* was an Onondaga chief who enjoyed a position of honor in the Confederate Council. His name became an honorific, or traditional title, for Iroquois leaders.
2. *Firekeepers* were important chiefs who oversaw the Council Fire, which symbolized the confederacy.
3. *Globe thistle* is a plant that has prickly leaves and blue flowers. Like a dandelion, the flower becomes a mass of white, silky fuzz, or down, when it goes to seed.

---

1 Author's Purpose *Based on this statement, what do you think is Dekanawida's purpose in writing this piece?*

Vocabulary

disposition (dis´ pə zish´ ən) *n.* one's general way of thinking or feeling

---

Draw Conclusions About Culture *What can you conclude about the Iroquois attitude toward strangers or outsiders?* **2**

The Sacred Earth and the Power of Storytelling *How does the opening of a council meeting reflect the importance of storytelling in Native American culture?* **3**

DEKANAWIDA **49**

Approaching Level

DIFFERENTIATED INSTRUCTION

SMALL GROUP

Established Divide the class into seven or fourteen groups. Assign each group one section of the selection. Have students discuss and record the main idea of the section. Then have them record at least two possible reasons that the author chose to include the section in the constitution. Have the groups present their reasons to the class.

AAVE Have approaching-level students who are users of African American Vernacular English (AAVE) read aloud a section of Dekanawida's constitution. Reading offers practice with certain sounds that may cause difficulty, such as the *-th* sound in words such as *feathery, north, south,* and *beneath.* Direct students to think about where they should pause, emphasize words, or use gestures.

Teach

Reading Strategy 1

Draw Conclusions

Ask: Based on the first full paragraph, what conclusions can you draw about the Five Nations? *(Students might note, based on the groupings, that the Mohawk and Seneca, and the Oneida and Cayuga, seem more closely allied, and the Onondaga seem most powerful.)*

Reading Strategy 2

Draw Conclusions

Answer: *Traditionally, Native Americans believed that land did not belong to one person or group. Dekanawida states that clans will own the land. Perhaps the Iroquois fought with European settlers over land and adopted the idea of ownership to protect themselves.*

Political History ☆

Firekeeper At the time of this meeting, Adodarho was chief of the Onondaga nation. As the Chief Firekeeper, he was called on to decide whether a council should meet when the Confederate Council was not officially in session.

---

water, the pools, the springs and the lakes, to the maize[4] and the fruits, to the medicinal herbs and trees, to the forest trees for their usefulness, to the animals that serve as food and give their pelts for clothing, to the great winds and the lesser winds, to the Thunderers, to the Sun, the mighty warrior, to the moon, to the messengers of the Creator who reveal his wishes and to the Great Creator who dwells in the heavens above, who gives all the things useful to men, and who is the source and the ruler of health and life.

1 All the business of the Five Nations' Confederate Council shall be conducted by the two combined bodies of Confederate Lords. First the question shall be passed upon by the Mohawk and Seneca Lords; then it shall be discussed and passed by the Oneida and Cayuga Lords. Their decisions shall then be referred to the Onondaga Lords (Firekeepers) for final judgment. ☆

When the Council of the Five Nation Lords shall **convene,** they shall appoint a speaker for the day. He shall be a Lord of either the Mohawk, Onondaga, or Seneca Nation.

No individual or foreign nation interested in a case, question, or proposition shall have any voice in the Confederate Council except to answer a question put to him or them by the speaker for the Lords.

If the conditions which shall arise at any future time call for an addition to or change of this law, the case shall be carefully considered, and if a new beam seems necessary or beneficial, the proposed change shall be voted upon and, if adopted, it shall be called, "Added to the Rafters."[5]

---

4. *Maize* is corn.
5. The Iroquois leaders thought of their confederacy of five nations as a longhouse, a communal Iroquois dwelling with an east door, a west door, and a central fire. The terms *beam* and *Added to the Rafters* continue this comparison.

Vocabulary

convene (kən vēn′) *v.* to come together; assemble

The Clans

Among the Five Nations and their **posterity** there shall be the following original clans: Great Name Bearer, Ancient Name Bearer, Great Bear, Ancient Bear, Turtle, Painted Turtle, Standing Rock, Large Plover, Little Plover, Deer, Pigeon Hawk, Eel, Ball, Opposite-Side-of-the-Hand, and Wild Potatoes. These clans, distributed through their respective Nations, shall be the sole owners and holders of the soil of the country, and in them is it vested as a birthright.

People of the Five Nations [who are] members of a certain clan shall recognize every other member of that clan, irrespective of the Nation, as relatives.

The lineal descent of the people of the Five Nations shall run in the female line. Women shall be considered the progenitors[6] of the Nation. They shall own the land and the soil. Men and women shall follow the status of the mother.

The Leaders

The Lords of the Confederacy of the Five Nations shall be mentors[7] of the people for all time. The thickness of their skin shall be seven spans—which is to say that they shall be proof against anger, offensive actions, and criticism. Their hearts shall be full of peace and good will and their minds filled with a yearning for the welfare of the people of the Confederacy. With endless patience they shall carry out their duty,

---

6. *Progenitors* are direct ancestors or originators of an ancestral line.
7. *Mentors* are wise and trusted advisers.

Draw Conclusions About Culture *What shift in traditional attitudes toward the land is shown here and what conclusion might you draw from it?* **2**

Vocabulary

posterity (pos ter′ ə tē) *n.* generations of the future; all of one's descendants

---

Reading Practice

SPIRAL REVIEW Compare and Contrast
Have students compare and contrast the sections of the Iroquois constitution listed here with the U.S. Constitution and other American laws and customs. Focus comparisons by supplying topics such as the organization of government (the confederate council *vs.* the three branches of the U.S. government), property rights, qualifications for public office, national holidays, and national symbols. Draw attention to a major cultural difference: The Iroquois trace their lineage through the mother's line, while the American practice (drawn from European settlers) is to trace lineage through the father's line. Direct students to record their findings in a Venn Diagram.

and their firmness shall be **tempered** with a tenderness for their people. Neither anger nor fury shall find lodgment in their minds, and all their words and actions shall be marked by calm **deliberation**.

The Festivals

The rites and festivals of each Nation shall remain undisturbed and shall continue as before because they were given by the people of old times as useful and necessary for the good of men.

The recognized festivals of Thanksgiving shall be the Midwinter Thanksgiving, the Maple or Sugar Making Thanksgiving, the Raspberry Thanksgiving, the Strawberry Thanksgiving, the

---

3 | **Author's Purpose** *How does Dekanawida's lengthy description of the traits of the Lords of the Confederacy reinforce his purpose for writing the constitution?*

Vocabulary

temper (tem´ pər) *v.* to modify or moderate; soften
deliberation (di lib´ ə rā´ shən) *n.* careful consideration

Corn Planting Thanksgiving, the Corn Hoeing Thanksgiving, the Little Festival of Green Corn, the Great Festival of Ripe Corn, and the complete Thanksgiving for the Harvest.

The Symbols

A large bunch of shell strings, in the making of which the Five Nations' Confederate Lords have equally contributed, shall symbolize the completeness of the union and certify the pledge of the Nations represented by the Confederate Lords of the Mohawk, the Oneida, the Onondaga, the Cayuga, and the Seneca, that all are united and formed into one body or union called the Union of the Great Law, which they have established.

Five arrows shall be bound together very strong, and each arrow shall represent one nation. As the five arrows are strongly bound, this shall symbolize the complete union of the nations. Thus are the Five Nations united completely and enfolded together, united into one head, one body, and one mind. Therefore they shall labor, legislate, and council together for the interest of future generations.

DEKANAWIDA **51**

After You Read

Assess

1. Dekanawida is a great peace-maker. His plan is thorough.

2. Peace and strength

3. (a) Changes should be decided by the council. (b) He had excellent judgment.

4. Shell strings and an arrow from each nation show the unity of the tribes.

5. (a) Each tribe shares its judgment; firekeepers pass final judgment. Speakers rotate among three tribes. (b) This process promoted peace.

6. Traits: Selfless, peaceful, caring, patient; a leader needs these traits to keep the nations united.

7. The opening ceremony and the nature metaphors display reverence for nature.

8. The Iroquois traced their ancestry through the women.

For additional assessment, see Assessment Resources, pp. 65–66.

Progress Check

Can students identify the author's purpose?

If No → See Unit 1 Teaching Resources Book, p. 51.

After You Read

Respond and Think Critically

Respond and Interpret

1. What is your opinion of Dekanawida's abilities as a peacemaker? Explain.

2. What does Dekanawida say is the nature of the roots of the Tree of the Great Peace?

3. (a)Describe the rules Dekanawida includes about making changes to the law. (b)Given these rules, how would you characterize Dekanawida's skills as a planner?

4. Explain the symbols of the confederacy described on page 51. In what way, do you think, does the design of the symbols reflect Dekanawida's vision for the confederacy?

Analyze and Evaluate

5. (a)How does the constitution divide authority among the five nations? (b)How did structuring decision making this way benefit the Iroquois?

6. What do you think were important leadership qualities in the confederacy? Explain.

Connect

7. **Big Idea** The Sacred Earth and the Power of Storytelling How is reverence for nature reflected in the Iroquois Constitution? Explain.

8. **Connect to the Author** Dekanawida gives women a great deal of power. Why might he have assigned women these roles?

Literary Element Author's Purpose

After forming your initial idea of the **author's purpose**, double-check your notion against the information in the piece.

1. What is Dekanawida's basic purpose in creating the Iroquois Constitution?

2. What different comparisons does he introduce to convey his ideas of peace and unity?

Reading Strategy Draw Conclusions About Culture

To **draw conclusions** about the Iroquois, think about how the details tell you something about Iroquois society. Review your chart on page 48 and the passage about women's roles on page 50. What conclusions do you draw about the importance of women in Iroquois society?

Vocabulary Practice

Practice with Synonyms Match each vocabulary word below with its synonym on the right. You will not use all the answer choices. Check your answers in a thesaurus or dictionary.

1. disposition   a. moderate
2. convene   b. congregate
3. posterity   c. contemplation
4. temper   d. journey
5. deliberation   e. temperament
                        f. imprisonment
                        g. descendants

LOG ON ▶ Literature Online

Selection Resources For Selection Quizzes, eFlash-cards, and Reading-Writing Connection activities, go to glencoe.com and enter QuickPass code GLA9800u1.

Writing

Write a Letter Imagine that you were a guest at the meeting at which the Constitution was presented. Write a letter to your friends giving your evaluation of Dekanawida's proposal.

Reading Strategy

Students may conclude that women are of great importance because they own the land and determine family status.

Literary Element

1. To persuade the Iroquois to unite and stop fighting among themselves
2. He compares the confederacy to a great tree and to a bundle of five arrows bound together.

Vocabulary

1. e 2. b 3. g 4. a 5. c

Writing

Students' letters should reflect an understanding of the Iroquois Constitution and Dekanawida's purpose in writing it.

Vocabulary Workshop

Academic Vocabulary

What Is Academic Vocabulary? Words that are commonly used in academic texts such as textbooks, directions, and tests are called **academic vocabulary.** Learning academic vocabulary is important; it will help you read, write, and research in many academic areas. These words will also help you do well on standardized tests.

Specific and General Academic Vocabulary Some words are specific to certain disciplines, or areas of study. For example, the words *iambic*, *denouement*, and *soliloquy* pertain to literature. Other words, such as *function*, *evidence*, and *theory*, are used in many areas of study. The charts below show more examples of both kinds of words.

Discipline-Specific Academic Vocabulary

Discipline	Words
Math	hypotenuse, polynomial, pi, epicycloid
Science	hypothalamus, electrodynamics, igneous, Pleistocene
Social Studies	egalitarian, servitude, judiciary, anthropology

General Academic Vocabulary

derived	framework	procedure	aggregate
foundation	focus	domain	paradigm

Multiple-Meaning Words Many academic vocabulary words, such as *foundation*, have more than one meaning. The first meaning is a literal, more common definition that you may already be familiar with: "the solid slab on which a building is constructed." An example is the foundation of a house. The second definition is more academic and may be unfamiliar to you: "the assumptions or evidence underlying a theory or belief." These two definitions are related, however. The ideas that support the theory are its foundation. The chart on the following page lists additional examples of academic words with more than one meaning.

Learning Objectives

For pages 53–54
In this workshop, you will focus on the following objectives:

Vocabulary:
Understanding academic vocabulary. Using context clues to determine the meanings of words with multiple meanings.

Test-Taking Tip

These key academic vocabulary words often appear on standardized tests.

- **Analyze:** to systematically and critically examine all parts of an issue or event

- **Classify or categorize:** to put people, things, or ideas into groups based on common characteristics

- **Compare:** to show how things are alike

- **Contrast:** to show how things are different

- **Describe:** to present a sketch or an impression

- **Discuss:** to systematically write about all sides of an issue or event

- **Evaluate:** to make a judgment and support it with evidence

- **Explain:** to clarify, give reasons for, or elaborate

Focus

Explain to students that academic vocabulary words are useful tools for discussing or writing about material they read. Help students understand that these words are used in the process of critical thinking. **Say:** Determine what the word *critical* means in this sentence: Reading literature requires critical thinking. *(characterized by careful evaluation and judgment)*

Teach

Vocabulary

Multiple-Meaning Words
Some terms that are used to refer to physical things—*foundation, framework*—are useful when discussing concepts that are intangible. **Ask:** What tangible things are the words *foundation* and *framework* used to describe? *(the base and skeleton of houses and other buildings)* **Ask:** What might serve as the foundation for an essay? *(a philosophy or set of political or moral beliefs)*

English Learners

DIFFERENTIATED INSTRUCTION

PARTNERS **Intermediate** Explain that academic words are often multisyllabic and may seem intimidating. Remind students to break these long words into parts in order to understand them. Have each student choose a word from the General Academic Vocabulary list to look up in the dictionary. Have pairs of students work together to explain both the common and the academic definitions of the words they have chosen.

For example, *domain*'s root means "lord" or "master." A domain is the territory over which control is exercised. When the word is used in the academic sense, a domain is a person's field or area of expertise, such as American history or physics or modern poetry. The word has additional meanings in science and math.

Teach

Vocabulary

Multiple-Meaning Words

Explain that the academic definition of a word often differs from its common meaning when used in test instructions. **Ask:** If a test asked you to "illustrate" how American Indians viewed animals, what would the test likely be asking for? *(several examples of their interactions with animals)* **Ask:** What is the common meaning of the word *justify*? *(to defend or make an excuse)*

Assess

Practice

1. Students should infer that *casualty* used figuratively means "something that is harmed or destroyed as a result of something else."

2. Students should infer that *aristocracy* here means "a gathering of people with superior talents."

 For additional vocabulary practice, see Glencoe Interactive Vocabulary CD-ROM.

Academic vocabulary words appearing often on standardized tests, continued.

- **Illustrate:** to provide examples or to show with a picture or another graphic

- **Infer:** to read between the lines or to use knowledge or experience to draw conclusions, make generalizations, or form predictions

- **Justify:** to prove or to support a position with specific facts and reasons

- **Predict:** to tell what will happen in the future based on an understanding of prior events and behaviors

- **State:** to briefly and concisely present information

- **Summarize:** to give a brief overview of the main points of an event or issue

- **Trace:** to present the steps or stages in a process or an event in sequential or chronological order

For a complete list of academic vocabulary words, see pages R89–R91.

LOG ON ▶ **Literature** Online

Vocabulary For more vocabulary practice, go to glencoe.com and enter QuickPass code GLA9800u1.

Academic Vocabulary with Multiple Meanings

Word	Definitions	Relationship
authority	*n.* person or group in charge *n.* person or source of information considered to be knowledgeable and accurate	Both definitions involve making final decisions
illustrate	*v.* to create pictures of something *v.* to explain something by giving examples or presenting case studies	Both definitions involve showing and clarifying
role	*n.* a part in a drama *n.* the responsibility or contribution of a person or thing in a particular activity	Both definitions involve acting in a way that contributes to a whole

Academic Vocabulary in This Book You will learn all three types of academic vocabulary words in this book. Words that are specific to literature and language arts will most often be introduced and explained in Literary Element and Reading Strategy features connected with specific reading selections. You will encounter more general and multiple-meaning academic vocabulary words in a feature called Academic Vocabulary that appears after many literature selections.

As you encounter academic vocabulary words in this book, you will master the words through various activities. You'll have a chance to practice these activities in the exercise below.

Practice Follow the instructions to complete each exercise.

1. *The judge feared that civil rights would become a* **casualty** *of emergency security measures.*

   Casualty is an academic word with more than one meaning. Speaking literally, someone might say that the terrible automobile accident didn't result in a single **casualty**. Using context clues, try to infer the more figurative meaning of *casualty* in the sentence above. Check your inference in a dictionary.

2. *Thomas Jefferson called America's early political leadership a "natural* **aristocracy**" *of talent.*

   Aristocracy is an academic word with more than one meaning. Speaking literally, someone might say that the British royal family are members of the **aristocracy**. Using context clues, try to infer the more figurative meaning of *aristocracy* as used by Jefferson in the sentence above. Check your inference in a dictionary.

Vocabulary Practice

PARTNERS **Multiple Meanings** Have each student choose five academic vocabulary words that have multiple meanings. **Say:** Write a sentence using each word. After you have written your sentences, exchange papers with a partner. Partners should add a sentence for each word, using a different meaning for each word. Work together to mark sentences that use the words with their academic meanings. *(Multiple meaning words include most of the words listed on page 53 under General Academic Vocabulary and most of the words listed on pages 53 and 54 under Test-Taking Tip. Additional words students might use are narrative, character, myth, central, and action.)*

→ **Part 2** ←

LIFE IN THE NEW WORLD

Self-portrait, c. 1680. Thomas Smith. Oil on canvas, 24¾ x 23¾ in. Worcester Art Museum, Worcester, MA.

 View the Art Smith's self-portrait includes a skull sitting on top of a poem that contrasts the sorrows of Earthly existence with the joys of eternal life. Why might the artist have included these elements? ★

"For we must consider that we shall be as a city upon a hill. The eyes of all people are upon us." **1**

—John Winthrop, *A Model of Christian Charity*

Approaching Level

DIFFERENTIATED INSTRUCTION

Emerging Ask students to discuss the meaning of the phrase "a city upon a hill." *(The colony will be highly visible to everyone and will be a model community.)* Ideas can be listed on the board. Direct students to paraphrase the quotation, using complete sentences.

Established Have students infer details about Smith's character from the painting.
Ask: What conclusion can you draw about Smith from his portrait? *(formal, serious, dignified)* Have students write a description of the painting, stating their impression of Smith.

Analyze and Extend

| **Reading Strategy** | **1** |

Evaluate Direct students to read the quotation by John Winthrop. Explain that Winthrop, born in England in 1588, was a key figure in the shaping of Puritan New England. Winthrop composed his sermon "A Model of Christian Charity" in 1630, while he was sailing to the New World.

Ask: How might Winthrop's notion of a city upon a hill be a symbol of Puritan values? *(The ideal Puritan community was a harmonious society that would be an example for all people.)*

 ★

Answer: *To emphasize the shortness of life.*

Thomas Smith was a naval officer, painter, and poet. The painting shows Smith's own hair rather than a wig, a sign of the Puritan preference for plainness. The skull rests on a poem that he wrote about the acceptance of mortality.

Ask: What images appear in the painting's inset? What do they reveal about Smith's life? *(The naval battle and the fort may relate to his career.)*

 For additional support for English Learners, see Unit 1 Teaching Resources Book, p. 59.

Focus

Bellringer Options

Selection Focus Transparency 4

Daily Language Practice Transparency 6

Or display a world map and a map of the solar system. Point out that explorers during the Age of Discovery (roughly, the 1400s and 1500s) risked their lives to face the unknown.

Ask: What personal qualities are needed by explorers at any time in history—for example, those who explore outer space and the ocean floors today? As they read, have students consider the character traits that Cabeza de Vaca and his men must have needed to survive.

Before You Read

from *La Relación*

Meet **Álvar Núñez Cabeza de Vaca** (1490–1556)

F ew adventurers have faced greater odds than the Spanish explorer Álvar Núñez Cabeza de Vaca (äl´ vär nōō´ nyez   kä bā´ zä   dä   bä´ kä). Stranded and defenseless in the vast wilderness of the New World, he had only a slim chance of surviving. His tale of the journey, *La Relación*, was the first European account of the interior of what is now the United States.

In 1527, Cabeza de Vaca left Spain as a career soldier on an expedition to occupy North America and discover riches for the king. The expedition, which landed in 1528 at what is today Tampa Bay, Florida, was a disaster. Boat accidents, faulty judgment, and disease led to the deaths of many of the 600 men. The survivors developed a fruitful relationship with the Apalachee tribe, but the situation soured when the Spaniards took the tribe's leader hostage. The Spaniards ended up cowering in a coastal swamp, eating horseflesh to survive. Finally, led by Cabeza de Vaca, the explorers constructed basic rafts from horsehide and trees and set sail, praying they could reach Cuba. Wracked by starvation and thirst, the 80 men who managed to cling to the rafts were buffeted by a hurricane and deposited near present-day Galveston, Texas, on the Gulf of Mexico.

Adaptation The expedition landed in November. By the following spring, there were 15 men alive. Eventually, Cabeza de Vaca and three others were the only survivors. Cabeza de Vaca lived among the nomadic Native Americans in east Texas—the Karankawa, the Mariames, the Yguazes—for four years, adapting to their ways of life and morphing from conquistador to trader and physician in order to survive. The Native Americans were not as lucky. Many perished as a result of a stomach virus that the Spaniards unwittingly carried with them.

Trailblazer Cabeza de Vaca traveled south and west, hoping to find a Spanish outpost. He was the first European to trek through present-day Texas. He continued west through northern Mexico and then turned south, finally running into a band of Spanish slave traders in the present-day Mexican state of Sinaloa. His countrymen were flabbergasted when Cabeza de Vaca stood before them naked and filthy. Eight years had passed since he had landed in Florida—during that time, he had traveled approximately 2,500 miles, mostly on foot.

> "We were entering a land for which we had no description . . ."
>
> —Álvar Núñez Cabeza de Vaca
> from *La Relación*

During his travels, Cabeza de Vaca proved to be a masterful ethnologist. He lived among Native Americans before they had been influenced by European culture. His writings detail the unique customs of many tribes. Unlike other early explorers, he called for tolerance and justice for Native Americans.

 Literature Online

Author Search For more about Álvar Núñez Cabeza de Vaca, go to glencoe.com and enter QuickPass code GLA9800u1.

Selection Skills

Literary Element
- Point of View (SE pp. 57, 60, 61)

from La Relación

Writing Skills/Grammar
- Write a Story (SE p. 61)
- Evaluate (TE p. 60)

Reading Skills
- Recognize Bias (SE pp. 57, 61; TE p. 60)
- Sequence of Events (TE p. 58)

Vocabulary Skills
- Practice with Synonyms (SE p. 61)
- Words with Many Uses (TE p. 57)

Listening/Speaking/Viewing Skills
- Analyze Art (SE p. 60)

Literature and Reading Preview

Connect to the Narrative

Have you ever had to rely on someone you didn't know? Write a journal entry describing such a situation, and the result. Consider what forced you to trust that person and how you felt.

Build Background

In the early 1500s, Spanish conquistadores began exploring and invading Central and South America, searching for gold and other riches. The indigenous people were baffled and frightened by the sudden appearance of the Spanish. The Spanish had weapons that ensured victory in war: horses, war dogs, guns, and cannons. As a result of Spanish occupation, indigenous societies and cultures were often decimated.

Set Purposes for Reading

Big Idea Life in the New World

As you read, ask yourself, What does this narrative imply about the Spaniards' view of their own culture in comparison with that of the indigenous people they met in the New World?

Literary Element Point of View

Point of view is the relationship of the narrator to the story. In a narrative with a first-person point of view, the narrator is a character in the story and uses the words *I* and *me*. As you read, ask yourself, How does Cabeza de Vaca's first-person point of view affect his description of people and events?

Reading Strategy Recognize Bias

Bias refers to an author's inclination toward a particular opinion or position. As you read, ask yourself, What do Cabeza de Vaca's descriptions reveal about his biases?

Tip: Take Notes Use a chart to record instances of bias and what they suggest about Cabeza de Vaca.

Quote	Bias
p. 60 "Crude and untutored people, who were like brutes"	Cabeza de Vaca assumes indigenous people are unintelligent and unschooled.

Learning Objectives

For pages 56–61

In studying this text, you will focus on the following objectives:

Literary Study: Analyzing point of view.

Reading: Recognizing bias.

Writing: Writing a story.

Vocabulary

ration (rash′ ən) *n.* fixed portion or share; p. 58 *The campers ate their entire day's ration and were still hungry.*

rouse (rouz) *v.* to awaken from sleep; p. 58 *They had gone to bed late, and it was difficult to rouse them.*

revive (ri vīv′) *v.* to give new strength, or awaken; p. 58 *The lifeguard was able to revive the unconscious swimmer.*

embark (em bärk′) *v.* to set out on a venture; p. 59 *The hunting party mounted their horses and prepared to embark.*

Before You Read

Focus

Summary

After four days at sea, Cabeza de Vaca's ship is caught in a storm. When the ship runs aground on an island, the men fear they will be sacrificed by Native Americans. However, the Native Americans are sympathetic. The Spaniards set sail again but are shipwrecked a second time. The Native Americans weep for the misfortunes of the sailors and hold a great celebration.

 For summaries in languages other than English, see Unit 1 Teaching Resources Book, pp. 60–65.

Vocabulary

Words with Many Uses

Say: To discover the different meanings a word may have, check a dictionary. Direct students to check the meanings of *revive*. Have them use the word in three different contexts. *(revive someone who has fainted; revive a play; revive an idea)*

APPROACHING **Ask:** Which word can be used as a noun and a verb? *(ration)* Have students use the word as a noun and as a verb.

 For additional vocabulary practice, see Unit 1 Teaching Resources Book, p. 68.

 For additional context, see Glencoe Interactive Vocabulary CD-ROM.

English Learners

DIFFERENTIATED INSTRUCTION

Intermediate Explain to students that although this narrative is nonfiction, the narrator, Cabeza de Vaca, is still a character in the story. Direct them to create a chart and take notes about Cabeza de Vaca as they read. Ask them to use these headings for their charts:

- His description of people and events
- His actions
- How others respond to him

After completing their reading, have students orally summarize the character of Cabeza de Vaca, referring to specific details.

Teach

Life in the New World

Say: Keep the following questions in mind as you read. What assumptions does Cabeza de Vaca make about the native people? How do those assumptions change? *(He refers to his own men as "Christians" to distinguish them from the "pagan" native people, who he believes have no morals. He learns, though, that many Native Americans are hospitable and compassionate.)*

Readability Scores

Dale-Chall: 6.1
DRP: 55
Lexile: 1100

---

from LA RELACIÓN

Álvar Núñez Cabeza de Vaca
Translated by Martin A. Favata
and José B. Fernández

1 We sailed in this manner together for four days, eating a daily **ration** of half a handful of raw corn. After four days a storm came up and caused the other boat to be lost. We did not sink because of God's great mercy. The weather was rough, very cold, and wintery. We had been suffering from hunger for many days and had been pounded so much by the sea that the following day many men began to faint. By nightfall all the men in my boat had passed out, one on top of another, so near death that few of them were conscious and fewer than five were still upright. During the night only the sailing master and I were left to sail the boat. Two hours after nightfall he told me I should take over because he was in such a condition that he thought he would die that very night; so I took the tiller. In the middle of the night, I went to see if the sailing master had died, but he told me that he was better and that he would steer until daybreak. At that time I certainly would have rather died than see so many people before me in that condition. After the sailing master took over the boat, I tried to rest some but could not, and sleep was the furthest thing from my mind.

Near dawn I thought I heard the roar of the breakers[1] near shore, which was very loud because the coast was low. Surprised by this, I **roused** the sailing master, who said he thought we were near land. We took a sounding and found that the water was seven fathoms[2] deep. He thought that we should stay out until dawn. So I took an oar and rowed along the coast, which was a league[3] distant. Then we set our stern[4] to sea.

Near land a great wave took us and cast the boat out of the water as far as a horseshoe can be tossed. The boat ran aground with such force that it **revived** the men on it who were almost dead. When they saw they were near land they pushed themselves overboard and crawled on their hands and knees. When they got to the beach, we lit a fire by some rocks and toasted some of the corn we had and found rain water.

---

1. *Breakers* are waves that foam as they break.
2. A *fathom* is a linear measure equal to six feet.
3. A *league* is a measure of distance of about three miles.
4. The *stern* is the rear part of a boat or ship.

Vocabulary

rouse (rouz) *v.* to awaken from sleep
revive (ri vīv´) *v.* to give new strength, or awaken

Vocabulary

ration (rash´ ən) *n.* fixed portion or share

Reading Practice

SPIRAL REVIEW **Sequence of Events** Have students read silently, paying careful attention to the order in which events occur. Draw a timeline on the board and provide the first and last events:

Help students identify four or five events that occurred between June 1527 and April 1528. Then have students determine the correct order of events.

June 1527 ———————————————— April 1528

Cabeza de Vaca's
expedition sets sail
from Spain

The 60 remaining men
of the expedition
arrive in Florida

With the warmth of the fire, the men revived and began to regain some of their strength. We arrived at this place on the sixth of November.

☆ Once our people had eaten, I sent Lope de Oviedo, who was stronger and fitter than the rest of us, to climb one of the trees nearby to sight the land and find out something about it. He did this and saw that we were on an island, and that the land appeared to have been trampled by livestock. He thought for this reason that it must be a country of Christians, and told us so. I told him to look again very carefully to see if there were any paths that could be followed, but not to go too far because of possible danger. He found a path and followed it for half a league and found some unoccupied Indian huts, for the Indians had gone into the fields. He took a pot from one of them, a small dog and some mullet[5] and started back.

We thought he was taking a long time to return, so I sent two other Christians to look for him and find out what had happened to him. They found him near there, pursued by three Indians with bows and arrows. They were calling out to him and he was trying to speak to them through sign language. He got to where we were and the Indians stayed back a bit seated on the same shore. Half an hour later another one hundred Indian bowmen appeared. We were so scared that they seemed to us to be giants, whether they were or not. They stopped near us, where the first three were. We could not even think of defending ourselves, since there were scarcely six men who could even get up from the ground. The Inspector and I went towards them and called them, and they approached us. As best we could we tried to reassure them and ourselves, and gave them beads and little bells. Each of them gave me an arrow, which is a sign of

friendship. In sign language they told us that they would return in the morning and bring us food, since they did not have any at the time. The following day at sunrise, at the time the Indians had indicated, they came to us as promised, bringing us much fish, some roots which they eat, the size of walnuts, some larger or smaller. Most of these are pulled with great difficulty from under the water. In the evening they returned to bring us more fish and the same kind of roots. They had their women and children come to see us and they considered themselves rich with little bells and beads that we gave them. The following days they returned to visit with the same things as before.

Seeing that we were provisioned with fish, roots, water, and the other things we requested, we agreed to **embark** on our voyage once again. We dug up the boat from the sand. We had to strip naked and struggle mightily to launch it, because we were so weak that lesser tasks would have been enough to exhaust us. Once we were out from the shore the distance of two crossbow shots, a wave struck us quite a blow and got us all wet. Since we were naked and it was very cold, we let go of the oars. Another strong wave caused the boat to capsize. The Inspector and two other men held on to it to survive, but quite the opposite occurred because the boat pulled them under and they drowned. Since the surf was very rough, the sea wrapped all the men in its waves, except the three that had been pulled under by the boat, and cast them on the shore of the same island. Those of us who survived were as naked as the day we were born and had lost everything we had. Although the few things we had were of little value, they meant a lot to us.

It was November then and the weather was very cold. We were in such a state that our bones

5. A *mullet* is a type of fish.

2 Life in the New World *How does Lope de Oviedo's assumption reflect the Spaniards' expectations?*

Vocabulary
embark (em bärk´) *v.* to set out on a venture

ÁLVAR NÚÑEZ CABEZA DE VACA **59**

Teach

Big Idea **2**

Life in the New World
Answer: *Because he finds something that seems familiar to him— land trampled by livestock—he assumes that the people who live there must be like him—Christian.*

Writer's Technique ☆

Style Cabeza de Vaca's account is simple and straightforward. His narrative reveals his training as a mariner and his instincts as an explorer. The experiences he and his men endure—storms, starvation, exhaustion, death, and encounters with native peoples—are described in credible detail.

Approaching Level

DIFFERENTIATED INSTRUCTION

Emerging Remind students that a subordinate clause has a subject and a verb but cannot stand alone as a sentence. **Ask:** Find a subordinate clause in this sentence: Each of them gave me an arrow, which is a sign of friendship. *(which is a sign of friendship)* Point out that *which* is a relative pronoun. List relative pronouns used to begin subordinate clauses: *that, which, who, whom, whose.* Have students locate several sentences in the selection that have relative pronouns. Direct them to copy each clause, circling the relative pronoun and underlining the subject once, the verb twice.

Advanced Learners

DIFFERENTIATED INSTRUCTION

Correct Bias Have students choose short passages from *La Relación* to rewrite as bias-free newspaper articles. Review examples of bias, such as charged words, faulty reasoning, stereotyping, and exaggeration. Have students check their own articles for examples of bias.

Teach

Reading Strategy 1

Recognize Bias Cabeza de Vaca gives accounts of suffering throughout the selection. In this passage, he tells how the explorers were cold and naked, and so hungry that their bones could be counted.

Ask: Do you consider Cabeza de Vaca a credible witness? (*We are told that Cabeza de Vaca wrote this account for the king of Spain. He probably wanted to please or impress the king with his bravery, so he may have exaggerated these events.*)

Literary Element 2

Point of View Answer: *Cabeza de Vaca's description of his own food rations can be generalized to apply to all of the men.*

For additional practice using the reading skill or strategy, see Unit 1 Teaching Resources Book, p. 67.

View the Art ★

Answer: *The men look weary and forlorn. They gaze out at the distance, but seem contemplative rather than hopeful.*

To check students' understanding of the selection, see Unit 1 Teaching Resources Book, p. 71.

---

could easily be counted and we looked like the picture of death. I can say for myself that I had not eaten anything but parched corn since the previous May, and sometimes I had to eat it raw. Although the horses were slaughtered while we were building the boats, I was never able to eat them, and I had eaten fish fewer than ten times. This is but a brief comment, since anyone can **1** imagine what shape we were in. On top of all this, the north wind began to blow, and so we were closer to death than to life. It pleased our Lord to let us find some embers among the coals of the fire we had made, and we made large fires. In this way we asked our Lord's mercy and the forgiveness of our sins, shedding many tears, with each man pitying not only himself but all the others who were in the same condition.

At sunset the Indians, thinking that we had not gone, looked for us again and brought us food. When they saw us in such a different state of attire and looking so strange, they were so frightened that they drew back. I went out to them and called them and they returned very frightened. I let them know through sign language that one of our boats had sunk and that three of our men had drowned. And there before their very eyes they saw two of the dead men, and those of us who were alive seemed as if we would soon join them.

The Indians, seeing the disaster that had come upon us and brought so much misfortune and misery, sat down with us. They felt such great pain and pity at seeing us in such a state that they all began to cry so loudly and sincerely that they could be heard from afar. This went on for more than half an hour. In fact, seeing that these crude and untutored people, who were like brutes, grieved so much for us, caused me and the others in my company to suffer more and think more about our misfortune. When their crying ceased, I told the Christians that, if they agreed, I would ask those Indians to take us to their lodges. And some who had been in New Spain[6] responded

---

6. *New Spain* was a part of the Spanish Empire in the 1500s. It included Venezuela, Florida, Mexico, and Central America.

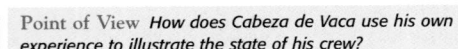
2 Point of View *How does Cabeza de Vaca use his own experience to illustrate the state of his crew?*

60 UNIT 1 EARLY AMERICA

View the Art This painting shows Cabeza de Vaca and the three remaining members of his crew. How would you describe the men's mood in this depiction? ★

that we should not even think about it, because if they took us to their lodges they would sacrifice us to their idols.[7] But seeing that we had no other recourse and that any other action would certainly bring us closer to death, I did not pay attention to what they were saying and I asked the Indians to take us to their lodges. They indicated that they would be very pleased to do this. They asked us to wait a bit and then they would do what we wanted. Then thirty of them loaded themselves with firewood and went to their lodges, which were far from there. We stayed with the others until nearly nightfall, when they held on to us and took us hastily to their lodges. Since it was so cold and they feared that someone might feint or die on the way, they had provided for four or five large fires to be placed at intervals, and they warmed us at each one. Once they saw that we had gained some strength and gotten warmer, they took us to the next one so rapidly that our feet scarcely touched the ground. In this way we went to their lodges and found that they had one ready for us with many fires lighted in it. Within an hour of our arrival they began to dance and have a great celebration that lasted all night. For us there was no pleasure nor celebration nor sleep because we were waiting to see when they would sacrifice us. In the morning they again gave us fish and roots and treated us so well that we were a little reassured and lost some of our fear of being sacrificed.

---

7. *Idols* are images of gods used as objects of worship.

Writing Practice

SPIRAL REVIEW **Evaluate** Cabeza de Vaca says that he and his men were "a little reassured" by how the Native Americans had treated them. **Ask:** What treatment did the Spaniards expect to receive? (*They thought they would be sacrificed to pagan idols.*) Ask students to write a paragraph evaluating how the men were treated. Be sure students refer to specific examples from the selection. Have students consider the attitudes European Christians of the sixteenth century held toward people in the New World. Students should assess how beliefs were shaped by the religious and philosophical influences of the historical period.

After You Read

Respond and Think Critically

Respond and Interpret

1. After reading Cabeza de Vaca's account, what questions might you ask him?

2. (a)Why do the Native Americans chase Lope de Oviedo? (b)How does the behavior of Oviedo and his pursuers reveal each group's assumptions about the other?

3. (a)In what ways do the Native Americans help Cabeza de Vaca and his companions? (b)What do you think prompts them to give assistance?

Analyze and Evaluate

4. How do Cabeza de Vaca's descriptions of his own and his men's suffering contribute to the effectiveness and emotional impact of this account?

5. How do de Vaca's references to God's mercy affect your impression of him and his mission?

Connect

6. **Big Idea** **Life in the New World** What does Cabeza de Vaca's narrative indicate about the difficulties of first encounters between Native Americans and Europeans?

7. **Connect to the Author** De Vaca makes several judgmental remarks about Native Americans. Yet he also called for tolerance and justice for them. How do you reconcile these seemingly opposite perspectives?

Literary Element Point of View

The narrator tells what happens in a story from his or her **point of view.** Narratives of the same events written from a third-person omniscient point of view, or by a different "first person," may reflect different details, feelings, and ideas.

1. How might the story have been different if one of de Vaca's men had told it?

2. Cabeza de Vaca portrays himself as a heroic character. What details create this image?

Reading Strategy Recognize Bias

De Vaca's account contains considerable **bias.** To detect bias, look for oversimplification and stereotyping, analyze the writer's reasoning, and identify emotionally charged language.

1. Refer to the chart you made and identify two examples of bias in Cabeza de Vaca's narrative.

2. Write the strategy that helped you recognize the bias and the word clues that helped you.

Vocabulary Practice

Practice with Synonyms Match each boldfaced vocabulary word below with its synonym on the right. You will not use all the answer choices. Check your answers in a thesaurus or dictionary.

1. ration   a. seek
2. rouse   b. stimulate
3. revive   c. allowance
4. embark   d. launch
                   e. stir
                   f. storm

Writing

Write a Story Rewrite the first meeting of the two cultures from the Native American perspective, detailing your thoughts, feelings, and reactions.

LOG ON **Literature** Online

Selection Resources For Selection Quizzes, eFlash-cards, and Reading-Writing Connection activities, go to glencoe.com and enter QuickPass code GLA9800u1.

After You Read

Assess

1. Questions should refer to experiences Cabeza de Vaca describes.

2. (a) He is a stranger who may have stolen from them. (b) Native Americans assume the Spaniards are thieves; Spaniards assume Native Americans are savages.

3. (a) They give him food and shelter. (b) They may trust them.

4. His descriptions stir feelings of sympathy and compassion, underscoring the seriousness of their condition.

5. He seems to be a religious man who may feel that his mission has been sanctioned by God.

6. Language barriers, different social customs

7. They helped Cabeza de Vaca and his crew, so he hopes that they are treated well. Conversely, he sees the Native Americans poorly because their culture is different.

Progress Check

Can students identify point of view?

If No → See Unit 1 Teaching Resources Book, p. 66.

For additional assessment, see Assessment Resources, pp. 67–68.

Writing

Students' answers should reflect an understanding of Native American culture as it is depicted in Cabeza de Vaca's account.

Literary Element

1. One of the men might have shown frustration with the conditions on the voyage.

2. His mention of his hunger, his ability to survive hardships, and his decision to go to the lodges.

Vocabulary

1. c **2.** e **3.** b **4.** d

Reading Strategy

1. Examples include emotionally charged words, such as "picture of death," "misery," and "pity," to describe the crew, and his characterization of the Native Americans as "crude and untutored."

2. Students may refer to the strategy of taking notes to record instances of bias.

Before You Read

Focus

Bellringer Options

**Selection Focus
    Transparency 5**
**Daily Language Practice
    Transparency 7**

Or display newspaper articles that describe people suffering extreme hardship (earthquake, war, illness). **Ask:** What qualities do people need to endure hardship? As they read, have students consider the qualities that might have helped the Pilgrims get through hardships.

Cultural History ☆

Passengers on the *Mayflower*

Of the 102 passengers aboard the *Mayflower,* there were 50 men and 19 women, 14 teenage passengers, and 19 children under twelve. Most wished to join the settlement for economic reasons, while a minority were Separatists.

Before You Read

from *Of Plymouth Plantation*

Meet **William Bradford**
(1590–1657)

It was 1620, and the passengers aboard the *Mayflower* were traveling to the Americas. Violent storms tossed the creaking ship and blew it far off course. Among the passengers was thirty-year-old William Bradford.

Born in Yorkshire, England, in 1590, Bradford was orphaned as an infant and brought up by relatives. As a youth, he studied the Bible and became a Separatist. Like the Puritans, Separatists sought reforms in the Church of England. Rather than try to "purify" it, however, the Separatists broke away. In 1609, Bradford expatriated, moving to Leiden in Holland with the congregation and its leader, John Robinson. Fearing they might become assimilated into Dutch culture and lose their identity, the Separatists decided to go to the Americas. John Carver, a successful businessman, attained financial backing and chartered the *Mayflower.* Nearly 500 miles northeast of their intended destination, the Separatists landed in Provincetown, Massachusetts, on Cape Cod on November 21, 1620. On December 26, the 102 settlers disembarked nearby at a site they named Plymouth, after the town where they had set sail. Before leaving the *Mayflower,* the men in the group drafted and signed the historic Mayflower Compact, the colony's rules of government.

The First Winter The group of about 100 settlers, known today as the Pilgrims, elected Bradford leader after John Carver, the first governor, died. The voyage had been harsh. They arrived with little or no food at the onset of winter and had no wilderness survival skills. They constructed crude shelters, hoping to make it through the winter. Nearly half the colonists died of scurvy, pneumonia, fever, or starvation.

Governor The colony survived and in time grew into a thriving community under Bradford's leadership. He was reelected governor for thirty one-year terms between 1622 and 1656. In his gubernatorial years, he served as chief magistrate, high judge, and treasurer. He also presided over the community's legislature, known as the General Court. Unlike the Massachusetts Bay Colony, which was a Bible commonwealth, Plymouth was fairly egalitarian for its day, allowing Presbyterians and maverick non-believers to live in the community without forcing them to practice in Congregationalist or Separatist churches. To ensure a peaceable, organized society, Bradford distributed parcels of land equally to all settlers, even non-believers.

> "All great and honorable actions are accompanied with great difficulties . . ."
> —William Bradford

In 1630, Bradford started to compile *Of Plymouth Plantation, 1620–1647.* The chronicle is unique in that it separates religious commentary from historical commentary. Certain narratives published by Puritans who had arrived during the Great Migration deemed colonial life as God's plan. Bradford made no such doctrinaire claims. Instead, he steered a middle course between a Bible commonwealth and a secular society that made for a prosperous Plymouth.

 Literature Online

Author Search For more about William Bradford, go to glencoe.com and enter QuickPass code GLA9800u1.

Selection Skills

Literary Elements
- Diction (SE pp. 63, 65, 68)
- Point of View (TE p. 65)

from
Of Plymouth Plantation

Reading Skills
- Monitor Comprehension (SE pp. 63, 64, 66, 68)
- Connotation (TE p. 64)
- Make Critical Judgments (TE p. 67)

Vocabulary Skills
- Context Clues (SE p. 68)
- Create Analogies (TE p. 63)

Writing Skills/Grammar
- Write a Letter (SE p. 68)
- Graphic Aids (TE p. 66)

Literature and Reading Preview

Connect to the History

How important are your beliefs and your ability to share them with others? Would you put everything on the line for a particular cause? Discuss these questions with a partner.

Build Background

Sea voyages were extremely dangerous in the 1600s. The wooden ships were easily damaged when they hit shoals (sandbars or shallow spots in the water). Sometimes, strong waves caused ships to "seele," or lurch suddenly from side to side. In fierce winds, sails were lowered by heavy ropes called "halyards," and ships would have to "hull" or drift at sea.

Set Purposes for Reading

Big Idea Life in the New World

As you read Bradford's description of Plymouth Plantation, ask yourself, How do the colonists demonstrate their values in their daily effort to survive in a harsh environment?

Literary Element Diction

Diction is a writer's choice of words, an important element of the writer's voice or style. As you read, ask yourself, How does Bradford's diction express the values of his time?

Reading Strategy Monitor Comprehension

Bradford's writing style, while typical of his time, can be hard to understand today because he uses archaic idioms and vocabulary and long, complex sentences. As you read, try breaking long sentences into smaller parts. Ask yourself, What is Bradford trying to say in this passage?

Tip: Take Notes Choose three of Bradford's challenging sentences and rewrite them using everyday contemporary words.

Sentence	Revision
"At length they understood by discourse with him, that he was not of these parts, but belonged to the eastern parts where some English ships come to fish."	"After talking with him for a while, they found out that he lived in the east near the ocean where the English had come to fish."

Learning Objectives

For pages 62–68

In studying this text, you will focus on the following objectives:

Literary Study: Analyzing diction.

Reading: Monitoring comprehension by breaking down sentences.

Writing: Writing a letter.

Vocabulary

resolve (ri zolv′) *v.* to decide; determine; p. 65 *After failing two driving tests, Candy resolved to pass her third.*

providence (prov′ ə dəns) *n.* divine care or guidance; foresight; p. 65 *We trusted to providence that it would not rain on graduation day.*

procure (prə kyoor′) *v.* to obtain by care or effort; p. 67 *Sam set out to procure some dry wood for the campfire.*

commodity (kə mod′ ə tē) *n.* a product or economic good; an article of trade; p. 67 *Our town's most important commodity is cranberries.*

feigned (fānd) *adj.* fictitious; not genuine; p. 67 *The actress was so convincing that it was hard to believe her emotions were feigned.*

WILLIAM BRADFORD **63**

Before You Read

Focus

Summary

In 1620, a group of Separatists now called the Pilgrims set sail from Holland for Virginia. A storm blows the *Mayflower* off course, and the ship lands in what is now Massachusetts. A few months after their arrival, nearly half the 100 Pilgrims have died of disease. Some Native Americans befriend the settlers. Squanto becomes an interpreter, guide, and teacher for the Pilgrims, who learn to provide for themselves and celebrate a "First Thanksgiving" after the harvest.

For summaries in languages other than English, see Unit 1 Teaching Resources Book, pp. 73–78.

Vocabulary

Create Analogies Explain that a verbal analogy expresses a relationship between two pairs of words. The relationship may involve synonyms, antonyms, cause and effect, grammatical function, or something else. **Say:** Identify the relationship of the two pairs of words in this verbal analogy: *Feigned is to pretended as genuine is to authentic.* (Both pairs of words are synonyms.)

English Learners

DIFFERENTIATED INSTRUCTION

Beginning Have students locate the places named in Bradford's history on a map. As they read, ask them to take notes connecting the places to the events described by Bradford. They can use library sources and the Internet to obtain additional information.

Intermediate Direct students to assume the identity of a passenger aboard the *Mayflower* and to keep a journal as they read the selection. Ask them to recount these events from their own point of view and to explain what the events reveal about the lives of the Pilgrims.

For additional vocabulary practice, see Unit 1 Teaching Resources Book, p. 81.

For additional context, see Glencoe Interactive Vocabulary CD-ROM.

Teach

Reading Strategy | 1

Monitor Comprehension
Answer: *Some storms were so strong that all of the sails had to be taken down from the ships' masts.*

 For additional practice using the reading skill or strategy, see Unit 1 Teaching Resources Book, p. 80.

Big Idea | 2

Life in the New World
Ask: What does Bradford's use of the phrase "profitable member" imply about the values the Pilgrims brought to their life in the New World? *(The phrase implies a practical outlook that valued hard work and success.)*

Cultural History ☆

The Puritans Puritans held to a strict work ethic. In England, the calendar year included about 240 working days, but the Puritans in America worked at least 300 days a year, taking holidays only on the Sabbath, election day, Harvard College commencement day, and public thanksgiving days.

Readability Scores

Dale-Chall: 11.6
DRP: 62
Lexile: 1430

 For an audio recording of this selection, use Listening Library Audio CD-ROM.

The Mayflower on Her Arrival in Plymouth Harbor, 1882. William Formsby Halsall. Oil on canvas. Pilgrim Hall Museum, Plymouth, MA.

from

OF PLYMOUTH PLANTATION   William Bradford

from Chapter 9
Of Their Voyage, and How They Passed the Sea; and of Their Safe Arrival at Cape Cod

In sundry[1] of these storms the winds were so fierce and the seas so high, as they could not bear a knot of sail, but were forced to hull for divers[2] days together. And in one of them, as they thus lay at hull in a mighty storm, a lusty[3] young man called John Howland, coming upon some occasion above the gratings was, with a seele of the ship, thrown into sea; but it pleased God that he caught hold of the topsail halyards which hung overboard and ran out at length. Yet he held his hold (though he was sundry fathoms under water) till he was hauled up by the same rope to the brim of the water, and then with a boat hook and other means got into the ship again and his life saved. And though he was something ill with it, yet he lived many years after and became a profitable member both in church and commonwealth. In all this voyage there died but one of the passengers, which was William Butten, a youth, servant to Samuel Fuller, when they drew near the coast.

But to omit other things (that I may be brief) after long beating at sea they fell with that land which is called Cape Cod; the which being made

---

1. *Sundry* refers to an indefinite number.
2. *Divers* means "several."
3. *Lusty* here means "strong."

1 Monitor Comprehension *How would you rephrase this passage in modern English?*

64 UNIT 1 EARLY AMERICA

Reading Practice

SPIRAL REVIEW **Connotation** Explain that a writer's diction, or choice of words, sometimes has subtle effects on readers because words differ in their connotations, or emotional overtones. In the first sentence of his account, if Bradford had described the storms as *big,* rather than *fierce,* we would have a different impression of them.

Ask students to read the second paragraph on this page, beginning "But to omit other things . . ." Then have them discuss the connotations of the following words: *joyful, deliberation, resolved, roaring, entangled.*

and certainly known to be it, they were not a little joyful. After some deliberation had amongst themselves and with the master of the ship, they tacked about and **resolved** to stand for the southward (the wind and weather being fair) to find some place about Hudson's River for their habitation. But after they had sailed that course about half the day, they fell amongst dangerous shoals and roaring breakers, and they were so far entangled therewith as they conceived themselves in great danger; and the wind shrinking upon them withal,[4] they resolved to bear up again for the Cape and thought themselves happy to get out of those dangers before night overtook them, as by God's good **providence** they did. And the next day they got into the Cape Harbor where they rid[5] in safety. . . .

Being thus arrived in a good harbor, and brought safe to land, they fell upon their knees and blessed the God of Heaven who had brought them over the vast and furious ocean, and delivered them from all the perils and miseries thereof, again to set their feet on the firm and stable earth, their proper element. And no marvel if they were thus joyful, seeing wise Seneca[6] was so affected with sailing a few miles on the coast of his own Italy, as he affirmed, that he had rather remain twenty years on his way by land than pass by sea to any place in a short time, so tedious and dreadful was the same unto him.

But here I cannot but stay and make a pause, and stand half amazed at this poor people's present condition; and so I think will the reader, too, when he well considers the same. Being

---

4. *Also* is another word for *withal*.
5. *Rid* means "rode."
6. *Seneca* was a Roman philosopher and writer.

3 Diction *How does this phrase reflect Bradford's beliefs?*

Vocabulary

resolve (ri zolv´) *v.* to decide; determine
providence (prov´ ə dəns) *n.* divine care or guidance; foresight

---

thus passed the vast ocean, and a sea of troubles before in their preparation (as may be remembered by that which went before), they had now no friends to welcome them nor inns to entertain or refresh their weatherbeaten bodies; no houses or much less towns to repair to, to seek for succor.[7] It is recorded in Scripture[8] as a mercy to the Apostle and his shipwrecked company, that the barbarians showed them no small kindness in refreshing them, but these savage barbarians, when they met with them (as after will appear) were readier to fill their sides full of arrows than otherwise. And for the season it was winter, and they that know the winters of that country know them to be sharp and violent, and subject to cruel and fierce storms, dangerous to travel to known places, much more to search an unknown coast.

from Chapter 11
The Starving Time

But that which was most sad and lamentable was, that in two or three months' time half of their company died, especially in January and February, being the depth of winter, and wanting houses and other comforts; being infected with the scurvy[9] and other diseases which this long voyage and their inaccommodate condition had brought upon them. So as there died some times two or three of a day in the foresaid time, that of 100 and odd persons, scarce fifty remained. And of these, in the time of most distress, there was but six or seven sound persons who to their great commendations, be it spoken, spared no pains night nor day, but with abundance of toil and hazard of their own health, fetched them wood, made them **4**

---

7. *Succor* means "assistance in a time of need; relief."
8. The reference here to *Scripture,* or the Bible, is Acts of the Apostles 28, which tells of the kindness shown to St. Paul and his companions by the natives of Malta after they were shipwrecked on that island.
9. A severe lack of vitamin C causes a disease called *scurvy.*

Diction *What idea about life in the New World is reinforced by the adjectives in this passage?* **5**

WILLIAM BRADFORD **65**

Teach

English Learners

DIFFERENTIATED INSTRUCTION

SMALL GROUP **Beginning** Explain that although Bradford's seventeenth-century English is challenging, readers can use context clues and a dictionary for help. Divide the class into groups and direct each group to rephrase one or more of the following brief excerpts, using context clues and a dictionary to check unfamiliar words. Have them share their answers with the class.

- "after long beating at sea" (p. 64)
- "they fell amongst dangerous shoals and roaring breakers" (p. 65)
- "nor inns to entertain or refresh their weatherbeaten bodies" (p. 65)
- "spared no pains night nor day" (p. 65)

Intermediate Ask students to rephrase, in contemporary English, the sentence from Bradford's history that begins "But here I cannot but stay and make a pause . . ."

Teach

Reading Strategy   1

Monitor Comprehension
Answer: *This passage suggests that this "certain Indian" is from a different area—one where British fishing boats docked.*

View the Art ★

Answer: *The emphasis is on the peaceful and reflective tone of the moment. Though most of the Native Americans are not seated at the table, the tone seems respectful.*

The First Thanksgiving at Plymouth, Massachusetts, 1914. Jennie Brownscombe. Oil on canvas. The Granger Collection.

View the Art What aspects of the colonists' first Thanksgiving do you think the artist wanted to emphasize in this painting? ★

fires, dressed them meat, made their beds, washed their loathsome clothes, clothed and unclothed them. In a word, did all the homely[10] and necessary offices for them which dainty and queasy stomachs cannot endure to hear named; and all this willingly and cheerfully, without any grudging in the least, showing herein their true love unto their friends and brethren; a rare example and worthy to be remembered. Two of these seven were Mr. William Brewster, their reverend Elder, and Myles Standish, their Captain and military commander, unto whom myself and many others were much beholden in our low and sick condition. And yet the Lord so upheld these persons as in this general calamity they were not at all infected either with sickness or lameness. . . .

Indian Relations

All this while the Indians came skulking about them, and would sometimes show themselves aloof off, but when any approached near them, they would run away; and once they [the Indians] stole away their [the colonists'] tools where they had been at work and were gone to dinner. But about the 16th of March, a certain Indian came boldly amongst them and spoke to them in broken English, which they could well understand but marveled at it. At length they understood by discourse with him, that he was not of these parts, but belonged to the eastern parts where some English ships came to fish, with whom he was acquainted and could

Monitor Comprehension *What does this passage say about this "certain Indian"?*   **1**

---

10. *Homely* here means "domestic."

Writing Practice

SPIRAL REVIEW **Graphic Aids** Maps and timelines can help students gain perspective on the difficulties of the Pilgrims' travels. After students have read the selection, have them create a timeline of the events. Tell students that Bradford grew up in Yorkshire, England, and then moved with other Separatists to a small town nearby. Fearing persecution, the group then crossed the North Sea to Holland. After 12 years there, the group sailed to the New World, landing at Cape Cod. Hand out a map that shows the United States, the Atlantic Ocean, England, and Holland, and have students trace Bradford's travels.

name sundry of them by their names, amongst whom he had got his language. He became profitable to them in acquainting them with many things concerning the state of the country in the east parts where he lived, which was afterwards profitable unto them; as also of the people here, of their names, number and strength, of their situation and distance from this place, and who was chief amongst them. His name was Samoset. He told them also of another Indian whose name was Squanto, a native of this place, who had been in England and could speak better English than himself.

Being, after some time of entertainment and gifts dismissed, a while after he came again, and five more with him, and they brought again all the tools that were stolen away before, and made way for the coming of their great Sachem, called Massasoit. Who, about four or five days after, came with the chief of his friends and other attendance, with the aforesaid Squanto. With whom, after friendly entertainment and some gifts given him, they made a peace with him (which hath now continued this 24 years) in these terms:

2   1. That neither he nor any of his should injure or do hurt to any of their people.

2. That if any of his did hurt to any of theirs, he should send the offender, that they might punish him.

3. That if anything were taken away from any of theirs, he should cause it to be restored; and they should do the like to his.

4. If any did unjustly war against him, they would aid him; if any did war against them, he should aid them.

5. He should send to his neighbors confederates to certify them of this, that they might not wrong them, but might be likewise comprised in the conditions of peace.

6. That when their men came to them, they should leave their bows and arrows behind them.

After these things he returned to his place called Sowams, some 40 miles from this place, but Squanto continued with them and was their interpreter and was a special instrument sent of God for their good beyond their expectation. He directed them how to set their corn, where to take fish, and to <u>procure</u> other <u>commodities,</u> and was also their pilot to bring them to unknown places for their profit, and never left them till he died.

from Chapter 12
First Thanksgiving

They began now to gather in the small harvest they had, and to fit up their houses and dwellings against winter, being all well recovered in health and strength and had all things in good plenty. For as some were thus employed in affairs abroad, others were exercised in fishing, about cod and bass and other fish, of which they took good store, of which every family had their portion. All the summer there was no want; and now began to come in store of fowl, as winter approached, of which this place did abound when they came first (but afterward decreased by degrees). And besides waterfowl there was great store of wild turkeys, of which they took many, besides venison, etc. Besides they had about a peck of meal a week to a person, or now since harvest, Indian corn to that proportion. Which made many afterwards write so largely of their plenty here to their friends in England, which were not <u>feigned</u> but true reports. ✍

Life in the New World *How did life for the settlers change so drastically since their bleak arrival in the New World?* **3**

Vocabulary

procure (prə kyoor′) *v.* to obtain by care or effort
commodity (kə mod′ ə tē) *n.* a product or economic good; an article of trade
feigned (fānd) *adj.* fictitious; not genuine

Reading Strategy   **2**

Making Critical Judgments
Ask: Do you think the six peace terms are reasonable? Why or why not? *(Students might point out that the terms would encourage peaceful relations between the two groups.)*

Big Idea   **3**

Life in the New World
Answer: *By the settlers' second winter in the New World, they had been able to gather enough food to avoid the hardships of the previous winter.*

> To check students' understanding of the selection, see Unit 1 Teaching Resources Book, p. 84.

Progress Check

Can students analyze diction?

If No → See Unit 1 Teaching Resources Book, p. 79.

Approaching Level

DIFFERENTIATED INSTRUCTION

SMALL GROUP

Emerging Have students work in small groups to paraphrase the list of peace terms. Have each student read one term aloud to the group to improve students' **reading fluency.** Have them rewrite each rule as if it were for a peace treaty today. Also, have groups discuss whether they think the peace terms would be effective. They should add one or two terms of their own that they believe would strengthen a peace treaty. Ask representatives from each group to read their revised rules to the class. Discuss group answers.

AAVE Use the First Thanksgiving section with approaching-level students who are users of African American vernacular English (AAVE) to work on subject-verb agreement. Have students replace the third person plural with third person singular. Have pairs record all the words that change as a result.

67

After You Read

Assess

1. Winter, lack of food, disease.
2. *Mayflower:* storms, disease; Plymouth: some Native Americans, hunger, disease, weather
3. (a) They were blown off course by storms. (b) They were without shelter in winter weather.
4. (a) The selfless effort of the few who escaped disease (b) They worked without complaint.
5. (a) Samoset taught the Pilgrims about the land and helped negotiate peace. Squanto was an interpreter and an advisor on fishing, farming, and hunting. (b) They might not have survived.
6. (a) Each side would not harm the other, and they would become allies if others waged war. (b) Possible answer: It was a good plan: they could live without fearing each other.
7. (a) Hunting, fishing, good harvest. (b) They and Squanto deserve credit.
8. Possible answer: Today some Americans struggle with hunger and lack shelter.
9. Students may mention *Night* or *Into Thin Air.*

 For additional assessment, see Assessment Resources, pp. 69–70.

After You Read

Respond and Think Critically

Respond and Interpret

1. If you had been a Plymouth settler, what do you think would have been your greatest challenge?
2. What hardships did the Pilgrims face aboard the *Mayflower* and in Plymouth?
3. (a)What caused the Pilgrims to land on Cape Cod, in Massachusetts, instead of farther south, near the Hudson River? (b)How did this event affect the expedition?
4. (a)What enabled the Pilgrims to survive "the Starving Time"? (b)What do Bradford's comments reveal about the Pilgrims' character?
5. (a)What did Samoset and Squanto accomplish? (b)What do you think might have happened to the Pilgrims without Squanto's help?

Analyze and Evaluate

6. (a)What were the six terms of peace meant to accomplish? (b)In your opinion, was this plan a good one? Explain.
7. (a)What enabled the Pilgrims to survive and celebrate their "First Thanksgiving"? (b)How much credit do you give the Pilgrims for this success?

Connect

8. **Big Idea** **Life in the New World** Do the experiences of the Pilgrims have any connection to our society today? Explain.
9. **Connect to Today** What are some modern-day examples of survival stories? Why do you think people are so attracted to write—and read—this type of story?

Literary Element Diction

Diction is a writer's choice of words. Diction contributes to a writer's voice or style. Paraphrase the first sentence on page 65 paragraph 1, which begins "Being thus arrived . . . " How would you describe the style of this sentence?

Reading Strategy Monitor Comprehension

Bradford's writing style involves obscure idioms, archaic vocabulary, and long, complex sentences. In the description of the sea journey, he also uses jargon. You learned several of these words on page 63. Using the chart you made, figure out a few on your own.

 Literature Online

Selection Resources For Selection Quizzes, eFlashcards, and Reading-Writing Connection activities, go to glencoe.com and enter QuickPass code GLA9800u1.

Vocabulary Practice

Practice with Context Clues Identify the context clues that help you determine the meaning of each boldfaced vocabulary word.

1. When I was young, stickers were valuable **commodities**; I traded them for candy.
2. I knew my sister had taken my sweater because she **feigned** surprise so poorly when I found a stain on it.
3. Last month I **resolved** to run a mile a day, but I haven't followed through with it.
4. It took a lot of determination, but I **procured** two tickets to the sold-out concert.
5. It was sheer **providence**, or fate, that I ran into Amanda at the library.

Writing

Write a Letter Imagine you are one of the colonists. Write a letter describing life in Plymouth. Explain whether you believe your religious freedom and other benefits were worth the sacrifice.

Literary Element

Now that they had found a good harbor and reached land, they fell on their knees and thanked God for bringing them across the ocean through many dangers to set them again on land, where they belonged. Students may judge the style to be formal and stately.

Vocabulary

1. Students should infer that *commodities* are items of trade.
2. The sister's surprise must be unreal—or *feigned*—because that is how the speaker finds out she took it.
3. The phrase "made a decision" defines the word *resolved.*
4. Students should note that as the task is difficult and the show is sold out, the action of *procuring* is to acquire.
5. The restatement "or fate" defines *providence.*

Writing

Students' letters should reflect an understanding of life on Plymouth Plantation and should use proper sentence structure and grammar.

Before You Read
from *The Life of Olaudah Equiano*

Meet **Olaudah Equiano**
(1745–1797)

The life of Olaudah Equiano (ō lau´ dä e kwē ä´ nō) was a mixture of tragedy, struggle, and great achievement. The son of an Ibo chieftain, Equiano was born in Essaka, a village in what is now Nigeria. His village was a considerable distance from the coast, and as a child he had never heard of the sea or of the people who lived beyond it. When he was eleven, he had a terrifying introduction to both when he and his sister were kidnapped by slave traders. They were separated, and Equiano was sold to Europeans and packed onto a slave ship headed for the Caribbean island of Barbados. The horrors he witnessed on the ship haunted him for the rest of his life.

In the years after being captured, Equiano spent time in Virginia and England, where he was owned by an officer of the British Royal Navy. Equiano served in the British navy with this officer from 1758 to 1762, during the French and Indian War. Over the years, the officer baptized him, renamed him Gustavus Vassa, and taught him seafaring skills as well as how to read and write. These skills would serve Equiano well after the officer sold him to a merchant in the West Indies in 1763.

Sailor and Trader As a slave to the merchant, Equiano worked on trading ships between the West Indies and mainland American colonies. In 1766, at the age of 21, he used money he had made to buy his freedom. He spent the next several years working on ships and traveling.

While sailing, Equiano realized that life as a free man was in many respects no easier than his life as a slave had been. Freed slaves in the British colonies had no legal rights and were often treated miserably. Soon after he was freed, he wrote, "Hitherto I had thought only slavery dreadful; but the state of the free negro appeared to me now equally so at least, and in some respects even worse."

> "... I might say my sufferings were great; but when I compare my lot with that of most of my countrymen, I regard myself as a particular favorite of heaven. ..."
>
> —Olaudah Equiano

Freedom Fighter In 1776 Equiano settled in England to campaign against slavery. He helped organize several antislavery organizations in London and, along with other abolitionists, petitioned the British parliament to end the slave trade. Equiano was also part of the Committee for Relief of the Black Poor in London and a leader in the Sierra Leone recolonization project, a failed attempt to bring former slaves back to Africa. His greatest contribution to the abolitionist cause, however, was his 1789 autobiography, *The Interesting Narrative of the Life of Olaudah Equiano, or Gustavus Vassa, the African*. Its graphic and powerful descriptions of the inhumanity Equiano and other slaves suffered helped further the abolitionist cause throughout Europe and the United States.

 Literature Online

Author Search For more about Olaudah Equiano, go to glencoe.com and enter QuickPass code GLA9800u1.

OLAUDAH EQUIANO **69**

Before You Read
Focus

Bellringer Options

Selection Focus
 Transparency 6
Daily Language Practice
 Transparency 8

Or display images showing flags of the United States and other nations.

Ask: What does freedom mean? How do the freedoms you enjoy compare with freedoms in other countries? **Say:** Consider the nature of freedom as you read.

Cultural History ☆

Records of the Slave Trade In addition to firsthand accounts of former slaves like Equiano, historians consult primary sources about slave ships that identify the type of ship, the ports and dates of arrival, the number of days of voyage, and the number of slaves. They also refer to documents such as advertisements for slave auctions, letters of slave dealers, and property records.

Selection Skills

Literary Elements
- Slave Narrative
  (SE pp. 70–72, 76, 78)
- Characterization (TE p. 74)

from **The Life of Olaudah Equiano**

Reading Skills
- Respond (SE pp. 70–71, 74–76, 78)
- Make Critical Judgments (TE p. 70)

Listening/Speaking/ Viewing Skills
- Analyze Art (SE pp. 72, 74)

Writing Skills/Grammar
- Report Main Ideas or Events (SE p. 79)
- Evaluate (TE p. 70)
- Compound Subjects (TE p. 74)
- Write Questions (TE p. 76)

Vocabulary Skills
- Academic Vocabulary (SE p. 78)
- Word Origins (SE p. 78; TE p. 70)

Before You Read

Focus

Summary

In this excerpt, Olaudah Equiano recounts his experiences traveling as a kidnapped, enslaved person on a ship from Africa to Barbados in the West Indies. Using vivid details and straightforward language, Equiano reveals the horrors on the slave ship and the degradation he endured.

 For summaries in languages other than English, see Unit 1 Teaching Resources Book, pp. 86–91.

Vocabulary

Etymology Explain that learning the etymology, or origin, of a word can provide insights into the word's connotation. *Clamor,* for example, has the same root as the word *claim:* the Latin verb *clamare,* which means "to cry out." *Clamor* is used to describe shouting that shows dissatisfaction or displeasure, not joy. Have students explore the etymology of each word and write a sentence connecting the word and its origins.

 For additional vocabulary practice, see Unit 1 Teaching Resources Book, p. 94.

 For additional context, see Glencoe Interactive Vocabulary CD-ROM.

Literature and Reading Preview

Connect to the Autobiography

How do you respond when people restrict your freedom? Freewrite for a few minutes about a time when someone imposed rules on you that you considered unjust. Discuss your feelings and reactions.

Build Background

From the 1500s to the 1800s, approximately ten million Africans suffered miserable treatment on the forced journey from their homes to enslavement in the Western Hemisphere. The most arduous portion of the journey, known as the Middle Passage, was a two-month voyage from West Africa to the West Indies. Some two million Africans died from malnutrition, disease, suffocation, beatings, and despair during the journey.

Set Purposes for Reading

Big Idea Life in the New World

As you read from Equiano's autobiography, ask yourself, What does this selection reveal about the suffering endured by many of the Africans who helped build the United States?

Literary Element The Slave Narrative

A **slave narrative** is an autobiographical account of a formerly enslaved person's life. Slave narratives helped abolitionists expose slavery's cruelty. As you read, ask yourself, How successful is Equiano in making readers aware of slavery's injustice?

Reading Strategy Respond

Responding is explaining what you think about a selection and how it affects you. Responding personally includes describing what you like, dislike, or find interesting in a selection and how these aspects of the work relate to your own life. More analytical responses deal with giving your opinion on aspects such as the behavior of the characters or stylistic techniques used by the author. As you read, ask yourself, What thoughts and feelings does the selection envoke? What factors contribute to my response?

....

Tip: Take Notes As you read the selection, jot down quick notes about the passages you think are especially moving or intense.

Learning Objectives

For pages 69–79

In studying this text, you will focus on the following objectives:

Literary Study: Analyzing autobiography.

Reading: Responding to events.

Vocabulary

apprehension (ap´ ri hen´ shən) *n.* fear of what may happen in the future; anxiety; p. 73 *Sam thought of his upcoming speech with apprehension.*

copious (kō´ pē əs) *adj.* large in quantity; plentiful; p. 74 *Copious amounts of food were served at the banquet.*

gratify (grat´ ə fī´) *v.* to satisfy or indulge; p. 75 *Our walks outside gratify my craving for sunlight.*

clamor (klam´ ər) *n.* confused, insistent shouting; p. 76 *The clamor woke Kim from her sleep.*

scruple (skrōō´ pəl) *n.* moral principle that restrains action; p. 76 *Without a scruple, Nina stole the bike.*

Writing Practice

SPIRAL REVIEW **Evaluate** Discuss with students the ways in which an autobiographical account teaches lessons that an encyclopedia or other secondary source does not. **Ask:** What makes a good autobiography? What should an autobiography convey about a subject that might not be found in other pieces of writing? *(Autobiography conveys the feelings and thoughts of a person who lived through an experience.)* Have students examine the methods Equiano uses to present his ideas. Direct them to write an evaluation of his account, supporting their arguments with precise details from the selection.

from The Life of Olaudah Equiano

Olaudah Equiano

The first object which saluted[1] my eyes when I arrived on the coast, was the sea, and a slave ship, which was then riding at anchor, and waiting for its cargo. These filled me with astonishment, which was soon converted into terror, when I was carried on board. I was immediately handled, and tossed up to see if I were sound, by some of the crew; and I was now persuaded that I had gotten into a world of bad spirits, and that they were going to kill me. Their complexions, too, differing so much from ours, their long hair, and the language they spoke, (which was very different from any I had ever heard) united to confirm me in this belief. Indeed, such were the horrors of my views and fears at the moment, that, if ten thousand worlds had been my own, I would have freely parted with them all to have exchanged my condition with that of the meanest[2] slave in my own country. When I looked round the ship too, and saw a large furnace of copper boiling, and a multitude of black people of every description chained together, every one of their countenances[3] expressing dejection and sorrow, I no longer doubted of my fate; and, quite overpowered with horror and anguish, I fell motionless on the deck and fainted. When I recovered a little, I found some black people about me, who I believed were some of those who had brought me on board, and had been receiving their pay; they talked to me in order to cheer me, but all in vain.[4] I asked them if we were not to be eaten by those white men with horrible looks, red faces, and long hair. They told me I was not: and one of the crew brought me a small portion of spirituous liquor in a wine glass, but, being afraid of him, I would not take it out of his hand. One of the blacks, therefore, took it from him and gave it to me, and I took a little down my palate,[5] which, instead of reviving me, as they thought it would, threw me into the greatest consternation[6] at the strange feeling it produced, having never tasted any such liquor before. Soon after this, the blacks who brought me on board went off, and left me abandoned to despair.

I now saw myself deprived of all chance of returning to my native country, or even the least glimpse of hope of gaining the shore, which I now considered as friendly; and I even wished for my former slavery[7] in preference to

---

1. Here, *saluted* means "became noticeable to" or "struck."
2. Here, *meanest* means "of the lowest social position or rank."
3. *Countenance* means "face" or "facial expression."

---

4. Something done *in vain* is done without effect or success.
5. The *palate*, here, is the mouth and throat.
6. *Consternation* is paralyzing dismay or fear.
7. Equiano refers to a brief period of time he spent as a slave to the Africans who kidnapped him and eventually sold him. In his experience, slavery in Africa was far less brutal than slavery in the New World.

1 Slave Narrative *Why might Equiano have included these details?*

2 Respond *What about this passage makes it striking or memorable?*

Teach

Literary Element | 1

Slave Narrative Answer: *The details about people who are so different from the people with whom he is familiar emphasize his confusion and fear.*

Reading Strategy | 2

Respond Answer: *The description of so many people chained together and of their expressions creates a horrific image.*

(**ENGLISH LEARNERS**) Have students locate words that express Equiano's feelings. Direct students to use a dictionary to find the meanings of unfamiliar words. (*Examples:* astonishment, terror, horrors, overpowered, anguish, despair)

 For an audio recording of this selection, use Listening Library Audio CD-ROM.

Readability Scores

Dale-Chall: 7.6
DRP: 59
Lexile: 1250

English Learners

DIFFERENTIATED INSTRUCTION

Intermediate Help students analyze Equiano's long sentences. Using the sentence beginning "When I looked round the ship," indicates the relationship of the ideas to follow.

When he looked round the ship,

  What he saw
  ▪ a furnace of copper boiling
  ▪ a large number of people chained together

  ▪ their faces expressing sorrow

  How he reacted
  ▪ He became sure of his fate.
  ▪ He became overwhelmed with emotion and fainted on the deck.

Advanced Learners

DIFFERENTIATED INSTRUCTION

Research Have students investigate the case of the *Zong,* a slave ship that was transporting slaves to Jamaica in 1781. Direct students to prepare a brief presentation by formulating several key research questions and seeking at least three sources to provide answers and information.

Teach

Literary Element   1

Slave Narrative Answer:
Seeing slavery through Equiano's eyes captures the experience vividly. Such a perspective can be far more powerful than reading facts or statistics.

View the Art ★

Answer: *Since the slave trade had been abolished, this ship was likely not designed to carry slaves. That would explain why these slaves seem to have more room than Equiano described in his narrative.*

In 1845, the British ship *Albatross* captured the Brazilian slave ship *Albaroz*. Francis Meynell was a mate on the *Albatross*.

The Slavedeck of the Albaroz, Prize to the H.M.S. Albatross, 1846. Francis Meynell. Watercolor. National Maritime Museum, London.

View the Art Francis Meynell was both a painter and a sailor—he served on an anti-slavery ship that patrolled the waters after the British Parliament abolished slave trading in 1807. How does Equiano's description of slave ship conditions compare to this painting? ★

my present situation, which was filled with horrors of every kind, still heightened by my ignorance of what I was to undergo. I was not long suffered[8] to indulge my grief; I was soon put down under the decks, and there I received such a salutation in my nostrils as I had never experienced in my life: so that, with the loathsomeness of the stench, and crying together, I became so sick and low that I was not able to eat, nor had I the least desire to taste any thing. I now wished for the last friend, death, to relieve me; but soon, to my grief, two of the white men offered me eatables; and, on my refusing to eat, one of them held me fast by the hands, and laid me across, I think the windlass,[9] and tied my feet, while the other flogged me severely. I had never experienced any thing of this kind before, and although not being used to the water, I naturally feared that element the first time I saw it, yet, nevertheless, could I have got over the nettings,[10] I would have jumped over the side, but I could not; and besides, the crew used to watch us very closely who were not chained down to the decks, lest we should leap into the water; and I have seen some of these poor African prisoners most severely cut, for attempting to do so, and hourly whipped for not eating. This indeed was

8. Here, *suffered* means "allowed."

1   **Slave Narrative** *How does the point of view affect the message of this selection?*

9. A *windlass* is a type of crank with a handle. It is used to raise or lower a heavy object such as an anchor.
10. *Nettings* were networks of small ropes on the sides of a ship. On slave ships, nettings were used to prevent captives from jumping overboard.

72   UNIT 1   EARLY AMERICA

Reading Practice

Changes in English Note instances in Equiano's account that reveal how the English language has changed over time. For example, the word *suffered* on page 72 means "allowed" not "endured pain."
Ask: What other differences do you notice between Equiano's English and modern American English? *(Students may say that Equiano's English sounds* more formal.) What similarities do you notice? *(Students may say that most of the words and sentence structures of colonial English are similar to today.)* As students read pages 72‑73, have them develop a list of words and phrases from the selection that are rarely used today. *(Possible responses: "salutation" and "eatables" on p. 72; "brute" and "quar-* tered" on p. 73.) Clarify and discuss the meanings of unfamiliar words. (salutation means "greeting"; eatables means "food"; brute means "beast"; quartered means "sheltered.")*

often the case with myself. In a little time after, amongst the poor chained men, I found some of my own nation, which in a small degree gave ease to my mind. I inquired of these what was to be done with us? They gave me to understand, we were to be carried to these white people's country to work for them. I then was a little revived, and thought, if it were no worse than working, my situation was not so desperate; but still I feared I should be put to death, the white people looked and acted, as I thought, in so savage a manner; for I had never seen among any people such instances of brutal cruelty; and this not only shown towards us blacks, but also to some of the whites themselves. One white man in particular I saw, when we were permitted to be on deck, flogged so unmercifully with a large rope near the foremast, that he died in consequence of it; and they tossed him over the side as they would have done a brute. This made me fear these people the more; and I expected nothing less than to be treated in the same manner. I could not help expressing my fears and **apprehensions** to some of my countrymen; I asked them if these people had no country, but lived in this hollow place? (the ship) they told me they did not, but came from a distant one. "Then," said I, "how comes it in all our country we never heard of them?" They told me because they lived so very far off. I then asked where were their women? had they any like themselves? I was told they had. "And why," said I, "do we not see them?" They answered, because they were left behind. I asked how the vessel could go? they told me they could not tell; but that there was cloth put upon the masts by the help

of the ropes I saw, and then the vessel went on; and the white men had some spell or magic they put in the water when they liked, in order to stop the vessel. I was exceedingly amazed at this account, and really thought they were spirits. I therefore wished much to be from amongst them, for I expected they would sacrifice me; but my wishes were vain—for we were so quartered that it was impossible for any of us to make our escape.

While we stayed on the coast I was mostly on deck; and one day, to my great astonishment, I saw one of these vessels coming in with the sails up. As soon as the whites saw it, they gave a great shout, at which we were amazed; and the more so, as the vessel appeared larger by approaching nearer. At last, she came to an anchor in my sight, and when the anchor was let go, I and my countrymen who saw it, were lost in astonishment to observe the vessel stop—and were now convinced it was done by magic. Soon after this the other ship got her boats out, and they came on board of us, and the people of both ships seemed very glad to see each other. Several of the strangers also shook hands with us black people, and made motions with their hands, signifying I suppose, we were to go to their country, but we did not understand them.

At last, when the ship we were in, had got in all her cargo, they made ready with many fearful noises, and we were all put under deck, so that we could not see how they managed the vessel. But this disappointment was the least of my sorrow. The stench of the hold while we were on the coast was so intolerably loathsome, that it was dangerous to remain there for any time, and some of us had been permitted to stay on the deck for the fresh air; but now that the whole ship's cargo were confined together, it became absolutely pestilential.[11] The closeness of the place, and the heat of the climate, added to the number in the ship, which was so crowded that each had scarcely room to turn himself, almost

2 Life in the New World *What kind of mood does Equiano create here?*

3 Life in the New World *Why might Equiano have included a description of this event?*

Vocabulary

apprehensions (ap´ ri hen´ shənz) *n.* fears of what may happen in the future; anxieties

11. *Pestilential* means "poisonous" or "likely to cause disease or death."

OLAUDAH EQUIANO **73**

Teach

Big Idea	**2**

Life in the New World
Answer: *The mood is one of confusion, fear, and despair. By describing how he felt, Equiano shows the confusion of the situation and the horror of being held captive by cruel strangers.*

Big Idea	**3**

Life in the New World
Answer: *He is exposing the brutality of the white people on the ship. They are cruel not only to the Africans but also to each other, suggesting that they have no regard for people in general.*

Writer's Technique ☆

Purpose Ask: What purpose could Equiano have had for writing this narrative? Which reason do you think was foremost in Equiano's mind? *(Many students may say that Equiano wanted to expose the horrors of slavery in order to support its abolition.)*

Approaching Level

DIFFERENTIATED INSTRUCTION

Emerging Have students use Equiano's punctuation as an aid to decoding his long sentences. Point out that both commas and semicolons indicate pause, but that the semicolon indicates a stronger pause, often to separate clauses. Call on a volunteer to read the sentence on page 72 that begins "I now wished for the last friend . . ."

Direct students to restate the sentence in their own words. **Ask:** What words can you substitute for *eatables* and *flogged*? *(food, whipped)* Have students read their paraphrases aloud to compare responses.

AAVE Approaching level students who use AAVE may use two negatives where only one is needed. Have them find the single negative in Equiano's words.

- if it were no worse than working
- I expected nothing less than to be treated in the same manner

Teach

Reading Strategy | 1

Respond Answer: *Students will likely say they feel anger toward the slave traders and disbelief that the traders could treat other people so inhumanely.*

Literary Element | 2

Characterization Discuss with the class what sort of person the writer reveals himself to be. What actions, comments, or descriptions can help the reader make valid inferences about Equiano's personality? *(He is observant—he can remember in vivid detail events that happened to him long ago. He is also very curious when he watches the sailors use their strange instrument. Despite the staggering hardships of the journey, he seems resilient.)*

View the Art ★

Answer: *Students may say that the intense red and orange suggest violence and death, the small size of the ship in comparison to the vastness of the sea suggests man's powerlessness over nature, the lack of a distinct horizon suggests chaos, and the drowning slaves in the foreground represent the slave traders' cruelty and disregard for human life.*

The English painter J. M. W. Turner (1775–1851) was known for his seascapes and landscapes in oil and watercolor and for his ability to show weather. The subtitle of this painting is "Slavers Throwing Overboard the Dead and Dying—Typhoon Coming On."

The Slave Ship, 1840. Joseph Mallord William Turner. Oil on canvas. Museum of Fine Arts, Boston.

View the Art ★ This painting was based on the story of a captain who reportedly threw sick and dying slaves overboard to collect insurance money for slaves "lost at sea," as well as a poem about a slave ship caught in a typhoon. What visual techniques does the painter use to capture the horror of such a situation?

suffocated us. This produced **copious** perspirations, so that the air soon became unfit for respiration, from a variety of loathsome smells, and brought on a sickness among the slaves, of which many died—thus falling victims to the improvident[12] avarice,[13] as I may call it, of their purchasers. This wretched situation was again aggravated by the galling[14] of the chains, now became insupportable; and the filth of the necessary tubs,[15] into which the children often fell,

and were almost suffocated. The shrieks of the women, and the groans of the dying, rendered[16] the whole a scene of horror almost inconceivable. Happily perhaps, for myself, I was soon reduced so low here that it was thought necessary to keep me almost always on deck; and from my extreme youth I was not put in fetters.[17] In this situation I expected every hour to share the fate of my companions, some of whom were almost daily brought upon deck at the point of death, which I began to hope would soon put an end to my miseries. Often did I think many of the inhabitants of the deep much more happy than myself. I envied them the freedom they enjoyed, and as often wished I could change my condition for theirs. Every circumstance I met with, served only to render my state more painful, and heightened my apprehensions, and my opinion of the cruelty of the whites.

---

12. *Improvident* means "lacking foresight" or "not providing for the future."
13. *Avarice* is greed.
14. *Galling* is the chafing or rubbing that causes irritation of the skin.
15. *Necessary tubs* are containers for bodily waste.

1 | Respond *After reading this passage, what feelings and thoughts do you have about the slave traders?*

Vocabulary

copious (kō′ pē əs) *adj.* large in quantity; plentiful

---

16. *Render* means "to cause to be" or "to make."
17. *Fetters* are leg irons.

74 UNIT 1 EARLY AMERICA

Vocabulary Practice

SPIRAL REVIEW **Compound Subjects** Point out that a compound subject is composed of two or more nouns or pronouns. The nouns or pronouns have the same verb, and they are joined by a conjunction such as *and*. In a two-part compound subject no comma is used before the conjunction. Have students look through the autobiography to find examples of sentences with compound subjects. Ask students why a writer might choose to use them. *(to sound more natural; to express more complicated ideas)*

One day they had taken a number of fishes; and when they had killed and satisfied themselves with as many as they thought fit, to our astonishment who were on deck, rather than give any of them to us to eat, as we expected, they tossed the remaining fish into the sea again, although we begged and prayed for some as well as we could, but in vain; and some of my countrymen, being pressed by hunger, took an opportunity, when they thought no one saw them, of trying to get a little privately; but they were discovered, and the attempt procured them some very severe floggings. One day, when we had a smooth sea and moderate wind, two of my wearied countrymen who were chained together, (I was near them at the time,) preferring death to such a life of misery, somehow made through the nettings and jumped into the sea: immediately, another quite dejected fellow, who, on account of his illness, was suffered to be out of irons, also followed their example; and I believe many more would very soon have done the same, if they had not been prevented by the ship's crew, who were instantly alarmed. Those of us that were the most active, were in a moment put down under the deck, and there was such a noise and confusion amongst the people of the ship as I never heard before, to stop her, and get the boat out to go after the slaves. However, two of the wretches were drowned, but they got the other, and afterwards flogged him unmercifully, for thus attempting to prefer death to slavery. In this manner we continued to undergo more hardships than I can now relate, hardships which are inseparable from this accursed trade. Many a time we were near suffocation from the want of fresh air, which we were often without for whole days together. This, and the stench of the necessary tubs, carried off many.

During our passage, I first saw flying fishes, which surprised me very much; they used frequently to fly across the ship, and many of them fell on the deck. I also now first saw the use of the quadrant; I had often with astonishment seen the mariners make observations with it, and I could not think what it meant.

They at last took notice of my surprise; and one of them, willing to increase it, as well as to **gratify** my curiosity, made me one day look through it. The clouds appeared to me to be land, which disappeared as they passed along. This heightened my wonder; and I was now more persuaded than ever, that I was in another world, and that every thing about me was magic. At last, we came in sight of the island of Barbadoes, at which the whites on board gave a great shout, and made many signs of joy to us. We did not know what to think of this; but as the vessel drew nearer, we plainly saw the harbor, and other ships of different kinds and sizes, and we soon anchored amongst them, off Bridgetown.[18] Many merchants and planters now came on board, though it was in the evening. They put us in separate parcels,[19] and examined us attentively. They also made us jump, and pointed to the land, signifying we were to go there. We thought by this, we should be eaten by these ugly men, as they appeared to us; and, when soon after we were all put down under the deck again, there was much dread and trembling among us, and nothing but bitter cries to be heard all the night from these apprehensions, insomuch, that at last the white people got some old slaves from the land to pacify us. They told us we were not to be eaten, but to work, and were soon to go on land, where we should see many of our country people. This report eased us much. And sure enough, soon after we were landed, there came to us Africans of all languages.

We were conducted immediately to the merchant's yard, where we were all pent up together,

---

18. *Bridgetown* is the capital of Barbados.
19. Here, *parcels* means "groups."

Respond *Does this passage affect your perception of the slave traders? Why or why not?* **3**

Vocabulary

gratify (grat´ ə fī´) *v.* to satisfy or indulge

OLAUDAH EQUIANO **75**

Teach

Literary Element   1

Slave Narrative **Answer:**
The tone changes from a first-person account to direct address—an appeal to those in power to make changes. Equiano appeals to these people's own religious beliefs by quoting the Bible, to emphasize the importance of abolishing slavery.

Reading Strategy   2

Respond **Answer:** *Equiano's use of the word* refinement *undermines the traders' belief that they are more civilized than the slaves and instead highlights their ability to inflict new kinds of cruelty.*

To check students' understanding of the selection, see Unit 1 Teaching Resources Book, p. 97.

like so many sheep in a fold, without regard to sex or age. As every object was new to me, every thing I saw filled me with surprise. What struck me first, was, that the houses were built with bricks and stories, and in every other respect different from those I had seen in Africa; but I was still more astonished on seeing people on horseback. I did not know what this could mean; and, indeed, I thought these people were full of nothing but magical arts. While I was in this astonishment, one of my fellow-prisoners spoke to a countryman of his, about the horses, who said they were the same kind they had in their country. I understood them, though they were from a distant part of Africa; and I thought it odd I had not seen any horses there; but afterwards, when I came to converse with different Africans, I found they had many horses amongst them, and much larger than those I then saw.

We were not many days in the merchant's custody, before we were sold after their usual manner, which is this:—On a signal given, (as the beat of a drum,) the buyers rush at once into the yard where the slaves are confined, and make choice of that parcel they like best. The noise and **clamor** with which this is attended, and the eagerness visible in the countenances of the buyers, serve not a little to increase the apprehension of terrified Africans, who may well be supposed to consider them as the ministers of that destruction to which they think themselves devoted. In this manner, without **scruple,** are relations and friends separated, most of them never to see each other again. I remember, in the vessel in which I was brought over, in the men's apartment, there were several brothers, who, in the sale, were sold in different lots; and

A Slave Auction in the Deep South, c. 1850. American School. Coloured engraving.

it was very moving on this occasion, to see and hear their cries at parting. O, ye nominal[20] Christians! might not an African ask you—Learned you this from your God, who says unto you, Do unto all men as you would men should do unto you?[21] Is it not enough that we are torn from our country and friends, to toil for your luxury and lust of gain? Must every tender feeling be likewise sacrificed to your avarice? Are the dearest friends and relations, now rendered more dear by their separation from their kindred, still to be parted from each other, and thus prevented from cheering the gloom of slavery, with the small comfort of being together, and mingling their sufferings and sorrows? Why are parents to lose their children, brothers their sisters, or husbands their wives? Surely, this is a new refinement in cruelty, which, while it has no advantage to atone[22] for it, thus aggravates distress, and adds fresh horrors even to the wretchedness of slavery. ✑

---

20. *Nominal* means "in name only."

21. "Therefore all things whatsoever ye would that men should do to you, do ye even so to them." (Matthew 7:12)
22. *Atone* means "to make amends" or "to compensate for."

Vocabulary

clamor (klam′ ər) n. confused, insistent shouting
scruple (skrōō′ pəl) n. moral principle

Slave Narrative *How is this section different from the rest of the work? Why does Equiano make this change?*   1

Respond *How does Equiano's use of the word* refinement *strengthen the impact of this sentence?*   2

76 UNIT 1   EARLY AMERICA

Writing Practice

SMALL GROUP

Questions Remind students that three types of questions are frequently used with literature.

- Literal questions ask readers to recall facts stated in the text. (*What did Equiano observe from the ship?*)
- Interpretive questions ask readers to explain the meaning of the words and require the reader to draw inferences. (*What does Equiano imply about himself*

when he says, "At last, when the ship we were in, had got in all her cargo"?)
- Evaluative questions ask readers to go beyond the text by making outside connections or offering personal opinions or ideas that cannot be inferred from the text. (*How does reading about this time period from the perspective of Equiano make you feel about American history?*)

Have students work in groups to write

one of each type of question about the passage. When each group has finished, redistribute the questions to new groups to answer the questions. Solicit examples of questions from the class and discuss which type of question each is and why.

After You Read

Respond and Think Critically

Respond and Interpret

1. What was your reaction to the description of life on a slave ship?

2. (a)What does Equiano fear will happen to him when he is taken aboard the ship? (b)Why?

3. (a)In spite of his fear, Equiano displays great curiosity. Relate an incident that reveals this curiosity. (b)What might the incident reveal about his character?

4. (a)What phrases does Equiano use to describe his feelings about slavery's separation of loved ones? (b)Why does he regard it as he does?

Analyze and Evaluate

5. (a)How does Equiano's tone in the last paragraph shift? (b)What is the effect of this change?

6. Equiano's book was a best seller in its time. (a)Why do you think his story so successfully captured the public's interest? (b)Why would his story have been useful to the cause of abolition?

Connect

7. **Big Idea** **Life in the New World** How has reading this work affected your attitudes about personal freedom, human nature, or our nation's history of enslavement of Africans? Explain, using details from the selection.

8. **Connect to the Author** Equiano was only eleven years old when slave traders kidnapped him. From his narrative, are you able to picture both the young, scared boy and the middle-aged writer and abolitionist? Explain.

Primary Visual Artifact

A Nightmarish Journey

Enslaved African men, women, and children endured brutal, inhuman conditions as they were shipped across the Atlantic to the Americas. Crammed against one another below deck, they could neither stand up nor turn over. During the day, they were sometimes brought on deck, where they would be forced to do exercises while shackled in iron chains. The filthy conditions below deck caused widespread disease, and an estimated 13 percent of the captives on these ships died before reaching their destination. This model, created in the late eighteenth century, depicts the interior of one such ship.

Group Activity Discuss the following questions with your classmates.

1. (a)What effect does the scale on which the people in the model are represented have? (b)How might the effect have been created?

2. (a)How does this image compare to the one you imagined as you read? (b) How does viewing this image inform your understanding of the selection?

Assess

1. Students should support their responses with details.

2. (a) He fears the white men will kill and eat him (b) His youth; never having seen a white person before

3. (a) Equiano observes the sailors who are using a navigation instrument (b) He remains curious and eager to learn.

4. (a) "A new refinement in cruelty"; "adds fresh horrors even to the wretchedness of slavery." (b) Slavery is made even more horrible without family support.

5. (a) From matter-of-fact to impassioned as Equiano directly challenges those who trade and hold slaves (b) To provide a call to action

6. (a) The book described slavery through the eyes of a real-life slave. (b) It showed the victims of slavery to be human beings with the same right to dignity as other people.

7. Students may say that the graphic images of a slave ship were shocking, making them realize the cruelty that people are capable of.

8. Students may say that Equiano's refined language make it easier to picture him as a writer and abolitionist, rather than as an 11-year-old boy.

For additional assessment, see Assessment Resources, pp. 71–72.

Primary Visual Artifact

1. (a)The scale is disturbing because each person seems to be a tiny piece of cargo, rather than an individual. (b)This indicates that the slave trade dehumanized captives and treated them as commodities.

2. (a)Students may have envisioned suffering individuals, rather than rows of identical captives. (b)The image illustrates the unbearably cramped conditions on the ships, as well as suggesting the dehumanizing lens through which slave traders viewed their captives.

After You Read

Literary Element

ACT Skills Practice

1. **A** is the correct answer because Equiano's personal experiences are what distinguish his slave narrative from an opinion statement and strengthen its message.

2. **H** is the correct answer because often one person's courage in speaking out makes it easier for others to step forward as well.

Progress Check

Can students identify a slave narrative?

If No → See Unit 1 Teaching Resource Book, p. 77.

Review: Point of View

1. Students should note that the first-person point of view captures the horror and trauma of the slave ships in a very personal way.

2. A third-person narrative would seem more removed from the events.

Progress Check

Can students respond to literature?

If No → See Unit 1 Teaching Resource Book, p. 78.

Literary Element The Slave Narrative

ACT Skills Practice

1. Which elements of Equiano's narrative might have made it a more effective condemnation of slavery than a direct statement of opinion?

   I. The first-person point of view
   II. The vivid personal details
   III. The reliable facts and statistics

   A. II only
   B. III only
   C. I and III only
   D. II and III only

2. The publication of Equiano's account might have motivated other African Americans to share their slave narratives because:

   F. their suffering was more severe than his.
   G. they felt he had misrepresented the experience of slavery.
   H. his narrative validated and ennobled their own stories.
   J. they realized that slavery would soon be abolished.

Review: Point of View

As you learned in Part One, **point of view** is the relationship of the narrator to the story. Olaudah Equiano narrates his own life story using the words *I* and *me*, which means he writes from the first-person point of view. Discuss the following questions with a partner:

1. How does Equiano's point of view affect the credibility and impact of his narrative?

2. How might the story have been different written from another point of view?

LOG ON ▶ **Literature** Online

Selection Resources For Selection Quizzes, eFlashcards, and Reading-Writing Connection activities, go to glencoe.com and enter QuickPass code GLA9800u1.

Reading Strategy Respond

Responding to literature is reacting in a personal way to what you read. Look back at the notes you took while reading Equiano's narrative. To which aspects of slavery did you react most strongly? Why? Use a chart like the one shown to record your responses.

Vocabulary Practice

Practice with Word Origins Create a word map like the one below for each of these vocabulary words. Use a dictionary for help.

apprehension   copious   gratify
clamor   scruple

EXAMPLE:

Definition: punishment in return for wrongdoing

Etymology: Latin *vindicare*, meaning "to lay claim to, avenge"

vengeance

Sample Sentence: The king sought vengeance against the invaders who had destoyed his lands.

Academic Vocabulary

In this passage from Equiano's autobiography, he details the mental and physical anguish he experienced on the journey from Africa.

Physical is an academic word. More familiar words that are similar in meaning are *concrete* and *tangible*. Using context clues, try to figure out the meaning of *physical* in the sentence below.

1. **Physical** education is included in the school curriculum to promote fitness and keep students engaged bodily as well as mentally.

For more on academic vocabulary, see pages 53–54.

Vocabulary Practice

apprehension—Etymology: Latin *apprehendere*, meaning "to grasp" Sample sentence: Because the doctor had given her a shot on the last visit, Maeve felt apprehension about tomorrow's appointment.

clamor—Etymology: Latin *clamare*, meaning "to cry out" Sample sentence: We knew the strikers had arrived because we could hear a clamor in front of the building.

copious—Etymology: Latin *copia*, meaning "abundance" Sample sentence: He took copious notes during the lecture so that he would remember every detail.

scruple—Etymology: Latin *scrupulus*, meaning a small weight or measure Sample sentence: A scruple might prevent you from being cruel to someone you do not like.

gratify—Etymology: Latin *gratus*, meaning "pleasing" Sample sentence: If you gratify a child's every wish, the child may not learn to amuse himself.

Academic Vocabulary

Physical in this sentence means "having to do with the body."

Respond Through Writing

Summary

Report Main Ideas or Events When you write a summary of a piece of nonfiction, you restate the main ideas or events in a short version of the original. A summary does not include personal opinions. In about 100 words, summarize this passage from *The Life of Olaudah Equiano*.

Prewrite Make a timeline of the events in this passage. The example below refers to Bradford's *Of Plymouth Plantation* (pages 62–68).

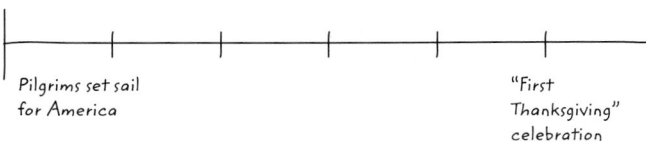

Pilgrims set sail for America

"First Thanksgiving" celebration

Draft Using your timeline, summarize the events of this passage. Avoid inserting your own opinions. Use transitional phrases to make the order of events clear. Below is a sample summary of Bradford's narrative.

In his account, William Bradford details the experience of the Pilgrims aboard the Mayflower. In 1620 they leave Europe to live in America where they can practice their religion freely. Bradford describes the harsh conditions the crew endures during the journey, which ends off the coast of Cape Cod. The Pilgrims settle in Plymouth (present-day Massachusetts), and nearly half of the 100 Pilgrims die in the first few months because they lack shelter and resources. A turning point occurs when the Pilgrims meet the Native Americans Samoset and Squanto. The Pilgrims and Native Americans form a peace treaty, and the Native Americans teach the settlers to farm, fish, and hunt. After nearly a year in America, the Pilgrims celebrate their good harvest with the "First Thanksgiving."

Revise Exchange your summary with a peer. Did you and your partner include the same events? If not, discuss your choices.

Edit and Proofread Proofread your paper, correcting any errors in spelling, grammar, and punctuation.

Learning Objectives

In this assignment, you will focus on the following objectives:

Writing: Writing a summary.
Grammar: Understanding parts of speech.

> **Grammar Tip**

Parts of Speech

A noun is a word that names a person, place, thing, idea, quality, or characteristic. The following are all nouns: *ship, Africa, slavery.*

An adjective is a word that modifies a noun or pronoun by limiting its meaning. An adjective may tell *what kind, which one, how many,* or *how much.* The following are all adjectives: *dejected, sorrowful, severe.*

In a short piece of writing such as a summary, using a lot of adjectives to modify nouns can take up valuable space. Instead, choose specific nouns to achieve the same effect using fewer words. Compare these two sentences to see this idea in action.

- *The hold smelled like a cesspit.*

- *The hold smelled like a squalid, filthy, rotting pit.*

After You Read

 ## Respond Through Writing

Students' summaries should reflect a clear understanding of main themes and events in Equiano's text. Students should use transitional phrases and correct sentence structure and grammar.

Assess students' performance in the following categories using the scoring guide at the bottom of the page. The work:

- shows a comprehensive understanding of the text
- shows a clear understanding of the main ideas and events
- summarizes the main ideas thoroughly
- provides a variety of sentence types; uses precise, descriptive language
- follows English language conventions
- avoids inserting personal opinions

 For grammar practice, see Unit 1 Teaching Resources Book, p. 96.

Scoring Guide	4	3	2	1
Grasp of text	thoughtful and comprehensive	comprehensive	limited	minimal
Understanding of main themes and events	clear	general	limited	minimal
Summary of main themes	comprehensive	generally covered	limited coverage	minimal coverage
Language	varied, precise, descriptive	varied, somewhat descriptive	predictable, basic	not varied, limited
Convention errors	few or none	several	many	serious
Personal opinions	totally absent	mostly absent	few	many

Before You Read

Focus

Bellringer Options

Selection Focus Transparency 7

Daily Language Practice Transparency 9

Or have students write a private entry in their journal, about a time when they were in a frightening situation involving strangers. What first impressions did they have? Did anything change those impressions? As they read the selection, have students consider the ways in which Mary Rowlandson was able to avoid breaking down under pressure.

Literary History ☆

The Captivity Narrative Most but not all of what came to be known as "Indian-captivity narratives" were written by women. The captivity stories tended to stereotype Native Americans and settlers.

Before You Read

from *A Narrative of the Captivity and Restoration of Mrs. Mary Rowlandson*

Meet **Mary Rowlandson**
(1636–1710)

In 1675, a long period of relative peace between the Native Americans and Europeans in New England ended in the bloody conflict known as King Philip's War. King Philip was the white settlers' name for Metacom, the *Sachem* or leader of the Wampanoag people, who vowed to halt European expansion into his lands. The war began as a series of Native American sieges on colonial towns in present-day Massachusetts, Connecticut, and Rhode Island. Lancaster, a frontier town in central Massachusetts, was one of the last to be ransacked.

At dawn on February 10, 1676, a party of Wampanoag warriors took 24 prisoners from Lancaster, including Mary Rowlandson, her six-year-old daughter, and her older son and daughter. Rowlandson was the wife of Reverend Joseph Rowlandson, the first minister in Lancaster, and many of the townspeople had been using their home as a safe haven. But the Wampanoag quickly overwhelmed the defenders of this makeshift garrison. Both Rowlandson and her six-year-old daughter were wounded during the fray, and the child died eight days later. After being captured, Rowlandson was separated from her two surviving children and allowed only short, sporadic contact with them.

Survival as a Prisoner The Wampanoag killed many of the prisoners, but Rowlandson was spared because she was adept at sewing and knitting. She was held captive for three months. Her wounds healed, and she adapted to the Wampanoags' meager diet. She often bartered her skills as a seamstress for food, knitting a pair of socks for a quart of peas or making a shirt for a hunk of bear meat. The Wampanoag were constantly on the move, traveling as far north as New Hampshire while Rowlandson was being held captive. She had become disoriented early on, and fleeing was not an option, especially because she could not bear to leave her surviving children in the hands of the Wampanoag. A stolen Bible one of the Wampanoag had given her and the small portions of food she managed to procure were all that sustained her.

Reunited with Family In May 1676, Reverend Joseph Rowlandson paid a £20 ransom for the release of his wife and children, and Rowlandson was finally reunited with her family.

> *"I had often before this said, that if the Indians should come, I should choose rather to be killed by them than taken alive; but when it came to the trial my mind changed. . . ."*
>
> —Mary Rowlandson

Rowlandson's account of her ordeal was published in 1682. It received high acclaim and prompted many imitations. Her memoir is the first—and widely considered the best—example of an American literary form, the so-called ☆ Indian-captivity narrative.

 Literature Online

Author Search For more about Mary Rowlandson, go to glencoe.com and enter QuickPass code GLA9800u1.

Selection Skills

Literary Elements
- Allusion (SE pp. 81, 82, 85, 86)
- Characterization (TE p. 84)

from **A Narrative of the Captivity and Restoration of Mrs. Mary Rowlandson**

Writing Skills/Grammar
- Write a List (SE p. 86)
- Interjections (TE p. 82)
- Character Study (TE p. 84)

Reading Skills
- Analyze Historical Context (SE pp. 81–83, 86; TE p. 84)

Vocabulary Skills
- Word Usage (SE p. 86)
- Parts of Speech (TE p. 81)

Literature and Reading Preview

Connect to the Narrative

How did you handle and adapt to unfamiliar situations and surroundings as a kid? Write a journal entry about your responses to being in a strange place.

Build Background

As a child, the Wampanoag chief Metacom had watched his father, Massasoit, help the Pilgrims who arrived on the *Mayflower*. By 1675, there were about 50,000 Puritans in the Massachusetts Bay Colony. With each passing year, more Puritans arrived, encroaching on the Native Americans' land and disrupting their way of life. Metacom began forming alliances against the settlers. In 1675, after three Wampanoag were executed by the Puritans, a swift, desperate war broke out.

Set Purposes for Reading

Big Idea Life in the New World

As you read Rowlandson's narrative, ask yourself, How did the deep cultural conflict between New England's Native American and European inhabitants affect the lives of both groups?

Literary Element Allusion

An **allusion** is a reference to a well-known character, place, or situation from history or from music, art, or another literary work. As you read, ask yourself, What allusions does Rowlandson use? What purpose do they serve?

Reading Strategy Analyze Historical Context

Analyzing historical context involves gathering background information and exploring social forces that influenced the writing of a literary work. As you read Rowlandson's account, ask yourself, How did cultural conflicts between Native Americans and Europeans lead to King Philip's War?

Tip: Take Notes Use a timeline like the one started below to record the sequence of events that led to King Philip's War.

Learning Objectives

For pages 81–86

In studying this text, you will focus on the following objectives:

Literary Study: Analyzing text structure.

Reading: Analyzing historical content.

Writing: Writing a list.

Vocabulary

desolation (des´ə lā´ shən) *n.* devastation; misery; sadness; p. 82 *The survivors of the hurricane in Florida experienced great desolation when they found their homes destroyed.*

daunt (dônt) *v.* to overcome with fear; to intimidate; p. 82 *A visit to the dentist would always daunt her.*

compassion (kəm pash´ ən) *n.* deep awareness of another's suffering with a desire to help; p. 82 *The compassion of the doctor earned the gratitude of his patients.*

discern (di surn´) *v.* to recognize as different and distinct; distinguish; p. 84 *He could barely discern the boat on the horizon.*

lament (lə ment´) *v.* to express deep sorrow or grief; p. 84 *The dead child's mother began to weep and lament.*

Before You Read

Focus

Summary

Mary Rowlandson and the survivors of a Wampanoag attack are taken into the wilderness. Forced to travel on foot, Rowlandson carries her wounded six-year-old child, who dies soon after their capture. Rowlandson's captors treat her better than she expects. Throughout her account, she thanks God for sparing her life.

 For summaries in languages other than English, see Unit 1 Teaching Resources Book, pp. 99–104.

Vocabulary

Parts of Speech Help students with proper usage of vocabulary words. Students may have heard the adjective *daunting,* meaning "overwhelming," but may not realize that it is related to the verb *daunt. Lament* may be used as a noun as well as a verb. Have students discuss other parts of speech that are related to the vocabulary words.

For additional vocabulary practice, see Unit 1 Teaching Resources Book, p. 107.

Advanced Learners

DIFFERENTIATED INSTRUCTION

Genre Characteristics Explain that the Indian-captivity narrative is a literary genre that has certain features in common with the slave narrative. As students read, direct them to analyze characteristics that both types of captivity narrative share. Ask them to put this information in the form of a graphic that can be shared with the rest of the class. For example, students could create a two-column chart or a Venn diagram.

Approaching Level

DIFFERENTIATED INSTRUCTION

Emerging Students should note the order of events as they read. Have them summarize the major incidents of the narrative. Ask them to conclude their summaries with a sentence that states Rowlandson's purpose in writing the narrative.

Teach

Literary Element | 1

Allusion Answer: *The writer is a devout person familiar with the Bible; she believes that misfortune does not happen randomly but is an act of God.*

📁 For additional literary element practice, see Unit 1 Teaching Resources Book, p. 105.

Reading Strategy | 2

Analyze Historical Context
Answer: *Since Rowlandson "often" talked about what she would do if the Indians came, attacks by the Indians must have been fairly common. If she would rather have been killed than taken alive, it's likely she had heard horrible accounts of what happened to people after they were captured.*

Writer's Technique ☆

Tone Somewhat surprisingly, the author's tone in this selection is not bitter. Instead, her faith strengthens her—she seems to feel she has much to be thankful for. By the end of the narrative, she has no hatred for her captors; in fact, she acknowledges the kindness of some.

 For an audio recording of this selection, use Listening Library Audio CD-ROM.

Readability Scores

Dale-Chall: 7.9
DRP: 57
Lexile: 1030

---

from

A Narrative of the Captivity and Restoration of Mrs. Mary Rowlandson

Mary Rowlandson

Oh the doleful sight that now was to behold at this house! *Come, behold the works of the Lord, what* **desolation** *he has made in the earth.*[1] Of thirty seven persons who were in this one house, none escaped either present death or a bitter captivity, save only one, who might say as he, *Job*[2] i. 15, *And I only am escaped alone to tell the news.* There were twelve killed, some shot, some stabbed with their spears, some knocked down with their hatchets. When we are in prosperity, oh, the little that we think of such dreadful sights; and to see our dear friends and relations lie bleeding out their heart-blood upon the ground! . . .

I had often before this said, that if the Indians should come, I should choose rather to be killed by them than taken alive; but when it came to the trial my mind changed; their glittering weapons so **daunted** my spirit, that I chose rather to go . . . than that moment to end my days. And that I may the better declare what happened to me during that grievous captivity, I shall particularly speak of the several removes[3] we had up and down the wilderness.

There remained nothing to me but one poor wounded babe, and it seemed at present worse than death that it was in such a pitiful condition, bespeaking **compassion**, and I had no refreshing ☆ for it, nor suitable things to revive it . . .

The second remove.—But now (the next morning) I must turn my back upon the town,

---

1. The author is quoting Psalms 46:8.
2. In the Bible, *Job* is a good man. His faith in God is tested by many afflictions. Messengers bring word of catastrophes affecting his possessions and family members. Each messenger tells Job that he alone has escaped to tell the news.

1 **Allusion** *What does this allusion reveal immediately about the writer?*

Vocabulary

desolation (des´ ə lā´ shən) *n.* devastation; misery; sadness

3. Here, *removes* means "changes of residence"; we would say *moves* today.

Analyze Historical Context *What clues does this statement offer about the historical context?* **2**

Vocabulary

daunt (dônt) *v.* to overcome with fear; to intimidate
compassion (kəm pash´ ən) *n.* deep awareness of another's suffering with a desire to help

82 UNIT 1   EARLY AMERICA

Grammar Practice

SPIRAL REVIEW 🌀 **Interjections Say:** Interjections are words or phrases that express emotion or feeling. In the first paragraph of the excerpt from Mary Rowlandson's narrative, for example, she uses interjections:

- "O[h] the doleful sight"
- "Oh, the little that we think of such dreadful sights"

Explain that an interjection is usually followed by a comma or an exclamation point. Other examples of interjections include *wow, aha, um, oops, shh,* and *eek.* Direct students to rewrite another paragraph of the selection, using one or two interjections at appropriate points.

and travel with them into the vast and desolate wilderness, I know not whither.[4] It is not my tongue or pen can express the sorrows of my heart and bitterness of my spirit that I had at this departure: but God was with me in a wonderful manner, carrying me along, and bearing up my spirit, that it did not quite fail. One of the Indians carried my poor wounded babe upon a horse: it went moaning all along, I shall die, I shall die! I went on foot after it, with sorrow that cannot be expressed. At length I took it off the horse, and carried it in my arms, till my strength failed, and I fell down with it. Then they set me upon a horse, with my wounded child in my lap. . . .

Thus nine days I sat upon my knees, with my babe in my lap, till my flesh was raw again. My child, being even ready to depart this sorrowful world, they bid me carry it out to another wigwam; (I suppose because they would not be troubled with such spectacles;) whither I went with a very heavy heart, and down I sat with the picture of death in my lap. About two hours in the night, my sweet babe, like a lamb, departed this life, on Feb. 18, 1675 [1676] it being about six years and five months old. It was nine days (from the first wounding) in this miserable condition, without any refreshing of one nature or other, except a little cold water. I cannot but take notice how, at another time, I could not bear to be in the room where any dead person was; but now the case is changed; I must and could lie down by my dead babe, side by side, all the night after. I have thought since of the wonderful goodness of God to me, in preserving me so in the use of my reason and senses in that distressed time, that I did not use wicked and violent means to end my own miserable life. In the morning, when they understood that my child was dead, they sent for me home to my master's wigwam; (by my master, in this writing, must be understood Quannopin, who was a Saggamore,[5] and

married King Philip's wife's sister; not that he first took me, but I was sold to him by another Narrhaganset Indian, who took me when first I came out of the garrison).[6] I went to take up my dead child in my arms to carry it with me, but they bid me let it alone; there was no resisting, but go I must and leave it. When I had been a while at my master's wigwam, I took the first opportunity I could get to go look after my dead child. When I came, I asked them what they had done with it. They told me it was upon the hill; then they went and shewed me where it was, where I saw the ground was newly dug, and there they told me they had buried it; there I left that child in the wilderness, and must commit it, and myself also, in this wilderness condition, to Him who is above all.

. . . During my abode in this place Philip spake to me to make a shirt for his boy, which I did; for which he gave me a shilling;[7] I offered the money to my master, but he bade me keep it; and with it I bought a piece of horse flesh. Afterwards I made a cap for his boy, for which he invited me to dinner; I went, and he gave me a pancake about as big as two fingers; it was made of parched wheat, beaten and fried in bear's grease, but I thought I never tasted pleasanter meat in my life. There was a squaw who spake to me to make a shirt for her sannup; for which she gave me a piece of bear. Another asked me to knit a pair of stockings, for which she gave me a quart of peas. I boiled my peas and bear together, and invited my master and mistress to dinner; but the proud gossip, because I served them both in one dish, would eat nothing, except one bit that he gave her upon the point of his knife. Hearing that my son was come to this place, I went to see him, and found him lying flat upon the ground; I asked him how he could

6. A *garrison* is a military post.
7. A *shilling* was an English or early American coin, whose value was 20 pence (pennies) or 1/20 pound.

Analyze Historical Context *Why does the author include this information?* **3**

4. *Whither* means "to what place."
5. A *Saggamore* was a subordinate chief in the hierarchy of various Native American peoples.

MARY ROWLANDSON **83**

Teach

Reading Strategy	3

Analyze Historical Context Answer: *Rowlandson is trying to place the story in historical context. The reference to King Philip helps to place the events at the time of King Philip's War.*

Political History ☆

Colonial Garrisons The "garrison" to which Rowlandson refers was the group of homes in her settlement designated as a fortress during invasions. Different families were assigned to different houses. At the time of this invasion, 37 people were seeking shelter in Rowlandson's home, which was part of the designated garrison.

English Learners

DIFFERENTIATED INSTRUCTION

Beginning Ask students to select a brief passage of the narrative and rewrite it from the third person point of view. Have students compare their versions with the originals. Ask them to decide how the passage changes when the narrative voice changes.

SMALL GROUP
Intermediate Because of the time period and context, Rowlandson uses words from Native American languages, such as *wigwam* and *sannup.* Have students work in pairs or groups to find other words that are specific to Rowlandson's historical era. *(garrison, shilling)* Direct students to derive meanings of the words from context and to check their responses in a dictionary. Ask

students to paraphrase the sentences in the text where the words appear. Have pairs or groups exchange their sentences for review and revision.

Teach

Big Idea | 1

Life in the New World
Answer: *Rowlandson's son must hide his praying, which suggests that he would be punished by the Native Americans for doing so. His devotion to God, however—like that of most early settlers—leads him to risk injury in order to pray.*

Reading Strategy | 2

Analyze Historical Context
Ask: *How do these details show Rowlandson's accurate perception of her own circumstances? (She realizes that the Native Americans need gunpowder to support the war effort and might be willing to sell her back to a white purchaser in Albany in exchange for powder. She also realizes that the availability of horses might solve the practical difficulty of her getting away on foot.)*

Literary Element | 3

Characterization **Say:**
Rowlandson's details in this passage reflect well on her captors. Why do you think she includes these positive details? (She may have included the details simply because she was an honest person or because she wanted to show the power and goodness of God.)

(**ENGLISH LEARNERS**) Discuss the meanings of the terms piety and courage. Have students orally give evidence of these two qualities of Rowlandson's.

The Indian captivity of Mrs. Mary Rowlandson during King Philip's War in 1676, c. 19th century. Color engraving. The Granger Collection, NY.

sleep so? he answered me, that he was not asleep, but at prayer; and lay so, that they might not observe what he was doing. I pray God he may remember these things, now he is returned in safety. At this place (the sun now getting higher) what with the beams and heat of the sun, and the smoke of the wigwams, I thought I should have been blind; I could scarce **discern** one wigwam from another. There was here one Mary Thurston of Medfield, who, seeing how it was with me, lent me a hat to wear; but as soon as I was gone, the squaw (who owned that Mary Thurston) came running after me, and got it away again. Here there was a squaw who gave

---

1 Life in the New World *How does this short passage illustrate the cultural differences between the Native Americans and the European settlers?*

Vocabulary

discern (di surn′) *v.* to recognize as different and distinct; distinguish

84 UNIT 1 EARLY AMERICA

---

me one spoonful of meal;[8] I put it in my pocket to keep it safe; yet, notwithstanding, somebody stole it, but put five Indian corns in the room of it; which corns were the greatest provision I had in my travel for one day.

The Indians returning from Northampton, brought with them some horses and sheep, and other things which they had taken; I desired them that they would carry me to Albany upon one of those horses, and sell me for powder; for so they had sometimes discoursed.[9] I was utterly hopeless of getting home on foot the way that I came. I could hardly bear to think of the many weary steps I had taken to come to this place.

. . . My son being now about a mile from me, I asked liberty to go and see him; they bade me go, and away I went; but quickly lost myself, travelling over hills and through swamps, and could not find the way to him. And I cannot but admire at the wonderful power and goodness of God to me, in that though I was gone from home, and met with all sorts of Indians, and those I had no knowledge of, and there being no Christian soul near me; yet not one of them offered the least imaginable miscarriage to me. I turned homeward again, and met with my master; he showed me the way to my son: when I came to him I found him not well; and withal he had a boil on his side, which much troubled him; we bemoaned one another a while, as the Lord helped us, and then I returned again. When I was returned, I found myself as unsatisfied as I was before. I went up and down moaning and **lamenting;** and my spirit was ready to sink with the thoughts of my poor children; my son was ill, and I could not but think of his mournful looks; and no Christian friend was near him to do any office of love for him, either for soul or body.

---

8. *Meal* is coarsely ground grain.
9. *Discoursed* means "discussed."

Life in the New World *Why is it important to Rowlandson that her son have a "Christian friend" near him?* **4**

Vocabulary

lament (lə ment′) *v.* to express deep sorrow or grief

Writing Practice

SPIRAL REVIEW **Character Study** Ask students to name the qualities that Rowlandson shows in her narrative. Have them identify examples of traits other Puritans would have admired, such as piety and perseverance. Have them create a graphic such as a cluster diagram to connect Rowlandson's character traits with specific evidence. For example, to illustrate the quality of perseverance, they could cite her continued patience in caring for her sick child, enduring a long journey, and suffering from food deprivation. Have them write a character study, including a topic sentence that sums up Rowlandson's most significant qualities.

And my poor girl, I knew not where she was, nor whether she was sick or well, or alive or dead. I repaired under these thoughts to my Bible (my great comforter in that time) and that scripture came to my hand, *Cast thy burden upon the Lord, and he shall sustain thee.* Psal. lv. 22.

But I was fain[10] to go and look after something to satisfy my hunger; and going among the wigwams, I went into one, and there found a squaw who showed herself very kind to me, and gave me a piece of bear. I put it into my pocket, and came home; but could not find an opportunity to broil it, for fear they would get it from me, and there it lay all that day and night in my stinking pocket. In the morning I went again to the same squaw, who had a kettle of ground nuts boiling; I asked her to let me boil my piece of bear in her kettle, which she did, and gave me some ground nuts to eat with it, and I cannot but think how pleasant it was to me. I have seen bear baked very handsomely amongst the English, and some liked it, but the thoughts that it was bear made me tremble: but now that was savory to me that one would think was enough to turn the stomach of a brute creature.

One bitter cold day I could find no room to sit down before the fire; I went out, and could not tell what to do, but I went into another wigwam where they were also sitting round the fire; but the squaw laid a skin for me, and bid me sit down; and gave me some ground nuts, and bade me come again; and told me they would buy me if they were able; and yet these were strangers to me that I never knew before.

. . . *The fourteenth remove.*—Now must we pack up and be gone from this thicket, bending our course towards the bay-towns. I having nothing to eat by the way this day, but a few crumbs of cake, that an Indian gave my girl the same day we were taken. She gave it

---

10. In this instance, *fain* means "obliged."

5 Allusion *Why do these words help Rowlandson feel better about her son and daughter?*

6 Life in the New World *How does Rowlandson suggest that life in the New World has changed her?*

---

me, and I put it into my pocket; there it lay till it was so moldy (for want of good baking) that one could not tell what it was made of; it fell all to crumbs, and grew so dry and hard, that it was like little flints;[11] and this refreshed me many times when I was ready to faint. It was in my thoughts when I put it into my mouth; that if ever I returned, I would tell the world what a blessing the Lord gave to such mean food. As we went along, they killed a deer, with a young one in her; they gave me a piece of the fawn, and it was so young and tender, that one might eat the bones as well as the flesh, and yet I thought it very good. When night came on we sat down; it rained, but they quickly got up a bark wigwam, where I lay dry that night. I looked out in the morning, and many of them had lain in the rain all night. I saw by their reeking.[12] Thus the Lord dealt mercifully with me many times; and I fared better than many of them.

. . . O the wonderful power of God that I have seen, and the experiences that I have had! I have been in the midst of those roaring lions and savage bears, that feared neither God nor man, nor the devil, by night and day, alone and in company, sleeping all sorts together; and yet not one of them ever offered the least abuse or unchastity to me in word or action. Though some are ready to say I speak it for my own credit; but I speak it in the presence of God, and to His glory.

. . . If trouble from smaller matters begins to arise in me, I have something at hand to check myself with, and say when I am troubled, it was but the other day, that if I had had the world, I would have given it for my freedom. . . . I have learned to look beyond present and smaller troubles, and to be quieted under them, as *Moses* said, *Exod.* xiv. 13, *Stand still, and see the salvation of the Lord.*
FINIS[13]

---

11. *Flints* refers to pieces of flint, a very hard type of quartz.
12. *Reeking* here means "steaming"; that is, water was evaporating from their hair and clothing.
13. *Finis* means "The End."

MARY ROWLANDSON **85**

Teach

Big Idea | **4**

Life in the New World
Answer: *She wants her son to be cared for in the way she would care for him, by taking care of his wounds and also by reminding him to find strength in God.*

Literary Element | **5**

Allusion **Answer:** *The passage she quotes reaffirms the ideas behind her faith: that God will help her if she shares her troubles, and that she can find "great comfort" in the Bible.*

Big Idea | **6**

Life in the New World
Answer: *Being in a rougher environment has led her to accept things that she would never have considered acceptable before.*

To check students' understanding of the selection, see Unit 1 Teaching Resources Book, p. 110.

Literary History

The Redeemed Captive Almost as popular as Rowlandson's narrative was an account by Reverend John Williams, *The Redeemed Captive, Returning unto Zion* (1707). His book tells of a forced march to Canada after a raid on a frontier village by French and Native American forces. Williams spent eight weeks with Abenaki Indians and more than two years among the French.

Progress Check

Can students analyze historical context?

If No → See Unit 1 Teaching Resources Book, p. 106.

After You Read

Assess

1. Students should identify an incident and provide support.
2. (a) She would rather be killed than taken alive. (b) She may have been too frightened to resist.
3. (a) Praying but pretending to sleep (b) Wampanoags frowned on displays of piety by captives.
4. (a) She resents being denied adequate food and is upset about the lack of care for her children. But, she notes acts of kindness. (b) Students may say she gives a balanced portrayal.
5. (a) Strength, religious faith (b) Her ability to cope with her ordeal may seem surprising.
6. Such accounts may have deepened settlers' mistrust of Native Americans and led to harsh policies.
7. Students answers will vary, but should point to the initial act and the retributive act.

> For additional assessment, see Assessment Resources, pp. 73–74.

Literary Element

1. She uses biblical allusions to create powerful imagery and to stress God's providence.
2. It emphasizes her sufferings.

Writing

Students' should list sensible options with clear explanations of how these options would be helpful.

After You Read

Respond and Think Critically

Respond and Interpret

1. What incident or observation in Rowlandson's account surprised or moved you most?
2. (a) What does Rowlandson say that she always intended to do if Native Americans attacked? (b) Why do you think she changes her mind?
3. (a) When Rowlandson first visits her son, what does she find him doing? (b) What might this episode suggest about the attitude of the Wampanoag?

Analyze and Evaluate

4. (a) How does Rowlandson portray her captors? (b) In your opinion, is this portrayal fair?

5. (a) What qualities or behaviors help Rowlandson survive her ordeal? (b) What did you find most puzzling about her behavior? Explain.

Connect

6. **Big Idea** **Life in the New World** Captivity narratives were a popular literary genre in early America. What effect do you think they might have had on attitudes toward Native Americans?
7. **Connect to Today** Retribution—taking revenge—has long been a part of cultural clashes. What current conflicts seem to you to be fueled by a desire for retribution?

Literary Element Allusion

The Bible shaped the Puritan culture of early New England. Rowlandson's biblical **allusions** would be readily understood by the first readers of her account.

1. What are some reasons for her biblical allusions?
2. What is the effect of alluding to the Book of Job?

Reading Strategy Analyze Historical Context

SAT Skills Practice

1. Rowlandson's account suggests that the settlers in King Philip's War were
   (A) master strategists
   (B) aggressive allies
   (C) vulnerable victims
   (D) outside agitators
   (E) skilled consultants

LOG ON **Literature** Online

Selection Resources For Selection Quizzes, eFlashcards, and Reading-Writing Connection activities, go to glencoe.com and enter QuickPass code GLA9800u1.

Vocabulary Practice

Practice with Word Usage Respond to these statements to help you explore the meanings of vocabulary words from the selection.

1. Name someone in current events for whom you have felt **compassion**.
2. Give examples of things that might **daunt** you if you found yourself in a foreign country.
3. Describe a situation in which you might experience **desolation**.
4. Give an example from a book or movie in which a character **laments**.
5. Explain how you **discern** good music from bad.

Writing

Write a List In response to a series of painful and terrifying events, Mary Rowlandson wrote a memoir. What are some other ways to deal with and work through difficult experiences? Make a list of options. Next to each, jot down why it might be helpful.

Vocabulary

1. Refugees, people who have experienced a natural disaster
2. Not knowing the language might daunt them.
3. A situation that would leave them miserable
4. A book or movie in which a character expresses deep sorrow or grief
5. What they look for in music

Grammar Workshop

Sentence Combining

Literature Connection Mary Rowlandson was not a professional writer, but she had to make choices about how to express herself. Consider the passage below:

> *"Hearing that my son was come to this place, I went to see him, and found him lying flat upon the ground . . ."*
>
> —Mary Rowlandson, from *A Narrative of the Captivity and Restoration of Mrs. Mary Rowlandson*

Rowlandson could have written the passage above in the following manner: *I heard that my son was come to this place. I went to see him. I found him lying flat upon the ground.* Instead she chose to combine these ideas into one sentence.

To write effectively, you must make similar choices about sentence length and structure. Making short sentences into longer ones helps you develop your own writing style. Sentence combining is a research-tested writing strategy that enables you to explore options and develop style.

Strategies for Sentence Combining

Here are some specific ways to help you combine sentences.

▶ Use a **prepositional phrase**, a group of words that begins with a preposition and ends with a noun or a pronoun.

Original: *Mary searched for her son. She went over hills and through swamps.*

Combined with prepositional phrases: *Mary searched for her son over hills and through swamps.*

▶ Use an **appositive**, a noun or pronoun placed next to another noun or pronoun to give additional information about it. An **appositive phrase** is an appositive plus any words that modify it.

Original: *One woman gave Mary a spoonful of meal. Meal is a coarse flour made from corn.*

Combined with an appositive phrase: *One woman gave Mary a spoonful of meal, a coarse flour made from corn.*

Learning Objectives

For pages 87–88

In this workshop, you will focus on the following objectives:

Grammar:
Recognizing the function of phrases, conjunctions, and clauses in sentence combining.
Combining sentences using a variety of techniques.

Drafting Tip

Vary the length and structure of your sentences. Work for a rhythmic, interesting balance of long and short sentences, remembering that brevity often has dramatic force. By using different kinds of sentence openers—and by sometimes tucking information in the middle of a sentence—you can create stylistic interest.

Revising Tip

Read your draft aloud, stopping now and then to experiment with clusters of sentences. Whisper them to yourself in various combinations. As you read, listen to which version sounds most effective. This process is faster than rewriting and helps you decide on a "best sentence" to write down.

Approaching Level

DIFFERENTIATED INSTRUCTION

 Emerging Review some of the grammatical constructions that students can use to combine sentences. Remind them that a prepositional phrase does not have a subject or a verb. Have students work in pairs to create prepositional phrases using the prepositions *over, under, through,* and *around.* To help students with appositives, have them combine the following sentences by making one sentence an appositive:

Acorns come from oak trees.

Acorns are a type of nut.

(Acorns, a type of nut, come from oak trees.)

Focus

Write the following sentences on the board:

My bike is brand new.

I trust Oren.

I let Oren borrow my bike.

Ask: How could you combine these sentences into one? *(Although my bike is brand new, I let Oren borrow it because I trust him.)*

Teach

Sentence Combining Point out that combining sentences requires students to think about the relationship between the two sentences. **Say:** When you combine sentences, you often eliminate the subject and verb from one sentence. Sometimes there are several ways to combine sentences. **Write the following sentences on the board:**

Joel's friend danced gracefully.

She used to be a ballerina.

Ask: How could you combine these sentences? *(Joel's friend, a former ballerina, danced gracefully. Joel's friend danced gracefully because she used to be a ballerina.)*

 For additional grammar practice, see Unit 1 Teaching Resources Book, p. 112.

Grammar Workshop

Teach

Conjunctions Help students review the differences between coordinating and subordinating conjunctions.

Ask: What is the meaning of the prefixes *co-* and *sub-*? *(together and under)* Remind students that these prefixes can help them remember that coordinating conjunctions join groups of words with equal weight, while subordinating conjunctions join clauses so that one is dependent on the other.

Assess

Practice

1. Mary had never eaten bear meat or ground nuts before, but she made them into a delicious stew.

2. The Indians returned from Northampton with sheep and horses that they had stolen.

3. Traveling with her captors, Mary remained dry at night because she slept in a bark wigwam.

Test-Taking Tip

Remember that there are many ways to combine sentences. When deciding which solution works best, ask yourself the following questions:

- Is my solution free of excess words?

- Does my solution emphasize the important idea of the sentence?

- Does my solution flow naturally when I read it aloud?

- Is my solution a complete sentence with a subject and predicate and not just a long fragment?

LOG ON **Literature** Online

Grammar For more grammar practice, go to glencoe.com and enter QuickPass code GLA9800u1.

▶ Use a **participial phrase.** A **participle** is a verb form, often ending in *–ing* or *–ed,* that functions as an adjective or adverb. A participial phrase—which includes a participle and its related words—also functions as an adjective or adverb.

Original: *Mary grieved for her child. She visited the grave.*

Combined with a participial phrase: *Grieving for her child, Mary visited the grave.*

▶ Use a **coordinating conjunction** to join words or groups of words with equal grammatical weight in a sentence. Coordinating conjunctions include words such as *and, but, or, so, nor, for,* and *yet.*

Original: *Mary was always hungry. She was often physically exhausted. Her captors did not injure her.*

Combined with coordinating conjunctions: *Mary was always hungry and often physically exhausted, but her captors did not injure her.*

▶ Use a **subordinating conjunction** to join two clauses, or ideas, so that one is dependent upon the other. Subordinating conjunctions include words such as *after, although, as, because, if, since,* and *when.*

Original: *Mary was often afraid. Her strength and faith supported her.*

Combined with a subordinating conjunction: *Although Mary was often afraid, her strength and faith supported her.*

▶ Use an **adjective clause,** a group of words with a subject and a predicate that modifies a noun or a pronoun. Adjective clauses often begin with *who, whom, whose, that,* and *which.*

Original: *King Philip was their leader. His real name was Metacom.*

Combined with an adjective clause: *King Philip, whose real name was Metacom, was their leader.*

Practice

1. Use coordinating conjunctions to combine these sentences: *Mary had never eaten bear meat before. She had never eaten ground nuts. She made them into a delicious stew.*

2. Use a prepositional phrase and an adjective clause to combine these sentences: *The Indians returned from Northampton. They had sheep and horses. They had stolen the sheep and horses.*

3. Use a participial phrase and a subordinating conjunction to combine the following sentences: *Mary traveled with her captors. She remained dry at night. She slept in a bark wigwam.*

Grammar Practice

SMALL GROUP **Conjunctions** Have students work with a partner. **Say:** Each of you should write a sentence that will cause your partner to ask a question. Then exchange papers and your partner will add a question. Exchange papers again, and write one sentence that includes your initial statement as well as your answer. Use either a coordinat-ing or a subordinating conjunction in your final sentence. Give students the following model:

- Initial sentence: My father does not like to cook.
- Question: Why?
- Final sentence: My father does not like to cook because he often gets distracted and the food burns.

Have students share their final sentences with the class, explaining whether they combined their sentences with a coordinating or subordinating conjunction.

Before You Read
Upon the Burning of Our House and *To My Dear and Loving Husband*

Meet **Anne Bradstreet**
(1612–1672)

> "[Anne Bradstreet wrote] . . . the first good poems in America, while rearing eight children, lying frequently sick, keeping house at the edge of the wilderness, [and] managed a poet's range and extension within confines as severe as any American poet has confronted."
>
> —Adrienne Rich

A nne Bradstreet was the first published poet in America—a remarkable accomplishment considering that writing was thought improper for a woman at that time.

From England to the New World Anne Bradstreet (born Dudley) was born and raised in England. At age 16, Anne married Simon Bradstreet, a friend of the family. Two years later, Anne, her husband, and her parents boarded the *Arbella* as members of John Winthrop's party and sailed to the Massachusetts Bay Colony to join the Puritan community there. At first, Bradstreet was appalled by the crude life of the settlement, but she soon adjusted. She wrote, "I changed my condition and was married, and came into this country, where I found a new world and new manners, at which my heart rose [reacted angrily]. But after

I was convinced it was the way of God, I submitted to it and joined to the church at Boston."

In Massachusetts, Bradstreet began to write poetry. At first, she imitated the lofty style of established male poets. As a result, her early poems contain many wooden lines and do not reveal her deeper emotions. Bradstreet wrote for her own satisfaction and shared her poems only with her family and friends. Nonetheless, her brother-in-law, the Reverend John Woodbridge, took fifteen of her poems to England without her knowledge and had them published as *The Tenth Muse Lately Sprung Up in America*. (The nine Muses were ancient Greek goddesses who inspired writers and artists.)

A Change of Style When Bradstreet saw *The Tenth Muse* in print, she was dissatisfied with her ☆ work and stopped writing imitative verse. Instead, she started writing poetry about her experiences as a woman in seventeenth-century New England. Bradstreet's best poems explore her love for her husband, her sadness at the death of her parents, and her struggle to accept the losses she suffered. Six years after Bradstreet's death, an American edition of *The Tenth Muse* appeared under the new title *Several Poems Compiled with Great Variety of Wit and Learning*.

ANNE BRADSTREET **89**

Before You Read

Focus

Language History ☆

Plain Style Most Puritan writers preferred to use simple words in clear order. They believed that a plain style would be understood by all people. They avoided elaborate images and figurative language.

Selection Skills

Literary Elements
- Metaphor (SE pp. 90, 91, 93; TE p. 90)
- Author's Purpose (SE p. 93)
- Speaker (TE p. 91)

Vocabulary Skills
- Synonyms (SE p. 94)
- Academic Vocabulary (SE p. 94)
- Adjectives (TE p. 90)

Upon the Burning of Our House/To My Dear and Loving Husband

Reading Skills
- Draw Conclusions (SE pp. 90, 91, 94)

Study Skills/Research/Assessment
- Short Response (TE p. 94)

Listening/ Viewing/ Speaking Skills
- Analyze Art (TE p. 92)

Writing Skills/Grammar
- Write an Extended Metaphor (SE p. 94)
- Inverted Syntax (TE p. 92)

Before You Read

Focus

Summary

In "Upon the Burning of Our House," Anne Bradstreet comes to terms with the loss of her home and her possessions to a fire. In "To My Dear and Loving Husband," she rejoices in her love for her husband.

 For summaries in languages other than English, see Unit 1 Teaching Resources Book, pp. 113–118.

Teach

Vocabulary

Adjectives Point out that *bereft* is an alternative form of the past participle *bereaved*. *Bereaved* is typically used to describe a person whose loved one has died. *Bereft* describes a loss of anything precious—a person, a feeling, or property.

 For additional context, see Glencoe Interactive Vocabulary CD-ROM.

Literature and Reading Preview

Connect to the Poems

What possessions and people do you most value? Make a list of them. Next to each, describe how you would feel if you were to lose that person or thing forever.

Build Background

Bradstreet's husband and father were both governors of the Massachusetts Bay Colony. Their prominence resulted in frequent moves and separations. This instability, along with the daily tragedies of colonial life and Bradstreet's Puritan beliefs, likely influenced her sense of impermanence.

Set Purposes for Reading

▌Big Idea▐ Life in the New World

As a Puritan, Bradstreet viewed all events within the context of God's divine plan. She found similarities between the domestic details of daily life and the spiritual details of her religious life. As you read, ask yourself, How did Bradstreet's religious beliefs affect her relationships and her interactions with the harsh circumstances of early American life?

▌Literary Element▐ Metaphor

A **metaphor** is a figure of speech that compares or equates two seemingly unlike things. As you read, ask yourself, What metaphors does Bradstreet use? What do they add to her work?

▌Reading Strategy▐ Draw Conclusions About Author's Beliefs

When you **draw a conclusion,** you make a general statement based on the information in a text. For example, you might conclude that the author of an essay about the beauty of a prairie would support prairie conservation efforts. As you read Bradstreet's poems, ask yourself, What conclusions can I draw about Bradstreet's personal and religious beliefs from the text?

Tip: Graphic Organizer Use a two-column chart to record details from the poems and the conclusions you draw from them.

Detail	Conclusion
p. 91, line 54 "My hope and treasure lies above."	Bradstreet valued the afterlife more than earthly existence.

Learning Objectives

For pages 89–94

In studying these texts, you will focus on the following objectives:

Literary Study: Analyzing metaphor.

Reading: Drawing conclusions about author's beliefs.

Writing: Applying extended metaphor in a poem.

Vocabulary

bereft (bi reft´) *adj.* deprived of the possession or use of something; p. 91 *The foul weather left him bereft of his usual good mood.*

chide (chīd) *v.* to find fault with or to blame; p. 91 *The teacher chided the class for not completing their homework.*

recompense (rek´ əm pens´) *n.* something given in return for something else; compensation; p. 92 *When the soles of his new shoes came apart, the athlete requested recompense from the shoe company.*

Reading Practice

Metaphor Prepare students to read and respond to the metaphors in Bradstreet's poetry by asking students to define and give examples of metaphors. A metaphor expresses an imaginative comparison that should not be interpreted literally. List some metaphors and have students explain the types of comparisons:

- It's raining cats and dogs.
- The moon was a golden coin in the sky.
- We are in the springtime of life.

Invite students to provide other examples of metaphors from everyday expressions or from their reading.

Have students create a chart to analyze and paraphrase metaphors in Bradstreet's poetry.

Upon the Burning of Our House		
Line	Metaphor	Paraphrase
45	"With glory richly furnished"	Filled with God's glory

90

Upon the Burning of Our House
July 10th, 1666

Anne Bradstreet

In silent night when rest I took
For sorrow near I did not look
I wakened was with thund'ring noise
And piteous shrieks of dreadful voice.
5   That fearful sound of "Fire!" and "Fire!"
Let no man know is my desire.
I, starting up, the light did spy,
And to my God my heart did cry
To strengthen me in my distress
10   And not to leave me succorless.[1]
Then, coming out, beheld a space
The flame consume my dwelling place.
And when I could no longer look,
I blest His name that gave and took,[2]
15   That laid my goods now in the dust.
Yea, so it was, and so 'twas just.
It was His own, it was not mine,
Far be it that I should repine;[3]
He might of all justly **bereft**
20   But yet sufficient for us left.
When by the ruins oft I past
My sorrowing eyes aside did cast,
And here and there the places spy
Where oft I sat and long did lie:
25   Here stood that trunk, and there that chest,
There lay that store I counted best.

My pleasant things in ashes lie,
And them behold no more shall I.
Under thy roof no guest shall sit,
30   Nor at thy table eat a bit.
No pleasant tale shall e'er be told,
Nor things recounted done of old.
No candle e'er shall shine in thee,
Nor bridegroom's voice e'er heard shall be.
35   In silence ever shall thou lie,
Adieu, Adieu,[4] all's vanity.[5]
Then straight I 'gin my heart to **chide**,
And did thy wealth on earth abide?
Didst fix thy hope on mold'ring dust?
40   The arm of flesh didst make thy trust?
Raise up thy thoughts above the sky
That dunghill mists away may fly.
Thou hast an house on high erect,
Framed by that mighty Architect,
45   With glory richly furnished,
Stands permanent though this be fled.
It's purchased and paid for too
By Him who hath enough to do.
A price so vast as is unknown
50   Yet by His gift is made thine own;
There's wealth enough, I need no more,
Farewell, my pelf,[6] farewell my store.
The world no longer let me love,
My hope and treasure lies above.

---

1. *Succorless* means "without assistance" or "helpless."
2. Refers to Job 1:21, "the Lord gave, and the Lord hath taken away; blessed be the name of the Lord."
3. *Repine* means "to express unhappiness."

Draw Conclusions About Author's Beliefs *What conclusions can you draw about Bradstreet's faith in God from these lines?*

1

---

4. *Adieu* (ə dyō̄o) is French for "good-bye."
5. *All's vanity* is a reference to Ecclesiastes 1:2 and 12:8.
6. *Pelf* is a term for wealth, often used disapprovingly.

Metaphor *Who is the "mighty Architect" in this metaphor?*

3

ANNE BRADSTREET **91**

Reading Strategy   1

Draw Conclusions
Answer: *She believes that God is responsible for all things, good and bad, and that she must trust God's will.*

Literary Element   2

Speaker Say: The speaker is the voice of a poem, similar to the narrator in a work of prose. Sometimes the speaker's voice is that of the poet; sometimes, it is that of a fictional person—or even a thing. **Ask:** How does the structure of these lines suggest that the speaker is presenting a dialogue or debate with herself—possibly as a result of her internal conflict triggered by the fire? *(In lines 27–36, her thoughts focus on the tragic destruction of her material possessions. In line 37, however, she reproves or "chides" her own heart, as she recalls that true wealth does not abide on earth.)*

Literary Element   3

Metaphor Answer: *The "mighty Architect" is God.*

Interactive Read and Write

Other options for teaching this selection can be found in

- Interactive Read and Write for EL Students, pp. 17–24
- Interactive Read and Write for Approaching-Level Students, pp. 17–24
- Interactive Read and Write for On-Level Students, pp. 17–24

Approaching Level

DIFFERENTIATED INSTRUCTION

Established Predicting helps students identify their expectations for what they will read before they begin. As they read, students can compare their expectations with the text, enhancing their comprehension and involvement with the content. Explain that "Upon the Burning of Our House" tells how a woman reacts when she loses all her possessions. Ask students to write a paragraph predicting her possible reac-

tions. After reading, students can compare their ideas with those in the poem.

Ask: How do such comparisons help you draw conclusions about the author's beliefs? *(By considering personal reactions to a situation, a context is created to which a comparison can be made.)*

Teach

Life in the New World
Answer: *Only God, or the heavens, has the power to reward her husband appropriately.*

View the Art ★

This house and garden sampler made of wool and silk was created in 1785 by an unknown British artist. This type of embroidery was a popular form of folk art in colonial America. The alphabet at the top indicates that this sampler had an educational as well as an ornamental function.

Ask: How might the subject of the art connect with the subject of the poem? *(The art portrays a scene of domestic tranquility, shown by the animals and the well-tended landscaping; this connects with the speaker's inner contentment and tranquility.)*

 For an audio recording of this selection, use Listening Library Audio CD-ROM.

 To check students' understanding of the selection, see Unit 1 Teaching Resources Book, p. 122.

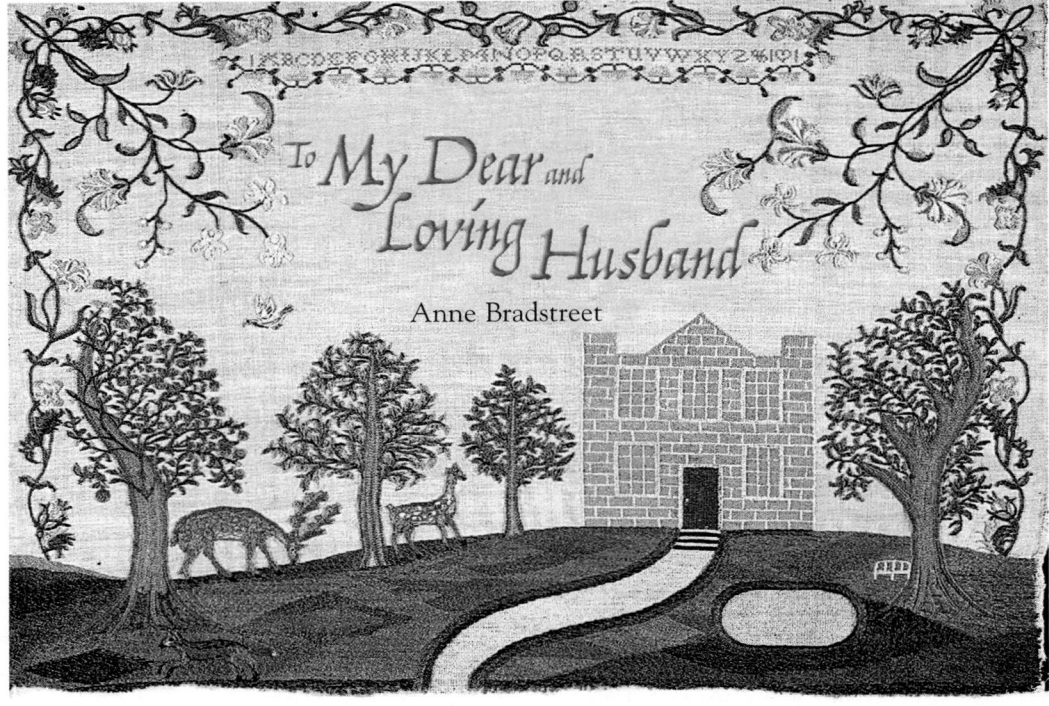

To My Dear and Loving Husband
Anne Bradstreet

★

    If ever two were one, then surely we.
If ever man were loved by wife, then thee;
If ever wife was happy in a man,
Compare with me, ye women, if you can.
5 I prize thy love more than whole mines of gold
Or all the riches that the East doth hold.
My love is such that rivers cannot quench,
Nor ought[1] but love from thee, give **recompense.**
Thy love is such I can no way repay,
10 The heavens reward thee manifold,[2] I pray.
Then while we live, in love let's so persevere[3]
That when we live no more, we may live ever.

---

1. *Ought* means "anything."
2. Here, *manifold* means "in many different ways."

Vocabulary

recompense (rek´ əm pens´) *n.* something given in return for something else; compensation

3. In the 1600s, the word *persevere* was pronounced *per sé ver,* with the accent on the second syllable. Therefore, it rhymes with *ever* in the following line.

Life in the New World *How does Bradstreet's description of her love for her husband reflect her religious beliefs?*

  1

92 UNIT 1 EARLY AMERICA

Grammar Practice

SPIRAL REVIEW **Inverted Syntax** Explain that poets often reverse the conventional word order of a sentence. Inversion may be used to emphasize a word or phrase, or it may be used for the sake of rhyme. **Ask:** How would you rephrase the opening line of "Upon the Burning of Our House" in conventional word order? *(In silent night when I took rest.)*

Ask: How does the line change when the word order is changed? Have students practice changing word order by creating "found poems." Have students select one sentence from a newspaper, a textbook, or any accessible printed source. Have students take the sentence and write it in poetic form by rearranging the words and dividing it into lines. The sentence "She shared her poems with family and friends" might become

  With family and friends
    Her poems she shared
Have students share their "found poems" with the class.

After You Read

Respond and Think Critically

Respond and Interpret

1. Which Bradstreet poem did you find more poignant? Explain.

2. (a)How did the speaker in "Upon the Burning of Our House" feel about her possessions before the fire? How does she feel afterward? (b)What do you think brought about the change in her perspective?

3. (a)In the final line, where does the speaker say her "hope and treasure" are? (b)What does this suggest about the speaker's home and possessions?

4. (a)In "To My Dear and Loving Husband," what does the speaker prize "more than whole mines of gold"? (b)Why do you think she compares the way she feels to mines of gold?

Analyze and Evaluate

5. In "Upon the Burning of Our House," how effective are Bradstreet's frequent references to her faith in conveying the poem's meaning? Explain.

6. How effective is the repetition in the opening lines of "To My Dear and Loving Husband"? Explain.

Connect

7. **Big Idea** **Life in the New World** How do Bradstreet's Puritan beliefs affect her perception of the world as represented by these poems?

8. **Connect to the Author** After reading *The Tenth Muse*, Bradstreet's poetic style changed (see page 89). What evidence of that do you see in these poems?

Literary Element Metaphor

SAT Skills Practice

1. The author uses the extended metaphor in lines 43–50 of "Upon the Burning of Our House" to describe

   (A) the specifications for rebuilding her house

   (B) her heavenly home built by God

   (C) her hope for recovering her lost money and furnishings

   (D) God's motivation for burning her house

   (E) her confusion at being homeless while God lives in glory

2. In line 7 of "To My Dear and Loving Husband" ("My love . . . cannot quench") the author is suggesting that her love is like a

   (A) boundless ocean

   (B) cascading waterfall

   (C) thirsty traveler

   (D) blazing fire

   (E) fertile breeding ground

Review: Author's Purpose

As you learned on page 48, an **author's purpose** is his or her intent in writing a literary work. Authors typically write for one or more of the following purposes: to persuade, to inform, to explain, to entertain, or to describe.

Partner Activity Meet with a classmate and discuss Bradstreet's purpose. Work with your partner to infer what Bradstreet's purpose was for writing each poem. Include details from the poem that you think reveal information about her purpose.

 Literature Online

Selection Resources For Selection Quizzes, eFlashcards, and Reading-Writing Connection activities, go to glencoe.com and enter QuickPass code GLA9800u1.

ANNE BRADSTREET **93**

Literary Element

1. B is the correct answer because that interpretation supports the message of the poem—the author's realization that her true home is with God.

2. D is the correct answer because the only thing a river possibly could quench is a fire.

Review: Author's Purpose

Sample answers:
"Upon the Burning of Our House"
Detail: "There's wealth enough, I need no more"
Purpose: To explain her beliefs
"To My Dear and Loving Husband"
Detail: "Thy love is such I can no way repay,"
Purpose: To show that she is overjoyed by her husband's love

After You Read

Assess

1. Students' answers will vary. They should cite evidence from the poems to support their opinion.

2. (a) The possessions were important to her; her "sorrowing eyes" look over the ashes and mourn for all the "pleasant things." Later, she decides that her possessions really belong to God. (b) She thought about what is most important in life.

3. (a) She says they are "above," or in heaven. (b) This statement suggests that her home and possessions are impermanent and not her own.

4. (a) Her husband's love (b) She wants to show how deeply she values this love.

5. Some may say that the references make Bradstreet's life and hardships appear universal or ordered by providence.

6. Repetition creates a musical effect and also rhetorically strengthens the speaker's claim.

7. Her beliefs cause her to see the world as both divinely preordained and as transient. Thus, she is willing to accept her fate.

8. Answers will vary, but students should cite evidence from Bradstreet's poem.

For additional assessment, see Assessment Resources, pp. 75–76.

Progress Check

Can students analyze a metaphor?

If No → See Unit 1 Teaching Resources Book, p. 119.

After You Read

Assess

Reading Strategy

1. She feels that they are impermanent—that ultimately all is God's.

2. Students' answers will vary. They might point to Bradstreet's claim that "all's vanity," that "My hope and treasure lies above," and that the "house on high erect,/ Framed by that mighty Architect . . . stands permanent though this be fled."

Vocabulary

1. e 2. c 3. a

Academic Vocabulary

Students should state that site means the location of a building or structure.

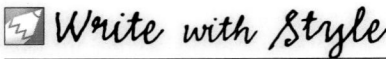 Write with Style

Students' writing should reflect an understanding of extended metaphors. Their metaphors should be meaningful and should reflect their personal style.

Reading Strategy Draw Conclusions About Author's Beliefs

Authors often incorporate their own beliefs into their writing. Sometimes they state these beliefs explicitly. Other times it might be possible to infer the author's beliefs only by examining their word choice, use of figurative language, or rhetorical techniques. Review the chart you made on page 90. Then answer the following questions.

1. How does Bradstreet feel about worldly things?

2. List three pieces of evidence to support your opinion.

Vocabulary Practice

Practice with Synonyms With a partner, match each boldfaced vocabulary word below with its synonym on the right. Use a thesaurus or dictionary to check your answers.

1. bereft
2. chide
3. recompense

a. payment
b. aggravated
c. scold
d. revenge
e. stripped

Academic Vocabulary

*Passing the **site** of her former home, Bradstreet reminisces about her life there.*

Site is an academic word. In more casual usage, you might say workers are erecting a skyscraper at a building **site**. Using context clues, try to figure out the meaning of the word in the sentence about Bradstreet above. Check your definition in a dictionary.

For more on academic vocabulary, see pages 53–54.

Write with Style

Apply Extended Metaphor

Assignment Writers often use metaphors to explain ideas and convey feelings. Review the extended metaphor in "Upon the Burning of Our House" (lines 43–50). Then write one of your own to explain an idea and how you feel about it.

Get Ideas Think of a comparison between what you want to talk about and some other thing it is like. For example, you might sometimes think your school is like a zoo. Then brainstorm some ways the two things could be compared. For example, you might compare students to zoo animals. Finally, think of some examples for each comparison. Use a word web to keep track of your ideas.

EXAMPLE:

My School

Some animals just sit all day looking beautiful, and some do tricks to show how smart they are or act scary so people leave them alone. Others try to blend in with the rocks or leaves so it looks as though no one is home.

Give It Structure Choose your line breaks carefully to give your images maximum impact.

Look at Language Be careful not to take an extended metaphor too far. A few comparisons go a long way.

Assessment Practice

Short Response Remind students that answers to short-response questions are evaluated on the basis of their insightfulness and the evidence drawn from the text to support them.

Ask: Which of the two poems shows Bradstreet's Puritan philosophy more clearly? Provide evidence for your answer. *(Students should offer citations from their chosen poem to support their answers.)*

 To create custom assessments using software, use ExamView Assessment Suite.

 To create custom assessments online, go to Progress Reporter Online Assessment.

Before You Read

from *Sinners in the Hands of an Angry God*

Meet **Jonathan Edwards**
(1703–1758)

Jonathan Edwards was a Puritan theologian, preacher, and philosopher who captivated congregations with his "preaching of terror," a brand of sermonizing aimed at shaking the faith of unrepentant sinners and saving them from eternal damnation. His sermons hinge on fire-and-brimstone depictions of hell and visions of churchgoers dangling by tenuous threads over the depths of hell, held by the hand of an angry God. "I think it is a reasonable thing to fright persons away from hell," Edwards explained. "Is it not a reasonable thing to fright a person out of a house on fire?"

As a child, the precocious Edwards used his vivid imagination and shrewd, analytical mind to write scientific essays on insects, colors, and rainbows. At 13, he matriculated at Yale. He intended to use his education to publish works refuting natural philosophy and its key doctrines of materialism and atheism.

> *"O sinner! consider the fearful danger you are in: it is a great furnace of wrath, a wide and bottomless pit, full of the fire of wrath, that you are held over in the hand of that God…"*
>
> —Jonathan Edwards

Conversion Edwards was a religious young man, due to his Puritan upbringing, but he had qualms about predestination, the doctrine that claims it is predetermined whether an individual will go to heaven or hell. But in 1721, while studying divinity, he underwent a religious conversion that confirmed his belief in God as omnipotent, total, and in control of all things, including human destiny. Edwards subsequently thought of the revelation of God in intuitive terms—God the divine conveyed directly to the individual soul.

In 1729, Edwards succeeded his grandfather at the pulpit in Northampton, Massachusetts. In his sermons, he attributed New England's ailing morality to its moral and religious independence and its incomplete acceptance of faith as the sole means to salvation.

Great Awakening Between 1730 and 1750, a religious revival known as the Great Awakening swept through the colonies. Preachers attracted people in droves and brought about ecstatic emotional reactions and frenzied mass conversions with their sermons. Edwards sought to keep his audiences calm, but his sermons were equally effective. His sermons were reproduced and read across Britain and other regions in America. However, by 1750 some of Northampton's Puritans objected to Edwards's extreme teachings and removed him from his post. He went into exile for several years, during which he served as a missionary to Native Americans in the frontier village of Stockbridge. He then became president of what is now Princeton University, but he died of smallpox shortly thereafter. Edwards is widely considered the most influential American writer before Benjamin Franklin.

> **LOG ON** ▶ **Literature** Online
>
> **Author Search** For more about Jonathan Edwards, go to glencoe.com and enter QuickPass code GLA9800u1.

JONATHAN EDWARDS **95**

Before You Read

Focus

Bellringer Options

Selection Focus
 Transparency 9
Daily Language Practice
 Transparency 11

Or **display** magazine ads, appealing to reason and emotion.

Ask: Which is a more powerful strategy in persuasion, an appeal to reason or an appeal to emotion? As they read, students should consider Edwards' persuasive skills.

Cultural History

The Puritan Concept of Grace
Puritans believed that God granted certain people the gift of grace—the ability to live righteously and receive salvation. Puritans constantly examined their lives for outward signs of being God's elect. They felt that people could not achieve grace through prayer or through attendance at church. Their inner spiritual lives could be transformed only by God.

Selection Skills

Literary Elements
- Imagery (SE pp. 96, 98–100; TE p. 97)
- Repetition (TE p. 99)

> *from* Sinners in the Hands of an Angry God

Writing Skills/Grammar
- Apply Diction (SE p. 101)

Reading Skills
- Examine Connotation (SE pp. 96, 99, 101)

Listening/Speaking/Viewing Skills
- Analyze Art (SE p. 98)

Before You Read

Focus

Summary

Jonathan Edwards preaches a fiery sermon, invoking images of hell and punishment. He says that God is angry with the sinners who have not received God's grace. The members of the congregation have an opportunity to turn to God and enter God's kingdom. Edwards asks the members of the congregation how they can remain in this condition, knowing they could be saved.

 For summaries in languages other than English, see Unit 1 Teaching Resources Book, pp. 124–129.

Vocabulary

Persuasive Words Explain that when the vocabulary words are in the hands of Jonathan Edwards, they take on a strong moral connotation. While to *appease* a child implies comforting, to *appease* God's anger does not mean to comfort God. Have students find additional synonyms for the word. **Ask:** What might Edwards mean when he says sinners have done nothing to *appease* God's anger? *(to pacify, conciliate, or make up for)*

 For additional vocabulary practice, see Unit 1 Teaching Resource Book, p. 132.

 For additional context, see Glencoe Interactive Vocabulary CD-ROM.

Literature and Reading Preview

Connect to the Sermon

What methods would you use if you were trying to convert someone to your way of thinking? Discuss this question with a partner, including any examples from your own experience.

Build Background

This sermon, which Jonathan Edwards delivered in 1741, remains the most famous literary monument to the Great Awakening. Edwards upheld strict Calvinism, which taught that human nature is essentially evil and that God predestines only a select few to be saved from eternal punishment.

Set Purposes for Reading

Big Idea **Life in the New World**

As you read, ask yourself, What does this sermon reveal about the importance of religion in colonial America?

Literary Element **Imagery**

Imagery refers to the set of mental pictures that writers create by using **sensory details,** or descriptions that appeal to one or more of the senses. As you read, ask yourself, What images does Edwards use to stir fear in the hearts of his listeners? How effective are these images?

Reading Strategy **Examine Connotation**

Connotation refers to the implied or suggested meanings associated with a word beyond its denotation, or literal meaning. For example, the words *statesman* and *politician* have similar denotations but very different connotations. Connotation is subtle, but often potent in its emphasis of the writer's points. As you read, ask yourself, How does Edwards use specific connotations to emphasize his ideas?

Tip: Take Notes Use a chart to record the denotations and connotations of three words Edwards uses to describe the plight of sinners.

Word	Denotation	Connotation
p. 97 sentenced	having had a sentence imposed, as in a trial	The word *sentenced* suggests the finality of a court trial.

Learning Objectives

For pages 95–101

In studying this text, you will focus on the following objectives:

Literary Study: Analyzing imagery.

Reading: Examining connotation.

Writing: Applying diction in a persuasive essay.

Vocabulary

appease (ə pēz′) *v.* to bring to a state of peace or quiet; soothe; p. 97 *He tried to appease the sobbing child with a toy.*

abate (ə bāt′) *v.* to lessen or reduce in force or intensity; p. 97 *Did the storm abate after the sun came out?*

prudence (prōōd′ əns) *n.* exercise of good and cautious judgment; p. 98 *Showing prudence, the motorist slowed as she neared the school zone.*

abhor (ab hôr′) *v.* to regard with disgust; p. 98 *After working in a candy store, she began to abhor sweets.*

abominable (ə bom′ ə nə bəl) *adj.* disgusting; detestable; p. 98 *Stealing from the poor is an abominable crime.*

Listening Practice

Persuasive Connotation Explain that a sermon is an example of persuasive writing. The preacher wishes to convert his audience or to convince them to renounce their sins. Have students listen to an audio recording of the sermon and create a chart where they can record their answers to the following questions:

- What comparisons are used to express God's wrath?

- What images of doom and destruction are used to appeal to the audience's emotions?
- What hope of God's mercy does Edwards offer repentant sinners?

Ask students to summarize orally how Edwards uses figures of speech and connotative language as a means of persuasion and the impact it has on the listener.

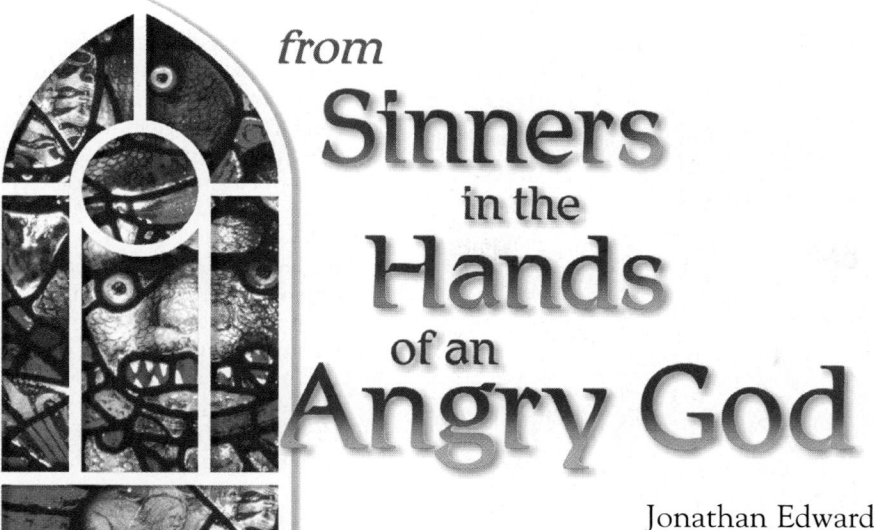

from

Sinners
in the
Hands
of an
Angry God

Jonathan Edwards

Red Devil Window (detail), 1500–1517. Bernard Flower. Stained glass.
St. Mary's Church, Fairford, Gloucestershire, Great Britain.

1 So that thus it is, that natural men[1] are held in the hand of God over the pit of hell; they have deserved the fiery pit, and are already sentenced to it; and God is dreadfully provoked, his anger is as great towards them as to those that are actually suffering the executions of the fierceness of his wrath in hell, and they have done nothing in the least, to **appease** or **abate** that anger, neither is God in the least bound by any promise to hold them up one moment; the devil is waiting for them, hell is gaping for them, the flames gather and flash about them, and would fain[2] lay hold on them and swallow them up; the fire pent up in their own hearts is struggling to break out; and they have no interest in any Mediator, there are no means within reach that can be any security to them. In short, they have no refuge, nothing to take hold of; all that preserves them every moment is the mere arbitrary will, and uncovenanted, unobliged forbearance of an incensed God.

Application

The use may be of awakening to unconverted persons in this congregation. This that you have heard is the case of every one of you that are out of Christ.[3] That world of misery, that lake of burning brimstone, is extended abroad under you. There is the dreadful pit of the glowing flames of the wrath of God; there is hell's wide gaping mouth open; and you have nothing to stand upon, nor any thing to take hold of. There is nothing between you and hell but the air; it is only the power and mere pleasure of God that holds you up.

You probably are not sensible of this; you find you are kept out of hell, but do not see the hand of God in it; but look at other things, as the good state of your bodily constitution, your care of your own life, and the means you use for your own

---

1. *Natural men* are those who have not received God's grace. They are "out of Christ."
2. Here, *fain* means "willingly" or "gladly."

Vocabulary

appease (ə pēz´) *v.* to bring to a state of peace
abate (ə bāt´) *v.* to lessen or reduce in force

---

3. Those who are *out of Christ* are not in God's grace.

JONATHAN EDWARDS **97**

Teach

Literary Element | 1

Imagery Answer: *The image of a fragile spider's web torn by a falling rock vividly suggests the danger facing those who are "unconverted."*

Big Idea | 2

Life in the New World
Answer: *It indicates that religion was a regular part of the lives of most colonial families.*

View the Art ★

Answer: *Students may say that Whitefield's outstretched arms and intense expression show the dramatic tone of sermons and the power of the preacher. Alternatively, they may say that Whitefield looks still and posed, so he does not look as if he is delivering an impassioned speech.*

John Wollaston came to America from England in 1749. His works have a heightened sense of line and surface design. His portraits are famous for graceful poses and elaborate costumes.

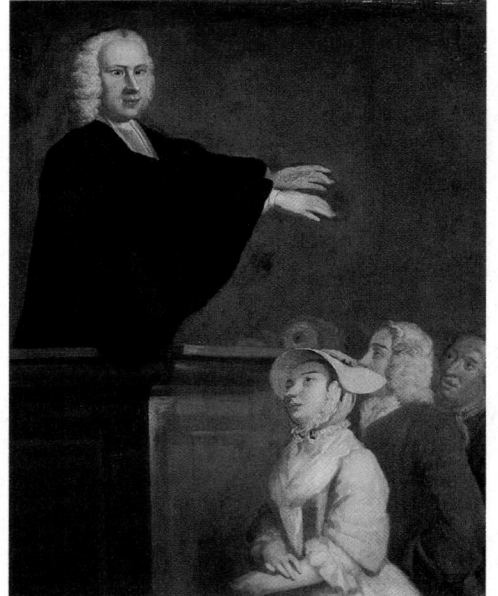

George Whitefield, c. 1742. John Wollaston. Oil on canvas, 32⅝ x 26 in. National Portrait Gallery, London.

View the Art George Whitefield, like Jonathan Edwards, was a minister during the Great Awakening. What does his portrait suggest about sermons of this period? ★

preservation. But indeed these things are nothing; if God should withdraw his hand, they would avail no more to keep you from falling, than the thin air to hold up a person that is suspended in it.

Your wickedness makes you as it were heavy as lead, and to tend downwards with great weight and pressure towards hell; and if God should let you go, you would immediately sink and swiftly descend and plunge into the bottomless gulf, and your healthy constitution, and your own care and **prudence,** and best contrivance,[4] and all your righteousness, would have no more influence to uphold you and keep you out of hell, than a spider's web would have to stop a falling rock.

---

4. A *contrivance* is a clever scheme or plan.

1 | Imagery *Why does Edwards introduce this image?*

Vocabulary

prudence (prōōd′ əns) *n.* exercise of good judgment

The bow of God's wrath is bent, and the arrow made ready on the string, and justice bends the arrow at your heart, and strains the bow, and it is nothing but the mere pleasure of God, and that of an angry God, without any promise or obligation at all, that keeps the arrow one moment from being made drunk with your blood.

Thus are all you that never passed under a great change of heart, by the mighty power of the Spirit of God upon your souls; all that were never born again, and made new creatures, and raised from being dead in sin, to a state of new, and before altogether unexperienced light and life, (however you may have reformed your life in many things, and may have had religious affections, and may keep up a form of religion in your families and closets,[5] and in the houses of God, and may be strict in it) you are thus in the hands of an angry God; it is nothing but his mere pleasure that keeps you from being this moment swallowed up in everlasting destruction.

The God that holds you over the pit of hell, much as one holds a spider, or some loathsome insect, over the fire, **abhors** you, and is dreadfully provoked; his wrath towards you burns like fire; he looks upon you as worthy of nothing else, but to be cast into the fire; he is of purer eyes than to bear to have you in his sight; you are ten thousand times so **abominable** in his eyes, as the most hateful and venomous serpent is in ours.

O sinner! consider the fearful danger you are in: it is a great furnace of wrath, a wide and bottomless pit, full of the fire of wrath, that you are held over in the hand of that God, whose wrath is provoked and incensed as much against you, as against many of the damned in

---

5. Here, *closets* refers to small rooms used especially for prayer and meditation.

Life in the New World *What does Edwards's observation indicate about the place of religion in the American colonies?* **2**

Vocabulary

abhor (ab hôr′) *v.* to regard with disgust
abominable (ə bom′ ə nə bəl) *adj.* disgusting; detestable

Reading Practice

Changes in English Note instances in Edwards's sermon that reveal how the English language has changed over time. For example, the word *closets* on page 98 refers to prayer chambers, not to places in which clothing is stored. **Say:** Although Edwards's English sounds more formal than modern American English does, much of his language is similar. Only a few of his expressions are rarely seen today. As students read on, have them develop a list of words and phrases from the selection that are no longer commonly used. *(Possible responses: "O sinner!" on p. 98; "'Tis doubtless the case," "heretofore," and "lest you be consumed" on p. 99.)* Clarify and discuss the meanings of unfamiliar words. *(heretofore means "up to this time"; lest means "for fear that.")*

hell: you hang by a slender thread, with the flames of divine wrath flashing about it, and ready every moment to singe it, and burn it asunder;[6] and you have no interest in any **3** Mediator, and nothing to lay hold of to save yourself, nothing to keep off the flames of wrath, nothing of your own, nothing that you ever have done, nothing that you can do, to induce God to spare you one moment.

There is reason to think, that there are many in this congregation now hearing this discourse, that will actually be the subjects of this very misery to all eternity. We know not who they are, or in what seats they sit, or what thoughts they now have. It may be they are now at ease, and hear all these things without much disturbance, and are now flattering themselves that they are not the persons; promising themselves that they shall escape. If we knew that there was one person, and but one, in the whole congregation, that was to be the subject of this misery, what an awful thing it would be to think of! If we knew who it was, what an awful sight would it be to see such a person! How might all the rest of the congregation lift up a lamentable and bitter cry over him! But alas! Instead of one, how many is it likely will remember this discourse in hell! And it would be a wonder, if some that are now present should not be in hell in a very short time, before this year is out. And it would be no wonder if some persons, that now sit here in some seats of this meeting-house in health, and quiet and secure, should be there before to-morrow morning.

Those of you that finally continue in a natural condition, that shall keep out of Hell longest, will be there in a little time! Your damnation does not slumber; it will come swiftly, and in all probability very suddenly upon many of you. You have reason to wonder that you are not already in Hell. 'Tis doubtless the case of some that heretofore you have seen and known, that never deserved Hell more than you, and that heretofore appeared as likely to have been now alive as you: Their case is past all hope. They are crying in extreme misery and perfect despair. But here you are in the land of the living, and in the house of God, and have an opportunity to obtain salvation. What would not those poor damned, helpless souls give for one day's such opportunity as you now enjoy!

And now you have an extraordinary opportunity, a day wherein Christ has flung the door of mercy wide open, and stands in the door calling and crying with a loud voice to poor sinners; a day, wherein many are flocking to Him, and pressing into the kingdom of God. Many are daily coming from the east, west, north and south; many that were very lately in the same miserable condition that you are in, are in now a happy state, with their hearts filled with love to Him that has loved them and washed them from their sins in His own blood, and rejoicing in hope of the Glory of God.[7] How awful is it to be left behind at such a day! To see so many others feasting, while you are pining and perishing! To see so many rejoicing and singing for joy of heart, while you have cause to mourn for sorrow of heart and howl for vexation of spirit! How can you rest one moment in such a condition? . . .

Therefore let everyone that is out of Christ now awake and fly from the wrath to come. The wrath of Almighty God is now undoubtedly hanging over a great part of this congregation: Let everyone fly out of Sodom![8] *Haste and escape for your lives, look not behind you, escape to the mountain, lest you be consumed.*

---

7. The author is referring to the many people who were part of the Great Awakening, a movement that urged people to experience religion on a personal, emotional level.
8. In Genesis 19:15–17, angels warn Lot, the only virtuous inhabitant of the sinful city of Sodom, to flee the city before it is destroyed.

---

6. *Asunder* means "into separate pieces."

4 Imagery *Which senses does this image appeal to? What emotions does it stir?*

Examine Connotation *How does the connotation of the word* flocking *contribute to Edwards's point?* **5**

Teach

Literary Element | 3

Repetition Say: In this paragraph, Edwards repeats the word *nothing* several times. **Ask:** What is the effect of this repetition? *(The repetition emphasizes that human beings are powerless, while God is omnipotent.)*

Literary Element | 4

Imagery Answer: *Appeals to the senses of sight and touch; stirs emotions of fear*

Reading Strategy | 5

Examine Connotation Answer: *It conveys a sense of joy and peace. It also suggests the loyalty of sheep following a shepherd.*

 For additional practice using the reading skill or strategy, see Unit 1 Teaching Resources Book, p. 131.

For additional practice to check students' understanding of the selection, see Unit 1 Teaching Resources Book, p. 135.

English Learners

DIFFERENTIATED INSTRUCTION

Advanced Say: As a preacher, Edwards knew how to use sound as well as sense to capture his audience's attention. Call attention to techniques such as alliteration, repetition, parallelism, and connotation, which are effective in oral delivery. Provide examples and ask students to find other effective examples.

Alliteration: In the opening sentence of the selection, Edwards uses alliteration to link *held, hand,* and *hell.*

Repetition: Edwards repeats the word *wrath* a number of times: "fierceness of his *wrath*"; "glowing flames of the *wrath* of God"; "The bow of God's *wrath* is bent."

Parallelism: Edwards repeats patterns in phrases and clauses: "nothing to lay hold of . . .," "nothing to keep off the flames," "nothing of your own . . ."

Connotation: Edwards chooses words to describe hell that make it sound as if it is alive and active: *waiting, gaping, lay hold, swallow, consumed.*

After You Read

Assess

1. Some may be frightened; others may be repelled.

2. (a) All those who have not been "born again" deserve the punishment of hell. (b) He wants the members of the congregation to be aware of their peril.

3. (a) He compares the sinner to a spider about to be thrown into a fire. (b) It underscores the loathsomeness of sin and the peril of the sinner.

4. (a) He says that Christ has opened the door of mercy for his congregation. (b) Humanity is hopeless without an all-powerful God, who offers mercy to sinners who convert.

5. (a) Edwards's message is addressed to each member of the congregation. (b) *A sinner* would have been more impersonal and therefore weaker.

6. Some people would be frightened into a "change of heart." Others might have been repelled by the vision of a God who regards human beings as loathsome insects.

7. They might have contributed to the fierce, uncompromising aspects of Edwards's message.

8. Modern speakers with similar reputations include Garrison Keillor, Nelson Mandela, and Queen Rania of Jordan. Students should note the specific qualities the speaker they chose exhibits.

Progress Check

Can students analyze imagery?

If No → See Unit 1 Teaching Resources Book, p. 130.

100

After You Read

Respond and Think Critically

Respond and Interpret

1. Imagine that you are in the congregation, listening to Edwards's sermon. How might you respond?

2. (a) In the first paragraph, what generalization does Edwards make about all people? (b) Why do you think Edwards makes this statement?

3. (a) To what does Edwards compare the unrepentant sinner in paragraph seven? (b) What is the effect of this comparison?

4. (a) Near the end of the sermon, what does Edwards say Christ has done? (b) How would you describe Edwards's view of the relationship between God and humanity?

Analyze and Evaluate

5. (a) What is the effect of Edwards's repetition of *you*? (b) How would the effect have been different if he had replaced *you* with *a sinner*?

6. What effects—intended and unintended—do you think this sermon might have had on listeners?

Connect

7. **Big idea** **Life in the New World** How might the conditions of colonial life have contributed to the impact of Edwards's message?

8. **Connect to Today** Edwards was known as a powerful, convincing speaker. What public figures have a similar reputation today? Explain.

Literary Element **Imagery**

SAT Skills Practice

1. The author uses the imagery of a bow and arrow in the second full paragraph on page 98 to convey which attribute of God?

   (A) his unerring aim
   (B) his understanding of human activities
   (C) his ability to punish
   (D) his superhuman strength
   (E) his infinite flexibility

2. At the top of page 99, the "slender thread" that the author says sinners hang by suggests their

   (A) frailty
   (B) simplicity
   (C) beauty
   (D) preciousness
   (E) materialism

Review: Archetype

As you learned on page 23, an **archteype** is a character type, a descriptive detail, an image, or a story pattern that recurs frequently in the literature from many cultures and evokes strong psychological and emotional responses.

Partner Activity Discuss the following questions:

1. What aspects of Edwards's description of Hell do you think could be described as archetypal?

2. Why might this archetype have a strong psychological and emotional impact on listeners or readers?

Be prepared to share your answers with the class.

 Literature Online

Selection Resources For Selection Quizzes, eFlashcards, and Reading-Writing Connection activities, go to glencoe.com and enter QuickPass code GLA9800u1.

Literary Element

SAT Skills Practice

1. C is correct because it supports the author's view of an angry God.

2. A is correct because a thread is fragile and easily consumed by fire.

Reading Strategy

1. *Abominable, hateful, venomous,* and *serpent* have negative connotations.

2. The absolute repugnance of unrepentant sinners.

> For additional assessment, see Assessment Resources, pp. 77–78.

Reading Strategy — Examine Connotation

Words may have different associations, or **connotations**. In describing sinners, Edwards uses the word *howl*, which suggests an animal in distress.

1. Identify connotations in this passage: "you are ten thousand times so abominable in his eyes, as the most hateful and venomous serpent is in ours."

2. How do these connotations reinforce Edwards's message?

Vocabulary Practice

Practice with Word Origins Create a word map like the one shown for each vocabulary word below. Use a dictionary for help.

appease   prudence   abominable
abate   abhor

EXAMPLE:

> Definition: a gloomy and pensive state of mind

> Etymology: From Greek *melas*, "black" + *khole*, "bile"

> melancholy

> Sample Sentence: April's melancholy did not fit the month she was named after.

Academic Vocabulary

In this sermon, Edwards gives his parishioners **guidelines** *for avoiding damnation.*

Guidelines is an academic word. A teacher might give **guidelines** for writing essays. To further explore the meaning of this word, answer the following question: If you were asked to give **guidelines** to incoming freshman, what advice would you give?

For more on academic vocabulary, see pages 53–54.

Write with Style

Apply Diction

Assignment Through his use of emotionally charged diction—including vivid sensory details—Edwards attempts to convince his audience to repent and follow God. Write a short essay using strong words and details to make an emotional appeal. Make sure you carefully consider your audience and spell out your call to action.

Get Ideas Think of a subject that is important to you. What emotions do you want your readers to feel and what words will evoke those emotions? Create a word web to explore these connections.

> Language: cities drowning as the glaciers melt and the seas rise

> Issue: dangers of global warming
> Emotion: fear

> Language: dead silence, where birds once sang

Give It Structure Begin with some of the charged language from your diagram to capture your readers' attention. Then state your main idea, or thesis. Follow with sentences that support your thesis. Include more details from your diagram to target your readers' emotions and convince them of your argument or idea. Conclude with a sentence supporting your thesis.

Look at Language Appealing to multiple senses strengthens the emotional influence of your diction. The example about global warming appeals to a reader's sense of sight, hearing, and touch with specific, evocative words. As you revise your essay, make sure you have engaged at least three senses. If you need to, use a thesaurus to find words with the greatest impact.

JONATHAN EDWARDS **101**

After You Read

Assess

Vocabulary

- **appease**—Etymology: Latin *pax*, "peace" Sentence: No one could appease Jake's anger when the umpire said he was out.
- **abate**—Etymology: Latin *battuere*, "to beat" Sentence: We hoped the noise would abate when the construction crew stopped.
- **prudence**—Etymology: Latin *providere*, "to provide for" Sentence: Jenna showed prudence when she decided not to ski.
- **abhor**—Etymology: Latin *horrere*, "to shudder" Sentence: I left the room because I abhor reality tv.
- **abominable**—Etymology: Latin *abominari*, "to abhor" Sentence: A group of students protested the abominable conditions.

Academic Vocabulary

I would advise incoming freshmen to get involved in extracurricular activities.

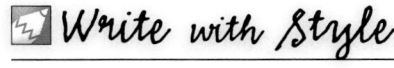

Write with Style

Essays should:

- Use vivid sensory details that appeal to at least three senses.
- Have a clear goal for the piece, pursued throughout the work.
- Use appropriate diction to make an effective emotional appeal.

Scoring Guide	4	3	2	1
Presentation of thesis	thoughtful and comprehensive	comprehensive	limited	minimal
Support of thesis	specific	general	little or none	none
Understanding of complexities	clear	generally	limited	minimal
Language	varied, precise, descriptive	varied, somewhat descriptive	predictable, basic	not varied, limited
Convention errors	few or none	several	many	serious
Emotional appeal	thoughtfully addressed	addressed	may be partially addressed	not addressed

Vocabulary Workshop

Dictionary Use

Focus

Ask: How do you figure out the meaning of an unknown word? *(Students may say they use context clues to figure out the meaning of the word or they look up the word in a dictionary.)*

Teach

Vocabulary

Use a Dictionary Remind students that when looking up a word, they sometimes have to determine its part of speech. Words such as *incense* and *will* have the same spelling as nouns and as verbs. The noun and verb forms each have their own separate main entries in the dictionary. **Ask:** After reading the quote, can you tell what part of speech the word *incensed* belongs to? *(It is a verb being used as an adjective.)* Remind students that most words have several subentries.

 For additional vocabulary practice, see Glencoe Interactive Vocabulary CD-ROM.

Tip

Specialized dictionaries provide in-depth information about words in a particular field. There are dictionaries of biography, place names, slang, historic documents, politics, art, and many other subjects. Ask your librarian to help you find the right dictionary for your research.

Technology

Using an online dictionary, you simply enter a search word to find its definition. Online dictionaries also offer features such as illustrations, word games, language tips, and fun facts.

Vocabulary For more vocabulary practice, go to glencoe.com and enter QuickPass code GLA9800u1.

Vocabulary Workshop

Dictionary Use

Literature Connection In reading literature, history, and politics, you will find a dictionary invaluable. The passage below contains several words not common today.

> "... all that preserves them every moment is the mere arbitrary will, and uncovenanted, unobliged forbearance of an incensed God."
>
> —Jonathan Edwards, from "Sinners in the Hands of an Angry God"

What does *incensed* mean, for example? Isn't that something you burn?

Looking for a Word Guide words at the top of each dictionary page tell you the first and last words listed on the page to help you locate the word you need alphabetically. As you can see from the excerpt below, *incense* means "to make someone angry," so *incensed* means "angered."

Main Entry Each word in a dictionary has a main entry. Sometimes a word appears to have more than one main entry. *Incense* appears twice in the excerpt below. The small raised numbers indicate that it is two separate words with different meanings. The word **incense**[1] is something you burn; **incense**[2] is the word used in the quotation above.

Subentries Each main entry often includes different related meanings of the same word. Below, **incense**[1] has three subentries.

Additional Word Information In addition to a word's meaning or meanings, dictionary entries can show you how it is divided into syllables, how it is pronounced, what part of speech it is, its etymology (or origin and history), and how the word is correctly used.

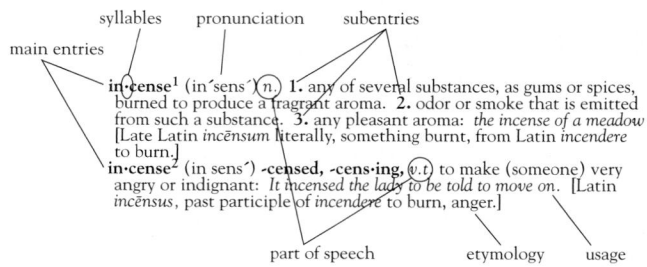

Exercise Use the excerpt above to answer the following questions.

1. How are the verb and noun forms of *incense* pronounced differently?
2. Compare and contrast the etymologies of **incense**[1] and **incense**[2].
3. What synonym for *incensed* might Edwards have used in the passage above? Why do you suppose he chose to use *incensed*?

Vocabulary Practice

Homonyms Students may confuse the words *homonyms*, *homophones*, and *homographs*. Remind students that *homonyms* are words with the same spelling and pronunciation but different meanings and different main entries in the dictionary. *Homophones* are words with the same pronunciation but different meanings. *Homographs* are words that are spelled the same but have different meanings.

Have students practice using the dictionary by looking up these homonyms: *bear, base, grate, lay, root.* Then have students practice using the different meanings of these words in conversation.

THE ROAD TO INDEPENDENCE

Spirit of '76, 1891. Archibald M. Willard. Lithograph. 36 x 50 in. Private collection.

 View the Art How do you think the artist intended the three drum-and-fife players in this painting to illustrate the spirit of '76? ★

"These are the times that try men's souls." **1**

—Thomas Paine, *The Crisis*, No. 1

103

Analyze and Extend

Reading Strategy **1**

Evaluate Direct students to read the quotation. **Ask:** How does the painting relate to the quotation? *(The painting depicts men marching to war; a time of war is "trying.")*

View the Art ★

Answer: *The drummer in the middle shows courage and determination; one of the men is old and one is wounded, yet they carry on.*

This lithograph is based on the painting originally known as Yankee Doodle, which was created by the Ohio artist Archibald M. Willard (1836–1918).

 For additional support for English Learners, see Unit 1 Teaching Resources Book, p. 138.

Approaching Level
DIFFERENTIATED INSTRUCTION

Emerging Read the quotation from *The Crisis* aloud to students. Explain that the word *try* has two meanings: "to test" and "to attempt." **Ask:** What does Paine mean by the word *try*? How does his choice of this word convey his overall meaning? *(He means that war will test people's character. The word shows Paine's belief that the American colonists' struggle for independence will be difficult.)*

English Learners
DIFFERENTIATED INSTRUCTION

Intermediate Explain that the authors in this part played an important role in the struggle for American independence. Thomas Paine wanted to inspire people to action. Discuss the different meanings of the word *soul,* including its meaning in Paine's quote. *(character or inner self)*

103

Bellringer Options

**Selection Focus
Transparency 10**

**Daily Language Practice
Transparency 12**

Or **write** the Benjamin Franklin quotation on the board.

Ask: What are some of your favorite sayings or "words to live by"? Have students discuss their favorite sayings. Have students restate the sayings in their own words and explain why they like the sayings.

Before You Read
from *The Autobiography of Benjamin Franklin* and from *Poor Richard's Almanack*

Meet **Benjamin Franklin**
(1706–1790)

I magine a senator who invented the Internet and a new kind of electric guitar, spoke many languages, wrote poetry, started a successful corporation, founded a college, and helped write some of the world's most important political documents. If you can imagine such a person today, then you are beginning to understand just how remarkable Benjamin Franklin was in his time.

> "*Dost though love life? Then do not squander time; for that's the stuff life is made of.*"
>
> —Benjamin Franklin
> from *Poor Richard's Almanack*

Printer and Scientist Franklin was born into a poor Boston family, the tenth of seventeen children. His formal education ended when he was only ten. By the age of twelve, he was an apprentice in his brother James's print shop, and over the next five years he mastered this trade, which eventually gave him financial security. By the time Franklin was twenty-six, he was operating his own printing firm in Philadelphia and was writing and publishing *Poor Richard's Almanack*, one of the most popular and influential works of its time.

In middle age, Franklin became more involved in civic affairs and scientific research. He helped to found both the first public library in America and the Academy of Philadelphia, which became the University of Pennsylvania. In 1746 and 1747, Franklin's groundbreaking investigations of electrical phenomena brought him international fame. He also invented bifocal glasses, the Franklin stove, daylight saving time, and the lightning rod.

Diplomat and Revolutionary As a representative of the Pennsylvania Assembly, Franklin spent much of the period from 1757 to 1775 in London. He also acted as an agent for the colonies and argued against the hated Stamp Act. While Franklin had always opposed this tax, he did not, at first, support American independence. Instead, Franklin imagined a British empire made up of many self-governing nations. By 1775, however, his hopes for reconciliation had vanished. He left Britain for Philadelphia to prepare for the coming war. Within days, Franklin was made a delegate to the Continental Congress for which he helped draft the Declaration of Independence.

Franklin's greatest contribution to the Revolution took place from 1776 to 1785, during his diplomatic mission to France. Franklin, whose charm and wit were famous, became a celebrity almost immediately. The American cause was soon adopted by the French government, which pledged funds and more than 40,000 troops. French support, secured by Franklin's diplomacy, was vital in achieving American independence.

 Literature Online

Author Search For more about Benjamin Franklin, go to glencoe.com and enter QuickPass code GLA9800u1.

Literary Elements
- Autobiography
  (SE pp. 105, 106, 108, 109)

from **The Autobiography of Benjamin Franklin**

Listening/Speaking/ Viewing Skills
- Analyze Art (SE p. 107)

Reading Skills
- Analyze Voice (SE pp. 105, 106, 108, 109)
- Question (TE p. 106)
- Visualize (TE p. 107)

Vocabulary Skills
- Word Parts (SE p. 109)
- Nouns (TE p. 105)

Writing Skills/Grammar
- Conjunctions (TE p. 108)

Literature and Reading Preview

Connect to the Autobiography

When you travel, how does the way you are treated by the people you meet affect your impression of that town, city, or country? Write a journal entry in which you discuss these questions. If you can, relate your response to a specific experience.

Build Background

The passage from Franklin's autobiography begins with his arrival in Philadelphia in the 1720s. Franklin published *Poor Richard's Almanack* in Philadelphia every year for the 25 years between 1733 and 1758. Almanacs were one of the earliest types of reading material to be published and were the forerunners of today's magazines. Colonial almanacs provided a wide variety of material, including puzzles, both serious and humorous articles, and common-sense aphorisms, or witty sayings, of the type that made Franklin famous.

Set Purposes for Reading

Big Idea The Road to Independence

As you read these two excerpts, ask yourself, What role did Franklin play in the colonists' struggle for independence?

Literary Element Autobiography

An **autobiography** is a nonfiction narrative in which the author tells the story of his or her own life. As you read Franklin's autobiography, ask yourself, How did his experience in Philadelphia help shape him as a person?

Reading Strategy Analyze Voice

Voice is the distinctive use of language that conveys the author's or narrator's personality. Word choice, tone, and sentence structure contribute to voice.

Tip: Take Notes In a chart, describe the effect of Franklin's word choice, tone, and sentence structure on voice.

Example	Effect
"ambulatory quack doctor"	vivid, humorous observation

Learning Objectives

For pages 104–111

In studying these texts, you will focus on the following objectives:

Literary Study:
Analyzing autobiography.
Analyzing aphorism.

Reading:
Analyzing voice.
Connecting to personal experience.

Writing:
Writing a journal entry.
Writing an article.

Vocabulary

indentured (in den´ chərd) *adj.* bound to serve for a time; p. 106 *The indentured servant completed a six-year term.*

ambulatory (am´ byə lə tôr´ ē) *adj.* moving from place to place; p. 106 *The ambulatory news correspondent traveled all over Europe.*

ingenious (in jēn´ yəs) *adj.* creative; inventive; p. 106 *Ani used an ingenious marketing strategy.*

infidel (in´ fə del´) *n.* an unbeliever; p. 106 *Those who did not regularly attend church were considered infidels.*

mortification (môr´ tə fi kā´ shən) *n.* feeling of shame or embarrassment; p. 107 *My speech was pure mortification.*

Before You Read

Focus

Summary

Although recovering from a fever, Benjamin Franklin sets out to walk 50 miles to Burlington, New Jersey, and then travel by boat to Philadelphia. Along the way he befriends the roguish innkeeper Dr. Brown. Despite his lack of funds and makeshift travel arrangements, Franklin finally arrives in Philadelphia, where he obtains something to eat and falls asleep at a Quaker meetinghouse.

 For summaries in languages other than English, see Unit 1 Teaching Resources Book, pp. 139–144.

Vocabulary

Nouns Elicit that nouns can name people, places, objects, or feelings and ideas. **Ask:** Which vocabulary word names a feeling? *(mortification)* Tell students that nouns that name feelings and ideas often include the suffix *-tion*, which creates a noun from a verb. The verb in this case is *mortify.* **Ask:** Based on the meaning of *mortification*, what does *mortify* mean? *(Mortify means "to cause a feeling of shame, humiliation, or embarrassment.")*

English Learners

 DIFFERENTIATED INSTRUCTION

Advanced Students may benefit from further explanation of the autobiography genre. Write the word *autobiography* on the board and underline the parts *auto, bio,* and *graph.* Clarify the meaning of each word part: *auto* means "self," *bio* means "life," and *graph* means "write." In an autobiography, the author writes about his or her own life. Explain that autobiography is usually written in the first-person point of view, using the pronouns *I, me,* or *myself.* This point of view allows readers to step inside the writer's experience but limits what readers learn to what the narrator chooses to share. As students read, have them identify places where they notice Franklin's use of first-person point of view.

Teach

from The Autobiography of Benjamin Franklin

Benjamin Franklin

East Prospective View of Philadelphia, published 1778. Lithograph.

In the evening I found myself very feverish and went to bed; but having read some where that cold water drunk plentifully was good for fever, I followed the prescription and sweat plentifully most of the night. My fever left me, and in the morning, crossing the ferry, I proceeded on my journey on foot, having fifty miles to go to Burlington,[1] where I was told I should find boats that would carry me the rest of the way to Philadelphia.

It rained very hard all the day; I was thoroughly soaked, and by noon a good deal tired; so I stopped at a poor inn, where I stayed all night, beginning now to wish I had never left home. I made so miserable a figure, too, that I found, by the questions asked me, I was suspected to be some runaway **indentured** servant and in danger of being taken up on that suspicion. However, I proceeded next day and got in the evening to an inn within eight or ten miles of Burlington, kept by one Dr. Brown. He entered into conversation with me while I took some refreshment, and finding I had read a little, became very obliging and friendly. Our acquaintance continued all the rest of his life. He had been, I imagine, an **ambulatory** quack doctor, for there was no town in England nor any country in Europe of which he could not give a very particular account. He had some letters,[2] and was **ingenious,** but he was an **infidel,** and wickedly undertook, some years after, to turn the Bible into doggerel[3] verse,

---

1. Burlington, New Jersey, is not far from Philadelphia, on the opposite side of the Delaware River.
2. Here, *letters* means "education or knowledge, especially of literature."
3. English poet Charles Cotton (1630–1687) wrote a *doggerel* version, or parody, of Virgil's epic poem the *Aeneid*.

1 Autobiography *What does Franklin reveal about himself in this passage?*

Vocabulary

indentured (in den´ chərd) *adj.* bound by contract to serve someone for a time

2 Analyze Voice *What do Franklin's word choice and tone suggest about his attitude toward his new friend?*

Vocabulary

ambulatory (am´ byə lə tôr´ ē) *adj.* moving from place to place

ingenious (in jēn´ yəs) *adj.* exhibiting creative ability; inventive

infidel (in´ fə del´) *n.* an unbeliever

106 UNIT 1 EARLY AMERICA

Reading Practice

Benjamin Franklin, Printer, c. 1928. John Ward Dunsmore. Oil on canvas, 28 x 36 in. The New York Historical Society, New York.

<u>View the Art</u> As a colonial tradesman, Benjamin Franklin printed everything from translations of Cicero to hymnals to paper currency. What might Franklin have been discussing with the other people in this scene?

as Cotton had formerly done with Virgil. By this means he set many facts in a ridiculous light, and might have done mischief with weak minds if his work had been published; but it never was.

3 At his house I lay that night, and arrived the next morning at Burlington, but had the **mortification** to find that the regular boats were gone a little before, and no other expected to go before Tuesday, this being Saturday. Wherefore I returned to an old woman in the town, of whom I had bought some gingerbread to eat on the water, and asked her advice. She proposed to

lodge me till a passage by some other boat occurred. I accepted her offer, being much fatigued by traveling on foot. Understanding I was a printer, she would have had me remain in that town and follow my business, being ignorant what stock was necessary to begin with. She was very hospitable, gave me a dinner of oxcheek with great good-will, accepting only of a pot of ale in return; and I thought myself fixed till Tuesday should come. However, walking in the evening by the side of the river, a boat came by, which I found was going toward Philadelphia with several people in her. They took me in, and as there was no wind we rowed all the way; and

The Road to Independence *How does this description reveal the spirit of people who will fight for independence?* **4**

BENJAMIN FRANKLIN **107**

Teach

Teach

Reading Strategy 1

Analyze Voice Answer:
He is good-natured and willing to poke fun at himself.

Literary Element 2

Autobiography Answer: *He is being ironic.*

Some students find the concept of irony difficult to grasp. Irony is a contrast or discrepancy between appearance and reality. The "house" Franklin "slept in" was really a Quaker meetinghouse where he fell asleep. Franklin uses irony as a form of humor.

Cultural History

Quakers George Fox founded the Society of Friends in England. Committed to peace and simple living, the sect spread to other countries, including the United States.

> To check students' understanding of the selection, see Unit 1 Teaching Resources Book, p. 150.

108

---

about midnight, not having yet seen the city, some of the company were confident we must have passed it and would row no further; the others knew not where we were, so we put toward the shore, got into a creek, landed near an old fence, with the rails of which we made a fire, the night being cold, in October, and there we remained till daylight. Then one of the company knew the place to be Cooper's Creek, a little above Philadelphia, which we saw as soon as we got out of the creek, and arrived there about eight or nine o'clock on the Sunday morning and landed at Market Street wharf.

I have been the more particular in this description of my journey, and shall be so of my first entry into that city, that you may in your mind compare such unlikely beginnings with the figure I have since made there. I was in my working dress, my best clothes coming round by sea. I was dirty, from my being so long in the boat. My pockets were stuffed out with shirts and stockings, and I knew no one nor where to look for lodging. Fatigued with walking, rowing, and the want of sleep, I was very hungry; and my whole stock of cash consisted in a single dollar, and about a shilling[4] in copper coin, which I gave to the boatmen for my passage. At first they refused it, on account of my having rowed; but I insisted on their taking it. Man is sometimes more generous when he has little money than when he has plenty; perhaps to prevent his being thought to have but little.

I walked toward the top of the street, gazing about till near Market Street, when I met a boy with bread. I had often made a meal of dry bread, and inquiring where he had bought it, I went immediately to the baker's he directed me to. I asked for biscuits, meaning such as we had at Boston; that sort, it seems, was not made at Philadelphia. I then asked for a threepenny loaf and was told they had none. Not knowing the different prices nor the names of the different sorts of bread,

I told him to give me threepenny worth of any sort. He gave me accordingly three great puffy rolls. I was surprised at the quantity, but took it, and having no room in my pockets, walked off with a roll under each arm and eating the other. Thus I went up Market Street as far as Fourth Street, passing by the door of Mr. Read, my future wife's father; when she, standing at the door, saw me, and thought I made, as I certainly did, a most awkward, ridiculous appearance. Then I turned and went down Chestnut Street and part of Walnut Street, eating my roll all the way; and coming round found myself again at Market Street wharf, near the boat I came in, to which I went for a draught[5] of the river water; and being filled with one of my rolls, gave the other two to a woman and her child that came down the river in the boat with us and were waiting to go further.

Thus refreshed I walked again up the street, which by this time had many clean-dressed people in it, who were all walking the same way. I joined them, and thereby was led into the great meeting-house of the Quakers,[6] near the market. I sat down among them, and after looking round a while and hearing nothing said,[7] being very drowsy through labor and want of rest the preceding night, I fell fast asleep and continued so till the meeting broke up, when some one was kind enough to rouse me. This, therefore, was the first house I was in, or slept in, in Philadelphia. ❧

---

4. A *shilling* is a British coin equal to one-twentieth of a pound.

5. Here, *draught* means "a gulp" or "a swallow."
6. *Quakers* are members of the Society of Friends, a Christian religious group founded in the seventeenth century.
7. Quaker religious meetings often include long periods of silence.

Analyze Voice *What does Franklin reveal about his personality with this passage?* **1**

Autobiography *Why might have Franklin chosen to include this detail in his autobiography?* **2**

Grammar Practice

 Conjunctions Remind students that conjunctions join sentence elements and that they also show relationships between the elements. Coordinating conjunctions join words and word groups that have equal grammatical weight (salt *and* pepper); subordinating conjunctions join clauses in a way that makes one clause grammatically dependent on the other (*although* I had taken a nap, I was tired).

Have students work in small groups to identify sentences on this page that contain coordinating and subordinating conjunctions, and then list the conjunctions. Have groups identify whether conjunctions are coordinating or subordinating. (*shirts <u>and</u> stockings; <u>but</u> took it*)

After You Read

Respond and Think Critically

Respond and Interpret

1. How would you have felt if, like Franklin, you arrived in an unfamiliar city with little money, no job, and no place to live?

2. (a)What people does Franklin meet before he takes the boat to Philadelphia? (b)What do you learn about Franklin from these encounters?

3. (a)Why do the boatmen at first refuse to accept money from Franklin? (b)Why do you think he offers to pay?

4. (a)What does Franklin do during the Quakers' meeting? (b)What do you think the last sentence of this selection reveals about Franklin?

Analyze and Evaluate

5. (a)How does an autobiography differ from a biography? (b)How should this difference affect one's evaluation of Franklin's autobiography?

6. (a)Why do you think Franklin emphasizes self-reliance? (b)Do you think self-reliance is as important today as it was in Franklin's time?

Connect

7. **Big Idea** The Road to Independence How might the colonists' reaction to Franklin's arrival indicate a desire for independence?

8. **Connect to the Author** What one word might you use to describe Benjamin Franklin? Explain, using details from what you have read.

Literary Element Autobiography

An **autobiography** is the story an author writes about his or her own life.

1. Why do you think Franklin thought it was important to write his autobiography? Explain.

2. Do you think that Franklin presented himself as he really was or from a biased perspective? Support your response with details from the selection.

Reading Strategy Analyze Voice

Voice is determined by sentence structure, tone, and word choice.

1. According to your notes, what are some of the features of Franklin's voice?

2. Judging by Franklin's literary voice, what sort of personality do you imagine he possessed?

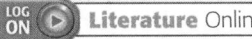 **Literature** Online

Selection Resources For Selection Quizzes, eFlashcards, and Reading-Writing Connection activities, go to glencoe.com and enter QuickPass code GLA9800u1.

Vocabulary Practice

Practice with Word Parts Use a dictionary to find the meaning of each vocabulary word's root and any prefixes or suffixes it has. Record the meanings in a diagram like the one shown. Then write a sentence using the word correctly.

indentured	ingenious	mortification
ambulatory	infidel	

EXAMPLE:

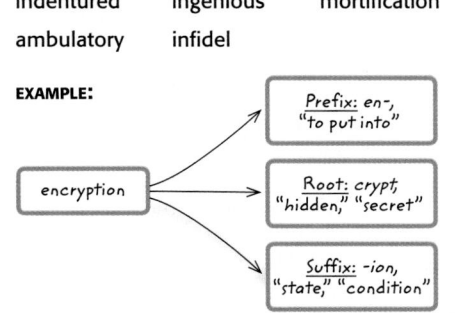

encryption →
- Prefix: en-, "to put into"
- Root: crypt, "hidden," "secret"
- Suffix: -ion, "state," "condition"

After You Read

Assess

1. Students may say "frightened."

2. (a) Dr. Brown and an old woman (b) He is observant, conversational, and friendly.

3. (a) He helped to row the boat. (b) He is generous and wants to show others he is not poor.

4. (a) Falls asleep (b) His wit in his pun on the word *house*

5. (a) An autobiography is the life of its writer; a biography is of someone other than its writer (b) Franklin might want readers to think well of him.

6. (a) It helped him succeed. (b) Answers will vary.

7. They are friendly, are eager to help, and have faced the challenge of surviving in a new place.

8. Students may say *resourceful*, given Franklin's ability to find food, shelter, and friendship.

Literary Element

1. Franklin was aware that his life was part of an important historical period.

2. He seems candid and true to life, but there may have some bias, such as his description of himself.

Progress Check

Can students analyze an autobiography?

If No → See Unit 1 Teaching Resources Book, p. 145.

Reading Strategy

1. Conversational, humorous; varied word choice and sentence structure.

2. Congenial and witty

Vocabulary

indentured: root *endenter*, "to indent a document"; suffix *-ed*, "past participle"; The indentured servant was eager to earn his freedom.

ingenious: root *ingenium*, "natural capacity"; suffix *-ous*, "having"; The ingenious engineer came up with an elegant solution.

mortification: root *mortificare*, "deaden"; suffix *-ion*, "process of"; The embarrassed actor's facial expression was full of mortification.

ambulatory: root *ambulare*, "to walk"; suffix *-ory*, "relating to"; After a week, the bedridden patient became ambulatory.

infidel: prefix *in-*, "not"; root *fid-*, "faith"; The infidel did not celebrate religious holidays.

Summary

In a group of aphorisms excerpted from *Poor Richard's Almanack*, Benjamin Franklin offers observations about life.

Teach

Reading Strategy 1

Connect **Write** on the board: "The worst wheel of the cart makes the most noise." Have students give an example that shows what this means.

(ENGLISH LEARNERS) Explain that in Franklin's time, people moved heavy things by using carts pulled by horses. Roads were poor, so wheels wore out quickly.

Reading Strategy 2

Connect **Answer:** *Students should describe times when they or others had to work very hard to achieve something.*

Literary Element Aphorism

An **aphorism** is a short, pointed statement that expresses a wise or clever observation about human experience. As you read, ask yourself, Which aphorisms are my most and least favorite, and why?

Reading Strategy Connect

Connecting means linking what you read to events in your own life. As you read, connect Franklin's aphorisms to your own experiences. Then make a list of the aphorisms that you have found to be true.

from Poor Richard's Almanack

Benjamin Franklin

If you would keep your secret from an
   enemy, tell it not to a friend.
1 The worst wheel of the cart makes the
   most noise.
He that cannot obey, cannot command.
No gains without pains.
'Tis easier to prevent bad habits than to
   break them.
A rolling stone gathers no moss.
Today is yesterday's pupil.
Most fools think they are only ignorant.[1]
An empty bag cannot stand upright.
Well done is better than well said.
What you would seem to be, be really.

Honesty is the best policy.
Dost thou love life? Then do not squander
   time; for that's the stuff life is made of.
Beware of little expenses, a small leak will
   sink a great ship.
A penny saved is a penny earned.
Don't count your chickens before they are
   hatched.
Buy what thou hast no need of; and e'er
   long thou shalt sell thy necessaries.
Not to oversee workmen, is to leave them
   your purse open.
Fish and visitors smell in three days.
Quarrels never could last long, if on one
   side only lay the wrong.
Love thy neighbor; yet don't pull down your
   hedge.

---

1. *Ignorant* means "uneducated" or "uninformed."

2 Connect *What is a real-life example of this aphorism?*

Selection Skills

Literary Elements
- Aphorism (SE pp. 110, 111)

→ *from* Poor Richard's Almanack ←

Writing Skills/Grammar
- Write an Article (SE p. 111)

Reading Skills
- Connect (SE pp. 110, 111)

After You Read

Respond and Think Critically

Respond and Interpret

1. Which of the aphorisms from *Poor Richard's Almanack* were your favorites? Explain.

2. (a)According to Franklin, how can a secret be kept from an enemy? (b)Describe in your own words the advice given in the second aphorism.

3. (a)What does Franklin say will sink a great ship? (b)What do you think he means by this aphorism?

4. (a)In the final aphorism, what does Franklin say about "thy neighbor"? (b)What might he mean by "don't pull down your hedge"?

Analyze and Evaluate

5. Which of Franklin's aphorisms do you think would be most relevant in today's society?

6. Would any of these aphorisms be irrelevant in today's society? Explain.

Connect

7. **Big Idea** The Struggle for Independence Which aphorisms would have been most relevant to the struggle for independence? Explain.

8. **Connect to Today** How popular do aphorisms seem to be today? Why do you think that is?

Literary Element Aphorism

Franklin's **aphorisms** reflect his clever use of language. For example, the saying "An empty bag cannot stand upright" presents a humorous metaphor for a person who lacks substance or conviction.

1. Explain how Franklin's use of language contributes to the impact of one of his aphorisms.

2. Using modern language and references to contemporary life, reword one of Franklin's aphorisms.

Reading Strategy Connect

You can recall ideas from a reading selection better by **connecting** them to your own life. What connections can you make between your life and *Poor Richard's Almanack?*

Writing

Write an Article Today we are more likely to read advice columns in the newspaper than aphorisms. Select a letter written to an advice columnist and write a response. Include an original aphorism that sums up your advice to the letter writer.

Academic Vocabulary

In his aphorisms, Franklin places an **emphasis** on prudence and hard work.

Emphasis is an academic word. A coach might put **emphasis** on the importance of regular training. To study this word further, fill out the graphic organizer below.

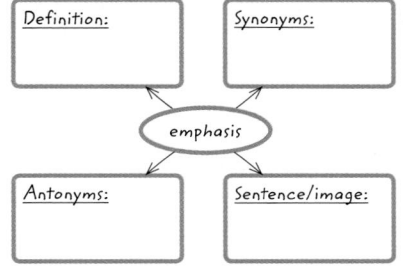

For more on academic vocabulary, see pages 53–54.

 Literature Online

Selection Resources For Selection Quizzes, eFlashcards, and Reading-Writing Connection activities, go to glencoe.com and enter QuickPass code GLA9800u1.

BENJAMIN FRANKLIN **111**

After You Read

Assess

1. Students' answers will vary.
2. (a) A secret can be kept by not telling anyone, even a friend. (b) People who shout the loudest usually have the least worthwhile things to say.
3. (a) A small leak (b) He means that little expenses can ruin a person over time.
4. (a) You should love him or her. (b) He means that it is good to have some privacy and some space to call your own.
5. Students' answers will vary.
6. Students' answers will vary, but most students should agree that each aphorism is at least somewhat relevant today.
7. "Fish and visitors smell in three days"; "No gains without pains." Franklin could have intended the first as a way of humorously asserting that the British troops should leave the colonies. The second could mean that going to war is difficult but that the rewards will be great.
8. Students should provide examples to support their positions.

For additional assessment, see Assessment Resources, pp. 81–82.

Literary Element

Students' answers will vary.

Writing

Help students find samples of advice columns in the newspaper or on an Internet blog, or have them create a question of their own for their column. Students' advice columns should include an aphorism and be well-organized and insightful.

Progress Check

Can students analyze an aphorism?

If No → See Unit 1 Teaching Resources Book, p. 158.

Reading Strategy

Students' connections should be relevant to the reading selection.

Academic Vocabulary

emphasis

Definition: a stress on the importance of something

Synonyms: stress, accent, importance

Antonyms: negativity, unimportance

Sentence/image: The emphasis of the course is learning to speak the language.

111

Focus

Learning Objectives

For pages 112–113

In studying this text, you will focus on the following objectives:

Literary Study:
Analyzing literary periods. Evaluating historical influences.

Bellringer Options

**Daily Language Practice
Transparency 13**

Or **ask:** Why is the ability to persuade others to adopt a course of action important in a democracy?

Teach

View the Art ★

Answer: *Henry seems to be delivering an impassioned call to action, as he does in his famous speech.*

Clyde DeLand was an American painter and illustrator of the late 1800s and early 1900s.

The Rhetoric of Revolution

THAT THE UNITED STATES WON independence from British colonial rule is as much a result of effective writers and powerful speakers as of General Washington and his brave army. Patrick Henry, Thomas Paine, and Thomas Jefferson were all highly skilled in rhetoric, the art of persuasion. Persuasion is often based on three types of appeal:

- appeal to reason, logic, and evidence
- appeal to emotions, such as fear, pride, or hate
- ethical appeal, or persuasion based on what we ourselves, moral philosophers, or the majority of people in our culture think is right

Rhetorical Devices

No matter what kinds of appeals speakers and writers focus on, they rely on a number of **rhetorical devices.** For example, making an ethical and emotional appeal in his pamphlet *The Crisis, No. 1,* Thomas Paine uses imagery, a type of figurative language, to illustrate his understanding of patriotism.

"The summer soldier and the sunshine patriot will, in this crisis, shrink from the service of his country; but he that stands it now, deserves the love and thanks of man and woman."

Another common device is **hyperbole,** or exaggeration. In the following quotation, Thomas Paine uses hyperbole to enhance an emotional appeal.

"The heart that feels not now is dead . . ."

Many speakers use **rhetorical questions,** or questions that emphasize the obvious answer to what is asked. Patrick Henry's "Speech to the Second Virginia Convention" contains more than twenty rhetorical questions. This technique builds to an emotional climax and makes a strong impression on the listeners.

Patrick Henry's Famous Speech, 1915. Clyde DeLand. Oil on canvas.

View the Art Patrick Henry's famous speech helped convince a majority of his fellow delegates at the Second Virginia Convention to support military resistance against Britain. Does this painting reflect the tone of that speech? Explain. ★

Listening and Speaking Practice

PARTNERS Faulty Reasoning Explain that people seeking to persuade often use faulty reasoning. Discuss these two common types:

- **Circular reasoning** is an argument that moves in a circle, assuming what it claims to prove, as in "Pablo Picasso was a genius because his paintings show extraordinary talent."

- **Bandwagon reasoning** appeals to the actions or thoughts of a group, as in "You should let me go to the party because all of the other kids' parents are letting them go."

Have students work in pairs to develop their own examples of faulty reasoning. They should develop arguments for or against independence from Britain and then present these to another team that must identify the flaw in their thinking.

"Not only do I want a cracker—we all want a cracker!"

 Analyze Political Cartoons Like many political cartoons, this one has a serious message. What does it say about a speaker's ability to sway audiences?

"They tell us, sir, that we are weak; unable to cope with so formidable an adversary. But when shall we be stronger? Will it be the next week, or the next year? Will it be when we are totally disarmed, and when a British guard shall be stationed in every house?"

In the following passage, Patrick Henry uses the rhetorical device **parallelism** for emphasis. Parallelism is the use of a series of words, phrases, or sentences that have similar grammatical form. Henry's series reaches a powerful climax with a reference to the English king. The appeal is to reason and emotion.

"Our petitions have been slighted; our remonstrances have produced additional violence and insult; our supplications have been disregarded; and we have been spurned, with contempt, from the foot of the throne."

Thomas Jefferson also uses parallelism in the Declaration of Independence to list the colonial grievances against King George III. Additionally, in the following excerpt, Jefferson uses another powerful rhetorical device, **connotative language,** to make an emotional and ethical appeal.

"He has plundered our seas, ravaged our coasts, burned our towns, and destroyed the lives of our people."

Connotations are the suggested or implied meanings associated with a word. Here, Jefferson uses verbs with strong negative connotations. Earlier in the Declaration, Jefferson refers to "swarms of officers" sent to "harass our people." How different the statement would have been had he written, "A lot of soldiers were sent to bother us"!

While Thomas Paine, Patrick Henry, and Thomas Jefferson did not cause the American Revolution with their rhetoric, they did rally the colonists to their side. Paine's pamphlet *Common Sense* sold 100,000 copies in three months. Before its publication, Benjamin Franklin observed that he had heard no American speaking in favor of independence. Six months after *Common Sense* was published in Philadelphia, the Declaration of Independence was signed there. **1**

LOG ON ▶ **Literature** Online

Literature and Reading For more about the rhetoric of revolution, go to glencoe.com and enter QuickPass code GLA9800u1.

Respond and Think Critically

1. What answers is Patrick Henry expecting to his rhetorical questions quoted above? Explain.

2. What connotation is suggested by Thomas Jefferson's phrase "swarms of officers"?

3. Which type of persuasive appeal—appeal to reason, appeal to emotion, or appeal based on ethics—most influences your political views? Explain.

LITERARY HISTORY **113**

Approaching Level

DIFFERENTIATED INSTRUCTION

Emerging Explain to students that they may find text features such as boldface type and colored type helpful when they are answering questions about a selection. Boldface type can help them quickly locate important terms. For example, if students cannot immediately answer question 1, they can find the term *rhetorical questions* in bold type and reread the text that follows.

AAVE Have approaching-level students who are users of African American vernacular English read the quotations in blue italic type and write down the uses of the verbs *to be* and *to have* to practice these constructions that may cause difficulty.

Before You Read

Focus

Bellringer Options

Selection Focus
Transparency 11

Daily Language Practice
Transparency 14

Or read aloud the Patrick Henry quotation displayed on this page. Have students discuss in small groups what freedoms they enjoy every day and what life might be like without those freedoms.

APPROACHING If students have difficulty thinking of examples of freedom, have them work together to list public places they can enter freely. *(parks, libraries, stores)* Then have students list the things they are free to do in each of these places. *(walk, run, read, borrow, browse, buy)*

Before You Read
Speech to the Second Virginia Convention

Meet **Patrick Henry**
(1736–1799)

On March 23, 1775, Patrick Henry stood before fellow delegates at the Second Virginia Convention and thundered his famous challenge, "Give me liberty, or give me death!" Thomas Marshall, a delegate to the convention, recalled that Henry's speech was "one of the most bold, vehement, and animated pieces of eloquence that had ever been delivered."

Henry was born in Hanover County, Virginia. After a series of unsuccessful ventures as a storekeeper and farmer, he began to study law. Henry was admitted to the bar in 1760 and within several years began to prosper. In 1765, at the age of twenty-nine, he became a member of the House of Burgesses, the representative assembly in colonial Virginia. That same year, England passed the Stamp Act, an extremely unpopular tax. When Henry attacked the act in a fiery speech in the House of Burgesses, several members interrupted him with accusations of treason. Henry replied, "If this be treason, make the most of it."

> "I know not what course others may take; but as for me, give me liberty, or give me death."
>
> —Patrick Henry

Governor and Legislator In 1776, as the battles of the Revolution raged around them, the citizens of Virginia elected Henry to be the first governor of the commonwealth under its new constitution. He served three consecutive one-year terms as governor from 1776 through 1778. As wartime governor, Henry vigorously supported General George Washington and his army.

High Standards In 1787, Henry turned down an offer to attend the Philadelphia Constitutional Convention. Although he had toiled as a lawyer, legislator, and governor to uphold inalienable rights, Henry initially opposed the ratification of the U.S. Constitution. What seemed a contradiction, even an insult, to his critics was really Henry's unwillingness to compromise his high ethical standards. Henry championed American independence, but he believed that the Constitution as written did not sufficiently secure the rights of states or those of individuals. Henry also feared that under the Constitution, Spain might retain control of the Mississippi River and its lucrative commerce routes.

The Constitution was published in 1787, but the nation remained divided in two camps. The Federalists supported the Constitution, and the Anti-Federalists did not. Henry was the nation's leading Anti-Federalist, and he and his supporters lobbied for amendments. The Constitution was ratified in Virginia in 1788 by the narrow margin of 89 to 79. The arguments that Henry and his faction of Anti-Federalists made during the debate eventually led to the Bill of Rights. Henry refused several high positions in the new federal government due to his ailing health and family responsibilities. He died at the age of 63 and was interred at Red Hill, his Virginia home.

 Literature Online

Author Search For more about Patrick Henry, go to glencoe.com and enter QuickPass code GLA9800u1.

Selection Skills

Literary Elements
- Rhetorical Question (SE pp. 115, 117–119)

Speech to the Second Virginia Convention

Reading Skills
- Analyze Figures of Speech (SE pp. 115, 117–119)
- Evaluate Persuasive Writing (TE p. 118)

Vocabulary Skills
- Antonyms (SE p. 119)
- Intensity (TE p. 115)

Listening/Speaking/Viewing Skills
- Reasoning and Propositions (TE p. 116)

Writing Skills/Grammar
- Write a Speech (SE p. 119)

Literature and Reading Preview

Connect to the Speech

What does the phrase "give me liberty, or give me death" mean to you? Do you find it persuasive? Discuss these questions in a small group.

Build Background

The British parliament passed a series of taxes on its colonies. American colonists protested these taxes, and thousands of British troops were sent to Boston to preserve order. Patrick Henry was one of the leaders of the growing opposition to British rule. The speech you are about to read would firmly establish Henry's reputation as a forceful proponent of liberty.

Set Purposes for Reading

Big Idea The Road to Independence

As you read this speech, ask yourself, What does Henry imply about the American colonists' disagreement regarding independence from British rule?

Literary Element Rhetorical Question

A **rhetorical question** is one to which no answer is expected. It is used to emphasize the obvious answer to what is asked. As you read, ask yourself, How does Henry use rhetorical questions? What effect do they have?

Reading Strategy Analyze Figures of Speech

Figurative language is used for descriptive effect, in order to convey ideas or emotions. Figurative expressions are not literally true but express some truth beyond the literal level. A **figure of speech** is a specific device or kind of figurative language, such as allusion, assonance, hyperbole, metaphor, metonymy, personification, simile, or symbol. As you read, ask yourself, How does Patrick Henry use figures of speech?

Tip: Take Notes Use a chart to record examples of figures of speech and to restate them in your own words.

Figure of Speech	Restatement
"Suffer not yourselves to be betrayed with a kiss."	

Learning Objectives

For pages 114–119

In studying this text, you will focus on the following objectives:

Literary Study: Analyzing rhetorical question.

Reading: Analyzing figures of speech.

Writing: Writing a speech.

Vocabulary

arduous (är′ jŏŏ əs) *adj.* requiring great exertion or endurance; difficult; p. 117 *Running the marathon was too arduous for eight of the contestants.*

insidious (in sid′ ē əs) *adj.* slyly treacherous and deceitful; deceptive; p. 117 *The candidate used insidious methods, such as bribery, to get elected.*

subjugation (sub′ jə gā′ shən) *n.* act of bringing under control; domination; p. 117 *No one liked being under the subjugation of an evil ruler.*

remonstrate (ri mon′ strāt) *v.* to object; to protest; p. 118 *The whole country will remonstrate if taxes are raised again.*

Before You Read

Focus

Summary

In this speech to the Second Virginia Convention, Henry passionately speaks out against British injustices. Likening Americans to enslaved people, he challenges his fellow colonists to defend themselves. Henry asserts that not only is war justifiable, it is inevitable.

 For summaries in languages other than English, see Unit 1 Teaching Resources Book, pp. 165–170.

Vocabulary

Intensity Verbs and adjectives can have varying intensity, or strength of meaning. Choosing the correct word requires an understanding of that intensity. **Ask:** What is a less intense word for *insidious*? *(sneaky)*

APPROACHING **Ask:** Which word in this selection's vocabulary is a more intense word for *challenging*? *(arduous)*

 For additional vocabulary practice, see Unit 1 Teaching Resources Book, p. 173.

 For additional context, see Glencoe Interactive Vocabulary CD-ROM.

English Learners

DIFFERENTIATED INSTRUCTION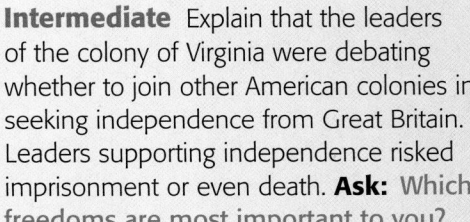

Intermediate Explain that the leaders of the colony of Virginia were debating whether to join other American colonies in seeking independence from Great Britain. Leaders supporting independence risked imprisonment or even death. **Ask:** Which freedoms are most important to you?

Approaching Level

DIFFERENTIATED INSTRUCTION

AAVE Have approaching-level students who are users of African American Vernacular English (AAVE) practice forming the past tense of verbs. Make sure students practice with verbs that end in *-ed,* making sure the final syllable is pronounced.

Teach

Reading Strategy   1

Predict Have students read the first paragraph of Henry's speech. **Ask:** What tone do you expect the rest of the speech to have? *(The last sentences hint at a blunt and outspoken tone.)*

ENGLISH LEARNERS Remind students that *tone* is an author's or speaker's attitude toward the topic. Words, such as "freely" and "without reserve," hint at Henry's tone.

View the Art ★

In the 1763 "parson's cause" case, Patrick Henry argued that the colonial government, not the British government, should set the price of tobacco paid to the clergy for their services. Henry won the case.

 For an audio recording of this selection, use Listening Library Audio CD-ROM.

Readability Scores

Dale-Chall: 8.4
DRP: 60
Lexile: 930

Patrick Henry Arguing the Parson's Cause at the Hanover County Courthouse, 1834. ★
George Cooke. Oil on canvas. Virginia Historical Society, Richmond.

Speech to the Second Virginia Convention

Patrick Henry

Mr. President:[1] No man thinks more highly than I do of the patriotism, as well as abilities, of the very worthy gentlemen who have just addressed the house. But different men often see the same subject in different lights; and, therefore, I hope it will not be thought disrespectful to those gentlemen, if, entertaining,[2] as I do, opinions of a character very opposite to theirs, I shall speak forth my sentiments freely and without reserve. This is no time for ceremony.

The question before the house is one of awful moment[3] to this country. For my own part, I consider it as nothing less than a question of freedom or slavery. And in proportion to the magnitude of the subject ought to be the

---

1. *Mr. President* refers to the president of the Convention.
2. In this case, *entertaining* means "having in mind."
3. Here, *of awful moment* means "of great consequence."

Listening and Speaking Practice

  SPIRAL REVIEW   SMALL GROUP

Reasoning and Propositions Break the speech into sections and have a different student read each part aloud. Ask students whether Henry is using inductive reasoning (specific to general) or deductive reasoning (general to specific) to support each argument.

Explain that a proposition is a statement that focuses a discussion or debate. There are propositions of fact (provable asser-

tions), value (opinions), and policy (courses of action). Have student groups discuss the major propositions in Patrick Henry's speech and identify whether each is a proposition of fact, of value, or of policy.

freedom of the debate. It is only in this way that we can hope to arrive at truth, and fulfill the great responsibility which we hold to God and our country. Should I keep back my opinions at such a time, through fear of giving offense, I should consider myself as guilty of treason toward my country, and of an act of disloyalty toward the Majesty of Heaven, which I revere above all earthly kings.

Mr. President, it is natural for man to indulge in the illusions of hope. We are apt to shut our eyes against a painful truth, and listen to the song of that siren, till she transforms us into beasts. Is this the part of wise men, engaged in a great and **arduous** struggle for liberty? Are we disposed to be of the number of those who, having eyes, see not, and having ears, hear not, the things which so nearly concern their temporal[4] salvation? For my part, whatever anguish of spirit it may cost, I am willing to know the whole truth; to know the worst and to provide for it.

I have but one lamp by which my feet are guided; and that is the lamp of experience. I know of no way of judging of the future but by the past. And judging by the past, I wish to know what there has been in the conduct of the British ministry for the last ten years to justify those hopes with which gentlemen have been pleased to solace themselves and the

> # Give me liberty, or give me death!

House? Is it that **insidious** smile with which our petition has been lately received? Trust it not, sir; it will prove a snare to your feet. Suffer not yourselves to be betrayed with a kiss. Ask yourselves how this gracious reception of our petition comports with these warlike preparations which cover our waters and darken our land. Are fleets and armies necessary to a work of love and reconciliation? Have we shown ourselves so unwilling to be reconciled, that force must be called in to win back our love?

Let us not deceive ourselves, sir. These are the implements of war and **subjugation;** the last arguments to which kings resort. I ask gentlemen, sir, what means this martial array,[5] if its purpose be not to force us to submission? Can gentlemen assign any other possible motives for it? Has Great Britain any enemy, in this quarter of the world, to call for all this accumulation of navies and armies? No, sir, she has none. They are meant for us; they can be meant for no other. They are sent over to bind and rivet upon us those chains which the British ministry have been so long forging. And what have we to oppose to them? Shall we try argument? Sir, we have been trying that for the last ten years. Have we

---

5. A *martial array* is a military display.

Rhetorical Question *How does Henry build on this rhetorical question several sentences later?* **3**

Analyze Figures of Speech *Explain Henry's use of metaphor in this sentence.* **4**

Vocabulary

insidious (in sid′ ē əs) *adj.* slyly treacherous
subjugation (sub′ jə gā′ shən) *n.* act of bringing under control; domination

---

4. The word *temporal* means "in time; earthly."

2 Analyze Figures of Speech *What is being compared in this metaphor?*

Vocabulary

arduous (är′ jōō əs) *adj.* exhausting; difficult

PATRICK HENRY **117**

Teach

Reading Strategy **2**

Analyze Figures of Speech
Answer: *Henry is comparing experience to a lamp that illuminates one's path.*

Ask: How does using a metaphor help Henry make his meaning clear? *(It gives readers a concrete image to link to Henry's ideas.)*

(APPROACHING) **Ask:** What is a metaphor? *(It is a figure of speech that compares or equates two seemingly unlike things.)*

Literary Element **3**

Rhetorical Question
Answer: *He later identifies the British fleets and armies as "implements of war and subjugation."*

Reading Strategy **4**

Analyze Figures of Speech
Answer: *Henry is likening the British use of military force against the colonists to the chaining of enslaved people.*

Teach

Big Idea   1

The Road to Independence
Answer: *He wants to remind his fellow delegates of Britain's repeated refusals to negotiate with the colonists.*

Literary Element   2

Rhetorical Question
Answer: *He is nearing the end of his speech and wants to produce an emotional effect on his audience.*

To check students' understanding of the selection, see Unit 1 Teaching Resources Book, p. 176.

Progress Check

Can students identify a rhetorical question?

If No → See Unit 1 Teaching Resources Book, p. 171.

anything new to offer on the subject? Nothing. We have held the subject up in every light of which it is capable; but it has been all in vain. Shall we resort to entreaty[6] and humble supplication?[7] What terms shall we find which have not been already exhausted? Let us not, I beseech you, sir, deceive ourselves longer. Sir, we have done everything that could be done to avert the storm which is now coming on. We have petitioned; we have **remonstrated;** we have supplicated; we have prostrated[8] ourselves before the tyrannical hands of the ministry and parliament. Our petitions have been slighted; our remonstrances have produced additional violence and insult; our supplications have been disregarded; and we have been spurned,[9] with contempt, from the foot of the throne. In vain, after these things, may we indulge the fond[10] hope of peace and reconciliation. There is no longer any room for hope. If we wish to be free—if we mean to preserve inviolate[11] those inestimable privileges for which we have been so long contending—if we mean not basely[12] to abandon the noble struggle in which we have been so long engaged, and which we have pledged ourselves never to abandon until the glorious object of our contest shall be obtained, we must fight! I repeat it, sir, we must fight! An appeal to arms and to the God of Hosts is all that is left us!

They tell us, sir, that we are weak; unable to cope with so formidable an adversary. But when shall we be stronger? Will it be the next week, or the next year? Will it be when we are totally dis-

armed, and when a British guard shall be stationed in every house? Shall we gather strength by irresolution and inaction? Shall we acquire the means of effectual resistance by lying supinely on our backs, and hugging the delusive phantom of hope, until our enemies shall have bound us hand and foot? Sir, we are not weak, if we make a proper use of the means which the God of nature hath placed in our power. Three millions of people, armed in the holy cause of liberty, and in such a country as that which we possess, are invincible by any force which our enemy can send against us. Besides, sir, we shall not fight our battles alone. There is a just God who presides over the destinies of nations; and who will raise friends to fight our battles for us. The battle, sir, is not to the strong alone; it is to the vigilant, the active, the brave. Besides, sir, we have no election.[13] If we were base enough to desire it, it is now too late to retire from the contest. There is no retreat but in submission and slavery! Our chains are forged! Their clanking may be heard on the plains of Boston! The war is inevitable—and let it come! I repeat it, sir, let it come!

It is in vain, sir, to extenuate[14] the matter. Gentlemen may cry peace, peace—but there is no peace. The war is actually begun! The next gale that sweeps from the North will bring to our ears the clash of resounding arms![15] Our brethren are already in the field! Why stand we here idle? What is it that gentlemen wish? What would they have? Is life so dear, or peace so sweet, as to be purchased at the price of chains and slavery? Forbid it, Almighty God! I know not what course others may take; but as for me, give me liberty, or give me death! ∾

---

6. An *entreaty* is a plea or request.
7. Here, *supplication* means "begging."
8. *Prostrated* means "bowed down."
9. *Spurned* means "rejected with disdain."
10. Here, *fond* means "foolish."
11. The word *inviolate* means "unharmed and intact."
12. Here, *basely* means "dishonorably."

---

1   **The Road to Independence** *Why does Henry refer to these past events?*

Vocabulary

remonstrate (ri mon´ strāt) *v.* to object; to protest

---

13. In this instance, *election* means "choice."
14. Here, *extenuate* means "to debate; offer excuses."
15. A *gale* is a strong wind. Colonists in Massachusetts were already engaged in open opposition to the British.

Rhetorical Question *Why does Henry use so many rhetorical questions in this paragraph?*   **2**

Reading Practice

 SMALL GROUP

Evaluate Persuasive Writing Patrick Henry's speech was designed to persuade his listeners to join the cause against the British.
Ask: How effective are Henry's arguments? Would his words motivate you to join his cause? Have groups of students evaluate Henry's speech. Do they think his arguments are sound? Why or why not?

Ask: When you read a piece of persuasive writing, how do you decide whether to accept its arguments? Have students develop lists of evaluation criteria, such as "Arguments are logical."

After You Read

Respond and Think Critically

Respond and Interpret

1. Imagine that you were a delegate at the Second Virginia Convention. How do you think you would have reacted to Henry's speech?

2. (a)According to Henry, what is the question "of awful moment" to the country? (b)Why do you think Henry offers several reasons to support his speaking out?

3. (a)What does Henry say about Britain's military and naval forces? (b)Why does he introduce this point?

4. (a)According to Henry, what makes Americans "invincible"? (b)Why does Henry say that God is on the side of the colonists?

Analyze and Evaluate

5. (a)Which emotions are expressed in the speech? (b)In your opinion, does Henry's passion add to his effectiveness? Explain.

6. (a)Why does Henry suggest that the colonists have only two choices—liberty or death? (b)Are there other options? Explain.

Connect

7. **Big Idea** **The Road to Independence** What steps do you think Henry wanted Virginia to take in reponse to this speech?

8. **Connect to the Author** Do you find Patrick Henry's presentation of the situation as a choice between extremes—liberty or death—effective? Explain.

Literary Element Rhetorical Question

A rhetorical question presumes that listeners agree with the speaker. The speaker can use this persuasive technique as an emotional appeal designed to achieve solidarity with his or her audience or as a device to lead the audience to accept the speaker's beliefs.

1. What is the effect of the rhetorical questions in the last paragraph of Henry's speech?

2. Name one idea or belief that Henry wants his audience to accept.

Reading Strategy Analyze Figures of Speech

In classical mythology (for example, in Homer's *Odyssey*), a siren was a sea goddess who lured sailors to their doom with her beautiful song.

1. What does Henry compare to the siren's song?

2. Why do you think he uses this metaphor?

Vocabulary Practice

Practice with Antonyms With a partner, brainstorm three antonyms for each boldfaced vocabulary word below. Then discuss your choices with your classmates. Be prepared to explain why you chose your words.

arduous   insidious
subjugation   remonstrate

EXAMPLE: morose
Antonyms: cheerful, happy, joyous
Sample explanation: A person who is morose is very gloomy, but a cheerful person is not.

Writing

Write a Speech Patrick Henry's famous speech expresses a great deal of personal feeling. Consider a contemporary issue about which you feel strongly and write a short speech in support of your position, including a call to action. Use rhetorical questions to give your speech added emotional appeal.

PATRICK HENRY **119**

Vocabulary

arduous Antonyms: easy, effortless, simple; Sample explanation: An *arduous* task is very difficult; an easy task is not.

insidious Antonyms: straightforward, honest, forthright; Sample explanation: An *insidious* person is deceitful, but an honest person is not.

subjugation Antonyms: emancipation, freedom, independence; Sample

explanation: People who live under the *subjugation* of a ruler are dominated by that ruler; people who live in independence are not.

remonstrate Antonyms: agree, consent, laud; Sample explanation: When people, *remonstrate*, they object to something; when they agree, they are of the same opinion.

After You Read

Assess

1. Students' answers will vary.

2. (a) Whether to fight for freedom from British rule (b) To ingratiate himself with a hostile audience

3. (a) Britain is increasing these forces in the colonies (b) He claims the forces' only purpose is to subjugate the colonies.

4. (a) They are armed in a good cause. (b) To incite them to war

5. (a) Patriotism, desire for freedom, bravery, and fervor (b) Students' answers will vary.

6. (a) To eliminate all options but war (b) Students may suggest alternatives to war.

7. To join the Massachusetts colonists in preparing to fight the British

8. Students may say that it underscores the powerful emotions and opinions behind his words.

> For additional assessment, see Assessment Resources, pp. 83–84.

Literary Element

1. They build to a powerful climax.

2. Possible answer: Peace without freedom is worse than death.

Reading Strategy

1. The illusions of hope

2. To suggest how foolish false hope can be.

Writing

Students' speeches should clearly relate to a contemporary issue and should use persuasive techniques.

Before You Read

Focus

Bellringer Options

Selection Focus
  Transparency 12
Daily Language Practice
  Transparency 15

Or **write on the board:** How much freedom should an individual or country have? What, if anything, should limit freedom? Have groups of students imagine they are the Founding Fathers in order to brainstorm freedoms to include in the country's constitution. Have each group make a word web, with "Freedom" in the center and their ideas about individual and national freedoms in circles around it.

Before You Read

Declaration of Independence

Meet **Thomas Jefferson**
(1743–1826)

Honoring Nobel Prize winners at the White House in 1962, President John F. Kennedy observed, "I think this is the most extraordinary collection of talent, of human knowledge, that has ever been gathered together at the White House, with the possible exception of when Thomas Jefferson dined alone." Kennedy was referring to Jefferson's amazing mastery of at least a dozen different professions. He was an architect, inventor, lawyer, surveyor, musician, and botanist, to name but six. Ultimately he became president of the United States.

Jefferson was born in 1743, in Albemarle County, Virginia, to Peter and Jane Jefferson. In 1760 he enrolled in the College of William and Mary in Williamsburg, where he studied mathematics, science, and law. He began to practice law in 1767 and was elected to the Virginia House of Burgesses in 1769. In 1772 he married a widow, Martha Wayles Skelton. They had six children, but only two survived. Martha herself died in 1782.

> *"The spirit of resistance to government is so valuable on certain occasions that I wish it to be always kept alive. . . . I like a little rebellion now and then."*
>
> —Thomas Jefferson,
> from a letter to Abigail Adams, 1787

Jefferson the Writer As a delegate to the Second Continental Congress in 1776, Jefferson drafted what many believe to be the most powerful argument for freedom ever written. As the delegates debated breaking away from Britain, they turned to Jefferson to commit their ideas about equality and liberty to writing. He expressed those ideas eloquently in the Declaration. Though others edited, revised, and deleted portions of the draft, the final version was essentially Jefferson's.

Jefferson the Leader Jefferson succeeded Patrick Henry as governor of Virginia but served again in the congress from 1783 to 1784. After his appointment as U.S. ambassador to France, he became George Washington's secretary of state and then vice president under John Adams. In 1803, during the first of his two terms as president, Jefferson made a decision that changed the nation forever. He arranged to purchase the Louisiana Territory from France. The Louisiana Purchase cost the nation $11.25 million plus $3.75 million in French debts it agreed to pay but doubled the size of the United States. Jefferson then sent a scientific expedition headed by Meriwether Lewis and William Clark to explore these new lands and continue on to the Pacific Ocean.

Thomas Jefferson spent his last years at the Virginia home he designed, built, and rebuilt—Monticello. In 1819 he founded the University of Virginia at nearby Charlottesville. He died on July 4, 1826, exactly fifty years after the signing of the Declaration. A man of contradictions, Jefferson opposed slavery in principle but owned slaves himself. His epitaph, which he composed himself, cited his writing of the Declaration of Independence among his achievements but made no reference to his presidency.

LOG ON ▶ **Literature** Online

Author Search For more about Thomas Jefferson, go to glencoe.com and enter QuickPass code GLA9800u1.

Selection Skills

Literary Elements
- Text Structure (SE pp. 121, 124, 126)
- Tone (TE p. 123)

Reading Skills
- Evaluate Argument (SE pp. 121, 122, 126)
- Predict (TE p. 122)

Declaration of Independence

Vocabulary Skills
- Context (SE p. 126)

Listening/Speaking/Viewing Skills
- View Art (SE p. 123)

Writing Skills/Grammar
- Persuasive Essay (SE p. 127)
- Identify Bias (TE p. 124)

Literature and Reading Preview

Connect to the Text

If your freedom was severely limited by the government, what would you do? Would you protest, move, or do something else entirely? Make a list of possible actions you might take.

Build Background

On June 11, the delegates of the Second Continental Congress had appointed a five-member committee to draft a statement declaring independence from Britain. The committee included Benjamin Franklin, John Adams, and Jefferson, but Jefferson was called upon to do the writing. Some of his ideas were not new. According to John Locke's theory of "natural law," which Jefferson had studied, human beings are "by nature free, equal and independent." Following Locke, Jefferson stressed that the American Revolution was a struggle for the rights of all people.

Set Purposes for Reading

Big Idea **The Road to Independence**

As you read the Declaration of Independence, ask yourself, How does Jefferson describe the challenges the colonists faced in their struggle for independence?

Literary Element **Text Structure**

Text structure is the way the parts of a text are organized and related to each other. In the Declaration of Independence, Jefferson structures his text in terms of **problem and solution.** As you read, ask yourself, What problem does Jefferson identify? What solution does he propose?

Reading Strategy **Evaluate Argument**

To **evaluate arguments,** you need to distinguish valid from invalid reasoning. In **deductive reasoning,** a writer argues from general principles to specific conclusions. A **syllogism** is a form of deduction that has three parts: a major premise, a minor premise, and a conclusion. A syllogism is valid if its conclusion follows logically from its premises. Here is an example:

- Major premise: All human beings are mortal.
- Minor premise: Jefferson is a human being.
- Conclusion: Jefferson is mortal.

As you read the Declaration of Independence, notice how Jefferson uses deductive reasoning to develop his argument.

Vocabulary

usurpation (ū′ sər pā′ shən) *n.* the act of seizing power without right or authority; p. 122 *Civil disorder led to a usurpation of power by military leaders.*

endeavor (en dev′ ər) *v.* to make an effort; to try; p. 123 *The student endeavored to finish his paper on time.*

tenure (ten′ yər) *n.* duration or terms of a position or office; p. 123 *The tenure of an elected judge depends on performance.*

acquiesce (ak′ wē es′) *v.* to consent or agree to, despite objections; to comply passively; p. 124 *Ling decided to acquiesce to her friend's plans for the evening.*

rectitude (rek′ tə tōōd′) *n.* uprightness of moral character; honesty; p. 124 *Known for his rectitude, Thomas was put in charge of the club's finances.*

THOMAS JEFFERSON **121**

English Learners

DIFFERENTIATED INSTRUCTION

Advanced Have students generate a list of ideas or beliefs about the most important things in life. *(Students might say family, job, friends, health, or wealth.)* From the list, ask students to write down which idea is the most important to them. Have students list underneath the idea two or three reasons that their selection is the best choice. *(Possible answer: family, because it provides support, love, and* trust.) Then have students think about what might be most important for an entire country. Tell them to keep these thoughts in mind as they read the selection.

Before You Read

Focus

Summary

The Declaration of Independence explains precisely why the colonists believed they deserved their freedom and lays the groundwork for establishing the basic freedoms that are the foundation of our democracy.

 For summaries in languages other than English, see Unit 1 Teaching Resources Book, pp. 178–183.

Vocabulary

Noun Suffixes Tell students that the suffix *-tion* means "the act or state of." It is added to a verb to create a noun. **Ask:** Which word in this selection's vocabulary is the noun form of a verb? *(usurpation)*

ADVANCED Point out to advanced learners that some verbs are changed to nouns by adding other suffix endings, such as *-ence.* **Ask:** What noun is created by adding *-ence* to the verb *acquiesce*? What does the noun mean? *(acquiescence; the act of consenting or agreeing silently.)*

 For additional vocabulary practice, see Unit 1 Teaching Resources Book, p. 186.

 For additional context, see Glencoe Interactive Vocabulary CD-ROM.

Teach

Reading Strategy | **1**

Evaluate Argument
Answer: *The basic principles are that governments are instituted to secure basic human rights and that governments derive their just powers from the consent of the governed.*

Big Idea | **2**

The Road to Independence
Answer: *Jefferson's statement emphasizes that the colonists have been suffering for some time under an unfair system of government, that they have been patient, and that their patience has come to an end.*

Political History ☆

Colonial Legislatures The first colonial assemblies modeled their governments on the British Parliament. The assemblies dealt with internal matters, such as raising taxes, forming armies, and overseeing the courts.

 For an audio recording of this selection, use Listening Library Audio CD-ROM.

Readability Scores
Dale-Chall: 12.6
DRP: 71
Lexile: 1360

122

Declaration of Independence

In Congress, July 4, 1776

Thomas Jefferson

When, in the course of human events, it becomes necessary for one people to dissolve the political bands which have connected them with another, and to assume, among the powers of the earth, the separate and equal station to which the laws of nature and nature's God entitle them, a decent respect to the opinions of mankind requires that they should declare the causes which impel them to the separation.

We hold these truths to be self-evident: that all men are created equal, that they are endowed by their Creator with certain unalienable rights;[1] that among these are life, liberty, and the pursuit of happiness; that to secure these rights, governments are instituted among men, deriving their just powers from the consent of the governed; that whenever any form of government becomes destructive of these ends, it is the right of the people to alter or to abolish it, and to institute new government, laying its foundation on such principles, and organizing its powers in such form, as to them shall seem most likely to effect their safety and happiness. Prudence,[2] indeed, will dictate that governments long established should not be changed for light and transient causes; and accordingly all experience hath shown that mankind are more disposed to suffer, while evils are sufferable, than to right

themselves by abolishing the forms to which they are accustomed. But when a long train of abuses and **usurpations,** pursuing invariably the same object, evinces[3] a design to reduce them under absolute despotism,[4] it is their right, it is their duty, to throw off such government, and to provide new guards for their future security.

Such has been the patient sufferance of these colonies; and such is now the necessity which constrains[5] them to alter their former systems of government. The history of the present King of Great Britain is a history of repeated injuries and usurpations, all having in direct object the establishment of an absolute tyranny[6] over these states. To prove this, let facts be submitted to a candid world.

He has refused his assent[7] to laws, the most wholesome and necessary for the public good.

He has forbidden his governors to pass laws of immediate and pressing importance, unless suspended in their operation till his assent

---

1. *Unalienable rights* cannot be taken away.
2. The exercise of good judgment is called *prudence*.

1 | **Evaluate Argument** *Which of the basic principles stated earlier support this argument?*

---

3. *Evinces* means "makes clear or evident."
4. *Despotism* is government by a ruler of absolute authority.
5. *Constrains* means "forces."
6. The arbitrary or oppressive exercise of power is *tyranny*.
7. *Assent* is agreement.

The Road to Independence *In what way does this statement shed light on what the colonists have endured in their struggle for independence?* **2**

Vocabulary
usurpation (yū´ sər pā´ shən) *n.* the act of seizing power without right or authority

122 UNIT 1 EARLY AMERICA

Reading Practice

SPIRAL REVIEW **Predict** Explain to students that the first sentence of the Declaration acts like a thesis statement. Ask a student to read the sentence aloud. Have students restate the sentence in their own words. Then ask them what information they think Jefferson will convey. *(Possible response: He will show why it is neces-* *sary for the colonists to dissolve political ties, why the laws of God and nature entitle them to independence, and why they are taking action.)*

should be obtained; and when so suspended, he has utterly neglected to attend to them.

He has refused to pass other laws for the accommodation of large districts of people, unless those people would relinquish the right of representation in the legislature, a right inestimable to them, and formidable to tyrants only.

He has called together legislative bodies at places unusual, uncomfortable, and distant from the depository of their public records, for the sole purpose of fatiguing them into compliance with his measures.

He has dissolved representative houses repeatedly, for opposing, with manly firmness, his invasions on the rights of the people.

He has refused, for a long time after such dissolutions, to cause others to be elected; whereby the legislative powers, incapable of annihilation, have returned to the people at large for their exercise; the state remaining, in the meantime, exposed to all the dangers of invasion from without and convulsions within.

He has **endeavored** to prevent the population of these states; for that purpose obstructing the laws for naturalization[8] of foreigners, refusing to pass others to encourage their migrations hither, and raising the conditions of new appropriations of lands.

He has obstructed the administration of justice, by refusing his assent to laws for establishing judiciary powers.

He has made judges dependent on his will alone for the **tenure** of their offices, and the amount of payment of their salaries.

He has erected a multitude of new offices, and sent hither swarms of officers to harass our people and eat out their substance.

He has kept among us, in times of peace, standing armies, without the consent of our legislatures.

---

8. *Naturalization* is the process by which foreigners become citizens of another country.

Drafting of the Declaration of Independence, c. 1900. Jean-Léon Gérome Ferris.

 View the Art Do you find this painting a believable depiction of the drafting of the Declaration of Independence? Explain. ★

He has affected to render the military independent of, and superior to, the civil power.

He has combined with others to subject us to a jurisdiction foreign to our constitution and unacknowledged by our laws, giving his assent to their acts of pretended legislation:

For quartering[9] large bodies of armed troops among us;

For protecting them, by a mock trial, from punishment for any murders which they should commit on the inhabitants of these states;

For cutting off our trade with all parts of the world;

For imposing taxes on us without our consent;

For depriving us, in many cases, of the benefits of trial by jury;

For transporting us beyond seas, to be tried for pretended offenses;

---

9. Here, *quartering* means "providing with lodging."

THOMAS JEFFERSON **123**

Teach

Big Idea 1

The Road to Independence

Ask: How does the last sentence in the Declaration show the seriousness of the colonists' act of declaring independence? *(It expresses the need to repy on a higher power in the undertaking, as well as the signers' certainty and their willingness to risk everything—their lives, their fortunes, and their honor—rather then continue to live under British rule.)*

Literary Element 2

Text Structure Answer:
Since the King has not just failed to protect the colonists' rights, but actually violated those rights, the colonists have decided to declare independence and set up their own government to protect their rights and interests.

> To check students' understanding of the selection, see Unit 1 Teaching Resources Book, p. 189.

For abolishing the free system of English laws in a neighboring province,[10] establishing therein an arbitrary government, and enlarging its boundaries, so as to render it at once an example and fit instrument for introducing the same absolute rule into these colonies;

For taking away our charters, abolishing our most valuable laws, and altering fundamentally the forms of our governments;

For suspending our own legislatures, and declaring themselves invested with power to legislate for us in all cases whatsoever.

He has abdicated government here, by declaring us out of his protection and waging war against us.

He has plundered our seas, ravaged our coasts, burned our towns, and destroyed the lives of our people.

He is at this time transporting large armies of foreign mercenaries[11] to complete the works of death, desolation, and tyranny already begun with circumstances of cruelty and perfidy[12] scarcely paralleled in the most barbarous ages, and totally unworthy the head of a civilized nation.

He has constrained our fellow-citizens, taken captive on the high seas, to bear arms against their country, to become the executioners of their friends and brethren, or to fall themselves by their hands.

He has excited domestic insurrections among us, and has endeavored to bring on the inhabitants of our frontiers, the merciless Indian savages, whose known rule of warfare is an undistinguished destruction of all ages, sexes, and conditions.

In every stage of these oppressions we have petitioned for redress[13] in the most humble terms; our repeated petitions have been answered only by repeated injury. A prince whose character is thus marked by every act which may define a tyrant is unfit to be ruler of a free people.

Nor have we been wanting in our attentions to our British brethren. We have warned them,

---

10. The *neighboring province* is Quebec, Canada.
11. *Mercenaries* are paid soldiers in a foreign army.
12. *Perfidy* means "a deliberate betrayal of trust."
13. A compensation for a wrong done is a *redress*.

from time to time, of attempts by their legislature to extend an unwarrantable jurisdiction over us. We have reminded them of the circumstances of our emigration and settlement here. We have appealed to their native justice and magnanimity;[14] and we have conjured[15] them, by the ties of our common kindred, to disavow these usurpations, which would inevitably interrupt our connections and correspondence. They, too, have been deaf to the voice of justice and consanguinity.[16] We must, therefore, **acquiesce** in the necessity which denounces[17] our separation, and hold them, as we hold the rest of mankind, enemies in war, in peace, friends.

We, therefore, the representatives of the United States of America, in General Congress assembled, appealing to the Supreme Judge of the world for the **rectitude** of our intentions, do, in the name and by the authority of the good people of these colonies, solemnly publish and declare that these United Colonies are, and of right ought to be, free and independent states; that they are absolved from all allegiance to the British crown, and that all political connection between them and the state of Great Britain is, and ought to be, totally dissolved; and that, as free and independent states, they have full power to levy war, conclude peace, contract alliances, establish commerce, and do all other acts and things which independent states may of right do. And for the support of this declaration, with a firm reliance on the protection of Divine Providence, we mutually pledge to each other our lives, our fortunes, and our sacred honor. ♋

1

---

14. *Magnanimity* means "nobility of mind and heart."
15. Here, *conjured* means "solemnly appealed to."
16. *Consanguinity* is a blood relationship.
17. Here, *denounces* means "announces" or "proclaims."

> **Text Structure** *How is this declaration and the ones that follow a solution to the problems Jefferson has described?*

2

Vocabulary

acquiesce (ak´ wē es´) *v.* to consent or agree to, despite objections; to comply passively
rectitude (rek´ tə to͞od´) *n.* uprightness of moral character; honesty

---

Writing Practice

Identify Bias Remind students that bias is the favoring of one side of an argument over the other. **Say:** Skim the Declaration to find words and phrases that reveal bias against the British. **Ask:** How do the words "He has refused his assent to laws, the most wholesome and necessary for the public good" on page 122 accomplish Jefferson's goal? *(Calling the laws "wholesome" and "necessary" casts the colonists in the best possible light.)* Have students write a one-page analysis of bias in the Declaration. Analyses should include a thesis about Jefferson's bias and discussion of at least two more examples.

After You Read

Respond and Think Critically

Respond and Interpret

1. How has reading the Declaration of Independence affected your ideas about freedom?

2. (a)What is the purpose of the document? (b)To which "opinions of mankind" might Jefferson be referring?

3. (a)According to Jefferson, which human rights are "unalienable"? (b)How do you interpret the phrase "pursuit of happiness"?

4. (a)How have the colonists met with "these oppressions"? (b)Why might the king have ignored the colonists' petitions for redress?

Analyze and Evaluate

5. (a)In what ways does Jefferson emphasize that the colonists' complaints are against the king of England, not against the British people? (b)Why

do you think Jefferson went to such lengths to emphasize this distinction?

6. (a)What method of organization did Jefferson use in creating this document? (b)How effective is this method of organization?

Connect

7. **Big Idea** **The Road to Independence** (a)What does the Declaration of Independence stress about the dangers of changing a form of government? (b)What does this indicate about the process that led to the American Revolution?

8. **Connect to Today** Jefferson chose his words with great care. Do you think politicians today put the same amount of thought into their words, either spoken or written? Explain.

Primary Source Quotation

Liberty for All?

Although Jefferson owned slaves, he included a scathing condemnation of slavery in his original draft of the Declaration. However, John Adams and Benjamin Franklin feared alienating slave-holding colonists, whose support of the revolution was desperately needed. At his colleagues' urging, Jefferson deleted this material, which is excerpted below.

"He [King George] has waged cruel war against human nature itself, violating its most sacred rights of life and liberty in the persons of a distant people who never offended him, captivating and carrying them into slavery in another hemisphere, or to incur miserable death in their transportation

thither . . . He has [stopped] every legislative attempt to prohibit or to restrain this execrable commerce determining to keep an open market where [people] should be bought and sold . . ."

Group Activity Discuss the following questions with your classmates.

1. How do you think the principles of the Declaration could be applied to slavery?

2. How does the fact that Jefferson owned slaves affect your reading of this quotation?

3. Was the deletion of this material from the Declaration an inexcusable mistake or a justifiable strategy for gaining wider support for the cause of revolution? Explain.

Primary Source Quotation

1. The Declaration of Independence states that "all men are created equal" and are entitled to the same "unalienable rights," so it would follow that enslaved Africans should have the same rights as anyone else.

2. Some students might say that this information reveals both Jefferson and the Declaration of Independence to be hypo-

critical. Others might argue that Jefferson should be admired for holding views that were innovative for his time—even if he did not model them in his behavior.

3. Some students might say that it was justified because drafters were acting pragmatically to gain widespread support for declaring independence. Others might argue that this deletion was unconscionable and contributed to the continued suffering of thousands of people.

After You Read

Assess

1. Students' answers will vary.

2. (a) It explains and justifies the colonists' declaring their independence. (b) To the view that it is wrong to rebel against a government without good cause

3. (a) Life, liberty, and the pursuit of happiness (b) Students may say it is what people can do to better their lot without harming others.

4. (a) They have asked to be rightfully compensated, and then warned of more severe action. (b) He may not have believed that the colonists had the right to make demands.

5. (a) Jefferson never once mentions the British people. (b) He may have wanted to gain the British people's support for the colonists' cause.

6. (a) He begins with an introduction that establishes basic principles, then presents a list of violations of the principles, and then concludes with the colonists' response to the violations. (b) Very effective, because it follows a clear pattern of deductive reasoning

7. (a) That such a change is dangerous and to be undertaken only as a last resort (b) It indicates that the break with Britain was not a step the colonists took lightly.

8. Students' answers will vary, but may mention that politicians today do choose their words carefully to avoid ridicule.

 For additional assessment, see Assessment Resources, pp. 85–86.

After You Read

Literary Element

1. Jefferson devotes almost two-thirds of the Declaration to the colonists' problems. This list justifies Jefferson's argument that the King has trampled on natural rights and that the colonists are justified.

2. Jefferson declares that the colonists should have the right to form their own governments and set up their own laws. The King has taken away all these rights from the colonists.

3. Jefferson uses deductive reasoning. First, he lays out his major premise that people have the right to overthrow a government that does not derive power from its subjects. Then, he spells out specific grievances against the King. Finally, he concludes that independence is the only logical solution to the colonists' problems.

Review: Author's Purpose

Jefferson and his compatriots wrote the Declaration to justify their arguments for declaring independence and to show the legitimacy of their actions.

Reading Strategy

SAT Skills Practice

1. E is the correct answer because a deductive argument moves from general principles to specific conclusions.

Progress Check

Can students evaluate an argument?

If No → See Unit 1 Teaching Resources Book, p. 154.

126

Literary Element Text Structure

Jefferson structures the Declaration in terms of problem and solution.

1. How much space does Jefferson devote to stating the problems faced by the colonists? What is the effect of this list?

2. In what ways does Jefferson declare the Colonies independent of Britain? How are these declarations related to the abuses he has described?

3. Why do you think Jefferson structures the Declaration of Independence in the way he does?

Review: Author's Purpose

Understanding an author's purpose does not mean interviewing the author or trying to read his or her mind. Purpose is something that can be inferred from the text itself. Based on your reading of the Declaration of Independence, what can you infer about Jefferson's and his compatriots' purpose in writing the document?

Reading Strategy Evaluate Argument

SAT Skills Practice

1. An example of deductive reasoning in the "Declaration of Independence" is

   (A) the presentation of the self-evident truths.

   (B) the enumeration of Britain's abuse of the self-evident truths.

   (C) the declaration of independence from Britain.

   (D) the argument from the specific self-evident truths to the general conclusion—independence.

   (E) the argument from the general self-evident truths to the specific conclusion—independence.

 Literature Online

Selection Resources For Selection Quizzes, eFlash-cards, and Reading-Writing Connection activities, go to glencoe.com and enter QuickPass code GLA9800u1.

Vocabulary Practice

Practice with Context Identify the context clues in the following sentences that help you determine the meaning of each boldfaced vocabulary word.

1. Though the group **endeavored** to make it to the top of the mountain, they had to give up when a storm came.

2. Because of her **rectitude,** no one ever questions the truth of Sarah's statements.

3. Craig's absence at several practices resulted in Andy's **usurpation,** or seizure, of the position of captain.

4. Though my brother didn't want me to drive his car, he **acquiesced** when I promised to do his chores for a month.

5. With the approach of the next contest, Elaine's **tenure** as Miss America was coming to a close.

Academic Vocabulary

The Declaration of Independence is greatly influenced by the political **philosophy** *of John Locke.*

Philosophy is an academic word. Someone who has ambitions to become a doctor might live by a **philosophy** of working hard, learning constantly, and helping others.

To study this word further, answer the following question: What is your personal **philosophy**? Write a list of the principles by which you live your life.

For more on academic vocabulary, see pages 53–54.

Vocabulary

1. The group's aim was to make it to the top; therefore, *endeavored* means that they tried.

2. The quality that makes people believe whatever she says is her *rectitude;* therefore, it means honesty and moral firmness.

3. Andy seizes the power from Craig, or *usurps* it.

4. The promise of doing the chores makes the brother give in, or *acquiesce.*

5. Miss America has the title for the year between contests, which is her *tenure.*

Academic Vocabulary

Students should mention the system of thought or principles by which they conduct their life. For example, a student might mention that she lives by the belief that she should always be honest.

Respond Through Writing

Persuasive Essay

Argue a Position How relevant is the Declaration of Independence to Americans today? In a persuasive essay, identify themes in the Declaration and argue for or against the relevance of these themes to contemporary American society.

Understand the Task In a **persuasive essay**, you use reason, evidence, and appropriate emotional appeals to convince your reader to adopt a certain position. A **theme** is the main idea or message a literary work conveys.

Prewrite Before you draft your essay, create a chart like the one below to identify key themes in the Declaration, examples of these themes in the text, and evidence for whether these themes remain relevant.

Theme	Example	Relevance
government by the people	based on "the consent of the governed"	yes; participation of Americans in their government —as measured by voting—is declining

Draft Create a logical structure of arguments and ideas supported with precise and relevant evidence. Strengthen your arguments with an effective and appropriate use of persuasive techniques, such as parallelism, connotative language, symbolism, appeals to authority, and rhetorical questions. (See page R60 for more on using these techniques.) Try using the following sentence frame to help conclude your essay with a call to action: In conclusion, because of _____ I believe we should _____.

Revise Ask your partner if your essay addresses opposing arguments and anticipates the concerns of your audience. You can also use the checklist on page 154. Refine your draft based on your partner's feedback.

Edit and Proofread Proofread your paper, correcting any errors in spelling, grammar, and punctuation.

THOMAS JEFFERSON **127**

Learning Objectives

In this assignment, you will focus on the following objectives:

Writing: Write a persuasive essay.

Grammar: Citing source information correctly.

> **Grammar Tip**

Parentheses

When you quote or refer to the Declaration of Independence or another source in support of your thesis, remember to enclose source information in parentheses. Here are two examples of in-text citations.

"Nor have we been wanting in our attentions to our British brethren" (Declaration of Independence 124).

Many scholars believe that the idea of people being born with the right to life, liberty, and the pursuit of happiness remains the most American of all ideals (Jenkins 492–494).

The use of an author's last name or the name of the work is typically related to an entry in a works-cited list. See page R31 for more on citing sources.

After You Read

 ## Respond Through Writing

Persuasive Essay: Argue a Position

Students should clearly state a position for or against the relevance of the Declaration of Independence. Assess students' essays using the scoring guide at the bottom of the page. Students' essays should

- provide a well-reasoned, focused argument
- support the argument with convincing evidence
- show understanding of the contemporary issues related to the Declaration of Independence
- use effective persuasive techniques and rhetorical devices
- follow standard English language conventions
- be well-organized with a clear structure that lays out the argument and supporting evidence in a logical order

Scoring Guide	4	3	2	1
Argument/Reasoning	authoritative	general	little or none	none
Evidence	convincing	somewhat convincing	little or none	none
Understanding of complexities of theme	clear	general	limited	minimal
Language	varied, precise, persuasive	varied, somewhat persuasive	predictable, basic	limited, unpersuasive
Convention errors	few or none	several	many	serious
Structure and organization	logical, very clear	somewhat logical, clear	little or none	none

Focus

Summary

This article describes the drafting and revision of the Declaration of Independence. As chairman of the Declaration committee, Jefferson was responsible for drafting the document. As editor, Franklin made a few changes, such as changing an appeal to religion to an appeal to reason. The Continental Congress made additional changes before signing the document.

Teach

Reading Strategy | 1

Preview the Article

1. It might be about why the people who wrote the Declaration used the words they did. I know that the American colonists struggled to break free from Britain during this period.

2. The author's use of *immortal* suggests that he considers Franklin's editing very important.

 For an activity related to this selection, see Unit 1 Teaching Resources Book, pp. 191–196.

Readability Scores

Dale-Chall: 7.9
DRP: 68
Lexile: 1200

Set a Purpose for Reading

Read to learn about the the roles of Franklin and Jefferson in writing the Declaration of Independence.

1 #### Preview the Article

1. From the title, what do you think this article will be about? What do you already know about this subject?

2. Read the *deck,* or the sentence in large type that appears below the title. How does the author feel about Franklin's edits?

Reading Strategy

Determine the Main Idea and Supporting Details

The *main idea* of a text is the most important thing that the writer wants to convey. Ask yourself: What main idea does the author wish to convey? What details support this idea?

As you read, create a graphic organizer like the one below.

> Main Idea:
> • Supporting detail 1: Benjamin Franklin made important changes to the document.
> • Supporting detail 2:

128 UNIT 1

TIME

How They Chose These WORDS

Jefferson wrote the Declaration's first draft, but it was Franklin's editing that made a phrase immortal.

By WALTER ISAACSON

AS THE CONTINENTAL CONGRESS PREPARED TO VOTE on the question of American independence in 1776, it appointed a committee for a job that no one at the time thought was very important. The task, however, would turn out to be a momentous one: drafting a declaration that explained the decision. The committee included Benjamin Franklin, of course, and Thomas Jefferson and John Adams, as well as Connecticut merchant Roger Sherman and New York lawyer Robert Livingston.

How was it that Jefferson, at age 33, got the honor of drafting the document? His name was listed first on the committee, signifying that he was the chairman, because he had gotten the most votes and because he was from Virginia, the colony that had proposed the resolution. His four colleagues had other committee assignments that they considered to be more important. None of them realized that the document would eventually come to be viewed as a cornerstone of American politics. As for Franklin, he was still laid up in bed with boils and gout when the committee first met.

And thus it fell to Jefferson to compose, on a little lap desk he had designed, some of the most famous phrases in history while sitting alone in a second-floor room of a house on Market Street in Philadelphia just a block from Franklin's house. "When, in the course of human events . . . ," he famously began.

Taking a Page from Franklin
The document Jefferson drafted was in some ways similar to what Franklin would have written. It

---

Writing Practice

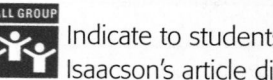 #### Draft and Revise

SMALL GROUP Indicate to students that Walter Isaacson's article discusses how Jefferson drafted the Declaration and Franklin edited it. Emphasize that most writers edit their own work first. Drafting is a time for trial and error. Students should use this writing phase to focus on ideas, rather than on grammar or literary techniques. Write on the board, or **say:** Name a freedom that people in the United

States enjoy and explain why it is important. Have students write a paragraph about this topic. Then have small groups exchange paragraphs and suggest edits for each other's work.

A Declaration by the Representatives of the UNITED STATES OF AMERICA, in General Congress assembled.

DEFT TOUCH Franklin changed the phrase "sacred and undeniable" to "self-evident," an assertion of rationality.

contained a highly specific bill of particulars against the British. It also recounted, as Franklin had often done, the details of America's attempts to make peace despite England's unbending attitude. Indeed, Jefferson's words echoed some of the language that Franklin had used, earlier that year, in a draft resolution that he never published: "Whereas, whenever kings, instead of protecting the lives and properties of their subjects, as is their bounden duty, do endeavor to perpetrate the destruction of either, they thereby cease to be kings, become tyrants, and dissolve all ties of allegiance between themselves and their people."

Jefferson's writing style, however, was different from Franklin's. It was graced with rolling rhythms and smooth phrases, soaring in their poetry and powerful despite their polish. In addition, Jefferson drew on a depth of philosophy not found in Franklin. He echoed both the language and grand theories of English and Scottish Enlightenment thinkers. Having read John Locke's *Second Treatise on Government* at least three times, Jefferson was most notably influenced by Locke's concept of natural rights. And Jefferson built his case, in a manner more sophisticated than Franklin would have, on a contract between government and the governed that was founded on the consent of the people. Jefferson also, it should be noted, borrowed freely from the phrasings of others, including the resounding Declaration of Rights in the new Virginia constitution. Today, this kind of borrowing might lead to accusations of plagiarism, but back then it was considered not only proper but learned.

When he had finished a draft and included some changes from Adams, Jefferson sent it to Franklin on the morning of Friday, June 21. "Will Doctor Franklin be so good as to peruse it," he wrote in his cover note, "and suggest such alterations as his more enlarged view of the subject will dictate?" People were much more polite to editors back then.

Change for the Better?
Franklin made only a few changes, some of which can be viewed written in his hand on what Jefferson referred to as the "rough draft" of the Declaration. The most important of his edits was small but significant. He crossed out, using the heavy backslashes that he often employed, the last three words of Jefferson's phrase "We hold these truths to be sacred and undeniable." Franklin changed them to the words now enshrined in history: "We hold these truths to be self-evident."

The idea of "self-evident" truths drew on the rational view of the world held by Isaac Newton and

---

TIME

Teach

Big Idea   2

The Road to Independence
Ask: How might Jefferson's and Franklin's writing styles have inspired the colonists? (*Possible answer: Jefferson's graceful, polished style appealed to the educated, whereas Franklin's more succinct style appealed to the working class.*)

Vocabulary   3

Plagiarism Remind students that plagiarism is the act of presenting someone else's ideas or words as one's own. **Ask:** What's the difference between quoting from a source and plagiarizing? (*When you quote from a source, you identify the source. When you plagiarize, you take credit for the writing.*)

> **Interactive Read and Write**
> Other options for teaching this selection can be found in
> - Interactive Read and Write for EL Students , pp. 25–36
> - Interactive Read and Write for Approaching-Level Students, pp. 25–36
> - Interactive Read and Write for On-Level Students, pp. 25–36

Approaching Level
DIFFERENTIATED INSTRUCTION

Emerging Read aloud the first three sentences in the section headed "Taking a Page from Franklin." Then **ask:** What did Jefferson borrow from Franklin? (*a list of British offenses and a list of American peace attempts*)

English Learners
DIFFERENTIATED INSTRUCTION

Intermediate Have students reread the subsection "Change for the Better?" Record some of the changes. Then **ask:** What is the main difference? (*Franklin took out the element of religion.*) Why might Franklin have done this? (*To create a separation of church and state*)

TIME

Assess

1. Possible response: I would like some of the changes that Franklin made, such as "We hold these truths to be self-evident." However, I might think that the changes made by the Continental Congress were excessive.

2. (a) John Locke's *Second Treatise on Government* (b) It taught Jefferson the concept of natural rights, convincing him that a government should be guided by the will of the people.

3. (a) The criticism of the King for continuing the slave trade was deleted. (b) This shows that some people were in favor of slavery; it also suggests that the proslavery forces were powerful.

4. Editing played an important role in the crafting of the Declaration of Independence.

5. The article points out how much even minor revisions can improve a document.

6. Writing is powerful because it can influence and give shape to public opinion; the Declaration of Independence helped the American colonists understand what they were fighting for.

Franklin's close friend David Hume. The great Scottish philosopher Hume had developed a theory that distinguished between truths that describe matters of fact (such as "London is bigger than Philadelphia") and truths that are declared so through reason and definition ("the angles of a triangle total 180 degrees"; "all bachelors are unmarried"). He referred to the latter type of axioms as "self-evident" truths. By using the word sacred, Jefferson had implied, intentionally or not, that the principle in question—the equality of men and their endowment by their creator with inalienable rights—was a matter of religion. Franklin's edit turned it instead into a matter of reason and rationality.

Franklin's other edits were less suitable. He changed Jefferson's "reduce them to arbitrary power" to "reduce them under absolute despotism," and he took out the literary flourish in Jefferson's "invade and deluge us in blood" to make it more sparse: "invade and destroy us." And a few of his changes seemed stodgy and unnecessary. "Amount of their

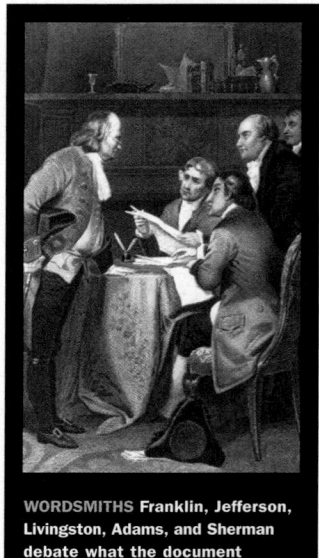

WORDSMITHS Franklin, Jefferson, Livingston, Adams, and Sherman debate what the document should say.

Archive Photos/NewsCom

salaries" became "amount and payment of their salaries."

Congress Makes Cuts
After the Continental Congress voted for independence from England, it formed itself into a committee to consider Jefferson's draft Declaration. The members were not so light in their editing as Franklin had been. Large sections were sliced out, most notably the one that criticized the king for continuing the slave trade. Congress also, to its credit, cut by more than half the draft's final five paragraphs, in which Jefferson had begun to ramble in a way that detracted from the document's power. Jefferson was upset. "I was sitting by Dr. Franklin," he recalled, "who perceived that I was not insensible to these mutilations." Franklin did his best to console him.

At the official signing of the parchment copy on August 2, John Hancock, the president of the Congress, penned his name with his famous flourish. "There must be no pulling different ways," he declared. "We must all hang together." Supposedly, Franklin replied, "Yes, we must, indeed, all hang together, or most assuredly we shall all hang separately." Their lives, as well as their sacred honor, had been put on the line.

—Updated 2005, from TIME, July 7, 2003

Respond and Think Critically

Respond and Interpret

1. If you had drafted the Declaration, what would you think of the revisions it underwent?

2. (a)What book influenced Thomas Jefferson as he drafted the Declaration? (b)How did this book shape Jefferson's political beliefs?

3. (a)What criticism of the king did the Continental Congress delete from the draft? (b)What does this tell you about society during this time period?

Analyze and Evaluate

4. How would you describe in your own words the main idea of the reading selection?

5. (a)What does the effect of Franklin's revisions say about the importance of the revision process?

Connect

6. Why do you think a written document played so important a role in the battle for independence?

Progress Check

Can students identify the main idea and details?

If No → See Unit 1 Teaching Resources Book, p. 197.

 For additional assessment, see Assessment Resources, pp. 87–88.

Vocabulary Workshop

Word Origins: Political Science

Literature Connection Thomas Jefferson's words helped to "dissolve the political bands" between England and its American colonies.

> *"Whenever any form of government becomes destructive of these ends, it is the right of the people to alter or to abolish it."*
>
> —Thomas Jefferson, from the Declaration of Independence

Much of the political language Jefferson used, and that we still use today, traces its origins to ancient Greek and Latin.

Many dictionaries display the etymology, or origin and history, of a word in brackets before or after its definition. For example, the following entry contains the etymology of the word *govern*. Note that the symbol < means "comes from."

govern (guv′ ərn) *v.* to exercise political authority over: *to govern a nation.* [ME < OF *gouverner* < L *gubernāre* to steer (a ship) < Gk *kybernān* to steer]

The entry indicates that the word *govern* comes from a Middle English (ME) word, which comes from the Old French (OF) word *gouverner,* which comes from the Latin word *gubernāre,* which comes from the Greek *kybernān,* meaning "to steer." Knowing the etymology of the word *govern* not only enhances your understanding of the word's origins but may also help you understand other related words, such as *government* and *governor.*

Practice Use a dictionary to research the origins of the following political terms that appear in the Declaration of Independence. In a chart, copy the etymology for each word and write an explanation, similar to the one above, of its origin. How might knowing a word's etymology help you understand the meanings of other words?

Word	Etymology	Explanation
liberty		
jurisdiction		
usurp		

Learning Objectives

In this workshop, you will focus on the following objectives:

Vocabulary:
Understanding multiple-meaning words.
Understanding language resources.

Vocabulary Terms

A **prefix** is an attachment at the *beginning* of a word. It adds to or changes the word's meaning.

A **suffix** is an attachment at the *end* of a word. It adds to or changes the word's meaning.

A **word root** is the part of the original word to which a prefix or suffix is attached.

A **base word** is the original word to which a prefix or suffix may be attached.

Tip

Analyzing word parts can help you determine the meanings of words and increase your vocabulary. If you memorize common prefixes and suffixes, you will be more prepared when taking standardized tests.

 Literature Online

Vocabulary For more vocabulary practice, go to glencoe.com and enter QuickPass code GLA9800u1.

English Learners

DIFFERENTIATED INSTRUCTION

Intermediate If students struggle, review basic dictionary skills. Provide a list of numbered steps for reference, and then have students practice it with the word *liberty.*

1. Identify the first letter of the word: *l.*
2. Search for that letter using page tabs or headings.
3. Identify the first three letters: *lib.*
4. Use guidewords to locate the correct page: *liberal–liberty tea.*
5. Skim the page for the word: *liberty.*

Vocabulary Workshop

Word Origins: Politics

Focus

Ask students what languages they speak or are studying; list these on the board. Point out that studying other languages can help students expand their English vocabulary. Ask them to list words they use that come from other languages. *(Possible responses: regime, ballet [from French]; rodeo, tortilla [from Spanish]; prima donna, spaghetti, pizza, piano [from Italian])*

Teach

Word Origins Say: Many English words come from Latin. A knowledge of Latin roots can help you decode these words.

(ENGLISH LEARNERS) Tell English learners who speak Latin-based languages to use cognates to help them define English words with Latin roots. Have them identify cognates for the word *govern* in their home languages. *(Spanish, gobernar; French, gouverner; Italian, governare; Portuguese, governar)*

Practice
Possible etymologies:

liberty: *ME* liberte < *OF* < *L* lībertās < līber, *free*

jurisdiction: *ME* jurisdiccioun < *OF* juridicion, < *L* iūrisdictiō, iūrisdictiōn-: iūris, *genitive of* iūs, *law* + dictiō, dictiōn-, *declaration*

usurp: *ME* usurpen < *OF* usurper < *L* ūsūrpāre, *to take into use, usurp*

 For additional vocabulary practice, see Glencoe Interactive Vocabulary CD-ROM.

Before You Read

Focus

Bellringer Options

Selection Focus
   Transparency 13
Daily Language Practice
   Transparency 16
Or write on the board: "These are the times that try men's souls." Remind students that the quotation appeared on page 103, as an element in the Part 3 introduction. Have students discuss the quotation. **Ask:** Is Paine referring to everyday nuisances like a flat tire, or is he referring to something more serious? *(Students may say that although a flat tire could be irritating, it wouldn't affect one's soul.)* What are some modern examples of "trying" experiences? *(Possible responses: war; poverty; diseases)*

Before You Read

from *The Crisis, No. 1*

Meet **Thomas Paine**
(1737–1809)

Corset maker, cobbler, teacher, tax collector—Thomas Paine failed miserably at every line of work he attempted in his native England. Finally, at age thirty-seven, Paine set sail for the colonies to start a new life. It was 1774, and the colonists were weighing the pros and cons of a break with England. Always a friend of the "little guy," Paine sympathized with the revolutionary forces.

> "Had it not been for America, there had been no such thing as freedom left throughout the whole universe."
>
> —Thomas Paine
> from *The Crisis, No. 5*

Success in America In January 1776, Paine anonymously published the pamphlet *Common Sense*, a cry for complete independence from Britain. Paine argued that England was a mother country "devouring her young." The pamphlet quickly sold more than 100,000 copies. Paine enlisted in Washington's army and began to write the first pamphlet of a series of sixteen called *The Crisis*. Washington ordered that this first pamphlet be read aloud at every military campground. From 1777 to 1779, Paine served as secretary to the Committee on Foreign Affairs of the Continental Congress. After American independence was won, Paine returned to private life.

Troubles in England and France Paine eventually returned to Europe—and to trouble. In the early 1790s, he wrote a defense of the French Revolution called *The Rights of Man*, in which he argued against the rule of kings and for legislation to help the poor. Although Paine had already escaped to France, he was tried for treason and outlawed by the British. After he was made a citizen by the French assembly, he became an elected official. Unfortunately, he associated with the wrong political party. When that party fell during the French Revolution, he was thrown into prison and stripped of citizenship. After almost a year, and with the help of James Monroe, U.S. minister to France, he was released. Paine returned to the United States in 1802, but he received no hero's welcome. Many Americans misunderstood his later writings and branded him an atheist, although Thomas Jefferson remained a good friend.

When Paine's life ended, he was poor, alone, and swollen with dropsy, a disease of the body's connective tissue. Even after his death, the insults continued. He was buried on his farm in New Rochelle, New York. Ten years later, William Cobbett, a British admirer of Paine, dug up his remains and transported them to England, after which they disappeared. (Cobbett apparently intended a memorial that never came to pass.) Paine achieved his successes with a pen only, but his contribution to the cause of freedom is incalculable. *Common Sense* inspired even the most reluctant to rebel against what Paine called the "tyranny of Britain."

 Literature Online

Author Search For more about Thomas Paine, go to glencoe.com and enter QuickPass code GLA9800u1.

Selection Skills

Literary Elements
- Tone (SE pp. 133, 135–137)
- Diction (SE p. 137)

from **The Crisis, No. 1**

Writing Skills/Grammar
- Apply Tone (SE p. 138)

Reading Skills
- Summarize (SE pp. 133, 135, 136, 138)
- Analyze Arguments (TE p. 134)

Vocabulary Skills
- Denotation and Connotation (SE p. 138)
- Related Words (TE p. 133)

Listening/Speaking/Viewing Skills
- Analyze Art (SE p. 136)
- Presentation (TE p. 136)

Literature and Reading Preview

Connect to the Essay

Have you ever gotten so fed up with something or someone that you felt forced to say, "Enough is enough!"? Write a journal entry about such a situation. Explain what caused your reaction and its result.

Build Background

In *The Crisis*, Paine applies a seventeenth-century idea—that if a government oversteps its bounds, people can voluntarily end it—to British rule in the American colonies.

Set Purposes for Reading

Big Idea **The Road to Independence**

In their struggle with the British, the American colonists were fighting for a cause. As you read, ask yourself, How does Paine encourage his readers' devotion to the struggle for freedom?

Literary Element **Tone**

An author's attitude toward his or her subject matter or toward the audience is conveyed through **tone**. Tone consists of such elements as word choice, sentence structure, and figures of speech. As you read, ask yourself, How does Paine's tone convey his attitude?

Reading Strategy **Summarize**

To **summarize** what you have read is to state the main ideas in your own words and in a logical sequence. A summary is much shorter than the original. Summarizing can help you focus your understanding and remember what you have read.

....

Tip: Outline Look for main ideas and supporting details as you read. Putting them in a simple outline form will help you construct a summary after you read.

> 1. Britain's actions are tyrannical.
>   a. Britain has declared a right to tax us.
>   b.
>   c.

Learning Objectives

For pages 132–138

In studying this text, you will focus on the following objectives:

Literary Study: Analyzing tone.

Reading: Summarizing.

Writing: Applying tone.

Vocabulary

tyranny (tir′ ə nē) *n.* cruel use of authority; oppressive power; p. 134 *In order to regain their rights, the villagers rebelled against the tyranny of the king.*

resolution (rez′ ə loo′ shən) *n.* firmness of purpose; p. 135 *My resolution to study harder resulted in better grades.*

petrified (pet′ rə fīd) *adj.* paralyzed with fear; p. 135 *Caught in our headlights, the deer seemed petrified and unable to move.*

exploit (eks′ ploit) *n.* notable, heroic deed; feat; p. 135 *Reading about superheroes can be fun, but I prefer learning about the exploits of real people.*

hypocrisy (hi pok′ rə sē) *n.* an expression of feelings or beliefs not actually possessed or held; p. 135 *The politician revealed his hypocrisy when he did not fulfill his campaign promises.*

English Learners

DIFFERENTIATED INSTRUCTION

Intermediate Remind students that an outline is a structured list of main ideas and supporting details. Outlines can be used as reading tools or as prewriting tools. Clarify that each numbered outline entry corresponds to a main idea. The lettered entries under each main idea correspond to supporting details. Have students create an outline, entering ideas and details in sentence form. As students read, have them note sentences they want to enter in the outline and label each M for main idea or SD for Supporting Detail.

Before You Read

Focus

Summary

In his essay, Paine calls on every reader to join in the noble struggle for independence from Britain. Paine asserts that the war is just—that the British king is a murderer and thief. Paine castigates people who do not act.

For summaries in languages other than English, see Unit 1 Teaching Resources Book, pp. 200–205.

Vocabulary

Related Words Words often have different forms for different parts of speech. The related words all share an origin, such as a Latin or Greek root. Explain that recognizing the root and building word families can help students define unfamiliar words and understand complex text. For example, the word *tyranny* comes from the Latin *tyrannus*. **Ask:** What other English words share this root? *(tyrant, tyrannical)* **Ask:** What words are related to *resolution*? *(resolve, resolute)*

For additional vocabulary practice, see Unit 1 Teaching Resources Book, p. 208.

For additional context, see Glencoe Interactive Vocabulary CD-ROM.

Teach

The Road to Independence

Answer: *Paine makes this comparison because it ennobles the colonial struggle. The conflict is elevated from an argument over taxes to a struggle for freedom and independence.*

Political History ☆

The Stamp Act In March 1766, the Stamp Act of 1765 was repealed. This had been the fourth Stamp Act passed by the British Parliament. It had levied a tax on, among other things, all legal documents, newspapers, pamphlets, and playing cards in the American colonies. The colonists were so incensed by the taxes that they threatened the tax collectors. The resistance was strong enough that the tax was never enforced.

 For an audio recording of this selection, use Listening Library Audio CD-ROM.

Readability Scores

Dale-Chall: 8.8
DRP: 62
Lexile: 1050

Washington Crossing the Delaware, 1851. Emanuel Gottlieb Leutze. Oil on canvas, 12²/₅ x 21¹/₄ in. Metropolitan Museum of Art, NY.

from

The Crisis, No. 1

Thomas Paine

These are the times that try men's souls. The summer soldier and the sunshine patriot will, in this crisis, shrink from the service of his country; but he that stands it now, deserves the love and thanks of man and woman. **Tyranny,** like hell, is not easily conquered; yet we have this consolation with us, that the harder the conflict, the more glorious the triumph. What we obtain too cheap, we esteem[1] too lightly: it is dearness only that gives everything its value.

Heaven knows how to put a proper price upon its goods; and it would be strange indeed if so celestial an article as freedom should not be highly rated. Britain, with an army to enforce her tyranny, has declared that she has a right (not only to tax) but "to bind us in all cases whatsoever";[2] and if being bound in that manner is not slavery, then is there not such a thing as slavery upon earth. Even the

---

1. *Esteem* means "to value" or "to appreciate."

Vocabulary

tyranny (tir´ ə nē) *n.* cruel use of authority; oppressive power

---

2. In March 1766, the British parliament repealed the Stamp Act but also passed the Declaratory Act, which extended its right to impose taxes on the colonies and *"to bind [the colonies] in all cases whatsoever."*   ☆

The Road to Independence *Why does Paine compare taxation without representation to slavery?*   **1**

134 UNIT 1   EARLY AMERICA

Reading Practice

SPIRAL REVIEW **Analyze Arguments** Have students analyze Paine's reasoning in the first paragraph. **Ask:** What is Paine's main point? *(These are difficult times that require much of people.)* Then point out that Paine uses contrasts to support his point. **Ask:** What contrasts does Paine describe? *(Tyranny is hell, whereas freedom is heaven; the harder the conflict, the more glorious is the triumph.)* **Ask:** Do you agree that the

harder a problem is to solve, the greater the satisfaction in solving it? Explain. *(Most students will agree, citing personal experiences as evidence.)* Students should use their own life experiences, as well as text evidence, to evaluate author's arguments.

expression is impious;[3] for so unlimited a power can belong only to God.

Whether the independence of the continent was declared too soon, or delayed too long, I will not now enter into as an argument; my own simple opinion is, that had it been eight months earlier it would have been much better. We did not make a proper use of last winter; neither could we, while we were in a dependent state. However, the fault, if it were one, was all our own; we have none to blame but ourselves. But no great deal is lost yet. All that Howe[4] has been doing for this month past is rather a ravage than a conquest, which the spirit of the Jerseys[5] a year ago would have quickly repulsed, and which time and a little **resolution** will soon recover.

I have as little superstition in me as any man living; but my secret opinion has ever been, and still is, that God Almighty will not give up a people to military destruction, or leave them unsupportedly to perish, who have so earnestly and so repeatedly sought to avoid the calamities of war, by every decent method which wisdom could invent. Neither have I so much of the infidel[6] in me as to suppose that He has relinquished the government of the world, and given us up to the care of devils; and as I do not, I cannot see on what grounds the king of Britain can look up to heaven for help against us: a common murderer, a highwayman,[7] or a housebreaker, has as good a pretense as he.

It is surprising to see how rapidly a panic will sometimes run through a country. All nations and ages have been subject to them: Britain has trembled like an ague[8] at the report of a French fleet of flat-bottomed boats; and in the fourteenth century the whole English army, after ravaging the kingdom of France, was driven back like men **petrified** with fear; and this brave **exploit** was performed by a few broken forces collected and headed by a woman, Joan of Arc. Would that heaven might inspire some Jersey maid to spirit up her countrymen, and save her fair fellow sufferers from ravage and ravishment! Yet panics, in some cases, have their uses; they produce as much good as hurt. Their duration is always short; the mind soon grows through them, and acquires a firmer habit than before. But their peculiar advantage is, that they are the touchstones[9] of sincerity and **hypocrisy,** and bring things and men to light, which might otherwise have lain forever undiscovered. In fact, they have the same effect on secret traitors which an imaginary apparition[10] would have upon a private murderer. They sift out the hidden thoughts of man, and hold them up in public to the world. Many a disguised tory has lately shown his head, that shall penitentially solemnize[11] with curses the day on which Howe arrived upon the Delaware.

---

8. An *ague* is a fit of shivering.
9. A *touchstone* is anything that tests the quality or genuineness of something.
10. An *apparition* is a ghost.
11. A colonist who supported British rule was a *tory*. *Penitentially solemnize* means "to celebrate formally with sorrow and regret."

> **The Road to Independence** *What does Paine feel is missing from the colonists' struggle?* **3**

> **Summarize** *Briefly, what does Paine say about the effect of panics on British sympathizers?* **4**

Vocabulary

petrified (pet′ rə fīd) *adj.* paralyzed with fear; stiff or like stone
exploit (eks′ ploit) *n.* notable, heroic deed; feat
hypocrisy (hi pok′ rə sē) *n.* an expression of feelings or beliefs not actually possessed or held

---

3. *Impious* (im′ pē əs) means "lacking in reverence for God."
4. Major General Sir William Howe was commander in chief of the British forces in America during part of the Revolutionary War.
5. At one time New Jersey was divided into two sections, East Jersey and West Jersey. The two parts were reunited as a royal colony in 1702.
6. Here, *infidel* means "someone who does not believe in God."
7. A thief who stole from travelers on a public road was a *highwayman.*

2 Tone *Does Paine seem objective and removed here, or subjective and emotional? Explain.*

Vocabulary

resolution (rez′ ə lōō′ shən) *n.* firmness of purpose

Teach

Literary Element | **2**

Tone Answer: *Paine's tone seems objective and removed as he expresses his "simple opinion."*

Big Idea | **3**

The Road to Independence Answer: *Paine feels that the colonists need a symbol of hope and strength, like Joan of Arc.*

Reading Strategy | **4**

Summarize Answer: *If the Americans appear to be losing the war, British sympathizers will reveal themselves.*

For additional practice using the reading skill or strategy, see Unit 1 Teaching Resources Book, p. 207.

Political History

Joan of Arc Joan (1412?–1431) was a French peasant who became a military leader and led French troops in victories against the English, saving her country from English rule. She was declared a saint after her death.

English Learners

DIFFERENTIATED INSTRUCTION

Intermediate Ask: To whom does the word *men's* in the first line of Paine's essay refer? *(It refers to both men and women.)* Discuss the convention of using male nouns and pronouns to refer to people of both genders, pointing out that it has fallen out of favor with many writers today.

Approaching Level

DIFFERENTIATED INSTRUCTION

Emerging Students may need help paraphrasing Paine's complex language. Work with students sentence by sentence, separating long sentences into shorter ones. Explain that a paraphrase should be roughly the same length as the original text, but use the student's own words.

Advanced Learners

DIFFERENTIATED INSTRUCTION

Ask: What is a symbol? How do symbols inspire people? *(Symbols are tangible representations of abstract ideas, such as hope or patriotism. They bind people together in service of a common goal.)*

Teach

Literary Element 1

Tone Answer: *People who do not act might as well be dead; future generations will curse their cowardice. Paine's tone becomes much more forceful and threatening.*

Reading Strategy 2

Summarize Answer: *Nothing would cause me to start a war, because that is murder. However, when someone threatens me and my property, I will fight back, whether he is a common criminal or the king.*

View the Art ★

Answer: *Yorn depicts the soldier realistically. The soldier looks cold, not even having enough rags to completely cover his skin. By representing the soldier realistically, willing to tolerate such conditions, Yorn conveys each American soldier's determination to fight for independence.*

. . . Quitting this class of men, I turn with the warm ardor of a friend to those who have nobly stood, and are yet determined to stand the matter out: I call not upon a few, but upon all: not on *this* State or *that* State, but on *every* State: up and help us; lay your shoulders to the wheel; better have too much force than too little, when so great an object is at stake. Let it be told to the future world that in the depth of winter, when nothing but hope and virtue could survive, that the city and the country, alarmed at one common danger, came forth to meet and to repulse it. Say not that thousands are gone—turn out your tens of thousands; throw not the burden of the day upon Providence, but *"show your faith by your works,"*[12] that God may bless you. It matters not where you live, or what rank of life you hold, the evil or the blessing will reach you all. The far and the near, the home counties and the back, the rich and poor, will suffer or rejoice alike. The heart that feels not now is dead; the blood of his children will curse his cowardice who shrinks back at a time when a little might have saved the whole, and made *them* happy. I love the man that can smile in trouble, that can gather strength from distress and grow brave by reflection. It is the business of little minds to shrink; but he whose heart is firm, and whose conscience approves his conduct, will pursue his principles unto death. My own line of reasoning is to myself as straight and clear as a ray of light. Not all the treasures of the world, so far as I believe, could have induced[13] me to support an

Winter at Valley Forge, 1898. F. C. Yorn.

View the Art In this painting the artist represents the troops at Valley Forge by focusing on a single soldier. How does he depict the soldier? What is the effect of this approach? ★

offensive war, for I think it murder; but if a thief breaks into my house, burns and destroys my property, and kills or threatens to kill me or those that are in it, and to *"bind me in all cases whatsoever"* to his absolute will, am I to suffer[14] it? What signifies[15] it to me, whether he who does it is a king or a common man; my countryman or not my countryman; whether it be done by an individual villain, or an army of them? If we reason to the root of things we shall find no difference; neither can any just cause be assigned why we should punish in the one case and pardon in the other. . . . ∾

---

12. Here, *Providence* means "God." The quotation is from the New Testament Book of James.
13. *Induced* means "persuaded."

1 **Tone** *What does Paine imply about those people who do not act? How does this contribute to his tone?*

2 **Summarize** *Summarize the passage beginning "Not all the treasures of the world . . ."*

---

14. Here, *suffer* means "to put up with."
15. Here, *signifies* means "makes important."

Listening and Speaking Practice

SMALL GROUP

Presentation Form students into groups. To each group, assign one section of Paine's *Crisis* essay to present as a speech. A group may read the section in unison or assign lines to each member. Have students paraphrase their sections and be prepared to explain them to the rest of the class. As they rehearse, have students advise one another on tone, speed, and volume. Then have each group present its section.

After You Read

Respond and Think Critically

Respond and Interpret

1. Suppose you were going to choose a sentence from Thomas Paine's essay to put on a bulletin board as a memorable quotation. Which sentence would you choose? Why?

2. Which Americans does Paine criticize in his essay? Which does he praise?

3. (a)To whom does Paine compare the English king? (b)What emotions does Paine appeal to when describing the king?

4. What connection do you think Paine sees between the panics in European history Paine describes and the experience the colonists were facing?

5. (a)Paine suggests that this is not an "offensive" war. Why does he feel this way? (b)Why do you think Paine might have chosen this analogy as his final argument?

Analyze and Evaluate

6. (a)How does Paine use religion as part of his argument? (b)How effective is this approach in persuading the reader?

7. (a)In what ways does Paine express the Enlightenment idea that government should operate by "the consent of the governed"? (b)Do you agree with this idea?

Connect

8. **Big Idea** **The Road to Independence** Paine encourages his fellow citizens to defend themselves against British tyranny. (a)What kinds of qualities does Paine encourage the colonists to have? (b)How might these qualities help to define the new nation?

9. **Connect to the Author** From what you've read, do you think Thomas Paine's early failures influence his later ideas and actions? Explain.

Literary Element | Tone

SAT Skills Practice

1. The tone of this essay suggests that Paine's attitude toward his audience is

   (A) respectful but provocative

   (B) disparaging but hopeful

   (C) compassionate but disappointed

   (D) ironic but judgmental

   (E) nostalgic but different

2. The first sentence in the second column on page 135 ("It is surprising . . . a country") conveys a tone of

   (A) disbelief.

   (B) disdain.

   (C) objectivity.

   (D) terror.

   (E) boredom.

Review: Diction

Diction is a writer's choice of words, an important element in the writer's voice or style.

Partner Activity With a classmate, choose two or three sentences that seem typical of Paine's writing. Analyze the sentences, paraphrasing them where appropriate and substituting your own words. Working with your partner, create a chart like the one below. Then write a paragraph describing Paine's diction.

Sentence	Paraphrase

Assess

1. Students' choices will vary.

2. He criticizes the "summer soldier," the "sunshine patriot," and the "disguised tory." He praises supporters of freedom.

3. (a) A murderer, highwayman, or housebreaker (b) Disgust and hatred

4. Panics bring people together, reveal those unwilling to fight.

5. (a) Since the King acts like a thief, he should be punished like one. (b) To show the colonists not to be intimidated by the King's status

6. (a) Only God can rule a people "in all cases"; God would not desert a people who have tried to avoid war (b) Students' answers will vary.

7. (a) By criticizing Britain for denying the colonists' right to agree or disagree with governing policies (b) Many students will agree.

8. (a) courage, support for the revolutionary cause, understanding of the danger of British tyranny. (b) The new nation would uphold similar values of strength and freedom.

9. Paine's early failures likely helped him identify with the common person and to better understand the effects of British tyranny on the everyday life of colonial citizens.

Literary Element

1. A is the correct answer because Paine presents logical yet strongly persuasive arguments geared toward his audience's intellect.

2. C is the correct answer because the statement is an observation made without judgment or emotion.

Review: Diction

Students may paraphrase Paine's statement "What signifies it to me, whether he who does it is a king or a common man; my countryman or not my countryman; whether it be done by an individual villain, or an army of them?" as "What do I care whether the thief is a king or a commoner, a single person or an army?"

Progress Check

Can students analyze tone?

If No → See Unit 1 Teaching Resources Book, p. 206.

 For additional assessment, see Assessment Resources, pp. 89–90.

After You Read

Assess

Reading Strategy

1. The reader must remain courageous and defy Britain's threats.
2. Britain is trying to gain complete control over us.

Vocabulary

The words *tyranny* and *domination* have a similar denotation, "control," but *tyranny* has a stronger connotation, suggesting cruelty and coercion.

The words *resolution* and *aim* have a similar denotation, "determination," but *resolution* has a stronger connotation, suggesting a stronger commitment.

The words *petrified* and *scared* have a similar denotation, "frightened," but *petrified* has a stronger connotation, suggesting an extreme degree of fear.

The words *exploit* and *deed* have a similar denotation, "accomplishment," but *exploit* has a stronger connotation, suggesting a difficult feat.

The words *hypocrisy* and *insincerity* have a similar denotation, "dishonesty," but *hypocrisy* has a stronger connotation, suggesting a more calculated effort to appear to be the opposite of what one is.

Academic Vocabulary

Possible answer: Funding for the sports programs was the issue that came before the school committee.

Reading Strategy | Summarize

To summarize is to put the main ideas of a reading in your own words and in a logical sequence. Since most persuasion encourages people to act or think in a certain way, you can write a summary of a persuasive essay by answering two questions:

1. What does the writer want the reader to think or do?
2. What reasons does the writer give to support this proposal?

Write a very brief summary (two or three sentences) of this excerpt from Paine's *The Crisis, No. 1*. Be sure to include answers to the two questions above.

Vocabulary Practice

Practice with Denotation and Connotation
Denotation is the literal, or dictionary, meaning of a word. **Connotation** is the implied, or cultural, meaning of a word. For each vocabulary word below, identify a word with a similar denotation. Then explain which word has the stronger connotation and why.

tyranny	petrified	hypocrisy
resolution	exploit	

EXAMPLE: The words *hot* and *torrid* have a similar denotation, "very warm," but *torrid* has a stronger connotation, suggesting visceral, scorching heat.

Academic Vocabulary

This selection from Paine's The Crisis, No. 1 *deals with the* **issue** *of States' support for the war.*

Issue is an academic word. In the sentence above *issue* means a topic and the unresolved questions and problems surrounding it. Write a sentence of your own in which you use *issue* in the academic sense explained above.

For more on academic vocabulary, see pages 53–54.

Write with Style

 Apply Tone

Assignment: Review the overall tone in "The Crisis, No. 1." Using a similar emotional yet respectful tone, write a paragraph about a topic on which you have a strong viewpoint.

Get Ideas: Make lists of things that create strong emotions in you: things that delight you, inspire you, annoy you, or enrage you. Look through personal journals and recall recent conversations or events to complete your lists. Choose one thing from the lists to write about.

Give It Structure: Begin your paragraph with a topic sentence stating your main idea, which in this case is your thesis. Follow with sentences that support that thesis. End with a sentence that restates it.

Look at Language: Tone is conveyed through various elements of style, including word choice. Use a thesaurus to find words that help to convey your tone. If you have decided to write about something that annoys you, for example, find words that respectfully express irritation and frustration. Jot them down to choose from as you write your paragraph. As you revise, change words or phrases that might be insulting to your audience. Look at Paine's work for inspiration and guidance.

EXAMPLE:

> complaining   express
> Girls should stop ~~whining~~ that guys don't ~~go on and on about~~ their feelings as girls do.

In this sentence, for example, *complaining* and *express* convey a more respectful tone than the words they replace.

LOG ON ▶ **Literature** Online

Selection Resources For Selection Quizzes, eFlashcards, and Reading-Writing Connection activities, go to glencoe.com and enter QuickPass code GLA9800u1.

 ## Write with Style

Students should give clear and logical support for their thesis, should use words that convey an emotional connection to this thesis, and should avoid words that would offend readers.

To His Excellency, General Washington

Meet **Phillis Wheatley**
(1753–1784)

> *"We whose Names are underwritten, do assure the World, that the Poems . . . were (as we verily believe) written by Phillis, a young Negro Girl, who . . . [is] under the Disadvantage of serving as a Slave. . . ."*
>
> — *Poems on Various Subjects*

In 1773 most readers would have doubted that an enslaved woman had written a book of poetry. The above statement was taken from the introduction to Phillis Wheatley's book of poetry, *Poems on Various Subjects, Religious and Moral,* published when Wheatley was only nineteen or twenty years old. Signed by eighteen of "the most respectable characters in Boston," including John Hancock and the royal governor, the statement was testimony to the authenticity of the poems. Wheatley was the first African American to publish a book of poetry.

Wheatley was born in the Senegal/Gambia region on the west coast of Africa around 1753. In 1761, when she was just seven or eight, she was captured by slave traders and brought to New England on the slave ship *Phillis.* John and Susanna Wheatley, wealthy Bostonians, purchased her to be a personal attendant for Mrs. Wheatley.

Early Promise The young girl was often seen trying to form letters on the wall with a piece of chalk or charcoal. When the Wheatley family recognized Phillis's intelligence, they did not give her menial tasks. Instead, she was taught to read and write by Mrs. Wheatley's daughter. Phillis gained use of the home library, mastered English and Latin, read many ancient Greek and Latin classics, and studied the Bible.

Wheatley first published a poem in 1767, when she was thirteen years old. Three years later, she published a poem honoring the famous evangelist Reverend George Whitefield, which garnered her favorable publicity.

Book Published In May of 1773, the Wheatleys sent Phillis to London. There, Wheatley was able to publish her first and only volume of poetry. Many of the poems contained pleas for justice, as shown in these lines from her poem "To the Right Honourable William, Earl of Dartmouth": "That from a father seiz'd his babe belov'd: / Such, such my case. And can I then but pray / Others may never feel tyrannic sway?"

Freedom When Phillis returned from England, the family freed her from enslavement. However, she remained in the Wheatley household until John Wheatley died in 1778. In April of that same year, she married John Peters, a freed African American. Her husband's business failed, and their two children died as infants. In 1784, alone and working as a servant, she wrote her last poem. Her husband died in debtor's prison, and on December 5, she died of malnutrition when she was only thirty-one. A brief announcement in Boston's *Independent Chronicle* read, "Last Lord's Day, died Mrs. Phillis Peters (formerly Phillis Wheatley), aged thirty-one, known to the world by her celebrated miscellaneous poems."

 Literature Online

Author Search For more about Phillis Wheatley, go to glencoe.com and enter QuickPass code GLA9800u1.

PHILLIS WHEATLEY **139**

Bellringer Options

Selection Focus
Transparency 14

Daily Language Practice
Transparency 17

Or note that modern popular songs may be considered poetry. Form student groups and ask them to brainstorm lists of performers and songs that make statements about the condition of the world. Have them explain their choices.

Selection Skills

Literary Elements
- Couplet (SE pp. 140, 142, 143)

To His Excellency, General Washington

Vocabulary Skills
- Academic Vocabulary (SE p. 143)

Writing Skills/Grammar
- Poem (SE p. 143)

Reading Skills
- Analyze Structure (SE pp. 140, 141, 143)
- Paraphrase (TE p. 140)
- Visualize (TE p. 142)

Before You Read

Focus

Summary

When Washington took command of the Continental Army in 1775, Phillis Wheatley wrote a letter and a poem to him. The letter entreats him to overlook the inadequacies of the poem. The poem glorifies Washington and the American fight for freedom.

 For summaries in languages other than English, see Unit 1 Teaching Resources Book, pp. 213–218.

Literature and Reading Preview

Connect to the Poem

If you were to write a letter to a politician or other authority figure, whom would you choose? What would you say? Discuss these questions with a partner.

Build Background

When General George Washington traveled to Boston in 1775 to assume leadership of the Continental Army and to rid the city of occupying British soldiers, Phillis Wheatley wrote to him. Her letter and poem to the general were sent to his headquarters in nearby Cambridge. Washington was so impressed by Wheatley's poem that he invited her to visit him.

Set Purposes for Reading

Big Idea **The Road to Independence**

Some people have criticized Phillis Wheatley for writing a poem that glorifies freedom while failing to speak out against slavery. Others see Wheatley's choice as a necessity for maintaining support among her readers. As you read this poem, ask yourself, How did Wheatley's experience as a slave affect her reaction to the American Revolution?

Literary Element **Couplet**

A **couplet** is two consecutive, paired lines of poetry, usually rhyming and often forming a stanza. As you read, ask yourself, How does Wheatley use couplets in this poem? What effects does she achieve?

Reading Strategy **Analyze Structure**

Poets often use **inversion,** or reversal of the usual word order, for emphasis or variety or to maintain a rhyme scheme. For example, look at this line in Wheatley's poem: "Thy ev'ry action let the goddess guide." In normal word order, this line would be "Let the goddess guide thy ev'ry action." Look for other examples of inversion.

Tip: Understand Inverted Sentences To better understand the meaning of the poem, copy it onto a sheet of paper, changing each inversion to a more natural word order. Then compare the rhyme, rhythm, and emphasis in your modified version with the rhyme, rhythm, and emphasis in Wheatley's original poem.

Learning Objectives

For pages 139–143
In studying this text, you will focus on the following objectives:

Literary Study: Analyzing couplets.

Reading: Analyzing structure.

Writing: Writing a poem.

George Washington. Artist unknown, after Charles Wilson Peale. Oil on canvas. Chateau de Versailles, France.

Reading Practice

SPIRAL REVIEW **Paraphrase** Ask students to paraphrase the material in the Build Background and Set Purposes for Reading sections. Remind them that paraphrasing involves putting others' writing into your own words. Have volunteers share their paraphrases. *(Possible answers:* Build Background— *When George Washington became the leader of the colonial army, Phillis Wheatley wrote to him. Washington liked the poem that she sent him and invited her to visit.* Set Purposes for Reading— *Wheatley described the United States as a goddess of liberty. Readers disagree about whether this was appropriate, because slavery was legal in the United States at that time.)*

To His Excellency, General Washington

Phillis Wheatley

Sir,

I Have taken the freedom to address your Excellency in the enclosed poem, and entreat your acceptance, though I am not insensible of its inaccuracies. Your being appointed by the Grand Continental Congress to be Generalissimo of the armies of North America, together with the fame of your virtues, excite sensations not easy to suppress. Your generosity, therefore, I presume, will pardon the attempt. Wishing your Excellency all possible success in the great cause you are so generously engaged in. I am,

Your Excellency's most obedient humble servant,
Phillis Wheatley.

Providence, Oct. 26, 1775.
His Excellency Gen. Washington.

> Celestial choir! enthron'd in realms of light,
>   Columbia's scenes of glorious toils I write.
> While freedom's cause her anxious breast alarms,
> She flashes dreadful in refulgent[1] arms.
> 5   See mother earth her offspring's fate bemoan,
> And nations gaze at scenes before unknown!
> See the bright beams of heaven's revolving light
> Involved in sorrows and the veil of night!

---

1. *Refulgent* means "radiant."

Analyze Structure *How would you change the inversion in this passage to a more natural word order?*

Teach

Reading Strategy   1

Predict **Ask** students to read the letter that precedes the poem. On the basis of the letter, what can they predict about the poem's content and tone? *(Students may predict that the poem will praise Washington and his cause and that the tone will probably be formal.)*

For students who are struggling, point out clues in the letter.

(APPROACHING) **Ask:** To whom is the letter addressed? *(George Washington)* What attitude do the words "fame of your virtues," "excite sensations," and "generosity" suggest? *(admiration)*

Reading Strategy   2

Analyze Structure
Answer: *See mother earth bemoan her offspring's fate*

> **For additional practice using the reading skill or strategy, see Unit 1 Teaching Resources Book, p. 220.**

> **For an audio recording of this selection, use Listening Library Audio CD-ROM**

English Learners

DIFFERENTIATED INSTRUCTION

SMALL GROUP

Advanced Organize students in groups to paraphrase each line or couplet of the poem. Students should begin by identifying each example of figurative language.

Approaching Level

DIFFERENTIATED INSTRUCTION

Emerging Some students may find it easier to understand the poem if they map actions that take place. For example, in the first seven lines, "Columbia" worries about freedom, "mother earth" worries over what will happen to humans, and people in nations everywhere are stunned by war and other new events. Have students create a character and action chart where they can map actions as they read.

Character	Action
Columbia	worries about freedom's cause

Teach

Literary Element | 1

Couplet **Answer:** *The second line answers the question in the first to form a complete idea. The speaker need not praise the soldiers to Washington because he can see at first hand, in battle, how great they are.*

Big Idea | 2

The Road to Independence
Answer: *She is referring to the mounting losses that Britain is suffering at the hands of the colonists.*

Point out that the ancient Greek city of Athens was the first democracy in history. Have students note that many of Wheatley's images evoke ancient Greece.

(ADVANCED) Ask students to find images in Wheatley's poems that evoke ancient Greece, and to use research to explain these images to the class.

 To check students' understanding of the selection, see Unit 1 Teaching Resources Book, p. 221.

The goddess comes, she moves divinely fair,
10 Olive and laurel binds her golden hair:
Wherever shines this native of the skies,
Unnumber'd charms and recent graces rise.
    Muse!² bow propitious³ while my pen relates
How pour her armies through a thousand gates,
15 As when Eolus⁴ heaven's fair face deforms,
Enwrapp'd in tempest and a night of storms;
Astonish'd ocean feels the wild uproar,
The refluent⁵ surges beat the sounding shore;
Or thick as leaves in Autumn's golden reign,
20 Such, and so many, moves the warrior's train.
In bright array they seek the work of war,
Where high unfurl'd the ensign⁶ waves in air.
Shall I to Washington their praise recite?
Enough thou know'st them in the fields of fight.
25 Thee, first in peace and honours,—we demand
The grace and glory of thy martial band.
Fam'd for thy valour, for thy virtues more,
Hear every tongue thy guardian aid implore!
    One century scarce perform'd its destined round,
30 When Gallic⁷ powers Columbia's fury found;
And so may you, whoever dares disgrace
The land of freedom's heaven-defended race!
Fix'd are the eyes of nations on the scales,
For in their hopes Columbia's arm prevails.
35 Anon⁸ Britannia⁹ droops the pensive head,
While round increase the rising hills of dead.
Ah! cruel blindness to Columbia's state!
Lament thy thirst of boundless power too late.
    Proceed, great chief, with virtue on thy side,
40 Thy ev'ry action let the goddess guide.
A crown, a mansion, and a throne that shine,
With gold unfading, WASHINGTON! be thine.

---

2. The poet asks for aid from a *Muse.* In Greek mythology, the Muses (goddesses) preside over arts and sciences.
3. Here, *propitious* means "favorably."
4. In Greek mythology, *Eolus* is the god of the winds.
5. *Refluent* means "back-flowing."
6. The *ensign* here is a flag.
7. *Gallic* means "French." Washington had fought the French during the French and Indian War (1754–1763).
8. *Anon* means "soon."
9. *Britannia* is Great Britain, personified as a goddess.

1 Couplet *How does this couplet work to form one complete idea?*

2 The Road to Independence *What does the speaker mean by the "rising hills of dead"?*

Reading Practice

Visualize Wheatley uses striking visual images to describe the colonists' quest for freedom. Visualizing as they read or hear the poem will help students better understand Wheatley's view of her country. Explain that visualizing means using the poet's descriptive language to create mental pictures. **Ask:** What do you see when you hear the line "While freedom's cause her anxious breast alarms"? *(Possible response: a motherly figure who might be holding her hand over her heart in concern)* Have students sketch what they visualize as Wheatley's vision of America. Drawings might include Columbia, Britannia, or a victorious Washington. **Ask:** What feelings or emotions do your drawings convey? Do you think Wheatley's images produce the effect she desires? *(Answers will vary.)*

After You Read

Respond and Think Critically

Respond and Interpret

1. What is your impression of Phillis Wheatley from reading her letter and poem?

2. (a)In your own words, restate the message in Wheatley's letter to General Washington. (b)Based on the letter, what can you infer about her opinion of Washington?

3. (a)How is Columbia is described in lines 9–12? (b)What does that image convey about the speaker's view of America?

4. (a)In lines 13–22, to what things does the speaker compare the colonial army? (b)Why might Wheatley have chosen these images?

Analyze and Evaluate

5. (a)To whom are lines 29–38 addressed? (b)How does this section of the poem differ from the rest?

6. Do Wheatley's allusions to mythology strengthen or weaken the meaning of the poem? Explain.

Connect

7. **Big Idea** **The Road to Independence** How do you think Wheatley's experience of being enslaved affected her attitude toward the colonial cause of freedom?

8. **Connect to Today** Few people in the 1770s would have thought an enslaved woman could write poetry—a perspective that reveals the deep prejudices of the time. Can you think of any social groups today that are considered by many to be incapable of achieving certain goals? What does this reveal about our society?

Literary Element | Couplet

A **couplet** is two consecutive lines of poetry that rhyme. A **heroic couplet** (commonly used in epic poems) has a specific rhythm, or meter, called **iambic pentameter:** each line has five units, or feet, and each foot has two syllables, an unstressed one followed by a stressed one.

1. Read aloud three heroic couplets from the poem. In your opinion, does this form add to or detract from the meaning of the poem?

2. Why do you think Wheatley might have chosen to write this poem in heroic couplets?

Reading Strategy | Analyze Structure

Wheatley uses inversion in each of the following lines. Rewrite each without the use of inversion.

1. How pour her armies through a thousand gates, As when Eolus heaven's fair face deforms . . .

2. Shall I to Washington their praise recite?

Academic Vocabulary

Wheatley's ode to Washington has a regular metrical **structure.**

Structure is an academic word. More familiar words with similar meanings are shape, composition, framework, and organization. Using context clues, try to figure out the meaning of *structure* in each sentence below:

1. Researchers studied the **structure** of families in various cultures to find similarities.

2. Epithelial tissues are arranged in a **structure** like a sheet that protects underlying cells.

Writing

Write a Poem Using Wheatley's work as an example, write a poem of praise addressed to someone you consider to be a great leader or role model. Use heroic couplets in your poem and imitate Wheatley's elevated diction and style.

After You Read

Assess

1. Some students may say she believes fully in the cause.

2. (a) The country has confidence in Washington. (b) He is a man of great virtue.

3. (a) Columbia wears symbols of peace and victory. (b) America is strong but not warlike.

4. (a) A storm at sea and autumn leaves (b) She wanted to suggest the army's power and numbers.

5. (a) To all potential enemies of the American colonists, particularly Great Britain (b) The tone is threatening.

6. The references to Columbia, Britannia, a Muse, and Eolus give it an added sense of grandeur.

7. Students may feel that her experience made her enthusiastic about the Revolution. Some may sense irony in a formerly enslaved person's enthusiasm for a leader who did not intend to free enslaved Africans.

8. Answers will vary.

> For additional assessment, see Assessment Resources, pp. 91–92.

Progress Check

Can students identify a couplet?

If No → See Unit 1 Teaching Resources Book, p. 219.

Literary Element

1. Students may note that the regularity of the couplets creates a rational, dignified tone, which adds both gravity and intensity to the poem.

2. Students may say that Wheatley saw General Washington and his cause as heroic, so she chose a form that was used to record heroic deeds.

Reading Strategy

1. How her armies pour through a thousand gates, / As when Eolus deforms heaven's fair face . . .

2. Shall I recite their praise to Washington?

Writing Skills

Students should focus on a specific role model, emulating Wheatley's style and using heroic couplets.

Academic Vocabulary

1. In this statement about sociology, *structure* means the "interrelated arrangement of or relationship between members of a family."

2. In this statement about biology, *structure* means "the arrangement and construction of tissues, organs, and parts."

Before You Read

Focus

Bellringer Options

Literature Launchers:
  Pre-Reading Videos DVD,
  Selection Launcher
Selection Focus
  Transparency 15
Daily Language Practice
  Transparency 18
Ask: What challenges might
women have faced during the
Revolutionary War? *(Possible
responses: being separated from
husbands; lack of education)*

Interactive Read and Write
Other options for teaching this
selection can be found in

- Interactive Read and Write for
  EL Students, pp. 37–44
- Interactive Read and Write for
  Approaching-Level Students,
  pp. 37–44
- Interactive Read and Write for
  On-Level Students, pp. 37–44

Before You Read

Letter to John Adams

Meet **Abigail Adams**
(1744–1818)

In her day, Abigail Adams was known to the world as the loyal wife of John Adams, second president of the United States. Today she is just as famous for her brilliant mind. Adams participated in the events of some of the most tumultuous years of the nation, writing about them with sparkling wit.

A Happy Childhood The daughter of an accomplished Massachusetts minister, Adams grew up surrounded by people who valued strong principles and enjoyed defending them. Adams was passionate for knowledge and pursued her education in secret. She gained a wide knowledge of literature, but lamented what she felt was her ignorance. In letters to her husband, she argued that women deserved education and the right to own property.

> *"I desire you would remember the ladies, and be more generous and favorable to them than your ancestors."*
>
> —Abigail Adams, Letter to John Adams

Wife and Mother Adams met John Adams, a Harvard-trained lawyer, when she was fifteen. In 1764 the two married and went to live on John's farm at Braintree (later Quincy), Massachusetts. John Adams soon rose to prominence as a believer in American independence, requiring him to spend years in Philadelphia at the Continental Congress. Abigail, deeply supportive of the cause, stayed in Braintree to raise their five children. Outwardly cheerful, she felt, but rarely expressed, deep pain at being separated from her husband.

After some months spent without a word from him, she finally wrote: "I pray my guardian generous to waft me the happy tidings of your safety and welfare . . . Difficult as the day is, cruel as this war has been, separated as I am on account of it from the dearest connection in life, I would not exchange my country for the wealth of the Indies, or be any other than an American."

Later Years After the war, John Adams was selected as the first U.S. ambassador to England, later became the first vice president of the United States, and succeeded George Washington as president from 1797 to 1801. After John Adams lost the presidency, he and Abigail retired to Quincy. Their eldest son, John Quincy, went on to become the sixth president of the United States in 1825.

Letters That Endure Abigail Adams's letters vibrate with personality. She could be unapologetically opinionated, seeking to enlarge her husband's sense of morality: "You know my mind upon this subject," she wrote him regarding slavery. "I wish most sincerely there was not a slave in the province. It always appeared a most iniquitous scheme to me—fight ourselves for what we are daily robbing and plundering from those who have as good a right to freedom as we have." Her most famous observations relate to women, who she felt needed expanded legal rights and education. "If we mean to have heroes, statesmen, and philosophers, we should have learned women," she said.

 Literature Online

Author Search For more about Abigail Adams, go to glencoe.com and enter QuickPass code GLA9800u1.

Selection Skills

Literary Elements
- Description
  (SE pp. 145, 147, 148)

Reading Skills
- Recognize Author's Purpose
  (SE pp. 145, 147, 148)
- Preview (TE p. 146)

Letter to John Adams

Vocabulary Skills
- Analogies (SE p. 148)
- Sentences (TE p. 145)

**Listening/Speaking/
Viewing Skills**
- View Art (TE p. 146)

Writing Skills/Grammar
- Letter (SE p. 148)

Literature and Reading Preview

Connect to the Letters

Is it important to you to keep in touch with relatives or friends who live far away? Why? Reflect on these questions in a journal entry.

Build Background

With the onset of war in 1775, the Continental Congress became the provisional government for the American side. While John Adams labored at the Congress, war raged in Massachusetts. Troops occupied Boston for nearly a year, forcing Bostonians to house them. The British retreated just a few days before Abigail wrote her March 31, 1776, letter.

Set Purposes for Reading

Big Idea The Road to Independence

As you read, ask yourself, How does this letter reflect ideals of the time, such as self-reliance and human rights?

Literary Element Description

Description is the use of details to give the reader a vivid impression of a person, place, or thing. Good descriptive writing contributes to the overall purpose of a piece and avoids irrelevant details. As you read, ask yourself, Which details give you a sense of being in colonial Boston? Why?

Reading Strategy Recognize Author's Purpose

The **author's purpose** is the author's intent in writing a work. Authors usually write to persuade, to inform, to explain, to entertain, or to describe. As you read, consider what Adams describes and what opinions she expresses. What does her inclusion of these details tell you about her purpose for writing?

....

Tip: Double-Entry Journal Use a double-entry journal to help you think about Adams's purpose.

Questions to ask	Answers
What does Adams's word choice suggest about her attitude toward her readers?	

Learning Objectives

For pages 144–148

In studying this text, you will focus on the following objectives:

Literary Studies: Analyzing description.

Reading: Recognizing author's purpose.

Vocabulary

deprive (di prīv´) *v.* to take away from; to keep from enjoying or having; p. 146 *Students should not deprive themselves of education.*

tyrant (tī´ rənt) *n.* a ruler who exercises power or authority in an unjust manner; one who has absolute power; p. 147 *Many colonists felt that King George was a tyrant.*

foment (fō ment´) *v.* to promote the development or growth of; p. 147 *The cruelty of the guards fomented discontent in the inmates.*

vassal (vas´ əl) *n.* a person in a subservient position; p. 147 *The vassals, who vowed loyalty to their feudal lord, were nearly slaves.*

Tip: Analogies Analogies are comparisons based on relationships between words. For example:

deprive : rob :: supply : provide

To finish an analogy, decide on the relationship between the first two words. Then apply that relationship to the second set of words.

Before You Read

Focus

Summary

In a letter to her husband written in 1776, Abigail Adams describes damage done by British troops to Massachusetts homes. She also requests that the Continental Congress create a government that respects the rights of women.

 For summaries in languages other than English, see Unit 1 Teaching Resources Book, pp. 223–228.

Vocabulary

Sentences Ask students to create a sentence that uses two of the vocabulary words to describe the relationship between the colonists and King George. *(The colonists viewed King George as a tyrant who had deprived them of inalienable rights.)*

APPROACHING Specific verbs often have more general synonyms, such as *walk* for *stroll*. **Ask:** Which verb is a synonym for *deprive: remove* or *supply*? *(remove)*

 For additional vocabulary practice, see Unit 1 Teaching Resources Book, p. 231.

 For additional context, see Glencoe Interactive Vocabulary CD-ROM.

English Learners

DIFFERENTIATED INSTRUCTION

Intermediate Review the words that describe reasons for writing. **Ask:** Why might a writer want to persuade? *(to get a result)* Inform? *(to provide facts)* Explain? *(to teach how to do something)* Entertain? *(to get a reader's attention)* Describe? *(to share an experience)* As students read, have them pause to restate main ideas and then use these restatements to infer Adams's purpose for writing.

Advanced Remind students that descriptive details may be adjectives, nouns, or verbs. Have students create a map to keep track of descriptive details in Adams's writing.

Teach

Reading Strategy | 1

Draw Conclusions **Ask:** Why does Abigail Adams say that the colony has been duped by Dunmore? *(Adams believes that Dunmore was devious in offering freedom to slaves who fought for the British.)*

[ENGLISH LEARNERS] Provide students with a synonym for *duped*, and then have them use it in place of *duped* in the sentence to build meaning. **Ask:** What does *duped* mean? *(fooled, tricked)*

For additional practice using the reading skill or strategy, see Unit 1 Teaching Resources Book, p. 230.

Big Idea | 2

The Road to Independence
Answer: *As a principle, Adams believes that all who fight in the name of freedom should be willing to grant freedom and human rights to others.*

View the Art ★

The older house in this painting, on the right, was built in 1681. John Adams lived there until he and Abigail were married. Then they moved into the house next door, where their son John Quincy was born.

For an audio recording of this selection, use Listening Library Audio CD-ROM.

Readability Scores
Dale-Chall: 8.8
DRP: 62
Lexile: 1350

146

Letter to John Adams

Abigail Adams

Birthplaces of John Adams and John Quincy Adams, 1849. G. N. Frankenstein. Watercolor. Courtesy of the Adams National Historic Site, National Park Service. ★

Braintree, March 31, 1776

I wish you would ever write me a letter half as long as I write you; and tell me if you may where your fleet are gone? What sort of defense Virginia can make against our common enemy? Whether it is so situated as to make an able defense? Are not the gentry[1] lords and the common people vassals?[2] Are they not like the uncivilized natives Britain represents us to be? I hope their rifle men,[3] who have shown themselves very savage and even bloodthirsty, are not a specimen of the generality of the people.

I am willing to allow the colony great merrit for having produced a Washington, but they have been shamefully duped by a Dunmore.[4]

---

1. *Gentry* means the "upper," or "ruling," class.
2. Here, a *vassal* is someone in a subordinate or inferior position.
3. *Rifle men* refers to British soldiers and Loyalists fighting pro-independence forces.
4. The Earl of *Dunmore* was Virginia's last royal governor. He promised freedom to slaves who would fight against the Continental Congress and for England's king, thus angering American patriots.

146 UNIT 1 EARLY AMERICA

I have sometimes been ready to think that the passion for liberty cannot be equally strong in the breasts of those who have been accustomed to **deprive** their fellow creatures of theirs. Of this I am certain: that it is not founded upon the generous and Christian principle of doing to others as we would that others should do unto us.

Do not you want to see Boston; I am fearful of the small pox, or I should have been in before this time. I got Mr. Crane to go to our house and see what state it was in. I find it has been occupied by one of the doctors of a regiment, very dirty, but no other damage has been done to it. The few things which were left in it are all gone. Crane has the key, which he never delivered up. I have wrote to him for it

---

The Road to Independence *How does Adams's criticism reflect her belief in human rights?* **2**

Vocabulary

deprive (di prīv´) *v.* to take away from; to keep from enjoying or having

---

Reading Practice

 SMALL GROUP
Preview and Make Inferences Explain that Abigail Adams was a prolific letter writer. Her letters reflect the thoughts and feelings of a woman whose intelligence transcended her lack of formal education. Elicit discussion by asking these questions:

- How can a lack of education hinder people?
- How can people compensate for a lack of formal schooling?

Tell students to begin reading the letter. Have them make inferences as they read to identify the traits that Abigail Adams possessed. Then organize students in small groups to exchange and defend their inferences. Students must identify a trait and then point to specific evidence in the letter that supports the inference.

and am determined to get it cleaned as soon as possible and shut it up. I look upon it a new acquisition of property, a property which one month ago I did not value at a single shilling, and could with pleasure have seen it in flames.

The town in general is left in a better state than we expected, more owing to a precipitate[5] flight than any regard for the inhabitants, though some individuals discovered a sense of honor and justice and have left the rent of the houses in which they were for the owners and the furniture unhurt, or if damaged sufficient to make it good.

Others have committed abominable ravages. The mansion house of your president[6] is safe and the furniture unhurt, whilst both the house and the furniture of the Solicitor General have fallen a prey to their own merciless party. Surely the very fiends feel a reverential awe for virtue and patriotism, whilst they detest the parricide[7] and traitor.

I feel very differently at the approach of spring to which I did a month ago. We knew not then whether we could plant or sow with safety, whether when we had toiled we could reap the fruits of our own industry, whether we could rest in our own cottages, or whether we should not be driven from the sea coasts to seek shelter in the wilderness, but now we feel as if we might sit under our own vine and eat the good of the land.

I feel a gaieté de coeur[8] to which before I was a stranger. I think the sun looks brighter, the birds sing more melodiously, and nature puts on a more cheerful countenance. We feel

a temporary peace, and the poor fugitives are returning to their deserted habitations.

Though we felicitate ourselves, we sympathize with those who are trembling lest the lot of Boston should be theirs. But they cannot be in similar circumstances unless pusillanimity[9] and cowardice should take possession of them. They have time and warning given them to see the evil and shun it.—I long to hear that you have declared an independency—and by the way, in the new Code of Laws which I suppose it will be necessary for you to make, I desire you would remember the ladies, and be more generous and favorable to them than your ancestors. Do not put such unlimited power into the hands of the husbands. Remember, all men would be **tyrants** if they could. If particular care and attention is not paid to the ladies, we are determined to **foment** a rebellion, and will not hold ourselves bound by any laws in which we have no voice, or representation.

That your sex are naturally tyrannical is truth so thoroughly established as to admit no dispute, but such of you as wish to be happy willingly give up the harsh title of master for the more tender and endearing one of friend. Why, then, not put it out of the power of the vicious and the lawless to use us with cruelty and indignity with impunity. Men of sense in all ages abhor those customs which treat us only as the **vassals** of your sex. Regard us then as beings placed by providence under your protection, and in imitation of the Supreme Being, make use of that power only for our happiness.

Abigail

---

5. *Precipitate* means "sudden" or "hasty."
6. John Hancock was the president of the Continental Congress. When the British occupied Boston, General William Howe took Hancock's house as his headquarters.
7. Here, *parricide* means "a person who commits the crime of treason."
8. *Gaieté de coeur* (gā ə tā də koer) is a French idiom meaning "lightheartedness" or "playfulness."

3 Recognize Author's Purpose *Why might Adams have included this information?*

4 Description *How do these details express the emotional pitch of Adams's situation?*

9. *Pusillanimity* (pū′ sə lə nim′ ə tē) means "cowardliness" or "faintheartedness."

Vocabulary

tyrant (tī′ rənt) *n.* a ruler who exercises power or authority in an unjust manner; one who has absolute power

foment (fō ment′) *v.* to promote the development or growth of

vassal (vas′ əl) *n.* a person in a subservient position

ABIGAIL ADAMS **147**

Teach

Reading Strategy 3

Recognize Author's Purpose **Answer:** *Adams wanted her husband to know about the condition of his hometown.*

Literary Element 4

Description **Answer:** *These details show Adams's tremendous relief after having lived through a very uncertain time.*

To check students' understanding of the selection, see Unit 1 Teaching Resources Book, p. 234.

Approaching Level

DIFFERENTIATED INSTRUCTION

Emerging For students still struggling to identify descriptive language, work through the text word by word. Identify descriptive details and **ask:** What does this word make you think of? What do you see or hear? What feelings do you associate with these ideas? *(Possible responses: The sun coming out of the clouds and birds singing; feelings of happiness and relief)*

Established To help students respond to the Literary Element question, review the text with them. Point out a few examples of descriptive details, and then ask students to identify additional examples. Have students indicate to what sense the details appeal and then describe the images they visualize as a result of Adams's description.

After You Read

Assess

1. Students' answers will vary.

2. (a) The occupation of Boston left many homes ruined; Dunmore angered patriots by offering freedom to slaves who would fight for the British; many people feared that the British might take over their towns. (b) Adams is concerned about the effects of the war on people's lives. She is impressed with the leadership of Washington and disappointed in Dunmore.

3. (a) The rights of women (b) If women are ignored, they will organize a rebellion.

4. Men would rather dominate women than consider them their equals. Students' answers will vary.

5. Students are likely to say that Adams's opinions are fair.

6. Adams's letters show a world in turmoil before the Revolution and a much calmer, yet still developing, culture after the war.

7. People can now get in touch with other people much more quickly via telephone and e-mail, but interpersonal relationships are not necessarily closer than those in Adams's time.

 For additional assessment, see Assessment Resources, pp. 93–94.

Progress Check

Can students analyze a description?

If No ➔ See Unit 1 Teaching Resources Book, p. 229.

After You Read

Respond and Think Critically

Respond and Interpret

1. Would you like to have known Abigail Adams? Why or why not?

2. (a)From reading this letter, what details did you learn about the British occupation of Boston, the role of Dunmore, and "those who are trembling lest the lot of Boston should be theirs"? (b)What are Adams's attitudes toward the conflict and the various people mentioned? Explain.

3. (a)What does Adams urge her husband to consider as he creates a new code of laws? (b)What reasons does she give for urging this consideration?

Analyze and Evaluate

4. What do you think Adams means when she says that "all men would be tyrants if they could"? Do you agree?

5. Do Adams's opinions seem fair to you? Explain.

Connect

6. **Big Idea** The Road to Independence What does this letter tell you about life before and after the American Revolution?

7. **Connect to Today** How have the changes in long-distance communication since Abigail Adams wrote this letter affected people's relationships and sense of connectedness?

Literary Element Description

Good descriptive writing gives the reader a picture of a person, place, or thing. Did Adams's descriptions bring war-torn Boston to life for you? Explain why or why not. If so, be sure to include specific examples of details that appealed to your senses.

Reading Strategy Recognize Author's Purpose

You can get a sharper idea of Abigail Adams's purposes for writing by considering the context in which she wrote. Think of what you know about John Adams's responsibilities as well as the issues faced by colonists. What would you say is one purpose of Adams's letter to her husband?

Vocabulary Practice

Practice with Analogies Choose the word pair that best completes each analogy.

1. deprive : provide ::
   a. abuse : berate
   b. aid : help
   c. comfort : console
   d. defend : attack

2. tyrant : abuse ::
   a. manager : mislead
   b. expert : speculate
   c. benefactor : aid
   d. mentor : learn

3. foment : growth ::
   a. nourish : hunger
   b. injure : pain
   c. bankrupt : wealth
   d. succeed : defeat

4. vassal : servant ::
   a. nurse : caregiver
   b. doctor : medicine
   c. zoologist : animals
   d. baby : mother

Writing

Write a Letter Imagine you know someone who is about to move to your neighborhood. Write this person an informal letter giving an accurate description of the area, including the pros and cons of living there. Include sensory details to make your description more vivid.

LOG ON ▶ **Literature** Online

Selection Resources For Selection Quizzes, eFlashcards, and Reading-Writing Connection activities, go to glencoe.com and enter QuickPass code GLA9800u1.

Reading Strategy

Students' answers will vary.

Literary Element

Students' answers will vary.

Vocabulary

1. d 2. c 3. b 4. a

Writing

Students should follow the conventions of letter writing; they should include clear pros and cons and interesting sensory details.

Grammar Workshop

Clauses as Modifiers

Literature Connection In the quotation below, both sentences are made up of two clauses, each of which has a subject and a predicate and expresses a complete thought. The main (independent) clause can stand alone, but the subordinate (dependent) clause needs the main clause to complete its meaning.

> *"Remember, all men would be tyrants if they could. . . . Men of sense in all ages abhor those customs which treat us only as the vassals of your sex."*
>
> —Abigail Adams, from *Letter to John Adams*

In the first sentence, the subordinate clause *if they could* acts as an adverb by answering the question *Under what conditions?* of the verb *would be.* (An adverb clause may also modify an adjective or an adverb.) In the second sentence, the subordinate clause *which treat us only as the vassals of your sex* acts as an adjective by modifying the noun *customs.*

Examples

- Crane has the key, <u>which he never delivered up.</u>

  The underlined adjective clause modifies the noun *key* by providing additional information about it.

- <u>Although the poor fugitives are returning,</u> we cannot feel peaceful.

  The underlined adverb clause answers the question *Under what conditions?* It modifies the verb *cannot.* Adverb clauses may also answer the questions *how?, when?, where?, why?, how often?,* or *how much?*

Revise Write two new sentences to expand each main clause below. In one new sentence use an adverb clause and in the other use an adjective clause. Underline each clause and identify the word or words that the clause modifies. For adverb clauses, identify the question each answers.

1. Some individuals discovered a sense of honor and justice.
2. Others have committed ravages.
3. The mansion house of your president proved safe.
4. I long to hear that you have declared an independency.
5. I hope their rifle men do not represent the people in general.

Learning Objectives

In this workshop, you will focus on the following objectives:

Grammar: Understanding how to use clauses as modifiers. Punctuating subordinate clauses.

Punctuating Clauses

When a subordinate clause introduces a sentence, it is set off from the main clause with a comma. In other positions, only nonessential elements, like *which he never delivered up* in the first example at left, are set off with commas. Essential elements, such as the clause beginning *which treat us only* in the Adams quotation, are not set off with commas.

Tip

Adjective clauses are often introduced by relative pronouns (*who, whom, which,* and *that*). Adverb clauses are often introduced by subordinating conjunctions such as *after, although, as, because, if,* and *when.*

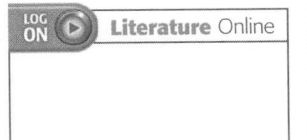

Literature Online

GRAMMAR WORKSHOP **149**

Grammar Workshop

Clauses as Modifiers

Focus

Write on the board: The students feel nervous about their English test, which will account for 20 percent of their grade. Point out that the subordinate clause is acting as an adjective modifying the noun *test.*

Teach

Nonessential Clauses Tell students that they can tell whether a subordinate clause is nonessential if the meaning of the sentence does not change when the clause is removed from the sentence. Nonessential clauses must be set off from the main clause with commas.

Assess

In their sentences, students should correctly use adverb and adjective clauses, identify what each clause modifies, and tell what question each adverb clause answers.

 For additional grammar practice, see Unit 1 Teaching Resources Book, p. 233.

Approaching Level

DIFFERENTIATED INSTRUCTION

Emerging Help students work through the exercise in the Revise section. Remind students that adjective clauses modify nouns or pronouns and adverb clauses modify verbs, adjectives, or adverbs. Have students read the first sentence in the exercise aloud. **Ask:** Which of the words in this sentence are nouns or pronouns? (*individuals, honor, justice*) Which are verbs, adjectives, or adverbs? (*some,* *discovered*) Ask students to pick one of the nouns and write an adjective clause that gives additional information about the noun. Have students put together their first sentence by picking a suitable relative pronoun to join their adjective clause to the main clause. Students should then write an adverb clause that may modify the verb and pick a subordinating conjunction to join their adverb clause to the main clause for their second sentence. Help students work on the rest of the sentences in the exercise in the same systematic manner.

149

Focus

Summary

McCullough paints a vivid portrait of Abigail and John Adams, describing the mutual admiration and respect that sustained their marriage despite much separation. McCullough writes about Abigail's intelligence and competence and the equal partnership that made their marriage a success. McCullough also describes the Adamses' happy domestic life before John's ambition took him away from his home and family.

Teach

| Literary Element | 1 |

Description **Ask:** How does McCullough convey information about Abigail's character? *(Students may say that his vivid description of her face and facial expressions makes it clear that she was a strong, intelligent woman.)*

(ENGLISH LEARNERS) Remind students that many English words have multiple meanings. Ask students to think of two meanings for *stiff* (one meaning is "not easily bent;" the other is "reserved, lacking in grace"). Ask how McCullough uses the word to describe the portrait of Abigail Adams. *(reserved, lacking in grace)*

For an audio recording of this selection, use Listening Library Audio CD-ROM.

Readability Scores

Dale-Chall: 9.9
DRP: 64
Lexile: 1270

Historical Perspective
on *John Adams*

from

John Adams

Pulitzer Prize Winner   David McCullough

Learning Objectives

For pages 150–153
In studying this text, you will focus on the following objectives:

Reading:
Analyzing informational text.
Analyzing biographical narrative.

Build Background

Letters between John and Abigail Adams provide insights into their lives, the Revolutionary War, and the career of the second president. This excerpt, from historian David McCullough's biography *John Adams,* frequently refers to their correspondence.

Set a Purpose for Reading

Read to discover biographical information about Abigail and John Adams.

Reading Strategy

Analyze a Biographical Narrative

As you read, take notes about what the selection reveals about Abigail and John. Use word webs like the one below to help you.

Of the courtship Adams had said not a word in his diary. Indeed, for the entire year of 1764 there were no diary entries, a sure sign of how preoccupied he was.

At their first meeting, in the summer of 1759, Abigail had been a shy, frail fifteen-year-old. Often ill during childhood and still subject to recurring headaches and insomnia, she appeared more delicate and vulnerable than her sisters. By the time of her wedding, she was not quite twenty, little more than five feet tall, with dark brown hair, brown eyes, and a fine, pale complexion. For a rather stiff pastel portrait, one of a pair that she and John sat for in Salem a few years after their marriage, she posed with just a hint of a smile, three strands of pearls at the neck, her hair pulled back with a blue ribbon. But where the flat, oval face in her husband's portrait conveyed nothing of his bristling intelligence and appetite for life, in hers there was a strong, unmistakable look of good sense and character. He could have been almost any well-fed, untested young man with dark, arched brows and a grey wig, while she was distinctly attractive, readily identifiable, her intent dark eyes clearly focused on the world.

One wonders how a more gifted artist might have rendered Abigail. Long years afterward,

 1

Reading Practice

Compare and Contrast Point out to students that McCullough compares and contrasts Abigail and John Adams by describing their looks and expressions. Have each student make a two-column chart of their traits, with one column for Abigail's and one for John's. Have students point out the similarities and differences between the traits. Then ask students to describe each of the Adamses in a short summary sentence or two. Have students use their lists and sentences to draw conclusions about why Abigail and John Adams had such an enduring marriage.

Gilbert Stuart,[1] while working on her portrait, would exclaim to a friend that he wished to God he could have painted Mrs. Adams when she was young; she would have made "a perfect Venus,"[2] to which her husband, on hearing the story, expressed emphatic agreement.

Year after year through the long courtship, John trotted his horse up and over Penn's Hill[3] by the coast road five miles to Weymouth[4] at every chance and in all seasons. She was his Diana, after the Roman goddess of the moon. He was her Lysander, the Spartan hero. In the privacy of correspondence, he would address her as "Ever Dear Diana" or "Miss Adorable." She nearly always began her letters then, as later, "My Dearest Friend." She saw what latent abilities and strengths were in her ardent suitor and was deeply in love. Where others might see a stout, bluff[5] little man, she saw a giant of great heart, and so it was ever to be.

Only once before their marriage, when the diary was still active, did Adams dare mention her in its pages, and then almost in code:

Di was a constant feast. Tender, feeling, sensible, friendly. A friend. Not an imprudent, not an indelicate, not a disagreeable word or action. Prudent, soft, sensible, obliging, active.

She, too, was an avid reader and attributed her "taste for letters" to Richard Cranch,[6] who, she later wrote, "taught me to love the poets and put into my hands, Milton, Pope, and Thompson,[7] and Shakespeare." She could quote poetry more readily than could John

Adams, and over a lifetime would quote her favorites again and again in correspondence, often making small, inconsequential mistakes, an indication that rather than looking passages up, she was quoting from memory.

Intelligence and wit shined in her. She was consistently cheerful. She, too, loved to talk quite as much as her suitor, and as time would tell, she was no less strong-minded.

Considered too frail for school, she had been taught at home by her mother and had access to the library of several hundred books accumulated by her father. A graduate of Harvard, the Reverend Smith[8] was adoring of all his children, who, in addition to the three daughters, included one son, William. They must never speak unkindly of anyone, Abigail remembered her father saying repeatedly. They must say only "handsome things," and make topics rather than persons their subjects—sensible policy for a parson's family. But Abigail had views on nearly everything and persons no less than topics. Nor was she ever to be particularly hesitant about expressing what she thought.

Open in their affections for one another, she and John were also open in their criticisms. "Candor is my characteristic," he told her, as though she might not have noticed. He thought she could improve her singing voice. He faulted her for her "parrot-toed" way of walking and for sitting cross-legged. She told him he was too severe in his judgments of people and that to others often appeared haughty.[9] Besides, she chided[10] him, "a gentleman has no business to concern himself about the legs of a lady."

During the terrible smallpox epidemic of 1764, when Boston became "one great hospital," he went to the city to be inoculated, an often harrowing, potentially fatal ordeal extending over many days. Though he sailed through with little discomfort, she worried excessively, and they corresponded nearly every day, Adams reminding her to be sure to have his letters "smoked," on the chance they carried contamination.

---

1. Born in Rhode Island, *Gilbert Stuart* (1755–1828) was the most highly regarded American portrait painter of his time.
2. *Venus* was the Roman goddess of love and beauty, associated with the Greek goddess Aphrodite.
3. *Penn's Hill* is a hill near Boston.
4. *Weymouth,* a town in eastern Massachusetts, was Abigail Adams's birthplace.
5. Here, *bluff* means "outspoken and frank."
6. *Richard Cranch* was Abigail Adams's brother-in-law.
7. John *Milton* (1608–1674), Alexander *Pope* (1688–1744), and James *Thomson* (1700–1748)—whose name Abigail misspells—were all prominent British poets.

---

8. *The Reverend William Smith* was Abigail's father.
9. *Haughty* means "disdainfully proud."
10. *Chided* means "scolded constructively."

DAVID McCULLOUGH **151**

Teach

Reading Strategy   2

Context Clues **Say:** Use context clues to determine the meanings of the following words: *emphatic, latent, ardent.* Identify the context clues you used. If you cannot determine the meaning of a word, use a dictionary for help.

(APPROACHING) Read each context sentence aloud with students. Ask them to suggest a meaning, and then have them read aloud dictionary definitions and etymologies. Have students explain how the etymology informs the usage in context.

Cultural History ☆

Women's Education Before the American Revolution, most colonists believed that girls needed only the most basic education in reading, writing, music, dancing, and needlework. After the Revolution, people began to place a higher value on girls' education. Dr. Benjamin Rush of Philadelphia played a key role in implementing educational reform that benefited girls.

For an activity related to this selection, see Unit 1 Teaching Resources Book, pp. 237–245.

English Learners

DIFFERENTIATED INSTRUCTION

Intermediate Help students appreciate the light-hearted banter between Abigail and John. Post the phrases "parrot-toed" and "cross-legged." Ask students to describe, draw, or demonstrate these. **Ask:** What is John saying to Abigail? *(that she is unladylike and awkward in her posture)* What is she saying in reply? *(that it is not polite for him to look at her legs anyway)*

Advanced List words from the selection containing prefixes and suffixes, such as *unkindly, discomfort, disagreeable, indelicate,* and *imprudent.* Circle the affixes and ask students to define them. (un-, dis-, in-, *and* im- *all mean "not"; * -ly *means "in the manner of";* -able *means "capable of being."*) Have students locate the words in the selection and explain their meaning.

Teach

Block Quotations Point out the long quotation on this page. Explain that lengthy quotations are indented in this manner to make them easier to read and to emphasize that they include primary source material.

Make Inferences Have students identify the characteristics that McCullough associates with a "New England woman." Ask whether the expression has a positive connotation.

ADVANCED Have students explain why McCullough contrasts Abigail's knowledge of English poetry and literature with her Yankee speech patterns. Ask them to infer McCullough's attitude toward the Yankee speech patterns.

Informational Text

The rambling, old-fashioned parsonage at Weymouth and its furnishings were a step removed from the plain farmer's cottage of John's boyhood or the house Abigail would move to once they were married. Also, two black slaves were part of the Smith household.

According to traditional family accounts, the match was strongly opposed by Abigail's mother. She was a Quincy, the daughter of old John Quincy, whose big hilltop homestead, known as Mount Wollaston, was a Braintree[11] landmark. Abigail, it was thought, would be marrying beneath her. But the determination of both Abigail and John, in combination with their obvious attraction to each other—like steel to a magnet, John said—were more than enough to carry the day.

A month before the wedding, during a spell of several weeks when they were unable to see one another because of illness, Adams wrote to her:

> Oh, my dear girl, I thank heaven that another fortnight[12] will restore you to me—after so long a separation. My soul and body have both been thrown into disorder by your absence, and a month or two more would make me the most insufferable cynic in the world. I see nothing but faults, follies, frailties and defects in anybody lately. People have lost all their good properties or I my justice or discernment.
>
> But you, who have always softened and warmed my heart, shall restore my benevolence as well as my health and tranquility of mind. You shall polish and refine my sentiments of life and manners, banish all the unsocial and ill natured particles in my composition, and form me to that happy temper that can reconcile a quick discernment with a perfect candor.
>
> Believe me, now and ever your faithful
> Lysander

---

11. *Braintree,* a town in eastern Massachusetts, was John Adams's birthplace.
12. A *fortnight* is two weeks.

His marriage to Abigail Smith was the most important decision of John Adams's life, as would become apparent with time. She was in all respects his equal, and the part she was to play would be greater than he could possibly have imagined, for all his love for her and what appreciation he already had of her beneficial, steadying influence.

Bride and groom moved to Braintree the evening of the wedding. There was a servant to wait on them—the same Judah who had been the cause of the family row years before—who was temporarily on loan from John's mother.[13] But as the days and weeks passed, Abigail did her own cooking by the open hearth, and while John busied himself with his law books and the farm, she spun and wove clothes for their everyday use.

Her more sheltered, bookish upbringing notwithstanding, she was to prove every bit as hardworking as he and no less conscientious about whatever she undertook. She was and would remain a thoroughgoing New England woman who rose at five in the morning and was seldom idle. She did everything that needed doing. All her life she would do her own sewing, baking, feed her own ducks and chickens, churn her own butter (both because that was what was expected and because she knew her butter to be superior). And for all her reading, her remarkable knowledge of English poetry and literature, she was never to lose certain countrified Yankee patterns of speech, saying "Canady" for Canada, as an example, using "set" for sit, or the old New England "aya," for yes.

To John's great satisfaction, Abigail also got along splendidly with his very unbookish mother. For a year or more, until Susanna Adams was remarried to an older Braintree man named John Hall, she continued to live with her son Peter in the family homestead next door, and the two women grew extremely fond of one another. To Abigail her mother-in-law was a cheerful, open-minded person of "exemplary benevolence,"

---

13. *Judah* was a homeless woman who, being unable to care for herself, had been brought to the Adamses' household by Braintree officials. Her arrival had caused a family argument.

Writing Practice

 Summarize

SMALL GROUP Remind students that summarizing a passage is a helpful way to reinforce the main ideas and details it contains. Tell students to write a summary of this. Suggest that they create an outline before they begin writing. Tell students that their summary should include the main ideas and the central events and characters. It should also answer the questions *who, what, where, when, why,* and *how.*

Students may want to answer the 5Ws and H questions before they begin writing their summaries to ensure that this information is included. When students are finished, pair them to compare summaries. Have students work together to resolve any discrepancies in their grasp of the facts.

dedicated heart and soul to the welfare of her family, which was more than her eldest son ever committed to paper, even if he concurred.

John and Abigail's own first child followed not quite nine months after their marriage, a baby girl, Abigail or "Nabby," who arrived July 14, 1765, and was, her mother recorded, "the dear image of her still dearer Papa."

A second baby, John Quincy, was born two years later, in 1767, also in mid-July, and Adams began worrying about college for Johnny, fine clothes for Nabby, dancing schools, "and all that." To Abigail, after nearly three years of marriage, her John was still "the tenderest of husbands," his affections "unabated."[14]

For Adams, life had been made infinitely fuller. All the ties he felt to the old farm were stronger now with Abigail in partnership. She was the ballast[15] he had wanted, the vital center of a new and better life. The time he spent away from home, riding the court circuit, apart from her and the "little ones," became increasingly difficult. "God preserve you and all our family," he would write.

But in 1765, the same year little Abigail was born and Adams found himself chosen surveyor of highways in Braintree, he was swept by events into sudden public prominence. His marriage and family life were barely under way when he began the rise to the fame he had so long desired. "I never shall shine 'til some animating occasion calls forth all my powers," he had written, and here now was the moment.

"I am . . . under all obligations of interest and ambition, as well as honor, gratitude and duty, to exert the utmost of abilities in this important cause," he wrote, and with characteristic honesty he had not left ambition out. **3** ∾

---

14. *Unabated* means "at full strength."
15. Here, *ballast* means "something that provides stability."

Respond and Think Critically

Respond and Interpret

1. In what ways do you think that the relationship between John and Abigail Adams is like relationships between married people today? How is it different?

2. (a)What nicknames taken from the classical world did John and Abigail give each other? (b)How do these names reveal the perceptions each had of the other?

3. At the beginning of this excerpt, what inferences does McCullough draw about John's and Abigail's characters from their portrait? How do these inferences contribute to his portrayal of the couple?

Analyze and Evaluate

4. Do you agree with McCullough when he calls Adams's marriage to Abigail the "most important decision of John Adams's life"? Explain.

5. McCullough writes that "life had become infinitely fuller" for John Adams after his marriage and the birth of his children. Do you think that Adams considered his marriage more fulfilling than his career? Why or why not?

Connect

6. Abigail's letters are notable partly because of their plea for protections for women's rights in the new American government. How does her reasoning resemble the views of other writers involved in the struggle for American independence?

DAVID McCULLOUGH **153**

Historical Perspective
on *John Adams*

Teach

Big Idea	3

The Road to Independence
Point out to students that the closing quotation lists the motivating forces that drew John Adams away from his family.

(APPROACHING) Ask students to identify the "important cause."

Cultural History ☆
Class and Marriage Abigail's mother opposed her marriage to John. Explain that John's relatives were farmers, whereas Abigail's father, William Smith, was a Congregational minister. Many highly educated guests spent time at the Smith home. Class distinctions were especially acute during the colonial period, and Abigail's parents felt themselves superior to the Adams family.

Assess

1. They expressed affection for each other and criticized each other as a modern couple would. Their extensive correspondence sets their relationship apart from most modern ones.

2. (a) Diana and Lysander. (b) She glowed with beauty, like the moon; he was heroic.

3. He infers that Abigail possessed good character and that John had not yet proven himself. He portrays Abigail as bright and confident and John as still seeking a channel for his ambition.

4. Students are likely to agree. According to McCullough, Abigail proved to be a competent woman who became the center of "a new and better life."

5. Students may say that he found marriage as fulfilling as career.

6. Abigail hated tyranny and was willing to go out on a limb to fight for the values she believed in.

 For additional assessment, see Assessment Resources, pp. 95–96.

Writing Workshop

Write a Persuasive Speech

Focus

Bellringer

Say: There are many controversial issues involving our school and community. Think about some issues that you feel strongly about. Tell students to list a few issues and then to jot down arguments on both sides of each issue.

Summary

In this workshop, students will write and present persuasive speeches. They will follow the stages of the writing process, including prewriting, drafting, revising, and proofreading. In addition, the workshop provides two mini-lessons, one on supporting reasons with evidence and one on parallelism.

Learning Objectives

For pages 154–161

In this workshop, you will focus on the following objectives:

Writing: Writing a persuasive speech as an instrument for change in your community or the world, including a clearly stated opinion supported by relevant evidence.

▶ Writing Process

At any stage of a writing process you may think of new ideas. Feel free to return to earlier stages as you write.

Prewrite

Draft

Revise

Focus Lesson: Use Evidence

Edit and Proofread

Focus Lesson: Parallelism

Present

LOG ON ▶ **Literature** Online

Writing and Research For prewriting, drafting, and revising tools, go to glencoe.com and enter QuickPass code GLA9800u1.

 Writing Workshop

Persuasive Speech

Literature Connection Patrick Henry's direct and passionate "Speech to the Second Virginia Convention" is a memorable example of persuasive speaking and the effective use of rhetorical devices.

> *"Is life so dear, or peace so sweet, as to be purchased at the price of chains and slavery?"*

To write a successful persuasive speech, review "The Rhetoric of Revolution" on pages 112–113 and the following goals and strategies of effective persuasive writing.

Checklist

Goals	Strategies
To present a clearly stated opinion	☑ Choose an issue that has opposing viewpoints
	☑ Clearly state your thesis
To present a logically organized argument	☑ Give reasons for your opinion
	☑ Use precise, relevant evidence to support your reasons
	☑ Analyze evidence to show how it supports your reasons
	☑ End with a call to action
To demonstrate understanding of your audience, purpose, and form	☑ Acknowledge and refute opposing arguments
	☑ Maintain a tone that matches your audience and purpose
	☑ Use point of view to achieve your purpose
To convince an audience that a particular point of view is correct	☑ Use appeals to logic, ethics, and emotion
	☑ Employ rhetorical devices and vivid language to strengthen your argument

Workshop Resources

Print Materials

- Unit 1 Teaching Resources, pp. 247–249
- Writing Kit
- Success in Writing: Research and Reports

Technology

- Literature Online: Writing Resources and Grammar Resources, www.glencoe.com
- Online Essay Grader, www.glencoe.com
- Student Presentation Builder on Student-Works Plus CD-ROM
- Media Workshop DVD
- Online Student Edition

Assignment: Support an Opinion

Write a persuasive speech of at least 1,500 words about a situation in your school or community that you wish to change. As you work, keep your audience and purpose in mind.

Audience: your school or community

Purpose: to persuade others to improve a situation in the school or the community

Analyze a Professional Model

In her persuasive speech, Becky Cain, the president of the League of Women Voters, urges members of the House of Representatives to abolish the Electoral College. As you read the following passage, notice how Cain clearly presents the debate and her position, supports her position with strong evidence, and urges her audience to act. Pay close attention to the comments in the margin. They point out features to include in your own persuasive speech.

From *"Proposals for Electoral College Reform"* by Becky Cain, President, League of Women Voters

I am pleased to be here today to express the League's support for a constitutional amendment to abolish the electoral college and establish the direct election of the President and Vice President of the United States by popular vote of the American people.

The electoral college system is fundamentally unfair to voters. In a nation where voting rights are grounded in the one-person, one-vote principle, the electoral college is a hopeless anachronism.

The current system is unfair for two reasons.

First, a citizen's individual vote has more weight if he or she lives in a state with a small population than if that citizen lives in a state with a large population.

For example, each electoral vote in Alaska is equivalent to approximately 112,000 people. Each electoral vote in New York is equivalent to approximately 404,000 eligible people (based on 1990 census data). And that's if everyone votes!

Persuasion

Real-World Connection

If you have addressed a community problem, send your speech to your local newspaper for publication. If you have addressed a school problem, submit your speech to your school or community newspaper. Be sure to learn the publication's requirements for submission first.

Introduction

Identify and explain the problem or the situation you are addressing, and propose a solution. State your thesis.

Appeals

Appeal to your audience's emotions and logic.

Supporting Evidence/ Statistics

Support your reasons with strong evidence, attributing sources of information as needed.

WRITING WORKSHOP **155**

Writing Workshop

Write a Persuasive Speech

Teach

Big Idea

The Road to Independence
Help students make a connection between the persuasive speech and American independence. Explain that many prominent colonists delivered persuasive speeches during the struggle for independence. **Ask:** What was the role of the persuasive speech in the struggle for independence? *(To succeed, the patriots had to persuade others that independence from Britain was a cause worth fighting for.)*

Political History ☆
The League of Women Voters
Since 1920, the League of Women Voters has worked to encourage citizens to participate in elections and to take an active role in government. The league is active in all 50 states and is nonpartisan, not supporting any particular candidates for public office.

Approaching Level
DIFFERENTIATED INSTRUCTION 🐾

Emerging Have students read editorials from newspapers or magazines. If possible, use local periodicals. Then have students work in small groups to identify the stated position, the supporting evidence, and the call to action.

English Learners
DIFFERENTIATED INSTRUCTION 🐾

Intermediate Before students begin, review terms used to discuss elements of a persuasive speech. A *position* is the statement of the writer's point of view. The *supporting evidence* is the reasons, facts, examples, and details that explain why the writer believes the position is valid. Speeches may also have a *call to action,* which is the action or response the writer wants from the reader. For example, a call

to action might include writing a letter to a local politician in support of a new law. Give students one simple editorial from a school or local newspaper. Have them identify the three elements discussed.

155

Write a Persuasive Speech

Teach

Writing Skills

Support Emphasize that students must support an argument with facts. An emotional plea alone is not strong enough to convince an audience to embrace a point of view. Students should expect to do some research in preparation for writing a persuasive speech.

Audience and Purpose/Tone
Remind students to choose words carefully to convey the appropriate tone to the audience. For example, if students are speaking to a group of parents, they should use a more formal tone. They may use a more casual tone when making a speech in front of other students.

Persuasive Technique Explain that, after presenting factual information, students should make an emotional appeal to their audience. One way to touch people's emotions is by describing what might happen if no one takes action.

(APPROACHING) For students who are struggling, clarify that emotional appeals address readers' feelings. To persuade readers to act, writers often appeal to fear, to pride, or to a sense of fairness. Have students identify other emotions that could motivate readers to act.

Reasons/Support
Structure paragraphs to present clear reasons followed by precise, relevant evidence.

Facts/Support
Support your reasons with facts to appeal to your audience's sense of logic.

Audience and Purpose/Tone
Invite your audience to identify and empathize with the negative consequences of inaction. Keep your tone consistent with your purpose and audience.

Persuasive Techniques
Put short sentences, repetition, emotional appeals, and connotation to work for you.

Conclusion
End your argument with a call to action.

The system is also unfair because a citizen's individual vote has more weight if the percentage of voter participation in the state is low. For example, if only half of all people in Alaska vote, then each electoral vote is equivalent to roughly 56,000 people.

Moreover, the electoral vote does not reflect the volume of voter participation within a state. If only a few voters go to the polls, all the electoral votes of the state are still cast.

Finally, the electoral college system is flawed because the Constitution does not bind presidential electors to vote for the candidates to whom they have been pledged. For example, in 1948, 1960, and 1976, individual electors pledged to the top two vote getters cast their votes for third-place finishers and also-rans. Defecting electors in a close race could cause a crisis of confidence in our electoral system.

For all these reasons, the League believes that the presidential election method should incorporate the one-person, one-vote principle. The President should be directly elected by the people he or she will represent, just as the other federally elected officials are in this country. Direct election is the most representative system. It is the only system that guarantees the President will have received the most popular votes. It also encourages voter participation by giving voters a direct and equal role in the election of the President. . . .

The time has come to take the next step to ensure a broad-based, representative democracy. Fairness argues for it. Retaining the fragile faith of American voters in our representative system demands it. We urge the House and the Senate to pass a constitutional amendment abolishing the electoral college system and establishing the direct popular election of our President and Vice President.

Reading-Writing Connection Think about the writing techniques that you have just encountered and try them out in the persuasive speech you write.

Writing Practice

Call to Action Recall that persuasive speeches should end with a call to action. Stress that such a call must be persuasive and clear so that readers in fact follow its direction. Have a student read aloud the conclusion to Becky Cain's speech. **Ask:** What word does Becky use to call readers to action? *(urge)* Then have students brainstorm to compile a list of strong verbs for *request,* such as *urge, implore, appeal, press,* and *beg.*

Have them create a list of such verbs that are less urgent, such as *recommend, wish, invite, ask,* and *call.* Tell students to refer to these lists and choose strong verbs as they write the conclusion of their speech.

Prewrite

Choose an Issue Think of a situation you would like to change. Have you noticed a rule or policy that is ineffective or unfair? Enacting change requires you to persuade others that a situation can and should be improved, and that your solution is the right one.

▶ The **purpose** of a persuasive speech is to inform and influence.

▶ Determine your **audience.** Your audience should include people who have the power to improve the situation you describe.

Clarify Your Position In one or two sentences, state the issue and your opinion about it. This is your **thesis.**

Support Your Position To be persuasive, you need to give reasons and support them with relevant evidence. You should make appeals to logic, ethics, and emotions. Defend your reasons with precise and accurate evidence, such as facts, expert opinions, statistics, and examples.

Outline Your Argument Make an outline to organize your reasons and evidence. Your introduction should describe the issue and your proposal. (For more information on types of proposals, see "Persuasive Speech" on page 154.) In each body paragraph, include a reason and relevant evidence. In your conclusion, summarize your position and end with a call to action.

Introduction • Thesis		
Body Paragraph(s) • Reasons • Evidence • Analysis	• Reason:	The electoral college system is flawed because the Constitution does not bind presidential electors to vote for the candidates to whom they have been pledged.
	• Evidence:	For example, in 1948, 1960, and 1976, individual electors pledged to the top two vote getters cast their votes for third-place finishers and also-rans.
Conclusion • Call to Action	• Analysis:	Defecting electors in a close race could cause a crisis of confidence in our electoral system.

Discuss Your Ideas When you finish your outline, share your ideas with a partner. To develop your writing voice and to become more comfortable speaking in front of others, read your thesis and reasons. Be sure that each part is clear and that your tone suits your purpose and audience.

Persuasion

Rhetorical Devices

Here are some other rhetorical devices you could use:

Repetition Repeat a word or phrase for emphasis. *"I came, I saw, I conquered."* —Julius Caesar

Rhetorical Question These questions are asked to emphasize the obvious. *"If you wrong us, shall we not revenge?"* —William Shakespeare

Metaphor Metaphors compare two seemingly unlike things. *"No man is an island."* —John Donne

Avoid Plagiarism

When doing Internet research, make notes in your own words rather than cutting and pasting.

Write a Persuasive Speech

Teach

Writing Process

Prewrite Have small groups generate ideas for their speeches. **Say:** List at least six topics. After each topic, write down the specific audience you will be writing for. Keep this audience in mind as you begin to write.

ADVANCED Remind students that in order to support a position with facts, they will need to spend some time doing research. **Say:** In the course of gathering evidence, you may find information that persuades you to change your position. Be sure you are clear about your final position and will be able to argue your case convincingly.

Peer Review Direct partners to provide supportive but honest feedback. Suggest that students listen closely and that they offer ideas for more persuasive language, stronger reasons, or more effective emotional appeals.

English Learners
DIFFERENTIATED INSTRUCTION

Beginning Consult with students individually if possible. Help them develop their position and list their supporting reasons or evidence. Have them look up pronunciations of unfamiliar words. Have students read portions of their speeches aloud to you as they progress through the writing process.

Approaching Level
DIFFERENTIATED INSTRUCTION

Established Spend a class period in the library or media center with students who have limited experience with research. Outline major sources for information, such as Web sites, books, and periodicals. Locate and demonstrate the use of search tools to find information in each major source area. Have students list other ways to gather information on their topic, such as interviews or surveys.

Emerging Review outline methods and rules, and then provide a template outline that students can complete. If you prefer sentence outlining, demonstrate this technique. Have students exchange outlines with a partner and highlight areas where their partners need to gather more evidence.

Write a Persuasive Speech

Teach

Writing Process

Draft Remind students that the most important part of the drafting process is to get all their ideas on paper, including their central thesis and supporting evidence. Students will be able to refine and reorganize their argument when they revise their drafts.

Writing Skills

Audience and Purpose/Tone
Answer: *Discussion of the haunted house creates mystery and suspense. It will probably grab the audience's attention and draw people to listen to the speech.*

Thesis Answer: *The house shouldn't be torn down. Instead, it should be renovated and used as a museum.*

Supporting Evidence/Expert Opinion Answer: *An expert's opinion could persuade the audience that the writer's point is valid.*

Writing Frames

As you read the workshop model, think about the writer's use of the following frames:

Instead of _____, we should _____.

Some critics may argue that _____ …

Let's … _____. _____ is the first step.

Consider using frames like these in your own speech.

Audience and Purpose/Tone

How does this opening use content and tone to lure the audience and help achieve the purpose?

Thesis

What is the thesis?

Supporting Evidence/Expert Opinion

How does this attributed evidence help persuade?

Draft

Don't Get Stuck Writers often modify their original thesis after developing the rest of their argument. Keep in mind that it may be easier to start with a very general thesis, to draft your body paragraphs, and to go back to clarify your thesis afterward. Whichever order you choose, you will be able to revise your thesis later to make your position clear.

Analyze a Workshop Model

Here is a final draft of a persuasive speech. Read the speech and answer the questions in the margin. Use the answers to these questions to guide you as you write your own speech.

Haunted House or Historical Attraction?

Hauntingly beautiful, perhaps—but not a haunted house!

Some neighbors claim that they hear strange sounds at night from the old Dillard mansion at the end of Briar Street. Others complain that with the sprawling weeds, teetering fence, and peeling paint, the house might just as well be haunted. Now the Briar Street Neighborhood Association is pressuring the city government to bulldoze the old house.

The Dillard mansion has been empty since 1971, and no doubt the neglect has made it quite an eyesore. Still, the house remains one of the town's oldest standing structures, and a decision to tear it down should not be made without considering other options. Instead of destroying an important part of Dillard history, we should attempt to renovate and restore it. The renovated mansion would serve as an ideal site for a town museum.

Many of our citizens recognize that Dillard needs a town museum. In fact, the Dillard Historical Society has been talking about building a museum for some time now. As historian and Society member Adam Frasier explains, "With no central location, Dillard's historic objects risk being damaged or lost. There is no systematic organization in place. The longer we postpone the decision,

---

Writing Practice

Use Transitions Discuss the importance of using transition words, especially in writing that is intended to be presented to an audience orally. Tell students that a speech flows more smoothly when one thought leads naturally to the next and when the connections between the thoughts are made clear. Have the class make a list of transition words that they can refer to as they write.

Post students' ideas on the board. Then discuss categories of transition words. For example, *first, next,* and *last* are sequence transition words. *Most important, in addition,* and *finally* are order-of-importance transition words. Other categories include cause-effect and comparison-contrast transition words. Have students categorize the posted words, and then identify and categorize transition words in the Work-

shop model. (*Examples include some … other, comparison = contrast;* however, *for contrast;* but, *for contrast*).

the worse it will get." In July 2004, the *Dillard Post* noted that an estimated 65 percent of archived material is currently in storage, unavailable to the public or even most researchers. Why not solve this need for a public museum by restoring the Dillard mansion?

Some critics may argue that the cost of restoring the old house would outweigh the benefits. The town would need to replace the existing plumbing and electricity to bring it up to safety codes. A complete restoration would require expensive specialists and hours of costly research. However, the cost of building a new museum from the ground up would probably be more expensive overall. The town would need not only to purchase all new materials, fixtures, and labor, but also to pay for an architect and for land to build on. Moreover, a newer building could not achieve the look and atmosphere of an authentically historic space.

Records at Dillard City Hall indicate that the town's founder, Evan Dillard, built the house in 1798. Not only is the house more than 200 years old, it includes a number of architectural features that cannot be found anywhere else in the city. A hidden staircase leads to a secret room, and rare amethyst-glass windows and unexpected gables decorate the roof. Such a unique museum would appeal to both experts and amateurs, and it would probably draw tourists from all over the state.

Let's preserve the cultural heritage, deep history, and unique architecture of our town. Let's turn the Dillard eyesore into a historical attraction. Renovating—not bulldozing—the Dillard mansion is the first step.

Persuasion

Persuasive Technique
How does this rhetorical question help achieve the writer's purpose?

Opposing Arguments
How does the writer acknowledge and refute an opposing argument?

Reasons/Support
What evidence does the writer provide? How does this evidence appeal to both logic and emotion? How does it support the thesis?

Persuasive Techniques
How does the writer use sentence structure, parallelism, word choice, repetition, a call to action, and an emotional appeal to persuade?

🖥 Writing Workshop

Write a Persuasive Speech

Teach

Writing Skills

Persuasive Technique
Answer: *The question invites the audience to agree with the speaker.*

Opposing Arguments
Answer: *The writer reasons that more money would be needed to build a new museum than to renovate the old house to be a museum.*

Reasons/Support
Answer: *The writer appeals to the audience emotionally by inviting the audience to feel protective of an important piece of town history. The appeal to logic lies in the reasoning that the town would benefit financially as tourists would be lured to the unique building. Both appeals support the thesis that the building should be saved.*

Persuasive Techniques
Answer: *The writer connects to the audience by starting the first two sentences with the word "Let's" and using words such as "cultural heritage," and "deep history." The writer ends the speech by inviting the audience to take action.*

English Learners

DIFFERENTIATED INSTRUCTION 🔁

Intermediate Clarify that a counterargument is the argument that an opponent might make. **Ask:** What does the word *counter* mean in this term? (*Counter means "opposite" in this case.*)

Advanced Learners

DIFFERENTIATED INSTRUCTION 🔁

Models of Persuasion Have students read famous persuasive speeches as additional models for their own writing. Tell them to think about topics they have studied, such as slavery, suffrage, and civil rights. Then have them use the library or the Internet to find speeches on these topics. (Direct students to www.americanrhetoric.com which has a speech bank of famous American speeches, some of which include audio

files.) Have students identify thesis, counterarguments, logical or emotional appeals, and rhetorical devices such as parallelism or rhetorical questions in one of the speeches.

159

Writing Workshop

Teach

Writing Process

Revise After students finish writing their persuasive speeches, tell them to wait a couple of days before revising. They will approach their work with renewed vision and clarity after some time away from their writing.

Writing Skills

Reliable Sources Caution students to be critical of the sources of the facts they use to support their arguments. Emphasize that what is found on Web sites may not be accurate. Tell them to focus on sites that are produced by governments and educational institutions.

(APPROACHING) For students who are struggling, review how to recognize sites sponsored by government or educational institutions. Explain that students can identify such sites by .gov or .edu in the URL. In addition, students may be able to use advanced search features to find only these sites.

Traits of Strong Writing

Include these traits of strong writing to express your ideas effectively.

Ideas message or theme and the details that develop it
Organization arrangement of main ideas and supporting details
Voice writer's unique way of using tone and style
Word Choice vocabulary a writer uses to convey meaning
Sentence Fluency rhythm and flow of sentences
Conventions correct spelling, grammar, usage, and mechanics
Presentation the way words and design elements look on a page

For more information on using the Traits of Strong Writing, see pages R30–R32.

Word Choice

Academic vocabulary in the student model:

structure (strǝk' shǝr) *n.* 1. a building or other construction; 2. coherent form and organization, as in a piece of writing; *Still, the house remains one of the town's oldest standing structures.* Using academic vocabulary may strengthen your writing. Try to use one or two academic vocabulary words in your persuasive speech. See the list on R89–R91.

Revise

Use the checklist below to evaluate your writing.

Checklist
☑ Do you clearly state your thesis?
☑ Do you use a point of view and tone that matches your purpose and audience?
☑ Do you present precise, relevant evidence to support your thesis?
☑ Do you use rhetorical devices and vivid language to strengthen your argument?
☑ Do you use appeals to logic, ethics, and emotion?
☑ Do you present and respond to opposing arguments in a respectful tone?
☑ Do you end with a call to action?

> **Focus Lesson**

Support Reasons with Evidence

A well-supported reason will demonstrate that you are informed about your subject and that your argument is logical and valid. Make sure to support your reasons with convincing evidence from reliable sources. Here is a sentence from the Workshop Model followed by three kinds of supporting evidence—example, expert opinion, statistic—that you may want to use in your persuasive speech.

Draft:

Many of our citizens recognize that Dillard needs a town museum.

Revision:

Many of our citizens recognize that Dillard needs a town museum. In fact, the Dillard Historical Society has been talking about building a museum for some time now.[1] As historian and Society member Adam Frasier explains, "With no central location, Dillard's historic objects risk being damaged or lost. There is no systematic organization in place. The longer we postpone the decision, the worse it will get."[2] In July 2004, the Dillard Post noted that an estimated 65 percent of archived material is currently in storage, unavailable to the public or even most researchers.[3]

1: Example   **2: Expert Opinion**   **3: Statistic**

160 UNIT 1 EARLY AMERICA

Writing Practice

Review Discuss the importance of reviewing a piece of writing before deciding that it is finished. In the case of a speech, students should read their work aloud, thinking about which words to emphasize, how to pace the speech, and when to increase or reduce the volume of their voice. Suggest that students work in pairs to review their speeches. Partners should first listen for clarity of argument. Then, on a second hearing, partners should listen for presentation. Have students then exchange tips for final text revision and for improving presentation.

Edit and Proofread

Get It Right Proofread your speech for errors in grammar, usage, mechanics, and spelling. See the Language Handbook, pages R42–R61.

> ### Focus Lesson
>
> ### Parallelism
>
> Parallelism is the use of a series of words, phrases, or sentences that have similar grammatical form. To write a parallel sentence, balance each item in a series by using the same grammatical construction.
>
> **Original:** In this sentence, similar ideas are not connected or emphasized.
>
> *Let's preserve <u>the cultural heritage</u> and <u>the deep history</u> of our town, as well as <u>its architecture</u>, which is unique.*
>
> **Improved:** Create parallel phrases to reflect the parallel meaning.
>
> *Let's preserve the <u>cultural heritage</u>, <u>deep history</u>, and <u>unique architecture</u> of our town.*
>
> **Original:** In this sentence, the series does not use parallel grammatical forms.
>
> *Others complain that with <u>weeds</u>, <u>teetering fence</u>, and <u>paint that is cracked and peeling</u>, the house might just as well be haunted.*
>
> **Improved:** Edit the sentence so that all items are parallel in form.
>
> *Others complain that with the <u>sprawling weeds</u>, <u>teetering fence</u>, and <u>peeling paint</u>, the house might just as well be haunted.*

Present

Preparing Your Persuasive Speech Once you have finished your persuasive speech, think about how you'll present it. Many speakers read from note cards instead of from the paper itself. If you prefer reading from the paper, you may wish to increase the type size and spacing, or add notes in the margins. Your teacher may ask for a clean copy of your speech to grade, so be sure to check the presentation guidelines.

Peer Review Tips

A classmate may ask you to read his or her speech. Take your time and jot down notes as you read so you can give constructive feedback. Use the following questions to get started:

- Can you state the writer's thesis and identify clear reasons and support for it?

- Which persuasive techniques do you see, and how effective do you think they are?

Word-Processing

The title of your speech should appear at the top of the page, in the same font as the rest of your work, without quotation marks. Leave a line of space between the title and the first line of your speech. Double-space the body of your speech, but do not add extra spaces between paragraphs. Use a uniform indent for all paragraphs of about one-half inch.

Writer's Portfolio

Place a copy of your persuasive speech in your portfolio to review later.

Teach

Writing Process

Edit and Proofread After students edit and proofread their own work, have them trade speeches with a partner. Have partners check each other's speeches for errors in grammar, punctuation, and mechanics.

ENGLISH LEARNERS Pair English learners with native English speakers. Have English speakers explain each change they make so that English learners understand the language convention behind the change.

Present Presentation guidelines can be adapted from the rubric on page 163. Have students make two copies of their speech—one to hand in and another to read from. They should mark up the copy that they will use for their oral presentation with notes about which words to emphasize, when to read more slowly, and when to increase their volume.

English Learners

DIFFERENTIATED INSTRUCTION

Intermediate Provide extra time for students to practice reading their speeches aloud. Set up a special session in which students can rehearse their speeches in front of a small group. Have students focus on using standard English grammatical forms and on speaking naturally and clearly. Tell listeners not to interrupt but to take notes as they listen. Have them focus on identifying the main arguments and determining if speakers have included sufficient supporting evidence to be persuasive. Ask listeners to share their comments clearly and supportively with speakers.

Focus

Summary

In this workshop, students will learn techniques for planning, rehearsing, and delivering a persuasive speech.

Teach

Speaking Skills

Model Speech To give students a model of effective speaking, play an audiotape or a videotape of a particularly good speech. After you have played the speech, ask students to read the chart on the next page and identify techniques that make the speech effective.

 For help with creating presentations, see Student Presentation Builder on StudentWorks Plus.

Learning Objectives

For pages 162–163
In this workshop, you will focus on the following objectives:

Speaking and Listening:
Delivering a persuasive presentation that develops a logical argument.
Providing feedback on a presentation.
Using visual media to support an oral presentation.

Speaking, Listening, and Viewing Workshop

Persuasive Speech

Literature Connection In 1799, George Washington needed help. Supporters of state independence were resisting the federal union. Fearing that "the tranquility of the Union [was] hastening to an awful crisis," Washington turned to Patrick Henry, who spoke passionately for the inviolability of the Union. Henry's last speech turned sullen opponents into cheering supporters.

> **Assignment** **Deliver your persuasive speech to an audience.**

Plan Your Presentation

Reread your speech, making sure you have used opportunities for deduction, induction, syllogism, or analogy. Avoid logical fallacies such as an ad hominem attack, a false cause, or a red herring. Determine whether you have presented a proposition of fact, value, policy, or problem, and be sure that you have the organization and support appropriate for this type of speech. (See pages R62–R65 for help.)

Next, decide where your speech is most powerful and convincing and why. Speculate on its probable effect on a live audience. Then look for places to increase its effectiveness by adding or amplifying the following:

- **Rhetorical devices:** Where appropriate, consider inserting a rhetorical question, parallel structure, figurative language, vivid action verbs, and other choices that will make your speech more forceful and memorable.
- **Appeals:** Add appropriate logical, ethical, and emotional appeals.
- **Level of language:** If appropriate, raise or lower your level of formality. If you need technical language for accuracy, use it. Otherwise, for clarity and effectiveness, use standard English.

stunning bell-cast eaves and interior bead molding
It includes a number of architectural features that cannot be found anywhere else in the city.

Listening and Speaking Practice

SMALL GROUP
Reread Tell students to read their speeches several times until they have almost memorized them. First, they should read their speeches to themselves. Tell students to rehearse independently in front of a mirror. Students should explore and select gestures, facial expressions, and body movements that enhance and emphasize the points of their arguments. If students include quotations in their speeches, tell them to find out through research the correct way to pronounce names or dialect. Then have students work with partners to practice presenting the speeches aloud and to exchange helpful pointers that they can use to improve their presentation.

Rehearse

Rehearse your speech both in private and in front of friends and family. Ask your listeners for feedback on your pronunciation, enunciation, gestures, and movement. If you will be fielding questions from your audience, ask your listeners for practice questions. Keep your answers focused and to the point. If possible, watch a videotape of a famous speech, such as Kennedy's 1961 inaugural, or turn on the television to view politicians and world leaders. Identify strategies to emulate.

Use some of the verbal and nonverbal techniques below.

Techniques for Delivering a Speech

Verbal Techniques	Nonverbal Techniques
☑ **Volume** Speak loudly enough so that everyone can hear you.	☑ **Posture** Stand up tall with your head straight.
☑ **Pronunciation** Speak clearly, pronouncing all the words.	☑ **Eye Contact** Make eye contact with people throughout your audience.
☑ **Pace** Speak at a moderate speed but vary the rate and use pauses.	☑ **Facial Expressions** Vary your facial expressions to reflect what you are saying.
☑ **Tone** Speak in an animated voice.	☑ **Gestures** Use natural gestures to reinforce your ideas.
☑ **Emphasis** Stress important words and ideas.	☑ **Visual Aids** Use photographs or other visuals to enhance your presentation.

Listen and Evaluate

As others present their speeches, use these listening techniques:

- Focus on the speaker.
- Sit up straight; keep your head up; do not fidget.
- Respond: if the speaker uses humor, laugh or smile; if the speaker poses a question, react to or consider it in some visible way.

To evaluate others' speeches, use the presentation tips in the side column. In addition, jot down notes about the speaker's word choice and sentence structure. Note how these choices affected you or other members of the audience.

Sound Check

Record your presentation and play it back to check on whether your voice expresses the right mood and your words are understandable.

Speaking Frames

Consider using the following frames in your persuasive speech:
- My own view is that _____ because _____.
- While it is true that _____, it does not necessarily mean that _____.

Presentation Tips

Use the following checklist to evaluate your speech.
- ☑ Did you command your audience's attention throughout the speech? What evidence did you see of audience response?
- ☑ Did you use appeals, rhetorical devices, and levels of language to help persuade your audience?

 Literature Online

Speaking, Listening, and Viewing For project ideas, templates, and presentation tips, go to glencoe.com and enter QuickPass code GLA9800u1.

Teach

Speaking Skills

Visual Aids Students may wish to use visual aids to emphasize or illustrate one or two key points of their speech. Explain that a visual aid should be clearly relevant to the intent of the speech and not distract the audience from paying attention to the speaker. Remind students that their visual aids must be displayed so that audience members sitting at the back and to the sides of the room can see the details of the visual aid clearly.

Listening Skills

Peer Assessment Ask students to use the following criteria to evaluate one another's speeches:
- Does the speech give clear reasons to persuade listeners to take action?
- Does the speaker present his or her main points in a clear and convincing manner?

Approaching Level

DIFFERENTIATED INSTRUCTION

Emerging To help students evaluate their presentation, have them demonstrate the techniques listed in the chart. For example, you might have students speak at a volume they think is appropriate. Ask other students to build consensus on appropriate volume. Repeat the process for the remaining techniques. As each is discussed, ask students to provide specific comments on how to use each effectively.

Established Tell students to mark their written speeches to indicate which words and phrases to stress. Students might highlight the parts they want to read with greater emphasis. Before students mark text, ask them to identify types of text that merit emphasis and to explain their thinking.

Focus

Summary

These pages highlight some of the literature that will enrich students' understanding of Native American cultures, colonial times, and the founding of the nation. These books include *The First Americans: Spirit of the Land and the People; Words That Make America Great;* an anthology of Native American Literature; *The Scarlet Letter;* Benjamin Franklin's autobiography; and a historical novel called *The Rising Shore: Roanoke.*

To create customized reading lists from a database of more than 30,000 titles, use BookLink K–12 CD-ROM.

Early America

THE LITERATURE OF EARLY AMERICA reflects the diversity of its people and their experiences. Native American myths, the journals of European explorers, slave narratives, political treatises, and contemporary historical fiction all tell a piece of the country's story. Explore these selections to expand your understanding of America from the pre-Colonial era through independence from Great Britain.

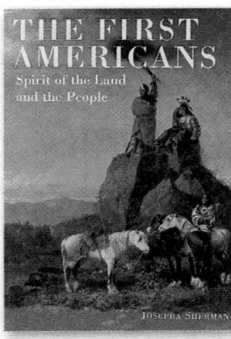

The First Americans: Spirit of the Land and the People

Josepha Sherman

An intelligent and vividly illustrated overview of Native American cultures, this book includes information about customs, beliefs, living conditions, and contact with white settlers. The illustrations include artwork and portraits of Native Americans in traditional clothing.

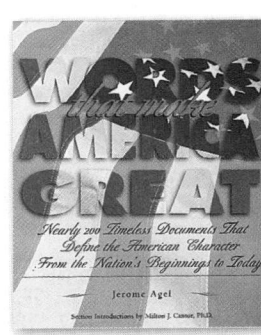

Words That Make America Great

Jerome Agel, Editor

This book presents 200 documents that have helped define America's character and ideals from its earliest days to the present. Included are many documents of the years 1750–1850, from the Declaration of Independence to the earliest rules of baseball. The book also includes commentaries on the significance of each document.

Writing Practice

SMALL GROUP

Book Review Help students understand that book reviews go beyond the question of whether the reader liked the book. Have students find book reviews in a local paper, a magazine, or online. Have them work in small groups to analyze some of the characteristics of a review. For example, have them discuss the ways authors summarize the basic idea of the book without revealing too much about the story. Have them discuss how the length of the review affects the depth of the writer's analysis.

GLENCOE LITERATURE LIBRARY

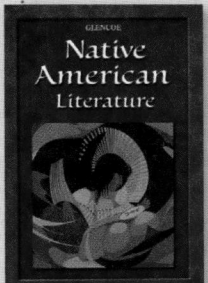

Native American Literature: An Anthology

Lawana Trout, Editor

This rich collection features writers such as William Least Heat-Moon, Leslie Marmon Silko, Michael Dorris, N. Scott Momaday, and many more.

The Scarlet Letter

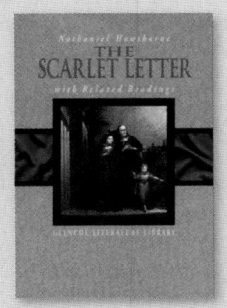

Nathaniel Hawthorne

Set in Colonial Boston in the mid-1600s, *The Scarlet Letter* tells the story of Hester Prynne, who has committed adultery and must wear a scarlet letter "A" publicly as punishment.

The Autobiography of Benjamin Franklin

Benjamin Franklin

The life of this amazing American—scientist, statesman, philosopher, businessman, civic leader, author—is an enduring source of inspiration.

CRITICS' CORNER

"Homsher's novel gives life to the few scraps of historical documentation of the Roanoke colony and creates strong characters that grab your attention and make you dream of an altered history."

—Catherine Perk,
Historical Novels Review Online

The Rising Shore: Roanoke

Deborah Homsher

This historical novel tells the story of Elenor, the daughter of Roanoke Governor John White. It also explores the mystery of this early American colony, which vanished without explanation.

Write a Review

Imagine you are the book reviewer for a newspaper or magazine. Read one of these books and write a review for your publication. Share your assessment with your class. Make sure to address whether you would recommend the book to others, and how it affects your understanding of early America.

INDEPENDENT READING **165**

English Learners

DIFFERENTIATED INSTRUCTION

Intermediate When reading Catherine Perk's words from "Historical Novels Review Online," English learners may need help with phrases such as "gives life to the few scraps of historical documentation" and "make you dream of an altered history." Have students break down these phrases into parts and discuss what Perk means. **Ask:** What does "gives life" mean in this quote? *(makes lively or real)* **Ask:** What are the scraps that she is talking about? *(small amounts of information found in various places)* Remind students that a historical novel uses a real setting and some real events, but the novelist must imagine many of the details.

Independent Reading

Teach

Cultural History ☆

American Puritanism *The Scarlet Letter* is set in seventeenth-century Puritan New England. Puritans first came to North America in 1620, establishing Plymouth Colony in New England. Puritans had an intense devotional life. Because Bible study was central to their life, Puritan society was highly literate. Puritan ideals of self-reliance and the virtues of frugality and hard work became defining characteristics of the American way of life.

Glencoe Literature Library

Glencoe Literature Library offers an extensive collection of hardcover books that help you encourage your students to read independently. Choose among the more than 120 full-length literary works—novels, novellas, plays, and nonfiction. Each book includes related readings

Write a Review Evaluate students' reviews for the following:
- a clear summary of the book
- an evaluation of the book's execution
- reference to the book's contribution to an understanding of history

 For access to all study guides for the Glencoe Literature Library, see the Literature Library Teacher Resources CD-ROM.

165

Focus

Bellringer

Say: In the next two years, you will take many tests in your classes, and you will take tests as you apply for college. To improve your results, learn test-taking strategies and apply them in test situations. Have students list some of the test-taking strategies that they have already learned.

Teach

Assessment

Tell students that this Assessment will provide reinforcement in general test-taking strategies and will test them in the skills and vocabulary taught in this unit. Students will read a nonfiction selection and will answer context, comprehension, and inference questions. Then they will choose answers for ten paragraph-improvement questions. Finally, they will write a short persuasive essay.

Assessment Practice

Paraphrase Directions Explain that instructors often give test directions orally and students need to understand these directions accurately and quickly. Clarify that restating or paraphrasing information is a strategy for checking comprehension. Students may apply the strategy orally or in writing. Ask students to listen carefully as you read aloud the directions at the top of this page, and then to restate them in writing. Tell students to focus on identifying the verbs that indicate required actions and on descriptive language that highlights details of the task. As needed, point out the words *read, use context clues, meaning of words, author's main idea,* and *rhetorical devices,* as well as the page numbers where questions appear. For additional practice, preview the directions on pages 169 and 171, providing clarification as needed. Have students rewrite each set of directions.

Assessment

English Language Arts

Reading: Nonfiction

Carefully read the following passage. Use context clues to determine the meaning of words that you are unfamiliar with. Pay close attention to the author's main idea and use of rhetorical devices. Then answer the questions on pages 167–168.

from *The Whistle* by Benjamin Franklin

line

When I was a child of seven years old, my friends, on a holiday, filled my pocket with coppers. I went directly to a shop where they sold toys for children; and being charmed with the sound of a *whistle,* that I met by the way in the hands of another boy, I voluntarily offered and gave all my money for one. I then came home, and went whistling all over the house, much pleased with my *whistle,* but disturbing

5 all the family. My brothers, and sisters, and cousins, understanding the bargain I had made, told me I had given four times as much for it as it was worth; put me in mind what good things I might have bought with the rest of the money; and laughed at me so much for my folly, that I cried with vexation; and the reflection gave me more chagrin than the *whistle* gave me pleasure.

This, however, was afterwards of use to me, the impression continuing on my mind; so that often,

10 when I was tempted to buy some unnecessary thing, I said to myself, *Don't give too much for the whistle;* and I saved my money.

As I grew up, came into the world, and observed the actions of men, I thought I met with many, very many, *who gave too much for the whistle.*

When I saw one too ambitious of court favor, sacrificing his time in attendance on levees, his repose,

15 his liberty, his virtue, and perhaps his friends, to attain it, I have said to myself, *This man gives too much for his whistle.*

When I saw another fond of popularity, constantly employing himself in political bustles, neglecting his own affairs, and ruining them by that neglect, *He pays, indeed,* said I, *too much for his whistle.*

If I knew a miser, who gave up every kind of comfortable living, all the pleasure of doing good to

20 others, all the esteem of his fellow-citizens, and the joys of benevolent friendship, for the sake of accumulating wealth, *Poor man,* said I, *you pay too much for your whistle.*

When I met with a man of pleasure, sacrificing every laudable improvement of the mind, or of his fortune, to mere corporeal sensations, and ruining his health in their pursuit, *Mistaken man,* said I, *you are providing pain for yourself, instead of pleasure; you give too much for your whistle.*

(continued)

25 If I see one fond of appearance, or fine clothes, fine houses, fine furniture, fine equipages, all above his fortune, for which he contracts debts, and ends his career in a prison, *Alas!* say I, *he has paid dear, very dear, for his whistle.*

When I see a beautiful sweet-tempered girl married to an ill-natured brute of a husband, *What a pity,* say I, *that she should pay so much for a whistle!*

30 In short, I conceive that great part of the miseries of mankind are brought upon them by the false estimates they have made of the value of things, and by their giving too much for their whistles.

1. From whom did Franklin get the whistle?
   A. a shop
   B. friends on a holiday
   C. another boy
   D. a peddler

2. Which rhetorical device is most evident in the sentence beginning on line 5?
   A. hyperbole
   B. rhetorical question
   C. connotative language
   D. parallelism

3. From the context, what does the word *folly* in line 7 mean?
   A. a good deal
   B. an agreement
   C. a mistake
   D. good sense

4. From the context, what does the word *reflection* in line 8 mean?
   A. likeness
   B. mirror image
   C. possibility
   D. thought

5. The word **whistle,** in line 11, is an example of which rhetorical device?
   A. connotative language
   B. hyperbole
   C. parallelism
   D. figurative language

6. According to Franklin, what will happen if people overvalue popularity?
   A. Their affairs will suffer.
   B. They will succeed in politics.
   C. They will become popular.
   D. They will give up comfortable living.

7. In line 18, which literary device does Franklin use in the phrase *said I*?
   A. allusion
   B. aphorism
   C. inversion
   D. meter

8. In the paragraph beginning on line 19, which is an example of connotative language?
   A. pleasure
   B. miser
   C. wealth
   D. friendship

Literature Online

Assessment For additional test practice, go to glencoe.com and enter QuickPass code GLA9800u1.

Assessment

Assess
Reading

1. **A** is the correct answer because Franklin says "I went directly to a shop . . . and gave all my money for one." (DOK 2)

2. **D** is the correct answer because Franklin uses three parallel clauses to describe the actions of his siblings and cousins. (DOK 4)

3. **C** is the correct answer because Franklin learns that he paid four times what the whistle was worth. (DOK 1)

4. **D** is the correct answer because Franklin was thinking about his mistake. (DOK 1)

5. **D** is the correct answer because Franklin uses the word *whistle* as a metaphor for something that is not worth its price. (DOK 4)

6. **A** is the correct answer because Franklin states in line 18 that "neglecting his own affairs" is one price to be paid for being "fond of popularity." (DOK 1)

7. **C** is the correct answer because Franklin precedes the subject *I* with its verb *said*. (DOK 4)

8. **B** is the correct answer because the word *miser* carries a negative connotation. (DOK 4)

English Learners

DIFFERENTIATED INSTRUCTION

Intermediate Clarify with students that while they need to understand the passage, they will receive points only for correctly answering questions. As a result, students should use the questions to guide their reading. Point out that most of the questions refer test-takers to specific line numbers in the passage. Have students locate the line numbers in the passage and in the questions. After reading the passage through quickly for general understanding, students should focus on reading the questions. They can return to the passage to find the specific details they need in order to answer the questions.

Assessment

Assess

9. C is the correct answer because *elegant* means "of high quality." `DOK 1`

10. D is the correct answer because, in line 26, Franklin says such a person "ends his career in prison." `DOK 1`

11. A is the correct answer because, in lines 30–31, Franklin says "the false estimates they have made of the value of things" are the cause of mankind's miseries. `DOK 1`

12. D is the correct answer because Franklin repeats variations of the expression "gave too much for the whistle." `DOK 4`

13. A is the correct answer because Franklin uses an aphorism, or moral, to state a basic principle of life. `DOK 4`

14. B is the correct answer because Franklin wants to persuade readers not to falsely value things. `DOK 2`

15. C is the correct answer because it restates Franklin's conclusion in lines 30–31. `DOK 2`

9. From the context, what does the word *fine* in line 25 mean?
   A. penalty
   B. satisfactory
   C. elegant
   D. thin

10. Where does Franklin say one who "lives above his fortune" may end his career?
   A. with a fine house
   B. without benevolent friendship
   C. in ruined health
   D. in prison

11. From where does Franklin say most of the "miseries of mankind" come?
   A. false estimates of value
   B. the high value of things
   C. ill-natured brutes
   D. contracted debts

12. Starting with the second paragraph, which literary or rhetorical device does Franklin employ at the end of each paragraph?
   A. allusion
   B. hyperbole
   C. connotative language
   D. repetition

13. On the basis of this passage, what is the overall tone of this piece?
   A. aphoristic
   B. ironic
   C. angry
   D. formal

14. Which of the following best describes the author's purpose?
   A. to explain
   B. to persuade
   C. to entertain
   D. to describe

15. What is the main idea of this passage?
   A. Never spend money on things you cannot afford.
   B. Avoid wasting time.
   C. Always be aware of the true cost of your desires.
   D. Always listen to advice from concerned family members.

Main Idea and Supporting Details

Tell students that one way to sharpen their reading skills is to focus on the main idea of each paragraph. When taking a test, students may create their own systems to identify main ideas and details—for example, they could draw wavy lines under main ideas and straight lines under details. By focusing on the main ideas, they will be better able to see the underlying organization of the author's thoughts.

Have students use magazine or newspaper articles to practice this technique. Have students share their methods with a small group, and then choose and practice a second method learned in the group discussion.

Vocabulary Skills: Sentence Completion

For each item in the Vocabulary Skills section, choose the word or words that best complete the sentence.

1. In the end, England's attempts to _____ the colonists' demand for representation were unsuccessful.
   A. abate
   B. rouse
   C. convene
   D. lament

2. The _____ in Boston Harbor frightened soldiers and woke many people.
   A. commodity
   B. ration
   C. clamor
   D. scruple

3. There were no _____ reactions to Patrick Henry's powerful speech to the Second Virginia Convention, which greatly _____ the delegates.
   A. petrified . . . alighted
   B. obliging . . . deprived
   C. feigned . . . roused
   D. ingenious . . . gratified

4. Jonathan Edwards believed that his sermons could help repair the _____ in people's souls.
   A. desolation
   B. prudence
   C. vault
   D. conjurer

5. Persecution in England motivated the Pilgrims to _____ on a very _____ voyage across the Atlantic Ocean.
   A. temper . . . abominable
   B. embark . . . arduous
   C. revive . . . copious
   D. abhor . . . insidious

6. The Native Americans viewed the Pilgrims with a great deal of _____, especially after so many began to arrive.
   A. apprehension
   B. compassion
   C. subjugation
   D. providence

7. The Native American oral tradition is populated with powerful _____, animals, and ancestral spirits.
   A. vaults
   B. mortifications
   C. scruples
   D. conjurers

8. According to Olaudah Equiano, the Africans, who were shown no _____ during the Middle Passage, were _____ by their captors' use of violence.
   A. mischief . . . appeased
   B. hypocrisy . . . daunted
   C. tyranny . . . spurned
   D. compassion . . . petrified

9. Thomas Jefferson hoped to protect America's _____ from tyranny when he drafted the Declaration of Independence.
   A. resolutions
   B. infidels
   C. rations
   D. posterity

10. During his lifetime, Benjamin Franklin created many _____ things.
    A. copious
    B. petrified
    C. ingenious
    D. insidious

ASSESSMENT **169**

Assessment

Assess

1. **A** is the correct answer because the English wanted to end the colonists' demand for representation. **DOK 1**

2. **C** is the correct answer because it is the only option that might frighten soldiers and wake people. **DOK 1**

3. **C** is the correct answer because Henry's speech roused the delegates. **DOK 2**

4. **A** is the correct answer because it is the only option that makes sense in this context. **DOK 1**

5. **B** is the correct answer because it is the only option that makes sense in this context. **DOK 2**

6. **A** is the correct answer because the arrival of many Pilgrims would cause the Native Americans to be apprehensive. **DOK 1**

7. **D** is the correct answer because it is the only option that makes sense in this context. **DOK 1**

8. **D** is the correct answer because *compassion* is the only option that makes sense in the first answer blank. **DOK 2**

9. **D** is the correct answer because Jefferson intended the Declaration of Independence to protect future generations. **DOK 1**

10. **C** is the correct answer because Franklin was a creative inventor. **DOK 1**

Approaching Level

DIFFERENTIATED INSTRUCTION

Emerging If students struggle with revising paragraphs, tell them to silently read the sentence in question, along with the sentence before and after it. They should ask themselves what sounds or looks incorrect. Then substitute each answer choice, reading it silently, and "listen" to how it sounds. Have students read the questions first and go back to the passage in search of the answer.

Assess

Grammar and Writing

1. **C** is the correct answer because the second sentence works best as the topic sentence of the paragraph. **DOK 2**

2. **B** is the correct answer because the introductory phrase should be followed by a comma. **DOK 1**

Grammar and Writing Skills: Paragraph Improvement

The following is the rough draft of a student's report, which may contain errors. Read through it carefully; then answer the questions below.

[1] *Of all of those who signed this document, though, Benjamin Franklin was certainly the most important.* [2] *There are many important Americans whose names appear on the Declaration of Independence.* [3] *No other figure from this period is as interesting or as consistently relevant as Franklin continues to be.*

[4] *Unlike many of the other founders Franklin was from a modest background and was largely self-educated.* [5] *He did not have the kinds of advantages that Jefferson, and Washington took for granted.* [6] *Amazingly, his formal education ended when he was only ten years old.*

[7] *Franklin's background is startling when one considers his accomplishments.* [8] *No other founder can claim the same number of achievements in so many different fields of study.* [9] *Franklin was a great scientist, writer, politician, philosopher, and diplomat.*

[10] *What is truly incredible, though, is that so many of his inventions and concepts are still useful today.* [1] *For example, Franklin was responsible for bifocal glasses, the lightning rod, the Franklin stove the first North American volunteer fire department, and the first North American public library.*

[12] *While the other founders were important figures who played prominent roles in the shaping of this country, none was as exciting, were as diverse in talents, or had as much foresight as Benjamin Franklin.*

1. Which of the following sequences of sentences will make paragraph 1 most logical?
   A. NO CHANGE
   B. 3, 1, 2
   C. 2, 1, 3
   D. 3, 2, 1

2. Which of the following is the best way to improve sentence 4?
   A. NO CHANGE
   B. Unlike many of the other founders, Franklin was from a modest background
   C. Unlike other founders Franklin was from a modest background
   D. Many of the other founders came from modest backgrounds

Assessment Practice

Rearrange Tell students that paragraph-improvement exercises are like puzzles. Students will have to read the passage more than once to figure out the most logical sequence of sentences and paragraphs. To help students become more comfortable with these exercises, provide practice models students can work on during free time. Take a passage from a book that the class is reading and rearrange the sentences. Have students sequence the sentences in an order that makes sense. Tell students to pay attention to tone and voice as clues to sequence and meaning. Details added to a passage must match the tone and voice of the section to which they are added.

3. Which of the following is the best revision of sentence 5?
A. NO CHANGE
B. Washington, and Jefferson
C. Jefferson and Washington
D. Jefferson, Washington

4. Which of the following is the best way to write sentence 9?
A. NO CHANGE
B. Franklin was a great scientist, writer, politician and philosopher, diplomat.
C. Franklin was a great scientist and diplomat.
D. Franklin was a scientist and writer and a politician, and philosopher, and diplomat

5. Which of the following sentences, if inserted at the beginning of paragraph 4, would provide the most effective transition?
A. Benjamin Franklin was a good inventor.
B. Franklin's inventions and scientific findings were groundbreaking in the 1700s.
C. There were many things that Franklin knew, even without a strong formal education.
D. In the long run, Franklin's formal education wasn't that important.

6. Which of the following is the best revision of the end of sentence 11?
A. NO CHANGE
B. the Franklin stove the first North American volunteer fire department and the first public library in North America.
C. the Franklin stove and the first volunteer fire department and public library.
D. the Franklin stove, the first North American volunteer fire department, and the first North American public library.

7. Which of the following is the best way to improve sentence 12?
A. NO CHANGE
B. was as diverse in talents, or had as much foresight
C. is as diverse in talents, or had as much foresight
D. that could be as diverse in talents, or have as much insight

8. What could have been added to the last paragraph to make it stronger?
A. a summary of the key points
B. the introduction of new information
C. the introduction of opposing viewpoints
D. a visual aid

Questions 9 and 10 ask about the essay as a whole.

9. The writer intends to add a paragraph concerning Franklin's contribution to the Revolutionary War. The most logical place to insert this paragraph is:
A. before the third paragraph
B. after the last paragraph
C. before the second paragraph
D. after the third paragraph

10. What information could have been added to this essay to make it more convincing?
A. rebuttals of specific arguments against the author's position
B. further examples of Franklin's inventions
C. a thorough description of everyday life in America during the 1700s
D. an account of Franklin's time in Paris

3. **C** is the correct answer because a comma is not needed. DOK 1

4. **A** is the correct answer because the sentence is correct as it stands. DOK 1

5. **C** is the correct answer because the previous sentence is about the end of Franklin's formal education. DOK 2

6. **D** is the correct answer because items in a series must be separated by commas. DOK 1

7. **B** is the correct answer because the singular verb *was* is consistent with the first verb in the series and agrees with the subject, *none*. DOK 1

8. **A** is the correct answer because a summary of key points is an effective way to end the paragraph. DOK 4

9. **D** is the correct answer because information about Franklin's wartime contributions should directly follow mention of his political and diplomatic roles. DOK 4

10. **A** is the correct answer because countering arguments that Franklin *wasn't* the most important signer of the Declaration of Independence would strengthen the writer's position. DOK 4

Essay

Evaluate essays for the following:
- a clear thesis statement fully supported by specific examples and details
- effective voice, word choice, and sentence variety
- effective presentation, with attention to grammar and spelling conventions
DOK 3

English Learners

DIFFERENTIATED INSTRUCTION

Intermediate Remind students that they will need a thesis or main idea in order to write a persuasive essay. Model the strategy of creating a thesis or main idea from the essay question. For example, use the following template sentence for the essay question: Benjamin Franklin's view that giving up liberty to gain safety leads to the loss of both _____. Students would fill in their point of view in the blank line or use the template sentence to construct their own thesis. Point out that the thesis includes the important content from the essay question but restates it in the essay writer's own words. Then have students create a brief outline before beginning to write. Review outline techniques and allow students time to outline or make notes prior to writing their essays.

Skills Scope and Sequence

Readability Scores Key: Dale-Chall/DRP/Lexile

PART 1: Individualism, Optimism, and Nature

Selections and Features	Literary Elements
Unit Introduction pp. 172-186	Romanticism **SE** pp. 178-179 Transcendentalism **SE** p. 180 Gothic **SE** p. 184
Essay *from* **Nature,** by Ralph Waldo Emerson **8.9/61/960** pp. 188-193	Theme **SE** p. 189
Essay *from* **Self Reliance,** by Ralph Waldo Emerson **10.2/64/1030** pp. 194-197	Figurative Language **SE** p. 194 Tone (review) **SE** p. 196
Informational Text **TIME**: **The Biology of Joy,** by Michael D. Lemonick **11.9/68/1110** pp. 198-202	
Essay *from* **Woman in the Nineteenth Century,** by Margaret Fuller **8.2/65/1340** pp. 203-209	Thesis **SE** p. 204
Literary History The Fireside Poets pp. 210-211	Poetry **SE** p. 210
Memoir *from* **Walden,** by Henry David Thoreau **6.3/58/1260** pp. 212-219	Metaphor **SE** p. 213
Comparing Literature *from* **Civil Disobedience** (essay), by Henry David Thoreau **7.7/63/1110** **On the Eve of Historic Dandi March** (speech), by Mohandas K. Gandhi **6.8/59/950** *from* **Long Walk to Freedom** (autobiography), by Nelson Mandela **6.8/59/950** pp. 220-236	Argument **SE** p. 221

PART 2: The Dark Side of Romanticism

Literary History American Short Stories pp. 238-239	Short Story **SE** p. 238
Short Story The Devil and Tom Walker, by Washington Irving **8.4/64/1220** pp. 240-253	Characterization **SE** p. 241 Archetype (review) **SE** p. 252

Reading Skills and Strategies	Vocabulary	Writing / Grammar	Speaking, Listening, and Viewing
Analyze Graphic Information **TE** p. 176 Analyze Historical Context **SE** p. 178 Summarize **TE** p. 186	Compound Words **TE** p. 178	Create Graphic Organizers **TE** pp. 174, 180 Write an Expository Essay **TE** p. 182, **SE** p. 186 Commas in Appositives **TE** p. 184	Analyze Art **SE** p. 172 Presentation **SE** p. 186 Diagram **SE** p. 186
Recognize Author's Purpose **SE** p. 189 Reread **TE** p. 192	Word Usage **SE** p. 193	Write a Description **TE** p. 190 Write a Journal Entry **SE** p. 193	
Draw Conclusions **SE** p. 194	Context Clues **SE** p. 197 Academic Vocabulary **SE** p. 197	Write a Persuasive Speech **SE** p. 197	Persuasive Speech **SE** p. 197
Analyze Cause-and-Effect Relationships **SE** p. 198 Preview **SE** p. 198 Analyze Text Features **TE** p. 200		Write a Paragraph **TE** p. 198	
Summarize **SE** p. 204 Analyze Structure **TE** p. 206	Word Usage **SE** p. 209	Linking Verbs **TE** p. 208 Write a Letter **SE** p. 209	Analyze Art **SE** p. 205
Analyze Poetic Characteristics **SE** p. 211		Write a Description **TE** p. 210	Analyze Art **SE** p. 210
Connect **SE** p. 213 Skim and Scan **TE** p. 216	Context Clues **SE** p. 219	Write a Comparison-Contrast Essay **TE** p. 214 Write a Summary **TE** p. 218	Analyze Art **SE** p. 216
Compare and Contrast **SE** p. 220 Evaluate Evidence **SE** p. 221 Recognize Bias **TE** p. 232	Negative Prefixes **TE** p. 226 Antonyms **SE** p. 228	Transitions **TE** p. 224 Write a Summary **SE** p. 228 Write an Expository Essay **SE** p. 236	Analyze Art **SE** p. 225 Discussion **SE** p. 236 Collage **SE** p. 236
Analyze Fiction **SE** p. 239		Create a Story Map **TE** p. 238	
Make and Verify Predictions **SE** p. 241 Visualize **TE** p. 242	Analogies **SE** p. 252 Academic Vocabulary **SE** p. 252	Absolute Phrases **TE** p. 246 Action Verbs **TE** p. 250 Write a Summary **SE** p. 253 Verb Tenses **SE** p. 253	Analyze Art **SE** p. 245 Oral Presentation **TE** p. 248 Discussion **SE** p. 251

Readability Scores Key: Dale-Chall/DRP/Lexile

PART 2: The Dark Side of Romanticism *(continued)*

Selections and Features	Literary Elements
Poem The Raven, by Edgar Allan Poe pp. 254-261	Narrative Poem **SE** p. 255
Short Story The Pit and the Pendulum, by Edgar Allan Poe **9.0/65/1010** pp. 262-276	Suspense **SE** p. 262 Point of View (review) **SE** p. 275
Vocabulary Workshop p. 277	
Short Story The Minister's Black Veil, by Nathaniel Hawthorne **8.0/66/1240** pp. 278-292	Symbol **SE** p. 279 Characterization (review) **SE** p. 291
Grammar Workshop p. 293	
Novel *from* **Moby-Dick,** by Herman Melville **9.0/67/1150** pp. 294-305	Motivation **SE** p. 295 Metaphor (review) **SE** p. 304
Historical Perspective *from* **In the Heart of the Sea,** by Nathaniel Philbrick **9.0/67/1150** pp. 306-309	
Writing Workshop pp. 310-317	
Speaking, Listening, and Viewing Workshop pp. 318-319	
Independent Reading pp. 320-321	
Assessment pp. 322-327	

Reading Skills and Strategies	Vocabulary	Writing / Grammar	Speaking, Listening, and Viewing
Analyze Sound Devices **SE** p. 255 Classify **TE** p. 256	Synonyms **SE** p. 261	Combining Sentences **TE** p. 260 Write a Summary **SE** p. 261	

Identify Sequence **SE** p. 262
Evaluate Tone **TE** p. 272
	Context Clues **TE** p. 264
	Word Origins **SE** p. 275
	Academic Vocabulary
	   SE p. 275
		Write a Literary Analysis
		   TE p. 266
		Write a Description **TE** p. 268
		Dashes **TE** p. 270
		Write an Expository Essay
		   SE p. 276
		Apostrophes **SE** p. 276
			Analyze Art **SE** p. 263
			Discussion **SE** p. 274

	Context Clues **SE** p. 277		

Make Inferences **SE** p. 279
Analyze Mood **TE** p. 280
	Connotation **TE** p. 282
	Synonyms **SE** p. 291
	Academic Vocabulary
	   SE p. 291
		Dangling Participles **TE** p. 286
		Write a Letter **TE** p. 288
		Write an Expository Essay
		   SE p. 292
			Analyze Art **SE** p. 283
			Discussion **SE** p. 290

		Misplaced and Dangling Modifiers **SE** p. 293	

Monitor Comprehension **SE** p. 295
Preview **TE** p. 296
	Antonyms **SE** p. 305
	Academic Vocabulary
	   SE p. 305
		Write a Character Sketch
		   TE p. 298
		Write Research Questions
		   TE p. 300
			Performance **TE** p. 302
			Oral Report **SE** p. 305

Analyze Historical Context **SE** p. 306		Write a Research Report **TE** p. 308	Analyze Art **SE** p. 307
		Create an Outline **TE** p. 312 Prewrite **SE** p. 313 Draft **SE** p. 314 Passive Voice **TE** p. 314 Revise **SE** p. 316 Adjectives **TE** p. 316 Write a Reflective Essay **SE** p. 317	
Analyze Cultural Context **SE** p. 320		Revise **SE** p. 319 Write an Outline **TE** p. 319	Reflective Presentation **SE** p. 319
		Write a Research Report **TE** p. 320	Collage **SE** p. 321
		Write a Reflective Essay **SE** p. 327	

Focus

Independence (Squire Jack Porter), 1858. Frank Blackwell Mayer. Oil on paperboard, 12 x 15⅞ in. Smithsonian American Art Museum, Washington, DC.

View the Art One definition of *squire* is "the chief landowner in a district." Why do you think the painter chose Squire Jack Porter to represent independence? ★

172

Unit Introduction Skills

**American Romanticism
1800–1860**

Reading Skills
- Analyze Graphic Information (SE pp. 174–177)
- Analyze Cause and Effect (SE p. 181)
- Interpret (SE p. 183; TE p. 182)
- Compare and Contrast (SE p. 185)
- Draw Conclusions (TE p. 176, 178, 180)

Vocabulary Skills
- Compound Words (TE p. 178)

Writing Skills/Grammar
- Write an Essay (SE p. 186)
- Graphic Organizers (TE p. 174)
- Interpret Literature (TE p. 182)
- Commas in Appositives (TE p. 184)

Listening/Speaking/Viewing Skills
- Analyze Art (SE pp. 172; TE pp. 173, 177, 181, 183, 185)

AMERICAN ROMANTICISM

1800-1860

Looking Ahead

Powerful forces marked the period that produced the first great American literature. The arrival of the European cultural movement known as Romanticism strongly influenced many American writers of this time. These writers also responded to social forces, including an outburst of reform movements, the spread of industry, and the increasing sectional strife that would soon bring the Civil War.

Keep the following questions in mind as you read:

➥ How do you think the big ideas that shaped this period continue to affect American culture today?

➥ Which of the writers of this period reflect the positive side of Romanticism? Which reflect its dark side?

➥ In what ways does the Romantic period seem better than the contemporary American period? In what ways does it seem worse?

173

Focus
Summary

This introduction begins with an overview of the political, social, and cultural history of the United States from 1800 to 1860. It focuses on the effects of the Industrial Revolution, the growth of sectional strife that would lead to the Civil War, the social reform movements that began with the Second Great Awakening, and the major features of American Romanticism: optimism and individualism, the idealization of nature, and the darkness of the Gothic imagination.

View the Art

Answer: *A squire is a country gentleman, a person of some wealth and importance. Squire Jack Porter seems completely at ease here. He represents an American who is proud of the land he owns and has the time to sit and admire it.*

The American painter Frank Blackwell Mayer (1827–1899) is well known for his realistic scenes of everyday life. His subject was seventy-five years old when Mayer painted him. Porter had been a captain in the War of 1812.

 For diagnostic and end-of-unit assessment, see Assessment Resources, pp. 9–16, 333–334.

Unit Resources

Print Materials
- Unit 2 Teaching Resources, pp. 1–216
- Interactive Read and Write (On Level, Approaching, EL), pp. 45–98
- Novel Companion, pp. 75–118
- Bellringer Option Transparencies: Selection Focus 16–19; Daily Language Practice 19–29
- Assessment Resources, Selection Assessment, pp. 97–120

Technology
- TeacherWorks Plus CD
- StudentWorks Plus CD
- Literature Launchers: Pre-Reading Videos DVD, Unit 2
- Literature Online
- Interactive Vocabulary CD-ROM
- Listening Library CD-ROM
- ExamView CD-ROM
- Skill Level Up! CD-ROM

Teach

Use the Timeline Help students read the timeline.

- Explain that this unit covers the era from the territorial expansion of the Louisiana Purchase to the eve of the U.S. Civil War.
- Have students find a United States or world event that they know.

Ask: How might that event have affected writers? *(The Underground Railroad, for example, might have inspired someone to write about slavery.)*

Language History ☆

Rise of American English

Noah Webster (1758–1843) was inspired to write his *American Dictionary of the English Language* to help standardize and simplify spelling. (For example, he replaced the English spelling *honour* with *honor.*) He also added new words, such as *skunk* and *squash,* from Native American languages.

TIMELINE 1800–1860

Godey's Lady's Book ▼

AMERICAN LITERATURE   1

1800	1810	1820	1830
1800 Library of Congress founded	**1819** *The Sketch Book* by Washington Irving (which includes tales such as "Rip Van Winkle")	**1828** Noah Webster's first dictionary of American English ☆▼	**1831** Ralph Waldo Emerson resigns from the ministry
1805 Red Jacket, a Seneca chief, gives a speech defending Native American beliefs			**1836** Transcendental Club founded
Chief Red Jacket ▶			**1837** Sarah Josepha Hale is made editor of *Godey's Lady's Book;* it becomes one of the most influential literary magazines of the century

UNITED STATES EVENTS

1800	1810	1820	1830
1803 United States buys Louisiana Territory from France, more than doubling the size of the U.S.	**1812–1815** United States and Great Britain fight War of 1812	**1820** Missouri Compromise preserves balance of slave and free states	**1831** Cyrus H. McCormick invents the mechanical reaper
1807 Robert Fulton builds the *Clermont,* the first successful steamboat	**1814** Francis Scott Key writes "The Star-Spangled Banner"	**1825** Erie Canal opens, linking Atlantic Ocean and Great Lakes	**1833** The American Anti-Slavery Society is founded in Philadelphia; by 1838 there are 250,000 members
	1815 Victory over British at New Orleans makes Andrew Jackson a national hero	**1828** Andrew Jackson elected president	**1838** Cherokees are driven west along the Trail of Tears

WORLD EVENTS

1800	1810	1820	1830
1804 Napoleon crowned emperor of France	**1810** Miguel Hidalgo begins revolution in Mexico	**1821** Mexico declares independence from Spain	**1837** Victoria crowned queen of Great Britain ▼
1805 Reign of Muhammad Ali begins in Egypt	**1815** Napoleon defeated at the Battle of Waterloo	**1825** World's first railway line opens in England	
		1829 Greece wins independence from Turkey	

LOG ON ▶ **Literature** Online

Literature and Reading To explore the Interactive Timeline, go to glencoe.com and enter QuickPass code GLA9800u2.

Writing Practice

Create Graphic Organizers Explain that a timeline is one kind of chart that presents a sequence of events. Another kind of diagram that serves this function is a flowchart. Flowcharts can help students organize material in preparation for writing assignments. To construct a flowchart, arrange events in order. Then draw arrows to show how one event flows into another.

Have students create flowcharts that correctly sequence the following events from the timeline:

- Thoreau writes novel about living alone at Walden Pond *(3)*
- Transcendental Club founded *(1)*
- Transcendentalists establish Brook Farm *(2)*

◄ Masthead from the
North Star newspaper

1840

1840
Tales of the Grotesque and Arabesque by Edgar Allan Poe

1841
Social reformers establish Brook Farm, an experiment in communal living

1841
Essays by Ralph Waldo Emerson

1845
The Raven and Other Poems by Edgar Allan Poe

1845
Woman in the Nineteenth Century, an early work of feminism, by Margaret Fuller

1847
Frederick Douglass begins publishing the *North Star*, an abolitionist newspaper

1850

1850
The Scarlet Letter by Nathaniel Hawthorne

1851
Moby-Dick by Herman Melville

1852
Uncle Tom's Cabin by Harriet Beecher Stowe ☆

1854
Walden by Henry David Thoreau

1855
The Song of Hiawatha by Henry Wadsworth Longfellow

1855
Leaves of Grass by Walt Whitman

1840

1844
Samuel Morse demonstrates the first telegraph by sending a message from Washington, D.C., to Baltimore

Gold pan and nuggets ▼

1846–1848
Mexican-American War fought; Mexico cedes territory in Southwest to United States

1848
First women's rights convention held in Seneca Falls, New York

1849
California gold rush begins

1850

1850
Fugitive Slave Act, forcing return of escaped slaves to their owners, inflames sectional conflict

1857
In *Dred Scott* case, Supreme Court rules that slaves and former slaves are not U.S. citizens

1859
Antislavery activist John Brown is hanged for raiding federal arsenal at Harpers Ferry, Virginia

1840

1845
Potato famine begins in Ireland, leading to mass immigration to America

1848
Revolutions sweep Europe; Karl Marx and Friedrich Engels publish the *Communist Manifesto*

1850

1850
Taiping Rebellion begins in China

▲
1859
Charles Darwin publishes his theory of evolution

▲ *The Irish Famine*, 1850. George Frederick Watts. Oil on canvas. Watts Gallery, Compton, Surrey, UK.

Reading Check

Analyzing Graphic Information What relationship can you see between the events in U.S. history in 1815 and 1828 as they are related to the career of Andrew Jackson?

INTRODUCTION **175**

Approaching Level

DIFFERENTIATED INSTRUCTION

Emerging Explain to students that information in the timeline will help them understand how literature connects to the political and social events of the time. **Ask:** What events in the United States might connect to Henry David Thoreau's choice to live in solitude and to write *Walden*, the book that describes his life in the woods and his thoughts on nature? *(The many industrial and technological advances, such as the* mechanical reaper and the telegraph, may have caused Thoreau to long for a quieter, more natural life.) What event in the United States might be related to Margaret Fuller's essay *Woman in the Nineteenth Century*? *(the women's rights convention held in 1848)* What events in the United States might have prompted Harriet Beecher Stowe to write *Uncle Tom's Cabin*? *(the Missouri Compromise in 1820, the founding of the American*

Teach

Reading Check

Answer: *In 1815, Jackson became a war hero. People often vote for someone who has shown leadership in crisis and courage in battle. Many people had heard of Jackson, so he was a popular choice for president in the 1828 election.*

Reading Strategy | 2

Make Inferences **Ask:** What historical events can you find that might make a writer long to return to a simpler way of life in which he is closer to nature? *(Inventions that change the way people do things—steamboat, mechanical reaper, telegraph— quicken the pace of life and can lead to stress. Warfare could make people long for a peaceful life.)*

Literary History ☆

Uncle Tom's Cabin The controversy produced by Harriet Beecher Stowe's best-selling antislavery novel contributed to one of the main conflicts leading to the Civil War. Stowe wrote her novel in response to the passing of the Fugitive Slave Act of 1850.

Anti-Slavery Society in 1833, and the Fugitive Slave Act in 1850)

Teach

Draw Conclusions **Ask:** If you compare immigration from 1841 to 1860 with immigration during the twenty years before that, by what factor did immigration increase? *(By more than 5)* Point out the Voter Participation chart. **Ask:** What conclusions can you draw from the rise in voter participation in 1840? *(Perhaps people felt that the outcome of the election would affect them personally. Perhaps the election campaign was exciting and the candidates were appealing.)*

Political History ☆

Log Cabin Election The U.S. presidential election of 1840 was between incumbent Martin Van Buren and William Henry Harrison, a military hero. In their "Log Cabin and Hard Cider" campaign, Harrison and his running mate, John Tyler, presented themselves as common folk—like those who lived in log cabins and drank hard cider. Harrison and Tyler won the election.

BY THE NUMBERS

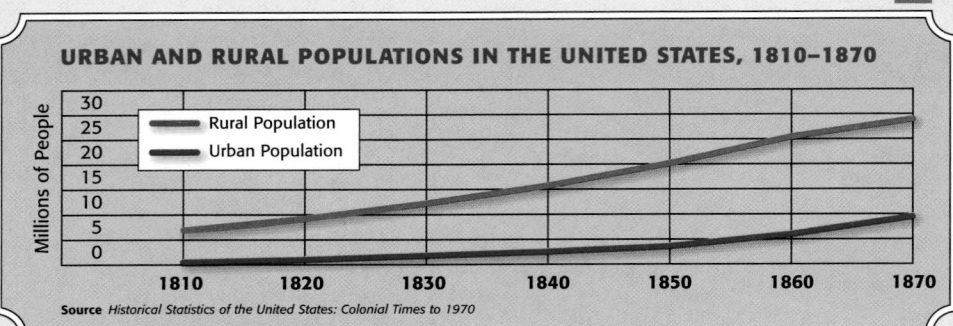

URBAN AND RURAL POPULATIONS IN THE UNITED STATES, 1810–1870

Source *Historical Statistics of the United States: Colonial Times to 1970*

Purchasing Power

In 1851, a male textile worker earned $6.50 a week, a shoemaker or printer between $4 and $6 a week, and an unskilled laborer about $1 a week. Only a small group of skilled workers were able to make at least $10.38 per week, the amount reformer Horace Greeley calculated that a family of five needed to make ends meet (see list below).

Weekly Needs

Flour	.63
Sugar	.32
Butter	.63
Milk	.14
Butcher's meat	$1.40
Potatoes	.50
Tea and coffee	.25
Candles and oil	.14
Fuel	.40
Sundries	.40
Household articles	.25
Bedding	.20
Rent	$3.00
Wearing apparel	$2.00
Newspapers	.12
TOTAL	**$10.38**

BIG CITIES OF 1830

City	Population
New York	200,000
Baltimore	80,000
Philadelphia	80,000
Boston	60,000

IMMIGRATION

- Between 1821 and 1840, 751,000 immigrants entered the United States.
- Between 1841 and 1860, more than 4 million immigrants came to the U.S. (most from Great Britain, Ireland, and Germany).

EDUCATION

- In 1850, 64.9 percent of white children and 31.3 percent of African American children attended school.
- In 1860, more than half of the 321 high schools in the U.S. were in Massachusetts, New York, and Ohio.

RAILROAD

In 1833, there were 380 miles of rails in the United States. By 1860, there were more than 30,000 miles of rails in the United States.

FACTORIES

In 1840, U.S. factories and mills produced goods valued at less than $500 million. In 1850, they produced goods valued at more than $1 billion.

VOTER PARTICIPATION, 1824–1840 ☆

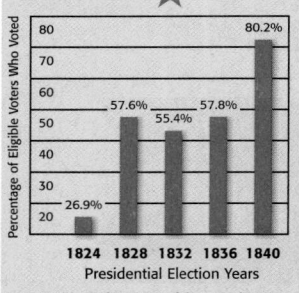

Source *Historical Statistics of the United States: Colonial Times to 1970*

Reading Practice

Use a Graph Have students read "Purchasing Power" and create a graph that summarizes the information in that paragraph. Discuss the difference between incomes and the cost of living. Point out that most people did not have enough income to support a family of five. Then have students create a bar graph showing the levels of income of the four types of workers mentioned versus Greeley's cost of living in 1851. *(Students' bar graphs should resemble the example.)*

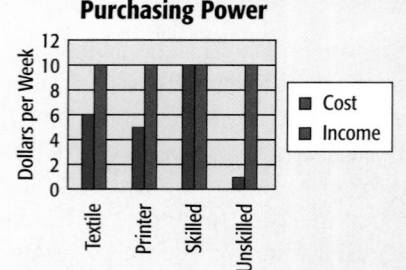

Purchasing Power

BEING THERE

The major American writers of the period 1800–1860 lived in the northeastern United States, roughly the area from Maryland to New England. These images provide a glimpse of this area.

A *Boston as the Eagle and the Wild Goose See It*, 1860, James Wallace Black. Photograph. This photo of Boston is the first aerial photograph taken in the United States.

B *Market Street, Baltimore*, 1850. Unknown artist. Colored lithograph. Enoch Pratt Free Library, Baltimore MD. Painting of downtown Baltimore.

C *Brook Farm*, 1844. Josiah Wolcott. Oil on panel. Massachusetts Historical Society, Boston, MA. Painting of a Transcendentalist community outside Boston.

LOG ON ▶ **Literature** Online

Literature and Reading For more about the history and literature of this period, go to glencoe.com and enter QuickPass code GLA9800u2.

Reading Check

Analyzing Graphic Information

1. In which presidential election year during this period did voter participation increase the most from the previous one?

2. How many more U.S. citizens lived in rural areas than in urban areas in 1850?

3. What large cities are located on the map? Judging by the images, how were the cities of the period like and unlike big U.S. cities today?

INTRODUCTION **177**

Teach

Reading Check

Answers:

1. *Voter participation increased most from 1824 to 1828.*

2. *Approximately 16 million*

3. *Six cities are shown on the map. The pictures show buildings close together, but no skyscrapers.*

Reading Strategy | 2

Use Maps Point out that the large map shows the part of the United States where the writers in this unit lived.

Ask: What does the small locator map indicate? (It shows the portion of the continental United States occupied by the area of the larger map.)

View the Art ★

A. Black took his photograph from a balloon tethered over Boston.

B. The Baltimore Museum and Gallery of Fine Arts is pictured on the right.

C. Wolcott's painting of Brook Farm shows the entrance to the community.

177

Teach

Reading Strategy | 1

Draw Conclusions Have students read "The Industrial Revolution" subsection.

Ask: Which workers' jobs have disappeared or radically changed since the 1750s? Why? *(Workers whose jobs have disappeared or changed include blacksmiths, weavers, shoemakers, and wagon builders. Machines have changed the way people work.)*

Reading Strategy | 2

Connect **Say:** Social issues are often reflected in works of fiction. **Ask:** What social issues are reflected in books, movies, and TV programs today? *(Students may list issues that include crime, unemployment, abuse, substance addiction, and poverty.)*

Learning Objectives

For pages 178–186
In studying this text, you will focus on the following objectives:

Literary Study:
Analyzing literary periods.
Analyzing literary genres.
Evaluating historical influences.
Connecting to the literature.

AMERICAN ROMANTICISM
1800-1860

Historical, Social, and Cultural Forces

The Industrial Revolution

In the mid-1700s, a huge economic change known as the Industrial Revolution began in Britain. Manufacturing shifted from skilled workers using hand tools to unskilled laborers tending large, complex machines. Factories, some housing hundreds of machines and workers, replaced home-based workshops. Manufacturers sold their goods nationwide or abroad instead of just locally.

The Industrial Revolution soon spread to the United States, where it caused tremendous economic growth and transformed American society. Hundreds of new factories were built. The Boston Manufacturing Company, for example, employed thousands of women and children, who worked for lower wages than men and in often dangerous conditions. An expanding network of roads and canals united different sections of the country. Two new inventions—the steamboat and the railroad—revolutionized transportation.

The Industrial Revolution brought economic growth, but it also helped divide Americans into two nations. The North had large cities and an economy based on manufacturing. The South had few large cities and a farming economy dominated by a single crop—cotton. Much of this cotton was grown on large plantations worked by slaves. In time, these divisions would bring the Civil War.

The Age of Reform

In the 1820s, idealistic Americans produced an outburst of reform movements. Many of these reformers were inspired by the Second Great Awakening, a major religious movement that reached its peak in the 1820s and 1830s. During the Age of Reform, Americans banded together in dozens of organizations to end slavery, stop drunkenness, secure women's rights, provide better care for the mentally ill, and improve prisons.

In the 1840s, railroads reduced the travel time from New York to Boston from a week (by stagecoach) to less than 12 hours.

Vocabulary Practice

Compound Words Remind students that a compound word is made up of two or more words put together. Readers can increase their understanding of familiar words by examining the meaning of the separate parts.

Examples in the introduction include *steamboat, railroad,* and *nationwide.*

Give students practice by asking them to define these compound words: *smokescreen, newspaper, gingerbread, nightfall, daybreak, horseshoe, basketball, playground.*

Roots of Romanticism

Optimism and Individualism

Romanticism was a movement in art and thought that dominated Europe and the United States throughout much of the 1800s. Romantic writers valued imagination and feeling over intellect and reason. Some celebrated individualism and freedom; they believed in the basic goodness and equality of human beings and in their right to govern themselves. Others took a more pessimistic view of human life. Overall, Romanticism reflected a division between a "bright" and a "dark" vision of the world.

Kinship with Nature

Another attitude that the Romantics shared was a belief in the importance of nature. In the 1700s, many European thinkers had believed that nature was merely a wilderness to be tamed. In opposition to this view, the Romantics celebrated the beauty, power, and wonder of the natural world. They also stressed the value of nature as a spiritual and moral guide for humanity. The Romantics'

reverence for nature also caused them to fear the destructive effects of industry.

> "A man should learn to detect and watch that gleam of light which flashes across his mind from within."
>
> —Ralph Waldo Emerson

The Power of Darkness

Many Romantics were drawn to the nonrational side of human nature, such as the emotions, imagination, intuition—even evil and insanity. They were also fascinated by remote periods of history and exotic places. These interests came together in Gothic literature—literature with a brooding atmosphere that emphasizes the unknown and inspires fear. Gothic novels typically feature wild and remote settings, such as haunted castles or wind-blasted moors, and their plots involve violent or mysterious events. **3**

 PREVIEW **Big Ideas** of American Romanticism

1 Optimism and Individualism	**2** Kinship with Nature	**3** The Power of Darkness
Optimism is the belief that the world around us is always improving. Some American Romantics presented an optimistic view of the possibility of human progress, based in part on a democratic confidence in the ability of ordinary individuals to better themselves, their political system, and society. **See pages 180–181.**	Many American Romantics believed in the beneficial effects of a close link between humanity and nature. This belief coexisted with a concern that the spread of industry and new technology threatened the natural world and isolated people from it. **See pages 182–183.**	There was a dark underside to American Romanticism. It took a variety of forms, including a fascination with disease, madness, death, evil, the supernatural, and the destructive aspects of nature. **See pages 184–185.**

Literary Element | 3

Romanticism Ask: What were the values of the Romantic writers? *(Imagination, feeling, individuality, freedom, human goodness, equality, self-government, and the importance of nature)*

Ask: What characterized the dark side of Romanticism? *(The supernatural, nature's destructiveness, evil, insanity, remote periods in history, and exotic places)*

Literary History ☆

American Gothic Gothic fiction by British writers became wildly popular in the United States in the 1790s. American writers followed the trend. Charles Brockden Brown's *Wieland, or The Transformation,* published in 1798, took the familiar elements of European Gothic fiction—strange buildings, mysterious deaths, unearthly voices, and madness—and transferred them to an American setting.

English Learners

DIFFERENTIATED INSTRUCTION

 Intermediate To help students understand the paragraph "Optimism and Individualism," ask them to list the words and phrases that describe the attitudes Romantic writers shared. Ask students to work in small groups to restate or give examples to show they understand the meanings of *imagination, feeling, individualism, freedom, basic goodness, equality of human beings,* and *right to govern themselves.*

For the paragraph "Kinship with Nature," have students clarify the meanings of *nature, wilderness, tamed, celebrated, spiritual, humanity,* and *reverence.*

Lastly, for the paragraph "The Power of Darkness," have students determine the meanings of *nonrational, emotions, imagination, intuition, exotic, brooding,* and *Gothic.*

Have students look up unfamiliar terms in a dictionary. Have groups share their findings with each other.

Teach

Draw Conclusions **Ask:**
How might a rise in the power of common people change literary history? *(More power might lead to greater literacy and wealth, which could both expand the reading public and increase demands for certain types of writing, such as works of entertainment or self-help books.)*

Writer's Technique ☆
Emerson's Informal Style
During much of his career, Emerson spread his ideas by giving public lectures. In writing his essays, Emerson often drew on the notes he used as a lecturer. When he spoke, Emerson often reshuffled the pages of his manuscript, reading from different sections as ideas struck him. The literary style of Emerson's essays retains something of this spontaneous, improvised quality.

Big Idea 1
Optimism and Individualism

ach of us has ambitions and plans, hopes and dreams. Our beliefs affect how we feel about what we can achieve as individuals and citizens. Optimists believe they can reach their goals in life. Ralph Waldo Emerson (see pages 188–197) was a lifelong optimist. He also celebrated the individual, proclaiming that by being true to their innermost selves, people could accomplish great things.

1 Rise of the Common People
Beginning in the 1820s, the American belief in the power of the ordinary citizen had a huge impact on both political and social life. Changes in voting laws expanded the electorate to include nearly all white males. In 1828, these voters elected frontiersman Andrew Jackson as president, marking the arrival of the common people in American politics. Americans of this period also became involved in a broad range of reform movements. These ordinary citizens formed associations, raised money, wrote pamphlets, held rallies, gave speeches, and worked to pass laws designed to improve American society.

> *"All that Adam had, all that Caesar could, you have and can do."*
>
> —Ralph Waldo Emerson

Transcendentalism
In the 1830s, the influence of Romanticism began to be felt in the United States. One result was Transcendentalism, a loosely organized movement that embodied the ideas of thinkers who were active in New England in the 1830s and 1840s. Emerson was a leading figure in this group, which began as an informal discussion club. Among those who participated in the talks at the Transcendental Club were Margaret Fuller, Henry David Thoreau, and Nathaniel Hawthorne.

The essence of Transcendentalism was the philosophy known as Idealism. For Idealists, such as the German philosopher Immanuel Kant, reality is not "out there" in material objects but instead exists in our ideas about those objects. The Transcendentalists believed that intuition is a more valuable guide than sensory experience in grasping what nature really is.

Emerson's Outlook
Emerson's optimism convinced him that the universe existed for humanity's benefit. He told people that they simply needed to look within themselves to awaken a sense of wonder and recover their oneness with the universe: "Every spirit builds itself a house, and beyond its house a world, and beyond its world a heaven. Know then that the world exists for you." He believed that ordinary human beings had limitless potential. His avid reading of mystical Hindu philosophy influenced his conviction that humans are divine because they share in the Over-soul, Emerson's name for the spirit that pervades the universe. Emerson summed up his ideas by saying that he had really taught only one thing, that every person was infinite.

Emerson's Essays ☆
Emerson is best known for his essays, such as "Self-Reliance." Essays can range from serious, formal analyses to light, personal reflections. Although Emerson's essays are formal, they are not tightly unified around a single topic. Instead, he presented his thoughts in a loosely organized series of striking sentences. "The maker of a sentence," he observed, "launches out into the infinite."

Organize Ideas To help students keep track of the ideas presented on this page, have them make a concept map for each major heading. An example follows.

Supporting Detail	**Main Idea: Transcendentalism**	Supporting Detail
• Transcendental Club members: Margaret Fuller Henry David Thoreau Nathaniel Hawthorne		• Intuition is better than sensory experience for grasping reality.

Supporting Detail	Supporting Detail
• Ralph Waldo Emerson, a leading figure	• Philosophy of Idealism: Reality exists in our ideas about objects.

The Jolly Flatboatmen, 1877–78. George Caleb Bingham. Oil on canvas, 26¹⁄₁₆ x 36³⁄₈ in. Daniel J. Terra Acquisition Endowment Fund, 1992. Terra Foundation for American Art, Chicago, IL.

from *Self-Reliance* by Ralph Waldo Emerson

Our houses are built with foreign taste; our shelves are garnished with foreign ornaments; our opinions, our tastes, our faculties, lean, and follow the Past and the Distant. The soul created the arts wherever they have flourished. It was in his own mind that the artist sought his model. It was an application of his own thought to the thing to be done and the conditions to be observed. And why need we copy the Doric or the Gothic model? Beauty, convenience, grandeur of thought, and quaint expression are as near to us as to any, and if the American artist will study with hope and love the precise thing to be done by him, considering the climate, the soil, the length of the day, the wants of the people, the habit and form of the government, he will create a house in which all these will find themselves fitted, and taste and sentiment will be satisfied also.

Insist on yourself; never imitate.

Reading Check

Analyzing Cause and Effect Why would Emerson's optimism have made him a reformer?

Approaching Level

DIFFERENTIATED INSTRUCTION

Emerging Point out the main heads, subheads, displayed quotation, and the excerpt on pages 180-181. **Ask:** Without reading the text, what information do the subheadings give about Emerson? *(He was a transcendentalist.)* How can you tell that the text on this page is an excerpt from an Emerson essay? *(Emerson's name and the title of the essay are above the excerpt.)*

Established Explain to students that Emerson is asking readers to rely on their own experience. Ask them to make two lists from the excerpt: (1) words that promote self-reliance (2) words that promote dependence on foreign influences.

Teach

Reading Check

Answer: *He would have believed that the world could be made a better place through reform.*

Literary Element   2

Aphorism **Say:** An aphorism is a short, pointed statement that expresses a wise or clever observation about human experience. Emerson's writing is full of aphoristic statements. Identify observations in this passage that might stand alone as aphorisms. *("The soul created the arts wherever they have flourished." "Insist on yourself; never imitate.")* What do these statements say about life and the human experience? *(Students may say that these statements encourage people to be individuals and not imitators.)*

View the Art

George Caleb Bingham (1811–1879) grew up along the Missouri River. Today he is best known for his paintings of frontier life.

Ask: Why might pioneers such as these flatboatmen tend to be optimistic? *(People with the self-confidence needed to face the challenges of settling a frontier would probably possess optimism.)*

181

Teach

Reading Strategy | 1

Connect **Ask:** What do you feel should be the human response to nature? Does nature exist primarily for our use, or do we have the responsibility to preserve the natural world? Have students give examples from what they have read so far to support their answers.

Reading Strategy | 2

Evaluate Discuss with students the comment in paragraph 2 by Luther Standing Bear. Ask them how much they think that the attitude he attributed to white people has contributed to today's environmental problems. Ask students to give specific examples to support their opinions about Luther Standing Bear's comment.

Literary History ☆

The Influence of Thoreau
Thoreau is one of the most influential and admired of American writers. His nature writing has made him a hero to the modern environmental movement. Thoreau's political writings, particularly his essay "Civil Disobedience," helped shape the nonviolent civil rights campaigns of both the Indian nationalist Mohandas K. Gandhi and Martin Luther King Jr.

Big Idea 2
Kinship with Nature

Today, many people are concerned about the effects of civilization on the wilderness. How important is nature, and what can we learn from it? In the 1800s, Henry David Thoreau (see pages 212–228) revealed his thoughts about this question in his journal. Thoreau believed that contact with wild nature refreshed the human spirit. Nature can also teach us respect for its destructive ways and remind us that, though we try, we can never wholly subdue its powerful forces.

> *"I would rather sit on a pumpkin, and have it all to myself, than be crowded on a velvet cushion."*
>
> —Henry David Thoreau

America—Garden or Wilderness?

The natural environment of America has produced very different responses in different people. Luther Standing Bear, a Teton Sioux, explained the Native American view: "We did not think of the great open plains, the beautiful rolling hills, and winding streams with tangled growth as 'wild.' Only to the white man was nature a 'wilderness'. . . . To us it was tame."

The first European explorers and settlers viewed America as both a paradise to be enjoyed and a wilderness to be tamed. Many were amazed and delighted at the number of animals and plants that were unknown in Europe. But to others, such as Pilgrim leader William Bradford, arriving in 1620, America was a place to be feared: "What could they see but a hideous and desolate wilderness, full of wild beasts and wild men?"

Thoreau and Nature

Another New Englander, Emerson's friend Thoreau, also rejected a conventional life. Like Emerson, Thoreau championed American individualism. He spent two years in a cabin he built at Walden Pond near his home of Concord, Massachusetts. Thoreau sharply observed the natural surroundings there. "For many years," he wrote, "I was self-appointed inspector of snow storms and rain storms and did my duty faithfully." Thoreau was not fond of luxuries and not afraid of striking out on his own.

Emerson's and Thoreau's concept of the natural world had much in common with the Native American viewpoint. Both traditions found harmony and purpose in the unspoiled earth. At Walden, Thoreau communed with nature. He wrote, "You only need sit still long enough in some attractive spot in the woods that all its inhabitants may exhibit themselves to you by turns." Leslie Marmon Silko, a contemporary Native American author, expresses a similar view. She writes, "I never feel lonely when I walk alone in the hills: I am surrounded with living beings, with these sandstone ridges and lava rock hills full of life."

Thoreau and Politics ☆

Thoreau's extreme individualism led him to take certain radical political positions. In the 1840s, as the southern states became more determined to protect and extend slavery, he came to regard all government as a threat to liberty. During the Mexican-American War (1846–1848), which many opponents of slavery believed was being fought to establish slavery in the West, Thoreau wrote his essay "Civil Disobedience." He argued that the individual conscience is more important than the law: "Law never made men a whit more just; and by means of their respect for it, even the well-disposed are daily made the agents of injustice."

Writing Practice

⚡ **Interpret Literature** Remind students that studying literature is not just reading stories; it is also confronting and interpreting powerful, thought-provoking ideas. Ask students to think about the highlighted Thoreau quote. Ask them to make some notes about possible interpretations of Thoreau's statement. Then tell them to write a two-paragraph explanatory essay. The first paragraph should offer an interpretation of Thoreau's words, and the second paragraph should explain what this quote tells them about the man.

Teach

Reading Check

Answer: *He wanted to live in harmony with nature, with as much freedom as possible. He felt government could threaten people's freedom.*

Literary Element | 3

Style **Ask:** How would you describe the style of this passage from Thoreau's journal? *(Informal, passionate)*

Cathedral Forest, Albert Bierstadt. Private collection. ⭐

Thoreau's Journals

Many of Thoreau's writings, including *Walden*, are based on his journal entries. Thoreau kept a journal from the time he was twenty and reshaped and revised it throughout his life. When he died at forty-four, the journal ran to 7,000 manuscript pages containing nearly two million words.

Thoreau's journal provides insights into the extraordinary richness of his mind. In one entry, he observed, "My Journal is that of me which would else spill over and run to waste, gleanings from the field which in action I reap."

---

from *The Journal*
by Henry David Thoreau

March 5. [1858] . . . We would fain know something more about these animals and stones and trees around us. We are ready to skin the animals alive to come at them. Our scientific names contain a very partial information only. It does not occur to me that there are other names for most of these objects, given by a people who stood between me and them, who had better senses than our race. . . . No science does more than arrange what knowledge we have of any class of objects. But, generally speaking, how much more conversant was the Indian with any wild animal or plant than we are, and in his language is implied all that intimacy, as much as ours is expressed in our language. How many words in his language about moose, or birch bark, and the like! The Indian stood nearer to wild nature than we. The wildest and noblest quadrupeds, even the largest fresh-water fishes, some of the wildest and noblest birds and fairest flowers have actually receded as we advanced, and we have but the most distant knowledge of them. A rumor has come down to us that the skin of a lion was seen and his roar heard here by an early settler. But there was a race here that slept on his skin. It was a new light when my guide gave me Indian names for things for which I had only scientific ones before. In proportion as I understood the language, I saw them from a new point of view. **3**

Reading Check

Interpreting How did Thoreau's individualism affect his attitude toward nature and politics?

INTRODUCTION **183**

View the Art ⭐

Albert Bierstadt (1830–1902) traveled west with a government expedition and began to paint the dramatic landscapes of the American wilderness for which he is best known.

Ask: What sense of the human presence in nature is expressed by Bierstadt's painting? *(Human beings seem dwarfed by the magnificence of nature.)*

English Learners

DIFFERENTIATED INSTRUCTION

Beginning Point out the quotation in the box on the previous page, and ask students to write a similar statement about themselves. Tell them to begin with the words "I would rather." When students have written their sentences, have them read their statements orally to the class.

Intermediate Preteach the words *fain, conversant,* and *quadrupeds* from Thoreau's journal excerpt. *Fain* means "gladly or willingly." *Conversant* means "familiar." Urge students to try to determine the meaning of *quadruped* by studying the parts of the word. If necessary, have a student look up the word's meaning in a dictionary and read it aloud. Then read

the journal entry aloud and have different students look up unfamiliar words. Discuss their meanings as a class.

Reading Strategy   1

Connect As students read "The Power of Darkness," discuss how political, religious, and social ideals of the time period influenced writers. **Ask:** Which category of evils mentioned here—the known or the unknown—seems more fearful to you?

Reading Strategy   2

Question Urge students to ask questions as they read. As an example, point to this quotation from Poe and tell students that questions to clarify meaning might include these:

- Which kinds of terrors did Poe link to Germany?
- What does "terror of the soul" mean?

Discuss with students the answers to these and other questions about Poe's quotation on this page and the excerpt on the following page.

Writer's Technique ☆

Hawthorne's Notebooks

Throughout his career, Hawthorne recorded ideas for stories in notebooks—for example,

- "A physician for the cure of moral diseases."
- "A person who has all the qualities of a friend, except that he invariably fails you at the pinch."

O ur experience of life and the world has a dark side. We fear the evils we know—poverty, violence, disease, madness, death—and are troubled by nameless terrors that might lurk in the shadows beyond our knowledge. Not all the important American writers of Emerson's time shared his optimism. Nathaniel Hawthorne (see pages 278–292) admired Emerson but thought him unrealistic. To Herman Melville (see pages 294–305), Emerson's optimism was "nonsense" that ignored the "disagreeable facts" of life.

Hawthorne and Melville ☆

Almost all of Hawthorne's fiction is based on stories of the past, particularly the history and legends of his Puritan ancestors in New England. In Puritan New England, he found a strange, stark world that provided a richly textured background for the explorations of the nature of good and evil in his fiction. Hawthorne's friend Melville first gained a literary reputation for romantic tales of adventure in the South Seas. In succeeding books, he used his sea stories to explore the mystery of the evil that he saw in both human life and the forces of nature. In Melville's masterpiece, *Moby-Dick*, Ahab, the crazed captain of a whaling ship, sees evil personified in a huge white whale.

Gothic Horror

The dark side of European Romanticism can be seen in the tradition of Gothic literature. A classic example from nineteenth-century England is Mary Shelley's *Frankenstein*, a novel about a monster that destroys its creator. The American Romantics also recognized the power of darkness. Gothic horror relies chiefly on atmosphere, or mood, to achieve its effects. Writers create an atmosphere of horror through plot, characters, and settings that most people find chilling. Plots often focus on mysterious happenings, tragic events, and hideous

outcomes. Characters are often mad, half-mad, or frightened to death. They may exhibit strange behavior and physical traits. Settings are dark and often contain decayed dwellings with shadowy passageways, haunting sounds, and damp rooms.

Poe and the Terror of the Soul

A European tradition of Gothic literature existed long before Edgar Allan Poe (see pages 254–275), but he was the first American master of this type of horror. In his poems and stories, Poe often bettered earlier Gothic writers in achieving spine-tingling effects. Most of his stories and poems deal with loss and sorrow, ruin and revenge, disease and death. Poe's literary works reflected his own troubles and fears, but many readers responded favorably to his subject matter and to the mood of his works, thus confronting their own fears. Emerson and the Transcendentalists believed that humans are inherently good. By contrast, Poe seems to have had an instinctive feel for the dark impulses of human nature. Poe observed, "The terror of which I write is not of Germany [the setting of much Gothic fiction], but of the soul." He expressed this spiritual terror in haunting literary works.

Poe's Short Stories

Poe was a master of the short story. In addition to writing many Gothic tales of terror, he invented a new type of short fiction, the detective story. His first detective story, "The Murders in the Rue Morgue," combines Gothic horror with solid reasoning by Poe's fictional detective, Dupin.

Poe's stories illustrate his idea that any artistic composition should have a single, unique effect. This effect is evident in the gloomy, ominous beginning of his short story "The Fall of the House of Usher," guaranteed to make the reader long for sunshine or the comfort of his or her own room.

Grammar Practice

Commas in Appositives Have students notice the use of commas to set off explanatory information:

- "In Melville's masterpiece, *Moby-Dick*, Ahab, the crazed captain of a whaling ship, sees all evil embodied in a huge white whale."

Ask students to use commas to set off the appositives in these sentences:

1. One important writer of Emerson's time Nathaniel Hawthorne did not share his optimism.
2. Hawthorne wrote about the early colonists in New England the region where he lived.

Abbey in an Oak Forest, 1810. Caspar David Friedrich. Oil on canvas. Nationalgalerie, Staatliche Museen zu Berlin, Berlin.

from *The Fall of the House of Usher* by Edgar Allan Poe

During the whole of a dull, dark, and soundless day in the autumn of the year, when the clouds hung oppressively low in the heavens, I had been passing alone, on horseback, through a singularly dreary tract of country; and at length found myself, as the shades of the evening drew on, within view of the melancholy House of Usher. I know not how it was—but, with the first glimpse of the building, a sense of insufferable gloom pervaded my spirit. I say insufferable; for the feeling was unrelieved by any of that half-pleasurable, because poetic, sentiment, with which the mind usually receives even the sternest natural images of the desolate or terrible. I looked upon the scene before me—upon the mere house, and the simple landscape features of the domain—upon the bleak walls—upon the vacant eye-like windows—upon a few rank sedges—and upon a few white trunks of decayed trees—with an utter depression of soul . . . **3**

Reading Check

Comparing and Contrasting In what sense were Poe and Emerson both Romantics (see pages 180–181)? How did their Romanticism differ?

Advanced Learners

DIFFERENTIATED INSTRUCTION

Tone Say: A writer's tone is his or her attitude toward the subject and the audience. Writers establish tone through the words they choose, the point of view they use, and the level of formality they employ. The tone of a piece of literature can be angry, hesitant, friendly, regretful, fearful, or many other attitudes. What do you think is Poe's tone in the excerpt on this page? *(Fearful or hesitant)*

To give students practice establishing tone in their writing, ask them to write a few paragraphs describing a place. Tell students to choose vivid and fresh words that convey whatever tone they choose. Have students read their paragraphs aloud and ask the rest of the class to identify the tone of the work.

Teach

Reading Check

Answer: *Both Emerson and Poe valued imagination and feeling. Both were individualists, but Poe wrote of the dark side of Romanticism. He was neither an optimist nor a reformer.*

Literary Element | 3

Setting Poe often used details of time and place to create a gloomy or threatening mood in his stories. **Say:** Find specific details in this passage that Poe uses to develop the setting of his story. *(These details include "dull, dark, and soundless day," "clouds hung oppressively low," "dreary tract of country," "bleak walls," "rank sedges," and "decayed trees.")* **Ask:** What mood and tone does Poe create through the use of these details of setting? *(The mood is melancholy or sad, and the tone is frightened.)*

View the Art ★

Caspar David Friedrich (1774–1840) was a painter of the Romantic movement in Germany. Ruins, cemeteries, and solitary figures are the subjects of many of his works.

Ask: What words describe the mood of this painting? *(Students might use words such as somber, ominous, eerie, weird, gloomy.)*

Assess/Close

Legacy of the Period

Refer students to Abraham Lincoln's words, "the last, best hope of earth." **Ask:** Does the United States still have a responsibility to serve as a model community for the rest of the world?

Cultural and Literary Links

Suggest that as students read the unit, they look for ways in which its authors have influenced today's writers.

Connect to Today

1. **Speaking/Listening** Each member of the group might concentrate on one of the four categories suggested.

2. **Visual Literacy** As an alternative, students can make a "color meter" showing degrees of brightness and darkness in Romanticism, with a movable arrow.

 3. **Writing** Students' comparisons should provide concrete examples from both time periods to support their point of view.

FOLDABLES
Study Organizer

4. Have students make and label the Three-Pocket Foldable. Then have them write notes about the Big Ideas on note cards to insert in the pockets of their Foldables.

WRAP-UP

Legacy of the Period

Some characteristics of American Romanticism—optimism, individualism, and the impulse to reform—had shaped American experience from the time of the first explorers and settlers. The colonists saw their experiment as a model for the rest of the world to imitate. This sense of the United States as a nation with a reforming mission—what Abraham Lincoln described as "the last, best hope of earth"—continues today.

The Romantic view of human kinship with nature has had a limited influence on American culture. Americans have typically viewed the land as something to be "tamed." However, the modern environmental movement is an important legacy of Romanticism, together with the nature writing of authors such as Gary Snyder, N. Scott Momaday, John McPhee, and Annie Dillard.

Cultural and Literary Links

 The essays of Ralph Waldo Emerson (1801–1882) had a great influence on Walt Whitman (1819–1892), who later said, "I was simmering, simmering, simmering. Emerson brought me to a boil."

The writings of Henry David Thoreau (1817–1862) are among the basic texts of the American environmental movement. John Muir, founder of the Sierra Club (1892), shared the basic outlook that Thoreau expressed: "In wildness lies the preservation of the world."

As a pioneer of detective, horror, and science fiction writing, Edgar Allan Poe (1809–1849) has had a huge impact on popular culture worldwide.

LOG ON ▶ **Literature** Online

Unit Resources For additional skills practice, go to glencoe.com and enter QuickPass code GLA9800u2.

Connect to Today ▶▶

Choose one of the following activities to explore and develop as you read this unit.

1. **Speaking/Listening** Working with several other students, create a brief presentation for your class about how one of this period's big ideas affects American culture today. You can use examples from literature, fine art, music, movies, or other kinds of expression.

2. **Build Visual Literacy** Create an illustrated diagram showing the bright and dark sides of Romanticism. For example, you might present your diagram in the form of a color spectrum on which you position cultural ideas and values, works of art, and writers associated with Romanticism's two aspects.

3. **Writing** Taking into account the political, social, economic, and cultural characteristics of this period, do you think the United States was a better place to live in then or now? Write a brief essay exploring this question.

4. **Take Notes** Use this graphic organizer to keep track of the three big ideas in this unit. File note cards and other information in each pocket.

FOLDABLES
Study Organizer

THREE-POCKET BOOK

Big Idea 1   Big Idea 2   Big Idea 3

Reading Practice

Summarize Have students write a summary of the information about Romanticism. Provide these tips:

- Identify the main ideas and supporting details.
- Relate the main ideas and the essential details in a logical sequence.
- Use your own words.

PART 1

Individualism and Nature

Kindred Spirits, 1849. Asher Durand. Oil on canvas. The New York Public Library, NY.

 Asher Durand's painting captures an imagined moment in the friendship of American painter Thomas Cole and American poet William Cullen Bryant. What does Durand suggest about the relationship between, nature, art, and literature?

"We see the world piece by piece, as the sun, the moon, the animal, the tree; but the whole, of which these are the shining parts, is the soul." **1**

—Emerson, "The Over-Soul"

187

Analyze and Extend

Reading Strategy | 1

Evaluate Direct students to read the quotation by Emerson. Explain that the Over-Soul was a Transcendentalist concept referring to a universal mind that unified the entire cosmos. Emerson described the Over-Soul as "the universal beauty to which every part and particle is equally related."

Say: Explain Emerson's quotation in your own words. *(Emerson says that most people see the world in its small parts, yet all of these parts fit together in unity to create the whole, which is what he calls the Over-Soul.)*

For additional support for English Learners, see Unit 2 Teaching Resources Book, p. 19.

View the Art ★

Answer: *The natural world with all of its beauty is an appropriate subject for both art and literature.*

English Learners

DIFFERENTIATED INSTRUCTION

Beginning Read the quotation from "The Over-Soul" aloud to students. Have each student take a turn reading the quotation aloud. **Ask:** What do you think Emerson means by "the world"? *(He is referring to both the physical and spiritual parts of the universe.)*

Intermediate Some students may be unfamiliar with the early American history. Explain that in the 1800s much of the country was still unexplored. **Ask:** Based on the painting, how do you think America in the 1800s was different? *(Less populated, connected to nature)*

Before You Read

Focus

Bellringer Options

Daily Language Practice Transparency 20

Tell students that peace and solitude were important ideas to Emerson. He believed that peace and solitude were best found in nature.

Ask: Do you think that people can find solitude in the city as well as in nature? As they read, have students consider how their answers compare with Emerson's views of how people find peace and solitude.

Before You Read

from *Nature*, from *Self-Reliance*

Meet **Ralph Waldo Emerson**
(1803–1882)

Ralph Waldo Emerson was the central figure of American Romanticism. His ideas about the individual, claims about the divine, and attacks on society were revolutionary.

Emerson's father was a Unitarian minister and his mother a devout Anglican. When Emerson was only eight years old, his father died, and Mrs. Emerson was forced to open a boarding-house. At the age of 14, Emerson entered Harvard College. After graduation, he studied at Harvard Divinity School. By 1829, Emerson had been ordained a Unitarian minister and was preaching in Boston's Second Church.

In 1831 Ellen Tucker, Emerson's wife, died suddenly. Emerson had already been questioning his religious convictions, and after Ellen's death, he experienced intense grief that further eroded his faith. Eventually, Emerson left the church to embark on a career as a writer.

A Controversial Career In 1833 Emerson settled in Concord, Massachusetts, and began writing *Nature*. This slim book was to become one of Emerson's most influential works. Two years later, Emerson married Lydia Jackson, whom he called "Lidian." Emerson and Lydia had four children.

During the late 1830s, Emerson gained fame for his lectures—notably "The American Scholar" and "The Divinity School Address." These speeches, delivered at Harvard, rejected organized religion and undue reverence for the past. Harvard's conservative administration was outraged. As a result, he was not invited to speak at the college for the next 30 years.

While Emerson's ideas enraged some, they excited many others and helped create the transcendentalist movement, of which Emerson was the spokesperson. Optimism, self-reliance, intuition, and idealism formed the core of transcendentalist thought. Idealism is a philosophy that maintains the belief that reality is created by the mind.

Challenges to Optimism Emerson's own optimism was challenged when his son Waldo died of scarlet fever in 1842. Two years later, Emerson's essay "The Tragic" appeared in *The Dial*, a transcendentalist magazine he had co-founded. In this essay, Emerson claimed that the arts and the intellect can "ravish us into a region whereinto these passionate clouds of sorrow cannot rise."

After 1870, his memory began to fail and the quality of his essays diminished. He stayed in Concord and wrote little in his last years; he died of pneumonia at the age of 79.

Emerson influenced writers as diverse as essayist Henry David Thoreau (page 212), novelist Louisa May Alcott, and poets Robert Frost (page 714), Wallace Stevens (page 699), and Hart Crane. Emerson was a radical individualist, and his impact on American thought can still be felt today. As modern critic Harold Bloom wrote, ". . . no single sage, not Dr. Johnson nor Coleridge, is as inescapable as Emerson goes on being for American poets and storytellers."

 Literature Online

Author Search For more about Ralph Waldo Emerson, go to glencoe.com and enter QuickPass code GLA9800u2.

Selection Skills

Literary Elements
- Theme (SE pp. 189, 192, 193)

from **Nature**

Listening/Speaking/Viewing Skills
- Analyze Art (SE p. 190)

Reading Skills
- Recognize Author's Purpose (SE pp. 189, 191, 193)
- Rereading (TE p. 192)

Vocabulary Skills
- Word Usage (SE p. 193)
- Synonyms (TE p. 189)

Writing Skills/Grammar
- Journal Entry (SE p. 193)
- Describe a Scene (TE p. 190)

Literature and Reading Preview

Connect to the Essay

How do you interact with nature in your daily life? How does your mood affect the way you see the world? Discuss these questions with a partner.

Build Background

The Romantics tended to emphasize two aspects of nature—beauty and power. The darker Romantics, such as the Melville of *Moby-Dick,* stressed nature's destructive power. Although Emerson was sensitive to the power of the untamed American wilderness, he chose to dwell on the beauty of nature.

Set Purposes for Reading

Big Idea Kinship with Nature

As you read this selection from *Nature,* ask yourself, How does Emerson link nature to optimism and individualism?

Literary Element Theme

Theme is the central message of a work of literature that readers can apply to life. As you read, ask yourself, What is the central theme of Emerson's essay?

Reading Strategy Recognize Author's Purpose

The **author's purpose** is the author's intent in writing a piece of literature. Authors typically write to persuade, to inform, to explain, to entertain, or to describe. While reading, ask yourself, What is Emerson's purpose in writing this essay?

··

Tip: Ask Questions It might be useful as you read to ask yourself questions such as the following:

- What is the thesis or main idea statement?
- How do the details support the thesis statement?
- What are Emerson's special concerns? Does he show any biases or prejudices? If so, what are they?

Learning Objectives

For pages 188–197

In studying these texts, you will focus on the following objectives:

Literary Study: Analyzing theme.

Reading: Recognizing author's purpose.

Writing: Writing a journal entry.

Vocabulary

perpetual (pər pech´ ōō əl) *adj.* lasting forever; eternal; p. 191 *The leaders had hoped to create a perpetual union of states.*

integrate (in´ tə grāt´) *v.* to bring all parts together into a whole; p. 191 *Can we integrate some new members into the community?*

perennial (pə ren´ ē əl) *adj.* continuing year after year; enduring; p. 192 *Art is a perennial joy.*

blithe (blīth) *adj.* lighthearted and carefree; p. 192 *He was blithe in the company of his grandchildren.*

occult (ə kult´) *adj.* beyond human understanding; mysterious; p. 192 *The old doctor was interested in strange, occult research.*

Before You Read

Focus

Summary

Emerson makes an argument for solitude in communion with nature as a way to achieve inner peace. According to Emerson, nature will never fail to nourish and strengthen us if we contemplate it from the perspective of a child whose inner and physical senses are attuned to the natural world.

 For summaries in languages other than English, see Unit 2 Teaching Resources Book, pp. 20–25.

Vocabulary

Use Synonyms Synonyms have similar meanings and are the same part of speech. Ask students to write sentences using each adjective in the vocabulary list and one of its synonyms to describe a person, place, thing, or feeling.

(APPROACHING) For students having difficulty explain that because synonyms have the same meaning, they are often used to define each other. For example, the word *eternal* is a synonym of *perpetual* and it is also used in the definition.

 For additional vocabulary practice, see Unit 2 Teaching Resources Book, p. 28.

 For additional context, see Glencoe Interactive Vocabulary CD-ROM.

English Learners

DIFFERENTIATED INSTRUCTION

Advanced Read "Connect to the Essay" aloud. **Ask:** What do you predict the theme of this selection will be? *(Students might say the theme is that each person has a unique relationship with nature.)*

Approaching Level

DIFFERENTIATED INSTRUCTION

Emerging Remind students that the theme is a literary work's central message, which readers may be able to apply to their lives. **Ask:** Based on the title, what do you think this selection will be about? *(Emerson will share his thoughts about nature.)*

Teach

View the Art ★

Answer: *Yes; Cole's depiction of himself painting a landscape suggests that he believed in the importance of observing nature closely, as did Emerson.*

Thomas Cole (1801–1848) was one of the leading American landscape painters of the nineteenth century. His works emphasize nature's untamed beauty.

💿 For an audio recording of this selection, use Listening Library Audio CD-ROM.

Readability Scores

Dale-Chall: 8.9
DRP: 61
Lexile: 960

View from Mount Holyoke, Northampton, Massachusetts, after a Thunderstorm—The Oxbow, 1836.
Thomas Cole. Oil on canvas, 51½ x 76 in. Metropolitan Museum of Art, NY.

View the Art Hidden in the shadows of this painting is an image of the painter himself, Thomas Cole, painting this very scene. Based on that information and the visual elements of this painting, do you think Cole would have agreed with Emerson's views on nature? Explain.

Writing Practice

SPIRAL REVIEW **Describe a Scene** Read aloud several descriptive scenes taken from Emerson's *Nature.* Discuss how Emerson brings natural images to life through the use of imagery and sensory details. Also point out that Emerson expresses his thoughts and feelings about nature within his essay. Have students write a descriptive paragraph of a nature scene they have recently experienced. Students should give concrete details that activate the senses by describing the sights, sounds, and smells of the scene. They should also include their thoughts and feelings at the time they observed the scene.

Ralph Waldo Emerson

To go into solitude, a man needs to retire as much from his chamber as from society. I am not solitary whilst I read and write, though nobody is with me. But if a man would be alone, let him look at the stars. The rays that come from those heavenly worlds will separate between him and what he touches. One might think the atmosphere was made transparent with this design, to give man, in the heavenly bodies, the **perpetual** presence of the sublime. Seen in the streets of cities, how great they are! If the stars should appear one night in a thousand years, how would men believe and adore; and preserve for many generations the remembrance of the city of God which had been shown! But every night come out these envoys[1] of beauty, and light the universe with their admonishing[2] smile.

The stars awaken a certain reverence, because though always present, they are inaccessible; but all natural objects make a kindred impression, when the mind is open to their influence. Nature never wears a mean[3] appearance. Neither does the wisest man extort her secret, and lose his curiosity by finding out all her perfection. Nature never became a toy to a wise spirit. The flowers, the

animals, the mountains, reflected the wisdom of his best hour, as much as they had delighted the simplicity of his childhood.

When we speak of nature in this manner, we have a distinct but most poetical sense in the mind. We mean the integrity of impression made by manifold[4] natural objects. It is this which distinguishes the stick of timber of the wood-cutter from the tree of the poet. The charming landscape which I saw this morning is indubitably[5] made up of some twenty or thirty farms. Miller owns this field, Locke that, and Manning the woodland beyond. But none of them owns the landscape. There is a property in the horizon which no man has but he whose eye can **integrate** all the parts, that is, the poet. This is the best part of these men's farms, yet to this their warranty-deeds[6] give no title.

To speak truly, few adult persons can see nature. Most persons do not see the sun. At least they have a very superficial seeing. The sun illuminates only the eye of the man, but shines into the eye and the heart of the child. The lover of nature is he whose inward and

---

1. *Envoys* are those sent as representatives of another.
2. *Admonishing* means "gently warning" or "scolding."
3. Here, *mean* means "poor," "inferior," or "shabby."

 Kinship with Nature *How does Emerson's statement relate nature to his belief in individualism?*

Vocabulary

perpetual (pər pech´ ōō əl) *adj.* lasting forever; eternal

---

4. *Manifold* means "many kinds or varieties."
5. *Indubitably* means "without a doubt" or "certainly."
6. *Warranty-deeds* are legal documents that state ownership of property.

Recognize Author's Purpose *What does this statement suggest to you about Emerson's purpose?*

Vocabulary

integrate (in´ tə grāt´) *v.* to bring all parts together into a whole

RALPH WALDO EMERSON **191**

Teach

Literary Element 1

Theme Answer: *Emerson uses the woods as a metaphor for nature itself. By returning people to reason and faith, nature promotes optimism.*

ENGLISH LEARNERS Remind students that a metaphor directly compares two things. Write the following sentence on the board, "Alex was a tiger on the soccer field." Explain to students that Alex is being compared to a tiger because of his aggressive play. Ask students to write their own simple metaphors and read them to the class.

Literary Element 2

Theme Answer: *Earlier, Emerson says that a person in touch with nature has the inward and outward senses adjusted to each other; thus, the inward mood will affect how nature is perceived by the outward senses.*

 To check students' understanding of the selection, see Unit 2 Teaching Resources Book, p. 31.

Progress Check

Can students analyze the theme of the essay?

If No → See Unit 2 Teaching Resources Book, p. 26.

outward senses are still truly adjusted to each other; who has retained the spirit of infancy even into the era of manhood. His intercourse with heaven and earth becomes part of his daily food. In the presence of nature a wild delight runs through the man, in spite of real sorrows. Nature says,—he is my creature, and maugre[7] all his impertinent[8] griefs, he shall be glad with me. Not the sun or the summer alone, but every hour and season yields its tribute of delight; for every hour and change corresponds to and authorizes a different state of the mind, from breathless noon to grimmest midnight. Nature is a setting that fits equally well a comic or a mourning piece. In good health, the air is a cordial[9] of incredible virtue. Crossing a bare common,[10] in snow puddles, at twilight, under a clouded sky, without having in my thoughts any occurrence of special good fortune, I have enjoyed a perfect exhilaration. I am glad to the brink of fear. In the woods, too, a man casts off his years, as the snake his slough, and at what period soever of life is always a child. In the woods is perpetual youth. Within these plantations of God, a decorum and sanctity reign, a **perennial** festival is dressed, and the guest sees not how he should tire of them in a thousand years. In the woods, we return to reason and faith. There I feel that nothing can befall me in life,—no disgrace, no calamity (leaving me my eyes), which nature cannot repair. Standing on the bare ground,— my head bathed by the **blithe** air and uplifted into infinite space,—all mean egotism van-

ishes. I become a transparent eyeball; I am nothing; I see all; the currents of the Universal Being circulate through me; I am part or parcel of God. The name of the nearest friend sounds then foreign and accidental: to be brothers, to be acquaintances, master or servant, is then a trifle and a disturbance. I am the lover of uncontained and immortal beauty. In the wilderness, I find something more dear and connate[11] than in streets or villages. In the tranquil landscape, and especially in the distant line of the horizon, man beholds somewhat as beautiful as his own nature.

The greatest delight which the fields and woods minister is the suggestion of an **occult** relation between man and the vegetable. I am not alone and unacknowledged. They nod to me, and I to them. The waving of the boughs in the storm is new to me and old. It takes me by surprise, and yet is not unknown. Its effect is like that of a higher thought or a better emotion coming over me, when I deemed I was thinking justly or doing right.

Yet it is certain that the power to produce this delight does not reside in nature, but in man, or in a harmony of both. It is necessary to use these pleasures with great temperance. For nature is not always tricked[12] in holiday attire, but the same scene which yesterday breathed perfume and glittered as for the frolic of the nymphs is overspread with melancholy today. Nature always wears the colors of the spirit. To a man laboring under calamity, the heat of his own fire hath sadness in it. Then there is a kind of contempt of the landscape felt by him who has just lost by death a dear friend. The sky is less grand as it shuts down over less worth in the population. ✍

---

7. *Maugre* means "in spite of."
8. *Impertinent* means "irrelevant."
9. A *cordial* is a stimulant, such as a drink or medicine.
10. A *common* is community property, such as a park, owned or used by the public.

1 **Theme** *What does this statement tell you about Emerson's theme?*

Vocabulary

perennial (pə ren´ ē əl) *adj.* continuing year after year; enduring
blithe (blīth) *adj.* lighthearted and carefree

192 UNIT 2   AMERICAN ROMANTICISM

---

11. *Connate* means "being in harmony or sympathy."
12. Here, *tricked* means "dressed."

Theme *Why does Emerson hold this belief?* **2**

Vocabulary

occult (ə kult´) *adj.* beyond human understanding; mysterious

Reading Practice

Rereading Remind students that rereading Emerson's selection will help them identify the theme and supporting evidence, as well as the author's purpose. Have the students write down the following note headings:

- Theme and supporting evidence
- Author's purpose
- Unfamiliar words

Have students use these headings to direct their note taking as they reread the selection.

After You Read

Respond and Think Critically

Respond and Interpret

1. (a)Which of Emerson's ideas do you think are true in light of your own experience? (b)With which ideas do you disagree?

2. (a)What does Emerson say would happen if the stars appeared only one night in a thousand years? (b)What does his comment suggest about human nature?

3. (a)In Emerson's view, how do adults and children differ in the way they view nature? (b)What does Emerson suggest accounts for this difference?

4. (a)According to Emerson, what effect does the experience of nature have on him? (b)What conclusion does he draw from that effect?

Analyze and Evaluate

5. (a)In this essay, how does Emerson personify, or give human traits to, nature? (b)Does Emerson's personification of nature strengthen or weaken his arguments? Explain.

6. How is Emerson's idealism shown in this essay?

Connect

7. **Big Idea** **Kinship with Nature** How do your feelings about nature compare with those of Emerson?

8. **Connect to the Author** Emerson's first profession was that of a preacher. What impact, if any, do you think Emerson's religious background might have had on his writing? Explain.

Literary Element Theme

While themes can be stated, they are more often implied through events, dialogue, or description.

1. What is the central theme in *Nature*? Is this theme stated or implied? Explain.

2. How is the theme of this essay consistent with Emerson's transcendentalism?

Reading Strategy Recognize Author's Purpose

Sometimes an author will have more than one purpose for writing. However, authors generally consider one purpose more important than the others.

1. What do you think Emerson's main purpose was for writing *Nature*?

2. In support of your opinion, list three details from the essay.

 Literature Online

Selection Resources For Selection Quizzes, eFlashcards, and Reading-Writing Connection activities, go to glencoe.com and enter QuickPass code GLA9800u2.

Vocabulary Practice

Practice with Word Usage Respond to these statements to help you explore the meanings of vocabulary words from this selection.

1. Name something that is **perpetual.**

2. Describe a time when you helped **integrate** various members into a group.

3. Give an example of a **perennial** problem.

4. Describe a time when you felt **blithe.**

5. Name a creature that appears **occult** in its behavior.

 Writing

Write a Journal Entry Emerson asserts that few people can appreciate, or truly "see," the glory of nature. Write a journal entry in which you describe an encounter with the outdoors.

After You Read

Assess

1. Answers will vary.

2. (a) People might think that the sublime is transient and rare. (b) We tend to take natural beauty for granted.

3. (a) Adults see with the eye; children see with both the eye and the heart. (b) Children's senses work in harmony.

4. (a) All of his egotism vanishes. (b) Nature can make one "part or parcel with God."

5. (a) The boughs of trees "nod" to him, and "nature is not always tricked in holiday attire." (b) Students should support their opinions.

6. Emerson sees immersion in nature as the way to true happiness. He writes that "In the woods . . . I feel that nothing can befall me in life . . . which nature cannot repair."

7. Students may express positive feelings about nature, but they may not equate nature with reason or faith.

8. Students may say that his religious background impacted his writings, particularly his connections between reason and faith.

For additional assessment, see Assessment Resources, pp. 97–98.

Literary Element

1. Nature allows people to become "part or parcel of God"; stated

2. Advocates kinship with nature, optimism, and individualism

Writing

Be sure students describe a specific positive or negative encounter.

Reading Strategy

1. To persuade the reader of nature's beauty and power.

2. Possible answers: The "lover of nature is he whose inward and outward senses are truly adjusted to each other"; the power that produces this delight "does not reside in nature, but in man, or in a harmony of both."

Vocabulary

1. Earth's turning is *perpetual.*

2. I helped *integrate* the new information into the financial report.

3. Global warming is a *perennial* problem.

4. I felt *blithe* at the homecoming dance.

5. Witches and vampires are often described as *occult.*

Literary Element Figurative Language

Figurative language is descriptive language used to convey ideas or emotions. Figurative expressions reach beyond the literal level. As you read, ask yourself, How does Emerson use figurative language to help his readers understand abstract ideas?

Reading Strategy Draw Conclusions

Drawing a conclusion is using details from the text to arrive at a general statement. As you read "Self-Reliance," use the details Emerson presents as the basis for drawing a conclusion about his beliefs.

from Self-Reliance

Ralph Waldo Emerson

I read the other day some verses written by an eminent[1] painter which were original and not conventional. Always the soul hears an **admonition** in such lines, let the subject be what it may. The sentiment they instill is of more value than any thought they may contain. To believe your own thought, to believe that what is true for you in your private heart, is true for all men,—that is genius. Speak your **latent** conviction and it shall be the universal sense; for always the inmost becomes the outmost,—and our first thought is rendered back to us by the trumpets of the Last Judgment. Familiar as the voice of the mind is to each, the highest merit we ascribe to Moses, Plato, and Milton is that they set at naught books and traditions, and spoke not what men, but what they thought. A man should learn to detect and watch that gleam of light which flashes across his mind from within, more than the lustre of the firmament of bards[2] and sages. Yet he dismisses without notice his thought, because it is his. In every work of genius we recognize our own rejected thoughts: they come back to us with a certain alienated majesty. Great works of art have no more affecting lesson for us than this. They teach us to abide by our spontaneous impression with good humored inflexibility then most when the whole cry of voices is on the other side. Else, tomorrow a stranger will say with masterly good sense precisely what we have thought and felt all the time, and we shall be forced to take with shame our own opinion from another.

There is a time in every man's education when he arrives at the conviction that envy is ignorance; that imitation is suicide; that he must take himself for better, for worse, as his portion; that though the wide universe is full of good, no kernel of nourishing corn can come to him but through his toil bestowed on that plot of ground

---

1. *Eminent* means "distinguished" or "prominent."

Vocabulary

admonition (ad´ mə nish´ ən) *n.* a warning
latent (lā´ tənt) *adj.* present but not evident; hidden

---

2. *Bards* are poets.

Draw Conclusions *What does Emerson mean by this?*

194 UNIT 2 AMERICAN ROMATICISM

---

which is given to him to till. The power which resides in him is new in nature, and none but he knows what that is which he can do, nor does he know until he has tried. Not for nothing one face, one character, one fact makes much impression on him, and another none. It is not without preëstablished harmony, this sculpture in the memory. The eye was placed where one ray should fall, that it might testify of that particular ray. Bravely let him speak the utmost syllable of his confession. We but half express ourselves, and are ashamed of that divine idea which each of us represents. It may be safely trusted as proportionate and of good issues, so it be faithfully imparted, but God will not have his work made **manifest** by cowards. It needs a divine man to exhibit any thing divine. A man is relieved and gay when he has put his heart into his work and done his best; but what he has said or done otherwise, shall give him no peace. It is a deliverance which does not deliver. In the attempt his genius deserts him; no muse[3] befriends; no invention, no hope.

Trust thyself: every heart vibrates to that iron string. Accept the place the divine Providence[4] has found for you; the society of your contemporaries, the connection of events. Great men have always done so and confided themselves childlike to the genius[5] of their age, betraying their perception that the Eternal was stirring at their heart, working through their hands, predominating[6] in all their being. And

we are now men, and must accept in the highest mind the same transcendent[7] destiny; and not pinched in a corner, not cowards fleeing before a revolution, but redeemers and **bene-factors,** pious aspirants[8] to be noble clay plastic under the Almighty effort, let us advance and advance on Chaos and the Dark. . . .

Society everywhere is in conspiracy against the manhood of every one of its members. Society is a joint-stock company in which the members agree for the better securing of his bread to each shareholder, to surrender the liberty and culture of the eater. The virtue in most request is conformity. Self-reliance is its aversion. It loves not realities and creators, but names and customs.

Whoso would be a man must be a nonconformist. He who would gather immortal palms[9] must not be hindered by the name of goodness, but must explore if it be goodness. Nothing is at last sacred but the **integrity** of your own mind. . . .

What I must do, is all that concerns me, not what the people think. This rule, equally arduous[10] in actual and in intellectual life, may serve for the whole distinction between greatness and meanness.[11] It is the harder, because you will always find those who think they know what is your duty better than you know it. It is easy in the world to live after the world's opinion; it is easy in solitude to live after our own; but the great man is he who in the midst of the crowd keeps with perfect sweetness the independence of solitude.

3. In Greek mythology, the Muses were goddesses who presided over the arts and sciences.
4. The *divine Providence* is God.
5. Here, *genius* means "the predominant spirit."
6. *Predominating* means "having controlling influence."

> **Figurative Language** *What comparison is Emerson making here?*

> **Draw Conclusions** *According to Emerson, what is the cause of our shame?*

Vocabulary

manifest (man´ ə fest´) *adj.* apparent to the eye or the mind; evident; obvious

7. *Transcendent* means "concerned with a spiritual reality beyond the limits of experience."
8. *Aspirants* are those who seek, or aspire to, advancement or honors.
9. *Palm* leaves are a traditional symbol of victory or success.
10. *Arduous* means "difficult."
11. Here, *meanness* means "the state of having little importance, worth, or consequence."

> **Optimism and Individualism** *What does Emerson think about relationships between individuals?*

Vocabulary

benefactor (ben´ ə fak´ tər) *n.* one who gives help
integrity (in teg´ rə tē) *n.* moral uprightness; honesty

RALPH WALDO EMERSON **195**

Approaching Level

DIFFERENTIATED INSTRUCTION

AAVE Read the final sentence in the selection. Note the phrase "It is easy." Approaching-level students who are users of African American vernacular English (AAVE) may forget to use *is* or *are* between a pronoun subject, such as *it*, and a noun or adjective, such as *easy*. Give students a few other examples: *She is my sister. They are friends.* Then provide students with a list of pronoun subjects (you,

he, she, it, we, they) and a list of adjectives or predicate nouns (funny, happy, my friend, and so on) and have them join one word from each list using either is or are, as appropriate.

Teach

Literary Element | 2

Figurative Language
Answer: *He is comparing the benefits of farming one's own land to the benefits of individualism.*

(APPROACHING) Figurative language is often used to compare an intangible concept to something tangible. Readers may relate to the real, physical thing, and thereby begin to understand the concept.
Ask: Why do you think Emerson compares individualism to farming? *(Many people farmed during Emerson's time, so they could relate to the rewards of hard work on the land.)*

Reading Strategy | 3

Draw Conclusions
Answer: *We are too modest and timid to trust and express our God-given original ideas.*

Big Idea | 4

Optimism and Individualism **Answer:**
Relationships have the potential to destroy individuality and self-reliance.

> To check students' understanding of the selection, see Unit 2 Teaching Resources Book, p. 44.

After You Read

Assess

1. (a) Answers will vary. (b) Answers should show an understanding of Emerson's idea of nonconformity.

2. (a) Believing your own thoughts (b) The individualist cares about what is true for him or her.

3. (a) With willingness, confidence, and determination to do his or her best (b) Intellectual and spiritual activity and the way to lead one's life

4. (a) A "joint-stock company" (b) Society penalizes those who don't conform.

5. (a) Transcendental thought and religion are intertwined. (b) These references add a sense of importance.

6. (a) Metaphor and hyperbole; he refers to society as a company and to individuals as "divine." (b) It is very effective.

7. (a) Students' opinions will vary. (b) Metaphor, hyperbole, connotative language, and appeals to emotion and reason

8. Encourage students to consider the cost of individualism and nonconformity to the collective sense of community.

9. Students may say that Emerson's life reflected his message: he quit preaching to become a writer and gave speeches that challenged conventional ideas.

Literary Element

1. He is using a metaphor.
2. Students might point to any number of examples. However, make sure that they demonstrate an understanding of how each example functions in context.

After You Read

Respond and Think Critically

Respond and Interpret

1. (a) What was your reaction to Emerson's discussion of nonconformity? (b) In your experience, how valuable a trait is the type of nonconformity that Emerson recommends?

2. (a) According to Emerson, what is genius? (b) How does his definition of genius relate to his belief in individualism?

3. (a) According to Emerson, in what way should a person approach his or her work? (b) What kind of "work" do you think he is describing?

4. (a) To what does Emerson compare society? (b) How does society affect what people value?

Analyze and Evaluate

5. Emerson uses many religious references throughout the essay. (a) Why do you think he does so? (b) How do they affect the essay's meaning and tone?

6. (a) What kinds of figurative language does Emerson use to describe both society and the individual? (b) How effective is his use of figurative language?

7. (a) What parts of Emerson's essay did you find most persuasive? (b) What techniques did he use to convince you of his arguments?

Connect

8. **Big Idea** Optimism and Individualism Do you think it is possible for people to live as individuals and nonconformists in modern society? Why or why not?

9. **Connect to the Author** Did Emerson's own life reflect his message in *Self-Reliance*? Support your answer using what you learned about Emerson's life as well as details from the text.

Literary Element Figurative Language

There are many different kinds of **figurative language.** Examples include imagery, personification, metaphor, metonymy, simile, and symbol. An author can use each of these devices to generate various moods, effects, or ideas. For example, when Emerson says that a person "should learn to detect and watch that gleam of light which flashes across the mind from within," he is using a metaphor that compares a sudden idea to a flash of lightning.

1. When Emerson writes, "Trust thyself: every heart vibrates to that iron string," what kind of figurative language is he using?

2. Find at least two other examples of figurative language in the excerpt from "Self-Reliance." Tell how each helps to explain an idea or make it more concrete.

Review: Tone

As you learned in a previous lesson, **tone** is the reflection of a writer's attitude toward his or her subject matter, as conveyed through word choice, punctuation, sentence structure, and figures of speech.

Partner Activity Pair up with a classmate and discuss the tone of "Self-Reliance." Working with your partner, create a two-column chart similar to the one below. Fill in the left-hand column with examples from the text that demonstrate a particular tone. In the right-hand column, label each example with an adjective that describes the tone.

Examples	Tone
"It is a deliverance which does not deliver."	Resolute

Progress Check

Can students analyze figurative language?

If No → See Unit 2 Teaching Resources Book, p. 39.

Review: Tone

Pairs of students should give accurate examples from the text, along with appropriate tones.

Reading Strategy — Draw Conclusions

ACT Skills Practice

From the statements in this essay, you can conclude Emerson believes that:

   I. people are untrustworthy.

  II. solitude and independence destroy the structure of society.

 III. God has a plan for people's lives.

A. I only	**C.** II and III only
B. III only	**D.** I and III only

Vocabulary Practice

Practice with Context Clues In the following sentences, identify context clues to the meaning of each boldfaced vocabulary word.

1. Mom gave me the **admonition** that if I did not work, I would not be able to go skiing.

2. One of Kyle's **latent**—or hidden—talents was his ability to country line dance.

3. To Adriana, the solution to the equation seemed quite clear—almost **manifest**.

4. My uncle, a very generous **benefactor**, is sending me to soccer camp in Brazil.

5. My friend's **integrity** is so solid that her parents never doubt her.

Academic Vocabulary

Evidence of the theme of Emerson's essay "Self-Reliance" can be found in its title.

Evidence is an academic word. To further explore the meaning of this word, answer the questions below.

1. What **evidence** does Emerson present in "Self-Reliance" to support his theme?

2. Emerson directly addresses his reader. What **evidence** does this provide about his belief in personal responsibility?

For more on academic vocabulary, see pages 53–54.

Speaking and Listening

Deliver a Persuasive Speech

Assignment Emerson argues that people should follow their own convictions—not imitate other people's beliefs and ideas. Practically speaking, what does that mean? Write and deliver a persuasive speech in which you argue for why—and how—people should practice self-reliance.

Prepare As you plan your speech, note how Emerson employs figurative language to convey his ideas and persuade his audience. Using figurative language can also help you support your argument. Appealing to your audience logically, ethically, and emotionally can also help set a tone for your speech and reinforce your message. As you write your speech, fill out a chart like the one below to help you develop logical and ethical appeals.

Emotional Appeal	Ethical Appeal
Do you want to take charge of your life?	According to Emerson, a great person is as independent in a crowd as when alone. This is an ideal we should all follow.

Deliver As you deliver your speech, pay attention to verbal and nonverbal techniques such as eye contact, body language, and tone of voice. Ask a friend to watch you rehearse and give feedback to make sure your voice, posture, and gestures match the tone of your speech.

Evaluate After delivering your speech, use the list on page 163 to write a short critique of your presentation. Note what you think you did well and what you could improve for next time.

 LOG ON ▶ **Literature** Online

Selection Resources For Selection Quizzes, eFlashcards, and Reading-Writing Connection activities, go to glencoe.com and enter QuickPass code GLA9800u2.

RALPH WALDO EMERSON **197**

Reading Strategy

ACT Skills Practice

1. B is the correct answer, since the ideas in sentences I and II are not examined in *Self-Reliance*.

Vocabulary

1. The fact that the speaker cannot go on the trip without a job indicates that her mom is probably giving her a warning or *admonition*.

2. *Hidden* is given as a synonym or definition for *latent*.

3. *Clear* is given as a synonym for *manifest*.

4. The uncle pays for the camp, which is the definition of *benefactor*.

5. The friend's moral uprightness makes the parents trust her without question.

Academic Vocabulary

1. Possible answer: "It is easy in the world to live after the world's opinion; but the great man is he who in the midst of the crowd keeps with perfect sweetness the independence of solitude."

2. By addressing the reader as "you," Emerson commands the individual to take responsibility for his or her actions.

 Speaking and Listening

Students' speeches should include persuasive techniques, such as logical and emotional appeals, and should be delivered using verbal and nonverbal techniques.

📁 For additional assessment, see Assessment Resources, pp. 99–100.

Focus

Summary

The article begins with Dr. Richard Davidson studying the brain waves of a monk. Davidson is interested in learning if there are any changes in the monk's brain activity when he meditates. Research performed by Davidson and other scientists shows a connection between happiness and health.

Teach

Reading Strategy	1

Analyze Cause-and-Effect Relationships Point out that writers use different ways of organizing cause-and-effect arguments. A writer may first present an effect and then provide its causes; or a writer may present causes and conclude with their effect.

[APPROACHING] **Ask:** According to the first page of this article, what effect does happiness seem to have on health? *(Happiness seems to help people stay healthier.)*

Readability Scores

Dale-Chall: 11.9
DRP: 68
Lexile: 1110

Learning Objectives

For pages 198–202

In studying this text, you will focus on the following objectives:

Reading:
Analyzing informational text.
Analyzing cause-and-effect relationships.

Set a Purpose for Reading

Read to discover the biological roots of positive emotion and to connect these ideas with the optimism of Emerson and Thoreau.

Preview the Article

1. Analyze the photos of the monk on page 199 and the babies on page 200. What might these tell you about the article?

2. Skim the first paragraph. What connection do you think the writer is going to make between biology and joy?

| Reading Strategy | Analyze Cause-and-Effect Relationships |

1 **Cause and effect** describes the relationship between an action and its consequence. The cause, or action, directly results in the effect, or consequence. As you read, ask yourself, What cause-and-effect relationships are discussed in this article and why are they important?

Cause	Effect

198 UNIT 2

The Biology of JOY

Scientists know plenty about depression. Now they are starting to understand the roots of positive emotion.

By MICHAEL D. LEMONICK

IT ALL BEGAN WITH RICHARD DAVIDSON, A PROFESSOR OF psychology and psychiatry at the University of Wisconsin. Davidson was in a lab observing a Buddhist monk sink deep into blissful meditation when he noticed something that sent his own pulse racing. Davidson checked the data streaming to his computer from electrodes attached to the monk's skull. Electrical activity in the left prefrontal lobe of the monk's brain was shooting up at a tremendous rate. "It was exciting," Davidson recalls. "We didn't expect to see anything that dramatic."

When Davidson made his discovery, he had been studying the link between prefrontal-lobe activity and the bliss deep meditators experience. But even for someone with his experience, watching the brain crackle with activity as a person entered a trancelike state was something never seen before. It made clear, says Davidson, that happiness isn't just a vague feeling. Instead it's a physical state of the brain—one that you can bring on deliberately.

That's not all. As researchers have gained an understanding of the physical characteristics of a happy brain, they have come to see that those traits have a powerful influence on the rest of the body. Scientists have **2** discovered that happiness or feelings of hopefulness, optimism, and contentment appear to lessen the risk or limit the severity of cardiovascular disease, lung disease, diabetes, high blood pressure, and colds. According to a Dutch study of elderly patients, those upbeat mental states reduced an individual's risk of death 50%.

Doctors have known for years that clinical depression—the

Writing Practice

Achieve Unity Explain to students that a paragraph is unified when all of its sentences support the main idea of the paragraph, usually expressed in the topic sentence. Ask students to state the main idea of paragraph three on this page that begins "That's not all…." *(Sentence two in paragraph three is the main idea)* Then ask them to point out the details that support the main idea. *(Lessen risk of diseases, colds, and death)* Finally, ask students to write a paragraph about what makes them optimistic. Remind them that the paragraph should have a clearly stated main idea that is supported by relevant details.

NIRVANA CHECK
Davidson, right, prepares to record the brain activity of a Buddhist monk entering a state of blissful meditation.

 We're just beginning to apply a lens to all those parts of the nervous system in which the positive emotions are embodied. This is really neat territory.
—DACHER KELTNER,
University of California, Berkeley

THE BIOLOGY OF JOY **199**

TIME

Teach

Big Idea | 2

Optimism and Individualism Point out to students that Ralph Waldo Emerson placed great importance on the value of optimism. "The Biology of Joy" shows the positive effects optimism and happiness can have on one's health.

Cultural History ☆

Buddhism Buddhism was founded in northern India in the sixth century B.C. by Gautama, called the Buddha ("Enlightened One") by his followers. The Buddha preached that detachment from worldly goods and desires was the key to human happiness.

 For activities related to this selection, see Unit 2 Teaching Resources Book, p. 46–54.

 For an audio recording of this selection, use Listening Library Audio CD-ROM.

English Learners

DIFFERENTIATED INSTRUCTION

Advanced Explain to students that it is helpful to look for context clues when reading. Context clues are the surrounding words and information that can help you figure out the meaning of unfamiliar words. For example, write the following sentence on the chalkboard: Neuroscientists have studied the brain intensely over the past several years. Students may not know the meaning of the word *neuroscientist*, but if they examine the surrounding words, they can see that neuroscientists study the brain and thus can conclude that a neuroscientist is a scientist who studies the functions of the brain.

TIME

Teach

Analyze Cause-and-Effect Relationships Ask: Look at the quote above the split image of the smiling and crying babies. What cause/effect relationship is described? *(Happiness may be an inborn result of levels of brain activity.)* What is the cause in this relationship? *(Higher left prefrontal brain activity in some children)* What is the effect? *(No crying when their mothers left the room)*

Cultural History ☆

Pavlov's Dogs The experiments of the Russian physiologist Ivan Pavlov (1849–1935) in the study of conditioned reflexes are among the most famous in the history of science. The expression "like Pavlov's dogs" has come to describe any reaction that seems to be so automatic as to be involuntary.

Informational Text

ROBERT FROST ▶

"Happiness makes up in height for what it lacks in length."

Bettmann/CORBIS

BENJAMIN FRANKLIN

"Happiness consists more in small conveniences or pleasures that occur every day, than in great pieces of good fortune that happen but seldom to a man in the course of his life."

extreme opposite of happiness— can worsen heart disease and other illnesses. But the neurochemistry of depression is much better known than that of happiness, mostly because depression has been studied more intensively and for much longer. Until about 10 years ago, says Dacher Keltner, a psychologist at the University of California, Berkeley, "90% of emotion research focused on the negative. There still are all of these interesting questions about the positive state."

Happiness on the Brain

A growing number of researchers exploring the physiology and neurology of happiness are starting to answer those questions. Perhaps most basic of all is what happiness is, in a clinical sense. At this point, nobody can say exactly. The word *happiness*, Davidson observes, "is kind of a placeholder for a group of positive emotional states. It's a state of well-being where individuals are usually not motivated to change the way they are feeling. They're motivated to preserve it." But, Davidson notes, there is much more that scientists must learn about the qualities and effects of happiness in humans. Much of that information lies in a part of the brain called the left prefrontal cortex, the brain's major center of happiness.

Is happiness wired in from the beginning?

A cheerful outlook may be inborn. Babies with less activity in the left prefrontal cortex tend to cry when their mothers leave the room; those with more activity stay content. By looking at brain scans, researchers could predict which infants would cry.

Penny Gentieu (2)

1

Scientists want to know if the prefrontal cortex creates the sensation of happiness or whether it merely reflects a person's more general emotional state. Davidson thinks the answer is both: "We're confident that this part of the brain is the cause of at least certain kinds of happiness." That suggests some

people are genetically predisposed to be happy by virtue of their busy prefrontal cortexes, and research in infants confirms it. Davidson first measured left prefrontal activity in babies less than a year old. Then he gave them a test in which their mothers left the room briefly. "Some babies will cry hysterically the instant the mom leaves," he says. "Others are more resilient." It turns out that the babies with the higher left prefrontal activity are the ones who don't cry. "We were actually able to predict which infants would cry in response to that brief but significant stress."

In short, some babies are just born happy. But neuroscientists have also learned that the brain is highly adaptable. It rewires itself in response to experience, and that's especially true before the age of puberty. One might assume, therefore, that negative experiences might destroy a happy personality—and if they're extreme and frequent enough, that might be true. Davidson has learned, however, that mild to moderate doses of negative experience are helpful. The reason, he believes, is that stressful events give us practice at bouncing back from unpleasant emotions. They're like an exercise to strengthen our happiness muscles.

200 UNIT 2   AMERICAN ROMANTICISM

Pictures and Text Point out the quotes and images that appear at the top of this page and the next. Have different volunteers read each quote aloud. **Ask:** What do you think is the purpose of this information? *(Humor; draw attention to the article; provide a break in the text)* Also point out the picture of the babies

and the related text in the middle of this page. **Ask:** What is the purpose of this information? *(To capture the reader's attention; to present a main idea quickly)*

◄ EDITH WHARTON

"If only we'd stop trying to be happy we'd have a pretty good time."

◄ MARK TWAIN

"Happiness ain't a thing in itself—it's only a contrast with something that ain't pleasant."

The Chemistry of Happiness

Exactly what is the physical difference, though, between a left prefrontal cortex that leans towards happiness and one that doesn't? It almost certainly has in part to do with neurotransmitters. These chemicals ferry signals from one neuron to the next. Davidson believes that one of these chemicals, dopamine, may be significant. Researchers are studying the relationship of dopamine levels to feelings of extreme happiness and depression.

Dopamine pathways may be especially important in aspects of happiness associated with moving toward some sort of goal such as monks achieving a meditative state. "People have made progress telling the difference between the positive feeling you get when you approach a goal, which maps onto dopamine, and the sensory pleasure of enjoying something, which maps onto the opioid system," says Berkeley's Keltner. "This is really neat territory."

Among those exploring that territory is Brian Knutson, an assistant professor of psychology and neuroscience at Stanford, who monitors the brains of test subjects. The mental mode he studies is anticipation. "When people think of happiness," says Knutson, "they think of feeling good. But a big part of happiness is also looking forward to something." Knutson's research was inspired by the classic work of Ivan Pavlov, who trained dogs to salivate at the sound of a bell, which they associated with mealtime.

Instead of food, Knutson used money—a small cash payoff if subjects won a video game. "When we looked at their brains just before they got the reward," he says, "we saw this spark that clearly had to do with how positive the idea of making money was." The spark showed up not in the left prefrontal cortex but in the nucleus accumbens, located in the subcortex, at the bottom of the brain. The bigger the prize, Knutson found, "the more activation." Knutson believes he is looking at the kind of happy feelings we experience as excitement. The primary focus of his work is to understand how emotion and reason work together as people make choices. But it could also be a key to mapping out the brain's broader happiness circuitry. **2**

Happiness and Physical Health

Understanding brain changes when a person feels good is one aspect of happiness research. Another is understanding how positive emotion affects the rest of the body. As with the brain studies, researchers tend to focus on specific aspects of happiness.

Harvard psychologist Laura Kubzansky is studying optimism. In a large study she tracked 1,300 men for 10 years and found that heart-disease rates among men who called themselves optimistic were half the rates for men who didn't.

"It was a much bigger effect than we expected," she says. Kubzansky also looked at pulmonary function, since poor pulmonary function can signal a range of problems, including early death and cardiovascular disease. Again, optimists did much better. "I'm an optimist," she says, "but I didn't expect results like this."

In a separate study, Kubzansky, working with Duke psychologist Laura Richman, looked at hopefulness and curiosity—mental states that overlap with optimism in some ways. "We found them to be protective against hypertension, diabetes, and upper-respiratory infection," she says. Such protective effects may explain the longevity advantage found in that Dutch study of the elderly—an advantage for happy optimists that persisted even when researchers corrected for diet, education, and other factors.

Exactly how states of mind affect the body's biochemistry is still far from clear. Optimists may simply feel less stress than pessimists and so they can avoid the noxious biochemical cascades

THE BIOLOGY OF JOY **201**

Reading Strategy **2**

Analyze Cause-and-Effect Relationships **Say:** Try stopping after each subsection of the article to review the causes and effects the writer has presented.

[APPROACHING] Ask students having difficulty to work in small groups to complete their cause-and-effect charts from page 198 as they read. Have groups read the article aloud, pausing after each subsection to list the causes and effects presented.

Approaching Level

DIFFERENTIATED INSTRUCTION

Emerging A root is an element that conveys the basic meaning of a word. Knowing roots can be useful when reading challenging material. For example, if students understand that the Greek root *bio* means "life" and *-logy* means "study," they are likely to understand that *biology* is the study of life.

Ask students to determine the meanings of the words on the left, given the meanings of their Greek roots on the right.

cardiology	kardi	"heart"
psychology	psych	"soul"
ichthyology	ikhthu	"fish"

As students read the article, ask them to look for other scientific terms. Have them attempt to figure out the meaning of the words using the root.

TIME

Reading Strategy 1

Analyze Cause-and-Effect Relationships

Ask: What did the "grateful" group do that the other groups did not do? *(They recorded each day the things for which they were grateful.)* What was the effect? *(They were happier and took better care of their health.)*

Assess

1. Yes; I didn't think there could be any connection between my attitude and my health. No; when I am sick I am often in a bad mood, and when I am happy I usually feel healthy.

2. They are more likely to exercise, have regular medical check ups, and practice preventive health actions, such as wearing sunscreen.

3. (a) Meditation produces an intense experience of happiness. (b) People who achieve elevated levels of happiness in periods of peak performance (for example, dancers, artists, and athletes)

4. (a) Results of experiments conducted by scientific researchers (b) Science is revealing a link between happiness and brain activity.

5. Students may feel that some of the activities Emerson and Thoreau pursued (both were enthusiastic walkers and kept journals) helped encourage their optimistic outlook.

that stress is known to trigger. Another likely factor: optimistic, happy types seem to take better care of themselves than sad sacks do. Many studies—and common sense—suggest that to be the case.

In a series of studies begun in 1998, psychologist Robert Emmons of the University of California at Davis has found further evidence that happy people are better at keeping themselves in good shape. Emmons randomly assigned 1,000 adults to one of three groups. The first group kept daily journals of their moods and rated them on a scale of 1 to 6. The second group did that and listed the things that annoyed or hassled them throughout their day. The third group kept a journal but added an activity that has repeatedly been shown to improve one's sense of satisfaction with life: they were asked to write down every day all the things for which they were grateful.

Despite being assigned randomly, the last group not only had the predicted jump in their overall feelings of happiness, says Emmons, but were also found to spend more time exercising, be more likely to have regular medical checkups, and routinely take preventive health actions like wearing sunscreen. Overall, the "gratitude" group were promoting better health. "They rate themselves as more energetic, more enthusiastic, more alert," Emmons reports. In short, keeping the diaries contributed to their physical and emotional well-being.

Not surprisingly, the advantages were greatest when compared with the group that focused on life's hassles. "People who are grateful tend to view their body a certain way," says Emmons. "They see life as a gift, health as a gift. So they want to take certain measures to preserve it." Reminding yourself of what you're grateful for is a technique open to anyone, but more sophisticated methods of manipulating happiness are showing promise as well. Behavior therapy and medication, for example, are used mostly to fight depression, but they may also be useful in enhancing happiness.

Such positive results gratify happiness scientists. Thanks to Keltner, Davidson, and others, those findings have gained the field a degree of respectability that's long overdue—and that ultimately could make all of us a whole lot happier.

—From **TIME**, January 17, 2005

Respond and Think Critically

Respond and Interpret

1. Were you surprised at the findings of the scientists? Why or why not?

2. What are some reasons given in the article for why happier people live longer?

3. (a) Why did Davidson use a monk for his study? (b) What other professions or types of people would also be suitable for his experiment?

Analyze and Evaluate

4. (a) What kinds of evidence does the writer use to support his point? (b) Why is the writer's choice of evidence appropriate to his purpose?

5. How is your appreciation of Emerson and Thoreau affected by the possibility that their optimism may have been biologically determined?

Connect

6. **Connect to Today** Pretend that you are Emerson and write a letter to the editor agreeing or disagreeing with the findings in "The Biology of Joy." Try to imitate Emerson's tone and language, using the excerpt from "Self-Reliance" on pages 194–195 as a guideline. Be sure to support your conclusions with evidence from the article.

For additional assessment, see Assessment Resources, pp. 101–102.

6. Answers will vary, but students may say that Emerson thinks that the article is correct because his journals and reflections help him feel optimistic. Be sure students imitate Emerson's tone and writing. Check that students have supported their conclusions with evidence from the article.

Before You Read

from *Woman in the Nineteenth Century*

Meet **Margaret Fuller**
(1810–1850)

New England socialite, expatriate revolutionary, transcendentalist, author, feminist—all of these labels describe Margaret Fuller. Born in Cambridgeport, Massachusetts, Fuller received an extensive education in literature, languages, and the arts from her father, Timothy Fuller Jr., a congressman from Massachusetts. She was a very precocious child and continued to educate herself after attending several local academies. After her father's sudden death in 1835, she became responsible for the education of her eight younger siblings.

> "When people keep telling you that you can't do a thing, you kind of like to try it."
>
> —Margaret Fuller

Feminist and Intellectual In 1836, Fuller first met Ralph Waldo Emerson (page 188) and stayed at his house in Concord while he was finishing his essay *Nature*. On first acquaintance he was uninterested in Fuller, put off by what he described as her "extreme plainness." However, he soon changed his opinion and developed great respect for Fuller. They became close friends, and Fuller eventually joined his Transcendentalist Club.

In 1839 Fuller moved to Boston and began a series of language classes and formal conversations for women on topics such as literature, education, mythology, and philosophy. She was described as a dazzling discussion leader, and these meetings attracted many intellectuals and social activists. Fuller's meetings provided an opportunity for women to discuss their ideas and speak their thoughts freely. These meetings gave her a formidable reputation, and in 1840 she was invited to edit *The Dial*, a transcendentalist magazine, in which she published her essay "The Great Lawsuit." She later expanded this essay into her groundbreaking feminist work, *Woman in the Nineteenth Century*. Her book reveals her extensive knowledge of literature and philosophy. It gained a wide audience and is an impressive argument for the equal status of women.

Activism Abroad In 1846 Fuller went to Europe as the first female foreign correspondent for the *New York Tribune*. While in Rome, she was involved with Italian aristocrat and revolutionary Giovanni Angelo Ossoli and eventually had a child with him. Ossoli was active in the Risorgimento, a movement to overthrow Rome's papal state and to unify Italy; Fuller vigorously supported the movement. She felt at home in Italy and saw the Risorgimento as an opportunity for women and the laboring class to gain freedom and human rights. When the 1848 revolution broke out, Fuller volunteered in a hospital and sent vivid reports home to the *Tribune* while Ossoli fought. The revolution failed, and in 1850 Fuller and Ossoli fled to the United States with their infant son, Angelo. Tragically, their ship sank off the coast of New York, and all three were killed.

Fuller's life is well summed up by her memorial in Cambridge: "in youth an insatiable student . . . in riper years teacher, writer, critic . . . in maturer age . . . earnest reformer in America and Europe."

LOG ON ▶ **Literature** Online

Author Search For more about Margaret Fuller, go to glencoe.com and enter QuickPass code GLA9800u2.

Before You Read

Focus

Bellringer Options

Daily Language Practice Transparency 21

Or write on the board: Women are not capable of making important decisions. Explain that most people in the nineteenth century believed this idea.

Ask: How do you feel about this idea? If you lived in the nineteenth century, how might you change people's perceptions about women? Have students discuss the answers to these questions.

Literary History ☆
Summer on the Lakes, in 1843 Margaret Fuller's trip around the Great Lakes in 1843 was the topic of her first book. In the book, Fuller describes scenes from nature, the people she encountered, and her thoughts during the journey.

Selection Skills

Literary Elements
- Thesis (SE pp. 204, 207, 209)

Reading Skills
- Summarize (SE pp. 204, 205, 209)
- Analyze (TE pp. 206, 207)

from Woman in the Nineteenth Century

Listening/Speaking/ Viewing Skills
- Analyze Art (SE pp. 205, 206)

Writing Skills/Grammar
- Letter (SE p. 209)
- Take Notes (TE p. 204)
- Linking Verbs (TE p. 208)

Vocabulary Skills
- Word Usage (SE p. 209)
- Nouns (TE p. 204)

Before You Read

Focus

Summary

In her essay, Margaret Fuller focuses on women's social status in the nineteenth century. She demonstrates the hypocrisy of society for allowing women to apply their talents to some roles but not to others. Fuller concludes that women's issues cannot be advanced unless women represent themselves publicly.

 For summaries in languages other than English, see Unit 2 Teaching Resources Book, pp. 55–60.

Vocabulary

Nouns Remind students that concrete nouns name something that can be seen, heard, touched, smelled, or tasted. Abstract nouns name an idea or feeling that cannot be directly sensed. **Ask:** Are *lot* and *reverence* concrete or abstract nouns? *(Both nouns are abstract.)* Have students explain the abstract nouns used in the example sentences.

[APPROACHING] Have students identify nouns from the essay as concrete or abstract: respect *(abstract);* wife *(concrete);* woman *(concrete);* words *(concrete);* beauty *(abstract);* dignity *(abstract)*

 For additional context, see Glencoe Interactive Vocabulary CD-ROM.

Literature and Reading Preview

Connect to the Essay

Do you have any unpopular or controversial opinions? What are they? Freewrite for a few minutes about the pros and cons of sharing these views with other people.

Build Background

Fuller was one of the earliest and most vocal supporters of women's rights in the United States. She was writing at a time when women were gaining more legal rights. Shortly before *Woman in the Nineteenth Century* was published, for example, laws were passed in some states allowing married women to own property separately from their husbands. Fuller's book laid the groundwork for the women's suffrage movement that in 1920 resulted in the Nineteenth Amendment to the Constitution, which guarantees women's right to vote.

Set Purposes for Reading

Big Idea Optimism and Individualism

As you read this excerpt from *Woman in the Nineteenth Century,* ask yourself, How is Fuller's feminism an extension of Emerson's belief in the divinity of the individual?

Literary Element Thesis

A **thesis** is the main idea of a work of nonfiction. The thesis may be stated directly or implied. As you read this essay, ask yourself, What is Fuller's thesis?

Reading Strategy Summarize

Summarizing is briefly stating the main ideas of a selection in your own words and in a logical sequence. Summarizing what you have read is an excellent tool for understanding and remembering a passage. As you read, summarize Fuller's ideas to better understand this selection.

204 UNIT 2   AMERICAN ROMANTICISM

Learning Objectives

For pages 203–209

In studying this text, you will focus on the following objectives:

Literary Study: Analyzing thesis.

Reading: Summarizing.

Writing: Writing a letter.

Vocabulary

ludicrous (lōō′ də krəs) *adj.* laughable; foolish; false; p. 206 *It would be ludicrous to go camping during this blizzard.*

commensurate (kə men′ sər it) *adj.* equal to; proportionate; p. 207 *Our effort in this project was commensurate with yours.*

arbitrary (är′ bə trer′ ē) *adj.* of a random or unreasonable character; p. 207 *The organization of the police roadblocks appeared to be arbitrary.*

lot (lot) *n.* way of life or purpose as determined by fate; fortune; p. 208 *The lot of the poor family was full of hardship.*

reverence (rev′ ər əns) *n.* a feeling of deep affection; p. 208 *The congregation had a great deal of reverence for their minister.*

Writing Practice

Take Notes Tell students that rereading a passage and taking notes will help them identify its main idea and supporting details, the author's tone and purpose, rhetorical or literary devices, and unfamiliar words. Write the following headings on the board, and have students copy them onto a piece of paper to guide their note taking.

- Main Idea and Supporting Details
- Tone
- Author's Purpose
- Rhetorical and Literary Devices
- Unfamiliar Words

As they read, tell students to stop at the end of each page to take notes using the headings they wrote down.

WOMAN IN THE NINETEENTH CENTURY

Margaret Fuller

Mr. and Mrs. I. N. Phelps Stokes, 1897. John Singer Sargent. Oil on canvas, 84¼ x 39¾ in. The Metropolitan Museum of Art, NY.

 View the Art John Singer Sargent painted many portraits of the "modern" nineteenth-century woman. What elements in this painting suggest a more progressive view of women and their role in society? How does this compare with Fuller's message? ★

Knowing that there exists in the minds of men a tone of feeling toward women as toward slaves, such as is expressed in the common phrase, "Tell that to women and children"; that the infinite soul can only work through them in already ascertained limits; that the gift of reason, Man's highest prerogative,[1] is allotted to them in much lower degree; that they must be kept from mischief and melancholy by being constantly engaged in active labor, which is to be furnished and directed by those better able to think, etc., etc.,—we need not multiply instances, for who can review the experience of last week without recalling words which imply, whether in jest or earnest, these views, or views like these,—knowing this, can we wonder that many reformers think that measures are not likely to be taken in behalf of women, unless their wishes could be publicly represented by women?

"That can never be necessary," cry the other side. "All men are privately influenced by women; each has his wife, sister, or female friends, and is too much biased by these relations to fail of representing their interests; and, if this is not enough, let them propose and enforce their wishes with the pen. The beauty of home would be destroyed, the delicacy of the sex be violated, the dignity of halls of legislation degraded, by an attempt to introduce

---

1. *Prerogative* means "right."

Summarize *Summarize this statement in your own words.* **1**

MARGARET FULLER **205**

Approaching Level

DIFFERENTIATED INSTRUCTION

Emerging Have students create an outline of the essay, working in pairs or groups. Their outlines should list the main ideas and supporting details y. After students have completed their outlines, have them write a thesis statement that reflects Fuller's overall argument.

AAVE Approaching level students who are users of AAVE sometimes use the word *it* where they should be using the word *there* in sentences. Have a volunteer read the first sentence aloud to the class. Point out the phrase "there exists." Help students use *there* in their own sentences.

Teach

Analyze **Say:** Fuller uses principles of logic when presenting her argument. Explain Fuller's reasoning, giving examples from the text. *(Fuller identifies opponents' inconsistencies. For example, to those who say that women are too weak to go to work, Fuller gives examples of women who show great physical strength.)*

View the Art ★

Answer: *Students may say that a scene of women going to work suggests that the role of women changed after the Civil War—more women went to work to support their families. The strong morning light illuminates the central figure, echoing Fuller's positive portrayal of women.*

The Morning Bell (a.k.a. The Old Mill), 1871. Winslow Homer. Oil on canvas, 24 x 38⅛ x 1 in. Yale University Art Gallery.

View the Art In this painting, Homer shows several young women on their way to work in a New England mill. What does this painting suggest about the role of women in society? ★

them there. Such duties are inconsistent with those of a mother;" and then we have **ludicrous** pictures of ladies in hysterics at the polls, and senate-chambers filled with cradles.

But if, in reply, we admit as truth that Woman seems destined by nature rather for the inner circle, we must add that the arrangements of civilized life have not been, as yet, such as to secure it to her. Her circle, if the duller, is not the quieter. If kept from "excitement," she is not from drudgery. Not only the Indian squaw carries the burdens of the camp, but the favorites of Louis XIV[2] accompany him in his journeys, and the washerwoman stands at her tub, and carries home her work at all seasons, and in all states of health. Those who think the physical circumstances of Woman would make a part in the affairs of national government unsuitable, are by no means those who think it impossible for negresses[3] to endure fieldwork, even during pregnancy, or for sempstresses[4] to go through their killing labors.

As to the use of the pen, there was quite as much opposition to Woman's possessing herself of that help to free agency as there is now to

her seizing on the rostrum[5] or the desk; and she is likely to draw, from a permission to plead her cause that way, opposite inferences to what might be wished by those who now grant it.

As to the possibility of her filling with grace and dignity any such position, we should think those who had seen the great actresses, and heard the Quaker preachers of modern times, would not doubt that Woman can express publicly the fulness of thought and creation, without losing any of the peculiar beauty of her sex. What can pollute and tarnish is to act thus from any motive except that something needs to be said or done. Woman could take part in the processions, the songs, the dances of old religion; no one fancied her delicacy was impaired by appearing in public for such a cause.

As to her home, she is not likely to leave it more than she now does for balls, theatres, meetings for promoting missions, revival meetings, and others to which she flies,[6] in hope of an animation for her existence **commensurate** with what she sees enjoyed by men. Governors of ladies'-fairs are no less engrossed by such a charge, than the governor of a state by his;

---

2. *Louis XIV* was the king of France from 1638 to 1715.
3. *Negresses:* (archaic) women of black African descent.
4. *Sempstresses* are "seamstresses."

Vocabulary

ludicrous (lōō′ də krəs) *adj.* laughable; foolish; false

---

5. A *rostrum* is a platform for speakers.
6. Here, *flies* means "rushing toward."

Vocabulary

commensurate (kə men′ sər it) *adj.* equal to; proportionate

206 UNIT 2   AMERICAN ROMANTICISM

Reading Practice

SPIRAL REVIEW **Analyze Structure** Students may not be able to determine how Fuller organizes her argument. Remind students that Fuller presents an opposing argument to her thesis in the second paragraph on page 205. Have students read the first sentence of the next five paragraphs, beginning with the paragraph "But if, in reply." **Ask:** How do these five paragraphs relate to the second paragraph on page 205? What

clues tell you about the relationship? *(The paragraphs systematically refute each part of the opposing argument presented in the second paragraph. Each paragraph begins by quoting the specific part of the argument Fuller is trying to refute.)* As students read on, remind them to analyze how each paragraph fits in the structure of Fuller's argument.

presents of Washingtonian societies[7] no less away from home than presidents of conventions. If men look straitly to it, they will find that, unless their lives are domestic, those of the women will not be. A house is no home unless it contain food and fire for the mind as well as for the body. The female Greek, of our day, is as much in the street as the male to cry, "What news?" We doubt not it was the same in Athens of old. The women, shut out from the marketplace, made up for it at the religious festivals. For human beings are not so constituted that they can live without expansion. If they do not get it in one way, they must in another, or perish.[8]

As to men's representing women fairly at present, while we hear from men who owe to their wives not only all that is comfortable or graceful, but all that is wise, in the arrangement of their lives, the frequent remark, "You cannot reason with a woman,"—when from those of delicacy, nobleness, and poetic culture, falls the contemptuous[9] phrase "women and children," and that in no light sally[10] of the hour, but in works intended to give a permanent statement of the best experiences,—when not one man, in the million, shall I say? no, not in the hundred million, can rise above the belief that Woman was made *for Man*,—when such traits as these are daily forced upon the attention, can we feel that Man will always do justice to the interests of Woman? Can we think that he takes a sufficiently discerning and religious view of her office and destiny ever to do her justice, except when prompted by sentiment,—accidentally or transiently, that is, for the sentiment will vary according to the relations in which he is placed? The lover, the poet, the artist, are likely to view her nobly. The father and the philosopher have some chance of liberality; the man of the world, the legislator for expediency, none.

Under these circumstances, without attaching importance, in themselves, to the changes demanded by the champions of Woman, we hail them as signs of the times. We would have every **arbitrary** barrier thrown down. We would have every path laid open to Woman as freely as to Man. Were this done, and a slight temporary fermentation[11] allowed to subside, we should see crystallizations more pure and of more various beauty. We believe the divine energy would pervade nature to a degree unknown in the history of former ages, and that no discordant collision, but a ravishing harmony of the spheres,[12] would ensue.

Yet, then and only then will mankind be ripe for this, when inward and outward freedom for Woman as much as for Man shall be acknowledged as a right, not yielded as a concession. As the friend of the Negro assumes that one man cannot by right hold another in bondage, so should the friend of Woman assume that Man cannot by right lay even well-meant restrictions on Woman. If the Negro be a soul, if the woman be a soul, apparelled in flesh, to one Master only are they accountable. There is but one law for souls, and, if there is to be an interpreter of it, he must come not as man, or son of man, but as son of God.

Were thought and feeling once so far elevated that Man should esteem himself the brother and friend, but nowise[13] the lord and tutor, of Woman,—were he really legally bound with her in equal worship,—arrangements as to function and employment would be of no

---

11. Here, *fermentation* means "unrest."
12. The ancients believed that the stars and planets created a perfect music, known as "the music of the spheres."
13. *Nowise* means "not at all."

Optimism and Individualism *How does this statement relate to transcendentalism?* **3**

Thesis *What details support this statement?* **4**

Vocabulary

arbitrary (är′ bə trer′ ē) *adj.* of a random or unreasonable character

---

7. *Washingtonian societies* were patriotic groups.
8. Fuller is suggesting here that the women of ancient Greece, although excluded from male society, were able to find alternative modes of expression.
9. *Contemptuous* means "scornful."
10. Here, *sally* means "witty remark."

MARGARET FULLER **207**

Teach

Reading Strategy **2**

Analyze Have students reread the sentence containing the word *arbitrary*. **Ask:** How does the author's use of the adjective *arbitrary* to modify the noun *barrier* reflect her beliefs? *(The author believes the obstacles to women's equality are irrational.)*

Big Idea **3**

Optimism and Individualism
Answer: *This statement links optimism about the future with the freedom of the individual.*

Literary Element **4**

Thesis **Answer:** *It is supported by Fuller's claims about equality among the sexes and her statement that the body is just the "soul, apparelled in flesh."*

Cultural History ☆

Women's Rights In 1848, the first women's rights convention in the United States was held in Seneca Falls, New York. Meetings were then held on a regular basis.

English Learners

DIFFERENTIATED INSTRUCTION

Intermediate Write these words on the board: *fermentation, discordant, unimpeded,* and *unfold.* Explain that it is easier to understand these words if they are broken into parts. Have partners work together to find and break unfamiliar words into parts and decide what the parts mean.

Advanced Learners

DIFFERENTIATED INSTRUCTION

Oral Response Ask advanced learners to prepare oral responses to Fuller's essay. Their oral presentations should include three elements: the thesis of Fuller's essay; details and examples from the essay which support the thesis; and their logical response in support of or against Fuller's thesis. Have students share their oral responses with the rest of the class.

Teach

Literary Element   1

Thesis **Ask:** How does Fuller's example of Miranda reinforce the thesis of this essay? *(Miranda proved herself to be equal to men in thought and ability. She was an example of a woman who broke the limits put upon women and was respected by men and women alike.)*

📁 To check students' understanding of the selection, see Unit 2 Teaching Resources Book, p. 66.

Progress Check

Can students identify a thesis?

If No → See Unit 2 Teaching Resources Book, p. 61.

---

consequence. What Woman needs is not as a woman to act or rule, but as a nature to grow, as an intellect to discern, as a soul to live freely and unimpeded, to unfold such powers as were given her when we left our common home. If fewer talents were given her, yet if allowed the free and full employment of these, so that she may render back to the giver his own with usury,[14] she will not complain; nay, I dare to say she will bless and rejoice in her earthly birth-place, her earthly **lot.** Let us consider what obstructions impede this good era, and what signs give reason to hope that it draws near.

I was talking on this subject with Miranda,[15] a woman, who, if any in the world could, might speak without heat and bitterness of the position of her sex. Her father was a man who cherished no sentimental reverence for Woman, but a firm belief in the equality of the sexes. She was his eldest child, and came to him at an age when he needed a companion. From the time she could speak and go alone, he addressed her not as a plaything, but as a living mind. Among the few verses he ever wrote was a copy addressed to this child, when the first locks were cut from her head; and the **reverence** expressed on this occasion for that cherished head, he never belied.[16] It was to him the temple of immortal intellect. He respected his child, however, too much to be an indulgent parent. He called on her for clear judgment, for courage, for honor and fidelity;

---

14. Here, *usury* means "interest."
15. *Miranda* is a fictional character based on the author.
16. *Belied* means "betrayed" or "misrepresented."

Vocabulary

lot (lot) *n.* way of life or purpose as determined by fate; fortune
reverence (rev´ ər əns) *n.* a feeling of respect or deep affection

---

in short, for such virtues as he knew. In so far as he possessed the keys to the wonders of this universe, he allowed free use of them to her, and, by the incentive of a high expectation, he forbade, so far as possible, that she should let the privilege lie idle.

Thus this child was early led to feel herself a child of the spirit. She took her place easily, not only in the world of organized being, but in the world of mind. A dignified sense of self-dependence was given as all her portion, and she found it a sure anchor. Herself securely anchored, her relations with others were established with equal security. She was fortunate in a total absence of those charms which might have drawn to her bewildering flatteries, and in a strong electric nature, which repelled those who did not belong to her, and attracted those who did. With men and women her relations were noble,—affectionate without passion, intellectual without coldness. The world was free to her, and she lived freely in it. Outward adversity came, and inward conflict; but that faith and self-respect had early been awakened which must always lead, at last, to an outward serenity and an inward peace.

Of Miranda I had always thought as an example, that the restraints upon the sex were insuperable[17] only to those who think them so, or who noisily strive to break them. She had taken a course of her own, and no man stood in her way. Many of her acts had been unusual, but excited no uproar. Few helped, but none checked her; and the many men who knew her mind and her life, showed to her confidence as to a brother, gentleness as to a sister. And not only refined, but very coarse men approved and aided one in whom they saw resolution and clearness of design. Her mind was often the leading one, always effective. ✎

---

17. *Insuperable* means "insurmountable."

Grammar Practice

SPIRAL REVIEW 🌀 **Linking Verbs** Explain that a linking verb joins the subject of a sentence with a word or expression that identifies or describes the subject. The most common linking verbs are *be* and its forms, such as *am, is, are, was,* and *were. Appear, become, grow,* and *seem*—as well as words associated with the senses, such as *look, smell,* or *feel*—can also serve as linking verbs. Have students find sentences with linking verbs and identify the words that are linked. *(Example: "It was to him the temple of immortal intellect." The phrase "temple of immortal intellect" identifies the subject "it.")* Then have students write a brief paragraph summarizing Fuller's description of Miranda. Ask students to use and underline linking verbs in their paragraphs.

After You Read

Respond and Think Critically

Respond and Interpret

1. Which of Fuller's arguments do you find most convincing? Explain.

2. (a)Fuller says that women are kept from excitement. In her judgment, what are they not kept from? (b)Based on this judgment, what can you infer about the true motives of those opposed to women's rights?

3. (a)What are two examples that Fuller gives of women who fill public positions with "grace and dignity"? (b)How do these examples strengthen Fuller's argument?

4. (a)How do men respond to Miranda? (b)What is the reason for their response, and what does it suggest about women's education?

Analyze and Evaluate

5. Fuller makes an analogy between the plight of women and that of enslaved African Americans. Is this a valid analogy? Why or why not?

6. (a)Why do you think Fuller introduces Miranda into this essay? (b)Does Miranda help advance Fuller's arguments? Explain.

Connect

7. **Big Idea** Optimism and Individualism How does Fuller's feminism draw on the transcendentalist belief in optimism and individualism?

8. **Connect to Today** What are some issues related to women's rights today? Do you think these issues are being addressed adequately?

Literary Element Thesis

The **thesis** statement in a nonfiction piece may be stated directly, or it may be implied. Writers often state the thesis in the opening paragraph. However, if the thesis is implied, the reader must closely examine the facts, details, and rhetorical devices used by the author to determine the thesis statement.

1. What is the thesis of this essay?

2. Is Fuller's thesis stated directly or implied?

Reading Strategy Summarize

Summarizing can help you come to a conclusion about an author's beliefs. Briefly summarize the main ideas of this essay. On the basis of your summary, state two of Fuller's beliefs.

 Literature Online

Selection Resources For Selection Quizzes, eFlash-cards, and Reading-Writing Connection activities, go to glencoe.com and enter QuickPass code GLA9800u2.

Vocabulary Practice

Practice with Word Usage Respond to the following to practice using selection vocabulary.

1. Describe a school rule that is **arbitrary**.
2. Answer the following question with a **ludicrous** response: "When were you born?"
3. Explain how you would show **reverence** for a great leader.
4. Give an example of a character from literature whose **lot** in life is sad.
5. Explain how you would gain privileges **commensurate** to your grade level in school.

 Writing

Write a Letter Would Fuller be pleased with women's opportunities today? Write a letter to Fuller discussing this question and comparing the roles of women now and 150 years ago. Refer to specific passages in the text when making your comparisons.

After You Read

Assess

1. Students' answers should support their choice.

2. (a) Drudgery (b) Men opposed to women's rights are mainly interested in women's labor.

3. (a) Actresses and preachers (b) They show women can be successful in public positions.

4. (a) Men approve of her resolution and clear design. (b) She is educated; all women could receive this respect if allowed the opportunity to be educated.

5. Students may say the analogy is exaggerated because women enjoyed more rights than enslaved African Americans.

6. (a) To illustrate her arguments with concrete examples (b) Students should offer support for their opinions.

7. Students may say that her arguments stem from her conviction that all individuals are divine.

8. Students may note issues such as wages.

> For additional assessment, see Assessment Resources, pp. 103–104.

Reading Strategy

Students should properly summarize Fuller's ideas in a logical manner.

Writing

Students' letters should address issues related to women's rights.

Literary Element

1. "Yet, then and only then will mankind be ripe for this, ... concession."
2. Fuller's thesis is directly stated.

Vocabulary

1. Allowing some students to go off campus is an arbitrary school rule.
2. I was never born.
3. Writing a paper about a great leader would show reverence for that person.
4. Tom Walker's lot in life is sad.
5. You gain privileges by acting responsibly.

Focus

Bellringer Options

Daily Language Practice Transparency 22

Or say: Imagine it is a chilly, dark winter evening. What would you do to entertain yourselves? *(Possible responses: watch TV; play a board game; listen to music)* **Say:** In the nineteenth century, American families entertained themselves by reading poetry aloud.

Teach

Literary Element   1

Poetry Ask: What characteristics of poetry are different from prose? *(Many poems are divided into stanzas and use patterns of rhyme and meter; poems use imaginative language and rely more on figures of speech than prose does.)*

ENGLISH LEARNERS Give English learners an opportunity to discuss the characteristics of poetry further.

Ask: What elements of poetry make it easier to memorize than prose? Why? *(Rhyme, rhythm, repetition, and stanzas make poetry easier to memorize because they give it a more musical quality.)*

View the Art ★

Born in England, Thomas Birch settled in Philadelphia in 1794. He painted portraits, landscapes, and miniatures—but he is most admired for his seascapes and portraits of ships.

210

Learning Objectives

For pages 210–211

In studying this text, you will focus on the following objectives:

Literary Study:
Analyzing literary periods.
Analyzing literary genres.

The Fireside Poets

IN THE MID-1800S, A GROUP OF HIGHLY popular American writers became known as the "Fireside Poets" because it was thought that families often sat by the fire and read or recited their poems aloud. Eager to help establish a truly national literature, these poets frequently created vivid pictures of the New England countryside in their lyrics or of famous events from American history in their narrative poems.

William Cullen Bryant (1794–1878) was the oldest of the Fireside Poets. Though his background was Puritan, Bryant was influenced by the English Romantic poets, such as William Wordsworth. He was the first to portray the American landscape in words. In such famous poems as "To a Waterfowl" and "To the Fringed Gentian," Bryant wrote of the wildlife he encountered while he was hiking through the Berkshire Mountains in western Massachusetts.

Henry Wadsworth Longfellow (1807–1882) entered Bowdoin College at the age of fifteen and graduated in the same class as Nathaniel Hawthorne. In his poetry, such as the narrative poems *Evangeline* and *The Song of Hiawatha*, he mythologized the American past by using rhyme and simple verse. *Tales of a Wayside Inn* (1863), a collection of stories in verse supposedly told by various people at an inn, includes one of Longfellow's best-known poems, "Paul Revere's Ride." He was the first American to have a bust placed in the Poet's Corner of England's Westminster Abbey.

John Greenleaf Whittier (1807–1892) came from a poor Quaker farm family. His first book, *Legends of New England*, was published in 1831, but he became nationally famous with the work *Snow-Bound*, published in 1866. "Storytelling was a necessary resource in the long winter evenings," Whittier wrote, and *Snow-Bound* tells of a family isolated and telling stories during a storm. Whittier was devoted to the abolitionist movement, and much of his poetry, including "The Hunters of Men" and "Massachusetts to Virginia," reflects his stance against racism and slavery.

210 UNIT 2 AMERICAN ROMANTICISM

USS Constitution vs. HMS Guerriere, 1813. Attributed to Thomas Birch. Oil on canvas. US Naval Academy Museum, Annapolis, MD.

Oliver Wendell Holmes (1809–1894) studied both law and medicine but opted for a medical career. Among his best-known poems are "The Chambered Nautilus" and "Old Ironsides," the nickname for the famous American warship, the USS *Constitution*. Rumors that the ship was about to be scrapped inspired Holmes's poem, which roused public sentiment in support of saving it.

James Russell Lowell (1819–1891) objected to slavery and the war with Mexico. In 1846 the first of *The Biglow Papers*, his antislavery and antiwar poetry series, was published to great acclaim. Lowell created the voice of a rural Yankee, Hosea Biglow, who expressed Lowell's views with wit and humor. Lowell became the first editor of the *Atlantic Monthly* in 1857.

Writing Practice

⚡ **Use Sensory Details** Tell students that well-chosen sensory details can help readers experience a scene or an incident just as the writer did. Remind them that sensory details appeal to sight, hearing, smell, touch, and taste. Have students scan the poems on the following page and list the words and phrases that appeal to the senses. Then ask students to write a descriptive paragraph that uses sensory details to paint a vivid picture of a person, place, or thing. Before writing, tell students to jot down at least one sensory detail for each of the five senses. They should also brainstorm possible adjectives to describe each sensory detail.

Americans responded enthusiastically to the Fireside Poets, in part because their works celebrated the values of ordinary people—regard for hard work, respect for family, courage in the face of danger, love of one's country, and love of nature.

Because Americans also believed that these writers were the equals of the British poets of the time, they became more confident about the future of their country's culture.

To the Fringed Gentian
William Cullen Bryant

Thou blossom bright with autumn dew,
And colored with the heaven's own blue,
That openest when the quiet light
Succeeds the keen and frosty night—

5   Thou comest not when violets lean
O'er wandering brooks and springs unseen,
Or columbines, in purple dressed,
Nod o'er the ground-bird's hidden nest.

Thou waitest late and com'st alone,
10   When woods are bare and birds are flown,
And frosts and shortening days portend
The aged year is near his end.

Then doth thy sweet and quiet eye
Look through its fringes to the sky,
15   Blue—blue—as if that sky let fall
A flower from its cerulean wall.

I would that thus, when I shall see
The hour of death draw near to me,
Hope, blossoming within my heart,
20   May look to heaven as I depart.

 Literature Online

Literature and Reading For more about the Fireside Poets, go to glencoe.com and enter QuickPass code GLA9800u2.

Old Ironsides
Oliver Wendell Holmes

Ay, tear her tattered ensign down!
Long has it waved on high,
And many an eye has danced to see
That banner in the sky;
5   Beneath it rung the battle shout,
And burst the cannon's roar; —
The meteor of the ocean air
Shall sweep the clouds no more.

Her deck, once red with heroes' blood,
10   Where knelt the vanquished foe,
When winds were hurrying o'er the flood,
And waves were white below,
No more shall feel the victor's tread,
Or know the conquered knee; —
15   The harpies of the shore shall pluck
The eagle of the sea!

Oh, better that her shattered hulk
Should sink beneath the wave;
Her thunders shook the mighty deep,
20   And there should be her grave;
Nail to the mast her holy flag,
Set every threadbare sail,
And give her to the god of storms,
The lightning and the gale!

Respond and Think Critically

1. What do lines 9–12 add to your understanding of the speaker's attitude towards the gentian?

2. How does Bryant use personification in lines 13 and 14? How do these lines relate to the end of the poem?

3. What does the speaker's description of events that have taken place on the ship suggest about his attitude towards it?

4. In "Old Ironsides," explain the terms of the metaphor in lines 15–16.

Assess

1. The gentian blooms when it is almost winter. The speaker associates the flower with hope in the face of death.

2. Bryant describes the flower as if it has an eye. At the end of the poem, the speaker says that he would like to look to heaven with the same hopefulness as his own death approaches.

3. The phrases "battle shout," "cannon's roar," and "heroes' blood" suggest respect for the ship.

4. In Greek mythology, a harpy was part bird and part woman. In English, the term has come to mean a predatory person. The "harpies of the shore" are those who want to scrap Old Ironsides.

 For an activity related to this selection, see Unit 2 Teaching Resources Book, pp. 68–69.

 For an audio recording of this selection, use Listening Library Audio CD-ROM.

English Learners
DIFFERENTIATED INSTRUCTION

Intermediate Point out the archaic ending -est on the verb openest. Tell students to read the word simply as opens. Have them identify words with archaic endings and read them in modern English. (comest, com'st—come; o'er—over; waitest—wait; doth—does)

Approaching Level
DIFFERENTIATED INSTRUCTION

 SMALL GROUP **Emerging** To help students understand the poems' sensory details, have students create five-column charts and label each column with one of the five senses (sight, sound, smell, touch, taste). Ask students to work in small groups to read each poem aloud and list details in the appropriate columns. For example, they would list "blossom bright" from the poem "To the Fringed Gentian"

under sight. Discuss the sensory details to help students understand the images.

Before You Read

Focus

Bellringer Options

Selection Focus
Transparency 16
Daily Language Practice
Transparency 23

Or show students a page in a date book or other objects that indicate a busy life. **Ask:** How might you simplify your life? *(Answers might include turning off phone for certain hours, spending time alone, or watching less TV.)* Point out that Thoreau urges people to simplify their lives in order to live more fully.

Literary History ☆

Beyond Nature Though Thoreau is most well known for writing *Walden,* he was a man of diverse interests. In *Civil Disobedience,* he discussed America's involvement in the Mexican War. In *Slavery in Massachusetts,* he spoke against the enslavement of other people.

Before You Read

from *Walden*

Meet **Henry David Thoreau**
(1817–1862)

Although he is best known for his simple lifestyle at Walden Pond, Henry David Thoreau was a complex man: opinionated, cranky, nonconformist, compassionate, and subtly humorous. He was an unconventional thinker who expressed his ideas about major issues such as war, slavery, wealth, taxes, friendship, vegetarianism, and the lessons that nature can teach, yet he also wrote about topics as simple as hoeing his garden and walking in the woods. Much of what Thoreau did, thought about, or saw—and he was a keen observer—later took the form of a journal entry, an essay, or part of a book. ☆

Thoreau was born in Concord, Massachusetts, and lived there most of his life. He graduated from Harvard University in 1837 and took a teaching job at his old grammar school. However, he refused to physically discipline his students and quickly resigned. Thoreau founded a progressive school with his brother John in Concord the next year. Although the school was successful, it had to close in 1841 because of his brother's poor health.

> *"In Wildness is the preservation of the world."*
>
> —Thoreau, *Walking*

Life in the Woods While at Harvard, Thoreau was influenced by the works of Ralph Waldo Emerson, and the two men became friends. From 1841 to 1843, Thoreau lived with the Emerson family, assisting as a handyman. During this time he contributed a variety of works to *The Dial,* a

Transcendentalist magazine, including poetry, literary essays, and the first of his nature essays. In 1845, he built a cabin on land that Emerson owned at Walden Pond near Concord. Thoreau lived there for more than two years, spending most of his time reading, writing (including his most famous book, *Walden*), observing nature, and meditating.

Thoreau was deeply affected by his brother's death in 1842, and three years later decided to write an account of a camping and canoeing trip they had taken, referring to notes he had made along the way. The account became his first book, *A Week on the Concord and Merrimack Rivers,* published in 1849. The publisher returned the unsold copies, prompting Thoreau to later observe, "I now have a library of nearly nine hundred volumes, over seven hundred of which I wrote myself."

Thoreau's most famous book, *Walden, or, Life in the Woods,* was first published in 1854 and has become an American classic. *Walden* reflects Thoreau's personal philosophies and his response to industrialization, as well as the changing New England in which he lived. Through *Walden* and his other works, Thoreau helped inspire a long tradition of nature writing in the United States. He remains an inspiration for environmentalists everywhere.

 Literature Online

Author Search For more about Henry David Thoreau, go to glencoe.com and enter QuickPass code GLA9800u2.

Selection Skills

Literary Elements
- Metaphor (SE pp. 213, 215, 217–219)
- Tone (TE p. 218)

Writing Skills/Grammar
- Compare Literature (TE p. 214)
- Summarize (TE p. 218)

from **Walden**

Vocabulary Skills
- Context Clues (SE p. 219)
- Modifiers (TE p. 213)

Reading Skills
- Connect (SE pp. 213–214, 218, 219)
- Vary Reading Rate (TE p. 216)

Listening/Speaking/Viewing Skills
- Analyze Art (SE p. 216)

Literature and Reading Preview

Connect to the Essay

In a journal entry, describe your ideal place to go to be alone and get away from it all. Why is this the place you would choose?

Build Background

Thoreau lived at Walden Pond for two years, two months, and two days in a rugged cabin that measured ten feet by fifteen feet. The cabin, which he built himself, was simple and sturdy, with plastered walls and a shingled roof. He made his own furniture, including a bed, table, desk, and three chairs. At Walden, Thoreau devoted himself to observing the seasons, the animals, the plants and to writing his journals.

Set Purposes for Reading

Big Idea Kinship with Nature

As you read this selection from *Walden*, ask yourself, How does Thoreau stress the importance of a close relationship with nature?

Literary Element Metaphor

A **metaphor** is a figure of speech that compares or equates two seemingly unlike things. Unlike a **simile**, a metaphor implies the comparison instead of stating it directly, and does not use the connectives *like* or *as.* For example, Thoreau uses the metaphor "this chopping sea of civilized life" to suggest the perils and difficulties of modern living. As you read, identify other metaphors Thoreau uses to convey his ideas. Ask yourself, What theme, or message about life, is Thoreau trying to suggest with this metaphor? Why does he use a metaphor rather than literal language?

Reading Strategy Connect

When you connect to personal experience, you relate what you read to your own life. As you read, look for connections between Thoreau's observations and your own experiences and list ones that you find.

Learning Objectives

For pages 212–219

In studying this text, you will focus on the following objectives:

Literary Study: Analyzing metaphor.

Reading: Connecting to personal experience.

Writing: Writing a speech.

Vocabulary

deliberately (di lib′ ər it lē) *adv.* in a careful, thoughtful way; p. 214 *Thoreau deliberately nailed in place the roof to his cabin.*

resignation (rez′ ig nā′ shən) *n.* unresisting acceptance; submission; p. 214 *He practiced calm resignation to life's troubles.*

sublime (səb līm′) *adj.* of great spiritual or intellectual value; noble; p. 214 *To Emerson, intuition was a sublime power.*

rudiment (rōō′ də mənt) *n.* an imperfect or undeveloped part; p. 215 *Though the rudiments of the plan look interesting, it needs more elaboration and detail.*

myriad (mir′ ē əd) *adj.* countless, innumerable; p. 215 *There were myriad efforts to improve society during the Age of Reform.*

HENRY DAVID THOREAU **213**

English Learners

DIFFERENTIATED INSTRUCTION

Intermediate Display these words from the essay: *sturdily, simplicity.* Ask students to identify other forms of these words. *(sturdy, simple)* Have students create a four-column chart, with the headings *Noun, Verb, Adjective, Adverb,* and write the various word forms in the columns. As they read, have them write in forms of these words that Thoreau uses: *calculator, communications, memorable, application.*

Advanced Students may find Thoreau hard to read because he uses long, complex sentences. Have them read the essay aloud for practice. Remind students to pace themselves, to use expression, and to pause at commas and periods.

Before You Read

Focus

Summary

Rejecting a life of needless complexity, Thoreau goes into the woods to live more simply. He belittles those who complicate their lives by hurrying, working too hard, and trying to keep track of the latest news. He believes these things limit the time people have for what is important. When he leaves the woods, his belief in simplicity is confirmed and his insight into life is deepened.

 For summaries in languages other than English, see Unit 2 Teaching Resources Book, pp. 70–75.

Vocabulary

Modifiers Remind students that adjectives modify nouns or pronouns. Adverbs modify verbs, adjectives, and other adverbs. Have students fill in each blank with a vocabulary word:

- _____ ants crawled on the discarded piece of bread.
- Alicia knew she had done the right thing, so she had a _____ look on her face.
- Antonio _____ crossed the street to help an elderly man carry his groceries.

 For additional context, see Glencoe Interactive Vocabulary CD-ROM.

Teach

Big Idea   1

Kinship with Nature   Say:
Keep the following questions in mind as you read. Why did Thoreau go to Walden? *(He went to discover "the essential facts of life.")* How did he want to live his life? *(He wanted to live life deeply, without being distracted by trivial things.)* What did Thoreau find in nature? *(Thoreau found fulfillment in living a simple life close to nature.)*

[APPROACHING] Ask students for sentences that show Thoreau's desire to live simply, to live intensely, and to live in nature.

Reading Strategy   2

Connect   Answer: *Students may suggest such things as following rigid schedules or worrying about things that cannot be changed.*

[ENGLISH LEARNERS] Help English learners navigate the third sentence. **Ask:** What is Thoreau saying about life and his response to it? *(Thoreau does not want to die without having experienced life to its fullest.)*

 For additional practice using the reading skill or strategy, see Unit 2 Teaching Resources Book, p. 77.

 For an audio recording of this selection, use Listening Library Audio CD-ROM.

Readability Scores
Dale-Chall: 6.3
DRP: 58
Lexile: 1260

from WALDEN
Henry David Thoreau

from
Where I Lived and What I Lived For

1 I went to the woods because I wished to live **deliberately,** to front only the essential facts of life, and see if I could not learn what it had to teach, and not, when I came to die, discover that I had not lived. I did not wish to live what was not life, living is so dear; nor did I wish to practice **resignation,** unless it was quite necessary. I wanted to live deep and suck out all the marrow[1] of life, to live so sturdily and Spartanlike[2] as to put to rout all that was not life, to cut a broad swath and shave close,[3] to drive life into a corner, and reduce it to its lowest terms, and, if it proved to be mean,[4] why then to get the whole and genuine meanness of it, and publish its meanness to the world; or if

it were **sublime,** to know it by experience, and be able to give a true account of it in my next excursion. For most men, it appears to me, are in a strange uncertainty about it, whether it is of the devil or of God, and have *somewhat hastily* concluded that it is the chief end of man here to "glorify God and enjoy him forever."

Still we live meanly, like ants; though the fable tells us that we were long ago changed into men;[5] like pygmies we fight with cranes;[6] it is error upon error, and clout upon clout, and our best virtue has for its occasion a superfluous and evitable[7] wretchedness. Our life is frittered away by detail. An honest man has hardly need to count more than his ten fingers, or in extreme cases he may add his ten toes, and lump the rest. Simplicity, simplicity, simplicity! I say, let your affairs be as two or three, and not a hundred or a thousand; instead of a million count half a dozen, and keep your accounts on your thumb nail. In the midst of this chopping sea of civilized life, such are the clouds and

---

1. *Marrow* is the soft tissue inside bones. It also means "the best or most essential part."
2. Spartans were inhabitants of the ancient Greek city-state of Sparta. *Spartanlike* means "simple, economical, and disciplined."
3. [*to cut . . . close*] means "to gather as much of the essence of life as possible."
4. Here, *mean* means "of little importance, worth, or consequence" or "ignoble."

2   Connect   *In what ways might people today "live what [is] not life"?*

Vocabulary
deliberately (di lib´ ər it lē) *adv.* in a careful, thoughtful way
resignation (rez´ ig nā´ shən) *n.* unresisting acceptance; submission

---

5. The *fable* referred to is a Greek myth in which Zeus changes *ants* into *men.*
6. In Homer's *Iliad,* the Trojans are compared to *cranes* battling *pygmies.*
7. *Evitable* means "avoidable."

Vocabulary
sublime (səb līm´) *adj.* of great spiritual or intellectual value; noble

Writing Practice

 Compare Literature Lead a class discussion comparing the tone of this essay with that of Emerson's *Nature.* Draw a Venn diagram on the board to note similarities and differences. **Ask:** What are the major themes found in each essay? What is each author saying about life? Guide students to note that the themes of the writers are similar (the glory of the individual, the beauty of nature) and that both writers are exuberant and forceful in

their presentation of ideas. Thoreau, however, is more blunt and more critical. Have students write a summary of the similarities and differences, supporting their ideas with examples from both texts.

storms and quicksands and thousand-and-one items to be allowed for, that a man has to live, if he would not founder[8] and go to the bottom and not make his port at all, by dead reckoning,[9] and he must be a great calculator indeed who succeeds. Simplify, simplify. Instead of three meals a day, if it be necessary eat but one; instead of a hundred dishes, five; and reduce other things in proportion. . . .

Why should we live with such hurry and waste of life? We are determined to be starved before we are hungry. Men say that a stitch in time saves nine, and so they take a thousand stitches today to save nine tomorrow. As for *work*, we haven't any of any consequence. We have the Saint Vitus' dance,[10] and cannot possibly keep our heads still. If I should only give a few pulls at the parish bell-rope, as for a fire, that is, without setting the bell, there is hardly a man on his farm in the outskirts of Concord, notwithstanding that press of engagements which was his excuse so many times this morning, nor a boy, nor a woman, I might almost say, but would forsake all and follow that sound, not mainly to save property from the flames, but, if we will confess the truth, much more to see it burn, since burn it must, and we, be it known, did not set it on fire,—or to see it put out, and have a hand in it, if that is done as handsomely; yes, even if it were the parish church itself. Hardly a man takes a half hour's nap after dinner, but when he wakes he holds up his head and asks, "What's the news?" as if the rest of mankind had stood his sentinels. Some give directions to be waked every half hour, doubtless for no other purpose; and then, to pay for it, they tell what they have dreamed. After a night's sleep the news is as indispensable as the breakfast. "Pray tell me any thing new that has happened to a man any where on this globe,"—and he reads it over his coffee

8. *Founder* means "to sink, as a boat."
9. *Dead reckoning* is a method of navigation used by sailors when the stars cannot be seen.
10. *Saint Vitus' dance* is a nervous disorder characterized by involuntary twitching of the muscles in the face, arms, and legs.

and rolls, that a man has had his eyes gouged out this morning on the Wachito River;[11] never dreaming the while that he lives in the dark unfathomed mammoth cave of this world, and has but the **rudiment** of an eye himself.

For my part, I could easily do without the post-office. I think that there are very few important communications made through it. To speak critically, I never received more than one or two letters in my life—I wrote this some years ago—that were worth the postage. The penny-post is, commonly, an institution through which you seriously offer a man that penny for his thoughts which is so often safely offered in jest. And I am sure that I never read any memorable news in a newspaper. If we read of one man robbed, or murdered, or killed by accident, or one house burned, or one vessel wrecked, or one steamboat blown up, or one cow run over on the Western Railroad, or one mad dog killed, or one lot of grasshoppers in the winter,—we never need read of another. One is enough. If you are acquainted with the principle, what do you care for a **myriad** instances and applications? . . .

Time is but the stream I go a-fishing in. I drink at it; but while I drink I see the sandy bottom and detect how shallow it is. Its thin current slides away, but eternity remains. I would drink deeper; fish in the sky, whose bottom is pebbly with stars. I cannot count one. I know not the first letter of the alphabet. I have always been regretting that I was not as wise as the day I was born. The intellect is a cleaver; it discerns and rifts its way into the secret of things. I do not wish to be any more busy with my hands than is necessary. My head is hands and feet. I feel all my best faculties **3**

---

11. The *Wachito River* (now called the Ouachita) flows from southern Arkansas into northern Louisiana. People in Thoreau's time thought that criminals went to that region to escape from the law.

Metaphor *What comparison is Thoreau making here?* **4**

HENRY DAVID THOREAU **215**

Teach

A Cabin on Greenwood Lake, 1879. Jasper Francis Cropsey. Oil on canvas, 23.3 x 41.4 cm. Private collection.

View the Art The Hudson River painters—including Jasper Francis Cropsey—created works that were visual parallels to the ideas of Emerson, Thoreau, and other transcendentalists. How does this painting reflect the themes in *Walden*? ★

concentrated in it. My instinct tells me that my head is an organ for burrowing, as some creatures use their snout and fore-paws, and with it I would mine and burrow my way through these hills. I think that the richest vein is somewhere hereabouts; so by the divining rod[12] and thin rising vapors I judge; and here I will begin to mine.

from **Brute Neighbors**

1 It is remarkable how many creatures live wild and free though secret in the woods, and still sustain themselves in the neighborhood of towns, suspected by hunters only. How retired the otter manages to live here! He grows to be four feet long, as big as a small boy, perhaps without any human being getting a glimpse of him. I formerly saw the raccoon in the woods behind where my house is built, and probably still heard their whinnering at night. Commonly I rested an hour or two in the shade at noon, after planting, and ate my lunch, and read a little by a spring which was the source of a swamp and of a brook, oozing from under Brister's Hill, half a mile from my field. The approach to this was through a succession of descending grassy hollows, full of young pitch pines, into a larger wood about the swamp. There, in a very secluded and shaded spot, under a spreading white pine, there was yet a clean firm sward[13] to sit on. I had dug out the spring and made a well of clear gray water, where I could dip up a pailful without roiling it, and thither I went for this purpose almost every day in mid-summer, when the pond was warmest. Thither too the woodcock led her brood, to probe the mud for worms, flying but a foot above them down the bank, while they ran in a troop beneath; but at last, spying me, she would leave her young and circle round and round me, nearer and nearer till within four or five feet, pretending broken wings and legs, to attract my attention, and get off her young, who would already have taken up their march, with faint wiry peep, single file through the swamp, as she directed. Or I heard the peep of the young when I could not see the parent bird. There too the turtle-doves sat over the spring, or fluttered from bough to bough of the soft white pines over my head; or the red squirrel, coursing down the nearest bough, was particularly familiar and inquisitive. You only need sit still long enough in some attractive spot in the woods that all its inhabitants may exhibit themselves to you by turns.

I was witness to events of a less peaceful character. One day when I went out to my wood pile, or rather my pile of stumps, I observed two large ants, the one red, the other much larger, nearly half an inch long, and black, fiercely contending with one another. Having once got hold they never let go, but struggled and wrestled and rolled on the chips incessantly. Looking farther, I was

---

12. A *divining rod* is a forked stick believed to indicate the presence of underground minerals or water.
13. *Sward* means a "grassy piece of land."

Kinship with Nature *How would you compare this suggestion with Thoreau's comments in the chapter "Where I Lived and What I Lived For"?* **2**

Reading Practice

SPIRAL REVIEW **Vary Reading Rate** Discuss the different ways students can approach reading the excerpt from "Brute Neighbors." (a) *Skimming* is for previewing and reviewing. (b) *Scanning* is for finding specific facts or topics. (c) *In-depth reading* gives thorough knowledge of material. Before students begin reading, ask them to skim the selection by reading the first sentence of each paragraph and looking quickly through the paragraphs.

After they skim the selection to get a general idea of the content, ask students to write down the main idea of this excerpt. Then have them scan the text to locate specific passages or ideas that support their conclusion. Finally, have them read the excerpt carefully and confirm their assumptions.

surprised to find that the chips were covered with such combatants, that it was not a *duellum*, but a *bellum*, a war between two races of ants, the red always pitted against the black, and frequently two red ones to one black. The legions of these Myrmidons[14] covered all the hills and vales in my wood-yard, and the ground was already strewn with the dead and dying, both red and black. It was the only battle which I have ever witnessed, the only battlefield I ever trod while the battle was raging; internecine[15] war; the red republicans on the one hand, and the black imperialists on the other. On every side they were engaged in deadly combat, yet without any noise that I could hear, and human soldiers never fought so resolutely. I watched a couple that were fast locked in each other's embraces, in a little sunny valley amid the chips, now at noonday prepared to fight till the sun went down, or life went out. The smaller red champion had fastened himself like a vice to his adversary's front, and through all the tumblings on that field never for an instant ceased to gnaw at one of his feelers near the root, having already caused the other to go by the board; while the stronger black one dashed him from side to side, and, as I saw on looking nearer, had already divested him of several of his members. They fought with more pertinacity than bulldogs. Neither manifested the least disposition to retreat. It was evident that their battle-cry was Conquer or die. In the meanwhile there came along a single red ant on the hillside of this valley, evidently full of excitement, who either had despatched his foe, or had not yet taken part in the battle; probably the latter, for he had lost none of his limbs; whose mother had charged him to return with his shield or upon it. Or perchance he was some Achilles,[16] who had nourished his wrath apart, and had now come to

avenge or rescue his Patroclus.[17] He saw this unequal combat from afar—for the blacks were nearly twice the size of the red—he drew near with rapid pace till he stood on his guard within half an inch of the combatants; then, watching his opportunity, he sprang upon the black warrior, and commenced his operations near the root of his right foreleg, leaving the foe to select among his own members; and so there were three united for life, as if a new kind of attraction had been invented which put all other locks and cements to shame. I should not have wondered by this time to find that they had their respective musical bands stationed on some eminent chip, and playing their national airs the while, to excite the slow and cheer the dying combatants. I was myself excited somewhat even as if they had been men. The more you think of it, the less the difference. And certainly there is not the fight recorded in Concord history, at least, if in the history of America, that will bear a moment's comparison with this, whether for the numbers engaged in it, or for the patriotism and heroism displayed. For numbers and for carnage it was an Austerlitz or Dresden.[18] Concord Fight! Two killed on the patriots' side, and Luther Blanchard wounded! Why here every ant was a Buttrick—"Fire! for God's sake fire!"—and thousands shared the fate of Davis and Hosmer.[19] There was not one hireling there. I have no doubt that it was a principle they fought for, as much as our ancestors, and not to avoid a three-penny tax on their tea;[20] and the

---

17. *Patroclus* was Achilles' cousin and constant companion.
18. *Austerlitz* refers to the Battle of Austerlitz, one of Napoleon's greatest victories. *Dresden* refers to the Battle of Dresden, Napoleon's last big victory over Germany. *Concord* refers to the Battle of Concord, April 19, 1775, one of the opening battles of the Revolutionary War.
19. *Luther Blanchard* was a fifer who was killed at the Battle of Concord. *Buttrick* refers to Major John Buttrick, an American commander at Concord. *Davis* and *Hosmer* refer to Captain Isaac Davis and Abner Hosmer, two American soldiers who died at the Battle of Concord.
20. *Three-penny tax on their tea* refers to the tea tax portion of the Townshend Acts, designed by the English Parliament to collect revenue from the American colonies.

Metaphor *How effective is this extended metaphor comparing the battling ants to human warfare?* **3**

---

14. The *Myrmidons* were a legendary group of Thessalians who followed their king, Achilles, in the Trojan War. In modern English, *Myrmidon* can refer to any devoted, unquestioning follower.
15. *Internecine* means "deadly" or "marked by destruction."
16. In Greek mythology, *Achilles* was king of the Myrmidons. A handsome warrior reknowned for his bravery and greatness, he died in battle during the Trojan War.

Teach

Metaphor Answer: *Students may suggest that the comparison adds drama and connects the events of nature more closely with those of people. Others may argue that the comparisons become ridiculous.*

[APPROACHING] Explain to approaching level students that personification is a type of metaphor in which human characteristics are given to nonhuman things. **Ask:** How does Thoreau personify the ants? *(He names the different groups of ants and describes the ant's mother sending him off to war.)*

English Learners

DIFFERENTIATED INSTRUCTION

Beginning The use of subordinate clauses may be confusing to English language learners. Explain that compound and complex sentences can often be rewritten as groups of shorter sentences. Write the following example on the board: "On every side they were engaged in deadly combat, yet without any noise that I could hear, and human soldiers never fought so resolutely." Students can simplify these sentences as

follows: "On every side they were engaged in deadly combat. I could not hear them making any noise. Human soldiers never fought so resolutely." Have students work with a partner to rewrite sentences from the selection.

Advanced Learners

DIFFERENTIATED INSTRUCTION

Creative Writing Ask advanced students to imitate Thoreau's ant metaphor and write an essay comparing people to some element in nature. Students should use figurative language and descriptive details.

Teach

Literary Element 1

Tone **Ask:** What is the tone of the last paragraph on this page? How does the tone shift from that of the previous paragraph? *(The tone of the last paragraph is lofty, and forcefully optimistic, as opposed to the previous paragraph, which is more reflective and personal.)*

Literary Element 2

Metaphor **Answer:** *Thoreau is continuing his argument for living life to its fullest. Most students will say that the metaphor is effective because it includes a powerful image—that of being on deck and seeing one's surroundings versus being in a dark room below deck.*

Reading Strategy 3

Connect **Answer:** *Students should suggest concrete ways in which they might make their dreams or plans come to fruition.*

> To check students' understanding of the selection, see Unit 2 Teaching Resources Book, p. 81.

---

results of this battle will be as important and memorable to those whom it concerns as those of the battle of Bunker Hill,[21] at least.

I took up the chip on which the three I have particularly described were struggling, carried it into my house, and placed it under a tumbler on my window sill, in order to see the issue. Holding a microscope to the first-mentioned red ant, I saw that, though he was assiduously gnawing at the near foreleg of his enemy, having severed his remaining feeler, his own breast was all torn away, exposing what vitals he had there to the jaws of the black warrior, whose breastplate was apparently too thick for him to pierce; and the dark carbuncles[22] of the sufferer's eyes shone with ferocity such as war only could excite. They struggled half an hour longer under the tumbler, and when I looked again the black soldier had severed the heads of his foes from their bodies, and the still living heads were hanging on either side of him like ghastly trophies at his saddle-bow, still apparently as firmly fastened as ever, and he was endeavoring with feeble struggles, being without feelers and with only the remnant of a leg, and I know not how many other wounds, to divest himself of them; which at length, after half an hour more, he accomplished. I raised the glass, and he went off over the window sill in that crippled state. Whether he finally survived that combat, and spent the remainder of his days in some Hôtel des Invalides,[23] I do not know; but I thought that his industry would not be worth much thereafter. I never learned which party was victorious, nor the cause of the war; but I felt for the rest of that day as if I had had my feelings excited and harrowed by witnessing the struggle, the ferocity and carnage, of a human battle before my door.

---

21. *Bunker Hill* was the first major battle of the American Revolutionary War. It was fought in Charlestown (now Boston, Massachusetts) on June 17, 1775.
22. Here, *carbuncle* means a type of red precious stone.
23. The *Hôtel des Invalides* is a famous complex in Paris, France. Louis XIV founded the hospital to accommodate 7,000 elderly or injured veterans. Today, it houses several museums and a church.

from **Conclusion**

. . . I left the woods for as good a reason as I went there. Perhaps it seemed to me that I had several more lives to live, and could not spare any more time for that one. It is remarkable how easily and insensibly we fall into a particular route, and make a beaten track for ourselves. I had not lived there a week before my feet wore a path from my door to the pond-side; and though it is five or six years since I trod it, it is still quite distinct. It is true, I fear that others may have fallen into it, and so helped to keep it open. The surface of the earth is soft and impressible by the feet of men; and so with the paths which the mind travels. How worn and dusty, then, must be the highways of the world, how deep the ruts of tradition and conformity! I did not wish to take a cabin passage,[24] but rather to go before the mast and on the deck of the world, for there I could best see the moonlight amid the mountains. I do not wish to go below now.

I learned this, at least, by my experiment; that if one advances confidently in the direction of his dreams, and endeavors to live the life which he has imagined, he will meet with a success unexpected in common hours. He will put some things behind, will pass an invisible boundary; new, universal, and more liberal laws will begin to establish themselves around and within him; or the old laws be expanded, and interpreted in his favor in a more liberal sense, and he will live with the license of a higher order of beings. In proportion as he simplifies his life, the laws of the universe will appear less complex, and solitude will not be solitude, nor poverty poverty, nor weakness weakness. If you have built castles in the air, your work need not be lost; that is where they should be. Now put the foundations under them. . . . ❧

---

24. A person who took a *cabin passage* on a sailing ship would travel in a private compartment, sheltered from the weather.

Metaphor *Why might Thoreau have chosen to use this metaphor?* **2**

Connect *How might you apply Thoreau's advice in your own life?* **3**

Writing Practice

 SPIRAL REVIEW Summarize Have students write a paragraph summarizing one excerpt from *Walden* other than the "Conclusion" excerpt to help fill in confusing details about the selection. Tell students that after they read the excerpt from "Conclusion," they will be asked to relate the main ideas of the essay in their own words. Suggest that they take notes as they read to remember key points such as *who, what, when, where, how,* and *why.* Ask volunteers to read their summaries to the class.

218

After You Read

Respond and Think Critically

Respond and Interpret

1. With which of Thoreau's ideas do you strongly agree? With which ideas do you strongly disagree?

2. (a)What did Thoreau hope to do at Walden? (b)How could being at Walden help him achieve his goal?

3. (a) What are Thoreau's views of the news and the mail? (b)What do these views tell you about his values?

4. (a)Summarize the battle between the ants that Thoreau describes. (b)Why do you think he becomes so fascinated with this battle?

Analyze and Evaluate

5. (a)How does Thoreau characterize the animals he observes? (b)Do you agree with his observations?

6. (a)Why does Thoreau insist that people need to simplify their lives? (b)Is he a credible speaker on this topic? Explain.

7. (a)What is Thoreau's central message in *Walden*? (b)Does Thoreau's decision to leave Walden affect your evaluation of his message?

Connect

8. **Big Idea** **Kinship with Nature** (a)What does Thoreau learn at Walden? (b)What role does nature play in what he learns?

9. **Connect to the Author** Do you think it would be possible to live a happy, successful life by following Thoreau's philosophy? Explain.

Literary Element Metaphor

Thoreau frequently uses **metaphor** and other types of figurative language to help convey his ideas. For example, the metaphor "Time is but the stream I go a-fishing in" (p. 215) compares time to a stream, suggesting that one moment follows another in an uninterrupted flow. Sometimes, Thoreau develops a metaphor throughout an entire paragraph—a technique called **extended metaphor**.

1. Why does Thoreau say he goes "a-fishing" in time?

2. Give an example of another metaphor from the reading.

Reading Strategy Connect

Connect to Personal Experience What are some of the things that surround us in the United States today about which Thoreau might cry, "Simplify, simplify"?

Vocabulary Practice

Context Clues In the following sentences, identify context clues to the meaning of each boldfaced vocabulary word.

1. Trying not to jostle the ants, Thoreau very **deliberately** lifted the chip they were on.

2. Realizing his guilt, the man bowed his head and listened with **resignation** to the verdict.

3. Mozart's music seems **sublime**, as if created by a higher power.

4. He thought it was a story, but it was merely the **rudiments** of a character sketch.

5. Thoreau must have had **myriad** reflections on nature before completing *Walden*.

HENRY DAVID THOREAU **219**

Assess

1. Students should state Thoreau's ideas and provide support.

2. (a) To discover the essence of life (b) It offered a place for a simple life, time for reflection.

3. (a) He disdains news and mail, viewing them as unimportant. (b) He values deeper knowledge.

4. (a) A large black ant defeats two smaller red ants after a long struggle. (b) He is amazed at their intensity and ferocity.

5. (a) Self-reliant and brave (b) Students should give support.

6. (a) People are immersed in meaningless activities. (b) Yes, he simplified his own life.

7. (a) Simplify life; follow dreams with confidence. (b) Students may say that Thoreau decided to follow his own dreams.

8. (a) The practical and the philosophical essentials of life (b) Being close to nature expanded his awareness and taught him "the essential facts of life."

9. Students may say that the text is insightful, but hard to follow.

Vocabulary

1. The contrast of "jostle" to "deliberately" helps identify the meaning of the word as "in a careful, thoughtful way."

2. It can be inferred that "resignation" means "submission or acceptance."

3. The phrase "higher power" suggests "of great spiritual value."

4. The contrast of "story" to "character sketch" defines "rudiments" as "undeveloped parts."

5. The plural of the word "reflections" indicates that "myriad" is also plural.

Reading Strategy

Students may say that Thoreau would decry the use of cell phones and other electronic devices that complicate our lives.

Progress Check

Can students analyze a metaphor?

If No → See Unit 2 Teaching Resources Book, p. 76.

219

Focus

Bellringer Options

Literature Launchers:
    Pre-Reading Videos DVD,
    Selection Launcher
Daily Language Practice
    Transparency 24

Or tell students that the power of individualism has motivated people to seek reform in their governments. **Ask:** What do you know about social protest? How can individuals protest peacefully?

Compare Literature About Protesting Injustice

Allow students to share their responses to the opening question. Then have students discuss what they already know about the authors Henry David Thoreau, Mohandas Gandhi, and Nelson Mandela.

Comparing Literature

Across Time and Place

Learning Objectives

For pages 220–236
In studying these texts, you will focus on the following objectives:

Literary Studies:
Comparing cultural context. Comparing themes. Analyzing argument.

Compare Literature About Protesting Injustice

How far would you go to carry out your principles? The writers compared here—Henry David Thoreau, Mohandas K. Gandhi, and Nelson Mandela—spoke out against the oppression they witnessed during their lifetimes.

from *Civil Disobedience*

by Henry David Thoreau..essay 222

On the Eve of Historic Dandi March

by Mohandas K. Gandhi.. speech 229
INDIA, 1930

from *Long Walk to Freedom*

by Nelson Mandela .... autobiography 231
SOUTH AFRICA, 1994

COMPARE THE `Big Idea` **Optimism and Individualism**

Some of the major American Romantic writers celebrated the spirit of individualism and optimism. Thoreau, for instance, believed that ordinary citizens can better themselves, their political system, and their society. Gandhi and Mandela, reformers from other cultures and eras, shared Thoreau's belief in the power of the individual to bring about change peacefully. As you read, ask yourself, What passages convey the power of the individual as a catalyst for social reform?

COMPARE Persuasive Messages

Thoreau, Gandhi, and Mandela tried to sway audiences to adopt their views or to take action. Each of these leaders used persuasive appeals to convey his message with clarity and force. As you read, ask yourself, What arguments do these writers make to influence the audience?

COMPARE Cultures

Thoreau, Gandhi, and Mandela belonged to different cultures and fought injustices that were unique to their surroundings. Social and historical circumstances presented each of them with distinct challenges. In meeting those challenges, they left their mark on their particular cultures—and changed the course of history. As you read, ask yourself, What social and historical forces helped shape each writer's message?

South Africa, 1994

220 UNIT 2 AMERICAN ROMANTICISM

Selection Skills

Literary Elements
 ▪ Argument (SE pp. 221, 222, 228)
 ▪ Description (TE p. 232)

Reading Skills
 ▪ Evaluate (SE pp. 221, 223, 228)
 ▪ Preview (TE p. 222)
 ▪ Compare (TE p. 230)

Comparing Literature

Vocabulary Skills
 ▪ Antonyms (SE p. 228)
 ▪ Connotation (TE p. 221)
 ▪ Context Clues (TE p. 222)
 ▪ Negative Prefixes (TE p. 226)
 ▪ Multiple Meanings (TE p. 226)

Writing Skills/Grammar
 ▪ Summary (SE p. 228)
 ▪ Quickwrite (SE p. 230, 235)
 ▪ Essay (SE p. 236)
 ▪ Transitions (TE p. 224)

Listening/Speaking/ Viewing Skills
 ▪ Analyze Art (SE p. 225)
 ▪ Use Transitions (TE p. 233)

Before You Read

Civil Disobedience

Connect to the Essay

What risks would you be willing to take to stand up for something you believe in? Discuss this question with a partner or a small group of classmates.

Build Background

As a protest against slavery and the U.S. war with Mexico, Thoreau refused to pay a poll tax—and was arrested. In "Civil Disobedience," he reflects on the night he spent in jail and criticizes the government for straying from its true purpose—to serve the people.

Set Purposes for Reading

Big Idea Optimism and Individualism

Thoreau's outlook reflected the Romantic spirit of optimism and individualism—the belief that ordinary citizens could better themselves, their political system, and their society. As you read, ask yourself, How does Thoreau feel about putting limitations on personal freedom?

Literary Element Argument

An **argument** is a form of persuasion that uses logic, reasons, and evidence. In "Civil Disobedience," Thoreau argues for limiting the power of government. As you read, ask yourself, How does Thoreau develop his argument?

Reading Strategy Evaluate Evidence

One way of evaluating the **evidence** presented in an argument is to distinguish between facts and opinions. Facts are statements that can be proved true, while opinions are statements that are based on personal beliefs. As you read, ask yourself, Do the facts seem relevant, reliable, and accurate? Do the opinions seem based on facts and thoughtful observations?

Vocabulary

din (din) *n.* loud, continuous noise; p. 222 *The din of the children kept me from concentrating.*

alacrity (ə lak´ rə tē) *n.* speed; swiftness; p. 222 *She plays the fiddle with great alacrity.*

expedient (ek spē´ dē ənt) *adj.* convenient or efficient for a certain purpose; p. 223 *During Thoreau's era, the railroad was the most expedient means of traveling from Boston to New York.*

blunder (blun´ dər) *n.* a serious error or mistake; p. 224 *The police officer's blunder allowed the criminal to escape through the back door.*

sanction (sangk´ shən) *n.* approval or support; p. 227 *The troops awaited sanction from their commanding officer before continuing their mission.*

HENRY DAVID THOREAU **221**

English Learners

DIFFERENTIATED INSTRUCTION

 SMALL GROUP

Beginning Have students create an outline of the main ideas in Thoreau's essay as they read. Have them work with a partner to identify and state the main idea of each paragraph. Their outlines should include the major claim (thesis) and supporting evidence.

Intermediate Have students read the first paragraph. **Ask:** What is Thoreau's major claim? *(The government's power should be limited.)* What evidence does he give to support this claim? *(He uses the Mexican War as an example of the power of the few.)*

Before You Read

Focus

Summary

Thoreau's night in jail confirms his belief that the government can control people's bodies, but not their minds or souls. He argues that the government's actions diverge from the will of the people. Though imprisoned, Thoreau feels freer than those outside because he follows his own conscience rather than the law.

> For summaries in languages other than English, see Unit 2 Teaching Resources Book, pp. 84–89.

Vocabulary

Connotation Explain that connotation refers to the meaning or emotions associated with a word. For example, the words *mature* and *old* may refer to an elderly person; however, *mature* has a positive connotation where *old* is more negative. **Ask:** Which words in this vocabulary list have a more negative connotation? *(din, blunder)* Which words in this vocabulary list have a more positive connotation? *(alacrity, expedient, sanction)*

 For additional context, see Glencoe Interactive Vocabulary CD-ROM.

Comparing Literature

Teach

Literary Element | 1

Argument **Answer:** *Thoreau presents evidence to support his argument, saying a few people seized the power of the entire government in waging the Mexican War.*

Vocabulary | 2

Context Clues **Say:** Describe how "complicated machinery" helps you to understand the meaning of *din*. (The context suggests the sound of loud, metal-on-metal grinding.)

> **Interactive Read and Write**
>
> Other options for teaching this selection can be found in
>
> - Interactive Read and Write for EL Students, pp. 45–78
> - Interactive Read and Write for Approaching-Level Students, pp. 45–78
> - Interactive Read and Write for On-Level Students, pp. 45–78

For an audio recording of this selection, use Listening Library Audio CD-ROM.

Readability Scores

Dale-Chall: 7.7
DRP: 63
Lexile: 1110

from
Civil Disobedience

Henry David Thoreau

I heartily accept the motto, "That government is best which governs least"; and I should like to see it acted up to more rapidly and systematically. Carried out, it finally amounts to this, which also I believe—"That government is best which governs not at all"; and when men are prepared for it, that will be the kind of government which they will have. Government is at best but an expedient;[1] but most governments are usually, and all governments are sometimes, inexpedient. The objections which have been brought against a standing army, and they are many and weighty, and deserve to prevail, may also at last be brought against a standing government. The standing army is only an arm of the standing government. The government itself, which is only the mode which the people have chosen to execute their will, is equally liable to be abused and perverted before the people can act through it. Witness the present Mexican war, the work of comparatively a few individuals using the standing government as their tool;

for, in the outset, the people would not have consented to this measure.

This American government—what is it but a tradition, though a recent one, endeavoring to transmit itself unimpaired to posterity,[2] but each instant losing some of its integrity? It has not the vitality and force of a single living man; for a single man can bend it to his will. It is a sort of wooden gun to the people themselves. But it is not the less necessary for this; for the people must have some complicated machinery or other, and hear its **din,** to satisfy that idea of government which they have. Governments show thus how successfully men can be imposed on, even impose on themselves, for their own advantage. It is excellent, we must all allow. Yet this government never of itself furthered any enterprise, but by the **alacrity** with which it got out of its way. *It* does not keep the country free. *It* does not settle the

---

1. *Expedient* means "something employed to bring about a desired result; a means to an end."

1 **Argument** *How does Thoreau support his argument?*

---

2. *Posterity* means "future generations."

> **Vocabulary**
>
> **din** (din) *n.* loud, continuous noise
> **alacrity** (ə lak′ rə tē) *n.* speed; swiftness

Reading Practice

SPIRAL REVIEW **Preview** Point out to students that they can anticipate the tone and content of Thoreau's essay by looking over the art, displayed quotations, highlighted passages, and bottom-of-the-page questions before reading. Have students create a chart with things they know about Thoreau, things they anticipate will be in his essay, and things they would like to know. Then have them use the information in their chart to set a purpose for their reading.

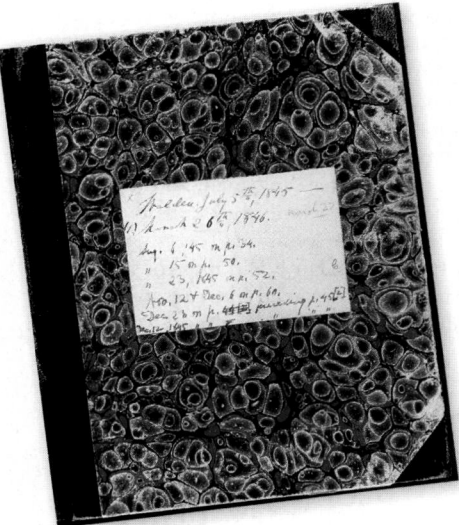

One of the notebooks in which Thoreau kept his journal

 West. *It* does not educate. The character inherent in the American people has done all that has been accomplished; and it would have done somewhat more, if the government had not sometimes got in its way. For government is an expedient by which men would fain[3] succeed in letting one another alone; and, as has been said, when it is most **expedient,** the governed are most let alone by it. Trade and commerce, if they were not made of india-rubber, would never manage to bounce over the obstacles which legislators are continually putting in their way; and if one were to judge these men wholly by the effects of their actions and not partly by their intentions, they would deserve to be

---

3. *Fain* means "gladly" or "willingly."

Vocabulary

expedient (ek spē′ dē ənt) *adj.* convenient or efficient for a certain purpose

---

classed and punished with those mischievous persons who put obstructions on the railroads.

But, to speak practically and as a citizen, unlike those who call themselves no-government men, I ask for, not at once no government, but *at once* a better government. Let every man make known what kind of government would command his respect, and that will be one step toward obtaining it.

After all, the practical reason why, when the power is once in the hands of the people, a majority are permitted, and for a long period continue, to rule is not because they are most likely to be in the right, nor because this seems fairest to the minority, but because they are physically the strongest. But a government in which the majority rule in all cases cannot be based on justice, even as far as men understand it. Can there not be a government in which majorities do not virtually decide right and wrong, but conscience?—in which majorities decide only those questions to which the rule of expediency is applicable? Must the citizen ever for a moment, or in the least degree, resign his conscience to the legislator? Why has every man a conscience, then? I think that we should be men first, and subjects afterward. It is not desirable to cultivate a respect for the law, so much as for the right. The only obligation which I have a right to assume is to do at any time what I think right. It is truly enough said that a corporation has no conscience; but a corporation of conscientious men is a corporation *with* a conscience. Law never made men a whit[4] more just; and, by means of their respect for it, even the well-disposed are daily made the agents of injustice. . . .

Some years ago, the State met me in behalf of the Church, and commanded me to pay a

---

4. *Whit* means "a tiny amount" or "a bit."

Evaluate Evidence *Is Thoreau's opinion of majority rule fair or unfair? Explain.*

HENRY DAVID THOREAU **223**

Comparing Literature

Teach

| **Reading Strategy** | **3** |

Evaluate Evidence Answer:
Thoreau makes a distinction between ruling by conscience and ruling by force. He aslo states that majority rule is unfair "in all cases."
Ask: What does Thoreau suggest is the first step toward making sure government acts with a conscience? *(Each and every person should "make known what kind of government would command his respect, and that will be one step toward obtaining it.")*

📁 **For additional practice using the reading skill or strategy, see Unit 2 Teaching Resources Book, p. 91.**

Political History ☆

Manifest Destiny America went to war with Mexico partly because of an idea called Manifest Destiny. American political leaders in the 1840s believed that it was America's destiny to expand from the east coast to the west coast. In order to achieve this goal, America went to war with Mexico to gain the territory that now includes Texas, New Mexico, Arizona, and California.

Approaching Level

DIFFERENTIATED INSTRUCTION 🔁

Emerging Students' comprehension may improve if they read, summarize, and predict. Have students read the last paragraph on page 223 and the first full paragraph on page 224. Ask them to summarize Thoreau's argument. Next have them list facts and opinions that are given as evidence. Then ask them to predict how Thoreau will get out of jail.

Established Point out the ellipsis points at the end of the last full paragraph on this page. Explain that this punctuation indicates that part of Thoreau's essay has been omitted. **Ask:** What might this indicate about the subject of the next paragraph? *(A new thought is coming.)* What are the main ideas of the paragraphs before and after the ellipsis?

(The paragraph before is about the unfairness of majority rule and the idea that people should rule by their consciences. The paragraph after the ellipsis is about an unfair tax that Thoreau refused to pay.)

Comparing Literature

Teach

Big Idea   1

Optimism and Individualism

Answer: *Though imprisoned, Thoreau feels freer than those outside the jail because he follows his own conscience rather than the law. He believes his mind is free—and therefore can go places that his fellow villagers' minds cannot—though his body is in jail.*

(APPROACHING) **Ask:** What does Thoreau think about the government that has imprisoned him? *(He believes the government wants to change his attitudes and ideas, but since it is unable to change him, it attacks his physical body instead. He only pities the government rather than respecting it.)*

---

certain sum toward the support of a clergyman whose preaching my father attended, but never I myself. "Pay," it said, "or be locked up in the jail." I declined to pay. But, unfortunately, another man saw fit to pay it. I did not see why the schoolmaster should be taxed to support the priest, and not the priest the schoolmaster; for I was not the State's schoolmaster, but I supported myself by voluntary subscription. I did not see why the lyceum[5] should not present its tax-bill, and have the State to back its demand, as well as the Church. However, at the request of the selectmen,[6] I condescended to make some such statement as this in writing: "Know all men by these presents, that I, Henry Thoreau, do not wish to be regarded as a member of any incorporated society which I have not joined." This I gave to the town clerk; and he has it. The State, having thus learned that I did not wish to be regarded as a member of that church, has never made a like demand on me since; though it said that it must adhere to its original presumption that time. If I had known how to name them, I should then have signed off in detail from all the societies which I never signed on to; but I did not know where to find a complete list.

I have paid no poll-tax[7] for six years. I was put into a jail once on this account, for one night; and, as I stood considering the walls of solid stone, two or three feet thick, the door of wood and iron, a foot thick, and the iron grating which strained the light, I could not help being struck with the foolishness of that institution which treated me as if I were mere flesh and blood and bones, to be locked up. I wondered that it should have concluded at length that this was the best use it

---

5. A *lyceum* is an organization that sponsors educational programs, such as concerts and lectures.
6. *Selectmen* refers to a group of elected local officials.
7. A *poll tax*, now illegal, was a tax on people (not property). Payment was often required in order to vote.

could put me to, and had never thought to avail itself of my services in some way. I saw that, if there was a wall of stone between me and my townsmen, there was a still more difficult one to climb or break through, before they could get to be as free as I was. I did not for a moment feel confined, and the walls seemed a great waste of stone and mortar. I felt as if I alone of all my townsmen had paid my tax. They plainly did not know how to treat me, but behaved like persons who are underbred. In every threat and in every compliment there was a **blunder;** for they

> ## They only can force me who obey a higher law than I.

thought that my chief desire was to stand the other side of that stone wall. I could not but smile to see how industriously they locked the door on my meditations, which followed them out again without let[8] or hindrance, and *they* were really all that was dangerous. As they could not reach me, they had resolved to punish my body; just as boys, if they cannot come at some person against whom they have a spite, will abuse his dog. I saw that the State was half-witted, that it was timid as a lone woman with her silver spoons, and that it did not know its friends from its foes, and I lost all my remaining respect for it, and pitied it.

Thus the State never intentionally confronts a man's sense, intellectual or moral,

---

8. Here, *let* means "an obstruction" or "an obstacle."

Optimism and Individualism *Why does Thoreau believe he is freer than his "townsmen"?*   **1**

Vocabulary

blunder (blun´ dər) *n.* a serious error or mistake

Writing Practice

SPIRAL REVIEW **Transitions** Remind students to use transitions to make clear connections between the ideas in their writing. Point out that transitions show various relationships:

- movement in time *(before, during, first, second, soon, then, next, later)*
- location in space *(beyond, farther, in front of, between, near, under)*
- similarities and differences *(also, in the same way, but, however)*

- emphasis *(in fact, especially, above all)*

Have students supply a transitional word in the following sentences:

1. Jail can be a harsh place; _____ Thoreau found it a good place to reflect. *(however)*
2. _____ his time in jail, Thoreau felt freer than the other people in his community. *(During)*

Have students write a paragraph about their schedule for the rest of the day using an example of each type of transition listed above.

Teach

Stump Speaking, 1853–54, George Caleb Bingham. Oil on canvas, 108 x 147 cm. Private collection.

View the Art George Caleb Bingham not only painted political scenes; he was also a politician. In this scene, what does he suggest about the relationship between citizens and government in Thoreau's era?

but only his body, his senses. It is not armed with superior wit or honesty, but with superior physical strength. I was not born to be forced. I will breathe after my own fashion. Let us see who is the strongest. What force has a multitude? They only can force me who obey a higher law than I. They force me to become like themselves. I do not hear of *men* being *forced* to live this way or that by masses of men. What sort of life were that to live? When I meet a government which says to me, "Your money or your life," why should I be in haste to give it my money? It may be

in a great strait, and not know what to do: I cannot help that. It must help itself; do as I do. It is not worth the while to snivel about it. I am not responsible for the successful working of the machinery of society. I am not the son of the engineer. I perceive that, when an acorn and a chestnut fall side by side, the one does not remain inert to make way for the other, but both obey their own laws, and spring and grow and flourish as best they can, till one, perchance, overshadows and destroys the other. If a plant cannot live according to its nature, it dies; and so a man.

HENRY DAVID THOREAU **225**

Literary Element 2

Argument Ask: Why might Thoreau go into so much detail about how he spent his time in jail? *(to show that his punishment had little effect)*

View the Art ★

Answer: *Bingham presents a spirited political scene in which ordinary people are participating. In his essay, Thoreau says that political decisions are made without the input of ordinary people.*

Ask: How does the image contrast with political speeches of today? *(Bingham's painting shows a close connection between the public and the politician; the public has direct access to speak to the politician on the stage. Modern security needs make this unworkable in many situations.)*

English Learners

DIFFERENTIATED INSTRUCTION

Intermediate After students have read to the end of the first full paragraph on page 226, have them create a four-column chart for notetaking about the theme, supporting evidence, setting, and people. Prompt ideas by asking questions and having students take notes during the discussion. **Ask:** What is the theme of Thoreau's essay so far? *(Thoreau believes the power of the government should be more* limited.*)* What evidence does Thoreau give to support this theme? *(Thoreau discusses the Mexican war, the power of the minority, an unfair church tax, not paying a poll tax, and a night in jail.)* What setting has Thoreau described? *(Thoreau describes his jail cell.)* What people has Thoreau discussed? *(Thoreau mentions himself, the government, the American people, a clergyman, the jailer, and his* cellmate.*)* What do you predict might happen? *(Thoreau will get out of jail and continue not paying his poll tax.)*

Comparing Literature

Teach

Vocabulary | 1

Multiple Meanings Students may recognize a different usage of the word *sanction* than the way Thoreau uses it in the essay. Today, *sanction* often refers to "an economic or militarily coercive measure adopted by several nations to deter another nation from violating international law."

(**ENGLISH LEARNERS**) Have students read the sentence in which sanction appears. **Ask:** What context clue helps you understand the meaning of the word *sanction*? (*The word "consent" gives a synonym for* sanction.)

The night in prison was novel and interesting enough. The prisoners in their shirtsleeves were enjoying a chat and the evening air in the doorway, when I entered. But the jailer said, "Come, boys, it is time to lock up"; and so they dispersed, and I heard the sound of their steps returning into the hollow apartments. My room-mate was introduced to me by the jailer as "a first-rate fellow and a clever man." When the door was locked, he showed me where to hang my hat, and how he managed matters there. The rooms were whitewashed once a month; and this one, at least, was the whitest, most simply furnished, and probably the neatest apartment in

> **I saw yet more distinctly the State in which I lived.**

the town. He naturally wanted to know where I came from, and what brought me there; and, when I had told him, I asked him in my turn how he came there, presuming him to be an honest man, of course; and, as the world goes, I believe he was. "Why," said he, "they accuse me of burning a barn; but I never did it." As near as I could discover, he had probably gone to bed in a barn when drunk, and smoked his pipe there; and so a barn was burnt. He had the reputation of being a clever man, had been there some three months waiting for his trial to come on, and would have to wait as much longer; but he was quite domesticated and contented, since he got his board for nothing, and thought that he was well treated.

He occupied one window, and I the other; and I saw that if one stayed there long, his principal business would be to look out the window. I had soon read all the tracts[9] that were left

there, and examined where former prisoners had broken out, and where a grate had been sawed off, and heard the history of the various occupants of that room; for I found that even here there was a history and a gossip which never circulated beyond the walls of the jail. Probably this is the only house in the town where verses are composed, which are afterward printed in a circular form, but not published. I was shown quite a long list of verses which were composed by some young men who had been detected in an attempt to escape, who avenged themselves by singing them.

I pumped my fellow-prisoner as dry as I could, for fear I should never see him again; but at length he showed me which was my bed, and left me to blow out the lamp. It was like traveling into a far country, such as I had never expected to behold, to lie there for one night. It seemed to me that I never had heard the town clock strike before, nor the evening sounds of the village; for we slept with the windows open, which were inside the grating. It was to see my native village in the light of the Middle Ages, and our Concord was turned into a Rhine[10] stream, and visions of knights and castles passed before me. They were the voices of old burghers[11] that I heard in the streets. I was an involuntary spectator and auditor[12] of whatever was done and said in the kitchen of the adjacent village inn—a wholly new and rare experience to me. It was a closer view of my native town. I was fairly inside of it. I never had seen its institutions before. This is one of its peculiar institutions; for it is a shire town.[13] I began to comprehend what its inhabitants were about.

In the morning, our breakfasts were put through the hole in the door, in small

---

9. *Tracts* are leaflets or pamphlets, especially those on religious or political topics.

10. *Concord* refers to the Concord River. The *Rhine* River flows through Germany and the Netherlands.
11. *Burghers* is a term for inhabitants of a city.
12. Here, *auditor* means "someone who hears," or "a listener."
13. A *shire town*, or county town, is similar to a county seat.

Vocabulary Practice

SPIRAL REVIEW **Negative Prefixes** Point out that negative prefixes such as *un-, im-, in-, il-, dis-, a-,* and *ir-* change base words to antonyms. Examples include *happy/unhappy, legal/illegal,* and *natural/ unnatural.* Have students add a negative prefix to each base word in parentheses.

1. The court order was (typical). (*atypical*)

2. Considering the blunder was his fault, the judge was surprisingly (apologetic). (*unapologetic*)

3. The investigation showed the mayor had been (honest) about his past. (*dishonest*)

Ask students to identify other words on this spread that contain negative prefixes and to explain their meanings. (*involuntary—"not voluntary"; impure—"not pure"; independent—"not dependent"; inconsistent—"not consistent"*) oblong-square tin pans, made to fit, and holding a pint of chocolate, with brown bread, and an iron spoon. When they called for the vessels again, I was green enough to return what bread I had left; but my comrade seized it, and said that I should lay that up for lunch or dinner. Soon after he was let out to work at haying in a neighboring field, whither he went every day, and would not be back till noon; so he bade me good-day, saying that he doubted if he should see me again.

When I came out of prison—for some one interfered, and paid that tax—I did not perceive that great changes had taken place on the common, such as he observed who went in a youth and emerged a tottering and grayheaded man; and yet a change had to my eyes come over the scene—the town, and State, and country—greater than any that mere time could effect. I saw yet more distinctly the State in which I lived. . . .

The authority of government, even such as I am willing to submit to—for I will cheerfully obey those who know and can do better than I, and in many things even those who neither know nor can do so well—is still an impure one: to be strictly just, it must have the **sanction** and consent of the governed. It can have no pure right over my person and property but what I concede to it.

1

The progress from an absolute to a limited monarchy, from a limited monarchy to a democracy, is a progress toward a true respect for the individual. Even the Chinese philosopher[14] was wise enough to regard the individual as the basis of the empire. Is a democracy, such as we know it, the last improvement possible in government? Is it not possible to take a step further towards recognizing and organizing the rights of man? There will never be a really free and enlightened State until the State comes to recognize the individual as a higher and independent power, from which all its own power and authority are derived, and treats him accordingly. I please myself with imagining a State at least which can afford to be just to all men, and to treat the individual with respect as a neighbor; which even would not think it inconsistent with its own repose[15] if a few were to live aloof from it, not meddling with it, nor embraced by it, who fulfilled all the duties of neighbors and fellow-men. A State which bore this kind of fruit, and suffered it to drop off as fast as it ripened, would prepare the way for a still more perfect and glorious State, which also I have imagined, but not yet anywhere seen.

---

14. The *Chinese philosopher* is Confucius (c. 551–479 B.C.)
15. Here, *repose* refers to the state's "peace of mind."

Optimism and Individualism *What type of freedom does Thoreau desire?* **2**

Optimism and Individualism
Answer: *Thoreau desires the freedom to follow his own conscience and to live apart from society and its laws. He believes as long as he does no harm to other people, the state should allow him to live as he chooses.*

Literary History

Publishing Background
Thoreau wrote "Civil Disobedience" for a Concord Lyceum lecture he delivered on January 26, 1848. In May 1849, the essay was first published as "Resistance to Civil Government." The title changed in *Yankee in Canada, with Anti-Slavery and Reform Papers,* an 1866 collection of Thoreau's writings. Historians are unsure if Thoreau himself ever actually used the term "civil disobedience."

To check students' understanding of the selection, see Unit 2 Teaching Resources Book, p. 95.

Progress Check

Can students analyze an argument?

If No → See Unit 2 Teaching Resources Book, p. 90.

English Learners

DIFFERENTIATED INSTRUCTION

Intermediate English learners may benefit from help with some of Thoreau's idiomatic expressions. Have pairs of students read pages 226 and 227 to identify words or phrases they find confusing. Have students write down these words or phrases. Give students some examples, such as the word *domesticated* and the phrase "He occupied one window," both in the lefthand column on page 226. Explain that when

Thoreau says his fellow prisoner was "quite domesticated," he means that he seemed calm and at home living in jail. When he says that they each occupied a window, he means they stood at the window and looked out. Have partners work together to find the meanings using the context and a dictionary.

Comparing Literature

Assess

1. He makes logical points about the value of one's conscience.

2. (a) He did not pay his poll tax. (b) His beliefs were powerful.

3. (a) For burning down a barn (b) That his cellmate accidentally caused the fire

4. (a) Enjoys fellow inmates and the chance to reflect (b) He makes the best of an experience.

5. Still idealistic, but more cynical about the prospects for government's becoming truly just

6. Some may say he should not have let someone pay his tax.

7. (a) Answers will vary. (b) Responses should cite Thoreau's use of facts. (c) Arguments against the Mexican War, majority rule, and taxation

8. (a) Dedication, courage, ability to inspire others (b) Dedication

9. Students may say that this fact gives his arguments validity because he clearly adheres to the principles of his essay.

Vocabulary

Possible answers:

alacrity <u>Antonyms</u>: slowness, hesitation; <u>Explanation</u>: A decision made with alacrity comes quickly, while hesitation makes it take a long time.

expedient <u>Antonyms</u>: inefficient, slow, impractical <u>Explanation</u>: Something that is expedient is convenient and efficient, not slow.

sanction <u>Antonyms</u>: disapproval, veto <u>Explanation</u>: I have my parents' sanction to buy a car, but I couldn't buy it if I had their disapproval.

blunder <u>Antonym</u>: correction <u>Explanation</u>: A blunder is an error, and a correction amends the error.

228

After You Read

Respond and Think Critically

Respond and Interpret

1. What was your reaction to Thoreau's opinion on disobeying the government?

2. (a) Why was Thoreau jailed? (b) What does this tell you about Thoreau's beliefs?

3. (a) Why is Thoreau's cellmate in prison? (b) What does Thoreau presume about his cellmate's conviction?

4. (a) How does Thoreau react to his night in jail? (b) What does this say about his personality?

Analyze and Evaluate

5. How does Thoreau's perspective change when he is released from prison?

6. How does the fact that Thoreau spent only one night in jail affect your evaluation of his opinions?

7. (a) How do you evaluate Thoreau's criticism of democracy? (b) Is it accurate; is it fair? (c) Cite evidence from the story to support your opinion.

Connect

8. **Big Idea** Optimism and Individualism (a) What do you think are some essential qualities for an individual who wishes to reform society or the government? (b) Which of these qualities does Thoreau possess?

9. **Connect to the Author** Does Thoreau's spending a night in jail in protest give his arguments in this essay more validity than they would have otherwise? Explain your response.

Literary Element Argument

A valid **argument** relies on logic—clear, well-organized thinking leading to a reasonable conclusion.

Partner Activity Discuss what Thoreau concludes about freedom and the role of government.

Reading Strategy Evaluate Evidence

A successful persuasive essay relies on various kinds of supporting evidence, such as facts and opinions.

1. What kind of evidence does Thoreau rely on more—facts or opinions?

2. Was the evidence presented in the essay strong enough to persuade you to agree with Thoreau's viewpoints? Why or why not?

LOG ON Literature Online

Selection Resources For Selection Quizzes, eFlashcards, and Reading-Writing Connection activities, go to glencoe.com and enter QuickPass code GLA9800u2.

Vocabulary Practice

Practice with Antonyms An antonym is a word that has a meaning opposite to that of another word. With a partner, brainstorm antonyms for each boldfaced vocabulary word below. Then discuss your choices with your classmates. Be prepared to explain why you chose your words.

| alacrity | sanction |
| expedient | blunder |

EXAMPLE: wise

<u>Antonyms</u>: ignorant, foolish, naïve
<u>Explanation</u>: Wise people learn from their experiences, but foolish people make the same mistakes over and over.

Writing

Write a Summary In about 100 words, summarize this excerpt from "Civil Disobedience."

Reading Strategy

1. Thoreau relies more on opinions based on observations and logic.

2. Responses should include students' interpretation of the essay.

Writing

Students' summaries should include only the main ideas of the text, not opinions.

Literary Element

He concludes that the best government would allow the individual freedom if no harm is done to others.

On the Eve of Historic DANDI MARCH

Mohandas K. Gandhi

Build Background

Known as Mahatma, or "Great-Souled," Gandhi opposed British rule in early twentieth-century India using *satyagraha*—"truth persistence"—nonviolent resistance to injustice. Gandhi's "salt march" in 1930 protested the salt monopoly, which required Indians to buy taxed salt from the British government. To demonstrate opposition marchers to the Arabian Sea defied British law by extracting salt from seawater.

In all probability this will be my last speech to you. Even if the Government allow me to march tomorrow morning, this will be my last speech on the sacred banks of the Sabarmati.[1] Possibly these may be the last words of my life here.

I have already told you yesterday what I had to say. Today I shall confine myself to what you should do after my companions and I are arrested. The program[2] of the march to Jalalpur[3] must be fulfilled as originally settled. The enlistment of the volunteers for this purpose should be confined to Gujarat[4] only. From what I have seen and heard during the last fortnight, I am inclined to believe that the stream of civil resisters will flow unbroken.

But let there be not a semblance of breach of peace even after all of us have been arrested. We have resolved to utilize all our resources in the pursuit of an exclusively nonviolent strug-gle. Let no one commit a wrong in anger. This is my hope and prayer. I wish these words of mine reached every nook and corner of the land. My task shall be done if I perish and so do my comrades. It will then be for the Working Committee of the Congress[5] to show you the way and it will be up to you to follow its lead. So long as I have not reached Jalalpur, let nothing be done in contravention to the authority vested in me by the Congress. But once I am arrested, the whole responsibility shifts to the Congress. No one who believes in nonviolence, as a creed, need, therefore, sit still. My compact with the Congress ends as soon as I am arrested. In that case there should be no slackness in the enrolment of volunteers. Wherever possible, civil disobedience of salt laws should be started. These laws can be violated in three ways. It is an offense to manufacture salt wherever there are facilities for doing so. The possession and sale of contraband salt,

---

1. The *Sabarmati* is a river in western India.
2. Here, *program* means "mission."
3. *Jalalpur,* a city in India, was the last stop before Dandi.
4. *Gujarat* is a state in western India.

---

5. By *Congress,* Gandhi is referring to the Indian National Congress, a political party he led in the 1920s and '30s.

MOHANDAS K. GANDHI **229**

Advanced Learners

DIFFERENTIATED INSTRUCTION

Persuasive Writing Students might enhance their exploration by researching Hinduism and the political, social, and cultural forces in India—including the caste system. Next have students write an essay agreeing or disagreeing with Gandhi's statement: "I have faith in the righteousness of our cause and the purity of our weapons. And where the means are clean, there God is undoubtedly present with His blessings. And where these three combine, there defeat is an impossibility." Remind students to use evidence from this speech, from other writings by Gandhi, and from their background research to support their claims. Students may present their essays to the class.

Comparing Literature

Focus

Summary

Gandhi outlines his strategy for challenging the British monopoly on the salt industry as part of his campaign for Indian self-rule. This strategy comprises manufacturing, buying, selling, and transporting homemade salt in defiance of British law. Gandhi impels his listeners to carry on this campaign if British forces arrest him, or worse. He also tells his audience to hold firm to nonviolent protest methods even in the face of physical confrontation.

Political History ☆

Civil Disobedience Gandhi believed in peaceful protest and desired to end the British rule of India. In order to live his beliefs, Gandhi chose to break unfair laws as a nonviolent method of opposing the government. He predicted in the opening of this speech that the Dandi March would end with his arrest or death. Gandhi was arrested just outside of Dandi and, without a trial, was jailed for eight months. In addition to this incident, Gandhi was arrested twelve more times.

 For an audio recording of this selection, use Listening Library Audio CD-ROM.

Readability Scores

Dale-Chall: 6.8
DRP: 59
Lexile: 950

Comparing Literature

Teach

Quickwrite

Student responses should make a connection between self-confidence and nonviolence.

Reading Strategy · 1

Compare Ask: How do Gandhi's ideas about individuality and reform compare to Thoreau's? (*Gandhi suggests that Indians rise up against the ruling British government. Thoreau discusses his desire to live apart from government, while Gandhi proposes a method of engaging and opposing the government.*)

Cultural History ☆

An Epic Speech Gandhi delivered his "salt march" speech to a crowd of 10,000 on the banks of the Sabarmati River. The following morning, Gandhi and 78 followers started the 24-day trek to Dandi. On the morning of April 6, 1930, about 2,000 fellow protestors accompanied Gandhi as he waded into the sea.

---

which includes natural salt or salt earth, is also an offense. The purchasers of such salt will be equally guilty. To carry away the natural salt deposits on the seashore is likewise violation of law. So is the hawking of such salt. In short, you may choose any one or all of these devices to break the salt monopoly.

1 We are, however, not to be content with this alone. There is no ban by the Congress and wherever the local workers have self-confidence other suitable measures may be adopted. I stress only one condition, namely, let our pledge of truth and nonviolence as the only means for the attainment of Swaraj[6] be faithfully kept. For the rest, every one has a free hand. But, that does not give a license to all and sundry to carry on on their own responsibility. Wherever there are local leaders, their orders should be obeyed by the people. Where there are no leaders and only a handful of men have faith in the program, they may do what they can, if they have enough self-confidence. They have a right, nay it is their duty, to do so. The history of the world is full of instances of men who rose to leadership, by sheer force of self-confidence, bravery and tenacity. We too, if we sincerely aspire to Swaraj and are impatient to attain it, should have similar self-confidence. Our ranks will swell and our hearts strengthen, as the number of our arrests by the Government increases.

Much can be done in many other ways besides these. The liquor and foreign cloth shops can be picketed. We can refuse to pay taxes if we have the requisite strength. The lawyers can give up practice. The public can boycott the law courts by refraining from litigation. Government servants can resign their posts. In the midst of the despair reigning all round people quake with fear of losing employment. Such men are unfit for Swaraj. But why this despair? The number of Government servants in the country does not exceed a few hundred thou-

sand. What about the rest? Where are they to go? Even free India will not be able to accommodate a greater number of public servants. A Collector then will not need the number of servants he has got today. He will be his own servant. Our starving millions can by no means afford this enormous expenditure. If, therefore, we are sensible enough, let us bid goodbye to Government employment, no matter if it is the post of a judge or a peon. Let all who are cooperating with the Government in one way or another, be it by paying taxes, keeping titles, or sending children to official schools, etc. withdraw their cooperation in all or as many ways as possible. Then there are women who can stand shoulder to shoulder with men in this struggle.

You may take it as my will. It was the message that I desired to impart to you before starting on the march or for the jail. I wish that there should be no suspension or abandonment of the war that commences tomorrow morning or earlier, if I am arrested before that time. I shall eagerly await the news that ten batches are ready as soon as my batch is arrested. I believe there are men in India to complete the work begun by me. I have faith in the righteousness of our cause and the purity of our weapons. And where the means are clean, there God is undoubtedly present with His blessings. And where these three combine, there defeat is an impossibility. A Satyagrahi,[7] whether free or incarcerated, is ever victorious. He is vanquished only when he forsakes truth and nonviolence and turns a deaf ear to the inner voice. If, therefore, there is such a thing as defeat for even a Satyagrahi, he alone is the cause of it. God bless you all and keep off all obstacles from the path in the struggle that begins tomorrow. ⟋

---

6. *Swaraj* means "home rule." It refers to Indians' desire to rule themselves, rather than be ruled by the British.

7. A *Satyagrahi* embodies Gandhi's ideals of nonviolence.

📝 Quickwrite

Gandhi insists his followers must have self-confidence to succeed. Why is this important when using nonviolence as a tool for social justice?

Reading Practice

Compare and Contrast Point out that a Venn diagram is one way to organize thoughts when asked to compare and contrast selections. Have students make a list of things that they know about Thoreau's cultural background, beliefs, and purpose for writing. After they read this selection, have them do the same for Gandhi, and then fit things that are similar in the overlapping portion of the diagram and things that seem different on the outside.

Thoreau   Gandhi

from
Long Walk to Freedom

Nelson Mandela

Focus

Summary

This excerpt from Nelson Mandela's autobiography begins at the former South African president's inauguration day. He discusses the difficulties of serving both his family as a father and his country as a reformer. The autobiography refers to Mandela's fellow activists and expresses his belief that adversity strengthens the individual. According to Mandela, acts of racism hurt both the oppressor and the oppressed. At the end of this excerpt, Mandela tells the reader that he has a long way to go on his journey to improve his country.

Build Background

From prisoner to president of South Africa, Nelson Mandela was one of the political miracles of the twentieth century. In 1944 he became a leader in the African National Congress (ANC), a political party that opposed apartheid, South Africa's policy of racial segregation. After a massacre of unarmed Africans in 1960, Mandela dropped his nonviolent reform method in favor of supporting acts of sabotage against the government. In 1962 he was jailed and, after a widely publicized trial, was sentenced to life in prison in 1964. Over the years, Mandela became the world's best-known political prisoner, gaining international support in his fight against apartheid.

May 10 dawned bright and clear. For the past few days, I had been pleasantly besieged by arriving dignitaries[1] and world leaders who were coming to pay their respects before the inauguration.[2] The inauguration would be the largest gathering ever of international leaders on South African soil.

The ceremonies took place in the lovely sandstone amphitheater formed by the Union Buildings in Pretoria.[3] For decades, this had been the seat of white supremacy, and now it was the site of a rainbow gathering of different colors and nations for the installation of South Africa's first democratic, nonracial government.

On that lovely autumn day I was accompanied by my daughter Zenani. On the podium, Mr. de Klerk[4] was first sworn in as second deputy president. Then Thabo Mbeki[5] was

---

1. *Dignitaries* are people who hold a rank of dignity, or honor.
2. An *inauguration* is a ceremonial induction into office, or a formal beginning.

3. *Pretoria* is the administrative capital of South Africa.
4. *F. W. de Klerk* served as president of South Africa from 1989 to 1994.
5. *Thabo Mbeki* is a politician who became the president of South Africa in 1999.

NELSON MANDELA **231**

Political History

Establishment of Apartheid

When it took control of the government in the 1940s, the Afrikaner National Party created a system of apartheid to solidify its power. The goal of apartheid was to give power to Caucasian people and to repress other races. The government passed apartheid laws that instituted racial discrimination and segregation as a way of life.

For an audio recording of this selection, use Listening Library Audio CD-ROM.

Readability Scores

Dale-Chall: 6.8
DRP: 59
Lexile: 950

English Learners

DIFFERENTIATED INSTRUCTION

Beginning Compound adjectives such as best-known or dark-skinned are hyphenated to show that they work together to modify the noun that follows. Have students place the hyphen in this sentence: *The long standing bans on voting were repealed.*

Intermediate Have students paraphrase Mandela's inauguration speech.
Ask: What is Mandela referring to when he uses the following terms: *human disaster, human dignity,* and *human achievement*? (*apartheid, the African people, overcoming apartheid*)

Comparing Literature

Teach

Literary Element 1

Description Say: Analyze Mandela's use of description in the paragraph beginning with "A few moments later." To which senses does this passage appeal? *(Fighter jets and generals wearing medals and ribbons appeal to sight; the sound of the jets performing a flyover appeals to hearing.)*

Ask: Why does Mandela find it ironic that the generals are saluting him? *(The same people who are saluting Mandela now would have arrested him a few years earlier.)*

Political History ☆

Apartheid Laws Apartheid became an official government policy in 1948. It was fortified by laws such as the Group Areas Act of 1950 and the Land Acts of 1954 and 1955, which led to white control of more than 80 percent of the nation's land. In 1990 F. W. de Klerk repealed the laws that sustained apartheid.

232

---

sworn in as first deputy president. When it was my turn, I pledged to obey and uphold the constitution and to devote myself to the well-being of the republic and its people. To the assembled guests and the watching world, I said:

Today, all of us do, by our presence here . . . confer[6] glory and hope to newborn liberty. Out of the experience of an extraordinary human disaster that lasted too long, must be born a society of which all humanity will be proud.

. . . We, who were outlaws not so long ago, have today been given the rare privilege to be host to the nations of the world on our own soil. We thank all of our distinguished international guests for having come to take possession with the people of our country of what is, after all, a common victory for justice, for peace, for human dignity.

We have, at last, achieved our political emancipation.[7] We pledge ourselves to liberate all our people from the continuing bondage of poverty, deprivation, suffering, gender, and other discrimination.

Never, never, and never again shall it be that this beautiful land will again experience the oppression of one by another. . . . The sun shall never set on so glorious a human achievement.

Let freedom reign. God bless Africa!

---

6. *Confer* means "to bestow, or give, an honor."
7. *Emancipation* means "the process of becoming free from restraint or control."

232 UNIT 2 AMERICAN ROMANTICISM

A few moments later we all lifted our eyes in awe as a spectacular array of South African jets, helicopters, and troop carriers roared in perfect formation over the Union Buildings. It was not only a display of pinpoint precision and military force, but a demonstration of the

Nelson Mandela visits schoolchildren in South Africa.

military's loyalty to democracy, to a new government that had been freely and fairly elected. Only moments before, the highest generals of the South African Defense Force and police, their chests bedecked[8] with ribbons and medals from days gone by, saluted me and pledged their loyalty. I was not unmindful of the fact that not so many years before they would not have saluted but arrested me. Finally a chevron of Impala jets[9] left a smoke trail of the black, red, green, blue, white, and gold of the new South African flag.

---

8. *Bedecked* means "adorned or clothed."
9. Here, *chevron* is a V-shaped pattern; an *Impala jet* is a military fighter plane.

Reading Practice

Detecting Bias Explain that persuasive messages, such as advertisements, editorials, and political campaigns, appeal heavily to an audience's emotions. A bandwagon appeal attempts to make you think everyone else is doing something. Loaded language is words with strong connotations. Testimonials supply endorsements from experts or celebrities. Polling results offer numbers to show support for a certain viewpoint.

Have students compare Gandhi's speech with the excerpt from Mandela's autobiography. Ask them to identify whether bias appears in either work or whether the political and philosophical ideas each man presented are clear and accurate.

The day was symbolized for me by the playing of our two national anthems, and the vision of whites singing *"Nkosi Sikelel' iAfrika"* and blacks singing *"Die Stem,"* the old anthem of the republic. Although that day, neither group knew the lyrics of the anthem they once despised, they would soon know the words by heart.

On the day of the inauguration, I was overwhelmed with a sense of history. In the first decade of the twentieth century, a few years after the bitter Anglo-Boer War[10] and before my own birth, the white-skinned peoples of South Africa patched up their differences and erected a system of racial domination against the dark-skinned peoples of their own land. The structure they created formed the basis of one of the harshest, most inhumane societies the world has ever known. Now, in the last decade of the twentieth century, and my own eighth decade as a man, that system had been overturned forever and replaced by one that ☆ recognized the rights and freedoms of all peoples regardless of the color of their skin.

That day had come about through the unimaginable sacrifices of thousands of my people, people whose suffering and courage can never be counted or repaid. I felt that day, as I have on so many other days, that I was simply the sum of all those African patriots who had gone before me. That long and noble line ended and now began again with me. I was pained that I was not able to thank them and that they were not able to see what their sacrifices had wrought.[11]

The policy of apartheid created a deep and lasting wound in my country and my people. All of us will spend many years, if not generations, recovering from that profound hurt. But the decades of oppression and brutality had another, unintended effect, and that was that it produced the Oliver Tambos, the Walter Sisulus, the Chief Luthulis, the Yusuf Dadoos, the Bram Fischers, the Robert Sobukwes[12] of our time—men of such extraordinary courage, wisdom, and generosity that their like may never be known again. Perhaps it requires such depth of oppression to create such heights of character. My country is rich in the minerals and gems that lie beneath its soil, but I have always known that its greatest wealth is its people, finer and truer than the purest diamonds.

It is from these comrades in the struggle that I learned the meaning of courage. Time and again, I have seen men and women risk and give their lives for an idea. I have seen men stand up to attacks and torture without breaking, showing a strength and resiliency that defies the imagination. I learned that courage was not the absence of fear, but the triumph over it. I felt fear myself more times than I can remember, but I hid it behind a mask of boldness. The brave man is not he who does not feel afraid, but he who conquers that fear.

2

I never lost hope that this great transformation would occur. Not only because of the great heroes I have already cited, but because of the courage of the ordinary men and women of my country. I always knew that deep down in every human heart, there is mercy and generosity. No one is born hating another person because of the color of his skin, or his background, or his religion. People must learn to hate, and if they can learn to hate, they can be taught to love, for love comes more naturally to the human heart than its opposite. Even in the grimmest times in prison, when my comrades and I were pushed to our limits, I would see a glimmer of humanity in one of the guards, perhaps just for a second, but it was enough to reassure me and keep me going. Man's goodness is a flame that can be hidden but never extinguished.

---

10. The *Anglo-Boer War* (1899–1902) was fought between Great Britain and the Boers, who are South Africans of Dutch descent.

11. Here, *wrought* means "made."

12. The people Mandela refers to—*Tambo, Sisulu, Luthuli, Dadoo, Fischer,* and *Sobukwe*—are fellow South African reformers and opponents of apartheid.

NELSON MANDELA **233**

Comparing Literature

Teach

Reading Strategy | 1

Understand Cause and Effect Ask: How does Mandela argue that oppression affects more than just the person who is oppressed? *(Mandela says that someone who engages in racist acts is a "prisoner of hatred." He says he cannot rest until the people of his country are free from hatred.)* How did this cause Mandela to make sacrifices? *(Mandela notes that he was forced to take time away from his family and abandon his law career in the pursuit of social reform.)*

Cultural History ☆

Mandela's Retirement Mandela retired from politics in 1999, devoting himself to other reform efforts. In 2005, he was the host of a benefit concert for women with HIV. The concert was named 46664, in honor of Mandela's number while a prisoner.

We took up the struggle with our eyes wide open, under no illusion that the path would be an easy one. As a young man, when I joined the African National Congress,[13] I saw the price my comrades paid for their beliefs, and it was high. For myself, I have never regretted my commitment to the struggle, and I was always prepared to face the hardships that affected me personally. But my family paid a terrible price, perhaps too dear a price for my commitment.

In life, every man has twin obligations— ☆ obligations to his family, to his parents, to his

The oppressed and the oppressor alike are robbed of their humanity.

wife and children; and he has an obligation to his people, his community, his country. In a civil and humane society, each man is able to fulfill those obligations according to his own inclinations and abilities. But in a country like South Africa, it was almost impossible for a man of my birth and color to fulfill both of those obligations. In South Africa, a man of color who attempted to live as a human being was punished and isolated. In South Africa, a man who tried to fulfill his duty to his people was inevitably ripped from his family and home and was forced to live a life apart, a twilight existence of secrecy and rebellion. I did not in the beginning choose to place my people above my family, but in attempting to serve my people, I found that I was prevented from fulfilling my obligations as a son, a brother, a father, and a husband.

In that way, my commitment to my people, to the millions of South Africans I would never know or meet, was at the

---

13. The *African National Congress* (ANC) is a South African political party founded by blacks in 1912.

---

expense of the people I knew best and loved most. It was as simple and yet as incomprehensible as the moment a small child asks her father, "Why can you not be with us?" And the father must utter the terrible words: "There are other children like you, a great many of them . . ." and then one's voice trails off.

I was not born with a hunger to be free. I was born free—free in every way that I could know. Free to run in the fields near my mother's hut, free to swim in the clear stream that ran through my village, free to roast mealies[14] under the stars and ride the broad backs of slow-moving bulls. As long as I obeyed my father and abided by the customs of my tribe, I was not troubled by the laws of man or God.

It was only when I began to learn that my boyhood freedom was an illusion, when I discovered as a young man that my freedom had already been taken from me, that I began to hunger for it. At first, as a student, I wanted freedom only for myself, the transitory freedoms of being able to stay out at night, read what I pleased, and go where I chose. Later, as a young man in Johannesburg, I yearned for the basic and honorable freedoms of achieving my potential, of earning my keep, of marrying and having a family—the freedom not to be obstructed in a lawful life.

But then I slowly saw that not only was I not free, but my brothers and sisters were not free. I saw that it was not just my freedom that was curtailed, but the freedom of everyone who looked like I did. That is when I joined the African National Congress, and that is when the hunger for my own freedom became the greater hunger for the freedom of my people. It was this desire for the freedom of my people to live their lives with dignity and self-respect that animated my life, that transformed a frightened young man into a bold one, that drove a law-abiding attorney

---

14. A *mealie* is an ear of Indian corn.

Speaking and Listening Practice

Use Transitions Discuss the importance of transitions in a speech. Transitional words, such as *first, second, finally, most importantly,* and *in conclusion* serve as signposts, cuing the audience and guiding them through a speech. In the introduction of an oral presentation, it helps to preview the main points that will be discussed so that the audience can anticipate the speech's direction. Have students prepare an oral response to the three essays in this section. Students should compare and contrast the writers' attitudes toward government and their ideas about social protest. Have students use examples and evidence from the three texts to support their conclusions.

Mandela, 1993. Bayo Iribhogbe. Oil on board, 58.4 x 73.6 cm. Private Collection.

to become a criminal, that turned a family-loving husband into a man without a home, that forced a life-loving man to live like a monk. I am not more virtuous or self-sacrificing than the next man, but I found that I could not even enjoy the poor and limited freedoms I was allowed when I knew my people were not free. Freedom is indivisible; the chains on any one of my people were the chains on all of them, the chains on all of my people were the chains on me.

It was during those long and lonely years that my hunger for the freedom of my own people became a hunger for the freedom of all people, white and black. I knew as well as I knew anything that the oppressor must be liberated just as surely as the oppressed. A man who takes away another man's freedom is a prisoner of hatred, he is locked behind the bars of prejudice and narrow-mindedness. I am not truly free if I am taking away someone else's freedom, just as surely as I am not free when my freedom is taken from me. The oppressed and the oppressor alike are robbed of their humanity.

When I walked out of prison, that was my mission, to liberate the oppressed and the oppressor both. Some say that has now been achieved. But I know that is not the case. The truth is that we are not yet free; we have merely achieved the freedom to be free, the right not to be oppressed. We have not taken the final step of our journey, but the first step on a longer and even more difficult road. For to be free is not merely to cast off one's chains, but to live in a way that respects and enhances the freedom of others. The true test of our devotion to freedom is just beginning.

I walked that long road to freedom. I have tried not to falter; I have made missteps along the way. But I have discovered the secret that after climbing a great hill, one only finds that there are many more hills to climb. I have taken a moment here to rest, to steal a view of the glorious vista[15] that surrounds me, to look back on the distance I have come. But I can rest only for a moment, for with freedom come responsibilities, and I dare not linger, for my long walk is not yet ended.

---

15. Here, *vista* means a "wide viewpoint of history."

Quickwrite

What qualities and values distinguish Nelson Mandela as a leader of the people? Write a paragraph describing these qualities and values. Use evidence from his autobiography to support your position.

NELSON MANDELA **235**

Teach

Quickwrite

Students should discuss Mandela's belief in serving both family and country and his idea that an essential feature of bravery is acknowledging one's fears.

Cultural History ☆

The ANC Nelson Mandela's presidential victory in 1994 was part of a sweep for the African National Congress, a political party founded in 1912. The group was energized in the 1940s by Mandela and other such leaders, then banned by the South African government in 1960 until it was reinstated by President F. W. de Klerk in 1990. Today the ANC remains the dominant party of South Africa.

Approaching Level

DIFFERENTIATED INSTRUCTION

Emerging Have students reread the last paragraph. **Ask:** How does the last paragraph sum up the theme of this excerpt? *(Throughout the excerpt Mandela has discussed gaining freedom from an oppressive government. In the last paragraph, he looks at where he has been and where he is going.)* How does Mandela use the imagery of hills in this paragraph? *(The hills are an extended metaphor for* the hard or difficult challenges in life. The "great hill" Mandela climbed was overcoming apartheid and seeing his country freed.)* How does the imagery of the hills fit with the overriding imagery of a "long walk"? *(The "long walk" is an extended metaphor for Mandela's journey through life. The hills represent the challenges in life and the top of a hill represents accomplishment and rest.)*

Assess

🗂 Compare the Big Idea

Evaluate using these criteria:

- Do students discuss both the theories presented and the actions taken by each writer?
- Do they find similarities and differences among Thoreau, Gandhi, and Mandela?

Have students decide how they will organize their comparisons before they begin to write their essays.

Compare Persuasive Messages

1. Thoreau: The State must respect the individual as a higher power than itself; Gandhi: Indians must fight oppression with non-violence; Mandela: His country cannot be free until both the oppressor and the oppressed escape hatred. Context, Thoreau: industrialization and the era of reform; Gandhi: British colonialism; Mandela: era of apartheid.

2. Students should include an evaluation of the evidence presented by each writer.

3. Students might point to Thoreau's argument that rule by majority can never be fair by nature or Mandela's point about the negative effects of hatred.

Compare Cultures

Each panel might include different colors or textures that help contrast the three writers.

- **from *Civil Disobedience*** by Henry David Thoreau
- ***On the Eve of Historic Dandi March*** by Mohandas K. Gandhi
- **from *Long Walk to Freedom*** by Nelson Mandela

COMPARE THE Big Idea **Optimism and Individualism**

Writing Activity Henry David Thoreau, Mohandas K. Gandhi, and Nelson Mandela reflect the spirit of optimism and individualism in these selections. Write a brief essay discussing each writer's message about the power of the individual to bring about social reform. In your essay, be sure to describe the historical context that frames each writer's message. Cite evidence from the selections to support your ideas.

COMPARE Persuasive Messages

Group Activity Thoreau, Gandhi, and Mandela craft different arguments for social reform and develop them by using a variety of persuasive techniques. With a small group discuss the following questions. Cite evidence from the selections to support your answers.

1. What is each writer's main message or philosophical assumption? What is the historical context that shapes each writer's message?

2. Evaluate the effectiveness of each writer's argument for both friendly and hostile audiences. Which writer best succeeds at stating his case? Why?

3. Which of the reading selections challenged you to think in a new way? Explain.

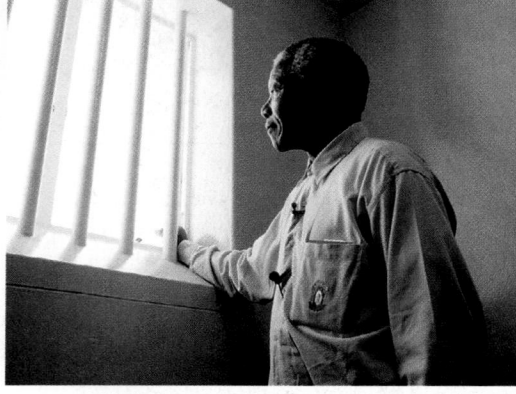

Former South African President Nelson Mandela gazes through the bars of the jail cell he spent more than two decades in as a political prisoner.

COMPARE Cultures

Visual Display Cultural, social, and political forces influenced all of these writers. Thoreau was influenced by American Romanticism and the Reform Era; Gandhi, by British colonialism in India; Mandela, by African tribal culture and apartheid. Create a three-panel collage of images—one panel for each writer—that illustrate these cultural, historical, and political forces.

Literature Online

Selection Resources For Selection Quizzes, eFlashcards, and Reading-Writing Connection activities, go to glencoe.com and enter QuickPass code GLA9800u2.

236 UNIT 2   AMERICAN ROMANTICISM

Assessment Practice

Short Response Remind students that answers to short-response questions are evaluated based on their insightfulness and the evidence drawn from the text to support them. For example, in order to answer question 3 above, students should decide which selection presented them with a new idea, and then find the particular words that challenged them to think in a new way.

PART 2

The Dark Side of Romanticism

The Fog Warning, 1885. Winslow Homer. Oil on canvas. Museum of Fine Arts, Boston.

 Homer's painting seems to capture a moment in a story. What might be some main events in the story and what does it suggest about the relationship between humans and nature?

> "All that we see or seem
> Is but a dream within a dream." **1**
>
> —Edgar Allan Poe

237

Analyze and Extend

Literary Element 1

Create a Mood Have a student read aloud the quotation on this page. Discuss what Poe's words mean. *(Students may say that Poe means reality is an illusion or a dream.)* **Ask:** What mood do these lines create? *(Students may say that they create a mood of sadness and strangeness by blurring the line between what is real and what is imagined.)*

View the Art

Answer: *The main idea might be that the fisherman has gone far from his ship to harvest nature's bounty, but now he might fear that he cannot overcome the rough sea to get back to his ship. Nature gives and takes.*

The American artist Winslow Homer (1836–1920) is known for his powerful paintings of the sea. His seascapes, based on direct observations of nature, show men challenging the power of the ocean. The subjects in his paintings perceive the dangers of dark, turbulent, and overwhelming natural forces and struggle to survive.

 For additional support for English Learners, see Unit 2 Teaching Resources Book, p. 100.

Approaching Level

DIFFERENTIATED INSTRUCTION

Emerging Some students may not be familiar with examining fine art and responding to it. Encourage them to examine the painting and then write down adjectives and phrases that describe the sea and the man in the boat. *(Students may say that the sea looks angry, rough, dark, threatening, dangerous, or frightening and that the man is rowing hard, watching the sky and sea, and looking* *worried.)* **Ask:** How does the mood of this painting compare with the mood created in the quotation by Poe? *(Both moods are dark and somewhat eerie.)*

Focus

Bellringer Options

Daily Language Practice Transparency 25

Or write on the board: What makes a good adventure story? Horror story? Mystery? Guide the discussion to help students realize that every story contains basic elements: setting, plot, characters, point of view, and theme.

Teach

Literary Element

Short Story A short story is a brief fictional narrative written in prose. It generally includes a plot (sequence of events), a setting (time and place in which events occur), characters, a point of view (relationship of the narrator to the story), and a theme (central message).

View the Art ★

John Quidor (1801–1881) was both a painter and an artisan. Of his 35 known paintings, 17 depict subjects from Washington Irving's stories.

 For an activity related to this selection, see Unit 2 Teaching Resources Book, pp. 98–99.

238

Learning Objectives

For pages 238–239

In studying this text, you will focus on the following objectives:

Literary Study:
Analyzing literary periods.
Analyzing literary genres.

Literary History

American Short Stories

As THE AMERICAN NOVELIST and critic Henry James observed, "It takes a great deal of history to produce a little literature." At the beginning of the 1800s, the United States was still a very young country. American writers of the time were painfully conscious of the lack of a native literary tradition. This was particularly true in the area of fiction. Dominated by Puritanism, early American culture had no place for made-up stories created largely for the purpose of entertainment.

This attitude toward fiction lingered for a long time. It was not until the period of American Romanticism that Washington Irving, Nathaniel Hawthorne, and Edgar Allan Poe laid the foundations of the American short story. In the process, they created literary forms and ideas about how to write short stories that remain important today.

> *"It has been a matter of marvel, to my European readers, that a man from the wilds of America should express himself in tolerable English."*
>
> —Washington Irving

Literary Pioneers

Irving, the first American writer to become famous outside the U.S., transplanted traditional European narratives and gave them American settings. For example, he based "Rip Van Winkle" on legends about people captured by fairies. Hawthorne used both European material and the histories and legends of Puritan New England as the basis for fiction. Poe helped develop the new American literary magazines into mass-circulation marketplaces for short stories. More importantly, he was a true innovator who pioneered new literary genres—mysteries (or detective stories) and science fiction.

The Headless Horseman Pursuing Ichabod Crane, 1858. John Quidor. Oil on canvas, 68 x 86 cm. Smithsonian American Art Museum, Washington, DC.

★

Mysteries and Science Fiction

Tales of robbery and murder had always existed. Poe's brilliant innovation was to combine such stories with a skilled detective using reasoning to investigate a crime. This new investigative approach had not existed until the appearance of the first professional police forces in the early 1800s. In "The Murders in the Rue Morgue," Poe established many of the basic conventions that mystery writers have followed ever since:

- the brilliant, eccentric detective (Dupin)
- his less-gifted partner, who is an admiring foil
- the blundering official police force
- the "impossible crime" taking place in a locked room

Writing Practice

Evaluate Elements Remind students of the devices that Poe developed (the eccentric detective, blundering police force). Tell students that many of the conventions of these early writers survive today in television programs and movies. Discuss a detective or crime program and write a brief list of elements from that show (noting the major characters, plot, setting). Ask students to look for these story elements in the works of literature they read. For information about characters, remind students to look for what the characters say and do. Remind students that the writers discussed in this introduction often focused on New England settings. Have students create a story map to track the basic conventions of mystery writers.

Poe also has a claim to be the "father of science fiction." In stories such as "A Descent into the Maelstrom," he created Romantic tales of terror with an emphasis on factual detail that anticipated later science fiction. Poe so realistically portrayed a transatlantic balloon flight in one of his stories that it was widely believed actually to have taken place.

Theory and Practice

Poe believed that the most effective short stories are those that can be read in a single sitting. He theorized that every detail in a well-constructed story contributes to the creation of a certain unique and single effect. By effect, Poe meant the overall impact that the story makes upon the reader. Some favorite effects that Poe tried to achieve in his stories were feelings of dread, horror, and suspense. Poe's theory of a unique single effect remains a fundamental principle of short-story writing today.

Although Hawthorne's stories were finely crafted, he showed little interest in constructing literary theories. Hawthorne chose to focus on moral and psychological themes, such as the struggle between good and evil and the isolation of people from their fellow human beings. Unlike his friend Emerson, Hawthorne saw life as essentially tragic. His pessimistic view of human nature gave his stories a dark, shadowy quality that Poe criticized as "a somewhat too general or prevalent tone—a tone of melancholy and mysticism." Hawthorne's mystical outlook led him to rely heavily on symbolism and allegory to convey his meaning, often at the expense of a realistic rendering of

Literature Online

Literature and Reading For more about American short stories, go to glencoe.com and enter QuickPass code GLA9800u2.

everyday life. His distinguishing feature is his probing exploration of the role of guilt in the inner lives of human beings—an obsession that he inherited from his Puritan ancestors.

Short Story Elements

The short story generally includes these elements.

Setting: the time and place in which the events occur

Characters: the participants in the story. The main character is the **protagonist.** There may be an **antagonist,** a character in conflict with the protagonist.

Point of view: the perspective of the storyteller, or narrator

Theme: the central message of the story that readers can apply to life. A theme may be stated clearly or implied.

Plot: the sequence of related events in a story. Most plots deal with a problem and develop around a conflict, a struggle between opposing forces.

Poster for Universal film *Murders in the Rue Morgue,* unknown artist, 1932.

Respond and Think Critically

1. What was the attitude of readers in early American culture toward fiction? Why do you think early American readers had this attitude?

2. What materials did Irving use as the basis of his fiction? How did he use these materials?

3. Compare and contrast Poe's and Hawthorne's attitudes toward literary theory and practice. Name one literary achievement that each author is famous for today.

4. **Connect to Today** What were Poe's important innovations in literary form? Explain how these innovations can be seen in literature today.

Assess

1. They generally did not read fictional stories for entertainment. American culture was dominated by Puritanism, which discouraged the use of art forms for enjoyment.

2. Irving combined European material and the legends of New England, putting traditional European narratives into American settings.

3. Poe thought that a short story should create a single effect on the reader. Hawthorne focused on moral and psychological themes. Poe's theory of a unique effect continues to influence short story writers today. Hawthorne is known for his deep exploration of the role of guilt in people's inner lives.

4. Detective stories and science fiction; today, conventions such as the brilliant private detective who outsmarts the police force and the "impossible crime" that takes place in a locked room are still found in such stories.

Approaching Level

DIFFERENTIATED INSTRUCTION

Established To help students keep track of these three authors, have them make a chart similar to the one shown. Tell them to look for personal, historical, religious, and cultural influences on each author's writing. An example of how students might use the chart is shown.

	Personal Influences	Historical Influences	Religious and Cultural Influences
Washington Irving	*His fiancée died; focused on writing*		
Edgar Allan Poe			
Nathaniel Hawthorne			*Read widely about dark Puritan past*

Before You Read

Focus

Bellringer Options

Selection Focus Transparency 17

Daily Language Practice Transparency 26

Or tell students about a difficult decision you have made—such as changing careers or moving to a new town—and the effects of that decision. Ask students to give examples of decisions they have made and to share the consequences of their decisions.

Ask: What is the most difficult aspect of making an important decision? *(not being able to predict the outcome)*

Before You Read

The Devil and Tom Walker

Meet **Washington Irving**
(1783–1859)

Named after his country's first president, Washington Irving won the battle for America's literary independence. He was the first American storyteller to be internationally recognized as a man of letters.

> "[Washington Irving is] the first ambassador from the New World of Letters to the Old."
>
> —William Makepeace Thackeray

Lawyer and Writer The youngest of eleven children, Irving was born in New York City to a wealthy family with strict moral values. Though he had little formal education, he took an interest in the study of law, later working in the law office of Josiah Hoffman. Irving and Hoffman's daughter Matilda fell in love, and they were engaged.

His interest in law began to dwindle, however, and in 1802 he started to write, publishing satirical essays in a New York newspaper. He soon began to publish a series of periodical essays called *Salmagundi*. The success of *Salmagundi* steered Irving away from law and toward writing.

Success and Heartbreak In 1809, under the pseudonym Diedrich Knickerbocker, he published his most popular work, Knickerbocker's *A History of New York from the Beginning of the World to the End of the Dutch Dynasty*. This book was a humorous combination of history, folklore, and opinion that delighted readers with sketches of the customs and families of old New York. That same year, however, Matilda died suddenly of

tuberculosis. Overwhelmed by grief, Irving put his writing on hold. Haunted by the memory of his lost fiancée, he was never to marry.

During this dark period, Irving traveled often, eventually moving to Europe to manage his brother's business interests. In 1818, after the family business went bankrupt, Irving resumed writing.

International Acclaim *The Sketch Book of Geoffrey Crayon, Gent* (1819–1820) established Irving's literary reputation in Europe. The book included two stories that later became classics, "The Legend of Sleepy Hollow" and "Rip Van Winkle." Irving borrowed the plots of these stories from two German folktales and then placed them in the Hudson Valley.

Irving eventually returned to the United States, where he continued writing—travel books, histories, biographies of Columbus and Washington, and more tales and sketches. His enormous popularity earned him recognition as the father of American letters. Irving's distinctively American settings and character types later influenced a range of authors, including Romantics, such as Nathaniel Hawthorne and Edgar Allan Poe, and regionalist writers, such as Mark Twain and William Faulkner.

 Literature Online

Author Search For more about Washington Irving, go to glencoe.com and enter QuickPass code GLA9800u2.

Selection Skills

Literary Elements
- Characterization (SE pp. 241, 242, 244, 245, 247–249, 252)

The Devil and Tom Walker

Writing Skills/Grammar
- Summary (SE p. 252)
- Appositives and Appositive Phrases (TE p. 244)
- Absolute Phrases (TE p. 246)
- Action Verbs (TE p. 250)

Reading Skills
- Make Predictions (SE pp. 241, 243, 246, 247, 249, 252)
- Visualize (TE p. 242)

Vocabulary Skills
- Analogies (SE pp. 241, 252)
- Academic Vocabulary (SE p. 252)

Listening/Speaking/Viewing Skills
- Analyze Art (SE pp. 245, 247, 250)
- Oral Presentation (TE p. 248)

Literature and Reading Preview

Connect to the Story

Have you ever made a decision that you later regretted? Have you ever made a commitment to do something and then later changed your mind? Discuss these questions in a small group.

Build Background

"The Devil and Tom Walker" takes place in New England in the 1720s—when Puritanism was fading and commercialism was on the rise. The story is an adaptation of the old German legend of Faust, a sixteenth-century astronomer who sold his soul to the devil.

Set Purposes for Reading

Big Idea **The Power of Darkness**

As you read "The Devil and Tom Walker," ask yourself, What elements of Romanticism does this story reflect?

Literary Element **Characterization**

Characterization refers to the methods a writer uses to reveal the personality of a character. In **direct characterization** the writer makes explicit statements about a character. In **indirect characterization** the writer reveals a character through the character's words and actions and through what other characters think and say about that character. As you read, ask yourself, How does Irving characterize Tom Walker? What details about Walker's character stand out to you most?

Reading Strategy **Make and Verify Predictions**

Predicting is making an educated guess about what will happen in a story. Predicting helps you anticipate events and appreciate less obvious parts of a story. To make predictions, combine clues the author provides with your own understanding of characters and events. Adjust or change your predictions as you continue to read and discover more clues.

....

Tip: Predict Ask yourself, "How do I think this situation will be resolved based on the clues I have discovered so far?" Write down your ideas. After reading, review your work to see whether your predictions were correct.

Learning Objectives

For pages 240–252

In studying this text, you will focus on the following objectives:

Literary Study: Analyzing characterization (direct and indirect).

Reading: Making and verifying predictions about plot.

Vocabulary

prevalent (prev´ ə lent) *adj.* widespread; p. 242 *Flu was so prevalent that all the kids were sick.*

discord (dis´ kôrd) *n.* lack of agreement or harmony; conflict; p. 243 *There was discord in the court when the verdict was read.*

melancholy (mel´ ən kol´ ē) *adj.* depressing; dismal; gloomy; p. 243 *The dark clouds made us melancholy.*

surmise (sər mīz´) *v.* to infer from little evidence; to guess; p. 245 *She surmised that the roses came from a secret admirer.*

speculate (spek´ yə lāt´) *v.* to engage in risky business ventures, hoping to make quick profits; p. 248 *He speculated by purchasing older houses cheaply and then reselling them at high prices.*

....

Tip: Analogies Analogies are matching relationships between word pairs, for example, *Weak is to strong as dark is to _____.* To complete an analogy, use the relationship between the first two words to find a partner for the third (*light*).

English Learners

DIFFERENTIATED INSTRUCTION

Advanced Remind students that "characterization" refers to the various ways an author or narrator introduces a character to the reader. In this selection, the narrator uses mostly direct characterization by making statements about the characters. For example, Tom Walker is described as "a meager, miserly fellow." Tell students to use a sticky note to mark examples of indirect characterization. Have them look for the following clues to indirect characterization:

- quotation marks (what a character says and what others say about the character)
- verbs (actions a character takes that reveal something about his or her personality)

Before You Read

Focus

Summary

One day, the devil offers Tom Walker a pirate's treasure. When Tom's greedy wife urges him to accept the deal, he refuses out of spite; so she tries to make her own bargain with the devil—but she disappears. Tom then accepts the devil's offer and becomes a rich moneylender who preys on those in need. When a borrower asks Tom for an extension on a loan, he replies, "The devil take me if I have made a farthing." The devil whisks Tom away, and his riches turn to cinders.

 For summaries in languages other than English, see Unit 2 Teaching Resources Book, pp. 101–106.

Vocabulary

Make Analogies Write these examples on the board.

1. peace : war ::
  harmony : discord

2. enjoyable : thrilling ::
  unpleasant : melancholy

Have students describe the relationship between the first pair of words in each set and use that information to help them understand the relationship between the vocabulary words in the second pair in each set. (1. *opposites* 2. *degree or intensity*)

 For additional vocabulary practice, see Unit 2 Teaching Resources Book, p. 109.

 For additional context, see Glencoe Interactive Vocabulary CD-ROM.

Teach

Reading Strategy   1

Make Predictions Help students predict the direction the story will take by focusing on the first four paragraphs.

 For additional practice using the reading skill or strategy, see Unit 2 Teaching Resources Book, p. 108.

Literary Element   2

Characterization Answer: *Both Tom and his wife are so greedy that they even cheat each other. They appear to have no love for each other.*

Literary History ☆

Captain Kidd In 1695, the king of England commissioned Captain William Kidd to arrest all pirates in the eastern seas. When Kidd arrived at the Comoro Islands, however, he joined the pirates instead of hunting them.

 For an audio recording of this selection, use Listening Library Audio CD-ROM.

Readability Scores

Dale-Chall: 8.4
DRP: 64
Lexile: 1220

The Devil and Tom Walker

Washington Irving

A few miles from Boston, in Massachusetts, there is a deep inlet, winding several miles into the interior of the country from Charles Bay, and terminating in a thickly wooded swamp or morass. On one side of this inlet is a beautiful dark grove; on the opposite side the land rises abruptly from the water's edge into a high ridge, on which grow a few scattered oaks of great age and immense size.

Under one of these gigantic trees, according to old stories, there was a great amount of treasure buried by Kidd the pirate. The inlet allowed a facility to bring the money in a boat, secretly and at night, to the very foot of the hill; the elevation of the place permitted a good lookout to be kept that no one was at hand; while the remarkable trees formed good landmarks by which the place might easily be found again. The old stories add, moreover, that the devil presided at the hiding of the money, and took it under his guardianship; but this, it is well known, he always does with buried treasure, particularly when it has been ill gotten. Be that as it may, Kidd never returned to recover his wealth, being shortly after seized at Boston, sent out to England, and there hanged for a pirate.

About the year 1727, just at the time that earthquakes were **prevalent** in New England and shook many tall sinners down upon their knees, there lived near this place a meager, miserly fellow, of the name of Tom Walker. He had a wife as miserly as himself; they were so miserly that they even conspired to cheat each other. Whatever the woman could lay hands on she hid away; a hen could not cackle but she was on the alert to secure the new laid egg. Her husband was continually prying about to detect her secret hoards, and many and fierce were the conflicts that took place about what ought to have been common property. They lived in a forlorn-looking house that stood alone and had an air of starvation. A few straggling savin trees, emblems of sterility, grew near it; no smoke ever curled from its chimney, no traveler stopped at its door. A miserable horse, whose ribs were as articulate as the bars of a gridiron, stalked about a field where a thin carpet of moss, scarcely covering the ragged beds of pudding stone,[1] tantalized and balked his hunger; and sometimes he would lean his head over the fence, look piteously at the passer-by, and seem to petition deliverance from this land of famine.

The house and its inmates had altogether a bad name. Tom's wife was a tall termagant,[2] fierce of temper, loud of tongue, and strong of arm. Her voice was often heard in wordy warfare with her husband, and his face sometimes showed signs that their conflicts were not confined to words. No one ventured, however, to interfere between **1**

---

1. *Pudding stone* is a rock consisting of pebbles and gravel embedded in cement, like plums in a pudding.
2. A *termagant* is a quarrelsome, scolding woman.

 Vocabulary

prevalent (prev´ ə lent) *adj.* widespread

Characterization *What does this detail tell you about Tom Walker and his wife?* **2**

Reading Practice

SPIRAL REVIEW **Visualize Sensory Details** Explain to students that this selection requires the reader to pay attention to the setting to understand the interactions among the characters. The inlet, Tom's house, the swamp, and other locations inform the actions and inner thoughts of the characters. **Ask:** What does Tom's house look like? *(bare, forlorn)* How do he and his wife behave with each other? *(miserly with each other)* Ask students to list each place or scene as they read and to write sensory details about it. Have students note the specific actions and feelings of the characters that have been influenced by each place or scene.

242

them. The lonely wayfarer shrunk within himself at the horrid clamor and clapperclawing,[3] eyed the den of **discord** askance, and hurried on his way, rejoicing, if a bachelor, in his celibacy.

One day that Tom Walker had been to a distant part of the neighborhood, he took what he considered a short cut homeward, through the swamp. Like most short cuts it was an ill-chosen route. The swamp was thickly grown with great gloomy pines and hemlocks, some of them ninety feet high, which made it dark at noonday, and a retreat for all the owls of the neighborhood. It was full of pits and quagmires, partly covered with weeds and mosses, where the green surface often betrayed the traveler into a gulf of black, smothering mud; there were also dark and stagnant pools, the abodes of the tadpole, the bullfrog, and the water snake, where the trunks of pines and hemlocks lay half drowned, half rotting, looking like alligators sleeping in the mire.

Tom had long been picking his way cautiously through this treacherous forest, stepping from tuft to tuft of rushes and roots, which afforded precarious footholds among deep sloughs, or pacing carefully, like a cat, along the prostrate[4] trunks of trees, startled now and then by the sudden screaming of the bittern or the quacking of a wild duck rising on the wing from some solitary pool. At length he arrived at a firm piece of ground, which ran out like a peninsula into the deep bosom of the swamp. It had been one of the strongholds of the Indians during their wars with the first colonists. Here they had thrown up a

kind of fort, which they had looked upon as almost impregnable, and had used as a place of refuge for their squaws and children. Nothing remained of the old Indian fort but a few embankments, gradually sinking to the level of the surrounding earth, and already overgrown in part by oaks and other forest trees, the foliage of which formed a contrast to the dark pines and hemlocks of the swamp.

Visual Vocabulary
A *bittern* is a marsh-dwelling wading bird with mottled brownish plumage and a deep, booming cry.

It was late in the dusk of evening when Tom Walker reached the old fort, and he paused there awhile to rest himself. Any one but he would have felt unwilling to linger in this lonely, **melancholy** place, for the common people had a bad opinion of it, from the stories handed down from the time of the Indian wars, when it was asserted that the savages held incantations[5] here, and made sacrifices to the evil spirit.

Tom Walker, however, was not a man to be troubled with any fears of the kind. He reposed himself for some time on the trunk of a fallen hemlock, listening to the boding cry of the tree toad, and delving with his walking staff into a mound of black mold at his feet. As he turned up the soil unconsciously, his staff struck against something hard. He raked it out of the vegetable mold, and lo! a cloven[6] skull, with an Indian tomahawk buried deep in it, lay before him. The rust on the weapon showed the time that had elapsed since this death blow

---

3. *Clapperclawing* is scratching or clawing with the fingernails.
4. *Prostrate* means "lying down."

4 Make and Verify Predictions *How does this detail of the setting help you predict what might happen to Tom?*

5 Make and Verify Predictions *What purpose might this fort serve in the story? What clues lead you to this prediction?*

Vocabulary

discord (dis′ kôrd) *n.* lack of agreement or harmony; conflict

---

5. *Incantations* are the recitations of verbal charms or spells to produce a magical effect.
6. *Cloven* means "split" or "divided."

6 The Power of Darkness *How does Irving's description reflect Romanticism's interest in exotic settings?*

Vocabulary

melancholy (mel′ ən kol′ ē) *adj.* depressing; dismal; gloomy

WASHINGTON IRVING **243**

Literary Element 3

Simile Explain that a simile is a comparison between two seemingly unlike things, containing the word *like* or *as*. **Ask:** What are some of the similes in the first column on this page? (*Possible answers: "trunks of pines . . . looking like alligators"; "pacing carefully, like a cat"*)

Reading Strategy 4

Make and Verify Predictions Answer: *"Ill-chosen route" suggests that something bad might happen to Tom.*

Reading Strategy 5

Make and Verify Predictions Answer: *The fort might represent evil, since Tom has taken "an ill-chosen route" to get there.*

Big Idea 6

The Power of Darkness Answer: *Irving's description shows nature in its wildest, most exotic state. His choice of an Indian fort as part of the setting also reveals his interest in the exotic.*

Approaching Level

DIFFERENTIATED INSTRUCTION

SMALL GROUP

emerging Have students work in small groups to analyze the role that the forest and thick woods play in setting the tone and mood of the scenes. **Ask:** What does Tom find in the woods from the colonists' wars with the Indians? (*He finds an old fort once used as a place of refuge.*) Who lived here and what happened? (*The squaws and children lived in the fort. The colonists killed and drove out the Indians.*)

How does this history contribute to the mood? (*The woods seem haunted and frightening.*) Have students find descriptions of the woods that contribute to the dark tone and mood.

Teach

Make Predictions Tom learns that the tall trees, "fair and flourishing without," are actually "rotten at the core." **Ask:** What do you think is the link between these trees and Crowninshield? *(Crowninshield, rich through piracy, was morally as rotten as the trees.)*

Characterization Answer: *Tom is comfortable talking to Old Scratch in a casual manner because he is so corrupt that he finds nothing to fear in the devil himself.*

---

had been given. It was a dreary memento of the fierce struggle that had taken place in this last foothold of the Indian warriors.

"Humph!" said Tom Walker, as he gave it a kick to shake the dirt from it.

"Let that skull alone!" said a gruff voice. Tom lifted up his eyes, and beheld a great black man seated directly opposite him on the stump of a tree. He was exceedingly surprised, having neither heard nor seen any one approach, and he was still more perplexed on observing, as well as the gathering gloom would permit, that the stranger was neither negro nor Indian. It is true he was dressed in a rude, half Indian garb,[7] and had a red belt or sash swathed round his body, but his face was neither black nor copper color, but swarthy and dingy, and begrimed with soot, as if he had been accustomed to toil among fires and forges. He had a shock of coarse black hair, that stood out from his head in all directions, and bore an ax on his shoulder.

He scowled for a moment at Tom with a pair of great red eyes.

"What are you doing on my grounds?" said the black man, with a hoarse, growling voice.

"Your grounds!" said Tom with a sneer, "no more your grounds than mine; they belong to Deacon Peabody."

"Deacon Peabody be d——d," said the stranger, "as I flatter myself he will be if he does not look more to his own sins and less to those of his neighbors. Look yonder, and see how Deacon Peabody is faring."

Tom looked in the direction that the stranger pointed, and beheld one of the great trees, fair and flourishing without, but rotten at the core, and saw that it had been nearly hewn through, so that the first high wind was likely to blow it down. On the bark of the tree was scored the name of Deacon Peabody, an eminent man who had waxed[8] wealthy by driving shrewd bargains with the Indians. He now looked around, and found most of the tall trees marked with the name of some great man of

1

the colony, and all more or less scored by the ax. The one on which he had been seated, and which had evidently just been hewn down, bore the name of Crowninshield, and he recollected a mighty rich man of that name, who made a vulgar display of wealth which it was whispered he had acquired by buccaneering.[9]

1

"He's just ready for burning!" said the black man, with a growl of triumph. "You see I am likely to have a good stock of firewood for winter."

"But what right have you," said Tom, "to cut down Deacon Peabody's timber?"

"The right of a prior claim," said the other. "This woodland belonged to me long before one of your white-faced race put foot upon the soil."

"And pray, who are you, if I may be so bold?" said Tom.

"Oh, I go by various names. I am the wild 'huntsman' in some countries, the 'black miner' in others. In this neighborhood I am known by the name of the 'black woodsman.' I am he to whom the red men consecrated this spot, and in honor of whom they now and then roasted a white man, by way of sweet-smelling sacrifice. Since the red men have been exterminated by you white savages, I amuse myself by presiding at the persecutions of Quakers and Anabaptists;[10] I am the great patron and prompter of slave dealers, and the grand master of the Salem witches."

"The upshot of all which is that, if I mistake not," said Tom sturdily, "you are he commonly called 'Old Scratch.'"[11]

"The same, at your service!" replied the black man, with a half civil nod.

Such was the opening of this interview, according to the old story, though it has almost too familiar an air to be credited. One would think that to meet with such a singular personage, in this wild, lonely place, would have shaken any man's nerves; but Tom was a hard-minded fellow,

---

7. *Garb* means "clothing" or "attire."
8. Here, *waxed* means "grown" or "become."

9. *Buccaneering* is robbing ships at sea (piracy).
10. The *Quakers* and the *Anabaptists* were two religious groups in Massachusetts that were persecuted for their beliefs.
11. *Old Scratch* is a nickname for the devil.

Characterization *What does the manner in which Tom speaks to Old Scratch reveal about Tom's character?* **2**

Grammar Practice

SPIRAL REVIEW **Appositives and Appositive Phrases** Display and explain the following definitions:

- appositive: a noun or pronoun that further identifies another noun or pronoun
- appositive phrase: an appositive plus its modifiers

Explain that nonessential appositive phrases are set off with commas. Write the following example and direct attention to the commas:

"On the bark of the tree was scored the name of Deacon Peabody, an eminent man . . . ." Explain that "an eminent man" is nonessential because it describes the deacon, but it does not single him out. Write these nonessential appositive phrases for students:

Tom, a simple man; Absalom Crowninshield, the rich buccaneer; Old Scratch, the devil. Have students write sentences using each of these phrases. Have them

exchange sentences with other students to check for correct punctuation.

not easily daunted, and he had lived so long with a termagant wife that he did not even fear the devil.

It is said that after this commencement they had a long and earnest conversation together, as Tom returned homeward. The black man told him of great sums of money buried by Kidd the pirate under the oak trees on the high ridge, not far from the morass. All these were under his command, and protected by his power, so that none could find them but such as propitiated[12] his favor. These he offered to place within Tom Walker's reach, having conceived an especial kindness for him; but they were to be had only on certain conditions. What these conditions were may be easily **surmised,** though Tom never disclosed them publicly. They must have been very hard, for he required time to think of them, and he was not a man to stick at trifles when money was in view. When they had reached the edge of the swamp the stranger paused. "What proof have I that all you have been telling me is true?" said Tom. "There's my signature," said the black man, pressing his finger on Tom's forehead. So saying, he turned off among the thickets of the swamp, and seemed, as Tom said, to go down, down, down into the earth, until nothing but his head and shoulders could be seen, and so on, until he totally disappeared.

When Tom reached home he found the black print of a finger burned, as it were, into his forehead, which nothing could obliterate.

The Devil and Tom Walker, 1856. John Quidor. Oil on canvas. The Cleveland Museum of Art. Cleveland, OH.

View the Art John Quidor's best-known paintings were inspired by Washington Irving's stories. Do you find this painting to be a faithful depiction of Tom Walker's encounter with the devil? Explain. ★

The first news his wife had to tell him was the sudden death of Absalom Crowninshield, the rich buccaneer. It was announced in the papers with the usual flourish, that a great man had fallen in Israel.[13]

Tom recollected the tree which his black friend had just hewn down, and which was ready for burning. "Let the freebooter[14] roast," said Tom; "who cares!" He now felt convinced that all he had heard and seen was no illusion.

He was not prone to let his wife into his confidence, but as this was an uneasy secret he willingly shared it with her. All her avarice was awakened at the mention of hidden gold, and she urged her husband to comply with the black

---

12. *Propitiated* means "won over" or "gained by pleasing acts."

---

13. Here, *Israel* is a biblical reference to 2 Samuel 3:38: "Know ye not that there is a prince and a great man fallen this day in Israel?" The Puritans referred to New England as "Israel," their Promised Land.
14. A *freebooter* is a pirate.

Characterization *How does Irving use the attitudes of Tom and his wife toward the devil to develop their characters? Is this direct or indirect characterization?* **4**

WASHINGTON IRVING **245**

Teach

Reading Strategy 1

Make and Verify Predictions Answer: *Some students may reply that Tom's wife was killed by the devil while trying to make a deal with him.*

Ask: Do you think Tom's uneasiness is caused by a genuine concern for his wife's safety? Why or why not? *(Some students may argue that he is concerned that an unscrupulous thief stole the goods and did away with his wife. Others may think that Tom worries more about the loss of property than the loss of his wife.)*

---

man's terms, and secure what would make them wealthy for life. However Tom might have felt disposed to sell himself to the devil, he was determined not to do so to oblige his wife, so he flatly refused, out of the mere spirit of contradiction. Many and bitter were the quarrels they had on the subject, but the more she talked the more resolute was Tom not to be damned to please her.

At length she determined to drive the bargain on her own account, and, if she succeeded, to keep all the gain to herself. Being of the same fearless temper as her husband, she set off for the old Indian fort towards the close of a summer's day. She was many hours absent. When she came back she was reserved and sullen in her replies. She spoke something of a black man whom she had met about twilight hewing at the root of a tall tree. He was sulky, however, and would not come to terms; she was to go again with a propitiatory offering, but what it was she forbore to say.

The next evening she set off again for the swamp, with her apron heavily laden. Tom waited and waited for her, but in vain; midnight came, but she did not make her appearance; morning, noon, night returned, but still she did not come. Tom now grew uneasy for her safety, especially as he found she had carried off in her apron the silver teapot and spoons and every portable article of value. Another night elapsed, another morning came, but no wife. In a word, she was never heard of more.

What was her real fate nobody knows, in consequence of so many pretending to know. It is one of those facts which have become confounded by a variety of historians. Some asserted that she lost her way among the tangled mazes of the swamp, and sank into some pit or slough; others, more uncharitable, hinted that she had eloped with the household booty,[15] and made off to some other province; while others surmised that the tempter had decoyed her into a dismal quagmire, on the top of which her hat was

---

15. *Booty* is stolen goods.

 1 Make and Verify Predictions *What do you think has happened to Tom's wife?*

---

found lying. In confirmation of this it was said a great black man, with an ax on his shoulder, was seen late that very evening coming out of the swamp, carrying a bundle tied in a check apron, with an air of surly triumph.

The most current and probable story, however, observes that Tom Walker grew so anxious about the fate of his wife and his property that he set out at length to seek them both at the Indian fort. During a long summer's afternoon he searched about the gloomy place, but no wife was to be seen. He called her name repeatedly, but she was nowhere to be heard. The bittern alone responded to his voice, as he flew screaming by, or the bullfrog croaked dolefully from a neighboring pool. At length, it is said, just in the brown hour of twilight, when the owls began to hoot and the bats to flit about, his attention was attracted by the clamor of carrion crows[16] hovering about a cypress tree. He looked up, and beheld a bundle tied in a check apron and hanging in the branches of the tree, with a great vulture perched hard by, as if keeping watch upon it. He leaped with joy, for he recognized his wife's apron and supposed it to contain the household valuables.

"Let us get hold of the property," said he consolingly to himself, "and we will endeavor to do without the woman."

As he scrambled up the tree the vulture spread its wide wings and sailed off, screaming, into the deep shadows of the forest. Tom seized the check apron, but, woeful sight! found nothing but a heart and liver tied up in it!

Such, according to this most authentic old story, was all that was to be found of Tom's wife. She had probably attempted to deal with the black man as she had been accustomed to deal with her husband; but though a female scold is generally considered a match for the devil, yet in this instance she appears to have had the worst of it. She must have died game, however, for it is said Tom noticed many prints of cloven feet deeply stamped about the tree, and found handfuls

---

16. *Carrion crows* are crows that feed on dead or decaying flesh.

Grammar Practice

SMALL GROUP

Absolute Phrases Point out to students that an absolute phrase consists of a noun or pronoun that is modified by a participle or a participial phrase. An absolute phrase is used as a modifier. It may modify an entire sentence. For example, the sentence *His wife being ill-tempered, Tom was not saddened to lose her* contains an absolute phrase (underlined).

Organize the class into small groups, and have each student write and share a sentence containing an absolute phrase. Discuss and rewrite problem sentences.

Swamp Sunset. Harold Rudolph. Oil on canvas. The Ogden Museum of Southern Art, University of New Orleans, LA.

View the Art What mood does this painting evoke? Would the mood be different if the artist had called it *Swamp Sunrise*? How does the scene in the painting compare with Irving's description of the one where Tom Walker and the devil first meet? ★

of hair that looked as if they had been plucked from the coarse black shock of the woodman. Tom knew his wife's prowess by experience. He shrugged his shoulders as he looked at the signs of a fierce clapperclawing. "Egad," said he to himself, "Old Scratch must have had a tough time of it!"

Tom consoled himself for the loss of his property with the loss of his wife, for he was a man of fortitude. He even felt something like gratitude towards the black woodman, who, he considered, had done him a kindness. He sought, therefore, to cultivate a further acquaintance with him, but for some time without success; the old blacklegs played shy, for whatever people may think, he is not always to be had for calling for; he knows how to play his cards when pretty sure of his game.

At length, it is said, when delay had whetted Tom's eagerness to the quick, and prepared him to agree to anything rather than not gain the promised treasure, he met the black man one

evening in his usual woodman's dress, with his ax on his shoulder, sauntering along the swamp, and humming a tune. He affected to receive Tom's advances with great indifference, made brief replies, and went on humming his tune.

By degrees, however, Tom brought him to business, and they began to haggle about the terms on which the former was to have the pirate's treasure. There was one condition which need not be mentioned, being generally understood in all cases where the devil grants favors; but there were others about which, though of less importance, he was inflexibly obstinate. He insisted that the money found through his means should be employed in his service. He proposed, therefore, that Tom should employ it in the black traffic,—that is to say, that he should fit out a slave ship. This, however, Tom resolutely refused; he was bad enough, in all conscience, but the devil himself could not tempt him to turn slave trader.

Finding Tom so squeamish on this point, he did not insist upon it, but proposed, instead, that he should turn usurer,[17] the devil being extremely anxious for the increase of usurers, looking upon them as his peculiar[18] people.

To this no objections were made, for it was just to Tom's taste.

"You shall open a broker's shop in Boston next month," said the black man.

---

2 Characterization *Why does Irving use humor to describe the disappearance of Tom's wife? How does this reflect on Tom?*

3 Make and Verify Predictions *What will be the outcome of this relationship?*

---

17. A *usurer* is a person who lends money, especially at an excessive or unlawfully high rate of interest.
18. Here, *peculiar* means "special."

WASHINGTON IRVING **247**

Teach

Literary Element | 2

Characterization Answer: *Irving's humor helps convey the character of both Tom and his wife. Tom is not distressed about his wife's disappearance; in fact, he is rather amused at the devil's struggle to capture her, as he knows that she is no easy match. The reader learns that Tom's wife is so greedy that she will tackle the devil. Irving gives the reader permission to laugh at the misfortune they have brought upon themselves.*

Reading Strategy | 3

Make Predictions Answer: *Students may say that anyone with such a relationship will eventually lose his soul.*

View the Art ★

Answer: *This painting's mood might change from melancholy to hopeful if it were named* Swamp Sunrise. *The scene is similar to Irving's descriptions of the swamp, including the rushes, weeds, and tree trunks.*

Harold Rudolph began his career by painting portraits. He then turned his attention to landscapes, particularly those of Louisiana.

Approaching Level

DIFFERENTIATED INSTRUCTION

Established Make sure that students understand that when words in a selection are footnoted, numbers are used to identify both the words in the text and the corresponding notes at the bottom of the page. Explain that the term *carrion crows* on page 246 is superscripted—and carries a corresponding footnote at the bottom of the page. The phrase *cloven feet* in the same column is not footnoted.

Tell students that a cloven foot is one that is split or divided, such as a sheep's hoof. **Ask:** What else might have cloven feet? *(the devil)* Have students suggest additional words or phrases that could be footnoted and write their own footnotes.

247

Teach

| Literary Element | 1 |

Characterization Answer:
Irving shows that Tom is more than willing to cheat people out of money.

| Reading Strategy | 2 |

Make Inferences Ask students whether Tom is a hypocrite. *(yes)* **Ask:** What details support your inference? *(Tom's public appearance masks his real self. Instead of being a "universal friend of the needy," he squeezes his customers dry; his "vast house" is actually "unfinished and unfurnished," and he owns a carriage but starves his horses.)*

"I'll do it tomorrow, if you wish," said Tom Walker.

"You shall lend money at two percent a month."

"Egad, I'll charge four!" replied Tom Walker.

"You shall extort[19] bonds, foreclose mortgages, drive the merchants to bankruptcy—"

"I'll drive them to the d—l!" cried Tom Walker.

"You are the usurer for my money!" said blacklegs with delight. "When will you want the rhino?"[20]

"This very night."

"Done!" said the devil.

"Done!" said Tom Walker. So they shook hands and struck a bargain.

A few days' time saw Tom Walker seated behind his desk in a countinghouse in Boston.

His reputation for a ready-moneyed man, who would lend money out for a good consideration, soon spread abroad. Everybody remembers the time of Governor Belcher,[21] when money was particularly scarce. It was a time of paper credit. The country had been deluged with government bills; the famous Land Bank[22] had been established; there had been a rage for **speculating;** the people had run mad with schemes for new settlements, for building cities in the wilderness; land jobbers[23] went about with maps of grants and townships and Eldorados,[24] lying nobody knew where, but which everybody was ready to purchase. In a word, the great speculating fever which breaks out every now and then in the country had raged to an alarming degree, and everybody was dreaming of making sudden fortunes from nothing. As usual the fever had subsided, the dream had gone off, and the imaginary fortunes with it; the patients were left in doleful plight, and the whole country resounded with the consequent cry of "hard times."

> His reputation for a ready-moneyed man, who would lend money out for a good consideration, soon spread abroad.

At this propitious time of public distress did Tom Walker set up as usurer in Boston. His door was soon thronged by customers. The needy and adventurous, the gambling speculator, the dreaming land jobber, the thriftless tradesman, the merchant with cracked credit,— in short, everyone driven to raise money by desperate means and desperate sacrifices hurried to Tom Walker.

Thus Tom was the universal friend of the needy, and acted like a "friend in need"; that is to say, he always exacted good pay and good security. In proportion to the distress of the applicant was the hardness of his terms. He accumulated bonds and mortgages, gradually squeezed his customers closer and closer, and sent them at length, dry as a sponge, from his door.

19. *Extort* means "to obtain by threats, force, or other types of oppression."
20. *Rhino* is a slang term for money.
21. Jonathan *Belcher* was governor of Massachusetts and New Hampshire from 1730 to 1741.
22. Boston merchants organized the *Land Bank* in 1739. Landowners could borrow money in the form of mortgages on their property and then repay the loans with cash or manufactured goods. When the bank was outlawed in 1741, many colonists lost money.
23. *Land jobbers* are people who buy and sell land for profit.

1 Characterization *What does Irving show about Tom's character with this dialogue?*

Vocabulary

speculate (spek′ yə lāt′) *v.* to engage in risky business ventures, hoping to make quick profits

24. *Eldorados* are places of great wealth or opportunity. The term comes from the name El Dorado, a legendary region of South America sought by Spanish explorers for its gold and jewels.

Speaking and Listening Practice

Oral Presentation Ask each student to assume the identity of a Boston citizen who has had an encounter with Tom Walker and who will now testify for or against him in court—for example, a borrower, a neighbor, a churchgoer, or a stable boy.

Establish guidelines for a two-minute student presentation. Students should

• identify their character by name
• state the character's relationship to Tom

• memorize their "testimony" or use note cards rather than read a prepared text
• use vocal tone and gestures to imply the character's attitude toward Tom.

Have each student deliver, in character, a two-minute statement to the class. Have students critique presentations for accurate tone and content to match the character.

In this way he made money hand over hand, became a rich and mighty man, and exalted his cocked hat upon 'Change.[25] He built himself, as usual, a vast house, out of ostentation,[26] but left the greater part of it unfinished and unfurnished, out of parsimony. He even set up a carriage in the fullness of his vainglory,[27] though he nearly starved the horses which drew it; and as the ungreased wheels groaned and screeched on the axletrees you would have thought you heard the souls of the poor debtors he was squeezing.

As Tom waxed old, however, he grew thoughtful. Having secured the good things of this world, he began to feel anxious about those of the next. He thought with regret on the bargain he had made with his black friend, and set his wits to work to cheat him out of the conditions. He became, therefore, all of a sudden, a violent churchgoer. He prayed loudly and strenuously, as if heaven were to be taken by force of lungs. Indeed, one might always tell when he had sinned most during the week by the clamor of his Sunday devotion. The quiet Christians who had been modestly and steadfastly traveling Zionward,[28] were struck with self-reproach at seeing themselves so suddenly outstripped in their career by this new-made convert. Tom was as rigid in religious, as in money, matters; he was a stern supervisor and censurer of his neighbors, and seemed to think every sin entered up to their account became a credit on his own side of the page. He even talked of the expediency of reviving the persecution of Quakers and Anabaptists. In a word, Tom's zeal became as notorious as his riches.

Still, in spite of all this strenuous attention to forms, Tom had a lurking dread that the devil, after all, would have his due. That he might not be taken unawares, therefore, it is said he always

carried a small Bible in his coat pocket. He had also a great folio Bible on his countinghouse desk, and would frequently be found reading it when people called on business. On such occasions he would lay his green spectacles in the book, to mark the place, while he turned round to drive some usurious bargain.

Some say that Tom grew a little crack-brained in his old days, and that, fancying his end approaching, he had his horse new shod, saddled, and bridled, and buried with his feet uppermost, because he supposed that at the last day the world would be turned upside down, in which case he should find his horse standing ready for mounting, and he was determined at the worst to give his old friend a run for it. This, however, is probably a mere old wives' fable. If he really did take such a precaution it was totally superfluous; at least, so says the authentic old legend, which closes his story in the following manner.

One hot summer afternoon in the dog days,[29] just as a terrible, black thunder gust was coming up, Tom sat in his countinghouse, in his white linen cap and India silk morning gown. He was on the point of foreclosing a mortgage, by which he would complete the ruin of an unlucky land speculator for whom he had professed the greatest friendship. The poor land jobber begged him to grant a few months' indulgence. Tom had grown testy and irritated, and refused another day.

"My family will be ruined and brought upon the parish," said the land jobber.

"Charity begins at home," replied Tom; "I must take care of myself in these hard times."

"You have made so much money out of me," said the speculator.

Tom lost his patience and his piety. "The devil take me," said he, "if I have made a farthing."[30]

Just then there were three loud knocks at the street door. He stepped out to see who was

---

25. The 'Change, or Exchange, was a financial center where merchants, bankers, and brokers met to do business.
26. Ostentation means "a display meant to impress others."
27. Vainglory is boastful, undeserved pride in one's accomplishments or qualities.
28. Zionward means "toward heaven."

29. Dog days are the hot, sultry days of summer.
30. A farthing was a British coin worth one-fourth of a penny.

3 Make and Verify Predictions *Do you think Tom will succeed in cheating the devil?*

Characterization *How does this statement develop Tom's character?* **4**

Reading Strategy 3

Make Predictions Answer: *Tom will not, because he has not really had a change of heart. He merely uses the trappings of religion in a superstitious attempt to outwit a power greater than himself and to protect his own interests.*

Literary Element 4

Characterization Answer: *It reinforces the hypocrisy of Tom's religious pursuits.*

Approaching Level

DIFFERENTIATED INSTRUCTION

Established Have groups of students review the text on this page, and then reread the Big Ideas of American Romanticism on page 179. Have groups select one of the Big Ideas and discuss how this section of the story represents one of the ideas. Ask each group to prepare a five-minute presentation explaining their connections. Tell students to support their findings with text from the reading.

Teach

View the Art ★

Answer: *Students may say that the exaggerated representation of the characters and their actions reflects the fantastic nature of Irving's story.*

Say: Some of John Quidor's critics thought that the gestures and expressions in his works were so dramatic that he must have based his paintings on theatrical productions. Have students discuss their reactions to this painting and the one on page 245.

 To check students' understanding of the selection, see Unit 2 Teaching Resources Book, p. 112.

Tom Walker's Flight, 1856. John Quidor. Oil on canvas, 23³/₄ x 33³/₄ in. The Fine Arts Museum of San Francisco.

View the Art   Review the description of the devil on page 244. Is Quidor's painting a good illustration of the text? How does it compare with the way you pictured the devil when you first read Irving's description? ★

there. A black man was holding a black horse, which neighed and stamped with impatience.

"Tom, you're come for," said the black fellow gruffly. Tom shrank back, but too late. He had left his little Bible at the bottom of his coat pocket, and his big Bible on the desk buried under the mortgage he was about to foreclose; never was sinner taken more unawares. The black man whisked him like a child into the saddle, gave the horse a lash, and away he galloped, with Tom on his back, in the midst of the thunderstorm. The clerks stuck their pens behind their ears, and stared after him from the windows. Away went Tom Walker, dashing down the streets, his white cap bobbing up and down, his morning gown fluttering in the wind, and his steed striking fire out of the pavement at every bound. When the clerks turned to look for the black man he had disappeared.

Tom Walker never returned to foreclose the mortgage. A countryman, who lived on the border of the swamp, reported that in the height of

the thunder gust he had heard a great clattering of hoofs and a howling along the road, and running to the window caught sight of a figure such as I have described, on a horse that galloped like mad across the fields, over the hills, and down into the black hemlock swamp towards the old Indian fort, and that shortly after, a thunderbolt falling in that direction seemed to set the whole forest in a blaze.

The good people of Boston shook their heads and shrugged their shoulders, but had been so much accustomed to witches and goblins, and tricks of the devil, in all kinds of shapes, from the first settlement of the colony, that they were not so much horror-struck as might have been expected. Trustees were appointed to take charge of Tom's effects. There was nothing, however, to administer upon. On searching his coffers,[31] all his bonds and mortgages were found reduced to cinders. In place of gold and silver his iron chest was filled with chips and shavings; two skeletons lay in his stable instead of his half starved horses; and the very next day his great house took fire and was burned to the ground.

Such was the end of Tom Walker and his ill-gotten wealth. Let all griping money brokers lay this story to heart. The truth of it is not to be doubted. The very hole under the oak trees, whence he dug Kidd's money, is to be seen to this day, and the neighboring swamp and old Indian fort are often haunted in stormy nights by a figure on horseback, in morning gown and white cap, which is doubtless the troubled spirit of the usurer. In fact, the story has resolved itself into a proverb, and is the origin of that popular saying, so prevalent throughout New England, of "the devil and Tom Walker." ✒

---

31. *Coffers* are strongboxes used to hold money or other valuables.

1   **The Power of Darkness** *What is the effect of including details of the thunderstorm?*

The Power of Darkness *Why do you think Irving adds this detail?*   **2**

Grammar Practice

Action Verbs Explain that writers choose strong verbs to describe dramatic actions. Ask students to identify verbs that Irving uses to describe Tom's last earthly ride. *(whisked, galloped, dashing, bobbing fluttering, striking)* Tell students that these are examples of strong, specific verbs. Explain that general verbs are not as strong or specific. List these general verbs for students: *ran, said, looked, asked, walked out.* Ask students to write a sentence for each of these words and then rewrite each sentence using a stronger, more specific verb.

After You Read

Respond and Think Critically

Respond and Interpret

1. (a)What was your reaction to Tom Walker at the beginning of the story? (b)Did your opinion of him change by the end?

2. (a)How does Tom react to the devil and his offer? (b)What does this tell you about Tom?

3. (a)What kind of person is Tom's wife? (b)How does she contribute to Tom's downfall?

4. (a)What eventually happens to Tom's wife? (b)Which version of what happened to her does the narrator want the readers to believe? Explain.

5. How do you interpret what happens to Tom Walker and his possessions?

Analyze and Evaluate

6. (a)The narrator often uses disclaimers by saying "people said" or "it is said." Why might Irving have used this tactic? (b)How trustworthy does the narrator appear to be?

7. **Satire** is a form of writing that uses humor as a way of criticizing someone or something. (a)In what ways is this story a satire? (b)Do you agree with Irving's implied criticisms?

Connect

8. **Big Idea** **The Power of Darkness** Irving wrote "The Devil and Tom Walker" when Puritanism was fading and the urge to acquire wealth was growing. How does Irving portray the dark side of both religion and wealth in his story?

9. **Connect to Today** Is Irving's fantastic depiction of the result of greed applicable in a realistic way to people's behavior today? Explain.

You're the Critic

How Creative Was Irving?

Some of Washington Irving's most famous stories, such as "The Devil and Tom Walker," are adaptations of European folktales. As a result, some critics have faulted Irving for a lack of originality, while others applaud his ability to synthesize something new.

> *"It has been said that Irving lacked imagination. . . . Now, it seems to me that the transmutation of the crude and heretofore unpoetical materials which he found in the New World into what is as absolute a creation as exists in literature, was a distinct work of the imagination."*
>
> —Charles Dudley Warner

> *"[In 'The Devil and Tom Walker,'] Irving began with the legends of Captain Kidd and his buried treasure and . . . he grafted upon this material a much wider variety of motifs drawn from German folklore. . . . The devil himself, for example, is a compound of German, American Indian, and Puritan elements."*
>
> —Edward Wagenknecht

Group Activity Discuss the questions below. Refer to these quotations and evidence from the story.

1. How imaginative is Irving's story?

2. How important is it for a writer to be completely original in creating a literary work?

Group Activity

1. Irving adapts an old tale, making it seem fresh and new to readers through characterization, setting, and dialogue. The story also teaches a moral lesson.

2. A story based on an old favorite can be successful if it has some originality. A writer can bring values and style to a familiar story to make it seem fresh.

 For additional assessment, see Assessment Resources, pp. 109–110.

After You Read

Assess

1. (a) Students may not like Tom because he did not care about other people. (b) Students' opinions may be lower at the end because he had cheated others.

2. (a) Tom asks for time to consider the devil's offer. (b) Although Tom is tempted by the devil's offer, he does not want to make a rash decision.

3. (a) Loud, physically abusive, and greedy (b) She encourages Tom to cultivate a friendship with the devil.

4. (a) She most likely tried to make a deal with the devil in the forest and was killed. (b) The narrator wants readers to believe that Tom's wife was involved in a fight with the devil, because that is the version that is described in greatest detail.

5. He is whisked away by the devil, and his wealth is reduced to cinders.

6. (a) To establish the credibility of the narrator (b) The narrator seems to be careful to distinguish fact from hearsay.

7. (a) The story satirizes marriage, the expectation that characters will be heroes, and the social institutions fostering greed. (b) Students' responses will vary.

8. Tom represents the evil side of both—he is greedy and concerned with money over all else, and he takes up religion only to try to save himself from being taken by the devil.

9. Students may note that while the depiction of the devil kidnapping a person may not be realistic, greedy people often do face consequences for their behavior in modern society.

After You Read

Assess

Literary Element

Characterization

1. Possible response: *Direct:* "Tom was a hard-minded fellow"; *Indirect:* "Any one but he would have felt unwilling to linger in this lonely, melancholy place." Direct characterization reveals what readers must know to interpret characters and events as the author intended. Indirect characterization shows more than it tells, allowing readers to interpret characters and events.

2. The narrator gives us information that Tom cannot. Tom's wife shows how greedy Tom is. Tom shows the reader the moral of the story.

Progress Check

Can students identify character?

If No → See Unit 2 Teaching Resources Book, p. 107.

Review: Archetype

Irving uses the archetype of the villain. Also, the setting of a dark forest is archetypal. Archetypes stir deep emotions in the reader.

Literary Element Characterization

In "The Devil and Tom Walker," Irving uses either direct or indirect characterization at different points in the story. Through these methods of characterization, he creates dramatic effects, generates humor, and foreshadows future events.

1. Identify examples of both indirect and direct characterization used in "The Devil and Tom Walker." Record these details in a chart like the one shown below. Why do you think Irving chose each method in each instance?

Tom Walker	
Direct Characterization	Indirect Characterization
p. 242 "... a meager, miserly fellow"	p. 246 "He leaped with joy, for he recognized his wife's apron and supposed it to contain the household valuables."

2. If characters are tools used by the author to develop a story, in what ways did Irving use the narrator? Tom's wife? Tom?

Review: Archetype

As you learned in Unit One, an **archetype** is a character type, a setting, an image, or a story pattern that occurs frequently in literature across many cultures and evokes strong emotional responses. For example, heroes like Luke Skywalker are archetypal figures, as are evil-hearted villains like Darth Vader. What archetypes does Irving use in "The Devil and Tom Walker"? Why do you think he chose to use them?

Literature Online

Selection Resources For Selection Quizzes, eFlashcards, and Reading-Writing Connection activities, go to glencoe.com and enter QuickPass code GLA9800u2.

252 UNIT 2 AMERICAN ROMANTICISM

Reading Strategy Make and Verify Predictions

Making Predictions About Plot An inference involves using reasoning and experience to come up with an idea based on what a writer implies or suggests but does not directly state. A **prediction** is a type of inference, one that involves making an educated guess about what will happen in a story.

1. How did you use your own experiences and reasoning to predict the outcome of the story? Was the outcome of the story different from your original prediction? Explain.

2. List details in "The Devil and Tom Walker" that Irving uses to **foreshadow** later events in the story.

Vocabulary Practice

Practice with Analogies Choose the word that best completes each analogy.

1. prevalent : common :: continual :
   a. low **b.** nonstop **c.** fast

2. war : discord :: famine :
   a. abundance **b.** scarcity **c.** happiness

3. surmise : evidence :: prove :
   a. facts **b.** ideas **c.** questions

4. preserve : save :: speculate :
   a. predict **b.** rebuild **c.** gamble

Academic Vocabulary

In this story, Tom Walker's wife seeks to **benefit** by cheating her husband.

Benefit is an academic word. If you gain something from a set of circumstances, you **benefit** from it. To further explore the meaning of the word, answer the questions below.

1. How does the devil **benefit** from his pact with Tom Walker?

2. Why does Tom Walker ultimately not **benefit** from his "ill-gotten wealth"?

For more on academic vocabulary, see pages 53–54.

Reading Strategy

1. Students may have predicted that Tom would get what he deserved in the end because bad deeds are often punished. They may have been surprised that Tom's wife disappeared and Tom became religious.

2. "He was sulky . . . and would not come to terms" hints that Tom's wife will have trouble making a deal with Old Scratch.

"Still, in spite of all this strenuous attention to forms, Tom had a lurking dread that the devil, after all, would have his due" foreshadows Tom's being whisked off by the devil.

Vocabulary

1. b **2.** b **3.** a **4.** c

Academic Vocabulary

1. The devil benefits by gaining a moneylender with whom he can torment desperate people.

2. Tom Walker ultimately does not benefit from his "ill-gotten wealth" because he loses his home in a fire and his soul to the devil.

⚡ Respond Through Writing

Summary

Report Story Events When summarize a story, you tell a short version of the original and report its main events in sequence. A summary does not include personal opinions. In about 100 words, write a plot summary of "The Devil and Tom Walker." Write in the present tense.

Prewrite Skim the text to review the main events in the plot. Then complete a sequence notes chart like the one below, which is based on "How the World Was Made" (see pages 24–25).

> Animals living in the sky determine they need more room, but all is water.

⬇

> The Water-beetle stirs up mud to form land on which the animals can settle.

⬇

> Plants grow on the land, followed by the emergence of humans.

Draft As you draft your summary, draw upon the sequence of events you made. Be sure to distinguish between major and minor events. Example:

> The Cherokee creation myth "How the World Was Made" describes the formation and population of the earth. In this myth water surrounds the earth, which hangs from cords attached to a rock in the sky. (When the earth grows old, it will sink.) In the early stages of this myth, animals living in the sky seeking more space send the Water-beetle to explore an area underwater. The beetle discovers soft mud, which it pulls to the surface. This mud expands to form the earth. Animals then settle on the land and set the height and movement of the sun. Plants grow on the land, and finally humans emerge after the development of both plants and animals.

Revise Have a partner read your summary and ask him or her to circle the basic elements of the plot you included. If your partner cannot recognize these events, revise your summary so that the major plot points are clear.

Edit and Proofread Proofread your paper, correcting grammar, spelling, and punctuation. Use the Grammar Tip in the side column for help.

▶ Grammar Tip

Verb Tenses

The tense of a verb indicates when the action or state of being occurs. **Present tense** expresses a constant, repeated, or habitual action or condition. It also expresses an action or condition that exists only now. When writing about a literary work—such as in your summary of Irving's story—use the present tense. For example:

In "The Devil and Tom Walker," Tom's wife is greedy.

Past tense is used to express an action or condition started and completed in the past. **Future tense** expresses an action or condition that will occur in the future.

After You Read

Assess

⚡ Writing

Evaluate students' writing using the following criteria. Students' reports should:

- summarize the story in sequence of events
- avoid mentioning personal opinions
- be written in present tense

Scoring Guide

- Students who meet all of these criteria should receive the equivalent of a 4-point response.
- Students who fully meet two or partially meet three of these criteria should receive the equivalent of a 3-point response.
- Student who fully meet one or partially meet two of these criteria should receive the equivalent of a 2-point response.
- Students who partially meet one of these criteria should receive the equivalent of a 1-point response.

Approaching Level

DIFFERENTIATED INSTRUCTION

AAVE For approaching level students who are users of AAVE, the past tense may present two types of difficulties. Some consonant clusters may be pronounced without the *-ed* sound, so past tense may sound like present tense in verbs such as *stamped* or *scrambled*. Also AAVE speakers may need practice using the standard forms of irregular verbs in the past tense. While students will write their summaries

in the present tense, they will need to use the past tense in some places. Have students who use AAVE practice forming the past tense by replacing the verb in parentheses with the simple past tense in these sentences.

- Tom wonders if the devil (to kill) his wife.
- He thinks she (to talk) to the Devil the same way she (to speak) to him.

- Tom suspects his wife (to quarrel) with the devil.

(killed, talked, spoke, quarrelled)

253

Literature Launchers:
Pre-Reading Videos DVD,
Selection Launcher

Selection Focus
Transparency 18

Daily Language Practice
Transparency 27

Or display images of a variety of Gothic structures, such as mansions and castles.

Say: Poe used these types of settings to create atmosphere in his poems and stories.

Ask: How do these images make you feel? What type of mood do these images convey?

List students' responses on the board. Tell students that Poe developed stories of horror and violence with a focus on the supernatural. Have students note the details of each setting and how the setting contributes to the mood in Poe's poem and story.

Selection Skills

Before You Read

The Raven and
The Pit and the Pendulum

Meet **Edgar Allan Poe**
(1809–1849)

Today's authors might well envy Edgar Allan Poe. More than 150 years after his death, he is still one of the world's most popular writers. Known primarily as a master of horror and suspense tales, he is also credited with inventing the detective story and contributing to the development of science fiction. Despite his talent, Poe led a troubled life marked by poverty, restlessness, and loneliness.

Poe's Early Life Poe was born in Boston, the son of traveling actors. His father abandoned the family when Poe was an infant, and his mother died a year later. John and Frances Allan, a wealthy couple from Richmond, Virginia, became his foster parents. Though Poe got along well with his foster mother, he and John Allan frequently quarreled. Allan refused to pay for Poe's education because of his gambling debts and wild life. Later, when Poe was expelled from West Point for breaking rules, his relationship with his foster father ended.

Penniless, Poe moved to Baltimore, where he lived with his aunt and her daughter, Virginia Clemm. He had already published three volumes of poems and now began to write short stories. In 1835 he returned to Richmond, where he edited the *Southern Literary Messenger* and married his cousin Virginia.

Poe's World During Poe's lifetime, the literary world in the United States was centered in Boston, New York, and Philadelphia. Poe contributed to an assortment of journals in these cities. Still, he spent much of his life struggling for financial stability.

In 1847, just as Poe seemed to be gaining recognition for his writing, his world collapsed. His wife died at the age of twenty-four, and Poe plunged into a sorrow too deep to bear. Two years after his wife's death, Poe was found delirious on the streets of Baltimore and died shortly thereafter, completely alone.

Poe's Influence To the Irish poet W. B. Yeats, Poe was "certainly the greatest of American poets." Poe's story "The Unparalleled Adventures of One Hans Pfaal" influenced Jules Verne and other science-fiction writers. Fictional detectives such as Sherlock Holmes and Hercule Poirot are modeled after C. Auguste Dupin, the detective Poe introduced in "The Murders in the Rue Morgue." Modern writers of horror influenced by Poe include Richard Matheson, Anne Rice, and Stephen King.

> "They who dream by day are cognizant of many things which escape those who dream only by night."
>
> —Edgar Allan Poe, from "Eleonora"

The Mystery Writers of America (MWA) annually confers the Edgar Allan Poe Awards® to recognize outstanding achievement in the mystery genre. The award is a statuette of Poe. But perhaps the strongest proof of Poe's enduring popularity is the name of the National Football League team in Baltimore—the Ravens.

 Literature Online

Author Search For more about Edgar Allan Poe, go to glencoe.com and enter QuickPass code GLA9800u2.

Literary Elements
- Narrative Poem
  (SE pp. 255. 257, 260, 261)

The Raven

Writing Skills/Grammar
- Write a Summary (SE p. 261)
- Combine Main Clauses
  (TE p. 260)

Reading Skills
- Analyze Sound Devices
  (SE pp. 255, 257–261)
- Classify (TE p. 256)

Vocabulary Skills
- Synonyms (SE p. 255, 258, 261)

Literature and Reading Preview

Connect to the Poem

Make a list of songs, movies, or stories you know that deal with strong emotions. Underneath each one, write down the emotion(s) that were portrayed and how you responded.

Build Background

Poe wrote that in this poem he set out to create a melancholy effect and that *nevermore* was the first word that came into his mind, both for its sound and for its meaning. The subject of the poem, he decided, would be the death of a beautiful woman, "unquestionably, the most poetical topic in the world."

Set Purposes for Reading

Big Idea The Power of Darkness

As you read, ask yourself, How does "The Raven" reflect the Romantics' fascination with madness and death?

Literary Element Narrative Poem

A **narrative poem** is a poem that tells a story. Although the poem may include figurative language, imagery, rhythm, and rhyme, it also includes story elements such as setting, characters, and plot. As you read, ask yourself, How is telling a story in a poem similar to and different from telling one in prose?

Reading Strategy Analyze Sound Devices

Poets take advantage of words' sounds as well as their meanings. Two common sound devices are the repetition of words and **alliteration,** the repetition of consonant sounds at the beginnings of words. For example, Poe uses alliteration to create an almost hypnotic effect in phrases like "weak and weary." As you read, look for examples of these sound devices.

Tip: Take Notes On a chart, list examples of repetition and alliteration and describe their effects.

Sound Devices	Examples	Effects
alliteration	"nodded, nearly napping"	

Learning Objectives

For pages 254–261

In studying these texts, you will focus on the following objectives:

Literary Study:
Analyzing narrative poetry.
Analyzing sound devices.

Writing: Writing a summary.

Vocabulary

lattice (laˊ təs) *n.* a structure of crisscrossed strips forming a pattern of openings; p. 258 *The dog tried to push its nose through the fence lattice.*

beguile (bi gīlˊ) *v.* to influence by deceit; to trick; p. 258 *The amateur magician's tricks beguiled only the children in the audience.*

placid (plaˊ səd) *adj.* calm; peaceful; undisturbed; p. 259 *The placid lake reflected the blue sky.*

respite (resˊ pət) *n.* a period of rest or relief, as from work or sorrow; p. 259 *The students looked forward to the respite of vacation.*

balm (bäm) *n.* something that heals or soothes, as an ointment; p. 260 *The aloe gel was a balm.*

Before You Read

Focus

Summary

In "The Raven," the speaker is a melancholy man who has lost his beloved Lenore. Late one night, while he is grieving, he is visited by an eerie and mysterious raven. The man questions the raven about Lenore, but the raven's only response is "Nevermore." The poem shows how loneliness and excessive grieving drive the man to madness.

 For summaries in languages other than English, see Unit 2 Teaching Resources Book, pp. 114–119.

Vocabulary

Word Origins Explain that the word *placid* comes from the Latin *placere,* meaning "to please." **Ask:** What is the connection between the Latin meaning of *placere* and the meaning of *placid*? (*Both connote calm, peace.*)

(ADVANCED) Have students explain the connection between the vocabulary words and their derivations: lattice (*from Old French* lath—*a thin piece of wood*); respite (*from Latin* respectus, *the act of looking back*); balm (*from Greek* balsamon, *a substance used for soothing ointments*)

 For additional vocabulary practice, see Unit 2 Teaching Resources Book, p. 122.

 For additional context, see Glencoe Interactive Vocabulary CD–ROM.

English Learners

DIFFERENTIATED INSTRUCTION

Intermediate Some students may have difficulty with Poe's language. Help students by providing an overview of the poem. Explain that it is a narrative (story) told in the first person. The speaker refers to himself as "I" or "me." Each stanza, or group of lines, includes an event in the "plot" of the poem. Display the first line of the poem: "Once upon a midnight dreary, while I pondered weak and weary." Explain that this line can be rewritten in simpler terms as follows: It is midnight and the speaker is sad and thoughtful. As students read, ask them to think of each stanza as an event in the plot. Have them restate the events of the poem's "plot" in simple terms.

Teach

Reading Strategy | 1

Analyze Sound Devices

Have a volunteer read the first two stanzas aloud. **Say:** Poets often use internal rhyme, or rhyming words within individual lines, to emphasize ideas. **Ask:** What are the internal rhymes in lines 1, 3, 7, and 9? *(dreary/weary; napping/tapping; remember/December; morrow/borrow)*

Literary History ☆

Ravens Ravens have a long literary history. They are often, like Poe's raven, viewed as birds of ill omen. They appear as tricksters in many Native American myths. The raven also plays a role in Aesop's fables.

 For an audio recording of this selection, use Listening Library Audio CD–ROM.

The Raven

Edgar Allan Poe

256

Reading Practice

Classify Tell students that as they read "The Raven," they should try to recreate the poem's sensory images in their imaginations. Write the following images from "The Raven" on the board:

- "a tapping, / As of someone gently rapping"
- "each separate dying ember wrought its ghost upon the floor"
- "silken, sad, uncertain rustling"
- "Deep into that darkness peering"

- "the air grew denser, perfumed from an unseen censer"

Have students identify the sense to which each image appeals. *("Tapping" and "rustling" appeal to the sense of sound; "dying ember" and "darkness" appeal to the sense of sight; "perfumed from an unseen censer" appeals to the sense of smell)*

256

O nce upon a midnight dreary, while I pondered, weak and weary,
Over many a quaint and curious volume of forgotten lore—
While I nodded, nearly napping, suddenly there came a tapping,
As of someone gently rapping, rapping at my chamber[1] door.
5 "'Tis some visitor," I muttered, "tapping at my chamber door—
        Only this and nothing more."

Ah, distinctly I remember it was in the bleak December;
And each separate dying ember wrought its ghost upon the floor.
Eagerly I wished the morrow;—vainly I had sought to borrow
10 From my books surcease[2] of sorrow—sorrow for the lost Lenore—
For the rare and radiant maiden whom the angels name Lenore—
        Nameless *here* for evermore.

And the silken, sad, uncertain rustling of each purple curtain
Thrilled me—filled me with fantastic terrors never felt before;
15 So that now, to still the beating of my heart, I stood repeating
"'Tis some visitor entreating entrance at my chamber door—
Some late visitor entreating entrance at my chamber door;—
        This it is and nothing more."

Presently my soul grew stronger; hesitating then no longer,
20 "Sir," said I, "or Madam, truly your forgiveness I implore;
But the fact is I was napping, and so gently you came rapping,
And so faintly you came tapping, tapping at my chamber door,
That I scarce was sure I heard you"—here I opened wide the door;—
        Darkness there and nothing more.

25 Deep into that darkness peering, long I stood there wondering, fearing,
Doubting, dreaming dreams no mortal ever dared to dream before;
But the silence was unbroken, and the stillness gave no token,
And the only word there spoken was the whispered word, "Lenore!"
This I whispered, and an echo murmured back the word, "Lenore!"
30   Merely this and nothing more.

1. A *chamber* is a room.
2. *Surcease* means "an end."

Narrative Poem *What element of storytelling is established in these lines?* **2**

Analyze Sound Devices *Why might Poe have used alliteration in this line?* **3**

EDGAR ALLAN POE **257**

Teach

Reading Strategy 1

Analyze Sound Devices

Answer: *The repetition emphasizes the fact that the speaker would have to walk underneath the raven in order to leave the room.*

(ENGLISH LEARNERS) **Say:** Give an example of alliteration in these lines. *(The p sound is repeated.)* Remind students that alliteration is the repetition of initial vowel sounds.

Big Idea 2

The Power of Darkness

Answer: *The lines include a reference to Pluto, the god of the dead; the words* ghastly, grim, *and* ancient *all evoke dark, sinister elements. "Nightly shore" may refer to death.*

(ADVANCED) **Ask:** How might the raven's perching above the door affect the speaker? *(The presence of the raven is a reminder of the speaker's loss of Lenore.)*

Cultural History ☆

Athena Athena was also a goddess of war and the patron of the city of Athens. She is sometimes depicted wearing armor and a helmet.

Back into the chamber turning, all my soul within me burning,
Soon again I heard a tapping somewhat louder than before.
"Surely," said I, "surely that is something at my window **lattice**;
Let me see, then, what thereat is, and this mystery explore—
35 Let my heart be still a moment and this mystery explore;—
       'Tis the wind and nothing more!"

Open here I flung the shutter, when, with many a flirt and flutter
In there stepped a stately Raven of the saintly days of yore.[3]
Not the least obeisance[4] made he; not a minute stopped or stayed he;
40 But, with mien of lord or lady, perched above my chamber door—
Perched upon a bust of Pallas[5] just above my chamber door—
       Perched, and sat, and nothing more.

Then this ebony bird **beguiling** my sad fancy into smiling,
By the grave and stern decorum of the countenance[6] it wore,
45 "Though thy crest be shorn and shaven, thou," I said, "art sure no craven,
Ghastly grim and ancient Raven wandering from the Nightly shore—
Tell me what thy lordly name is on the Night's Plutonian[7] shore!"
       Quoth the Raven "Nevermore."

Much I marveled this ungainly fowl to hear discourse so plainly,
50 Though its answer little meaning—little relevancy bore;
For we cannot help agreeing that no living human being
Ever yet was blessed with seeing bird above his chamber door—
Bird or beast upon the sculptured bust above his chamber door,
       With such name as "Nevermore."

---

3. *Days of yore* means "days of long ago." Here Poe is referring to a Bible story in which ravens feed the Hebrew prophet Elijah during a sojourn in the wilderness. (1 Kings 17:1–7)
4. *Obeisance* means "a movement or gesture, such as a bow, that expresses respect."
5. A *bust* is a statue of someone's head and shoulders. *Pallas* refers to Pallas Athena, the Greek goddess of wisdom. ☆
6. Here, *countenance* means "facial expression."
7. *Plutonian* refers to Pluto, the Roman god of the dead and ruler of the underworld.

 1   Analyze Sound Devices   *What effect does Poe create by repeating the description "above my chamber door"?*

2   The Power of Darkness   *How does this bit of dialogue reflect the dark side of Romanticism?*

Vocabulary

lattice (la′ təs) *n.* a structure of crisscrossed strips forming a pattern of openings
beguile (bi gīl′) *v.* to influence by deceit; to trick

Vocabulary Practice

SPIRAL REVIEW   **Synonyms** Point out that many words in this poem are no longer commonly used. Most of these words have synonyms that are used today. Identifying synonyms of these words will help students better understand the poem and Poe's meaning.

Write the following words on the board. Have students use a dictionary or a thesaurus to locate synonyms of each word.

- chamber *(room)*
- obeisance *(bow)*
- yore *(past)*
- quaff *(drink)*
- balm *(ointment)*

55 But the Raven, sitting lonely on the **placid** bust, spoke only ▶ **3**
    That one word, as if his soul in that one word he did outpour.
    Nothing farther then he uttered—not a feather then he fluttered—
    Till I scarcely more than muttered "Other friends have flown before—
    On the morrow *he* will leave me, as my Hopes have flown before."
60   Then the bird said "Nevermore."

    Startled at the stillness broken by reply so aptly spoken,
    "Doubtless," said I, "what it utters is its only stock and store ▶ **4**
    Caught from some unhappy master whom unmerciful Disaster
    Followed fast and followed faster till his songs one burden bore—
65 Till the dirges[8] of his Hope that melancholy burden bore
        Of 'Never—nevermore.' "

    But the Raven still beguiling all my fancy into smiling,
    Straight I wheeled a cushioned seat in front of bird, and bust and door;
    Then, upon the velvet sinking, I betook myself to linking
70 Fancy unto fancy, thinking what this ominous bird of yore—
    What this grim, ungainly, ghastly, gaunt, and ominous bird of yore
        Meant in croaking "Nevermore."

    This I sat engaged in guessing, but no syllable expressing
    To the fowl whose fiery eyes now burned into my bosom's core;
75 This and more I sat divining,[9] with my head at ease reclining
    On the cushion's velvet lining that the lamplight gloated o'er,
    But whose velvet violet lining with the lamplight gloating o'er,
        She shall press, ah, nevermore!

    Then, methought, the air grew denser, perfumed from an unseen censer[10]
80 Swung by Seraphim[11] whose foot-falls tinkled on the tufted floor.
    "Wretch," I cried, "thy God hath lent thee—by these angels he hath sent thee
    Respite—**respite** and nepenthe[12] from thy memories of Lenore;
    Quaff,[13] oh quaff this kind nepenthe and forget this lost Lenore!"
        Quoth the Raven "Nevermore."

---

8. *Dirges* are slow, mournful pieces of music, such as funeral hymns.
9. *Divining* means "knowing through insight or intuition" or "guessing."
10. A *censer* is a container in which incense is burned.
11. *Seraphim* are angels of the highest rank.
12. The ancient Greeks believed the drug *nepenthe* (ni pen' thē) would ease pain and grief by causing forgetfulness.
13. *Quaff* means "to drink heartily and deeply."

> Analyze Sound Devices *How is this repetition of the word* nevermore *different than others in the poem, and what is the significance of that difference?* ▶ **5**

Vocabulary

placid (pla´ səd) *adj.* calm; peaceful; undisturbed
respite (res´ pət) *n.* a period of rest or relief, as from work or sorrow

EDGAR ALLAN POE **259**

Teach

Vocabulary   3

Synonyms Say: Read the definition of *placid* on this page. The word is defined by synonyms. **Ask:** What is a synonym of *placid*? (*Possible answers: quiet; tranquil*)

Literary Element   4

Narrative Poem Ask: Why is the speaker "startled" in line 61? (*The bird speaks the word* nevermore *as if in answer to the speaker's thoughts.*)

Reading Strategy   5

Analyze Sound Devices
Answer: *Here,* nevermore *is not said by the bird but is a part of the speaker's thoughts. He has connected the repeated word to the haunting memory of his lost love.*

Say: Many of the poem's stanzas end in *nevermore*. What is the effect of this repetition? (*Hypnotic; it emphasizes the mournful mood of the poem.*)

Approaching Level

DIFFERENTIATED INSTRUCTION

Emerging To help students keep track of the sequence of events in this poem, show them how to complete a sequence map as they continue to read. In the first box, display the following sentences retelling the first event in the poem: *It is midnight and the speaker is alone. He is sad about his lost love Lenore. The speaker hears a rustling at the curtains.* In the second box, write *He opens the shutter and lets the Raven inside his room.* **Ask:** What does the speaker say to the Raven? What does he do? Ask students to write their answers in boxes on their sequence maps.

English Learners

DIFFERENTIATED INSTRUCTION

Intermediate Remind students to use the footnotes at the bottom of the page. Have students find the meanings of *ominous, gaunt,* and *syllable* and record them in their two-column charts.

Teach

Reading Strategy   1

Analyze Sound Devices
Answer: *The repetition of the commands "take thy beak from" and "take thy form from" emphasizes the speaker's frustration and agitation.*

Literary Element   2

Narrative Poem **Answer:**
The end of the poem ties up the narrative. The story peaks, or reaches its climax, in the second-to-last stanza. The last lines present the final resolution to the story.

Language History

Biblical Allusions Literature is peppered with allusions to persons, places, and events in—as well as quotations from—the Bible. When Poe uses the phrase "balm in Gilead," he expects readers to be familiar with the Biblical prophet Jeremiah, who calls out for relief from pain.

To check students' understanding of the selection, see Unit 2 Teaching Resources Book, p. 124.

85 "Prophet!" said I, "thing of evil!—prophet still, if bird or devil!—
      Whether Tempter[14] sent, or whether tempest tossed thee here ashore,
      Desolate yet all undaunted, on this desert land enchanted—
      On this home by Horror haunted—tell me truly, I implore—
      Is there—*is* there **balm** in Gilead?[15]—tell me—tell me, I implore!"
90   Quoth the Raven "Nevermore."

      "Prophet!" said I, "thing of evil!—prophet still, if bird or devil!
      By that Heaven that bends above us—by that God we both adore—
      Tell this soul with sorrow laden if, within the distant Aidenn,[16]
      It shall clasp a sainted maiden whom the angels name Lenore—
95   Clasp a rare and radiant maiden whom the angels name Lenore."
           Quoth the Raven "Nevermore."

      "Be that word our sign of parting, bird or fiend!" I shrieked, upstarting—
      "Get thee back into the tempest and the Night's Plutonian shore!
      Leave no black plume as a token of that lie thy soul hath spoken!
100 Leave my loneliness unbroken!—quit the bust above my door!
      Take thy beak from out my heart, and take thy form from off my door!"
           Quoth the Raven "Nevermore."

      And the Raven, never flitting, still is sitting, *still* is sitting
      On the pallid[17] bust of Pallas just above my chamber door;
105 And his eyes have all the seeming of a demon's that is dreaming,
      And the lamp-light o'er him streaming throws his shadow on the floor;
      And my soul from out that shadow that lies floating on the floor
           Shall be lifted—nevermore!

Le Corbeau (The Raven), 1875.
Edouard Manet. Lithograph.
Hamburger Kunsthalle, Germany.

---

14. *Tempter* refers to the devil.
15. *Gilead* was a region in ancient Palestine. Here Poe paraphrases a line from the Bible (Jeremiah 8:22): "Is there no balm in Gilead?" By this he means, "Is there no relief from my suffering?"
16. *Aidenn* means "Eden."
17. *Pallid* means "lacking in color" or "pale."

Analyze Sound Devices *What is the effect of the repetition in this line?*   **1**

Narrative Poem *How is the end of this poem similar to the end of a short story?*   **2**

Vocabulary
balm (bäm) *n.* something that heals or soothes, as an ointment

260 UNIT 2   AMERICAN ROMANTICISM

Writing Practice

SPIRAL REVIEW **Combine Sentences** Explain to students that a main clause has a subject and a verb and expresses a complete thought. Closely related main clauses can be combined to form a compound sentence. Write these two main clauses on the board: **Poe's father abandoned his family when Poe was an infant. His mother died a year later.** Show students that these two main clauses can be combined using a coordinating conjunction preceded by a comma: **Poe's father abandoned his family when Poe was an infant, and his mother died a year later.** Have students write a summary of one stanza from "The Raven" using coordinating conjuctions to combine two main clauses.

After You Read

Respond and Think Critically

Respond and Interpret

1. In your opinion, what is the most haunting image in this poem?

2. (a)Why is the speaker reading at the beginning of the poem? (b)How would you describe his emotional state in the first six stanzas?

3. (a)What is the speaker's first reaction to the raven's entrance? (b)Why does he react this way?

4. (a)What will never be lifted from the raven's shadow? (b)What does the future hold for him?

Analyze and Evaluate

5. What is the effect of the repetition of *nevermore*?

Literary Element Narrative Poem

Narrative poems include a narrator, or speaker.

1. Who is the "I" in "The Raven"?

2. What words would you use to describe this speaker?

Reading Strategy Analyze Sound Devices

The music of Poe's verses derives from his use of sound devices, most of which are kinds of repetition.

1. What is the effect of the repetition of the word *tapping*?

2. The words *grim, ungainly, ghastly,* and *gaunt* describe the raven. How do these words contribute to the meaning of the poem?

 LOG ON **Literature** Online

Selection Resources For Selection Quizzes, eFlash-cards, and Reading-Writing Connection activities, go to glencoe.com and enter QuickPass code GLA9800u2.

6. (a)How would you describe Poe's purpose in writing this poem? (b)Did he achieve his purpose? Explain.

Connect

7. **Big Idea** The Power of Darkness Which details contribute to the mood of this poem, and how do they illustrate the dark side of Romanticism?

8. **Connect to the Author** As you read on page 254, Poe's life was full of both tragedy and controversy—including heavy gambling and marriage to his 13-year-old cousin. In your opinion, how did his experiences and his lifestyle affect his literary efforts and career?

Vocabulary Practice

Practice with Synonyms With a partner, match each boldfaced vocabulary word below with its synonym. (You will not use all options.) Check your work with a thesaurus or dictionary.

1. lattice   **a.** evade
2. beguile   **b.** net
3. placid   **c.** charm
4. respite   **d.** lull
5. balm   **e.** chaotic
               f. serene
               g. ointment

Writing

Write a Summary Narrative poems contain elements of both poetry and storytelling. Summarize the plot in "The Raven," making sure to identify the climax, or point of greatest emotional intensity. Remember that a summary should be shorter than the original because the purpose is to highlight main points. For help summarizing, see page 79.

After You Read

Assess

1. Students' answers will vary.

2. (a) To distract himself from his sorrow (b) He moves from grief to curiosity to fear.

3. (a) He is startled and amused. (b) He is relieved to be distracted from his melancholy.

4. (a) The speaker's soul (b) The future will be one of despair.

5. It unifies the poem and adds to the mystery of the raven's arrival and ability to speak.

6. (a) Students may say that Poe's purpose was to write a poem that would create a mood of melancholy and a speaker haunted by memories. (b) Students may point to the poem's enduring popularity as evidence that Poe achieved his purpose.

7. Details such as "darkness," "midnight dreary," "fantastic terrors," and "ominous bird," as well as details about the speaker's distress, create a haunting, mysterious mood that reflects Romanticism's dark side.

8. Students may say that his father's disappearance and his mother's death likely affected the themes of death and mystery that permeate his works.

> For additional assessment, see Assessment Resources, pp. 111–112.

Progress Check

Can students analyze sound devices?

If No → See Unit 2 Teaching Resources Book, p. 121.

Literary Element

1. The "I" is the lover of Lenore.

2. Students might suggest *obsessed, tortured, depressed, melancholy, grieving,* and *distracted*.

Writing

Students' summaries should clearly identify the climax and main points of the poem.

Vocabulary

1. b **2.** c **3.** f **4.** d **5.** g

Before You Read

Focus

Summary

A soldier is sentenced to death by the Spanish Inquisition but escapes a sharp swinging pendulum. Just as he is about to be forced into a pit by heated metal walls, French soldiers enter the city, and he is saved.

 For summaries in languages other than English, see Unit 2 Teaching Resources Book, pp. 126–131.

Vocabulary

Synonyms and Antonyms
Say: Look at the definition for *deduce.* The word *conclusion* is in the definition. A synonym for *deduce* is *conclude.* **Ask:** What is an antonym for *impede*? *(help, assist)* Ask students to find a synonym and/or antonym for each word in the vocabulary list.

 For additional vocabulary practice, see Unit 2 Teaching Resources Book, p. 134.

Before You Read

The Pit and the Pendulum

Connect to the Story

Why do certain things terrify some people more than they do others? Freewrite for a few minutes about personal phobias and what might cause them.

Build Background

This story is set during the last years of the Spanish Inquisition (1478–1834). Established in 1231 by the Roman Catholic Church, the Inquisition was a court that arrested and tried suspected heretics, or those who opposed Church teaching. Those convicted of heresy were imprisoned for life or sentenced to death. Today, the Inquisition is remembered as a period of mercilessness and brutality.

Set Purposes for Reading

Big Idea **The Power of Darkness**

As you read, ask yourself, How are psychological darkness and terror—two topics that fascinated some Romantics—portrayed in this story?

Literary Element **Suspense**

Suspense is a feeling of curiosity, uncertainty, or even dread about what is going to happen next. Writers heighten the suspense in a story by creating a threat to the central character, or protagonist, and giving readers clues about what might happen. As you read "The Pit and the Pendulum," ask yourself, How does Poe create suspense?

Reading Strategy **Identify Sequence**

Sequence is the logical order of ideas or events. To indicate time order, writers often use signal words or phrases, such as *before, earlier that morning,* or *after that.* As you read Poe's story, look for signal words that indicate the sequence of events.

Tip: Take Notes Use a chart to record the sequence of events.

Learning Objectives

For pages 262–275

In studying this text, you will focus on the following objectives:

Literary Study: Analyzing sequence.

Reading: Identifying sequence.

Vocabulary

deduce (di dōōs´) *v.* to draw a conclusion from something known or assumed; p. 265 *Several clues helped us deduce the location of the runaways.*

impede (im pēd´) *v.* to slow or block progress or action; obstruct; p. 265 *Road construction will impede travel this summer.*

lethargy (leth´ ər jē) *n.* sluggish inactivity or drowsiness; p. 268 *Dad told Bill to be active and get over his lethargy.*

proximity (prok sim´ ə tē) *n.* closeness in space, time, sequence, or degree; nearness; p. 271 *The proximity of the cobra made us nervous.*

diffuse (di fūz´) *v.* to spread widely; to scatter in all directions; p. 273 *Green dye was diffused into the river on St. Patrick's Day.*

Selection Skills

Literary Elements
▪ Suspense (SE pp. 262, 263, 266, 267, 269, 273, 275)

The Pit and the Pendulum

Writing Skills/Grammar
▪ Write an Essay (SE p. 276)
▪ Analyze Description (TE p. 266)
▪ Imagine (TE p. 268)
▪ Use the Dash (TE p. 270)

Reading Skills
▪ Identify Sequence (SE pp. 262, 265, 267–271, 275)
▪ Evaluate Tone (TE p. 272)

Vocabulary Skills
▪ Word Origins (SE p. 275)
▪ Context Clues (TE p. 264)

Listening/Speaking/Viewing Skills
▪ Analyze Art (SE pp. 266, 270, 274)

The Pit and the Pendulum

Edgar Allan Poe

Inquisition Scene, 1816. Francisco Goya. Oil on canvas, 46 x 73 cm. Real Academia de Bellas Artes de San Fernando, Madrid.

I was sick—sick unto death with that long agony; and when they at length unbound me, and I was permitted to sit, I felt that my senses were leaving me. The sentence—the dread sentence of death—was the last of distinct accentuation which reached my ears. After that, the sound of the inquisitorial voices seemed merged in one dreamy indeterminate hum. It conveyed to my soul the idea of *revolution*—perhaps from its association in fancy with the burr of a millwheel. This only for a brief period; for presently I heard no more. Yet, for a while, I saw; but with how terrible an exaggeration! I saw the lips of the black-robed judges. They appeared to me white—whiter than the sheet upon which I trace these words—and thin even to grotesqueness;[1] thin with the intensity of their expression of firmness—of immovable resolution—of stern contempt of human torture. I saw that the decrees of what to me was Fate, were still issuing from those lips. I saw them writhe with a deadly locution.[2] I saw them fashion the syllables of my name; and I shuddered because no sound succeeded. I saw, too, for a few moments of delirious horror, the soft and nearly imperceptible waving of the sable draperies which enwrapped the walls of the apartment. And then my vision fell upon the seven tall candles upon the table. At first they wore the aspect of charity, and seemed white slender angels who would save me; but then, all at once, there came a most deadly nausea over my spirit, and I felt every

---

1 Suspense *The narrator obviously lives to tell his story despite his death sentence. How do you think the author will maintain interest in his tale?*

2 The Power of Darkness *What is the effect of Poe's description of extreme whiteness here?*

---

1. *Grotesqueness* is the state of being distorted or unnatural in shape or appearance.
2. *Locution* is a form or style of verbal expression.

EDGAR ALLAN POE **263**

Teach

Identify Sequence Read the bracketed passage aloud.

Say: In this passage, the narrator is describing his descent into a lower dungeon. **Ask:** What words and phrases describe the sequence of the descent? *(Possible answers: "down—down—still down"; "Then comes"; "After this")*

(APPROACHING) Ask students whether the descent took place slowly or quickly. *(The repetition of the word down suggests that it felt like a long time to the narrator.)*

StdNA

Literary History ☆

The Gothic Tradition Dark, mysterious, and often ghastly settings and subjects are part of the Gothic literary tradition. Mary Shelley's *Frankenstein* and Bram Stoker's *Dracula* are two of the most famous British Gothic novels. In the United States, Poe and Nathaniel Hawthorne were the two most famous authors to write in the Gothic tradition.

---

fiber in my frame thrill as if I had touched the wire of a galvanic battery,[3] while the angel forms became meaningless specters,[4] with heads of flame, and I saw that from them there would be no help. And then there stole into my fancy, like a rich musical note, the thought of what sweet rest there must be in the grave. The thought came gently and stealthily, and it seemed long before it attained full appreciation; but just as my spirit came at length properly to feel and entertain it, the figures of the judges vanished, as if magically, from before me; the tall candles sank into nothingness; their flames went out utterly; the blackness of darkness supervened; all sensations appeared swallowed up in a mad rushing descent as of the soul into Hades.[5] Then silence, and stillness, and night were the universe.

☆   I had swooned; but still will not say that all of consciousness was lost. What of it there remained I will not attempt to define, or even to describe; yet all was not lost. In the deepest slumber—no! In delirium—no! In a swoon—no! In death—no! even in the grave all *is not* lost. Else there is no immortality[6] for man. Arousing from the most profound[7] of slumbers, we break the gossamer web of *some* dream. Yet in a second afterward, (so frail may that web have been) we remember not that we have dreamed. In the return to life from the swoon there are two stages; first, that of the sense of mental or spiritual; secondly, that of the sense of physical, existence. It seems probable that if, upon reaching the second stage, we could recall the impressions of the first, we should find these impressions eloquent in memories of the gulf beyond. And that gulf is—what? How at least shall we distinguish

> Very suddenly there came back to my soul motion and sound . . . .

its shadows from those of the tomb? But if the impressions of what I have termed the first stage, are not, at will, recalled, yet, after long interval, do they not come unbidden, while we marvel whence they come? He who has never swooned, is not he who finds strange palaces and wildly familiar faces in coals that glow; is not he who beholds floating in midair the sad visions that the many may not view; is not he who ponders over the perfume of some novel[8] flower—is not he whose brain grows bewildered with the meaning of some musical cadence which has never before arrested his attention.

Amid frequent and thoughtful endeavors to remember; amid earnest struggles to regather some token of the state of seeming nothingness into which my soul had lapsed, there have been moments when I have dreamed of success; there have been brief, very brief periods when I have conjured up remembrances which the lucid reason of a later epoch assures me could have had reference only to that condition of seeming unconsciousness. These shadows of memory tell, indistinctly, of tall figures that lifted and bore me in silence down—down—still down—till a hideous dizziness oppressed me at the mere idea of the interminableness[9] of the descent. They tell also of a vague horror at my heart, on account of that heart's unnatural stillness. Then comes a sense of sudden motionlessness throughout all things; as if those who bore me (a ghastly train!) had outrun, in their descent, the limits of the limitless, and paused from the wearisomeness of their toil. After this I call to mind flatness and dampness; and that all is *madness*—the madness of a memory which busies itself among forbidden things.

Very suddenly there came back to my soul motion and sound—the tumultuous motion of

---

3. In a *galvanic battery,* direct electric current is produced by means of chemical action.
4. *Specters* are ghosts or ghostly visions.
5. In Greek myth, *Hades* is the underground place of the dead.
6. Here, *immortality* means "eternal life."
7. Here, *profound* means "complete" or "deep."
8. A *novel* flower is new and unusual.
9. *Interminableness* means "endlessness."

Vocabulary Practice

SPIRAL REVIEW **Context Clues** Tell students that many words have multiple meanings. Readers must rely on context clues to determine which meanings authors intend. For example, *brief* can mean "short in length" or "a summary of the main points of a law case." Context determines its meaning.

Point out the word *stole* in the fifth line from the beginning of this page. **Ask:** What context clues help you determine the meaning of the word? *(The words* gently *and* stealthily *and the phrase "it seemed long . . . appreciation" are clues that the meaning is "came gradually and secretly.")*

the heart, and, in my ears, the sound of its beating. Then a pause in which all is blank. Then again sound, and motion, and touch—a tingling sensation pervading my frame. Then the mere consciousness of existence, without thought—a condition which lasted long. Then, very suddenly, *thought*, and shuddering terror, and earnest endeavor to comprehend my true state. Then a strong desire to lapse into insensibility.[10] Then a rushing revival of soul and a successful effort to move. And now a full memory of the trial, of the judges, of the sable draperies, of the sentence, of the sickness, of the swoon. Then entire forgetfulness of all that followed; of all that a later day and much earnestness of endeavor have enabled me vaguely to recall.

So far, I had not opened my eyes. I felt that I lay upon my back, unbound. I reached out my hand, and it fell heavily upon something damp and hard. There I suffered[11] it to remain for many minutes, while I strove to imagine where and *what* I could be. I longed, yet dared not to employ my vision. I dreaded the first glance at objects around me. It was not that I feared to look upon things horrible, but that I grew aghast lest there should be *nothing* to see. At length, with a wild desperation at heart, I quickly unclosed my eyes. My worst thoughts, then, were confirmed. The blackness of eternal night encompassed me. I struggled for breath. The intensity of the darkness seemed to oppress and stifle me. The atmosphere was intolerably close. I still lay quietly, and made

effort to exercise my reason. I brought to mind the inquisitorial proceedings,[12] and attempted from that point to **deduce** my real condition. The sentence had passed; and it appeared to me that a very long interval of time had since elapsed. Yet not for a moment did I suppose myself actually dead. Such a supposition, notwithstanding what we read in fiction, is altogether inconsistent with real existence;—but where and in what state was I? The condemned to death, I knew, perished usually at the *autos-da-fé*,[13] and one of these had been held on the very night of the day of my trial. Had I been remanded to my dungeon, to await the next sacrifice which would not take place for many months? This I at once saw could not be. Victims had been in immediate demand. Moreover, my dungeon, as well as all the condemned cells at Toledo,[14] had stone floors, and light was not altogether excluded.

A fearful idea now suddenly drove the blood in torrents upon my heart, and for a brief period, I once more relapsed into insensibility. Upon recovering, I at once started to my feet, trembling convulsively in every fiber. I thrust my arms wildly above and around me in all directions. I felt nothing; yet dreaded to move a step, lest I should be **impeded** by the walls of the *tomb*. Perspiration burst from every pore and stood in cold big beads on my forehead. The agony of suspense grew at length intolerable, and I cautiously moved forward, with my arms extended, and my eyes straining from their

---

10. The narrator is describing his wish to return to unconsciousness *(insensibility)*.
11. Here, *suffered* means "allowed."

Identify Sequence Note the number of times the narrator repeats the word *then* in this paragraph. What does this repetition tell you about the stages the narrator goes through as he gradually regains consciousness?

3 The Power of Darkness How does the narrator's description of his surroundings reflect the Gothic tradition?

12. During the Inquisition, a person's refusal to confess was taken as evidence of guilt.
13. Often, the sentence was to be burned alive in public ceremonies called *autos-da-fé* (ô′ tōz də fā′). The phrase is Portuguese for "acts of faith," referring to the Inquisitors' faith that the condemned persons were guilty as charged.
14. The Spanish city of *Toledo* was important during the Inquisition.

Vocabulary

deduce (di doōs′) *v.* to draw a conclusion from something known or assumed
impede (im pēd′) *v.* to slow or block progress or action; obstruct

Identify Sequence Answer: *He alternates between extreme awareness of his predicament and blankness, thoughtlessness, and forgetfulness.*

| Big Idea | 3 |

The Power of Darkness Answer: *The author mentions the "intensity of the darkness" and uses the words* blackness, shadows, tomb, dampness, madness, fear, *and* eternal night—*all Gothic details.*

English Learners

DIFFERENTIATED INSTRUCTION

Beginning Explain that an adverb describes a verb, an adjective, or another adverb. Many adverbs end in *-ly.* The word *heavily* (describes the verb *fell*) is an example of an adverb. Ask students to identify other adverbs and the words they describe on this page.

Approaching Level

DIFFERENTIATED INSTRUCTION

Emerging Explain to students that the narrator describes how all of his senses are taking in this horrible experience. For example, he refers to the sense of touch in this line: "I felt that I lay upon my back, unbound." Ask students to make a five-column "Senses" chart and use it to identify descriptions that show how the speaker's sight, hearing, smell, taste, and touch are affected in the dungeon.

Teach

sockets, in the hope of catching some faint ray of light. I proceeded for many paces; but still all was blackness and vacancy. I breathed more freely. It seemed evident that mine was not, at least, the most hideous of fates.

And now, as I still continued to step cautiously onward, there came thronging upon my recollection a thousand vague rumors of the horrors of Toledo. Of the dungeons there had been strange things narrated— fables I had always deemed them—but yet strange, and too ghastly to repeat, save in a whisper. Was I left to perish of starvation in the subterranean[15] world of darkness; or what fate, perhaps even more fearful, awaited me? That the result would be death, and a death of more than customary bitterness, I knew too well the character of my judges to doubt. The mode and the hour were all that occupied or distracted me.

My outstretched hands at length encountered some solid obstruction. It was a wall, seemingly of stone masonry—very smooth, slimy, and cold. I followed it up; stepping with all the careful distrust with which certain antique narratives had inspired me. This process, however, afforded me no means of ascertaining the dimensions of my dungeon; as I might make its circuit, and return to the point whence I set out, without being aware of the fact; so perfectly uniform seemed the wall. I therefore sought the knife which had been in my pocket, when led into the inquisitorial chamber; but it was gone; my clothes had been exchanged for a wrapper of coarse serge. I had thought of forcing the blade in some minute crevice of the masonry, so as to identify my point of departure. The difficulty, nevertheless, was but triv-

---

15. *Subterranean* describes things that exist or occur below the earth's surface.

1 Suspense *How do the narrator's physical and psychological torments add to the suspense?*

2 Suspense *How does this sentence build tension?*

Half length portrait of a man bending over, 18th c. Giovanni Battista Piranesi. Pen and ink on paper, 15.8 x 21.6 cm. Hamburger Kunsthalle, Hamburg, Germany.

View the Art Giovanni Battista Piranesi uses lines to create areas of light and shadow in his portrait rather than sharp outlines. How does this technique compare with Poe's narration in this story? ★

ial; although, in the disorder of my fancy, it seemed at first insuperable.[16] I tore a part of the hem from the robe and placed the fragment at full length, and at right angles to the wall. In groping my way around the prison I could not fail to encounter this rag upon completing the circuit. So, at least I thought: but I had not counted upon the extent of the dungeon, or upon my own weakness. The ground was moist and slippery. I staggered onward for some time, when I stumbled and fell. My excessive fatigue induced me to remain prostrate; and sleep soon overtook me as I lay.

Upon awakening, and stretching forth an arm, I found beside me a loaf and a pitcher with water. I was too much exhausted to reflect upon this circumstance, but ate and drank with avidity.[17] Shortly afterward, I resumed my tour around the prison, and with much toil, came at last upon the fragment of the serge. Up to the period when I fell I had counted fifty-two paces,

---

16. Something that's *insuperable* cannot be overcome.
17. *Avidity* is eagerness and enthusiasm.

Writing Practice

⚡ Analyze Description Explain to students that descriptive writing is controlled by a dominant impression that functions as a thesis. Details in the description should reinforce the dominant impression. Have students identify the dominant impression in one paragraph from Poe's story and write an analysis of the description. The analysis should identify the dominant impression Poe creates, explain how the descriptive details are organized, and point out the senses to which the description appeals.

and upon resuming my walk, I counted forty-eight more;—when I arrived at the rag. There were in all, then, a hundred paces; and admitting two paces to the yard, I presumed the dungeon to be fifty yards in circuit. I had met, however, with many angles in the wall, and thus I could form no guess at the shape of the vault; for vault I could not help supposing it to be.

I had little object—certainly no hope—in these researches; but a vague curiosity prompted me to continue them. Quitting the wall, I resolved to cross the area of the enclosure. At first I proceeded with extreme caution, for the floor, although seemingly of solid material, was treacherous with slime. At length, however, I took courage, and did not hesitate to step firmly; endeavoring to cross in as direct a line as possible. I had advanced some ten or twelve paces in this manner, when the remnant of the torn hem of my robe became entangled between my legs. I stepped on it, and fell violently on my face.

In the confusion attending my fall, I did not immediately apprehend a somewhat startling circumstance, which yet, in a few seconds afterward, and while I still lay prostrate, arrested my attention. It was this—my chin rested upon the floor of the prison, but my lips and the upper portion of my head, although seemingly at a less elevation than the chin, touched nothing. At the same time my forehead seemed bathed in a clammy vapor, and the peculiar smell of decayed fungus arose to my nostrils. I put forward my arm, and shuddered to find that I had fallen at the very brink of a circular pit, whose extent, of course, I had no means of ascertaining at the moment. Groping about the masonry just below the margin, I succeeded in dislodging a small fragment, and let it fall into the abyss.[18] For many seconds I hearkened to its reverberations as it dashed against the sides of the chasm in its descent; at length there was a sullen plunge into water, succeeded by loud echoes. At the same moment there came a sound resembling the quick opening, and a rapid closing of a door overhead, while a faint gleam of light flashed suddenly through the gloom, and as suddenly faded away.

I saw clearly the doom which had been prepared for me, and congratulated myself upon the timely accident by which I had escaped. Another step before my fall, and the world had seen me no more. And the death just avoided, was of that very character which I had regarded as fabulous and frivolous[19] in the tales respecting the Inquisition. To the victims of its tyranny, there was the choice of death with its direst physical agonies, or death with its most hideous moral horrors. I had been reserved for the latter. By long suffering my nerves had been unstrung, until I trembled at the sound of my own voice, and had become in every respect a fitting subject for the species of torture which awaited me.

Shaking in every limb, I groped my way back to the wall; resolving there to perish rather than risk the terrors of the wells, of which my imagination now pictured many in various positions about the dungeon. In other conditions of mind I might have had courage to end my misery at once by a plunge into one of these abysses; but now I was the veriest of cowards. Neither could I forget what I had read of these pits—that the *sudden* extinction of life formed no part of their most horrible plan.

Agitation of spirit kept me awake for many long hours; but at length I again slumbered. Upon arousing, I found by my side as before, a loaf and a pitcher of water. A burning thirst consumed me, and I emptied the vessel at a draught. It must have been drugged; for

---

18. Here, *abyss* (ə bis′) refers to "an extremely deep hole."

  Identify Sequence *What signal words indicate the sequence of events in this paragraph?*

19. Here, *fabulous* means "fictional," and *frivolous* means "silly" or "unimportant."

Suspense *How do the opening and closing of a door overhead help create suspense?* **4**

The Power of Darkness *How does this sentence reflect Romanticism's fascination with disease and madness?* **5**

EDGAR ALLAN POE **267**

Teach

Reading Strategy   3

Identify Sequence Answer: *Signal words include* at first *and* at length*.* **Ask:** What is the narrator attempting to do at this time? *(He is attempting to walk directly across the dungeon rather than feel his way along the wall.)*

(ADVANCED) Ask students to identify and record other words and structures that signal sequence as they continue to read.

Literary Element   4

Suspense Answer: *It is ominous that the narrator is being observed. It is a mystery that urges the reader onward to discover the answer.*

Big Idea   5

The Power of Darkness
Answer: *The narrator's nerves are unstrung; even the sound of his own voice makes him tremble. These are indications that he is breaking down physically and mentally.*

English Learners

DIFFERENTIATED INSTRUCTION

Intermediate Help students visualize this dungeon scene by identifying some of the spatial relationships that the narrator describes. Display the following passages from the story:

- "fallen at the very brink of a circular pit"
- "closing of a door overhead"
- "groped my way back to the wall"
- "began my tour with the wall to the left"
- "ended . . . with the wall to the right"

Have students explain what each of the passages tells about the narrator's movement or location within the dungeon.

Advanced Learners

UNIVERSAL ACCESS

Spanish Inquisition Have students research these questions and share their findings: Who did the Inquisition target? How did the Inquisition period end? How does the story relate to the Inquisition?

Teach

Reading Strategy | 1

Identify Sequence Answer:
Constant activity in chronological sequence would be as wearying for the reader as for the narrator. Both the reader and the narrator need time to rest and reflect on the rhythmic series of events.

Ask: What event has occurred while the narrator slept? *(The room has been lighted.)*

Literary History

The Detective Story Critics consider Poe the father of the mystery/detective story. "The Murders in the Rue Morgue," his first mystery, was published in 1841, the same year as "The Pit and the Pendulum." "The Murders in the Rue Morgue," along with "The Mystery of Marie Roget" and "The Purloined Letter," features the brilliant and eccentric detective C. Auguste Dupin, who is considered one of the prototypes for the great fictional detective Sherlock Holmes. As he does in "The Pit and the Pendulum," Poe stresses close observation of details and logical deduction in his detective stories.

---

scarcely had I drunk, before I became irresistibly drowsy. A deep sleep fell upon me—a sleep like that of death. How long it lasted of course, I know not; but when, once again, I unclosed my eyes, the objects around me were visible. By a wild sulphurous luster, the origin of which I could not at first determine, I was enabled to see the extent and aspect of the prison.

In its size I had been greatly mistaken. The whole circuit of its walls did not exceed twenty-five yards. For some minutes this fact occasioned me a world of vain trouble; vain indeed! for what could be of less importance, under the terrible circumstances which environed[20] me, than the mere dimensions of my dungeon? But my soul took a wild interest in trifles, and I busied myself in endeavors to account for the error I had committed in my measurement. The truth at length flashed upon me. In my first attempt at exploration I had counted fifty-two paces, up to the period when I fell; I must then have been within a pace or two of the fragments of serge; in fact, I had nearly performed the circuit of the vault. I then slept, and upon awaking, I must have returned upon my steps—thus supposing the circuit nearly double what it actually was. My confusion of mind prevented me from observing that I began my tour with the wall to the left, and ended it with the wall to the right.

I had been deceived, too, in respect to the shape of the enclosure. In feeling my way around I had found many angles, and thus deduced an idea of great irregularity; so potent is the effect of total darkness upon one arousing from **lethargy** or sleep! The angles were simply those of a few slight depressions, or niches, at odd intervals. The general shape of the prison

---

20. To *environ* is to encircle or surround.

1 Identify Sequence *Why does the author alternate periods of activity with periods of inaction?*

Vocabulary

lethargy (leth′ ər jē) *n.* sluggish inactivity or drowsiness

---

was square. What I had taken for masonry seemed now to be iron, or some other metal, in huge plates, whose sutures or joints occasioned the depression. The entire surface of this metallic enclosure was rudely daubed in all the hideous and repulsive devices[21] to which the charnel[22] superstitions of the monks has given rise. The figures of fiends in aspects of menace, with skeleton forms, and other more really fearful images, overspread and disfigured the walls. I observed that the outlines of these monstrosities were sufficiently distinct, but that the colors seemed faded and blurred, as if from the effects of a damp atmosphere. I now noticed the floor, too, which was of stone. In the center yawned the circular pit from whose jaws I had escaped; but it was the only one in the dungeon.

All this I saw distinctly and by much effort: for my personal condition had been greatly changed during slumber. I now lay upon my back, and at full length, on a species of low framework of wood. To this I was securely bound by a long strap resembling a surcingle.[23] It passed in many convolutions about my limbs and body, leaving at liberty only my head, and my left arm to such extent that I could, by dint of much exertion, supply myself with food from an earthen dish which lay by my side on the floor. I saw, to my horror, that the pitcher had been removed. I say to my horror; for I was consumed with intolerable thirst. This thirst it appeared to be the design of my persecutors to stimulate: for the food in the dish was meat pungently seasoned. ☆

Looking upward I surveyed the ceiling of my prison. It was some thirty or forty feet overhead, and constructed much as the side walls. In one of its panels a very singular figure riveted my whole attention. It was the painted figure of Time as he is commonly represented, save that, in lieu of[24] a scythe, he held what, at a casual

---

21. Here, the *devices* are ornamental designs.
22. Here, *charnel* means "gruesome" or "deathlike." As a noun, it refers to a vault where bones or bodies are placed.
23. A *surcingle* is a belt or band used to hold a saddle or pack on a horse or pack animal.
24. *In lieu* (in lōō) *of* means "in place of" or "instead of."

Writing Practice

Imagine Explain that imagining the sights, sounds, smells, tastes, and feel of objects will help the reader appreciate the horror of Poe's story. Poe offers many descriptive details, but he also leaves many details to readers' imaginations.

Have students write their responses to the following questions:

- What does the dungeon smell like?
- What sounds are made by the rats and the moving pendulum?
- What sensations does the narrator feel from his bindings?

glance, I supposed to be the pictured image of a huge pendulum such as we see on antique clocks. There was something, however, in the appearance of this machine which caused me to regard it more attentively. While I gazed directly upward at it (for its position was immediately over my own) I fancied that I saw it in motion. In an instant afterward the fancy was confirmed. Its sweep was brief, and of course slow. I watched it for some minutes, somewhat in fear, but more in wonder. Wearied at length with observing its dull movement, I turned my eyes upon the other subjects in the cell.

A slight noise attracted my notice, and, looking to the floor, I saw several enormous rats traversing it. They had issued from the well, which lay just within view to my right. Even then, while I gazed, they came up in troops, hurriedly, with ravenous eyes, allured by the scent of the meat. From this it required much effort and attention to scare them away.

It might have been half an hour, perhaps even an hour, (for I could take but imperfect note of time) before I again cast my eyes upward. What I then saw confounded and amazed me. The sweep of the pendulum had increased in extent by nearly a yard. As a natural consequence, its velocity was also much greater. But what mainly disturbed me was the idea that it had perceptibly *descended*. I now observed—with what horror it is needless to say—that its nether extremity[25] was formed of a crescent of glittering steel, about a foot in length from horn to horn; the horns upward, and the under edge evidently as keen as that of a razor. Like a razor also, it seemed massy and heavy, tapering from the edge into a solid and broad structure above. It was appended to a weighty rod of brass, and the whole *hissed* as it swung through the air.

I could no longer doubt the doom prepared for me by monkish ingenuity[26] in torture. My cognizance of the pit had become known to the inquisitorial agents—*the pit* whose horrors had been destined for so bold a recusant[27] as myself—*the pit*, typical of hell, and regarded by rumor as the Ultima Thule[28] of all their punishments. The plunge into this pit I had avoided by the merest of accidents, and I knew that surprise, or entrapment into torment, formed an important portion of all the grotesquerie of these dungeon deaths. Having failed to fall, it was no part of the demon plan to hurl me into the abyss; and thus (there being no alternative) a different and a milder destruction awaited me. Milder! I half smiled in my agony as I thought of such application of such a term.

What boots it[29] to tell of the long, long hours of horror more than mortal, during which I counted the rushing vibrations of the steel! Inch by inch—line by line—with a descent only appreciable at intervals that seemed ages—down and still down it came! Days passed—it might have been that many days passed—ere it swept so closely over me as to fan me with its acrid breath. The odor of the sharp steel forced itself into my nostrils. I prayed—I wearied heaven with my prayer for its more speedy descent. I grew frantically mad, and struggled to force myself upward against the sweep of the fearful scimitar.[30] And then I fell suddenly calm, and lay smiling at the glittering death, as a child at some rare bauble.[31]

---

25. The pendulum's *nether extremity* is its lower end.

26. *Ingenuity* (in′ jə nōō′ ə tē)—the noun form of *ingenious*—is creative ability or inventiveness.
27. A *recusant* (re′ kyə zənt) is one who refuses to accept or obey established authorities.
28. Here, *Ultima Thule* (ul′ tə mə thōō lē) means "extreme limit" or "greatest degree." In ancient times, this was the name of the northernmost part of the known world.
29. *What boots it* is an expression meaning "What good is it?"
30. A *scimitar* is a curved, single-edged sword of Asian origin.
31. A *bauble* is any showy but worthless trinket.

2 Identify Sequence *How does this reference to the passage of time contribute to the suspense of the following sentence?*

Suspense *What is to be his fate? Why is the destruction "milder?"* **3**

EDGAR ALLAN POE **269**

Reading Strategy	2

Identify Sequence Answer: *The reference reinforces the fact that the narrator has been looking away from the ceiling long enough for a startling change to have taken place there.*

Literary Element	3

Suspense Answer: *His fate will apparently not include being hurled into the abyss; therefore, some other form of "destruction" is in store. That destruction is milder only because the narrator so dreads the pit.*

Advanced Learners

DIFFERENTIATED INSTRUCTION

Physics of a Pendulum Explain to students that the narrator is describing the frightening swings of a pendulum. Have students find photos of pendulums and research the factors (weight, length, amplitude) that affect a pendulum's swing and answer these questions:

- What is the length of time of a pendulum swing in a standard wall clock? *(about one second)*

- What is the length of time of a pendulum swing in a standard grandfather clock? *(about two seconds)*
- How long is a pendulum in a standard grandfather clock? *(between two and three feet)*
- What factor or factors affect the period of time it takes for a pendulum to go back and forth? *(length of the pendulum)*

Teach

Identify Sequence Answer:
The repetition of again *indicates that the action of the pendulum is unceasing.*

Ask: When the narrator repeats the word *again*, what is he anticipating will happen to him? *(He anticipates that the pendulum will continue to lower until it slowly cuts through his chest and kills him.)*

[ADVANCED] **Say:** The text says that the sweep of the pendulum is some thirty feet or more. **Ask:** What would you estimate the pendulum's length to be? *(It is at least about ten feet long.)*

View the Art ★

Answer: *The prison in the illustration—apparently like that in the story—is vast, oppressive, and equipped with elaborate mechanisms.*

Piranesi created a series of etchings of imaginary prisons that influenced contemporary stage designers, artists, and Gothic novelists. The influence of these etchings continued into the 20th century, when they inspired designers of sets for horror films.

There was another interval of utter insensibility; it was brief; for, upon again lapsing into life there had been no perceptible descent in the pendulum. But it might have been long; for I knew there were demons who took note of my swoon, and who could have arrested the vibration at pleasure. Upon my recovery, too, I felt very—oh, inexpressibly sick and weak, as if through long inanition.[32] Even amid the agonies of that period, the human nature craved food. With painful effort I outstretched my left arm as far as my bonds permitted, and took possession of the small remnant which had been spared me by the rats. As I put a portion of it within my lips, there rushed to my mind a half formed thought of joy—of hope. Yet what business had I with hope? It was, as I say, a half formed thought— man has many such which are never completed. I felt that it was of joy—of hope; but I felt also that it had perished in its formation. In vain I struggled to perfect—to regain it. Long suffering had nearly annihilated all my ordinary powers of mind. I was an imbecile—an idiot.

The vibration of the pendulum was at right angles to my length. I saw that the crescent was designed to cross the region of the heart. It would fray the serge of my robe—it would return and repeat its operations—again—and again. Notwithstanding its terrifically wide sweep (some thirty feet or more) and the hissing vigor

Carceri d'Invenzione, Plate XIII, 1780. Giovanni Battista Piranesi. Etching, 16 x 22 in. Private collection.

View the Art In a series called *Carceri,* Giovanni Battista Piranesi invented elaborate, ominous prison scenes—much as Poe does in this story. What in this illustration suggests a setting similar to the one described by the story's narrator?

of its descent, sufficient to sunder these very walls of iron, still the fraying of my robe would be all that, for several minutes, it would accomplish. And at this thought I paused. I dared not go farther than this reflection. I dwelt upon it with a pertinacity[33] of attention—as if, in so dwelling, I could arrest *here* the descent of the steel. I forced myself to ponder upon the sound of the crescent as it should pass across the garment—upon the peculiar thrilling sensation which the friction of cloth produces on the nerves. I pondered upon all this frivolity until my teeth were on edge.

Down—steadily down it crept. I took a frenzied pleasure in contrasting its downward with its lateral velocity. To the right—to the left—far and wide—with the shriek of a damned spirit; to my heart with the stealthy pace of the tiger! I alternately laughed and howled as the one or the other idea grew prominent.

---

32. **The exhaustion caused by a lack of food or water is called** *inanition.*

1 Identify Sequence *How does the repetition of the signal word* again *heighten the feeling of terror?*

33. *Pertinacity* is stubborn persistence.

Grammar Practice

SPIRAL REVIEW **The Dash** Point out that Poe punctuates many sentences with dashes. A dash is used to signal a change in thought or to emphasize parenthetical material.

Tell students that a good test of the correct use of dashes for parenthetical material is to delete the information that the dashes set off. If the remaining sentence keeps its basic meaning, then the dashes were properly used.

Have students apply this test to two sentences on this page. Have them explain how the sentences retain their meaning when the material enclosed by dashes is removed.

Down—certainly, relentlessly down! It vibrated within three inches of my bosom! I struggled violently, furiously, to free my left arm. This was free only from the elbow to the hand. I could reach the latter, from the platter beside me, to my mouth, with great effort, but no farther. Could I have broken the fastenings above the elbow, I would have seized and attempted to arrest the pendulum. I might as well have attempted to arrest an avalanche!

Down—still unceasingly—still inevitably down! I gasped and struggled at each vibration. I shrunk convulsively at its every sweep. My eyes followed its outward or upward whirls with the eagerness of the most unmeaning despair; they closed themselves spasmodically at the descent, although death would have been a relief, oh! how unspeakable! Still I quivered in every nerve to think how slight a sinking of the machinery would precipitate that keen, glistening axe upon my bosom. It was *hope* that prompted the nerve to quiver—the frame to shrink. It was *hope*—the hope that triumphs on the rack[34]—that whispers to the death-condemned even in the dungeons of the Inquisition.

I saw that some ten or twelve vibrations would bring the steel in actual contact with my robe, and with this observation there suddenly came over my spirit all the keen, collected calmness of despair. For the first time during many hours—or perhaps days—I *thought*. It now occurred to me that the bandage, or surcingle, which enveloped me, was *unique*. I was tied by no separate cord. The first stroke of the razor-like crescent athwart any portion of the band, would so detach it that it might be unwound

They were wild, bold, ravenous . . . .

from my person by means of my left hand. But how fearful, in that case, the **proximity** of the steel! The result of the slightest struggle how deadly! Was it likely, moreover, that the minions of the torturer had not foreseen and provided for this possibility! Was it probable that the bandage crossed my bosom in the track of the pendulum? Dreading to find my faint, and, as it seemed, my last hope frustrated, I so far elevated my head as to obtain a distinct view of my breast. The surcingle enveloped my limbs and body close in all directions—*save in the path of the destroying crescent.*

Scarcely had I dropped my head back into its original position, when there flashed upon my mind what I cannot better describe than as the unformed half of that idea of deliverance to which I have previously alluded, and of which a moiety[35] only floated indeterminately through my brain when I raised food to my burning lips. The whole thought was now present—feeble, scarcely sane, scarcely definite,—but still entire. I proceeded at once, with the nervous energy of despair, to attempt its execution.

For many hours the immediate vicinity of the low framework upon which I lay, had been literally swarming with rats. They were wild, bold, ravenous; their red eyes glaring upon me as if they waited but for motionlessness on my part to make me their prey. "To what food," I thought, "have they been accustomed in the well?"

They had devoured, in spite of all my efforts to prevent them, all but a small remnant of the contents of the dish. I had fallen into an habitual seesaw, or wave of the hand about the platter: and, at length, the unconscious uniformity

---

34. The *rack* was an instrument of torture used to stretch or pull a victim's body in different directions.

35. A *moiety* of something is a portion of it.

[2] Identify Sequence *How does the repetition of the word* down *at the beginning of each of three paragraphs indicate the passing of time?*

EDGAR ALLAN POE **271**

Reading Strategy [2]

Identify Sequence Answer: *Each time the pendulum moves down, a little more time has passed.*

Ask: What sequence of events is occurring in the three paragraphs beginning with the word *down*? (*The pendulum is slowly descending, and the narrator is becoming more terrified.*)

Vocabulary [3]

Context Clues Ask: How do the phrases "how fearful" and "result of the slightest struggle how deadly" help you understand the meaning of *proximity*? (*The context shows that the pendulum is getting very close to the narrator.*)

English Learners
DIFFERENTIATED INSTRUCTION

Intermediate Explain that Poe uses many terms to refer to the same object. Draw a word map and write *rats* in the center. In outer circles write *ravenous animals; wild, bold; vermin; deliverers.* Have students make a word map for *pendulum* with Poe's terms in the outer circles.

Approaching Level
DIFFERENTIATED INSTRUCTION

Emerging Explain that the narrator's emotions range from scared and depressed to wildly excited. Show students how this range might look on a line graph with high points for excitement and surprise and low points for sadness and terror. Have students make a graph using a vertical axis of 0–5 for emotional level. They should label the horizontal axis points with the page and paragraph number. Have students make a line graph of the emotions the narrator experiences on this page, and then make predictions about the next series of emotions the narrator may feel.

Teach

Reading Strategy   1

Identify Sequence
Say: Describe the sequence of events in this passage. *(The narrator rubs his greasy hands on his bindings, then lies perfectly still, waiting for the rats to gnaw the bindings. The rats at first are frightened, but then they swarm over him.)*

[ENGLISH LEARNERS] To help English learners follow the developments in the sequence, be sure they understand these terms: *voracity* (greediness in eating), *writhed* (twisted and turned), and *severed* (cut through).

Big Idea   2

The Power of Darkness
Answer: *Nature is presented as malevolent.*

of the movement deprived it of effect. In their voracity the vermin frequently fastened their sharp fangs into my fingers. With the particles of the oily and spicy viand which now remained, I thoroughly rubbed the bandage wherever I could reach it; then, raising my hand from the floor, I lay breathlessly still.

At first the ravenous animals were startled and terrified at the change—at the cessation of movement. They shrank alarmedly back; many sought the well. But this was only for a moment. I had not counted in vain upon their voracity. Observing that I remained without motion, one or two of the boldest leaped upon the frame-work, and smelt at the surcingle. This seemed the signal for a general rush. Forth from the well they hurried in fresh troops. They clung to the wood—they overran it, and leaped in hundreds upon my person. The measured movement of the pendulum disturbed them not at all. Avoiding its strokes they busied themselves with the anointed bandage. They pressed—they swarmed upon me in ever accumulating heaps. They writhed upon my throat; their cold lips sought my own; I was half stifled by their thronging pressure; disgust, for which the world has no name, swelled my bosom, and chilled, with a heavy clamminess, my heart. Yet one minute, and I felt that the struggle would be over. Plainly I perceived the loosening of the bandage. I knew that in more than one place it must be already severed. With a more than human resolution I lay *still*.

Nor had I erred in my calculations—nor had I endured in vain. I at length felt that I was *free*. The surcingle hung in ribands from my body. But the stroke of the pendulum already pressed upon my bosom. It had divided the serge of the robe. It had cut through the linen beneath. Twice again it swung, and a sharp sense of pain shot through every nerve. But the moment of escape had arrived. At a wave of my hand my deliverers hurried tumultuously away. With a

steady movement—cautious, sidelong, shrinking, and slow—I slid from the embrace of the bandage and beyond the reach of the scimitar. For the moment, at least, *I was free*.

Free!—and in the grasp of the Inquisition! I had scarcely stepped from my wooden bed of horror upon the stone floor of the prison, when the motion of the hellish machine ceased and I beheld it drawn up, by some invisible force through the ceiling. This was a lesson which I took desperately to heart. My every motion was undoubtedly watched. Free!—I had but escaped death in one form of agony, to be delivered unto worse than death in some other. With that thought I rolled my eyes nervously around the barriers of iron that hemmed me in. Something unusual—some change which at first I could not appreciate distinctly—it was obvious, had taken place in the apartment. For many minutes in a dreamy and trembling abstraction,[36] I busied myself in vain, unconnected conjecture.[37] During this period, I became aware, for the first time, of the origin of the sulphurous light which illuminated the cell. It proceeded from a fissure, about half an inch in width, extending entirely around the prison at the base of the walls, which thus appeared, and were completely separated from the floor. I endeavored, but of course in vain, to look through the aperture.

As I arose from the attempt, the mystery of the alteration in the chamber broke at once upon my understanding. I have observed that, although the outlines of the figures upon the walls were sufficiently distinct, yet the colors seemed blurred and indefinite. These colors had now assumed, and were momentarily assuming, a startling and most intense brilliancy, that gave to the spectral and fiendish portraitures an aspect that might have thrilled even firmer nerves than my own. Demon eyes, of a wild and ghastly vivacity, glared upon me in a thousand directions, where none had been

---

2   **The Power of Darkness** *What view of nature is presented here?*

36. *Abstraction* is the state of being lost in thought.
37. *Conjecture* is the forming of an opinion without definite or sufficient evidence.

Reading Practice

SPIRAL REVIEW **Evaluate Tone** Guide students to evaluate the tone of "The Pit and the Pendulum." Explain that the rhythm of the sentences is established by the punctuation and length of the sentences. **Ask:** How does Poe use sentence structure (or style) to show the horror of the speaker's situation? What makes the speaker sound frightened and desperate? *(repetition and dashes reveal uncertainty; exclamation points reveal desperation)* Have students support their evaluation of tone with five examples from the text.

visible before, and gleamed with the lurid lus-ter[38] of a fire that I could not force my imagination to regard as unreal.

Unreal!—Even while I breathed there came to my nostrils the breath of the vapor of heated iron! A suffocating odor pervaded the prison! A deeper glow settled each moment in the eyes that glared at my agonies! A richer tint of crimson **diffused** itself over the pictured horrors of blood. I panted! I gasped for breath! There could be no doubt of the design of my tormentors—oh! most unrelenting! oh! most demoniac of men! I shrank from the glowing metal to the center of the cell. Amid the thought of the fiery destruction that impended, the idea of the coolness of the well came over my soul like balm.[39] I rushed to its deadly brink. I threw my straining vision below. The glare from the enkindled roof illumined its inmost recesses. Yet, for a wild moment, did my spirit refuse to comprehend the meaning of what I saw. At length it forced—it wrestled its way into my soul—it burned itself in upon my shuddering reason.—Oh! for a voice to speak! oh! horror!—oh! any horror but this! With a shriek, I rushed from the margin, and buried my face in my hands—weeping bitterly.

The heat rapidly increased, and once again I looked up, shuddering as with a fit of the ague.[40] There had been a second change in the cell—and now the change was obviously in the *form*. As before, it was in vain that I, at first, endeavoured to appreciate or understand what was taking place. But not long was I left in doubt. The Inquisitorial vengeance had been hurried by my two-fold escape, and there was

to be no more dallying with the King of Terrors.[41] The room had been square. I saw that two of its iron angles were now acute—two, consequently, obtuse. The fearful difference quickly increased with a low rumbling or moaning sound. In an instant the apartment had shifted its form into that of a lozenge. But the alteration stopped not here—I neither hoped nor desired it to stop. I could have clasped the red walls to my bosom as a garment of eternal peace. "Death," I said, "any death but that of the pit!" Fool! might I have not known that *into the pit* it was the object of the burning iron to urge me? Could I resist its glow? or, if even that, could I withstand its pressure? And now, flatter and flatter grew the lozenge, with a rapidity that left me no time for contemplation. Its center, and of course, its greatest width, came just over the yawning gulf. I shrank back—but the closing walls pressed me resistlessly onward. At length for my seared and writhing body there was no longer an inch of foothold on the firm floor of the prison. I struggled no more, but the agony of my soul found vent in one loud, long, and final scream of despair. I felt that I tottered upon the brink—I averted my eyes—

There was a discordant hum of human voices! There was a loud blast of many trumpets! There was a harsh grating as of a thousand thunders! The fiery walls rushed back! An outstretched arm caught my own as I fell, fainting, into the abyss. It was that of General Lasalle.[42] The French army had entered Toledo. The Inquisition was in the hands of its enemies.

---

38. The eyes are full of life (*vivacity*), with a fiery, reddish glare (a *lurid* luster).
39. Although destruction was about to occur (*impended*), the idea of coolness seemed to be something calming or soothing (a *balm*).
40. *Ague* (ā′ gū) is a fever accompanied by chills and shivering.

41. The *King of Terrors* could be either the "Inquisitorial vengeance" or death.
42. *Lasalle* was an officer of the French emperor Napoleon Bonaparte, whose army invaded Spain in 1808.

Suspense *How has the mystery of the pit heightened the suspense throughout the story?* **3**

The Power of Darkness *An atmosphere of horror is essential to Gothic fiction. How does this passage create a sense of horror?* **4**

EDGAR ALLAN POE **273**

Teach

Literary Element **3**

Suspense Answer: *The reader is never certain whether the narrator will meet his end at the bottom of the pit. This uncertainty hovers over the entire story.*

(**ENGLISH LEARNERS**) Check to make sure that English learners understand the three dangers involved in his uncertainty: the demon eyes of the rats, the darkness, and the pit.

Big Idea **4**

The Power of Darkness
Answer: *The passage creates a sense of horror by depicting the narrator shrinking in terror as he is about to topple into the pit.*

To check students' understanding of the selection, see Unit 2 Teaching Resources Book, p. 137.

Approaching Level

DIFFERENTIATED INSTRUCTION

AAVE Read the following sentence in the selection: *I saw that two of its iron angles were now acute—two, consequently, obtuse.* Note the phrase *two angles were acute.* Approaching level students who are users of AAVE may not follow subject-verb agreement with irregular verbs. For example, they might say *two angles was acute.* Give students a few correct examples: *She were my friend, They was happy, My*

friends has gone. Then provide students with a list of pronoun subjects (you, he, she, it, we, they) and a list of adjectives or nouns (funny, happy, my friend, etc.) and have them join one word from each list using either *was* or *were*, as appropriate. Provide students with lists of words that they can use to practice the correct use of *does, do, have, has.*

After You Read

Assess

1. (a) Horror, sympathy (b) Students may have been surprised by how the narrator is rescued.

2. (a) Death (b) He is so fearful that he cannot hear the judges; then he faints.

3. (a) He walks around the walls, counting his steps. (b) He wants to know what fate awaits him.

4. (a) A death of "hideous moral horrors," like hell (b) Its depth and contents are unknown.

5. (a) He is strapped down beneath a gradually descending pendulum. (b) Students may mention the narrator's hope and his renewed ability to think.

6. (a) Above all, the narrator fears the pit. (b) Yes: words like *shriek* and *shuddering* convey terror.

7. (a) Even the most rational people are subject to mental distress in extreme situations. (b) Many will say his attempts to escape death are realistic.

8. Frightening and macabre; Poe uses concise details to describe the setting, build suspense, and portray fear.

9. Answers will vary. Students may note that, in America today, certain groups do suffer because of the suspicion, fear, and misunderstanding of other citizens.

 For additional assessment, see Assessment Resources, pp. 113–114

Progress Check

Can students identify sequence?

If No → See Unit 2 Teaching Resources Book, p. 133.

After You Read

Respond and Think Critically

Respond and Interpret

1. (a) What emotions did you experience while reading this story? (b) Were you surprised by the ending? Why or why not?

2. (a) To what fate has the narrator been sentenced? (b) What does his immediate reaction tell you about his state of mind?

3. (a) How does the narrator determine the size of his prison? (b) Why might he feel that he must find out about his surroundings?

4. (a) What kind of death does he associate with the pit? (b) Why might the pit put him in such a state of terror?

5. (a) What horror does the narrator face after avoiding the pit? (b) Why do you think the narrator responds as he does to the second horror?

Analyze and Evaluate

6. (a) Why is the third method of torture especially frightening for the narrator? (b) Is Poe's portrayal of the third method as the most horrible convincing?

7. (a) What do the narrator's struggles and thoughts throughout his ordeal tell you about Poe's view of human nature? (b) Do you think the narrator's actions are realistic given his situation? Explain.

Connect

8. **Big Idea** **The Power of Darkness** How would you describe the mood or atmosphere of this story? How does Poe achieve this effect?

9. **Connect to Today** Could the Spanish Inquisition—or something like it—occur today? Explain your response.

Primary Visual Artifact

Attacking the Inquisition

The artist Francisco de Goya (1746–1828) was a fierce critic of the Spanish Inquisition. Many of his works deal with the suffering it caused, including the series of prints, *Los caprichos (The Caprices)*, published in 1799. Number 23 of the series, *Aquellos polbos (Those Specks of Dust)*, depicts a disabled woman arrested for selling love potions. Dressed in the typical robe and conical hat worn by condemned heretics, she slumps before the officers of the Inquisition.

Group Activity Discuss the following questions:

1. Why do you think Goya might have chosen to depict the trial of this woman?

2. How would you compare and contrast Poe's and Goya's portrayals of the Inquisition?

Los caprichos, Plate 23, 1799. Francisco de Goya. Etching, 22 x 15 cm. Private Collection.

Group Activity

1. Her disability and her trivial offense show that she is a victim of a brutal institution.

2. Both show the Inquisition as brutal; Poe's story shows an impersonal, sadistic power, whereas Goya's print puts a face on the terror.

Literary Element Suspense

Suspense generally increases as the plot of a story moves toward its climax. In "The Pit and the Pendulum," Poe generates tension and uncertainty by pitting the narrator against one horror after another. The reader becomes more and more involved in the story and concerned about what will happen to the narrator.

1. The narrator undergoes moments of both physical and psychological torment. Give two examples of each. Describe the event, and tell how each event heightens the story's suspense.

2. In your opinion, what is the most suspenseful moment in the story? Explain your choice.

Review: Point of View

As you learned in Unit One, **point of view** refers to the perspective from which a story is told. Poe's story is told in the first-person point of view. The narrator is a character in the story who uses the pronouns *I, me,* and *my.* Everything that the reader learns is filtered through the eyes, ears, and thoughts of the narrator.

Partner Activity With another classmate discuss how the story's point of view contributes to its mood of suspense. Create a list of examples in which the first-person point of view limits your knowledge of events, characters, and setting. Then, explain how each example helps create suspense. If possible, share your findings with the class.

Reading Strategy Identify Sequence
ACT Skills Practice

1. The ending of "The Pit and the Pendulum" represents:

   A. a logical progression of events.

   B. an improbable solution to the narrator's plight.

   C. the triumph of the Inquisition.

   D. the negation of the narrator's premonitions and fears.

Vocabulary Practice

Practice with Word Origins Create a word map like the one shown for each selection vocabulary word. Use a dictionary for help.

deduce	proximity	lethargy
impede	diffuse	

Definition: a peculiarity of constitution or temperament

Etymology: Greek *idiosynkrasia* means "to blend"

idiosyncrasy

Sample Sentence: Her habit of making sarcastic comments during serious occasions was definitely an idiosyncrasy.

Academic Vocabulary

The action of "The Pit and the Pendulum" unfolds in an **environment** *that is filled with mystery and terror.*

The word *environment* can have different meanings in different subject areas. Use context clues to infer the meaning of *environment* in the sentence above. Check your inference in a dictionary.

For more on academic vocabulary, see pages 53–54.

After You Read

Assess

Literary Element

1. Being tied to a table and being cut by the pendulum; the darkness and the rats. As each horror is overcome, another, more terrifying one looms ahead.

2. When the pendulum cuts through the narrator's clothing; when the heated walls move

Review: Point of View

Events: The narrator does not give details about the "long agony" he suffered prior to his trial; details of the trial are not made clear; what caused the French to rescue the narrator is not revealed.

Characters: People watching the narrator in the dungeon are unknown.

Setting: Details about the building that houses the dungeon are not revealed.

Vocabulary

impede Definition: to slow progress or action; Etymology: Latin *impedire* means "to hobble"; Sample Sentence: The curb impeded the driver from backing up.

deduce Definition: to draw a conclusion from something known or assumed; Etymology: Latin *deduco* means "to bring down"; Sample Sentence: From studying the patient's symptoms, the doctor was able to deduce a diagnosis.

lethargy Definition: sluggish inactivity or drowsiness; Etymology: Greek *lethargus* means "drowsiness"; Sample Sentence: Her lethargy prevented her from doing her chores.

proximity Definition: closeness in space, time, sequence, or degree; Etymology: Latin *proximitas* means "nearness"; Sample Sentence: The proximity of fast food was apparent from the smell.

diffuse Definition: to spread widely; to scatter in all directions; Etymology: Latin *diffusilis* means "capable of spreading"; Sample Sentence: The campaign manager tried to diffuse news of her candidate's lead in the polls.

After You Read

Assess

 ### Respond Through Writing

Students' expository essays should have a clear thesis that examines the story sequence, supported by evidence from the text. Assess students' essays in the following categories using the rubric at the bottom of the page:

- Addresses all parts of the writing task.
- Provides a meaningful thesis, maintains focus and organization.
- Supports the thesis with details and examples.
- Provides a variety of sentence types; uses precise, descriptive language.
- Follows English language conventions.
- Makes a logical, convincing analysis.

For grammar practice, see Unit 2 Teaching Resources Book, p. 136.

Respond Through Writing

Expository Essay

Analyze Sequence "The Pit and the Pendulum" is full of suspense, despite its confined setting and single character. To keep the reader interested, Poe unfolds his tale very carefully. In an expository essay, analyze how Poe uses this story's sequence to create suspense.

Understand the Task When you **analyze** something, you identify its parts to find meaning in their relationship to the whole. **Sequence** is the logical order of ideas or events.

Prewrite Look back at the notes you took (page 262) to record the sequence of events in "The Pit and the Pendulum." Then create a chart like the one below to analyze how Poe indicates sequence through techniques such as signal words or words that indicate the passage of time. Find examples of these techniques in the text. Examine where these instances occur in relation to the story's suspenseful passages. Note your observations on the relationship of sequence and suspense.

Sequence Indicator	Example	Relationship to Suspense
signal words	• "After that..." • "And then..."	
passage of time		

Draft Using your work from the prewriting step, craft your thesis. In your essay, remember to both describe Poe's sequencing techniques and make a claim about how those techniques affect the story's suspense. Try using the following sentence frame to express your ideas.

Poe uses _____ and _____ to create suspense by _____.

Revise Consider how the sequence of "The Pit and the Pendulum" differs from that of other stories you have read. As you revise your essay, emphasize what makes Poe's use of sequence unique.

Edit and Proofread Proofread your paper, correcting any errors in spelling, grammar, and punctuation. Review the Grammar Tip in the side column for help using apostrophes.

Grammar Tip

Apostrophes

To show possession, add an apostrophe and an *s* ('s) to all singular nouns, including those ending with an *s* (such as *Jones*), and plural nouns that do not end in *s*:

The story's mood is tense.

That is Ms. Jones's book.

There is the mice's hole.

Add only an apostrophe to a plural noun ending in *s*.

Where is the kids' mother?

Do not add an apostrophe to a possessive adjective:

It is hers, not theirs.

Scoring Guide	4	3	2	1
Task addressed	fully	mostly	partially	barely
Themes	meaningful	provided	partial	weak
Support	thoughtful	provided	limited	weak
Language	varied, descriptive	varied, often descriptive	predictable, imprecise	repetitive, limited
Convention errors	few or none	several	many	serious
Analysis is	convincing	mostly convincing	partially convincing	not convincing

Vocabulary Workshop

Context Clues

Literature Connection What does *swooned* mean in the quotation below?

> *"I had swooned; but still will not say that all of consciousness was lost."*
>
> —Edgar Allan Poe, from "The Pit and the Pendulum"

Sometimes the context in which a word appears provides clues to its meaning. That the narrator "will not say that all of consciousness was lost" is a clue that *swooned* means "to fall in a faint."

One or more kinds of context clues may be provided.

- Context sometimes provides an **example** of a word's meaning:
  Falling into a dark pit would certainly be a calamity.

- Context may provide a restatement or a **definition** of a word:
  Tom Walker was gullible, and his wife was just as easy to fool.

- Context may provide a **synonym** for the unfamiliar word:
  The money was sufficient—enough for everyone there.

- Context may also supply an antonym—a word or phrase with an opposite meaning—to **contrast** with the unfamiliar word.
  Many would fear a talking raven, but not the dauntless narrator.

Practice Use *context* clues to infer the **meaning** of each underlined word. Identify the type of context clue used to uncover its meaning.

1. Edgar Allan Poe is credited with writing the first crime stories that use <u>ratiocination</u>, or logical thinking, to solve a mystery.
   a. reasoning **b.** characters **c.** mathematics **d.** footprints

2. In one of Poe's stories, "The <u>Purloined</u> Letter," a detective is asked to get the document back that was taken without consent.
   a. ancient **b.** personal **c.** damaged **d.** stolen

3. Other characters may think that a problem is <u>inexplicable</u>, but Poe's detective, C. Auguste Dupin, finds it easy to understand.
   a. mysterious **b.** boring **c.** simple **d.** dangerous

4. Many modern <u>sleuths</u>, from Nancy Drew to the police investigators on TV crime shows, owe their methods to Dupin.
   a. criminals **b.** readers **c.** detectives **d.** authors

 Literature Online

Vocabulary For more vocabulary practice, go to glencoe.com and enter QuickPass code GLA9800u2.

Learning Objectives

In this workshop, you will focus on the following objectives:

Vocabulary: Inferring meaning from context clues.

Vocabulary Terms

The **context** of a word refers to the words and sentences surrounding a given word. **Synonyms** are words that have similar meanings.

Tip

When you are asked for the meaning of a word that appears in a reading passage, you will usually find one or more context clues near the word.

Vocabulary Workshop

Context Clues

Focus

Context Clues Say: When you meet an unfamiliar word in a sentence, you should check the sentence before and the sentence after to see if they contain context clues to the word's meaning.

Teach

Have students identify the context clues offered for the underlined words in the **Practice** sentences:

    sentence 1: logical thinking
    sentence 2: taken without consent
    sentence 3: easy to understand
    sentence 4: investigators

Then have them figure out the meanings of the underlined words.

Assess

Practice

1. a; definition

2. d; synonym

3. a; antonym

4. c; example

 For additional vocabulary practice, see Glencoe Interactive Vocabulary CD–ROM.

English Learners

DIFFERENTIATED INSTRUCTION

Intermediate English language learners may be unsure of the meaning of such academic vocabulary as *definition, synonym, antonym,* and *example.* If so, work through the exercise as a way of helping them grasp the meanings of these terms.

Before You Read

Focus

Bellringer Options

**Selection Focus
  Transparency 19**
**Daily Language Practice
  Transparency 28**

Or display images of different types of masks (such as those worn by athletes and medical personnel, Halloween masks, and African and Native American masks).

Ask: What is the same about all masks? What are some of the purposes masks serve? Have students consider as they read how the minister's black veil is like and unlike other masks.

Before You Read

The Minister's Black Veil

Meet **Nathaniel Hawthorne**
(1804–1864)

What do you think it would be like to spend a dozen years in self-imposed solitude? Nathaniel Hawthorne did just that, reading widely in New England history and perfecting his skills as a writer. The dark Puritan past haunted Hawthorne's imagination. His ancestors included one judge who had prosecuted Quakers in the 1650s and another who had served in the notorious witchcraft trials at Salem, Massachusetts, in 1692. No churchgoer, Hawthorne was still as keenly aware of problems of sin and guilt as any early Puritan. He explored complex questions of right and wrong in tales he called "allegories of the heart"—stories that teach a moral principle.

Habits of Solitude Born in Salem, young Hawthorne was an avid reader of poetry and stories of adventure. He also spent long periods alone in the remote Maine woods, where "I first got my cursed habits of solitude." After attending college in Maine, Hawthorne returned to Salem, where he secluded himself at home for the "twelve lonely years" of his apprenticeship as a writer. He produced two books, first a novel titled *Fanshawe* and later a collection of short stories, *Twice-Told Tales*. The novel was a failure, but reviewers praised *Twice-Told Tales*, and the book sold well. In the late 1830s, as Hawthorne was beginning to establish his reputation as a writer, he met and fell in love with Sophia Peabody, whom he married in 1842. The couple moved to Concord, where Hawthorne socialized with Ralph Waldo Emerson and Henry David Thoreau. However, Hawthorne was not in sympathy with Emerson's optimistic outlook and goals of reforming society.

Literary Success Unable to support his growing family as a writer, Hawthorne returned to Salem and took a government job that he disliked. When he lost the job, he turned again to writing, completing his masterpiece, *The Scarlet Letter*, in early 1850. The book was a sensation, and Hawthorne soon followed it with another successful novel, *The House of the Seven Gables*. During this period, he moved his family from Salem to the countryside, where a close neighbor was the writer Herman Melville. The two writers, who shared a dark view of human life, spent a great deal of time together.

> *"What other dungeon is so dark as one's own heart! What jailer so inexorable as one's self!"*
>
> —Nathaniel Hawthorne
> from *The House of the Seven Gables*

In ill health, struggling to continue writing, and depressed, Hawthorne died in 1864 while on a journey. In his writing, he tried to create "a neutral ground where the Actual and the Imaginary might meet." When he succeeds, his fiction has, as the literary critic Alfred Kazin observes, "the mysterious authenticity and the self-sufficient form of a dream."

 Literature Online

Author Search For more about Nathaniel Hawthorne, go to glencoe.com and enter QuickPass code GLA9800u2.

Selection Skills

Literary Elements
- Symbol (SE pp. 279, 281, 283, 285, 286, 288, 289, 291; TE p. 284)

← **The Minister's Black Veil** →

Listening/Speaking/Viewing Skills
- Analyze Art (SE pp. 283, 287)

Reading Skills
- Make Inferences (SE pp. 279, 281, 286, 288, 291)
- Analyze Mood (TE p. 280)

Vocabulary Skills
- Synonyms (SE p. 291)
- Academic Vocabulary (SE p. 291)
- Affixes (TE pp. 279, 287)
- Connotations (TE p. 282)

Writing Skills/Grammar
- Expository Essay (SE p. 292)
- Dangling Participles (TE p. 284)
- Write a Letter (TE p. 288)

Literature and Reading Preview

Connect to the Story

Do you ever wear a "mask" in order to hide or distance yourself from other people? Why or why not? Reflect on these questions in a journal entry. Refer to specific situations if possible.

Build Background

"The Minister's Black Veil" is set in a small town in Puritan New England in the early 1700s. Puritans believed that human beings were sinful by nature and deserved eternal punishment but that God had "elected" some people to be saved. Puritans fought the "natural" tendency to sin and felt responsible for the moral welfare of others. The subtitle of "The Minister's Black Veil" is "A Parable." A parable is a story meant to illustrate a moral lesson.

Set Purposes for Reading

Big Idea The Power of Darkness

As you read, ask yourself, How is the Romantics' fascination with the strange and sinister represented in the "The Minister's Black Veil"?

Literary Element Symbol

A **symbol** is a person, place, or thing that has meaning in itself and also stands for something other than itself. A crossroads, for example, may symbolize choices in life. A symbol in a literary work may be unique to that work, or it may be an **archetype**— a symbol that has universal meaning and appears in many cultures and historical periods. Hawthorne develops the meaning of the veil in ways that are specific to this story's characters and action. However, darkness has a symbolic meaning that is archetypal—it can be found in literature and art of many times and traditions. As you read, ask yourself, How does Hawthorne develop the symbolic meaning of the black veil?

Reading Strategy Make Inferences

To **infer** is to make a reasonable guess about the meaning of a literary work from what a writer implies. In a symbolic story such as "The Minister's Black Veil," we must observe details to infer the writer's meaning.

Learning Objectives

For pages 278–291

In studying this text, you will focus on the following objectives:

Literary Study: Analyzing symbols.

Reading: Making inferences about theme.

Vocabulary

venerable (ven´ ər ə bəl) *adj.* deserving respect because of age, character, or position; p. 281 *The people relied on the venerable judge's wisdom.*

iniquity (in ik´ wə tē) *n.* sin; p. 282 *He was too steeped in iniquity to tell right from wrong.*

sagacious (sə gā´ shəs) *adj.* having or showing wisdom and keen perception; p. 282 *The sagacious man often gave very good advice.*

irreproachable (ir´ i prō´ chə bəl) *adj.* free from blame; faultless; p. 288 *The lawyer's handling of the case was irreproachable.*

zealous (zel´ əs) *adj.* filled with enthusiastic devotion; passionate; p. 288 *The zealous music fan had attended hundreds of concerts.*

NATHANIEL HAWTHORNE **279**

When Parson Hooper arrives in church to preach his Sunday sermon, he is wearing a black veil that hides much of his face. His congregation is deeply troubled by the veil, but no one is willing to ask him why he wears it. As the years pass, the minister's veil remains an object of dread but also makes him a more effective clergyman.

For summaries in languages other than English, see Unit 2 Teaching Resources Book, pp. 139–144.

Vocabulary

Understand Affixes Point out the adjective suffixes in this list: *-able* ("worthy or capable of being") and *-ous* ("full of"). Explain that adding the suffix *-ous* to *iniquity* changes the noun to its adjective form *iniquitous,* which means "full of sin, wicked." Ask students to identify the roots of *venerable, sagacious, irreproachable,* and *zealous. (venerate, sagacity, reproach, zeal)*

For additional vocabulary practice, see Unit 2 Teaching Resources Book, p. 147.

For additional context, see Glencoe Interactive Vocabulary CD–ROM.

Approaching Level

DIFFERENTIATED INSTRUCTION

Emerging Remind students that they learned about the Puritans in Unit One. Although this story was written in 1836, it is set in the 1700s, nearly one hundred years earlier. Ask students to recall details about the time period. Direct students back to the Timeline on pages 6–7 to stimulate their thinking. **Ask:** What questions might a writer ask to help him or her write a story set in a historic time

period? *(How did people live, work, and talk? What did people believe in? How were people's lives different from our lives today?)*

Teach

Big Idea　1

The Power of Darkness

Say: Why might Hawthorne introduce hints of the supernatural into this story? *(He was fascinated with the dark side of Romanticism.)* How does this supernaturalism emphasize the sinister nature of the black veil? *(It suggests an unobservable evil lurking behind the veil.)*

APPROACHING **Ask:** Why would a person wear a veil or a mask? *(to hide something)*

Cultural History ☆

Architecture In the 1700s, small towns and villages had meeting-houses. The meetinghouse was often the only public gathering place. The community used this public "house" as a church, a school, and a gathering place for social and governmental functions. The style of these buildings was similar to that of the colonists' houses; it did not necessarily look like what we consider a "church."

For an audio recording of this selection, use Listening Library Audio CD-ROM

Readability Scores

Dale-Chall: 8.0
DRP: 66
Lexile: 1240

A PARABLE

The Minister's Black Veil

Nathaniel Hawthorne

1

☆ The sexton[1] stood in the porch of Milford meeting-house, pulling busily at the bell-rope. The old people of the village came stooping along the street. Children, with bright faces, tripped merrily beside their parents, or mimicked a graver gait, in the conscious dignity of their Sunday clothes. Spruce[2] bachelors looked sidelong at the pretty maidens, and fancied that the Sabbath sunshine made them prettier than on week days. When the throng had mostly streamed into the porch, the sexton began to toll the bell, keeping his eye on the Reverend Mr. Hooper's door. The first glimpse of the clergyman's figure was the signal for the bell to cease its summons.

"But what has good Parson Hooper got upon his face?" cried the sexton in astonishment.

All within hearing immediately turned about, and beheld the semblance of

Mr. Hooper, pacing slowly his meditative way towards the meeting house. With one accord[3] they started,[4] expressing more wonder than if some strange minister were coming to dust the cushions of Mr. Hooper's pulpit.[5]

"Are you sure it is our parson?" inquired Goodman[6] Gray of the sexton.

"Of a certainty it is good Mr. Hooper," replied the sexton. "He was to have exchanged pulpits with Parson Shute, of Westbury; but Parson Shute sent to excuse himself yesterday, being to preach a funeral sermon."

The cause of so much amazement may appear sufficiently slight. Mr. Hooper, a gentlemanly person, of about thirty, though still a bachelor, was dressed with due clerical neatness, as if a careful wife had starched his band,

---

1. A *sexton* is a church employee who cares for church property and who may also ring the bells and dig graves.
2. *Spruce* means "neat and trim in appearance" or "dapper."
3. *With one accord* means "with complete agreement" or "with unity."
4. Here, *started* means "made a sudden involuntary movement, as from fear or surprise."
5. A *pulpit* is a raised structure from which a minister delivers a sermon or conducts a worship service.
6. *Goodman* is a title of polite address similar to "Mister."

280　UNIT 2　AMERICAN ROMANTICISM

Reading Practice

SPIRAL REVIEW **Analyze Mood** Point out the sexton's reaction to Mr. Hooper's face (page 281): "I can't really feel as if good Mr. Hooper's face was behind that piece of crepe." Also note the words "set all the congregation astir." Explain that this story deals with judgment. **Ask:**

- Have you ever judged someone incorrectly on the basis of appearance?
- What assumptions have you made based on someone's clothing or hairstyle?

As they read, have them consider how the mood of each scene is created by the judgments of the congregation.

and brushed the weekly dust from his Sunday's garb. There was but one thing remarkable in his appearance. Swathed about his forehead, and hanging down over his face, so low as to be shaken by his breath, Mr. Hooper had on a black veil. On a nearer view it seemed to consist of two folds of crepe,[7] which entirely concealed his features, except the mouth and chin, but probably did not intercept his sight, further than to give a darkened aspect to all living and inanimate things. With this gloomy shade before him, good Mr. Hooper walked onward, at a slow and quiet pace, stooping somewhat, and looking on the ground, as is customary with abstracted[8] men, yet nodding kindly to those of his parishioners who still waited on the meeting-house steps. But so wonder-struck were they that his greeting hardly met with a return.

"I can't really feel as if good Mr. Hooper's face was behind that piece of crepe," said the sexton.

"I don't like it," muttered an old woman, as she hobbled into the meeting-house. "He has changed himself into something awful, only by hiding his face."

> **"He has changed himself into something awful, only by hiding his face."**

"Our parson has gone mad!" cried Goodman Gray, following him across the threshold.

A rumor of some unaccountable phenomenon had preceded Mr. Hooper into the meeting-house, and set all the congregation astir. Few could refrain from twisting their heads towards the door; many stood upright, and turned directly about; while several little boys clambered upon the seats, and came down again with a terrible racket. There was a general bustle, a rustling of the women's gowns and shuffling of the men's feet, greatly at variance with that hushed repose which should attend the entrance of the minister. But Mr. Hooper appeared not to notice the perturbation[9] of his people. He entered with an almost noiseless step, bent his head mildly to the pews on each side, and bowed as he passed his oldest parishioner, a white-haired great-grandsire, who occupied an arm-chair in the center of the aisle. It was strange to observe how slowly this **venerable** man became conscious of something singular in the appearance of his pastor. He seemed not fully to partake of the prevailing wonder, till Mr. Hooper had ascended the stairs, and showed himself in the pulpit, face to face with his congregation, except for the black veil. That mysterious emblem was never once withdrawn. It shook with his measured breath, as he gave out the psalm; it threw its obscurity between him and the holy page, as he read the Scriptures; and while he prayed, the veil lay heavily on his uplifted countenance.[10] Did he seek to hide it from the dread Being whom he was addressing?

Such was the effect of this simple piece of crepe, that more than one woman of delicate nerves was forced to leave the meeting-house. Yet perhaps the pale-faced congregation was almost as fearful a sight to the minister, as his black veil to them.

Mr. Hooper had the reputation of a good preacher, but not an energetic one: he strove to

---

9. *Perturbation* (pur′ tər bā′ shən) means "agitation" or "uneasiness."
10. *Countenance* means "face."

 Make Inferences Why do you think Mr. Hooper may find his congregation a fearful sight? **4**

Vocabulary

venerable (ven′ ər ə bəl) *adj.* deserving respect because of age, character, or position

---

7. *Crepe* is a light, soft fabric with a crinkled surface.
8. Here, *abstracted* means "lost in thought" or "preoccupied."

 Symbol How does Mr. Hooper's veil affect the way he views the world around him?

NATHANIEL HAWTHORNE **281**

NATHANIEL HAWTHORNE **281**

Reading Strategy 2

Make Inferences Have students examine the description of Mr. Hooper. **Ask:** Why is wearing the black veil out of character for him? (*The minister is neat, thoughtful, and quiet. He is not the type of person who would call attention to himself.*)

 For additional practice using the reading skill or strategy, see Unit 2 Teaching Resources Book, p. 146.

Literary Element 3

Symbol Answer: *He views the world as dark and shadowy.*

Ask: What does this suggest about the veil as a symbol? (*It symbolizes guilty human nature and the eerie aspect of the natural world at night.*)

(ENGLISH LEARNERS) Ensure that students understand the meaning of *veil* and can visualize a *veil* in front of the man's face.

Reading Strategy 4

Make Inferences
Answer: *He is shy and fears their reactions; their uneasy response to his veil seems a sign of guilt to him.*

English Learners

DIFFERENTIATED INSTRUCTION

Intermediate Direct students' attention to *Sabbath* in the first paragraph of the story and **Ask:** What term in the previous sentence is a clue to the meaning of "Sabbath"? (*The clue is "Sunday clothes"; Sabbath refers to Sunday.*) Ask students to find a clue for "clergyman." (*Reverend*)

Advanced Learners

DIFFERENTIATED INSTRUCTION

Analyze Contrasts Explain that the complex characters and settings include contrasts: light/dark, real/unreal, past/present, beauty/horror, ordinary/extraordinary, and good/evil. **Ask:** Can people be both good and bad, beautiful and plain? As students read, ask them to identify the contrasts in the story and explain how Hawthorne uses them to develop a theme.

Teach

Literary History ☆

Hawthorne and Original Sin

In a review, Herman Melville commented on the source of the darkness in Hawthorne's nature: "This great power of blackness in him derives its force from its appeals to that Calvinistic sense of Innate Depravity and Original Sin, from whose visitations, in some shape or other, no deeply thinking mind is always and wholly free. For, in certain moods, no man can weigh this world, without throwing in something, somehow like Original Sin, to strike the uneven balance."

---

win his people heavenward by mild, persuasive influences, rather than to drive them thither by the thunders of the Word. The sermon which he now delivered was marked by the same characteristics of style and manner as the general series of his pulpit oratory. But there was something, either in the sentiment of the discourse itself, or in the imagination of the auditors,[11] which made it greatly the most powerful effort that they had ever heard from their pastor's lips. It was tinged, rather more darkly than usual, with the gentle gloom of Mr.

☆ Hooper's temperament. The subject had reference to secret sin, and those sad mysteries which we hide from our nearest and dearest, and would fain[12] conceal from our own consciousness, even forgetting that the Omniscient[13] can detect them. A subtle power was breathed into his words. Each member of the congregation, the most innocent girl, and the man of hardened breast, felt as if the preacher had crept upon them, behind his awful veil, and discovered their hoarded **iniquity** of deed or thought. Many spread their clasped hands on their bosoms. There was nothing terrible in what Mr. Hooper said, at least, no violence; and yet, with every tremor of his melancholy voice, the hearers quaked. An unsought pathos[14] came hand in hand with awe. So sensible were the audience of some unwonted[15] attribute in their minister, that they longed for a breath of wind to blow aside the veil, almost believing that a stranger's visage[16] would be discovered, though the form, gesture, and voice were those of Mr. Hooper.

At the close of the services, the people hurried out with indecorous confusion, eager to communicate their pent-up amazement, and

---

11. *Auditors* are "those who hear" or "listeners."
12. *Fain* means "gladly" or "willingly."
13. *The Omniscient* is "the all-knowing," or God.
14. *Pathos* is a feeling of pity, compassion, or sorrow.
15. *Unwonted* means "not customary" or "unusual."
16. *Visage* means "face."

Vocabulary

iniquity (in ik′ wə tē) *n.* sin

---

conscious of lighter spirits the moment they lost sight of the black veil. Some gathered in little circles, huddled closely together, with their mouths all whispering in the center; some went homeward alone, wrapt in silent meditation; some talked loudly, and profaned the Sabbath day with ostentatious laughter. A few shook their **sagacious** heads, intimating that they could penetrate the mystery; while one or two affirmed that there was no mystery at all, but only that Mr. Hooper's eyes were so weakened by the midnight lamp, as to require a shade. After a brief interval, forth came good Mr. Hooper also, in the rear of his flock. Turning his veiled face from one group to another, he paid due reverence to the hoary heads,[17] saluted the middle aged with kind dignity as their friend and spiritual guide, greeted the young with mingled authority and love, and laid his hands on the little children's heads to bless them. Such was always his custom on the Sabbath day. Strange and bewildered looks repaid him for his courtesy. None, as on former occasions, aspired to the honor of walking by their pastor's side. Old Squire Saunders, doubtless by an accidental lapse of memory, neglected to invite Mr. Hooper to his table, where the good clergyman had been wont[18] to bless the food, almost every Sunday since his settlement. He returned, therefore, to the parsonage, and, at the moment of closing the door, was observed to look back upon the people, all of whom had their eyes fixed upon the minister. A sad smile gleamed faintly from beneath the black veil, and flickered about his mouth, glimmering as he disappeared.

"How strange," said a lady, "that a simple black veil, such as any woman might wear on her bonnet, should become such a terrible thing on Mr. Hooper's face!"

---

17. *Hoary heads* are white-haired heads.
18. *Wont* means "accustomed."

Vocabulary

sagacious (sə gā′ shəs) *adj.* having or showing wisdom and keen perception

---

Vocabulary Practice

SPIRAL REVIEW **Connotations** Beyond their literal meaning, words carry feelings called connotations. *Sagacious* and *shrewd* both mean "wise." However, *sagacious* carries the sense of "farsighted" or "prudent," whereas *shrewd* often has a connotation of "cunning" or "tricky."

In the following sentences, have students select the word whose connotations best fit the context.

1. The (sagacious/shrewd) salesperson can persuade a customer to buy. *(shrewd)*
2. The government created by the (sagacious/shrewd) statesmen endured for centuries. *(sagacious)*

Give students practice using words with different connotations. Ask them to write new sentences using the following word pairs: shroud/cloth; portend/warning.

The Sermon, 1886. Julius Gari Melchers. Oil on canvas, 62⅝ x 86½ in. Smithsonian American Art Museum, Washington, DC.

View the Art Gari Melchers's credo was "Waar en Klaar," Dutch for "True and Clear." What connections can you make between Melchers' painting and credo and Hawthorne's story? ★

"Something must surely be amiss with Mr. Hooper's intellects," observed her husband, the physician of the village. "But the strangest part of the affair is the effect of this vagary,[19] even on a sober-minded man like myself. The black veil, though it covers only our pastor's face, throws its influence over his whole person, and makes him ghostlike from head to foot. Do you not feel it so?"

"Truly do I," replied the lady; "and I would not be alone with him for the world. I wonder he is not afraid to be alone with himself!"

"Men sometimes are so," said her husband.

The afternoon service was attended with similar circumstances. At its conclusion, the bell tolled for the funeral of a young lady. The relatives and friends were assembled in the house, and the more distant acquaintances stood about the door, speaking of the good qualities of the deceased, when their talk was interrupted by the appearance of Mr. Hooper, still covered with his black veil. It was now an appropriate emblem. The clergyman stepped into the room where the corpse was laid, and bent over the coffin, to take a last farewell of his deceased parishioner. As he stooped, the veil hung straight down from his forehead, so that, if her eyelids had not been closed forever, the dead maiden might have seen his face. Could Mr. Hooper be fearful of her glance, that he so hastily caught back the black veil? A person who watched the interview between the dead and living, scrupled[20] not to affirm, that, at the instant when the clergyman's features were disclosed, the corpse had slightly shuddered, rustling the shroud[21] and muslin cap, though the countenance retained the composure of death. A superstitious old woman was the only witness of this prodigy.[22] From the coffin Mr. Hooper passed into the chamber of the mourners, and thence to the head of the staircase, to make the funeral prayer. It was a tender and heart-dissolving prayer, full of sorrow, yet so imbued with celestial hopes, that the music of a heavenly harp, swept by the fingers of the dead, seemed faintly to be heard among the saddest accents of the minister. The people trembled, though they but darkly understood him when he prayed that they, and himself, and all of mortal race, might be ready, as he trusted this young maiden had been, for the dreadful hour that should snatch the veil from their faces. The bearers went heavily forth, and the mourners followed, saddening all the street, with the dead before them, and Mr. Hooper in his black veil behind.

---

19. A *vagary* is an odd or erratic action or idea.

1 | Symbol *What meaning does this comment give to the symbolism of the veil?*

---

20. *Scrupled* means "hesitated."
21. A *shroud* is a cloth used to wrap a dead body for burial.
22. Here, *prodigy* means "an extraordinary event that causes amazement."

NATHANIEL HAWTHORNE **283**

Teach

Literary Element | 1

Symbol Answer: *It strengthens the association of the veil with the spiritual identity of its wearer.*

Ask: How do the comments in the next two paragraphs strengthen this link? *(They emphasize the weird effect of the veil, especially by the alarming possibility that Hooper, when alone, is forced to confront a ghostly double.)*

ADVANCED **Ask:** What classic elements of Gothic fiction are evident in Hawthorne's symbol of the veil? *(the ghostly double, or doppelgänger; the supernatural)*

View the Art ★

Answer: *Students may say that the painting and the story share religion as their subject; both portray churchgoers as somber people. Melchers' credo suggests that he believes in honesty, accuracy, and candor. This is in opposition to Hooper's dying words, that few people can or will reveal their innermost selves to others.*

Born in Detroit, Michigan, Julius Gari Melchers (1860–1932) is known primarily for his portraits and murals, or wall paintings. Melcher's portraits include one of President Theodore Roosevelt, and his murals decorate the Library of Congress in Washington, D.C.

Teach

The Power of Darkness

Answer: *Ghosts and other supernatural apparitions were a common feature of Gothic fiction.*

Ask: How does the dialogue of the mourners reinforce the ambiguity of the story's meaning? *(The dialogue reinforces the earlier supernatural hint of the shuddering corpse and anticipates the bride's sensations and the minister's odd reaction in the next paragraph. However, what Hawthorne means by these hints remains unclear.)*

APPROACHING **Say:** The people at the wedding make a connection between the previous day's funeral and this event. What is the mood at this wedding? Why? *(The mood at this wedding is dark and gloomy because of Mr. Hooper's presence and because of the thought that the bride is the spirit of the woman whose funeral was held earlier.)*

"Why do you look back?" said one in the procession to his partner.

"I had a fancy," replied she, "that the minister and the maiden's spirit were walking hand in hand."

"And so had I, at the same moment," said the other.

That night, the handsomest couple in Milford village were to be joined in wedlock. Though reckoned a melancholy man, Mr. Hooper had a placid cheerfulness for such occasions, which often excited a sympathetic smile where livelier merriment would have been thrown away. There was no quality of his disposition which made him more beloved than this. The company at the wedding awaited his arrival with impatience, trusting that the strange awe, which had gathered over him throughout the day, would now be dispelled. But such was not the result. When Mr. Hooper came, the first thing that their eyes rested on was the same horrible black veil, which had added deeper gloom to the funeral, and could portend[23] nothing but evil to the wedding. Such was its immediate effect on the guests that a cloud seemed to have rolled duskily from beneath the black crepe, and dimmed the light of the candles. The bridal pair stood up before the minister. But the bride's cold fingers quivered in the tremulous hand[24] of the bridegroom, and her deathlike paleness caused a whisper that the maiden who had been buried a few hours before was come from her grave to be married. If ever another wedding were so

dismal, it was that famous one where they tolled the wedding knell.[25] After performing the ceremony, Mr. Hooper raised a glass of wine to his lips, wishing happiness to the new-married couple in a strain of mild pleasantry that ought to have brightened the features of the guests, like a cheerful gleam from the hearth. At that instant, catching a glimpse of his figure in the looking-glass, the black veil involved his own spirit in the horror with which it overwhelmed all others. His frame shuddered, his lips grew white, he spilt the untasted wine upon the carpet, and rushed forth into the darkness. For the Earth, too, had on her Black Veil.

The next day, the whole village of Milford talked of little else than Parson Hooper's black veil. That, and the mystery concealed behind it, supplied a topic for discussion between acquaintances meeting in the street, and good women gossiping at their open windows. It was the first item of news that the tavern-keeper told to his guests. The children babbled of it on their way to school. One imitative little imp covered his face with an old black handkerchief, thereby so affrighting his playmates that the panic seized himself, and he well-nigh lost his wits by his own waggery.[26]

It was remarkable that of all the busybodies and impertinent people in the parish, not one ventured to put the plain question to Mr. Hooper, wherefore he did this thing. Hitherto, whenever there appeared the slightest call for such interference, he had never lacked advisers, nor shown himself averse to be guided by their judgment. If he erred at all, it was by so

> **For the Earth, too, had on her Black Veil.**

---

23. *Portend* means "to be a warning or an indication of."
24. A *tremulous hand* is one that is trembling or shaking.

1   **Power of Darkness** *How does Hawthorne's description of the imaginings of those at the funeral service link his story to Gothic literature?*

---

25. Hawthorne is referring to his own short story "The Wedding Knell." A *knell* is the solemn sound of a bell ringing, as at a funeral.
26. *Waggery* is mischievous or joking behavior.

Reading Practice

SMALL GROUP

Symbol Discuss with students the significance of the minister's wearing something that allows him to see out but does not allow others to see in.
Ask: How does the veil give the minister power? *(It puts him in control of what is seen by others, while he can see what he wants to see.)* What are some powerful things that an unseen or hiding person can do? *(An unseen person can surprise another person, invade another person's* privacy, or make another person feel suspicious.) Have students brainstorm in small groups and make a list of how they might feel if they knew someone was hiding in a room that they were in. Then as a class discuss how these feelings relate to the feelings people have toward the minister.

painful a degree of self-distrust, that even the mildest censure would lead him to consider an indifferent action as a crime. Yet, though so well acquainted with this amiable weakness, no individual among his parishioners chose to make the black veil a subject of friendly remonstrance. There was a feeling of dread, neither plainly confessed nor carefully concealed, which caused each to shift the responsibility upon another, till at length it was found expedient to send a deputation[27] of the church, in order to deal with Mr. Hooper about the mystery, before it should grow into a scandal. Never did an embassy so ill discharge its duties. The minister received them with friendly courtesy, but became silent, after they were seated, leaving to his visitors the whole burden of introducing their important business. The topic, it might be supposed, was obvious enough. There was the black veil swathed round Mr. Hooper's forehead, and concealing every feature above his placid mouth, on which, at times, they could perceive the glimmering of a melancholy smile. But that piece of crepe, to their imagination, seemed to hang down before his heart, the symbol of a fearful secret between him and them. Were the veil but cast aside, they might speak freely of it, but not till then. Thus they sat a considerable time, speechless, confused, and shrinking uneasily from Mr. Hooper's eye, which they felt to be fixed upon them with an invisible glance. Finally, the deputies returned abashed[28] to their constituents, pronouncing the matter too weighty to be handled, except by a council of the churches, if, indeed, it might not require a

☆ general synod.[29]

But there was one person in the village unappalled by the awe with which the black veil had impressed all beside herself. When the deputies returned without an explanation, or even venturing to demand one, she, with the calm energy of her character, determined to chase away the strange cloud that appeared to be settling round Mr. Hooper, every moment more darkly than before. As his plighted wife,[30] it should be her privilege to know what the black veil concealed. At the minister's first visit, therefore, she entered upon the subject with a direct simplicity, which made the task easier both for him and her. After he had seated himself, she fixed her eyes steadfastly upon the veil, but could discern nothing of the dreadful gloom that had so overawed the multitude: it was but a double fold of crepe, hanging down from his forehead to his mouth, and slightly stirring with his breath.

"No," said she aloud, and smiling, "there is nothing terrible in this piece of crepe, except that it hides a face which I am always glad to look upon. Come, good sir, let the sun shine from behind the cloud. First lay aside your black veil: then tell me why you put it on."

Mr. Hooper's smile glimmered faintly.

"There is an hour to come," said he, "when all of us shall cast aside our veils. Take it not amiss, beloved friend, if I wear this piece of crepe till then."

"Your words are a mystery, too," returned the young lady. "Take away the veil from them, at least."

"Elizabeth, I will," said he, "so far as my vow may suffer me. Know, then, this veil is a type and a symbol, and I am bound to wear it ever, both in light and darkness, in solitude and before the gaze of multitudes, and as with strangers, so with my familiar friends. No mortal eye will see it withdrawn. This dismal shade must separate me from the world: even you, Elizabeth, can never come behind it!"

"What grievous affliction hath befallen you," she earnestly inquired, "that you should thus darken your eyes forever?"

"If it be a sign of mourning," replied Mr. Hooper, "I, perhaps, like most other mortals, have sorrows dark enough to be typified by a black veil."

---

27. A *deputation* is a delegation.
28. *Abashed* means "ashamed" or "embarrassed."
29. A *synod* is a council of church officials or a governing body of all churches.

---

30. *Plighted wife* means "intended wife," or "fiancée."

Symbol *How does Mr. Hooper's reply to Elizabeth indicate another view of the veil's meaning?* | 2

NATHANIEL HAWTHORNE **285**

Literary Element | 2

Symbol **Answer:** *The minister's reply, which associates the veil with the separation of body and soul at death, seems to point to the veil as a symbol of mortal life.*

(APPROACHING) **Say:** The veil symbolizes two ideas. Hooper thinks it represents one, Elizabeth and the congregation think it means something else. Name two things that the veil represents. *(The veil represents shame or evil; it represents moral life.)*

Cultural History ☆

Early Puritanism Hawthorne was descended from one of the judges who presided at the Salem witchcraft trials in 1692. Salem was a small town in the Massachusetts Bay Colony that had been founded as a religious community by Puritans in the early 1600s. By the end of the century, many Puritans felt they were losing hold of their religious ideals, helping to create a climate of guilt and blame that encouraged accusations of witchcraft in Salem. Hundreds of people were accused and 20 were executed before the hysteria ceased.

Approaching Level

DIFFERENTIATED INSTRUCTION

Emerging To help them follow the events, have students make a two-column list with the heads "What people say" and "What people do." Suggest that they start their lists with these items: adults gossip about the veil; children make fun of Mr. Hooper and the veil.

Established Hawthorne places the paragraphs about the funeral and the wedding one after the other. Have students compare and contrast the events by completing a chart like the one shown.

	Funeral	Wedding
Behavior of Hooper		
Hooper's effect on event		
Reactions of those present		

Teach

Literary Element | 1

Symbol Answer: *The minister's "sad smile" seems to be a profound reflection of his personality. Its association with the veil emphasizes the symbolism of the veil as an element that obscures the deepest self.*

Reading Strategy | 2

Make Inferences

Answer: *She is repelled by his decision to wear the veil. She has made an important request of him, which he has refused. She has begun to share the fear (an emotion she despises) that the veil inspires in others.*

Literary History ☆

Hawthorne's Source Hawthorne included a footnote suggesting one source for "The Minister's Black Veil": "Another clergyman in New England, Mr. Joseph Moody, of York, Maine, who died about eighty years since, made himself remarkable by the same eccentricity that is here related of the Reverend Mr. Hooper. In his case, however, the symbol had a different import. In early life he had accidentally killed a beloved friend, and from that day till the hour of his own death, he hid his face from men."

"But what if the world will not believe that it is the type of an innocent sorrow?" urged Elizabeth. "Beloved and respected as you are, there may be whispers that you hide your face under the consciousness of secret sin. For the sake of your holy office, do away this scandal!"

The color rose into her cheeks as she intimated the nature of the rumors that were already abroad in the village. But Mr. Hooper's mildness did not forsake him. He even smiled again—that same sad smile, which always appeared like a faint glimmering of light, proceeding from the obscurity beneath the veil.

"If I hide my face for sorrow, there is cause enough," he merely replied; "and if I cover it for secret sin, what mortal might not do the same?"

And with this gentle, but unconquerable obstinacy did he resist all her entreaties.[31] At length Elizabeth sat silent. For a few moments she appeared lost in thought, considering, probably, what new methods might be tried to withdraw her lover from so dark a fantasy, which, if it had no other meaning, was perhaps a symptom of mental disease. Though of a firmer character than his own, the tears rolled down her cheeks. But, in an instant, as it were, a new feeling took the place of sorrow: her eyes were fixed insensibly on the black veil, when, like a sudden twilight in the air, its terrors fell around her. She arose, and stood trembling before him.

"And do you feel it then, at last?" said he mournfully.

She made no reply, but covered her eyes with her hand, and turned to leave the room. He rushed forward and caught her arm.

"Have patience with me, Elizabeth!" cried he, passionately. "Do not desert me, though this veil must be between us here on earth. Be mine, and hereafter there shall be no veil over my face, no darkness between our souls! It is but a mortal veil—it is not for eternity! O! you know not how lonely I am, and how fright-

ened, to be alone behind my black veil. Do not leave me in this miserable obscurity forever!"

"Lift the veil but once, and look me in the face," said she.

"Never! It cannot be!" replied Mr. Hooper.

"Then farewell!" said Elizabeth.

She withdrew her arm from his grasp, and slowly departed, pausing at the door, to give one long shuddering gaze, that seemed almost to penetrate the mystery of the black veil. But, even amid his grief, Mr. Hooper smiled to think that only a material emblem had separated him from happiness, though the horrors, which it shadowed forth, must be drawn darkly between the fondest of lovers.

From that time no attempts were made to remove Mr. Hooper's black veil, or, by a direct appeal, to discover the secret which it was supposed to hide. By persons who claimed a superiority to popular prejudice, it was reckoned merely an eccentric whim, such as often mingles with the sober actions of men otherwise rational, and tinges them all with its own semblance of insanity. But with the multitude, good Mr. Hooper was irreparably a bugbear.[32] He could not walk the street with any peace of mind, so conscious was he that the gentle and timid would turn aside to avoid him, and that others would make it a point of hardihood[33] to throw themselves in his way. The impertinence of the latter class compelled him to give up his customary walk at sunset to the burial ground; for when he leaned pensively over the gate, there would always be faces behind the gravestones, peeping at his black veil. A fable went the rounds that the stare of the dead people drove him thence. It grieved him, to the very depth of his kind heart, to observe how the children fled from his approach, breaking up their merriest sports, while his melancholy figure was yet afar off. Their instinctive dread caused him to feel more strongly

---

31. *Entreaties* are pleas.

 1 **Symbol** *Hawthorne closely links the minister's black veil with his "sad smile." How does this affect the meaning of the symbol?*

---

32. A *bugbear* is a real or imaginary object of fear.
33. *Hardihood* is offensive boldness or daring.

Make Inferences *Why do you think Elizabeth decides to break off her engagement with Mr. Hooper?* **2**

Grammar Practice

SPIRAL REVIEW 🌀 **Dangling Participles** A participle is a verb form that can function as an adjective, and a participial phrase contains a participle plus any complements and modifiers of it. A participial phrase at the beginning of a sentence must modify the sentence's subject.

Write on the board:

Rising over the horizon, the Reverend Mr. Hooper saw the morning sun.

Veiling the minister's countenance, I saw a piece of somber black cloth.

Have students rewrite each sentence to eliminate the dangling phrase.

<u>View the Art</u> One example of American colonial craft is the tombstone, which typically displays the sense of the nearness of death that was a part of this culture. How does this image affect your view of Puritan daily life? ★

than aught else, that a preternatural[34] horror was interwoven with the threads of the black crepe.

In truth, his own antipathy[35] to the veil was known to be so great, that he never willingly passed before a mirror, nor stooped to drink at a still fountain, lest, in its peaceful bosom, he should be affrighted by himself. This was what gave plausibility to the whispers, that Mr. Hooper's conscience tortured him for some great crime too horrible to be entirely concealed, or otherwise than so obscurely intimated. Thus, from beneath the black veil, there rolled a cloud into the sunshine, an ambiguity of sin or sorrow, which enveloped the poor minister, so that love or sympathy could never reach him. It was said that ghost and fiend consorted with him there. With self-shudderings and outward terrors, he walked continually in its shadow, groping darkly within his own soul, or gazing through a medium that saddened the whole world. Even the lawless wind, it was believed, respected his dreadful secret, and never blew aside the veil. But still good Mr. Hooper sadly smiled at the pale visages of the worldly throng as he passed by.

Among all its bad influences, the black veil had the one desirable effect, of making its wearer a very efficient clergyman. By the aid of his mysterious emblem—for there was no other apparent cause—he became a man of

awful power over souls that were in agony for sin. His converts always regarded him with a dread peculiar to themselves, affirming, though but figuratively, that, before he brought them to celestial light, they had been with him behind the black veil. Its gloom, indeed, enabled him to sympathize with all dark affections. Dying sinners cried aloud for Mr. Hooper, and would not yield their breath till he appeared; though ever, as he stooped to whisper consolation, they shuddered at the veiled face so near their own. Such were the terrors of the black veil, even when Death had bared his visage! Strangers came long distances to attend service at his church, with the mere idle purpose of gazing at his figure, because it was forbidden them to behold his face. But many were made to quake ere they departed! Once, during Governor Belcher's[36] administration, Mr. Hooper was appointed to preach the election sermon.[37] Covered with his black veil, he stood before the chief magistrate, the council, and the representatives,

---

34. *Preternatural* means "supernatural."
35. *Antipathy* is a feeling of intense dislike.

36. Jonathan *Belcher* was governor of Massachusetts and New Hampshire from 1730 to 1741.
37. Mr. Hooper was given the honor of preaching at the governor's inaugural ceremony.

Make Inferences *What does Hawthorne mean by "dark affections"? Why has Mr. Hooper come to understand or share these emotions?* 3

NATHANIEL HAWTHORNE **287**

Teach

Teach

Suffixes Knowing the meaning of suffixes can help students understand unfamiliar words. The suffix -*ous* means "full of"; therefore, *zealous* means "full of zeal" or "passionate." **Ask:** What does *calamitous* mean? (*"dreadful"* or *"unfortunate"*) .

(ENGLISH LEARNERS) Ensure that students know the meaning of *calamity* (a great misfortune that causes damage or suffering). Lead them to see that *calamitous* literally means "full of calamity" or "unfortunate."

Literary Element | 2

Symbol Answer: *Referring to the movement of the veil caused by the minister's breathing both makes the piece of cloth seem like a living thing and links it to the minister's own life force.*

Writing Practice

🖊 **Compose a Letter**
Have students imagine they are Mr. Clark of Westbury, the minister at Mr. Hooper's deathbed. As Mr. Clark, have them write a letter to a friend, describing his mood, his feelings about being there, what he hopes to accomplish, and his expectations about Mr. Hooper's final moments. Tell students to use the story as a guide for descriptions, tone, and mood.

288

---

and wrought[38] so deep an impression, that the legislative measures of that year were characterized by all the gloom and piety of our earliest ancestral sway.[39]

In this manner Mr. Hooper spent a long life, **irreproachable** in outward act, yet shrouded in dismal suspicions; kind and loving, though unloved, and dimly feared; a man apart from men, shunned in their health and joy, but ever summoned to their aid in mortal anguish. As years wore on, shedding their snows above his sable veil,[40] he acquired a name throughout the New England churches, and they called him Father Hooper. Nearly all his parishioners, who were of mature age when he was settled, had been borne away by many a funeral: he had one congregation in the church, and a more crowded one in the churchyard; and having wrought[41] so late into the evening, and done his work so well, it was now good Father Hooper's turn to rest.

Several persons were visible by the shaded candlelight, in the death chamber of the old clergyman. Natural connections[42] he had none. But there was the decorously grave, though unmoved physician, seeking only to mitigate[43] the last pangs of the patient whom he could not save. There were the deacons, and other eminently pious members of his church. There, also, was the Reverend Mr. Clark, of Westbury, a **[1]** young and **zealous** divine, who had ridden in haste to pray by the bedside of the expiring minister. There was the nurse, no hired handmaiden of death, but one whose calm affection had endured thus long in secrecy, in solitude, amid

---

38. Here, *wrought* means "made."
39. Here, *sway* means "influence."
40. *[As years … veil]* This phrase refers to the fact that his hair was turning white with time.
41. Here, *wrought* means "worked."
42. *Natural connections* are relatives.
43. *Mitigate* means "to make less intense, severe, or painful."

Vocabulary

irreproachable (ir´ i prō´ chə bəl) *adj.* free from blame; faultless
zealous (zel´ əs) *adj.* filled with enthusiastic devotion; passionate

---

---

the chill of age, and would not perish, even at the dying hour. Who, but Elizabeth! And there lay the hoary head of good Father Hooper upon the death pillow, with the black veil still swathed about his brow, and reaching down over his face, so that each more difficult gasp of his faint breath caused it to stir. All through life that piece of crepe had hung between him and the world: it had separated him from cheerful brotherhood and woman's love, and kept him in that saddest of all prisons, his own heart; and still it lay upon his face, as if to deepen the gloom of his darksome chamber, and shade him from the sunshine of eternity.

For some time previous, his mind had been confused, wavering doubtfully between the past and the present, and hovering forward, as it were, at intervals, into the indistinctness of the world to come. There had been feverish turns, which tossed him from side to side, and wore away what little strength he had. But in his most convulsive struggles, and in the wildest vagaries of his intellect, when no other thought retained its sober influence, he still showed an awful solicitude[44] lest the black veil should slip aside. Even if his bewildered soul could have forgotten, there was a faithful woman at his pillow, who, with averted eyes, would have covered that aged face, which she had last beheld in the comeliness of manhood. At length the death-stricken old man lay quietly in the torpor[45] of mental and bodily exhaustion, with an imperceptible pulse, and breath that grew fainter and fainter, except when a long, deep, and irregular inspiration seemed to prelude the flight of his spirit.

The minister of Westbury approached the bedside.

"Venerable Father Hooper," said he, "the moment of your release is at hand. Are you

---

44. *Solicitude* means "concern" or "anxiety."
45. *Torpor* is a state of being unable to move or feel.

Symbol *Several times a narrator describes the movement of the veil caused by Mr. Hooper's breath. What quality does this give to the symbol?* **[2]**

ready for the lifting of the veil that shuts in time from eternity?"

Father Hooper at first replied merely by a feeble motion of his head; then, apprehensive, perhaps, that his meaning might be doubted, he exerted himself to speak.

"Yea," said he, in faint accents, "my soul hath a patient weariness until that veil be lifted."

"And is it fitting," resumed the Reverend Mr. Clark, "that a man so given to prayer, of such a blameless example, holy in deed and thought, so far as mortal judgment may pronounce; is it fitting that a father in the church should leave a shadow on his memory, that may seem to blacken a life so pure? I pray you, my venerable brother, let not this thing be! Suffer us to be gladdened by your triumphant aspect as you go to your reward. Before the veil of eternity be lifted, let me cast aside this black veil from your face!"

And thus speaking, the Reverend Mr. Clark bent forward to reveal the mystery of so many years. But, exerting a sudden energy, that made all the beholders stand aghast, Father Hooper snatched both his hands from beneath the bedclothes, and pressed them strongly on the black veil, resolute to struggle, if the minister of Westbury would contend with a dying man.

"Never!" cried the veiled clergyman. "On earth, never!"

"Dark old man!" exclaimed the affrighted minister, "with what horrible crime upon your soul are you now passing to the judgment?"

Father Hooper's breath heaved; it rattled in his throat; but, with a mighty effort, grasping forward with his hands, he caught hold of life, and held it back till he should speak. He even raised himself in bed; and there he sat, shivering with the arms of death around him, while the black veil hung down, awful, at that last moment, in the gathered terrors of a lifetime. And yet the faint, sad smile, so often there, now seemed to glimmer from its obscurity, and linger on Father Hooper's lips.

"Why do you tremble at me alone?" cried he, turning his veiled face round the circle of pale spectators. "Tremble also at each other! Have men avoided me, and women shown no pity, and children screamed and fled, only for my black veil? What, but the mystery which it obscurely typifies, has made this piece of crepe so awful? When the friend shows his inmost heart to his friend; the lover to his best beloved; when man does not vainly shrink from the eye of his Creator, loathsomely treasuring up the secret of his sin; then deem me a monster, for the symbol beneath which I have lived, and die! I look around me, and, lo! on every visage a Black Veil!"

While his auditors shrank from one another, in mutual affright, Father Hooper fell back upon his pillow, a veiled corpse, with a faint smile lingering on the lips. Still veiled, they laid him in his coffin, and a veiled corpse they bore him to the grave. The grass of many years has sprung up and withered on that grave, the burial stone is moss-grown, and good Mr. Hooper's face is dust; but awful is still the thought that it moldered[46] beneath the Black Veil!

---

46. *Moldered* means "turned to dust" or "crumbled."

Symbol *To what "mystery" do you think the minister is referring?* **3**

The Power of Darkness *How does this final detail reflect the dark side of Romanticism?* **4**

"Are you ready for the lifting of the veil that shuts in time from eternity?"

Teach

Literary Element **3**

Symbol **Answer:** *In his last words, the minister seems to link the veil with the final "mystery" of our innermost selves, which few will reveal to another.*

Big Idea **4**

The Power of Darkness
Answer: *The dark side of Romanticism, particularly the Gothic literary tradition, emphasized such images of death and decay.*

 To check students' understanding of the selection, see Unit 2 Teaching Resources Book, p. 150.

English Learners

DIFFERENTIATED INSTRUCTION

Intermediate Help students break down sentences into manageable pieces of information. Take the full sentence beginning "'And is it fitting,' resumed the Reverend Mr. Clark," on page 289.

Write on the board "It is fitting that . . ." and then make a chart to sort out the remainder of the sentence. Start with these entries:

Subject:	a man
Modifiers:	so given to prayer
	of such a blameless example
	holy in deed and thought, so far as mortal judgment may pronounce
Verb:	should leave
Object:	a shadow

Guide students in completing the analysis of this sentence and restating it in their own words.

After You Read

Assess

1. Students' answers will vary.

2. (a) They are surprised, and fearful that he is insane. (b) It is unusual and seems sinister. They may recognize that they too have secret sins.

3. (a) The subject is secret sin. (b) They suspect that he has a secret sin.

4. (a) Summaries should include (at least) the Sunday sermon, funeral, wedding, meeting with Elizabeth, and death scene. (b) Answers will vary.

5. (a) The veil makes Mr. Hooper a very effective clergyman. (b) It frightens children and timid people. It prompts bolder people to confront him. It surrounds him with sinister rumors.

6. (a) Elizabeth's decision to break off their engagement confirms her firmness of character. Her care for him at his time of death reveals the depth of her feeling for him. (b) Answers will vary.

7. (a) Students will probably be most puzzled by Mr. Hooper's original decision to wear the veil. (b) Possible question: "What prompted Mr. Hooper to put on the veil in the first place?"

8. Hawthorne shows the Romantic view in the value Mr. Hooper puts on feelings and on the importance of his spiritual life, which transcends daily human concerns.

9. Students should be able to support their points with relevant examples. Students might say that the parable is still relevant because people in modern society still have difficulty revealing their true selves and are often judged on the way they choose to present themselves.

After You Read

Respond and Think Critically

Respond and Interpret

1. (a) What was your first reaction to the minister's black veil? (b) Did your reaction change as the story developed?

2. (a) How do the townspeople react when they first see Mr. Hooper wearing the black veil? (b) Why might the veil affect them as it does?

3. (a) What is the subject of Mr. Hooper's sermon on the first day he wears the black veil? (b) What do you think is the association between the veil and congregation's interpretation of the sermon?

4. (a) Briefly retell in your own words the main events of the story. (b) Which of these events was most surprising?

Analyze and Evaluate

5. (a) What is "the one desirable effect" that the veil has on Mr. Hooper? (b) What are the negative effects?

6. (a) What does Elizabeth's changing relationship with Mr. Hooper reveal about her personality? (b) Do you find her a sympathetic character? Explain.

7. (a) What do you think was most puzzling about the story? (b) Write your thoughts down in the form of question.

Connect

8. **Big Idea** The Power of Darkness The Puritan view of sin and human nature is a basic element of this story. How is the Romantic view of human nature also shown?

9. **Connect to Today** In your opinion, is "The Minister's Black Veil" a relevant parable for today? Explain.

You're the Critic: Different Viewpoints

How Pessimistic Was Hawthorne?
How do the viewpoints expressed below differ?

"What pleased [Hawthorne in gloomy subjects] was their picturesqueness, their rich duskiness of color, their chiaroscuro; but they were not the expression of a hopeless...feeling about the human soul."
—Henry James

"...this black conceit [Original Sin] pervades [Hawthorne's writing].... You may be witched by his sunlight,—transported by the bright gildings in the skies he builds over you; but... even his bright gildings but fringe and play upon the edges of thunder-clouds."
—Herman Melville

Group Activity Discuss the following questions. Cite evidence from "The Minister's Black Veil."

1. Do you think James or Melville comes closer in assessing Hawthorne's pessimism? Explain.

2. Chiaroscuro is the use of strongly contrasting light and dark areas in visual art. How might this technique apply to Hawthorne?

Group Activity

1. Melville views Hawthorne as more of a pessimist than James does. Answers will vary.

2. The blend of light and shade resembles the mixture of good and evil that for Hawthorne was fundamental to human nature.

 For additional assessment, see Assessment Resources, pp. 115–116.

Literary Element Symbol

There are two basic types of symbols—traditional and original. Traditional symbols usually have a single meaning. For example, the theater masks shown here are traditional symbols representing the two sides of drama—comedy and tragedy.

In contrast, writers often create original symbols that have no familiar meanings to readers. This allows writers more freedom to develop what the symbols represent.

1. What kind of symbol—traditional or original—does Hawthorne use in "The Minister's Black Veil"? Explain.

2. What different meanings do you think the black veil represents for Mr. Hooper, Elizabeth, and the townspeople?

Review: Characterization

Characterization refers to the methods a writer uses to develop the personality of a character.

Partner Activity Create a web diagram like the one below. Then fill it in with an example for each method of characterization that Hawthorne uses.

 Literature Online

Selection Resources For Selection Quizzes, eFlash-cards, and Reading-Writing Connection activities, go to glencoe.com and enter QuickPass code GLA9800u2.

Reading Strategy Make Inferences

ACT Skills Practice

1. The theme of "The Minister's Black Veil" is the:

    A. paralyzing terror of the hidden and unknown.

    B. inescapable guilt that drives people's actions.

    C. inability of people to reveal their true natures.

    D. omnipresence of the supernatural in human life.

Vocabulary Practice

Practice with Synonyms A *synonym* is a word that has the same or nearly the same meaning as another word. With a partner, match each boldfaced vocabulary word below with its synonym. Use a thesaurus or dictionary to check your answers.

1. venerable   a. wise
2. iniquity   b. reckless
3. sagacious   c. faultless
4. irreproachable   d. esteemed
5. zealous   e. enthusiastic
                      f. uncaring
                      g. wickedness

Academic Vocabulary

Strict interpretation of the Bible and belief in punishment were **cultural** *convictions of the Puritans in New England in the early 1700s.*

Cultural is an academic word. In more casual conversation, someone might say that a person of a certain ethnicity practices the **cultural** traditions of that ethnicity. Using context clues, try to figure out the meaning of the word in the sentence above describing the setting and characters of "The Minister's Black Veil." Check your conclusion in a dictionary.

For more on academic vocabulary, see pages 53–54.

NATHANIEL HAWTHORNE **291**

Review: Characterization

physical appearance

Mr. Hooper's faint, sad smile that glimmers in the shadow of his black veil

actions

Making a wedding toast, Mr. Hooper catches a glimpse of himself in a mirror and is so frightened he spills his wine.

spoken words

"O! you know not how lonely I am, and how frightened . . . behind my black veil."

other characters' comments

"I wonder he is not afraid to be alone with himself!"

narrator's comments

"It grieved him . . . to observe how the children fled from his approach, breaking up their merriest sports, while his melancholy figure was yet afar off."

After You Read

Assess

Literary Element

1. Although some students may recall traditional blindfolded figures (such as Justice or Cupid), Hawthorne creates an original symbol in "The Minister's Black Veil."

2. For Mr. Hooper, the veil seems to represent guilt; for Elizabeth, perhaps the unknowable secret self of Mr. Hooper; for the townspeople, many things, including guilt, sin, madness, and the terrifying unknown.

3. By providing no final explanation of what caused Mr. Hooper's decision, Hawthorne makes the veil a more mysterious symbol.

Progress Check

Can students interpret a symbol?

If No → See Unit 2 Teaching Resources Book, p. 145.

Reading Strategy

1. H is the correct answer because the point of the story is that everyone has a hidden sin.

Vocabulary

1. d **2.** g **3.** a **4.** c **5.** e

Academic Vocabulary

The words *interpretation, belief,* and *punishment* should help students deduce that the word *cultural* describes the customs and beliefs shared by the people of a certain social, ethnic, or religious group.

After You Read

Assess

Respond Through Writing

Students' essays should draw clear connections between the veil and the reactions it inspired and use these connections to analyze the meaning of the story. To evaluate the essays, use the scoring guide below.

Prewrite

Help students determine how many characters they will include in their essays and how they will go about gathering the information they need in order to fill in a cause-and-effect diagram for each character. Explain to students that the first box in the diagram is already determined by the assignment. Remind them that the second box will be an effect of the first box, but it will also be a cause of the event in the third box. Students may use more than four boxes in their diagrams.

 For grammar practice, see Unit 2 Teaching Resources Book, p. 149.

Respond Through Writing

Expository Essay

Analyze Cause and Effect Write an expository essay in which you analyze the effect Mr. Hooper's black veil has on different people (including him) in the story. Then explain how these different cause-and-effect relationships contribute to the overall meaning of Hawthorne's "parable."

Understand the Task An **expository essay** is a piece of writing that explains or informs. When you **analyze** something, you identify the parts to find meaning in their relationship to the whole.

Prewrite Before you draft your essay, make a cause-and-effect diagram like the one below for each main character or group of characters. Examine three periods in the story: when Mr. Hooper first appears wearing his black veil; when his persistence in wearing it gains him notoriety; and when he is on his deathbed.

Elizabeth

Mr. Hooper appears with a black veil → She confronts Mr. Hooper → Mr. Hooper refuses to remove veil → She abandons Mr. Hooper

Draft Use your diagrams to gather and organize evidence in support of a thesis. Sometimes it helpful to use sentence frames as you draft your essay. For example, your thesis might be stated as follows:

In "The Minister's Black Veil," Hawthorne introduces a single cause—a simple veil—that presents a complex effect of _____, _____, and _____.

Revise Anticipate and address readers' potential misunderstandings, biases, and expectations by offering evidence supporting the cause-and-effect relationships you identify. Consider using computer publishing software to introduce your diagrams as visual aids. If you use technical terms or words your reader might not encounter everyday, such as *pulpit,* make sure you are using them correctly.

Edit and Proofread Proofread your paper, correcting any errors in spelling, grammar, and punctuation. Review the Grammar Tip in the side column for information on degrees of comparison with modifiers.

Learning Objectives

In this assignment, you will focus on the following objectives:

Writing: Writing an expository essay.

Grammar: Using comparative and superlative forms of modifiers.

Grammar Tip

Degrees of Comparison

When modifiers are used in a comparison, their form changes to reflect the number of things being compared. How many things are being compared in each of the following sentences?

Elizabeth sat nearer to the pulpit than Squire Sanders.

Elizabeth sat nearest to the pulpit of all the members of the congregation.

With two things, use the **comparative** form of a modifier *(better, worse, farther).* With more than two things, use the **superlative** form *(best, worst, farthest).* Remember that the comparative form often ends in *–er,* while the superlative form often ends in *–st.*

Scoring Guide	4	3	2	1
Task addressed	fully	mostly	partially	barely
Thesis	meaningful	provided	partial	weak
Support	thoughtful	provided	partial	weak
Language	varied, descriptive	varied, often descriptive	predictable, imprecise	repetitive, limited
Convention errors	few or none	several	many	serious
Analysis is	convincing	mostly convincing	partially convincing	not convincing

Grammar Workshop

Misplaced and Dangling Modifiers

Literature Connection In the quotation below, Hawthorne places the phrase *with bright faces* directly after the noun it modifies, *children*.

> "Children, *with bright faces*, tripped merrily beside their parents…"
>
> —Nathaniel Hawthorne, from "The Minister's Black Veil"

If Hawthorne had written *Children tripped merrily beside their parents, with bright faces*, one could interpret *with bright faces* as modifying *parents*. A modifier placed in such a way that it appears to modify something it does not is a **misplaced modifier**.

To correct a misplaced modifier, move it closer in the sentence to the word or phrase that it modifies.

Misplaced: Children tripped merrily beside their parents, with bright faces. (It sounds as though the parents have bright faces.)

Corrected: Children, with bright faces, tripped merrily beside their parents. (It is clear that the children have bright faces.)

A modifier that does not clearly or logically modify *any* word in a sentence is a **dangling modifier**: *Passing into the chamber, the funeral prayer created a solemn mood.* What does *Passing into the chamber* modify?

To correct a dangling modifier, add to the sentence a word or phrase that the modifier goes with.

Dangling: Passing into the chamber, the funeral prayer created a solemn mood. (What is passing into the chamber is not stated.)

Corrected: Passing into the chamber, Hooper spoke the funeral prayer, which created a solemn mood. (It is clear that Hooper is passing.)

Revise Correct the following misplaced or dangling modifiers.

1. Looking for movie ideas, Poe's stories were discovered one day.
2. Working feverishly, the script was finally finished.
3. Watching the 1926 film *The Scarlet Letter,* the theater was filled with people.
4. Admitted to the theater late, the lights were out.

Learning Objectives

In this workshop, you will focus on the following objective:

Grammar: Understanding how to avoid misplaced and dangling modifiers.

Prepositional and Participial Phrases as Modifiers

Prepositional phrases can act as adjectives or adverbs. *With bright faces* in the example at left is a prepositional phrase acting as an adjective.

A **participle** is a verb form that ends in *–ed* or *–ing.* **Participial phrases** always act as adjectives. *Passing into the chamber* in the example at left is a participial phrase.

Language Handbook

For more on modifiers, see Language Handbook pp. R42–R61.

Literature Online

Grammar For more grammar practice, go to glencoe.com and enter QuickPass code GLA9800u2.

Grammar Workshop

Misplaced and Dangling Modifiers

Focus

Write this sentence on the board:

After reading the directions, the machine was ready to assemble.

Discuss why this sentence is confusing. Remind students that the sequence, or order, of words in a sentence determines the meaning of the sentence.

Teach

Participles Point out that participial phrases that appear at the beginning of a sentence must be followed immediately by the subject.

Assess

Possible rewrites:

1. Looking for movie ideas, the director discovered Poe's stories.
2. Working feverishly, the screenwriter finally finished the script.
3. Watching the 1926 film *The Scarlet Letter,* the audience filled the theater.
4. The audience smiled at the silent film actress, who was gesturing wildly.

Approaching Level

DIFFERENTIATED INSTRUCTION

Emerging Misplaced and dangling modifiers create confusion and misunderstanding. Examples, such as the following, are sometimes found in newspaper headlines:

- Confused Minister Injures Governor with Phone
- Miners Refuse to Work After Death
- Two Sisters Reunite After Eighteen Years at College

Ask students to identify the misplaced or dangling modifiers and to rewrite the headlines to make them clear and sensible.

Before You Read

Focus

Before You Read

from *Moby-Dick*

Meet **Herman Melville**
(1819–1891)

"NO! in thunder." This, according to Herman Melville, is what the true writer says. With his own great "NO!" Melville set himself against the optimism of the Transcendentalists and rejected the idea of progress and prosperity that dominated the American mind in the 1800s.

Adventure and Fame Born in New York City, Melville faced many misfortunes in his youth despite being the son of a wealthy merchant. He was forced to leave school at the age of twelve and began focusing on finding a profession. Unable to do so, in 1841 he became a sailor aboard the whale ship *Acushnet*, bound for the South Pacific.

During his time as a sailor, Melville jumped ship and lived for a month with the Typee, a tribe that treated him graciously. He also took part in a mutiny and spent time in jail on the island of Tahiti. These sailing years gave him the background knowledge of ships and exotic islands that served him well in his first two novels, *Typee* (1846) and *Omoo* (1847), both popular tales of adventure.

The success of these novels brought temporary stability into Melville's life. In 1847, he married Elizabeth Shaw, the daughter of the chief justice of Massachusetts. He became a literary celebrity in both England and America, but his sudden success was short-lived. His third novel, *Mardi* (1849), written in an allegorical style, was poorly received because it was not the adventure story that readers had expected.

Critical Neglect In 1850, Melville purchased a farm near Pittsfield, Massachusetts, and befriended Nathaniel Hawthorne, who lived just six miles away. The two writers shared the Puritan view of humanity as inherently evil, and they wrote fiction that explored the dark side of life.

Hawthorne's influence can be seen in Melville's later work, beginning with *Moby-Dick*, a whaling story of complexity and power, meant to rival the work of Shakespeare. Published in 1851, this tale of Captain Ahab and his search for the white whale is now regarded as one of the greatest American novels. When the novel first appeared, however, it met with neither critical nor popular acclaim.

The commercial failure of his next two works convinced Melville that he could not support his family by writing. He sold his farm and spent nearly twenty years as a customs inspector in New York City. In his later years, he published poems, which were overlooked by the public. At his death he left behind the manuscript of his last work, the novel *Billy Budd*. It was published posthumously in 1924.

During his life, Herman Melville achieved fame and then watched it fade to nothing. His most important achievements were ridiculed by critics and ignored by the public. Nathaniel Hawthorne, however, asserted that no "writer ever put . . . reality before his reader more unflinchingly" than did Herman Melville. Generations later, readers began to discover the depth and power of his writing and to accept his bold rendering of reality.

Selection Skills

Literary Elements
- Motivation (SE pp. 295, 296, 298, 299, 302, 304)

Reading Skills
- Monitor Comprehension (SE pp. 295, 296, 298, 301, 303, 305)
- Preview (TE p. 296)

from **Moby-Dick**

Vocabulary Skills
- Antonyms (SE p. 305; TE p. 295)

Writing Skills/Grammar
- Literary Criticism (SE p. 305)
- Character Sketch (TE p. 298)

Listening/Speaking/Viewing Skills
- Analyze Art (SE p. 300)
- Dramatic Presentation (TE p. 296)

Literature and Reading Preview

Connect to the Story

Think of someone you know who has a magnetic personality. What gives him or her that quality? To explore this question, make a word web. In the center of a page, write the person's name. List the person's engaging traits or behaviors in surrounding circles.

Build Background

Melville's novel is set in the early 1800s. It describes the voyage of the *Pequod,* a whale ship, which hunts and kills sperm whales for their oil. Ishmael, the young sailor who narrates the book, signs on because he is penniless but curious to find out what life aboard a whale ship is like. Despite dangerous work, fierce weather, low pay, bad food, and harsh treatment, Americans and foreigners alike were drawn to whaling.

Set Purposes for Reading

Big Idea The Power of Darkness

As you read, ask yourself, Why does Captain Ahab consider the white whale Moby Dick to be evil?

Literary Element Motivation

Motivation refers to the stated or implied reason or cause for a character's actions. A character's motivation helps the reader understand why he or she behaves in a certain way. In a great literary work such as *Moby-Dick,* the main character's motivation is complex, but comprehensible. As you read, ask yourself, Why does Captain Ahab act as he does?

Reading Strategy Monitor Comprehension

Monitoring comprehension is a helpful way to make sure that you understand what you are reading. Melville's style is highly ornate, with long, complicated passages and sentences rich in descriptive detail. To get the most from this selection, reread challenging passages and break down difficult sentences.

....

Tip: Break Down Difficult Sentences Use the following tips to break down difficult sentences:

1. Identify the subject.
2. Isolate the verb or verb phrase.
3. Rephrase the sentence in your own words.

Learning Objectives

For pages 294–305
In studying this text, you will focus on the following objectives:
Literary Study: Analyzing motivation.
Reading: Monitoring comprehension.
Writing: Writing a literary critical response.

Vocabulary

fortitude (fôr´ tə tōōd´) *n.* strength, particularly strength of mind that enables one to encounter danger or bear adversity with courage; p. 298 *The soldier showed fortitude in facing the enemy.*

genial (jēn´ yəl) *adj.* mild or friendly; p. 298 *Despite her severe illness, my grandmother remained genial.*

recluse (rek´ lōōs) *n.* someone who leads a secluded or solitary life; p. 298 *The author was considered a recluse because he granted no interviews and never spoke in public.*

misanthropic (mis´ ən throp´ ik) *adj.* having hatred for humankind; p. 298 *Lack of compassion may be a sign of a misanthropic cast of mind.*

inscrutable (in skrōō´ tə bəl) *adj.* mysterious, or not able to be interpreted or understood; p. 301 *Her actions may be clear, but her intentions are inscrutable.*

HERMAN MELVILLE **295**

English Learners

DIFFERENTIATED INSTRUCTION

Advanced Give students help with the nautical terms in this selection. Write these words on the board: *cabin, captain, deck, harpooners, crew, southward, latitude, plank.* Have students sort them into these three categories: people, ship, navigation. You may refer to a photo or illustration of a nineteenth-century whaling ship and have students label or point out the parts mentioned in the selection. Students may clarify the navigational terms by referring to a map.

Before You Read

Focus

Summary

Moby-Dick is the story of a man's obsessive desire for vengeance against a white whale that took off one of his legs. In this excerpt, the ship *Pequod* has just set sail, with its crew believing that they are on a routine whaling voyage. In the first days of the voyage, Captain Ahab quickly shows himself to be a stern, joyless, obsessed man. The crew soon learn the true purpose of the voyage—to "hunt Moby Dick to his death."

 For summaries in languages other than English, see Unit 2 Teaching Resources Book, pp. 153–158.

Vocabulary

Antonyms Explain to students that all of the words in the vocabulary list can describe people. Ask students to provide an antonym for each word. For example, an antonym for *genial* is *unfriendly.*

(ADVANCED) Ask students to use each word and its antonym in a sentence describing a character from a story. (*Mr. Hooper in "The Minister's Black Veil" is genial at the outset, but he becomes more unfriendly when he puts on the veil.*)

 For additional vocabulary practice, see Unit 2 Teaching Resources Book, p. 161.

 For additional context, see Glencoe Interactive Vocabulary CD-ROM.

Teach

Literary Element | **1**

Motivation **Answer:** *Ahab feels superior to the crew and stays aloof, letting the mates attend to the ship's business early in the voyage. By remaining in his cabin, Ahab instills a sense of wonder and awe in the crew.*

Reading Strategy | **2**

Monitor Comprehension **Answer:** *Ishmael describes the harpooneers and the ship's crew.*

 For additional practice using the reading skill or strategy, see Unit 2 Teaching Resources Book, p. 160.

 For an audio recording of this selection, use Listening Library Audio CD–ROM.

Readability Scores

Dale-Chall: 9.0
DRP: 67
Lexile: 1150

from
Moby-Dick

Herman Melville

Capturing a Sperm Whale, published 1835. J. Hill. Engraving, 47.1 x 61.5 cm. Peabody Essex Museum, Salem, MA.

Ahab

For several days after leaving Nantucket, nothing above hatches[1] was seen of Captain Ahab. The mates regularly relieved each other at the watches, and for aught[2] that could be seen to the contrary, they seemed to be the only commanders of the ship; only they sometimes issued from the cabin with orders so sudden and peremptory, that after all it was plain they but commanded vicariously. Yes, their supreme lord and dictator was there, though hitherto unseen by any eyes not permitted to penetrate into the now sacred retreat of the cabin.

Every time I ascended to the deck from my watches below, I instantly gazed aft[3] to mark if any strange face were visible; for my first vague disquietude touching the unknown captain, now in the seclusion of the sea, became almost a perturbation. This was strangely heightened at times by the ragged Elijah's diabolical incoherences uninvitedly recurring to me, with a subtle energy I could not have before conceived of. But poorly could I withstand them, much as in other moods I was almost ready to

smile at the solemn whimsicalities of that outlandish prophet of the wharves.[4] But whatever it was of apprehensiveness or uneasiness—to call it so—which I felt, yet whenever I came to look about me in the ship, it seemed against all warranty to cherish such emotions. For though the harpooneers, with the great body of the crew, were a far more barbaric, heathenish, and motley set than any of the tame merchant-ship companies which my previous experiences had made me acquainted with, still I ascribed this—and rightly ascribed it—to the fierce uniqueness of the very nature of that wild Scandinavian vocation in which I had so abandonedly embarked. But it was especially the aspect of the three chief officers of the ship, the mates, which was most forcibly calculated to allay these colorless misgivings, and induce confidence and cheerfulness in every presentment of the voyage. Three better, more likely sea-officers and men, each in his own different way, could not readily be found, and they were every one of the Americans; a Nantucketer, a Vineyarder, a Cape man. Now, it being

---

1. *Above hatches* means "on deck."
2. Here, *aught* means "anything" or "all."
3. *Aft* means "the rear section of a ship."

4. Before the *Pequod* set sail, an odd sailor, Elijah, warned Ishmael about Captain Ahab.

1 Motivation *Why does Ahab isolate himself from his crew?*

Monitor Comprehension *Whom does Ishmael describe in this passage?* **2**

296 UNIT 2 AMERICAN ROMANTICISM

Previewing This story deals with a man obsessed with his quest for vengeance and tells how he engages others in his mission. Have students discuss these questions.

- Have you ever known or read about someone who seemed irrationally obsessed with a thing or an idea?
- Was the person able to convince others to share his or her obsession?

As students read the selection, they should note how Ahab draws others into his plans. Encourage students to think about how they might react if they were a crew member. Have students also preview the illustrations and captions and scan the footnotes and questions at the bottoms of pages to get a sense of the content of this selection.

Christmas when the ship shot from out her harbor, for a space we had biting Polar weather, though all the time running away from it to the southward; and by every degree and minute of latitude which we sailed, gradually leaving that merciless winter, and all its intolerable weather behind us. It was one of those less lowering, but still grey and gloomy enough mornings of the transition, when with a fair wind the ship was rushing through the water with a vindictive sort of leaping and melancholy rapidity, that as I mounted to the deck at the call of the forenoon watch, so soon as I levelled my glance towards the taffrail, foreboding shivers ran over me. Reality outran apprehension; Captain Ahab stood upon his quarter-deck.[5]

There seemed no sign of common bodily illness about him, nor of the recovery from any. He looked like a man cut away from the stake, when the fire has overrunningly wasted all the limbs without consuming them, or taking away one particle from their compacted aged robustness. His whole high, broad form, seemed made of solid bronze, and shaped in an unalterable mould, like Cellini's cast Perseus.[6] Threading its way out from among his grey hairs, and continuing right down one side of his tawny scorched face and neck, till it disappeared in his clothing, you saw a slender rod-like mark, lividly whitish. It resembled that perpendicular seam sometimes made in the straight, lofty trunk of a great tree, when the upper lightning tearingly darts down it, and without wrenching a single twig, peels and grooves out the bark from top to bottom, ere running off into the soil, leaving the tree still greenly alive, but branded. Whether that mark was born with him, or whether it was the scar left by some desperate wound, no one could certainly say.

By some tacit consent, throughout the voyage little or no allusion was made to it, especially by the mates. But once Tashtego's senior, an old Gayhead Indian[7] among the crew, superstitiously asserted that not till he was full forty years old did Ahab become that way branded, and then it came upon him, not in the fury of any mortal fray, but in an elemental strife at sea. Yet, this wild hint seemed inferentially negatived, by what a grey Manxman[8] insinuated, an old sepulchral man, who, having never before sailed out of Nantucket, had never ere this laid eye upon wild Ahab. Nevertheless, the old sea-traditions, the immemorial credulities, popularly invested this old Manxman with preternatural powers of discernment. So that no white sailor seriously contradicted him when he said that if ever Captain Ahab should be tranquilly laid out—which might hardly come to pass, so he muttered—then, whoever should do that last office for the dead, would find a birthmark on him from crown to sole.

So powerfully did the whole grim aspect of Ahab affect me, and the livid[9] brand which streaked it, that for the first few moments I hardly noted that not a little of this overbearing grimness was owing to the barbaric white leg upon which he partly stood. It had previously come to me that this ivory leg had at sea been fashioned from the polished bone of the sperm whale's jaw. "Aye, he was dismasted[10] off Japan," said the old Gayhead Indian once; "but like his dismasted craft, he shipped another mast without coming home for it. He has a quiver of 'em."

I was struck with the singular posture he maintained. Upon each side of the Pequod's quarter deck, and pretty close to the mizen shrouds,[11] there was an auger hole, bored

---

5. The *quarter-deck* is the part of a ship set aside by the captain for official use.
6. *Cellini's cast Perseus* refers to Benvenuto Cellini's bronze statue that shows Perseus, a Greek mythological hero, holding Medusa's severed head.

 3 | The Power of Darkness *How does this detail suggest that Ahab is strange, perhaps even unnatural?*

7. *Gayhead Indian* refers to a Native American from Gayhead, a town in Martha's Vineyard, Massachusetts.
8. A *Manxman* is someone from the Isle of Man, an island in the Irish Sea.
9. Here, *livid* means "pale."
10. Literally, *dismasted* means "with the mast removed or broken off." This term is used figuratively to describe Ahab's loss of his leg.
11. *Shrouds* means "sails."

HERMAN MELVILLE **297**

The Power of Darkness
Answer: *Ahab's body looks as though it has been pulled from a fire but not completely burned. He seems at odds with nature, but nature has been unable to destroy him.*

Cultural History ☆

Ship's Captain The author refers to Ahab as a "supreme lord and dictator." At the time this story is set, the captain of a ship was the absolute authority on board. The crew was bound to follow the captain's orders without question. The captain had the authority to administer harsh punishment for any infractions.

Approaching Level
DIFFERENTIATED INSTRUCTION

Established Students may find it difficult to follow Melville's long complex sentences. Display this sentence from this page: "So powerfully did the whole grim aspect . . . ." Help students find the main clause's subjects (*aspect* and *brand*), verb (*did affect*) and direct object (*me*). Then have them state the basic parts of sentences in conventional sentence order.

Emerging To help students understand information that is implied, not stated, guide them in formulating questions as they read, such as "What theories are given about how Ahab got his scar?" and "What is his white leg made of?" Help them make inferences to answer the questions and have them write the answers.

Teach

Motivation Answer: *The "crucifixion in his face" and the "overbearing dignity of some mighty woe" suggest a terrible suffering, perhaps unmerited, that continues to afflict him. This suffering may cause him to act in irrational ways.*

Ask: How would you explain the metaphor "a crucifixion in his face"? (*Crucifixion was a Roman punishment that caused great suffering. The metaphor means that Ahab's face bears the signs of great suffering.*)

Reading Strategy | 2

**Monitor Comprehension
Answer:** *The* Pequod *is not yet in a whaling area, so Ahab is not needed to direct the crew; he is alone with his troubled thoughts.*

Literary History ☆

The *Pequod* Tell students that the *Pequod* set sail from Nantucket on Christmas Day, at the beginning of winter. As the ship sails south toward the equator, the weather gradually becomes warmer. In the Southern Hemisphere, December begins the summer season.

Writing Practice

Character Sketch Have students write a brief character sketch of Ahab. Their sketches should include both his physical and his personality traits. Remind students that Melville reveals Ahab's character both directly and indirectly. Students should include evidence of characterization, both direct and indirect, to support their statements about his character.

298

---

about half an inch or so, into the plank. His bone leg steadied in that hole; one arm elevated, and holding by a shroud; Captain Ahab stood erect, looking straight out beyond the ship's ever-pitching prow. There was an infinity of firmest **fortitude,** a determinate, unsurrenderable wilfulness, in the fixed and fearless, forward dedication of that glance. Not a word he spoke; nor did his officers say aught to him; though by all their minutest gestures and expressions, they plainly showed the uneasy, if not painful, consciousness of being under a troubled master-eye. And not only that, but moody stricken Ahab stood before them with a crucifixion in his face; in all the nameless regal overbearing dignity of some mighty woe.

Ere long, from his first visit in the air, he withdrew into his cabin. But after that morning, he was every day visible to the crew; either standing in his pivot-hole, or seated upon an ivory stool he had; or heavily walking the deck. As the sky grew less gloomy; indeed, began to grow a little **genial,** he became still less and less a **recluse;** as if, when the ship had sailed from home, nothing but the dead wintry bleakness of the sea had then kept him so secluded. And, by and by, it came to pass, that he was almost continually in the air; but, as yet, for all that he said, or perceptibly did, on the at last sunny deck, he seemed as unnecessary there as another mast. But the Pequod was only making a passage now; not regularly cruising; nearly all whaling preparatives needing supervision the mates were fully competent to, so that there was little or noth-

ing, out of himself to employ or excite Ahab, now; and thus chase away, for that one interval, the clouds that layer upon layer were piled upon his brow, as ever all clouds choose the loftiest peaks to pile themselves upon.

Nevertheless, ere long, the warm, warbling persuasiveness of the pleasant, holiday weather we came to, seemed gradually to charm him from his mood. For, as when the red-cheeked, dancing girls, April and May, trip home to the wintry, **misanthropic** woods; even the barest, ruggedest, most thunder-cloven old oak will at least send forth some few green sprouts, to welcome such glad-hearted visitants; so Ahab did, in the end, a little respond to the playful allurings of that girlish air. More than once did he put forth the faint blossom of a look, which, in any other man, would have soon flowered out in a smile.

As the Pequod sails farther south, Ahab ☆ *grows increasingly restless. He paces the deck even in the dead of night when most of the crew are asleep. No longer able to relax and enjoy simple pleasures, he tosses his pipe into the sea.*

The Quarter-Deck

(*Enter Ahab: Then, all.*)

It was not a great while after the affair of the pipe, that one morning shortly after breakfast, Ahab, as was his wont, ascended the cabin-gangway to the deck. There most sea-captains usually walk at that hour, as country gentlemen, after the same meal, take a few turns in the garden.

---

1 | Motivation *What is revealed about Ahab's past that may help explain his present or future actions?*

Vocabulary

fortitude (fôr´ tə tōōd´) *n.* strength, particularly strength of mind that enables one to encounter danger or bear adversity with courage
genial (jēn´ yəl) *adj.* mild or friendly
recluse (rek´ lōōs) *n.* someone who leads a secluded or solitary life

Monitor Comprehension *What is happening in this sentence? Rephrase the sentence in your own words.* | **2**

The Power of Darkness *What effect does Melville create by describing the routine walks of other sea captains and country gentlemen before describing Ahab's pacing?* | **3**

Vocabulary

misanthropic (mis´ ən throp´ ik) *adj.* having hatred for humankind

Soon his steady, ivory stride[12] was heard, as to and fro he paced his old rounds, upon planks so familiar to his tread, that they were all over dented, like geological stones, with the peculiar mark of his walk. Did you fixedly gaze, too, upon that ribbed and dented brow; there also, you would see still stranger foot-prints—the foot-prints of his one unsleeping, ever-pacing thought.

But on the occasion in question, those dents looked deeper, even as his nervous step that morning left a deeper mark. And, so full of his thought was Ahab, that at every uniform turn that he made, now at the main-mast and now at the binnacle,[13] you could almost see that thought turn in him as he turned, and pace in him as he paced; so completely possessing him, indeed, that it all but seemed the inward mould of every outer movement.

"D'ye mark him, Flask?" whispered Stubb; "the chick that's in him pecks the shell. 'Twill soon be out."

The hours wore on;—Ahab now shut up within his cabin; anon, pacing the deck, with the same intense bigotry of purpose[14] in his aspect.

It drew near the close of day. Suddenly he came to a halt by the bulwarks,[15] and inserting his bone leg into the auger-hole there, and with one hand grasping a shroud, he ordered Starbuck to send everybody aft.

"Sir!" said the mate, astonished at an order seldom or never given on shipboard except in some extraordinary case.

"Send everybody aft," repeated Ahab. "Mast-heads, there! come down!"

When the entire ship's company were assembled, and with curious and not wholly unappre-

hensive faces, were eyeing him, for he looked not unlike the weather horizon when a storm is coming up, Ahab, after rapidly glancing over the bulwarks, and then darting his eyes among the crew, started from his stand-point; and as though not a soul were nigh[16] him resumed his heavy turns upon the deck. With bent head and half-slouched hat he continued to pace, unmindful of the wondering whispering among the men; till Stubb cautiously whispered to Flask, that Ahab must have summoned them there for the purpose of witnessing a pedestrian feat. But this did not last long. Vehemently pausing, he cried:—

"What do ye do when ye see a whale, men?"

"Sing out for him!" was the impulsive rejoinder[17] from a score of clubbed voices.

"Good!" cried Ahab, with a wild approval in his tones; observing the hearty animation into which his unexpected question had so magnetically thrown them.

"And what do ye next, men?"

"Lower away, and after him!"

"And what tune is it ye pull to, men?"

"A dead whale or a stove boat!"[18]

More and more strangely and fiercely glad and approving grew the countenance[19] of the old man at every shout; while the mariners began to gaze curiously at each other, as if marvelling how it was that they themselves became so excited at such seemingly purposeless questions.

But, they were all eagerness again, as Ahab, now half-revolving in his pivot-hole, with one hand reaching high up a shroud, and tightly, almost convulsively grasping it, addressed them thus:—

"All ye mast-headers have before now heard me give orders about a white whale. Look ye! d'ye see this Spanish ounce of gold?"—holding

---

12. *Ivory stride* refers to Ahab's walking with an artificial leg made from a whale's jawbone.
13. A *binnacle* is a compartment on a ship for the ship's lamp and compass.
14. *Bigotry of purpose* refers to Ahab's fierce single-mindedness.
15. The sides of a ship above the upper deck are known as the *bulwarks*.

4 Motivation *Why does Ahab pace the deck so resolutely?*

16. Here, *nigh* means "close" or "near."
17. An *impulsive rejoinder* is a spontaneous response or reply.
18. *A dead whale or a stove boat!* is a whaler's motto meaning, "We kill a whale or wreck our boat in the attempt!"
19. *Countenance* refers to the appearance or expression of the face that reveals mood or emotion.

HERMAN MELVILLE **299**

Teach

Big Idea 3

The Power of Darkness
Answer: *Melville creates a contrast between the others' relaxed walks and Ahab's anxious pacing, which creates dents upon the planks. This contrast further establishes Ahab's mood as unusual.*

Literary Element 4

Motivation Answer: *His outward movements suggest that his thoughts are stuck in a groove. They go back and forth over the same issue endlessly.*

Ask: What does Melville mean by the metaphor in this sentence? *(The thought or feeling in Ahab's mind is striving to come out into the open, like a chick pecking its way out of an egg.)*

(ENGLISH LEARNERS) **Say:** Visualize the way Ahab is walking. Why would his steps make footprints and deep marks on the planks of the deck? *(Walking over the same place again and again would wear marks into the surface.)*

English Learners

DIFFERENTIATED INSTRUCTION

Intermediate Have English learners work with a partner to interpret and explain the meaning of these figurative expressions: "the chick that's in him pecks the shell"; "not unlike the weather horizon when a storm is coming up."

Approaching Level

DIFFERENTIATED INSTRUCTION

Emerging Explain that Melville writes with great detail. Help readers sort out main ideas from additional descriptive detail. Read aloud the paragraph that begins "It was not a great while after the affair . . . ." Explain that the main idea of this paragraph is that Ahab goes up to the deck for a walk. As extra detail, Melville compares Ahab to a country gentleman who takes a walk after his breakfast. As

students continue to read, ask them to separate the main idea in each paragraph from details that illustrate or help them visualize the scenes.

Teach

View the Art ★

Answer: *Students' answers will vary, but they should express plausible views of Ahab's character and of the attitude of the man depicted in the artwork.*

Prior to 1712, the British hunted whales off the coast of the North American colonies. In 1712, a ship sailing out of Nantucket was the first to kill a sperm whale, which produced far more oil and other valuable products than other kinds of whales. Sperm whales had a wide range, from the cold waters of the North Atlantic to the warmer southern waters. With the promise of high profits from sperm whales, whaling voyages extended far into the Pacific, sometimes lasting as long as four years. When a crew spotted a whale, a six-man group set out in a boat to pursue it. The whale was struck with harpoons with coiled ropes attached and held until it tired. A whaler then used a hand lance to kill the whale.

Man in Boat Looking at White Whale. Christopher Zacharow.

View the Art This painting focuses on the man and the whale, with few other elements included. How does the image correspond to your view of Ahab's character? ★

up a broad bright coin to the sun—"it is a sixteen dollar piece, men,—a doubloon. D'ye see it? Mr. Starbuck, hand me yon topmaul."

While the mate was getting the hammer, Ahab, without speaking, was slowly rubbing the gold piece against the skirts of his jacket, as if to heighten its lustre, and without using any words was meanwhile lowly humming to himself, producing a sound so strangely muffled and inarticulate that it seemed the mechanical humming of the wheels of his vitality in him.

Receiving the topmaul from Starbuck, he advanced towards the main-mast with the hammer uplifted in one hand, exhibiting the gold with the other, and with a high raised voice exclaiming: "Whosoever of ye raises[20] me a white-headed whale with a wrinkled brow and a crooked jaw; whosoever of ye raises me that white-headed whale, with three holes punctured in his starboard fluke[21]—look ye, whosoever of ye raises me that same white whale, he shall have this gold ounce, my boys!"

"Huzza! huzza!" cried the seamen, as with swinging tarpaulins they hailed the act of nailing the gold to the mast.

"It's a white whale, I say," resumed Ahab, as he threw down the topmaul; "a white whale. Skin your eyes for him, men; look sharp for white water; if ye see but a bubble, sing out."

All this while Tashtego, Daggoo, and Queequeg[22] had looked on with even more intense interest and surprise than the rest, and at the mention of the wrinkled brow and crooked jaw they had started as if each was separately touched by some specific recollection.

"Captain Ahab," said Tashtego, "that white whale must be the same that some call Moby Dick."

"Moby Dick?" shouted Ahab. "Do ye know the white whale then, Tash?"

"Does he fan-tail a little curious, sir, before he goes down?" said the Gayheader deliberately.

"And has he a curious spout, too," said Daggoo, "very bushy, even for a parmacetty,[23] and mighty quick, Captain Ahab?"

"And he have one, two, tree—oh! good many iron in him hide, too, Captain," cried Queequeg disjointedly, "all twiske-tee betwisk, like him—him—" faltering hard for a word, and screwing his hand round and round as though uncorking a bottle—"like him—him—"

"Corkscrew!" cried Ahab, "aye, Queequeg, the harpoons lie all twisted and wrenched in him;[24] aye, Daggoo, his spout is a big one, like a whole shock of wheat, and white as a pile of our Nantucket wool after the great annual sheep-shearing; aye, Tashtego, and he fan-tails like a split jib in a squall.[25] Death and devils! men, it is Moby Dick ye have seen—Moby Dick—Moby Dick!"

---

20. To *raise* a whale is to spot or identify it in the sea.
21. *Starboard fluke* means "the right half of a whale's tail."

---

22. *Tashtego, Daggoo, and Queequeg* are the harpooneers on the *Pequod;* Ishmael befriended Queequeg in Nantucket before signing up for the voyage.
23. *Parmacetty* (or spermaceti) is a white, waxy solid found in the oil of whales. Here, it refers to the whale itself.
24. Moby Dick has survived many attacks and bears the wounds (and mangled harpoons) inflicted by those who failed to kill him.
25. *Like a split jib in a squall* means "like a torn sail in a storm."

Writing Practice

SPIRAL REVIEW **Research Questions** Moby Dick is a sperm whale, a kind of whale that was frequently hunted because of its great commercial value. Encourage students to research the sperm whale.

Before students begin, help them formulate research questions. To get students started, offer these questions:

- What is the range of the sperm whale?
- What is its size?
- Why was it commercially valuable?
- What were its products used for?

"Captain Ahab," said Starbuck, who, with Stubb and Flask, had thus far been eyeing his superior with increasing surprise, but at last seemed struck with a thought which somewhat explained all the wonder. "Captain Ahab, I have heard of Moby Dick—but it was not Moby Dick that took off thy leg?"

"Who told thee that?" cried Ahab; then pausing, "Aye, Starbuck; aye, my hearties all round; it was Moby Dick that dismasted me; Moby Dick that brought me to this dead stump I stand on now. Aye, aye," he shouted with a terrific, loud, animal sob, like that of a heart-stricken moose; "Aye, aye! it was that accursed white whale that razeed[26] me; made a poor pegging lubber of me for ever and a day!" Then tossing both arms, with measureless imprecations he shouted out: "Aye, aye! and I'll chase him round Good Hope, and round the Horn, and round the Norway Maelstrom, and round perdition's[27] flames before I give him up. And this is what ye have shipped for, men! to chase that white whale on both sides of land, and over all sides of earth, till he spouts black blood and rolls fin out. What say ye, men, will ye splice hands on it, now? I think ye do look brave."

"Aye, aye!" shouted the harpooneers and seamen, running closer to the excited old man: "A sharp eye for the White Whale; a sharp lance for Moby Dick!"

"God bless ye," he seemed to half sob and half shout. "God bless ye, men. Steward! go draw the great measure of grog.[28] But what's this long face about, Mr. Starbuck; wilt thou not chase the white whale? art not game for Moby Dick?"

"I am game for his crooked jaw, and for the jaws of Death too, Captain Ahab, if it fairly comes in the way of the business we follow; but I came here to hunt whales, not my commander's vengeance. How many barrels will thy ven-

geance yield thee even if thou gettest it, Captain Ahab? it will not fetch thee much in our Nantucket market."

"Nantucket market! Hoot! But come closer, Starbuck; thou requirest a little lower layer. If money's to be the measurer, man, and the accountants have computed their great counting-house the globe, by girdling it with guineas, one to every three parts of an inch; then, let me tell thee, that my vengeance will fetch a great premium *here*!"

"He smites[29] his chest," whispered Stubb, "what's that for? methinks it rings most vast, but hollow."

"Vengeance on a dumb brute!" cried Starbuck, "that simply smote thee from blindest instinct! Madness! To be enraged with a dumb thing, Captain Ahab, seems blasphemous."

"Hark ye yet again,—the little lower layer. All visible objects, man, are but as pasteboard masks. But in each event—in the living act, the undoubted deed—there, some unknown but still reasoning thing puts forth the mouldings of its features from behind the unreasoning mask. If man will strike, strike through the mask! How can the prisoner reach outside except by thrusting through the wall? To me, the white whale is that wall, shoved near to me. Sometimes I think there's naught beyond. But 'tis enough. He tasks me; he heaps me; I see in him outrageous strength, with an inscrutable malice sinewing it. That **inscrutable** thing is chiefly what I hate; and be the white whale agent, or be the white whale principal, I will wreak that hate upon him. Talk not to me of blasphemy, man; I'd strike the sun if it insulted me. For could the sun do that, then could I do the other; since there is

---

29. To *smite* is to strike sharply.

Monitor Comprehension *Whom does Ahab describe in this passage?* 2

Vocabulary

inscrutable (in skrōō′ tə bəl) *adj.* mysterious, or not able to be interpreted or understood

HERMAN MELVILLE **301**

---

26. A *razee* is a "cut-off" ship, or a ship with its upper decks removed. Ahab, too, has had a part of himself removed, namely, his leg.

27. Here, *perdition* is hell.

28. *Grog* is alcoholic liquor, such as rum, often diluted with water.

1

Teach

Big Idea | 1

The Power of Darkness

Say: In this passage, Ahab—with great emotion—reveals to his crew the true reason for their voyage. Have a volunteer read the passage aloud, with feeling. (You may wish to allow the volunteer a brief time to prepare by reading the passage silently.) **Ask:** What dark and brooding element of his spirit does Ahab reveal in this speech? (*Ahab reveals a soul tormented by hatred and a thirst for vengeance. He acknowledges that he will go to any lengths to kill Moby Dick.*)

APPROACHING **Say:** Ahab lists many places around the world, including the Cape of Good Hope in South Africa and the Norway Maelstrom. He also mentions hell. What do these references tell you about Ahab's past experience on the sea and his present plans? (*Ahab has sailed in many parts of the world. He will go anywhere to get the white whale.*)

Reading Strategy | 2

Monitor Comprehension

Answer: *Ahab is describing the whale, Moby Dick.*

Ask: What actions or characteristics does Captain Ahab attribute to Moby Dick in this passage? (*Ahab characterizes Moby Dick as immensely strong and deliberately malicious.*)

English Learners

DIFFERENTIATED INSTRUCTION

Intermediate English learners may have trouble with the archaic language in the dialogue on this page. Tell students that this language is no longer commonly used. Review the following words and phrases with students:

thee, ye	"you"
aye	"yes"
wilt thou not	"won't you"
art	"are"
thou, thy	"you," "your"
methinks	"it seems to me"
hark ye	"listen"

Encourage students to write down these words and their meanings for reference as they continue to read.

Teach

The Power of Darkness
Answer: *Expressions such as "Starbuck now is mine" suggest a growing madness in Ahab. Also, the imagery Ahab uses to describe his influence on Starbuck ("Something shot from my dilated nostrils, he has inhaled it in his lungs") is strange and demonic.*

Literary Element   2

Motivation **Answer:** *Ahab believes that Starbuck is "his" and will not oppose him. Lost in his own obsessions, Ahab is oblivious to everything else.*

Reading Strategy   3

Monitor Comprehension
Answer: *The leader of the prairie wolves rushes after bison but gets caught in the Indian's snare (trap). Ahab is compared to the wolves' leader.*

Ask: What does this passage suggest about Ahab's power over his crew? *(It suggests that Ahab has a mysterious, almost mesmerizing power over the crew.)*

---

ever a sort of fair play herein, jealousy presiding over all creations. But not my master, man, is even that fair play. Who's over me? Truth hath no confines. Take off thine eye! more intolerable than fiends' glarings is a doltish stare! So, so; thou reddenest and palest; my heat has melted thee to anger-glow. But look ye, Starbuck, what is said in heat, that thing unsays itself. There are men from whom warm words are small indignity.[30] I meant not to incense[31] thee. Let it go. Look! see yonder Turkish cheeks of spotted tawn—living, breathing pictures painted by the sun. The Pagan[32] leopards—the unrecking and unworshipping things, that live; and seek, and give no reasons for the torrid life they feel! The crew, man, the crew! Are they not one and all with Ahab, in this matter of the whale? See Stubb! he laughs! See yonder Chilean! he snorts to think of it. Stand up amid the general hurricane, thy one tost sapling cannot, Starbuck! And what is it? Reckon it. 'Tis but to help strike a fin; no wondrous feat for Starbuck. What is it more? From this one poor hunt, then, the best lance out of all Nantucket, surely he will not hang back, when every foremast-hand has clutched a whetstone? Ah! constrainings seize thee; I see! the billow lifts thee! Speak, but speak!—Aye, aye! thy silence, then, *that* voices thee. (*Aside*) Something shot from my dilated nostrils, he has inhaled it in his lungs. Starbuck now is mine; cannot oppose me now, without rebellion."

"God keep me!—keep us all!" murmured Starbuck, lowly.

But in his joy at the enchanted, tacit acquiescence of the mate, Ahab did not hear his foreboding invocation;[33] nor yet the low laugh from

the hold; nor yet the presaging vibrations of the winds in the cordage;[34] nor yet the hollow flap of the sails against the masts, as for a moment their hearts sank in. For again Starbuck's downcast eyes lighted up with the stubbornness of life; the subterranean[35] laugh died away; the winds blew on; the sails filled out; the ship heaved and rolled as before. Ah, ye admonitions and warnings! why stay ye not when ye come? But rather are ye predictions than warnings, ye shadows! Yet not so much predictions from without, as verifications of the foregoing things within. For with little external to constrain us, the innermost necessities in our being, these still drive us on.

"The measure! the measure!" cried Ahab.

Receiving the brimming pewter, and turning to the harpooneers, he ordered them to produce their weapons. Then ranging them before him near the capstan,[36] with their harpoons in their hands, while his three mates stood at his side with their lances, and the rest of the ship's company formed a circle round the group; he stood for an instant searchingly eyeing every man of his crew. But those wild eyes met his, as the bloodshot eyes of the prairie wolves meet the eye of their leader, ere he rushes on at their head in the trail of the bison; but, alas! only to fall into the hidden snare of the Indian.

"Drink and pass!" he cried, handing the heavy charged flagon to the nearest seaman. "The crew alone now drink. Round with it, round! Short draughts—long swallows, men; 'tis hot as Satan's hoof. So, so; it goes round excellently. It spiralizes in ye; forks out at the serpent-snapping eye. Well done; almost drained. That way it went, this way it comes. Hand it me—here's a hollow! Men, ye seem the years; so brimming life is gulped and gone. Steward, refill!

---

30. An *indignity* is an insult.
31. *Incense* means "to cause extreme anger."
32. Here, *Pagan* describes someone with little or no religion.
33. An *invocation* is the act of calling on an authority for help or support.

---

1 **The Power of Darkness** *What does this passage suggest about Ahab?*

2 **Motivation** *Why does Ahab not hear Starbuck's invocation?*

---

34. *Cordage* is the rope used in a ship's rigging.
35. Here, *subterranean* refers to something below the deck of the ship.
36. A *capstan* is a vertical drum around which a cable is turned to move or raise weights.

Monitor Comprehension *What happens to the leader of the prairie wolves in this comparison? Who on the ship is compared to that leader?*   **3**

Listening and Speaking Practice

Dramatic Presentation Pages 301–303 include a pivotal scene that reveals Ahab's character. Form the class into small groups to present a dramatic reading of this scene, starting with the next to last paragraph on page 301, the paragraph beginning "Vengeance on a dumb brute!" and ending after the first full paragraph on page 303.

Each group should have a reader for Ahab's dialogue, one for Starbuck's

dialogue, and one for the narrator. Have students present their readings before the class.

Scrimshaw on Whalebone. New Bedford Whaling Museum, New Bedford, MA.

"Attend now, my braves. I have mustered ye all round this capstan; and ye mates, flank me with your lances; and ye harpooneers, stand there with your irons; and ye, stout mariners, ring me in, that I may in some sort revive a noble custom of my fisherman fathers before me. O men, you will yet see that—Ha! boy, come back? bad pennies come not sooner. Hand it me. Why, now, this pewter had run brimming again, wert not thou St. Vitus' imp—away, thou ague![37]

"Advance, ye mates! Cross your lances full before me. Well done! Let me touch the axis." So saying, with extended arm, he grasped the three level, radiating lances at their crossed centre; while so doing, suddenly and nervously twitched them; meanwhile, glancing intently from Starbuck to Stubb; from Stubb to Flask. It seemed as though, by some nameless, interior volition,[38] he would fain[39] have shocked into them the same fiery emotion accumulated within the Leyden jar[40] of his own magnetic life. The three mates quailed before his strong, sustained, and mystic aspect. Stubb and Flask looked sideways from him; the honest eye of Starbuck fell downright.

"In vain!" cried Ahab; "but, maybe, 'tis well. For did ye three but once take the full-forced shock, then mine own electric thing, *that* had perhaps expired from out me. Perchance, too, it would have dropped ye dead. Perchance ye need it not. Down lances! And now, ye mates, I do appoint ye three cup-bearers to my three pagan kinsmen there—yon three most honorable gentlemen and noblemen, my valiant harpooneers. Disdain the task? What, when the great Pope washes the feet of beggars, using his tiara for ewer? Oh, my sweet cardinals![41] your own condescension, *that* shall bend ye to it. I do not order ye; ye will it. Cut your seizings and draw the poles, ye harpooneers!"

Silently obeying the order, the three harpooneers now stood with the detached iron part of their harpoons some three feet long, held, barbs up, before him.

"Stab me not with that keen steel! Cant them; cant them over! know ye not the goblet end? Turn up the socket! So, so; now, ye cup-bearers, advance. The irons! take them; hold them while I fill!" Forthwith, slowly going from one officer to the other, he brimmed the harpoon sockets with the fiery waters from the pewter.

"Now, three to three, ye stand. Commend the murderous chalices! Bestow them, ye who are now made parties to this indissoluble league. Ha! Starbuck! but the deed is done! Yon ratifying sun now waits to sit upon it. Drink, ye harpooneers! drink and swear, ye men that man the deathful whaleboat's bow—Death to Moby Dick! God hunt us all, if we do not hunt Moby Dick to his death!" The long, barbed steel goblets were lifted; and to cries and maledictions[42] against the white whale, the spirits were simultaneously quaffed down with a hiss. Starbuck paled, and turned, and shivered. Once more, and finally, the replenished pewter went the rounds among the frantic crew; when, waving his free hand to them, they all dispersed; and Ahab retired within his cabin.

---

37. *St. Vitus'* or *St. Vitus' Dance* is a nervous disorder that causes shaking of the limbs. Ahab mocks the steward for having a shaky hand and spilling some of the liquor. An *ague* is a fever.
38. *Volition* is an act of choosing or willing something.
39. Here, *fain* means "rather."
40. A *Leyden jar* is a form of capacitor, or "electrical circuit element that can store an electrical charge temporarily."

41. *Cardinals* are high officials of the Roman Catholic Church; Ahab addresses his three mates as cardinals.
42. A *malediction* is a curse.

The Power of Darkness *How does Ahab's use of religious language and ritual reveal the darker side of his intention?* **4**

HERMAN MELVILLE **303**

Teach

Big Idea	4

The Power of Darkness
Answer: *Ahab subverts religious ritual and language, using them to induce his crew to accept his mission as their own. Although he manipulates his crew, he maintains that they have chosen this mission of their own free will, as though they were aware of his intent from the outset of the voyage.*

Cultural History ☆

Movies Even though *Moby-Dick* is a literary classic, Hollywood has been reluctant to adapt the novel for film. The best-known movie version of *Moby-Dick* was released in 1956. Its director, John Huston, tried for three years to convince studios to produce the film. Hollywood's complaint was that *Moby-Dick* is a depressing tale without a female character and with no love story.

To check students' understanding of the selection, see Unit 2 Teaching Resources Book, p. 164.

Approaching Level

DIFFERENTIATED INSTRUCTION

SMALL GROUP

Emerging Explain to students that Ahab is inspiring his crew with a speech as a military leader does before a battle or as a coach does before a big game. He wants them to commit to his goal of catching the white whale. Have students work in pairs or small groups to interpret and summarize each paragraph—what Ahab says and what he does. Remind them to use the footnotes and questions at the bottoms of these pages.

After You Read

Assess

1. Students should show insight into Ahab's character.

2. (a) He notices Ahab's scar and artificial leg. (b) His injuries reveal the savage nature of Ahab's fight with the whale and escape from death.

3. (a) He stands erect, looking straight ahead. (b) His stance suggests he is fearless.

4. (a) Starbuck opposes Ahab's intention. (b) He wants to make money, and Ahab's mission is unprofitable.

5. (a) To Ahab, Moby Dick represents "inscrutable malice"; to Starbuck, a "dumb brute"; to the rest of the crew, an adventure. (b) Melville suggests that Ahab's perspective is not the only valid one.

6. (a) Ahab is seeking revenge against a brute that acted from instinct. (b) Ahab shows a lack of reverence by usurping God's role and engaging in a mock-religious ritual.

7. (a) Ahab's passion is contagious. (b) His passion exerts an almost physical force on the crew.

8. Students may say the crew seems just as devoted as Ahab, or may cite Ahab's apparent madness.

9. Ahab perceives him as an unknowable evil that confronts him and mankind.

10. Students may note that it has validity today, as people become obsessed with finding someone or something.

 For additional assessment, see Assessment Resources, pp. 117–118.

After You Read

Respond and Think Critically

Respond and Interpret

1. Would you want to sail with a captain like Ahab? Explain.

2. (a) What does Ishmael notice about Ahab's appearance? (b) How does Ahab's appearance influence Ishmael's impression of him?

3. (a) Describe Ahab's posture as he stands on the quarter-deck. (b) How does his stance affirm his position as captain?

4. (a) What is Starbuck's reaction to Ahab's intention to hunt Moby Dick? (b) Why does he react this way?

Analyze and Evaluate

5. (a) What does Moby Dick represent to Ahab, Starbuck, and the crew of the *Pequod*? (b) Why does Melville present different perceptions of the whale?

6. (a) Why does Starbuck accuse Ahab of blasphemy? (b) Is Ahab guilty of blasphemy or not? Explain.

7. (a) Why does the crew choose to follow Ahab in his mission to kill Moby Dick? (b) How do you account for the "magnetism" between Ahab and his crew?

8. Is Ahab justified in not revealing the *Pequod*'s mission until the voyage is underway? Support your answer with evidence from the story.

Connect

9. **Big Idea** **The Power of Darkness** How does Melville use Ahab and his mission as a means of exploring the mystery of evil in the world?

10. **Connect to Today** Does Melville's depiction of obsession have validity in today's world? Explain.

Literary Element | Motivation

Motivation is a central feature of psychological realism, the attempt to portray characters in a plausible, objective manner. Above all else, psychological realism insists that characters be clearly motivated; they should not act without apparent reason.

In *Moby-Dick*, Ahab's words and actions as well as the words and thoughts of the other characters, particularly Ishmael, provide clues to Ahab's motivation.

1. Are Ahab's motivations clearly depicted? Support your answer.

2. Is Ahab's motivation in hunting Moby Dick purely revenge? Explain.

Review: Metaphor

A **metaphor** is a figure of speech in which two seemingly unlike things are equated. In a metaphor the comparison is implied, rather than stated directly.

Metaphor	What Is Compared	Why It Is Appropriate
p. 301 "it was Moby Dick that dismasted me"		

LOG ON ▶ **Literature** Online

Selection Resources For Selection Quizzes, eFlash-cards, and Reading-Writing Connection activities, go to glencoe.com and enter QuickPass code GLA9800u2.

304 UNIT 2 AMERICAN ROMANTICISM

Literary Element

1. Yes, Ahab states that he hates the white whale.

2. Students' answers will vary. Some students will argue that Ahab is a complex character whose motivations run deeper than revenge. Other students will argue that revenge is the single motivating factor in Ahab's hunt for Moby Dick.

Progress Check

Can students analyze motivation?

If No → See Unit 2 Teaching Resources Book, p. 159.

Reading Strategy · Monitor Comprehension

Reread this passage from page 302. Then break it down and answer the questions below.

"And what is it? Reckon it. 'Tis but to help strike a fin; no wondrous feat for Starbuck. What is it more? From this one poor hunt, then, the best lance out of all Nantucket, surely he will not hang back, when every foremast-hand has clutched a whetstone?"

1. To whom is Ahab speaking?
2. What is Ahab trying to do?
3. How would you summarize the passage?

Vocabulary Practice

Practice with Antonyms An **antonym** is a word that has a meaning opposite to that of another word. With a partner, match each bold-faced vocabulary word below with its antonym. You will not use all of the options. Check your answers in a thesaurus or dictionary.

1. fortitude   **a.** morose
2. recluse   **b.** clear
3. misanthropic   **c.** bizarre
4. inscrutable   **d.** cowardice
5. genial   **e.** friendly
                    f. busy
                    g. socialite

Academic Vocabulary

*In Moby-Dick, Captain Ahab exercises a passionate **authority** over his crew.*

Authority is an academic word. It can mean "direct power to command," but also "trusted source of information." To further explore the meaning of this word, complete the sentence below.

Her main **authority** for her claims about the causes of the War of 1812 was _____.

For more on academic vocabulary, see pages 53–54.

Research and Report

 Literary Criticism

Assignment Evaluate a passage of literary criticism about Melville's work. Write a short response in which you explain whether you agree or disagree that the criticism applies to the selection from *Moby-Dick*. Deliver your response to the class.

Prepare Read the following passage from a review of *Moby-Dick* in the *London Leader*, November 8, 1851. (Cetology is the branch of zoology that deals with whales and other sea mammals. One definition of romance is "a prose narrative treating imaginary characters involved in events remote in time or place and usually heroic, adventurous, or mysterious.")

"The book is not a romance, nor a treatise on cetology. It is something of both: a strange, wild work with the tangled overgrowth and luxuriant vegetation of American forests, not the trim orderliness of an English park. Criticism may pick many holes in this work; but no criticism will thwart its fascination."

To help you evaluate this statement, use a simple chart like the one below. In one column, record details from *Moby-Dick* that convey information about whaling. In the other, record details that fit the description of romance. When you have completed the chart, review it and decide how well the story supports the review. Then craft a thesis statement and write your response.

Whaling	Romance

Report When you deliver your response, make eye contact, speak loudly and clearly, and maintain good posture to reflect confidence. Use appropriate tones of voice to clarify logical appeals and enhance emotional ones.

Evaluate Write a paragraph evaluating your delivery of your response. When your classmates present their reports, offer oral feedback on their performances. Use the checklist on page 624 for help in your evaluation.

HERMAN MELVILLE **305**

After You Read

Assess

Review: Metaphor

Possible answers:

Metaphor: p. 296, "their supreme lord and dictator was there"; *What Is Compared:* Captain Ahab is compared to a king and a dictator; *Why It Is Appropriate:* Like a king or dictator, the captain of a ship commands the absolute obedience of others.

Metaphor: p. 303, "Oh, my sweet cardinals!"; *What Is Compared:* The mates are compared to cardinals, high officials of the Catholic Church; *Why It Is Appropriate:* The mates are high officials under Ahab, just as cardinals are under the pope.

Reading Strategy

1. Ahab is speaking to Starbuck.
2. Ahab is trying to convince Starbuck to join the hunt for Moby Dick.
3. Ahab boosts Starbuck's ego by calling him "the best lance out of all Nantucket," de-emphasizes the danger of the hunt, and mentions the crew's endorsement of the mission.

Vocabulary

1. d **2.** g **3.** e **4.** b **5.** a

Academic Vocabulary

Possible answer: Her main authority for her claims about the causes of the War of 1812 was a general who left behind a careful account of the war.

Research and Report

Students should express a clear evaluation of the literary criticism and use evidence from the selection to support opinions. Students should effectively use verbal and nonverbal techniques in their presentation.

Focus

Summary

A day after their whaling ship has sunk, the survivors are divided among three small boats in the middle of the Pacific. They plan how to seek help and how to divide up their food.

Teach

Analyze Historical Context Before students read this passage, encourage them to recall the details they found most memorable in the excerpts of *Moby-Dick* they have read. These details will be useful in constructing their two-column charts.

 For an activity related to this selection, see Unit 2 Teaching Resources Book, pp. 166–174.

 For an audio recording of this selection, use Listening Library Audio CD-ROM.

Readability Scores

Dale-Chall: 9.0
DRP: 67
Lexile: 1150

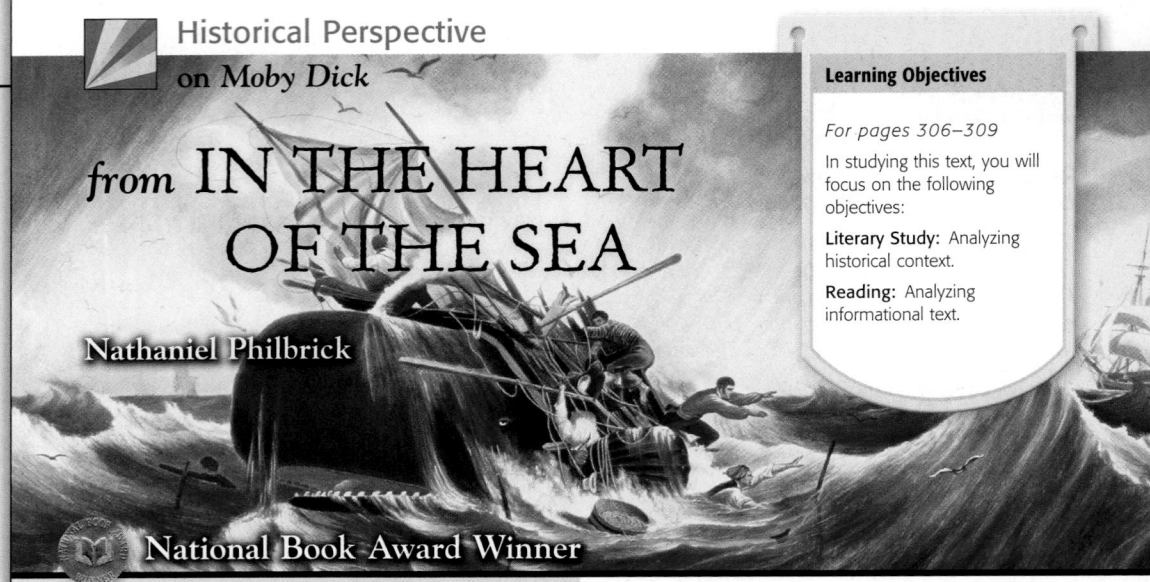

Historical Perspective on *Moby Dick*

from IN THE HEART OF THE SEA

Nathaniel Philbrick

National Book Award Winner

Set a Purpose for Reading

Read to discover the historical basis for Melville's novel *Moby-Dick*.

Build Background

In 1820 a sperm whale sank the Nantucket whaling ship *Essex*. The crew was lost at sea for four months; eight survived. This event inspired Herman Melville's *Moby-Dick*. In the chapters "Ahab" and "The Quarter-Deck" (see pages 296–303), Melville models his portrayal of Captain Ahab on first mate Owen Chase's account of the tragedy. The following selection, from historian Nathaniel Philbrick's non-fiction book, describes the *Essex* crew's first days stranded at sea.

Reading Strategy Analyze Historical Context

Analyzing **historical context** involves gathering background information and exploring social forces that influenced the writing of a literary work. As you read, take notes on the historical context for Melville's tale. Use a two-column chart like the one below.

World of Ahab	World of Owen Chase

The Sperm Whale in a Flurry (showing reversed) from *The Whale Fishery*, published by Currier & Ives. After Louis Ambroise Garneray. Colour lithograph. Peabody Essex Museum, Salem, MA.

As darkness approached at the end of the first day, the wind built steadily, kicking up a steep, irregular chop.[1] The *Essex* whaleboats were hybrids—built for rowing but now adapted to sail—and the men were still learning how they handled. Instead of a rudder, each boat was equipped with a steering oar. This eighteen-foot lever enabled a rowed whaleboat to spin around in its own length, but it was not so effective in guiding a sailboat, and required the helmsman to stand at the cumbersome oar. At this early stage in the voyage, the whaleboats were dangerously overloaded. Instead of five hundred pounds of whaling equipment, each boat contained close to a thousand pounds of bread, water, and tortoises,[2] and waves broke over the built-up gunnels[3] and soaked the men. The boats were also without centerboards or skegs[4] to help them track through the water, forcing the helmsmen to tug

---

1. Here, *chop* means "waves."
2. *Tortoises* were commonly kept aboard whaleships to be used as food for the crew.
3. A *gunnel* is the upper edge of a boat's side.
4. A *skeg* is the rear, or stern, of a ship's keel, or main timber. A *centerboard* is a retractable keel.

Vocabulary Practice

Context Clues Remind students that context clues sometimes take the form of definitions. Write these examples on the board and have students identify the definitions of the underlined words:

- When ships met at sea, the sailors held a get-together, or <u>gam</u>. *(get-together)*
- The boat hung from the side of the ship on a <u>davit</u>, a type of crane. *(a type of crane)*

- The whales scooped up <u>brit</u>—tiny sea animals floating near the surface. *(tiny sea animals floating near the surface)*

Have students pick several words from the selection and write sentences containing context clues.

and push their steering oars as their little, deeply laden boats corkscrewed in the turbulent seas.

Each boat-crew was divided into two watches. While half the men attempted to rest—curling up with the Galapagos tortoises in the bilge[5] or leaning uncomfortably against the seats—the others steered, tended the sails, and bailed. They also attempted to keep an eye on the other boats, which would sometimes disappear entirely from view when they dipped down into the trough of a wave.

2 At the start it had been decided that every effort would be made to keep the three boats together. Together they could help if one of them ran into trouble; together they could keep one anothers' spirits up. "[U]naided, and unencouraged by each other," Chase[6] observed, "there were with us many whose weak minds, I am confident, would have sunk under the dismal retrospections of the past catastrophe, and who did not possess either sense or firmness enough to contemplate our approaching destiny, without the cheering of some more determined countenance than their own."

There was also a more practical reason for staying together: there was not enough navigational equipment to go around. Pollard[7] and Chase each had a compass, a quadrant, and a copy of *Bowditch's Navigator,* but Joy[8] had nothing. If his boat-crew should become separated from the other two, they would be unable to find their way across the ocean.

Night came on. Although moon and starlight still made it possible to detect the ghostly paleness of the whaleboats' sails, the men's field of vision shrank dramatically in the darkness even as their perception of sounds was heightened.

First Mate Owen Chase

---

5. In this context *bilge* means "the lowest part of a ship's hull."
6. Owen *Chase* was the first mate aboard the *Essex.*
7. George *Pollard* was the captain of the *Essex.*
8. Matthew *Joy* was second mate aboard the *Essex.*

The whaleboats' clinker, or lapstrake, construction (with planks overlapping, resembling the clapboards of a house) made them much noisier than a smooth-bottomed boat, and the fussy, fluted sound of water licking up against their boats' lapped sides would accompany them for the duration of the voyage.

Even at night the crews were able to maintain a lively three-way conversation among the boats. The subject on everyone's mind was of course the "means and prospects of our deliverance." It was agreed that their best chance of survival lay in happening upon a whaleship. The *Essex* had sunk about three hundred miles north of the Offshore Ground.[9] They still had about five days of sailing before they entered the Ground, where, they desperately hoped, they would come across a whaler.

A circumstance in their favor was that, unlike merchant vessels, whaleships almost always had a lookout posted at the masthead, so in whaling territory they had a better chance of being seen. Against them was the immensity of the Offshore Ground. It encompassed an enormous amount of ocean—more than twice the area of the state of Texas, a rectangle about three hundred miles north to south and almost two thousand miles from east to west. There were at least seven whaleships on the Offshore Ground at this time. But even if there were double that number, the odds were poor that three whaleboats sailing along a straight line through the Ground (which might take only four or five days to cross) would be spotted by a ship.

One possibility was to extend their time in the Offshore Ground and actively search for whalers. But that was a gamble. If they searched the region and didn't find a ship, they would jeopardize their chances of reaching

---

9. The *Offshore Ground* was a heavily whaled expanse of ocean off the coast of Peru.

NATHANIEL PHILBRICK **307**

Teach

Big Idea	2

The Power of Darkness

Explain to students that the crew of the *Essex* faced a terrible fate after their ship was sunk. Some survivors committed murder, some went insane, many engaged in cannibalism, and most died from starvation.

Write these questions on the board and ask students to keep the questions in mind as they read:

- How do real-life tragedies, such as the Essex disaster, affect my view of Emerson's optimism?
- What was it about these events that attracted Melville's imagination?

(APPROACHING) Encourage students to copy these questions on paper before they begin reading.

View the Art ★

Capturing a Sperm Whale is a colored engraving made from a painting by the American artist William Page (1811–1885), who based his image on a sketch drawn in the 1830s by the whaler C. B. Hulsart.

English Learners

DIFFERENTIATED INSTRUCTION

Advanced Explain that conditional sentences present events linked by cause-effect relationships: If A happens, then B will follow. Give this example: "If his boat-crew should become separated from the other two, they would be unable to find their way across the ocean." Ask students for other examples from the selection.

Approaching Level

DIFFERENTIATED INSTRUCTION

Emerging Explain that this excerpt describes the crew lost at sea after their ship, the *Essex,* sank. Guide comprehension by having students find answers to these questions:

- How were the smaller *Essex* whaleboats outfitted?
- How is the crew divided for the search?
- Why do they keep the three boats together?

- Why are they looking for a whaleship?
- What problems do they have?

Ask students to use sticky notes to mark places in the text with answers to the questions.

Teach

Reading Strategy   1

Analyze Historical Context   **Ask:** Why do you think Melville limited his adaptation of the *Essex* tragedy to those events related to the ship's sinking? *(Students might argue that Melville was more interested in the allegory of the whale than in the human tragedy that followed. Students might also point out that disasters at sea were common, but the sinking of a ship by a whale was unique.)*

Cross-Curricular Link ☆

Biology The sperm whale's skull contains the spermaceti organ. This massive organ can extend through 40 percent of the whale's length and hold upwards of 530 gallons of sperm oil. Sperm oil was used widely during earlier eras in fuels, lubricants, and cosmetics.

Informational Text

The sea chest of
Captain George Pollard

South America before their food supplies ran out. As it was, they would be entering the western extreme of the Ground and would have a difficult time heading east against the southeasterly trades.[10]

There was another factor influencing their decision to continue on with the original plan. After having fallen victim to such a seemingly random and inexplicable attack, the men felt an overpowering need to reclaim at least some control of their own destiny. Being sighted by a whaleship would, according to Chase, not "depend on our own exertions, but on chance alone." Reaching South America, on the other hand, depended "on our own labors." From Chase's perspective, this made all the difference and demanded that they not "lose sight, for one moment, of the strong probabilities which, under Divine Providence, there were of our reaching land by the route we had prescribed to ourselves."

The plan had one iron requirement: they had to make their provisions last two months. Each man would get six ounces of hardtack and half a pint of water a day. Hardtack was a simple dried bread made out of flour and water. Baked into a moisture-free rock to prevent spoilage, hardtack had to be broken into small pieces or soaked in water before it was eaten, if a sailor didn't want to crack a tooth.

The daily ration was equivalent to six slices of bread, and it provided about five hundred calories. Chase estimated that this amounted

to less than a third of the nourishment required by "an ordinary man." Modern dietary analysis indicates that for a five-foot, eight-inch person weighing 145 pounds, these provisions met about a quarter of his daily energy needs. True, the men of the *Essex* had more than just bread; they had tortoises. Each tortoise was a pod of fresh meat, fat, and blood that was capable of providing as many as 4,500 calories per man—the equivalent of nine days of hardtack. Yet, even augmented by the tortoises, their daily rations amounted to a starvation diet. If they did succeed in reaching South America in sixty days, each man knew he would be little more than a breathing skeleton.

But as they would soon discover, their greatest concern was not food but rather water. The human body, which is 70 percent water, requires a bare minimum of a pint a day to remove its waste products. The men of the *Essex* would have to make do with half that daily amount. If they experienced any hot weather, the deficit would only increase.

That first night of their journey, Chase, Pollard, and Joy distributed the rations of bread and water to their boat-crews. It was two days after the sinking now, and the men's interest in food had finally returned; the bread was quickly eaten. There was something else they craved: tobacco. A whaleman almost always had a quid[11] of tobacco in his mouth, going through more than seventy pounds of it in a single voyage. In addition to all their other woes, the crew of the *Essex* had to contend with the jittery withdrawal symptoms associated with nicotine addiction.

After the meager meal, the men not on watch went to sleep. "Nature became at last worn out with the watchings and anxieties of the two preceding nights," Chase recalled, "and sleep came insensibly upon us." But as his men fell into what he judged to be a dreamless stupor, Chase found himself in the middle of a waking nightmare.

Unable to sleep for the third night in a row, he continued to dwell obsessively on the circumstances of the ship's sinking. He could not

---

10. The *trades* are trade winds, or winds that always move in the same direction.

11. A *quid* means "a cut of something chewable."

308 UNIT 2   AMERICAN ROMANTICISM

Writing Practice

Analyze Data Display this sentence for students: "Modern dietary analysis indicates that for a five-foot, eight-inch person weighing 145 pounds, these provisions met about a quarter of his daily energy needs." Explain to students that 2,000 calories per day is an average—and that active people and athletes often need more than 2,000 calories per day to fuel their bodies.

Ask students to complete a three-column chart with these heads: "Rations," "Calories per Ration," "Calories per Day Needed to Survive." For example, the third column would indicate that a man needs at least 2,000 calories per day. Remind students that the crew had to make their provisions last for two months. Tell students to also do some research on the effects of starvation and malnutrition.

Have students use the data from their charts and from their research to write a paragraph drawing conclusions about the effect of the crew's diet and its possible outcome.

Sketch of the attack by cabin boy Thomas Nickerson

get the creature out of his mind: "[T]he horrid aspect and revenge of the whale, wholly engrossed my reflections." In his desperate attempts to find some explanation for how a normally passive creature could suddenly become a predator, Chase was plagued by what psychologists call a "tormenting memory"—a common response to disasters. Forced to relive the trauma over and over again, the survivor finds larger, hidden forces operating through the incident. The philosopher William James felt this compulsion firsthand some years later. After the San Francisco earthquake of 1906, he wrote: "I realize now how inevitable were men's earlier mythological versions [of disaster] and how artificial and against the grain of our spontaneous perceiving are the later habits which science educates us."

For most disaster victims, the repeated flashbacks of a tormenting memory have a therapeutic value, gradually weaning the sufferer from anxieties that might otherwise interfere with his ability to survive. There are some, however, who cannot rid themselves of the memory. Melville, building upon Chase's account, would make his Captain Ahab a man who never emerged from the psychic depths in which Chase had writhed these three nights. Just as Chase was convinced that the whale that attacked the Essex exhibited "decided, calculating mischief," so was Ahab haunted by a sense of the white whale's "outrageous strength, with an inscrutable malice sinewing[12] it."

Locked in his own private chamber of horrors, Ahab resolved that his only escape was through hunting down and killing Moby Dick: "How can the prisoner reach outside except by thrusting through the wall? To me, the white whale is that wall, shoved near to me." Chase, on a tiny boat a thousand miles from land, did not have the possibility of revenge. Ahab was fighting a symbol; Chase and his shipmates were fighting for their lives. ॐ

1

---

12. *Sinewing* means "supporting."

Respond and Think Critically

Respond and Interpret

1. Are you surprised that the whale's attack on the *Essex* haunted Chase? Why or why not?

Analyze and Evaluate

2. After the attack, the *Essex* crew "felt an overpowering need to reclaim at least some control of their own destiny." Do you think that this need for control drove Ahab's obsessive quest? Explain.

Connect

3. In an interview, Philbrick states, "I think all of us wonder while reading a survival tale, what would I have done in this situation?" What questions did you think about as you read the story? Explain.

NATHANIEL PHILBRICK **309**

Writing Workshop

Reflective Essay

Focus

Bellringer

Display word images of nature, such as photographs of forest fires, thunderstorms, birds in flight, or trees lining a city street.

Ask: What feelings or thoughts do these images of nature evoke? How do different aspects of nature affect our lives?

Ask students to reflect on their most memorable experiences with nature as they learn how to write a reflective essay about nature.

Summary

In this workshop, students will write and present a reflective essay. Students will follow the stages of the writing process, including prewriting, drafting, revising, and editing. In addition, two mini-lessons on elaborating ideas and correcting comma splices are provided.

Learning Objectives

For pages 310–317

In this workshop, you will focus on the following objective:

Writing: Writing a reflective essay using the writing process.

> **Writing Process**
>
> At any stage of a writing process, you may think of new ideas. Feel free to return to earlier stages as you write.
>
> **Prewrite**
>
> **Draft**
>
> **Revise**
>
> Focus Lesson: Elaborate Ideas
>
> **Edit & Proofread**
>
> Focus Lesson: Comma Splices
>
> **Present**

> **LOG ON** ▶ **Literature** Online
>
> **Writing and Research** For prewriting, drafting, and revising tools, go to glencoe.com and enter QuickPass code GLA9800u2.

Writing Workshop

Reflective Essay

Literature Connection In "Nature," as in other writing, Emerson often looks back, or reflects, on his experiences and uses them as jumping-off places for exploring his thoughts on a subject.

> *"Crossing a bare common, in snow puddles, at twilight, under a clouded sky, without having in my thoughts any occurrence of special good fortune, I have enjoyed a perfect exhilaration."*

In a reflective essay, you narrate and describe a personal experience to show both what the experience taught you and what it might teach others. To write a successful essay, you will need to learn the goals of reflective writing and the strategies to achieve those goals.

Checklist: Features of Reflective Essays

Goals	Strategies
To retell a personal experience	☑ Use narrative details to tell a story with a clear beginning, middle, and end
	☑ Include precise, relevant details
To connect with an audience	☑ Use first-person point of view
	☑ Use fresh, natural, vivid language and varied sentences
	☑ Use effective rhetorical devices, such as parallelism, repetition, and analogy
To reflect on a personal experience	☑ Explore the significance
	☑ Connect the experience to broader themes or abstract concepts

> **Assignment: Write a Reflective Essay**
>
> Write a reflective essay of about 1,500 words that describes one of your experiences and expresses the insight you gained. As you work, keep your audience and purpose in mind.
>
> **Audience:** peers and classmates
>
> **Purpose:** to explore the significance of a personal experience

Workshop Resources

Print Materials

- Unit 2 Teaching Resources pp. 176-178
- Writing Kit
- Success in Writing: Research and Reports

Transparencies

- Grammar and Language Transparency 67
- Writing Transparency 11, 12, 13, 14, 15

Technology

- Literature Online: Writing Resources and Grammar Resources, www.glencoe.com
- Online Essay Grader, www.glencoe.com
- Student Presentation Builder on Student-Works Plus CD-ROM
- Media Workshop DVD
- Online Student Edition

Analyze a Professional Model

In her autobiography, Pulitzer Prize-winning author Annie Dillard reflects on the significance of a childhood encounter with a moth. As you read the following passage, note how Dillard uses both narrative and descriptive details to convey her unique voice. Pay close attention to the comments in the margin. They point out features that you might want to include in your own reflective essay.

From *An American Childhood* by Annie Dillard

At school I saw a searing sight. It turned me to books; it turned me to jelly; it turned me much later, I suppose, into an early version of a runaway, a scapegrace. It was only a freshly hatched Polyphemus moth crippled because its mason jar was too small.

The mason jar sat on the teacher's desk; the big moth emerged inside it. The moth had clawed a hole in its hot cocoon and crawled out, as if agonizingly, over the course of an hour, one leg at a time; we children watched around the desk, transfixed. After it emerged, the wet, mashed thing turned around walking on the green jar's bottom, then painstakingly climbed the twig with which the jar was furnished.

There, at the twig's top, the moth shook its sodden clumps of wings. When it spread those wings—those beautiful wings—blood would fill their veins, and the birth fluids on the wings' frail sheets would harden to make them tough as sails. But the moth could not spread its wide wings at all; the jar was too small. The wings could not fill, so they hardened while they were still crumpled from the cocoon. A smaller moth could have spread its wings to their utmost in that mason jar, but the Polyphemus moth was big. Its gold furred body was almost as big as a mouse. Its brown, yellow, pink, and blue wings would have extended six inches from tip to tip, if there had been no mason jar. It would have been as big as a wren.

The teacher let the deformed creature go. We all left the classroom and paraded outside behind the teacher with pomp and

Real-World Connection

Some magazines and Web sites offer opportunities for high-school students to publish essays and creative writing. Use a search engine to locate reputable publishers, or ask a reference librarian for help.

First-Person Point of View

Use the pronoun *I* to speak directly to your reader

Audience

Use fresh, natural, vivid language and varied sentences.

Narrative Details

Include precise, relevant details.

Descriptive Details

Show, don't tell. Use vivid details to create a clear picture.

Writing Workshop

Reflective Essay

Teach

Big Idea

Optimism and Individualism Have students make a connection between the reflective essay and optimism and individualism. Explain that Romantic writers such as Emerson and Thoreau often used reflective writing in their journals and observations.

Ask: What connection exists between the reflective essay and Romanticism's emphasis on individualism? *(Individualism stresses the value of the ordinary person and his or her views on life.)*

English Learners

DIFFERENTIATED INSTRUCTION

Advanced Ask students what words they see within the words *reflective (reflect)* and *individualism (individual)*. Help students remember the meaning of the words *suffix* and *root word*. The additions *-ive* and *-ism* are suffixes. Discuss the meaning of the word *reflect* and associated terms such as *reflection* (in a mirror). Ask them to describe an *individual*. Discuss *individualism*. Tell students to reflect on their personal experiences as they write to find characteristics that make them an individual.

Approaching Level

DIFFERENTIATED INSTRUCTION

Emerging Explain that adjectives are words that describe people, things, actions, and feelings. Display the sentence: "After it emerged, the wet, mashed thing . . . ." Have students point out the adjectives.

Writing Workshop

Teach

Writing Skills

Show vs. Tell The writing principle of "show vs. tell" means that a writer should show readers the setting, plot, and details through descriptive imagery rather than simply tell them. Ask students to point out examples of how *An American Childhood* shows rather than tells. *(Dillard does not say that she feels sorry for the moth, but implies it with her vivid description of the insect's emergence from its cocoon.)*

Sentence Variety Say: Reread the paragraph that ends, "I watched it go." Note how Dillard creates fluency and drama in her writing by varying her sentence length.

Cross-Curricular Link ☆

Biology The Polyphemus moth feeds on tree leaves such as oak and maple. The insect's green-and-white larva eventually metamorphoses into the colorful moth Dillard describes. Some varieties of the Polyphemus moth are used for commercial silk.

Rhetorical Devices

Use repetition, parallelism, analogies, or other devices to retell your experience.

Significance

Connect your experience to broader themes or abstract concepts; make or imply a generalization about life.

circumstance. She bounced the moth from its jar and set it on the school's asphalt driveway. The moth set out walking. It could only heave the golden wrinkly clumps where its wings should have been; it could only crawl down the school driveway on its six frail legs. The moth crawled down the driveway toward the rest of Shadyside, an area of fine houses, expensive apartments, and fashionable shops. It crawled down the driveway because its shriveled wings were glued shut. It crawled down the driveway toward Shadyside, one of several sections of town where people like me were expected to settle after college, renting an apartment until they married one of the boys and bought a house. I watched it go.

I knew that this particular moth, the big walking moth, could not travel more than a few yards before a bird or cat began to eat it, or a car ran over it. Nevertheless, it was crawling with what seemed wonderful vigor, as if, I thought at the time, it was still excited from being born. I watched it go till the bell rang and I had to go in. I have told this story before, and may yet tell it again, to lay the moth's ghost, for I still see it crawl down the broad black driveway, and I still see its golden wing clumps heave.

Reading-Writing Connection Think about the writing techniques that you just encountered and try them out in the reflective essay that you write.

Writing Practice

Create Outlines An outline like this allows students to brainstorm ideas and map out a sequence of events at the same time:

1. I found injured bird.
   A. I called veterinarian.
   B. I took bird to animal rescuer.
2. Bird could not be saved.
   A. Bird was old.
   B. Animal rescuer helped other animals.
3. Concern for animals can coexist with tough-mindedness.

Have students create an outline of the Dillard selection.

Prewriting

Gather Ideas Prewriting is the stage of the writing process during which you generate ideas. You can use many different strategies:

▶ If you keep a journal, you might review it for ideas. Thoreau referred to his journal as he wrote *Walden*.

▶ Look at family videos or photograph albums to recall important or formative events in your life.

▶ Find memory triggers. Start by dividing your life into a series of stages. For each stage, list one or more key personal experiences that you can recall and briefly state why they were significant.

Age/Stage in Life	Experience	Significance
Up to Kindergarten	Fight with my best friend Tris over his robots	Learned that I couldn't have everything my friends had
Elementary School	Sat the bench all season in Minor A baseball	Learned to value the team more than my own efforts
High School	Found injured starling	Learned different ways of caring about nature

Choose a Subject After reviewing some of your experiences, choose one of them as a subject for your reflective essay.

Talk About Your Ideas Meet with a partner to help focus on what you will say to your readers and how you will say it. Think about your essay as a conversation on the page in which you, the writer, do all the talking. To help develop your writing voice, take turns telling each other the most vivid details of your experience. As you and your partner speak, listen to the style of your language and your original approach to ideas. Jot down notes and refer to them when you are developing your essay.

Next, explore the significance of your experience.

▶ How did you feel about your experience at the time?

▶ Looking back, do you feel different about your experience now?

Sequence the Events

Test your idea for writing by making a sequence chain or storyboard. Before you begin drafting, decide whether you can retell a clear series of events that leads you to a specific realization about life.

Avoid Plagiarism

An older friend or sibling may have written on this topic for the same class last year. Resist the temptation to resubmit someone else's work! For one thing, your teacher may recall it and fail your work as a result. You will also forego an important opportunity to develop your own writing skills.

WRITING WORKSHOP **313**

Writing Workshop

Reflective Essay

Teach

Writing Process

Prewrite Some students find it difficult to recognize how their own experiences have caused them to change. These students will benefit from class time spent brainstorming about the kinds of experiences in nature that are most likely to influence a young person, such as moving to a new place where the landscape is very different; starting a new outdoor activity that becomes very important; or experiencing an unexpected success or failure that is influenced by an event in nature.

Writing Skills

Observation Dillard used close observation to help her describe her subject. She watched the moth as long as she could, "till the bell rang," and described each detail she observed. Tell students to think back as if they are "watching" the subject they are writing about, and to record each detail with close observation.

Approaching Level

DIFFERENTIATED INSTRUCTION

Emerging Have students work in small groups to brainstorm ideas for their essays. Have each student fill in a cluster diagram as group members volunteer ideas. Remind students that there are no bad ideas in brainstorming. They can select the ideas that work best for them after they write down many ideas. Give students some examples of times they might write about:

- when nature took care of them
- when nature seemed to be against them
- when they noticed something in nature for the first time
- when they first saw a landscape that was very different from the one they knew

Have pairs of students exchange webs and ask each other questions that will help them narrow down their ideas.

313

Teach

Writing Process

Draft Direct students to the opening sentence of the model essay. Explain that the opening should catch readers' attention and make them want to continue. Have students create alternate opening sentences for the model and share their ideas with the class.

Writing Skills

First-Person Point of View

Answer: *The first-person point of view helps you understand the author's thoughts and feelings. If this were written in third-person, readers might not feel as much empathy for the bird.*

[ENGLISH LEARNERS] Make sure that English learners know which pronouns indicate first-person point of view. **Ask:** What words tell you this is first-person point of view? *(I, my, me)*

Rhetorical Devices

Answer: *Asking a question engages the reader; it encourages the reader to think of a response, thus making the tone more conversational.*

Narrative Purpose

Answer: *The writer structures the essay chronologically.*

Writing Frames

As you read the workshop model, think about the writer's use of the following frames:

Along the way, I began to think about _____. Thinking about _____ later, it was clear that _____. My _____ taught me that _____.

Consider using frames like these in your own reflective essay.

First-Person Point of View

What are the advantages of using the first-person point of view? What effect would these sentences have if they were written in the third-person?

Rhetorical Devices

How does asking a question invite the audience's participation?

Narrative Purpose

How does the writer structure the essay?

Draft

Just Jump In When you begin writing, don't get bogged down trying to find the perfect word or to make your sentences flow smoothly. You can revise later. Do stop occasionally and reflect on your work. If your writing is going in an unexpected direction, you may want to follow it. You could gain new insights about your experience—and yourself.

Analyze a Workshop Model

Here is a final draft of a reflective essay. Read it, and use your answers to the questions in the margins to guide you as you write.

Animal 911

I generally like nature to keep its distance—wild things belong outside. So when I saw a white-flecked feather on the stairs leading up to the second floor, I knew it was a bad sign. I followed the trail of fluff to the kitchen, where I found the rest of the bird. I didn't know what kind of bird it was—just a small round creature with a long bill. It had somehow survived a meeting with our family cat. By the time I managed to corner and capture the bird, it seemed to be in deep shock. I wasn't feeling too well myself.

I had no way of knowing how seriously injured the poor creature was. Should I simply put the bird outside on the porch and let nature—the neighborhood cats—take its course? I called the vet. He suggested I get in touch with a Mrs. Roberts, who lived not far away. This woman took in injured animals that people brought her and cared for them until they were well enough to return to the wild. She sounded like just the person I needed. I put my injured bird into a shoe box lined with tissue and took the bus to see her.

Along the way, I began to think about the person I was about to meet. What would Mrs. Roberts look like? Since she was in the business of looking after hurt animals, I began to picture her as a very sweet and gentle sort of person—sort of cuddly. I was wrong.

When I got to her house, I rang the bell, then walked around to the back. I knew immediately I had come to the right place. There were large screened-in areas, where I could see different

Writing Practice

Passive Voice Explain that students should avoid passive voice in writing and instead use active voice. In active voice, the subject performs an action. Passive voice, the opposite of active voice, tends to overuse linking verbs such as *am, is, was, were, be* and *been*, thus confusing the reader.

Write out the following examples:
Shawn ate the last slice of pizza. (active)

The last slice of pizza was eaten by Shawn. (passive)

Ask students to write a sentence with passive voice and a second version of the same sentence using an active voice.

animals, including a deer. A large, fierce-looking bird—some kind of hawk, I guess—sat on a post. It glared at me as if I were a mouse. As I waited, I was startled by a clear, low voice behind me.

"May I help you?" I spun around, nearly dropping my shoe box.

"Mrs. Roberts?" She simply nodded in reply. My cuddly fantasy of an animal rescuer was quickly replaced by a far tougher reality. She was an old woman but still very strong and sturdy, with dark eyes and sharp features. She looked a bit like a hawk herself.

"I have an injured bird here," I began, offering her my shoe box.

As she took the box and removed the lid, she seemed to smile. It may have been the sight of the tissue paper I had used. She probably thought it looked like a doll bed created by a little kid. She picked up the bird in one strong, brown hand and studied it for a time before returning it to the box and replacing the cover.

"It's a starling," Mrs. Roberts said, as if she understood I wouldn't know. "I'm afraid there's nothing I can do for it."

"Really?" I asked, feeling a sharp stab of disappointment.

"It's a very old bird," she explained.

This comment was also a bit of shock. During my bus ride, I had decided—based on no knowledge at all—that the bird was young. Part of my fantasy had been visiting the bird as it got better.

"People bring me so many animals that I have to limit myself to aiding those that are worth saving," Mrs. Roberts explained. "This starling just isn't. Sorry. I'll dispose of the bird for you."

I was grateful she had relieved me of responsibility for the injured bird, but I still felt that somehow Mrs. Roberts didn't "care" for nature in the way I had expected. She wasn't cuddly. Thinking about her later, however, it was clear that she cared very much; but she only applied her concern to creatures that could benefit from it. My meeting with Mrs. Roberts taught me that to love nature does not mean to be sentimental about wild creatures. You can be both realistic and caring.

Narration / Description

Narrative Details

In what ways are these details relevant and precise?

Audience

How do variations in sentence structure and the use of fresh, natural language help to create interest?

Narrative Details/ Significance

How does the use of dialogue show your readers what is happening? How does the writer use it to relate the incidents to more abstract ideas?

Teach

Writing Skills

Narrative Details
Answer: *The author uses descriptive words that help the reader see what is happening. The words that describe the bird—fierce-looking, gripped, glared—create a feeling of tension.*

Audience
Answer: *The writer avoids the use of clichés, which are overused phrases in writing such as "tried-and-true" or "as easy as taking candy from a baby." Fresh language keeps the audience curious about what the writer will say next.*

Narrative Details/Significance
Answer: *Dialogue helps readers feel as if they are experiencing the scene as it happens, putting them in the middle of the action. The dialogue demonstrates the contrast between the narrator's expectations and reality.*

English Learners

DIFFERENTIATED INSTRUCTION

Beginning Explain that students can write descriptive details using figurative language to compare unlike things. For example, the line "She looked a bit like a hawk herself" uses figurative speech—a simile. Encourage students to compare two unlike things by using the connecting words *like* or *as.*

Intermediate Explain how to write dialogue by pointing out phrases and writing them on the board:
- To show that Mrs. Roberts is speaking: "It's a starling," Mrs. Roberts said.
- To show order of punctuation: "Really?" I asked. The question mark appears before the quotation mark.

- To add details to describe how something is said: "Really?" I asked, feeling a sharp stab of disappointment. The final phrase helps the reader understand how the word *"Really"* is expressed.

315

Reflective Essay

Teach

Writing Process

Revise Writing workshops can create a sense of community in the classroom. After students have revised their reflective essays, ask volunteers to read their work aloud. If time permits, place students into small groups and have them read each other's essays.

Writing Skills

Elaborate with Details

Tell students that elaboration is the support or development of a main idea with facts, statistics, sensory details, or examples. Ask students how Dillard uses sensory details in her essay to make the moth appealing to the reader. Encourage students to elaborate in their own writing using details that appeal to the five senses.

(APPROACHING) Explain the sensory details in the revision example: "the sight of the tissue paper" (sight, touch); "injured bird" (sight, touch); "doll bed created by a little kid" (sight, touch).

Traits of Strong Writing

Include these traits of strong writing to express your ideas effectively.

Ideas
Organization
Voice
Word Choice
Sentence Fluency
Conventions
Presentation

For more information on using the Traits of Strong Writing, see pages R30–R32.

Word Choice

This academic vocabulary appears in the student model:

benefit (be' nə fit) *v.* 1. to draw an advantage from; 2. to promote the well-being of; *She only applied her concern to creatures that could benefit from it.* Using academic vocabulary may help strengthen your writing. Try to use one or two academic vocabulary words in your reflective essay. See the complete list on pages R89–R91.

LOG ON ▶ **Literature** Online

Writing and Research For editing **and publishing** tools, go to glencoe.com and enter QuickPass code GLA9800u2.

Revise

Peer Review Ask a peer reviewer to help you assess your essay. Talk over your ideas and ask your partner for feedback. Identify any strengths and weaknesses you find. Remember to refer to the traits of strong writing. Use the checklist below to evaluate and strengthen each other's writing.

Checklist

☑ Do you tell a story with a clear beginning, middle, and end?

☑ Do you include precise, relevant details?

☑ Do you vividly describe the details and vary your sentences?

☑ Do you use first-person point of view?

☑ Do you include effective rhetorical devices?

☑ Do you connect the experience to broader themes or abstract concepts?

▶ **Focus Lesson**

Elaborate Ideas

Give your readers a detailed picture of what is happening and when. Elaboration is a technique you can use to include details that develop, support, or explain the ideas presented in your essay. Here is a sentence from the Workshop Model followed by three kinds of elaboration—reasons, descriptions, and dialogue—you might want to try.

Draft:

As she took the box and removed the lid, I noticed she seemed to smile.

Revision:

As she took the box and removed the lid, I noticed she seemed to smile. It might have been the sight of the tissue paper I had used.[1] She probably thought it looked like a doll bed created by a little kid.[2] "It's a starling," Mrs. Roberts said.[3]

1: Reasons   **2: Descriptions**   **3: Dialogue**

Writing Practice

Describe Art and Photographs

To help students gain practice in developing details, have them describe art or photographs using adjectives. Provide magazines and books, and ask students to describe an image that appeals to them. Ask them to make a list of five adjectives using the five senses for each piece of art or photograph. To get students started, offer these questions:

- What subjects are in the image? How are light and color used for effect?
- Can you feel anything from the image? Is it cool or hot?
- Does the image suggest any of the other senses—how something might taste, sound, or smell?

Edit and Proofread

Get It Right Proofread your final draft for errors in grammar, usage, mechanics, and spelling. See Language Handbook, pages R42–R61.

> **Focus Lesson**
>
> ### Correct Comma Splices
>
> A comma splice is a type of run-on sentence that occurs when two main clauses are joined only by a comma.

Comma Splice:

I was grateful she had relieved me of responsibility for the injured bird, I still felt that somehow Mrs. Roberts didn't "care" for nature in the way I had expected.

Solution A: Replace the comma with end punctuation, such as a period or a question mark, and begin a new sentence.

I was grateful she had relieved me of responsibility for the injured bird. I still felt that somehow Mrs. Roberts didn't "care" for nature in the way I had expected.

Solution B: Place a semicolon between the two main clauses.

I was grateful she had relieved me of responsibility for the injured bird; I still felt that somehow Mrs. Roberts didn't "care" for nature in the way I had expected.

Solution C: Add a coordinating conjunction after the comma.

I was grateful she had relieved me of responsibility for the injured bird, but I still felt that somehow Mrs. Roberts didn't "care" for nature in the way I had expected.

Present

Appearance Matters Make your essay inviting to read. Handwritten papers should be neat and legible. If you are working on a word processor, double-space the lines of text and use a readable font, or typeface. Other design elements—such as boldfaced headings—can help you present information effectively and make your essay look more appealing. Be sure to check with your teacher about presentation guidelines.

Peer Review Tips

A classmate may ask you to read his or her reflective essay. Take your time and jot down notes as you read so you can give constructive feedback. Use the following questions to get started:

- Can you identify a story with a clear beginning, middle, and end?

- Do you understand the significance of the events and their connection to broader ideas and concepts?

Word-Processing

Did you know that font helps to convey tone? Some fonts telegraph a message of playfulness or friendliness; others evoke computer systems or laws inscribed on stone tablets from the days of the ancient Greeks. For most essay writing, choose common, conservative, highly readable fonts such as those found in your textbooks and newspapers.

Writer's Portfolio

Place a copy of your reflective essay in your portfolio to review later.

 Writing Workshop

Reflective Essay

Teach

Writing Skills

Edit Explain to students that commas and semicolons organize ideas and show the relationship between ideas. Remind students that a semicolon is needed when separating two related sentences and that a comma should be used to separate a related phrase.

(**ENGLISH LEARNERS**) Check to make sure that English learners understand the difference between the comma and semicolon by providing them with the symbols. Explain the difference between a colon and a semicolon.

Writer's Technique ☆

Dillard on Revision "You must demolish the work and start over. You can save some of the sentences, like bricks. It will be a miracle if you can save some of the paragraphs, no matter how excellent in themselves or hard won. You can waste a year worrying about it, or you can get it over with now."

—Annie Dillard

Approaching Level
DIFFERENTIATED INSTRUCTION

Emerging Help students by listing the main rules for commas as outlined here. Then read each corresponding example sentence aloud and leave pauses for the commas. Ask students to explain where the commas should appear in the sentences. Have students write the sentences with the commas inserted.

- Items in a series: *Birds, squirrels, and rabbits live here.*
- Long introductory prepositional phrases: *In the early days of spring, the birds fly north.*
- Introductory participles: *Fearing the worst, I took the bird to her house.*
- Before *and, or,* or *but* to join main clauses: *Caring for animals is rewarding, but it is hard work.*

Have students work with a partner to exchange work and identify places where commas may be necessary or misplaced in their own essays.

317

Speaking, Listening, and Viewing Workshop

Reflective Presentation

Focus

Summary

In this workshop, students will learn techniques for planning, rehearsing, and delivering a presentation of a reflective essay.

Teach

Speaking Skills

Ease Stage Fright Some students may be nervous about speaking in front of the class. Share the following strategies to ease students' stage fright:

- Be well prepared, with note cards if needed.
- Imagine you are having a casual conversation with friends.
- Rehearse the speech often.
- Make eye contact with the friendliest faces in the classroom, such as a teacher or friends.

Literature Connection During Ralph Waldo Emerson's lifetime, more Americans probably became acquainted with his ideas from hearing him lecture than from reading his essays. After he spoke in Cincinnati, a newspaper there observed that "without his own language, his manner, his delivery," no report could really convey the effect he created. Emerson's speaking style was very much a part of the appeal of his thoughts. In this workshop, you will deliver an oral presentation of your reflective essay.

> **Assignment** **Present your reflective essay to the class.**

Plan Your Presentation

When you wrote your reflective essay, you were addressing an audience of readers. When you deliver your reflective presentation, you will be addressing an audience of listeners. Use your essay as a starting point.

- Read your essay aloud to a peer. Discuss which ideas you should keep or delete and how you might adjust the language to fit the purpose. For example, you might add informal expressions, vary sentence structure, or increase the amount of narration or description.
- Jot down vivid details, striking dialogue, and key ideas on note cards. Arrange the note cards in the same order as the elements appear in your essay. Use your note cards as a speaking prompt.
- Strike a balance between narrating the personal experience and relating it to broader themes or generalizations about life.

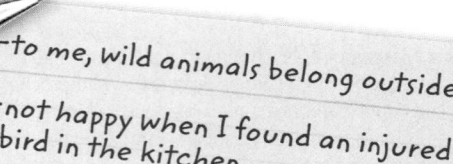

—to me, wild animals belong outside

—not happy when I found an injured bird in the kitchen

Writing Practice

Plan a Presentation Explain to students that writing key ideas on note cards is similar to developing an outline. The main ideas are the roman numerals (I, II) and the details are listed below the main ideas (A, B). Have students practice by writing an outline for the sample reflective essay "Animal 911." To help them get started, provide the following:

Animal 911

I. Bird found
   A. In deep shock, injured
   B. Help, or not?

After students complete their outlines, tell them to use the outlines as a guide for identifying the most important information and details from their essays.

Create Your Visual Media

Think about how visual media, such as a photograph, collage, drawing, or computer presentation, can make your ideas clearer. Reflect on how symbols, colors, and organization may work within your visual to effectively convey your point. Use the chart below to brainstorm ideas.

Which parts of my essay best reflect my experience or its broader meaning? } What images can I create of my essay to illustrate these parts? } How will I use my choice of media to balance retelling with reflection?

Rehearse

Rehearsing your speech with a partner will strengthen your speaking and listening skills. Your partner can help you identify any flaws that you missed. As you listen to your partner's speech, practice these skills:

- Show your interest by looking at the speaker and maintaining an upright, slightly forward posture.
- Show understanding by responding appropriately with subtle changes in your facial expression or slight movements of your head or hands.

Use some of the verbal and nonverbal techniques below to ensure that your audience understands you and is engaged in what you have to say.

Techniques for Delivering a Reflective Presentation

Verbal Techniques	Nonverbal Techniques
☑ **Volume** Speak loudly enough so that everyone can hear you.	☑ **Posture** Stand up tall with your head straight.
☑ **Pronunciation** Speak clearly, pronouncing all the words.	☑ **Eye Contact** Make eye contact with people throughout your audience.
☑ **Pace** Speak at a moderate speed, but vary the rate and use pauses to convey your meaning.	☑ **Facial Expressions** Vary your facial expressions to reflect what you are saying.
☑ **Emphasis** Stress important words and ideas.	☑ **Gestures** Use natural gestures to reinforce your ideas.

Use a Mirror

Practice your gestures in front of a mirror until your body language looks natural.

Speaking Frames

Consider using the following frames in your reflective presentation:

Looking back on it now, I think _____.

At the time, _____, but now _____.

Presentation Tips

Use the following checklist to evaluate your reflective presentation.

Did you effectively adjust your language to turn an essay into an oral presentation?

Did you use visuals to enhance your presentation and to reflect both the experience and its broader meanings?

Did you listen attentively and responsively to others?

 Literature Online

Speaking, Listening, and Viewing For project ideas, templates, and presentation tips, go to glencoe.com and enter QuickPass code GLA9800u2.

Teach
Speaking Skills

Use Models Have students listen to an oral reading, such as "Total Eclipse" by Annie Dillard. Ask them to describe Dillard's speaking skills, including her word choice and use of tone and rhythm. Have students include these skills in their own presentations.

(ENGLISH LEARNERS) Check to make sure that English learners understand the difference between *verbal* and *nonverbal* techniques. Explain that they communicate verbally with words and their voices, and nonverbally with the rest of the body.

Listening Skills

Peer Assessment Ask students to respond to each other's speeches, using the following criteria:

- Is there a clear account of the details of the incident?
- Does the speech illustrate feelings as well as actions?
- Does the speech show evidence of self-discovery?
- Does the speaker follow the Techniques for Delivering a Presentation?

English Learners
DIFFERENTIATED INSTRUCTION

Intermediate Students may have trouble with the vocabulary in the techniques chart. Explain the terms using visual and auditory clues. For example, read a paragraph on this page with a high and low volume to explain *volume.* Demonstrate the terms *pronunciation, pace, tone,* and *emphasis* as you read. Have students repeat examples back to you. For *posture, eye contact, facial expressions,* and *gestures* use body language to define these terms. Ask students to give you examples to show that they understand each term.

Approaching Level
DIFFERENTIATED INSTRUCTION

Emerging Have students present their speech to a partner. Have the listener take notes on these topics: clear order of information, clear enunciation, eye contact and posture, and use of visual aids. Have students switch roles.

Focus

Summary

These pages summarize some of the best-known novels of the early 1800s, including *The Last of the Mohicans* and *The Scarlet Letter*. There is also an excerpt from Anthony Trollope's 1879 review of *The Scarlet Letter.* Annie Dillard's 1974 work, *Pilgrim at Tinker Creek,* is a twentieth-century *Walden.*

Teach

Literary History ☆

Clarissa Samuel Richardson's novel *Clarissa* was an enormous success; it was widely read and critically acclaimed during the Romantic period. *Clarissa* is an epistolary novel, that is, it is told in the form of letters, written mainly by the heroine. Samuel Johnson said the novel was "the first book in the world for the knowledge it displays of the human heart."

Independent Reading

American Writing: From Novel to Nature

I N THE LATE 1700s, READERS AND CRITICS BEGAN, FOR THE FIRST TIME, to accept the novel as a legitimate literary form. This shift can be attributed partly to the novels of English author Samuel Richardson, which became popular in the mid-1700s. ☆

By the 1820s, however, the first truly American novels emerged. Romanticism started to take hold in Europe, and American writers embraced the movement's celebration of the individual, freedom from old forms, and love of nature.

But it was not only American fiction that thrived in this era—essays by Transcendentalists such as Henry David Thoreau and Ralph Waldo Emerson have inspired both novelists and nonfiction writers from the mid-1800s through today.

The Last of the Mohicans

James Fenimore Cooper

James Fenimore Cooper's *The Leatherstocking Tales*, about wilderness scout Natty Bumppo, contains the first novels to depict realistic American frontier scenes and characters. *The Last of the Mohicans*, the second in the series, is set during the French and Indian War and portrays a group of Native Americans whose way of life is quickly disappearing. The novel offers thrills and adventure galore, while presenting a serious contrast of two ways of life: the Native Americans' freedom and reverence for nature, and the settlers' drive to build farms and towns.

Pilgrim at Tinker Creek

by Annie Dillard

Dillard's book is as much a meditation on spirituality as it is a piece of *Walden*-inspired American nature writing. The nonfiction work details Dillard's explorations in her neighborhood near Roanoke, Virginia, over the course of a year, and her reflections about her findings. In chapter one, she writes: "I propose to keep here what Thoreau called a 'meteorological journal of the mind.'" As Dillard observes the birds, trees, frogs, flowers, and insects which inhabit the seasons of Tinker Creek, she ponders both nature's and God's purposes. The widely acclaimed book won a Pulitzer Prize for Nonfiction in 1975.

Writing Practice

Report Tell students that understanding the historical period in which a book was written can help them when they compare books from two different periods of time. The world that Henry David Thoreau describes in *Walden* and the one Annie Dillard describes in *Pilgrim at Tinker Creek* are very different places. Have students research and write a paragraph summarizing the political climate or the role of technology in Thoreau's time,

the 1840s. Then have students do the same for Dillard's time, the 1970s. Students may use these questions to guide their research:

- What wars or political disputes might have influenced each writer?
- What technologies were developing at the time?

Have students discuss their findings.

Teach

Glencoe Literature Library

Glencoe Literature Library offers an extensive collection of hardcover books that help you encourage your students to read independently. Choose among the more than 120 full-length literary works—novels, novellas, plays, and nonfiction. Each book includes related readings from a broad range of genres. Go to www.glencoe.com for more information.

Make a Collage

Evaluate students' collages on the following:

- effective representation of the book's theme through elements in the collage
- well-organized explanation
- effective presentation with attention to grammar and spelling conventions

For access to all study guides for the Glencoe Literature Library Teacher Resources CD-ROM.

To create customized reading lists from a database of more than 30,000 titles, use BookLink K-12 CD-ROM.

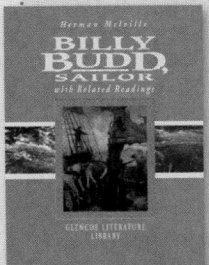

Billy Budd

Herman Melville

An industrious young sailor accidentally kills the tyrannical master-at-arms who victimized him.

The House of the Seven Gables

Nathaniel Hawthorne

For two centuries, the inhabitants of a New England mansion experience mysterious misfortunes that stem from the moral corruption of its first owner.

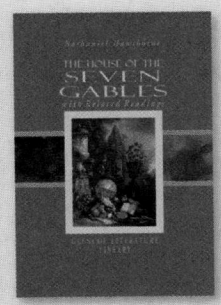

Walden

Henry David Thoreau

Thoreau abandons society and its comforts to pursue a solitary and independent life in the woods.

CRITICS' CORNER

"[The Scarlet Letter] *is so terrible in its pictures of diseased human nature as to produce most questionable delight. The reader's interest never flags for a moment. There is nothing of episode or digression. The author is always telling his one story with a concentration of energy which, as we can understand, must have made it impossible for him to deviate. The reader will certainly go on with it to the end very quickly, entranced, excited, shuddering, and at times almost wretched. His consolation will be that he too has been able to see into these black deeps of the human heart."*

—Anthony Trollope, *The North American Review*
September 1879

The Scarlet Letter

Nathaniel Hawthorne

Rooted in American Puritanism, this tragic tale of colonial New England examines three complex characters—a woman who follows her heart rather than Puritan standards of behavior, a minister torn by guilt, and a husband consumed by hatred and revenge. Hawthorne, who called this a novel of "frailty and human sorrow," peers deeply into the mind and heart of each character to reveal tortuous moral dilemmas.

 Make a Collage

Read one of the books listed on this page. Then make a collage to represent your interpretation of the book's main message or theme. Present your collage to the class, explaining how the images you chose relate to ideas in the book.

English Learners

DIFFERENTIATED INSTRUCTION

Intermediate When reading the excerpt of the review by Anthony Trollope, English learners may have trouble understanding comments such as "diseased human nature" and "black deeps of the human heart." Encourage students to review some of the material about Puritans that appears in Part 1 of Unit One, especially "Sinners in the Hands of an Angry God," by Jonathan Edwards. You might also obtain a copy of an overview of *The Scarlet Letter.* Read students the overview. Then lead a discussion of Trollope's comments.

Focus

Bellringer

Say: In addition to helping you to be successful students, knowing test-taking strategies can help you obtain certifications and other benefits throughout your lives. Have students brainstorm a list of test-taking strategies they have learned so far.

Teach

Assessment Tell students that the Assessment features will help them prepare for the SAT and ACT tests and for state assessments. This practice will also help them review the skills and vocabulary taught in each unit. For this test, they will read a nonfiction selection and answer comprehension, analysis, and vocabulary questions about it. Then they will answer questions dealing with the process and conventions of writing, and respond to a reflective-essay prompt.

Reread Tell students that rereading a passage like the one on this page will help them identify the passage's main ideas and supporting details, the author's tone and purpose for writing, and any rhetorical or literary devices used. Write the following note headings on the board:

Assessment

English–Language Arts

Reading: Nonfiction

Carefully read the following passage. Use context clues to help you define any words with which you are unfamiliar. Pay close attention to the author's main idea and use of rhetorical devices. Then, on a separate sheet of paper, answer the questions on pages 323–324.

from *Self-Reliance* by Ralph Waldo Emerson

line

Society is a wave. The wave moves onward, but the water of which it is composed does not. The same particle does not rise from the valley to the ridge. Its unity is only phenomenal. The persons who make up a nation to-day, next year die, and their experience with them.

5 And so the reliance on Property, including the reliance on governments which protect it, is the want of self-reliance. Men have looked away from themselves and at things so long, that they have come to esteem the religious, learned, and civil institutions as guards of property, and they deprecate assaults on these, because they feel them to be assaults on property. They measure their esteem of each other by what each has, and not by what each is. But a cultivated man becomes ashamed of his property, out of new respect for his nature. Especially he hates what he has, if he see that it is

10 accidental,—came to him by inheritance, or gift, or crime; then he feels that it is not having; it does not belong to him, has no root in him, and merely lies there, because no revolution or no robber takes it away. But that which a man is does always by necessity acquire, and what the man acquires is living property, which does not wait the beck of rulers, or mobs, or revolutions, or fire, or storm, or bankruptcies, but perpetually renews itself wherever the man breathes. . . . It is only as a man puts

15 off all foreign support, and stands alone, that I see him to be strong and to prevail. He is weaker by every recruit to his banner. Is not a man better than a town? Ask nothing of men, and, in the endless mutation, thou only firm column must presently appear the upholder of all that surrounds thee. He who knows that power is inborn, that he is weak because he has looked for good out of him and elsewhere, and so perceiving, throws himself unhesitatingly on his thought, instantly rights himself,

20 stands in the erect position, commands his limbs, works miracles; just as a man who stands on his feet is stronger than a man who stands on his head.

So use all that is called Fortune. Most men gamble with her, and gain all, and lose all, as her wheel rolls. But do thou leave as unlawful these winnings, and deal with Cause and Effect, the chancellors of God. In the Will work and acquire, and thou hast chained the wheel of Chance, and shalt sit

25 hereafter out of fear from her rotations. A political victory, a rise of rents, the recovery of your sick, or the return of your absent friend, or some other favorable event, raises your spirits, and you think good days are preparing for you. Do not believe it. Nothing can bring you peace but yourself. Nothing can bring you peace but the triumph of principles.

Main Ideas and Supporting Details
Tone
Author's Purpose
Rhetorical and Literary Devices
Unfamiliar Words

Have students copy these headings onto a piece of paper to guide their notetaking as they reread.

1. What literary or rhetorical device does Emerson use in the first sentence?
   (A) parallelism
   (B) connotative language
   (C) hyperbole
   (D) metaphor
   (E) rhetorical question

2. What type or types of rhetorical appeal does Emerson make in the first paragraph?
   (A) ethical appeal
   (B) rational appeal
   (C) emotional appeal
   (D) emotional and ethical appeals
   (E) emotional and rational appeals

3. According to Emerson, why do people deprecate assaults on religious, learned, and civil institutions?
   (A) They hate property.
   (B) They believe that these assaults are on property.
   (C) They believe in self-reliance.
   (D) They believe that people should rely solely on the government.
   (E) They are afraid of all criticism.

4. Why does the cultivated man become ashamed of his property?
   (A) No robber or revolution has taken it away.
   (B) He has stolen his property.
   (C) His property comes from an inheritance.
   (D) He realizes that property is alien to his true nature.
   (E) He has allowed his property to deteriorate.

5. From the context, what does the word *beck* in line 13 mean?
   (A) command
   (B) failure
   (C) creation
   (D) loss
   (E) help

6. What can you infer from the sentence *He is weaker by every recruit to his banner* in lines 15 and 16?
   (A) The individual should look for support from others.
   (B) The individual cannot help but receive support from others.
   (C) The individual becomes weak from relying on the support of others.
   (D) Every cause is weakened by the individual.
   (E) Only the individual can prevail.

7. What literary or rhetorical device does Emerson use in the sentence *Is not a man better than a town?* in line 16?
   (A) parallelism
   (B) connotative language
   (C) metaphor
   (D) rhetorical question
   (E) allusion

8. To what does *endless mutation*, in lines 16 and 17, refer?
   (A) constant change
   (B) random accident
   (C) perpetual motion
   (D) steady equilibrium
   (E) inborn power

9. From the context, what does the word *rights* in line 19 mean?
   (A) justifies
   (B) subjects
   (C) corrects
   (D) claims as true
   (E) liberates

 Literature Online

Assessment For additional test practice, go to glencoe.com and enter QuickPass code GLA9800u2.

ASSESSMENT **323**

Assessment

Assess

Reading

1. **(D)** is the correct answer because Emerson directly compares society to a wave. (DOK 2)

2. **(B)** is the correct answer because Emerson appeals to reason by making an analogy between the people who constitute a society and the particles of water that constitute a wave. (DOK 2)

3. **(B)** is the correct answer because Emerson says in line 7, "they feel them to be assaults on property." (DOK 1)

4. **(D)** is the correct answer because Emerson says in line 11 that property "has no root in him." (DOK 1)

5. **(A)** is the correct answer because beck means "a summons or command." (DOK 1)

6. **(C)** is the correct answer because Emerson is emphasizing his earlier statement that a man becomes strong only when he "puts off all foreign support." (DOK 4)

7. **(D)** is the correct answer because Emerson asks a question for effect. (DOK 2)

8. **(A)** is the correct answer because mutation means "alteration." (DOK 1)

9. **(C)** is the correct answer because rights means "to redress injury." (DOK 1)

English Learners

DIFFERENTIATED INSTRUCTION

Emerging You may wish to discuss with English learners the specific features of your state's exam. If possible, provide them with sample questions and review the particulars. Provide one-on-one instructions for students who need extra help.

Assessment

Assess

10. (C) is the correct answer because Emerson refers to a popular gambling device. **[DOK 2]**

11. (D) is the correct answer because Emerson occasionally uses a short sentence to contrast with his longer sentences. **[DOK 4]**

12. (B) is the correct answer because Emerson wants to convince readers to agree with his position. **[DOK 4]**

13. (B) is the correct answer because Emerson is supporting the ability of the individual to be self-reliant. **[DOK 4]**

14. (C) is the correct answer because Emerson does not acknowledge the validity of opposing viewpoints. **[DOK 4]**

15. (E) is the correct answer because it restates Emerson's conclusion in line 27, "Nothing can bring you peace but yourself." **[DOK 2]**

10. By referring to the wheel of fortune, what literary technique is Emerson using?
   (A) foreshadowing
   (B) irony
   (C) allusion
   (D) motif
   (E) analogy

11. Which trait of good writing is Emerson demonstrating in the sentence *Do not believe it*, in line 27?
   (A) organization
   (B) presentation
   (C) word choice
   (D) sentence variety
   (E) voice

12. What type of essay is this?
   (A) informal
   (B) persuasive
   (C) expository
   (D) narrative
   (E) personal

13. On the basis of this passage, with which of the following statements would Emerson be most likely to agree?
   (A) People are generally solitary.
   (B) Individuals are stronger than communities.
   (C) There is no such thing as community.
   (D) Only governments can protect private property.
   (E) Private property must be outlawed.

14. On the basis of this passage, what is the overall tone of this essay?
   (A) despairing
   (B) ironic
   (C) authoritative
   (D) angry
   (E) sarcastic

15. What is the main idea of this passage?
   (A) The individual is greedy and corrupt.
   (B) Individuals should reject society.
   (C) Individuals must look to themselves to be free.
   (D) There is no such thing as chance.
   (E) People must reject governments and property.

Vocabulary Practice

Context Clues Explain that standardized tests often assess a student's ability to determine the meaning of unfamiliar words. Clues to a word's meaning can often be found in the context of that word. Write the following sentence on the board:

> After their team's victory, the football fans waved their banners and hands <u>exultantly</u>.

Have students read the sentence and use context clues to determine the meaning of the underlined word.

Vocabulary Skills: Sentence Completion

For each item in the Vocabulary Skills section, choose the word or words that best complete the sentence. Write your answers on a separate sheet of paper.

1. For the writers of the era, Romanticism was a way to _____ political and literary values.
   (A) surmise
   (B) speculate
   (C) integrate
   (D) beguile
   (E) impede

2. The agrarian South had few cities, whereas the _____ cities in the North were heavily industrialized.
   (A) manifest
   (B) inherent
   (C) myriad
   (D) blithe
   (E) latent

3. The Age of Reform saw the rise of many _____ religious organizations that hoped to increase the overall _____ of America.
   (A) melancholy . . . lethargy
   (B) perennial . . . cognizance
   (C) expedient . . . alacrity
   (D) deliberately . . . resignation
   (E) zealous . . . integrity

4. The _____ and clamor of the cities drove Thoreau into nature and a life of seclusion.
   (A) wealth
   (B) size
   (C) greed
   (D) din
   (E) pollution

5. Thoreau's life at Walden Pond was a response to his own _____ to live simply and deliberately.
   (A) iniquity
   (B) cognizance
   (C) decorum
   (D) admonition
   (E) discord

6. In their writings, Poe and Hawthorne often deal with evil, or _____.
   (A) expedient
   (B) admonition
   (C) iniquity
   (D) lethargy
   (E) torpor

7. Individualism, the _____ concern of the Transcendentalists, remains an important issue to this day.
   (A) diffuse
   (B) occult
   (C) impregnable
   (D) perennial
   (E) melancholy

8. Poe crafted his _____ stories of the _____ in order to convey a sense of horror to the reader.
   (A) melancholy . . . occult
   (B) irreproachable . . . culture
   (C) sublime . . . sage
   (D) sagacious . . . culture
   (E) prevalent . . . sublime

9. Ralph Waldo Emerson was a _____ writer and philosopher, known as "The Sage of Concord."
   (A) pessimistic
   (B) venerable
   (C) popular
   (D) sinister
   (E) superficial

10. Hawthorne was drawn to the moral _____ of the Puritan's past.
    (A) discord
    (B) iniquity
    (C) fortitude
    (D) torpor
    (E) pollution

DIFFERENTIATED INSTRUCTION

Intermediate Students still acquiring English will likely have a difficult time with choosing the best way to fill in the missing words. Explain that it is often possible to determine the correct answer by reading each choice, eliminating any unlikely answers, and then choosing the sentence that sounds best.

Assessment

Assess

Vocabulary

1. **(B)** is the correct answer because it is the only option makes sense in this context. **DOK 1**
2. **(C)** is the correct answer because no other option conveys a meaning opposite to *few*. **DOK 1**
3. **(D)** is the correct answer because it is the only option that makes sense in this context. **DOK 2**
4. **(B)** is the correct answer because *clamor* suggests that the missing word should have something to do with sound. **DOK 1**
5. **(C)** is the correct answer because the context suggests that the missing word should be a synonym of *advice*. **DOK 1**
6. **(C)** is the correct answer because the context suggests that the missing word should be a synonym of *evil*. **DOK 1**
7. **(D)** is the correct answer because it is the only option that makes sense in this context. **DOK 1**
8. **(A)** is the correct answer because it is the only option that indicates a sense of horror. **DOK 2**
9. **(B)** is the correct answer because it is the only option that reflects the status of a sage. **DOK 1**
10. **(C)** is the correct answer because it is the only option that goes with *drawn*. **DOK 1**

Assessment

Assess

Grammar and Writing

1. (B) is the correct answer because the context suggests that the missing word should be a synonym of belief. DOK1

2. (C) is the correct answer because no other option conveys a meaning opposite to few. DOK1

3. (C) is the correct answer because it is the only answer that makes sense in this context. DOK1

Grammar and Writing Skills: Paragraph Improvement

Paragraph Improvement As you read the following paragraphs from the first draft of a student's reflective essay, pay close attention to the writer's use of grammar, parallel construction, modifiers, and adjectives. Then answer the questions below. Write your answers on a separate sheet of paper.

---

(1) *I've always thought of myself as an optimistic person.* (2) *When troubles emerge.* (3) *I try my hardest to make those troubles work to my advantage.* (4) *I can remember plenty of times throughout my life when things seem particularly gloomy.* (5) *However, I improved the situation by looking at it in another way.*

(6) *I was on summer break.* (7) *Just before my sophomore year.* (8) *My mom, dad, and sister have gone to visit my grandmother, who had recently moved to Alaska.* (9) *Stuck having rehearsal for jazz band, Alaska was so far away.* (10) *It was horrible!* (11) *Even my mom's most trustworthy promise—to take us to visit grandma that following Christmas—was not enough to get rid of my deep disappointment.*

(12) *They were going to be gone for two whole weeks, to go fishing, hike, and white-water rafting, while I stayed at home, practicing my drums.* (13) *If things weren't bad enough, all of my friends were either on vacation with their families, or too busy with summer jobs, to notice that I was all by myself.*

---

1. Which of the following is the best way to write sentences 2 and 3?
   - **(A)** When troubles emerge; I try my hardest to make those troubles work to my advantage.
   - **(B)** When troubles emerge, I try my hardest to make them work to my advantage.
   - **(C)** I try my hardest to make those troubles work to my advantage—when troubles emerge.
   - **(D)** I try my hardest to make troubles work to my advantage—when those troubles emerge.
   - **(E)** Emerging troubles, I try my hardest to turn to my advantage.

2. Which of the following is the best revision of sentence 4?
   - **(A)** I can remember plenty of times during my life when things seem particularly gloomy.
   - **(B)** There have been plenty of times during my life, when thing seemed particularly gloomy.
   - **(C)** I can remember plenty of times throughout my life when things seemed particularly gloomy.
   - **(D)** Plenty of times throughout my life, that I can remember, seem gloomy.
   - **(E)** There are many times that seem gloomy.

3. Which of the following is the best way to improve sentence 5?
   - **(A)** Change *improved* to *improve*.
   - **(B)** Change *However* to *Although*.
   - **(C)** Change *I improved* to *I was usually able to improve*.
   - **(D)** Change *improved* to *seldom improved*.
   - **(E)** Change *I improved* to *couldn't possibly improve*.

Grammar Practice

Subject-Verb Agreement Explain that standardized tests regularly assess a student's ability to identify and correct sentences lacking subject-verb agreement.

Write these sentences on the board:

The cat on the basement steps were clawing at the door.

John, Patrick, and I was stuck in the snow for most of the afternoon.

Over by the girls stand the mathematics instructor.

Have students identify the subject and verb of each sentence. Then have them rewrite to create agreement between the subject and verb.

326

4. Which of the following sentences could the writer insert at the start of the second paragraph to improve the essay's organization?
   (A) Lots of bad things have happened to me.
   (B) In general I've been pretty lucky in the past.
   (C) Sometimes bad things happen to good people.
   (D) A different perspective can be a really good thing.
   (E) One occasion in particular springs to mind.

5. Which of the following is the best way to write sentences 6 and 7?
   (A) I was on summer break, just before my sophomore year.
   (B) Around the start of my sophomore year—I was on summer break.
   (C) Just as my sophomore year was getting ready to start, I had summer break.
   (D) In August, before the start of my sophomore year in high school, I had summer break.
   (E) Just before the start of my sophomore year—I had summer break.

6. Which of these errors appears in sentence 8?
   (A) run-on sentence
   (B) incorrect parallelism
   (C) fragment
   (D) incorrect verb tense
   (E) misplaced modifier

7. Which of the following is the best revision of sentence 9?
   (A) Stuck having rehearsal for jazz band, Alaska stays far away.
   (B) Because I was stuck with rehearsal for jazz band, I couldn't go to Alaska.

   (C) Because there was rehearsal for jazz band, Alaska was far away from me.
   (D) I have rehearsal for jazz band, so Alaska was far away.
   (E) Jazz band rehearsal had me stuck, so Alaska was so far away.

8. Which of the following sentences could replace sentence 10 to illustrate better the reason for the writer's feelings?
   (A) Alaska was so far away!
   (B) I'd never been outside of my home state, and Alaska sure seemed exciting.
   (C) I was pretty sure that Alaska wasn't horrible.
   (D) Going to Alaska is about as exciting as going to jazz band.
   (E) It is really unfair—my family should never have gone to Alaska.

9. Which of these errors appears in sentence 12?
   (A) run-on sentence
   (B) misplaced modifier
   (C) fragment
   (D) incorrect verb tense
   (E) incorrect parallelism

10. While writing the concluding paragraphs of this draft, what information should the writer include to illustrate the essay's general idea?
    (A) examples of other people wasting their free time
    (B) how to get a summer job
    (C) how the writer's optimism improved the situation
    (D) details about band rehearsal
    (E) details about his family's trip to Alaska

Essay

Ralph Waldo Emerson claimed that "nothing can bring you peace but yourself." Do you agree with this statement? Write a short reflective essay that expresses your ideas about individualism and Emerson's claim. As you write, keep in mind that your essay will be checked for **ideas, organization, voice, word choice, sentence fluency, conventions,** and **presentation.**

English Learners

DIFFERENTIATED INSTRUCTION

Intermediate Tell students that while demonstrating a command of sophisticated vocabulary is good, error-free writing and logical organization are more important. Remind students that creating an outline can improve the organization of their writing a great deal.

Have students write an outline for a three-paragraph reflective essay. They should include a thesis statement and at least three pieces of evidence in support of this thesis. Because students are being asked to write a reflective essay, the evidence that they use should come largely from their own experiences.

Assessment

Assess

4. **(E)** is the correct answer because it creates a transition between the introductory paragraph and the first body paragraph. [DOK4]
5. **(A)** is the correct answer because no other option corrects the fragment in sentence 7 as efficiently. [DOK1]
6. **(D)** is the correct answer because the sentence requires a past perfect verb, *had gone,* to indicate that this event took place before the past tense of the narrative. [DOK2]
7. **(B)** is the correct answer because it corrects the dangling modifier without awkwardness. [DOK1]
8. **(B)** is the correct answer because it provides evidence that supports the writer's feeling of disappointment. [DOK4]
9. **(E)** is the correct answer because *hike* is not parallel with *fishing* and *white-water rafting.* [DOK1]
10. **(C)** is the correct answer because it is needed to support the main idea of the essay as stated in the topic sentence of the first paragraph. [DOK2]

Essay

Evaluate essays for the following:

- clearly stated main ideas supported by good reasons and details
- effective voice, word choice, and sentence variety
- effective presentation with attention to grammar and spelling conventions
  [DOK3]

Skills Scope and Sequence

Readability Scores Key: Dale-Chall/DRP/Lexile

PART 1: Resistance to Slavery

Selections and Features	Literary Elements
Unit Introduction pp. 328–342	Allusion **TE** p. 337, **TE** p. 339 Figurative Language. **TE** p. 340 Imagery **TE** p. 340, **SE** p. 341 Metaphor **SE** p. 341, Poetic Language **TE** p. 341
Songs Swing Low, Sweet Chariot; Go Down, Moses; and Keep Your Hand on the Plow pp. 344–349	Refrain **SE** p. 345
Comparing Literature from **My Bondage and My Freedom** (autobiography), by Frederick Douglass **6.6/63/1160** **Frederick Douglass** (poem), by Robert Hayden **In Texas Grass** (poem), by Quincy Troupe pp. 350–361	Autobiography **SE** p. 352
Literary History Slave Narratives and Civil War Memoirs, Letters, and Diaries pp. 362–363	
Informational Text TIME: Slavery Under Glass, by Richard Lacayo **8.8/68/1240** pp. 364–367	
Speech And Ain't I a Woman?, by Sojourner Truth **3.7/49/750** pp. 368–371	Oratory **SE** p. 369 Rhetorical Question **TE** p. 370
Vocabulary Workshop p. 372	

Reading Skills and Strategies	Vocabulary	Writing / Grammar	Speaking, Listening, and Viewing
Use Timelines **TE** p. 330 Analyze Graphic Information **SE** p. 331 Use Bar Graphs **TE** p. 332 Analyze Cause and Effect **TE** p. 336 Analyze Author's Purpose **SE** p. 337 Summarize Main Idea **SE** p. 339		Summarize **TE** p. 334 Write an Essay **TE** p. 338	Analyze Art **SE** and **TE** p. 328 Oral Interpretation **SE** p. 342 Create a Timeline **SE** p. 342
Analyze Historical Context **SE** p. 345 Evaluate **TE** p. 348	Academic Vocabulary **SE** p. 349	Write a List **SE** p. 349	Analyze Art **SE** and **TE** p. 343

Analyze Cause-and-Effect
    Relationships **SE** and **TE** p. 352
	Denotation and Connotation,
	    SE p. 352
		Write a Critical Response
		    TE p. 354
		Write a Dialogue **SE** p. 358
		Analyze Imagery **TE** p. 360
			Analyze Art **TE** p. 355

		Write Interview Questions **TE** p. 362	Analyze Art **TE** p. 363

		Write Persuasive Letters
		    TE p. 364
		Write a Journal Entry
		    TE p. 366
			Analyze Art **TE** p. 366

Evaluate Argument **SE** p. 369	Multiple-Meaning Words **TE** p. 369 Word Usage **SE** p. 371	Write a Speech **SE** p. 371	
	Denotation and Connotation **SE** p. 372		

Readability Scores Key: **Dale-Chall**/**DRP**/Lexile

PART 2: The Civil War: A Nation Divided

Selections and Features	Literary Elements
Memoir *from* **Mary Chesnut's Civil War,** by Mary Chesnut **6.9**/**52**/680 pp.373–380	Journal **SE** p. 375
Grammar Workshop p. 381	
Letter Letter to His Son, by Robert E. Lee **9.9**/**64**/1130 pp. 382–386	Diction **SE** p. 383
Short Story An Occurrence at Owl Creek Bridge, by Ambrose Bierce **7.3**/**63**/1000 pp. 387–399	Point of View **SE** p. 388
Speech The Gettysburg Address, by Abraham Lincoln **9.3**/**62**/1490 pp. 400–403	Parallelism **SE** p. 401
Political Perspective *from* **Lincoln at Gettysburg: The Words that Remade America,** by Garry Wills **10.4**/**68**/1250 pp. 404–406	

PART 3: A Poetic Revolution

Selections and Features	Literary Elements
Poems I Hear America Singing and **When I Heard the Learn'd Astronomer,** by Walt Whitman pp. 407–412	Free Verse **SE** p. 409
Poems A Sight in Camp in the Daybreak Gray and **Dim and Beat! Beat! Drums!,** by Walt Whitman pp. 413–415	Alliteration **TE** p. 414 Free Verse **SE** p. 415
Memoir *from* **Specimen Days,** by Walt Whitman **5.8**/**62**/1410 pp. 416–419	Historical Narrative **SE** and **TE** p. 416
Poem *from* **Song of Myself,** by Walt Whitman pp. 420–429	Voice **SE** p. 420 Parallelism **TE** p. 422 Author's Purpose **TE** p. 428
Historical Perspective *from* **Walt Whitman: A Life,** by Justin Kaplan **8.4**/**68**/1390 pp. 430–436	

Reading Skills and Strategies	Vocabulary	Writing Grammar	Speaking, Listening, and Viewing
Distinguish Fact and Opinion **SE** p. 375 Analyze Point of View **TE** p. 378	Word Parts **TE** p. 375 Context Clues **SE** p. 380	Sentence Fragments **TE** p. 376	Analyze Art **SE** and **TE** p. 379
		Transitional Expressions **SE** p. 381	
Determine Main Idea and Supporting Details **SE** p. 383 Analyze Cause and Effect **TE** p. 384	Diction **TE** p; 383 Word Parts **SE** p. 383	Write a Summary **SE** p. 386	
Make and Verify Predictions **SE** p. 388 Chronological Order **TE** p. 388 Identify Sequence **TE** p. 390 Make Inferences **TE** p. 392	Synonyms **TE** p. 396, **SE** p. 398 Academic Vocabulary **SE** p. 398	Conjunctions **SE** p. 399 Write an Expository Essay **SE** p. 399	Analyze Art **TE** p. 389
Analyze Style **SE** p. 401 Identify Main Idea **TE** p. 402	Synonyms **TE** p. 401 Analogies **SE** p. 403	Write an Interior Monologue **SE** p. 403	
Connect to Political Context **SE** and **TE** p. 404		Primary and Secondary Sources **TE** p. 404	

Reading Skills and Strategies	Vocabulary	Writing Grammar	Speaking, Listening, and Viewing
Paraphrase **SE** p. 409	Word Parts **TE** p. 409	Sentence Fragments **TE** p. 410 Write a Poem **SE** p. 412	Analyze Art **TE** p. 410
Paraphrase **SE** p. 414		Run-on Sentences **TE** p. 414 Write an Essay **SE** p. 415	Analyze Art **TE** p. 413
	Context Clues **SE** p. 419 Academic Vocabulary **SE** p. 419	Write a Journal Entry **SE** p. 419	Analyze Art **TE** p. 418
Draw Conclusions **SE** p. 420 Parallelism **TE** p. 422	Academic Vocabulary **SE** and **TE** p. 428	Write a Reflective Essay **SE** p. 429 Hyphens **SE** p. 429	Analyze Art **SE** and **TE** p. 422
Synthesize Information **SE** and **TE** p. 430 Interpret **TE** p. 432		Subject-Verb Agreement **TE** p. 434	

Readability Scores Key: Dale-Chall/DRP/Lexile

PART 3: A Poetic Revolution *(continued)*

Selections and Features	Literary Elements
Poems If you were coming in the Fall, My Life closed twice, and **The Soul selects,** by Emily Dickinson pp. 437–441	Rhyme **SE** p. 438
Poems Much Madness is divinest Sense and **Success is counted sweetest,** by Emily Dickinson pp. 442–444	Imagery **SE** p. 443 Rhyme **SE** p. 444
Poems I heard a fly buzz and **The Bustle in a House,** by Emily Dickinson pp. 445–447	Irony **SE** p. 445 Rhyme **SE** p. 447
Poem Because I could not stop for Death, by Emily Dickinson pp. 448–449	Personification **SE** p. 448
Poems There's a certain Slant and **This is my letter to the World,** by Emily Dickinson pp. 450–454	Rhyme **SE** p. 450 Personification (review) **SE** p. 453
Historical Perspective Emily Dickinson: An Introduction, by Billy Collins **10.6/66/1360** pp. 455–457	
Writing Workshop pp. 458–467	
Speaking, Listening, and Viewing Workshop pp. 468–471	
Independent Reading pp. 472–473	
Assessment pp. 474–479	

Reading Skills and Strategies	Vocabulary	Writing Grammar	Speaking, Listening, and Viewing
Analyze Sound Devices **SE** p. 438		Write a Paraphrase **TE** p. 440 Write a Journal Entry **SE** p. 441	
Analyze Sound Devices **SE** p. 442		Ellipses **TE** p. 442 Write a Poem **SE** p. 444	Analyze Art **SE** p. 443
Respond to Poetry **TE** p. 446 Analyze Sound Devices **SE** p. 447		Write an Essay **SE** p. 447	Analyze Art **TE** p. 445
Clarify Meaning **SE** p. 448	Word Origins **TE** p. 448	Write a Paragraph **SE** p. 449	

Connect **TE** p. 450	Word Usage **SE** p. 453
	Academic Vocabulary
	   SE p. 453
		Write an Expository Essay
		   SE p. 454
		Dashes **SE** p. 454
			Analyze Art **TE** p. 450
			Discussion **SE** p. 452

Analyze Literary Criticism **SE** p. 455 Identify Main Idea **TE** p. 456		Write a Summary **SE** p. 457	

Draw Conclusions **TE** p. 464		Prewrite **SE** p. 459
		Thesis Statement **TE** p. 460
		Draft **SE** p. 461
		Works Cited Page **TE** p. 462
		Revise **SE** p. 466
		Coherent Paragraphs
		   SE p. 466
		Sentence Variety **TE** p. 466
		Write a Historical Investigation
		   Report **SE** p. 467	

		Create a Storyboard
		   SE p. 470
			Multimedia Presentation
			   SE p. 468

		Write Research Questions **TE** p. 472 Write a Review **SE** p. 473	
		Write a Persuasive Essay **SE** p. 479	

UNIT THREE

Focus

Bellringer Options

Literature Launcher DVD
    Pre-Reading Video: Unit 3
Daily Language Practice
    Transparency 30

Or **say:** Imagine you are on a sports team or the school newspaper. What kinds of issues might cause divisiveness within the group? *(Ideas about how the team should be led; ideas about how to accomplish goals)* **Ask:** What might cause citizens to begin a war against another region of the country? *(Disputes over land, wealth, power, or beliefs)*

Answer: *People's faces are painted as if a light is shining on them. Their expressions show great respect toward Lincoln.*

Lincoln's Drive Through Richmond, 1866. Dennis Malone Carter. Oil on canvas, 77.5 x 19.9 cm. Chicago Historical Society, IL.

View the Art The setting of this painting is Richmond, Virginia, the capital of the Confederacy, following the end of the Civil War. How does the artist depict the feelings of the people in this painting? Why do you think he might have done so? ★

328

Unit Introduction Skills

Reading Skills
- Analyze Graphic Information (SE pp. 331, 333)
- Analyze Author's Purpose (SE p. 337)
- Summarize Main Idea (SE p. 339)
- Analyze Imagery and Metaphor (SE p. 341)
- Analyze Cause and Effect (TE p. 336)
- Use Bar Graphs (TE p. 332)

The Civil War Era

Writing Skills/Grammar
- Summarize (TE p. 334)
- Write an Essay (TE p. 338)

Literary Elements
- Imagery (SE p. 341)
- Metaphor (SE p. 341; TE p. 337)
- Allusion (TE p. 339)
- Poetic Language (TE p. 341)

Listening/Speaking/Viewing Skills
- Give an Oral Interpretation (SE p. 342)
- Create a Timeline (SE p. 342)
- Analyze Art (SE p. 328; TE pp. 329, 333, 334, 337, 339, 341)

The Civil War Era

1850-1880

Looking Ahead

By the 1850s, the Southern states had become increasingly isolated from the rest of the country because of their support of slavery and their exclusion from the industrial boom in the North. Tensions between the North and South grew, and the end of the Union—or a war to preserve it—hovered on the horizon. Writers responded to the issues of slavery, regional conflict, and eventually the Civil War. Many moved from Romanticism to a realistic portrayal of the problems confronting the nation. Two major poets of the period also found inspiration in personal feelings and ordinary events.

Keep the following questions in mind as you read:

◇ How did the slavery question lead to the Civil War?

◇ How was the Civil War reflected in the writing of the period?

◇ What made the poetry of Whitman and Dickinson revolutionary?

Focus

Summary

This introduction relates the historical, social, and cultural forces of the American Civil War era, 1850–1880, to the literature of this period. It connects the religious traditions and narratives of enslaved Africans to growing tensions between the North and the South. It considers how the speeches and memoirs of the war's participants influenced American values, attitudes, and beliefs. It also looks at how two major writers spurred sweeping changes in the art of writing poetry.

For diagnostic and end-of-unit assessment, see Assessment Resources, pp. 17–24, 345–346.

For school-to-home activities, see Unit 3 Teaching Resources Book, pp. 5–11.

For students who would profit from independent novel study, see Novel Companion, pp. 119–162.

329

Unit Resources

Print Materials

- Unit 3 Teaching Resources, pp. 1–262
- Interactive Read and Write (On Level, Approaching, EL), pp. 99–146
- Novel Companion, pp. 119–162
- Bellringer Option Transparencies: Selection Focus 20–29; Daily Language Practice 30–40
- Literary Element Transparencies 16, 46, 49, 55, 72, 77, 88, 107

- Assessment Resources, Unit Assessment, pp. 17–24, 345–346
- Assessment Resources, Selection Assessment, pp. 121–160

Technology

- TeacherWorks Plus CD
- StudentWorks Plus CD
- Literature Launchers: Pre-Reading Videos DVD, Unit 3
- Literature Online

- Visual Vocabulary CD-ROM
- Listening Library CD-ROM
- ExamView CD-ROM
- Skill Level Up! CD-ROM

UNIT THREE

Teach

Reading Strategy | 1

Use the Timeline Connect works of literature to historical events.

Ask: How do the following works written between 1850 and 1865 reflect the events in the United States at that time?

- *My Bondage and My Freedom* by Frederick Douglass
- Lincoln's Gettysburg Address

(Douglass's autobiography reflects the ongoing controversy about slavery; Lincoln's address is connected with the Battle of Gettysburg.)

Literary History ☆

A Little Woman and a Great War Outraged by the Fugitive Slave Act of 1850, Harriet Beecher Stowe (1811–1896) wrote *Uncle Tom's Cabin,* a novel depicting the suffering and human dignity of an African American slave. Stowe's book influenced the nation's move toward war. Stowe was about five feet tall, and when President Lincoln met her in person during the Civil War, he reportedly said, "So you're the little woman who wrote the book that started this great war!"

Timeline 1850-1880

AMERICAN LITERATURE | 1

 Uncle Tom's Cabin

1850

1852
Harriet Beecher Stowe's *Uncle Tom's Cabin* is published ☆

1855
Walt Whitman's *Leaves of Grass* is published

1855
Frederick Douglass's autobiography, *My Bondage and My Freedom*, is published

1858
Abraham Lincoln gives A House Divided speech

1860

1859–1865
Emily Dickinson writes more than eight hundred poems

1861
Harriet Jacobs's *Incidents in the Life of a Slave Girl* is published under the pseudonym Linda Brent

1862
Julia Ward Howe's "Battle Hymn of the Republic" is published

1863
Abraham Lincoln delivers the Gettysburg Address

1865
Walt Whitman's *Drum-Taps* is published

UNITED STATES EVENTS

1850

1850
Compromise of 1850 strengthens Fugitive Slave Act

1854
Congress passes Kansas-Nebraska Act

1857
Dred Scott decision makes slavery legal in all territories

1859
John Brown raids federal arsenal at Harpers Ferry, VA

1860

◀ **1860–1861**
Pony Express runs from Missouri to California

1860
Abraham Lincoln wins presidential election

1860
South Carolina secedes from the Union

1861
Jefferson Davis becomes the Confederate president

1861
Confederate forces fire on Fort Sumter, SC, starting the Civil War

1861
First Battle of Bull Run

1862
Richard Gatling patents the first practical machine gun

1863
Union collects income tax to fund the Civil War

WORLD EVENTS

1850

1850
Chinese Taiping Rebellion

1853
Commodore Perry opens Japan to world trade

1857
Flaubert's *Madame Bovary*

1858 ▶
Benito Juárez becomes president of Mexico

1860

1861
Alexander II, czar of Russia, frees serfs

1861
Burke and Wills expedition reaches Australia

1865
Lewis Carroll's *Alice's Adventures in Wonderland*

1867
Alfred Nobel receives British patent on dynamite

1868
Meiji Restoration reforms Japan's government

LOG ON ▶ **Literature** Online

Literature and Reading To explore the Interactive Timeline, go to glencoe.com and enter QuickPass code GLA9800u3.

330 UNIT 3 THE CIVIL WAR ERA

Writing Practice

Use Timelines Remind students that timelines help us track the chronological sequence of events (the order in which events occur), examine the importance of each event, and see how one event leads to another. Have students research one of the following people:

- Walt Whitman
- Emily Dickinson
- Abraham Lincoln

Instruct students to create a timeline that includes the date and a brief description of at least five significant events in the life of the person.

330

◀ Medal of Honor

1870

1873
Henry Timrod's "Cotton Boll" is published

1875
Mary Baker Eddy's *Science and Health with Key to the Scriptures* is published

1876
Mark Twain's *Adventures of Tom Sawyer* is published

1878
Henry James's *Daisy Miller* and *The Europeans* are published

1879
George W. Cable's *Old Creole Days* is published

▲ **1868**
Louisa May Alcott's *Little Women* is published
☆

War Department, Washington, April 20, 1865.
$100,000 REWARD!
THE MURDERER
Of our late beloved President, Abraham Lincoln,
IS STILL AT LARGE.
$50,000 REWARD
$25,000 REWARD
$25,000 REWARD

1863
Emancipation Proclamation declares freedom for enslaved persons in the Confederate states

1863
Battle of Gettysburg

1864
Abraham Lincoln is reelected president

1865
Lincoln is assassinated by John Wilkes Booth

1865
Civil War ends

1866
Ku Klux Klan organizes in Tennessee

1868
Ulysses S. Grant is elected president; he holds office until 1877

1870
Hiram Revels becomes the first African American elected to the U.S. Senate

1876
Battle of the Little Bighorn (Custer's Last Stand)

1877
Reconstruction ends

1870

Ferdinand de Lesseps, engineer for Suez Canal

1869
Suez Canal opens in Egypt

1869
Mohandas K. Gandhi is born

1870

1870
Franco-German War begins

1872
Claude Monet completes *Impression: Sunrise*

1874
The Three-Cornered Hat by Pedro Antonio de Alarcón y Ariza is published

1879
Henrik Ibsen's *A Doll's House* is published

Reading Check
Analyze Graphic Information:
1. How long did the Civil War last?
2. Did the Emancipation Proclamation come before or after the freeing of the serfs in Russia?

English Learners

DIFFERENTIATED INSTRUCTION

Intermediate To familiarize students with the format of a timeline, ask several questions about the information and the images on this spread. **Ask:** Who is being sought by the "wanted poster" shown on this page? *(The murderer of President Lincoln)* In what year did the *Dred Scott* decision occur? *(1857)* The Pony Express ran between which two states?

(Missouri and California) What book did Mark Twain publish in 1876? *(The Adventures of Tom Sawyer)*

Teach
Reading Check

Answers: *1. 1861 to 1865 2. The serfs were freed in Russia (1861) before the Emancipation Proclamation was issued (1863).*

Reading Strategy

Connect Help students connect their prior knowledge of the literature and events on the timeline to historical periods and events unfamiliar to them. **Ask:** Which of the people, places, and events listed on the timeline have you heard of before? What do you know about them? *(Allow students to share their prior knowledge with the rest of the class.)*

Literary History ☆
Louisa May Alcott
Alcott's popular novel *Little Women* (1868–1869) is an autobiographical work about her childhood. In addition to being an author, Alcott worked as a nurse in a Union hospital and was later involved in the women's suffrage movement.

Teach

Draw Conclusions Have students note the difference in resources available to the North and the South. Then direct them to compare a Confederate soldier's monthly income with the prices for common goods.

Ask: Why were these goods so expensive? (*Students might say the Civil War caused serious problems for the Southern economy, including shortages.*)

[**ENGLISH LEARNERS**] Have students look up and discuss synonyms for the economic terminology used on this page: *resources (support, supplies); production (output); capital (money to invest),* and *inflation (rising prices).*

Political History ☆

Economy and War Regional economic differences helped bring about the outbreak of the Civil War. In the South, enslaved Africans provided the labor that maintained the agricultural economy. In the North, free people, including African Americans, worked for wages in a growing industrial economy.

By the Numbers

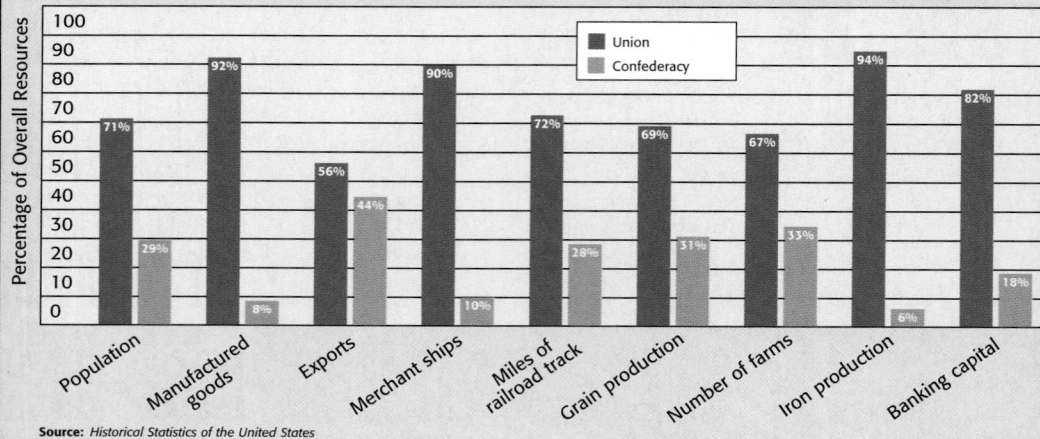

DIVISION OF RESOURCES BETWEEN THE UNION AND THE CONFEDERACY ☆

Legend: ■ Union ■ Confederacy

Y-axis: Percentage of Overall Resources (0–100)

Resource	Union	Confederacy
Population	71%	29%
Manufactured goods	92%	8%
Exports	56%	44%
Merchant ships	90%	10%
Miles of railroad track	72%	28%
Grain production	69%	31%
Number of farms	67%	33%
Iron production	94%	6%
Banking capital	82%	18%

Source: *Historical Statistics of the United States*

---

1 Inflation in the South

Limited resources caused severe inflation in the South during the war. Compare the income of a Confederate soldier with the prices for these goods:

Monthly income: $18.00

Pound of coffee:	$12.00
Quart of milk:	$10.00
Pound of butter:	$6.25
Dozen eggs:	$6.00

SLAVERY

At the start of the 1800s, there were 700,000 enslaved persons in the South. By 1860, there were four million.

CIVIL WAR FORCES

Union

Troops:	2,100,000
Casualties:	634,703
Military Deaths:	360,222

Confederate

Troops:	800,000
Casualties:	483,000
Military Deaths:	260,000

POPULATION

Most populous states in 1880:

New York	5,082,871
Pennsylvania	4,282,891
Ohio	3,198,062
Illinois	3,077,871
Missouri	2,168,380

AFRICAN AMERICAN SOLDIERS

- 180,000 served in the Union army.
- There were 66 all-black Union regiments.
- Twenty-three were awarded the Medal of Honor.

Source: *For the Common Defense*

Reading Practice

Bar Graphs Direct students' attention to the bar graph that shows the division of resources between the North and South. The graph breaks down the totals of various types of resources, comparing the percentages held by each side in the Civil War. **Ask:** Which three resources were held most heavily by the Union? (*Manufactured goods, merchant ships, and iron production*) Which three resources did the Confederacy hold more than 30 percent of? (*Exports, grain production, number of farms*) What do these numbers tell you about the South's dependence on slavery? (*The South's economy was based on agriculture, which had grown through the labor of enslaved people.*)

A *Plantation on the Mississippi,* nineteenth century. Currier & Ives. Color lithograph. Museum of the City of New York.

Being There

Before South Carolina seceded in December 1860, the nation stood on the brink of destruction. After secession began, the tensions between the industrial North and the agricultural South came to a violent head. ★

B Wounded Union soldiers being cared for by nurse Anne Bell, 1861–1865. Photograph.

C *The Battle of Antietam,* 1862. Captain James Hope. Oil on canvas. U.S. Department of the Interior, Washington, DC.

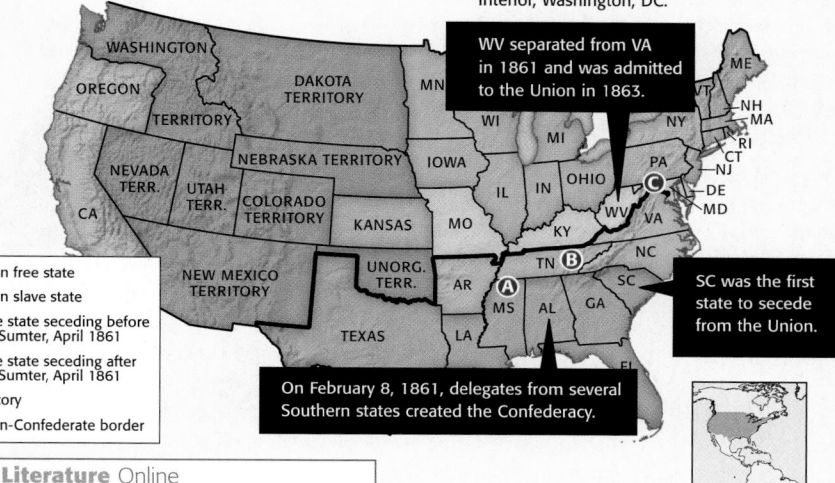

WV separated from VA in 1861 and was admitted to the Union in 1863.

SC was the first state to secede from the Union.

On February 8, 1861, delegates from several Southern states created the Confederacy.

- Union free state
- Union slave state
- Slave state seceding before Fort Sumter, April 1861
- Slave state seceding after Fort Sumter, April 1861
- Territory
- Union-Confederate border

LOG ON ▶ **Literature** Online

Literature and Reading For more about the history and literature of this period, go to glencoe.com and enter QuickPass code GLA9800u3.

Reading Check

Analyze Graphic Information:

1. In which category in the bar graph on page 332 is the difference between the resources of the Union and the Confederacy greatest?

2. How many slave states seceded, as shown on the map, before the firing on Fort Sumter?

3. How do the political boundaries west of the Mississippi River during the Civil War compare with those in the present-day United States?

Teach

Reading Check

Answers: *1. Iron production— Union 94 percent versus Confederacy 6 percent*
2. Seven states—Texas, Louisiana, Mississippi, Alabama, Georgia, South Carolina, and Florida
3. The territories controlled by the United States had not yet been divided into the states we have today.

View the Art ★

A. Plantation owners formed the ruling class in Southern society, and much of the South's economy depended on the slave labor required to operate the plantations.

B. The Civil War death toll was nearly as great as that for all other American wars combined, from the Revolutionary War through the Vietnam War.

C. More than 4,000 Northern and Southern soldiers died on the first day of fighting at Antietam, making it the single bloodiest day of the Civil War.

Approaching Level

DIFFERENTIATED INSTRUCTION

Emerging Draw students' attention to the Civil War map of the states. Ask them to point out the five Union slave states. *(Missouri, Kentucky, West Virginia, Maryland, Delaware)* Why do you think these states are known as "border states"? *(These states create a border or dividing line between the Union and the Confederacy.)*

Established Point out to students the different connotations of the terms *Union* and *Confederacy.* Explain that *Union* emphasizes the binding of states into a single national unit. *Confederacy* suggests a voluntary association of states that keep important rights and independence. (Remind students, if necessary, that at first the United States operated as a confederation of states.) Despite the Confederacy's

strong emphasis on state's rights, its constitution was almost identical to the U.S. Constitution.

333

Teach

Reading Strategy | 1

Predict Have students read the headings to themselves and think about what they might read about in each of the five sections.

Ask: Which section would most likely contain information about the Underground Railroad? *(This information is given in the section entitled Antislavery Movement.)*

View the Photograph ★

In 1862, American photographer Mathew Brady (1823–1896) formed a team of photographers who would document all the major engagements of the war, as well as Union camp life. This effort led to Brady's financial ruin, and though his photographs are highly valued today, Brady died a pauper in a New York poorhouse.

Ask: How do photos like this one help us better understand the Civil War era? *(Students may say that the photos help us visualize the events of the war.)*

Writing Practice

Summarize Have students write a two-sentence summary for each section on pages 334 and 335. Tell students that in order to write an accurate summary, they must first identify the main idea of a passage. Review The Path to War section as a class, pointing out the differing goals of the North and the South. Then write this sample summary on the board: *The North wanted to stop slavery's spread,*

Learning Objectives

For pages 334–342
In studying this text, you will focus on the following objectives:

Literary Study: Analyzing literary periods. Evaluating historical influences.

Reading: Connecting to the literature.

The Civil War Era
1850–1880

Historical, Social, and Cultural Forces

The Path to War 1

As the nation expanded westward, it became evident that the legality of slavery in the new territories would have to be determined. Northerners in Congress pushed to prohibit it in new territories, while Southern senators argued that such a move would deny slaveholders their constitutional rights. In 1850, Senator Henry Clay, in an effort to save the Union, proposed several compromise measures. For the North, Congress admitted California as a free state. To appease the South, Congress passed the Fugitive Slave Act. This law mandated the return of enslaved Africans who had fled to the North and penalized individuals who helped them escape. The Compromise of 1850 averted immediate disaster for the Union but it proved to be only a temporary solution to the problem.

Antislavery Movement

Most Northerners opposed the Fugitive Slave Act, and most free-state legislatures passed laws in an attempt to block it. The Underground Railroad, a secret network that aided enslaved fugitives escaping to the North, became more active than ever.

In 1852, Harriet Beecher Stowe's best-selling novel *Uncle Tom's Cabin* depicted the cruelty of slavery and the fight for freedom. Abolitionists hailed the book; one review proclaimed, "A slaveholder might read it without anger, but not easily without a secret abhorrence of the system which he himself upholds."

Abraham Lincoln with General George Brinton McClellan talking in a tent at the Antietam battlefield. Mathew Brady. ★

Secession

As the 1860 presidential election approached, the Republican Party nominated Abraham Lincoln. Lincoln was not an outright abolitionist; he simply believed that slavery should be excluded from the new territories. With Lincoln's victory, many Southern states, anticipating the abolition of slavery, felt that they had no choice but to leave the

but Southerners insisted that new states should have the right to allow slavery. To satisfy both sides, Henry Clay proposed the Compromise of 1850. Next have students work independently to summarize the next four sections. Invite volunteers to share their summaries with the class.

Union. On December 20, 1860, South Carolina seceded. Six more states soon followed. These states formed the Confederate States of America, or the Confederacy, which included eleven states by the start of the war. In Lincoln's inaugural address, he pleaded for the North and South to avoid bloodshed and violence. His plea was not heeded, and on April 12, 1861, Confederate troops attacked Fort Sumter in the harbor of Charleston, South Carolina. The Civil War had begun.

> ☆ *"We failed, but in the good providence of God apparent failure often proves a blessing."*
>
> —Confederate General Robert E. Lee

War

The South's long tradition of military service gave the Confederate army an early advantage over the Union. As the war continued, however, the Union grew stronger, while Confederate losses weakened the South. To win the war, Union General Ulysses S. Grant finally began to attack Southern resources as well as Confederate forces.

President Lincoln, assassinated on April 14, 1865, did not witness the end to the struggle that had divided the nation. After more than 600,000 deaths on both sides, the last Confederate soldiers surrendered in May. The Thirteenth Amendment became law in December, officially ending slavery in the nation. The North's victory in the Civil War destroyed the South's slave economy.

Reconstruction

Although the fighting had ended, the period of Reconstruction involved more than rebuilding and repairing the South. It would take years to restructure Southern society, grant rights to those who had been enslaved, and readmit the Southern states to the Union. Congress passed the Civil Rights Act in 1866 and then the Fourteenth Amendment—redefining citizenship to include African Americans and requiring their equal protection under the law—but the nation did little to help those who had been freed. After Reconstruction, the new South was in some ways similar to the pre-Civil War South: White Southern Democrats returned to power, and African Americans lost many of their civil rights.

PREVIEW **Big Ideas** of the Civil War Era

1 Resistance to Slavery	**2** A Nation Divided	**3** A Poetic Revolution
The culture of African Americans was shaped by their struggle against slavery. Spirituals and slave narratives testified to the harshness of slavery and African Americans' fierce resistance to it. **See pages 336–337.**	During the Civil War, Americans created a literary record that ranged from vivid accounts of wartime life to profound expressions of faith in American ideals. **See pages 338–339.**	Poets Walt Whitman and Emily Dickinson experimented with new verse forms during this period. In divergent ways, they explored the self and its relation to the world. **See pages 340–341.**

INTRODUCTION **335**

Reading Strategy 2

Make Inferences

Ask: After the war, what do you think life was like for African Americans in the South? In the North? *(Possible answers: In the South, African Americans were no longer slaves, but they faced poverty, racism, and lack of rights. In the North, life for African Americans was probably about the same as before; perhaps there was more optimism because slavery had been abolished.)*

Political History ☆

Lee's Dilemma Unlike many Southerners, General Robert E. Lee (1807–1870) at first did not support secession. Rising tensions forced Lee to weigh his love for his native Virginia against his love for the Union. To avoid fighting against his relatives, Lee sided with the South and became its military commander. By resigning his commission as a career military officer in the United States Army, Lee said goodbye to and then fought brilliantly against many of his longtime comrades from the North.

Approaching Level

DIFFERENTIATED INSTRUCTION

Emerging To help students keep track of the three Big Ideas covered in this unit, draw a three-column chart on the board and use the three Big Ideas as column heads. Have students copy the chart and tell them to use it to make notes as they read the rest of the introduction. As the class completes each Big Idea section, have students volunteer to share the important ideas with the class, using their notes to support their answers. For example, after students read the Resistance to Slavery section, students should know that spirituals and slave narratives raised peoples' awareness of the horrors of slavery.

UNIT THREE

Teach

Reading Strategy | 1

Evaluate Sources **Ask:** What is one advantage and one disadvantage of using an eyewitness account as a source? *(Advantage: It gives a personal, emotional account of an event. Disadvantage: It is limited to one person's point of view.)*

[ENGLISH LEARNERS] Have English learners orally paraphrase the Slave Narratives section to increase comprehension.

Writer's Technique ☆

The Narrative Form A narrative is a piece of writing or a speech that tells a story and is an important element in nonfiction. Narratives include biographies, autobiographies, memoirs, and essays. Two narratives were the inspiration for Harriet Beecher Stowe's novel *Uncle Tom's Cabin*: Frederick Douglass's *Narrative of the Life of Frederick Douglass, an American Slave* (1845), and Josiah Henson's *The Life of Josiah Henson* (1849).

Big Idea 1
Resistance to Slavery

Suppose you were not allowed to read or write or own property. Picture being whipped for disobeying or hunted after running away. Imagine being sold away from your family. Such was slave-life.

> *"There is no Negro problem. The problem is whether the American people have loyalty enough, honor enough, patriotism enough, to live up to their own Constitution."*
>
> —Frederick Douglass

The Realities of Slavery

Southern plantation owners purchased Africans to work in the fields. The law made enslaved people property for life. It was illegal to teach them to read or write; owners feared that knowledge would bring revolt. Escape was difficult, and captured fugitives might be whipped or even killed.

Slavery was legal in the North, too; however, conditions were different. Slaves could work in industrial trades, and in some states marry and own property. They could be punished, but an owner who killed one could be charged with murder. Religious groups had always opposed slavery, and many Northerners came to believe it was wrong.

Strength in Religion

Enslaved Africans combined traditional African music with Christian hymns to create spirituals, or songs of salvation and religious beliefs (see pages 344–349). Much of the imagery in spirituals was drawn from the Bible, as slaves likened their situation to that of the Jews held captive in Egypt.

Many songs had a dual meaning, expressing both religious faith and a hunger for freedom. Some also served as encoded messages. The first line of "Follow the Drinking Gourd"—"When the sun comes back and the first quail calls"—refers to late winter. "Conductors" on the Underground Railroad found that it took about a year for escapees to journey from the South to the Ohio River and that crossing the river was easiest during winter, when the river was frozen. Thus, the song suggests that enslaved Africans make their escape during winter and follow the "Drinking Gourd"—the Big Dipper constellation, whose cup points to the North Star.

Frederick Douglass

Frederick Douglass (see pages 351–358) was born on a Maryland plantation and was separated from his mother soon after birth. Early on, Douglass realized that education was the path to freedom. As he taught himself to read and write, he grew determined to gain that freedom. After Douglass escaped at age twenty, he spoke at an antislavery meeting, launching his career as a powerful orator and an influential member of the abolitionist movement. In 1845, he authenticated his life story and the brutality he had endured by writing *Narrative of the Life of Frederick Douglass, an American Slave*, later expanded into *My Bondage and My Freedom* and *Life and Times of Frederick Douglass*. ☆

Slave Narratives

Slave narratives became increasingly popular in the decades before the Civil War. In addition to Frederick Douglass, writers William Wells Brown, Solomon Northup, and Sojourner Truth (see pages 368–371) sold tens of thousands of copies of their life stories. They not only provided Northerners and abolitionists with glimpses of the horrors of slavery but also contradicted the claims of slave owners. Through these narratives, slaves could be seen as people rather than property. [1]

336 UNIT 3 THE CIVIL WAR ERA

Reading Practice

Analyze Cause and Effect Have students practice finding cause-and-effect relationships. Tell students to create a two-column chart with the headings Cause and Effect. Have students reread this page to find cause-and-effect relationships and record them on their chart. Give these examples:

Cause: The Ohio River freezes in winter.

Effect: Escape to the North was easier in winter when slaves could walk across the Ohio River.

Cause: Frederick Douglass realized that education could lead to freedom.

Effect: He taught himself to read and write.

336

The Hour of Emancipation, 1863. William Tolman Carlton. Oil on canvas. Private collection.

Frederick Douglass gave a speech to a white audience in Rochester, New York, on July 5, 1852. The following paragraphs are taken from that speech.

from *The Meaning of July Fourth for the Negro* by Frederick Douglass

The blessings in which you, this day, rejoice, are not enjoyed in common. The rich inheritance of justice, liberty, prosperity and independence, bequeathed by your fathers, is shared by you, not by me. The sunlight that brought light and healing to you has brought stripes and death to me. This Fourth July is *yours,* not *mine. You* may rejoice, *I* must mourn. . . .

What, to the American slave, is your fourth of July? I answer, a day that reveals to him, more than all other days in the year, the gross injustice and cruelty to which he is the constant victim. To him, your celebration is a sham; your boasted liberty, an unholy license; your national greatness, swelling vanity; your sounds of rejoicing are empty and heartless; your

denunciation of tyrants, brass fronted impudence; your shouts of liberty and equality, hollow mockery; your prayers and hymns, your sermons and thanksgivings, with all your religious parade and solemnity, are, to him mere bombast, fraud, deception, impiety, and hypocrisy—a thin veil to cover up crimes which would disgrace a nation of savages. There is not a nation on earth guilty of practices more shocking and bloody than are the people of the United States, at this very hour.

Reading Check

Analyze Author's Purpose How did Douglass try to persuade his white readers and listeners to fight against slavery?

Teach

Reading Check

Answer: *Douglass showed them slavery and its horrors, which often contradicted the claims made by slave owners. He also showed his readers and listeners that slaves were real people, rather than mere property.*

Literary Element	2

Metaphor Say: A metaphor is a figure of speech that compares two seemingly unlike things without using the word *like* or *as.* Read Douglass's July Fourth speech and identify the key metaphor. *(Sunlight is a metaphor for independence from Great Britain.)*

View the Art

President Lincoln issued the Emancipation Proclamation in two parts. In September 1862, he proclaimed that if the Confederate states did not return to the Union by 1863, he would issue a declaration freeing all of their slaves. This declaration was issued on January 1, 1863. Carlton's painting depicts a group of slaves gathered around a watch on the night that emancipation was declared.

English Learners

DIFFERENTIATED INSTRUCTION

SMALL GROUP

Advanced Douglass's language in this speech is both deeply emotional and highly formal, characterized by powerful word choices, parallel sentence structure, and elliptical clauses. Have students work together to determine the meaning of words and expressions that may be unfamiliar. Point out that in the second paragraph, Douglass sometimes omits repetitive words when his meaning is clear, using a comma to indicate the omission. To help students identify patterns, write this example on the board, using brackets to show the words that are omitted. Example: ". . . your boasted liberty [is] an unholy license; your national greatness [is] swelling vanity."

337

Teach

Reading Strategy | 1

Connect Ask: If you were asked to record your life experiences from the last month, what events would you choose to emphasize? *(Students should share significant life events and respond to those of others.)*

Ask: How might the events of the Civil War era have influenced the letters, journals, and speeches written at this time? *(Students might say that the struggles and demands of the time occupied people's thoughts and were expressed in their private and public writings.)*

Political History ☆

War Begins In April 1861, the newly declared Confederacy refused to allow provisions to be delivered to Fort Sumter in South Carolina. Instead, General P.G.T. Beauregard demanded that the Union surrender the fort. Rather than acknowledge Southern autonomy, Lincoln ordered that provisions be sent to the men. Beauregard's troops opened fire on the fort, and on the second day, with Fort Sumter badly damaged, U.S. Army Major Robert Anderson surrendered.

Big Idea 2
A Nation Divided

Fighting any war brings fear, loss, suffering, and death, but a war that turns the people of a country against each other is doubly bitter. In the American Civil War, communities and sometimes even families became divided by the conflict. Letters home were written from places most people had never heard of—Shiloh, Antietam, Gettysburg, and Chickamauga—all sites of major battles where thousands of soldiers were wounded or killed.

> *"Many are the hearts that are weary tonight, Wishing for the war to cease,"*
>
> —from the Civil War song "Tenting on the Old Campground" by Walter C. Kittredge

Revolution or Treason?

When Abraham Lincoln (see pages 400–403) was elected to the U.S. Congress in 1846, he voted against abolishing slavery, because he thought it would destroy the Union. Still, he opposed its spreading to new territories, believing they should remain "places for poor people to go and better their condition." In his speech A House Divided in 1858, Lincoln warned of the possible end of the Republic:

> "We are now far into the fifth year, since a policy was initiated with the avowed object and confident promise of putting an end to slavery agitation. . . . In my opinion, it will not cease until a crisis shall have been reached, and passed—'A house divided against itself cannot stand.'"

When Lincoln was elected president in 1860, his words proved true. The North saw secession as an act of treason. The South believed that it had launched a second American revolution, and the Civil War began soon after Lincoln took office. ☆

Mary Chesnut's World

Mary Boykin Miller Chesnut (see pages 374–380) grew up in luxury on a large South Carolina plantation. Although she personally hated slavery, her family owned hundreds of slaves, and both her father and husband served as proslavery senators. Chesnut had little choice but to remain loyal to the South, but she documented the brutal cost of the war in her journal:

> July 1st [1862] . . . Edward Cheves, only son of John Cheves, killed. His sister kept crying, 'Oh, mother, what shall we do; Edward is killed,' but the mother sat dead still, white as a sheet, never uttering a word or shedding a tear. Are our women losing the capacity to weep?

Chesnut visited hospitals, rejoiced with friends at Confederate victories, and cried over Confederate losses. Through it all, she detailed the cruelties and evils of war in her journal. Her story told of her own fears and reactions, the devaluation of Confederate currency, and the inflation that forced families into starvation.

Lincoln's Vision and Words

Abraham Lincoln initially wished only to limit slavery and to preserve the Union, but he came under increasing pressure to turn the war into a campaign against slavery. He cautiously committed himself to eliminating slavery throughout the country, beginning with the Emancipation Proclamation, which announced that he would free the enslaved people in the South on January 1, 1863. The proclamation turned the war into a moral battle that aroused not only the spirit of the North but also the spirits of those who were enslaved. Lincoln's speeches reflected his dedication to the preservation of the Union and his desire to heal the nation. When Lincoln delivered the Gettysburg Address in 1863, he expressed a new vision of the United States. **1**

Writing Practice

🖊 **Compare Songs** Point out that Julia Ward Howe's song "Battle Hymn of the Republic," noted on the timeline on page 330, came to be regarded as the anthem of the Union cause during the war. Similarly, "Dixie," a minstrel-show song written before the war, became the anthem of the Confederate cause. Ask students to listen to versions of both songs and to compare the first verses and choruses of each. Point out that both songs have strong, steady rhythms that make them ideal for marching soldiers.

Ask: What other similarities and differences do you find in the music and the language? In imagery and theme? Ask students to write an essay comparing the two Civil War anthems.

Civilians at 31st Pennsylvania Infantry Camp, 1862. Black and white photograph. Medford Historical Society Collection.

from *Second Inaugural Address, March 4, 1865* by Abraham Lincoln

2 The Almighty has his own purposes. "Woe unto the world because of offenses! for it must needs be that offenses come; but woe to that man by whom the offense cometh!" If we shall suppose that American slavery is one of those offenses which, in the providence of God, must needs come, but which, having continued through His appointed time, He now wills to remove, and that He gives to both North and South, this terrible war, as the woe due to those by whom the offense came, shall we discern therein any departure from those divine attributes which the believers in a Living God always ascribe to Him? Fondly do we hope—fervently do we pray—that this mighty scourge of war may speedily pass away. Yet, if God wills that it continue, until all the wealth piled by the bond-man's two hundred and fifty years of unrequited toil shall be sunk, and until every drop of blood drawn with the lash, shall be paid by another drawn with the sword, as was said three thousand years ago, so still it must be said, "the judgments of the Lord, are true and righteous altogether." **2**

With malice toward none; with charity for all; with firmness in the right, as God gives us to see the right, let us strive on to finish the work we are in; to bind up the nation's wounds; to care for him who shall have borne the battle, and for his widow, and his orphan—to do all which may achieve and cherish a just and lasting peace, among ourselves, and with all nations.

Reading Check

Summarize Main Ideas What are the main ideas of each of the two paragraphs from Lincoln's Second Inaugural Address?

INTRODUCTION **339**

Teach

Reading Check

Answers: *1. God's will shall be done, and the length of the war shall be determined by it. 2. The country must both carry out the war and prepare to reunite with the enemy in peace.*

Literary Element 2

Allusion Say: When writing to persuade, authors often make allusions to famous works to support their positions. In the excerpt from Lincoln's second inaugural address, there are two quotations. **Ask:** Where do these quotations come from? *(Both come from the Bible.)*

View the Photograph ★

Ask: How does this photograph make the Civil War more real? *(Students may say that the image of people of different genders, races, and ages conveys a feeling of everyday life in the scene. Objects such as the tools suggest the work that waits to be done. The young child could belong to the woman at the left, or she might have been orphaned.)*
Say: Photographs like this one are valuable contributions to the historical record of the Civil War.

Teach

Reading Strategy   1

Connect **Ask:** What does Whitman mean when he says, "The genius of the United States is . . . most in the common people"? *(Students might point out that the United States is a democracy, and so the common people deserve credit for the country's achievements.)*

Literary History ☆

Poet of Controversy Walt Whitman (1819–1892) wrote innovative poetry, and the subject of his writing was sometimes controversial because some of his poems celebrated the human body. While some people hailed Whitman as a prophet and genius, others viewed him as crude and unseemly. In the same year that he wrote his great elegy to Lincoln, Whitman was fired from his job as a government clerk, reportedly because the new secretary of the interior, James Harlan, hated Whitman's poetry.

Reading Practice

Imagery and Figurative Language
Define *imagery* as descriptive language that evokes an emotional response and appeals to the senses. Define *figurative language* as words not meant to be read literally (e.g., simile, metaphor, personification). Have students find examples of imagery and figurative language in the two poems on this spread. Tell them to

list their findings on a two-column chart. Examples:

Imagery
- *arms flash in the sun; the musical clank*

Figurative Language
- *Tables in the sky; awful Cutlery*

Big Idea 3
A Poetic Revolution

In the middle of the 1800s, two poets with dramatically contrasting lives and writing styles altered the course of American poetry. Walt Whitman and Emily Dickinson explored their emotions through poetry that broke with traditional themes and forms. Their work created two diverse inspirations for poets to this day.

> *"The genius of the United States is not best or most in its executives or legislatures, nor in its ambassadors or authors or colleges . . . but always most in the common people."* **1**
>
> —Walt Whitman

Whitman's World

Walt Whitman (see pages 408–429) found poetry in the lives of everyday Americans. He took daily walks to absorb the sights and sounds of Brooklyn and its people, especially blue-collar workers. Whitman used his experiences as a reporter, teacher, laborer, and Civil War nurse to create his poetry. His distinctive style is marked by long, rollicking lines written in free verse—poetry based on the irregular rhythms of speech, rather than on traditional poetic meter. Whitman imagined his work as one long, boundless poem that expressed his all-embracing view of the world. *Leaves of Grass* captured the colorful speech and brash, optimistic spirit of a vital young nation. In an essay on the ideal poet, Ralph Waldo Emerson had observed: "The poet has a new thought; he has a whole new experience to unfold; he will tell us how it was with him, and all men will be the richer in his fortune." Inspired by Emerson's vision, Whitman saw himself as this poet.

Whitman on the War

When the Civil War came, Whitman's work reflected his sympathies for the struggles of the Union. The poems in *Drum-Taps* reflect his changing attitudes and experiences as a nurse. Whitman cared for both Union and Confederate soldiers in war hospitals. Being on the scene was essential to him, whether he was sharing the energy of city life or the grief of battle casualties. In President Abraham Lincoln, Whitman found an American hero. He celebrated the "Rail-Splitter" who had emerged from humble origins to unify the nation and felt profound grief when Lincoln was assassinated. In the elegy "When Lilacs Last in the Dooryard Bloom'd," Whitman addresses the nature of grief and embraces a theme of renewal in spite of the tragic assassination.

Dickinson's Introspection

While Whitman experienced America and its people, Emily Dickinson (see pages 437–454) observed the life of Amherst, Massachusetts, from her bedroom window, composing poetry that could turn the ordinary into the deeply meaningful. Dickinson wrote approximately 1,775 poems, though less than a dozen were published in her lifetime. She suggested that her work had to make its points subtly: "The Truth must dazzle gradually / Or every man be blind." Although Dickinson created poetry during the Civil War, her poems do not place the reader on the battlefield and in the action as Whitman's do. Instead, her themes connect the reader to moments and feelings.

In her poem on the following page, Dickinson describes the time before darkness envelops the day. Her metaphor relates sunset and darkness to death. Though this poem is not about the Civil War, it conveys a fear of dying, appropriate to a period of war. Dickinson has been described as an expert miniaturist because of the depth of expression contained in her tightly constructed poems.

Central Park, 20th century. George Luks. Oil on canvas, 31.5 x 34.4 in. Private collection.

"Cavalry Crossing a Ford"
by Walt Whitman

    A line in long array where they wind betwixt
      green islands,
    They take a serpentine course, their arms flash
      in the sun—hark to the musical clank,
    Behold the silvery river, in it the splashing
      horses loitering stop to drink,
    Behold the brown-faced men, each group, each
      person a picture, the negligent rest on the
      saddles,
5 Some emerge on the opposite bank, others are
      just entering the ford—while,
    Scarlet and blue and snowy white,
    The guidon flags flutter gayly in the wind. **2**

"The Lightning is a yellow Fork"
by Emily Dickinson

    The Lightning is a yellow Fork
    From Tables in the sky
    By inadvertent fingers dropt
    The awful Cutlery

5 Of mansions never quite disclosed
    And never quite concealed
    The Apparatus of the Dark
    To ignorance revealed.

Reading Check

Analyze Imagery How does Whitman convey a sense of motion in his poem? To how many senses does this poem appeal and in what lines?

Analyze Metaphor What two things does Dickinson compare in her poem?

INTRODUCTION **341**

Teach

Reading Check

Analyze Imagery
Answers: *Whitman conveys a sense of motion through long lines with an irregular rhythm. The imagery shows multiple perspectives of the cavalry, providing a sense of moving with the troops. The poem appeals to sight (lines 1–5) and hearing (lines 2 and 3).*

Analyze Metaphor
Answer: *A storm and a heavenly dinner party*

Literary Element   2

Poetic Language Poetry expresses experiences or insights through the imaginative use of language. **Say:** Review the poem by Whitman. How does he describe usual things in unusual ways? (*He gives them particular attention—for example, the shining weapons and the snakelike appearance of the column of men on horseback.*)

View the Art ★

In addition to painting, George Luks (1867–1933) led a colorful life as a war correspondent in Cuba, a cartoonist, and a boxer. His subjects were often society's social outcasts. Like Walt Whitman, Luks looked to the lives of common people for his inspiration.

Assess/Close

Legacy of the Period

Refer students to the quotation by Whitman: "The United States themselves are essentially the greatest poem." **Ask:** Since Whitman lived during a time when the nation's future seemed bleak, what might have caused him to make this statement? *(Whitman had faith in the nation's people and character.)*

Cultural and Literary Links

Suggest that students look for music, art, or literature that was influenced by the Civil War era.

Activities

1. **Follow up** The South believed it was a constitutional right to allow slavery, while the North disagreed. The Civil War became a focal point for many of the writings from this period. Whitman and Dickinson revolutionized poetry by breaking traditional forms and themes.

2. **Contrast Literary Periods** Students should use specific examples to support how one of the Big Ideas reflects American culture today.

3. **Visual Literacy** Students could create a timeline of landmark events in the struggle against slavery.

4. **Take Notes** Students should use the study organizer to identify main ideas in this unit and hone their note taking skills.

FOLDABLES
Study Organizer

Have students make and label the Three-Tab Book, and then write notes about the people, places, and events for each Big Idea beneath each tab.

Wrap-Up

Legacy of the Period

Up to and during the Civil War, writers shifted from Romanticism to Realism in response to the cultural and social forces affecting the nation. Depictions of slavery, and of fugitives from slavery, by Frederick Douglass and others stirred the Northern conscience and infuriated Southern planters.

Eventually, the North's resistance to slavery and the South's insistence on states' rights resulted in a bloody conflict that tore the nation apart. Civil War cemeteries and battlefields throughout Eastern and Southern states today are grim reminders of lives shattered or ended.

Walt Whitman claimed that "the United States themselves are essentially the greatest poem." Poets continue to emulate the free verse of Whitman and his exploration of the self in relationship to the world. Emily Dickinson is now recognized as one of the greatest American poets.

Her work—with its concise style, experimental grammar and punctuation, and everyday subjects transformed into the meaningful and universal—has influenced poets worldwide.

Cultural and Literary Links

◇ Whitman has influenced scores of poets, including Allen Ginsberg, who called him "dear father, graybeard, lonely old courage-teacher."

◇ One of the most famous movies ever made, *Gone with the Wind*, was based on a 1936 novel about the Civil War and Reconstruction by Southerner Margaret Mitchell.

 Literature Online

Unit Resources For additional skills practice, go to glencoe.com and enter QuickPass code GLA9800u3.

Activities

 Choose one of the following activities to explore and develop as you read this unit.

1. Follow Up Go back to the Looking Ahead section on page 329 and answer the questions.

2. Contrast Literary Periods Working in a small group, create a brief presentation for your class about how one of this time period's big ideas is reflected in American culture today. Focus your presentation on one aspect of contemporary culture, such as art, music, literature, or politics.

3. Visual Literacy Create a timeline that represents the American people and the struggles they faced during the Civil War. Use works of art, photographs, advertisements, book covers, and posters

in your presentation. Include brief descriptions of how these works reflect the period.

4. Take Notes Use this study organizer to record information about the people, settings, and events you read about in this unit.

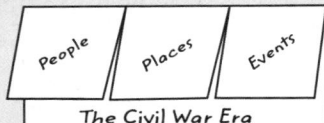
FOLDABLES
Study Organizer   **THREE-TAB BOOK**

People / Places / Events

The Civil War Era

Speaking Practice

Persuasive Language Ask students to practice their persuasive skills by responding to the following statement: "Abraham Lincoln was the greatest president in American history." Tell students to research both sides of the issue in order to argue in a classroom "town meeting." Suggest that they come prepared to state why their position is right. Tell students to use study

strategies, such as note taking, outlining, and asking questions, to understand their research materials. Suggest that they write down opposing arguments and prepare notes in defense.

PART 1

Resistance to Slavery

A Ride for Liberty, or The Fugitive Slaves, 1862. J. Eastman Johnson. 55.9 x 66.7 cm. Brooklyn Museum of Art, New York.

 View the Art Eastman Johnson claimed he based this painting on an event he witnessed near a Virginia battlefield in 1862. Scholars believe Johnson never exhibited this work because it was too controversial. What aspects of this painting might have aroused controversy in the 1860s?

"You have seen how a man was made a slave;
you shall see how a slave was made a man."

—Frederick Douglass **1**
Narrative of the Life of Frederick Douglass, an American slave

343

English Learners

DIFFERENTIATED INSTRUCTION

Intermediate Ask students to make a list of the details they notice in the painting. *(Three people on a horse; man, woman, and child; woman appears Caucasian while the man and child appear African American; woman is looking backwards; horse is moving quickly; the landscape is blurred, reddish color; the sky appears cloudy)* Discuss the details and what each might suggest about the meaning of the painting. Ask students to write two sentences describing the painting and their interpretation of the painting's meaning. Read the Frederick Douglass quotation aloud. Discuss connections between the quotation and the painting. Have students write a sentence explaining a connection.

UNIT THREE

PART 1

Analyze and Extend

Reading Strategy   1

Connect **Say:** Frederick Douglass became a powerful orator for the abolitionist cause. Yet many doubted such an educated man could ever have been a slave. This led Douglass to write his autobiography. Direct students to read the quotation from Douglass.

Ask: How does this quotation explain Douglass's purpose for writing his biography? *(Douglass intends to show how he developed into an independent person out of the conditions of slavery.)*

View the Art

Answer: *The painting would have been controversial because the man is African American and the woman is white, and because in the South, slaves' escape was illegal.*

Jonathan Eastman Johnson (1824–1906) was born in Maine and studied in the Netherlands. He became known as the American Rembrandt. His paintings are noted for their detail and their storytelling quality.

> For additional support for English Learners, see Unit 3 Teaching Resources Book, p. 19.

343

Before You Read

Focus

Bellringer Options

**Selection Focus
    Transparency 20**

**Daily Language Practice
    Transparency 31**

Or play recordings of African American spirituals other than those included in this anthology. Possibilities include "Go Tell It on the Mountain," "Deep River," and "Wade in the Water." Tell students to listen for similarities. **Ask:** What do these spirituals have in common? *(Students might point out rhythm or references to God, Jesus, and the Bible.)*

Before You Read

Three Spirituals

The Life of Harriet Tubman, #4, 1940. Jacob Lawrence. Casein tempera on hardboard, 12 x 17⅞ in. Hampton University Museum, Hampton, VA.

Who Wrote the Spirituals?

The spirituals featured here came out of the oral tradition of African Americans enslaved in the South before the outbreak of the Civil War. These "sorrow songs," as they were called, were created by anonymous artists and transmitted by word of mouth. As a result, several versions of the same spiritual may exist. According to the Library of Congress, more than six thousand spirituals have been documented, though some are not known in their entirety.

Cultures Old and New African American spirituals combined the tunes and texts of Christian hymns with the rhythms, finger-snapping, clapping, and stamping of traditional African music. The spirituals allowed enslaved Africans to retain some of the culture of their homelands and forge a new culture while facing the hardships of captive life in the United States. Many spirituals followed a call-and-response pattern in which a leader sang the verses and was answered by a group of singers. The singers often improvised the songs by changing words or adding new verses.

> *"Every tone [in the spirituals] was a testimony against slavery, and a prayer to God for deliverance from chains."*
>
> —Frederick Douglass

Enslaved African Americans sang spirituals both in worship and while laboring in the field. Many of the songs have a dual meaning, expressing both religious faith and a hunger for freedom. The *New York Tribune* published "Go Down, Moses" after Reverend Lewis Lockwood heard African Americans singing it on September 3, 1861, and submitted the lyrics.

Encoded Messages Some spirituals served as encoded messages by which enslaved field workers, forbidden to speak to each other, could communicate practical information about escape plans. Some typical code words included *Egypt,* referring to the South or the state of bondage, and the *promised land* or *heaven,* referring to the North or freedom. To communicate a message of hope, spirituals frequently recounted Bible stories about people liberated from oppression through divine intervention. The spiritual "Keep Your Hand on the Plow," for example, tells the story of Paul and Silas, who were released from prison after God sent an earthquake to free them.

Saved from Obscurity The spirituals were saved from obscurity after the Civil War by the Jubilee Singers of Fisk University in Nashville, Tennessee. To raise money for the school during a time of financial hardship, the small university choir sang spirituals to church groups around the country. The Jubilee Singers were soon in demand and eventually performed the spirituals for President Ulysses S. Grant and England's Queen Victoria.

The spirituals became a part of American pop culture, paving the way for other musical forms including blues and jazz and influencing poets such as James Weldon Johnson. When Martin Luther King Jr. led the march in Washington, D.C., for civil rights in March 1963, he quoted from the spiritual "Free at Last": "You can hinder me here, but you can't hinder me there."

Selection Skills

Literary Elements
- Refrain (SE pp. 345, 346, 349)

Three Spirituals

Listening/Speaking/Viewing Skills
- Analyze Art (TE pp. 346–348)

Reading Skills
- Analyze Historical Context (SE pp. 345, 348, 349)
- Evaluate (TE p. 342)

Writing Skills/Grammar
- Write a List (SE p. 349)
- Compare Songs and Poems (TE p. 346)

Vocabulary Skills
- Academic Vocabulary (SE p. 349)

Literature and Reading Preview

Connect to the Spirituals

What music do you turn to for inspiration or comfort? Why do you think it helps you? Discuss these questions with a partner.

Build Background

For many enslaved African Americans, the situation of the Jews in the Bible was especially poignant. According to the Bible, the Jews were forced into slavery by a pharaoh, or ruler, of Egypt. Moses, a leader of the Jews, asked the pharaoh to free his people, warning that otherwise God would send ten plagues upon the Egyptians. The plagues came, and the pharaoh released the Jews. After Egyptian soldiers chased the Jews to the shores of the Red Sea, Moses called upon God to part the waters so his people could cross. The sea rolled back for the Jews to pass but closed in on the Egyptian soldiers. When the Jews "reached the other shore," they were free people once again.

Set Purposes for Reading

Big Idea **Resistance to Slavery**

As you read, ask yourself, What role did spirituals play in the African American struggle for freedom?

Literary Element **Refrain**

A **refrain** is a line or lines repeated in a poem or song. For example, the line "Let my people go" is repeated in every stanza of the spiritual "Go Down, Moses." As you read, ask yourself, How do the refrains in each spiritual help emphasize a central idea?

Reading Strategy **Analyze Historical Context**

Understanding the context in which the spirituals were created can help you better appreciate them. Enslaved African Americans toiled long hours, were barred from communicating with each other, and were frequently threatened with violence. In spirituals, African Americans were depicted as the beloved children of a just and mighty God, destined for freedom.

Spirituals were a fundamental part of slave life. They were sung during worship, rest, work, and play. As you read the spirituals, jot down your thoughts about how they reflect the hopes and beliefs of slaves.

Learning Objectives

For pages 344–349

In studying these texts, you will focus on the following objectives:

Literary Study: Analyzing repetition.

Reading: Analyzing historical context.

Writing: Writing a list.

Before You Read

Focus

Summary

The three spirituals reproduced here represent part of the body of "sorrow songs" created by African Americans during their enslavement of more than 200 years. All three have roots in an oral tradition that combined the traditions of Christian faith and those of African music. Sung during work, during worship, and for secret communication, the spirituals are a rich part of the cultural heritage of the United States.

 For summaries in languages other than English, see Unit 3 Teaching Resources Book, pp. 20–25.

Literary History

Symbols in Spirituals In spirituals, *Egypt* and *Pharaoh* represent the South, slavery, and the slave master. *Canaan, the Promised Land, heaven* and *home* represent freedom, the North, and an end to trouble and pain. *Crossing the Jordan River* has a dual meaning: making a risky move and entering a new and better life.

Approaching Level

DIFFERENTIATED INSTRUCTION

Emerging Some students may be more familiar with *chorus* than its synonym *refrain.* Ask them to think of refrains from pop or folk songs they know. Point out that a refrain is a memory device that reinforces the main idea or emotion of a song or poem. Ask them to focus on repeated lines in the spirituals to identify the idea or emotion that is being emphasized.

Established Have students make a three-column chart or other graphic organizer to keep track of the details of each song as they read. When you begin to read the selection, model for students an example of your own response to a detail from "Swing Low, Sweet Chariot." Then, tell students to continue using the chart as they read the spirituals.

Teach

Big Idea

Resistance to Slavery

Say: How can singing be a form of resistance? (Music can bring people dignity when they are mistreated; music lifts spirits; music can communicate through rhythm or symbolic lyrics.)

Literary Element | 1

Refrain Answer: *It is part of the call-and-response structure; it emphasizes the singers' longing to be "home."*

View the Art ★

William H. Johnson (1901–1970) was a master of several artistic styles. In the 1930s he began to use a distinctive folk style to reflect the African American experience.
Ask: What specific elements of "Swing Low, Sweet Chariot" are shown in the painting? *(Students should identify the band of angels, the chariot, and the Jordan River.)* What emotion does the figure in the foreground seem to be expressing? *(Students may say that the figure seems to be welcoming or embracing the arrival of the chariot and angels.)*

Swing Low, Sweet Chariot

Swing Low, Sweet Chariot, 1944. William H. Johnson. Oil on board, 28½ x 26½ in. National Museum of American Art, Washington, DC.

Swing low, sweet chariot,
Coming for to carry me home,
Swing low, sweet chariot,
Coming for to carry me home.

5 I looked over Jordan[1] and what did I see,
Coming for to carry me home?
A band of angels coming after me,
Coming for to carry me home.

If you get there before I do,
10 Coming for to carry me home,
Tell all my friends I'm coming too;
Coming for to carry me home.

I'm sometimes up, I'm sometimes down,
Coming for to carry me home,
15 But still my soul feels heavenly bound;
Coming for to carry me home.

Swing low, sweet chariot,
Coming for to carry me home,
Swing low, sweet chariot,
20 Coming for to carry me home.

---

1. *Jordan* refers to the Jordan River. In the Book of Exodus in the Bible, when the Jews were fleeing from slavery in Egypt, they had to cross the Jordan to reach their Promised Land.

Refrain *How does the refrain function in the spiritual?* **1**

Writing Practice

Compare Songs and Poems Initiate a brief discussion. **Ask:** In what ways are songs similar to poems? *(Students might say that both contain stanzas and refrains, and both use rhyme, rhythm, repetition, figurative language, and imagery.)* Point out that spirituals can be experienced by reading them, singing them, or listening to them.

Say: Which way of experiencing the spirituals do you prefer? Write a paragraph explaining your preference.

Harriet Tubman Series No. 11, 1939-40. Jacob Lawrence. Casein tempera on gessoed hardboard, 12 x 17⅞ in. Hampton University Museum, Hampton, VA.

Go Down, Moses

Go down, Moses,
'Way down in Egypt's land;
Tell ole Pharaoh
Let my people go.

5 When Israel was in Egypt's land,
Let my people go;
Oppressed so hard they could not stand,
Let my people go.

Thus saith the Lord, bold Moses said,
10 Let my people go;
Let them come out with Egypt's spoil,
Let my people go.

The Lord told Moses what to do,
Let my people go;
15 To lead the children of Israel thro',
Let my people go.

When they had reached the other shore,
Let my people go;
They sang a song of triumph o'er.
20 Let my people go.

Go down, Moses,
'Way down in Egypt's land;
Tell ole Pharaoh
Let my people go.

Resistance to Slavery *How does this biblical allusion reflect the enslaved people's desire to escape slavery?* **2**

Big Idea | 2

Resistance to Slavery
Answer: *Enslaved people would have drawn a parallel between the Israelites' escape from Egypt and their own escape from slavery.*

View the Art ★

Jacob Lawrence (1917–2000), whose work is featured in Part 3 of Unit Five, is one of the most well-known African American artists of the 1900s. Lawrence created several series of paintings showing scenes from African American history. **Ask:** What details in this painting remind you of the spirituals sung by African American slaves? *(Students might say that the painting draws attention to the sky, particularly the stars, where the slaves looked for direction as they escaped toward the North.)*

 For an audio recording of this selection, use Listening Library Audio CD-ROM.

English Learners

DIFFERENTIATED INSTRUCTION

Intermediate Some students may have difficulty making detailed analogies between the slavery experience of the Israelites and that of African Americans. Review the basic parallels: *Egypt's land* represents the South; *Pharoah* represents slave owners; *my people* (the Israelites) represent people enslaved in America. **Ask:** What is "the other shore" in line 17? What does that phrase mean to the people singing the song? *(Students should recognize that the shore is the other side of the Jordan River, in the Promised Land. For African Americans in slavery, the other shore is the land of freedom.)*

Teach

Big Idea | 1

Resistance to Slavery
Answer: *These lines connect bondage with the hope of salvation.*

Reading Strategy | 2

Analyze Historical Context
Answer: *In the antebellum South, slavery was a form of both physical and psychological bondage. Enslaved people would have made the connection between their bondage and Paul and Silas's time in jail.*

 For additional practice using the reading skill or strategy, see Unit 3 Teaching Resources Book, p. 27.

View the Art ★

William H. Johnson (1901–1970) learned to draw by copying comics. His pursuit of a career in painting led him to Paris, Denmark, and North Africa. He focused his art on reworking traditional religious images in African American culture. **Ask:** What religious traditions of African American culture are depicted in the painting? *(The family is dressed up for church, and the entire family is going to church together.)*

 To check students' understanding of the selection, see Unit 3 Teaching Resources Book, p. 28.

Going to Church, 1940–1941. William H. Johnson. Oil on burlap, 38⅛ x 45½ in. Smithsonian American Art Museum, Washington, DC. ★

Keep Your Hand on the Plow

Mary wo' three links of chain,
Ev'ry link was Jesus' name.
Keep your hand on the plow,
Hold on.

CHORUS
5   Hold on, hold on,
Keep your hand on the plow,
Hold on.

Paul and Silas bound in jail,[1]
Had nobody for to go their bail,
10 Keep your hand on the plow,
Hold on.

Paul and Silas began to shout,
Jail doors opened and they walked out . . .

Peter was so nice and neat,[2]
15 Wouldn't let Jesus wash his feet . . .

Jesus said, "If I wash them not,
You'll have no father in this lot" . . .

Peter got anxious and he said,
"Wash my feet, my hands and head," . . .

20 Got my hand on the gospel plow,
Wouldn't take nothin' for my journey now, . . .

---

1. In the Bible (Acts 16:16–40) the Apostle *Paul* and his companion *Silas* are imprisoned, but an earthquake shakes the prison and releases them.
2. In the Bible (John 13:4–20) the Apostle *Peter* objects at first when Jesus wants to wash his feet.

Resistance to Slavery *How might these lines have helped singers and listeners endure slavery?* **1**

Analyze Historical Context *Why might enslaved people have connected with these lines in the spiritual?* **2**

Reading Practice

Evaluate Frederick Douglass wrote of spirituals, "Every tone was a testimony against slavery and a prayer to God for deliverance from chains." **Ask:** How does this spiritual support what he wrote? *(Students might say that the reference to Mary's chain and the imprisonment of Paul and Silas point to the injustice of slavery; the allusion to Jesus and Peter suggests the freedom the slaves could hope for.)*

After You Read

Respond and Think Critically

Respond and Interpret

1. Which phrases or lines from these spirituals did you find most comforting or inspiring?

2. (a)What feelings does the speaker express in lines 13–16 of "Swing Low, Sweet Chariot"? (b)Why do you think the speaker's "soul feels heavenly bound"?

3. (a)In lines 1–8 of "Go Down, Moses," what is the speaker asking Moses to do? (b)What might these lines say about the experiences and hopes of enslaved African Americans?

4. (a)Summarize the two Bible stories retold in "Keep Your Hand on the Plow." (b)Why do you think these particular stories were included in a spiritual? Explain.

Analyze and Evaluate

5. (a)What do you think is the meaning of lines 1–3 of "Keep Your Hand on the Plow"? (b)In what way do these lines illuminate the **theme**, or overall message, of the song?

6. Describe the **mood**, or overall feeling, created by each of the spirituals. Use specific examples from each song to support your response.

Connect

7. **Big Idea** **Resistance to Slavery** What elements of the spirituals helped singers and listeners endure and overcome slavery? Include details from the spirituals in your answer.

8. **Connect to the Author** From what you have read, what do you think the authors of the spirituals were like? Explain.

Literary Element Refrain

Spirituals usually contain at least one refrain that emphasizes the central idea, or **theme**, and that also helps establish the **mood**.

1. What mood is created by the refrain in "Swing Low, Sweet Chariot"?

2. In "Go Down, Moses," what impact does the repetition of "Let my people go" create?

Reading Strategy Analyze Historical Context

Spirituals often combined phrases from English hymns with harmonies and rhythms found in African music. How do spirituals reflect the history of African Americans?

 Literature Online

Selection Resources For Selection Quizzes, eFlashcards, and Reading-Writing Connection activities, go to glencoe.com and enter QuickPass code GLA9800u3.

Academic Vocabulary

*The South's economic **reliance** on slavery made the prospect of abolition an unsavory one.*

Reliance is an academic word. In more casual conversation, someone might say a man with terrible eyesight has an unavoidable **reliance** on his glasses.

To study the word further, finish the sentence below.

A person who has a **reliance** on _____ needs it/them for _____ .

Writing

Write a List Think about a modern-day issue that might be the subject of a spiritual. Write a list of five refrains that you think represent that issue. Remember that a refrain contributes to theme, mood, and rhythm. Next to each refrain, jot down a reason for your choice.

THREE SPIRITUALS **349**

Reading Strategy

They tell of enslavement and hardship. They are reminders of a difficult past.

Academic Vocabulary

Sample Sentence: *A person who has a **reliance** on an inhaler needs it for easing asthma attacks.*

Writing

Students' lists and reasons will vary. Some students may say their issues would work in a spiritual because they deal with injustice or discrimination, just as the original spirituals did.

After You Read

Assess

1. Sample answers: "Carry me home" and "heavenly bound"

2. a) Sometimes feels all right, sometimes depressed; always believes he/she will attain freedom (b) The speaker has faith.

3. (a) Demand freedom for the Jews (b) That they suffered and desired liberation

4. (a) Paul and Silas were in prison; freed by God. Peter first refuses to let Jesus wash his feet, then lets him do so. (b) To encourage people to have faith

5. (a) Remain hopeful that escape is possible (b) Faith in God helps overcome hard times.

6. Plaintive, hopeful; people are unjustly oppressed but supported by faith; students should provide details for support.

7. Comfort, hope, advice about escape; students should provide details for support.

8. Students may say the authors felt oppressed by slavery but drew strength from their religious faith and their sense of community.

> For additional assessment, see Assessment Resources, pp. 121–122.

Literary Element

1. Anticipation, hopefulness
2. Adds power to the demand

Progress Check

Can students identify a refrain?

If No → See Unit 3 Teaching Resources Book, p. 26.

Focus

Bellringer Options

**Literature Launchers DVD:
   Pre-Reading Videos**

**Selection Focus
   Transparency 21**

**Daily Language Practice
   Transparency 32**

Or on the board, **write:**
Knowledge is power.
Ask: How can education help
a person who is oppressed?
*(Students may say that learn-
ing can help one become more
persuasive and influence others
to help; education makes people
proud of their abilities.)*

Connect to the Reading Selections

Ask students if they know people
who have struggled or are struggling under oppression. Allow them
to share their responses with the
class. Then have students discuss
what they already know about
Frederick Douglass and slavery in
the American South.

Selection Skills

Comparing Literature
Across Time and Place

Learning Objectives

For pages 350–361

In studying these texts, you
will focus on the following
objectives:

Literary Study:
Comparing cultural contexts.
Comparing historical contexts.

Compare Literature About Racial Oppression

What characteristics are vital in someone who battles oppression?
The three authors compared here—Frederick Douglass, Robert Hayden,
and Quincy Troupe—portray people struggling against limitations placed
on them by society. The works of these writers show both the stubbornness of racial oppression and the potential for individuals to overcome
oppressive traditions.

from *My Bondage and My Freedom*
by Frederick Douglass..................................... autobiography 353

Frederick Douglass by Robert Hayden..................... poem 359

In Texas Grass by Quincy Troupe................................ poem 360

COMPARE THE Big Idea Resistance to Slavery

The struggle against slavery has shaped African American culture. Literature
about slavery and its legacy illustrates the resilient spirit that has helped
African Americans endure hard times with dignity, overcome slavery, and
resist the lingering effects of racism and discrimination. As you read, ask
yourself, What is each writer's attitude toward slavery or its legacy?

COMPARE Portrayals of People

A portrayal reveals the essential qualities of an individual or a group. By taking
an individual as the subject, the writer of a literary portrayal explores that individual's character and personality, in addition to the social and cultural forces
that shaped his or her life. A group portrayal reveals the traits that members
of the group have in common. As you read, ask yourself, What traits distinguish the individuals and groups portrayed in these selections?

COMPARE Historical Context

Works of literature often reflect the historical events that shape the way
people see the world and live their lives. Recognizing the historical backdrop of a selection can increase your understanding of its themes and
messages, as well as the author's purpose. As you read, ask yourself,
How would you describe the historical context of each selection?

Literary Elements
- Autobiography (SE pp. 352, 354, 358)

Reading Skills
- Analyze Cause and Effect (SE pp. 352, 356, 358; TE p. 352)

from **My Bondage and My Freedom**

Writing Skills/Grammar
- Write a Dialogue (SE p. 358)
- Critical Response (TE p. 354)
- Analyze Imagery (TE p. 360)

Study Skills/Research/Assessment
- Short Answer Questions (TE p. 356)

Listening/Speaking/Viewing Skills
- Analyze Art (TE p. 355)

Vocabulary Skills
- Connotation (SE p. 352)
- Transitive Verbs (TE p. 352)

Before You Read
from *My Bondage and My Freedom*

Meet **Frederick Douglass**
(1818–1895)

Of all of the voices raised against slavery, few were as powerful as that of Frederick Douglass's. He was, as women's rights activist Elizabeth Cady Stanton wrote, "conscious of his dignity and power, grand in his proportions, majestic in his wrath."

> *"Where justice is denied, where poverty is enforced, where ignorance prevails, and where any one class is made to feel that society is in an organized conspiracy to oppress, rob, and degrade them, neither persons nor property will be safe."*
>
> —Frederick Douglass

From Bondage to Freedom Douglass was born on a Maryland plantation and given the name Frederick Bailey. When Frederick was eight years old, he went to work as a house servant for the Auld family in Baltimore. Mrs. Auld decided to teach Frederick how to read, which violated a Maryland state law. When her husband discovered what was happening, he forbade any further reading lessons. Frederick then secretly continued his education on his own. At the age of twenty, Frederick Bailey finally escaped to freedom and changed his name to Douglass to avoid capture.

In 1841 Douglass's life took a remarkable turn. He was asked to speak at an antislavery convention in Nantucket, Massachusetts. Although he was

nervous about speaking, Douglass's speech about his experiences as a slave was so eloquent that it prompted abolitionist leaders to ask him to work as an agent for the Massachusetts Anti-Slavery Society. While Douglass toured for the society, his reputation quickly grew.

Public Life In 1845 Douglass wrote his autobiography, *Narrative of the Life of Frederick Douglass, an American Slave.* Because Douglass identified his former owner in the book, he sailed to Great Britain to avoid capture. Abolitionists welcomed Douglass and raised money to enable him to buy his freedom and return home in 1847. That same year he started publishing a newspaper, *The North Star.* The paper's masthead read: "Right is of no Sex— Truth is of no Color," proclaiming both Douglass's abolitionism and his support for women's rights.

At the outbreak of the Civil War in 1861, President Lincoln appointed Douglass one of his advisers. After the war, he remained a staunch supporter of civil rights for formerly enslaved people. Before his death in 1895, Douglass served as the marshal and recorder of deeds in Washington, D.C., and as consul general to Haiti. He also revised and republished his autobiography as *My Bondage and My Freedom* in 1855, and then again as *Life and Times of Frederick Douglass* in 1882. Douglass's autobiography remains one of the most important chronicles of the enslaved person's experience and displays the brilliance of Douglass's literary mind.

Literature Online

Author Search For more about Frederick Douglass, go to glencoe.com and enter QuickPass code GLA9800u3.

FREDERICK DOUGLASS **351**

Comparing Literature

Focus

Summary

Douglass tells of his struggle to learn to read and write. At first Mrs. Auld is happy to teach him, but then her husband insists she stop. Douglass turns to his white friends to continue learning. They help him in return for "fees" of food. Douglass's newfound knowledge creates in him a deep scorn for the institution of slavery, because he sees that it harms both the enslaved person and the slaveholder.

 For summaries in languages other than English, see Unit 3 Teaching Resources Book, pp. 31–36.

Vocabulary

Transitive Verbs Point out to students that the verbs *induce*, *vanquish*, and *censure* are transitive verbs, that is, verbs that act upon a direct object. **Ask:** Which verb would you be most likely to use for an action upon an enemy, foe, or opponent? *(vanquish)* Which verb would you use for an action upon a listener or audience? *(induce)* Which verb would you use for an action upon one who has done wrong or made a error. *(censure)*

 For additional context, see Glencoe Interactive Vocabulary CD-ROM.

Literature and Reading Preview

Connect to the Autobiography

What would your life be like if you couldn't read? Freewrite for a few minutes about the effects illiteracy might have on you.

Build Background

As a result of restrictive slave laws, Douglass had to improvise to improve his reading and writing skills. For example, while running errands for workers in the Baltimore shipyards, he observed carpenters who were painting signs on boards.

Set Purposes for Reading

Big Idea **Resistance to Slavery**

In this excerpt, Douglass reveals his thoughts about his life as an enslaved African American. As you read, ask yourself, What role does he believe that education plays in fighting slavery?

Literary Element **Autobiography**

An **autobiography** is a narrative that a person writes about his or her life. Douglass wrote about his own life in the wider historical context of slavery. As you read, ask yourself, What was Douglass's purpose in writing about his experiences?

Reading Strategy **Analyze Cause and Effect**

Analyzing cause-and-effect relationships means figuring out how a writer arranges details to show that certain events and ideas can *cause*, or bring about, certain results or *effects*. As you read, ask yourself the following questions:

- What major events does Douglass write about?
- What effects were caused by these major events?

Tip: Take Notes Use a chart to record the cause-and-effect relationships you find in the selection.

Cause	Effect
Mrs. Auld introduces Douglass to reading.	Douglass determines to attain knowledge at any cost.

Vocabulary

benevolent (bə nev´ ə lənt) *adj.* doing or desiring to do good; kind; p. 353 *The benevolent girl helped the woman who was struggling to carry bags of groceries.*

depravity (di prav´ ə tē) *n.* the state of being morally bad or corrupt; p. 353 *The brutal tactics of slave traders showed a depravity that has shocked modern citizens.*

induce (in doos´) *v.* to lead by persuasion or influence; p. 354 *The powerful speaker tried to induce the members of his audience to change their minds on the issue.*

vanquish (vang´ kwish) *v.* to defeat; p. 356 *President Lincoln decided that military force would be the only way to vanquish slavery in the South.*

censure (sen´ shər) *v.* to express disapproval of; to find fault with; to blame; p. 357 *The writer decided to censure the government policy in her report.*

Tip: Denotation and Connotation Some words that have the same dictionary definition can have different cultural definitions. For example, *benevolent* and *nice* have a similar meaning, but *benevolent* has a stronger connotation.

Reading Practice

 Analyze Cause and Effect Cause-and-effect relationships can work in a variety of ways. Explain to students that some examples of causal relationships are

- one cause can have multiple effects
- multiple causes can lead to one effect
- a causal chain can be created with one cause producing an effect, which then becomes the cause of another effect, creating a chain of events

Have students work in small groups to create examples for these relationships, starting with the statement "I overslept." As students read, have them analyze cause and effect. *(Douglass will show that several factors combined to produce the total change in Mrs. Auld's attitude toward him.)*

from

MY BONDAGE *and* MY FREEDOM

Frederick Douglass

Series No. 8. Jacob Lawrence. Casein tempera on gessoed hardboard, 12 x 17⅞ in. Hampton University Museum, VA.

I lived in the family of master Hugh, at Baltimore, seven years, during which time—as the almanac[1] makers say of the weather—my condition was variable. The most interesting feature of my history here, was my learning to read and write, under somewhat marked disadvantages. In attaining this knowledge, I was compelled to resort to indirections by no means congenial to my nature, and which were really humiliating to me. My mistress—who, as the reader has already seen, had begun to teach me—was suddenly checked in her **benevolent** design, by the strong advice of her husband. In faithful compliance with this advice, the good lady had not only ceased to instruct me, herself, but had set her face as a flint against my learning to read by any means. It is due, however, to my mistress to say, that she did not adopt this course in all its stringency at the first. She either thought it unnecessary, or she lacked

the **depravity** indispensable to shutting me up in mental darkness. It was, at least, necessary for her to have some training, and some hardening, in the exercise of the slaveholder's prerogative, to make her equal to forgetting my human nature and character, and to treating me as a thing destitute of a moral or an intellectual nature. Mrs. Auld—my mistress—was, as I have said, a most kind and tender-hearted woman; and, in the humanity of her heart, and the simplicity of her mind, she set out, when I first went to live with her, to treat me as she supposed one human being ought to treat another.

It is easy to see, that, in entering upon the duties of a slaveholder, some little experience is needed. Nature has done almost nothing to prepare men and women to be either slaves or slaveholders. Nothing but rigid training, long persisted in, can perfect the character of the one or the other. One cannot easily forget to love freedom; and it is as hard to cease to respect that natural love in our fellow creatures. On entering upon the career of a slave-

---

1. An *almanac* is an annual publication that includes calendars, weather forecasts, and other information.

Vocabulary

benevolent (bə nev´ ə lənt) *adj.* doing or desiring to do good; kind

Vocabulary

depravity (di prav´ ə tē) *n.* the state of being morally bad or corrupt

FREDERICK DOUGLASS **353**

Advanced Learners

DIFFERENTIATED INSTRUCTION

Douglass's Use of Irony In the first paragraph, Douglass introduces his quest for an education as a means of rising above the condition of slavery. He also ironically describes the education Mrs. Auld receives in order to become a "hardened" slaveholder. **Ask:** According to Douglass, what "training" did Mrs. Auld need? (*She needed to forget Douglass's status as a human being and to learn to treat him as*

a "thing" without character or intellect.) How does Douglass's ironic reference to Mrs. Auld's "education" make a larger point about slavery? (*Students may say that the reference suggests that slavery is unnatural and that it requires that slaveholders learn to ignore their natural impulses and to harden themselves.*)

Teach

Big Idea

Resistance to Slavery Say: Keep the following questions in mind as you read. What does Douglass do to resist oppression? (*He took every possible opportunity to learn how to read; he argued the issue of slavery with white children.*) How does slavery affect the oppressor? (*Students might note the change in attitude and behavior of Mrs. Auld.*)

 For an audio recording of this selection, use Listening Library Audio CD-ROM.

Readability Scores

Dale-Chall: 6.6
DRP: 63
Lexile: 1160

Comparing Literature

Teach

Reading Strategy   1

Clarify Ask: Why did Mr. Douglass's mistress go beyond her husband's instructions and try to prohibit Douglass from learning altogether? (Students may say that the mistress was persuaded that slaves should not learn, or that she wanted to show her husband that she took his concerns seriously.)

Literary Element   2

Autobiography Answer:
Slavery prevented him from obtaining an education because it corrupted Mrs. Auld, who at one time was eager to teach him.

For additional practice using the reading skill or strategy, see Unit 3 Teaching Resources Book, p. 38.

---

holding mistress, Mrs. Auld was singularly deficient; nature, which fits nobody for such an office, had done less for her than any lady I had known. It was no easy matter to **induce** her to think and to feel that the curly-headed boy, who stood by her side, and even leaned on her lap; who was loved by little Tommy, and who loved little Tommy in turn; sustained to her only the relation of a chattel.[2] I was *more* than that, and she felt me to be more than that. I could talk and sing; I could laugh and weep; I could reason and remember; I could love and hate. I was human, and she, dear lady, knew and felt me to be so. How could she, then, treat me as a brute, without a mighty struggle with all the noble powers of her own soul. That struggle came, and the will and power of the husband was victorious. Her noble soul was overthrown; but, he that overthrew it did not, himself, escape the consequences. He, not less than the other parties, was injured in his domestic peace by the fall.

When I went into their family, it was the abode of happiness and contentment. The mistress of the house was a model of affection and tenderness. Her fervent piety and watchful uprightness made it impossible to see her without thinking and feeling—*"that woman is a Christian."* There was no sorrow nor suffering for which she had not a tear, and there was no innocent joy for which she had not a smile. She had bread for the hungry, clothes for the naked, and comfort for every mourner that came within her reach. Slavery soon proved its ability to divest her of these excellent qualities, and her home of its early happiness. Conscience cannot stand much violence. Once thoroughly broken down, *who* is he that can repair the damage? It may be broken toward the slave, on Sunday, and toward the

---

2. *Chattel* is property, such as furniture or livestock. Enslaved people were sometimes referred to as *chattel*.

Vocabulary

induce (in dōōs′) *v.* to lead by persuasion or influence

---

master on Monday. It cannot endure such shocks. It must stand entire, or it does not stand at all. If my condition waxed bad, that of the family waxed not better. The first step, in the wrong direction, was the violence done to nature and to conscience, in arresting the benevolence that would have enlightened my young mind. In ceasing to instruct me, she must begin to justify herself *to* herself; and, once consenting to take sides in such a debate, she was riveted to her position. One needs very little knowledge of moral philosophy, to see *where* my mistress now landed. She finally became even more violent in her opposition to my learning to read, than was her husband himself. She was not satisfied with simply doing as *well* as her husband had commanded her, but seemed resolved to better his instruction. Nothing appeared to make my poor mistress—after her turning toward the downward path—more angry, than seeing me, seated in some nook or corner, quietly reading a book or a newspaper. I have had her rush at me, with the utmost fury, and snatch from my hand such newspaper or book, with something of the wrath and consternation which a traitor might be supposed to feel on being discovered in a plot by some dangerous spy.   **1**

Mrs. Auld was an apt woman, and the advice of her husband, and her own experience, soon demonstrated, to her entire satisfaction, that education and slavery are incompatible with each other. When this conviction was thoroughly established, I was most narrowly watched in all my movements. If I remained in a separate room from the family for any considerable length of time, I was sure to be suspected of having a book, and was at once called upon to give an account of myself. All this, however, was entirely *too late*. The first, and never to be retraced, step had been taken. In teaching me the alphabet, in the days of her simplicity and

---

Autobiography *What is Douglass saying here about the effects of slavery on his own life?*   **2**

Writing Practice

Critical Response Explain to students that Douglass sought to tell his life story and to argue against slavery. Elicit examples from the selection that show each purpose and discuss how effective the examples are. **Write the following question on the board:** How does Douglass use details from his life story to argue against slavery? Have students write a paragraph that uses a declarative form of the question as the topic sen-

tence. Have them use specific examples from the text.

The Life of Frederick Douglass #29: The war was over. The slaves were literally turned out by their masters into a world unknown to them. They had ceased to be slaves of man and became slaves of nature, 1939. Jacob Lawrence. Casein tempera on hardboard, 17 x 12. Hampton University Museum, Hampton, VA.

kindness, my mistress had given me the *"inch,"* and now, no ordinary precaution could prevent me from taking the *"ell."*[3]

Seized with a determination to learn to read, at any cost, I hit upon many expedients to accomplish the desired end. The plea which I mainly adopted, and the one by which I was most successful, was that of using my young white playmates, with whom I met in the street, as teachers. I used to carry, almost constantly, a copy of Webster's spelling book in my pocket; and, when sent of errands, or when play time was allowed me, I would step, with my young friends, aside, and take a lesson in

---

3. An *ell* is equal to forty-five inches. Douglass is referring to the adage "give him an inch, and he'll take an ell."

spelling. I generally paid my *tuition fee* to the boys, with bread, which I also carried in my pocket. For a single biscuit, any of my hungry little comrades would give me a lesson more valuable to me than bread. Not every one, however, demanded this consideration, for there were those who took pleasure in teaching me, whenever I had a chance to be taught by them. I am strongly tempted to give the names of two or three of those little boys, as a slight testimonial of the gratitude and affection I bear them, but prudence forbids; not that it would injure me, but it might, possibly, embarrass them; for it is almost an unpardonable offense to do any thing, directly or indirectly, to promote a slave's freedom, in a slave state. It is enough to say, of my warm-hearted little play fellows, that they lived on Philpot street, very near Durgin & Bailey's shipyard.

Although slavery was a delicate subject, and very cautiously talked about among grown up people in Maryland, I frequently talked about it—and that very freely—with the white boys. I would, sometimes, say to them, while seated on a curb stone or a cellar door, "I wish I could be free, as you will be when you get to be men." "You will be free, you know, as soon as you are twenty-one, and can go where you like, but I am a slave for life. Have I not as good a right to be free as you have?" Words like these, I observed, always troubled them; and I had no small satisfaction in wringing from the boys, occasionally, that fresh and bitter condemnation of slavery, that springs from nature, unseared and unperverted. Of all consciences, let me have those to deal with which have not been bewildered by the cares of life. I do not remember ever to have met with a *boy*, while I was in slavery, who defended the slave system; but I have often had boys to console me, with the hope that something would yet occur, by which I might be made free. Over and over again, they have told me, that "they believed *I* had as good a right to be free as *they* had"; and that "they did not believe God ever made any one to be a slave." The reader will

---

Comparing Literature

Teach

Literary Element   3

Autobiography **Ask:** How does Douglass's choice of the genre of autobiography enhance the impact of this statement? *(Douglass's description of boys' refusing to defend slavery gives his point more impact and credibility than if it had been presented in a work of fiction or in an essay. He is presenting information gained from personal experience.)*

View the Art ★

Lawrence used tempera paint, a mixture of pigment and water-soluble materials, such as egg yolk, to depict enslaved persons and important figures in the struggle against slavery, including Harriet Tubman and Frederick Douglass. Have students read the caption beneath the painting. **Ask:** What might the next painting in this series depict? *(Students might say it will show how African Americans struggled to make a living in a world where few cared what happened to them.)*

English Learners

DIFFERENTIATED INSTRUCTION

Intermediate Point out to students that the idiomatic expression "give him an inch and he'll take an ell" is more commonly known today as "give him an inch and he'll take a mile." Ask students if they have a saying in their home language that has a similar meaning. Such sayings usually imply a negative meaning of greediness or exploitation. However, they can imply a positive meaning of ambition and full use of opportunities. **Ask:** Do you think Douglass uses this expression in a positive or negative way? *(Students may say that Douglass is using the saying in a positive way, emphasizing his powerful ambition to learn.)*

Comparing Literature

Teach

Reading Strategy | 1

Analyze Cause and Effect
Answer: *The ironic effect was that Douglass's reading about the free states, which might have given him hope, made him feel even worse about being enslaved.*

Reading Strategy | 2

Analyze Cause and Effect
Ask: What effect did reading this anecdote about the slave and his master have on Douglass? *(His reading of this anecdote had a profound effect on him. He became hopeful that some day he too would be able to argue eloquently against slavery.)*

Literary History ☆

Return to Africa? Harriet Beecher Stowe suggested that African Americans, once freed from slavery, should find their own homeland in Africa. In a letter to Stowe, Douglass said, "The truth is, dear madame, we are here, and here we are likely to remain."
Ask: Why would Douglass have disagreed with Stowe? *(Americans who were formerly enslaved would be outsiders in Africa too—especially if they had been born in the United States.)*

---

easily see, that such little conversations with my play fellows, had no tendency to weaken my love of liberty, nor to render me contented with my condition as a slave.

When I was about thirteen years old, and had succeeded in learning to read, every increase of knowledge, especially respecting the FREE STATES, added something to the almost intolerable burden of the thought—"I AM A SLAVE FOR LIFE." To my bondage I saw no end. It was a terrible reality, and I shall never be able to tell how sadly that thought chafed my young spirit. Fortunately, or unfortunately, about this time in my life, I had made enough money to buy what was then a very popular school book, viz:[4] the "Columbian Orator." I bought this addition to my library, of Mr. Knight, on Thames street, Fell's Point, Baltimore, and paid him fifty cents for it. I was first led to buy this book, by hearing some little boys say that they were going to learn some little pieces out of it for the Exhibition. This volume was, indeed, a rich treasure, and every opportunity afforded me, for a time, was spent in diligently perusing it. Among much other interesting matter, that which I had perused and reperused with unflagging satisfaction, was a short dialogue between a master and his slave. The slave is represented as having been recaptured, in a second attempt to run away; and the master opens the dialogue with an upbraiding speech, charging the slave with ingratitude, and demanding to know what he has to say in his own defense. Thus upbraided, and thus called upon to reply, the slave rejoins, that he knows how little anything that he can say will avail, seeing that he is completely in the hands of his owner; and with noble resolution, calmly says, "I submit to my fate." Touched by the slave's answer, the master insists upon his further speaking, and recapitu-

lates the many acts of kindness which he has performed toward the slave, and tells him he is permitted to speak for himself. Thus invited to the debate, the quondam[5] slave made a spirited defense of himself, and thereafter the whole argument, for and against slavery, was brought out. The master was **vanquished** at every turn in the argument; and seeing himself to be thus vanquished, he generously and meekly emancipates the slave, with his best wishes for his prosperity. It is scarcely necessary to say, that a dialogue, with such an origin, and such an ending—read when the fact of my being a slave was a constant burden of grief—powerfully affected me; and I could not help feeling that the day might come, when the well-directed answers made by the slave to the master, in this instance, would find their counterpart in myself. . . .

I had now penetrated the secret of all slavery and oppression, and had ascertained their true foundation to be in the pride, the power and the avarice of man. The dialogue and the speeches were all redolent of the principles of liberty, and poured floods of light on the nature and character of slavery. . . . Nevertheless, the increase of knowledge was attended with bitter, as well as sweet results. The more I read, the more I was led to abhor and detest slavery, and my enslavers. "Slaveholders," thought I, "are only a band of successful robbers, who left their homes and went into Africa for the purpose of stealing and reducing my people to slavery." I loathed them as the meanest and the most wicked of men. As I read, behold! the very discontent so graphically predicted by Master Hugh, had already come upon me. I was no longer the light-hearted, gleesome boy, full of mirth and play, as when I landed first at Baltimore. Knowledge had come; light had penetrated the moral dungeon where I dwelt; and,

---

4. *Viz* is an abbreviation for the Latin word *videlicet,* meaning "namely" or "that is."

1 Analyze Cause and Effect *What was the ironic effect of Douglass's learning to read?*

5. *Quondam* means "that once was" or "former."

Vocabulary
vanquish (vang′ kwish) *v.* to defeat

Assessment Practice

 SPIRAL REVIEW **Short-Answer Questions** Short-answer questions on tests often ask students to use critical thinking skills and to cite support from the text. Present the following as a sample short-answer question: What does the way Douglass spent his money reveal about his character? *(Students might say that Douglass's choice to spend his money on a schoolbook indicates that he valued education over almost anything else.)*

☆ behold! there lay the bloody whip, for my back, and here was the iron chain; and my good, *kind master*, he was the author of my situation. The revelation haunted me, stung me, and made me gloomy and miserable. As I writhed under the sting and torment of this knowledge, I almost envied my fellow slaves their stupid contentment. This knowledge opened my eyes to the horrible pit, and revealed the teeth of the frightful dragon that was ready to pounce upon me, but it opened no way for my escape. I have often wished myself a beast, or a bird—anything, rather than a slave. I was wretched and gloomy, beyond my ability to describe. I was too thoughtful to be happy. It was this everlasting thinking which distressed and tormented me; and yet there was no getting rid of the subject of my thoughts. All nature was redolent of it. Once awakened by the silver trump[6] of knowledge, my spirit was roused to eternal wakefulness. Liberty! the inestimable birthright of every man, had, for me, converted every object into an asserter of this great right. It was heard in every sound, and beheld in every object. It was ever present, to torment me with a sense of my wretched condition. The more beautiful and charming were the smiles of nature, the more horrible and desolate was my condition. I saw nothing without seeing it, and I heard nothing without hearing it. I do not exaggerate, when I say, that it looked from every star, smiled in every calm, breathed in every wind, and moved in every storm.

I have no doubt that my state of mind had something to do with the change in the treatment adopted, by my once kind mistress toward me. I can easily believe, that my leaden, downcast, and discontented look, was very offensive to her. Poor lady! She did not know my trouble, and I dared not tell her. Could I have freely made her acquainted with the real state of my mind, and given her the reasons therefor, it might have been well for both of us. Her abuse of me fell upon me like

the blows of the false prophet upon his ass; she did not know that an *angel* stood in the way;[7] and—such is the relation of master and slave—I could not tell her. Nature had made us *friends*; slavery made us *enemies*. My interests were in a direction opposite to hers, and we both had our private thoughts and plans. She aimed to keep me ignorant; and I resolved to know, although knowledge only increased my discontent. My feelings were not the result of any marked cruelty in the treatment I received; they sprung from the consideration of my being a slave at all. It was *slavery*—not its mere *incidents*—that I hated. I had been cheated. I saw through the attempt to keep me in ignorance; I saw that slaveholders would have gladly made me believe that they were merely acting under the authority of God, in making a slave of me, and in making slaves of others; and I treated them as robbers and deceivers. The feeding and clothing me well, could not atone for taking my liberty from me. The smiles of my mistress could not remove the deep sorrow that dwelt in my young bosom. Indeed, these, in time, came only to deepen my sorrow. She had changed; and the reader will see that I had changed, too. We were both victims to the same overshadowing evil—*she*, as mistress, *I*, as slave. I will not **censure** her harshly; she cannot censure me, for she knows I speak but the truth, and have acted in my opposition to slavery, just as she herself would have acted, in a reverse of circumstances.

---

7. Douglass refers to a Bible story (Numbers 22:21–35) in which a donkey, despite being beaten by its master, Balaam, cannot go forward because its way is blocked by an angel whom Balaam cannot see.

Resistance to Slavery *What does this statement say about the institution of slavery?* **3**

Vocabulary

censure (sen′ shər) *v.* to express disapproval of; to find fault with; to blame

6. *Trump* is a trumpet.

FREDERICK DOUGLASS **357**

Comparing Literature

Teach

Big Idea 3

Resistance to Slavery
Answer: *Slavery hurts both the enslaved person and the slaveholder. The enslaved person is a victim, deprived of liberty and the ability to reach his or her potential. The slaveholder is a victim, having become dehumanized and morally corrupt.*

Political History ☆

Slavery and Civil War Douglass believed that the Union could not be saved without overthrowing slavery. He wrote dozens of editorials and speeches asserting that slavery was the cause of the conflict and that victory was impossible without emancipation.

 To check students' understanding of the selection, see Unit 3 Teaching Resources Book, p. 42.

Approaching Level

DIFFERENTIATED INSTRUCTION

 Established In the paragraph beginning "I had now penetrated the secret," Douglass describes slave owners as "a band of robbers." Point out that this metaphor expresses Douglass's deep disgust. Assign students to work in pairs to find at least one other metaphor in the paragraph that expresses Douglass's feelings about slavery. ("moral dungeon," "horrible pit")

Emerging Students may be surprised that knowledge only increases Douglass's gloom and anger. As a class, reread the paragraph on pages 356–357 that begins "I had now penetrated the secret." **Ask:** What has Douglass learned that deepens his unhappiness? (*Knowledge has given Douglass insights into the hateful nature of slavery, slave owners, and his own circumstance. Everything he sees and*

experiences reminds him that he is hopelessly trapped in a "wretched condition.")

Comparing Literature

After You Read

Assess

1. Students should compare their lives with Douglass's life.
2. (a) She helps him learn to read. (b) Uncorrupted human nature prompts people to treat each other as equals.
3. (a) She stops teaching and becomes cruel. (b) He says that slavery had made them enemies.
4. (a) White children (b) They believe he has "a right to be free."
5. (a) It is "in the pride, the power, and the avarice of man." (b) Students should provide support with their answers.
6. Some may say the Aulds have lost their conscience.
7. By not being brainwashed and by reading and thinking
8. They gave a firsthand look at the horrors of slavery.
9. Students who say they would choose as Douglass did may say the truth is worth sacrificing for. Students who say they would choose differently may say that he should have put his freedom and survival above all else.

Literary Element

1. Slavery victimizes both the enslaved person and the slaveholder.
2. Students' answers will vary.

Progress Check

Can students identify an autobiography?

If No → See Unit 3 Teaching Resources Book, p. 37.

After You Read

Respond and Think Critically

Respond and Interpret

1. How did this narrative affect your appreciation of your personal freedom?
2. (a)How does Mrs. Auld treat Douglass when he first arrives? (b)What does Douglass infer from her initial attitude toward him?
3. (a)How does Mrs. Auld's behavior toward Douglass change? (b)What does Douglass infer from these changes?

Analyze and Evaluate

4. (a)From his reading, what conclusion does Douglass draw about the foundation of slavery? (b)Do you agree with his analysis? Explain.

5. In your opinion, who is hurt more by the system of slavery—Douglass or the Auld family? Explain.

Connect

6. **Big Idea** **Resistance to Slavery** Why do you think that slave narratives such as Douglass's were an important part of the antislavery effort?

7. **Connect to the Author** Frederick Douglass was committed to the truth—so much so that he identified his former owner in his autobiography, even though doing so forced him to flee the country. Why do you think Douglass did this? Would you have made the same choice? Explain.

Literary Element Autobiography

Douglass's **autobiography** recounts his experiences during his enslavement and as a free man.

1. What do you think is Douglass's main idea or purpose in this excerpt from his autobiography?

2. Do you think Douglass presents himself as he was, or is his view biased, or one-sided? Explain.

Reading Strategy Analyze Cause and Effect

A cause can have more than one effect. An effect can also have multiple causes.

1. What effect did learning to read have on Douglass's ideas and behavior?

2. What effect did his learning have on U.S. society?

Vocabulary Practice

Denotation is the literal meaning of a word. **Connotation** is its implied, or cultural, meaning. *Mischievous* and *devilish* have similar denotations, but *mischievous* has a stronger connotation. For each pair of words with similar denotations, choose the word that has a stronger connotation.

1. benevolent   kind
2. depravity   badness
3. induce   manipulate
4. vanquish   defeat
5. censure   condemn

Writing

Write a Dialogue Imagine Frederick Douglass meeting Mrs. Auld again later in life, when he is a famous writer and a free man. What might they talk about? Write the dialogue that might ensue.

LOG ON ▶ **Literature** Online

Selection Resources For Selection Quizzes, eFlashcards, and Reading-Writing Connection activities, go to glencoe.com and enter QuickPass code GLA9800u3.

358 UNIT 3   THE CIVIL WAR ERA

Reading Strategy

1. He understood relations between enslaved persons and slaveholders, was inspired to learn more, and was discontent because of his knowledge.

2. Mrs. Auld's submission to her husband's order; the system of slavery that required people to be treated as less than human.

Vocabulary

1. benevolent   4. vanquish
2. depravity   5. condemn
3. manipulate

Writing

Students' dialogues should reflect their understanding of Douglass's and Auld's personalities and of how Douglass has changed as a free man.

Build Background

Born in Detroit, Michigan, in 1913, Robert Hayden viewed history "as a long, tortuous, and often bloody process of becoming, of psychic evolution." He created elegant, well-crafted poetry, much of it concerned with African American history and featuring prominent African American historical figures such as Nat Turner, Frederick Douglass, and Malcolm X.

Hayden wanted to be known as a poet rather than as a black poet. He believed that racial labeling restricted African American poets, placing them "in a kind of literary ghetto," where the standards of other writers were not applied to them. In 1976 Hayden was the first African American poet to be appointed poetry consultant to the Library of Congress. He died in 1980. ☆

Frederick Douglass

Robert Hayden

When it is finally ours, this freedom, this liberty, this beautiful
and terrible thing, needful to man as air,
usable as earth; when it belongs at last to all,
when it is truly instinct, brain matter, diastole,[1] systole,[2]
5 reflex action; when it is finally won; when it is more
than the gaudy mumbo jumbo of politicians:
this man, this Douglass, this former slave, this Negro
beaten to his knees, exiled, visioning a world
where none is lonely, none hunted, alien,
10 this man, superb in love and logic, this man
shall be remembered. Oh, not with statues' rhetoric,
not with legends and poems and wreaths of bronze alone,
but with the lives grown out of his life, the lives
fleshing his dream of the beautiful, needful thing.

---

1. *Diastole* (dī as' tə lē') is the period of normal relaxation of the heart between beats.
2. *Systole* (sis' tə lē) is the period of normal contraction between diastoles.

ROBERT HAYDEN **359**

> **⚙ Quickwrite**
>
> From reading this poetic portrayal, what did you learn about Frederick Douglass? Write a paragraph explaining what you learned about Douglass, using examples from the text to support your points.

Focus

Summary

Hayden's poem memorializes Frederick Douglass to all who continue to struggle for human freedom. The poem confronts the rhetoric of politicians and envisions a time when there will truly be freedom for all.

Teach

Literary Element

Repetition Writers sometimes repeat sounds, words, phrases, or stanzas in a piece of writing. Repetition increases the unity in a work and calls attention to particular ideas. **Ask:** What words or phrases does Hayden repeat in his poem? *(this, needful, beautiful, when it, the lives, and this man)*

Literary History ☆

Hayden's Achievement Just as Frederick Douglass won distinction as the first African American to consult with an American president, Robert Hayden was honored to be the first African American poetry consultant to the Library of Congress, a position that is now known as poet laureate. Hayden served so effectively he was appointed to a second term.

Comparing Literature

Focus

Summary

"In Texas Grass" depicts a nation's negligence with regard to its resources, particularly its people. Troupe uses the imagery of decay and death to communicate the sense of a people waiting in vain for compensation that may never come.

Teach

Literary Element	1

Alliteration When writers repeat consonant sounds at the beginning of words, they are using alliteration. **Ask:** Where does Troupe use alliteration in his poem? *("tracks of texas / old train cars lay" and "like photos fading")*

Build Background

Poet Quincy Troupe, born in St. Louis, Missouri, in 1939, experienced firsthand the limitations that racial discrimination placed on generations of African Americans.

In the following poem, "In Texas Grass," Troupe alludes to a "promise of forty acres & a mule." At the end of the Civil War, General William T. Sherman promised that freed African Americans would receive forty acres of land and a mule. However, few formerly enslaved African Americans ever received land, or even a mule, from the government. As a result, that phrase came to represent the failure of Reconstruction to assist African Americans emerging from slavery.

In Texas Grass

Quincy Troupe

all along the railroad
tracks of texas   **1**
old train cars lay
rusted & overturned
5   like new african governments
long forgotten by the people
who built & rode them
till they couldn't run no more
& they remind me of old race horses
10 who've been put out to pasture
amongst the weeds
rain, sleet & snow
till they die & rot away   **1**
like photos fading
15 in grandma's picture book
of old black men & women, in mississippi
texas, who sit on dilapidated porches
that fall away
like dead man's skin
20 like white people's eyes
& inside the peeling photos
old men sit, sad eyed
& waiting, waiting for worm dust
thinking of the master & his long forgotten

25 promise of forty acres & a mule
& even now, if you pass across
this bleeding flesh
ever changing landscape
you will see the fruited
30 countryside, stretching, stretching
& old black men & young black
men, sitting on porches, waiting
waiting for rusted trains
silent in texas grass

💬 Discussion Starter

Although this poem is set after the end of slavery in the United States, it describes in vivid and poignant detail slavery's legacy. With a small group, discuss the literal and figurative examples the poem gives of the conditions African Americans experienced after slavery. What conclusions about the journey from slavery to equality can you draw from these examples? Share your group's conclusions with the rest of the class.

Writing Practice

Analyze Imagery Quincy Troupe uses vivid images to appeal to readers' compassion for the ignored and oppressed. Tell students to reread the poem and find three images that elicit emotion. For each image, they should write a brief explanation of the emotional effects of the words. Ask students to compare the images they find and state what they have in common.

Wrap-Up: Comparing Literature

Across Time and Place

- from *My Bondage and My Freedom* by Frederick Douglass

- *Frederick Douglass* by Robert Hayden

- *In Texas Grass* by Quincy Troupe

COMPARE THE Big Idea Resistance to Slavery

Writing About Literature In the three selections you have read, each writer uses a different **tone**, or attitude toward his subject. How would you describe the tone used by each writer? Whose tone is most optimistic? Whose is most bitter? Write a brief essay in which you compare the tone used by each writer. Cite evidence from the selections to support your conclusions.

COMPARE Portrayals of People

Speaking and Listening With a partner, review the three selections to identify several passages that portray an individual, such as Frederick Douglass in the excerpt from his autobiography or in Hayden's poem, or a group, such as the African Americans "waiting for rusted trains / silent in Texas grass" in Troupe's poem. Discuss how each passage relates to the oppression of slavery or racial discrimination. Then share your conclusions with the class in an oral report.

COMPARE Historical Context

Group Activity These selections treat both the progress and the setbacks in the journey of African Americans toward liberty and equality. With a small group, discuss the following questions.

1. What is the historical context that shapes each selection?

2. How effective is each writer's use of historical background? Which author presents the most compelling rendition of historical events?

3. Which of the selections most sparked your interest in the historical context? Explain.

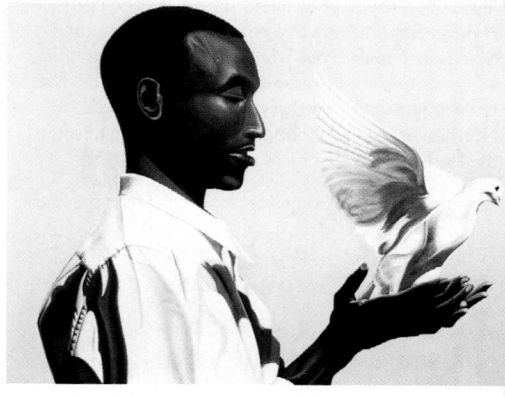

Be Free Three, 21st c. Kaaria Mucherera. Oil and acrylic on canvas, 30 x 40 in. Private collection.

 Literature Online

Selection Resources For Selection Quizzes, eFlashcards, and Reading-Writing Connection activities, go to glencoe.com and enter QuickPass code GLA9800u3.

COMPARING LITERATURE **361**

Assess

Compare the Big Idea

 Writing About Literature

When evaluating essays, make sure that students understand the concept of tone and that they offer support from the text.

Compare Portrayals of People

Speaking and Listening

Instruct partners to share ideas and to support conclusions by citing evidence from the selections.

Compare Historical Context

Group Activity

Make sure that all students in the group are given a chance to express their views and that all students support their opinions by citing evidence from the text.

View the Art

Mucherera's painting shows a black man setting loose a dove. **Ask:** How does this painting reflect the themes addressed by the three selections? *(The dove in this painting is a symbol of peace and freedom, which connects with the themes of an oppressed people seeking freedom.)*

For additional assessment, see Assessment Resources, pp. 123–124.

Approaching Level

DIFFERENTIATED INSTRUCTION

Emerging To help students organize their Writing About Literature essays, tell them to use a four-column graphic organizer to record evidence as they review the tone in the three selections they have read. Students should use the first column to set the categories: Evidence of Optimistic Tone, Evidence of Bitter Tone. They should record related details from the three poems in the three remaining columns.

The Douglass selection is far longer than the two poems and may naturally produce more evidence. Remind students that the purpose of the essay is to compare quality of tone—optimism or bitterness of tone—rather than quantity of material.

Focus

Literary History

Bellringer Options

Daily Language Practice Transparency 33

Or lead a discussion on the importance of eyewitness testimony. **Ask:** How does eyewitness testimony affect one's understanding of a crime, an accident, or a historical event? *(Students may say that eyewitnesses provide factual details about events as well as personal impressions that make events more vivid and real to others.)*

View the Photograph ★

In Sarah Gudger's interview, recorded in 1937, Gudger recalls the backbreaking labor and chronic cruelty of slavery, but she also mentions a childhood memory of a night when stars fell like rain: the famous meteor shower of 1833. **Ask:** Why was it fortunate that WPA writers were able to record stories such as these in the 1930s? *(By then, few survivors of slavery were left, so it was fortunate that WPA writers were able to record the remaining survivors' tales before they were lost.)*

 For an activity related to this selection, see Unit 3 Teaching Resources Book, pp. 44–45.

Learning Objectives

For pages 362–363

In studying this text, you will focus on the following objectives:

Literary Study: Analyzing literary periods.

Reading: Evaluating historical influences.

Slave Narratives and Civil War Memoirs, Letters, and Diaries

I N THE NINETEENTH CENTURY, MANY writers shared their personal accounts of the two major issues of the day—slavery and the Civil War. These writings, which recount the emotions their authors felt, the details they saw, and the battles they fought, contribute much to the understanding of this tumultuous time in the United States.

Accounts of Slavery

Nineteenth-century African American writers, such as Frederick Douglass (pp. 351–358) and Sojourner Truth (pp. 368–371), told variations of one compelling story—the story of life in slavery, escape from bondage, and life as a free person. These accounts, called **slave narratives,** were written as early as 1760 and continued to be written after the Civil War. The pre-war narratives were in part intended to recruit Northerners to the abolitionist cause, especially after the Fugitive Slave Act was passed in 1850. **1**

> *"Reader, be assured this narrative is no fiction. I am aware some of my adventures may seem incredible; but they are, nevertheless, strictly true."*
>
> —Harriet Jacobs
> from Preface to *Incidents in the Life of a Slave Girl,* 1861

After the Civil War, emancipated slaves, such as Elizabeth Keckley, who had worked for Mary Todd Lincoln as a dressmaker, continued to write autobiographies. Many writers hoped to show how well they had succeeded in a free society after the war. Others, especially those later in the century, expressed disappointment with the restrictions they still encountered.

Sarah Gudger, age 121. North Carolina. Library of Congress photo. ★

From 1936 to 1938, during the Depression, writers and journalists from the Works Progress Administration (WPA) interviewed more than 2,300 former slaves and recorded their memories of the past. These narratives are a rich source of details about life on plantations and in cities.

Slave narratives have had an influence on modern literature as well, in the works of such writers as Richard Wright (pp. 899–908), Ernest J. Gaines, Alice Walker (pp. 1161–1165), and Toni Morrison (pp. 1308–1314).

362 UNIT 3   THE CIVIL WAR ERA

Writing Practice

Write Interview Questions Have students assume the role of writers and journalists from the Works Progress Administration. Their assignment is to interview former slaves. Tell students to prepare for the interviews by writing a list of ten questions that they may ask. Students may wish to do some research on the historical period and on slave narratives in order to write more informed and more specific questions for the interview. Remind students that their questions should be tactful and respectful.

> "I hope both you and Johnston will write the history of your campaigns. Every one should do all in his power to collect and disseminate the truth, in the hope that it may find a place in history and descend to posterity."
>
> —Robert E. Lee
> letter to Confederate General
> P. G. T. Beauregard, 1865

Memoirs, Letters, and Diaries

Many who lived through the Civil War felt that it was the central event of their lives. Writers on both sides composed memoirs, letters, and diaries. These accounts ranged from those of generals recollecting great battles, to soldiers commenting on life on the battlefields, to civilians recounting details from the home front, especially in the South, where the battlefield and the home front were side-by-side.

Mark Twain persuaded his friend Ulysses S. Grant to write his acclaimed *Personal Memoirs*, which he completed a week before he died in 1885. Union Generals William T. Sherman, Philip H. Sheridan, and George B. McClellan also published memoirs.

The letters of Confederate General Robert E. Lee were saved and published after his death. Some letters, such as his letter to Grant agreeing to release prisoners of war on both sides, give details of the war

 Literature Online

Literature and Reading For more about slave narratives and Civil War memoirs, letters, and diaries, go to glencoe.com and enter QuickPass code GLA9800u3.

and its aftermath. Others, such as his letters to his family, including the letter to his son (pp. 382–386), express concern and describe the hardships of his troops, many of whom had no shoes.

Soldiers—often farm boys who had never been away from home—also wrote to their families describing the excitement, horrors, and hardships of war as well as their longing for home.

Diarists such as Mary Chesnut (pp. 374–380) and Rachel Cormany documented everyday events along with the worries, loneliness, and difficulties caused by the war. Chesnut recounts her fear as the Union army swept through the South. These diaries provide rich detail about life on the home front.

These first-person accounts of slavery and the Civil War provide insight into what it was like to be enslaved, to face an enemy who was also a countryman, and to remain on the home front as family and friends left for war. Nineteenth-century writers documented their tumultuous lives and times to understand and preserve their stories. Today, their work offers us great historical insights.

Ulysses S. Grant, American Civil War general, and later president, writing his memoirs at Mount McGregor, New York, 1885.

Respond and Think Critically

1. How might slave narratives have influenced the abolitionist cause?

2. A memoir, unlike an autobiography, focuses on only part of the writer's life, often a significant part. What are some reasons a person might choose to write a memoir? Explain.

3. Why are personal diaries and letters often of interest to general readers in later times?

LITERARY HISTORY **363**

363

Focus

Summary

The article showcases the Underground Railroad Freedom Center in Cincinnati, Ohio. It begins by examining contemporary feelings about American slavery. It then gives details about the museum experience: the brutality of American slavery is presented in two exhibits, along with an exhibit that concentrates on the struggles against bondage and oppression today.

 For summaries in other languages and for activities related to this selection, see Unit 3 Teaching Resources Book, pp. 46–54.

Reading Strategy | 1

Question To ask good questions about a text, a student should skim it first. This type of quick reading prepares students to read the text more thoroughly the second time. This second reading will yield more substantive questions. Remind students that when they are pre-reading, it is not necessary to understand every word or idea.

 For an audio recording of this selection, use Listening Library Audio CD-ROM.

Readability Scores

Dale-Chall: 8.8
DRP: 68
Lexile: 1240

Learning Objectives

For pages 364–367

In studying this text, you will focus on the following objectives:

Reading:
Analyzing and evaluating informational text. Connecting to contemporary issues.

Set a Purpose for Reading

As you read, ask, How do these museums educate us about slavery and the struggle for freedom?

Preview the Article

1. What clues to the content of the article do the photographs on pages 365–367 provide?
2. Skim the first paragraph. From it, what do you think that this article might teach you about slavery?

Reading Strategy Question

As you read, ask these questions:

1 • How is this idea important? Why?
  • Do I understand this passage?
  • How does this information relate to what I already know?

Record your answers in a chart.

Question	Answer
How is this idea important?	

Slavery Under
GLASS

New African American–history museums try to balance authenticity and to uplift.

By RICHARD LACAYO

THE GLASS-WALLED MAIN ENTRY OF THE UNDERGROUND Railroad Freedom Center in Cincinnati, Ohio, faces south across the banks of the Ohio River. The center faces that direction for good reason—the river is at the heart of the story of the Underground Railroad. Separating free-soil Ohio from slave-holding Kentucky, the Ohio River was a desperate crossing point for runaway slaves. The river's north banks were the site of persistent low-intensity warfare between abolitionists and armed slave owners, who were permitted by law to pursue their human "property" into free states. In that era of escalating confrontation, Cincinnati and nearby towns became important way stations in the Underground Railroad. This informal network of safe houses, sympathetic whites, and free African Americans helped conduct escaped slaves to safety.

African American Life in Focus

The Freedom Center is part of a wave of more than 20 new museums dedicated to African American history that are in development around the country. They include the U.S. National Slavery Museum in Fredericksburg, Virginia, the International African American Museum in Charleston, South Carolina, the National Museum of African American History and Culture in Washington, D.C., and the Reginald F. Lewis Museum of Maryland African History and Culture in Baltimore, Maryland. In addition, numerous locales from the 20th century civil rights movement, like the Montgomery, Alabama, bus stop

---

Writing Practice

Persuasive Letter After students have learned the purpose and features of the Underground Railroad Freedom Center, discuss with the class the educational benefits of the museum to students.

Say: Write a persuasive letter to your teacher or school principal, proposing that your class make a field trip to the Freedom Center. Tell students to develop arguments that will particularly appeal to their audience and to emphasize features of the Freedom Center that support those points. If necessary, have students do additional research into the current exhibits at the Freedom Center. Briefly review the form of a business letter before students begin to write.

where Rosa Parks was arrested, are being turned into monuments and pilgrimage points. Clearly, the story of African American life, for so long passed over in near silence, is finally being set down in stone.

The Delicate Subject of Slavery

All the same, telling the part of that story concerning slavery can be tricky. Any museum needs to inspire and instruct. It also needs to bring in paying customers. Slavery is one of the most shameful chapters of American history, but shameful stories are not the kind that everybody wants to pay money to hear.

"There is a reluctance on the part of African Americans and whites to deal with slavery," says former Virginia Governor Doug Wilder. He conceived the National Slavery Museum, scheduled to open in 2007. "People don't want to discuss it. 'Let's get past it,' they say. Well, I say that attitude is insulting to our history. We need to develop a conscious awareness of how far we've come and who we are."

The museum envisioned by Wilder, a descendant of enslaved persons, will unabashedly be a museum about the brutal merchandising of human beings. The Freedom Center in Cincinnati, which cost $110 million to build and hopes to attract 250,000 visitors each year, is more cautious about its approach to a difficult subject. Even the center's name sidesteps the loaded word slavery. By taking the Underground Railroad as its focus, the center gets to emphasize biracial resistance, not racial victimization.

The Underground Railroad was a rare triumph of African American and white cooperation in those days, not the far more usual story of white oppression. "The story of the Underground Railroad allows you to talk about slavery in a way that's productive, positive, and uplifting," says Ed Rigaud, the center's president. ☆

Using the Past to Heal the Present

The project was first conceived 11 years ago by Robert C. Harrod. He is the executive director of the regional chapter of what was then called the National Conference of Christians and Jews, now the National Conference of Community and Justice. His hope was that it could help improve race relations in Cincinnati—it was only in 2002 that the Ku Klux Klan stopped its annual mounting

of a Christmas tree in the city's main square. The desire for reconciliation is built into the center's mission. Its focus, says Spencer Crew, its executive director, "is not about finger pointing."

More than that, it also aims to be America's first museum intended not just to arouse feelings but also to resolve them safely. Concerned that people might exit the exhibition galleries with feelings of guilt (whites), anger (African Americans), and resentment (both), the center offers a final room that is not a gallery of any kind but a space for discussion. Trained facilitators will encourage visitors to examine their feelings and share them.

"Productive, positive, uplifting"—is this any way to tell a story so full of suffering? Well, maybe it is. For one thing, the

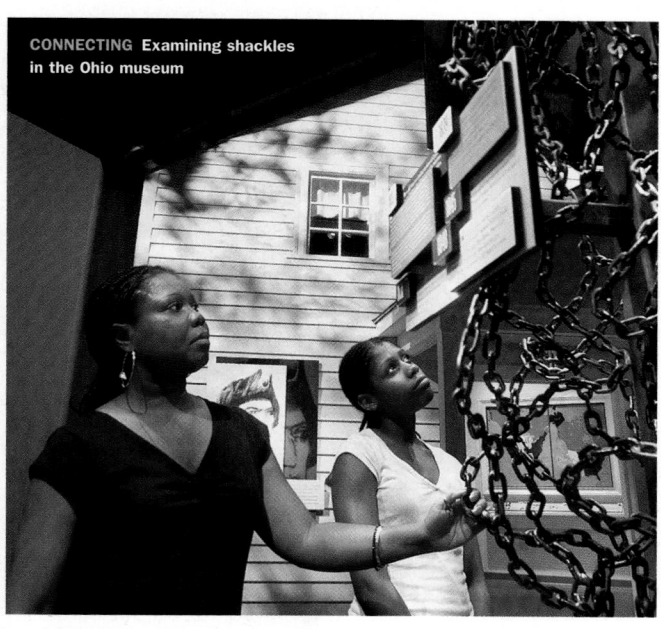
CONNECTING Examining shackles in the Ohio museum

SLAVERY UNDER GLASS **365**

TIME

Teach

Reading Strategy

Connect Say: Recall an event that caused someone you know to suffer deeply, and imagine how the person would feel if he or she were not allowed to talk about it. Allow students to share their experiences. Then ask if these experiences help them understand former governor Wilder's comment.

Political History ☆
Abolitionism Prominent African Americans, such as Frederick Douglass and Sojourner Truth, worked to fight slavery. Douglass became a member of the Massachusetts Anti-Slavery Society, and Truth was appointed by President Lincoln as a counselor to escaped slaves in Washington, D.C.

Approaching Level

DIFFERENTIATED INSTRUCTION

Emerging Point out that subheads provide useful prompts for questions about the text. Read the first subhead with the class and model how you would ask a question based on that subhead. *(Possible question: How is African American life being put into focus?)* As a class, read the first subsection to see how the text offers an answer to the question.

Established Explain that a "loaded word" is one that conveys a strong emotional impression in addition to its literal meaning. Often, loaded words carry an extremely negative emotional meaning. **Ask:** Why is *slavery* a loaded word? Have students answer the question by drawing a concept map and filling it with the impressions and associations they have for the word.

TIME

Teach

A STARRY OPENING GALA

Joining in the center's festivities were Courtney Vance (left), Angela Bassett, and Oprah Winfrey, who said the Freedom Center honors those who "paid the price for me to be who I am."

Reading Strategy

Question The author suggests that despite its fame, the Underground Railroad succeeded on only a small scale. **Say:** Let's think of some questions that might help us understand why this was so. Tell students to consider what it might have been like to manage the Underground Railroad: the communication required and the large number of slaves involved. Students may jot down notes as ideas come to mind. Have them use their notes to pose questions aloud. Guide students to see how asking questions can lead to a deeper understanding of a subject.

View the Photograph ★

Structures like this served as holding pens for slaves who were being sold or as temporary housing for slaves traveling with their masters. The structures were also used to confine and punish slaves who had angered their masters. **Ask:** What features of this building would make it an unpleasant place to be? (The building has few openings; it would be dark, hot, and suffocating for those inside.)

Freedom Center is in many respects still the thing it claims not to be: a museum of slavery. Its largest feature is a two-story, rough-hewn log cabin rescued from a Kentucky farm. Built by slave trader Captain John W. Anderson, the structure held dozens of men and women waiting to be sold, shackled in pairs to a central chain and confined to sitting or lying. It lets visitors imagine themselves in the cramped space where enslaved persons were crammed. Carl Westmoreland, a historian and preservationist, was responsible for rescuing the cabin. The great-grandson of an enslaved blacksmith, Westmoreland says, "It's a place that's ugly and dark. But you've got to look at the ugly side of the journey to see the glory of our emergence."

Eyes Still on the Prize

The longest of the center's display areas is a series of galleries devoted to the history of slave labor, the miseries of the Middle Passage across the Atlantic from Africa, and the resistance struggles that eventually led to emancipation. Visitors can see an image of the scarred back of a whipped enslaved person and hear actors reading the testimonies of enslaved people who described the suffering they endured.

AS IT STOOD It took six years to dismantle and reassemble the pen.

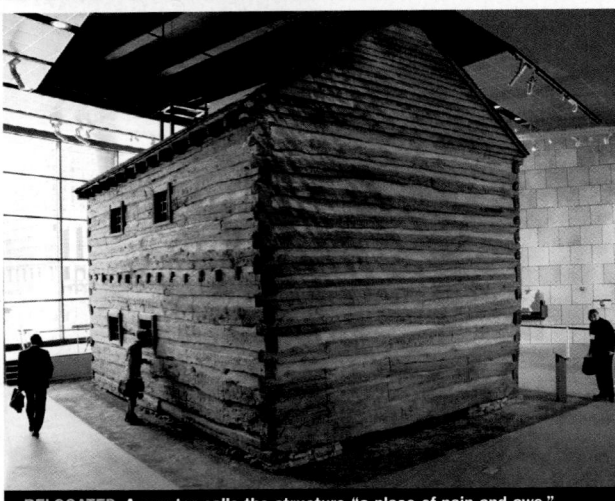

RELOCATED A curator calls the structure "a place of pain and awe."

Writing Practice

 Journal Entry Direct students to study the photograph of the slave pen. **Say:** What would it be like to be locked inside such a place? Write a journal entry of a freed slave remembering the day when he or she arrived there. Prompt students' thinking by asking what the occupants might see inside such a building. What would the temperature and air quality be like? Encourage students to use sensory details to help their readers imagine what someone would see, hear, smell, and feel in the pen.

CINCINNATI A gallery at the Underground Railroad Freedom Center

By placing so much stress on the system of escape routes for runaways, the center takes the risk of inflating the real importance of the Underground Railroad. By some estimates, of the 4 million enslaved persons in the United States when the Civil War began, no more than 100,000 benefited from the system. But that emphasis is essential for the center to sustain its uplifting message. Its next significant section of exhibits is the "Hall of Everyday Freedom Heroes." It offers portraits and touch-screen information about a whole spectrum of figures from throughout the world who fought for the rights of religious and racial minorities, women, and just about anyone who ever stood up against an oppressive system.

That leads in turn to a final area, called "The Struggle Continues." Here interactive computer displays allow you to learn about ongoing efforts against oppression, hunger, illiteracy, bigotry, and modern-day slavery.

So you may well leave the last galleries with your mind far from the horrors of the slave experience or even the struggles against it. But the center will also have temporary exhibitions that will expand on both themes. "We will prove ourselves to be the museum of the future," promises Naomi Nelson, the center's director of education. She may be right about that. If it also always manages to do justice to the past, the future looks O.K.

— UPDATED 2006, from TIME, August 30, 2004, and People, September 6, 2004

Respond and Think Critically

Respond and Interpret

1. Write a brief summary of the main ideas in this article before you answer the following questions. For help on writing a summary, see page 79.

2. What was your initial reaction to the idea of creating museums dedicated to the experience of slavery? How did your reaction change after reading the article?

3. (a)What is the emphasis of the Freedom Center? (b)Why do you think this approach is favored?

4. (a)What role did Cincinnati play in the antislavery movement? (b)How is the struggle for freedom a contemporary issue as well as a historical one?

Analyze and Evaluate

5. According to the article, why is it difficult to create a successful museum dedicated to the subject of slavery?

6. (a)How do you think the author feels that the goals of the Freedom Center compare with those of other slavery museums? (b)What evidence from the text supports your answer?

Connect

7. How do you think Frederick Douglass, Sojourner Truth, and other abolitionists would want the subject of slavery to be taught today? How do you think it should be taught?

SLAVERY UNDER GLASS **367**

Advanced Learners

DIFFERENTIATED INSTRUCTION

Multimedia Presentation Assign students to work in groups to prepare a multimedia presentation about the Freedom Center. Tell students to develop a three-minute commercial for the Center, using text, images, and sound. Students should use the Internet and other sources to gather material for their presentation. Their target audience is parents, and the purpose is to encourage them to bring

their children to the museum. The presentation should include practical details about the museum's location and hours of operation as well as information about the purposes and nature of its exhibits.

TIME

Assess

1. Students' summaries should accurately describe all the main points of the article.

2. Students should describe their reactions and explain how their reactions changed.

3. (a) To teach about cooperative resistance to slavery (b) The Freedom Center wants to uplift people by teaching them about how some enslaved persons escaped.

4. (a) It was a meeting point for the Underground Railroad. (b) People continue to struggle against oppression, hunger, illiteracy, and slavery.

5. Slavery is a sensitive topic in American history. Some people will not visit a museum that makes them upset or angry.

6. (a) The author feels that the Freedom Center is more cautious than other slavery museums. (b) The author mentions that the center's mission includes the desire for reconciliation.

7. Students may say that Douglass, Truth, and other abolitionists would want slavery to be presented with accuracy. Students should support their ideas with well-reasoned thoughts.

For additional assessment, see Assessment Resources, pp. 125–126.

Before You Read

Focus

Bellringer Options

Selection Focus
   Transparency 22
Daily Language Practice
   Transparency 34

Or point out that the Fifteenth Amendment to the U.S. Constitution states that citizens can vote regardless of their "race, color, or previous condition of servitude." The amendment does not mention women, who would not win the right to vote for 55 years.

Literary History ☆

Speaking Truth When Sojourner Truth rose to speak, some women feared she would focus on antislavery issues and distract attention from women's rights. They urged Frances Gage, who was presiding at the meeting, not to let her speak. Gage did otherwise.

Before You Read

And Ain't I a Woman?

Meet **Sojourner Truth**
(1797–1883)

Armed with common sense and sharp wit, Sojourner Truth spent her long life battling slavery and demanding voting rights for women. Nearly six feet tall, Truth had a deep, smooth voice that quieted rowdy crowds and won devoted supporters. She believed that resisting injustice was her divinely ordained duty.

Sojourner Truth, whose given name was Isabella, was born into slavery in Ulster County, New York, a Dutch-speaking region. She endured cruel slave owners, backbreaking work, and harsh beatings until, at age twenty-nine, she escaped. Given refuge by Isaac and Maria Van Wagener, she took the

> "There is no use in one man, or one nation, to try to do or be everything. It is a good thing to be dependent on each other for something, it makes us civil and peaceable."
>
> —Sojourner Truth

name Isabella Van Wagener. Since childhood, Isabella had believed she saw visions and heard messages sent from God. In about 1843, she changed her name to Sojourner Truth—meaning that she would become a sojourner, or visiting traveler, spreading the truth of God—and started to preach throughout the northeastern United States. Before long, she began to weave antislavery messages into her preaching.

Truth also became an ardent champion of women's rights. In 1850 she began traveling the Midwest, attracting large crowds wherever she spoke. On this tour, in Akron, Ohio, she delivered what would become her most famous address, "And Ain't I a Woman?" Truth then moved to Battle Creek, Michigan, where she continued to agitate for women's rights and abolition. After the start of the Civil War in 1861, Truth worked to gather supplies and funds for black volunteer regiments. Toward the end of the war, Truth moved to Washington, D.C., where she accepted a job with the National Freedmen's Relief Association, counseling former slaves. At the age of seventy-eight, Truth returned to Battle Creek, where she remained until her death.

Literature Online

Author Search For more about Sojourner Truth, go to glencoe.com and enter QuickPass code GLA9800u3.

Selection Skills

Reading Skills
- Evaluate Argument (SE pp. 369–371; TE p. 370)

← **And Ain't I a Woman?** →

Writing Skills/Grammar
- Persuasive Speech (SE p. 371)

Literary Elements
- Oratory (SE pp. 369, 371)
- Rhetorical Question (TE p. 369)

Vocabulary Skills
- Word Usage (SE pp. 369, 371)
- Multiple Meanings (TE p. 369)

Literature and Reading Preview

Connect to the Speech

Can one person's stand against injustice make a difference? Discuss your opinion with a partner. Use examples from your own experience to support your views.

Build Background

On the second day of the 1851 Women's Rights Convention where Truth gave her speech, a number of male ministers spoke, insisting that women were too weak and intellectually inferior to vote. One man gave religious reasons against women's suffrage, or right to vote. Truth's speech is her answer to these critics. Her speech was not written or rehearsed, so many versions have survived—some in what might be interpreted as the dialect of an enslaved person from the South. In reality, Truth spoke Standard English and was from New York.

Set Purposes for Reading

Big Idea **Resistance to Slavery**

As you read, ask, What obstacles and challenges did Sojourner Truth face as she spoke out against injustices of the time?

Literary Element **Oratory**

Oratory is the art of effective public speaking, or the use of persuasive skills when speaking. Oratory is common in politics, law, and religion. As you read the speech, ask yourself, How does Truth use persuasive devices, such as providing evidence from her personal experience, to achieve her purpose?

Reading Strategy **Evaluate Argument**

To **evaluate** is to make a judgment or form an opinion about something you read. Evaluating a persuasive text means determining whether its arguments are convincing. Think about how effective Truth is in convincing you to adopt her positions.

Tip: Take Notes Use a chart to evaluate Truth's arguments.

Assertion	Reason	Effective?
I have ploughed and planted, and gathered into barns, and no man could head me!	To prove that she is as physically strong as a man	

Learning Objectives

For pages 368–371

In studying this text, you will focus on the following objectives:

Literary Study: Analyzing oratory.

Reading: Evaluating argument.

Writing: Writing a speech.

Vocabulary

racket (rak´ it) *n.* loud noise; clamor; din; p. 370 *We couldn't hear over the racket of the saw.*

borne (bôrn) *v.* past participle of bear; given birth to; produced; p. 370 *The peach trees have not borne any fruit yet.*

oblige (ə blīj´) *v.* to make grateful or indebted; to do a favor or service for; p. 370 *I would be obliged if you would remove your hat.*

Tip: Word Usage When you encounter new words, it might help you to answer a specific question about the word. Example: *What is something that makes a **racket**?*

Before You Read

Focus

Summary

In this famous speech supporting women's rights, Sojourner Truth recites commonly accepted arguments against women's rights—and then destroys each one by reference to personal experience, logic, and common sense.

 For summaries in languages other than English, see Unit 3 Teaching Resources Book, pp. 49–52.

Vocabulary

Multiple Meanings Point out to students that *racket* has several meanings. It refers to a loud noise, to a criminal scheme, or to an item of sporting equipment. When confronted with words with multiple meanings, readers should pay close to the context of the word. **Ask:** In the first sentence of Sojourner Truth's speech, what is *racket* referring to? *(The noise generated by a large group of people)*

 For additional context, see Glencoe Interactive Vocabulary CD-ROM.

Interactive Read and Write

Other options for teaching this selection can be found in

- Interactive Read and Write for English Learners, pp. 115–122
- Interactive Read and Write for Approaching-Level Learners, pp. 115–122
- Interactive Read and Write for On-Level Learners, pp. 115–122

 For a pre-reading video for this selection, use Literature Launchers DVD: Selection Launcher.

English Learners

DIFFERENTIATED INSTRUCTION

Beginning Sojourner Truth's speech contains some idioms that may be unfamiliar to students. Have students work together to interpret the meanings of these expressions: "out of kilter," "in a fix," and "bear the lash." Then ask volunteers to explain the meanings.

Intermediate The ministers made three assertions: women were physically weak, less intelligent, and Christ was a man. Have students note Truth's responses to these three points. Ask them to explain why her arguments are persuasive.

Teach

Big Idea 1

Resistance to Slavery
Answer: *Her experience of slavery showed that men and women are equal. She held up just as well as any man under slavery.*

Reading Strategy 2

Evaluate Argument **Answer:**
He is one of the male speakers who insisted that women are not intelligent enough to vote. Truth addresses him because she is exhibiting her intelligence.

Literary Element 3

Rhetorical Question
Ask: What rhetorical questions does Truth use to persuade her audience? *("Ain't I a woman?" and "Where did your Christ come from?")*

 For additional literary element practice, see Unit 3 Teaching Resources Book, p. 61.

 For an audio recording of this selection, use Listening Library Audio CD-ROM.

Readability Scores

Dale-Chall: 3.7
DRP: 49
Lexile: 750

 To check students' understanding of the selection, see Unit 3 Teaching Resources Book, p. 65.

Anna Washington Derry, 1927. Laura Wheeler Waring. Oil on canvas, 20 x 16 in. Gift of the Harmon Foundation. Smithsonian American Art Museum, Washington, DC.

And Ain't I a Woman?

Address to the Ohio Women's Rights Convention, 1851

Sojourner Truth

1 **Resistance to Slavery** *How does Truth connect slavery and women's rights?*

2 **Evaluate Argument** *Who is the "little man in black"? Why is it appropriate that she addresses him during her speech?*

Vocabulary

racket (rak´ it) *n.* loud noise; clamor; din
borne (bôrn) *v. past participle of* bear; given birth to; produced
oblige (ə blīj´) *v.* to make grateful or indebted; to do a favor or service for

Well, children, where there is so much **racket** there must be something out of kilter.[1] I think that 'twixt[2] the Negroes of the South and the women at the North, all talking about rights, the white men will be in a fix pretty soon. But what's all this here talking about? That man over there says that women need to be helped into carriages, and lifted over ditches, and to have the best place everywhere. Nobody ever helps me into carriages, or over mud-puddles, or gives me any best place! And ain't I a woman? Look at me! Look at my arm. I have ploughed and planted, and gathered into barns, and no man could head[3] me! And ain't I a woman? I could work as much and eat as much as a man—when I could get it—and bear the lash as well! And ain't I a woman? I have **borne** thirteen children, and seen them most all sold off to slavery, and when I cried out with my mother's grief, none but Jesus heard me! And ain't I a woman?

Then they talk about this thing in the head; what's this they call it? [Intellect, someone whispers.] That's it, honey. What's that got to do with women's rights or Negroes' rights? If my cup won't hold but a pint, and yours holds a quart, wouldn't you be mean not to let me have my little half-measure full?

Then that little man in black there, he says women can't have as much rights as men, 'cause Christ wasn't a woman! Where did your Christ come from? Where did your Christ come from? From God and a woman! Man had nothing to do with Him.

If the first woman God ever made was strong enough to turn the world upside down all alone, these women together ought to be able to turn it back, and get it right side up again! And now they is asking to do it, the men better let them.

Obliged to you for hearing me, and now old Sojourner ain't got nothing more to say. ∾

1. The phrase *out of kilter* means "out of order" or "mixed up."
2. *'Twixt* is a shortened form of *betwixt,* an Old English word meaning "between."
3. Here, Truth uses *head* to mean "to do better than" or "to get ahead of."

Reading Practice

Evaluate an Argument Point out that in addressing arguments made by male ministers, Truth twice refers to the Bible for evidence. **Ask:** What does Truth mean by stating that man had nothing to do with Christ? *(According to the Bible, Jesus Christ did not have a human father.)* Who is Truth referring to as "the first woman God ever made" ? *(Eve, who according to the Bible, first ate forbidden fruit in the Garden of Eden and changed the destiny of the human race)* Why would Truth's choice of evidence be effective in an argument with ministers? *(By using details from the Bible, the ministers might find it difficult to refute.)*

After You Read

Respond and Think Critically

Respond

1. Imagine you are attending the Women's Rights Convention in 1851. How might you respond to Sojourner Truth's speech?

Recall and Interpret

2. (a)How does Truth refute the first three reasons given against women's suffrage? (b)What does Truth's response tell you about her character?

3. What is the effect of the **repetition** Truth uses in the first part of her argument?

4. (a)How does Truth answer the religious argument against letting women vote? (b)What does her argument tell you about her religious beliefs?

Analyze and Evaluate

5. (a)What allusion to the Bible does Truth make in the paragraph just before her closing statement? (b)Evaluate the impact of that allusion on her message.

Connect

6. **Big Idea** **Resistance to Slavery** (a)How does Truth introduce the antislavery message into her speech? (b)How appropriate is this message, given the purpose of the convention?

7. **Connect to Today** Are Sojourner Truth's arguments about equality for women and minorities still relevant today? Explain.

Literary Element Oratory

Oratory is the art of effective public speaking, or the use of persuasive skills when speaking. Identify the qualities that you think make this speech effective and help Truth achieve her purpose. Use details from the speech to support your answer.

Reading Strategy Evaluate Argument

Evaluate one of Truth's arguments by analyzing her reasoning. Do you agree with her reasoning? Why or why not?

Vocabulary

Practice with Word Usage Respond to these statements to help you explore the meanings of vocabulary words from the selection.

1. Give an example of an environment in which you would hear a **racket.**

2. What is one responsibility you have **borne**?

3. Describe a situation from your life wherein you have **obliged** someone.

Writing

Write a Speech Sojourner Truth supports the rights of women and slaves—both marginalized groups in the mid-1850s. Think of a group of people today that lacks equal rights. Write a brief speech championing that group's rights, using persuasive skills.

LOG ON **Literature** Online

Selection Resources For Selection Quizzes, eFlash-cards, and Reading-Writing Connection activities, go to glencoe.com and enter QuickPass code GLA9800u3.

SOJOURNER TRUTH **371**

Literary Element

Truth's emotional appeal in describing her experiences as a slave and her allusions to the Bible are effective in refuting opponents' arguments and in persuading the audience to support women's rights.

 For additional assessment, see Assessment Resources, pp. 127–128.

Vocabulary

1. You would hear a **racket** on a construction site.

2. A student may have **borne** certain responsibilities in doing chores at home.

3. A student might mention having **obliged** a peer by helping with a cleanup project.

After You Read

Assess

1. Students may respond sympathetically.

2. (a) She says nobody has helped her into carriages or over mud puddles or has given her the best place. (b) She is strong.

3. It underscores the inaccuracy of her opponent's assertions.

4. (a) Christ was born of God and a woman. (b) She is deeply familiar with the Bible.

5. (a) Adam and Eve (b) Strong; speakers opposing women's suffrage had referred to the Bible.

6. (a) She refers to the backbreaking work she did when she was enslaved. (b) Linking "Negroes of the South" and "women at the North" makes her message appropriate.

7. Students may say that women and minorities still face discrimination in some situations.

Writing

Students' speeches should incorporate persuasive techniques such as the use of personal experiences, rhetorical questions, and logical arguments.

Progress Check

Can students evaluate an argument?

If No → See Unit 3 Teaching Resources Book, p. 62.

Focus

Write these words and their synonyms on the board:
short (squat, petite); **tall** (lanky, towering).

Ask students which synonyms have positive connotations and which have negative connotations.

Teach

Denotation Work through the Denotation column of the chart as a class, asking volunteers to check the accuracy of each definition with a dictionary.

 For additional context, see Glencoe Interactive Vocabulary CD-ROM.

Assess

Practice

1. *Grief* conveys deep and powerful suffering. *Sorrow* conveys an enduring sense of loss or guilt. *Regret* conveys disappointment or remorse. Sojourner Truth was trying to convey deep distress at the loss of her children, so *grief* seems most appropriate.

2. Students might find similar words in the spirituals (pages 346–348) or in the excerpt from Frederick Douglass's autobiography (pages 353–357). Answers will vary but should reflect an understanding of the denotations and connotations of the words selected.

Denotation and Connotation

The **denotation** of a word is its literal meaning; the **connotation** of a word is its implied meaning.

Tip

If, during a test, you are asked what the denotation of a word is, think about how you would define the word for someone else. To describe the word's connotations, think about the images and ideas the word brings to mind.

LOG ON ▶ **Literature** Online

Vocabulary For more vocabulary practice, go to glencoe.com and enter QuickPass code GLA9800u3.

Vocabulary Workshop

Denotation and Connotation

Literature Connection Sojourner Truth recounts the experience of watching helplessly as her children are sold into slavery.

> "And when I cried out with my mother's grief, none but Jesus heard me!"
>
> —Sojourner Truth, from "And Ain't I a Woman?"

Truth could have used words other than *grief*. She could have spoken of *sorrow* or *regret*—after all, those words have a meaning similar to *grief*. But they also convey subtle differences. Words can have similar **denotations** (dictionary definitions) but different **connotations** (ideas, images, or feelings suggested by the word). The power of a word to suggest an array of connotations contributes to precision in speaking and in writing.

A chart like the one below can help you analyze the words *grief, sorrow,* and *regret*—their similarities, their differences, and their shades of meaning. Follow these instructions to create the chart:

- Place the words to be analyzed in the left-hand column.
- Look up different definitions, or denotations, for each word.
- In the second column, record the definition for each term.
- In the third column, list ideas, images, or feelings that you associate with each word.

Semantic Features Chart

	Denotation	Connotation
Grief		
Sorrow		
Regret		

Practice

1. Complete the chart. With your classmates, discuss the denotations and connotations of the three words. Why do you think Truth chose to describe her feeling as *grief* and not as *sorrow* or *regret*? Explain.

2. Find three or four words that have denotations similar to each other in other selections in Unit 3, Part 1. Fill in a semantic features chart using these words. Explain how the connotations of these words help the authors to suggest different shades of meaning.

Vocabulary Practice

Connotation Students may sometimes find it helpful to figure out a word's connotation by trying out the word on themselves. **Say:** Consider the words *clever* and *sly*. Which of these would you prefer to apply to yourself? Why? (*Students may prefer* clever, *noting that* sly *has a slightly less positive connotation.*) Have students use the same technique to identify connotations for the following word pairs: *slim* or *skinny; timid* or *prudent; cheap* or *thrifty; unaware* or *ignorant; rigid* or *firm.* (*Students may select* slim, prudent, thrifty, unaware, *and* firm *as words having the more positive connotation.*)

PART 2

The Civil War: A Nation Divided

The Old Flag Never Touched The Ground. Rick Reeves.

 View the Art Following this 1863 battle at Fort Wagner, a soldier named William Carney was given the Congressional Medal of Honor—the first African-American to receive this award. A song was also written in 1901 commemorating this event. Why do you think these artists felt the need to record and preserve Carney's achievement?

> "*Many are the hearts that are weary tonight,
> Wishing for the war to cease . . .*" **1**

— Walter C. Kittredge, "Tenting on the Old Campground"

373

English Learners

DIFFERENTIATED INSTRUCTION

Intermediate Read the Kittredge quotation aloud to students. **Ask:** What does Kittredge mean by "the hearts that are weary"? *(He is referring to people who have struggled for a long time.)* Point out that Kittredge is using a particular kind of figurative language, using a part to represent the whole. In referring to people as "hearts," feeling is emphasized. A writer might refer to people as "minds" or "hands" to emphasize thinking or action. Ask students to think of other examples of this type of figurative language in daily use.

Analyze and Extend

Reading Strategy 1

Connect Direct students to read the quotation from Kittredge's song. Remind them that most soldiers and nearly all civilians affected by the Civil War—on both sides—were American.

Ask: Why are Kittredge's lines especially true for Americans during the Civil War? *(Possible response: Americans fought on both sides, with families and communities sometimes divided.)*

View the Art

Answer: *Carney's achievement is an important milestone in African American history.*

Rick Reeves (1959–), a former commercial artist, specializes in military-historical art. "The Old Flag Never Touched the Ground" shows an attack on Fort Wagner, a Confederate stronghold near Charleston, South Carolina, by the 54th Massachusetts Infantry, one of the first units of African American soldiers to see combat. This costly 1863 battle has also been depicted in the movie *Glory* (1989).

> For additional support for English Learners, see Unit 3 Teaching Resources Book, p. 68.

Before You Read

Focus

Before You Read

from
Mary Chesnut's Civil War

Meet **Mary Chesnut**
(1823–1886)

Mary Boykin Chesnut's life was one of opposites. Before the Civil War, she was the privileged daughter of Stephen Miller, a wealthy plantation owner in South Carolina. When the war ended, however, she and her husband were financially ruined. Although she abhorred slavery, her family owned hundreds of slaves, and her father was a pro-slavery congressman, senator, and governor. Chesnut's observant nature, education, and social position made her an excellent chronicler of the South during the Civil War.

Education Unlike many women of her era, Chesnut received a formal education. She attended Madame Talvande's French School for Young Ladies in Charleston, South Carolina, where she was an excellent student. During her time at Madame Talvande's, she met James Chesnut Jr., a lawyer from a neighboring plantation. The couple married just after Chesnut turned seventeen years old. When James was elected to the Senate in 1858, the Chesnuts moved to Washington, D.C., where they entertained politicians who would become the leading figures of the Confederacy, such as Jefferson Davis, the future president of the Confederacy. When she was not charming her friends with her sharp wit, Chesnut immersed herself in reading history books and English and French novels.

When the war broke out, Chesnut remained loyal to the South despite her opposition to slavery. Her husband had relinquished his seat in the U.S. Senate in 1860 after the ideological differences between the North and South became too extreme. Afterward, he was a prominent figure in the Confederacy, and as a result the Chesnuts traveled throughout the South. Throughout the Civil War, Chesnut lamented the cruelties and evils of war in detailed journals that reflected what people of the time believed, thought, and said.

Publication After the war ended, Chesnut and her family came upon difficult times. They lost their plantation due to debt, and James died in 1884. After his death, Chesnut was left alone to oversee their struggling dairy farm. Despite these hardships, she still worked to publish her memoirs. Similar to many other works of the Civil War era, Chesnut's "diary" is actually a compilation of journal entries recorded during the war and recollections written after it ended. Chesnut wrote her memoirs between 1881 and 1884. Unfortunately, she died of a heart attack before it could reach publication. The first public version of her journals, *A Diary from Dixie,* was published almost twenty years later. Today it is lauded for its vivid descriptions and details of a life in the Confederacy.

Literature Online

Author Search For more about Mary Chesnut, go to glencoe.com and enter QuickPass code GLA9800u3.

Selection Skills

Literary Elements
- Journal (SE pp. 375, 378, 379, 380)
- Point of View (TE p. 378)

Reading Skills
- Distinguish Fact and Opinion (SE pp. 375, 377, 378, 380)

from **Mary Chesnut's Civil War**

Vocabulary Skills
- Context Clues (SE pp. 375, 380)
- Latin Word Parts (TE p. 375)

Writing Skills/Grammar
- Sentence Fragments (TE p. 376)

Listening/Speaking/Viewing Skills
- Analyze Art (SE p. 379; TE p. 376)

Literature and Reading Preview

Connect to the Journal

Why do people keep journals? Why do we like to *read* other people's journals? Compile a list of possible answers to these two questions.

Build Background

The passage you are about to read from Chesnut's journal describes the outbreak of the Civil War. By early 1861, South Carolina had seceded from the Union and claimed ownership of all federal property within the state. Only Fort Sumter, located in Charleston Harbor, remained under federal control. Confederate authorities demanded the removal of U.S. troops from the fort. President Lincoln refused their request, and on April 12, 1861, Confederate cannons opened fire on the fort. The Civil War had begun.

Set Purposes for Reading

Big Idea A Nation Divided

As you read these journal entries, ask yourself, What conflicting feelings might Chesnut and other Southerners have felt about supporting the Confederacy?

Literary Element Journal

A **journal** is a daily record of events by a participant in those events or a witness to them. Journals are subjective, which means that they reflect the writer's personal perspective. As you read, ask yourself, What do Chesnut's journal entries reveal about her personality and character?

Reading Strategy Distinguish Fact and Opinion

A **fact** is a statement that can be validated with proof, while an **opinion** offers a personal point of view or feeling. As you read Chesnut's journal, note where she offers an opinion rather than presenting the facts.

....

Tip: Identify Opinion Statements Adverbs and adjectives, such as *delightfully, silly,* and *horrible,* are often indicators of opinion statements.

Vocabulary

allusion (ə loo´ zhən) *n.* an indirect or casual reference; an incidental mention; p. 377 *She ignored his allusion to her tardiness.*

audaciously (ô dā´ shəs lē) *adv.* boldly; arrogantly; p. 377 *He audaciously interrupted the teacher.*

prostrate (pros´ trāt) *adj.* stretched out with face to the ground in humility, adoration, or submission; p. 377 *The priest was prostrate before the altar.*

delusion (di loo´ zhen) *n.* a false impression or belief; p. 378 *The defeated candidate still had the delusion that he could win.*

pervade (pər vād´) *v.* to spread through every part; p. 378 *Dampness pervaded the old castle.*

....

Tip: Context Clues To help you determine the meaning of an unfamiliar word, it helps to examine its context clues—such as the surrounding phrases. For example, in the sentence *But tea trays pervade the corridors, going everywhere* on page 378, it is clear that to **pervade** means *to be present everywhere.*

MARY CHESNUT **375**

Mary Chesnut's husband served as the Confederate president Jefferson Davis's liaison with Major Robert Anderson, commander of the Union forces at Fort Sumter. This excerpt covers the events leading up to the outbreak of the Civil War. In these entries, Chesnut writes about preparations for the attack, her concern for her husband, and the excitement of the surrender.

 For summaries in languages other than English, see Unit 3 Teaching Resources Book, pp. 69–74.

Vocabulary

Latin Word Parts Ask: Which two words share the same root and suffix? *(allusion, delusion).* Tell students that the suffix *-ion* changes a verb form into a noun. *Allusion* and *delusion* share the Latin root *ludere,* meaning "to play; to jest."

(ADVANCED) Ask: What other words in English share this same Latin root? *(Possible responses: prelude, preclude, elude, collude, and interlude)*

 For additional context, see Glencoe Interactive Vocabulary CD-ROM.

Interactive Read and Write
Other options for teaching this selection can be found in

- Interactive Read and Write for English Learners, pp. 123–132
- Interactive Read and Write for Approaching-Level Learners, pp. 123–132
- Interactive Read and Write for On-Level Learners, pp. 123–132

Approaching Level
DIFFERENTIATED INSTRUCTION

Established Explain that people in the Civil War era had strong, patriotic attachment to their home states because they spent their whole lives in those states.

English Learners
DIFFERENTIATED INSTRUCTION

Advanced Point out that facts often involve dates, numbers, or actions that have taken place and can be verified. Opinions cannot be checked or proved; they are personal ideas or feelings. Tell students to look for these signals of opinion:

- words expressing approval or disapproval
- statements with "should" or "should not"
- intensifiers such as "too, "very," or "overly"

Teach

Big Idea   1

A Nation Divided   **Say:**
Keep these questions in mind as you read: Where do Mary Chesnut's loyalties lie? *(Her loyalties are to her husband and the Confederacy.)* How might this affect her writing? *(It might cause her writing to be biased or slanted, unfairly favoring the Confederate cause.)*

Big Idea   2

A Nation Divided   **Answer:**
Although Chesnut makes a negative comment about Union leaders, she wants peace. Like many Southerners, she feels resentment toward the North but does not relish the violence of war.

View the Art ★

The medallions depict the well-known Confederate generals Thomas "Stonewall" Jackson, Robert E. Lee, and Joseph Johnston.

Ask: What attitude do these medallions express toward their subjects? *(They seem to honor their subjects in a favorable way.)* How does this attitude compare to Chesnut's feelings for the South? *(She is dedicated to the South and to the Confederacy.)*

 For an audio recording of this selection, use Listening Library Audio CD-ROM.

Readability Scores

Dale-Chall: 6.9
DRP: 52
Lexile: 680

376

---

from

Mary Chesnut's Civil War

Mary Chesnut

1 April 7, 1861. . . . Today things seem to have settled down a little. One can but hope still. Lincoln or Seward[1] have made such silly advances and then far sillier drawings back. There may be a chance for peace, after all.

Things are happening so fast.

My husband has been made an aide-de-camp[2] of General Beauregard.[3] Three hours ago we were quietly packing to go home. The convention has adjourned.

Now he tells me the attack upon Fort Sumter may begin tonight. Depends upon Anderson and the fleet outside. The *Herald* says that this show of war outside of the bar[4] is intended for Texas.[5]

John Manning came in with his sword and red sash. Pleased as a boy to be on Beauregard's staff while the row goes on. He has gone with Wigfall to Captain Hartstene with instructions.

Mr. Chesnut[6] is finishing a report he had to make to the convention.

Mrs. Hayne called. She had, she said, "but one feeling, pity for those who are not here."

---

1. *William Henry Seward* was U.S. Secretary of State from 1861 to 1869.
2. An officer who serves as an assistant to a superior officer is an *aide-de-camp.*
3. *General Beauregard* commanded the Confederate forces surrounding Fort Sumter.

2 **A Nation Divided** *How does this statement show the conflicting feelings of Southerners during the Civil War?*

---

4. *Bar* refers to a sandbar.
5. Texas, a pro-slavery state, had recently voted to secede from the Union.
6. *Mr. Chesnut* (also called Colonel Chesnut) refers to Mary's husband, James, who served as the liaison between Confederate President Jefferson Davis and Major Robert Anderson.

376   UNIT 3   THE CIVIL WAR ERA

Grammar Practice

SPIRAL REVIEW   **Sentence Fragments** Explain that journal writers often write in sentence fragments to allow their thoughts to flow freely. Explain that a sentence fragment is an incomplete sentence punctuated as if it were a complete sentence. A sentence fragment lacks a subject or a verb or is a subordinate clause. Have students rewrite the following passage, eliminating the sentence fragment:

"By 1860 the United States was a nation divided. Eighteen free states and 15 slave states. Abraham Lincoln won the election that year." *(By 1860 the United States was a nation divided. There were eighteen free states and fifteen slave states. Abraham Lincoln won the election that year.)*

Jack Preston, Willie Alston—"the take-life-easys," as they are called—with John Green, "the big brave," have gone down to the island—volunteered as privates.

Seven hundred men were sent over. Ammunition wagons rumbling along the streets all night. Anderson burning blue lights—signs and signals for the fleet outside, I suppose.

Today at dinner there was no **allusion** to things as they stand in Charleston Harbor. There was an undercurrent of intense excitement. There could not have been a more brilliant circle. In addition to our usual quartet (Judge Withers, Langdon Cheves, and Trescot) our two governors dined with us, Means and Manning.

These men all talked so delightfully. For once in my life I listened.

That over, business began. In earnest, Governor Means rummaged a sword and red sash from somewhere and brought it for Colonel Chesnut, who has gone to demand the surrender of Fort Sumter.

— ★ —

And now, patience—we must wait.

— ★ —

 Why did that green goose Anderson go into Fort Sumter? Then everything began to go wrong.

Now they have intercepted a letter from him, urging them to let him surrender. He paints the horrors likely to ensue if they will not.

He ought to have thought of all that before he put his head in the hole.

April 12, 1861. . . . Anderson will not capitulate.

— ★ —

Yesterday was the merriest, maddest dinner we have had yet. Men were more **audaciously** wise and witty. We had an unspoken foreboding it was to be our last pleasant meeting. Mr. Miles dined with us today. Mrs. Henry King rushed in: "The news, I come for the latest news—all of the men of the King family are on the island"—of which fact she seemed proud.

While she was here, our peace negotiator—or envoy—came in. That is, Mr. Chesnut returned—his interview with Colonel Anderson had been deeply interesting—but was not inclined to be communicative, wanted his dinner. Felt for Anderson. Had telegraphed to President Davis for instructions.

What answer to give Anderson, &c&c.[7] He has gone back to Fort Sumter, with additional instructions.

When they were about to leave the wharf, A. H. Boykin sprang into the boat, in great excitement; thought himself ill-used. A likelihood of fighting—and he to be left behind!

— ★ —

I do not pretend to go to sleep. How can I? If Anderson does not accept terms—at four—the orders are—he shall be fired upon.

I count four—St. Michael chimes. I begin to hope. At half-past four, the heavy booming of a cannon.

I sprang out of bed. And on my knees—**prostrate**—I prayed as I never prayed before.

There was a sound of stir all over the house—pattering of feet in the corridor—all seemed hurrying one way. I put on my double gown and a shawl and went, too. It was to the housetop.

The shells were bursting. In the dark I heard a man say "waste of ammunition."

---

3 Distinguish Fact and Opinion **Is Chesnut presenting here a fact or an opinion?**

Vocabulary

allusion (ə loo´ zhən) n. an indirect or casual reference; an incidental mention

7. &c&c means "et cetera" or "and others."

Vocabulary

audaciously (ô dā´ shəs lē) adv. boldly; arrogantly
prostrate (pros´ trāt) adj. stretched out with face to the ground in humility, adoration, or submission

MARY CHESNUT **377**

Advanced Learners

DIFFERENTIATED INSTRUCTION

Analyze Historical Accounts Chesnut's journal is a jumble of incidental detail, rumor, and opinion, yet it still manages to give readers a "front row seat" to a historically momentous event: the start of the Civil War. Ask students to review each passage of Chesnut's journal to identify the historically important information. When they have done so, ask them to read at least two other brief historical accounts of the Fort Sumter attack. Then have students write an analysis of the benefits of each perspective on the Sumter event.

Teach

Reading Strategy | 3

Distinguish Fact and Opinion **Answer:** *Opinion: Mary Chesnut is expressing a judgment on Major Anderson's decision to go into Fort Sumter. The word* ought *shows that this is her opinion.* Explain to students that Chesnut refers to Anderson as "Colonel," but that he was actually a major.

ENGLISH LEARNERS Some students may have difficulty interpreting some of Chesnut's expressions in the sentences that precede the highlighted one. Point out that *goose* means "a silly person." Ask what *green* might mean. *(Green is a figurative expression meaning "inexperienced.")*

 For additional practice using the reading skill or strategy, see Unit 3 Teaching Resources Book, p. 76.

Political History ☆

Fort Sumter Amazingly, no one was killed on either side during the thirty-four-hour bombardment, though a Union soldier died afterward in an accidental explosion during the firing of a salute. Anderson and his men were allowed to return to the North. In 1865, exactly four years after he lowered his colors, Anderson, now Major General, raised the same flag over Fort Sumter, which was once again the property of the United States.

Teach

378

I knew my husband was rowing about in a boat somewhere in that dark bay. And that the shells were roofing it over—bursting toward the fort. If Anderson was obstinate—he was to order the forts on our side to open fire. Certainly fire had begun. The regular roar of the cannon—there it was. And who could tell what each volley accomplished of death and destruction.

The women were wild, there on the housetop. Prayers from the women and imprecations[8] from the men, and then a shell would light up the scene. Tonight, they say, the forces are to attempt to land. The Harriet Lane[9] had her wheelhouse smashed and put back to sea.

Visual Vocabulary
The *wheelhouse* is the enclosed area on the deck of a ship that shelters the steering equipment and the pilot.

 — ★ —

We watched up there—everybody wondered. Fort Sumter did not fire a shot.

— ★ —

Today Miles and Manning, colonels now—aides to Beauregard—dined with us. The latter hoped I would keep the peace. I give him only good words, for he was to be under fire all day and night, in the bay carrying orders, &c.

— ★ —

Last night—or this morning truly—up on the housetop I was so weak and weary I sat down on something that looked like a black stool.

"Get up, you foolish woman—your dress is on fire," cried a man. And he put me out. It was a chimney, and the sparks caught my clothes. Susan Preston and Mr. Venable then ☆ came up. But my fire had been extinguished before it broke out into a regular blaze.

---

8. *Imprecations* are curses.
9. The *Harriet Lane* was a federal ship that brought provisions to the troops at Fort Sumter.

1 Journal *How might a soldier describe this situation differently?*

378 UNIT 3 THE CIVIL WAR ERA

 — ★ —

Do you know, after all that noise and our tears and prayers, nobody has been hurt. Sound and fury, signifying nothing.[10] A **delusion** and a snare. . . .

— ★ —

Somebody came in just now and reported Colonel Chesnut asleep on the sofa in General Beauregard's room. After two such nights he must be so tired as to be able to sleep anywhere. . . .

APRIL 13, 1861. . . . Nobody hurt, after all. How gay we were last night.

Reaction after the dread of all the slaughter we thought those dreadful cannons were making such a noise in doing.

Not even a battery[11] the worse for wear.

Fort Sumter has been on fire. He has not yet silenced any of our guns. So the aides—still with swords and red sashes by way of uniform—tell us.

But the sound of those guns makes regular meals impossible. None of us go to table. But tea trays **pervade** the corridors, going everywhere.

Some of the anxious hearts lie on their beds and moan in solitary misery. Mrs. Wigfall and I solace ourselves with tea in my room.

These women have all a satisfying faith. . . .

APRIL 15, 1861. . . . I did not know that one could live such days of excitement.

They called, "Come out—there is a crowd coming."

A mob indeed, but it was headed by Colonels Chesnut and Manning.

---

10. "Sound and fury, signifying nothing" is taken from *Macbeth* (act 5, scene 5, lines 27–28), a play by Shakespeare.
11. A *battery* is an artillery unit.

Distinguish Fact and Opinion *Do you think that this statement is based on factual information, or is it Chesnut's opinion?* **2**

Vocabulary

delusion (di lōō′ zhen) *n.* a false impression or belief
pervade (pər vād′) *v.* to spread through every part

Sunset at Fort Sumter, 1863. Conrad Wise Chapman.

 Conrad Wise Chapman didn't have to seek out war scenes to paint—he encountered them daily as a Confederate soldier stationed in South Carolina. What do the details of this painting reveal about the situation at Fort Sumter at this time?

The crowd was shouting and showing these two as messengers of good news. They were escorted to Beauregard's headquarters. Fort Sumter had surrendered.

Those up on the housetop shouted to us, "The fort is on fire." That had been the story once or twice before.

— ★ —

When we had calmed down, Colonel Chesnut, who had taken it all quietly enough—if anything, more unruffled than usual in his serenity—told us how the surrender came about.

Wigfall was with them on Morris Island when he saw the fire in the fort, jumped in a little boat and, with his handkerchief as a white flag, rowed over to Fort Sumter. Wigfall went in through a porthole.

When Colonel Chesnut arrived shortly after and was received by the regular entrance, Colonel Anderson told him he had need to pick his way warily, for it was all mined.

As far as I can make out, the fort surrendered to Wigfall.

But it is all confusion. Our flag is flying there. Fire engines have been sent to put out the fire.

Everybody tells you half of something and then rushes off to tell something else or to hear the last news. . . . ◈

> Journal *Would a member of the Confederate army or a Confederate official agree that "it is all confusion"?* **3**

MARY CHESNUT **379**

Approaching Level

DIFFERENTIATED INSTRUCTION

Emerging To help students track the events at Fort Sumter through Chesnut's journal, organize the class into groups. Assign each group one journal entry. Have them identify important events that relate to the developing attack on the fort. Ask a volunteer from each group to orally describe the sequence of events on a given date. As a class, create a timeline of the attack.

Established Point out to students that the journal does not report everything that happened to Chesnut, only events she chose to record. Explain that each blue star indicates a break in the narrative. Tell students to pause at each blue star.

Teach

Literary Element 3

Journal Answer: *War is inherently confusing, so even those in the military might agree that "it is all confusion." However, a soldier or an official would have more information than Chesnut and would find the situation less confusing than she does.*

View the Art

Answer: *The painting shows a tattered Confederate flag, a broken wall, an abandoned cannon. These details, plus the title,* Sunset at Fort Sumter, 1863, *suggest that the Confederacy is losing the war.*

Conrad Wise Chapman (1842–1913) is known for his paintings of the Civil War. He made many paintings during his time as a Confederate soldier on the South Carolina coast. Point out that this painting was created two years after the events described in Mary Chesnut's journal.

 To check students' understanding of the selection, see Unit 3 Teaching Resources Book, p. 80.

Progress Check

Can students analyze a journal?

If No → See Unit 3 Teaching Resources Book, p. 75.

379

After You Read

Assess

1. Possible response: People had varied feelings and perspectives about the war.
2. (a) Soldiers assembling, ammunition wagons moving (b) Hope for peace
3. (a) Fort Sumter was fired upon. (b) Foreboding and fear
4. (a) Restrained excitement (b) No, since war means death.
5. (a) To show her status in sharing meals with prominent people (b) They show how war affects everyday lives.
6. Yes, Anderson had a chance to surrender before the fighting began.
7. Support for those close to her, such as her husband

Literary Element

1. It is less objective.
2. Possible answers: formal; eloquent; hurried

Reading Strategy

Facts: "The convention has adjourned"; "Seven hundred men were sent over"; "Fort Sumter has been on fire." Opinions: "There could not have been a more brilliant circle"; "These men all talked so delightfully"; "But it is all confusion."

Writing

Answers will vary. Students should use a standard memo format, address a specific audience, and provide reasons for their opinions.

After You Read

Respond and Think Critically

Respond and Interpret

1. What insights about the Civil War did these journal entries give you?
2. (a)What activities in Chesnut's entry for April 7 suggest that war is about to begin? (b)What attitude does Chesnut express toward these activities?
3. (a)What major event takes place on April 12? (b)What hopes and fears does Chesnut convey in the entry for that day?

Analyze and Evaluate

4. (a)Describe the **tone**, the writer's feelings about the topic, in the first journal entry. (b)Is this what you might expect under the circumstances? Explain your response.

Literary Element Journal

Along with recording daily events, a **journal** writer includes thoughts, observations, and feelings.

1. How is Chesnut's journal different from a history or memoir that a politician or military officer of the time might have written?
2. How would you describe Chesnut's writing style?

Reading Strategy Distinguish Fact and Opinion

A personal diary account of a historic event, such as this one by Mary Chesnut, is likely to contain both **fact** and **opinion**. Review the excerpt and identify at least three statements of fact and three opinions.

LOG ON ▶ **Literature** Online

Selection Resources For Selection Quizzes, eFlashcards, and Reading-Writing Connection activities, go to glencoe.com and enter QuickPass code GLA9800u3.

---

5. Many of Chesnut's entries document meals and the people who were present at them. (a)Why might she have documented these meals? (b)In what ways do they contribute to the impact of her journal?

Connect

6. **Big Idea** A Nation Divided Chesnut writes, "There may be a chance for peace, after all." From your reading here, do you think the events that took place at Fort Sumter could have been avoided? Explain your response.
7. **Connect to the Author** Although Chesnut did not approve of slavery, she believed in the Confederate cause. What factors might have motivated her to support the Confederacy?

Vocabulary Practice

Practice with Context Clues Look back at the text to find context clues for the vocabulary words below. Record your findings as shown.

allusion   delusion   audaciously
pervade   prostrate

EXAMPLE:
Word: pervade
Textual Clues: "Tea trays pervade the corridors, going everywhere..."
Meaning: to spread through every part

📝 Writing

Write a Memo Would you publish Chesnut's journals? Answer this question in a formal memo to Chesnut.

Vocabulary

allusion; Textual Clues: At dinner, no one mentioned the situation at Charleston Harbor; Meaning: an indirect reference

delusion; Textual Clues: All the "sound and fury" was a delusion because no one was hurt; Meaning: a false impression or belief

audaciously; Textual Clues: "Men were more audaciously wise and witty"

at an especially merry dinner; Meaning: boldly; arrogantly

prostrate; Textual Clues: Chesnut says, "on my knees—prostrate—I prayed as I never prayed before." She is lying on the ground; Meaning: stretched out with face to the ground

 For additional assessment, see Assessment Resources, pp. 129–130.

380

Grammar Workshop

Transitional Expressions

Literature Connection In the passage below, Mary Chesnut uses **transitional expressions** to show connections between ideas.

> *"My husband has been made an aide-de-camp of General Beauregard. Three hours ago we were quietly packing to go home. The convention has adjourned.*
> *"Now he tells me the attack upon Fort Sumter may begin tonight."*
>
> —Mary Chesnut, from "Mary Chesnut's Civil War"

The transitional phrase *three hours ago* tells when Chesnut and her husband were packing. The transitional word *now* tells when she hears about the attack. Both expressions show time relationships. Transitional words and phrases can clarify not only time order but other relationships as well. Each of those relationships uses particular transitions.

Relationship	Transitional Words and Phrases
Time	*first, next, now, today, yesterday, meanwhile*
Importance	*especially, above all, in fact, primarily, more importantly*
Cause and Effect	*because, as a result, consequently*
Contrast	*but, yet, now, on the other hand, however, nevertheless*
Example	*namely, for instance, that is, for example*

Examples

• <u>Because</u> Anderson refused to surrender Fort Sumter, the battle began. [*Because* shows a cause/effect relationship.]

• The cannon fire was intense; <u>however</u>, no one was hurt. [*However* shows a contrast relationship.]

Revise Add a transitional expression to show the relationship between sentences in each pair. Underline the transition and explain the relationship.

1. Many Charleston men were exhausted during the battle. Colonel Chesnut fell asleep on a sofa in the commanding general's quarters.
2. Mrs. Auld began to teach Frederick Douglass to read. She became angry when she saw him reading.
3. "Swing Low, Sweet Chariot" was sung in worship. It carried a coded meaning.

Transitions

Transitional expressions may be used between parts of sentences, between paragraphs, or between sections of text.

Tip

To identify transitions in a test-taking situation, skim the text for key terms shown in the chart.

Dashes

Dashes are used to add emphasis. Dashes that set off text signify a sudden change or an abrupt interruption in thought. Therefore, in some cases a dash may be used in place of a semicolon before a transitional expression.

Language Handbook

For more about transitions, see Writing Handbook, p. R31.

Literature Online

Grammar For more grammar practice, go to glencoe.com and enter QuickPass code GLA9800u3.

Approaching Level

 UNIVERSAL ACCESS

AAVE Approaching level students who use AAVE may have difficulty with the proper placement of adverbs in writing. Transitional adverbs, such as those listed above, often appear at the beginning of a sentence. Adverbs which appear in the middle of a sentence, such as "always," "never," or "probably," are placed after "to be" verbs, but before other verbs. For example: "He is always going to school," and "He always goes to school," show the correct placement of the adverb. Have

students insert adverbs into the following sentences.
1. He is studying at home. (always)
2. She earns high grades. (always)
3. He walks the dog. (never)
4. She is at the office. (never)

Grammar Workshop

Transitional Expressions

Focus

Write on the board: Tomorrow there will be a quiz on content, but the test on Friday will also include grammar.

Discuss how the transition *tomorrow* helps readers understand time and how *but* signals a contrast between the quiz and the test.

Teach

Transitions Have students list additional examples of transitions and write sentences using them. Discuss how each transition clarifies meaning.

ENGLISH LEARNERS Students may be unfamiliar with such transitional terms as *meanwhile, primarily,* and *consequently.* Define these terms and model their use in sentences.

Assess

Revise

1. Many Charleston men were exhausted during the battle. <u>For instance</u> [example], Colonel Chesnut fell asleep on a sofa in the commanding general's quarters.
2. Mrs. Auld began to teach Frederick Douglass to read. <u>Later, however</u> [time, contrast], she became angry when she saw him reading.
3. "Swing Low, Sweet Chariot" was sung in worship. <u>More importantly</u> [importance], it carried a coded message.

 For additional grammar practice, see Unit 3 Teaching Resources Book, p. 68.

Before You Read

Focus

Bellringer Options

Selection Focus
   Transparency 24
Daily Language Practice
   Transparency 36

Or list some common conflicts that students might face, such as a disagreement between friends or between family members. **Ask:** What underlying emotions create conflicts? How do these conflicts demonstrate the strength of people's attachments? As they read, students should consider the challenges that divided loyalties pose to people in all time periods.

Political History ☆

Lee's Choice Lee was not alone in his decision. Hundreds of Southern-born officers trained at West Point chose to serve their home states. One notable exception was Virginia-born George Thomas, considered one of the best Union generals of the war.

Before You Read

Letter to His Son

Meet **Robert E. Lee**
(1807–1870)

Adored by his troops and respected by his enemies, Robert E. Lee remains a symbol of Southern and American dignity. He was born into the famous Lee family of Virginia, who, according to President John Adams, had "more men of merit in it than any other family." His father was a cavalry commander during the Revolutionary War, a governor of Virginia, and a friend to George Washington. As a student at West Point, Lee earned many honors, including a commission to the elite Army Corps of Engineers. During the Mexican War (1846–1848), he rose to the rank of captain. General Winfield Scott said that Lee was "the very best soldier I ever saw in the field."

A Difficult Decision In 1861 Lee faced an agonizing decision. President Lincoln asked him to command the Union forces in the Civil War. Unwilling to fight against his state, Lee declined

and resigned his position in the United States Army. He had been in the army for thirty-six years. Lee then joined the Confederate forces and took command of the Army of Northern Virginia in 1862.

Within three weeks of taking command, Lee had organized his troops, improved discipline and morale, and convinced his soldiers of his authority. Nevertheless, he knew that the powerful Union forces far outnumbered his own and had no doubt that his regiment would be crushed in the open battlefield.

> "There was not a man in the Confederacy whose influence with the whole people was as great as his."
>
> —Ulysses S. Grant

Victory and Defeat Lee achieved brilliant victories at the battles of Second Manassas, Fredericksburg, and Chancellorsville. Then, in order to keep fighting off of Virginia soil, Lee pushed north into Maryland and Pennsylvania, engaging the U.S. Army at Antietam and Gettysburg in June and July of 1863. However, after Gettysburg, the Union forces began to prevail. Lee's forces were malnourished and undersupplied, while those of Union General Grant had a fresh batch of recruits, superior armaments, and an impressive cavalry. Grant's troops progressed farther and farther into Virginia. On April 9, 1865, seeing that the end had come, Lee surrendered to General Grant at Appomattox. After the war Lee urged his fellow Southerners to put their bitterness behind them. An enduring U.S. hero, Lee was a brilliant soldier with a noble spirit and a chivalric manner.

LOG ON **Literature** Online

Author Search For more about Robert E. Lee, go to glencoe.com and enter QuickPass code GLA9800u3.

382 UNIT 3   THE CIVIL WAR ERA

Selection Skills

Literary Elements
- Diction (SE pp. 383, 385, 386)

← **Letter to His Son** →

Writing Skills/Grammar
- Summary (SE p. 386)

Reading Skills
- Determine Main Idea and Supporting Details (SE pp. 383, 386)
- Cause and Effect (TE p. 384)

Vocabulary Skills
- Word Parts (SE pp. 383, 386)
- Diction (TE p. 383)

Literature and Reading Preview

Connect to the Letter

Whom would you contact if you needed to talk about two conflicting loyalties or a tough decision? How would you expect this person to respond?

Discuss these questions with a partner. Refer to personal experiences if possible.

Build Background

In the days before telephones and e-mail, letters were the most common way to communicate at a distance. Robert E. Lee's letters are of interest because they throw light on historic events and reveal the mind and heart of a great leader. Lee wrote this letter on January 23, 1861. South Carolina had seceded from the Union in December 1860, followed quickly by Mississippi, Florida, and Alabama. Lee's home state of Virginia would secede approximately three months later, on April 17, 1861.

Set Purposes for Reading

Big Idea **A Nation Divided**

As you read, ask yourself, How does Lee's personal conflict reflect the sharp divide between the North and South?

Literary Element **Diction**

Diction is a writer's choice of words, an important element in the writer's "voice" or style. As you read, ask yourself, How does Lee's choice of words express his concerns shortly before the outbreak of the Civil War?

Reading Strategy **Determine Main Idea and Supporting Details**

The **main idea** in a paragraph is the guiding thought that all of the sentences in the paragraph support. As you read, identify Lee's main ideas and the **details** that **support** them.

Tip: Take Notes Use a chart to record main ideas and details.

Main Idea	Supporting Details

Vocabulary

perusal (pə rōō′ zəl) *n.* the process of examining carefully; p. 385 *Her perusal of the essay revealed errors.*

anarchy (an′ ər kē) *n.* the absence of government; p. 385 *Without lawmen, anarchy frequently ruled.*

array (ə rā′) *v.* to place in proper or methodical order; p. 385 *The chess pieces were arrayed correctly.*

redress (rē′ dress′) *n.* compensation, as for wrong done; p. 385 *The victim demanded redress.*

contend (kən tend′) *v.* to argue; dispute; p. 385 *Martin contends that he is a master at checkers.*

Tip: Word Parts Word roots, prefixes, and suffixes can help with unfamiliar words. **Anarchy,** for example, has the prefix *an*–, "without," and the root *–arch*, "ruler."

ROBERT E. LEE **383**

English Learners

DIFFERENTIATED INSTRUCTION

Beginning Students may need background on the figures Lee mentions. Ask students to identify George Washington *(led the American army and became the first president),* Thomas Jefferson *(wrote the Declaration of Independence),* Alexander Hamilton, and James Madison *(played key roles in shaping and passing the Constitution).*

SMALL GROUP
Intermediate Help students comprehend Lee's letter by clarifying some of his figurative and idiomatic expressions. Have students find and read the lines in which these expressions occur: "fruit of his deeds," "gulf of revolution," "resort to force." Put students in groups to discuss the meanings of these expressions.

Before You Read

Focus

Summary

Robert E. Lee's letter expresses dismay at the state of the Union. He calls civil war an "evil," but fears it is likely. Lee believes the South has been subjected to aggression by the North. He concludes that if war comes, he will return to Virginia and will draw his sword only to defend himself.

 For summaries in languages other than English, see Unit 3 Teaching Resources Book, pp. 83–88.

Vocabulary

Diction Point out that each of the vocabulary words represents a high level of formality that contributes to the lofty tone Lee uses in his letter. In ordinary conversation, one would likely say "careful reading" rather than "perusal."

Ask: What informal words would you use in conversation for the following: *anarchy, array, redress, contend?* (*Possible answers:* lawlessness, arrange, compensation, argue)

 For additional vocabulary practice, see Unit 3 Teaching Resources Book, p. 91.

 For additional context, see Glencoe Interactive Vocabulary CD-ROM.

Teach

Big Idea

A Nation Divided **Say:**

Keep these questions in mind as you read: How could Lee praise the Union but plan to fight for the Confederacy? *(His loyalty to his state is greater than his admiration for his nation.)* What problems might this cause for Lee and for others in his situation? *(He might lose his rank in the military.)*

Political History ☆

Harper's Ferry Robert E. Lee was involved in a violent prologue to the Civil War. Abolitionist John Brown tried to ignite an insurrection by raiding the federal arsenal at Harper's Ferry, Virginia, in 1859. Lee was given command of the federal response. Lee's troops overwhelmed the raiders' position, captured John Brown, and restored order.

 For an audio recording of this selection, use Listening Library Audio CD-ROM.

Readability Scores

Dale-Chall: 9.9
DRP: 64
Lexile: 1130

Reading Practice

SPIRAL REVIEW **Cause and Effect** Discuss Lee's strong opinions about the causes of the impending Civil War and its probable devastating effects. Ask students to examine Lee's letter and to identify any cause-and-effect relationships among the events mentioned. In Lee's opinion, what will have caused the war? What will cause him to return to his native state? What would be the effects of a reunited nation?

General Robert E. Lee, 1869. Frank Buchser. Oil on canvas. Kunstmuseum, Bern, Switzerland.

Letter to His Son

Robert E. Lee

Have students list the causes and effects in a chart.

Cause	Effect

I received Everett's[1] *Life of Washington* which you sent me, and enjoyed its **perusal.** How his spirit would be grieved could he see the wreck of his mighty labors! I will not, however, permit myself to believe, until all ground of hope is gone, that the fruit of his noble deeds will be destroyed, and that his precious advice and virtuous example will so soon be forgotten by his countrymen. As far as I can judge by the papers, we are between a state of **anarchy** and civil war. May God avert[2] both of these evils from us! I fear that mankind will not for years be sufficiently Christianized to bear the absence of restraint and force. I see that four states[3] have declared themselves out of the Union; four more will apparently follow their example.

Then, if the border states are brought into the gulf of revolution, one half of the country will be **arrayed** against the other. I must try and be patient and await the end, for I can do nothing to hasten or retard it.

The South, in my opinion, has been aggrieved by the acts of the North, as you say. I feel the aggression and am willing to take every proper step for **redress.** It is the principle I **contend** for,

---

1. Edward *Everett* was a noted American politician and orator.
2. Here, *avert* means "to ward off."
3. The first *four states* to secede from the Union were South Carolina, Mississippi, Florida, and Alabama. With Georgia, Louisiana, Texas, Virginia, Arkansas, Tennessee, and North Carolina, these states would make up the Confederate States of America.

1 Diction *What does Lee's choice of adjectives indicate about his feelings toward George Washington?*

Vocabulary

perusal (pə rōō´ zəl) *n.* the process of examining carefully

anarchy (an´ ər kē) *n.* the absence of government

array (ə rā´) *v.* to place in proper or methodical order

redress (rē´ dress´) *n.* compensation, as for wrong done

contend (kən tend´) *v.* to argue; dispute

---

not individual or private benefit. As an American citizen, I take great pride in my country, her prosperity and institutions, and would defend any state if her rights were invaded. But I can anticipate no greater calamity for the country than a dissolution of the Union. It would be an accumulation of all the evils we complain of, and I am willing to sacrifice everything but honor for its preservation. I hope, therefore, that all constitutional means will be exhausted before there is a resort to force. Secession is nothing but revolution. The framers of our Constitution never exhausted so much labor, wisdom, and forbearance in its formation, and surrounded it with so many guards and securities, if it was intended to be broken by every member of the Confederacy at will. It was intended for "perpetual union," so expressed in the preamble, and for the establishment of a government, not a compact, which can only be dissolved by revolution or the consent of all the people in convention assembled. It is idle to talk of secession. Anarchy would have been established, and not a government, by Washington, Hamilton, Jefferson, Madison, and the other patriots of the Revolution. . . . Still, a Union that can only be maintained by swords and bayonets,[4] and in which strife and civil war are to take the place of brotherly love and kindness, has no charm for me. I shall mourn for my country and for the welfare and progress of mankind. If the Union is dissolved, and the government disrupted, I shall return to my native state and share the miseries of my people; and, save in defense, will draw my sword on none. ❧

---

4. A *bayonet* is a large knife or dagger that can be attached to the muzzle of a rifle.

A Nation Divided *What does this statement reveal about Lee's personal response to the imminent war?*

Teach

Literary Element | 1

Diction Answer: *The words* noble, precious, *and* virtuous *all indicate Lee's high esteem for Washington.*

Big Idea | 2

A Nation Divided Answer: *Despite the fact that he was a military man, Lee was hesitant to go to war because he knew the reality of war was grim.*

Literary History ☆

Edward Everett The man who wrote the biography of George Washington that Lee so admired would later deliver a grand oration at the dedication of a cemetery on the Gettysburg battlefield, the site of Lee's most significant defeat of the war. Everett's speech is not well remembered because Abraham Lincoln delivered the Gettysburg Address on the same occasion.

📁 To check students' understanding of the selection, see Unit 3 Teaching Resources Book, p. 94.

Approaching Level

DIFFERENTIATED INSTRUCTION ♻

Established Students may need help in using the note-taking chart for main ideas on page 383. Model the use of the chart on the board by putting "Breaking up the Union would be a disaster for the country" in the *Main Idea* column and listing two details from Lee's letter in the *Supporting Details* column.

Emerging Lee's highly formal style produces long, complicated sentences that include many modifiers and descriptions that may be unfamiliar to students. Tell students to locate the subject, the verb, and the object in each sentence and to use these to understand the sentence's main intent. Model this strategy by reading and paraphrasing the third sentence of Lee's letter, beginning "I will not, however . . ."

A basic restatement of that sentence would be: *I refuse to think that results of Washington's great work will be ruined and that his ideas and example will be forgotten.*

After You Read

Assess

1. Why is the South "aggrieved"? What principles do you stand for?

2. (a) As a man of "mighty labors," "noble deeds," "precious advice," and "virtuous example" (b) Lee admires people of great character.

3. (a) Anarchy and civil war (b) Strict laws and the military are needed to hold society together.

4. (a) If the Union is dissolved, Lee will return to Virginia and fight only in self-defense. (b) Patriotic; opposed to secession; loyal to Virginia.

5. (a) Since the Constitution was not arrived at easily, it should not be set aside easily. (b) He wants to preserve the Union.

6. Torn between love for the Union and belief that the North mistreated the South

7. He would want to defend our nation and Constitution.

Literary Element

1. A breakup of the Union is the worst thing that could happen.
2. A serious and formal tone

Progress Check

Can students analyze diction?

If No → See Unit 3 Teaching Resources Book, p. 89.

Reading Strategy

1. Ending the Union is the worst possible outcome for the nation.
2. Secession is revolution; it is not an option in the Constitution.

Writing

Students' summaries should be about 100 words long, include the main ideas, and omit opinions.

386

After You Read

Respond and Think Critically

Respond and Interpret

1. What questions would you like to ask Robert E. Lee after reading his letter?

2. (a) How does Lee describe George Washington? (b) What do you learn about Lee's character from his description of Washington?

3. (a) What two evils does Lee say the country is between? (b) What do you think Lee means when he says, "I fear that mankind will not for years be sufficiently Christianized to bear the absence of restraint and force"?

4. (a) What decision does Lee announce at the end of the letter? (b) What kind of person does this letter reveal Lee to be?

Analyze and Evaluate

5. (a) How does Lee support his opinions about secession? (b) What can you infer from this about Lee's attitude toward his country?

Connect

6. **Big Idea** **A Nation Divided** Mary Custis Lee wrote to a friend, "My husband has wept tears of blood over this terrible war, but as a man of honor and a Virginian, he must follow the destiny of his state." How was Lee's dilemma comparable to the one facing the country as a whole?

7. **Connect to Today** How do you think Lee might react to events taking place today? Explain.

Literary Element · Diction

Diction is a writer's choice of words, one tool used to convey **tone** and meaning. For example, Lee wrote, "But I can anticipate no greater calamity for the country than a dissolution of the Union."

1. Restate the above sentence using contemporary, informal diction.

2. What does Lee's diction contribute to the impact of his letter?

Reading Strategy · Determine Main Idea and Supporting Details

Determining the main idea helps you discover an author's purpose for writing.

1. What is Lee's main idea in the passage beginning "But I can anticipate. . ." and concluding ". . . and the other patriots of the Revolution"?

2. What details support this main idea?

LOG ON ▶ **Literature** Online

Selection Resources For Selection Quizzes, eFlashcards, and Reading-Writing Connection activities, go to glencoe.com and enter QuickPass code GLA9800u3.

386 UNIT 3 THE CIVIL WAR ERA

Vocabulary Practice

Practice with Word Parts For each word in the left column, identify the related word with a shared root in the right column. Write each word pair, underlining the root. Then use a dictionary to define the related word and explain how it is related to the vocabulary word.

1. perusal   tense
2. anarchy   dressage
3. array   persuasion
4. redress   raiment
5. contend   monarch

EXAMPLE: approximate, proximity
Proximity means "nearness." Something that is **approximate** is nearly correct or exact.

Writing

Write a Summary When you write a summary of nonfiction, you restate the main ideas or events in a short version of the original. A summary does not include personal opinions. In about 100 words, summarize Lee's letter to his son.

Vocabulary

1. *perusal*, persuasion: root meaning "to examine." Persuasion involves examining an argument and *perusal* is the process of examining.

2. *anarchy*, monarch: A monarch is the head of state. *Anarchy* is a state without a leader.

3. *array*, raiment: Raiment is clothing; to *array* is to make sure it looks right.

4. *redress*, dressage: Horses' movements are corrected in a dressage. *Redress* is correction for wrong done.

5. *contend*, tense: Tense means "stretched tight or in a strained state." When you *contend*, you oppose.

For additional assessment, see Assessment Resources, pp. 131–132.

Before You Read

An Occurrence at Owl Creek Bridge ☆

Meet **Ambrose Bierce**
(1842–1914)

A mbrose Bierce did not trust people. Nor did he trust governments, businesses, or churches. Most of all, "Bitter Bierce," as he was known, did not trust easy answers or sentimentality. As his biographer Carey McWilliams wrote, Bierce was "idealistic, cynical, morose . . . a realist who wrote romances, a fine satirist and something of a charlatan."

"Nothing is so improbable as what is true."

—Ambrose Bierce, "The Short Story"

Soldier and Civilian Ambrose Bierce was born into an impoverished Ohio farm family. He was the tenth of thirteen children. After one year of high school at the Kentucky Military Institute, Bierce became a printer's apprentice for a newspaper in Indiana.

At the outbreak of the Civil War, Bierce enlisted in the Ninth Indiana Volunteers. He fought in several important battles, including Shiloh and Chickamauga. At the battle of Kennesaw Mountain in 1864, Bierce suffered a severe head wound. He would later say that the bullet "crushed my skull like a broken walnut."

After the war, Bierce settled in San Francisco, California. For the next two years, he worked as a guard at the mint and studied for long periods of time at the public library. In 1868 Bierce landed a position at the *San Francisco News Letter and Commercial Advertiser*, a financial weekly. He was put in charge of the paper's humor section, "The Town Crier." Bierce's columns often consisted of

satirical attacks against politicians and business leaders, attracting great notoriety for himself and the *News Letter*.

Nuggets and Dust In 1872 Bierce and his wife, Mary Ellen, traveled to England. While overseas, he published three books of fiction, *The Fiend's Delight, Nuggets and Dust Panned Out in California*, and *Cobwebs from an Empty Skull*. In 1875 Bierce returned to San Francisco, but his life continued to be restless and dissatisfied. He quit his job as editor for the *Argonaut* and traveled to the Dakota Territory. There Bierce worked as a manager for a mining firm that was losing money. The firm collapsed and he returned to San Francisco. From 1881 to 1886, Bierce wrote for *Wasp*, a humor magazine. From 1887 to 1908, Bierce worked as a columnist for the *San Francisco Examiner*.

In 1914 Bierce disappeared in Mexico, which was then in the midst of a revolution. In a letter to a friend, he wrote, "Goodbye, if you hear of my being stood up against a Mexican stone wall and shot to rags please know that I think it a pretty good way to depart this life. It beats old age, disease, or falling down the cellar stairs." His disappearance and death remain a mystery.

 Literature Online

Author Search For more about Ambrose Bierce, go to glencoe.com and enter QuickPass code GLA9800u3.

Before You Read

Focus

Bellringer Options

**Selection Focus
   Transparency 25**
**Daily Language Practice
   Transparency 37**

Or write on the board: panic, sharpened mind, quick reflexes, religious thoughts, important memories. **Ask:** Which of these expressions best describe how people respond to life-threatening situations? What words or phrases would you add to this list? Have students consider, as they read, how Peyton Farquhar responds to a threat against his life.

Cultural History ☆

Bierce on Film At least three film versions have been made of "Occurrence at Owl Creek Bridge." The most recent version was released in 2005. An earlier French film was adapted into an episode of *The Twilight Zone*.

Selection Skills

Literary Elements
- Point of View (SE pp. 388, 389, 393, 396, 398)

Reading Skills
- Make and Verify Predictions (SE pp. 388, 391–393, 398)
- Chronological Order (TE p. 388)
- Identify Steps in a Process (TE p. 390)
- Make Inferences (TE p. 392)

An Occurrence at
Owl Creek Bridge

Vocabulary Skills
- Synonyms
  (SE p. 398; TE p. 396)

Writing Skills/Grammar
- Coordinating Conjunctions (SE p. 399)
- Expository Essay (SE p. 399)

Listening/Speaking/Viewing Skills
- Analyze Art (SE p. 394; TE pp. 389, 391, 396)
- Group Discussion (SE p. 397)

Before You Read

Focus

Summary

A man is about to be hanged from a railroad bridge in northern Alabama. The platform he stands on is released. In a flashback, the reader learns the man is Peyton Farquhar, a wealthy Southern planter. A disguised Union spy has tricked him into attempting to burn the Owl Creek Bridge. As Farquhar is plunging to his death, the rope appears to break, and he escapes. Just as he is about to reach his loving wife's arms, the noose takes his life. The reader learns that the escape was an elaborate, split-second fantasy.

 For summaries in languages other than English, see Unit 3 Teaching Resources Book, pp. 96–101.

Vocabulary

Pronunciation Draw attention to *poignant,* a word often mispronounced. Model the correct pronunciation, and then have the class repeat the word aloud several times. Point out that the three verbs on the list, *protrude, adorn,* and *assent,* are each accented on the second syllable. Have the class pronounce the words aloud.

 For additional vocabulary practice, see Unit 3 Teaching Resources Book, p. 104.

 For additional context, see Glencoe Interactive Vocabulary CD-ROM.

388

Literature and Reading Preview

Connect to the Story

How much of reality is constructed by our own minds? Is it possible to use the imagination to protect oneself in an unpleasant situation? Explore these questions in a journal entry.

Build Background

This story, set during the Civil War in rural Alabama, was inspired by events that Bierce witnessed at the Battle of Shiloh. Union troops, encamped at Pittsburg Landing in southwestern Tennessee, were planning a southward offensive, when Confederate troops unexpectedly attacked. In two days, 20,000 soldiers were killed. This battle shocked both sides and anticipated the enormous loss of life that was still to come.

Set Purposes for Reading

Big Idea **A Nation Divided**

As you read, ask yourself, How are Bierce's attitudes toward the Civil War reflected in this story?

Literary Element Point of View

Point of view is the relationship of the narrator, or storyteller, to the story. A story with a **first-person point of view** is told by one of the characters. In a story with **third-person limited point of view,** the narrator is outside the story and reveals the thoughts, feelings, and observations of only one character. In a story with an **omniscient,** or all-knowing, point of view, the narrator is outside the story and knows everything about all of the characters and events in the story. As you read, ask, How does Bierce use point of view? What effects does he achieve?

Reading Strategy Make and Verify Predictions

To **predict** means to make an educated guess about what will happen based on the clues that a writer provides. As you read, verify, adjust, or change your predictions as you get new information.

Tip: Take Notes Use a chart to record your predictions and the evidence on which you base those predictions.

Prediction	Evidence
Things are not what they seem. Something is wrong with the character's perceptions.	"great golden stars looking unfamiliar and grouped in strange constellations"

388 UNIT 3 THE CIVIL WAR ERA

Reading Practice

SPIRAL REVIEW **Chronological Order** The action in "An Occurrence at Owl Creek Bridge" moves forward and backward in time. To help students comprehend the sequence in which the events occur, have them list the main events as they read. When they have finished, they can organize the events into a timeline. Explain that the beginning of the timeline will not coincide with the beginning of the story.

Learning Objectives

For pages 387–398

In studying this text, you will focus on the following objectives:

Literary Study: Analyzing point of view.

Reading: Making and verifying predictions.

Vocabulary

protrude (prō trōōd´) *v.* to stick out; to project; p. 390 *After the accident, the victim had a large bump protruding from his forehead.*

adorn (ə dôrn´) *v.* to make beautiful; to decorate; p. 390 *The vain man adorned himself with jewelry and expensive clothes.*

ardently (ärd´ ent lē) *adv.* passionately; enthusiastically; p. 391 *The man ardently pursued the woman he loved.*

assent (ə sent´) *v.* to express agreement; p. 392 *After meeting for three hours, the committee finally assented to the chairman's proposal.*

poignant (poin´ yənt) *adj.* sharp; severe; causing emotional or physical anguish; p. 392 *Dan experienced a poignant loss when his grandmother died.*

An Occurrence at Owl Creek Bridge

Ambrose Bierce

I

1 A man stood upon a railroad bridge in northern Alabama, looking down into the swift water twenty feet below. The man's hands were behind his back, the wrists bound with a cord. A rope closely encircled his neck. It was attached to a stout cross-timber above his head and the slack fell to the level of his knees. Some loose boards laid upon the sleepers supporting the metals of the railway supplied a footing for him and his executioners—two private soldiers of the Federal army, directed by a sergeant who in civil life may have been a deputy sheriff. At a short remove upon the same temporary platform was an officer in the uniform of his rank, armed. He was a captain. A sentinel[1] at each end of the bridge stood with his rifle in the position known as "support," that is to say, vertical in front of the left shoulder, the hammer[2] resting on the forearm thrown straight across the chest—a formal and unnatural position, enforcing an erect carriage of the body. It did not appear to be the duty of these two men to know what was occurring at the

---

1. A *sentinel* is a soldier who guards a point of passage.
2. A *hammer* is the part of a gun that helps to ignite the cartridge.

Point of View *What does this detail tell the reader about the narrative point of view at this point in the story?* **2**

English Learners

DIFFERENTIATED INSTRUCTION

Intermediate Tell students that during the Civil War, several synonyms applied to each side. *Federal* was used interchangeably with the words *Union* and *Northern*. Here the term *Federal army* refers to Union soldiers. Similarly, *Confederate* was synonymous with *secessionist* and *Southern*.

Approaching Level

DIFFERENTIATED INSTRUCTION

Emerging Ask students to evaluate the first paragraph in terms of creating a suspenseful mood. **Ask:** What is happening in the first paragraph? *(A bound man is about to be hanged; soldiers are carrying out the execution.)* Do you think the story will be about what caused the man to be in this situation or about what happens to him next? Ask volunteers to share their predictions with the class.

Teach

Big Idea 1

A Nation Divided Answer:
He is a civilian Southern planter being hanged by Union troops; therefore, he has probably committed an act of subversion against the Union army.

Writer's Technique ☆

Tone Dry cynicism is a hallmark of Ambrose Bierce's writing. Cynicism is an attitude based on a belief that all actions are rooted in selfish motives. Bierce, in his *Devil's Dictionary*, defines a *cynic* as "a blackguard whose faulty vision sees things as they are, not as they ought to be."

Reading Practice

Identifying Steps in a Process Explain that military activities of all types are carried out in precise, predetermined steps. The steps are called a **sequence**. As students read the story, have them use a chart to note the steps involved in Farquhar's hanging.

Suggest that students use their notes to explain the process of a military hanging during the Civil War.

---

center of the bridge; they merely blockaded the two ends of the foot planking that traversed it.

Beyond one of the sentinels nobody was in sight; the railroad ran straight away into a forest for a hundred yards, then, curving, was lost to view. Doubtless there was an outpost farther along. The other bank of the stream was open ground—a gentle acclivity³ topped with a stockade of vertical tree trunks, loop-holed for rifles, with a single embrasure through which **protruded** the muzzle of a brass cannon commanding the bridge. Midway of the slope between bridge and fort were the spectators—a single company of infantry in line, at "parade rest," the butts of the rifles on the ground, the barrels inclining slightly backward against the right shoulder, the hands crossed upon the stock. A lieutenant stood at the right of the line, the point of his sword upon the ground, his left hand resting upon his right. Excepting the group of four at the center of the bridge, not a man moved. The company faced the bridge, staring stonily, motionless. The sentinels, facing the banks of the stream, might have been statues to **adorn** the bridge. The captain stood with folded arms, silent, observing the work of his subordinates, but making no sign. Death is a dignitary who when he comes announced is to be received with formal manifestations of respect, even by those most familiar with him. In the code of military etiquette silence and fixity⁴ are forms of deference.

The man who was engaged in being hanged was apparently about thirty-five years of age. He was a civilian, if one might judge from his habit,⁵

---

3. An *acclivity* is an upward slope.
4. *Fixity* refers to a steady and unmoving stance.
5. *Habit* refers to a distinctive manner of dress or type of clothing.

1 **A Nation Divided** *What does the condemned man's position in life suggest about the possible causes for his execution?*

Vocabulary

protrude (prō trōōd´) *v.* to stick out; to project
adorn (ə dôrn´) *v.* to make beautiful; to decorate

---

which was that of a planter. His features were good—a straight nose, firm mouth, broad forehead, from which his long, dark hair was combed straight back, falling behind his ears to the collar of his well-fitting frock-coat. He wore a mustache and pointed beard, but no whiskers; his eyes were large and dark gray, and had a kindly expression which one would hardly have expected in one whose neck was in the hemp. Evidently this was no vulgar assassin. The liberal military code makes provision for hanging many kinds of persons, and gentlemen are not excluded. ☆

The preparations being complete, the two private soldiers stepped aside and each drew away the plank upon which he had been standing. The sergeant turned to the captain, saluted and placed himself immediately behind that officer, who in turn moved apart one pace. These movements left the condemned man and the sergeant standing on the two ends of the same plank, which spanned three of the cross-ties⁶ of the bridge. The end upon which the civilian stood almost, but not quite, reached a fourth. This plank had been held in place by the weight of the captain; it was now held by that of the sergeant. At a signal from the former the latter would step aside, the plank would tilt and the condemned man go down between two ties. The arrangement commended itself to his judgment as simple and effective. His face had not been covered nor his eyes bandaged. He looked a moment at his "unsteadfast footing," then let his gaze wander to the swirling water of the stream racing madly beneath his feet. A piece of dancing driftwood caught his attention and his eyes

Visual Vocabulary
A *frock-coat* is a man's coat that reaches to the knees. Popular in the nineteenth century, it is usually double-breasted and fitted at the waist.

---

6. *Cross-ties* are the wooden pieces to which railroad rails are secured.

The Red Bridge, 1896. Julian Alden Weir. Oil on canvas, 24¼ x 33¾ in. The Metropolitan Museum of Art, New York.

followed it down the current. How slowly it appeared to move! What a sluggish stream!

2 He closed his eyes in order to fix his last thoughts upon his wife and children. The water, touched to gold by the early sun, the brooding mists under the banks at some distance down the stream, the fort, the soldiers, the piece of drift—all had distracted him. And now he became conscious of a new disturbance. Striking through the thought of his dear ones was a sound which he could neither ignore nor understand, a sharp, distinct, metallic percussion like the stroke of a blacksmith's hammer upon the anvil; it had the same ringing quality. He wondered what it was, and whether immeasurably distant or near by—it seemed both. Its **3** recurrence was regular, but as slow as the tolling of a death knell.[7] He awaited each stroke with impatience and—he knew not why—apprehension. The intervals of silence grew progressively longer; the delays became maddening. With their greater infrequency the sounds increased in strength and sharpness. They hurt his ear like the thrust of a knife; he feared he would shriek. What he heard was the ticking of his watch.

---

7. A *knell* is the solemn sound of a bell ringing.

He unclosed his eyes and saw again the water below him. "If I could free my hands," he thought, "I might throw off the noose and spring into the stream. By diving I could evade the bullets and, swimming vigorously, reach the bank, take to the woods and get away home. My home, thank God, is as yet outside their lines; my wife and little ones are still beyond the invader's farthest advance."

As these thoughts, which have here to be set down in words, were flashed into the doomed man's brain rather than evolved from it the captain nodded to the sergeant. The sergeant stepped aside.

II

Peyton Farquhar was a well-to-do planter, of an old and highly respected Alabama family. Being a slave owner and like other slave owners a politician he was naturally an original secessionist[8] and **ardently** devoted to the Southern cause. Circumstances of an imperious nature, which it is unnecessary to relate here, had prevented him from taking service with the gallant army that had fought the disastrous campaigns ending with the fall of Corinth, and he chafed[9] under the inglorious restraint, longing for the release of his energies, the larger life of the soldier, the opportunity for distinction. That opportunity,

---

8. A *secessionist* was one in favor of breaking away from the Union.
9. *Chafe* means "to fret; to feel irritation."

Make and Verify Predictions *What can the reader predict about the condemned man from this statement?* **4**

Vocabulary

ardently (ärd´ ent lē) *adv.* passionately; enthusiastically

AMBROSE BIERCE **391**

Teach

Literary Element | **2**

Point of View Ask: What insights does this sentence provide about the condemned man? *(The sentence provides insight into the condemned man's thoughts and personality.)*

Reading Strategy | **3**

Make Inferences Ask: What is happening to the man's perception of time? *(The intervals of silence between the sounds of his watch ticking are growing longer. Time is moving more slowly.)*

For additional practice using the reading skill or strategy, see Unit 3 Teaching Resources Book, p. 103.

Reading Strategy | **4**

Make and Verify Predictions Answer: *The word* doomed *suggests that Farquhar will not escape death.*

View the Art

Julian Alden Weir (1852–1919) learned to paint from his father, the landscape painter Robert Walter Weir. In works such as *The Red Bridge,* the younger Weir focused on variations in light and confluences of angles. The real Red Bridge spanned the Connecticut River near a farm Weir owned.

Ask: How does the style of this painting compare or contrast with scenes Bierce describes in the story? *(Some students may say the soft visual style matches Farquhar's impressionistic descriptions. Others may say that the painting's style is in contrast to the sharply observed physical details of the story.)*

English Learners

DIFFERENTIATED INSTRUCTION

Intermediate The powerful opening of "An Occurrence at Owl Creek Bridge" is filled with military terminology. Have volunteers identify military terms in section I of the story. Write them on the board and help students build meanings from context. Add any of the following terms the class did not identify: *private soldiers, Federal army, captain, sentinel, outpost, stockade, loop-holed, muzzle, company, infantry,* *stock, lieutenant, subordinates, sergeant.* Have the class use dictionaries to verify their definitions and then read section I again with knowledge of meaning.

Teach

Make and Verify Predictions Answer: *The sentence suggests that Farquhar is being betrayed by a Union spy and that his mission will be unsuccessful.*

he felt, would come, as it comes to all in war time. Meanwhile he did what he could. No service was too humble for him to perform in aid of the South, no adventure too perilous for him to undertake if consistent with the character of a civilian who was at heart a soldier, and who in good faith and without too much qualification **assented** to at least a part of the frankly villainous dictum[10] that all is fair in love and war.

One evening while Farquhar and his wife were sitting on a rustic bench near the entrance to his grounds, a gray-clad[11] soldier rode up to the gate and asked for a drink of water. Mrs. Farquhar was only too happy to serve him with her own white hands.[12] While she was fetching the water her husband approached the dusty horseman and inquired eagerly for news from the front.

"The Yanks are repairing the railroads," said the man, "and are getting ready for another advance. They have reached the Owl Creek bridge, put it in order and built a stockade[13] on the north bank. The commandant has issued an order, which is posted everywhere, declaring that any civilian caught interfering with the railroad, its bridges, tunnels or trains will be summarily[14] hanged. I saw the order."

"How far is it to the Owl Creek bridge?" Farquhar asked.

"About thirty miles."

> *As Peyton Farquhar fell straight downward through the bridge he lost consciousness . . .*

"Is there no force on this side the creek?"

"Only a picket post[15] half a mile out, on the railroad, and a single sentinel at this end of the bridge."

"Suppose a man—a civilian and student of hanging—should elude the picket post and perhaps get the better of the sentinel," said Farquhar, smiling, "what could he accomplish?"

The soldier reflected. "I was there a month ago," he replied. "I observed that the flood of last winter had lodged a great quantity of driftwood against the wooden pier at this end of the bridge. It is now dry and would burn like tow."[16]

The lady had now brought the water, which the soldier drank. He thanked her ceremoniously, bowed to her husband and rode away. An hour later, after nightfall, he repassed the plantation, going northward in the direction from which he had come. He was a Federal scout.[17]

III

As Peyton Farquhar fell straight downward through the bridge he lost consciousness and was as one already dead. From this state he was awakened—ages later, it seemed to him—by the pain of a sharp pressure upon his throat, followed by a sense of suffocation. Keen, **poignant**

---

10. A *dictum* is a formal, authoritative pronouncement.
11. Confederate soldiers wore *gray* uniforms.
12. [*Mrs. Farquhar . . . hands*] Ordinarily, a servant or slave would have served the guest. In this case, Mrs. Farquhar brought the soldier a drink of water.
13. A *stockade* is an enclosure made of posts in which prisoners may be kept.
14. *Summarily* means "without delay; arbitrarily."

Vocabulary

assent (ə sent´) *v.* to express agreement

---

15. A *picket post* is a group of soldiers sent ahead to watch for and to warn of a surprise attack.
16. *Tow* (tō) is the coarse fibers of flax or hemp used to make yarn and twine.
17. Here, a *Federal scout* is a Union spy.

Make and Verify Predictions *What does this sentence enable the reader to predict about the outcome of Farquhar's mission to burn the bridge?* | **1**

Vocabulary

poignant (poin´ yənt) *adj.* sharp; severe; causing emotional or physical anguish

Reading Practice

Make Inferences Have students read the first paragraph of section II. Then challenge them to infer the identity of the condemned man from this passage. Have them list the information they might use to support an inference that the condemned man is Peyton Farquhar:

- The man on the bridge is a civilian who looks like a planter. He is about to be hanged by the Federal army.

- Peyton Farquhar is a civilian and a planter. He is eager to serve the Confederate cause.

agonies seemed to shoot from his neck downward through every fiber of his body and limbs. These pains appeared to flash along well-defined lines of ramification[18] and to beat with an inconceivably rapid periodicity.[19] They seemed like streams of pulsating fire heating him to an intolerable temperature. As to his head, he was conscious of nothing but a feeling of fullness—of congestion. These sensations were unaccompanied by thought. The intellectual part of his nature was already effaced; he had power only to feel, and feeling was torment. He was conscious of motion. Encompassed in a luminous cloud, of which he was now merely the fiery heart, without material substance, he swung through unthinkable arcs of oscillation,[20] like a vast pendulum. Then all at once, with terrible suddenness, the light about him shot upward with the noise of a loud plash;[21] a frightful roaring was in his ears, and all was cold and dark. The power of thought was restored; he knew that the rope had broken and he had fallen into the stream. There was no additional strangulation; the noose about his neck was already suffocating him and kept the water from his lungs. To die of hanging at the bottom of a river!—the idea seemed to him ludicrous. He opened his eyes in the darkness and saw above him a gleam of light, but how distant, how inaccessible! He was still sinking, for the light became fainter and fainter until it was a mere glimmer. Then it began to grow and brighten, and he knew that he was rising toward the surface—knew it with reluctance, for he was now very comfortable. "To be hanged and drowned," he thought, "that is not so bad; but I do not wish to be shot. No; I will not be shot; that is not fair."

He was not conscious of an effort, but a sharp pain in his wrist apprised him that he was trying to free his hands. He gave the struggle his atten-

tion, as an idler[22] might observe the feat of a juggler, without interest in the outcome. What splendid effort!—what magnificent, what superhuman strength! Ah, that was a fine endeavor! Bravo! The cord fell away; his arms parted and floated upward, the hands dimly seen on each side in the growing light. He watched them with a new interest as first one and then the other pounced upon the noose at his neck. They tore it away and thrust it fiercely aside, its undulations[23] resembling those of a water-snake. "Put it back, put it back!" He thought he shouted these words to his hands, for the undoing of the noose had been succeeded by the direst pang that he had yet experienced. His neck ached horribly; his brain was on fire; his heart, which had been fluttering faintly, gave a great leap, trying to force itself out at his mouth. His whole body was racked and wrenched with an insupportable anguish! But his disobedient hands gave no heed to the command. They beat the water vigorously with quick, downward strokes, forcing him to the surface. He felt his head emerge; his eyes were blinded by the sunlight; his chest expanded convulsively, and with a supreme and crowning agony his lungs engulfed a great draft of air, which instantly he expelled in a shriek!

He was now in full possession of his physical senses. They were, indeed, preternaturally[24] keen and alert. Something in the awful disturbance of his organic system had so exalted and refined them that they made record of things never before perceived. He felt the ripples upon his face and heard their separate sounds as they struck. He looked at the forest on the bank of the stream, saw the individual trees, the leaves and the veining of each leaf—saw the very insects upon them: the locusts, the brilliant-bodied flies, the gray spiders stretching their webs from twig to twig. He noted the prismatic colors in all the dewdrops

---

18. Here, *ramification* means "the act of branching out."
19. *Periodicity* means "recurrence at regular intervals."
20. *Oscillation* is swinging back and forth with regular rhythm.
21. *Plash* is a splash or the sound of a splash.

22. An *idler* is a person who is lazy or not employed.
23. *Undulations* are regular movements that come in waves.
24. *Preternaturally* (prē′ tər nach′ ər əl ē) means "going beyond what is normal" or "extraordinarily."

Point of View *What does this statement tell the reader about the narrator's point of view?*

Make and Verify Predictions *What does this statement suggest about Farquhar's attempt to escape?*

Literary Element   2

Point of View Answer: *Because the narrator reveals only Farquhar's thoughts, Bierce is using a third-person limited point of view at this point in the story.*

Reading Strategy   3

Make and Verify Predictions Answer: *The word* preternaturally *suggests that Farquhar's attempt to escape possesses an aura of unreality.*

Cultural History ☆

Hanging Peyton Farquhar is being hanged for a crime. Hanging was a legal means of execution during the Civil War and continues to be a lawful alternative to lethal injection in some states. The last execution by hanging in the United States occurred in Delaware in 1996.

Advanced Learners
DIFFERENTIATED INSTRUCTION

Eyewitness Account Say: Write a Federal soldier's account of the incident at the bridge. Write your account as an officer's official report or a journal entry.

Approaching Level
DIFFERENTIATED INSTRUCTION

Emerging Approaching-level students may have difficulty with the use of multiple negatives. Explain to students that there are many ways to make a sentence negative, but as in mathematics, two negatives produce a positive. Review the sentence, "As to his head, he was conscious of nothing but a feeling of fullness." Point out that this sentence uses a single negative term "nothing." Ask students to add a second

negative term to the sentence, such as, "As to his head, he was not conscious of nothing…" Discuss with students how the second negative term changes the sentence's meaning.

Teach

Literary Element   1

Point of View **Ask:** What parts of this descriptive passage are specific physical details? What parts represent Farquhar's personal impressions? *(Farquhar notices such specific details as the bridge, the fort, and soldiers by rank and by number. He hears the men's shouts and sees their actions. Farquhar's impressions are reflected in his sense of a turning motion and his view that the soldiers were "gigantic" and their actions "grotesque and horrible.")*

View the Art ★

Answer: *The bridge and type of foliage depicted in this painting are consistent with what is described in the story. The painting's dark and somber mood also reflects the mood of the story.*

George Rodrigue (1944–) was born in southern Louisiana and began his career by painting the scenes and people of this region. These paintings were dark and brooding.

Sugar Bridge Over Coulee, 1973. George Rodrigue. Oil on canvas, 48 x 75 in. Private collection.

View the Art Fascinated by the Louisiana live oak, George Rodrigue painted hundreds of studies of his native ground, sky, and trees, often in shadowy, sepia tones. Does this painting look as if it could depict a scene from "An Occurrence at Owl Creek Bridge"? Explain.

upon a million blades of grass. The humming of the gnats that danced above the eddies[25] of the stream, the beating of the dragon-flies' wings, the strokes of the water-spiders' legs, like oars which had lifted their boat—all these made audible music. A fish slid along beneath his eyes and he heard the rush of its body parting the water.

He had come to the surface facing down the stream; in a moment the visible world seemed to wheel slowly round, himself the pivotal point, and he saw the bridge, the fort, the soldiers upon the bridge, the captain, the sergeant, the two privates, his executioners. They were in silhouette against the blue sky. They shouted and gesticulated, pointing at him. The captain had drawn his pistol, but did not fire; the others were unarmed. Their movements were grotesque and horrible, their forms gigantic.

Suddenly he heard a sharp report[26] and something struck the water smartly within a few inches of his head, spattering his face with spray. He heard a second report, and saw one of the sentinels with his rifle at his shoulder, a light cloud of blue smoke rising from the muzzle. The man in the water saw the eye of the man on the bridge gazing into his own through the sights of the rifle. He observed that it was a gray eye and remembered having read that gray eyes were keenest, and that all famous marksmen had them. Nevertheless, this one had missed.

A counter-swirl had caught Farquhar and turned him half round; he was again looking into the forest on the bank opposite the fort. The sound of a clear, high voice in a monotonous singsong now rang out behind him and came across the water with a distinctness that pierced and subdued all other sounds, even the beating of the ripples in his ears. Although no soldier, he had frequented camps enough to know the dread significance of that deliberate, drawling, aspirated[27] chant; the lieutenant on shore was taking a part in the morning's work. How coldly and pitilessly—with what an even, calm intonation, presaging,[28] and enforcing tranquillity in the men—with what accurately measured intervals fell those cruel words:

"Attention, company! . . . Shoulder arms! . . . Ready! . . . Aim! . . . Fire!"

Farquhar dived—dived as deeply as he could. The water roared in his ears like the voice of

---

25. *Eddies* are currents that move contrary to the main current in a river or stream, usually in a circular motion.
26. Here, a *report* is an explosive sound or noise, especially from a rifle or a pistol when fired.

27. Here, *aspirated* refers to a breathy sort of speech.
28. *Presaging* means "acting as a sign or a warning of."

Speaking and Listening Practice

SPIRAL REVIEW **Motivation** Point out that in attempting to destroy the bridge as a civilian, Farquhar was taking a far greater risk than if he had been acting as a uniformed soldier. A soldier would have the benefit of military training and, if captured, could not be executed for attacking an enemy position. **Ask:** If Farquhar loved his wife and children so much, why did he take such extraordinary risks? Why did he act so abruptly, so alone, and with so little preparation? In small groups, have students discuss Farquhar's motivation and intention before he left on his mission. After students have had time to discuss, select a student volunteer to stand up and explain Farquhar's reasoning by pretending to be Farquhar. The rest of the class can ask questions to the student acting as Farquhar, who should answer questions based on what has been learned about the character. Tell students that they may add imagined details from Farquhar's past that might explain his motives as long as the details fit with his character. Have several students take turns role playing.

Niagara, yet he heard the dulled thunder of the volley[29] and, rising again toward the surface, met shining bits of metal, singularly flattened, oscillating slowly downward. Some of them touched him on the face and hands, then fell away, continuing their descent. One lodged between his collar and neck; it was uncomfortably warm and he snatched it out.

As he rose to the surface, gasping for breath, he saw that he had been a long time under water; he was perceptibly farther down stream—nearer to safety. The soldiers had almost finished reloading; the metal ramrods[30] flashed all at once in the sunshine as they were drawn from the barrels, turned in the air, and thrust into their sockets. The two sentinels fired again, independently and ineffectually.

The hunted man saw all this over his shoulder; he was now swimming vigorously with the current. His brain was as energetic as his arms and legs; he thought with the rapidity of lightning.

"The officer," he reasoned, "will not make that martinet's[31] error a second time. It is as easy to dodge a volley as a single shot. He has probably already given the command to fire at will. God help me, I cannot dodge them all!"

An appalling plash within two yards of him was followed by a loud, rushing sound *diminuendo*,[32] which seemed to travel back through the air to the fort and died in an explosion which stirred the very river to its deeps! A rising sheet of water curved over him, fell down upon him, blinded him, strangled him! The cannon had taken a hand in the game. As he shook his head free from the commotion of the smitten[33] water he heard the deflected shot humming through the air ahead, and in an instant it was cracking and smashing the branches in the forest beyond.

"They will not do that again," he thought; "the next time they will use a charge of grape.[34] I must keep my eye upon the gun; the smoke will apprise me—the report arrives too late; it lags behind the missile. That is a good gun."

Suddenly he felt himself whirled round and round—spinning like a top. The water, the banks, the forests, the now distant bridge, fort and men—all were commingled and blurred. Objects were represented by their colors only; circular horizontal streaks of color—that was all he saw. He had been caught in a vortex[35] and was being whirled on with a velocity of advance and gyration that made him giddy and sick. In a few moments he was flung upon the gravel at the foot of the left bank of the stream—the southern bank—and behind a projecting point which concealed him from his enemies. The sudden arrest of his motion, the abrasion of one of his hands on the gravel, restored him, and he wept with delight. He dug his fingers into the sand, threw it over himself in handfuls and audibly blessed it. It looked like diamonds, rubies, emeralds; he could think of nothing beautiful which it did not resemble. The trees upon the bank were giant garden plants; he noted a definite order in their arrangement, inhaled the fragrance of their blooms. A strange, roseate[36] light shone through the spaces among their trunks and the wind made in their branches the music of æolian harps.[37] He had no wish to perfect his escape—was content to remain in that enchanting spot until retaken.

A whiz and rattle of grapeshot among the branches high above his head roused him from his dream. The baffled cannoneer had fired him a random farewell. He sprang to his feet,

---

29. Here, a *volley* is a discharge of bullets in rapid succession.
30. *Ramrods* are rods used for stuffing the charge down the barrel of a rifle that is loaded from the muzzle.
31. A *martinet* is one who stresses strict attention to forms and rules.
32. *Diminuendo* (di min´ ū en´ dō) is a musical term that describes a gradual decrease in volume.
33. Here, *smitten* means that the water has been bombarded with ammunition from the cannon.

3 A Nation Divided *How do you think Bierce's actual experiences in the war affected his descriptions of combat?*

---

34. *Grape* refers to grapeshot, a cluster of small iron balls that disperse when shot from a cannon.
35. Here, a *vortex* is a whirling mass of water that pulls everything to its center.
36. *Roseate* means "rose-colored."
37. *Æolian harps* produce musical sounds when air passes through the strings.

AMBROSE BIERCE **395**

Teach

Literary Element   1

Point of View Answer: *The statement suggests that the narrator has been intentionally misleading the reader about the reality of Farquhar's escape.*

View the Photograph ★

Point out the yellowish tone of this photograph and the stark contrast between the light sky and the dark trees. **Ask:** How does this image relate to Farquhar's experiences? *(It suggests the distortion of his reality.)*

 To check students' understanding of the selection, see Unit 3 Teaching Resources Book, p. 107.

---

rushed up the sloping bank, and plunged into the forest.

All that day he traveled, laying his course by the rounding sun. The forest seemed interminable; nowhere did he discover a break in it, not even a woodman's road. He had not known that he lived in so wild a region. There was something uncanny[38] in the revelation.

By nightfall he was fatigued, footsore, famishing. The thought of his wife and children urged him on. At last he found a road which led him in what he knew to be the right direction. It was as wide and straight as a city street, yet it seemed untraveled. No fields bordered it, no dwelling anywhere. Not so much as the barking of a dog suggested human habitation. The black bodies of the trees formed a straight wall on both sides, terminating on the horizon in a point, like a diagram in a lesson in perspective. Overhead, as he looked up through this rift in the wood, shone great golden stars looking unfamiliar and grouped in strange constellations. He was sure they were arranged in some order which had a secret and malign[39] significance. The wood on either side was full of singular noises, among which—once, twice, and again—he distinctly heard whispers in an unknown tongue.

His neck was in pain and lifting his hand to it he found it horribly swollen. He knew that it had a circle of black where the rope had

Somerset Place at Creswell, North Carolina. ★

bruised it. His eyes felt congested; he could no longer close them. His tongue was swollen with thirst; he relieved its fever by thrusting it forward from between his teeth into the cold air. How softly the turf had carpeted the untraveled avenue—he could no longer feel the roadway beneath his feet!

Doubtless, despite his suffering, he had fallen asleep while walking, for now he sees another scene—perhaps he has merely recovered from a delirium. He stands at the gate of his own home. All is as he left it, and all bright and beautiful in the morning sunshine. He must have traveled the entire night. As he pushes open the gate and passes up the wide white walk, he sees a flutter of female garments; his wife, looking fresh and cool and sweet, steps down from the veranda to meet him. At the bottom of the steps she stands waiting, with a smile of ineffable[40] joy, an attitude of matchless grace and dignity. Ah, how beautiful she is! He springs forward with extended arms. As he is about to clasp her he feels a stunning blow upon the back of the neck; a blinding white light blazes all about him with a sound like the shock of a cannon—then all is darkness and silence!

Peyton Farquhar was dead; his body, with a broken neck, swung gently from side to side beneath the timbers of the Owl Creek bridge. ∾

---

40. *Ineffable* means "indescribable" or "unspeakable."

Point of View *What does this statement suggest to the reader about the reliability of the narrator in Part III of the story?* **1**

---

38. *Uncanny* means "eerie" or "weird."
39. *Malign* (mə līn') means "evil or harmful in nature or effect."

Vocabulary Practice

 Synonyms Review that synonyms are words with the same or similar meaning. Many words could describe Farquhar's attempt to escape in this story. For example, the words *evade, elude, circumvent,* and *skirt* all convey the idea of avoiding or escaping.

Have students find pairs of synonyms in this list, using a dictionary if needed:

destroyed   daringly
obstinate   confiscate
seize   criticize
upbraid   obliterated
boldly   stubborn

(destroyed—obliterated; obstinate—stubborn; seize—confiscate; upbraid—criticize; boldy—daringly)

After You Read

Respond and Think Critically

Respond and Interpret

1. What was your reaction to the end of the story?

2. (a)Summarize the scene in the story's first two paragraphs. Who is involved? What reactions does the narrator describe? (b)Why do the observers of the event respond to it in the way they do?

3. (a)In sections I and II, what do you learn about Farquhar's appearance, personality, and background? (b)What can you infer about the narrator's attitude toward Farquhar from these descriptions?

4. (a)Describe the specific physical sensations that Farquhar experiences in section III. (b)How do his sensations change during the course of this section? (c)What do these changes suggest?

Analyze and Evaluate

5. (a)What literary device does Bierce use in section II of the story? (b)Did you find this literary device to be effective? Explain.

6. Do you think that the description of Farquhar's final thoughts is realistic? Explain.

Connect

7. **Big Idea** A Nation Divided How do you think Bierce's war experiences affected his attitude toward the events in this story? What view of people's desire to fight wars do you think Bierce expresses in this selection?

8. **Connect to Today** (a)Are Bierce's ideas relevant to today? Why or why not? (b)If Bierce were writing about a contemporary conflict, how might his story be the same or different? Explain.

You're the Critic

Bierce's Obsession With Death

Read the following excerpts of literary criticism. Consider how these critics share similar assumptions but differ in their conclusions.

> "But eventually . . . the obsession with death becomes tiresome. If we try to read these stories in bulk, they get to seem not merely disgusting but dull . . . the trick repeated again and again. The executioner Death comes to us from outside our human world and, capriciously, gratuitously, cruelly, slices away our lives. It is an unpleasant limitation of Bierce's treatment of violent death that it should seem to him never a tragedy, but merely a bitter jest."
> —Edmund Wilson

> "One might quibble with the charge that Bierce's stories lack sympathy; they are, in their way enormously sympathetic, but it is the understated and unspoken sympathy of the modern stylist, not the breathy sentimentality of the Victorian. Besides, Bierce might have answered, such sentimental bosh is what got the soldiers in his stories into their deadly predicaments in the first place. It is not sympathy that Bierce is after, but clarity."
> —Roy Morris Jr.

Group Activity

Discuss the following questions. How do these two critics agree and differ in their conclusions about Bierce? Which critic do you think comes closer to accurately assessing Bierce's attitude?

AMBROSE BIERCE **397**

Group Activity

Possible answers: *Wilson:* Bierce lacks sympathy for his characters' violent deaths; *Morris:* Bierce expresses sympathy without sentimentality, but clarity is his main goal; *Both:* Bierce is obsessed with death.

Possible answer: Morris more accurately assesses Bierce's unsentimental attitude.

> For additional assessment, see Assessment Resources, pp. 133–134.

After You Read

Assess

1. Students may say they were surprised and shocked by his death.

2. (a) Federal soldiers are about to execute a man by hanging. Those watching are mostly emotionless. (b) Codes of military discipline probably dictate that observers remain quiet during an execution.

3. (a) He is a wealthy planter devoted to the Southern cause and wants a part in the conflict. (b) It is sympathetic but faintly ironic; it subtly hints that Farquhar's effort to burn the bridge is futile.

4. (a) A sense of suffocation; pain in his neck (b) His sensations heighten—for example, he sees the tiny veins and insects upon each leaf of a tree. (c) They suggest a lapse into fantasy.

5. (a) Flashback (b) Yes, a flashback creates suspense and supplies information the reader needs to interpret the story.

6. Encourage students to appreciate that Bierce's juxtaposition of realism and fantasy is what makes this story compelling.

7. Bierce's war experiences left him disillusioned about the value of heroism and the glory of war. He believes that the desire to fight is misguided and tragic.

8. (a) Students who think Bierce's ideas are relevant to today may mention current wars and violence. (b) Students may say the story might have been the same in its bleak portrayal of war or different in that the setting would be somewhere other than America and the weapons and technology would be more advanced.

After You Read

Assess

Literary Element

1. Sections of the story that focus on characters other than Farquhar are told from a third-person omniscient point of view. Most of the story, which focuses on Farquhar's thought processes, is told from a third-person limited point of view.

2. Students should realize Bierce's use of the third-person limited point of view allows the narrator to convey Farquhar's thought processes without commentary, thus intentionally misleading the reader and setting up the surprise ending.

Progress Check

Can students identify point of view?

If No → See Unit 3 Teaching Resources Book, p. 102.

Reading Strategy

1. Farquhar's exaggerated perceptions near the end of the story; the unusually loud ticking of his watch; the narrator's statement (at the beginning of section III) that as Farquhar falls through the bridge, he is "as one already dead"

2. The somber tone of the opening section; the description of "grotesque" and "gigantic" figures of soldiers in the third section

 To create custom assessments using software, use ExamView Assessment Suite.

Literary Element Point of View

Authors will sometimes shift the narrative **point of view** during a story. The shift might be dramatic, such as a change from the first- to the third-person point of view, or it might be a subtle shift from the third-person omniscient to the third-person limited point of view.

1. How does Bierce shift the point of view in this story? Explain.

2. What does Bierce achieve by using the third-person limited point of view for most of the story?

Review: Description

As you learned in Unit One, **description** is the use of details to give the reader a vivid picture of a person, place, thing, or event.

Partner Activity Meet with a classmate and discuss the descriptions used in section III of the story. Pay attention to Bierce's use of precise and vivid adjectives, nouns, and verbs and sensory details, such as color, texture, or smell. Working with your partner, create a list of those descriptions that you found most compelling. Be sure to take note of what the author is describing and what kind of details he uses to describe it. Use a simple table, such as the one shown below.

What Is Described	Details
the lieutenant's order to fire	vivid adjectives: "deliberate" "drawling" "aspirated"

 Literature Online

Selection Resources For Selection Quizzes, eFlash-cards, and Reading-Writing Connection activities, go to glencoe.com and enter QuickPass code GLA9800u3.

Reading Strategy Make and Verify Predictions

Predictions can be made about various aspects of a text. In "An Occurrence at Owl Creek Bridge," Bierce intentionally misleads the reader to make the ending a surprise. However, Bierce does provide clues to help the reader predict the plot's outcome.

1. What images, details, or descriptions do you notice that foreshadow the story's conclusion?

2. List any clues that you did not notice initially that now can be seen to foreshadow the conclusion.

Vocabulary Practice

Practice with Synonyms With a partner, match each boldfaced vocabulary word below with its synonym. Use a thesaurus or dictionary to check your answers.

1. protrude
2. adorn
3. ardently
4. assent
5. poignant

  a. sentimental
  b. passsionately
  c. severe
  d. send
  e. embellish
  f. jut
  g. concur

Academic Vocabulary

*Bierce relates the **sequence** of events leading to Peyton Farquhar's hanging.*

Sequence is an academic word. It can have different meanings in different subject areas. Use context clues to infer its meaning in each sentence below.

1. The movie opened with a **sequence** showing the main character's wedding preparations.

2. Beethoven's *Symphony No. 1* features the repetition of the harmonies in **sequence** that explore the musical subject.

For more on academic vocabulary, see pages 53–54.

Vocabulary

1. f **2.** e **3.** b **4.** g **5.** c

Academic Vocabulary

1. In this sentence about film, *sequence* means a series of scenes or shots that together make up an episode of the movie's narrative.

2. In this sentence about music, *sequence* means a pattern, melodic or harmonic, that is repeated at least three times throughout a piece of music at different pitches.

Respond Through Writing

Expository Essay

Analyze Point of View Most fiction writers maintain the same point of view throughout a story. But in "An Occurrence at Owl Creek Bridge," Bierce dramatically shifts point of view. Write an essay analyzing this technique. Discuss Bierce's purpose in using this technique, as well as its effect on the story.

Understand the Task When you **analyze,** you identify the parts to understand their relationships to the whole. **Point of view** is the standpoint from which a story is told (see page 388).

Prewrite Before you begin, make some notes about how point of view affects the story. You might record your notes in a three-column chart like the one below. To clarify your points, refer to direct quotations in the text.

Point of view	Quotation	Effect
third person omniscient	"At a short remove upon the same temporary platform was an officer in the uniform of his rank, armed."	factual, detached

To help you understand Bierce's purpose, you might also ask yourself questions such as, How did I react to the shift in point of view as I read this story? Did this technique affect my ability to predict the story's outcome? How would the story have been different written from another point of view?

Draft After you consider your purpose and audience, craft your thesis—your central idea or unifying point. You might phrase your thesis like this: *In "An Occurrence at Owl Creek Bridge," Bierce shifts the point of view within the story in order to* _____ .

Revise Ask a partner to read your draft. Ask whether your ideas are clear, and whether the quotations you used from the text are accurate. Revise your draft based on the feedback you get.

Edit and Proofread Proofread your paper, correcting any errors in grammar, spelling, and punctuation. Use the Grammar Tip in the side column for help with conjunctions.

Learning Objectives

In this assignment, you will focus on the following objectives:

Writing: Writing an expository essay.

Grammar: Using conjunctions.

> ### Grammar Tip
>
> #### Conjunctions
>
> Coordinating conjunctions (such as *and, but, or, nor, for, yet*) join phrases or clauses that have equal grammatical weight in a sentence:
>
> *Farquhar had a moustache* **and** *beard* **yet** *no whiskers.*
>
> *He was from a prestigious family,* **yet** *Farquhar had a difficult life.*
>
> Subordinating conjunctions (such as *because, since, who, that,* and *how*) join phrases or clauses so that one is grammatically dependent on the other:
>
> **Because** *of his prestigious family, Farquhar had a lot to lose.*

After You Read

Assess

Writing

Make sure students' essays address the story's shifting point of view. Check that students discuss the effects of the shifting perspective in their essays.

Scoring Guide

Assess students' performance in the following categories using the scoring guide at the bottom of the page:

- Addresses all parts of the writing task.
- Provides a meaningful thesis, maintains focus and organization.
- Supports the thesis with details and examples.
- Provides a variety of sentence types; uses precise, descriptive language.
- Follows English language conventions.
- Makes a logical, convincing analysis.

 For grammar practice, see Unit 3 Teaching Resources Book, p. 106.

Scoring Guide	4	3	2	1
Task addressed	fully	mostly	partially	barely
Thesis	meaningful	provided	partial	weak
Support	thoughtful	provided	limited	weak
Language	varied, descriptive	varied, often descriptive	predictable, imprecise	repetitive, limited
Convention errors	few or none	several	many	serious
Analysis is	convincing	mostly convincing	partially convincing	not convincing

Before You Read

Focus

Bellringer Options

Selection Focus
  Transparency 26
Daily Language Practice
  Transparency 38

Or display several images of Abraham Lincoln. **Ask:** What kind of man was Abraham Lincoln? What did he accomplish? Why are his accomplishments important today? Have students consider, as they read, the challenges that leaders face, especially in wartime.

Political History ☆

Lincoln's Illness Lincoln grew feverish on his return trip to the capital after he delivered the Gettysburg Address. He was ill for the three weeks with what was diagnosed as a mild form of smallpox. Some medical researchers now contend that Lincoln actually had a more serious form of the disease.

Before You Read

The Gettysburg Address

Meet **Abraham Lincoln**
(1809–1865)

Abraham Lincoln's impact on the history and culture of the United States has been immeasurable. He is a familiar figure to all Americans—even small children recognize his trademark hat. One of the United States' greatest presidents, Lincoln led the country through the Civil War, helping to preserve the Union and to end slavery. Lincoln and the United States showed the world that democracy can be a durable form of government.

Politician Born in Hardin County, Kentucky, Lincoln grew up mainly on frontier farms in Indiana, where he worked as a rail-splitter, flat-boatman, storekeeper, surveyor, and postmaster. Lincoln's parents were nearly illiterate and Lincoln received no formal education. Nevertheless, he developed a hunger for learning and read every book he could find. Following a move to New Salem, Illinois, Lincoln began to study law. At twenty-five, he was elected to the Illinois state legislature, marking the beginning of an astounding political career. In 1836, the self-taught Lincoln passed the bar examination and began to practice law. Twenty-four years later, after gaining national political prominence, he was nominated as the Republican presidential candidate. Lincoln won the election on November 6, 1860.

President and Commander in Chief Because Lincoln believed that Congress should prevent the spread of slavery, his victory prompted seven Southern states to secede from the Union. As a result the nation plunged into the Civil War. A man who had once described military glory as "that attractive rainbow that rises in showers of blood—that serpent's eye that charms to destroy" became a great war leader only because it was necessary to preserve the Union. Lincoln believed quite strongly that a Confederate victory would

> *"A new nation, conceived in liberty, and dedicated to the proposition that all men are created equal."*
>
> —Abraham Lincoln
> The Gettysburg Address

most likely have resulted in at least two separate nations. That, he felt, would have marked the failure of our nation's democracy. His policies as president proved shrewd, and the war ended on April 9, 1865, with victory for the North.

Public Speaker Lincoln's tragic and dramatic assassination cemented his place as a U.S. legend. His fame stems largely from the enduring power of his words, and the Gettysburg Address and his Second Inaugural Address are perhaps the most notable examples of Lincoln's mastery of public speaking. These speeches forcefully convey Lincoln's deepest convictions in spare, highly evocative language. Both speeches have had a vast influence on the language of U.S. politics.

 Literature Online

Author Search For more about Abraham Lincoln, go to glencoe.com and enter QuickPass code GLA9800u3.

Selection Skills

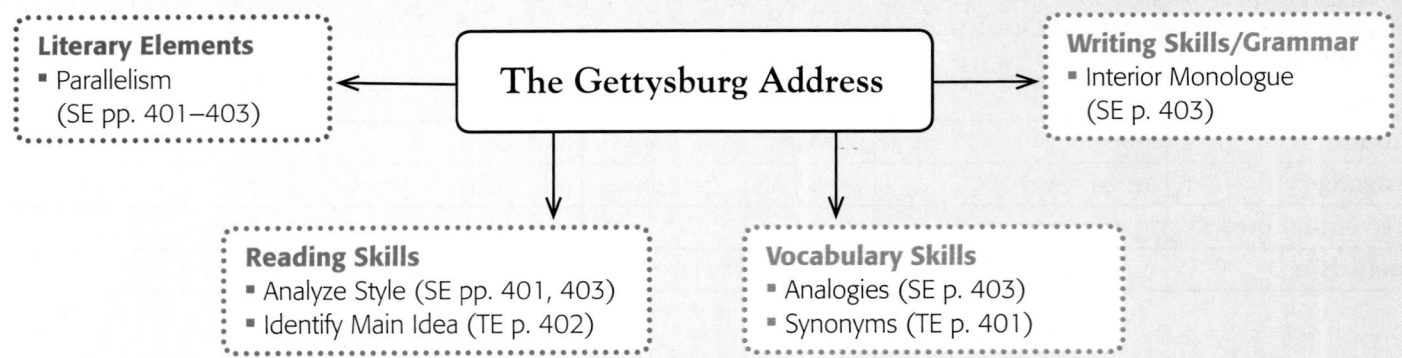

Literary Elements
- Parallelism
  (SE pp. 401–403)

The Gettysburg Address

Writing Skills/Grammar
- Interior Monologue
  (SE p. 403)

Reading Skills
- Analyze Style (SE pp. 401, 403)
- Identify Main Idea (TE p. 402)

Vocabulary Skills
- Analogies (SE p. 403)
- Synonyms (TE p. 401)

Literature and Reading Preview

Connect to the Speech

Imagine you have lost a loved one in a war and are attending a memorial service for that person. What words of comfort would you expect to hear? What rhetorical skills would you find appropriate for such an occasion? Discuss these questions with a small group of classmates.

Build Background

Lincoln delivered the Gettysburg Address on November 19, 1863, at the dedication of a military cemetery in Gettysburg, Pennsylvania. The main speaker was Edward Everett, one of the most famous orators of the time. Everett spoke first—for two hours. Lincoln spoke for approximately two minutes. Everett wrote to Lincoln afterward, "I should be glad if I could flatter myself that I came as near to the central idea of the occasion in two hours as you did in two minutes."

Set Purposes for Reading

Big Idea A Nation Divided

As you read, ask yourself, How does Lincoln stress the way the Civil War has tested the United States' democracy?

Literary Element Parallelism

Parallelism is the use of a series of words, phrases, or sentences that have similar grammatical form. As you read, ask yourself, How does Lincoln use parallelism as a rhetorical technique?

Reading Strategy Analyze Style

Style is a term that denotes the expressive qualities that distinguish an author's work. As you analyze Lincoln's style in this speech, note his word choice, the structure and length of his sentences, and his figurative language.

Tip: Take Notes Use a chart to record examples of Lincoln's style.

Style Element	Example
word choice	dedicate
repetition	consecrate

Learning Objectives

For pages 400–403

In studying this text, you will focus on the following objectives:

Literary Study: Analyzing parallelism.

Reading: Analyzing style.

Writing: Writing an interior monologue.

Vocabulary

score (skôr) *n.* a group of twenty items; p. 402 *Ben ordered ten tablecloths and six score of napkins.*

consecrate (kon´ sə krāt´) *v.* to set apart as sacred; to make or declare holy; p. 402 *A ceremony was held to consecrate the young couple's marriage.*

hallow (hal´ ō) *v.* to make or select as holy; to regard or honor as sacred; p. 402 *The church stands on hallowed ground.*

perish (per´ ish) *v.* to pass from existence; to disappear; p. 402 *Thousands of animals perish in forest fires.*

Before You Read

Focus

Summary

Lincoln agrees that the dedication of a cemetery at Gettysburg is "altogether fitting and proper" because of what the soldiers accomplished. The living, however, should dedicate themselves to "government of the people, by the people, for the people."

 For summaries in languages other than English, see Unit 3 Teaching Resources Book, pp. 109–114.

Vocabulary

Synonyms Point out that *consecrate* and *hallow* are synonyms. They are also similar in meaning to *dedicate,* a word that appears in some form six times in Lincoln's short speech. **Ask:** Why are these words appropriate in speaking at a cemetery on the site of an important battlefield? *(They are appropriate both in their literal meaning of setting something apart for a purpose and in their formal tone, which honors the soldiers' sacrifice.)*

[ADVANCED] Which words sound especially formal because they are no longer in common use? *(score, hallow)*

 For additional context, see Glencoe Interactive Vocabulary CD-ROM.

English Learners

DIFFERENTIATED INSTRUCTION

Intermediate Ask students to explain the source of the phrase "all men are created equal." If necessary, remind them that it is from the Declaration of Independence. Explain that Lincoln's reference to these words expresses his view of what is at stake in the war.

Approaching Level

DIFFERENTIATED INSTRUCTION

Emerging Tell students that Lincoln's style is very formal. Instead of saying "eighty-seven," he says "four score and seven." Ask students to for examples when they use a different level of formality. Explain that Lincoln's purpose at Gettysburg required the most serious tone and loftiest language at his command.

Teach

Big Idea 1

A Nation Divided Say:
Keep this question in mind as you read: To whom is Lincoln's message figuratively addressed? *(to all Americans, even those not present)*

Big Idea 2

A Nation Divided Answer:
A Southerner might have denied that the war was a civil war, considering it a war of aggression against the Confederacy.

Literary Element 3

Parallelism Answer: *The words "what we say here" and "what they did here" are similar grammatical constructions.*

Have students analyze the impact of Lincoln's use of parallelism by listening to an audio version of the speech.

 For additional literary element practice, see Unit 3 Teaching Resources Book, p. 115.

 For an audio recording of this selection, use Listening Library Audio CD-ROM.

Readability Scores

Dale-Chall: 9.3
DRP: 62
Lexile: 1490

THE GETTYSBURG ADDRESS

Abraham Lincoln

1 FOUR SCORE AND SEVEN YEARS AGO OUR fathers brought forth on this continent, a new nation, conceived in liberty, and dedicated to the proposition that all men are created equal.

Now we are engaged in a great civil war, testing whether that nation or any nation so conceived and so dedicated, can long endure. We are met on a great battle-field of that war. We have come to dedicate a portion of that field, as a final resting place for those who here gave their lives that that nation might live. It is altogether fitting and proper that we should do this.

> **2** **A Nation Divided** *How do you think someone living in a Confederate state might have perceived this statement? Explain.*

> **Vocabulary**
>
> **score** (skôr) *n.* a group of twenty items
> **consecrate** (kon´ sə krāt´) *v.* to set apart as sacred; to make or declare holy
> **hallow** (hal´ ō) *v.* to make or select as holy; to regard or honor as sacred
> **perish** (per´ ish) *v.* to pass from existence; to disappear

But, in a larger sense, we can not dedicate—we can not **consecrate**—we can not **hallow**—this ground. The brave men, living and dead, who struggled here, have consecrated it, far above our poor power to add or detract. The world will little note, nor long remember what we say here, but it can never forget what they did here. It is for us the living, rather, to be dedicated here to the unfinished work which they who fought here have thus far so nobly advanced. It is rather for us to be here dedicated to the great task remaining before us—that from these honored dead we take increased devotion to that cause for which they gave the last full measure of devotion—that we here highly resolve that these dead shall not have died in vain—that this nation, under God, shall have a new birth of freedom—and that government of the people, by the people, for the people, shall not **perish** from the earth.

> **Parallelism** *How is this sentence an example of parallelism?* **3**

Reading Practice

SPIRAL REVIEW Identify Main Idea Remind students that sometimes an author states a main idea directly—often in the first or last sentence of a work—and sometimes readers must infer the main idea from many parts of the work. Have students read the speech several times to identify Lincoln's main point. Highlight sentences that point to the main idea (the need for Americans to dedicate themselves to the preservation of freedom and the Union), such as "It is rather for us to be here dedicated. . . ."

After You Read

Respond and Think Critically

Respond and Interpret

1. Which part of this speech made the greatest impression on you? Why?

2. (a)In the opening sentence, what words does Lincoln use to describe the United States? (b)What does this sentence tell you about Lincoln's concept of government?

3. (a)According to Lincoln, why are he and those in the audience gathered together? (b)In what way does Lincoln believe that the battlefield has already been consecrated?

Analyze and Evaluate

4. This speech is often quoted. What, in your opinion, makes it so memorable and inspiring?

5. What is unintentionally ironic about Lincoln's statement that "The world will little note, nor long remember what we say here"?

Connect

6. **Big Idea** A Nation Divided Why did Lincoln consider the Civil War a test of U.S. democracy?

7. **Connect to Today** Does the United States face tests of its democracy today? Explain.

Literary Element Parallelism

The expression "of the people, by the people, for the people" is a famous example of parallelism in American literature. The grammatical structure that is repeated is the prepositional phrase. Find another example of parallelism in this speech and identify the grammatical structure that is repeated.

Reading Strategy Analyze Style

SAT Skills Practice

1. The last sentence of Lincoln's address serves to

   (A) reiterate and elaborate on Lincoln's main ideas

   (B) confuse and bore listeners with its repetition

   (C) build momentum toward an emotional climax

   (D) leave listeners breathless and relieved to hear the last word

   (E) symbolize the intricacy and weight of the issues facing the nation

 Literature Online

Selection Resources For Selection Quizzes, eFlash-cards, and Reading-Writing Connection activities, go to glencoe.com and enter QuickPass code GLA9800u3.

Vocabulary Practice

Practice with Analogies Choose the pair that best completes each analogy.

1. **twenty : score ::**
   a. four : quarter   c. hundred : millennium
   b. twelve : dozen   d. twice : three

2. **consecrate : church ::**
   a. sterilize : hospital   c. discuss : school
   b. sport : stadium   d. plan: schedule

3. **hallow : holy ::**
   a. relax : stressed   c. disrespect : ashamed
   b. celebrate : unite   d. freeze : solid

4. **perish : survive ::**
   a. soar : sail   c. defeat : lose
   b. fail : succeed   d. blaze : fire

 Writing

Write an Interior Monologue Write an interior monologue describing the thoughts and feelings of someone present during Lincoln's speech.

ABRAHAM LINCOLN **403**

After You Read

Assess

1. Students may say the first and last sentences.

2. (a) "A new nation, conceived in liberty, and dedicated to the proposition that all men are created equal" (b) It should be dedicated to the democratic principles of liberty and equality.

3. (a) To dedicate a cemetery for the Union soldiers killed in the Battle of Gettysburg (b) Soldiers have consecrated it with their heroic sacrifices.

4. Students should quote memorable lines and discuss the powerful emotions they evoke.

5. Lincoln did not know that his speech would be as famous as the Battle of Gettysburg.

6. The Civil War tested the concepts on which U.S. democracy was founded—liberty and equality.

7. Students may mention political polarization or the threat of terrorism. Or, they may mention ways our political system is designed to deal with such challenges.

> For additional assessment, see Assessment Resources, pp. 135–136.

Writing

Students' monologues should include thoughts and feelings related to Lincoln's speech, and evaluate Lincoln's style.

Progress Check

Can students analyze style?

If No → See Unit 3 Teaching Resources Book, p. 116.

Literary Element

Possible answer: "we can not dedi-cate—we can not consecrate—we can not hallow"; The parallel structure unifies key ideas by emphasizing them.

Vocabulary

1. b 2. a 3. d 4. b

Reading Strategy

1. **C** is the correct answer because the parallel structure of the extended phrases sweeps readers toward the powerful conclusion.

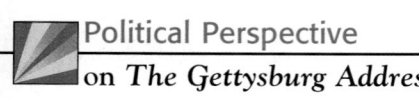

Political Perspective
on *The Gettysburg Address*

Focus

Summary

This passage from *Lincoln at Gettysburg: The Words that Remade America* begins by describing Lincoln's appearance at the dedication of the cemetery and the audience's response to his speech. It goes on to analyze how contemporaries of Lincoln perceived the speech.

 For activities related to this selection, see Unit 3 Teaching Resources Book, pp. 122–130.

Teach

Reading Strategy | 1

Connect to Political Context Before students read the passage, encourage them to recall the events Lincoln discusses in his speech and the background that they learned on page 401.

 For an audio recording of this selection, use Listening Library Audio CD-ROM.

Readability Scores

Dale-Chall: 10.4
DRP: 68
Lexile: 1250

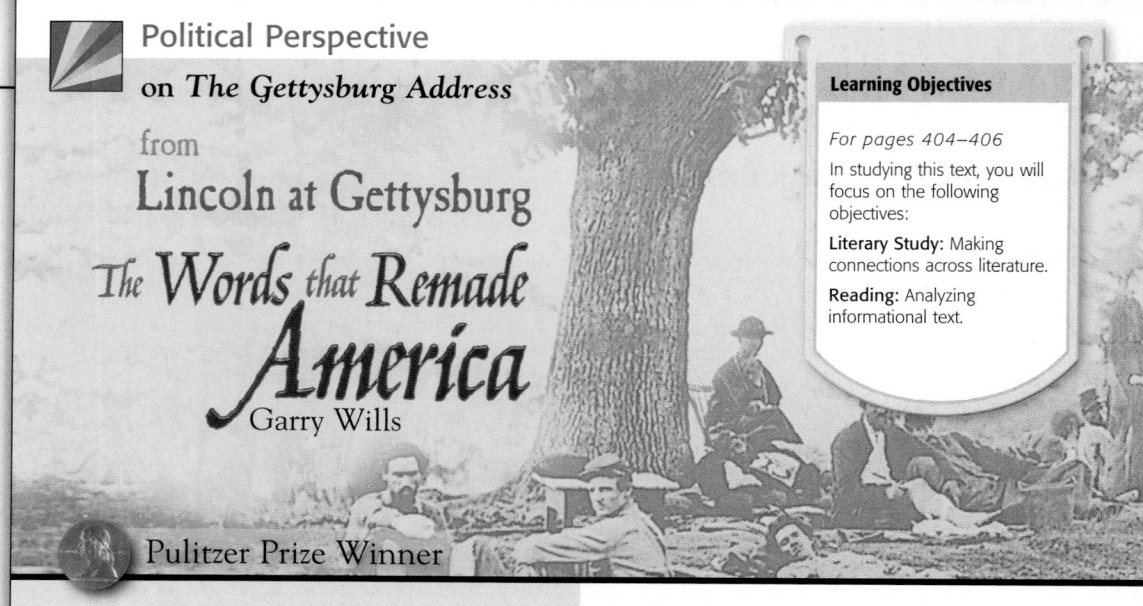

from
Lincoln at Gettysburg
The *Words that Remade* *America*
Garry Wills

Pulitzer Prize Winner

Set a Purpose for Reading
Read to discover the significance of the Gettysburg Address and why it remains important today.

Build Background
In the following passage, historian Garry Wills closely examines the continuing significance of Lincoln's Gettysburg Address, which is considered one of the greatest speeches ever given by an American president. In Wills's Pulitzer Prize–winning book, he discusses the meaning of Lincoln's words, their long-term effect, and the historical environment in which Lincoln delivered the address. Wills maintains that the importance of Lincoln's brief 272-word speech is nearly unparalleled.

Reading Strategy Connect to Political Context

When you **connect to political context,** you examine the political assumptions that influenced the writing of a literary work. As you read this selection, look for the answer to this question: What is the basic political assumption that Wills attributes to Lincoln in the Gettysburg Address? Cite evidence from the text to support your answer.

1

404 UNIT 3 THE CIVIL WAR ERA

When Lincoln rose, it was with a sheet or two, from which he read—as had the minister who offered the invocation. Lincoln's three minutes would, ever after, be obsessively contrasted with Everett's[1] two hours in accounts of this day. It is even claimed that Lincoln disconcerted the crowd with his abrupt performance, so that people did not know how to respond ("Was that all?"). Myth tells of a poor photographer making leisurely arrangements to take Lincoln's picture, expecting him to be there for some time. But it is useful to look at the relevant part of the program as Wills's[2] committee printed it:

> *Music,* by BIRGFIELD'S Band.
> *Prayer,* by REV. T. H. STOCKTON, D.D.
> *Music,* by the Marine Band.
> *Oration,* by Hon. EDWARD EVERETT.
> *Music,* Hymn composed by
> B. B. FRENCH, Esq.

---

1. Edward *Everett,* who delivered the previous oration, had been president of Harvard University, a member of Congress, and the governor of Massachusetts. He was one of the most well-known speakers of his day.
2. David *Wills* was a prominent citizen of Gettysburg, Pennsylvania, and responsible for organizing the interstate commission that created the Gettysburg National Cemetery.

Writing Practice

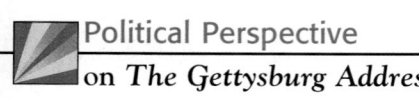 **Primary and Secondary Sources** Tell students that primary sources are firsthand accounts or records of events, whereas secondary sources are written by people who did not experience or influence the events. **Ask:** Is this selection a primary or a secondary source? *(Secondary)* What two primary sources does Garry Wills refer to in his discussion? *(The program of the organizing committee and an article from the* New York Times*)* Have students write a paragraph explaining how reading both a primary source (The Gettysburg Address) and a secondary source helps them to understand a historical event more fully.

Dedicatory Remarks, by the PRESIDENT OF THE UNITED STATES.
Dirge, sung by Choir selected for the occasion.
Benediction, by REV. H. L. BAUGHER, D.D.

There was only one "oration" announced or desired here. Though we call Lincoln's text *the* Gettysburg Address, that title clearly belongs to Everett. Lincoln's contribution, labeled "remarks," was intended to make the dedication formal (somewhat like ribbon-cutting at modern "openings"). Lincoln was not expected to speak at length, any more than Reverend Stockton was (though Stockton's prayer *is* four times the length of the President's remarks). In fact, Lincoln's contribution was as ancillary to Everett's as were those of Reverend Baugher and B. B. French (Lamon's friend, who rushed in where Longfellow, Bryant, and Whittier feared to tread[3]). Lincoln's text had about the same number of words as French's, and twice the number of Dr. Baugher's. It is instructive to look at *The New York Times'* coverage of the events in Gettysburg. It ranked Lincoln's talk, about which it had good things to say, with two given the night before in response to roving serenaders,[4] rather than with Everett's, which was kept in a category of its own. The headline reads:

IMMENSE NUMBERS OF VISITORS
ORATION BY HON. EDWARD EVERETT—
SPEECHES OF PRESIDENT LINCOLN,
MR. SEWARD AND GOVERNOR SEYMOUR

Lincoln was briefer, even, than New York's Governor Seymour had been the night before; but comparison with him was more natural at the time than with the designated orator of the

---

3. Ward *Lamon* was Lincoln's friend and bodyguard; Henry Wadsworth *Longfellow* (1807–1882), William Cullen *Bryant* (1794–1878), and John Greenleaf *Whittier* (1807–1892) were all famous poets (see pages 210–211).
4. The night before the address, serenaders wandered through Gettysburg's crowded town square. The crowds prompted speeches from Lincoln's secretary of state, William Seward, and New York's governor, Horatio Seymour.

---

day. A contrast of length with Everett's talk raises a false issue. Lincoln's text *is* startlingly brief for what it accomplished, but that would be equally true if Everett had spoken for a shorter time or had not spoken at all.

The contrast in other ways was strong. Everett's voice was sweet and expertly modulated; Lincoln's was high to the point of shrillness, and his Kentucky accent offended some Eastern sensibilities. But Lincoln derived an advantage from his high tenor voice—carrying power. If there is agreement on any one aspect of Lincoln's delivery, at Gettysburg and elsewhere, it is his audibility. Modern impersonators of Lincoln, like Walter Huston, Raymond Massey, Henry Fonda, and the various actors who give voice to Disneyland animations of the President, bring him before us as a baritone, which is considered a more manly or heroic voice—though both the Roosevelt presidents of our century were tenors. What should not be forgotten is that Lincoln was himself an actor, an expert raconteur[5] and mimic, and one who spent hours reading speeches out of Shakespeare to any willing (and some unwilling) audiences. He knew a good deal about rhythmic delivery and meaningful inflections. John Hay,[6] who had submitted to many of those Shakespeare readings, gave high marks to his boss's performance at Gettysburg. He put in his diary at the time that "the President, in a fine, free way, with more grace than is his wont, said his half dozen words of consecration." Lincoln's text was polished, his delivery emphatic, he was interrupted **2** by applause five times. Read in a slow, clear way to the farthest listeners, the speech would take about three minutes. It is quite true that the audience did not take in all that happened in that short time—we are still trying to weigh the consequences of that amazing performance. But the myth that Lincoln was disappointed in the result—that he told the unreliable Lamon that his speech, like a bad plow, "won't scour"—has no basis. He had done what he wanted to do,

---

5. A *raconteur* is a storyteller.
6. John *Hay* was President Lincoln's personal secretary.

GARRY WILLS **405**

Teach

Big Idea　　2

A Nation Divided Explain that for many Americans, Lincoln's leadership and eloquence were key elements in reuniting the divided nation.

Write on the board:

- How can strong leaders change our view of events?
- How did the combination of words and military actions win the Civil War for the North?

Tell students to keep these questions in mind as they read.

English Learners

DIFFERENTIATED INSTRUCTION

Intermediate To help students understand how Wills dismisses "myths" about Lincoln's speech, write the following two statements on the board:

> The audience was surprised by the shortness of the speech. Lincoln was disappointed by the audience's reaction to his speech.

Then have students respond to simple comprehension questions. **Ask:** How does the printed program describe Lincoln's role at the dedication? *(Lincoln is to make "dedicatory remarks," not an oration, or long speech.)* Who quoted Lincoln as saying his speech "won't scour"? What is Wills's opinion of this person? *(Ward Lamon is the source of the quote. Wills describes Lamon as "unreliable.")* After discussing Wills's treatment of these myths, ask students if they think Wills is successful in showing the two "myths" to be false.

Political Perspective
on *The Gettysburg Address*

Teach

Reading Strategy 1

Connect to Political Context Point out the words *testing* and *proposition*, which appear in Lincoln's speech.
Ask: What assumption does Lincoln make about the value of such a test? (*Such a test is vital for the nation.*)

Political History ☆

Turning Point The Battle of Gettysburg was a turning point in the war, even before Lincoln's dedication. Robert E. Lee's Southern army was devastated, suffering 25,000 to 28,000 casualties. Gettysburg was the last major attack that Lee could mount.

Assess

1. Students' summaries should be about 100 words long and include the main ideas of the article. The summaries should not include personal opinions.

2. Answers will vary. Students may mention the brevity of Lincoln's speech and people's reactions.

3. (a) They were meant to serve different purposes—one an oration and the other "remarks"— and were never meant to be compared. (b) The brevity is important; Lincoln expressed powerful sentiments in few words.

4. (a) *Voice:* high, shrill, audible; *Delivery:* polished and emphatic (b) He was an actor and expert storyteller.

Informational Text

and Hay shared the pride his superior took in an important occasion put to good use.

At the least, Lincoln had far surpassed David Wills's hope for words to disinfect the air of Gettysburg. The tragedy of macerated[7] bodies, the many bloody and ignoble aspects of this inconclusive encounter, are transfigured in Lincoln's rhetoric, where the physical residue of battle is volatilized as the product of an experiment *testing* whether a government can maintain the *proposition* of equality. The stakes of the three days' butchery are made intellectual, with abstract truths being vindicated. Despite verbal gestures to "that" battle and the men who died "here," there are no particulars mentioned by Lincoln—no names of men or sites or units, or even of sides (the Southerners are part of the "experiment," not foes mentioned in anger or rebuke). Everett succeeded with his audience by being thoroughly immersed in the details of the event he was celebrating. Lincoln eschews[8] all local emphasis. His speech hovers far above the carnage. He lifts the battle to a level of abstraction that purges it of grosser matter—even "earth" is mentioned as the thing from which the tested form of government shall

---

7. *Macerated* means "wasted away."
8. *Eschew* means "to avoid."

not perish. More than William Saunders[9] himself, Lincoln has aligned the dead in ranks of an ideal order. The nightmare realities have been etherealized[10] in the crucible of his language.

But that was just the beginning of this complex transformation. Lincoln did for the whole Civil War what he accomplished for the single battlefield. He has prescinded[11] from messy squabbles over constitutionality, sectionalism, property, states. Slavery is not mentioned, any more than Gettysburg is. The discussion is driven back and back, beyond the historical particulars, to great ideals that are made to grapple naked in an airy battle of the mind. Lincoln derives a new, a transcendental, significance from this bloody episode. Both North and South strove to win the battle for *interpreting* Gettysburg as soon as the physical battle had ended. Lincoln is after even larger game—he means to "win" the whole Civil War in ideological terms as well as military ones. And he will succeed: the Civil War *is*, to most Americans, what Lincoln wanted it to *mean*. Words had to complete the work of the guns. ᔜ

---

9. *William Saunders* designed the Gettysburg National Cemetery.
10. *Etherealized* means "eliminated physical properties."
11. *Prescinded* means "removed from thought."

Respond and Think Critically

Respond and Interpret

1. Write a brief summary of the main ideas in this selection before answering the following questions. For help writing a summary, see page 79.

2. What did you find most interesting in this excerpt?

3. (a)Why does Wills say that comparing the lengths of Lincoln's address and Everett's oration "raises a false issue"? (b)How important to Wills is the length of the Gettysburg Address?

4. (a)What does Wills tell us about Lincoln's voice and delivery? (b)To what personal fact about Lincoln does Wills attribute the effectiveness of his speech?

Analyze and Evaluate

5. (a)According to Wills, how did Lincoln elevate the discussion of the Civil War? (b)What evidence does Wills present to support this contention? (c)What effect do you think the speech has had on historians' interpretation of the war?

Connect

6. Wills says that, because of the Gettysburg Address, "the Civil War *is*, to most Americans, what Lincoln wanted it to *mean*." How has the Gettysburg Address influenced what the Civil War means to you?

---

5. (a) Lincoln elevates the Civil War to an intellectual plane of abstract idealism. (b) Lincoln never refers to slavery, sectionalism, or the name of the battlefield. (c) Lincoln influenced historians to concentrate on the war's ideological issues.

6. Students should explain how they view the Civil War and cite Lincoln's speech to support their points.

 For additional assessment, see Assessment Resources, pp. 137–138.

A Poetic Revolution

The Girl I Left Behind Me, 1870–75. J. Eastman Johnson. Oil on canvas, 42 x 34⁷/₈ in. Smithsonian American Art Museum, Washington, DC.

 View the Art The woman in this painting is the young wife of a Civil War soldier. What is the mood of the painting? What might the painting suggest about the couple's—and the country's—future? Explain.

"*A child said* What is the grass? *fetching it to me with full hands;*
How could I answer the child? I do not know what it is any more than he." **1**

—Walt Whitman, "Song of Myself"

Analyze and Extend

Reading Strategy   1

Evaluate Read the quotation from Walt Whitman. **Ask:** What does Whitman mean by saying he does not know what grass is? *(He may mean that even common things in nature, such as grass, are full of mystery.)*

View the Art

Answer: *The woman's tense pose, the ominous wind, and the darkening sky all suggest that the future may be dark and uncertain.*

Eastman Johnson (1824–1906) took the title for this painting from a popular Irish ballad.

> For additional support for English Learners, see Unit 3 Teaching Resources Book, p. 132.

English Learners

DIFFERENTIATED INSTRUCTION

Intermediate Point out that *revolution* is a cognate in other languages—for example, *revolución* in Spanish or *revoluzione* in Italian. Have students list words they associate with revolution *(change, war, history)* and predict what a poetic revolution might be like.

Approaching Level

DIFFERENTIATED INSTRUCTION

Emerging Explain that *revolution* has different meanings. In science, *revolution* refers to the way one object moves around another. In history, a *revolution* is a sudden change in events. Ask students to think of historical revolutions they may have studied *(American Revolution, Industrial Revolution).* Then ask students to explain how the word *revolution* is used in the title of Part 3.

407

Meet **Walt Whitman**
(1819–1892)

When Walt Whitman first published *Leaves of Grass* in 1855, it marked the beginning of a revolution in poetry. At the time, however, few people noticed the young poet's radical work—and most of those who did were either dismayed or offended. Whitman's poetry was realistic, free flowing, and shockingly candid. He was the first poet in English to write extensively in free verse, an open, unregulated form that reflected the cadences of everyday speech. Although it took decades for his poetry to be broadly accepted, *Leaves of Grass* eventually became an enduring symbol of the democratic spirit it celebrated.

An American Voice As a young man, Whitman loved to wander through the streets of Manhattan, a section of New York City. As he walked, he jotted down his impressions of the city's sights, sounds, and array of characters. A great reader, Whitman was nurtured by the transcendentalists, yet he was no country dweller delighting in the quiet joys of nature. Instead, he believed in gathering a wide range of experiences, so he held numerous jobs: office boy, doctor's helper, printer's assistant, journalist, typesetter, and printer. He also traveled down the Mississippi River, listening to the talk of working people, farmers, and soldiers. Whitman used his experiences to create a new kind of poetry that celebrated the multifaceted spirit of his country.

The first edition of *Leaves of Grass* contained just twelve poems, but they were enough to convince Ralph Waldo Emerson, the most famous literary figure of his day, of the unknown poet's genius. In a letter to Whitman, Emerson said the collection was "the most extraordinary piece of wit and wisdom that America has yet contributed." With the encouragement of a small group of admirers,

Whitman pressed on with his life's work: revising, rearranging, and adding to *Leaves of Grass*, envisioning all of his work as one vast poem.

Witness to War Like all Americans, Whitman was deeply distressed by the Civil War. In 1862, he traveled to the Virginia battlefront to care for his brother George, who had been wounded in the first battle of Fredericksburg. Deeply moved by the suffering he encountered and finding his brother's condition stable, Whitman went on to Washington, D.C., to work as a volunteer nurse in army hospitals. His experiences during the war inspired some of his greatest works, including "When Lilacs Last in the Door-yard Bloom'd," his elegy to President Lincoln.

> *"The United States themselves are essentially the greatest poem."*
>
> —Walt Whitman

Even in old age, Whitman kept writing, attempting to put "a Person, a human being (myself, in the latter half of the Nineteenth Century, in America) freely, fully, and truly on record." The final, "deathbed" edition of *Leaves of Grass* (1891), which contained 383 titled poems, put on record the man who had become America's national poet.

Literature Online

Author Search For more about Walt Whitman, go to glencoe.com and enter QuickPass code GLA9800u3.

Bellringer Options

Literature Launchers DVD:
Pre-Reading Video
Selection Focus
Transparencies 27, 28
Daily Language Practice
Transparency 39

Or write on the board the quotation from Whitman displayed on this page. **Ask:** What traditional qualities of the United States and of individual Americans might make them an appropriate subject for a great poem?

Cultural History ☆

New York City Whitman's experiences and observations of life in New York City led him to believe that a democratic society is a vital, though imperfect, creation.

Selection Skills

Literary Elements
- Free Verse (SE pp. 409, 410, 412, 415)

I Hear America Singing/When I Heard . . . /A Sight in Camp . . . / Beat! Beat! Drums!

Writing Skills/Grammar
- Write a Poem (SE p. 412)
- Write an Essay (SE p. 415)
- Sentence Fragments (TE p. 410)
- Run-on Sentences (TE p. 414)

Vocabulary Skills
- Word Parts (TE p. 409)

Reading Skills
- Paraphrase (SE pp. 409, 411, 412, 414, 415)

Listening/Speaking/Viewing Skills
- Analyze Art (TE pp. 410, 411, 413)

Literature and Reading Preview

Connect to the Poems

To Whitman, working people were the essence of America. How do the people you know seem to feel about their jobs? How do you hope to feel about your own profession someday? Freewrite for ten minutes on these questions and the relationships between people and their work.

Build Background

Whitman wrote "I Hear America Singing" just before the Civil War and "When I Heard the Learn'd Astronomer" at its end. "A Sight in Camp in the Daybreak Gray and Dim" captures one of the poet's experiences in army hospitals. "Beat! Beat! Drums!" is Whitman's response to the defeat of the Union army by the Confederate forces in the first battle of Bull Run. All four poems reflect themes he explored during the Civil War.

Set Purposes for Reading

Big Idea A Poetic Revolution

As you read, ask yourself, How does Whitman use ordinary details and sprawling lines to create a new kind of poetry?

Literary Element Free Verse

Whitman is famous for using **free verse**—a type of poetry that does not have a regular pattern of rhythm or rhyme. As you read, ask yourself, What effects does Whitman create by using free verse?

Reading Strategy Paraphrase

When you **paraphrase**, you put something you have read into your own words. As you read the poems, break down long sentences and restate them in your own words.

....

Tip: Take Notes Use a chart to record your paraphrases.

> Original
>
> "How soon unaccountable I became tired and sick..."
>
> Paraphrase

Learning Objectives

For pages 408–419

In studying this text, you will focus on the following objectives:

Literary Study:
Analyzing free verse.
Analyzing historical narratives.

Reading: Paraphrasing.

Writing:
Writing a poem.
Writing an essay.
Writing a journal entry.

Vocabulary

impromptu (im promp′ tōō, -tū) *adv.* done on the spur of the moment; p. 416 *The committee held an impromptu meeting.*

incredulity (in′ krə dōō′ lə tē) *n.* disbelief; p. 417 *Skeptics felt only incredulity when the team won.*

subsequently (sub′ sə kwent′ lē) *adv.* at a later time; p. 417 *She had cash and subsequently lost it.*

susceptible (sə sep′ tə bəl) *adj.* easily influenced or affected; p. 417 *Dogs do not sweat, so they are more susceptible to overheating.*

convalescent (kon′ və le′ sənt) *n.* a person who is recovering from illness or injury; p. 418 *The visit cheered the convalescent.*

WALT WHITMAN **409**

Before You Read

Focus

Summary

In "I Hear America Singing," the speaker presents a catalog of the rich diversity of American life. In "When I Heard the Learn'd Astronomer," the speaker records his response to a dry lecture that seems to deprive nature of its grandeur and mystery. The speaker in "A Sight in Camp in the Daybreak Gray and Dim" describes three dead soldiers in the Civil War. In "Beat! Beat! Drums!" the speaker tells of the power of war to overwhelm all other elements of society.

 For summaries in languages other than English, see Unit 3 Teaching Resources Book, pp. 133–148.

Vocabulary

Word Parts Prefixes and suffixes affect the meaning and part of speech of a word. **Ask:** Which prefix in the vocabulary list means "not"? *(in-)* Which suffix indicates a noun form? *(-ity)* Which vocabulary words can be changed into another word by changing a prefix or suffix? *(incredulity— incredulous; subsequently, consequently; susceptible—susceptibility; convalescent—convalescence)*

For additional context, see Glencoe Interactive Vocabulary CD-ROM.

 Interactive Read and Write
Other options for teaching this selection can be found in

- Interactive Read and Write for English Learners, pp. 133–138
- Interactive Read and Write for Approaching-Level Learners, pp. 133–138
- Interactive Read and Write for On-Level Learners, pp. 133–138

409

English Learners

DIFFERENTIATED INSTRUCTION

SMALL GROUP **Intermediate** Help students understand the term *free verse* by having them work in groups to brainstorm for two word webs. One should focus on words or concepts associated with *free;* the other should focus on *verse.* Bring students together to share webs and to compare their ideas to the definition of free verse on this page.

SMALL GROUP **Advanced** Ask students to explain what they expect when they listen to a traditional poem. *(regular rhymes and rhythms or sing-song sounds)* Have students work in pairs to preview Whitman's poems and talk about how the poems' appearance surprises them.

Teach

A Poetic Revolution **Say:** In free verse, two key elements are repetition and parallelism. In line 1, what phrase does Whitman repeat? *("I hear")* In lines 3–6, what structure does Whitman use to begin the lines the same way? *("The [noun] singing")*

ADVANCED **Ask:** What effect does the repetition have on readers? *(It helps establish rhythm; it makes the reader expect to read about a different kind of singer at the beginning of each line.)*

Literary Element   2

Free Verse **Answer:** *Whitman describes everyday people at work. Free verse captures the rhythms of everyday speech better than formal poetry does.*

View the Art ★

Thomas Hart Benton (1889–1975), like Walt Whitman, celebrated the American worker in his art. Unlike Whitman, Benton lived well into the twentieth century, a time shaped by industrialization and urban growth. **Ask:** Do you think the subjects of this painting would fit in Whitman's poem? Why? *(The workers in his poem, like the harvesters in the painting, are working honestly and hard.)*

For an audio recording of this selection, use Listening Library Audio CD-ROM.

Village Carpenter, 1899. Edward Henry Potthast. Oil on canvas. ★ Private Collection.

I Hear America Singing

Walt Whitman

I hear America singing, the varied carols I hear,
Those of mechanics, each one singing his as it should be blithe[1] and strong,
The carpenter singing his as he measures his plank or beam,
The mason singing his as he makes ready for work, or leaves off work,
5 The boatman singing what belongs to him in his boat,
    the deckhand singing on the steamboat deck,
The shoemaker singing as he sits on his bench, the hatter singing as he stands,
The wood-cutter's song, the ploughboy's on his way in the morning,
    or at noon intermission or at sundown,
The delicious singing of the mother, or of the young wife at work,
    or of the girl sewing or washing,
Each singing what belongs to him or her and to none else,
10 The day what belongs to the day—at night the party of young fellows,
    robust, friendly,
Singing with open mouths their strong melodious songs.

1 (in right margin)

---

1. *Blithe* means "lighthearted" or "cheerful."

2 **Free Verse** *Why is free verse appropriate for the descriptions in this poem?*

410   **UNIT 3**   THE CIVIL WAR ERA

Grammar Practice

SPIRAL REVIEW ⟳ **Sentence Fragments** Point out that a sentence fragment is punctuated as though it were a complete sentence but is missing a subject or a verb or is a dependent clause. To fix the sentence fragment "Because Whitman wrote free verse," delete *because* or connect the fragment to another sentence. Ask students to rewrite each of the following as a complete sentence:

1. Which they sang as they worked. *(They enjoyed the songs, which they sang as they worked.)*

2. Singing as he sits on his bench. *(I see the shoemaker singing as he sits on his bench.)*

When I Heard the Learn'd Astronomer

The Life of Harriet Tubman, #31, 1940. Jacob Lawrence. Casein tempera on hardboard, 17⅞ x 12 in. Hampton University Museum.

Walt Whitman

When I heard the learn'd astronomer,
When the proofs, the figures, were ranged in columns before me,
When I was shown the charts and diagrams, to add, divide, and measure them,
When I sitting heard the astronomer where he lectured with much applause
    in the lecture-room,
5 How soon unaccountable I became tired and sick,
Till rising and gliding out I wander'd off by myself,
In the mystical moist night-air, and from time to time,
Look'd up in perfect silence at the stars.

Paraphrase *How would you rephrase these lines in your own words?* **3**

Teach

Reading Strategy **3**

Paraphrase **Answer:** *I became tired and bored while sitting and listening to the astronomer, who was applauded by the audience.*

📁 For additional practice using the reading skill or strategy, see Unit 3 Teaching Resources Book, p. 140.

View the Art ★

Although African American painter Jacob Lawrence (1917–2000) was born long after the end of slavery, the Abolitionist movement was central to much of his art. He created several series of paintings that depicted the efforts of anti-slavery heroes such as Harriet Tubman, who led slaves to freedom along the Underground Railroad, and Frederick Douglass, the former slave turned orator. **Ask:** How does Lawrence's painting connect to the feelings expressed by the speaker in Whitman's poem? *(The painting captures the "mystical" nature and "perfect silence" of a night sky that the narrator yearns for.)*

 To check students' understanding of the poems, see Unit 3 Teaching Resources Book, p. 141.

Approaching Level

DIFFERENTIATED INSTRUCTION

Established Read the poem aloud to students. After each line, ask students "What happened?" Suggest that they replace each use of the word *when* with sequence words, such as *first, second, next,* and *last.* Finally, ask volunteers to give oral retellings of what happens in the poem using their own words.

AAVE Remind approaching level students who are users of African American vernacular English (AAVE) to use the past tense in their responses. When using past tense verbs, students should be careful to pronounce the *-ed* sound at the end of the verb. For example, students should say, "He walked outside," instead of "He walk outside."

After You Read

Assess

1. Students should offer evidence to support their opinions.

2. (a) Mechanic, carpenter, mason, boatman, deckhand, shoemaker, hatter, wood-cutter, ploughboy, mother, young wife at work, and girl sewing or washing (b) Labor makes the country strong. (c) Their work is satisfying and meaningful.

3. (a) Young fellows socialize and sing. (b) It takes many workers to make a strong America.

4. (a) Catalog of occupations (b) Images make the poem more immediate.

5. Common people

6. (a) Using mathematics, charts, diagrams (b) His approach is analytical and impersonal.

7. (a) It leads to direct spiritual knowledge. (b) It implies knowledge gained through emotional or spiritual means.

8. (a) It is spontaneous, mysterious, and emotional. (b) He values artistic experience and emotions over scientific analysis.

9. Students may say that Whitman wanted to highlight the accomplishments of everyday citizens, or to write in a new form of poetry.

> For additional assessment, see Assessment Resources, pp. 139–140.

 Writing

Students' poems should be in free verse form and incorporate everyday scenes that depict modern culture.

After You Read

Respond and Think Critically

I Hear America Singing
Respond and Interpret

1. Which of these poems do you prefer, and why?

2. (a) What occupations does the speaker say represent America? (b) What do these occupations suggest about Whitman's view of his country? (c) What do the laborers' songs suggest about the work they do?

3. (a) What happens at night? (b) Why do you think the poem ends the way it does?

Analyze and Evaluate

4. (a) What **catalog**, or list of images and details, is included in this poem? (b) What effect does the catalog have on your reading of the poem?

5. What about America does Whitman seem to be celebrating in this poem?

When I Heard the Learn'd Astronomer
Respond and Interpret

6. (a) How does the astronomer present information? (b) What does this suggest about the astronomer's approach to his subject?

7. (a) Why is the night air "mystical"? (b) What is implied by this word?

Analyze and Evaluate

8. (a) How does the speaker's method for "studying" the stars differ from the astronomer's? (b) What difference in values does this imply?

Connect

9. **Connect to the Author** Based on these poems, what can you infer about Whitman's beliefs and values?

Literary Element Free Verse

Free verse lacks a regular pattern of stressed and unstressed syllables. The lengths of the lines usually differ, and the lines may not be grouped together in stanzas. Instead, the way words and phrases are arranged and repeated creates a natural, conversational rhythm in the poem.

1. With a partner, read one of Whitman's poems aloud. Do you find the rhythm of the poem similar to that of everyday speech? Explain.

2. In what ways might "I Hear America Singing" have a different effect if it were written in a regular pattern?

Reading Strategy Paraphrase

Paraphrasing can help you judge whether you understand what you have read. This strategy also helps you appreciate particular words or phrases in the poem. Reread the following lines:

Till rising and gliding out I wander'd off by myself,
In the mystical moist night-air, and from time to time,
Look'd up in perfect silence at the stars.

1. How would you paraphrase these lines?

2. What is lost in your paraphrase?

 Writing

Write a Poem In "I Hear America Singing," Whitman uses several snapshot descriptions to evoke nineteenth-century life. Following Whitman's example, write a free verse poem describing twenty-first-century America. Think about scenes you encounter every day to help you represent modern culture.

> **LOG ON** **Literature** Online
>
> **Selection Resources** For Selection Quizzes, eFlashcards, and Reading-Writing Connection activities, go to glencoe.com and enter QuickPass code GLA9800u3.

Literary Element

1. Yes; this is characteristic of free verse.
2. A regular rhythm might contradict the spirit at the heart of this poem.

Progress Check

Can students identify free verse?

If No → See Unit 3 Teaching Resources Book, p. 139.

Reading Strategy

1. Until I rose from my seat and left the room, wandering away alone and occasionally looking at the stars and taking in their mystery
2. Rhythm, precision of image, voice, and eloquence

Encampment of Duryea's Zouaves, Virginia. 1862. William MacIlvaine the younger. Watercolor and gouache on paper, 18.1 x 27.3 in. New York Historical Society, NY. ★

A Sight in Camp in the Daybreak Gray and Dim

Walt Whitman

A sight in camp in the daybreak gray and dim,
As from my tent I emerge so early sleepless,
As slow I walk in the cool fresh air the path near by the hospital tent,
Three forms I see on stretchers lying, brought out there untended lying,
5 Over each the blanket spread, ample brownish woolen blanket,
Gray and heavy blanket, folding, covering all.

Curious I halt and silent stand,
Then with light fingers I from the face of the nearest the first just lift the blanket;
Who are you elderly man so gaunt and grim, with well-gray'd hair, and flesh all sunken
    about the eyes?
10 Who are you my dear comrade?

Then to the second I step—and who are you my child and darling?
Who are you sweet boy with cheeks yet blooming?

Then to the third—a face nor child nor old, very calm, as of beautiful yellow-white ivory;
Young man I think I know you—I think this face is the face of the Christ himself,
15 Dead and divine and brother of all, and here again he lies.

A Poetic Revolution *How is this description different from what you might read in poems from an earlier era?*

WALT WHITMAN **413**

Teach

Big Idea 1

A Poetic Revolution Have students discuss why Whitman seems to condemn the Civil War itself, rather than the Union or the Confederate side. **Ask:** Why is this view a revolutionary approach to war? *(It transcends the issues on both sides and questions the violence and destruction of war.)*

Literary Element 2

Alliteration Point out Whitman's use of alliteration—a repetition of consonant sounds at the beginning of words—in the final stanza. **Ask:** How does Whitman's repetition of the *m* sound *(make, mind, man, mother's)* affect the reader's response to the poem? *(The repetition of the m sound sets up a kind of hum or moan, which is appropriate to the weeping that is a response to the destruction of war.)*

Reading Strategy 3

Paraphrase Answer: *Students' paraphrases will be much longer than this line. Most will say that a paraphrase would not work because it would be too cumbersome.*

Progress Check

Can students paraphrase?

If No → See Unit 3 Teaching Resources Book, p. 150.

Beat! Beat! Drums!

Walt Whitman

The Wounded Drummer Boy, 1871. J. Eastman Johnson. Oil on canvas, 40 x 36 in. The Brooklyn Museum of Art, New York.

Beat! beat! drums!—blow! bugles! blow!
Through the windows—through doors—burst like a ruthless force,
Into the solemn church, and scatter the congregation,
Into the school where the scholar is studying;
5 Leave not the bridegroom quiet—no happiness must he have now with his bride,
Nor the peaceful farmer any peace, ploughing his field or gathering his grain,
So fierce you whirr and pound you drums—so shrill you bugles blow.

Beat! beat! drums!—blow! bugles! blow!
Over the traffic of cities—over the rumble of wheels in the streets;
10 Are beds prepared for sleepers at night in the houses? no sleepers must sleep in those beds,
No bargainers' bargains by day—no brokers or speculators[1]—would they continue?
Would the talkers be talking? would the singer attempt to sing?
Would the lawyer rise in the court to state his case before the judge?
1 Then rattle quicker, heavier drums—you bugles wilder blow.

15 Beat! beat! drums!—blow! bugles! blow!
Make no parley—stop for no expostulation,[2]
Mind not the timid—mind not the weeper or prayer,
Mind not the old man beseeching the young man,
Let not the child's voice be heard, nor the mother's entreaties,
20 Make even the trestles[3] to shake the dead where they lie awaiting the hearses,
So strong you thump O terrible drums—so loud you bugles blow.

---

1. *Speculators* are people who engage in risky business ventures hoping to make quick or large profits.
2. A *parley* is a conference between enemies to discuss terms of a truce or an agreement. *Expostulation* is the act of reasoning with a person to correct or dissuade him or her.
3. *Trestles* are structures in which a beam is supported by four diverging legs.

3 Paraphrase *Would your paraphrase of this line work with the rest of the poem?*

414 UNIT 3   THE CIVIL WAR ERA

Grammar Practice

SPIRAL REVIEW **Run-on Sentences** A run-on sentence is two or more sentences written as one sentence. Correct a run-on by joining the sentences with a semicolon or a comma and a coordinating conjunction or by breaking the run-on into two or more sentences.

Have students correct these sentences:

1. He took books from the library none of them were returned overdue. *(He took books from the library, and none of them were returned overdue.)*

2. She searched for information about Whitman, the library had 20 of his books. *(She searched for information about Whitman. The library had 20 of his books.)*

After You Read

Respond and Think Critically

A Sight in Camp in the Daybreak Gray and Dim

Respond and Interpret

1. Which image or idea from these two poems stands out in your mind? Why?

2. (a)What item does the speaker describe in lines 5–6? (b)Why might the speaker have focused on this item?

3. (a)Describe the first two soldiers. (b)What do the speaker's questions imply about his feelings toward the soldiers?

Analyze and Evaluate

4. Why do you think Whitman presents the three soldiers in this order?

5. (a)What comparison does Whitman make in the last stanza? (b)What is the effect of comparing the third soldier to Christ?

Beat! Beat! Drums!

Respond and Interpret

6. (a)What instruments are mentioned in this poem? (b)What might they represent?

7. (a)What kinds of activities do the instruments interrupt? (b)What does the variety of activities suggest to you about the speaker's message?

Analyze and Evaluate

8. (a)Why might the people in stanza 3 be praying, beseeching, and so on? (b)What message does this stanza convey? Explain your answer.

9. (a)What attitude toward war does the poem express? (b)Is the poem effective? Explain.

Connect

10. **Connect to Today** Do you think the views regarding war expressed in these two poems are applicable today? Support your answer.

Literary Element **Free Verse**

Whitman's poetry is an example of **free verse** at its most impressive. Free verse is poetry that has an irregular rhythm and line length and attempts to avoid any predetermined verse structure. Despite this lack of regularity, free verse does have a structure, which seems to "grow" organically to fit its subject matter. Whitman pioneered this form and made it important in American poetry.

1. Find examples of rhythm and repetition in "Beat! Beat! Drums!" In particular, consider the effect of lines 1, 8, and 15.

2. How do these examples reinforce the meaning of the poem?

 Literature Online

Selection Resources For Selection Quizzes, eFlashcards, and Reading-Writing Connection activities, go to glencoe.com and enter QuickPass code GLA9800u3.

Reading Strategy **Paraphrase**

In "Beat! Beat! Drums!" the sound effects reinforce the meaning of the poem. One way to appreciate these effects is to **paraphrase** selected lines and then compare your paraphrases with Whitman's original lines. Refer to the notes you took while reading to help you answer these questions.

1. How would you paraphrase the last line of the first stanza?

2. How do the verbs and adjectives that describe the drums and bugles suggest that their sound is a "ruthless force"?

Writing

Write an Essay In describing the Civil War, Whitman often writes about subjects on the periphery (sidelines) rather than the battle itself. Why do you think he does this? Write a brief essay answering this question. Use examples from the poems to support your views.

WALT WHITMAN **415**

Literary Element

1. The line "Beat! beat! drums!—blow! bugles! blow!" is repeated at the beginning of each stanza. The rhythm of this line derives from the heavily stressed, monosyllabic words *beat, drums,* and *blow,* and the repetition of the *b* sound.

2. They echo the unrelenting force of war.

Reading Strategy

1. You drums make a such a wild and rapid beat; you bugles make such a harsh, unpleasant sound.

2. Words such as *beat, blow, burst,* and *shrill* suggest a savage force.

 For additional assessment, see Assessment Resources, pp. 141–142.

After You Read

Assess

1. Answers will vary.

2. (a) The blanket that covers the dead (b) It is a sign of respect and hides the dead.

3. (a) Older man, gaunt, grim, gray-haired; rosy-cheeked boy (b) The deaths *are* personal, even though he does not know the victims.

4. It builds toward a dramatic and emotional high point.

5. (a) Whitman compares the soldier to Christ. (b) It emphasizes Whitman's sorrow for the soldier's death, making it a tragedy for all humankind.

6. (a) Drums and bugles (b) War's invasion of every aspect of life

7. (a) Sleeping, praying, ploughing, studying, talking, and singing (b) War disrupts all aspects of life.

8. (a) They are praying for loved ones not to go to war or to return safely from it. (b) War is oblivious to reason and emotion.

9. (a) The speaker's attitude is bitterly ironic; war bursts "like a ruthless force" over all aspects of life, and humans are powerless to stop it. (b) Yes, it expresses the speaker's attitude powerfully.

10. Students may agree that war causes unnecessary death, but may say that war is not necessarily inevitable.

Writing

Students' essays should answer the question in the prompt and include details from Whitman's poems as support.

415

Summary

In these excerpts from his Civil War diary, Whitman chronicles the outbreak of war and the attitudes of Northerners toward the South, gives his personal impressions of the front, and pays a poignant tribute to Abraham Lincoln a few weeks after the president's assassination in April 1865.

 For summaries in languages other than English, see Unit 3 Teaching Resources Book, pp. 153–158.

Teach

Literary Element   **1**

Historical Narrative
Answer: *The description of the newsboys running "furiously" through the streets creates a sense of heightened tension.*

 For an audio recording of this selection, use Listening Library Audio CD-ROM.

Readability Scores
Dale-Chall: 5.8
DRP: 62
Lexile: 1410

Selection Skills

from Specimen Days

Walt Whitman

Before You Read

Build Background

While serving as a volunteer nurse during the Civil War, Whitman recorded his experiences in the form of journal entries. Writing about this experience, Whitman noted, "I supply often to some of these dear suffering boys . . . that which doctors nor medicines nor skill nor any routine assistance can give. . . . There is something in . . . the magnetic flood of sympathy that does, in its way, more good than all the medicine in the world."

Literary Element   Historical Narrative

A **historical narrative** is a nonfiction work that tells the story of important historical events or developments. Often told from an individual's point of view, historical narratives provide a "you-are-there" perspective, allowing readers to experience history deeply and personally. As you read these excerpts from *Specimen Days,* ask yourself, How does Whitman bring the Civil War home to his readers?

Opening of the Secession War

News of the attack on fort Sumter and *the flag* at Charleston harbor, S. C., was receiv'd in New York city late at night (13th April, 1861,) and was immediately sent out in extras of the newspapers. I had been to the opera in Fourteenth street that night, and after the performance was walking down Broadway toward twelve o'clock, on my way to Brooklyn, when I heard in the distance the loud cries of the newsboys, who came presently tearing and yelling up the street, rushing from side to side even more furiously than

usual. I bought an extra and cross'd to the Metropolitan hotel (Niblo's) where the great lamps were still brightly blazing, and, with a crowd of others, who gather'd **impromptu**, read the news, which was evidently authentic. For the benefit of some who had no papers, one of us read the telegram aloud, while all listen'd silently and attentively. No remark was made by any of the crowd, which had increas'd to thirty or forty, but all stood a minute or two, I remember, before they dispers'd. I can almost see them there now, under the lamps at midnight again.

1   *Historical Narrative* How does this description set the tone for this entry?

Vocabulary
impromptu (im promp′ too͞, -tū) *adv.* done on the spur of the moment

Literary Elements
- Historical Narrative (SE pp. 416, 419)

Study Skills/Research/ Assessment
- Text Aids (TE p. 418)

from **Specimen Days**

Vocabulary Skills
- Context Clues (SE p. 419)
- Academic Vocabulary (SE p. 419)

Writing Skills/Grammar
- Journal Entry (SE p. 419)

Listening/Speaking/Viewing Skills
- Analyze Art (TE p. 418)

Contemptuous Feeling

Even after the bombardment of Sumter, however, the gravity of the revolt, and the power and will of the slave States for a strong and continued military resistance to national authority, were not at all realized at the North, except by a few. Nine-tenths of the people of the free States look'd upon the rebellion, as started in South Carolina, from a feeling one-half of contempt, and the other half composed of anger and **incredulity**. It was not thought it would be join'd in by Virginia, North Carolina, or Georgia. A great and cautious national official predicted that it would blow over "in sixty days," and folks generally believ'd the prediction. I remember talking about it on a Fulton ferry-boat with the Brooklyn mayor, who said he only "hoped the Southern fire-eaters would commit some overt act of resistance, as they would then be at once so effectually squelch'd, we would never hear of secession again—but he was afraid they never would have the pluck to really do anything." I remember, too, that a couple of companies of the Thirteenth Brooklyn, who rendezvou'd at the city armory, and started thence as thirty days' men, were all provided with pieces of rope, conspicuously tied to their musket-barrels, with which to bring back each man a prisoner from the audacious South, to be led in a noose, on our men's early and triumphant return!

Down at the Front

Falmouth, Va., opposite Fredericksburgh, December 21, 1862.—Begin my visits among the camp hospitals in the army of the Potomac. Spend a good part of the day in a large brick mansion on the banks of the Rappahannock, used as a hospital since the battle—seems to have receiv'd only the worst cases. Out doors, at the foot of a tree, within ten yards of the front of the house, I notice a heap of amputated feet, legs, arms, hands, &c., a full load for a one-horse cart. Several dead bodies lie near,

each cover'd with its brown woolen blanket. In the door-yard, towards the river, are fresh graves, mostly of officers, their names on pieces of barrel-staves or broken boards, stuck in the dirt. (Most of these bodies were **subsequently** taken up and transported north to their friends.) The large mansion is quite crowded upstairs and down, everything impromptu, no system, all bad enough, but I have no doubt the best that can be done; all the wounds pretty bad, some frightful, the men in their old clothes, unclean and bloody. Some of the wounded are rebel soldiers and officers, prisoners. One, a Mississippian, a captain, hit badly in leg, I talk'd with some time; he ask'd me for papers, which I gave him. (I saw him three months afterward in Washington, with his leg amputated, doing well.) I went through the rooms, downstairs and up. Some of the men were dying. I had nothing to give at that visit, but wrote a few letters to folks home, mothers, &c. Also talk'd to three or four, who seem'd most **susceptible** to it, and needing it.

After First Fredericksburg

December 23 to 31.—The results of the late battle are exhibited everywhere about here in thousands of cases, (hundreds die every day,) in the camp, brigade, and division hospitals. These are merely tents, and sometimes very poor ones, the wounded lying on the ground, lucky, if their blankets are spread on layers of pine or hemlock twigs, or small leaves. No cots; seldom even a mattress. It is pretty cold. The ground is frozen hard, and there is occasional snow. I go around from one case to another. I do not see that I do much good to these wounded and dying; but I cannot leave them. Once in a while some youngster holds on to me convulsively, and I do what I can for him; at any

---

Teach

Historical Narrative Have students characterize Whitman's attitude here toward visiting the wounded in the camp hospitals. (*Although the realities of war are gruesome, Whitman is compassionate and seems at ease among the men.*) **Ask:** What do Whitman's actions and comments here and throughout the selection suggest about his political assumptions about war? (*Whitman seems to care only about the soldiers, not about the reasons they are fighting. He sees the soldiers from both sides as human beings.*)

English Learners

DIFFERENTIATED INSTRUCTION

Advanced Remind students that this selection is taken from the author's journal in which he jotted down his observations quickly and informally. Point out that often journal writers use sentence fragments and abbreviations because they do not expect others to read their writing. Ask students to identify the letters that are replaced by apostrophes or ideas that are indicated by "&c," which means "et cetera," or "and

so on" and is used at the end of a list to indicate that the list continues.

Explain that Whitman's contemporaries would have understood many of the idioms and terms he uses. Work with students to decode unfamiliar words or phrases, such as "fire-eaters," "rendezvous'd," or "barrel staves."

Advanced Learners

DIFFERENTIATED INSTRUCTION

Fredericksburg The battle at Fredericksburg, Virginia, was supposed to have ended the Civil War. Have students research what happened there from both the Union and Confederate perspectives and share the information with classmates.

Teach

Literary Element 1

Characterization Ask: What aspect of his own personality does Whitman convey in this passage? How do others regard him? *(He portrays himself as friendly and sympathetic. By saying that he is always well used," he implies that others regard him the same way.)*

 To check students' understanding of the selection, see Unit 3 Teaching Resources Book, p. 163.

View the Art ★

Challenge students to think of words that describe the scene depicted in the artwork. *(serene, calm, orderly)* **Ask:** How does the artwork fit in with the world that Whitman describes in his journal entries? *(The artwork does not convey the pain or fear that Whitman encounters, nor does it give a sense of the humanity that he appreciates.)*

Progress Check

Can students identify a historical narrative?

If No → See Unit 3 Teaching Resources Book, p. 159.

Howard's Grove Hospital Near Richmond, Virginia, artist unknown, c. 19th century. Oil on canvas. The Chicago Historical Society.

★

rate, stop with him and sit near him for hours, if he wishes it.

Besides the hospitals, I also go occasionally on long tours through the camps, talking with the men, &c. Sometimes at night among the groups around the fires, in their shebang enclosures of bushes. These are curious shows, full of characters and groups. I soon get acquainted anywhere in camp, with officers or men, and am always well used. Sometimes I go down on picket with the regiment I know best. As to rations, the army here at present seems to be tolerably well supplied, and the men have enough, such as it is, mainly salt pork and hard tack. Most of the regiments lodge in the flimsy little shelter-tents. A few have built themselves huts of logs and mud, with fire-places.

No Good Portrait of Lincoln

Probably the reader has seen physiognomies (often old farmers, sea-captains, and such) that, behind their homeliness, or even ugliness, held superior points so subtle, yet so palpable, making the real life of their faces almost as impossible to depict as a wild perfume or fruit-taste, or a passionate tone of the living voice—and such was Lincoln's face, the peculiar color, the lines of it, the eyes, mouth, expression. Of technical beauty it had nothing—but to the eye of a great artist

it furnished a rare study, a feast and fascination. The current portraits are all failures—most of them caricatures.

A Soldier on Lincoln

May 28.—As I sat by the bedside of a sick Michigan soldier in hospital to-day, a **convalescent** from the adjoining bed rose and came to me, and presently we began talking. He was a middle-aged man, belonged to the 2d Virginia regiment, but lived in Racine, Ohio, and had a family there. He spoke of President Lincoln, and said: "The war is over, and many are lost. And now we have lost the best, the fairest, the truest man in America. Take him altogether, he was the best man this country ever produced. It was quite a while I thought very different; but some time before the murder, that's the way I have seen it." There was deep earnestness in the soldier. (I found upon further talk he had known Mr. Lincoln personally, and quite closely, years before.) He was a veteran; was now in the fifth year of his service; was a cavalry man, and had been in a good deal of hard fighting. ∾

Vocabulary

convalescent (kon və le′ sənt) n. a person who is recovering from an illness or injury.

Study Skills Practice

SPIRAL REVIEW **Text Aids** Remind students to make use of the many study aids that the text provides to help their reading comprehension. Draw students' attention to the subheadings and the identifications of place names and dates in this selection. Ask how these features help. *(The subheadings break up the text, and they can be used as heads for notetaking. The places and dates help to sequence the excerpts and categorize the content.)* Remind students also to use the vocabulary definitions at the bottom of the pages to clarify meaning and the study questions to guide their reading.

After You Read

Respond and Think Critically

Respond and Interpret

1. What is your impression of the Civil War after reading these excerpts?

2. (a)How has the soldier from the Virginia regiment changed his mind about Lincoln? (b)Why is Whitman fascinated by this soldier's story?

3. (a)Describe the attitude of many people in the North toward the South at the start of the war. (b)How would you account for this attitude?

4. (a)In "After First Fredericksburg," where does Whitman find the wounded soldiers lying? (b)Why do you think he includes this detail?

Analyze and Evaluate

5. (a)In "Down at the Front," what is Whitman's main theme? (b)How does he convey this theme?

6. (a)How would you describe the tone of "After First Fredericksburg"? (b)Do you think the tone is appropriate to the subject matter?

7. **Connect to Today** If you could read a first-person narrative about a current event or issue, what would it be? Why? What would you hope to learn that you couldn't get from a news report or a textbook entry?

Literary Element **Historical Narrative**

Historical narratives can provide compelling and intense portrayals of historical developments. One reason why these accounts can be so compelling is that they show large events from a human perspective. Seeing events through one person's eyes helps the reader experience what happened at a particular moment in history.

1. Why do you think Whitman chose to publish his journal notes?

2. How does reading Whitman's historical narrative compare with reading an account of the Civil War in a history book?

Vocabulary Practice

Practice with Context Clues Look at pages 416–418 to find context clues for the vocabulary words below. Write a list of these clues.

impromptu   susceptible   incredulity
convalescent   subsequently

Academic Vocabulary

*Whitman's **interaction** with Northern and Southern soldiers shows that he seeks to help them, no matter their political affiliation.*

Interaction is an academic word. When you talk to a friend, you have an **interaction** with him or her. To further explore the meaning of this word, answer the following question: Of all the **interactions** in your life, which do you look forward to the most?

📝 Writing

Write a Journal Entry In the historical narrative *Specimen Days*, Whitman describes his experiences during and feelings about the Civil War. Think about an influential or historic event in your lifetime. Write a journal entry describing your experiences during that occurrence and how it affected you emotionally.

After You Read

Assess

1. Students may say it conveys the suffering caused by war.

2. (a) The soldier did not like Lincoln before, but now calls Lincoln "the best man this country ever produced." (b) Whitman greatly admires Lincoln.

3. (a) Northerners felt contempt for the South and thought that it would be over quickly. (b) They failed to understand the determination of the Southerners.

4. (a) On the ground, most without even a mattress (b) The detail shows the extreme suffering of the wounded and the army's lack of supplies.

5. (a) The grotesqueness of the injuries and the suffering of the soldiers (b) His images are brutally candid—for example, the heap of amputated limbs.

6. (a) The tone is one of futility. (b) Students may say that the tone is appropriate.

7. Students may say they hope to get a personal, unfiltered perspective on their subject.

📝 Writing

Students' journal entries should describe their emotional reaction to their experiences.

Literary Element

1. To tell people about the suffering and sacrifices made by the soldiers

2. Students may say that this is more focused on how war affected people.

Vocabulary

- **impromptu** (The crowd gathered because the newsboys were yelling.)
- **incredulity** (Northerners did not think that other states would join the conflict, which they looked upon with contempt, anger, and incredulity.)
- **subsequently** (Bodies were buried, but subsequently they were dug up and brought north.)
- **susceptible** (The speaker talks to dying men who are most susceptible to his company.)
- **convalescent** (He was by the bedside of a sick soldier in the hospital.)

Academic Vocabulary

Possible answer: Having lunch with my best friend the most

Before You Read

Focus

Summary

In section 1, the speaker declares his goal to "sing myself" and to celebrate his kinship with the reader. In section 6, he ponders the grass as a symbol of regeneration. In section 16, he uses a series of paradoxes to emphasize his own diversity and sympathies. Section 17 asserts the universality of human thought, and section 46 pictures the speaker as a traveler who invites the reader to join him on his journey. In section 51, the speaker exhorts the listener to join him in a dialogue. In section 52, the speaker asserts the authenticity of his poetic voice, as he takes his leave of the reader.

 For summaries in languages other than English, see Unit 3 Teaching Resources Book, pp. 165–170.

Literary History ☆

The *Divine Comedy* Italian writer Dante completed *Divine Comedy* in 1321. The epic poem, a masterpiece of Western literature, tells of a man's spiritual development as he journeys through Hell, Purgatory, and Paradise.

Before You Read

from *Song of Myself*

Connect to the Poem

What might it mean to feel "connected" to nature and to all of humankind? Discuss this question in a small group.

Build Background

When Whitman was young, he read Dante's classic epic poem the *Divine Comedy*. Several years later Whitman would create his own epic poem—*Song of Myself*. Like the *Comedy*, this poem describes the development of a hero whose quest is at once physical, poetic, and spiritual.

Set Purposes for Reading

Big Idea A Poetic Revolution

As you read, ask yourself, How does Whitman use irregular lines and rhythms to give form to his poem?

Literary Element Voice

Voice is the distinctive use of language that conveys the author's or speaker's personality to the reader. Voice is determined by several elements, including word choice and tone. In *Song of Myself*, Whitman set out to create a unique poetic voice—one that would reflect the nation as a whole and the language of the common people in particular. As you read, ask yourself, What characteristics describe Whitman's voice?

Reading Strategy Draw Conclusions

Drawing conclusions about a text involves using pieces of given information to make a general statement about the meaning of a line, passage, or section. Many elements in a literary work—including word choice, voice, imagery, and figurative language—contribute to the meaning. In a long poem such as *Song of Myself*, it is important to identify these elements from time to time and to use them to draw conclusions about the poem's meaning.

Learning Objectives

For pages 420–428

In studying this text, you will focus on the following objectives:

Literary Study: Analyzing voice.

Reading: Drawing conclusions.

LOG ON ▶ **Literature** Online

Author Search For more about Walt Whitman, go to glencoe.com and enter QuickPass code GLA9800u3.

420 UNIT 3 THE CIVIL WAR ERA

Selection Skills

Literary Elements
- Voice (SE pp. 420, 423, 425, 426, 428)
- Author's Purpose (SE p. 428)
- Parallelism (TE p. 422)

from **Song of Myself**

Reading Skills
- Draw Conclusions (SE pp. 420, 422, 424, 426, 428)

Vocabulary Skills
- Academic Vocabulary (SE p. 428)
- Study Skills (TE p. 424)

Writing Skills/Grammar
- Reflective Essay (SE p. 429)
- Hyphens (SE p. 429)
- Free Verse (TE p. 426)

Listening/Speaking/ Viewing Skills
- Analyze Art (SE pp. 422, 426)

from Song of Myself

Walt Whitman

1

I celebrate myself, and sing myself,
And what I assume you shall assume,
For every atom belonging to me as good belongs to you.

I loafe and invite my soul,
5   I lean and loafe at my ease observing a spear of summer grass.

My tongue, every atom of my blood, form'd from this soil, this air,
Born here of parents born here from parents the same, and their parents the same,
I, now thirty-seven years old in perfect health begin,
Hoping to cease not till death.

10   Creeds and schools in abeyance,[1]
Retiring back a while sufficed at what they are, but never forgotten,
I harbor for good or bad, I permit to speak at every hazard,
Nature without check with original energy.

6

A child said *What is the grass?* fetching it to me with full hands;
15   How could I answer the child? I do not know what it is any more than he.

I guess it must be the flag of my disposition, out of hopeful green stuff woven.

Or I guess it is the handkerchief of the Lord,
A scented gift and remembrancer[2] designedly dropt,
Bearing the owner's name someway in the corners, that we may see and remark,
    and say *Whose?*

---

1. *In abeyance* means "suspended" or "in a state of being undetermined."
2. A *remembrancer* is a reminder.

 A Poetic Revolution *In line 14 the rhythmic pattern creates a rising and falling effect, ending in a stop. What pattern does Whitman use in line 15?*

Teach

A Poetic Revolution
Answer: *He uses the same pattern: The rhythm rises with the question "How could I answer the child?" then falls with "I do not know what it is any more than he."*

Literary History ☆

Naming "Song of Myself" The first edition of *Leaves of Grass* was published in 1855. The poem "Song of Myself," which did not even have a title at that point, served as a rambling introduction to the book. Over the years, Whitman gave the poem several titles, including "A Poem of Walt Whitman," "An American," and "Walt Whitman." The poet finally settled on the title "Song of Myself" in 1881. In the final edition of *Leaves of Grass,* published in 1892, "Song of Myself" concludes the first section of the book.

 For an audio recording of this selection, use Listening Library Audio CD-ROM.

English Learners
DIFFERENTIATED INSTRUCTION

Intermediate Point out that the poem repeats key words and often uses variations of the words. *Hoping* in line 9, for example, is followed by *hopeful* in line 16. Have students list repeated words and their variations in the poem.

Approaching Level
DIFFERENTIATED INSTRUCTION

SMALL GROUP
Emerging Students may need help seeing the sentence structure within the form of free verse. Point out that the poet expresses a complete thought in each grouping of lines and has inserted a space between each "sentence." Have students work in small groups and take turns reading each "sentence" aloud and discussing its meaning. Ask students how the poem's structure affects the way they read it.

Teach

Reading Strategy   1

Draw Conclusions Answer:
The smallest sprout of grass convinces him that life, not death, is the ultimate reality.

(APPROACHING) **Ask:** What words or phrases does the speaker repeat on this page? *("What do you think," "become of," "and," and "life.")* Why does the speaker repeat these words? *(to suggest that the speaker thinks it is important to ask about life and about what may come afterward)*

For additional practice using the reading skill or strategy, see Unit 3 Teaching Resources Book, p. 172.

View the Art ★

Answer: *In the poem, Whitman celebrates the diverse people and occupations of our country as he rejoices in their connectedness. Homer also celebrates his subject, a farmer gathering hay, by depicting him peacefully working in a warm and appealing setting.*

Winslow Homer (1835–1910), born in Boston, is considered by many to have been the greatest American artist of his time. Homer's paintings mainly depict people at work and play, Civil War scenes, and dramatic seascapes.

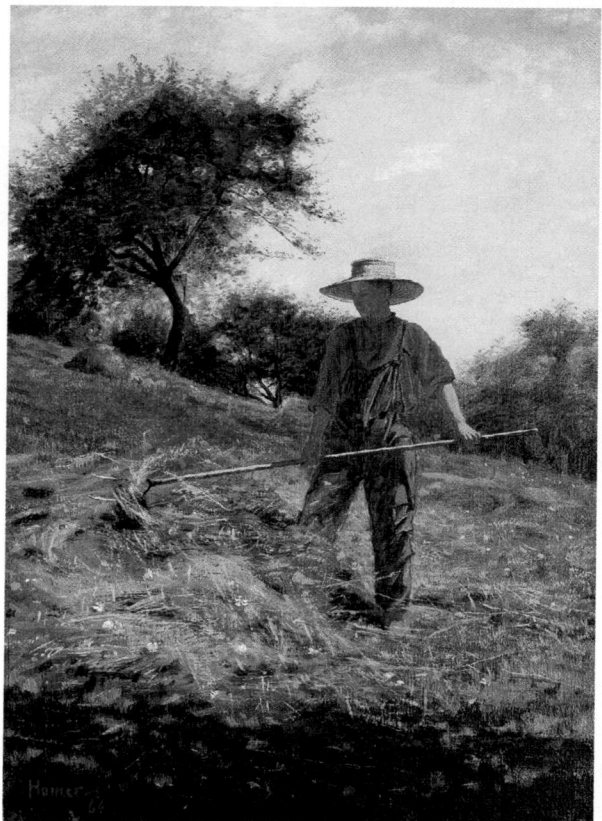

Haymaking, 1864. Winslow Homer. Oil on canvas. The Columbus Museum of Art, Columbus, OH.

View the Art Most of Winslow Homer's early works included people, unlike many of his nineteenth-century contemporaries, who focused on landscapes. In what ways does this painting capture the mood of *Song of Myself*? Explain, using details from both the painting and the poem.

20   What do you think has become of the young and old men?
    And what do you think has become of the women and children?

    They are alive and well somewhere,
    The smallest sprout shows there is really no death,
    And if ever there was it led forward life, and does not wait at the end to arrest it,
25   And ceas'd the moment life appear'd.

    All goes onward and outward, nothing collapses,
    And to die is different from what any one supposed, and luckier.

1   Draw Conclusions *Why is the speaker convinced that death does not exist?*

422   UNIT 3   THE CIVIL WAR ERA

Reading Practice

SPIRAL REVIEW **Parallelism** Explain that Whitman uses parallel structure to create a rhythmic effect that emphasizes his ideas. Parallelism is the repetition of phrases or sentences with similar structures. Direct students' attention to the example in lines 20 and 21, where he repeats the phrase "what do you think." Have students identify other examples of parallelism throughout the poem.

16

I am of old and young, of the foolish as much as the wise,
Regardless of others, ever regardful of others,
30   Maternal as well as paternal, a child as well as a man,
Stuff'd with the stuff that is coarse and stuff'd with the stuff that is fine,
One of the Nation of many nations, the smallest the same and the largest the same,
A Southerner soon as a Northerner, a planter nonchalant[3] and hospitable down by the
    Oconee[4] I live,
A Yankee bound my own way ready for trade, my joints the limberest joints on earth and
    the sternest joints on earth,
35   A Kentuckian walking the vale of the Elkhorn in my deer-skin leggings, a Louisianian
    or Georgian,
A boatman over lakes or bays or along coasts, a Hoosier, Badger, Buckeye;[5]
At home on Kanadian snow-shoes or up in the bush, or with fishermen off Newfoundland,
At home in the fleet of ice-boats, sailing with the rest and tacking,
At home on the hills of Vermont or in the woods of Maine, or the Texan ranch,
40   Comrade of Californians, comrade of free North-Westerners, (loving their big proportions,)
Comrade of raftsmen and coalmen, comrade of all who shake hands and welcome
    to drink and meat,
A learner with the simplest, a teacher of the thoughtfullest,
A novice beginning yet experient of myriads of seasons,
Of every hue and caste am I, of every rank and religion,
45   A farmer, mechanic, artist, gentleman, sailor, quaker,
Prisoner, fancy-man, rowdy,[6] lawyer, physician, priest.

I resist any thing better than my own diversity,
Breathe the air but leave plenty after me,
And am not stuck up, and am in my place.

50   (The moth and the fish-eggs are in their place,
The bright suns I see and the dark suns I cannot see are in their place,

The palpable[7] is in its place and the impalpable is in its place.)

17

These are really the thoughts of all men in all ages and lands, they
    are not original with me,
If they are not yours as much as mine they are nothing, or next to nothing,

---

3. *Nonchalant* means "showing a lack of interest or enthusiasm."
4. The *Oconee* is a river in Georgia.
5. *Hoosier, Badger,* and *Buckeye* are nicknames for natives or residents of Indiana, Wisconsin, and Ohio, respectively.
6. A *rowdy* is a rough, disorderly person.
7. *Palpable* means "able to be touched or felt."

4   Voice *What do these lines convey about the speaker's personality?*

WALT WHITMAN **423**

Teach

Literary Element | 1

Style Remind students that style involves the choice and arrangement of words in a written work. **Ask:** How does Whitman's choice of everyday language in section 46 reinforce his theme? *(Whitman's words are appropriate for a conversation among friends and for his message about the connectedness of all people.)*

[APPROACHING] **Ask:** What do you notice about the speaker's choice of words in section 46? How would you describe them? *(Most of the words are simple, ordinary words. A few, such as per-petual and continents, are longer; a few, like duds and orbs, are unusual.)*

Reading Strategy | 2

Draw Conclusions
Answer: *Only the reader can discover and travel his or her path in life.*

---

55 If they are not the riddle and the untying of the riddle they are nothing,
    If they are not just as close as they are distant they are nothing.

    This is the grass that grows wherever the land is and the water is,
    This is the common air that bathes the globe.

46

    I know I have the best of time and space, and was never measured and
        never will be measured.

60 I tramp a perpetual journey, (come listen all!)
    My signs are a rain-proof coat, good shoes, and a staff cut from the woods,
    No friend of mine takes his ease in my chair,
    I have no chair, no church, no philosophy,
    I lead no man to a dinner-table, library, exchange,
65 But each man and each woman of you I lead upon a knoll,[8]
    My left hand hooking you round the waist,
    My right hand pointing to landscapes of continents and the public road.

    Not I, not any one else can travel that road for you,
    You must travel it for yourself.

70 It is not far, it is within reach,
    Perhaps you have been on it since you were born and did not know,
    Perhaps it is everywhere on water and on land.

    Shoulder your duds[9] dear son, and I will mine, and let us hasten forth,
    Wonderful cities and free nations we shall fetch as we go.

75 If you tire, give me both burdens, and rest the chuff of your hand[10] on my hip,

    And in due time you shall repay the same service to me,
    For after we start we never lie by again.

    This day before dawn I ascended a hill and look'd at the crowded heaven,
    And I said to my spirit *When we become the enfolders of those orbs, and the pleasure and
        knowledge of every thing in them, shall we be fill'd and satisfied then?*
80 And my spirit said *No, we but level that lift to pass and continue beyond.*
    You are also asking me questions and I hear you,
    I answer that I cannot answer, you must find out for yourself.

1

---

8. A *knoll* is a small, rounded hill.
9. *Duds* are personal belongings.
10. *Chuff of your hand* refers to the fat part of the palm.

2 Draw Conclusions *What message does the speaker convey about the reader's path in life?*

Vocabulary Practice

[SPIRAL REVIEW] **Study Skills** Tell students that one type of vocabulary question on standardized tests asks them to recognize which meaning of a multiple-meaning word is the same as that in a given sentence. In the following example, tell students to choose the sentence in which the underlined word is used in the same way as in the line from Whitman's poem:

1. It is not far, it is within reach. (line 70)

   A The temperature will reach 75° today.

   B His unrealistic goals were out of reach.

   C The jury is expected to reach a verdict today.

   D Support organizations reach out to those in need.

The correct answer is **B**; the meaning is "achievable."

Sit a while dear son,
Here are biscuits to eat and here is milk to drink,
85 But as soon as you sleep and renew yourself in sweet clothes, I kiss you with a good-by kiss
    and open the gate for your egress hence.[11]

Long enough have you dream'd contemptible dreams,
Now I wash the gum from your eyes,
You must habit yourself to the dazzle of the light and of every moment of your life.

Long have you timidly waded holding a plank by the shore,
90 Now I will you to be a bold swimmer,
    To jump off in the midst of the sea, rise again, nod to me, shout, and laughingly dash with
        your hair.

 51

The past and present wilt—I have fill'd them, emptied them,
And proceed to fill my next fold of the future.

Listener up there! what have you to confide to me?
95 Look in my face while I snuff the sidle of evening,[12]
    (Talk honestly, no one else hears you, and I stay only a minute longer.)

Do I contradict myself?
Very well then I contradict myself,
(I am large, I contain multitudes.)

100 I concentrate toward them that are nigh,[13] I wait on the door-slab.

Who has done his day's work? who will soonest be through with his supper?
Who wishes to walk with me?

Will you speak before I am gone? will you prove already too late?

52

The spotted hawk swoops by and accuses me, he complains of my gab and my loitering. **3**

105 I too am not a bit tamed, I too am untranslatable,
    I sound my barbaric yawp[14] over the roofs of the world.

---

11. *Egress hence* means "departure from this place."
12. *Snuff the sidle of evening* means "to put out the last light of the day, which is moving sideways across the sky."
13. *Nigh* means "near."
14. A *yawp* is a loud, sharp cry.

4 Voice *How would you describe the intended relationship between the speaker and the reader of this poem?*

Teach

Literary Element 3

Personification Remind students that personification is the giving of human characteristics to inanimate objects or animals. **Ask:** How does Whitman's use of personification in line 104 contribute to the poem's message? *(Personification reinforces Whitman's theme of the link between people and nature.)*

(APPROACHING) **Ask:** What object or animal acts like a human being in line 104? What does it do? *(A hawk. It "accuses" and "complains.")*

Literary Element 4

Voice Answer: *The relationship is one of deep and tender intimacy, like that between a parent and child.*

Literary History ☆

Egress The word *egress* (line 86), originally from the Latin word *egressus,* means "the act of going forth or leaving." It was often used in legal documents and referred to the right of people, such as immigrants or travelers, to leave or pass through a place. Today the word is rarely used. **Ask:** What word do we use now to refer to the act of leaving? *(exit)*

English Learners

 DIFFERENTIATED INSTRUCTION

Intermediate Students may have trouble understanding the metaphors in line 92. Work with students to help them make connections. Read aloud line 92. Then ask students to identify things that wilt. *(flowers, vegetables, clothing, and people on hot days)* Ask students to use the information in the second part of the line to paraphrase the metaphor. *(Memories and the present moment fade or wilt like flowers in a vase.)*

425

Teach

Reading Strategy   1

Draw Conclusions
Answer: *The speaker is about to leave the reader. He has reached the final stage of his life in the flesh.*

Literary Element   2

Voice Answer: *The poet longs to connect with the reader and hopes that some lines of the poem will resonate with the reader's spirit.*

View the Art ★

Answer: *The painting depicts robust, hard-working Americans, just as Whitman conveys the spirit of a powerful, young, and hard-working nation.*

Writer's Technique ☆

Whitman's Philosophy The optimism expressed as the speaker leaves the world at the end of the poem reflects Whitman's own philosophy. In an afterword to the final edition of *Leaves of Grass*, Whitman expresses satisfaction with his life's work, explaining that his book "ought to emanate buoyancy and gladness legitimately enough, for it was grown out of those elements, and has been the comfort of my life since it was originally commenced."

To check students' understanding of the selection, see Unit 3 Teaching Resources Book, p. 173.

The Sand Team, 1917. George Bellows. Oil on canvas. The Brooklyn Museum of Art, New York.

View the Art Critics dubbed George Bellows and his colleagues the "Ashcan" school because their work—realistic portrayals of early twentieth-century social conditions—was considered crude. What spirit of America does this particular painting convey? How is it similar to or different from Whitman's view of the American spirit? ★

The last scud[15] of day holds back for me,
It flings my likeness after the rest and true as any on the shadow'd wilds,
It coaxes me to the vapor and the dusk.

110 I depart as air, I shake my white locks at the runaway sun,
I effuse[16] my flesh in eddies, and drift it in lacy jags.

I bequeath myself to the dirt to grow from the grass I love,
If you want me again look for me under your boot-soles.

You will hardly know who I am or what I mean,
115 But I shall be good health to you nevertheless,
And filter and fibre your blood.

Failing to fetch me at first keep encouraged,
Missing me one place search another,
I stop somewhere waiting for you.

---

15. *Scud* refers to wind-driven clouds or rain.
16. *Effuse* means "to pour out or forth."

1 Draw Conclusions *What stage of his journey has the speaker reached?*

2 Voice *How would you describe the poet's voice in the closing lines of the poem?*

Writing Practice

📝 **Free Verse** Have students pick their favorite section of "Song of Myself" and discuss in small groups what may have influenced Whitman to write these particular lines. After this activity, have students write their own poems in free verse, using lines of Whitman's poem as springboards. For example, a student might imitate line 114 and begin their poem with "You will hardly know who I am . . . ." The student may then write the rest of the poem using their own ideas. When they have finished writing, have volunteers read their poems to the class.

After You Read

Respond and Think Critically

Respond and Interpret

1. How did you react to the speaker in the poem? Explain your answer.

2. What do lines 10–13 and 20–27 suggest about the speaker's view of life and death?

3. (a)A **paradox** is a seemingly contradictory statement. What paradoxes does Whitman list in section 16? (b)What do these lines suggest about Whitman's attitude toward himself?

Analyze and Evaluate

4. (a)How does the speaker view himself in relation to nature and to the rest of the world? (b)Would you call the speaker a hero? Explain.

5. Why do you think the speaker gives his "son" the advice he does in lines 73–91? Explain.

6. (a)What does the image of the grass in sections 6 and 52 have to do with life and death? (b)Why might Whitman have called his volume of poetry *Leaves of Grass*?

Connect

7. **Big Idea** **A Poetic Revolution** Why is free verse particularly well suited to Whitman's ideas?

8. **Connect to Today** Whitman's poetry was a radical departure in both form and content. What are some examples of contemporary "radical" artists or movements that you know?

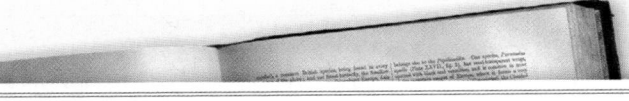

You're the Critic

Responses to Whitman

It took several years for the American public to embrace Whitman's poetry. At first, most readers—and there were few of them—were shocked by the unconventional subject matter, the unusual forms, and the break with standard rhyme and meter. A famous poet of that time, John Greenleaf Whittier, threw his copy of *Leaves of Grass* into his fireplace in disgust.

Whitman, however, did have some early supporters besides Ralph Waldo Emerson. They included Horace Traubel, an American, and John Addington Symonds, an Englishman. Each expressed a different view about what is most important in Whitman's work. As you read the two excerpts, notice their different perspectives.

"That's what Leaves of Grass all comes to. The declaration that the people are first. Not a portion of the people. Not the saving remnant. But the everyday people. The vast overflowing populations."
—Horace Traubel, 1912

"We can trace an order in [Whitman's] ideas. First comes religion or the concept of the universe; then personality, or the sense of self . . .; then love . . . and comradely emotions; then democracy, or the theory of human equality and brotherhood."
—John Addington Symonds, 1893

1. Find passages in *Song of Myself* that support the views of these critics.

2. Which of the two views do you think is more accurate? Explain.

 For additional assessment, see Assessment Resources, pp. 145–146.

You're the Critic

1. To support Traubel's view, students may choose a section from lines 28–46. Students may choose lines 78–80 to support Symonds's view.

2. Students should provide lines that support their points of view.

After You Read

Assess

1. Some students may say that the speaker's words are inspirational. Others may say that he is irresponsible.

2. In lines 10–13, the speaker is putting aside formal education to experience all the good and bad life has to offer. The speaker believes in the continuity of life. For him, death is not an end. In death, we are reunited with nature and continue to live.

3. (a) Being both old and young, foolish and wise, careful and careless, male and female, coarse and cultured (b) He embraces all of himself and humanity, including contradictions.

4. (a) In harmony with nature and the world (b) Some students may say that anyone who accepts the risks Whitman does must be heroic; others may say that a real hero has other qualities that he does not mention.

5. The speaker enjoins his "son" to put on traveler's clothing and follow him, to hand over his burdens, to savor life, and to find his own answers. The speaker wants to share his excitement about society, its multitudes, and the boundless human spirit that can be found there.

6. (a) The grass is both the final resting place for mortal life and an affirmation of the renewal of life. (b) The book contains "leaves" (pages) that he associates with grass on literal and symbolic levels. Grass represents the essence of life and death.

7. Free verse allows Whitman to break standard forms, thereby capturing his enthusiasm, informality, and individuality.

8. Answers will vary.

After You Read

Assess

Literary Element

1. C is the correct answer because, in the first lines of the poem, Whitman's voice actively engages readers and addresses them directly.

2. H is the correct answer because the energy and positivity of Whitman's voice help lend weight to his message.

Progress Check

Can students analyze voice?

If No → See Unit 3 Teaching Resources Book, p. 171.

Reading Strategy

1. In line 26, the speaker says that the universe is eternal and boundless. Given this, one can interpret line 27 to mean that the speaker believes we go beyond death to something eternal.

2. Students should be encouraged to explore their own ideas about what lines 47–49 mean. Given that the speaker has said in the earlier lines that all life "goes onward," he may be saying that his life, and the diverse lives of the people of America, are all equal parts of a larger whole. He does not want to be set apart from that whole. He wants to breathe the air but leave plenty for others now and in the future, as life goes on.

Literary Element Voice

ACT Skills Practice

1. Whitman's voice in the opening lines of the poem is

  I. selfish.
  II. engaging.
  III. personal.

  A. I only
  B. II only
  C. II and III only
  D. I, II, and III

2. How does Whitman's voice affect the impact of his message?

  F. Its colloquialism conflicts with Whitman's individualism and confuses readers.
  G. Its self-absorption offends readers and lessens the effectiveness of Whitman's ideas.
  H. Its confidence and urgency underscore the significance of Whitman's view of life.
  J. Its poetic pretension detracts from the seriousness of Whitman's commitment.

Review: Author's Purpose

Once you understand the **author's purpose,** or intent in writing, you can better evaluate what you are reading and respond appropriately.

Partner Activity With a partner, identify and discuss the different themes, or messages, in *Song of Myself*. With your partner, create a web diagram. In the outer boxes, list the themes you discussed. Then, in the center, write down an overarching theme, or Whitman's main message in the poem.

428 UNIT 3 THE CIVIL WAR ERA

Reading Strategy Draw Conclusions

Skillful readers are always **drawing conclusions** and, in doing so, understand much more than an author says directly. This process is similar to that used by a detective solving a mystery. You examine evidence that the author provides—for example, word choice or imagery—and then combine it with your own experiences to reach a conclusion. Since poets imply more than they state directly, drawing conclusions is an especially useful tool for interpreting poetry. When you come upon difficult lines or passages in a poem, examine the surrounding lines to see if they provide any clues to help you figure out the meaning.

1. How does line 26 of *Song of Myself* help you interpret line 27?

2. How do lines 26 and 27 help you draw conclusions about the meaning of lines 47–49?

Academic Vocabulary

In *Song of Myself*, Whitman glorifies man as an **individual** as well as a universal entity.

Individual is an academic word. In more casual conversation, someone might say that a person who distinguishes him- or herself from the crowd in dress and behavior is an **individual.**

Using context clues, try to figure out the meaning of *individual* in each sentence and explain the difference between the two meanings:

1. I painted a different type of rose on each **individual** plate.

2. My best friend's band's music is quite **individual;** it's unlike any I've heard before.

For more on academic vocabulary, see pages 53–54.

 Literature Online

Selection Resources For Selection Quizzes, eFlashcards, and Reading-Writing Connection activities, go to glencoe.com and enter QuickPass code GLA9800u3.

Academic Vocabulary

1. Each separate plate is painted; in this sentence, *individual* means "distinct from the group."

2. The music has qualities different from all other music; in this sentence, *individual* means "distinguished by singular characteristics."

Review: Author's Purpose

Themes that students might list include exploring the meaning of self, celebrating the human spirit, embracing the common people, and exploring the relationship between humans and nature. Students may say that the author's purpose is to express the essence of America.

Respond Through Writing

Reflective Essay

Explore Theme Whitman's purpose in writing *Song of Myself* is to explore a range of themes that relate both to himself and to his country. If you were to write your own *Song of Myself,* what would your purpose and themes be? How do they compare with Whitman's? Explore these questions in a reflective essay.

Understand the Task A **reflective essay** explores the broader meaning and effect of specific details, observations, or experiences. The **author's purpose** refers to a writer's reason for creating a literary work; authors typically write to persuade, to entertain, or to explain.

Prewrite Review the author's purpose/theme diagram you filled out on page 428. Then create your own diagram using that one as a model. You might detail a significant experience, a question you often ask yourself, a strong belief, or an observation about the world that would be essential in your own epic poem. Each example should support one of your main themes, and all of your themes should contribute to your purpose. You can use your diagram as a blueprint for your essay.

Draft In your essay, explain the significance of the examples you have chosen from your life. What would your "song" say about how you view yourself and your place in the world? You might use phrases like this:

Doing ——————— has taught me the importance of
———————, and that my role in life is ———————.

As you write, make sure that your tone and word choice support your themes and purpose, and that you draw comparisons between your priorities and Whitman's.

Revise Use the checklist on page 310 to evaluate your reflective essay. As you reread and revise your essay, focus on your use of metaphor, repetition, and anecdote. These elements and other rhetorical devices will help emphasize your ideas and themes, and can help show readers what they can learn from your experience.

Edit and Proofread Proofread your paper, correcting any errors in spelling, grammar, and punctuation. Review the Grammar Tip in the side column for information on the correct use of hyphens.

Learning Objectives

In this assignment, you will focus on the following objectives:

Writing: Writing a reflective essay.

Grammar: Using hyphens.

> **Grammar Tip**

Hyphens

Hyphens are used with
- some compound words: *so-called; ice-cold; fish-fry; self-knowledge; president-elect*
- multiple words used as modifiers: *ice-cream cone; two-and-a-half year old*

Tip: Compound words can be written with hyphens, as a single word, or as separate words: *ice-free, icemaker,* and *ice cream* are all correct.

After You Read

Assess

Writing

Students' essays should include personal experiences that support the essay's themes. Students should also pursue a purpose throughout their esssays and employ suitable rhetorical devices that highlight their ideas.

Scoring Guide

Assess students' performance in the following categories using the scoring guide at the bottom of the page:

- Addresses all parts of the writing task.
- Explains themes and purpose of the "song" they would write.
- Supports their themes and purpose with examples from their lives or with their own observations of the world.
- Employs rhetoric devices that support their ideas and themes.
- Provides a variety of sentence types, uses precise and thoughtful language.
- Follows English language conventions.

Scoring Guide	4	3	2	1
Task addressed	fully	mostly	partially	barely
Themes	fully explained and developed	somewhat explained and developed	partially developed	incoherent and undeveloped
Support	relevant examples from life	somewhat relevant examples from life	few relevant examples from life	irrelevant examples
Rhetoric devices	well employed	employed	few employed	none
Language	varied, precise, thoughtful	varied, somewhat thoughtful	predictable, basic	not varied, limited
Convention errors	few or none	several	some	many

Focus

Summary

This passage from Justin Kaplan's biography addresses the initial public reception of *Leaves of Grass,* as well as Whitman's strategies for promoting his own work.

 For summaries in languages other than English, see Unit 3 Teaching Resources Book, pp. 175–180.

Teach

Reading Strategy | 1

Synthesize Information

Remind students of the differences between primary and secondary sources. Primary sources are first-hand accounts of events; secondary sources are written after events by people who did not witness them; secondary sources incorporate, or synthesize, ideas from primary sources. After students begin reading the selection, **Ask:** Is the selection a primary or secondary source? How do you know? *(Secondary—the writer relies on primary sources such as letters and diary entries to tell about Whitman.)*

 For an audio recording of this selection, use Listening Library Audio CD-ROM.

Readability Scores

Dale-Chall: 8.4
DRP: 68
Lexile: 1390

430

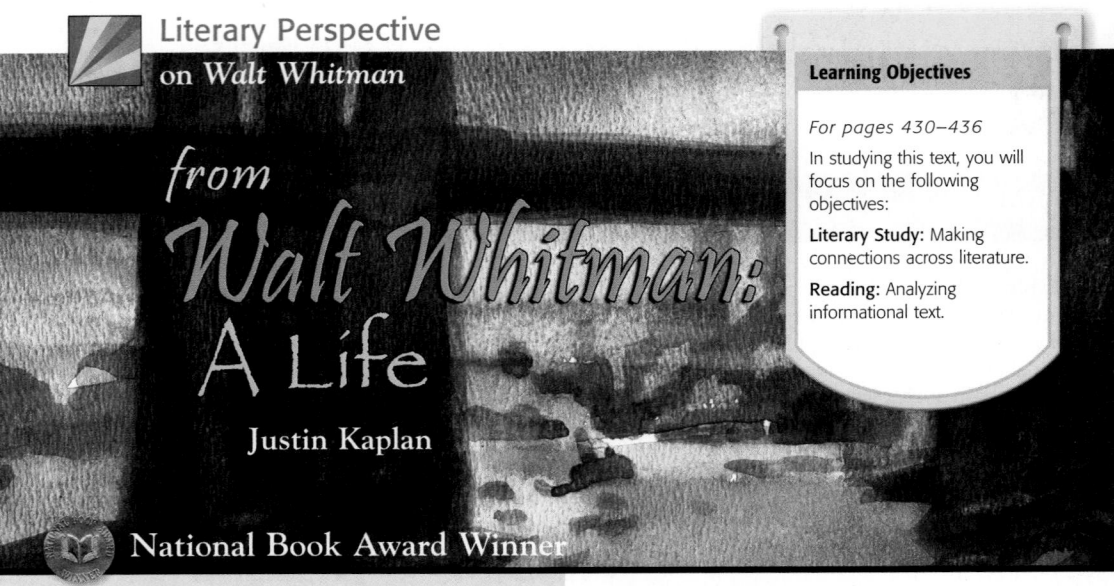

from Walt Whitman: A Life

Justin Kaplan

National Book Award Winner

Learning Objectives

For pages 430–436
In studying this text, you will focus on the following objectives:

Literary Study: Making connections across literature.

Reading: Analyzing informational text.

Under Brooklyn Bridge. Robert McIntosh.

Set a Purpose for Reading

As you read, ask yourself, How did critics review *Leaves of Grass* when it first was published? How did Whitman attempt to publicize his book?

Build Background

Today Walt Whitman is celebrated as one of the most original poets of the nineteenth century. When *Leaves of Grass* was first published in 1855, however, it received mixed reviews and little fanfare. Undaunted, Whitman set out to convince the public that his work was a literary sensation. In the following selection, historian and biographer Justin Kaplan describes how Whitman promoted his work and launched his career.

Reading Strategy Synthesize Information

1 **Synthesizing** is combining ideas to create something new. To synthesize information from varied sources, follow these steps:

- interpret the information
- identify similarities and differences between ideas
- combine ideas to create new knowledge

As you read this selection, take notes about Walt Whitman. Then generate new ideas about this poet by relating your notes to the information you derived from other sources in this unit.

"The beginning of a great career"

I

Do you take it I would astonish?
Does the daylight astonish? or the early red-
start twittering through the woods?
Do I astonish more than they?

Reading these lines at his desk in Concord, in a complimentary copy sent him by an anonymous author, Emerson almost believed he had seen salvation and could depart in peace. "In raptures," as a visitor noted, Emerson pointed to a certain "oriental largeness of generalization" as evidence that an American Buddha, the long-awaited national poet, had spoken at last. "So extraordinary," he told a Boston friend, Samuel Gray Ward, "I must send it to you, & pray you to look it over." He wondered whether the author had not been "hurt by hard life & too animal experience," but still praised *Leaves of Grass* as "wonderful," "the American poem," "a nondescript monster," as he wrote to Carlyle,[1]

---

1. Thomas *Carlyle* (1795–1881) was a British historian and essayist.

Research Practice

Citing Evidence Point out that throughout the selection, the writer uses a variety of techniques to cite supporting evidence from primary sources. For example, he combines direct quotations with indirect statements when he discusses Ralph Waldo Emerson's reaction to *Leaves of Grass.* Some quotations are from conversations; others are from correspondence with people other than Whitman. The writer also quotes an entire letter Emerson wrote to Whitman. Tell students that in full biographies, writers use footnotes or endnotes to identify their sources. Have students practice using citations by writing a one-paragraph review of *Leaves of Grass* that cites at least two critics or reviewers quoted in the selection. Remind students to try different techniques—direct quotations, indirect quotations, and lengthy passages.

"which yet had terrible eyes and buffalo strength." After some puzzlement over the identity and whereabouts of the new poet, Emerson composed a letter to Walter Whitman, Esq., in care of Fowler and Wells[2] in New York.

Concord Massachusetts 11 July 1855

DEAR SIR,

I am not blind to the worth of the wonderful gift of "Leaves of Grass." I find it the most extraordinary piece of wit & wisdom that America has yet contributed. I am very happy in reading it, as great power makes us happy. It meets the demand I am always making of what seemed the sterile & stingy Nature, as if too much handiwork or too much lymph[3] in the temperament were making our western wits fat & mean.

I give you joy of your free & brave thought. I have great joy in it. I find incomparable things said incomparably well, as they must be. I find the courage of *treatment*, which so delights us, & which large perception only can inspire.

I greet you at the beginning of a great career, which yet must have had a long foreground somewhere, for such a start. I rubbed my eyes a little to see if this sunbeam were no illusion; but the solid sense of the book is a sober certainty. It has the best merits, namely, of fortifying & encouraging.

I did not know until I, last night, saw the book advertised in a newspaper, that I could trust the name as real & available for a Post-office. I wish to see my benefactor, & have felt much like striking my tasks, & visiting New York to pay you my respects.

R. W. EMERSON

MR. WALTER WHITMAN.

---

2. *Fowler and Wells* was the publishing firm that printed the second edition of *Leaves of Grass*.
3. *Lymph* is a clear liquid that travels through the human lymphatic system, removing fat from the intestines.

I find it the most extraordinary piece of wit & wisdom that America has yet contributed.

This five-page salute, Whitman later said, was the charter of "an emperor"—"I supposed the letter was meant to be blazoned." In the annals of literary partisanship and the laying-on of hands, Emerson's words are unmatched for their generosity and force, their shrewdness and simple justice. Another insurgent scripture, *Walden*, published the summer before, had drawn only qualified praise from Emerson. Now he proclaimed the greatness of *Leaves of Grass* to friends, casual visitors, and far-flung acquaintances. "Toward no other American, toward no contemporary excepting Carlyle, had Emerson used such strong expressions," said Moncure Conway, the young Harvard Divinity School graduate who was to be Emerson's first legate[4] to the new poet. "Emerson had been for many years our literary banker; paper that he had inspected, coin that had been rung on his counter, would pass safely anywhere." Stripped of its marketplace metaphors the same idea was echoed on the other side of the Atlantic by William Howitt, reviewer for the *London Weekly Dispatch*—"What Emerson has pronounced to be good must not be lightly treated." Even the *Criterion*, a high-toned New York weekly that dismissed Whitman's book as "a mass of stupid filth," had to acknowledge, apologetically, the quality of its credentials—"an unconsidered letter of introduction has oftentimes procured the admittance of a scurvy fellow into good society."

Emerson's letter admitted *Leaves of Grass* to a meeting of Philadelphia abolitionists where Lucretia Mott, the Quaker preacher, heard it discussed and praised. "R. W. Emerson calls it 'the book of the age,'" she wrote to her sister. "It is something Emersonian in style—a kind of unmeasured poetry in praise of America & telling what true poetry is." She had no objection to the purchase of a copy for her seventeen-year-

---

4. A *legate* is an official representative.

JUSTIN KAPLAN **431**

431

Literary Perspective on *Walt Whitman*

Teach

Reading Strategy 2

Interpret Author's Argument Point out to students that this paragraph contains the writer's main point. **Ask:** What point does the writer make about the impact of Emerson's opinion on Whitman's book? (*Emerson's praise positively influenced other reviewers and critics—even those who did not like the book.*) Ask students to identify details that support their assertion. (*Students should cite quotations from reviewers and people who knew Emerson.*)

Text Element 3

Displayed Quotations Draw students' attention to the text in the shaded box between the columns. Explain that this is a quotation from the selection. **Ask:** What is the effect and purpose of displaying quotations from text in this way? (*They draw attention and give you insight into the text.*)

For activities related to this selection, see Unit 3 Teaching Resources Book, pp. 181–182.

English Learners

DIFFERENTIATED INSTRUCTION

Intermediate Help students get the gist of Emerson's letter by making lists of the words that suggest positive feelings (*happy, power, free, brave, joy, sunbeam*) and negative feelings (*fat, mean, stingy, sober.*) Have students look up unfamiliar words and assign them to each list. Ask students for an overall impression of Emerson's feelings based on their lists.

Advanced Ask students to interpret two metaphors. First, have students reread Emerson's letter and explain "this sunbeam." (*Emerson thinks Whitman's poem is as delightful as a sunbeam.*) Then have them explain how Emerson is a "literary banker." (*Like a banker who inspects good and bad [counterfeit] bills, Emerson knows good poetry from bad.*)

Teach

Big Idea	1

A Poetic Revolution Ask:

What phrases in the reviews by Charles Eliot Norton and Edward Everett Hale reveal these critics' perceptions of Whitman's "newness" or novelty? *("preposterous yet somehow fascinating"; "freshness, simplicity, and reality")*

Reading Strategy	2

Interpret Information

Ask: How does the writer interpret the change in attitude of both William Swayne and Samuel Wells toward Whitman's work? *(He believes that the men's attitudes were affected by negative comments by Charles Dana.)* Have students reread Dana's comments. **Ask:** How would you interpret Dana's comments? *(Students should point out that Dana praises Whitman's boldness and sense of beauty but criticizes his rough language.)*

Informational Text

old granddaughter. The patrician[5] critic and scholar Charles Eliot Norton told his friend James Russell Lowell[6] that he had been alerted to the existence of this "literary curiosity" by the revered Emerson, who had apparently written a letter to the author "expressing the warmest admiration and encouragement." In his unsigned review in the September *Putnam's Monthly* Norton described *Leaves of Grass* as "preposterous yet somehow fascinating," a surprisingly harmonious fusion of "Yankee transcendentalism and New York rowdyism" that at times exhibited, in the "rough and ragged thicket of its pages," undeniable boldness and originality. Norton confessed that he had had to overcome his distaste for the book's "disgusting" and "intolerable" coarseness. "One cannot leave it about for chance readers,"

1 he told Lowell, "and would be sorry to know that any woman had looked into it past the title-page. I have got a copy for you, for there are things in it you will admire." ("No, no," Lowell replied, "the kind of thing you describe won't do.") Another member of Emerson's circle, the clergyman Edward Everett Hale, future author of *The Man Without a Country*, praised Whitman (in the January 1856 *North American Review*) for his "remarkable power," his "freshness, simplicity, and reality," and for living up to the claims made in the preface. Half a century later Hale was still congratulating himself for having written this review, the first that, in Whitman's recollection, had done his book anything close to justice.

In the summer of 1855, when he returned from his vacation on eastern Long Island, he had been greeted by a review of a different sort, prominent but grudging and even mischievous, by Charles A. Dana of the *Tribune*, Horace

---

5. Here, *patrician* means "aristocratic."
6. *James Russell Lowell* (1819–1891) was a famed American Fireside poet.

432 UNIT 3 THE CIVIL WAR ERA

Greeley's[7] managing editor. A one-time member of the Brook Farm commune[8] who had lived on admiring terms with its founder, George Ripley, and with Margaret Fuller and Nathaniel Hawthorne, Dana had retrieved some remnants of idealism from the ruins of that experiment in plain living and high thinking. In the "nameless bard" of *Leaves of Grass* he recognized an oafish descendant of Emerson, Bronson Alcott[9], and other "prophets of the soul." He too praised Whitman's "bold, stirring thoughts," "genuine intimacy with nature," and "keen appreciation of beauty." But he argued that "the essential spirit of poetry" had found "an uncouth and grotesque embodiment." "His independence often becomes coarse and defiant. His language is too frequently reckless and indecent," Dana said, sounding the cry that Whitman was to hear to the end of his days, "and will justly prevent his volume from free circulation in scrupulous circles." Because of such objections William Swayne, the Fulton Street bookseller listed in the original announcements in the *Tribune*, had withdrawn *Leaves of Grass* from his stock and his name from Fowler and Wells's advertisements. Even *Life Illustrated*, the firm's own "Family Newspaper," said the book was "perfect nonsense," "a series of *utterances*" that the public was advised to take or leave, "just as they prefer." Soon Samuel Wells, more of a businessman and less of a crusader than his partner Orson Fowler, suggested that Whitman omit "certain objectionable passages" or look for another publisher.

2

> Norton confessed that he had had to overcome his distaste for the book's "disgusting" and "intolerable" coarseness.

---

7. *Horace Greeley* (1811–1872) was an abolitionist and the founder of the *New York Tribune*.
8. The *Brook Farm commune* was an experimental utopian community in West Roxbury, Massachusetts, from 1841 to 1847.
9. *Bronson Alcott* (1799–1888) was a Transcendentalist, a radical educator, and the father of novelist Louisa May Alcott.

Writing Practice

Research Allusions Remind students that an allusion is an indirect reference to a well-known person, place, historical event, or literary work. Kaplan's mention of Concord, Massachusetts—the home of Ralph Waldo Emerson, the leading writer of the generation preceding Whitman—carries with it the association of the town where the American Revolution began.

Tell students that context clarifies some allusions and that footnotes may explain others. Ask them to write a paragraph explaining the allusions in these phrases using information from the text and their own research and ideas:

- "an American Buddha had spoken at last"
- "this Ali Baba formula"

*W W from life
one hot July forenoon 1855
Brooklyn N Y*

At Mickle Street[10] Whitman made an almost casual thing of it when he explained how Emerson's letter, a private and privileged communication, came to be published in the New York *Tribune* without the writer's permission or foreknowledge. He said that when he was walking down the street in New York he happened to run into Dana, who had heard about the letter along the transcendental grapevine, was eager to print it in his newspaper, and wanted Whitman to release the text to him. Whitman refused, but a week or so later changed his mind, with some justification, as "a friend of Mr. Emerson" and therefore in a responsible position to decide what was legitimate and proper for everyone concerned. He printed the letter in the *Tribune* on October 10 and prefaced it with a brief paragraph that suggested a turning-point in the public fortunes of *Leaves of Grass:*

> We sometime since had occasion to call the attention of our readers to this original and striking collection of poems, by Mr. Whitman

of Brooklyn. In so doing we could not avoid noticing certain faults which seemed to us to be prominent in the work. The following opinion, from a distinguished source, views the matter from a more positive and less critical standpoint.

At first cautious and reluctant, just as his phrenological chart[11] had said, Whitman could justifiably claim to have been, up to this point, the unoffending victim of Dana's good intentions and unreliable assurances.* But once the letter was released he fell on it like a hawk—"I too am not a bit tamed." The life of his sacred book was in the balance. He sent the *Tribune* clipping to Longfellow and other celebrities, arranged to have the letter printed in *Life Illustrated,* and eventually distributed it to editors and critics in the form of a small broadside he printed up. It was headed "Copy for the convenience of private reading only" and changed Emerson's formal "Mr. Walter Whitman" to "Walt Whitman."

The letter became part of the fabric of his plans as he prepared the second edition of his book during 1855 and 1856. "Make no puns / funny remarks / Double entendres / 'witty' remarks / ironies / Sarcasms," he instructed himself in his notebook. "Only that which / is simply earnest, / meant,—harmless / to any one's feelings / —unadorned / unvarnished / nothing to / excite a / laugh / silence / silence / silence / silence / laconic[12] / taciturn,"[13] He vows to "Avoid all the 'intellectual / subtleties,' and 'withering doubts' and 'blasted hopes' and

---

11. A *phrenological chart* describes an individual's personality on the basis of the shape of his or her skull. Whitman believed in phrenology.

* The official version of the episode, laid out by Bucke in 1883 with Whitman's approval, even denied there had been any evidence "that the letter was meant to be private." Whitman became more circumspect about such matters. In 1871, after he received a flattering letter from Tennyson, he cautioned a newspaper friend, "I rely on your promise not to publish the letter, nor any thing equivalent to it." But he had no objection to printing the news that he had received such a letter. (Richard Maurice Bucke, M.D., *Walt Whitman* [Philadelphia, 1883], p. 139.)

12. *Laconic* means "using few words."

13. *Taciturn* means "quiet."

---

10. *Mickle Street* in Camden, New Jersey, was the location of Whitman's house, which he purchased in 1884.

JUSTIN KAPLAN **433**

Literary Perspective
on *Walt Whitman*

Teach

Reading Strategy **3**

Synthesize Information
Point out to students that the writer draws information from several sources in his discussion of Emerson's letter. Ask students to identify at least three sources. *(clippings from the* New York Tribune, *Whitman's notebooks, a book by Richard Maurice Bucke)* **Ask:** What assertion does the writer support with those sources? *(Although Whitman once pretended that he did not think it appropriate to publish Emerson's private letter, he planned all along to use it as part of his publicity.)*

(APPROACHING) Ask students to think about Whitman's reasons for publishing Emerson's letter. Point out that the writer says that "the life of [Whitman's] sacred book was in the balance." Ask students to interpret the writer's comment. *(Whitman would do anything to get his book published and sold.)*

Approaching Level

DIFFERENTIATED INSTRUCTION

SMALL GROUP **Emerging** Remind students that signal words reveal the organization of a work. Have students work in pairs to identify words on this page that indicate sequence *(when, at first, up to this point, eventually)* and contrast *(but)* and to draw conclusions from them. Students may conclude that the author conveys Whitman's lack of consistency over time.

SMALL GROUP **Established** Students may benefit from creating a timeline that charts what happened to Emerson's letter. Have students work in pairs to skim the selection for dates and events. Tell students to draw a timeline and write down dates above the line and key events below the line.

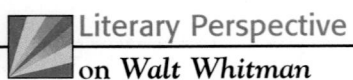
Teach

Reading Strategy | 1

Make Inferences **Ask:**
From Whitman's parenthetical comments in his list of casual acquaintances, what can you infer about how he classified people? *(He seems to have noted physical characteristics, such as height, clothing, country of origin, and headgear, as well as professions or trades.)*

[APPROACHING] **Ask:** What conclusion can you draw about the people Whitman meets? *(They are ordinary people—workers and tourists.)*

Reading Strategy | 2

Compare and Contrast **Ask:**
What contemporary methods of promotion might you compare and contrast with Whitman's strategies? *(Students might mention newspaper advertisements, book-jacket blurbs, and author tours featuring radio and television appearances.)*

Informational Text

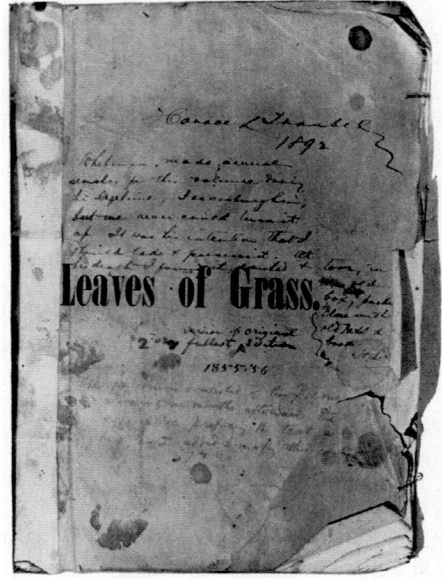

'unre-quited / loves,' and 'ennui'[14] and 'wretch-edness' and the whole of the lurid and artistical and melo-dramatic / effects.—Preserve perfect calmness and sanity." He lists some of his casual acquaintances in New York—

1
> Sam (with black eyes & cap)
> Nick (black eyes 40th st—small)
> Joe (Canadian-Montreal)
> Bill Young (milkman & driver)
> George Applegate (tallest)
> English Johnny (49th st Jockey cap)
> Sam (49th st round shoulders light clothes)

—and also sketches out, in the pride of creation and mastery, his "Sun-Down Poem" ("Crossing Brooklyn Ferry") of 1856:

> Poem of passage / the scenes on the river / as I cross the / Fulton ferry / Others will see the flow / of the river, also, / Others will see on both / sides the city of / New York and the city / of Brooklyn / a hundred years hence oth-

---

14. *Ennui* means "weariness."

---

ers / will see them . . . The continual and hurried crowd of / men and women crossing / The reflection of the sky / in the water—the blinding / dazzle in a track from / the most declined sun, / The lighters—the sailors / in their picturesque costumes / the nimbus[15] of light / around the shadow of my / head in the sunset

Further on, along with trial passages for another major new poem of 1856, "Song of the Broad-Axe," is an entry of a different sort. Enclosed within a large bracket, it occupies a page to itself:

> "I greet you at the beginning of a great career"
> R. W. EMERSON

Whitman made several layouts of these words on binder's paper left over from the first edition before he had them stamped in gold on the spine of the second edition around August 1856. Torn out of context, gaudily displayed, this Ali Baba[16] formula appeared to be an endorsement even of new poems Emerson could not possibly have seen. And further compounding what a Boston paper had called "the grossest violation of literary comity[17] and courtesy that ever passed under our notice," at the end of the book Whitman once again printed the entire letter along with a vaunting[18] essay in the form of a public thank-you:

2

> Brooklyn *August 1856*.
> Here are thirty-two poems, which I send you, dear Friend and Master, not having found how I could satisfy myself with sending any usual acknowledgement of your letter. The first edition, on which you mailed me that till now unanswered letter, was twelve poems—I printed a thousand copies, and they readily sold; these thirty-two Poems I stereotype, to print several thousand copies

---

15. A *nimbus* is a cloud or an atmosphere.
16. *Ali Baba* is a woodcutter in *The Arabian Nights' Entertainments*, or *The Thousand and One Nights*, a collection of Asian stories. He gains access to the cave of the Forty Thieves by saying the magic phrase "open sesame."
17. *Comity* means "courteousness."
18. *Vaunting* means "boasting."

Grammar Practice

Subject-Verb Agreement Remind students to pay particular attention to subject-verb agreement in sentences with inverted word order or with phrases intervening between subjects and verbs. Write the following on the board and have students rewrite the sentences, using the correct verb in each.

1. Further on, along with trial passages for another major new poem, (is/are) an entry of a different sort. *(is)*

2. At the end of the book (appear/appears) the entire letter. *(appears)*

3. Here (is/are) thirty-two poems, which I send to you, dear Friend and Master. *(are)* of. I much enjoy making poems. Other work I have set for myself to do, to meet people and The States face to face, to confront them with an American rude tongue; but the work of my life is making poems. I keep on till I make a hundred, and then several hundred—perhaps a thousand. A few years, and the average annual call for my Poems is ten or twenty thousand—more, quite likely. Why should I hurry or compromise? . . . Master, I am a man of perfect faith.

Even the loyal and resourceful Bucke,[19] utterly flummoxed[20] for once, had to admit that Whitman's "they readily sold" was "a plain lie." According to Bucke's information, the first edition had "no sale" and the second "little or no sale." "If the reader goes to a bookstore," Hale had pointed out in his review, "he may expect to

be told, at first, as we were, that there is no such book, and has not been." Whitman himself said he doubted "if even ten were sold" and that he ended up giving away almost all of his first edition to "friends and relatives"—"Oh, as a money matter, the book was a dreadful failure." It was a "failure" despite the vigorous deployment of his talents as an impresario[21] with one lifelong act to manage. The lessons of P. T. Barnum's American Museum, General Tom Thumb and the Swedish Nightingale had not been wasted on him.[22]

Whitman supplied friendly journals with the information that *Leaves of Grass* created "an extraordinary sensation in the literary world on

3

---

19. Richard Maurice *Bucke* was a longtime friend and the first biographer of Whitman.
20. *Flummoxed* means "confused."

21. An *impresario* is a theatrical manager or producer.
22. *P. T. Barnum* (1810–1891) was an American showman who helped popularize the three-ring circus. His *American Museum* in New York City displayed curiosities. Charles S. Stratton, named *General Tom Thumb* by Barnum, was a 25-inch-tall performer. Jenny Lind, a Swedish soprano, was promoted by Barnum as the *Swedish Nightingale.*

JUSTIN KAPLAN **435**

Literary Perspective
on *Walt Whitman*

Teach

Reading Strategy **3**

Synthesize Information

Ask: How are the details that Whitman provides in his anonymous "reviews" consistent with characteristics of *Leaves of Grass*? *(Students might mention such qualities as the speaker's brashness, his bold originality, and his enthusiastic endorsement of American democracy.)*

(ADVANCED) **Ask:** What style elements are obviously the same in Whitman's poetry and his anonymous endorsements? *(The poet's use of dashes and exclamation points, his inverted syntax, and the way he celebrates coarseness and ordinary people.)*

Assess

1. Students' summaries should represent the main ideas of the selection in a short, concise manner. The summaries should not contain personal opinions.

2. Students may say that they are surprised that Whitman's poetry was initially scrutinized heavily by critics.

3. (a) Emerson responded enthusiastically. (b) Emerson valued originality and hoped that an original poetic voice would arise in the United States. In Whitman, Emerson believed he had found such a voice.

4. (a) Whitman allowed Charles A. Dana to publish the letter, placed a quotation from the letter on the spine of the 1856 edition of *Leaves of Grass*, reprinted the entire letter at the back of that edition, and included a thank-you letter to Emerson. (b) Whitman's motives were self-promotional, suggesting that a deep bond existed between Emerson and himself when that was not actually the case.

5. Some students may say that Whitman was dishonest in writing favorable reviews of his own work and then passing them off as the responses of objective critics. Other students may say that Whitman had to break the rules to ensure that the public would not dismiss his work.

6. Students may say that Lucretia Mott's comment that Whitman's work is "a kind of unmeasured poetry in praise of America" captures the essence of *Leaves of Grass*.

both sides of the Atlantic"—"the emphatic commendation of America's greatest critic has been ratified by the public." And it was Whitman who wrote three anonymous reviews of *Leaves of Grass* that appeared around the end of 1855. "An American bard at last!" he announced in the *United States Review*. "Politeness this man has none, and regulation he has none. A rude child of the people!—No imitation—No foreigner—but a growth and idiom of America," he wrote in the Brooklyn *Daily Times*, and in support of these and similar claims he subjoined Lorenzo Fowler's[23] reading of the bard's skull and personality. In the *American Phrenological Journal*, a Fowler and Wells enterprise, he cited Tennyson's poetry with admiring tolerance but predicted his own, riding the wave of the future, might yet prove "the most glorious of triumphs, in the known history of literature."

Skillfully managed, Whitman's homemade appreciations made news in their own right. A friendly journalist, William Swinton, praised him in the New York *Times* for the "manly vigor" and "brawny health" of *Leaves of Grass*. "This man has brave stuff in him. He is truly

---

23. *Lorenzo Fowler* was a phrenologist and the founder of Fowler and Wells, a publishing house.

astonishing." In the course of several thousand words of careful and sensitive discussion, Swinton reported that "proof slips of certain articles written about *Leaves of Grass*" had been delivered to the *Times* office together with a copy of the first edition bound in green and gold and the printed text of a letter in which Ralph Waldo Emerson complimented the author "on the benefaction conferred on society":

On subsequently comparing the critiques from the *United States Review* and the *Phrenological Journal* with the Preface of *Leaves of Grass* we discovered unmistakable evidence that Mr. Walt Whitman, true to the character of a Kosmos, was not content with writing a book, but was also determined to review it, so Mr. Walt Whitman has concocted both those criticisms of his own work, treating it we need not say how favorably.

Sensation generated sensation, Whitman had learned. So did neglect, if it was conspicuous enough. Later he tended to favor a history in which *Leaves of Grass*, far from "an extraordinary sensation," had been greeted in total silence or with howls of derision. ◆

Respond and Think Critically

Respond and Interpret

1. Write a brief summary of the main ideas in this excerpt before you answer the following questions. For help on writing a summary, see page 79.

2. How did you react to Kaplan's perspective on Walt Whitman?

3. (a)How did Emerson respond to Whitman's *Leaves of Grass*? (b)Why do you think Emerson responded this way?

4. (a)What did Whitman do with the letter that Emerson had sent him? (b)What do Whitman's actions reveal about his motives?

Analyze and Evaluate

5. Did Whitman do the right thing in writing his own reviews of *Leaves of Grass*? Explain.

6. Which of the early comments on *Leaves of Grass* do you think sheds the most light on Whitman's work?

7. (a)Why does Kaplan compare Whitman to the showman P. T. Barnum? (b)Is Kaplan's comparison fair or not? Support your answer.

Connect

8. How would you compare the speaker in *Leaves of Grass* with Whitman himself, as depicted in Kaplan's perspective?

7. (a) Kaplan compares Whitman to Barnum to support his point that Whitman knew the importance of advertisement and self-promotion. (b) Students may say that the comparison is fair, since Whitman wrote favorable reviews of his own work and exploited Emerson's letter to enhance his literary reputation.

8. Students may say that the speaker in *Leaves of Grass* is unconventional, self-assured, and aggressive—qualities characteristic of Whitman himself in his efforts to publicize his own work.

 For additional assessment, see Assessment Resources, pp. 147–148.

Before You Read

Dickinson's Poetry

Meet **Emily Dickinson**
(1830–1886)

Virtually unknown during her lifetime, Emily Dickinson now stands as a giant of American literature. Her stark, concise poems speak in an instantly recognizable voice, reflecting a sense of style as individual as a fingerprint. In spare, chiseled verses, Dickinson upended convention, posing the great questions of life in the form of riddles for the reader.

> "I conclude that space and time are things of the body and have little or nothing to do with ourselves. My Country is Truth . . . I like Truth— it is a free Democracy."
>
> —Emily Dickinson

Formative Years Dickinson was born into a distinguished and prosperous family in Amherst, Massachusetts. Her father was a lawyer who served in Congress. Though stern, he was a kind man whose integrity deeply influenced Dickinson.

At Amherst Academy and Mount Holyoke Female Seminary, Dickinson was a serious student with a mischievous streak. Her intensely religious family pressured her to be an outspoken Christian. Despite her reverence for the Bible, she refused. She had strong religious feelings and equally strong doubts all her life, sharing her thoughts on the matter with only a few close friends.

In her late teens and twenties, Dickinson read authors considered by her parents to be shockingly secular: William Shakespeare, Ralph Waldo Emerson, George Eliot, and Charlotte and Emily

Brontë. She also formed friendships with lawyers and ministers whose intelligence attracted her. In her late twenties or early thirties, Dickinson seems to have had a devastating emotional experience, related perhaps to a disappointment in love. She began to spend much time alone in her Amherst home. Dickinson seemed fully content with her solitary existence, telling a friend, "I find ecstasy in living—the mere sense of living is joy enough."

Greatness Achieved Dickinson seems to have dreamed of public acclaim, but she gave up these dreams when her friend Thomas Wentworth Higginson, editor of the *Atlantic Monthly*, urged her not to publish. While ceasing attempts to publish, Dickinson continued to write as she pleased. She preferred obscurity to compromise.

After Dickinson's death from kidney failure, her sister Lavinia published the poems, but in altered form. Dashes were eliminated, capitalizations were undone, and some words were completely changed. In 1955, scholar Thomas H. Johnson began to publish the poems as Dickinson had written them. Dickinson has come to be recognized for what she was: a great American nonconformist and poet of rare purity.

 Literature Online

Author Search For more about Emily Dickinson, go to glencoe.com and enter QuickPass code GLA9800u3.

Bellringer Options

**Literature Launches
    Pre-reading Videos DVD**
**Selection Focus
    Transparency 29**
**Daily Language Practice
    Transparency 40**

Or explain that although Dickinson rarely left her home, her poems touch on universal themes. **Ask:** How important is it for a writer to have much worldly experience? *(Since much poetry is about the inner world of experience, worldly experience may be less important.)*

Interactive Read and Write

Other options for teaching this selection can be found in

- Interactive Read and Write for English Learners, pp. 139–146
- Interactive Read and Write for Approaching-Level Learners, pp. 139–146
- Interactive Read and Write for On-Level Learners, pp. 139–146

Selection Skills

Reading Skills
- Analyze Sound Devices (SE pp. 438, 440-442, 444, 446, 447, 453)
- Clarify Meaning (SE pp. 448, 449)
- Read Poetic Lines (TE p. 438)
- Paraphrase (TE p. 440)
- Respond to Poetry (TE p. 446)

Dickinson's Poetry

Literary Elements
- Rhyme (SE pp. 438–453)
- Personification (SE pp. 448, 449, 453)

Vocabulary Skills
- Word Usage (SE p. 453)
- Academic Vocabulary (SE p. 453)
- Explore Latin Roots TE p. 448)

**Listening/Speaking/
Viewing Skills**
- Analyze Art (SE p. 443; TE pp. 445, 446, 450)

Writing Skills/Grammar
- Journal Entry (SE p. 441)
- Poem (SE p. 444)
- Essay (SE p. 447, 454)
- Paragraph (SE p. 449)

Before You Read

Focus

Summary

In "If you were coming …," the speaker ponders the impermanence of human life. In "My life closed twice …," the speaker meditates on parting, and in "The Soul selects …," she focuses on choice. "Much Madness …" and "Success is counted sweetest" center on paradoxes. "I Heard a Fly buzz …" zeroes in on the moment of death; "The Bustle …" conjures up death's effects on survivors. "Because I could not …" expresses the speaker's realization that death has stopped for her. In "There's a certain …," the speaker evokes feelings of fear. "This is my letter …" asserts the speaker's links to nature.

 For summaries in languages other than English, see Unit 3 Teaching Resources Book, pp. 184–229.

Vocabulary

Suffixes Point out that *-al* on the end of *cathedral* is not a suffix. It is, however, an adjective suffix on *imperial*. Challenge students to think of science or math words with this suffix. (*medical, technological, biological, mathematical*)

 For additional context, see Glencoe Interactive Vocabulary CD-ROM.

Literature and Reading Preview

Connect to the Poems

Dickinson's poetry explores the complexity of the human soul in verses that are concise yet powerful. What does it feel like to experience loss and longing? What is success? What is wisdom? Discuss these questions with a partner.

Build Background

Much of Dickinson's poetry features an unconventional use of grammar, punctuation, and form. Dashes may suddenly interrupt a thought or rhythm, or call attention to the words they enclose. Capitalized common nouns create emphasis. Dickinson's choice of meter—that of Protestant hymns rather than iambic pentameter, the dominant meter of the day—echoes the rhythms of great hymn composers such as Isaac Watts.

Set Purposes for Reading

Big Idea A Poetic Revolution

As you read, ask yourself, How does Dickinson experiment with rhyme, rhythm, and punctuation to create a new poetic style?

Literary Element Rhyme

A **full rhyme** is the repetition of the same stressed vowel sounds and any succeeding sounds in two or more words. For example, *notation* rhymes with *vacation*. **Slant rhyme** occurs when the rhyme of two words depends on sounds that are similar but not identical. For instance, Dickinson rhymes *today* with *victory*. As you read, ask yourself, How does Dickinson's use of slant rhymes add tension and interest?

Reading Strategy Analyze Sound Devices

Sound devices are techniques that appeal to the ear. Poets use sound devices to create a sense of rhythm, emphasize particular sounds, or add to the musical quality of writing. Rhyme is one sound device. Others include **alliteration** (repeated consonant sounds at the beginnings of words), **assonance** (repeated vowel sounds), and **consonance** (repeated consonant sounds in the middle or at the ends of words). As you read, notice the rhythms and changes in emphasis that sound devices create.

Tip: Close Reading To analyze sound devices, first read closely for specific examples.

Learning Objectives

For pages 437–453

In studying these texts, you will focus on the following objectives:

Literary Study:
Analyzing rhyme.
Analyzing personification.

Reading:
Analyzing sound devices.
Clarifying meaning.

Writing:
Writing a journal entry.
Writing a poem.
Writing a paragraph.

Vocabulary

heave (hēv) *n.* an upward motion, or an effort to raise; p. 445 *With a heave, Lana lifted the huge box into her car.*

interpose (in´ tər pōz´) *v.* to intrude, intervene, or to put oneself between; p. 445 *Don't interpose yourself in this argument.*

cathedral (ke thē´ drəl) *n.* a church that is the official seat of a bishop; p. 450 *We visited the lovely cathedral of Notre Dame.*

imperial (im pēr´ ē əl) *adj.* of or relating to an empire or emperor; p. 450 *In A.D. 200, imperial Rome stretched across several continents.*

affliction (ə flik´ shən) *n.* great suffering, distress, or its cause; p. 450 *The nation was reeling from the affliction of tuberculosis.*

Reading Practice

Read Poetic Lines Tell students that when reading poetry, it is not necessary to stop at the end of every line. They should use punctuation and meaning as a guide for pauses. Suggest that they read the lines with the same intonation they would read sentences. Model the process with these lines from the poem, "If you were coming in the Fall":

> I'd brush the Summer by
> With half a smile, and half a spurn,

Point out that there is no punctuation after *by* and therefore no reason to pause or stop there. The line should be read as if it were written as a sentence: I'd brush the Summer by with half a smile . . . . Reading Dickinson's poems this way will help students comprehend their meaning.

Waiting, 1885. Clement Rollins Grant. Oil on canvas, 20 x 30 in. Private collection.

If you were coming in the Fall

Emily Dickinson

If you were coming in the Fall,
I'd brush the Summer by
With half a smile, and half a spurn,
As Housewives do, a Fly.

5   If I could see you in a year,
I'd wind the months in balls—
And put them each in separate Drawers,
For fear the numbers fuse—

If only Centuries, delayed,
10   I'd count them on my Hand,
Subtracting, till my fingers dropped
Into Van Dieman's Land.[1]

If certain, when this life was out—
That yours and mine, should be
15   I'd toss it yonder, like a Rind,
And take Eternity—

But, now, uncertain of the length
Of this, that is between,
It goads me, like the Goblin Bee— **2**
20   That will not state—its sting.

---

1. *Van Dieman's Land* is the former name for Tasmania, an island that is part of Australia.

1 Rhyme *What is the rhyme scheme of this stanza?*

EMILY DICKINSON **439**

Teach

Big Idea   1

A Poetic Revolution
Answer: *The speaker experienced devastating losses or partings that prompted the feelings expressed in the poem.*

Reading Strategy   2

Analyze Sound Devices
Answer: *In this poem, the Soul makes a definitive decision. She chooses one from "an ample nation," then closes "the Valves of her attention"—no longer focusing her attention on the outside world, the world of Society. The phrase "Choose One" emphasizes that the decision is irreversible. The final line, "Like Stone—," shows that the decision is complete.*

Progress Check

Can students analyze sound devices?

If No → See Unit 3 Teaching Resources Book, p. 191.

Writer's Technique ☆

Ambiguity Dickinson often uses words in her poetry that have more than one meaning and could be interpreted in more than one way. *Society* has several meanings that could apply to the poem: a group of people who share certain interests; an exclusive organization; the upper class; and the company of others. Point out the irony or contradiction here: "In seeking its own society, the Soul is turning away from others rather than joining them."

To check students' understanding of the selection, see Unit 3 Teaching Resources Book, p. 192.

440

My life closed twice before its close

Emily Dickinson

My life closed twice before its close—
It yet remains to see
If Immortality unveil
A third event to me

5   So huge, so hopeless to conceive
As these that twice befell.
Parting is all we know of heaven,
And all we need of hell.

1   **A Poetic Revolution** *Why did events not described in the poem prompt the speaker to express these feelings in lines 7 and 8?*

The Soul selects her own Society

Emily Dickinson

The Soul selects her own Society— ☆
Then—shuts the Door—
To her divine Majority—
Present no more—

5   Unmoved—she notes the Chariots—pausing—
At her low Gate—
Unmoved—an Emperor be kneeling
Upon her Mat—

   I've known her—from an ample nation—
10   Choose One—
Then—close the Valves of her attention—
Like Stone—

2   **Analyze Sound Devices** *How does the length of lines 10 and 12 reinforce the meaning of the stanza?*

Writing Practice

Paraphrase Remind students that a paraphrase is a restatement of a line in a poem, not an interpretation. Explain that paraphrasing helps a reader understand what a poet is saying and how the poet creates layers of meaning. Tell students to write a paraphrase of the poem "My life closed twice before its close." Have volunteers read their paraphrases, and have the class discuss how the paraphrases differ from the poem and what they reveal about the poem.

After You Read

Respond and Think Critically

If you were coming in the Fall
Respond and Interpret

1. (a)What periods of time does the speaker describe in each of the first four stanzas? (b)Describe the actions the speaker imagines taking in each of these stanzas.

Analyze and Evaluate

2. How effective is the simile in the last verse of the poem at conveying suspense? Explain.

My life closed twice before its close
Respond and Interpret

3. (a)How does the speaker define parting? (b)How, in your opinion, do partings affect the speaker?

Analyze and Evaluate

4. How do the dash and the capitalization of "Immortality" affect the meaning of the poem? Explain.

The Soul selects her own Society
Respond and Interpret

5. (a)In your own words, explain what the soul selects. (b)From how many does the soul choose just one? Tell what you think this suggests about the soul.

Analyze and Evaluate

6. The last verse includes a **metaphor** describing the soul closing "the Valves of her attention." In your opinion, is this verse a fitting end given the content of the previous stanzas? Explain why or why not.

Connect

7. Connect to the Author At Thomas Higginson's recommendation, Dickinson stopped trying to publish her work. Why might she have followed this advice? Does knowing she did affect how you view her poetry? Explain.

Literary Element Rhyme

Slant rhyme refers to words at the ends of lines of poetry that almost—but don't quite—rhyme, for example, "be" and "fly." Dickinson makes repeated use of slant rhymes in her poems. When you come across slant rhyme, you may notice that it heightens tension or the element of surprise.

1. Review "The Soul selects her own Society" and identify the example of slant rhyme in the second stanza.

2. In the last stanza, notice the contrast between the soft *o* sound of "One" and the longer, heavier *o* sound of "Stone." How does this final slant rhyme help reinforce the meaning of the poem?

 Literature Online

Selection Resources For Selection Quizzes, eFlashcards, and Reading-Writing Connection activities, go to glencoe.com and enter QuickPass code GLA9800u3.

Reading Strategy Analyze Sound Devices

Sound devices create rhythm, highlight particular words and sounds, and add to the musical quality of poetry. The sound of a poem and the poem's meaning are closely linked, even inseparable.

1. Record examples of **internal rhyme** (rhyme occurring within a single line) and **assonance** (repeated vowel sounds) in the last stanza of "If you were coming in the Fall." How do these techniques contribute to the poem's meaning?

2. (a)What words does the use of **alliteration** draw attention to in "My life closed twice before its close"? (b)Why are these words emphasized?

Writing

Write a Journal Entry Write a journal entry in which you reflect on one of these poems and how it connects to your own life. Refer to specific lines to make your comparisons clear.

EMILY DICKINSON **441**

After You Read

Assess

1. (a) Fall, summer; a year; centuries; a lifetime. (b) The speaker imagines brushing the seasons away, tracking months, counting centuries on her fingers, and trading her life for eternity.

2. Students may compare waiting for a loved one to waiting for a "Goblin Bee" to "state its sting."

3. (a) The speaker says that "Parting is all we know of heaven / And all we need of hell." (b) Students may say that partings devastate the speaker.

4. Students may say that the dash emphasizes the abrupt close, or death of the speaker, and that the capitalization of "Immortality" transforms a passive state of being into an active character.

5. (a) The soul selects its own society, or company. (b) The soul selects just one from her "divine Majority." This may suggest that the soul is given many options.

6. Students may note the connection between the Valves of the final stanza and the Door of the first stanza and the Gate of the second stanza.

7. Some students may say Dickinson "preferred obscurity to compromise" (from page 437), and her artistic integrity should be admired.

For additional assessment, see Assessment Resources, pp. 149–150.

 Writing

Students should justify reflections and comparisons with references to specific lines in the poem.

Literary Element

1. The slant rhyme is created by the words *gate* and *mat.*

2. Students may say that the longer, heavier sound reinforces the heaviness of the stone, thus dramatizing the finality of the Soul's choice.

Reading Strategy

1. Internal rhyme: "me/Bee." Assonance: the long *e* in *between, me,* and *Bee.* The internal rhyme reinforces the connection between *me, Bee,* and *between.*

2. (a) *Huge, hopeless, heaven,* and *hell.* (b) *Huge* and *hopeless* suggest despair. Heaven and hell are themes of the poem.

Teach

Reading Strategy   **1**

Analyze Sound Devices
Answer: *Consonance reinforces the speaker's point that, in society, assenting is equated with being sane, while demurring is equated with being dangerous.*

ENGLISH LEARNERS For the benefit of English learners, read the poem aloud, stressing the sounds made by the letters *s* and *d*. Ask students what impression they get from your reading.

Writer's Technique ☆

Paradox A *paradox* is a statement that seems to contradict itself but nevertheless suggests an important truth. Dickinson often uses paradoxes in her poetry—for example, in the line "Much Madness is divinest Sense—." Ask students to explain the truth contained in this apparent contradiction. (*Unusual thinking and actions, which might be construed as madness, often reflect a higher order of sense than is commonly recognized.*)

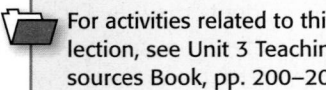
For activities related to this selection, see Unit 3 Teaching Resources Book, pp. 200–202.

For an audio recording of this selection, use Listening Library Audio CD-ROM.

442

Much Madness is divinest Sense

Emily Dickinson

Woman Sitting in Darkness, Kari Van Tine.

Much Madness is divinest Sense— ☆
To a discerning Eye—
Much Sense—the starkest Madness—
'Tis the Majority
5   In this, as All, prevail—
Assent—and you are sane—
Demur[1]—you're straightway dangerous—
And handled with a Chain—

---

1. *Demur* means "to hesitate" or "to protest."

Analyze Sound Devices *What is the effect of the repeated consonant sounds in* assent *and* sane? *In* demur *and* dangerous?   **1**

Grammar Practice

Elliptical Constructions Point out that Dickinson often uses elliptical constructions, in which words are left out and must be inferred by the reader. Model such a construction by reading lines 1–3. Students should realize that in line 3, the verb *is* is understood, so that the sentence is parallel to the statement in line 1. Have students supply the missing words in line 5 (*that*) and lines 6–7 (*if you*).

Success is counted sweetest

Emily Dickinson

Success is counted sweetest
By those who ne'er succeed.
To comprehend a nectar[1]
Requires sorest need.

5 Not one of all the purple Host[2]
Who took the Flag today
Can tell the definition
So clear of Victory

  As he defeated—dying—
10 On whose forbidden ear
The distant strains of triumph
Burst agonized and clear!

---

1. *Nectar* is a sweet liquid secreted by plants and used by bees in the making of honey. In Greek mythology, nectar is the drink of the gods that makes all who drink it immortal.
2. *Purple Host* means "winning army."

3   **A Poetic Revolution** *Why does the poet enclose the word* dying *in dashes in line 9?*

Taps, c. 1907–1909. William Gilbert Gaul. Oil on canvas, 32¾ x 43 in. The Birmingham Museum of Art, AL.

 View the Art In this painting the artist presents a poignant and ironic contrast between a fallen soldier and his faithfully waiting horse. How does the artist's vision of defeat compare with Dickinson's? ★

EMILY DICKINSON   **443**

After You Read

Assess

1. Students may say they were surprised by the unexpected truths Dickinson reveals.

2. (a) Madness (b) A discerning person

3. (a) A person who disagrees with accepted ideas is chastised by the majority. (b) *Chain* suggests that such a person is persecuted.

4. Dickinson expresses disagreement with this concept.

5. (a) A conquering army (b) The defeated know how awful it feels not to have victory.

6. (a) Stanzas two and three illustrate the point made in lines 1–2. (b) Dickinson uses war imagery to suggest that the struggle to gain success and to avoid failure is inherently unfair.

7. (a) Only those who do not attain success can fully understand its meaning. (b) Students may think of examples from real life that support or contradict the poem.

8. Students may say that Dickinson may have believed that society considered her "mad" (as in "Much Madness is divinest Sense").

 For additional assessment, see Assessment Resources, pp. 151–152.

Literary Element

Students should provide support for their answers.

Reading Strategy

Mŭch mádnĕss ĭs dĭvínĕst Sénse—
Tŏ á dĭscérnĭng Éye—
Mŭch Sénse—thĕ stárkĕst Mádnĕss—

After You Read

Respond and Think Critically

Much Madness is divinest Sense

Respond and Interpret

1. Were you surprised by Dickinson's ideas about madness and success? Explain why or why not.

2. (a)According to the speaker, in lines 1–3, with what is sense often confused? (b)Who does the speaker say knows the difference?

3. (a)How is a person who disagrees with accepted ideas regarded? (b)What does the last word of the poem suggest about what happens to such a person?

Analyze and Evaluate

4. How would you describe the poet's attitude toward the popular concept of sanity?

Success is counted sweetest

Respond and Interpret

5. (a)What example of success is given in the second stanza? (b)In the third stanza, why do you think the poem calls the "defeated" one's perception of victory "agonized" and "clear"?

Analyze and Evaluate

6. (a)How is the observation about soldiers and armies in stanzas two and three related to lines 1–2? (b)Why, in your opinion, did Dickinson choose to use war **imagery** in a poem about success? Explain what this choice might suggest about Dickinson's views of the world or of personal fulfillment.

7. (a)What paradox lies at the heart of this poem? (b)Do you agree with the observation about success and human nature in the poem?

Connect

8. **Connect to the Author** What connections, if any, do you see between Dickinson's life experiences and these two paradoxical poems? Explain, referring to the biographical information on page 437 as needed.

Literary Element Rhyme

Dickinson tended to write in **axioms,** or sayings meant to express a truth. Her use of rhythm and rhyme makes these axioms easy to remember.

(a)In your opinion, which lines or verses in these poems are made especially memorable by rhyme? (b)Explain the importance of these lines and verses for the poem in which they are included.

Reading Strategy Analyze Sound Devices

Meter is the pattern of stressed (´) and unstressed (˘) syllables that gives a line of poetry a more or less predictable **rhythm.** The basic unit of meter is a group of syllables known as the **foot.** In most of Dickinson's poems, every line is iambic (an unstressed syllable followed by a stressed one) and contains either three or four feet. Lines of four feet generally alternate with lines of three feet.

Write "Much Madness is divinest Sense" and mark the pattern of stressed and unstressed syllables for the whole poem. Is the pattern that Dickinson follows regular or does it occasionally deviate to become irregular? Explain how you think the rhythm affects the poem's meaning. Does it lend a musical quality? Does it emphasize certain words or ideas?

 Literature Online

Selection Resources For Selection Quizzes, eFlashcards, and Reading-Writing Connection activities, go to glencoe.com and enter QuickPass code GLA9800u3.

Writing

Write a Poem Come up with an original axiom that has personal significance for you. Write a short poem based on your saying. Use rhyme to emphasize your intended meaning and make your saying more memorable.

'Tĭs thĕ Májŏrĭty
Ĭn thĭs, ăs Áll, prĕvaíl—
Ăssént—ănd yoŭ áre sáne—
Dĕmúr—yoŭ're straíghtwăy dángĕroŭs—
Ănd hándlĕd wĭth ă Chaín—

At the third line, Dickinson begins to diverge from her usual pattern of alternating lines of eight syllables and six syllables. The irregular rhythm creates drama, interest, and a sense of surprise.

Writing

Each axiom and poem should express a message that is personally significant to the student, and should incorporate rhyme to emphasize that meaning.

I heard a Fly buzz when I died

Emily Dickinson

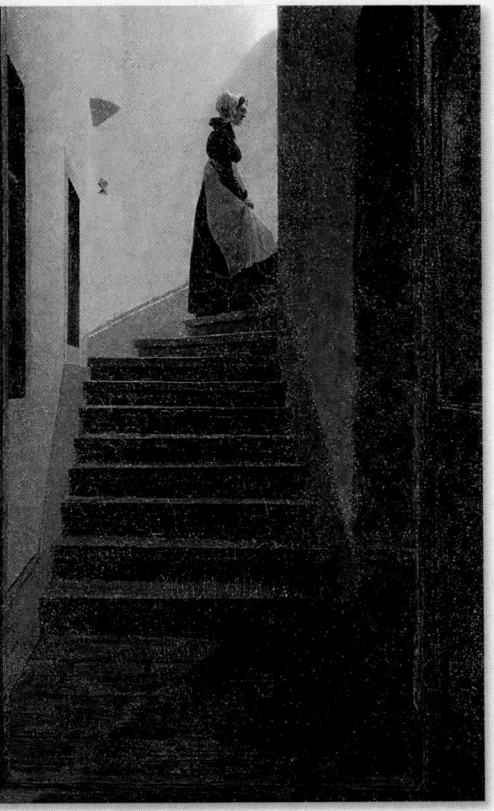

Caroline Auf Der Treppe. Caroline on the Stairs, 1825. Caspar David Friedrich. Oil on canvas, 29 x 20.3 in. Private collection.

I heard a Fly buzz—when I died—
The Stillness in the Room
Was like the Stillness in the Air—
Between the **Heaves** of Storm—

5 The Eyes around—had wrung them dry—
And Breaths were gathering firm
For that last Onset—when the King
Be witnessed—in the Room—

I willed my Keepsakes—Signed away
10 What portion of me be
Assignable—and then it was
There **interposed** a Fly—

With Blue—uncertain stumbling Buzz—
Between the light—and me—
15 And then the Windows failed—and then
I could not see to see—

Rhyme *How is the rhyme scheme in the final stanza different from the rhyme scheme of earlier stanzas?* **2**

Vocabulary

heave (hēv) *n.* an upward motion, or an effort to raise
interpose (in´ tər pōz´) *v.* to intrude, intervene, or to put oneself between

EMILY DICKINSON **445**

Teach

Reading Strategy 1

Compare and Contrast
Ask: How would you compare the view of death expressed in "The Bustle in a House" with that in "I heard a Fly buzz when I died"? *(The view in "I heard a Fly buzz when I died" creates doubt about life beyond death; "The Bustle in a House" suggests that love is stored to use again for loved ones after death.)*

Reading Strategy 2

Analyze Sound Devices
Answer: *In both stanzas, the first, second, and last lines have the same short length. Students may say that this helps emphasize the contrast between earthly life and eternity.*

View the Art ★

Patrick William Adam (1854–1929) was born in Edinburgh, Scotland. He painted portraits, landscapes, and still lifes, but is best remembered for his interior scenes. **Ask:** How does the painting connect to the poem? *(The painting suggests that domestic life may be framed by shadow. The poem also suggests that ordinary life is overshadowed by grief.)*

The Bustle in a House

Emily Dickinson

Interior, Morning. Patrick William Adam. Oldham Art Gallery, Lancashire, UK. ★

The Bustle in a House
The Morning after Death
Is solemnest of industries
Enacted upon Earth—

5   The Sweeping up the Heart
And putting Love away
We shall not want to use again
Until Eternity. **1**

2 Analyze Sound Devices *How does line length function in this poem?*

Reading Practice

Respond to Poetry Tell students that their own responses to a poem or other work of literature are an important way to connect with the literature. Have students make a two-column chart in which to respond to Dickinson's poems. In the left column, they should copy words, phrases, or lines from the poem that are meaningful or appealing to them. In the right column, they should write their response to the quotation. Students may respond by interpreting the words, connecting them to their own lives, questioning them, or commenting on them.

After You Read

Respond and Think Critically

I heard a Fly buzz when I died
Respond and Interpret

1. Which images in these poems did you find especially striking? Why?

2. In the first stanza of "I heard a Fly buzz when I died," to what is the atmosphere in the room compared?

3. (a)In lines 5 and 6, what are the "Eyes" and "Breaths" doing? (b)What do they await? Explain.

4. Summarize the last two stanzas. Explain what impression of death you received from these lines.

Analyze and Evaluate

5. (a)Why do you think the speaker calls his or her belongings "Keepsakes"? (b)What other words or phrases in the poem seem to indicate an implied truth about life, death, or the human soul?

6. How does Dickinson's account of someone dying compare with other representations of death?

The Bustle in a House
Respond and Interpret

7. (a)What words does the speaker use that suggest everyday household chores? (b)To what type of chores is Dickinson really referring?

8. (a)According to the second stanza, when will we again "use" the love we put aside on the morning after death? (b)What might this suggest about Dickinson's religious faith? Explain.

Analyze and Evaluate

9. (a)What **analogy** does the speaker make in this poem? (b)What does this analogy suggest about human reactions and needs after a death?

Connect

10. **Connect to Today** In these two poems, Dickinson offers very different perspectives on death. In your opinion, which of the poems more accurately reflects how our society perceives death? Explain.

Literary Element Rhyme

The sounds and images of a poem work together to create meaning. The jarring effect of a slant **rhyme** can underscore a word's importance.

1. In "The Bustle in a House," which words does Dickinson draw attention to through slant rhyme?

2. The poem contrasts the mundane with the elevated and abstract. How does the use of slant rhyme reinforce this dual aspect of the poem?

Writing

Write an Essay Dickinson's original poems were untitled, so they are usually referenced by their first lines. Write a title for each of these two poems based on your interpretations of their themes. In a brief essay, explain your choice.

Reading Strategy Analyze Sound Devices

Assonance is the repetition of similar vowel sounds, as in this example:

The S<u>ou</u>l selects her <u>ow</u>n Society—

Consonance is the repetition of similar consonant sounds, typically within or at the ends of words.

Much Ma<u>dn</u>ess is divi<u>n</u>est Se<u>n</u>se—

Find examples of assonance and consonance in "The Bustle in a House." You may want to copy the poem and use different colored pens to underline examples. In your opinion, what does the poem gain from the use of consonance and assonance?

LOG ON **Literature** Online

Selection Resources For Selection Quizzes, eFlashcards, and Reading-Writing Connection activities, go to glencoe.com and enter QuickPass code GLA9800u3.

EMILY DICKINSON **447**

Literary Element

1. Death/Earth; away/Eternity
2. Death, unimaginable and final, is contrasted with Earth, which is familiar. "Putting Love away" is a way to cope with everyday loss, whereas Eternity is a grand concept.

Reading Strategy

Assonance: the long *e* sound in *industries, Sweeping,* and *Eternity*; Consonance: the *n* sound in *Morning, industries, Enacted.* These give unity to the poem and enhance its hymnlike qualities.

After You Read

Assess

1. Answers will vary.
2. A tense anticipation
3. (a) The Eyes are being wiped dry after crying, and Breaths are trying to become steady. (b) The death of the speaker
4. The speaker wills away worldly possessions and then dies. Death is uncertain, mysterious, or mundane.
5. (a) *Keepsakes* suggests that belongings are fragile and, in the end, trivial. (b) The focus on the fly suggests that until the end, only material aspects can be perceived with clarity.
6. The account is unsentimental.
7. (a) Terms such as *bustle, industries, sweeping,* and *putting away* suggest household chores. (b) The chores that consume families after a death
8. (a) In eternity (b) Dickinson's belief in an afterlife
9. (a) Between cleaning up a house and experiencing grief (b) Humans need activity and order to recover from grief. Students should provide support for their evaluations.
10. The first reflects people who question the idea of an afterlife. The second reflects a belief in heaven and hell.

> For additional assessment, see Assessment Resources, pp. 153–154.

Writing

Each essay should include an original title related to one of the poem's themes and explain why that title is appropriate.

447

Teach

Big Idea | 1

A Poetic Revolution Have students discuss whether Dickinson's view of death might have represented a new way of thinking about death in the mid-1800s. You may wish to review with students the views of other authors of the time.

Literary Element | 2

Personification Answer: *In the previous stanza, the speaker says, "We passed the Setting Sun." In the next line, He, the Sun, is passing the speaker and Death. Suddenly, the speaker has gone from acting to being acted upon.*

ENGLISH LEARNERS **Ask:** What inanimate objects in the poem act like human beings? What do they do? *(Death stops and waits, passes, and pauses. The dews quiver and feel cold.)*

Language History ☆

Gossamer The word *gossamer* comes from Middle English. The word is really a combination of two ordinary words—*goose* and *summer*. The word refers to fabric or cobweb strands that are light, airy, and delicate—like the downy feathers that geese shed during late summertime and early autumn.

 For activities related to this selection, see Unit 3 Teaching Resources Book, pp. 220–222.

For an audio recording of this selection, use Listening Library Audio CD-ROM.

Before You Read

Literary Element **Personification**

Personification is a figure of speech in which an animal, an object, a force of nature, or an idea is given human characteristics. As you read, ask yourself, What are specific ways in which Death resembles a person?

Reading Strategy **Clarify Meaning**

To **clarify meaning,** go back and reread confusing sections of the poem more slowly. This will help you notice ideas you may have previously missed.

Because I could not stop for Death

Emily Dickinson

Because I could not stop for Death—
He kindly stopped for me—
The Carriage held but just Ourselves—
And Immortality.

5 We slowly drove—He knew no haste
And I had put away
My labor and my leisure too,   **1**
For His Civility[1]—

We passed the School, where Children strove
10 At Recess—in the Ring—
We passed the Fields of Gazing Grain—
We passed the Setting Sun—

Or rather—He passed Us—
The Dews drew quivering and chill—
15 For only Gossamer, my Gown—   ☆
My Tippet—only Tulle[2]—

We paused before a House that seemed
A Swelling of the Ground—
The Roof was scarcely visible—
20 The Cornice—in the Ground—

Since then—'tis Centuries—and yet
Feels shorter than the Day
I first surmised the Horses' Heads
Were toward Eternity—

---

1. An old meaning of *civility* is "a community of citizens." Among the more modern meanings is "courtesy."
2. *Gossamer* is a light gauzelike fabric. A *tippet* is a scarf for the neck and shoulders with loose ends that hang down in front. *Tulle* is fine netting used for scarves and veils.

Personification *How does the personification of the sun (he) introduce a shift in the poem?* **2**

448 UNIT 3 THE CIVIL WAR ERA

Vocabulary Practice

SPIRAL REVIEW **Explore Latin Roots** Many English words have Latin roots. The root is usually combined with a prefix, a suffix, or both. The meaning of the English word is related to the meaning of its root. For example, the word *immortality* (line 4) contains the prefix *im-*, meaning "not" and the Latin root *mort*, meaning "death." *Immortality* thus means "the state of being deathless." Define each of the following words, using a dictionary if necessary, and discuss the Latin root for each one.

1. labor   3. visible
2. civility   4. centuries

Have students use this knowledge to define these words: *civic, civilization, laboratory, collaborate, per cent, centigrade.*

After You Read

Respond and Think Critically

Respond and Interpret

1. What were your first reactions upon reading this poem? Explain.

2. (a)According to lines 1–2, why does "Death" stop for the speaker? Explain what these lines suggest about human behavior. (b)According to lines 3–4, what does "Death's" carriage hold?

3. (a)What places and things does the speaker pass in the third stanza? (b)What might these places and things represent?

4. What is the "House" in the ground described in the fifth stanza? Explain how you know.

5. (a)According to the sixth stanza, how much time has passed since the day of "Death's" visit? (b)Why did that day seem so long to the speaker? Support your answer with details from the poem.

Analyze and Evaluate

6. Reread lines 9–16. (a)How does the poem shift at line 13? (b)What effect is created by this? Explain your answer.

7. (a)How would you describe the **mood**, or emotional quality and atmosphere, of this poem? (b)Which **images** or details help to create this mood? Explain.

8. One critic says that in this poem, the question of death is presented "without making any final statement about it. There is no solution to the problem . . . the idea of immortality is confronted with the fact of physical disintegration. We are not told what to think; we are told to look at the situation." Do you agree? Explain why or why not.

Connect

9. **Connect to the Author** Raised in a religious family, Dickinson experienced both intense faith and intense doubt throughout her life. In your opinion, where does this poem fit within that spectrum? Explain.

Literary Element Personification

Dickinson uses **personification** when she portrays death as a gentlemanly carriage driver with human characteristics.

1. What other object or idea is personified?

2. What is the effect of this personification? Explain.

3. Why do you think Dickinson chooses to portray death as she does? Use details from the poem to support your answer.

 Literature Online

Selection Resources For Selection Quizzes, eFlashcards, and Reading-Writing Connection activities, go to glencoe.com and enter QuickPass code GLA9800u3.

Reading Strategy Clarify Meaning

When you **clarify meaning**, you reread difficult sections of a text to figure out the meaning.

1. What is the relationship between the "Horses" in the last stanza and "Death"? To clarify, reread the poem.

2. What other points in the poem were clarified for you by rereading? Explain.

 Writing

Write a Paragraph Through personification, Dickinson gives form to death—something we can't see, but will all experience. Write a brief, descriptive paragraph in which you personify something that is unseen yet influential. You might choose an emotion, an idea, or a force of nature.

EMILY DICKINSON **449**

Literary Element

1. The grain is personified as gazing.
2. Students may say this heightens the discrepancy between the speaker, who is dying, and the world as it goes on without her.
3. Students may say that Dickinson wanted to suggest that Death is the kindly guide that takes us to Eternity.

Reading Strategy

1. The Horses are part of Death's carriage, headed toward Eternity.
2. Answers will vary. Students should support their answers.

After You Read

After You Read

Assess

1. Students should support their answers.
2. (a) Death stops for the speaker because the speaker could not stop for death. This suggests that humans are never fully prepared for death. (b) The speaker, Death, and Immortality
3. (a) Children, fields of grain, and the setting sun (b) Childhood, maturity, and old age
4. The House is a burial chamber. It is described as a "Swelling of the Ground," suggesting that something is buried inside.
5. (a) Centuries (b) Death is mysterious when it happens.
6. (a) At line 13, the poem diverges from the rhythm it had until that point. (b) This shift creates drama.
7. (a) Eerie (b) The image of Death as a driver, or the images of the carriage ride and cemetery
8. Students should support their answers with details.
9. Students may say she neither endorses nor refutes religion in this poem, and therefore is expressing her own uncertainty.

For additional assessment, see Assessment Resources, pp. 155–156.

Writing

Students should use descriptive language to give human characteristics to a non-human form, such as an animal or object.

Teach

Reading Strategy | 1

Connect The speaker describes how an external condition of nature causes a certain emotional state. Have students identify weather conditions that affect their moods. **Ask: What is the time of year, time of day, and the mood of the speaker?** *(It is winter and late afternoon, when the light is waning. The mood is painfully oppressive, hopeless, and despairing.)*

Literary Element | 2

Rhyme Answer: *The slant rhymes are* listens *and* Distance.

[ENGLISH LEARNERS] Ask English learners to think of words that they associate with the winter season. Point out connections between their answers and the poem.

View the Art ★

In *A Woman Sewing in an Interior*, Danish painter Vilhelm Hammershoi (1864–1916) captures the brilliant sunlight filtering through an otherwise dark room. **Ask: What is the mood of the painting?** *(The mood is quiet and reflective, exuding a sense of stillness and concentration.)*

For activities related to this selection, see Unit 3 Teaching Resources Book, pp. 230–234.

450

There's a certain Slant of light

Emily Dickinson

A Woman Sewing in an Interior, 1901. Vilhelm Hammershoi. Oil on canvas, 29 x 28 in. Detroit Institute of Arts. Founders Society Purchase, Robert H. Tannahill Foundation Fund.

★

There's a certain Slant of light,
Winter Afternoons—
That oppresses, like the Heft[1]
Of **Cathedral** Tunes—

5 Heavenly Hurt, it gives us—
We can find no scar,
But internal difference,
Where the Meanings, are—

None may teach it—Any—
10 'Tis the Seal[2] Despair—
An **imperial affliction**
Sent us of the Air—

When it comes, the Landscape listens—
Shadows—hold their breath—
15 When it goes, 'tis like the Distance
On the look of Death—

1

1. Here, *heft* means "heaviness."
2. Here, *seal* means "emblem."

Rhyme *Where are the slant rhymes in the last stanza?* **2**

Vocabulary

cathedral (ke thē´ drəl) *n.* a church that is the official seat of a bishop

imperial (im pēr´ ē əl) *adj.* of or relating to an empire or emperor

affliction (ə flik´ shən) *n.* great suffering, distress, or its cause

450 UNIT 3 THE CIVIL WAR ERA

Grammar Practice

SPIRAL REVIEW **Use Dashes** Dashes are a hallmark of Emily Dickinson's style. Point out that dashes indicate an abrupt break or change in thought or add emphasis. Have students write at least three original sentences in which they use dashes either for emphasis or to indicate an abrupt change. Have volunteers read their sentences aloud for the class and use their voice and facial expressions to convey the meanings of the dashes. Lead the class in a discussion of what dashes add to a written or spoken composition. *(Students may suggest that the dashes add energy or a sense of suspense or mystery to the writing.)*

This is my letter to the World

Emily Dickinson

At The Window, 1870. Karl Harald Alfred Broge. Oil on canvas, 21 x 17¼ in. Private collection.

This is my letter to the World
That never wrote to Me—
The simple News that Nature told—
With tender Majesty

5 Her Message is committed[1]
To Hands I cannot see—
For love of Her—Sweet—countrymen—
Judge tenderly—of Me

---

1. *Committed* means "entrusted."

3   A Poetic Revolution *Why does the poet capitalize maj-esty in line 4?*

A Poetic Revolution
Answer: *Students may say that the poet wishes to emphasize the power or omnipotence of nature. Students may also say that the poet wishes to create symmetry with the capitalized* Me *two lines before.*

ENGLISH LEARNERS Have students list the capitalized words in the poem. Guide students to come up with a generalization about the capitalized words. *(Most are nouns or pronouns—except for* Sweet *and* Judge.*)*

Writer's Technique ☆

Dickinson's Style Explain to students that this poem has all the hallmarks readers expect to find in a Dickinson poem—regular rhythm, a mixture of regular and slant rhyme, four-line stanzas, and the use of nonstandard dashes and capitalization. Lead students in a discussion of what makes Dickinson's style and voice unique.

> For an audio recording of this selection, use Listening Library Audio CD-ROM.

Advanced Learners

DIFFERENTIATED INSTRUCTION

SMALL GROUP **Nature in Poetry** Remind students that nature has always been a favorite subject of poets in almost every culture. Some poets, like the English Romantics of the late eighteenth and early nineteenth centuries, celebrated nature's power and mystery. For others, nature inspires them to analyze or express their own emotions and experiences. Ask students to consider how nature is depicted in Dickinson's poems. Ask them to work with partners to identify images of nature and to come up with a generalization about what nature means to Dickinson as a poet. For example, is nature a powerful force or just an object she describes? Does nature inspire her or is it merely a convenient metaphor? Remind students to draw on other traditions of nature poetry they may have read. Ask volunteers from each pair to share their ideas orally with the class.

After You Read

Assess

1. Answers will vary. Students should support their answers.
2. (a) Heavenly Hurt (b) It brings a feeling of oppression and heaviness.
3. (a) The speaker observes the slant of light in winter. (b) Winter might suggest that the slant of light comes at a moment of weakness or death.
4. The slant of light may represent death or the premonition of death. The last lines compare the waning light to the gap separating the living and the dead.
5. (a) Students may say that these words evoke depression, fear, or vulnerability. (b) Students should support their answers with examples.
6. (a) The letter may be Dickinson's poetry. (b) What nature has expressed, taught, or given to the speaker
7. (a) The speaker begs to be judged leniently. (b) Dickinson's poetry expresses what she has learned from nature.
8. For the speaker, life itself provides no easy answers.
9. Students should support their answers with examples.
10. Students may say that Dickinson wrote "There's a certain Slant of light" to express her own feelings of sadness. They may say that she wrote "This is my letter to the World" to articulate her respect for nature.

After You Read

Respond and Think Critically

There's a certain Slant of light
Respond and Interpret

1. What did you most like about these poems?
2. (a) What does the slant of light give us, according to the speaker? (b) Describe the **mood**, or feeling, that the slant of light brings.
3. (a) When does the speaker observe the slant of light? (b) Why is this significant? Explain.
4. What does the light seem to represent to the speaker? Explain how lines 15–16 reinforce this.

Analyze and Evaluate

5. (a) What feelings does Dickinson evoke with her descriptions of a "Heavenly Hurt" and "the Seal Despair"? (b) Does Dickinson bring out these feelings effectively?

This is my letter to the World
Respond and Interpret

6. (a) What might "my letter" refer to? (b) What "News" does the letter contain?
7. (a) What plea does the speaker make in stanza 2? (b) Why does she make this plea?

Analyze and Evaluate

8. What does the fact that the world never wrote to her suggest about the speaker?

Connect

9. **Big Idea** A Poetic Revolution How would you summarize Dickinson's poetic innovations?
10. **Connect to the Author** What connections might these poems have to Dickinson's life?

You're the Critic

What is Dickinson's true worth?
Read the following two excerpts of literary criticism.

> "She was an independent spirit. She did her best to get away from too strict an interpretation. . . . And she followed the American idiom. . . . She speaks the spoken language, the idiom, which would be deformed by Oxford English. . . . She was a real good guy."
> —William Carlos Williams

> "Emily Dickinson cuts things off very short, and that always seems to me rather shocking. She ends poems too soon for me."
> —Helen Vendler

Group Activity Discuss the following questions with your classmates. Refer to the two quotes and cite evidence from Dickinson's poems for support.

- Which aspects of Dickinson's poetry are praised by Williams? Which aspects are criticized by Vendler?
- Which of the critical assessments do you agree with more? Explain.

Caroline Auf Der Treppe. Caroline on the Stairs, 1825 (detail). Caspar David Friedrich. Oil on canvas, 29 x 20.3 in. Private collection.

You're the Critic

- Williams praises Dickinson's American diction. Vendler criticizes Dickinson's brevity.
- Students should support their opinions.

 For additional assessment, see Assessment Resources, pp. 157–158.

Literary Element | Rhyme

Through the skillful manipulation of **rhyme**, poets can achieve subtle emotional effects. Aware that readers have a tendency to expect perfect, or full, rhymes as they read, poets may decide to delay the expression of a full rhyme in order to create tension. When the full rhyme arrives later than expected, the overall effect may be to provide satisfaction and to emphasize a certain meaning.

1. How is the strategy described above illustrated in "This is my letter to the World"?

2. What effect does **internal rhyme**, or rhyme that occurs within a line of poetry, have on the poem?

Review: Personification

Personification is a figure of speech in which an animal, an object, a force of nature, or an idea is given human characteristics.

Partner Activity With a partner, examine "There's a certain Slant of light" and "This is my letter to the World." Working with your partner, create two web diagrams like the one below, and fill them in with examples of personification from each poem. Then discuss which examples you found most memorable or effective. Also discuss why Dickinson uses personification as she does.

 Literature Online

Selection Resources For Selection Quizzes, eFlashcards, and Reading-Writing Connection activities, go to glencoe.com and enter QuickPass code GLA9800u3.

Reading Strategy | Analyze Sound Devices

Alliteration refers to the repetition of similar consonant sounds at the beginnings of words. It is often used to emphasize certain words or ideas.

1. List three instances of alliteration in "There's a certain Slant of light." What is the effect of each on the sound and meaning of the poem?

2. What effect might Dickinson have intended to create with the repetition of the *m* sound in "This is my letter to the World"? Explain.

Vocabulary Practice

Practice with Word Usage Respond to these statements to help you explore the meanings of vocabulary words from the selections.

1. Explain a situation in which a **heave** might help you.

2. Describe an occurrence in your life when you have had to **interpose** yourself between people.

3. Name things you would find in a **cathedral**.

4. Identify a country or culture that has, at one point, had an **imperial** government.

5. Name a character from a book or movie who suffers from an **affliction**.

Academic Vocabulary

In Dickinson's poems, there is a sharp **contrast** *between her world and the external world.*

Contrast is an academic word. The poem "Much Madness is divinest Sense" depends on the usual contrast between "madness" and sense." To further explore the meaning of *contrast*, complete the sentence below.

In contrast to Whitman's expansive, outgoing, sociable poetic persona, that of Emily Dickinson could be described as _____ .

For more on academic vocabulary, see pages 53–54.

EMILY DICKINSON **453**

After You Read

Assess

Literary Element

1. The full rhyme arrives only at the end of each stanza; the first and third lines do not rhyme.

2. The internal rhyme of *tenderly* and *me* gives emphasis and character to the final line.

Review: Personification

"There's a certain Slant of light"
(1) "Slant of light, / Winter Afternoons— / That oppresses"
(2) "Shadows—hold their breath—"

"This is my letter to the World"
(1) "the World / That never wrote to Me—"
(2) "The simple News that Nature told—"

Reading Strategy

1. Examples include *Heft* and *Heavenly Hurt*; *Landscape listens* and *look*; and *Despair, Distance*, and *Death*. Students should provide support for their analysis.

2. Students may say she wished to emphasize *Me* by including other words that begin with *m*.

Vocabulary

1. Students may say having to lift furniture.

2. Students may provide a scenario wherein they had to come between friends to stop them from fighting.

3. Students may say stained glass, an altar, statues, pews, and tourists.

4. Students should name a country or cul-

ture that has practiced imperialism, such as the Roman Empire, China, England, or France.

5. Students should name a character who undergoes great physical or emotional distress. Examples include Ophelia in *Hamlet* or the narrator of "The Pit and the Pendulum."

Academic Vocabulary

Possible answers: introspective, shy, private, reserved.

After You Read

Assess

Respond Through Writing

Students' essays should analyze and evaluate Dickinson's nonstandard punctuation and spelling. Have students revise their drafts to strengthen the thesis and address the topic as needed.

Scoring Guide

Assess students' performance in the following categories using the scoring guide at the bottom of the page:

- Addresses all parts of the writing task.
- Provides a meaningful thesis, maintains focus and organization.
- Supports the thesis with details and examples.
- Provides a variety of sentence types; uses precise, descriptive language.
- Follows English language conventions.
- Makes a logical, convincing analysis.

Respond Through Writing

Expository Essay

Learning Objectives

In this assignment, you will focus on the following objectives:

Writing: Writing an expository essay.

Grammar: Using dashes.

Analyze Style Dickinson uses capitalization and dashes to achieve complex effects and add nuances to her poetry. In an expository essay, analyze and evaluate her nonstandard punctuation and spelling.

Understand the Task A **nuance** is subtle quality or variation. When you **analyze** a literary work, you methodically examine it by separating the selection into parts and studying the interrelations between those parts. To **evaluate** means to form opinions and make judgments about the effectiveness of certain parts of a literary work.

Prewrite Reread the poems both silently and out loud. Pay special attention to the effects created by the dashes and capitalizations and how they are connected with imagery and sound devices. Jot down some notes on these effects, and what you think Dickinson was trying to achieve, using a two-column chart like the one below. It has been started for you. You can use this chart to help you write your thesis and organize your essay.

Device	Effect
Em Dashes	Adds break in rhythm and shifts in thought
Slant Rhyme	Connects separate lines and the thoughts they contain

Draft In your thesis, explain Dickinson's use of nonstandard spelling and punctuation and its effects. In supporting paragraphs, include specific references to the text. Elaborate on each quotation you choose and show how it supports your thesis. Try using the sentence frame below to present your supporting details.

Dickinson's use of _____ expresses _____, _____, and _____.

Revise Reread your essay. Do you address how Dickinson's individual use of spelling and punctuation adds complexity to her writing? If not, make any necessary changes to your draft to address this point. Be sure your main points are emphasized and supported by evidence.

Edit and Proofread Proofread your paper, correcting any errors in grammar, spelling, and punctuation. Use the Grammar Tip in the side column for help with using dashes.

Grammar Tip

Dashes

Em dashes (—) can indicate an abrupt break or change in thought:

Dickinson's poetry is untraditional—but it explores universal themes.

Em dashes can be used to set off a parenthetical statement:

Dickinson's closest literary friend—and a person she trusted—encouraged her not to publish her work.

Em dashes can also be used to set off appositives:

Dickinson's gift to the world—her poetry—is highly regarded.

Scoring Guide	4	3	2	1
Task addressed	fully	mostly	partially	barely
Thesis	meaningful	provided	partial	weak
Support	thoughtful	provided	limited	weak
Language	varied, descriptive	varied, often descriptive	predictable, imprecise	repetitive, limited
Convention errors	few or none	several	many	serious
Analysis is	convincing	mostly convincing	partially convincing	not convincing

Emily Dickinson: An Introduction

Billy Collins

Poet Laureate 2001–2003

Interior With A Woman Reading A Letter, Strandgade 30 (detail), 1899. Vilhelm Hammershoi.

Learning Objectives

For pages 455–457

In studying this text, you will focus on the following objectives:

Literary Study: Making connections across literature.

Reading:
Analyzing informational text.
Analyzing literary criticism.

Set a Purpose for Reading

As you read, ask yourself, How does the author of this selection interpret Emily Dickinson's life and poems?

Build Background

Known for his witty, accessible poetry, Billy Collins served as the nation's poet laureate from 2001 to 2003. In the following passage from his introduction to *The Selected Poems of Emily Dickinson*, Collins discusses the myth that surrounds Emily Dickinson's life, the enduring power of her work, and the tools that she used in crafting her poems.

Reading Strategy Analyze Literary Criticism

Analyzing **literary criticism** involves recognizing the main ideas and supporting details in a piece of criticism in order to compare the critic's response to a piece of literature with your response. As you read, take notes on Collins's literary criticism. Use a two-column chart like the one below.

Critic's Response	My Response
zigzag logic in poems	

Today Emily Dickinson is recognized not only as a major poet of the American nineteenth century but also as one of the most intriguing poets of any place or time, in both her art and her life. The outline of her biography is well known. She was born in Amherst, Massachusetts, in 1830 and, except for a few excursions to Philadelphia, Washington, and Boston, spent her entire life there, increasingly limiting her activities to her father's house. "I do not cross my Father's ground to any House or Town," she wrote, referring to a personal reclusiveness that was noticeable even to her contemporaries. In the front corner bedroom of that house on Main Street, Dickinson wrote over 1,700 poems, often on scraps of paper and on the backs of grocery lists, only a handful of which were published in her lifetime and then anonymously. She was known to give poems to friends and neighbors, often as an accompaniment to the cakes and cookies she baked, sometimes lowering them from an upstairs window in a basket. Her habit of binding groups of poems together into little booklets called fascicles might indicate she felt her poems were presentable, but most of her poems never went farther than her desk drawer where they were discovered by her sister after Dickinson's death in 1886 of kidney failure.

BILLY COLLINS **455**

Focus

Summary

In this excerpt, the poet Billy Collins discusses some of the mysteries of Dickinson's "private existence," and some features of Dickinson's poetry—including common meter and "zigzag logic."

 For activities related to this selection, see Unit 3 Teaching Resources Book, pp. 236–244.

Teach

Reading Strategy

Set a Purpose for Reading

Have students summarize their responses to the subject matter, themes, form, figurative language, imagery, and sound effects of Dickenson's poetry. Have students compare their responses with those of Billy Collins.

For an audio recording of this selection, use Listening Library Audio CD-ROM.

Readability Scores

Dale-Chall: 10.6
DRP: 66
Lexile: 1360

Approaching Level

DIFFERENTIATED INSTRUCTION

Emerging Review the purpose of literary criticism with students. Much literary criticism does more than analyze a work of literature. It may also introduce new ideas about a writer and his or her work and support those ideas by citing other critics. Explain that Collins cites several other critics' ideas about Dickinson's life and work. Some critics he uses to support his own ideas; other critics he refutes. Tell students to make a checklist with the following three items: *Dickinson's poetry, Collins's ideas,* and *Other critics' ideas.* Each time they read about Dickinson's poetry, an original idea expressed by Collins, or a citation of another critic's thoughts, students should put a checkmark next to the item on the list. After reading the selection, ask students to discuss how the writer balanced the three elements. Ask students how well Collins supported his ideas by citing other critics and Dickinson's poetry.

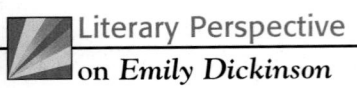
Teach

Reading Strategy

Analyze Literary Criticism

Have students reread the first complete paragraph on this page, beginning "It is fascinating to consider the case." Point out that Collins refers to several interpretations of Dickinson's life. Collins's survey of these interpretations seems reasonably objective. However, he concludes that the poet's separateness "took extreme forms." **Ask:** What details does he use to support this judgment? *(Details include her exclusive preference for white clothing and her reluctance to write addresses on envelopes.)*

APPROACHING Point out to students how the writer lets readers know when he is citing other people's ideas. Tell them to look for phrases such as "Some critics valorize . . ." and "Others make her out . . ." and "Still others believe . . . ." **Ask:** Does the writer agree with the ideas of the other critics? *(He does not. He states his own idea at the end of the paragraph. He suggests that Dickinson's withdrawal from the world "took extreme form.")*

Reading Practice

Connect the Main Idea Point out that Collins singles out brevity and conciseness as two of Dickinson's outstanding characteristics. Collins sums up this idea in a statement that is both figurative and concise: "Dickinson does not knock before entering."

Have students discuss what this statement means and how it captures the main idea of the paragraph. Then have students explain how this main idea connects to Collins's central thesis, or his purpose for writing the article.

Informational Text

In her lifetime, her poetry remained unknown, and although a few small editions of her poems were published in the 1890s, it was not until 1955 that a reliable scholarly edition appeared, transcribing the poems precisely from the original manuscripts and preserving all of Dickinson's typographical eccentricities. Convincingly or not, she called publication "the auction of the mind" and compared the public figure to a frog croaking to the admiring audience of a bog.

It is fascinating to consider the case of a person who led such a private existence and whose poems remained unrecognized for so long after her death, as if she had lain asleep only to be awakened by the kiss of the twentieth century. The quirky circumstances of her life have received as much if not more commentary than the poems themselves. Some critics valorize[1] her seclusion as a form of female self-sufficiency; others make her out to be a victim of her culture. Still others believe that her solitariness has been exaggerated. She did attend school, after all, and she maintained many intimate relationships by letter. Moreover, it was less eccentric in her day than in ours for one daughter—she had a brother who was a lawyer and a sister who married—to remain home to run the household and assist her parents. Further, all writers need privacy; all must close the door on the world to think and compose. But Dickinson's separateness—which has caused her to be labeled a homebody, a spinster, and a feminist icon among other things—took extreme forms. She was so shy that her sister Lavinia would be fitted for her clothes; she wore only white for many years ("Wear nothing commoner than snow"); and she rarely would address an envelope, afraid that her handwriting would be seen by the eyes of strangers. When asked of her companions, she replied in a letter to Thomas Wentworth Higginson[2], "Hills, sir, and the sundown, and a dog large as myself that my father bought me."

However tempting it is to search through the biographical evidence for a solution to the enigma[3] of Emily Dickinson's life, we must remember that no such curiosity would exist were it not for the poems themselves. Her style is so distinctive that anyone even slightly acquainted with her poems would recognize a poem on the page as an Emily Dickinson poem, if only for its shape. Here is a typical example:

> 'Tis little I could care for pearls
>   Who own the ample sea;
> Or brooches[4] when the Emperor
>   With rubies pelteth me;
>
> Or gold, who am the Prince of Mines;
>   Or diamonds, when I see
> A diadem[5] to fit a dome
>   Continual crowning me.

Such a short form leads to concision and quick-wittedness, her poems standing as dramatic examples of poetry's ability to compress wide meaning into small spaces. She was also fond of the riddle. The diadem that crowns her always is the sky. With the dome of earth overhead, the little poem wants to ask, who needs the grosser[6] riches of pearls, rubies, gold, or diamonds? The modest size of her poems (most are shorter than a sonnet) matches the modest space of house and garden in which she chose to live. The poems are also short because she does not waste time introducing the poem. She neither provides the details of a physical setting, as a conventional nature poem might do, nor does she explain the poem's occasion. The poems begin suddenly, often with a declaration ("Superiority to fate / Is difficult to learn") or a definition ("Hope is a subtle glutton"). Dickinson does not knock before entering, so the reader may feel swept up into the center of the poet's thought process without warning. To open a poem by saying "I felt a cleavage in my mind / As if my brain had split" is to thrust the reader into a psychic intimacy with the fractured speaker. Also, her poems tend to end abruptly and decisively, often

---

1. *Valorize* means to "attach value or worth to something."
2. *Thomas Wentworth Higginson* was a noted abolitionist, ordained minister, and editor for the *Atlantic Monthly*.
3. An *enigma* is something puzzling or mysterious.
4. A *brooch* is a piece of jewelry that is fastened by a pin.
5. *Diadem* means "crown."
6. Here, *grosser* mean "less fine."

with epigrammatic[7] authority ("The only secret people keep / Is Immortality").

Her tiny, untitled poems may fit her sensibility and provide the verbal equivalent of a home's safe enclosure—a room within a room—but the shortness of her lines is due to something else: her preference for common meter, the meter of ballads and Protestant hymns, and even of nursery rhymes. In common meter, a line of four beats is followed by a line of three beats.

> Amazing grace, how sweet the sound
> That saved a wretch like me.

---

7. *Epigrammatic* means "in the manner of a pithy, wise saying."

Or, more speedily,

> Old King Cole was a merry old soul
> And a merry old soul was he.

Or, with Dickinson,

> A thought went up my Mind to-day
> That I have had before, . . .

Rhythmically, the three-beat line sounds like an answer to the four-beat line, and it also provides a one-beat pause at the end, a space to breathe. Dickinson used other kinds of cadences, but common meter is the usual gait[8] of her poetry. Almost every Dickinson poem can be sung—like it or not—to the tune of "The Yellow Rose of Texas," a song in common meter. But unlike that song, her poems also include a counter-rhythm she created by interrupting the regular beat with dashes—her obsessive type of punctuation—and by her sudden jumps of thought. Instead of a steady run of meaning, the Dickinson poem hops from one figure to another in a kind of zigzag logic that requires not just our concentration but our own agility in making imaginative and grammatical leaps. Even her obituary in the *Springfield Republican* noted that she was "quick as the electric spark in her intuitions."

---

8. Here, *gait* means "rhythm."

Respond and Think Critically

Respond and Interpret

1. Write a brief summary of the main ideas in this excerpt before you answer the following questions. For help on writing a summary, see page 79.

2. How did you respond to Emily Dickinson's seclusion?

3. (a)To what does Dickinson compare the public figure? (b)How would you explain her disdain for public opinion?

4. Collins asserts that the meter of Dickinson's poems creates "the verbal equivalent of a home's safe enclosure." Why else do you think Dickinson may have used this meter?

Analyze and Evaluate

5. What does Collins suggest about the "commentary" related to Dickinson's seclusion?

6. Collins states that in her poetry Dickinson "compress[es] wide meaning into small spaces" and that Dickinson's poems require an agile reader who can make "imaginative and grammatical leaps"? Do you agree with his statement?

Connect

7. **Big Idea** A Poetic Revolution In what ways do you think Dickinson's poetic innovations are related to her separation from the world?

BILLY COLLINS **457**

Literary Perspective
on *Emily Dickinson*

Teach

View the Photograph ★

The Homestead was built in 1813 and was likely the first brick house in Amherst, Massachusetts. The house was a center for Amherst society and even hosted some of Amherst College's receptions. As an adult, Emily Dickinson confined herself to the Homestead and the grounds; after the late 1860s, she never left the property. Today, both this house and the house built next door for her brother and sister-in-law have been preserved as the Emily Dickinson Museum.

Ask: How does the author characterize Dickinson's desire to seclude herself in her home? Does he think she is being revolutionary? *(He suggests that all writers need privacy and seclusion. He suggests that she went to an extreme, which is not the same thing as being revolutionary.)*

For additional assessment, see Assessment Resources, pp. 159–160.

Assess

1. Students' summaries should represent the main ideas and should not contain personal opinions.

2. Students may express surprise at the extent to which Dickinson cloistered herself.

3. (a) Dickinson compares the public figure to a frog croaking in a bog. (b) Students may say that the primary reason is that society can inhibit individuality. Other may argue that she preferred seclusion because she was shy.

4. Students may argue that she chose this meter because of her familiarity with it. Others may say she chose it for its musical qualities.

5. Collins suggests that the commentary is dependent on, and of secondary importance to, the poems.

6. Students should realize that poetic compression often requires unique grammatical phrasing and a zigzag logic.

7. Students may say that Dickinson's separation provided the isolation necessary for her to create a unique poetic style.

Research Report

Focus

Bellringer Options

Have students look back through the pages of this unit for images that depict life during the Civil War. **Ask:** When you look at the images, what questions come to mind? What resources do you think would help you find answers to those questions?

Have students consider what they would like to learn about the Civil War as they learn how to write a research report.

Summary

In this workshop, students will write and present research reports. They will follow the stages of the writing process, including prewriting, drafting, revising, and editing. In addition, two mini-lessons, on paragraph coherence and correct quotation use, are provided.

Writing Process

At any stage of the writing process you may think of new ideas. Feel free to return to earlier stages as you write.

Prewrite

Draft

Revise

Focus Lesson: Coherent Paragraphs

Edit & Proofread

Focus Lesson: Quotations

Present

Writing Workshop

Research Report

Literature Connection Chesnut's diary is an example of a primary source, or a source that provides a firsthand account of events.

> *"Prayers from the women and imprecations from the men, and then a shell would light up the scene. Tonight, they say, the forces are to attempt to land."*
>
> —Mary Chesnut, from "Mary Chesnut's Civil War"

A secondary source is a source created after an event and is often based upon primary sources. In a **research report**, a writer presents facts and ideas gathered from various primary and secondary sources about a specific topic or issue.

Checklist: Features of Research Reports

Goals	Strategies
To present a strong, focused thesis	☑ Use multiple sources to draw a central conclusion about your topic and state it in your introduction
To develop and elaborate on main ideas that support the thesis	☑ Quote, paraphrase, and summarize information from a variety of primary and secondary sources ☑ Assess and comment on the relative value of your sources
To employ an effective, logical order	☑ Maintain a focus on your thesis ☑ Supply transitions to create clear relationships between main ideas ☑ Support main ideas with substantial, specific, and relevant examples
To create precision and interest	☑ Use precise language and a variety of sentence structures
To use sources honestly and correctly	☑ Attribute all sources ☑ Use standardized citations correctly

Workshop Resources

Print Materials

- Unit 3 Teaching Resources pp. 246–252
- Writing Kit
- Success in Writing: Research and Reports

Technology

- Literature Online: Writing Resources and Grammar Resources, www.glencoe.com
- Online Essay Grader, www.glencoe.com
- Student Presentation Builder on StudentWorks Plus CD-ROM
- Media Workshop DVD
- Online Student Edition

Assignment: Write a Research Report

Write a research report of at least 1,500 words in which you synthesize information from a variety of sources, draw conclusions, and discuss related insights. As you write, keep your audience and purpose in mind.

Audience: classmates and teacher

Purpose: to investigate a topic and report your conclusions

Prewrite

Schedule the Assignment Create a time frame for completing each stage of your writing process.

Investigate and Narrow a Topic Find a subject area and topic that interest you. Then narrow or expand your topic as needed.

▶ **Ask Questions** Think of a research report as a well-documented response to a significant question. List several research questions. As you learn more, refine your research questions and focus on a central idea.

▶ **Focus Your Topic** Use your questions to determine the scope of your topic. The topic should not be so broad that you will be writing in generalities nor so narrow that you cannot find adequate sources.

Compare the topics in the chart below to see the differences between topics that are too broad, too narrow, and appropriately limited.

Too Broad	Appropriately Limited	Too Narrow
Civil War photography	Civil War photography of Mathew Brady	Mathew Brady's photographs of the battles of Bull Run
Women during the Civil War	Women soldiers during the Civil War	Women soldiers of the 95th Illinois Infantry Regiment

Gather Evidence After you narrow your topic, try to answer your research questions. Pay attention to your topic's context and background.

▶ **Find Reliable Sources** Evaluate your sources to make sure that they are not outdated, biased, or based on faulty data. Personal Web sites may promote personal agendas and not facts. Books published by well-known publishers or universities are generally reliable.

▶ **Consider Different Perspectives** Keep in mind that people can have different perspectives on events. Consider perspectives that are often overlooked in the study of your topic.

Real-World Connection

You will use research and documentation skills in a variety of workplace documents, including statistical and annual reports. For now, you can publish your findings by presenting an oral report about them.

The Right Tone

Consider the purpose of your paper and how best to address your audience. Use a formal and objective tone to show that your research is serious and unbiased. Avoid slang and contractions. Use the third-person point of view.

 Writing Workshop

Research Report

Teach

Big Idea

A Nation Divided Talk with students about issues and events that divided the nation during the Civil War era. Explain that people had many different views about those issues, just as people differ on issues today. **Say:** The literary materials created in the Civil War era typically reflect the strong sectional viewpoints of their writers.

Writing Process

Prewriting Have students work in groups to generate questions and develop their ideas. Tell them to review the Unit Three selections and look for issues of interest.

Cultural History

Mathew Brady Mathew Brady (c. 1823–1896) opened his photography studio in 1844. In less than ten years, Brady's eyesight deteriorated so badly that, after 1851, he hired other photographers to take most of his pictures. Still, Brady's commitment to recording the events of the Civil War has made him one of America's best-known photographers. Brady's photographs were among the first ever to record a war as it raged. Have students imagine the impact his photographs had on viewers who had never seen war up close before.

Approaching Level

DIFFERENTIATED INSTRUCTION

Emerging Less proficient readers may gain a basic understanding of a particular event or issue from reference materials in the young-adult section of the library. Once they have identified a research question, they can start using more sophisticated sources for their research.

English Learners

DIFFERENTIATED INSTRUCTION

Intermediate Remind students that *perspective* has multiple meanings. Clarify that here it means "point of view." Illustrate point of view by having volunteers stand in different places around the room and describe the room from their viewpoint. Each description of the room should be slightly different. Explain that in writing a research report, students will read different perspectives or viewpoints on the same event.

Research Report

Focus

Writing Skills

Take Notes Suggest that students use colored note cards or highlighter pens to group notes for various subtopics. They might also use colored sticky notes to mark pages in reference sources.

Make a Plan Review possible ways to organize main ideas, such as chronological, comparison-contrast, and cause-and-effect orders. Point out that different organizational plans fit different topics. Students should look at their central research question, decide what organizational plan the question suggests, and then plan their paper accordingly.

Language History ☆

Plagiarism Tell students that this term comes from the Latin word *plagiarius,* which means "kidnapper" or "plunderer." It is used today to mean "literary thievery."

Take Notes As you read through various sources, note important ideas, facts, and quotations. Record this information on note cards, in a notebook, or in separate computer files. Make sure to keep your information organized. For each source, record full publishing information (see the guidelines on pages R33–R39) and assign it a number or the author's last name. Then use this number or name as you label any notes taken from the source. This will save time and help you compile your Works Cited page(s) later. As you find information you want to include, decide how to best incorporate it into your paper.

▶ **Quote** Record direct quotations exactly as they appear, including punctuation. Use quotations sparingly.

▶ **Paraphrase** Restate someone else's original idea in your own words, giving credit to the author whose idea it is.

▶ **Summarize** Condense information to its key points and details.

Avoid Plagiarism

Plagiarism is using another writer's words or ideas without giving proper credit. Be careful not to plagiarize unintentionally. For example, paraphrasing another writer's words too closely is plagiarism—*even if you cite the source.* Avoid this by fully rewriting information in your own words as well as citing the source.

Give Due Credit

Cite sources within your paper as close to the end of the borrowed information as possible, usually before a period or comma. The first citation consists of the author's last name and the page number(s) within parentheses: **(Burgess 7).** Give full bibliographic information on the Works Cited page at the end of the paper.

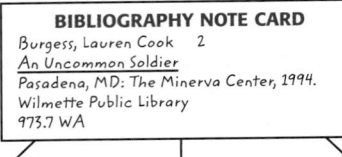

BIBLIOGRAPHY NOTE CARD
Burgess, Lauren Cook   2
An Uncommon Soldier
Pasadena, MD: The Minerva Center, 1994.
Wilmette Public Library
973.7 WA

PARAPHRASE NOTE CARD
Women Disguised as Soldiers 2
Women from poorer and more rural backgrounds tended to succeed at disguising themselves because they had more experience with physical labor and thus were able to blend in more easily with the men. (paraphrase) page 7

DIRECT QUOTATION NOTE CARD
Women Disguised as Soldiers 2
"Poor immigrant women from the cities worked at hard, physical labor and possessed none of the refined sensibilities of their 'betters.' Women such as these, who were confident of their survival skills, would have few qualms about their ability to measure up with the men in the military." (quotation) page 7

SUMMARY NOTE CARD
Women Disguised as Soldiers 2
Often rural women disguised as men could pass as male soldiers. (summary) page 7

Analyze Information Once you have gathered a number of primary and secondary sources, look for patterns and similarities as well as contradictions. Organize your information around main ideas. Remember that a successful research report synthesizes ideas and presents new conclusions rather than simply stringing quotations together.

Make a Plan Once you are familiar with several expert perspectives on your topic, write a **thesis statement.** Use your notes to help you make an outline. Include only information that is relevant to your thesis. Choose an effective way to order the main ideas and keep related ideas together.

Writing Practice

Thesis Statement Tell students that a thesis is a central idea that guides a research report. Since every element of a report must support its thesis statement, it is important to keep the thesis statement in mind throughout the research process. Have students write their proposed thesis statements on note cards and tape the cards to their research binders. Then work with students to develop a research strategy—a preliminary list of paper, online, and real-life sources they might consult for information on their topics. Remind students to revise their statements and strategies as they research.

Draft

Make Connections Start writing by following your outline and note cards. If you find it easier, write the body paragraphs before you write the introduction. Consider how each point in your outline relates to other points and to your thesis statement. Remember to explain those relationships to your reader.

Analyze a Workshop Model

Here is a final draft of a historical research report. Read the research report and pay close attention to the comments in the margin. They point out features that you might want to include in your own paper. Answer the questions in the margin, and use the answers to guide you as you write your own draft.

On the Front Lines: Women Soldiers in the Civil War

Often disguised as men, women who fought on the front lines in the Civil War defied feminine stereotypes and nineteenth-century expectations. Unfortunately, these stereotypes labeled women who fought or attempted to fight in the Civil War as scandalous and criminal, yet their reasons for fighting were often not much different from those of male soldiers. Despite discrimination, women fought in the Civil War out of patriotism, love, and a desire for independence, adventure, and better status and pay.

Women had been fighting in wars and battles long before the Civil War. Joan of Arc's fifteenth-century battles may be the most famous, but other women warriors fought throughout history. Matilda of Tuscany fought for Pope Gregory VII in the eleventh and twelfth centuries, and Lakshmi Bai led the Bengal army against the British in India just before the American Civil War (Hall xi–xii). American women also took part in earlier wars. For example, Pennsylvanian Margaret Cochran Corbin joined the Continental army with her husband in 1776, and Mary Hays took over her husband's duties as gunner when he was injured in 1778

Thesis Statement

State your topic and your perspective on it in the thesis statement. What information do you expect to see in this paper?

Main Ideas

Develop main ideas and organize them effectively to support your thesis successfully. Why does the writer begin the paper with this main idea?

 Writing Workshop

Research Report

Teach

Writing Process

Draft Show students an inverted triangle to illustrate a possible organization for an introductory paragraph. Students may start with general information about their topic, such as a striking quotation, and then narrow down to the thesis statement. This plan places the thesis statement last in the paragraph, so it leads immediately into the first body paragraph.

Writing Skills

Main Proposition/Thesis Statement Answer: *I expect to see the reasons why women fought in the Civil War and to learn that their reasons were often not very different from those of male soldiers.* Remind students to return periodically to this sentence and consider how each part of the paper supports the thesis statement.

Logical Structure

Answer: *This main idea gives historical background on the topic. Placing this paragraph at the beginning helps the writer establish an effective chronological order.*

Teach

Writing Skills

Paraphrase Offer students the following rule for quotations: "If you cannot express a thought more clearly or vividly than the source, quote from it." Otherwise it is better to paraphrase. Remind students not to string together many quotations. **Answer:** *The source material might not tell the facts as succinctly as the writer's paraphrase does.*

[ENGLISH LEARNERS] Remind students to be certain that they understand exactly what the words in a quotation mean before including them in their writing.

Direct Quotations

Answer: *In this paragraph, the details show some of the obstacles that women had to overcome to serve in the military.*

Supporting Details

Supporting Details Tell students to vary supporting details, such as reasons, statistics, and factual descriptions. **Answer:** *The main idea is that women were legitimately involved in the Civil War; the details specify the ways in which women were involved.*

Transitions

Answer: *It clearly marks a turning point from the historical background to the paper's main argument.*

Paraphrase

Paraphrase information rather than quote from an unremarkable passage. Do not use quotation marks. Why might the writer avoid a direct quotation here?

Direct Quotations

Use direct quotations to retain the author's exact wording and to highlight particularly striking or meaningful phrases. What effect do these direct quotations have?

Supporting Details

Support your main ideas with relevant details. How do these details support the main idea of the paragraph?

Transitions

Shift gears by using transitional phrases or sentences that explain your thought process. Is this transition effective?

(Leonard 102–104). Therefore, by the opening salvos of the Civil War, women had been fighting in armies for centuries.

The Civil War, however, was different. Neither the Union army nor the Confederate army allowed women to enlist (Blanton, Part 1, 2). Most newspaper stories of the time about women found in the armies were neutral or positive, but some suggest that the women were considered to be "of very bad character, indeed" (Burgess 6). When sisters Mary and Mollie Bell were discovered in 1864, they were accused of being prostitutes, arrested, and described as "manifestly crazy" (Burgess 6). Despite the restrictions and the threat of personal attacks, many women still enlisted. According to Mary Livermore, a women's rights activist of the time, there were about four hundred female soldiers during the Civil War (Hattaway 135). The more modern estimate is that between four hundred and six hundred women campaigned during the Civil War (Wagner 445).

Although enlistment was technically forbidden, there were many other legitimate ways for women to involve themselves in the war and support the army. Many Union women were considered *vivandières* or *cantinières*, women who assisted the troops by providing water and aid and carrying messages between commanders and soldiers (Varhola 120). Other women—more than three thousand in the Northern states—served as nurses and helped ill or injured soldiers. These nurses had to endure low pay and abysmal working conditions. Southern women also supported the troops by working as nurses, although they faced criticism for attending to "ruffians" (Ward 149). Still, women did not allow their roles as nurses to inhibit their involvement in combat.

However, for some women, working as a nurse or helping as a vivandière did not satisfy their motivations, so they turned toward disguise. In the Victorian age, gender was closely linked to exterior characteristics, such as clothing and hair. For example, if a person was seen wearing pants, "most people of the period would naturally have assumed that the person was a man" (Burgess 3).

Writing Practice

Document Sources Review that a direct quotation needs to be credited. Other information that should be credited includes:

- another writer's opinion
- a generalization that someone else has analyzed
- statistics that are not common knowledge

Remind students to prepare a Works Cited page as they research. Then, when they

need to credit a source, they can easily find and copy the information they need.

Such attitudes made it easy for women to disguise themselves as men. In addition, women cut their hair, wore fake mustaches, and, to create the illusion of muscles, padded their uniforms. Those who did not sport false facial hair found it easy to blend in among the boys and young men who were also fighting in the war. Women also created male pseudonyms—and army officials never asked for official identification (Blanton, Part 1, 2–3). Women from poorer and more rural backgrounds tended to succeed at disguise because they had more experience with physical labor and thus were able to blend in more easily with the men (Burgess 7). Yet some of the women, despite their best attempts at disguise, were discovered. Most were found out when they visited a hospital after becoming sick or wounded (Commager 241). For example, one woman was discovered only when she fainted after an injury (Hall 158). Many—both successfully and unsuccessfully—tried to reenlist in different regiments after their discovery.

There were many reasons for women to get involved in the Civil War, either in legitimate ways or by sneaking their way into battle, and many of these reasons did not differ from the motivations for men. Elizabeth D. Leonard, a prominent scholar, explains that, as with their male counterparts, "the traditional explanation has centered on pure, unadulterated patriotism" (227). The Civil War was a philosophical conflict as well as a military one. Many abolitionists were women. They identified with the fight for equality. For many women in the North, this was the first time that they had ever felt such intense loyalty to their country.

In addition, as Frank Moore noted in 1866, some women went to war because they could not bear separation from loved ones, while others went out of "a pure love of romance and adventure" (17). For instance, when her husband became a private, Bridget Divers joined the First Michigan Cavalry as a nurse. Her efforts extended into direct combat. She was known for helping move wounded men off the battlefield, rallying soldiers to retreat, and even occasionally fighting with the troops (Faust 221). Leonard explains:

Interest

Create interest through precise language and a variety of sentence structures, as well as through substantial, specific, and relevant examples. Which word choices and examples are especially apt here?

Sources

Attribute your sources. How does the writer also comment on the relative value of this source?

Transitions

Show relationships between main ideas. Where else do you find an effective use of transitional words and phrases?

Secondary Sources

Use a combination of primary and secondary sources. Why might the writer have chosen to use a secondary source?

Writing Workshop

Teach

Writing Skills

Interest
Answer: *The phrase "sport false facial hair" has a playful quality, which points to the slightly humorous lengths to which women would go in order to serve.*

Sources Say: Look at the Works Cited list on page 465.
Answer: *The Works Cited list indicates that Leonard has written a 1999 book on the subject.*

Transitions
Answer: *On page 464, the first full paragraph's opening sentence effectively transitions from the more philosophical reasons for going to war to a pratical reason: money.*

Sources Say: Look again at the Works Cited list on page 465.
Answer: *The sources for this section are Moore, an 1866 book that probably included quotes from primary sources; Faust, whose information comes from primary sources—newspapers of the time; and Leonard, a secondary source.*

English Learners

DIFFERENTIATED INSTRUCTION

Intermediate Suggest that English learners limit their research to answering one question using only a few sources. Also, limit the number of pages and citations in the report. Work directly with students to find reliable sources at an appropriate reading level.

Advanced Explain that the phrase "heat of battle" is an idiom that means the highest degree of intensity in a situation or action. Think of how "heat" or the highest degree of intensity may evoke an image of weapons constantly firing during the "battle." Tell students that they should avoid using any idioms in research papers unless they have looked up the idiom's meaning and understand how it should be used.

Research Report

Focus

Writing Skills

Long Quotations Say: Limit block quotations to one a page, and use one only when the entire passage supports the text. **Answer:** *The quotation presents an expert's explanation of Divers's importance.*

Coherent Paragraphs

Answer: *The author summarizes the points made in the earlier paragraph by using the words "patriotism, love, and adventure." Then, by saying these were not the only reasons, the author opens the possibility that there is yet another reason: the practical need to earn money.*

Draw Conclusions Tell students that it is their job as writers to draw conclusions. Readers should not have to wonder what conclusion to draw. **Answer:** *They synthesize source information, draw conclusions about the quotation's meaning, and link the quotation to the paper's thesis.*

Restate Thesis Answer: *Restating the thesis enables the reader to reconsider the main point after reading all the supporting evidence.*

Adding Insight Answer: *The writer extends the conclusion beyond its historical context and examines current situations. The reader then thinks about how the past and present differ or have similarities.*

464

Long Quotations

For quotations four lines or longer, start a new line and indent the entire quotation ten spaces. Do not use quotation marks. What is the effect of the long quotation used here?

Coherent Paragraphs

Use transitions and repeat key words and phrases to help make your paragraphs coherent. How does the author connect this paragraph to the one before it?

Draw Conclusions

Synthesize the information from your sources and draw your own conclusions about what it means. How do the sentences after the long quotation strengthen the writer's point?

Restate Thesis

In your conclusion, restate your thesis and summarize your main points. Why would the writer want to restate the thesis at the end of the paper?

Adding Insight

In your conclusion, draw inferences and add relevant insight. What does the writer leave the reader to think about?

Bridget Divers became widely known for her valiant efforts on behalf of the wounded, for her courage under fire in battle, and . . . for her willingness to position herself in such a way as to generate among the men in the ranks the greatest enthusiasm that they could muster for the fight (123). Interestingly, in the heat of battle it did not matter to the other combatants that Bridget Divers was a woman. She still had the ability to inspire and help her fellow Americans.

Patriotism, love, and adventure were not the only reasons women became soldiers, however, and historians have only recently addressed the more practical motivations. Another major reason that women—and men—joined the army was for the money. As Leonard asserts, a woman's service in the Civil War, "however patriotic in its essential motivation, however exciting in comparison with what most mid-century American women could expect from their normal daily lives, was compensated by wages" (230). A military salary was particularly attractive to women, who typically earned far less than men. Higher wages offered women independence that would have been otherwise unheard of in the 1860s. Implicitly, then, women were fighting to complete the promise of equality put forth during the American Revolution.

The women who fought in the Civil War, often in disguise, exhibited courage and persistence and had to overcome substantial obstacles as a result of their gender. Their reasons for fighting included love and adventure but also more practical reasons. Today, U.S. women soldiers serve bravely alongside men in the armed forces. However, official rules still bar women from positions that involve direct combat. Although nearly 150 years have passed since the Civil War, women still face discrimination; yet female soldiers of today share many qualities—integrity, bravery, and determination—with those who fought in the Civil War. In essence, one of the lessons we can learn from the Civil War is that there are few differences in motivation and abilities between men and women in battle.

Reading Practice

Draw Conclusions Explain that drawing a conclusion involves using facts and general knowledge of human behavior to make an inference.

As students read different perspectives on the same historical event, they will draw their own conclusions about what happened. Remind them to share those conclusions with their readers. After students write a first draft, ask them to write a brief statement about the conclusions they drew from their research and what they want readers to understand from reading their reports.

Works Cited

Blanton, DeAnne. "Women Soldiers of the Civil War." <u>Prologue Magazine</u> 25.1 Spring 1993 <http://www.archives.gov/publications/prologue/1993/spring/women-in-the-civil-war-1.html>.

Burgess, Lauren Cook, ed. <u>An Uncommon Soldier: The Civil War Letters of Sarah Rosetta Wakeman, alias Private Lyons Wakeman, 153rd Regiment, New York State Volunteers</u>. Pasadena, MD: The Minerva Center, 1994.

Commager, Henry Steele, ed. <u>The Civil War Archive: The History of the Civil War in Documents</u>. New York: Black Dog & Leventhal, 2000.

Faust, Patricia L., ed. "Divers, Bridget." <u>Historical Times Illustrated Encyclopedia of the Civil War</u>. New York: Harper & Row, 1986.

Hall, Richard. <u>Patriots in Disguise: Women Warriors of the Civil War</u>. New York: Paragon, 1993.

Hattaway, Herman. <u>Shades of Blue and Gray: An Introductory Military History of the Civil War</u>. Columbia, MO: Missouri, 1997.

Leonard, Elizabeth D. <u>All the Daring of the Soldier: Women of the Civil War Armies</u>. New York: Norton, 1999.

Moore, Frank. <u>Women of the War: Their Heroism and Self-Sacrifice</u>. 1866. Reprint. Alexander, NC: Blue/Gray, 1997.

Varhola, Michael J. <u>Everyday Life During the Civil War</u>. Cincinnati: Writer's Digest, 1999.

Wagner, Margaret E., Gary W. Gallagher, and Paul Finkelman, eds. <u>Civil War Desk Reference</u>. New York: Grand Central, 2002.

Ward, Geoffrey C. <u>The Civil War: An Illustrated History</u>. New York: Knopf, 1990.

Exposition

Reliable Sources

Internet sources may be less reliable than published sources. What indicates that this source should be reliable?

Primary Sources

Use primary sources to give original accounts of events, but check that they are reliable. How can you tell whether a primary source is reliable?

Encyclopedia Sources

Use encyclopedias and similar reference materials for general background and research. When would you use an encyclopedia as a source? When would you not?

Variety of Sources

Use a variety of sources from all perspectives in your research. How would you assess the relative value of this source?

Research Report

Teach

Writing Skills

Reliable Sources

Answer: *It is a U.S. government site.* Talk with students about why some online sources may be less reliable. *(They are not necessarily written by experts and are often not fact-checked.)* **Say:** Use a print source to verify Internet sources other than encyclopedias or government sites.

Primary Sources

Answer: *Consider the purpose, tone, and perspective of the source and its acceptance by secondary sources on the topic.*

Encyclopedia Sources

Answer: *I would use encyclopedias and similar sources for general background information, and other sources for more specific, detailed information.*

Variety of Sources

Answer: *This outdated source is valuable because it gives the perspective of a different era and can be used to show how opinions may have changed. It can provide a glimpse into what people knew and thought in an earlier time.*

Approaching Level

DIFFERENTIATED INSTRUCTION

Emerging Explain that electronic sources often contain formal citations. Students should copy these citations onto note cards. Point out that there are different citation format styles. Tell students which style to use, and provide guidance in following the format.

Advanced Learners

DIFFERENTIATED INSTRUCTION

Annotated Bibliography Tell students that a Works Cited page or bibliography is a valuable research tool for readers who want to know more. Have advanced students create an annotated bibliography, complete with comments that assess the usefulness of each source.

Research Report

Focus

Writing Process

Revise When students exchange papers, they may benefit from their partner's expertise or insight into a topic. You might post all students' topics and pair students with strong backgrounds in each other's topics.

Writing Process

Make Paragraphs Coherent
Walk students through the revisions of the incoherent paragraph. Explain how each revision affects the paragraph. Point out that each detail in the revised paragraph ties to the idea that money was a strong motivator for women to join the army.

Writer's Technique ☆

Revision If students are using word-processing programs, they might use a Track Changes feature as they revise. This allows them to see both old and new versions simultaneously.

Traits of Strong Writing

Include these traits of strong writing to express your ideas effectively.

Ideas
Organization
Voice
Word Choice
Sentence Fluency
Conventions
Presentation

For more information on using the traits of strong writing, see pages R30–R32.

Word Choice

This academic vocabulary word appears in the student model:

despite (di spīt') *prep.* in spite of; even though; *Despite discrimination, women fought in the Civil War.* Using academic vocabulary may help strengthen your writing. Try to use one or two academic vocabulary words in your historical investigation report. See the complete list on pages R88–R90.

Revise

Peer Review After drafting, exchange papers with a partner. Use the checklist below to evaluate and strengthen each other's writing.

Checklist

- ☑ Do you begin with a strong, focused thesis statement?
- ☑ Do you use a variety of sources and assess, comment on, and correctly attribute them?
- ☑ Do you support main ideas with substantial, relevant examples?
- ☑ Do you present ideas in a logical order and use transitions?
- ☑ Do you quote, paraphrase, summarize, and cite sources correctly?
- ☑ Do you explain varying perspectives?
- ☑ Do you create interest through sentence variation and effective word choice?

> **Focus Lesson**

Make Paragraphs Coherent

To make your writing coherent, choose an organizational scheme, eliminate unrelated information, and use transitional expressions.

Draft: Incoherent paragraph

Sarah Rosetta Wakeman disguised herself and joined the army to help her family pay off debts (Burgess 18). As a child, Wakeman hunted squirrels. A military salary was particularly attractive to women, who typically earned far less than men.

Revision: Revise and reorganize the paragraph to make it coherent.

Another major reason that women—and men—joined the army was for the money.[1] Sarah Rosetta Wakeman, for example,[2] disguised herself and joined the army to help her family pay off debts (Burgess 18). As a child, Wakeman hunted squirrels.[3] A military salary was particularly attractive to women, who typically earned far less than men. Higher wages offered women independence that would have been otherwise unheard of in the 1860s.[4]

1: **Begin with a topic sentence**   3: **Eliminate unrelated information**
2: **Give an example**   4: **Analyze details**

Writing Practice

Sentence Variety Sentence variety adds interest and appeal to writing. Review the different types of sentences (simple, compound, complex, and compound-complex) students can use. Then discuss how to vary sentence structure. For example, writers can add subordinate clauses to the end of sentences. They can also use parentheses or dashes to include asides. Challenge students to rewrite at least three of the sentences in their drafts, changing the type of sentence. Then ask them how the revisions affected their writing.

Edit and Proofread

Get It Right Proofread the draft for errors in grammar, mechanics, and spelling. Refer to the Language Handbook, pages R42–R61, as a guide.

> **Focus Lesson**

Use Quotations Correctly

Check to make sure that your quotations are cited correctly. Analyze the quotation in your own words so that its significance is clear.

Problem: Too many direct quotations break up the flow of the paper.

"Although most accounts were neutral or complementary, some newspaper reports about women discovered in the ranks implied that they were of very bad character, indeed" (Burgess 6).

Solution A: Quote indirectly, using your own words.

Most newspaper stories of the time about women in the armies were neutral or positive, but some suggested that the women were "of very bad character, indeed" (Burgess 6).

Solution B: Quote a sentence but introduce it in your own words.

Historian Lauren Cook Burgess notes, "Although most accounts were neutral or complementary, some newspaper reports about women discovered in the ranks implied that they were of very bad character, indeed" (6).

Solution C: Omit words or sentences and use ellipses. Place brackets around any words you insert in place of omitted words or sentences. Be careful not to change the meaning of the quotation.

As historian Lauren Cook Burgess notes, "some newspaper reports about [disguised] women . . . implied that they were of very bad character, indeed" (6).

Present

Prepare Your Historical Research Paper Before you turn in your final paper, make sure that it is formatted correctly and that you are handing in a clean copy, including the Works Cited page. Check the indentation of long quotations. Ask your teacher about any additional presentation guidelines.

> **Exposition**

Peer Review Tips

A classmate may ask you to read his or her research report. Take your time and jot down notes as you read so you can give constructive feedback. Use the following questions to get started:

- Can you identify a variety of primary and secondary, as well as reliable sources?

- Where do you find a thoughtful examination of varying perspectives?

Word-Processing Tip

Put your sources on a separate page called "Works Cited." Begin each entry at the left margin and indent all turn lines five spaces. Double-space the list; do not add extra lines of space between entries or between the centered title of the page and the first entry.

Writer's Portfolio

Place a clean copy of your research report in your portfolio to review later.

LOG ON ▶ **Literature** Online

Writing and Research For editing and publishing tools, go to glencoe.com and enter QuickPass code GLA9800u3.

Writing Workshop

Research Report

Teach

Writing Process

Edit and Proofread Suggest that students proofread their work several times, first focusing on errors in structure and reasoning, then focusing on grammar, and finally focusing on spelling and punctuation.

Writing Skills

Use Quotations Correctly

When quoting a single source several times in a paragraph, a writer may include only one citation, at the end of the paragraph, as long as no other sources are quoted in that paragraph.

(APPROACHING) Remind students that it is perfectly acceptable for them to paraphrase or summarize information in their own words, as long as they give credit to the source of the idea. Remind students that long quotations should be used sparingly; otherwise, the quotations overshadow students' own ideas and writing style.

Approaching Level

DIFFERENTIATED INSTRUCTION 🐟

Emerging Remind students that visual aids can deepen a reader's comprehension of ideas. Suggest that students add visuals, such as photographs, charts, graphs, or illustrations, to their reports. Provide specific guidelines for the use of the visuals. For example, tell students that the visuals should appear near the text that they support. Students should also include credit lines for the visuals. Review with students how to prepare and place such credits in the document.

Focus

Summary

In this workshop, students will learn techniques for planning, developing, rehearsing, and delivering a multimedia presentation of their historical investigation reports.

Teach

Speaking Skills

Plan Your Presentation Depending on the time available for creating the presentation, you may decide to have students work in pairs or small groups. Some students may have multimedia resources available to them at home and may be willing to make these available to other students. Ask for volunteers to research the availability of various types of both low- and high-tech equipment at school. Students may need help initiating conversations with the people in the school who can help them set up a multimedia presentation.

 For help with creating presentations, see Student Presentation Builder on StudentWorks Plus.

Learning Objectives

For pages 468–471
In this workshop, you will focus on the following objective:

Speaking and Listening: Delivering multimedia presentations.

Workshop Model

In this workshop, note the examples used from a multimedia presentation titled "Women Soldiers in the Civil War." You might try out some of the techniques shown in the multimedia presentation that you create.

Real-World Connection

Computer slide and other multimedia presentations are commonly presented in offices, conference rooms, and auditoriums to inform and persuade.

Speaking, Listening, and Viewing Workshop

Multimedia Presentation

Literature Connection If modern media had been available to Walt Whitman and he had done *Leaves of Grass* as a multimedia presentation, what images and sounds do you think he might have chosen to go with his grand poem? In this workshop, you will create a modern multimedia presentation of your historical investigation report.

> **Assignment** **Plan and deliver a multimedia presentation of your historical investigation report. As you develop your presentation, keep your audience and purpose in mind.**
>
> **Audience:** classmates and teacher
>
> **Purpose:** to inform and describe; to engage

Plan Your Presentation

Multimedia is the merging of text, sound, and images (art, photos, video clips, animation, and print) into a single presentation, such as a narrated slide or transparency presentation, a Web site, or a webcast.

Study the chart on the next page. Consider the type of presentation that appeals to you, and find out whether you might be able to do it at your school. If you want to do a low-tech presentation using an overhead projector, chances are good that one is available at your school. Nevertheless, you may have to get permission to use a projector, or you may need to reserve it for a certain day. Some schools may also offer access to digital or video cameras, as well as audio equipment.

For a high-tech presentation, start by asking about available computer hardware. Look carefully at the computer memory too. Then check with your school media or IT (information technology) person to find out which, if any, photo, graphics, or animation programs, or other authorship programs specific to multimedia, might be available to you. Also inquire about how much learning or training you will need to use them, and factor that information into your choice. Finally, ask a librarian or other specialist to point you in the direction of available databases or free, downloadable software for audio and video clips.

Listening and Viewing Practice

Choose Media Suggest that students think about the topic of their historical report and ask themselves what types of images they would like to see or sounds they would like to hear if they could be transported back to the time described in the report. Have them make a list of these images and sounds. Then have students think about the best way to convey a sense of "being there" to the students who will be listening to their presentation. They should ask themselves what role music might play; whether their topic needs illustrations, maps, or photos; and so on.

Ways to Create a Multimedia Presentation

Equipment		Application
Low-tech ↓ **High-tech**	Camera, slide or overhead projector, and tape recorder	Use 35-mm slides or overhead transparencies for the visuals—images or text, or images with text
	Computer with speakers, monitor, and microphone	Use presentation software to create a slide show.
	Computer with speakers, monitor, a microphone plus a digital camera, video camera, and scanner	Use a hypertext program to combine text, graphics, and sounds to create "cards" with hyperlinks that make different sequences possible.

Choose Your Media

Once you have selected a type of presentation, examine your historical investigation report for ways in which to incorporate a variety of sounds and images. One way to do this is by returning to your outline and highlighting or annotating main ideas and details, as this model shows.

Color Code: ▓▓▓ = image   ▓▓▓ = sound

I. Introduction
   Dramatic reading—introductory paragraph
   Sounds—marching music, military drums or fife and drums, bugle
   A. Thesis
   B. Background Information: early female soldiers
   Photos/Drawings—Joan of Arc, Lakshmi Bai, Margaret Cochran Corbin
II. Some women supported the army
   Images—Confederate and Union flags, or other emblems of Civil War
   A. Nurses
   B. "Vivandieres"
   Photos/Drawings—Women as nurses, water carriers, messengers
III. Some women disguised themselves as soldiers and fought for various reasons
   A. Patriotism
      Sounds—a few bars of "The Star Spangled Banner"
   B. Could not be separated from loved ones
   Dramatic Reading—Quote from Leonard about Bridget Divers
   C. Adventure
   D. Money
   Dramatic Reading—words of Sarah Rosetta Wakeman

Select Appropriate Media

Keep in mind the standards of reliability and validity you used as you selected sources for your historical investigation report. Apply similar criteria to your media. Think carefully about the authorship and purpose of any site or source from which you draw. Also, determine whether editing and oversight occurred before the item was published or released.

Edit the Media

Your text, images, and sounds must support a single controlling idea, which is your thesis. Choose only those portions of the media that explain, support, or enhance the presentation of your thesis. Remember that the sounds and images will not communicate everything by themselves and must be linked by careful, meaningful narration.

SPEAKING, LISTENING, AND VIEWING WORKSHOP **469**

Teach

Speaking Skills

Ways to Create a Multimedia Presentation Tell students to plan how they will use each type of media during their presentation. They may want to show a photograph when speaking of a historical figure or trace the course of a battle on a map. They can also pass out visual materials as they speak. Their goal is to use visual material to illustrate what they say.

APPROACHING Remind students that some visuals may be text-based, such as bulleted lists or important quotations. Text-based visuals will help listeners and viewers focus and take notes.

Choose Your Media Suggest that students make a clean copy of their outline or report, then highlight in one or two colors appropriate places to add media. Students might also identify interesting information to illustrate by:

- reviewing the note cards or other notes they used for writing
- asking a friend or family member to read the report and identify areas of high interest

APPROACHING If students included visual aids in their written reports, they might use them as the starting point for their multimedia presentations. The presentation should make logical and clear connections to the visual aids.

English Learners

DIFFERENTIATED INSTRUCTION

Beginning Help English learners review their reports for sections that they might emphasize in their multimedia presentations. Bulleted lists may be particularly useful, so encourage students either to turn some of their paragraphs into bulleted lists, or to use their outlines to make bulleted lists. These lists can serve as their notes for the presentation, which may be highly visual and aural. Have students work in pairs to practice reading aloud the verbal part of their presentation.

Speaking, Listening, and Viewing Workshop

Multimedia Presentation

Teach

Speaking Skills

Develop Your Presentation

Remind students that what they do not include in their presentation is as important as what they include. Give students a time limit for their presentations so that they can work within boundaries. Tell them that news segments on radio shows are often only a minute long, because it is possible to pack a lot of information into a short period of time.

Develop Your Presentation

- *Evaluate and edit appropriate images and sounds.* Incorporate only high-quality, reliable information. Be selective about the amount of each sound clip, video clip, or other media you use.
- *Recall your purpose.* Your primary goal is to deliver an accurate, clear presentation that informs your audience. Because the basis of your information is your research, be sure to scan in or otherwise incorporate some of the historical records that you used to write your report. Consider displaying title pages or examples of variable information on your topic. Your listeners can focus on this information as you explain possible reasons for the similarities and differences—of fact, perspective, reliability, and validity—that you found among your sources. You may be able to use a scanner to create images of these sources; otherwise, you can photocopy them and enlarge or reduce them as needed.
- *Stay focused on the audience and occasion.* Develop a clear narrative that will complement and link your images, as well as support your thesis. State the thesis at or near the beginning of your presentation, and recall it in the middle and at the end. Remember that your audience is hearing this information for the first time, so provide necessary background information and explanation. Throughout your presentation, use persuasive, narrative, and descriptive elements to create interest as well as to inform.

Avoid Plagiarism

Credit all your sources for images, sound, and video, as well as the original sources, in a complete, correctly formatted Works Cited slide at the end of your presentation. (See pages R33–39 for standardized citation styles.)

Organize Your Presentation

Put your ideas in order by making a storyboard that shows text, images, and sounds for each slide, card, or transparency you will use. Begin with a title slide that identifies your presentation and its creator. Add slides with text and visuals. Include sound elements where appropriate. End with a Works Cited list that includes all your research sources, as well as all your visual and sound sources.

• title 1 • picture—female Civil War soldier <u>marching drumbeat</u>	<u>bring drumbeat</u> 2 <u>down</u> • read introduction • display thesis	• drawings: female 3 soldiers in history • narration: women couldn't enlist in Civil War • cite numbers: women in Civil War	• Photos: nurses, 4 helpers, water carriers <u>sound effects—</u> <u>battlefield</u>
• Reasons to fight 5 — adventure, love, $, love of country <u>patriotic music</u>	• Women soldiers 6 — video clip from *The Civil War* — images: disguises	Images of women 7 who fought — read Wakeman's letter — add narration	• thesis 8 • Works Cited <u>patriotic music or</u> <u>battle sounds</u>

Writing Practice

Organize Your Presentation Tell students that a storyboard can be thought of as a way to break their presentation into chunks. Each chunk should consist of one central visual or sound that a listener can absorb in a short period of time. The storyboard is a form of outline that lists all the elements that the listener will see or hear at one time. It is helpful to make the storyboard in such a way that scenes can be rearranged to find the best order.

Female volunteers in the Civil War.

Civil War vivandière. Vivandières followed a regiment, acting as nurses.

Rehearse and Deliver Your Presentation

Successfully delivering a multimedia presentation depends a great deal on timing. All the elements have to appear in the right order and at precisely the right moment. Getting this timing down will probably require several rounds of practice. When you are satisfied that you have combined all the elements smoothly and effectively, deliver the presentation to a small audience of classmates, family members, or friends. Ask them where you need to adjust your pace, your volume, or the size or quality of your images. Also ask them for feedback on anything that wasn't clear in your narration or on any images or sounds that did not make sense to them.

As you rehearse and deliver your presentation, keep the presentation techniques below in mind. When you are an audience member, keep the listening and viewing techniques in mind.

Techniques for a Multimedia Presentation

Presentation Techniques	Listening and Viewing Techniques
☑ **Pace** Allow the audience enough time to view and hear each piece of your exhibit.	☑ **Body Language** Encourage the presenter by using your body language to show respect.
☑ **Volume** Keep both your words and music loud enough so that your entire audience can hear them.	☑ **Facial Expression and Movement** Show that you are listening and understanding. Provide cues such as an occasional nod.
☑ **Eye Contact** Look at your images as you direct audience attention to them.	☑ **Focus** Keep your eyes on the presenter or on the images.

Evaluation Checklist

☑ How well does the presentation meet the purpose of informing?

☑ How well does the presentation engage the audience?

☑ Is the thesis clear at all times?

☑ Do the text, images, and sounds clearly support the thesis and main ideas?

☑ Do any of the text elements, sounds, or images need editing?

☑ Does the presentation flow smoothly from beginning to end?

Teach

Speaking Skills

Rehearse and Deliver Your Presentation Remind students that they can rehearse in front of a mirror until they feel ready to rehearse in front of other people. Explain that the technology they have chosen to use should be tested in the place where they will give the presentation if at all possible. Students will then know whether they need to gather extension cords, power strips, batteries, or bulbs before the actual presentation.

Listening Skills

Pay Attention Tell students that closely watching a speaker or the screen on which the presentation is shown is a good way for them to increase their listening comprehension. If they cannot hear the speaker or see visual aids, they should let the speaker know promptly.

English Learners

DIFFERENTIATED INSTRUCTION

Intermediate Tell students that rehearsal time is when they can improve their fluency and pronunciation. Tell students to enlist the help of a trusted friend or family member and work with a tape recorder. Students should record a practice presentation and then listen to the tape with their friend or family member. They should identify places in the presentation where difficult words cause the speaker to stumble or misspeak. Students should practice those sections several times until their speaking is fluent and clear.

Focus

Summary

The purpose of the Independent Reading is to encourage students to read literature from or about the time period that they have learned about in this unit.

Teach

Literary History ☆

Louisa May Alcott Like the sisters in *Little Women,* Alcott and her sisters grew up in Massachusetts. Their father was Bronson Alcott, a noted intellectual. Some of the great thinkers and writers of the time were friends of the Alcott family. The character of Jo March is patterned after Louisa, who helped support her financially struggling family with her writing.

Independent Reading

The Civil War Era

THE CIVIL WAR'S BRUTALITY SHOCKED THE NATION. IN ITS WAKE, WRITERS LOST interest in Romantic depictions of exotic or idealized situations. They turned instead to Realism, writing that portrayed everyday situations and people, as well as the imperfections of life. Many of the great Realist novels analyze economic conditions and conflicts between people from different social classes. Conflicts are presented in an accurate and plausible way. Realist writers frequently focused on middle- and working-class settings and characters, often with the intent to spur reform.

Little Women

by Louisa May Alcott ☆

This tale of four sisters growing up in Concord, Massachusetts, during the Civil War era has become one of the best-loved American novels about the transition from adolescence to adulthood. Each sister in the March family has a distinctive personality. Meg, the oldest, is the most refined. Jo, fiery and independent, wants to be a writer. Beth is shy and musical. Amy, the youngest and most sensible, is the most beautiful. Alcott modeled the sisters, their levelheaded mother, and their idealistic father on her own family.

Harriet Tubman

by Ann Petry

Harriet Tubman, herself an escaped slave, was a "conductor" on the Underground Railroad— the network of travel routes, safe havens, and good Samaritans that helped numerous runaway slaves find their way safely to free states. While Tubman's ways were not always gentle, they were effective. In this biography of Tubman, Petry, herself an African American woman, explores the life of this real-life heroine of the Civil War era.

Study and Research Practice

Gathering Information Review with students some ways to obtain more information about the authors and books listed here:

- Do an Internet search, with the author or book title as the keyword.
- Use print biographical reference sources.
- Consult literary encyclopedias, such as *The Readers' Encyclopedia.*

Have partners or groups research several of the books discussed on these pages, take notes on the information, and report their findings to the class.

Narrative of the Life of Frederick Douglass

by Frederick Douglass

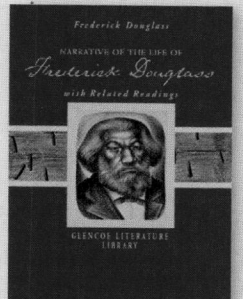

The acclaimed autobiography of Frederick Douglass, a formerly enslaved man who escaped to freedom and became a renowned orator and abolitionist

Great Expectations

by Charles Dickens

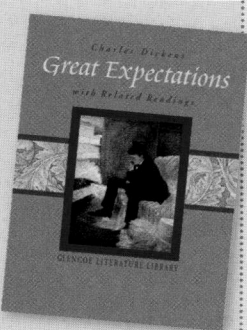

The orphaned Pip falls in love with the wealthy Estella and struggles to attain status in nineteenth-century England. ☆

The Brothers Karamazov

by Fyodor Dostoevsky

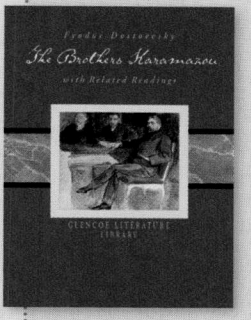

The tragic and dramatic story of the murdered Fyodor Karamazov and his culpable sons

CRITICS' CORNER

"In the execution of her very difficult task, Mrs. Stowe has displayed rare descriptive powers, a familiar acquaintance with slavery under its best and worst phases, uncommon moral and philosophical acumen, great facility of thought and expression, feelings and emotions of the strongest character. . . . [W]e confess to the frequent moistening of our eyes, and the making of our heart grow liquid as water, and the trembling of every nerve within us, in the perusal of the incidents and scenes so vividly depicted in her pages."

—*Liberator Review*, March 26, 1852

Uncle Tom's Cabin

by Harriet Beecher Stowe

When Arthur Shelby decides to sell Uncle Tom and Harry, Harry's mother, Eliza, runs away with Harry, making her way to the free state of Ohio. Tom is put on a riverboat to be sold farther south. Stowe's depiction of slaves' suffering made *Uncle Tom's Cabin* highly influential in stirring abolitionist sentiment.

 Write a Review

Read one of the books listed on these two pages and write a review of it for your classmates. Explain why you think they might enjoy the book or how they might overcome difficulties in reading it. If possible, present your review orally.

English Learners

DIFFERENTIATED INSTRUCTION

Intermediate Allow students to read these books in their first languages before discussing them in English. If students prefer, they might listen to audio recordings of the works in English. Students might also watch film versions of some of the works to increase their comprehension.

Approaching Level

DIFFERENTIATED INSTRUCTION

Emerging Tell students that these works are challenging. Encourage them to access online or print study guides, such as those in the Glencoe Literature Library. Guided-reading questions, graphic organizers, and background information can help them.

Teach

Literary History ☆
Novels of the World

Point out that neither *Great Expectations* nor *The Brothers Karamazov* was written by an American. Dickens's book, however, explores issues of status in society that can be related to the struggle to define the status of African Americans during the Civil War era. Dostoevsky's book has had a powerful influence on modern American literature.

 Review

Evaluate students' reviews by considering the following:

- clearly stated summary
- effective evaluation
- attention to grammar and spelling conventions

 Glencoe Literature Library

Glencoe Literature Library offers an extensive collection of hardcover books that help you encourage your students to read independently. Choose among the more than 120 full-length literary works—novels, novellas, plays, and nonfiction. Each book includes related readings from a broad range of genres. Go to www.glencoe.com for more information.

 For access to all study guides for the Glencoe Literature Library, see the literature Library Teacher Resources CD-ROM.

 To create customized reading lists from a database of more than 30,000 titles, use BookLink K-12 CD-ROM.

473

Focus

Bellringer

Say: You will take many tests in your life, from standardized exams to those for getting a driver's license or job certification. Many strategies apply to a range of test-taking situations. Have students discuss test-taking strategies that have worked for them in the past.

Teach

Assessment Tell students that this practice assessment will provide reinforcement in general test-taking strategies and will test the skills and vocabulary taught in this unit. Students will first be asked to read a nonfiction selection and answer comprehension, context clues, and inference questions. Then they will be asked to complete ten paragraph-improvement questions and to respond to a short reflective-essay question.

Set a Purpose Tell students that in a test situation, their reading purpose must be to answer the test questions. Tell them that previewing the questions before reading the passage will help them read effectively and efficiently. Have students read through the questions on pages 475–476 and note the kinds of information they require, such as the words to be defined. Students can then read the passage with their notes as a guide.

Assessment

English Language Arts

Reading: Nonfiction

Carefully read the following passage. Use context clues to help define any words with which you are unfamiliar. Pay close attention to the author's main idea and use of literary devices. Then answer the questions on pages 475–476 on a sheet of paper.

from *My Bondage and My Freedom* by Frederick Douglass

line

If at any one time of my life, more than another, I was made to drink the bitterest dregs of slavery, that time was during the first six months of my stay with Mr. Covey. We were worked all weathers.
5 It was never too hot or too cold; it could never rain, blow, snow, or hail too hard for us to work in the field. Work, work, work, was scarcely more the order of the day than the night. The longest days were too short for him, and the shortest
10 nights were too long for him. I was somewhat unmanageable when I first went there; but a few months of this discipline tamed me. Mr. Covey succeeded in breaking me. I was broken in body, soul and spirit. My natural elasticity was crushed;
15 my intellect languished; the disposition to read departed; the cheerful spark that lingered about my eye died; the dark night of slavery closed in upon me; and behold a man transformed into a brute!

Sunday was my only leisure time. I spent
20 this in a sort of beast-like stupor, between sleep and wake, under some large tree. At times, I would rise up, a flash of energetic freedom would dart through my soul, accompanied with a faint beam of hope, that flickered for a moment, and then vanished. I sank
25 down again, mourning over my wretched condition. I was sometimes prompted to take my life, and that of Covey, but was prevented by a combination of hope and fear. My sufferings on this plantation seem now like a dream rather than a stern reality.

30 Our house stood within a few rods of the Chesapeake bay, whose broad bosom was ever

white with sails from every quarter of the habitable globe. Those beautiful vessels, robed in purest white, so delightful to the eye of freemen, were to
35 me so many shrouded ghosts, to terrify and torment me with thoughts of my wretched condition. I have often, in the deep stillness of a summer's Sabbath, stood all alone upon the banks of that noble bay, and traced, with saddened heart and tearful eye, the
40 countless number of sails moving off to the mighty ocean. The sight of these always affected me powerfully. . . .

I shall never be able to narrate the mental experience through which it was my lot to pass
45 during my stay at Covey's. I was completely wrecked, changed and bewildered; goaded almost to madness at one time, and at another reconciling myself to my wretched condition. Everything in the way of kindness, which I had experienced at
50 Baltimore; all my former hopes and aspirations for usefulness in the world, and the happy moments spent in the exercises of religion, contrasted with my then present lot, but increased my anguish.

I suffered bodily as well as mentally. I had
55 neither sufficient time in which to eat or to sleep, except on Sundays. The overwork, and the brutal chastisements of which I was the victim, combined with that ever-gnawing and soul-devouring thought—*"I am a slave—a slave for life—a slave*
60 *with no rational ground to hope for freedom"*—rendered me a living embodiment of mental and physical wretchedness.

1. What does Douglass say the "longest days" were to Mr. Covey?
   A. like Sunday
   B. like nights
   C. too long
   D. too short

2. From the context, what can you infer that the word *discipline* in line 12 means?
   A. specialty
   B. suffering
   C. transformation
   D. training

3. According to Douglass, what caused his transformation "into a brute"?
   A. Mr. Covey's success at breaking him
   B. the death of the spark in his eye
   C. the crushing of his elasticity
   D. the departure of his inclination to read

4. How did Douglass spend his Sundays?
   A. at work
   B. in a stupor
   C. reading
   D. exercising his religious beliefs

5. What literary device is Douglass using when he writes that his sufferings were "like a dream"?
   A. allusion
   B. personification
   C. simile
   D. irony

6. What literary device is Douglass using when he writes that the Chesapeake Bay has a "broad bosom"?
   A. allusion
   B. personification
   C. simile
   D. irony

 Literature Online

Assessment For additional test practice, go to glencoe.com and enter QuickPass code GLA9800u3.

---

7. What can you infer about the source of Douglass's feelings concerning the ships in Chesapeake Bay?
   A. The ships reminded him of the freedom that he did not have.
   B. To Douglass, the ships represented Mr. Covey's cruelty.
   C. The ships carried enslaved people and so reminded Douglass of his own condition.
   D. Because the ships were ghostlike, they terrified Douglass.

8. From the context, what can you infer that the word *present* in line 53 means?
   A. exhibited
   B. previous
   C. granted
   D. current

9. What effect did Douglass's memories of Baltimore have on him?
   A. They drove him to the brink of madness.
   B. They increased his anguish.
   C. They gave him hope.
   D. They made him exercise his religion.

10. From the context, what does the word *ground* in line 60 mean?
    A. land
    B. position
    C. floor
    D. reason

11. In this passage how does Douglass reveal the personality of Mr. Covey?
    A. through direct characterization
    B. through indirect characterization
    C. through metaphor
    D. through symbols

12. What is the overall tone of this passage?
    A. authoritative
    B. ironic
    C. despairing
    D. sarcastic

Assessment

Assess

1. **D** is the correct answer because in line 9, Douglass states that "the longest days were too short." **DOK 2**

2. **D** is the correct answer because *discipline* in this context means "control gained by forced obedience." **DOK 1**

3. **A** is the correct answer because the other options are effects, not causes. **DOK 1**

4. **B** is the correct answer because in line 20, Douglass says he spent Sundays "in a sort of beast-like stupor." **DOK 1**

5. **C** is the correct answer because Douglass's use of the word *like* identifies the comparison as a simile. **DOK 2**

6. **B** is the correct answer because Douglass attributes a human characteristic to a place. **DOK 2**

7. **A** is the correct answer because the ships remind him that free men, unlike slaves, are able to travel and come and go as they please. **DOK 4**

8. **D** is the correct answer because *current* here means "occurring at the same time." **DOK 1**

9. **B** is the correct answer because Douglass states that his positive memories of Baltimore "increased [his] anguish" in his present condition. **DOK 1**

10. **D** is the correct answer because *ground* in this context means "a basis for belief." **DOK 1**

11. **A** is the correct answer because Douglass reveals Covey's personality by stating his thoughts and actions. **DOK 2**

12. **C** is the correct answer because the tone expresses hopelessness. **DOK 4**

English Learners

DIFFERENTIATED INSTRUCTION

Intermediate States are required to offer English language learners access to standardized tests. Options for services vary from state to state and population to population. For Spanish speakers, many states offer translated tests. For speakers of other languages, states may offer individual translators or other services. Provide students with information on how to access tests in your state, as provided by the state department of education.

Assessment

Assess

13. **D** is the correct answer because Douglass's purpose is to inform the reader about the experience of slavery. **[DOK4]**

14. **A** is the correct answer because Douglass uses the first-person pronouns *I, me,* and *my.* **[DOK2]**

15. **D** is the correct answer because options A, B, and C are too narrow to cover the entire autobiography. **[DOK2]**

 To create custom assessments online, go to Progress Reporter Online Assessment.

 To create custom assessments using software, use ExamView Assessment suite.

13. Which of the following best describes the author's purpose in this passage?
    - **A.** to entertain
    - **B.** to persuade
    - **C.** to solve a problem
    - **D.** to explain

14. From what point of view is this passage written?
    - **A.** first person
    - **B.** second person
    - **C.** third-person omniscient
    - **D.** third-person limited

15. According to this passage, which of the following best describes the main idea of *My Bondage and My Freedom?*
    - **A.** Slavery was common in Baltimore.
    - **B.** Mr. Covey, for a time, broke Frederick Douglass.
    - **C.** Mr. Covey was an evil man.
    - **D.** Slavery is an evil institution that must be resisted.

Point of View Post the four answer choices from question 14. Help students define them:

- **first person**—the narrator is a character in the story, describing events from his or her own point of view and using the pronoun *I.*
- **second person**—this is not typically used in literary writing.
- **third-person omniscient**—the narrator knows all and describes the feelings, actions, and words of all characters.
- **third-person limited**—the narrator focuses on the thoughts, feelings, and actions of one character.

Vocabulary Skills: Sentence Completion

For each question in the Vocabulary Skills section, choose the best word to complete the sentence.

1. Robert E. Lee feared that the secession of the Southern states would result in lawlessness and _____ throughout the country.
   A. depravity
   B. anarchy
   C. perusal
   D. rackets

2. A series of misjudgments and military failures _____ the Confederacy to surrender in 1865.
   A. consecrated
   B. arrayed
   C. induced
   D. censured

3. Frederick Douglass and Sojourner Truth both fought to _____ slavery.
   A. vanquish
   B. consecrate
   C. pervade
   D. adorn

4. Because he had witnessed the horrors of combat, Ambrose Bierce rejected the idea that there could be a/an _____ war.
   A. imperial
   B. prostrate
   C. poignant
   D. benevolent

5. In the nineteenth century, many people believed that Walt Whitman's poems were filled with _____ and that his books should be banned.
   A. scores
   B. redress
   C. depravity
   D. allusions

6. Many soldiers _____ at the Battle of Gettysburg, which was one of the war's bloodiest.
   A. hallowed
   B. perished
   C. assented
   D. censured

7. Robert E. Lee was responsible for some of the Civil War's most brilliant and _____ military maneuvers.
   A. audacious
   B. imperial
   C. prostrate
   D. poignant

8. A common _____ of slave owners was that they were "civilizing" the people they held in bondage.
   A. cathedral
   B. perusal
   C. allusion
   D. delusion

9. In the end, the South could not _____ with the North's overwhelming force.
   A. protrude
   B. assent
   C. induce
   D. contend

10. There was little actual _____ for those who had suffered so severely under slavery.
    A. heave
    B. redress
    C. affliction
    D. score

Assess

Vocabulary

1. **B** is the correct answer because *anarchy* best pairs with *lawlessness*. DOK 1
2. **C** is the correct answer because the failures influenced the decision to surrender.
3. **A** is the correct answer because they both fought to end slavery. DOK 1
4. **D** is the correct answer because *horrors* suggests that combat is not kind. DOK 1
5. **C** is the correct answer because a book might be banned if people believe it is morally corrupt. DOK 1
6. **B** is the correct answer because the word *bloodiest* suggests that many died. DOK 1
7. **A** is the correct answer because Lee was a bold leader. DOK 1
8. **D** is the correct answer because the context suggests that slave owners' beliefs were wrong. DOK 1
9. **D** is the correct answer because it is the only option that makes sense in this context. DOK 1
10. **B** is the correct answer because it there was no compensation for their suffering. DOK 1

English Learners

DIFFERENTIATED INSTRUCTION

Emerging Tell students to use context clues and etymology to narrow down words' meanings. Students should begin by reading a sentence and thinking of a simple word that could complete its meaning. Next students should compare that word with the options listed. If any are similar in meaning, they should be seriously considered. Students can also look at word roots for clues to meaning. For example, the word *anarchy* contains the root *arch,* meaning "chief" or "ruler." This links anarchy to the context clue *lawlessness* because both relate to order in society.

Assessment

Assess

1. C is the correct answer because it is the only option that corrects the lack of subject-verb agreement between *period* and were. `DOK 1`

2. C is the correct answer because it is the only option that corrects the lack of subject-verb agreement between *consequences* and *was*. `DOK 1`

3. B is the correct answer because the subject *war* lacks a predicate. `DOK 2`

Grammar and Writing Skills:
Paragraph Improvement

Read carefully through the following passage from the first draft of a student's research essay. Pay close attention to the writer's use of subordinate clauses, quotation marks, and commas. Then answer the questions below.

> *(1) The period of the Civil War and Reconstruction were an important time in American history. (2) No other event has had so many long-term effects on American politics, the arts in America, and the development of equipment and techniques of war.*
>
> *(3) The consequences of the war for American law and politics was profound. (4) The war directly responsible for the thirteenth, fourteenth, and fifteenth constitutional amendments, which freed enslaved people and guaranteed them citizenship and the right to vote. (5) The conflict changed how people thought about their culture. (6) Furthermore, the outcome of the war essentially swept away the old political squabbles that had gripped the nation for so long. (7) Regionalism would no longer be the central source of national conflict.*
>
> *(8) The Civil War helped launch photography as a vital tool for relaying newsworthy images, it established photography as a new form of art. (9) Literature too was changed by the war. (10) The massive loss of life was partly responsible for romanticism's end and the rise of both realism and naturalism. (11) As Walt Whitman said, a great literature will . . . arise out of that era.*
>
> *(12) Often called the "first modern war" the Civil War was the first to use equipment that became common during the 1900s. (13) This was the first war in which the telegraph, the machine, and shell gun, surveillance balloons, the submarine, ironclad ships, and land mines were extensively used.*

1. Which of the following is the best revision of sentence 1?
   A. The period of the Civil War and Reconstruction were an important times in American history.
   B. The period of the Civil War and Reconstruction was important times in American history.
   C. The period of the Civil War and Reconstruction was an important time in American history.
   D. The period of the Civil War and Reconstruction were important times in American history.

2. Which of the following is the best revision of sentence 3?
   A. The consequences of the war was profound.
   B. The war's consequences for American law and politics was profound.
   C. The consequences of the war for American law and politics were profound.
   D. The consequences for American law and politics was profound.

3. Which of the following errors appears in sentence 4?
   A. run-on sentence
   B. fragment
   C. misplaced modifier
   D. incorrect parallelism

Subject-Verb Agreement
Explain that correcting subject-verb agreement problems is a common test item. Often sentences with compound subjects or collective nouns are used. Review these general rules:

- Use a plural verb when *and* links the parts of a compound subject.

- Match the verb to the closest noun when *or* or *nor* links the parts of a compound subject.

- Choose a singular verb if a collective noun (family, group, staff) describes a single unit and a plural verb when it describes a collection of separate units.

4. Which sentence is not related to the main idea of paragraph 2?
   A. 3
   B. 4
   C. 5
   D. 6

5. Which of the following is the best revision of sentence 8?
   A. The Civil War helped launch photography as a vital tool for relaying newsworthy images, and it established photography as a new form of art.
   B. The Civil War helped launch photography.
   C. The Civil War launched photography as a vital tool for relaying newsworthy images, it established photography as a new form of art.
   D. The Civil War helped launch photography as a new form of art.

6. Which of the following is the best revision of sentence 11?
   A. As Walt Whitman said, a great literature will arise out of that era.
   B. A great literature will . . . arise out of that era.
   C. "As Walt Whitman said, a great literature will . . . arise out of that era."
   D. As Walt Whitman said, "A great literature will . . . arise out of that era."

7. Which of the following is the best revision of sentence 12?
   A. The "first modern war," the Civil War, used modern equipment.
   B. Often called the "first modern war," the Civil War was the first to use equipment that became common during the 1900s.

C. Often called the "first modern war." The Civil War was the first to use equipment that became common during the 1900s.
D. Often called the first modern war the Civil War was the first to use equipment that became common during the 1900s.

8. Which of the following is the best revision of sentence 13?
   A. This was the first war in which the telegraph, the machine and shell gun, surveillance balloons, the submarine, ironclad ships, and land mines were extensively used.
   B. This was the first war in which the telegraph, the machine, and shell gun, surveillance balloons, and the submarine, and ironclad ships, and land mines were extensively used.
   C. This was the first war in which the telegraph and the machine were extensively used.
   D. This was the first war in which the telegraph was extensively used.

9. What is most notably missing from this essay?
   A. a concluding paragraph
   B. an opening paragraph
   C. evidence
   D. a visual aid

10. Which of the following titles would best suit this essay?
    A. "America at War"
    B. "Nineteenth-Century Combat"
    C. "American Innovation"
    D. "The Effects of the Civil War"

Writing: Essay

By the time students enter high school, they have learned how many events in history have influenced our world today. Think about the issue of slavery in the United States. Write an essay in which you consider how the issue of slavery divided the United States and how it eventually changed our country.

English Learners

DIFFERENTIATED INSTRUCTION

Intermediate Stress the importance of answering the essay prompt. Point out the words *divided* and *changed,* and explain that this item asks for a cause-effect discussion. Essays should define the cause (slavery) and the effects (division, change). Urge students to use cause-effect transition words.

Assessment

Assess

4. **C** is the correct answer because the other options are related to the main idea of the paragraph—the effects of the war on politics. Sentence 5 is about culture. **DOK4**

5. **A** is the correct answer because no other option corrects the comma splice while preserving the original meaning. **DOK1**

6. **D** is the correct answer because it is the only option that supplies the correct use of quotation marks. **DOK1**

7. **B** is the correct answer because it adds a comma after the introductory participial phrase. **DOK1**

8. **B** is the correct answer because it corrects the faulty parallelism while preserving the original meaning. **DOK1**

9. **A** is the correct answer because the essay ends abruptly without a concluding paragraph that sums up the main points. **DOK4**

10. **D** is the correct answer because it reflects the thesis statement of the essay regarding the "long-term effects" of the Civil War. **DOK2**

 Essay

Evaluate essays for:

- clearly stated main ideas supported by good reasons and details
- effective voice, word choice, and sentence variety
- effective presentation with attention to grammar and spelling conventions

Skills Scope and Sequence

Readability Scores Key: Dale-Chall/DRP/Lexile

PART 1: Regionalism and Local Color

Selections and Features	Literary Elements
Unit Introduction pp. 480–494	Regionalism and Realism **SE** pp. 481, 486–491 Dialect **TE** p. 488 Imagery **TE** p. 491 Naturalism **SE** p. 492
Short Story The Celebrated Jumping Frog of Calaveras County, by Mark Twain **10.2/59/**1410 pp. 496–503	Dialect **SE** p. 497
Memoir *from* **Two Views of the River,** by Mark Twain **7.7/63/**1130 pp. 504–507	Analogy **SE** p. 504 Tone (review) **SE** p. 506
Informational Text TIME: Life Along the Mississippi, by Nancy Gibbs **7.1/62/**1120 pp. 508–513	Text Structure **TE** p. 508 Persuasion **TE** p. 510
Poems Lucinda Matlock and Fiddler Jones, by Edgar Lee Masters pp. 514–518	Dramatic Monologue **SE** p. 515
Short Story A Wagner Matinee, by Willa Cather **10.5/63/**1410 pp. 519–529	Point of View **SE** p. 520 Voice (review) **SE** p. 528
Grammar Workshop p. 530	
Speech I Will Fight No More Forever, by Chief Joseph **3.0/41/**380 pp. 531–534	Tone **SE** p. 532

PART 2: Realism and Naturalism

Selections and Features	Literary Elements
Literary Periods The Two Faces of Urban America pp. 536–537	Stream of Consciousness **TE** p. 536
Short Story April Showers, by Edith Wharton **5.8/60/**1020 pp. 538–548	Flashback **SE** p. 539 Characterization **TE** p. 546 Theme (review) **SE** p. 547
Vocabulary Workshop p. 549	

Reading Skills and Strategies	Vocabulary	Writing / Grammar	Speaking, Listening, and Viewing
Analyze Graphic Information **TE** p. 482 Draw Conclusions **TE** p. 484 Summarize **TE** p. 486 Compare and Contrast **SE** p. 493	Word Meanings **TE** p. 486	Apply Figurative Language **TE** p. 492	Analyze Art **TE** p. 481 Create a Graph **TE** p. 484
Analyze Comic Devices **SE** p. 497 Classify **TE** p. 498 Analyze Author's Purpose **TE** p. 502	Word Origins **SE** p. 503	Write a Story **SE** p. 503	Analyze a Photograph **TE** p. 501
Compare and Contrast Language **SE** p. 504	Academic Vocabulary **SE** p. 507	Create a Travel Brochure **SE** p. 507	Analyze Art **TE** p. 504
Preview **SE** p. 508 Clarify Meaning **SE** p. 508	Compound Words **TE** p. 512	Write a Summary **SE** p. 513	Analyze a Photograph **TE** p. 511
Draw Conclusions About Characters **SE** p. 515	Word Usage **SE** p. 518	Take Notes **TE** p. 516 Write a Poem **SE** p. 518	Analyze Art **TE** p. 516
Identify Sequence **SE** p. 520 Analyze Flashback **TE** p. 521 Make Inferences **TE** p. 522 Analyze Comparisons **TE** p. 526	Analogies **SE** p. 528 Academic Vocabulary **SE** p. 528	Analyze Imagery **TE** p. 522 Write a Reflective Essay **SE** p. 529 Absolute Phrases **SE** p. 529	Analyze Art **TE** p. 521 Analyze Music **TE** p. 524
		Appositives **SE** p. 530	
Evaluate Style **SE** p. 532 Predict **TE** p. 532	Academic Vocabulary **SE** p. 534	Write a Journal Entry **SE** p. 534	Analyze Art **TE** p. 533

Reading Skills and Strategies	Vocabulary	Writing / Grammar	Speaking, Listening, and Viewing
			Analyze Art **TE** p. 537
Make and Verify Predictions **SE** p. 539 Preview **TE** p. 540	Synonyms **TE** p. 539 Word Choice **TE** p. 543 Denotation and Connotation **SE** p. 548 Context Clues **SE** p. 548	Summarize **TE** p. 542 Write a Narrative **SE** p. 548	Analyze a Photograph **TE** p. 544
	Thesaurus Usage **SE** p. 549		

Selections and Features	Literary Elements
Comparing Literature **The Story of an Hour** (short story) by Kate Chopin **7.3/57/970** **The Darling** (short story), by Anton Chekhov **7.3/57/1100** **Richness** (poem), by Gabriela Mistral pp. 550–567	Social Context **SE** p. 550 Conflict **SE** p. 552 Characterization **TE** p. 558 Literary Allusion **TE** p. 559 Repetition **TE** p. 560 Theme **TE** p. 566
Poems Douglass and **We Wear the Mask,** by Paul Laurence Dunbar pp. 568–572	Rhyme Scheme **SE** p. 569 Sonnet **TE** p. 570
Poems Richard Cory and **Miniver Cheevy,** by Edwin Arlington Robinson pp. 573–577	Irony **SE** p. 574
Short Story The Open Boat, by Stephen Crane **7.6/60/980** pp. 578–600	Author's Purpose **SE** p. 579 Figurative Language **TE** p. 581 Foreshadowing **TE** p. 585 Suspense **TE** p. 586 Dialogue **TE** p. 588 Climax **TE** p. 595 Conflict (review) **SE** p. 599
Short Story To Build a Fire, by Jack London **6.1/59/970** pp. 601–616	Setting **SE** p. 602 Simile **TE** p. 609 Suspense (review) **SE** p. 615
Geographical Perspective *from* **Arctic Dreams: Imagination and Desire in a Northern Landscape,** by Barry Lopez **8.0/60/1130** pp. 617–623	
Writing Workshop pp. 624–633	
Speaking, Listening, and Viewing Workshop pp. 634–635	
Independent Reading pp. 636–637	
Assessment pp. 638–633	

Reading Skills and Strategies	Vocabulary	Writing / Grammar	Speaking, Listening, and Viewing
Compare and Contrast **SE** p. 550 Apply Background Knowledge **SE** p. 552 Analyze Author's Viewpoint **TE** p. 558 Predict **TE** p. 562	Word Usage **SE** p. 556 Context Clues **TE** p. 563	Write a Journal Entry **TE** p. 552 Write an Interior Monologue **SE** p. 556 Subordinate Clauses **TE** p. 558 Write a Short-Response Essay **SE** p. 567	Analyze Art **TE** p. 553 Oral Interpretation **TE** p. 566 Discussion **SE** p. 567
Clarify Meaning **SE** p. 569	Denotation and Connotation **SE** p. 572	Write a Letter **SE** p. 572	Analyze Art **TE** p. 570
Make Inferences About Characters **SE** p. 574	Word Origins **TE** p. 574 Denotation and Connotation **SE** p. 577	Write a Poem **SE** p. 577	Analyze Art **TE** p. 575
Summarize **SE** p. 579	Adjectives and Adverbs **TE** p. 584 Context Clues **SE** p. 599 Academic Vocabulary **SE** p. 599	Evaluate a Story **SE** p. 588 Write an Essay **TE** p. 594 Write a News Story **TE** p. 596 Write a Story Review **SE** p. 600 Semicolons **SE** p. 600	Analyze Art **TE** p. 583 Interview **TE** p. 592
Analyze Cause-and-Effect Relationships **SE** p. 602 Analyze Setting **TE** p. 602 Analyze Sequence **TE** p. 604 Analyze Character **TE** p. 606	Adjectives **TE** p. 606 Word Origins **SE** p. 616 Academic Vocabulary **SE** p. 616	Write a Narrative Account **TE** p. 612 Write a Descriptive Essay **SE** p. 616	Analyze a Photograph **TE** p. 607
Analyze Setting **SE** p. 617 Compare and Contrast **TE** p. 622		Write a Paper **TE** p. 620	Use Visual Aids **TE** p. 618
		Prewrite **SE** p. 628 Draft **SE** p. 629 Revise **SE** p. 632 Write a Response to Literature **SE** p. 633 Subject-Verb Agreement **SE** p. 633	
			Oral Response to Literature **SE** p. 634
Analyze Plot **TE** p. 636		Keep a Journal **SE** p. 637	
	Context Clues **TE** p. 638	Write an Essay **SE** p. 643	

UNIT FOUR

Focus

Bellringer Options

Literature Launcher
Pre-Reading Video: Unit 4

Daily Language Practice
Transparency 41

Or Say: Describe how realists differ from romantics. *(Students may say that realists see life as it really is but romantics see life as they wish or imagine it could be.)* The literary term *Realism* refers to a movement away from romantic ideals toward an examination of real people and real life.

 For school-to-home activities, see Unit 4 Teaching Resources Book, pp. 5–11.

 For students who would profit from independent novel study, see Novel Companion pp. 163–206.

Breezing Up (A Fair Wind), 1873–1876. Winslow Homer. Oil on canvas, 24⅛ x 38⅛ in. National Gallery of Art, Washington, DC. Gift of the W. L. and May T. Mellon Foundation.

View the Art Winslow Homer completed this painting as the country was celebrating its centennial. In this scene, what does Homer suggest about life in America one hundred years after independence? Do you find his depiction believable? Explain. ★

Unit Introduction Skills

Reading Skills
- Analyze Graphic Information (SE pp. 483, 485; TE p. 482)
- Generalize (SE p. 489)
- Cause and Effect (SE p. 491)
- Compare and Contrast (SE p. 493)
- Make Inferences (TE p. 482)
- Draw Conclusions (TE p. 484)
- Use Maps (TE p. 485)
- Summarize (TE p. 486)

Regionalism and Realism

Listening/Speaking/Viewing Skills
- Analyze Art (SE p. 480; TE pp. 485, 486, 489, 493)
- Visual Literacy (SE p. 494)

Writing Skills/Grammar
- Create a Graph (TE p. 484)
- Figurative Language (TE p. 492)

Literary Elements
- Dialect (TE p. 488)
- Cultural Characteristics (TE p. 489)
- Imagery (TE p. 491)
- Relate to the Text (TE p. 493)

Regionalism and Realism

~ 1880–1910 ~

Looking Ahead

The United States changed rapidly after the Civil War. American writers reacted to these changes by turning away from Romanticism toward Realism, a literary movement whose writers depicted life as they saw it, not as they imagined it to be. A literary movement that was akin to Realism was Regionalism, sometimes known as the local color movement, whose writers portrayed the distinctive traits of particular areas of the United States. A later, more extreme movement was Naturalism, whose writers sought to describe with scientific objectivity the effects of environment and heredity on character.

Keep the following questions in mind as you read:

⇒ How was the United States changing between 1880 and 1910?

⇒ What are the basic characteristics of Realism, Regionalism, and Naturalism?

⇒ How do you think the historical and cultural trends of this period continue to affect the United States today?

481

Unit Resources

Print Materials

- Unit 4 Teaching Resources, pp. 1–214
- Interactive Read and Write (On Level, Approaching, EL), pp. 147–178
- Novel Companion, pp. 163–206
- Bellringer Option Transparencies: Selection Focus 34–43; Daily Language Practice 41–54
- Assessment Resources, Selection Assessment, pp. 161–186

Technology

- TeacherWorks Plus CD
- StudentWorks Plus CD
- Literature Launchers: Pre-Reading Videos DVD, Unit 4
- Literature Online
- Visual Vocabulary CD-ROM
- Listening Library CD-ROM
- ExamView CD-ROM
- Skill Level Up! CD-ROM

Focus

Summary

This introduction describes the historical, social, and cultural forces that led to three literary movements: Regionalism, Realism, and Naturalism. After the Civil War the United States underwent great changes: expansion westward, the growth of population and industry in the East, and the struggles of diverse groups for social and economic rights. Essays about each literary movement tell how national and world events influenced writers of the time.

View the Art ★

Answer: *Winslow suggests that life is easygoing and that there is plenty of leisure time. Some students may say that his depiction, based on the relaxed appearance of the people on the boat, is believable; however, others may say that it is not believable because of the struggle to catch wind on the sail.*

Winslow Homer (1836–1910) began his career as an illustrator for magazines. In 1873 Homer visited Gloucester, Massachusetts, a fishing port, where he began to create watercolors. In 1876 he reworked one of the Gloucester watercolors, *Breezing Up,* into the oil painting shown here. Homer's interest in the sea intensified and became the primary focus of his work.

 For diagnostic and end-of-unit assessment, see Assessment Resources, pp. 25–32, 337–338.

Teach

Reading Strategy | 1

Analyze Graphic Information
Much of the literature written between 1880 and 1910 relates to what was happening politically and culturally at that time.

Ask: Using prior knowledge and any clues in the titles, look for relationships between United States and world events and literature in the following areas:

- African Americans
- Women
- Expansion, inventions, and technology
- People and nature

(Students familiar with Up from Slavery *or* The Souls of Black Folk *should connect those works to African Americans; students may use title clues to predict that* The Call of the Wild *connects to people and nature.)*

Reading Strategy | 2

Make Inferences
Ask students to infer which two events on the World Events timeline appear to be most closely related. *(The 1904 and 1905 entries: the Russo-Japanese war led to the Russian strikes and protests of 1905.)*

Timeline ◦ 1880–1910 ◦

AMERICAN LITERATURE 1

1880

1881
Henry James's *The Portrait of a Lady* is published

1884
Helen Hunt Jackson's *Ramona* is published

1884
Mark Twain's *The Adventures of Huckleberry Finn* is published

1885
W. D. Howells's *The Rise of Silas Lapham* is published

1886
Sarah Orne Jewett's "A White Heron" is published

1890

1896
Paul Laurence Dunbar's *Lyrics of a Lowly Life* is published

1898
Stephen Crane's "The Open Boat" is published

1899
Kate Chopin's *The Awakening* is published

1899
Charles Waddell Chesnutt's *The Conjure Woman* is published

Queen Liliuokalani ▲

UNITED STATES EVENTS

1880

1881
Clara Barton founds American Association of the Red Cross

1881
Booker T. Washington founds Tuskegee Institute

1884
George Eastman designs roll film for cameras

1885
William Le Baron Jenney builds the first skyscraper in Chicago

1886
President Grover Cleveland dedicates the Statue of Liberty in New York

1890

1890
Wounded Knee Massacre takes place

1891
James A. Naismith invents basketball

1892
Immigration center opens on Ellis Island

1893
Americans overthrow Queen Liliuokalani of Hawaii

1896
Plessy v. Ferguson case is tried

1896
Klondike gold rush begins

1898
Spanish-American War is fought

WORLD EVENTS

1880

1883
Krakatoa volcano erupts; ensuing tsunami kills over 36,000 people

1883
Standard time divides Earth into 24 time zones

1885
Indian National Congress is founded

1890

1890
German chancellor Otto von Bismarck resigns, due to conflicts with Kaiser Wilhelm II

1895
Lumière Brothers introduce motion pictures

1896
First modern Olympic Games are held in Athens

1896
Famine that will kill millions of people begins in India

1898
Marie and Pierre Curie discover radium

LOG ON ▶ **Literature** Online

Literature and Reading To explore the Interactive Timeline, go to glencoe.com and enter QuickPass code GLA9800u4.

482 UNIT 4 REGIONALISM AND REALISM

Reading Practice

Analyze Graphic Information Explain to students that the information on the three timelines shown on these pages could be subsumed into a single timeline. Ask student pairs to put all events shown for the 1880s in order on a single timeline. Discuss the pros and cons of presenting the same information on a single timeline or on parallel timelines.

THE JUNGLE
BY
UPTON SINCLAIR

DOUBLEDAY PAGE & Co.
NEW YORK

1900

1900
L. Frank Baum's *The Wonderful Wizard of Oz* is published

1900
Theodore Dreiser's *Sister Carrie* is published

1900
Zitkala-Sa's (Gertrude Bonnin) *Impressions of an Indian Childhood* is published ▶

1901
Frank Norris's *The Octopus* is published ☆

1901
Booker T. Washington's *Up from Slavery* is published

1903
W. E. B. Du Bois's *The Souls of Black Folk* is published

1903
Jack London's *The Call of the Wild* is published

1904
Henry James's *The Golden Bowl* is published

1906 ▲
Upton Sinclair's *The Jungle* is published

1909
Gertrude Stein's *Three Lives* is published

1900

1900
Hawaii becomes a territory of the United States

1901
President McKinley is assassinated; Theodore Roosevelt becomes president

1903
Wright Brothers make first airplane flight ▶

1903
The Great Train Robbery, first narrative film, is shown

1904
The United States begins construction of the Panama Canal

1906
San Francisco earthquake takes place

1908
Ford Motor Company produces the Model T Ford

1908
Electric washing machine is invented

1909
National Association for the Advancement of Colored People (NAACP) is founded

1910
Angel Island facility for Asian immigrants is opened

1900

Pierre and Marie Curie

1900
Boxer Rebellion against European influence begins in China

1904
Russo-Japanese War begins

1905
Strikes and mass protests begin reform in Russia

1906
Finland is first European country to grant woman suffrage

1908
Oil is discovered in the Middle East

1910
Mexican Revolution begins

2 **Reading Check**
Analyze Graphic Information Which events on the timeline continue to shape the daily life of people in the United States today?

Teach

Reading Check

Answer: *Almost all of the events continue to shape the daily lives of people today in some way, but perhaps those with the greatest impact involve airplane flight, automobile production, movies, washing machines, the NAACP, women's suffrage, the Panama Canal, and oil in the Middle East. Students should provide support for their choices.*

Cultural History ☆
Railroads and Growth
The Octopus concerns the power of railroads. The railroads wielded immense power in the U.S. economy of the late 1800s. They carried settlers west. They also facilitated the rapid growth of population and industry. For example, between 1880 and 1910, the population of California nearly tripled.

Approaching Level

DIFFERENTIATED INSTRUCTION

Established Make sure that students understand the significance of events on the timeline. For example, the Tuskegee Institute was a school for African Americans; the *Plessy* v. *Ferguson* case affirmed the constitutionality of racial segregation; and *The Weavers*, a German play, dramatized the true story of an 1844 weavers' revolt. Have students research and share one event with the class.

Emerging Tell students that reading and analyzing a timeline can help them understand history. Point out entries on the timeline that are related to demographic changes in the United States. In 1892, an immigration center opened on Ellis Island; in 1896, the Klondike gold rush began; and in 1910, the Angel Island facility for Asian immigrants opened. **Ask:** What changes were occurring in the U.S. population during this time period? *(People emigrated from other countries to the United States, and some Americans moved westward across North America looking for land and gold.)*

Teach

Draw Conclusions Have students trace the rise of immigration to the United States from central and eastern Europe on the graph.

Ask: How would you use the graph to research some of the reasons for the rise of immigration? *(To find the countries people came from and to research the conditions in those countries that led people to leave)*

[ENGLISH LEARNERS] Remind students that *immigration* refers to the movement into a country (prefix *in-*, meaning "into"), whereas *emigration* (prefix *ex-*, meaning "out") refers to movement out of a country.

Literary History ☆

Children's Literature

Largely because of the growing concern for education, the number of books being written and printed for children skyrocketed during the late 1800s. At first most books were designed to provide moral instruction. Books intended for pleasure and entertainment appeared later.

By the Numbers

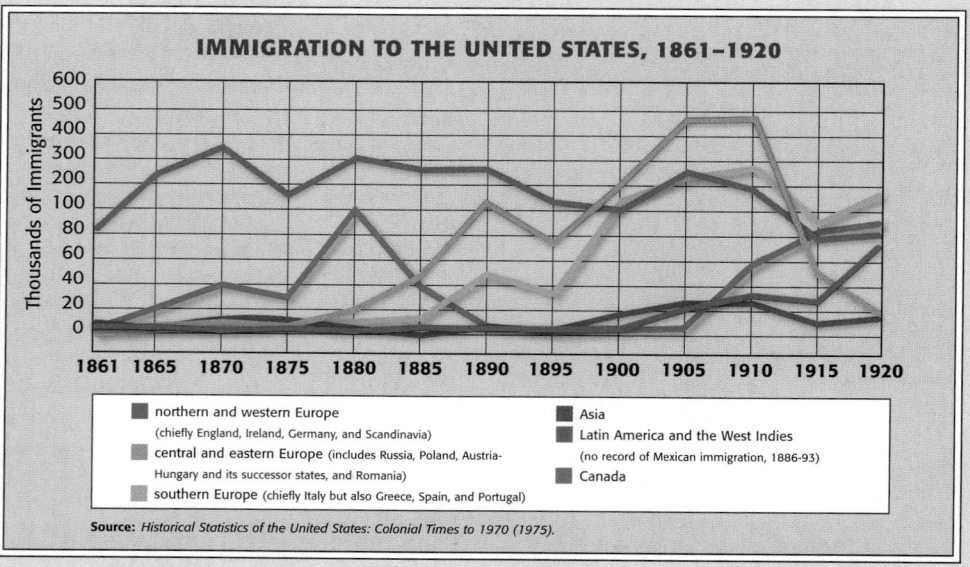

IMMIGRATION TO THE UNITED STATES, 1861–1920

- ■ northern and western Europe (chiefly England, Ireland, Germany, and Scandinavia)
- ■ central and eastern Europe (includes Russia, Poland, Austria-Hungary and its successor states, and Romania)
- ■ southern Europe (chiefly Italy but also Greece, Spain, and Portugal)
- ■ Asia
- ■ Latin America and the West Indies (no record of Mexican immigration, 1886–93)
- ■ Canada

Source: *Historical Statistics of the United States: Colonial Times to 1970 (1975).*

Railroad Time

Before the 1880s, each community set its clocks by the sun's position at high noon. Local time interfered with train scheduling and even threatened passenger safety: when two trains traveled on the same track, collisions could result from scheduling errors. In 1883, to make rail service safer and more reliable, the American Railway Association divided the country into four time zones, each with its own standard time. The federal government ratified the change in 1918.

STEEL PRODUCTION, 1865–1900

Source: *Historical Statistics of the United States: Colonial Times to 1970.*

EDUCATION ☆

The number of public schools multiplied after the Civil War.

- In 1870 around 6,500,000 children attended school.
- By 1900 the number of children attending school had risen to over 17,300,000.

LIFE AND DEATH

- In 1900 the average life expectancy for an American was 47.3 years. Today it is more than 77 years.

INEQUALITY OF WAGES

In the late 1890s, women were paid much less than men for the same type of work and the same hours. In the woolen industry, for example, male spinners made $7.50 per week in 1890; by 1900 this wage had risen to $9.50. By contrast, female spinners made only $5.50 a week in 1890; by 1900 this wage had only risen to $6.00.

Writing Practice

Create a Graph Tell students that creating a graph from written information helps them gain a visual picture of the written word. Read the section "Inequality of Wages" aloud. Then have students use the information to create a line graph, modeled after the "Immigration to the United States" graph, or a double-bar graph. Have students write a paragraph about the conclusions that can be drawn from their graphs.

Being There

Between the Civil War and World War I, the growth of mining, ranching, and farming brought settlement to the West. At the same time, populations of cities in the East swelled as immigrants poured into the United States and job seekers from rural areas sought employment in industry.

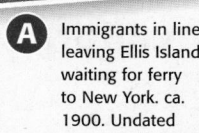

A Immigrants in line leaving Ellis Island, waiting for ferry to New York. ca. 1900. Undated photograph.

B A group of cowboys sit on the grass beside their horses and a chuck wagon to eat. Western United States.

C Ranch located in Nebraska, 1887. Photograph. Library of Congress, Washington, DC.

UNITED STATES, 1900

LOG ON ▶ **Literature** Online

Literature and Reading For more about the history and literature of this period, go to glencoe.com and enter QuickPass code GLA9800u4.

Reading Check

Analyze Graphic Information

1. Between what years did immigration from central and eastern Europe reach its peak?

2. In 1900, roughly how many times greater was school attendance than it had been in 1870?

3. What change did the western and eastern parts of the U.S. have in common during this time?

INTRODUCTION **485**

Teach

Reading Check

Answers:

1. *Immigration to the United States from central and eastern Europe reached its peak between 1905 and 1910.*
2. *Roughly three times greater*
3. *Population growth*

Reading Strategy 2

Use Maps **Ask:** How is this map of the United States in 1900 different from a map of the United States today? *(Arizona and New Mexico are not yet states; what is now Oklahoma then consisted of the Oklahoma Territory and the Indian Territory; Alaska and Hawaii are not included.)*

View the Photograph ★

A. Between 1892 and 1954, Ellis Island, a U.S. immigration station, processed over 12 million immigrants.

B. Cowboys often spent their days herding large numbers of cattle over long distances. A typical meal on the trail consisted of bread, meat, beans, and coffee.

C. Due to a lack of other building materials on the prairie, many Nebraska settlers built houses out of sod blocks cut from the ground. These houses generally had dirt floors and thick walls.

Ask: Why might these photos be more appropriate for illustrating realistic rather than romantic writing? *(These photos show real people living or working in difficult circumstances and under harsh conditions.)*

Teach

Summarize Have students read the first paragraph of the section titled "Westward Expansion."

Ask: What are the main ideas and the main supporting details in this passage? *(Many Americans were hesitant to move to the Great Plains. Then railroads, the Homestead Act, and improvements in farming inspired many to move west. Pioneer life on the Great Plains was demanding.)*

Write a class summary. Then have students continue reading and summarizing pages 486–487 on their own.

View the Art ★

Fanny Palmer created this illustration in 1868. It shows a railroad train passing through a frontier settlement as it continues on to the West.

Ask: How do you think this image represents America's expansion westward? *(Students may note that the railroad is bringing settlers and goods to the frontier.)*

Learning Objectives

For pages 486–494
In studying this text, you will focus on the following objectives:

Literary Study:
Analyzing literary periods.
Evaluating historical influences.
Connecting to the literature.

Regionalism and Realism

◦⊂ 1880–1910 ⊃◦

Historical, Social, and Cultural Forces

Westward Expansion

For a time during the early nineteenth century, American settlement paused at the edge of the Great Plains. Settlers felt challenged by these vast, treeless grasslands, which had little rainfall, a fierce climate, and soil that was very fertile but difficult to plow. But beginning in the 1860s, improvements in farming equipment, the expansion of the railroads, and the Homestead Act, which enabled settlers to claim public land, made more Americans willing to move to the Great Plains. However, these prairie farmers—or "sodbusters"—still faced constant toil, drought, extreme temperatures, blizzards, tornadoes, grass fires, locusts, and a social and cultural isolation that broke many homesteaders' spirits.

Across the Continent, Westward the Course of Empire Takes Its Way. Color lithograph. Museum of the City of New York. ★

The West's rich deposits of gold, silver, and copper served the needs of growing industries in the East. The lure of these precious metals brought the first wave of settlers that populated what would become the mountain states of the West.

Westward expansion was a disaster for the Native Americans of the region. Each new group of settlers further encroached on Native Americans' traditional ways of life. The Native Americans of the Great Plains had long depended on the herds of buffalo for food, clothing, and shelter. By the 1880s, the destruction of these herds by white hunters had doomed this way of life. After the Civil War, the policy of the U.S. government was to move Native Americans onto reservations, which were large tracts of land set aside for them. Resistance by some Native Americans led to armed clashes with U.S. troops.

The Gilded Age

As the Great Plains and the West were being settled, cities in the East and Midwest were also growing. New inventions, such as the electric light and the telephone, improved economic efficiency and created new jobs. Thousands of Americans moved to cities in search of work, and millions of immigrants arrived, many of them from southern and eastern Europe. By the early 1900s, Americans had transformed the United States into the world's leading industrial nation. However, this rapid growth had a social cost.

Vocabulary Practice

Word Meanings Have students use the dictionary and context clues to figure out the meaning of the word *gilded* in the phrase "the Gilded Age." *(Something that is gilded is covered with a thin layer of gold or something that looks like gold.* Gilded *can mean "superficial" or "deceptive." Historians called this period "the Gilded Age" because beneath the glittering surface of prosperity there were people who lived in crowded, dirty, and unsafe tenements in overpopulated cities.)*

Beneath the glittering surface of prosperity, corruption in business and politics became so widespread that historians often refer to this period as the Gilded Age, a reference to Mark Twain's scathing social satire of the same name, which described the greed and corruption of the time. The gap between rich and poor Americans widened greatly, and a few so-called robber barons became enormously wealthy as a result of the labors of their employees. Cities were overpopulated, and the poor were forced to live in tenement houses that were crowded, dirty, and unsafe.

Reformers and writers tried to improve working and housing conditions. Jane Addams founded Hull House, a settlement house to serve immigrants and poor working people in Chicago. Hull House offered hot lunches for factory workers and classes in English for foreign-language speakers. Some journalists—later called muckrakers—exposed the social problems brought on by industrialization and urbanization. Ida Tarbell analyzed the way in which the Standard Oil Company had come to control 95 percent of the country's oil-refining capacity. In his novel *The Jungle*, Upton Sinclair shocked and sickened readers with a graphic account of the filthy and unsafe conditions in Chicago's stockyards and meatpacking plants.

Women's Rights

After the Civil War, reformers such as Susan B. Anthony realized that women would remain powerless until they could own property and vote. With Elizabeth Cady Stanton, Anthony formed the National Woman Suffrage Association in 1869. Although the federal government balked at giving women the right to vote and own property, individual states in the West were more progressive. When Wyoming joined the union in 1890, it became the first state to give women the right to vote. By 1914, women could vote in fifteen states. It was not until 1920 that the Nineteenth Amendment guaranteed voting rights for all American women.

Regionalism, Realism, Naturalism

Writers known as Regionalists or local color writers created vivid portrayals of their own regions. Another movement, Realism, attempted to portray people as they actually were. As novelist and critic William Dean Howells observed, "Realism is nothing more and nothing less than the truthful treatment of material." Naturalist writers were influenced by the theories of scientists such as Charles Darwin.

 PREVIEW | **Big Ideas**

Regionalism, Realism, and Naturalism ☆

1 Regionalism	**2** Realism	**3** Naturalism
Following the Civil War, some American writers concentrated on the unique characteristics, or local color, of a particular region of the country. They attempted to portray the landscape, speech, customs, and other cultural details of their chosen region. **See pages 488–489**	Writers of this period turned away from Romanticism and attempted to create the appearance of ordinary life. Known as Realists, these writers aimed not to transcend reality but to render the truth of everyday experience as they saw, heard, and felt it. **See pages 490–491**	Naturalism, a more extreme movement, grew out of Realism. Naturalist writers, influenced by scientists such as Charles Darwin, believed that human beings are shaped by heredity and environment and dominated by economic, social, or natural forces. **See pages 492–493**

INTRODUCTION **487**

UNIT FOUR

Teach

Big Idea   2

Regionalism Some writers of this time period were most interested in a particular region of the country. They fed Americans' curiosity about other parts of the country. For example, Mark Twain conveys the social attitudes and behavior of people along the Mississippi River in the pre-Civil War era.

Ask: Why might today's readers be less interested in Regionalist writers than readers in the late 1800s were? *(We have fewer regional differences today. We watch the same movies and news programs, buy the same products, and can travel quickly and easily from one place to another.)*

Literary History ☆
Realism and Naturalism
These literary movements are sometimes confused for each other. Both portray nature and human lives as faithfully as possible. The realist, however, believes that people can choose a direction in life and make choices that shape it. The naturalist, on the other hand, believes that human life is determined by heredity and environment—that individuals are trapped in predestined lives that they cannot change.

Advanced Learners/Pre-AP

DIFFERENTIATED INSTRUCTION

Research Challenge advanced students to investigate the scientific progress of the period. Have students work as a group to identify significant American scientists and scientific breakthroughs between 1880 and 1910. Students can return to the timeline on pages 482–483 for ideas. Have each student learn about one topic and its impact on the society, the culture, and the literature of the time. Have students as a group present their findings to the class.

487

Teach

Literary Element   1

Dialect Tell students that many regionalist writers, including Mark Twain, used dialect to make their characters more authentic.

Ask: How would you define *dialect*? (a variation of language spoken by a particular group, often within a particular region and time)

Ask: What are some examples of dialect that you have encountered? (Students may mention a Southern dialect, a New England dialect, and others.)

Literary History ☆

Twain's Inspirations
Samuel Langhorne Clemens (1835–1910), whose pseudonym was Mark Twain, grew up in the Mississippi River town of Hannibal, Missouri, during the age of the steamboat. The Mississippi provides the setting for some of his major works, including *The Adventures of Huckleberry Finn* (1855). His pen name derives from a term used by riverboat men to measure depth. "Mark twain" means the water is two fathoms deep—just deep enough for navigation.

Big Idea 1
Regionalism

1 Influenced by such factors as public education and mass media, culture in the United States today is probably more uniform than at any other time in our history. In the past, cultural differences among people from various parts of the United States were more marked. After the Civil War, a new group of American writers, known as Regionalists or local colorists, emphasized local cultures. Not all of these Regionalist writers were born and educated in the East, as most previous American writers had been. Many came from the South, Midwest, or West. Under the influence of the new emphasis on Realism in art and literature, they did not present the unusual characters and exotic settings familiar in Romanticist writing. Instead, local colorists depicted the ordinary people and everyday places around them.

In their writing, the local colorists emphasized setting, and their characters tended to be typical of a particular region, which was clear from their speech and beliefs. Often the narrator was an outsider who observed a world filled with unfamiliar or outdated characteristics and customs. This outsider frequently revealed the tension between the new and old, the modern and the old-fashioned. The mood of local color writing was sometimes nostalgic, serving as a reminder of a time before mass production and noisy urban life. At other times, the mood was more somber, presenting a criticism of habits and ideas considered long outmoded.

☆ ### Mark Twain's Mississippi River
Born in a small Missouri town on the Mississippi River, Mark Twain (see pages 496–507) vividly evoked the world of that river in a series of works, including his masterpiece *The Adventures of Huckleberry Finn*. In this novel, an orphaned boy and a runaway slave flee down the Mississippi in a raft. Through their innocent eyes, Twain presented a piercing view of American society in the pre-Civil War era and revealed the injustices of slavery

and the culture that enforced it. He also employed a lively sense of humor and a fine ear for American dialect. His editor and friend William Dean Howells was the first to realize that Twain was more than a humorist or local colorist. In *The Adventures of Huckleberry Finn*, Twain had transformed our literature by writing a true American novel, in which the setting, subject matter, characters, and style were unmistakably American. Howells claimed Twain to be an American genius, hailing him as "incomparable, the Lincoln of our literature."

Bret Harte's Far West
Bret Harte told stories of the rude, lawless life of the California gold-mining country while describing places few people had ever seen. One of his earliest stories, "The Luck of Roaring Camp," made Harte famous. Readers in both the United States and Britain enthusiastically read about the gamblers, thieves, and social misfits that populate his work. Harte distinguished himself from other writers of the West by his ironic tone. His unsavory characters frequently undergo an unexpected reformation, which provides the narrator with an opportunity to make wry comments on their sudden changes of heart.

Willa Cather's Great Plains
When she was nine years old, Willa Cather's family left Virginia and moved to the open prairie of Nebraska—a move that would change her life dramatically. Cather's writing (see pages 520–530) reflects her memories of prairie life, and many of her early works focus on the harshness and isolation of pioneers' lives. In her novel *O Pioneers!* she depicted immigrant farmers in Nebraska, whose tough yet sensitive natures and determination made their survival possible. In other works, such as *My Ántonia*, she celebrated the pioneer lifestyle for its freedom and simplicity.

Study Skills Practice

Text Organizers Have students list the headings on this page, then write each section's main idea.

Regionalism
Writers influenced by this literary movement depicted ordinary people and everyday places in certain areas.

Mark Twain's Mississippi River
Many of Twain's works focused on life along the Mississippi River.

Bret Harte's Far West
Harte wrote about life in gold-mining country.

Willa Cather's Great Plains
Cather's writing about pioneers reflects her memories of prairie life.

Old Kentucky Home Life in the South, 1859. J. Eastman Johnson. Oil on canvas. Brooklyn Museum of Art, NY.

from *O Pioneers!* by Willa Cather 2

For the first three years after John Bergson's death, the affairs of his family prospered. Then came the hard times that brought every one on the Divide to the brink of despair; three years of drought and failure, the last struggle of a wild soil against the encroaching plowshare. The first of these fruitless summers the Bergson boys bore courageously. The failure of the corn crop made labor cheap. Lou and Oscar hired two men and put in bigger crops than ever before. They lost everything they spent. The whole country was discouraged. Farmers who were already in debt had to give up their land. A few foreclosures demoralized the county. The settlers sat about on the wooden sidewalks in the little town and told each other that the country was never meant for men to live in; the thing to do was to get back to Iowa, to Illinois, to any place that had been

proved habitable. The Bergson boys, certainly, would have been happier with their uncle Otto, in the bakery shop in Chicago. Like most of their neighbors, they were meant to follow in paths already marked out for them, not to break trails in a new country. A steady job, a few holidays, nothing to think about, and they would have been very happy. It was no fault of theirs that they had been dragged into the wilderness when they were little boys. A pioneer should have imagination, should be able to enjoy the idea of things more than the things themselves.

Reading Check

Generalize How would you describe the overall goals of the local color movement?

INTRODUCTION **489**

English Learners

DIFFERENTIATED INSTRUCTION

Beginning Choose several difficult words from the Cather excerpt: *prospered, encroaching, habitable.* Have each student choose two words to locate in a dictionary and define for the class.

Intermediate Before students read the essay on Regionalism, ask them to predict the meaning of unfamiliar words. For example, **Ask:** What does the word *humor* mean? *(something funny)* Then what is a *humorist*? *(a person who specializes in humor).* Have students consult a dictionary for the meaning of these words.

Teach
Reading Check

Answer: *Students might suggest that the overall goal of the local color movement was to accurately reflect life in a particular region. To do this, writers used dialect; described the details of everyday life and of the physical environment; and told about the customs, dress, and beliefs of the people.*

Literary Element   2

Cultural Characteristics
Have students read the excerpt from *O Pioneers!*

Ask: What unique characteristics of pioneer culture are revealed in the excerpt? *(The pioneers faced hard circumstances in nature, including drought, "wild soil," and failed crops. They faced emotional hardships and longed for an easier life back East.)*

View the Art

A native of Maine, J. Eastman Johnson earned fame as a painter of sentimental subjects. His father operated a hotel, which gave the artist exposure to a variety of people. **Ask:** How does the artist's representation of his subjects compare with Cather's portrayal of the Bergson boys? *(Johnson paints country life as relaxed and carefree, but Cather suggests that pioneer life is very difficult for the Bergson boys.)*

Teach

Realism Say: Before the Civil War, most fiction and poetry depicted imaginary people and situations.

Ask: Why do you think Realism replaced Romanticism after the Civil War? *(The reality of how hard and cruel life can be—especially during a war—may have caused writers to no longer want to portray life with Romantic ideals.)*

Cultural History ☆

Moving Away from Romanticism The horrors of the Civil War and the impersonal nature of the country's growing industrial base made Romantic literature less attractive. Novels like *The Adventures of Huckleberry Finn* brought in a new note of Realism, and later works like *The Red Badge of Courage* revealed characters in the grip of emotional and economic forces beyond their control.

Study Skills Practice

Organize Information Remind students that taking notes will help them remember important information for tests. Students can organize their notes as an outline or as a summary. Notes should contain main ideas and supporting details.

For example, for the first paragraph on this page, students could take these notes:

I. Realism was in part a reaction to Romanticism.

A. Romanticism glorified the imagination.
B. Realists portrayed real people.
C. Important Realist writers
    1. Henry James
    2. O. Henry
    3. William Dean Howells

Have students take notes as they read the remainder of this essay.

Big Idea 2
Realism

The emergence of American Realism in the second half of the 1800s was in part a reaction to the Romanticism of the previous era. Romanticism's glorification of the imagination became unappealing to Realists, who wanted to explore the motivations, behaviors, and actions of real people. Some of the most important writers of the time were considered Realists, including fiction writers Henry James, O. Henry, and William Dean Howells.

The Birth of Realism

Before Realism appeared in America, it was already flourishing in Europe. French novelist Honoré de Balzac is commonly considered the father of Realism. His masterpiece *The Human Comedy* is a massive collection of ninety novels and novellas that detail the panorama of French society. Balzac did not limit the scope of his masterpiece to one class of people or cultural environment. Instead he invented a complex and textured fictional world based on all levels of society.

Advanced by such authors as Gustave Flaubert, Leo Tolstoy, George Eliot, and Charles Dickens, Realism soon became the most prominent literary movement in Europe. These novelists examined the psychology of human behavior and created characters who struggle with problems that nineteenth-century readers would have recognized in their own lives or in the lives of their contemporaries.

The rise of Realism in the United States can be traced to disillusionment following the Civil War. For many, the war had destroyed the Romantic view of humanity. Like Mathew Brady in his famous photographs of the Civil War dead or Jacob Riis in his portraits of New York slum children, the Realists wanted to present life as it actually was—often cruel and never embellished. Photography enabled artists to capture and convey, with stark objectivity, the world as it appeared through the camera's lens. Many Realist writers aspired to adapt this kind of photographic realism to their literary works.

Kate Chopin and Women

During her lifetime, Kate Chopin was widely criticized for her realistic portrayal of women. She was the first American woman to write frankly about the suppressed passion and discontentment of women who were confined to the traditional roles of wives and mothers. She believed that the role of an artist was to rebel. As a character in her novel *The Awakening* observes, an artist must have "a soul that dares and defies." Chopin wrote of women "awakening" to their confined state and challenging the social values and patriarchal rules that defined and limited them. Chopin is sometimes considered to be a Regionalist writer, because in some of her stories she depicted the customs of Creoles and Cajuns in Louisiana, using their language and describing their lifestyles. She made their world real and confirmed their humanity by refusing to judge their lives or their struggles.

Paul Laurence Dunbar and African Americans

Paul Laurence Dunbar was one of the earliest African American poets to gain widespread recognition. William Dean Howells's favorable review of Dunbar's book *Majors and Minors* in *Harper's Weekly* helped to establish Dunbar as an international literary figure. While Dunbar wrote the bulk of his verse in the lofty poetic diction of his day, he is best known for his use of rural African American dialect. Dunbar's dialect poems depict the post-war lives of African Americans and reflect their frustrated aspirations in an era of white dominance. Throughout his life, Dunbar tried to strike a balance between the conventions of the European literary tradition and those of African American folk culture.

The City of Ambition, 1910. Alfred Stieglitz. Photogravure, 13⅜ x 10¼ in. Réunion des Musées Nationaux, France.

Edith Wharton and the Upper Classes

The characters in Edith Wharton's fiction, like Wharton herself, inhabited the upper crust of New York society. Crafted with penetrating psychological insight, her stories and novels depict the desires, prejudices, and foibles of her privileged and affluent characters. In two of her most famous novels, *The Age of Innocence* and *The House of Mirth,* Wharton presents a culture that devalues the individual in favor of class divisions, social status, and the pursuit and enjoyment of wealth. Her best fiction satirizes the hypocrisy of the American aristocracy of which she was a member.

from *The Awakening* by Kate Chopin 2

It was then past midnight. The cottages were all dark. A single faint light gleamed out from the hallway of the house. There was no sound abroad except the hooting of an old owl in the top of a water-oak, and the everlasting voice of the sea, that was not uplifted at that soft hour. It broke like a mournful lullaby upon the night.

The tears came so fast to Mrs. Pontellier's eyes that the damp sleeve of her *peignoir* no longer served to dry them. She was holding the back of her chair with one hand; her loose sleeve had slipped almost to the shoulder of her uplifted arm. Turning, she thrust her face, steaming and wet, into the bend of her arm, and she went on crying there, not caring any longer to dry her face, her eyes, her arms. She could not have told why she was crying. Such experiences as the foregoing were not uncommon in her married life. They seemed never before to have weighed much against the abundance of her husband's kindness and a uniform devotion which had come to be tacit and self-understood.

An indescribable oppression, which seemed to generate in some unfamiliar part of her consciousness, filled her whole being with a vague anguish. It was like a shadow, like a mist passing across her soul's summer day. It was strange and unfamiliar; it was a mood. She did not sit there inwardly upbraiding her husband, lamenting at Fate, which had directed her footsteps to the path which they had taken. She was just having a good cry all to herself. The mosquitoes made merry over her, biting her firm, round arms and nipping at her bare insteps.

Reading Check

Analyze Cause and Effect What cultural shifts and historical events contributed to the rise of American Realism?

Approaching Level

DIFFERENTIATED INSTRUCTION

Emerging Students may better understand the realism in Chopin's excerpt if they create a mental image of the scene. Have them reread each paragraph aloud and discuss how the image develops. Make sure they note that Mrs. Pontellier is alone and barefoot in her bathrobe, crying into the crook of her arm. The mosquitoes seem to be taking advantage of her vulnerability and adding discomfort to her

sadness. **Ask:** What is realistic about the picture the author makes? *(It describes how someone might really look and feel. The description of the mosquitoes biting the woman's skin is a realistic detail.)*

Teach

Reading Check

Answer: *European writers who were already writing realistic fiction influenced American writers. Because of the Civil War, many Americans lost faith in Romantic ideals.*

Literary Element 2

Imagery Ask: In the excerpt from *The Awakening,* what emotions do you feel and which images cause you to feel this way? *(sadness, conveyed by the sounds of the owl and the sea; loneliness, due to the hour of the night, the darkness, and the single light).*

ENGLISH LEARNERS Help students break some of the longer words into their roots and affixes: *everlasting, foregoing, self-understood, indescribable, oppression, upbraiding.*

View the Art ★

Photographer Alfred Stieglitz (1864–1946) documented the rapid changes in New York City as new construction materials and technologies led to the creation of buildings that seemed to scrape the sky. Stieglitz was the first American photographer whose work was considered a serious art form.

Teach

Big Idea 1

Naturalism Explain to students that Naturalism is a literary movement characterized by a belief that people have little control over their own lives. Naturalist writers focus on the powerful economic, social, and environmental forces that shape the lives of individuals.

Ask: How do Naturalist and Realist writers differ? *(Naturalists and Realists both wrote about ordinary people and everyday life, but Naturalists also focused on the pointless fights of individuals against "a brutal society or an indifferent universe.")*

Cultural History ☆

Psychology One factor that influenced the novels of this period was the development of psychology. William James, Carl Jung, and Sigmund Freud all investigated whether people's lives were determined by biological and environmental factors or whether people could act out of free will. Among themselves, these men agreed on little, but together they made people more aware of the human mind and its mysterious workings.

Big Idea 3
Naturalism

What do you think contributes most to shaping a person's life? Is it the biological factor of heredity? Is it the social and economic factor of environment? Or is it the result of other factors, such as an individual's own will? Realistic writers, for the most part, did not concern themselves with these philosophical questions. Toward the end of the 1800s, however, a group of writers known as Naturalists, who were strongly influenced by Charles Darwin's scientific theory of evolution by natural selection, adopted the view that people had little control over their own lives. They believed that human destiny was shaped by powerful forces, including heredity, social and economic pressures, and the natural environment. Like the Realists, Naturalists wrote about ordinary people, but often focused on the working class and the poor, depicting the futile battles of individuals against a brutal society or an indifferent universe. ☆

Edwin Arlington Robinson and Fate

Edwin Arlington Robinson said he felt "doomed, or elected, or sentenced for life, to the writing of poetry." His most famous poems are set in fictional Tilbury Town, which was modeled on his childhood hometown of Gardiner, Maine. The characters in his poems, like Robinson himself, are often loners or misfits. They live in communities where people feel pressure to conform and where creativity is misunderstood or simply ignored. Robinson's poems focus almost exclusively on an individual or on individual relationships. His tone is a blend of irony and compassion toward his characters, many of whose lives end in personal failure and despair.

Jack London and Nature

From the age of nine, Jack London helped to support his family through hard physical labor. His early experiences made him sympathetic toward the working class and convinced him that capitalist society was brutal and repressive. London was also drawn to social Darwinism, a movement that attempted to apply Darwin's biological theories to human behavior. These ideas are important in several of London's works, including his most popular novels, *The Call of the Wild* and *The Sea-Wolf*. London spent time in the Alaskan wilderness and the South Seas, and many of his stories demonstrate the power of nature over civilization.

> A man said to the universe:
> "Sir, I exist!"
> "However," replied the universe,
> "The fact has not created in me
> A sense of obligation."
>
> —Stephen Crane

Stephen Crane and War

Though the Civil War had ended six years before Crane was born, he used it as the subject of his best-known book, *The Red Badge of Courage*. Later short stories express Crane's belief in the necessity of courage, honesty, and poise in the face of an indifferent universe. In "The Blue Hotel," Crane described humans as so many lice clinging "to a whirling, fire-smote, ice-locked, disease-stricken, space-lost bulb." The pathos of human helplessness in the face of brute fact closes the story "An Episode of War" as a young officer reacts to the loss of his arm: "'Oh, well,' he said, standing shamefaced amid these tears. 'I don't suppose it matters so much as all that.'" In *The Red Badge of Courage*, Crane presents his hero, a young recruit named Henry Fleming, who responds to his first experience of a new, violent environment—battle.

Writing Practice

⚡ **Use Figurative Language** After students have read the excerpt by Stephen Crane, have them identify some of the similes and metaphors Crane uses to convey his character's actions and emotions. These include references to a carpenter, hot stones, a pestered animal, a driven beast, battle phantoms, and a smothered baby. Discuss how these comparisons enhance the meaning of the passage. Instruct students to write their own one-page narratives about a real or imagined person facing a difficult situation. Have them use similes and metaphors to describe the person's state of mind. Have students read their narratives aloud to the class.

Newspaper boys, one missing a leg, stand on the steps of a bank near a busy trolley junction in Jersey City, NJ. 1912. Lewis Wickes Hine. ★

from *The Red Badge of Courage* by Stephen Crane **2**

He was at a task. He was like a carpenter who has made many boxes, making still another box, only there was furious haste in his movements. He, in his thoughts, was careering off in other places, even as the carpenter who as he works whistles and thinks of his friend or his enemy, his home or a saloon. And these jolted dreams were never perfect to him afterward, but remained a mass of blurred shapes.

Presently he began to feel the effects of the war atmosphere—a blistering sweat, a sensation that his eyeballs were about to crack like hot stones. A burning roar filled his ears.

Following this came a red rage. He developed the acute exasperation of a pestered animal, a well-meaning cow worried by dogs. He had a mad feeling against his rifle, which could only be used against

one life at a time. He wished to rush forward and strangle with his fingers. He craved a power that would enable him to make a world-sweeping gesture and brush all back. His impotency appeared to him, and made his rage into that of a driven beast.

Buried in the smoke of many rifles his anger was directed not so much against the men whom he knew were rushing toward him as against the swirling battle phantoms which were choking him, stuffing their smoke robes down his parched throat.

Reading Check

Compare and Contrast How did the attitude of the Naturalists toward the place of humanity in the universe differ from that of the Transcendentalists?

INTRODUCTION **493**

Teach
Reading Check

Answer: *Naturalists denied the existence of the supernatural and saw human beings as alone in the universe. They thought that forces outside a person's control shaped life. Transcendentalists believed people could shape their lives through intuition, self-reliance, and inspiration. They also believed in the supernatural.*

Literary Element	2

Relate to the Text Have students read the excerpt from *The Red Badge of Courage.*

Ask: Has there ever been a time in your life when you felt overwhelming emotions? How did it feel? *(Students may say that they felt paralyzed—they couldn't walk or speak.)*

View the Photograph ★

Lewis Wickes Hine (1874–1940) was the National Child Labor Committee photographer for ten years.

Ask: How might the Committee use this photograph? *(It may be part of a collection showing children's working conditions.)*

English Learners

DIFFERENTIATED INSTRUCTION

Intermediate Help students understand metaphors used by the author in the essay on Naturalism. Explain that metaphors cannot be interpreted literally, but are used to help describe or explain something. Have students read the first sentence in the Robinson section aloud. Then explain that in reality he was not *elected* or *sentenced* to write poetry as a criminal would be sentenced to time in prison. Instead, he is

saying that fate has given him no choice. He feels an overwhelming need to write. Continue by examining the quotes by London and Crane and elicit the meaning of different words and phrases from students. For example, **Ask:** What is the meaning of London's phrase *heaven's artillery*? *(thunder).* **Ask:** Why does London refer to the ocean tides and the weather as *tricks*? *(He portrays nature as a powerful*

magician.) **Ask:** What does Crane mean by the universe's response to the man? *(He thinks humans are insignificant to nature.)*

Assess

Legacy of the Period

Ask: Why did New England writers no longer dominate American literature? *(Responses will vary but may include westward expansion and immigration.)*

Cultural and Literary Links

Students should look for ways that these three literary movements have influenced today's writers.

Have students make and label the Three-Pocket Foldable. Then have them write notes about each Big Idea on note cards to insert in the pockets of their Foldables.

Wrap-Up

Legacy of the Period

Between 1880 and 1910, writers from the Midwest, the Great Plains, and the West enriched our country's literature with new kinds of American landscapes, characters, and styles of speech.

The effects of Realism are widespread and can be seen in journalism, film, the novel, and painting. By challenging the conventions of Romanticism, writers like Wharton, Chopin, and Dunbar redefined the boundaries of acceptable content in literature and paved the way for future workers.

Beginning in the 1890s, literary Naturalism shone a bright but harsh light on the human condition. Naturalist writers presented life as a brutal, losing battle between individuals and the forces of their environments, which could be as diverse as an Alaskan wilderness or a Chicago factory.

Cultural and Literary Links

⟹ The influence of the American Regionalist writers on subsequent American literature has been enormous. Ernest Hemingway once said, "All modern American literature comes from one book by Mark Twain called *Huckleberry Finn.*"

⟹ Kate Chopin's work is valued for its portrayals of attitudes toward race, class, ethnicity, and gender relations.

⟹ Stephen Crane was neglected for a time after his death in 1900 until writers began to recognize his experiments with subject, theme, and form.

Literature Online

Unit Resources For additional skills practice, go to glencoe.com and enter QuickPass code GLA9800u4.

Activities

Choose one of the following activities to explore and develop as you read this unit.

1. Follow Up Go back to the Looking Ahead on page 481 and answer the following questions.

2. Contrast Literary Periods Like the Transcendentalists of the mid-nineteenth century, the Naturalists were interested in the interactions between people and the natural world. Working with a partner, compare and contrast these two groups' views of nature and how their members represented nature in literature. Present your findings to your class.

3. Visual Literacy Create a map showing the regions of the country that were represented by Mark Twain, Willa Cather, and Kate Chopin. For

each area, create an icon to represent the author and the region.

4. Take Notes Use this organizer to explore your personal responses to the poetry, short stories, and nonfiction in this unit.

 BOUND BOOK

Nonfiction / Drama / Poems

Reader-Response Journal

Activities

1. **Following Up** Have students choose a question to keep in mind as they read.

2. **Contrasting Literary Periods** Have students look back at some of the Transcendentalist writers in Unit 2. Have them keep a list of points of comparison between the Unit 2 writers and the Naturalists in Unit 4.

3. **Visual Literacy** Students' works should focus on just one section of the country and its main authors.

4. **Take Notes** Have students make the graphic organizer before they begin to read the selections.

PART 1

Regionalism and Local Color

Red Pepper Time, c. 1930. Oscar Edmund Berninghaus. Oil on canvas, 25 x 30¹/₁₆ in. Gift of Arvin Gottlieb. Smithsonian American Art Museum, Washington, DC.

View the Art Oscar Edmund Berninghaus came to love the West—especially Taos, New Mexico—when the Denver and Rio Grande Railroad sent him to capture the scenery along the railroad's western route. What aspects of this painting capture the flavor of the region? What can you infer about life in this part of the country?

> *"Elsewhere the sky is the roof of the world;*
> *but here the earth is the floor of the sky."*
>
> —Willa Cather, *Death Comes for the Archbishop*

495

Analyze and Extend

Reading Strategy

Interpret Meaning Direct students to read the Willa Cather quotation. **Say:** Explain Cather's meaning in your own words. *(Cather says that in the West, the sky is greater than in other places and that people feel exposed rather than covered.)*

View the Art ★

Answer: *The people in the painting seem small and insignificant, whereas the sky seems vast and expansive. Life was greatly affected by nature and the environment.*
Oscar Berninghaus (1874–1952) is known for his landscapes, especially those depicting the American Southwest.

English Learners

DIFFERENTIATED INSTRUCTION

Intermediate Some students may be unfamiliar with the history of American settlement. In 1804 President Jefferson appointed Meriweather Lewis and William Clark to lead an exploration of the unclaimed land in the West. Later, in 1848, Mexico surrendered its claim to all the territories north of its current border. This entitled the United States to take possession of this land and enabled pioneers to move westward and settle in these territories. Other events, such as the California Gold Rush in 1849, encouraged settlers to move to the West. Point out that many settlers came from crowded cities or wooded land. **Ask:** Why might the sky seem more like a roof in one place than in another? *(Possible answers: Crowds of people, buildings, and trees could give a person the feeling of being covered with a roof. In a place without close surroundings, the sky might seem open, endless.)*

For additional support for English Learners, see Unit 4 Teaching Resources Book, p. 19.

Before You Read

Focus

Before You Read
The Celebrated Jumping Frog of Calaveras County

Meet **Mark Twain**
(1835–1910)

"When I was born I was a member of a firm of twins," Twain told an audience in 1901. "And one of them disappeared." Although not actually a twin, Twain did have two sides. Born Samuel Langhorne Clemens, he took as his pen name a term used by riverboat pilots in navigation: *Mark Twain.*

Missouri Boyhood Samuel Clemens spent his early life in Missouri, chiefly in Hannibal on the west bank of the Mississippi River. Life there was full of adventure, but the death of Clemens's father when the boy was just eleven forced him to curtail his childhood escapades and his schooling in order to work as a printer's apprentice. At twenty-one, Clemens fulfilled his lifelong dream of becoming a riverboat pilot on the Mississippi. As he declared, "a pilot was the only unfettered and entirely independent being that lived on the earth."

> "My books are water; those of the great geniuses are wine. Everybody drinks water."
>
> —Mark Twain

Travels When the Civil War closed the Mississippi to commercial traffic, Clemens headed for Nevada in hopes of striking it rich. He eventually settled in San Francisco, where he met author Bret Harte, lectured, and worked as a journalist. During this time, Twain wrote the story that brought him his first taste of fame: "The Celebrated Jumping Frog of Calaveras County." In 1867, as a traveling correspondent for the *Alta California*, Twain set out for Europe and the Middle East. This journey provided the material for *The Innocents Abroad; or, The New Pilgrim's Progress* (1869), which poked fun at inexperienced American travelers and quickly became a best seller.

Literary Success In 1870 Twain married Olivia Langdon, a wealthy easterner. They settled in Hartford, Connecticut, where Twain met William Dean Howells, the most influential literary critic of the day. In Howells's *Atlantic Monthly,* Twain recounted his experiences as a riverboat pilot in a series called "Old Times on the Mississippi," which he embellished and published eight years later as *Life on the Mississippi* (1883). *The Adventures of Tom Sawyer* (1876) established Twain as a master of fiction, and its sequel, *The Adventures of Huckleberry Finn* (1884), cemented Twain's place as one of the greatest novelists the United States has ever produced. His use of realism and detail influenced many later writers of American fiction, including Ernest Hemingway, who stated that "all modern American literature comes from one book by Mark Twain called *Huckleberry Finn.*"

Plagued by financial misfortunes and the deaths of loved ones, Twain's later years found him frequently embittered. In some of his later works, Twain brooded over the dark side of human nature. Today, however, he is remembered for capturing the brash, optimistic spirit and youthful vitality of his fellow Americans.

Literature Online

Author Search For more about Mark Twain, go to glencoe.com and enter QuickPass code GLA9800u4.

Selection Skills

Literary Elements
- Dialect (SE pp. 497, 499, 502, 503)

The Celebrated Jumping Frog...

Listening/Speaking/Viewing Skills
- Analyze Art (SE p. 501)

Vocabulary Skills
- Word Origins (SE p. 503)
- Visual Vocabulary (SE pp. 499–500)
- Use Adjectives (TE p. 497)

Reading Skills
- Analyze Comic Devices (SE pp. 497, 500–503; TE p. 498)
- Classify (TE p. 498)
- Dialect (TE p. 500)
- Infer (TE p. 502)

Writing Skills/Grammar
- Write a Story (SE p. 503)

Literature and Reading Preview

Connect to the Story

Which of your friends or family members is the best storyteller? What makes this person's stories effective? Discuss these questions with a partner.

Build Background

In 1848 James W. Marshall discovered rich deposits of gold at Sutter's Mill, near Coloma. This discovery led to the California gold rush, during which many adventurous people thronged to California to prospect for gold, hoping to "strike it rich." In the remote mining camps and frontier towns, life was hard and entertainment was scarce. For fun, people invented tall tales—stories filled with humorous exaggerations.

Set Purposes for Reading

Big Idea Regionalism

As you read, ask yourself, What techniques does Twain use to give you the flavor of the Old West during the Gold Rush?

Literary Element Dialect

Dialect is a variation of a language spoken by a particular group, often within a specific region and time. Dialects may differ from the standard form of a language in vocabulary, pronunciation, or grammatical form. As you read, ask yourself, What are some examples of dialect in this story? What effect does Twain's use of dialect achieve?

Reading Strategy Analyze Comic Devices

In addition to dialect, Twain uses several other devices to create humor, including absurd situations, comic characters, and exaggerations.

....

Tip: Take Notes Use a web diagram to help you record details about each comic device listed.

Learning Objectives

For pages 496–503

In studying this text, you will focus on the following objectives:

Literary Study: Analyzing dialect.

Reading: Analyzing comic devices.

Writing: Writing a story.

Vocabulary

garrulous (gar´ ə ləs) *adj.* talkative; p. 498 *Our garrulous neighbor went on with his story, never pausing for breath.*

conjecture (kən jek´ chər) *v.* to form an opinion without definite evidence; to guess; p. 498 *Not really sure, I conjectured that she meant more than she said.*

dilapidated (di lap´ ə dā´ tid) *adj.* fallen into ruin or decay; shabby; p. 498 *Pigeons flew through the holes in the dilapidated roof.*

interminable (in tur´ mi nə bəl) *adj.* seemingly endless; p. 499 *The dull speech lasted only fifteen minutes, but seemed interminable.*

enterprising (en´ tər prī´ zing) *adj.* showing energy and initiative, especially in beginning new projects; p. 502 *The enterprising class planned to raise money in a new way—by having a silent auction.*

Before You Read

Focus

Summary

Simon Wheeler tells the narrator the colorful story of Jim Smiley, who loved to gamble so much that he would take any side in a bet. Smiley is eventually outwitted by a stranger who agrees to bet on a frog-jumping competition. As Smiley leaves in search of a frog to compete against his own frog, Dan'l Webster, the stranger fills Dan'l's stomach with small metal pellets. The stranger wins the bet because Dan'l becomes so heavy he cannot jump.

For summaries in languages other than English, see Unit 4 Teaching Resources Book, pp. 20–25.

Vocabulary

Apply Meaning Have students think of people, places, or activities that can be described using one of the vocabulary words. Volunteers should suggest their ideas while other students guess the matching vocabulary word. For example: "A haunted house" might be described as "dilapidated." "A wait in a doctor's office" could be called "interminable."

For additional vocabulary practice, see Unit 4 Teaching Resources Book, p. 28.

For additional context, see Glencoe Interactive Vocabulary CD-ROM.

English Learners

DIFFERENTIATED INSTRUCTION

Intermediate Explain that Twain uses dialect to give his characters personality, but that such use of the language would be considered incorrect when writing or speaking formally. Point out that Mr. Wheeler is telling a story and that his sentences seem to go on and on, as if he is thinking aloud. His dialect would have been very common among the people of Angel's Camp but sounds very distinctive to a modern reader. Have students read the first sentence of Mr. Wheeler's story and identify deviations from standard or common English usage. (He uses "feller" in place of fellow and "curiosest" rather than most curious or strange.) Have students suggest synonyms for any other nonstandard words they encounter as they read.

Teach

Big Idea   1

Regionalism Say: Keep these questions in mind as you read: How do the setting details suggest a specific local community? *(Details paint a vivid picture of a western mining camp.)* How are Twain's characters unique to their local place? *(They speak in dialect and use unique local words such as* straddle-bug.*)*

Reading Strategy   2

Analyze Comic Devices
Have students examine the prediction about Simon Wheeler. **Ask:** How does Twain use exaggeration to create humor here? *(He suggests that Wheeler will bore the narrator "nearly to death.")*

Big Idea   3

Regionalism Answer: *It would be stark and unsophisticated—perhaps even dangerous.*

Readability Scores

Dale-Chall: 10.2
DRP: 59
Lexile: 1410

The Country Store, 1872. Winslow Homer. Oil on board, 11½ x 18 in.

The Celebrated Jumping Frog of Calaveras County

Mark Twain

1 In compliance with the request of a friend of mine, who wrote me from the East, I called on good-natured, **garrulous** old Simon Wheeler, and inquired after my friend's friend, *Leonidas W. Smiley*, as requested to do, and I hereunto append[1] the result. I have a lurking suspicion that *Leonidas W. Smiley* is a myth; that my friend never knew such a personage; and that he only **conjectured** that, if I asked old Wheeler about him, it would remind him of his infamous *Jim* Smiley, and he would go to **2** work and bore me nearly to death with some infernal[2] reminiscence of him as long and tedious as it should be useless to me. If that was the design, it certainly succeeded.

I found Simon Wheeler dozing comfortably by the bar-room stove of the old **dilapidated**

----

1. *Append* means "to add as a supplement" or "to attach."
2. *Infernal* means "awful" or "thoroughly unpleasant."

Vocabulary

garrulous (gar´ ə ləs) *adj.* talkative

conjecture (kən jek´ chər) *v.* to form an opinion without definite evidence; to guess

dilapidated (di lap´ə dā´tid) *adj.* fallen into ruin or decay; shabby

498   UNIT 4   REGIONALISM AND REALISM

tavern in the ancient mining camp of Angel's,[3] and I noticed that he was fat and bald-headed, and had an expression of winning gentleness and simplicity upon his tranquil countenance.[4] He roused up and gave me good-day. I told him a friend of mine had commissioned me to make some inquiries about a cherished companion of his boyhood named *Leonidas W. Smiley—Rev. Leonidas W. Smiley*—a young minister of the Gospel, who he had heard was at one time a resident of Angel's Camp. I added that, if Mr. Wheeler could tell me any thing about this Rev. Leonidas W. Smiley, I would feel under many obligations to him.

Simon Wheeler backed me into a corner and blockaded me there with his chair, and then sat me down and reeled off the monotonous narrative which follows this paragraph. He never smiled, he never frowned, he never changed his voice from the gentle-flowing key to which he

----

3. *Angel's* refers to Angel's Camp.
4. A *tranquil countenance* is a calm face.

Regionalism *What sort of atmosphere would you expect to find in a mining camp?* **3**

Reading Practice

Classify Good writers create well-rounded characters by describing their actions, appearances, and personalities. Ask students to read the second and third paragraphs of this story, looking for descriptions of Simon Wheeler. Have students classify the descriptions in a chart like the one below.

After students have completed the chart, **Ask:** Through whose eyes does the reader see Wheeler's character? *(through the eyes of the narrator)* **Ask:** Does the description of Wheeler seem positive or negative? Explain. *(Students may say that the description is negative because it makes Wheeler appear lazy and simple.)*

Action	Appearance	Personality

tuned the initial sentence, he never betrayed the slightest suspicion of enthusiasm; but all through the **interminable** narrative there ran a vein of impressive earnestness and sincerity, which showed me plainly that, so far from his imagining that there was any thing ridiculous or funny about his story, he regarded it as a really important matter, and admired its two heroes as men of transcendent[5] genius in finesse.[6]

To me, the spectacle of a man drifting serenely along through such a queer yarn without ever smiling, was exquisitely absurd. As I said before, I asked him to tell me what he knew of Rev. Leonidas W. Smiley, and he replied as follows. I let him go on in his own way, and never interrupted him once:

☆ There was a feller here once by the name of

Visual Vocabulary
A *flume* is a trough or chute, often inclined, that carries water.

Jim Smiley, in the winter of '49—or may be it was the spring of '50—I don't recollect exactly, somehow, though what makes me think it was one or the other is because I remember the big flume wasn't finished when he first came to the camp; but any way, he was the curiosest man about always betting on any thing that turned up you ever see, if he could get any body to bet on the other side; and if he couldn't he'd change sides. Any way that suited the other man would suit him—any way just so's he got a bet, *he* was satisfied. But still he was lucky, uncommon lucky; he most always come out winner. He was always ready and laying for a chance; there couldn't be no solitry thing mentioned but that feller'd offer to bet on

---

5. *Transcendent* means "surpassing others" or "superior."
6. *Finesse* is the smooth or artful handling of a situation.

4 **Dialect** *How would you characterize Wheeler's use of language?*

Vocabulary

interminable (in tur´mi nə bəl) *adj.* seemingly endless

---

it, and take any side you please, as I was just telling you. If there was a horse race, you'd find him flush,[7] or you'd find him busted at the end of it; if there was a dog-fight, he'd bet on it; if there was a cat-fight, he'd bet on it; if there was a chicken-fight, he'd bet on it; why, if there was two birds setting on a fence, he would bet you which one would fly first; or if there was a camp-meeting,[8] he would be there reg'lar, to bet on Parson Walker, which he judged to be the best exhorter[9] about here, and so he was, too, and a good man. If he even seen a straddle-bug[10] start to go anywheres, he would bet you how long it would take him to get wherever he was going to, and if you took him up, he would foller that straddle-bug to Mexico but what he would find out where he was bound for and how long he was on the road. Lots of the boys here has seen that Smiley, and can tell you about him. Why, it never made no difference to *him*—he would bet on *any* thing—the dangdest feller. Parson Walker's wife laid very sick once, for a good while, and it seemed as if they warn't going to save her; but one morning he come in, and Smiley asked how she was, and he said she was considerable better—thank the Lord for his inf'nit mercy—and coming on so smart that, with the blessing of Prov'dence,[11] she'd get well yet; and Smiley, before he thought, says, "Well, I'll risk two-and-a-half[12] that she don't, any way."

Thish-yer[13] Smiley had a mare—the boys called her the fifteen-minute nag, but that was only in fun, you know, because, of course, she was faster than that—and he used to win money

---

7. Here, *flush* means "having a large amount of money" or "rich."
8. A *camp-meeting* is an outdoor religious gathering, sometimes held in a tent.
9. An *exhorter* is someone who urges by giving strong advice or warnings; here, a preacher.
10. A *straddle-bug* is a long-legged beetle.
11. *Prov'dence* (Providence) is God.
12. *Risk two-and-a-half* means "risk, or bet, $2.50."
13. *Thish-yer* is dialect for "this here."

Regionalism *How does Twain evoke the region in this passage?* **5**

Intermediate Write on the board: "I don't recollect," "couldn't be," and "he'd bet." Explain that the underlined words are contractions created by joining words and using apostrophes in place of omitted letters. Write the expanded version of each contraction and show the changes made (don't comes from do not, and so on.) Have students find other examples in the text, and then discuss how Twain uses

---

Teach

Literary Element **4**

Dialect **Answer:** *Wheeler's language is characterized by contractions, regionalisms, and nonstandard usage.*

(ENGLISH LEARNERS) Ask students to point out some of Wheeler's contractions and explain what the apostrophe stands for. (so's *for* so as; feller'd *for* fellow would; reg'lar *for* regular)

Big Idea **5**

Regionalism **Answer:** *Students might mention that the straddle-bug is a species found in the West or that Smiley's curious behavior is a product of the West.*

Writer's Technique ☆

Frame Story A frame story is a story that frames, or surrounds, another story. In a frame story, a writer may set up a situation that allows the narrator to comment on the internal story.

Interactive Read and Write

Other options for teaching this selection can be found in

- Interactive Read and Write for EL Students pp. 147–158
- Interactive Read and Write for Approaching-Level Students, pp. 147–158
- Interactive Read and Write for On-Level Students, pp. 147–158

Teach

Reading Strategy 1

Evaluate **Ask:** Do you think this story rings true? Why do you think Wheeler tells it? How does the story's style add to its humor? *(Students may say that this story is a tall tale told simply to amuse or entertain the stranger. The exaggeration in a tall tale creates the humor.)*

Reading Strategy 2

Analyze Comic Devices
Answer: *It is an exaggeration; it is very unlikely that a dog with no hind legs could win a fight or that a dog would die of a broken heart after losing a fight.*

For additional practice using the reading skill or strategy, see Unit 4 Teaching Resources Book, p. 27.

Political History ☆
President Jackson

Andrew Jackson was president of the United States in the 1830s. He was known for his toughness, his military experience, and the time he had spent on the frontier. **Ask:** How does Twain evoke the character of Calaveras County by naming the dog Andrew Jackson? *(Students may say that the county is tough, like Jackson.)*

on that horse, for all she was so slow and always had the asthma, or the distemper, or the consumption,[14] or something of that kind. They used to give her two or three hundred yards start, and then pass her under way; but always at the fag-end[15] of the race she'd get excited and desperate-like, and come cavorting[16] and straddling up, and scattering her legs around limber, sometimes in the air, and sometimes out to one side amongst the fences, and kicking up m-o-r-e dust, and raising m-o-r-e racket with her coughing and sneezing and blowing her nose—and always fetch up at the stand[17] just about a neck ahead, as near as you could cipher it down.[18]

And he had a little small bull pup, that to look at him you'd think he wan't worth a cent, but to set around and look ornery, and lay for a chance to steal something. But as soon as money was up on him, he was a different dog; his under-jaw'd begin to stick out like the fo'castle of a steamboat, and his teeth would uncover, and shine savage like the furnaces. And a dog might tackle him, and bully-rag[19] him, and bite him, and throw him over his shoulder two or three times, and Andrew Jackson—which was the name of the pup—Andrew Jackson would never let on but what *he* was satisfied, and hadn't expected nothing else—and the bets being doubled and doubled on the other side all the time, till the money was all up; and then all of a sudden he would grab that other dog jest by the j'int of his hind leg and freeze to it—not chaw, you understand, but only jest grip and hang on till they

Visual Vocabulary
The *fo'castle*, or forecastle (fōk′ səl), of a steamboat is a raised deck at the front of the boat.

14. *Consumption* is another name for tuberculosis.
15. The *fag-end* is the last part.
16. *Cavorting* means "running and jumping around playfully."
17. *Fetch up at the stand* means "arrive at the grandstand," which was placed at the finish line.
18. *Cipher it down* means "calculate it."
19. *Bully-rag* means "to intimidate" or "to abuse."

throwed up the sponge,[20] if it was a year. Smiley always come out winner on that pup, till he harnessed[21] a dog once that didn't have no hind legs, because they'd been sawed off by a circular saw, and when the thing had gone along far enough, and the money was all up, and he come to make a snatch for his pet holt,[22] he saw in a minute how he'd been imposed on, and how the other dog had him in the door,[23] so to speak, and he 'peared surprised, and then he looked sorter discouraged-like, and didn't try no more to win the fight, and so he got shucked out[24] bad. He give Smiley a look, as much as to say his heart was broke, and it was *his* fault, for putting up a dog that hadn't no hind legs for him to take holt of, which was his main dependence in a fight, and then he limped off a piece and laid down and died. It was a good pup, was that Andrew Jackson, and would have made a name for hisself if he'd lived, for the stuff was in him, and he had genius—I know it, because he hadn't had no opportunities to speak of, and it don't stand to reason that a dog could make such a fight as he could under them circumstances, if he hadn't no talent. It always makes me feel sorry when I think of that last fight of his'n, and the way it turned out.

Well, thish-yer Smiley had rat-tarriers,[25] and chicken cocks,[26] and tom-cats, and all them kind of things, till you couldn't rest, and you couldn't fetch nothing for him to bet on but he'd match you. He ketched a frog one day, and took him home, and said he cal'klated[27] to edercate him; and so he never done nothing for three months but set in his back yard and

1

20. *Throwed up the sponge* means "gave up the contest."
21. Here, *harnessed* means "set up a fight with."
22. A *pet holt* is a favorite hold.
23. *Had him in the door* means "had him at a disadvantage or in a tight place."
24. *Shucked out* means "beaten" or "defeated."
25. *Rat-tarriers* are dogs (terriers) once used for catching rats.
26. *Chicken cocks* are adult male chickens (roosters) that are trained to fight.
27. *Cal'klated* is dialect for calculated, meaning "planned."

Analyze Comic Devices *What makes this situation humorous?* 2

Reading Practice

Dialect When reading stories containing dialect, students may want to read the text aloud. Suggest that they identify the colloquialisms and other elements of dialect in the text before they read. Refer them to the footnotes for help in understanding particular words and phrases.

Urge students to use Twain's unusual spellings as a guide for pronouncing the dialect. Point out that reading aloud will give them a sense of the rhythm of the

speech and thus help them better appreciate Twain's story.

learn[28] that frog to jump. And you bet you he *did* learn him, too. He'd give him a little punch behind, and the next minute you'd see that frog whirling in the air like a doughnut—see him turn one summerset, or may be a couple, if he got a good start, and come down flat-footed and all right, like a cat. He got him up so in the matter of catching flies, and kept him in practice so constant, that he'd nail a fly every time as far as he could see him. Smiley said all a frog wanted was education, and he could do most any thing—and I believe him. Why, I've seen him set Dan'l Webster[29] down here on this floor—Dan'l Webster was the name of the frog—and sing out, "Flies, Dan'l, flies!" and quicker'n you could wink, he'd spring straight up, and snake a fly off'n the counter there, and flop down on the floor again as solid as a gob of mud, and fall to scratching the side of his head with his hind foot as indifferent as if he hadn't no idea he'd been doin' any more'n any frog might do. You never see a frog so modest and straightfor'ard as he was, for all he was so gifted. And when it come to fair and square jumping

28. Here, *learn* means "teach."
29. *Dan'l Webster* refers to Daniel Webster (1782–1852), a famous orator who served as a U.S. senator and a U.S. secretary of state.

3 Analyze Comic Devices *How does Twain create humor in this passage?*

on a dead level, he could get over more ground at one straddle[30] than any animal of his breed you ever see. Jumping on a dead level was his strong suit, you understand; and when it come to that, Smiley would ante up[31] money on him as long as he had a red.[32] Smiley was monstrous proud of his frog, and well he might be, for fellers that had traveled and been everywheres, all said he laid over any frog that ever *they* see.

Well, Smiley kept the beast in a little lattice box, and he used to fetch him down town sometimes and lay for a bet. One day a feller—a stranger in the camp, he was—come across him with his box, and says:

"What might it be that you've got in the box?"

And Smiley says, sorter indifferent like, "It might be a parrot, or it might be a canary, may be, but it an't—it's only just a frog."

And the feller took it, and looked at it careful, and turned it round this way and that, and says, "H'm—so 'tis. Well, what's *he* good for?"

"Well," Smiley says, easy and careless, "He's good enough for *one* thing, I should judge—he can outjump any frog in Calaveras county."

The feller took the box again, and took another long, particular look, and give it back to Smiley, and says, very deliberate, "Well, I

30. Here, *straddle* means "to jump."
31. *Ante up* means "to put into the pool" or "to bet."
32. *A red* refers to a red cent, meaning "any money at all."

Teach

Approaching Level

Teach

Reading Strategy | 1

Analyze Comic Devices
Answer: *By filling Dan'l Webster with quail shot, the stranger will make the frog too heavy to jump.*

Literary Element | 2

Dialect **Answer:** *Well, this Smiley had a yellow one-eyed cow that had no tail, only a short stump like a banana, and* _____

 To check students' understanding of the selection, see Unit 4 Teaching Resources Book, p. 28.

Progress Check

Can students analyze dialect?

If No → See Unit 4 Teaching Resources Book, p. 26.

don't see no p'ints[33] about that frog that's any better'n any other frog."

"May be you don't," Smiley says, "May be you understand frogs, and may be you don't understand 'em; may be you've had experience, and may be you an't only a amature, as it were. Anyways, I've got *my* opinion, and I'll risk forty dollars that he can outjump any frog in Calaveras county."

And the feller studied a minute, and then says, kinder sad like, "Well, I'm only a stranger here, and I an't got no frog; but if I had a frog, I'd bet you."

And then Smiley says, "That's all right—that's all right—if you'll hold my box a minute, I'll go and get you a frog." And so the feller took the box, and put up his forty dollars along with Smiley's, and set down to wait.

So he set there a good while thinking and thinking to hisself, and then he got the frog out and prized his mouth open and took a teaspoon and filled him full of quail shot[34]—filled him pretty near up to his chin—and set him on the floor. Smiley he went to the swamp and slopped around in the mud for a long time, and finally he ketched a frog, and fetched him in, and give him to this feller, and says:

"Now, if you're ready, set him alongside of Dan'l, with his fore-paws just even with Dan'l, and I'll give the word." Then he says, "One—two—three—jump!" and him and the feller touched up the frogs from behind, and the new frog hopped off, but Dan'l give a heave, and hysted up his shoulders—so—like a Frenchman, but it wan't no use—he couldn't budge; he was planted as solid as an anvil, and he couldn't no more stir than if he was anchored out. Smiley was a good deal surprised, and he was disgusted too, but he didn't have no idea what the matter was, of course.

The feller took the money and started away; and when he was going out at the door, he sorter jerked his thumb over his shoulders—this way—at Dan'l, and says again, very deliberate, "Well, *I* don't see no p'ints about that frog that's any better'n any other frog."

Smiley he stood scratching his head and looking down at Dan'l a long time, and at last he says, "I do wonder what in the nation that frog throw'd off for—I wonder if there an't something the matter with him—he 'pears to look mighty baggy, somehow." And he ketched Dan'l by the nap of the neck, and lifted him up and says, "Why, blame my cats, if he don't weigh five pound!" and turned him upside down, and he belched out a double handful of shot. And then he see how it was, and he was the maddest man—he set the frog down and took out after that feller, but he never ketched him. And—

[Here Simon Wheeler heard his name called from the front yard, and got up to see what was wanted.] And turning to me as he moved away, he said: "Just set where you are, stranger, and rest easy—I an't going to be gone a second."

But, by your leave, I did not think that a continuation of the history of the **enterprising** vagabond *Jim* Smiley would be likely to afford[35] me much information concerning the Rev. *Leonidas W.* Smiley, and so I started away.

At the door I met the sociable Wheeler returning, and he buttonholed[36] me and recommenced:

"Well, thish-yer Smiley had a yaller one-eyed cow that didn't have no tail, only jest a short stump like a bannanner, and——"

"Oh! hang Smiley and his afflicted cow!" I muttered, good-naturedly, and bidding the old gentleman good-day, I departed. ❧

---

35. *Afford* means "to give" or "to provide."
36. *Buttonholed* means "detained in conversation."

Dialect *How would you express Wheeler's statement in Standard English?* | 2

Vocabulary

enterprising (en´ tər prī´ zing) *adj.* showing energy and initiative, especially in beginning new projects

---

33. *P'ints* is dialect for points, meaning "qualities" or "characteristics."
34. *Quail shot* is ammunition made up of small lead pellets.

1 Analyze Comic Devices *How might the stranger's action bring about an absurd situation?*

Reading Practice

SPIRAL REVIEW **Author's Purpose** Explain to students that some people interpret Twain's humor as criticism of particular people or groups of people. **Ask:** Who do you think is the target in this story and why? *(People from the West, from Smiley's overconfident attitude and people from the East from the narrator's arrogance.)* **Say:** Compare the lives of the narrator and Smiley.

(The narrator is from the East and has probably never worked in a mining town. Smiley leads a rougher life and has probably worked in the mines.) **Ask:** What might Twain be suggesting about some Easterners' opinions of Westerners? *(Twain may be suggesting that Easterners consider Westerners uncultured and of a lower status.)*

After You Read

Respond and Think Critically

Respond and Interpret

1. What questions would you like to ask Simon Wheeler?

2. (a)How does the narrator come to meet Simon Wheeler and to hear his story? (b)What can you infer about the narrator's attitude toward Wheeler?

3. (a)Why does Wheeler call Smiley "the curiosest man"? (b)What conclusions can you draw about Smiley's character, based on the tale Wheeler tells?

4. (a)What does Smiley entice the stranger to do? (b)What event or events determine the outcome of the encounter with the stranger? Explain your answer.

Analyze and Evaluate

5. Why do you think Wheeler tells his listener about the mare and bull pup first, before focusing on the frog?

6. Who is the main character in this story? Explain.

7. (a)In this selection, one story serves as a frame for another story. Which story is the frame? (b)Why might Twain have chosen this structure?

Connect

8. **Big Idea** Regionalism How does Twain capture the flavor of the Old West in this story?

9. **Connect to Today** Think of some humorous stories, movies, or television shows you know. How does Twain's brand of humor compare with theirs?

Literary Element Dialect

Twain uses **dialect** to evoke the region and the people he is writing about, as in this example: "He ketched a frog one day, and took him home, and said he cal'klated to edercate him. . . ."

1. What words in the example above does Wheeler pronounce differently from Standard English?

2. What is the difference between Wheeler's language and the narrator's? What does this difference suggest about them?

Reading Strategy Analyze Comic Devices

Mark Twain first achieved fame as a western humorist, and his humor is irresistible. He once wrote, "The humorous story may be spun out to great length and may wander around as much as it pleases, and arrive nowhere in particular."

1. Does this story fit Twain's description of a comic story?

2. What elements of humor in this story do you find most effective?

Vocabulary Practice

Practice with Word Origins Studying the etymology, or origins, of a word can help you understand its meaning. Create a chart with the headings *Word, Definition, Etymology*. Fill it in with information on the vocabulary words from the selection. Use a dictionary for help.

garrulous   conjecture   dilapidated
interminable   enterprising

 Writing

Write a Story In a few paragraphs, finish Wheeler's story about the "yaller one-eyed cow," making sure to reflect Twain's use of regional dialect and humor. Refer to your web diagram from page 497 to review how Twain creates humor.

LOG ON ▶ **Literature** Online

Selection Resources For Selection Quizzes, eFlashcards, and Reading-Writing Connection activities, go to glencoe.com and enter QuickPass code GLA9800u4.

MARK TWAIN **503**

Reading Strategy

1. Yes, because Wheeler's tale has no real purpose. It recounts a number of incidents in a meandering way and ends only because the narrator leaves.

2. Answers might include specific examples of exaggeration and parts of the characterization of Smiley.

Vocabulary

The etymology of the vocabulary follows: *garrulous*: Latin *garrire* means "to chatter"; *interminable*: Latin *interminabilis* means "not (in-) relating to or making boundaries (-terminalis)"; *conjecture*: Latin *conjectura* means "guess"; *enterprising*: Middle English *enterpris* means "to undertake"; *dilapidated*: Latin *dīlapidāre* means "to demolish or destroy."

After You Read

Assess

1. Possible answers: Did Smiley really exist? What happened to Smiley's one-eyed cow?

2. (a) The narrator's friend tells him to call on Wheeler to ask after Leonidas W. Smiley. (b) Wheeler is boring, ignorant.

3. (a) Smiley will take either side of a bet. (b) He is obsessed with gambling and is insensitive.

4. (a) Enter a frog-jumping contest (b) The stranger weights the frog.

5. Wheeler wants to establish Smiley's gambling obsession and his use of animals and tricks.

6. Simon Wheeler, the one who tells funny stories about Smiley

7. (a) The narrator's story about meeting Wheeler (b) He can comment on the story and contrast both speakers' language.

8. In his depiction of Wheeler, a westerner who loves to talk

9. Students may mention the use of exaggeration in current films and characters whose dialect may seem out of place.

> 📁 **For additional assessment, see Assessment Resources, pp. 161–162.**

Literary Element

1. *ketched* ("caught"), *cal'klated* ("calculated"), and *edercate* ("educate")

2. Wheeler speaks a regional dialect and the narrator Standard English with a large vocabulary. The narrator is more educated.

⚡ Writing

Students should imitate Wheeler's dialect and create an exaggerated event involving Smiley's gambling and ability to cooperate with animals.

503

Focus

Summary

As a riverboat pilot, Mark Twain came to know the Mississippi River intimately. He began to view the river as a road to navigate, not as the romantic natural phenomenon he had seen before.

 For activities related to this selection, see Unit 4 Teaching Resources Book, pp. 33–44.

Teach

View the Art ★

Steamboats were invented in the late 1700s and came into regular use in the early 1800s on rivers that included the Mississippi. **Ask:** How does this picture show both the river's romantic aspects and its practical uses? *(Students may say that the picture shows boats using the river for transportation and that the shadows give it a mystical appearance.)*

Readability Scores

Dale-Chall: 7.7
DRP: 63
Lexile: 1130

Selection Skills

from

Two Views of the River

Mark Twain

Before You Read

Literary Element Analogy

Writers use **analogies** to make experiences more vivid for the reader or to explain unfamiliar things by comparing them to familiar things. As you read, ask yourself, What analogy does Twain use in this memoir about his experiences as a riverboat pilot? What feelings does this comparison evoke?

Reading Strategy Compare and Contrast Language

Twain's first two sentences in this part of *Life on the Mississippi* suggest a contrast: ". . . I had made a valuable acquisition. But I had lost something, too." As you read, ask, What diction, or choice of words, does Twain use to develop this contrast?

1 Now when I had mastered the language of this water and had come to know every trifling feature that bordered the great river as familiarly as I knew the letters of the alphabet, I had made a valuable acquisition. But I had lost something, too. I had lost something which could never be restored to me while I lived. All the grace, the beauty, the poetry had gone out of the majestic river! I still keep in mind a certain wonderful sunset which I witnessed when steamboating was new to me. A broad expanse of the river was turned to blood; in the middle distance the red

hue brightened into gold, through which a solitary log came floating, black and conspicuous; in one place a long, slanting mark lay sparkling upon the water; in another the surface was broken by boiling, tumbling rings, that were as many-tinted as an opal; where the ruddy flush was faintest, was a smooth spot that was covered with graceful circles and radiating lines, ever so delicately traced; the shore on our left was densely wooded, and the somber shadow that fell from this forest was broken in one place by a long, ruffled trail that shone like silver; and high

504 UNIT 4 REGIONALISM AND REALISM

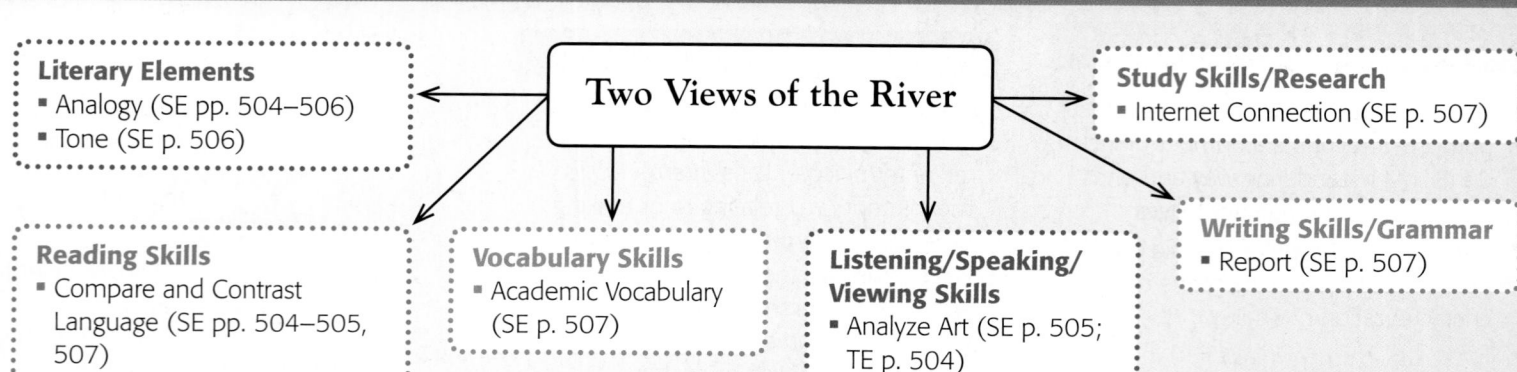

Literary Elements
- Analogy (SE pp. 504–506)
- Tone (SE p. 506)

Reading Skills
- Compare and Contrast Language (SE pp. 504–505, 507)

Vocabulary Skills
- Academic Vocabulary (SE p. 507)

Two Views of the River

Listening/Speaking/ Viewing Skills
- Analyze Art (SE p. 505; TE p. 504)

Study Skills/Research
- Internet Connection (SE p. 507)

Writing Skills/Grammar
- Report (SE p. 507)

above the forest wall a clean-stemmed dead tree waved a single leafy bough that glowed like a flame in the unobstructed splendor that was flowing from the sun. There were graceful curves, reflected images, woody heights, soft distances; and over the whole scene, far and near, the dissolving lights drifted steadily, enriching it, every passing moment, with new marvels of coloring.

I stood like one bewitched.[1] I drank it in, in a speechless rapture. The world was new to me, and I had never seen anything like this at home. But as I have said, a day came when I began to cease from noting the glories and the charms which the moon and the sun and the twilight wrought[2] upon the river's face; another day came when I ceased altogether to note them. Then, if that sunset scene had been repeated, I should have looked upon it without rapture, and should have commented upon it, inwardly, after this fashion: This sun means that we are going to have wind tomorrow; that floating log means that the river is rising, small thanks to it; that slanting mark on the water refers to a bluff reef which is going to kill somebody's steamboat one of these nights, if it keeps on stretching out like that; those tumbling "boils" show a dissolving bar and a changing channel there; the lines and circles in the slick water over yonder are a warning that that troublesome place is shoaling up[3] dangerously; that silver streak in the shadow of the forest is the "break" from a new snag, and he has located himself in the very best place he could have found to fish for steamboats; that tall dead tree, with a single living branch, is not going to last long, and then how is a body ever going to get through this blind place at night without the friendly old landmark?

No, the romance and the beauty were all gone from the river. All the value any feature of it had for me now was the amount of usefulness

---

1. *Bewitched* means "captivated" or "entranced."
2. *Wrought* means "created."
3. To *shoal up* means "to become shallow."

2 Compare and Contrast Language *How has Twain's perspective of the tree changed?*

Mark Twain on Ship Deck, March 15, 1901.

View the Art This photo shows Twain in a reflective mood on a voyage. How do you think he might have been feeling when the photo was taken? What might he have been doing? ★

it could furnish toward compassing the safe piloting of a steamboat. Since those days, I have pitied doctors from my heart. What does the lovely flush in a beauty's cheek mean to a doctor but a "break" that ripples above some deadly disease? Are not all her visible charms sown thick with what are to him the signs and symbols of hidden decay? Does he ever see her beauty at all, or doesn't he simply view her professionally, and comment upon her unwholesome condition all to himself? And doesn't he sometimes wonder whether he has gained most or lost most by learning his trade? ✎

Analogy *What do doctors and riverboat pilots have in common?* **3**

MARK TWAIN **505**

Teach

Big Idea 1

Regionalism Say: Keep this question in mind as you read: How does Twain capture the world of the Mississippi River in this excerpt? (*Students may notice his vivid details.*)

Reading Strategy 2

Compare and Contrast Language Answer: *Twain no longer perceives the tree as something beautiful. It has become only a useful landmark for navigation.*

Literary Element 3

Analogy Answer: *Their training and experience blind them to beauty.*

View the Photograph ★

Answer: *He may have been reflecting on his life, travels, and literary success, or thinking about his next literary endeavor.*

Advanced Learners/Pre-AP

DIFFERENTIATED INSTRUCTION

Identify the Theme Remind students that the theme is the central idea or message. Rather than state themes directly, authors may imply them through elements such as diction, images, and structure. **Ask:** What message do you think Twain may be trying to express in this essay? (*Students may say that knowledge and experience result in both losses and gains.*) **Say:** Identify details in the passage that support the theme. Include examples of word choice and imagery. (*Students may say that once Twain mastered the river, he had "made a valuable acquisition"; however, he notes that "I had lost something which could never be restored to me while I lived." He suggests that he gained practical knowledge of the river but lost appreciation for its beauty.*)

Point out the similarities in the structures of the first and second paragraphs. Discuss the effect of connecting a long string of images with semicolons to describe the river in both paragraphs. **Ask:** Why does Twain use a similar structure but very different diction and images? (*Students may say that Twain wants to show that he has changed but that the river has not.*)

After You Read

Assess

1. Twain was perceptive, sensitive to beauty, realistic, and introspective.

2. (a) The "language" includes the details that make the river seem beautiful but also signal danger. (b) As with a foreign language, it takes skill to "read" the river correctly.

3. (a) Twain refers to the glorious impression the river makes on an observer, as when a sunset turns it blood-red and gold. (b) As a riverboat pilot, Twain must look out for anything that will imperil his journey. The river's beautiful features could signal disaster.

4. (a) Technical terms include *bluff reef, bar, channel,* and *shoaling up.* (b) He includes these terms to show that he views the river as a trained professional. The terms add credibility to his memoir.

5. Students should support their views with evidence and note that Twain lost his rapture but gained valuable knowledge.

6. Twain's main purpose was to examine a defining moment in his own life and to convey that learning a skill entails both gain and loss.

7. Possible answer: No, he makes the job sound difficult and dangerous.

8. Navigating the Mississippi River takes skill, experience, and an eye for the traps that lie beneath its beauty.

9. As a riverboat pilot, Twain visited many towns and met different people. Twain tried to capture the dialect and setting of what he heard and saw so that his readers and audiences could share in his travels and experiences.

After You Read

Respond and Think Critically

Respond and Interpret

1. What are your impressions of Mark Twain's personality?

2. (a)What is "the language of this water" that Twain masters? (b)Why does he suggest that learning how to navigate the river is like mastering a foreign language?

3. (a)What does Twain mean by "the romance and the beauty" of the river? (b)Why does he lose the ability to see these special qualities forever?

4. (a)What terms does Twain use that would be familiar mainly to riverboat pilots or people living along the river? (b)Why does Twain include these terms in this memoir?

Analyze and Evaluate

5. Do you think that Twain gained more or lost more by learning the trade of a riverboat pilot?

6. What do you think was Twain's main purpose for writing this memoir?

7. Does Twain make the job of riverboat pilot sound appealing?

Connect

8. **Big Idea** Regionalism What did you learn about the challenges of life on the Mississippi?

9. **Connect to the Author** How did Twain's travels and experiences as a riverboat pilot affect his writing?

Literary Element Analogy

SAT Skills Practice

1. By concluding this section with an analogy, Twain
   (A) appeals to the widest possible audience
   (B) confesses that he suffers from a grave illness
   (C) ennobles the profession of riverboat pilot
   (D) expresses regret at not becoming a doctor
   (E) emphasizes his deep sense of loss

2. Which of the following would have been the best substitute for the profession of doctor in Twain's analogy?
   (A) farmer due to the need to anticipate problems in nature
   (B) musician due to the long training and practice required
   (C) train engineer due to the exposure to different landscapes
   (D) stagecoach driver due to the transportation of goods and people
   (E) factory worker due to the repetitive labor involved

Review: Tone

As you learned in Unit One, **tone** is the attitude that a writer expresses toward his or her subject matter. Tone is conveyed through elements such as word choice, punctuation, sentence structure, and figures of speech. A writer's tone may convey a variety of attitudes, such as sympathy, objectivity, or humor.

Partner Activity Meet with a classmate and discuss the tone of Twain's memoir. Fill in a chart like the one below with elements from the story that convey tone. Based on these elements, list the tone of the memoir at the top.

Tone:		
word choice	sentence structure	figures of speech

Literary Element

1. **E** is the correct answer because the analogy with a familiar profession helps readers understand the loss he feels.

2. **A** is the correct answer because the analogy is meant to express Twain's sadness at not seeing the beauty in nature after being trained to look for problems.

Review: Tone

Twain's tone is resigned and a little sad.

Progress Check

Can students analyze analogies?

If No → See Unit 4 Teaching Resources Book, p. 39.

Reading Strategy — Compare and Contrast Language

In this section of *Life on the Mississippi*, Twain describes how his perspective of the river shifted from the poetic to the practical as he learned the trade of a riverboat pilot.

1. What words in the first paragraph capture "the romance and the beauty" of the river?
2. What words in the second paragraph convey a practical view of the river?

Academic Vocabulary

*Mark Twain captures the character of a **region** in his writings about life along the Mississippi River.*

Region is an academic word. More familiar words that are similar in meaning are *area, territory,* and *province.* To further explore the meaning of this word, answer the questions below.

1. What traits of the people of the Mississippi River **region** does Mark Twain depict in his writings?
2. How do the environmental aspects of a **region** define the character of its inhabitants?

For more on academic vocabulary, see pages 53–54.

Research and Report

 Internet Connection

Assignment People still travel the Mississippi River by boat, just as in Twain's time. Use the Internet to research a short stretch of the river. Then use the computer to design a travel brochure describing a boat trip in that area. Include the distance traveled, cardinal (north, south, east, and west) and ordinal (northeast, southeast, northwest, and southwest) directions of travel, landmarks, and a map or photos.

Get Ideas Focus on choosing a manageable section of the river. For example, you might research the region known as the "Mississippi Delta" (the section between the cities of Memphis and Vicksburg, known especially for its connection to music). Once you have determined your focus, give your brochure an appropriate title.

EXAMPLE:

Visit the Mississippi Delta
∾ Home of the Blues ∾

Then, using search terms related to your particular focus, do your Internet research.

Research Strategies As you gather your information, carefully evaluate it for objectivity and reliability. For example, Web sites operated by the National Park Service or state tourism boards would be reliable sources of information. Keep a list of your sources.

Report Once you have gathered your information, use the computer to create your travel brochure. Make an effective use of typefaces and graphics.

 Literature Online

Selection Resources For Selection Quizzes, eFlashcards, and Reading-Writing Connection activities, go to glencoe.com and enter QuickPass code GLA9800u4.

MARK TWAIN **507**

After You Read

Assess

Reading Strategy

1. *grace, beauty, poetry, majestic,* and *sparkling*
2. *kill, warning, troublesome, dangerously,* and *blind place*

Progress Check

Can students compare and contrast language?

If No → See Unit 4 Teaching Resources Book, p. 40.

Academic Vocabulary

1. Twain captures the community of mining camp workers and their pastime of telling tales.
2. The environment defines the types of industry that exist there. People in the Old West and the Mississippi region mined in camps and transported goods along the river, defining their belief in hard work and camaraderie.

 For additional assessment, see Assessment Resources, pp. 163–164.

Research and Report

Use these criteria when evaluating students' travel brochures:

- Did the student focus on a manageable and identifiable portion of the Mississippi?
- Did the student identify a key feature or characteristic of the region to promote?
- Did the student use reliable and appropriate Internet sources?
- Did the student effectively use the computer in laying out the brochure?
- Did the student use descriptive language to entice visitors?

For grammar practice, see Unit 4 Teaching Resources Book, p. 42.

Focus

Summary

The article begins with the writer's noting how difficult it is to see the Mississippi River from the ground. As she explores the river and its communities more closely, she discovers its unique personality and her poignant desire to preserve a rich history. While she discovers terrible poverty in towns abandoned by industry, she also finds economic development through tourism and historic recreation.

> For activities related to this selection, see Unit 4 Teaching Resources Book, pp. 45–53.

Teach

Reading Strategy | 1

Clarify Meaning Review the two Preview questions with students, making sure that they understand each one. Then point out strategies for building meaning, such as using subheads to identify main ideas, defining unfamiliar words to clarify sentence meanings, and examining visuals and their captions to gain understanding. Have students create a graphic organizer where they can list questions and answers.

Readability Scores

Dale-Chall: 7.1
DRP: 62
Lexile: 1120

Learning Objectives

For pages 508–513

In studying this text, you will focus on the following objectives:

Reading:
Clarifying meaning.
Analyzing informational text.
Using text features.

Set a Purpose for Reading

As you read, ask, How have communities along the Mississippi changed since Mark Twain's time?

Preview the Article

1. What have you already learned about life on the Mississippi from reading Twain's work?

2. Read the article's section headings. What clues do these provide about the content?

Reading Strategy Clarify Meaning

When you **clarify the meaning** of a text, you reread individual sections or paragraphs for deeper understanding. As your read, create a chart like the one started below.

1

Questions	Answers
What does this section mean?	
How does this relate to the main idea?	

TIME

Life Along the
Mississippi

By NANCY GIBBS

UNLESS YOU ARE DRIVING ACROSS IT OR FLYING OVER it or floating down it, it is hard to see the actual Mississippi. Anyone who had anything to do with the river discovered long ago that this huge continental drainpipe was too powerful to leave alone. So the great engineers designed the levees and locks and dams that reduced the number of ships that sank and towns that vanished. But their work also hid the river behind its walls and left the rest to the imagination.

Aside from Mark Twain's *Huckleberry Finn*, the imagination may be the best guide for exploring the Mississippi River. Otherwise you need both a boat and a car, maybe a canoe and a bicycle too, for the skinny inlets and alleys along the way, and a lot of time and patience. We could at best splash in it a little, to see what it felt like and what we might learn—and unlearn—by stopping along the way. It was worth remembering Huck Finn's lesson: The river is the sanctuary; the shore is where you get into trouble.

In a country where travelers lament that every town looks the same—Where's Taco Bell? Where's Home Depot?—it's easy to assume that no region is really distinct anymore. We're all online now, and even in Baton Rouge, Louisiana, a local observes, the kids don't say "y'all" anymore. They say, "you guys," just like on TV.

Reading Practice

 SPIRAL REVIEW **Text Structure** Have students read the title and the first subhead of the article. **Ask:** What do you think the main focus of this article will be? *(Students may say that the main focus will be people living near the Mississippi.)* Point out that text made to stand out in some way, such as the sentence printed across the picture on page 509, also gives the reader clues to the main ideas in an article. Have students read the sentence. **Ask:** What issue or problem is this article likely to analyze? *(Students should note that the article will explain some of the economic issues that trouble the people living on the Mississippi.)*

Let us take you on a trip down America's great river, where we explore the troubles and triumphs of people trying to catch up with the new economy.

TIME

Teach

Big Idea   2

Regionalism Remind students that Mark Twain grew up in a town on the Mississippi River. "Life Along the Mississippi" shows that many of the characteristics Twain wrote about are still to be found in the Mississippi River region. There is still a strong sense of community and a divide between white people and African Americans. Ask students to suggest ways that the region probably has changed since Twain's time.

Heading South

2 So we were surprised, everywhere we went. The more you explore the communities along the river, and the farther south you travel down into the Mississippi Delta, more than one thing becomes clear: This is still a land unto itself, defined by its colorful, bloody past. It is a land apart from the region that cradles the early stretches of the river itself,

the Midwestern states of Minnesota, Wisconsin, and Iowa. While these states have reinvented themselves three times in a half century, moving from agriculture to industry to high technology, many communities in the Mississippi Delta have wrestled with the explosion of progress and prosperity.

The South is where the country's two wars were fought: the Civil

War and, a century later, the battle for civil rights. "Of course the war is not over," says our 87-year-old guide in Vicksburg, Mississippi. Now there is a quieter conflict raging, not on the broad political stage but in the particulars of individual lives. Along the river, people hear about the new economy, but they don't have a ticket to get there. Information superhighway? Progress

Cultural History ☆

Two Wars The Civil War lasted from 1861 to 1865 and caused terrible devastation in the American South. A key issue was the institution of slavery, which was entrenched in the Southern economy and opposed by most Northerners. Conflict between white Americans and African Americans continued with the Civil Rights Movement of the 1950s and 1960s. A key component of this movement was the passage of the Civil Rights Act of 1964, which outlawed discrimination on the basis of race.

LIFE ALONG THE MISSISSIPPI   **509**

Approaching Level
UNIVERSAL ACCESS

Established Have students read the first section of the article, stopping at the first subhead. Make sure that students are aware of the article's connection to the theme of Regionalism. **Ask:** What details suggest that the country no longer has distinct regions? (Students may say that many businesses are the same across the country or that young people are less likely to use regional expressions now.)

Have students make and support a prediction about whether Gibbs's article will explain what makes the towns along the Mississippi distinctive. (Students may point out that the text across the photo on the second page of the article suggests that the southern Mississippi region has distinct-ive troubles and triumphs.)

509

TIME

Reading Strategy | 1

Clarify Meaning Have students reread the text under the subhead "A Terrible Beauty." **Ask:** How has the farming industry changed since Mark Twain's lifetime? *(Fewer people are needed to farm the land.)* Upon what do local economies now depend? *(Towns rely on factories for jobs.)* What is the main idea of this section? *(The main idea is that parts of the Mississippi River region are very poor.)*

Cultural History ☆

Mississippi Like its regional neighbor Arkansas, Mississippi has struggled economically. The state's economic growth has not kept up with that of the rest of the nation, and it appears near the bottom of many economic and social indexes.

In 2005 Hurricane Katrina devastated several communities in Mississippi—particularly on the Biloxi-Gulfport coastline, where 90 percent of the buildings were destroyed.

---

here is a back road, winding, scenic, and personal, but slow by the standards of a country that hurries into the future.

Even progress on race comes in the most intimate gestures: Last December, as Elnora Littleton in Rosedale, Mississippi, tells it, she became the first African American woman in those parts ever to preach at a white man's funeral. In this part of the country, she says, it is a milestone worth noting. "I made history," she says.

A Terrible Beauty

In the South, the river is the color of *café au lait* (coffee with milk). Down toward the mouth of the Mississippi, the land was formed of sedimentary deposits from farther upriver, including the rich topsoil blown from the hills of Wyoming into the Missouri and acres of Kansas prairie swallowed by flooding and swept downstream. Mark Twain's characters claimed that a man who drank the water could grow corn in his stomach. You know all this, and yet you are unprepared for the Delta, otherworldly and flat, the best place to grow cotton on this earth. It was once a hellish jungle, cleared by the backbreaking labor of enslaved persons and sharecroppers. It's like a wet western Kansas—beautiful, flat, and fertile.

The difference, of course, is that when faced with the shrinking labor needs of modern farming, the good people of western Kansas simply moved away in search of better lives elsewhere. While this happened in the Delta as well, a large number of people chose to stay in one of the poorest regions in the U.S. The average family of four here has an income of $16,538,

Riverfront architecture in the Mississippi River town of Alton, Illinois, reflects the river's colorful past.

slightly more than half the national average. In Mississippi County, Arkansas, 35% of kids live in poverty, and 40% of adults don't have a high school diploma.

If the new economy has not yet flowed downstream, there are lots of people who will tell you no one

is even looking for it here. Whether or not a town stays afloat has a lot to do with whether the local factory is still open—the fate of the town rests in the hands of Continental Concrete, Sparta Printing, the Mississippi Lime Co., Tower Rock Quarry, Ralston

510 UNIT 4 REGIONALISM AND REALISM

Writing Practice

Cause and Effect Have students examine the causes and effects of the changes occurring in towns along the Mississippi River. **Ask,** According to the author, what has caused the deterioration of these towns? *(Factory closures, discrimination)* What are the effects of the declining economies in the towns? *(Although there are no jobs, many people*

have not moved away creating high levels of poverty.) Have students write a three- to five-paragraph essay explaining the causes that have led to the current situation in towns along the Mississippi and how the people of these towns have been affected. Have them analyze the connections between the causes and effects, using support from the article.

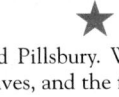

Purina, and Pillsbury. When one of these leaves, and the farms start to fail, an entire town can shrivel and die. Laid-off workers lose their livelihood. Retired workers lose their health insurance.

Town and Out?

We were left asking the same question all these towns face as the ground shifts beneath their feet: What's it going to be? Change? Or die? Is there maybe another choice? The towns individually try to reinvent themselves, and the region as a whole tries to reinvent itself. As you move farther south, many towns don't have the roads or infrastructure to recruit some big new car plant or distribution center. The idea of luring a nice little software company is years away.

Suppose you have lost your brickyard, and the tugs no longer stop at your town, and the interstate has drawn the megastores, and even the schools and churches move away, and the young people leave, and Main Street is on life support. The Chamber of Commerce gets together and daydreams: What would it take to bring life back to this town? Or do we just roll up the streets and move on?

For many towns, the answer is to attract tourists. They say, if we can't find some big new employer to bring the new economy to town, how about reverting to the old economy—the very old one? In this polished and pasteurized vision, Main Street becomes a theme park of 19th-century life, with women wearing petticoats and shops selling candlesticks and lemon drops. Kimmswick, Missouri, was almost dead after the lumberyard and the brickyard closed—until 7-Up heiress Luci Anna Ross began buying up collapsing buildings and renting them out as gift shops and bed-and-breakfasts. Now there is the Kimmswick Korner gift shop and lots of places to buy apple butter or have your horse reshod. The annual Apple Butter Festival gets

40,000 people. More than 100,000 come to Hannibal, Missouri, for Tom Sawyer Days on the Fourth of July weekend. Disney even sent a representative to Hannibal to learn how to re-create Tom Sawyer for its theme parks. Having developed everyplace else, Americans are homesteading the past.

Inventing History/Prettifying the Past

But because this re-creation of the past is for tourists, it's an airbrushed souvenir postcard. You see only the good side of a town's history—or a distorted version of that history. In Nauvoo, Illinois, the Mormons celebrate their 19th-century village life as they rebuild the town and its temple as a pilgrimage spot. Glossed over are the bloody religious battles that led to their being pillaged and expelled in the first place. The hotel owner in Kimmswick says the town's latest scheme is reenactments of the Civil War battle there. Was there ever really a Battle of Kimmswick? He concedes that it was, in his words, "just a skirmish that involved three Confederate soldiers hiding in a cave." Whatever.

This sort of thing is what social critics denounce as the strip-mining of history to market a version of the past that has a special appeal. This is not re-creating the past, they say, so much as distorting it. Back when life in these towns was real, it wasn't always quaint—yet quaint is what sells now. Create a time that feels sweet and simple, and you don't have to smell the horses or die of cholera.

Cairo's "Main" Dilemma

If you want to visit the most unusual theme park in America, try the

LIFE ALONG THE MISSISSIPPI **511**

TIME

Teach

Reading Strategy

Clarify Meaning Point out that the final sentences of an article often focus on the most important ideas. Students can clarify meaning by reading the final sentences and connecting them to the text they have already read.

View the Photograph ★

Many forms of American music originated in the South, including the blues, which many see as the parent of jazz and rock. The blues can be traced to songs and shouts that enslaved Africans used in the fields and to the "down-home" songs of the Mississippi Delta.

Informational Text

IN FORT MADISON, IOWA, a town that has found a way to revive downtown, residents gather for a band concert.

Main Street in Cairo, Illinois. It is a water slide of desolation, one abandoned building after another, with 90% of the storefronts dark and boarded over.

If Cairo is a ghost town, it was the fight for justice that killed it. "It used to be called Little Chicago," says Deputy Mayor Judson Childs, walking a couple of visitors to the town center, where civil rights battles flared in the 1960s. African Americans boycotted stores that discriminated; whites retaliated with violence; federal authorities intervened. But most whites chose to shut down their stores and leave Cairo rather than integrate. Over time the streets of Cairo became empty. Now if you want gas, you have to get it before 8 at night. To shop or go to a movie means driving 30 or 40 miles into Kentucky or Missouri. A woman in her late 20s sadly remarks, "This town is trapped in the past."

Maybe it's natural to try to market Cairo. Just turn the 1872 cus-tomhouse into a museum, get a big grant to repave the center of town with cobblestones and fake streetcar lines, peddle the old glory days of the big river town, and hope no one asks how it died. There is lots of history here, all fascinating but not pretty. So some residents aren't sure that the buses will ever come rolling in or the hotels ever reopen. "You ask the average person on the street what Cairo needs," says Mayor James Wilson, "and they'll say a McDonald's and a Wal-Mart."

512 UNIT 4 REGIONALISM AND REALISM

Vocabulary Practice

SPIRAL REVIEW **Compound Words** Remind students that a compound word is made up of two or more smaller words. Compounds can be categorized as open, such as *ice cream;* closed, such as *headache;* and hyphenated, such as *well-known.* Readers can infer their meanings from the words that make up the compound. Ask students to find examples of compound words throughout this selection, to categorize them, and to infer their meanings. *(Examples include* theme park *[open];* downstream *[closed]; and* laid-off *[hyphenated].)*

512

Home of the Blues

The future of Clarksdale, Mississippi, is also tied to its past. This Delta town is trying to find its way by reengineering its cash crop, the blues. There is the newly reopened Delta Blues Museum, which honors such hometown heroes as Charley Patton, Son House, Robert Johnson, Muddy Waters, and John Lee Hooker. The history of the music is the story of the people who invented it and the suffering that created it. Without African American workers to clear the thickly wooded Delta plain and sharecroppers to pick the cotton, there would have been no plantation economy; without African Americans to sing the work songs and field chants and play diddley bows and mail-order guitars, there would be no Delta blues.

Without the blues, there would be no rock 'n' roll to conquer the world and help sell all those burgers and jeans. The poorest, most oppressed people in America created its richest cultural legacy, and that, of course, yields all kinds of lessons for anyone willing to listen closely.

"Are you going to find anything good to write about?" people ask again and again. They are aware of how things must look to a bunch of outsiders. The natives know that much of what is great and sweet and honorable in these places never makes headlines. The Cairo deputy fire chief will tell you how many people appear in an instant when a windstorm sweeps through town and smashes a block of homes. Anyplace you have good friends is a place worth staying. Here and elsewhere, there are big groups of

people—ministers and teachers and store owners and bureaucrats—who are prepared to give all their time and muscle to putting things right, making a place better. To the outsider, it would seem so much easier just to pick up and move on. Trying to stay, and to change, is an act of faith.

**–Updated 2005,
from TIME, July 10, 2000**

Respond and Think Critically

Respond and Interpret

1. Write a brief summary of the main ideas in this article before you answer the following questions. For help on writing a summary, see page 79.

2. How did this article make you feel about the situation that many of the small towns along the Mississippi face?

3. (a)What is the "new economy" the author refers to? (b)Why are the communities along the Mississippi not yet a part of this?

4. (a)What kinds of businesses have found success in many of the small towns along the Mississippi River? (b)Why might the towns want to "prettify" their past?

Analyze and Evaluate

5. (a)Return to the graphic organizer you created to clarify meaning. What ideas does the author express in the subsection "Home of the Blues"? (b)Why does the author claim that the past is connected to the future of the Mississippi Delta?

6. (a)How would you describe Gibbs's tone, or attitude toward her subject, in this article? Support your response with details from the text. (b)How might this **tone** contribute to an overall **bias**, or inclination toward a certain opinion?

Connect

7. Compare and contrast Mark Twain's and Nancy Gibbs's portrayals of the Mississippi Delta region. What are their similarities and differences?

LIFE ALONG THE MISSISSIPPI **513**

Assess

1. Students should refer to article subheadings to help them organize and write summaries.

2. Answers will vary.

3. (a) A high-tech, global economy (b) Area towns are far from interstate highways and are damaged by local industry failures.

4. (a) Tourist-oriented businesses (b) Tourism thrives when towns focus on their "quaint" history.

5. (a) She describes how a blues museum has increased tourism in Clarksdale, Mississippi. She also notes African American contributions to the local economy and culture. (b) Small towns promote their past in order to gain economic prosperity.

6. (a) Frank, skeptical, and sometimes disdainful, as evidenced by expressions such as "Americans are homesteading the past" (b) Gibbs seems biased against some economic development.

7. Twain lived by the Mississippi; Gibbs is an outside observer.

 For additional assessment, see Assessment Resources, pp. 165–166.

English Learners

 UNIVERSAL ACCESS

Intermediate Identify some of the figurative and idiomatic expressions in the section called "Home of the Blues" and help English learners decode them. Write the following expressions on the board:

- future . . . is tied to its past
- its cash crop, the blues
- plantation economy
- play diddley bows and mail-order guitars

- no rock 'n' roll to conquer the world and help sell all those burgers and jeans
- never makes headlines
- an act of faith

Help students by having them volunteer the literal meanings of these expressions and by then discussing with them how the literal meaning has migrated into a figurative meaning. Explain, for example, that a word such as *tie* can be used not only to mean

"to fasten with string," but also to mean "to bind together in a relationship." A diddley bow is a homemade stringed instrument. Have students consult a dictionary for the meanings of any unfamiliar words.

Before You Read

Focus

**Selection Focus
Transparency 32**

**Daily Language Practice
Transparency 44**

Or describe a basic and familiar philosophy of living, such as "Live and let live" or "Live every day to the fullest."

Ask: What are some philosophies of living that you have heard? Have students consider, as they read, how the philosophies expressed in these poems are similar to and different from philosophies they know.

Before You Read
Lucinda Matlock and
Fiddler Jones

Meet **Edgar Lee Masters**
(1868–1950)

Edgar Lee Masters's *Spoon River Anthology* took early twentieth-century readers by surprise. Published in 1915, the anthology is a collection of free-verse first-person monologues spoken by the people of a small Midwestern town, who are now "sleeping on the hill." Masters called the poems epitaphs.

The realism and irony expressed in *Spoon River Anthology* were at odds with the romantic and sentimental poetry popular at the time. Though some critics questioned this new type of poetry, the book sold thousands of copies, is still in print, and has even been adapted for the stage. After the anthology's publication, Ezra Pound wrote of Masters, "At last! America has discovered a poet."

> "It is all very well, but for
> myself I know
> I stirred certain vibrations in
> Spoon River
> Which are my true epitaph,
> more lasting than stone."
>
> —Edgar Lee Masters
> "Percival Sharp"

From Small Town to Supreme Court Masters grew up in the small Illinois towns of Petersburg and Lewistown. As a boy, he spent time at his grandfather's farm, where he fished, rode horses, and read Charles Dickens and Ralph Waldo Emerson. After he graduated from high school, he worked as an apprentice for a local printer and attended Knox College for one year.

Although Masters wanted to be a writer, his father pushed him toward a career in law. Masters eventually took up both pursuits and established his first law office in Chicago in 1893. He married Helen M. Jenkins in 1898, and they had three children. Masters was a successful attorney and argued some cases before the U.S. Supreme Court.

Literary Success Masters's first book, *A Book of Verses*, was published in 1898, and he published a number of other poetry books, a collection of essays, and several plays over the next sixteen years. Through his writing, he became friends with Carl Sandburg and Harriet Monroe, the editor of *Poetry* magazine. Masters later separated from his family and moved to New York City. He married Elaine Coyne, a teacher, in 1926.

Spoon River Anthology was well received both critically and commercially. Masters was later awarded the Poetry Society of America Award, the Mark Twain silver medal, and the Shelley Memorial Award. By the end of his life, Masters had published more than fifty volumes, including poetry collections, plays, novels and biographies. *Spoon River*, however, remained his only literary success.

 Literature Online

Author Search For more about Edgar Lee Masters, go to glencoe.com and enter QuickPass code GLA9800u4.

514 UNIT 4 REGIONALISM AND REALISM

Selection Skills

Literary Elements
- Dramatic Monologue (SE pp. 515, 516, 518; TE p. 517)

```
Lucinda Matlock and
Fiddler Jones
```

Writing Skills/Grammar
- Write a Poem (SE p. 518)

Reading Skills
- Draw Conclusions About Character (SE pp. 515, 517, 518)

Vocabulary Skills
- Word Usage (SE pp. 515, 518)

Literature and Reading Preview

Connect to the Poems

If you had to sum up your life so far, what experiences would you focus on? What did those experiences mean to you? Discuss these questions with a partner or small group.

Build Background

When Masters read the epigrams from the *Greek Anthology*—an ancient collection of poems—he was struck by their brevity, wit, and irony. He decided to write a similar collection of free-verse epitaphs in the form of monologues. The result was *Spoon River Anthology*. Masters's characters were inspired by people he knew. Many of the monologues in *Spoon River Anthology* are related, so a complex history of numerous families unfolds.

Set Purposes for Reading

Big Idea Regionalism

As you read, ask yourself, What do these two poems reveal about the customs and lifestyle of the people in Masters's fictional Midwestern town?

Literary Element Dramatic Monologue

Each of these poems is a **dramatic monologue,** a form of dramatic poetry in which the speaker addresses a silent listener. The speaker in these poems is not Masters but a character he created. As you read the poems, ask yourself, What philosophy of life does each character express?

Reading Strategy Draw Conclusions About Character

When you **draw a conclusion,** you use various pieces of information to make a general statement about people, places, events, and ideas. As you read the poems, look for specific details about each speaker. These details can be the basis for a general statement about each speaker's character. You can use a chart like the one below to keep track of these details.

Learning Objectives

For pages 514–518

In studying these texts, you will focus on the following objectives:

Literary Study: Analyzing dramatic monologue.

Reading: Drawing conclusions about characters.

Writing: Writing a poem.

Vocabulary

repose (ri pōz′) *n.* relaxation; tranquility; eternal rest; p. 516 *Unafraid of death, the woman welcomed the idea of repose.*

degenerate (di jen′ ər it) *adj.* having declined in condition or character; deteriorated; p. 516 *Despite spending time in jail, the thief continued to live a degenerate lifestyle.*

ruinous (rōō′ i nəs) *adj.* causing ruin; destructive; p. 517 *The extreme weather in Alaska can have a ruinous effect on highways there.*

....

Tip: Word Usage When you encounter a new word, it might help you to answer a specific question about the word. Example: *How would someone look who is in a state of repose?* Someone in a state of **repose** would appear relaxed and calm.

EDGAR LEE MASTERS **515**

Before You Read

Focus

Summary

In "Lucinda Matlock," the speaker recounts her long, full family life, ending with her death at age 96. She observes that today's youngsters complain too much and fail to live fully.

In "Fiddler Jones," the speaker recalls his life as one in which music was always more important than getting other work done. He has no regrets about his life.

 For summaries in languages other than English, see Unit 4 Teaching Resources Book, pp. 54-59.

Vocabulary

Vocabulary Practice Help students better understand the new vocabulary words. **Ask:** Which vocabulary word best completes this sentence: He does not wish to be disturbed while in _____. *(repose)* Then have students state their own fill-in-the-blank sentences for classmates to complete. Work with students to discuss how each vocabulary word is used.

For additional context, see Glencoe Interactive Vocabulary CD-ROM.

 For additional vocabulary practice, see Unit 4 Teaching Resources Book, p. 62.

English Learners

DIFFERENTIATED INSTRUCTION

Intermediate Remind students that the poems they are about to read are written in free verse. Explain that free verse has no fixed meter, rhyme, line length, or stanza arrangement but is still poetry rather than prose by virtue of its rhythm and the pacing of words and ideas. Have English learners take turns reading all or parts of the poems aloud.

Ask: How did reading these poems differ from reading poems with rhymes? Why might free verse be particularly suited to a dramatic monologue, in which a speech is delivered to a silent listener? *(Students may say that free verse sounds like natural speech.)*

Teach

Big Idea | 1

Regionalism **Say:** How does Masters's description of Lucinda Matlock convey the character of Spoon River? *(Lucinda Matlock is an unpretentious rural woman who speaks plainly and works hard. These characteristics might also describe Spoon River.)*

(APPROACHING) Reread the poem and look for examples of how Lucinda speaks without elaborate descriptions, how she works hard without complaint, and how humble she seems.

Literary Element | 2

Dramatic Monologue
Answer: *One needs a positive attitude and a strong spirit to enjoy life.*

View the Art ★

A triptych (from the Greek words for *three* and *fold*) is a work of art presented in three panels. Typically the center panel is the largest and is connected to the outer panels by hinges. Many triptychs were created for religious buildings during the Renaissance.

For an audio recording of this selection, use Listening Library Audio CD-ROM.

Contemplating Life, 1903.
Richard Pfeiffer.

Lucinda Matlock

Edgar Lee Masters

I went to the dances at Chandlerville,
And played snap-out[1] at Winchester.
One time we changed partners,
Driving home in the moonlight of middle June,
5   And then I found Davis.
We were married and lived together for seventy years,
Enjoying, working, raising the twelve children,
Eight of whom we lost
Ere I had reached the age of sixty.
10 I spun, I wove, I kept the house, I nursed the sick,
I made the garden, and for holiday
Rambled over the fields where sang the larks,

And by Spoon River gathering many a shell,
And many a flower and medicinal weed—
15 Shouting to the wooded hills, singing to the green valleys.
At ninety-six I had lived enough, that is all,
And passed to a sweet **repose.**
What is this I hear of sorrow and weariness,
Anger, discontent and drooping hopes?
20 **Degenerate** sons and daughters,
Life is too strong for you—
It takes life to love Life.   **1**

Dramatic Monologue *What does this line tell you about the speaker's philosophy of life?*   **2**

Vocabulary

repose (ri pōz´) *n.* relaxation; tranquility; eternal rest
degenerate (di jen´ ər it) *adj.* having declined in condition or character; deteriorated

---

1. *Snap-out* (also known as crack-the-whip) is a game in which players link hands in a line and then run or skate so as to shake off those at the end of the line.

516   UNIT 4   REGIONALISM AND REALISM

Reading Practice

SPIRAL REVIEW **Take Notes** Remind students that customs are the traditional social practices in a society and that lifestyle is the way an individual lives. As students read the two poems, have them write down what each narrator does for leisure and what each does for work. Ask students to write down phrases that reveal each narrator's attitude toward life. Have students refer to the notes when drawing conclusions about the customs and lifestyles of the people in Masters's fictional Midwestern town.

Fiddler Jones

Edgar Lee Masters

Pop and the Boys, 1963. Thomas Hart Benton. Oil on canvas, 67.7 x 47.7 cm. Fundación Colección Thyssen-Bornemisza, Madrid, Spain.

The earth keeps some vibration going
There in your heart, and that is you.
And if the people find you can fiddle,
Why, fiddle you must, for all your life.
5   What do you see, a harvest of clover?
Or a meadow to walk through to the river?
The wind's in the corn; you rub your hands
For beeves[1] hereafter ready for market;
Or else you hear the rustle of skirts
10   Like the girls when dancing at Little Grove.
To Cooney Potter a pillar of dust
Or whirling leaves meant **ruinous** drouth;[2]
They looked to me like Red-Head Sammy
Stepping it off, to "Toor-a-Loor."[3]
15   How could I till my forty acres
Not to speak of getting more,
With a medley of horns, bassoons and piccolos
Stirred in my brain by crows and robins
And the creak of a wind-mill—only these?
20   And I never started to plow in my life
That some one did not stop in the road
And take me away to a dance or picnic.
I ended up with forty acres;
I ended up with a broken fiddle—
25   And a broken laugh, and a thousand memories,
And not a single regret.

---

1. *Beeves* is the plural form of *beef;* here, it refers to beef cattle.
2. A *drouth* (also *drought*) is a long period of dry weather.
3. *Toor-a-Loor* refers to a phrase in an Irish folk song.

> Draw Conclusions About Character *What do these details suggest about the speaker's character?*

> **Vocabulary**
>
> **ruinous** (roō′ i nəs) *adj.* causing ruin; destructive

EDGAR LEE MASTERS   **517**

Teach

Reading Strategy   3

Draw Conclusions About Characters **Answer:** *These details suggest that the character is an exuberant, gregarious person who took advantage of opportunities to have fun in life. They also suggest that he may have been irresponsible.*

View the Art

Thomas Hart Benton (1889–1975) lived in Missouri and is known for his paintings of the region. Many of his works feature laborers and everyday people at their daily work.

 To check students' understanding of the selection, see Unit 4 Teaching Resources Book, p. 63.

Progress Check

Can students draw conclusions about character?

If No → See Unit 4 Teaching Resources Book, p. 61.

Approaching Level

DIFFERENTIATED INSTRUCTION

Emerging Tell students that the speaker in each of these two poems is not the author but the title character. The thoughts and feelings expressed in the poems are those of the characters, and the words they use help convey their attitudes toward life. Have students reread lines 11–15 of "Lucinda Matlock." Point out words such as *holiday, sang, flower, shouting,* and *singing.* Explain that the words Lucinda Matlock uses help express how she feels about the life she has led. Ask students how they think she feels. (*Students may say that she thinks she has led a good life.*)

Established Have students reread lines 16 and 17 in "Lucinda Matlock." **Ask:** What words show that Lucinda Matlock accepts death without fear? (*"I had lived enough, that is all," "sweet repose"*)

After You Read

Assess

1. Answers will vary.
2. (a) She spent her life caring for her family. (b) *Joys:* family and nature; *sorrows:* losing children
3. (a) Contented and matter-of-fact (b) Serious and reprimanding—she disapproves of complainers.
4. (a) Some people see "a harvest of clover" but others "a meadow to walk through." Cooney Potter saw drought where Fiddler Jones saw dancing. (b) People's attitudes affect their perceptions.
5. (a) What is the key to your happiness? Did you ever feel that your life has been too hard? (b) "Keep life simple"; "enjoy the good and don't dwell on the bad."
6. (a) Be positive and enjoy life, even if your choices do not make you rich. (b) Possible answer: His philosophy is wise but might not work for those who must support others.
7. Possible answers: The characters would have had less peaceful lives in a city; philosophy, not place, defined these characters.
8. Masters could show a variety of perspectives in the small town by using many characters.

> For additional assessment, see Assessment Resources, pp. 167–168.

 Writing

Students should create a distinct speaker and address a specific life lesson in the poem each writes.

518

After You Read

Respond and Think Critically

Respond and Interpret

1. Have you ever known anyone whose outlook on life resembles that of Lucinda Matlock or Fiddler Jones? Explain.
2. (a) Describe how Lucinda Matlock spent her life. (b) What were her joys and her sorrows?
3. (a) Describe Lucinda's **tone**, or attitude toward her subject and audience, in lines 1–17. (b) How does her tone change in lines 18–22? What might you infer about her character from this change?
4. In lines 5–14 of "Fiddler Jones," Fiddler describes different ways of perceiving the same things. (a) Summarize these descriptions. (b) What point do you think he is trying to make?

Analyze and Evaluate

5. (a) If you could interview Lucinda Matlock, what questions would you ask about facing life's ups and downs? (b) How might she answer you?
6. (a) What is Fiddler's philosophy of life? (b) What do you think of Fiddler's philosophy? Explain.

Connect

7. **Big Idea** Regionalism In your opinion, how might Lucinda Matlock's and Fiddler Jones's philosophies be different if they had spent their lives in a busy city instead of a rural area?
8. **Connect to the Author** Why might Masters have used characters as the speakers in his poems rather than speaking in his own voice? Do you find this technique effective? Explain.

Literary Element Dramatic Monologue

The speakers in these poems want to share the lessons they have learned with their audience.

1. What general statement sums up the philosophy of life these two monologues share?
2. Do you think this work would be as effective in prose as it is in poetry? Explain your response.

Reading Strategy Draw Conclusions About Character

Review the notes you took for your chart on page 515. Then answer the following questions.

1. Why does Lucinda Matlock disapprove of the younger generation?
2. What do you think was Fiddler Jones's greatest joy?

 Literature Online

Selection Resources For Selection Quizzes, eFlash-cards, and Reading-Writing Connection acivities, go to glencoe.com and enter QuickPass code GLA9800u4.

Vocabulary Practice

Practice with Word Usage Respond to these statements to help you explore the meanings of vocabulary words from the selection.

1. Explain what you would be doing if you were in a deep **repose**.
2. Describe a **degenerate** lifestyle.
3. Give an example of a **ruinous** aspect of the Industrial Revolution.

Writing

Write a Poem Masters uses dramatic monologue to express a philosophy about life. Think of a life lesson you have learned and want to share with others. Write a dramatic monologue in which you create a speaker who explains that lesson to a silent listener. For your poem's title, use the name of the speaker in your poem.

Literary Element

1. Life is precious, and a positive attitude will improve its quality.
2. Answers will vary.

Reading Strategy

1. They do not appreciate being alive.
2. He enjoyed fiddling for people.

Vocabulary

1. Students should say that they would be relaxing or resting soundly.
2. Students may describe a lifestyle that demonstrates poor self-care or criminal activity.
3. Students may identify pollution or the negative effects of assembly-line labor on workers.

Meet **Willa Cather**

(1873–1947)

Readers best remember Willa Cather for her portrayal of the pioneer life and landscape. During the mid-twentieth century, the connection between Cather's writing and the prairie that inspired her began to undermine her literary status. Critics labeled her a regional writer, criticizing her for "escapism" and for romanticizing the past. Nonetheless, Cather's books have never gone out of print, and there has been a renewed interest in her work over the past few decades. She is now recognized as a writer who explored the complexities of American life and showed how the tendency to link one's life to the past adds meaning—though not always happiness—to life in the present.

> "So the country and I had it out together and by the end of the first autumn the shaggy grass country had gripped me with a passion that I have never been able to shake. It has been the happiness and curse of my life."
>
> —Willa Cather

The Vast Frontier Cather's family moved from the Shenandoah Valley of Virginia to rural Red Cloud, Nebraska, when she was nine. She remarked that she felt "a kind of erasure of personality" as she first encountered the Nebraskan prairie, a feeling that would later permeate the characters in her fiction. In Red Cloud, Cather gained insight into pioneer life and the intricate histories of her European immigrant neighbors. She learned French, German, Latin, and Greek, participated in plays, and attended local opera performances. In high school, she gained a reputation as both a remarkable student and a nonconformist. She enrolled at the University of Nebraska in 1891 and supported herself by writing literary reviews that won statewide recognition.

Returning East After graduating in 1895, Cather moved to Pittsburgh to begin editing for *Home Monthly*. She published her first book of poetry, *April Twilights*, in 1903 and one of stories, *The Troll Garden*, which includes "A Wagner Matinée," in 1905. The head of the progressive magazine *McClure's* was so impressed by the latter that he offered Cather a job in New York City. She became managing editor by 1908 but felt unfulfilled because her position left little time to work on her own writing. In 1911, at the urging of her friend and mentor Sarah Orne Jewett, Cather left journalism to write fiction exclusively.

Cather's memories of the vast prairie and the endurance of its people inspired *O Pioneers!* (1913), *Song of the Lark* (1915), and *My Ántonia* (1918). In her earlier stories, Cather focused on the desolation of pioneer life. In later works, however, she celebrated the prairie landscape and the powerful dreams and illusions of those who attempted to cultivate it. Cather is recognized for her complex treatment of human emotion, her understanding of darker American themes, and her carefully crafted writing style.

 Literature Online

Author Search For more about Willa Cather, go to glencoe.com and enter QuickPass code GLA9800u4.

WILLA CATHER **519**

Bellringer Options

Literature Launchers:
   Pre-Reading Videos DVD, Selection Launcher

Selection Focus Transparency 33

Daily Language Practice Transparency 46

Or play clips of music from different genres or different time periods **Ask:** What places, emotions, or sensations do you feel when you listen to this music?

As they read, students should keep in mind the power of music to evoke memories and emotions.

Interactive Read and Write

Other options for teaching this selection can be found in

- Interactive Read and Write for EL Students, pp. 159–170
- Interactive Read and Write for Approaching-Level Students, pp. 159–170
- Interactive Read and Write for On-Level Students, pp. 159–170

Selections Skill

Literary Elements
- Point of View (SE pp. 520, 522, 525, 526, 528)
- Voice (SE p. 528)

A Wagner Matinée

Writing Skills/Grammar
- Reflective Essay (SE p. 529)
- Absolute Phrases (SE p. 529)
- Imagery (TE p. 523)

Reading Skills
- Identify Sequence (SE pp. 520, 521, 524)
- Identify and Analyze Flashback (TE p. 521)
- Make Inferences (TE pp. 522)

Vocabulary Skills
- Analogies (SE p. 528)
- Adverbs (TE p. 520)

Listening/Speaking/Viewing Skills
- Analyze Art (SE p. 523; TE p. 521)
- Analyze Music (TE p. 525)

Before You Read

Focus

Summary

A young man named Clark takes his visiting aunt, Georgiana, to a concert. Georgiana is a music teacher who has not been to Boston or heard a concert since she married and moved to a remote Nebraska farm many years ago. She has arrived in Boston exhausted and still focused on the country life she has temporarily left behind. As the music fills the theater, however, she becomes entranced and is greatly saddened when the performance ends.

 For summaries in languages other than English, see Unit 4 Teaching Resources Book, pp. 65–70.

Vocabulary

Use Adverbs Remind students that adverbs usually modify verbs by telling how, when, where, or to what extent. Adverbs can also modify adjectives, other adverbs, and groups of words. Give pairs of students five minutes to complete the following sentences in as many ways as possible: *Doggedly describes how . . .* and *Obliquely describes how . . . (Possible answers: serious athletes train; books on the shelf lean.)* Have each group read a couple of their sentences aloud while classmates decide whether the sentences were completed correctly.

 For additional vocabulary practice, see Unit 4 Teaching Resources Book, p. 73.

Literature and Reading Preview

Connect to the Story

How does it feel to return to a place you have not been in a long time? Write a short journal entry to explore this question. Refer to specific situations from your life if possible.

Build Background

The title "A Wagner Matinée" refers to the German opera composer Wilhelm Richard Wagner (1813–1883). Willa Cather based this story on her Aunt Franc's and Uncle George's experience of moving to Nebraska after the passage of the Homestead Act in 1862.

Set Purposes for Reading

Big Idea Regionalism

As you read, ask, What role does each character's choice of where to live play in this story? What opportunities are opened or closed to each character as a result of that choice?

Literary Element Point of View

Point of view refers to the relationship of the narrator to the story. In **first-person point of view,** the story is told by one of the characters, referred to as "I," and the reader sees everything through that character's eyes. In **third-person limited point of view,** the narrator reveals the thoughts and feelings of only one character, referred to as "he" or "she." In an **omniscient point of view,** the narrator knows everything about the characters and events. As you read, ask yourself, How does point of view influence my understanding of the story?

Reading Strategy Identify Sequence

Identifying sequence means determining the order of ideas or events. Main events are often told in chronological order, but authors sometimes reveal important events and details through flashbacks.

Tip: Chart Story Sequence Make a diagram like the one shown to organize the events of the story into chronological order.

Vocabulary

legacy (leg´ ə sē) *n.* an inheritance; p. 521 *Paul's generous grandfather left him a legacy when he died.*

reproach (ri prōch´) *n.* an expression of disapproval; a reprimand; p. 522 *Kim missed curfew and suffered her mother's reproach.*

doggedly (dô´ gid lē) *adv.* in a stubbornly persistent manner; obstinately; p. 522 *The salesman doggedly pursued customers, even when they rebuffed him.*

trepidation (trep´ ə dā´ shən) *n.* nervous anticipation; anxiety; p. 523 *Dana could not shake her feeling of trepidation about the next day's exam.*

obliquely (ō blēk´ lē) *adv.* in a slanting or sloping direction; p. 525 *Her hair hung obliquely across her face, hiding her left eye.*

Reading Practice

Identify and Analyze Flashback

Sometimes a writer uses a flashback to present events that occurred earlier than the main story. Cather includes flashbacks of the narrator's experiences in his aunt's home. Rather than describe the memories, the narrator presents himself as that young boy. This technique helps readers experience the memories with Clark and understand his perception of them. Have students record details that reveal Clark's attitude toward farm life. *(Students may say that words such as* scourged, chilblains, cracked *and* sore *suggest that farm life was torturous for Clark.)* Have students note other flashbacks and the attitude or message that each conveys.

A Wagner Matinée

Willa Cather

In the Loge, 1879. Mary Cassatt. Oil on canvas, 32 x 36 in. The Hayden Collection. Museum of Fine Arts, Boston.

1 I received one morning a letter, written in pale ink on glassy, blue-lined note-paper, and bearing the postmark of a little Nebraska village. This communication, worn and rubbed, looking as if it has been carried for some days in a coat pocket that was none too clean, was from my uncle Howard, and informed me that his wife had been left a small **legacy** by a bachelor relative, and that it would be necessary for her to go to Boston to attend to the settling of the estate. He requested me to meet her at the station and render[1] her whatever services might be necessary. On examining the date indicated as that of her arrival, I found it to be no later than tomorrow. He had characteristically delayed writing until, had I been away from home for a day, I must have missed my aunt altogether.

The name of my Aunt Georgiana opened before me a gulf of recollection so wide and deep that, as the letter dropped from my hand,

I felt suddenly a stranger to all the present conditions of my existence, wholly ill at ease and out of place amid the familiar surroundings of my study. I became, in short, the gangling farmer-boy my aunt had known, scourged[2] with chilblains[3] and bashfulness, my hands cracked and sore from the corn husking. I sat again before her parlour organ, fumbling the scales with my stiff, red fingers, while she, beside me, made canvas mittens for the huskers.

The next morning, after preparing my landlady for a visitor, I set out for the station. When the train arrived I had some difficulty in finding my aunt. She was the last of the passengers to alight, and it was not until I got her into the carriage that she seemed really to recognize me. She had come all the way in a day coach; her linen duster[4] had become black with soot and

---

1. *Render* means "to make available" or "to provide."

Vocabulary

legacy (leg´ ə sē) *n.* an inheritance

2. *Scourged* means "afflicted."
3. *Chilblains* are red, swollen sores on the skin caused by exposure to the cold.
4. A *duster* is a long, lightweight coat worn to protect one's clothing from dust.

> Identify Sequence *How does the narration shift after Clark sees Aunt Georgiana's name in the letter?* **2**

WILLA CATHER   **521**

English Learners

DIFFERENTIATED INSTRUCTION

Intermediate To help English learners better understand the story, preteach the following vocabulary phrases: "none too clean" *(not very clean);* "ill at ease" *(awkward, uneasy, uncomfortable in a situation);* "in short" *(to summarize a situation);* "the upshot of this" *(the conclusion to a situation)* "at the mercy of" *(under the power of [someone or something].)* To reinforce comprehension, ask students

questions, using the vocabulary phrases. For example, **Ask:** When might a person call something "none too clean"? When might a person feel "ill at ease"? Have students answer your questions, using the new vocabulary phrases and complete sentences.

Teach

Big Idea   1

Regionalism Say: Keep these questions in mind as you read: Why does Cather contrast Georgiana's Nebraska home with the Boston opera house? *(The contrast highlights the importance of setting in Georgiana's life.)* **Ask:** How are Georgiana's emotions affected by her surroundings? *(Being in the opera house brings back fond memories.)*

Reading Strategy   2

Identify Sequence Answer: *Clark's memories of his childhood are sparked when he sees Georgiana's name.*

View the Art

Mary Cassatt (1844–1926) grew up in Pennsylvania and is best known for her compositions depicting mothers and children. This painting has an alternative title: *At the Opera.*

Ask: How does the painting help you understand the story's title? *(It suggests that the matinée will be of a play or musical performance.)*

For an audio recording of this selection, use Listening Library Audio CD-ROM.

Readability Scores

Dale-Chall: 10.5
DRP: 63
Lexile: 1410

Teach

Reading Strategy | 1

Make Inferences Discuss Clark's description of his aunt's marriage. **Ask:** From his description of it here, what can you infer about Clark's opinion of his aunt's marriage? *(Students may say that his reference to "infatuation" implies that he does not think his aunt should have married the young and impetuous Howard Carpenter.)*

Literary Element | 2

Point of View Answer: *The story is told from Clark's perspective, a first-person point of view, so the exact meaning and intention of Georgiana's words are ambiguous.*

ENGLISH LEARNERS Point out that Georgiana uses the word "it" and does not specify what was taken away from her. The pronoun *it* may stand for anything from music to Georgiana's old life in Boston.

her black bonnet grey with dust during the journey. When we arrived at my boarding-house the landlady put her to bed at once and I did not see her again until the next morning.

Whatever shock Mrs. Springer experienced at my aunt's appearance, she considerately concealed. As for myself, I saw my aunt's battered figure with that feeling of awe and respect with which we behold explorers who have left their ears and fingers north of Franz-Joseph-Land,[5] or their health somewhere along the Upper Congo.[6] My Aunt Georgiana had been a music teacher at the Boston Conservatory, somewhere back in the latter sixties. One summer, while visiting in the little village among the Green Mountains[7] where her ancestors had dwelt for generations, she had kindled the callow[8] fancy of my uncle, Howard Carpenter, then an idle, shiftless boy of twenty-one. When she returned to her duties in Boston, Howard followed her, and the upshot of this infatuation was that she eloped with him, eluding the **reproaches** of her family and the criticism of her friends by going with him to the Nebraska frontier. Carpenter, who, of course, had no money, took up a homestead in Red Willow County, fifty miles from the railroad. There they had measured off their land themselves, driving across the prairie in a wagon, to the wheel of which they had tied a red cotton handkerchief, and counting its revolutions. They built a dug-out in the red hillside, one of those cave dwellings whose inmates so often reverted to primitive conditions. Their water they got from the lagoons where the buffalo drank, and their slender stock of provisions was always at the mercy of bands of roving Indians. For thirty years my aunt had not been farther than fifty miles from the homestead.

---

5. *Franz-Joseph-Land* is a group of islands in the Arctic Ocean.
6. The *Congo* River in central Africa is also called the Zaire River.
7. The *Green Mountains* extend from western Massachusetts through Vermont and into Canada.
8. *Callow* means "inexperienced" or "immature."

Vocabulary

reproach (ri prōch´) *n.* an expression of disapproval; a reprimand

I owed to this woman most of the good that ever came my way in my boyhood, and had a reverential[9] affection for her. During the years when I was riding herd for my uncle, my aunt, after cooking the three meals—the first of which was ready at six o'clock in the morning—and putting the six children to bed, would often stand until midnight at her ironing-board, with me at the kitchen table beside her, hearing me recite Latin declensions and conjugations,[10] gently shaking me when my drowsy head sank down over a page of irregular verbs. It was to her, at her ironing or mending, that I read my first Shakespere, and her old text-book on mythology was the first that ever came into my empty hands. She taught me my scales and exercises on the little parlor organ which her husband had bought her after fifteen years, during which she had not so much as seen a musical instrument. She would sit beside me by the hour, darning and counting, while I struggled with the "Joyous Farmer."[11] She seldom talked to me about music, and I understood why. Once when I had been **doggedly** beating out some easy passages from an old score of *Euryanthe*[12] I had found among her music books, she came up to me and, putting her hands over my eyes, gently drew my head back upon her shoulder, saying tremulously,[13] "Don't love it so well, Clark, or it may be taken from you."

---

9. *Reverential* means "with a feeling of deep respect and awe."
10. *Declensions* are different forms of nouns, pronouns, and adjectives. *Conjugations* are different forms of verbs. Students often memorize these forms when learning a new language.
11. "*Joyous Farmer*" is one of a series of compositions for children by Robert Shumann (1810–1856).
12. *Euryanthe* (ā ûr i än tā) is an opera by the German composer Carl Maria von Weber (1786–1826).
13. *Tremulously* means "in a trembling or shaking manner."

Point of View *How is your understanding of this passage affected by the point of view of the story?* | 2

Vocabulary

doggedly (dô´ gid lē) *adv.* in a stubbornly persistent manner; obstinately

Writing Practice

Imagery Point out Cather's use of color throughout this story. Have students look for references to colors in the descriptions of the women in the concert hall and of Georgiana's home in Nebraska. Then ask students to make a table contrasting the different uses of color.

After completing the table, have students write a one-paragraph response to the following questions: Why did the author include these details about color? How do they convey the meaning of the story?

Dark Colors	Bright Colors
Georgiana's clothes	Colorful frocks at opera

When my aunt appeared on the morning after her arrival in Boston, she was still in a semi-somnambulant[14] state. She seemed not to realize that she was in the city where she had spent her youth, the place longed for hungrily half a lifetime. She had been so wretchedly train-sick throughout the journey that she had no recollection of anything but her discomfort, and, to all intents and purposes, there were but a few hours of nightmare between the farm in Red Willow County and my study on Newbury Street. I had planned a little pleasure for her that afternoon, to repay her for some of the glorious moments she had given me when we used to milk together in the straw-thatched cowshed and she, because I was more than usually tired, or because her husband had spoken sharply to me, would tell me of the splendid performance of the *Huguenots*[15] she had seen in Paris, in her youth.

At two o'clock the Symphony Orchestra was to give a Wagner program, and I intended to take my aunt; though, as I conversed with her, I

14. *Semi-somnambulant* (sem´ ē som nam´ byə lənt) means "bewildered or dazed, as if sleepwalking."
15. *Huguenots* (hū´ gə nots´) is a French opera by the German composer Giacomo Meyerbeer (1791–1864).

Boston Common, 1901. Childe Hassam. Oil on canvas, 16 x 20 in. David David Gallery, Philadelphia.

View the Art In contrast to Aunt Georgiana's city-to-country transition, Boston Common underwent the opposite transformation—from a field of grazing cattle to a landscaped city park. Suppose Aunt Georgiana saw a scene like this one when she arrived in Boston. How might she have reacted? Explain. ★

grew doubtful about her enjoyment of it. I suggested our visiting the Conservatory and the Common[16] before lunch, but she seemed altogether too timid to wish to venture out. She questioned me absently about various changes in the city, but she was chiefly concerned that she had forgotten to leave instructions about feeding half-skimmed milk to a certain weakling calf, "old Maggie's calf, you know, Clark," she explained, evidently having forgotten how long I had been away. She was further troubled because she had neglected to tell her daughter about the freshly-opened kit of mackerel in the cellar, which would spoil if it were not used directly.

I asked her whether she had ever heard any of the Wagnerian operas, and found that she had not, though she was perfectly familiar with their respective situations, and had once possessed the piano score of *The Flying Dutchman*. I began to think it would be best to get her back to Red Willow County without waking her, and regretted having suggested the concert.

From the time we entered the concert hall, however, she was a trifle less passive and inert, and for the first time seemed to perceive her surroundings. I had felt some **trepidation** lest she might become aware of her queer, country clothes, or might experience some painful embarrassment at stepping suddenly into the world to which she had been dead for a quarter

16. *Common* refers to Boston Common, a public park.

Regionalism How does the concert hall draw Georgiana's attention away from the farm in a way the city could not? **3**

Vocabulary

trepidation (trep´ ə dā´ shən) *n.* nervous anticipation; anxiety

WILLA CATHER **523**

Teach

Reading Strategy | 1

Identify Sequence Answer:
Through the flashbacks, readers learn what Clark knows of Georgiana's background. They also allow readers to understand the concert's significance to Georgiana as Clark understands it.

Cultural History ☆

Richard Wagner Nineteenth-century German composer Richard Wagner is known not only for his innovation in the art of opera but also for his controversial political views. Some views expressed in his writings are considered antisemitic.

---

of a century. But, again, I found how superficially I had judged her. She sat looking about her with eyes as impersonal, almost as stony, as those with which the granite Rameses[17] in a museum watches the froth and fret that ebbs and flows[18] about his pedestal. I have seen this same aloofness in old miners who drift into the Brown hotel at Denver, their pockets full of bullion,[19] their linen soiled, their haggard faces unshaven; standing in the thronged corridors as solitary as though they were still in a frozen camp on the Yukon.[20]

The matinée audience was made up chiefly of women. One lost the contour of faces and figures, indeed any effect of line whatever, and there was only the color of bodices past counting, the shimmer of fabrics soft and firm, silky and sheer; red, mauve, pink, blue, lilac, purple, écru,[21] rose, yellow, cream, and white, all the colors that an impressionist[22] finds in a sunlit landscape, with here and there the dead shadow of a frock coat. My Aunt Georgiana regarded them as though they had been so many daubs of tube-paint on a palette.

When the musicians came out and took their places, she gave a little stir of anticipation, and looked with quickening interest down over the rail at that invariable grouping, perhaps the first wholly familiar thing that had greeted her eye since she had left old Maggie and her weakling calf. I could feel how all those details sank into her soul, for I had not forgotten how they had sunk into mine when I came fresh from ploughing forever and forever between green aisles of corn, where, as in a treadmill, one might walk from daybreak to dusk without perceiving a shadow of change.

---

17. *Rameses* (ram' ə sēz) is the name shared by several kings of ancient Egypt.
18. *[froth and fret . . . flows]* This phrase refers to the general busy activity that would come and go past a museum statue.
19. Here, *bullion* (bool' yən) is gold.
20. *Yukon* refers to the Yukon River, a major route to the Klondike gold fields in Canada.
21. *Écru* (ā' krōō) is beige.
22. An *impressionist* is a member of a movement in French painting that emphasized the play of light and color.

The clean profiles of the musicians, the gloss of their linen, the dull black of their coats, the beloved shapes of the instruments, the patches of yellow light on the smooth, varnished bellies of the 'cellos and the bass viols in the rear, the restless, wind-tossed forest of fiddle necks and bows—I recalled how, in the first orchestra I ever heard, those long bow-strokes seemed to draw the heart out of me, as a conjurer's stick reels out yards of paper ribbon from a hat.

The first number was the *Tannhauser* overture. When the horns drew out the first strain of the Pilgrim's chorus, Aunt Georgiana clutched my coat sleeve. Then it was I first realized that for her this broke a silence of thirty years. I saw again the tall, naked house on the prairie, black and grim as a wooden fortress; the black pond where I had learned to swim, its margin pitted with sun-dried cattle tracks; the rain gullied clay banks about the naked house, the four dwarf ash seedlings where the dish-cloths were always hung to dry before the kitchen door. The world there was the flat world of the ancients;[23] to the east, a cornfield that stretched to daybreak; to the west, a corral that reached to sunset; between, the conquests of peace, dearer-bought than those of war.

The overture closed, my aunt released my coat sleeve, but she said nothing. She sat staring dully at the orchestra. What, I wondered, did she get from it? She had been a good pianist in her day, I knew, and her musical education had been broader than that of most music teachers of a quarter of a century ago. She had often told me of Mozart's operas and Meyerbeer's, and I could remember hearing her sing, years ago, certain melodies of Verdi.[24] When I had fallen ill with a fever in her house she used to sit by my cot in the evening—

---

23. *The ancients* refers to those who lived in classical Greece and Rome.
24. Wolfgang Amadeus *Mozart* (woolf' gang˙ ä' mə dā' əs mōt' särt) (1756–1791) was an Austrian composer. Giuseppe *Verdi* (jōō zep' pe˙ ver' dē) (1813–1901) was an Italian composer of opera.

Identify Sequence *How do the flashbacks contribute to the effect of Clark's realizations about his aunt?* | **1**

Listening Practice

Analyze Music Point out to students that they hear music all around them, far more than people in Georgiana's time did. To respond thoughtfully to music, have students analyze its content. Have students use these questions to help them analyze a favorite piece of music:

- How does the music affect my mood? What emotions do I associate with the music?
- How do the melody and lyrics contribute to the mood of the music?
- What instruments are used to perform the music? What is the tempo of the music?

when the cool, night wind blew in through the faded mosquito netting tacked over the window and I lay watching a certain bright star that burned red above the cornfield—and sing "Home to our mountains, O, let us return!" in a way fit to break the heart of a Vermont boy near dead of homesickness already.

I watched her closely through the prelude to *Tristan and Isolde*, trying vainly to conjecture what that seething turmoil of strings and winds might mean to her, but she sat mutely staring at the violin bows that drove **obliquely** downward, like the pelting streaks of rain in a summer shower. Had this music any message for her? Had she enough left to at all comprehend this power which had kindled the world since she had left it? I was in a fever of curiosity, but Aunt Georgiana sat silent upon her peak in Darien.[25] She preserved this utter immobility throughout the number from *The Flying Dutchman*, though her fingers worked mechanically upon her black dress, as if, of themselves, they were recalling the piano score they had once played. Poor hands! They had been stretched and twisted into mere tentacles to hold and lift and knead with; on one of them a thin, worn band that had once been a wedding ring. As I pressed and gently quieted one of those groping hands, I remembered with quivering eyelids their services for me in other days.

Soon after the tenor began the "Prize Song," I heard a quick drawn breath and turned to my aunt. Her eyes were closed, but the tears were glistening on her cheeks, and I think, in a moment more, they were in my eyes as well. It never really died, then—the soul which can suffer so excruciatingly and so interminably; it withers to the outward eye only; like that strange moss which can lie on a dusty shelf half a century and yet, if placed in water, grows green again. She wept so throughout the development and elaboration of the melody.

During the intermission before the second half, I questioned my aunt and found that the "Prize Song" was not new to her. Some years before there had drifted to the farm in Red Willow County a young German, a tramp cowpuncher,[26] who had sung in the chorus at Bayreuth[27] when he was a boy, along with the other peasant boys and girls. Of a Sunday morning he used to sit on his gingham-sheeted bed in the hands' bedroom which opened off the kitchen, cleaning the leather of his boots and saddle, singing the "Prize Song," while my aunt went about her work in the kitchen. She had hovered over him until she had prevailed upon him to join the country church, though his sole fitness for this step, in so far as I could gather, lay in his boyish face and his possession of this divine melody. Shortly afterward, he had gone to town on the Fourth of July, been drunk for several days, lost his money at a faro[28] table, ridden a saddled Texas steer on a bet, and disappeared with a fractured collar-bone. All this my aunt told me huskily, wanderingly, as though she were talking in the weak lapses of illness.

"Well, we have come to better things than the old *Trovatore*[29] at any rate, Aunt Georgie?" I queried, with a well meant effort at jocularity.[30]

Her lip quivered and she hastily put her handkerchief up to her mouth. From behind it

---

25. The phrase *"peak in Darien"* (dãr′ ē en′) alludes to the poem "On First Looking into Chapman's Homer" by John Keats. The poem describes Spanish explorers on a mountain in Darien, now Panama, who stand silently and in awe, as the first Europeans to view the Pacific Ocean.

2 | Point of View *What effect does the first-person point of view have on the depiction of the concert?*

3 | Regionalism *What does the description of Georgiana's hands reveal about the difference between Boston and the Nebraska farm, according to Clark?*

Vocabulary

obliquely (ō blēk′ lē) *adv.* in a slanting or sloping direction

---

26. *Cowpuncher* means "cowboy."
27. *Bayreuth* (bī roit′) is a German city famous for its annual Wagnerian music festival.
28. *Faro* (fār′ ō) is a gambling game played with a deck of cards.
29. *Trovatore* (tro və tōr′e) refers to *Il Trovatore*, an opera by Giuseppe Verdi.
30. *Jocularity* means "joking" or "humor."

WILLA CATHER **525**

Teach

Teach

Literary Element   1

Point of View Answer: *He has experienced both city life and farm life, so he can empathize with his aunt.*

 To check students' understanding of the selection, see Unit 4 Teaching Resources Book, p. 76.

Baritone Bryn Terfel as Wolfram in Wagner's *Tannhäuser* at the Metropolitan Opera.

she murmured, "And you have been hearing this ever since you left me, Clark?" Her question was the gentlest and saddest of reproaches.

The second half of the program consisted of four numbers from the *Ring,* and closed with Siegfried's funeral march. My aunt wept quietly, but almost continuously, as a shallow vessel overflows in a rain-storm. From time to time her dim eyes looked up at the lights, burning softly under their dull glass globes.

The deluge of sound poured on and on; I never knew what she found in the shining current of it; I never knew how far it bore her, or past what happy islands. From the trembling of her face I could well believe that before the last number she had been carried out where the myriad[31] graves are, into the grey, nameless burying grounds of the sea; or into some world of death vaster yet, where, from the beginning of the world, hope has lain down with hope and dream with dream and, renouncing,[32] slept.

The concert was over; the people filed out of the hall chattering and laughing, glad to relax and find the living level again, but my kinswoman made no effort to rise. The harpist slipped the green felt cover over his instrument; the flute-players shook the water from their mouthpieces; the men of the orchestra went out one by one, leaving the stage to the chairs and music stands, empty as a winter cornfield.

I spoke to my aunt. She burst into tears and sobbed pleadingly. "I don't want to go, Clark, I don't want to go!"

I understood. For her, just outside the concert hall, lay the black pond with the cattle-tracked bluffs; the tall, unpainted house, with weather-curled boards, naked as a tower; the crook-backed ash seedlings where the dish-cloths hung to dry; the gaunt,[33] moulting turkeys picking up refuse about the kitchen door. ∽

---

31. *Myriad* means "countless" or "innumerable."
32. *Renouncing* means "giving up."

33. *Gaunt* means "extremely thin."

Point of View *How does Clark know what his aunt is feeling?*   1

526 UNIT 4 REGIONALISM AND REALISM

Reading Practice

Compare *Comparison* refers to an expression of either similarity or difference. In literary works, metaphors are often used to develop subtle and complex comparisons. Work with students to find examples of metaphors and comparisons in the story—of colors, of the ways Georgiana's hands function, of the similarity of Nebraska life to prehistoric times or to a prison. Urge students to list as many comparisons and metaphors as they can. Discuss generalizations students can make about the comparisons—for instance, that they mostly favor Boston.

After You Read

Respond and Think Critically

Respond and Interpret

1. How did the story affect your impressions of nineteenth-century frontier life?

2. (a)How does Clark react to the letter from his uncle? (b)Why does he react so strongly to the letter?

3. The narrator says that he owed to his aunt "most of the good that ever came my way in my boyhood." How is her influence apparent in his adult life?

4. (a)How does Georgiana behave after the concert ends? (b)What might the concert hall symbolize for her?

Analyze and Evaluate

5. Georgiana seldom talks to Clark about music. Why then does she tell Clark about the *Huguenots* performance she saw in Paris?

6. After his experience with Georgiana, how might Clark perceive his access to concerts?

Connect

7. **Big Idea** Regionalism In what ways is this story regional? In what ways is it universal?

8. **Connect to the Author** How is Cather's ambivalence toward Nebraska reflected in this story? Explain, using details from the story.

Primary Source Quotation

Growing Up in Red Cloud

Cather moved to Nebraska with her family when she was nine. Prairie homesteaders endured severe conditions in a barren landscape. Due to the scarcity of trees, many lived in sod houses like the one shown below right. Despite hardships, Cather enjoyed riding her pony and hearing the stories of European immigrants. She learned Greek and Latin, and attended theatrical and opera performances. Prairie life inspired Cather to write novels and short stories.

"So the [Nebraska] country and I had it out together and by the end of the first autumn, that shaggy grass country had gripped me with a passion I never have been able to shake. It has been the happiness and curse of my life."

—Willa Cather

Group Activity Discuss the following questions with your classmates.

Based on what you have read, how do you think Cather's experience of prairie life influenced her writing of "A Wagner Matinée"? How might these experiences have shaped her different portrayals of Aunt Georgiana and the narrator?

Primary Source Quotation

1. Students should be able to compare the rugged characteristics of the narrator in "A Wagner Matinée" to the life of someone living on the prairie. They may also see a relationship between Cather's interest in theater and opera as a girl.

2. Prairie life subjected people to conditions such as living in sod houses, loneliness, and harsh weather. Aunt Georgiana was brought up in Boston; she was exposed to a more cosmopolitan lifestyle in her early youth.

After You Read

Assess

1. Possible answer: I gained new insight into the difficulties of frontier life and the sacrifices people made to live it.

2. (a) He feels like a shy farm boy again. (b) Clark has been deeply affected by his aunt's kindness to him. He also realizes that this trip may be significant for her.

3. Georgiana's influence is apparent in Clark's appreciation of culture and in his choice of city life over country life.

4. (a) She cries because she does not want to go return to a life so lacking in culture. (b) The concert hall symbolizes her youth and her lost opportunities.

5. She wants to console Clark and distract him from his own pain.

6. Clark will appreciate even more his access to cultural events.

7. The story is regional in its depiction of Aunt Georgiana, scenes from her pioneer life, and scenes from her visit to Boston, where she is now an outsider. As a story about choices and regrets, it is a universal story.

8. The narrator's admiration for Aunt Georgiana and a few of his recollections about the farm convey the author's appreciation for her life as a pioneer. However, Aunt Georgiana's desire to stay in Boston and the narrator's recollections of the harshness of the pioneer life suggest the author's appreciation for city life.

 For additional assessment, see Assessment Resources, pp. 169–170.

After You Read

Assess

Literary Element

1. Clark grew up close to Georgiana, knows the details of her background, and cares about her feelings.
2. Her comments about the concert seem to confirm Clark's inferences.

Progress Check

Can students analyze point of view?

If No ➔ See Unit 4 Teaching Resources Book, p. 71.

Review: Voice

1. Clark is curious about what Georgiana is thinking.
2. That he is sensitive to music's powerful effect on his aunt
3. Clark's voice reveals that he is sensitive, passionate, educated, and observant.

Reading Strategy

1. **C** is the correct answer because the use of flashbacks enables Cather to extend readers' knowledge of the characters into the past while centering the action in the present.

Progress Check

Can students identify sequence?

If No ➔ See Unit 4 Teaching Resources Book, p. 72.

Literary Element Point of View

"A Wagner Matinée" is written from the **first-person point of view.** The story is filtered through the sensations, thoughts, and memories of Clark, the narrator. The use of pronouns such as *I, you,* and *me* also indicates first-person point of view.

In stories told in the first person, the narrator is a character in the story, and the story is limited to his or her knowledge, experience, and biases. The narrator may not be reliable, so judge whether his or her interpretation of events is accurate. Use details in the story to help evaluate narrator reliability and to infer events the narrator may not know or share.

1. Why might the reader trust Clark's interpretation of Georgiana?
2. What details about Georgiana confirm Clark's interpretation of her?

Review: Voice

Voice refers to the distinctive language that conveys the author's or narrator's personality to the reader. Voice is determined by elements of style such as word choice, sentence structure, and tone.

Partner Activity Discuss how Clark's voice is conveyed in the excerpt below and answer the questions.

1. What does Clark's use of questions reveal?
2. What do words such as *power, kindled,* and *fever* and the Darien allusion reveal about Clark?
3. How does Clark's voice convey his personality?

> "Had this music any message for her? Had she enough left to at all comprehend this power which had kindled the world since she had left it? I was in a fever of curiosity, but Aunt Georgiana sat silent upon her peak in Darien."

LOG ON ▶ **Literature** Online

Selection Resources For Selection Quizzes, eFlashcards, and Reading-Writing Connection activities, go to glencoe.com and enter QuickPass code GLA9800u4.

528 UNIT 4 REGIONALISM AND REALISM

Reading Strategy Identify Sequence

ACT Skills Practice

1. Cather might have used flashbacks instead of presenting events chronologically to
   I. provide important background information about the characters.
   II. maintain the focus of the action on Georgiana's visit to Boston.
   III. create a sense of what might happen after the story ends.

   A. I only   **C.** I and II only
   B. III only   **D.** I, II, and III

Vocabulary Practice

Practice with Analogies Choose the word that best completes each analogy.

1. grandparent : legacy :: groom :
   a. house   **c.** bride
   b. ring   **d.** husband
2. quickly : fast :: doggedly :
   a. stubborn   **c.** obediently
   b. proud   **d.** docile
3. reproach : disapproval :: compliment :
   a. criticism   **c.** affection
   b. approval   **d.** attention
4. sweat : trepidation :: wink :
   a. anxiety   **c.** mischief
   b. blink   **d.** eye
5. obliquely : direction :: passionately :
   a. reason   **c.** spontaneous
   b. instinct   **d.** feeling

Academic Vocabulary

*Aunt Georgiana has an internal response to the **external** stimulus of music.*

External has many meanings. Using context clues, infer its meaning in each sentence below.

1. The skin is an **external** feature of the body.
2. Despite her **external** composure, Deepali was so on edge she could barely breathe.

Vocabulary

1. b **2.** a **3.** b **4.** c **5.** d

Academic Vocabulary

1. In this sentence, *external* means "exterior."
2. In this sentence, *external* means "superficial or appearing merely as such."

Respond Through Writing

Reflective Essay

Compare and Contrast Hearing Wagner once again in a concert hall has a powerful effect on Aunt Georgiana. Write a reflective essay about a time when a particular piece of music or art had a strong effect on you. Compare and contrast your experiences with the events in "A Wagner Matinée." Why did this experience affect you strongly? What generalizations about the nature of art can you make based on your experience?

Understand the Task In a **reflective essay,** you describe an experience to better understand what it means personally and what it might teach others. It is important to develop a **theme,** or central message about life, in your essay.

Prewrite Brainstorm, look over old journal entries, revisit some of your favorite music or art, or talk to friends to help you recall the experience you wish to describe. Consider how it shaped your views.

Draft Compare your experience to Aunt Georgiana's response to hearing Wagner in the story. Pay attention to your word choice, sentence structure, and tone. In "A Wagner Matinée," Cather uses details and evocative images to describe Georgiana's memories. This specificity helps the reader glean more abstract ideas about Georgiana's life. Include details and imagery that highlight the significance of the event to you so that the reader can draw more abstract ideas and themes from your reflection.

Event	Significance	Details and Images

Revise Exchange papers with a partner. Ask your partner to underline your essay's thesis and circle its supporting details. Ask him or her if your experience relates to a broader theme or idea. Based on your partner's feedback, revise your draft.

Edit and Proofread Proofread your paper, correcting any errors in grammar, spelling, and punctuation. See the Grammar Tip in the side column for help using absolute phrases.

WILLA CATHER **529**

Learning Objectives

In this assignment, you will focus on the following objectives:

Writing: Writing a reflective essay.

Grammar: Using absolute phrases.

▶ Grammar Tip

Absolute Phrases

Absolute phrases modify an entire sentence rather than a specific word. They consist of nouns or pronouns modified by participles or participial phrases. In the following example, the absolute phrase is underlined:

- *The concert drawing to a close,* Aunt Georgiana began to dread leaving.

- *His aunt overwhelmed with emotion,* Clark found it hard to talk to her.

Sometimes the participle *being* is understood:

- *His aunt [being] near the end of her life,* Clark knew change would be hard.

After You Read

Teach

 ## Writing

Students' reflective essays should relate a significant event and compare that event to themes in "A Wagner Matinée." Essays should also relate to broader themes or abstract ideas and should employ emotional language and descriptions.

For grammar practice, see Unit 4 Teaching Resources Book, p. 75.

Scoring Guide

Assess students' performance in the following categories with reference to the scoring guide at the bottom of the page:

- Addresses all parts of the writing task.
- Provides a meaningful thesis; maintains focus and organization.
- Supports the thesis with details and examples.
- Provides a variety of sentence types; uses precise, descriptive language.
- Observes English language conventions.

Scoring Guide	4	3	2	1
Task addressed	fully	mostly	partially	barely
Thesis	meaningful	provided	partial	weak
Support	thoughtful	provided	limited	weak
Language	varied, descriptive	varied, often descriptive	predictable, imprecise	repetitive, limited
Convention errors	few or none	several	many	serious

Focus

Write this sentence on the board:

Your substitute teacher, a retired college professor, will administer the exam.

Discuss how the substitute teacher's being a retired professor is an extra detail.

Teach

Essential/Nonessential One way to classify an appositive is to remove it. If the meaning of the sentence is still clear, the appositive is nonessential. **Ask:** Does the posted sentence contain an essential or a nonessential appositive? Explain. *(Nonessential: if the appositive "a retired college professor" is removed, the sentence is still clear.)*

Assess

Revise

1. Willa Cather, a prolific writer, was known for her portrayal of pioneer life.

2. "A Wagner Matinée" appeared in *The Troll Garden,* a collection of stories.

3. The music evoked nostalgia that brought the woman, Clark's aunt, to tears.

4. A cowpuncher, a young German who had sung at Bayreuth, had drifted in.

5. Correct

Learning Objectives

In this assignment, you will focus on the following objectives:

Grammar:
Distinguishing between essential and nonessential appositives.
Using commas with nonessential elements.

Appositives

An **appositive** is a noun, pronoun, or noun phrase that identifies another noun, pronoun, or a noun phase.

Restrictive (essential) appositives are not set off with commas. (My brother *Alfred* is a poet.)

Nonrestrictive (nonessential) appositives are set off with commas. (Alfred, *our family poet,* has never been published.)

Tip

To determine whether to set off an appositive with commas, try reading the sentence without it. If the appositive is not needed to identify a noun, add commas.

Language Handbook

For more on appositives, see Language Handbook pp. R42–R61.

Grammar Workshop

Appositives

Literature Connection In the following quotation, *Howard Carpenter* is an appositive—a noun, a pronoun, or a noun phrase that further identifies another noun, pronoun, or noun phrase.

> *"One summer . . . she had kindled the callow fancy of my uncle, Howard Carpenter, then an idle, shiftless boy of twenty-one."*
>
> —Willa Cather, from "A Wagner Matinée"

The appositive is set off with commas because it is **nonessential** (or nonrestrictive). Removing it would not change the meaning of *my uncle*; it simply adds information—the uncle's name. If Cather had written *she had kindled the fancy of my uncle Howard,* the appositive *Howard* would be **essential** (or restrictive); it would provide essential information, specifying which uncle the speaker is referring to.

Examples

Cather's experiences inspired the novels My Ántonia and O Pioneers!

Here, the appositive *My Ántonia and O Pioneers!* specifies which novels—it is essential to the meaning of the sentence.

She was in the city where she had spent her youth, a place longed for.

Here, the appositive *a place longed for* is nonessential. It supplies information about *city,* but does not change its meaning. Notice that the appositive comes after an adjective clause *(where she had spent her youth)* modifying *city.*

Revise Write the five sentences below, adding commas as necessary. One sentence needs no commas.

1. Willa Cather a prolific writer was known for her portrayal of pioneer life.

2. "A Wagner Matinée" appeared in *The Troll Garden* a collection of stories.

3. The music evoked nostalgia that brought the woman Clark's aunt to tears.

4. A cowpuncher a young German who had sung at Bayreuth had drifted in.

5. The aria "The Prize Song" is from Wagner's opera *Die Meistersinger.*

Approaching Level

DIFFERENTIATED INSTRUCTION

Emerging To decide whether an appositive is essential, students should ask themselves whether taking out the appositive changes the meaning of the sentence. Write the following sentence on the board: *My sister Jessica runs track.* **Ask:** Which is the appositive? *(Jessica)* Erase the word *Jessica.* Point out that the sentence still makes sense but that its meaning has changed in that it does not tell which sister runs track. The appositive is therefore essential to the sentence. Have students complete the "Revise" exercise on this page and remind them to insert commas around nonessential appositives. Afterwards, have students read each exercise sentence aloud. Then have them read the sentence again without the appositive and decide whether removing the appositive changed the meaning of the sentence.

Before You Read

I Will Fight No More Forever

Meet **Chief Joseph**
(ca. 1840–1904)

Chief Joseph—whose given name was Hinmaton Yalaktit (hin mə tō´ yä läkh´ tet) or "Thunder Rolling Down the Mountain"—was born in the Wallowa Valley in what is now northeastern Oregon. When his father died in 1871, Joseph was elected to succeed him as a chief of the Nez Percé (nez´ purs´), the largest and most powerful of the Sahaptin-speaking tribes that lived in present-day central Idaho and contiguous areas in Oregon and Washington. Other Sahaptin-speaking tribes include the Cayuse, Tenino, Wallawalla, and Yakima.

The Nez Percé were more warlike than neighboring tribes, especially after acquiring the horse from the Plains Indians in the early eighteenth century. However, they had maintained peace with the whites for decades, ever since the Lewis and Clark expedition in 1805, which was their first significant contact with whites. Nevertheless, Joseph inherited a volatile situation. In 1863, following a gold rush into Nez Percé territory, the U.S. government had reclaimed three quarters of the land it had ceded to the tribe in an 1855 treaty. Chief Joseph successfully resisted efforts to remove his band from the Wallowa Valley until 1877, when the government threatened removal by force.

> *"Hear me, my chiefs. I am tired; my heart is sick and sad."*
>
> —Chief Joseph

Cooperator and Leader To avoid bloodshed, Chief Joseph decided to cooperate, but as he led his band toward a reservation in Idaho, he learned that three of his braves, enraged at the government's action, had killed a group of white settlers and prospectors. To escape retaliation by the U.S. Army, Chief Joseph led his people—some 200 to 300 warriors and their families—on a long, grueling march toward the Canadian border. They trekked through Oregon, Washington, Idaho, and Montana for nearly three months, covering 1,000 miles as the warriors successfully fought off U.S. troops. Within forty miles of their destination, in the Bear Paw mountains of Montana, the Nez Percé were surrounded and forced to surrender. The chase and intermittent skirmishes had claimed the lives of 239 Nez Percé, many of them women and children, as well as the lives of 266 U.S. Army personnel.

Lasting Legacy Although Chief Joseph had thought his people would be able to return home, they were removed to Indian Territory, or present-day Oklahoma, where many fell ill and died. In 1885 some of the survivors were returned to the Pacific Northwest, but about half, including Chief Joseph, were taken to Colville reservation, a non-Nez Percé reservation in Washington State. There Chief Joseph died, according to his doctor, "of a broken heart." At a ceremony honoring him, a Nez Percé chief named Yellow Bull said, "Joseph is dead, but his words will live forever."

 Literature Online

Author Search For more about Chief Joseph, go to glencoe.com and enter QuickPass code GLA9800u4.

Before You Read

Focus

Selection Skills

```
Literary Elements          I Will Fight No More Forever          Writing Skills/Grammar
• Tone (SE pp. 532, 534)                                          • Journal Entry (SE p. 534)


   Reading Skills              Vocabulary Skills          Listening/Speaking/
   • Evaluate Style            • Academic Vocabulary      Viewing Skills
     (SE pp. 532–534)            (SE p. 534)              • Analyze Art (TE p. 531)
   • Predict (TE p. 532)
```

Before You Read

Focus

Summary

In the midst of his tribe's desperate flight to Canada, Chief Joseph realizes that many of the tribe's leaders are dead and that the women and children are freezing and starving. After years of fighting with white people to protect the Nez Perce land and way of life, he concludes that it is time to stop fighting.

Cultural History ☆

Media Influence The national press followed the Nez Perce retreat closely. By the time of surrender, Chief Joseph had earned the respect and admiration not only of his opponents but also of a great many others. He did not mistreat his prisoners, and he showed great leadership and empathy in his care for the women, the children, and the elderly. Also, instead of stealing supplies, he bought them from ranches and stores as the Nez Perce retreated.

 For an audio recording of this selection, use Listening Library Audio CD-ROM.

Readability Scores

Dale-Chall: 3.0
DRP: 41
Lexile: 380

Literature and Reading Preview

Connect to the Speech

What does it mean to lose with dignity? Discuss this question with a partner.

Build Background

The Nez Percé was the southeasternmost tribe in the Plateau culture, which developed on the plateaus between the coastal mountain ranges and the Rocky Mountains. In the winter, the Plateau tribes lived by rivers. In the summer, they moved to mountain valleys to hunt and gather roots. By the time Chief Joseph came to power, the Nez Percé had strayed away from the Plateau culture and adopted many cultural components of the Plains Indians, including the war bonnet and the teepee.

Set Purposes for Reading

Big Idea Regionalism

As you read, ask yourself, How were the Native Americans affected by westward expansion?

Literary Element Tone

Tone is the writer's attitude toward the subject of a work. Writers create the tone of a work primarily through diction, or word choice. As you read, ask yourself, How does Chief Joseph's diction contribute to the tone of his speech?

Reading Strategy Evaluate Style

Style refers to the way that a writer uses language. Elements of style include tone, diction, sentence length, and imagery. When you evaluate style, you make a judgment about it based on the application of appropriate standards. As you read, evaluate how individual elements contribute to Chief Joseph's style.

Tip: Take Notes Use a chart to record examples of different elements of Chief Joseph's style. In the right-hand column, explain briefly how the elements work.

Element	Example	Effect
Tone	"Maybe I shall find [the children] among the dead."	

Reading Practice

SPIRAL REVIEW **Predict** Ask students to reread the quotation by Chief Joseph and the paragraph titled "Cooperator and Leader" on page 531. Then have students study the painting on page 533 and imagine how Chief Joseph must have felt as he rode forward to surrender.
Ask: What do you think the tone of the speech will be? *(sad, weary)* Have students describe the people in the painting. Tell students to use the clues from the text and the painting to brainstorm about possible reasons for Chief Joseph's decision to surrender.

Learning Objectives

For pages 531–534

In studying this text, you will focus on the following objectives:

Literary Study: Analyzing tone.

Reading: Evaluating style.

Writing: Writing a journal entry.

Chief Joseph Rides to Surrender, 1979. Howard Terpning. Oil on canvas. ©1979 Howard Terpning. ©1979 The Greenwich Workshop® Inc. Courtesy of The Greenwich Workshop Inc., Shelton, CT. ⭐

I Will Fight No More Forever

Chief Joseph

"Tell General Howard[1] I know his heart. What he told me before, I have in my heart. I am tired of fighting. Our chiefs are killed. Looking Glass[2] is dead. Too Hul Hul Suit[3] is dead. The old men are all dead. It is the young men who say yes and no. He who led on the young men is dead.[4] It is cold and we have no blankets. The little children are freezing to death. My people, some of them, have run away to the hills and have no blankets, no food; no one knows where they are—perhaps freezing to death. I want to have time to look for my children and see how many I can find. Maybe I shall find them among the dead. Hear me, my chiefs. I am tired; my heart is sick and sad. From where the sun now stands I will fight no more forever."

1

---

1. *General* (Oliver Otis) *Howard* (1830–1909) had been a Union general in the Civil War. He sent troops to fight the Nez Percé in the Battle of White Bird Canyon.
2. *Looking Glass* was a respected leader of the Nez Percé. He took part in the 1877 retreat.
3. *Too Hul Hul Suit,* or Tu Ku Lxu C'uut (tœ kœl´ hu sœt´), leader of the White Bird tribe, was a member of the negotiating team that met with General Howard. He favored fighting for the Nez Percé land rather than moving to a reservation.
4. *[He who led . . . dead.]* refers to Chief Joseph's younger brother, Ollikut (ōl okh' ut).

Evaluate Style *What do the form and content of these two sentences emphasize? How do you think they affect the listener or reader?*

2

CHIEF JOSEPH **533**

Teach

Big Idea · 1

Regionalism Say: Keep these questions in mind as you read: How does Chief Joseph's speech suggest the time and place of its writing? *(It describes the cold and barren surroundings and the moment of despair facing the Nez Perce.)* What has happened to the community of the Nez Perce? *(The community is broken and some members are lost.)*

Reading Strategy · 2

Evaluate Style Answer: *The parallel structure of the sentences emphasizes the deaths of two individuals close to Joseph. Joseph's use of the chiefs' names makes it easier for the listener or reader to connect to his message.*

View the Art ⭐

Howard Terpning (1927–) was born and educated in Illinois and later lived in Arizona. He has painted many aspects of Native American life and the Old West. His paintings are much sought after by collectors.

Approaching Level

UNIVERSAL ACCESS

Emerging Help students analyze Chief Joseph's reasons for surrendering so close to the Canadian border. **Ask:** What does Chief Joseph hope to achieve by giving this speech? *(He hopes for peace and the chance to find rest for his people.)* What reasons does he give for his decision to surrender? *(The chiefs and all of the old men are dead, and the children are freezing to death. He wants to look for his missing people, and he is tired and full of sorrow.)*

After You Read

Assess

1. Students may wish that they could have asked whether he had ever regretted his decision or what General Howard said.

2. (a) They have all died. (b) They may have discouraged Joseph and convinced him that it was time for the next generation to lead.

3. (a) *Sick* and *sad* (b) His sorrow is the cause of his decision to stop fighting.

4. (a) They have fled to the hills and are suffering from exposure. (b) He is the father of his people, so he wants to help them.

5. (a) He repeats the phrases "is dead" and "freezing to death." (b) The repetition reinforces his sorrow at the many deaths.

6. Possible answer: The speech effectively expresses the chief's feelings. The shortness of the speech suggests his weariness.

7. (a) He uses words such as "know," "no blankets," and "death," indicating finality. (b) honor, bravery, and dignity

8. Students may discuss political candidates' calling their opponents to concede an election, a confrontation's arising, or an important decision to be made.

 For additional assessment, see Assessment Resources, pp. 171–172.

After You Read

Respond and Think Critically

Respond and Interpret

1. If you could speak to Chief Joseph, what would you say?

2. (a)What has happened to the chiefs and the old men of the tribe? (b)How might these circumstances have affected Chief Joseph's decision to surrender?

3. (a)What words does Chief Joseph use to describe his heart? (b)How does this description help you better understand his decision?

Analyze and Evaluate

4. (a)What does Chief Joseph say about his children? (b)Why does he want to look for them?

5. (a)What words or phrases does Chief Joseph repeat? (b)What effect does this repetition create?

6. In this short speech, Chief Joseph explains a decision that will have an enormous impact on the lives of his people. Would a longer, more detailed speech have been more effective? Explain.

Connect

7. **Big Idea** **Regionalism** According to one critic, this speech "is a classic statement of Native American pride and resolve in the midst of terrible suffering." (a)How does Chief Joseph display pride and resolve in this speech? (b)Which values of the Nez Percé does this speech reveal?

8. **Connect to Today** Think of a contemporary example of someone conceding defeat. How was this person's reaction similar to or different from Chief Joseph's? Which do you find more honorable or appealing? Explain.

Literary Element Tone

In "I Will Fight No More Forever," the tone conveys feelings of weariness, resignation, sadness, and dignity. Chief Joseph's use of simple, direct language and brief sentences reinforces this sense of loss.

1. What phrases help create the tone?

2. Find examples of simple, direct language and brief sentences. How do they affect the tone?

Reading Strategy Evaluate Style

Tone, diction, syntax, sentence length, imagery, and figurative language all contribute to style. To evaluate Chief Joseph's style, refer to the chart you made (page 532) and answer these questions:

1. Is the style appropriate for the message?

2. Does the style reveal the writer's personality?

 Literature Online

Selection Resources For Selection Quizzes, eFlash-cards, and Reading-Writing Connection activities, go to glencoe.com and enter QuickPass code GLA9800u4.

Academic Vocabulary

*In 1863, the United States government **imposed** territorial restrictions upon the Nez Percé tribe.*

Imposed is an academic word. In more casual conversation, a guest at a party might have **imposed** on his host by bringing additional guests with him. Using context clues, try to figure out the meaning of the word in the sentence about the Nez Percé above. Check your inference in a dictionary.

For more on academic vocabulary, see pages 53–54.

Writing

Write a Journal Entry In this speech, Chief Joseph explains his decision to surrender. Think about a time when you had to defend your actions. Write a journal entry in which you describe the situation and your feelings, and explain why you acted as you did. Try to write in a tone that reflects your emotions at the time.

Literary Element

1. "I am tired of fighting"; "I am tired; my heart is sick and sad."

2. "The old men are all dead"; the repetition of "dead" and "freezing." Both contribute to the sad, resigned tone of the speech.

Reading Strategy

1. Yes. It vividly portrays their stark plight.
2. Yes. It reflects his dignity and anguish.

Progress Check

Can students analyze tone?

If No → See Unit 4 Teaching Resources Book, p. 85.

Academic Vocabulary

Students should be able to deduce from the context that *impose* means "to apply authority" or "to bring about by force."

Writing

Students might write about a conflict with an authority figure such as a parent, a teacher, or a coach; how they felt during the conflict; and how it was resolved.

Realism and Naturalism

Mrs. Charles Thursby, 1897–1898. John Singer Sargent. Oil on canvas, 78 x 39¾ in. Collection of The Newark Museum, NJ.

 View the Art One of the most famous portraitists of his time, John Singer Sargent was known for capturing the personality of his subjects. Looking at this painting, what impressions do you have of the woman pictured? What details contribute to your impressions?

"There are two ways of spreading light: to be The candle or the mirror that reflects it." **1**

—Edith Wharton, "Vesalius in Zante"

535

Analyze and Extend

Literary Element   1

Figurative Language **Ask:** What might *spreading light* be a metaphor for? What might *candle* and *mirror* be metaphors for? *(Spreading light suggests sharing knowledge. A candle provides light directly and a mirror indirectly.)*

Say: People used the quotation to comment on the human responsibility to make new discoveries or to inspire others to improve human life. **Ask:** What human conditions needed improvement during this period? *(urban poverty and women's rights)*

View the Art

Answer: *The woman looks confident and assertive. She is sitting with her legs crossed, hands on her hips, leaning forward in her chair.*

John Singer Sargent (1856–1925) was known for his portrait painting. **Ask:** How do you think this portrait relates to the quotation? *(The woman looks strong and capable of having and sharing knowledge.)*

English Learners

DIFFERENTIATED INSTRUCTION

Intermediate Ask: How would you know what to call an adult you meet? *(Ask what the person would like to be called; notice how someone introduces himself or herself.)* Explain that in the past, a married woman in the United States was referred to by her husband's name—for example, Mrs. Charles Thursby.

Approaching Level

DIFFERENTIATED INSTRUCTION

Emerging To make the quotation by Wharton more meaningful, ask students to write down examples of direct light and examples of reflected light. **Ask:** Which kind of light is better? *(They are different, but both are beneficial.)*

For additional support for English Learners, see Unit 4 Teaching Resources Book, p. 94.

Focus

Bellringer Options

Daily Language Practice
Transparency 48

Or have students discuss this question: Is the United States a classless society? (*Students may say that today's classes are defined by family income, "white collar" versus "blue collar" jobs, and level of education.*)

Say: As you read the essay, consider to what extent these class differences exist today and how social reform has helped diminish them.

Teach

Literary Element

Stream of Consciousness
Read students the passage on page 586 from Stephen Crane's "The Open Boat": "If I am going to be drowned . . . "

Ask: Why is stream of consciousness an appropriate technique of Realism? (*Inner monologues realistically portray free-flowing human thoughts.*)

Study Skills Practice

Urban America's Two Faces

IN THE LATE NINETEENTH AND EARLY twentieth centuries, despite the growing middle class, rapid industrialization created two sharply contrasting urban classes: wealthy entrepreneurs and poor immigrants from Europe and Asia who provided them with cheap labor. Although dependent upon each other, these groups seldom met, living in starkly different neighborhoods. Wealthy families established fashionable districts in the hearts of cities, where they built fabulous mansions.

By contrast, the majority of factory workers squeezed into dark, overcrowded tenements where crime, violence, fire, and disease were constant threats. U.S. writers of the time responded to and reflected these urban conditions.

> "The entire metropolitan center possessed a high and mighty air calculated to . . . make the gulf between poverty and success seem both wide and deep."
>
> —Theodore Dreiser
> *Sister Carrie*

Picnicking in Central Park, 1885. Robert L. Bracklow. Black and white photograph.

The Face of the Urban Rich

Two major Realist writers from the upper class who reflected and criticized its values were the famous literary friends Edith Wharton and Henry James.

Edith Wharton was born in 1862 into one of New York's most prominent families. Her interest in architecture prompted her to criticize and satirize the "conspicuous consumption" (a term coined by social critic Thorstein Veblen) that led to the fashionable, cluttered interior decoration favored by her social class. In Wharton's early novel *The House of Mirth* (1905), heroine Lily Bart's descent from wealth into poverty is mirrored by a decline in the houses she is forced to inhabit.

Wharton's older contemporary and friend Henry James was born into a distinguished Boston family in 1843. James became the master chronicler of the

inner lives of his characters, and his subtle innovations in narrative point of view contributed to the literary technique that his brother William, the famous psychologist, called "the stream of consciousness." James used this technique to probe the complex relationship between wealth and culture. One of his favorite themes was the confrontation between naïve, wealthy, uncultured Americans and highly cultivated and sophisticated Europeans, whose aristocratic civilization was in decline. James's treatment of this theme reached its zenith in his late novel *The Ambassadors* (1903).

536 UNIT 4 REGIONALISM AND REALISM

Track Terminology Ask students the following questions about the term *conspicuous consumption* and the man who coined it. Encourage students to use a history textbook, a source of quotations, a biographical dictionary, a regular dictionary, and reliable Web sites to find the answers.

- What was the title of Thorstein Veblen's now-famous 1902 book in which he

coined the term *conspicuous consumption*? (*The Theory of the Leisure Class*)
- What are two definitions of *conspicuous*? (*"attracting attention" and "violating good taste"*)
- How would you paraphrase the following line by Veblen: "Conspicuous consumption of valuable goods is a means of reputability to the gentleman of leisure"? (*Rich people buy expensive things to impress others.*)

The Face of the Urban Poor

The plight of the urban poor was a favorite subject of the new group of Naturalist writers. Stephen Crane's *Maggie: A Girl of the Streets* is a bleak study of life in the slums of New York City.

Some writers focused their attention on the hardships of immigrants and ethnic groups who faced bigotry and discrimination as well as poverty in U.S. cities. Anzia Yezierska and Abraham Cahan wrote about the social, cultural, and political tensions experienced by Eastern European Jews living in New York's Lower East Side.

Men gather in an alley called "Bandit's Roost" in Manhattan's Little Italy. Around the turn of the century, this part of Mulberry Bend was a notoriously dilapidated and dangerous section of New York City. ca. 1890s. Jacob August Riis.

View the Art How do the people in this scene compare with those of the previous page?

Perhaps the most famous writer to address the socioeconomic plight of the urban poor was Theodore Dreiser. In his first and perhaps greatest novel, *Sister Carrie* (1900), Carrie Meeber, a naïve country girl, comes to Chicago looking for work. There she endures the impersonal cruelty and loneliness of a large U.S. city at the turn of the century.

Reformers and Muckrakers

In the late nineteenth century, a social reform movement arose that was dedicated to providing better conditions for the urban working class. Perhaps the most prominent reformer was Jane Addams. In *Twenty Years at Hull-House* (1910), she tells how she turned an old home in an immigrant neighborhood in Chicago into a settlement house where residents could learn to speak English, discuss political events, and hold celebrations.

Journalists and novelists known as "muckrakers" began to criticize the social, economic, and political system creating the gulf between rich and poor. In *How the Other Half Lives* (1890), Jacob Riis alerted President Roosevelt to the squalor of New York City slum tenements. Improvements in the water supply, child labor laws, and other areas resulted. *The Jungle* (1906), Upton Sinclair's exposé of brutal working conditions in meatpacking, led to the 1906 Meat Inspection and the Pure Food and Drug Acts.

LOG ON **Literature** Online

Literature and Reading For more about the literature of urban America, go to glencoe.com and enter QuickPass code GLA9800u4.

Respond and Think Critically

1. In Dreiser's *Sister Carrie*, the protagonist believes that the city will provide her with new opportunities and a new life. Would you have wanted to live in a large city at the turn of the twentieth century? Why or why not?

2. What were Edith Wharton's and Henry James's main criticisms of the wealthy upper class in the United States?

3. How would you compare and contrast Realist and Naturalist Fiction with their predecessor, Romantic Fiction?

English Learners

UNIVERSAL ACCESS

Advanced Read short sections of "The Two Faces of Urban America" aloud to students. After reading the section called The Face of the Urban Rich, **ask:** What does the author mean when he says that Henry James was the "master chronicler of inner lives?" *(He wrote about people's thoughts and feelings.)* After reading The

Face of the Urban Poor section, **ask:** What do you think the "impersonal cruelty and loneliness of the big city" means? *(the harshness of living alone, without support, and unknown by others)* After reading the final section, **ask:** What do you think "the other half" means in the Riis book title? *(the very poor people)*

Teach

View the Art ★

Answer: *The general mood and scenery of this candid photograph contrasts with the formal pose and park setting shown in the photograph on page 536. This group's clothes are plainer, and the view shows laundry and rubbish, instead of "the great outdoors."*

Assess

1. Some students may say that they would have been attracted by the city's opportunities and excitement. Others may think that most people in cities suffered dehumanizing conditions.

2. Wharton satirized their conspicuous consumption and aggressiveness. James criticized them for lack of culture and sophistication.

3. Romantic Fiction glorified the imagination; Realist and Naturalist Fiction explored the motivations, actions, and behaviors of real people. The real people whom Naturalists focused on were generally poor or working-class individuals, waging hopeless battles against an unresponsive society or universe.

 For activities related to this selection, see Unit 4 Teaching Resources Book, pp. 93–94.

Focus

April Showers

Bellringer Options

**Daily Language Practice
Transparency 49**

Or remind students that American women did not have the right to vote until passage of the Nineteenth Amendment in 1920 and had few opportunities for educational development or economic independence.

Ask: What do you think life was like for women at this time? What do you think young women at this time hoped for?

As they read, have students consider Theodora's hopes and the realities of her life. Have students research the Nineteenth Amendment and compare the intentions of the Amendment to her life.

Meet **Edith Wharton**
(1862–1937)

Edith Wharton is best known for her novels depicting the intricate codes of conduct that ruled the lives of New York City's aristocracy at the end of the 1800s. She felt that the upper-class discouraged both art and the artist.

> "Mrs. Ballinger is one of the ladies who pursue Culture in Bands, as though it were dangerous to meet it alone."
>
> —Edith Wharton
> *Xingu and Other Stories*, 1916

A Privileged Youth Edith Newbold Jones was born into one of New York City's wealthiest and most distinguished families. Taught by private tutors, she received an excellent education both in the United States and abroad. When she was sixteen, Edith privately published her first book. Her mother may have arranged the publication, hoping that Edith would feel fulfilled, stop writing, and take up interests considered more suited to her social position.

In 1885 Edith married Edward Wharton, a wealthy Boston banker. Shortly after, he began to suffer from both mental and physical illnesses. It was during this time that Wharton began seriously writing fiction with the intention of publishing. She modeled her work mostly after novelist Henry James—combining complicated psychological portraits with critiques of social convention. Throughout the 1890s, she contributed to various magazines and produced two collections of short stories.

A Novelist Abroad Wharton's first novel, *The Valley of Decision*, was published in 1902. In 1905 the acclaimed novel *The House of Mirth* appeared.

In 1907, after selling her home and separating from her husband, Wharton permanently settled in Paris, where she felt female artists were more accepted.

As World War I raged, Wharton worked in support of the French—aiding Belgian refugees and raising money from Americans. For this she was given the Cross of the Legion of Honor, the highest honor awarded to a foreigner in France.

During this time Wharton published some of her greatest novels: *Ethan Frome*, *The Reef*, *The Custom of the Country*, and *Summer*. For *The Age of Innocence* (1920), probably her best-known work, Wharton became the first woman to be awarded a Pulitzer Prize for fiction.

Wharton's greatness came from her ability to depict the interplay between the life of the mind and of society. Alternately tragic and satiric, Wharton's incisive fiction helped to establish Realism as the most important movement of her day.

 Literature Online

Author Search For more about Edith Wharton, go to glencoe.com and enter QuickPass code GLA9800u4.

Selection Skills

Literary Elements
- Flashback (SE pp. 539, 540, 545, 547)
- Theme (SE p. 547)
- Characterization (TE p. 546)
- Sentence Fragments (TE p. 544)

April Showers

Reading Skills
- Make and Verify Predictions (SE pp. 539, 541, 543, 545, 546, 548)
- Preview (TE p. 540)

Vocabulary Skills
- Denotation and Connotation (SE pp. 548)
- Synonyms (TE p. 539)

Writing Skills/Grammar
- Point of View (SE p. 548)
- Summarize (TE p. 542)

Listening/Speaking/ Viewing Skills
- Analyze Art (TE p. 544)

Literature and Reading Preview

Connect to the Story

Have you ever neglected your responsibilities in order to devote yourself to a project you felt passionately about? What was the result? Freewrite for ten minutes on this subject.

Build Background

"April Showers" is set in Massachusetts in the early 1900s. At the time, novels were often printed in magazines in serial form, appearing in weekly or monthly installments.

Set Purposes for Reading

Big Idea Realism

As you read, ask yourself, How is Realism's focus on psychology and human behavior displayed in "April Showers"?

Literary Element Flashback

A **flashback** is an interruption in the chronological order of a narrative to show an event that happened earlier. A writer may use the flashback structure to give readers information that explains the main events of a story. As you read, ask yourself, How does Wharton's use of flashbacks help the reader better understand Theodora's character and the story's events?

Reading Strategy Make and Verify Predictions

To **predict** means to make an educated guess about what will happen in a text, using the clues that a writer provides. Predicting will help you stay engaged in the plot of a story as it evolves. While you read "April Showers," verify, adjust, or change your predictions as new information emerges in the text.

Tip: Take Notes Use a chart to record your predictions and the evidence on which you base those predictions.

Prediction	Evidence
Theodora's obsession with her novel will come back to haunt her.	Theodora is neglecting her family obligations.

Learning Objectives

For pages 538–548

In studying this text, you will focus on the following objectives:

Literary Study: Analyzing flashback.

Reading: Making and verifying predictions.

Writing: Applying point of view in a brief narrative.

Vocabulary

prosperous (pros′ pər əs) *adj.* wealthy or successful; p. 540 *The Smiths, who owned a factory, were the most prosperous family in town.*

obscure (əb skyoor′) *adj.* little known or having an insignificant reputation; p. 541 *The more obscure painters were overlooked in the student's research paper.*

stupor (stoo′ pər) *n.* a confused or dazed state of mind; p. 543 *Jack was in a stupor after having his tonsils removed the day before.*

calamity (kə lam′ ə tē) *n.* an unfortunate event or disaster; p. 543 *The hurricane was a terrible calamity for the small coastal town.*

EDITH WHARTON **539**

Before You Read

Focus

Summary

Seventeen-year-old Theodora Dace ignores her responsibilities in order to write a novel. When her novel is apparently accepted, she becomes a local celebrity. After a misunderstanding, Theodora confronts the publisher and retrieves her manuscript. At the end, she learns something about her father's aspirations.

 For summaries in languages other than English, see Unit 4 Teaching Resources Book, pp. 95–100.

Vocabulary

Synonyms Have students name two new synonyms for each vocabulary word. *(prosperous: rich, affluent; obscure: hidden, unknown; stupor: trance, daze; calamity: catastrophe, tragedy.)*

(**ENGLISH LEARNERS**) Explain that the roots of words can help distinguish one synonymous word from another. For example, a synonym for the word *stupor* is *daze*, whose root means "to become weary." Someone who is not paying attention might be described as "in a daze." The word *stupor* comes from a Latin root that means "numb" or "stunned." **Ask:** Which is more extreme, a daze or a stupor? *(stupor)*

 For additional vocabulary practice, see Unit 4 Teaching Resources Book, p.103.

 For additional context, see Glencoe Interactive Vocabulary CD-ROM.

English Learners

DIFFERENTIATED INSTRUCTION

Intermediate On page 538 it says that Wharton's work contained "complicated psychological portraits" and "critiques of social convention." Explain that the first phrase means that her characters are like real people: neither all good nor all bad. **Say:** Think of a fairy tale or comic book character such as Superman. **Ask:** How does this character compare to someone you know? *(The figure always does good things, while the person they know does not.)* Explain the meaning of "critiques of social convention": Wharton wrote honestly about the damaging restrictions that upper-class society placed on people. Have students use sticky notes to mark this sort of commentary as they read.

Teach

Big Idea | 1

Realism Answer: *This comment suggests that Theodora is confident in her abilities as a writer. She may, in fact, be overly confident.*

Say: Remember that Realists attempted to re-create the appearance of ordinary lives in their writing.

Literary Element | 2

Flashback Answer: *This sentence gives the reader clues that what is being described happened in the past and that this is a flashback.*

Ask: What information does this flashback provide? *(It tells the reader what Theodora's world is like.)*

Language History ☆

A-one The expression *A-one* means "excellent, superior, or first class." It comes from the world of transatlantic shipping, in which the term referred to the condition of first-class ships. The expression can also be written *A 1* or *A number 1*.

For an audio recording of this selection, use Listening Library Audio CD-ROM.

Readability Scores

Dale-Chall: 5.8
DRP: 60
Lexile: 1020

540

April Showers

Edith Wharton

Girl Sitting in a Sunlit Room. Carl Holsoe. Private collection.

"But Guy's heart slept under the violets on Muriel's grave."

It was a beautiful ending; Theodora had seen girls cry over last chapters that weren't half as pathetic. She laid her pen aside and read the words over, letting her voice linger on the fall of the sentence; then, drawing a deep breath, she wrote across the foot of the page the name by which she had decided to become known in literature—Gladys Glyn.

Downstairs the library clock struck two. Its muffled thump sounded like an admonitory knock against her bedroom floor. Two o'clock! and she had promised her mother to be up early enough to see that the buttons were sewn on Johnny's reefer,[1] and that Kate had her cod-liver oil[2] before starting for school!

Lingeringly, tenderly she gathered up the pages of her novel—there were five hundred of them—and tied them with the blue satin ribbon that her Aunt Julia had given her. She had meant to wear the ribbon with her new dotted muslin on Sundays, but this was putting it to a

nobler use. She bound it round her manuscript, tying the ends in a pretty bow. Theodora was clever at making bows, and could have trimmed hats beautifully, had not all her spare moments been given to literature. Then, with a last look at the precious pages, she sealed and addressed the package. She meant to send it off next morning to the *Home Circle.* She knew it would be hard to obtain access to a paper which numbered so many popular authors among its contributors, but she had been encouraged to make the venture by something her Uncle James had said the last time he had come down from Boston.

He had been telling his brother, Doctor Dace, about his new house out at Brookline. Uncle James was **prosperous**, and was always moving into new houses with more "modern improvements." Hygiene was his passion, and he migrated in the wake of sanitary plumbing.

---

1. A *reefer* is a short, heavy jacket.
2. *Cod-liver oil* is an unpleasant-tasting liquid rich in vitamins A and D.

1 | **Realism** *What can you infer about Theodora's view of herself from this comment?*

Flashback *What does this sentence indicate about the paragraphs following it?* | **2**

Vocabulary

prosperous (pros´ pər əs) *adj.* wealthy or successful

540 UNIT 4 REGIONALISM AND REALISM

Reading Practice

Preview Explain that this story focuses on the discrepancy between a young woman's hopes and the reality of daily life. Theodora dreams of becoming a famous writer, but the real world intrudes upon her fantasies. **Ask:** Have you ever gotten so lost in your dreams or expectations that you missed what was really happening? Have students take notes as they read in order to answer the following questions: At which points in the story is Theodora

lost in her fantasy world? *(while she prepares to mail her manuscript; while waiting to hear about its acceptance; after she receives the acceptance letter)* At which points in the story does she awaken to reality? *(when the editor explains the mistake)*

"The bathrooms alone are worth the money," he was saying, cheerfully, "although it *is* a big rent. But then, when a man's got no children to save up for—" he glanced compassionately round Doctor Dace's crowded table "—and it *is* something to be in a neighborhood where the drainage is A-one. That's what I was telling our neighbor. Who do you suppose she is, by the way?" He smiled at Theodora. "I rather think that young lady knows all about her. Ever hear of Kathleen Kyd?"

Kathleen Kyd! The famous "society novelist," the creator of more "favorite heroines" than all her predecessors put together had ever turned out, the author of *Fashion and Passion, An American Duchess, Rhona's Revolt.* Was there any intelligent girl from Maine to California whose heart would not have beat faster at the mention of that name?

"Why, yes," Uncle James was saying, "Kathleen Kyd lives next door. Frances G. Wollop is her real name, and her husband's a dentist. She's a very pleasant, sociable kind of woman; you'd never think she was a writer. Ever hear how she began to write? She told me the whole story. It seems she was a saleswoman in a store, working on starvation wages, with a mother and a consumptive sister to support. Well, she wrote a story one day, just for fun, and sent it to the *Home Circle.* They'd never heard of her, of course, and she never expected to hear from them. She did, though. They took the story and passed their plate for more. She became a regular contributor and eventually was known all over the country. Now she tells me her books bring her in about ten thousand a year. Rather more than you and I can boast of, eh, John? Well, I hope *this* household doesn't contribute to her support." He glanced sharply at Theodora. "I don't believe in feeding youngsters on sentimental trash; it's like sewer gas—doesn't smell bad, and infects the system without your knowing it."

Theodora listened breathlessly. Kathleen Kyd's first story had been accepted by the *Home Circle,* and they had asked for more!

Why should Gladys Glyn be less fortunate? Theodora had done a great deal of novel reading—far more than her parents were aware of—and felt herself competent to pronounce upon the quality of her own work. She was almost sure that "April Showers" was a remarkable book. If it lacked Kathleen Kyd's lightness of touch, it had an emotional intensity never achieved by that brilliant writer. Theodora did not care to amuse her readers; she left that to more frivolous talents. Her aim was to stir the depths of human nature, and she felt she had succeeded. It was a great thing for a girl to be able to feel that about her first novel. Theodora was only seventeen; and she remembered, with a touch of retrospective compassion, that George Eliot[3] had not become famous till she was nearly forty.

No, there was no doubt about the merit of "April Showers." But would not an inferior work have had a better chance of success? Theodora recalled the early struggles of famous authors, the notorious antagonism[4] of publishers and editors to any new writer of exceptional promise. Would it not be wiser to write the book down to the average reader's level, reserving for some later work the great "effects" into which she had thrown all the fever of her imagination? The thought was sacrilege! Never would she lay hands on the sacred structure she had reared; never would she resort to the inartistic expedient of modifying her work to suit the popular taste. Better **obscure** failure than a vulgar triumph. The great authors never stooped to such concessions, and Theodora felt

---

3. *George Eliot* (1819–1880) was the pen name of famed British novelist Mary Ann Cross.
4. *Antagonism* means "hostility."

Make and Verify Predictions *What is your prediction of Gladys Glyn's success?* **3**

Vocabulary

obscure (əb skyoor´) *adj.* little known or having an insignificant reputation

Reading Strategy 3

Make and Verify Predictions **Answer:**
Students might feel this statement is ironic and that Gladys Glyn will not experience much success.

Ask: On what do you base your prediction? *(Students may suggest that Theodora's youth and romantic ideas about writing set her up for disappointment.)*

 For additional practice using the reading skill or strategy, see Unit 4 Teaching Resources Book, p. 102.

Literary History ☆

George Eliot Theodora's allusion to George Eliot is ironic. Eliot was one of the great British writers of the nineteenth century. Her realistic works examined the lives of people in an industrialized and socially stratified Britain. Eliot wrote serious novels, including *Middlemarch, The Mill on the Floss,* and *Daniel Deronda.* She was the antithesis of a young Romantic writer like Theodora.

English Learners

DIFFERENTIATED INSTRUCTION

Intermediate Have students create a chart with these headings: *Unfamiliar Word, What I Think It Means,* and *Meaning.* Have students fill in the first two columns as they read, using context clues to fill in the second. Have students use a dictionary to complete the third column.

Approaching Level

DIFFERENTIATED INSTRUCTION

Emerging Explain that predictions are statements about future events based upon observations, experience, or reason. For example, you might have guessed that Theodora would not sew on her brother's buttons; she was preoccupied with her book. **Ask:** What is Uncle James's opinion of romantic novels? *(dislikes them; calls them "sentimental trash"; compares them to sewer gas)* **Ask:** What do you think his reaction would be to Theodora writing a book? *(Students may guess that he will disapprove.)*

Teach

Realism Answer: *In some books written by Romantic authors, characters might not behave in a realistic way. Most students will think that characters in this story are portrayed in a realistic way.*

Ask: What is realistic about the way Theodora is portrayed? *(Theodora's romantic ideas and irresponsible behavior suggest that she is a typical teenager.)*

Cultural History ☆

Medicine in the Early 1900s
In the early twentieth century, the practice of medicine was not highly developed. Local doctors visited patients in their homes but sometimes could offer little help to very sick ones. Effective medicines and treatments were not available for some diseases at the time.

Writing Practice

Summarize Remind students that summarizing is a skill that can help them read fiction. Review that a summary is a short restatement of main ideas and key details in a passage. **Say:** The first full paragraph on page 543 shows how Theodora is handling her responsibilities at home. Reread the paragraph and then write a summary of it. Students' summaries should mention Theodora's reactions to the postman and her fam-

542

---

herself included in their ranks by the firmness with which she rejected all thought of conciliating[5] an unappreciative public. The manuscript should be sent as it was.

She woke with a start and a heavy sense of apprehension. The *Home Circle* had refused "April Showers"! No, that couldn't be it; there lay the precious manuscript, waiting to be posted. What was it, then? Ah, that ominous thump below stairs—nine o'clock striking! It was Johnny's buttons!

She sprang out of bed in dismay. She had been so determined not to disappoint her mother about Johnny's buttons! Mrs. Dace, helpless from chronic rheumatism,[6] had to entrust the care of the household to her eldest daughter; and Theodora honestly meant to see that Johnny had his full complement of buttons, and that Kate and Bertha went to school tidy. Unfortunately, the writing of a great novel leaves little time or memory for the lesser obligations of life, and Theodora usually found that her good intentions matured too late for practical results.

Her contrition[7] was softened by the thought that literary success would enable her to make up for all the little negligences of which she was guilty. She meant to spend all her money on her family; and already she had visions of a wheeled chair for her mother, a fresh wallpaper for the doctor's shabby office, bicycles for the girls, and Johnny's establishment at a boarding school where sewing on his buttons would be included in the curriculum. If her parents could have guessed her intentions, they would not have found fault with her as they did; and Doctor Dace, on this particular morning, would

> "I suppose you didn't get home from the ball till morning?"

not have looked up to say, with his fagged,[8] ironical air:

"I suppose you didn't get home from the ball till morning?"

Theodora's sense of being in the right enabled her to take the thrust with a dignity that would have awed the unfeeling parent to fiction.

"I'm sorry to be late, father," she said.

Doctor Dace, who could never be counted on to behave like a father in a book, shrugged his shoulders impatiently.

"Your sentiments do you credit, but they haven't kept your mother's breakfast warm."

"Hasn't mother's tray gone up yet?"

"Who was to take it, I should like to know? The girls came down so late that I had to hustle them off before they'd finished breakfast, and Johnny's hands were so dirty that I sent him back to his room to make himself decent. It's a pretty thing for the doctor's children to be the dirtiest little savages in Norton!"

Theodora had hastily prepared her mother's tray, leaving her own breakfast untouched. As she entered the room upstairs, Mrs. Dace's patient face turned to her with a smile much harder to bear than her father's reproaches.

"Mother, I'm *so* sorry—"

"No matter, dear. I suppose Johnny's buttons kept you. I can't think what that boy does to his clothes!"

Theodora sat the tray down without speaking. It was impossible to own to having forgotten Johnny's buttons without revealing the cause of her forgetfulness. For a few weeks longer she

---

5. *Conciliating* means "appeasing."
6. *Rheumatism* is an illness that causes discomfort in the joints or muscles.
7. *Contrition* means "remorse."

8. *Fagged* means "tired" or "weary."

Realism *How might a person's behavior in reality differ from his or her behavior in a book? Are the characters in this story portrayed realistically?* **1**

---

ily. **Ask:** What does this paragraph say about Theodora's home life and her role in it? *(It is chaotic and falling apart, and Theodora is doing little to help.)*

must bear to be misunderstood; then—ah, then if her novel were accepted, how gladly would she forget and forgive! But what if it were refused? She turned aside to hide the dismay that flushed her face. Well, then she would admit the truth—she would ask her parents' pardon, and settle down without a murmur to an obscure existence of mending and combing.

She had said to herself that after the manuscript had been sent, she would have time to look after the children and catch up with the mending; but she had reckoned without the postman. He came three times a day; for an hour before each ring she was too excited to do anything but wonder if he would bring an answer this time, and for an hour afterward she moved about in a leaden **stupor** of disappointment. The children had never been so trying. They seemed to be always coming to pieces, like cheap furniture; one would have supposed they had been put together with bad glue. Mrs. Dace worried herself ill over Johnny's tatters, Bertha's bad marks at school, and Kate's open abstention[9] from cod-liver oil; and Doctor Dace, coming back late from a long round of visits to a fireless office with a smoky lamp, called out furiously to know if Theodora would kindly come down and remove the "East, West, home's best" that hung above the empty grate.

In the midst of it all, Miss Sophy Brill called. It was very kind of her to come, for she was the busiest woman in Norton. She made it her duty to look after other people's affairs, and there was not a house in town but had the benefit of her personal supervision. She generally came when things were going wrong, and the sight of her bonnet on the doorstep was a surer sign of **calamity** than a crepe bow[10] on the bell.

---

9. *Abstention* means "the act of refraining from something."
10. A *crepe bow* is a piece of black fabric displayed as a sign of mourning.

Vocabulary

stupor (stōō´ pər) *n.* a confused or dazed state of mind
calamity (kə lam´ ə tē) *n.* an unfortunate event or disaster

After she left, Mrs. Dace looked very sad, and the doctor punished Johnny for warbling down the entry:

"Miss Sophy Brill
Is a bitter pill!"

while Theodora, locking herself in her room, resolved with tears that she would never write another novel.

The week was a long nightmare. Theodora could neither eat nor sleep. She was up early enough, but instead of looking after the children and seeing that breakfast was ready, she wandered down the road to meet the postman, and came back wan and empty-handed, oblivious of her morning duties. She had no idea how long the suspense would last; but she didn't see how authors could live if they were kept waiting more than a week.

Then suddenly, one afternoon—she never quite knew how or when it happened—she found herself with a *Home Circle* envelope in her hands, and her dazzled eyes flashing over a wild dance of words that wouldn't settle down and make sense.

"Dear Madam:" (They called her *Madam!* And then; yes, the words were beginning to fall into line now.) "Your novel, 'April Showers,' has been received, and we are glad to accept it on the usual terms. A serial on which we were counting for immediate publication has been delayed by the author's illness, and the first chapters of 'April Showers' will therefore appear in our midsummer number. Thanking you for favoring us with your manuscript, we remain," and so forth.

Theodora found herself in the wood beyond the schoolhouse. She was kneeling on the ground, brushing aside the dead leaves and pressing her lips to the little bursting green things that pushed up eager tips through last year's decay. It was spring—spring! Everything was crowding toward the light and in her own heart hundreds of germinating hopes had burst

---

Make and Verify Predictions *What news do you think the envelope will contain?* **3**

EDITH WHARTON **543**

Teach

| **Vocabulary** | **2** |

Word Choice Ask: Why does Wharton repeat *obscure* here? *(Being obscure is what Theodora dreads and is probably what her future holds.)*

| **Reading Strategy** | **3** |

Make and Verify Predictions Answer: *Some students may expect the envelope to contain good news; others will expect it to contain notice of the novel's rejection.*

Writer's Technique

Voice The publisher's letter provides Wharton an opportunity to use an outsider's voice in the story. The language in the letter is formal and businesslike.

Ask: How does the voice in the letter compare with Theodora's? *(It is a mature and businesslike voice unlike Theodora's, but it is still somewhat flowery.)*

Approaching Level
DIFFERENTIATED INSTRUCTION

Emerging Students may be confused by the use of flashbacks. Have students create a timeline that indicates when each event takes place. Remind them to look for clue words and shifts in verb tense that indicate when an event occurs.

English Learners
DIFFERENTIATED INSTRUCTION

Intermediate To help students understand unfamiliar words, remind them to use their knowledge of word parts. Point out that *manuscript* is made up of two Latin roots: *manu,* meaning "hand," and *script,* meaning "writing." **Ask:** What do you think the meaning of manuscript is? *(writing done by hand)* Point out that today the word refers to typed as well as handwritten documents.

Teach

Big Idea   1

Realism **Answer:** *These descriptions suggest that most people are impressed by success. Some students may say that some people pay attention only to important people.*

Say: Describe how people's attitudes toward Theodora changed. *(Her parents have become more lenient, and people outside the family have become more respectful of and interested in Theodora.)*

View the Photograph

In 1870 approximately 53,000 miles of railroads connected the regions of the United States. By 1916 there were 254,000 miles of track. The train was the most practical way for Theodora to get to Boston quickly.

Trains at Paddington Station, London, 1910.

into sudden leaf. She wondered if the thrust of those little green fingers hurt the surface of the earth as her springing raptures hurt—yes, actually hurt!—her hot, constricted breast! She looked up through interlacing boughs at a tender, opaque blue sky full of the coming of a milky moon. She seemed enveloped in an atmosphere of loving comprehension. The brown earth throbbed with her joy, the treetops trembled with it, and a sudden star broke through the branches like an audible "I know!"

Theodora, on the whole, behaved very well. Her mother cried, her father whistled and said he supposed he must put up with grounds in his coffee now, and be thankful if he ever got a hot meal again; while the children took the most deafening and harassing advantage of what seemed a sudden suspension of the laws of nature.

Within a week everybody in Norton knew that Theodora had written a novel, and that it was coming out in the *Home Circle*. On Sundays, when she walked up the aisle, her friends dropped their prayer books and the soprano sang false in her excitement. Girls with more pin money than Theodora had ever dreamed of copied her hats and imitated her way of speaking. The local paper asked her for a poem; her old school teachers stopped to shake hands and grew shy over their congratulations; and Miss Sophy Brill came to call. She

had put on her Sunday bonnet and her manner was almost abject.[11] She ventured, very timidly, to ask her young friend how she wrote, whether it "just came to her," and if she had found that the kind of pen she used made any difference; and wound up by begging Theodora to write a sentiment in her album.

Even Uncle James came down from Boston to talk the wonder over. He called Theodora a "sly baggage," and proposed that she should give him her earnings to invest in a new patent greasetrap company. From what Kathleen Kyd had told him, he thought Theodora would probably get a thousand dollars for her story. He concluded by suggesting that she should base her next romance on the subject of sanitation, making the heroine nearly die of sewer gas poisoning because her parents won't listen to the handsome young doctor next door, when he warns them that their plumbing is out of order. That was a subject that would interest everybody, and do a lot more good than the sentimental trash most women wrote.

At last the great day came. Theodora had left an order with the bookseller for the midsummer number of the *Home Circle* and before the shop was open she was waiting on the sidewalk. She clutched her precious paper and ran home without opening it. Her excitement was almost more than she could bear. Not heeding her father's call to breakfast, she rushed upstairs and locked herself in her room. Her hands trembled so that

1   **Realism** *What do these descriptions of people's reactions to Theodora's success suggest about human behavior?*

11. *Abject* means "miserable."

544   UNIT 4   REGIONALISM AND REALISM

Reading Practice

SPIRAL REVIEW   **Sentence Fragments** Explain that writers often use sentence fragments to convey the way people actually speak. To illustrate, have students identify sentence fragments in the second to the last full paragraph on p. 545. An example is "Mrs. Kyd's new serial?" Ask students to rewrite the paragraph as a complete dialogue between Theodora and the publisher at *Home Circle*. Then have a few volunteers read their dialogues aloud to the class. Ask students to compare their dialogues with Wharton's. *(Wharton's is more realistic. Full dialogue slows the pace of the flashback.)*

she could hardly turn the pages. At last—yes, there it was: "April Showers."

The paper dropped from her hands. What name had she read beneath the title? Had her emotion blinded her?

"April Showers, by *Kathleen Kyd*."

Kathleen Kyd! Oh, cruel misprint! Oh, dastardly typographer! Through tears of rage and disappointment Theodora looked again; yes, there was no mistaking the hateful name. Her glance ran on. She found herself reading a first paragraph that she had never seen before. She read farther. All was strange. The horrible truth burst upon her: *It was not her story!*

2 She never knew how she got back to the station. She struggled through the crowd on the platform, and a gold-banded arm pushed her into the train just starting for Norton. It would be dark when she reached home; but that didn't matter—nothing mattered now. She sank into her seat, closing her eyes in the vain attempt to shut out the vision of the last few hours; but minute by minute memory forced her to relive it; she felt like a rebellious schoolchild dragged forth to repeat the same detested "piece."

Although she did not know Boston well, she had made her way easily enough to the *Home Circle* building; at least, she supposed she had, since she remembered nothing till she found herself ascending the editorial stairs as easily as one does incredible things in dreams. She must have walked very fast, for her heart was beating furiously, and she had barely breath to whisper the editor's name to a young man who looked out at her from a glass case, like a zoological specimen. The young man led her past other glass cases containing similar specimens to an inner enclosure which seemed filled by an enormous presence. Theodora felt herself enveloped in the presence, submerged by it, gasping for air as she sank under its rising surges.

Gradually fragments of speech floated to the surface. "'April Showers?' Mrs. Kyd's new serial? *Your* manuscript, you say? You have a letter from me? The name, please? Evidently some unfortunate misunderstanding. One moment." And then a bell ringing, a zoological specimen ordered to unlock a safe, her name asked for again, the manuscript, her own precious manuscript, tied with Aunt Julia's ribbon, laid on the table before her, and her outcries, her protests, her interrogations, drowned in a flood of bland apology: "An unfortunate accident—Mrs. Kyd's manuscript received the same day—extraordinary coincidence in the choice of a title—duplicate answers sent by mistake—Miss Dace's novel hardly suited to their purpose—should of course have been returned—regrettable oversight—accidents would happen—sure she understood."

The voice went on, like the steady pressure of a surgeon's hand on a shrieking nerve. When it stopped she was in the street. A cab nearly ran her down, and a car bell jangled furiously in her ears. She clutched her manuscript, carrying it tenderly through the crowd, like a live thing that had been hurt. She could not bear to look at its soiled edges and the ink stain on Aunt Julia's ribbon.

The train stopped with a jerk and she opened her eyes. It was dark, and by the windy flare of gas on the platform she saw the Norton passengers getting out. She stood up stiffly and followed them. A warm wind blew into her face the fragrance of the summer woods, and

> The voice went on, like the steady pressure of a surgeon's hand on a shrieking nerve.

---

3 Making and Verifying Predictions *How does this turn of events compare with your predictions about Theodora's success?*

Flashback *What clues does this give you about the chronology of the story?* **4**

EDITH WHARTON **545**

Teach

Literary Element 2

Flashback Point out that the story jumps abruptly forward at this point.

Ask: Why did the author break up the narrative in this way? (*The flashback is more efficient. Wharton does not have to tell how Theodora got to Boston; she can cover only the most important parts.*)

(APPROACHING) **Ask:** What in the text indicates that the author is writing a flashback? (*She gets on the train "just starting for Norton" before you know she had traveled to Boston.*)

Reading Strategy 3

Make and Verify Predictions Answer: *Students' answers will vary. Some will be surprised that Theodora's success was actually a mistake. Others may have suspected that her good fortune would change.*

Literary Element 4

Flashback Answer: *The previous action happened earlier in the story, and the narration has now returned to the present.*

Ask: How does the flashback affect the tone or feeling of the story? (*The flashback is fast-paced and filled with sentence fragments and sensory details. It changes the tone from hopefulness to anxiety.*)

English Learners

DIFFERENTIATED INSTRUCTION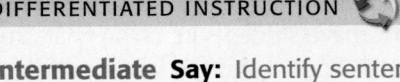

Intermediate Say: Identify sentences on this page that contain similes. (*For example, "The voice went on, like the steady pressure of a surgeon's hand on a shrieking nerve" and "She clutched her manuscript, carrying it tenderly through the crowd, like a live thing that had been wounded."*) Discuss the literal and figurative meanings of these expressions.

Teach

Reading Strategy   1

Make and Verify Predictions **Answer:**
Students' answers will vary. Most students would not have expected Doctor Dace to be sympathetic.

Ask: Why do you think Doctor Dace is now sympathetic to Theodora? *(He may have remembered that he was like Theodora when he was younger; he may understand her disappointment.)*

ENGLISH LEARNERS Theodora's father showed "a face of unexpected participation" while walking Theodora home from the train station. Students may be confused by this phrase. Have students replace the word *participation* with the synonym *sympathy,* and then describe his face using their own words.

> To check students' understanding of the selection, see Unit 4 Teaching Resources Book, p. 106.

Progress Check

Can students analyze a flashback?

If No → See Unit 4 Teaching Resources Book, p. 101.

she remembered how, two months earlier, she had knelt among the dead leaves, pressing her lips to the first shoots of green. Then for the first time she thought of home. She had fled away in the morning without a word, and her heart sank at the thought of her mother's fears. And her father—how angry he would be! She bent her head under the coming storm of his derision.

The night was cloudy, and as she stepped into the darkness beyond the station a hand was slipped in hers. She stood still, too weary to feel frightened, and a voice said, quietly:

"Don't walk so fast, child. You look tired."

"Father!" Her hand dropped from his, but he recaptured it, and drew it through his arm. When she found voice, it was to whisper, "You were at the station?"

"It's such a good night I thought I'd stroll down and meet you."

Her arm trembled against his. She could not see his face in the dimness, but the light of his cigar looked down on her like a friendly eye, and she took courage to falter out: "Then you knew—"

"That you'd gone to Boston? Well, I rather thought you had."

They walked on slowly, and presently he added, "You see, you left the *Home Circle* lying in your room."

How she blessed the darkness and the muffled sky! She could not have borne the scrutiny of the tiniest star.

"Then mother wasn't very much frightened?"

"Why, no, she didn't appear to be. She's been busy all day over some toggery¹² of Bertha's."

---

12. *Toggery* means "clothes."

Theodora choked. "Father, I'll—" She groped for words, but they eluded her. "I'll do things—differently; I haven't meant—" Suddenly she heard herself bursting out: "It was all a mistake, you know—about my story. They didn't want it; they won't have it!" and she shrank back involuntarily from his impending mirth.

She felt the pressure of his arm, but he didn't speak, and she figured his mute hilarity. They moved on in silence. Presently he said:

"It hurts a bit just at first, doesn't it?"

"O Father!"

He stood still, and the gleam of his cigar showed a face of unexpected participation.

"You see I've been through it myself."

"You, Father? You?"

"Why, yes. Didn't I ever tell you? I wrote a novel once. I was just out of college, and didn't want to be a doctor. No; I wanted to be a genius, so I wrote a novel."

The doctor paused, and Theodora clung to him in a mute passion of commiseration.¹³ It was as if a drowning creature caught a live hand through the murderous fury of the waves.

"Father—O Father!"

"It took me a year—a whole year's hard work; and when I'd finished it the public wouldn't have it, either; not at any price and that's why I came down to meet you, because I remembered my walk home." ✑

---

13. *Commiseration* means "sympathy."

> Make and Verify Predictions *Is this a comment you would have expected from Doctor Dace? Why or why not?*

Reading Practice

 SPIRAL REVIEW **Characterization** Review with students the methods Wharton uses to give readers a sense of who Theodora Dace and her father are. In *direct characterization,* the writer makes explicit statements about a character. In *indirect characterization,* the writer reveals a character through his or her words and actions. Have students draw a two-column chart that has the headings *Beginning* and *Ending*. Under each heading, have students jot down character traits of Theodora and her father as they are perceived in the beginning of the story and then at the end of the story. Have students identify the character trait as the result of direct or indirect characterization.

Respond and Think Critically

Respond and Interpret

1. (a)How do you feel about Theodora? (b)Do you think she is a sympathetic character? Explain.

2. (a)At the start of "April Showers," how does Theodora feel about her novel? (b)How do you think the narrator feels about it? Explain.

3. (a)Describe Theodora's reaction to both the letter she receives from *Home Circle* and to the midsummer issue of the magazine. (b)In what ways are these reactions similar? What does this tell you about Theodora's character?

4. (a)When Theodora goes to Boston, what explanation does the editor at *Home Circle* give her for the confusion over the novel? (b)What does this suggest to you about the quality of Theodora's novel?

Analyze and Evaluate

5. (a)What tone does the narrator take toward Theodora? (b)Is the tone appropriate? Explain.

6. (a)How does Theodora feel about neglecting her responsibilities at home? (b)Is she right to feel this way? Explain.

7. (a)What is ironic about Theodora's father meeting her at the station? (b)How does your perception of his character change at the end of the story?

Connect

8. **Big Idea** Realism In what ways does this story demonstrate the techniques of Realism?

9. **Connect to Today** Is it easier or harder for young adults to make names for themselves today than in Wharton's time? Explain.

Literary Element Flashback

SAT Skills Practice

1. What does Theodora's reference to her uncle's visit ("He had been . . . Brookline") signal?

   (A) A return to the present time

   (B) A projection into the future

   (C) A description of past events

   (D) A shift in narrator

   (E) The climax of the story

2. The flashbacks in "April Showers" serve to

   (A) foreshadow the similarity of Theodora's and her father's experiences

   (B) highlight the depth of Theodora's desire to become a published writer

   (C) shift the point of view to reveal Theodora's unconscious feelings

   (D) show the competition between Theodora's uncle and father for her affection

   (E) create tension that involves the reader in Theodora's experiences

Review: Theme

The **theme** of a piece of literature is a dominant idea, often a universal message about life, that the writer communicates to the reader. Most short stories have one main, or central, theme. They may also have secondary themes.

Partner Activity Meet with a classmate to identify the central theme of "April Showers." Working with your partner, create a web diagram like the one below. First, write the theme in the center oval. Then fill in the outer ovals with evidence that supports the theme.

EDITH WHARTON **547**

Literary Element

1. **C** is the correct answer because the visit took place in the past and explains Theodora's confidence in submitting her novel for publication.

2. **E** is the correct answer because the flashbacks jar readers from the chronological sequence of events in an engaging way.

Review: Theme

Theme: A writer's life is filled with highs and lows.

Evidence: Theodora is thrilled by her celebrity status.

Evidence: Theodora is crushed by her rejection.

Evidence: The doctor once tried to write but was disappointed too.

After You Read

Assess

1. (a) Sympathetic (b) Yes; she has remorse and good intentions.

2. (a) Rapturous (b) The narrator is more skeptical. The opening line is meant to be ironic, as are Theodora's romantic exclamations.

3. (a) She is thrown into a rapture and kisses the ground. When she sees Kyd's story, she is shocked. (b) Both are exaggerated; they suggest that Theodora is melodramatic.

4. (a) He tells her that Kathleen Kyd submitted a story on the same day with the same title. (b) It may not be as memorable as she has thought.

5. (a) The narrator is sympathetic but also critical of and amused by Theodora. (b) It is an appropriate balance of sympathy and skepticism.

6. (a) She feels guilty but thinks literary success will make up for her neglectfulness. (b) Students may argue that her family should be her first priority.

7. (a) He had been critical of her earlier. (b) He is sympathetic now because he once went through the same experience as Theodora.

8. Wharton's exploration of Theodora's inner life, her attention to detail, and her balanced presentation are characteristics of Realism.

9. Students might comment on the increased competition for fame and success today; yet with many more magazines, cable television, and the internet, more people can gain access to the media.

After You Read

Assess

Reading Strategy

1. The realistic images of plumbing and sewing buttons, the reference to George Eliot, and the details about Theodora's family life all hint at the disappointment she will experience.

2. Students may see that the title of Theodora's story hints at a sad ending.

Vocabulary

1. prosperous
2. insignificant
3. stupor
4. calamity

Academic Vocabulary

1. The weather is not conducive to swimming, so *notion* means "a whim or fancy."

2. The uncle has a theory that vitamins can prevent all disease, so here *notion* means "a belief held by a person or group."

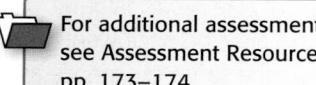

For additional assessment, see Assessment Resources, pp. 173–174.

Reading Strategy Make and Verify Predictions

Predictions About Plot Inevitably, the predictions you make will sometimes be wrong. In this story, Wharton intentionally withholds information in order to increase the dramatic tension. However, she does provide clues throughout the text that make it possible to predict the plot's outcome.

1. What images, details, or descriptions did you notice that seemed to hint at the story's conclusion?

2. List any details you did not notice while reading that may seem relevant now.

Vocabulary Practice

Denotation and Connotation Denotation is the literal, or dictionary, meaning of a word. **Connotation** is the implied, or cultural, meaning of a word. For example, the words *pleased* and *ecstatic* have a similar denotation, "happy," but they have different connotations:

Weaker	Stronger
pleased	ecstatic

For each pair below, choose the word that has the stronger connotation.

1. prosperous — well-off
2. obscure — insignificant
3. stupor — haze
4. calamity — misfortune

Academic Vocabulary

*Theodora has the **notion** that she could be a great author.*

Notion is an academic word. Using context clues, infer its meaning in these sentences.

1. Lawrence had the **notion** to go swimming, even though it was still winter.

2. My uncle has the **notion** that vitamins can prevent all illnesses.

For more on academic vocabulary, see pages 53–54.

Write with Style

 Apply Point of View

Assignment By cruel coincidence, Theodora is mistakenly led to believe that *Home Circle* will publish her novel. Because this story is told from the third person limited point of view, the reader discovers the story's twist at the same time as Theodora. Think of an experience from your own life when things didn't turn out as expected. Write a narrative of this experience, using third person limited point of view.

Get Ideas Look over old journal entries or talk to friends to help you think of instances in which things didn't turn out as expected. Choose the experience that you find most compelling.

Give It Structure Use a plot diagram like the one below to chart the course of events of your story. Think about which character you would like to follow in your point of view. Use your diagram to guide you as you write.

Look at Language Note the variety in Wharton's sentences and her careful diction. Emulate these qualities in your writing. After you have written your story, review it and see if you can further vary the lengths of your sentences or add more precise words to your descriptions.

 Literature Online

Selection Resources For Selection Quizzes, eFlashcards, and Reading-Writing Connection activities, go to glencoe.com and enter QuickPass code GLA9800u4.

 Writing

Students' stories should

- use the third person limited point of view
- use a variety of sentences structures
- use precise diction

For grammar practice, see Unit 4 Teaching Resources Book, p. 105.

Vocabulary Workshop

Thesaurus Use

Literature Connection In "April Showers," a character describes author Kathleen Kyd as a "pleasant, sociable kind of woman." *Pleasant* and *sociable* are **synonyms**. Some synonyms are practically interchangeable, but many convey subtle differences in meaning or connotation. Recognizing such distinctions can improve your reading, writing, listening, and speaking.

A **thesaurus** is a dictionary used to find synonyms, alternative expressions, or information about specialized terminology. Thesauruses are available on CD-ROM, as part of word-processing software, on the Internet, or in print form.

Organization Thesauruses are organized two ways. The traditional style of organization is by concept (because you may not know the word you want to find). In Example 1 below, a search for names of basketball shots begins with the concept of sports and leads to a thesaurus listing of names of basketball shots. If you know a key word for your search, you can also begin with the index, an alphabetical list of terms, as in Example 2.

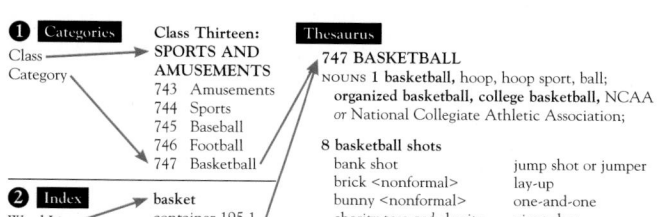

Thesauruses can also be organized like dictionaries, with words and synonyms listed together in alphabetical order.

Practice

1. Using a thesaurus, find two synonyms for each word below. Then find the precise meaning for each synonym in a dictionary.
   a. pathetic   **b.** linger   **c.** prosperous
2. Using the above list of words and the synonyms you have found, use each word in a sentence. Be sure that your sentences reflect the slight differences in meaning within each group of synonyms.

Learning Objectives

In this workshop, you will focus on the following objective:

Vocabulary: Understanding language resources.

Synonyms and Antonyms

Synonyms are words that have similar meanings but possibly different connotations. **Antonyms** are words that have opposite meanings. Both synonyms and antonyms are always the same part of speech.

Tip

Many Internet and CD-ROM thesauruses have extra features such as audio pronunciation and the ability to define a word within an entry.

LOG ON **Literature** Online

Vocabulary For more vocabulary practice, go to glencoe.com and enter QuickPass code GLA9800u4.

Vocabulary Workshop

Thesaurus Use

Focus

Ask: When do you as a writer need to find a synonym? *(Students may suggest needing synonyms when they have used a given word too often.)*

Teach

Thesaurus Usage Caution students to be selective with synonyms and to consider their audience, purpose, and tone when choosing. Their synonym choice should rest on connotation, the associations a word has beyond its literal meaning.

Assess

Practice

1. Possible synonyms:
   a. mournful, pitiable
   b. continue, persevere
   c. wealthy, affluent
2. Answers will vary.

 For additional vocabulary practice, see Glencoe Interactive Vocabulary CD-ROM.

Approaching Level

DIFFERENTIATED INSTRUCTION

Emerging Explain that synonyms are important because writers often want to substitute a long, fancy word for a perfectly good short word for literary purposes. The key to selecting a synonym is knowing whether it achieves the desired connotation.

Have students try each synonym for *kind* in the sentence. Ask them to choose those that fit well in the sentence. Then discuss the connotations of each synonym.

Synonyms for *kind*

benign	charitable	supportive
benevolent	considerate	tender
caring	genial	thoughtful

Although the little boy is often rude, he is _____ toward his mother and kittens.

Focus

Learning Objectives

For pages 550–567

In studying these texts, you will focus on the following objectives:

Literary Study:
Comparing cultural context.
Comparing historical context.

Bellringer Options

**Selection Focus
Transparency 35**

**Daily Language Practice
Transparency 50**

Or ask students to consider the dynamics of marriage.
Ask: What adjustments might a man and a woman have to make when they get married? (Changing daily routines and habits to fit each other's schedules and personalities.) **Ask:** In what ways do people react at the end of a relationship? (Some students may say that it is best to move on it "wasn't meant to be"; feelings of loss heal only with time.)

Compare Literature About Relationships

Allow students to share their responses to the questions. Then have students discuss what they know about Kate Chopin, Anton Chekhov, and Gabriela Mistral.

Compare Literature About Relationships

Have you ever had a relationship too complex to describe? Perhaps you have had a friendship that ended in a way you did not expect. The three works compared here—by Kate Chopin, Anton Chekhov, and Gabriela Mistral—attempt to re-create the eccentric behaviors and passionate reactions of people in pivotal moments of a relationship. The fictional worlds in these selections analyze how human interactions continue to surprise us.

The Story of an Hour by Kate Chopin............short story 553
UNITED STATES, 1894

The Darling by Anton Chekhov...........................short story 557
RUSSIA, 1899

Richness by Gabriela Mistral..poem 566
CHILE, 1922

COMPARE THE `Big Idea` Realism

Writers associated with Realism chose to depict life as they saw it rather than in a romanticized or idealized way. Characters in Realistic literature are often ordinary people who encounter struggles familiar to many people. Kate Chopin, Anton Chekhov, and Gabriela Mistral reveal insights about characters that often contrast with their outward appearances. As you read, ask yourself, What insights do you learn about the characters?

COMPARE Narratives About Relationships

Relationships are complex; two people can view the same relationship in vastly different ways. These selections explore the interactions between people and the way these interactions connect to larger themes about individuality and society. As you read, ask yourself, What do these interactions reveal about the main character's relationships?

COMPARE Social Context

In these selections, the social context—the common values, habits, and beliefs of a certain society—provides a way of understanding characters' actions. In some cases, society creates roles that limit the potential of the individual. At other times, social interaction is the saving grace in a character's existence. As you read, ask yourself, What role does the social context play in each selection?

 Literature Online

Author Search For more about Kate Chopin, Anton Checkhov, and Gabriela Mistral, go to glencoe.com and enter QuickPass code GLA9800u4.

550 COMPARING LITERATURE

Skills Practice

Literary Elements
- Conflict (SE pp. 552, 554, 556)

Comparing Literature

Reading Skills
- Apply Background Knowledge (SE pp. 552, 554–556)
- Author's Viewpoint (TE p. 558)

Vocabulary Skills
- Word Usage (SE p. 556)
- Context Clues (TE p. 563)
- Titles of Respect (TE p. 565)

Writing Skills/Grammar
- Interior Monologue (SE p. 556)
- Journal Entry (TE p. 552)
- Adapt a Short Story to Drama (TE p. 554)

Listening/Speaking/Viewing Skills
- Oral Interpretation (TE p. 566)
- Analyze Art (TE pp. 559, 562)

Before You Read

The Story of an Hour

Meet **Kate Chopin**

(1850–1904)

Kate Chopin (shō´ pan) was the first female writer in the U.S. to portray frankly the passions and discontents of women confined to traditional roles as wives and mothers. Critics condemned her, focusing their wrath on her novel *The Awakening*, the story of a woman who abandons her husband and children to find her identity. They called it shocking, morbid, coarse, and vulgar.

Strong, Independent Women Chopin was born Katherine O'Flaherty in St. Louis, Missouri. She grew up in the late Victorian period, a time when the ideal woman devoted herself to the will of her husband and to the welfare of her children. When Chopin was five, her father died in a railroad accident. For the next two years she studied at home with her mother, grandmother, and great-grandmother. Growing up among strong, independent women shaped Chopin as a person and a writer.

> *"The artist must possess the courageous soul that dares and defies."*
>
> —Kate Chopin, *The Awakening*

At twenty, Kate married Oscar Chopin and moved to New Orleans. Business problems soon forced them to move to Oscar's hometown Cloutierville, Louisiana, which later inspired many of her stories. Oscar died in 1882, leaving Chopin with children to raise and support. She soon moved back to St. Louis to be near her family. When her mother died a year later, she was overwhelmed with grief. At her doctor's advice, she turned to writing and published her first work in 1889.

Daring Pieces During the next ten years, Chopin published over 100 short stories, two story collections, and two novels. She earned praise for early stories that captured the local color of Louisiana. In later stories, she explored women's issues considered controversial in her time. She took inspiration from the work of Guy de Maupassant, the French master of the Realist short story. Not surprisingly, she had difficulty finding publishers for her most daring pieces, including "The Story of an Hour."

Chopin was not prepared for the reaction to *The Awakening* in 1899. The deluge of negative reviews destroyed her spirit. She continued to write, but by 1903 her health was failing. After visiting the 1904 St. Louis World's Fair, Chopin complained of head pain. Two days later she died of a cerebral hemorrhage.

Lonely Pioneer For more than fifty years, Chopin's works were ignored. Then, in 1969, as the women's movement in the U.S. gained momentum, Per Seyersted published Chopin's biography and complete works. His efforts galvanized modern readers hungry to learn more about the woman who, according to scholar Emily Toth, had written "the most radical novel of the 1890s." Today *The Awakening* is one of the most read novels in colleges and universities across the U.S. Kate Chopin is celebrated as a lonely pioneer who dared to write realistic portraits of women trapped and stifled by the social conventions of their time.

KATE CHOPIN **551**

Comparing Literature

Before You Read

Focus

Read aloud the following statements and ask students to make an informed guess about whether each statement is true or false for women in the late 1800s.

1. Women had the right to vote. *(F)*
2. Married women could own property. *(F)*
3. Generally, the husband was considered the one and only head of the household. *(T)*

Cultural History

Women's Career Choices In the late 1800s, women had few career choices. For example, in 1872, Myra Bradwell was denied entry to the state bar even though she had passed the exam. When her appeal to the U.S. Supreme Court failed, Justice Joseph P. Bradley wrote: "The natural and proper timidity and delicacy which belongs to the female sex evidently unfits it for many of the occupations of civil life."

Approaching Level

DIFFERENTIATED INSTRUCTION

Emerging Review with students the definitions of an external conflict and an internal conflict. Explain that an external conflict is a character's disagreement or struggle with an external force, while an internal conflict is a character's struggle within his or her mind. Ask students to classify each of these conflicts as external or internal: (1) A woman feels both proud and jealous of her friend who has just won an award. *(internal)* (2) A father gets lost in the mountains and is struggling to survive in the wilderness. *(external)* (3) A woman is successful in business despite the fact that her previous business failed. *(external)* (4) A boy is torn between playing basketball with friends and spending time with visiting grandparents. *(internal)* As students read the story, ask them to look for potential conflicts by noting the main character's interactions with other characters and the main character's thoughts and feelings.

551

Comparing Literature

Before You Read

Focus

Summary

When Mrs. Mallard hears about her husband's death in an accident, she becomes emotional. However, in the privacy of her room, she realizes that his death comes with a benefit: her freedom from the demands and expectations of a husband. Mrs. Mallard becomes enamored of this thought. When it turns out that her husband is still alive, she feels such intense shock that her heart gives out.

 For summaries in languages other than English, see Unit 4 Teaching Resources Book, pp. 93–97.

Vocabulary

The Suffix -ly The suffix -ly can be added to certain adjectives to form adverbs. **Ask:** What adverbs can you form from the vocabulary words or a word in their word families by adding the suffix -ly? (elusively, exaltedly, perceptively, persistently)

 For additional context, see Glencoe Interactive Vocabulary CD-ROM.

 For additional vocabulary practice, see Unit 4 Teaching Resources Book, p. 117.

Literature and Reading Preview

Connect to the Story

What are some advantages and disadvantages of having others depend on you for their happiness? Freewrite on this topic for fifteen minutes. Then discuss the question and your answers with a small group of classmates. Explore this question by making a chart like the one below.

Build Background

Some women in the 1890s attended college and entered professions previously open only to men, but many others were told that "the woman's place" was in the home. Although society glorified the roles of wives and mothers, women had few legal rights. For example, when her husband died, Chopin had to petition the court to be appointed the legal guardian of her own children. In much of Chopin's fiction, she criticized the institution of marriage and wrote about women who struggled against social convention in expressing their individuality.

Set Purposes for Reading

Big Idea Realism

As you read the story, ask yourself, What details does Chopin use to create a realistic description of Mrs. Mallard's thoughts and emotions?

Literary Element Conflict

Conflict is the central struggle between two opposing forces in a literary work. **External conflict** exists when a character struggles against an outside force, such as a person, nature, society, or fate. **Internal conflict** takes place within the mind of a character who is torn between opposing feelings, desires, or goals. As you read, ask, What types of conflict operate in this story?

Reading Strategy Apply Background Knowledge

Knowing the historical, social, and cultural forces that influenced an author can help you understand his or her writing. As you read "The Story of an Hour," ask yourself these questions:

* How does the information you have read about Kate Chopin affect your understanding of the story?
* If you knew nothing about Chopin or her time, how might your opinion of the characters be different?

552 UNIT 4 REGIONALISM AND REALISM

Vocabulary

elusive (i lōō′ siv) adj. difficult to explain or grasp; p. 554 *The speaker's elusive argument left the audience scratching their heads.*

tumultuously (tōō mul′ chōō əs lē) adv. in an agitated manner; violently; p. 554 *The wind swirled tumultuously across the plains.*

exalted (ig zôl′ təd) adj. elevated; p. 555 *The film actress enjoyed the exalted status of a star.*

perception (pər sep′ shən) n. an awareness; an insight; p. 555 *The musician responded modestly to the applause to avoid giving the perception that he was conceited.*

persistence (pər sis′ təns) n. stubborn or determined continuance; p. 555 *The newspaper reporters pursued the politician with a persistence that frustrated his campaign workers.*

Writing Practice

SPIRAL REVIEW **Journal Entry** Have students read Kate Chopin's biography and the Build Background section on this page. Then ask students to write a short journal entry from the point of view of a married woman in the late 1800s who has just learned of her husband's death. Have students imagine the characters of the woman and her husband and the kind of marriage they had. Ask them to consider the feelings the woman might have had about her marriage. Have students give details in their journal entries about how the woman felt when she learned of her husband's death. Remind them to write from a first-person point of view.

The Story of an Hour

Kate Chopin

The Lady Anne, 1899. Edwin Austin Abbey. Oil on canvas, 48 x 24 in. The Butler Institute of American Art, Youngstown, OH.

KATE CHOPIN **553**

Teach

View the Art ★

Edwin Austin Abbey loved history—particularly the medieval period. As such, he was a Romantic even in the age of Realism. Lady Anne does in fact assume a Romantic pose: her hair fading into the dark background, her hands theatrical. Lady Anne led a dramatic life. She was the widow of Edward, Prince of Wales, who was murdered by Richard III of England (who reigned from 1483 to 1485). Nevertheless, Anne later agreed to marry Richard.

 For an audio recording of this selection, use Listening Library Audio CD-ROM.

Readability Scores
Dale-Chall: 7.3
DRP: 57
Lexile: 970

Approaching Level

DIFFERENTIATED INSTRUCTION

Emerging Help students better comprehend the story and improve **reading fluency** by asking them questions. Have students read the first paragraph of the story on the next page. Point out that the paragraph succinctly lays out the Who? What? Where? When? Why? and How?

Ask: Who are the characters introduced in the first paragraph? (*Mrs. Mallard, Mr. Mallard, her sister Josephine, her hus-* band's friend Richards) Where does the story take place? (*Mrs. Mallard's home*) What has happened to Mrs. Mallard's husband? (*He has died in a railroad disaster.*) How does Richards find out about Mr. Mallard's death? (*A list of people "killed" in a railroad disaster is sent to the newspaper office. Richards then double-checks to be sure that Mr. Mallard is dead by sending a second telegram.*)

Tell students that as they read the rest of the story, they should pause every so often to ask themselves questions about what is happening in the story. This will help them keep track of the events.

Comparing Literature

Teach

Literary Element | 1

Conflict Answer: *This passage directly follows mention of Mrs. Mallard's sister, so the conflict could be between them. It seems more likely, however, that it will be an internal conflict because Mrs. Mallard goes to her room alone.*

Literary Element | 2

Conflict Answer: *Clearly, there is internal conflict. Mrs. Mallard is struggling with an approaching thought that scares her.*

Reading Strategy | 3

Apply Background Knowledge Answer: *During the Victorian era, women did not have many rights and were expected to do as their husbands said. For Mrs. Mallard to whisper "free, free, free!" shows that she looks forward to a major change in her lifestyle.*

 For additional practice using the reading skill or strategy, see Unit 4 Teaching Resources Book, p. 116.

Cultural History ☆

Telegram Remind students of communication technology in the late 1800s. A telegram is a paper printout of a message sent by telegraph; telegraphy is a system of communication, invented in 1837, that was based on coded electrical pulses.

Knowing that Mrs. Mallard was afflicted with a heart trouble, great care was taken to break to her as gently as possible the news of her husband's death. It was her sister Josephine who told her, in broken sentences; veiled[1] hints that revealed in half concealing. Her husband's friend Richards was there, too, near her. It was he who had been in the newspaper office when intelligence of the railroad disaster was received, with Brently Mallard's name leading the list of "killed." He had only taken the time to assure himself of its truth by a second telegram, and had hastened to forestall[2] any less careful, less tender friend in bearing the sad message.

She did not hear the story as many women have heard the same, with a paralyzed inability to accept its significance. She wept at once, with sudden, wild abandonment, in her sister's arms. When the storm of grief had spent[3] itself she went to her room alone. She would have no one follow her.

There stood, facing the open window, a comfortable, roomy armchair. Into this she sank, pressed down by a physical exhaustion that haunted her body and seemed to reach into her soul.

She could see in the open square before her house the tops of trees that were all aquiver with the new spring life. The delicious breath of rain was in the air. In the street below a peddler was crying his wares. The notes of a distant song which some one was singing reached her faintly, and countless sparrows were twittering in the eaves.

There were patches of blue sky showing here and there through the clouds that had met and piled one above the other in the west facing her window.

---

1. *Veiled* means "disguised" or "obscure."
2. *Forestall* means "to hinder by action taken beforehand."
3. Here, *spent* means "exhausted."

1 Conflict *Based on this passage, what do you think the main conflict will be?*

She sat with her head thrown back upon the cushion of the chair, quite motionless, except when a sob came up into her throat and shook her, as a child who has cried itself to sleep continues to sob in its dreams.

She was young, with a fair, calm face, whose lines bespoke repression and even a certain strength. But now there was a dull stare in her eyes, whose gaze was fixed away off yonder on one of those patches of blue sky. It was not a glance of reflection, but rather indicated a suspension of intelligent thought.

There was something coming to her and she was waiting for it, fearfully. What was it? She did not know; it was too subtle and **elusive** to name. But she felt it, creeping out of the sky, reaching toward her through the sounds, the scents, the color that filled the air.

Now her bosom rose and fell **tumultuously**. She was beginning to recognize this thing that was approaching to possess her, and she was striving to beat it back with her will—as powerless as her two white slender hands would have been.

When she abandoned herself a little whispered word escaped her slightly parted lips. She said it over and over under her breath: "free, free, free!" The vacant stare and the look of terror that had followed it went from her eyes. They stayed keen and bright. Her pulses beat fast, and the coursing[4] blood warmed and relaxed every inch of her body.

She did not stop to ask if it were or were not a monstrous joy that held her. A clear and

---

4. *Coursing* means "swiftly moving."

2 Conflict *How does this passage complicate the conflict?*

3 Apply Background Knowledge *What knowledge about the Victorian era helps you understand this passage?*

Vocabulary

elusive (i lōō′ siv) *adj.* difficult to explain or grasp
tumultuously (tōō mul′ chōō əs lē) *adv.* in an agitated manner; violently

---

Writing Practice

 Adapt a Short Story to Drama
Have students dramatize the second and final page of the story. They should designate part of Chopin's text as dialogue and part as stage direction. They will have to generate some material from scratch—perhaps converting some of Mrs. Mallard's inner thoughts into a spoken monologue. Students will also have to decide where to end the story—at the point of Mrs. Mallard's collapse or of the doctors' explanation of her death.

exalted perception enabled her to dismiss the suggestion as trivial.

She knew that she would weep again when she saw the kind, tender hands folded in death; the face that had never looked save[5] with love upon her, fixed and gray and dead. But she saw beyond that bitter moment a long procession of years to come that would belong to her absolutely. And she opened and spread her arms out to them in welcome.

There would be no one to live for her during those coming years; she would live for herself. There would be no powerful will bending hers in that blind persistence with which men and women believe they have a right to impose a private will upon a fellow-creature. A kind intention or a cruel intention made the act seem no less a crime as she looked upon it in that brief moment of illumination.

And yet she had loved him—sometimes. Often she had not. What did it matter! What could love, the unsolved mystery, count for in face of this possession of self-assertion which she suddenly recognized as the strongest impulse of her being!

"Free! Body and soul free!" she kept whispering.

Josephine was kneeling before the closed door with her lips to the keyhole, imploring

> "Free! Body and soul free!" she kept whispering.

for admission. "Louise, open the door! I beg; open the door—you will make yourself ill. What are you doing, Louise? For heaven's sake open the door."

"Go away. I am not making myself ill." No; she was drinking in a very elixir of life[6] through that open window.

Her fancy was running riot along those days ahead of her. Spring days, and summer days, and all sorts of days that would be her own. She breathed a quick prayer that life might be long. It was only yesterday she had thought with a shudder that life might be long.

She arose at length and opened the door to her sister's importunities.[7] There was a feverish triumph in her eyes, and she carried herself unwittingly like a goddess of Victory. She clasped her sister's waist, and together they descended the stairs. Richards stood waiting for them at the bottom.

Some one was opening the front door with a latchkey. It was Brently Mallard who entered, a little travel-stained, composedly carrying his grip-sack[8] and umbrella. He had been far from the scene of accident, and did not even know there had been one. He stood amazed at Josephine's piercing cry; at Richards' quick motion to screen him from the view of his wife.

But Richards was too late.

When the doctors came they said she had died of heart disease—of joy that kills.

5. Here, *save* means "except."

4 Realism *Why does Chopin include this information?*

Vocabulary

exalted (ig zôl´ təd) *adj.* elevated
perception (pər sep´ shən) *n.* an awareness; an insight
persistence (pər sis´ təns) *n.* stubborn or determined continuance

6. An *elixir* (i lik´ sər) *of life* is a substance thought to prolong life indefinitely.
7. *Importunities* are persistent requests or demands.
8. A *grip-sack* is a small traveling bag.

Apply Background Knowledge *How does this passage reflect what you know about Chopin's writing?* **5**

KATE CHOPIN **555**

Comparing Literature

Teach

Big Idea **4**

Realism **Answer:** *Chopin presents a realistic view of marriage as she sees it—marked by love but not necessarily by all-abiding love. Without this insight by Mrs. Mallard, the reader could not fully understand her feelings toward widowhood.*

Reading Strategy **5**

Apply Background Knowledge **Answer:** *This is an example of the type of writing for which Chopin was criticized—a realistic description of women's frustration with their status in the world.*

Cultural History ☆

Nike The Greek goddess of victory and triumph was Nike, who was known primarily for her speed. When Chopin compared Mrs. Mallard to "a goddess of Victory," she may have been thinking about the eight-foot marble statue *Nike of Samothrace* (c. 200–190 B.C.). The statue is considered by some to be the greatest masterpiece of Hellenistic sculpture.

English Learners

DIFFERENTIATED INSTRUCTION

Intermediate Help students understand the conflict in this story. **Ask:** What does Mrs. Mallard do when she hears that her husband has died? What does her action tell you about her feelings? *(She weeps; this suggests that she feels grief.)* Then ask students to read the paragraph starting with the words "When she abandoned herself . . ." **Ask:** What word does Mrs. Mallard repeat? What does this suggest about how she feels? *(She repeats the word* free; *this suggests that she feels relief.)* Point out that Mrs. Mallard's conflicting feelings reflect an internal conflict.

Comparing Literature

After You Read

Assess

1. At the news of her husband's death; at the discovery that her marriage was not happy. Students may feel surprised.
2. (a) She grieves. (b) She will miss him.
3. (a) She realizes that she will be free. (b) It is socially unacceptable; later on, freedom appeals to her.
4. She feels trapped by marriage.
5. She may have a good reason for her feelings, but her feelings about her husband's death may be troubling.
6. In writing about Mrs. Mallard's struggle, Chopin realistically describes the character's thoughts.

Progress Check

Can students analyze conflict?

If No → See Unit 4 Teaching Resources Book, p. 115.

After You Read

Respond and Think Critically

Respond and Interpret

1. At what points in the story did you feel sorry for Mrs. Mallard? Explain. How did the end of the story affect you?
2. (a) How does Mrs. Mallard first react to the news about her husband? (b) What does her reaction indicate about her feelings toward him?
3. (a) How do Mrs. Mallard's feelings change while she is in her room? (b) Why might she fear this change at first but later welcome it?

Analyze and Evaluate

4. What is your opinion of Mrs. Mallard? Support your evaluation with details from the story.
5. How does Mrs. Mallard's admission that often she had not loved her husband affect your evaluation of her character?

Connect

6. **Big Idea** **Realism** How does the central conflict of this story illustrate the idea that Chopin wrote realistic portraits of women's lives?

Literary Element Conflict

The events of a story develop its **conflict**. The conflict builds until the story reaches a **climax**, which is the point of greatest emotional intensity. The story then concludes with the **resolution**, or the final outcome of the conflict.

1. Identify the conflict in Chopin's story. Is this conflict external or internal? Explain why.
2. At what point does the conflict reach its climax?
3. What is the resolution of the conflict?

Reading Strategy Apply Background Knowledge

Applying background knowledge is a reading strategy that can help you infer the commentary that Chopin's story makes about the institution of marriage in Victorian America.

Partner Activity Review your answers to the Reading Strategy questions on page 552. Meet with another classmate to compare how you each applied background information to the selection.

Vocabulary Practice

Practice with Word Usage Respond to the following to explore the meanings of the vocabulary words from the selection.

1. Give an example of an **elusive** concept.
2. What might behave **tumultuously?**
3. Why is a person who is knighted **exalted?**
4. Describe a time when you had the incorrect **perception** of a situation.
5. Name a famous person who you think has shown **persistence.**

 Writing

Write an Interior Monologue Imagine what might have been going through Mrs. Mallard's head the moment she saw her husband walk through the door. Write down her possible thoughts in the form of an interior monologue. Address how her death relates to the story's main conflict.

LOG ON ▶ **Literature** Online

Selection Resources For Selection Quizzes, eFlashcards, and Reading-Writing Connection activities, go to glencoe.com and enter QuickPass code GLA9800u4.

Literary Element

1. Mrs. Mallard's struggle to embrace the knowledge that she is free; internal
2. Chopin describes Mrs. Mallard's thoughts: shock and grief, then joy. The climax occurs when Mrs. Mallard sees her husband.
3. She dies, perhaps from the shocking disappointment of seeing her husband.

Vocabulary

1. String Theory is an elusive concept.
2. A hurricane may behave tumultuously; it can cause much damage.
3. A knighted person has an elevated status, so he can be seen as exalted.
4. I had the mistaken perception that my teacher did not like my essay.
5. Abraham Lincoln was persistent in his campaign for president because initially he was not popular.

Reading Strategy

Chopin critcizes marriage: Mrs. Mallard tastes freedom before realizing that she is still trapped in a unfulfilling marriage.

Writing

Students' monologues should connect to events in the stories and be written from the perspective of Mrs. Mallard.

The Darling

Anton Chekhov

Translated by Harvey Pitcher

Open-air Theater of Acrobats. Boris Kustodiev. Russian State Museum, St. Petersburg, Russia.

Focus

Summary

Olga Semyonovna marries a theater manager. She comes to love the theater and lives happily until her husband dies suddenly. Then she marries the manager of a lumberyard and helps her husband run his business. He too dies. She begins spending time with a veterinarian, but he moves away. When he returns many years later, Olga helps him raise his son. Her love for the child restores happiness and purpose to her life.

 For an audio recording of this selection, use Listening Library Audio CD-ROM.

Build Background

Anton Chekhov studied both medicine and literature. He eventually focused on his literary pursuits, becoming a master of the short story as well as Russia's most revered playwright. His realistic stories, which focus on atmosphere and character rather than plot and action, became an essential influence on modern literature. Chekhov's substantial place in literature comes in part from his ability to reveal how ordinary events can have a huge impact on people's lives.

Olenka,[1] the daughter of retired collegiate assessor Plemyannikov, sat on the porch in her yard, lost in thought. It was hot, the flies wouldn't leave her alone, and it was bliss to think it would soon be evening. Dark rain-clouds were moving up from the east, preceded by occasional wafts of humid air.

In the middle of the yard Snookin, manager-proprietor of the Tivoli Pleasure Gardens, who lodged across the yard in Olenka's fliegel,[2] stood gazing at the sky.

"Not again!" he was saying in despair. "Not rain again! Day after day, day after day, rain, rain, rain! Just my luck! What I have to put up with! I'm ruined! I'm losing huge sums every day!"

Throwing up his hands, he turned to Olenka and said:

---

1. *Olenka* is a nickname for *Olga.* In Russia, people are often informally referred to by their given name and then a patronymic, which is a variation of their father's given name. If the father's name were Ivan, the son's patronymic name would be Ivanovich, and the daughter's would be Ivanovna. *Semyonovna* is Olga's patronymic.

2. A *fliegel* is a small house that is on the property of a larger house and might be rented out.

ANTON CHEKHOV **557**

Readability Scores
Dale-Chall: 7.3
DRP: 57
Lexile: 1100

Comparing Literature

Teach

Literary Element | 1

Characterization Ask: What does Snookin reveal about himself through his speech? *(He presents himself as a man with high standards who has to put up with the whims of nature and with a shallow public.)*

Reading Strategy | 2

Author's Viewpoint Explain that the way Chekhov portrays his characters reveals his opinion of married life. **Ask:** How do you think Chekhov felt about the relationship between Olenka and Snookin? Explain. *(He thinks the relationship is unhealthy—one feels pity for Olenka when she readily adopts her husband's opinions as her own.)*

(ADVANCED) Challenge students to find the topic sentence that sums up Olenka's character in the paragraph that begins "Olenka said nothing." *("She was constantly in love with someone and could not live otherwise.")*

---

1 "You see what our life's like, Olga Semyonovna. Enough to make you weep! You work hard and do your best, you worry and have sleepless nights, you're always thinking of improvements—and what's the result? Take audiences for a start. They're nothing but ignorant savages. I give them the best operetta and pantomime, top-quality burlesque,³ but is that what they want? Do they appreciate it? No, they want some vulgar little peepshow. Then take the weather. Rain almost every evening. May 10th it started, and it's been at it right through May and June. Appalling! The public stays away, but who has to pay the rent, I ask you? Who has to pay the performers?"

Clouds began gathering at the same time next day.

"Oh yes, let it all come!" Snookin said, laughing hysterically. "Let it flood the whole Gardens and take me with it! I don't deserve any happiness in this world or the next! Let the performers take me to court! Why stop at that? Make it penal servitude in Siberia! The scaffold!⁴ Ha-ha-ha!"

It was the same next day. . . .

Olenka said nothing but listened to Snookin gravely, and sometimes tears came to her eyes. In the end his misfortunes moved her and she fell in love with him. He was short and skinny, with a sallow complexion and hair **2** combed back off the temples, he spoke in a high-pitched tenor, twisting his mouth as he did so, and his face wore an expression of permanent despair—yet he aroused in her deep and genuine emotion. She was constantly in love with someone and could not live otherwise. Previously she had loved her Papa, now

an invalid sitting in his armchair in a darkened room and breathing with difficulty; then she had loved her aunt, who came to visit them every other year from Bryansk;⁵ and earlier still she had loved the French master at her school. She was a quiet, good-natured, tender-hearted girl, with soft gentle eyes, and in the best of health. Looking at her plump rosy cheeks and soft white neck with its dark birthmark, at the innocent, kindly smile on her face whenever she was listening to something pleasant, men said to themselves, "yes, not a bad one, that," and smiled, too, while her female visitors could not refrain from seizing her by the hand in the middle of a conversation and exclaiming with delight:

"You're such a darling!"

The house she had lived in all her life and was due to inherit stood on the edge of town in Gypsy Lane, not far from the Tivoli, so that in the evenings and at night, hearing the band playing and the rockets going off with a bang, she imagined this was Snookin challenging his fate and taking his chief enemy, the indifferent public, by storm; her heart would melt, she didn't feel a bit sleepy, and when he returned home in the early hours, she would knock softly on her bedroom window and, letting him see through the curtains only her face and one shoulder, smile affectionately. . . .

He proposed and they were married. Now that he could see her neck and both her plump healthy shoulders properly, he threw up his hands and said:

"You darling, you!"

He was happy, but since it rained on the wedding day *and* on the wedding night, the look of despair never left his face.

Life went well after the marriage. She sat in his box office, supervised the Gardens, wrote down expenses and paid out salaries, and you'd catch a glimpse of her rosy cheeks and sweetly innocent, radiant smile at the box office window one moment, behind stage

---

3. An *operetta* is a form of opera that includes elaborate dancing and music, as well as a romantic, usually comic plot. A *pantomime* relies on body movement to tell a story. A *burlesque,* usually a series of comic short skits, uses exaggeration to ridicule.
4. The governments of Imperial Russia and the Soviet Union sent criminals to *Siberia,* an area known for being remote and having a harsh climate. Here, *scaffold* refers to the platform on which a criminal is executed.

5. *Bryansk* is a Russian city southwest of Moscow.

Grammar Practice

SPIRAL REVIEW **Subordinate Clauses** Review with students that a subordinate clause is a group of words that has a subject and a predicate but cannot stand alone as a sentence. A subordinate clause can be used as an adjective. Adjective clauses begin with a relative pronoun such as *which, who, whom, whose,* or *that.* **Ask:** What is the subordinate clause in this sentence: "She was like the hens, she thought, which stay awake all night and are restive when the cock isn't in the henhouse." What word signals the beginning of the subordinate clause? *(which stay awake all night and are restive when the cock isn't in the henhouse; the word which)* Have students practice using subordinate clauses by writing sentences about the story.

the next, and now in the refreshment bar. Already she was telling her friends that nothing in the world was so remarkable, so important and necessary as the theatre, and only in the theatre could you experience real enjoyment and become an educated, civilized human being.

"But does the public appreciate that?" she would say. "What they want is a peepshow. Yesterday we did *Faust Inside Out* and almost all the boxes were empty, but if we'd put on something vulgar, me and Vanya,[6] we'd have been packed out, I can tell you. Tomorrow we're doing *Orpheus in the Underworld*, me and Vanya, why don't you come?"

Whatever Snookin said about the theatre and the actors, she repeated. Like him, she despised the public for its indifference to art and its ignorance, interfered in rehearsals, corrected the actors and made sure the musicians behaved, and whenever there was a bad notice in the local press, she would cry and then go round to the editorial office to have it out with them.

The actors were fond of her and called her "Me and Vanya" and "The Darling." She felt sorry for them and gave them small loans, and if they let her down, she just had a quiet cry and said nothing to her husband.

Life went well that winter, too. They hired the town theatre for the whole season and rented it out for short periods to a Ukrainian troupe, a conjuror, and the local amateur dramatic company. Olenka put on weight and positively radiated well-being, but Snookin looked thin and sallow, and complained of huge losses, even though business was quite good all winter. At night he coughed and she

Russian Woman at the Window, 1923. Boris Kustodiev. Watercolor over pencil on paper, 24.3 x 21.5 cm. Museum of Fine Arts, Kostroma, Russia. ★

gave him raspberry or lime-blossom tea to drink, rubbed him with eau-de-Cologne and wrapped him in her soft shawls.

"My wonderful little man!" she would say with complete sincerity, as she stroked his hair. "My handsome little man!"

During Lent[7] he went off to Moscow to engage a new company, and in his absence she couldn't sleep, but sat by the window looking at the stars. She was like the hens, she thought, which stay awake all night and are restive when the cock isn't in the henhouse. Snookin was delayed in Moscow but said he'd be back by Easter, and his letters were already giving her instructions about the Tivoli. But on the Sunday before Easter, late at night, there was a sudden ominous knocking outside. Someone was banging on the gate until it started booming like a barrel. The

---

6. *Vanya* is a nickname for Ivan, which is Snookin's given name.

7. *Lent* is a period of fasting and self-denial prior to the celebration of Easter that is observed by some Christian denominations.

ANTON CHEKHOV **559**

Comparing Literature

Teach

Big Idea ▏3

Realism Here Olenka is saying exactly the sort of thing Snookin said earlier. **Ask:** What does this fact suggest about nineteenth-century married life? (*Wives presented themselves not as individuals but as extensions of their husbands.*)

Literary Element ▏4

Literary Allusion In medieval literature, Faust is a philosopher who sells his soul to the devil in exchange for power. In Greek mythology, Orpheus is a genius musician. **Ask:** Do you think Olenka has ever read the plays? (*No, Olenka is just repeating her husband's words. She probably has not read the plays.*)

View the Art ★

Boris Kustodiev (1878–1927) was known for his colorful, joyful paintings—even at this point in his career, when he had become paralyzed. Confined to his studio, he painted scenes from his memory. **Ask:** What, if anything, about this painting looks Russian? (*Some may say the woman's hairstyle and the lace curtains seem Russian; others may say the scene could be from anywhere.*)

Comparing Literature

Teach

Literary Element | 1

Repetition Say: On this page we read that "life went well for Pustovalov and Olenka after their marriage." We also learn that the timber business "was the most vitally important thing in life" for Olenka. Where have you read such statements before? *(Students should recognize that Olenka expressed similar sentiments about the business of her first husband. Students may comment on an emerging pattern.)*

---

sleepy cook ran to answer, her bare feet splashing in the puddles.

"Open up, please!" someone outside was saying in a deep bass. "Telegram for you!"

Olenka had received telegrams from her husband before, but now for some reason she felt petrified. She opened it with trembling hands and read as follows:

"Ivan Petrovich[8] died suddenly today suchly await instructions funreal Tuesday."

That was what the telegram said, "funreal" and the other meaningless word "suchly"; it was signed by the producer of the operetta company.

"My darling!" Olenka sobbed. "My sweet darling little Vanya! Why did I ever meet you? Why did I come to know you and love you? Who's going to look after your poor wretched Olenka now you've abandoned her?"

Snookin was buried on the Tuesday at the Vagankovo Cemetery in Moscow. Olenka returned home on Wednesday and as soon as she entered her room, flung herself down on the bed and sobbed so loudly she could be heard in the street and the neighboring yards.

"Poor darling!" the women neighbors said, crossing themselves. "She *is* taking it badly, poor darling Olga Semyonovna!"

Three months later Olenka, in full mourning, was returning home sadly one day from church. It so happened that a neighbor of hers, Vasily Andreich Pustovalov, manager of the merchant Babakayev's timber yard, was also returning from church and walking alongside her. He was wearing a straw hat and a white waistcoat[9] with a gold watch-chain, and looked more like a landowner than a tradesman.

"Everything has to take its proper course, Olga Semyonovna," he was saying soberly, with a sympathetic note in his voice, "and if someone dear to us dies, that means it is God's wish, so we must contain ourselves and bear it with resignation."

---

8. *Ivan Petrovich* is Snookin's name.
9. A *waistcoat* is an ornamental vest worn under a jacket.

After seeing Olenka to her gate, he said goodbye and walked on. For the rest of the day she kept hearing that sober voice, and she had only to close her eyes to picture his dark beard to herself. She liked him very much. Evidently she had made an impression on him, too, for not long afterwards an elderly lady, whom she scarcely knew, came to drink coffee with her, and had no sooner sat down at the table than she started talking about Pustovalov, what a good, reliable man he was and how any young lady would be delighted to have him for a husband. Three days later Pustovalov himself paid her a visit, stayed no more than about ten minutes and said little, but Olenka fell for him so completely that she lay awake all night feeling hot and feverish, and next morning sent for the elderly lady. The match was quickly arranged, then came the wedding.

Life went well for Pustovalov and Olenka after their marriage. He would usually stay at the timber yard until lunch and then go out on business, whereupon Olenka would take his place and stay in the office until evening, doing the accounts and dispatching orders.

"Timber's going up by twenty percent a year now," she would tell customers and friends. "In the past we used to get our timber locally, but now, imagine, my Vasya[10] has to fetch it every year from Mogilyov Province. And the freight charges!" she would say, covering both cheeks with her hands in horror. "The freight charges!"

She felt that she had been dealing in timber for ages and ages, and it was the most vitally important thing in life, and the words joist, batten, offcut, purlin,[11] round beam, short beam, frame and slab, were like dear old friends to her. At night she dreamed of whole mountains of boards and battens, of never-ending convoys of carts carrying timber somewhere far beyond the town; she dreamed of a

1

---

10. *Vasya* is a nickname for Vasily.
11. A *joist* is a type of wood beam; a *batten* is a piece of wood used on a boat or in a floor; an *offcut* is a small piece of wood; a *purlin* is a piece of wood used in a roof.

Reading Practice

SPIRAL REVIEW Understand Footnotes Have students identify the kind of information that is presented in the footnotes. *(The footnotes provide definitions of foreign and unfamiliar words and terms used in the text. They also explain cultural references and present other information related to the text.)*
Ask: Why is certain information provided in footnotes instead of in the main text of a selection? *(The information is not essential to the story's theme and may distract from the flow of the story.)*

whole regiment of beams, thirty feet by nine inches, marching upright into battle against the timber yard, and how beams, joists and slabs banged together with the resounding thud of dry wood, falling over and then righting themselves, piling up on top of each other. Olenka would cry out in her sleep and Pustovalov would say to her tenderly:

"What's the matter, Olenka dear? Better cross yourself!"[12]

Whatever thoughts her husband had, she had also. If he thought the room was too hot or business had become quiet, she thought the same. Her husband did not like any entertainments and on holidays stayed at home; so did she.

"You're always at home or in the office," friends said to her. "You should go to the theatre, darling, or the circus."

"Me and Vasya have no time for theatres," she replied soberly. "We're working folk, we can't be bothered with trifles. What do people see in those theatres, anyway?"

On Saturdays she and Pustovalov attended the all-night vigil, and on feast days early-morning service. Afterwards, walking home side by side, they both looked deeply moved, they smelt fragrant, and her silk dress rustled agreeably. At home they drank tea, with rich white bread and various jams, then they had pie. Every day at noon the yard and the street outside the gates were filled with the appetizing smell of borsch[13] and roast lamb or duck, or fish on fast days, and no one could walk past without beginning to feel hungry. In the office the samovar[14] was always on the boil, and customers were treated to tea and buns. Once a week the couple went to the baths and walked home side by side, both red in the face.

"We're not complaining," Olenka told her friends. "Life's going well, praise be to God.

May God grant everyone as good a life as me and Vasya."

When Pustovalov went off to Mogilyov Province for timber, she missed him terribly and could not sleep at night for crying. Sometimes she had an evening visit from the young man renting her fliegel, a regimental vet[15] called Smirnin. He would tell her about something or they'd play cards, and this cheered her up. She was particularly interested to hear about his own family life: he was married with a son, but had separated from his wife because she'd been unfaithful, and now he hated her and sent her forty roubles[16] a month for the boy's maintenance. As she listened, Olenka sighed and shook her head, and felt sorry for him.

"The Lord be with you," she would say, bidding him good night and lighting him to the top of the stairs with a candle. "It was kind of you to while away your time with me, may God and the Holy Mother watch over you. . . ."

She always expressed herself in the same sober, judicious tones, imitating her husband. The vet was already disappearing behind the downstairs door when she would call him back and say:

"Vladimir Platonych,[17] don't you think you should make it up with your wife? Forgive her, if only for your son's sake! That little chap knows just what's going on, be sure of that."

When Pustovalov returned, she would tell him in a hushed voice about the vet and his unhappy family situation, and both would sigh, shake their heads and talk of how the boy must be missing his father; then, by some strange association of ideas they would both kneel before the icons,[18] prostrate themselves and pray that God might send them children.

---

12. Pustovalov is suggesting that Olenka make the sign of a cross to help keep away her nightmare.
13. Borsch is beet soup.
14. A samovar is a type of urn used to make tea in Russia.

15. Here, vet is short for veterinarian.
16. Roubles is an alternate spelling of rubles, Russian currency.
17. Vladimir Platonych is Smirnin's formal name.
18. Here, icons refers to religious images, often painted on wood and used in religious practices.

ANTON CHEKHOV **561**

Comparing Literature

Teach

Literary Element 2

Characterization Explain that when Olenka denigrates the theater, which was previously the center of her life, Chekhov expects the reader to find the character silly.

(ENGLISH LEARNERS) Help students understand Olenka's words. Explain that *trifle* means "something of little value." The question "What do people see in those theatres, anyway?" means "Why do people want to go to the theater, anyway?"

English Learners

DIFFERENTIATED INSTRUCTION

Beginning Explain that an idiom is a saying that has a meaning that is different from the meaning of the individual words that make up the saying. **Say:** Look at the dialogue of the neighbor women on page 560. What do they say that may be an idiom? *("taking it badly")* **Ask:** Can you find another idiom a few paragraphs later? *("made an impression on him")* Discuss the meanings of these

idioms. *("Taking it badly" means experiencing difficult emotions in response to something. "Making an impression" is not making a physical mark on someone but having an effect or influencing someone's mind, feelings, or senses.)*

Comparing Literature

Teach

Literary Element | 1

Repetition Say: Identify an example of repetition on this page. *(When Pustovalov dies, Olenka sobs, "Who will look after me now?" Excessive mourning and lamenting were also characteristics of Olenka when her first husband died).*

Reading Strategy | 2

Predict Point out that Olenka's behavior follows a pattern. **Ask:** What do you think will happen now that Pustovalov is dead? *(Olenka may marry Smirnin.)*

[ADVANCED] **Ask:** What clues in the story hint that the relationship between Olenka and Smirnin may break Olenka's pattern? *(Smirnin was married before and has a son; Olenka had pushed for Smirnin to reconcile with his wife.)*

Portrait of Vasily Mathé, 1902. Boris Kustodiev. Oil on canvas, 125 x 151 cm. Russian State Museum, St. Petersburg, Russia. ★

Thus did the Pustovalovs live for six years, quietly and peacefully, in love and complete harmony. But one winter's day at the yard Vasily Andreich went out bare-headed to dispatch some timber after drinking hot tea, caught cold and fell ill. He was treated by the best doctors, but the illness took its course and he died four months later.

Olenka had become a widow again.

"Who will look after me now, my darling?" she sobbed, after burying her husband. "How can I possibly live without you? I'm so wretched and unhappy! Pity me, good people, I'm all alone now. . . ."

She wore a black dress with weepers,[19] having vowed never to wear a hat or gloves again, went out seldom and then only to church or to her husband's grave, and lived at home like a nun. Six months passed before she discarded the weepers and began opening her shutters. Some mornings she was to be seen shopping for food in the market with her cook, but people could only surmise how she was living

19. Here, *weepers* means "a veil worn as a symbol of mourning."

now and what her domestic arrangements were. They surmised when they saw her, for example, sitting in her little garden drinking tea with the vet while he read the newspaper out to her, and also when she bumped into a female friend at the post office and was heard to say:

"Our town has no proper veterinary inspection and that gives rise to many illnesses. You're always hearing of people being infected by milk or catching diseases from horses and cows. We really ought to treat the health of domestic animals as seriously as we do that of human beings."

She repeated the vet's thoughts and now shared his opinions on everything. It was clear that she could not survive even for a year without an attachment and had found her new happiness in the fliegel next door. Anyone else would have been condemned for this, but no one could think ill of Olenka, her whole life was so transparent. She and the vet did not tell anyone about the change that had taken place in their relationship and tried to conceal it, but without success, because Olenka could not keep a secret. When regimental colleagues came to visit him and she was pouring out their tea or serving supper, she would start talking about cattle plague, pearl disease,[20] and the municipal slaughterhouses. This made him terribly embarrassed, and as they were leaving, he would seize her by the arm and hiss angrily:

"Haven't I told you before not to talk about things you don't understand? When we vets are talking shop, please don't butt in. It's extremely tedious."

She would look at him in alarm and astonishment, and say:

20. *Pearl disease* is a blood disease in cattle.

View the Art ★

The subject of the painting, Vasily Mathé, was one of Kustodiev's teachers. Mathé had taught the artist etching in St. Petersburg. Note that the portrait is from the same era as Chekhov's story.

Reading Practice

SPIRAL REVIEW Characterization Challenge students to discuss how Olenka's character changes in the course of this page. Ask students to find two contrasting portrayals of Olenka. *(Olenka "lived at home like a nun;" Olenka "found her new happiness in the fliegel next door.")*

Then review with students the methods Chekhov uses to give readers a sense of Olenka. The narrator makes direct statements about the character's appearance and mood; the author shows us the character's statements and actions.

"But Volodya[21] dear, what *am* I to talk about?!"

With tears in her eyes she embraced him and begged him not to be angry, and they were both happy.

But this happiness did not last long. The vet departed with his regiment, and since they had been transferred somewhere very distant, practically to Siberia, his departure was permanent.

Olenka was left on her own.

This time she was completely on her own. Her father had long since died, and his armchair, with one leg missing, was gathering dust in the attic. She became plain and thin, and people meeting her in the street no longer looked at her and smiled as they used to; her best years were evidently gone for good, now a new, unknown life was beginning that did not bear thinking about. In the evenings Olenka sat on her porch and could hear the band playing and the rockets going off at the Tivoli, but this no longer made her think of anything. She gazed apathetically at her empty yard, had no thoughts or desires, and when night fell, went to bed and dreamed of her empty yard. She seemed reluctant even to eat or drink.

But the worst thing of all was no longer having any opinions. She saw objects round her and understood everything that was going on, but she could not form opinions about anything and did not know what to talk about. How awful it is not to have an opinion! You see a bottle, for example, standing there, or the rain falling, or a peasant going along in his cart, but what the bottle or rain or peasant are for, what sense they make, you can't say and couldn't say, even if they offered you a thousand roubles. In Snookin's and Pustovalov's time, and then with the vet, Olenka could explain everything and give her opinion on any subject you liked, whereas now her mind and heart were as empty as the yard outside. It was a horrible, bitter sensation, like a mouthful of wormwood.[22]

The town has gradually expanded in all directions. Gypsy Lane is now called a street, and where the Tivoli and the timber yards once stood, houses have sprung up and there are a number of side streets. How time flies! Olenka's house looks dingy, the roof has rusted, the shed is leaning to one side, and the yard is completely overgrown with weeds and stinging nettles.[23] Olenka herself has grown older and plainer. In summer she sits on her porch, with the same feeling of emptiness, boredom, and bitterness in her soul as before, in winter she sits by her window gazing at the snow. If she feels the breath of spring, or hears the sound of cathedral bells carried on the wind, memories suddenly flood in, tugging at her heart-strings, and copious tears stream down her face; but this lasts only a minute, then the same emptiness and sense of futility returns. Her black cat Bryska snuggles up to her, purring softly, but Olenka is unmoved by these feline caresses. Is that what she needs? No, she needs the kind of love that will possess her completely, mind and soul, that will provide her with thoughts and a direction in life, and warm her aging blood. She bundles black Bryska off her lap and says irritably:

"Go away . . . I don't want you here!"

It's the same day after day, year after year—she doesn't have a single joy in life or a single opinion. Whatever Mavra the cook says is good enough.

One hot July day, towards evening, when the town cattle were being driven past and clouds of dust had filled the yard, all of a sudden someone knocked at the gate. Olenka went to open it herself, took one look and was completely dumbfounded: Smirnin the vet was standing there, grey-haired and in civilian clothes. Suddenly everything came back to her, she broke down and burst into tears, laid her head on his chest without saying a word, and was so overcome that afterwards she had

---

21. *Volodya* is Smirnin's nickname (his first name is Vladimir).
22. *Wormwood* is a plant that produces a bitter oil.

23. *Stinging nettles* are a perennial herb with sharp leaves and white flowers.

ANTON CHEKHOV **563**

Context Clues **Ask:** How can you figure out the meaning of the word *apathetically* from reading the previous sentence, the sentence containing the word, and the following sentence? *(All three sentences tell the reader about Olenka's lack of desire and interest in the world, so* apathetically *must mean "without interest or emotion.")* Have students practice using the word *apathetically* in sentences.

[ENGLISH LEARNERS] Help students figure out the meaning of the word *apathetically.* Have students reread the three sentences again and write down phrases that tell of Olenka's lack of interest in the world. *("no longer made her think of anything," "had no thoughts or desires," "reluctant to eat or drink")* Tell students that looking for context clues while reading is a good way to figure out new vocabulary words.

English Learners

DIFFERENTIATED INSTRUCTION

Intermediate Have students read aloud what Smirnin says to Olenka on page 562: "When we vets are talking shop, please don't butt in. It's extremely tedious." Explain that while *talking shop* and *butt in* are informal expressions, the phrase *extremely tedious* is more formal. It is unlikely that these three expressions would appear together in the speech of native English speakers. Remind students that this story has been translated from Russian and that it can be difficult for translators to find a balanced mix of formal and informal English. Ask students to rewrite the first sentence in formal English.

Comparing Literature

Teach

Big Idea   1

Realism Chekhov depicts Olenka as acting totally subservient to Vladimir Platonych. She sacrifices herself so that he and his family will be comfortable. **Ask:** What view is Chekhov underscoring here? (*He is underscoring his view that women did not look out for themselves in the late nineteenth and early twentieth centuries.*) **Ask:** How does that compare with married women you know today? (*Women today are more independent, more educated, and often have careers of their own.*)

Writer's Technique ☆

Author's Voice After describing Olenka's willingness to give her life away for her new love, the narrator asks the reader directly, "Why? Who can possibly say why?" Explain to students that although less common in modern literature, there is a tradition of authors directly addressing their readers in order to draw readers' attention to a specific comment or issue.

no recollection of how they went into the house together and sat down to drink tea.

"Vladimir Platonych," she murmured, trembling with joy, "dearest! Whatever brings you here?"

"I'd like to settle down here permanently," he told her. "I've resigned my commission and come to try my luck as a civilian, leading a settled life. Then there's my son, he's growing up and it's time he went to grammar school. I've made it up with my wife, you know."

"And where is she now?" Olenka asked.

"At the hotel with the boy while I go round looking for lodgings."

"But good heavens, have *my* house, dear! Far better than lodgings. Oh heavens above, I don't want any rent," Olenka went on, becoming agitated and bursting into tears again. "You live here and the fliegel will do for me. Wonderful!"

Next day they were already painting the roof and whitewashing the walls, and Olenka was walking about the yard, arms on hips, giving orders. Her face shone with its old smile, and everything about her was fresh and lively, as if she had just woken from a long sleep. The vet's wife arrived, a thin, unattractive woman with short hair and a peevish expression. With her came the boy, Sasha, who was small for his age (he was over nine) and chubby, with bright blue eyes and dimpled cheeks. He had no sooner set foot in the yard than he began chasing the cat, and his merry, joyful laughter rang out.

"Is that your cat, Auntie?" he asked Olenka. "When it has babies, will you give us one, please? Mamma's scared stiff of mice."

Olenka chatted to him and gave him tea, and suddenly felt a warm glow and pleasurable tightening in her heart, as if this boy were her own son. And when he was sitting in the dining-room repeating his lessons in the evenings, she would look at him with tenderness and pity, and whisper:

"My darling, my pretty little child. . . . You're so clever and your skin is so fair."

"An island," he read out, "is an area of dry land surrounded on all sides by water."

"An island is an area of dry land . . ." she repeated, and this was the first opinion she had expressed with confidence after all those years of silence and emptiness of mind.

Now she had her own opinions and talked to Sasha's parents over supper about how hard children had to work at grammar school these days, but all the same a classical education was better than a modern one, because every career was open to you afterwards—doctor, engineer, whatever you wished.

Sasha had begun attending the grammar school. His mother went away to her sister's in Kharkov and did not come back, his father went off somewhere every day to inspect herds and might be away for three days at a time, and Olenka felt that Sasha was being completely neglected, his parents didn't want him and he must be starving to death; so she transferred him to her fliegel and fixed him up in a little room there.

Six months have now passed since Sasha began living in her fliegel. Every morning Olenka goes into his room: he is fast asleep with his hand under his cheek, breathing imperceptibly. She is sorry to have to wake him.

"Sashenka," she says sadly, "get up, dear! Time for school."

He gets up, dresses, says his prayers, and then sits down to drink tea; he drinks three glasses and consumes two large rolls and half a French loaf with butter. Still not fully awake, he is in a bad mood.

"You didn't learn your fable properly, you know, Sashenka," Olenka says, looking at him as if about to see him off on a long journey. "What a worry you are to me. You *must* make an effort to learn, dear, and do as the teachers say."

"Oh, stop nagging!" says Sasha.

Then he walks along the street to school, a small boy in a big cap, with a satchel on his back. Olenka follows silently behind.

"Sashenka-a!" she calls.

Writing Practice

Journal Entry Have students write a couple of journal entries as Olenka. The first entry takes place after the vet is transferred to somewhere distant, leaving Olenka alone. The second entry should be set when Smirnin and his family move back to the area. The journal entries should use sensory details to describe Olenka's life when she apathetically isolates herself in her house and her life when she starts to devote herself to caring for Sasha. Tell students to look for clues in the story and write about Olenka's feelings. Remind students that Olenka's feelings should be different in the two journal entries.

He looks round, and she pops a date or a caramel into his hand. When they turn into the school street, he feels ashamed at being followed by this tall, stout woman, looks round and says:

2 "You go home now, Auntie, I'll do the last bit on my own."

She stops and keeps her eyes fixed on him until he disappears through the school entrance. Oh, how she loves him! Not one of her previous attachments has been so deep, never before has she surrendered herself so wholeheartedly, unselfishly and joyfully as now, when her maternal feelings are being kindled more and more. For this boy, who is not hers, for his cap and his dimpled cheeks, she would give away her whole life, and do so with gladness and tears of emotion. Why? ☆ Who can possibly say why?

After seeing Sasha off, she returns home quietly, feeling so calm and contented, and overflowing with love. In these last six months her face has become younger, she is smiling and radiant, and people meeting her in the street feel pleasure as they look at her, and say:

"Olga Semyonovna darling, good morning! How are you, darling?"

"They have to work so hard at grammar school these days," she tells them in the market. "It's no laughing matter. Yesterday the first year had a fable to learn by heart *and* a Latin translation *and* a math problem. . . . How can a small boy cope?"

She goes on to talk about teachers and lessons and textbooks—repeating exactly what Sasha tells her.

Between two and three they have their meal together, and in the evening they do Sasha's homework together and cry. Putting

him to bed, she spends a long time making the sign of the cross over him and whispering a prayer, then, on going to bed herself, she pictures that distant hazy future when Sasha has finished his degree and become a doctor or an engineer, has his own large house with horses and a carriage, marries and has children. . . . She falls asleep still thinking about it all, and tears run down her cheeks from her closed eyes. The black cat lies purring by her side: mrr, mrr, mrr. . . .

Suddenly there's a loud knock at the gate. Olenka wakes up, too terrified to breathe. Her heart is thumping. Half a minute passes, then there's another knock.

"It's a telegram from Kharkov," she thinks, beginning to tremble all over. "Sasha's mother wants him to live with her in Kharkov. . . . Oh heavens!"

She is in despair. Her head, arms and legs turn cold, she feels the unhappiest person in the world. But another minute passes and she hears voices. It's the vet, he's come back from his club.

"Oh, thank God," she thinks.

Gradually the pressure on her heart eases and she feels relaxed again. She lies down and thinks of Sasha, who is sleeping soundly in the room next door. From time to time he starts talking in his sleep:

"I'll show you! Get out! Stop fighting!" ॐ

> *Suddenly there's a loud knock at the gate. Olenka wakes up, too terrified to breathe. Her heart is thumping. Half a minute passes, then there's another knock.*

🐾 Quickwrite

Olenka is described as being "constantly in love" and unable to live without love. How does love affect Olenka? In what ways is her need for love both beneficial and detrimental to her? Write a short response explaining your views.

ANTON CHEKHOV **565**

Comparing Literature

Teach

Vocabulary	2

Titles of Respect Sasha calls Olenka "Auntie" not because they are relatives but as a sign of respect toward an elder. Elicit from students the titles used in their home cultures when a young person addresses an older person.

Quickwrite

Students may say that Olenka bases her identity on the person she loves. Each time she loses her beloved, she also loses her thoughts and opinions. This trait benefits her when she is with someone who loves her, but she suffers when she is alone.

Approaching Level

DIFFERENTIATED INSTRUCTION 🔁

Established Point out to students that although Olenka does not marry the vet as predicted, her character has not changed at the end of the story. Have students reread the paragraph beginning "She goes on to talk about . . . ."

Ask: What is one hint that Olenka has not changed? *(Olenka repeats the opinions of Sasha, just as she used to repeat her husbands' opinions.)*

 SMALL GROUP

Emerging Have students form small discussion groups to answer the following questions: Why does Olenka break into a cold sweat when there is a knock on the door? *(She is afraid she will lose Sasha.)* Is it a happy ending when the vet appears at the door? *(No. Olenka is temporarily happy, but her happiness is still dependent on others.)* What prediction can you make for Olenka's future?

(She will lose Sasha eventually and she will go into despair again.) Is it healthy to depend on others for your happiness? Explain. *(No, other people may not always be around.)*

Comparing Literature

Focus

Read the famous line by Tennyson in its modernized form: "It's better to have loved and lost than never to have loved at all." Ask students whether they agree with the statement.

Teach

Literary Element

Theme Ask: What the meaning of "Richness" is? *(Life is complex; we experience deep feelings of happiness and deep feelings of sadness, sometimes at the same time.)*

APPROACHING **Ask:** What lines are repeated in the poem? *("I have a faithful joy and a joy that is lost.")* Explain that these lines stand for the theme: happiness and sadness are both part of life.

Quickwrite

Mistral links the contrasting "richness" of joy and sorrow through contrasting similes—the "faithful joy" is like a rose and the "joy that is lost" is like a thorn.

Tête De Jeune Fille, 1916. Amedeo Modigliani. Oil on canvas. Private collection.

Build Background

Gabriela Mistral (gä brē ā′ lä   mēs träl′) became the first Latin American writer to receive the Nobel Prize in Literature. Many of her poems explore themes of suffering and compassion, and the Bible was one of her most important influences.

Quickwrite

Mistral describes two sides of experience in this poem—joy and sorrow. She suggests the "richness" of life includes both of these feelings. Describe how the poem links joy and sorrow, exploring how the imagery adds to the theme. Cite evidence from the poem in your response.

Richness

Gabriela Mistral
Translated by Doris Dana

I have a faithful joy
and a joy that is lost.
One is like a rose,
the other, a thorn.
5 The one that was stolen
I have not lost.
I have a faithful joy
and a joy that is lost.
I am as rich with purple
10 as with sorrow.
Ay! How loved is the rose,
how loving the thorn!
Paired as twin fruit,
I have a faithful joy
15 and a joy that is lost.

Listening and Speaking Practice

SMALL GROUP

Oral Interpretation To help students understand the poem, have two students read the poem aloud, alternating lines as follows: the first to read lines 1, 3, 5–7, 9, 11, and 13–14; the other to read lines 2, 4, 8, 10, 12, and 15. With two voices reading different lines in the poem, students may better see and understand the poem's rich and unique contrasts.

Students may have trouble understanding how a thorn can represent joy and love. Split them into groups and have them discuss how thorns or difficult, sharp things in life can also represent joy and love. Have students share their answers with the class. *(Thorns keep roses safe, just as parents sometimes do things that seem harsh in order to protect their children.)*

Wrap-Up: Comparing Literature

Across Time and Place

- *The Story of an Hour* by Kate Chopin

- *The Darling* by Anton Chekhov

- *Richness* by Gabriela Mistral

A Friendly Call, 1895. William Merritt Chase. Oil on canvas, 76.5 x 122.5 cm. National Gallery of Art, Washington, DC.

COMPARE THE Big Idea Realism

Speaking and Listening In creating **verisimilitude,** or the illusion of reality in a literary work, Realist writers tend to focus more on the motivations of characters than on advancing a plot. These writers strive to portray the confusion and contradiction of their characters. With a small group, discuss how Mrs. Mallard in "The Story of an Hour," Olenka in "The Darling," and the speaker in "Richness" each respond to their problems.

1. Do you find their circumstances and their responses realistic?

2. What contradictions do you find in their thoughts and behaviors?

3. What misconceptions might other characters have about them?

Choose one person to summarize the group's conclusions for the class.

COMPARE Narratives About Relationships

Writing Activity Realist writers explore the complexity of close relationships, a mixture of good and bad, an amalgam of benefits and difficulties. Write a short-response essay in which you describe the complexity of the relationships involving Mrs. Mallard, Olenka, and the speaker in "Richness." Cite evidence from the selections to support your ideas.

COMPARE Social Context

Partner Activity Social context, or the values and morals of society, plays a role in each of these selections. Chopin and Chekhov both use the actions and dialogue of various characters to reveal social context. However, Mistral renders the feelings of the poem's speaker in isolation from social context. With a partner, discuss the following questions:

1. Compare and contrast the use of social context in the stories by Chopin and Chekhov.

2. How does the lack of social context affect the reader's understanding of Mistral's poem?

Literature Online

Selection Resources For Selection Quizzes, eFlashcards, and Reading-Writing Connection activities, go to glencoe.com and enter QuickPass code GLA9800u4.

COMPARING LITERATURE **567**

Assess

Compare the Big Idea

Speaking and Listening

1. Students should discuss how the circumstances are portrayed in each selection and how they themselves would act.

2. Discussions should cover Mrs. Mallard's initial apprehension at embracing her new freedom, Olenka's shifts in loyalty, and the dual nature of the comments in "Richness."

3. Josephine has no idea of Mrs. Mallard's joy; Sasha doesn't understand his importance to Olenka; an observer of the speaker in "Richness" might not understand the comfort she finds in loss.

Compare Narratives About Relationships

 Writing Activity

Students should note Mrs. Mallard's anguish and new sense of freedom; the sustenance and then the emptiness Olenka feels; and the joy and the sorrow that the speaker in "Richness" feels.

For additional assessment, see Assessment Resources, pp. 175–176.

Compare Social Context

Partner Activity

1. Students should address the conventions governing marriage and women's behavior in Victorian culture. Students may say that social context helps increase the serious realism in "The Story of an Hour" and the humorous realism in "The Darling."

2. Students may say that the lack of social context in "Richness" makes the speaker's circumstances less clear. This confusion may either frustrate the reader or allow the reader to make a more personal connection to the poem.

Douglass and *We Wear the Mask*

Meet **Paul Laurence Dunbar**
(1872–1906)

These words aptly describe the complex plight of Paul Laurence Dunbar. To reach an audience for his poetry, he often felt he had to "sing" within the constraints of the taste and prejudice that dominated his times.

A Midwestern Childhood One of the first African American writers to attain national recognition, Dunbar was the son of formerly enslaved people. He grew up hearing their stories of pre-Emancipation days, which would later provide a wealth of material for his work. Dunbar had a close relationship with his mother throughout his life, but his father died when Dunbar was only twelve years old.

Dunbar was the only African American student at his Dayton, Ohio, high school. He excelled at his studies, edited the school paper, wrote plays for the drama club, and became class president. Despite his success in school, he could not afford college and had trouble finding a job in a newspaper or a legal office. He worked instead as an elevator operator and spent time writing between calls for the elevator. With help from the Wright Brothers—who owned a printing business in addition to pioneering aviation—he published the *Dayton Tattler*, an African American newsletter.

Dunbar the Poet Dunbar took out a loan in 1893 to publish his first volume of poetry, *Oak and Ivy*, which he sold to elevator passengers and at recitals. After it was published, he joined Frederick Douglass at the Chicago World's Fair, where he gave recitations of his poetry. His second volume, *Majors and Minors*, came out in 1895 and was followed by *Lyrics of a Lonely Life* in 1896. He married Alice Ruth Moore, an African American poet, in 1898. When the influential writer and critic William Dean Howells favorably reviewed *Majors and*

> *"I know why the caged bird sings, ah me, . . . When he beats his bars and he would be free. . . ."*
>
> —Paul Laurence Dunbar, "Sympathy"

Minors, Dunbar found himself famous and in great demand across the United States and in England as a reader.

Much to Dunbar's despair, the poems he wrote in black dialect were his best-received works. He also wrote novels, librettos, short stories, and Standard English poems, but these received little attention from critics and readers. His poetry eventually garnered him a clerkship at the Library of Congress. Toward the end of his life, he told James Weldon Johnson, "I have never really gotten to the things I really wanted to do." Despite this sentiment, he was the first African American who was able to live solely on the profits of his writing, and his home became the first state memorial to an African American.

 Literature Online

Author Search For more about Paul Laurence Dunbar, go to glencoe.com and enter QuickPass code GLA9800u4.

Bellringer Options

Literature Launchers:
  Pre-Reading Videos DVD,
  Selection Launcher
Selection Focus
  Transparency 36
Daily Language Practice
  Transparency 51

Or **ask:** Do you sometimes feel you have to "wear" more than one face? Are you one person at home, another at school, and yet another when out with friends? Have students consider their different "masks" as they read "We Wear the Mask."

Interactive Read and Write

Other options for teaching this selection can be found in

- Interactive Read and Write for EL Students, pp. 171–178
- Interactive Read and Write for Approaching-Level Students, pp. 171–178
- Interactive Read and Write for On-Level Students, pp. 171–178

Selection Skills

Literary Elements
- Rhyme Scheme (SE pp. 569, 571, 572)
- Sonnet (TE p. 570)

Douglass/We Wear the Mask

Listening/Speaking/ Viewing Skills
- Analyze Art (TE pp. 570, 571)
- Compare Poetry (TE p. 570)

Reading Skills
- Clarify Meaning (SE pp. 569, 570, 572)

Vocabulary Skills
- Denotation and Connotation (SE p. 572)

Writing Skills/Grammar
- Write a Letter (SE p. 572)

Literature and Reading Preview

Connect to the Poems

What are the advantages and disadvantages of wearing a "mask"? In what situations do you wear a mask? Explore these questions in a short journal entry.

Build Background

Dunbar wrote two kinds of poetry. He was known and loved for his sentimental verse, written in dialect, about an idyllic, pastoral, pre-Civil War plantation life. However, this portion of his work has led some to criticize him for failing to confront the issues of racial stereotypes and discrimination. Dunbar also produced less popular poems in Standard English that meditate on love, nature, or death; express pride in African Americans; or lament thwarted efforts to live and create freely. "Douglass" and "We Wear the Mask" are examples of his Standard English poems.

Set Purposes for Reading

Big Idea Naturalism

Naturalism held that people often faced challenges beyond their control. As you read, ask yourself, How much control does Dunbar seem to have felt over his own life and challenges?

Literary Element Rhyme Scheme

The pattern formed by end rhymes in a stanza or poem is called a **rhyme scheme.** If you assign a different letter to each ending *sound* in "Douglass," you can chart the rhyme scheme like this: *abba, abba, cdcdcd.* As you read, ask yourself, What is the rhyme scheme of "We Wear the Mask"?

Reading Strategy Clarify Meaning

If you have trouble understanding a passage, carefully reread it to better comprehend its meaning. Be sure to read any footnotes and definitions that accompany the text and look for **context clues** to define unfamiliar words.

Tip: Paraphrase You can clarify meaning by **paraphrasing,** or stating a passage in your own words. When paraphrasing a poem, look for natural breaks in thoughts—at the ends of lines or stanzas and at end punctuation. Paraphrase sections, then combine them to form complete thoughts. Here is one paraphrase of lines 11–14 of "Douglass": *Today, with so much disagreement and no leaders whom we can trust, we need your clear voice, guiding arm, and inspiring presence.*

Learning Objectives

For pages 568–572

In studying these texts, you will focus on the following objectives:

Literary Study: Analyzing rhyme scheme.

Reading: Clarifying meaning.

Writing: Writing a letter.

Vocabulary

salient (sāl′ yənt) *adj.* prominent or conspicuously noticeable; p. 570 *Arrogance was a salient aspect of his personality.*

tempest (tem′ pist) *n.* a violent storm; p. 570 *The trees shook wildly in the tempest.*

dissension (di sen′ shən) *n.* disagreement or discord; p. 570 *There was dissension in the drama club over which play to perform.*

guile (gīl) *n.* deceit or slyness; p. 571 *She swayed the jury with her guile.*

vile (vīl) *adj.* repulsive or digusting; p. 571 *The smell of the rotten fish was vile.*

Before You Read

Focus

Summary

In "Douglass," the speaker notes that the struggles of his day are even harsher than those that Frederick Douglass (1817?–1895) faced as an enslaved person. He wishes that Douglass were alive to guide his people. "We Wear the Mask" describes the jolting contrast between the inner and outer lives of African Americans.

 For summaries in languages other than English, see Unit 4 Teaching Resources Book, pp. 122–127.

Vocabulary

Write a Short Story Have groups of students practice using the vocabulary words by writing a short story. Students should use at least four of the vocabulary words in their story. Have students read their stories to the class and discuss their use of the vocabulary words.

 For additional vocabulary practice, see Unit 4 Teaching Resources Book, p. 130.

English Learners

DIFFERENTIATED INSTRUCTION

Intermediate Explain to students that poets sometimes use archaic English words and contracted forms of words in their poems. **Write these words on the board:** thou, thee, thy, fall'n, didst, amaze, lieth, o'er, nay. Explain that *thou* is the form of the word "you" when used as the subject of a sentence. *Thee* is the form of "you" when used as the object of a sentence. *Thy* means "your." *Fall'n* is the con- tracted form of the word "fallen." *Didst* is a form of the word "did." *Amaze* in modern English is used as a verb but it was also used as a noun meaning "amazement" a long time ago. *Lieth* is a poetic way to say "lies down." *O'er* is the contracted form of the word "over." *Nay* means "no." Help students better remember these words by having them translate modern English sentences into archaic English. For exam- ple, "You did a great job" would translate to "Thou didst a great job." Give students other sentences to practice with, such as "Your mother asked you to help her after she had fallen" which would translate to "Thy mother asked thee to help her after she had fall'n."

Teach

Literary Element `1`

Sonnet Explain that a sonnet is a fourteen-line poem, typically with five stresses in each line: an unstressed syllable followed by a stressed one. The first stanza (eight lines) presents a situation, a question, or an idea. The second stanza (six lines) provides a resolution, an answer, or a comment.

Reading Strategy `2`

Clarify Meaning Answer: *The speaker says that life is full of more evil than in Douglass's time.*

Big Idea `3`

Naturalism Answer: *The speaker's cry clearly suggests that the speaker does not feel in control of his life.*

View the Art ★

Jacob Lawrence is famous for his series of paintings based on Frederick Douglass's autobiography.
Ask: How is Lawrence's view of Douglass similar to Dunbar's view? *(Both see Douglass as a large, dominant figure.)*

Douglass

Paul Laurence Dunbar

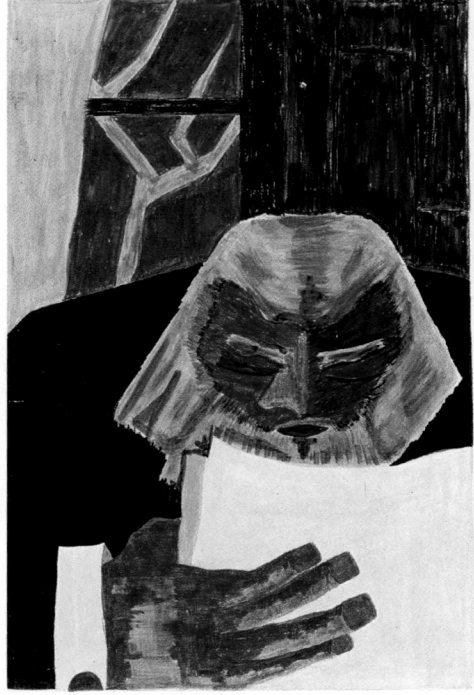

The Life of Frederick Douglass #30, 1939. Jacob Lawrence. © ARS, NY. Casein tempera on hardboard, 12 x 17⅞ in. Hampton University Museum. ★

Ah, Douglass,[1] we have fall'n on evil days, `1`
  Such days as thou, not even thou didst know,
  When thee, the eyes of that harsh long ago
Saw, **salient,** at the cross of devious ways,
5 And all the country heard thee with amaze.
  Not ended then, the passionate ebb and flow,[2]
  The awful tide that battled to and fro;
We ride amid a **tempest** of dispraise.

Now, when the waves of swift **dissension** swarm,
10 And Honor, the strong pilot, lieth stark,[3]
Oh, for thy voice high-sounding o'er the storm,
  For thy strong arm to guide the shivering bark,[4]
The blast-defying power of thy form,
  To give us comfort through the lonely dark.

---

1. Frederick *Douglass* escaped from slavery and became a great speaker and leader in the abolition movement.
2. *Ebb and flow* means "fall and rise."
3. *Stark* means "stiffly" or "rigidly."
4. A *bark* is a type of boat.

Clarify Meaning *What does the speaker tell Douglass in the first two lines?* `2`

Naturalism *From this statement, do you think that the speaker feels like he has control over his circumstances?* `3`

Vocabulary

salient (sāl´ yənt) *adj.* prominent or conspicuously noticeable
tempest (tem´ pist) *n.* a violent storm
dissension (di sen´ shən) *n.* disagreement or discord

570 UNIT 4 REGIONALISM AND REALISM

Listening and Speaking Practice

Compare Poetry Have students turn to page 359 to read a poem titled "Frederick Douglass" by Robert Hayden. Hayden's poem was published in 1946, more than forty years after "Douglass" by Paul Laurence Dunbar was published (1903). Have students create a Venn diagram with the title "Dunbar" over the left circle and "Hayden" over the right. Have a student reread Dunbar's poem aloud while students create a list of observa- tions in the left circle. Then, as a student volunteer reads Hayden's poem aloud, students should create a list of observa- tions about the poem in the right circle. Discuss with students the similarities and differences in the poems. Students should pay attention to word choice *(Dunbar's use of old English),* form *(both are fourteen lines),* and purpose *(Dunbar calls on Douglass for inspiration; Hayden honors his memory).* Through discussion of the two poems, create a list of similari- ties to place in the overlapping section of the diagram. **Ask:** Are the two poems more alike than different? Have stu- dents explain their answers using specific examples.

We Wear the Mask

Paul Laurence Dunbar

We wear the mask that grins and lies,
It hides our cheeks and shades our eyes,—
This debt we pay to human **guile**;
With torn and bleeding hearts we smile,
5   And mouth with myriad[1] subtleties.[2]

Why should the world be overwise,
In counting all our tears and sighs?
Nay, let them only see us, while
      We wear the mask.

10   We smile, but, O great Christ, our cries
To thee from tortured souls arise.
We sing, but oh the clay is **vile**
Beneath our feet, and long the mile;
But let the world dream otherwise,
15   We wear the mask!

---

1. *Myriad* means "countless" or "innumerable."
2. *Subtleties* are things so slight that they are barely perceptible.

4 Rhyme Scheme *What is the rhyme scheme of this poem? What is the effect of the word* mask?

Vocabulary

guile (gīl) *n.* deceit or slyness
vile (vīl) *adj.* repulsive or disgusting

Back Home from Up the Country. Romare Bearden. Romare Bearden Foundation. Licensed by VAGA, New York.

Teach

Literary Element   4

Rhyme Scheme **Answer:** *aabba aabc aabbac. The sound of the word* mask *breaks the rhyme pattern but then is repeated at the end of the poem.*

View the Art ★

Romare Bearden (1911–1988), an African American artist who focused on cultural and historical themes, is best known for his collages, such as the one on this page. **Say:** Explain why this collage works well as an illustration for this particular poem. *(Several of the figures' faces are constructed in a way that makes them look like masks.)*

To check students' understanding of the selection, see Unit 4 Teaching Resources Book, p. 132.

Progress Check

Can students analyze rhyme scheme?

If No → See Unit 4 Teaching Resources Book, p. 128.

Approaching Level

DIFFERENTIATED INSTRUCTION

Emerging To create rhyme and maintain rhythm, poets sometimes use inverted sentences that do not follow the usual subject-verb-object word order. To improve **reading fluency,** have students restate line 3 of "We Wear the Mask" in standard word order. *(We pay this debt to human guile.)*

Established Explain that personification is figurative language that gives human characteristics to an inanimate object. **Ask:** How does Dunbar use personification in this poem? *(Dunbar makes the mask an animate object by saying that it "grins and lies.")* Where in the poem does the poet explain why we wear the mask? What is the reason? *(second stanza; so that others cannot see the tears or hear the sighs)* Based on this poem, what is Dunbar's view on life? *(Life is hard and full of sorrow, but people put on an act and pretend they are fine.)*

After You Read

Assess

1. Students may cite "Mask" lines ". . . our cries/To thee from tortured souls arise."

2. (a) The "evil days" the speaker is living through are worse than those days that Douglass lived through. (b) Return and lead his people through these times

3. (a) The mask "grins and lies" and "hides." (b) African Americans wear it to hide their suffering.

4. (a) The mask hides a grim reality. (b) "Tears and sighs"; "torn and bleeding hearts"

5. To awaken in readers the memory of this strong leader

6. A tempest is a powerful and violent force. The speaker sees opposition to African Americans as strong and violent; therefore, the metaphor is appropriate.

7. The message remains relevant because people today still hide their suffering.

8. Douglass desired to challenge injustice; the speaker in "Douglass" sees the need for another leader to do this. In "We Wear the Mask," people "grin" and "lie" in order to conform.

9. Students may say that writing the poem contradicts what one who wears a mask would do.

After You Read

Respond and Think Critically

Respond and Interpret

1. Which lines in these poems had the greatest emotional impact on you? Explain your choices.

2. (a)According to the speaker in "Douglass," how does the present time compare to Douglass's time? (b)What does the speaker wish that Douglass could do?

3. (a)What words does the speaker in "We Wear the Mask" use to describe the mask? (b)Who wears the mask, and why must it be worn?

4. (a)What reality is hidden behind the mask? (b)What words and images describe this reality?

Analyze and Evaluate

5. The speaker in "Douglass" addresses his words directly to Frederick Douglass, even though Douglass had died by the time the poem was written. What is the purpose of this **apostrophe,** or direct address to an absent person?

6. Evaluate how well the extended metaphor used by the speaker in "Douglass" represents the struggle the speaker is describing.

7. Do you think the **theme,** or central message, of "We Wear the Mask" is relevant today? Explain.

Connect

8. **Big Idea** Naturalism Naturalist writers believed social pressures shaped human destiny. Do you see evidence of this belief in Dunbar's poems? Explain.

9. **Connect to the Author** In your opinion, was Dunbar speaking from personal experience when he wrote "We Wear the Mask"? Explain.

Literary Element Rhyme Scheme

A **rhyme scheme** is the pattern formed by end rhymes in a stanza or a poem.

1. Compare the rhyme scheme of "We Wear the Mask" with that of "Douglass." How do the rhyme schemes in the poems differ?

2. What letter in "We Wear the Mask" represents an entire repeated line, or **refrain**?

Reading Strategy Clarify Meaning

Paraphrase lines 3–5 of "We Wear the Mask." It will be easier to paraphrase if you refer to the poem to **clarify** the context.

Vocabulary Practice

Practice with Denotation and Connotation
Denotation is the literal, or dictionary, meaning of a word. **Connotation** is its implied, or cultural, meaning. Each vocabulary word below is listed with a word that has a similar denotation. Choose the word that has the stronger connotation.

1. salient   noticeable
2. storm   tempest
3. dissension   disagreement
4. guile   slyness
5. gross   vile

 Writing

Write a Letter In "Douglass," the speaker addresses Douglass directly, longing for the leader's presence. Have you ever longed for someone who was gone? Write a letter to that person, expressing why you wish he or she was here now.

 Literature Online

Selection Resources For Selection Quizzes, eFlashcards, and Reading-Writing Connection activities, go to glencoe.com and enter QuickPass code GLA9800u4.

Reading Strategy

To lie about our pain, we must smile, though our hearts are torn and bleeding, and we must speak with care.

 For additional assessment, see Assessment Resources, pp. 177–178.

Literary Element

1. In "Douglass," end rhymes alternate; in "We Wear the Mask," end rhymes are paired, with variations in the last lines of the stanzas.

2. The letter c

Vocabulary

1. salient **2.** tempest **3.** dissension **4.** guile **5.** vile

 Writing

Students' letters should be addressed to a person of significance in their lives.

Before You Read

Richard Cory and Miniver Cheevy

Meet **Edwin Arlington Robinson** (1869–1935)

Describing his childhood in Gardiner, Maine, as stark and unhappy, Edwin Arlington Robinson once wrote to a friend that by the time he was six years old he wondered why he had been born. He began writing at an early age because he felt "doomed, or elected, or sentenced for life, to the writing of poetry." As a high school student, he practiced intricate verse forms under the guidance of a local poet. He continued to write during the two years he attended Harvard University until family financial problems forced him to leave and return to a troubled home. Robinson's father died in 1892, and his mother died of diphtheria in 1896. One of Robinson's brothers became a drug addict, and the other became an alcoholic; both died early.

> "I used to read about clearness, force, and elegance in the rhetoric books, but I'm afraid I go in chiefly for force. . ."
>
> —Edwin Arlington Robinson

Hope and Despair Robinson's characters are often people who feel defeated or frustrated by life and who lack a sense of direction. Most of his poems are written in an ironic tone, with philosophical themes, and tragic ending. However, Robinson was not a true pessimist. He believed that life has meaning despite its hardships and that there is hope beyond "the black and awful chaos of the night." Most of Robinson's early poems are dramatic lyrics, and he became known for his poetic structure based on natural diction and skillful rhyming patterns within stanzas. His later works include several long narrative poems

in blank verse, which were often expanded versions of the psychological portraits he wrote during his earlier period. Robinson was not an experimental poet, yet his poems do break with the traditions of nineteenth-century romantic verse in their use of conversational language and irregular lines.

Struggle for Recognition Robinson's first books of poems, *The Torrent and the Night Before* and *The Children of the Night*, were published in 1896 and 1897 at his friends' expense. He moved to New York City in 1897 when he was twenty-eight and poverty-stricken. He held a variety of jobs there but made little money and was unable to publish more poetry. He was rescued from his desperate state by President Theodore Roosevelt, who had read and admired his work. Roosevelt arranged a position for Robinson at the U.S. Customs House in New York, an easy job that enabled him to write without worrying about money. Robinson dedicated his third collection, *The Town Down by the River*, to the president. He left his position at the Customs House in 1909 to devote himself entirely to writing. Robinson was generally ignored by both critics and the public until relatively late in his career. His first critical acclaim came with *The Man Against the Sky* (1916). His later works include a trilogy based on Arthurian legend, *Merlin*, *Lancelot*, and *Tristram*, which became a big critical and popular success. Eventually, Robinson won three Pulitzer Prizes and became one of America's favorite poets.

LOG ON ▶ **Literature** Online

Author Search For more about Edwin Arlington Robinson, go to glencoe.com and enter QuickPass code GLA9800u4.

Before You Read

Focus

Selection Skills

Literary Elements
- Irony (SE pp. 574, 576, 577; TE p. 574)

Richard Cory/Miniver Cheevy

Reading Skills
- Make Inferences About Characters (SE pp. 574, 575, 577; TE p. 576)

Vocabulary Skills
- Denotation and Connotation (SE p. 577)
- Word Origins (TE p. 574)

Writing Skills/Grammar
- Write a Poem (SE p. 577)
- Poetry (TE p. 576)

Listening/Speaking/Viewing Skills
- Analyze Art (TE p. 575)

Before You Read

Focus

Summary

In the first poem, Richard Cory, rich and kingly, is much admired by the working class. One night, Cory goes home and shoots himself. In the second poem, Miniver Cheevy, an idle, unhappy man, dreams of ancient and more glorious times.

 For summaries in languages other than English, see Unit 4 Teaching Resources Book, pp. 134–139.

Vocabulary

Word Origins Ask students to look up the words *imperially, assail,* and *incessantly* in the dictionary and find out the origins of these words. *(Imperially is from the Latin word* imperium *meaning "command, empire." Assail is from the Latin prefix* ad- *plus the verb* salire *meaning "to leap." Incessantly is from the Latin prefix* in- *plus the word* cessant- *meaning "to delay.")* Have students practice using these new vocabulary words in sentences.

[APPROACHING] Because in AAVE there is often no distinction between /i/ and /e/ before /m/ and /n/, some students may pronounce the word *imperially* as emperially. Model the pronunciation for students. Then have students repeat the word aloud and use the word in a sentence.

 For additional context, see Glencoe Interactive Vocabulary CD-ROM.

Literature and Reading Preview

Connect to the Poems

How much control do you think people have over their lives and their feelings? How much is outside of our control? Discuss these questions in a small group.

Build Background

More than sixty of Robinson's earliest and best-known poems are set in Tilbury Town, a fictional setting modeled on the poet's hometown, Gardiner, Maine. Robinson is daringly realistic in his portrayal of the town and its inhabitants.

Set Purposes for Reading

Big Idea Naturalism

Robinson's poetry often focuses on characters who seem to have little control over their lives or the scientific, social, and environmental forces that affect them. As you read, ask, How do Richard Cory and Miniver Cheevy react to these forces?

Literary Element Irony

Irony is a discrepancy between appearance and reality. In literature it is often accompanied by grim humor. As you read, ask, How is appearance different from reality in these poems?

Reading Strategy Make Inferences About Characters

You **make inferences** when you use reason and your experience to understand meaning that is implied but not stated directly. As you read Robinson's portraits of Richard Cory and Miniver Cheevy, look for the clues that the poet offers about each man's public and private "faces"—how they appear to the world around them and how they appear to themselves.

Tip: Take Notes Use a chart to record the inferences you draw from the details presented.

Detail	Inference
p. 575 "He was a gentleman from sole to crown"	Richard Cory takes care of his appearance and dresses appropriately.

Learning Objectives

For pages 573–577

In studying these texts, you will focus on the following objectives:

Literary Study: Analyzing irony.

Reading: Making inferences about characters.

Writing: Writing a poem.

Vocabulary

imperially (im pēr´ ē əl ē) *adv.* majestically; magnificently; p. 575 *The queen walked imperially into the palace.*

assail (ə sāl´) *v.* to attack violently; p. 576 *The ship was assailed by the heavy storm.*

fragrant (frā´ grənt) *adj.* having a strong, pleasant smell; p. 576 *The fragrant roses made the apartment look and smell lovely.*

incessantly (in ses´ ənt lē) *adv.* continually; happening over and over without interruption; p. 576 *Alison's brother incessantly asked for a cookie.*

scorn (skôrn) *v.* to treat with open contempt; reject something as worthless; p. 576 *The angry citizens scorned the mayor's proposal.*

Reading Practice

Situational Irony Review with students that situational irony occurs when something happens that is the opposite of what the readers expect. A classic example of situational irony is O. Henry's story "The Gift of the Magi." In the story, a couple is too poor to buy each other Christmas gifts. The wife cuts and sells her beautiful hair to buy her husband a watch chain. He sells his gold watch to buy her combs for her hair. **Ask:** How is this situation ironic? *(The husband no longer has a watch to use with the watch chain and the wife no longer has the long hair to wear the combs.)*

Richard Cory

Edwin Arlington Robinson

Man with the Cat (Henry Sturgis Drinker), 1898.
Cecilia Beaux. Oil on canvas, 48 x 34⁵/₈ in. Bequest
of Henry Ward Ranger through the National Academy
of Design. Smithsonian American Art Museum,
Washington, DC.

Whenever Richard Cory went down town,
We people on the pavement looked at him:
He was a gentleman from sole to crown,
Clean favored,[1] and **imperially** slim.

5 And he was always quietly arrayed,[2]
And he was always human when he talked;
But still he fluttered pulses when he said,
"Good-morning," and he glittered when he walked.

And he was rich—yes, richer than a king—
10 And admirably schooled in every grace:
In fine,[3] we thought that he was everything
To make us wish that we were in his place.

So on we worked, and waited for the light,
And went without the meat, and cursed the bread;
15 And Richard Cory, one calm summer night,
Went home and put a bullet through his head.

---

1. *Clean favored* means "having a tidy appearance."
2. *Arrayed* means "dressed."
3. *In fine* means "in short."

> Make Inferences About Characters *What can you infer about Richard Cory's relationship with the people based on the speaker's description?* **2**

Vocabulary

imperially (im pēr′ ē əl ē) *adv.* majestically; magnificently

EDWIN ARLINGTON ROBINSON **575**

Teach

Make Inferences About Characters Have students paraphrase lines 13–16 to better understand the meaning of those lines. *(Miniver misses the days of famous successful people. Romantic and artistic feelings, he claims, are no more.)* **Ask:** Based on the paraphrase, what can you infer about Cheevy? (He seems to see the world in black and white: the past was great; the present is not.)

Literary Element | 2

Irony Answer: *The character thinks of armor as graceful when, in reality, it is uncomfortable and makes smooth movement impossible.*

Writer's Technique ☆

What's in a Name? Writers often give hints about a character's nature by giving that character a particular name. *Miniver* is the name of a white fur trim on robes worn by medieval nobles.

To check students' understanding of the selection, see Unit 4 Teaching Resources Book, p. 144.

Miniver Cheevy ☆

Edwin Arlington Robinson

Miniver Cheevy, child of scorn,
    Grew lean while he **assailed** the seasons;
He wept that he was ever born,
    And he had reasons.

5 Miniver loved the days of old
    When swords were bright and steeds were prancing;
The vision of a warrior bold
    Would set him dancing.

Miniver sighed for what was not,
10   And dreamed, and rested from his labors;
He dreamed of Thebes[1] and Camelot,[2]
    And Priam's[3] neighbors.

Miniver mourned the ripe renown
    That made so many a name so **fragrant;**
15 He mourned Romance, now on the town,[4] **| 1**
    And Art, a vagrant.

Miniver loved the Medici,[5]
    Albeit he had never seen one;
He would have sinned **incessantly**
20   Could he have been one.

Miniver cursed the commonplace
    And eyed a khaki suit with loathing;
He missed the mediæval grace
    Of iron clothing.

25 Miniver **scorned** the gold he sought,
    But sore annoyed was he without it;
Miniver thought, and thought, and thought,
    And thought about it.

Miniver Cheevy, born too late,
30   Scratched his head and kept on thinking;
Miniver coughed, and called it fate,
    And kept on drinking.

Vocabulary

assail (ə sāl´) *v.* to attack violently
fragrant (frā´ grənt) *adj.* having a strong, pleasant smell
incessantly (in ses´ ənt lē´) *adv.* continually; happening over and over without interruption
scorn (skôrn) *v.* to treat with open contempt; reject something as worthless

---

1. *Thebes* (thēbz) was a city-state in ancient Greece.
2. *Camelot* is the legendary site of King Arthur's court.
3. In Homer's *Iliad, Priam* was the king of Troy.
4. *On the town* means "on welfare."
5. *Medici* (med´ i chē) refers to a noble, rich, and powerful family in Florence, Italy (1300–1500).

Irony *What is the verbal irony in these lines?* **2**

Writing Practice

SMALL GROUP
Poetry Have students analyze the rhythm of the poem:

˘ / ˘ / ˘ / ˘ /
Miniver loved the days of old

˘ / ˘ / ˘ / ˘
When swords were bright and steeds were

/ ˘
prancing;

Then have them analyze rhyme *(abab)* and imagery. *(Flashing swords and prancing horses convey a romantic attitude toward the past.)* After students analyze the poem, have them work in groups to write a poem in the style of Robinson's work. Remind students to create their own unhappy characters and suitable images to describe these characters before they start writing their poems.

After You Read

Respond and Think Critically

Respond and Interpret

1. What was your reaction to the last line in each poem? Give reasons for your answer.

2. (a)Summarize the speaker's description of Richard Cory. (b)In what ways does Cory's life differ from the lives of the "people on the pavement"?

3. (a)What does Richard Cory do "one calm summer night"? (b)What does this action suggest about Cory's quality of life?

4. (a)What does Miniver Cheevy blame for his unhappiness? (b)What do you think is the real reason he is unhappy? Explain.

Analyze and Evaluate

5. (a)What is ironic about Cory's life and death? (b)Can you sympathize with him? Explain.

6. (a)What is the speaker's **tone,** or attitude, toward Miniver Cheevy? (b)How does the speaker's tone affect your attitude toward him?

Connect

7. **Big Idea** **Naturalism** According to Robinson, why do money and art not always make people happy or help them overcome limitations?

8. **Connect to Today** Do you think any of these poems' themes is relevant to today? Explain.

Literary Element   Irony

Situational irony occurs when the actual outcome of a situation is the opposite of what is expected. **Verbal irony** occurs when the meaning of a statement is the opposite of what is said.

Partner Activity Discuss this question: How does Robinson use situational and verbal irony to reveal details about the various characters?

Reading Strategy   Make Inferences About Characters

Refer to your chart from page 574 to help you answer the following questions.

1. What clues indicate that the townspeople regard Richard Cory as many people regard royalty?

2. What details lead you to understand that Miniver Cheevy is an unhappy person who is unable or unwilling to improve his life?

LOG ON   Literature Online

Selection Resources For Selection Quizzes, eFlashcards, and Reading-Writing Connection activities, go to glencoe.com and enter QuickPass code GLA9800u4.

Vocabulary Practice

Denotation and Connotation **Denotation** is the literal, or dictionary, meaning of a word. **Connotation** is the implied, or cultural, meaning. For example, *determined, stubborn,* and *unshakeable* have similar denotation—"unwilling to change"—but different connotations:

Negative	*Neutral*	*Positive*
stubborn	determined	unshakeable

From each pair below, choose the word with a more neutral or positive connotation.

1. imperially   majestically
2. assail   apprehend
3. fragrant   odoriferous
4. incessantly   continually
5. scorn   dislike

Writing

Write a Poem Robinson uses irony to comment on the people and culture of his time. Using his work as an example, write a poem in which you use verbal or situational irony to reveal something about today's society.

EDWIN ARLINGTON ROBINSON   **577**

Literary Element

Situational irony occurs in line 16 of "Richard Cory." Envying Cory is ironic: the townspeople's lives were more satisfying than his. Verbal irony in "Miniver Cheevy" includes the statement that "he had reasons" to regret being born.

Vocabulary

1. majestically
2. apprehend
3. fragrant
4. continually
5. disliked

Writing

Students' poems should be about modern society and contain irony.

After You Read

Assess

1. Students may be surprised by the last line of each poem.

2. (a) He is rich, well-dressed, and educated. (b) He lives luxuriously.

3. (a) He shoots himself. (b) This action suggests that his life was not a happy one.

4. (a) The fact that the present is not like the past (b) Students should provide support for their opinions.

5. (a) His wealth cannot relieve the unhappiness that leads him to suicide. (b) Some students may sympathize with Cory's depression; others may feel that Cory should have appreciated all that he had.

6. (a) Sarcastic and critical (b) It causes readers to have negative feelings toward Cheevy.

7. Wealth and art do not give people control over their personal anxieties or disappointments.

8. Students' connections will vary.

For additional assessment, see Assessment Resources, pp. 179–180.

Reading Strategy

1. "[A] gentleman from sole to crown," "imperially slim," and "richer than a king"

2. Cheevy regrets being born; he wishes he could wear armor; he drinks instead of living life.

Progress Check

Can students analyze irony?

If No → See Unit 4 Teaching Resources Book, p. 152.

Before You Read

Focus

Bellringer Options

Selection Focus
 Transparency 38
Daily Language Practice
 Transparency 53

Or have students read the lines that are printed in large type on this page.

Ask: What do these lines suggest about the quality of Crane's work? Given these lines, how would you interpret the statement that Crane "lived quickly and wrote fast"?

Before You Read

The Open Boat

Meet **Stephen Crane**
(1871–1900)

By the time he reached college, Stephen Crane was better known for his baseball-playing skills than for his scholarly achievements. Within a decade, however, Crane's rebelliousness toward his schooling, his upbringing, and society at large would help shape a short but prolific literary career. In his work, Crane embraced a pessimistic realism that undermined earlier, romanticized visions of human experiences. In fiction, as in journalism, Crane portrayed life as it was, not as one wished it were.

"Stephen Crane was a craftsman. The stones he put in the wall are still there."

—Sherwood Anderson

Bowery Life The fourteenth child of a Methodist minister and his devout wife, Crane chafed against the constraints of structured family life. University life left him with much the same feeling, and he attended classes sporadically before leaving college entirely to work as a newspaper writer. As a freelance reporter, Crane lived in the Bowery district of Manhattan, reporting on the poverty of the district's slums through firsthand experience. His observations of Bowery life eventually became the basis for his controversial first novel, *Maggie: A Girl of the Streets* (1893). Crane's sympathetic but starkly realistic portrayal of New York slum life repelled publishers; he finally published the novel at his own expense under the pseudonym Johnston Smith. Crane's harsh story did not sell well. However, critics Hamlin Garland and William Dean Howells noticed Crane's talent and became his mentors.

Live Quick; Write Fast Crane's second novel, *The Red Badge of Courage: An Episode of the American Civil War*, appeared first as a syndicated newspaper feature in 1894 and became a bestseller in 1895. At age twenty-four, the struggling journalist had reached international fame with the novel's success. In *The Red Badge of Courage*, Crane turned his power for acute observation inward, exploring the psychology of a Civil War soldier who grapples with his fear, cowardice, and pride in battle. Ironically, Crane became famous for his realistic portrayal of a soldier during battle even though he had not yet experienced war firsthand and was born six years after the Civil War ended. Nonetheless, many veterans applauded his ability to re-create the internal tension experienced during combat. In late 1895, Crane published a book of poems, *The Black Riders and Other Lines*, to less favorable reviews.

Fascinated with danger and war, Crane covered the Greco-Turkish War in Greece and the Spanish-American War in Cuba. He then settled in Sussex, England, in 1899, heavily in debt and ill with tuberculosis and recurrent malarial fever. Years of exposure, poor food, and lack of treatment ended Crane's life at twenty-eight.

Crane is known as a man who "lived quickly and wrote fast." Despite a brief literary career, his studies of characters overwhelmed by uncontrollable circumstances still resonate today.

LOG ON ▶ **Literature** Online

Author Search For more on Stephen Crane, go to glencoe.com and enter QuickPass code GLA9800u4.

Selection Skills

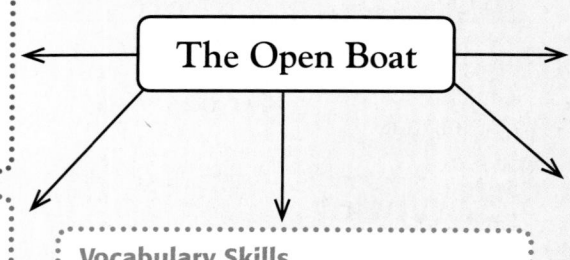

Literary Elements
- Author's Purpose (SE pp. 579, 581, 584, 586, 588, 591, 595, 599; TE p. 586)
- Conflict (SE p. 599)

Reading Skills
- Summarize (SE pp. 579, 582, 584, 586, 588, 591, 592, 594, 596, 599)
- Visualize (TE p. 580)

The Open Boat

Vocabulary Skills
- Context Clues (SE pp. 579, 599)
- Adjectives and Adverbs (TE p. 584)

Listening/Speaking/Viewing Skills
- Analyze Art (SE pp. 587, 593, 598; TE pp. 583, 590, 593)
- Interview (TE p. 592)

Writing Skills/Grammar
- Story Review (SE p. 600)
- Evaluate a Story (TE p. 588)
- Research (TE p. 594)
- News Story (TE p. 596)

Literature and Reading Preview

Connect to the Story

How do one's priorities change in times of great danger? List what your own priorities would be in such a situation.

Build Background

As a war correspondent, Crane traveled from Jacksonville, Florida, to Cuba aboard the steamship *Commodore* in January 1897. The ship sank, and Crane and three others faced the raging Atlantic in a ten-foot dinghy until they managed to reach the Florida coast. Afterward, Crane published a fictionalized account in *Scribner's Magazine*. The tale became the title story in his book *The Open Boat and Other Tales of Adventure*.

Set Purposes for Reading

Big Idea Naturalism

Like other Naturalists, Crane does not soften his depiction of the struggle his characters face. As you read, ask yourself, How does Crane depict the relationship between his characters in "The Open Boat" and their environment?

Literary Element Author's Purpose

An **author's purpose** is his or her intent in writing a literary work. For example, an author may want to inform, entertain, persuade, or express an opinion. An author's purpose may be expressed through direct commentary, through the dialogue, actions, and thoughts of the characters, or through tone, word choice, and narrative point of view. As you read, ask yourself, Where in this story does Crane reveal his purpose?

Reading Strategy Summarize

Summarizing means stating the main ideas of a selection or passage in your own words and in a logical sequence. Summarizing will help you understand and think about what you have read.

Tip: Answer the 5 Ws Use a chart to help you answer who, what, where, when, and why questions about the passage you're summarizing.

Quotation:				
Who	What	Where	When	Why

Vocabulary

uncanny (un ka´ nē) *adj.* strangely unsettling; eerie; p. 582 *Yoshi found the presence of two dead birds on the path uncanny.*

emphatic (em fa´ tik) *adj.* forceful; p. 582 *Jon gave one last emphatic push, and the door opened.*

ingenuously (in jen´ ū əs lē) *adv.* honestly; frankly; p. 585 *The child talked ingenuously to the doctor about his broken arm.*

impudently (im´ pyə dənt lē) *adv.* in an offensively bold manner; p. 585 *The politician spoke so impudently that few voters trusted him.*

coerce (kō urs´) *v.* to force; p. 595 *The boy coerced his sister into giving him all her candy.*

Tip: Context Clues Use words and sentences that come before and after an unfamiliar word to infer information about its meaning.

STEPHEN CRANE **579**

Before You Read

Focus

Summary

Four men—a cook, an oiler, a captain, and a newspaper correspondent—are stranded in a small rowboat after their ship sinks off the coast of Florida. The crew eventually sights land, but there are no rescue brigades. The crew spends a long night on the open water. In the morning, the men get as close to shore as they can and then swim the rest of the way. Only three men survive the ordeal.

> For summaries in languages other than English, see Unit 4 Teaching Resources Book, pp. 146–151.

Vocabulary

Reinforce Meaning

Ask: Would you need to *coerce* your friends to eat ice cream? If someone gives an *emphatic* "no" for an answer, is she likely to change her mind? Explain.

What might happen if a student spoke *impudently* to the principal? Explain.

(APPROACHING) Caution students not to confuse *ingenuously* ("honestly; frankly") with *ingeniously* ("in a clever and inventive manner"). Students who are users of AAVE may not distinguish between /i/ and /e/ before /m/ or /n/, so *pin* and *pen* sound the same. Model the correct pronunciation of *emphatic*, with a focus on the /e/ at the beginning of the word. Provide other examples, such as *tent* and *tint, imagine,* and *empathy.*

English Learners

DIFFERENTIATED INSTRUCTION

SMALL GROUP
Intermediate To help English learners understand and visualize the setting of this story, present the following terms:

- "the hue of slate"
- "froth-top"
- "broken sea"
- "thin little oar"
- "seat upon a bucking bronco"

Allow students to work together in small groups to determine the meanings of these phrases. When students have worked out the meanings, ask what impression they convey about the setting of the story. Then have students predict what the story might be about based on their impressions.

Teach

Big Idea 1

Naturalism Say: Before you answer the question, remember that Crane combines realistic details and events with a depiction of nature as indifferent to humanity's needs and hopes.

Answer: *The passage presents humans as powerless victims of indifferent natural and social forces.*

Literary History ☆

The Sinking of the *Commodore* According to newspaper reports of the incident, as Crane and the others in the dinghy left the ship, they joked about whether or not it would sink. As they looked back at the ship, however, they were horrified to discover that seven crewmen were still on board. **Ask:** How might this experience have influenced Crane's writing?

 For an audio recording of this selection, use Listening Library Audio CD-ROM.

Readability Scores

Dale-Chall: 7.6
DRP: 60
Lexile: 980

Reading Practice

SPIRAL REVIEW Visualize Spatial Relationships The story takes place almost entirely within the confines of a crowded rowboat. Visualizing the boat will help students understand the men's predicament. After students read part I of the story, ask four students to demonstrate the amount of room in the dinghy by measuring a space of 10 by 5 feet and seating themselves as the men were seated. Ask students to visualize the boat in relation to the ocean. Ask students to explain how the exercise increased their understanding of the characters' situation. Encourage them to continue visualizing the situation as they read.

the Open Boat

Stephen Crane

A tale intended to be after the fact. Being the experience of four men from the sunk steamer Commodore . . . ☆

I

None of them knew the color of the sky. Their eyes glanced level, and were fastened upon the waves that swept toward them. These waves were of the hue of slate, save for the tops, which were of foaming white, and all of the men knew the colors of the sea. The horizon narrowed and widened, and dipped and rose, and at all times its edge was jagged with waves that seemed thrust up in points like rocks.

Many a man ought to have a bathtub larger than the boat which here rode upon the sea. These waves were most wrongfully and barbarously abrupt and tall, and each froth-top was a problem in small boat navigation.

The cook squatted in the bottom and looked with both eyes at the six inches of gunwale[1] which separated him from the ocean. His sleeves were rolled over his fat forearms, and the two flaps of his unbuttoned vest dangled as he bent to bail out the boat. Often he said: "Gawd! That was a narrow clip." As he remarked it he invariably gazed eastward over the broken sea.

The oiler,[2] steering with one of the two oars in the boat, sometimes raised himself suddenly to keep clear of water that swirled in over the stern.[3] It was a thin little oar and it seemed often ready to snap.

The correspondent, pulling at the other oar, watched the waves and wondered why he was there.

The injured captain, lying in the bow, was at this time buried in that profound dejection and indifference which comes, temporarily at least, to even the bravest and most enduring when, willy nilly,[4] the firm fails, the army loses, the ship goes down. The mind of the master of a vessel is rooted deep in the timbers

---

1. A *gunwale* is the upper edge of the side of a boat.
2. The *oiler* is the person responsible for oiling machinery in the engine room on a ship.
3. The *stern* is the rear part of a boat or ship.
4. *Willy nilly* means "whether one wishes it or not."

Naturalism *How does this passage reflect characteristics of Naturalism?* **1**

of her, though he command for a day or a decade, and this captain had on him the stern impression of a scene in the grays of dawn of seven turned faces, and later a stump of a top-mast with a white ball on it that slashed to and fro at the waves, went low and lower, and down. Thereafter there was something strange in his voice. Although steady, it was deep with mourning, and of a quality beyond oration[5] or tears.

"Keep'er a little more south, Billie," said he.

"'A little more south,' sir," said the oiler in the stern.

A seat in this boat was not unlike a seat upon a bucking bronco, and, by the same token, a bronco is not much smaller. The craft pranced and reared, and plunged like an animal. As each wave came, and she rose for it, she seemed like a horse making at a fence outrageously high. The manner of her scramble over these walls of water is a mystic thing, and, moreover, at the top of them were ordinarily these problems in white water, the foam racing down from the summit of each wave, requiring a new leap, and a leap from the air. Then, after scornfully bumping a crest, she would slide, and race, and splash down a long incline and arrive bobbing and nodding in front of the next menace.

A singular disadvantage of the sea lies in the fact that after successfully surmounting one wave you discover that there is another behind it just as important and just as nervously anxious to do something effective in the way of swamping boats. In a ten-foot dinghy one can get an idea of the resources of the sea in the line of waves that is not probable to the average experience, which is never at sea in a dinghy. As each slaty[6] wall of water approached, it shut all else from the view of the men in the boat, and it was not difficult to imagine that

5. An *oration* is a formal speech.
6. *Slaty* means "having the bluish gray color of slate."

3 Author's Purpose *Why does Crane have the narrator address the reader in this paragraph?*

this particular wave was the final outburst of the ocean, the last effort of the grim water. There was a terrible grace in the move of the waves, and they came in silence, save for the snarling of the crests.

In the wan[7] light, the faces of the men must have been gray. Their eyes must have glinted in strange ways as they gazed steadily astern. Viewed from a balcony, the whole thing would doubtlessly have been weirdly picturesque. But the men in the boat had no time to see it, and if they had had leisure there were other things to occupy their minds. The sun swung steadily up the sky, and they knew it was broad day because the color of the sea changed from slate to emerald green, streaked with amber lights, and the foam was like tumbling snow. The process of the breaking day was unknown to them. They were aware only of this effect upon the color of the waves that rolled toward them.

In disjointed sentences the cook and the correspondent argued as to the difference between a lifesaving station and a house of refuge. The cook had said: "There's a house of refuge just north of the Mosquito Inlet Light, and as soon as they see us, they'll come off in their boat and pick us up."

"As soon as who see us?" said the correspondent.

"The crew," said the cook.

"Houses of refuge don't have crews," said the correspondent. "As I understand them, they are only places where clothes and grub are stored for the benefit of shipwrecked people. They don't carry crews."

"Oh, yes, they do," said the cook.

"No, they don't," said the correspondent.

"Well, we're not there yet, anyhow," said the oiler, in the stern.

"Well," said the cook, "perhaps it's not a house of refuge that I'm thinking of as being near Mosquito Inlet Light. Perhaps it's a lifesaving station."

"We're not there yet," said the oiler, in the stern.

7. *Wan* means "pale."

STEPHEN CRANE **581**

Literary Element	2

Figurative Language **Say:** Notice how Crane compares the boat to a bucking bronco.

Ask: What figure of speech does Crane use here and how does it reveal Crane's use of Naturalism? *(It is a simile that makes the boat seem like an untamed animal and that gives a sense of how the men are not in control.)*

Literary Element	3

Author's Purpose **Answer:** *Crane wishes to inform the reader about the sea's devastating power.*

Ask: What figure of speech does Crane use at the end of this paragraph? *(He uses a metaphor to compare the waves to a graceful, snarling animal.)*

Writer's Technique ☆

Narrator's Perspective In this passage, the narrator is trying to imagine his situation from the perspective of an outsider. For the most part, though, the narrator focuses only on details the men themselves would notice, such as the color of the waves.

Approaching Level

DIFFERENTIATED INSTRUCTION

Emerging To give students practice in summarizing, ask them to list the most important information from part I. Remind students that a summary includes all important information, but not all details. Students' lists should include the characters, the situation they are in, the reason they are in the situation, the dangers of their predicament, and their goal. Help students who include other information to see that additional details are not critical to a basic plot summary.

Advanced Learners

UNIVERSAL ACCESS

Analysis Have advanced learners analyze Crane's use of description to set the mood. Emphasize that descriptive details may appeal to all senses. Suggest that students first identify relevant details, and then explain how these details create mood.

Teach

Reading Strategy | 1

Summarize Answer: *The men are stubborn and try to think optimistically, but they are also aware of the reality of their situation. They seem to feel hope and despair equally, so instead of expressing either they do not say anything.*

Ask: What do you learn about the men based on your summary? *(Students may say that the men think alike and are working as a unit; all the men are realistic and responsible.)*

For additional practice using the reading skill or strategy, see Unit 4 Teaching Resources Book, p. 153.

II

As the boat bounced from the top of each wave, the wind tore through the hair of the hatless men, and as the craft plopped her stern down again the spray slashed past them. The crest of each of these waves was a hill, from the top of which the men surveyed, for a moment, a broad tumultuous[8] expanse, shining and wind-riven. It was probably splendid. It was probably glorious, this play of the free sea, wild with lights of emerald and white and amber.

"Bully good thing it's an onshore wind,"[9] said the cook. "If not, where would we be? Wouldn't have a show."

"That's right," said the correspondent.

The busy oiler nodded his assent.

Then the captain, in the bow, chuckled in a way that expressed humor, contempt, tragedy, all in one. "Do you think we've got much of a show, now, boys?" said he.

Whereupon the three were silent, save for a trifle of hemming and hawing. To express any particular optimism at this time they felt to be childish and stupid, but they all doubtless possessed this sense of the situation in their mind. A young man thinks doggedly[10] at such times. On the other hand, the ethics of their condition was decidedly against any open suggestion of hopelessness. So they were silent.

"Oh, well," said the captain, soothing his children, "we'll get ashore all right."

But there was that in his tone which made them think, so the oiler quoth: "Yes! If this wind holds!"

The cook was bailing. "Yes! If we don't catch hell in the surf."

Canton flannel gulls[11] flew near and far. Sometimes they sat down on the sea, near

patches of brown seaweed that rolled over the waves with a movement like carpets on a line in a gale. The birds sat comfortably in groups, and they were envied by some in the dinghy, for the wrath of the sea was no more to them than it was to a covey of prairie chickens a thousand miles inland. Often they came very close and stared at the men with black bead-like eyes. At these times they were **uncanny** and sinister[12] in their unblinking scrutiny, and the men hooted angrily at them, telling them to be gone. One came, and evidently decided to alight on the top of the captain's head. The bird flew parallel to the boat and did not circle, but made short sidelong jumps in the air in chicken-fashion. His black eyes were wistfully fixed upon the captain's head. "Ugly brute," said the oiler to the bird. "You look as if you were made with a jackknife." The cook and the correspondent swore darkly at the creature. The captain naturally wished to knock it away with the end of the heavy painter,[13] but he did not dare do it, because anything resembling an **emphatic** gesture would have capsized this freighted boat, and so with his open hand, the captain gently and carefully waved the gull away. After it had been discouraged from the pursuit the captain breathed easier on account of his hair, and others breathed easier because the bird struck their minds at this time as being somehow gruesome and ominous.

In the meantime the oiler and the correspondent rowed. And also they rowed.

They sat together in the same seat, and each rowed an oar. Then the oiler took both oars; then the correspondent took both oars; then the oiler; then the correspondent. They rowed

---

8. *Tumultuous* means "agitated" or "turbulent."
9. An *onshore wind* is one that blows toward the shore.
10. *Doggedly* means "in a stubbornly persistent manner."
11. *Canton flannel gulls* are gulls whose feathers resemble Canton flannel, a strong cotton fabric that is soft on one side and ribbed on the other.

---

12. *Sinister* means "evil" or "ominous."
13. A *painter* is a rope attached to the front of a boat, used for tying up to a dock.

Naturalism *How is the influence of Naturalism reflected in this passage?* | 2

Vocabulary

uncanny (un ka´ nē) *adj.* strangely unsettling; eerie
emphatic (em fa´ tik) *adj.* forceful

1 **Summarize** *How would you summarize the thoughts of the four men at this point?*

Reading Practice

 SPIRAL REVIEW Descriptive Language Explain that good writers use precise words to convey specific ideas or images. Write the following sentence from the story on the board: "After [the bird] had been discouraged from the pursuit the captain breathed easier on account of his hair, and others breathed easier because the bird struck their minds at this time as being somehow gruesome and ominous." Direct students' attention to the words *gruesome* and *ominous*. **Ask:** What mood is created by these words? *(eerie, scary, tense)* Ask students to identify other descriptive words that contribute to this mood. *(Possible responses: hopelessness, uncanny, sinister, wrath of the sea)*

Moonlit Shipwreck at Sea, 1901. Thomas Moran. Oil on canvas, 30 x 40¼ in. Private collection.

and they rowed. The very ticklish part of the business was when the time came for the reclining one in the stern to take his turn at the oars. By the very last star of truth, it is easier to steal eggs from under a hen than it was to change seats in the dinghy. First the man in the stern slid his hand along the thwart[14] and moved with care, as if he were of Sèvres.[15] Then the man in the rowing seat slid his hand along the other thwart. It was all done with the most extraordinary care. As the two sidled past each other, the whole party kept watchful eyes on the coming wave, and the captain cried: "Look out now! Steady there!"

The brown mats of seaweed that appeared from time to time were like islands, bits of earth. They were traveling, apparently, neither one way nor the other. They were, to all intents, stationary. They informed the men in the boat that it was making progress slowly toward the land.

The captain, rearing cautiously in the bow, after the dinghy soared on a great swell, said that he had seen the lighthouse at Mosquito Inlet. Presently the cook remarked that he had seen it. The correspondent was at the oars, then, and for some reason he too wished to look at the lighthouse, but his back was toward the far shore and the waves were important, and for some time he could not seize an opportunity to turn his head. But at last there came a wave more gentle than the others, and when at the crest of it he swiftly scoured the western horizon.

"See it?" said the captain.

"No," said the correspondent, slowly, "I didn't see anything."

"Look again," said the captain. He pointed. "It's exactly in that direction."

---

14. A *thwart* is a seat going across a boat, on which a rower or passenger sits.
15. *Sèvres* (sev′ rə) refers to fine porcelain made in Sèvres, France.

STEPHEN CRANE **583**

Teach

Big Idea   2

Naturalism Answer: *The passage indicates the indifference of nature toward the men. The sea is a natural force that could prove fatal to the crew, but the "wrath" the men associate with the sea is not a threat to the birds.*

Ask: Is the narrator's depiction of the birds in the paragraph realistic, naturalistic, or both? *(The birds are described realistically and naturalistically; while they are indifferent to the men's situation, they also have an aura of cruelty.)*

View the Art ★

Thomas Moran was a member of the Hudson River school. The school was a style specific to a group of nineteenth-century American artists who painted landscapes. Through large, detailed, and highly romanticized depictions, they conveyed the majesty, wildness, and potential power of the new country. The group took its name from the Catskill region of New York State, an area that was still wild in the early 1800s. Thomas Moran was best known for his paintings of the American West.

Teach

Literary Element　1

Author's Purpose　Answer:
The captain's reply gives hope to the other men and creates suspense for the reader. **Say:** Notice how the correspondent has broken the unspoken rule of the boat of not voicing optimism or fatalism when he asks the captain to comment on their chances of survival.

Reading Strategy　2

Summarize　Answer: *From the crew's perspective, the boat appears to be making little progress in the vast ocean.*

Literary History ☆

Author's Purpose As Crane was writing "The Open Boat," he met with Edward Murphy, captain of the *Commodore*. Crane read Murphy the first part of the story and said to him, "Listen, Ed, I want to have this *right*, from your point of view. How does it sound so far?" Murphy is said to have replied, "You've got it, Steve."

At the top of another wave, the correspondent did as he was bid, and this time his eyes chanced on a small still thing on the edge of the swaying horizon. It was precisely like the point of a pin. It took an anxious eye to find a lighthouse so tiny.

"Think we'll make it, Captain?"

"If this wind holds and the boat don't swamp, we can't do much else," said the captain.

The little boat, lifted by each towering sea, and splashed viciously by the crests, made progress that in the absence of seaweed was not apparent to those in her. She seemed just a wee thing wallowing, miraculously, top up, at the mercy of five oceans. Occasionally, a great spread of water, like white flames, swarmed into her.

"Bail her, cook," said the captain, serenely.

"All right, Captain," said the cheerful cook.

III

It would be difficult to describe the subtle brotherhood of men that was here established on the seas. No one said that it was so. No one mentioned it. But it dwelt in the boat, and each man felt it warm him. They were a captain, an oiler, a cook, and a correspondent, and they were friends, friends in a more curiously iron-bound degree than may be common. The hurt captain, lying against the water jar in the bow, spoke always in a low voice and calmly, but he could never command a more ready and swiftly obedient crew than the motley three of the dinghy. It was more than a mere recognition of what was best for the common safety. There was surely in it a quality that was personal and heartfelt. And after this devotion to the commander of the boat there was this comradeship that the correspondent, for instance, who had been taught to be cynical of men,

---

1 Author's Purpose *What is the function of the captain's optimistic reply to the correspondent?*

2 Summarize *What is the main idea expressed in this paragraph?*

knew even at the time was the best experience of his life. But no one said that it was so. No one mentioned it.

"I wish we had a sail," remarked the captain. "We might try my overcoat on the end of an oar and give you two boys a chance to rest." So the cook and the correspondent held the mast and spread wide the overcoat. The oiler steered, and the little boat made good way with her new rig. Sometimes the oiler had to scull[16] sharply to keep a sea from breaking into the boat, but otherwise sailing was a success.

Meanwhile the lighthouse had been growing slowly larger. It had now almost assumed color, and appeared like a little gray shadow on the sky. The man at the oars could not be prevented from turning his head rather often to try for a glimpse of this little gray shadow.

At last, from the top of each wave the men in the tossing boat could see land. Even as the lighthouse was an upright shadow on the sky, this land seemed but a long black shadow on the sea. It certainly was thinner than paper. "We must be about opposite New Smyrna,"[17] said the cook, who had coasted this shore often in schooners. "Captain, by the way, I believe they abandoned that lifesaving station there about a year ago."

"Did they?" said the captain.

The wind slowly died away. The cook and the correspondent were not now obliged to slave in order to hold high the oar. But the waves continued their old impetuous swooping at the dinghy, and the little craft, no longer under way, struggled woundily over them. The oiler or the correspondent took the oars again.

Shipwrecks are *apropos*[18] of nothing. If men could only train for them and have them occur when the men had reached pink condition, there would be less drowning at sea. Of the

3

---

16. *Scull* means "to propel a boat forward by moving a single oar from side to side over the stern of a boat."

17. *New Smyrna* refers to the town of New Smyrna Beach, on the east coast of Florida.

18. *Apropos* means "relevant" or "pertinent."

Vocabulary Practice

SPIRAL REVIEW **Adjectives and Adverbs** Explain that adjectives and adverbs add vivid detail to Crane's descriptions. They help readers imagine the scene. Tell students to draw a two-column chart with the headings *Adjectives* and *Adverbs*. Select a paragraph or two from the passage, and ask students to identify all the adjectives and adverbs and write them in the appropriate columns in the chart. Review students' answers as a class.

Discuss the effect of these adjectives and adverbs on the story.

four in the dinghy none had slept any time worth mentioning for two days and two nights previous to embarking in the dinghy, and in the excitement of clambering about the deck of a foundering[19] ship they had also forgotten to eat heartily.

For these reasons, and for others, neither the oiler nor the correspondent was fond of rowing at this time. The correspondent wondered **ingenuously** how in the name of all that was sane could there be people who thought it amusing to row a boat. It was not an amusement; it was a diabolical punishment, and even a genius of mental aberrations could never conclude that it was anything but a horror to the muscles and a crime against the back. He mentioned to the boat in general how the amusement of rowing struck him, and the weary-faced oiler smiled in full sympathy. Previously to the foundering, by the way, the oiler had worked doublewatch in the engineroom of the ship.

"Take her easy, now, boys," said the captain. "Don't spend yourselves. If we have to run a surf you'll need all your strength, because we'll sure have to swim for it. Take your time."

Slowly the land arose from the sea. From a black line it became a line of black and a line of white—trees and sand. Finally, the captain said that he could make out a house on the shore. "That's the house of refuge, sure," said the cook. "They'll see us before long, and come out after us."

The distant lighthouse reared high. "The keeper ought to be able to make us out now, if

> *"Funny they don't see us," said the men.*

he's looking through a glass," said the captain. "He'll notify the lifesaving people."

"None of those other boats could have got ashore to give word of the wreck," said the oiler, in a low voice. "Else the lifeboat would be out hunting us."

Slowly and beautifully the land loomed out of the sea. The wind came again. It had veered from the northeast to the southeast. Finally, a new sound struck the ears of the men in the boat. It was the low thunder of the surf on the shore. "We'll never be able to make the lighthouse now," said the captain. "Swing her head a little more north, Billie."

"'A little more north,' sir," said the oiler.

Whereupon the little boat turned her nose once more down the wind, and all but the oarsman watched the shore grow. Under the influence of this expansion doubt and direful apprehension was leaving the minds of the men. The management of the boat was still most absorbing, but it could not prevent a quiet cheerfulness. In an hour, perhaps, they would be ashore.

Their backbones had become thoroughly used to balancing in the boat and they now rode this wild colt of a dinghy like circus men. The correspondent thought that he had been drenched to the skin, but happening to feel in the top pocket of his coat, he found therein eight cigars. Four of them were soaked with seawater; four were perfectly scatheless. After a search, somebody produced three dry matches, and thereupon the four waifs[20] rode **impudently** in their little boat, and with an assurance of an impending rescue shining in their eyes, puffed

---

19. *Foundering* means "sinking."

---

20. *Waifs* are persons having no apparent home.

STEPHEN CRANE **585**

Teach

Literary Element | 1

Suspense Say: Suspense is the tension that readers feel when they do not know the outcome of a story.

Ask: How has the narrator built up suspense in the story so far? *(He has described the power of the waves; he has mentioned the men's weakness; he has suggested that there may not be a rescue crew at the lighthouse.)*

Say: Pace is part of building suspense. The narrator gives us a break from the suspense by allowing the men to relax for a moment.

Reading Strategy | 2

Summarize Answer: *The crew does not realize that there is not a lifesaving station anywhere near them. They curse the missing "lifesavers" as though the lifesavers are on shore but do not see the dinghy.*

Big Idea | 3

Naturalism Answer: *A Naturalist might say that the crew's response is unwarranted. They should understand that their situation is merely the result of factors beyond their control, and they should accept the inevitability of their fate.* **Say:** The crew's response characterizes the forces of nature as inherently unjust. When the crew thinks fate will win, they resort to calling it names. **Ask:** How do the crew members characterize fate? *(They imply that fate is stupid and without purpose by calling it an "old ninny-woman" and an "old hen.")*

at the big cigars and judged well and ill of all men. Everybody took a drink of water.

IV

[1] "Cook," remarked the captain, "there don't seem to be any signs of life about your house of refuge."

"No," replied the cook. "Funny they don't see us!"

A broad stretch of lowly coast lay before the eyes of the men. It was of dunes topped with dark vegetation. The roar of the surf was plain, and sometimes they could see the white lip of a wave as it spun up the beach. A tiny house was blocked out black upon the sky. Southward, the slim lighthouse lifted its little gray length.

Tide, wind, and waves were swinging the dinghy northward. "Funny they don't see us," said the men.

The surf's roar was here dulled, but its tone was, nevertheless, thunderous and mighty. As the boat swam over the great rollers, the men sat listening to this roar. "We'll swamp sure," said everybody.

It is fair to say here that there was not a lifesaving station within twenty miles in either direction, but the men did not know this fact and in consequence they made dark and opprobrious[21] remarks concerning the eyesight of the nation's lifesavers. Four scowling men sat in the dinghy and surpassed records in the invention of epithets.[22]

"Funny they don't see us."

The light-heartedness of a former time had completely faded. To their sharpened minds it was easy to conjure pictures of all kinds of incompetency and blindness and, indeed, cowardice. There was the shore of the populous land, and it was bitter and bitter to them that from it came no sign.

---

21. *Opprobrious* (ə prō′ brē əs) means "derogatory."
22. *Epithets* are descriptive, sometimes abusive, words or phrases used with or in place of a name.

[2] **Summarize** *In your own words, summarize what is happening in this paragraph.*

"Well," said the captain, ultimately, "I suppose we'll have to make a try for ourselves. If we stay out here too long, we'll none of us have strength left to swim after the boat swamps."

And so the oiler, who was at the oars, turned the boat straight for the shore. There was a sudden tightening of muscles. There was some thinking.

"If we don't all get ashore—" said the captain. "If we don't all get ashore, I suppose you fellows know where to send news of my finish?"

They then briefly exchanged some addresses and admonitions.[23] As for the reflections of the men, there was a great deal of rage in them. Perchance they might be formulated thus: "If I am going to be drowned—if I am going to be drowned—if I am going to be drowned, why, in the name of the seven mad gods who rule the sea,[24] was I allowed to come thus far and contemplate sand and trees? Was I brought here merely to have my nose dragged away as I was about to nibble the sacred cheese of life? It is preposterous. If this old ninny-woman, Fate,[25] cannot do better than this, she should be deprived of the management of men's fortunes. She is an old hen who knows not her intention. If she has decided to drown me, why did she not do it in the beginning and save me all this trouble. The whole affair is absurd. . . . But, no, she cannot mean to drown me. She dare not drown me. She cannot drown me. Not after all this work." Afterward the man might have had an impulse to shake his fist at the clouds. "Just you drown me, now, and then hear what I call you!"

---

23. *Admonitions* are warnings or advice.
24. *[seven . . . the sea]* This description probably refers to the seven major seas, each at the mercy of a deity.
25. *Fate* implies a supernatural power guiding one to an inevitable end. In classical mythology, the three Fates were portrayed as old women.

Naturalism *What might the response of a Naturalist be to this question?* **3**

Author's Purpose *Why does Crane have the narrator attribute this sentiment to the men in the boat?* **4**

Reading Practice

Understand Author's Purpose In a class discussion, have students review what they have learned about Crane's life as well as what they know about Realism and Naturalism. Then write the following questions on the board:

- Why do you think Crane decided to write a fictional account of his experience on a lifeboat?

- What ideas do you think Crane intended readers to take away from his story?

Have students write their responses to these questions.

586

Lord Ullin's Daughter, before 1907. Albert Pinkham Ryder. Oil on canvas, 20½ x 18⅜ in. Smithsonian American Art Museum, Gift of John Gellatly.

 In an attempt to create visual depth and intensity, Albert Pinkham Ryder applied multiple layers of paint colors—often so thick that the paint failed to dry, cracking over time. How does this painting convey a sense of the power of the sea? ★

The billows that came at this time were more formidable. They seemed always just about to break and roll over the little boat in a turmoil of foam. There was a preparatory and long growl in the speech of them. No mind unused to the sea would have concluded that the dinghy could ascend these sheer heights in time. The shore was still afar. The oiler was a wily[26] surfman. "Boys," he said, swiftly, "she won't live three minutes more and we're too far out to swim. Shall I take her to sea again, Captain?"

"Yes! Go ahead!" said the captain.

This oiler, by a series of quick miracles, and fast and steady oarsmanship, turned the boat in the middle of the surf and took her safely to sea again.

---

26. *Wily* means "cunning" or "sly."

There was a considerable silence as the boat bumped over the furrowed sea to deeper water. Then somebody in gloom spoke. "Well, anyhow, they must have seen us from the shore by now."

The gulls went in slanting flight up the wind toward the gray desolate east. A squall,[27] marked by dingy clouds, and clouds brick-red, like smoke from a burning building, appeared from the southeast.

"What do you think of those lifesaving people? Ain't they peaches?"

"Funny they haven't seen us."

"Maybe they think we're out here for sport? Maybe they think we're fishin'. Maybe they think we're damned fools."

It was a long afternoon. A changed tide tried to force them southward, but wind and wave said northward. Far ahead, where coastline, sea, and sky formed their mighty angle, there were little dots which seemed to indicate a city on the shore.

"St. Augustine?"

The captain shook his head. "Too near Mosquito Inlet."

And the oiler rowed, and then the correspondent rowed. Then the oiler rowed. It was a weary business. The human back can become the seat of more aches and pains than are registered in books for the composite anatomy of a regiment. It is a limited area, but it can become the theater of innumerable muscular conflicts, tangles, wrenches, knots, and other comforts.

"Did you ever like to row, Billie?" asked the correspondent.

"No," said the oiler. "Hang it."

When one exchanged the rowing-seat for a place in the bottom of the boat, he suffered a

---

27. A *squall* is a short, sudden, strong windstorm, often accompanied by rain or snow.

STEPHEN CRANE **587**

Teach

Literary Element 1

Dialogue Say: The narrator does not always specify which of the four men is speaking in this section of the story.

Ask: Why doesn't the narrator tell who is speaking? *(He may want to indicate that all of the men are experiencing similar periods of surprise, shock, and anger. He may also wish to emphasize their shared feelings of confusion and exhaustion.)*

Reading Strategy 2

Summarize Answer: *The oiler and the correspondent are so weary from rowing that they feel relief while resting at the bottom of the boat, despite the cold and wetness. At this point in the trip, the thought that the boat might capsize even seems comforting.*

Literary Element 3

Author's Purpose Answer: *Crane wishes to show how the men's feelings vacillate between hope and despair.*

Ask: What do you think is happening in this scene? Are the people on shore stupid or just playing around? *(Students should suggest that people on shore may feel concern for the crew but are unable to communicate this concern across the water. They may be signaling for the crew to row further north.)*

bodily depression that caused him to be careless of everything save an obligation to wiggle one finger. There was cold seawater swashing to and fro in the boat, and he lay in it. His head, pillowed on a thwart, was within an inch of the swirl of a wave crest, and sometimes a particularly obstreperous[28] sea came inboard and drenched him once more. But these matters did not annoy him. It is almost certain that if the boat had capsized he would have tumbled comfortably out upon the ocean as if he felt sure that it was a great soft mattress.

"Look! There's a man on the shore!"

"Where?"

"There! See 'im? See 'im?"

"Yes, sure! He's walking along."

"Now he's stopped. Look! He's facing us!"

"He's waving at us!"

"So he is! By thunder!"

"Ah, now, we're all right! Now we're all right! There'll be a boat out here for us in half an hour."

"He's going on. He's running. He's going up to that house there."

The remote beach seemed lower than the sea, and it required a searching glance to discern the little black figure. The captain saw a floating stick and they rowed to it. A bathtowel was by some weird chance in the boat, and, tying this on the stick, the captain waved it. The oarsman did not dare turn his head, so he was obliged to ask questions.

"What's he doing now?"

"He's standing still again. He's looking, I think. . . . There he goes again. Toward the house. . . . Now he's stopped again."

"Is he waving at us?"

"No, not now! he was, though."

"Look! There comes another man!"

"He's running."

"Look at him go, would you."

"Why, he's on a bicycle. Now he's met the other man. They're both waving at us. Look!"

28. *Obstreperous* (əb strep′ ər əs) means "unruly."

2 Summarize *Summarize this paragraph in your own words.*

"There comes something up the beach."

"What the devil is that thing?"

"Why, it looks like a boat."

"Why, certainly it's a boat."

"No, it's on wheels."

"Yes, so it is. Well, that must be the lifeboat. They drag them along shore on a wagon."

"That's the lifeboat, sure."

"No, by——, it's—it's an omnibus."[29]

"I tell you it's a lifeboat."

"It is not! It's an omnibus. I can see it plain. See? One of those big hotel omnibuses."

"By thunder, you're right. It's an omnibus, sure as fate. What do you suppose they are doing with an omnibus? Maybe they are going around collecting the lifecrew, hey?"

"That's it, likely. Look! There's a fellow waving a little black flag. He's standing on the steps of the omnibus. There come those other two fellows. Now they're all talking together. Look at the fellow with the flag. Maybe he ain't waving it!"

"That ain't a flag, is it? That's his coat. Why, certainly, that's his coat."

"So it is. It's his coat. He's taken it off and is waving it around his head. But would you look at him swing it!"

"Oh, say, there isn't any lifesaving station there. That's just a winter resort hotel omnibus that has brought over some of the boarders to see us drown."

"What's that idiot with the coat mean? What's he signaling, anyhow?"

"It looks as if he were trying to tell us to go north. There must be a lifesaving station up there."

"No! He thinks we're fishing. Just giving us a merry hand. See? Ah, there, Willie."

"Well, I wish I could make something out of those signals. What do you suppose he means?"

"He don't mean anything. He's just playing."

29. An *omnibus*, or bus, would have been pulled by horses during this time period.

Author's Purpose *What is the function of these lines at this point in the story?* 3

Writing Practice

Evaluate a Story Remind students that when they interpret a work of literature, they do more than simply read it. They consider the author's message, or theme, and the literary elements he or she uses to convey it, such as setting, imagery, character, plot, and conflict. Have students write a paragraph examining Crane's use of one of these elements and its significance in the story. Remind students to include specific examples from the story.

"Well, if he'd just signal us to try the surf again, or to go to sea and wait, or go north, or go south, or go to hell—there would be some reason in it. But look at him. He just stands there and keeps his coat revolving like a wheel. The ass!"

"There come more people."

"Now there's quite a mob. Look! Isn't that a boat?"

"Where? Oh, I see where you mean. No, that's no boat."

"That fellow is still waving his coat."

"He must think we like to see him do that. Why don't he quit it. It don't mean anything."

"I don't know. I think he is trying to make us go north. It must be that there's a lifesaving station there somewhere."

"Say, he ain't tired yet. Look at 'im wave."

"Wonder how long he can keep that up. He's been revolving his coat ever since he caught sight of us. He's an idiot. Why aren't they getting men to bring a boat out. A fishing boat—one of those big yawls[30]—could come out here all right. Why don't he do something?"

"Oh, it's all right, now."

"They'll have a boat out here for us in less than no time, now that they've seen us."

A faint yellow tone came into the sky over the low land. The shadows on the sea slowly deepened. The wind bore coldness with it, and the men began to shiver.

"Holy smoke!" said one, allowing his voice to express his impious mood, "if we keep on monkeying out here! If we've got to flounder out here all night!"

"Oh, we'll never have to stay here all night! Don't you worry. They've seen us now, and it won't be long before they'll come chasing out after us."

The shore grew dusky. The man waving a coat blended gradually into this gloom, and it swallowed in the same manner the omnibus and the group of people. The spray, when it dashed uproariously over the side, made the voyagers shrink and swear like men who were being branded.

"I'd like to catch the chump who waved the coat. I feel like soaking him one, just for luck."

"Why? What did he do?"

"Oh, nothing, but then he seemed so damned cheerful."

In the meantime the oiler rowed, and then the correspondent rowed, and then the oiler rowed. Gray-faced and bowed forward, they mechanically, turn by turn, plied the leaden oars. The form of the lighthouse had vanished from the southern horizon, but finally a pale star appeared, just lifting from the sea. The streaked saffron[31] in the west passed before the all-merging darkness, and the sea to the east was black. The land had vanished, and was expressed only by the low and drear thunder of the surf.

"If I am going to be drowned—if I am going to be drowned—if I am going to be drowned, why, in the name of the seven mad gods who rule the sea, was I allowed to come thus far and contemplate sand and trees? Was I brought here merely to have my nose dragged away as I was about to nibble the sacred cheese of life?"

The patient captain, drooped over the water jar, was sometimes obliged to speak to the oarsman.

"Keep her head up! Keep her head up!"

"'Keep her head up,' sir." The voices were weary and low.

This was surely a quiet evening. All save the oarsman lay heavily and listlessly in the boat's bottom. As for him, his eyes were just capable of noting the tall black waves that swept forward in a most sinister silence, save for an occasional subdued growl of a crest.

The cook's head was on a thwart, and he looked without interest at the water under his nose. He was deep in other scenes. Finally he spoke. "Billie," he murmured, dreamfully, "what kind of pie do you like best?"

---

31. Here, *saffron* means "yellow-orange in color."

Author's Purpose *Why does Crane repeat this speech verbatim from page 586?* **4**

STEPHEN CRANE **589**

---

30. A *yawl* is a sailboat with two masts, the large mast near the front of the boat and the smaller one near the back.

Literary Element 4

Author's Purpose Answer: *Crane wants to underscore his theme that much of human life is determined by chance, not justice or reason.*

Say: The narrator uses a metaphor here, comparing man's quest for survival to a mouse nibbling at "the sacred cheese of life." The metaphor emphasizes the Naturalist belief that humans are as small and insignificant as mice, compared to the forces of nature.

English Learners

DIFFERENTIATED INSTRUCTION

Beginning Many of the nautical words in the story, such as *bow, stern, rollers,* and *row,* have other meanings as well. Have students explain the nautical meaning of these words as well as another meaning. Urge them to list other words with a nautical meaning in this story that also have another meaning.

Students might wish to find a picture of a rowboat and label the bow and stern, as well as any other parts they have learned about in this story, such as the gunwale.

Teach

Naturalism Answer: *A Naturalist might argue that in extreme situations, people act instinctively to satisfy hunger. The oiler and the correspondent are doing their best not to let their instincts make them act irrationally, so they want to avoid any mention of food.*

Say: It is natural for the cook to be thinking about food. For him food is a source of enjoyment, but for the oiler and the correspondent it is a dangerous distraction from their efforts at self-control.

View the Art ★

Unlike the Hudson River school painters who were his contemporaries, Albert Pinkham Ryder did not glorify nature in his art. More a Naturalist than a Romantic, Ryder emphasized nature's power and forcefulness. In the painting here, the boat is depicted in the same dark colors as the water. It is as if the dark water were swallowing the boat, just as the night swallowed the people standing on the shore in the story.

Moonlight, 1885. Albert Pinkham Ryder. Oil on canvas, 16 x 17¾ in. Smithsonian American Art Museum, ★ Washington, DC.

V

"Pie," said the oiler and the correspondent, agitatedly. "Don't talk about those things, blast you!"

"Well," said the cook, "I was just thinking about ham sandwiches, and—"

A night on the sea in an open boat is a long night. As darkness settled finally, the shine of the light, lifting from the sea in the south, changed to full gold. On the northern horizon a new light appeared, a small bluish gleam on the edge of the waters. These two lights were the furniture of the world. Otherwise there was nothing but waves.

---

2   **Naturalism** *From your understanding of Naturalism, why might discussion of food be dangerous, rather than pleasantly distracting, given the circumstances?*

Two men huddled in the stern, and distances were so magnificent in the dinghy that the rower was enabled to keep his feet partly warmed by thrusting them under his companions. Their legs indeed extended far under the rowing seat until they touched the feet of the captain forward. Sometimes, despite the efforts of the tired oarsman, a wave came piling into the boat, an icy wave of the night, and the chilling water soaked them anew. They would twist their bodies for a moment and groan, and sleep the dead sleep once more, while the water in the boat gurgled about them as the craft rocked.

The plan of the oiler and the correspondent was for one to row until he lost the ability, and then arouse the other from his seawater couch in the bottom of the boat.

The oiler plied the oars until his head drooped forward, and the overpowering sleep blinded him. And he rowed yet afterward. Then he touched a man in the bottom of the boat, and called his name. "Will you spell me for a little while?" he said, meekly.

"Sure, Billie," said the correspondent, awakening and dragging himself to a sitting position. They exchanged places carefully, and the oiler, cuddling down in the seawater at the cook's side, seemed to go to sleep instantly.

The particular violence of the sea had ceased. The waves came without snarling. The obligation of the man at the oars was to keep the boat headed so that the tilt of the rollers would not capsize her, and to preserve her from filling when the crests rushed past. The black

---

Study Skills Practice

SPIRAL REVIEW   **Use Text Structure** Point out that "The Open Boat" is a long story. Crane has made it more manageable by dividing it into seven sections. Have students construct informal outlines as they read "The Open Boat." Their outlines should have seven headings that correspond to the seven sections of the story. Under each heading, students should jot down notes on plot, character, point of view, and tone, or on any other element they find in the story. When they have completed their notes, students should review them to discern the significant developments in each section that combine to reveal the theme or meaning of the story. Have students discuss this question: What view of life is revealed by the events in this story? *(Students may discuss some aspect of the naturalists' view of the power of nature and the powerlessness of humans.)*

waves were silent and hard to be seen in the darkness. Often one was almost upon the boat before the oarsman was aware.

In a low voice the correspondent addressed the captain. He was not sure that the captain was awake, although this iron man seemed to be always awake. "Captain, shall I keep her making for that light north, sir?"

The same steady voice answered him. "Yes. Keep it about two points off the port bow."[32]

The cook had tied a life belt around himself in order to get even the warmth which this clumsy cork contrivance could donate, and he seemed almost stove-like when a rower, whose teeth invariably chattered wildly as soon as he ceased his labor, dropped down to sleep.

The correspondent, as he rowed, looked down at the two men sleeping under foot. The cook's arm was around the oiler's shoulders, and, with their fragmentary clothing and haggard faces, they were the babes of the sea, a grotesque rendering of the old babes in the wood.[33]

Later he must have grown stupid at his work, for suddenly there was a growling of water, and a crest came with a roar and a swash into the boat, and it was a wonder that it did not set the cook afloat in his life belt. The cook continued to sleep, but the oiler sat up, blinking his eyes and shaking with the new cold.

"Oh, I'm awful sorry, Billie," said the correspondent, contritely.

"That's all right, old boy," said the oiler, and lay down again and was asleep.

Presently it seemed that even the captain dozed, and the correspondent thought that he was the one man afloat on all the oceans. The wind had a voice as it came over the waves, and it was sadder than the end.

---

32. The *bow* is the forward part of a boat or ship. The *port bow,* then, would be the left side of the forward part.

33. In the fairy tale "Babes in the Wood," two children are left after their parents die. An uncle tries to have them killed, but the children are spared. Alone in the woods, the children are lulled to sleep by birds.

2 Summarize *Summarize this paragraph. How have the crew's challenges changed?*

There was a long, loud swishing astern of the boat, and a gleaming trail of phosphorescence, like blue flame, was furrowed on the black waters. It might have been made by a monstrous knife.

Then there came a stillness, while the correspondent breathed with the open mouth and looked at the sea.

Suddenly there was another swish and another long flash of bluish light, and this time it was alongside the boat, and might almost have been reached with an oar. The correspondent saw an enormous fin speed like a shadow through the water, hurling the crystalline spray and leaving the long glowing trail.

The correspondent looked over his shoulder at the captain. His face was hidden, and he seemed to be asleep. He looked at the babes of the sea. They certainly were asleep. So, being bereft[34] of sympathy, he leaned a little way to one side and swore softly into the sea.

But the thing did not then leave the vicinity of the boat. Ahead or astern, on one side or the other, at intervals long or short, fled the long sparkling streak, and there was to be heard the whiroo of the dark fin. The speed and power of the thing was greatly to be admired. It cut the water like a gigantic and keen projectile.

The presence of this biding thing did not affect the man with the same horror that it would if he had been a picnicker. He simply looked at the sea dully and swore in an undertone.

Nevertheless, it is true that he did not wish to be alone with the thing. He wished one of his companions to awaken by chance and keep him company with it. But the captain hung motionless over the water jar and the oiler and the cook in the bottom of the boat were plunged in slumber.

---

34. *Bereft* means "lacking something needed."

3 Author's Purpose *Why does Crane have the correspondent react this way to the shark?*

STEPHEN CRANE **591**

Teach

Reading Strategy | 1

Summarize Answer: *The correspondent imagines the dying soldier and realizes that he feels sorry for this anonymous man. After experiencing the terrible indifference of nature himself, the correspondent can now relate to the soldier in the verse. The correspondent comprehends for the first time that death affects everyone.*

Literary History ☆
Misquotation of the Poem

Crane actually misquotes the poem, omitting about twenty words. Critics have argued over whether Crane omits the words on purpose or whether he simply forgets them. He may have deleted them to show how the narrator's indifference as a child has made him misremember the poem that means so much to him now.

VI

"If I am going to be drowned—if I am going to be drowned—if I am going to be drowned, why, in the name of the seven mad gods who rule the sea, was I allowed to come thus far and contemplate sand and trees?"

During this dismal night, it may be remarked that a man would conclude that it was really the intention of the seven mad gods to drown him, despite the abominable injustice of it. For it was certainly an abominable injustice to drown a man who had worked so hard, so hard. The man felt it would be a crime most unnatural. Other people had drowned at sea since galleys[35] swarmed with painted sails, but still—

When it occurs to a man that nature does not regard him as important, and that she feels she would not maim the universe by disposing of him, he at first wishes to throw bricks at the temple, and he hates deeply the fact that there are no bricks and no temples. Any visible expression of nature would surely be pelleted with his jeers.

Then, if there be no tangible thing to hoot he feels, perhaps, the desire to confront a personification and indulge in pleas, bowed to one knee, and with hands supplicant, saying: "Yes, but I love myself."

A high cold star on a winter's night is the word he feels that she says to him. Thereafter he knows the pathos[36] of his situation.

The men in the dinghy had not discussed these matters, but each had, no doubt, reflected upon them in silence and according to his mind. There was seldom any expression upon their faces save the general one of complete weariness. Speech was devoted to the business of the boat.

To chime the notes of his emotion, a verse mysteriously entered the correspondent's head. He had even forgotten that he had forgotten this verse, but it suddenly was in his mind.

---

35. A *galley* is a medieval ship propelled by sails and a row (or rows) of oars on either side.
36. *Pathos* means "deep sadness."

A soldier of the Legion[37] lay dying in ☆ Algiers,[38]
There was lack of woman's nursing, there was dearth of woman's tears;
But a comrade stood beside him, and he took that comrade's hand,
And he said: "I never more shall see my own, my native land."[39]

In his childhood, the correspondent had been made acquainted with the fact that a soldier of the Legion lay dying in Algiers, but he had never regarded it as important. Myriads of his schoolfellows had informed him of the soldier's plight, but the dinning[40] had naturally ended by making him perfectly indifferent. He had never considered it his affair that a soldier of the Legion lay dying in Algiers, nor had it appeared to him as a matter for sorrow. It was less to him than the breaking of a pencil's point.

Now, however, it quaintly came to him as a human, living thing. It was no longer merely a picture of a few throes[41] in the breast of a poet, meanwhile drinking tea and warming his feet at the grate; it was an actuality—stern, mournful, and fine.

The correspondent plainly saw the soldier. He lay on the sand with his feet out straight and still. While his pale left hand was upon his chest in an attempt to thwart the going of his life, the blood came between his fingers. In the far Algerian distance, a city of low square forms was set against a sky that was faint with the last sunset hues. The correspondent, plying the oars and dreaming of the slow and slower movements of the lips of the soldier, was moved by a profound

---

37. *Legion* refers to the French Foreign Legion, an army composed mainly of foreign volunteers.
38. *Algiers* (al jērz′) is the capital of Algeria, a country in northern Africa that was once ruled by France.
39. This verse compresses the first stanza of "Bingen on the Rhine" by English poet Caroline E. S. Norton (1808–1877).
40. *Dinning* means "insistent repetition."
41. *Throes* are pains.

Summarize *Summarize this passage. Why has the correspondent's reaction to the poem changed since he was a child?* | 1

Listening and Speaking Practice

SMALL GROUP

Interview Role-playing an interview with a character will give students an opportunity to consider the events of the story both as an outsider and as a character. After students have read the story, have them work in groups of three, with one student playing the role of interviewer, one playing one of the men in the story, and one as notetaker.

The interviewer should pose up to five questions about the man's experiences and thoughts. The student playing the character should answer in that character's voice, while the third student records responses. Encourage interviewers to prepare thoughtful questions that encourage the respondent to think about the meaning of his experience.

and perfectly impersonal comprehension. He was sorry for the soldier of the Legion who lay dying in Algiers.

The thing which had followed the boat and waited had evidently grown bored at the delay. There was no longer to be heard the slash of the cut water, and there was no longer the flame of the long trail. The light in the north still glimmered, but it was apparently no nearer to the boat. Sometimes the boom of the surf rang in the correspondent's ears, and he turned the craft seaward then and rowed harder. Southward, some one had evidently built a watch fire on the beach. It was too low and too far to be seen, but it made a shimmering, roseate reflection upon the bluff back of it, and this could be discerned from the boat. The wind came stronger, and sometimes a wave suddenly raged out like a mountain cat and there was to be seen the sheen and sparkle of a broken crest.

The captain, in the bow, moved on his water jar and sat erect. "Pretty long night," he observed to the correspondent. He looked at the shore. "Those lifesaving people take their time."

"Did you see that shark playing around?"

"Yes, I saw him. He was a big fellow, all right."

"Wish I had known you were awake."

Later the correspondent spoke into the bottom of the boat.

"Billie!" There was a slow and gradual disentanglement. "Billie, will you spell me?"

"Sure," said the oiler.

As soon as the correspondent touched the cold comfortable seawater in the bottom of the boat, and had huddled close to the cook's life belt he was deep in sleep, despite the fact that his teeth played all the popular airs. This sleep was so good to him that it was but a moment before he heard a voice call his name in a tone

Veiled Moon, 1995. Jane Wilson. Oil on linen, 18 x 18 in. Fischbach Gallery, NY.

View the Art Inspired by the light and landscape of Long Island, New York, Jane Wilson creates luminous paintings that appear universal enough to come from almost anywhere. How does Wilson portray nature in this painting? ★

that demonstrated the last stages of exhaustion. "Will you spell me?"

"Sure, Billie."

The light in the north had mysteriously vanished, but the correspondent took his course from the wide-awake captain.

Later in the night they took the boat farther out to sea, and the captain directed the cook to take one oar at the stern and keep the boat facing the seas. He was to call out if he should hear the thunder of the surf. This plan enabled the oiler and the correspondent to get respite together. "We'll give those boys a chance to get into shape again," said the captain. They curled down and, after a few preliminary chatterings and trembles, slept once more the dead sleep. Neither knew they had bequeathed to the cook the company of another shark, or perhaps the same shark.

As the boat caroused on the waves, spray occasionally bumped over the side and gave

STEPHEN CRANE **593**

View the Art ★

Answer: *The painting depicts nature as serene and beautiful, if indifferent.*

Say: There are no humans in the painting, so it is difficult to gauge nature in relationship to us. To a viewer outside the painting, it appears beautiful.

Iowa native Jane Wilson specializes in dreamy, impressionistic nature scenes that often depict a cloud-obscured sky.

Approaching Level

DIFFERENTIATED INSTRUCTION

Emerging Students may need assistance in understanding the meaning of the poem and its relevance to the story. Tell them to use the footnotes for explanations of unfamiliar terms. Read the poem aloud, and discuss the meaning of each line. Ask students what the poem means to them. Is their reaction to the poem more like that of the correspondent as a child or of the adult correspondent in the boat? Then ask them what the poem may mean to the correspondent in his present situation.

Teach

Reading Strategy   1

Summarize **Answer:** *The men are so exhausted that they are numb to the effects of the wind and water.*

Ask: How are the men like mummies? *(They have bodies but have no feelings or reactions to their surroundings.)*

Literary Element   2

Suspense As the story approaches its climax, Crane goes into more detail about the actions of the men.

Ask: How does providing more detail help to build suspense? *(It gives the reader a clearer picture of the situation; it also delays the outcome.)*

(APPROACHING) Ask students to identify the specific details that create suspense.

Big Idea   3

Naturalism **Answer:** *The correspondent perceives nature as indifferent to the fate of human beings.*

Say: People often "make a deal" when they are faced with the possibility of death. For example, they promise a higher power that they will change or improve themselves in exchange for survival.

them a fresh soaking, but this had no power to break their repose. The ominous slash of the wind and the water affected them as it would have affected mummies.

"Boys," said the cook, with the notes of every reluctance in his voice, "she's drifted in pretty close. I guess one of you had better take her to sea again." The correspondent, aroused, heard the crash of the toppled crests.

As he was rowing, the captain gave him some whiskey and water, and this steadied the chills out of him. "If I ever get ashore and anybody shows me even a photograph of an oar—"

At last there was a short conversation.

"Billie . . . Billie, will you spell me?"

"Sure," said the oiler.

VII

When the correspondent again opened his eyes, the sea and the sky were each of the gray hue of the dawning. Later, carmine and gold was painted upon the waters. The morning appeared finally, in its splendor, with a sky of pure blue, and the sunlight flamed on the tips of the waves.

On the distant dunes were set many little black cottages, and a tall white windmill reared above them. No man, nor dog, nor bicycle appeared on the beach. The cottages might have formed a deserted village.

The voyagers scanned the shore. A conference was held in the boat. "Well," said the captain, "if no help is coming, we might better try a run through the surf right away. If we stay out here much longer we will be too weak to do anything for ourselves at all." The others silently acquiesced in this reasoning. The boat was headed for the beach. The correspondent wondered if none ever ascended the tall wind-tower, and if then they never looked seaward. This tower was a giant, standing with its back to the plight of the ants. It represented in a degree, to the correspondent, the

serenity of nature amid the struggles of the individual—nature in the wind, and nature in the vision of men. She did not seem cruel to him then, nor beneficent, nor treacherous, nor wise. But she was indifferent, flatly indifferent. It is, perhaps, plausible that a man in this situation, impressed with the unconcern of the universe, should see the innumerable flaws of his life and have them taste wickedly in his mind and wish for another chance. A distinction between right and wrong seems absurdly clear to him, then, in this new ignorance of the grave-edge, and he understands that if he were given another opportunity he would mend his conduct and his words, and be better and brighter during an introduction, or at a tea.

"Now, boys," said the captain, "she is going to swamp sure. All we can do is to work her in as far as possible, and then when she swamps, pile out and scramble for the beach. Keep cool now, and don't jump until she swamps sure."

The oiler took the oars. Over his shoulders he scanned the surf. "Captain," he said, "I think I'd better bring her about, and keep her head-on to the seas and back her in."

"All right, Billie," said the captain. "Back her in." The oiler swung the boat then and, seated in the stern, the cook and the correspondent were obliged to look over their shoulders to contemplate the lonely and indifferent shore.

The monstrous inshore rollers heaved the boat high until the men were again enabled to see the white sheets of water scudding[42] up the slanted beach. "We won't get in very close," said the captain. Each time a man could wrest his attention from the rollers, he turned his glance toward the shore, and in the expression of the eyes during this contemplation there was a singular quality. The correspondent, observing the others, knew that they were not afraid,

42. *Scudding* means "moving swiftly."

1 Summarize **What is the main idea expressed in this paragraph?**

Naturalism **How is Naturalism apparent in the correspondent's attitude in this paragraph?**   3

594 UNIT 4   REGIONALISM AND REALISM

Writing Practice

SPIRAL
REVIEW **Research** *The Open Boat* is a fictionalized account of the sinking of the *Commodore*. Have students use the Internet and other resources to learn more about the actual shipwreck. Have them consult the article "Stephen Crane's Own Story," which appeared in *The New York Press* on January 7, 1897. Have students write a brief essay, comparing the article with the short story. In their essay, students should identify the

events in Crane's article that do not appear in the story. They should also compare the tone and style of the article to the short story.

but the full meaning of their glances was shrouded.

As for himself, he was too tired to grapple fundamentally with the fact. He tried to **coerce** his mind into thinking of it, but the mind was dominated at this time by the muscles, and the muscles said they did not care. It merely occurred to him that if he should drown it would be a shame.

There were no hurried words, no pallor,[43] no plain agitation. The men simply looked at the shore. "Now, remember to get well clear of the boat when you jump," said the captain.

Seaward the crest of a roller suddenly fell with a thunderous crash, and the long white comber[44] came roaring down upon the boat.

"Steady now," said the captain. The men were silent. They turned their eyes from the shore to the comber and waited. The boat slid up the incline, leaped at the furious top, bounced over it, and swung down the long back of the wave. Some water had been shipped and the cook bailed it out.

But the next crest crashed also. The tumbling boiling flood of white water caught the boat and whirled it almost perpendicular. Water swarmed in from all sides. The correspondent had his hands on the gunwale at this time, and when the water entered at that place he swiftly withdrew his fingers, as if he objected to wetting them.

The little boat, drunken with this weight of water, reeled and snuggled deeper into the sea.

"Bail her out, cook! Bail her out," said the captain.

"All right, Captain," said the cook.

"Now, boys, the next one will do for us, sure," said the oiler. "Mind to jump clear of the boat."

4 The third wave moved forward, huge, furious, implacable.[45] It fairly swallowed the din-

ghy, and almost simultaneously the men tumbled into the sea. A piece of life belt had lain in the bottom of the boat, and as the correspondent went overboard he held this to his chest with his left hand.

The January water was icy, and he reflected immediately that it was colder than he had expected to find it off the coast of Florida. This appeared to his dazed mind as a fact important enough to be noted at the time. The coldness of the water was sad; it was tragic. This fact was somehow so mixed and confused with his opinion of his own situation that it seemed almost a proper reason for tears. The water was cold.

When he came to the surface he was conscious of little but the noisy water. Afterward he saw his companions in the sea. The oiler was ahead in the race. He was swimming strongly and rapidly. Off to the correspondent's left, the cook's great white and corked back bulged out of the water, and in the rear the captain was hanging with his one good hand to the keel[46] of the overturned dinghy.

There is a certain immovable quality to a shore, and the correspondent wondered at it amid the confusion of the sea.

It seemed also very attractive, but the correspondent knew that it was a long journey, and he paddled leisurely. The piece of life preserver lay under him, and sometimes he whirled down the incline of a wave as if he were on a hand-sled.

But finally he arrived at a place in the sea where travel was beset with difficulty. He did not pause swimming to inquire what manner of current had caught him, but there his progress ceased. The shore was set before him like a bit of scenery on a stage, and he looked at it and understood with his eyes each detail of it.

As the cook passed, much farther to the left, the captain was calling to him, "Turn over on

---

43. *Pallor* is paleness or the lack of natural or healthy color.
44. A *comber* is a long, rolling wave that curls and breaks.
45. *Implacable* means "unrelenting" or "unyielding."

Vocabulary

coerce (kō urs′) *v.* to force

---

46. The *keel* runs along the center of the bottom of a boat. It supports the boat's frame and gives the boat stability.

Author's Purpose *Why do you think Crane chose to narrate this part of the story from the correspondent's point of view?* **5**

Literary Element 4

Climax Point out to students that the story reaches its climax with the sentence, "The third wave moved forward, huge, furious, implacable.

Ask: Why is this climax particularly appropriate to a Naturalist work of literature? *(At the climax, nature is in full control and the men are helpless.)*

APPROACHING Remind students that the climax is the turning point in the action. **Ask:** What do you think will happen now? *(The men will either drown or be rescued. There will be no more waiting.)*

Literary Element 5

Author's Purpose Answer: *Students may note that, because the correspondent is a newspaper reporter, he is trained to be a keen observer of events. Also, because the correspondent is a sensitive and educated person, his impressions of the events are bound to be more articulate and informative than those of his companions.*

Approaching Level

UNIVERSAL ACCESS

AAVE Read the last sentence on page 594. Note the phrase *they were not afraid*. Approaching level students who use African American vernacular English (AAVE) may use *was*, instead of *were*, in the plural. Give students a few other examples: *We were happy, They were my friends*. Then give students a list of pronoun subjects (I, you, he, she, it, we, they) and a list of adjectives and predicate nouns (happy, my family, your friend, friendly, etc.) and have them join words from each list using either *was* or *were*, as required.

Teach

Literary Element | 1

Conflict **Say:** The correspondent must now battle an internal conflict, as well as his external conflict with the sea. In this passage, the thought of respite from his struggle, even death, seems appealing.

Ask: Do you think the correspondent will give up? *(The correspondent's earlier anger at the possibility that he might drown will drive him to continue swimming.)*

Reading Strategy | 2

Summarize **Answer:** *The correspondent is swimming toward the captain and the boat. His main goal now is not survival but avoiding pain.*

your back, cook! Turn over on your back and use the oar."

"All right, sir." The cook turned on his back, and, paddling with an oar, went ahead as if he were a canoe.

Presently the boat also passed to the left of the correspondent with the captain clinging with one hand to the keel. He would have appeared like a man raising himself to look over a board fence, if it were not for the extraordinary gymnastics of the boat. The correspondent marvelled that the captain could still hold to it.

They passed on, nearer to shore—the oiler, the cook, the captain—and following them went the water jar, bouncing gayly over the seas.

The correspondent remained in the grip of this strange new enemy—a current. The shore, with its white slope of sand and its green bluff, topped with little silent cottages, was spread like a picture before him. It was very near to him then, but he was impressed as one who in a gallery looks at a scene from Brittany[47] or Holland.

He thought: "I am going to drown? Can it be possible? Can it be possible? Can it be possible?" Perhaps an individual must consider his own death to be the final phenomenon of nature.

But later a wave perhaps whirled him out of this small deadly current, for he found suddenly that he could again make progress toward the shore. Later still, he was aware that the captain, clinging with one hand to the keel of the dinghy, had his face turned away from the shore and toward him, and was calling his name. "Come to the boat! Come to the boat!"

1 In his struggle to reach the captain and the boat, he reflected that when one gets properly

> *Perhaps an individual must consider his own death to be the final phenomenon of nature.*

wearied, drowning must really be a comfortable arrangement, a cessation of hostilities accompanied by a large degree of relief, and he was glad of it, for the main thing in his mind for some moments had been horror of the temporary agony. He did not wish to be hurt.

Presently he saw a man running along the shore. He was undressing with most remarkable speed. Coat, trousers, shirt, everything flew magically off him.

"Come to the boat," called the captain.

"All right, Captain." As the correspondent paddled, he saw the captain let himself down to bottom and leave the boat. Then the correspondent performed his one little marvel of the voyage. A large wave caught him and flung him with ease and supreme speed completely over the boat and far beyond it. It struck him even then as an event in gymnastics, and a true miracle of the sea. An overturned boat in the surf is not a plaything to a swimming man.

The correspondent arrived in water that reached only to his waist, but his condition did not enable him to stand for more than a moment. Each wave knocked him into a heap, and the undertow pulled at him.

Then he saw the man who had been running and undressing, and undressing and running, come bounding into the water. He dragged ashore the cook, and then waded toward the captain, but the captain waved him away, and sent him to the correspondent. He was naked, naked as a tree in winter, but a halo was about his head, and he shone like a saint. He gave a strong pull, and a long drag, and a bully heave at the correspondent's hand. The correspondent, schooled in the minor formulæ, said: "Thanks, old man." But suddenly the man

47. *Brittany* is a region in northwestern France.

596 UNIT 4 REGIONALISM AND REALISM

Summarize *Summarize this paragraph and explain how the correspondent's goals have changed.* **2**

Writing Practice

News Story Have students imagine that they are reporters for a newspaper and write a news story about the rescue of the men in the boat. Remind students that news stories report the five Ws and an H: who, what, when, where, why, and how. After this basic information is covered, the news story may elaborate with additional background, such as what caused their ship to sink. News stories may also include interviews with the rescued men. *(Students may use interview material developed in the previous Skills Practice.)*

Moonrise on the Seashore, 1821. Caspar David Friedrich. Oil on canvas, 22½ x 28½ in. Hermitage, St. Petersburg, Russia.

cried: "What's that?" He pointed a swift finger. The correspondent said: "Go."

In the shallows, face downward, lay the oiler. His forehead touched sand that was periodically, between each wave, clear of the sea.

The correspondent did not know all that transpired afterward. When he achieved safe ground he fell, striking the sand with each particular part of his body. It was as if he had dropped from a roof, but the thud was grateful to him.

It seems that instantly the beach was populated with men with blankets, clothes, and flasks, and women with coffeepots and all the remedies sacred to their minds. The welcome of the land to the men from the sea was warm and generous, but a still and dripping shape was carried slowly up the beach, and the land's welcome for it could only be the different and sinister hospitality of the grave.

When it came night, the white waves paced to and fro in the moonlight, and the wind brought the sound of the great sea's voice to the men on shore, and they felt that they could then be interpreters. ❧

---

3 Naturalism **What ironic prophecy is fulfilled by the oiler's death?**

STEPHEN CRANE **597**

Teach

Big Idea · 3

Naturalism Answer: *Students may identify the following passage as a prophecy: ". . . if I am going to be drowned, why, in the name of the seven mad gods who rule the sea, was I allowed to come thus far and contemplate sand and trees?"*

 To check students' understanding of the selection, see Unit 4 Teaching Resources Book, p. 157.

View the Art ★

Caspar David Friedrich was a pioneer of the Romantic movement in Germany. His paintings often contain religious symbols and a sense of alienation.

Ask: Does this painting provide a sense of hope? *(Students may say that the light on the horizon provides a sense of hope. The landscape is desolate, but the people seem to be relying on each other.)*

English Learners

DIFFERENTIATED INSTRUCTION

SMALL GROUP **Intermediate** After students have completed the story, divide them into groups of four. Assign one character from the story to each student. Have students review the story and take notes on their assigned character in a three-column chart with the heads *Actions,* *Words,* and *Thoughts.* When students have completed their charts, have them write sentences about the key traits of their character. Then have them present their descriptions orally to their groups.

After You Read

Assess

1. Some may feel the oiler's death is unjustified; others may say this emphasizes the indifference of nature.

2. (a) They are stranded at sea in a ten-foot dinghy after their ship sinks. (b) The cook is optimistic; the correspondent is not; the oiler is both cautious and optimistic.

3. (a) The captain is awake and silent. The correspondent is silent as he rows. He and the oiler row until the captain orders the cook to steer while the rowers rest. (b) The captain and the cook are considerate; the oiler and the correspondent are determined; the captain and the correspondent are thoughtful.

4. (a) The men swim ashore. All but the oiler survive. (b) The strongest and most sympathetic man dies.

5. (a) boat and bronco (simile), water and flames (simile), men to mice and ants (metaphors) (b) They help the reader visualize the dangers of the sea and emphasize the connection between the men and nature.

6. Literary devices give the story emotional impact.

7. The crew accepts that nature has no stake in their survival.

8. Some people may identify with the idea that humans are at the mercy of an indifferent universe.

For additional assessment, see Assessment Resources, pp. 181–182.

After You Read

Respond and Think Critically

Respond and Interpret

1. How did you react when you realized the correspondent survives but the oiler does not?

2. (a)Summarize the situation of the four men in part I. (b)From the discussion that three of the men have at the end of part I, what might you infer about each man's character?

3. (a)How does each man behave during the night at sea (parts V and VI)? (b)What can you infer about their characters from their actions?

4. (a)What is the outcome of the story? (b)How is the outcome ironic, and what might this imply about nature?

Analyze and Evaluate

5. (a)List several similes and metaphors Crane uses in the story. (b)What effect do these comparisons have on the reader?

6. Could the emotional effect of this story be conveyed just as well in the form of a newspaper article about the shipwreck and the men's struggle to survive? Explain.

Connect

7. **Big Idea** Naturalism How might being lost at sea influence the crew's view of nature in a way that another type of mishap might not?

8. **Connect to Today** People today still identify with Crane's stories, characters, and themes. Why do you think this is?

Visual Literacy

Fine Art

Moonlit Shipwreck at Sea, 1901. (detail) Thomas Moran. Oil on canvas, 30 x 40¼ in. Private Collection.

Thomas Moran belonged to the Hudson River school, a group of painters who attempted to evoke specific moods and emotional states, often to express the sublime—that which is awe-inspiring—in nature.

Answer these questions about Moran's painting: (see page 583 for a larger version)

1. (a)What is the subject of the painting? (b)How is the human element treated?

2. (a)What is the effect of the light and shadow in the painting? (b)How is this effect comparable to Crane's literary effects in "The Open Boat"?

3. (a)From what perspective is the viewer watching this scene? (b)How does this perspective contribute to the mood of the painting?

Visual Literacy

1. (a) A shipwreck (b) The only trace of humans is the tiny boat. (c) Like the dinghy in the story, the boat is outmatched by the sea.

2. (a) The dramatic contrast shows both the power and splendor of the sea. (b) Crane uses contrast to help reveal how the crew's feelings about the sea shift from anger to acceptance.

3. (a) From a great distance (b) It creates feelings of helplessness and awe.

Literary Element | Author's Purpose

An author can have more than one purpose in writing a literary work. For example, a short story writer's main purpose might be to convey an idea or present a philosophical view of life. In addition, the writer might have several other purposes, such as to construct a suspenseful plot, to create sympathetic characters, or to entertain the reader through humor, irony, or figurative language.

1. (a) What do you think was Crane's main purpose in writing "The Open Boat"? (b) Identify at least one of Crane's other purposes.

2. On page 584, the narrator says of the crew, ". . . there was this comradeship that the correspondent, for instance, who had been taught to be cynical of men, knew even at the time was the best experience of his life." What might Crane's purpose have been in having the narrator make this statement?

Review: Conflict

As you learned on page 552, **conflict** refers to the central struggle between two opposing forces in a story. **External conflict** exists when a character struggles against an outside force, such as another person, nature, society, or fate. **Internal conflict** is a struggle between two opposing thoughts or desires within the mind of a character.

Partner Activity With a partner, discuss the conflicts that the correspondent faces in "The Open Boat." Which type of conflict—internal or external—is more prevalent? With your partner, discuss whether one type of conflict is more prevalent or they are about equal.

LOG ON ▶ **Literature** Online

Selection Resources For Selection Quizzes, eFlashcards, and Reading-Writing Connection activities, go to glencoe.com and enter QuickPass code GLA9800u4.

Reading Strategy | Summarize

Summarize Theme By analyzing the elements of a story, you can piece together the author's message about life. Refer to your chart you made on page 579 as you respond to the following:

1. Summarize the theme of Crane's story.

2. What story details support your summary?

Vocabulary Practice

Practice with Context Clues Identify the context clues in the following sentences that help you determine the meaning of each bold-faced vocabulary word.

1. An **emphatic** crash in the alley jolted Miranda awake.

2. The feeling that he had the same conversation with his friend earlier, even though he knew he hadn't, was **uncanny**.

3. When diagnosing the patient, it was important for the doctor to talk frankly, or **ingenuously**.

4. At the political rally, some citizens behaved politely, whereas others acted **impudently**.

5. In order to restrain the rabid dog, the animal control officer had to **coerce** it into the back of his van.

Academic Vocabulary

Stephen Crane uses naturalistic **techniques,** *such as focusing on the sky and the waves, to illustrate the characters' struggle.*

Technique is an academic word. In more casual conversation, someone might say a dancer uses excellent or poor **techniques.**

To study this word further, use context clues to figure out the meaning of the word *technique* in the sentence above. Then check your inference in a print or online dictionary.

For more on academic vocabulary, see pages 53–54.

STEPHEN CRANE **599**

After You Read

Assess

Literary Element

1. (a) Students may say that Crane's main purpose was to demonstrate the Naturalistic belief that nature is indifferent to human life. (b) A purpose may have been to entertain the reader with a suspenseful plot.

2. Students may say that it shows how people bond together in a crisis and put aside their differences in the interest of a shared humanity.

Progress Check

Can students interpret the author's purpose?

If No ➔ See Unit 4 Teaching Resources Book, p. 152.

Review: Conflict

External Conflicts: ocean waves, cold, wind, night, seabirds, shark

Internal Conflicts: fear, physical exhaustion, hunger, desire for sleep and for relief from pain

Reading Strategy

1. Nature is indifferent toward people, and people are insignificant in the universe.

2. The narrator notes, "…it occurs to a man that nature does not regard him as important, and that she feels she would not maim the universe by disposing of him.…" The sinister description of the birds on page 582, the relentless churning of the waves, and the inability of the people on shore to rescue the men indicate a similar indifference.

Vocabulary

1. The context of the sentence and the use of the word "jolted" imply that the meaning of *emphatic* is "forceful."

2. The feeling is eerie, or *uncanny.*

3. The synonym of *ingenuously,* which is "frankly," is used in the sentence.

4. The antonym of *impudently,* which is "politely," is used in the sentence; therefore, *impudently* means "in an impulsive bold manner."

5. The context of the sentence and the use of the word "restrain" implies that the meaning of *coerce* is "to force."

Academic Vocabulary

An example of naturalistic technique is given. Students should infer that "technique" means "the manner in which something is treated."

599

After You Read

Assess

 Writing

Students' reviews should present ideas and arguments in a logical way, supported by evidence from the text or excerpts of other literary criticism. Reviews should also refute possible counterarguments.

Scoring Guide

Assess students performance in the following categories using the scoring guide at the bottom of the page:

- Addresses all parts of the writing task.
- Provides a meaningful thesis, maintains focus and organization.
- Supports the thesis with details and examples.
- Provides a variety of sentence types; uses precise, descriptive language.
- Follows English language conventions.
- Makes a logical, convincing argument.

 For grammar practice, see Unit 4 Teaching Resources Book, p. 156.

Respond Through Writing

Story Review

Persuasion and Audience This short story is often included in literature textbooks. Do you think it deserves to remain in the literary canon? Write a review in which you address this question. Use specific examples from the story to support your opinions.

Understand the Task A **review** is an analysis and interpretation of a subject presented through the mass media. The **literary canon** refers to the set of works widely acknowledged as the best representatives in a given area of literature, such as American literature.

Prewrite Before you begin writing, consider the individuals in your audience. For example, are you writing for fellow students or for readers of a literary magazine? Thinking about this will help you determine the tone and language you use.

Draft In your review, structure your ideas and arguments in a logical way. Use rhetorical devices such as parallelism, repetition, hyperbole, analogy, or irony to strengthen your essay. Include supporting evidence, such as passages from the text or excerpts of literary criticism, that reinforce your views. You might phrase your supporting evidence in a sentence like this one:

Some examples of _____ in the story are _____, _____, and _____.

Revise If you used sources outside the text for supporting evidence, check that you have cited them correctly. Also, make sure you have identified and refuted possible counterarguments from your intended audience. Exchange papers with a classmate and evaluate one another's work. Use the checklist on page 624 to help you evaluate your peer's essay. Revise your review as necessary.

Edit and Proofread Proofread your paper, correcting any errors in spelling, grammar, and punctuation. Review the Grammar Tip in the side column for help using semicolons.

600 UNIT 4 REGIONALISM AND REALISM

Learning Objectives

In this assignment, you will focus on the following objectives:

Writing: Writing a review.

Grammar Tip

Semicolons

Semicolons typically connect two main clauses that are not joined by a coordinating conjunction, two main clauses joined by a conjunctive adverb, or two main clauses joined by an expression such as *for example* or *that is.* For example:

Many things could have gone wrong; for example, the boat could have capsized.

In your writing, try using semicolons to connect clauses that have closely-related ideas.

Rowing the boat is exhausting work; the moment the rower is relieved, he immediately falls asleep.

Scoring Guide	4	3	2	1
Task addressed	fully	mostly	partially	barely
Thesis	meaningful	provided	partial	weak
Support	thoughtful	provided	limited	weak
Language	varied, descriptive	varied, often descriptive	predictable, imprecise	repetitive, limited
Convention errors	few or none	several	many	serious
Argument is	convincing	mostly convincing	partially convincing	not convincing

Before You Read

To Build a Fire

Meet **Jack London**
(1876–1916)

I n 1897 Jack London left college and went to the Yukon to join the Klondike gold rush. He never found gold, but he did find something that proved more precious to him: a wealth of raw material for the stories that eventually made him famous.

> "I would rather be ashes than dust!"
>
> —Jack London

An Adventurous Life Born in 1876 in San Francisco to an unstable mother and a father who refused to claim him, London was raised mainly by a family friend and a stepsister. From the age of eleven, he worked to earn money to help put food on his family's table. London loved the sea, so he hung around the harbor, doing odd jobs and learning to be an expert sailor. While still in his teens, he signed on to a schooner sailing to Siberia. From that adventure came his first published story.

At eighteen, London set off to ride the rails, living the life of a drifter as he traveled across the country on freight trains. This journey became a turning point in his life as he saw up close the raw, painful lives of men and women who did not seem to belong anywhere in society. As a result of the conditions he saw, London vowed to educate himself so he could survive by his mental powers rather than by his physical strength.

After completing high school in just one year, London attended the University of California at Berkeley for a semester before rushing off to the Klondike. He failed to strike it rich, however, so he came home and turned to writing for his livelihood. In 1903, London published *The Call of the Wild*, the novel that firmly established his reputation. Before long, he became the country's highest-paid author—a stunning reversal of fortune for the once-impoverished writer.

Struggle to Make Ends Meet Throughout his life, London worked under pressure to support not only himself but also numerous family members and friends. He set himself the task of writing at least a thousand publishable words every day, and he rarely deviated from that schedule. But despite publishing more than fifty books and becoming the country's first millionaire author, London habitually spent more money than he earned, and he often wrote stories in order to pay off urgent debts.

In the last years of his life, London bought a ranch in northern California and began building his dream house, Wolf House, on it. In 1913, shortly before he was to move into the newly completed house, it burned down. The fire devastated London both emotionally and financially. He continued to live on the ranch but never rebuilt the house. Three years later, plagued by severe health problems and financial difficulties, London died. He was only forty years old.

 Literature Online

Author Search For more about Jack London, go to glencoe.com and enter QuickPass code GLA9800u4.

Before You Read

Focus

Bellringer Options

**Selection Focus
  Transparency 39**

**Daily Language Practice
  Transparency 54**

Or pass around news articles or photographs depicting people in places with extreme weather conditions, such as the Arctic, a desert, or a coastline in the aftermath of a hurricane or tsunami.

Write this statement on the board: Human beings can use their intelligence to overcome the extremities of nature.

Have students agree or disagree with this statement and explain their reasoning. Tell them to keep their response in mind and see if they feel the same way after reading this story.

Selection Skills

Literary Elements
- Setting (SE pp. 602–604, 607, 612, 614, 615; TE p. 602)

Reading Skills
- Cause and Effect (SE pp. 602, 604, 606, 608, 610, 611, 613, 616)
- Sequence (TE p. 604)

To Build a Fire

Vocabulary Skills
- Word Origins (SE p. 616, TE p. 602)
- Academic Vocabulary (SE p. 616)
- Adjectives (TE p. 606)

Listening/Speaking/ Viewing Skills
- Analyze Art (SE p. 607)

Writing Skills/Grammar
- Descriptive Essay (SE p. 616)
- Cause and Effect (TE p. 610)
- Narrative Account (TE p. 612)

Study Skills/Research/ Assessment
- Assessment (TE p. 608)

Before You Read

Focus

Summary

A man travels with his dog across the Yukon in temperatures reaching −75°F. He makes a fatal mistake when he steps into a spring and exposes his feet to the cold water. His one chance for survival is to remove his shoes and warm his feet by building a fire. When his fire is extinguished, he realizes that he has lost his only hope for survival. He makes an attempt to run for the camp but collapses and dies in the wilderness.

 For summaries in languages other than English, see Unit 4 Teaching Resources Book, pp. 159–164.

Vocabulary

Word Roots Have students identify the words in the vocabulary list that have these roots:

Latin *tangere:* to touch *(tangible)*

Latin *mors:* death *(immortality)*

Greek *pathos:* suffering, feeling *(apathetically)*

[ADVANCED] Challenge students to share other words they know that contain these roots. *(Possible responses: tangent; morbid, postmortem; sympathy, pathology)*

 For additional vocabulary practice, see Unit 4 Teaching Resources Book, p. 167.

 For additional context, see Glencoe Interactive Vocabulary CD-ROM.

Literature and Reading Preview

Connect to the Story

Think about a time you took on a task that turned out to be much more difficult than you had thought. How did it affect you physically and emotionally? Explore this question in a brief journal entry.

Build Background

In 1896, miners discovered gold in a tributary of the Klondike River. By 1898, thousands of prospectors had poured into what is now Canada's Yukon Territory. Many of the prospectors were unprepared for the brutal conditions in the north, where temperatures could sink below minus fifty degrees Fahrenheit.

Set Purposes for Reading

Big Idea Naturalism

A battle with nature is a common conflict in literature, particularly in Naturalist literature. As you read, ask yourself, Do humans ever win such a battle?

Literary Element Setting

The **setting** is the time and place in which the events of a literary work occur. Naturalist writers generally emphasize the setting, focusing on the importance of the environment in defining human character. As you read, ask yourself, How does London use the setting to develop plot and character?

Reading Strategy Analyze Cause-and-Effect Relationships

In a **cause-and-effect** relationship, one event brings about another. The second event occurs not only after the first but as a consequence of it. A cause may have several effects, and an effect may, in turn, cause other events to happen. In "To Build a Fire," cause-and-effect relationships are essential to the plot.

Tip: Take Notes Use a diagram to record causes and effects.

Cause	Effect
The temperature is colder than fifty below zero.	The man's spittle crackles in the air before falling to the snow.

602 UNIT 4 REGIONALISM AND REALISM

Vocabulary

intangible (in tan′ jə bəl) *adj.* not easily defined or evaluated by the mind; p. 603 *Volunteer work brings not money but intangible benefits.*

immortality (im′ ôr tal′ ə tē) *n.* the condition of having eternal life; p. 604 *Unlike mortals, who live and then die, the gods in Greek myths enjoyed immortality.*

compel (kəm pel′) *v.* to force; p. 606 *His tardiness and lack of hustle compelled the coach to bench him.*

intervene (in′ tər vēn′) *v.* to come or lie between; p. 607 *He decided to intervene to prevent the quarrel between the angry motorists from escalating.*

apathetically (ap′ ə thet′ i kal ē) *adv.* in a manner showing little interest or concern; p. 612 *Apathetically, she cast her vote, not really caring who would win or lose.*

Reading Practice

Effect of Setting Tell students that the setting in this story is a critical factor. This is a story that could not take place in a different setting. Prepare students to examine the effects of the setting as they read. Have them divide a sheet of notebook paper into three sections, and label them *Setting, Effects on Action,* and *Effects on Character.* As they read, have students use this organizer to record notes on the details of the setting, the way the setting affects the development of the action, and the way the setting affects the character. Their notes will help them to see causes and effects and to discuss the setting when they have finished reading.

to Build a Fire

Jack London

Intermediate After English learners have read the Build Background section on page 602, draw their attention to the words "brutal conditions." Explain that *brutal* means "harsh" or "extremely difficult." Ask students what might make up brutal conditions in this environment. (*Possible responses: ice, snow, extreme cold, wind*)

Day had broken cold and gray, exceedingly cold and gray, when the man turned aside from the main Yukon[1] trail and climbed the high earth-bank, where a dim and little-traveled trail led eastward through the fat spruce timberland. It was a steep bank, and he paused for breath at the top, excusing the act to himself by looking at his watch. It was nine o'clock. There was no sun nor hint of sun, though there was not a cloud in the sky. It was a clear day, and yet there seemed an **intangible** pall over the face of things, a subtle gloom that made the day dark, and that was due to the absence of sun. **1**

This fact did not worry the man. He was used to the lack of sun. It had been days since he had seen the sun, and he knew that a few more days must pass before that cheerful orb,

---

1. Here, *Yukon* refers to the Yukon River. The river was a major route to the Klondike goldfields.

Setting *What mood do these details create?* **2**

Vocabulary

intangible (in tan´ jə bəl) *adj.* not easily defined or evaluated by the mind

JACK LONDON **603**

Teach

Literary Element   1

Setting **Answer:** *The details suggest that the temperature is dangerously cold, even life-threatening. The Yukon River is frozen to a depth of three feet.*

Reading Strategy   2

Cause and Effect **Answer:** *A good imagination helps one anticipate dangers and foresee the consequences of actions in this life-threatening environment.*

 For additional practice using the reading skill or strategy, see Unit 4 Teaching Resources Book, p. 166.

Writer's Technique ☆

Omniscient Narrator The narrator of this story is omniscient, or all-knowing, and able to see into the minds of both the man and the dog. This point of view gives readers an opportunity to see events from two perspectives.

---

due south, would just peep above the skyline and dip immediately from view.

The man flung a look back along the way he had come. The Yukon lay a mile wide and hidden under three feet of ice. On top of this ice were as many feet of snow. It was all pure white, rolling in gentle undulations[2] where the ice jams of the freeze up had formed. North and south, as far as his eye could see, it was unbroken white save for a dark hairline that curved and twisted from around the spruce-covered island to the south, and that curved and twisted away into the north, where it disappeared behind another spruce-covered island. This dark hairline was the trail—the main trail—that led south five hundred miles to the Chilkoot Pass, Dyea, and saltwater; and that led north seventy miles to Dawson, and still on to the north a thousand miles to Nulato,[3] and finally to St. Michael on Bering Sea, a thousand miles and half a thousand more.

But all this—the mysterious, far-reaching hairline trail, the absence of sun from the sky, the tremendous cold, and the strangeness and weirdness of it all—made no impression on the man. It was not because he was long used to it. He was a newcomer in the land, a *chechaquo*,[4] and this was his first winter. The trouble with him was that he was without imagination. He was quick and alert in the things of life, but only in the things, and not in the significances. Fifty degrees below zero meant eighty-odd degrees of frost. Such fact impressed him as being cold and uncomfortable, and that was all.

---

2. *Undulations* are rippling or wavelike forms or outlines.
3. *Dyea* (dī´ ä) was a mining village in Alaska at the beginning of the route to the goldfields. The trail led through the *Chilkoot Pass* and to northern gold-mining centers in the Yukon such as *Dawson* and *Nulato* (nōō lä´ tō).
4. In the language of the Chinook, Native Americans of the Pacific Northwest, a *chechaquo* (chē chä´ kō) is a "newcomer" or a "tenderfoot."

1   Setting *Why does the author include these details?*

2   Cause and Effect *Why is a good imagination especially important in this environment?*

It did not lead him to meditate upon his frailty in general, able only to live within certain narrow limits of heat and cold; and from there on it did not lead him to the conjectural[5] field of **immortality** and man's place in the universe. Fifty degrees below zero stood for a bite of frost that hurt and that must be guarded against by the use of mittens, earflaps, warm moccasins, and thick socks. Fifty degrees below zero was to him just precisely fifty degrees below zero. That there should be anything more to it than that was a thought that never entered his head.

As he turned to go on, he spat speculatively. There was a sharp, explosive crackle that startled him. He spat again. And again, in the air, before it could fall to the snow, the spittle crackled. He knew that at fifty below spittle crackled on the snow, but this spittle had crackled in the air. Undoubtedly it was colder than fifty below—how much colder he did not know. But the temperature did not matter. He was bound for the old claim[6] on the left fork of Henderson Creek, where the boys were already. They had come over across the divide[7] from the Indian Creek country, while he had come the roundabout way to take a look at the possibilities of getting out logs in the spring from the islands in the Yukon. He would be in to camp by six o'clock; a bit after dark, it was true, but the boys would be there, a fire would be going, and a hot supper would be ready. As for lunch, he pressed his hand against the protruding bundle under his jacket. It was also under his shirt, wrapped up in a handkerchief and lying against the naked skin. It was the only way to keep the biscuits from freezing. He smiled agreeably to himself as he thought of those biscuits, each cut open and sopped in

---

5. *Conjectural* means "based on guesswork or indefinite evidence."
6. A *claim* is a piece of land registered for mining rights.
7. A *divide* is a ridge of land that separates two river drainage systems.

Vocabulary

immortality (im´ ôr tal´ ə tē) *n.* the condition of having eternal life

---

Reading Practice

SPIRAL REVIEW **Sequence** London's story mainly progresses in straightforward chronological order. Although the main character occasionally thinks of someone he met before starting his trek, the action moves forward without any significant flashbacks.

Have students take notes to keep track of the story's major events and the order in which they occur. Explain that sometimes the man's thoughts or realizations—not happenings in the outside world—are major events. Students' notes should provide a rough outline of the story, telling essentially what happens and why. When students have finished the story, draw a timeline on the board. Have students consult their notes to identify the important events to enter on the timeline.

bacon grease, and each enclosing a generous slice of fried bacon.

He plunged in among the big spruce trees. The trail was faint. A foot of snow had fallen since the last sled had passed over, and he was glad he was without sled, traveling light. In fact, he carried nothing but the lunch wrapped in the handkerchief. He was surprised, however, at the cold. It certainly was cold, he concluded, as he rubbed his numb nose and cheekbones with his mittened hand. He was a warm-whiskered man, but the hair on his face did not protect the high cheekbones and the eager nose that thrust itself aggressively into the frosty air.

 At the man's heel trotted a dog, a big native husky, the proper wolf dog, gray-coated and without any visible or temperamental difference from its brother, the wild wolf. The animal was depressed by the tremendous cold. It knew that it was no time for traveling. Its instinct told a truer tale than was told to the man by the man's judgment. In reality, it was not merely colder than fifty below zero; it was colder than sixty below, than seventy below. It was seventy-five below zero. Since the freezing point is thirty-two above zero, it meant that one hundred and seven degrees of frost obtained. The dog did not know anything about thermometers. Possibly in its brain there was no sharp consciousness of a condition of very cold such as was in the man's brain. But the brute had its instinct. It experienced a vague but menacing apprehension that subdued it and made it slink along at the man's heels, and that made it question eagerly every unwonted[8] movement of the man as if expecting him to go into camp or to seek shelter some-

where and build a fire. The dog had learned fire, and it wanted fire, or else to burrow under the snow and cuddle its warmth away from the air.

The frozen moisture of its breathing had settled on its fur in a fine powder of frost, and especially were its jowls, muzzle, and eyelashes whitened by its crystalled breath. The man's red beard and mustache were likewise frosted, but more solidly, the deposit taking the form of ice and increasing with every warm, moist breath he exhaled. Also, the man was chewing tobacco, and the muzzle of ice held his lips so rigidly that he was unable to clear his chin when he expelled the juice. The result was that a crystal beard of the color and solidity of amber was increasing its length on his chin. If he fell down it would shatter itself, like glass, into brittle fragments. But he did not mind the appendage.[9] It was the penalty all tobacco-chewers paid in that country, and he had been out before in two cold snaps. They had not been so cold as this, he knew, but by the spirit thermometer[10] at Sixty Mile he knew they had been registered at fifty below and at fifty-five.

> *The dog had learned fire, and it wanted fire, or else to burrow under the snow and cuddle its warmth away from the air.*

He held on through the level stretch of woods for several miles and dropped down a ☆ bank to the frozen bed of a small stream. This was Henderson Creek, and he knew he was ten miles from the forks. He looked at his watch. It was ten o'clock. He was making four miles an hour, and he calculated that he would arrive at

---

9. An *appendage* is something that is added on or attached.
10. A *spirit thermometer* is an alcohol thermometer. It is used in areas of extreme cold, where the more common mercury thermometer would freeze.

Naturalism *Why does the man still chew tobacco even after ice forms on his chin?* **3**

---

8. *Unwonted* means "unusual."

Big Idea	3

Naturalism Answer: *The man is in a battle with nature and wants to spite nature. Also, the tobacco chewing gives him solace in the harsh environment.*

Writer's Technique ☆

Conflict To make plots compelling, writers include various types of conflict. **Ask:** What is the main conflict in this story? (*a battle between nature and man*) How does London use the relationship of the man and the dog to explore the conflict between nature and humanity? (*The dog is closely connected to nature and instinctively knows how to protect itself. The man relies on intellect and does not know how cold it really is, thus putting himself at risk.*)

English Learners

UNIVERSAL ACCESS 🐟

SMALL GROUP

Beginning After students have read the first few pages, have them meet in small groups to share what they know about the man based on what they have read so far. Then have each student make a statement about about one of his characteristics and support it with evidence from the story. (*Sample response: He does not have good judgment; starting out on his journey in these conditions was not wise.*)

Advanced Students may find it easier to understand the symbolism in the story if they explore cultural symbols with which they are already familiar. Explain that a symbol is an object, person, place, or experience that represents something else. Ask students to share familiar symbols they know. Then **ask:** What does fire symbolize in this story? (*life*)

Teach

Reading Strategy | **1**

Cause and Effect Answer:
The man is unimaginative, proud, and unresponsive to the signs of danger.

Reading Strategy | **2**

Analyze Character Point out that experts emphasize the importance of keeping dry in very cold temperatures, because water draws heat away from the body 25 times faster than air does. **Ask:** What does the man's situation tell you about his character flaws? *(He does not foresee consequences; he lacks vision and imagination.)*

the forks at half-past twelve. He decided to celebrate that event by eating his lunch there.

The dog dropped in again at his heels, with a tail drooping discouragement, as the man swung along the creek bed. The furrow[11] of the old sled trail was plainly visible, but a dozen inches of snow covered the marks of the last runners. In a month no man had come up or down that silent creek. The man held steadily on. He was not much given to thinking, and just then particularly he had nothing to think about save that he would eat lunch at the forks and that at six o'clock he would be in camp with the boys. There was nobody to talk to; and, had there been, speech would have been impossible because of the ice muzzle on his mouth. So he continued monotonously to chew tobacco and to increase the length of his amber beard.

Once in a while the thought reiterated[12] itself that it was very cold and that he had never experienced such cold. As he walked along he rubbed his cheekbones and nose with the back of his mittened hand. He did this automatically, now and again changing hands. But rub as he would, the instant he stopped his cheekbones went numb, and the following instant the end of his nose went numb. He was sure to frost his cheeks; he knew that, and experienced a pang of regret that he had not devised a nose strap of the sort Bud wore in cold snaps. Such a strap passed across the cheeks, as well, and saved them. But it didn't matter much, after all. What were frosted cheeks? A bit painful, that was all; they were never serious.

Empty as the man's mind was of thoughts, he was keenly observant, and he noticed the changes in the creek, the curves and bends and timber jams, and always he sharply noted where he placed his feet. Once, coming around the bend, he shied[13] abruptly, like a startled horse, curved away from the place where he

---

11. A *furrow* is a long, narrow groove or depression.
12. *Reiterated* means "repeated."
13. *Shied* means "moved suddenly, as in fear."

1 Cause and Effect *Why doesn't the man seek shelter and build a fire?*

had been walking, and retreated several paces back along the trail. The creek he knew was frozen clear to the bottom—no creek could contain water in that arctic winter—but he knew also that there were springs that bubbled out from the hillsides and ran along under the snow and on top the ice of the creek. He knew that the coldest snaps never froze these springs, and he knew likewise their danger. They were traps. They hid pools of water under the snow that might be three inches deep, or three feet. Sometimes a skin of ice half an inch thick covered them, and in turn was covered by the snow. Sometimes they were alternate layers of water and ice skin, so that when one broke through he kept on breaking through for a while, sometimes wetting himself to the waist.

That was why he had shied in such panic. He had felt the give under his feet and heard the crackle of a snow-hidden ice skin. And to get his feet wet in such a temperature meant trouble and danger. At the very least it meant delay, for he would be forced to stop and build a fire, and under its protection to bare his feet while he dried his socks and moccasins. He stood and studied the creek bed and its banks, and decided that the flow of water came from the right. He reflected awhile, rubbing his nose and cheeks, then skirted to the left, stepping gingerly and testing the footing for each step. Once clear of the danger, he took a fresh chew of tobacco and swung along at his four-mile gait. **2**

In the course of the next two hours he came upon similar traps. Usually the snow above the hidden pools had a sunken, candied appearance that advertised the danger. Once again, however, he had a close call; and once, suspecting danger, he **compelled** the dog to go on in front. The dog did not want to go. It hung back until the man shoved it forward, and then it went quickly across the white, unbroken surface. Suddenly it broke through, floundered to one side, and got away to firmer footing. It had

Vocabulary

compel (kəm pel′) *v.* to force

Vocabulary Practice

SPIRAL REVIEW **Adjectives** Tell students that good writers include vivid details to make their descriptions come to life. Adjectives make the text more immediate. Have students reread the paragraph beginning "In the course of the next two hours" and make a list of the adjectives that help the reader "see" the scene. *(Adjectives include* hidden, sunken, candied, white, unbroken, sore, mysterious, deep, astonished, *and* swift.) Then ask students to explain how each word appeals to readers' senses.

Glacier, 1964. Sir Sidney Nolan. Oil on board. Private collection.

View the Art As you look at this painting, jot down the first five words that come to mind. Which of these words seems most applicable to the story? Explain. ★

Setting Answer: *The man still does not have the proper respect for the environment. He is astonished, but he should not be surprised that nature has the upper hand.*

Naturalism Ask: What is the symbolic meaning of the fact that the man casts no shadow? (In this vast environment, the man has no importance; nature makes his shadow disappear.) Explain that the symbolism here might be even more important to a Naturalist writer than the scientific reason for the missing shadow.

View the Art ★

Answer: *Possible words include* majestic, serene, brilliant, vast, crisp. *The photograph is beautiful, but the story has a foreboding mood. In other words, there is a discrepancy between the image and what it signifies. Similarly, the man has not yet understood the seriousness of his situation.*

wet its forefeet and legs, and almost immediately the water that clung to it turned to ice. It made quick efforts to lick the ice off its legs, then dropped down in the snow and began to bite out the ice that had formed between the toes. This was a matter of instinct. To permit the ice to remain would mean sore feet. It did not know this. It merely obeyed the mysterious prompting that arose from the deep crypts[14] of its being. But the man knew, having achieved a judgment on the subject, and he removed the mitten from his right hand and helped tear out the ice particles. He did not expose his fingers more than a minute, and was astonished at the swift numbness that smote[15] them. It certainly was cold. He pulled on the mitten hastily, and beat the hand savagely across his chest.

14. Here, *crypts* means "hidden recesses."
15. *Smote* (past tense of smite) means "afflicted" or "attacked."

3 | **Setting** *What do these details suggest about the relationship of the man and the environment?*

At twelve o'clock the day was at its brightest. Yet the sun was too far south on its winter journey to clear the horizon. The bulge of the earth **intervened** between it and Henderson Creek, where the man walked under a clear sky at noon and cast no shadow. At half-past twelve, to the minute, he arrived at the forks of the creek. He was pleased at the speed he had made. If he kept it up, he would certainly be with the boys by six. He unbuttoned his jacket and shirt and drew forth his lunch. The action consumed no more than a quarter of a minute, yet in that brief moment the numbness laid hold of the exposed fingers. He did not put the mitten on, but, instead, struck the fingers a dozen sharp smashes against his leg. Then he sat down on a snow-covered log to eat. The sting that followed upon the striking of his fingers against his leg ceased so quickly that he was startled. He had

4

Vocabulary

intervene (in´ tər vēn´) *v.* to come or lie between

Naturalism Challenge advanced students to analyze this story in its larger literary context. Explain that London was a Naturalist, a follower of a movement that began in France during the nineteenth century. Have students read about the ideas of the Naturalists in references such as the *Oxford Companion to American Literature* and online. Then have students write essays connecting this story to the literary trends of the time, paying particular attention to the role nature plays in the man's life and death.

Teach

had no chance to take a bite of biscuit. He struck the fingers repeatedly and returned them to the mitten, baring the other hand for the purpose of eating. He tried to take a mouthful, but the ice muzzle prevented. He had forgotten to build a fire and thaw out. He chuckled at his foolishness, and as he chuckled he noted the numbness creeping into his exposed fingers. Also, he noted that the stinging which had first come to his toes when he sat down was already passing away. He wondered whether the toes were warm or numb. He moved them inside the moccasins and decided that they were numb.

He pulled the mitten on hurriedly and stood up. He was a bit frightened. He stamped up and down until the sting returned into the feet. It certainly was cold, was his thought. That man from Sulphur Creek had spoken the truth when telling how cold it sometimes got in the country. And he had laughed at him at the time! That showed one must not be too sure of things. There was no mistake about it, it *was* cold. He strode up and down, stamping his feet and threshing his arms, until reassured by the returning warmth. Then he got out matches and proceeded to make a fire. From the undergrowth, where high water of the previous spring had lodged a supply of seasoned twigs, he got his firewood. Working carefully from a small beginning, he soon had a roaring fire, over which he thawed the ice from his face and in the protection of which he ate his biscuits. For the moment the cold of space was outwitted. The dog took satisfaction in the fire, stretching out close enough for warmth and far enough away to escape being singed. **1**

When the man had finished, he filled his pipe and took his comfortable time over a smoke. Then he pulled on his mittens, settled the earflaps of his cap firmly about his ears, and took the creek trail up the left fork. The dog was disappointed and yearned back toward the fire. This man did not know cold. Possibly all the genera-

tions of his ancestry had been ignorant of cold, of real cold, of cold one hundred and seven degrees below freezing point. But the dog knew; all its ancestry knew, and it had inherited the knowledge. And it knew that it was not good to walk abroad in such fearful cold. It was the time to lie snug in a hole in the snow and wait for a curtain of cloud to be drawn across the face of outer space whence this cold came. On the other hand, there was no keen intimacy between the dog and the man. The one was the toil slave of the other, and the only caresses it had ever received were the caresses of the whiplash and of harsh and menacing throat sounds that threatened the whiplash. So the dog made no effort to communicate its apprehension to the man. It was not concerned in the welfare of the man; it was for its own sake that it yearned back toward the fire. But the man whistled, and spoke to it with the sound of whiplashes, and the dog swung in at the man's heels and followed after.

The man took a chew of tobacco and proceeded to start a new amber beard. Also, his moist breath quickly powdered with white his mustache, eyebrows, and lashes. There did not seem to be so many springs on the left fork of the Henderson, and for half an hour the man saw no signs of any. And then it happened. At a place where there were no signs, where the soft, unbroken snow seemed to advertise solidity beneath, the man broke through. It was not deep. He wet himself to the knees before he floundered out to the firm crust. **3**

He was angry, and cursed his luck aloud. He had hoped to get into camp with the boys at six o'clock, and this would delay him an hour, for he would have to build a fire and dry out his foot gear. This was imperative[16] at that low temperature—he knew that much; and he turned aside to the bank, which he climbed. On top, tangled in the underbrush about the trunks of several small spruce trees, was a high-water deposit of dry fire-

---

16. *Imperative* means "absolutely necessary."

2 Cause and Effect *Why does the man suddenly recall the man from Sulphur Creek?*

Naturalism *What view of nature is suggested by this passage?* **4**

Assessment Practice

wood—sticks and twigs, principally, but also larger portions of seasoned branches and fine, dry, last-year's grasses. He threw down several large pieces on top of the snow. This served for a foundation and prevented the young flame from drowning itself in the snow it otherwise would melt. The flame he got by touching a match to a small shred of birch bark that he took from his pocket. This burned even more readily than paper. Placing it on the foundation, he fed the young flame with wisps of dry grass and with the tiniest dry twigs.

He worked slowly and carefully, keenly aware of his danger. Gradually, as the flame grew stronger, he increased the size of the twigs with which he fed it. He squatted in the snow, pulling the twigs out from their entanglement in the brush and feeding directly to the flame. He knew there must be no failure. When it is seventy-five below zero, a man must not fail in his first attempt to build a fire—that is, if his feet are wet. If his feet are dry, and he fails, he can run along the trail for half a mile and restore his circulation. But the circulation of wet and freezing feet cannot be restored by running when it is seventy-five below. No matter how fast he runs, the wet feet will freeze the harder.

All this the man knew. The old-timer on Sulphur Creek had told him about it the previous fall, and now he was appreciating the advice. Already all sensation had gone out of his feet. To build the fire he had been forced to remove his mittens, and the fingers had quickly gone numb. His pace of four miles an hour had kept his heart pumping blood to the surface of his body and to all the extremities. But the instant he stopped, the action of the pump eased down. The cold of space smote the unprotected tip of the planet, and he, being on that unprotected tip, received the full force of the blow. The blood of his body recoiled before it. The blood was alive, like the dog, and like the dog it wanted to hide away and cover itself up from the fearful cold. So long as he walked four miles an hour, he pumped that blood, willy-nilly,[17] to the surface; but now it ebbed[18]

---

17. *Willy-nilly* means "without choice."
18. *Ebbed* means "flowed back" or "receded."

away and sank down into the recesses of his body. The extremities were the first to feel its absence. His wet feet froze the faster, and his exposed fingers numbed the faster, though they had not yet begun to freeze. Nose and cheeks were already freezing, while the skin of all his body chilled as it lost its blood.

But he was safe. Toes and nose and cheeks would be only touched by the frost, for the fire was beginning to burn with strength. He was feeding it with twigs the size of his finger. In another minute he would be able to feed it with branches the size of his wrist, and then he could remove his wet foot gear, and, while it dried, he could keep his naked feet warm by the fire, rubbing them at first, of course, with snow. The fire was a success. He was safe. He remembered the advice of the old-timer on Sulphur Creek, and smiled. The old-timer had been very serious in laying down the law that no man must travel alone in the Klondike after fifty below. Well, here he was; he had had the accident; he was alone; and he had saved himself. Those old-timers were rather womanish, some of them, he thought. All a man had to do was to keep his head, and he was all right. Any man who was a man could travel alone. But it was surprising, the rapidity with which his cheeks and nose were freezing. And he had not thought his fingers could go lifeless in so short a time. Lifeless they were, for he could scarcely make them move together to grip a twig, and they seemed remote from his body and from him. When he touched a twig, he had to look and see whether or not he had hold of it. The wires were pretty well down between him and his finger-ends.

All of which counted for little. There was the fire, snapping and crackling and promising life with every dancing flame. He started to untie his moccasins. They were coated with ice; the thick German socks were like sheaths of iron halfway to the knees; and the moccasin strings were like rods of steel all twisted and knotted as by some conflagration. For a moment he tugged with his numb fingers, then, realizing the folly of it, he drew his sheath-knife.

But before he could cut the strings, it happened. It was his own fault or, rather, his mis-

Big Idea 4

Naturalism Answer: *The man is caught in one of nature's traps. Nature is indifferent and does not regard him as a special creature.*

Reading Strategy 5

Draw Conclusions Ask: What conclusions can you draw about the man, based on his comment about the old-timer from Sulphur Creek? *(He lives only in the moment; he is arrogant.)*

Literary Element 6

Simile Remind students that a simile is a comparison between two unlike things that contains the word *like* or *as*. Ask students to identify the similes in this passage and tell why the author includes them. *(London compares the man's socks to "sheaths of iron" and his moccasin strings to "rods of steel." These similes emphasize the difficulties the man encounters in trying to remove his socks and shoes.)*

English Learners

UNIVERSAL ACCESS

Intermediate Help English learners clarify the following expressions on this page and the next:

- "old-timer" *(old man or someone out of touch with the present times)*
- "keep his head" *(stay calm and think clearly)*
- "the fire . . . promising life" *(the fire gives the man hope)*

- "each bough was fully freighted" *(each tree branch had a full load or burden)*
- "sentence of death" *(death sentence, handed down by a court as a punishment for a crime. In this case, the man realizes he is going to die.)*

Teach

Reading Strategy | 1

Cause and Effect Answer:
The man's lack of imagination and pursuit of his own comfort finally catch up with him. He should have thought about the consequences of building a fire under a tree rather than out in the open.

take. He should not have built the fire under the spruce tree. He should have built it in the open. But it had been easier to pull twigs from the brush and drop them directly on the fire. Now the tree under which he had done this carried a weight of snow on its boughs. No wind had blown for weeks, and each bough was fully freighted. Each time he had pulled a twig he had communicated a slight agitation to the tree—an imperceptible agitation, so far as he was concerned, but an agitation sufficient to bring about the disaster. High up in the tree one bough capsized its load of snow. This fell on the boughs beneath, capsizing them. This process continued, spreading out and involving the whole tree. It grew like an avalanche, and it descended without warning upon the man and the fire, and the fire was blotted out! Where it had burned was a mantle of fresh and disordered snow.

There was the fire, snapping and crackling and promising life with every dancing flame.

The man was shocked. It was as though he had just heard his own sentence of death. For a moment he sat and stared at the spot where the fire had been. Then he grew very calm. Perhaps the old-timer on Sulphur Creek was right. If he had only had a trail mate he would have been in no danger now. The trail mate could have built the fire. Well, it was up to him to build the fire over again, and this second time there must be no failure. Even if he succeeded, he would most likely lose some toes. His feet must be badly frozen by now, and there would be some time before the second fire was ready.

Such were his thoughts, but he did not sit and think them. He was busy all the time they were passing through his mind. He made a new foundation for a fire, this time in the open, where no treacherous tree could blot it out. Next, he gathered dry grasses and tiny twigs from the high-water flotsam.[19] He could not bring his fingers together to pull them out, but he was able to gather them by the handful. In this way he got many rotten twigs and bits of green moss that were undesirable, but it was the best he could do. He worked methodically, even collecting an armful of the larger branches to be used later when the fire gathered strength. And all the while the dog sat and watched him, a certain yearning wistfulness[20] in its eyes, for it looked upon him as the fire provider, and the fire was slow in coming.

When all was ready, the man reached in his pocket for a second piece of birch bark. He knew the bark was there, and, though he could not feel it with his fingers, he could hear its crisp rustling as he fumbled for it. Try as he would, he could not clutch hold of it. And all the time, in his consciousness, was the knowledge that each instant his feet were freezing. This thought tended to put him in a panic, but he fought against it and kept calm. He pulled on his mittens with his teeth, and threshed his arms back and forth, beating his hands with all his might against his sides. He did this sitting down, and he stood up to do it; and all the while the dog sat in the snow, its wolf brush of a tail curled around warmly over its forefeet, its sharp wolf ears pricked forward intently as it watched the man. And the man, as he beat and threshed with his arms and hands, felt a great surge of envy as he regarded

---

1 Cause and Effect *Why does the man make a crucial mistake when his life is on the line?*

19. *Flotsam* (flot' səm) is floating debris, here left behind by a river or stream in the spring when the water rises with the runoff from melting snow and ice.
20. *Wistfulness* means "thoughtful sadness."

Writing Practice

Cause and Effect Remind students that when they read, they should look for signal words to identify relationships in text. Tell them that when they write, they should provide those signal words to show relationships among their ideas. List the following words and phrases on the board:

because	so
because of	so that
as a result	consequently
in order to	therefore

Tell students that these words often signal a cause and effect relationship.

Have students write three or four sentences explaining causes and effects in this story and using words that signal the cause or effect.

the creature that was warm and secure in its natural covering.

After a time he was aware of the first faraway signals of sensation in his beaten fingers. The faint tingling grew stronger till it evolved into a stinging ache that was excruciating, but which the man hailed with satisfaction. He stripped the mitten from his right hand and fetched forth the birch bark. The exposed fingers were quickly going numb again. Next he brought out his bunch of sulphur matches. But the tremendous cold had already driven the life out of his fingers. In his effort to separate one match from the others, the whole bunch fell in the snow. He tried to pick it out of the snow, but failed. The dead fingers could neither touch nor clutch. He was very careful. He drove the thought of his freezing feet, and nose, and cheeks, out of his mind, devoting his whole soul to the matches. He watched, using the sense of vision in place of that of touch, and when he saw his fingers on each side of the bunch, he closed them—that is, he willed to close them, for the wires were down, and the fingers did not obey. He pulled the mitten on the right hand, and beat it fiercely against his knee. Then, with both mittened hands, he scooped the bunch of matches, along with much snow, into his lap. Yet he was no better off.

After some manipulation he managed to get the bunch between the heels of his mittened hands. In this fashion he carried it to his mouth. The ice crackled and snapped when by a violent effort he opened his mouth. He drew the lower jaw in, curled the upper lip out of the way, and scraped the bunch with his upper teeth in order to separate a match. He succeeded in getting one, which he dropped on his lap. He was no better off. He could not pick it up. Then he devised a way. He picked it up in his teeth and scratched it on his leg. Twenty

times he scratched before he succeeded in lighting it. As it flamed he held it with his teeth to the birch bark. But the burning brimstone[21] went up his nostrils and into his lungs, causing him to cough spasmodically.[22] The match fell into the snow and went out.

The old-timer on Sulphur Creek was right, he thought in the moment of controlled despair that ensued;[23] after fifty below, a man should travel with a partner. He beat his hands, but failed in exciting any sensation. Suddenly he bared both hands, removing his mittens with his teeth. He caught the whole bunch between the heels of his hands. His arm muscles not being frozen enabled him to press the hand heels tightly against the matches. Then he scratched the bunch along his leg. It flared into flame, seventy sulphur matches at once! There was no wind to blow them out. He kept his head to one side to escape the strangling fumes, and held the blazing bunch to the birch bark. As he so held it, he became aware of sensation in his hand. His flesh was burning. He could smell it. Deep down below the surface he could feel it. The sensation developed into pain that grew acute. And still he endured it, holding the flame of the matches clumsily to the bark that would not light readily because his own burning hands were in the way, absorbing most of the flame.

At last, when he could endure no more, he jerked his hands apart. The blazing matches fell sizzling into the snow, but the birch bark was alight. He began laying dry grasses and the tiniest twigs on the flame. He could not pick and choose, for he had to lift the fuel between the heels of his hands. Small pieces of rotten wood and green moss clung to the twigs, and he bit them off as well as he could with his teeth. He cherished the flame carefully and awkwardly. It

---

21. **Brimstone** is sulfur.
22. **Spasmodically** means "in a sudden, violent manner" or "convulsively."
23. **Ensued** means "happened afterward" or "followed."

2 **Naturalism** *Why is the dog better adapted to survive in this environment? Explain.*

3 **Naturalism** *Why does the author use the phrase* **the wires were down?**

Cause and Effect *What will be the likely consequences of the man's failure to build a fire a second time?* **4**

JACK LONDON **611**

Big Idea | 2

Naturalism Answer: *The dog is better adapted to survive because its fur protects it from the cold and its instincts guide its actions.*

Big Idea | 3

Naturalism Answer: *The phrase equates the man's body to an electrical system that has broken down as a result of the extreme weather.*

Reading Strategy | 4

Cause and Effect Answer: *The man cannot make a third attempt because he has no more matches and has lost control of his hands. He will not be able to thaw out his wet and frozen feet and is likely to freeze to death in the wilderness.*

ENGLISH LEARNERS Ensure that English learners know the meaning of *consequences*. Clarify that the man's failure to build a fire is a cause, and the consequence is the effect, or what will happen as a result.

Approaching Level

UNIVERSAL ACCESS

Emerging Remind students that conflict in a story is the struggle between opposing forces. Conflict can be either external—such as a character struggling against another character or against nature—or internal—a character struggling against something within himself or herself. Tell them that this story contains both external and internal conflicts. **Ask:** What is the external conflict the man is involved in? *(He is struggling against the environment to stay alive.)* What is his internal conflict? *(He is struggling to stay calm, focused, and in control.)*

611

Teach

Vocabulary   1

Word Parts **Ask:** What is the root of the word *apathetically,* and what does it mean? *(The root is path, meaning "emotion.")* What does the prefix *a-* generally mean? *(not)* What does the *-ly* ending mean? *(that the word is an adverb)* Have students put the word parts together to come up with a meaning for *apathetically.* *("in a manner that shows no emotion")*

Reading Strategy   2

Analyze Conflict By this point, students should be fully aware of the external conflict that London has created. **Say:** Describe the second conflict going on. It is an internal conflict. *(Students should observe the man's difficulty in staying calm as he realizes what is happening to him.)* **Ask:** Is one conflict more significant to London? Explain. *(Some students will say that London is more interested in the man's internal conflict.)*

Literary Element   3

Setting **Answer:** *The fire represents life, so the setting must represent death.*

---

meant life, and it must not perish. The withdrawal of blood from the surface of his body now made him begin to shiver, and he grew more awkward. A large piece of green moss fell squarely on the little fire. He tried to poke it out with his fingers, but his shivering frame made him poke too far, and he disrupted the nucleus of the little fire, the burning grasses and tiny twigs separating and scattering. He tried to poke them together again, but in spite of the tenseness of the effort, his shivering got away with him, and the twigs were hopelessly scattered. Each twig gushed a puff of smoke and went out. The fire provider had failed. As he looked **apathetically** about

1 him, his eyes chanced on the dog, sitting across the ruins of the fire from him, in the snow, making restless, hunching movements, slightly lifting one forefoot and then the other, shifting its weight back and forth on them with wistful eagerness.

The sight of the dog put a wild idea into his head. He remembered the tale of the man, caught in a blizzard, who killed a steer and crawled inside the carcass, and so was saved. He would kill the dog and bury his hands in the warm body until the numbness went out of them. Then he could build another fire. He spoke to the dog, calling it to him; but in his voice was a strange note of fear that frightened

2 the animal, who had never known the man to speak in such way before. Something was the matter, and its suspicious nature sensed danger—it knew not what danger, but somewhere, somehow, in its brain arose an apprehension of the man. It flattened its ears down at the sound of the man's voice, and its restless, hunching movements and the liftings and shiftings of its

Wolves hunting an explorer, c. 1900. H. Morgal. Watercolour and pencil. Private collection.

---

forefeet became more pronounced; but it would not come to the man. He got on his hands and knees and crawled toward the dog. This unusual posture again excited suspicion, and the animal sidled mincingly[24] away.

The man sat up in the snow for a moment and struggled for calmness. Then he pulled on his mittens, by means of his teeth, and got upon his feet. He glanced down at first in order to assure himself that he was really standing up, for the absence of sensation in his feet left him unrelated to the earth. His erect position in itself started to drive the webs of suspicion from the dog's mind; and when he spoke peremptorily,[25] with the sound of whiplashes in his voice, the dog rendered its customary allegiance and came to him. As it came within reaching distance, the man lost his control. His arms flashed out to the dog, and he experienced genuine surprise when he discovered that his hands could not clutch, that there was neither bend nor feeling in the fingers. He had forgotten for the moment that they were frozen and that they were freezing more and more. All this happened

---

3   Setting *What does this detail tell you about the setting?*

Vocabulary

apathetically (ap´ ə thet´ i kal ē) *adv.* in a manner showing little interest or concern

---

24. *Sidled mincingly* means "moved sideways in a careful manner."
25. *Peremptorily* (pə remp´ tə rə lē) means "authoritatively" or "dictatorially."

Skills Practice

⚡ WRITING: Narrative Account

Have students imagine that they are one of the miners in the camp where the man in this story was heading. Eventually this miner is out in the woods and comes across the man's body. Have students write the first-person account that the finder tells others when he returns to camp. Students should include not only what he sees but his conclusions about what happened based on the evidence nearby.

quickly, and before the animal could get away, he encircled its body with his arms. He sat down in the snow, and in this fashion held the dog, while it snarled and whined and struggled.

But it was all he could do, hold its body encircled in his arms and sit there. He realized that he could not kill the dog. There was no way to do it. With his helpless hands he could neither draw nor hold his sheath knife nor throttle the animal. He released it, and it plunged wildly away, with tail between its legs, and still snarling. It halted forty feet away and surveyed him cautiously, with ears sharply pricked forward. The man looked down at his hands in order to locate them, and found them hanging on the ends of his arms. It struck him as ☆ curious that one should have to use his eyes in order to find out where his hands were. He began threshing his arms back and forth, beating the mittened hands against his sides. He did this for five minutes, violently, and his heart pumped enough blood up to the surface to put a stop to his shivering. But no sensation was aroused in the hands. He had an impression that they hung like weights on the ends of his arms, but when he tried to run the impression down, he could not find it.

A certain fear of death, dull and oppressive, came to him. This fear quickly became poignant[26] as he realized that it was no longer a mere matter of freezing his fingers and toes, or of losing his hands and feet, but that it was a matter of life and death with the chances against him. This threw him into a panic, and he turned and ran up the creek bed along the old, dim trail. The dog joined in behind and kept up with him. He ran blindly, without intention, in fear such as he had never known in his life. Slowly, as he ploughed and floundered through the snow, he began to see things again—the banks of the creek, the old timber

---

26. *Poignant* (poin´ yənt) means "sharply felt" or "intensely distressing."

4 Cause and Effect *Why does the man forget that his hands are frozen?*

jams, the leafless aspens, and the sky. The running made him feel better. He did not shiver. Maybe, if he ran on, his feet would thaw out; and, anyway, if he ran far enough, he would reach camp and the boys. Without doubt he would lose some fingers and toes and some of his face; but the boys would take care of him, and save the rest of him when he got there. And at the same time there was another thought in his mind that said he would never get to the camp and the boys; that it was too many miles away, that the freezing had too great a start on him, and that he would soon be stiff and dead. This thought he kept in the background and refused to consider. Sometimes it pushed itself forward and demanded to be heard, but he thrust it back and strove to think of other things.

It struck him as curious that he could run at all on feet so frozen that he could not feel them when they struck the earth and took the weight of his body. He seemed to himself to skim along above the surface, and to have no connection with the earth.

Somewhere he had once seen a winged Mercury, and he wondered if Mercury felt as he felt when skimming over the earth.

His theory of running until he reached camp and the boys had one flaw in it: he lacked the endurance. Several times he stumbled, and finally he tottered, crumpled up, and fell. When he tried to rise, he failed. He must sit and rest, he decided, and next time he would merely walk and keep on going. As he sat and regained his breath, he noted that he was feeling quite warm and comfortable. He was not shiver-

Visual Vocabulary
In Roman mythology, *Mercury* is the messenger of the gods. He is portrayed wearing a winged hat and winged sandals.

Cause and Effect *Why does the man try to repress thoughts of his impending death?* **5**

JACK LONDON **613**

Reading Strategy 4

Cause and Effect **Answer:**
The man no longer feels any sensation in his hands.

Reading Strategy 5

Cause and Effect **Answer:**
The man is afraid that such thoughts will make him panic. Even with death near, he refuses to think of his fate and recognize the power of nature.

Language History ☆

Hypothermia The character in this story is experiencing hypothermia, a condition of dangerously low body temperature. Explain that the word comes from *hypo-*, meaning "below," and *therme*, meaning "heat." The man's extreme shivering, the numbness in his hands and feet, and his inability to use his muscles properly are symptoms. As he continues to chill, he will become confused, and before long his organs will fail, resulting in his death.

Approaching Level

UNIVERSAL ACCESS

Established To reinforce the concept of cause and effect, present the following example: Judy was late to school because she overslept. She overslept because she stayed up late the night before reading a good book. **Ask:** What happened first? *(Judy read a good book.)* **Say:** Judy's reading a book is a cause. What did it cause to happen? *(Judy went to bed late.)* **Say:** Going to bed late was the

effect of her reading. It was also a cause. What did it cause? *(Judy overslept.)* What was the final effect? *(She was late for school.)*

Teach

Big Idea   1

Naturalism **Answer:** *The man's ability to cope with the cold is decreasing. He now feels he has lost control over his condition.*

Literary Element   2

Setting **Answer:** *There is no mourning for the man's death. On the contrary, it is as if nature is celebrating a victory.*

(ADVANCED) Ask advanced students to explain the irony in this description. *(Leaping and dancing are activities associated with life, not with death.)*

 To check students' understanding of the selection, see Unit 4 Teaching Resources Book, p.170.

Progress Check

Can students analyze setting?

If No → See Unit 4 Teaching Resources Book, p. 165.

---

ing, and it even seemed that a warm glow had come to his chest and trunk. And yet, when he touched his nose or cheeks, there was no sensation. Running would not thaw them out. Nor would it thaw out his hands and feet. Then the thought came to him that the frozen portions of his body must be extending. He tried to keep this thought down, to forget it, to think of something else; he was aware of the panicky feeling that it caused, and he was afraid of the panic. But the thought asserted itself, and persisted, until it produced a vision of his body totally frozen. This was too much, and he made another wild run along the trail. Once he slowed down to a walk, but the thought of the freezing extending itself made him run again.

And all the time the dog ran with him, at his heels. When he fell down a second time, it curled its tail over its forefeet and sat in front of him, facing him, curiously eager and intent. The warmth and security of the animal angered him, and he cursed it till it flattened down its ears appeasingly. This time the shivering came more quickly upon the man. He was losing in his battle with the frost. It was creeping into his body from all sides. The thought of it drove him on, but he ran no more than a hundred feet, when he staggered and pitched headlong. It was his last panic. When he had recovered his breath and control, he sat up and entertained in his mind the conception of meeting death with dignity. However, the conception did not come to him in such terms. His idea of it was that he had been making a fool of himself, running around like a chicken with its head cut off—such was the simile that occurred to him. Well, he was bound to freeze anyway, and he might as well take it decently. With this newfound peace of mind came the first glimmerings of drowsiness. A good idea, he thought, to sleep off to death. It was like taking an anaesthetic.[27] Freezing was not so bad as people thought. There were lots worse ways to die.

He pictured the boys finding his body next day. Suddenly he found himself with them,

coming along the trail and looking for himself. And, still with them, he came around a turn in the trail and found himself lying in the snow. He did not belong with himself any more, for even then he was out of himself, standing with the boys and looking at himself in the snow. It certainly was cold, was his thought. When he got back to the States he could tell the folks what real cold was. He drifted on from this to a vision of the old-timer on Sulphur Creek. He could see him quite clearly, warm and comfortable, and smoking a pipe.

"You were right, old hoss; you were right," the man mumbled to the old-timer on Sulphur Creek.

Then the man drowsed off into what seemed to him the most comfortable and satisfying sleep he had ever known. The dog sat facing him and waiting. The brief day drew to a close in a long, slow twilight. There were no signs of a fire to be made, and, besides, never in the dog's experience had it known a man to sit like that in the snow and make no fire. As the twilight drew on, its eager yearning for the fire mastered it, and with a great lifting and shifting of its forefeet, it whined softly, then flattened its ears down in anticipation of being chidden[28] by the man. But the man remained silent. Later, the dog whined loudly. And still later it crept close to the man and caught the scent of death. This made the animal bristle and back away. A little longer it delayed, howling under the stars that leaped and danced and shone brightly in the cold sky. Then it turned and trotted up the trail in the direction of the camp it knew, where were the other food providers and fire providers. ✖

---

27. An *anaesthetic* is something that produces a loss of sensation.
28. *Chidden* (past participle of *chide*) means "scolded."

1 **Naturalism** *What do these thoughts tell us about the man as he faces this hostile environment?*

Setting *Why does the author describe the stars as leaping and dancing?* **2**

Writing Practice

SPIRAL REVIEW **Avoid Clichés** Point out the simile "running around like a chicken with its head cut off." Ask students to explain the image. Then explain to them that this simile is a cliché, an overused and unoriginal expression. Ask them for other examples of clichés that they know, either in English or in their native languages. Tell them that it is best to avoid clichés in writing. Point out that London is not suggesting that a cliché is acceptable in a literary story; he is putting the cliché into his character's thoughts. His character, as he has already demonstrated, lacks imagination.

After You Read

Respond and Think Critically

Respond and Interpret

1. Which images from the story do you find the most vivid and memorable?

2. (a)Where is the man going and what is his attitude toward his journey? (b)What can you infer about the man's personality and character based on the first five paragraphs?

3. (a)Describe how the man's dog behaves. (b)What event does the dog's behavior foreshadow?

4. (a)What mishap occurs shortly after the man eats lunch and resumes his journey? (b)What external and internal forces must the man struggle against?

5. (a)What happens to the man and his dog at the end of the story? (b)What lesson or lessons might be learned from reading this story?

Analyze and Evaluate

6. How are the events of the story reflected in the change of mood as the story develops?

7. (a)What contrasting qualities do the dog and the man have? (b)What does the ending suggest about London's view of these qualities in relation to survival in the natural world?

Connect

8. **Big Idea** Naturalism (a)What elements of Naturalism does the story contain? (b)How might the story have been different if it had been written by a Romantic writer?

9. **Connect to Today** In an age of computers, cellular phones, and GPS devices, do you think the theme of man battling against nature is still relevant? Explain.

Literary Element Setting

"To Build a Fire" is set in a specific historical time and place. The setting of London's story is well-defined and essential; without the **setting**, this particular story could not have been written.

1. (a)How does the setting of the story establish the central conflict? (b)How does it influence the resolution, or final outcome, of this conflict?

2. How does London reveal the man's character through his interactions with the physical environment? Give specific examples.

3. How would you describe the relationship between humans and the environment in this story?

Review: Suspense

Suspense is a feeling of curiosity, anticipation, or even dread about what is going to happen next. Writers can increase suspense by creating a threat to the central character, or **protagonist**, and by giving readers clues as to what might happen.

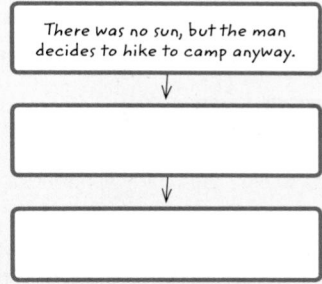

> There was no sun, but the man decides to hike to camp anyway.

Group Activity With a small group of classmates, discuss how each event in "To Build a Fire" builds suspense, ultimately leading to the final scene. Create a flow chart like the one started below.

After You Read

Assess

1. Burning hands, imposing setting

2. (a) He is going to Henderson Creek and feels no danger. (b) He is arrogant and does not prepare well.

3. (a) The dog fears the man, whom he associates with whippings, and wants to dig in, knowing that the temperature is too low for traveling. (b) The man's death is foreshadowed.

4. (a) The man accidentally gets his feet wet. (b) He fights nature and his fear.

5. (a) The man dies; the dog heads toward camp. (b) One must listen to experts and prepare; instincts are survival tools.

6. The changing mood reflects the man's increasing desperation.

7. (a) The man ignores common sense and dies; the dog follows instinct and survives. (b) Instinct prevails over flawed reason.

8. (a) The man struggles against forces that are beyond his control; the tone lacks sentiment. (b) A Romantic writer might have portrayed nature as vengeful rather than indifferent.

9. Most students will probably agree that nature is still a force greater than man. They may mention events such as hurricanes, tsunamis, earthquakes, or other natural disasters.

 For additional assessment, see Assessment Resources, pp. 183–184.

Literary Element

1. (a) The frigid snowy environment is the man's major antagonist. (b) Environmental factors prevent the man from building a life-saving fire.

2. The man lacks respect for the cold; he builds his fire too close to a tree.

3. Humans are victims, not masters, of the environment.

Review: Suspense

Possible answer: The man breaks through the ice and gets his feet wet; the man builds a fire that is extinguished by snow that falls from a tree.

Allow students to include more than three entries in their charts.

After You Read

Assess

Reading Strategy

1. **D** is the correct answer because having another person with him would have enabled the man to avoid or make up for his other mistakes.

Vocabulary

- **intangible:** not easily defined or evaluated by the mind (from Latin *tangibilis,* meaning "that may be touched"); Some people do not believe in *intangible* things that they cannot observe with their five senses.
- **immortality:** the condition of having eternal life (from Latin *mort,* meaning "death"); In some tales, the characters' wish for *immortality* backfires as their loved ones die.
- **compel:** to force (from Latin *pellere,* meaning "to drive"); The defense argued that police *compelled* the defendant to falsely confess.
- **intervene:** to come or lie between (from Latin *venire,* meaning "to come"); School security had to *intervene* when a fight broke out in the hallway.
- **apathetically:** in a manner showing little interest or concern (from Latin *pathein,* meaning "to suffer"); We knew the play was a flop when the audience responded *apathetically.*

Reading Strategy Analyze Cause-and-Effect Relationships

ACT Skills Practice

1. What was the greatest mistake made by the man in the story?
   - **A.** Not having an imagination
   - **B.** Not bringing water with him
   - **C.** Getting his feet wet
   - **D.** Traveling alone

Vocabulary Practice

Practice with Word Origins Studying the origins of a word can help you understand and explore its meaning. Create a word map, like the one below, for each of these vocabulary words from the selection. Use a dictionary for help.

intangible   immortality   compel
intervene   apathetically

EXAMPLE:

Definition: to mislead; to lead astray by underhandedness

Etymology: Latin *decipere* means "to ensnare"

deceive

Sample sentence: He deceived his teacher by forging a note from his mother.

Academic Vocabulary

*In order to survive, the man in "To Build a Fire" relies **solely** on his ability to make fire.*

Solely is an academic word. Using context clues, try to figure out the meaning of *solely* in the sentence above. Check your inference in a print or online dictionary.

For more on academic vocabulary, see pages 53–54.

616 UNIT 4 REGIONALISM AND REALISM

Write with Style

 Apply Imagery

Assignment Setting is an integral part of this story. Think of a place that is special to you and, with London's work as an example, write a descriptive essay about that place.

Get Ideas Gather information about your place: review journal entries, look at photo albums, or jot down ideas about when and why you go there. If you can, visit the setting and note specific details you observe. Then make a graphic organizer like the one started below. At the center, write the name of your setting. Around the central circle, write several elements of your setting. Extending from each element, list specific sensory details.

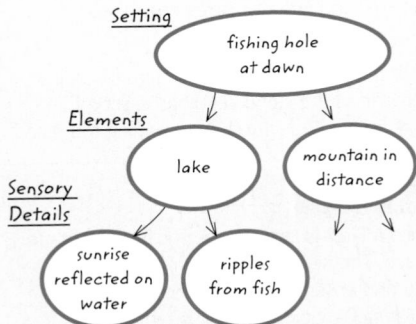

Give It Structure Consider the different ways you could structure your essay, such as spatially, chronologically, or in order of importance. Put a number next to each element in your chart indicating the order in which you will include it in your essay. Use your graphic organizer to help you write your draft.

Look at Language After you finish writing, reread your essay and evaluate your word choice. Make sure your words reflect the mood of your setting and the impression you want to create.

LOG ON ▶ **Literature** Online

Selection Resources For Selection Quizzes, eFlashcards, and Reading-Writing Connection activities, go to glencoe.com and enter QuickPass code GLA9800u4.

Academic Vocabulary

The man must rely only on his ability because he is alone in the wilderness; this implies that *solely* means "exclusively."

 For grammar practice, see Unit 4 Teaching Resources Book, p. 169.

Writing

Use these criteria when evaluating students' writing:

- Does the writer use specific sensory details to describe the setting?
- Does the writer's word choice create an appropriate mood for the setting?
- Does the writer give a full sensory picture of the setting?

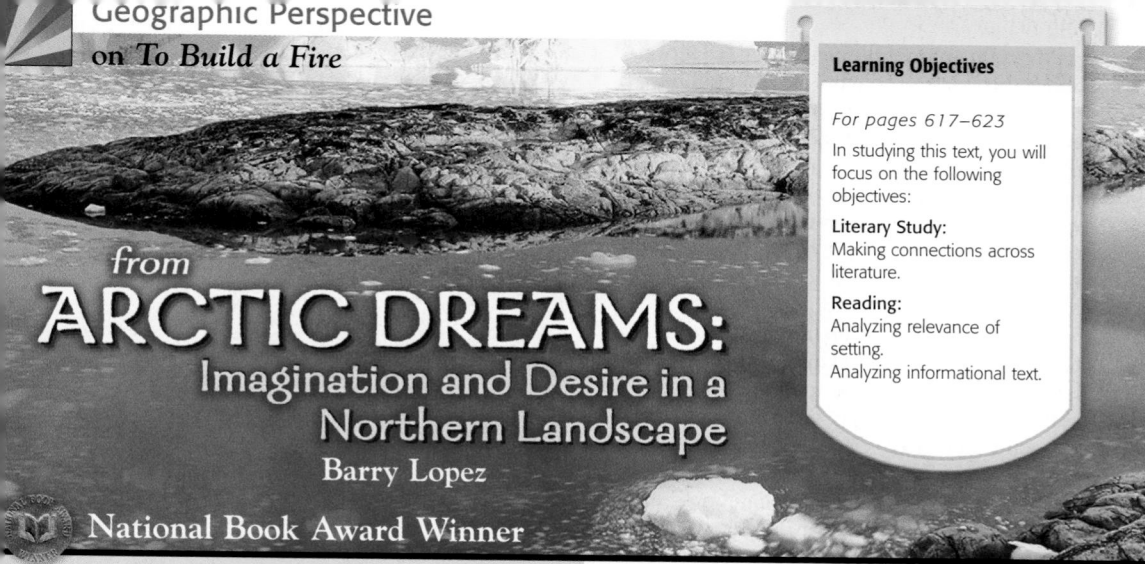

from

ARCTIC DREAMS:
Imagination and Desire in a Northern Landscape
Barry Lopez

National Book Award Winner

Set a Purpose for Reading

As you read, ask yourself, What might compel a person to venture into the Arctic? How do people survive the harsh conditions there?

Build Background

Writer and photographer Barry Lopez finds many of the subjects for his writing in nature and the environment. He is often drawn to extreme locales, describing his own experiences in those harsh regions. In the following passage from *Arctic Dreams*, Lopez describes his experiences working with scientists in the Arctic Ocean.

Reading Strategy

1 **Analyze Relevance of Setting**

Analyzing the **relevance of setting** involves gathering information about the importance of time and place in a literary work. Remember that setting is not limited to the characters' physical surroundings. As you read, take notes about the setting of both *Arctic Dreams* and "To Build a Fire." Use a two-column chart like the one below.

Setting of "To Build a Fire"	Setting of *Arctic Dreams*

 e left our camp on Pingok Island[1] one morning knowing a storm was moving in from the southwest, but we were not worried. We were planning to work in open water between the beach and the edge of the pack ice,[2] only a few miles out, making bottom trawls[3] from an open 20-foot boat. The four of us were dressed, as usual, in heavy clothes and foul-weather gear.

You accept the possibility of death in such situations, prepare for it, and then forget about it. We carried emergency and survival equipment in addition to all our scientific gear—signal flares, survival suits, a tent, and each of us had a pack with extra clothing, a sleeping bag, and a week's worth of food. Each morning we completed a checklist of the boat and radioed a distant base camp with our day plan. When we departed, we left a handwritten note on the table in our cabin, saying what time we left, the compass bearing we were taking, and when we expected to return.

---

1. *Pingok Island* lies in the Beaufort Sea, which is a part of the Arctic Ocean.
2. *Pack ice* is ice formed in the sea from the crashing together of floes and other ice masses.
3. *Trawls* are large nets that are dragged along the bottom of a body of water to gather marine life.

BARRY LOPEZ **617**

Learning Objectives

For pages 617–623
In studying this text, you will focus on the following objectives:

Literary Study:
Making connections across literature.

Reading:
Analyzing relevance of setting.
Analyzing informational text.

English Learners

DIFFERENTIATED INSTRUCTION

Beginning Preview some of the vocabulary students may not be able to determine from context. For example, to learn the meaning of *prow* (the forward part of a ship) and *floe* (a sheet of floating ice), students need to use a dictionary. Tell students to refer to a dictionary for the meaning of all unfamiliar words that cannot be determined by using context clues.

Focus
Summary

Barry Lopez travels with a group of scientists to the Arctic. One day, after the scientists accomplish their research goals in the Beaufort Sea, they set out to search for seals. They soon find that their boat is trapped by ice. The group works its way back to the open sea only to confront a fierce storm. Back at camp, with the storm dying down, Lopez takes a walk and reflects on the motivations of earlier Arctic explorers, and on their dreams and desires.

Teach

Reading Strategy | **1**

Analyze Relevance of Setting Before students read this selection, encourage them to recall the details of the setting in "To Build a Fire." Those details will help them construct their two-column charts.

> For an audio recording of this selection, use Listening Library Audio CD-ROM.

Readability Scores

Dale-Chall: 8.0
DRP: 60
Lexile: 1130

> For activities related to this selection, see Unit 4 Teaching Resources Book, pp. 172–180.

Teach

Big Idea   1

Naturalism Point out that nature cooperates with the group at first, and then rather suddenly shuts them off from the sea.
Say: This view of nature as indifferent to humans is a major theme of Naturalist writers. Ask students to think about this question as they read: Is the author a Naturalist?

Cultural History ☆

Arctic Seal Hunting In the third paragraph on this page, the author refers to a search for seals. He does not say anything about hunting or killing them. Until late into the twentieth century, the native peoples of the Arctic freely hunted seals for food and for skins. They sold the sealskins to Russians and others. After decades of such hunting, the fur seal population has diminished to the point where major restrictions have been placed on the commercial hunting of seals.

Informational Text

My companions, all scientists, were serious about this, but not solemn or tedious. They forestalled trouble by preparing for it, and were guided, not deterred, by the danger inherent in their work. It is a pleasure to travel with such people. As in other walks of life, the person who feels compelled to dramatize the risks or is either smugly complacent or eager to demonstrate his survival skills is someone you hope not to meet.

Our camaraderie came from our enthusiasm for the work and from exhilaration with the landscape, the daily contact with seabirds, seals, and fish. We rarely voiced these things to each other; they surfaced in a word of encouragement or understanding around rough work done in unending dampness and cold. Our mutual regard was founded in the accomplishment of our tasks and was as important to our survival as the emergency gear stowed in a blue box forward of the steering console.

☆ We worked through the morning, sorting the contents of bottom trawls and vertical plankton tows.[4] Around noon we shut the engines off and drifted under overcast skies, eating our lunch. The seas were beginning to slap at the hull, but we had another couple of hours before they built up to three or four feet—our match, comfortably. We decided, then, to search for seals in the ice front before heading in. An hour later, by a movement of the ice so imperceptible it was finished before we realized it, we were cut off from the sea. The wind, compacting the ice, was closing off the channels of calm water where we had been cruising. We were suddenly 200 yards from open water, and a large floe, turning off the wind and folding in from the west, threatened to close us off even deeper in the pack. Already we had lost steerageway[5]—the boat was pinned at that moment on all four sides.

---

4. *Vertical plankton tows* are funnel-shaped nets that are dropped into the water and lifted straight up to collect samples, such as plankton, from the water.
5. *Steerageway* is the minimum rate of movement needed to make a boat respond to its rudder.

In those first hours we worked wordlessly and diligently. We all knew what we faced. Even if someone heard our distress call over the radio, we could not tell him precisely where we were, and we were in pack ice moving east. A three-day storm was coming on. The floes might crush the boat and drive it under, or they could force it out of the water where we would have it for shelter.

We took advantage of any momentary opening in the ice to move toward open water, widening the channels with ice chisels, pushing with the twin 90-horsepower engines, the four of us heaving at the stern and gunnels.[6] We were angling for a small patch of water within the pack. From there, it seemed, after a quick reconnoiter[7] ahead on foot, we might be able to get out to the open sea. Thirty feet shy of our patch of water, we doubted the wisdom of taking ice chisels to one particular chunk of weathered pressure ice that blocked our path. Fractured the wrong way, its center of gravity would shift and the roll could take the boat under. The only way around it was to pull the boat, which weighed

---

6. The *stern* is the rear of a boat. The *gunnel,* or gunwale, is the upper edge of the side of a ship.
7. *Reconnoiter* means "to survey."

Use Visual Aids Ask students to locate Pingok Island on a map. Explain that students can use the map as a visual aid to help them follow Lopez's narrative. They should also locate other places Lopez mentions: Harrison Bay, Melville Island, and the Chukchi Sea.

Encourage students to search for map projections that show the relationship of the Arctic to the lands from which its early explorers came, according to Lopez: Scandinavia (Norway, Sweden, and Denmark), Iceland, Ireland, Great Britain, and Russia.

Small boat by iceberg in Disko Bay, Greenland.

3000 pounds, completely out of the water. With an improvised system of ice anchors, lines, and block and tackle,[8] and out of the terrific desire to get free, we set to. We got the boat up on the floe, across it, and back into the water.

Had that been open water, we would have cheered. As it was, we exchanged quick glances of justifiable but not foolish hope. While we had been winching the boat over the ice toward it, this patch of water had been closing up. And another large floe still separated us from the ocean. Where the surf broke against it, it fell a sheer four feet to the sea. Even if we got the boat over that ice, we could never launch it from such a precipice.

Two stayed in the boat. I and one other went in opposite directions along the floe. Several hundred yards to the east I found a channel. I looked it over quickly and then signaled with the upraised shaft of my ice chisel for the others. It was barely negotiable to begin with, and in the few minutes it took to get the boat there, the channel closed. We put the prow[9] of the boat against the seaward floe and

8. A *block and tackle* is a series of pulleys used to pull or lift a heavy object.
9. The *prow,* or bow, is the front of a boat.

Informational Text

brought both engines up to full power, trying to hold it against the wind. The ice beside it continued to move east. The channel started to open. With the engines roaring, the gap opened to six feet. With a silent, implicit understanding each of us acted decisively. The man at the helm reversed the engines, heeled the boat around, and burst up the channel. We made 20 quick feet, careened the boat over on its port[10] gunnel, and pivoted through a 120° turn. One ran ahead, chopping swift and hard at the closing ice with a chisel. Two of us heaved, jumping in and out of the boat, stabbing at chunks of ice closing on the props.[11] One man remained at the throttles. Suddenly he lunged away, yanking the starboard[12] engine clear of fouling ice. The man ahead threw his ice chisel into the boat and jumped across to help lift at the port gunnel. We could *feel* how close. The starboard side of the boat slid off the ice, into the water. The bow lifted on the open sea. There was nothing more for our legs to strain against. We pulled ourselves over the gunnel and fell into the boat, limp as feed sacks. Exhausted. We were out.

We were out, and the seas were running six feet. And we were miles now from a shore that we could not see. In the hours we had been in the ice, the storm had built considerably, and we had been carried we did not know how far east. The seas were as much as the boat could handle, and too big to quarter[13]—we had to take them nearly bow-on. The brief views from wave crests showed us nothing. We could not see far enough through the driving sleet and spray, and the arctic coast here lies too low, anyway. We could only hope we were east of Pingok, the westernmost of the barrier islands, and not to the west, headed down into Harrison Bay,[14] where the wind has a greater fetch[15] and the shore is much farther on.

10. *Port* is a ship's left side.
11. Here, *props* means "propellers."
12. *Starboard* is a ship's right side.
13. Here, *quarter* means "to travel in a crisscross manner."
14. *Harrison Bay* is a shallow inlet of the Beaufort Sea.
15. Here, *fetch* means "intensity."

BARRY LOPEZ **619**

Geographical Perspective
on *To Build a Fire*

Teach

Reading Strategy   2

Analyze Relevance of Setting Help students picture what the men went through to get the boat into open water. Starting with the paragraph that begins "Had that been open water," have students discuss such things as why they could not winch the boat across the ice floe as they had done over the previous ice floe; why some men stayed in the boat and others got out; how they managed to break through the ice.

View the Photograph ★

Ask: How would you feel if you were on the boat in this photograph? *(Awed by the view; frightened by the ice cliffs)*

English Learners

DIFFERENTIATED INSTRUCTION

Intermediate Remind students to look for context clues when they encounter unfamiliar words. Draw their attention to *not deterred* at the top of page 618. Tell them that *guided* in the same sentence provides a clue to meaning. **Ask:** What do you think deter means? *(to discourage from doing something)*

Ask students to infer the meaning of these terms from the context:
- camaraderie *(a friendly relationship)*
- imperceptible *(hardly noticeable)*

Remind students that they should verify the meanings in a dictionary.

Teach

Analyze Relevance of Setting **Say:** The physical setting does not change between these paragraphs—Lopez and two others are still standing on the deck of their boat. Why, then, does Lopez switch from the pronoun *we* to the pronoun *I*? *(Students may point out that although the physical setting has not changed, Lopez has gone somewhere else mentally. No longer working nonstop with the others, he is no longer part of a "we" and is only himself.)* Use this passage to introduce the notion that setting can involve more than real time and place.

Tourist on Ellesmere Island.

We took water over the bow and shouted strategy to each other over the wind and the sound of engines screaming as the props came out of the water. We erected a canvas shelter forward to break the force of the sea and shed water. We got all the weight we could out of the bow. A resolute steadiness came over us. We were making headway. We were secure. If we did not broach[16] and if we were far enough to the east, we would be able to run up on a lee-ward[17] shore somewhere and wait out the storm.

We plowed ahead. Three of us stood hunched backward to the weather.

1 I began to recognize in the enduring steadiness another kind of calmness, or relief. The distance between my body and my thoughts slowly became elongated, and muffled like a dark, carpeted corridor. I realized I was cold, that I was shivering. I sensed the dry pits of warmth under my clothes and, against this, an opening and closing over my chest, like cold breath. I realized with dreamlike stillness that the whole upper right side of my body was soaked. The shoulder seams of my foul-weather gear were torn open.

I knew I had to get to dry clothes, to get them on. But desire could not move my legs or arms. They were too far away. I was staring at someone, then moving; the soaked clothes were coming off. I could not make a word in my mouth. I felt suspended in a shaft in the earth, and then imagined I was sitting on a bare earthen floor somewhere within myself. The knowledge that I was being slammed around like a wooden box in the bottom of the boat was like something I had walked away from.

In dry wool and protected by a tarp from the seas, I understood that I was safe; but I could not understand the duration of time. I could not locate any visual image outside myself. I concentrated on trying to gain a sense of the boat; and then on a rhythmic tensing and loosening of my muscles. I kept at it and at it; then I knew time was passing.

---

16. Here, *broach* means "to be turned broadside into the wind."
17. *Leeward,* or the lee side, means "facing the same direction toward which the wind is blowing."

Writing Practice

Synthesize Ideas Jack London and Barry Lopez have both written about the Arctic wilderness, London in fiction and Lopez in nonfiction. Ask students to write a paper summarizing what they have learned about the Arctic wilderness from these two selections. Students may describe the environment, discuss its appeal to humans, or examine the challenges it presents. Tell them to include a thesis statement in which they present their main point and to refer to specific details or information from both selections in their papers.

There was a flow of time again. I heard a shout. I tried to shout myself, and when I heard an answer I knew that I was at the edge of time again, and could just step into it. I realized I was sitting up, that I was bracing myself against heavy seas.

The shouts were for the coast. We had found Pingok.

We anchored the boat under the lee shore and went into the cabin and changed clothes and fixed dinner. Our sense of relief came out in a patter of jokes at each other's expense. We ate quietly and went to bed and slept like bears in winter.

The storm blew for two days. We nearly lost the boat when an anchor line parted, and got wet and cold again trying to secure it; but that seemed no more than what we had chosen by coming here. I went for a long walk on the afternoon of the second day, after the storm had become only fretful gusts and sunlight threatened to break through the low clouds.

I still felt a twinge of embarrassment at having been reduced from a state of strength to such an impassive weight, to a state of disassociation, so quickly. But I did not dwell on it long. And we would go out again, when the seas dropped. We would go into the ice again. We would watch more closely; but nothing, really, had changed.

 With the experience so fresh in my mind, I began thinking of frail and exposed craft as I walked down the beach, of the Irish carraughs and Norse knarrs[18] that brought people across the Atlantic, bucking pack ice streaming southward on the East Greenland Current. My God, what had driven them? All we know is what we have deduced from the records of early historians. And the deference those men showed to their classical predecessors, to Ptolemy, Solinus, and Isidore,[19] their own nationalism and religious convictions, their vanity, and the shape of the ideas of their age—all this affected what they expressed. And when it was translated, or when they them-

selves translated from others, interpolations, adaptation, and plain error colored the historical record further. So the early record of arctic exploration is open to interpretation. And this refined history is less real, less harrowing than what had happened to us in the boat. It is events mulled and adjudicated.[20]

I wanted to walk the length of the seaside beach on Pingok, knowing the storm was dying away. I brooded over the fates of those early immigrants, people whose names no one knows, who sailed in ships of which there are neither descriptions nor drawings, through ice and storms like this one—but so much farther from a shore, with intentions and dreams I could only imagine.

The earliest arctic voyages are recorded in the Icelandic sagas and Irish imramha. But they were written down hundreds of years after the fact by people who did not make the journeys, who only heard about them. The Norse Eddas[21] and Icelandic sagas, wrote the arctic explorer and historian Fridtjof Nansen, are "narratives somewhat in the light of historical romances, founded upon legend and more or less uncertain traditions." The same can be said of the imramha and the records of Saint Brendan's voyage,[22] though in tone and incident these latter are different from the sagas.

In the following ages, beginning in a time before the sagas, the notion of a road to Cathay, a Northwest Passage,[23] emerges. The quest for such a corridor, a path to wealth that had to be followed through a perilous landscape, gathers the dreams of several ages. Rooted in this search is one of the oldest of all

---

18. *Carraughs* and *knarrs* are both types of ships.
19. *Ptolemy* (c. A.D. 85–165) was a geographer and astronomer; Gaius Julius *Solinus* (third century A.D.) was a Latin grammarian who wrote a book titled *The Wonders of the World;* Saint *Isidore* of Seville (A.D. 560–636) was a Spanish theologian and historian.
20. *Adjudicated* means "settled" or "judged."
21. The *sagas, imramha,* and *Eddas* are all tales of sea voyages.
22. *Saint Brendan* (c. A.D. 484–578) was an Irish monk who is said to have gone on a seven-year sea voyage in search of the Garden of Eden. Some believe he found North America during this voyage.

BARRY LOPEZ **621**

Informational Text

Geographical Perspective
on *To Build a Fire*

Teach

Political History ☆
Exploration Chronology Lopez switches from a personal narrative to a contemplation of earlier human motivations for exploring the Arctic. Make sure that students read the footnotes to follow the chronology, beginning with Norse and Irish voyages, including that of Saint Brendan, and ending in the twentieth century.

Approaching Level

DIFFERENTIATED INSTRUCTION

Emerging Point out that Barry Lopez's text is densely packed with ideas and information. When students encounter text like this, they must slow down, read carefully, and reread. Tell them that it is normal not to understand everything on a first reading, and that rereading is an effective strategy. Have them work with partners to read aloud sentences or short passages and then restate what they just read. The partners can work together to clarify meaning as necessary.

Advanced Learners/Pre-AP

DIFFERENTIATED INSTRUCTION

Research Have advanced students choose one of the early explorers Lopez mentions and consult several electronic and print resources to write reports about him. They should include a formal bibliography, citing their research sources.

621

Teach

Literary History ☆

Writers Inspiring Writers
Lopez mentions his own reading of travel logs and histories of explorers. These writings inspired him and helped motivate him to explore the Arctic and write about his experiences.

---

human yearnings—finding the material fortune that lies beyond human struggle, and the peace that lies on the other side of hope.

I should emphasize two points. Few original documents point up the unadorned character, the undisguised sensibilities, of the participants in these dramas. And the most common simile of comparison for these journeys—the exploits of astronauts—falls short. The astronaut is suitably dressed for his work, professionally trained, assiduously looked after en route, and nationally regarded. He possesses superb tools of navigation and observation. The people who first came into the Arctic had no photograph of the far shore before they left. They sailed in crude ships with cruder tools of navigation, and with maps that had no foundation or geographic authority. They shipwrecked so often that it is difficult to find records of their deaths, because shipwreck and death were unremarkable at the time. They received, for the most part, no support—popular or financial. They suffered brutally and fatally from the weather and from scurvy,[24] starvation, Eskimo hostility, and thirst. Their courage and determination in some instances were so extreme as to seem eerie and peculiar rather than heroic. Visions of achievement drove them on. In the worst moments they were held together by regard for each other, by invincible bearing, or by stern naval discipline. Whether one finds such resourceful courage among a group of young monks on a spiritual voyage in a carraugh, or among worldly sailors with John Davis in the sixteenth century, or in William Parry's[25] snug winter quarters on Melville Island in 1819–20, it is a sterling human quality.

☆ In the journals and histories I read of these journeys I was drawn on by a sharp leaning in

the human spirit: pure desire—the complexities of human passion and cupidity. Someone, for example, had to pay for these trips; and whoever paid was looking for a way to be paid back. Rarely was the goal anything as selfless as an increase in mankind's geographical knowledge. An arctic voyage in quest of unknown riches, or of a new passage to known riches, could mean tangible wealth for investors, and it could mean fame and social position for a captain or pilot. For a common seaman the reward might only mean some slip of the exotic, or a chance at the riches himself—at the very least a good story, probably something astounding. Enough, certainly, to sign on.

As I read, I tried to imagine the singular hunger for such things, how desire alone might convey a group of people into those fearsome seas. The achievement of one's desires may reveal what one considers moral; but it also reveals the aspiration and tack of an individual life, and the tenor of an age. In this light, one can better understand failures of nerve in the Arctic, such as Bering's in the Chukchi Sea in 1728—he simply did not have Peter the Great's[26] burning desire to define eastern Russia. And one can better understand figures in arctic exploration so obsessed with their own achievement that they found it irksome to acknowledge the Eskimos, unnamed companions, and indefatigable dogs who helped them.

Arctic history became for me, then, a legacy of desire—the desire of individual men to achieve their goals. But it was also the legacy of a kind of desire that transcends heroics and which was privately known to many—the desire for a safe and honorable passage through the world.

As I walked the beach I stopped now and then to pick over something on the storm-hardened shore—bits of whale vertebrae, water-

---

23. *Cathay* is an old name for China; the *Northwest Passage* is a route through the Arctic that passes from the Atlantic Ocean to the Pacific Ocean.
24. *Scurvy* is a disease brought on by lack of vitamin C.
25. Sir *William Parry* (1790–1855), a British explorer, discovered and named several islands in the Arctic, including the inhospitable Melville Island, where he and his group were forced to spend a winter because of sea ice.

26. Vitus *Bering* (1681–1741) was a Danish-born Russian explorer. The Russian tsar *Peter the Great* chose Bering to discover whether Asia and North America were connected. Heavy fog caused Bering to return to Russia, where he was criticized for not actually seeing the American coast.

Reading Practice

Compare and Contrast Have students reread Lopez's comparison of Arctic explorers and space explorers on pages 621–622. Draw a Venn diagram on the board and fill it in with the aid of the class, noting similarities and differences. Infer Lopez's attitude toward those who explore the Arctic. Students may also make a similar comparison between Lopez's exploration group and the early explorers.

Arctic Explorer   **Space Explorer**

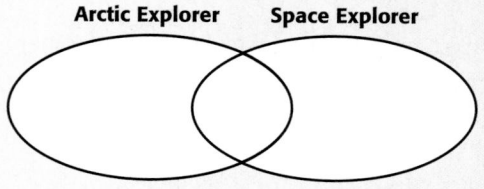

logged feathers, the odd but ubiquitous piece of plastic, a strict reminder against romance.

The narratives I carried in my head that afternoon fascinated me, but not for what they recorded of geographic accomplishment or for how they might be used in support of one side or another of a controversy, such as whether Frederick Cook or Robert Peary[27] got to the Pole first. They held the mind because of what they said about human endeavor. Behind the polite and abstemious journal entries of British naval officers, behind the self-conscious prose of dashing explorers, were the lives of courageous, bewildered, and dreaming people. Some reports suggest that heroic passage took place for many just offstage. They make clear that others struggled mightily to find some meaning in what they were doing in those regions, for the very act of exploration seemed to them at times completely mad. They wanted to feel that what they were doing was necessary, if not for themselves then for the nation, for mankind.

The literature of arctic exploration is frequently offered as a record of resolute will before the menacing fortifications of the landscape. It is more profitable I think to disregard this notion—that the land is an adversary bent on human defeat, that the people who came and went were heroes or failures in this. It is better to contemplate the record of human longing to achieve something significant, to be free of some of the grim weight of life. That weight was ignorance, poverty of spirit, indolence, and the threat of anonymity and destitution. This harsh landscape became the focus of a desire to separate oneself from those things and to overcome them. In these arctic narratives, then, are the threads of dreams that serve us all.

1

---

27. *Frederick Cook* (1865–1940) and *Robert Peary* (1856–1920) were both American explorers. While Peary is usually listed as the first person to reach the North Pole (in April 1909), Cook claimed to have reached it in 1908.

Respond and Think Critically

Respond and Interpret

1. Write a brief summary of the main ideas in this article before you answer the following questions. For help on writing a summary, see page 79.

2. What part of this narrative did you find the most engaging? Explain.

3. (a) How does Lopez feel about the scientists with whom he worked? (b) Why is the quality of their relationships important?

4. (a) How does the boat become stuck in the ice? (b) What does this incident suggest about the arctic environment? (c) What does it suggest about the expedition?

Analyze and Evaluate

5. How do Lopez's descriptions at the end of this excerpt compare with Jack London's descriptions at the end of "To Build a Fire"?

6. Lopez recounts the stories of earlier arctic explorers. Do you agree that in these stories are "the threads of dreams that serve us all"? Why or why not?

Connect

7. Briefly describe some of the differences and similarities in the settings of *Arctic Dreams* and "To Build a Fire." How do these settings affect the events of each?

BARRY LOPEZ **623**

---

6. Students may suggest that the stories are too far removed from their own experience, or they may suggest that the stories illustrate longings that all people share.

7. Both are set in the Arctic, but the action in *Arctic Dreams* takes place on the open water, whereas "To Build a Fire" takes place on land. The characters have different motives for their actions and relate to their environments in differ-

ent ways, even though they face similar struggles. The settings have a profound effect on the events, leading to the death of the man in "To Build a Fire" and giving purpose to the characters in *Arctic Dreams*.

 For additional assessment, see Assessment Resources, pp. 185–186.

Geographical Perspective
on *To Build a Fire*

Teach

Big Idea	1

Naturalism Even though Lopez is writing a century after the Naturalist movement, he avoids romanticizing nature. **Ask:** What are some examples of Naturalist language in this passage? *(Possible answers: "menacing fortifications of the landscape"; "that the land is an adversary bent on human defeat")*

Assess

1. Students should identify key events such as leaving camp to search for seals, getting trapped by the ice, returning to camp, reflecting on the challenges, dreams, and desires of early Arctic explorers.

2. The suspense of getting the boat through the ice is likely to have engaged many students.

3. (a) He feels an unspoken camaraderie with them. (b) They are often forced to depend on one another.

4. (a) The wind shifts the ice, which cuts off the route back to the sea. (b) The environment is unpredictable and dangerous. (c) The crew, no matter how diligent, cannot avoid all dangers.

5. Lopez describes feeling that his body and mind have been disconnected. This is similar to London's portrayal of the freezing man's thoughts at the end of "To Build a Fire."

Writing Workshop

Literary Analysis

Focus

Bellringer Options

Display works of art, such as the paintings on pages 583, 587, and 590 of the selection "The Open Boat." **Ask:** What is your response to the art? What elements in the works make you feel as you do? By examining an artwork and considering the different elements that make up the image, students are analyzing it. In a similar way, they will learn how to write a literary analysis by examining a literary work.

Summary

In this workshop, students will write and present literary analyses. They will follow the stages of the writing process, including prewriting, drafting, revising, and editing. In addition, the workshop provides a mini-lesson on subject-verb agreement.

Learning Objectives

For pages 624–633

In this workshop, you will focus on the following objectives:

Writing: Writing a literary analysis.

Grammar: Maintaining subject-verb agreement.

▶ Writing Process

At any stage of a writing process, you may think of new ideas to include. Feel free to return to earlier stages as you write.

Prewrite

Draft

Revise

Edit & Proofread

Focus Lesson:
Subject-Verb Agreement

Present

Writing Workshop

Literary Analysis

Literature Connection In a well-known quotation Mark Twain emphasizes the importance of precise word choice in writing.

"The difference between the almost right word and the right word . . . is the difference between the lightning-bug and the lightning."

—Mark Twain, Letter to George Bainton

Analyzing word choice is a kind of **literary analysis**—a close-up view of a literary work. When writing a literary analysis, first consider your immediate impression of the work. Then as you reread, you can look for themes and techniques that contributed to your impression. By analyzing these elements, you will clarify the deeper meanings and understand how they are revealed. Study the checklist below to learn the goals and strategies for writing a successful literary analysis.

Checklist: Features of Literary Analysis Writing

Goals	Strategies
To analyze one element or aspect of a short story	☑ Demonstrate an understanding of the story as a whole
	☑ Show appreciation for the author's style
	☑ Find a single, narrow aspect of the story to focus on
	☑ Adopt and maintain a third-person point of view
To state and support a clear, insightful thesis	☑ Maintain a consistent focus on your thesis throughout your essay
	☑ Quote directly from the story to support your main ideas
	☑ Elaborate on main ideas with substantial, specific, and relevant details
	☑ Establish a logical pattern of organization
To reflect a careful, thoughtful reading	☑ Make inferences; explain subtle details and complex ideas
To demonstrate a command of language	☑ Use action verbs and other precise or creative language
	☑ Vary sentences

Workshop Resources

Print Materials

📁 Unit 4 Teaching Resources pp. 182–184

📁 Writing Kit

📁 Success in Writing: Research and Reports

💻 Technology

- Literature Online: Writing Resources and Grammar Resources, www.glencoe.com
- Online Essay Grader, www.glencoe.com
- Student Presentation Builder on Student-Works Plus CD-ROM
- Media Workshop DVD
- Online Student Edition

Assignment: Analyze a Short Story

Write a literary analysis of about 1,500 words from the unit. Show how the author's language, characters, plot, setting, themes, or other elements of the text contribute to the story's meaning. As you work, keep your audience and purpose in mind.

Audience: peers, classmates, and teachers who are familiar with the story

Purpose: to demonstrate an understanding of the author's style and appreciation of the effects created

Analyze a Professional Model

In her literary analysis essay, Bettina L. Knapp analyzes the effects of terror on the crew in Stephen Crane's "The Open Boat." As you read the following passage, note how Knapp uses direct evidence from the story and explains the significance of that evidence. Pay close attention to the comments in the margin. They point out features to include in your own literary analysis.

From *Stephen Crane: Tales of Adventure*
by Bettina L. Knapp

"None of them knew the color of the sky," is perhaps one of the most celebrated opening lines of any short story. The opening line conveys the fierce struggle between finite man and the infinitude that engulfs him—as in Melville's *Moby-Dick*. The sea for Crane, as it is for Melville, is "the image of the ungraspable phantom of life."

The men's agony at not knowing their fate is underscored by the power of those surging waters—waves that could sweep the men under at any moment. "The horizon narrowed and widened, and dipped and rose, at all times its edge was jagged with waves that seemed thrust up in points like rocks."

Man, like the helpless survivors in the boat, is thrust here and there and floats about in utter helplessness. No matter how hard people try to fix and direct themselves, they are castaways. Salvation—if there is one—lies in the bonds between men that assuage their implacable solitude.

Real-World Connection

Publish your response by reading it aloud to or exchanging it with members of your class who wrote about the same story. Discuss new insights you developed while writing about the story and listening to the work of others.

Thesis

Make a concise judgment that analyzes a literary element, such as theme, throughout the story.

Major Points

Make sure that your major points support your thesis.

Command of Language/ Point of View

Use action verbs and other precise words. Maintain the third-person point of view.

Literature Online

Writing and Research For prewriting, drafting, and revising tools, go to glencoe.com and enter QuickPass code GLA9800u4.

WRITING WORKSHOP **625**

Approaching Level

DIFFERENTIATED INSTRUCTION

Emerging Writing an effective literary analysis requires a clear understanding of the literary elements in a work of literature. Make sure students understand the nature of the basic literary elements—character, plot, setting, theme, and conflict—before they begin preparing their analyses. Help students identify the elements of the model that they should include in their own analyses. Knapp's analysis, like any good composition, contains a clear thesis, ideas and evidence that develop the thesis, explanations of the evidence, and a conclusion.

 Writing Workshop

Teach

Big Idea

Realism Have students make a connection between literary analysis and Realism. Explain that Realist writers focused on details, characters, and ideas that reflected real life.

Ask: What connection exists between literary analysis and Realism's emphasis on detail and character? (*Students may say that Realist writers carefully analyzed the world around them in order to include details and behaviors that mirrored the way people and the world really were. A writer of a literary analysis must look closely at a work of literature to understand how its parts fit together.*)

Literary History ☆

Bettina L. Knapp Bettina L. Knapp (1926–) is a respected literary critic, educator, and scholar. She is best known for her insights into French literature and world mythology. Knapp often considers how culture affects writers. Her study of modern writers suggests that they are deeply influenced by the world in which they live.

Teach

Writing Skills

Literary Elements Have students identify the literary elements that Knapp addresses in her essay. **Ask:** What literary element of Crane's writing does Knapp illustrate with the first excerpt on this page? *(the rhythm and vividness of his language)* Which of Crane's words do you think convey the terror and utter senselessness that she refers to? *(reared, plunged, outrageously high, mystic, problems in white water, racing down from the summit, a leap from the air)*

Primary Source To support her point about Crane's use of irony and humor, Knapp includes a long quotation from "The Open Boat." This use of Crane's own words is a more effective way of showing his sense of humor than retelling or summarizing his writing would be. **Ask:** What is humorous in the passage Knapp quotes? *(The speaker calls fate silly and insulting names.)* Knapp allows readers to identify the humor themselves.

Literary Elements

Analyze language, setting, character, and unique aspects of the text to show how these elements contribute to the story's meaning as a whole and to show appreciation for the author's style.

Primary Source

Support your analysis with direct evidence from the story.

Support

Make accurate and detailed references to the story.

The craft pranced and reared, and plunged like an animal. As each wave came, and she rose for it, she seemed like a horse making at a fence outrageously high. The manner of her scramble over these walls of water is a mystic thing, and moreover, at the top of them were ordinarily these problems in white water, the foam racing down from the summit of each wave, requiring a new leap, and a leap from the air.

Crane's use of changing rhythms throughout the tale points up the terror of the dinghy's passengers and exemplifies the utter senselessness of existence itself.

Crane suggests that if an observer were to look upon the events objectively, viewing them "from a balcony, the whole thing would doubtless have been weirdly picturesque. But the men in the boat had no time to see it, and even if they had had leisure, there were other things to occupy their minds." Values of virtue, bravery, integrity were once of importance, but now are meaningless in a godless universe where nature observes impassively human despair and frustration. Yet, the harrowing sea journey creates a new morality, which gives fresh meaning to life: "the brotherhood of men . . . was established on the seas. No one said that it was so. No one mentioned it. But it dwelt in the boat, and each man felt it warm him." Comfort and feelings of well-being emerge as each helps the other assuage his growing terror.

In the midst of fear and harrowing terror, there is also irony and humor:

If I am going to be drowned—if I am going to be drowned—if I am going to be drowned, why, in the name of the seven mad gods who rule the sea, was I allowed to come thus far and contemplate sand and trees? Was I brought here merely to have my nose dragged away as I was about to nibble the sacred cheese of life? It is preposterous. If this old ninny-woman, Fate, cannot do better than this, she should be deprived of the management of men's fortunes. She is an old hen who knows not her intention. If she has decided to drown me, why did she not do it in the beginning and save me all this trouble. The whole affair is absurd. . . . But, no, she cannot mean to drown me. Not after all this work.

Listening and Speaking Practice

SMALL GROUP

Oral Prewriting Students may find that an effective prewriting strategy is to explain the plan of their essays aloud to a partner. Pair students and have partners present their theses to each other before they put their ideas on paper. Encourage the listening partners to ask probing questions. Remind students that it is especially important to ask where in the text the writer finds evidence that supports his or her interpretation of the story.

A mystical relationship exists between the men in the dinghy—and the sea and heavens. Crane feels compelled to point out man's smallness, to set him back into nature and reduce him to size.

Conversations between the oiler and the cook, seemingly trivial, since they revolve around food—"What kind of pie do you like best?"—serve in reality to point out the absurdity of humankind's preoccupations. They also act as a way of dispelling progressive terror. As for the captain, he is ridiculed; the men laugh at him, again distracting themselves from their great fear of death.

The sight of a shark heightens the men's dreadful tension. Crane does not mention the shark by name, but the reader can almost hear the shark's fin cut the water's surface and see its phosphorescent gleaming body. Like the survivors of "Raft of the Medusa," whose harrowing episode is famous in French maritime history, the men in the dinghy do not know there is a lifesaving station twenty miles away.

When the ordeal is over, the men, safely on land, look back at the water: "white waves paced to and fro in the moonlight, and the wind brought the sound of the great sea's voice to the men on shore, and they felt that they could then be interpreters." The narrator's voice withdraws, as it were, from the chaotic drama, introducing a sense of spatial and temporal distance. Comfortable on land, the narrator can indulge in the luxury of waxing poetic and thus transform subjective emotions into a work of art.

Its poetry and rhythmic schemes make "The Open Boat" the match of Melville's "White Jacket" and the best of Jack London and Joseph Conrad. This tale's unusually punctuated sentences of contrasting length simulate the heart beat of a man under extreme stress, producing an incantatory quality. Crane's sensual images of man struggling against the sea remain vivid long after the reading of "The Open Boat." The salt spray and deafening roar of the waves pounding against the dinghy can almost be tasted and heard.

Reading-Writing Connection Think about the writing techniques that you just encountered and try them out in your own literary analysis.

Exposition

Explanation of Ambiguities
Identify and explain ambiguities, complexities, and nuances in the text to reveal additional layers of meaning.

Organization
Order your response in a logical, effective way, such as by chronological order.

Explanation of Evidence
Draw your own conclusions about your evidence, making sure to connect it to your thesis.

Conclusion
Summarize your thesis and major points, and leave your reader with something to think about.

WRITING WORKSHOP **627**

Literary Analysis

Teach

Writing Skills

Explanation of Ambiguities In the second paragraph on this page, Knapp introduces her interpretation of the conversation about food. Remind students that in a literary analysis, the thesis must be supported with evidence from the literary work.

Ask: What is Knapp's interpretation, and how does she relate it to her thesis? *(Her interpretation is that the talk of food, although absurd in these circumstances, provides a distraction that helps the men cope with their fears. Knapp's interpretation supports her idea that the men in the boat are insignificant in the natural world.)*

Explanation of Evidence Point out to students that their first impressions of a story may change. They may discover new meanings as they analyze the language and literary elements. They should study the literary work carefully, and formulate an interpretation based on evidence in the text.

Literary History ☆
Word Origins The word *analyze* comes from an ancient Greek word meaning "to loosen or undo." An analysis "undoes" a piece of literature when the analyst takes it apart and examines how the different elements work together.

Approaching Level

DIFFERENTIATED INSTRUCTION

SMALL GROUP
Emerging Have students work in small groups to analyze works of literature. Have each student select one literary element (language, setting, plot, character) and examine its use in and effect on the story. Students should share their findings and work together to develop a thesis.

Teach

Writing Process

Clarify Your Thesis Explain to students that their thesis is a summary of the point they intend to make in their essay. It is possible that they will write their thesis, and then, as they begin to gather evidence, they will want to revise their thesis. **Say:** Write down the basic idea of your thesis, but do not worry about the precise wording at this point. You may revise or rewrite it once you have begun to gather evidence. Explain that it is important not to become so attached to your thesis that you are unwilling to revise it as you learn and understand more during the writing process.

Prewrite Suggest that students organize material in order of importance, beginning with a discussion of the literary elements that best support the thesis and then going on to mention less important elements. They should restate the thesis in the conclusion. A graphic organizer may help them put their evidence in order.

Avoid Plagiarism

To complete this assignment, it is not necessary to consult outside sources. If you do, however, remember that both honesty and the law require you to cite them.

Multiple Interpretations

Keep in mind that great stories usually have many valid interpretations. In your literary analysis, briefly address other interpretations or counterarguments but keep your analysis focused. Use words such as *suggests* in your analysis to acknowledge that there may be other valid interpretations.

Prewrite

Choose a Story to Analyze First decide which story in the unit to analyze. It need not be the story you liked best or the one you understood the best. In fact, the best essays often analyze challenging stories that initially leave the reader with mixed feelings or unanswered questions. Choose a story that left you with a strong impression and will give you enough to talk about in your analysis.

Explore Your Story Once you select your story, review it to gain a comprehensive understanding of the text. Remember that *analyzing* a text means looking at its separate parts individually and then determining how the parts work together as a whole. Focus on a literary element—such as character, setting, plot, theme, point of view, or style—or another aspect of the work, such as language, to examine significant ideas apparent throughout the text. For example, think about how a character changes or how the setting or point of view influences the meaning of the story. As you explore your story, look for patterns and recurring themes that contribute to its overall meaning.

Clarify Your Thesis In a literary analysis essay, your thesis should be a concise judgment that interprets, analyzes, and evaluates a specific element throughout the entire story. Your one- to two-sentence thesis statement should include the element you will analyze and the conclusion you reached about the story.

Gather Evidence As you develop your major points, remember to support your ideas and viewpoints with evidence—accurate, detailed references to the story. The story will be your primary source, but you can use secondary sources such as dictionaries and literary criticism to reinforce your claims. A strong argument depends on the ability to make

Wagner= life, passion, music

Georgiana on arrival= black with soot, battered, somnambulant

matinée/concert hall=art, leisure, rich fabrics, colors

Georgiana's home= cave dwelling, black pond, dishcloths

Georgiana's past= Paris, Boston Conservatory, pianist

Georgiana's life= black dress, treadmill, ploughing forever

Analysis: Word choice shows character, setting, and theme through contrast.

628 UNIT 4 REGIONALISM AND REALISM

Assessment Practice

Formulate a Plan Standardized tests may call for students to analyze works of literature. Tell students that after reading a selection, they should identify some of its literary elements. Then they can develop a thesis about the work's theme, or message. This thesis must be supported by evidence in the text. Finally, they should locate in the work specific passages that support the thesis and incorporate these as quotations in an analysis. Have students write down the steps to follow in a test.

clear to the reader connections between such evidence and the thesis. After giving evidence, explain its significance to your argument, noting other possible interpretations.

Organize Your Major Points In the body of your essay, organize your major points in an effective, logical order. If you are analyzing a change that occurs in the story, use chronological order. In other analyses, you may prefer to use order of importance. Adjust the order to maximize the impact of your points.

Draft

Present and Expand Your Points Present your major points in a straightforward, logical way and back them up with direct evidence from the story. Maintain the present tense throughout your literary analysis. Use direct quotations where appropriate, especially to emphasize a point. As you discuss more complex interpretations and connections, explain the significance of your evidence to the reader and clarify how it supports your thesis. Using your thesis as a guide, revise your writing as necessary.

Analyze a Workshop Model

Here is a final draft of a literary analysis essay. Read the essay and answer the questions in the margin. Use the answers to these questions to guide you as you write your own essay.

Word Choice in "A Wagner Matinée"

Not much happens in "A Wagner Matinée" by Willa Cather. A summary of the action might read, "A woman arrives in Boston after a long train trip from Nebraska. She is so worn out she goes straight to bed. The next day, her nephew takes her to an afternoon concert. She listens as the orchestra plays the music of Wagner, and she cries a lot. She says she does not want to go home." Yet, "A Wagner Matinée" is a great story. One of the aspects of Cather's craft that transforms the story from a bare-bones sequence of humdrum events into a compelling work of literature is word choice. Word choice sheds light on the characters and settings of the story, and also develops its themes, primarily through contrast.

Exposition

Writing Frames

As you read the workshop model, think about the writer's use of the following frames:

- _____ sheds light on the _____ of the story, and also _____.

- In contrast, <the main character> _____.

- _____ also helps illuminate _____.

Consider using frames like these in your own literary analysis.

Point of View/Thesis

What aspect of the story will the writer focus on? What insight do you find in the thesis? What is the writer's point of view?

Teach

Writing Process

Draft Point out that in the first paragraph, the writer tells the reader what Cather's story is *not*, and by extension, what the thesis is *not*. **Say:** Summarize what the writer thinks is not remarkable about Cather's story. *(the plot, the action)*

Ask: What is the thesis, or main idea, of the paragraph? *(The thesis is stated in the final sentence.)*

Writing Skills

Writing Frames Model for students how they might use the writing frames suggested on the page. **Say:** If I were to analyze the point of view in "A Wagner Matinée," I might say, "Cather's choice of Clark as the storyteller sheds light on the contrast between the past and the present in the story. " Have volunteers complete the remaining frames.

Point of View/Thesis

Answer: *The writer will focus on specific word choices that contribute to a reader's understanding of the characters and theme. The thesis points out how the use of contrasting words can convey the stark contrast between the prairie and the city, and therefore about different aspects of Georgiana. The writer's point of view is that Cather's word choice is responsible for making the story compelling.*

Writing Workshop

Teach

Writing Process

Support

Answer: *The reference to her black dusty clothing supports the thesis because the words shed light on Georgiana's state of mind. The rest of the paragraph points out the contrast between her state of mind and the vibrant opera that she is about to attend.*

Consistent Focus

Answer: *After examining the significance of the word* Wagner *in the title, the writer examines another word choice,* matinée.

Command of Language

Answer: *Parallel elements: people of leisure, ladies of leisure; the means and time on their hands. The active verbs* contains, comes, says, have, attend, causes, seek, *and* enjoy *are all used in sentences in the active voice. The paragraph contains simple, compound, and complex sentences.*

Support

How does the quoted evidence support the thesis? What other references to the text also support the thesis?

Consistent Focus

How does the writer demonstrate a consistent focus?

Command of Language

Where do you find parallel elements, active verbs, the active voice, and varied sentences in this paragraph?

The most powerful and important word choices of all may lie in the title. First, there's the name *Wagner*. Wagner was a great composer whose music is full of emotional intensity and passion. He is not just any composer, nor a composer of tuneful, orderly delights as, for example, Bach was. Instead, he is composer of operas, great emotional works for the stage, and his work is full of ideas about freedom. At the time when Cather wrote, few people could have been further from the American prairie than Wagner was.

In contrast, Georgiana has become the human embodiment of the American prairie, at least in the eyes of the author. She has come to Boston because someone has died, and she arrives in a nearly dead state. Her long coat, a duster that seems a lot like a shroud, has become "black with soot," and her black bonnet has turned grey with dust. She is so sick from her journey or even deathly looking that the narrator's landlady experiences "shock at her appearance" and puts her "to bed at once." The narrator's assessment of his aunt when he first sees her in Boston is that she is a "battered figure," the opposite of a bright, bold figure out of a Wagner opera, alive with emotion and intensity. The next morning she remains in "a semi-somnambulant state." She says almost nothing and does almost nothing. When she does speak, it is to show her concern for details of farm life. Everything the reader learns about her at the beginning of the story is in stark contrast to the bold intensity associated with the word *Wagner*.

The title also contains the word *matinée*. A matinée is an afternoon performance. This word, which comes from French, is often associated with people of leisure, and perhaps especially in Cather's time, with ladies of leisure. In fact, the narrator says that the "matinée audience was chiefly made up of women." This audience of members of the leisure class have the means and time on their hands to attend an afternoon arts event.

People who attend matinées also have the appreciation of music, theater, or another performing art that causes them to seek and enjoy the diversion of an afternoon performance. The word choices Cather

Writing Practice

Use Precise Language Students sometimes have difficulty using precise language. They can deploy a more extensive and specific vocabulary by replacing general terms with more specific ones. Draw a T-bar diagram or a two-column chart on the board with the headings *General* and *Specific*. Write the word *sad* under the first heading. Have students supply more specific synonyms, such as *depressed, blue,* and *melancholy.* Then have students repeat this exercise with other words, such as *angry, big,* and *said.* Explain that specific terms make a writer's meaning clearer and a work more engaging.

uses to describe the matinée audience further this impression of rich women at leisure. She refers to the "color of bodices past counting." She evokes the "fabrics soft and firm, silky and sheer," as well as the rainbow of colors that include "red, mauve, pink, blue, lilac, purple, écru, rose, yellow, cream, and white." In this audience are life, color, exuberance, frills, and luxury. In contrast, Georgiana is dressed once again in black. Furthermore, details of her farm life suggest anything but silk and sheer, or pink and écru, fabrics. Instead, the details paint a picture of Georgiana doing the backbreaking work of drawing water from the dirty "lagoons where the buffalo drank." Instead of associating Georgiana with the matinée in the concert hall, the reader associates her with the "cave dwelling," a word choice Cather selects to rename Georgiana's sod home on the prairie.

Word choice also helps illuminate who Georgiana became in Nebraska—in stark contrast with the woman she might have become. Cather uses only a few words to describe Howard Carpenter, the man Georgiana married, but two of them are "shiftless, idle." When the narrator reflects on his own past in Nebraska, the reader learns that Carpenter had "spoken sharply" to him. These two words also speak volumes, for if Carpenter had "spoken sharply" to a young boy, what might he have said over the years of hard work to his wife? The narrator also reflects on what his days on the farm were like; his words no doubt describe the texture, if not the exact activities, of Georgiana's days, too. The narrator recalls "ploughing forever and forever between green aisles of corn, where, as in a treadmill, one might walk from daybreak to dusk without perceiving a shadow of change." Grim word choices like *treadmill* contrast starkly with the words *Wagner* and *matinée*. Word choices also give clues to who or what Georgiana might have become if she had never gone to Nebraska with Howard Carpenter. For example, there is the word Paris, the place Georgiana visited as a youth, and the place where she saw opera; there are the words *Boston Conservatory*, the place where she taught; and there is the word *pianist*, her great talent. All of these words evoke associations with a world of privilege, culture, music, society, and art.

Exposition

Author's Style

How does the writer show appreciation for the author's style?

Teach

Writing Skills
Author's Style
Answer: *The author analyzes Cather's word choices in detail, showing an appreciation for the impact that each word has on the reader. The quotes chosen as examples are clear examples of words that evoke associations and feelings. The author also uses descriptive precise words in the essay: "grim word choices," "contrast starkly."*

Cultural History ☆
Role of Critics Literary critics help define and maintain artistic standards, and they reflect the culture of their time. Critics have biases, so readers should be sensitive to underlying reasons for a critic's like or dislike of a particular work.

Advanced Learners

DIFFERENTIATED INSTRUCTION

Reading Literary Criticism Encourage students to use the Internet and other resources to find critical essays that discuss the stories and authors they are analyzing. Students may find it helpful to see what others have observed about particular writers or works.

Advanced students may be interested in developing a class literary magazine. The staff should choose an editor, a designer, and a technical expert. Encourage the staff to decide on the magazine's focus and to include an introductory essay that identifies a theme in the essays included in the issue.

Writing Workshop

Teach

Writing Process

Shades of Meaning

Answer: *The writer understands that the way Georgiana's voice sounds is not just a descriptive detail, but an indication of the emotion she feels. The writer associates words such as "primitive" and "inmate" with the barrenness of Georgiana's life in Nebraska.*

Organization

Answer: *The essay is organized as a series of contrasts between words, starting with the title of the essay and ending with an analysis of the final section of the essay.*

Revise Have students meet in small groups and circulate their essays among group members. Each student should make comments and suggestions on self-stick notes or an attached page. These notes should be as specific as possible.

Writer's Technique ☆

Voice Point out to students that the voice of their essays should be more formal than that which appears in their other writing. They are offering their interpretations of another person's work, so they should use language that is respectful and appropriate.

Shades of Meaning

How does the reader reflect a careful reading? In what ways does the writer find meaning in subtle details?

Organization

How is this essay organized?

Traits of Strong Writing

Include these traits of strong writing to express your ideas effectively.

Ideas
Organization
Voice
Word Choice
Sentence Fluency
Conventions
Presentation

For more information on using the Traits of Strong Writing, see pages R30–R32.

Writer's Portfolio

Place a copy of your literary analysis in your portfolio to review later.

LOG ON ▶ **Literature** Online

Writing and Research For editing and publishing tools, go to glencoe.com and enter QuickPass code GLA9800u4.

Near the end of the story, one word choice, *huskily*, speaks volumes about Georgiana. This word describes the tone of voice in which Georgiana relates to the narrator the story of the young German who briefly brought music back into her life in Nebraska. As Georgiana tells her nephew Clark about the man, her voice is husky with emotion, with the thrill of music relived, of "divine melody." Yet, in the grim "primitive" land of Nebraska, where Georgiana lives like an "inmate," nothing so grand, so full of life and passion, so uplifting and romantic, can survive.

Cather's story tells the story of a pioneer woman who has had her life drained by a life of toil on the frontier. The story does not rely on plot to convey its theme of the harsh reality of pioneer life and the life-giving powers of music, however. Instead, through a careful selection of detail, apt characterization, details about setting, as well as compelling word choice, Cather conveys all the reader wants to know—and perhaps far more—about a life without music on the Nebraska plains.

Revise

Peer Review Exchange drafts with a partner to help you identify areas of your essay that can be improved. Use the checklist below to evaluate and strengthen each other's writing.

Checklist: Writing an Effective Literary Analysis Essay

☑ Do you present a clear, insightful thesis about one aspect of the story in your introduction?

☑ Do you use substantial, specific, and relevant details to support your thesis?

☑ Do you maintain a consistent point of view and focus?

☑ Do you establish a logical pattern of organization?

☑ Do you show a command of language through precise word choice and varied sentences?

☑ Do you demonstrate a careful, thoughtful reading and an appreciation for the author's style?

Writing Practice

 Conclusions Emphasize that a conclusion should be more than a simple restatement of the main idea. Refer students to the final paragraph of Bettina L. Knapp's analysis of "The Open Boat," on page 627. Then give students the following suggestions for creating an effective conclusion:

- End with an overarching comment about the text or the writer. (Knapp says that Crane is as good as the other literary giants of his day.)

- End with an image from the story that illustrates your idea. (Knapp says that readers can almost taste the salt and hear the roar of the ocean.)

Edit and Proofread

Get It Right When you have completed the final draft of your essay, proofread for errors in grammar, usage, mechanics, and spelling. Refer to the Language Handbook, pages R42–R61, as a guide.

> **Focus Lesson**

Subject-Verb Agreement

A collective noun names a group. Common collective nouns are *team, audience, class, jury, army, club, committee, crowd, group, flock,* and *orchestra.* Usually, a collective noun that refers to a group as a whole is considered singular. If the collective noun is the subject of the sentence or clause, the verb must agree.

Problem: A collective-noun subject is treated as a plural and the verb does not agree.

She watches as the orchestra play the music of Wagner.

Solution: Make the verb agree with the singular subject.

She watches as the orchestra plays the music of Wagner.

Problem: A collective noun is incorrectly identified as the subject and the verb does not agree.

Members of the leisure class has the means and time to attend afternoon arts events.

Solution: Correctly identify the subject of the sentence.

Members of the leisure class have the means and time to attend afternoon arts events.

Present

Make It Legible If you are writing your essay by hand, be sure to use blue or black ink and extremely neat, legible handwriting. If you have torn the pages from a spiral-bound notebook, trim them with scissors to create a perfectly even edge. If you are word-processing, follow your teacher's manuscript or format guidelines.

Word Choice

This academic vocabulary word appears in the student model:

sequence (se′ kwən(t)s) *n.* 1. a related series; 2. related shots or scenes in a film or story that create a distinct episode or part; *Cather's craft transforms the story from a barebones sequence of humdrum events into a compelling work of literature.* Using academic vocabulary may help strengthen your writing. Try to use one or two academic vocabulary words in your literary analysis. See the complete list on pages R89–R91.

Peer Review Tips

Take your time and jot down notes as you read so you can give constructive feedback. Use the following questions to get started:

- Does the writer prove the thesis? Where is the support most detailed, thoughtful, and convincing?

- How does the writer increase your understanding of the story and/or your appreciation for the writer's style?

Word-Processing Tips

Headers and footers give you choices for pagination, as well as for other elements that might appear at the top or bottom of each page.

Writing Workshop

Literary Analysis

Teach

Writing Process

Edit Explain that subject-verb agreement problems are often hard to pinpoint. Suggest that students go through their essays and circle all the subjects in the sentences and underline the corresponding verbs. Students should consult a usage handbook to learn which collective nouns are always considered plural.

Remind students of the rules for capitalizing the titles of short stories, book, and articles. They should demonstrate correct capitalization when referencing works of literature in their papers. For additional support, see the Language Handbook, pages R55 and R58.

Proofread Discuss with students the reasons for careful proofreading.

Ask: What happens when mechanical errors appear in the final copy of an essay? *(Students may say that these distract readers from the ideas in the essay.)*

English Learners

DIFFERENTIATED INSTRUCTION

Intermediate Students may have trouble mastering the formal tone of critical writing. You may help them by reading aloud sections of the models on pages 625–627 and 629–632. After you read, discuss the writers' tone and word choices. Encourage students to reflect that tone in their own writing. Point out to students that neither literary analysis attempts to explain every aspect of a story. Remind students of the literary elements that they might choose to focus on.

Focus

Summary

In this workshop, students will learn techniques for organizing, preparing for, contributing to, participating in, and evaluating an oral response to literature.

Teach

Speaking Skills

Improve Delivery Help students hone their speaking skills by discussing these tips and having each student rehearse with a partner.

- Organize in your mind the main idea you wish to state. Plan how to build on small points to convey the main idea.
- Speak clearly and slowly.
- Establish eye contact with your listeners.
- Be expressive and show interest in the subject. The audience will react to your enthusiasm.

Learning Objectives

For pages 634–635

In this workshop, you will focus on the following objectives:

Listening and Speaking: Delivering an oral response to literature.
Listening to and evaluating a presentation.

Setting Time Limits

Set time limits for your group to ensure that enough time is allowed for discussion of each idea or topic.

Speaking, Listening, and Viewing Workshop

Oral Response to Literature

Literature Connection After reading thought-provoking literature such as "To Build a Fire," readers often enjoy expressing their opinions and interpretations. Participating in group discussion is a useful way for people to express their responses to literature and enhance their understanding of a piece of writing. Discussion helps people solve problems, explore ideas, and exchange information.

> **Assignment** Working in groups, discuss and respond to the major themes in "To Build a Fire" or another literary work.

Organizing a Discussion Group

When you participate in a group discussion, each member contributes ideas. Assign roles, such as facilitator and recorder, to members of your group. Each group member is to be equally responsible for discussion.

This chart will help you understand these roles.

Facilitator	
☑ Introduces the discussion topic	☑ Keeps track of the time
☑ Invites each participant to speak	☑ Helps participants arrive at a consensus
☑ Keeps the discussion focused and interactive	

Group Participants (All)	
☑ Form ideas and questions about the literature before discussion	☑ Support any opinions with detailed references to the work
☑ Contribute throughout the discussion	☑ Listen carefully to other group members
☑ Avoid repeating what has been said earlier	☑ Evaluate and respect the opinions of others

Recorder	
☑ Helps the group leader form conclusions based on the discussion	☑ Keeps track of the most important points
	☑ Helps summarize the discussion

Listening and Speaking Practice

Set a Purpose Review the purpose of the group discussion: to share responses and form conclusions. This will help each participant stay focused. Point out that each student may respond differently to the literature and that it is important to listen to the contributions of all members of the group. Encourage students to listen carefully to others' points of view and to extend, agree, or disagree with these points in their follow-up comments.

Prepare for Discussion

- Reread. Jot down one or more themes that you find in the work.
- Think about ways to narrate, explain, or describe how the author expressed the themes. List details about characters, setting, or events of the plot that help show the theme. Also, list stylistic choices, such as imagery and word choice, that help express the theme.
- Consider the ways in which the theme arises out of associations you bring to the text and judgments you make. For example, which word choices convey a broad range of connotations or nuances? Where do you find ambiguous details or events to interpret in more than one way? How does that affect your understanding of the work and your appreciation of it?

The more you think through your own ideas before the discussion starts, the better prepared you will be to make insightful, well-supported contributions and to respond thoughtfully to the ideas of others.

Participate

Taking part in a discussion is more than just presenting. You must also listen effectively and evaluate what you hear. Follow these guidelines.

- Direct your attention on the group member who is speaking.
- Respond to comments you do not understand by asking for elaboration or clarification. If you agree, say or show it.
- If you disagree, do so respectfully. Politely state your own ideas, providing evidence for them from the text.
- Engage with others in keeping the discussion focused and on track or by responding right away to any signal that you are moving off track.

Techniques for Discussing Oral Responses to Literature

☑ **Pacing** Allow each group member time to voice his or her opinion.	☑ **Listening** Remain quiet until it is your turn to speak.
☑ **Discussion** Ask open-ended questions to promote discussion.	☑ **Poise** Use nonverbal communication to show you understand what the speaker is saying.
☑ **Evaluation** Set aside some time after discussion to evaluate the group's ability to work together.	☑ **Gestures** Avoid nervous habits and other movements that may distract the speaker.

Speaking Frames

Consider using the following frames in the group discussion:

- One reason for my opinion is found in the part of the story when _____.
- I see your point, but doesn't the passage/story/character say _____?
- Yes, I know what you mean. The part of the story in which _____ also demonstrates _____.

Presentation Tips

Use the following checklist to evaluate your group discussion.

- Did everyone participate, both by presenting and by responding to the ideas of others?
- Did everyone both listen and respond respectfully?
- What would you do differently if the group met again?

 Literature Online

Speaking, Listening, and Viewing For project ideas, templates, and presentation tips, go to glencoe.com and enter QuickPass code GLA9800u4.

English Learners

DIFFERENTIATED INSTRUCTION

Intermediate English learners may use one of these techniques to improve their oral response to literature: work with a partner to formulate an oral response, practice speaking before a full-length mirror, or use a tape recorder to improve their ability to express their ideas.

Teach

Speaking Skills

Vary the Tone As students respond to literature, remind them to vary their tone as they speak. Explain that speaking in a monotone makes for a boring presentation. Students should deliberately vary their volume and intonation to hold their listeners' attention.

Listening Skills

Show Politeness Emphasize that students should listen to a classmate until he or she is finished—they should not interrupt a speaker. Suggest that they raise a hand if they have a question or comment to make while someone is speaking. Every student should have the opportunity to contribute to the discussion.

Cultural History ☆

Ways of Listening Explain that people in different countries have different rules about how to listen. In some cultures, it is impolite for a child to look at an adult who is speaking. In other cultures, it is considered rude to look away as an adult speaks. In the United States, it is considered acceptable for people of any age to look attentively at a speaker.

Focus

Summary

The purpose of Independent Reading is to encourage students to read novels from the time period they have learned about in this unit, as well as current novels that have been influenced by the period.

Teach

Literary History ☆

Compare Novels Have students who have read novels written in the early 1900s recall the subject matter of those works.

Ask: What were the authors' views of human nature and society? Were the characters real and believable? Point out that gradual changes occurred in writing during this time period. Guide students to a realization that these novels focus on believable characters living in a realistic society.

Independent Reading

Regionalist and Realist Fiction

THE LATE 1800S AND EARLY 1900S SAW GREAT DEVELOPMENTS IN TECHNOLOGY, ☆ industry, and science. As the world changed, novelists found inspiration in various places. Some, like Henry James, turned inward. These writers used insights from the developing field of psychology and focused on the thoughts and perceptions of their characters. Other writers, like Frank Norris, were struck by the turmoil of rapid industrialization and portrayed the vast, impersonal economic forces that were overwhelming individuals. Still others, such as Mark Twain, focused on reflecting the regional lifestyles in the United States, using humor to portray greater truths about human nature and U.S. culture. The themes, styles, and techniques of these authors continue to influence writers today.

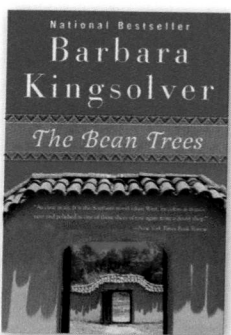

The Bean Trees

Barbara Kingsolver

Like the Regionalist writer Mark Twain, Barbara Kingsolver evokes a strong sense of place in her work. Her first novel, *The Bean Trees*, is set in Tucson, Arizona, where Kingsolver herself lived for more than 25 years. The book centers on Taylor Greer, who escapes rural Kentucky life for the freedom and anonymity of the Southwest. But when Greer unexpectedly acquires a three-year-old girl named Turtle, Greer must face the very issues she was running from—motherhood, love, abandonment, and finding a place to belong.

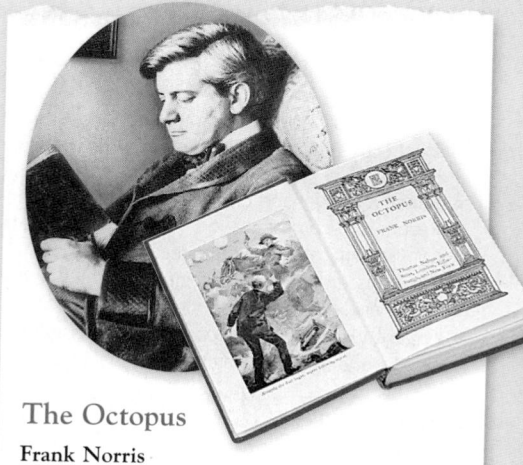

The Octopus

Frank Norris

Frank Norris was the first notable Naturalist writer in the United States. *The Octopus* was the opening novel in an unfinished trilogy—he died before the final book was written—that examines the social forces that drive agriculture and industry. In *The Octopus*, Norris describes the struggle between the railroad companies and California wheat farmers. The railroads have become a multi-tentacled monster, dominating every aspect of life, from the state legislature to the very land the farmers work. Farmers fight back, only to learn that the railroads have become the masters of those they were intended to serve.

636 UNIT 4 REGIONALISM AND REALISM

Reading Practice

Plot Have students, as they read novels independently, examine the plots of the works. Remind them that a plot is the sequence of events in a dramatic or narrative work of fiction. The plot begins with exposition, which introduces the story's characters, setting, and situation. The rising action builds to a climax, or the point of highest emotional pitch. The falling action is the logical result of the climax. The resolution, or denouement, presents the final outcome.

Have each student create a plot diagram for the novel he or she reads. Tell students to note the following events in a plot:

- exposition
- rising action
- climax
- falling action
- resolution

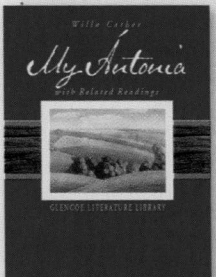

My Ántonia

Willa Cather

A young boy moves west from Virginia to the Nebraska plains and must adjust to life on the American frontier.

The Jungle

Upton Sinclair

This shocking story of an immigrant family working in Chicago's meatpacking industry led to the establishment of the Food and Drug Administration.

Heart of Darkness

Joseph Conrad

In this symbolic tale, a man describes a dark and dangerous trip he took to investigate a Belgian trader in the Congo.

CRITICS' CORNER

"The Concord, Mass. Public Library committee has decided to exclude Mark Twain's latest book from the library. One member of the committee says that, while he does not wish to call it immoral, he thinks [it] contains but little humor, and that of a very coarse type. He regards it as the veriest trash. The librarian and the other members of the committee entertain similar views, characterizing it as rough, coarse and inelegant, dealing with a series of experiences not elevating, the whole book being more suited to the slums than to intelligent, respectable people."

—*The Boston Transcript,* March 17, 1885

The Adventures of Huckleberry Finn

Mark Twain

In his novel *The Adventures of Huckleberry Finn,* Mark Twain describes the travels of the runaway orphan Huck and his new friend Jim, an African American fleeing slavery and the South. The episodic story moves between satire, slapstick, and touching portrayals of the relationship between Huck and Jim.

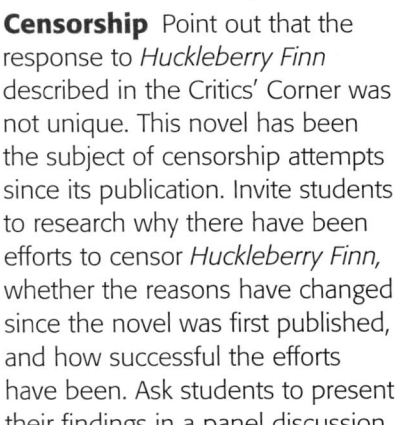

Mark Twain, 1903. Isaac Radu.

 Keep a Journal

Read one of the books listed here and record your responses and questions in a journal. After you finish the book and your journal, type up your notes and share them with your class.

Approaching Level

DIFFERENTIATED INSTRUCTION

Established To help less proficient readers understand the novels they read, have them look for the authors' purposes and the novels' themes. Often an author's reason for writing will help reveal the theme of a literary work. Remind them that a theme is the central message of a work of literature.

Independent Reading

Teach

Cultural History ☆

Censorship Point out that the response to *Huckleberry Finn* described in the Critics' Corner was not unique. This novel has been the subject of censorship attempts since its publication. Invite students to research why there have been efforts to censor *Huckleberry Finn,* whether the reasons have changed since the novel was first published, and how successful the efforts have been. Ask students to present their findings in a panel discussion.

📓 Journal

Evaluate students' journals by considering the following:

- clearly stated responses to literature
- effective use of questions
- attention to grammar and spelling conventions

📚 Glencoe Literature Library

Glencoe Literature Library offers an extensive collection of hardcover books that help you encourage your students to read independently. Choose among the more than 120 full-length literary works—novels, novellas, plays, and nonfiction. Each book includes related readings from a broad range of genres. Go to www.glencoe.com for more information.

> **For access to all study guides for the Glencoe Literature Library, see the Literature Library Teacher Resources CD-ROM.**

Bellringer Options

Say: A part of the practice test you will take today is a multiple-choice test. Your job as the test-taker is to choose each correct answer from the choices provided. Have students name other types of tests (*essay, true or false, short answer*) and describe the characteristics of each test.

Teach

Assessment Tell students that this assessment will provide reinforcement in general test-taking strategies and will test the skills and vocabulary taught in this unit. Students will first be asked to read a selection and answer comprehension, context-clue, and inference questions. Then they will be asked to answer sentence-improvement questions. Finally they will write an explanatory essay in answer to a prompt.

Writing Practice

Use Context to Discover Meaning
When students look for clues to an unfamiliar word's meaning, they are using context. Tell students to connect what they know about the surrounding words with what the author has written.

Suggest these strategies.
- Look for a synonym or antonym nearby.
- Notice whether the text relates the word's meaning to another word.
- Check for a description of an action associated with the word.
- Look for an idea related to the word.

Assessment

Assessment For additional test practice, go to glencoe.com and enter QuickPass code GLA9800u4.

English–Language Arts

Reading: Fiction

Carefully read the following passage. Use context clues to help you define any words with which you are unfamiliar. In each selection, pay close attention to the author's purpose, main idea, and use of literary or rhetorical devices. Then, on a separate sheet of paper, answer the questions on pages 639–640.

from *The Jungle* by Upton Sinclair

line

When he opened his eyes again it was to the clanging of the bell of an ambulance. He was lying in it, covered by a blanket, and it was threading its way slowly through the holiday-shopping crowds. They took
5 him to the county hospital, where a young surgeon set his arm; then he was washed and laid upon a bed in a ward with a score or two more of maimed and mangled men.
    Jurgis spent his Christmas in this hospital,
10 and it was the pleasantest Christmas he had had in America. Every year there were scandals and investigations in this institution, the newspapers charging that doctors were allowed to try fantastic experiments upon the patients; but Jurgis knew
15 nothing of this—his only complaint was that they used to feed him upon tinned meat, which no man who had ever worked in Packingtown would feed to his dog. Jurgis had often wondered just who ate the canned corned beef and "roast beef" of the
20 stockyards; now he began to understand—that it was what you might call "graft meat," put up to be sold to public officials and contractors, and eaten by soldiers and sailors, prisoners and inmates of institutions, "shantymen" and gangs of railroad laborers.
25   Jurgis was ready to leave the hospital at the end of two weeks. This did not mean that his arm

was strong and that he was able to go back to work,
but simply that he could get along without further
attention, and that his place was needed for some
30 one worse off than he. That he was utterly helpless,
and had no means of keeping himself alive in the
meantime, was something which did not concern
the hospital authorities, nor any one else in the city.
   As it chanced, he had been hurt on a
35 Monday, and had just paid for his last week's board
and his room rent, and spent nearly all the balance
of his Saturday's pay. He had less than seventy-five
cents in his pockets, and a dollar and a half due him
for the day's work he had done before he was hurt.
40 He might possibly have sued the company, and got
some damages for his injuries, but he did not know
this, and it was not the company's business to tell him.
He went and got his pay and his tools, which
he left in a pawnshop for fifty cents. Then he went
45 to his landlady, who had rented his place and had no
other for him; and then to his boardinghouse keeper,
who looked him over and questioned him. As he must
certainly be helpless for a couple of months, and had
boarded there only six weeks, she decided very
50 quickly that it would not be worth the risk to keep him
on trust.
   So Jurgis went out into the streets, in a most
dreadful plight. It was bitterly cold, and a heavy
snow was falling, beating into his face. He had no
55 overcoat, and no place to go, and two dollars and
sixty-five cents in his pocket, with the certainty that
he could not earn another cent for months.

1. In the context of line 3, what does the word
    threading mean?
    A. sewing
    B. winding
    C. whirling
    D. racing

2. What can you infer about Jurgis from the
    sentence that begins the second paragraph?
    F. He does not enjoy Christmas.
    G. He is a new arrival to the United
         States.
    H. He has never celebrated Christmas.
    J. He is surprised to learn that Christmas
         is celebrated in the United States.

Assessment

Teach

Literary History ☆
Upton Sinclair Sinclair (1878–
1968) was an American novelist,
journalist, and social reformer. He
was a pioneer in a kind of investigative journalism called muckraking, which sought to expose social
injustice. He received a Pulitzer
Prize for a novel about Hitler's rise
to power in Germany.

Assess
Reading

1. **B** is the correct answer because
   threading in this context means
   "passing through and between."
   (DOK 1)

2. **G** is the correct answer because
   the sentence clearly implies that
   Jurgis is a new arrival. (DOK 4)

To create custom assessments
online, go to Progress Reporter
Online Assessment.

To create custom assessments
using software, use ExamView
Assessment Suite.

Approaching Level
DIFFERENTIATED INSTRUCTION

Established When confronted with a
reading selection on a test, students may
use the following tips:
- Read slowly and carefully.
- Reread difficult passages.
- Take careful notes or construct a graphic
  as an aid to recalling main ideas and
  details.

Emphasize that students must pace
themselves whenever they need to read
a selection and answer questions within a
limited time frame.

Assessment

Assess

3. D is the correct answer because *fantastic* in this context means "bizarre" or "grotesque."

(**DOK 1**)

4. F is the correct answer because the narrator states in lines 20–24 that "graft meat" is produced to make a profit for public officials and contractors who feed the meat to members of the armed forces, inmates of institutions, and impoverished laborers. (**DOK 1**)

5. C is the correct answer because the narrator states in lines 28–29 that Jurgis was released because "he could get along without further attention."

(**DOK 1**)

6. F is the correct answer because the narrator states in lines 30–31 that Jurgis was "utterly helpless, and had no means of keeping himself alive." (**DOK 1**)

7. B is the correct answer because the narrator states in lines 37–39 that Jurgis had "less than seventy-five cents in his pockets and a dollar and a half due him for the day's work he had done before he was hurt." (**DOK 1**)

8. J is the correct answer because there is no information in the selection to indicate that Jurgis was untrustworthy or dangerous or wanted to live rent-free. (**DOK 4**)

9. D is the correct answer because the selection focuses on social injustice. (**DOK 2**)

10. G is the correct answer because the narrator reveals Jurgis's personality through Jurgis's actions and other people's reactions to him. (**DOK 2**)

11. D is the correct answer because although the narrator adheres closely to Jurgis's thought processes, the narrator

3. In the context of line 13, what does the word *fantastic* mean?
   A. wonderful
   B. amazing
   C. zealous
   D. strange

4. What is Jurgis's only complaint about the hospital?
   F. The quality of the tinned meat is poor.
   G. The doctors perform experiments.
   H. Scandals are reported.
   J. The young doctor is a poor surgeon.

5. Why does Jurgis leave the hospital after two weeks?
   A. He is completely healed.
   B. He is eager to return to his work.
   C. He can get along without further attention.
   D. He needs to speak with the boardinghouse keeper.

6. Which of the following is an effect of Jurgis's injury?
   F. He loses his ability to work.
   G. He is released too soon from the hospital.
   H. He sues the company.
   J. He spends all his Saturday pay.

7. Why did Jurgis leave his tools in the pawnshop?
   A. He didn't need them any longer.
   B. He needed the money the pawnbroker paid for them.
   C. They had been damaged in the accident.
   D. They were a painful reminder of his misfortune.

8. What can you infer from the phrase ". . . [his boardinghouse keeper] decided very quickly that it would not be worth the risk to keep him on trust"?
   F. Jurgis was untrustworthy.
   G. Jurgis was a dangerous man.
   H. Jurgis wanted to live at the boardinghouse free of charge.
   J. Jurgis was not likely to earn enough money for his rent any time soon.

9. What is the central conflict presented in this passage?
   A. man versus nature
   B. man versus man
   C. man versus fate
   D. man versus society

10. In this passage, how does Sinclair reveal the personality of Jurgis?
   F. direct characterization
   G. indirect characterization
   H. metaphor
   J. symbol

11. From what point of view is this passage written?
   A. first person
   B. second person
   C. third-person limited
   D. third-person omniscient

12. What is the overall tone of this passage?
   F. reportorial
   G. comic
   H. ironic
   J. angry

13. What does this passage strongly suggest?
   A. Industrialization had overwhelmingly positive results.
   B. Packing houses had stringent standards of quality.
   C. The poor received inferior health care.
   D. The economic system was often brutal and unforgiving.

14. Which story element in this passage affects all the others?
   F. the setting
   G. the plot
   H. the characters
   J. the dialogue

15. Which of the following do you think best describes Sinclair's purpose in *The Jungle*?
   A. to entertain
   B. to persuade
   C. to describe
   D. to explain

knows things about the hospital that Jurgis does not know. (**DOK 2**)

12. F is the correct answer because, despite the trenchant social criticism implied in the excerpt, the narrator maintains an objective tone. (**DOK 4**)

13. D is the correct answer because Jurgis's dire plight is due to the exploitation of workers under industrial capitalism. (**DOK 4**)

14. F is the correct answer because the setting in the hospital is the focal point of Jurgis's predicament. (**DOK 4**)

15. B is the correct answer because Sinclair's purpose is to expose a social problem and, by implication, to persuade people to do something about it. (**DOK 4**)

Vocabulary Skills: Sentence Completion

For each question in the Vocabulary Skills section, choose the best word to complete the sentence.

1. In his novel *The Jungle*, Upton Sinclair exposed the _____ conditions in the meat-packing industry.
   A. palpable
   B. wallowing
   C. degenerate
   D. venerable

2. He wanted to change public _____ and arouse empathy for the workers' plight to inspire concrete action.
   F. poise
   G. perception
   H. valedictory
   J. reverence

3. The meat-packers often would _____ processes that would have protected the health of the workers and wholesomeness of their products.
   A. covet
   B. vindicate
   C. stipulate
   D. scorn

4. Many _____ and inappropriate products often found their way into the meat processed in the plants.
   F. transformed
   G. vile
   H. perennial
   J. vivid

5. Hundreds of people refused _____ to eat meat again after reading *The Jungle*.
   A. doggedly
   B. abjectly
   C. sluggishly
   D. exclusively

6. Across the country, disgust, wariness, and mistrust of many processed foods became _____.
   F. arduous
   G. tactful
   H. incessant
   J. occult

7. Many normally _____ people became militant in their condemnation of the meat-packing industry.
   A. exalted
   B. subverting
   C. presumptuous
   D. apathetic

8. There was remarkable _____ among those responding to the urgency of Sinclair's message.
   F. disposition
   G. repose
   H. persistence
   J. depravity

9. Public outrage grew as people became _____ in their support of change.
   A. misanthropic
   B. emphatic
   C. elusive
   D. premeditated

10. The uproar incited by Sinclair's book eventually caused the government to _____ and pass the Pure Food and Drug Act.
   F. intervene
   G. interpose
   H. reprieve
   J. tarnish

Assess

Vocabulary

1. **B** is the correct answer because it is the only option that describes conditions. `DOK 1`

2. **G** is the correct answer because is the only option that goes with *public*. `DOK 1`

3. **D** is the correct answer because the context clue *that would have prevented* implies that the missing word means "did not take seriously." `DOK 1`

4. **G** is the correct answer because it is the only option that fits with the context clue *inappropriate*. `DOK 1`

5. **A** is the correct answer because it is the only option that makes sense in this context. `DOK 1`

6. **H** is the correct answer because it is the only option that fits with the context clue *across the country*. `DOK 1`

7. **D** is the correct answer because the missing word must be an antonym of *militant*. `DOK 1`

8. **H** is the correct answer because it is the only option that makes sense in this context. `DOK 1`

9. **B** is the correct answer because it is the only option that makes sense in this context. `DOK 1`

10. **F** is the correct answer because it is the only option that makes sense in this context. `DOK 1`

English Learners

DIFFERENTIATED INSTRUCTION

Intermediate Tell students to use context clues and etymology to narrow down the meaning of difficult words. Students should begin by reading a sentence and thinking of a familiar word that could complete the sentence. Next students should compare that word with the answer choices. If any are similar in meaning, they should be seriously considered. Students can also look at word roots for clues to meaning. For example, the word *zealous* contains the root *zeal,* meaning "fervor" or "passion." This links *zealous* to the context clue *outrage* because both relate to extreme emotions.

Assess

Grammar and Writing

1. **C** is the correct answer because it is the only option that corrects the sentence fragment without introducing other errors. `DOK 1`

2. **H** is the correct answer because the writer needs to define the unfamiliar term *muckraking* for readers. `DOK 4`

3. **D** is the correct answer because the adverbial clause *when he was a boy* should be next to *began,* the verb it modifies. `DOK 2`

4. **J** is the correct answer because the selfishness of other people is irrelevant to the essay about Jacob Riis. `DOK 4`

Grammar and Writing Skills: Paragraph Improvement

Read carefully through the following passage from the first draft of a student's essay. Pay close attention to verb tense, the use of modifying phrases, and sentence fragments. Then, on a separate sheet of paper, answer the questions below.

(1) During the early 1900s, many authors began focusing on social problems. (2) The reformer, journalist, and photographer Jacob Riis was influential to initiate. (3) The tradition called muckraking.

(4) Riis immigrated to the United States from Denmark in 1870. (5) His concern began when he was a boy with those less fortunate than himself. (6) According to legend, one Christmas, he gave all his money to a family that had even less than the Riis's. (7) In contrast, there are many people who are terribly selfish and only look out for themselves.

(8) Once in America, Riis lived for many years in extreme poverty, unable to find work. (9) Ultimately becoming a reporter for a New York newspaper, he used his skills to investigate and educate people about the fix of the poor. (10) One of Riis most influential books was *How the Other Half Lives.* (11) In this work, he exposed in the city the deplorable living conditions of the poor. (12) These slums included lodging-houses that often offered no more than a rat-infested mattress. (13) Many people could not even afford the few cents for a bed, though. (14) They slept in alleys wrapped up in newspapers or blankets. (15) Riis continued to write on the problems of the poor; and also gave lectures. (16) His photographs and magic-lantern shows added immeasurably to the effect of his words.

1. Which of the following is the best way to combine sentences 2 and 3?
   A. To initiate the tradition, called muckraking, the reformer, journalist, and photographer Jacob Riis was influential.
   B. The tradition called muckraking, was what the reformer, journalist, and photographer Jacob Riis was influential to initiate.
   C. The reformer, journalist, and photographer Jacob Riis was influential in initiating the tradition called muckraking.
   D. Initiating the tradition called muckraking, was what the reformer, journalist, and photographer Jacob Riis influenced.

2. What details should be inserted after sentence 3 to make the essay more informative?
   F. other traditions of the time
   G. Riis's specific influence on muckraking
   H. a definition of "muckraking"
   J. a list of other muckrakers

3. Which of the following errors appears in sentence 5?
   A. sentence fragment
   B. incorrect verb tense
   C. incorrect parallelism
   D. misplaced modifier

4. Which sentence in the second paragraph is not relevant to this essay?
   F. 4
   G. 5
   H. 6
   J. 7

Writing Practice

Paragraph Improvement Explain to students that questions that ask how best to revise a sentence typically refer to one error in that sentence. They should read the sentence to identify the place that sounds awkward or wrong. Tell them to rewrite the sentence in their minds and then look at the answer choices to find the one that revises the error without introducing another error. If a sentence revises some part of the sentence that was not incorrect, they should quickly skip that choice.

5. Which of the following is the best replacement for the word "fix" in sentence 9?
   A. plight
   B. case
   C. matter
   D. mode

6. Which of the following is the best revision of sentence 10?
   F. One of Riis most influential books, was *How the Other Half Lives.*
   G. One of Riis's most influential books was *How the Other Half Lives.*
   H. One of Riis' most influential books was, *How the Other Half Lives.*
   J. One of Riis' most influential, books was, *How the Other Half Lives.*

7. In sentence 11, which of the following is the best position for the phrase "in the city"?
   A. after "work"
   B. between "living" and "conditions"
   C. between "the" and "poor"
   D. after "poor"

8. Between which sentences should the writer begin a new paragraph?
   F. 10 and 11.
   G. 11 and 12.
   H. 12 and 13.
   J. 14 and 15.

9. Which of the following is the best revision of sentence 15?
   A. Riis continued to write and lecture on the problems of the poor.
   B. Continuing to write on the problems of the poor, Riis also was giving lectures.
   C. The problems of the poor continued to occupy Riis in both writing and lecturing.
   D. Continuously, also giving lectures, Riis wrote on the problems of the poor.

10. Which of the following is the best title for this essay?
   F. "The Muckrakers"
   G. "Jacob Riis: Reformer"
   H. "The Problems of the Poor"
   J. "Nineteenth-Century Danish Immigration"

Essay

Injustice has been an ongoing characteristic of human society. The authors featured in this unit used their works to inform readers of the realities of injustices such as war, racism, and poverty. Write an essay in which you explain what it means to struggle against injustice. Support your explanation with examples and details from the works in the unit as well as your own experiences. As you write, keep in mind that your essay will be checked for **ideas, organization, voice, word choice, sentence fluency, conventions,** and **presentation.**

Approaching Level

DIFFERENTIATED INSTRUCTION

Emerging Remind students about the response to literature they wrote in the Writing Workshop and explain that that was an example of one kind of explanatory writing. Suggest that they include the same elements they used in their analyses—a thesis, an organized series of major points, supporting evidence, and an effective conclusion—in their explanatory essays here. Tell them to remember to vary their sentence structure and to proofread their essays for mechanical errors.

Assessment

Assess

5. **A** is the correct answer because the negative connotations of *plight* most vividly capture the difficult situation of the poor. `DOK 1`

6. **G** is the correct answer because it is the only option that correctly spells the possessive of Riis without introducing other errors. `DOK 1`

7. **D** is the correct answer because it places the prepositional phrase *in the city* next to the collective noun that it modifies, *poor.* `DOK 1`

8. **J** is the correct answer because sentence 15 begins the concluding paragraph. `DOK 4`

9. **A** is the correct answer because it is the most economical way of stating the idea while correcting the misuse of the semicolon. `DOK 1`

10. **G** is the correct answer because it is the only option that focuses on Jacob Riis, the subject of the essay. `DOK 2`

Essay

Evaluate essays for the following:

- a clearly stated explanation of what the struggle against injustice means to the writer, well-organized and supported by relevant examples and details from literary works in the unit and from the writer's experiences
- effective voice, word choice, and sentence variety
- effective presentation, with attention to grammar and spelling conventions
`DOK 3`

Skills Scope and Sequence

Readability Scores Key: Dale-Chall/DRP/Lexile

PART 1: Modern Poetry

Selections and Features	Literary Elements
Unit Introduction pp. 644–658	
Literary Periods Symbolist and Imagist Poetry pp. 660–661	Symbolism **TE** p. 660
Poems In a Station of the Metro and **A Pact,** by Ezra Pound pp. 662–665	Imagery **SE** p. 663
Poem The Love Song of J. Alfred Prufrock, by T. S. Eliot pp. 666–675	Allusion **SE** p. 667 Dramatic Monologue (review) **SE** p. 674
Poems The Red Wheelbarrow and **This is Just to Say,** by William Carlos Williams pp. 676–680	Form **SE** p. 677
Vocabulary Workshop p. 681	
Poems Summer Rain and Fireworks, by Amy Lowell pp. 682–686	Structure **SE** p. 683

Comparing Literature
   Ars Poetica (poem), by Archibald MacLeish
   from **Letters to a Young Poet** (letter), by Rainer Maria Rilke **8.3/59/860**
   Eating Poetry (poem), by Mark Strand
   beware: do not read this poem (poem), by Ishmael Reed pp. 687–698
	Theme **SE** pp. 689–691
	Simile **TE** p. 690

Poems Study of Two Pears and *from* **The Man with the Blue Guitar,** by Wallace Stevens pp. 699–703	Tone **SE** p. 700

Reading Skills and Strategies	Vocabulary	Writing Grammar	Speaking, Listening, and Viewing
Analyze Graphic Information **SE** pp. 647, 649 Summarize **SE** p. 653 Analyze Cause and Effect **SE** pp. 655, 657	Context Clues **TE** p. 656	Create a Graph **TE** p. 648 Note Taking **TE** p. 650 Create Graphic Organizers **TE** p. 652	Analyze Art **TE** p. 645 Oral Interpretation **SE** p. 658
		Connect to Poetry **TE** p. 660	Analyze Art **TE** p. 660; **SE** p. 661
Question **SE** p. 663 Visualize **TE** p. 664	Multiple-Meaning Words **TE** p. 663 Context Clues **SE** p. 665	Paraphrase **TE** p. 664 Write a Poem **SE** p. 665	
Connect to Cultural Context **SE** p. 667 Identify Sequence **TE** p. 668	Analogies **TE** p. 667 Antonyms **SE** p. 674	Write a Short Story **SE** p. 675 Run-on Sentences **SE** p. 675	Analyze Art **SE** p. 673
Recognize Author's Purpose **SE** p. 677 Activate Prior Knowledge **TE** p. 678	Synonyms **SE** p. 677 Word Parts **TE** p. 677	Write a List **SE** p. 680	Analyze Art **TE** p. 679
	Compound Words **SE** p. 681		
Interpret Imagery **SE** p. 683	Synonyms **TE** p. 683 Context Clues **SE** p. 686	Voice **TE** p. 684 Write a Dialogue **SE** p. 686	
Analyze Style **SE** p. 689 Reread **TE** p. 694	Word Roots **TE** p. 689 Analogies **SE** p. 691	Verbs as Adjectives **TE** p. 688 Author's Purpose **TE** p. 692 Identify a Literary Trend **SE** p. 698	
Recognize Author's Purpose **SE** p. 700 Interpret **TE** p. 702	Word Origins **SE** p. 703 Synonyms **TE** p. 700	Write a Journal Entry **SE** p. 703	Analyze Art **TE** p. 701

Readability Scores Key: Dale-Chall/DRP/Lexile

PART 1: Modern Poetry *(continued)*

Selections and Features	Literary Elements
Poems somewhere I have never travelled, gladly beyond and **anyone lived in a pretty how town,** by e. e. cummings pp. 704–708	Rhythm **SE** p. 705
Poems Chicago and Grass, by Carl Sandburg pp. 709–713	Apostrophe **SE** p. 710
Poems **Mending Wall,** Birches, **Stopping By Woods on a Snowy Evening, Acquainted with the Night,** and **The Death of the Hired Man,** by Robert Frost pp. 714–734	Blank Verse **SE** p. 715 Rhyme Scheme **SE** pp. 722, 724
Political Perspective Remarks at Amherst College, by President John F. Kennedy **9.7/65/1270** pp. 735–738	

PART 2: Modern Fiction

Selections and Features	Literary Elements
Literary Periods The Modern American Short Story pp. 740–741	Antihero **TE** p. 741
Short Story In Another Country, by Ernest Hemingway **4.7/54/1050** pp. 742–750	Style **SE** p. 743
Grammar Workshop p. 751	
Short Story Winter Dreams, by F. Scott Fitzgerald **7.9/60/1080** pp. 752–772	Motivation **SE** p. 753 Conflict (review) **SE** p. 771
Short Story The Jilting of Granny Weatherall, by Katherine Anne Porter **4.6/50/820** pp. 773–784	Stream of Consciousness **SE** p. 774 Characterization (review) **SE** p. 783

Reading Skills and Strategies	Vocabulary	Writing / Grammar	Speaking, Listening, and Viewing
Analyze Style **SE** p. 705	Multiple-Meaning Words **TE** p. 705 Analogies **SE** p. 708	Write a Character Sketch **SE** p. 708	Analyze Art **TE** p. 706
Make Inferences About Theme **SE** p. 710 Recognize Author's Purpose **TE** p. 712	Denotation and Connotation **SE** p. 713 Adjectives **TE** p. 710	Write a Poem **SE** p. 713	Analyze Art **TE** p. 712
Compare and Contrast Speakers **SE** p. 715	Concrete and Abstract Nouns **TE** p. 715 Synonyms **SE** p. 720 Academic Vocabulary **SE** p. 724	Write a Dialogue **SE** p. 722 Write a List **SE** p. 724 Write a Poem **SE** p. 734	Analyze Art **SE** p. 716 Choral Reading **TE** p. 718
Analyze Philosophical Assumptions **TE** p. 738		Research Statistics **TE** p. 736	

Reading Skills and Strategies	Vocabulary	Writing / Grammar	Speaking, Listening, and Viewing
			Analyze Art **TE** p. 740
Recognize Author's Purpose **SE** p. 743 Identify Writer's Technique **TE** p. 744	Parts of Speech **TE** p. 743 Antonyms **SE** p. 750 Academic Vocabulary **SE** p. 750	Research and Report **TE** p. 746 Write a Personal Response **TE** p. 748 Apply Diction **SE** p. 750	Analyze Art **TE** p. 744; **SE** p. 746
		Coordinating Conjunctions **SE** p. 751	
Evaluate Sensory Details **SE** p. 753 Preview **TE** p. 754	Synonyms **SE** p. 771 Academic Vocabulary **SE** p. 771	Dramatize a Scene **TE** p. 756 Write a College Application Essay **TE** p. 764 Write a Short Story **SE** p. 772	Discussion **TE** p. 762
Monitor Comprehension **TE** p. 774 Draw Conclusions About the Protagonist **SE** p. 77	Suffixes **TE** p. 774 Context Clues **SE** p. 784	Write a Eulogy **TE** p. 776 Make a Timeline **TE** p. 778 Write a Monologue **SE** p. 784	Analyze Art **SE** p. 779 Discussion **TE** p. 780 Perform a Monologue **SE** p. 784

Readability Scores Key: Dale-Chall/DRP/Lexile

PART 3: The Harlem Renaissance

Selections and Features	Literary Elements
Poem My City, by James Weldon Johnson pp. 786–789	Sonnet **SE** p. 787
Autobiography *from* **Dust Tracks on a Road,** by Zora Neale Hurston **5.1/53/920** pp. 790–799	Voice **SE** p. 791 Allusion (review) **SE** p. 798
Vocabulary Workshop p. 800	
Poems If We Must Die and **The Tropics of New York,** by Claude McKay pp. 801–805	Meter **SE** p. 802
Informational Text TIME: Stanzas from a Black Epic, by Robert Hughes **9.8/68/1240** pp. 806–809	
Poems I, Too and **The Negro Speaks of Rivers,** by Langston Hughes pp. 810–814	Repetition **SE** p. 811
Autobiography When the Negro Was in Vogue, by Langston Hughes **6.1/64/1290** pp. 815–823	Juxtaposition **SE** p. 816 Historical Narrative (review) **SE** p. 822
Poem A black man talks of reaping, by Arna Bontemps pp. 824–827	Metaphor **SE** p. 825 Allusion **TE** p. 826
Poem Any Human to Another, by Countee Cullen pp. 828–831	Stanza **SE** p. 829
Writing Workshop pp. 832–839	
Speaking, Listening, and Viewing Workshop pp. 840–841	
Independent Reading p. 842–843	
Assessment pp. 844–849	

Reading Skills and Strategies	Vocabulary	Writing Grammar	Speaking, Listening, and Viewing
Interpret Imagery **SE** p. 787	Antonyms **SE** p. 787	Write a Brochure **SE** p. 789	Analyze Art **TE** p. 788
Analyze Language **SE** p. 791 Predict **TE** p. 792 Connect **TE** p. 796	Synonyms and Antonyms **TE** p. 791 Analogies **SE** p. 791	Point of View **TE** p. 794 Apply Allusion **SE** p. 799	Analyze Art **TE** p. 792; **SE** p. 795
	Homonyms **SE** p. 800		
Identify Author's Purpose **TE** p. 802 Analyze Tone **SE** p. 802	Synonyms **TE** p. 802 Word Origins **SE** p. 805	Write a Poem **SE** p. 805	Analyze Art **TE** p. 804
Preview **TE** p. 806		Write a List **TE** p. 806	Analyze Art **TE** p. 808
Make Predictions About Theme **SE** p. 811	Analogies **SE** pp. 811, 814	Write a Poem **TE** p. 812 Write an Essay **SE** p. 814	
Analyze Concrete Details **SE** p. 815	Word Roots **TE** p. 818 Synonyms **SE** p. 822	Write an Essay **TE** p. 820 Write an Essay **SE** p. 823 Ellipses **SE** p. 823	Design a Poster **TE** p. 816 Analyze Art **TE** p. 818
Connect to Personal Experience **SE** p. 825	Context Clues **SE** p. 825		Analyze Art **TE** p. 826
Connect to Contemporary Issues **SE** p. 829 Analyze Text Structure **TE** p. 830	Antonyms **SE** p. 829	Write a Journal Entry **SE** p. 831	Analyze Art **TE** p. 830
	Multiple-Meaning Words **TE** p. 836	Abstract vs. Concrete Nouns **TE** p. 838 Write an Essay **SE** pp. 839	
Scan **TE** p. 840			Oral Interpretation **SE** p. 840
			Discussion **TE** p. 842 Create a Book Jacket **SE** p. 843
		Write an Essay **SE** p. 849	

Focus

Bellringer Options

Literature Launcher
Pre-Reading Video: Unit 5

Daily Language Practice
Transparency 55

Or **say:** Contrast how people live during hard times and during prosperous times. *(Students may say that in hard times people cannot find work, so they they have less money. In prosperous times, people spend money more freely.)* From 1910 to 1930, people in the United States experienced both hard times because of World War I and good times with a booming economy, rapid industrialization, advances in technology, and social change.

For school-to-home activities, see Unit 5 Teaching Resources Book, pp. 5–11.

The Great White Way, Times Square, c. 1925. Howard A. Thain. Oil on canvas, New York Historical Society.

View the Art In 1925, the year Howard Thain painted this night scene of Times Square, New York surpassed London as the most populous city in the world. What does Thain seem to suggest about city life during this era? ★

644

Unit Introduction Skills

Reading Skills
- Analyze Graphic Information (SE pp. 647, 649)
- Summarize (SE p. 653)
- Analyze Cause and Effect (SE pp. 655, 657)
- Use Graphic Organizers (TE p. 646)
- Outline (TE p. 654)

Beginnings of the Modern Age

Study Skills/Research/Assessment
- Note Taking (TE p. 650)
- Create Graphic Organizers (TE p. 652)

Vocabulary Skills
- Use Context Clues (TE p. 656)

Writing Skills/Grammar
- Create a Graph (TE p. 648)
- Organize Information (TE p. 658)

Listening/Speaking/Viewing Skills
- Give an Oral Interpretation (SE p. 658)
- Analyze Art (TE pp. 645, 651, 655, 657)

BEGINNINGS OF THE MODERN AGE
1910-1930s

Looking Ahead

Modern American literature developed in a turbulent era characterized by extremes—both despair and exuberance. The violence of World War I caused many people to lose faith in traditional values. Following the war, an economic boom ushered in an age of prosperity and confidence. Writers of the time created new literary works that mirrored this period of rapid change and clashing values.

Keep the following questions in mind as you read:

≈ How did World War I change Americans' view of the world?

≈ How was Modernism a departure from the American literary tradition?

≈ What social and cultural forces shaped the Harlem Renaissance?

645

Focus
Summary

This introduction begins with an overview of the historical, social, and cultural forces in the United States from 1910 to 1930. It focuses on the effects of World War I, the Roaring Twenties, women's rights, the Great Depression, and the major features of the modern age in American literature: the new poetics, modern fiction, and the Harlem Renaissance.

View the Art ★

Answer: *The scene suggests prosperity: bright lights, people in formal clothing, and crowds entering theatres.*

The Modernist painter Howard A. Thain (1891–1959) was born in Dallas, Texas, but later lived in New York City, where he studied art at the Art Students League. He is best known for his New York cityscapes. Explain that "The Great White Way" is a nickname for Broadway, the home of many theaters.

For students who would profit from independent novel study, see Novel Companion pp. 207–251.

Unit Resources

Print Materials

- Unit 5 Teaching Resources, pp. 1–310
- Interactive Read and Write (On Level, Approaching, EL), pp. 179–212
- Novel Companion, pp. 207–251
- Bellringer Option Transparencies: Selection Focus 40–52; Daily Language Practice 55–77
- Assessment Resources, Selection Assessment, pp. 187–234

Technology

- TeacherWorks Plus CD
- StudentWorks Plus CD
- Literature Launchers: Pre-Reading Videos DVD, Unit 5
- Literature Online
- Visual Vocabulary CD-ROM
- Listening Library CD-ROM
- ExamView CD-ROM
- Skill Level Up! CD-ROM

Teach

Reading Strategy | 1

Use the Timeline Have students examine the timeline and relate key events in American literature to events in the United States and around the world.

Say: During this time period, World War I occurred, along with other historic events, such as the sinking of the *Titanic,* the ratification of the Nineteenth Amendment, and the stock market crash.

Ask: What other events of this time have you heard about? *(Answers will vary. Students may say that they know about Henry Ford's assembly lines, Prohibition, or Babe Ruth.)*

Political History ☆

Women Get the Vote In 1920, the states ratified the Nineteenth Amendment, which granted women the right to vote. For Carrie Chapman Catt, a feminist leader, the amendment was the result of 25 years of work. Before her marriage to George Catt in 1890, she demanded a prenuptial agreement guaranteeing that for four months each year she could devote herself to women's suffrage.

TIMELINE 1910–1930s

AMERICAN LITERATURE | 1

1910

1910
Twenty Years at Hull-House by Jane Addams

1912
Harriet Monroe founds *Poetry: A Magazine of Verse*

1913
A Boy's Will poetry collection by Robert Frost

1914
Tender Buttons by Gertrude Stein

1916
Chicago Poems by Carl Sandburg

1919
Winesburg, Ohio by Sherwood Anderson published

1920

1920
The Age of Innocence by Edith Wharton

1920
Main Street by Sinclair Lewis

1921
American Indian Stories by Zitkala-Sa

UNITED STATES EVENTS

1910

1910
W. E. B. Du Bois founds the *Crisis* magazine

1911
National Urban League formed

1911
The Nestor Company builds the first Hollywood film studio

1913
Henry Ford introduces assembly-line productivity

1913
U.S. mint issues first "buffalo," or "Indian head," nickel

1914
Marcus Garvey founds Universal Negro Improvement Association

1916
Great Migration begins

1917
United States declares war on Germany

1919
Black Sox Scandal rocks American baseball

1920

1920
Prohibition Amendment outlaws the sale of alcohol

1920
Nineteenth Amendment gives women the right to vote ☆

1920
The nation's first commercial radio station, KDKA, begins broadcasting in Pittsburgh

WORLD EVENTS

1910

1910
Mexican Revolution begins

1912
Native American Jim Thorpe stars at the Olympic games

1912
Titanic sinks after striking an iceberg near Newfoundland

1913
The Rite of Spring by Russian composer Igor Stravinsky heralds Modernism in music

1914 ▲
Panama Canal opens

1914
World War I begins

1918
Armistice signed in France, ending WW I

1920

1920
First meeting of the League of Nations in Geneva, Switzerland

1921
Diego Rivera begins his first mural in Mexico

1921
Mongolia gains independence from China

LOG ON ▶ **Literature** Online

Literature and Reading To explore the Interactive Timeline, go to glencoe.com and enter QuickPass code GLA9800u5.

Reading Practice

Use Graphic Organizers Explain that graphic organizers provide an opportunity to see information at a glance. Charts allow students to analyze and compare information. Give students the following tips for reading a chart:

- Examine the title, labels, and other explanatory features.
- Study how the labels clarify the information in the chart.

Guide students through a discussion of the timeline, using the steps listed above. Have students choose one event from the timeline and write one or two sentences about the event. Have them share their writing with the class.

Langston Hughes, 1932. Carl van Vechten. Photograph, gelatin silver print, 14.1 x 21.4 cm. Gift of Prentiss Taylor. National Portrait Gallery, Smithsonian Institution, Washington, DC.

Teach

Reading Check

Answer: *Two: Mexico and Mongolia*

Reading Strategy   2

Draw Conclusions

Ask: What conclusion can you draw about the women of the time based on the information provided in the timeline? *(Students may say that women's roles were changing, perhaps due to women's rights activists.)* What information in the timeline led you to your conclusion? *(Many female writers are being published; women are given the right to vote.)*

1930

1921
All–African American musical *Shuffle Along* opens on Broadway

1922
The Waste Land by T. S. Eliot

1922
The Enormous Room by E. E. Cummings

1923
Edna St. Vincent Millay wins Pulitzer Prize in poetry

1925
The New Yorker magazine established

1925
The Great Gatsby by F. Scott Fitzgerald

1926
The Weary Blues by Langston Hughes ▲

1926
The Sun Also Rises by Ernest Hemingway

1928
Home to Harlem by Claude McKay

1930
Flowering Judas by Katherine Anne Porter

1936
Eugene O'Neill wins Nobel Prize in Literature

1930

1924
☆ Immigration Act bars nearly all Asians

1925
Schoolteacher John Scopes goes on trial for teaching evolution in Tennessee

1926
Jelly Roll Morton and his Red Hot Peppers begin a series of jazz recordings

1927
Conclusion of Sacco-Vanzetti murder trial draws world attention

1927 ▲
Charles Lindbergh flies the first nonstop solo flight across the Atlantic Ocean

1927
Babe Ruth hits 60 home runs, a record until 1961

1927
First feature-length talking motion picture, or "talkie," *The Jazz Singer,* is released

1929
League of United Latin American Citizens founded

1929
The stock market crashes; Great Depression begins

1931
"The Star-Spangled Banner" becomes national anthem

1935
George H. Gallup begins the Gallup Poll

1938
Minimum wage is established in the Fair Labor Standards Act

2

Cultural History ☆

Closing the Door Congress continued to close the celebrated "open door" to the United States during the 1920s by passing the Immigration Act. Immigration restrictions in 1921 and 1924 targeted Asians and southern and eastern Europeans.

1930

1922
Irish writer James Joyce publishes *Ulysses*

1922
Insulin isolated and used to save a life, first successful diabetes treatment

1926
Economic turmoil leads to a general strike in Britain

1928
Fifteen countries sign the Kellogg-Briand Pact, condemning war

1928
Joseph Stalin starts eliminating private businesses in Soviet Union

▲ Mohandas K. Gandhi

1930
Mohandas K. Gandhi leads protest against British salt monopoly in India

Reading Check

Analyze Graphic Information How many changes of government throughout the world are shown on this timeline?

Approaching Level

DIFFERENTIATED INSTRUCTION

SMALL GROUP **Established** Explain some timeline events that students may not recognize. For example, explain that the "Gallup Poll" is a public opinion poll. Have small groups research and share information about one unfamiliar event with the class.

Advanced Learners

DIFFERENTIATED INSTRUCTION

Assembly Line Production Have students research the effect of Henry Ford's use of the assembly line in the manufacture of automobiles. Ask students to focus on one topic: effect on labor, effect on where people lived, or effect on streetcar and train transportation. Students must consult at least two reputable sources.

Have students write a report that identifies a main idea and supporting examples. Then have them report their results to the class.

Teach

Make Inferences In the chart "World War I Military Deaths," have students compare the number of deaths of United States military personnel with the number of deaths of personnel from other countries.

Ask: Why do you think there were fewer American deaths than German, French, and Russian deaths? *(Students may say that the United States entered the war at a later date than these countries; the major battles were fought in Europe, while no battles took place in the United States.)*

Cultural History ☆

Car Culture In 1910 there were about 500,000 cars in the United States. By 1920 there were more than 8 million. By 1925 nearly 20 million cars traveled on the nation's roads. Before World War I, almost no one borrowed money to buy a car. By 1925, 75 percent of all cars were purchased on the installment plan.

BY THE NUMBERS

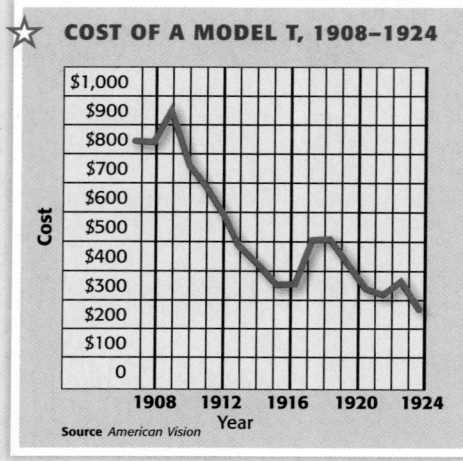

☆ COST OF A MODEL T, 1908–1924

(Line graph showing Cost in dollars, from $0 to $1,000, against Year from 1908 to 1924. Cost peaks around $900 near 1908–1909 and declines to roughly $250 by 1924, with a brief rise around 1916.)

Source *American Vision*

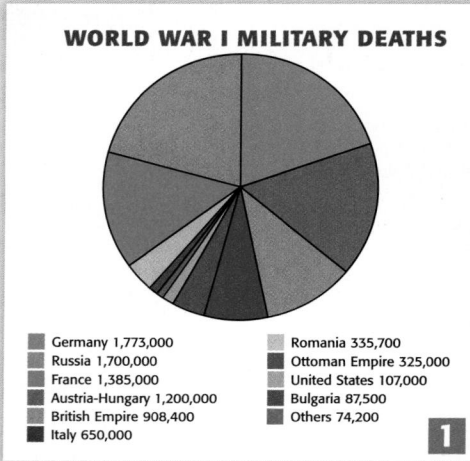

WORLD WAR I MILITARY DEATHS

- Germany 1,773,000
- Russia 1,700,000
- France 1,385,000
- Austria-Hungary 1,200,000
- British Empire 908,400
- Italy 650,000
- Romania 335,700
- Ottoman Empire 325,000
- United States 107,000
- Bulgaria 87,500
- Others 74,200

1

Back in My Day

The value of a dollar and the cost of goods changed dramatically in the twentieth century. Here are some statistics from 1915:

Average Yearly Income

- Workers in finance, insurance, and real estate $1,040
- Industrial workers $687
- Retail trade workers $510
- Farm laborers $355
- Domestic servants $342
- Public school teachers $328

Price of Goods

- Bicycle $11.95
- Baseball $1.15
- Dozen eggs .39
- Glass of cola .50

HERO'S WELCOME

Charles Lindbergh thrilled people in the United States and abroad in 1927 with his nonstop, 33½-hour flight from New York to Paris.

GREAT MIGRATION

- In 1910, 75 percent of African Americans lived on farms, and 90 percent lived in the South.

- In the late 1910s and the 1920s, 1.5 million Southern blacks moved to cities—a movement called the "Great Migration."

- During this period, Chicago's black population increased by 148%, Cleveland's by 307%, and Detroit's by 611%.

IMMIGRATION

- More than 17 million immigrants entered the United States in the first quarter of the twentieth century.

- In 1921 the Emergency Quota Act restricted newcomers from Europe to 3% of a nationality's U.S. population in the 1910 census.

THE SHORTENING SKIRT

- In 1919, the average skirt hem height above the ground in proportion to a woman's height was 10%.

- In 1924, it was 15%.

- In 1925, it was 20%.

- In 1927, it surpassed 25%, reaching the knee.

Skills Practice

 Make a Graph

 SMALL GROUP Refer students to the "Price of Goods" list under "Back in My Day." Ask students to estimate today's average price for the goods listed. Then have students create a bar graph of 1915 and 2007 prices using their estimates or the following data:

Goods	1915 Price	Today's Price
Bicycle	$11.95	$90.00
Baseball	$1.15	$14.00
Hotel room	$1.00	$80.00
Dozen eggs	$.39	$4.00
Glass of cola	$.50	$2.00

Students' graphs should include a descriptive title, clear labels, and any other necessary explanatory features. Tell students to make their graphs accurate and easy to read. Have partners write a conclusion paragraph based on their observations of the data and share what they learned about the changing value of the dollar.

BEING THERE

At the beginnings of the modern era there was war, economic boom and collapse, and the rise of an international culture. These images show the East Coast of the United States, an area strongly affected by these developments.

A A 1910s farmhouse in rural New England, similar to the one in Derry, New Hampshire, in which Robert Frost lived and wrote.

B Women Walking with Girls in Harlem, ca. 1920. Underwood & Underwood. Black and white photograph.

C Fifth Avenue at 42nd Street in New York City, 1924. Photograph. In 1920, for the first time a majority of U.S. citizens lived in cities instead of in rural areas.

(Map of northeastern United States showing: MAINE, VERMONT, NEW HAMPSHIRE, NEW YORK, Lake Ontario, Rochester, Buffalo, MASSACHUSETTS, Boston, RHODE ISLAND, CONNECTICUT, New York City, PENNSYLVANIA, NEW JERSEY, Philadelphia, Baltimore, MARYLAND, DELAWARE)

LOG ON **Literature** Online

Literature and Reading For more about the history and literature of this period, go to glencoe.com and enter QuickPass code GLA9800u5.

Reading Check

Analyze Graphic Information

1. Which nation had the greatest number of military deaths during World War I?

2. How much less did a Model T cost in 1920 than in 1910?

3. What can you infer about the literature in this unit from the images of Harlem and a rural farmhouse in New Hampshire?

Teach

Make Predictions

Have students read only the red headings on these two pages.

Say: Describe what you think changed during the Roaring Twenties. *(Students may say that "roaring" might indicate a lot of action or noise, and so life may have become more exciting.)*

Ask: What might have happened during the Great Migration? *(Students may say that many people moved from one place to another.)*

Cultural History ☆

Three Tragedies In 1911 a fire at New York City's Triangle Shirtwaist Company killed 146 employees—most of them young women—who had been working in unsafe conditions. The next year the *Titanic*, a luxury ship on its first voyage, hit an iceberg and sank. About 1,500 of its 2,200 passengers died. In 1918 a deadly influenza epidemic killed about 500,000 people in the United States, and an estimated 30 million people worldwide—about three times the number killed in World War I.

Learning Objectives

For pages 650–658

In studying this text, you will focus on the following objectives:

Literary Study:
Analyzing literary periods.
Analyzing literary genres.
Evaluating historical influences.
Connecting to the literature.

BEGINNINGS OF THE MODERN AGE

1910–1930s ☆

Historical, Social, and Cultural Forces

1 World War I

Europe exploded into war after the assassination of Austria-Hungary's Archduke Franz Ferdinand in 1914. Complex military alliances and national rivalries quickly divided European countries into two opposing forces: the Allies (Britain, France, Russia, and Italy) and the Central Powers (Germany, Austria-Hungary, and the Ottoman Empire). For three years, massive armies fought each other all over Europe. The U.S. joined the war in 1917, in part because a German submarine had sunk an unarmed British ship, the *Lusitania*, in the Atlantic in 1915. On November 11, 1918, the Allies emerged victorious. Ten million soldiers died in World War I; more lives were lost than in all wars during the century before. The staggering rate of casualties is attributed to the introduction of tanks, warplanes, machine guns, and poison gas.

The Roaring Twenties

After the war, the U.S. entered the Roaring Twenties, a decade marked by a booming economy, jazz, and late-night parties where people danced the Charleston. Many were unsettled by what they saw as society's loosening morals. Congress had passed the National Prohibition Act in 1919. It did little to limit drinking, but contributed to the rise of gangsters such as Al Capone, who secretly transported liquor and ran "speakeasies," nightclubs where people could drink illegally.

Women's Rights

The push for women's right to vote, or suffrage, grew stronger in the early twentieth century. The work of reformer Carrie Chapman Catt led to some states in the Midwest and West granting women the right to vote. However, the move toward a nationwide amendment to the Constitution stalled. In 1917, suffragist leaders such as Alice Paul picketed the White House and went on hunger strikes when they were jailed for their protests. Women finally got the vote when the Nineteenth Amendment became law in 1920.

The Great Migration

African Americans left the rural South for northern cities in huge numbers during the 1910s and 1920s. A labor shortage caused by men's leaving to fight in World War I and new limits on immigration from Europe opened up many well-paying jobs for African Americans in cities and industrial areas. Brutal southern segregation policies and widespread crop failure also drove blacks north. With its affordable housing and thriving cultural life, New York City's Harlem was an especially good place to relocate. This largely African American neighborhood was the center of an explosion of creativity in the 1920s, which became a cultural movement known as the Harlem Renaissance.

Study Skills Practice

Study Questions Guide students in creating study questions that will help them take notes on the material presented on these pages. Before students read about the modern age, have them scan the red headings and write study questions based on the headings. For example, for the heading "World War I," a student might write, "What effect did World War I have on the beginning of the modern age?" After students have

written their questions, have them read the material silently to find the answers. They may revise any questions for which they cannot find answers. After students have answered their questions, divide them into groups to share what they have learned about the modern age.

Suzette Dewey, daughter of Charles Dewey, posed beside roadster, c. 1926. Herbert E. French. Photographic print, Library of Congress.

2 Popular Culture

In the 1920s, U.S. popular culture was transformed by the automobile, radio, movies, advertising, and other innovations. Henry Ford's introduction of the assembly line in 1913 enabled factories to pro-duce cars at prices the average person could afford. During the 1920s, radios became a fixture in U.S. homes, allowing people across the country to tune in to soap operas, comedies, sports, and music. People in the U.S. became fascinated with the exploits of popular heroes such as baseball star Babe Ruth, tennis champion Bill Tilden, and avia-tor Charles Lindbergh—who flew the first solo, nonstop transatlantic flight from New York to Paris. Even before the first feature-length "talk-ing" picture in 1927, movies were essential to U.S. life. Attendance continued to rise in the 1930s, as movies provided a temporary escape from the hard times of the Depression.

The Great Depression

The stock market crash on October 29, 1929, ended the prosperity of the Roaring Twenties. Market conditions were ripe for a collapse, as investors bought stock on credit, and banks did not have enough money in reserve to cover all their customers' deposits. In 1929, investors became worried that their stocks were overvalued and began selling at a frantic pace. Disastrously, no one was buying. By 1933, about a quarter of the population was unemployed, and many fami-lies became homeless, depending on soup kitchens and migrant camps for food and shelter.

PREVIEW **Big Ideas** of the Modern Age

1 New Poetics	**2** Modern Fiction	**3** The Harlem Renaissance
In the first part of the twen-tieth century, American poetry pushed the boundar-ies of subject matter, form, and style. Poets in this era found inspiration in a wide range of sources and cre-ated new ways to capture individual experience. **See pages 652–653.**	World War I created a gen-eration of writers who questioned traditional val-ues. As a result, many of them focused on social problems, a loss of belief in the old truths, and human despair. **See pages 654–655.**	African Americans who flocked to New York City's Harlem turned it into a cen-ter of creativity. Out of this cultural whirlwind came lit-erature that both celebrated African American culture and emphasized the strug-gle against racial prejudice. **See pages 656–657.**

INTRODUCTION **651**

UNIT FIVE

Teach

Reading Strategy | 2

Preread Discussion Before students read the section "Popu-lar Culture," have them describe today's popular culture. **Ask:** What inventions or innovations have transformed our culture in the past three decades? *(Students may answer that computers, cell phones, the Internet, and satel-lite technology have transformed our culture.)* Who are the most popular people in our culture? *(Students may mention movie stars, athletes, musicians, or spiri-tual leaders.)* After the discussion, have students read the section "Popular Culture" to discover some of the inventions and people who transformed the 1920s.

View the Photograph ★

The photo of Suzette Dewey was taken in 1926. She illustrates the appearance of a "flapper" in the 1920s. Her father, Charles Dewey, was assistant secretary of the trea-sury in the federal government.

Ask: What details stand out in this photo? *(Students may say that the clothing and the cars stand out.)*

English Learners

DIFFERENTIATED INSTRUCTION

Advanced Students may be confused by the meaning of the word *depression* in the phrase *The Great Depression*. Tell students that *depression* is the noun form of the verb *depress*, which has multiple meanings. Have student volunteers use a dictionary to look up the definitions for *depress* and read them aloud to the class. Elicit from students the fact that the differ-ent meanings of *depress* all involve making something lower. Explain that the term *depression* as used here refers to a low level of business and trade activity along with high unemployment. **Say:** Words used to describe economic conditions are often easier to remember if you understand the physical phenomenon that they also describe. Have students look up the words *inflation, recession, boom,* and *bust* in a dictionary.

Beginning Choose difficult words such as *attributed, exploits,* and *overvalued* from the essay. Have each student look up two words in a dictionary and define them for the class.

651

Teach

Write Summaries Guide students in summarizing the section titled "New Directions."

Ask: What is the main idea of this section? *(Poets of the modern age sought to make their work different and new.)* What details support this main idea? *(Poets found inspiration in new places and did not use the same sources as those of traditional poetry.)*

Cultural History ☆

A New Art With their belief in human reason shaken by a horrible war, artists looked for new ways to portray the world. Pablo Picasso, instead of reproducing what he saw from a single perspective, showed multiple perspectives in one painting. The composer Arnold Schoenberg abandoned the traditional 8-note scale and created music using a 12-tone scale. Writers such as James Joyce, T. S. Eliot, and E. E. Cummings also discarded traditional conventions to create new and different styles of writing.

Big Idea 1
New Poetics

Shortly before the turn of the twentieth century, many U.S. poets tried new ways to express their feelings and observations. Their new, experimental ways of writing became known as Modernism. Some people thought the new poetics, or methods for writing poetry, were an assault on literature. To others, modern poetry spoke eloquently about the mind and the heart of the individual, doing so in new ways linked to the groundbreaking work of earlier poets Walt Whitman and Emily Dickinson (see pages 408–454). ☆

1 New Directions

Writers in this period believed that American poetry had become stagnant. As Ezra Pound (see pages 662–665) said, the modern poets sought to "Make it new!" Modern poets found inspiration in a wide range of sources beyond the traditional lyric and Romantic poetry of England. The French Symbolist poets, avant-garde, or experimental, painters such as Pablo Picasso, traditional Chinese and Japanese poetry, and everyday life all influenced the new poets.

> "A classic is classic not because it conforms to certain structural rules, or fits certain definitions (of which its author had quite probably never heard). It is classic because of a certain external and irrepressible freshness.
>
> —Ezra Pound
> from *ABC of Reading*

The Imagists

The Imagist movement (see pages 660–661), largely founded by Ezra Pound, flourished after 1910. Imagist poets believed that traditional poetry wasted energy by describing, generalizing, and rhyming. To reform poetry, they insisted on direct presentation of images. "An 'Image' is that which presents an intellectual and emotional complex in an instant of time," Pound wrote. He and other Imagist poets, such as Amy Lowell (see pages 682–686) and H.D. (Hilda Doolittle), also wrote manifestos, statements explaining their artistic philosophy. Imagism strongly influenced William Carlos Williams (see pages 676–680), among others, to expand the subject matter of poetry to include visual impressions that capture the mysterious power of ordinary experience.

Eliot's Perspective

Modernism took a different form in the poetry of T. S. Eliot (see pages 666–675). Wide-ranging allusions—references to history, art, and literature—are a fundamental part of his poetic method. Eliot said: "The poet must become more and more comprehensive, more allusive, more indirect, in order to force, to dislocate if necessary, language into its meaning." Eliot believed that war and industry had shattered the human spirit. *The Waste Land* (1922), which takes a pessimistic view of civilization, is considered the most influential poem of this period.

Breaking the Rules

E. E. Cummings (see pages 704–708) didn't care for the literary conventions that govern the arrangement of words, punctuation, and capitalization—or for the increasing conformity of individuals in U.S. society. He insisted on an irregular use of capital and lowercase letters, creating poems that looked ungrammatical, and celebrating the individual—especially the artist.

Study Skills Practice

Create Graphic Organizers Help students take notes on pages 652–653 in a concept map similar to this one:

Imagists
They believed poetic images should be presented directly.

Frost's New England
He followed traditional forms but used colloquial speech and focused on the individual.

New Poetics

Eliot's Perspective
He used many allusions and had a pessimistic view.

Breaking the Rules
Cummings ignored conventions of grammar and mechanics.

Telegraph Poles with Buildings, 1917. Joseph Stella. Oil on canvas, 36¼ x 30¼ in. Daniel J. Terra Collection, Terra Foundation for American Art, Chicago, IL. ★

Frost's New England

One major poet of this period, Robert Frost (see pages 714–734), did not follow Modernist poetics. He held firm to traditional New England settings for inspiration, and his lyric poetry is often traditional in form as well. Frost relied largely on rhyme and regular meter, and his language is frequently colloquial. Several of his poems are written as dialogue between two people. Frost often wrote of the loneliness and isolation of the individual, a typical theme in modern poetry.

from *I: Six Nonlectures*
by E. E. Cummings

Poetry is being, not doing. If you wish to follow, even at a distance, the poet's calling (and here, as always, I speak from my own totally biased and entirely personal point of view) you've got to come out of the measurable doing universe into the immeasurable house of being. I am quite aware that, wherever our socalled civilization has slithered, there's every reward and no punishment for unbeing. But if poetry is your goal, you've got to forget all about punishments and all about rewards and all about selfstyled obligations and duties and responsibilities etcetera ad infinitum and remember one thing only: that it's you—nobody else—who determine your destiny and decide your fate. Nobody else can be alive for you; nor can you be alive for anybody else. Toms can be Dicks and Dicks can be Harrys, but none of them can ever be you. There's the artist's responsibility; and the most awful responsibility on earth. If you can take it, take it—and be. **2**

Reading Check

Summarize How were the goals of the Modernist poets different from those of more traditional American poetry?

Advanced Learners

DIFFERENTIATED INSTRUCTION

Research World and national events during the period 1910–1930 contributed to an outpouring of innovative work in literature, music, and art. Invite students to examine the effects that this work had on later generations of artists. For example, they can collect information about the influence of Schoenberg's 12-tone scale or Picasso's cubist paintings or Joyce's stream-of-consciousness writing. Have students prepare brief reports to share with the class. Encourage them to include audio-visual materials with their reports.

Teach

Reading Check

Answer: *The Modernist poets wanted to "make it new." These poets developed their own styles while creating a distinctive voice for American poetry.*

Literary Element | 2

Tone and Mood Ask students to examine the passage by E. E. Cummings with a partner.

Say: Each of you will practice reading aloud the excerpt from *I: Six Nonlectures* to your partner. You and your partner should decide what the author's tone and mood are in this passage and express these in your reading.

When everyone has had time to practice the reading, invite volunteers to read a few lines from the piece to the class.

Say: Cummings's first sentence sets up a contrast between being and doing. **Ask:** Where else in the poem does he compare being with doing? *(the measurable doing universe versus the immeasurable house of being; doing is referred to as unbeing)*

View the Art ★

Joseph Stella (1877–1946) was born in Italy. He came to the United States in 1896. He studied medicine and pharmacology, and then attended the Art Students League. He was an illustrator from 1900 to 1909 and later became a painter.

Reading Strategy | 1

Determine Main Ideas
Have students read "The Jazz Age" on page 654.

Ask: Who or what is this paragraph about? *(F. Scott Fitzgerald and the period 1918–1929)* Why is Fitzgerald a focus of the paragraph? *("Fitzgerald embodied the frantic pace and social ambitions typical of the Jazz Age.")*

Literary History ☆

A Common Theme A theme common in literature of this period was high society and how to succeed within it. Writers brought different perspectives to this theme. In *The Great Gatsby,* Fitzgerald paints an intriguing picture of wealth and deception. In contrast, Edith Wharton, in novels like *The Age of Innocence,* depicts the suffocating effects of society, social climbing, and wealth in the 19th century. In such Hemingway novels as *The Sun Also Rises,* the characters are outside the mainstream of society, in search of an identity.

---

 hat is the best way to tell a story? Modernist fiction writers broke from tradition, as they omitted standard beginnings, transitions, and endings in order to tell stories that reproduced the complex ways in which people think. ☆

The Shadow of War

World War I prompted many writers to question cultural traditions and the meaning of life, turning quite a few youthful optimists into premature cynics. One of them, John F. Carter, wrote in the *Atlantic Monthly,* "The older generation had certainly pretty well ruined this world before passing it on to us. They give us this thing, knocked to pieces, leaky, red-hot, threatening to blow up; and then they are surprised that we don't accept it with the same attitude of pretty, decorous enthusiasm with which they received it." With this shattered world in view, modern fiction writers probed the complex inner workings of the mind and the breakdown of traditional values in their era.

The Lost Generation

Many writers left the U.S. during this period and established lives in Europe, leading to a international perspective very different from post-Civil War regionalism. American poet Gertrude Stein, a longtime resident of Paris, remarked to a new American expatriate, Ernest Hemingway (see pages 742–750), that young people of the time were a "lost generation." This description became famous as a label for those who had lost faith in U.S. society and didn't know where to turn. The main character in Hemingway's *The Sun Also Rises* comments: "You can't get away from yourself by moving from one place to another. There's nothing to that." In modern fiction, themes of change, indecision, and broken attachments often replace those of stability, heroism, and love.

The Jazz Age · 1

F. Scott Fitzgerald (pages 752–772) gave the label "the Jazz Age" to the period between World War I and the Great Depression. Fitzgerald embodied the frantic pace and social ambitions typical of the Jazz Age. Yet he believed that the United States was fundamentally in disarray. He said there was a new "generation grown up to find all Gods dead, all wars fought, all faiths in man shaken." Desire for consumer goods soared after the war, and symbols of success, such as cars, were everywhere. But many writers were disgusted by what they viewed as shallow materialism. In *The Great Gatsby,* Fitzgerald created glamorous and wealthy characters who dash from one party to the next, yet cannot find happiness.

> *"It seemed only a question of a few years before the older people would step aside and let the world be run by those who saw things as they were."*
>
> —F. Scott Fitzgerald
> from *Echoes of the Jazz Age*

Hemingway's Prose

Ernest Hemingway's spare style was markedly different from the elaborate prose that short-story writers and novelists had often used in the 1800s. Through understatement and irony, Hemingway's fiction suggests connections that the reader is left to infer. "I always try to write on the principle of the iceberg," he said. "There is seven-eighths of it underwater for every part that shows." His first novel, *The Sun Also Rises,* is about the lost generation. It is told by Jake Barnes, an American newspaperman who has been wounded in World War I.

Reading Practice

Outline To help students take notes and study the material on pages 654 and 655, have them write outlines using the title and headings on the pages. A partial example follows.

Modern Fiction

 I. The Shadow of War
    A. World War I made writers question traditional beliefs.
    B. Writers looked at the workings of the mind and the breakdown of values.

II. The Lost Generation
    A. Writers left for Europe.
    B. They developed international perspectives.

III. The Jazz Age
    A. Like many others of his time, Fitzgerald lived at a hectic pace.
    B. Many people were disgusted with the shallow materialism of the time.

New York, 1911. George Bellows. Oil on canvas, 42 x 60 in. National Gallery of Art, Washington, DC. Collection of Mr. and Mrs. Paul Mellon.

from *The Sun Also Rises* by Ernest Hemingway

Enjoying living was learning to get your money's worth and knowing when you had it. You could get your money's worth. The world was a good place to buy in. It seemed like a fine philosophy. In five years, I thought, it will seem just as silly as all the other fine philosophies I've had.

Perhaps that wasn't true, though. Perhaps as you went along you did learn something. I did not care what it was all about. All I wanted to know was how to live in it. Maybe if you found out how to live in it you learned from that what it was all about.

Reading Check

Analyze Cause and Effect How did World War I affect fiction writing?

Approaching Level

DIFFERENTIATED INSTRUCTION

Established Have a student volunteer read aloud the excerpt from *The Sun Also Rises*. Have students paraphrase the first sentence. **Ask:** What is important about this sentence? (*The sentence acts as a thesis statement: it announces what Hemingway is talking about in the following paragraph. It also sets the tone.*) **Ask:** What is the speaker—Jake Barnes—talking about when he refers to "it"? (*"Knowing when you had it" means knowing that you have gotten your money's worth. In the second paragraph, it refers to life.*)

Teach

Reading Check

Answer: *Writers turned their dismay with society into works that broke with tradition and explored the inner lives of their characters.*

Literary Element	2

Style, Form, and Impact

Read the excerpt from *The Sun Also Rises*. **Ask:** What is the author's style of writing? (*Hemingway's writing is concise and direct.*) Which sentence shows irony? (*"In five years, I thought, it will seem just as silly as all the other fine philosophies I've had."*)

ENGLISH LEARNERS	**Ask:**

What is an author's style? (*the unique way an author expresses himself or herself*)

View the Art ★

George Bellows (1882–1925) was born in Columbus, Ohio, and became a major American artist of the early 20th century. He was an instructor at the Art Students League in New York and at the Art Institute of Chicago.

Ask: What mood does this painting of New York City portray? (*Students may say that the city is crowded with many people, and much of the painting seems dark. This gives the painting a somber mood.*)

Teach

Preview and Brainstorm

Before students read pages 656 and 657, have them preview and brainstorm questions that they may have about the essay.

APPROACHING **Say:** Look at the title, the headings, and the painting; then read the first sentence in each section. List ideas about what the text might be about. Have volunteers share their lists.

Political History ☆

Moving to Harlem The Harlem Renaissance was a result of several issues that arose after the Civil War. Reconstruction increased tension between freed African Americans and white Southerners. Hate groups committed acts of violence against African Americans.

Restrictions on immigrants created worker shortages in the North, and factory owners became willing to hire African Americans. Low prices, floods, and insect infestations created hardship for Southern sharecroppers. Thousands of Southern African Americans moved north to find a better life; many settled in Harlem.

Big Idea 3
The Harlem Renaissance

1 Music inspires many of today's writers and artists, just as it did during the Harlem Renaissance. Artists fed off the energy of jazz and their community and changed American art. The Harlem Renaissance represented the coming-of-age of African American culture and the flowering of the community's creative impulses, especially for southern blacks, who had been exploited for generations.

> *Good morning, daddy!*
> *Ain't you heard*
> *The boogie-woogie rumble*
> *Of a dream deferred?*
>
> —Langston Hughes
> from *Montage of a Dream Deferred*

Blues to Jazz

Out of the African American tradition of spirituals and work songs came blues music. Influenced by blues, jazz later developed in New Orleans as a type of music that combined West African rhythms, ragtime, and some European instruments, such as the string bass. Jazz was largely improvisational, or spontaneous, within a rhythmic framework. Langston Hughes (see pages 810–823) transposed themes and rhythms from blues and jazz into poems that celebrated the everyday life of African Americans and their strength in the face of oppression. Hughes said, "I tried to write poems like the songs they sang on Seventh Street." Jazz inspired an energetic social life and filled clubs. Hughes reported that at one Harlem party thrown by black socialite A'Lelia Walker, it was so crowded that even a Scandinavian prince couldn't get in;

he could only have a beverage delivered to his car idling outside the apartment building.

The Neighborhood

Harlem became a main destination during the Great Migration. Word about the vibrant community life and affordable rents in this New York neighborhood quickly spread, attracting writers, artists, and musicians. It was a haven where African Americans could escape the restrictions they faced in the rest of society. In 1929, when the whole country felt the economic shock of the stock market crash, there was less money available to spend on the arts—and as a result, the Harlem Renaissance was over. However, writers in the 1930s and 1940s such as Richard Wright (see pages 899–908) and Ralph Ellison continued the artistic coming-of-age that this movement had begun.

The Deferred Dream

W. E. B. Du Bois's magazine of the NAACP, the *Crisis*, brought racial issues to the forefront of U.S. culture. He wrote that the "problem of the twentieth century is the problem of the color-line." Racial segregation was widespread, and Du Bois said this created a veil of perception that forced African Americans to see themselves through the eyes of whites. The African American "simply wishes to make it possible for a man to be both a Negro and an American, . . . without having the doors of Opportunity closed roughly in his face," Du Bois said. Racial identity became a pivotal issue for writers in this period. For example, Countee Cullen (see pages 828–831) believed that race was a huge issue, but that a poet's race should not determine how he or she writes or how readers and critics understand him or her. Other writers, such as Arna Bontemps (see pages 824–827), believed that a writer's work could not be separated from his or her racial identity.

Vocabulary Practice

Context Clues Remind students that they use context clues to find the meaning of an unknown word when they look at the surrounding words and sentences. In definition clues, writers provide the meaning of the word. Inference clues enable readers to deduce the meaning from the context. Contrast clues show what the word does not mean. Ask students to figure out the type of clue and definition for each of these words, found in the essay above.

1. **exploited** *(contrast: taken advantage of contrasts with coming-of-age and flowering community)*

2. **improvisational** *(definition: spontaneous)*

3. **perception** *(inference: "to see themselves" implies the word means how a person views something)*

from "The Negro Artist and the Racial Mountain" by Langston Hughes

Most of my own poems are racial in theme and treatment, derived from the life I know. In many of them I try to grasp and hold some of the meanings and rhythms of jazz. I am as sincere as I know how to be in these poems and yet after every reading I answer questions like these from my own people: Do you think Negroes should always write about Negroes? I wish you wouldn't read some of your poems to white folks. How do you find anything interesting in a place like a cabaret? Why do you write about black people? You aren't black. What makes you do so many jazz poems?

But jazz to me is one of the inherent expressions of Negro life in America; the eternal tom-tom beating in the Negro soul—the tom-tom of revolt against weariness in a white world, a world of subway trains, and work, work, work; the tom-tom of joy and laughter, and pain swallowed in a smile. . . .

We younger Negro artists who create now intend to express our individual dark-skinned selves without fear or shame. If white people are pleased we are glad. If they are not, it doesn't matter. We know we are beautiful. And ugly too. The tom-tom cries and the tom-tom laughs. If colored people are pleased we are glad. If they are not, their displeasure doesn't matter either. We build our temples for tomorrow, strong as we know how, and we stand on top of the mountain, free within ourselves.

2

The Janitor Who Paints, ca. 1937. Palmer Hayden. Oil on canvas, 39⅛ x 32⅞ in. Smithsonian American Art Museum, Washington, DC.

Hurston's Folklore

Zora Neale Hurston (see pages 790–799) explored the folklore of African Americans and the building of community in the South during Reconstruction. A student of anthropology, she applied her training to her own experiences growing up in southern African American communities in works such as *Dust Tracks on a Road.* Hurston first went to Harlem at sixteen when she was traveling as a member of a theater group. Although her work became associated with the Harlem Renaissance, she resisted being classified by any artistic movement. "All clumps of people turn out to be individuals on close inspection," she said.

Reading Check

Analyze Cause and Effect How did the Harlem Renaissance contribute to the beginnings of the modern age in literature?

INTRODUCTION **657**

Teach

Reading Check

Answer: *The writers of the Harlem Renaissance created bold, experimental works that captured the psychology of their subjects and used new, freer, and everyday language in ways that contrasted with traditional literature.*

Reading Strategy ┃ 2

Make Connections

Ask: How does music affect and inspire you? *(Students may say that music affects their moods or that it inspires them to be more creative.)* **Say:** Describe a time when you felt you were treated unfairly. *(Students may describe an incident in which a peer, their parents, or a stranger treated them unfairly.)*

ENGLISH LEARNERS Hughes describes jazz as "the eternal tom-tom beating in the Negro soul." Have students guess the meaning of *tom-tom*, and then use a dictionary to define it. *(a drum or steady beat)*

View the Art ★

Palmer Hayden (1890–1973) lived in New York and painted many scenes of Harlem. He studied art abroad and won awards for his paintings.

Ask: Why do you think the painter portrayed here is a janitor? *(Students may say that the painter could not support himself through his artwork, or that people from all walks of life could be artists.)*

Assess/Close

Legacy of the Period

Read the third paragraph.

Ask: How has the fight for civil rights affected our culture? *(Job discrimination and segregation are illegal now.)*

Cultural and Literary Links

Suggest students look for ways unit authors have influenced today's writers.

Activities

1. **Follow Up** To help answer the questions, have students list some of the changes that came about in this period.

2. **Contrast Literary Periods** Responses should include specific examples of creative work in each period.

3. **Visual Literacy** Remind students of the types of graphic organizers that they might create.

4. **Take Notes** Remind students that they can go back and skim the introduction to make notes.

FOLDABLES®
Study Organizer

Have students make and label the Three-Pocket Foldable. They can put note cards about each Big Idea in the three pockets.

WRAP-UP

Legacy of the Period

The writers who created Modernism challenged the traditional values of society and forms of literature. They believed their innovations brought literature closer to capturing human experience. Today, writers such as Dave Eggers, Jhumpa Lahiri, and Sherman Alexie take on the challenge of portraying reality in the twenty-first century.

Modern poets' use of imagery and everyday speech further convinced people that a poem could be about any subject. The poetry and manifestos of the Imagist movement provided inspiration for many groundbreaking poets of the 1950s and 1960s, including Anne Sexton (see pages 1208–1212) and Sylvia Plath (see pages 1226–1231).

The Harlem Renaissance was an influential time in African American and United States history. The leading figures in the movement blazed a trail for later African American writers, such as James Baldwin and Ralph Ellison, and helped to push forward the battle for civil rights in the 1960s.

Cultural and Literary Links

- The "little magazines" such as *Poetry* that sprouted up during the period championed modern Imagism and other Modernist experimentation. *Poetry*'s founder, Harriet Monroe, wrote, "The Open Door will be the policy of this magazine—may the great poet we are looking for never find it shut, or half-shut, against his ample genius!" Today, *Poetry* receives about 90,000 submissions per year.

- William Carlos Williams influenced the Beat Generation writers of the 1950s with his accessible language and experimentation with form.

- The Harlem Renaissance has influenced modern African American poets and hip-hop artists who strive to be leaders for the black community.

 Literature Online

Unit Resources For additional skills practice, go to glencoe.com and enter QuickPass code GLA9800u5.

Activities

Choose one of the following activities to explore and develop as you read this unit.

1. Follow Up Go back to the Looking Ahead section on page 645 and answer the questions.

2. Contrast Literary Periods Working with a partner, create a brief presentation for your class comparing and contrasting the Harlem Renaissance era with contemporary hip-hop culture.

3. Visual Literacy Create an illustrated graphic organizer that shows the influences of World War I on American literature and culture. You might show how writers responded to the effects of war, as well as to the postwar economic boom.

4. Take Notes Use this study organizer to keep track of the big ideas in this unit.

FOLDABLES
Study Organizer

THREE-TAB BOOK

Big Idea 1   Big Idea 2   Big Idea 3

Writing Practice

Organizing Information If students are not sure which activity to choose, discuss with them some of the organizational work that they will need to do for each activity. If they choose one of the follow-up questions, they will need to gather their notes about World War I, Modernism, or the Harlem Renaissance, propose how this event or movement contrasted with the period that preceded it, and how it influenced the period after it.

To compare literary periods, they will need to research examples from hip-hop culture for comparison. For the graphic organizer, they will need to find the right level of detail so that their organizer is useful and readable. For taking notes, they will need to determine the most important points on each page of the introduction.

658

MODERN POETRY

American Landscape, c. 1930. Charles Sheeler. Oil on canvas, 24 x 31 in. The Museum of Modern Art, New York.

View the Art One hallmark of Charles Sheeler's paintings is his use of precise, geometric forms and lines. What do you think he was trying to achieve with this technique? Explain.

> "Poetry is the opening and closing of a door,
> leaving those who look through to guess about
> what is seen during a moment." **1**

—Carl Sandburg, "Poetry Considered"

659

UNIT FIVE

PART 1

Analyze and Extend

Reading Strategy   1

Evaluate Direct students to read the Carl Sandburg quotation. **Ask:** When a door opens and closes, will all viewers see the same items in the moment that the door is open? Why or why not? *(No; different viewers will focus on different items.)* **Ask:** What is Sandburg saying about the experience of reading poetry? *(Sandburg is saying that the experience of reading poetry is different for each reader; each reader will see something different.)*

View the Art

Answer: *The lines are moving up and to the left, which suggests the landscape is shrinking. The lines are harsh and severe.*

Charles Sheeler (1883–1965) often used photographs of industrial subjects to plan his paintings.

English Learners

DIFFERENTIATED INSTRUCTION

Intermediate On the board, **write:** In the 1900s, the United States experienced a growth in factories, technology, and cities. There were also many social changes and significant political events such as World Wars I and II. Have students orally restate the main ideas in their own words. Then lead students to predict how such changes and events may have affected the way that people viewed

the world and the subjects that writers chose to address. Provide sentence starters such as the following: *When people began working in factories, they may have felt _____ . Technology such as subways may have caused people to _____ . Because there were more cities, people may have faced problems such as _____ . Political events such as the World Wars may have caused people to _____ . These changes*

and events may have caused writers to address subjects such as _____ .

Focus

Bellringer Options

Daily Language Practice Transparency 56

Or tell students that Symbolist poets focused on the mind, whereas Imagist poets focused on sensory experience. **Ask:** How would a Symbolist's poem about Steichen's photograph differ from an Imagist's poem? (*A Symbolist poem would explore the meaning of the image. An Imagist poem would describe the photo with sensory details.*)

Teach

Literary Element   1

Symbolism Ask: What style elements did Symbolist poets use in their poems? (*suggestion, metaphor, symbols*)

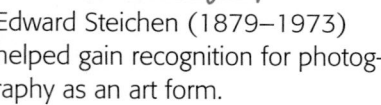 ★
Edward Steichen (1879–1973) helped gain recognition for photography as an art form.

Learning Objectives

For pages 660–661

In studying this text, you will focus on the following objectives:

Literary Study:
Analyzing literary periods.
Analyzing literary genres.
Evaluating historical influences.

Reading: Connecting to the literature.

Symbolist and Imagist Poetry

PHOTOGRAPHERS CAPTURE MOMENTS in time. Painters depict visual ideas through arrangements of colors and shapes. What methods allow writers to use words as someone else might use a camera or a paintbrush? In the beginning of the modern age, a group of poets called the Imagists developed new, influential techniques for presenting visual impressions. Much of their inspiration came from the Symbolists, across the Atlantic Ocean, in France.

The Symbolist Foundation

The avant-garde, or experimental, Symbolist movement in Paris dominated French poetry and art in the late 1800s and inspired the Imagists. Symbolist poets such as Charles Baudelaire, Stéphane Mallarmé, Arthur Rimbaud, and Paul Verlaine reacted against Realism by focusing their attention inward on moods and sensations. These poets believed that direct explanation could not capture emotion. They sought access to the inner workings of the mind through suggestion, metaphor, and symbols. The Symbolists took inspiration from Edgar Allan Poe, whose work is rich in symbolism.

The American Imagists

Contrasting with the Symbolists' abstract poetry, the Imagists presented a concrete, tangible image that appeared frozen in time. "Essentially, it is a moment of revealed truth," wrote critic William Pratt.

"In a Station of the Metro" by Ezra Pound (see page 664) is a classic Imagist poem. Responding to the sight of faces in a train station, Pound condensed a first draft of thirty lines into two lines of fourteen words and two striking images. He believed that the poet should "use no superfluous word, no adjective which does not reveal something." He found a model for this intense compression in Asian poetry, such as in this haiku by Japanese poet Basho:

The Flatiron Building, Evening, from *Camera Work*, April, 1906. Edward Steichen. ★

> *On a dead limb*
> *squats a crow—*
> *Autumn night.*
>   *(Lucien Stryk translation)*

In 1912 Pound submitted three poems by H.D. (Hilda Doolittle) to *Poetry: A Magazine of Verse*.

Study Skills Practice

Connect to Poetry Explain that readers can connect to poetry in several ways. They can draw on personal knowledge and experiences that the details or images of a poem bring to mind. Forming mental images based on the writer's words is another helpful way to understand a poem. Students may also use idea webs and other graphic organizers to decode figurative language and make emotional associations. Have students use these strategies as they study the poems throughout Part 1.

Sudden Rain Shower on Ohashi Bridge, from *One Hundred Views of Famous Places in Edo,* 1850. Ando Hiroshige. Woodblock print. Musée des Arts Asiatiques-Guimet, Paris.

View the Art This wood-block print recalls the style of Japanese haiku masters such as Basho. What does this print have in common with Imagism?

One of the published poems was "Oread" (following). In Greek mythology, the Oreads were nymphs, minor female divinities of nature, from the mountains. Notice the irregular, jagged look of the lines and how the line breaks are determined by the poet's sense of imagery.

Whirl up, sea—
Whirl your pointed pines,
Splash your great pines
On our rocks.
Hurl your green over us—
Cover us with your pools of fir.

H.D. and Amy Lowell were central figures in the Imagist movement. At a poetry reading, Lowell reportedly said to her audience, "Well, clap or hiss, I don't care which, but . . . do something!" Such bold statements energized American poetry, which often displays the Imagist method of compressing an emotion or idea into a sharply observed image.

Imagist Principles

The Imagists issued manifestos, or public declarations on their poetic principles. The following are sample manifestos in the style of those issued:

- The image is the essence, the raw material, of poetry.
- Poetry should be expressed in brief, clear, concrete language that forms precise images.
- These images should instantly convey to the reader the poem's meaning and emotion.
- The language of these poetic images should sound like simple speech—not be made up of predictable rhythms and rhymes.
- Topics for poems need not be high-minded or "poetic." No topic is unsuitable for a poem.

LOG ON ▶ **Literature** Online

Literature and Reading For more about Symbolist and Imagist Poetry, go to glencoe.com and enter QuickPass code GLA9800u5.

Respond and Think Critically

1. Who were some of the French poets who formed the Symbolist movement in reaction to Realism?

2. Why did the Symbolist poets refrain from directly explaining their themes?

3. What did the Imagists want to eliminate from poetry? Why?

4. Compare and contrast the ways in which the poems on these two pages reflect the themes of Imagist poets. Which do you find most interesting?

LITERARY HISTORY **661**

Teach

Big Idea 2

New Poetics Explain that early 20th-century poets experimented with new forms as a way to express feelings and make observations.

View the Art ★

Answer: *It depicts a moment frozen in time.*

Ando Hiroshige (1797–1858) was a Japanese painter and printmaker.

Assess

1. Baudelaire, Mallarmé, Rimbaud, Verlaine

2. They believed poetry should suggest emotions through creative use of language.

3. They wanted to eliminate sentimentality. They wrote poetry that used simple speech.

4. Each poem captures a moment in time. The haiku captures a still image; H.D.'s poem captures movement.

For activities related to this selection, see Unit 5 Teaching Resources Book, pp. 20–21.

Approaching Level

DIFFERENTIATED INSTRUCTION

Established Explain to students that when they are asked to analyze imagery in a poem, they may want to use a graphic organizer to create associative word lists. For example, help them identify the three natural elements used in the poem on this page: water, pine trees, and rocks. Make sure that students understand the comparison H.D. makes. Have students write these elements as headings in three-column charts. Below each heading, tell students to list every word in the poem that is associated with each element. For example, in the *Water* column, students might list *whirl, sea, splash,* and *pools.* At the bottom of each column, have them note the associations that the word grouping evokes.

Before You Read

Focus

Bellringer Options

Selection Focus
Transparency 40
Daily Language Practice
Transparency 57

Or display several images that capture moments in time that students can relate to on subjective and emotional levels (such as the climactic moment of an athletic contest or a dramatic scene from an important current event).

Ask: How can these images be compared with Imagist poetry? Have students consider the similarities and differences between the images and Ezra Pound's poetry, focusing on his directness, exactness, emotion, and the reinvention of the past.

Before You Read
In a Station of the Metro and A Pact

Meet Ezra Pound
(1885–1972)

Ezra Pound's friend and protégé William Carlos Williams once wrote, "Pound is a fine fellow, but not one person in a thousand likes him, and a great many people detest him." Nevertheless, T. S. Eliot claimed Pound was "more responsible for the twentieth-century revolution in poetry than [was] any other individual."

Imagism Pound was born in a small town in Idaho. When he was still young, he determined that "at thirty [he] would know more about poetry than any living man." Pound entered the University of Pennsylvania at age fifteen but completed his undergraduate education at Hamilton College. As a student, he immersed himself in the Latin, Greek, and French classics.

> "I have weathered the storm,
> I have beaten out my exile."
>
> —Ezra Pound, "The Rest"

After receiving his master's degree in 1906, Pound briefly taught languages at a small Presbyterian college in Indiana. His eccentric manner did not fit well with the school's character, and, at 23, Pound left for Europe. He settled first in London, then Paris, and finally in Italy. There he wrote poetry and criticism and translated verse from nine languages. He also served as an overseas editor for *Poetry* magazine—a position he used to nurture the careers of Robert Frost and T. S. Eliot, among others. In 1912, Pound helped establish Imagism's manifesto. It called for "direct treatment of the 'thing'" and the use of "the language of common speech, but . . . always the exact word."

A Complex Writer Though Pound declared that writers should "Make it new!" he did not believe in newness for its own sake and relied heavily on the literature of the past. In *The Cantos*, his longest and best-known work, Pound combined materials from different cultures and languages, historical texts, and newspaper articles. *The Cantos* is an extremely complex work, notorious for its difficulty and uneven quality.

Politics, Prison, and Exile During World War II, Pound supported Fascist Italian dictator Benito Mussolini and made radio broadcasts openly criticizing the United States and the efforts of the Allies in the war. After Italy fell, Pound spent six months as a prisoner of war near Pisa. Here he wrote *The Pisan Cantos*, generally considered the greatest section of his long work.

After being declared mentally unfit to stand trial for treason, Pound was sent to St. Elizabeth's Hospital for the criminally insane in Washington, D.C. He spent the next twelve years at the hospital, after which the charges against him were dropped. Pound then left the United States, returning to Italy, where he stayed until his death in Venice in 1972.

 Literature Online
Author Search For more about Ezra Pound, go to glencoe.com and enter QuickPass code GLA9800u5.

Selection Skills

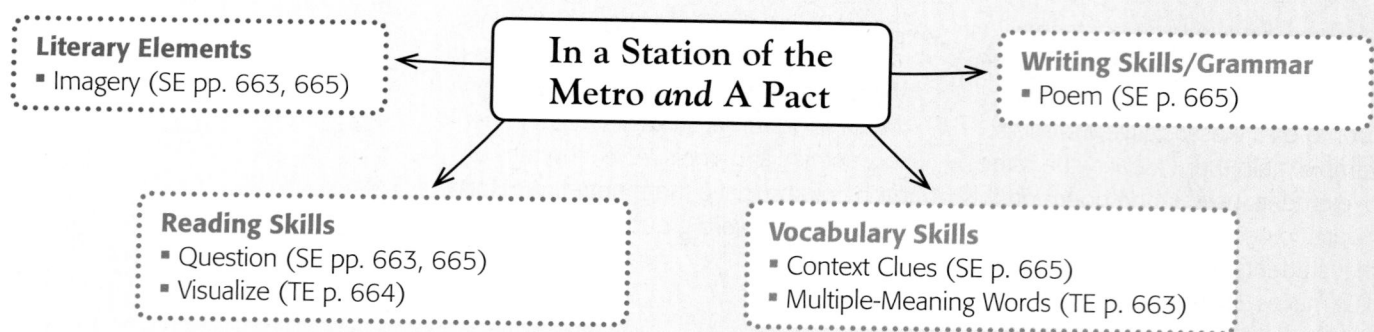

Literary Elements
- Imagery (SE pp. 663, 665)

In a Station of the Metro *and* A Pact

Writing Skills/Grammar
- Poem (SE p. 665)

Reading Skills
- Question (SE pp. 663, 665)
- Visualize (TE p. 664)

Vocabulary Skills
- Context Clues (SE p. 665)
- Multiple-Meaning Words (TE p. 663)

Literature and Reading Preview

Connect to the Poems

Have you ever looked at something that you see every day as if for the first time? Explore this question in a brief journal entry.

Build Background

"In a Station of the Metro" and "A Pact" were originally published together in *Poetry* in 1916. Pound was impressed with the brief but evocative Japanese haiku form (see Literary Terms Handbook, p. R9). After experiencing the moment that inspired "In a Station of the Metro," Pound composed a thirty-line poem. He destroyed this first attempt, calling it a work "of second intensity." After two other tries, he created a short, haiku-like poem with a single powerful image.

Set Purposes for Reading

Big Idea New Poetics

As you read, ask yourself, How does Pound employ free verse and the rules of Imagism in his work?

Literary Element Imagery

Imagery is the "word pictures" that writers create to make their subject more vivid or to evoke an emotional response in the reader. In creating effective images, writers use sensory details, or descriptions that appeal to one or more of the five sense: sight, hearing, touch, taste, and smell. As you read, ask yourself, How does Pound use imagery to heighten the effect of his words?

Reading Strategy Question

Questioning is asking yourself regularly whether you've understood what you have read. In an Imagist poem such as "In a Station of the Metro," it is important to use questioning to slow down your reading in order to fully understand the poet's meaning.

....

Tip: Take Notes As you read "In a Station of the Metro" and "A Pact," note in a double-entry journal any questions that occur to you.

Questions	Answers
How does Pound feel about Walt Whitman?	

Learning Objectives

For pages 662–665

In studying these texts, you will focus on the following objectives:

Literary Study: Analyzing imagery.

Reading: Questioning.

Writing: Writing a poem.

Vocabulary

detest (di test´) *v.* to greatly dislike or loathe; p. 664 *I have detested television ever since my favorite show was canceled.*

sap (sap) *n.* a watery source of nutrients that flows through a plant's circulatory system; p. 664 *I decided never to park under a tree again after finding my car covered in sap.*

commerce (kom´ ərs) *n.* exchange of ideas and opinions; p. 664 *Through lively debate and commerce, the two opposing political sides were able to reach an agreement.*

apparition (ap´ ə rish´ ən) *n.* a ghostlike or nearly invisible appearance; p. 664 *Those who saw the shadowy apparition in the cemetery believed it was a ghost.*

bough (bou) *n.* tree branch; p. 664 *The baby bird clung to the bough as it waited for food.*

EZRA POUND **663**

English Learners

DIFFERENTIATED INSTRUCTION

Intermediate Using the following headings, create a three-column chart on the board: Word/phrase, Sense(s), Emotion(s). Write the phrase "broke the new wood" from the poem "A Pact" in the first column. Explain that this phrase appeals to the sense of touch as people must use their hands to break wood. Explain that the idea of cutting new wood represents the excitement of starting a new project. Record these ideas in the sense and emotion columns. Have students record their ideas in the appropriate columns.

Before You Read

Focus

Summary

In "A Pact," Ezra Pound comes to terms with Walt Whitman's legacy. "In a Station of the Metro" presents a momentary vision in a Paris subway—an instant when a familiar sight captures Pound's attention in a new way.

 For summaries in languages other than English, see Unit 5 Teaching Resources Book, pp. 23–28.

Vocabulary

Multiple-Meaning Words

Tell students that many English words have more than one meaning. For example, the word *sap* may refer to the nutrient system of a plant or to a foolish or gullible person. Readers must use context to determine which meaning of a word an author intends.

Ask: What does the word *commerce* mean in each of the following sentences?

- The *commerce* at the political convention was lively and insightful. *(exchange of ideas and opinions)*
- The decline in *commerce* led to an economic depression. *(the buying and selling of goods between cities, states, or nations)*

 For additional vocabulary practice, see Unit 5 Teaching Resources Book, p. 31.

Teach

Big Idea 1

New Poetics Answer: *It suggests Pound believes that Whitman laid the groundwork for Modernism.*

Reading Strategy 2

Visualize After students read the poem "In a Station of the Metro," have them describe the image they visualize and the emotions they associate with it. *(Possible answers: the faces of people speeding by in subway cars; isolation, loneliness.)*

 For additional practice using the reading skill or strategy, see Unit 5 Teaching Resources Book, p. 30.

Writer's Technique ☆

Apostrophe Tell students that apostrophe is a writer addressing a dead person or an object as if it could respond. **Ask:** How does Pound use apostrophe in "A Pact" and to what effect? *(Possible answer: to address Walt Whitman as though speaking directly to him; Walt Whitman comes alive for readers)*

 For an audio recording of this selection, use Listening Library Audio CD-ROM.

A Pact

Ezra Pound

I make a pact with you, Walt Whitman— ☆
I have **detested** you long enough.
I come to you as a grown child
Who has had a pig-headed father;
5 I am old enough now to make friends.
It was you that broke the new wood,
Now is a time for carving.
We have one **sap** and one root—
Let there be **commerce** between us.

Vocabulary

detest (di test´) *v.* to greatly dislike or loathe
sap (sap) *n.* a watery source of nutrients that flows through a plant's circulatory system
commerce (kom´ ərs) *n.* exchange of ideas and opinions

1 **New Poetics** *What does line 6 suggest about Pound's understanding of Walt Whitman's relationship to modern poetry?*

In a Station of the Metro [1]

Ezra Pound

The **apparition** of these faces in the crowd;
Petals on a wet, black **bough.** **2**

1 The *Metro* refers to the Paris subway.

Vocabulary

apparition (ap´ ə rish´ ən) *n.* a ghostlike or nearly invisible appearance
bough (bou) *n.* tree branch

Study Skills Practice

 Paraphrase Tell students that paraphrasing is a useful way to study and understand poetry. Remind them that when they paraphrase, they restate the writer's ideas in their own words. For example, a paraphrase of "In a Station of the Metro" might be as follows: The ghostly faces of people in the crowd look like flower petals blown against a tree branch.

Have students reread "A Pact," clarifying the meaning of any lines or phrases that might not be clear. Then have them write a paraphrase of it. Students can then form small groups in which they read and critique each other's paraphrases.

After You Read

Respond and Think Critically

Respond and Interpret

1. (a)In the first line of "In a Station of the Metro," what word does the speaker use to describe how the faces look to him? (b)What might that word suggest about the faces?

2. (a)In the second line, to what image does the speaker compare the faces? (b)From this image, what can you infer about the speaker's feelings?

3. (a)In "A Pact," to whom is the poem addressed? In what way have the speaker's feelings changed about that person? (b)What might be the reason?

4. (a)What is the **extended metaphor** used in the last four lines of "A Pact"? (b)What idea do you think the speaker expresses in these lines?

Analyze and Evaluate

5. Pound once wrote, "The image is the poet's pigment." How is "In a Station of the Metro" like a painting? Explain.

6. (a)Briefly describe the most important differences in tone, form, and content of these two poems. (b)Which poem seems more compelling? Explain.

Connect

7. **Big Idea** New Poetics How do these poems embody the values and stylistic goals of Modernism and Imagism?

8. **Connect to the Author** Which of these poems do you think reveals more about the poet? Explain.

Literary Element Imagery

While most **imagery** appeals to the sense of sight, images can appeal to all five senses. The same image may also involve more than a single sense.

1. Which senses does Pound appeal to in "In a Station of the Metro"?

2. Identify one image from "A Pact" that appeals to the sense of sight.

Reading Strategy Question

Questioning To understand an author's purpose, ask yourself questions as you read:

1. What do you think was Pound's purpose for writing "A Pact"?

2. Write and answer two questions about the poem that could help you determine Pound's purpose.

LOG ON ▶ **Literature** Online

Selection Resources For Selection Quizzes, eFlash-cards, and Reading-Writing Connection activities, go to glencoe.com and enter QuickPass code GLA9800u5.

Vocabulary Practice

Practice with Context Clues Identify context clues to the meaning of each vocabulary word.

1. We need **commerce,** or an exchange of ideas and opinions, to solve the problem.

2. I highly doubt that some ghostly **apparition** stole your homework.

3. The heavy storm caused the **bough** of a tree to fall and crash into my windshield.

4. I have never enjoyed travel in an airplane; in fact, I have always **detested** it.

5. Parked under the tree, my car was covered in **sap** that had dripped from its branches.

🖋 Writing

Write a Poem Review the journal entry you were asked to complete on page 663 under Connect to the Poems. Using "In a Station of the Metro" as an example, write a short, descriptive poem about the experience you described.

EZRA POUND **665**

After You Read

Assess

1. (a) *Apparition* (b) They are ghostlike and hazy.

2. (a) Petals on a wet branch (b) He sees them as a contrast to their surroundings.

3. (a) Walt Whitman, whom the speaker no longer detests (b) Pound's development as a poet and reader has allowed him to accept Whitman.

4. (a) Poetry as wood (b) Whitman developed a new form of poetry, which the speaker will now refine.

5. It presents the poet's idea in visual terms.

6. (a) "In a Station . . ." evokes an emotional response with images. "A Pact" is longer and contains more explicit content. (b) Students' answers will vary.

7. "In a Station . . ." epitomizes the Imagist aesthetic, and the tone, content, and open form of "A Pact" reflect Modernist tendencies.

8. Students might choose "A Pact" because the speaker is more defined, though "Metro" creates a strong tone which could be revealing.

Literary Element

1. Sight

2. Possible answer: the "new wood"

Progress Check

Can students analyze imagery?

If No → See Unit 5 Teaching Resources Book, p. 29.

🖋 Writing

Students' poems should be short but include strong descriptive images.

Reading Strategy

1. To define himself as a Modernist poet in relation to Walt Whitman

2. What does Pound think of Whitman? Why is Pound making a pact?

Vocabulary

1. The definition of *commerce* is provided in the phrase, "exchange of ideas and opinions."

2. *Apparition* is modified by "ghostly," giving a clue that an *apparition* has a ghostlike appearance.

3. During storms, tree branches, a synonym of *bough,* tend to fall.

4. The sentence indicates that *detested,* has an opposite meaning to the word "enjoyed."

5. Based on the context, *sap* is a sticky liquid that a tree produces.

665

Before You Read

Focus

Bellringer Options

Literature Launchers:
   Pre-Reading Videos DVD,
   Selection Launcher
Selection Focus
   Transparency 41
Daily Language Practice
   Transparency 58

Or have students discuss what they know about love songs.
Ask: What are some common characteristics of love songs? What are some different themes in love songs?

Have students consider, as they read, to what extent those characteristics appear in "The Love Song of J. Alfred Prufrock."

Literary History ☆

Poetry Founded in 1912, *Poetry* magazine was devoted entirely to the publication and criticism of new poetry. Many poets of the early twentieth century were first published in this magazine.

Before You Read

The Love Song of J. Alfred Prufrock

Meet **T. S. Eliot**
(1888–1965)

T. S. Eliot revolutionized poetry more than any other twentieth-century writer. His experiments in language and form and his introduction of the scenes and concerns of everyday life into poetry changed literary tastes and influenced future poets.

Eliot was born in St. Louis, Missouri, into a distinguished family that provided him with the best education available. In 1906 he matriculated at Harvard, where he steeped himself in literature and published his first poems. At Harvard, he studied under Irving Babbitt, the New Humanist critic of Romanticism, who helped Eliot develop his taste for classicism in literature. Eliot then studied philosophy at the Sorbonne in Paris, at Harvard, and at Oxford. He eventually settled in England.

The First Modernist Poet In his youth, Eliot was influenced by the French Symbolists. In England, he met Ezra Pound, another American expatriate. Pound had an even stronger influence on Eliot. He championed Eliot's writing and served as his editor. In 1915 Pound persuaded *Poetry* magazine to publish "The Love Song of J. Alfred Prufrock." Often called the first Modernist poem, "Prufrock" captures the emptiness and alienation many people experienced while living in impersonal modern cities. The poem baffled and angered many readers, who found its subject matter "unpoetic," its fragmented structure off-putting, and its allusions difficult to understand.

The outbreak of World War I prevented Eliot's return to Harvard for his final doctoral examinations. He remained in England, where he married Vivien Haigh-Wood, taught school, and worked for Lloyds Bank. He also continued to write poetry and literary essays. His best-known work, *The Waste Land*, was published in 1922; in it he expresses the disillusionment that many people felt after World War I and decries the inability to find meaning and purpose in life. The work brought him international acclaim, but not happiness. Eliot was facing great strain in his marriage and in his job.

> *"Genuine poetry can communicate before it is understood."*
>
> —T. S. Eliot

Finding a Purpose Eventually, Eliot began a new, more satisfying career as a book editor and joined the Church of England. In Christianity he found a purpose in life, and in his poems, such as "The Hollow Men," "Ash Wednesday," and *Four Quartets*, he described the importance and difficulty of belief in a spiritually impoverished world.

Eliot received the Nobel Prize in Literature in 1948. His poetry has been praised for the power of its symbolism, its precise language, and its mastery of form. At the time of his death in 1965, Eliot was considered by many to be the most important and influential poet and critic writing in the English language.

LOG ON ▶ **Literature** Online

Author Search For more about T. S. Eliot, go to glencoe.com and enter QuickPass code GLA9800u5.

Selection Skills

Literary Elements
- Allusion (SE pp. 667, 671, 672, 674)
- Dramatic Monologue (SE p. 674)

← **The Love Song of J. Alfred Prufrock** →

Writing Skills/Grammar
- Short Story (SE p. 675)
- Run-on Sentences (SE p. 675)
- Mood of Verbs (TE p. 670)

Vocabulary Skills
- Antonyms (SE p. 674)
- Analogies (TE p. 667)

Reading Skills
- Connect to Cultural Context (SE pp. 667, 669–671, 674)
- Sequence (TE p. 668)
- Personal Response (TE p. 672)

Listening/Speaking/ Viewing Skills
- Analyze Art (SE p. 673; TE pp. 668, 671)

Literature and Reading Preview

Connect to the Poem

In Eliot's poem, the speaker asks himself, "Do I dare?" about several things. Do you ever ask yourself that same question? How do you answer? Discuss this subject with a partner or small group.

Build Background

When Eliot wrote "The Love Song of J. Alfred Prufrock," cities were growing at a rapid rate. In many countries, city dwellers outnumbered those inhabiting rural areas. Factories overran residential neighborhoods, and people crowded into huge tenement buildings. Factory owners amassed great wealth at the expense of workers who toiled under miserable conditions. In his poems, Eliot expressed the feelings of loneliness, alienation, and frustration that came with these changes.

Set Purposes for Reading

Big Idea New Poetics

As you read, ask yourself, In what ways does Eliot reject some of the conventions of traditional poetry?

Literary Element Allusion

An **allusion** is an indirect reference to a character, a place, or a situation from history, art, music, or literature. For example, "The Love Song of J. Alfred Prufrock" can be seen as an extended allusion to Dante's *Inferno*. By quoting Dante in the epigraph, Eliot suggests that Prufrock's journey with a companion through the streets of London to "the room" is similar to the journey that Dante and Virgil make through the underworld to the center of hell. As you read, ask yourself, What purpose do Eliot's allusions serve?

Reading Strategy Connect to Cultural Context

A piece of writing is more meaningful to you when you place it in its **cultural context.** Think about the society in which the writer lived, the technologies that surrounded the writer, and the historical forces that influenced the writer's choice of subject matter, point of view, and tone. "Prufrock," like much of Eliot's work, is set in the cultural context of England's upper-middle-class society in London before, during, and after World War I.

Learning Objectives

For pages 666–674

In studying this text, you will focus on the following objectives:

Literary Study: Analyzing allusion.

Reading: Connecting to cultural context.

Vocabulary

tedious (tē´ dē əs) *adj.* tiresome because of length; boring; p. 668 *After an hour, my uncle's talk on fly fishing became tedious.*

presume (pri zōōm´) *v.* to expect something without justification; to take for granted; p. 670 *The employee presumed she would be promoted because her boss liked her.*

digress (dī gres´) *v.* to depart from the main subject; to ramble; p. 670 *The teacher digressed by telling the class amusing anecdotes.*

malinger (mə ling´ gər) *v.* to pretend incapacity or illness to avoid work; p. 670 *To avoid Eva, John malingered, staying home.*

deferential (def´ ə ren´ shəl) *adj.* yielding to someone else's opinions or wishes; p. 672 *Sam was always deferential toward his father.*

T. S. ELIOT **667**

Approaching Level

DIFFERENTIATED INSTRUCTION

Established Explain to students that when writers make allusions, they expect the readers to recognize these references. To prepare students to read the poem, write the following references in idea webs on the board: Dante's Inferno, Michelangelo, John the Baptist, Lazarus, and Hamlet. Ask students to tell what they already know about each term, and record the information in the radiating circles.

As students read, they can use the side column notes and information from class discussions to add to these webs.

Before You Read

Focus

Summary

As the character of J. Alfred Prufrock is developed, he is revealed to be a person of low self-esteem who is an observer of life rather than an active participant in it.

 For summaries in languages other than English, see Unit 5 Teaching Resources Book, pp. 35–40.

Vocabulary

Analogies Tell students that antonyms often appear in word analogies, or groups of words that are related in the same ways. For example: cold : hot :: insidious : honest. **Ask:** Which vocabulary word best completes this analogy: up : down :: disrespectful : _____? *(deferential)* Which vocabulary word best completes this analogy: back : forward :: focus : _____? *(digress)*

 For additional vocabulary practice, see Unit 5 Teaching Resources Book, p. 43.

Interactive Read and Write

Other options for teaching this selection can be found in

- Interactive Read and Write for EL Students, pp. 179–188
- Interactive Read and Write for Approaching-Level Students, pp. 179–188
- Interactive Read and Write for On-Level Students, pp. 179–188

Teach

Reading Strategy | 1

Connect to Cultural Context Explain that Dante's epigraph prepares readers for a literary journey to hell. Remind students that World War I was fought between 1914 and 1918. Eliot's poem was published in 1919.
Ask: What might Eliot be saying about the effect of World War I on modern life? *(Possible answer: World War I created a kind of hell on Earth because people felt disenchanted, spiritually dead, and isolated.)*

Big Idea | 2

New Poetics Answer: *It captures the emptiness and sense of isolation many people feel in an impersonal modern city.*

View the Art ★

Although born in Nuremberg, Germany, Stefan Hirsch (1899–1964) was considered an American artist.
Ask: How does Hirsch's painting capture the mood of the opening lines of the poem? *(Possible answer: The dark colors and shadows capture the ominous feelings expressed in the opening lines.)*

The Love Song of J. Alfred Prufrock

T. S. Eliot

Winter Night, 1928. Stefan Hirsch. Oil on panel, 22½ x 19¾ in. Collection of the Newark Museum.

1 S'io credessi che mia resposta fosse
a persona che mai tornasse al mondo,
questa fiamma staria senza più scosse.
Ma per ciò che giammai di questo fondo
non tornò vivo alcun, s'i'odo il vero,
senza tema d'infamia ti respondo.[1]

Let us go then, you and I,
When the evening is spread out against the sky
Like a patient etherised[2] upon a table;
Let us go, through certain half-deserted streets,
5   The muttering retreats
Of restless nights in one-night cheap hotels
And sawdust restaurants with oyster-shells:
Streets that follow like a **tedious** argument
Of insidious intent

2 New Poetics *How is this simile an example of Modernism in poetry?*

Vocabulary

tedious (tē′ dē əs) *adj.* tiresome because of length; boring

1. The epigraph is from Dante's *Inferno,* Canto XXVII, in which a condemned spirit in hell confesses his sins. He says, "If I thought that I was speaking / to someone who would go back to the world, / this flame would shake no more. / But since nobody has ever / gone back alive from this place, if what I hear is true, / I answer you without fear of infamy."
2. *Etherised* (etherized) (ē′ thə rīzd′) means "anesthetized with ether, as before an operation"; in other words, "made insensitive to pain."

668 UNIT 5   BEGINNINGS OF THE MODERN AGE

Reading Practice

SMALL GROUP
Sequence Point out some ways in which Eliot links the seemingly disparate stanzas in this poem. Examples: the words "In the room" (line 13) answer the question of where the speaker intends to visit (line 12). Lines 15–22 extend the description of evening in lines 2–3. Line 37 picks up the idea of time, repeating line 23. Tell students that understanding the links will help them understand the structure of the poem. Have students work in pairs to identify other links between phrases and lines in the poem. Encourage them to create sequence chains that show how the phrases and lines connect.

10   To lead you to an overwhelming question . . .
    Oh, do not ask, 'What is it?'
    Let us go and make our visit.
    In the room the women come and go
    Talking of Michelangelo.[3]

15   The yellow fog that rubs its back upon the window-panes,
    The yellow smoke that rubs its muzzle on the window-panes,
    Licked its tongue into the corners of the evening,
    Lingered upon the pools that stand in drains,
    Let fall upon its back the soot that falls from chimneys,
20   Slipped by the terrace, made a sudden leap,
    And seeing that it was a soft October night,
    Curled once about the house, and fell asleep.
    And indeed there will be time
    For the yellow smoke that slides along the street
25   Rubbing its back upon the window-panes;
    There will be time, there will be time
    To prepare a face to meet the faces that you meet;
    There will be time to murder and create,
    And time for all the works and days of hands
30   That lift and drop a question on your plate;
    Time for you and time for me,
    And time yet for a hundred indecisions,
    And for a hundred visions and revisions,
    Before the taking of a toast and tea.

35   In the room the women come and go
    Talking of Michelangelo.

    And indeed there will be time
    To wonder, 'Do I dare?' and, 'Do I dare?'
    Time to turn back and descend the stair,
40   With a bald spot in the middle of my hair—
    (They will say: 'How his hair is growing thin!')
    My morning coat,[4] my collar mounting firmly to the chin,
    My necktie rich and modest, but asserted[5] by a simple pin—
    (They will say: 'But how his arms and legs are thin!')
45   Do I dare
    Disturb the universe?

Connect to Cultural Context *What is the cultural difference between this room and the streets through which Prufrock has traveled?* **4**

New Poetics *How does Eliot disregard traditional poetic elements in these lines? What traditional element does he keep?* **5**

3. *Michelangelo* Buonarroti (mī' kəl an' jə lō bwô nä rô' tē) (1475–1564) was a gifted Italian sculptor and painter.

3

4. A *morning coat* is a man's jacket that slopes away from a front button at the waist to tails at the back. It was worn for formal daytime dress.
5. Here, *asserted* means "made more bold" or "enhanced."

T. S. ELIOT **669**

Teach

Literary Element 3

Metaphor Discuss the metaphor developed in lines 15–22. **Ask:** What animal is the fog and smoke compared to? *(a cat)* How does this metaphor compare with the simile of the "tedious argument of insidious intent" in lines 8–9? *(Both imply stealth and furtiveness.)* What emotion does this metaphor evoke? *(fear)*

 For additional literary element practice, see Unit 5 Teaching Resources Book, p. 41.

Reading Strategy 4

Connect to Cultural Context **Answer:** *The room is filled with cultured conversation, unlike the seedy "cheap hotels" and "sawdust restaurants."*

[APPROACHING] **Ask:** What is the difference between the people who attend a tea party to talk about art and the people who go to "one-night cheap hotels" and "sawdust restaurants"?

Big Idea 5

New Poetics **Answer:** *The lines are of irregular length and rhythm; the phrase "there will be time" is repeated not as a refrain but as a nagging reminder. The use of rhyme (street/meet) is traditional but is not part of a conventional rhyme scheme.*

Approaching Level

DIFFERENTIATED INSTRUCTION

SMALL GROUP

Emerging Provide student pairs with two-column charts. Make the first column heading "What do we know about . . ." and the second column "Answers." Fill in these completions for the question in the first row:

. . . the streets?

. . . Prufrock—both physically and emotionally?

. . . Prufrock's companion?

. . . the room?

. . . the people in the room?

Have the students reread the poem and record the answers to these questions in the second column using textual support. Have each pair share their information aloud with the class.

Teach

Reading Strategy | 1

Draw Conclusions Have students discuss the meaning of lines 73–74. **Ask:** What is Prufrock's opinion of himself? What image reveals that opinion? *(The image of a "scuttling" ocean creature reveals that Prufrock has low self-esteem.)* **Ask:** What emotion does this image evoke in readers toward Prufrock? *(pity)*

Reading Strategy | 2

Connect to Cultural Context Answer: *The people in the society that Prufrock inhabits are consumed by tedious and trivial rituals.*

In a minute there is time
For decisions and revisions which a minute will reverse.

For I have known them all already, known them all—
50 Have known the evenings, mornings, afternoons,
I have measured out my life with coffee spoons;
I know the voices dying with a dying fall
Beneath the music from a farther room.
    So how should I **presume**?

55 And I have known the eyes already, known them all—
The eyes that fix you in a formulated[6] phrase,
And when I am formulated, sprawling on a pin,
When I am pinned and wriggling on the wall,
Then how should I begin
60 To spit out all the butt-ends of my days and ways?
    And how should I presume?
And I have known the arms already, known them all—
Arms that are braceleted and white and bare
(But in the lamplight, downed with light brown hair!)?
65 Is it perfume from a dress
That makes me so **digress**?
Arms that lie along a table, or wrap about a shawl.
    And should I then presume?
    And how should I begin?
70 Shall I say, I have gone at dusk through narrow streets
And watched the smoke that rises from the pipes
Of lonely men in shirt-sleeves, leaning out of windows? . . . [1]
I should have been a pair of ragged claws
Scuttling across the floors of silent seas.
75 And the afternoon, the evening, sleeps so peacefully!
Smoothed by long fingers,
Asleep . . . tired . . . or it **malingers**,
Stretched on the floor, here beside you and me.
Should I, after tea and cakes and ices,
80 Have the strength to force the moment to its crisis?
But though I have wept and fasted, wept and prayed,

[6] *Formulated* means "reduced to or expressed as a formula," thereby losing individuality.

---

[2] Connect to Cultural Context *What does this metaphor tell the reader about the society that Prufrock inhabits?*

Vocabulary

presume (pri zōōm′) *v.* to expect something without justification; to take for granted
digress (dī gres′) *v.* to depart from the main subject; to ramble
malinger (mə ling′ gər) *v.* to pretend incapacity or illness to avoid work

670 UNIT 5 BEGINNINGS OF THE MODERN AGE

Grammar Practice

Mood of Verbs Point out that in addition to tense and voice, verbs also express mood. The two most common are the indicative mood and the imperative mood. The **indicative** makes a statement or asks a question. The **imperative** gives a command. Write these examples on the board:

Indicative: "So how should I presume?"
Imperative: "Oh, do not ask, 'What is it?'"
Have students list other examples of indicative and imperative verbs in "The Love Song of J. Alfred Prufrock."

670

Rainy Night, 1929–1930.
Charles Burchfield.
Watercolor, 30 x 42 in.
San Diego Museum of Art,
CA. Gift of Anne R. and
Amy Putnam. ★

Though I have seen my head (grown slightly bald) brought in
    upon a platter[7]
I am no prophet[8]—and here's no great matter;
I have seen the moment of my greatness flicker,
85 And I have seen the eternal Footman[9] hold my coat, and snicker,
And in short, I was afraid.

And would it have been worth it, after all,
After the cups, the marmalade, the tea,
Among the porcelain, among some talk of you and me,
90 Would it have been worth while,
To have bitten off the matter with a smile,
To have squeezed the universe into a ball

To roll it towards some overwhelming question,
To say: 'I am Lazarus, come from the dead,[10]
95 Come back to tell you all, I shall tell you all'—
If one, settling a pillow by her head,
    Should say: 'That is not what I meant at all.
    That is not it, at all.'
And would it have been worth it, after all,
100 Would it have been worth while,
After the sunsets and the dooryards and the sprinkled streets,

7. [head . . . platter] This biblical reference is to the beheading of the prophet John the Baptist (Matthew 14:1–11). King Herod was so pleased with the dancing of Salome, his stepdaughter, that he promised her anything she desired. Prompted by her mother, Salome asked for the head of John on a platter. Herod granted her request.
8. A *prophet* is a person who predicts the future or who speaks by divine inspiration.
9. The *eternal Footman* is Death.
10. [*I am Lazarus . . . dead*] This biblical reference is to John 11:1–44 in which Jesus restores his friend Lazarus to life after he has been dead for four days.

Allusion *Although he claims not to be a prophet, Prufrock compares himself to John the Baptist. In what sense does Prufrock envision his head "brought in upon a platter"?* **3**

Connect to Cultural Context *How does this symbol characterize the cultural context of the poem?* **4**

T. S. ELIOT **671**

Teach

To check students' understanding of the selection, see Unit 5 Teaching Resources Book, p. 45.

Literary Element | 1

Allusion Answer: *Prufrock does not see himself as a heroic figure like Hamlet but as a foolish and ridiculous figure.*

[APPROACHING] Explain that Prufrock understands life to be similar to a stage play. Some people such as Hamlet are heroes; some people such as Polonius are needless advisors; and some people such as Prufrock are fools.

Big Idea | 2

New Poetics Answer: *The line undercuts any sense of romance in the image of the mermaids. Although it is a perfect example of iambic pentameter, it is not part of any overall metrical pattern; it stands alone.*

Ask: How is the form of this poem different from the forms of poems from earlier time periods? *(Possible answer: The stanzas are of unequal length, and rhyme and meter are used irregularly.)*

After the novels, after the teacups, after the skirts that trail along
    the floor—
And this, and so much more?—
It is impossible to say just what I mean!

105 But as if a magic lantern[11] threw the nerves in patterns on a screen:
Would it have been worth while
If one, settling a pillow or throwing off a shawl,
And turning toward the window, should say:
    'That is not it at all,
110   That is not what I meant, at all.'

No! I am not Prince Hamlet,[12] nor was meant to be;
Am an attendant lord, one that will do
To swell a progress,[13] start a scene or two,
Advise the prince; no doubt, an easy tool,
115 **Deferential,** glad to be of use,
Politic,[14] cautious, and meticulous;
Full of high sentence, but a bit obtuse;[15]
At times, indeed, almost ridiculous—
Almost, at times, the Fool.

120 I grow old . . . I grow old . . .
I shall wear the bottoms of my trousers rolled.

Shall I part my hair behind? Do I dare to eat a peach?
I shall wear white flannel trousers, and walk upon the beach.
I have heard the mermaids singing, each to each.

125 I do not think that they will sing to me.

I have seen them riding seaward on the waves
Combing the white hair of the waves blown back
When the wind blows the water white and black.

We have lingered in the chambers of the sea
130 By sea-girls wreathed with seaweed red and brown
Till human voices wake us, and we drown.

---

11. The *magic lantern,* a forerunner of the modern slide projector, was a device for projecting enlarged images.

12. *Prince Hamlet* is the Prince of Denmark, the tragic hero of Shakespeare's play *Hamlet.*

13. *To swell a progress* is to participate in, and thereby increase (swell) the number of people in a royal procession or a play.

14. *Politic* (po' lə tik) means "characterized by prudence or shrewdness in managing, dealing, or promoting a policy."

15. *High sentence* is fancy, pompous speech full of advice, like that of the old counselor Polonius in *Hamlet. Obtuse* (əb tōōs') means "slow in understanding" or "dull."

---

1 Allusion *What does this allusion tell the reader about how Prufrock sees himself?*

2 New Poetics *How is this line an example of the new poetics of Modernism?*

Vocabulary

deferential (def´ ə ren´ shəl) *adj.* yielding to someone else's opinions or wishes

Reading Practice

Personal Response *Participants* are active readers who interact with texts; *spectators* are passive readers. When asked to write a personal response, a participant has difficulty choosing among various responses, and a spectator has difficulty finding something to say.

- Ask students to write personal responses to the poem, using at least one of the following active-reading strategies: listen, imagine, clarify, interpret.
- Encourage students to develop a question related to each strategy to guide them as they write.

Have student volunteers share their personal responses to the poem with the class.

After You Read

Respond and Think Critically

Respond and Interpret

1. What image does the name *J. Alfred Prufrock* conjure up for you? How does Prufrock, as his character and personality are expressed throughout the poem, illustrate this image?

2. (a)In lines 1–9, what do the images Prufrock uses to describe the evening and the places he will travel through evoke? (b)What do the images suggest about his state of mind?

3. (a)What kinds of activities does Prufrock say he will have time for in lines 26–48? (b)What does he mean by "Do I dare/Disturb the universe"?

4. (a)How does Prufrock describe himself and his life in lines 49–74? (b)What does Prufrock's description of his life suggest about his personal self-assessment?

Analyze and Evaluate

5. In lines 26–27, what does Prufrock mean when he says that there will be time "To prepare a face to meet the faces that you meet"?

6. What, in your opinion, is Prufrock's "overwhelming question" (lines 10, 93)?

7. (a)What do the mermaids (124–130) suggest about Prufrock's state of mind? (b)What is the function of the final line of the poem?

Connect

8. **Big Idea** New Poetics (a)How does this "love song" differ from traditional love poetry? (b)How is the title of the poem ironic?

9. **Connect to Today** What aspects of life cause alienation and frustration today? Explain.

Visual Literacy

Fine Art

Study the painting *Rainy Night* at right. (A larger version appears on page 671.) Charles Burchfield (1893–1967) painted this work in 1930. It is representative of the second phase of the artist's career, when he painted scenes depicting the bleakness of city life.

1. What is your overall impression of the painting? Cite details in the painting that contribute to your impression.

2. Which images or lines from "The Love Song of J. Alfred Prufrock" might you use to describe this painting? Explain.

Rainy Night, 1929–1930. Charles Burchfield. Watercolor, 30 x 42 in. San Diego Museum of Art, CA. Gift of Anne R. and Amy Putnam.

T. S. ELIOT **673**

Fine Art

1. Possible answer: It is sad and depressing. Students may cite the rainy street, the gloomy colors, and the lack of much human activity.

2. Possible answers: "the evening is spread out against the sky"; "half-deserted streets"

 For additional assessment, see Assessment Resources, pp. 189–190.

After You Read

Assess

1. The name is stuffy and comical. Prufrock is indecisive, insecure, afraid of aging.

2. (a) Sickliness, loneliness, and sordidness (b) He sees himself as a helpless "patient," traveling hopelessly through life.

3. (a) Preparing a face; murdering and creating; indecisions, visions, and revisions; wondering "Do I dare?"; turning back and descending the stair (b) Any expression of truth or strong emotion would disturb the shallow inhabitants of his social "universe."

4. (a) He cannot "begin" or "presume" to express himself or declare love, and fears becoming one of the "lonely men in shirt-sleeves." (b) He is unable to improve his dreary life.

5. He means that there will be time to create a superficial "face" to make a good impression.

6. A question about life's meaning

7. (a) He has an erotic fantasy about the mermaids, but he fears they will not sing to him. (b) It sums up Prufrock's life view—we live trivial, purposeless lives, and then we die.

8. (a)The poem is not traditional because the speaker cannot make a declaration of love. (b) His "love song" is actually a lament that expresses his inability to express his feelings.

9. Students may say people in cities are isolated from their neighbors and that the intrusion of technology into daily life causes frustration for some people.

After You Read

Assess

Literary Element

1. Prufrock feels that he is not the "hero" of his own life. He does not have the rank of a prince, and although Hamlet eventually acts, Prufrock does not.

2. John, Lazarus, and Hamlet are impressive figures who are taken seriously. They contrast with Prufrock, who is unable to rise above mediocrity.

3. The allusions add richness and complexity to the poem and enlarge its artistic compass.

Review: Dramatic Monologue

1. Possible answers: the reader of the poem; Prufrock's alter ego; an unidentified companion

2. The "you" in the epigraph refers to Dante and Virgil, to whom the speaker confides. The use of "you" in line 1 therefore implies that Prufrock will similarly confide in the reader.

3. Prufrock maintains a fairly even tone—one of quiet despair.

Vocabulary

1. e 2. g 3. a 4. b 5. f

Progress Check

Can students connect to a cultural context?

If No → See Unit 5 Teaching Resources Book, p. 42.

Literary Element Allusion

An **allusion** can add richness and depth to a work of literature through its association of ideas. For example, lines 92–93 contain an allusion to Andrew Marvell's poem "To His Coy Mistress," in which the speaker says, "Let us roll all our strength and all / Our sweetness into one ball, / And tear our pleasures with rough strife / Through the iron gates of life." This allusion is ironic because Prufrock, after squeezing "the universe into a ball," is unable to "roll it towards some overwhelming question."

1. In the allusion to Shakespeare in lines 111–119, why does Prufrock claim he is *not* Prince Hamlet?

2. In the poem, Prufrock makes allusions to John the Baptist, Lazarus, and Hamlet. What do these characters have in common? How do they relate to Prufrock?

3. In your opinion, what is the overall effect of Eliot's use of allusions in this poem?

Review: Dramatic Monologue

As you learned on page 515, a **dramatic monologue** is an extended speech by a literary character to a silent listener. When that silent listener is the reader, the speech takes the form of an interior monologue, also known as **stream of consciousness**, a term first used by the psychologist William James to describe the spontaneous flow of a person's random thoughts and feelings. Some readers have interpreted "Prufrock" as a stream-of-consciousness monologue in which Prufrock addresses his *alter ego,* or the opposite side of his personality.

Partner Activity Meet with a classmate and talk about the function of the dramatic monologue in "The Love Song of J. Alfred Prufrock." Address these questions during your discussion:

1. Who is the "you" in line 1?

2. What is the relationship between the "you" in the poem and the "you" in the epigraph from Dante's *Inferno?*

3. Does Prufrock maintain the same tone throughout the poem? Explain.

Reading Strategy Connect to Cultural Context

The lines "In the room the women come and go/ Talking of Michelangelo" (lines 13–14, 35–36) refer to the great Italian Renaissance painter.

1. What can you infer about these women?

2. Why do you think that the lines are repeated? What can you infer from this repetition about the nature of the women's conversations?

Vocabulary Practice

Practice with Antonyms An antonym is a word that has a meaning opposite to that of another word. With a partner, match each bold-faced vocabulary word below with its antonym. You will not use all the answer choices. Use a thesaurus or dictionary to check your answers.

1. tedious	a. focus
2. presume	b. persevere
3. digress	c. candid
4. malinger	d. pretend
5. deferential	e. interesting
	f. disobedient
	g. know

Academic Vocabulary

In "The Love Song of J. Alfred Prufrock," Eliot *comments* on the hopelessness of modern life.

Comment is an academic word. A reporter looking for a quotation for a story might take notes as a politician **comments** on an election.

To further explore the meaning of this word, answer the following question: If you were to write a poem similar to this one about modern life, how would you **comment** on your world?

For more on academic vocabulary, see pages 53–54.

LOG ON ▶ **Literature** Online

Selection Resources For Selection Quizzes, eFlash-cards, and Reading-Writing Connection activities, go to glencoe.com and enter QuickPass code GLA9800u5.

Reading Strategy

1. B is the correct answer because the reference to Michelangelo suggests the women's familiarity with art, but their coming and going suggests a lack of serious concentration.

Academic Vocabulary

Students might mention greed or the sense of danger and claustrophobia in cities.

Respond Through Writing

Short Story

Apply Mood Write a short story narrated from the first-person point of view of a modern-day teen Prufrock. Decide whether you want your readers to feel sympathy for your character. Keep that purpose in mind as you write, selecting an appropriate tone, mood, and language.

Understand the Task **Tone** is the writer's attitude toward the subject or audience, as conveyed through elements such as word choice, punctuation, sentence structure, and figures of speech. **Mood** is the general emotional quality of a piece of writing.

Prewrite What kind of life would Prufrock live if he were a modern-day teenager? Brainstorm a list of events that might happen during a normal day in his life. Then choose the events you think would most strongly illustrate his character. Next, make a list of words and phrases that your character would use in reacting and responding to these events.

Draft As you draft your story, present events in a logical sequence. Make sure each event you describe contributes to the overall mood you want to create, and that each is consistent with the impression you want your audience to have of your character. Remember to also use concrete sensory details to describe the character's specific movements and thoughts. To plan your story, make a chart like the one below:

Events	Character's responses/thoughts	Effects on mood
Opportunity to audition for school play	It's pointless; I might embarrass myself	Creates feeling of bleakness

Revise Exchange stories with a classmate. After reading each other's work, discuss whether each of you was successful in your writing purpose. If not, discuss revisions you might make to strengthen your story.

Edit and Proofread Proofread your paper, correcting any errors in spelling, grammar, and punctuation. Review the Grammar Tip in the side column for help avoiding run-on sentences.

Learning Objectives

In this assignment, you will focus on the following objectives:

Writing: Writing a short story.

Grammar: Correcting run-on sentences.

> ### Grammar Tip
>
> **Run-on Sentences**
>
> *I arrived at the test I did not want to go through with it.*
>
> This is a run-on sentence, because two sentences are joined without a transition. One solution: change one sentence to a subordinate clause: *When I arrived at the test, I did not want to go through with it.* You can also join the sentences using a coordinating conjunction: *I arrived at the test, but I did not want to go through with it.*

After You Read

Assess

Writing

Students' stories should develop a distinct tone and be organized in a logical sequence. Stories should also include concrete sensory details and be free of run-on sentences and other grammatical errors.

Scoring Guide

Assess students' performance in the following categories using the scoring guide at the bottom of the page:

- Addresses all parts of the writing task.
- Conveys a certain tone through use of word choice, punctuation, sentence structure and figures of speech.
- Describes and develops characters and events to communicate a consistent mood to readers.
- Employs concrete sensory details that illustrate characters' thoughts and actions.
- Provides a variety of sentence types; uses precise, descriptive language.
- Follows English language conventions.

T. S. ELIOT **675**

Scoring Guide	4	3	2	1
Task addressed	fully	mostly	partially	barely
Tone	consistent and well conveyed	somewhat consistent and conveyed	partially conveyed	no particular tone
Character, events	well developed and described	somewhat developed and described	partially developed and described	not developed or described
Sensory details	well employed	employed	few employed	none
Language	varied, precise, descriptive	varied, somewhat descriptive	predictable, basic	not varied, limited
Convention errors	few or none	several	some	many

Before You Read

Focus

Bellringer Options

Selection Focus
   Transparency 42
Daily Language Practice
   Transparency 59

Or have students scan the classroom for objects that catch their interest. Then have them discuss the relationship between what they observe and Williams's statement, "Eyes stand first in the poet's equipment."

Writer's Technique ☆

Form and Content During his writing career, Williams continually experimented with rhythm and line arrangement. Most of his poems are not written in traditional meters; they are more organic in their rhythms. Their forms are shaped by the impressions he received from everyday experiences and conversations.

Before You Read
The Red Wheelbarrow and *This Is Just to Say*

Meet **William Carlos Williams**
(1883–1963)

Williilliam Carlos Williams led a double life as a doctor and an award-winning poet. Often he would write between seeing patients, sometimes even jotting down poems on prescription pads. Despite the fact that his attention was divided, Williams managed to write some of the most memorable poems of the Imagist movement. In his poetry, he captured America's colloquial speech and presented everyday events in powerful, compact lines.

> "*Eyes stand first in the poet's equipment.*"
>
> —William Carlos Williams

Doctor and Poet Williams was born in Rutherford, New Jersey, and came from a diverse background: his mother was born in Puerto Rico, and his father was British. Williams began writing poetry in high school and soon settled on the goal of becoming both a doctor and a writer.

While attending the University of Pennsylvania Medical School, Williams wrote many of the poems that would appear in his first book, *Poems*, published in 1909. At school he also met and befriended the poet Ezra Pound. Pound would become a great influence on the young Williams, even arranging for the publication of his second collection, *The Tempers*, in 1913.

After completing his internship in New York and further study in advanced pediatrics in Leipzig, Germany, Williams returned to Rutherford, where he began his medical practice and continued to write. In his next book, *Al Que Quiere!* (*To Him*

Who Wants It!), published in 1917, Williams drew upon his Spanish and Puerto Rican heritage and established himself as a major voice in modern poetry. However, he soon began to drift away from Pound and Imagism. He felt that Pound's ideas were too rooted in the cultural values of Europe, not those of the United States, which Williams so adored.

During the 1920s and 1930s, Williams published several books, including two collections of poetry, *Kora in Hell* and *Spring and All*; a book of essays, *In the American Grain*; and a novel, *White Mule*. From 1946 through 1958, Williams worked on his masterpiece, *Paterson*. This nine-volume epic poem mythologizes northern New Jersey. In 1963 Williams was awarded a posthumous Pulitzer Prize for his collection *Pictures from Brueghel and Other Poems*.

Visionary and Legacy Believing that poetry should be grounded in everyday things and scenes, Williams was famous for saying, "No ideas but in things." He explored the world around him, writing of New Jersey's gritty, industrial landscape and of his patients and neighbors, many of whom were impoverished immigrants struggling to succeed in the United States. Williams left an impressive legacy of work that had an enormous influence on the writers of the 1950s and 1960s and continues to be very important to poets today. Somehow, while accomplishing so much as a writer, he also managed to deliver more than two thousand babies.

LOG ON **Literature** Online

Author Search For more about William Carlos Williams, go to glencoe.com and enter QuickPass code GLA9800u5.

676 UNIT 5   BEGINNINGS OF THE MODERN AGE

Selection Skills

Reading Skills
- Recognize Author's Purpose (SE pp. 677, 679, 680)
- Activate Prior Knowledge (TE p. 678)

The Red Wheelbarrow *and* **This Is Just to Say**

Writing Skills/Grammar
- Write a List (SE p. 680)

Literary Elements
- Form (SE pp. 677, 678, 680)

Vocabulary Skills
- Synonyms (SE pp. 677, 680)
- Roots and Affixes (TE p. 677)

Literature and Reading Preview

Connect to the Poems

What ordinary objects, sounds, or scenes inspire you? Freewrite for ten minutes about the first few items that come to mind.

Build Background

Imagism's influence is obvious in "The Red Wheelbarrow" and "This Is Just to Say." About writing in this style, Williams wrote, "Cut and cut again whatever you write—while you leave by your art no trace of your cutting—and the final utterance will remain packed with what you have to say."

Set Purposes for Reading

Big Idea New Poetics

As you read, ask yourself, How does Williams's spare style exemplify Imagism and evoke the American landscape?

Literary Element Form

The **form** of a poem is its prescribed pattern, usually involving meter, rhyme, rhyme scheme, and structure. Many contemporary writers use loosely structured poetic forms instead of following stricter, more traditional patterns. One way Williams creates a loose, informal structure is by using **enjambment,** the continuation of a sentence from one line of a poem to the next. As you read, ask yourself, How does Williams both use and break with traditional forms to add depth and complexity? What purpose does his use of enjambment serve?

Reading Strategy Recognize Author's Purpose

An **author's purpose** is the author's intent in writing a piece of literature. Authors typically write in order to persuade, inform, explain, entertain, or describe. While reading these poems, try to determine Williams's purpose for writing them.

···

Tip: Take Notes List questions to ask as you read. As you think about your answers, consider the author's purpose or argument.

Question	Answer	Evidence
What did I learn that I didn't already know?	I learned that simple things can leave a lasting impression.	The poem is about a simple red wheelbarrow in the rain.

Learning Objectives

For pages 676–680

In studying these texts, you will focus on the following objectives:

Literary Study: Analyzing form.

Reading: Recognizing author's purpose.

Writing: Writing a list.

Vocabulary

depend (di pend´) *v.* to rely on; p. 678 *In football, the whole team depends on the quarterback to get the ball to the end zone.*

glazed (glāzd) *adj.* covered with a smooth, glossy coating; p. 678 *The cinnamon rolls were glazed with icing.*

delicious (di lish´ əs) *adj.* having a very pleasing taste; p. 679 *I love all kinds of ice cream flavors but I find chocolate to be the most delicious.*

Tip: Synonyms Understanding words that are similar in meaning to an unfamiliar word, or **synonyms,** can help you learn the word. Example: *Glazed and coated* are synonyms; they both mean "to be covered with something."

Before You Read

Focus

Summary

In "The Red Wheelbarrow," the speaker describes a red wheelbarrow in the rain next to white chickens. In the Imagist manner, Williams uses only a few words to create this image.

He takes a similar approach in "This Is Just to Say," in which the speaker apologizes for eating plums meant for breakfast.

 For summaries in languages other than English, see Unit 5 Teaching Resources Book, pp. 47–52.

Vocabulary

Roots and Affixes **Ask:** What suffixes can you add to the verb *depend* to form adjectives? What are the meanings of the words formed? *(-able, dependable: "reliable"; -ent, dependent: "needing to rely on someone or something")*

ENGLISH LEARNERS **Ask:** What prefixes can you add to these words to make them opposites? *(un-, in-; undependable, independent)*

 For additional context, see Glencoe Interactive Vocabulary CD-ROM.

Approaching Level

DIFFERENTIATED INSTRUCTION

 Established Emphasize that the form of a poem is the way that the words and lines are arranged on a page.

Write the following words on separate note cards: *depends, red, wheelbarrow, glazed, rain, water, white,* and *chickens.* Have student pairs work together to create several different poems with these words by arranging and rearranging the words on desktops. Tell students that they may add words or change the forms of words as necessary for meaning.

When students have finished, lead them to discuss how they used form to create different poems even though they were working with a relatively constant word set.

Teach

New Poetics Ask: How does Williams use imagery and sensory details to turn an ordinary object into the subject of a poem? *(Possible answer: He calls attention to an ordinary scene by emphasizing visual details. He contrasts the glistening, rain-covered wheelbarrow with the white chickens.)* **Ask:** What is the effect of this image on readers? *(Possible answer: Readers hope for a new beginning.)*

Literary Element **2**

Form Answer: *Students may point out that the separation makes the pace more deliberate and forces readers to listen to each word and respond to the meaning of each word part.*

ENGLISH LEARNERS Explain that *wheelbarrow* is a compound word that should be joined. Here, Williams splits the compound word into two words: *wheel* and *barrow*. **Ask:** How is the word *wheelbarrow* (a small cart with wheels, pushed by hand) different from the words *wheel* and *barrow*? *(Possible answer: A wheelbarrow is a single object that viewers might observe as one thing. The words* wheel *and* barrow *describe two separate objects, forcing viewers to look at the parts of the whole.)*

Wheelbarrow, 1934.
Morris Graves.
Oil on canvas, 31⅛ x 35⅛ in.
Smithsonian American Art Museum,
Washington, DC.

The Red Wheelbarrow

William Carlos Williams

so much **depends**
upon

a red wheel
barrow

5   **glazed** with rain
water

beside the white
chickens.   **1**

> **Form** *What effect does the break between the words* wheel *and* barrow *have?*   **2**

Vocabulary

depend (di pend´) *v.* to rely on
glazed (glāzd) *adj.* covered with a smooth, glossy coating

678 UNIT 5 BEGINNINGS OF THE MODERN AGE

Reading Practice

SPIRAL REVIEW Activate Prior Knowledge
What readers already know contributes to their understanding of literature. Although students may not have seen a red wheelbarrow and white chickens in the rain, you can create an experience that will help them understand the poem. Display a wet object such as an apple or a cup. Have students write descriptions of the object using concrete sensory details that appeal to the senses of sight, sound, smell, touch, and taste. Ask students to say how the wetness of the object changes its appearance and captures viewers' attention. Students should also include their emotional responses to the object and the significance of their observations.

Plums and Pears. Paul Cezanne. Oil on canvas, 7¾ x 14 in.
The Barnes Foundation Collection, Merion Station, PA.

This Is Just to Say

William Carlos Williams

I have eaten
the plums
that were in
the icebox

5   and which
you were probably
saving
for breakfast

Forgive me
10 they were **delicious**
so sweet
and so cold

3

Recognize Author's Purpose *What does line 9
suggest about the author's purpose?* **4**

Vocabulary

delicious (di lish′ əs) *adj.* having a very pleasing taste

WILLIAM CARLOS WILLIAMS **679**

Reading Strategy | 3

Connect Ask: How are Williams's two poems similar? *(Possible answer: Both capture the beauty and uniqueness of ordinary objects.)*

APPROACHING Draw a Venn diagram on the board. Label one circle "Wheelbarrow/chickens," and label the other circle "Plums." Ask students to identify similarities and differences between these objects. Students can use these notes to draw conclusions.

Reading Strategy | 4

Recognize Author's Purpose Answer: *The speaker's apology may indicate that he feels guilty for having eaten the plums.*

View the Art

The French painter Paul Cézanne (1839–1906), like Williams, was inspired by everyday objects.
Ask: How does Cézanne portray the subject of plums and pears? *(Possible answer: The plums and pears are not realistic. Instead they appear as patches of color within a confined space.)*

English Learners

UNIVERSAL ACCESS

SMALL GROUP
Intermediate English learners may find the sentence structures in poetry difficult to decode. The simple structures of Williams's poems provide students with an opportunity to apply their knowledge of English conventions as a way to understand how meaning is expressed in poetry.

Have students write the text of "This Is Just to Say" in sentence form, adding punctuation where appropriate. Have student pairs work together to identify subjects and predicates. Point out the conjunction *and* in the second stanza and explain that it connects two clauses. Lead students to discuss how the revised sentence structure and punctuation clarify the meaning of the poem.

After You Read

Assess

1. Students' answers should identify specific feelings evoked by the poems.

2. The speaker sees something important in the scene he is about to describe.

3. (a) Rainwater and chickens (b) He asks readers to see beauty in ordinary things.

4. (a) The speaker has eaten the plums belonging to "you." (b) The speaker is close to the person.

5. (a) Forgiveness (b) The pleasure that the speaker has in eating the plums is described. The description justifies eating the plums.

6. (a) It forces readers to respond to the meaning of each word part. (b) Most students will appreciate the technique.

7. (a) The tone is calm and honest. (b) The tone is appropriate to a speaker who is sincerely apologetic.

8. They focus on concrete objects rather than lofty ideals or abstract concepts.

9. Students may connect his appreciation for useful objects with an appreciation for the usefulness of the human body.

✍ Writing

Students should list compound nouns that would make sense even when broken into two separate words.

Progress Check

Can students analyze form?

If No → See Unit 5 Teaching Resources Book, p. 53.

After You Read

Respond and Think Critically

Respond and Interpret

1. What feelings do the images, tones, and word choice in these poems evoke?

2. What do the first two lines of "The Red Wheelbarrow" suggest about the speaker's response to the scene?

3. (a) What does Williams describe in stanzas 3 and 4? (b) What do you think Williams is saying by introducing these elements into his poem?

4. (a) In "This Is Just to Say," what does the speaker admit to in the first two lines of the poem? (b) What does this admission suggest about the speaker's relationship with the person being addressed?

5. (a) What is described in the final lines of the poem? (b) Why do you think it is described?

Analyze and Evaluate

6. (a) Williams carefully arranges his words, including breaking up the words *rainwater* and *wheelbarrow*. How, in your opinion, does the breaking of these words across lines affect their meaning? (b) What do you think of this technique? Explain.

7. (a) What is the tone of "This Is Just to Say"? (b) Why is this tone appropriate?

Connect

8. **Big Idea** **New Poetics** How are these poems innovative in their subject matter and style?

9. **Connect to the Author** What, if any, effects do you think Williams's experiences as a doctor had on his writing, and vice versa? Explain.

Literary Element | Form

One way Williams creates a distinctive form is by using enjambment to isolate images. For example, in "The Red Wheelbarrow," the words *a red wheel* appear on a line by themselves.

1. What other images does Williams create using enjambment?

2. Is his use of this technique effective? Explain.

Reading Strategy | Recognize Author's Purpose

Writers of fiction or nonfiction generally have purposes that can be easily identified. This is not always true of poets.

1. What do you think is the author's purpose in "The Red Wheelbarrow"? Support your answer.

2. What do you think is the author's purpose in "This Is Just to Say"? Support your answer.

Vocabulary Practice

Synonyms Synonyms are words with the same or nearly the same meaning. With a partner, match each boldfaced vocabulary word below with one synonym. Use a dictionary or thesaurus to check your work.

1. depend   a. delectable
2. glazed   b. varnished
3. delicious   c. dreamy
               d. rely
               e. sweet

✍ Writing

Write a List Williams breaks *wheelbarrow* into two words to achieve a poetic effect. Write a list of compound nouns that one could use in a similar way.

 Literature Online

Selection Resources For Selection Quizzes, eFlashcards, and Reading-Writing Connection activities, go to glencoe.com and enter QuickPass code GLA9800u5.

Literary Element

1. Answers will vary. Students may say that Williams isolates the images "glazed with rain," the white color of the chickens, and the three adjectives used to describe the taste of the plums.

2. Answers will vary. Students should identify and explain the effectiveness of the uses of enjambment.

Reading Strategy

1. He is demonstrating the beauty in the everyday.

2. He apologizes but explains how one gets pleasure from ordinary things.

Vocabulary

1. d 2. b 3. a

Vocabulary Workshop

Compound Words

Literature Connection In the quotation below, *wheelbarrow* is a **compound word,** a word made up of two words that together have a meaning different from the meaning of each word individually. Compound words may be spelled open (*magic lantern*), closed (*sawdust*), or hyphenated (*half-deserted*). A dictionary will give the correct form.

> so much depends
> upon
>
> a red wheel
> barrow

—William Carlos Williams, from "The Red Wheelbarrow"

Williams writes *wheelbarrow* as an open compound for poetic effect.

The meanings of many compound words are obvious from the parts that make up the word.

- What is *sawdust*?
  It is the dust created by sawing wood.

- What is a *look-alike*?
  It is something that looks just like something else.

- What is a *natural resource*?
  It is a naturally occurring material that is useful to humans.

To learn the meaning of less familiar compound words, consult a dictionary.

Practice

A. Match each compound word with its definition.

1. elbow room	**a.** underwater plant
2. seaweed	**b.** metal screen or grating
3. grillwork	**c.** mistreated
4. swaybacked	**d.** adequate space
5. ill-used	**e.** having a sagging spine

B. Use their parts to define the following compound words. Discuss your definitions with a partner. Check your work in a dictionary.

1. ivory tower	**3.** icebox
2. dark horse	**4.** green revolution

Learning Objectives

In this workshop, you will focus on the following objectives:

Vocabulary:
Understanding compound words.
Understanding language resources.

Grammar Tip

Compound Words

A **compound word** is made of two separate words that each have a different meaning standing alone.

Tip

If a compound word does not appear in a dictionary, it is most likely to be correctly spelled open.

Reading Handbook

For more about compound words, see Reading Handbook, p. R61.

 Literature Online

Vocabulary For more vocabulary practice, go to glencoe.com and enter QuickPass code GLA9800u5.

Vocabulary Workshop

Compound Words

Focus

Have students note how the definition of each example word contains the separate parts of the compound.

Teach

Define Compound Words Remind students that the meaning of a compound word cannot always be inferred from the meanings of its parts.

Assess

Practice

A. 1. d **2.** a **3.** b **4.** e **5.** c

B. Actual definitions:

1. A place or situation remote from practical concerns and considerations

2. An improbable winner

3. A refrigerator

4. A radical increase in environmental awareness

 For additional vocabulary practice, see Glencoe Interactive Vocabulary CD-ROM.

English Learners

DIFFERENTIATED INSTRUCTION

Intermediate Many languages other than English use compound words, many of which have no equivalents in English. An example is the Chinese character for *crisis,* which is composed of the characters for *danger* and *opportunity.* Invite English learners to list examples of compound words from languages other than English. Have them check a dictionary to determine whether equivalent English compounds exist. Then point out to students that items 1, 2, and 4 in Exercise B on this page have figurative meanings. They will need to check a dictionary for the meanings of these terms.

Before You Read

Focus

Bellringer Options

Daily Language Practice Transparency 60

Or display images with clear central focuses or themes, such as exploding fireworks, a fire, or a sleeping child. **Ask:** If these images were meant to depict feelings, what might those feelings be? Have students consider as they read how Amy Lowell uses imagery or word pictures to evoke emotional responses in readers.

Before You Read

Summer Rain and *Fireworks*

Meet **Amy Lowell**
(1874–1925)

Amy Lowell was a brash, controversial, uncompromising woman, and one of the most important and best-known poets of the Imagist movement and of her generation.

Lowell was born in Brookline, Massachusetts, of a wealthy and socially prominent family, which included Fireside poet James Russell Lowell (see pages 210–211). Lowell spent her first twenty-eight years like most women in her social set. She traveled, was educated in private schools in Boston, and considered prospects for marriage. However, in 1902, Lowell chose a new path and dedicated her life to poetry.

An Imagist Poet In 1913 Lowell read several poems by Imagist poet H.D. (Hilda Doolittle) in *Poetry* magazine. Lowell connected immediately to the Imagist style. She traveled to England that same year, met Ezra Pound (page 662), and joined his Imagist circle. The first anthology of Imagist poetry, *Des Imagistes*, edited by Pound, appeared the next year and included a poem by Lowell. Also in 1914, Lowell published her book *Sword Blades and Poppy Seed*.

Lowell also began to make friends with many literary figures, including Robert Frost (page 714) and D. H. Lawrence. In 1915 she helped launch Frost's career with a favorable review of his collection *North of Boston* in the *New Republic*.

Poetic Influence Lowell's growing influence within the Imagist movement caused Pound to remove himself from it. He would later sarcastically refer to the group as "Amygism" after it had fully come under Lowell's influence. Over the next several years, she edited three volumes of the annual anthology *Some Imagist Poets*. Before 1920 she published many more books of poetry and prose, including *Can Grande's Castle*, *Tendencies in Modern American Poetry*, and *Men, Women, and Ghosts*.

> "Why should one read Poetry? That seems to me a good deal like asking: Why should one eat?"
>
> —Amy Lowell

Inspired by a lecture she gave about John Keats in 1921 and by a lifelong fascination with the English Romantic poet, Lowell published a biography of Keats. This, unfortunately, would be her last publication during her life. In 1925 Lowell died of a cerebral hemorrhage. One volume of her poetry, *What's O'Clock*, appeared after her death and was awarded the Pulitzer Prize.

Lowell is important not just for her literary contributions, but also for her promotion of the poetic innovation of Imagism. Fellow Modernist T. S. Eliot called her "the demon saleswoman of poetry." Through her tenacity, her brilliant mind, and her poems, Lowell helped to define the texture of twentieth-century verse.

 Literature Online

Author Search For more about Amy Lowell, go to glencoe.com and enter QuickPass code GLA9800u5.

Selection Skills

Literary Elements
- Structure (SE pp. 683, 685, 686)

→ **Summer Rain** *and* **Fireworks** →

Writing Skills/Grammar
- Dialogue (SE p. 686)
- Voice (TE p. 684)

Reading Skills
- Interpret Imagery (SE pp. 683–686)

Vocabulary Skills
- Context Clues (SE p. 686)
- Synonyms (TE p. 683)

Literature and Reading Preview

Connect to the Poems

How would you describe your strongest feelings using concrete images, sounds, or colors? Explore this question by making a word web like the one below.

Build Background

"Summer Rain" and "Fireworks" appeared in *Pictures of the Floating World*, a collection of imagistic free-verse poems. The poems in the first section, "Lacquer Prints," closely resemble haiku, a Japanese poetic form. "Summer Rain" and "Fireworks" are from the second section, "Planes of Personality," which celebrates intense emotions such as love, hate, and longing.

Set Purposes for Reading

Big Idea New Poetics

As you read, ask yourself, How does Lowell use imagery to convey emotions and ideas?

Literary Element Structure

Poetic structure is created through the organization of images, ideas, words, and lines. As you read, ask, How does Lowell's use of structure enhance the meaning of the poems?

Reading Strategy Interpret Imagery

Imagery is the "word pictures" authors use to evoke emotional responses in the reader. Poets may create images using figures of speech, including metaphors, similes, and personification.

....

Tip: Take Notes Use a chart like the one below to record your interpretations of Lowell's imagery.

Imagery	Interpretation
p. 685: "It spits and sparkles in stars and balls, / Buds into roses— and flares, and falls."	The speaker is filled with intense emotion upon seeing this hated person.

AMY LOWELL **683**

Learning Objectives

For pages 682–686

In studying these texts, you will focus on the following objectives:

Literary Study: Analyzing structure.

Reading: Interpreting imagery.

Writing: Writing a dialogue.

Vocabulary

pepper (pe´ pər) *v.* to shower with small objects; p. 685 *The crowd was peppered with candy from the passing parade floats.*

crimson (krim´ zən) *adj.* a bright purplish red; p. 685 *The girl's crimson coat caught the eye of many people.*

azure (azh´ ər) *adj.* a light purplish blue; p. 685 *The azure sky was a beautiful sight.*

mount (mount) *v.* to ascend or to soar; p. 685 *As the rocket mounted, the crowd began to cheer.*

Before You Read

Focus

Summary

Lowell evokes different emotional responses in these poems. In "Summer Rain" she writes about "red-gold and crocus-colored brightness" against the backdrop of a rainstorm. In "Fireworks" she uses the metaphor of exploding fireworks to describe antagonism between two people.

 For summaries in languages other than English, see Unit 5 Teaching Resources Book, pp. 58–63.

Vocabulary

Synonyms Explain to students that there are three primary colors: red, blue, and yellow. However, there are many shades or variations in the intensities of these three colors. Point out that *crimson* and *azure* describe shades of red and blue. **Ask:** What other words describe shades of red? (*scarlet, ruby, burgundy, cherry*) What other words describe shades of blue? (*cobalt, navy, sapphire, cerulean, indigo*)

 For additional vocabulary practice, see Unit 5 Teaching Resources Book, p. 66.

 For additional context, see Glencoe Interactive Vocabulary CD-ROM.

English Learners

DIFFERENTIATED INSTRUCTION

Intermediate Display the following lines, and have students discuss the comparisons and sounds in each:

- The rain drops rang like little metal disks on the tin roof.
- The slats of the shutters danced.
- Ping! Ping!
- We are fireworks.

Then have students use detailed sentences to orally identify and explain the following elements of imagery in these lines: simile, metaphor, personification, and sound.

Teach

Big Idea   1

New Poetics Say: Keep this question in mind as you read. How do Lowell's poems exemplify the principles of Imagist poetry? *(Possible answer: Both poems use clear, concrete language to convey their images. "Summer Rain" focuses on an ordinary event rather than a more abstract topic; "Fireworks" evokes intense emotions from its opening lines.)*

Reading Strategy   2

Interpret Imagery Answer: *The speaker's feelings for the person are passionate and intimate. The contrast between the dark, loud rain outside and the bright, whispering fire inside may suggest that the speaker is keeping these feelings hidden—as exposing them to the outside world might cause them to be extinguished.*

 For additional practice using the reading skill or strategy, see Unit 5 Teaching Resources Book, p. 65.

 For an audio recording of this selection, use Listening Library Audio CD-ROM.

Dusk Outside the Town, 1885. Isaak Ilich Levitan. Oil on canvas, 49.5 x 61.5 cm.

Summer Rain

Amy Lowell

      1

All night our room was outer-walled with rain.
Drops fell and flattened on the tin roof,
And rang like little disks of metal.
Ping!—Ping!—and there was not a pinpoint of silence between them.
5   The rain rattled and clashed,
And the slats of the shutters danced and glittered.
But to me the darkness was red-gold and crocus-coloured
With your brightness,
And the words you whispered to me
10 Sprang up and flamed—orange torches against the rain.
Torches against the wall of cool, silver rain!

> **Interpret Imagery** *What does this image tell you about how the speaker views the other occupant of the room?*   2

684   UNIT 5   BEGINNINGS OF THE MODERN AGE

Writing Practice

SPIRAL REVIEW **Voice** Explain that a writer's "voice" is his or her distinctive use of language. To characterize a writer's voice, you would examine word choice, tone, sound devices, and even the vowel and consonant sounds of the words. Ask volunteers to locate examples of words and phrases that echo the speaker's emotions in each poem.

Have students freewrite for ten minutes on subjects that stir strong emotions in them. Then have them choose images and expressions they like best from their notes and draft poems that express their feelings.

684

Fireworks

Amy Lowell

Fighting Couple. Jami Jennings.

You hate me and I hate you,
And we are so polite, we two!

But whenever I see you, I burst apart
And scatter the sky with my blazing heart. **3**
5 It spits and sparkles in stars and balls,
Buds into roses—and flares, and falls.

Scarlet buttons, and pale green disks,
Silver spirals and asterisks,
Shoot and tremble in a mist
10 **Peppered** with mauve and amethyst.

I shine in the windows and light up the trees,
And all because I hate you, if you please.

And when you meet me, you rend asunder[1]
And go up in a flaming wonder
15 Of saffron[2] cubes, and **crimson** moons,
And wheels all amaranths[3] and maroons.

Golden lozenges and spades,
Arrows of malachites[4] and jades,
Patens[5] of copper, **azure** sheaves.
20 As you **mount**, you flash in the glossy leaves.

Such fireworks as we make, we two!
Because you hate me and I hate you.

---

1. *Rend asunder* means "to tear apart."
2. Here, *saffron* refers to an orange-yellow color.
3. Here, *amaranth* refers to a reddish purple color.
4. *Malachite* is a deep green stone.
5. *Patens* are small metal plates.

Interpret Imagery *What do you think the imagery in these lines means?* **4**

Structure *What structural elements can you identify in this poem?* **5**

Vocabulary

pepper (pe´ pər) *v.* to shower with small objects
crimson (krim´ zən) *adj.* a bright purplish red
azure (azh´ ər) *adj.* a light purplish blue
mount (mount) *v.* to ascend or to soar

AMY LOWELL **685**

Teach

Literary Element	**3**

Metaphor Have students discuss the effectiveness of Lowell's use of metaphor to create an image of the intense feelings that exist between the speaker and the person being addressed. *(The metaphor of exploding fireworks creates a clear and precise image of the feelings described in the poem.)*

(APPROACHING) **Ask:** What are the similarities between the relationship and the fireworks? *(Both are fiery, passionate, dangerous, and beautiful.)* **Ask:** What emotions does this metaphor evoke in readers? *(Possible answer: Readers may feel that the couple does not appreciate the passion that exists between them.)*

Reading Strategy	**4**

Interpret Imagery Answer: *The imagery suggests strong emotion that is also somewhat ambiguous. The expressions "burst apart" and "blazing heart" are ambivalent in that they might suggest love cloaked in hatred.*

Literary Element	**5**

Structure Answer: *Lowell uses contrasting images and feelings (love/hate, spits/sparkles), stanzas to separate images, and consistent rhyme and rhythm patterns.*

Progress Check

Can students analyze structure?

If No → See Unit 5 Teaching Resources Book, p. 64.

Approaching Level

UNIVERSAL ACCESS

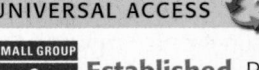

Established Point out that the speaker makes a comparison between the way the two characters behave toward each other and the way the two characters really feel about each other in lines 1 through 4. Suggest that students draw two boxes, one for each character. Outside the boxes, tell students to write words and images that might illustrate this "polite" external behavior. Inside the boxes, have students use the words and images in the poem to illustrate what the two characters are feeling internally during these polite exchanges. Finally, have students present and explain their diagrams to partners.

After You Read

Assess

1. Answers will vary.
2. (a) As ringing like "little disks of metal," making a "Ping!—Ping!" sound, and rattling and crashing (b) The speaker may not enjoy the sound.
3. (a) As "red-gold and crocus-colored" (b) The speaker loves the person.
4. (a) As polite (b) The fireworks may not symbolize anger.
5. (a) "Shine in the windows and light up the trees" (b) This image suggests that hate makes the speaker beautiful.
6. (a) The rhyming in "Fireworks" is regular. (b) Many students will prefer the regular rhymes.
7. (a) The quatrains are devoted to description and metaphor; the couplets to the speaker's feelings. (b) It effectively adds to the poem's complexity.
8. Modernism is seen in the bold imagery and use of free verse in "Summer Rain." The regular rhyme and stanza patterns in "Fireworks" is traditional poetry.
9. Students might say stories with an action-filled plot or graphic novels have similarities to video.

Literary Element

Students should discuss the structure of these poems.

Reading Strategy

The tone of "Summer Rain" is loving and passionate (slats dancing, red-gold and crocus-colored darkness, words springing up as torches). The tone of "Fireworks" is both humorous and angry (heart bursting into roses and flares, hated person being torn apart, speaker lighting up trees and windows).

After You Read

Respond and Think Critically

Respond and Interpret

1. In your opinion, which poem expresses the speaker's emotion most effectively? Explain.
2. (a) In "Summer Rain," in what ways does the speaker describe the sound of the rain? (b) What do these descriptions suggest about the speaker's feelings for the rain?
3. (a) How does the speaker see "the darkness"? (b) What does this suggest about the speaker's feelings for the person addressed?
4. (a) In the first couplet of "Fireworks," besides hate, how does the speaker characterize the relationship described in the poem? (b) What does this description suggest about the poem's "fireworks"?
5. (a) What does the speaker claim to do in the window and to the trees? (b) In your opinion, how does this image affect the following line?

Analyze and Evaluate

6. (a) How does the rhyme scheme in "Fireworks" differ from that in "Summer Rain"? (b) Which poem's rhyme scheme do you prefer? Explain.
7. (a) In what way does the content of the couplets in "Fireworks" differ from that in the quatrains? (b) Is the variation in stanza length effective?

Connect

8. **Big Idea** New Poetics In your opinion, how are the ideals of Modernism reflected in these poems? How are the more classical ideas and techniques reflected?
9. **Connect to Today** In Lowell's day, photography was the visual sister of literature's Imagism; both offered their audiences a vivid picture of a moment frozen in time. Can you imagine a literary parallel to the contemporary visual art of video? What would it look like?

Literary Element Structure

In each of these poems, Lowell uses poetic structure—the organization of images, ideas, words, and lines—to contribute to the poem's meaning.

Partner Activity Jot down notes on the structure of each poem. Then meet with a classmate to discuss how Lowell's use of structure affects meaning in the two poems.

Reading Strategy Interpret Imagery

The **imagery** in a poem can contribute to its tone. Refer to the imagery chart you created on page 683. How would you describe the tone in each of these poems? Support your opinion with examples.

Vocabulary Practice

Context Clues Identify context clues to the meaning of each boldfaced vocabulary word.

1. After the party, my sweater was **peppered** with the confetti that had been released.
2. I knew he was guilty, because when I asked him about it, he blushed a bright **crimson**.
3. Meredith's eyes are such a beautiful shade of **azure** that her family calls her "Bluebell."
4. At dawn the sun begins to **mount** the sky.

 Writing

Write a Dialogue In "Fireworks," Lowell uses vivid imagery to describe the intensity of her feelings toward another person. Imagine that Lowell and this person meet. Write a dialogue detailing what they might say to each other. Use your imagery interpretation chart from page 683 to help you get started.

Vocabulary

1. The context of the sentence shows that the sweater was sprinkled randomly with small pieces of paper.
2. Crimson is a bright shade of red, the color of a blush.
3. A synonym for *azure,* "blue," is included in the sentence. The description "beautiful shade" provides further context.

4. At dawn, the sun rises, so *mount* must mean "to ascend."

Writing

Students' dialogues should describe Lowell's relationship with the person in the poem and use imagery and sensory details to illustrate their feelings.

Comparing Literature

Across Time and Place

Compare Literature About the Experience of Poetry

How does one distinguish between what is ordinary and what is poetic? The four writers compared here—Archibald MacLeish, Rainer Maria Rilke, Mark Strand, and Ishmael Reed—explore their enthusiasms for both reading and writing poetry in the following selections.

Ars Poetica by Archibald MacLeish .... poem 690
UNITED STATES, 1920s

from *Letters to a Young Poet*
by Rainer Maria Rilke .... letter 692
CZECHOSLOVAKIA, 1929

Eating Poetry by Mark Strand .... poem 694
UNITED STATES, 1968

beware : do not read this poem
by Ishmael Reed... poem 696
UNITED STATES, 1972

COMPARE THE [Big Idea] New Poetics

During the twentieth century, poets in the United States and elsewhere sought to capture individual experience by bending the traditional rules and conventions of poetic form. As you read, ask yourself, What does each poet suggest about the experience of poetry?

COMPARE Imagist Poetry

Modernist poets let content dictate form. In the early 1900s, the Imagists employed clear, concrete language to convey precise images. As you read, ask yourself, What images in these selections reflect the Imagists' principles?

COMPARE Literary Trends

Like other aspects of culture, literature has trends. However, sometimes a literary trend is not identified until years after it has passed. Distinct styles become apparent when one compares literary movements, such as local-color writing and Modernism. As you read, ask yourself, What literary trends do these writers represent?

COMPARING LITERATURE **687**

Learning Objectives

For pages 687–698

In studying these texts, you will focus on the following objectives:

Literary Study:
Comparing cultural context.
Comparing historical context.
Comparing themes.

Comparing Literature

Across Time and Place

Focus

Bellringer Options

Selection Focus
 Transparency 43

Daily Language Practice
 Transparency 61

Or display images of things that might be considered ordinary (for example, a telephone) and things that might be considered exhilarating (for example, an athlete in a moment of victory). **Ask:** Would you classify each image as exhilarating or as ordinary? What characteristics affected your classification? Was your classification based on objective or subjective reactions to the images?

Compare Literature About the Experience of Poetry

Allow students to share their responses to the opening question. Then have students discuss what they know about images, ideas, and emotions in poetry.

Selection Skills

Literary Elements
- Theme (SE pp. 689–691)
- Simile (TE p. 690)

Comparing Literature

Writing Skills/Grammar
- Literary Trend (SE p. 698)
- Verbs as Adjectives (TE p. 688)
- Author's Purpose (TE p. 692)

Reading Skills
- Analyze Style (SE pp. 689, 691)
- Reread (TE p. 694)

Vocabulary Skills
- Analogies (SE p. 691)
- Word Roots (TE p. 689)

Study Skills/Research/Assessment
- Short Response (TE p. 696)

Comparing Literature

Before You Read

Focus

Cultural History ☆

The New Deal One of Franklin Delano Roosevelt's campaign promises in 1932 was to create a "new deal," a plan for getting the country out of the Depression. Once elected, he kept his promise by creating a variety of programs to give people work, promote social reform, and prevent future economic recessions. Archibald MacLeish was active in supporting and promoting Roosevelt's reforms.

Before You Read

Ars Poetica

Meet **Archibald MacLeish**
(1892–1982)

Archibald MacLeish was a poet with a purpose. He believed that, through love and awareness, U.S. citizens could achieve the goals of freedom and equality set down in the Declaration of Independence. MacLeish's idealism is evident both in his poetry and in his public life.

> *"But what, then, is the business of poetry? Precisely to make sense of the chaos of our lives."*
>
> —Archibald MacLeish

Creative Echoes Born in the late 1800s in Glencoe, Illinois, MacLeish was keenly aware of both the traditional world and the constantly evolving cultural landscape of the early twentieth century. After attending Yale University, where he played football, MacLeish entered Harvard Law School at the age of twenty-three. Being at Harvard further enlivened his interest in, as MacLeish put it, "the vision of mental time, of the interminable journey of the human mind, the great tradition of the intellectual past which knows the bearings of the future." Within two years, he married singer Ada Hitchcock and enlisted in the army. After World War I, he became a successful lawyer, but he soon quit his job to move with his wife and two small children to Paris. There he pursued his writing and published four poetry collections in five years. In 1928 he returned with his family to the U.S., where he continued writing poetry. In 1933 he won a Pulitzer Prize for *Conquistador*, an epic poem about the conquest of Mexico.

Public Interests Concerned about the nation's social problems, MacLeish also wrote journalistic articles and supported President Franklin D. Roosevelt's New Deal economic reforms and anti-Hitler stance. In the 1940s, MacLeish served as director of a wartime office of propaganda, as assistant secretary of state, and as a librarian of Congress. He was also chairman of the U.S. delegation for the founding conference of UNESCO (the United Nations Educational, Scientific, and Cultural Organization) in 1945. During this time, he continued to write poetry as well as drama. MacLeish, who was also on the editorial board of the business magazine *Fortune*, lamented the hardship and despair brought on by the Depression. ☆

In the 1950s, MacLeish won two more Pulitzer Prizes: one for poetry and one for drama. Between 1944 and 1954 he published more than eighty poems. MacLeish's later works continued to explore both the poet's inner world and the core meaning of U.S. citizenship. Critic Hayden Carruth said, "MacLeish wrote not as a personal crusader, never as a political crank or lonely visionary, but instead as the spokesman of the people."

 Literature Online

Author Search For more about Archibald MacLeish, go to glencoe.com and enter QuickPass code GLA9800u5.

Grammar Practice

SPIRAL REVIEW **Verbs as Adjectives** In "Ars Poetica," MacLeish uses several verb forms as adjectives: *entangled* trees, *leaning* grasses, *worn* stone. As students read the poem, point out these examples, and tell them that present and past participles of verbs can function as adjectives. Remind students that present participles end in -*ing,* and past participles of regular verbs end in -*d* or -*ed*, but the past participles of irregular verbs have different endings. In the following pairs of sentences, have students identify the participle as part of the verb or as an adjective.

1. **a.** An ambulance was *speeding* down the street. *(verb)*
   b. A *speeding* ambulance came around the corner. *(adjective)*

2. **a.** The *crackled* surface made an interesting pattern. *(adjective)*
   b. The ice cubes *crackled* in the glass. *(verb)*

Have students look for other examples of participles as adjectives as they read.

Literature and Reading Preview

Connect to the Poem

How do you judge a work of art, be it literary, musical, or visual? Make a list of criteria you think would be helpful in evaluating the quality of a composition.

Build Background

Ars poetica, a Latin phrase meaning "the art of poetry," is the title of a work written around 13 B.C. by the Roman poet Horace. In this text, Horace laid down his own rules for writing poetry.

Set Purposes for Reading

Big Idea New Poetics

As you read, ask yourself, How does MacLeish's unique pattern of lines and creative, startling imagery add to his purpose?

Literary Element Theme

A **theme** is a central idea presented in a literary work. In some works the theme is stated directly, but in most works the theme is implied and revealed gradually. A literary work may have more than one theme. As you read "Ars Poetica," ask yourself, What events, dialogue, and description help develop the poem's theme?

Reading Strategy Analyze Style

Writers' **style** includes the expressive qualities that distinguish their work, such as word choice, the length and arrangement of sentences, and the use of figurative language and imagery. As you read "Ars Poetica," analyze MacLeish's style. Consider why he chose to break the lines the way he did and how the imagery and word choice contribute to the overall effect of the poem.

Tip: Take Notes Record the effects of MacLeish's style in a chart like the one below.

Author's Style	Overall Effect
Irregular line length	Helps emphasize certain words

Vocabulary

palpable (pal´ pə bəl) *adj.* tangible; able to be touched or felt; p. 690 *The tension was palpable in the team's locker room before the big game.*

mute (mūt) *adj.* silent; p. 690 *James hit the mute button on the television and decided to focus on his homework.*

entangled (en tan´ gəld) *adj.* twisted together; caught; p. 690 *The fish was entangled in the fisherman's net.*

Tip: Analogies An analogy is a type of comparison that is based on the relationships between things or ideas. To solve an analogy question, identify the relationship in the first pair of words.

ARCHIBALD MACLEISH **689**

Before You Read

Focus

Summary

"Ars Poetica" specifies what a poem should be. MacLeish expresses his definition in the form of a poem, using a series of images to illustrate his conclusion that "A poem should not mean / But be."

 For summaries in languages other than English, see Unit 5 Teaching Resources Book, pp. 71–76.

Vocabulary

Word Roots Draw students' attention to *palpable*. Explain that it derives from the Latin verb *palpare*, meaning "to touch or stroke." Ask students to determine the meanings of these words from the same root:

- palpate ("to examine medically by touch")
- palpitation ("throbbing or trembling, usually of the heart")

Approaching Level

DIFFERENTIATED INSTRUCTION

SMALL GROUP **Emerging** Guide students through "Ars Poetica" with the following procedure: Point out that MacLeish uses a repetitive sentence structure to define a poem: "A poem should be . . . ." Form three groups of students and assign the following lines for analysis, one set per group: 1–6; 7–8; and 9–16. Ask each group to identify the adjectives and the sensory images. Have someone from each group paraphrase each line grouping for the class. Point out that at lines 18 and 23, MacLeish introduces the word *not*. Instead of telling readers what a poem should be, he explores what a poem should not be. Ask students to identify the two things that a poem should not be. Discuss how the images in lines 20 and 22 could convey grief and love, respectively. Finally, ask groups to write statements of theme in which they explain MacLeish's ideas about poetry, citing examples from the poem to support their statements.

689

Teach

Big Idea   1

New Poetics Ask: What does MacLeish rely on to get his message across? *(Possible answer: He relies on imagery.)* How does the final stanza summarize the poet's theme? *(Possible answer: It makes clear that a poem should show, not tell, its ideas.)*

Literary Element   2

Theme Answer: *He compares poetry with a flight of birds.*

[APPROACHING] Write lines 7–8 on the board. Circle the two items the poet compares: a poem and the flight of birds. Underline the common descriptor, *wordless*. **Ask:** How is a flight of birds wordless? *(The flight of birds is a visual image or a physical action. It exists outside of language.)* **Ask:** If a poem is composed of words, how can it be word- less? *(If the imagery is powerful, readers will feel or experience the image and the words will become unnecessary.)*

Ars Poetica

Archibald MacLeish

A poem should be **palpable** and **mute**
As a globed fruit

Dumb[1]
As old medallions to the thumb

5 Silent as the sleeve-worn stone
Of casement[2] ledges where the moss has grown—

A poem should be wordless
As the flight of birds

A poem should be motionless in time
10 As the moon climbs

Leaving, as the moon releases
Twig by twig the night-**entangled** trees,

Leaving, as the moon behind the winter leaves,
Memory by memory the mind—

15 A poem should be motionless in time
As the moon climbs

A poem should be equal to:
Not true

For all the history of grief
20 An empty doorway and a maple leaf

For love
The leaning grasses and two lights above the sea—

A poem should not mean
But be

1

1. *Dumb:* here, unable to speak.

2. *casement:* a window that opens on hinges.

Theme *How does MacLeish develop the idea that a poem can be "wordless"?*   **2**

Vocabulary

palpable (pal´ pə bəl) *adj.* tangible; able to be touched or felt
mute (mūt) *adj.* silent
entangled (en tan´ gəld) *adj.* twisted together; caught

690 UNIT 5   BEGINNINGS OF THE MODERN AGE

Reading Practice

SPIRAL REVIEW   **Simile** MacLeish uses similes to describe what a poem should be. Remind students that a simile is a comparison using the word *like* or *as*. One element of the comparison is usually familiar to the reader. The comparison to something familiar provides insight into the less familiar thing or idea.

Have students find the similes used in the poem. Then have them describe the images and feelings that are evoked by each simile.

After You Read

Respond and Think Critically

Respond and Interpret

1. Which image in the poem could you see, feel, or hear most vividly in your imagination? Why?

2. (a)What five adjectives in lines 1–8 describe what a poem should be? (b)What is ironic about the use of these words to describe a poem?

3. (a)To what does the speaker compare poetry in lines 9–16? (b)What does this image suggest about the function of poetry?

4. (a)How does the speaker suggest that grief and love should be represented in poetry? (b)What can you infer from this suggestion about the way poems should express emotions?

Analyze and Evaluate

5. In your opinion, how effective are the images in this poem in appealing to the senses? Explain.

6. How does the repetition in lines 9–10 and lines 15–16 contribute to the poem?

7. In your opinion, do lines 20 and 22 adequately capture the emotions of grief and love? Why or why not?

8. A simile is a figure of speech in which things are compared through the use of words such as *like* or *as*. How do the similes in "Ars Poetica" contribute to the effectiveness of the poem?

Connect

9. **Big Idea** **New Poetics** MacLeish was a believer in both tradition and innovation. What traits of Modernism do you see in "Ars Poetica"?

10. **Connect to the Author** MacLeish published "Ars Poetica" in 1926—early in his writing career. Do you think the themes expressed would have been different if MacLeish had written the poem near the end of his career? Explain.

Literary Element Theme

The **themes** of a literary work are different from its topics. In "Ars Poetica," the topic is poetry, but the theme is a statement about poetry. How would you summarize this theme? Support your answer.

Reading Strategy Analyze Style

Style is made up of the expressive qualities that distinguish an author's work.

Group Activity With a group of classmates, discuss the elements of style in MacLeish's poem. Refer to the chart you made on page 689.

 Literature Online

Selection Resources For Selection Quizzes, eFlash-cards, and Reading-Writing Connection activities, go to glencoe.com and enter QuickPass code GLA9800u5.

Vocabulary Practice

Analogies Choose the word that best completes each analogy. To complete an analogy, decide on the relationship represented by the first pair of words. Then, apply that relationship to the second set of words.

1. palpable : real :: durable :
   a. lasting   c. stiff
   b. weak   d. boring

2. mute : noisy :: slowly :
   a. sluggishly   c. patiently
   b. quickly   d. irreverently

3. entangled : freed :: slumbering :
   a. awake   c. dormant
   b. asleep   d. enticed

ARCHIBALD MACLEISH   **691**

Comparing Literature

After You Read

Assess

1. "flight of birds"; "leaning grasses"

2. (a) *Palpable, mute, dumb, silent,* and *wordless* (b) They suggest that a poem should be silent, even though poetry is intended to be heard.

3. (a) The moon (b) Poetry should be unobtrusive while slowly illuminating its subject.

4. (a) They should be represented by images. (b) Emotions are best expressed through images.

5. Students may rate them highly for their evocative power.

6. It reinforces the concept of imperceptible motion and unifies the middle section of the poem.

7. Yes, the empty doorway and the lone leaf convey grief, and the two lights convey love; no, these images do not convey these powerful emotions.

8. They clarify the statements—for example, "as old medallions to the thumb" clarifies "dumb."

9. A desire to express private thoughts in a new way, irregular line length and meter, and a focus on imagery

10. Students might say that MacLeish would have a more defined sense of what a poem is and his tone may have changed later in his career.

Progress Check

Can students analyze theme?

If No → See Unit 5 Teaching Resources Book, p. 77.

Literary Element

Poetry takes on the form of its subject; a poem is an artifact, not a narrative. MacLeish directly states "A poem should not mean / But be" and also expresses the theme through imagery.

Reading Strategy

Students should cite evidence from the poem in their discussions.

Vocabulary

1. a 2. b 3. a

Comparing Literature

Before You Read

Focus

Summary

When Kappus asks whether he should write poetry, Rilke advises him to become introspective and to look toward nature and his everyday life, emotions, and thoughts for subject matter. Rilke tells him that in the poetry that arises he will find his answer. Rilke discourages Kappus from allowing outside opinions to influence him.

Literary History ☆

Franz Xaver Kappus At the time his correspondence with Rilke began, Kappus was a nineteen-year-old student at a military academy. An admirer of Rilke's poetry, he decided to send his attempts at poetry to Rilke after a professor told him that Rilke was a former student. Kappus thought that Rilke would respond to a young aspiring poet, and he did.

For an audio recording of this selection, use Listening Library Audio CD-ROM.

Readability Scores
Dale-Chall: 8.3
DRP: 59
Lexile: 860

Build Background

Rainer Maria Rilke was born in 1875 in Prague, which was then part of Austria-Hungary and is now the capital of the Czech Republic. In 1902 Rilke went to Paris to write a book about Auguste Rodin, the great French sculptor. Rodin quickly became Rilke's friend and mentor, sharing with the young poet a creative methodology based on an ethic of hard work and dedication to minute detail.

The following selection is from a collection of letters Rilke wrote to Franz Xaver Kappus, an aspiring poet, during a five-year period that started in 1903, when Rilke was in Paris.

from Letters to a Young Poet

Rainer Maria Rilke

The Heart Called Rancho Pastel, Jim Dine. Private collection. ★

You ask whether your poems are good. You send them to publishers; you compare them with other poems; you are disturbed when certain publishers reject your attempts. Well now, since you have given me permission to advise you, I suggest that you give all that up. You are looking outward and, above all else, that you must not do now. No one can advise and help you, no one.

There is only one way: Go within. Search for the cause, find the impetus[1] that bids you write. Put it to this test: Does it stretch out its roots in the deepest place of your heart?

Can you avow[2] that you would die if you were forbidden to write? Above all, in the most silent hour of your night, ask yourself this: *Must* I write? Dig deep into yourself for a true answer. And if it should ring its assent, if you can confidently meet this serious question with a simple, "I must," then build your life upon it. It has become your necessity. Your life, in even the most mundane and least significant hour, must become a sign, a testimony to this urge.

Then draw near to nature. Pretend you are the very first man and then write what you see

---

1. An *impetus* is a something that encourages or stimulates activity.

2. To *avow* is to declare openly.

Writing Practice

Author's Purpose Point out that looking at an author's subject matter, word choice, and sentence structure can help readers identify the author's purpose.
Ask: What was Rilke's purpose in writing this letter? *(Possible answers: to persuade Kappus to have confidence in his own abilities; to warn him about the dangers of being influenced by others; to express his ideas about the creative process)*

Have students write a statement of Rilke's purpose in this letter and cite specific passages that helped them determine his purpose. Guide them to locate evidence of tone, sentence structure, and choice of words.

and experience, what you love and lose. Do not write love poems, at least at first; they present the greatest challenge. It requires great, fully ripened power to produce something personal, something unique, when there are so many good and sometimes even brilliant renditions[3] in great numbers. Beware of general themes. Cling to those that your everyday life offers you. Write about your sorrows, your wishes, your passing thoughts, your belief in anything beautiful. Describe all that with fervent,[4] quiet, and humble sincerity. In order to express yourself, use things in your surroundings, the scenes of your dreams, and the subjects of your memory.

If your everyday life appears to be unworthy subject matter, do not complain to life. Complain to yourself. Lament that you are not poet enough to call up its wealth. For the creative artist there is no poverty—nothing is insignificant or unimportant. Even if you were in a prison whose walls would shut out from your senses the sounds of the outer world, would you not then still have your childhood, this precious wealth, this treasure house of memories? Direct your attention to that. Attempt to resurrect these sunken sensations of a distant past. You will gain assuredness. Your aloneness will expand and will become your home, greeting you like the quiet dawn. Outer tumult will pass it by from afar.

If, as a result of this turning inward, of this sinking into your own world, *poetry* should emerge, you will not think to ask someone whether it is good poetry. And you will not try to interest publishers of magazines in these works. For you will hear in them your own voice; you will see in them a piece of your life, a natural possession of yours. A piece of art is good if it is born of necessity. This, its source, is its criterion; there is no other.

1 Therefore, my dear friend, I know of no other advice than this: Go within and scale the depths of your being from which your

very life springs forth. At its source you will find the answer to the question, whether you *must* write. Accept it, however it sounds to you, without analyzing. Perhaps it will become apparent to you that you are indeed called to be a writer. Then accept that fate; bear its burden, and its grandeur, without asking for the reward, which might possibly come from without. For the creative artist must be a world of his own and must find everything within himself and in nature, to which he has betrothed[5] himself. **1**

It is possible that, even after your descent into your inner self and into your secret place of solitude, you might find that you must give up becoming a poet. As I have said, to feel that one could live without writing is enough indication that, in fact, one should not. Even then this process of turning inward, upon which I beg you to embark, will not have been in vain. Your life will no doubt from then on find its own paths. That they will be good ones and rich and expansive—that I wish for you more than I can say.

What else shall I tell you? It seems to me everything has been said, with just the right emphasis. I wanted only to advise you to progress quietly and seriously in your evolvement.[6] You could greatly interfere with that process if you look outward and expect to obtain answers from the outside—answers which only your innermost feeling in your quietest hour can perhaps give you. **2**

---

5. *Betrothed* means "engaged."
6. *Evolvement* is growth.

 Discussion Starter

In this letter, Rilke insists that the individual finds the most powerful means of expression by looking inward. He also says that a writer *must* write in order to express himself or herself, just as one must breathe in order to live. In what ways does Rilke's advice to the young poet apply to other aspirations people have in life?

RAINER MARIA RILKE **693**

---

3. *Renditions* are versions.
4. *Fervent* means "with intense feeling."

Reading Strategy **1**

Analyze Style **Ask:** What does Rilke's writing style reveal about his personality? *(Students may say Rilke is passionate about writing and is a supportive mentor.)*

ENGLISH LEARNERS Help students identify characteristics of Rilke's style: a serious tone, parallel sentence structure, rhetorical questions, formal language, and so on.

📁 **For additional practice using the reading skill or strategy, see Unit 5 Teaching Resources Book, p. 78.**

Literary Element **2**

Theme Explain that the central message of a work of literature is its theme. **Ask:** What is the theme of this letter? *(Possible answer: An individual must look within his or her heart to find the best, most honest, and most personal way to express his or her thoughts and desires.)*

View the Art ★

The heart shape is a recurring image in the art of Jim Dine (1935–). **Ask:** How does the artwork relate to Rilke's letter? *(It reflects the idea of going within to "the deepest place of [the] heart" to find the truth.)*

Comparing Literature

Before You Read

Focus

Summary

The setting of this poem is a library; the characters are a man, a librarian, and dogs. The man is happy because he has eaten (filled himself with) poetry; the librarian is at first bewildered, and then frightened, by the man's behavior.

Writer's Technique ☆

Ambiguity Ambiguity is a way of using language which is open to more than one interpretation. Poets like Mark Strand intentionally use ambiguity to express complex ideas and multiple levels of meaning. Readers should be aware that there is not one clear "right" explanation of a line or passage; various interpretations that can be supported by the text are acceptable.

Build Background

Mark Strand developed as a writer during the 1960s—a period when, he later noted, "Poets were underground pop stars."

Influenced by the work of Archibald MacLeish, Strand's poetry is noted for its surreal imagery and exploration of the power of presence and absence in life. Critic Jane Candia Coleman commented that although Strand's poetry can be abstract and difficult, "the reader who delves, who meets the poet halfway, will be rewarded by glimpses of a different world, that changeable one of dreams and the elusive beauty that haunts us all." ☆

House on Fire with People Inside. John Ritter.

Eating Poetry

Mark Strand

Reading Practice

Reread Tell students that rereading "Eating Poetry" will help them better understand the poem's imagery. Have students analyze the characters in the poem and consider whom or what each represents. Work with them to prepare a list of questions that will help focus their thinking.

Say: Here is one question: Are the dogs distinct characters in the poem, or are they a manifestation of some part of the man's mind? *(Students' answers will vary. Have them support their ideas with evidence from the poem.)*

Small Ferocious Dog.
John Ritter.

1 Ink runs from the corners of my mouth.
There is no happiness like mine.
I have been eating poetry.

The librarian does not believe what she sees.
5 Her eyes are sad
and she walks with her hands in her dress.

The poems are gone.
The light is dim.
The dogs are on the basement stairs and coming up.

10 Their eyeballs roll,
their blond legs burn like brush.
The poor librarian begins to stamp her feet and weep.

She does not understand.
When I get on my knees and lick her hand,
15 she screams.

I am a new man.
I snarl at her and bark.
I romp with joy in the bookish dark.   **2**

Quickwrite

Strand has said, "A poem may be the residue of an inner urgency, one through which the self wishes to register itself, write itself into being, and, finally, to charm another self, the reader, into belief." Strand's description of the speaker in "Eating Poetry" is purposefully ambiguous. Write a paragraph in which you interpret the character of the speaker. Cite evidence from the text to support your view.

MARK STRAND   **695**

Approaching Level

DIFFERENTIATED INSTRUCTION

SMALL GROUP

Emerging Have student pairs work together to list on a T-chart what is happening inside the speaker's head and what is happening in the external setting of the library. If students wish, they can make an open-mind diagram to illustrate what is happening in the speaker's head. For example, they might draw words running from the corners of the speaker's mouth. Have each pair present its findings to the class. Then discuss the emotions that the poem evokes. **Ask:** Do you envy the speaker, or do you fear him? Why?

Teach

Big Idea   1

New Poetics Have students consider the quotation from Jane Candia Coleman in the Before You Read text. **Ask:** What different world do you glimpse in "Eating Poetry"? *(Possible answer: The poem takes you inside the author's head, into a dream he is having.)*

Literary Element   2

Figurative Language Explain that in "Eating Poetry" Strand uses figurative language to convey his ideas and emotions. **Ask:** What devices of figurative language does Strand use in the poem? *(Possible answers: metaphor; personification)* Have students support their answers with examples from the text.

[APPROACHING] Read the first stanza aloud for students.
Ask: What is the poet comparing? *(The poet compares reading with eating.)* Point out that a metaphor forces readers to think about familiar topics such as reading in new ways. **Ask:** How is reading like eating? *(Possible response: Both activities are forms of nourishment.)*

Quickwrite

Students may say that the speaker is in fact a dog or that the speaker is a reader who is "a new man" after having an intense experience in reading poetry. They should support their views with evidence from the poem and address counterarguments.

Comparing Literature

Before You Read

Focus

Summary

The speaker compares what happens to the tenants of a house in a 1960s television show to what happens to the reader of this poem. He ends the poem with statistical information about missing persons in 1968.

Writer's Technique ☆

Poetic License Poets feel free to use language in unconventional ways. They may invent words or break rules of grammar, spelling, or punctuation. John Dryden, an English poet, playwright and critic, claimed that this practice was to liberate poetry from the strictness and severity of prose. Ask students to point out examples of Ishmael Reed's poetic license.

Build Background

Ishmael Reed has described his eclectic writing style as "Neoamerican hoodooism," an expression that implies a melding of the magic healing in African folk culture and many other U.S. cultural elements. Reed's style blends European and African traditions and showcases his broad-ranging cultural and historical knowledge.

In his poems, Reed's innovative approach is obvious. He purposely omits vowels, uses ampersands instead of the word *and,* and inserts punctuation at unexpected places. One effect of his techniques is to quicken and vary the pace of his poetry.

beware: do not read this poem

Ishmael Reed

Hallway, 1995. Mary Iverson.

```
     tonite ,          thriller¹ was
     abt an ol woman          ,so vain she
     surrounded herself w/
               many mirrors

  5  it got so bad that finally she
     locked herself indoors & her
     whole life became the
               mirrors

     one day the villagers broke
  10 into her house ,          but she was too
     swift for them .          she disappeared
               into a mirror

     each tenant who bought the house
     after that          ,          lost a loved one to
```

1. *Thriller* was a television show hosted by horror-film actor Boris Karloff that ran from 1960 to 1962. The hour-long episodes were divided between mystery and horror genres.

696   UNIT 5   BEGINNINGS OF THE MODERN AGE

Assessment Practice

Short Response Remind students that answers to short response questions are evaluated on the basis of their insightfulness and the evidence drawn from the text to support them. **Ask:** Which of the three poems in this lesson challenged you to think in a new way? Explain your response with examples of imagery, language, and theme. *(Students may cite the surrealistic poetry of Strand, because the symbolic meanings of the poem's images had to be interpreted before the poem could be understood.)*

Teach

15   the ol woman in the mirror :
    first a little girl
    then a young woman
    then the young woman/s husband

    the hunger of this poem is legendary
20   it has taken in many victims
    back off from this poem
    it has drawn in yr feet
    back off from this poem
    it has drawn in yr legs

25   back off from this poem
    it is a greedy mirror
    you are into this poem .   from
        the waist down
    nobody can hear you can they ?
30   this poem has had you up to here
        belch
    this poem aint got no manners
    you cant call out frm this poem
    relax now & go w/ this poem
35   move & roll on to this poem
    do not resist this poem
    this poem has yr eyes
    this poem has his head
    this poem has his arms
40   this poem has his fingers
    this poem has his fingertips
    this poem is the reader & the
    reader this poem

    statistic :   the us bureau of missing persons reports
45   that in 1968 over 100,000 people disappeared
    leaving no solid clues
        nor trace   only
    a space   in the lives of their friends

2

Literary Element   1

Author's Purpose **Ask:** What might be Reed's reasons for using unconventional spacing, grammar, spelling, and punctuation? *(Possible answer: The poem is written as though the poet is conversing with the reader in everyday language. The odd spacing and punctuation control the reader's pace so that the poem is read at the author's intended pace.)*

Reading Strategy   2

Compare Have students compare the author's purpose, form, and imagery of "Eating Poetry" with that of "beware: do not read this poem." *(Students may say that both poems are written in free verse, both contain precise images, and both treat topics that are not highly intellectual.)*

Quickwrite

Students should connect the anecdote in the first four stanzas and the "statistic" in the final stanza to Reed's comments in the middle of the poem about the way a poem draws in the reader.

Quickwrite

The title of this selection naturally attracts the reader's interest. Despite the fact that the title warns the reader not to continue reading, the poem focuses on the relationship that exists in poetry between the reader and the writer. Write a paragraph in which you discuss how this selection develops the idea that "this poem is the reader & the / reader this poem."

ISHMAEL REED **697**

English Learners

DIFFERENTIATED INSTRUCTION

Intermediate English learners may find Reed's idiosyncratic use of language and punctuation difficult to comprehend. To facilitate comprehension, work with students to rewrite the poem with conventional grammar, spelling, and punctuation. For example: Tonight, *Thriller* was about an old woman who was so vain that she surrounded herself with many mirrors. When students have completed rewriting the poem, have them compare the two versions, reading each aloud. Then lead them to discuss the effects of Reed's stylistic choices, focusing particularly on the sounds and rhythms of the language.

Assess

Compare the Big Idea

Group Activity

1. Each student should discuss what he or she believes poetry is, should be, or can be, relating the idea to one of the four selections in this section.

2. Students may respond that "Ars Poetica" and "Eating Poetry" both lack consistent patterns of meter and rhyme and that "beware: do not read this poem," in addition to lacking those characteristics, has unconventional punctuation, spelling, and capitalization.

3. MacLeish provides similes to clarify and expand upon his statements about what poetry should be; Rilke provides a way of determining whether one should pursue writing poetry; Strand describes the exhilaration of reading a poem; Reed describes a symbolic transaction between the reader and poetry.

Compare Imagist Poetry

Visual Display

Students' displays should relate to specific images found in the four selections.

Compare Literary Trends

 Writing

Use these criteria when evaluating students' writing:

- Does the essay connect trends in literature and culture to the styles and themes of the selections?

- *Ars Poetica* by Archibald MacLeish

- from *Letters to a Young Poet* by Rainer Maria Rilke

- *Eating Poetry* by Mark Strand

- *beware : do not read this poem* by Ishmael Reed

COMPARE THE Big Idea New Poetics

Group Activity Each of the writers compared here explains what he believes poetry should be. Review the four selections and then discuss the following questions with a group of classmates.

1. Which writer's statement about what poetry should be appeals to you most? Explain why.

2. In what ways does each selection break the traditional rules of poetry?

3. How does each writer demonstrate what the experience of poetry should be for both reader and writer, and how does each provide criteria for evaluating poetry?

COMPARE Imagist Poetry

Visual Display What images struck you most as you read the poems by MacLeish, Strand, and Reed, and the letter by Rilke? Create a visual display that represents the imagery you pictured in your mind as you read these selections.

COMPARE Literary Trends

Writing Research the literary trends associated with MacLeish, Rilke, Strand, and Reed. Write a short essay in which you discuss how each writer is a part of a literary trend.

Small Ferocious Dog. John Ritter.

- In describing the connection of the writers to literary trends, does the essay analyze specific features of the four selections?
- Does the essay show a thorough understanding of the themes and imagery in the selections?

Before You Read

Study of Two Pears and from The Man with the Blue Guitar

Meet Wallace Stevens
(1879–1955)

For a poet with such a powerful imagination, Wallace Stevens led an outwardly quiet and uneventful life. His entire professional career was spent as an employee of an insurance company. In his journals he expressed embarrassment about writing poems: "Keep all this a great secret. There is something absurd about all this writing of verses; but the truth is, it elates and satisfies me to do it."

> "How full of trifles everything is! It is only one's thoughts that fill a room with something more than furniture."
>
> —Wallace Stevens

Youth Stevens was born in Reading, Pennsylvania. His father was a country lawyer, and his mother was a teacher. Stevens enrolled at Harvard College in 1897, where he became friends with the philosopher George Santayana, who encouraged Stevens to publish his early poems in the *Harvard Advocate*. Stevens left school abruptly after only three years, failing to complete his degree. He moved to New York City and worked briefly as a reporter for the *Herald Tribune*. Then, after enrolling at the New York Law School, he acquired his degree and was admitted to the bar in 1904. Stevens worked for various law firms before moving to Connecticut where he worked for the Hartford Accident and Indemnity Company until his death.

In 1914 *Poetry* magazine published four of Stevens's poems. They were eventually included in his first book, *Harmonium* (1923). It was well received by critics but sold only one hundred copies. However, *Harmonium* contains some of Stevens's most recog-

nizable and important work. It shows the influence of the French Symbolists and the English Romantics, particularly Wordsworth and Coleridge. In this book, Stevens illustrates his belief that "the imagination is man's power over nature."

Maturity and Acceptance During the 1930s, Stevens published three more books, *Ideas and Order, Owl's Clover,* and *The Man with the Blue Guitar,* which reveal the progressive development of his poetic style. By the 1940s, Stevens had entered the most creatively fertile time in his life. He gradually abandoned the intricate forms and lavish imagery of his early work in favor of a more concise, abstract style. In 1954 Stevens's *Collected Poems* appeared. With this publication, shortly before his death, Stevens attracted widespread attention for the first time. The *Collected Poems* was awarded the Pulitzer Prize for Poetry in 1955.

Poet of the Imagination Central to all of Stevens's poetry is the primacy of the creative imagination. According to Stevens, the role of the poet is to use the imagination to "become the light in the minds of others" by helping people to discover new ways of viewing reality and to experience a sense of order in a chaotic world devoid of a clear spiritual definition. His best work explored the complex relationship between the shaping power of the imagination and the physical world.

LOG ON ▶ **Literature** Online

Author Search For more about Wallace Stevens, go to glencoe.com and enter QuickPass code GLA9800u5.

Before You Read

Focus

Bellringer Options

Daily Language Practice Transparency 62

Or display a common object, such as a cup or a flower, along with a painting and a photograph of a similar object. **Ask:** How does each of these three items represent "reality"? Which of the three is most "real"?

Tell students that the poet Wallace Stevens explores the nature of reality in many of his poems.

Selection Skills

Literary Elements
- Tone (SE pp. 700, 702, 703)

Study of Two Pears *and from* The Man with the Blue Guitar

Listening/Speaking/ Viewing Skills
- Analyze Art (SE p. 702; TE p. 701)

Reading Skills
- Recognize Author's Purpose (SE pp. 700, 701, 703)
- Interpret (TE p. 702)

Vocabulary Skills
- Word Origins (SE pp. 700. 703)
- Synonyms (TE p. 700)

Writing Skill/Grammar
- Journal Entry (SE p. 703)

Before You Read

Focus

Summary

In "Study of Two Pears," Wallace Stevens uses sensory details to describe a painting of pears. "The Man with the Blue Guitar" describes a man bent over a guitar who does not play "things exactly as they are." Both poems examine the nature of reality.

 For summaries in languages other than English, see Unit 5 Teaching Resources Book, pp. 82–87.

Vocabulary

Synonyms and Word Choice Ask students which words on the vocabulary list belong with the following groups of synonyms:

- protrude, stick out *(bulge)*
- sparkle, glint *(glisten)*
- narrow, shrink *(taper)*

Ask students to comment on the connotations of the words in each group. Then explain that poets look for precisely the right word to convey a specific idea or image.

Literature and Reading Preview

Connect to the Poems

When you view a physical object, how can you distinguish its appearance from its reality? Freewrite for ten minutes to explore this question.

Build Background

"The Man with the Blue Guitar" is the first stanza of a longer poem that appeared in 1937. It is tempting to connect the title of this poem to Pablo Picasso's famous painting *The Old Guitarist,* but Stevens claimed to have no particular painting in mind. However, he was deeply affected by the artistic experiments of Cubist painters like Picasso who subverted traditional perspective. Stevens's poetry, like Cubist painting, often mixes multiple points of view to create fresh perspectives on observed objects.

Set Purposes for Reading

Big Idea New Poetics

As you read, ask yourself, How do Stevens's poems encourage the reader to explore the way in which imagination can transform and deepen our perceptions of everyday experience?

Literary Element Tone

Tone is the author's attitude toward subject matter or audience. Writers convey tone through word choice, punctuation, sentence structure, and figures of speech. As you read, ask, How does Stevens convey tone in these poems?

Reading Strategy Recognize Author's Purpose

An **author's purpose** is the author's intent in writing a piece of literature. Authors typically write to persuade, to inform, to explain, to explore, to entertain, or to describe.

Tip: Double-Entry Journal Use a journal like the one started below to ask and answer questions about Stevens's purpose.

Questions to Ask	Answers
What is the tone?	
What kinds of details are there?	
What are some descriptive words?	

Learning Objectives

For pages 699–703

In studying these texts, you will focus on the following objectives:

Literary Study: Analyzing tone.

Reading: Recognizing author's purpose.

Writing: Writing a journal entry.

Vocabulary

bulge (bulj) *v.* to swell or curve outward; p. 701 *The shoplifter's shirt was bulging with the goods he had taken.*

taper (tā´ pər) *v.* to become progressively thinner or smaller; p. 701 *The river slowly tapered out as it entered the dry gorge.*

glisten (glis´ ən) *v.* to shine or to reflect light; p. 701 *All morning the dew was glistening on the grass.*

Tip: Word Origins Word origins, also called **etymologies,** are the history and development of words. They are often found in dictionary entries.

Vocabulary Practice

Word Origins Write the first line of "Study of Two Pears" on the board: *Opusculum paedagogum.* Point out the Latin meanings and roots of these words: *Opusculum,* meaning "small work," has the root *opus* (plural *opera*). *Paedagogum* is an adjective form referring to instruction or teaching.

Tell students that a number of English words have come from these two Latin words. Have students explain the meanings of the following terms and connect the meanings to their origins.

1. pedagogy
2. pedagogue
3. pedant
4. pedantic
5. operate
6. opera
7. *magnum opus*

700

Study of Two Pears

Wallace Stevens

Two Pears from the Jardinage, 2003. Simon Fletcher. Watercolor on paper. Private collection.

I

Opusculum paedagogum.[1]
The pears are not viols,[2]
Nudes or bottles.
They resemble nothing else.

II

They are yellow forms
Composed of curves
Bulging toward the base.
They are touched red.

III

They are not flat surfaces
Having curved outlines.
They are round
Tapering toward the top.

IV

In the way they are modelled
There are bits of blue.
A hard dry leaf hangs
From the stem.

V

The yellow glistens.
It **glistens** with various yellows,
Citrons,[3] oranges and greens
Flowering over the skin.

VI

The shadows of the pears
Are blobs on the green cloth.
The pears are not seen
As the observer wills.

1 **New Poetics** *What is the speaker saying in this stanza about the difference between art and physical reality?*

2 **Recognize Author's Purpose** *What do these lines suggest about Stevens's purpose for composing this poem?*

Vocabulary

bulge (bulj) *v.* to swell or curve outward
taper (tā´ pər) *v.* to become progressively thinner or smaller
glisten (glis´ ən) *v.* to shine or to reflect light

1. *Opusculum paedagogum* is Latin for "a small instructional text."
2. A *viol* is a bowed stringed instrument used chiefly in music of the sixteenth and seventeenth centuries.
3. *Citron* is a shade of yellowish green.

WALLACE STEVENS **701**

Approaching Level

DIFFERENTIATED INSTRUCTION

SMALL GROUP
Emerging Remind students to read Stevens's poems according to punctuation, not lines. Assist student pairs as they practice reading the poem aloud.

Advanced Learners

DIFFERENTIATED INSTRUCTION

Descriptive Writing Have students use Stevens's technique of contrasting what something is not with what something is to describe other still life scenes. Students may choose to write in prose or verse.

Teach

Literary Element 1

Tone Answer: *These lines state that the guitar player is not presenting things as they are. The poem's theme is that "things as they are" are inevitably changed by art.*

ENGLISH LEARNERS Discuss the meaning of the phrase "things as they are."

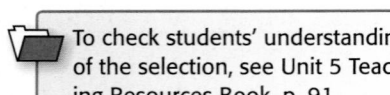

View the Art ★

Answer: *Students may say that the guitarist in the painting is bent over his guitar, like the one in the poem. They may contrast the moods of the painting and the poem.*

Pablo Picasso (1881–1973) was one of the most influential artists of the 20th century. Born in Spain, he moved to Paris, France, when he was 19. There, he experienced a period of melancholy (1901–1904), during which he used muted shades of blue in his work. He painted *The Old Guitarist* during this "blue period."

> To check students' understanding of the selection, see Unit 5 Teaching Resources Book, p. 91.

---

from The Man with the Blue Guitar

Wallace Stevens

I

The man bent over his guitar,
A shearsman[1] of sorts. The day was green.

They said, "You have a blue guitar,
You do not play things as they are."

The man replied, "Things as they are
Are changed upon the blue guitar."

And they said then, "But play, you must,
A tune beyond us, yet ourselves,

A tune upon the blue guitar
Of things exactly as they are."

The Old Guitarist, 1903–1904. Pablo Picasso ©ARS, NY. Oil on panel, 48¾ x 32½. The Art Institute of Chicago, IL.

View the Art During his Blue Period, Pablo Picasso painted melancholic themes, restricting his palette almost exclusively to shades of blue. How does the guitarist in this painting compare with your mental picture of the one described in the poem? ★

---

1. *Shearsman* refers to the posture of the guitarist, squatting like a tailor working on cloth.

1 **Tone** *What does the guitarist's response suggest about his attitude toward reality and perception?*

Reading Practice

SMALL GROUP

Interpret Explain to students that although this excerpt may seem simple, Stevens is attempting to explore an important philosophical issue.

Have students work in small groups to discuss the following questions:

- How is the poem about the nature of reality? *(Students may say that the poem shows that things are not always as they appear to be.)*

- How is the poem a philosophical statement? *(The poem implies that art can reveal a truth that transcends everyday notions of "things as they are.")*

Have a spokesperson from each group report the group's conclusions to the class.

After You Read

Respond and Think Critically

Respond and Interpret

1. Which of these poems do you prefer? Explain.

2. (a)In the final stanza of "Study of Two Pears," what does the speaker mean by saying that the pears are not seen as the observer wills? (b)How does this statement relate to the speaker's assertion in the first stanza?

3. (a)In "The Man with the Blue Guitar," what do the listeners accuse the guitarist of doing? How does the guitarist respond? (b)What does this exchange tell you about the guitar and the guitarist?

4. (a)What do the listeners tell the guitarist to do in the last two stanzas? (b)The guitarist does not reply. If he did reply, what do you think he would say?

Analyze and Evaluate

5. Why do you think Stevens chose to divide "Study of Two Pears" into multiple sections? How does this structure affect the poem's meaning?

6. How does Stevens use rhyme in "The Man with the Blue Guitar"? Why do you think that Stevens chose to employ this rhyme scheme?

7. In "The Man with the Blue Guitar," the listeners demand that the guitarist play "a tune beyond us, yet ourselves." What do they mean?

Connect

8. **Big Idea** **New Poetics** How do these two poems illustrate Modernism in poetry?

9. **Connect to the Author** Why do you think he was so drawn to stirring the imagination and exploring new ways of perceiving reality?

Literary Element Tone

Tone is the author's attitude toward his or her subject matter. A writer's tone might convey a variety of attitudes such as sympathy, objectivity, or humor.

1. How would you describe the tone in each of these poems? Refer to the poems for support..

2. Compare and contrast the tone in these poems.

Reading Strategy Recognize Author's Purpose

An **author's purpose** and the theme of a literary work are often interrelated. How would you summarize the theme in each of these poems? What can you infer about Stevens's purpose in writing?

LOG ON ▶ **Literature** Online

Selection Resources For Selection Quizzes, eFlashcards, and Reading-Writing Connection activities, go to glencoe.com and enter QuickPass code GLA9800u5.

Vocabulary Practice

Word Origins The etymology, or origin, of a word can help you better understand its meaning. For each vocabulary word below, use a dictionary to look up the etymology, then write a sentence explaining the connection between the word's definition and its origin.

bulge   taper   glisten

✍ Writing

Write a Journal Entry In "The Man with the Blue Guitar," Stevens suggests that music can have a meaning beyond literal lyrics and notes on a page. Think of a song that, for you, meets the listeners' demands of "A tune beyond us, yet ourselves." Write a journal entry about this song's significance to you.

WALLACE STEVENS **703**

After You Read

Assess

1. Answers will vary.

2. (a) The observer cannot change their essential nature. (b) The pears resemble nothing but themselves.

3. (a) Not playing things as they are. The guitarist claims that things "are changed upon the blue guitar." (b) Artists and art transform reality.

4. (a) To play a tune "beyond us," yet "of things exactly as they are" (b) That this is not the artist's role

5. Students may suggest that Stevens tried to "frame" each section like a still life. Each section provides a new perspective.

6. The rhymes reinforce the contrast between what "they" want and what the guitarist plays.

7. Listeners want an aesthetic experience, not divorced from reality.

8. Both poems present concrete images. Perspective, meaning, and the arts are Modernist concerns.

9. Students may say that he found a creative outlet in his poetry that he did not have in his career.

Progress Check

Can students analyze tone?

If No → See Unit 5 Teaching Resources Book, p. 88.

Literary Element

1. Students may describe the tone as challenging or provoking.

2. They are both challenging the way we see things.

Writing

Students' journal entries should relate a song to a personal experience.

Vocabulary

- *bulge* Etymology: Old French *bouge* means "leather bag"
- *taper* Etymology: Old English *tapur* refers to the wick of a candle
- *glisten* Etymology: Old English *glisian* means "to glitter"
- Students' sentences will vary.

Reading Strategy

The theme in "Study of Two Pears" is that perception does not change the essence of the thing perceived. Stevens wanted to show that essences are unchangeable. The theme in "The Man with the Blue Guitar" is that art can expose a truth that goes beyond our understanding of what is true. Stevens wanted to show that the imagination changes "things as they are."

703

Bellringer Options

Daily Language Practice Transparency 63

Or display several images of ordinary-looking people.
Ask: What qualities make a person unique?

Tell students that the poet E. E. Cummings believed that expressing one's uniqueness is the most difficult task. Encourage them to consider, as they read, how Cummings expresses his uniqueness—and disdain for conformity—in these two poems.

Before You Read

somewhere i have never travelled, gladly beyond and *anyone lived in a pretty how town*

Meet E. E. Cummings
(1894–1962)

Edward Estlin Cummings coined the term "mostpeople" to describe conformists. Throughout his life, Cummings rebelled against the authoritarian forces that tend to suppress uniqueness. Challenging the social norms of the day, he married three times and only briefly held a regular job. Friends and family came to his rescue when he needed money. "I'm living so far beyond my income," he once wrote, "that we may almost be said to be living apart." His rebellion against authority took radical form in his poetry. People often view language as a fixed system. Cummings saw language as a flexible tool. In his poems, he combined words, playing with punctuation and syntax to create unique forms of poetic expression.

> "To be nobody-but-myself—in a world which is doing its best, night and day, to make me everybody else—means to fight the hardest battle which any human being can fight and never stop fighting."
>
> —E. E. Cummings

Cummings was born in Cambridge, Massachusetts, the son of a Unitarian minister and a mother who encouraged him to write and keep a journal. A year after receiving a master's degree from Harvard University in 1916, Cummings volunteered to serve as an ambulance driver in World War I. He and a

friend were wrongly arrested and imprisoned in France on charges of spying. A few months later, they were released, and Cummings wrote about his experiences there in *The Enormous Room* (1922).

Art and Poetry After the war, Cummings settled in New York City's Greenwich Village, studied art in Paris, and published his first book of poetry, *Tulips and Chimneys* (1923). In New York City, he continued his experiments with free verse and painted in the Cubist style. In 1925, two more volumes of his verse were published, and Cummings received a $2,000 award from *Dial* magazine. In 1928 the Provincetown Playhouse produced a Cummings play called *Him*, which ran for 27 performances. Most critics hated it, but audience response was more favorable.

Applause at Last Cummings continued to publish his poetry throughout the 1930s and 1940s. His *Collected Poems* (1938) received generally good reviews but sold poorly. He had won a Guggenheim Fellowship in 1933, but it was not until the 1950s that he received more recognition, winning the Harriet Monroe Prize in 1950, another Guggenheim Fellowship in 1951, and the Bollingen Prize in Poetry in 1958. He also began to read his poetry to enthusiastic audiences, and in 1952–1953 he lectured at Harvard. Biographer Richard S. Kennedy summed up Cummings's work by writing "What he produced will long amuse, titillate, thrill, provoke, or enthrall his readers."

Literature Online

Author Search For more about E. E. Cummings, go to glencoe.com and enter QuickPass code GLA9800u5.

Selection Skills

Literary Elements
- Rhythm (SE pp. 705, 707, 708)

somewhere i have . . . / anyone lived in a pretty how town

Listening/Speaking/ Viewing Skills
- Analyze Art (TE p. 706)

Reading Skills
- Analyze Style (SE pp. 705–708)

Vocabulary Skills
- Analogies (SE p. 708; TE p. 706)
- Multiple Meanings (TE p. 705)

Writing Skills/Grammar
- Character Sketch (SE p. 708)

Literature and Reading Preview

Connect to the Poems

Do you think it is possible to convey emotions accurately through language? Discuss this question in a small group.

Build Background

Cummings's unusual arrangement of words, punctuation, and capitalization were his way of expressing his individuality and encouraging readers to look at the world in a new way.

Set Purposes for Reading

Big Idea New Poetics

Cummings was influenced by Imagist ideas, but he soon developed his own unique style, which to a great extent depended on visual images. As you read, ask yourself, How does Cummings use visual images in his poems?

Literary Element Rhythm

Rhythm is the arrangement of stressed and unstressed syllables. Regular rhythm has a predictable pattern, whereas irregular rhythm does not. Although both of these Cummings poems have irregular rhythm, the particular arrangement of stressed and unstressed syllables in the second poem plays an especially important role. As you read, ask yourself, What purpose does rhythm have in these poems?

Reading Strategy Analyze Style

Style refers to the expressive qualities that distinguish an author's work. Such things as word choice, figurative language, and imagery all help determine an author's style. Cummings's instantly recognizable style results in part from his arrangement of words on a page: his sentence patterns, use of parentheses, division of words, and capitalization or lack thereof.

Tip: Ask Questions As you read, note for later discussion any questions you have about Cummings's style.

1. In the first poem, who is being addressed?
2.
3.
4.
5.

Learning Objectives

For pages 704–708

In studying these texts, you will focus on the following objectives:

Literary Study: Analyzing rhythm.

Reading: Analyzing style.

Writing: Writing a character sketch.

Vocabulary

render (ren´ dər) *v.* to reproduce or depict in verbal or artistic form; p. 706 *The painting was the artist's attempt to render her emotional response to the tragedy.*

apt (apt) *adj.* likely; having a tendency; p. 707 *People's minds are apt to wander from doing homework on sunny days.*

English Learners

DIFFERENTIATED INSTRUCTION

Advanced Provide students with two-column charts. In the rows of the left column, record the following elements of style: unusual word choice; imagery; figures of speech such as similes, metaphors, or personification; and sounds. As they read the poems, have students record two examples of each style element in the corresponding rows in the right column. Then have students use detailed sentences to share aloud the entries in their charts.

Before You Read

Focus

Summary

In "somewhere i have never travelled,gladly beyond," Cummings describes the experience of love. The speaker describes himself as a fragile flower, which his lover has the power to open or close. In "anyone lived in a pretty how town," Cummings contrasts the harmony in the lives of "anyone" and "noone" with the ignorance and hostility of the "someones" in a small town.

 For summaries in languages other than English, see Unit 5 Teaching Resources Book, pp. 93–98.

Vocabulary

Multiple Meanings Point out that words on this vocabulary list have more than one meaning:

- *Render* can also mean "to cause or make" and "to give or do."
- *Apt* can mean "exactly right for a particular purpose or situation" or "able to learn or understand quickly."

Ask students to explain the words' meanings in the following sentences.

1. The award *rendered* Tyler speechless, but he finally managed to *render* thanks. *(made; give)*
2. Marla is a very *apt* pupil. "Excellent" is an *apt* description of her work. *(able to learn quickly; exactly right for the particular purpose)*

 For additional context, see Glencoe Interactive Vocabulary CD-ROM.

Teach

For additional practice using the reading skill or strategy, see Unit 5 Teaching Resources Book, p. 100.

Reading Strategy | 1

Analyze Style **Answer:** *You always open me petal by petal, as Spring opens her first rose with a skillful, mysterious touch.*

(APPROACHING) Remind students having difficulty to examine and revise capitalization, word order, word form, and spelling. Tell students that they may also add or delete words as necessary. Suggest that students work with partners to rewrite the sentence in several different ways.

Big Idea | 2

New Poetics **Answer:** *Images of opening and closing recur. The images are connected in their reference to the beloved's ability to open or close the speaker's heart.*

 View the Art ★

In this 20th-century oil painting, Konstantine Rodko (1908–1995) contrasts the deep colors of the room with the brilliant white of the beach. The wide-open doors invite the viewer into the bright, seemingly limitless world outside.
Ask: How does the artist use light, color, shape, or space to make the scene outside the door inviting? *(Possible answer: The artist uses warm colors and open space to suggest that the painting extends beyond itself.)*

706

Open Door on the Beach. Konstantine Rodko. Private collection. ★

somewhere i have never travelled, gladly beyond

E. E. Cummings

somewhere i have never travelled,gladly beyond
any experience, your eyes have their silence:
in your most frail gesture are things which enclose me,
or which i cannot touch because they are too near

5   your slightest look easily will unclose me
though i have closed myself as fingers,
you open always petal by petal myself as Spring opens
(touching skilfully,mysteriously) her first rose

or if your wish be to close me,i and
10 my life will shut very beautifully,suddenly,
as when the heart of this flower imagines
the snow carefully everywhere descending;

nothing which we are to perceive in this world equals
the power of your intense fragility:whose texture
15 compels me with the colour of its countries,
rendering death and forever with each breathing

(i do not know what it is about you that closes
and opens;only something in me understands
the voice of your eyes is deeper than all roses)
20 nobody,not even the rain,has such small hands

Analyze Style *Cummings purposefully plays with sentence structure. How would you untangle the syntax in these lines?* | 1

New Poetics *What images recur in this poem? How are these images connected?* | 2

Vocabulary

render (ren´ dər) *v.* to reproduce or depict in verbal or artistic form

Vocabulary Practice

SPIRAL REVIEW **Analogies** Remind students that analogies show relationships between ideas or things. Some analogies are based on antonyms or on synonyms.
Write the following on the board:
render : _____ :: _____ : _____
apt : _____ :: _____ : _____
Have students use words from this poem to complete the second half of each

analogy. *(Possible answers: render : reproduce :: careful : cautious; apt : likely :: little : small)* Then have students explain how Cummings uses analogies in his writing to explore what is familiar and unfamiliar.

anyone
lived in
a pretty
how town

E. E. Cummings

Jealousy, 1892. Tihamer Margitay. National Gallery, Budapest, Hungary.

anyone lived in a pretty how town
(with up so floating many bells down)
spring summer autumn winter
he sang his didn't he danced his did.

5 Women and men(both little and small)
cared for anyone not at all
they sowed their isn't they reaped their same
sun moon stars rain

children guessed(but only a few
10 and down they forgot as up they grew
autumn winter spring summer)
that noone loved him more by more

when by now and tree by leaf
she laughed his joy she cried his grief
15 bird by snow and stir by still
anyone's any was all to her

someones married their everyones
laughed their cryings and did their dance
(sleep wake hope and then)they
20 said their nevers they slept their dream

stars rain sun moon
(and only the snow can begin to explain
how children are **apt** to forget to remember
with up so floating many bells down)

25 one day anyone died i guess
(and noone stooped to kiss his face)
busy folk buried them side by side
little by little and was by was

all by all and deep by deep
30 and more by more they dream their sleep
noone and anyone earth by april
wish by spirit and if by yes.

Women and men(both dong and ding)
summer autumn winter spring
35 reaped their sowing and went their came
sun moon stars rain

Analyze Style *Cummings uses familiar words in unfamiliar ways. What effect does this stylistic element have on your understanding of the poem?* **3**

Rhythm *What effect does the rhythm have on the overall tone of the poem?* **4**

Vocabulary

apt (apt) *adj.* likely; having a tendency

E. E. CUMMINGS **707**

After You Read

Assess

1. Answers will vary.
2. The speaker is deeply affected by a "frail gesture" and a "slightest look."
3. (a) The speaker's heart is compared to a flower, and his beloved is compared to the weather. (b) Possible answer: Yes, love poems often contain images of flowers.
4. (a) The main character is "anyone"; his wife is "noone". (b) They suggest both anonymity and universality.
5. (a) They forget that "noone" loved "anyone." (b) Children are more observant and less comformist than adults.
6. Eyes can "speak," or convey a message, or be "silent."
7. (a) "Anyone" dies and "noone" follows. The townspeople seem indifferent. (b) Appropriate because of their anonymity
8. His poems look fragmented. Images and words are arranged in unconventional ways.
9. Students might suggest that how people dress or the activities in which they participate reveal individualism.

Vocabulary

1. d
2. b

🖋 Writing

Students' sketches should integrate personal beliefs with specific details and description to create a realistic character.

After You Read

Respond and Think Critically

Respond and Interpret

1. What was your first reaction to the strange syntax and the other unusual features in Cummings's poems?
2. In the first two stanzas of "somewhere i have never travelled,gladly beyond," how would you characterize the loved one's effect on the speaker?
3. (a)What metaphors are used throughout the poem, and what are they comparing? (b)Are the images presented in these metaphors typical for a love poem? Why or why not?
4. (a)In "anyone lived in a pretty how town," what is the name of the main character, and what is the name of his wife? (b)What do their names suggest to you?
5. (a)What happens to children as they grow up? (b)What is Cummings suggesting about the difference between children and adults?

Analyze and Evaluate

6. In "somewhere i have never travelled," how can eyes can be silent (line 2) or have a voice (line 19)?
7. (a)In "anyone lived in a pretty how town," what happens to the two main characters at the end and how do the townspeople react? (b)How is this an appropriate ending?

Connect

8. **Big Idea** **New Poetics** Painters known as Cubists painted objects that looked fragmented. How might these Cubist ideas in painting have influenced Cummings's ideas about poetry?
9. **Connect to Today** Cummings expressed his individuality through his writing style. What are some ways people you know express their uniqueness?

Literary Element **Rhythm**

Is the **rhythm** of "anyone lived in a pretty how town" regular or irregular? How does the rhythm support the meaning of the poem?

Reading Strategy **Analyze Style**

The speaker's tone can be an important part of a poem's style. How would you describe the tone and its effect on meaning in each of these poems?

🖋 Writing

Write a Character Sketch In "anyone lived in a pretty how town," Cummings expresses his thoughts about an "average" person's life. Write a character sketch in which you describe an "average" high school student. Incorporate your own views about individualism.

Vocabulary Practice

Practice with Analogies Choose the word that best completes each analogy. To complete an analogy, decide on the relationship represented by the first pair of words. Then, apply that relationship to the second set of words.

1. artist : render :: forecaster :
   a. formulate   c. weather
   b. tells   d. predict
2. apt : unlikely :: abstract :
   a. artistic   c. intellectual
   b. concrete   d. ideal

 Literature Online

Selection Resources For Selection Quizzes, eFlashcards, and Reading-Writing Connection activities, go to glencoe.com and enter QuickPass code GLA9800u5.

Literary Element

The rhythm is irregular: each line of the poem has four stresses, but the numbers of unstressed syllables differ. Students may say that the singsong rhythm reflects the ordinariness of the lives being described, or the natural cycle of life.

Reading Strategy

The tone of "somewhere I have never travelled,gladly beyond" is tender and vulnerable. The poem "anyone lived in a pretty how town" alternates between a positive and a negative tone, depending upon whether the poet is talking about "anyone" and "noone" or the "Women and men."

Before You Read

Chicago and Grass

Meet **Carl Sandburg**
(1878–1967)

Although influenced by Ezra Pound and the Imagists, Carl Sandburg sought to reach a wider audience—and he did. From the 1916 publication of *Chicago Poems* until his death, he was one of America's most popular and successful poets.

Carl Sandburg collected material for his poetry from his broad and varied life experience. Besides being a poet and biographer, he worked as a milk-truck driver, bricklayer, and traveling salesman.

Sandburg grew up in Galesburg, Illinois, the son of Swedish immigrants. He quit school after eighth grade and took odd jobs to help support his family. When he was nineteen, he set out to explore the United States, joining the many hoboes of the period who hitched rides on freight trains. Later he fought in the Spanish-American War, attended college, and then moved to Chicago. There he became a journalist, learning to write clearly and protesting social and racial injustices. He also began to contribute poems to *Poetry* magazine.

Literary Giant In the early twentieth century, Chicago was a vibrant place for a poet to live. It was home not only to the influential *Poetry* magazine, founded in 1912 by Harriet Monroe, but also to notable writers such as Sherwood Anderson, Theodore Dreiser, Vachel Lindsay, and Edgar Lee Masters. In 1914 *Poetry* magazine published six of Sandburg's poems, and with the publication of *Chicago Poems* two years later, Sandburg emerged as one of Chicago's literary giants. Dubbed "the Bard of the Midwest," he soon wrote three more volumes of poetry that established his national reputation: *Cornhuskers* (1918), *Smoke and Steel* (1920), and *Slabs of the Sunburnt West* (1922).

> *"Time is the coin of your life. It is the only coin you have, and only you can determine how it will be spent. Be careful lest you let other people spend it for you."*
>
> —Carl Sandburg

Critics, however, were divided over Sandburg's poetic merits. Supporters praised his original subject matter and voice, while detractors criticized his free-verse technique and focus on social issues.

The People's Poet A great admirer of Walt Whitman, Sandburg might be considered Whitman's successor in his enthusiasm for the common people. Sandburg's poems, like Whitman's, are noted for their use of the rhythms of everyday speech and for their democratic subjects and themes. They also include colorful use of sayings and anecdotes.

An extremely popular performer, Sandburg frequently traveled throughout the United States, lecturing on the lives of Whitman and Abraham Lincoln, reading his poems aloud, and singing folk songs while playing the guitar. Sandburg won the Pulitzer Prize for his biography of Lincoln in 1940 and for his *Complete Poems* in 1951. He continued to write throughout his final years.

 Literature Online

Author Search For more about Carl Sandburg, go to glencoe.com and enter QuickPass code GLA9800u5.

CARL SANDBURG **709**

Before You Read

Focus

Bellringer Options

Daily Language Practice Transparency 64

Or display several images of a bustling industrial city. **Ask:** If this city were a living being, what adjectives or phrases could you use to describe it? Encourage students to look for vivid images and adjectives in Carl Sandburg's poem describing Chicago.

Selection Skills

Literary Elements
- Apostrophe (SE pp. 710, 713; TE p. 711)

Chicago *and* Grass

Vocabulary Skills
- Denotation and Connotation (SE pp. 710, 713)
- Adjectives (TE p. 710)

Writing Skills/Grammar
- Poem (SE p. 713)

Reading Skills
- Make Inferences About Theme (SE pp. 710, 711, 713)
- Recognize Author's Purpose (TE p. 712)

Listening/Speaking/ Viewing Skills
- Analyze Art (TE p. 712)

Before You Read

Focus

Summary

In "Chicago," Carl Sandburg sings the praises of the vigorous city of Chicago and of its people. In "Grass," Sandburg uses muted understatement to convey the terrible cost and meaninglessness of war.

 For summaries in languages other than English, see Unit 5 Teaching Resources Book, pp. 104–109.

Vocabulary

Adjectives Write the word *husky* in the center of a word web on the board. Ask students to fill the radiating circles with items that they might describe as husky, such as football players, bears, and so on. Encourage students to move beyond stereotypical associations to unusual associations. Repeat the activity with the word *wanton*.

Literature and Reading Preview

Connect to the Poems

Are there situations or events in life that should never be forgotten? Are there things that are better forgotten? Discuss these questions with a partner.

Build Background

In 1896 Chicago's waterways and railroads united the nation, linking the wealth of the East with the agriculture of the West, Midwest, and South. But the city's rapid industrial growth also brought many labor disputes, including riots and a strike by railroad workers. During his years as a Chicago journalist, Sandburg saw firsthand the struggles and triumphs of the growing city.

Set Purposes for Reading

Big Idea **New Poetics**

As you read, ask yourself, How does Sandburg break new ground in these poems?

Literary Element **Apostrophe**

Apostrophe is a figure of speech in which a writer directly addresses an inanimate object, an idea, or an absent person. For example, in "Chicago," the speaker says to the city, "they tell me you are crooked." As you read, ask yourself, What are other examples of apostrophe in Sandburg's poems?

Reading Strategy **Make Inferences About Theme**

The **theme** is the central message of a work of literature. The theme of a poem is often implied rather than stated directly. You can infer the theme by analyzing elements such as diction, imagery, and figurative language. As you read, look for evidence in the poem that suggests the theme.

. . . .

Tip: Take Notes Use a diagram to record direct statements, images, and examples of figurative language that support a theme in these poems.

Learning Objectives

For pages 709–713

In studying these texts, you will focus on the following objectives:

Literary Study: Analyzing apostrophe.

Reading: Making inferences about theme.

Writing: Writing a poem.

Vocabulary

husky (hus´ kē) *adj.* strong; burly; p. 711 *He has a short, husky build.*

wanton (wont´ ən) *adj.* resulting from extreme cruelty or neglect; p. 711 *The house is in a state of wanton disrepair.*

sneer (snēr) *v.* to smile or laugh scornfully or critically; p. 711 *The bully did nothing but sneer at the other children.*

. . . .

Tip: Denotation and Connotation Some words that have the same dictionary definition can have different cultural definitions. For example, *husky* and *strong* have similar meanings, but *husky* has a stronger connotation.

Speaking Practice

SPIRAL REVIEW **Epithets** Read the first five lines of "Chicago" aloud. Have students respond to the meaning and images. Explain that Sandburg begins "Chicago" with a series of epithets, or short descriptive phrases that characterize a person or place. Sandburg uses these epithets to emphasize traits that he thinks are special to Chicago. Have students write a similar series of epithets about their town or city or another place they know. Invite them to share their epithets orally with the class and explain how these phrases express the special qualities of the places.

710

CHICAGO

Carl Sandburg

 Hog Butcher for the World,
Tool Maker, Stacker of Wheat,
Player with Railroads and the Nation's Freight Handler;
Stormy, **husky,** brawling,
5   City of the Big Shoulders:
They tell me you are wicked and I believe them, for I have seen your painted
    women under the gas lamps luring the farm boys.
And they tell me you are crooked and I answer: Yes, it is true I have seen the
    gunman kill and go free to kill again.
And they tell me you are brutal and my reply is: On the faces of women and
    children I have seen the marks of **wanton** hunger.
And having answered so I turn once more to those who **sneer** at this my city,
    and I give them back the sneer and say to them:
10 Come and show me another city with lifted head singing so proud to be alive
    and coarse and strong and cunning.
Flinging magnetic curses amid the toil of piling job on job, here is a tall bold
    slugger set vivid against the little soft cities;
Fierce as a dog with tongue lapping for action, cunning as a savage pitted
    against the wilderness,
        Bareheaded,
        Shoveling,
15   Wrecking,
        Planning,
        Building, breaking, rebuilding,
Under the smoke, dust all over his mouth, laughing with white teeth,
Under the terrible burden of destiny laughing as a young man laughs,
20 Laughing even as an ignorant fighter laughs who has never lost a battle,
Bragging and laughing that under his wrist is the pulse, and under his ribs the
    heart of the people,
        Laughing!
Laughing the stormy, husky, brawling laughter of Youth, half-naked, sweating,
    proud to be Hog Butcher, Tool Maker, Stacker of Wheat, Player
    with Railroads and Freight Handler to the Nation.

1

 2

Make Inferences About Theme *What does this phrase suggest about Chicago?*

Vocabulary

husky (hus´ kē) *adj.* strong; burly
wanton (wont´ ən) *adj.* resulting from extreme cruelty or neglect
sneer (snēr) *v.* to smile or laugh scornfully or critically

CARL SANDBURG   **711**

Teach

| Literary Element | 1 |

Apostrophe Read the bracketed passage aloud. **Ask:** In which lines does the speaker directly address the city? *(lines 6–8)* Whom does the speaker say he is addressing in line 10? *(those who sneer at the city)* What do lines 10–11 reveal about the speaker's attitude toward the city? *(that the speaker admires the city)* How do readers come to feel about Chicago? *(Readers may come to admire the city too.)*

| Reading Strategy | 2 |

Make Inferences About Theme Answer: *It suggests that Chicago is a noisy, energetic city.*

(APPROACHING) Write the words *noisy* and *energetic* in the center of an idea web on the board. Have students fill the radiating circles with words, phrases, or images from the poem that suggest noise and energy.

> For additional practice using the reading skill or strategy, see Unit 5 Teaching Resources Book, p. 111.

Cultural History ☆

Chicago's Stockyards During the 19th and 20th centuries, Chicago was an important meat-packing center. Supported by nine railroads and several of Chicago's leading meat packers, Union Stock Yards opened on Christmas Day, 1865. Not until August 1971 did all meat-processing activities cease at that location.

Approaching Level

DIFFERENTIATED INSTRUCTION

SMALL GROUP
Emerging Make sure that students understand that Sandburg describes what other people say about Chicago, and he acknowledges some truth in these claims. Then he goes on to describe the city in a positive way through action and sensory language. To help students analyze what Sandburg says about Chicago, have them work in pairs to identify the words and phrases that characterize the city. Remind them to look for verbs, such as *sneer*, and nouns, such as *curses*, as well as adjectives. When students have completed their lists, have them reread the lists to see how the words help focus a central idea, or theme.

Teach

Big Idea   1

New Poetics **Answer:** *The speaker is bitter that the sacrifices made by the dead soldiers are so quickly obscured and forgotten.*

APPROACHING Remind students having difficulty that speakers reveal attitude through word choice. Write the following phrases on the board: "pile the bodies," "shovel them under," "pile them high." **Ask:** How do these phrases make you feel? *(sad, bitter, angry)* Why don't the passengers on the train recognize the graveyards? *(They have forgotten about the soldiers and their sacrifices. The places no longer look like graveyards.)*

View the Art ★

Joan Mitchell (1926–1992) used vivid colors on huge canvases. Her work presents highly stylized images of landscapes, many of which, like *The Sky Is Blue, the Grass Is Green,* include large blocks of color. **Ask:** What elements of this painting can you relate to the poem "Grass"? *(The green and yellow-green blocks represent the grass, and the black block represents death.)*

 To check students' understanding of the selection, see Unit 5 Teaching Resources Book, p. 113.

The Sky Is Blue, the Grass Is Green, 1972. Joan Mitchell. Oil on canvas. Musee National d'Art Moderne, Centre Georges Pompidou, Paris. ★

Grass

Carl Sandburg

Pile the bodies high at Austerlitz and Waterloo.[1]
Shovel them under and let me work—
         I am the grass; I cover all.

And pile them high at Gettysburg[2]
5   And pile them high at Ypres and Verdun.[3]

Shovel them under and let me work.
Two years, ten years, and passengers ask the conductor:
         What place is this?
         Where are we now?

10   I am the grass.
         Let me work.

---

1. *Austerlitz and Waterloo* refer to battle sites in Moravia (part of the present-day Czech Republic) and Belgium during the Napoleonic Wars in the early 1800s.
2. *Gettysburg* refers to a battlefield in southern Pennsylvania where Union and Confederate forces fought a horrific battle in 1863 during the Civil War.
3. *Ypres and Verdun* refer to battle sites in Belgium and northern France where well over a million soldiers were slain in World War I.

New Poetics *How would you describe the speaker's attitude toward the dead?*   **1**

Reading Practice

SMALL GROUP
Recognize Author's Purpose Tell students that a poem's speaker may provide clues to an attitude or feeling that the poet wants readers to share. Have students explore these questions in small groups:

- Who is the speaker? *(grass)*
- What is shocking about the speaker's statements? *(The statements "shovel them under" and "pile them high" show a disregard for human life.)*

- How does the poet want readers to feel about war? *(He wants readers to feel the waste and horror of war.)*

After You Read

Respond and Think Critically

Respond and Interpret

1. Which images in these poems impress you the most? Explain.

Chicago

2. (a)What names does the speaker give Chicago in lines 1–5? (b)What do these names reveal?

3. (a)List positive adjectives the speaker uses to describe Chicago. (b)What do these words reveal about the city's inhabitants?

Analyze and Evaluate

4. How well does Sandburg's diction, or word choice, help create a vivid image of the city? Explain.

Grass

Recall and Interpret

5. (a)Who is the speaker in this poem? (b)What does the speaker want to do?

6. Why does the speaker mention famous battle sites from different wars?

Analyze and Evaluate

7. (a)Why does the speaker describe passengers on a train in lines 7–9? (b)How well does this image support the view of war presented?

Connect

8. **Big Idea** **New Poetics** Ezra Pound stated that modern poets should "Make it new!" What do you find new about Sandburg's poems?

9. **Connect to the Author** Sandburg once wrote that his goal as a poet was "to sing, blab, chortle, yodel, like people." Do you think he succeeded? Explain. Use examples from the text as support.

Literary Element Apostrophe

Poets often use **apostrophe** either to achieve a formal tone or to convey a sense of emotional immediacy.

1. In which lines in "Chicago" does the speaker address the city as "you"?

2. What effects do you think Sandburg's overall use of apostrophe creates? Explain.

Reading Strategy Make Inferences About Theme

On the basis of the evidence you listed in your diagram on page 710, how would you state the theme of "Chicago"?

Vocabulary Practice

Denotation and Connotation Denotation is the dictionary meaning of a word. **Connotation** is the implied, or cultural, meaning. For example, *criticize* and *condemn* have a similar denotation, "to disapprove," but very different connotations:

Negative	*More Negative*
criticize	condemn

Choose the word in each pair of synonyms below that that has the more negative connotation.

1. husky beefy
2. wanton abused
3. sneer smirk

Writing

Write a Poem Using "Chicago" as a model, write a poem defending your own city, town, or neighborhood. Incorporate apostrophe in your poem.

Literary Element

1. Lines 6–8
2. It creates a paradoxical effect: it entices the reader to share the speaker's feelings while distancing the reader with its artificiality.

Writing

Students' poems should incorporate different views of the city and use specific, vivid details.

Vocabulary

1. beefy
2. abused
3. sneer

After You Read

Assess

1. Answers will vary.

2. (a) Hog Butcher for the World; Tool Maker; Stacker of Wheat; Player with Railroads; Nation's Freight Handler; City of the Big Shoulders (b) The city is a commercial and industrial center.

3. (a) *Proud; strong; tall; bold* (b) They suggest that the people are energetic and vibrant and that the speaker admires them.

4. His choice of nouns and adjectives with powerful connotations helps create a vivid image of the city.

5. (a) The grass (b) It wants to cover the bodies from battlefields so that in the future people will have to ask what the places are.

6. The poet may want to emphasize that wars are recurrent.

7. (a) They are travelers who have forgotten the battles. (b) It supports the view that wars are forgotten and new wars are fought.

8. Students may say that Sandburg uses common, "unpoetic" language and images and irregular rhythms.

9. Students may say that Sandburg achieves his goal by varying his tone and word choice.

Reading Strategy

Answers will vary but students may say that celebrating the greatness of the city of Chicago is the theme of the poem.

Progress Check

Can students analyze apostrophe?

If No → See Unit 5 Teaching Resources Book, p. 110.

Bellringer Options

Selection Focus
 Transparency 44
Daily Language Practice
 Transparency 65

Or display images of several types of walls, large and small, made of different materials. Tell students that in "Mending Wall," Robert Frost says, "Good fences make good neighbors." Ask students to explain whether they agree or disagree with this idea.

Literary History ☆

John F. Kennedy's Inauguration
President John F. Kennedy asked Robert Frost to read a poem at his inauguration on January 20, 1961. Frost, age 87, frail, and blinded by the strong sunlight that day, was unable to read the poem he had written for the occasion. Instead, he recited from memory his poem "The Gift Outright."

Meet **Robert Frost**
(1874–1963)

Robert Frost was one of the most honored poets of the twentieth century. A four-time winner of the Pulitzer Prize for Poetry, Frost received special recognition from Congress in 1960. The following January, at age eighty-six, he had the honor of reciting his poem "The Gift Outright" at President John F. Kennedy's inauguration.

Although closely associated with New England, Frost spent his first eleven years in San Francisco. After his father died in 1885, his mother moved Frost and his sister to the gritty industrial city of Lawrence, Massachusetts. She taught school and wrote poetry, introducing Frost to the work of the English Romantic writers, the New England Transcendentalists, and the poets of her native Scotland. Frost graduated from high school and went off to Dartmouth College, but he left the school after less than a year.

Farming and Teaching Frost married Elinor White in 1895. (They had been co-valedictorians of their high school class.) They had six children, two of whom died young. Frost supported his family by farming and teaching school. At age twenty-six, Frost moved his family to a farm near Derry, New Hampshire.

There, between farm chores, Frost wrote poems describing the region's often harsh conditions and the experiences of his fellow New Englanders. In 1912, unable to get his poems published in the United States, he sold his farm and moved his family to England.

Success and Enduring Acclaim In London, Frost became acquainted with Ezra Pound and other Modernist poets. He was able to publish his first volume of poetry, *A Boy's Will*, in 1913, and *North of Boston* soon after. Praised by poet Amy Lowell in a review, *North of Boston* was soon published in the United States and sold well. By the time Frost returned to New England in 1915, at the start of the First World War, he was well on the road to fame. Prominent publishers backed his work, and prestigious universities sought him to teach.

> "[A poem] begins in delight and ends in wisdom . . . in a clarification of life—not necessarily a great clarification, . . . but in a momentary stay against confusion."
>
> —Robert Frost

Frost's later years were filled with accolades. He received more awards than any other twentieth-century poet and was chosen as poetry consultant to the Library of Congress. By the time of his death, his poetry had deeply embedded itself in the American imagination, and it continues to live there today.

 Literature Online

Author Search For more about Robert Frost, go to glencoe.com and enter QuickPass code GLA9800u5.

Selection Skills

Literary Elements
- Blank Verse (SE pp. 715, 717, 718, 720)
- Rhyme Scheme (SE pp. 722, 724)

Vocabulary Skills
- Synonyms (SE pp. 715, 720; TE p. 718)
- Academic Vocabulary (SE pp. 722, 724)
- Concrete and Abstract Nouns (TE p. 715)

Mending Wall/Birches/ Stopping by . . ./ Acquainted . . .

Listening/Speaking/ Viewing Skills
- Analyze Art (SE p. 716; TE pp. 718, 721, 723)
- Choral Reading (TE p. 718)

Writing Skills/Grammar
- Dialogue (SE p. 722)
- List (SE p. 724)

Reading Skills
- Compare and Contrast Speakers (SE pp. 715, 717, 719–724)
- Group Response (TE p. 716)

Literature and Reading Preview

Connect to the Poems

How would you describe the sights, smells, and sounds of where you live? Write a descriptive journal entry about your neighborhood, city, or region. Include concrete and sensory details to evoke a strong sense of place.

Build Background

From 1900 to 1909, Frost tried to earn a living on a small family farm he had bought in Derry, New Hampshire. Although Frost loved the outdoors, he did not enjoy farm life. Three years before leaving for England, Frost abandoned farming and resumed his teaching career. Despite his lack of success as a farmer, Frost drew inspiration for many poems from his memories of New England farm life.

Set Purposes for Reading

Big Idea **New Poetics**

Though Frost uses traditional forms for his poems, he often explores typical themes of modern poetry such as loneliness and isolation. As you read, ask yourself, How do "Mending Wall" and "Birches" reflect these themes?

Literary Element **Blank Verse**

Blank verse is poetry written in unrhymed iambic pentameter. Each line has a basic pattern of five pairs of syllables, with each pair made up of an unstressed syllable followed by a stressed syllable. As you read, ask yourself, What rhythms does Frost create by using blank verse?

Reading Strategy **Compare and Contrast Speakers**

The **speaker** is the voice of a poem, similar to the narrator in a work of prose. Sometimes the speaker's voice is that of the poet, and sometimes it is that of a fictional person or even a thing. The speaker's words communicate a particular **tone,** or attitude, toward the subject of a poem. As you read, ask yourself, How can comparing and contrasting the speakers of these poems help reveal the qualities that distinguish each one?

Tip: Use a Venn Diagram As you read, consider how the speakers of "Mending Wall" and "Birches" are similar and different. Use a Venn diagram to record your information.

Learning Objectives

For pages 714–733

In studying these texts, you will focus on the following objectives:

Literary Study:
Analyzing blank verse.
Analyzing narrative poetry.

Reading:
Comparing and contrasting speakers.
Evaluating characterization.

Writing:
Writing a dialogue.
Writing a list.

Vocabulary

enamel (i nam´ əl) *n.* a cosmetic or paint that gives a smooth, glossy appearance; p. 718 *The pot was covered in a dark blue enamel.*

bracken (bra´ kən) *n.* a type of fern that grows in humid, temperate areas; p. 718 *Bracken covered the forest floor in summer.*

poise (poiz) *n.* a state of balance; p. 719 *Her grace and poise made us think she must be a dancer.*

coax (kōks) *v.* to persuade gently; p. 726 *I tried to coax the cat out of the tree with a catnip toy.*

kin (kin) *n.* relatives, or a group of people with common ancestry; p. 730 *Sara had kin from four countries present at her wedding ceremony.*

Tip: Synonyms Understanding words that are similar in meaning to an unfamiliar word, or **synonyms,** can help you learn the new word. Example: *Poise and equilibrium are synonyms; they both refer to "a state of balance."*

ROBERT FROST **715**

Before You Read

Focus

Summary

In "Mending Wall," the speaker discusses his and his neighbor's views of walls and the "something" that doesn't love them. The speaker of "Birches" recalls his happy childhood. On his way home in the evening, the speaker of "Stopping by Woods on a Snowy Evening" pauses to observe the beauty of the dark woods, although he must soon continue his journey. The speaker of "Acquainted with the Night" describes his isolation and loneliness, which he seems to accept as part of life.

 For summaries in languages other than English, see Unit 5 Teaching Resources Book, pp. 115–120.

Vocabulary

Concrete and Abstract Nouns Point out that some nouns name concrete objects while others (abstract nouns) describe states of being or qualities. **Ask:** Which nouns on this vocabulary list are concrete—can be seen or touched? *(enamel, bracken, kin)* Which noun is abstract, describing a state of being? *(poise)* Ask student pairs to generate lists of nouns that describe states of being or qualities. *(Possible answers: beauty, happiness, sadness, goodness, honesty)*

English Learners

DIFFERENTIATED INSTRUCTION

Advanced Write on the board: "Something there is that doesn't love a wall." Use slash marks and tapping to show students that this line contains ten syllables. Then use slash marks to show students that there are five syllable pairs in the line. Point out that in each syllable pair, there is one unstressed syllable followed by a stressed syllable. Read the line aloud with exaggerated intonation so that students can hear the unstressed and stressed syllables. Invite students to echo your reading of the line several times. Then have pairs of students work together to mark syllables and stresses in the following line: "That sends the frozen-ground-swell under it."

Teach

Blank Verse Remind students that blank verse has five stressed syllables in each line. Read lines 1–4 aloud, exaggerating the stresses so that students can hear the rhythm clearly. Point out that the poem is nevertheless not meant to be read in a singsong manner. Read the passage again, following the punctuation and the natural sentence stresses. Finally, have students echo your reading of each line.

View the Art ★

Answer: *The wall resembles the one in the poem because it consists of a variety of boulders—"loaves" and "balls"—and appears to need repairing. It differs from the one in the poem because it includes a fence as well as the stones, making it an even more forbidding obstacle.*

Marsden Hartley (1877–1943) had his first major exhibition in 1909 at a gallery owned by the photographer Alfred Stieglitz. The Dogtown of the painting's title was an area of glacial boulders and deteriorating stone walls near Gloucester, Massachusetts.

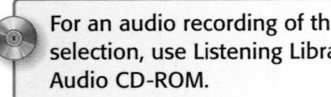

For an audio recording of this selection, use Listening Library Audio CD-ROM.

The Last Stone Walls, Dogtown, 1936–37. Marsden Hartley. Oil on canvas, 17½ x 23½ in. Yale University Art Gallery, New Haven, CT. Gift of Walter Bareiss, B.A. 1940.

View the Art Attracted to the Transcendentalist ideas of Emerson and Thoreau, Marsden Hartley frequently painted New England landscapes like this one. In what ways might this wall be similar to or different from the one in "Mending Wall"?

Mending Wall
Robert Frost

Something there is that doesn't love a wall,
That sends the frozen-ground-swell under it,
And spills the upper boulders in the sun;
And makes gaps even two can pass abreast.
5   The work of hunters is another thing:
I have come after them and made repair
Where they have left not one stone on a stone,
But they would have the rabbit out of hiding,
To please the yelping dogs. The gaps I mean,

1

Reading Practice

SPIRAL REVIEW **Group Response** Many readers find Frost's poems accessible because of their concrete language and vivid sensory details. Readers are able to visualize the characters and settings, and sense the moods Frost wishes to create.

Assign small groups to read "Mending Wall" and "Birches." Before class discussions of the poems, have the groups give brief multimedia presentations about what the language of the poems enables them to visualize and understand. A presentation might combine text, graphics, and sound.

> 10   No one has seen them made or heard them made,
>   But at spring mending-time we find them there.
>   I let my neighbour know beyond the hill;
>   And on a day we meet to walk the line
>   And set the wall between us once again.
> 15   We keep the wall between us as we go.
>   To each the boulders that have fallen to each.
>   And some are loaves and some so nearly balls
>   We have to use a spell to make them balance:
>   'Stay where you are until our backs are turned!'
> 20   We wear our fingers rough with handling them.
>   Oh, just another kind of out-door game,
>   One on a side. It comes to little more:
>   There where it is we do not need the wall:
>   He is all pine and I am apple orchard.
> 25   My apple trees will never get across
>   And eat the cones under his pines, I tell him.
>   He only says, 'Good fences make good neighbours.'
>   Spring is the mischief in me, and I wonder
>   If I could put a notion in his head:
> 30   'Why do they make good neighbours? Isn't it
>   Where there are cows? But here there are no cows.
>   Before I built a wall I'd ask to know
>   What I was walling in or walling out,
>   And to whom I was like to give offence.
> 35   Something there is that doesn't love a wall,
>   That wants it down.' I could say 'Elves' to him,
>   But it's not elves exactly, and I'd rather
>   He said it for himself. I see him there
>   Bringing a stone grasped firmly by the top
> 40   In each hand, like an old-stone savage armed.
>   He moves in darkness as it seems to me,
>   Not of woods only and the shade of trees.
>   He will not go behind his father's saying,
>   And he likes having thought of it so well
> 45   He says again, 'Good fences make good neighbours.'

New Poetics *What do these lines tell you about the relationship between the two neighbors?* **2**

Compare and Contrast Speakers *What do these lines reveal about the speaker?* **3**

Blank Verse *How does the rhythm of these lines help create a conversational tone?* **4**

ROBERT FROST **717**

For additional practice using the reading skill or strategy, see Unit 5 Teaching Resources Book, p. 121.

Teach

Big Idea 2

New Poetics Answer: *They are on good terms with each other but are not close friends.*

Reading Strategy 3

Compare and Contrast Speakers Answer: *The speaker does not see the need for a wall.*

Ask: Why do you think the speaker's neighbor insists on maintaining the wall? *(Some students may say he is doing what has always been done, probably at first to keep animals from straying.)*

Literary Element 4

Blank Verse Answer: *It reflects the natural rhythm of relaxed, informal speech and makes the words sound like a conversation.*

(APPROACHING) Students may benefit from listening to a recording or a reading of the poem while following along with the text. They will be able to hear how words are pronounced, which words are stressed, and where pauses occur. Afterwards, have them read the poem themselves.

Approaching Level

DIFFERENTIATED INSTRUCTION

SMALL GROUP

Emerging Point that that "Good fences make good neighbors" is an aphorism—a short, pointed sentence expressing a wise or clever observation or general truth about life. This aphorism means that clearly established boundaries help neighbors avoid disputes and thus remain on good terms. Point out to students that this statement comes from the speaker's neighbor. **Ask:** Does the speaker agree or disagree with this statement? How do you know? *(The speaker disagrees with this statement because he points out that nature works to bring down a wall.)* Have students work with a partner to write an aphorism that expresses the speaker's philosophy regarding walls. Be sure that students can defend their statements with evidence from the poem.

Teach

Literary Element | 1

Blank Verse Answer: *swing-, does-, bend, down, stay, ice-, do*
Point out that Frost follows the rhythmic regularity of the first four lines with the irregular lines 5–11.
Ask: What is the purpose of this shift? *(The shift underscores a change in subject. The first four lines tell what the speaker imagines; the following lines report facts.)*

Vocabulary | 2

Synonyms After students read the definition of enamel at the bottom of the page, refer them to the use of the word in line 9.
Ask: How does the poet use the word *enamel* in an unusual way? *(He refers to ice metaphorically as enamel, because it coats the tree branches with a shiny brittle surface.)*

[ENGLISH LEARNERS] Compare enamel to paint or nail polish. Have students work in pairs to list the similarities between ice and enamel.

View the Photograph ★

Ask: What characteristics of birches are evident in this photograph? *(They have whitish bark that breaks or peels. They are generally slender, not massive.)*

Birches
Robert Frost

When I see birches bend to left and right
Across the lines of straighter darker trees,
I like to think some boy's been swinging them.
But swinging doesn't bend them down to stay
5   As ice-storms do. Often you must have seen them
Loaded with ice a sunny winter morning
After a rain. They click upon themselves
As the breeze rises, and turn many-colored
As the stir cracks and crazes their **enamel**.
10 Soon the sun's warmth makes them shed crystal shells
Shattering and avalanching on the snow-crust—
Such heaps of broken glass to sweep away
You'd think the inner dome of heaven had fallen.
They are dragged to the withered **bracken** by the load,
15 And they seem not to break; though once they are bowed
So low for long, they never right themselves:
You may see their trunks arching in the woods
Years afterwards, trailing their leaves on the ground
Like girls on hands and knees that throw their hair

1 Blank Verse *Which syllables are stressed in this sentence?*

Vocabulary
enamel (i nam´ əl) *n.* a cosmetic or paint that gives a smooth, glossy appearance
bracken (bra´ kən) *n.* a type of fern that grows in humid, temperate areas
2

718 UNIT 5 BEGINNINGS OF THE MODERN AGE

Listening and Speaking Practice

SPIRAL REVIEW **Choral Reading** A choral reading provides a different way of experiencing a literary work. A "reading choir" can consist of many readers reading in unison, or it can be divided into high, medium, and low voices or into duets, trios, or quartets of balanced voices.

Organize students in groups and assign a part of "Birches" to each group. Have each group choose a director and separate its part into lines to be spoken by one or two individuals and lines to be spoken by the entire group. After students rehearse, have the groups present their choral readings.

20　Before them over their heads to dry in the sun.
　　But I was going to say when Truth broke in
　　With all her matter-of-fact about the ice-storm
　　I should prefer to have some boy bend them
　　As he went out and in to fetch the cows—
25　Some boy too far from town to learn baseball,
　　Whose only play was what he found himself,
　　Summer or winter, and could play alone.
　　One by one he subdued[1] his father's trees
　　By riding them down over and over again
30　Until he took the stiffness out of them,
　　And not one but hung limp, not one was left
　　For him to conquer. He learned all there was
　　To learn about not launching out too soon
　　And so not carrying the tree away
35　Clear to the ground. He always kept his **poise**
　　To the top branches, climbing carefully
　　With the same pains you use to fill a cup
　　Up to the brim, and even above the brim.
　　Then he flung outward, feet first, with a swish,
40　Kicking his way down through the air to the ground.
　　So was I once myself a swinger of birches.
　　And so I dream of going back to be.
　　It's when I'm weary of considerations,
　　And life is too much like a pathless wood
45　Where your face burns and tickles with the cobwebs
　　Broken across it, and one eye is weeping
　　From a twig's having lashed across it open.
　　I'd like to get away from earth awhile
　　And then come back to it and begin over.
50　May no fate willfully misunderstand me
　　And half grant what I wish and snatch me away
　　Not to return. Earth's the right place for love:
　　I don't know where it's likely to go better.
　　I'd like to go by climbing a birch tree,
55　And climb black branches up a snow-white trunk
　　Toward heaven, till the tree could bear no more,
　　But dipped its top and set me down again.
　　That would be good both going and coming back.
　　One could do worse than be a swinger of birches.

---

1. *Subdued* means "brought under control" or "conquered."

 New Poetics *Why does the poet include these details about the boy?*

Compare and Contrast Speakers *What does the speaker admire about the boy who swings on birches?* **4**

Vocabulary

poise (poiz) n. a state of balance

ROBERT FROST **719**

After You Read

Assess

1. Students should give reasons for their choices.

2. (a) "Something" that doesn't like walls (b) It might refer to a force of nature.

3. (a) Each replaces stones that have fallen on his side. (b) The speaker thinks the wall is unnecessary; the neighbor thinks walls make good neighbors.

4. (a) The neighbor refuses to change. (b) The speaker's lines reveals mischief, logic, imagination. The neighbor's line suggests he is rigid.

5. (a) He does not take the job seriously. (b) Barriers between people

6. (a) He wants to think that boys caused them to bend. The cause was ice storms. (b) He may be nostalgic.

7. (a) He compares the trunks and leaves to girls who throw their hair over their head to dry. (b) He sees them as beautiful, living things.

8. (a) Himself (b) Taking chances; mastering problems

9. Students may say that the simile is apt as life offers many paths but no assurance of where they will lead.

10. Students may say that technology such as e-mail and text messaging prevent people from talking face-to-face and getting beyond superficial conversations.

Progress Check

Can students analyze blank verse?

If No → See Unit 5 Teaching Resources Book, p. 121.

720

After You Read

Respond and Think Critically

Respond and Interpret

1. Which images from the poems do you find the most powerful? Explain.

Mending Wall

2. (a) According to the speaker, what causes a wall to fall apart? (b) To what might the "something" that "doesn't love a wall" refer?

3. (a) Describe how the speaker and the neighbor fix the wall. (b) How do their opinions differ?

Analyze and Evaluate

4. (a) What does the speaker suggest by describing the neighbor as "an old-stone savage"? (b) How does **dialogue** help emphasize the differences between the speaker and the neighbor?

5. (a) Why does the speaker refer to this spring ritual as "another kind of out-door game" (line 21)? (b) What might walls and fences **symbolize** in this poem?

Literary Element Blank Verse

To determine the rhythm of any line of poetry, mark its stressed and unstressed syllables:

When I see birches bend to left and right

Good poets always vary the rhythm in blank verse for emphasis and to reflect natural speech. How does Frost vary the rhythm in "Mending Wall"?

Reading Strategy Compare and Contrast Speakers

Refer to the Venn diagram you created on page 715 to answer the following questions:

1. How are the speakers of the poems similar and different?

2. How would you contrast the tone in the two poems?

Birches

Recall and Interpret

6. (a) What does the speaker want to think has caused the birches to bend? What has really caused them to bend? (b) Why might the speaker want to believe in the imaginary cause?

7. (a) What comparisons does the speaker use for the birches? (b) What can you infer from this about the speaker's feelings about the birches?

Analyze and Evaluate

8. (a) In describing the boy who lives "too far from town to learn baseball," whom is the speaker really describing? (b) What kinds of activities might swinging on birches represent?

9. **Big Idea** New Poetics Why, in "Birches," does Frost compare life to a pathless wood? Is this is an effective simile? Why or why not?

10. **Connect to Today** Do people today create "walls" between each other? Explain.

Vocabulary Practice

Practice with Synonyms With a partner, match each boldfaced vocabulary word below with its synonym. You will not use all the answer choices. Use a thesaurus or dictionary to check your answers.

1. enamel   a. bushes
2. bracken   b. pottery
3. poise   c. glaze
                d. rough
                e. balance

LOG ON ▶ **Literature** Online

Selection Resources For Selection Quizzes, eFlashcards, and Reading-Writing Connection activities, go to glencoe.com and enter QuickPass code GLA9800u5.

Literary Element

Frost imitates the rhythm of natural speech. He sometimes starts a line with a stressed syllable, and sometimes with an unstressed syllable.

Vocabulary

1. c **2.** a **3.** e

Reading Strategy

1. Both are farmers. The speaker of "Mending Wall" has a sense of humor; the speaker of "Birches" is nostalgic.

2. The tone of "Mending Wall" is lighthearted; that of "Birches" is thoughtful.

Winter Forest, 1991. Gerrit Greve.

Stopping by Woods on a Snowy Evening

Robert Frost

Whose woods these are I think I know.
His house is in the village though;
He will not see me stopping here
To watch his woods fill up with snow.

5 My little horse must think it queer
To stop without a farmhouse near
Between the woods and frozen lake
The darkest evening of the year.

He gives his harness bells a shake
10 To ask if there is some mistake.
The only other sound's the sweep
Of easy wind and downy flake.

The woods are lovely, dark and deep.
But I have promises to keep,
15 And miles to go before I sleep,
And miles to go before I sleep.

Compare and Contrast Speakers *What might "sleep" mean to the speaker?*

Reading Strategy   1

Compare and Contrast Speakers Answer: *"Sleep" might refer to the speaker's death.*

Ask: What conflicting feelings does the speaker reveal in the last stanza of the poem? *(He would like to stay and look at the woods, but he also feels he must meet his obligations.)*

APPROACHING **Ask:** What does the speaker want to do? *(stay in the woods and watch the snow fall)* What does the speaker have to do? *(keep a promise by traveling miles before bed time)*

View the Art

This image captures the poem's setting of dim, snowy woods.
Ask: How might a scene like this tempt a visitor to stay? *(Its mystery and peacefulness draw the visitor in, tempting him or her to walk deep into the woods.)*

> For activities related to this selection, see Unit 5 Teaching Resources Book, pp. 125–134.

English Learners

DIFFERENTIATED INSTRUCTION

Beginning Students may be confused by the syntax in the first line. Explain that *whose* is not a question word as they may expect. For clarity, have them read the sentence in normal word order, starting with the words "I think . . . ." *(I think I know whose woods these are.)*

Intermediate Show students how to mark the rhyme scheme of the poem. For example, *aaba, bbcb, ccdc, dddd*. Additionally, point out that Frost uses repetition in the final two lines. Read the poem aloud for students. Then have students echo your reading of line groupings, using the punctuation as a guide to determine units of meaning. **Ask:** What do you think is the effect of the sounds in this poem?

After You Read

Assess

1. Answers will vary.
2. (a) The owner lives in the village, so he will not see the speaker stop to view the woods. (b) The speaker may think that the owner would consider his actions foolish.
3. (a) The horse must find it odd to stop away from a farmhouse. (b) The horse's instinct is for food and shelter; the speaker wants to pause and enjoy his surroundings.
4. (a) *Lovely, dark,* and *deep* (b) Mystery and calm
5. The setting of dark woods and "frozen lake" on a winter evening adds to a sense of isolation.
6. (a) The speaker has obligations to fulfill. (b) When one reads line 15, one interprets it literally—the speaker has miles to travel to get home. The repetition of the line prompts one to extend the interpretation—perhaps the speaker is referring to what he must do before his death.
7. Life's mystery and the isolation of the individual
8. He seems familiar with the surroundings described in the poem.

Design

Definition: the arrangement of elements or details in a product or work of art

Synonyms: plan, outline, motif, blueprint

Antonyms: disorganization, randomness

Sentence: The design for the proposed memorial was impressive, but expensive.

After You Read

Respond and Think Critically

Respond and Interpret

1. Which lines from the poem did you find most powerful or meaningful? Explain.
2. (a) Where does the owner of the woods live, and what will he not see? (b) Why might the speaker care that the owner will not see this?
3. (a) According to the speaker, what must the horse think? (b) How might the horse's instincts differ from those of the speaker?
4. (a) What adjectives describe the woods in line 13? (b) What **mood** do these words create?

Analyze and Evaluate

5. How does the **setting** of the poem contribute to its meaning?

Literary Element Rhyme Scheme

"Mending Wall" and "Birches" are written in blank verse, but "Stopping by Woods on a Snowy Evening" has end rhymes and a rhyme scheme.

1. What is the rhyme scheme in stanzas 1–3? What is the effect of repeating a sound from each stanza in the one that follows it?
2. How does the change in rhyme scheme in the last stanza reinforce the meaning of the poem?

Reading Strategy Compare and Contrast Speakers

The speaker in "Stopping by Woods" is different from the speaker in "Mending Wall." How would you describe this difference? Support your response with specific examples from the poems.

 Literature Online

Selection Resources For Selection Quizzes, eFlash-cards, and Reading-Writing Connection activities, go to glencoe.com and enter QuickPass code GLA9800u5.

6. (a) Why does the speaker not embrace the peaceful escape offered by the woods? (b) How does the **repetition** in the final lines affect their meaning?

Connect

7. **Big Idea** **New Poetics** What themes of modern poetry does "Stopping by Woods on a Snowy Evening" reflect?
8. **Connect to the Author** Frost often used his own experiences and observations in his poems. What evidence of that do you see in "Stopping by Woods on a Snowy Evening"?

Academic Vocabulary

*The **design** of "Stopping by Woods on a Snowy Evening" enhances the poem's meaning.*

Design is an academic word. More familiar words that are similar in meaning are plan, outline, diagram, and blueprint.

To study this word further, fill out the graphic organizer below.

definition	synonyms
antonyms	sentence/image

For more on academic vocabulary, see pages 53–54.

 Writing

Write a Dialogue Imagine that the narrator and the owner of the woods cross paths. What would they say to each other? Write a dialogue in which you convey their respective attitudes toward the woods, and toward life. Use your interpretation of the poem's theme or themes to guide you.

Literary Element

1. The rhyme scheme is *aaba bbcb ccdc.* The effect is to tie the stanzas together and lead to the final stanza, which expresses the poem's theme.
2. The four rhymed lines of the last stanza signal that it sums up the poem's meaning.

Reading Strategy

The speaker in "Mending Wall" has a light-hearted attitude toward life whereas the speaker in "Stopping by Woods" is more serious and weary.

Writing

Students' dialogues should include two characters with differing views and an interpretation of the poem.

Acquainted with the Night

Robert Frost

I have been one acquainted with the night.
I have walked out in rain—and back in rain.
I have outwalked the furthest city light.

I have looked down the saddest city lane.
5 I have passed by the watchman on his beat
And dropped my eyes, unwilling to explain.

I have stood still and stopped the sound of feet
When far away an interrupted cry
Came over houses from another street,

1

10 But not to call me back or say good-bye;
And further still at an unearthly height,
One luminary¹ clock against the sky

Proclaimed² the time was neither wrong nor right.
I have been one acquainted with the night.

Park Row, Leeds, England, 1882. John Atkinson Grimshaw. Oil on canvas. Private collection.

---

1. *Luminary* means "giving light."
2. *Proclaimed* means "declared publicly."

> Compare and Contrast Speakers *What does this line tell you about the speaker's mood?* **2**

ROBERT FROST **723**

Teach

Reading Strategy   1

Compare and Contrast Speakers **Ask:** What is the speaker doing in lines 7–10? *(stopping to listen to a cry in the distance—a cry not addressed to the speaker)* What does this imply about the speaker's situation in life? *(The speaker is alone.)*

Reading Strategy   2

Compare and Contrast Speakers **Answer:** *The speaker feels isolated, outside of time.*

(APPROACHING) Write the following on the board: *not to call me back, good-bye, unearthly, luminary clock, night.* **Ask:** How do these words and phrases make you feel? *(lonely, disconnected from reality)*

View the Art ★

John Atkinson Grimshaw (1836–1893) was a self-taught artist undeterred by his parents' strong disapproval of his desire to paint. **Ask:** What is the mood of the painting, and how does Grimshaw achieve this mood? *(Grimshaw contrasts warm colors with cool colors and uses light and shadow to create an ominous mood.)*

Approaching Level

DIFFERENTIATED INSTRUCTION

 Emerging Remind students that the speaker in a poem is the "voice" that talks to readers. The speaker is not necessarily the writer. Ask students to work in small groups to characterize the speaker in this poem, referring to specific lines from the poem to support their ideas. **Ask:** What do you know about the speaker from what is stated directly? *(The speaker has walked alone at night before.)* What can you infer from what is not stated? *(Students may infer that the speaker walks alone to clear his or her mind.)* Have a student from each group share the group's findings with the class.

 For activities related to this selection, see Unit 5 Teaching Resources Book, pp. 135–144.

After You Read

Assess

1. Answers will vary.
2. (a) The speaker has walked at night, in the rain, to the edge of the city. In line 4, he says he has seen "the saddest city lane." (b) Students may suggest that he has something on his mind and cannot sleep.
3. (a) Drops his eyes (b) Perhaps he doesn't want to have to explain why he is out alone at night.
4. (a) That the time is neither right nor wrong (b) The time doesn't matter; it will not change the speaker's circumstances.
5. (a) Empty and depressing (b) It might symbolize loneliness or despair.
6. He wants to emphasize the speaker's isolation and loneliness.
7. The images of darkness, sad city lanes, and a distant cry that no one but the speaker seems to notice create a mood of loneliness and isolation.
8. Frost explores the theme of the isolation and the loneliness of the individual.
9. Students may say Frost was contrasting his work on nature by writing a poem about city life.

Academic Vocabulary

Round characterizations and witty dialogue are the most appealing features in a literary work to me.

> For additional assessment, see Assessment Resources, pp. 207–208.

724

After You Read

Respond and Think Critically

Respond and Interpret

1. Which image from this poem is most memorable?
2. (a) When and where has the speaker walked in lines 1–3? What has he seen in line 4? (b) Why might the speaker be out walking alone at night?
3. (a) What does the speaker do when passing the watchman? (b) Why does the speaker choose to do this?
4. (a) What does the clock proclaim? (b) Why does the speaker not reveal the exact time?

Analyze and Evaluate

5. (a) What is the night in this poem like? (b) What do you think "the night" **symbolizes**?
6. Why does Frost repeat line 1 in line 14?
7. How does Frost create a **mood** of loneliness or isolation in this poem?

Connect

8. **Big Idea** New Poetics What Modernist themes does Frost explore in this poem?
9. **Connect to the Author** In many ways, this poem is a departure from Frost's nature-focused work. Why might Frost have chosen to write about the city as well?

Literary Element Rhyme Scheme

In "Acquainted with the Night," Frost uses a traditional form, derived from Italian poetry, known as *terza rima.*

1. Based on stanzas 1–4, what is the rhyme scheme of terza rima?
2. What effects does Frost create in the final stanza?

Reading Strategy Compare and Contrast Speakers

Unlike the speakers in "Mending Wall," "Birches," and "Stopping by Woods on a Snowy Evening," the speaker in "Acquainted with the Night" is in an urban setting.

1. How would you characterize the speaker in this poem?
2. What other characteristics set this speaker apart from the other speakers created by Frost?

 Literature Online

Selection Resources For Selection Quizzes, eFlashcards, and Reading-Writing Connection activities, go to glencoe.com and enter QuickPass code GLA9800u5.

Academic Vocabulary

In "Acquainted with the Night," parallelism and rhyme are **features** *that contribute to the mood of the poem.*

Feature is an academic word. You might say loyalty and trustworthiness are **features** of a friend who will stand by you in any situation.

To further explore the meaning of this word, answer the following question: What **features** of a literary work are most appealing to you and why?

For more on academic vocabulary, see pages 53–54.

Writing

Write a List The speaker in this poem describes specific images to convey his feelings about night and to create a desired mood. Think about your feelings toward a specific time of day. Then brainstorm a list of specific images that capture those feelings. Pay attention to the mood you want your images to evoke.

Literary Element

1. It is *aba bcb cdc dad.*
2. The final stanza's two lines rhyme with (and the second one repeats) the first line of the poem. This gives the poem a circular structure.

Reading Strategy

1. He is lonely and avoids human contact.
2. He is self-absorbed.

Writing

Students' lists should reveal a particular time of the day and include strong, specific images.

A **narrative poem** tells a story. Like fictional prose, narrative poems often include story elements such as dialogue, description, characterization, plot, and conflict. Narrative poems also contain poetic elements such as line breaks, stanzas, and rhyme. As you read, ask yourself, Why does Frost tell this story in verse form?

Characterization is the techniques a writer uses to develop the personality of a character. In **direct characterization,** the narrator makes explicit statements about a character. In **indirect characterization,** the writer reveals a character through his or her words and actions and through those of other characters. As you read, ask yourself, What details does Frost use to convey the hired man's personality?

Focus

Summary

Silas, an elderly man, has returned to the farm of Warren and Mary, who have hired him in the past. Warren is concerned because Silas has often been lured away by other employers when Warren most needs his help. He is not convinced that they should take Silas in. Mary is concerned about preserving Silas's dignity. She argues that Silas is sick and weak, has no place to go, and considers their farm his home.

For summaries in languages other than English, see Unit 5 Teaching Resources Book, pp. 145–150.

The Death of the Hired Man

Robert Frost

> Mary sat musing[1] on the lamp-flame at the table
> Waiting for Warren. When she heard his step,
> She ran on tip-toe down the darkened passage
> To meet him in the doorway with the news
> 5   And put him on his guard. "Silas is back."
> She pushed him outward with her through the door
> And shut it after her. "Be kind," she said.
> She took the market things from Warren's arms
> And set them on the porch, then drew him down
> 10   To sit beside her on the wooden steps.
> "When was I ever anything but kind to him?
> But I'll not have the fellow back," he said.
> "I told him so last haying, didn't I?
> If he left then, I said, that ended it.

---

1. *Musing* means "meditating" or "pondering."

Narrative Poetry *What does this line of dialogue suggest about Mary's values?*

Teach

Literary Element 1

Narrative Poetry Answer:
It suggests that Mary is a kind person and believes people should be kind to one another. **Ask:** What do Mary's actions say about how she expects Warren to react to the news of Silas's return? *(Mary pushes Warren out the door because she expects Warren to react badly to this news.)*

Selection Skills

Literary Elements
- Narrative Poetry (SE pp. 725, 729, 733; TE p. 726)
- Blank Verse (SE p. 733)

The Death of the Hired Man

Writing Skills/Grammar
- Biographical Narrative (SE p. 734)
- Misplaced Modifiers (SE p. 734)
- Build Background (TE p. 726)
- Analyze a Poem (TE p. 730)

Reading Skills
- Evaluate Characterization (SE pp. 725–727, 731, 733; TE pp. 728, 730)
- Analyze Persuasion (TE p. 728)

Vocabulary Skills
- Word Usage (SE p. 733)
- Meaning in Context (TE pp. 727, 731)

Listening/Speaking/Viewing Skills
- Analyze Art (SE p. 730; TE p. 726)
- Group Activity (SE p. 732)

Teach

Narrative Poetry Call students' attention to the single and double quotation marks in lines 15–30. **Ask:** Why is the poem punctuated like this? *(The double quotation marks indicate that Warren is speaking. The single quotation marks enclose words that he is quoting from previous conversations.)*

APPROACHING Have students mark the double and single quotation marks with sticky notes, then read the lines aloud with their partners. One student should read the lines within double quotation marks, and the other student the lines within single quotation marks.

Reading Strategy | 2

Evaluate Characterization
Answer: *Silas leaves during haying time, when he is needed most, and then comes back in winter, when the haying is done.*

View the Photograph

Ask: How does this photograph relate to the poem? *(It shows an elderly man who could represent the character Silas.)* How would you describe the man in this photo? *(He looks sad and alone.)*

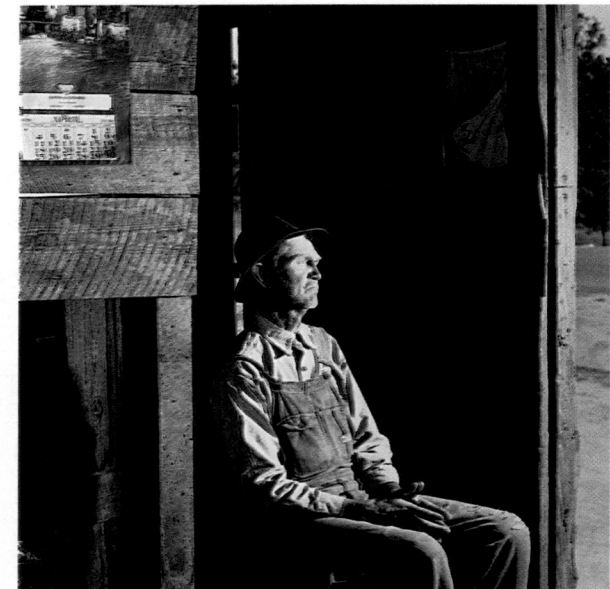

Meade Family (detail), 1941.
Jack Delano. Silver gelatin print.

15 What good is he? Who else will harbor[2] him
    At his age for the little he can do?
    What help he is there's no depending on.
    Off he goes always when I need him most.
    He thinks he ought to earn a little pay,
20 Enough at least to buy tobacco with,
    So he won't have to beg and be beholden.[3]
    'All right,' I say, 'I can't afford to pay
    Any fixed wages, though I wish I could.'
    'Someone else can.' 'Then someone else will have to.'
25 I shouldn't mind his bettering himself
    If that was what it was. You can be certain,
    When he begins like that, there's someone at him
    Trying to **coax** him off with pocket-money,—
    In haying time, when any help is scarce.
30 In winter he comes back to us. I'm done."

| 1 |

---

2. *Harbor* means "to give shelter or protection to."
3. *Beholden* means "obligated" or "indebted."

Evaluate Characterization *What are Warren's reasons for not wanting Silas back?* | 2 |

Vocabulary

coax (kōks) *v.* to persuade gently

Writing Practice

SPIRAL REVIEW **Build Background Say:** This narrative poem tells the story of an elderly man who returns to his former employer's farm because he has nowhere else to go. The farmer and his wife disagree about taking the man in.

Have students write brief essays responding to these questions: How are the elderly in our society treated? What should happen to elderly people who cannot care for themselves? After students read the poem, have them compare their essays with Warren's and Mary's arguments about Silas.

"Sh! not so loud: he'll hear you," Mary said.

"I want him to: he'll have to soon or late."

"He's worn out. He's asleep beside the stove.
When I came up from Rowe's I found him here,
35 Huddled against the barn-door fast asleep,
A miserable sight, and frightening, too—
You needn't smile—I didn't recognize him—
I wasn't looking for him—and he's changed.
Wait till you see."

40   "Where did you say he'd been?"

"He didn't say. I dragged him to the house,
And gave him tea and tried to make him smoke.
I tried to make him talk about his travels.
Nothing would do: he just kept nodding off."
45 "What did he say? Did he say anything?"

"But little."

              "Anything? Mary, confess
He said he'd come to ditch⁴ the meadow for me."

"Warren!"   **3**

50   "But did he? I just want to know."

"Of course he did. What would you have him say?
Surely you wouldn't grudge the poor old man
Some humble way to save his self-respect.
He added, if you really care to know,
55 He meant to clear the upper pasture, too.   **4**
That sounds like something you have heard before?
Warren, I wish you could have heard the way
He jumbled everything. I stopped to look
Two or three times—he made me feel so queer⁵—
60 To see if he was talking in his sleep.
He ran on⁶ Harold Wilson—you remember—

_____

4. Here, *ditch* means "to dig long, narrow channels." These channels, or
   ditches, are often used for drainage or irrigation.
5. *Queer* means "odd" or "strange."
6. *Ran on* means "talked continuously about."

Evaluate Characterization *What is happening to Silas?*   **5**

Literary Element | 3

Narrative Poetry Ask: What emotion does Mary convey when she exclaims "Warren!" in line 49? *(Possible answers: surprise; anger; reproof; warning; disappointment)*

Vocabulary | 4

Meaning in Context In line 55, Mary uses the verb *clear*. This word can refer to various farm activities, including the removal of trees, shrubs, and weeds or of the remains of harvested crops. In this case, it most likely refers to the removal of the rocks common in New England soil.

(ENGLISH LEARNERS) Have students write the word *clear* in the center of a word web and write the multiple meanings of it in the radiating circles, referring to a dictionary as necessary. Then help students determine the correct meaning for the word in line 55.

Reading Strategy | 5

Evaluate Characterization Answer: *Students may say that he is suffering from mental confusion associated with old age.*

Advanced Learners

DIFFERENTIATED INSTRUCTION

Musical Interpretation Musical students will find it interesting to analyze this poem in terms of musical moods. Have students find music to accompany excerpts of "The Death of the Hired Man." Encourage them to define and illustrate through music such elements as mood, tone, characters' thoughts and feelings, and plot. Then have them prepare multimedia presentations, combining text with sound, to explain their musical choices to the class.

Teach

Reading Strategy | 1

Evaluate Characterization

Read the bracketed passage aloud. **Ask:** What does Silas's concern about the past say about his state of mind? *(Students may say that his fixation on the past shows that age is causing him to be confused.)* Do you agree with Mary's statement in lines 79–80? *(Many students will say that they too have had this experience.)*

Reading Strategy | 2

Evaluate Characterization

Ask: What is your opinion of Silas's "one accomplishment"? *(Students may say the accomplishment is not very impressive and that it is sad that this is all Silas has to feel proud of and to teach.)*

[APPROACHING] Have pairs use two-column charts to list the ways that creating a perfect load of hay is both a grand and a sad accomplishment.

The boy you had in haying four years since.
He's finished school, and teaching in his college.
Silas declares you'll have to get him back.
65 He says they two will make a team for work:
Between them they will lay this farm as smooth!
The way he mixed that in with other things.
He thinks young Wilson a likely lad, though daft[7]
On education—you know how they fought
70 All through July under the blazing sun,
Silas up on the cart to build the load,
Harold along beside to pitch it on."

"Yes, I took care to keep well out of earshot."

"Well, those days trouble Silas like a dream.
75 You wouldn't think they would. How some things linger![8]
Harold's young college boy's assurance piqued[9] him.
After so many years he still keeps finding
Good arguments he sees he might have used.
I sympathize.[10] I know just how it feels
80 To think of the right thing to say too late.
Harold's associated in his mind with Latin.
He asked me what I thought of Harold's saying
He studied Latin like the violin
Because he liked it—that an argument!
85 He said he couldn't make the boy believe
He could find water with a hazel prong[11]—
Which showed how much good school had ever done him.
He wanted to go over that. But most of all
He thinks if he could have another chance
90 To teach him how to build a load of hay—"

"I know, that's Silas' one accomplishment.
He bundles every forkful in its place,
And tags and numbers it for future reference,
So he can find and easily dislodge[12] it
95 In the unloading. Silas does that well.
He takes it out in bunches like big birds' nests.
You never see him standing on the hay
He's trying to lift, straining to lift himself."

---

7. *Daft* means "foolish."
8. *Linger* means "to continue to exist" or "to endure."
9. *Piqued* means "aroused a feeling of anger or resentment in."
10. *Sympathize* means "to share in or to agree with the feelings or ideas of another."
11. A *hazel prong* is a stick believed to indicate the presence of underground water.
12. *Dislodge* means "to move or to force from a position."

Reading Practice

SMALL GROUP

Analyze Persuasion Point out to students that Mary and Warren are each speaking to persuade the other of a point of view. Mary works to persuade Warren to show compassion for Silas. Warren works to persuade Mary that Silas needs to go. Have students work with partners to analyze the persuasive techniques used by each speaker. Tell students to consider diction, syntax, patterns of organization, evidence, and appeals to ethics, logic, and emotion. One student should focus on Mary and the other student should focus on Warren. Have students record the results of their analyses in two-column charts and present their charts to the class.

"He thinks if he could teach him that, he'd be
100   Some good perhaps to someone in the world.
He hates to see a boy the fool of books.
Poor Silas, so concerned for other folk,
And nothing to look backward to with pride,
And nothing to look forward to with hope,
105   So now and never any different."

Part of a moon was falling down the west,
Dragging the whole sky with it to the hills.
Its light poured softly in her lap. She saw it
And spread her apron to it. She put out her hand
110   Among the harp-like morning-glory¹³ strings,
Taut¹⁴ with the dew from garden bed to eaves,
As if she played unheard some tenderness
That wrought¹⁵ on him beside her in the night.
"Warren," she said, "he has come home to die:
115   You needn't be afraid he'll leave you this time."

"Home," he mocked gently.

                        "Yes, what else but home?
It all depends on what you mean by home.
Of course he's nothing to us, any more
120   Than was the hound that came a stranger to us
Out of the woods, worn out upon the trail."

"Home is the place where, when you have to go there,
They have to take you in."

                        "I should have called it
125   Something you somehow haven't to deserve."

Warren leaned out and took a step or two,
Picked up a little stick, and brought it back

---

13. A *morning glory* is a vine that produces trumpet-shaped flowers.
    Gardeners often position a lattice or strings for a vine to grow along.
14. *Taut* means "stretched tight."
15. *Wrought* means "worked."

New Poetics *How is Silas depicted in these lines?*   **3**

Narrative Poetry *What does the description in these lines reveal about Mary?*   **4**

Narrative Poetry *What is the difference between Mary's view of a person's home and Warren's?*   **5**

Big Idea	3

New Poetics Answer: *Silas is depicted as a man who has achieved nothing of importance and who has no prospects for the future.*

Literary Element	4

Narrative Poetry Answer: *Mary is kind and tender-hearted, and she is able to influence Warren with her tenderness.*

Literary Element	5

Narrative Poetry Answer: *In Warren's view, "Home is the place where, when you have to go there, / They have to take you in." He implies a home only exists where there is a sense of obligation. Mary is more generous, arguing that home is "Something you somehow haven't to deserve."*

English Learners

DIFFERENTIATED INSTRUCTION

Intermediate Have students work in groups of three, with each student completing a character web. One student will focus on Mary, one on Warren, and one on Silas. Tell students to write the character's name in the center circle of the web. In the radiating circles, have students write what they know about the character. Remind students to examine the narration, dialogue, and action to glean information about each character. Then have students use the information in their character webs to orally describe the characters in complete sentences.

Teach

Evaluate Characterization

Ask: Why do you think Silas has not asked his brother for help? (*Possible answers: Silas is too proud to ask his brother; he may believe that his brother would refuse him.*) What does Mary mean by her statement in line 140 that Silas's brother "may be better than appearances"? (*She means that he may be kinder than he appears to be and he may take Silas in.*)

(APPROACHING) Tell students that "appearances" refers to the way that Silas's brother appears or looks to other people. **Ask:** How might a wealthy bank director appear to people like Mary and Warren? (*He may appear cold-hearted, removed, or arrogant.*)

View the Art ★

Answer: *The moods of both the painting and Mary reflect a sense that certain things, like the cosmos and death, are out of our control.*

Daniel Lang (1935–) began his career as an etcher and draftsman. Many of his paintings are landscapes, which he has "invented" on the basis of sketches and photographs he has taken in his travels.

Moonlight in Vermont. 1982. Daniel Lang. Oil on canvas, 48 x 72 in. Collection of Harrison Young, Beijing, China. Reproduced in *Spirit of Place* by John Arthur.

View the Art An avid world traveler, Daniel Lang bases many of his landscapes on sketches and snapshots from his trips. How does the mood of this painting compare with Mary's in lines 170–171? ★

> And broke it in his hand and tossed it by.
> "Silas has better claim on us you think
> 130 Than on his brother? Thirteen little miles
> As the road winds would bring him to his door.
> Silas has walked that far no doubt to-day.
> Why didn't he go there? His brother's rich,
> A somebody—director in the bank."
>
> 135 "He never told us that."
>
>   "We know it though."
>
> "I think his brother ought to help, of course.
> I'll see to that if there is need. He ought of right
> To take him in, and might be willing to—
> 140 He may be better than appearances.
> But have some pity on Silas. Do you think
> If he had any pride in claiming **kin**

1

Vocabulary

kin (kin) *n.* relatives, or a group of people with common ancestry

730   UNIT 5   BEGINNINGS OF THE MODERN AGE

Writing Practice

Analyze a Poem Frost wrote a number of dramatic poems including "The Mountain," "A Hundred Collars," "Home Burial," "Blueberries," "The Generations of Men," "The Housekeeper," and "The Fear" that reveal characters' personalities through dialogue, monologue, and description. Have students read some dramatic poems by Frost and write analyses of them.

Encourage students to compare and contrast the poems they select with "The Death of the Hired Man." Invite volunteers to read aloud the poems they selected and present their analyses.

Or anything he looked for from his brother,
He'd keep so still about him all this time?"

145   "I wonder what's between them."

                            "I can tell you.
Silas is what he is—we wouldn't mind him—
But just the kind that kinsfolk can't abide.[16]
He never did a thing so very bad.
150 He don't know why he isn't quite as good
As anybody. Worthless though he is,
He won't be made ashamed to please his brother."

        "I can't think Si ever hurt anyone."

        "No, but he hurt my heart the way he lay
155 And rolled his old head on that sharp-edged chair-back.
He wouldn't let me put him on the lounge.   **2**
You must go in and see what you can do.
I made the bed up for him there to-night.
You'll be surprised at him—how much he's broken.
160 His working days are done; I'm sure of it."

        "I'd not be in a hurry to say that."

        "I haven't been. Go, look, see for yourself.
But, Warren, please remember how it is:
He's come to help you ditch the meadow.
165 He has a plan. You mustn't laugh at him.
He may not speak of it, and then he may.
I'll sit and see if that small sailing cloud
Will hit or miss the moon."

                  It hit the moon.
170 Then there were three there, making a dim row,
The moon, the little silver cloud, and she.

Warren returned—too soon, it seemed to her,
Slipped to her side, caught up her hand and waited.

        "Warren?" she questioned.

175   "Dead," was all he answered.

---

16. *Abide* means "to put up with" or "to tolerate."

Evaluate Characterization   *Is Mary a good judge of Silas's character? Explain.*   **3**

Teach

Vocabulary   2

Meaning in Context The word *lounge* in line 156 refers to a sofa, often with a headrest and sometimes with no back. Consequently, it can be used as a bed.

Reading Strategy   3

Evaluate Characterization
Answer: *Most students will probably say that Mary is a good judge of Silas's character. She realizes that even though he has never accomplished much, he still has enough pride to prevent his asking his brother for help.*

Writer's Technique ☆

Diction By the words he chooses for her dialogue, Frost characterizes Mary as a woman who speaks in plain, often one-syllable, words. In line 150, the ungrammatical "He don't" achieves two purposes: It shows that Mary is a country woman who speaks nonstandard English, probably because she has not had much education, and it sustains the iambic rhythm of the poem. **Ask:** What other examples of diction characterize Mary as an uneducated country woman? (*Possible answer: kinsfolk*)

To check students' understanding of the selection, see Unit 5 Teaching Resources Book, p. 154.

Approaching Level

DIFFERENTIATED INSTRUCTION 🐾

SMALL GROUP

Established Students may have difficulty keeping track of who is speaking in this poem. To help them identify speakers, create an annotated script of the poem, marking the text according to the speakers and the narrator. Cross out the dialogue tags such as "she questioned" and so on. Give each student a copy of the script, and form groups of three students each. Have group members take the parts of Mary, Warren, and the narrator and read the poem aloud two or three times. Invite volunteers to perform readings aloud for the whole class.

After You Read

Assess

1. Students may say that they admire Mary's kindhearted and generous nature; they may like Warren, who is sensible but not unkind; and they feel pity for Silas.

2. (a) She meets Warren at the door, tells him Silas is back, pushes him onto the porch steps, and says, "Be kind." (b) She knows what Warren will say when he hears about Silas.

3. (a) Worn out and miserable (b) He knows that Silas is undependable.

4. (a) Wilson once worked with Silas on Warren's farm. Silas dislikes his love of books and learning. (b) Silas feels he is not as good as others; Harold reminds him of his failings.

5. (a) He "has come home to die." (b) It would shame him.

6. Mary is kind and soft-hearted; Warren is practical and unwilling to let people use him.

7. Students' answers will vary but should include reasons for their opinions.

8. It suggests that Warren feels some sympathy for Silas and is concerned about Mary's reaction to his death.

9. His reading illustrates the theme of isolation and loneliness. Some students may agree that Silas has no roots; others may say he has ties to Mary and Warren.

10. Students' answers will vary, but they should state the attitude in the poem that they think reflects society's treatment of the elderly and support their answers with real life examples.

732

After You Read

Respond and Think Critically

Respond and Interpret

1. How do you feel about the poem's characters?

2. (a)What does Mary do and say upon Warren's return in lines 1–10? (b)Why does she feel the need to put Warren "on his guard"?

3. (a)How does Silas look when Mary first sees him? (b)Why does Warren refuse to believe that Silas will tackle the chores he says he will?

4. (a)Who is Harold Wilson, and why does Silas dislike him? (b)What do Silas's feelings about Harold reveal about Silas's personality?

5. (a)According to Mary, why has Silas come to the house? (b)Why does Silas avoid asking his brother for help?

Analyze and Evaluate

6. Based on lines 1–30, how would you describe the differences between Mary and Warren?

7. In this poem Frost gives two different definitions of home. Which one do you prefer? Why?

8. What does the end of the poem suggest about Warren's feelings toward Silas?

Connect

9. **Big Idea** New Poetics "The Death of the Hired Man," contends scholar C. M. Bowra, "is about the pathos of men who have no roots and no ties and no firm grip on life." Which of the themes of modern poetry does Bowra's reading illustrate?

10. **Connect to Today** Which of the attitudes in the poem best reflects how our society treats elderly people?

Daily Life & Culture

New England in the Early 1900s

In the year 1900, when Robert Frost was twenty-six, most people in rural New England had neither electricity nor indoor plumbing. They heated their homes with a stove, often set up in the living room. Those fortunate enough to own a telephone shared a "party line" with several others. To make a call, a person first had to dial the operator. If there was someone else already on the line, the caller had to wait.

Boys and girls in rural areas combined schooling with chores at home. After leaving school at about age fourteen, boys often worked as farm laborers. Some became apprentices and learned trades or worked in stores. When they were not in school, girls helped with household chores such as cooking, sewing, and making cheese or butter.

Although a few people owned cars, horses were the usual method of transportation. They pulled wagons, carriages, and even fire engines and hearses. Of course, no one in 1900 had ever flown in a plane, listened to a radio, played a video game, or visited a mall.

Group Activity Discuss the following questions with your classmates.

1. How has life changed since 1900, and why?

2. Is today's society a better place to live compared with the early 1900s? Support your opinion.

Daily Life & Culture

1. Students may focus on technological changes and on the broadening of educational opportunities.

2. Some students may agree, citing lower infant mortality, longer lives, and technology. Those who disagree may cite more pollution and less time with one's family.

 For additional assessment, see Assessment Resources, pp. 209–210.

Literary Element | Narrative Poetry

In "The Death of the Hired Man," Frost tells the story of Silas, Mary, and Warren through dialogue, narration, and description.

1. How is this poem similar to a play?

2. Do you think this poem would have been as powerful if Frost had revealed Silas's personality through description only instead of dialogue and description together? Explain.

3. How does the language used in the dialogue between Mary and Warren differ from that used in the descriptive passages?

Review: Blank Verse

As you learned when studying the poems "Mending Wall" and "Birches," **blank verse** is unrhymed poetry that is written in a rhythmic pattern called **iambic pentameter.** In iambic pentameter, each line has five feet, or basic units of measurement of a line of metrical poetry; each foot contains an unstressed syllable followed by a stressed syllable. Pauses do not always come at the ends of lines but wherever they make sense.

Partner Activity With two classmates, read aloud the first fifty lines of "The Death of the Hired Man." One person should read the narrative or descriptive passages; the other two should read the lines of Mary and Warren. After your reading, discuss how iambic pentameter captures the cadences and rhythms of ordinary speech.

LOG ON ▶ **Literature** Online

Selection Resources For Selection Quizzes, eFlashcards, and Reading-Writing Connection activities, go to glencoe.com and enter QuickPass code GLA9800u5.

Reading Strategy | Evaluate Characterization

In "The Death of the Hired Man," Frost uses indirect characterization. Simply put, he shows rather than tells, letting the reader draw his or her own inferences about the characters from the details provided in the poem. Remarkably, though Silas remains offstage, the reader learns much about this hired man. Seeing him through Warren's and Mary's eyes, the reader learns about Silas's physical condition, his work habits, his interaction with Harold Wilson, his estrangement from his brother, and his motivation for his final return to the farm. Through his choice of details, Frost attempts to bring Silas to life in the reader's imagination.

1. Is Silas a realistic, well-developed character? Support your answer.

2. What does Frost accomplish by keeping Silas offstage?

Vocabulary Practice

Practice with Word Usage Respond to these statements to help you explore the meanings of vocabulary words from the selection.

1. Name people who make up your **kin** and describe their relation to you.

2. Describe an event in your life wherein you have **coaxed** someone or have been **coaxed.**

Academic Vocabulary

*Silas has come to Mary and Warren's house seeking a **task** in which he could be useful.*

Task is an academic word. More familiar words that are similar in meaning are *job, chore,* and *duty.*

To further explore the meaning of this word, complete this sentence: I enjoy **tasks** that _____, such as _____.

For more on academic vocabulary, see pages 53–54.

ROBERT FROST **733**

After You Read

Assess

Literary Analysis

1. Like a play, the poem has characters, dialogue, action, conflict, and a resolution.

2. Most students will say that the use of dialogue and description together is more powerful. The reader sees Silas through the eyes of Mary and Warren instead of learning about him from an impersonal narrator.

3. The dialogue is more informal and sometimes ungrammatical, reflecting the way two country people actually speak to each other.

Review: Blank Verse

Suggest that students record their reading and listen to the result before beginning the discussion.

You may wish to suggest that students tape-record readings of single paragraphs of prose works. (They might use "Remarks at Amherst College" on pages 735–738.) Have them compare the rhythm of the prose with the rhythm of Frost's blank verse.

Progress Check

Can students evaluate characterization?

If No → See Unit 5 Teaching Resources Book, p. 152.

Reading Strategy

1. Most students will say that Silas is a realistic and well-developed character. Frost reveals key details about his appearance and personality through his dealings with Mary, Warren, and others.

2. With Silas offstage, the reader gets the reactions of Mary and Warren.

Vocabulary

1. Students should name family members and identify how they are related to those people.

2. Students should mention a time they had to persuade someone to do something, or they were persuaded to do something.

Academic Vocabulary

Possible answer: I enjoy tasks that produce immediate results, such as cleaning my room and knitting.

After You Read

Assess

Writing

Students' poems should tell a story and include poetic elements such as line breaks, stanzas, and rhyme. Their poems should also incorporate strong, specific images.

Scoring Guide

Assess students' performance in the following categories using the scoring guide at the bottom of the page:

- Addresses all parts of the writing task.
- Character's life story is well narrated and characters are well fleshed out and developed.
- Describes setting and plot with concrete and sensory details.
- Employ sensory details and interior monologue to reinforce characterization.
- Provides a variety of sentence types; uses precise, descriptive language to convey certain moods.
- Follows English language conventions.

Respond Through Writing

Biographical Narrative

Apply Characterization In telling the story of Silas's life and death, Frost calls into question how our society values elderly people. Write a biographical narrative in verse form about someone you know. Your narrative poem should say something about how society treats that person's generation or age group, as Frost's does.

Understand the Task A **biographical narrative** is the story of a person's life written by someone other than the subject. **Narrative poetry** is verse that tells a story. In addition to conveying plot, setting, and characterization, narrative poetry also includes poetic elements, such as line breaks, stanzas, and rhyme.

Prewrite To stimulate your memory, review journal entries and flip through photo albums relating to your subject. Keep a list of images, ideas, and events you plan to include in your narrative. To help you stay organized, number the items on your list in the order you plan to present them in your narrative.

Draft As you record the important events in your subject's life story, remember to use concrete and sensory details that convey both characterization and appropriate mood. Below is a model you might use in writing your own narrative poem—it's the first stanza from Edna St. Vincent Millay's poem "That Courage That My Mother Had."

> The courage that my mother had
> Went with her, and is with her still:
> Rock from New England quarried;
> Now granite in a granite hill.

Revise Have a classmate read your poem and then ask him or her to describe its setting and plot. If your peer cannot give you an answer, or if the answer given is not what you intended, add concrete details to clarify these elements of your work. If you need to strengthen the characterization in your biographical narrative, incorporate an interior monologue to help depict your subject's inner thoughts.

Edit and Proofread Proofread your poem, correcting any errors in spelling, grammar, and punctuation. Use the Grammar Tip in the side column for help avoiding misplaced modifiers.

Scoring Guide	4	3	2	1
Task addressed	fully	mostly	partially	barely
Characterization	fully developed	somewhat developed	partially developed	not developed
Setting, Plot	well described with many details	somewhat described with some details	partially described with few details	not described
Sensory Details	well employed	employed	few employed	none
Language	varied, precise, thoughtful	varied, somewhat thoughtful	predictable, basic	not varied, limited
Convention errors	few or none	several	some	many

Remarks at
AMHERST COLLEGE

President John F. Kennedy

Pulitzer Prize Winner

Political Perspective

on *Robert Frost*

Learning Objectives

For pages 735–738

In studying this text, you will focus on the following objectives:

Literary Study: Making connections across literature.

Reading:
Analyzing informational text. Analyzing philosophical assumptions.

Set Purposes for Reading

As you read, ask yourself, What were the social and historical impacts of Robert Frost's poetry?

Build Background

In October 1963, President John F. Kennedy presented the following remarks at Amherst College, in Amherst, Massachusetts. The speech was given in honor of the groundbreaking of the Robert Frost Library, which was completed two years later. This would be one of Kennedy's last public appearances before his assassination less than a month later. Robert Frost, who died earlier in the year, had long been associated with Amherst College, having taught English there periodically throughout his career.

Reading Strategy Analyze Philosophical Assumptions

Analyzing philosophical assumptions involves gathering information to determine an author's implicit and explicit philosophical assumptions and beliefs about a subject. As you read, ask yourself, What does President Kennedy's speech reveal about his philosophical assumptions?

Mr. McCloy, President Plimpton, Mr. MacLeish,[1] *distinguished guests, ladies and gentlemen:*

I am very honored to be here with you on this occasion which means so much to this college and also means so much to art and the progress of the United States. This college is part of the United States. It belongs to it. So did Mr. Frost, in a large sense. And, therefore, I was privileged to accept the invitation somewhat rendered to me in the same way that Franklin Roosevelt rendered his invitation to Mr. MacLeish, the invitation which I received from Mr. McCloy.[2] The powers of the Presidency are often described. Its limitations should occasionally be remembered. And therefore when the Chairman of our Disarmament Advisory Committee, who has labored so long and hard, Governor Stevenson's[3] assistant during the very

---

1. John Jay *McCloy* (1895–1989), a diplomat and lawyer, served as an adviser to every president from Franklin Delano Roosevelt to Ronald Reagan. Calvin Hastings *Plimpton* was the president of Amherst College from 1960 to 1971. Archibald *MacLeish* (1892–1982) was a famed poet and playwright. MacLeish also served as a librarian of Congress and briefly as an assistant secretary of state.
2. Kennedy is referring to President Franklin Roosevelt's invitation to MacLeish to become a librarian of Congress.
3. Adlai *Stevenson* (1900–1965) served as governor of Illinois from 1948 to 1952 and as the U.S. delegate to the United Nations during the Kennedy administration. John McCloy served as Stevenson's assistant during the Cuban missile crisis.

JOHN F. KENNEDY **735**

Focus
Summary

In this speech honoring Robert Frost, President Kennedy emphasizes the responsibility of those who are privileged—such as students and alumni of Amherst College—to engage in public service. He praises Robert Frost for his contribution to the American spirit and emphasizes the importance of art in our culture. Kennedy concludes by outlining his vision for America.

Teach

Cultural History

"This College" Amherst College was established in 1821. One of its founders was Noah Webster, known for his *American Dictionary of the English Language*.

Originally Amherst was an all-male college, intended to train poor young men as ministers. Women were not admitted until 1975.

For an audio recording of this selection, use Listening Library Audio CD-ROM.

Readability Scores
Dale-Chall: 9.7
DRP: 6.5
Lexile: 1270

For activities related to this selection, see Unit 5 Teaching Resources Book, pp. 156–164.

English Learners

DIFFERENTIATED INSTRUCTION

 Intermediate Have students listen to a recording of the body of Kennedy's speech. Play the recording several times as students follow along with the text. Then have students work in pairs to identify and list the evidence that Kennedy presents to support the argument that those who lead a life of privilege have a responsibility to serve the national good.

Tell students to use simple sentences to orally critique or evaluate each of Kennedy's supporting points. **Ask:** Which points are convincing? Which points are not convincing? Why?

735

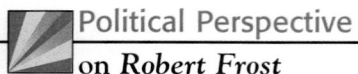
Teach

New Poetics Ask: How is this part of the speech by President Kennedy opposed to some characteristics of Modernism? *(Kennedy says that people should not remain isolated and concerned with only their private interests, whereas Modernism focused on the individual.)*

(APPROACHING) List attributes of Modernism on the board: individualism, disillusionment, and isolationism. Lead students to discuss how Kennedy speaks against these ideas.

Political History ☆

Cuban Missile Crisis On October 14, 1962, a U.S. spy plane photographed the building of nuclear-missile sites in communist Cuba by the Soviet Union. In response, President Kennedy set up a naval blockade to prevent more missiles from reaching Cuba and demanded that the Soviets remove the missiles already there.

For several days, the world seemed to be on the brink of nuclear war. Finally, on October 24, the Soviet ships headed for Cuba reversed their course. The Soviets agreed to withdraw the missiles if the United States promised never to invade Cuba.

President John F. Kennedy delivers a speech in 1962.

difficult days at the United Nations during the Cuban crisis, a public servant for so many years, asks or invites the President of the United States, there is only one response. So I am glad to be here.

Amherst has had many soldiers of the king since its first one, and some of them are here today: Mr. McCloy, who has long been a public servant; Jim Reed who is the Assistant Secretary of the Treasury; President Cole, who is now our Ambassador to Chile; Mr. Ramey, who is a Commissioner of the Atomic Energy Commission; Dick Reuter, who is head of the Food for Peace. These and scores of others down through the years have recognized the obligations of the advantages which the graduation from a college such as this places upon them to serve not only their private interest but the public interest as well.

Many years ago, Woodrow Wilson said, what good is a political party unless it is serving a great national purpose? And what good is a private college or university unless it is serving a great national purpose? The Library being constructed today, this college, itself—all of this, of course, was not done merely to give this school's graduates an advantage, an economic advantage, in the life struggle. It does do that. But in return for that, in return for the great opportunity which society gives the graduates of this and related schools, it seems to me incumbent[4] upon this and other schools' graduates to recognize their responsibility to the public interest.

Privilege is here, and with privilege goes responsibility. And I think, as your president said, that it must be a source of satisfaction to you that this school's graduates have recognized it. I hope that the students who are here now will also recognize it in the future. Although Amherst has been in the forefront of extending aid to needy and talented students, private colleges, taken as a whole, draw 50 percent of their students from the wealthiest 10 percent of our Nation. And even State universities and other public institutions derive 25 percent of their students from this group. In March 1962, persons of 18 years or older who had not completed high school made up 46 percent of the total labor force, and such persons comprised 64 percent of those who were unemployed. And in 1958, the lowest fifth of the families in the United States had 4½ percent of the total personal income, the highest fifth, 44½ percent. There is inherited wealth in this country and also inherited poverty. And unless the graduates of this college and other colleges like it who are given a running start in life—unless they are willing to put back into our society, those talents, the broad sympathy, the understanding, the compassion—unless they are willing to put those qualities back into the service of the Great Republic, then obviously the presuppositions upon which our democracy are based are bound to be fallible.

The problems which this country now faces are staggering, both at home and abroad. We

---

4. Here, *incumbent* means "imposed."

Research Practice

Statistics Have groups of students research whether education and income statistics have changed since 1958 and 1962. They should research these questions: What percentage of students in private colleges come from low-income homes? What percentage of students in state colleges come from low-income homes? What percentage of workers lack a high school diploma? What percentage of the unemployed lack a high school diploma? What percentage of the nation's total personal income belongs to the lowest one-fifth of the people? What percentage of the nation's total personal income belongs to the highest one-fifth of the people?

Have students present their findings in the form of charts, diagrams, or graphs.

need the service, in the great sense, of every educated man or woman to find 10 million jobs in the next 2½ years, to govern our relations—a country which lived in isolation for 150 years, and is now suddenly the leader of the free world—to govern our relations with over 100 countries, to govern those relations with success so that the balance of power remains strong on the side of freedom, to make it possible for Americans of all different races and creeds to live together in harmony, to make it possible for a world to exist in diversity and freedom. All this requires the best of all of us.

Therefore, I am proud to come to this college, whose graduates have recognized this obligation and to say to those who are now here that the need is endless, and I am confident that you will respond.

Robert Frost said:

> Two roads diverged in a wood, and I—
> I took the one less traveled by,
> And that has made all the difference.

I hope that road will not be the less traveled by, and I hope your commitment to the Great Republic's interest in the years to come will be worthy of your long inheritance since your beginning.

This day devoted to the memory of Robert Frost offers an opportunity for reflection which is prized by politicians as well as by others, and even by poets, for Robert Frost was one of the granite figures of our time in America. He was supremely two things: an artist and an American. A nation reveals itself not only by the men it produces but also by the men it honors, the men it remembers.

In America, our heroes have customarily run to men of large accomplishments. But today this college and country honors a man whose contribution was not to our size but to our spirit, not to our political beliefs but to our insight, not to our self-esteem, but to our self-comprehension. In honoring Robert Frost, we therefore can pay honor to the deepest sources of our national strength. That strength takes many forms, and the most obvious forms are

not always the most significant. The men who create power make an indispensable contribution to the Nation's greatness, but the men who question power make a contribution just as indispensable, especially when that questioning is disinterested, for they determine whether we use power or power uses us.

Our national strength matters, but the spirit which informs and controls our strength matters just as much. This was the special significance of Robert Frost. He brought an unsparing instinct for reality to bear on the platitudes and pieties of society. His sense of the human tragedy fortified him against self-deception and easy consolation. "I have been" he wrote, "one acquainted with the night." And because he knew the midnight as well as the high noon, because he understood the ordeal as well as the triumph of the human spirit, he gave his age strength with which to overcome despair. At bottom, he held a deep faith in the spirit of man, and it is hardly an accident that Robert Frost coupled poetry and power, for he saw poetry as the means of saving power from itself. When power leads man towards arrogance, poetry reminds him of his limitations. When power narrows the areas of man's concern, poetry reminds him of the richness and diversity of his existence. When power corrupts, poetry cleanses. For art establishes the basic human truth which must serve as the touchstone of our judgment.

The artist, however faithful to his personal vision of reality, becomes the last champion of the individual mind and sensibility against an intrusive society and an officious state. The great artist is thus a solitary figure. He has, as Frost said, a lover's quarrel with the world. In pursuing his perceptions of reality, he must often sail against the currents of his time. This is not a popular role. If Robert Frost was much honored in his lifetime, it was because a good many preferred to ignore his darker truths. Yet in retrospect, we see how the artist's fidelity has strengthened the fibre of our national life.

If sometimes our great artists have been the most critical of our society, it is because their sensitivity and their concern for justice, which

JOHN F. KENNEDY **737**

Political Perspective
on *Robert Frost*

Teach

| Reading Strategy | 1 |

Analyze Philosophical Assumptions Ask: What does President Kennedy mean by the phrase "our hold on this planet"? *(people's connection to the world around them)*

Assess

1. Students' summaries should include key points on responsibility and the American spirit.

2. Students' answers will vary but some may say that a society can only be truly democratic and free if artists are not censored and are allowed to follow their artistic visions freely. Others may say that there should be limits to artistic expression and that artists should not create art that deliberately insults and offends other people who live in this society.

3. (a) Of the individual mind against an intrusive society (b) The artist's critical and introspective stance allows him or her to serve truth and improve society.

4. Most students will agree that poems such as "The Death of the Hired Man" or the final lines of "Stopping by Woods on a Snowy Evening" contain "dark truths."

5. (a) Some students may say that Kennedy was simply beginning with a policy statement. Others will say the speech is about the advancement of the country through increasing cultural literacy and education. (b) Some will not find it interesting; others will like the ideas.

738

Informational Text

must motivate any true artist, makes him aware that our Nation falls short of its highest potential. I see little of more importance to the future of our country and our civilization than full recognition of the place of the artist.

If art is to nourish the roots of our culture, society must set the artist free to follow his vision wherever it takes him. We must never forget that art is not a form of propaganda; it is a form of truth. And as Mr. MacLeish once remarked of poets, there is nothing worse for our trade than to be in style. In free society art is not a weapon and it does not belong to the spheres of polemic and ideology. Artists are not engineers of the soul. It may be different elsewhere. But democratic society—in it, the highest duty of the writer, the composer, the artist is to remain true to himself and to let the chips fall where they may. In serving his vision of the truth, the artist best serves his nation. And the nation which disdains the mission of art invites the fate of Robert Frost's hired man, the fate of having "nothing to look backward to with pride, and nothing to look forward to with hope."

I look forward to a great future for America, a future in which our country will match its military strength with our moral restraint, its wealth with our wisdom, its power with our purpose. I look forward to an America which will not be afraid of grace and beauty, which will protect the beauty of our natural environment, which will preserve the great old American houses and squares and parks of our national past, and which will build handsome and balanced cities for our future.

I look forward to an America which will reward achievement in the arts as we reward achievement in business or statecraft. I look forward to an America which will steadily raise the standards of artistic accomplishment and which will steadily enlarge cultural opportunities for all of our citizens. And I look forward to an America which commands respect throughout the world not only for its strength but for its civilization as well. And I look forward to a world which will be safe not only for democracy and diversity but also for personal distinction.

Robert Frost was often skeptical about projects for human improvement, yet I do not think he would disdain this hope. As he wrote during the uncertain days of the Second War:

Take human nature altogether since time began . . .
And it must be a little more in favor of man,
Say a fraction of one percent at the very least . . .
Our hold on this planet wouldn't have so increased.

Because of Mr. Frost's life and work, because of the life and work of this college, our hold on this planet has increased. ∾ | **1**

Respond and Think Critically

Respond and Interpret

1. Write a brief summary of the main ideas in this excerpt before you answer the following questions. For help on writing a summary, see page 79.

2. What is your opinion of Kennedy's claim that "society must set the artist free to follow his vision wherever it takes him"? Are there limits to artistic expression? Explain.

3. (a) According to Kennedy, the artist becomes the last champion of what? (b) How might this championing help to bring about Kennedy's vision of America in the future?

Analyze and Evaluate

4. Do you agree with Kennedy that Frost's poems often hold "darker truths"? Why or why not?

5. (a) Why do you think Kennedy began his address by discussing economics and education? (b) What do you think of this portion of the address?

Connect

6. Briefly compare and contrast Kennedy's arguments about artists and society with the beliefs held by particular literary movements or with other arguments you've read by literary figures.

738 UNIT 5   BEGINNINGS OF THE MODERN AGE

---

6. Some students will say Kennedy's ideas are like those of Ralph Waldo Emerson and the Transcendentalists, who believed the artist should be a "champion of the individual mind." Others will compare his idea that the arts should be critical of culture to Realism.

 For additional assessment, see Assessment Resources, pp. 211–212.

MODERN FICTION

A Doughboy's Equipment, c. 1921. Charles A. Meurer. Oil on canvas, 68 x 40 in. Butler Institute of American Art, Youngstown, OH.

 View the Art As a master of *trompe l'œil*—from the French for "trick of the eye"—Charles Meuer was known for creating art that aimed to blur the lines between Realism and reality. What details from this painting bring it to life? What do they tell you about a typical World War I soldier?

> *"The hardest thing to do is to write straight honest prose on human beings."* **1**
>
> —Ernest Hemingway

739

Analyze and Extend

Reading Strategy **1**

Evaluate Direct students to read the quotation by Hemingway. Remind students that prose is ordinary language that reflects the way people express themselves. As a former journalist, Hemingway used everyday language to tell stories.

Ask: Why do you think Hemingway says that writing "straight, honest prose on human beings" is the hardest thing to do? *(Responses will vary. Students may say that people are complex and hard to write about simply, without embellishment.)*

View the Art

Answer: *The letter, other pieces of paper, and the medal show that the equipment belongs to a particular person. The soldier has taken care of his equipment; the medal shows courage; and the letter shows a connection with others. The static nature of the painting implies that the soldier is dead.* Charles A. Meurer (1865–1955) used the *trompe l'oeil* (pronounced trohmp loi) technique to create a memorial to the American soldiers of World War I.

Focus

Bellringer Options

Daily Language Practice Transparency 66

Or **ask:** How does a story without a plot reflect real life better than a story with a beginning, middle, and end? (*Students should understand that real lives do not have clear plots. Life is a series of episodes that may or may not be resolved.*)

Teach

Big Idea 1

Modern Fiction Say: After World War I, American writers questioned traditional values. **Ask:** Why do you think the war affected writers this way? (*Students may suggest that the war caused writers to become pessimistic and to look for different views of life.*)

View the Art ★

Edward Hopper (1882–1967) painted modern, everyday life. He used shadow, straight lines, and deep colors to reveal the inner lives of his subjects and to convey the human condition.

Learning Objectives

For pages 740–741

In studying this text, you will focus on the following objectives:

Literary Study:
Analyzing literary periods.
Analyzing literary genres.
Evaluating historical influences.
Connecting to the literature.

The Modern American Short Story

SINCE THE ERA of Poe, Hawthorne, and Irving, the short story has been one of the most popular genres among American writers. The early stories of American Romanticism featured supernatural plots and clear moral themes adapted from well-known European myths and tales. As literary styles and themes shifted in the 1800s during the movements of Realism and Naturalism, however, short story writers in the United States began to portray plots and characters that mirrored real life. Modernist writers continued this progression by experimenting with new ways of capturing the rich complexity of human life and by responding to a world that was just beginning to rise from the ashes of World War I. **1**

"There are no plot stories in life."
—Sherwood Anderson

Literary Mavericks

Writers such as Sherwood Anderson, Ernest Hemingway, F. Scott Fitzgerald, Henry James, and Katherine Anne Porter energized the short story in the early 1900s by peering into the private world of human thought. "The task of finding concrete ways to communicate emotional states becomes the central problem for most short story writers in the twentieth century," wrote critic Charles E. May. A representative example was Sherwood Anderson's *Winesburg, Ohio*, published in 1919. This groundbreaking collection of short stories explored the minds of characters that Anderson called "grotesque." Some of the stories, including "Hands," had previously appeared in a variety of journals that provided a forum for innovative stories. The characters in these stories are troubled by their difficult circumstances, yet endearing. Anderson's goal in portraying them was "to at last go out of myself, truly into others, the others I met constantly in the streets of the city, in the office where I then worked, and still others remembered out of my childhood in an American small town."

Room in New York, 1932. Edward Hopper. Oil on Canvas, 28½ x 35½ in. F.M. Hall Collection. ★

Stream of Consciousness

Many modernist short story writers in the early 1900s were influenced by the new psychological theories of the time, including those of Sigmund Freud, who sought unconscious causes for people's behavior. This interest in the mind spawned a new literary technique called **stream of consciousness,** an expression coined by American psychologist William James in 1890. He believed thought was a constant stream flowing through the minds without clear logic or order.

Listening and Speaking Practice

Oral Interpretation Ask volunteers to read aloud the first paragraph from "The Open Boat" (p. 580) and the first paragraph from "In Another Country" (p. 745). Tell students to listen for differences in the style and technique of each writer. (*Crane uses longer sentences, creates more suspense, focuses on the colors of the water and the movement of the boat; Hemingway uses short sentences, no colors, simple adjectives, and it's unclear* *what to focus on.*) After the paragraphs have been read, hold a class discussion contrasting the two stories. Read additional paragraphs from each story if needed. Students should recognize that Modernist stories like Hemingway's are leaner, with fewer details about the scene and the characters.

James Joyce, Virginia Woolf, William Faulkner, and Katherine Anne Porter (see page 773) are some of the notable practitioners of this method of narration. In stories that employ stream of consciousness, certain memories trigger seemingly random thoughts. Stream of consciousness stories include the following elements:

- first-person point of view
- a lack of conventional sentence structure or grammar
- "free associations" that flow through a character's mind and link distinctly separate events
- interior monologues

The Interior World

Modernist writers reacted against formulaic, plot-driven stories that dominated the early 1900s, including the surprise endings that made the fiction of O. Henry famous. Irish short-story writer Frank O'Connor explained that Modernists instead strove for the "artful approach to the significant moment." Another Irish writer, James Joyce, brought this idea of the moment charged with meaning to full effect in his 1914 short story collection *Dubliners*, in which he introduced the **epiphany,** or moment of revelation, and used it to redefine the short story.

Translations into English of the work of Russian writer Anton Chekhov (see page 557) between 1916 and 1923 brought his method of storytelling to the United States. Chekhov was a master at employing realistic detail and **understatement**—a de-emphasis on the importance of something or someone. He preferred to use "slice of life" anecdotes in his stories rather than traditional plots. Chekhov's stories, such as "Gooseberries," lack obvious external conflicts, action-packed events, and clear climaxes. Instead, the drama rages inside characters' minds. The protagonists in modern short stories, notably by

Hemingway and Fitzgerald, are often **antiheroes,** or conflicted characters engulfed by indecision.

The language in modern short stories is often subtle and poetic, and requires the reader to infer what is left unsaid. British short-story writer and critic H. E. Bates said, "It is no longer necessary to describe; it is enough to suggest. The full-length portrait, in full dress, with scenic background, has become superfluous; now it is enough that we should know a woman by the shape of her hands." Hemingway (see page 742), who was influenced by Chekhov's style, was also a master of understatement. Hemingway's terse, suggestive language was frequently imitated. Hemingway used the metaphor of an iceberg to explain his view of the short story. "There is seven-eighths of it underwater for every part that shows."

Features of the Modern Short Story

Note the following features of modern short stories to help enrich your understanding of these works.

- unspectacular, or everyday, settings
- themes of instability and loss
- plots without a clear climax or resolution
- understatement
- irony
- stream of consciousness
- antiheroes

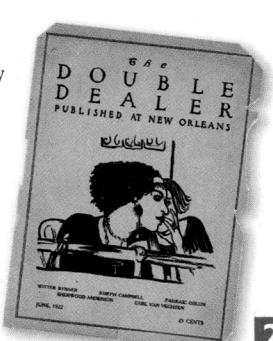

2

LOG ON ▶ **Literature** Online

Literature and Reading For more about the modern short story, go to glencoe.com and enter QuickPass code GLA9800u5.

Respond and Think Critically

1. (a) What is stream of consciousness? (b) What influenced its emergence in modern fiction?

2. The Russian writer Anton Chekhov influenced Modernist fiction. What are some characteristics of his short stories?

3. Look back at one of the short stories in Unit Two: American Romanticism. How is it similar to and different from one of the modern short stories in Unit Five?

LITERARY HISTORY **741**

Teach

Literary Element 2

Antihero Say: Modernist writers wrote about antiheroes, main characters who are conflicted and seldom act in heroic ways. Identify a character who is an antihero, and tell why he or she is an antihero. *(Students' choices will likely be characters who are more like real people than heroes.)*

Assess

1. (a) It is a literary technique that reflects the way people think—a steady and usually disorganized flow of thoughts. (b) Interest in the new field of psychology led writers to adopt stream of consciousness.

2. Realistic details, understatement, "slice of life" anecdotes, conflict within characters' minds

3. Stories written in the Romantic tradition often are dark and contain strong symbolism. Characters are often symbols or archetypes. Modernist short stories focus on the thoughts and problems of real people.

Approaching Level

DIFFERENTIATED INSTRUCTION

Emerging Engage students in a full discussion of the seven features of the Modernist short story. Instruct students to create a chart of the seven features, filling in definitions and examples of each feature, using the information on this spread and information gathered during the class discussion. Then have students add to their charts using the Literary Terms Handbook (pp. R1–R21), which will provide

students with additional examples and will direct students to selections that illustrate the devices. Finally, have students work in peer groups to compare the information and examples in their charts.

Before You Read

Focus

Bellringer Options

Selection Focus
Transparency 45

Daily Language Practice
Transparency 67

Or display images of war that are heroic, such as a photograph of the United States Marine Corps Memorial in Washington, D.C., which depicts the raising of the flag at Iwo Jima during World War II. **Ask:** How do heroic images of war affect us as individuals? Why are these images important to us as a nation?

Have students compare Hemingway's depiction of soldiers and war with those that appear in the images you show. Explain that the way Hemingway depicted soldiers and the war affected people's perspective. **Ask:** How does modern media affect the way you see soldiers and war?

Before You Read

In Another Country

Meet **Ernest Hemingway**
(1899–1961)

Big-game hunters, deep-sea fishermen, soldiers, boxers, bullfighters—these are the types of characters found in Ernest Hemingway's fiction. Strong but sensitive, brainy as well as brawny, the Hemingway hero is usually someone wounded by life, though he keeps his suffering to himself. Closely linked to Hemingway's own adventurous life and personality, the Hemingway hero captured the public's imagination and granted the author celebrity status beyond the literary world. His style and depiction of characters has been imitated by generations of writers.

Coming of Age Born in Oak Park, Illinois, Hemingway spent much of his childhood camping, hunting, and fishing with his father. He began writing in high school and upon graduating landed a job as a cub reporter for the *Kansas City Star.* Rejected by the military for service in World War I because of an eye defect, he volunteered to serve as a Red Cross ambulance driver near the battlefront in Italy, and was seriously wounded less than a month before he turned nineteen. The injury, said critic Alfred Kazin, "was a shock that went straight into Hemingway's early stories and fables of the war."

> *"A man can be destroyed but not defeated."*
>
> —Ernest Hemingway
> from *The Old Man and the Sea*

After recuperating, Hemingway took a job as foreign correspondent for the *Toronto Star* and joined the American writers and artists in Paris who, disillusioned by the war but reluctant to leave the continent where they had fought it, lived as expatriates. Many gathered at the Paris home of American author Gertrude Stein, who coined the term *lost generation* to describe them.

A Celebrity In 1925, Hemingway published *In Our Time,* a story collection that established him as an important new writer. He followed with *The Sun Also Rises* (1926), a novel of the lost generation in 1920s Paris and Spain, and *A Farewell to Arms* (1929), a tragic World War I love story.

Hemingway drew on his personal adventures as he wrote fiction and won fame for his lifestyle as much as for his writing. He wrote his bullfighting novel, *Death in the Afternoon* (1932), after attending bullfights in Spain, and his story "The Snows of Kilimanjaro" (1936) after he went on safari in Africa. In 1952 Hemingway published *The Old Man and the Sea,* a short novel that drew on his own experiences as a deep-sea fisherman off the coast of Cuba. In 1954 Hemingway won the Nobel Prize for Literature "for his mastery of the art of narrative, most recently demonstrated in *The Old Man and the Sea,* and for the influence that he has exerted on contemporary style."

 Literature Online

Author Search For more about Ernest Hemingway, go to glencoe.com and enter QuickPass code GLA9800u5.

Selection Skills

Literary Elements
- Style (SE pp. 743, 745, 746, 749)

Reading Skills
- Recognize Author's Purpose (SE pp. 743, 745, 748, 750)
- Identify Writer's Technique (TE p. 744)

In Another Country

Vocabulary Skills
- Antonyms (SE pp. 750)
- Academic Vocabulary (SE p. 750)
- Parts of Speech (TE p. 743)

Listening/Speaking/ Viewing Skills
- Analyze Art (SE p. 746; TE p. 744)

Writing Skills/Grammar
- Apply Diction (SE p. 750)
- Research and Report (TE p. 746)
- Personal Response (TE p. 748)

Literature and Reading Preview

Connect to the Story

Hemingway once defined "guts," or courage, as the ability to display "grace under pressure." How do you define courage? Discuss this question with a partner or small group.

Build Background

"In Another Country" takes place in the Italian city of Milan during World War I. The United States joined the Allied Powers only a year before the war ended, but Italy joined the Allied Powers in 1915. The war exacted a high toll of casualties; in fact, of the 65 million people who fought in World War I, over 10 million were killed, and more than 20 million more were wounded.

Set Purposes for Reading

Big Idea Modern Fiction

As you read, ask yourself, How does Hemingway's story differ from earlier fiction you have read, in terms of both subject matter and style?

Literary Element Style

Style is the writer's characteristic way of writing. It includes elements such as word choice, sentence structure, and tone. Hemingway, who was strongly influenced by his training as a journalist, pioneered a simple, unadorned style that has been frequently imitated. As you read, ask yourself, What are examples of Hemingway's simple, journalistic style?

Reading Strategy Recognize Author's Purpose

Writers have different **purposes,** or reasons, for writing. For some, the main purpose is to entertain. Others want to present stories with as much realism as possible. Some writers may also want to teach a lesson or present a set of values or an approach toward life. As you read Hemingway's story, ask yourself, What might his purpose have been?

Tip: Track Ideas Use a chart to note your ideas about the author's purposes.

Detail	Purpose
p. 745: "It was cold in the fall in Milan.... Beyond the old hospital were the new brick pavilions."	to portray the setting realistically

ERNEST HEMINGWAY **743**

Learning Objectives

For pages 742–750

In studying this text, you will focus on the following objectives:

Literary Study: Analyzing style.

Reading: Recognizing author's purpose.

Writing: Applying diction in a brief narrative.

Vocabulary

lurch (lurch) *v.* to move suddenly and unevenly; p. 745 *The dizzy man lurched across the room.*

withered (wi´ thərd) *adj.* shriveled; p. 745 *Fresh water did not revive the withered flowers.*

detached (di tacht´) *adj.* not involved emotionally; aloof; indifferent; p. 746 *I befriended him, but he remained detached.*

jostle (jo´ səl) *v.* to bump, push, or shove while moving, as in a crowd; p. 746 *Did the crowd jostle you, or did you trip on your own?*

resign (ri zīn´) *v.* to make oneself accept something; p. 748 *I must resign myself to the situation.*

Before You Read

Focus

Summary

During World War I, four Italian officers and the narrator—an American officer—meet regularly for physical therapy at an Italian hospital. The oldest officer, a major, offers the narrator lessons in Italian grammar and also advice. Later, the major's young wife dies. The major is inconsolable, and he loses interest in his rehabilitation and in his conversations with the narrator.

 For summaries in languages other than English, see Unit 5 Teaching Resources Book, pp. 169–174.

Vocabulary

Parts of Speech Explain that some words function as different parts of speech depending on how the word is used. **Ask:** What part of speech are the words *withered* and *detached* as defined in the vocabulary list? (*adjective*) **Ask:** Both of these words can also be used as what other part of speech? (*past tense form of verb*) Have students practice using these two vocabulary words as both adjectives and verbs.

 For additional vocabulary practice, see Unit 5 Teaching Resources Book, p. 177.

 For additional context, see Glencoe Interactive Vocabulary CD-ROM.

English Learners

DIFFERENTIATED INSTRUCTION

Intermediate The text refers to Hemingway's style as "journalistic." Ask students what they think that means. Explain that journalists tend to write without a lot of extra description because they usually are given limited space in their publication. They also tend to use simple sentence structures and shorter sentences. Instruct students to pay attention to the effect Hemingway's style has on them as they read.

Advanced Display the following from the first paragraph of the story:

It was a cold fall and the wind came down from the mountains.

Engage students in a discussion of how this sentence reflects Hemingway's journalistic sentence structure and word choice.

Teach

Big Idea   1

Modern Fiction Remind students that World War I had a major impact on American writers in the 1920s. Hemingway was seriously injured while serving as an ambulance driver in the war. **Ask:** How do you think Hemingway's experience during the war affected him as a writer? *(Students may suggest that Hemingway understood the random violence of war, and this influenced his writing.)*

View the Art ★

Russian artist B. V. Cerbakov (1916–) is a realist painter who has often focused on military themes. **Ask:** What do the man's pose and expression suggest about his feelings? *(The man seems composed, almost indifferent, as he sits among ruins.)* As students read, ask them to consider how the man in the artwork mirrors the narrator.

For an audio recording of this selection, use Listening Library Audio CD-ROM.

Readability Scores

Dale-Chall: 4.7
DRP: 54
Lexile: 1050

Reading Practice

Identify Writer's Technique Students may be confused by the story's lack of plot and conflict. They may also have difficulty identifying a theme. Explain that Hemingway uses literary devices that are often employed by poets, particularly imagery. Tell students to look for places where Hemingway presents images in a seemingly random way. Ask students to notice how the images suggest particular feelings and themes. Have students create a three-column chart with the headings Image, Feelings, and Themes and use the chart to make notes about images as they read. For example, the image of "deer hung stiff and heavy and empty" may make students feel grim, cold, lonely, and sad. The theme in this image could be the impersonal nature of death. After reading the story, have students use the charts and discuss how Hemingway uses images to evoke feelings and to hint at the themes of the story.

In Another Country

Ernest Hemingway

★ *The Invincible Soldier.* B.V. Cerbakov. Tretyakov Gallery, Moscow, Russia.

744 UNIT 5 BEGINNINGS OF THE MODERN AGE

1 In the fall the war[1] was always there, but we did not go to it any more. It was cold in the fall in Milan[2] and the dark came very early. Then the electric lights came on, and it was pleasant along the streets looking in the windows. There was much game[3] hanging outside the shops, and the snow powdered in the fur of the foxes and the wind blew their tails. The deer hung stiff and heavy and empty, and small birds blew in the wind and the wind turned their feathers. It was a cold fall and the wind came down from the mountains.

We were all at the hospital every afternoon, and there were different ways of walking across the town through the dusk to the hospital. Two of the ways were alongside canals, but they were long. Always, though, you crossed a bridge across a canal to enter the hospital. There was a choice of three bridges. On one of them a woman sold roasted chestnuts. It was warm, standing in front of her charcoal fire, and the chestnuts were warm afterward in your pocket. The hospital was very old and very beautiful, and you entered through a gate and walked across a courtyard and out a gate on the other side. There were usually funerals starting from the courtyard. Beyond the old hospital were the new brick pavilions, and there we met every afternoon and were all very polite and interested in what was the matter, and sat in the machines that were to make so much difference.

The doctor came up to the machine where I was sitting and said: "What did you like best to do before the war? Did you practice a sport?"

I said: "Yes, football."

"Good," he said. "You will be able to play football again better than ever."

My knee did not bend and the leg dropped straight from the knee to the ankle without a

---

1. The *war* is World War I (1914–1918). The United States, Italy, and other countries fought Germany and its allies.
2. *Milan* is a city in northern Italy.
3. Here, *game* refers to wild animals that have been hunted and killed for food.

2 Recognize Author's Purpose *What might be Hemingway's purpose in providing such a detailed description of the setting at the start of his story?*

---

calf, and the machine was to bend the knee and make it move as in riding a tricycle. But it did not bend yet, and instead the machine **lurched** when it came to the bending part. The doctor said: "That will all pass. You are a fortunate young man. You will play football again like a champion."

In the next machine was a major who had a little hand like a baby's. He winked at me when the doctor examined his hand, which was between two leather straps that bounced up and down and flapped the stiff fingers, and said: "And will I too play football, captain-doctor?" He had been a very great fencer, and before the war the greatest fencer in Italy.

The doctor went to his office in the back room and brought a photograph which showed a hand that had been **withered** almost as small as the major's, before it had taken a machine course, and after was a little larger. The major held the photograph with his good hand and looked at it very carefully. "A wound?" he asked.

"An industrial accident," the doctor said.

"Very interesting, very interesting," the major said, and handed it back to the doctor.

"You have confidence?"

"No," said the major.

There were three boys who came each day who were about the same age I was. They were all three from Milan, and one of them was to be a lawyer, and one was to be a painter, and one had intended to be a soldier, and after we were finished with the machines, sometimes we walked back together to the Café Cova, which was next door to the Scala.[4] We walked the short way through the communist quarter because we were four together. The people hated us because we were officers, and from a wine-shop some one would call out, "A basso

---

4. *The Scala* (skä′ lə) is Milan's world-famous opera house.

Style *How would you describe the style of the dialogue? What effect does it have on your sense of the characters?* **3**

Vocabulary

lurch (lurch) *v.* to move suddenly and unevenly
withered (wi′ thərd) *adj.* shriveled

ERNEST HEMINGWAY **745**

Teach

Reading Strategy 2

Recognize Author's Purpose **Answer:** *He may want to create a sense of reality and draw the reader in.*
Ask: What feelings does the description of the setting evoke in the second paragraph? *(comfortable, warm, enchanting)*
Ask: How do these details fit in with the details in the previous paragraph? *(The hospital seems inviting—a contrast to the cold weather and dead animals in the first paragraph.)*

 For additional practice using the reading skill or strategy, see Unit 5 Teaching Resources Book, p. 176.

Literary Element 3

Style **Answer:** *The dialogue is expressed in language that is ordinary, simple, and direct. It is even a bit repetitive and colorless, like everyday speech. The dialogue suggests that the characters are ordinary people with normal concerns.* **Say:** Hemingway uses dialogue to reveal his characters and their situations directly. The language is almost always simple and direct.

English Learners
DIFFERENTIATED INSTRUCTION

Beginning Although Hemingway writes many simple sentences, he also writes compound and compound-complex sentences. Review simple, compound, complex, and compound-complex sentences. Help students identify each type of sentence in the story. Refer students to the Language Handbook (p. R43) for an explanation of each type of sentence.

Approaching Level
DIFFERENTIATED INSTRUCTION

Emerging Help students improve their **reading fluency** to better understand the story. Have students reread the descriptions of the injuries and the promises the doctor makes to the soldiers. As students read aloud, pause and **ask:** What is the narrator's injury? *(He is missing the calf of one of his legs.)* How is the major's hand described? *(His hand is little "like a baby's" and "withered.")* Point out that

both the characters are permanently crippled and the machines will not give them back their limbs, only help them improve what is left. This is the reason the soldiers have no confidence in the machines.

Teach

Literary Element   1

Style Answer: *It is relayed in a matter-of-fact tone, with little emotion. This makes a hideous injury sound like a normal result of being in the war.* **Say:** Hemingway's use of understatement and tone often reveals surprises. For example, at the end of the paragraph, the narrator undermines the suspense of the story by explaining that the young man with no nose later went to work in a bank. This small detail lets readers know that both the narrator and the young man survive the war.

Vocabulary   2

Context Clues Say: Explain how the details about the movement of the people help you understand the meaning of the word *jostle.* *(The people are crowded together on a busy sidewalk, which helps to convey the idea that people bumped into one another.)* Have students practice using the word "jostle" in sentences.

Big Idea   3

Modern Fiction Answer: *The characters do not seem heroic but are emotionally numb; in some cases, they are disillusioned with the cause for which they fought.*

746

Piazza Corvetto in Genoa in 1918. Alessandro Milesi. Oil on canvas. Galleria d'Arte Moderna di Nervi, Genoa, Italy.

View the Art As an important Italian port city, Genoa played a key role in both World War I and II. In what ways does this painting reflect the sense of detachment that the characters feel in Hemingway's story? ★

gli ufficiali!"[5] as we passed. Another boy who walked with us sometimes and made us five wore a black silk handkerchief across his face because he had no nose then and his face was to be rebuilt. He had gone out to the front[6] from the military academy and been wounded within an hour after he had gone into the front line for the first time. They rebuilt his face, but he came from a very old family and they could never get the nose exactly right. He went to South America and worked in a bank. But this was a long time ago, and then we did not any of us know how it was going to be afterward. We only knew then that there was always the war, but that we were not going to it any more.

We all had the same medals, except the boy with the black silk bandage across his face, and he had not been at the front long enough to get any medals. The tall boy with a very pale face who was to be a lawyer had been a lieutenant of Arditi[7] and had three medals of the sort we each had only one of. He had lived a very long time with death and was a little **detached.** We were all a little detached, and there was nothing that held us together except that we met every afternoon at the hospital. Although, as we walked to the Cova through the tough part of town, walking in the dark, with light and singing coming out of the wine-shops, and sometimes having to walk into the street when the men and women would crowd together on the sidewalk so that we would have had to **jostle** them to get by, we   2
felt held together by there being something that had happened that they, the people who disliked us, did not understand.

---

7. The *Arditi* (ar dē′ tē) was a corps of soldiers specially selected for dangerous operations.

Modern Fiction *How is the portrayal of these characters different from portrayals of war heroes in literature from earlier periods?*   3

Vocabulary

detached (di tacht′) *adj.* not involved emotionally; aloof; indifferent
jostle (jo′ səl) *v.* to bump, push, or shove while moving, as in a crowd

---

5. In Italian, *A basso gli ufficiali!* (a bä′ sō lyē ō̄o̅ fē chä′ lē) means "Down with officers!"
6. The *front* is the line or area of conflict between opposing armies.

1   **Style** *How would you describe the tone in which this gruesome information is relayed?*

Writing Practice

Research and Report One of the few positive by-products of war is the advancement in the treatment of the wounded. Hemingway's characters illustrate this. They undergo physical therapy using innovative machines. Have students work in small groups to research medical advances that were developed during World War I. Their research might involve such fields as pharmaceuticals, anesthetics, plastic surgery, and field surgery. Have groups report their findings to the class. Have groups write a report on their findings. Remind them to use more than one source for their reports.

We ourselves all understood the Cova, where it was rich and warm and not too brightly lighted, and noisy and smoky at certain hours, and there were always girls at the tables and the illustrated papers on a rack on the wall. The girls at the Cova were very patriotic, and I found that the most patriotic people in Italy were the café girls—and I believe they are still patriotic.

The boys at first were very polite about my medals and asked me what I had done to get them. I showed them the papers, which were written in very beautiful language and full of *fratellanza* and *abnegazione*,[8] but which really said, with the adjectives removed, that I had been given the medals because I was an American. After that their manner changed a little toward me, although I was their friend against outsiders. I was a friend, but I was never really one of them after they had read the citations,[9] because it had been different with them and they had done very different things to get their medals. I had been wounded, it was true; but we all knew that being wounded, after all, was really an accident. I was never ashamed of the ribbons, though, and sometimes, after the cocktail hour, I would imagine myself having done all the things they had done to get their medals; but walking home at night through the empty streets with the cold wind and all the shops closed, trying to keep near the street lights, I knew that I would never have done such things, and I was very much afraid to die, and often lay in bed at night by myself, afraid to die and wondering how I would be when I went back to the front again.

The three with the medals were like hunting-hawks; and I was not a hawk, although I might seem a hawk to those who had never hunted; they, the three, knew better and so we drifted apart. But I stayed good friends with the boy who had been wounded his first day at the front, because he would never know now how he would have turned out; so he could never

be accepted either, and I liked him because I thought perhaps he would not have turned out to be a hawk either.

The major, who had been the great fencer, did not believe in bravery, and spent much time while we sat in the machines correcting my grammar. He had complimented me on how I spoke Italian, and we talked together very easily. One day I had said that Italian seemed such an easy language to me that I could not take a great interest in it; everything was so easy to say. "Ah, yes," the major said. "Why, then, do you not take up the use of grammar?" So we took up the use of grammar, and soon Italian was such a difficult language that I was afraid to talk to him until I had the grammar straight in my mind.

The major came very regularly to the hospital. I do not think he ever missed a day, although I am sure he did not believe in the machines. There was a time when none of us believed in the machines, and one day the major said it was all nonsense. The machines were new then and it was we who were to prove them. It was an idiotic idea, he said, "a theory, like another." I had not learned my grammar, and he said I was a stupid impossible disgrace, and he was a fool to have bothered with me. He was a small man and he sat straight up in his chair with his right hand thrust into the machine and looked straight ahead at the wall while the straps thumped up and down with his fingers in them.

"What will you do when the war is over if it is over?" he asked me. "Speak grammatically!"

"I will go to the States."

"Are you married?"

"No, but I hope to be."

"The more of a fool you are," he said. He seemed very angry. "A man must not marry."

"Why, Signor Maggiore?"[10]

---

10. *Signor Maggiore* (sē nyor′ ma jō′ rā) means "Mr. Major." In Italy, one said *Signor* before an officer's rank as a sign of respect.

Modern Fiction *How does the close proximity of these three unrelated statements reflect new ideas of Modernism?*

ERNEST HEMINGWAY **747**

---

8. *Fratellanza* (fra tāl än′ za) and *abnegazione* (ab nā ga tzyo′ nā) are Italian for "brotherhood" and "self-denial."
9. *Citations* are specific references to military achievements worthy of reward or praise.

747

Teach

Reading Strategy `1`

Recognize Author's Purpose **Answer:** *The author may have wanted to convey the randomness and the ironies of death. Instead of the major dying at war, his young wife died suddenly of pneumonia.*

Big Idea `2`

Modern Fiction **Answer:** *Hemingway includes only details that describe a particular moment in time. He is not interested in resolving all the questions at the end of the story.*

APPROACHING Remind students that Modernist stories do not have neat plots with a beginning, middle, and end. Instead, these stories capture moments in real life.

Cultural History ☆

Mourning Dress In the early twentieth century, widows wore black clothing and hats with veils for months at a time when mourning. Men wore black armbands on their upper left arms.

 To check students' understanding of the selection, see Unit 5 Teaching Resources Book, p. 180.

"Don't call me 'Signor Maggiore.'"

"Why must not a man marry?"

"He cannot marry. He cannot marry," he said angrily. "If he is to lose everything, he should not place himself in a position to lose that. He should not place himself in a position to lose. He should find things he cannot lose."

He spoke very angrily and bitterly, and looked straight ahead while he talked.

"But why should he necessarily lose it?"

"He'll lose it," the major said. He was looking at the wall. Then he looked down at the machine and jerked his little hand out from between the straps and slapped it hard against his thigh. "He'll lose it," he almost shouted. "Don't argue with me!" Then he called to the attendant who ran the machines. "Come and turn this thing off."

He went back into the other room for the light treatment and the massage. Then I heard him ask the doctor if he might use his telephone and he shut the door. When he came back into the room, I was sitting in another machine. He was wearing his cape and had his cap on, and he came directly toward my machine and put his arm on my shoulder.

"I am so sorry," he said, and patted me on the shoulder with his good hand. "I would not be rude. My wife has just died. You must forgive me."

"Oh—" I said, feeling sick for him. "I am *so* sorry."

He stood there biting his lower lip. "It is very difficult," he said. "I cannot **resign** myself."

> *A*nd then crying, his head up looking at nothing, carrying himself straight and soldierly, with tears on both his cheeks and biting his lips, he walked past the machines and out the door.

He looked straight past me and out through the window. Then he began to cry. "I am utterly unable to resign myself," he said and choked. And then crying, his head up looking at nothing, carrying himself straight and soldierly, with tears on both his cheeks and biting his lips, he walked past the machines and out the door.

The doctor told me that the major's wife, who was very young and whom he had not married until he was definitely invalided[11] out of the war, had died of pneumonia. She had been sick only a few days. No one expected her to die. The major did not come to the hospital for three days. Then he came at the usual hour, wearing a black band on the sleeve ☆ of his uniform. When he came back, there were large framed photographs around the wall, of all sorts of wounds before and after they had been cured by the machines. In front of the machine the major used were three photographs of hands like his that were completely restored. I do not know where the doctor got them. I always understood we were the first to use the machines. The photographs did not make much difference to the major because he only looked out of the window. ∾

11. *Invalided* means "removed from active duty because of sickness or disability."

Recognize Author's Purpose *What might the unexpected death of the major's wife reveal about the author's purpose?* `1`

Modern Fiction *How is Hemingway's omission of facts about the machines, the photos, and the fate of the major characteristic of the Modernist approach to fiction?* `2`

Vocabulary

resign (ri zīn´) *v.* to make oneself accept something

Writing Practice

SPIRAL REVIEW **Personal Response** Explain that Hemingway's style was unique in its day, and although it has been widely imitated, it remains undeniably his own. Have students write a short personal response to Hemingway's style based on their reading of "In Another Country." Remind students to respond to Hemingway's word choice, sentence structure, dialogue, details, characters, and lack of plot. Students should conclude their responses with an evaluation. Discuss whether Hemingway's reputation as an important modern writer is well deserved.

After You Read

Respond and Think Critically

Respond and Interpret

1. How did you react to the end of the story? Explain.

2. (a)Why do the narrator and the others go to the hospital every afternoon? (b)What might the machines represent?

3. (a)What is the effect of the narrator's grammar lessons? (b)Based on this effect, what generalization can you make about the narrator's views of the world?

4. (a)What makes the narrator suspicious of the machines? (b)What do his suspicions show about his attitude toward authority and the likelihood of his recovery?

Analyze and Evaluate

5. (a)To what type of bird does the narrator compare the three young Italian men with medals?

(b)How does this comparison affect your view of the three young men, and how does it stress the difference between them and the narrator?

6. (a)What is ironic about the bad news that the major receives? (b)How realistic do you find his reaction to this news?

7. (a)Besides their physical injuries, how might the narrator and the other soldiers be wounded? (b)How effectively does the story convey their attitudes?

Connect

8. **Big Idea** **Modern Fiction** How is the portrayal of war in this story different from heroic depictions in times past?

9. **Connect to Today** How does Hemingway's sparse writing style compare to journalism today?

Literary Element Style

When he began working for the *Kansas City Star*, Hemingway received a **style** sheet that instructed reporters to "avoid the use of adjectives, especially such extravagant ones as *splendid, gorgeous, grand, magnificent,* etc." Short sentences, brief opening paragraphs, and "vigorous English" were also required. Hemingway later called these "the best rules I ever learned for the business of writing."

1. What repeated words, images, and sentence rhythms appear in the opening paragraph? What effect do these elements have on the story's mood or tone?

2. How does Hemingway's style underscore the story's themes?

3. Do you think that Hemingway's journalistic tone, with its emphasis on reporting facts without emotion, robs the story of the emotion it otherwise would have? Why or why not? Support your opinion with examples.

Review: Setting

As you learned on page 602, **setting** is the time and place in which the events of a literary work occur.

Partner Activity Meet with another classmate to discuss the setting of "In Another Country." Consider the relevance of the story's title and how it highlights the situation of the narrator or the other characters. Also consider how the setting helps determine the story's plot events and themes. You might gather your ideas in a diagram like the one below.

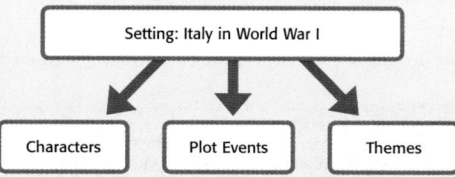

Setting: Italy in World War I → Characters / Plot Events / Themes

---

After You Read

Assess

1. Answers will vary.

2. (a) They go for treatment of their war injuries. (b) The machines might represent the dubious side of technology.

3. (a) The narrator realizes that the Italian language is not as easy as he thought. (b) The narrator has a detached view until he looks at life more closely; he realizes that it is difficult.

4. (a) He has been told that his group is the first to use the machines, yet he is shown pictures of other patients who recovered by using them. (b) His suspicions reflect his distrust of authority. He seems unconvinced that he will recover completely.

5. (a) He compares them to hunting-hawks. (b) It stresses the three men's valor as compared with that of the narrator, who says he received medals just for being an American.

6. (a) The major was more at risk of dying during the war than his wife was. (b) Students may find his reaction realistic because his wife was young and her death was unexpected.

7. (a) They have been emotionally wounded. (b) The narrator's detachment and the major's anger at him may be a result of their emotional wounds.

8. Instead of portraying war as an opportunity to prove one's honor or patriotism, Hemingway portrays it as a source of physical and emotional injury.

9. Students may say that today's journalists emulate Hemingway's dispassionate, spare style.

Literary Element

1. The words *cold* and *wind* create a dark mood, as do the images of the dark streets and the dead animals. The word *and* appears nine times; it connects the images.

2. The stark and detached style reinforces the narrator's emotional deadness and disenchantment with the war.

Review: Setting

Students should emphasize the physical and emotional damage done by being in a country torn by war.

Progress Check

Can students analyze style?

If No → See Unit 5 Teaching Resources Book, p. 175.

749

After You Read

Reading Strategy

1. E is the correct answer because the random structure of the story exemplifies Hemingway's belief in life's unpredictability.

Academic Vocabulary

Possible answer: Despite my inability to speak Spanish, I decided to study abroad in Peru for a semester.

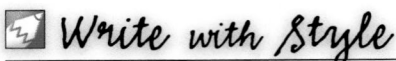 *Write with Style*

Use these criteria when evaluating students' writing:

- Does the writer use simple and compound sentences?
- Is the writer's word choice simple and clear?
- Does the writer accurately imitate Hemingway's style to relate an emotional experience from his or her past?

> For additional assessment, see Assessment Resources, pp. 213–214.

SAT Skills Practice

1. Hemingway's fragmentary presentation and lack of a clear resolution help to

   (A) reconcile readers to the death of the major's wife

   (B) explain why the major and the narrator survived the war

   (C) illustrate the chasm between the characters' cultures

   (D) emphasize the narrator's misplaced trust in the medical machines

   (E) convey the author's themes about the randomness and ironies of life

Vocabulary Practice

Practice with Antonyms Brainstorm antonyms for each vocabulary word below.

lurch   withered   detached   jostle   resign

EXAMPLE: modest
Antonyms: *arrogant, flashy, flamboyant*
Sample explanation: A modest person does not seek attention, but a flashy one does.

Academic Vocabulary

Despite the cultural differences between the narrator and the Italians, they are friends.

Despite is an academic word. Speaking casually, you might say that *despite* the rain, you were going to play soccer in the park. To further explore the meaning of this word, complete this sentence:
Despite my inability to _____, I _____.

For more on academic vocabulary, see pages 53–54.

> **LOG ON** ▶ **Literature** Online
>
> **Selection Resources** For Selection Quizzes, eFlashcards, and Reading-Writing Connection activities, go to glencoe.com and enter QuickPass code GLA9800u5.

Write with Style

 Apply Diction

Assignment Hemingway's style is characterized by simple and compound sentences, realistic dialogue, and clear, direct word choice. This style makes the narrator seem detached from the horrors of war. Using two or more of Hemingway's techniques, write a few paragraphs about an emotionally intense event.

Get Ideas Brainstorm to come up with a list of events to which you had a strong emotional reaction. Review journal entries, talk with a friend or relative, or review news articles to generate ideas.

Give It Structure Outline the main occurrences from this experience, especially encounters with others where you might include deceptively simple dialogue, like Hemingway's, which heightens emotional intensity for readers.

Look at Language As you review your piece, evaluate your word choice and sentence structure. Consider how the words you have chosen affect the mood of your piece. Do they suit the mood? Word choice is especially important in this sparse style. For instance, the use of the word *flapped* on page 745 has a very different effect than if Hemingway had said that the major's hand *waved* or *shook*. Choose key words from your piece and, in a chart like the one below, examine the connotation of the words you used versus similar words you could have used.

Word	Connotation	Alternative	Difference in Connotation
livid	explosive emotion	angry	less powerful or specific
bloom	lush flowers	bud	newer, less full flower
clatter	disruptive sound	noise	less specific, not negative

Also, try to make your sentences direct, like Hemingway's, to match his style. "It was a cold fall and the wind came down from the mountains" is very different from "That fall was chillingly cold, day in and day out, and the frigid wind blew down angrily from the snow-capped mountains."

Vocabulary

Antonyms for *lurch:* glide, move smoothly
Sample explanation: Something that lurches moves quickly and unevenly.
Antonyms for *withered:* ripened, thriving, lush
Sample explanation: A plant that is withered is dried and dying, whereas a plant that is thriving is growing and full of life.

Antonyms for *detached:* involved, concerned, caring
Sample explanation: A detached person does not get involved in emotional situations, but a concerned person does.
Antonyms for *jostle:* restrain
Sample explanation: To jostle is to move something around, but to restrain is to keep something in one place.

Antonyms for *resign:* refuse, deny
Sample explanation: A person who resigns himself accepts something, but a person who refuses does not.

> For additional grammar practice, see Unit 5 Teaching Resources Book, p. 179.

Grammar Workshop

Coordinating Conjunctions

Literature Connection A **coordinating conjunction** is a word, like *but* in the sentence below, that joins words or groups of words that are of equal grammatical importance in a sentence.

> *"In the fall the war was always there, but we did not go to it any more."*

> —Ernest Hemingway, "In Another Country"

Coordinating Conjunctions

and	but	or	nor	for	yet	so

Examples

Use coordinating conjunctions to join parts of a sentence.

He looked straight past me <u>and</u> out through the window.

The hospital was very old <u>and</u> very beautiful.

Use coordinating conjunctions to link short, choppy sentences or to connect sentences logically.

Hemingway was rejected by the military, <u>so</u> he became an ambulance driver.

In the fall the war was always there, <u>but</u> we did not go to it any more.

Practice Rewrite the following sentences, combining the sentence parts by using one of the coordinating conjunctions in parentheses.

1. A woman sold chestnuts, (and, but) we didn't buy them often.
2. The doctor told the men to exercise (or, and) face the consequences.
3. The hospital was old, (so, and) it was beautiful.
4. The major had neither confidence (or, nor) the ability to fence again.
5. We were glad to be in town, (so, for) there was fighting elsewhere.
6. The people hated us, (yet, so) they were not violent.
7. I could speak Italian, (but, and) the major corrected my grammar.
8. The major's wife had died, (for, so) he cried and looked out the window.

Commas and Coordinate Conjunctions

Use a comma before conjunctions when they join clauses that could stand on their own as complete sentences.

- He had complimented me on how I spoke Italian, and we talked together very easily.

Test-Taking Tip

Before handing in a written test, check to see that you have used appropriate coordinating conjunctions.

Language Handbook

For more on coordinating conjunctions, see Language Handbook, p. R43.

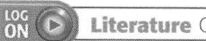

Literature Online

Grammar For more grammar practice, go to glencoe.com and enter QuickPass code GLA9800u5.

Approaching Level

DIFFERENTIATED INSTRUCTION

Established Remind students that conjunctions are words that join other words or groups of words. Write these sentences on the board:

- The man sold fruit and nuts.
- Al came, but he left early.

Ask: What are the conjunctions in the two sentences? *(and, but)* Point out that in the second sentence, the conjunction joins two groups of words or clauses.

Remind students that an independent clause is a group of words with a subject and a verb that can stand alone as a sentence. **Ask:** What are the two independent clauses in the second sentence? *(1. Al came; 2. He left early.)*

Grammar Workshop

Coordinating Conjunctions

Focus

Run-on Sentences

On the board, **write:** He went to the hospital every day and he used the physical therapy machines. He attended physical therapy every day but his leg did not improve. Discuss why each sentence needs a comma and where it should go.

Teach

Commas

Students may have trouble understanding when to insert a comma before a conjunction. If the conjunction is joining two nouns, verbs, or phrases, a comma should not be used. If the conjunction joins two independent clauses, a comma should go before the conjunction.

Assess

Practice

1. A woman sold roasted chestnuts, but we didn't buy them often.
2. The doctor told the men to exercise or face the consequences.
3. The hospital was old, and it was beautiful.
4. The major had neither confidence nor the ability to fence again.
5. We were glad to be in town, for there was fighting elsewhere.
6. The people hated us, yet they were not violent.
7. I could speak Italian, but the major corrected my grammar.
8. The major's wife had died, so he cried and looked out the window.

Before You Read

Focus

Bellringer Options

Selection Focus
Transparency 46

Daily Language Practice
Transparency 68

Or ask students to think of images they associate with winter in the northern part of the United States. If students need prompting, tell them to close their eyes and imagine a snow-covered scene.

As they read, have students compare their own winter-inspired feelings and wishes to those expressed by the characters in the story.

Before You Read

Winter Dreams

Meet **F. Scott Fitzgerald**
(1896–1940)

F Scott Fitzgerald once wrote that "all the stories that came into my head had a touch of disaster in them . . . I was pretty sure living wasn't the reckless, careless business these people thought." Many of Fitzgerald's stories and novels describe the reckless lifestyles of young, wealthy Americans in the 1920s.

> "Show me a hero and I will write you a tragedy."
>
> —F. Scott Fitzgerald, from *Notebooks*

Fitzgerald was born in St. Paul, Minnesota. He attended Princeton University, where he wrote for the newspaper and participated in the drama club. Fitzgerald joined the army before graduating, and while stationed in the South in 1918, he met Zelda Sayre at a country club dance. He fell in love, but Zelda was at first reluctant to marry him. That same summer, a New York publisher rejected the manuscript of his novel *The Romantic Egotist*.

Literary Success Following his stint in the army, Fitzgerald settled in New York City, working for an advertising agency, but he eventually returned to St. Paul to revise his novel. The publisher accepted the revision, retitled *This Side of Paradise*, and Fitzgerald was ecstatic. He and Zelda were married in 1920, and in 1921 they made their first trip to Europe, returning to St. Paul for the birth of their daughter Frances Scott (Scottie).

Fitzgerald's second novel, *The Beautiful and the Damned*, and "Winter Dreams" were published in 1922. While in France and Italy, he wrote and revised his most successful novel, *The Great Gatsby* (1925). He and Zelda lived lavishly, both in the United States and abroad, and spent most of the money Fitzgerald earned from his writing. They regularly moved from Paris to various cities on the French Riviera and then back to Paris. But when the frantic decade ended with the stock market crash in 1929, Fitzgerald's private life and prosperous career also crashed. His lucrative writing career began to dry up with the onset of the Depression. In 1930 Zelda suffered a series of nervous breakdowns and was hospitalized in Europe and the United States.

Later Years Though Fitzgerald struggled in the 1930s with alcoholism and with his marriage, he continued to write stories and novels. *Tender Is the Night* was published in 1934, and under contract with MGM, Fitzgerald worked on several screenplays in Hollywood. He was working on his fifth novel, *The Last Tycoon*, when he died in Hollywood of a heart attack at the age of 44. Zelda died in a hospital fire in North Carolina in 1948.

Fitzgerald's works, and his life with Zelda, have inspired more than twenty films of varying success. There have been three film versions of *The Great Gatsby* alone. Reviews were mixed of all of the movie versions of the novel. There are few dissenters about the book itself, however. Tobias Wolff says that Fitzgerald "saw our American world . . . with clearer eyes than any of his contemporaries."

LOG ON ▶ **Literature** Online

Author Search For more about F. Scott Fitzgerald, go to glencoe.com and enter QuickPass code GLA9800u5.

Selection Skills

Literary Elements
- Motivation (SE pp. 753, 755–757, 761, 762, 766, 767, 771)
- Conflict (SE p. 771)

Reading Skills
- Evaluate Sensory Details (SE pp. 753, 754, 758, 760, 763–765, 771)
- Preview (TE p. 754)

Vocabulary Skills
- Synonyms (SE p. 771)
- Academic Vocabulary (SE p. 771)

Winter Dreams

Listening/Speaking/ Viewing Skills
- Analyze Art (SE pp. 756, 760, 764, 766)
- Discussion (TE p. 762)

Writing Skills/Grammar
- Point of View (SE p. 772)
- Dramatize a Scene (TE p. 756)
- College Application Essay (TE p. 764)

Study Skills/Research
- The 1920s Economy (TE p. 758)
- Research the Author (TE p. 760)

Literature and Reading Preview

Connect to the Story

Do you think it is possible to love someone your entire life even though you are not with that person? Freewrite for ten minutes to explore this question.

Build Background

Many of Fitzgerald's stories are somewhat autobiographical. In 1915 he met Ginevra King at a party in St. Paul. The attraction was instant. Fitzgerald and Ginevra corresponded regularly, and Ginevra kept a diary in which she recorded that she was "madly in love with him." Ginevra had other boyfriends, however, and Fitzgerald was jealous. The romance was doomed. Ginevra ended up marrying a wealthy stockbroker, and shortly after, Scott married Zelda. Critics see aspects of Ginevra in most of Fitzgerald's heroines, however, including Judy Jones in "Winter Dreams."

Set Purposes for Reading

Big Idea Modern Fiction

As you read "Winter Dreams," ask yourself, What does this story reveal about romantic feelings and relationships during the Jazz Age?

Literary Element Motivation

Motivation refers to the stated or implied reason or cause for a character's actions. It is often revealed through a combination of the character's desires and morals and the circumstances in which the character finds himself or herself. As you read "Winter Dreams," ask yourself, What motivates the two main characters?

Reading Strategy Evaluate Sensory Details

Sensory details are details that appeal to one or more of the five senses. Writers use these details to help the reader imagine or experience more deeply the content of their work. As you read this story, ask yourself, How effective is Fitzgerald's use of sensory details?

Tip: Take Notes Use a chart like the one below to record the sensory details you find as you read.

Detail	Sense It Appeals To
"desolate sand-boxes knee-deep in crusted ice"	sight

Learning Objectives

For pages 752–771

In studying this text, you will focus on the following objectives:

Literary Study: Analyzing motivation.

Reading: Evaluating sensory details.

Vocabulary

grimace (grim´ is) *n.* facial expression showing contempt, disgust, or pain; p. 755 *Lee made a grimace at the horrible smell.*

ominous (om´ ə nəs) *adj.* threatening; p. 756 *Black clouds in the west looked ominous.*

perturbation (pur´ tər bā´ shən) *n.* state of being perturbed, anxious, or uneasy; p. 757 *The clerk showed perturbation when the police appeared.*

petulance (pech´ ə ləns) *n.* irritability; impatience; p. 761 *The child's petulance wore on the baby-sitter so much that she refused to return the following week.*

mundane (mun dān´) *adj.* ordinary; p. 761 *The mundane details disappointed them.*

Tip: Synonyms Understanding words that are similar in meaning to an unfamiliar word, or **synonyms,** can help you learn the word. Example: *Ominous* and *sinister* are synonyms; they both mean threatening.

Before You Read

Focus

Summary

Dexter Green, a boy from a middle-class family, works as a caddy at a local golf course. There he becomes obsessed with Judy Jones, the daughter of a wealthy businessman. Dexter's goal is to become rich, join high society, and win over Judy. A few years later, Judy accepts him as a suitor but treats him badly. Dexter tries to forget her, but Judy keeps him under her spell. At the end of the story, Dexter learns that Judy has married badly but is a devoted mother. Dexter cannot accept that his dreams have become old and faded.

For summaries in languages other than English, see Unit 5 Teaching Resources Book, pp. 183–188.

Vocabulary

Word Origins Have students use a dictionary to find the origins of vocabulary words. Then ask students to find connections between the meaning of the vocabulary words and the meaning of the words from which they were derived. Explain that finding connections will help them remember the meaning of the words.

(APPROACHING) Tell approaching level students that *ominous* comes from the Latin word *omen*, which means "forboding." **Ask:** What is an omen? Also point out that *mundane* comes from the Latin word *mundus*, which means "world."

For additional vocabulary practice, see Unit 5 Teaching Resources Book, p. 191.

Approaching Level

DIFFERENTIATED INSTRUCTION

Emerging Explain that while plot is about what happens in the story, motivation is about why things happen. Give the following example: Vinita is an 11th-grade student. Even though her classes are difficult this semester, she decides to take a part-time job at the local library. **Ask:** What are some possible reasons Vinita might have had for making this decision? *(She may have wanted to earn some pocket money or to save for college; she may be* thinking about working as a librarian, and she wanted some experience working in a library; she may enjoy being at the library; she may be able to do the library work and get her homework done while earning money.)* **Say:** You have described some of Vinita's possible *motivations.*

Teach

Reading Strategy · 1

Evaluate Sensory Details
Answer: *The details of winter's shutting like a box, Dexter's melancholy, the ragged birds, and the miserable wind all reinforce the gloominess of the setting.*

For additional practice using the reading skill or strategy, see Unit 5 Teaching Resources Book, p.190.

Writer's Technique ☆

Fitzgerald's Style The narrator offers a glimpse of happiness—the crispness of fall and bright colors of summer—amid a description of the misery of winter. Many of Fitzgerald's characters experience life similarly—as a plodding misery punctuated by brief flashes of happiness.

For an audio recording of this selection, use Listening Library Audio CD-ROM.

Readability Scores

Dale-Chall: 7.9
DRP: 60
Lexile: 1080

Winter Dreams

F. Scott Fitzgerald

Some of the caddies were poor as sin and lived in one-room houses with a neurasthenic[1] cow in the front yard, but Dexter Green's father owned the second best grocery-store in Black Bear—the best one was "The Hub," patronized by the wealthy people from Sherry Island—and Dexter caddied only for pocket-money.

☆ In the fall when the days became crisp and gray, and the long Minnesota winter shut down like the white lid of a box, Dexter's skis moved over the snow that hid the fairways of the golf course. At these times the country gave him a feeling of profound melancholy—it offended him that the links should be in enforced fallowness, haunted by ragged sparrows for the long season. It was dreary, too, that on the tees where the gay colors fluttered in summer there were now only the desolate sand-boxes knee-deep in crusted ice. When he crossed the hills the wind blew cold as misery, and if the sun was out he tramped with his eyes squinted up against the hard dimensionless glare.

In April the winter ceased abruptly. The snow ran down into Black Bear Lake scarcely tarrying for the early golfers to brave the season with red and black balls. Without elation, without an interval of moist glory, the cold was gone.

Dexter knew that there was something dismal about this Northern spring, just as he knew there was something gorgeous about the fall. Fall made him clinch his hands and tremble and repeat idiotic sentences to himself, and make brisk abrupt gestures of command to imaginary audiences and armies. October filled him with hope which November raised to a sort of ecstatic triumph, and in this mood the fleeting brilliant impressions of the summer at Sherry Island were ready

---

1. A *neurasthenic* cow is one that is thin and weak.

Evaluate Sensory Details *What details in this paragraph help you visualize the gloomy setting?* 1

Reading Practice

SPIRAL REVIEW **Preview** Explain that Fitzgerald's story follows one character as he strives to reach his goal of becoming rich and entering a higher social circle. Dexter Green is not content with a comfortable middle-class life and dreams of being something greater. On the board, write the following questions, and then ask students to keep them in mind as they read.

- Have you ever wanted to be someone completely different from who you are?
- Have you ever been obsessed by a goal that in the end was not right for you?

grist to his mill. He became a golf champion and defeated Mr. T. A. Hedrick in a marvellous match played a hundred times over the fairways of his imagination, a match each detail of which he changed about untiringly—sometimes he won with almost laughable ease, sometimes he came up magnificently from behind. Again, stepping from a Pierce-Arrow automobile, like Mr. Mortimer Jones, he strolled frigidly into the lounge of the Sherry Island Golf Club—or perhaps, surrounded by an admiring crowd, he gave an exhibition of fancy diving from the springboard of the club raft. . . . Among those who watched him in open-mouthed wonder was Mr. Mortimer Jones.

And one day it came to pass that Mr. Jones—himself and not his ghost—came up to Dexter with tears in his eyes and said that Dexter was the — — best caddy in the club, and wouldn't he decide not to quit if Mr. Jones made it worth his while, because every other — — caddy in the club lost one ball a hole for him—regularly——

2 "No, sir," said Dexter decisively, "I don't want to caddy any more." Then, after a pause: "I'm too old."

"You're not more than fourteen. Why the devil did you decide just this morning that you wanted to quit? You promised that next week you'd go over to the State tournament with me."

"I decided I was too old."

Dexter handed in his "A Class" badge, collected what money was due him from the caddy master, and walked home to Black Bear Village.

"The best — — caddy I ever saw," shouted Mr. Mortimer Jones over a drink that afternoon. "Never lost a ball! Willing! Intelligent! Quiet! Honest! Grateful!"

3 The little girl who had done this was eleven—beautifully ugly as little girls are apt to be who are destined after a few years to be inexpressibly lovely and bring no end of misery to a great number of men. The spark, however, was perceptible. There was a general ungodliness in the way her lips twisted down at the corners when she smiled,

4 Motivation *Why do you think Dexter has these particular daydreams?*

and in the—Heaven help us!—in the almost passionate quality of her eyes. Vitality is born in such women. It was utterly in evidence now, shining through her thin frame in a sort of glow. **3**

She had come eagerly out on to the course at nine o'clock with a white linen nurse and five small new golf-clubs in a white canvas bag which the nurse was carrying. When Dexter first saw her she was standing by the caddy houses, rather ill at ease and trying to conceal the fact by engaging her nurse in an obviously unnatural conversation graced by startling and irrelevant **grimaces** from herself.

"Well, it's certainly a nice day, Hilda," Dexter heard her say. She drew down the corners of her mouth, smiled, and glanced furtively around, her eyes in transit falling for an instant on Dexter.

Then to the nurse:

"Well, I guess there aren't very many people out here this morning, are there?"

The smile again—radiant, blatantly artificial—convincing.

"I don't know what we're supposed to do now," said the nurse, looking nowhere in particular.

"Oh, that's all right. I'll fix it up."

Dexter stood perfectly still, his mouth slightly ajar. He knew that if he moved forward a step his state would be in her line of vision—if he moved backward he would lose his full view of her face. For a moment he had not realized how young she was. Now he remembered having seen her several times the year before—in bloomers.[2]

Suddenly, involuntarily, he laughed, a short abrupt laugh—then, startled by himself, he turned and began to walk quickly away.

"Boy!"

Dexter stopped.

"Boy—"

Beyond question he was addressed. Not only that, but he was treated to that absurd smile, that

---

2. *Bloomers* are baggy trousers gathered at the knee and once worn by girls and women as an athletic costume.

Vocabulary

grimace (grim´ is) *n.* facial expression showing contempt, disgust, or pain

F. SCOTT FITZGERALD **755**

Teach

Reading Strategy 2

Make Inferences Point out that Dexter quitting as a caddy is a real event, not part of his daydream. **Ask:** Why do you think Dexter quits? *(He says he is too old, but in the previous paragraph he was daydreaming about beating a rich man at golf; Dexter may be thinking he is above his job as caddy.)*

APPROACHING **Ask:** What transitional phrase shows the story shift from Dexter's daydream to the reality of Mr. Jones speaking with him? *("And one day it came to pass")*

Literary Element 3

Character Tell students that Fitzgerald characterizes Judy Jones as a woman-child throughout the story even though she is only eleven years old when she first appears in the story. **Ask:** Which words from the story more typically describe a woman than a young girl? *(The narrator talks about the little girl's "spark," the "ungodliness" in her lips, and calls her eyes "passionate.")*

Literary Element 4

Motivation Answer: *He is imagining a future beyond his lowly job as caddy.*

Teach

Literary Element | 1

Motivation Answer: *Students will likely say that the girl's behavior is not justified; she is being bratty and bossy.*

[APPROACHING] **Ask:** What do Judy's actions reveal about her character? *(She is impulsive and bossy)* **Ask:** Why does Fitzgerald describe Dexter as feeling "a monstrous convictiton" that Judy is right in hitting her nurse? *(Dexter is immediately charmed by Judy's looks and antics at their first meeting.)*

View the Art ★

Answer: *The woman in the image is stylishly dressed and appears utterly self-assured.*

Portrait of a Woman Golfer by Maude Martin Ellis reinforces the image of golf as a sport for the wealthy.

Portrait of a Woman Golfer, 1922. Maude Martin Ellis. Private collection.

View the Art When Fitzgerald wrote this story, golf—a sport long dominated by men—was becoming popular with women as well. How does the woman in this picture compare with your image of Miss Jones? ★

preposterous smile—the memory of which at least a dozen men were to carry into middle age.

"Boy, do you know where the golf teacher is?"

"He's giving a lesson."

"Well, do you know where the caddy-master is?"

"He isn't here yet this morning."

"Oh." For a moment this baffled her. She stood alternately on her right and left foot.

"We'd like to get a caddy," said the nurse. "Mr. Mortimer Jones sent us out to play golf, and we don't know how without we get a caddy."

Here she was stopped by an **ominous** glance from Miss Jones, followed immediately by the smile.

Vocabulary

ominous (om′ ə nəs) *adj.* threatening

"There aren't any caddies here except me," said Dexter to the nurse, "and I got to stay here in charge until the caddy-master gets here."

"Oh."

Miss Jones and her retinue[3] now withdrew, and at a proper distance from Dexter became involved in a heated conversation, which was concluded by Miss Jones taking one of the clubs and hitting it on the ground with violence. For further emphasis she raised it again and was about to bring it down smartly upon the nurse's bosom, when the nurse seized the club and twisted it from her hands.

"You damn little mean old *thing!*" cried Miss Jones wildly.

Another argument ensued. Realizing that the elements of comedy were implied in the scene, Dexter several times began to laugh, but each time restrained the laugh before it reached audibility. He could not resist the monstrous conviction that the little girl was justified in beating the nurse.

The situation was resolved by the fortuitous appearance of the caddy-master, who was appealed to immediately by the nurse.

"Miss Jones is to have a little caddy, and this one says he can't go."

"Mr. McKenna said I was to wait here till you came," said Dexter quickly.

"Well, he's here now." Miss Jones smiled cheerfully at the caddy-master. Then she dropped her bag and set off at a haughty mince[4] toward the first tee.

"Well?" The caddy-master turned to Dexter. "What you standing there like a dummy for? Go pick up the young lady's clubs."

"I don't think I'll go out to-day," said Dexter.

"You don't—"

"I think I'll quit."

The enormity of his decision frightened him. He was a favorite caddy, and the thirty dollars a

---

3. A *retinue* is an attendant or a helper.
4. A *mince* is a proper, affected walk.

Motivation *Do you think Miss Jones's anger is justified? Why or why not?* | 1

Writing Practice

SMALL GROUP

Dramatize a Scene Have students imagine the scene with Dexter, Judy, and her nurse on the golf course as a moment on a television show. Have small groups of students write a one- or two-minute television script dramatizing this scene. Instruct students to include stage directions, dialogue, and an inner monologue for Dexter that he can speak out loud to the audience. After rehearsing, students can act out the scene.

month he earned through the summer were not to be made elsewhere around the lake. But he had received a strong emotional shock, and his **perturbation** required a violent and immediate outlet.

It was not so simple as that, either. As so frequently would be the case in the future, Dexter was unconsciously dictated to by his winter dreams.

II

Now, of course, the quality and the seasonability of these winter dreams varied, but the stuff of them remained. They persuaded Dexter several years later to pass up a business course at the State university—his father, prospering now, would have paid his way—for the precarious advantage of attending an older and more famous university in the East, where he was bothered by his scanty funds. But do not get the impression, because his winter dreams happened to be concerned at first with musings on the rich, that there was anything merely snobbish in the boy. He wanted not association with glittering things and glittering people—he wanted the glittering things themselves. Often he reached out for the best without knowing why he wanted it—and sometimes he ran up against the mysterious denials and prohibitions in which life indulges. It is with one of those denials and not with his career as a whole that this story deals.

He made money. It was rather amazing. After college he went to the city from which Black Bear Lake draws its wealthy patrons. When he was only twenty-three and had been there not quite two years, there were already people who liked to say: "Now *there's* a boy—" All about

him rich men's sons were peddling bonds precariously, or investing patrimonies[5] precariously, or plodding through the two dozen volumes of the "George Washington Commercial Course," but Dexter borrowed a thousand dollars on his college degree and his confident mouth, and bought a partnership in a laundry.

It was a small laundry when he went into it, but Dexter made a specialty of learning how the English washed fine woolen golf-stockings without shrinking them, and within a year he was catering to the trade that wore knickerbockers.[6] Men were insisting that their Shetland hose and sweaters go to his laundry, just as they had insisted on a caddy who could find golf-balls. A little later he was doing their wives' lingerie as well—and running five branches in different parts of the city. Before he was twenty-seven he owned the largest string of laundries in his section of the country. It was then that he sold out and went to New York. But the part of his story that concerns us goes back to the days when he was making his first big success.

When he was twenty-three Mr. Hart—one of the gray-haired men who liked to say "Now there's a boy"—gave him a guest card to the Sherry Island Golf Club for a week-end. So he signed his name one day on the register, and that afternoon played golf in a foursome with Mr. Hart and Mr. Sandwood and Mr. T. A. Hedrick. He did not consider it necessary to remark that he had once carried Mr. Hart's bag over this same links, and that he knew every trap and gully with his eyes shut—but he found himself glancing at the four caddies who trailed them, trying to catch a gleam or gesture that would remind him of himself, that would lessen the gap which lay between his present and his past.

It was a curious day, slashed abruptly with fleeting, familiar impressions. One minute he had the sense of being a trespasser—in the next he was impressed by the tremendous superiority he felt toward Mr. T. A. Hedrick, who was a bore and not even a good golfer any more.

---

 2 Modern Fiction *What is the "emotional shock" that has made Dexter quit caddying?*

3 Motivation *What is Dexter's motivation for seeking "the glittering things"?*

Vocabulary

perturbation (pur´ tər bā´ shən) *n.* state of being perturbed, anxious, or uneasy

---

5. A *patrimony* is an inheritance from a father.
6. *Knickerbockers* are full pants gathered just below the knee.

F. SCOTT FITZGERALD **757**

Teach

Big Idea   2

Modern Fiction
Answer: *The realization that a bratty 11-year-old girl is allowed to tell him what to do shocked him emotionally.*

Literary Element   3

Motivation Answer: *Having glittering things is part of Dexter's winter dreams.*

APPROACHING **Say:** Remember that Dexter's main motivation—his winter dreams—is not clearly stated. It is suggested by his daydreaming and his decisions to quit caddying and to attend a prestigious eastern school. Point out that Dexter is motivated to obtain the things that he is denied of when he is younger: wealth, prestige, the pretty rich girl.

Cultural History ☆

Golf in America Americans played informal rounds of golf as early as 1779. Players hit balls on playing fields for more than 100 years before clubs with groomed courses were created in the late 1800s.

English Learners

DIFFERENTIATED INSTRUCTION

Advanced Tell students that *malicious* is an adjective related to the noun *malice*. *Malice* means the desire to cause pain or injury to another. Have students guess the meaning of *malicious*.

Approaching Level

DIFFERENTIATED INSTRUCTION

SMALL GROUP **Established** Have students form small groups and assign passages to read aloud. Ask them to discuss what happens in the passage and what they noticed about Fitzgerald's use of language.

Teach

Literary Element   1

Character **Say:** Try to imagine Judy's tone of voice and facial expressions when she apologizes for having hit the man with her ball. **Ask:** Do you think the girl was sorry? *(Her casual glance and her desire to "play through" suggest that she is not sorry.)* **Ask:** Do you think the girl is ingenuous or malicious? *(Students may suggest that she is malicious; she seems to know exactly what she is doing.)*

Reading Strategy   2

Evaluate Sensory Details
Answer: *The description is appealing because it supports the previous statement that "she was arrestingly beautiful" and emphasizes her vibrancy. The description appeals to the senses of sight and touch.*

[ENGLISH LEARNERS] **Ask:** What do you think "high" color means? *(bright red)*

Reading Strategy   3

Evaluate Sensory Details
Answer: *Like the lake, Dexter becomes quiet and reflective at the thought of being near Judy. Both nature and Dexter experience a feeling of quiet anticipation at Judy's approach.*

Then, because of a ball Mr. Hart lost near the fifteenth green, an enormous thing happened. While they were searching the stiff grasses of the rough there was a clear call of "Fore!" from behind a hill in their rear. And as they all turned abruptly from their search a bright new ball sliced abruptly over the hill and caught Mr. T. A. Hedrick in the abdomen.

"By Gad!" cried Mr. T. A. Hedrick, "they ought to put some of these crazy women off the course. It's getting to be outrageous."

A head and a voice came up together over the hill:

"Do you mind if we go through?"

"You hit me in the stomach!" declared Mr. Hedrick wildly.

"Did I?" The girl approached the group of men. "I'm sorry. I yelled 'Fore!'"

Her glance fell casually on each of the men—then scanned the fairway for her ball.

"Did I bounce into the rough?"

It was impossible to determine whether this question was ingenuous or malicious. In a moment, however, she left no doubt, for as her partner came up over the hill she called cheerfully:

"Here I am! I'd have gone on the green except that I hit something."

As she took her stance for a short mashie[7] shot, Dexter looked at her closely. She wore a blue gingham dress, rimmed at throat and shoulders with a white edging that accentuated her tan. The quality of exaggeration, of thinness, which had made her passionate eyes and down-turning mouth absurd at eleven, was gone now. She was arrestingly beautiful. The color in her cheeks was centered like the color in a picture—it was not a "high" color, but a sort of fluctuating and feverish warmth, so shaded that it seemed at any moment it would recede and disappear. This color and the mobility of her mouth gave a continual impression of flux, of

---

7. A *mashie* is a five-iron used in playing golf.

Evaluate Sensory Details *Why is this a pleasing description of the girl's cheeks? To what sense does the description appeal?*   2

intense life, of passionate vitality—balanced only partially by the sad luxury of her eyes.

She swung her mashie impatiently and without interest, pitching the ball into a sand-pit on the other side of the green. With a quick, insincere smile and a careless "Thank you!" she went on after it.

"That Judy Jones!" remarked Mr. Hedrick on the next tee, as they waited—some moments—for her to play on ahead. "All she needs is to be turned up and spanked for six months and then to be married off to an old-fashioned cavalry captain."

"My God, she's good-looking!" said Mr. Sandwood, who was just over thirty.

"Good-looking!" cried Mr. Hedrick contemptuously. "She always looks as if she wanted to be kissed! Turning those big cow-eyes on every calf in town!"

It was doubtful if Mr. Hedrick intended a reference to the maternal instinct.

"She'd play pretty good golf if she'd try," said Mr. Sandwood.

"She has no form," said Mr. Hedrick solemnly.

"She has a nice figure," said Mr. Sandwood.

"Better thank the Lord she doesn't drive a swifter ball," said Mr. Hart, winking at Dexter.

Later in the afternoon the sun went down with a riotous swirl of gold and varying blues and scarlets, and left the dry, rustling night of Western summer. Dexter watched from the veranda of the Golf Club, watched the even overlap of the waters in the little wind, silver molasses under the harvest-moon. Then the moon held a finger to her lips and the lake became a clear pool, pale and quiet. Dexter put on his bathing-suit and swam out to the farthest raft, where he stretched dripping on the wet canvas of the springboard.

There was a fish jumping and a star shining and the lights around the lake were gleaming. Over on a dark peninsula a piano was playing the songs of last summer and of summers before that—songs from "Chin-Chin" and "The Count of Luxemburg" and "The Chocolate

Evaluate Sensory Details *How does this description reflect Dexter's feelings for Judy?*   3

Research Practice

SPIRAL REVIEW **The 1920s Economy** Dexter Green is able to become wealthy thanks to the economic boom that took place in urban areas in the years following World War I. Investing in stocks, trading bonds, and borrowing money became more common among the middle class. The widespread buying of stocks on credit, however, would eventually turn the boom into a devastating crash. Encourage interested students to research one impact of the economic boom on the American lifestyle in the 1920s. Have students write a paragraph about their research and share the information with the class.

The Music Pavilion. Henri Le Sidaner. Oil on canvas, 73 x 60.5 cm. Private collection.

Soldier"[8]—and because the sound of a piano over a stretch of water had always seemed beautiful to Dexter he lay perfectly quiet and listened.

The tune the piano was playing at that moment had been gay and new five years before when Dexter was a sophomore at college. They had played it at a prom once when he could not afford the luxury of proms, and he had stood outside the gymnasium and listened. The sound of the tune precipitated in him a sort of ecstasy and it was with that ecstasy he viewed what happened to him now. It was a mood of intense appreciation, a sense that, for once, he was magnificently attuned to life and that everything about him was radiating a brightness and a glamour he might never know again.

---

8. *"Chin-Chin," "The Count of Luxemburg,"* and *"The Chocolate Soldier"* are all musicals or light operas popular at the time of the story.

A low, pale oblong detached itself suddenly from the darkness of the Island, spitting forth the reverberated sound of a racing motor-boat. Two white streamers of cleft water rolled themselves out behind it and almost immediately the boat was beside him, drowning out the hot tinkle of the piano in the drone of its spray. Dexter raising himself on his arms was aware of a figure standing at the wheel, of two dark eyes regarding him over the lengthening space of water—then the boat had gone by and was sweeping in an immense and purposeless circle of spray round and round in the middle of the lake. With equal eccentricity one of the circles flattened out and headed back toward the raft.

"Who's that?" she called, shutting off her motor. She was so near now that Dexter could see her bathing-suit, which consisted apparently of pink rompers.[9]

The nose of the boat bumped the raft, and as the latter tilted rakishly he was precipitated toward her. With different degrees of interest they recognized each other.

"Aren't you one of those men we played through this afternoon?" she demanded.

He was.

"Well, do you know how to drive a motorboat? Because if you do I wish you'd drive this one so I can ride on the surf-board behind. My name is Judy Jones"—she favored him with an absurd smirk—rather, what tried to be a smirk, for, twist her mouth as she might, it was not grotesque, it was merely beautiful—"and I live in a house over there on the Island, and in that house there is a man waiting for me. When he drove up at the door I drove out of the dock because he says I'm his ideal."

There was a fish jumping and a star shining and the lights around the lake were gleaming. Dexter sat beside Judy Jones and she explained how her boat was driven. Then she was in the water, swimming to the floating surf-board with a sinuous crawl. Watching her was without effort to the eye, watching a branch waving or

---

9. *Rompers* are a one-piece outfit consisting of loose pants gathered at the knee.

F. SCOTT FITZGERALD **759**

Teach

Reading Strategy 4

Make Inferences Ask: What is Dexter's mood in this paragraph? What words indicate his mood? *(Dexter is lulled by the music into a brilliant mood. He is "magnificently attuned to life" and everything around him is "radiating a brightness and a glamour he might never know again.")* **Ask:** What might the words "radiating a brightness and a glamour he might never know again" be suggesting about Dexter's encounter with Judy? *(Dexter's late night encounter with Judy will be the pinnacle of happiness in his relationship with Judy. Dexter will never be able to recapture that same happiness in the rest of his encounters with Judy.)*

View the Art ★

French painter Henri Le Sidaner (1862–1939) adopted several styles during his career. Mid-career, he began to paint in broad brush strokes, as in this painting. He also painted his subjects from memory.

English Learners

DIFFERENTIATED INSTRUCTION

Intermediate Point out that Fitzgerald uses the word *sinuous* twice in one paragraph—once as an adjective (sinuous) and once as an adverb (sinuously)—to describe Judy's movements as she swims. **Say:** Fitzgerald also uses a metaphor to describe her movements: "Watching her was without effort to the eye, watching a branch waving or a seagull flying."

Ask: Given this metaphor, what do you think *sinuous* means? *(graceful, flexible)*

Teach

Reading Strategy   1

Evaluate Sensory Details

Answer: *Students may say that it appeals more to the sense of sight, since the narrator is describing Judy Jones's movements. Words like* stabbing *also appeal to the sense of touch.*

[APPROACHING] **Say:** Fitzgerald captured fleeting but important moments in his characters' lives. He focused on small, sensory details. The narrator does not have to explain the impact of Judy's appearance on Dexter; the details suggest that Dexter is deeply moved.

Big Idea   2

Modern Fiction **Answer:**

"His heart turned over" implies that Dexter has felt the stirrings of a strong attraction to Judy. The first "casual whim" had been her desire to play at the golf course where Dexter had been a caddy many years earlier.

View the Art ★

Answer: *The abundance of glittering, beautiful things, the richness of the people's dress, and the air of festivity and respectability might appeal to Dexter.*

Point out that the painting depicts the opulence and grandeur enjoyed by wealthy people around this time.

Victorian Ball. Vincent McIndoe.

View the Art Hosting—and attending—a ball like the one pictured here was a sign of affluence and respectability during the era when "Winter Dreams" takes place. What elements of high society depicted here might Dexter have found attractive?

He told her.

"Well, why don't you come to dinner to-morrow night?"

His heart turned over like the fly-wheel of the boat, and, for the second time, her casual whim gave a new direction to his life.

III

Next evening while he waited for her to come down-stairs, Dexter peopled the soft deep summer room and the sun-porch that opened from it with the men who had already loved Judy Jones. He knew the sort of men they were— the men who when he first went to college had entered from the great prep schools with graceful

a sea-gull flying. Her arms, burned to butternut, moved sinuously among the dull platinum ripples, elbow appearing first, casting the forearm back with a cadence of falling water, then reaching out and down, stabbing a path ahead.

They moved out into the lake; turning, Dexter saw that she was kneeling on the low rear of the now uptilted surf-board.

"Go faster," she called, "fast as it'll go."

Obediently he jammed the lever forward and the white spray mounted at the bow. When he looked around again the girl was standing up on the rushing board, her arms spread wide, her eyes lifted toward the moon.

"It's awful cold," she shouted. "What's your name?"

clothes and the deep tan of healthy summers. He had seen that, in one sense, he was better than these men. He was newer and stronger. Yet in acknowledging to himself that he wished his children to be like them he was admitting that he was but the rough, strong stuff from which they eternally sprang.

When the time had come for him to wear good clothes, he had known who were the best tailors in America, and the best tailors in America had made him the suit he wore this evening. He had acquired that particular reserve peculiar to his university, that set it off from other universities. He recognized the value to him of such a mannerism and he had

1 Evaluate Sensory Details **Does this description appeal more to the sense of sight or the sense of touch? Explain.**

Modern Fiction **What does "His heart turned over" imply? What was the first "casual whim" that affected Dexter?**   **2**

Study Skills Practice

Research the Author Fitzgerald based many of his stories and characters on his own experiences. Like Dexter Green, Fitzgerald was born and raised in the Midwest and struggled for years to earn enough money to win the rich girl of his dreams. Tell students to read about Fitzgerald's life, particularly his autobiographical works, such as *The Crack-Up* (1945). Tell students to look for comparisons between Fitzgerald and Dexter. Students can present their findings in an oral report.

adopted it; he knew that to be careless in dress and manner required more confidence than to be careful. But carelessness was for his children. His mother's name had been Krimplich. She was a Bohemian[10] of the peasant class and she had talked broken English to the end of her days. Her son must keep to the set patterns.

At a little after seven Judy Jones came downstairs. She wore a blue silk afternoon dress, and he was disappointed at first that she had not put on something more elaborate. This feeling was accentuated when, after a brief greeting, she went to the door of a butler's pantry and pushing it open called: "You can serve dinner, Martha." He had rather expected that a butler would announce dinner, that there would be a cocktail. Then he put these thoughts behind him as they sat down side by side on a lounge and looked at each other.

"Father and mother won't be here," she said thoughtfully.

He remembered the last time he had seen her father, and he was glad the parents were not to be here to-night—they might wonder who he was. He had been born in Keeble, a Minnesota village fifty miles farther north, and he always gave Keeble as his home instead of Black Bear Village. Country towns were well enough to come from if they weren't inconveniently in sight and used as footstools by fashionable lakes.

They talked of his university, which she had visited frequently during the past two years, and of the near-by city which supplied Sherry Island with its patrons, and whither Dexter would return next day to his prospering laundries.

During dinner she slipped into a moody depression which gave Dexter a feeling of uneasiness. Whatever **petulance** she uttered in her throaty voice worried him. Whatever she smiled at—at him, at a chicken liver, at nothing—it

disturbed him that her smile could have no root in mirth, or even in amusement. When the scarlet corners of her lips curved down, it was less a smile than an invitation to a kiss.

Then, after dinner, she led him out on the dark sun-porch and deliberately changed the atmosphere.

"Do you mind if I weep a little?" she said.

"I'm afraid I'm boring you," he responded quickly.

"You're not. I like you. But I've just had a terrible afternoon. There was a man I cared about, and this afternoon he told me out of a clear sky that he was poor as a church-mouse. He'd never even hinted it before. Does this sound horribly **mundane**?"

"Perhaps he was afraid to tell you."

"Suppose he was," she answered. "He didn't start right. You see, if I'd thought of him as poor—well, I've been mad about loads of poor men, and fully intended to marry them all. But in this case, I hadn't thought of him that way, and my interest in him wasn't strong enough to survive the shock. As if a girl calmly informed her fiancé that she was a widow. He might not object to widows, but—

"Let's start right," she interrupted herself suddenly. "Who are you, anyhow?"

For a moment Dexter hesitated. Then:

"I'm nobody," he announced. "My career is largely a matter of futures."

"Are you poor?"

"No," he said frankly, "I'm probably making more money than any man my age in the Northwest. I know that's an obnoxious remark, but you advised me to start right."

There was a pause. Then she smiled and the corners of her mouth drooped and an almost imperceptible sway brought her closer to him, looking up into his eyes. A lump rose in Dexter's

---

10. A *Bohemian* is a native of Bohemia, now part of the Czech Republic.

3 Motivation *What does Dexter's reason for giving Keeble as his home tell you about him?*

Vocabulary

petulance (pech´ ə ləns) *n.* irritability; impatience.

Motivation *What prompts Judy to smile and look into Dexter's eyes, when she has been moodily depressed up until this point?* **4**

Vocabulary

mundane (mun dān´) *adj.* ordinary

F. SCOTT FITZGERALD **761**

Teach

Literary Element | **3**

Motivation Answer: *Keeble is less unfashionable than Black Bear Village. Dexter wants to be fashionable and fit in with Judy's crowd and her family, even if it means being dishonest.*

[ENGLISH LEARNERS] Fitzgerald writes that "Country towns were well enough to come from if they weren't inconveniently in sight and used as footstools by fashionable lakes." **Ask:** What is a footstool? *(a stool for resting the feet when sitting)* **Ask:** What does this imply about the function of Black Bear Village for the wealthy people of Sherry Island? *(It served their needs.)*

Literary Element | **4**

Motivation Answer: *Dexter has just told her that he's making more money than any other man his age in the Northwest, in contrast to the man who earlier declared that he was "poor as a church-mouse."*

[ENGLISH LEARNERS] **Say:** Fitzgerald writes that Judy's kisses made Dexter feel, rather than hunger, "surfeit that would demand more surfeit." **Ask:** Can you guess the meaning of surfeit from this phrase? *(fullness)*

Approaching Level

DIFFERENTIATED INSTRUCTION

Established Students may benefit from a review of the meaning of *foreshadow:* a writer's use of clues or hints to prepare readers for later events in the story. **Ask:** Were you surprised that Judy is seeing men other than Dexter? Justify your answer with details from the text. (*Students may say no because Judy kisses Dexter when he tells her he is rich. Also, Judy does not seem to care about oth-* ers: *she doesn't seem to care that she hit another golfer with her golf ball. However, Fitzgerald has described the effect of Judy's beautiful features on men several times, so students may not be surprised.*)

Teach

Literary Element | 1

Motivation **Ask:** What effect do Judy's kisses have on Dexter? *(Her kisses make him want to kiss her even more. They make him realize that he has always been attracted to her.)*

Big Idea | 2

Modern Fiction **Answer:** *She seems unlikely to be true to one person. That Dexter is upset by the "varying dozen" bodes ill for their future relationship.*

Literary Element | 3

Motivation **Answer:** *The men seem to be completely engaged by her, and each one probably hopes that he will be the one she chooses.*

ADVANCED **Ask:** How would you characterize the way Judy handles men? *(She manipulates them; when they come on too strong, she changes her approach. The men all play her game.)*

throat, and he waited breathless for the experiment, facing the unpredictable compound that would form mysteriously from the elements of their lips. Then he saw—she communicated her excitement to him, lavishly, deeply, with kisses that were not a promise but a fulfilment. They aroused in him not hunger demanding renewal but surfeit that would demand more surfeit . . . kisses that were like charity, creating want by holding back nothing at all.

1 It did not take him many hours to decide that he had wanted Judy Jones ever since he was a proud, desirous little boy.

IV

It began like that—and continued, with varying shades of intensity, on such a note right up to the dénouement. Dexter surrendered a part of himself to the most direct and unprincipled personality with which he had ever come in contact. Whatever Judy wanted, she went after with the full pressure of her charm. There was no divergence of method, no jockeying for position or premeditation of effects—there was a very little mental side to any of her affairs. She simply made men conscious to the highest degree of her physical loveliness. Dexter had no desire to change her. Her deficiencies were knit up with a passionate energy that transcended and justified them.

When, as Judy's head lay against his shoulder that first night, she whispered, "I don't know what's the matter with me. Last night I thought I was in love with a man and to-night I think I'm in love with you——" —it seemed to him a beautiful and romantic thing to say. It was the exquisite excitability that for the moment he controlled and owned. But a week later he was compelled to view this same quality in a different light. She took him in her roadster to a picnic supper, and after supper she disappeared, likewise in her roadster, with another man. Dexter became enormously upset and was scarcely able to be decently civil to the other people present. When she assured him that she had not kissed the other man, he knew she was

lying—yet he was glad that she had taken the trouble to lie to him.

He was, as he found before the summer ended, one of a varying dozen who circulated about her. Each of them had at one time been favored above all others—about half of them still basked in the solace of occasional sentimental revivals. Whenever one showed signs of dropping out through long neglect, she granted him a brief honeyed hour, which encouraged him to tag along for a year or so longer. Judy made these forays upon the helpless and defeated without malice, indeed half unconscious that there was anything mischievous in what she did.

When a new man came to town every one dropped out—dates were automatically cancelled.

The helpless part of trying to do anything about it was that she did it all herself. She was not a girl who could be "won" in the kinetic sense—she was proof against cleverness, she was proof against charm; if any of these assailed her too strongly she would immediately resolve the affair to a physical basis, and under the magic of her physical splendor the strong as well as the brilliant played her game and not their own. She was entertained only by the gratification of her desires and by the direct exercise of her own charm. Perhaps from so much youthful love, so many youthful lovers, she had come, in self-defense, to nourish herself wholly from within.

Succeeding Dexter's first exhilaration came restlessness and dissatisfaction. The helpless ecstasy of losing himself in her was opiate rather than tonic.[11] It was fortunate for his work during the winter that those moments of ecstasy came infrequently. Early in their acquaintance it had seemed for a while that there was a deep and spontaneous mutual attraction—that first August,

---

11. *Opiate rather than tonic* means that Dexter's helpless ecstasy is numbing rather than stimulating.

Modern Fiction *What does Dexter's discovery foreshadow about his relationship with Judy?* **2**

Motivation *Why do Dexter and the other men tolerate Judy's behavior?* **3**

Listening and Speaking Practice

Formal Discussion Have students prepare for a formal discussion by writing the following question on the board: Are Dexter's feelings for Judy romantic or foolish? Require students to write down their first response to the question. Then have them gather evidence from the story, including specific quotes and examples, to support their opinions. Once students have enough evidence, begin the discussion by alternating between students who represent each side of the issue. For students struggling to pick sides, ask them to explain the distinction between these two characteristics and choose which Dexter is more like.

for example—three days of long evenings on her dusky veranda, of strange wan kisses through the late afternoon, in shadowy alcoves or behind the protecting trellises of the garden arbors, of mornings when she was fresh as a dream and almost shy at meeting him in the clarity of the rising day. There was all the ecstasy of an engagement about it, sharpened by his realization that there was no engagement. It was during those three days that, for the first time, he had asked her to marry him. She said "maybe some day," she said "kiss me," she said "I'd like to marry you," she said "I love you"—she said—nothing.

The three days were interrupted by the arrival of a New York man who visited at her house for half September. To Dexter's agony, rumor engaged them. The man was the son of the president of a great trust company. But at the end of a month it was reported that Judy was yawning. At a dance one night she sat all evening in a motorboat with a local beau, while the New Yorker searched the club for her frantically. She told the local beau that she was bored with her visitor, and two days later he left. She was seen with him at the station, and it was reported that he looked very mournful indeed.

On this note the summer ended. Dexter was twenty-four, and he found himself increasingly in a position to do as he wished. He joined two clubs in the city and lived at one of them. Though he was by no means an integral part of the stag-lines[12] at these clubs, he managed to be on hand at dances where Judy Jones was likely to appear. He could have gone out socially as much as he liked—he was an eligible young man, now, and popular with down-town fathers. His confessed devotion to Judy Jones had rather solidified his position. But he had no social aspirations and rather despised the dancing men who were always on tap for the Thursday or Saturday parties and who filled in at dinners

---

12. *Stag-lines* are lines of single men waiting for dance partners at the clubs.

Evaluate Sensory Details *What do the words* dusky, shadowy, *and* protecting trellises *imply about the nature of Dexter and Judy's relationship?*

---

with the younger married set. Already he was playing with the idea of going East to New York. He wanted to take Judy Jones with him. No disillusion as to the world in which she had grown up could cure his illusion as to her desirability.

Remember that—for only in the light of it can what he did for her be understood.

Eighteen months after he first met Judy Jones he became engaged to another girl. Her name was Irene Scheerer, and her father was one of the men who had always believed in Dexter. Irene was light-haired and sweet and honorable, and a little stout, and she had two suitors whom she pleasantly relinquished when Dexter formally asked her to marry him.

Summer, fall, winter, spring, another summer, another fall—so much he had given of his active life to the incorrigible lips of Judy Jones. She had treated him with interest, with encouragement, with malice, with indifference, with contempt. She had inflicted on him the innumerable little slights and indignities possible in such a case—as if in revenge for having ever cared for him at all. She had beckoned him and yawned at him and beckoned him again and he had responded often with bitterness and narrowed eyes. She had brought him ecstatic happiness and intolerable agony of spirit. She had caused him untold inconvenience and not a little trouble. She had insulted him, and she had ridden over him, and she had played his interest in her against his interest in his work—for fun. She had done everything to him except to criticise him—this she had not done—it seemed to him only because it might have sullied the utter indifference she manifested and sincerely felt toward him.

When autumn had come and gone again it occurred to him that he could not have Judy Jones. He had to beat this into his mind but he convinced himself at last. He lay awake at night for a while and argued it over. He told himself the trouble and the pain she had

---

Modern Fiction *Why do you think this is the only description of Irene, despite the fact that Dexter becomes engaged to her?*

Reading Strategy 4

Evaluate Sensory Details Answer: *The details suggest their romance is growing intensely and taking on a dreamlike quality for Dexter.*

(APPROACHING) **Ask:** How does Dexter's "winter self" differ from the way he is during his summer with Judy? *(During the winter, Dexter is a hard worker. During the summer, he allows himself to lose focus and fall under Judy's spell.)*

Big Idea 5

Modern Fiction Answer: *Dexter seems to take Irene for granted. She seems ordinary and arouses little passion in him.*

(ADVANCED) **Say:** Modern fiction captures the psychic and emotional restlessness of the "lost generation." **Ask:** Does it surprise you that Dexter has become engaged to another woman only eighteen months after meeting Judy Jones? *(Students may not be surprised because Judy is clearly unable to commit herself to Dexter. Or students may be surprised because Dexter seems so obsessed with Judy.)*

English Learners

DIFFERENTIATED INSTRUCTION

Intermediate Fitzgerald's use of adjectives may give English learners trouble—for example, *incorrigible, innumerable, ecstatic,* and *untold*. Tell students to identify adjectives that give them trouble. Have them work in pairs and use a dictionary to learn the meanings of these words.

Approaching Level

DIFFERENTIATED INSTRUCTION

Emerging Students may have trouble grasping Dexter's seemingly sudden shift from Judy to Irene. Work through the sequence of events with students and list the events on the board. Have students discover the time frame of the events (18 months), list details of what Dexter endured, and finally list details of how he made up his mind to let go of Judy.

Teach

Reading Strategy | 1

Evaluate Sensory Details

Answer: *These images are further evidence that Irene will be merely a backdrop to his life.*

(APPROACHING) **Ask:** What details in the paragraph establish Dexter's mood? *(The darkness and dampness reflect Dexter's depression.)*

View the Art ★

Answer: *Her suitors, like these men, are rich and have plenty of leisure time. The artwork offers a glimpse into the world of the rich gentlemen's club.*

French artist Jean Béraud (1849–1935?), who painted *Le Cercle* in 1911, was among the late Impressionists whose style was described by critics as polished or finished.

Le cercle, The Club, 1911. Jean Beraud. Oil on canvas, 61 x 73.5 cm. Musee d'Orsay, Paris.

View the Art When "Winter Dreams" was published in 1922, young adults had begun to reject formal courtship in favor of dating, which was more about socializing than settling down. However, men were still expected to initiate relationships. What might Judy's suitors have had in common with the two men in this painting? ★

caused him, he enumerated her glaring deficiencies as a wife. Then he said to himself that he loved her, and after a while he fell asleep. For a week, lest he imagined her husky voice over the telephone or her eyes opposite him at lunch, he worked hard and late, and at night he went to his office and plotted out his years.

At the end of a week he went to a dance and cut in on her once. For almost the first time since they had met he did not ask her to sit out with him or tell her that she was lovely. It hurt him that she did not miss these things—that was all. He was not jealous when he saw that there was a new man to-night. He had been hardened against jealousy long before.

He stayed late at the dance. He sat for an hour with Irene Scheerer and talked about books and about music. He knew very little about either. But he was beginning to be master of his own time now, and he had a rather priggish notion that he—the young and already fab-

ulously successful Dexter Green—should know more about such things.

That was in October, when he was twenty-five. In January, Dexter and Irene became engaged. It was to be announced in June, and they were to be married three months later.

The Minnesota winter prolonged itself interminably, and it was almost May when the winds came soft and the snow ran down into Black Bear Lake at last. For the first time in over a year Dexter was enjoying a certain tranquillity of spirit. Judy Jones had been in Florida, and afterward in Hot Springs, and somewhere she had been engaged, and somewhere she had broken it off. At first, when Dexter had definitely given her up, it had made him sad that people still linked them together and asked for news of her, but when he began to be placed at dinner next to Irene Scheerer people didn't ask him about her any more—they told him about her. He ceased to be an authority on her.

May at last. Dexter walked the streets at night when the darkness was damp as rain, wondering that so soon, with so little done, so much of ecstasy had gone from him. May one year back had been marked by Judy's poignant, unforgivable, yet forgiven turbulence—it had been one of those rare times when he fancied she had grown to care for him. That old penny's worth of happiness he had spent for this bushel of content. He knew that Irene would be no more than a curtain spread behind him, a hand moving among gleaming tea-cups, a voice calling to children . . . ☆

Evaluate Sensory Details *What do these two images tell you about Dexter's attitude toward Irene?* **1**

Writing Practice

College Application Essay Tell students that most colleges require applicants to write an essay. Often they request a specific topic. Have students write a 250–300 word essay analyzing "Winter Dreams." Suggest that they clearly identify the story's significance in the introductory paragraph, use details and quotations to support their points, and use vivid language to reveal their thoughts about the work. If time allows, ask students to exchange papers and offer constructive criticism.

fire and loveliness were gone, the magic of nights and the wonder of the varying hours and seasons . . . slender lips, down-turning, dropping to his lips and bearing him up into a heaven of eyes. . . . The thing was deep in him. He was too strong and alive for it to die lightly.

In the middle of May when the weather balanced for a few days on the thin bridge that led to deep summer he turned in one night at Irene's house. Their engagement was to be announced in a week now—no one could be surprised at it. And to-night they would sit together on the lounge at the University Club and look on for an hour at the dancers. It gave him a sense of solidity to go with her—she was so sturdily popular, so intensely "great."

He mounted the steps of the brownstone house and stepped inside.

"Irene," he called.

Mrs. Scheerer came out of the living-room to meet him.

"Dexter," she said, "Irene's gone up-stairs with a splitting head-ache. She wanted to go with you but I made her go to bed."

"Nothing serious, I—"

"Oh, no. She's going to play golf with you in the morning. You can spare her for just one night, can't you, Dexter?"

Her smile was kind. She and Dexter liked each other. In the living-room he talked for a moment before he said good-night.

Returning to the University Club, where he had rooms, he stood in the doorway for a moment and watched the dancers. He leaned against the door-post, nodded at a man or two—yawned.

"Hello, darling."

The familiar voice at his elbow startled him. Judy Jones had left a man and crossed the room to him—Judy Jones, a slender enamelled doll in cloth of gold: gold in a band at her head, gold in two slipper points at her dress's hem. The fragile glow of her face seemed to blossom as she smiled at him. A breeze of warmth and light blew

through the room. His hands in the pockets of his dinner-jacket tightened spasmodically. He was filled with a sudden excitement.

"When did you get back?" he asked casually.

"Come here and I'll tell you about it."

She turned and he followed her. She had been away—he could have wept at the wonder of her return. She had passed through enchanted streets, doing things that were like provocative music. All mysterious happenings, all fresh and quickening hopes, had gone away with her, come back with her now.

She turned in the doorway.

"Have you a car here? If you haven't, I have."

"I have a coupé."[13]

In then, with a rustle of golden cloth. He slammed the door. Into so many cars she had stepped—like this—like that—her back against the leather, so—her elbow resting on the door—waiting. She would have been soiled long since had there been anything to soil her—except herself—but this was her own self outpouring.

With an effort he forced himself to start the car and back into the street. This was nothing, he must remember. She had done this before, and he had put her behind him, as he would have crossed a bad account from his books.

He drove slowly down-town and, affecting abstraction, traversed the deserted streets of the business section, people here and there where a movie was giving out its crowd or where consumptive or pugilistic[14] youth lounged in front of pool halls. The clink of glasses and the slap of hands on the bars issued from saloons, cloisters of glazed glass and dirty yellow light.

She was watching him closely and the silence was embarrassing, yet in this crisis he could find no casual word with which to profane the hour. At a convenient turning he began to zigzag back toward the University Club.

"Have you missed me?" she asked suddenly.

"Everybody missed you."

He wondered if she knew of Irene Scheerer. She had been back only a day—her absence

2 Evaluate Sensory Details *What does this emphasis on gold seem to symbolize?*

---

13. A *coupé* is a small two-door car.
14. *Consumptive* means "wasteful," and *pugilistic* means "eager to fight."

F. SCOTT FITZGERALD **765**

Teach

Literary Element   **1**

Motivation Answer: *He may not wish to spoil the moment; he may lack the courage to tell her.*

[APPROACHING] **Say:** Judy has not seen Dexter in many months, and they meet almost by accident. **Ask:** Why do you think she says, "I wish you'd marry me"? *(Students should suggest that Judy is playing games with Dexter. She is pretending to want to marry him.)*

View the Art ★

Answer: *The painting reflects the grim side of Dexter's winter dreams.*

In this painting, American Leon Dabo (1865–1960) depicts a New England winter scene. **Ask:** What mood or feeling is conveyed in this artwork? *(The winter scene is gloomy. Winter seems endless and grim.)*

Winter Evening. Leon Dabo. Oil on canvas, 53.3 x 71.1 cm. Florence Griswold Museum, Old Lyme, CT.

View the Art Painter Leon Dabo was well known for his atmospheric landscapes of the Hudson River and his hazy lighting techniques. Do you think this painting might be a good representation of Dexter's winter dreams? Explain. ★

had been almost contemporaneous with his engagement.

"What a remark!" Judy laughed sadly—without sadness. She looked at him searchingly. He became absorbed in the dashboard.

"You're handsomer than you used to be," she said thoughtfully. "Dexter, you have the most rememberable eyes."

He could have laughed at this, but he did not laugh. It was the sort of thing that was said to sophomores. Yet it stabbed at him.

"I'm awfully tired of everything, darling." She called every one darling, endowing the endearment with careless, individual camaraderie. "I wish you'd marry me."

The directness of this confused him. He should have told her now that he was going to marry another girl, but he could not tell her. He could as easily have sworn that he had never loved her.

"I think we'd get along," she continued, on the same note, "unless probably you've forgotten me and fallen in love with another girl."

Her confidence was obviously enormous. She had said, in effect, that she found such a thing impossible to believe, that if it were true he had merely committed a childish

---

Motivation *Why do you think Dexter decides not to tell Judy that he is engaged?*   **1**

Listening and Speaking Practice

Pitch an Idea Point out that if Dexter were a celebrity today, dropping Irene for Judy would probably be a story on entertainment news. Have students imagine that they are part of the production team for an entertainment news show. Tell students that they have ten minutes to come up with a pitch for tonight's show. They have to decide how they will present Dexter's break-up and subsequent engagement. What facts will they emphasize, and what "spin" will they put on it? What kinds of shots, special effects, and music will they choose to achieve their goal? Will they use formal, journalistic language, or something more colloquial? Then have the students pitch their ideas to the class. Have the class compare and contrast how the groups' pitches differ in tone, style, and content from Fitzgerald's writing.

indiscretion—and probably to show off. She would forgive him, because it was not a matter of any moment but rather something to be brushed aside lightly.

"Of course you could never love anybody but me," she continued, "I like the way you love me. Oh, Dexter, have you forgotten last year?"

"No, I haven't forgotten."

"Neither have I!"

Was she sincerely moved—or was she carried along by the wave of her own acting?

"I wish we could be like that again," she said, and he forced himself to answer:

"I don't think we can."

"I suppose not. . . . I hear you're giving Irene Scheerer a violent rush."

There was not the faintest emphasis on the name, yet Dexter was suddenly ashamed.

"Oh, take me home," cried Judy suddenly; "I don't want to go back to that idiotic dance—with those children."

Then, as he turned up the street that led to the residence district, Judy began to cry quietly to herself. He had never seen her cry before.

The dark street lightened, the dwellings of the rich loomed up around them, he stopped his coupé in front of the great white bulk of the Mortimer Joneses' house, somnolent, gorgeous, drenched with the splendor of the damp moonlight. Its solidity startled him. The strong walls, the steel of the girders, the breadth and beam and pomp of it were there only to bring out the contrast with the young beauty beside him. It was sturdy to accentuate her slightness—as if to show what a breeze could be generated by a butterfly's wing.

He sat perfectly quiet, his nerves in wild clamor, afraid that if he moved he would find her irresistibly in his arms. Two tears had rolled down her wet face and trembled on her upper lip.

"I'm more beautiful than anybody else," she said brokenly, "why can't I be happy?" Her moist eyes tore at his stability—her mouth turned slowly downward with an exquisite sadness: "I'd

like to marry you if you'll have me, Dexter. I suppose you think I'm not worth having, but I'll be so beautiful for you, Dexter."

A million phrases of anger, pride, passion, hatred, tenderness fought on his lips. Then a perfect wave of emotion washed over him, carrying off with it a sediment of wisdom, of convention, of doubt, of honor. This was his girl who was speaking, his own, his beautiful, his pride.

"Won't you come in?" He heard her draw in her breath sharply.

Waiting.

"All right," his voice was trembling. "I'll come in."

V

It was strange that neither when it was over nor a long time afterward did he regret that night. Looking at it from the perspective of ten years, the fact that Judy's flare for him endured just one month seemed of little importance. Nor did it matter that by his yielding he subjected himself to a deeper agony in the end and gave serious hurt to Irene Scheerer and to Irene's parents, who had befriended him. There was nothing sufficiently pictorial about Irene's grief to stamp itself on his mind.

Dexter was at bottom hard-minded. The attitude of the city on his action was of no importance to him, not because he was going to leave the city, but because any outside attitude on the situation seemed superficial. He was completely indifferent to popular opinion. Nor, when he had seen that it was no use, that he did not possess in himself the power to move fundamentally or to hold Judy Jones, did he bear any malice toward her. He loved her, and he would love her until the day he was too old for loving—but he could not have her. So he tasted the deep pain that is reserved only for the strong, just as he had tasted for a little while the deep happiness.

Motivation *Why does Dexter agree to go in after his earlier doubts?* **3**

Big Idea **2**

Modern Fiction Say: Even though it appears that Dexter and Judy have made their choices at the end of section IV, keep in mind that indecision is an important theme in modern fiction. **Ask:** How have the characters demonstrated indecisiveness at the beginning of section V? *(Dexter has canceled his engagement to Irene, and Judy has ended her engagement to Dexter.)*

Literary Element **3**

Motivation Answer: *He is overcome with emotion; he may feel that he won't see her again.*

[APPROACHING] **Say:** Once Dexter has stopped the car, Judy does all the talking. **Ask:** How would you characterize Judy based on her remarks? *(Judy is self-absorbed, vain, and unhappy.)*

Cultural History ☆

Broken Engagements In the 1920s, breaking off an engagement had major social and financial consequences. For example, Irene and her parents might have invested considerable time and money in preparing a trousseau and planning a wedding.

Approaching Level

DIFFERENTIATED INSTRUCTION

AAVE Approaching level students who are users of African American vernacular English (AAVE) may not always use the right syntax when asking questions. For example, they may say: "Why Judy doesn't feel happy?" instead of "Why doesn't Judy feel happy?" Have students find and read aloud the questions on this page. Highlight the word order in the questions for students. Then have students practice using the correct syntax in asking questions by working in pairs to ask each other questions about the story so far. Work with each pair of students to make sure students are using correct Standard Academic English in their questions and answers.

Teach

Big Idea | 1

Answer: *He has been through a lot emotionally; he may be numb and incapable of showing strong feelings toward Judy.*

Literary Element | 2

Character Ask: What effect does Devlin's remark about Judy's current situation have on Dexter? (*Dexter is filled with disbelief and excitement. He wonders if he might still have a chance with Judy.*)

Even the ultimate falsity of the grounds upon which Judy terminated the engagement that she did not want to "take him away" from Irene—Judy, who had wanted nothing else—did not revolt him. He was beyond any revulsion or any amusement.

He went East in February with the intention of selling out his laundries and settling in New York—but the war[15] came to America in March and changed his plans. He returned to the West, handed over the management of the business to his partner, and went into the first officers' training-camp in late April. He was one of those young thousands who greeted the war with a certain amount of relief, welcoming the liberation from webs of tangled emotion.

VI

This story is not his biography, although things creep into it which have nothing to do with those dreams he had when he was young. We are almost done with them and with him now. There is only one more incident to be related here, and it happens seven years farther on.

It took place in New York, where he had done well—so well that there were no barriers too high for him. He was thirty-two years old, and, except for one flying trip immediately after the war, he had not been West in seven years. A

> *E*ven the ultimate falsity of the grounds upon which Judy terminated the engagement that she did not want to "take him away" from Irene—Judy, who had wanted nothing else—did not revolt him. He was beyond any revulsion or any amusement.

man named Devlin from Detroit came into his office to see him in a business way, and then and there this incident occurred, and closed out, so to speak, this particular side of his life.

"So you're from the Middle West," said the man Devlin with careless curiosity. "That's funny—I thought men like you were probably born and raised on Wall Street. You know— wife of one of my best friends in Detroit came from your city. I was an usher at the wedding."

Dexter waited with no apprehension of what was coming.

"Judy Simms," said Devlin with no particular interest; "Judy Jones she was once."

"Yes, I knew her." A dull impatience spread over him. He had heard, of course, that she was married— perhaps deliberately he had heard no more.

"Awfully nice girl," brooded Devlin meaninglessly, "I'm sort of sorry for her."

"Why?" Something in Dexter was alert, receptive, at once.

"Oh, Lud Simms has gone to pieces in a way. I don't mean he ill-uses her, but he drinks and runs around—"

"Doesn't she run around?"

"No. Stays at home with her kids."

"Oh."

"She's a little too old for him," said Devlin.

"Too old!" cried Dexter. "Why, man, she's only twenty-seven."

He was possessed with a wild notion of rushing out into the streets and taking a train to Detroit. He rose to his feet spasmodically.

"I guess you're busy," Devlin apologized quickly. "I didn't realize—"

---

15. *The war* refers to World War I, which the United States entered in 1917.

 Modern Fiction *Do you think Dexter really feels this way, or is he fooling himself?*

2

Listening and Speaking Practice

 SMALL GROUP Choral Reading A choral reading provides force to a literary work. Like a musical choir, choral readers work in unison. Organize students into three groups of varying sizes. Then assign each group one of the last three paragraphs of "Winter Dreams." Give students time to rehearse their group reading of the para-

graph, with one student serving as the director. The director should suggest phrasings, volume, and expressions that convey the meanings of the words. After rehearsing, the groups should present their choral readings to the class. Discuss with the class how the choral readings affected them. **Ask:** How did the readings

influence your understanding of the story? (*Students may say that it emphasized the sadness of the ending, and Dexter's loss.*)

"No, I'm not busy," said Dexter, steadying his voice. "I'm not busy at all. Not busy at all. Did you say she was—twenty-seven? No, I said she was twenty-seven."

"Yes, you did," agreed Devlin dryly.

"Go on, then, Go on."

"What do you mean?"

"About Judy Jones."

Devlin looked at him helplessly.

"Well, that's—I told you all there is to it. He treats her like the devil. Oh, they're not going to get divorced or anything. When he's particularly outrageous she forgives him. In fact, I'm inclined to think she loves him. She was a pretty girl when she first came to Detroit."

A pretty girl! The phrase struck Dexter as ludicrous.

"Isn't she—a pretty girl, any more?"

"Oh, she's all right."

"Look here," said Dexter, sitting down suddenly. "I don't understand. You say she was a 'pretty girl' and now you say she's 'all right.' I don't understand what you mean—Judy Jones wasn't a pretty girl, at all. She was a great beauty. Why, I knew her, I knew her. She was—"

Devlin laughed pleasantly.

"I'm not trying to start a row," he said. "I think Judy's a nice girl and I like her. I can't understand how a man like Lud Simms could fall madly in love with her, but he did." Then he added: "Most of the women like her."

Dexter looked closely at Devlin, thinking wildly that there must be a reason for this, some insensitivity in the man or some private malice.

"Lots of women fade just like *that*," Devlin snapped his fingers. "You must have seen it happen. Perhaps I've forgotten how pretty she was at her wedding. I've seen her so much since then, you see. She has nice eyes."

A sort of dullness settled down upon Dexter. For the first time in his life he felt like getting very drunk. He knew that he was laughing loudly at something Devlin had said, but he did not know what it was or why it was funny. When, in a few minutes, Devlin went he lay down on his lounge and looked out the window at the New York sky-line into which the sun was sinking in dull lovely shades of pink and gold.

He had thought that having nothing else to lose he was invulnerable at last—but he knew that he had just lost something more, as surely as if he had married Judy Jones and seen her fade away before his eyes.

The dream was gone. Something had been taken from him. In a sort of panic he pushed the palms of his hands into his eyes and tried to bring up a picture of the waters lapping on Sherry Island and the moonlit veranda, and gingham on the golf-links and the dry sun and the gold color of her neck's soft down. And her mouth damp to his kisses and her eyes plaintive with melancholy and her freshness like new fine linen in the morning. Why, these things were no longer in the world! They had existed and they existed no longer.

For the first time in years the tears were streaming down his face. But they were for himself now. He did not care about mouth and eyes and moving hands. He wanted to care, and he could not care. For he had gone away and he could never go back any more. The gates were closed, the sun was gone down, and there was no beauty but the gray beauty of steel that withstands all time. Even the grief he could have borne was left behind in the country of illusion, of youth, of the richness of life, where his winter dream had flourished.

"Long ago," he said, "long ago, there was something in me, but now that thing is gone. Now that thing is gone, that thing is gone. I cannot cry. I cannot care. That thing will come back no more."

Modern Fiction *What dream has gone, and why has it gone?* **3**

Teach

Big Idea **3**

Modern Fiction Answer:
Dexter has lost the dream of being with Judy. He realizes that time has passed, and with it, his and Judy's youth.

> To check students' understanding of the selection, see Unit 5 Teaching Resources Book, p. 194.

English Learners

DIFFERENTIATED INSTRUCTION

Intermediate The narrator says that Dexter felt neither revulsion nor amusement at the thought of Judy. Ask students to look up the meanings of *revulsion* and *amusement*, and ask them if they think the words are antonyms. Have students work in pairs to find words that are better antonyms.

Approaching Level

DIFFERENTIATED INSTRUCTION

Established Students who learn best by organizing information into patterns may find it useful to organize details about the characters and their actions. Suggest that students break the story into parts, such as sections, seasons, or years. Then have them jot down key details about the characters.

After You Read

Assess

1. Some students might tell him to forget the past. Others may be sympathetic toward him.

2. (a) He dreams of joining the privileged world. (b) He is envious of that world.

3. His job as a caddy separates him from the world he dreams about. By quitting, he takes his first step toward becoming part of that world.

4. (a) The point of view is third-person limited. (b) The reader can know only what Dexter is thinking and what he knows.

5. He wants to make money. Playing on the golf course leaves him feeling superior toward Mr. Hedrick.

6. (a) Dexter doesn't want to ruin his chances with Judy, so he is careful to fit in. (b) He knows that Judy doesn't like men who are poor.

7. To make Judy jealous; to be with someone more reliable than Judy

8. He has trouble facing his faded dreams.

9. (a) Students may suggest that he loves her for her beauty and excitement. (b) Students may suggest that Dexter would have been miserable because she would never have committed to him.

10. Real women in an earlier age would not have had the same freedoms, but literature from different time periods has examples of spirited, willful heroines.

11. Scott was strongly affected by his relationship with King.

After You Read

Respond and Think Critically

Respond and Interpret

1. At the end of the story, Dexter is obviously undergoing a significant life crisis. What would you tell him if you were with him?

2. (a) What are Dexter's winter dreams? (b) What do these dreams tell you about him?

3. In giving up caddying, "Dexter was unconsciously dictated to by his winter dreams." Explain how these dreams affected his decision.

4. (a) What is the point of view of this story? (b) How does this point of view affect the plot?

Analyze and Evaluate

5. How do Dexter's laundry business and his round of golf in Part II tell you that he is still under the influence of his winter dreams?

6. (a) In Part III, is Dexter becoming a snob, with his emphasis on clothes and his hometown, or is he simply trying to fit in? Explain. (b) Why does he tell Judy that he is making "more money than any man his age in the Northwest"?

7. Why do you think Dexter becomes engaged to Irene?

8. In Part VI, after Dexter learns about Judy's marriage, why is he so disturbed?

9. (a) Do you think Dexter really loves Judy? Explain. (b) Do you think Dexter would have been happier if he had married Judy? Why or why not?

Connect

10. **Big Idea** **Modern Fiction** Is Judy's reckless disregard for the feelings of others a symptom of the Jazz Age, or could her character appear in a story from any period? Explain.

11. **Connect to the Author** Why do you think Fitzgerald based aspects of so many of his heroines—including Judy Jones—on Ginevra King (see page 753)?

Daily Life & Culture

The Roaring Twenties

After World War I, radical social changes took place in the U.S. The attitude of the "Roaring Twenties" was embodied in the image of the "flapper"—an emancipated woman who cut her hair short, wore loose-fitting dresses, and danced with wild abandon. She could drive her own car, smoke and drink, and choose her own romantic partners without fear of social judgment. Yet this frivolity and conspicuous consumption masked a deep crisis in American society. Conservative values helped ratify the 18th Amendment that prohibited the making, sale, and distribution of alcohol, while liberal values helped gain popularity for the 19th

Amendment giving women the right to vote.

Group Activity
Discuss the following questions:

1. Why do you think the image of the flapper was so popular in the 1920s?

2. How might the Great Depression have affected people like Judy and Dexter?

Daily Life & Culture

1. The image appealed to women's growing sense of independence and took advantage of fluctuating social values.

2. Judy's family would probably have lost most of its money, thereby forcing her to live at a lower economic level; Dexter made his first fortune based on his own talents and started making a second fortune after the war. He could probably succeed again.

 For additional assessment, see Assessment Resources, pp. 215–216.

Literary Element — Motivation

In literature, **motivation** refers to the reasons or causes for a character's actions. The lack of clear motivation for characters' actions is considered a weakness in a story or play. Sometimes motivation is subtle, however, and may not be immediately apparent.

1. What is the chief motivation for most of Dexter's actions?

2. What do you think motivates Judy to behave as she does in her relationships with Dexter and others before she is married?

3. What is Judy's motivation in mentioning Irene to Dexter after he becomes engaged?

4. What do you think motivated Judy to get married?

Review: Conflict

As you learned in Unit Four, Part 2, **conflict** is the main struggle between two opposing forces in a story or drama. An **external conflict** is a struggle between a character and an outside force, such as another character. An **internal conflict** is a struggle between opposing thoughts in a character's mind.

Group Activity In a small group, discuss the nature of the conflict in "Winter Dreams." Answer these questions.

1. What is the conflict in "Winter Dreams"?

2. Is this conflict internal or external?

3. How is the conflict resolved?

> **LOG ON** ▶ **Literature** Online
>
> **Selection Resources** For Selection Quizzes, eFlashcards, and Reading-Writing Connection activities, go to glencoe.com and enter QuickPass code GLA9800u5.

Reading Strategy — Evaluate Sensory Details

Sensory details are details that appeal to the senses. Often, these details contribute to the meaning and mood, or atmosphere, of a story.

Partner Activity Refer to the chart you made on page 753 to help you answer these questions. A passage in the last part of "Winter Dreams" reads: "the sun was sinking in dull lovely shades of pink and gold." How does this passage seem to sum up Dexter's feelings and his life? What emotions does it stir up in you, the reader? Meet with another classmate to discuss these questions.

Vocabulary Practice

Practice with Synonyms With a partner, match each boldfaced vocabulary word below with its synonym. You will not use all the answer choices. Use a thesaurus or dictionary to check your answers.

1. grimace
2. ominous
3. perturbation
4. petulance
5. mundane

a. peevishness
b. artless
c. illness
d. commonplace
e. scowl
f. menacing
g. anxiety

Academic Vocabulary

*Judy **affects** all her suitors when she is young, and news of what she has become **affects** Dexter profoundly.*

Affect is an academic word. A doctor, writing a prescription, might warn her patient that the medicine she is recommending **affects** everyone differently.

To further explore the meaning of this word, answer the following question: How would you like to **affect** those around you?

For more on academic vocabulary, see pages 53–54.

F. SCOTT FITZGERALD **771**

After You Read

Literary Element

1. Dexter is chiefly motivated by his dream of being a part of a moneyed society and by his attraction to Judy.

2. She enjoys being sought after and admired. Her love seems to be for herself instead of others.

3. She is testing Dexter, trying to see whether she can lure him away from Irene.

4. Readers are not told whether she was truly in love with her husband; her age might have been her motivation. Also, she may have wanted to get revenge on Dexter.

Progress Check

Can students analyze motivation?

If No → See Unit 5 Teaching Resources Book, p. 189.

Review: Conflict

1. The conflict is Dexter's desire to be with Judy and to be accepted by high society. He is unable to manage to do either.

2. The conflict is internal.

3. The conflict is only resolved when he realizes that his dream has gone.

> To create custom assessments using software, use ExamView Assessment Suite.

> To create custom assessments online, go to Progress Reporter Online Assessment.

Reading Strategy

A setting sun is a traditional literary symbol of death. In Dexter's case, it is the death of a dream and of his youth. Before the sun sets, however, the sky, like Dexter's fading dream, is suffused with beauty.

Vocabulary

1. e 2. f 3. g 4. a 5. d

Academic Vocabulary

Students should describe what kind of influence they would like to have on others.

After You Read

Writing

Students' stories should use either the first- or third-person point of view consistently throughout. Students should also develop the character's motivation using details and use concrete details and images to develop setting, character, and tone in their stories.

Scoring Guide

Assess students' performances in the following categories using the scoring guide at the bottom of the page:

- Addresses all parts of the writing task.
- Develops believable and realistic characters and plot.
- Point of view in story is consistent, and narrator only talks about what he or she is allowed to know.
- Sensory details and techniques such as interior monologue add to the tone of the story and enhance understanding of the characters.
- Provides a variety of sentence types; uses precise, descriptive language.
- Follows English language conventions.

Respond Through Writing

Short Story

Apply Point of View When you consider how Judy treats Dexter in this story, it might seem hard to understand why he remains under her spell. Write a 1,500-word short story about someone who stays in a difficult relationship, explaining why he or she does so. Write your story from either the first-person or third-person point of view.

Understand the Task In a story with a **first-person point of view,** the narrator is a character in the story, and uses the words *I* and *me* to tell the story. In a story with a **third-person point of view,** the narrator is someone who stands outside the story and describes the characters and action. In a story with a third-person **limited point of view,** the narrator reveals the thoughts, feelings, and observations of only one character. In a story with a third-person **omniscient point of view,** the narrator knows everything that goes on—including the thoughts and feelings of every character.

Prewrite Detailing a character's motivation is key when writing about relationships. Each point of view allows you to give your readers different insight into why your main character acts as he or she does. When choosing a point of view, think about which one will help you to most effectively convey your main character's motivations.

Draft As you write, create a full world for your story. Use concrete details that appeal to multiple senses to establish the setting. Then, in your chosen point of view, narrate your character's story. Be sure to remain focused on significant events and details, and to allow the pace of the story to change to accommodate shifts in time and mood.

Revise Reread your story, looking closely at your descriptions. Are they vivid? Do they use concrete and sensory details to show the specific actions, movements, gestures, and feelings of the characters? If not, revise to give clearer descriptions. You might also incorporate interior monologues to help convey your characters' feelings and motivations. Below is an example of interior monologue told from a third-person point of view.

> **EXAMPLE:** I should be leaving, Marta told herself as she refilled her punch glass. I should just leave this horrid party right now and get back to my normal life. I don't belong here.

Edit and Proofread Proofread your paper, correcting any errors in spelling, grammar, and punctuation.

Learning Objectives

In this assignment, you will focus on the following objectives:

Writing: Writing a short story.

Grammar: Using pronouns to maintain consistent point of view.

Grammar Tip

Point of View

Avoid unintended shifts in point of view. Since your chosen point of view is the angle from which your reader sees people, objects, and events, switching your point of view within a story can create confusion.

Scoring Guide	4	3	2	1
Task addressed	fully	mostly	partially	barely
Characters, Plot	fully developed and believable	somewhat developed and believable	partially developed and realistic	unrealistic
Point of View	maintains one point of view	maintains one point of view	point of view changes occasionally	point of view changes often
Sensory Details	well employed	employed	few employed	none
Language	varied, precise, descriptive	varied, somewhat descriptive	predictable, basic	not varied, limited
Convention errors	few or none	several	some	many

Before You Read

The Jilting of Granny Weatherall

Meet **Katherine Anne Porter**
(1890–1980)

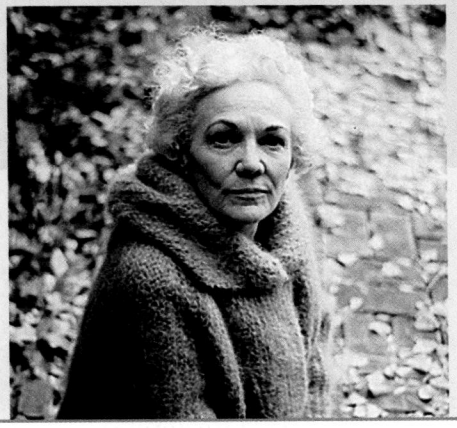

Katherine Anne Porter, who published her first collection of short stories when she was forty, described herself as "a late starter." But "a late finisher" might be more accurate. During her long career, she tended to write and rewrite her stories, sometimes putting them aside for many years. Porter sought to tell each story "as clearly and purely and simply as I can."

Experiences of Death and Near-Death
Katherine Anne Porter was born in a small log house on a farm in central Texas. Her mother died before she was two, and Porter and her four siblings were raised by one of their grandmothers. The grandmother's death when Porter was eleven had a powerful emotional impact on the family. Afterward, Porter's family moved to San Antonio, Texas, where she studied acting.

Shortly after moving to Dallas, Texas, in 1915, Porter became ill with tuberculosis and believed she had only a few months to live. She recovered only to be hit by the World War I flu epidemic, and she came so close to death that her family finalized her burial arrangements. Porter's struggle to survive, the close friendships she formed with other young women in a sanatorium in Texas, and the opportunities she had to reflect on her life during this period were to have a profound effect on her creative activities. She emerged from several years of illness with a new career goal: to be a writer.

A Creative Restlessness
Porter spent most of her thirties living abroad. She took on a range of writing projects and sought out the company of friends and circles of writers and artists who provided her with the intense interpersonal experiences that inspired her writing.

> "I knew what death was, and had almost experienced it. I had . . . the happy vision just before death. Now if you have had that, and survived it, come back from it, you are no longer like other people."
>
> —Katherine Anne Porter

Porter published several collections of short stories, starting with *Flowering Judas* (1929). Although it was her novel, *Ship of Fools* (1962), that became a best seller, Porter was primarily a practitioner of the short story. Many of her stories, including "The Jilting of Granny Weatherall," are set in the South and feature women who have profound self-realizations at crucial moments in their lives. At age seventy-six, two years after the publication of twenty-seven of her stories in *The Collected Stories of Katherine Anne Porter*, Porter received a Pulitzer Prize and the National Book Award.

 Literature Online

Author Search For more about Katherine Anne Porter, go to glencoe.com and enter QuickPass code GLA9800u5.

KATHERINE ANNE PORTER **773**

Before You Read

Focus

Bellringer Options

Literature Launchers:
   Pre-Reading Videos DVD,
   Selection Launcher
Selection Focus
   Transparency 47
Daily Language Practice
   Transparency 70

Or display images of weddings—pictures, cakes, rings, and decorations. **Ask:** What feelings do most people associate with weddings? Why are weddings important to people?

As they read, have students consider how the main character's disappointment at being left at the altar has affected her life.

Cultural History

1918 Influenza Pandemic In 1918, a flu virus spread around the world and became one of the deadliest disease outbreaks in human history. More people died from the flu than from World War I.

Selection Skills

Literary Elements
- Stream of Consciousness (SE pp. 774, 776, 777, 779, 780, 782, 783)
- Characterization (SE p. 783)

Vocabulary Skills
- Context Clues (SE pp. 784)
- Suffixes (TE p. 774)

The Jilting of Granny Weatherall

Reading Skills
- Draw Conclusions About the Protagonist (SE pp. 774–777, 780, 781, 784)
- Monitor Comprehension (TE p. 774)
- Draw Conclusions (TE p. 782)

Writing Skills/Grammar
- Monologue (SE p. 784)
- Eulogy (TE p. 776)
- Timeline (TE p. 778)

Listening/Speaking/Viewing Skills
- Analyze Art (SE p. 779)
- Monologue (SE p. 784)
- Literary Discussion (TE p. 780)

Before You Read

Focus

Summary

As feisty old Ellen Weatherall lies dying, she teases and scolds her daughter and her young doctor. As they come and go, her mind drifts between the present and the past. She remembers her husband, their children, and other details of her life. Now and then, she grieves over the painful memory of her humiliation sixty years earlier when her fiancé, George, jilted her on their wedding day. Her children arrive, the priest offers last rites, and then Granny drifts into death.

 For summaries in languages other than English, see Unit 5 Teaching Resources Book, pp. 196–201.

Vocabulary

Suffixes Ask students to look at the nouns and adjectives in the vocabulary list and identify the suffixes used to form these vocabulary words. *(-ful, -ty)* Have students use a dictionary to find the meanings of the suffixes. *(able to; state or quality)* Then have students list other words that use these suffixes.

(**ENGLISH LEARNERS**) Point out to students that when adding the suffix *-ful* to a noun ending in the letter *y*, the *y* changes to an *i*, as in the case of *dutiful*.

 For additional vocabulary practice, see Unit 5 Teaching Resources Book, p. 204.

774

Literature and Reading Preview

Connect to the Story

How would you feel if you were left waiting on your wedding day? How would you overcome that disappointment? Discuss these questions with a partner.

Build Background

This story is set in the South in the early twentieth century. Women of the time were often confined to the traditional roles of wife, mother, and homemaker. Roman Catholicism figures prominently in Porter's story. Granny Weatherall's religious beliefs and her ideas about guilt and forgiveness are important elements of the story.

Set Purposes for Reading

Big Idea Modern Fiction

As you read, ask, What Modernist techniques does Porter use?

Literary Element Stream of Consciousness

Stream of consciousness is a technique that a writer uses to imitate the flow of thoughts, feelings, images, and memories of a character. Stream of consciousness replaces traditional chronological order with a seemingly random collection of impressions, forcing the reader to piece together the plot or theme. Porter uses stream of consciousness to represent Granny's thoughts, memories, and state of mind. As you read, ask yourself, What is the chronological order of events in the story? How does this differ from the order Granny presents them?

Reading Strategy Draw Conclusions About the Protagonist

To **draw conclusions** means to use different pieces of information to make a general statement. A **protagonist** is the central character in a literary work, around whom the main conflict revolves. As Granny's thoughts skip from one person or subject to another, and back and forth in time, various clues about her past emerge. As you read, ask yourself, What clues and details can I use to draw conclusions about Granny's character?

Tip: Take Notes Use a chart to record details and draw conclusions based on them.

Details	Conclusion
Granny calls the doctor a brat.	Granny thinks of the doctor as a kid.

774 UNIT 5 BEGINNINGS OF THE MODERN AGE

Learning Objectives

For pages 773–784

In studying this text, you will focus on the following objectives:

Literary Study: Analyzing stream of consciousness.

Reading: Drawing conclusions about the protagonist.

Speaking and Listening: Performing a monologue.

Vocabulary

tactful (takt´ fəl) *adj.* able to speak or act without offending others; p. 776 *Southern women were expected to be tactful in their relations.*

dutiful (d<del>oo</del>´ ti fəl) *adj.* careful to fulfill obligations; p. 776 *Only a dutiful person could take care of a farm and raise several children.*

vanity (van´ i tē) *n.* excessive pride, as in one's looks; p. 779 *The man's vanity made it hard for him to see why he had not received the award.*

jilt (jilt) *v.* to drop or reject as a sweetheart; p. 779 *None of her children had been jilted; they had all married their first loves.*

piety (pī´ ə tē) *n.* religious devoutness; goodness; p. 780 *Piety was a common response to the moral issues raised by the war.*

Tip: Context Clues To learn a word's meaning, look at the other words in the sentence and try to predict a possible meaning.

Reading Practice

Monitor Comprehension Porter's stream-of-consciousness narrative may be challenging to some students. Encourage students to pause to ask questions while they read, particularly at points where they are confused. As students read the story, have them monitor their comprehension by asking themselves the following questions: *When did this event take place? To whom is Granny referring? What associa-* *tions does Granny make between past and present events? Is this event happening in the present, or is it a memory?* Tell students to record their answers and review and revise the answers as they read further.

The White Bed Jacket, c. 1905. Lilla Cabot Perry. Pastel on tan paper, 25½ x 31½ in. Hirschl & Adler Galleries Inc., NY.

The Jilting of Granny Weatherall

Katherine Anne Porter

 She flicked her wrist neatly out of Doctor Harry's pudgy careful fingers and pulled the sheet up to her chin. The brat ought to be in knee-breeches. Doctoring around the country with spectacles on his nose. "Get along now, take your schoolbooks and go. There's nothing wrong with me." **1**

Doctor Harry spread a warm paw like a cushion on her forehead where the forked green vein danced and made her eyelids twitch. "Now, now, be a good girl, and we'll have you up in no time."

"That's no way to speak to a woman nearly eighty years old just because she's down. I'd have you respect your elders, young man."

"Well, missy, excuse me." Doctor Harry patted her cheek. "But I've got to warn you, haven't I? You're a marvel,[1] but you must be careful or you're going to be good and sorry."

---

1. A *marvel* is a wonderful or astonishing thing.

Draw Conclusions About the Protagonist *"She" in this paragraph is Granny Weatherall. What can you infer about where she is and what she is like from this paragraph?* **2**

KATHERINE ANNE PORTER **775**

Teach

Literary Element 1

Stream of Consciousness
Answer: *Granny slips into the distant past, remembering long-ago illnesses. She forgets that she is weak and in bed. She tells the doctor that she is able to pay her own bills.*

Reading Strategy 2

Draw Conclusions About the Protagonist Answer: *Granny's wish to spank her grown daughter shows that her thoughts are in the past.*

ENGLISH LEARNERS Say: Granny's words offer clues to her character. Notice Granny's response to her daughter's kindness. Point out to students that the words *dutiful* and *good* are used as adjectives to praise people. However, Granny uses the words in a negative way and says that her daughter deserves a spanking for being *dutiful* and *good*. **Ask:** Why does Granny use adjectives that praise people in a negative way? *(She is teasing her daughter.)*

Interactive Read and Write

Other options for teaching this selection can be found in

- Interactive Read and Write for EL Students, pp. 189–202
- Interactive Read and Write for Approaching-Level Students, pp. 189–202
- Interactive Read and Write for On-Level Students, pp. 189–202

"Don't tell me what I'm going to be. I'm on my feet now, morally speaking. It's Cornelia. I had to go to bed to get rid of her."

Her bones felt loose, and floated around in her skin, and Doctor Harry floated like a balloon around the foot of the bed. He floated and pulled down his waistcoat[2] and swung his glasses on a cord. "Well, stay where you are, it certainly can't hurt you."

"Get along and doctor your sick," said Granny Weatherall. "Leave a well woman alone. I'll call for you when I want you . . . Where were you forty years ago when I pulled through milk-leg[3] and double pneumonia? You weren't even born. Don't let Cornelia lead you on," she shouted, because Doctor Harry appeared to float up to the ceiling and out. "I pay my own bills, and I don't throw my money away on nonsense!"

She meant to wave good-bye, but it was too much trouble. Her eyes closed of themselves, it was like a dark curtain drawn round the bed. The pillow rose and floated under her, pleasant as a hammock in a light wind. She listened to the leaves rustling outside the window. No, somebody was swishing newspapers: no, Cornelia and Doctor Harry were whispering together. She leaped broad awake, thinking they whispered in her ear.

"She was never like this, *never* like this!" "Well, what can we expect?" "Yes, eighty years old . . ."

Well, and what if she was? She still had ears. It was like Cornelia to whisper round doors. She always kept things secret in such a public way. She was always being **tactful** and kind. Cornelia was **dutiful;** that was the trouble with

---

2. A *waistcoat* is a vest.
3. *Milk-leg* is a painful swelling of the leg that may occur after childbirth.

1 **Stream of Consciousness** *How does this paragraph show that Granny's mind travels back and forth between the past and present?*

Vocabulary

tactful (takt´ fəl) *adj.* able to speak or act without offending others
dutiful (doo´ ti fəl) *adj.* careful to fulfill obligations

776 UNIT 5 BEGINNINGS OF THE MODERN AGE

---

her. Dutiful and good: "So good and dutiful," said Granny, "that I'd like to spank her." She saw herself spanking Cornelia and making a fine job of it.

"What'd you say, Mother?"

Granny felt her face tying up in hard knots. "Can't a body think, I'd like to know?"

"I thought you might want something."

"I do. I want a lot of things. First off, go away and don't whisper."

She lay and drowsed, hoping in her sleep that the children would keep out and let her rest a minute. It had been a long day. Not that she was tired. It was always pleasant to snatch a minute now and then. There was always so much to be done. Let me see: tomorrow.

Tomorrow was far away and there was nothing to trouble about. Things were finished somehow when the time came; thank God there was always a little margin over for peace: then a person could spread out the plan of life and tuck in the edges orderly. It was good to have everything clean and folded away, with the hairbrushes and tonic bottles sitting straight on the white embroidered linen; the day started without fuss and the pantry shelves laid out with rows of jelly glasses and brown jugs and white stone-china jars with blue whirligigs[4] and words painted on them: coffee, tea, sugar, ginger, cinnamon, allspice; and the bronze clock with the lion on the top nicely dusted off. The dust that lion could collect in twenty-four hours! The box in the attic with all those letters tied up, well, she'd have to go through that tomorrow. All those letters—George's letters and John's letters and her letters to them both—lying around for

Visual Vocabulary
Allspice, a spice thought to combine the flavors of cloves, cinnamon, and nutmeg, comes from the dried berries of the pimento tree.

---

4. *Whirligigs* (hwur´ li gigz´) are circular patterns, or swirls.

Draw Conclusions About the Protagonist *Do Granny's thoughts refer to the past or present? Explain.* **2**

Writing Practice

Eulogy A eulogy is a speech or written commendation praising the character and achievements of someone who has died. In the past, a eulogy was formal. Today, it can be formal or informal, with a serious or funny tone. A eulogy should contain the following elements:

- two or three characteristics of the person being eulogized
- supporting anecdotes or evidence

- achievements or honors of the deceased and their significance

Have students write a eulogy for Granny Weatherall based on details from the story. Ask volunteers to read their eulogies aloud.

the children to find afterwards made her uneasy. Yes, that would be tomorrow's business. No use to let them know how silly she had been once.

While she was rummaging round she found death in her mind and it felt clammy and unfamiliar. She had spent so much time preparing for death there was no need for bringing it up again. Let it take care of itself now. When she was sixty she had felt very old, finished, and went round making farewell trips to see her children and grandchildren, with a secret in her mind: This is the very last of your mother, children! Then she made her will and came down with a long fever. That was all just a notion like a lot of other things, but it was lucky too, for she had once for all got over the idea of dying for a long time. Now she couldn't be worried. She hoped she had better sense now. Her father had lived to be one hundred and two years old and had drunk a noggin[5] of strong hot toddy[6] on his last birthday. He told the reporters it was his daily habit, and he owed his long life to that. He had made quite a scandal and was very pleased about it. She believed she'd just plague Cornelia a little.

"Cornelia! Cornelia!" No footsteps, but a sudden hand on her cheek. "Bless you, where have you been?"

"Here, mother."

 "Well, Cornelia, I want a noggin of hot toddy."

"Are you cold, darling?"

"I'm chilly, Cornelia. Lying in bed stops the circulation. I must have told you that a thousand times."

Well, she could just hear Cornelia telling her husband that Mother was getting a little childish and they'd have to humor her. The thing that most annoyed her was that Cornelia thought she was deaf, dumb, and blind. Little hasty glances and tiny gestures tossed around

---

5. A *noggin* is a small mug or cup.
6. A *hot toddy* is a drink made with liquor, hot water, sugar, and spices.

3 Stream of Consciousness *In what way is this paragraph an unpredictable flow of feelings, thoughts, memories, and images?*

her and over her head, saying, "Don't cross her, let her have her way, she's eighty years old," and she sitting there as if she lived in a thin glass cage. Sometimes Granny almost made up her mind to pack up and move back to her own house where nobody could remind her every minute that she was old. Wait, wait, Cornelia, till your own children whisper behind your back!

In her day she had kept a better house and had got more work done. She wasn't too old yet for Lydia to be driving eighty miles for advice when one of the children jumped the track, and Jimmy still dropped in and talked things over: "Now, Mammy, you've a good business head, I want to know what you think of this . . . ?" Old. Cornelia couldn't change the furniture round without asking. Little things, little things! They had been so sweet when they were little. Granny wished the old days were back again with the children young and everything to be done over. It had been a hard pull, but not too much for her. When she thought of all the food she had cooked, and all the clothes she had cut and sewed, and all the gardens she had made—well, the children showed it. There they were, made out of her, and they couldn't get away from that. Sometimes she wanted to see John again and point to them and say, "Well, I didn't do so badly, did I?" But that would have to wait. That was for tomorrow. She used to think of him as a man, but now all the children were older than their father, and he would be a child beside her if she saw him now. It seemed strange and there was something wrong in the idea. Why, he couldn't possibly recognize her. She had fenced in a hundred acres once, digging the post holes herself and clamping the wires with just a Negro boy to help. That changed a woman. John would be looking for a young woman with the peaked Spanish comb in her hair and the painted fan. Digging post

Draw Conclusions About the Protagonist *How does Granny view herself as a mother?* **4**

KATHERINE ANNE PORTER **777**

Teach

Literary Element | 3

Stream of Consciousness
Answer: *The paragraph meanders through a series of seemingly unrelated thoughts—from memories of her pantry to the memory of love letters in the attic. Her memory of the letters reminds her to go through them so that her children will not read embarrassing parts.*

Reading Strategy | 4

Draw Conclusions About the Protagonist **Answer:**
Granny perceives herself as a hard-working mother who cooked, cleaned, raised her children, and ran a farm mostly by herself. She seems proud of her achievements.

ENGLISH LEARNERS Explain that when Granny says, "It had been a hard pull," she means that she had put a lot of effort into taking care of her children.

Language History ☆
Noggin and Toddy Granny Weatherall's choice of language shows that she is from another time. The words *noggin* and *toddy* were more commonly used in the 19th century. *Toddy* was first used to describe liquor made from tropical plants, such as a coconut and palm. The word dates back to the late 18th century. *Noggin* was first used to mean "a small drinking vessel" in the late 16th century.

English Learners
DIFFERENTIATED INSTRUCTION

Intermediate Explain that a simile is a figure of speech that compares unlike objects using *like* or *as*. Point out the simile "Doctor Harry floated like a balloon." Ask students to create similes that describe Granny Weatherall.

Approaching Level
DIFFERENTIATED INSTRUCTION

Emerging Have students read the paragraph beginning "In her day," aloud to increase **reading fluency**. Point out the lines in the passage that describe Granny.

Teach

Big Idea 1

Modern Fiction **Say:** Modernist fiction writers were familiar with psychology. They understood how the human mind drifts from one thought to another. They also understood the importance of symbols.
Ask: What might the fog stand for? *(The fog symbolizes Granny's unclear memories; it is also a real fog that Granny remembers, one that reminded her to call for her children and protect them.)*

Big Idea 2

Modern Fiction **Answer:**
The stream of consciousness method allowed modern writers to show the way people's minds flow from one thought or idea to another.

holes changed a woman. Riding country roads in the winter when women had their babies was another thing: sitting up nights with sick horses and sick Negroes and sick children and hardly ever losing one. John, I hardly ever lost one of them! John would see that in a minute; that would be something he could understand, she wouldn't have to explain anything!

It made her feel like rolling up her sleeves and putting the whole place to rights again. No matter if Cornelia was determined to be everywhere at once, there were a great many things left undone on this place. She would start tomorrow and do them. It was good to be strong enough for everything, even if all you made melted and changed and slipped under your hands, so that by the time you finished you almost forgot what you were working for. What was it I set out to do? she asked herself intently, but she could not remember. A fog rose over the valley, she saw it marching across **1** the creek swallowing the trees and moving up the hill like an army of ghosts. Soon it would be at the near edge of the orchard, and then it was time to go in and light the lamps. Come in, children, don't stay out in the night air.

Lighting the lamps had been beautiful. The children huddled up to her and breathed like little calves waiting at the bars in the twilight. Their eyes followed the match and watched the flame rise and settle in a blue curve, then they moved away from her. The lamp was lit, they didn't have to be scared and hang on to mother any more. Never, never, never more.

Lighting the lamps had been beautiful. The children huddled up to her and breathed like little calves waiting at the bars in the twilight.

God, for all my life I thank Thee. Without Thee, my God, I could never have done it. Hail, Mary, full of grace.[7]

I want you to pick all the fruit this year and see that nothing is wasted. There's always someone who can use it. Don't let good things rot for want of using. You waste life when you waste good food. Don't let things get lost. It's bitter to lose things. Now, don't let me get to thinking, not when I am tired and taking a little nap before supper . . .

The pillow rose about her shoulders and pressed against her heart and the memory was being squeezed out of it: oh, push down the pillow, somebody; it would smother her if she tried to hold it. Such a fresh breeze blowing and such a green day with no threats in it. But he had not come, just the same. What does a woman do when she has put on the white veil and set out the white cake for a man and he doesn't come? She tried to remember. No, I swear he never harmed me but in that. He never harmed me but in that . . . and what if he did? There was the day, the day, but a whirl of dark smoke rose and covered it, crept up and over into the bright field where everything was planted so carefully in orderly rows. That was hell, she knew hell when she saw it. For sixty years she had prayed against remembering him and against losing her

---

7. *Hail, Mary, full of grace* is the beginning of a Roman Catholic prayer to the Virgin Mary.

Modern Fiction *How is this method of showing Granny's thoughts related to Modernism?* **2**

778 UNIT 5 BEGINNINGS OF THE MODERN AGE

Writing Practice

Make a Timeline Because the writer uses stream of consciousness to convey the story, students may benefit from placing the main events of the story in chronological order. As they read, have them make a list of the main events. These will include the following:

- Granny is jilted by George.
- Granny raises her children by herself.

- Granny marries John.
- Father Connolly visits granny.
- Granny makes out a will.
- Granny sees Hapsy at her bedside.
- Granny gives birth to Hapsy.
- Cornelia washes Granny's face.

When students have finished reading the story, list the events students have identified on the board. Then have students write down the events in the order in which they occurred. Have volunteers share their answers with the class.

The Seamstress, 1914. Knud Larsen. Oil on canvas, 20 x 18½ in. Private collection.

View the Art Women of the early twentieth century often managed household tasks such as sewing. How might the woman in this painting be like Cornelia at that age?

soul in the deep pit of hell, and now the two things were mingled in one, and the thought of him was a smoky cloud from hell that moved and crept in her head when she had just got rid of Doctor Harry and was trying to rest a minute. Wounded **vanity,** Ellen, said a sharp voice in the top of her mind. Don't let your wounded vanity get the upper hand of you. Plenty of girls get **jilted.** You were jilted, weren't you? Then stand up to it. Her eyelids wavered and let in streamers of blue-gray light like tissue paper over her eyes. She must get up and pull the shades down or she'd never sleep. She was in bed again and the shades were not down. How could that happen? Better turn over, hide from the light; sleep-

ing in the light gave you nightmares. "Mother, how do you feel now?" and a stinging wetness on her forehead. But I don't like having my face washed in cold water!

Hapsy? George? Lydia? Jimmy? No, Cornelia, and her features were swollen and full of little puddles. "They're coming, darling, they'll all be here soon." Go wash your face, child, you look funny.

Instead of obeying, Cornelia knelt down and put her head on the pillow. She seemed to be talking but there was no sound. "Well, are you tongue-tied? Whose birthday is it? Are you going to give a party?"

Cornelia's mouth moved urgently in strange shapes. "Don't do that, you bother me, daughter."

"Oh, no, Mother. Oh, no . . ."

Nonsense. It was strange about children. They disputed your every word. "No what, Cornelia?"

"Here's Doctor Harry."

3 Stream of Consciousness *In writing that uses stream of consciousness, some information is often unclear. What is unclear here?*

Vocabulary

vanity (van´ i tē) *n.* excessive pride, as in one's looks
jilt (jilt) *v.* to drop or reject as a sweetheart

English Learners

DIFFERENTIATED INSTRUCTION

SMALL GROUP

Intermediate Students may have trouble with the disjointed sequence of Granny's thoughts. Break students into groups and assign each group one section of Granny's thoughts. Have each group work together to paraphrase their section. They may need to use a dictionary to look up any unfamiliar words. Then have a member of each group orally summarize their section for the class and tell whether Granny is thinking about the past, the present, or both.

Teach

Literary Element | 3

Stream of Consciousness

Answer: *Students may not understand that Granny is remembering the pain and humiliation of having been left at the altar sixty years before by her fiancé, George. This passage is the first time Granny refers to that time in the story.*

View the Art ★

Answer: *Students may say that Cornelia is described as "dutiful and good"—the woman in the painting appears to be dutiful and quiet as she bends over her needlework.*

Danish artist Knud Larsen (1865–1922) painted traditional landscapes, interiors, and genre paintings, such as *The Seamstress.*

Approaching Level

DIFFERENTIATED INSTRUCTION

Emerging Tell students to create a timeline of the events in Granny's life. They should include the following: Granny is jilted; she marries John and has children; John dies; Granny runs the farm; one child, Hapsy, dies young; the children grow up and seek her advice; Granny is dying.

Teach

Literary Element   1

Irony Ask: What is ironic when Granny tells Cornelia, "Find him and be sure to tell him I forgot him"? *(The irony is that Granny has not forgotten George or the pain he caused her.)*

Reading Strategy   2

Draw Conclusions About the Protagonist Answer: *Granny has drifted into the past; she remembers one of her children as a baby and then as an adult. Readers know that she is dreaming or remembering because it is Cornelia, not Hapsy, who is caring for Granny.*

Literary Element   3

Stream of Consciousness Answer: *She is experiencing pain related to a terrible memory. The pain has caused her to remember giving birth.*

(**ENGLISH LEARNERS**) Explain that while Granny is trying to remember everything she was able to have despite being jilted by George, her mind wanders to another memory. This is indicated by the ellipsis, which is punctuation used to indicate an omission or submission of words. At the end of the paragraph, when she says the phrase "my time has come," she is referring to going into labor.

780

"I won't see that boy again. He just left five minutes ago."

"That was this morning, Mother. It's night now. Here's the nurse."

"This is Doctor Harry, Mrs. Weatherall. I never saw you look so young and happy!"

"Ah, I'll never be young again—but I'd be happy if they'd let me lie in peace and get rested."

She thought she spoke up loudly, but no one answered. A warm weight on her forehead, a warm bracelet on her wrist and a breeze went on whispering, trying to tell her something. A shuffle of leaves in the everlasting hand of God, He blew on them and they danced and rattled. "Mother, don't mind, we're going to give you a little hypodermic." "Look here, daughter, how do ants get in this bed? I saw sugar ants yesterday." Did you send for Hapsy too?

It was Hapsy she really wanted. She had to go a long way back through a great many rooms to find Hapsy standing with a baby on her arm. She seemed to herself to be Hapsy also, and the baby on Hapsy's arm was Hapsy and himself and herself, all at once, and there was no surprise in the meeting. Then Hapsy melted from within and turned flimsy as gray gauze and the baby was a gauzy shadow, and Hapsy came up close and said, "I thought you'd never come," and looked at her very searchingly and said, "You haven't changed a bit!" They leaned forward to kiss, when Cornelia began whispering from a long way off, "Oh, is there anything you want to tell me? Is there anything I can do for you?"

Yes, she had changed her mind after sixty years and she would like to see George. I want you to find George. Find him and be sure to tell him I forgot him. I want him to know I had my husband just the same, and my children and my house, like any other woman. A good house too and a good husband that I loved and fine children out of him. Better than I hoped

for, even. Tell him I was given back everything he took away, and more. Oh, no, O God, no, there was something else besides the house and the man and the children. Oh, surely they were not all? What was it? Something not given back . . . Her breath crowded down under her ribs and grew into a monstrous frightening shape with cutting edges; it bored[8] up into her head, and the agony was unbelievable. Yes, John, get the doctor now, no more talk, my time has come.

When this one was born it should be the last. The last. It should have been born first, for it was the one she had truly wanted. Everything came in good time. Nothing left out, left over. She was strong, in three days she would be as well as ever. Better. A woman needed milk in her to have her full health.

"Mother, do you hear me?"

"I've been telling you—"

"Mother, Father Connolly's here."

"I went to Holy Communion only last week. Tell him I'm not so sinful as all that."

"Father just wants to speak to you."

He could speak as much as he pleased. It was like him to drop in and inquire about her soul as if it were a teething baby, and then stay on for a cup of tea and a round of cards and gossip. He always had a funny story of some sort, usually about an Irishman who made his little mistakes and confessed them, and the point lay in some absurd thing he would blurt out in the confessional[9] showing his struggles between native **piety** and original sin. Granny felt easy about her soul. Cornelia, where are your manners? Give Father Connolly a chair. She had her

---

8. Here, to *bore* means "to make a hole, as by drilling or pushing."
9. A *confessional* is a small booth in a Catholic church where a person confesses his or her sins to a priest and asks forgiveness from God through the priest.

Draw Conclusions About the Protagonist *In this paragraph, is Granny thinking about the past or present? How do you know?*   **2**

Stream of Consciousness *What causes this shift in Granny's thoughts?*   **3**

Vocabulary

piety (pī′ ə tē) *n.* religious devoutness; goodness

780   UNIT 5   BEGINNINGS OF THE MODERN AGE

Listening and Speaking Practice

SMALL GROUP

Literary Discussion Have students discuss "The Jilting of Granny Weatherall" in small groups, evaluating Porter's depiction of Granny and her thoughts. Remind students that good discussion should include evidence from the text. Students should also evaluate the story based on what they have seen and experienced in real life. Tell students that they need to express, argue, and support their opinions clearly in their contributions to the discussion. You might provide a statement to get students started, such as: *"The Jilting of Granny Weatherall" is a realistic depiction of an old woman facing death.* Tell students to consider the statement, adopt a position, and then discuss their reviews.

secret comfortable understanding with a few favorite saints who cleared a straight road to God for her. All as surely signed and sealed as the papers for the new Forty Acres. For ever . . . heirs and assigns[10] forever. Since the day the wedding cake was not cut, but thrown out and wasted. The whole bottom dropped out of the world, and there she was, blind and sweating, with nothing under her feet and the walls falling away. His hand had caught her under the breast, she had not fallen; there was the freshly polished floor with the green rug on it, just as before. He had cursed like a sailor's parrot and said, "I'll kill him for you." "Don't lay a hand on him, for my sake leave something to God." "Now, Ellen, you must believe what I tell you . . ."

So there was nothing, nothing to worry about any more, except sometimes in the night one of the children screamed in a nightmare, and they both hustled out shaking and hunting for the matches and calling, "There, wait a minute, here we are!" John, get the doctor now, Hapsy's time has come. But there was Hapsy standing by the bed in a white cap. "Cornelia, tell Hapsy to take off her cap. I can't see her plain."

Her eyes opened very wide and the room stood out like a picture she had seen somewhere. Dark colors with the shadows rising towards the ceiling in long angles. The tall black dresser gleamed with nothing on it but John's picture, enlarged from a little one, with John's eyes very black when they should have been blue. You never saw him, so how do you know how he looked? But the man insisted the copy was perfect, it was very rich and handsome. For a picture, yes, but it's not my husband. The table by the bed had a linen cover and a candle and a crucifix. The light was blue from Cornelia's silk lampshades. No sort of light at all, just frippery.[11] You had to live forty years with kerosene lamps to appreciate honest

electricity. She felt very strong and she saw Doctor Harry with a rosy nimbus[12] around him.

"You look like a saint, Doctor Harry, and I vow that's as near as you'll ever come to it."

"She's saying something."

"I heard you, Cornelia. What's all this carrying-on?"

"Father Connolly's saying—"

Cornelia's voice staggered and bumped like a cart in a bad road. It rounded corners and turned back again and arrived nowhere. Granny stepped up in the cart very lightly and reached for the reins, but a man sat beside her, and she knew him by his hands, driving the cart. She did not look in his face, for she knew without seeing, but looked instead down the road where the trees leaned over and bowed to each other and a thousand birds were singing a Mass. She felt like singing too, but she put her hand in the bosom of her dress and pulled out a rosary, and Father Connolly murmured Latin in a very solemn voice and tick-led her feet.[13] My God, will you stop that nonsense? I'm a married woman. What if he did run away and leave me to face the priest by myself? I found another a whole world better. I wouldn't have exchanged my husband for any-body except St. Michael[14] himself, and you may tell him that for me, with a thank you into the bargain.

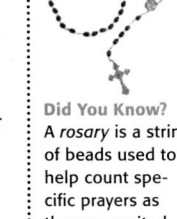

Did You Know?
A *rosary* is a string of beads used to help count spe-cific prayers as they are recited.

Light flashed on her closed eyelids, and a deep roaring shook her. Cornelia, is that light-ning? I hear thunder. There's going to be a storm. Close all the windows. Call the children

---

10. *Assigns* are people to whom property is legally transferred.
11. *Frippery* is a showy, useless display.

4 Draw Conclusions About the Protagonist *Besides the jilting, what events in Granny's life appear to have the most importance for her?*

---

12. A *nimbus* is a disk or ring of light; a halo.
13. The priest is administering the Sacrament of the Infirm, a Catholic ritual that includes saying prayers and applying oil to the many parts of a person's body.
14. *St. Michael* is an archangel, usually depicted as a handsome knight.

Modern Fiction *How is the characterization in this story different from traditional characterization?* **5**

Teach

Reading Strategy 4

Draw Conclusions About the Protagonist Answer:
The birth and premature death of Hapsy, her favorite child, are important to Granny.

(APPROACHING) **Ask:** How do you know these events have importance to Granny? (*Out of all the events of her life, these are the ones that she is focusing on in the last moments of her life, so they must be important to her.*)

Big Idea 5

Modern Fiction Answer:
The characterization is different because it is shown through the frenzied thoughts of a character that is dying.

Advanced Learners

DIFFERENTIATED INSTRUCTION

Journal Entry Invite students to write a journal entry from Cornelia's point of view. They should talk about Cornelia's feelings as she tries her best to take care of her mother and how Cornelia must have felt when she realized that her mother was dying. Instruct students to use details from the original story and to write in a stream of conscious-ness format. Students may wish to share their journal entries with the class.

Teach

Literary Element | 1

Stream of Consciousness
Answer: *It is unclear whose words are quoted or that Hapsy has died.*

Cultural History ☆

Marriage as Metaphor in the Bible Explain that in the Bible, God and Christ are referred to as bridegrooms, and that marriage is a metaphor used to describe the spiritual relationship between Christ and his followers. Tell students that some Christians believe that Christ escorts the recently deceased into the afterlife. Porter uses this belief in an ironic way. At the end, Granny is jilted a second time.

 To check students' understanding of the selection, see Unit 5 Teaching Resources Book, p. 207.

Progress Check

Can students identify stream of consciousness?

If No → See Unit 5 Teaching Resources Book, p. 202.

Illuminated dining room. Vicenzo Irolli. Pinacoteca Provinciale, Bari, Italy.

---

in . . . "Mother, here we are, all of us." "Is that you, Hapsy?" "Oh, no, I'm Lydia. We drove as fast as we could." Their faces drifted above her, drifted away. The rosary fell out of her hands and Lydia put it back. Jimmy tried to help, their hands fumbled together, and Granny closed two fingers round Jimmy's thumb. Beads wouldn't do, it must be something alive. She was so amazed her thoughts ran round and round. So, my dear Lord, this is my death and I wasn't even thinking about it. My children have come to see me die. But I can't, it's not time. Oh, I always hated surprises. I wanted to give Cornelia the amethyst[15] set—Cornelia, you're to have the amethyst set, but Hapsy's to wear it when she wants, and, Doctor Harry, do shut up. Nobody sent for you. Oh, my dear Lord, do wait a minute. I meant to do something about the Forty Acres, Jimmy doesn't need it and Lydia will later

---

15. *Amethyst* (am′ ə thist) is purple or violet quartz and is typically used in jewelry.

---

on, with that worthless husband of hers. I meant to finish the altar cloth and send six bottles of wine to Sister Borgia for her dyspepsia.[16] I want to send six bottles of wine to Sister Borgia, Father Connolly, now don't let me forget.

Cornelia's voice made short turns and tilted over and crashed. "Oh, Mother, oh, Mother, oh, Mother . . ."

"I'm not going, Cornelia. I'm taken by surprise. I can't go."

You'll see Hapsy again. What about her? "I thought you'd never come." Granny made a long journey outward, looking for Hapsy. What if I don't find her? What then? Her heart sank down and down, there was no bottom to death, she couldn't come to the end of it. The blue light from Cornelia's lampshade drew into a tiny point in the center of her brain, it flickered and winked like an eye, quietly it fluttered and dwindled. Granny lay curled down within herself, amazed and watchful, staring at the point of light that was herself; her body was now only a deeper mass of shadow in an endless darkness and this darkness would curl round the light and swallow it up. God, give a sign!

For the second time there was no sign. Again no bridegroom and the priest in the ☆ house. She could not remember any other sorrow because this grief wiped them all away. Oh, no, there's nothing more cruel than this—I'll never forgive it. She stretched herself with a deep breath and blew out the light. ∾

---

16. *Dyspepsia* is indigestion.

Stream of Consciousness *What is unclear about this moment in the story?* 1

Reading Practice

SPIRAL REVIEW **Draw Conclusions** When readers draw conclusions, they use evidence to infer new information. Readers can reach conclusions about why a writer wrote a piece of literature or why a character behaves in a certain way. Evidence may come from the selection and from the readers' experiences. Form small groups and ask students to draw conclusions to answer this question: What does "The Jilting of Granny Weatherall" say about the way people hold on to their memories? Have groups share their conclusions with the class.

After You Read

Respond and Think Critically

Respond and Interpret

1. What was your reaction to Granny Weatherall's train of thought throughout the story?

2. (a)At the beginning of the story, what attitudes does Granny have toward Dr. Harry, Cornelia, and her own illness? (b)What do Granny's attitudes reveal about her state of mind?

3. (a)Who is Hapsy, and where does Granny see her? (b)How does this experience relate to what occurs at the end of the story?

4. (a)Which event does Granny recall with particular anger and sadness? (b)What does her "message" for the person involved allow you to infer about her feelings toward him?

Analyze and Evaluate

5. (a)In your opinion, did Granny live a full life? Support your answer with details from the story. (b)What is symbolic about the name Weatherall?

6. (a)How do the present and past merge when the priest appears? (b)How does Porter use religion to add an extra layer of meaning to the story? Explain.

7. Evaluate whether Porter brings this story to an effective close. Explain your answer using details from the story.

Connect

8. **Big Idea** **Modern Fiction** How does the stream of consciousness technique that Porter uses to tell the story clarify the role that memories, experiences, and inner and outer worlds play in one's life?

9. **Connect to the Author** (a)What is the significance of Granny's name? (b)What connections, if any, do you make between Granny's life and Porter's?

Literary Element Stream of Consciousness

By using **stream of consciousness**, Porter takes the reader deep into the mind of Granny Weatherall and presents a vivid picture of death. Look back at the timeline you created as you answer the following questions:

1. What kinds of clues help the reader distinguish the past from the present?

2. Is stream of consciousness a good technique for telling the story of the hours and minutes leading up to death? Why or why not?

Review: Characterization

Characterization refers to the various methods that a writer uses to develop the personality of a character. These include description, dialogue, the character's actions, and sometimes, as in this story, the character's thoughts.

Partner Activity Work with a classmate to review how you learned about Cornelia as you read the story. Create a web diagram like the one below, adding new circles with specific information from the story.

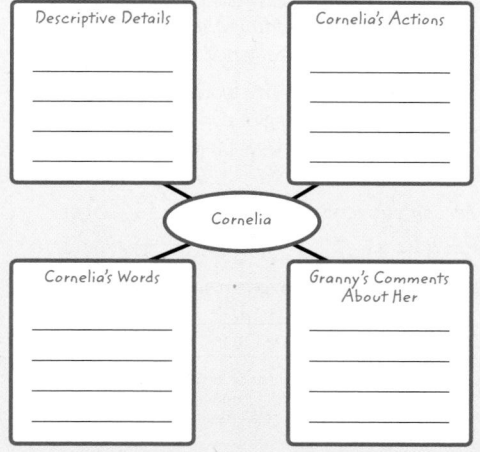

KATHERINE ANNE PORTER **783**

After You Read

Assess

1. Some students may think it is typical of how someone thinks. Others may dislike the style.

2. (a) Granny is irritated; she denies that she is ill. (b) She is rational enough to react to others but not aware she is dying.

3. (a) A daughter who has died; Granny visualizes Hapsy at her bedside. (b) Hapsy's appearance and words, "I thought you'd never come," lead to Granny's looking for Hapsy.

4. (a) Being jilted by her fiancé, George (b) She never got over the humiliation, but she does not want him to know.

5. (a) Students may say Granny has had a full and often difficult life. She raised her children and ran a farm after her husband's death. (b) Granny has weathered all the things, both good and bad, that have come her way.

6. (a) The priest reminds Granny of her wedding. (b) During her first engagement, Granny anticipated being joined with another under the eyes of God. As she dies, she expects a signal from God that she may rejoin Hapsy. In both cases, Granny is jilted.

7. Granny's death is the suitable ending. The irony and disappointment of her death mirror that of her being jilted years earlier.

8. Stream of consciousness allows Porter to show memories and feelings, which contrast with Granny's outer life.

9. (a) Granny has weathered both sorrows and joys in her life. (b) Students may say that both experienced intense realizations at critical points in their lives; Porter had a near-death experience.

Literary Element

1. Dialogue helps pinpoint Granny's place in time. For example, when she hears Cornelia's voice, she is in the present, but when she tells John to call the doctor, she is in the past.

2. Porter's use of stream of consciousness lets her portray the random thoughts of a dying person.

Review: Characterization

Possible responses:

Descriptive details: Cornelia's features are "swollen and full of little puddles."

Cornelia's words: "She was never like this, *never* like this!"

Cornelia's actions: She tries to make Granny as comfortable as possible.

Granny's comments: Cornelia is "dutiful and good."

After You Read

Reading Strategy

1. **A** is the correct answer because all of Granny's accomplishments that she remembers before dying happened because she rebounded and went on with her life.

Vocabulary

1. Annette's careful critique of her friends implies that she is sure to speak without offending.

2. It is the task of a caretaker to make sure his charges remain healthy, so *dutiful* refers to one who does his assigned job.

3. Though he has not heard the results, the uncle's excessive pride in himself makes him believe he will win.

4. The sister's emotional distress after the *jilting* implies that the boyfriend broke up with her.

5. Carrying a rosary, an item affiliated with religious worship, is characteristic of a devoutly spiritual person.

 For additional assessment, see Assessment Resources, pp. 217–218.

Reading Strategy Draw Conclusions About the Protagonist

SAT Skills Practice

1. Which event in Granny's life most powerfully illustrates her independence?

   (A) rebounding after being jilted

   (B) dying without forgiveness

   (C) digging post holes

   (D) plaguing Cornelia

   (E) playing cards with the priest

Vocabulary Practice

Practice with Context Clues Identify context clues to the meaning of each vocabulary word.

1. Annette was being **tactful** when she gave feedback on her friends' presentations.

2. We wanted to leave a **dutiful** caretaker in charge of the sensitive animals.

3. My uncle's **vanity** was great enough that he felt sure he had won the contest.

4. My sister cried for three days after her boyfriend **jilted** her and married another girl.

5. Joseph, who always carried a rosary, was known for his **piety**.

Academic Vocabulary

*Granny Weatherall's **dominant** thoughts are of her children and of the fiancé who left her.*

Dominant is an academic word. Using context clues, infer the meaning of *dominant* in the above sentence. Check your inference in a print or online dictionary.

For more on academic vocabulary, see pages 53–54.

LOG ON **Literature** Online

Selection Resources For Selection Quizzes, eFlash-cards, and Reading-Writing Connection activities, go to glencoe.com and enter QuickPass code GLA9800u5.

Speaking and Listening

 Performance

Assignment Imagine that George arrives in Granny's room or calls her on the phone. Write and perform a monologue in which Granny speaks to George. Review your details/conclusion chart from page 774 to help you understand what Granny would say to George and how she would act.

Prepare Before beginning to draft your monologue, use a word web such as the one below to help you analyze Granny's character. As you write Granny's speech, keep in mind the basic character traits you have identified.

Granny's character

Once you have drafted your monologue, read it aloud, both as an aid to revision and to begin rehearsing your delivery. Ask yourself if your monologue expresses the characteristics of Granny's personality and captures her voice. Once you are satisfied with the text of your monologue, rehearse it carefully. It is useful to rehearse in front of a family member or friend—you can practice eye contact and get feedback on details such as your pronunciation and pacing. You can also videotape your performance and provide your own evaluation.

Perform In performing your monologue, speak loudly enough to be heard, but vary the pacing and inflection of your voice to reflect the meaning of your words. Maintain eye contact with your audience. Use appropriate and natural facial expressions and gestures to reinforce the dramatic content of your monologue.

Evaluate Write a paragraph evaluating your delivery of your monologue. When your classmates present their monologues, offer oral feedback. Use the checklist on page 163 for help in your evaluation.

Academic Vocabulary

Students should infer from context that *dominant* means "in control over others."

 For help with creating presentations, see Student Presentation Builder on StudentWorks Plus.

Speaking and Listening

Use these criteria when evaluating students' monologues:

- Did the student use character analysis of Granny to prepare the monologue?
- Did the student's monologue capture Granny's character and voice?
- Did the student effectively use verbal and nonverbal techniques in delivering the monologue?

PART 3

THE HARLEM RENAISSANCE

The Bitter Nest, Part II: The Harlem Renaissance Party, c. 1988. Faith Ringgold. Acrylic on canvas with printed, dyed, and pieced fabric, 94 x 83 in. Smithsonian American Art Museum, Washington, DC.

View the Art Faith Ringgold explores feminism and racism through her painted story-quilts, which often incorporate both images and text. What story do you "read" from looking at this quilt? ⭐

"*I, too, am America.*"

—Langston Hughes, "I, Too"

785

Analyze and Extend

Reading Strategy **1**

Evaluate Explain that a *renaissance* is a period of rebirth or revival, or a period of artistic growth. *The Renaissance* refers most often to the European renaissance of the fourteenth through sixteenth centuries, which produced artists such as Michelangelo and Leonardo da Vinci. **Ask:** What connection can you infer between Langston Hughes's quote and a renaissance in the African American community of Harlem? *(As an African American Hughes contributes to American culture.)*

Literary Element **2**

Allusion Explain to students that the quotation is the last line of a poem by Hughes. The poem begins "I, Too, Sing America." This is an allusion to a poem from Walt Whitman's *Leaves of Grass*.

View the Art ⭐

Story Quilts Faith Ringgold (1930–) is an award-winning children's book illustrator, artist, and teacher. She is famous for her story quilts, which combine storytelling, painting, and quilted fabric. In this quilt, Ringgold includes some famous African American writers and artists.

 For additional support for English Learners, see Unit 5 Teaching Resources Book, p. 210.

English Learners
DIFFERENTIATED INSTRUCTION

Intermediate Explain that the 1920s are often referred to as the "Roaring Twenties," a period of prosperity and change for some Americans. Provide historical information for students to read and discuss. Ask why they think the term "Roaring Twenties" is used to describe this period.

Approaching Level
DIFFERENTIATED INSTRUCTION

Established Point out that Hughes wrote: "I, too, am America," not "I, too, am American." **Ask:** What is the difference? *(Stating "I am America" suggests that the speaker represents a larger group whereas "I am American" refers only to the speaker.)*

Before You Read

Focus

Bellringer Options

Selection Focus
   Transparency 48
Daily Language Practice
   Transparency 71

Or display images of major cities around the world, such as Paris, Shanghai, and Cairo.

Ask: If you could visit any city in the world, which would it be? Why?

Have students share their choices with the class. Encourage students to describe their city of choice and point out the imagery they use.

Before You Read

My City

Meet **James Weldon Johnson**
(1871–1938)

Both as an artist and an activist, James Weldon Johnson spent his life introducing the United States to the creative voice of African Americans while fighting the racism and the social injustices he believed hindered their progress. For Johnson, writing poetry and fighting for equality served the same goal: winning a respected place in society for African Americans.

Born in Jacksonville, Florida, Johnson grew up in a stable middle-class home and was raised to have an appreciation of the arts and a love of learning. Later, as a student at Atlanta University, he embraced the school's philosophy that educated African Americans should devote their lives to public service—and he did just that.

> *"I believe that the richest contributions the Negro poet can make to the American literature of the future will be the fusion into it of his own individual artistic gifts."*
>
> —James Weldon Johnson
> "Preface," *The Book of American Negro Poetry*

Born to be a New Yorker In 1900, he and his brother Rosamond composed the spiritual-influenced song "Lift Every Voice and Sing," which would later be referred to as "the Negro National Anthem." Shortly after that, the brothers began writing hit songs for Broadway musicals and the stage. By 1902, Johnson resigned his post as principal of Stanton School and the brothers relocated to New York City. For Johnson, New York City

proved "an alluring world, a tempting world, a world of greatly lessened restraints . . . but, above all, a world of tremendous artistic potentialities."

During the 1920s, Harlem became "the recognized Negro capital," and the passionate innovations in African American music, art, and literature that developed there became known as the Harlem Renaissance. Johnson was involved in the movement not only as an author but also as a mentor of young writers, such as Claude McKay and Langston Hughes. He urged artists to find their inspiration in real-life African American communities. In these artists he saw "a group whose ideals are becoming increasingly more vital than those of the traditionally artistic group, even if its members are less picturesque." In 1922, Johnson published his widely acclaimed anthology, *The Book of American Negro Poetry*.

Devoted to Public Service Johnson's work outside the creative sphere was equally impressive and, in some ways, groundbreaking. Johnson was the first African American lawyer to be admitted to the bar in Florida, and as a leader in the National Association for the Advancement of Colored People (NAACP), he was instrumental in helping the organization become a national force capable of lobbying in Washington. He played an integral role in bringing attention to the issues of desegregation and the abolishment of discrimination in housing, education, employment, and voting. Johnson's impact as a Civil Rights activist, poet, and novelist are still felt today.

 Literature Online

Author Search For more about James Weldon Johnson, go to glencoe.com and enter QuickPass code GLA9800u5.

Selection Skills

Literary Elements
- Sonnet (SE pp. 787, 789)

Listening/Speaking/Viewing Skills
- Analyze Art (TE p. 788)

My City

Reading Skills
- Interpret Imagery (SE pp. 787, 789)

Vocabulary Skills
- Antonyms (SE pp. 787, 789)
- Adjectives (TE p. 787)

Writing Skills/Grammar
- Write a Brochure (SE p. 789)
- Word Choice (TE p. 788)

Literature and Reading Preview

Connect to the Poem

What is your favorite place? Why? Make a list of your reasons. Use vivid language, imagery, and specific details.

Build Background

Johnson often crafted his early poetry using classical models—writing rhymed verse in traditional forms such as the sonnet. "My City" is an example of a Petrarchan sonnet, named for the Italian poet who developed the form in the 1300s.

Set Purposes for Reading

Big Idea The Harlem Renaissance

In "My City," Johnson celebrates Manhattan, the most well-known borough of New York City. Harlem is a neighborhood in Manhattan. As you read, ask, What does Johnson's poem say about the vitality of the city during the Harlem Renaissance?

Literary Element Sonnet

A **sonnet** is a lyric poem of fourteen lines, typically written in iambic pentameter. "My City" is a Petrarchan (or Italian) sonnet, which is divided into two stanzas, an eight-line *octave* and a six-line *sestet*. The octave often sets up a situation or poses a question that is responded to in the sestet. As you read, ask, What does Johnson accomplish by using this structure?

Reading Strategy Interpret Imagery

Imagery is the "word pictures" that a writer creates to make the text more vivid or evoke an emotional response. Writers often use sensory details to create effective images. As you read, ask, How does Johnson's imagery differ in each stanza?

Tip: Take Notes Create a chart like the one started below to analyze the impact of images in "My City." Consider both the impact on a reader's emotions and on the poem's meaning.

Image	Impact
endless night	

Learning Objectives

For pages 786–789

In studying this text, you will focus on the following objectives:

Literary Study: Analyzing a sonnet.

Reading: Interpreting imagery.

Writing: Writing a brochure.

Vocabulary

subtle (sə´ təl) *adj.* faint; barely noticeable; not obvious; p. 788 *Although her smirk was subtle, I saw it.*

stark (stärk) *adj.* absolute; complete; p. 788 *Pablo's opinion was in stark contrast to mine.*

unutterable (un ə´ tə rə bəl) *adj.* too deep or great to be put into words; p. 788 *The apprehended thief experienced unutterable regret.*

Tip: Antonyms Understanding an unfamiliar word's antonyms—words with opposite or nearly opposite meanings—and using them in a sentence can help you learn the new word. Example: *Overpowering is an antonym of subtle.* Sentence: When a dessert has a *subtle* mocha flavor, the taste of coffee is not too overpowering.

JAMES WELDON JOHNSON **787**

English Learners

DIFFERENTIATED INSTRUCTION

Intermediate Remind students that a writer uses *imagery* by creating "word pictures" to generate an emotional response. Write the word *imagery* on the board. Point out that the root of this word is *imāgō*, which is also the root of the word *image*. Ask students to define the word *image*. Then have them explain the differences between the words *image* and *imagery*. Help students brainstorm other words that have the same root and have them define the words. *(imagine, imaginary, imagination)* Write the words and the students' definitions on the board. Then have students use dictionaries to find the meanings of the words and compare them with their own definitions.

Before You Read

Focus

Summary

The sonnet begins with the speaker asking himself what he'll miss most when he dies. He ponders whether he will long for elements of nature, such as trees, birds, and streams. In the second stanza, he comes to the conclusion that he will miss Manhattan the most. He contrasts the delights of the borough with the elements of nature. He describes city sights and sounds and ends with a strong statement about how much he will miss them.

 For summaries in languages other than English, see Unit 5 Teaching Resources Book, pp. 211–216.

 For additional context, see Glencoe Interactive Vocabulary CD-ROM.

Vocabulary

Use Adjectives Explain to students that the word *stark* typically refers to a contrast or difference between things that are at opposite extremes, as opposed to the type of completeness that comes from having a full range of possibilities. **Ask:** What nouns might the word *stark* be used to modify? *(contrast, difference, justice)* What nouns might the word *stark* not be used to modify? *(compromise, well-being, joy)*

APPROACHING **Ask:** What is a feeling that could be described with the adjective *unutterable*? *(Despair, remorse, joy)*

The Harlem Renaissance
Answer: *The speaker loves all the features of Manhattan, including her shining towers and slums.*

<u>View the Art</u> ★

Jacob Lawrence (1917–2000) is one of the most famous African American artists. He is known for his depiction of important African American events. After making his name in Harlem, Lawrence achieved national acclaim in 1941 with his Migration series, featured on pages 807–809.

Ask: How does Lawrence's painting relate to Johnson's poem? *(Students may say it reflects the crowds and the "throbbing force" described in Johnson's poem.)*

For additional practice using the reading skill or strategy, see Unit 5 Teaching Resources Book, p. 218.

Progress Check

Can students analyze a sonnet?

If No → See Unit 5 Teaching Resources Book, p. 217.

My City

James Weldon Johnson

Fulton and Nostrand, 1958. Jacob Lawrence. Tempera on masonite, 24 x 30 in. Private collection. Courtesy Terry Dintenfass Gallery, NY. ★

When I come down to sleep death's endless night,
The threshold of the unknown dark to cross,
What to me then will be the keenest loss,
When this bright world blurs on my fading sight?
5 Will it be that no more I shall see the trees
Or smell the flowers or hear the singing birds
Or watch the flashing streams or patient herds?
No. I am sure it will be none of these.

But, ah! Manhattan's sights and sounds, her smells,
10 Her crowds, her throbbing force, the thrill that comes
From being of her a part, her **subtle** spells,
Her shining towers, her avenues, her slums—
O God! the **stark**, **unutterable** pity,

To

The Harlem Renaissance *How do you think the speaker feels toward Manhattan's "shining towers" and "slums"?*   **1**

Vocabulary

subtle (sə´ təl) *adj.* faint; barely noticeable; not obvious
stark (stärk) *adj.* absolute; complete
unutterable (un ə´ tə rə bəl) *adj.* too deep or great to be put into words

788 UNIT 5   BEGINNINGS OF THE MODERN AGE

Writing Practice

Word Choice Point out the importance of word choice in poetry. The condensed nature of poetry makes word choice essential. Note how words like *stark* and *unutterable* work well because they not only get their meaning across, but they also paint a vivid picture. Have students practice using imagery by writing a full description of the town in which they live. Instruct students to include favorite sights, sounds, and smells in their descriptions.

After You Read

Respond and Think Critically

Respond and Interpret

1. How did "My City" make you feel about New York City as it was during the Harlem Renaissance?

2. (a)What question does the speaker pose for himself at the beginning of the poem? (b)Is the speaker's age implied in this question? If so, how?

3. (a)What possible answers to his question does the speaker first explore? (b)Why might he propose these answers?

4. (a)What answer does the speaker finally provide? (b)What reasons does he give? (c)What does this answer tell you about the speaker's personality?

Analyze and Evaluate

5. (a)What, according to the speaker, is "the stark, unutterable pity" (line 13)? (b)Why might the speaker feel this way about the city?

6. (a)How does the rhyme scheme connect to the poem's meaning? (b)Would the poem have the same effect without a rhyme scheme? Explain.

Connect

7. **Big Idea** **The Harlem Renaissance** How does Johnson's poem reflect the general mood of the Harlem Renaissance?

8. **Connect to Today** Do people today feel as intense a connection to where they live as Johnson expresses in "My City"? Explain.

Literary Element **Sonnet**

Petrarchan **sonnets** have an octave and a sestet. After the octave establishes the main idea, the sestet can develop that idea or offer a new idea.

1. What relationship do the octave and sestet have in "My City"? Explain.

2. How does the division of this poem into an octave and a sestet contribute to its effectiveness?

Reading Strategy **Interpret Imagery**

Refer to your image and impact chart from page 787 as you answer the following questions.

1. How does the imagery change from the octave to the sestet?

2. How does the change support the poem's meaning?

LOG ON **Literature** Online

Selection Resources For Selection Quizzes, eFlashcards, and Reading-Writing Connection activities, go to glencoe.com and enter QuickPass code GLA9800u5.

Vocabulary Practice

Practice with Antonyms With a partner, brainstorm antonyms for each boldfaced vocabulary word below. Then discuss your choices with your classmates. Be prepared to explain why you chose your words.

subtle   stark   unutterable

EXAMPLE: ideal

Antonyms: *flawed, faulty, defective*

Sample explanation: An ideal vacation meets all possible hopes and expectations, but a flawed one does not.

Writing

Write a Brochure Using a map and tourist information about Manhattan, locate places that match Johnson's descriptions. Then create an illustrated tourism guide for "My City." Before you turn in your guide, share it with another student and ask for feedback on how well it expresses Johnson's love of Manhattan.

JAMES WELDON JOHNSON **789**

After You Read

Assess

1. Students may say that the poem expresses the excitement of living in New York.

2. (a) The speaker asks himself what he will miss most when he dies. (b) The speaker's age is not clear, but the question suggests that he is looking back over many years.

3. (a) He considers whether nature and pastoral scenes might be the answer. (b) These are conventional images of beauty.

4. (a) The speaker decides that he will miss Manhattan the most. (b) He loves the crowds and city life. (c) He enjoys the excitement and activity of city life.

5. (a) It is the sorrow the speaker feels because death will force him to give up Manhattan forever. (b) To the speaker, the city represents the best of life.

6. (a) The rhyme of the second stanza gives it a faster tempo, reflecting the rhythm and pace of the city. (b) A change would affect the tempo of one or both of the stanzas.

7. It celebrates a city where there was a great blossoming of African American culture.

8. Students may say that people feel less connected because they change cities more often.

Literary Element

1. Contradiction: The octave focuses on nature, and the sestet on civilization.

2. It creates a sharp distinction between pastoral prettiness and urban energy.

Writing

Make sure that students' citations of places match the images in the poem.

Reading Strategy

1. From rural imagery to urban imagery

2. The imagery evokes both the city and the author's feelings about it.

Vocabulary

subtle; Antonyms: obvious, overpowering, palpable; Sample explanation: A perfume that is subtle has a faint scent, whereas one that is overpowering can be smelled at a distance.

stark; Antonyms: incomplete; Sample explanation: Stark pity is absolute and whole, but incomplete pity is not.

unutterable; Antonyms: describable, imaginable; Sample explanation: Something that is unutterable cannot be described.

789

Before You Read

Focus

Bellringer Options

Selection Focus
  Transparency 49
Daily Language Practice
  Transparency 72

Or **write on the board:** What is your favorite book? How has it inspired you?

Display some popular books to start the discussion. Encourage students to share their favorite books with the class. Have volunteers give an oral review of their favorite book. They should include the title, author, and an explanation of why they enjoyed it or how it inspired them.

Before You Read

from *Dust Tracks on a Road*

Meet **Zora Neale Hurston**
(1891–1960)

I n 1973, writer Alice Walker traveled to Fort Pierce, Florida, to visit Zora Neale Hurston's grave. According to Walker, what she found looked "more like an abandoned field" than a cemetery. Walker ordered a headstone to mark Hurston's grave. "I wanted to mark Zora's grave so that one day all our daughters and sons would be able to locate the remains of a human mountain in Florida's and America's so frequently flat terrain," Walker explains.

Introduction to Folklore Zora Neale Hurston grew up in Eatonville, Florida, one of the first incorporated black towns in the United States, where her father was the mayor. Only thirteen years old when her mother died, Hurston spent the next two decades working as a waitress, a manicurist, and a maid, while trying to complete a high school education. Finally she enrolled in Howard University, and later Barnard College. There, she came to the attention of celebrated anthropologist Franz Boas, who invited Hurston to become formally trained as an anthropologist and a folklorist.

After completing her studies, Hurston used her training to collect the folklore of Eatonville and other southern African American communities. She later used this material as a source for much of the fiction writing she pursued when not documenting folklore.

Literary Success and Obscurity Although considered an important figure in the Harlem Renaissance, Hurston was a fierce individualist who resisted membership in any one school of thought. She once remarked, "I am so put together that I do not have much of a herd instinct. Or if I must be connected with the flock, let me be the shepherd my ownself. That is just the way I am made." Her ideas sometimes got her into trouble with her fellow writers, some of whom felt that documenting the speech and folkways of small-town African Americans could expose the community to ridicule. Over the years Hurston's popularity declined. By the time of her death in a Florida retirement home, she was penniless.

> *"There is no agony like bearing an untold story inside you."*
>
> —Zora Neale Hurston

Today, thanks to Walker and other admirers, Hurston's books are widely read. She is remembered for her ability to capture the traditions and poetic speech of southern African American culture. Her book *Mules and Men* is recognized as the first history of African American folklore written by an African American, and her novel *Their Eyes Were Watching God* has sold more than a million copies since its republication in 1969. In her autobiography, Hurston recalled, "I used to climb to the top of one of the huge chinaberry trees which guarded our front gate and look out over the world. The most interesting thing I saw was the horizon. . . . It grew upon me that I ought to walk out to the horizon and see what the end of the world was like."

 Literature Online

Author Search For more about Zora Neale Hurston, go to glencoe.com and enter QuickPass code GLA9800u5.

Selection Skills

Literary Elements
- Voice (SE pp. 791, 192, 791, 796, 797, 798)
- Allusion (SE p. 798)

Reading Skills
- Analyze Language (SE pp. 791, 793, 795, 796, 799)
- Predict (TE p. 792)
- Connect (TE, 796)

Dust Tracks on a Road

Listening/Speaking/ Viewing Skills
- Analyze Art (SE p. 795; TE p. 792)

Writing Skills/Grammar
- Apply Allusion (SE p. 799)
- Point of View (TE p. 794)

Vocabulary Skills
- Analogies (SE pp. 791, 799)
- Synonyms and Antonyms (TE p. 791)

Literature and Reading Preview

Connect to the Story

Have you ever received a gift that changed your perceptions of another person? Write a brief journal entry describing that situation.

Build Background

This excerpt takes place in about 1900 in Eatonville, Florida. Zora Neale Hurston frequently celebrated the customs and speech of her hometown in her writing. Although the autobiography *Dust Tracks on a Road* is fascinating for what it reveals about Hurston and her background, it conceals much about her life at the same time. Hurston never tells when she was born, never mentions her second marriage, and contradicts details about her life that she wrote about in private letters to friends.

Set Purposes for Reading

Big Idea **The Harlem Renaissance**

As you read, ask yourself, What details of Southern life did Hurston consider worthy of recording and celebrating?

Literary Element **Voice**

The **voice** of a literary work is the distinctive use of language that conveys the author's or narrator's personality to the reader. Voice is determined by elements of style such as word choice and tone. As you read, ask yourself, What does the narrator's voice reveal about her personality and background?

Reading Strategy **Analyze Language**

When you **analyze** a selection, you look at separate parts to see how they work together to produce an underlying meaning. As you read, ask yourself, How does Hurston use vivid words, dialect (local speech patterns), and regional expressions to create a rich portrait of childhood in Eatonville?

Tip: Read Slowly When you read material that contains unfamiliar words, phrases, or concepts, slow down your reading rate to aid comprehension.

ZORA NEALE HURSTON **791**

Learning Objectives

For pages 790–799

In studying this text, you will focus on the following objectives:

Literary Study: Analyzing voice.

Reading: Analyzing language.

Writing: Applying allusion in a paragraph.

Vocabulary

brazenness (brā´ zən nəs) *n.* defiant behavior; boldness; p. 792 *We laughed at the comic's brazenness when he ridiculed the mayor.*

exalt (ig zôlt´) *v.* to lift up; to put in high spirits; p. 794 *I always exalt the influence of my mother.*

snicker (sni´ kər) *n.* a snide, partly suppressed laugh, often expressing disrespect; p. 794 *When the actor forgot his lines, a man in the audience let out a snicker.*

indifferent (in dif´ ər ənt) *adj.* lacking feeling or concern; p. 796 *Jim played for the joy of it; he was completely indifferent to whether he won or lost.*

Tip: Analogies Analogies are comparisons that show similarities between two things that are otherwise dissimilar. An analogy can help explain something unfamiliar by comparing it to something familiar.

Before You Read

Focus

Summary

Hurston recalls an episode from her childhood that encouraged her interest in reading. When two white women visited her school in Eatonville, Florida—an African American town—they were impressed by her oral reading ability. They treated her to fancy food, clothes, and shiny new pennies; more importantly, they sent her a box of books. The books unlocked Hurston's imagination and inspired her deeply.

 For summaries in languages other than English, see Unit 5 Teaching Resources Book, pp. 222–227.

Vocabulary

Synonyms and Antonyms

Remind students that synonyms are words that have the same or similar meanings. Antonyms are words that have opposite or nearly opposite meanings. Synonyms and antonyms are always the same part of speech. Have students identify a synonym and an antonym for each of the four vocabulary words. Have students defend their choices.

(APPROACHING) Have students check the meanings of their synonyms and antonyms in the dictionary. Have them reevaluate whether or not they were correct choices.

 For additional vocabulary practice, see Unit 5 Teaching Resources Book, p. 230.

English Learners

DIFFERENTIATED INSTRUCTION

Intermediate Ask students to identify the most familiar use of the word *voice*. *(the sounds produced by a person)* Explain that a writer is said to have a distinctive voice just as an individual does. This voice comes through in the author's choice of words. Have students make a two-column chart, like the one at right, to record examples of the author's voice as they read the selection.

Word Choice	Narrator's Voice
The movement made me glad to see it.	Optimistic, open to adventure

Teach

Voice Answer: *Anecdotes such as the one about Hurston hitchhiking suggest that the young Hurston was likable, brash, and unafraid.*

View the Art ★

A library played an important part in Jacob Lawrence's artistic development. Lawrence was inspired by Professor Charles Seifert, who taught African American history at the 135th Street public library in Harlem. Due in part to Seifert's influence, Lawrence began painting the stories and histories of African Americans.

Ask: How might you take advantage of services provided by a library to further your own creative growth? *(Students may say that libraries offer free classes, Internet access, book clubs, and events.)*

For an audio recording of this selection, use Listening Library Audio CD-ROM.

Readability Scores

Dale-Chall: 5.1
DRP: 53
Lexile: 920

Harlem Series, no. 28: The Libraries Are Appreciated, 1943. Jacob Lawrence. Gouache on paper, 14½ x 21¼ in. Philadelphia Museum of Art, PA. ★

from Dust Tracks on a Road

Zora Neale Hurston

I used to take a seat on top of the gate-post and watch the world go by. One way to Orlando ran past my house, so the carriages and cars would pass before me. The movement made me glad to see it. Often the white travelers would hail[1] me, but more often I hailed them, and asked, "Don't you want me to go a piece of the way with you?" They always did. I know now that I must have caused a great deal of amusement among them, but my self-assurance must have carried the point, for I was always invited to come along. I'd ride up the road for perhaps a half-mile, then walk back. I did not do this with the permission of my parents, nor with their foreknowledge. When they found out about it later, I usually got a whipping. My grandmother worried about my forward ways a great deal. She had known slavery and to her my **brazenness** was unthinkable.

Voice *What does this passage suggest about the young Hurston's personality?* 1

Vocabulary

brazenness (brā´ zən nəs) *n.* defiant behavior; boldness

---

1. *Hail* means "to greet."

792 UNIT 5 BEGINNINGS OF THE MODERN AGE

Reading Practice

SMALL GROUP

Actively Read and Predict
Ask students to stop reading at the beginning of the first full paragraph on page 793. Divide students into groups. Based on what they have read so far, students hypothesize what they think might come next. Then, have them develop a list of questions that they would like answered as they read further.

Encourage students to look for the answers as they read further. This will help them set their own purposes for reading. When they finish the passage, have them compare their predictions with what actually happens.

"Git down offa dat gate-post! You li'l sow, you! Git down! Setting up dere looking dem white folks right in de face! They's gowine[2] to lynch you, yet. And don't stand in dat doorway gazing out at 'em neither. Youse too brazen to live long."

Nevertheless, I kept right on gazing at them, and "going a piece of the way" whenever I could make it. The village seemed dull to me most of the time. If the village was singing a chorus, I must have missed the tune.

Perhaps a year before the old man[3] died, I came to know two other white people for myself. They were women.

It came about this way. The whites who came down from the North were often brought by their friends to visit the village school. A Negro school was something strange to them, and while they were always sympathetic and kind, curiosity must have been present, also. They came and went, came and went. Always, the room was hurriedly put in order, and we were threatened with a prompt and bloody death if we cut one caper[4] while the visitors were present. We always sang a spiritual, led by Mr. Calhoun himself. Mrs. Calhoun always stood in the back, with a palmetto switch[5] in her hand as a squelcher. We were all little angels for the duration, because we'd better be. She would cut her eyes[6] and give us a glare that meant trouble, then turn her face towards the visitors and beam as much as to say it was a great privilege and pleasure to teach lovely children like us. They couldn't see that palmetto hickory in her hand behind all those benches, but we

knew where our angelic behavior was coming from.

Usually, the visitors gave warning a day ahead and we would be cautioned to put on shoes, comb our heads, and see to ears and fingernails. There was a close inspection of every one of us before we marched in that morning. Knotty heads, dirty ears and fingernails got hauled out of line, strapped and sent home to lick the calf[7] over again.

This particular afternoon, the two young ladies just popped in. Mr. Calhoun was flustered,[8] but he put on the best show he could. He dismissed the class that he was teaching up at the front of the room, then called the fifth grade in reading. That was my class.

So we took our readers and went up front. We stood up in the usual line, and opened to the lesson. It was the story of Pluto and Persephone.[9] It was new and hard to the class in general, and Mr. Calhoun was very uncomfortable as the readers stumbled along, spelling out words with their lips, and in mumbling undertones before they exposed them experimentally to the teacher's ears.

Then it came to me. I was fifth or sixth down the line. The story was not new to me, because I had read my reader through from lid to lid, the first week that Papa had bought it for me.

That is how it was that my eyes were not in the book, working out the paragraph which I knew would be mine by counting the children ahead of me. I was observing our visitors, who held a book between them, following the lesson. They had shiny hair, mostly brownish. One had a looping gold chain around her neck. The other one was dressed all over in black and white with a pretty finger ring on

---

2. *Gowine* is dialect for "going."
3. The *old man*, a white farmer who was a friend of Hurston's family, took Zora Neale fishing and gave her advice.
4. *Cut one caper* is slang for "play a trick or prank" or "behave extravagantly or noisily."
5. A *palmetto switch*, a whip used for discipline, was made from the flexible stem of a leaf from a palmetto palm.
6. *Cut her eyes* is slang for "look at with scorn or contempt."

7. *Lick the calf* is slang for "get cleaned up."
8. *Flustered* means "nervous" or "agitated."
9. The myth of *Pluto and Persephone* (pər sef′ ə nē) explains the origin of the seasons. Pluto is god of the underworld, and Persephone is his wife.

2 The Harlem Renaissance *What do these details reveal about the United States at the time?*

Analyze Language *Why does the author include phrases such as "lick the calf"?* **3**

ZORA NEALE HURSTON **793**

793

Teach

Big Idea 2

The Harlem Renaissance
Answer: *These details reveal that some Southern African Americans did not often come into contact with white people, especially with Northern whites. The details also suggest that the white visitors were motivated to visit the school both by kindness and by curiosity.*

Reading Strategy 3

Analyze Language **Answer:** *The inclusion of colloquial language adds authenticity and humor.*

 For additional practice using the reading skill or strategy, see Unit 5 Teaching Resources Book, p. 229.

English Learners

DIFFERENTIATED INSTRUCTION

Advanced Students may more readily understand this passage if they are familiar with some of the slang and dialect that Hurston uses. Preteach the following slang and unfamiliar terms from the story: *gowine, cut one caper, cut her eyes, lick the calf, flustered, passed,* and *roast.*

Have students pantomime each term or phrase. Once they understand the meaning of each one, reinforce comprehension by asking students questions such as the following:

Under what conditions would someone need to "lick the calf"? *(when visitors are coming)* What is another common or slang phrase with a meaning similar to "cut one caper"? *(cut up)* What is an example of a situation in which some-

one could feel flustered? *(when asked a difficult question)* When might a teacher "cut her eyes"? *(when students are whispering while she is talking)*

793

Teach

<table>
<tr><td>**Literary Element**</td><td>**1**</td></tr>
</table>

Point of View

Ask: What is first-person point of view in nonfiction? *(The story is told from the author's point of view.)* **Say:** An autobiography almost always uses first-person point of view. **Ask:** What might be an advantage and a disadvantage of this? *(Students may say that an advantage is they hear what the author thinks and feels, and a disadvantage is that they are limited because they only hear the author's side of the story.)*

<table>
<tr><td>**Literary Element**</td><td>**2**</td></tr>
</table>

Voice

Answer: *The word* exalted *conveys Hurston's feelings of being lifted into higher realms of experience through her reading of the myth.*

---

her left hand. But the thing that held my eyes were their fingers. They were long and thin, and very white, except up near the tips. There they were baby pink. I had never seen such hands. It was a fascinating discovery for me. I wondered how they felt. I would have given those hands more attention, but the child before me was almost through. My turn next, so I got on my mark, bringing my eyes back to the book and made sure of my place. Some of the stories I had re-read several times, and this Greco-Roman myth was one of my favorites. I was **exalted** by it, and that is the way I read my paragraph.

"Yes, Jupiter[10] had seen her (Persephone). He had seen the maiden picking flowers in the field. He had seen the chariot of the dark monarch pause by the maiden's side. He had seen him when he seized Persephone. He had seen the black horses leap down Mount Aetna's[11] fiery throat. Persephone was now in Pluto's dark realm and he had made her his wife."

The two women looked at each other and then back to me. Mr. Calhoun broke out with a proud smile beneath his bristly moustache, and instead of the next child taking up where I had ended, he nodded to me to go on. So I read the story to the end, where flying Mercury, the messenger of the Gods, brought Persephone back to the sunlit earth and restored her to the arms of Dame Ceres, her mother, that the world might have springtime and summer flowers, autumn and harvest. But because she had bitten the pomegranate while in Pluto's kingdom, she must return to him for three months of each year, and be his

1

queen. Then the world had winter, until she returned to earth.

The class was dismissed and the visitors smiled us away and went into a low-voiced conversation with Mr. Calhoun for a few minutes. They glanced my way once or twice and I began to worry. Not only was I barefooted, but my feet and legs were dusty. My hair was more uncombed than usual, and my nails were not shiny clean. Oh, I'm going to catch it now. Those ladies saw me, too. Mr. Calhoun is promising to 'tend to me. So I thought.

Then Mr. Calhoun called me. I went up thinking how awful it was to get a whipping before company. Furthermore, I heard a **snicker** run over the room. Hennie Clark and Stell Brazzle did it out loud, so I would be sure to hear them. The smart-aleck was going to get it. I slipped one hand behind me and switched my dress tail at them, indicating scorn.

"Come here, Zora Neale," Mr. Calhoun cooed as I reached the desk. He put his hand on my shoulder and gave me little pats. The ladies smiled and held out those flower-looking fingers towards me. I seized the opportunity for a good look.

"Shake hands with the ladies, Zora Neale," Mr. Calhoun prompted and they took my hand one after the other and smiled. They asked me if I loved school, and I lied that I did. There was *some* truth in it, because I liked geography and reading, and I liked to play at recess time. Whoever it was invented writing and arithmetic got no thanks from me. Neither did I like the arrangement where the teacher could sit up there with a palmetto stem and lick me whenever he saw fit. I hated things I couldn't do anything about. But I knew better than to bring that up right there, so I said yes, I *loved* school.

---

10. In Roman mythology, *Jupiter* is king of the gods and Pluto's brother.
11. *Mount Aetna* (et´ nə) (also spelled *Etna*) is a volcano in eastern Sicily, Italy.

2 **Voice** *What does the use of the word "exalted" convey about the feelings the myth stirs in the young Hurston?*

Vocabulary

exalt (ig zôlt´) *v.* to lift up; to put in high spirits

12. *Sandspurs* (also called *sandburs*) are spiny burs that grow on a grass of the same name.

Vocabulary

snicker (sni´ kər) *n.* a snide, partly suppressed laugh, often expressing disrespect

Writing Practice

SPIRAL REVIEW **Point of View** Have students practice using different points of view. Instruct students to write a paragraph describing what they did after school the previous day. Have students write the paragraph in first-person point of view. Then have students rewrite their paragraphs from the third-person point of view. Have students compare their two points of view and discuss how they differ.

Gwendolyn, 1918. John Sloan. Oil on canvas, 24 x 20 in. Smithsonian American Art Museum, Washington, DC. Gift of Mrs. John Sloan.

View the Art As a Realist, John Sloan often painted the gritty, hard side of life in New York City. How does the girl in his painting compare with your picture of the girl in Hurston's story? Support your response.

"I can tell you do," Brown Taffeta gleamed. She patted my head, and was lucky enough not to get sandspurs[12] in her hand. Children who roll and tumble in the grass in Florida are apt to get sandspurs in their hair. They shook hands with me again and I went back to my seat.

When school let out at three o'clock, Mr. Calhoun told me to wait. When everybody had gone, he told me I was to go to the Park House, that was the hotel in Maitland, the next afternoon to call upon Mrs. Johnstone and Miss Hurd. I must tell Mama to see that I

was clean and brushed from head to feet, and I must wear shoes and stockings. The ladies liked me, he said, and I must be on my best behavior.

The next day I was let out of school an hour early, and went home to be stood up in a tub of suds and be scrubbed and have my ears dug into. My sandy hair sported a red ribbon to match my red and white checked gingham dress, starched until it could stand alone. Mama saw to it that my shoes were on the right feet, since I was careless about left and right. Last thing, I was given a handkerchief to carry, warned again about my behavior, and sent off, with my big brother John to go as far as the hotel gate with me.

First thing, the ladies gave me strange things, like stuffed dates and preserved ginger, and encouraged me to eat all that I wanted. Then they showed me their Japanese dolls and just talked. I was then handed a copy of *Scribner's Magazine,* and asked to read a place that was pointed out to me. After a paragraph or two, I was told with smiles, that that would do.

I was led out on the grounds and they took my picture under a palm tree. They handed me what was to me then a heavy cylinder done up in fancy paper, tied with a ribbon, and they told me goodbye, asking me not to open it until I got home.

My brother was waiting for me down by the lake, and we hurried home, eager to see what was in the thing. It was too heavy to be candy

---

13. *Avarice* is greed, or excessive desire for wealth.

3 The Harlem Renaissance *What kinds of details about the old southern way of life does the author celebrate?*

Analyze Language *How would you characterize the language in this passage?* **4**

ZORA NEALE HURSTON **795**

Teach

Big Idea **3**

The Harlem Renaissance
Answer: *Hurston celebrates the intimate, rural way of life she knew through her use of details, such as colloquial speech.*

Reading Strategy **4**

Analyze Language **Answer:** *In this passage, Hurston uses more formal language. She may do this to convey her sense of being on top of the world after receiving the special gift from the two ladies.*

View the Art ★

Answer: *The girl in the painting is neatly dressed, sitting calmly and attentively with her hands folded in her lap. Like Zora, she seems eager to please. She looks similar to the way Zora might have looked when she went to the hotel to meet with the ladies.*

John Sloan (1871–1951) began his career as an illustrator and cartoonist. Influenced by art teacher Robert Henri, Sloan was part of the movement known as The Ashcan School. He and seven other artists became known as "The Eight," and they gained fame for their realist approach.

Approaching Level

DIFFERENTIATED INSTRUCTION

Emerging Help students explore the causes and effects of events in the passage to help them better understand its meaning. Ask students to describe what caused

- Zora's grandmother to worry about Zora's behavior in front of white people;
- Northerners to come to visit the school;
- Zora to have time to closely observe the two ladies who popped in; and

- Zora to receive attention from the two ladies.

Ask students to explain the effect of

- Zora receiving the new pennies;
- Mrs. Calhoun standing in the back of the room with a palmetto switch in her hand when visitors came; and
- Zora reading to the two lady visitors.

Teach

Literary Element | 1

Voice Answer: *Hurston's choice of words suggests she has strong faith in her own judgment. She is unafraid to reject the judgment of others in favor of her own.*

Reading Strategy | 2

Analyze Language Answer: *Humor includes exaggerated elements, such as the descriptions of the martyrs' "big, soulful, blue eyes," as well as the funny mixture of serious judgments with colloquial expressions, such as "had no meat on their bones."*

Literary History ☆

Hans and Robert Two of Hurston's favorite authors were Hans Christian Andersen (1805–1875), whose fairy tales include "The Ugly Duckling," and Robert Louis Stevenson (1850–1894), author of *Treasure Island*.

---

or anything like that. John insisted on toting it for me.

My mother made John give it back to me and let me open it. Perhaps, I shall never experience such joy again. The nearest thing to that moment was the telegram accepting my first book. One hundred goldy-new pennies rolled out of the cylinder. Their gleam lit up the world. It was not avarice[13] that moved me. It was the beauty of the thing. I stood on the mountain. Mama let me play with my pennies for a while, then put them away for me to keep.

That was only the beginning. The next day I received an Episcopal hymn-book bound in white leather with a golden cross stamped into the front cover, a copy of The Swiss Family Robinson, and a book of fairy tales.

I set about to commit the song words to memory. There was no music written there, just the words. But there was to my consciousness music in between them just the same. "When I survey the Wondrous Cross" seemed the most beautiful to me, so I committed that to memory first of all. Some of them seemed dull and without life, and I pretended they were not there. If white people liked trashy singing like that, there must be something funny about them that I had not noticed before. I stuck to the pretty ones where the words marched to a throb I could feel.

A month or so after the two young ladies returned to Minnesota, they sent me a huge box packed with clothes and books. The red coat with a wide circular collar and the red tam pleased me more than any of the other things. My chums pretended not to like anything that I had, but even then I knew that they were jealous. Old Smarty had gotten by them again. The clothes were not new, but they were very good. I shone like the morning sun.

---

14. In Norse mythology, *Thor* is the god of thunder. His magical hammer returns to him like a boomerang after being thrown.

 Voice *What does Hurston's choice of words suggest about her faith in her own sense of judgment?*

But the books gave me more pleasure than the clothes. I had never been too keen on dressing up. It called for hard scrubbings with Octagon soap suds getting in my eyes, and none too gentle fingers scrubbing my neck and gouging in my ears.

In that box were Gulliver's Travels, Grimm's Fairy Tales, Dick Whittington, Greek and Roman Myths, and best of all, Norse Tales. Why did the Norse tales strike so deeply into my soul? I do not know, but they did. I seemed to remember seeing Thor[14] swing his mighty short-handled hammer as he sped across the sky in rumbling thunder, lightning flashing from the tread of his steeds and the wheels of his chariot. The great and good Odin,[15] who went down to the well of knowledge to drink, and was told that the price of a drink from that fountain was an eye. Odin drank deeply, then plucked out one eye without a murmur and handed it to the grizzly keeper, and walked away. That held majesty for me.

Of the Greeks, Hercules moved me most. I followed him eagerly on his tasks. The story of the choice of Hercules as a boy when he met Pleasure and Duty, and put his hand in that of Duty and followed her steep way to the blue hills of fame and glory, which she pointed out at the end, moved me profoundly. I resolved[16] to be like him. The tricks and turns of the other Gods and Goddesses left me cold. There were other thin books about this and that sweet and gentle little girl who gave up her heart to Christ and good works. Almost always they died from ☆

---

15. *Odin* (ō´ din), the father of Thor, is the supreme god in Norse mythology and the creator of the first man and woman. Odin traded an eye for a drink from the well of wisdom, which was guarded by a giant.
16. *Resolved* means "decided."
17. *Passed* is short for "passed on" or "passed away" and means "died."

Analyze Language *Why is the language in this passage humorous?* **2**

Vocabulary

indifferent (in dif´ ər ənt) *adj.* lacking feeling or concern

---

Reading Practice

SMALL GROUP **SPIRAL REVIEW** **Connect** Many students are familiar with fairy tales by Andersen or by the Brothers Grimm. Point out that students have probably read many of the same stories that Hurston read. Have students break into groups, and have each group choose a favorite fairy tale. Have students come up with modern examples of their fairy tale. Have students write a modern version of their

fairy tale, using the same archetypal characters, and have each group present its story to the class.

David slaying Goliath. Pietro da Cortona. Pinacoteca, Vatican Museums, Vatican State.

Teach

Literary Element 3

Voice Answer: *Hurston liked forceful, active people.*

APPROACHING Ask students to rephrase the two sentences "Never a quiet moment. I liked him a lot" with one sentence that starts with the words "I liked him a lot because…"

Literary History ☆

Old Testament Refer students to Hurston's phrase "he smote 'em hip and thigh." This comes from the Book of Judges in the Old Testament: "And he smote them hip and thigh with great slaughter." The expressions *to smite hip and thigh* means "to attack unmercifully."

To check students' understanding of the selection, see Unit 4 Teaching Resources Book, p. 245.

wanted to hear and said it in a way that tingled me. Just a little below these friends was Rudyard Kipling in his Jungle Books. I loved his talking snakes as much as I did the hero.

I came to start reading the Bible through my mother. She gave me a licking one afternoon for repeating something I had overheard a neighbor telling her. She locked me in her room after the whipping, and the Bible was the only thing in there for me to read. I happened to open to the place where David[18] was doing some mighty smiting,[19] and I got interested. David went here and he went there, and no matter where he went, he smote 'em hip and thigh. Then he sung songs to his harp awhile, and went out and smote some more. Not one time did David stop and preach about sins and things. All David wanted to know from God was who to kill and when. He took care of

it, preaching as they passed.[17] I was utterly **indifferent** to their deaths. In the first place I could not conceive of death, and in the next place they never had any funerals that amounted to a hill of beans, so I didn't care how soon they rolled up their big, soulful, blue eyes and kicked the bucket. They had no meat on their bones.

But I also met Hans Andersen and Robert Louis Stevenson. They seemed to know what I

18. *David* was the second king of Judah and Israel. He killed the giant Goliath.
19. *Smiting* means "striking hard, as with a hand or a weapon, so as to cause serious injury or death."

20. *Luke* and *Paul* were authors of much of the New Testament of the Christian Bible.
21. *Laid about* means "hit out in all directions."
22. *Roast* is slang for "burn in hell."

Voice *What do you infer about Hurston from the language in this passage?* 3

ZORA NEALE HURSTON **797**

Advanced Learners

DIFFERENTIATED INSTRUCTION

Bibliography Ask students to create a bibliography of Hurston's short stories, novels, and plays. Annotate this bibliography by writing a brief summary of each work. For example, *John Redding Goes to Sea is a folktale about a larger-than-life character, John Redding, whose family prevents him from going to sea. While saving a bridge during a flood, Redding ironically gets his wish when he loses his life.*

Then have students identify three books or articles that critique Hurston's work, and three books or articles about her life. Tell them to annotate these sources, identifying distinguishing features among the sources.

After You Read

Assess

1. Students should cite passages from the selection for support.

2. (a) She sits on top of the gatepost, hailing travelers. She talks and often rides with them. (b) She is confident and curious.

3. (a) The students are told to come to school clean and to behave well. When the visitors come unannounced, the teacher and the students are nervous. (b) They are unsure of the white visitors' motives, but they know the importance of making a good impression.

4. (a) It is the books that she enjoys most. (b) She finds the books moving and uplifting, especially the myths.

5. Most students will think that she does a good job of portraying the setting and may cite her use of dialect and her descriptions.

6. Students may say that she gives the fifth-grade version of herself an adult point of view. Her comments on the books are more in keeping with an adult opinion.

7. (a) She shows that she is a good reader, is brave, and has a lively personality. (b) Students should cite specific examples from the story. They will likely view Hurston as intelligent and confident.

8. Many African American artists created work that spoke specifically to their heritage and experience. Hurston's story speaks specifically to her experiences growing up in a southern African American community.

9. Students may say that she is more interested in the meaning of the story than the facts.

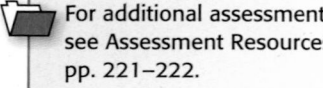
For additional assessment, see Assessment Resources, pp. 221–222.

798

After You Read

Respond and Think Critically

Respond and Interpret

1. How did you react to the narrator? Cite passages to support your response.

2. (a) What does the young Hurston do at the beginning of the selection? (b) What does this action tell you about her character?

3. (a) How do the teachers and students react to the white visitors? (b) Why do you think they behave this way?

4. (a) Which gifts from the white women does Hurston enjoy most? (b) What do those gifts provide for her that the other gifts do not?

Analyze and Evaluate

5. In your opinion, does Hurston do a good job of portraying the **setting** (the time and place) in which she grew up? Explain.

6. Think back to what you were like in the fifth grade. Do you think Hurston accurately recreates the thoughts of a fifth grader? Support your answer with examples.

7. (a) When Hurston reads aloud from the story of Persephone, what does she reveal about her personality and abilities? (b) Where else in the selection does she reveal these traits? Explain the overall impression of Hurston that you received.

Connect

8. **Big Idea** **The Harlem Renaissance** The Harlem Renaissance emphasized the value of African Americans' contributions to the country as a whole. How is this emphasis reflected in the selection? Explain.

9. **Connect to the Author** *Dust Tracks on a Road* presents an incomplete—at times even contradictory—account of Hurston's life. What connections, if any, do you make between this fact and Hurston's training as an anthropologist and a folklorist? Explain.

Literary Element Voice

ACT Skills Practice

1. Techniques that help give this excerpt from *Dust Tracks on a Road* its distinctive voice include:

   I. colloquial expressions.
   II. Biblical quotations.
   III. subtle humor.

   A. I only
   B. I and II only
   C. I and III only
   D. II and III only

2. The adjective phrase that best describes Hurston's voice in this selection is:

   F. dreamily unrealistic.
   G. gently sarcastic.
   H. precociously self-confident.
   J. boldly challenging.

798 UNIT 5 BEGINNINGS OF THE MODERN AGE

Review: Allusion

An **allusion** is a reference in a work of literature to a character, place, or situation from history or from music, art, or another work of literature.

Partner Activity Hurston makes an allusion to a figure in the Bible named David, a shepherd boy who grows up to become the king of Israel. In one of his many exploits, David kills the giant Goliath with a single stone fired from a sling. With a partner, reread the final paragraph of the selection. Make a web like the one below to show the character traits young Hurston may have felt she had in common with David.

Literary Element

1. **C** is the correct answer because Hurston's use of dialect and humor gives the work its distinctive voice of intelligent self-confidence.

2. **H** is the correct answer because Hurston's tone and use of language combine the innocence of a child with the wisdom of an adult.

Review: Allusion

Students might include traits such as fearlessness, a sense of purpose, and unflinching honesty.

Progress Check

Can students analyze voice?

If No → See Unit 4 Teaching Resources Book, p. 228.

Reading Strategy   Analyze Language

Hurston specialized in using colloquial, or everyday, language to bring to life the customs, geography, feelings, and way of speaking of the people she was writing about. In *Dust Tracks on a Road,* the inclusion of colorful regional expressions and local dialect lends the narration a powerful authenticity.

1. List examples of dialect or regional expressions that Hurston uses to evoke the people of Eatonville.

2. What ideas about or impressions of Eatonville do you glean from these examples? Explain.

Vocabulary Practice

Practice with Analogies Complete each analogy below using vocabulary words. Use a dictionary if you need help.

1. shyness : brazenness :: calmness :
   a. timidness **b.** serenity **c.** turbulence

2. snicker : laugh :: smirk :
   a. giggle **b.** grin **c.** frown

3. exalt : celebration :: weep :
   a. contest **b.** trial **c.** funeral

4. indifferent : fascinated :: ignorant :
   a. enlightened **b.** aggravated **c.** inundated

Academic Vocabulary

*As a child, Hurston had a **range** of literary interests, from Norse mythology to the Bible.*

Range is an academic word. To further explore the meaning of this word, complete this sentence:

*When I _____, I experience a **range** of emotions, from _____ to _____.*

For more on academic vocabulary, see pages 53–54.

 Literature Online

Selection Resources For Selection Quizzes, eFlash-cards, and Reading-Writing Connection activities, go to glencoe.com and enter QuickPass code GLA9800u5.

Write with Style

 Apply Allusion

Assignment In making an allusion to the Biblical figure David, Hurston reveals several things about herself as a young girl. Write a paragraph about yourself in which you incorporate an allusion to a character, place, or situation from history, music, art, or another piece of literature.

Get Ideas Think about a piece of literature, song, movie, historical event, or piece of art with which you identify. Why do you connect with it? What does it say about you? Look back at the word web you made about Hurston and David on page 798 and make a similar one for yourself and the subject of your allusion, noting what you and your subject have in common. Model it after the example below.

EXAMPLE:

Give It Structure Next, think about how you want to weave your allusion in to your writing. What is your purpose in using this allusion? Are you looking to make a direct comparison to yourself, as Hurston did, or does your allusion relate to a specific aspect of your life, such as your family? What do you want your audience to get from your piece? Is your allusion well known, or will you have to explain it? After considering these questions, write your paragraph.

Look at Language Review your paragraph and evaluate whether your use of allusion achieves your goal of revealing something about yourself or your life. Have you used precise language to convey your ideas, and a varied sentence structure to maintain a reader's interest? If not, revise your work, using a dictionary or thesaurus if necessary.

ZORA NEALE HURSTON **799**

Vocabulary Workshop

Focus

Remind students that words that are spelled the same but have different origins are homonyms. Have students look up the word *bear* to see the different meanings and etymology.

Teach

Write the homonyms *their, there* and *they're* on the board. Have students explain the difference among the words.

Suggest the following mnemonics:

Their contains *heir*. An heir gains possession of something.
There contains *here*, a place.
They're is correct only when it can be replaced by *they are*.

Have students use the words in sentences to clarify their different meanings and usages.

Assess

Practice

1. reel   **6.** tale
2. main   **7.** principal
3. bore   **8.** night
4. site   **9.** stares
5. scent   **10.** hoarse

Workshop Resources

Mnemonic Devices Write these pairs of sentences on the board:
The best <u>way</u> to go is through that door.
How much does the apple <u>weigh</u>?
The <u>principal</u> came to our class today.
He follows his <u>principles</u> and never lies.
What can you buy for just five <u>cents</u>?
The dog had lost its <u>sense</u> of hearing and did not hear the burglar.

Have pairs of students use context clues to find the meaning and pronunciation of each pair of words. Give an example of a mnemonic, e.g., "for" and "four" can be distinguished because "four" has 4 letters. Have teams generate mnemonics of their own for each word pair.

800

Learning Objectives

In this workshop, you will focus on the following objective:

Vocabulary: Understanding homonyms.

Homonyms

Homonyms are different words that sound alike and may be spelled alike. Homonyms are distinct from multiple-meaning words, which are single words with more than one meaning. In sentences 1–2 below, *bear* and *bear* are homonyms, because they are different words:

1. I can't **bear** it.
2. The **bear** growled.

In sentences 4–5, *bear* is one word with two different meanings:

4. I can't **bear** it.
5. I'm going to **bear** a child.

Tip

To determine the meaning of a homonym, use context clues.

Dictionary

To help you find word definitions, see p. 102..

 Literature Online

Vocabulary For more vocabulary practice, go to glencoe.com and enter QuickPass code GLA9800u5.

Vocabulary Workshop

Homonyms

Literature Connection Homonyms are different words that sound alike but have different meanings and sometimes different spellings. For example, *hail* can be either of two completely different words.

"Often the white travelers would hail me, but more often I hailed them, and asked, 'Don't you want me to go a piece of the way with you?'"

—Zora Neale Hurston, from *Dust Tracks on a Road*

Here *hail* means "to greet." *Hail* as a noun means "pellets of ice."

The English language is full of homonyms. Here is a sample list.

Word	Meaning	Example
bear bear	an animal to endure	The brown *bear* walked right into our campsite. The entire team must *bear* the burden of defeat.
bank bank	a mound or border a place to keep money	We stood on the river's *bank* and watched the current. My *bank* informed me my account was overdrawn.
break brake	to crack, split, or smash to stop a movement	Enslaved people endeavored to *break* their bonds. The negligent driver failed to *brake* for the pedestrian.
hear here	to listen in this place	In the village, we could *hear* the pealing church bells. I am resolved to remain *here* until I am evicted.
piece peace	a part of something tranquility	I completed the last *piece* of the puzzle. In the midst of war, people long for *peace*.
holy wholly holey	sacred completely full of holes	The pilgrims consider the shrine to be *holy*. I am not *wholly* convinced of your arguments. My *holey* socks are in need of repair.

Practice Choose the correct homonym to fit each sentence. Consult a dictionary if you need help.

1. The angler tried to (real, reel) in the fish.
2. The lion is the (main, mane) attraction at the zoo.
3. Most graduates considered the public speaker a (boar, bore).
4. This is a perfect (sight, site, cite) for the new museum.
5. The (scent, cent, sent) of spices wafted from the restaurant.
6. Upon his release, the prisoner told a (tail, tale) of woe.
7. Coffee is one of the (principle, principal) exports of Colombia.
8. One dark (knight, night), I lost my way.
9. The hostile (stares, stairs) of the judges unnerved the skater.

800 UNIT 5   BEGINNINGS OF THE MODERN AGE

If We Must Die and The Tropics in New York

Meet Claude McKay
(1890–1948)

Some critics think "If We Must Die" in 1919 was the spark that ignited the Harlem Renaissance. Though he was not an innovator in modern verse—his sonnets were strongly influenced by British literary traditions—McKay's focus on the African American experience distinguished him as a new, outspoken voice in American literature. The poets of the Harlem Renaissance hailed McKay as a leader because of his frank approach to racial and social issues.

McKay was born and educated in rural Jamaica. His brother Uriah Theophilus, a schoolteacher, and Englishman Walter Jekyll, a British scholar collecting Jamaican folklore, encouraged McKay's creativity. With access to their books, McKay read Victorian authors, as well as the medieval Italian writer Dante and the French poet Baudelaire.

Culture Shock After winning an award for his poetry in 1912, McKay used the money to come to the United States. McKay was drawn to this country, seeing it as "a new land to which all people who had youth and a youthful mind turned," and believing that "surely there would be opportunity in this land, even for a Negro." However, when McKay arrived, he was shocked by the blatant racism and violence he found, and he spent much of his life looking for ways to counter the "ignoble cruelty" of racism through his poetry and his actions.

McKay admired poets who wrote about their own struggles in society, and he strove to do the same in his own writing: "In their poetry I could feel their race, their class, their roots in the soil . . . I could not feel the reality of them without that. So likewise I could not realize myself writing without conviction." With its focus on the racial and social realities of the United States, *Home to Harlem* reached the best seller list—the first novel by an African American to do so.

> "All my life I have been a troubadour wanderer, nourishing myself mainly on the poetry of existence. And all I offer here is the distilled poetry of my experience."
>
> —Claude McKay

Lost and Then Found McKay truly represented the spirit of the "New Negro." Through his poem "If We Must Die," he captured a universal sentiment of resistance in the face of injustice. So universal was this theme that Winston Churchill quoted the poem to rally the British people during World War II.

By the time of his death, McKay had become virtually unknown. His work was later rediscovered and highly praised. In 1973 author Jean Wagner concluded that "McKay remains beyond a doubt the immediate forerunner and one of the leading forces of the Renaissance, the man without whom it could never have achieved what it did."

 Literature Online

Author Search For more about Claude McKay, go to glencoe.com and enter QuickPass code GLA9800u5.

CLAUDE MCKAY **801**

Bellringer Options

Selection Focus Transparency 50

Daily Language Practice Transparency 73

Or display images from various 1960s peace movements.

Ask: What modern injustices might your generation address? *(Students may mention genocide, poverty, and environmental destruction.)* Then, discuss with students which of these issues motivates them strongly enough that they could write poetry about them.

Selection Skills

Literary Elements
- Meter (SE pp. 802, 805)

If We Must Die / The Tropics in New York

Writing Skills/Grammar
- Write a Poem (SE p. 805)

Reading Skills
- Analyze Tone (SE pp. 802, 803, 805)
- Identify Author's Purpose (TE p. 802)

Vocabulary Skills
- Word Origins (SE p. 805)
- Synonyms (TE p. 802)

Listening/Speaking/ Viewing Skills
- Analyze Art (TE p. 804)
- Sound Devices (TE p. 804)

Before You Read

Focus

Summary

In "If We Must Die," McKay says that although African Americans are outnumbered, if they go down fighting, their deaths will not be in vain. In "The Tropics of New York," McKay describes exotic, luscious images from Jamaica. In the last four lines, he is so overcome that it brings him to tears.

 For summaries in languages other than English, see Unit 5 Teaching Resources Book, pp. 235–240.

Vocabulary

Synonyms Students may confuse the verb *constrained* with *restrained*. Both terms come from the Latin verb *stringere,* which means "to bind or draw tight." *Restrained* is a synonym for *constrained* when *constrained* means "limited" or "prevented": The belt restrained (or constrained) her lungs from expanding. However, *constrained* is more frequently used to mean "forced" and followed by the preposition *to.* Give students these examples:

Once they waved to him, Jack felt constrained to offer his friends a ride.

His father's direct question constrained Jack to confess that he had given his friends a ride.

 For additional vocabulary practice, see Unit 5 Teaching Resources Book, p. 243.

Literature and Reading Preview

Connect to the Poems

Have you or has someone you know ever faced prejudice? What is the best response in such a situation? Discuss these questions with a partner.

Building Background

"If We Must Die" reflects the racial strife in the United States just after World War I. During the summer of 1919, McKay worked as a waiter in a railroad dining car, and he and his coworkers feared being attacked. As McKay later wrote, "It was during those days that the sonnet, 'If We Must Die,' exploded out of me. And for it the Negro people unanimously hailed me as a poet."

Set Purposes for Reading

Big Idea The Harlem Renaissance

As you read, ask, How do these poems address social and cultural challenges faced by African Americans of the time?

Literary Element Meter

Meter is the regular pattern of stressed (´) and unstressed (ˇ) syllables that gives a line of poetry a predictable rhythm. The basic unit of meter is the foot, and the length of a metrical line can be expressed in terms of the number of feet it contains. As you read, ask, How does McKay use meter in these two poems?

Reading Strategy Analyze Tone

Tone is an author's attitude toward his or her subject matter. Authors convey tone through word choice, punctuation, sentence structure, and figures of speech. These two poems have very different tones. As you read, ask yourself, What is the tone of each poem? How does McKay convey that tone?

Tip: Compare and Contrast Use a chart to note the elements in each poem that contribute to the tone.

	"If We Must Die"	"The Tropics in New York"
Elements	simile—"like hogs hunted and penned"	
Tone		

Learning Objectives

For pages 801–805
In studying these texts, you will focus on the following objectives:

Literary Study: Analyzing meter.

Reading: Analyzing tone.

Writing: Writing a poem.

Vocabulary

nobly (noʹ blē) *adv.* with superior morals or character; p. 803 *The businessman nobly gave his fortune to the poor.*

constrain (kən strānʹ) *v.* to force or limit; p. 803 *In the 1800s strict laws constrained African Americans and women from voting.*

kinsmen (kinzʹ men) *n.* those who share the same racial or cultural background as another; p. 803 *Although not brothers by birth, the two friends were kinsmen by culture.*

benediction (benʹ ə dikʹ shən) *n.* a blessing or something that fosters goodness; p. 804 *The homeless shelter was a benediction for the men and women who needed it.*

Tip: Word Origins Word origins, also called **etymologies,** are the history and development of words. They are often found in dictionary entries.

Reading Practice

SPIRAL REVIEW **Identify Author's Purpose**
Explain that an author's purpose may be to entertain, to inform, to express an opinion, or to persuade. Readers can infer the author's purpose through careful reading. Ask students to examine "If We Must Die" for the author's purpose. Tell students to pay attention to how McKay stirs readers' thoughts and feelings. Then ask students to determine the author's purpose in "The Tropics in New York." Have students write a paragraph for each poem, explaining their conclusion and providing examples as supportive evidence.

802

Two Heads, 1946. Charles White. Watercolor, 16³/₄ x 24¹/₄ in. Collection of Martin & Sondra Sperber, New York. Courtesy Heritage Gallery, Los Angeles, CA.

If We Must Die

Claude McKay

If we must die, let it not be like hogs
Hunted and penned in an inglorious¹ spot,
While round us bark the mad and hungry dogs,
Making their mock at our accursed² lot.
5   If we must die, O let us **nobly** die,
So that our precious blood may not be shed
In vain; then even the monsters we defy
Shall be **constrained** to honor us though dead!
O **kinsmen**! we must meet the common foe!
10 Though far outnumbered let us show us brave,
And for their thousand blows deal one deathblow!
What though before us lies the open grave?
Like men we'll face the murderous, cowardly pack,
Pressed to the wall, dying, but fighting back!

1. *Inglorious* means "shameful" or "disgraceful."
2. *Accursed* (ə kur´ sid) means "being under a curse" or "doomed."

> **Analyze Tone** What tone does McKay establish here? What type of words does he use to achieve this? **2**

> **Vocabulary**
>
> **nobly** (no´ blē) *adv.* with superior morals or character
> **constrain** (kən strān´) *v.* to force or limit
> **kinsmen** (kinz´ men) *n.* those who share the same racial or cultural background as another

---

Teach

Literary Element   1

Analogies Ask: How does McKay describe his oppressors? *(as "mad and hungry dogs")* Discuss with students the effect this description has on the reader.

Reading Strategy   2

Analyze Tone Answer: *McKay evokes a bitter, but proud tone in these lines. He uses strong language, such as* murderous, cowardly, *and* fighting back *to emphasize the forcefulness of his tone.*
Ask: What other strong language does McKay use to emphasize his tone? *(McKay uses* nobly *and* honor *for proud;* inglorious, mock *and* accursed *for bitter;* defy *and* deathblow *for militant.)*

 For additional practice using the reading skill or strategy, see Unit 5 Teaching Resources Book, p. 242.

 For an audio recording of this selection, use Listening Library Audio CD-ROM.

English Learners
DIFFERENTIATED INSTRUCTION

Intermediate Have students read through each poem and write down unfamiliar words. Write these words on the board. Ask students to guess the meaning of each word, and then look it up in a dictionary. Have them compare the dictionary definition with their own and revise their definition as needed.

Approaching Level
DIFFERENTIATED INSTRUCTION

Emerging To reinforce the concept of tone, **ask:** What do you see or feel when you hear these phrases: a dark and stormy night *(fearful or curious)*; soothing, tropical breezes? *(content or relaxed)* Have students propose words or phrases that evoke emotions or images.

Teach

Big Idea | 1

The Harlem Renaissance

Answer: *This detail reveals McKay's longing for his former life in Jamaica and reflects the conflict that many African Americans felt between their home countries and life in the United States.*

View the Art ★

Hyacinth Manning is a contemporary painter based in St. Augustine, Florida. Like McKay, she is a native of Jamaica. Manning says, "With my figurative paintings in warm tropical colors and bold patterns, I hope to inspire emotions of comfort and love. I grew up in a bright and sunny Caribbean atmosphere." Discuss with students how Manning's use of darks and lights draws attention to the fruit at the center of the painting.

 To check students' understanding of the selection, see Unit 5 Teaching Resources Book, p. 245.

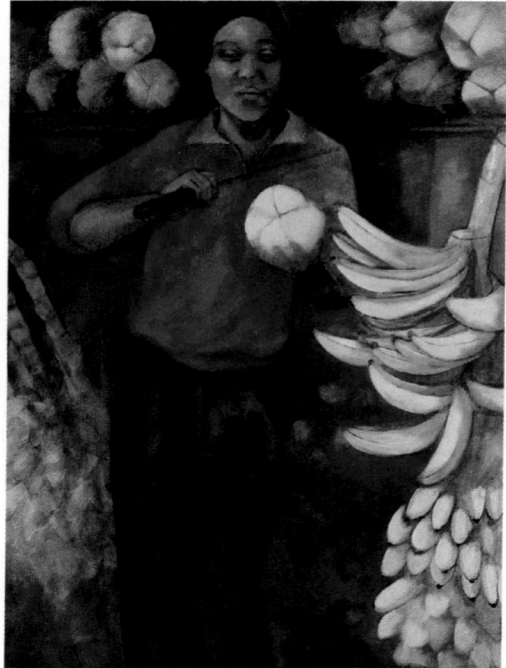

Fruit Stand Vendor, 1994. Hyacinth Manning. Acrylic on canvas. 28 x 22 in. Private collection. ★

The Tropics in New York

Claude McKay

Bananas ripe and green, and ginger-root,
   Cocoa in pods and alligator pears,
And tangerines and mangoes and grape fruit,
   Fit for the highest prize at parish fairs,

5 Set in the window, bringing memories
   Of fruit-trees laden by low-singing rills,
And dewy dawns, and mystical blue skies
   In **benediction** over nun-like hills.

My eyes grew dim, and I could no more gaze;
10   A wave of longing through my body

The Harlem Renaissance *How does this detail reflect the African American experience during the Harlem Renaissance?* **1**

Vocabulary

benediction (ben´ ə dik´ shən) *n.* a blessing or something that fosters goodness

Listening and Speaking Practice

 SMALL GROUP | SPIRAL REVIEW | **Sound Devices**

Say: Writers use sound devices to enhance the sense of rhythm, to emphasize particular sounds, or to add a musical quality to their writing. Review with students different sound devices from the Literary Terms Handbook, including alliteration, assonance, consonance, onomatopoeia, rhyme, and rhythm.

Divide the class into small groups. Have two students from each group read the two poems aloud to the group. Before the poems are read, tell students to keep these questions in mind as they listen:

- What sound devices are used in "If We Must Die"? What are some examples? *(Possible answers: alliteration:* mad, making, *and* mock; *rhyme:* in vain *and* constrained.)

- What sound devices are used in "The Tropics of New York"? What are some examples? *(Possible answers: alliteration:* dewy dawns; *assonance:* highest prize *or* parish fairs.)

Have students discuss their answers.

After You Read

Respond and Think Critically

Respond and Interpret

1. (a)Which images from the poems stand out in your mind? (b)What effects do these images have on you?

2. (a)In "If We Must Die," what two animals does the speaker name? Which animals are the hunters, and which are the hunted? (b)With which animals does the speaker identify? Explain.

3. (a)In "The Tropics in New York," what does the speaker see in the window? (b)What memories does that sight bring?

4. (a)How does the speaker react when he recalls his homeland? (b)Why might he have this reaction?

Analyze and Evaluate

5. Some critics believe "If We Must Die" marked the beginning of the Harlem Renaissance. Why might this poem have had a powerful impact?

6. In "The Tropics in New York," how do sensory details convey the author's meaning? Explain.

Connect

7. **Big Idea** **The Harlem Renaissance** What message about identity is implied in "The Tropics in New York"?

8. **Connect to Today** Does our culture deal today with social injustices comparable to those existing during the Harlem Renaissance?

Literary Element Meter

The metrical foot that McKay uses in both poems is the iamb: one unstressed syllable followed by one stressed syllable. Most lines have five iambic feet, or beats, to form **iambic pentameter.** How does the meter's effect differ in these poems?

Reading Strategy Analyze Tone

McKay uses very different **tones** in these poems.

1. Look at the chart you made on page 802. What words or images helped you understand the tone of each poem?

2. How would you describe the tone in each poem?

Vocabulary Practice

Word Origins For each vocabulary word, give the definition, summarize the etymology, and use the word correctly in a sentence. Use a dictionary for help.

nobly   constrained   kinsmen   benediction

> Definition: marked by hearty humor and joy
>
> Etymology: Latin jovialis means "of Jupiter"
>
> jovial
>
> Sample sentence: People love Randall because he is so jovial and ready to laugh.

Writing

Write a Poem A window display reminds the narrator in "The Tropics in New York" of a place he misses. Have you ever had a similar experience? Write a poem about how an everyday event or sight can awaken intense longing.

LOG ON **Literature** Online

Selection Resources For Selection Quizzes, eFlashcards, and Reading-Writing Connection activities, go to glencoe.com and enter QuickPass code GLA9800u5.

CLAUDE MCKAY **805**

Literary Element

In "If We Must Die," the meter creates a powerful dramatic feeling. In "The Tropics in New York," the meter has a more lilting, songlike quality.

📝 Writing

Students' poems should focus on an everyday event and use rhyme, alliteration, or meter.

Progress Check

Can students analyze meter?

If No → See Unit 5 Teaching Resources Book, p. 241.

After You Read

Assess

1. Students' answers will vary.

2. (a) Dogs are the hunters, and hogs are the hunted. (b) The speaker identifies with the hogs.

3. (a) Beautiful tropical fruit (b) The speaker's Caribbean homeland

4. (a) He cries. (b) Because of the ugliness of where he lives now

5. It encouraged African Americans to stand up for themselves.

6. The details present an image of a lost paradise.

7. There is a choice between retaining black identity and assimilation into white culture.

8. Students may say that poverty, racism, or sexism are injustices still faced today. Some people stage marches and picket events.

Reading Strategy

"If We Must Die": bitter, militant; "The Tropics in New York": nostalgic.

Vocabulary

nobly Definition: with superior morals or character; Etymology: Latin nobilis means "renowned, of superior birth"

constrained Definition: forced or limited; Etymology: Latin constringere means "to tie tightly together"

kinsmen Definition: those who share the same cultural background; Etymology: Old English cyn means "family"

benediction Definition: a blessing or something that fosters goodness; Etymology: Latin beneficium means "a kindness"

Focus

Summary

Robert Hughes describes the importance of Jacob Lawrence's *Migration* series. "Migration" refers to the exodus of many African Americans from the South to the North during the early decades of the twentieth century.

Teach

Reading Strategy   1

Preview

1. Explain that *epic* here refers to a work of art that depicts the legendary deeds of historical heroes.
2. The paintings deal with African Americans who faced hardship.

Historical Note ☆

Reconstruction Reconstruction was the effort to rebuild the South after the Civil War. After federal troops left the South in 1877, the South was allowed to continue segregation. Although the Thirteenth Amendment abolished slavery, most African Americans were treated as second-class citizens until the civil rights movement of the 1950s and 1960s.

 For activities related to this selection, see Unit 5 Teaching Resources Book, pp. 247–255.

Learning Objectives

For pages 806–809

In studying this text, you will focus on the following objectives:

Reading:
Using text features.
Analyzing informational text.
Scanning text.

Set a Purpose for Reading

As you read, ask yourself, How did Jacob Lawrence, a Harlem artist, view the African American experience?

Preview the Article

1. Examine the title. What might the author mean by a "black epic"?
2. Look at the paintings on pages 807–809. What can you predict about the content of the article from these images?

Reading Strategy

Scan Text to Find Specific Information

Scanning is the process of searching quickly through text for key words and specific information. Scan the article for the key words *Harlem* and *painting*. What do you learn about these topics? Use a graphic organizer to record information.

Word	Information
Harlem	Lawrence—younger than and different from Harlem Renaissance artists

Writing Practice

SPIRAL REVIEW **Make a List** Point out that Hughes refers to the Great Migration as "A Black Epic" in the title of this article. A story that resembles an epic, such as the *Iliad* or the *Odyssey*, is one that has heroic characters who endure many trials before they reach their goal. Have students write a list of the trials that African Americans went through that make the story of the Great Migration an epic.

STANZAS FROM A BLACK EPIC.₁

The 60 paintings in Jacob Lawrence's great *Migration* series present piercing images of the African American experience.

By ROBERT HUGHES

THE SIXTY PAINTINGS THAT MAKE UP JACOB LAWRENCE'S *Migration* series are works that anyone interested in African American cultural history—or, in a wider way, the story of American painting as a whole—should see.

More than 60 years have passed since Lawrence made these little pictures, on store-bought panels in his Harlem studio; and they are of far greater power than almost all the acreage of Works Progress Administration (WPA) murals that preceded them in the 1930s. They were almost immediately bought, half by the Phillips Collection in Washington, D.C., and half by the Museum of Modern Art (MOMA) in New York City, and were in fact the first paintings by a black artist to enter MOMA's collection. It seemed to the directors of both museums that Lawrence's series represented a unique combination of African American experience, history painting, and a modernist style. They were right. From Benjamin West to Robert Rauschenberg, American art is sown with attempts, varying between saccharine sentimentality and stunning success, to image forth the American story. And for reasons that are sadly obvious, few of these were created by African Americans, until Lawrence appeared.

Younger than the painters and writers who took part in the Harlem Renaissance of the 1920s, Lawrence was also at an angle to them: He was not interested in the kind of idealized portrayals of African Americans that others tended to produce. These fake-primitive images were being created as an antidote to the vile stereotypes with which white popular art had flooded the culture since Reconstruction. Nevertheless, Lawrence gained self-confidence from the cultural climate of Harlem—in particular, from Alain Locke, a Harvard-trained art critic. Locke believed strongly that art created by African Americans could speak explicitly to their community and still embody the values of modernism. Or, in Locke's words: "There is in truly great art no essential conflict between racial or national traits and universal human values."

2 The Great Migration

What are the paintings about? A huge subject, which no artist could touch and only an African American one could have handled with the depth of feeling it required. The migration of African Americans from the rural South to the industrial North, as it unfolded in the first decades of the 20th century, had an epic character. It was a collective Odyssey to match the Iliad of the Civil War. This migration was forced by the merciless Southern white reaction that came in the wake of Reconstruction. The African American population—all poor, nearly all rural—of the Southern states was plunged into a hell where their rights were abolished.

The Female Workers Were the Last to Arrive North Panel #57 from the *Migration* series. Jacob Lawrence. The Phillips Collection, Washington, DC.

In the South, 1900 to 1925 brought the high tide of Jim Crow laws, lynchings, and the terrorism of the Ku Klux Klan. Unable to vote, powerless to change their political status, Southern blacks voted with their feet. By the end of the 1930s more than a million of them (the exact figures will probably never be known) had flocked to mid-Atlantic, Northeastern, and Midwestern cities, looking for a

STANZAS FROM A BLACK EPIC **807**

TIME

Teach

Text Element 2

Subheads Explain that effective subheads point readers to the main idea of a section, are in the active voice if they include verbs, and often have parallel structure. Have students identify the subheads in the article, and then determine whether or not they have these characteristics. **Ask:** How do these subheads help the reader understand the text? (They give a quick overview.)

Literary History

Iliad* and *Odyssey Students may not be familiar with Homer's epic Greek poems the *Iliad* and the *Odyssey*. The *Iliad*, the first of the two poems, tells the story of the Trojan War. The *Odyssey* is the story of Odysseus' journey home after the war.

 For an audio recording of this selection, use Listening Library Audio CD-ROM.

Readability Scores
Dale-Chall: 9.8
DRP: 68
Lexile: 1240

TIME

Teach

Big Idea   1

The Harlem Renaissance

Point out to students that Hughes provides background about Lawrence's early years. **Ask:** How did the Harlem Renaissance affect Lawrence and his painting? *(Lawrence went to school in Harlem and grew up with people who had migrated.)*

Vocabulary   2

Context Clues Remind students that context clues can help them find the meaning of new or difficult vocabulary.

Ask: What kind of crowd is a *jeering* crowd? How can you tell from the context? *(Since the crowd is attending a hanging, they would be rowdy or unfriendly.)*

Ask: What kind of research is *painstaking*? How can you tell from the context? *(Since Lawrence spent months at it and got his facts right, it is thorough and accurate research.)*

Cultural History ☆

Cubism Pablo Picasso and Georges Braque founded Cubism in Paris in the early twentieth century. The Cubists broke down the subject matter into parts and then reassembled it in abstract forms. Cubism shows the subject from multiple angles and distances at the same time, usually resulting in many geometric shapes.

better America than the one they had known. Some of them no doubt imagined they were going to a promised land; and in this they were sharply disappointed, especially after 1929, when they arrived in a North economically devastated by the Depression. But there was no way back. The South was drained of its black workforce, while the North acquired a new one. From these migrants grew a radically altered conception of African American culture: distinctively urban but still Southern in its origins and collective memory. This was the culture that produced the Harlem Renaissance. In it, African Americans reinvented themselves.

A Harlem Education

1 Born in Atlantic City, New Jersey, in 1917, Lawrence was schooled in Harlem and grew up among migrants and their children. When, years later, he told an interviewer that "I am the black community," he was neither bragging nor kidding. He trained as a painter at the Harlem Art Workshop, inside the public library's 135th Street branch. Indeed the library itself, with its Schomburg Collection, Manhattan's chief archive on African American life and history, was to shape his series. Lawrence did months of painstaking research there to get the historical background right, even though the final paintings rarely allude to specific events. He took on the task with a youthful earnestness (he was in his early 20s) that remains one of the most touching aspects of the final work and goes far beyond self-expressiveness. You sense that

something is speaking through Lawrence.

One of the remarkable things about the *Migration* series is the language it does not use. Lawrence was not a propagandist. He avoided the caricatures used in Popular Front, Social Realist art, then at its peak in America. Considering the violence and suffering of so much of his subject matter—prisons, deserted communities, city slums, race riots, labor camps—his images are restrained, and all the more piercing. When he painted a lynching, for instance (No. 15), he left out the dangling body and the jeering crowd: there is only bare **2** earth, a branch, an empty noose, and the huddled lump of a grieving woman. He set aside the muralist influence that lay so heavily on other artists—he wasn't painting murals but images closer in size to single pages, no more than 18 inches by 12 inches.

Painting an Epic

Nevertheless, Lawrence imagined the paintings as integrally connected—a single work of art, no less united than a mural is, but portable. The *Migration* series has the effect of a visual ballad, with each painting a stanza: taut, compressed, pared down to the barest requirements of narration. Number 10, *They Were Very Poor*, takes the elements of a Southern sharecropper's life down to the static minimum. It shows a man and a woman staring at empty bowls on a bare brown plane and an empty basket hung on the wall by an enormous nail—the sort of nail you imagine in a crucifixion. There is no trace of sentimentality. Lawrence called his style "dynamic Cubism," and its debt to late Cubism is obvious—the flat, sharp overlaps of form, legible silhouettes, and generally high degree of abstraction in the color. Yet, his

They Were Very Poor Panel 10 from the *Migration* series. Jacob Lawrence. The Museum of Modern Art, NY.

Viewing Practice

Painters' Styles Hughes references Lawrence's style throughout his article. Students should be familiar with different styles in writing but may not have as much exposure to style in art. **Ask:** What are some different artistic styles? *(Impressionism, Cubism, Surrealism)*

Ask: How does Lawrence's style present the events of the Great Migration? *(Lawrence uses silhouettes, abstract colors and minimalist, sharp images*

that narrate the lives of those involved in the Great Migration.) Have students browse through the art in Unit 5 and select a painting with a style different from Lawrence's. Lead students in a discussion about the styles of painting they find.

And the Migration Spread Panel 23 from the *Migration* series. Jacob Lawrence. The Phillips Collection, Washington, DC.

style also tends to an Egyptian stillness, friezelike even when you know the subject was in motion, like the crowd surging into the narrow slot between two railroad cars in Number 23, *And the Migration Spread.*

Lawrence's style gives his pictures a solid gravity. His dense and well-locked compositions are prime illustrations of the permanence and resistance that are his key themes. These themes are integral to the African Americans depicted throughout

Lawrence's Migration series—the first, and arguably still the best, treatment of the African American historical experience by an African American artist.

—**Updated 2006, from TIME, December 6, 1993**

Respond and Think Critically

Respond and Interpret

1. Write a brief summary of the main ideas in this article before you answer the following questions. For help on writing a summary, see page 79.

2. How do you react to the paintings of Jacob Lawrence?

3. (a)What was the Great Migration? (b)How do Lawrence's paintings show this event?

4. (a)Name four or more subjects of the paintings in the *Migration* series. (b)How did Lawrence treat these subjects differently than others before him did?

5. (a)What is the artistic style of the paintings in the *Migration* series? (b)What is the effect of the style on the subject matter?

Analyze and Evaluate

6. (a)According to Hughes, why is the *Migration* series so important? (b)How well does Hughes back up his claim?

7. (a)What does Hughes mean by "stanzas from a black epic"? (b)How well does his title fit his essay? Explain.

8. The art critic Alain Locke said, "There is in truly great art no essential conflict between racial or national traits and universal human values." How is this idea evident in Lawrence's work?

Connect

9. How does this selection relate to the Harlem Renaissance? How does it go beyond it to tell more about African American history and culture?

STANZAS FROM A BLACK EPIC **809**

Advanced Learners

DIFFERENTIATED INSTRUCTION

Research Have students research Jacob Lawrence's paintings in books or on the Internet. Have students identify paintings that illustrate the ideas presented in the article. Then have students write a paragraph about each painting, explaining how it illustrates material in the article.

Assess

1. Students should use subheads to organize their summary of the main ideas in the article.

2. Students may react strongly to Lawrence's work.

3. (a) The Great Migration was a historic period in which African Americans moved from the South to the North. (b) His paintings show African Americans during the Great Migration.

4. (a) Female workers, a lynching, a sharecropper's life, and a crowd squeezed between two train cars (b) He combined African American experience and a Modernist style.

5. (a) The style is dynamic Cubism. (b) An Egyptian stillness

6. (a) It was the first and best depiction of the African American historical experience. (b) Hughes supports his claim well.

7. (a) Hughes is referring to specific events in African American history. (b) The title fits the essay well because each painting is like a stanza from African American history.

8. Lawrence appeals to the human race instead of any single race. He conveys ideas all people can relate to.

9. Lawrence's paintings depict southern African Americans whose culture made up the Harlem Renaissance.

 For additional assessment, see Assessment Resources, pp. 225–226.

Before You Read
Langston Hughes's Poetry and Prose

Meet **Langston Hughes**
(1902–1967)

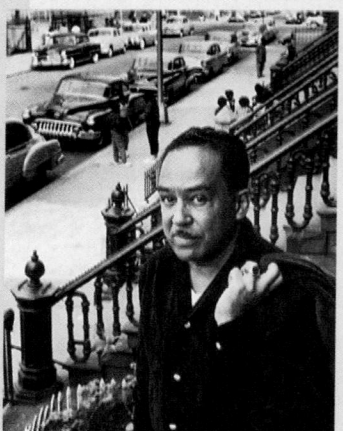

In 1921 Langston Hughes moved to New York City and enrolled at Columbia University to learn more about poetry—in the nightclubs and streets of Harlem. "To see *Shuffle Along* was the main reason I wanted to go to Columbia," Hughes said. "When I saw it, I was thrilled and delighted." Many African Americans were moving north for good-paying jobs and vibrant city life, yet Hughes knew their life was bittersweet. The remnants of slavery and the struggle with segregation held back African Americans from the American dream that was readily available to many whites during the Roaring Twenties.

Hughes's writing celebrated the dignity of ordinary, working-class African Americans, helping many realize that black was beautiful. "They seemed to me like the gayest and the bravest people possible—these Negroes from the Southern ghettos—facing tremendous odds, working and laughing and trying to get somewhere in the world," Hughes said. This sentiment fit the Modernist notion that everyday images, speech, and events belong in the highest forms of literature.

Many Homes Born in Joplin, Missouri, Hughes had lived in six different cities by the age of twelve. It was a childhood of books, music, and poverty.

His father moved to Mexico, and his mother moved frequently in search of employment. When his mother sought work, Hughes stayed in Lawrence, Kansas, with his grandmother.

After high school, he visited his father, who was by then a prosperous lawyer. Crossing the Mississippi on the train gave Hughes the inspiration for "The Negro Speaks of Rivers." "I put it down on the back of an envelope I had in my pocket, and within the space of ten or fifteen minutes, as the train gathered speed in the dusk, I had written this poem." His father offered to pay his college tuition if Hughes left the U.S., but Hughes wanted to try life in New York City. The city captivated him, but he was unhappy at school. He dropped out—later finishing his degree elsewhere—and did odd jobs while traveling to Africa and France.

Harlem's Bard Returning to the U.S., Hughes worked in a hotel in Washington, D.C. In 1925 he left three poems by the plate of well-known poet Vachel Lindsay. Newspapers reported the next day that Lindsay had discovered an astonishing poet, who happened to be an African American busboy. Hughes soon moved back to Harlem, able to support himself through his writing. Considered the poet laureate of Harlem, he also wrote novels, nonfiction, plays, and children's books. Even death could not dampen his sense of humor. He arranged for a jazz trio to play Duke Ellington's tune "Do Nothing Till You Hear from Me" at his funeral in New York City.

Hughes's legacy lives on in contemporary culture. Critic Kevin Powell writes, "The very people that he documented so well . . . were the people who created hip-hop. . . . We're still asking the same questions that Langston Hughes was asking."

 Literature Online

Author Search For more about Langston Hughes, go to glencoe.com and enter QuickPass code GLA3816u5.

Selection Skills

Literary Elements
- Repetition (SE pp. 811, 813, 814)

I, Too *and* **The Negro Speaks of Rivers**

Writing Skills/Grammar
- Essay (SE p. 814)
- Poetry (TE p. 812)

Reading Skills
- Make Predictions About Theme (SE pp. 811, 813, 814)

Vocabulary Skills
- Analogies (SE pp. 811, 814)
- Build Sentences (TE p. 811)

Literature and Reading Preview

Connect to the Poems

With what group of people do you feel most closely associated? What do you have in common with the other people in that group? Explore these questions in a brief journal entry.

Build Background

When Hughes began writing in the 1920s, little progress had been made in securing basic rights for African Americans. In the South, laws legalized segregation. In the North, African American workers were generally hired only for low-wage jobs. Hughes's father had left for Mexico because he was fed up with discrimination in the United States. Hughes's college-educated mother moved from city to city looking for work but found only menial jobs. In Harlem, many artists, writers, and intellectuals hoped their artistic movement would help bring about an end to such discrimination.

Set Purposes for Reading

Big Idea The Harlem Renaissance

As you read these poems, ask yourself, How does Hughes perceive African Americans and their rightful place in American culture?

Literary Element Repetition

Repetition is the recurrence of sounds, words, phrases, lines, and other elements in a literary work. Repetition increases the sense of unity in a work and can call attention to particular ideas, themes, or arguments. As you read these poems, ask yourself, What effect does Hughes's use of repetition and refrain have on his poems?

Reading Strategy Make Predictions About Theme

Making predictions about the theme, or message, of a literary work can help give you a purpose for reading. Verifying predictions can help you understand a work. Read the titles of the poems. What do you predict these poems will be about?

....

Tip: Use Titles to Make Predictions A title like "I, Too" implies a connection. Now complete the sentence to make predictions about the theme of the poem.

I, too, (am) _____ .

I, too, (can) _____ .

Learning Objectives

For pages 810–814

In studying these texts, you will focus on the following objectives:

Literary Study: Analyzing repetition.

Reading: Making predictions about theme.

Writing: Writing an essay.

Vocabulary

lull (lul) *v.* to soothe or cause to sleep; p. 813 *The mother rocked her baby to lull him to sleep.*

bosom (booz′ əm) *n.* the chest or heart; p. 813 *The frantic woman pressed her child to her bosom once she found him again.*

dusky (dus′ kē) *adj.* murky or dark in color; p. 813 *The sailors could not see the bottom of the muddy, dusky water.*

....

Tip: Analogies Comparisons based on relationships between words are known as **analogies**. For example, in the analogy *lull : agitate :: dark : light,* each pair of words is opposite in meaning. To complete an analogy, decide on the relationship represented by the first pair of words. Then apply that relationship to the second set of words.

Before You Read

Focus

Summary

In "I, Too," Hughes first paints a portrait of the African American as a second-class citizen, then presents his vision of future African Americans: allowed to sit at the table with whites and recognized as beautiful. In "The Negro Speaks of Rivers," Hughes uses rivers to portray African American history. The rivers he's "known" throughout time imbue him with a deep sense of history.

 For summaries in languages other than English, see Unit 5 Teaching Resources Book, pp. 256–261.

Vocabulary

Build Sentences Write the following words on the board: *conversation, apartment, time, family.* Have students write sentences that include one of these words and one of the vocabulary words. Have them use every vocabulary word on this page in their sentences.

ADVANCED Have students use the words on the board and the vocabulary words on this page to build sentences that form a story or a poem.

Approaching Level

DIFFERENTIATED INSTRUCTION

Emerging To understand the effects of rhythm and repetition in Hughes's poems, have student read the poems aloud in different ways, pausing in different places each time they read. Tell them to pay attention to the rhythm and repetition as they read. As students experiment, have them discuss these questions:

- Are there places in the poem where pauses seem to come more naturally?

- What is the natural rhythm of the poem? Does the poem imitate the rhythms of normal speech?

- How does repetition of certain words and phrases affect the rhythm? Does it help to emphasize the poet's theme?

Teach

Big Idea   1

The Harlem Renaissance

Answer: *These lines imply that conditions for African Americans are going to improve and that they will have opportunities equal to those of their white counterparts.*

(APPROACHING) Discuss with students the difference between sitting in the kitchen and sitting at the dining table when there is company at home.

Writer's Technique ☆

Allusion The Civil War–era poet Walt Whitman inspired Hughes to write "I, Too." Hughes's poem is a response to Whitman's "I Hear America Singing" (page 410), a celebratory portrayal of the unity of Americans.

Literary Element   2

Tone Have students suggest adjectives that describe the tone. *(optimistic, happy)* **Ask:** How does Hughes achieve a hopeful tone in the poem? *(The speaker hopes that "tomorrow," he will sit at the table, not in the kitchen.)*

(ENGLISH LEARNERS) Point out to that when Hughes uses the word "tomorrow," he does not literally mean the next day, but sometime in the future.

Against All Odds, 2003. Colin Bootman. Oil on board. Private collection.

I, Too

Langston Hughes

I, too, sing America. ☆

I am the darker brother.
They send me to eat in the kitchen
When company comes,
5   But I laugh,
And eat well,
And grow strong.

Tomorrow,
I'll be at the table   **2**
10 When company comes.
Nobody'll dare
Say to me,
"Eat in the kitchen,"
Then.

15 Besides,
They'll see how beautiful I am
And be ashamed—

I, too, am America.

---

1 The Harlem Renaissance *What do lines 8–10 imply about the future of African Americans?*

Writing Practice

Write Poetry Challenge students to write their own poems about America. Have students include repetition in their poems. Once they have completed first drafts, group students into pairs and have them read their poems to each other. Tell them to give feedback on the rhythm and flow of their partner's poem. Have students incorporate their partners' comments into their final drafts.

The Negro Speaks of Rivers

Langston Hughes

Rondout, New York, c. 1907. Leon Dabo. Oil on canvas.
Indianapolis Museum of Art, IN.

I've known rivers:
I've known rivers ancient as the world and older than the
    flow of human blood in human veins.

My soul has grown deep like the rivers. **3**

   I bathed in the Euphrates[1] when dawns were young.
5 I built my hut near the Congo[2] and it **lulled** me to sleep.
   I looked upon the Nile[3] and raised the pyramids above it.
   I heard the singing of the Mississippi when Abe Lincoln
      went down to New Orleans,[4] and I've seen its muddy
      bosom turn all golden in the sunset.

I've known rivers:
Ancient, **dusky** rivers.

10 My soul has grown deep like the rivers.

Make Predictions About Theme *What do you expect this poem to be about, after reading the title and the first line?* **4**

Repetition *What idea does the repetition in line 10 emphasize?* **5**

Vocabulary

lull (lul) *v.* to soothe or cause to sleep
bosom (booz′ əm) *n.* the chest or heart
dusky (dus′ kē) *adj.* murky or dark in color

1. The *Euphrates* (yoo frā′ tēz) River flows from Turkey through Syria and Iraq. Many ancient civilizations flourished in the area between the Euphrates and Tigris rivers.
2. The *Congo,* also called the Zaire, is a river in central Africa.
3. The *Nile,* which runs through northeast Africa, is the longest river in the world.
4. According to legend, Abraham Lincoln decided that slavery should be abolished after witnessing his first slave auction in *New Orleans,* Louisiana, along the Mississippi River.

LANGSTON HUGHES **813**

Teach

Literary Element   3

Analogy Remind students what an analogy is. **Ask:** What analogy does Hughes use in this poem? *(He compares his soul to rivers.)* Discuss with students why Hughes uses this analogy. *(He wants to express the depth of his soul and rivers are usually associated with depth.)*

(ENGLISH LEARNERS) Discuss how the word *deep* has a literal relation to a river, but it has a figurative relation to one's soul. Explain that the depth of a river is tangible, or having physical existence, while the depth of a soul is spiritual.

Reading Strategy   4

Make Predictions Answer: *The poem will probably be about rivers that African Americans have lived near and have gotten to know well.*

 For additional practice using the reading skill or strategy, see Unit 5 Teaching Resources Book, p. 263.

Literary Element   5

Repetition Answer: *The repetition of the line serves to emphasize the depth of history embodied in the rivers and reflected in the speaker's soul.*

Advanced Learners

DIFFERENTIATED INSTRUCTION

Compare and Contrast Provide students with a copy of Langston Hughes's poem, "Let America Be America Again." Have them compare and contrast this poem with the two in the textbook. Have them focus on literary elements such as repetition, tone, and the author's choice of words. Ask them to compare the themes of the poems and explain which poem they liked the best. Then have students choose one aspect of the poems (either a literary element or the theme) and write a paragraph comparing and contrasting the poems. Tell them to provide examples from the poems to support their analysis.

813

After You Read

Assess

1. Answers will vary.

2. (a) The speaker is an African American; "they" are white. (b) Separate

3. (a) As "ancient as the world" (b) To establish the long history of his race

4. (a) They suggest that Africans and African Americans have always been part of history. (b) They may symbolize the proud history of African Americans.

5. (a) Expectancy; anger; patience (b) Answers will vary.

6. (a) In the past, African Americans were forced into the background. (b) He embodies the experiences of his race.

7. The poems assert that African Americans have always been a part of American culture.

8. Students may say that Hughes felt the effects of racism during his childhood.

 For additional assessment, see Assessment Resources, pp. 227–228.

Literary Element

1. The words "I, too" and "America" are repeated. In the poem's first line, the speaker speaks as one man; in the last line, he speaks for his race.

2. It suggests that the speaker carries the accumulated experience and wisdom of his race.

Progress Check

Can students analyze repetition?

If No → See Unit 5 Teaching Resources Book, p. 262.

After You Read

Respond and Think Critically

Respond and Interpret

1. Which lines from the poems would you most like to have Langston Hughes explain? Put your response in the form of a question.

2. (a)What is the identity of the speaker and of the other people in "I, Too"? (b)Does the speaker feel at one with these people or separate from them?

3. (a)How does the speaker in "The Negro Speaks of Rivers" describe the rivers he has known? (b)For what reason might he emphasize their age?

4. (a)What do the activities associated with these rivers communicate about the history of African Americans? (b)In your opinion, what do the rivers **symbolize**, or stand for?

Analyze and Evaluate

5. (a)How would you describe the **mood** of "I, Too"? (b)What elements of the poem contribute to this mood?

6. (a)What historical realities does the poem "I, Too" reflect? (b)In what ways has the speaker in "The Negro Speaks of Rivers" been affected by the history of his people?

Connect

7. **Big Idea** **The Harlem Renaissance** How do these poems affirm the place of African Americans in the cultural history of this country?

8. **Connect to the Author** In what ways do you think Hughes's early experiences and family life influenced poems such as "I, Too" and "The Negro Speaks of Rivers"?

Literary Element Repetition

Repetition is the recurrence of sounds, words, phrases, lines, or other elements.

1. What words are repeated in two lines of "I, Too"? How does the difference between these lines develop the theme of the poem?

2. What does the **refrain** in "The Negro Speaks of Rivers" contribute to the theme of the poem?

Reading Strategy Make Predictions About Theme

Recall your **predictions** about the poems from page 811. How accurate were they?

Vocabulary Practice

Practice with Analogies Complete each analogy below. In each expression, : means "is to" and :: means "as."

1. lull : sleepy :: agitate :
   a. hungry   c. excited
   b. confused   d. ambivalent

2. bosom : torso :: knee :
   a. kneecap   c. joint
   b. leg   d. foot

3. dusky : bright :: glossy :
   a. matte   c. attractive
   b. shiny   d. opaque

LOG ON ▶ **Literature** Online

Selection Resources For Selection Quizzes, eFlashcards, and Reading-Writing Connection activities, go to glencoe.com and enter QuickPass code GLA3816u5.

Writing

Write an Essay Think about a person, place, or event that helped shape who you are. Write a brief essay describing how it affected your identity.

Reading Strategy

Students' answers will vary.

Vocabulary

1. c 2. b 3. a

Writing

Students' essays should identify a specific person, place, or event and relate it to the formation of identity.

When the Negro Was in Vogue

Connect to the Autobiography

Why do certain people and places become fashionable for a time and then just as suddenly fall out of favor? Freewrite three paragraphs in response to this question.

Build Background

Hughes's mentor Carl Van Vechten and publisher Alfred A. Knopf urged Hughes to write an autobiography. He replied, "I am still too much enmeshed in the effects of my young life to write about it." It was not until he was thirty-eight that he wrote *The Big Sea.*

Set Purposes for Reading

Big Idea **The Harlem Renaissance**

As you read, ask, Why was Harlem the center of the renaissance of African American arts in the 1920s and 1930s?

Literary Element **Juxtaposition**

The placing of two or more distinct things side by side is called **juxtaposition.** This is commonly done to contrast or compare the things and may evoke an emotional response in the reader. As you read, ask yourself, Why does Hughes juxtapose the Harlem natives with the "Nordics," or white tourists?

Reading Strategy **Analyze Concrete Details**

Good writers use **concrete,** or specific, **details** to help readers visualize scenes that they describe. As you read, ask, Why does Hughes want readers to visualize certain scenes or images?

Tip: Chart Details Create a chart like the one below to record concrete details you encounter as you read.

Thing Described	Concrete Details	Why Visualize

Vocabulary

scintillating (sin´ tə lā´ ting) *adj.* brilliant; sparkling; p. 816 *Her scintillating conversation drew a large number of partygoers to her side.*

vogue (vōg) *n.* fashion; style; p. 816 *It seems to be the vogue today to wear sunglasses indoors.*

patronage (pā´ trə nij) *n.* business; trade; custom; p. 817 *A large part of the restaurant's patronage comes from local people.*

influx (in´ fluks´) *n.* a continual coming in of people or things; p. 817 *The influx of patrons to the restaurant made waiting for a table a lengthy process.*

millennium (mi le´ nē əm) *n.* a period of great happiness, peace, or prosperity; p. 820 *For Roger, being a movie critic was like the millennium.*

Focus

Summary

Hughes describes the unprecedented milieu of Harlem in the 1920s. While African Americans enjoyed success in the arts, whites flocked to Harlem for entertainment. This unusual mingling of races was at times uncomfortable for the Harlem residents, who felt they were being scrutinized. To relax, they went to rent parties.

Vocabulary

Dialogues Have students work in pairs. Have one student make a statement that includes a vocabulary word, e.g., *I wear only clothes that are in vogue.* Have the other student ask a question that includes that word, e.g., *Why do you choose only clothes that are in vogue?* The dialogue may continue for several exchanges until they use all of the vocabulary words.

 For activities related to this selection, see Unit 5 Teaching Resources Book, pp. 267–279.

Selection Skills

Literary Elements
- Juxtaposition (SE pp. 815, 817, 819, 822)
- Historical Narrative (SE p. 822)

When the Negro Was in Vogue

Writing Skills/Grammar
- Persuasive Essay (SE p. 823)
- Ellipses (SE p. 823)
- Personal Opinion (TE p. 820)

Reading Skills
- Analyze Concrete Details (SE pp. 815, 819, 820, 822)

Vocabulary Skills
- Synonyms (SE p. 822)
- Word Roots (TE p. 818)

Study Skills/Research/Assessment
- Drama (TE p. 816)

Teach

816

When the Negro Was in Vogue

Langston Hughes

Aspects of Negro Life: Song of the Towers, 1934. Aaron Douglas. Oil on canvas, 9 x 9 ft. Manu Sassoonian. Schomburg Center for Research in Black Culture, The New York Public Library, NY. ★

The 1920's were the years of Manhattan's black Renaissance. It began with *Shuffle Along, Running Wild,* and the Charleston.[1] Perhaps some people would say even with *The Emperor Jones,* Charles Gilpin, and the tom-toms at the Provincetown. But certainly it was the musical revue, *Shuffle Along,* that gave a **scintillating** send-off to that Negro **vogue** in Manhattan, which reached its peak just before the crash of 1929, the crash that sent Negroes, white folks, and all rolling down the hill toward the Works Progress Administration.[2]

---

1. The *Charleston* is an energetic dance to jazz music. The Lindy Hop and the black-bottom, mentioned later, are similar dances.
2. The *Works Progress Administration* was a government agency established in 1935 to give employment to out-of-work people.

Vocabulary

scintillating (sin´ tə lā´ ting) *adj.* brilliant; sparkling
vogue (vōg) *n.* fashion; style

816 UNIT 5 BEGINNINGS OF THE MODERN AGE

Shuffle Along was a honey of a show. Swift, bright, funny, rollicking, and gay, with a dozen danceable, singable tunes. Besides, look who were in it: The now famous choir director, Hall Johnson, and the composer, William Grant Still, were a part of the orchestra. Eubie Blake and Noble Sissle wrote the music and played and acted in the show. Miller and Lyles were the comics. Florence Mills skyrocketed to fame in the second act. Trixie Smith sang "He May Be Your Man But He Comes to See Me Sometimes." And Caterina Jarboro, now a European prima donna,[3] and the internationally celebrated Josephine Baker were merely in the chorus. Everybody was in the audience—including me. People came back to see it innumerable times. It was always packed.

---

3. A *prima donna* (prē´ mə don´ ə) is a principal or featured woman singer.

was thrilled and delighted. From then on I was in the gallery of the Cort Theatre every time I got a chance. That year, too, I saw Katharine Cornell in *A Bill of Divorcement*, Margaret Wycherly in *The Verge*, Maugham's *The Circle* with Mrs. Leslie Carter, and the Theatre Guild production of Kaiser's *From Morn Till Midnight*. But I remember *Shuffle Along* best of all. It gave just the proper push—a pre-Charleston kick—to that Negro vogue of the 20's, that spread to books, African sculpture, music, and dancing.

Put down the 1920's for the rise of Roland Hayes, who packed Carnegie Hall, the rise of Paul Robeson in New York and London, of Florence Mills over two continents, of Rose McClendon in Broadway parts that never measured up to her, the booming voice of Bessie Smith and the low moan of Clara on thousands of records, and the rise of that grand comedienne of song, Ethel Waters, singing: "Charlie's elected now! He's in right for sure!" Put down the 1920's for Louis Armstrong and Gladys Bentley and Josephine Baker.

White people began to come to Harlem in droves.[4] For several years they packed the expensive Cotton Club on Lenox Avenue. But I was never there, because the Cotton Club was a Jim Crow[5] club for gangsters and monied whites. They were not cordial[6] to Negro **patronage**, unless you were a celebrity like Bojangles. So Harlem Negroes did not like the Cotton Club and never appreciated its Jim Crow policy in the very heart of their dark community. Nor did ordinary Negroes like the growing **influx** of whites toward Harlem after sundown, flooding the little cabarets and bars where formerly only colored people laughed and sang, and where now the strangers were given the best ringside tables to sit and stare at the Negro customers—like amusing animals in a zoo.

> *S*ome of the owners of Harlem clubs made the grievous error of barring their own race.

The Negroes said: "We can't go downtown and sit and stare at you in your clubs. You won't even let us in your clubs." But they didn't say it out loud—for Negroes are practically never rude to white people. So thousands of whites came to Harlem night after night, thinking the Negroes loved to have them there, and firmly believing that all Harlemites left their houses at sundown to sing and dance in cabarets, because most of the whites saw nothing but the cabarets, not the houses.

Some of the owners of Harlem clubs, delighted at the flood of white patronage,

---

4. *Droves* are large crowds.
5. *Jim Crow* refers to segregation or discrimination against African Americans.

2 The Harlem Renaissance *What factors helped make New York the center of African American culture?*

---

6. *Cordial* (kôr′ jəl) means "warm and friendly."

> Juxtaposition *How does the juxtaposition of whites and African Americans at the same Harlem nightclubs develop Hughes's theme?* **3**

Vocabulary

patronage (pā′ trə nij) *n.* business; trade; custom
influx (in′ fluks′) *n.* a continual coming in of people or things

LANGSTON HUGHES **817**

Big Idea **2**

The Harlem Renaissance
Answer: *Factors included the musical revue* Shuffle Along *and a number of other theatrical productions featuring African American performers.*

Literary Element **3**

Juxtaposition **Answer:** *It develops the theme that below the surface, things were not so great for most African Americans. Although whites had discovered African American musicians, dancers, and artists, whites were displacing African American patrons in their own clubs.*

Cultural History

The Cotton Club The legendary Cotton Club opened in 1923. All the performers were African American. Even though the club was located in Harlem, almost all the patrons were white. Many prominent African American performers got their start there, including Cab Calloway and Duke Ellington.

Approaching Level
DIFFERENTIATED INSTRUCTION

Established Point out to students that Hughes mentions many artists who lived in Harlem at the time in his essay. On the board make a three-column chart with the headings "Artist," "Type of Art," and "Other Facts." Have students review the essay to identify the artists Hughes mentions and, when provided, note down the type of artwork in which they were engaged and other facts about them.

Advanced Learners
DIFFERENTIATED INSTRUCTION

Research Have students research and write a report on Jim Crow laws. Tell them to find out when and where Jim Crow laws were passed, what activities the laws applied to, and the effects the laws had on African Americans.

Teach

Literary Element   1

Metaphor Tell students to reread the paragraph describing Gladys Bentley and find the metaphor Hughes uses to describe her. *("a perfect piece of African sculpture")* **Ask:** What does this metaphor tell us about how Hughes felt about Bentley's performances? *(Hughes greatly admired Bentley's energetic and powerful singing and thought that she was the epitome of African American culture in Harlem at that time.)*

View the Photograph ★

Have students examine the photograph on this page. **Ask:** What does the photograph show? *(It shows the entrance to the Cotton Club.)* What impression of the Cotton Club do you get from this photograph? *(There is a doorman standing at the entrance of the club. This shows that the club probably catered to the rich.)*

★

Some of the owners of Harlem clubs, delighted at the flood of white patronage, made the grievous error of barring their own race, after the manner of the famous Cotton Club. But most of these quickly lost business and folded up, because they failed to realize that a large part of the Harlem attraction for downtown New Yorkers lay in simply watching the colored customers amuse themselves. And the smaller clubs, of course, had no big floor shows or a name band like the Cotton Club, where Duke Ellington usually held forth, so, without black patronage, they were not amusing at all.

1 Some of the small clubs, however, had people like Gladys Bentley, who was something worth discovering in those days,

before she got famous, acquired an accompanist, specially written material, and conscious vulgarity. But for two or three amazing years, Miss Bentley sat, and played a big piano all night long, literally all night, without stopping—singing songs like "The St. James Infirmary," from ten in the evening until dawn, with scarcely a break between the notes, sliding from one song to another, with a powerful and continuous underbeat of jungle rhythm. Miss Bentley was an amazing exhibition of musical energy—a large, dark, masculine lady, whose feet pounded the floor while her fingers pounded the keyboard—a perfect piece of African sculpture, animated by her own rhythm.

1

818   UNIT 5   BEGINNINGS OF THE MODERN AGE

Vocabulary Practice

SPIRAL REVIEW **Word Roots** Remind students that knowing word roots can help them decode unfamiliar words. Point out that the word *millennium* on page 819 contains the Latin root *mill*, meaning "thousand." **Ask:** What is the word root in the word *century* and what do you think it means? *(The Latin root* cent *means "hundred.")* Point out that words like *centennial* and *centenarian* also contain this root. Have students

use a dictionary and look up number-related word roots for other words such as *pentameter, hexameter, septennial, octogenarian,* and *nonagenarian.* Tell students to make a table of number-related word roots and list other examples of words with these roots.

818

But when the place where she played became too well known, she began to sing with an accompanist, became a star, moved to a larger place, then downtown, and is now in Hollywood. The old magic of the woman and the piano and the night and the rhythm being one is gone. But everything goes, one way or another. The '20's are gone and lots of fine things in Harlem night life have disappeared like snow in the sun—since it became utterly commercial, planned for the downtown tourist trade, and therefore dull.

The lindy-hoppers at the Savoy even began to practise acrobatic routines, and to do absurd things for the entertainment of the whites, that probably never would have entered their heads to attempt merely for their own effortless amusement. Some of the lindy-hoppers had cards printed with their names on them and became dance professors teaching the tourists. Then Harlem nights became show nights for the Nordics.[7]

Some critics say that that is what happened to certain Negro writers, too—that they ceased to write to amuse themselves and began to write to amuse and entertain white people, and in so doing distorted and over-colored their material, and left out a great many things they thought would offend their American brothers of a lighter complexion. Maybe—since Negroes have writer-racketeers, as has any other race. But I have known almost all of them, and most of the good ones have tried to be honest, write honestly, and express their world as they saw it.

All of us know that the gay and sparkling life of the so-called Negro Renaissance of the '20's was not so gay and sparkling beneath the surface as it looked. Carl Van Vechten, in the character of Byron in *Nigger Heaven*, cap-tured some of the bitterness and frustration of literary Harlem that Wallace Thurman later so effectively poured into his *Infants of the Spring*—the only novel by a Negro about that fantastic period when Harlem was in vogue.

It was a period when, at almost every Harlem upper-crust dance or party, one would be introduced to various distinguished white celebrities there as guests. It was a period when almost any Harlem Negro of any social importance at all would be likely to say casually: "As I was remarking the other day to Heywood—," meaning Heywood Broun. Or: "As I said to George—," referring to George Gershwin. It was a period when local and visiting royalty were not at all uncommon in Harlem. And when the parties of A'Lelia Walker, the Negro heiress, were filled with guests whose names would turn any Nordic social climber green with envy. It was a period when Harold Jackman, a handsome young Harlem school teacher of modest means, calmly announced one day that he was sailing for the Riviera for a fortnight, to attend Princess Murat's yachting party. It was a period when Charleston preachers opened up shouting churches as sideshows for white tourists. It was a period when at least one charming colored chorus girl, amber enough to pass for a Latin American, was living in a pent house, with all her bills paid by a gentleman whose name was banker's magic on Wall Street. It was a period when every season there was at least one hit play on Broadway acted by a Negro cast. And when books by Negro authors were being published with much greater frequency and much more publicity than ever before or since in history. It was a period when white writers wrote about Negroes more successfully (commercially speaking) than Negroes did about themselves. It was the period (God help us!) when Ethel Barrymore appeared in blackface

---

7. *Nordics* usually refers to people of Scandinavia; here, the word means white people in general.

2 Analyze Concrete Details *What do the dancers' cards contribute to Hughes's criticism of Harlem nightlife?*

Juxtaposition *Hughes often juxtaposes two distinct people or situations. What is he saying about the situation in Harlem with this juxtaposition?* **4**

Reading Strategy **2**

Analyze Concrete Details
Answer: *The detail about the dancers' cards provides evidence that African Americans went to absurd lengths to entertain white people.*

Literary Element **3**

Repetition Point out that just as Hughes used repetition in his poetry, so he does here in prose. **Ask:** What is the effect of Hughes's use of repetition here? *(By repeating "it was a period when," Hughes reinforces his point, creates rhythm, and builds momentum.)*

Literary Element **4**

Juxtaposition **Answer:**
Hughes is saying that the cultural life in Harlem had reached a point where European nobility socialized with African American teachers. There was no telling where you might wind up if you were in the right club at the right time.

ENGLISH LEARNERS Explain that in the phrase "a handsome young Harlem teacher of modest means," the adjective *modest* means "being limited in amount." The noun *means* has the meaning of "a person's material resources." In other words, Hughes is saying that Harold Jackson was not a rich person.

English Learners

DIFFERENTIATED INSTRUCTION

 Intermediate English learners can benefit from reading aloud and paraphrasing the text in their own words. Have students work in pairs and read aloud portions of the passage to each other, helping each other with difficult pronunciations or unfamiliar words or phrases. Tell students to look up any unfamiliar terms not explained in the footnotes in the dictionary. Then ask students to orally paraphrase the section they have just read to each other.

The Harlem Renaissance

Answer: *He portrays the Harlem Renaissance as having little effect on society as a whole. Although African American actors and writers were in vogue, ordinary African Americans were not aware of what was going on in New York.*

Analyze Concrete Details

Answer: *The rent parties were events where unexpected talent would appear. There was a spontaneity about the parties that made them a big success.*

The Harlem Renaissance

Answer: *African Americans from all walks of life gathered at the rent parties. Because this sort of gathering happened in few other places, Harlem became the center of African American culture.*

---

in *Scarlet Sister Mary!* It was the period when the Negro was in vogue.

I was there. I had a swell time while it lasted. But I thought it wouldn't last long. (I remember the vogue for things Russian, the season the Chauve-Souris first came to town.) For how could a large and enthusiastic number of people be crazy about Negroes forever? But some Harlemites thought the **millennium** had come. They thought the race problem had at last been solved through Art plus Gladys Bentley. They were sure the New Negro would lead a new life from then on in green pastures of tolerance created by Countee Cullen, Ethel Waters, Claude McKay, Duke Ellington, Bojangles, and Alain Locke.

I don't know what made any Negroes think that—except that they were mostly intellectuals doing the thinking. The ordinary Negroes hadn't heard of the Negro Renaissance. And if they had, it hadn't raised their wages any. As for all those white folks in the speakeasies[8] and night clubs of Harlem—well, maybe a colored man could find *some* place to have a drink that the tourists hadn't yet discovered.

Then it was that house-rent parties began to flourish—and not always to raise the rent either. But, as often as not, to have a get-together of one's own, where you could do the black-bottom with no stranger behind you trying to do it, too. Non-theatrical, non-intellectual Harlem was an unwilling victim of its own vogue. It didn't like to be stared at

by white folks. But perhaps the downtowners never knew this—for the cabaret owners, the entertainers, and the speakeasy proprietors treated them fine—as long as they paid.

The Saturday night rent parties that I attended were often more amusing than any night club, in small apartments where God knows who lived—because the guests seldom did—but where the piano would often be augmented[9] by a guitar, or an odd cornet, or somebody with a pair of drums walking in off the street. And where awful bootleg[10] whiskey and good fried fish or steaming chitterling were sold at very low prices. And the dancing and singing and impromptu[11] entertaining went on until dawn came in at the windows.

These parties, often termed whist[12] parties or dances, were usually announced by brightly colored cards stuck in the grille of apartment house elevators. Some of the cards were highly entertaining in themselves.

Almost every Saturday night when I was in Harlem I went to a house-rent party. I wrote lots of poems about house-rent parties, and ate thereat many a fried fish and pig's foot—with liquid refreshments on the side. I met ladies' maids and truck drivers, laundry workers and shoe shine boys, seamstresses and porters. I can still hear their laughter in my ears, hear the soft slow music, and feel the floor shaking as the dancers danced. ∽

---

8. During Prohibition, *speakeasies* were secret clubs where alcoholic drinks were sold illegally.

The Harlem Renaissance *How does Hughes portray the effects of the Harlem Renaissance on society?*

1 | **Vocabulary**

millennium (mi le´ nē əm) *n.* a period of great happiness, peace, or prosperity

9. *Augmented* (ôg ment´ əd) means "accompanied; enlarged."
10. *Bootleg* means "made, transported, or sold illegally."
11. *Impromptu* (im promp´ tōō) means "offhand or without preparation."
12. *Whist* is a card game similar to bridge.

2

Analyze Concrete Details *What do the details Hughes shares about rent parties tell you about the reason for their success?*

3

The Harlem Renaissance *What does Hughes's experience at rent parties say about the reasons Harlem became the center of African American culture?*

Writing Practice

Personal Opinion Have students respond to these questions in a short essay: After reading Hughes's essay, what is your impression of the Harlem Renaissance? What positive and negative effects did the Harlem Renaissance have on African Americans?

Students may wish to do some additional research on the Harlem Renaissance before answering these questions. Remind students to support their opinions

with details from Hughes's essay and from other sources. After students finish their essays, have volunteers read their essays to the class.

After You Read

Respond and Think Critically

Respond and Interpret

1. If you had lived in Harlem in the 1920s, what aspect of its culture do you think you would have enjoyed most? Explain.

2. (a)How was the musical *Shuffle Along* instrumental in Hughes's move to Harlem? (b)According to Hughes, what was the musical's importance to the African American community?

3. (a)How did the Jim Crow policy operate in the Cotton Club? (b)How did the residents of Harlem respond to the Jim Crow policy?

4. (a)What were house-rent parties? (b)How does Hughes compare them to other forms of entertainment?

Analyze and Evaluate

5. (a)What did the "ordinary Negroes" who lived in Harlem think about the Renaissance? (b)Why?

6. According to Hughes, what did it mean for "the Negro" to be "in vogue"?

Connect

7. **Big Idea** **The Harlem Renaissance** How did some Harlemites expect the Renaissance to affect race relations? Was this realistic?

8. **Connect to Today** How might Hughes respond to African American artists today? Explain and support your response.

Daily Life & Culture

Harlem

By the middle of the 1920s, Harlem had become the largest community of people of African ancestry in the world. Laws were less oppressive in the North than in the South, but African Americans still faced prejudice. Hughes mentions the whites-only policy of the Cotton Club; other theaters and nightclubs had it also.

Employment opportunities were limited. Nearly half of African American men held service jobs as messengers, janitors, or waiters. Many others labored on the docks, loading and unloading ships. Few found work in the skilled trades, and many unions were closed to them. Over 60 percent of African American women were employed—far more than any other group of women at the time. More than half did laundry or worked as maids, both low-paying jobs.

Group Activity Discuss the following questions with classmates.

1. What opportunities and difficulties might a person from the rural South have faced in Harlem?

2. What problems might a young family have faced if both parents held jobs?

 For additional assessment, see Assessment Resources, pp. 229–230.

Daily Life & Culture

1. Their opportunities were limited by racism, segregation, and the lack of well-paying jobs.

2. The parents would not have the time or energy to devote to their children.

After You Read

Assess

1. Students' answers will vary.

2. (a) Hughes went to Columbia University in New York City so that he could see the show. (b) The show was the first musical written by, about, and for blacks, and it called attention to the vitality of African American music.

3. (a) The Cotton Club management disliked black patrons unless they were celebrities. (b) They resented such a policy in their own community.

4. (a) Parties at which food and drink were sold to anyone who wanted to attend, often to raise money to pay someone's rent. (b) He says that the rent parties were "more amusing than any night club."

5. (a) Many of them were unaware of the Harlem Renaissance. (b) The African American vogue did not affect their daily lives and did not raise their wages.

6. African American culture and art became fashionable among whites.

7. Some people in Harlem hoped that the Renaissance was the beginning of a millennium of racial tolerance. They were not realistic because their hopes proved to be illusory.

8. Hughes may admire the talent of African American artists today, but he might not like the fact that actors and singers have become "utterly commercial."

After You Read

Assess

Literary Element

1. These people were common people, not artists and intellectuals, out for fun on a Saturday night. The parties were democratic, including anyone and everyone.

2. Hughes thinks the intellectuals had unrealistic expectations, while the ordinary African Americans had no increased expectations because the Renaissance did not affect their lives.

Progress Check

Can students analyze juxtaposition?

If No → See Unit 5 Teaching Resources Book, p. 273.

Review: Historical Narrative

Students may say that the people Hughes mentions were so famous at the time he was writing that he did not need to identify them.

Literary Element Juxtaposition

Juxtaposition is the placing together of two or more distinct things for the purpose of comparing or contrasting them. In "When the Negro Was in Vogue," Langston Hughes juxtaposes people, places, and activities.

1. Why do you think Hughes juxtaposes "ladies' maids and truck drivers, laundry workers and shoe shine boys, seamstresses and porters" in his description of the house-rent parties?

2. What is Hughes's conclusion from his juxtaposition of the "intellectual" African Americans and the "ordinary" Harlem African Americans?

Review: Historical Narrative

As you learned on page 416, a **historical narrative** is a work of nonfiction that tells the story of important historical events or developments.

Partner Activity Meet with another classmate and talk about the many people that Hughes mentions in this historical narrative. Sort them out, as best you can, using the context in which Hughes mentions them. Use a chart like this one to take notes.

African Americans in Harlem

Writers & Poets	Singers & Actors	Musicians & Composers	Not Sure

When you have listed all the names, highlight any that you have heard of before. Why do you suppose Hughes does not identify each of the people he mentions, such as George Gershwin?

LOG ON **Literature** Online

Selection Resources For Selection Quizzes, eFlashcards, and Reading-Writing Connection activities, go to glencoe.com and enter QuickPass code GLA9800u5.

Reading Strategy Analyze Concrete Details

ACT Skills Practice

1. The concrete details Hughes gives about the rent parties appeal to the senses of:

   I. hearing
   II. smell / taste
   III. sight

   A. II only
   B. I and II only
   C. II and III only
   D. I, II, and III

Vocabulary Practice

Practice with Synonyms With a partner, match each vocabulary word with its synonym. You will not use all the answer choices. Use a thesaurus or dictionary to check your answers.

1. millennium
2. patronage
3. scintillating
4. vogue
5. influx

a. business
b. inflow
c. fashion
d. brilliant
e. time of happiness
f. unclear

Academic Vocabulary

Hughes **labels** the white tourists who flocked to Harlem for entertainment as "Nordics."

Label is an academic word. Using context clues, try to figure out the meaning of *label* in each sentence and explain the difference between the two meanings:

1. For my detention, my science teacher made me **label** slides with the names of the organisms they displayed.

2. The inventors **labeled** their new product "The Wingbat."

For more on academic vocabulary, see pages 53–54.

Vocabulary

1. e 2. a 3. d 4. c 5. b

Reading Strategy

1. D is the correct answer because Hughes describes the invitations, music, laughter, food, and drink of the rent parties.

Academic Vocabulary

1. The student is forced to copy the names down in order to identify the slides, so *label* means "to affix an identifying phrase to."

2. The inventors have to create an original name, so *label* means "to designate with an identifying phrase," not just to place a label with a preexisting name on an object.

Respond Through Writing

Persuasive Essay

Argue a Position Hughes examines both the artistic advances and social inequalities of the Harlem Renaissance. Overall, does he consider the movement to have had a positive or negative impact? Write a persuasive essay on this topic. Support your argument with details from the text, and include rhetorical devices to strengthen your argument.

Understand the Task When you **argue** persuasively, you use logic or reason to influence a reader's ideas or actions. **Rhetorical devices** include repetition, emotional appeal, hyperbole, and rhetorical questions.

Prewrite Fill in a chart with evidence that supports your argument. Make another chart with opposing arguments and evidence that supports them. Make sure to record any outside sources you use so you can properly attribute the information.

Argument	Evidence	Opposing Argument	Counter-Evidence

Draft Begin with your thesis, in which you will argue whether Hughes considered the Harlem Renaissance to have had a positive or negative impact. Your body paragraphs should all have topic sentences related to the thesis. Use evidence from your chart as support, and cite the page numbers for quotations. You might apply the sentence frame below to address opposing arguments:

While some might object that _____, I would reply that _____.

Revise Exchange papers with a partner. Evaluate each other's essay. Is the argument logical and well-supported? Does the essay refute counterarguments? Does the essay include persuasive techniques? Revise your essay based on the comments you receive.

Edit and Proofread Proofread your paper, correcting any errors in spelling, grammar, and punctuation. Use the Grammar Tip in the side column to help you with using ellipses.

Learning Objectives

In this assignment, you will focus on the following objectives:

Writing: Writing a persuasive essay.

Grammar: Using ellipses in quotations.

> **Grammar Tip**

Ellipses

Ellipsis points (. . .) are three spaced periods that indicate the omission of words within a text, such as a quotation. Ellipses are useful when you don't need to refer to the entirety of a quotation, just relevant portions:

Hughes claims it was white writers who benefited most: "White writers wrote about Negroes more successfully . . . than Negroes did about themselves."

When you use ellipses, make sure you do not alter the meaning of quotations by omitting key phrases or words. Do not use ellipses at the beginning of a quotation or at the end if the quotation reads as a complete sentence. In the second case, simply end the quotation with a period.

After You Read

Assess

 ## Respond Through Writing

Students' essays should

- Establish a clear position on the issue.
- Use logic and rhetorical strategies to persuade the reader.
- Be clearly and cohesively organized.

> For grammar practice, see Unit 5 Teaching Resources Book, p. 277.

Approaching Level

DIFFERENTIATED INSTRUCTION

AAVE Approaching level students who use African American vernacular English (AAVE) may have trouble with the verb "to be" in their writing. In their persuasive essays, help students recognize where they may make mistakes in Standard Academic English by omitting or misusing *is* or *are* with nouns and present participles. They may also sometimes omit *is* or *are* between pronoun subjects and predicate nouns or adjectives. For example, if students chose home as a setting, students may say "Home *be* comfortable and familiar" instead of "Home *is* comfortable and familiar." Work with students and help them find places in their persuasive essays where the verb "to be" is omitted or misused. Guide students in correcting their mistakes where necessary.

Bellringer Options

Daily Language Practice
Transparency 76

Or go over the vocabulary on the next page so that students are comfortable with the words *reap* and *sow*. **Ask:** What is the literal meaning of the biblical statement "you reap whatever you sow"? *(You will harvest the fruit of whatever seeds you plant.)* **Ask:** What is the figurative meaning of this statement? *(What you do comes back to you.)*

Discuss contemporary cases that illustrate the biblical idea, and ones that belie it.

Meet **Arna Bontemps**
(1902–1973)

Historian, educator, and author of poems, plays, and novels, Arna Bontemps helped draw attention to the misleading education he felt many U.S. citizens had received about the heritage and accomplishments of African Americans. He has been credited with helping to create the "trickle of interest in Negro American literature—that trickle which is now a torrent." He wrote, "Had I not gone home summers and hob-nobbed with Negroes, . . . I would have come out [of college] imagining that the story of the Negro could be told in two short paragraphs: a statement about jungle people in Africa and an equally brief account of the slavery issue in American history."

> "In the Harlem Renaissance poetry led the way for the other arts. It touched off the awakening that brought novelists, painters, sculptors, dancers, dramatists, and scholars of many kinds to the notice of a nation that had nearly forgotten about the gifts of its Negro people."
>
> —Arna Bontemps

A Childhood Teacher Bontemps was born in Alexandria, Louisiana, but racism there led his family to move to Los Angeles when Bontemps was three. During his childhood, his great-uncle Buddy shared with Bontemps a love of variety shows, folk stories, and dialect, all of which were staples of African American culture at the time. Bontemps

would go on to incorporate the cultural achievements of African Americans in his work.

When Bontemps was a student at UCLA, he discovered a book by Claude McKay, a poet whose work eventually helped to spark the Harlem Renaissance. Bontemps read McKay's book twice in one day and then "began telling everybody I knew about it." In 1923, when he moved to New York, he became friends with Langston Hughes, Countee Cullen, and other Harlem Renaissance artists.

Adult Achievements Bontemps's father wanted his son to become a mason, but Bontemps preferred to try his luck as a writer. Soon after his arrival in Harlem, he won recognition for his poetry and for his first novel, *God Sends Sunday*.

In 1943 Bontemps became the librarian at Fisk University in Nashville, Tennessee, where he devoted himself to recording the history of African Americans. He said that his book *The Story of the Negro* "consists mainly of things I learned after I left school that I wish I had known much earlier." Bontemps went on to write more than twenty-five books, including *The Harlem Renaissance Remembered* and *Golden Slippers*, the first children's anthology of African American poetry.

 Literature Online

Author Search For more about Arna Bontemps, go to glencoe.com and enter QuickPass code GLA9800u5.

Selection Skills

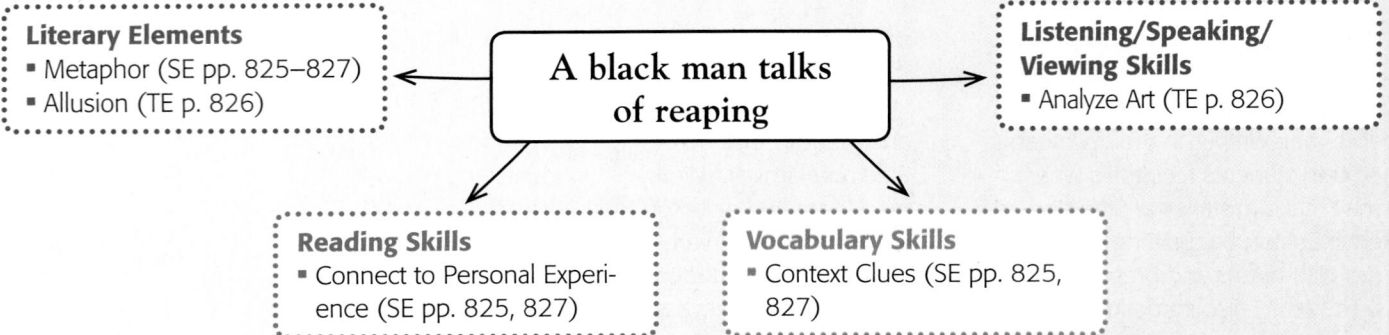

Literary Elements
- Metaphor (SE pp. 825–827)
- Allusion (TE p. 826)

A black man talks of reaping

Listening/Speaking/Viewing Skills
- Analyze Art (TE p. 826)

Reading Skills
- Connect to Personal Experience (SE pp. 825, 827)

Vocabulary Skills
- Context Clues (SE pp. 825, 827)

Literature and Reading Preview

Connect to the Poem

How you would feel if others benefited from your work but you did not? How would you feel if you unfairly benefited from someone else's work? Discuss these questions in a small group.

Build Background

The references to sowing in this poem are an extended metaphor, but the metaphor depends on some specific factual information about planting and harvesting. Because many things can go wrong before a seed becomes a harvestable plant, the results of sowing are unpredictable. Bontemps may have had in mind the New Testament parable of the Sower and the Seed (Matthew 13:3–9), which contains one of the best known examples of the metaphor.

Set Purposes for Reading

Big Idea The Harlem Renaissance

As you read, ask yourself, How does Bontemps's poem address the injustices stemming from racial inequality?

Literary Element Metaphor

A **metaphor** is a figure of speech that compares two seemingly unlike things. In contrast to a simile, a metaphor does not use the words *like* or *as* in making a comparison. For example, the phrase "the car was lightning and thunder" compares a noisy and speedy car to lightning and thunder. "A black man talks of reaping" includes an implied **extended metaphor**—a metaphor that is developed at length. As you read, ask, What does Bontemps accomplish by using an extended metaphor?

Reading Strategy Connect to Personal Experience

To **connect** the events and ideas of a literary work to your own life or to other works you've read, ask yourself, Do I know someone like this? Have I ever felt this way? What else have I read that reminds me of this poem?

....

Tip: Take Notes Use a chart like the one started below to record the connections you find.

Events, ideas, or feelings in the poem	My connections

Learning Objectives

For pages 824–827

In studying this text, you will focus on the following objectives:

Literary Study: Analyzing metaphors.

Reading: Connecting to personal experience.

Writing: Writing a letter.

Vocabulary

sown (sōn) *v.* planted; p. 826 *Two weeks after the seeds were sown, the plants sprouted.*

lean (lēn) *adj.* unproductive; lacking; p. 826 *The farmers fear that this year will be a lean one.*

reap (rēp) *v.* to gather or to harvest; p. 826 *Each fall, the farmers reap the grain in the fields.*

....

Tip: Context Clues To learn a word's meaning, look at the words surrounding it and try to predict its definition. Example: In lines 1–2, Bontemps writes, "I have *sown* beside all waters in my day / I planted deep, within my heart the fear." The placement of *sown* and *planted* suggests that the two words are synonyms.

Before You Read

Focus

Summary

The speaker is a black man who works the land but has little to show for his efforts. The first stanza tells about his efforts to ensure a good harvest. The second stanza describes the disappointing result. The third stanza points to the difference between those who work but have nothing to show for it and those who profit by the work of others.

 For summaries in languages other than English, see Unit 5 Teaching Resources Book, pp. 280–285.

Vocabulary

Perfect Tenses Explain to students that *sown* is a past participle form of the verb *to sow*. The word *sowed* may also be used: I have *sown* (or *sowed*) seeds in the fields. The tense used in this sentence is called the *present perfect*. This tense describes an action that is complete at the present time. It begins with *I have, you have, she has* and so on. Have students use the word *sown* in sentences in the present perfect.

(ADVANCED) Have students explain how the word *sown* is used in the future perfect and past perfect. Have them write a dialogue using all three forms of the perfect tense with this or other verbs.

 For additional context, see Glencoe Interactive Vocabulary CD-ROM.

Approaching Level

DIFFERENTIATED INSTRUCTION

Emerging Preteach these phrases from the poem: "beside all waters," "planted deep within my heart," "I scattered seed," "reaping only what the hand can hold at once," and "my children glean in fields they have not sown." Then have students explain each phrase in their own words.

Established Have students create a three-column chart with the headings "Questions," "Sowing," and "Reaping." In the first column have them list the questions Who? What? When? Where? and Why? They should answer these questions for sowing and reaping in the other two columns.

Teach

Big Idea | 1

The Harlem Renaissance
Say: Think about the Great Migration. Where might the speaker's children be working? *(Many African Americans had moved to Northern cities to find new jobs.)*

Literary Element | 2

Metaphor Answer: *Sharecroppers owed landowners so much for rent, tools, and seed that they saw little or no profit.*

> For additional literary element practice, see Unit 5 Teaching Resources Book, p. 286.

View the Art

Robert Gwathmey (1903–1988) was among the first white Americans to capture the hardships of blacks in rural Virginia. He depicted many scenes of sharecroppers who paid for the land they rented by giving most of their crop to the landowners.

Share Croppers, c. 1941. Robert Gwathmey. Watercolor, 45 x 32.4 cm. ©Estate of Robert Gwathmey/Licensed by VAGA, New York/San Diego Museum of Art. Museum purchase with funds provided by Mrs. Leon D. Bonnet.

A black man talks of reaping

Arna Bontemps

I have **sown** beside all waters in my day.
I planted deep, within my heart the fear
that wind or fowl would take the grain away.
I planted safe against this stark, **lean** year.

5 I scattered seed enough to plant the land
in rows from Canada to Mexico
but for my **reaping** only what the hand
can hold at once is all that I can show.

Yet what I sowed and what the orchard yields
10 my brother's sons are gathering stalk and root;
small wonder then my children glean[1] in fields | 1

---

1. *Glean* means "to gather grain left on a field after reaping."

Metaphor *What might be the underlying reason that the speaker has profited little from the hard work of sowing (lines 7–8)?* | 2

Vocabulary

sown (sōn) *v.* planted
lean (lēn) *adj.* unproductive; lacking
reap (rēp) *v.* to gather or to harvest

Reading Practice

Allusion Remind students that an author's indirect reference to a person, event, or another work of literature is called an *allusion*. Ask them how Bontemps alludes to Langston Hughes's "The Negro Speaks of Rivers" and to the Bible. *(Bontemp's "black man talks" calls to mind Hughes's "Negro speaks," his "reaping" alliterates with Hughes's "rivers," and his use of the terms "sown" and "reaping" allude to the Bible.)* Have students work in small groups to write a poem in which they allude to another work of literature, one in the text or one that is commonly known. Have groups read their poems and have the class determine the specific allusions they are making.

After You Read

Respond and Think Critically

Respond and Interpret

1. How did this poem affect you? Explain.

2. (a)What is the work done by the speaker in the poem? (b)How would you explain the fears and concerns expressed in the first stanza?

3. (a)Who are "my brother's sons," and what are they doing? (b)Why do you think they are able to act in such a way?

4. (a)What does the speaker mean by "my children glean in fields they have not sown"? (b)What might be the "bitter fruit" the children feed on? Explain.

Analyze and Evaluate

5. James Baldwin wrote, "Color is not a human or a personal reality; it is a political reality." How does this poem illustrate Baldwin's point?

6. How does the title of the poem help you understand the poem's overall meaning? Explain.

Connect

7. **Big Idea** **The Harlem Renaissance** How does this poem reflect both African American history and goals of the Harlem Renaissance?

8. **Connect to Today** Are the last two lines of the poem still applicable today? Explain.

Literary Element Metaphor

An **extended metaphor** is a metaphor that is developed over more than one line.

1. What comparison is Bontemps making?

2. What details in the poem convey the metaphor?

3. How does the metaphor help support the **theme**, or underlying message, of the poem?

Reading Strategy Connect to Personal Experience

Refer to your chart from page 825 to note connections to the poem.

1. How do your ideas and experiences compare with those Bontemps wrote about?

2. Think of a time you were treated unfairly. How did you feel and respond? Explain what you learned from this.

LOG ON **Literature** Online

Selection Resources For Selection Quizzes, eFlashcards, and Reading-Writing Connection activities, go to glencoe.com and enter QuickPass code GLA9800u5.

Vocabulary Practice

Practice with Context Clues Identify the context clues in the following sentences that help you determine the meaning of each boldfaced vocabulary word.

1. When it's time for the exam, I plan to **reap** the benefits of studying.

2. Our tomato plants produced far fewer tomatoes than they did last season; it was a **lean** crop.

3. When I looked out the window, I saw that the flowers I had **sown** last fall were just coming up.

Writing

Write a Letter In this poem, Bontemps raises awareness about the difficulties faced by African Americans. You can express your thoughts on injustice, too. Think about a troubling issue in your community. Write a letter to your state or national representative or senator describing the situation. Your style should be formal, like that of a business letter.

ARNA BONTEMPS **827**

After You Read

Assess

1. Students' responses will vary.

2. (a) Sowing and reaping (b) The speaker has feared that weather or birds would spoil his crop.

3. (a) The children of white people, who are taking the crops (b) The sharecropping system allows them to do so.

4. (a) A literal interpretation is that the speaker's children must search fields for unharvested grain. Metaphorically, they are working in other people's businesses. (b) Unfairness; prejudice

5. It shows that African Americans suffered from the politics of sharecropping.

6. The title presents the literal farming situation; metaphorically, work without reward.

7. The poem reflects the African American history of sharecropping. It reflects the Harlem Renaissance goal of bringing those concerns to the public.

8. Students may say that people have more choices today, so they are no longer forced to feed on "bitter fruit."

Writing

Students' letters should address a specific issue and have a formal and persuasive tone.

Literary Element

1. He is comparing the sharecropper's life to the results of racial prejudice.

2. Possible answers: "sown"; "planted deep"; "scattered seed"; "reaping"; "orchard"

3. It illustrates the theme of exploitation.

Reading Strategy

Students' answers will vary.

Progress Check

Can students connect the text to personal experience?

If No → See Unit 5 Teaching Resources Book, p. 287.

Vocabulary

1. Studying will help the student gain better grades on her exams, so *reap* means "to obtain or gather."

2. Because not many tomatoes were produced in the crop, *lean* means "not plentiful."

3. The flowers' growth is due to the fact that their seeds were *sown,* or planted, months before.

Before You Read

Any Human to Another

Meet **Countee Cullen**
(1903–1946)

Probably more than any other writer during the Harlem Renaissance, Countee Cullen embodied the ideal of the "New Negro" and fulfilled the goals of African American leaders W. E. B. DuBois and James Weldon Johnson. He successfully reached both African American and white audiences and eloquently addressed the issues of racism and injustice in the United States. Though some argued that Cullen spurned his African American heritage because he considered himself simply a *poet* and not an *African American poet*, he never denied his African American culture. His verse—even as it showed the influence of English Romantic poetry—echoed the struggle and violence of the times.

Cullen was born Countee Porter. His birthplace remains a mystery, but most scholars believe it was Louisville, Kentucky. Cullen was raised by a woman who was thought to be his grandmother, and when she died in 1917, he went to live with Reverend Frederick A. Cullen, pastor of the Salem Methodist Episcopal Church in Harlem, and his wife, Carolyn. Although not legally adopted by the Cullens, he eventually took their last name.

Cullen excelled in school and won several poetry awards, including a citywide contest. Before he graduated from New York University, his first book of poems, *Color*, was published to good reviews. By the time he received his master's degree from Harvard, Cullen had become the most esteemed African American poet of his time.

> "I shall not write of Negro subjects for the purpose of propaganda. That is not what a poet is concerned with. Of course, when the emotion rising out of the fact that I am a Negro is strong, I express it."
>
> —Countee Cullen

Contradictions Cullen wanted to prove that African Americans could write as well as whites. His belief in art's ability to unite people of all races prompted him to caution African American poets against becoming "racial poets." James Weldon Johnson understood Cullen's desire to avoid the "Negro poet" label, but he also noted a paradox: "Strangely, it is because Cullen revolts against… racial limitations—technical and spiritual—that the best of his poetry is motivated by race."

Legacy Cullen published several collections of poetry after *Color*. Although critical acclaim for his works waned in later years, his popularity never suffered, and today his literary legacy remains due to the eloquent, artfully crafted poems he wrote during the Harlem Renaissance.

Countee Porter Cullen, 1925. Winold Reiss. Pastel on artist board. National Portrait Gallery, Smithsonian Institution, Washington, DC.

 Literature Online

Author Search For more about Countee Cullen, go to glencoe.com and enter QuickPass code GLA9800u5.

Selection Skills

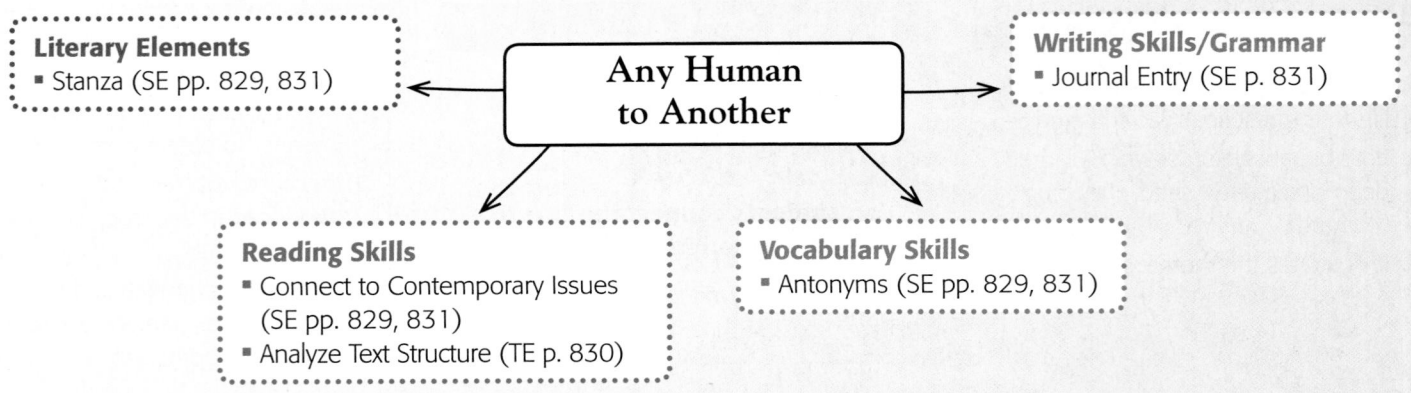

Literary Elements
- Stanza (SE pp. 829, 831)

Any Human to Another

Writing Skills/Grammar
- Journal Entry (SE p. 831)

Reading Skills
- Connect to Contemporary Issues (SE pp. 829, 831)
- Analyze Text Structure (TE p. 830)

Vocabulary Skills
- Antonyms (SE pp. 829, 831)

Literature and Reading Review

Connect to the Poem

How much can we empathize with—very deeply feel—another person's troubles? Freewrite for ten minutes on this topic.

Build Background

Growing up in Harlem, Cullen learned about African American pride, unity, and art. Yet he was also immersed in white culture: he was educated in white upper-class schools, read the works of European writers, and imitated John Keats and other English Romantic poets. This combination of influences—white and African American, formal and informal—is reflected in his work.

Set Purposes for Reading

Big Idea **The Harlem Renaissance**

As you read this poem, ask yourself, How did Cullen envision the role of art as a means of breaking down racial barriers?

Literary Element **Stanza**

A **stanza** is a group of lines forming a unit in a poem or song. A stanza tends to focus on a certain topic or feeling. Typically, stanzas are separated by a line space and often have the same number of lines, the same meter, and the same rhyme scheme. As you read, ask yourself, What is the focus of each stanza? How are the stanzas arranged?

Reading Strategy **Connect to Contemporary Issues**

Cullen's poem reflects his desire to see people as individuals rather than as representatives of a group and to focus on what unites them. As you read, ask, How are his beliefs relevant today?

....

Tip: Record Your Observations To assess the values you identify in Cullen's poem in the context of contemporary issues, record your observations in a chart like the one below:

Cullen's Beliefs	Contemporary Issues	Observations
Sorrow unites people	Terrorist attacks	Cullen would understand why people unite after terrorist attacks.

Learning Objectives

For pages 828–831

In studying this text, you will focus on the following objectives:

Literary Study: Analyzing stanzas.

Reading: Connecting to contemporary issues.

Writing: Writing a journal entry.

Vocabulary

fused (fūzd) *adj.* blended; p. 830
The jeweler crafted a bracelet made of fused metals.

diverse (di vurs´) *adj.* composed of different elements; p. 830
Because of newcomers from Asia and Latin America, the town had become more ethnically diverse.

unique (ū nēk´) *adj.* unusual; p. 830 *The artist generally paints religious paintings, so this landscape painting is unique.*

unsheathed (un shēthd´) *adj.* removed from a protective case; p. 830 *The unsheathed sword appeared both menacing and beautiful.*

....

Tip: Antonyms Understanding the opposite of an unfamiliar word, or its **antonym**, can help you learn the word. Example: *Unique* and *ordinary* are antonyms.

COUNTEE CULLEN **829**

Before You Read

Focus

Summary

The speaker points out that no person stands completely alone and that both joy and sorrow—the latter much more prevalent than the former—should be shared.

 For summaries in languages other than English, see Unit 5 Teaching Resources Book, pp. 291–296.

Vocabulary

Prefixes Two common prefixes are *un-* and *dis-*, both meaning "not," or "the opposite of." Give students the following list of words and have them affix the correct prefix: *reliable, comfort, prove, interesting, service, safe, place, appealing, interested.* Then have them check the meanings of the words in the dictionary.

[APPROACHING] Write the following words on the board: *unsheathed, unlikely, unpopular, unforeseen, unofficial, unnecessary.* Point out that when the first letter of the base word is *n*, you get a double letter. Have students identify the base word and its meaning using a dictionary. Have them predict the meaning of the words with the prefix. Have them use a dictionary to check their answers.

English Learners

DIFFERENTIATED INSTRUCTION

Intermediate To help students understand the poem, have them write out the individual stanzas as sentences without special capitalization. Then have them rearrange the words, add extra punctuation, or add pronouns or other words to make the sentences easier to understand. Have them read their sentences aloud and explain what each one means. Then have them return to the poem and read it aloud.

Advanced Have students read each stanza and identify and explain any metaphors or similes the poet uses. Have them discuss how each use of figurative language helps give the reader a better understanding of the poet's message.

Teach

For additional literary element practice, see Unit 5 Teaching Resources Book, p. 297.

Literary Element　　1

Stanza Ask: Would this work be better presented as a prose paragraph of six sentences? *(Some students may say the short lines and short stanzas help them understand the message and hear the music.)*

Big Idea　　2

The Harlem Renaissance
Answer: *Students may suggest race-proud whites (or blacks), class-conscious rich people, or people who seek to avoid human troubles.*

View the Art ★

The title of the artwork is a quotation from a 1933 speech by Jane Addams, a U.S. social worker.
Ask: What do the messages of Addams, the artist, and Cullen have in common? *(They all want humans to recognize what they share with one another.)*

Reading Practice

SPIRAL REVIEW Analyze Text Structure On first reading, students may have trouble following the sense of lines 1–6. One reason is syntax: The subject (*ills*) is separated from its verb (*pierce*) by two lines, and the verb's direct object (*me*), along with an adverb phrase (*like an arrow*), precedes the verb.

After pointing out this inverted syntax, ask students to write a paraphrase of the first stanza. Remind them that a paraphrase is a restatement of someone else's words in one's own words. Then ask for paraphrases of the remaining four stanzas of the poem. Have students read their paraphrases aloud for the class.

Civilization is a method of living, an attitude of equal respect for all men, from the series *Great Ideas of Western Man,* 1955. George Giusti. India ink and gouache on paper sheet, 24⁷⁄₈ x 18⁵⁄₁₆ in. National Museum of American Art, Smithsonian Institution, Washington, DC. ★

Any Human to Another

Countee Cullen

The ills I sorrow at
Not me alone
Like an arrow,
Pierce to the marrow,
5　Through the fat
And past the bone.

Your grief and mine
Must intertwine
Like sea and river,
10　Be **fused** and mingle,
Diverse yet single,
Forever and forever.

Let no man be so proud
And confident,
15　To think he is allowed
A little tent
Pitched in a meadow
Of sun and shadow
All his little own.

20　Joy may be shy, **unique,**
Friendly to a few,
Sorrow never scorned to speak
To any who
Were false or true.

25　Your every grief
Like a blade
Shining and **unsheathed**
Must strike me down.
Of bitter aloes¹ wreathed,
30　My sorrow must be laid
On your head like a crown. **1**

---

1. **Aloes** refers to the spiny leaves of the aloe plant, whose juices are used to make a bitter medicine.

Harlem Renaissance *What types of people might the speaker be referring to here?* **2**

Vocabulary

fused (fūzd) *adj.* blended
diverse (di vurs´) *adj.* composed of different elements
unique (ū nēk´) *adj.* unusual
unsheathed (un shēthd´) *adj.* removed from a protective case

After You Read

Respond and Think Critically

Respond and Interpret

1. (a)How did you respond to the title? (b)Did your response change after reading the poem?

2. (a)Who is the speaker in this poem? (b)Whom does the speaker address?

3. A **simile** is a comparison that uses words such as *like* or *as*. What similes does Cullen use in the first and second stanzas?

4. What image of human isolation and self-sufficiency does the speaker introduce in the third stanza, and what is his view of it?

5. (a)What point does the speaker make about joy in the fourth stanza? (b)How does the speaker contrast this point to the effect of sorrow?

Analyze and Evaluate

6. (a)What comparisons are introduced in stanza 5? (b)Why might Cullen have selected them?

7. In this poem, Cullen **personifies,** or gives human attributes to, the emotions of joy and sorrow. (a)What might be the purpose of this personification? (b)Is it effective? Explain.

Connect

8. **Big Idea** **The Harlem Renaissance** What attitude toward racism does this poem imply?

9. **Connect to the Author** Cullen did not want to be know as a "racial poet," yet much of his work explored the themes of race and racism. How do you explain this apparent contradiction?

Literary Element Stanza

Stanzas are often similar in structure, but some poems have stanzas with different numbers of lines, different rhyme schemes, or different meters.

1. (a)How many stanzas does this poem have? (b)How many lines are in each stanza? (c)How do the stanzas reflect the definition of a stanza?

2. What effect does Cullen create through his choice of stanza form?

Reading Strategy Connect to Contemporary Issues

Look back over the chart you made to record observations about values expressed in the poem.

1. What beliefs did you identify?

2. How relevant do you think the poem is today?

 Literature Online

Selection Resources For Selection Quizzes, eFlashcards, and Reading-Writing Connection activities, go to glencoe.com and enter QuickPass code GLA9800u5.

Vocabulary Practice

Practice with Antonyms An **antonym** is a word that has a meaning opposite to that of another word. With a partner, match each bold-faced vocabulary word below with its antonym. You will not use all the answer choices. Use a thesaurus or dictionary to check your answers.

1. fused
2. diverse
3. unique
4. unsheathed

a. common
b. protected
c. electrified
d. varied
e. separated
f. uniform

Writing

Write a Journal Entry In the third stanza of this poem, Cullen expresses his views on human isolation. Do you agree with his perspective? Do you ever isolate yourself? If so, what effect does that have? Describe your thoughts and feelings on isolation in a brief journal entry.

COUNTEE CULLEN **831**

After You Read

Assess

1. Answers will vary.

2. (a) Any human being (b) The reader, another human being

3. Stanza 1: Ills are compared to an arrow; stanza 2: Griefs are compared to a sea and a river.

4. The speaker describes a tent pitched in a meadow; he warns against seeking isolation.

5. (a) Joy is for the few. (b) Sorrow disdains no one.

6. (a) The reader's grief is compared to a blade; the speaker's sorrow is compared to a crown of aloes. (b) Cullen sees grief as piercing and sorrow as continual.

7. (a) To suggest that people have no control over their joys and sorrows (b) Students' answers will vary.

8. Cullen rejects any attitude that divides humans, including racism.

9. Students may say that Cullen was writing about his experiences and his life which were affected by race.

Literary Element

1. (a) Five (b) Six, six, seven, five, and seven (c) The stanzas vary slightly in number of lines, rhyme scheme, and meter, yet the ideas connect.

2. The effect of thinking through an idea

Reading Strategy

1. Possible answers: that sorrow unites humanity; that grief is unavoidable

2. Most will say that it is relevant.

Vocabulary

1. e **2.** f **3.** a **4.** b

Writing

Students' journal entries should make connections between Cullen's view on isolation and their personal thoughts and experiences.

Progress Check

Can students connect to contemporary issues?

If No → See Unit 5 Teaching Resources Book, p. 298.

Writing Workshop

Literary Analysis

Focus

Bellringer

This workshop reprints part of Lawrence Raab's analysis of "Mending Wall." His analysis points to questions the poem asks, various ways of interpreting certain lines in the poem, and some of the contradictions inherent in the poem. **Ask:** Do you think a poem can mean anything you want it to mean? Why do people sometimes take away different meanings from the same poem?

Summary

In this workshop, students will write and present analyses of poems. They will follow the stages of the writing process, including prewriting, drafting, revising, and editing. The workshop includes two mini-lessons, on precise word choice and the use of quotations.

Workshop Resources

Print Materials

- Unit 5 Teaching Resources pp. 304–306
- Writing Kit
- Success in Writing: Research and Reports

💻 Technology

- Literature Online: Writing Resources and Grammar Resources, www.glencoe.com
- Online Essay Grader, www.glencoe.com
- Student Presentation Builder on StudentWorks Plus CD-ROM
- Media Workshop DVD
- Online Student Edition

Learning Objectives

For pages 832–839

In this workshop, you will focus on the following objective:

Writing: Analyzing a poem to demonstrate understanding of the poem's meaning and appreciation of the effects that create that meaning.

> **Writing Process**
>
> At any stage of a writing process, you may think of new ideas to include and better ways to express them. Feel free to return to and revise earlier stages as you write.
>
> **Prewrite**
>
> **Draft**
>
> **Revise**
>
> Focus Lesson: Word Choice
>
> **Edit & Proofread**
>
> Focus Lesson: Embedding Quotations in Text
>
> **Present**

Writing Workshop

Literary Analysis

Literature Connection In this passage, John F. Kennedy examines aspects of Frost's character revealed through his poetry in order to honor Frost's achievement as a whole.

> *"[Robert Frost's] sense of the human tragedy fortified him against self-deception and easy consolation. 'I have been' he wrote, 'one acquainted with the night.' And because he knew the midnight as well as the high noon, because he understood the ordeal as well as the triumph of the human spirit, he gave his age strength with which to overcome despair."*
>
> —John F. Kennedy, from *"Remarks at Amherst College"*

Similarly, in a literary analysis, you examine the parts of a text to understand better the meaning of the text as a whole. The checklist below will help you learn the goals and strategies for writing a successful literary analysis of a poem.

Checklist: Features of Literary Analysis Essays

Goals	Strategies
To demonstrate understanding of a poem	☑ Analyze the form, language, meter, sound devices, or other aspects of a poem
	☑ Adopt and maintain a third-person point of view
To state a clear, insightful thesis	☑ State your own perspective on the meaning of the poem
	☑ Maintain a consistent focus throughout your essay
To support your thesis	☑ Quote directly from the poem to support your main ideas
	☑ Make substantial, specific, and relevant references to the poem
To use effective words and syntax	☑ Use precise, effective language
	☑ Vary sentences

Assignment: Analyze a Poem

Analyze a poem to interpret its meaning and write a literary analysis of about 1,500 words that explains how various techniques help create that meaning. Write with your audience and purpose in mind.

Audience: peers, classmates, and teachers familiar with the poem

Purpose: to demonstrate an understanding of the poem's meaning and an appreciation of the effects that create that meaning

Analyze a Professional Model

In his expository literary analysis, Lawrence Raab argues that Robert Frost's "Mending Wall" is less about revealing a particular meaning than showing the reader *how* to find meaning. As you read the analysis, pay attention to the comments in the margin. They point out features that you might want to include in your own literary analysis.

From **"Robert Frost's 'Mending Wall'"** by Lawrence Raab ☆

"Mending Wall" opens with a riddle: "Something there is . . ." And a riddle, after all, is a series of hints calculated to make us imagine and then name its hidden subject. The poem doesn't begin, "I hate walls," or even, "Something dislikes a wall." Its first gesture is one of elaborate and playful concealment, a calculated withholding of meaning. Notice also that it is the speaker himself who repairs the wall after the hunters have broken it. And it is the speaker each year who notifies his neighbor when the time has come to meet and mend the wall. Then can we safely claim that the speaker views the wall simply as a barrier between human contact and understanding?

Speaker and neighbor work together and equally. Although the job is tedious and hard, the speaker considers it "just another kind of outdoor game / One on a side." He acknowledges that his whimsical spell—"Stay where you are until our backs are turned!"'—is useless, and that the result is impermanent and perhaps less important than something else. For all practical purposes this particular wall is not needed. But the project of mending it has taken on significance: "Spring is the mischief in me, and I wonder / If I could put a notion in his head . . ."

The speaker's mischievous impulse is to plant an idea. He does not say that he wants to change his neighbor's mind, to make him believe

Real-World Connection

In the real world, whether you are making a recommendation for acquiring a business, advocating for a patient's care, or recommending a new dish for a menu, you are using the same skills you will practice in this workshop: explaining and supporting an opinion.

Introduction/Point of View

Engage your reader with an interesting introduction. State your own fresh perspective on the poem. Maintain the third-person point of view throughout your analysis.

Support

Use direct quotations from the poem to support your analysis.

 Literature Online

Writing and Research For prewriting, drafting, and revising tools, go to glencoe.com and enter QuickPass code GLA9800u5.

WRITING WORKSHOP **833**

📝 Writing Workshop

Teach

Big Idea

New Poetics Remind students that in this unit they have encountered poems that, when first published, pushed the boundaries of subject matter, form, and style. Other poems are more traditional. In their analyses, students should comment on the poems' relationship to tradition.

Writing Skills

Analyze a Professional Model Point out that one important way to become a better writer is to identify and imitate the practices of good writers. Have students bring in good writing models, similar to the Raab piece, that they find on their own.

Literary History ☆

Lawrence Raab Tell students that Raab is a respected poet who also teaches at Williams College in Massachusetts. A collection of his poems, titled *What We Don't Know About Each Other*, was a finalist for a National Book Award. This essay comes from *Touchstone: American Poets on a Favorite Poem* (1996).

Teach

Writing Skills

Purpose Point out that Raab uses the present tense in his analysis (for example, "He <u>does</u> not say that he <u>wants</u> to change his neighbor's mind"). Tell students that, in general, it is best to use the present tense in discussing authors' or characters' actions in works of literature. **Ask:** Why might the present tense be preferable in such cases? *(Possible answer: A work's actions are renewed as each reader experiences it.)*

Vivid Verbs Many students overuse the verb *to be*. Point out that Raab is not afraid to use *is* but also uses other verbs. **Ask:** What are some of his phrases with strong verbs? *(Possible answers: "nudge . . . imagination"; "irks the speaker"; "lures the unwary reader")*

Writer's Technique ☆

Direct Statement Point out the writer's statement of what he finds when he analyzes the poem: The poem is about thinking.

Purpose

Reflect your understanding of the poem by explaining its complexities and revealing its subtle meanings.

Command of Language

Vary sentences; use precise, effective language.

Purpose

Focus on specific literary elements—such as the speaker's point of view—and other unique aspects of the text. Support your ideas with accurate, detailed references to the poem.

Literary Analysis

Explain how quotations and examples support your major points.

Conclusion

Summarize your thesis in the conclusion and leave the reader with something to ponder.

---

what he himself believes. He wants to nudge the neighbor's imagination, just as a teacher might wish to challenge a student. So he asks questions: " '*Why* do they make good neighbors? Isn't it / Where there are cows? But here there are no cows.' " But the neighbor is unwilling to play this game of teacher and student. He won't answer the questions, or consider the riddle. . . .

This is the poem's essential challenge, which the neighbor will not accept. But the challenge is ours as well—our work, our play. The relationship between speaker and neighbor is like the relationship between poem and reader, another kind of indoor game, one on a side.

But this is a relationship between poem and reader, not poet and reader. Frost, I want to believe, is not the speaker *exactly*. He is behind the whole poem, rather than narrowly inside it. We need to be at least a little skeptical of the speaker and not associate him automatically with the side of upholding freedom, reason, and tolerance. At the end, because the neighbor won't play his game, the speaker imagines him as "an old-stone savage," a harsh judgment to apply even to the most recalcitrant student. Because the neighbor will only repeat what he remembers his father having said, he seems to "move in darkness . . . Not of woods only and the shade of trees." . . . It's his refusal to be playful and imaginative that irks the speaker, and his unwillingness to consider work as anything more than a job to be accomplished. The speaker, after all, does not ask the neighbor to give up his father's notion. He wants him to "go behind" it. If, as I want to suggest, the poem is about education, this distinction is important. The poem does not merely advocate one position over another. It asks neither for advocacy nor for application, but for investigation. It is not a statement but a performance. It enacts its meanings. . . .

"Mending Wall" is a poem that lures the unwary reader into believing that thinking is merely voting, choosing up sides, taking out of the poem what most fits our own preconceived ideas. It adopts this subversive tactic because its ultimate purpose is to challenge us to go behind what we might find initially appealing in the formulas that lie on its surface. "We ask people to think," Frost says, "and we don't show them what thinking is." "Mending Wall" is less a poem about what to think than it is a poem about what thinking is, and where it might lead. ☆

Reading-Writing Connection Think about the writing techniques you just encountered and try them out in the literary analysis you write.

Reading Practice

Speaker vs. Author Raab writes, "Frost, I want to believe, is not the speaker *exactly*." Help students understand the difference between a speaker or narrator and an author by asking them to think about clear-cut cases. **Say:** Look back at the biographical note about Arna Bontemps (page 824). Decide whether he is the speaker in the poem "A black man talks of reaping" on page 826. *(No, Bontemps was not a sharecropper.)*

Prewrite

Choose a Poem to Analyze Select a poem in this unit you find challenging and would like to understand better. Review your purpose and audience, and make a time frame for completing each stage of your writing process.

Explore Your Poem Explore the techniques used in the poem:

▶ Paraphrase the poem's general meaning. Then focus on specific words, punctuation, sounds, and figures of speech. Analyze how these elements contribute to the meaning. Then reread the poem.

▶ Focus on smaller sections of the poem in detail. Explore the images in each section and think about how they bring out the poet's message.

Analyze the Elements A chart like the one below can help you work out your analysis and can serve as evidence to support your thesis. ☆

Poem	"I, Too" by Langston Hughes
Form	5 stanzas; 18 lines
Rhyme Scheme	unrhymed
Repetition	Lines nearly repeat: "When company comes" (lines 4 and 10) and "eat in the kitchen" (lines 3 and 13).
Imagery	image of eating in kitchen in stanzas 2 and 3
Figurative Language	"I, too, sing America" (line 1); "I, too, am America" (line 18)
Speaker/ Characters	African American speaker; "They" (Americans excluding African Americans)
Tone	Confident in stanzas 1, 2, 3, 5; doubting in stanza 4
Theme	The speaker wants not only to be able to participate in what "America" is but also to be admired and seen as an individual.

Clarify Your Thesis Look at your analysis chart and decide which elements are most important in the poem you chose. Then examine your notes and sum up your interpretation of the poem in a thesis statement, explaining how literary elements contribute to the theme.

Make a Plan Use the elements in your chart to support your thesis. Organize your points so your analysis follows a logical, effective order.

Exposition

Every Word Counts

Poets choose each word in a poem specifically to give the poem meaning and impact. Always look for multiple meanings of a word and note how different meanings may enhance or complicate the meaning of the poem.

Avoid Plagiarism

If you consult outside sources to do this assignment, remember that work in both digital and print sources is usually copyrighted, which means that the author has the exclusive right to reproduce or recreate the work. Fair use laws allow you to copy small parts of a copyrighted work as long as you give complete and accurate credit to your sources.

Organization of Major Points

Use a graphic organizer to help you organize your body paragraphs.

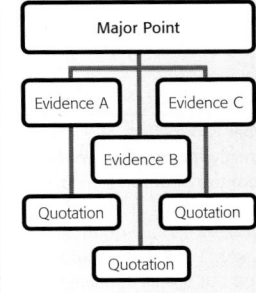

WRITING WORKSHOP **835**

Teach

Writing Process

Prewrite Model for students how they might mark up a copy of a poem under analysis. On an overhead transparency, show how an active reader underlines or checks key ideas, circles critical phrases, draws lines or arrows to connect related ideas, places a question mark beside confusing text, and so on.

(APPROACHING) Modify the instruction "think about a poem in this unit" by asking students to choose one of three poems that you have copied and to annotate it as part of their analysis.

Literary History ☆

Allusion On the next page, the workshop model calls Langston Hughes's "I, Too" (page 812) a response to Walt Whitman's "I Hear America Singing." A more literary term for Hughes's nod to Whitman's poem is *allusion*. Therefore, a student analyzing the Hughes poem might add a row labeled "Allusion" or "Other Literary Techniques" to a chart like the sample on this page.

English Learners

DIFFERENTIATED INSTRUCTION

SMALL GROUP **Intermediate** When students are writing their drafts, have them concentrate on recording their ideas on paper. Then have them read their drafts to a partner. Have them discuss the writer's intent and whether the listener has understood the point of the article. Instruct students to make helpful comments to each other and ask useful questions. Make sure students record any helpful ideas they receive. When they start revising, have them use these comments to help them clarify their work. Then have students read their essays to each other again. This time have them focus on their transitions. Have students discuss any problematic transitions and suggest improvements to each other.

Teach

Writing Process

Draft Here's what Lawrence Raab says to his Williams students about drafting: "Write your opening paragraph last, after you've discovered the ideas of your essay. Use the opening paragraph to get things started in an interesting way—with a provocative sentence, perhaps, or a challenging question. . . ." After students read the workshop model, ask volunteers to suggest alternative openings.

Writing Skills

Thesis/Point of View

Answer: *It gives an overall interpretation of the poem's meaning. The writer appears to agree with the thesis and is using a third-person point of view.*

Purpose

Answer: *The writer understands Whitman's poem, so he knows what Hughes means when he says that he, too, would like the opportunity to see himself as part of America, just as Whitman had. The writer discusses Whitman's reference to diversity, and shows how, ironically, Whitman's world does not include Hughes.*

Support

Answer: *The quotation supports the writer's point that the poem's speaker is part of America, yet different. The writer has woven the quote into a sentence. The line numbers in parentheses refer to specific lines in the poem.*

Writing Frames

As you read the workshop model, think about the writer's use of the following frames:

- The poem reflects _____.

- _____ can be interpreted as _____.

- The _____ stanza of the poem describes/shifts/continues _____.

- The speaker expresses/describes/wants/seems _____.

Consider using frames like these in your own literary analysis.

Thesis/Point of View

What makes this thesis effective? What is the writer's point of view?

Purpose

How does the writer demonstrate understanding of the poem? What unique aspect of the text or universal theme does the writer discuss?

Support

What is the effect of directly quoting the words from the poem here? How has the writer created coherence while quoting? How has the writer attributed the primary source?

Draft

Use Your Plan as a Guide Organize your main points in a straightforward way in the body of your essay, supporting each point with direct evidence from the poem. Explain the significance of quotations and examples and make clear how they support your thesis.

Analyze a Workshop Model

Here is the final draft of a literary analysis essay. Use your answers to the questions in the margins to guide you as you write your essay.

Part of America: Langston Hughes's "I, Too"

Langston Hughes's poem "I, Too" comments on the past, present, and possible future treatment of African Americans in the United States. The poem reflects the speaker's desire not only to be able to participate in what America is but also to be recognized as an individual, as part of the very definition of America.

Hughes's poem can be read as a direct response to Walt Whitman's poem "I Hear America Singing." Whitman writes about America's diversity by describing how each individual sings a unique song. In "I, Too" the speaker's response is a wish to be recognized as one of those individual voices. The opening line of the poem, set apart for emphasis, suggests a direct reply to Whitman. "I, too, sing America," proclaims the speaker, pleading for attention and recognition and wondering why he was excluded from Whitman's poetic list of Americans (line 1).

The second stanza of the poem describes the speaker's current situation. The line "I am the darker brother" implies that there is a relation to the rest of America, but by describing the speaker as "darker," Hughes identifies the speaker as an African American (line 2). Hughes describes an ambiguous "they" who send the speaker away "when company comes," segregating and hiding him from other people (lines 3, 4). Although he is shoved aside, he attempts to make the best of his situation by laughing, eating, and getting stronger (lines 5–7). Hughes illustrates how, even when they are being discounted, African Americans remain optimistic, knowing that a better future lies ahead.

836 UNIT 5

Vocabulary Practice

Multiple Meanings Six lines from the bottom of this page, the essay writer uses the word *ambiguous* to describe "they"— the people who "send [the speaker] to eat in the kitchen." Invite students to find two meanings of *ambiguous*. **Ask:** Which of the two meanings does the writer of the essay have in mind? *(One meaning is "having two or more possible meanings"; another is "not clear; indefinite; vague"—synonymous with* obscure. *Most students will decide that the writer of the essay is using* ambiguous *with the second meaning.)*

In the third stanza the speaker speculates on how the treatment of African Americans will change "Tomorrow." To highlight this shift, the speaker repeats the main image of the second stanza and follows a similar structure in both stanzas. The turning point, "When company comes," from line 4 is repeated exactly in line 10 but to a different effect. In the third stanza, the speaker looks forward to the day when he will sit at the table with everybody else, in a time when nobody will even consider telling him to "'Eat in the kitchen'" (line 13). In this stanza, Hughes cements the symbolism of "the table," which represents the basic rights and freedoms of a participating American.

In the fourth stanza the speaker further speculates on the changes the future will bring for African Americans. The three-line structure of this stanza sharply diverges from the structure of other stanzas, and the "Besides" introduces this stanza as an aside that similarly diverges from the main text of the poem (lines 15–17). In this stanza, the speaker shifts from affirming that "they" will allow him (and all African Americans) to participate, or "eat at the table," to affirming that "they" will eventually recognize him as *beautiful* and be ashamed of their past treatment of him (line 16–17). Therefore, the speaker wants—and expects—not only to be allowed to share the same freedoms and liberties as other American citizens, to participate in what "America" is, but also to be admired and seen as an individual. Line 17 ends abruptly with a dash, however, suggesting that the speaker suddenly doubts his own statement. This dash serves to undercut the proud, confident, determined tone of the speaker in the first three stanzas, each of which ends with a period. The speaker seems to acknowledge that the future he described may not happen.

With the final line, Hughes brings the poem full circle, concluding with "I, too, am America" (line 18). This line, in effect, repeats the opening of the poem, lending a sense of symmetry and closure to the whole. The speaker is not just participating in ("singing") America; he is also a part of it—he *is* America. Yet even this confident closing line cannot erase the hint of doubt from the preceding line. Placing the final line in the present tense, as if it were already true, emphasizes the pain behind the statement, as well as the insistence on strength and hope, even as "Tomorrow" seems further and further away.

Exposition

Organization
How is this essay organized, and why is this method effective?

Command of Language
Where is the language most effective or precise? How do the sentences vary?

Purpose
Why might the writer address the form of the poem here? How do the evidence and explanation support the writer's thesis?

Focus
How does the writer maintain a consistent focus?

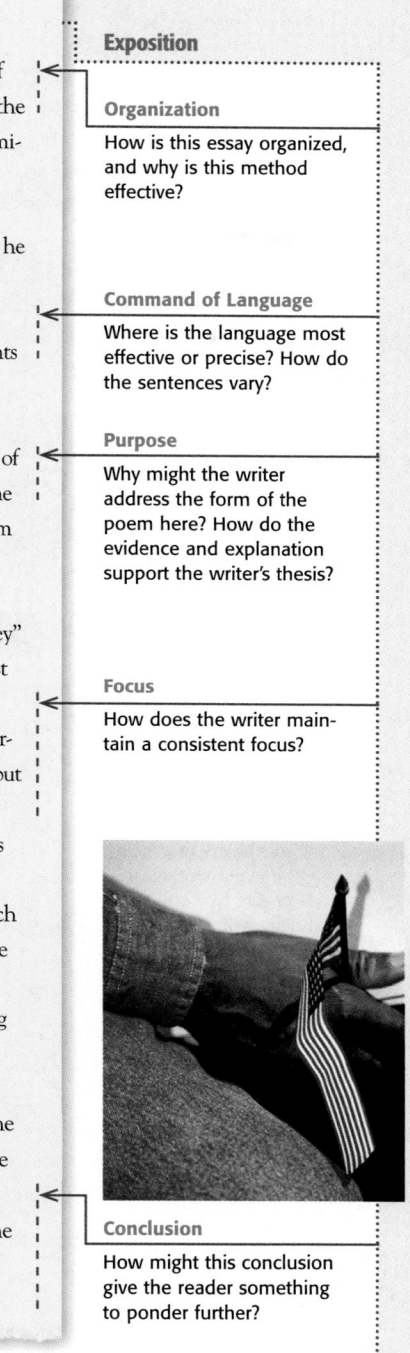

Conclusion
How might this conclusion give the reader something to ponder further?

Teach

Writing Skills

Organization/Appreciation
Answer: *It treats the poem's stanzas in order. The organization is effective because the writer's analysis points out the structure of the poem.*

Command of Language
Answer: *When the speaker of the poem talks about the possibilities of a better life in the future.*

Purpose
Answer: *The fourth stanza has a structure different from that of the preceding two stanzas. The writer supports the thesis that the speaker wants to be part of America.*

Focus
Answer: *It explains the basic motivation that underlies the speaker's statements in the poem.*

Conclusion
Answer: *It might make the reader wonder how much the situation of African Americans has changed since the poem was written.*

Approaching Level

DIFFERENTIATED INSTRUCTION

Emerging Raab suggests that students write their opening paragraph last.
Ask: How might you be able to start with your second paragraph before writing your first paragraph? *(Students may say that you can choose one line or stanza to write about; they may say that you can have an idea about your first paragraph, but still not write it until* later.*)* Have students examine the second paragraphs of the analyses of Frost's and Hughes's poem. Have them create a list of words and phrases they might use in the second paragraph of their essay.
Ask: What words in these paragraphs might be useful in analyzing any poem? *(speaker, considers, acknowledges, result, impermanent, important, practical, par-* *ticular, significance; interpreted, response, describing, recognized, voices, opening, line, emphasis, suggests, proclaims, pleading, wondering)* As students write their essays, remind them to use the words from the list.

Literary Analysis

Teach

Writing Process

Revise Remind students that as peer reviewers they should be coaches and cheerleaders as much as finders of errors. They should keep in mind that finding positive things to say about a classmate's writing is just as helpful as finding weaknesses.

Writing Skills

Conciseness Review the thesis statement in the workshop model on page 836. Ask students to contrast that sentence with the following one: "In this essay, I am going to talk about the main idea that I think is underlying this poem, which is the speaker's desire not only to be able to participate in what America is but also to be recognized as an individual, as part of the very definition of America."

Traits of Strong Writing

Include these traits of strong writing to express your ideas effectively.

Ideas
Organization
Voice
Word Choice
Sentence Fluency
Conventions
Presentation

For more information on using the Traits of Strong Writing, see pages R30–R32.

Word Choice

This academic vocabulary word appears in the student model:

individual (in´ də vij´ wəl, -vi´ jə wəl, -vi´ jū əl,) *n.* 1. one human being; 2. a person or thing existing in contrast to the group of which it may form a part; *The poem reflects the speaker's desire to be recognized as an individual.* Using academic vocabulary may help strengthen your writing. Try to use one or two academic vocabulary words in your literary analysis. See the complete list on pages R89–R91.

LOG ON ▶ **Literature** Online

Writing and Research For editing and publishing tools, go to glencoe.com and enter QuickPass code GLA9800u5.

Revise

Peer Review Exchange your finished draft with that of a partner to identify the strengths and weaknesses of each draft. Use the checklist below to evaluate and strengthen each other's writing.

Checklist

- ☑ Do you analyze the techniques in the poem to show how they contribute to the poem's meaning?
- ☑ Do you state your interpretation in a concise thesis statement?
- ☑ Do you explain subtle details and reveal complex meanings?
- ☑ Do you support your thesis with quotations and examples from the poem?
- ☑ Do you organize your response to literature in a logical, coherent way?
- ☑ Do you maintain a consistent point of view and focus?

Focus Lesson

Sharpen the Precision of Word Choice

In your essay, help your readers understand your ideas by replacing abstract statements with precise words and vivid examples.

Draft:

The poem, however, shifts toward a sense of doubt, suggesting that the speaker and his views have changed. The tone and the punctuation in the final stanza contribute to this effect.

Revision:

Line 17 ends abruptly with a dash,[1] however, suggesting that the speaker suddenly doubts his own statement.[2] This dash serves to undercut the proud, confident, determined tone of stanzas 1–3.[3]

1: Be concise and concrete.
2: Give specific rather than general explanations.
3: Replace vague examples with vivid, precise examples.

Writing Practice

Abstract vs. Concrete Nouns To give students practice in switching from abstract to concrete nouns (and vice versa), ask for concrete nouns to replace abstract nouns 1–3 below and for abstract nouns to replace concrete nouns 4–6. *Possible answers:*

1. warmth *(stove)*
2. poverty *(rags)*
3. insight *(teacher)*
4. motorcycle *(swiftness)*
5. laughter *(humor)*
6. eye *(insight)*

Edit and Proofread

Get It Right Proofread your draft for errors in grammar, usage, and spelling. Refer to the Language Handbook, pages R42–R61, as a guide.

> **Focus Lesson**
>
> ### Embed Quotations in Text
>
> Much of your direct evidence will be in the form of quotations embedded in your analysis. Place quotation marks around each quotation. Set off the quotation and line reference with commas.
>
> **Problem:** Direct evidence is not set off in quotation marks and is not set off with commas from the introductory remarks.
>
> *The turning point when company comes (line 4) is repeated.*
>
> **Solution:** Place quotation marks around the quotation and set off with commas the quotation from the surrounding remarks.
>
> *The turning point, "When company comes" (line 4), is repeated.* ☆
>
> **Problem:** Quotation marks include material not in the quotation.
>
> *Hughes describes an ambiguous "they who send the speaker away when company comes," hiding him from others (lines 3, 4).*
>
> **Solution:** Place quotation marks around only quoted material, using two or more sets of quotation marks if necessary.
>
> *Hughes describes an ambiguous "they" who send the speaker away "when company comes," hiding him from others (lines 3, 4).*

Present

The Final Touch Make sure your analysis is typed in a legible font and type size, with reasonable margins and spacing. If you are writing your analysis by hand, use clear, legible handwriting. Check with your teacher about any additional presentation guidelines.

Quoting Poetry

When you quote poetry, be sure to give the line numbers (rather than page numbers) in parentheses after each quotation. Use a slash (/) to indicate a line break. Example:

"Tomorrow, / I'll be at the table" (lines 8–9)

Peer Review Tips

A classmate may ask you to read his or her analysis. Jot down notes as you read so you can give constructive feedback. Use the following questions to get started:

- What is the writer's thesis? How well does the evidence support it?

- Does the writer increase your understanding of or appreciation for the poem and the author's style?

- Where has the writer used fresh, vivid language and rhetorical devices?

Word-Processing Tip

Select the header or footer option to number your pages. Put the number in the upper right-hand corner of the header, or center it in the footer.

Writer's Portfolio

Place a clean copy of your literary analysis in your portfolio to review later.

Advanced Learners

DIFFERENTIATED INSTRUCTION

Research Have students do independent research to find additional poems by the author of the poem they have chosen. Have them read and analyze these poems and use the information and understanding they gain about the author and the author's style and tone in their essay. As they write, instruct students to make use of a variety of techniques for providing supportive details, such as analogies, anecdotes, restatements, paraphrases, examples, and comparisons.

Teach

Writing Process

Edit and Proofread Alert students to the special care that even professional writers must take with quotation marks:

- Every opening quotation mark requires a closing quotation mark.
- In the United States, commas and periods almost always go inside closing quotation marks.

Remind students of the rules for capitalizing the titles of short stories, books, and articles. They should demonstrate correct capitalization when referencing works of literature in their papers. For additional support, see the Language Handbook, pages R55 and R58.

Language History ☆

Word Generalization Explain to students that one way word meanings have developed over time is through the process known as generalization—words that once had narrow meanings have taken on broader meanings. The word *company*, for example, can refer to a group of people or to a commercial enterprise. See whether students, using a good dictionary (perhaps the *Oxford English Dictionary* if a print or online edition is available), can figure out which meaning of *company* came first and which arose as a result of generalization.

Focus

Summary

In this workshop, students will plan, rehearse, and present an oral interpretation of a poem.

Teach

Speaking Skills

Keep Listeners on Track Remind students that just as they aim for coherence in their writing, they need, as speakers, to signal listeners when they move from one part of an oral presentation to another part. Discuss signals that speakers can use:

- pauses
- changes in posture, position, and tone of voice

 For help with creating presentations, see Student Presentation Builder on StudentWorks Plus.

Reading Practice

Scansion Remind students that to scan a line of poetry is to determine its meter or rhythm. Have students copy their poems and mark the stressed syllables with acute accents or capital letters and the unstressed syllables with breves or lowercase letters. Have them scan the lines from Claude McKay's "If We Must Die" on this page as practice. Note that some lines of poetry can be scanned in different ways—as in these two readings of line 1:

IF we must DIE, let it NOT be like HOGS

If WE must DIE, let it not BE like HOGS

Using Background Information

You can draw information from a poet's background into your interpretation. For example, many critics felt that T. S. Eliot's poem "The Love Song of J. Alfred Prufrock" reflected Eliot's sense of the growing alienation of modern industry. Elements such as economics, race, or politics can all influence a poet's work.

Speaking, Listening, and Viewing Workshop

Oral Interpretation of a Poem

Literature Connection Some poems, such as "Chicago," practically jump off the page into a setting and swing into action. Other poems, like "Stopping by Woods on a Snowy Evening," more subtly suggest a realm of actions—or inaction. All poems, however, can be the subject of dramatic interpretation—through music, movement, and images, as well as new words. In this workshop, you will work alone or with others to orally interpret a poem from this unit as a dramatic performance.

> **Assignment** Plan and deliver an oral interpretation of the subject of your literary analysis or another poem from this unit.

Plan Your Presentation

Follow these steps to get started:

Choose a poem and a purpose. Select a poem for your presentation, keeping in mind a workable length. For example, you might want something a bit longer than "This Is Just to Say," or you might want to excerpt stanzas from a long poem such as "The Love Song of J. Alfred Prufrock." Then select a purpose for your presentation, such as portraying the speaker, revealing or emphasizing the theme, expressing the mood, or recreating the musicality or lyricism of the poem.

Choose a type of oral interpretation or performance. Options for your oral interpretation include presenting a dramatic reading of the poem. If the poem has narrative elements, you might act them out instead. You might also use moving images, a computer slide presentation, and sound effects to interpret the poem in some way.

Consider audience and occasion. After you select a type of performance, carefully identify your audience and the site of your performance. Factors to consider include the size of the room and the technology you may or may not have available. Ask yourself how people might be seated and what kind of screen, stage, or other presentation space you will require for everyone to be able to see and hear easily. Think about the occasion, too. Is this to be an ordinary classroom performance, or will you perform for parents, other classes, or other guests?

Develop Your Presentation

To engage your audience, follow these guidelines:

- Open dramatically in order to capture your audience's attention from the first moment. For example, use sound effects that lure or jangle; a tone that startles or beguiles; or images that provoke or entertain.
- Create visual interest throughout your presentation:
  Computer slide show: Use elements of design, such as color, rules, shading, and other effects, to create interest.
  Dramatic reading: Make a backdrop, or bring in props to add interest.
  Audio broadcast: Consider projecting images your audience can watch as they listen.
  Adopting the persona of the speaker: Use a costume or makeup.
- Use your voice to its fullest effect. In a dramatic reading, use tone and volume to maximize, minimize, sugar-coat, or acidify meaning.
- Provide a satisfying and obvious sense of closure. Think carefully about your final words, pose, sound effect, bar of music, or image.

Rehearse

Rehearse your oral interpretation or dramatic presentation by performing it aloud on your own and then performing it for a small group. As you ask for feedback, keep the speaking techniques below in mind. As you offer feedback to others, keep the listening techniques below in mind.

Techniques for Dramatic Presentations

Speaking Techniques	Listening Techniques
☑ **Use Audience Feedback** Study the expressions on your listeners' faces for feedback that may tell you, for example, to slow down the rate of the images or to reduce the volume of the music or sound effects.	☑ **Focus** Look directly at the performers and images and concentrate on what they convey.
☑ **Volume** Adjust your volume to the size of your audience: no one should feel as if you're shouting for no reason, and no one should strain to hear you.	☑ **Respond** Show interest by responding to various effects as well as through upright posture and other posture that says, clearly, "I'm with you."
☑ **Entertain** Let go of the everyday you to slip into the role of performer.	☑ **Evaluate** Identify the most successful parts or aspects of the presentation.

Presentation Tips
Use the following checklist to evaluate your oral interpretation:

- Did you engage and entertain your audience from beginning to end?
- Did you achieve your purpose of conveying one central aspect of the poem?
- Did your oral interpretation suit the performance space and the occasion?

Listening Tips
Use the following checklist to evaluate your listening and viewing skills:

- Did you focus directly on the performance, showing respect and interest through focused attention and body language?
- Did you respond appropriately?
- Did you correctly interpret the purpose of the performance?
- Did you identify weaknesses and strengths of the performance?

Teach

Speaking Skills

Eye Contact Some presenters select a few individuals to make eye contact with while speaking; they move their eyes from one person to another and then back to the first again. Other presenters look at large areas of the audience, perhaps *slowly* moving their eyes (and their head) from the left side of the audience to the middle, to the right, and then back through the middle to the left. Ask students who have had prior experience speaking in public what they prefer to do with their eyes.

Listening Skills

Eye Contact Explain that good listeners, even when taking notes, try to make eye contact with presenters. Not only are they supporting the speakers, but by keeping themselves on task, these listeners are also guarding against losing their concentration. Ask for other suggestions on how listeners can make themselves concentrate on speakers.

Writing

After the students have recited their poems, have them write a reflection evaluating their preparation and the experience of speaking in front of an audience.

Intermediate To help English learners with pronunciation, intonation, and phrasing, read aloud—or provide an audio recording of—one or more poems to demonstrate techniques for oral interpretation. Reread each poem several times, demonstrating possible differences in the reading. First have students listen without the text in front of them, and then during the second or third reading, with the text in front of them. Then have students take turns reading the same poem after you, first to the group and then again in pairs for more practice.

Independent Reading

Focus

Summary

The purpose of Independent Reading is to encourage students to read novels from the time period that they have learned about in this unit, as well as recent novels that have been influenced by the period.

Teach

Cultural History ☆

From Book to Screen Many of the novels featured here have been adapted at least once for motion pictures or TV:

- *The Age of Innocence:* 1924, 1934, 1993
- *Their Eyes Were Watching God:* 2005
- *Ethan Frome:* 1993
- *All Quiet on the Western Front:* 1930, 1979
- *Heat and Dust:* 1983

If students have seen any of these, they may offer opinions on the pros and cons of adaptations.

Book Group Have students who read the same novel on their own discuss it as a group while the rest of the class listens. Instruct them to prepare discussion questions, follow a novel-discussion template that you provide, or select topics from publishers' discussion guides available in some versions of novels or online. After the discussion, have the listeners provide feedback to the group.

842

Independent Reading

The Modern Novel

MANY POST–WORLD WAR I WRITERS SAW THE WAR AS AN INDICATION OF the failure of the old ways and began to explore new subject matter, styles, and themes. As women marched and protested for the right to vote, stories focusing on women's lives began to reveal their struggles. Edith Wharton immerses readers in a world of scandal and deceit in the lives of the wealthy. Zora Neale Hurston creates a character of strength and passion who carves out a life of her own in a small town in the South. Ruth Prawer Jhabvala tells the story of a British woman in India whose independence leads to scandal and exile. The early twentieth century saw the acceptance of America into the literary conversation, with both women and men recognized for their contributions.

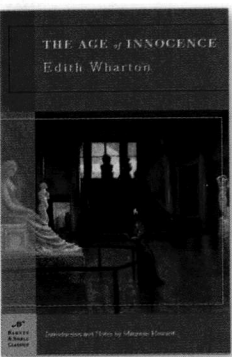

The Age of Innocence

Edith Wharton

Through the story of a doomed love, Edith Wharton presents an illuminating study of New York society in the 1870s. In an ideal match, worldly and wealthy Newland Archer is engaged to young and beautiful May Welland, a member of the same elite social circle. However, the presence of May's cousin, the exotic and aristocratic Ellen Olenska, disrupts the couple's perfect union. Wharton was awarded a Pulitzer Prize for this story of Archer's struggle between passion and society's conventions.

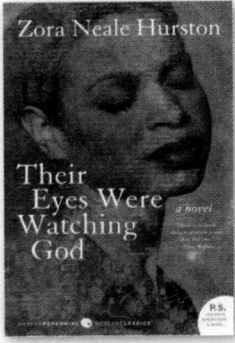

Their Eyes Were Watching God

Zora Neale Hurston

Janie Crawford journeys toward self-identity and love in Zora Neale Hurston's most famous novel. Hurston vividly captures the lives and aspirations of African American men and women in 1930s Florida. When the book was first published, Hurston was criticized for her use of southern dialect. Some critics believed it promoted black stereotypes. When the novel regained popularity in the 1970s, however, she was praised for her honest presentation of African American women. Oprah Winfrey produced a film version of the novel in 2005 starring Halle Berry.

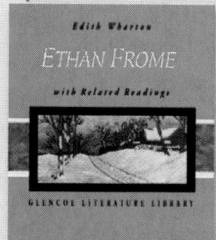

Ethan Frome
Edith Wharton

A tragic love triangle between the title character, his ailing wife, and her young cousin.

The Souls of Black Folk
W.E.B. DuBois

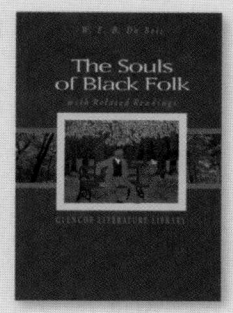

A guide for early twentieth-century black protest, these essays are essential to an understanding of African American history and the Civil Rights struggle.

All Quiet on the Western Front
Erich Maria Remarque

A German soldier experiences the horrors of battle during World War I and later struggles to adjust upon his return home.

GLENCOE LITERATURE LIBRARY

CRITICS' CORNER

"Jhabvala is a connoisseur of divided souls, conceiving characters whose inner longings are at odds with their outer protective coloration – Indians who covet and achieve more tidy, "modernized" existences, then feel as if someone had stolen their life force; Westerners who eagerly hand themselves over to India's chaotic bliss, then find it too rigorous to endure."

—*The New York Times*, November 29, 1993

"With the exception of E. M. Forster, no 20th-century writer has more eloquently described Westerners' attempts to grasp the ambiguities of Indian culture than Ruth Prawer Jhabvala."

—*The New York Times*, March 28, 1993

Heat and Dust
Ruth Prawer Jhabvala

Olivia is a beautiful and independent woman married to an important British official stationed in India in the 1920s. Inevitably, Olivia's free spirit clashes with the values of British colonial society.

Create a Book Jacket

Book jackets are designed to grab a potential reader's attention. Read one of the books listed on this page and design a new book jacket that will persuade your classmates to read it. Your book jacket should include a summary that does not reveal the ending, a description of the writer's style, and a short biography of the author with a picture if possible. Display your work for the class.

INDEPENDENT READING **843**

Approaching Level

DIFFERENTIATED INSTRUCTION

Emerging To encourage students in their reading, have them write response journals to connect the novel to their own lives. Possible questions for students to respond to include:

- How would you compare the characters to yourself, your family, and your friends?
- Could you be friends with any of the characters? Why or why not?
- How does your feeling about the book change as you read?
- How did you feel about the ending?
- What connections did you see between the book and your own life?
- What would you like to ask the author?

Independent Reading

Teach

Literary History

Ruth Prawer Jhabvala The author of *Heat and Dust*, which received the Booker Prize in 1975, is also a writer of screenplays. She won her first Oscar for her film adaptation of E. M. Forster's *A Room with a View*. Like her main character in *Heat and Dust*, Jhabvala knows what it means to live in a country where you were not born. She too moved to India from England when she married an Indian man in the early 1950s.

Book Jacket

Evaluate students' book jackets by considering the following:

- clearly stated summary
- effective use of details
- attention to grammar and spelling conventions

Glencoe Literature Library

Glencoe Literature Library offers an extensive collection of hardcover books that help you encourage your students to read independently. Choose among the more than 120 full-length literary works—novels, novellas, plays, and nonfiction. Each book includes related readings from a broad range of genres. Go to www.glencoe.com for more information.

Point out that some test takers can save time and better concentrate on reading a passage if they first scan the questions below the passage, whereas others, already familiar with the kinds of questions on a particular test, do not scan the questions first. **Say: Think about which approach will work for you.**

Teach

Assessment Tell students that this assessment is intended to reinforce general test-taking strategies as well as to test the skills and vocabulary covered in the unit. They will read a passage and answer comprehension and inference questions about it. They will read another short passage and answer ten paragraph-improvement questions. Finally, they will be asked to write a short persuasive essay.

Test Preparation Practice

Take Notes
Most reading tests ask questions about
- characters
- point of view
- plot
- theme
- setting

Students can prepare for such questions by tracking those elements while reading. Model how to take notes. Use the top half of a page for notes about characters, and divide the bottom half into four columns, one for each of the other elements. Direct students to take notes as they read "Early Autumn."

844

Assessment

English Language Arts

Reading: Short Stories

Carefully read the following passage. Use context clues to help you define any words with which you are unfamiliar. Pay close attention to the theme, use of literary devices, and tone. Then, on a separate sheet of paper, answer the questions on page 846.

Early Autumn by Langston Hughes

When Bill was very young, they had been in love. Many nights they had spent walking, talking together. Then something not very important had come between them, and they didn't speak.

5   Impulsively, she had married a man she thought she loved. Bill went away, bitter about women.

Yesterday, walking across Washington Square, she saw him for the first time in years.

"Bill Walker," she said.

10   He stopped. At first he did not recognize her, to him she looked so old.

"Mary! Where did you come from?"

Unconsciously, she lifted her face as though wanting a kiss, but he held out his hand. She took it.

15   "I live in New York now," she said.

"Oh"—smiling politely. Then a little frown came quickly between his eyes.

"Always wondered what happened to you, Bill."

20   "I'm a lawyer. Nice firm, way downtown."

"Married yet?"

"Sure. Two kids."

"Oh," she said.

A great many people went past them through
25   the park. People they didn't know. It was late afternoon. Nearly sunset. Cold.

"And your husband?" he asked her.

"We have three children. I work in the bursar's office at Columbia."

30   "You're looking very . . ." (he wanted to say
      old) ". . . well," he said.
          She understood. Under the trees in
      Washington Square, she found herself desperately
      reaching back into the past. She had been older than
35   he then in Ohio. Now she was not young at all. Bill
      was still young.
          "We live on Central Park West," she said.
      "Come and see us sometime."
          "Sure," he replied. "You and your husband
40   must have dinner with my family some night. Any
      night. Lucille and I'd love to have you."
          The leaves fell slowly from the trees in the
      Square. Fell without wind. Autumn dusk. She felt a
      little sick.
45   "We'd love it," she answered.
          "You ought to see my kids." He grinned.
          Suddenly the lights came on up the whole
      length of Fifth Avenue, chains of misty brilliance in
      the blue air.
50   "There's my bus," she said.
          He held out his hand, "Good-bye."
          "When . . . " she wanted to say, but the bus
      was ready to pull off. The lights on the avenue
      blurred, twinkled, blurred. And she was afraid to
55   open her mouth as she entered the bus. Afraid it
      would be impossible to utter a word.
          Suddenly she shrieked very loudly, "Good-
      bye!" But the bus door had closed.
          The bus started. People came between them
60   outside, people crossing the street, people they
      didn't know. Space and people. She lost sight of
      Bill. Then she remembered she had forgotten to
      give him her address—or to ask him for his—or tell
      him that her youngest boy was named Bill, too. **1**

Reading Strategy   **1**

Annotation An alternative
to taking notes in a chart during
a test is marking up a selection.
Advise students that they must not
write on test pages unless granted
permission to do so. **Ask: If you
could mark up the selection,
what might you write next to the
final line?** *(Possible responses:
"She still loves him!" "Wow,
I'm surprised." "How could she
forget?")*

Language History ☆

Fragments Acknowledge that
professional writers of fiction and
nonfiction do at times write sentence fragments—phrases that lack
subjects, predicates, or both—like
the two in line 43. Advertising copy
is also full of sentence fragments.
Caution students that most teachers and textbooks strongly advise
against the use of sentence fragments in essays written for class.

Approaching Level

DIFFERENTIATED INSTRUCTION

Established This piece of prose includes
many short speeches by both characters.
Tell students that authors use various
devices to help readers keep track of who
is speaking at each point in a back-and-
forth conversation:

- They begin a new paragraph when a different character begins speaking.
- They use tags such as "she said" or "he
  replied."
- They have one character use another
  character's name, as in "Always wondered
  what happened to you, Bill."

Assessment

Teach

Reading

1. D is the correct answer because options A and B are effects, not causes, and C is unrelated to their relationship. DOK1

2. A is the correct answer because Mary's love for Bill can be inferred from her actions, her disappointment at the end of the story, and because she named her youngest son Bill. DOK4

3. B is the correct answer because the relationship ended prematurely. DOK4

4. B is the correct answer because the paragraph describes the time, the temperature, and the strangers passing in the street. DOK2

5. B is the correct answer because she understands that Bill is pretending not to notice her departed youth. DOK2

6. A is the correct answer because the narrator says, "She had been older than he then in Ohio." DOK1

7. C is the correct answer because the narrator makes a direct comparison between rows of lights and "chains of misty brilliance." DOK2

8. D is the correct answer because *brilliance* in this context means "radiance, or great brightness." DOK1

9. C is the correct answer because the blurred lights suggest that Mary's eyes have begun to fill with tears. DOK4

10. C is the correct answer because *shrieked* strongly suggests hysterical emotion, while the other words are neutral. DOK2

1. Why did Bill and Mary end their relationship?
   - **A.** She impulsively married another man.
   - **B.** They stopped speaking.
   - **C.** They both moved to New York.
   - **D.** Something came between them.

2. Why do you think Mary unconsciously lifts her face as though wanting a kiss?
   - **A.** She is still in love with Bill.
   - **B.** She is unhappy to see Bill in New York.
   - **C.** She has momentarily forgotten the past.
   - **D.** She hopes to make Bill less bitter.

3. Of what is the title of the story most symbolic?
   - **A.** changing weather in New York
   - **B.** the changing of a relationship
   - **C.** the ages of Bill and Mary
   - **D.** the time of the meeting

4. To what element of the story does the paragraph beginning in line 24 contribute?
   - **A.** characters
   - **B.** setting
   - **C.** plot
   - **D.** conflict

5. What does Mary "understand" in line 32?
   - **A.** that Bill has a better life than hers
   - **B.** that Bill has noticed her age
   - **C.** that Bill is wealthy
   - **D.** that Bill is unhappy

6. Where did Mary and Bill first meet?
   - **A.** in Ohio
   - **B.** in Washington Square
   - **C.** in New York City
   - **D.** in Central Park

7. What literary element is most evident in the sentence beginning in line 47?
   - **A.** allusion
   - **B.** imagery
   - **C.** metaphor
   - **D.** simile

8. What does the word *brilliance* in line 48 mean?
   - **A.** intelligence
   - **B.** sharpness
   - **C.** preciousness
   - **D.** brightness

9. Why do you think Mary is "afraid it would be impossible to utter a word"?
   - **A.** She knows Bill is bitter toward women.
   - **B.** She is aware that Bill sees her as old.
   - **C.** She senses that they can no longer really communicate.
   - **D.** She thinks Bill will ignore her.

10. In the paragraph beginning in line 57, which is an example of connotative language?
    - **A.** very
    - **B.** closed
    - **C.** shrieked
    - **D.** good-bye

11. Of what are the "space and people" in line 61 most symbolic?
    - **A.** the emotional distance between Bill and Mary
    - **B.** Bill's and Mary's children and spouses
    - **C.** Bill and Mary's youthful relationship
    - **D.** the movement of the bus as it pulls away

12. In this passage, how does Hughes reveal the personality of Mary?
    - **A.** metaphor
    - **B.** symbolism
    - **C.** direct characterization
    - **D.** indirect characterization

13. From what point of view is this passage written?
    - **A.** first person
    - **B.** second person
    - **C.** third-person omniscient
    - **D.** third-person limited

14. What is the overall tone of this passage?
    - **A.** serious
    - **B.** humorous
    - **C.** mischievous
    - **D.** furious

846 UNIT 5 BEGINNINGS OF THE MODERN AGE

11. A is the correct answer because space and people (strangers) mirror Bill and Mary's alientation. DOK4

12. D is the correct answer because the author reveals Mary's personality through her actions, words, and thoughts. DOK2

13. C is the correct answer because the narrator knows what both characters think. DOK2

14. A is the correct answer because the tone suits the theme of lost love. DOK4

Vocabulary Skills: Sentence Completion

For each item in the Vocabulary Skills section, choose the best word or words to complete the sentence. Write your answers on a sheet of paper.

1. Ezra Pound believed that modern poetry should be built on the literature of the past and yet also _____.
   A. unique
   B. intimidated
   C. impeded
   D. haughty

2. Much of the U.S. public was _____ to the conflict in Europe until the United States entered the war.
   A. indifferent
   B. ingenious
   C. withered
   D. dutiful

3. Many critics were unimpressed by the bold declarations and _____ of some of the Modernist writers.
   A. piety
   B. hypocrisy
   C. brazenness
   D. snickers

4. The writers of the Harlem Renaissance refused to _____ themselves to second-class citizenship.
   A. jostle
   B. resign
   C. jilt
   D. exalt

5. In their writing, Imagists often tried to transform elements from the _____, everyday world into something remarkable.
   A. ominous
   B. mundane
   C. withered
   D. ingenious

6. With the spread of jazz came a great deal of _____ and disapproval among older people, who felt it was corrupting the youth.
   A. vanity
   B. piety
   C. patronage
   D. perturbation

7. The Jazz Age gradually eased, rather than _____, to a close as the Second World War approached.
   A. lurched
   B. exalted
   C. jilted
   D. jostled

8. There was a _____ on the face of many people in the United States on the day the stock market crashed.
   A. millennium
   B. snicker
   C. hemorrhage
   D. grimace

9. Many African Americans felt _____ and alienated from the mainstream culture in the United States.
   A. withered
   B. tactful
   C. dutiful
   D. detached

10. Many were impressed by E. E. Cummings's unusual and often _____ use of punctuation, grammar, and syntax.
    A. ominous
    B. withered
    C. scintillating
    D. tactful

Assess

Vocabulary Skills

1. **A** is the correct answer because it is the only option that makes sense in this context. (DOK 1)

2. **A** is the correct answer because it is the only option that makes sense with "to the conflict." (DOK 1)

3. **C** is the correct answer because the context suggests a synonym of *bold* is needed. (DOK 1)

4. **B** is the correct answer because it is the only option that makes sense in this context. (DOK 1)

5. **B** is the correct answer because the context suggests a synonym of *everyday* is needed. (DOK 1)

6. **D** is the correct answer because the context suggests a synonym of *disapproval* is needed. (DOK 1)

7. **A** is the correct answer because the context suggests an antonym of *eased* is needed. (DOK 1)

8. **D** is the correct answer because the stock market crash caused pain to many people. (DOK 1)

9. **D** is the correct answer because the context suggests a synonym of *alienated* is needed. (DOK 1)

10. **C** is the correct answer because it is the only option that makes sense in this context. (DOK 1)

English Learners

DIFFERENTIATED INSTRUCTION

Beginning The answers to some sentence-completion items are easier for students who have a good sense of which prepositions can idiomatically follow particular adjectives, nouns, and verbs. Give students practice in supplying the preposition that belongs in each blank:

admittance _____ the fair *(to)*
capable _____ great evil *(of)*
hinges _____ test results *(on)*
marred _____ a gash *(by)*
protest _____ authorities *(against)*
repent _____ a crime *(of)*
thrilled _____ the award *(by)*

847

Assessment

Assess

Grammar and Writing Skills

1. **C** is the correct answer because it sets off the three predicate nominative phrases with commas and encloses the words from the poem in quotation marks. (**DOK2**)

2. **B** is the correct answer because it is the only option that maintains consistency of verb tenses by using the present-tense verb *is*. (**DOK1**)

3. **A** is the correct answer because the sentence incorrectly joins two independent clauses with a comma. (**DOK2**)

Paragraph Improvement Remind students that unless one of the choices offered in sentence-improvement questions is either "NO CHANGE," or is a repetition of the sentence as it was written in the text, they must decide what is wrong with the sentence or paragraph in question. Having a clear idea where the error lies will help them quickly eliminate the wrong answer choices.

Grammar and Writing Skills:
Paragraph Improvement

Read carefully through the following passage from the first draft of a student's essay. Pay close attention to the verb tense, use of clauses, and commas. Then, on a separate sheet of paper, answer the questions below.

(1) The opening line immediately signals the reader that this poem will disclose something important. (2) That something—later revealed to be the wheelbarrow the white chickens, and rainwater—is supporting "so much." (3) The line stands out too, because it was the only line not dedicated to imagery. (4) Also, by never identifying what actually "depends," Williams creates a host of possible interpretations for his poem.

(5) Williams dedicates the next three stanzas almost entirely to the eye. (6) Each adds a detail to the poem's imagery, each drops another puzzle piece into place. (7) The wheelbarrow is presented first. (8) Williams described it outright, without embellishment. (9) However, he unexpectedly breaks the word wheelbarrow between two lines. (10) By breaking this compound noun into its composite parts, the poet draws the reader's attention to the word itself, more than to the word's meaning. (11) The wheelbarrow is simultaneously an actual physical thing and the words that are used to describe it.

(12) The next stanza, "which tells us that the wheelbarrow is glazed with rain / water," similarly breaks the word rainwater between lines. (13) This, even more than the last, creates a situation in which things, and the language used to describe those things, become confused. (14) Williams is aided by the closeness in meaning of the words rain and water. (15) One is a component of the other, rain itself can never really be separated from the water that makes it up.

(16) William Carlos Williams's "The Red Wheelbarrow" is a deceptively simple poem. (17) Deceptively simple in that, although it is succinct and its imagery plain and concrete, it expresses complex ideas. (18) Williams has written a very simple poem. (19) In eight lines Williams created a poem that shines a light on the underlying notions of language, literature, and representation.

1. Which of the following is the best revision of sentence 2?
   A. That something—later revealed to be the "wheelbarrow the white chickens and rainwater"—is supporting "so much."
   B. That something—later revealed to be the wheelbarrow the white chickens and rainwater—is supporting so much.
   C. That something—later revealed to be the wheelbarrow, the white chickens, and rainwater—is supporting "so much."
   D. That something later revealed to be the wheelbarrow the white chickens and rainwater is supporting "so much."

2. Which of the following is the best revision of sentence 3?
   A. The line stands out too, because it was not dedicated to imagery.
   B. The line stands out too, because it is the only line not dedicated to imagery.
   C. These lines were the only lines not dedicated to the creation of the poem's central image.
   D. This was the only line without imagery.

3. Which of the following errors appears in sentence 6?
   A. run-on sentence
   B. incorrect parallelism
   C. sentence fragment
   D. incorrect verb tense

4. Which of the following is the best revision of sentence 8?
   A. Williams describes it outright, without embellishment.
   B. Outright, Williams described it, without embellishment.
   C. Williams, describing it outright, without embellishment.
   D. Williams is without embellishment.

5. Which of the following errors appears in sentence 17?
   A. run-on sentence
   B. incorrect parallelism
   C. sentence fragment
   D. incorrect verb tense

6. Which of the following sentences adds the *least* to the last paragraph?
   A. 16
   B. 17
   C. 18
   D. 19

7. Which of the following is the best revision of sentence 19?
   A. Williams created a poem that shines a light on the underlying notions of language literature and representation.
   B. In eight lines Williams created a poem that shines a light on the underlying notions of language, and literature, and representation.
   C. Williams shines a light on the underlying notions of literature.
   D. In eight lines, Williams created a poem that shines a light on the underlying notions of language, literature, and representation.

8. What is noticeably missing from this essay?
   A. a concluding paragraph
   B. an opening paragraph
   C. evidence
   D. a visual aid

Writing: Essay

Imagine discussing with a Modernist writer the use of traditional forms in poetry. Think about how traditional forms, such as rhyme and meter, or the absence of these forms, function in a poem and their effect. Write an essay in which you argue for or against the use of these forms in modern poetry.

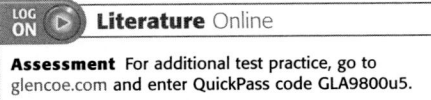

LOG ON **Literature** Online

Assessment For additional test practice, go to glencoe.com and enter QuickPass code GLA9800u5.

4. **A** is the correct answer because the present tense verb *describes* is necessary for consistency with the other verbs in the paragraph. **(DOK1)**

5. **C** is the correct answer because the sentence lacks a subject and a predicate in the main clause. **(DOK2)**

6. **C** is the correct answer because sentence 18 merely repeats the point made in the first two sentences of the paragraph. **(DOK4)**

7. **D** is the correct answer because the introductory phrase needs to be set off by a comma. **(DOK1)**

8. **B** is the correct answer because the passage does not include an introduction to the poem or a thesis statement. **(DOK4)**

Writing

Make sure students know how much time they have for the writing task, and approximately how long the essay should be. Remind students that they should try to recall work by poets who do not use traditional forms, as well as some who do, so that they can use these writers as examples.

Essay

Evaluate essays for:

- clearly stated main ideas supported by good reasons and details
- effective voice, word choice, and sentence variety
- effective presentation with attention to grammar and spelling conventions **(DOK3)**

DIFFERENTIATED INSTRUCTION

Established Some students practicing for standardized exams with essay questions will benefit from reminders about this first stage of the writing process. Encourage them to jot down—in any order—thoughts that address the writing prompt, then to reread their thoughts, cross out those that are irrelevant or dead ends, and add supporting details to those that seem significant. Finally, they should use letters or numbers to indicate the order in which they will treat the ideas and details in their drafts. Refer students to the Writing Workshop for further tips on writing an essay about literature.

Skills Scope and Sequence

Readability Scores Key: Dale-Chall/DRP/Lexile

PART 1: The New Regionalism and the City

Selections and Features	Literary Elements
Unit Introduction pp. 850-864	Regionalism **SE** p. 858 Urban Literature **SE** p. 860
Short Story Breakfast, by John Steinbeck **6.7/52/950** pp. 866-872	Implied Theme **SE** p. 867 Tone (review) **SE** p. 871
Vocabulary Workshop p. 873	
Short Story and Speech A Rose for Emily 5.9/60/1120 and **Address upon Receiving the Nobel Prize in Literature** 8.4/62/1170, by William Faulkner pp. 874-887	Foreshadowing **SE** p. 875 Flashback (review) **SE** p. 886
Short Story A Worn Path, by Eudora Welty **3.4/52/780** pp. 888-898	Description **SE** p. 889 Archetype (review) **SE** p. 897
Autobiography from **Black Boy,** by Richard Wright **5.6/57/970** pp. 899-908	Flash-forward **SE** p. 900 Autobiography (review) **SE** p. 907
Historical Perspective from **You Have Seen Their Faces,** by Erskine Caldwell and Margaret Bourke-White **11.7/63/1210** pp. 909-912	
Short Story The Life You Save May Be Your Own, by Flannery O'Connor **6.1/54/970** pp. 913-926	Dialogue **SE** p. 914 Foreshadowing (review) **SE** p. 925
Grammar Workshop p. 927	
Short Story The Second Tree from the Corner, by E. B. White **5.7/57/1110** pp. 928-936	Plot **SE** p. 929 Irony (review) **SE** p. 935
Poems The Bean Eaters and To Don at Salaam, by Gwendolyn Brooks pp. 937-941	Rhyme Scheme **SE** p. 938

Reading Skills and Strategies	Vocabulary	Writing / Grammar	Speaking, Listening, and Viewing
Use Graphic Information **TE** p. 852 Analyze Historical Context **SE** pp. 856, 862 Summarize **TE** p. 856		Write an Outline **TE** p. 860 Write a Research Report **TE** p. 862	Analyze Art **SE** p. 859 Musical Presentation **SE** p. 864 Photo Album **SE** p. 864
Connect to Personal Experience **SE** p. 867	Word Usage **SE** p. 872 Academic Vocabulary **SE** p. 872	Write a Narrative **TE** p. 868 Write a Report **SE** p. 872	
	Word Parts **SE** p. 873		
Identify Sequence **SE** p. 875 Make Inferences **TE** p. 878 Paraphrase **TE** p. 884	Denotation and Connotation **SE** p. 886 Academic Vocabulary **SE** p. 886	Adjectives **TE** p. 882 Write an Expository Essay **SE** p. 887	Oral Presentation **TE** p. 880 Analyze Art **SE** p. 881 Discussion **SE** p. 885
Visualize **SE** p. 889	Analogies **SE** p. 898 Academic Vocabulary **SE** p. 898	Create a Graphic Organizer **TE** p. 892 Write a Comparison-Contrast Essay **TE** p. 896 Apply Dialogue **SE** p. 898	Analyze Art **SE** p. 890 Readers Theater **TE** p. 894
Compare and Contrast Characters **SE** p. 900 Preview **TE** p. 900	Context Clues **SE** p. 908 Academic Vocabulary **SE** p. 908	Write a Letter **TE** p. 902 Write a Personal Essay **TE** p. 906	Analyze Art **SE** p. 903 Speech **SE** p. 908
Analyze the Purpose of Historical Texts and Photographs **SE** p. 909	Context Clues **SE** p. 910	Write a Summary **SE** p. 912	Analyze Art **TE** p. 911
Apply Background Knowledge **SE** p. 914 Visualize **TE** p. 916 Compare and Contrast **TE** p. 918 Analyze Irony **TE** p. 922	Double Negatives **TE** p. 914 Word Usage **SE** p. 925 Academic Vocabulary **SE** p. 925	Write a Scene **TE** p. 920 Write a Review **TE** p. 926	Analyze Art **TE** p. 921 Discussion **SE** p. 924
		Introductory Phrases and Clauses **SE** p. 927	
Analyze Text Structure **SE** p. 929 Draw Conclusions **TE** p. 930 Analyze Humor **TE** p. 932	Word Parts **SE** p. 936 Academic Vocabulary **SE** p. 936	Pronoun Antecedents **TE** p. 934 Apply Irony **SE** p. 936	
Evaluate Diction **SE** p. 938 Tone **TE** p. 940	Context Clues **SE** p. 941	Write a Personal Essay **SE** p. 941	Analyze Art **TE** p. 939

Readability Scores Key: Dale-Chall/DRP/Lexile

PART 1: The New Regionalism and the City *(continued)*

Selections and Features	Literary Elements
Short Story The Magic Barrel, by Bernard Malamud **6.3/62/1010** pp. 942-958	Dialect **SE** p. 943 Motivation (review) **SE** p. 957
Short Story The Rockpile, by James Baldwin **4.6/59/850** pp. 959-968	Foil **SE** p. 960

PART 2: The United States and the World

Selections and Features	Literary Elements
Speech War Message to Congress, by Franklin Delano Roosevelt **8.9/66/1280** pp. 970-974	Author's Purpose **SE** p. 971
Vocabulary Workshop p. 975	
Poem Death of the Ball Turret Gunner, by Randall Jarrell pp. 976-979	Imagery **SE** p. 977
Comparing Literature **All Rivers Run to the Sea** (memoir), by Elie Wiesel **6.1/53/860** *from* **Kubota** (memoir), by Garrett Hongo **9.0/63/1180** *from* **Maus** (graphic memoir), by Art Spiegelman pp. 980-1001	Narrator **SE** p. 982 Autobiography (review) **SE** p. 991
Essay *from* **Hiroshima,** by John Hersey **9.9/64/1260** pp. 1002-1016	Point of View **SE** p. 1003 Author's Purpose (review) **SE** p. 1015
Short Story The Portrait, by Tomas Rivera **4.5/47/760** pp. 1017-1023	Idiom **SE** p. 1018 Plot (review) **SE** p. 1022
Literary History Cultural Rebels: Writers of the Beat Generation pp. 1024-1025	

Reading Skills and Strategies	Vocabulary	Writing / Grammar	Speaking, Listening, and Viewing

Analyze Characterization **SE** p. 943
Compare and Contrast **TE** p. 944
Analyze Foreshadowing **TE** p. 954
Analyze Plot **TE** p. 956
	Word Roots **TE** p. 950
	Word Origins **SE** p. 958
	Academic Vocabulary
	   SE p. 958
		Write a Journal Entry
		   TE p. 948
		Write a Definition **TE** p. 952
			Analyze Art **TE** p. 946
			Debate **SE** p. 958

Make Generalizations About
   Characters **SE** p. 960
Analyze Sequence **TE** p. 962
Paraphrase **TE** p. 966
	Analogies **SE** p. 968	Create a Graphic Organizer
		   TE p. 960
		Double Negatives **TE** p. 964
		Write a Character Sketch
		   SE p. 968
			Analyze Art **TE** p. 965

Reading Skills and Strategies	Vocabulary	Writing / Grammar	Speaking, Listening, and Viewing

Distinguish Fact and Opinion
   SE p. 971
Analyze Speech **TE** p. 972
	Denotation and Connotation
	   SE p. 974
		Write a Press Release
		   SE p. 974	

	Word Origins **SE** p. 975		
Visualize **SE** p. 977	Context Clues **SE** p. 979	Write a Letter **TE** p. 978 Write a Journal Entry **TE** p. 979	

Compare and Contrast **SE** p. 980
Activate Prior Knowledge **SE** p. 982
Monitor Comprehension **TE** p. 984
Draw Conclusions **TE** p. 990
	Denotation and Connotation
	   SE p. 992
	Academic Vocabulary
	   SE p. 992
		Write a Biography **TE** p. 986
		Write a Description **TE** p. 994
		Write an Expository Essay
		   SE p. 1001
			Discussion **TE** pp. 988, 996,
			   1001
			Oral Report **SE** p. 992
			Performance **TE** p. 998
			Collage **SE** p. 1001

Draw Conclusions About Author's
   Beliefs **SE** p. 1003
Analyze Text Structure **TE** p. 1006
Distinguish Fact and Opinion
   TE p. 1008
Skim and Scan **TE** p. 1012
	Word Origins **SE** p. 1015
	Academic Vocabulary
	   SE p. 1015
		Create a Graphic Organizer
		   TE p. 1004
		Write an Editorial **TE** p. 1010
		Write an Expository Essay
		   SE p. 1016
		Underlining and Italics
		   SE p. 1016
			Discussion **TE** p. 1014

Respond to Plot and Characters
   SE p. 1018
Make Critical Judgments **TE** p. 1018
	Context Clues **SE** p. 1023
	Academic Vocabulary
	   SE p. 1023
		Write a Research Report
		   SE p. 1023	

Analyze Cultural Context **SE** p. 1024
Evaluate Literary Periods **SE** p. 1024
Evaluate Historical Influences
   SE p. 1025
		Write a Research Report
		   TE p. 1024	

Readability Scores Key: Dale-Chall/DRP/Lexile

PART 2: The United States and the World *(continued)*

Selections and Features	Literary Elements
Drama The Crucible, Act I, by Arthur Miller pp. 1026-1050	Dialogue **SE** p. 1027 Setting **TE** p. 1030 Irony **TE** p. 1044
Drama The Crucible, Act II, by Arthur Miller pp. 1051-1072	Stage Directions **SE** p. 1051
Drama The Crucible, Act III, by Arthur Miller pp. 1073-1095	Plot **SE** p. 1073 Dialogue **TE** p. 1074 Irony **TE** pp. 1088, 1094
Drama The Crucible, Act IV, by Arthur Miller pp. 1096-1115	Tragedy **SE** p. 1096 Irony **TE** p. 1102 Motif **TE** p. 1108 Climax **TE** p. 1110 Conflict (review) **SE** p. 1114
Literary History Modern American Drama pp. 1116-1117	Drama **SE** p. 1116 Musical Theater **SE** p. 1117
Writing Workshop pp. 1118-1125	Sensory Details **TE** p. 1122
Speaking, Listening, and Viewing Workshop pp. 1126-1127	
Independent Reading pp. 1128-1129	
Assessment pp. 1130-1135	

Reading Skills and Strategies	Vocabulary	Writing / Grammar	Speaking, Listening, and Viewing
Draw Conclusions About Characters **SE** p. 1027 Recognize Logical Fallacies **TE** p. 1032 Analyze Conflict **TE** p. 1048	Word Parts **SE** p. 1050	Write a Summary **TE** p. 1034 Write a Scene **TE** p. 1038 Active and Passive Voice **TE** p. 1040 Write a Dialogue **SE** p. 1050	Oral Report **TE** p. 1028 Analyze Art **TE** p. 1036 Readers Theater **TE** p. 1046
Analyze Historical Context **SE** p. 1051 Recognize Logical Fallacies **TE** p. 1056 Monitor Comprehension **SE** p. 1058	Analogies **SE** p. 1072	Write a Research Report **TE** pp. 1052, 1066 Exclamation Points **TE** p. 1054 Write a Definition **TE** p. 1064 Capitalization **TE** p. 1070 Write Stage Directions **SE** p. 1072	Mock Newscast **TE** p. 1060 Debate **TE** p. 1062 Analyze Art **SE** p. 1068
Evaluate Argument **SE** p. 1073 Make Inferences About Characters **TE** p. 1078 Analyze Dramatic Irony **TE** p. 1080	Context Clues **SE** p. 1095	Write a Research Report **TE** p. 1076 Inverted Sentences **TE** p. 1082 Write a Character Analysis **TE** p. 1086 Write an Application Letter **TE** p. 1092 Write a Summary **SE** p. 1095	Analyze Art **SE** p. 1081 Dramatic Reading **TE** p. 1084
Analyze Theme **SE** p. 1096 Compare and Contrast Characters **TE** p. 1100 Evaluate Argument **TE** p. 1104	Word Origins **TE** p. 1098 Word Usage **SE** p. 1114 Academic Vocabulary **SE** p. 1114	Write an Editorial **SE** p. 1115 Comparative and Superlative Adjectives **SE** p. 1115	Analyze Art **SE** p. 1101
Analyze Cultural Context **SE** p. 1116 Analyze Literary Periods **SE** p. 1116 Evaluate Historical Influences **SE** p. 1116			Dramatic Reading **TE** p. 1116
		Prewrite **SE** p. 1121 Draft **SE** p. 1122 Revise **SE** p. 1124 Avoid Stilted Language **SE** p. 1124 Write an Autobiographical Narrative **SE** p. 1125	
Analyze Images **SE** p. 1126			Photo Essay **SE** p. 1126
Respond to Experience **TE** p. 1128		Write an Advice Column **SE** p. 1129	
		Write an Autobiographical Narrative **SE** p. 1135	

Focus

Bellringer Options

Literature Launcher
  Pre-Reading Video: Unit 6
Daily Language Practice
  Transparency 78

Or **ask:** What is an economic depression? *(Students may say that it is a time when it is very difficult to find a job.)* **Say:** The term *depression* refers to a period of economic decline characterized by decreasing business activity, falling prices, and increased unemployment. **Ask:** What comes to mind when you hear the term "Great Depression"?

 For school-to-home activities, see Unit 6 Teaching Resources Book, pp. 5–11.

 For students who would profit from independent novel study, see Novel Companion pp. 251–294.

Baseball at Night, 1934. Morris Kantor. Oil on linen, 37 x 47¼ in. Smithsonian American Art Museum, Washington, DC.

View the Art Kantor painted this work after making several sketches of early night baseball games. Why might the artist have chosen this subject to reflect American culture during the middle part of the twentieth century?

Unit Introduction Skills

Reading Skills
- Analyze Graphic Information (SE pp. 853, 855)
- Make Inferences (SE p. 859)
- Analyze Cause and Effect (SE pp. 861, 863;)
- Use Timelines (TE p. 852)
- Summarize (TE p. 856)

From Depression to Cold War

Listening/Speaking/Viewing Skills
- Presentation on Music (SE p. 864)
- Photograph Murals (SE p. 864)
- Analyze Art (TE pp. 851, 856, 859, 861, 863)

Writing Skills/Grammar
- Graph Migration (TE p. 854)
- Organize and Support (TE p. 860)
- Present Research (TE p. 862)

Literary Elements
- Simile (TE p. 859)
- Rhyme Scheme (TE p. 861)

FROM DEPRESSION TO COLD WAR

1930s–1960s

Looking Ahead

During this period, the United States faced extraordinary challenges. In the 1930s, people in the United States struggled with the effects of the Great Depression, the worst economic crisis in U.S. history. U.S. entry into World War II in 1941 signaled the beginning of global responsibilities for the United States. The postwar world brought the United States an uneasy peace marked by anxiety about nuclear conflict.

Keep the following questions in mind as you read:

» How did the Depression encourage a revival of Regionalist literature?

» In what different ways did the writers of this period present urban life?

» How did the role of the United States in the world change as a result of World War II and the Cold War?

851

Unit Resources

Print Materials

- Unit 6 Teaching Resources, pp. 1–300
- Interactive Read and Write (On Level, Approaching, EL), pp. 213–254
- Novel Companion, pp. 251–294
- Bellringer Option Transparencies: Selection Focus 53–64; Daily Language Practice 78–95
- Assessment Resources, Selection Assessment, pp. 235–272

Technology

- TeacherWorks Plus CD
- StudentWorks Plus CD
- Literature Launchers: Pre-Reading Videos DVD, Unit 6
- Literature Online
- Visual Vocabulary CD-ROM
- Listening Library CD-ROM
- ExamView CD-ROM
- Skill Level Up! CD-ROM

Focus

Summary

The introduction describes the historical, social, and cultural forces that led to three literary responses: the revival of Regionalism, an examination of urban life, and a reaction to World War II and the Cold War. Following the optimism of the 1920s, a period of economic and social upheaval changed the outlook of the United States. Summaries of these events highlight their impact on writers of the time.

View the Art ★

Answer: *Baseball was one of the few signs of hope during the Great Depression. It was a form of entertainment known as the "American pastime."*

At the age of 15, Morris Kantor (1896–1974) moved from his birthplace in Minsk, Russia, to the United States. He studied art in New York and painted *Baseball at Night* in 1934, in the middle of the Great Depression. Most towns had a baseball team, and the first lighted games were played by these small-town teams.

For diagnostic and end-of-unit assessment, see Assessment Resources, pp. 41–48, 341–342.

Teach

Connect Timeline Information

Direct students to study the timeline to compare the literature of the time with the events happening in the United States and the world. Using a Reader's Encyclopedia, read aloud summaries of selected literary works found on the timeline. For each work, ask students to name a historical event that might have influenced the work.

Cultural History ☆

World War II Some historians call World War II the most significant episode in history. A total of 49 countries participated in the global conflict that resulted in more than $1 trillion in destruction and had long-lasting effects on people around the world. Popular novels based on the war include *The Naked and the Dead* (1948) by Norman Mailer and *The Caine Mutiny* (1951) by Herman Wouk. Individual soldiers' remembrances of the war filled magazines and books in the post-war years.

TIMELINE
1930s–1960s

THE GRAPES of WRATH
John Steinbeck

1 | AMERICAN LITERATURE

1930

1930
Sinclair Lewis becomes first U.S. citizen to win Nobel Prize for Literature

1936
Absalom, Absalom! by William Faulkner

1937
Their Eyes Were Watching God by Zora Neale Hurston

1938
Thornton Wilder stages *Our Town*

1939
The Grapes of Wrath by John Steinbeck

1940

1940
Native Son by Richard Wright

1943
Oklahoma! opens on Broadway

1945
Tennessee Williams stages *The Glass Menagerie*

1945
Black Boy by Richard Wright

1945
A Street in Bronzeville by Gwendolyn Brooks

1947
Tennessee Williams stages *A Streetcar Named Desire*

UNITED STATES EVENTS

1930

1930
Depression deepens; bank failures increase

1932
Franklin D. Roosevelt is elected president

1933
New Deal is launched

1934
Dust Bowl begins in the southern Great Plains

1935
Social Security Act is passed

1940

1941
Japan attacks Pearl Harbor; United States enters World War II ☆

1942
Internment of Americans of Japanese descent begins

1943
Race riots occur in Detroit; Zoot Suit Riots occur in Los Angeles

1944
D-Day invasion begins in northern France

1945
President Roosevelt dies; Vice President Harry S. Truman becomes president

1945
United States drops atomic bombs on Japan

Emblem required by Nazis to be worn by Jews

Jude

WORLD EVENTS

1930

1930
Mohandas Gandhi leads Salt March in India

1933
Adolf Hitler and Nazi party come to power in Germany

1935
Nazis deprive German Jews of citizenship

1939
Germany invades Poland; World War II begins

1940

1940
France surrenders to Germany

1940
Battle of Britain begins

1942
Nazi "final solution" establishes concentration and extermination camps for Jews

United Nations logo

1943
Soviets defeat Germans at Stalingrad

1945
Germany surrenders; Allied forces liberate Nazi death camps

LOG ON ▶ **Literature** Online

Literature and Reading To explore the Interactive Timeline, go to glencoe.com and enter QuickPass code GLA9800u6.

Reading Practice

Use Timelines Have students collaborate to research and prepare a biographical timeline of a writer from this era. The timeline should include such entries as birth and death dates, geographical moves, travels, meetings and relationships with other literary figures, publications of works, and awards. Encourage students to enhance their timelines with illustrations and quotations. To assist students with organization, provide printed timeline formats.

Franklin D. Roosevelt button

Jackie Robinson button

1950

1949
Arthur Miller's *Death of a Salesman* is staged

1949 ▼
William Faulkner wins Nobel Prize in Literature

1952
Invisible Man by Ralph Ellison ☆

1955
A Good Man Is Hard to Find by Flannery O'Connor

1960

1955
Notes of a Native Son by James Baldwin

1957
On the Road by Jack Kerouac

1959
Lorraine Hansberry's *A Raisin in the Sun* is staged

1960
To Kill a Mockingbird by Harper Lee

1961
Catch-22 by Joseph Heller

1950

1946
First electronic digital computer begins operation

1947
Jackie Robinson is first African American to play Major League Baseball

1949
North Atlantic Treaty Organization (NATO) is founded

1950
Senator McCarthy charges that Communists staff the U.S. State Department

1954
Supreme Court rules school segregation unconstitutional in *Brown v. Board of Education of Topeka*

1960

1955
Montgomery bus boycott begins

1962
Cuban Missile Crisis occurs

1963
President John F. Kennedy is assassinated; Vice President Lyndon Johnson becomes president

1950

1945
United Nations Charter

1945
Japan surrenders; World War II ends

1948
U.N. establishes Israel

1949
People's Republic of China established

1950
Korean War begins

1953 ▼
DNA code cracked

1960

1957 ▲
Sputnik 1 and *Sputnik 2*

1959
Fidel Castro takes Cuba

1961
Soviets erect Berlin Wall to separate East Germany from the West

Reading Check
Analyze Graphic Information Which events on the timeline show the effects of Nazi racial policies?

INTRODUCTION **853**

Teach

Reading Check

Answer: *1935—Nazis deprive German Jews of citizenship; 1942—Nazi "final solution" establishes concentration and extermination camps for Jews; 1945—Germany surrenders; Allied forces liberate Nazi death camps.*

Literary History ☆

Ralph Waldo Ellison Ralph Ellison (1914–1994) shares part of his name with an American literary voice—Ralph Waldo Emerson—from the previous century. Ellison's reputation rests on his novel *Invisible Man*, the story of an African-American man's search for identity. Ellison published numerous short stories and essays, and taught at several colleges and universities.

Approaching Level

DIFFERENTIATED INSTRUCTION

Emerging Explain to students that reading and analyzing a timeline can help them make connections as they read the unit. Have students hold a ruler vertically along one column of dates to see all the events that happened in a certain period of time. For example, reading down the second column of the timeline, they will see the relationship between John Steinbeck's *Grapes of Wrath* and the growth of the Dust Bowl.

Have them hold the ruler horizontally across a section to see a certain category of events over time. For example, have students find the events in Franklin Delano Roosevelt's presidency on the timeline (United States Events *rows, between 1932 and 1945*). **Ask:** Where on the timeline would you add the names of books published in 1962? (*In the* American Literature *section, in the* 1960 *column*)

Teach

Reading Strategy | 1

Draw Conclusions Have students examine the diagram, which shows one cyclical effect of the Great Depression.

Ask: In this diagram, what slowed industry? *(lower demand for materials, resulting from a decline in auto sales)* Clarify that a decline in auto sales was just one factor that slowed industry. Then examine the graphs depicting auto and tank production. **Ask:** How does the drop in automobile production after 1941 relate to the increase in tanks? *(Producing war materials required huge amounts of raw materials to be diverted from other industries. Automobile factories were converted into tank factories.)*

BY THE NUMBERS

Stock Market Crash

On October 29, 1929, 16 million stock shares were sold. By mid-November, stock prices were cut in half, costing investors about $30 billion—a sum that was equal to the total wages of all Americans for 1929. Nearly 1.5 million investors had previously purchased stock, and many lost everything. By 1933, more than 12 million people were unemployed, and between 1929 and 1932 the average family income dropped from $2,300 to $1,600 a year.

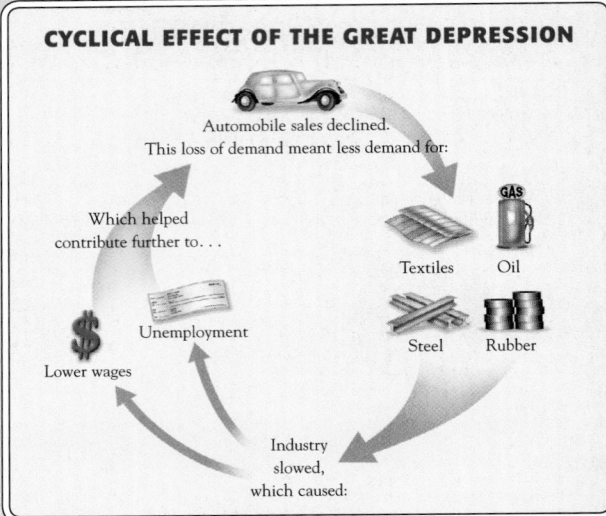

CYCLICAL EFFECT OF THE GREAT DEPRESSION

Automobile sales declined. This loss of demand meant less demand for: Textiles, Oil, Steel, Rubber

Industry slowed, which caused: Unemployment

Lower wages

Which helped contribute further to . . .

THE DUST BOWL

- In 1933 and 1935, dry weather desertified parts of the Great Plains. 1934 saw 22 dust storms; 1937 saw 72.

- Between 1934 and 1939, nearly 350,000 Dust Bowl families migrated to California.

- In the 1930s, millions of tons of topsoil kill crops and livestock.

THE SECOND GREAT MIGRATION

- The Depression slowed the Great Migration of rural African Americans from the South to the North.

- Production during World War II created new jobs, prompting a "Second Great Migration."

- Mechanization of Southern farming in the 1950s forced more rural Southern African Americans to move north seeking work.

- African American populations of big cities in the North and West grew dramatically; for example, in Chicago from 278,000 in 1940 to 813,000 in 1960.

AUTO PRODUCTION 1941–1945

Automobiles Produced (in millions)

1941: 3,779,628
1942: 222,862
1943: 139
1944: 610
1945: 70,001

Source *Historical Statistics of the United States: Colonial Times to 1970*

TANK PRODUCTION 1941–1945

Tanks Produced (in thousands)

1941: 4,203
1942: 23,884
1943: 29,497
1944: 17,565
1945: 11,184

Source *Historical Statistics of the United States: Colonial Times to 1970*

Writing Practice

Graph Migration Tell students to read "The Second Great Migration." Discuss the causes of the migration of African Americans to the North. Point out to students that the North's African American population more than doubled in twenty years, while the South's black population grew slowly. Then have students create a line or bar graph using the following data showing the African American population:

Year	North (millions)	South (millions)
1940	2.8	9.9
1950	4.2	10.2
1960	6.5	11.3

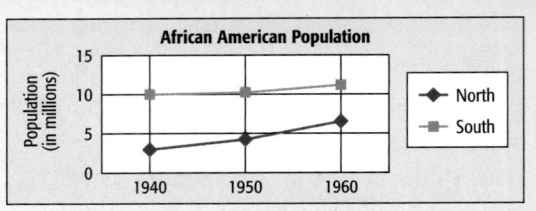

African American Population

Population (in millions)

North, South

1940, 1950, 1960

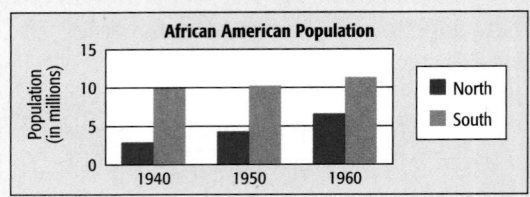

African American Population

Population (in millions)

North, South

1940, 1950, 1960

BEING THERE

In the 1930s, American artists, like American writers, were divided between Regionalists, who depicted rural life in the Midwest and West, and Social Realists, who focused on American cities, particularly New York.

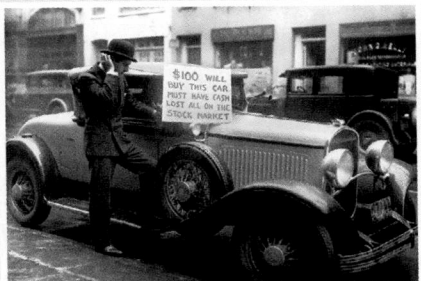

A *Against Barbwire Fence,* 1933. Arthur Rothstein. Black and white photograph.

B *Bankrupt Investor Walter Thornton Selling Roadster After Stock Market Crash,* 1929. Black and white photograph.

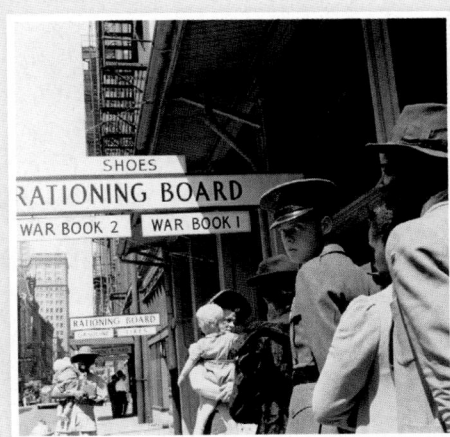

C *Line at Ration Board,* 1943. John Vachon. Black and white photograph.

Reading Check

Analyze Graphic Information:

1. How many more dust storms were there in 1937 than in 1934?

2. In what year during World War II were the fewest automobiles and the most tanks produced?

3. What effect did unemployment and lower wages have on automobile sales? See diagram on p. 854.

LOG ON ▶ **Literature** Online

Literature and Reading For more about the history and literature of this period, go to glencoe.com and enter QuickPass code GLA9800u6.

INTRODUCTION **855**

855

English Learners

DIFFERENTIATED INSTRUCTION

Intermediate With the class, brainstorm a list of economic terms, such as *stock, investor, shares,* and *income.* Have English learners create a two-column chart with the headers *Term* and *Meaning.* Have students list unfamiliar terms and consult a dictionary to find the meaning.

UNIT SIX

Teach

Reading Check

1. 50
2. 1943
3. Automobile sales continued to decline.

Reading Strategy 2

Use Maps Ask: What does this map reveal about the effects of the Great Depression and World War II? *(Students may say that the effects were not confined to a single region, but affected the entire nation.)*

View the Photograph ★

A. While working for the Federal Resettlement Administration, Arthur Rothstein became famous for his images of the Dust Bowl.

B. Speculation, the practice of engaging in risky stock market transactions, contributed to the stock market crash of 1929.

C. In order to fully supply the armed forces during WWII, the federal government used rationing to distribute scarce products to citizens at home. Coffee, sugar, shoes, and tires were rationed.

Teach

Reading Strategy | 1

Connect **Say:** Some people who lived through the Great Depression were reluctant to spend money for years after it was over. **Ask:** Why do you think they felt this way? *(They had seen rich people lose everything they had.)*

Reading Strategy | 2

Draw Conclusions **Ask:** Why did Franklin D. Roosevelt defeat President Herbert Hoover in the 1932 presidential election? *(Students may say that Hoover lost because the economy was in such bad shape.)*

View the Photograph ★

During World War I, many nations bought grain from U.S. farmers, who plowed more land to meet the increased demand. When the demand eased at the end of World War I, farmers with unpaid debts cultivated even more ground, leaving large areas stripped of ground cover. A severe drought and strong windstorms blew away millions of tons of topsoil.

Learning Objectives

For pages 856–864
In studying this text, you will focus on the following objectives:

Literary Study:
Analyzing literary periods.
Evaluating historical influences.
Connecting to the literature.

FROM DEPRESSION TO COLD WAR

1930s–1960s

Historical, Social, and Cultural Forces

1 The Depression

The stock market crashed in 1929, taking with it the optimism and prosperity of the 1920s. The crash started a chain reaction that cost millions of people their jobs and homes. Banks failed when loans could not be repaid. People frantically

Man in a Dust Storm, c. 1930. Black and white photograph. ★

removed their savings from banks, causing more banks to fail, which in turn caused factories and businesses to close. The popular song "Brother, Can You Spare a Dime?" captured the bleak spirit of the people of the United States, many of whom were now forced to sell their possessions, relinquish their homes, and stand in bread lines for food. When President Herbert Hoover ran for reelection in 1932, Franklin Delano Roosevelt defeated him **2** soundly, carrying 42 of the 48 states. Soon programs and policies aimed at economic recovery and social reform, which Roosevelt called the New Deal, offered some relief to the beleaguered nation.

The New Deal

New Deal agencies employed people in public works programs, such as reforestation; improved the nation's roads and schools; and built sidewalks, dams, and bridges. It played a role in the arts as well, employing out-of-work artists, writers, actors, and musicians to decorate public buildings and produce plays and musicals. Even with the new agencies, some people—dependent mothers, children, and the elderly—were unemployable. In 1935, Congress passed the Social Security Act, which offered unemployment insurance and retirement benefits that were financed through payroll taxes paid by employers and workers.

Reading Practice

Summarize **Say:** When you are studying a time period, you may find it helpful to summarize the most important points so that the information is more manageable. Have students create a two-column chart with the headers *Historical Events* and *Main Points*. Beneath the first column, students should list the five headings given in the selec-

tion. Have students read each of the five sections, stopping at the end of each to note the most important points in the second column.

Persistent Racism

Prejudice against African Americans and other minority groups continued. The New Deal failed to enact programs that challenged racism. Some agencies refused to hire African Americans, and others segregated them and paid them less. Violence, including lynching, remained widespread.

> "Dust storms are bringing distress and death to 300,000 square miles."
>
> —Margaret Bourke-White

The Dust Bowl

A combination of drought and poor farming methods during the 1920s turned a large area of the Great Plains into what became known as the Dust Bowl. Topsoil blew as far as the Atlantic coast. Many families left their farms and headed west in search of work. Not everyone found work, however, and the Farm Security Administration (FSA) built camps to house migrants. Those who stayed on their farms got help from the Soil Conservation Service (SCS), which advocated contour plowing to help keep the soil from blowing away.

World War II and the Cold War

In the 1930s, Italy's Fascists, Germany's Nazis, and Japan's military rulers formed an alliance known as the Axis Powers. Aggression by these countries led to World War II in 1939. Early in the war, the Axis forces overwhelmed their enemies, until only Britain still resisted. The U.S. entered the war on Britain's side after the Japanese attack on Pearl Harbor in December 1941. Nearly four years of global warfare followed, ending with the defeat of the Axis Powers in 1945. The end of the war left a world dominated by the U.S. and the Soviet Union. An intense political and economic rivalry developed between them, and the ensuing "Cold War" led to a massive buildup of armaments—including nuclear weapons.

PREVIEW **Big Ideas** of the Era of the Depression and the Cold War

1 Return to Regionalism	**2** Life in the City	**3** The United States and the World
The crisis of the Depression encouraged a revival of Regionalism in literature. Some writers saw the values of ordinary people in the United States as a source of strength in hard times. Other writers examined how characters' lives were shaped—and sometimes distorted—by the history and culture of their regions. **See pages 858–859.**	During the first half of the twentieth century, the big cities of the United States were magnets for foreign-born immigrants and rural U.S. citizens, who came seeking better lives for themselves and their families. Responding to modern urban life, American writers portrayed both its richness and its problems. **See pages 860–861.**	In 1941 aggression by the Axis Powers forced the United States to enter World War II. The end of the war saw the development of the Cold War between the United States and the Soviet Union. American writers examined both wartime struggles and postwar anxieties. **See pages 862–863.**

Teach

Literary Element

Historical Narrative Point out to students that World War II produced many examples of historical narrative, a work of nonfiction that tells the story of events and developments. Winston Churchill, prime minister of Great Britain throughout the war, penned the six-volume *History of the Second World War.*

Ask: Why is a narrative written by a participant in a historical event an important source of information? *(A narrative written by a participant may be more detailed than one written by someone who researched the event at a later time.)*

Cultural History

"Baby Boomers" The "baby boom" started in 1946—the year after World War II ended—as American soldiers returning from the war married and had families. The effect on the U.S. population was dramatic. In 1940, there were about 132 million Americans. By 1960, the population had grown to about 180 million people—an increase of nearly 40 percent.

Approaching Level

DIFFERENTIATED INSTRUCTION

Emerging To help students keep track of the three Big Ideas covered in this unit, have them make a chart similar to the one shown and use it to make notes as they read the rest of the introduction. An example of how students might use the chart is shown.

	Writers	Events	Ideas
Big Idea 1: Regionalism	*Steinbeck*	*Dust Bowl*	*hardship, discrimination*
Big Idea 2: City Life			
Big Idea 3: The World			

857

Reading Strategy   1

Connect Explain to students that regionalist writers were interested in how circumstances influenced character. **Ask:** What aspects of your own personal "setting" or circumstances make you who you are or influence what you do?

Literary Element   2

Setting Have students read the section called "Steinbeck's Migrant Workers." **Ask:** What aspects of the setting influenced Steinbeck's characterizations in *The Grapes of Wrath*? *(Steinbeck's characters were influenced by the dust storms in the Great Plains and by the difficulty of starting over in California.)*

Literary History ☆

Ordinary Heroes John Steinbeck's fiction sympathetically portrays the working class. In 1962, he published *Travels with Charley*, about a cross-country trip he took with his pet poodle. This work glows with an appreciation of ordinary Americans.

Big Idea 1
Return to Regionalism

The word "America" means something different to each person in the United States. Among the many factors that shape its meaning are the communities that people come from—their histories, traditions, customs, and values. During the Great Depression, some American writers rediscovered Regionalism, the literary movement that places emphasis on the themes, characters, and settings of a particular geographical region. Unlike the local colorists of the late 1800s, the Regionalists of the mid-twentieth century were less concerned with peculiarities of local dialect or dress than with the deeper impact of setting on character.

Steinbeck's Migrant Workers

During the Depression, the morale of people in the U.S. weakened and many lost faith in national institutions. Some writers turned to regional traditions and the values of ordinary people as sources of continuity and strength. California writer John Steinbeck (see pages 866–872) found enduring humanity in the struggles of Dust Bowl migrants. His most famous novel, *The Grapes of Wrath*, describes the effects of the Depression and Dust Bowl on farmers from the southern Great Plains who traveled westward to seek work as migrant laborers. Their toughness and optimism in the face of hardship and discrimination reflects the spirit of the New Deal era and Steinbeck's belief in the ability of ordinary people to defeat despair and rebuild their lives through community.

Faulkner's Yoknapatawpha County

The richness of modern Southern writing has caused some literary historians to speak of the Southern Literary Renaissance in the twentieth century. Many of these writers focused on the South's relationship to its complex, often bitter history and on the interaction between Southern whites and blacks. The most famous of these Southern writers, William Faulkner (see pages 874–887), used carefully detailed regional settings and situations to present universal themes, such as the burden of the past, the complexity of human relationships, the nature of time and history, and the loneliness and alienation of modern life. In order to analyze the effects that Southern history had on its people, Faulkner created a fictional Mississippi region he called Yoknapatawpha County. He populated it with former slaves, poor white families, wealthy businessmen, and plantation owners. As the county begins to change and slowly absorb Northern influences, its citizens struggle to either resist or keep up with the outside world. In his brilliant experimental novel *The Sound and the Fury*, Faulkner used a series of interior monologues to portray the psychological deterioration and moral decay of a once proud aristocratic family, the Compsons, whose members cannot face the changing realities of race, class, culture, and economics in the modern South.

O'Connor's Southern Gothic

One category of modern writing is sometimes referred to as Southern Gothic. Southern Gothic literature has some of the same elements as the Gothic literature of the Romantic period. The characters are similar to those in Edgar Allan Poe's stories: sometimes weird, alienated, and prone to strange actions and bizarre thoughts. Yet the reader is meant to feel sympathy for these characters and to understand what has blighted their lives. Another Southern writer, Flannery O'Connor (see pages 913–926), sought to shock her readers through "distortions of modern life." Her characters often encounter a force that threatens to change their lives and beliefs forever. When critics claimed that her stories were grotesque, O'Connor responded, "I have found that anything that comes out of the South is going to be called grotesque by the Northern reader, unless it is grotesque, in which case it is going to be called realistic."

Study Skills Practice

 SPIRAL REVIEW **Text Organizers** To help students remember the information on this page, have them make a concept map entitled "Return to Regionalism." Students should link three concept circles to the heading, one for each of the three authors described. Then have them link the important points about the authors to their respective circles. For example, Steinbeck could have the following information linked to his circle:

- *Grapes of Wrath*
- Dust Bowl
- Ordinary people overcome hardship and discrimination.

Valley Farms, 1933–34. Ross Dickinson. Oil on canvas, 39½ x 49⅗ in. Smithsonian American Art Museum, Washington, DC.

from *The Grapes of Wrath* by John Steinbeck

And they were lonely and perplexed, because they had all come from a place of sadness and worry and defeat, and because they were all going to a new mysterious place, they huddled together; they talked together, they shared their lives, their food, and the things they hoped for in the new country. Thus it might be that one family camped near a spring, and another camped for the spring and for company, and a third because two families had pioneered the place and found it good. And when the sun went down, perhaps twenty families and twenty cars were there.

In the evening a strange thing happened: the twenty families became one family, the children were the children of all. The loss of home became one loss, and the golden time in the West was one dream. And it might be that a sick child threw despair into the hearts of twenty families, of a hundred people; that a birth there in a tent kept a hundred people quiet and awestruck through the night and filled a hundred people with the birth-joy in the morning. A family which the night before has been lost and fearful might search its goods to find a present for the new baby. In the evening, sitting about the fires, the twenty were one.

3

Reading Check

Make Inferences Why do you think a preoccupation with the past was a major characteristic of Southern Regionalist writing?

Approaching Level

DIFFERENTIATED INSTRUCTION

Established Explain to students that Steinbeck describes people moving westward. They are moving not only from one place to another, but also from the old to the new, and from despair to hope. Students who have difficulty with Steinbeck's writing can benefit from making a two-column chart with the headings "From" and "To" or "Old" and "New."

Give students examples of Steinbeck's words, such as those shown in the chart. Have students list other words or phrases that are associated with each heading.

From	To
side roads	great cross-country highway
place of sadness, worry, and defeat	new mysterious place

Teach

Reading Check

Answer: *Southern writers were reflecting on the burden of the bitter past. Relationships between blacks and whites were a common theme as Southern writers tried to understand their troubled past.*

Literary Element | 3

Figurative Language Explain to students that Steinbeck intersperses figurative language with literal language throughout the excerpt. **Ask:** In the excerpt from *The Grapes of Wrath*, what do the families literally share? *(food, a spring, a place, goods)* **Ask:** What do the families share figuratively or symbolically? *(all the other aspects of life Steinbeck mentions: lives, hopes, one family, all the children, losses, dreams, despair, joy)*

View the Art ★

A native of Southern California, Ross Dickinson (1903–1978) was an artist and a teacher. He contributed many murals to Southern California's public buildings. This painting provides an idea of the California setting for Steinbeck's *Grapes of Wrath*.

Teach

Reading Strategy | 1

Connect **Ask:** If ten students were asked to describe life in your school, what might account for the differences in the descriptions? *(Possible answer: Different ages, genders, and backgrounds will result in different perceptions.)*

Reading Strategy | 2

Compare and Contrast

Ask: What circumstances might account for the different viewpoints of these writers on urban life? *(White, accepted in the mainstream culture, wrote from a perspective of relative security, while Ellison, Malamud, and Brooks—treated as outsiders—tried to find their way in more difficult circumstances.)*

Cultural History ☆

Jewish Experience Bernard Malamud (1914–1986) was the son of Russian-Jewish immigrant parents. He worked 16 hours a day in their small grocery store on New York City's East Side. Malamud wrote about Jews because he knew their history, experiences, beliefs, and literature best.

Big Idea 2
Life in the City

1 As the historian Richard Hofstadter famously observed in 1955, "The United States was born in the country and has moved to the city." Over the last hundred years, U.S. life has been shaped by cities, which have given direction to the economy, politics, and culture of the United States. The rapid urbanization of U.S. society had already begun in the late nineteenth century, as immigrants to the United States swelled urban populations and rural citizens also began migrating to the cities. By 1920, the urban population of the United States exceeded the rural population.

U.S. cities became busy, and exciting, but were also crowded, dirty, and dangerous. Large urban populations encouraged the growth of a varied, dynamic cultural life that ranged from museums and opera houses to movie theaters and nightclubs. However, the same rapid growth produced slums and crime. **2** In the twentieth century, many writers explored both the vitality and the malaise of U.S. cities.

> *"The city is like poetry: it compresses all life, all races and breeds, into a small island and adds music and the accompaniment of internal engines."*
>
> —E. B. White, "Here Is New York"

E. B. White and New York City

New York City was the center of modern U.S. culture, and the *New Yorker* magazine helped to set urban trends and styles for the rest of the country. While writing for the *New Yorker*, E. B. White (see pages 928–936) captivated the public with sophisticated essays and sketches. White's essays covered a range of topics, including personal experiences, the problems of urban living, and current events.

Ralph Ellison's Invisible Man

Decades after the Civil War, African Americans still suffered from prejudice and segregation. To Ralph Ellison, the African American man remained an "invisible man," marginalized by white society and uncertain of his own role and identity. The nameless narrator and protagonist of Ellison's award-winning novel *Invisible Man* struggles vainly to overcome racial and social stereotypes and to be perceived as an individual. Finally, he comes to realize the absurdity of his situation and goes underground, living in an abandoned basement that he symbolically fills with lightbulbs. "In my novel," Ellison wrote, "the narrator's development is one through blackness to light; that is, from ignorance to enlightenment: invisibility to visibility."

Bernard Malamud and Brooklyn ☆

The parents of Bernard Malamud (see pages 942–958) were Russian Jews who had emigrated to the U.S. and settled in Brooklyn. Malamud's fiction has typically focused on the experience of urban Jews. His work often combines sharply contrasting elements—humor and pain, fantasy and realism—as he explores a character's ability to overcome isolation and suffering. His family's difficult experiences in Brooklyn are clearly evident in his stories. "People say I write so much about misery, but . . . no matter how much happiness or success you collect, you cannot obliterate your early experience."

Gwendolyn Brooks and Bronzeville

Between World War I and the 1960s, more than 6 million African Americans migrated from the rural South to northern cities. Many of them settled on the south side of Chicago, forming the large African American community later known as Bronzeville. African American writer Gwendolyn Brooks (see pages 937–941) grew up in Bronzeville, which became the setting for much of her work.

Writing Practice

Organize and Support Direct students to use an informal outline, such as the one below, to compare the urban experiences and themes of each writer.

1. E. B. White
  - *The New Yorker*
  - essays and sketches
  - personal experience, urban problems, current events

2. Ralph Ellison
  - *Invisible Man*
  - identity of African American man
  - racial/social stereotypes

Have students create outlines for Malamud and Brooks, and then choose one of the writers to outline.

Subway, c. 1934. Lily Furedi. Oil on canvas, 39 x 48½ in. Smithsonian American Art Musuem, Washington, DC.

Her poetry and fiction are distinguished by a compassionate understanding of the lives of America's black urban poor, who struggle to survive both poverty and racism.

Suburbia

Despite the importance of cities in the development of the United States, a deep distrust of urban life also has been a part of the U.S. character. By 1900 U.S. cities were already ringed with suburbs. The growth of suburbia continued to accelerate throughout the twentieth century. For millions of people in the United States, a home in the suburbs came to symbolize the American dream. Nevertheless, some writers have depicted suburbia as a cultural wasteland inhabited by conformists. John Cheever and John Updike are two writers who have explored the culture of suburbs in the United States.

from *A Street in Bronzeville* by Gwendolyn Brooks

kitchenette building

We are things of dry hours and the involuntary plan,
Grayed in, and gray. "Dream" makes a giddy sound, not strong
Like "rent," "feeding a wife," "satisfying a man."

But could a dream send up through onion fumes
Its white and violet, fight with fried potatoes
And yesterday's garbage ripening in the hall,
Flutter, or sing an aria down these rooms

Even if we were willing to let it in,
Had time to warm it, keep it very clean,
Anticipate a message, let it begin?

We wonder. But not well! not for a minute!
Since Number Five is out of the bathroom now,
We think of lukewarm water, hope to get in it.

3

Reading Check

Analyze Cause and Effect How did cities affect the development of American literature in the mid-twentieth century?

English Learners

DIFFERENTIATED INSTRUCTION

Advanced To comprehend the text on these pages, students must understand difficult words, such as *urbanization, malaise, segregation,* and *stereotype.* Discuss these words, using roots and affixes to help them derive the meanings of the words.

Intermediate Have students use a dictionary to find the exact definitions of the four words listed in the Early Advanced section.

Teach

Reading Check

Answer: *As the urban population surged, writers explored the vitality of cities, as well as their problems.*

Literary Element   3

Rhyme Scheme Ask: What is the rhyme scheme for "kitchenette building"? Help students discern the scheme as follows:

- 1st stanza: *aba*
- 2nd stanza: *cdec*
- 3rd stanza: *fgf*
- 4th stanza: *hih*

[APPROACHING] Have students list the words that rhyme in each stanza. Explain how to assign a letter to each new word sound.

View the Art

Lily Furedi (1896–1969) was born in Hungary. This scene on a New York City subway is a snapshot of urban life during the Depression. **Ask:** How is this painting an effective portrayal of urban life in the 1930s? *(There are a variety of people on the train; some are dressed for work and some are dressed for a night on the town. Some of the people are traveling alone; others are in pairs.)*

Teach

Connect Ask: What is a "flashbulb memory" for you (other than 9/11)? How did it change your life? *(Answers will vary.)*

Analyze Cause and Effect
Tell students to review the summaries of world events from "The Good War" through "The Cold War."
Ask: How did these periods affect life in the United States? *(Possible answers: The Japanese attack on Pearl Harbor changed Americans' attitudes toward the war; racial tensions grew as a result of the migration of African Americans to the North.)*

Literary History ☆
Writers of the Holocaust
Much of what we know about the Nazi persecution of the Jews comes from writers who survived the Holocaust. Elie Wiesel (1928–) endured captivity at two Nazi concentration camps. Wiesel's book *Night* is an autobiographical account of his imprisonment. Anne Frank (1929–1945) wrote a diary of her family's two years in hiding, but died in a concentration camp.

Big Idea 3
The United States and the World

Can you remember where you were when you learned of the 9/11 terrorist attacks? Psychologists describe how a deeply felt or traumatic event can produce an intense "flashbulb memory." For millions in the U.S., the Japanese attack on Pearl Harbor, December 7, 1941, produced such a memory.

The Good War
World War II has become enshrined in American public memory as the "good war"—a heroic crusade against an evil enemy. However, most people in the U.S. were strongly opposed to military involvement following the outbreak of war in Europe in September 1939. This attitude changed abruptly after the Japanese attack on Pearl Harbor, and the U.S. mobilized for war against the Axis powers. On the battlefront, U.S. forces turned the tide in Europe and the Pacific and played a crucial role in the victory of the Allies. At home, U.S. workers quickly transformed the U.S. economy into the most productive and efficient war machine in the world.

> "We are now in this war. We are all in it—all the way. Every single man, woman, and child is a partner in the most tremendous undertaking of our American history."
>
> —Franklin D. Roosevelt, wartime radio broadcast December 9, 1941

Tension on the Home Front
Wartime production helped restore prosperity to the United States after the long Depression. Minorities shared in this wartime prosperity, but racism and ethnic animosities persisted. After Pearl Harbor, the U.S. gathered 120,000 people of Japanese ancestry—77,000 of whom were U.S. citizens—and forced them into internment camps in early 1942. The renewed migration of African Americans from the South to big cities in the North and West sometimes resulted in racial violence, as in Detroit, where 25 African Americans and 9 whites were killed during riots in June, 1943. During that same month, riots in Los Angeles occurred after hundreds of U.S. soldiers and sailors attacked a group of young Mexican American men.

The Holocaust
After seizing power in the 1930s, the Nazis began a brutal campaign of violence against Jews and other groups that they considered subhuman. During the early years of the war, Nazis rounded up and shot large numbers of Jews, Communists, Unitarians, Gypsies, and Slavs. Later, they expanded this program of genocide into the "final solution," a huge project of "ethnic cleansing" that involved a network of death camps in which millions of disabled persons, Jews, Poles, Russians, Gypsies, and other non-Aryans were systematically killed. In only a few years, Jewish communities in Europe that had existed for more than 1,000 years were obliterated in what has become known as the Holocaust.

The Cold War
The years after World War II brought changes to the U.S. Many began to challenge racial discrimination. Devastation in Europe allowed U.S. industries to dominate world markets, and the wartime economic boom continued through the 1950s. The U.S. and the Soviet Union, however—wartime allies against the Axis Powers—became tense rivals in a global power struggle between capitalism and communism. The two superpowers never went to war, but they developed and stockpiled nuclear weapons. An anxious world now lived under a new cloud—the mushroom cloud of the atomic age.

Writing Practice

Research To aid students' understanding of World War II and its aftermath, have students choose one of the subheads as a research topic. Tell students to use a variety of sources and include them in their reports:

- a bibliography of sources
- images of the time period with original captions
- a written summary of their research

Have students arrange their material on a large piece of poster board and make a presentation to the class.

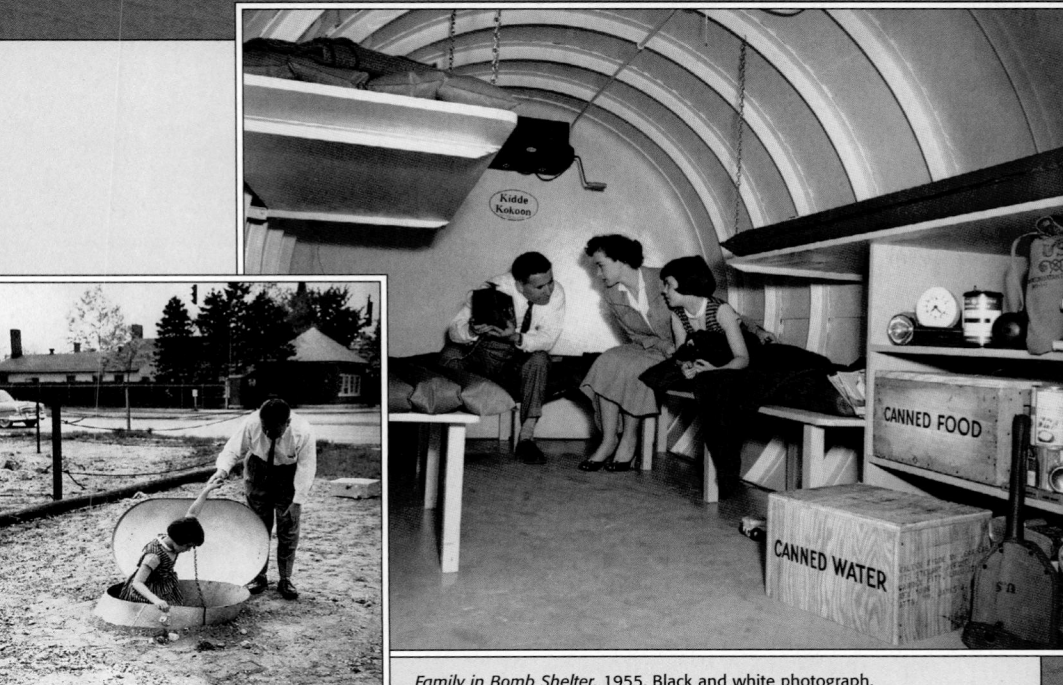

Family in Bomb Shelter, 1955. Black and white photograph.

Father and Daughter Entering Bomb Shelter, 1955. Black and white photograph.

from *"The Four Freedoms"* by Franklin D. Roosevelt

In the future days, which we seek to make secure, we look forward to a world founded upon four essential human freedoms.

The first is freedom of speech and expression—everywhere in the world.

The second is freedom of every person to worship God in his own way everywhere in the world.

The third is freedom from want, which, translated into world terms, means economic understandings which will secure to every nation a healthy peacetime life for its inhabitants everywhere in the world.

The fourth is freedom from fear—which, translated into world terms, means a worldwide reduction of armaments to such a point and in such a thorough fashion that no nation will be in a position to commit an act of physical aggression against any neighbor—anywhere in the world.

That is no vision of a distant millennium. It is a definite basis for a kind of world attainable in our own time and generation. That kind of world is the very antithesis of the so-called new order of tyranny which the dictators seek to create with the crash of a bomb.

3

Reading Check

Analyze Cause and Effect How did World War II lead to the development of the United States as a superpower?

Approaching Level

DIFFERENTIATED INSTRUCTION

Emerging Remind students that a good strategy to use when approaching a selection with unfamiliar elements is to vary reading rate. Instruct students to slow down to improve comprehension when the text is difficult and to read more quickly when the material contains familiar words and concepts. Ask students to make a note each time they encounter a difficult passage. After they have read the selection once, students should go back to the places they noted, carefully reading them again and paraphrasing to enhance comprehension.

Teach

Reading Check

Answer: *The United States became a superpower as a result of several factors: its crucial role in the victory of the Allies, its continued economic success after World War II, and its domination of world markets.*

Literary Element | 3

Structure The particular order or pattern a writer uses to present ideas is called *structure*. Depending on the writer's purpose and the genre, the structure may vary. Listing information or using cause and effect are two ways to present a topic. **Ask:** How does Roosevelt structure "The Four Freedoms" speech? *(He lists the freedoms he believes the world has a right to enjoy.)*

View the Photograph ★

Fear of nuclear war prompted some people to build underground bomb shelters. Civil defense plans were begun nationwide, and some high school students were required to monitor observation posts as part of an early warning system in case of an air attack.

Assess/Close

Legacy of the Period

Ask: In what ways does your own community affect your life and the lives of those around you? *(Students may discuss how the values they were brought up with reflect the values in their community.)*

Cultural and Literary Links

As students read the unit, suggest that they look for ways in which these authors have influenced today's writers.

Activities

1. **Follow Up** Have students discuss their answers with partners or in small groups. Each grouping can become experts on one question by returning to it throughout the unit and sharing their findings with the class.

2. **Musical Periods** Each member could focus on a specific artist or musical style. When presenting to the class, students should explain connections between the artist or musical style and the time period or geographic region.

3. **Visual Literacy** Students could create a slide show of their images. Students could also propose new art projects for their local community.

FOLDABLES
Study Organizer

Four-Tab Book Have students make and label the Four-Tab Book as shown. Then have them use it to organize information they learn about each literary genre.

WRAP-UP

Legacy of the Period

Beginning in the 1930s, Regionalism reasserted itself in the face of economic difficulties. Distrustful of big business and modern culture, some Regionalist writers found moral strength and universal significance in the lives and values of ordinary people in the United States. Other writers, particularly in the South, explored how their region's history and culture defined and distorted people's lives. Their focus on the macabre, which is often called Southern Gothic, had a significant influence on subsequent American literature.

The major global struggles of the period from the 1930s to the 1960s—World War II and the Cold War—shaped the contemporary world. The position of the United States as an economic and military superpower was established during this period and the nuclear arms race began. The Holocaust led to the founding of the State of Israel, which continues to be a source of tension and hostility in the Middle East.

Cultural and Literary Links

 John Steinbeck's Tom Joad, the main character of *The Grapes of Wrath*, was celebrated as a folk hero by American progressives such as Woody Guthrie, who wrote a ballad about him.

>> The influence of William Faulkner on both American and foreign writers has been enormous. Among the most prominent world writers who have acknowledged his influence are the Colombian writer Gabriel García Márquez and the Indian writer R. K. Narayan.

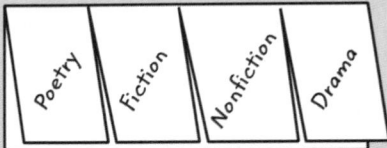
LOG ON ▶ **Literature** Online

Unit Resources For additional skills practice, go to glencoe.com and enter QuickPass code GLA9800u6.

Activities »

Choose one of the following activities to explore and develop as you read this unit.

1. **Follow Up** Go back to the Looking Ahead on page 851 and answer the questions.

2. **Contrast Musical Periods** Work with a small group to research music from one of the decades from the 1930s to 1960s. Find connections among the social, cultural, and musical styles of the decade that you choose. For example, you might research the songs of Woody Guthrie about the Dust Bowl period. Present your findings to the class, and, if possible, play recordings of some of the music.

3. **Build Visual Literacy** One of the New Deal's enduring cultural programs was the decoration of public buildings (often post offices) throughout the United States with murals and sculptures. View and take photographs of examples in your area of the art produced by the Works Progress Administration (WPA). Assemble a photo album to present to the class.

4. **Take Notes** Use this graphic organizer to keep track of the four literary genres in this unit.

FOLDABLES **Study Organizer** **FOUR-TAB BOOK**

Poetry | Fiction | Nonfiction | Drama

4. **Take Notes** Show students how to use the graphic organizer. Students could study their own community, report their findings, and propose a solution.

The New Regionalism and the City

American Gothic, 1930. Grant Wood. Oil on beaverboard, 29 x 25 in. Art Institute of Chicago.

 View the Art In this famous painting, Wood has chosen to portray his subjects as strong, restrained, and proud. How might these characteristics reflect the values of many Americans in urban and rural settings during the mid-twentieth century? ★

"*Not everything that is faced can be changed, but nothing can be changed until it is faced.*" **1**

—James Baldwin

Analyze and Extend

Reading Strategy **1**

Evaluate Direct students to read the quotation from James Baldwin. Explain that in his writing Baldwin portrayed the economic and emotional devastation brought about by racial prejudice. **Say:** Explain Baldwin's meaning in your own words. *(Baldwin says that people must face up to the need for change before change can take place.)*

 View the Art ★

Answer: *Americans had to be strong and restrained to live through the Great Depression and they were proud of the values they had stood up for in World War II.*

In *American Gothic,* Grant Wood portrayed his own region, the American midwest, in a style of painting he had learned in Europe.

865

English Learners

DIFFERENTIATED INSTRUCTION

Intermediate Explain that the word *gothic* in the painting's title refers to a style of architecture. Here, the word *style* refers to certain shapes and materials used at different times in history. The gothic style started in the twelfth century in France. Huge, ornate cathedrals were built with tall, pointed arches in the walls, ceilings, and windows. In the late nineteenth and early twentieth centuries, this style was revived in Britain and United States. Wood's title refers to this style, which was used in the design of the farmhouse's upper window. Have students look for and name other long, narrow shapes in the painting that are reminders of the gothic style. *(the farmer's faces, the pitchfork, the woman's brooch)*

For additional support for English Learners, see Unit 6 Teaching Resources Book, p. 19.

Before You Read

Focus

Bellringer Options

Selection Focus
   Transparency 53
Daily Language Practice
   Transparency 79

Or point out that some recollections are more vivid than others. Tell students that in this story, John Steinbeck uses sensory language to present a memory of the fictional narrator. **Ask:** What memories of people, places, or events are vivid in your mind? Why do you think particular memories remain strong?

Before You Read

Breakfast

Meet **John Steinbeck**
(1902–1968)

On October 25, 1962, during the Cuban missile crisis, John Steinbeck turned on his television set to see "if the world was still turning." He was greeted by a news flash announcing that he had just been awarded the Nobel Prize in Literature. Often during his long career, Steinbeck enjoyed both critical acclaim and enormous popularity.

> *"The writer is delegated to declare and to celebrate man's proven capacity for greatness of heart and spirit—for gallantry in defeat, for courage, compassion, and love."*
>
> —John Steinbeck
> from his Nobel Prize banquet speech

Crusader for Social Justice John Steinbeck was born and raised in Salinas, California, a small town nestled in a sprawling valley of lettuce farms. Bright and popular in high school, Steinbeck was accepted to Stanford University but yearned for more life experiences. He drifted in and out of college, never earning a degree. Instead he wrote and worked, taking an assortment of jobs that included ranch hand, fruit picker, factory worker, sales clerk, freelance newspaper writer, construction worker, and farm laborer.

These life experiences furnished Steinbeck with material for his novels and stories. His fourth work, the novel *Tortilla Flat* (1935), was his first to receive public acclaim. Set in his familiar Salinas Valley, it vividly and humorously depicted the joys and sorrows of a group of unemployed men. Several literary successes followed it: *In Dubious Battle* (1936), *Of Mice and Men* (1937), and *Travels with Charley* (1962).

Steinbeck's fiction offers a strong sense of social justice, a heightened sensitivity to the colors and textures of the U.S. landscape, and compelling plots. His characters often are society's forgotten people, struggling to survive and to preserve their humanity amid harrowing social and environmental conditions. Memorable and authentic, Steinbeck's characters seem to step right off the page.

Literary Distinction Steinbeck wrote his masterpiece, *The Grapes of Wrath* (1939), when the United States was recovering from the Great Depression of the 1930s. This 1940 Pulitzer Prize winner traces a dispossessed Oklahoma family's migration to California in search of a better life. There the family and others like it suffer tragically from injustice meted out by powerful landowners and corrupt officials. Today *The Grapes of Wrath* is universally respected for its depiction of the individual's quest for justice and dignity.

A little more than two decades after publishing *The Grapes of Wrath*, Steinbeck was awarded the Nobel Prize in Literature. Six years after receiving this award, Steinbeck died in New York City. He remains one of the most popular and respected authors of the twentieth century.

 Literature Online

Author Search For more about John Steinbeck, go to glencoe.com and enter QuickPass code GLA9800u6.

Selection Skills

Literary Elements
- Implied Theme (SE pp. 867 870, 871; TE p. 869)
- Tone (SE p. 871)

Vocabulary Skills
- Word Usage (SE pp. 867, 872)
- Academic Vocabulary (SE p. 872)

Breakfast

Writing Skills/Grammar
- Write a Report (SE p. 872)
- Historical Narrative (TE p. 868)
- Use *Good* and *Well* (TE p. 870)

Reading Skills
- Connect to Personal Experience (SE pp. 867-869, 872)

Literature and Reading Preview

Connect to the Story

When have you benefited from the kindness of strangers? Make a list of the five most significant experiences you can recall.

Build Background

This story is set in northern California in the 1930s. Steinbeck's odd jobs during the early 1920s gave him a firsthand look at the desperate working and living conditions forced upon most farm laborers. These observations helped Steinbeck develop the themes and plots of many of his major works. He wrote about the working person's quest for dignity and about the stark challenges presented by nature, society, and fate.

Set Purposes for Reading

Big Idea **Return to Regionalism**

As you read, ask yourself, What does Steinbeck reveal about the values of ordinary working people?

Literary Element **Implied Theme**

The theme of a piece of literature is a dominant idea—often a universal message about life—that the writer communicates to the reader. Authors rarely state a theme outright. Instead they use an **implied theme**, letting the main idea or message reveal itself through events, dialogue, or descriptions. As you read, ask yourself, What details suggest the author's message about life?

Reading Strategy **Connect to Personal Experience**

When you **connect to personal experience,** you link what you read to events in your own life or to other selections you've read. By connecting events, emotions, and characters to your own life, you create meaning in a selection and recall information and ideas better. To apply this strategy, ask yourself: Do I know someone like this? Have I ever felt this way? What else have I read that is like this selection?

....

Tip: **Note Familiar Details** Use a chart like the one below to record connections between your experiences and details in the story.

Story Details	My Experiences
encounter with a family camping out	Last summer I met other campers at a state park.

Learning Objectives

For pages 866–872

In studying this text, you will focus on the following objectives:

Literary Study: Analyzing theme.

Reading: Connecting to personal experience.

Writing: Writing a report.

Vocabulary

scuffle (skuf´ əl) *v.* to move with a slow, heavy, shuffling gait; p. 868 *The losing players lowered their eyes and scuffled down the ramp to the locker room.*

dissipate (dis´ ə pāt´) *v.* to cause to scatter and gradually vanish; to break up and drive off; p. 868 *As the fog slowly dissipated, more and more of the road ahead became visible.*

avert (ə vurt´) *v.* to turn away or aside; p. 869 *Terribly upset, the bystander averted her eyes from the car wreck.*

....

Tip: **Word Usage** When you encounter new words, it might help you to answer a specific question about the word. Example: *Name a situation where you might have to avert your eyes.* You might have to avert your eyes if a bright light shines in your face.

English Learners

DIFFERENTIATED INSTRUCTION

Intermediate Students may more readily visualize this breakfast scene if they are familiar with some of the gestures the narrator mentions. Preteach the following terms from the story:

"rubbed my hands"

"hunched my shoulders"

"scuffled my feet"

Have students demonstrate each gesture. Once students have grasped what each

gesture looks like, **ask** the following questions to reinforce comprehension:

In what situations might a person rub his or her hands?

What can it mean when a person hunches his or her shoulders?

Why would people scuffle their feet?

Before You Read

Focus

Summary

"Breakfast" describes an early-morning encounter in northern California during the Great Depression. The narrator comes across a family of migrant workers. A young mother is fixing breakfast. With her are a baby, an older man, and a younger man. The younger man kindly offers to help the narrator find a job. The narrator remembers the encounter as one "of great beauty" that gives him a "rush of warmth."

 For summaries in languages other than English, see Unit 6 Teaching Resources Book, pp. 20–25.

Vocabulary

Word Forms Point out that the three verbs in the vocabulary list have a noun form.

Ask: Which word is spelled the same as a noun and a verb? *(scuffle)* Which noun form ends in *-tion*? *(dissipation)*

ENGLISH LEARNERS **Ask:** Would you try to *scuffle, dissipate,* or *avert* an accident? *(avert)*

 For additional context, see Glencoe Interactive Vocabulary CD-ROM.

Teach

Reading Strategy   1

Predict **Ask:** On the basis of the first paragraph, the use of the word *curious,* and the title, what can you predict about the story? *(The tone will be pleasant, and the story will be a memory about a breakfast. The use of the word curious implies something special or unusual.)*

 For additional practice using the reading skill or strategy, see Unit 6 Teaching Resources Book, p. 27.

Reading Strategy   2

Connect to Personal Experience **Answer:** *Students should provide specific details in recounting their pleasant memories.*

Cultural History ☆

Homelessness The campsite in this story is, in fact, the family's home. During the Great Depression, many Americans were homeless and had to live in tents near wherever they could find work. They stayed as long as the work lasted and then moved on.

 For an audio recording of this selection, use Listening Library Audio CD-ROM.

Readability Scores

Dale-Chall: 6.7
DRP: 52
Lexile: 950

868

Breakfast

John Steinbeck

This thing fills me with pleasure. I don't know why, I can see it in the smallest detail. I find myself recalling it again and again, each time bringing more detail out of a sunken memory, remembering brings the curious warm pleasure.

It was very early in the morning. The eastern mountains were black-blue, but behind them the light stood up faintly colored at the mountain rims with a washed red, growing colder, grayer and darker as it went up and overhead until, at a place near the west, it merged with pure night.

And it was cold, not painfully so, but cold enough so that I rubbed my hands and shoved them deep into my pockets, and I hunched my shoulders up and **scuffled** my feet on the ground. Down in the valley where I was, the earth was that lavender gray of dawn. I walked along a country road and ahead of me I saw a tent that was only a little lighter gray than the ground. Beside the tent there was a flash of orange fire seeping out of the cracks of an old rusty iron stove. Gray smoke spurted up out of the stubby stovepipe, spurted up a long way before it spread out and **dissipated.**

2 Connect to Personal Experience *What pleasant memories can you recall in great detail?*

Vocabulary

scuffle (skuf′ əl) *v.* to move with a slow, heavy, shuffling gait

dissipate (dis′ ə pāt′) *v.* to cause to scatter and gradually vanish; to break up and drive off

Writing Practice

Historical Context The camp in this story reflects the plight of migrant laborers during the Depression. Have students imagine that, over breakfast, one of the family members talks to the narrator about his or her life both in the camp and before arriving in the camp. Tell students to put themselves in the place of that character and write a brief narrative, explaining what happened that brought the person to this place. Students may address such questions as these: What made the person move from his or her original home? How did the person get to California? What does he or she expect now? Students may make inferences from details in the story; they may also refer to the unit introduction for background.

I saw a young woman beside the stove, really a girl. She was dressed in a faded cotton skirt and waist.[1] As I came close I saw that she carried a baby in a crooked arm and the baby was nursing, its head under her waist out of the cold. The mother moved about, poking the fire, shifting the rusty lids of the stove to make a greater draft, opening the oven door; and all the time the baby was nursing, but that didn't interfere with the mother's work, nor with the light quick gracefulness of her movements. There was something very precise and practiced in her movements. The orange fire flicked out of the cracks in the stove and threw dancing reflections on the tent.

I was close now and I could smell frying bacon and baking bread, the warmest, pleasantest odors I know. From the east the light grew swiftly. I came near to the stove and stretched my hands out to it and shivered all over when the warmth struck me. Then the tent flap jerked up and a young man came out and an older man followed him. They were dressed in new blue dungarees[2] and in new dungaree coats with the brass buttons shining. They were sharp-faced men, and they looked much alike.

The younger had a dark stubble beard and the older had a gray stubble beard. Their heads and faces were wet, their hair dripped with water, and water stood out on their stiff beards and their cheeks shone with water. Together they stood looking quietly at the lightening east; they yawned together and looked at the light on the hill rims. They turned and saw me.

> The orange fire flicked out of the cracks in the stove and threw dancing reflections on the tent.

"Morning," said the older man. His face was neither friendly nor unfriendly.

"Morning, sir," I said.

"Morning," said the young man.

The water was slowly drying on their faces. They came to the stove and warmed their hands at it.

The girl kept to her work, her face averted and her eyes on what she was doing. Her hair was tied back out of her eyes with a string and it hung down her back and swayed as she worked. She set tin cups on a big packing box, set tin plates and knives and forks out too. Then she scooped fried bacon out of the deep grease and laid it on a big tin platter, and the bacon cricked[3] and rustled as it grew crisp. She opened the rusty oven door and took out a square pan full of high big biscuits.

When the smell of that hot bread came out, both of the men inhaled deeply.

The elder man turned to me, "Had your breakfast?"

"No."

"Well, sit down with us, then."

That was the signal. We went to the packing case and squatted on the ground about it. The young man asked, "Picking cotton?"

"No."

"We had twelve days' work so far," the young man said.

---

3. Here, *cricked* means "turned or twisted."

Return to Regionalism What does the young man's comment reveal about economic conditions for ordinary workers during the Great Depression? **5**

Vocabulary

avert (ə vurt´) *v.* to turn away or aside

---

1. Here, a *waist* is a blouse.
2. *Dungarees* are blue denim pants.

4 Connect to Personal Experience *Why do odors leave a lasting impression in one's memory?*

JOHN STEINBECK **869**

Teach

Literary Element 3

Implied Theme Point out that the theme of a work can be implied through details and descriptions. Here, Steinbeck paints an appealing picture of the campsite as a place of warmth and goodness. **Ask:** What are some of the ways Steinbeck establishes a theme? *(The mother nursing a baby, the aroma of the breakfast, the illumination of the scene by the dawn, and the stove all convey warmth and comfort.)*

Reading Strategy 4

Connect to Personal Experience Answer: *Students may respond that odors are powerful sensory stimuli and therefore are connected strongly with particular experiences.*

Big Idea 5

Return to Regionalism Answer: *It reveals that ordinary workers had difficulty finding steady work during the Great Depression.*

Approaching Level

DIFFERENTIATED INSTRUCTION

Emerging To help students identify an implied idea or theme, tell them that an idea that is implied is suggested or hinted at, not directly stated. Help students determine the message the author is suggesting by taking them through these steps:

1. Ask students to identify some of the words and phrases that appeal to the senses. Make a chart on the board to record the details:

Smells	Tastes	Feelings	Sights	Sounds

2. When students have listed several examples of each, **ask:** What is the general effect on the narrator of these details? *(The narrator finds them enjoyable and satisfying.)*

3. Ask students to summarize the way the family members behave toward the narrator. *(They are friendly and generous.)*

4. Then ask students to decide what message all of these details suggest or hint at. This is the implied theme. *(People can be warm and giving despite their own plight.)*

Teach

Return to Regionalism
Answer: *The family has struggled to earn enough money to buy food.*

(APPROACHING) Ask students to identify the sentence that suggests they had not been eating well until recently. *("The young man said 'We been eating good for twelve days.'" This sentence suggests that before twelve days ago they did not eat well.)*

Reading Strategy | 2

Summarize Ask: What are some of the reasons the narrator's experience was pleasant? *(The family was kind to the narrator; the family seemed happy even though they were poor; the breakfast was appetizing.)*

Literary Element | 3

Implied Theme Answer: *It suggests that the family's kindness deeply affected the narrator.*

> To check students' understanding of the selection, see Unit 6 Teaching Resources Book, p. 30.

The girl spoke from the stove. "They even got new clothes."

The two men looked down at their new dungarees and they both smiled a little.

The girl set out the platter of bacon, the brown high biscuits, a bowl of bacon gravy and a pot of coffee, and then she squatted down by the box too. The baby was still nursing, its head up under her waist out of the cold. I could hear the sucking noises it made.

We filled our plates, poured bacon gravy over our biscuits and sugared our coffee. The older man filled his mouth full and he chewed and chewed and swallowed. Then he said, "God Almighty, it's good," and he filled his mouth again.

The young man said, "We been eating good for twelve days."

We all ate quickly, frantically, and refilled our plates and ate quickly again until we were full and warm. The hot bitter coffee scalded our throats. We threw the last little bit with the grounds in it on the earth and refilled our cups.

There was color in the light now, a reddish gleam that made the air seem colder. The two men faced the east and their faces were lighted by the dawn, and I looked up for a moment and saw the image of the mountain and the light coming over it reflected in the older man's eyes.

Then the two men threw the grounds from their cups on the earth and they stood up together. "Got to get going," the older man said.

The younger turned to me. "'Fyou want to pick cotton, we could maybe get you on."

"No. I got to go along. Thanks for breakfast."

The older man waved his hand in a negative. "O.K. Glad to have you." They walked away together. The air was blazing with light at the eastern skyline. And I walked away down the country road.

That's all. I know, of course, some of the reasons why it was pleasant. But there was some element of great beauty there that makes the rush of warmth when I think of it. ∾ | 2

---

1 Return to Regionalism *What can you infer about the family's experiences until recently?*

Implied Theme *How does this detail provide a clue to the theme of the story?* **3**

Grammar Practice

 SPIRAL REVIEW Use *Good* and *Well* The words *good* and *well* pose a common usage challenge. Write the following sentence from "Breakfast" on the board: "We been eating good for twelve days." Focus attention on the misuse of the word *good*. Guide students to identify *good* as an adjective and not an adverb.

Then write the following sentences on the board and have students identify the correct word in each:

1. The child behaved (good, well). *(well)*
2. The coffee smelled (good, well). *(good)*
3. The new job paid (good, well). *(well)*

After You Read

Respond and Think Critically

Respond and Interpret

1. How did you react to the characters in this story? Explain.

2. (a)What are the first things the narrator describes? (b)What do these descriptions tell you about the narrator?

3. (a)What observations does the narrator make about the family of migrant workers? (b)What seems to be important to the family? Explain.

4. (a)What does the narrator say about his memory at the end of the story? (b)What might his attachment to this memory suggest about his life? What deeper understanding or awareness of life does he seem to gain?

Analyze and Evaluate

5. Steinbeck wrote about migrant workers who lived in small, supportive communities. In what ways does he portray the narrator as part of such a supportive community?

6. The reader never learns why the narrator is walking on a country road or where he is going. Why do you think Steinbeck chose not to reveal much about the narrator?

Connect

7. **Big Idea** **Return to Regionalism** Which values of migrant people does Steinbeck highlight in this story?

8. **Connect to Today** When do you think a group of people today might offer to share a meal with a stranger? Explain.

Literary Element Implied Theme

In "Breakfast," the **implied theme** is built around the narrator's warm recollection of an encounter with a family of migrant workers.

1. What is the implied theme, or message about life, in this selection?

2. What details and descriptions support this theme?

Review: Tone

As you learned on page 133, **tone** is a reflection of a writer's or a speaker's attitude toward the subject matter, as conveyed through elements such as word choice, punctuation, sentence structure, and figures of speech. A writer's tone might convey a variety of attitudes, such as sympathy, objectivity, or humor.

Partner Activity With a partner, examine the word choice and the dialogue in "Breakfast." Create a chart like the one started below, and fill it in with examples of effective word choice and dialogue. Then answer the following question: What tone is conveyed by the family's words and actions?

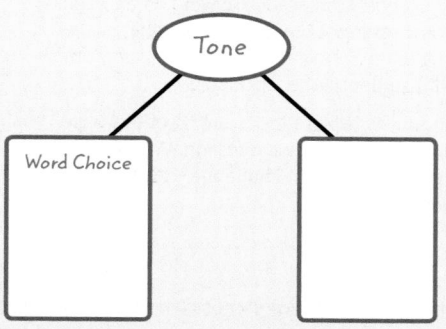

JOHN STEINBECK **871**

Progress Check

Can students identify an implied theme?

If No → See Unit 6 Teaching Resources Book, p. 26.

After You Read

Assess

1. Students may note that the characters are warm and generous; sharing their food with a stranger is impressive.

2. (a) The sunrise, the mountains, the temperature, and the family and its early-morning activities (b) He derives pleasure from simple sights.

3. (a) He notes their appearance, their demeanor, and their actions. (b) The family values work, basic needs, and food.

4. (a) The memory is pleasant and contains "some element of great beauty." (b) The narrator's life is hard; simple kindnesses are appreciated. He may realize that kindness gives life warmth.

5. The narrator does not hesitate to warm his hands at the fire. The family shares food and offers to help him find work.

6. The narrator becomes a universal figure who serves as the eyes and ears of the reader.

7. He highlights that they are hard-working, thankful, and generous. They willingly show hospitality to a stranger.

8. Some people would offer to share a meal or to give money if they saw a person was in need, but others might feel suspicious or cautious about the stranger's presence.

 For additional assessment, see Assessment Resources, pp. 235–236.

Review: Tone

The tone is pleasant, even optimistic, as the family enjoys and shares its meal and expresses thanks.

After You Read

Assess

Reading Strategy

1. Students may say that they related most strongly to the family's sharing their breakfast with a hungry stranger.
2. Students should mention specific insights about their personal experiences that have helped them understand the literary work and themselves better.

Vocabulary

1. I would walk slowly and heavily.
2. If a substance *dissipated* in water, it would scatter and disappear.
3. I would *avert* myself from a situation that would result in my punishment.

Academic Vocabulary

Trigonometry poses the greatest challenge to me, as I am not as capable in math as in other subjects.

 For grammar practice, see Unit 6 Teaching Resources Book, p. 29.

 To create custom assessments using software, use ExamView Assessment Suite.

Reading Strategy Connect to Personal Experience

Connecting to personal experience involves drawing parallels between the people, places, and events in the story and the people, places, and events in your own life. Review the chart you filled in as you read "Breakfast."

1. To which details in the story did you relate most strongly?
2. What new insights about your experiences did you discover by connecting them to people and events in this story?

Vocabulary Practice

Practice with Word Usage Respond to these statements to help you explore the meanings of vocabulary words from the selection.

1. Explain how you would walk if you **scuffled**.
2. Describe how a substance would appear if it **dissipated** in water.
3. Give an example of a situation that you might want to **avert**.

Academic Vocabulary

John Steinbeck captures the **challenge** *of surviving as a migrant worker in the Dust Bowl and the Great Depression.*

Challenge is an academic word. In an educational setting, a teacher may say that it is a **challenge** to maintain order in a classroom with students who lack discipline.

To further explore the meaning of this word, answer the following question: Which subject poses the greatest **challenge** to you as a student, and why?

For more on academic vocabulary, see pages 53–54.

LOG ON ▶ **Literature** Online

Selection Resources For Selection Quizzes, eFlash-cards, and Reading-Writing Connection activities, go to glencoe.com and enter QuickPass code GLA9800u6.

Connect to *Math*

 Write a Report

Assignment The Depression affected the economies of nations worldwide from 1929 to 1939. Millions were unemployed. Write a short report about the economic effects of the Depression in the U.S. Include a chart or graph with statistics on unemployment, wages, or homelessness during the 1930s. Compare these statistics to today.

Investigate Use more than one reliable source for statistics. Consult U.S. government Web sites, such as the Bureau of Labor Statistics or Census Bureau. Keep a bibliography of your sources.

Create Create a chart or graph of the statistics you discover. For example, place years on the x-axis and rates of unemployment or homelessness on the y-axis. If you create a chart, put years in one column and statistics in another. You may also want to include columns in your chart for the value of the dollar and the population during these years. Without considering inflation and population growth, your statistics may appear to be skewed. An example is provided below.

U.S. Unemployment Rates

Year	Unemployment rate	Population
1933	25%	125,578,763

Report If possible, use word-processing or spreadsheet software to make your chart look professional. Alongside your data, include a summary and analysis of the short-term and long-term effects of the Depression. Consider the impact it had on Americans' lives. Integrate any new math, historical, or sociological terms into your report.

Connect to *Math*

Evaluate students' reports based on these criteria:

- Does student provide statistics or estimates of unemployment, homelessness, or wages during the years of the Great Depression?
- Has the student researched reliable sources such as federal government Web sites or encyclopedias?
- Does the student's report include visual aids or media?

Vocabulary Workshop

Roots, Prefixes, and Suffixes

Literature Connection One way to determine the meaning of an unfamiliar word is to analyze its parts.

> *"The girl kept to her work, her face averted and her eyes on what she was doing."*

> —John Steinbeck, from "Breakfast"

The Latin **root** *vert* means "turn." It is a common root, found in the words *averse, aversion, reverse, subvert, divert,* and others. The **prefix** *a-* can mean "in the state or condition of"; and the **suffix** *-ed* shows past tense; so an *averted* face is turned away.

Recognizing some common Greek and Latin prefixes, suffixes, and word roots or base words will help you understand what you read.

Prefixes	Roots	Suffixes
geo- Earth	*graph* writing of	*-ical* having the nature of
dis- the reverse of	*place* position	*-ment* the condition of being
contra- against	*dic(t)* speak	*-tion* action or process of
in- within, into	*spir* breathe	*-ed* the past tense of a verb

Practice For each item below, refer to the prefixes, roots, and suffixes in the chart to help you select the best answer.

1. During the Great Depression, some authors wrote of particular **geographical** regions. Geographical regions are
   - **a.** particular times.
   - **b.** beside the ocean.
   - **c.** in the mountains.
   - **d.** particular places on Earth.

2. John Steinbeck writes about the human cost of the Dust Bowl migrants' **displacement** from their homes. *Displacement* means
   - **a.** being moved away.
   - **b.** being put in prison.
   - **c.** being confused.
   - **d.** being invited to stay.

3. Flannery O'Connor **contradicted** Northern critics who called her stories grotesque. O'Connor
   - **a.** agreed with her critics.
   - **b.** disagreed with them.
   - **c.** ignored them.
   - **d.** complimented them.

4. Steinbeck drew **inspiration** from the migrants who shared their breakfast with him. The migrants
   - **a.** gave him more spirit.
   - **b.** discouraged him.
   - **c.** frightened him.
   - **d.** did not impress him.

Learning Objectives

In this workshop, you will focus on the following objectives:

Vocabulary: Understanding word parts: roots, prefixes, and suffixes.

Affixes

A **prefix** is a word part that is inserted at the beginning of a word root or a base word to create a new meaning. A **suffix** is a combination of letters or a single letter added at the end of a base word or a word part. Prefixes and suffixes together are called **affixes**.

Tip

When you are asked for the meaning of a word that appears in a reading passage, check the word root, the prefix, and the suffix of the word. If you recognize the root, you can probably figure out what the word means.

Language Handbook

For more about prefixes and suffixes, see Language Handbook, p. R60.

Literature Online

Vocabulary For more vocabulary practice, go to glencoe.com and enter QuickPass code GLA9800u6.

VOCABULARY WORKSHOP **873**

Focus

Point out to students that prefixes are included alphabetically among the word entries in most dictionaries. Have students look up the prefixes *mis-*, *re-*, and *sub-* in a dictionary and identify their meanings.

Teach

Word Parts Ask volunteers for examples of words that contain the prefixes in the left-hand column of the chart (*geology, distract, contradict, inhabitant*) and of words that contain the roots in the middle column. (*graphic, placement, diction, respiration*)

Assess

Practice

1. d
2. a
3. b
4. a

For additional vocabulary practice, see Glencoe Interactive Vocabulary CD-ROM.

English Learners

DIFFERENTIATED INSTRUCTION

Advanced Students may need to review the terms *prefix, suffix,* and *word root*. Help students remember the meaning of the word *prefix* by explaining that *pre-* means "before." Have students place the prefix *pre-* in front of these words: *view, pay, arrange.* Have volunteers explain how the meaning of the prefix changes the meaning of the word.

Explain that a root may occur at various places in a word. For example, the root *scrib* or *script,* meaning "to write," is in the words *scribble, inscription,* and *describe.* Have students brainstorm words that can be formed from the roots *graph* and *spir.* (*photograph, graphic, inspire, spiritual*)

Meet **William Faulkner**
(1897–1962)

As a boy, William Faulkner did not seem destined for literary renown. He was both a high school and college dropout. His neighbors nicknamed him "Count No'count," and few guessed that this seemingly lazy youth was a literary genius who would capture the struggles of the human heart and immortalize a region of America.

Art Imitates Life Born in Albany, Mississippi, Faulkner moved when he was five with his family to Oxford, Mississippi, where his father could take advantage of his grandfather's connections.

Faulkner himself did not have the patience to deal with the monotony of steady work. One of his longest employments, almost three years, was as postmaster at the university in Oxford.

Although Faulkner read extensively, none of his reading concerned the history of the area where he lived. The flavor and settings of his stories were gleaned through word of mouth from the people around him.

Yoknapatawpha As a young man, Faulkner traveled abroad for some time and eventually landed in New Orleans, where he met Sherwood Anderson and other writers. It was here that he began to write seriously. His first book, a poetry collection entitled *The Marble Faun*, was less than successful. Anderson advised him to attempt fiction. Faulkner published his first novel, *Soldier's Pay*, in 1926, and his second novel, *Mosquitoes*, the following year.

> "I never read any history. I talked to people around who had lived through it, and I would pick it up—I was just saturated with it but never read about it."
>
> —William Faulkner

With his third novel, *Sartoris*, Faulkner found the formula that would place him among the greatest of American writers. He created the fictional world of Yoknapatawpha County, based on the region of northern Mississippi where he lived. Over the next thirty years, he explored the "history" of this county and its fictional inhabitants.

Faulkner's style can make his writing difficult to follow. He experimented with repetition, multiple points of view, and stream of consciousness. Because of the difficulty of his style, Faulkner was not widely read until *The Portable Faulkner* was published in 1946 and catapulted him to world fame. Three years later he won the Nobel Prize in Literature. Faulkner kept writing until his death.

 Literature Online

Author Search For more about William Faulkner, go to glencoe.com and enter QuickPass code GLA9800u6.

Selection Skills

Literary Elements
- Foreshadowing (SE pp. 875, 877, 878, 880, 882, 886)
- Flashback (SE p. 886)

Reading Skills
- Identify Sequence (SE pp. 875–877, 883, 886)
- Paraphrase (TE p. 884)

A Rose for Emily *and* Address upon Receiving...

Vocabulary Skills
- Denotation and Connotation (SE pp. 875, 886)

Writing Skills/Grammar
- Expository Essay (SE p. 887)
- Degrees of Comparison (TE p. 876)
- Use Adjectives (TE p. 882)

Listening/Speaking/Viewing Skills
- Analyze Art (TE pp. 878, 881, 883)
- Oral Presentation (TE p. 880)

Literature and Reading Preview

Connect to the Story

How different can a person's public identity be from his or her private identity? Discuss this question with a small group. Consider why people might have several layers.

Build Background

Faulkner's writings draw upon his knowledge of genteel aristocrats, unsophisticated sharecroppers, and Native Americans, as well as African Americans who had endured first the dehumanization of slavery and then the discrimination of Jim Crow. The language in Faulkner's work reflects this context. Modern readers may be shocked or offended by his use of racial slurs in this selection. Faulkner, like Mark Twain, does not use this language to offend or shock. He uses it merely to reflect the language of the time and place he describes.

Set Purposes for Reading

Big Idea Return to Regionalism

As you read, ask yourself, How does Faulkner present details that describe a small southern town from one hundred years ago?

Literary Element Foreshadowing

Foreshadowing is the use of clues by the author to prepare readers for events that will happen later in the story. In "A Rose for Emily," for example, the bad smell coming from Miss Emily's house foreshadows death and decay. As you read, ask yourself, Which events might foreshadow important plot developments?

Reading Strategy Identify Sequence

Faulkner shifts time frames so often in "A Rose for Emily" that it can be difficult for readers to understand exactly when the events in the story take place. As you read, ask yourself, What is happening? To keep track of what happens, list the events as they occur in the narrative and then number them in the sequence they occur in Emily's life.

Tip: Make a Sequence Chart Use a sequence chart to help you keep track of events. Order the events as they occur in Emily's life. Use the list you wrote above to guide you.

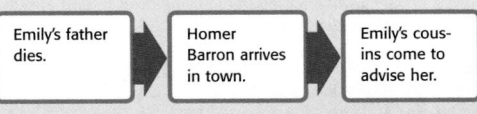

| Emily's father dies. | → | Homer Barron arrives in town. | → | Emily's cousins come to advise her. |

WILLIAM FAULKNER **875**

Vocabulary

sluggishly (slug´ ish lē) *adv.* slowly; without strength or energy; p. 877 *The weary hiker crawled sluggishly into his tent.*

vindicate (vin´ də kāt´) *v.* to justify; to prove correct in light of later circumstances; p. 879 *Winning the competition vindicated her efforts.*

haughty (hô´ tē) *adj.* conceited; arrogant; p. 880 *The haughty king would never admit a mistake.*

circumvent (sur´ kəm vent´) *v.* to get around or to avoid by clever maneuvering; p. 882 *We had to circumvent the usual procedure in order to finish the job.*

virulent (vir´ yə lənt) *adj.* extremely poisonous or harmful; p. 882 *After World War I, a virulent strain of influenza killed millions.*

Tip: Denotation and Connotation Words with the same dictionary definition can affect people differently. For example, *sluggishly* and *slowly* have similar meanings, but *sluggishly* has a stronger connotation.

Before You Read

Focus

Summary

After Miss Emily Grierson's death, flashbacks reveal details of her life. As a member of a prominent family, Emily has paid no taxes. A new generation of city officials unsuccessfully tries to collect them. After the death of her father, she had planned to marry a Yankee, but he disappeared. After her funeral, they find his remains in Emily's bed.

In his acceptance speech, Faulkner says that his award is not for him but for his work, which addresses the "universal truths" of the heart.

 For summaries in languages other than English, see Unit 6 Teaching Resources Book, pp. 32–37.

Vocabulary

Word Analysis Point out the prefix *circum-*, meaning "around," in *circumvent*. Students might recognize it in words from other subject areas. **Ask:** What math word describes the boundary of a circle? (*circumference*) What word from history would you use in discussing explorers? (*circumnavigate*)

APPROACHING **Ask:** Would you try to *circumvent* or *circumnavigate* a traffic jam? (*circumvent*)

 For additional vocabulary practice, see Unit 6 Teaching Resources Book, p. 40.

English Learners

DIFFERENTIATED INSTRUCTION

SMALL GROUP

Intermediate Faulkner's language and style are challenging. Present students with these words from the story:

decay; tarnished; vanquished; gross; insanity; despair; arsenic; acrid

Have them work in groups to determine meanings of the words using a dictionary. Then **ask:** Which words might be used in describing a setting for a story? *(decay, tarnished, gross, acrid)* Which words might refer to a character or a state of mind? *(vanquished, gross, insanity, despair)* Which word might suggest action? *(vanquished)*

Have them make predictions about the story, based on these words.

Teach

Reading Strategy | 1

Visualize Have students carefully read the description of Miss Emily's house. **Ask:** What impression do you have of Miss Emily's house? How is it like her? *(It is a decaying relic of a previous time, personified as "stubborn and coquettish.")*

 For additional practice using the reading skill or strategy, see Unit 6 Teaching Resources Book, p. 39.

Big Idea | 2

Return to Regionalism
Answer: *The town is small, and its citizens are interested in the affairs of their neighbors. There is still an apparent, though dwindling, respect for the upper class.*

Reading Strategy | 3

Identify Sequence Answer: *The story begins with Emily's funeral; here the word alive and the use of the past perfect tense signal a shift to an earlier time.*

 For an audio recording of this selection, use Listening Library Audio CD-ROM.

Readability Scores

Dale-Chall: 5.9
DRP: 60
Lexile: 1120

A Rose for Emily

William Faulkner

When Miss Emily Grierson died, our whole town went to her funeral: the men through a sort of respectful affection for a fallen monument, the women mostly out of curiosity to see the inside of her house, which no one save an old man-servant—a combined gardener and cook—had seen in at least ten years. It was a big, squarish frame house that had once been white, decorated with cupolas[1] and spires and scrolled balconies in the heavily lightsome style of the seventies,[2] set on what had once been our most select street. But garages and cotton gins had encroached and obliterated even the august[3] names of that neighborhood; only Miss Emily's house was left, lifting its stubborn and coquettish[4] decay above the cotton wagons and the gasoline pumps—an eyesore among eyesores. And now Miss Emily had gone to join the representatives of those august names where they lay in the cedar-bemused[5] cemetery among the ranked and anonymous graves of Union and Confederate soldiers who fell at the battle of Jefferson.

Alive, Miss Emily had been a tradition, a duty, and a care; a sort of hereditary obligation upon the town, dating from that day in 1894 when Colonel Sartoris, the mayor—he who fathered the edict that no Negro woman should appear on the streets without an apron—remitted her taxes, the dispensation dating from the death of her father on into perpetuity.[6] Not that Miss Emily would have accepted charity. Colonel Sartoris invented an involved tale to the effect that Miss Emily's father had loaned money to the town, which the town, as a matter of business, preferred this way of repaying. Only a man of Colonel Sartoris' generation and thought could have invented it, and only a woman could have believed it.

When the next generation, with its more modern ideas, became mayors and aldermen, this arrangement created some little dissatisfaction. On the first of the year they mailed her a tax notice. February came, and there was no

---

1. *Cupolas* are small, domed structures rising above a roof.
2. *Lightsome* means "light and graceful." *Seventies* refers to the 1870s.
3. *August* (ô gust') means "distinguished" or "prominent."
4. *Coquettish* (kō ket' ish) means "flirtatious."
5. *Cedar-bemused* means "lost among the cedar trees" (literally, "confused by cedars").

6. *[remitted . . . perpetuity]* This phrase means that Miss Emily was excused from paying taxes forever after her father's death.

Return to Regionalism *What does the opening of "A Rose for Emily" tell you about the town and the type of people who live there?* **2**

Identify Sequence *Which clues reveal that the narrator is moving into a flashback?* **3**

Grammar Practice

SPIRAL REVIEW Degrees of Comparison
Faulkner effectively uses adjectives and adverbs to create a striking picture of Emily's life. Remind students that the comparative and superlative forms of many modifiers are formed by adding -*er* and -*est*.

Create a chart on the board with columns headed "Positive," "Comparative," and "Superlative." Then ask volunteers to supply examples of modifiers from the selec-tion. Refer to page R42 of the Language Handbook to review adjective types. Guide students in identifying the proper column for each modifier. Challenge them to provide the other two forms of each.

reply. They wrote her a formal letter, asking her to call at the sheriff's office at her convenience. A week later the mayor wrote her himself, offering to call or to send his car for her, and received in reply a note on paper of an archaic[7] shape, in a thin, flowing calligraphy[8] in faded ink, to the effect that she no longer went out at all. The tax notice was also enclosed, without comment.

They called a special meeting of the Board of Aldermen.[9] A deputation[10] waited upon her, knocked at the door through which no visitor had passed since she ceased giving china-painting lessons eight or ten years earlier. They were admitted by the old Negro into a dim hall from which a stairway mounted into still more shadow. It smelled of dust and disuse—a close, dank smell. The Negro led them into the parlor. It was furnished in heavy, leather-covered furniture. When the Negro opened the blinds of one window, they could see that the leather was cracked; and when they sat down, a faint dust rose **sluggishly** about their thighs, spinning with slow motes[11] in the single sun-ray. On a tarnished gilt[12] easel before the fireplace stood a crayon portrait of Miss Emily's father.

They rose when she entered—a small, fat woman in black, with a thin gold chain descending to her waist and vanishing into her belt, leaning on an ebony cane with a tarnished gold head. Her skeleton was small and spare; perhaps that was why what would have been merely plumpness in another was obesity in her.

---

7. Here, *archaic* means "old-fashioned."
8. *Calligraphy* is an elegant type of handwriting.
9. The *Board of Aldermen* is the group formed by members of a city or town council.
10. A *deputation* is a "a small group that represents a larger one."
11. *Motes* are particles or specks, as of dust.
12. *Gilt* means "covered with gold."

4 Foreshadowing *What might the painting foreshadow?*

Vocabulary

sluggishly (slug′ ish lē) adv. slowly; without strength or energy

She looked bloated, like a body long submerged in motionless water, and of that pallid[13] hue. Her eyes, lost in the fatty ridges of her face, looked like two small pieces of coal pressed into a lump of dough as they moved from one face to another while the visitors stated their errand.

She did not ask them to sit. She just stood in the door and listened quietly until the spokesman came to a stumbling halt. Then they could hear the invisible watch ticking at the end of the gold chain.

Her voice was dry and cold. "I have no taxes in Jefferson. Colonel Sartoris explained it to me. Perhaps one of you can gain access to the city records and satisfy yourselves."

"But we have. We are the city authorities, Miss Emily. Didn't you get a notice from the sheriff, signed by him?"

"I received a paper, yes," Miss Emily said. "Perhaps he considers himself the sheriff . . . I have no taxes in Jefferson."

"But there is nothing on the books to show that, you see. We must go by the—"

"See Colonel Sartoris. I have no taxes in Jefferson."

"But, Miss Emily—"

"See Colonel Sartoris." (Colonel Sartoris had been dead almost ten years.) "I have no taxes in Jefferson. Tobe!" The Negro appeared. "Show these gentlemen out."

II

So she vanquished them, horse and foot, just as she had vanquished their fathers thirty years before about the smell. That was two years after her father's death and a short time after her sweetheart—the one we believed would marry her—had deserted her. After her father's death she went out very little; after her sweetheart went away, people hardly saw her at all. A few of the ladies had the temerity[14] to call,

---

13. *Pallid* means "lacking healthy color" or "pale."
14. *Temerity* (tə mer′ ə tē) is excessive boldness.

Identify Sequence *By the time Emily had "vanquished" the town officials about the "smell," what significant events had already occurred in Emily's life? List them in order.* **5**

Literary Element **4**

Foreshadowing **Answer:** *The prominent display and the gold easel suggest the importance and authority of Emily's father. The painting may foreshadow her father's presence as a haunting, overprotective figure in her life.*

Reading Strategy **5**

Identify Sequence **Answer:** *Her father had died; then her sweetheart had left her.*

Approaching Level

DIFFERENTIATED INSTRUCTION

 SMALL GROUP **Emerging** To help students grasp the sequence in this story, have them divide the events of the story into past and present, using a two-column chart, like the one shown. The starting event in the **Present** column is Miss Emily's funeral.

Past	Present
	Emily's funeral

Once students have identified the events that took place before Emily's funeral, they can go back through that list and number the events in order. Have students work in pairs or groups to complete this task. They can use their completed charts to develop a timeline for the story.

Teach

Literary Element   1

Foreshadowing **Answer:**
The statement seems to anticipate more connections between Emily and "the gross, teeming world." Possibly, the story will reveal the reason for the smell.

(**ENGLISH LEARNERS**) **Ask:** Does reference to Emily's "high and mighty" family carry a positive or negative connotation? *(negative)* What might the townspeople's attitude foreshadow? *(The townspeople would probably get satisfaction from something bad or unpleasant connected with the "high and mighty.")*

Big Idea   2

Return to Regionalism

Ask: How does Judge Stevens's remark capture the flavor of the American South in the early 1900s? *(The dialogue is passionate, yet also reflects the Southern emphasis on politeness.)*

(**APPROACHING**) Have students find another example of dialogue that shows politeness and concern. *("I'd be the last one in the world to bother Miss Emily, but . . . ")*

Language History ☆

Diction The use of an offensive word here is in keeping with the character and the specific historical time in which the story is set. It does not represent the author's own views or attitude.

Autumn Glory: The Old Mill, 1869. John Atkinson Grimshaw. Oil on canvas, 62.2 x 87.6 cm. Leeds Museums and Galleries, City Art Gallery, UK.

but were not received, and the only sign of life about the place was the Negro man—a young man then—going in and out with a market basket.

"Just as if a man—any man—could keep a kitchen properly," the ladies said; so they were not surprised when the smell developed. It was another link between the gross, teeming world and the high and mighty Griersons.

A neighbor, a woman, complained to the mayor, Judge Stevens, eighty years old.

"But what will you have me do about it, madam?" he said.

"Why, send her word to stop it," the woman said. "Isn't there a law?"

"I'm sure that won't be necessary," Judge Stevens said. "It's probably just a snake or a rat that nigger of hers killed in the yard. I'll speak ☆ to him about it."

The next day he received two more complaints, one from a man who came in diffident deprecation.[15] "We really must do something about it, Judge. I'd be the last one in the world to bother Miss Emily, but we've got to do something." That night the Board of Aldermen met—three graybeards and one younger man, a member of the rising generation.

"It's simple enough," he said. "Send her word to have her place cleaned up. Give her a certain time to do it in, and if she don't . . ."

"Dammit, sir," Judge Stevens said, "will you accuse a lady to her face of smelling bad?" **2**

So the next night, after midnight, four men crossed Miss Emily's lawn and slunk about the house like burglars, sniffing along the base of the brickwork and at the cellar openings while

---

1 Foreshadowing *What might this statement about the "smell" and Emily foreshadow?*

---

15. *Diffident deprecation* means "timid disapproval."

Reading Practice

 Make Inferences In this story, characters as well as readers must make inferences. Judge Stevens infers that the smell coming from Miss Emily's house is caused by a dead animal.
Ask: What leads him to make this inference? *(The ladies think that Emily's manservant does not keep up the place very well. The judge assumes that Emily's servant killed a small animal in the yard and the animal is decaying.)*

Ask: What further inference or prediction can you make, based on the foreshadowing hints and any other information you have? *Have students support their inferences by citing information in the text.*

one of them performed a regular sowing motion with his hand out of a sack slung from his shoulder. They broke open the cellar door and sprinkled lime there, and in all the outbuildings.[16] As they recrossed the lawn, a window that had been dark was lighted and Miss Emily sat in it, the light behind her, and her upright torso motionless as that of an idol. They crept quietly across the lawn and into the shadow of the locusts[17] that lined the street. After a week or two the smell went away.

That was when people had begun to feel really sorry for her. People in our town, remembering how old lady Wyatt, her great-aunt, had gone completely crazy at last, believed that the Griersons held themselves a little too high for what they really were. None of the young men were quite good enough for Miss Emily and such. We had long thought of them as a tableau,[18] Miss Emily a slender figure in white in the background, her father a spraddled[19] silhouette in the foreground, his back to her and clutching a horsewhip, the two of them framed by the backflung front door. So when she got to be thirty and was still single, we were not pleased exactly, but **vindicated**; even with insanity in the family she wouldn't have turned down all of her chances if they had really materialized.

When her father died, it got about that the house was all that was left to her; and in a way, people were glad. At last they could pity Miss Emily. Being left alone, and a pauper,[20]

---

16. *Outbuildings* are separate buildings, such as a woodshed or barn, associated with a main building.
17. *Locusts* are deciduous trees. Several varieties have thorns and fragrant flowers that hang down in clusters.
18. A *tableau* (tab lō′) is a striking or artistic grouping of people or objects.
19. *Spraddled* means "sprawled" or "spread wide apart."
20. A *pauper* is a very poor person.

 Return to Regionalism *What does this passage reveal about the social and economic status of most people in the town as opposed to that of Miss Emily?*

Vocabulary

vindicate (vin′ də kāt′) *v.* to justify; to prove correct in light of later circumstances

---

she had become humanized. Now she too would know the old thrill and the old despair of a penny more or less.

The day after his death all the ladies prepared to call at the house and offer condolence and aid, as is our custom. Miss Emily met them at the door, dressed as usual and with no trace of grief on her face. She told them that her father was not dead. She did that for three days, with the ministers calling on her, and the doctors, trying to persuade her to let them dispose of the body. Just as they were about to resort to law and force, she broke down, and they buried her father quickly.

We did not say she was crazy then. We believed she had to do that. We remembered all the young men her father had driven away, and we knew that with nothing left, she would have to cling to that which had robbed her, as people will.

III

She was sick for a long time. When we saw her again her hair was cut short, making her look like a girl, with a vague resemblance to those angels in colored church windows—sort of tragic and serene.

The town had just let the contracts for paving the sidewalks, and in the summer after her father's death they began the work. The construction company came with niggers and mules and machinery, and a foreman named Homer Barron, a Yankee—a big, dark, ready man, with a big voice and eyes lighter than his face. The little boys would follow in groups to hear him cuss the niggers, and the niggers singing in time to the rise and fall of picks. Pretty soon he knew everybody in town. Whenever you heard a lot of laughing anywhere about the square, Homer Barron would be in the center of the group. Presently we began to see him and Miss Emily on Sunday afternoons driving in the yellow-wheeled buggy and the matched team of bays from the livery stable.

Teach

Big Idea   3

Return to Regionalism
Answer: *The townspeople think that Emily holds too high an opinion of herself, so their economic status, and perhaps the social status of many, is probably not as high as hers.*

Literary Element   4

Characterization Have students compare what they know about Emily with the way Homer Barron is characterized.

Ask: Do the two seem a likely match? *(Possible response: Emily is characterized as reclusive; Barron is portrayed as remarkably outgoing. They seem an unlikely match.)*

[APPROACHING] Have students cite specific behaviors or traits of each character and contrast them. *(Emily doesn't accept visitors or respond to the townspeople; Homer enjoys being with groups of people and laughing a lot.)*

View the Art ★

John Atkinson Grimshaw (1836–1883) was a British artist whose most famous works are his "moonlights," seascapes painted on the Yorkshire coast in northern England. **Ask:** What mood or atmosphere does this painting evoke? *(Possible answers: mysterious, eerie, solemn)*

Teach

Return to Regionalism

Answer: *Southern aristocrats normally would not associate with a Northerner, particularly a workman. Emily's action is considered shocking, even though she may be desperate for companionship.*

(ADVANCED) Have students further explore the concept of *noblesse oblige.* Ask them to explain what it might mean in a social structure like Emily's and a society that values manners. *(Emily would be expected to be courteous and respectful to those of other classes.)*

Irony Ask: What is ironic about the label "For rats"? *(Homer Barron, who has made Emily a "fallen" woman in the eyes of the town, might be considered a "rat.")*

(APPROACHING) Remind students that irony is a contrast between what is stated or obvious and what the reader knows or thinks. **Ask: Why might Homer be considered a "rat," and who might think of him this way?** *(A "rat" is someone who is disloyal or who has deceived someone. Emily or readers might see him this way.)*

At first we were glad that Miss Emily would have an interest, because the ladies all said, "Of course a Grierson would not think seriously of a Northerner, a day laborer." But there were still others, older people, who said that even grief could not cause a real lady to forget *noblesse oblige*[21]—without calling it *noblesse oblige.* They just said, "Poor Emily. Her kinsfolk should come to her." She had some kin in Alabama; but years ago her father had fallen out with them over the estate of old lady Wyatt, the crazy woman, and there was no communication between the two families. They had not even been represented at the funeral.

And as soon as the old people said, "Poor Emily," the whispering began. "Do you suppose it's really so?" they said to one another. "Of course it is. What else could . . ." This behind their hands; rustling of craned[22] silk and satin behind jalousies closed upon the sun of Sunday afternoon as the thin, swift clop-clop-clop of the matched team passed: "Poor Emily."

She carried her head high enough—even when we believed that she was fallen. It was as if she demanded more than ever the recognition of her dignity as the last Grierson; as if it had wanted that touch of earthiness to reaffirm her imperviousness. Like when she bought the rat poison, the arsenic. That was over a year

Visual Vocabulary
Jalousies (jal′ ə sēz) are overlapping, adjustable slats that cover a door or window.

---

21. The French expression *noblesse oblige* (nō bles′ ō blēzh′) suggests that those of high birth or rank have a responsibility to act kindly and honorably toward others.
22. *Craned* means "stretched."

1 **Return to Regionalism** *What does this comment suggest about the southern aristocratic attitude toward northerners? What does it imply about Emily's interest in Homer Barron?*

---

after they had begun to say "Poor Emily," and while the two female cousins were visiting her.

"I want some poison," she said to the druggist. She was over thirty then, still a slight woman, though thinner than usual, with cold, **haughty** black eyes in a face the flesh of which was strained across the temples and about the eye-sockets as you imagine a lighthousekeeper's face ought to look. "I want some poison," she said.

"Yes, Miss Emily. What kind? For rats and such? I'd recom—"

"I want the best you have. I don't care what kind."

The druggist named several. "They'll kill anything up to an elephant. But what you want is—"

"Arsenic," Miss Emily said. "Is that a good one?"

"Is . . . arsenic? Yes, ma'am. But what you want—"

"I want arsenic."

The druggist looked down at her. She looked back at him, erect, her face like a strained flag. "Why, of course," the druggist said. "If that's what you want. But the law requires you to tell what you are going to use it for."

Miss Emily just stared at him, her head tilted back in order to look him eye for eye, until he looked away and went and got the arsenic and wrapped it up. The Negro delivery boy brought her the package; the druggist didn't come back. When she opened the package at home there was written on the box, under the skull and bones: "For rats." **2**

IV

So the next day we all said, "She will kill herself"; and we said it would be the best thing. When she had first begun to be seen with Homer Barron, we had said, "She will marry him." Then we said, "She will persuade him yet," because Homer himself had remarked—

Vocabulary
haughty (hô′ tē) adj. conceited; arrogant

Speaking Practice

SPIRAL REVIEW Oral Presentation The decaying Grierson family home is the centerpiece of the setting of "A Rose for Emily." In many communities across the country, similar Victorian-era mansions still stand. Many are in a state of disrepair, while others have been restored or remodeled.

Have students determine whether any such homes exist in their community or a nearby region. Then have students prepare and present oral reports on these houses, including visuals. Reports should answer the 5 Ws (who, what, where, when, why) about the houses and their history.

Day After the Funeral, 1925. Edward Hopper. Watercolor on paper. Private collection. James Goodman Gallery, NY.

Teach

Return to Regionalism
Answer: *The town has conservative morals and values, and people are uncomfortable seeing a woman and a man together unless they intend to marry. Emily, by riding in public with Barron, sets a bad example and undermines the town's conservative beliefs.*

View the Art ★
Edward Hopper (1882–1967) was the best-known American Realist of his time. During the 1920s and 1930s, he became famous for his stark portrayals of loneliness and alienation in American life.

Ask: What emotions do the figures in the painting suggest? *(Possible answers: grief; loneliness)*

he liked men, and it was known that he drank with the younger men in the Elks' Club—that he was not a marrying man. Later we said, "Poor Emily" behind the jalousies as they passed on Sunday afternoon in the glittering buggy, Miss Emily with her head high and Homer Barron with his hat cocked and a cigar in his teeth, reins and whip in a yellow glove.

Then some of the ladies began to say that it was a disgrace to the town and a bad example to the young people. The men did not want to interfere, but at last the ladies forced the Baptist minister—Miss Emily's people were Episcopal—to call upon her. He would never divulge what happened during that interview, but he refused to go back again. The next Sunday they again drove about the streets, and the following day the minister's wife wrote to Miss Emily's relations in Alabama.

So she had blood-kin under her roof again and we sat back to watch developments. At first nothing happened. Then we were sure that they were to be married. We learned that Miss Emily had been to the jeweler's and ordered a man's toilet set[23] in silver, with the letters H. B. on each piece. Two days later we learned that she had bought a complete outfit of men's clothing, including a nightshirt, and we said, "They are married." We were really glad. We were glad because the two female cousins were even more Grierson than Miss Emily had ever been.

So we were not surprised when Homer Barron—the streets had been finished some time since—was gone. We were a little disappointed that there was not a public blowing-off,[24] but we believed that he had

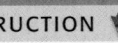

3 Return to Regionalism *What does the town's involvement in Emily's affairs suggest about its morals and values? Why is Emily a threat?*

23. A *toilet set* is a set of articles used for personal grooming (hairbrush, comb, etc.).
24. A *blowing-off* is a celebration.

WILLIAM FAULKNER **881**

Approaching Level
DIFFERENTIATED INSTRUCTION

Established Ask students to explain why the narrator and the townspeople thought Emily was married. *(She is doing things a married woman would do for a husband, buying him clothes and the toilet set.)* Then ask what these actions might foreshadow. *(Emily will still be involved with Homer Barron in some serious way.)*

English Learners
DIFFERENTIATED INSTRUCTION

Intermediate Have students note the use of two terms on this page: *people* and *blood-kin*. Have them determine what these terms mean in this context. *(These words refer to family members or relatives.)*

Teach

Literary Element   1

Foreshadowing Answer:
The sentences reveal that Barron and Emily drop from sight at the same time. This might foreshadow that their relationship is not over, even though the townspeople do not see them together.

gone on to prepare for Miss Emily's coming, or to give her a chance to get rid of the cousins. (By that time it was a cabal,[25] and we were all Miss Emily's allies to help **circumvent** the cousins.) Sure enough, after another week they departed. And, as we had expected all along, within three days Homer Barron was back in town. A neighbor saw the Negro man admit him at the kitchen door at dusk one evening.

And that was the last we saw of Homer Barron. And of Miss Emily for some time. The Negro man went in and out with the market basket, but the front door remained closed. Now and then we would see her at a window for a moment, as the men did that night when they sprinkled the lime, but for almost six months she did not appear on the streets. Then we knew that this was to be expected too; as if that quality of her father which had thwarted her woman's life so many times had been too **virulent** and too furious to die.

When we next saw Miss Emily, she had grown fat and her hair was turning gray. During the next few years it grew grayer and grayer until it attained an even pepper-and-salt iron-gray, when it ceased turning. Up to the day of her death at seventy-four it was still that vigorous iron-gray, like the hair of an active man.

From that time on her front door remained closed, save for a period of six or seven years, when she was about forty, during which she gave lessons in china-painting. She fitted up a studio in one of the downstairs rooms, where the daughters and granddaughters of Colonel Sartoris' contemporaries were sent to her with the same regularity and in the same spirit that they were sent to church on Sundays with a

---

25. A *cabal* (kə bäl´) is a group united in a secret plot.

1   **Foreshadowing** *What might the juxtaposition of these two sentences foreshadow about Emily and Homer Barron?*

Vocabulary
circumvent (sur´ kəm vent´) *v.* to get around or to avoid by clever maneuvering
virulent (vir´ yə lənt) *adj.* extremely poisonous or harmful

twenty-five-cent piece for the collection plate. Meanwhile her taxes had been remitted.

Then the newer generation became the backbone and the spirit of the town, and the painting pupils grew up and fell away and did not send their children to her with boxes of color and tedious brushes and pictures cut from the ladies' magazines. The front door closed upon the last one and remained closed for good. When the town got free postal delivery, Miss Emily alone refused to let them fasten the metal numbers above her door and attach a mailbox to it. She would not listen to them.

Daily, monthly, yearly we watched the Negro grow grayer and more stooped, going in and out with the market basket. Each December we sent her a tax notice, which would be returned by the post office a week later, unclaimed. Now and then we would see her in one of the downstairs windows—she had evidently shut up the top floor of the house—like the carven torso of an idol in a niche,[26] looking or not looking at us, we could never tell which. Thus she passed from generation to generation—dear, inescapable, impervious, tranquil, and perverse.

And so she died. Fell ill in the house filled with dust and shadows, with only a doddering Negro man to wait on her. We did not even know she was sick; we had long since given up trying to get any information from the Negro. He talked to no one, probably not even to her, for his voice had grown harsh and rusty, as if from disuse.

She died in one of the downstairs rooms, in a heavy walnut bed with a curtain, her gray head propped on a pillow yellow and moldy with age and lack of sunlight.

V

The Negro met the first of the ladies at the front door and let them in, with their hushed, sibilant[27] voices and their quick, curious glances, and then he disappeared. He walked

---

26. A *niche* (nich) is a recessed area in a wall, sometimes used for displaying a statue.
27. *Sibilant* (si´ bə lənt) means "making a hissing sound."

Writing Practice

Use Adjectives Draw students' attention to the list of adjectives describing Miss Emily in the right column of this page: *dear, inescapable, impervious, tranquil,* and *perverse.* Point out that two of these words have similar prefixes, *in-* and *im-.* Tell students that these have the same meaning.

Ask: What is the meaning? *(not)* Ask students to define *inescapable* and *impervious* with reference to Miss Emily. *(She is inescapable, meaning that although she does not interact with the townspeople, they cannot escape her presence. She is impervious because she is not affected or influenced by anything in the town.)* Have students list three words beginning with

in- or *im-* that they would use to describe themselves. Then have them write a brief character sketch of themselves using each word.

right through the house and out the back and was not seen again.

The two female cousins came at once. They held the funeral on the second day, with the town coming to look at Miss Emily beneath a mass of bought flowers, with the crayon face of her father musing profoundly above the bier[28] and the ladies sibilant and macabre;[29] and the very old men—some in their brushed Confederate uniforms—on the porch and the lawn, talking of Miss Emily as if she had been a contemporary of theirs, believing that they had danced with her and courted her perhaps, confusing time with its mathematical progression, as the old do, to whom all the past is not a diminishing road but, instead, a huge meadow which no winter ever quite touches, divided from them now by the narrow bottle-neck of the most recent decade of years.

Already we knew that there was one room in that region above stairs which no one had seen in forty years, and which would have to be forced. They waited until Miss Emily was decently in the ground before they opened it.

The violence of breaking down the door seemed to fill this room with pervading dust. A thin, acrid pall[30] as of the tomb seemed to lie everywhere upon this room decked and furnished as for a bridal:[31] upon the valance curtains of faded rose color, upon the rose-shaded lights, upon the dressing table, upon the delicate array of crystal and the man's toilet things backed with tarnished silver, silver so tarnished that the monogram was obscured. Among them lay a collar and tie, as if they had just been removed, which, lifted, left upon the surface a pale crescent in the dust. Upon a chair hung the suit, carefully folded; beneath it the two mute shoes and the discarded socks.

The man himself lay in the bed.

---

28. A *bier* is a stand for a coffin.
29. *Macabre* (mə kä′ brə) means "gruesome" or "suggesting the horror of death."
30. An *acrid pall* is a bitter-smelling covering.
31. Here, *bridal* means "wedding."

The Sunny Parlor, c. 1901. Wilhelm Hammershoi. Oil on canvas, 49.7 x 40 cm. Nationalgalerie, Staatliche Museen zu Berlin, Germany. ★

For a long while we just stood there, looking down at the profound and fleshless grin. The body had apparently once lain in the attitude of an embrace, but now the long sleep that outlasts love, that conquers even the grimace of love, had cuckolded[32] him. What was left of him, rotted beneath what was left of the nightshirt, had become inextricable from the bed in which he lay; and upon him and upon the pillow beside him lay that even coating of the patient and biding dust.

Then we noticed that in the second pillow was the indentation of a head. One of us lifted something from it, and leaning forward, that faint and invisible dust dry and acrid in the nostrils, we saw a long strand of iron-gray hair. ❧

---

32. *Cuckolded* means "betrayed," in the sense of a husband deceived by an unfaithful wife.

WILLIAM FAULKNER **883**

Teach

Big Idea — 1

Return to Regionalism
Answer: *At the core of "A Rose for Emily" is Emily's inner conflict caused by her sense of position in the town and her desire for love—a theme presented in a unique setting and circumstances.*

Reading Strategy — 2

Identify Sequence
Ask: How does the order in which Faulkner presents the ideas in his speech make the speech strong? *(Faulkner gives the audience a chance to understand the problem as he sees it and then to recognize the value of his solution. The audience is left with a strong impression of the power and necessity of the writer's transformative voice.)*

Readability Scores
Dale-Chall: 8.4
DRP: 62
Lexile: 1170

To check students' understanding of the selection, see Unit 6 Teaching Resources Book, p. 43.

Address upon Receiving the Nobel Prize in Literature

Stockholm, December 10, 1950

William Faulkner

I feel that this award was not made to me as a man, but to my work—a life's work in the agony and sweat of the human spirit, not for glory and least of all for profit, but to create out of the materials of the human spirit something which did not exist before. So this award is only mine in trust. It will not be difficult to find a dedication for the money part of it commensurate[1] with the purpose and significance of its origin. But I would like to do the same with the acclaim too, by using this moment as a pinnacle[2] from which I might be listened to by the young men and women already dedicated to the same anguish and travail,[3] among whom is already that one who will some day stand here where I am standing.

Our tragedy today is a general and universal physical fear so long sustained by now that we can even bear it. There are no longer problems of the spirit. There is only the question: When will I be blown up? Because of this, the young man or woman writing today has forgotten the problems of the human heart in conflict with itself which alone can make good writing because only that is worth writing about, worth the agony and the sweat.

He must learn them again. He must teach himself that the basest of all things is to be afraid; and, teaching himself that, forget it forever, leaving no room in his workshop for anything but the old verities and truths of the heart, the old universal truths lacking which any story is ephemeral[4] and doomed—love and honor and pity and pride and compassion and sacrifice. Until he does so, he labors under a curse. He writes not of love but of lust, of defeats in which nobody loses anything of value, of victories without hope and, worst of all, without pity or compassion. His griefs grieve on no universal bones, leaving no scars. He writes not of the heart but of the glands.

Until he relearns these things, he will write as though he stood among and watched the end of man. I decline to accept the end of man. It is easy enough to say that man is immortal simply because he will endure: that when the last ding-dong of doom has clanged and faded from the last worthless rock hanging tideless in the last red and dying evening, that even then there will still be one more sound: that of his puny inexhaustible voice, still talking. I refuse to accept this. I believe that man will not merely endure: he will prevail. He is immortal, not because he alone among creatures has an inexhaustible voice, but because he has a soul, a spirit capable of compassion and sacrifice and endurance. The poet's, the writer's, duty is to write about these things. It is his privilege to help man endure by lifting his heart, by reminding him of the courage and honor and hope and pride and compassion and pity and sacrifice which have been the glory of his past. The poet's voice need not merely be the record of man, it can be one of the props, the pillars to help him endure and prevail. ∾

---

1. *Commensurate* (kə men' sər it) means "of equal measure."
2. *Pinnacle* (pin' ə kəl) means "highest point" or "peak."
3. *Travail* (trə vāl') is exhausting mental or physical work.

1 **Return to Regionalism** *How might "A Rose for Emily" reflect Faulkner's desire to write about this problem?*

---

4. *Ephemeral* (i fem' ər əl) means "lasting a very brief time" or "short-lived."

Reading Practice

Paraphrase Remind students that a paraphrase is a restatement of a written or spoken passage in different words, conveying the same basic meaning. Paraphrasing is a useful tool for reviewing a speech, since it serves as a check on comprehension and can lead to greater understanding of the speaker's meaning.

Have students write paraphrases of Faulkner's speech. Their paraphrases should capture the essential meaning of Faulkner's speech but be written in the students' own words. Students should read their paraphrases aloud to partners.

After You Read

Respond and Think Critically

Respond and Interpret

1. Did the end of the story surprise you? Explain.

2. (a)How does Emily respond when asked to pay taxes? (b)What does this reveal about her?

3. (a)How does Emily respond when her house begins to smell and when her father dies? (b)How does the town interpret her response?

4. (a)In his Nobel address, what does Faulkner say modern writers are concerned with? (b)Why is this problematic?

5. In the speech, what does Faulkner say is the only thing worth writing about? Why?

Analyze and Evaluate

6. (a)How would you characterize the narrator of "A Rose for Emily"? (b)What do you infer about the narrator's attitude toward Emily? Explain.

7. (a)In Faulkner's speech, what is his view of our future and of the writer's role in that future? (b)Do you agree with this view? Explain.

Connect

8. **Big Idea** **Return to Regionalism** How do local traditions and attitudes affect Miss Emily?

9. **Connect to the Author** What events of Faulkner's time likely influenced his speech?

You're the Critic

Worth It?

Faulkner has a reputation for being difficult to follow. For one thing, his plots do not unfold in a linear way. As Dean Morgan Schmitter explains in "The Faulkner Legend":

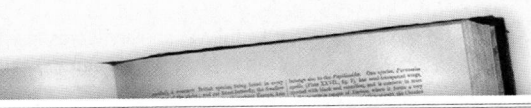

> "Another feature of Faulkner's style is the manner in which he releases information, sometimes preventing the reader from having full perspective on what is happening. Although the reader accumulates information as he goes along, often he must wait pages to find the facts he needs . . . ."

Another reason that Faulkner's writing is challenging is that his sentences are often long and rambling. As Conrad Aiken writes,

> "And at once, if one considers these queer sentences . . . in their relation to the book as a whole, one sees a functional reason and necessity for their being as they are. They parallel . . . the whole elaborate method of deliberately withheld meaning, of progressive and partial and delayed disclosure, which so often gives the characteristic shape of the novels themselves."

Group Activity Discuss the following.

1. What examples can you find of confusing sequences of events and rambling sentences in "A Rose for Emily"?

2. (a)Do you find the story difficult to follow? (b)Are your efforts rewarded by the end of the story? Explain.

You're the Critic

1. Students' answers will vary. One example could be the visit of the city officials about Emily's taxes, which occurs 30 years after the main events of the story but appears at the beginning of the story. A possible example of a difficult, rambling sentence is the second one in the second paragraph of part V.

2. Students' answers will vary, but should be supported by evidence from the story.

After You Read

Assess

1. Students may be shocked by some details, but they may have predicted Barron's death.

2. (a) She refuses to listen to their arguments. (b) She can be arrogant and stubborn.

3. (a) When her house smells, she does not seem to be bothered by it. When her father dies, she refuses to let anyone take care of his body for several days. (b) The townspeople think she has reasons for acting as she does.

4. (a) They are concerned with fear. (b) Fear is a base concern, disconnected from universal truths such as love, honor, and compassion.

5. The internal conflicts that people experience, since writing without such conflicts cannot endure

6. (a) The narrator uses the word *we* and speaks for the town. (b) The narrator thinks that her environment made Emily behave oddly.

7. (a) Human beings will prevail, and the writer reminds them of their past compassion, sacrifice, and endurance. (b) Students' answers will vary.

8. Emily can get away with things because of her status as a Grierson.

9. Students may note that the Cold War influenced the speech.

 For additional assessment, see Assessment Resources, pp. 237–238.

After You Read

Assess

Literary Element

1. **C** is the correct answer because the smell foreshadows the discovery of Barron's body.
2. **G** is the correct answer because the foreshadowing gives all the details readers need to understand Barron's fate.

Review: Flashback

Section 1: After Emily's funeral, the first flashback is Colonel Sartoris's edict that she owes no taxes; the second when town officials try to make her pay taxes.
Section 2: When Emily is younger, a group of men tries to remedy the smell; a second flashback shows Emily's father scaring off young men.
Section 3: After her father's death, Emily begins to see Homer Barron; a year later, Emily buys arsenic.
Sections 4 and 5: The flashbacks end as the narration returns to Emily's death.

Progress Check

Can students interpret foreshadowing?

If No → See Unit 6 Teaching Resources Book, p. 38.

Reading Strategy

1. Students' responses will vary but should show a grasp of the order of events.
2. Students may recognize that the sequence helps convey the significance of the discovery the town makes after Emily's death.

Literary Element Foreshadowing

ACT Skills Practice

1. The first event in the narrative that foreshadows Homer Barron's fate is
   - **A.** Emily Grierson's funeral.
   - **B.** the death of Emily's father.
   - **C.** the smell coming from Emily's house.
   - **D.** Emily's buying arsenic from the druggist.

2. Faulkner's use of foreshadowing is effective because it
   - I. is evident only after Barron's body is found.
   - II. provides concrete clues to Barron's death.
   - III. protects Emily's reputation and good name.
   - **F.** I only
   - **G.** II only
   - **H.** I and II only
   - **J.** II and III only

Review: Flashback

A **flashback** is an interruption in a plot to portray an incident that happened in the past.

Partner Activity Meet with another classmate to discuss Faulkner's use of flashback in "A Rose for Emily." Use the five sections as numbered by the author to determine where the flashbacks are and at what point in Emily's life each one occurs.

Section	Flashback
1	
2	

LOG ON ▶ **Literature** Online

Selection Resources For Selection Quizzes, eFlashcards, and Reading-Writing Connection activities, go to glencoe.com and enter QuickPass code GLA9800u6.

886 UNIT 6 FROM DEPRESSION TO COLD WAR

Reading Strategy Identify Sequence

Faulkner does not often take his readers on a chronological journey through his stories.

1. Use the list and the sequence chart that you made as you read the story to put the events in chronological order. Use sequencing words, such as *first, next, then,* and *finally.*

2. Explain how the convoluted sequence adds to or detracts from the story's meaning.

Vocabulary Practice

Practice with Denotation and Connotation
Denotation is the literal, or dictionary, meaning of a word. **Connotation** is the implied, or cultural, meaning of a word. For example, the words *enthusiasm* and *gusto* have a similar denotation, "great excitement," but they have different connotations:

Weaker	*Stronger*
enthusiasm	gusto

Each of the vocabulary words is listed with a word that has a similar denotation. Choose the word that has the stronger connotation.

1. sluggishly   inactively
2. circumvent   evade
3. harmful   virulent
4. avenge   vindicate
5. haughty   proud

Academic Vocabulary

Colonel Sartoris uses Emily's father's death as the **justification** *to permit her to not pay taxes.*

Justification is an academic word. If a student is caught cheating, he might use his desire to get into a good college as the **justification** for his mistake.

To further explore the meaning of this word, complete this sentence: His parents wanted an _____, not a *justification* for his deception.

For more on academic vocabulary, see pages 53–54.

Vocabulary

1. sluggishly
2. evade
3. virulent
4. vindicate
5. haughty

Academic Vocabulary

His parents wanted an apology, not a justification for his deception.

Respond Through Writing

Expository Essay

Analyze Symbolism In addition to using foreshadowing and flashback, Faulkner employs symbolism to add complexity to this story. Write an essay in which you analyze Faulkner's use of symbolism in "A Rose for Emily." In your essay, discuss how the symbolism contributes to the meaning of the story.

Understand the Task Symbolism is the author's use of an object, person, place, or experience to represent something else, usually something abstract. To write a **literary analysis** means to dissect a work of literature to better understand what it means and to comment on how it works.

Prewrite Jot down a list of objects, people, or experiences in "A Rose for Emily" that you think might be symbolic. Then consult sources that discuss the culture of the South during the early 1900s to generate ideas of what the symbols in the story might represent. Draw particularly upon stories of aristocrats, sharecroppers, and African Americans.

Draft Make sure to use proper citations in your discussion. An example is provided below.

EXAMPLE:

> Emily's house is a symbol of the Southern aristocracy that lost its prowess with the coming of the Civil War and Reconstruction. In the post-Civil War years, Southerners lost cropland (namely for cotton), livestock, and money in slave-related investments ("South, the." *Encyclopaedia Britannica*. 2007. Encyclopaedia Britannica Online. 16 July 2007). The "coquettish decay above the cotton wagons and gasoline pumps" of Emily's house mirrors this decline of the Southern aristocracy.

Revise Make sure you have used sources that help the reader better understand the meaning behind the symbolism in this story. Then evaluate your essay using the checklist on p. 624.

Edit and Proofread Proofread your essay, correcting any errors in spelling, grammar, and punctuation. Use the Grammar Tip in the side column to help you use paragraphing correctly.

Learning Objectives

In this assignment, you will focus on the following objective:

Writing: Writing an expository essay.

> **Grammar Tip**
>
> **Paragraphing**
> To enhance your writing, try to bring one idea into focus with each paragraph. All of the sentences in your paragraph should relate to that one main idea. Some paragraphing tips include the following:
>
> - Write a concise topic sentence that forms that paragraph's most important idea.
> - Elaborate on the topic sentence with supporting details.
> - Use transitions to link thoughts.
> - Include a conclusion statement to reiterate your main point.

After You Read

Assess

Writing

Evaluate students' essays based on the following criteria:

- Does the essay relate ideas from multiple sources and include proper citations to those sources?
- Does the essay support its thesis with evidence?
- Did the student use a rubric to evaluate and revise his or her essay?

For grammar practice, see Unit 6 Teaching Resources Book, p. 42.

WILLIAM FAULKNER **887**

Scoring Guide	4	3	2	1
Grasp of text	thoughtful and comprehensive	comprehensive	limited	minimal
Support of thesis	specific	general	little or none	none
Understanding of complexities	clear	general	limited	minimal
Language	varied, precise, descriptive	varied, somewhat descriptive	predictable, basic	not varied, limited
Convention errors	few or none	several	many	serious
Awareness of literary devices	clearly demonstrated	demonstrated	may be demonstrated	not demonstrated

Before You Read

Focus

Bellringer Options

Selection Focus
Transparency 55

Daily Language Practice
Transparency 81

Or **ask:** How far would you go to help someone else? Would you walk many miles through rough terrain? Would you go without food? Would you give up part of your home?

Have students discuss why people sometimes make great sacrifices for others.

For summaries in languages other than English, see Unit 6 Teaching Resources Book, pp. 45–50.

Before You Read

A Worn Path

Meet **Eudora Welty**
(1909–2001)

Eudora Welty admitted to living a sheltered life. Born and raised in Jackson, Mississippi, she lived in her family's house there until her death at age ninety-two. Welty maintained, though, that "a sheltered life can be a daring life as well. For all serious daring starts from within."

Pleasant Childhood Welty's parents filled their house with books and loved to read on their own and to their children. Once she learned to read herself, Welty read everything she could get her hands on. Her mother, however, put one restriction on her reading. She told the town librarian that Eudora could read anything in the library except the then-popular novel *Elsie Dinsmore*. When Eudora asked why, her mother explained that the main character fainted and fell off her piano stool after being made to practice for a long time. Her mother told Eudora that she was too impressionable: "You'd read that and the very first thing you'd do, you'd fall off the piano stool." Thereafter, Welty could never hear the word *impressionable* without calling up the image of falling off a piano stool.

> *"Writing a story is one way of discovering sequence in experience, of stumbling upon cause and effect in the happenings of a writer's own life. This has been the case with me. Connections slowly emerge."*
>
> —Eudora Welty

Work with the WPA Welty's love of reading and her lively imagination inspired her decision to become a writer for the Works Progress Administration (WPA). This government agency, founded during the Great Depression, gave people work on public projects, such as constructing roads and buildings, clearing trails in parks, and painting murals. Welty traveled around Mississippi and wrote articles about WPA projects in the state.

Successful Writing Career Welty had her first short story published when she was twenty-seven. Five years later, she published *A Curtain of Green*, a collection of short stories in which "A Worn Path" first appeared. In her thirties, she published her first novels, *The Robber Bridegroom* (1942) and *Delta Wedding* (1946). Welty went on to write award-winning fiction for many years, until severe arthritis forced her to give up writing at age eighty-five.

Southern Charm At Welty's funeral, her agent, Timothy Seldes, told a revealing story about Welty's last words. He said that when her doctor leaned over her bed and asked if there was anything he could do for her, she replied, "No, but thank you for inviting me to the party." This polite response illustrates Welty's southern charm and gracious warmth—qualities that Welty brought to her writing. Her compassionate portrayals of people living in the deep South powerfully illuminate their shared values and complicated history.

 Literature Online

Author Search For more about Eudora Welty, go to glencoe.com and enter QuickPass code GLA9800u6.

Selection Skills

Literary Elements
- Description (SE pp. 889, 891–894, 896, 897)
- Archetype (SE p. 897)

Reading Skills
- Visualize (SE pp. 889–891, 893, 895, 896, 898)

A Worn Path

Vocabulary Skills
- Analogies (SE p. 898)

Writing Skills/Grammar
- Dialogue (SE p. 898)
- Verb Usage (TE p. 890)
- Extended Metaphor (TE p. 892)

Listening/Speaking/Viewing Skills
- Analyze Art (SE pp. 892, 895)
- Readers Theater (TE p. 894)

Literature and Reading Preview

Connect to the Story

What would you do for someone you love? Write a journal entry in which you describe what you would do to help if someone you loved were sick.

Build Background

"A Worn Path" is set near the city of Natchez (nach' iz), Mississippi, around 1930. The Natchez Trace was an old trail that led from the Native American villages along the banks of the lower Mississippi River northeastward six hundred miles to settlements along the Cumberland River, in what is now Tennessee. Travelers who boated down the Mississippi had to walk or ride the Natchez Trace to return to locations upstream. Around the turn of the nineteenth century, the Natchez Trace was one of the most well-traveled trails in the United States. However, new, powerful steamships that could travel against the Mississippi's strong current were introduced and allowed river travelers to make their way upstream by boat. As a result, the Natchez Trace fell into disuse around 1820.

Set Purposes for Reading

Big Idea Return to Regionalism

As you read, ask yourself, How have the lives of the characters been shaped by the history and culture of the South?

Literary Element Description

Description is writing that captures the physical sensations of a place or of an experience. As you read, ask yourself, What details does Welty include to help readers imagine that they can see, hear, smell, taste, and feel what she is describing?

Reading Strategy Visualize

Visualizing is picturing a writer's ideas or descriptions in the mind's eye. Visualizing is one of the best ways to help you understand and remember information in a story. As you read, ask yourself, What do I see when I read each scene of this story?

Tip: Sketch On a separate sheet of paper, make quick sketches showing how you visualize each important scene that you read.

EUDORA WELTY **889**

Learning Objectives

For pages 888–898

In studying this text, you will focus on the following objectives:

Literary Study: Analyzing description.

Reading: Visualizing.

Writing: Applying dialogue.

Vocabulary

grave (grāv) *adj.* dignified and gloomy; somber; p. 890 *Mark delivered the eulogy with a grave look.*

vigorously (vig' ər əs lē) *adv.* with power, energy, and strength; p. 893 *Katie vigorously shook the rug to get the dust out.*

ceremonial (ser' ə mo' nē əl) *adj.* formal; p. 894 *The graduates wore ceremonial robes.*

solemn (sol' əm) *adj.* serious; somber; p. 895 *With a solemn face, the child tended her sick dog.*

comprehension (kom' pri hen' shən) *n.* the act of grasping mentally; understanding; p. 896 *Mia's comprehension of math is excellent.*

Tip: Analogies Comparisons that reveal the relationship between two words are **analogies**. When you identify the relationship in the first pair of words, you can apply that relationship to complete the second pair. If the first pair are synonymous, you can assume that the second pair will be the same.

EXAMPLE:

solemn : serious :: joyful : happy

Before You Read

Focus

Summary

"A Worn Path" tells of an elderly African American woman's journey from her home in the woods to the city of Natchez, Mississippi. Phoenix Jackson makes the difficult walk whenever she needs more medicine for her grandson, her only companion, whose throat was injured from accidentally swallowing lye. The walk is a metaphor for her life's journey, filled with hardships and triumphs.

Vocabulary

Suffixes Have students identify three suffixes in this vocabulary list. *(-ly, -al, -sion)* **Ask:** Which of these suffixes can you apply to two other words on the list? *(-ly)* To which two words can you apply it? *(grave, solemn)* How does this suffix change those words? *(The suffix changes the words from adjectives to adverbs.)*

ENGLISH LEARNERS **Ask:** Which word is correct in the following sentence: The principal spoke (solemn, solemnly) to the students' parents. *(solemnly)*

 For additional vocabulary practice, see Unit 6 Teaching Resources Book, p. 53.

English Learners

DIFFERENTIATED INSTRUCTION

Intermediate Explain that dialect is a specific form of language spoken by people in a region or group. A dialect may vary from standard English in vocabulary, pronunciation, and grammar. Give students this example from the story: "I in the thorny bush." Ask them to identify what is distinctive about this sentence. *(It omits the verb.)* Then ask them to restate the sentence in standard English. *(I am in the thorny bush.)* Guide them in translating these examples into standard English: "The time getting all gone here." "Who you watching?" "Ghost, who you be the ghost of?" "I the oldest people I ever know."

Teach

Reading Strategy | 1

Visualize **Answer:** *Students' perceptions will vary but should be based on details in the text.*
[APPROACHING] Guide students in locating details that describe Phoenix. Tell students to locate details about her clothing and the cane. Then, they should look for details about her facial features and the way she is walking.

For additional practice using the reading skill or strategy, see Unit 6 Teaching Resources Book, p. 52.

View the Photograph ★

A skilled photographer, Eudora Welty worked for the WPA for three years during the Great Depression. She traveled across Mississippi, taking photographs of the poor to document their terrible living conditions. **Ask:** What might this elderly woman be feeling at "day's end"? *(Possible answers: fatigue; relief)*

For an audio recording of this selection, use Listening Library Audio CD-ROM.

Readability Scores

Dale-Chall: 3.4
DRP: 52
Lexile: 780

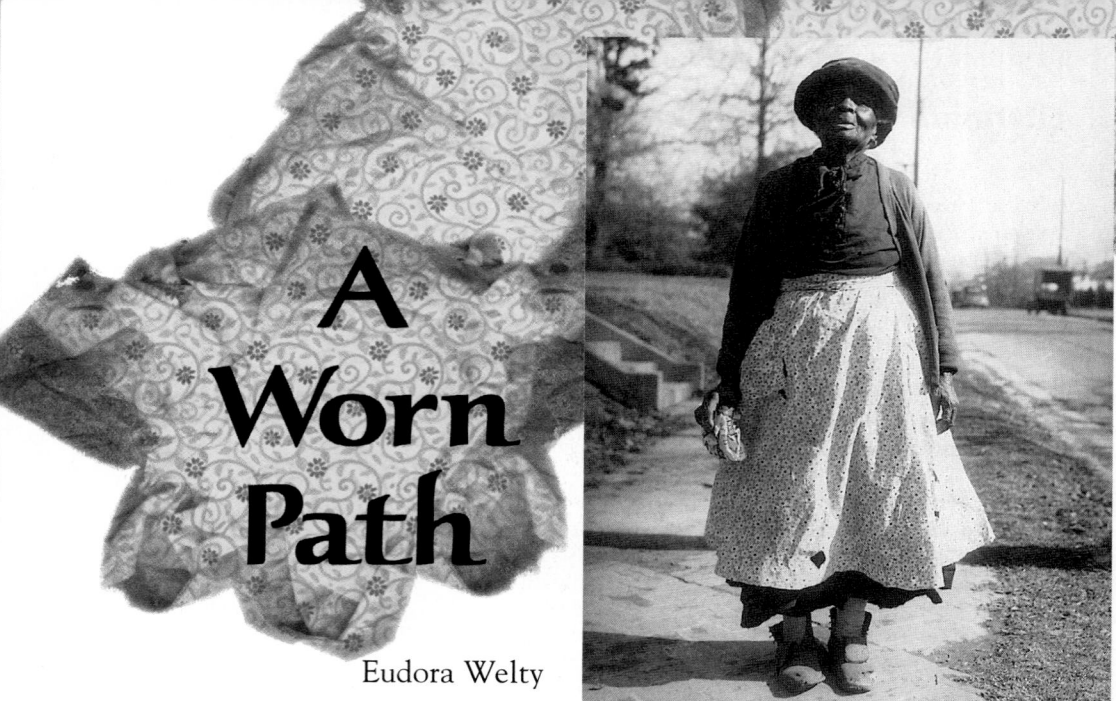

A Worn Path

Eudora Welty

Day's End, Jackson, 1930s. Eudora Welty. Photograph. Mississippi Department of Archives and History, Jackson, MS. Eudora Welty Collection. ★

It was December—a bright frozen day in the early morning. Far out in the country there was an old Negro woman with her head tied in a red rag, coming along a path through the pine-woods. Her name was Phoenix Jackson. She was very old and small and she walked slowly in the dark pine shadows, moving a little from side to side in her steps, with the balanced heaviness and lightness of a pendulum in a grandfather clock. She carried a thin, small cane made from an umbrella, and with this she kept tapping the frozen earth in front of her. This made a **grave** and persistent noise in the still air, that seemed meditative like the chirping of a solitary little bird.

She wore a dark striped dress reaching down to her shoe tops, and an equally long apron of bleached sugar sacks, with a full pocket: all neat and tidy, but every time she took a step she might have fallen over her shoelaces, which dragged from her unlaced shoes. She looked straight ahead. Her eyes were blue with age. Her skin had a pattern all its own of numberless branching wrinkles and as though a whole little tree stood in the middle of her forehead, but a golden color ran underneath, and the two knobs of her cheeks were illumined by a yellow burning under the dark. Under the red rag her hair came down on her neck in the frailest of ringlets, still black, and with an odor like copper.

Vocabulary

grave (grāv) *adj.* dignified and gloomy; somber

Visualize *Ask yourself what Phoenix Jackson looks like. Form a mental image of Phoenix based on the details you have read so far.* 1

890 UNIT 6 FROM DEPRESSION TO COLD WAR

Grammar Practice

Verb Usage In "A Worn Path," Phoenix Jackson's dialect includes many nonstandard usages, particularly verb usage. Many of these are mistakes in agreement, as when she says, "I doesn't mind asking a nice lady to tie up my shoe." Another of her errors is lack of an auxiliary verb, as when she says "I going to the store." Tell students to scan the story for her dialogue and identify examples of incorrect verb usage. Have them rewrite these sentences in standard English. Have students read her words aloud to help them recognize errors when they hear them.

890

Now and then there was a quivering in the thicket. Old Phoenix said, "Out of my way, all you foxes, owls, beetles, jack rabbits, coons and wild animals! . . . Keep out from under these feet, little bob-whites[1]. . . . Keep the big wild hogs out of my path. Don't let none of those come running my direction. I got a long way." Under her small black-freckled hand her cane, limber as a buggy whip, would switch at the brush as if to rouse up any hiding things.

On she went. The woods were deep and still. The sun made the pine needles almost too bright to look at, up where the wind rocked. The cones dropped as light as feathers. Down in the hollow[2] was the mourning dove—it was not too late for him.

The path ran up a hill. "Seem like there is chains about my feet, time I get this far," she said, in the voice of argument old people keep to use with themselves. "Something always take a hold of me on this hill—pleads I should stay."

After she got to the top she turned and gave a full, severe look behind her where she had come. "Up through pines," she said at length. "Now down through oaks."

Her eyes opened their widest, and she started down gently. But before she got to the bottom of the hill a bush caught her dress.

Her fingers were busy and intent, but her skirts were full and long, so that before she could pull them free in one place they were caught in another. It was not possible to allow the dress to tear. "I in the thorny bush," she said. "Thorns, you doing your appointed[3] work. Never want to let folks pass, no sir. Old eyes thought you was a pretty little *green* bush."

---

1. *Bob-whites,* also called quails or partridges, are birds with mottled brown plumage and white markings.
2. A *hollow* is a small valley.
3. *Appointed* means "assigned" or "designated."

 Description *Why does the author include details about the animals in the woods as well as about the silence and sunlight there?*

Finally, trembling all over, she stood free, and after a moment dared to stoop for her cane.

"Sun so high!" she cried, leaning back and looking, while the thick tears went over her eyes. "The time getting all gone here."

At the foot of this hill was a place where a log was laid across the creek.

"Now comes the trial," said Phoenix.

Putting her right foot out, she mounted the log and shut her eyes. Lifting her skirt, leveling her cane fiercely before her, like a festival figure in some parade, she began to march across. Then she opened her eyes and she was safe on the other side.

"I wasn't as old as I thought," she said.

But she sat down to rest. She spread her skirts on the bank around her and folded her hands over her knees. Up above her was a tree in a pearly cloud of mistletoe. She did not dare to close her eyes, and when a little boy brought her a plate with a slice of marble-cake on it she spoke to him. "That would be acceptable," she said. But when she went to take it there was just her own hand in the air.

So she left that tree, and had to go through a barbed-wire fence. There she had to creep and crawl, spreading her knees and stretching her fingers like a baby trying to climb the steps. But she talked loudly to herself: she could not let her dress be torn now, so late in the day, and she could not pay for having her arm or her leg sawed off if she got caught fast where she was.

At last she was safe through the fence and risen up out in the clearing. Big dead trees, like black men with one arm, were standing in the purple stalks of the withered cotton field. There sat a buzzard.

"Who you watching?"

Return to Regionalism *From what you have read so far, what do you infer about Phoenix Jackson's background as well as about her present life?*

Visualize *How do you imagine Phoenix Jackson looks and sounds as she goes through the fence?* **5**

Teach

Literary Element | 2

Characterization Ask: What can you infer about Phoenix's character from this paragraph? *(Her diction and grammar reveal her to be a rural Southerner with little education. Her words indicate a determination to proceed no matter what.)*

Literary Element | 3

Description Answer: *Students may say that these details make the scene seem vivid and real.*

Big Idea | 4

Return to Regionalism Answer: *Students may infer that Phoenix has lived in the South all her life and is deeply steeped in its ways. Though elderly, she is alone on a difficult errand, which may suggest poverty and a difficult life.*

Reading Strategy | 5

Visualize Answer: *Students' answers will vary but should be supported with details from the story .*

Teach

Literary Element | 1

Symbolism Ask: How might a field of corn with no path represent Phoenix's life? How might a maze be a symbol of a person's life? *(There was no one to guide Phoenix through life, so she had to find her own path. In life, as in a maze, people have to make their own choices and choose their paths.)*

Literary Element | 2

Description Answer: *These details help to evoke the Southern countryside. They may also contribute to the story's motifs of poverty and old age.*

View the Photograph ★

Answer: *The path in the photograph is old, sunken, and tree lined, like part of the path that Phoenix travels.*

Road Between High Banks, Hinds County, 1940s. Eudora Welty. Photograph. Mississippi Department of Archives and History, Jackson, MS. Eudora Welty Collection.

View the Photograph During the Great Depression, much of the country suffered from severe droughts that led to erosion, crop failure, and many other problems. In what ways is the path in the photograph similar to or different from the path in the story? ★

In the furrow[4] she made her way along.

"Glad this not the season for bulls," she said, looking sideways, "and the good Lord made his snakes to curl up and sleep in the winter. A pleasure I don't see no two-headed snake coming around that tree, where it come once. It took a while to get by him, back in the summer."

She passed through the old cotton and went into a field of dead corn. It whispered and shook and was taller than her head.

---

4. A *furrow* is a long, narrow channel in the ground made by a plow.

"Through the maze now," she said, for there was no path. **1**

Then there was something tall, black, and skinny there, moving before her.

At first she took it for a man. It could have been a man dancing in the field. But she stood still and listened, and it did not make a sound. It was as silent as a ghost.

"Ghost," she said sharply, "who be you the ghost of? For I have heard of nary[5] death close by."

But there was no answer—only the ragged dancing in the wind.

She shut her eyes, reached out her hand, and touched a sleeve. She found a coat and inside that an emptiness, cold as ice.

"You scarecrow," she said. Her face lighted. "I ought to be shut up for good," she said with laughter. "My senses is gone. I too old. I the oldest people I ever know. Dance, old scarecrow," she said, "while I dancing with you."

She kicked her foot over the furrow, and with mouth drawn down, shook her head once or twice in a little strutting way. Some husks blew down and whirled in streamers about her skirts.

Then she went on, parting her way from side to side with the cane, through the whispering field. At last she came to the end, to a wagon track where the silver grass blew between the red ruts. The quail were walking around like pullets,[6] seeming all dainty and unseen.

"Walk pretty," she said. "This the easy place. This the easy going."

She followed the track, swaying through the quiet bare fields, through the little strings of trees silver in their dead leaves, past cabins silver from weather, with the doors and windows boarded shut, all like old women under a spell

---

5. *Nary* means "not one."
6. *Pullets* are young hens.

Description *Why does the author include details of the scene such as "old cotton," "dead corn," and "ragged dancing in the wind"?* **2**

Writing Practice

Extended Metaphor Review with students that Phoenix's journey can be viewed as a metaphor for her own and others' passage through life. Have students write a paragraph explaining how Phoenix's journey represents the journey of life. Have them start by creating a three-column chart like the one shown here to identify and organize the details of the metaphor.

Event	Meaning for Phoenix	General Meaning
A thorny bush catches Phoenix's dress and she must free the dress without tearing it.	She keeps the bush from making her ragged, which would take away her dignity.	Even entangled in difficulties, one can patiently work one's way out with dignity.

The first column identifies the places or events of Phoenix's journey to town. The second column identifies the metaphorical meaning that each event or place might have in Phoenix's life. The third column lists general conclusions about life or human nature. Students can then use the details from the chart in the body of their papers.

892

sitting there. "I walking in their sleep," she said, nodding her head **vigorously.**

In a ravine[7] she went where a spring was silently flowing through a hollow log. Old Phoenix bent and drank. "Sweet-gum[8] makes the water sweet," she said, and drank more. "Nobody know who made this well, for it was here when I was born."

The track crossed a swampy part where the moss hung as white as lace from every limb. "Sleep on, alligators, and blow your bubbles." Then the track went into the road.

Deep, deep the road went down between the high green-colored banks. Overhead the live-oaks met, and it was as dark as a cave.

A black dog with a lolling tongue came up out of the weeds by the ditch. She was meditating, and not ready, and when he came at her she only hit him a little with her cane. Over she went in the ditch, like a little puff of milkweed.[9]

Down there, her senses drifted away. A dream visited her, and she reached her hand up, but nothing reached down and gave her a pull. So she lay there and presently went to talking. "Old woman," she said to herself, "that black dog come up out of the weeds to stall you off, and now there he sitting on his fine tail, smiling at you."

A white man finally came along and found her—a hunter, a young man, with his dog on a chain.

"Well, Granny!" he laughed. "What are you doing there?"

"Lying on my back like a June-bug waiting to be turned over, mister," she said, reaching up her hand.

---

7. A *ravine* is a deep, narrow valley, especially one eroded by running water.
8. The *sweet-gum* tree discharges a fragrant gum through cracks and crevices in its trunk.
9. The pods of a *milkweed* plant split open and release seeds with puffs of white, silky down.

Vocabulary

vigorously (vig´ ər əs lē) *adv.* with power, energy, and strength

He lifted her up, gave her a swing in the air, and set her down. "Anything broken, Granny?"

"No sir, them old dead weeds is springy enough," said Phoenix, when she had got her breath. "I thank you for your trouble."

"Where do you live, Granny?" he asked, while the two dogs were growling at each other.

"Away back yonder, sir, behind the ridge. You can't even see it from here."

"On your way home?"

"No sir, I going to town."

"Why, that's too far! That's as far as I walk when I come out myself, and I get something for my trouble." He patted the stuffed bag he carried, and there hung down a little closed claw. It was one of the bob-whites, with its beak hooked bitterly to show it was dead. "Now you go on home, Granny!"

"I bound to go to town, mister," said Phoenix. "The time come around."

He gave another laugh, filling the whole landscape. "I know you old colored people! Wouldn't miss going to town to see Santa Claus!"

But something held old Phoenix very still. The deep lines in her face went into a fierce and different radiation.[10] Without warning, she had seen with her own eyes a flashing nickel fall out of the man's pocket onto the ground.

"How old are you, Granny?" he was saying.

"There is no telling, mister," she said, "no telling."

Then she gave a little cry and clapped her hands and said, "Git on away from here, dog! Look! Look at that dog!" She laughed as if in admiration. "He ain't scared of nobody. He a big black dog." She whispered, "Sic him!"

"Watch me get rid of that cur," said the man. "Sic him, Pete! Sic him!"

---

10. Here, *radiation* means "a pattern of rays or waves."

Visualize *Picture the scene as the man helps Phoenix.* **4**

Description *What does the description of Phoenix suggest about her thoughts as she spies the nickel?* **5**

EUDORA WELTY **893**

Symbolism **Ask:** What might the spring symbolize? How can you interpret Phoenix's statement in light of this symbolism? *(The spring might symbolize life, since all living things need water. Phoenix's statement that the spring was there before she was born may suggest the continuity of life; individuals are born and die, but life itself continues.)*

Reading Strategy | **4**

Visualize Answer: *Students should describe their mental images of the scene.*

Literary Element | **5**

Description Answer: *Details such as "her face went into a fierce and different radiation" suggest that the appearance of the nickel is a notable event for Phoenix. She ignores the man's condescending remarks as she registers the presence of the nickel and secretly plots to take it.*

SMALL GROUP

Emerging Some learners may better understand the progress of the story by creating a map of Phoenix's journey. Have pairs of students work together to look through the story for clues and details that describe the terrain, distance, and directions. They should also indicate on the map where each event takes place and write down details of each event.

Teach

Big Idea　1

Return to Regionalism
Answer: *Students may say that this exchange suggests a paternalistic relationship. The white man is kind to Phoenix, but his kindness is tinged by condescension, and he lies to her about how much money he has in order to avoid helping her. Phoenix is outwardly deferential, but the story suggests that she behaves this way in order to survive.*

Literary Element　2

Characterization **Ask:** Why does Phoenix ask the woman to tie her shoe? What does the request reveal about her character? *(Phoenix doesn't want to be seen as a country woman, with her shoelaces untied. This indicates that although Phoenix generally seems humble, she also has pride.)*

Literary Element　3

Description **Answer:** *Students may point to the smell of the wood-smoke and the river around the cabins being in contrast to the electric lights that crisscrossed the paved city.*

Phoenix heard the dogs fighting, and heard the man running and throwing sticks. She even heard a gunshot. But she was slowly bending forward by that time, further and further forward, the lids stretched down over her eyes, as if she were doing this in her sleep. Her chin was lowered almost to her knees. The yellow palm of her hand came out from the fold of her apron. Her fingers slid down and along the ground under the piece of money with the grace and care they would have in lifting an egg from under a setting hen. Then she slowly straightened up, she stood erect, and the nickel was in her apron pocket. A bird flew by. Her lips moved. "God watching me the whole time. I come to stealing."

The man came back, and his own dog panted about them. "Well, I scared him off that time," he said, and then he laughed and lifted his gun and pointed it at Phoenix.

She stood straight and faced him.

"Doesn't the gun scare you?" he said, still pointing it.

"No, sir, I seen plenty go off closer by, in my day, and for less than what I done," she said, holding utterly still.

He smiled, and shouldered the gun. "Well, Granny," he said, "you must be a hundred years old, and scared of nothing. I'd give you a dime if I had any money with me. But you take my advice and stay home, and nothing will happen to you."

"I bound to go on my way, mister," said Phoenix. She inclined her head in the red rag. Then they went in different directions, but she could hear the gun shooting again and again over the hill.

She walked on. The shadows hung from the oak trees to the road like curtains. Then she smelled wood-smoke, and smelled the river, and she saw a steeple and the cabins on their steep steps. Dozens of little black children

1 Return to Regionalism *What does this exchange suggest about the way whites and African Americans in the town behaved toward each other?*

whirled around her. There ahead was Natchez shining. Bells were ringing. She walked on.

In the paved city it was Christmas time. There were red and green electric lights strung and crisscrossed everywhere, and all turned on in the daytime. Old Phoenix would have been lost if she had not distrusted her eyesight and depended on her feet to know where to take her.

She paused quietly on the sidewalk where people were passing by. A lady came along in the crowd, carrying an armful of red-, green- and silver-wrapped presents; she gave off perfume like the red roses in hot summer, and Phoenix stopped her.

"Please, missy, will you lace up my shoe?" She held up her foot.

"What do you want, Grandma?"

"See my shoe," said Phoenix. "Do all right for out in the country, but wouldn't look right to go in a big building."

"Stand still then, Grandma," said the lady. She put her packages down on the sidewalk beside her and laced and tied both shoes tightly.

"Can't lace 'em with a cane," said Phoenix. "Thank you, missy. I doesn't mind asking a nice lady to tie up my shoe, when I gets out on the street."

Moving slowly and from side to side, she went into the big building, and into a tower of steps, where she walked up and around and around until her feet knew to stop.

She entered a door, and there she saw nailed up on the wall the document that had been stamped with the gold seal and framed in the gold frame, which matched the dream that was hung up in her head.

"Here I be," she said. There was a fixed and **ceremonial** stiffness over her body.

3 Description *Which details evoke the contrast between the cabins near the river and the paved city?*

Vocabulary
ceremonial (ser´ ə mō´ nē əl) *adj.* formal

Speaking Practice

SMALL GROUP

Readers Theater Readers Theater is a cross between oral reading and dramatic presentation. Students assume the roles of characters and read passages in character, as if from a script. Assign students to work in groups of two or three to present the interaction between Phoenix and the hunter or the encounter at the doctor's office. Encourage students to stay in character during the presentation and to read their lines as realistically as possible.

School Children, Jackson, 1930s. Eudora Welty. Photograph. Mississippi Department of Archives and History, Jackson, MS. Eudora Welty Collection.

View the Photograph Many of Welty's stories are rooted in her experiences—and photographs—of Mississippi life during the Great Depression. Do you think Eudora Welty might have had her story "A Worn Path" in mind when she took this picture? Explain. ★

"A charity case, I suppose," said an attendant who sat at the desk before her.

But Phoenix only looked above her head. There was sweat on her face, the wrinkles in her skin shone like a bright net.

"Speak up, Grandma," the woman said. "What's your name? We must have your history, you know. Have you been here before? What seems to be the trouble with you?"

Old Phoenix only gave a twitch to her face as if a fly were bothering her.

"Are you deaf?" cried the attendant.

But then the nurse came in.

"Oh, that's just old Aunt Phoenix," she said. "She doesn't come for herself—she has a little grandson. She makes these trips just as regular as clockwork. She lives away back off the Old Natchez Trace." She bent down. "Well, Aunt Phoenix, why don't you just take a seat? We won't keep you standing after your long trip." She pointed.

The old woman sat down, bolt upright in the chair.

"Now, how is the boy?" asked the nurse. Old Phoenix did not speak.

"I said, how is the boy?"

But Phoenix only waited and stared straight ahead, her face very **solemn** and withdrawn into rigidity.

"Is his throat any better?" asked the nurse. "Aunt Phoenix, don't you hear me? Is your grandson's throat any better since the last time you came for the medicine?"

With her hands on her knees, the old woman waited, silent, erect and motionless, just as if she were in armor.

"You mustn't take up our time this way, Aunt Phoenix," the nurse said. "Tell us quickly

---

Visualize *Visualize the exchanges between Phoenix, the attendant, and the nurse. What attitudes toward Phoenix do the attendant and the nurse express?* **4**

Vocabulary

solemn (sol´ əm) *adj.* serious; somber

EUDORA WELTY **895**

Teach

Big Idea **1**

Return to Regionalism
Answer: *Students may infer that Phoenix and her grandson are penniless and isolated.*

Reading Strategy **2**

Visualize Answer: *Students may have the impression of a pitifully sick, but probably hopeful, boy. Phoenix's statement that she could "tell him from all the others in creation" conveys profound love for the boy.*

Literary Element **3**

Description Answer: *The details suggest Phoenix's pride, dignity, and compassion.*

 To check students' understanding of the selection, see Unit 6 Teaching Resources Book, p. 56.

about your grandson, and get it over. He isn't dead, is he?"

At last there came a flicker and then a flame of **comprehension** across her face, and she spoke.

"My grandson. It was my memory had left me. There I sat and forgot why I made my long trip."

"Forgot?" The nurse frowned. "After you came so far?"

Then Phoenix was like an old woman begging a dignified forgiveness for waking up frightened in the night. "I never did go to school, I was too old at the Surrender,"[11] she said in a soft voice. "I'm an old woman without an education. It was my memory fail me. My little grandson, he is just the same, and I forgot it in the coming."

"Throat never heals, does it?" said the nurse, speaking in a loud, sure voice to old Phoenix. By now she had a card with something written on it, a little list. "Yes. Swallowed lye. When was it?—January—two-three years ago—"

Phoenix spoke unasked now. "No, missy, he not dead, he just the same. Every little while his throat begin to close up again, and he not able to swallow. He not get his breath. He not able to help himself. So the time come around, and I go on another trip for the soothing medicine."

"All right. The doctor said as long as you came to get it, you could have it," said the nurse. "But it's an obstinate case."

"My little grandson, he sit up there in the house all wrapped up, waiting by himself," Phoenix went on. "We is the only two left in the world. He suffer and it don't seem to put

---

11. The *Surrender* of Robert E. Lee to Ulysses S. Grant in 1865 ended the Civil War.

1 **Return to Regionalism** *What do you infer about the situation of Phoenix and her grandson?*

Vocabulary

comprehension (kom′ pri hen′ shən) *n.* the act of grasping mentally; understanding

him back at all. He got a sweet look. He going to last. He wear a little patch quilt and peep out holding his mouth open like a little bird. I remembers so plain now. I not going to forget him again, no, the whole enduring time. I could tell him from all the others in creation."

"All right." The nurse was trying to hush her now. She brought her a bottle of medicine. "Charity," she said, making a check mark in a book.

Old Phoenix held the bottle close to her eyes, and then carefully put it into her pocket.

"I thank you," she said.

"It's Christmas time, Grandma," said the attendant. "Could I give you a few pennies out of my purse?"

"Five pennies is a nickel," said Phoenix stiffly.

"Here's a nickel," said the attendant.

Phoenix rose carefully and held out her hand. She received the nickel and then fished the other nickel out of her pocket and laid it beside the new one. She stared at her palm closely, with her head on one side.

Then she gave a tap with her cane on the floor.

"This is what come to me to do," she said. "I going to the store and buy my child a little windmill they sells, made out of paper. He going to find it hard to believe there such a thing in the world. I'll march myself back where he waiting, holding it straight up in this hand."

She lifted her free hand, gave a little nod, turned around, and walked out of the doctor's office. Then her slow step began on the stairs, going down. ∾

Visualize *After rereading the details of the grandson's appearance, picture him in your mind. What impressions do you have of the boy and of Phoenix's feelings about him?* **2**

Description *Notice the descriptions of Phoenix Jackson's manners, bearing, and plans she has for her money. What do these details suggest about her character?* **3**

Writing Practice

SPIRAL REVIEW **Compare and Contrast Characters** Point out that Phoenix Jackson encounters a number of people on her journey and when she arrives in town. Tell students to write an essay comparing and contrasting the secondary characters in the story. They should answer these questions in their essays: How does each character treat Phoenix Jackson? What do the encounters reveal about the personalities of Phoenix and the secondary characters? Why might the secondary characters treat Phoenix in the way they do?

Remind students that before they start writing, they should reread the passages describing Phoenix's encounters carefully and find details and examples to support their arguments in their essays. After students have completed their writing assignment, have volunteers read their essays to the class.

After You Read

Respond and Think Critically

Respond and Interpret

1. What is your favorite incident or image from "A Worn Path"? What is it about the image or incident that especially appeals to you?

2. (a)What does Phoenix Jackson look like? (b)What does Phoenix Jackson's appearance tell you about her?

3. (a)Describe in detail the path Phoenix is taking. (b)From its description, what can you infer about the path? Explain what the path may symbolize, or represent. Support your answer.

4. (a)What is Phoenix's destination and purpose? (b)At what point in the story do you learn this?

5. What does the purpose of Phoenix's trip tell you about her character?

Analyze and Evaluate

6. In Greek mythology, the **phoenix** is a bird that, at the end of its life, burns itself to death; from its ashes, a new phoenix rises. Why may Welty have named her main character Phoenix?

7. (a)An author uses **description** to create a picture of a person, place, or thing. In your opinion, how effective are Welty's descriptions in creating a believable portrait of Phoenix Jackson? (b)How effective is Welty's writing in creating a vivid picture of the "worn path"?

Connect

8. **Big Idea** **Return to Regionalism** What does "A Worn Path" reveal about the way conditions in the South during the 1930s affected the lives of people there?

9. **Connect to the Author** Welty lived in the same place for her entire life. How might this kind of life have affected her ability to observe people and events?

Literary Element Description

A **description** is a detailed portrayal of a person, place, or thing. When authors write descriptions, they may use details to describe tangible things, such as the appearance of a character, or use details to describe intangible things, such as a character's personality traits.

1. Identify details in the story that describe the countryside around the Natchez Trace. Which details do you consider most vivid or striking? Explain.

2. In the city, Phoenix Jackson speaks first to a woman carrying presents and later to an attendant and a nurse. How do the descriptions in these scenes help to suggest that Jackson has a certain amount of pride despite her humble situation?

Review: Archetype

As you learned on page 23, an **archetype** is an image, a character type, or a plot pattern that occurs frequently in literature, mythology, folklore, and religion. Archetypes call up strong—and sometimes illogical—emotions in the reader.

Group Activity Meet with a small group and discuss Eudora Welty's use of archetypes in "A Worn Path." Possible archetypes to discuss include the strong grandmother, the kind stranger, the poor but determined woman, and the sick child. Share your thoughts on Welty's use of these archetypes with the class.

After You Read

Assess

1. Students' answers will vary.

2. (a) She is a small, elderly African American woman whose hair is tied in a rag. Her eyes are blue and her skin is wrinkled. (b) She is old and poor.

3. (a) The path leads her through woods, over a creek, through a barbed-wire fence, through fields, past a spring, through a swampy area, and under trees to Natchez. (b) Students may infer that the path is one that Phoenix makes for herself, not a path laid out by someone else. It symbolizes Phoenix's difficult journey through life.

4. (a) A doctor's office, to obtain medicine for her grandson (b) Near the end

5. She is kind, self-sacrificing, and decent.

6. The name symbolizes her triumph over obstacles.

7. (a) Students will find the descriptions of Phoenix effective. (b) Students should describe the effectiveness of specific images in their answers.

8. The rural environment and poverty had a major impact on people's lives. For example, Phoenix Jackson has to walk far to obtain basic medical necessities.

9. Her observations were probably limited by the people she met and the areas she saw.

Literary Element

1. Students' answers will vary. They may cite the ominous "big, dead trees . . . standing in the purple stalks of the withered cotton field."

2. Even though she has less than these people, she interacts with them and asks for their help. When doing so, she is polite and acts in a dignified manner.

Review: Archetype

Other examples of archetypal characters might be the rugged outdoorsman and the helpful nurse. An archetypal plot pattern is the difficult journey, and an archetypal image is the person carrying Christmas packages.

Progress Check

Can students analyze description?

If No → See Unit 6 Teaching Resources Book, p. 51.

After You Read

Assess

Reading Strategy

The attendant is probably smiling and leaning toward Phoenix in a friendly way. Phoenix staring hard at the nickel and tilting her head to one side may indicate that she is thinking hard about how to spend the nickel.

Vocabulary

1. b **2.** a **3.** c **4.** a **5.** c

Academic Vocabulary

Possible answer: In this sense, *interactions* refers to a mutual relationship between two separate entities.

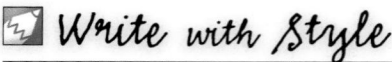

Use these criteria when evaluating students' writing:

- Does the student indirectly reveal character through dialogue?
- Does the student establish distinct, realistic characters?

Reading Strategy Visualize

Reread page 896, beginning, "Here's a nickel," and ending, "her head on one side." **Visualize** the facial expressions and body language of the characters.

Vocabulary Practice

Practice with Analogies Choose the word that best completes each analogy.

1. practice : competence :: study :
   a. books   c. mathematics
   b. comprehension
2. party : festive :: funeral :
   a. solemn   c. ceremony
   b. sermon
3. serious : trivial :: informal :
   a. tuxedo   c. ceremonial
   b. gathering
4. weakly : feebly :: forcefully :
   a. vigorously   c. reluctantly
   b. eagerly
5. lighthearted : cheerful :: somber :
   a. brokenhearted c. grave
   b. expressionless

Academic Vocabulary

*Old Phoenix comes across as stubborn and independent in her **interactions** with people.*

Interaction is an academic word. People might say that they meet new friends through social **interactions**. The word *interaction* is also used in the subjects of chemistry and biology. Using context clues, figure out the meaning of *interaction* in this sentence: *The immune system's defenses depend on cell-to-cell **interactions**.*

For more on academic vocabulary, see pages 53–54.

Write with Style

 Apply Dialogue

Assignment Welty breathes life into her characters through description and dialogue. Write a dialogue of your own that indirectly characterizes two people.

Get Ideas Decide who your characters are and what they are like. Think about real people you know or stories you have read to generate ideas. Then decide upon a scenario in which your characters will interact. To help you in your indirect characterization, create a chart like the one below.

Characteristic	How to describe through dialogue
friendly	initiates conversation, asks questions, listens attentively
smart	uses sophisticated language
new in town	refers to old house, old friends, old school, etc.
compassionate	notices an older woman and asks if she needs help crossing the street

Give It Structure As you write, refer back to your chart. Reveal character to your audience through what the characters say and how they say it.

Look at Language After you are done writing, have someone else read your work and discuss his or her impression of your characters. If they did not perceive your characters as you intended, revise your diction, tone, and sentence structure to more clearly establish your characterization.

LOG ON **Literature** Online

Selection Resources For Selection Quizzes, eFlash-cards, and Reading-Writing Connection activities, go to glencoe.com and enter QuickPass code GLA9800u6.

Writing Practice

SPIRAL REVIEW **Dialogue** Point out to students that writing a dialogue is like writing a skit—students have to create characters, setting, and a plot. In their charts about the characters, students should also jot down notes about where the characters meet, the circumstances in which they meet, whether the characters meet by chance or not, and whether the characters knew each other before they started talking. Tell students that once they have made notes on the characters and the setting, they should brainstorm possible topics of conversation between the characters based on their notes. For example, if their characters are strangers and they started a conversation because they are sitting next to each other on a train, the characters might make comments about the train and the train ride. Remind students that they should carefully pick the words they use in their dialogues to reflect the background and personalities of their characters.

Before You Read

from *Black Boy*

Meet **Richard Wright**
(1908–1960)

A s a writer, Richard Wright wanted to "wage a war with words," and he succeeded, becoming one of the first major African American literary figures. His books are raw and forceful—whether they are portraying life in the urban ghettos of the North or the oppression of African Americans in the South.

Wright's first book, *Uncle Tom's Children*, was praised by critics, and Malcolm Cowley of the *New Republic* claimed it was "heartening, as evidence of a vigorous new talent, and terrifying as the expression of a racial hatred that has never ceased to grow and gets no chance to die." However, Wright was dissatisfied with the book, because he felt that it did not adequately portray the reality of racism and violence in the United States. His next work was *Native Son*—a book that would change U.S. culture forever through its portrayal of a man who has suffered the injustices of racism, poverty, and despair.

Literature from Life In the opinion of many, *Black Boy* is Wright's most important work because it was not only his autobiography but a social documentary of the hardships caused by racism. Ralph Ellison, who was strongly influenced by Wright, claimed that "In *Black Boy* Wright has used his own life to probe what qualities of will, imagination, and intellect are required of a Southern Negro in order to possess the meaning of his life in the United States."

Born in 1908 in Mississippi, Wright experienced fear and oppression early. He first witnessed racial violence at the age of eight when his uncle was lynched by a group of white men. Throughout his life, Wright repeatedly saw members of his race degraded by whites, yet he refused to believe that African Americans were inferior. He began

> "It's strong, it's raw—but it's life as I see and lived it."
>
> —Richard Wright

reading and educating himself, and at nineteen he left for the North, mistakenly believing that he could live a life without discrimination there.

Outspoken Expatriate Realizing that social conditions for African Americans were not changing for the better, Wright moved his family to Paris, France, in 1947. He published no books for seven years but instead wrote articles on politics. While in France, he became friends with the writers Jean-Paul Sartre, Albert Camus, and André Gide. Their existential views influenced his later work.

Wright's reputation and literary influence declined during the 1950s, as young African American writers such as James Baldwin and Ralph Ellison emerged. Amid the Black Arts movement of the 1960s, however, Wright's work was rediscovered, inspiring and influencing a new generation of African Americans. Unfortunately, Wright died before he could take part in this emerging black unity and pride and the fight for equality that he yearned for.

 Literature Online

Author Search For more about Richard Wright, go to glencoe.com and enter QuickPass code GLA9800u6.

Before You Read

Focus

 For additional context, see Glencoe Interactive Vocabulary CD-ROM.

Selection Skills

Literary Elements
- Flash-forward (SE pp. 900, 906, 907)
- Autobiography (SE p. 907)

from **Black Boy**

Writing Skills/Grammar
- Speech (SE p. 908)
- Letter (TE p. 902)
- Connect (TE p. 906)

Reading Skills
- Compare and Contrast Characters (SE pp. 900–902, 905, 908)
- Visualize (SE p. 901)
- Preview (TE p. 900)

Vocabulary Skills
- Context Clues (SE pp. 900, 908)

Listening/Speaking/ Viewing Skills
- Analyze Art (SE p. 905)

Study Skills/Research/ Assessment
- Short-Answer Questions (TE p. 904)

Before You Read

Focus

Summary

This excerpt begins as Richard Wright's mother asks a judge to order her husband to provide financial support. The family faces extreme poverty. Wright's mother surrenders Richard and his brother to an orphan home. Richard runs away but is returned. Soon afterward, Richard's mother gets him to ask his father for support. Richard refuses the nickel that is offered. The tale flashes forward 25 years, when Richard next sees his father, by then a poor sharecropper.

 For summaries in languages other than English, see Unit 6 Teaching Resources Book, pp. 58–63.

Vocabulary

Adjectives Remind students that adjectives can describe people, things, actions, and feelings. Using an adjective correctly requires understanding what it can modify. **Ask:** Which word in this selection's vocabulary would not be used to describe a person? *(futile)*

[APPROACHING] Adjectives that are associated with strong feelings are often used to describe people and their actions. **Ask:** Which two words can describe either a person or an action? *(hostile, vindictive)*

 For additional vocabulary practice, see Unit 6 Teaching Resources Book, p. 66.

Literature and Reading Preview

Connect to the Story

How do you think your childhood will affect what you do later in life? List several events from your childhood and explain how they helped shape your beliefs or actions.

Build Background

Wright's father was a sharecropper near Natchez, Mississippi. He received a small cabin and some income from the cotton crop but had a difficult time making ends meet. Eventually he abandoned the family when Wright was six. Wright, his mother, and his brother were left with little income and a life marked by hunger and fear. Their struggles and the events following their abandonment are detailed in this excerpt from *Black Boy*.

Set Purposes for Reading

Big Idea Life in the City

As you read, ask yourself, How does Wright examine the impact of segregation and racism on his life?

Literary Element Flash-forward

A **flash-forward** is an interruption in the chronological sequence of a narrative to leap forward in time. A writer may signal a flash-forward with a new paragraph or with a description of a new setting. As you read, ask yourself, How does Wright use flash-forward to signal future events?

Reading Strategy Compare and Contrast Characters

When you **compare and contrast characters,** you note the similarities and differences between them. Comparing and contrasting can help you to better understand who the characters are and why they act in certain ways.

....

Tip: **Venn Diagrams** As you read, ask yourself, How are the characters similar and different? Use a Venn diagram to record your comparisons.

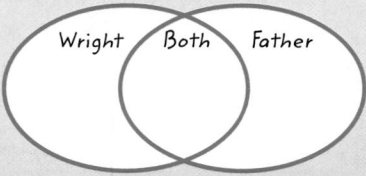

1. Physical Appearance

Wright   Both   Father

Learning Objectives

For pages 899–908
In studying this text, you will focus on the following objectives:

Literary Study: Analyzing sequence.

Reading: Comparing and contrasting characters.

Speaking and Listening: Delivering a speech.

Vocabulary

futile (fū´ til) *adj.* serving no practical purpose; useless; worthless; p. 902 *Trying to lift the chair was futile because it was nailed to the floor.*

hostile (host´ əl) *adj.* feeling or showing hatred; antagonistic; p. 902 *The woman became hostile when the salesclerk refused to answer her questions.*

vindictive (vin dik´ tiv) *adj.* desiring revenge; p. 902 *He was known for displaying vindictive behavior when he felt betrayed.*

poised (poizd) *adj.* having a calm, controlled, and dignified manner; composed; p. 906 *Though angry, she remained poised when her boss questioned her about her work.*

alien (ā´ lē ən) *adj.* strange; unfamiliar; foreign; p. 906 *The alien surroundings of her new town made her uncomfortable.*

....

Tip: **Context Clues** To learn a word's meaning, look at the other words in the sentence for clues.

Reading Practice

Preview Explain that this selection deals with the challenges of poverty—and especially the ways that poverty affects family relationships. Write the following connecting questions on the board for students to answer:

- Do you know of any other characters in literature or a movie who suffer from extreme poverty?
- How does the character's financial situation affect his or her family relationships?

Ask students to note the effects of poverty on Wright's relationship with his parents as they read the selection.

from Black Boy

Richard Wright

1 When I awakened one morning my mother told me that we were going to see a judge who would make my father support me and my brother. An hour later all three of us were sitting in a huge crowded room. I was overwhelmed by the many faces and the voices which I could not understand. High above me was a white face which my mother told me was the face of the judge. Across the huge room sat my father, smiling confidently, looking at us. My mother warned me not to be fooled by my father's friendly manner; she told me that the judge might ask me questions, and if he did I must tell him the truth. I agreed, yet I hoped that the judge would not ask me anything.

For some reason the entire thing struck me as being useless; I felt that if my father were going to feed me, then he would have done so regardless of what a judge said to him. And I did not want my father to feed me; I was hungry, but my thoughts of food did not now center about him. I waited, growing restless, hungry. My mother gave me a dry sandwich and I munched and stared, longing to go home. Finally I heard my mother's name called; she rose and began weeping so copiously[1] that she could not talk for a few moments; at last she managed to say that her husband had deserted her and her two children, that her children were hungry, that they stayed hungry, that she worked, that she was trying to raise them alone. Then my father was called; he came forward jauntily, smiling. He tried to kiss my mother, but she turned away from him. I only heard one sentence of what he said.

---

1. *Copiously* means "in great quantity."

2 Compare and Contrast Characters *How does Wright react to his parents' differences in court?*

"I'm doing all I can, Your Honor," he mumbled, grinning.

It had been painful to sit and watch my mother crying and my father laughing and I was glad when we were outside in the sunny streets. Back at home my mother wept again and talked complainingly about the unfairness of the judge who had accepted my father's word. After the court scene, I tried to forget my father; I did not hate him; I simply did not want to think of him. Often when we were hungry my mother would beg me to go to my father's job and ask him for a dollar, a dime, a nickel . . . But I would never consent to go. I did not want to see him.

My mother fell ill and the problem of food became an acute, daily agony. Hunger was with us always. Sometimes the neighbors would feed us or a dollar bill would come in the mail from my grandmother. It was winter and I would buy a dime's worth of coal each morning from the corner coalyard and lug it home in paper bags. For a time I remained out of school to wait upon my mother, then Granny came to visit us and I returned to school.

At night there were long, halting discussions about our going to live with Granny, but nothing came of it. Perhaps there was not enough money for railroad fare. Angered by having been hauled into court, my father now spurned us completely. I heard long, angrily whispered conversations between my mother and grandmother to the effect that "that woman ought to be killed for breaking up a home." What irked me was the ceaseless talk and no action. If someone had suggested that my father be killed, I would perhaps have become interested; if someone had suggested that his name never be mentioned, I would no

RICHARD WRIGHT **901**

Teach

Big Idea | 1

Life in the City Answer: *He might think that another city would not have the same problems—his father, an unfair judge, the cost of coal, and so on.*

(**APPROACHING**) Ask students for examples of sentences that show that the narrator is unhappy living in this city.

Reading Strategy | 2

Compare and Contrast Characters Answer: *He is always hungry, just like the other children, but his fear contrasts with their hostility and anger.*

Reading Strategy | 3

Compare and Contrast Characters Answer: *Wright is fearful of being abandoned. When his mother stops coming, he assumes that she has left him, just as his father did.*

Writing Practice

Letter Have students imagine that they are Wright living in the orphanage. **Say:** Write a letter to your mother, describing the conditions, your feelings about being there, and your hopes for how things will change. Tell students to use the story as a guide for descriptions and characterization. You may wish to extend the activity by having students write a response from Wright's mother.

902

---

doubt have agreed; if someone had suggested that we move to another city, I would have been glad. But there was only endless talk that led nowhere and I began to keep away from home as much as possible, preferring the simplicity of the streets to the worried, **futile** talk at home.

Finally we could no longer pay the rent for our dingy flat;[2] the few dollars that Granny had left us before she went home were gone. Half sick and in despair, my mother made the rounds of the charitable institutions, seeking help. She found an orphan home that agreed to assume the guidance of me and my brother provided my mother worked and made small payments. My mother hated to be separated from us, but she had no choice.

The orphan home was a two-story frame building set amid trees in a wide, green field. My mother ushered me and my brother one morning into the building and into the presence of a tall, gaunt, mulatto[3] woman who called herself Miss Simon. At once she took a fancy to me and I was frightened speechless; I was afraid of her the moment I saw her and my fear lasted during my entire stay in the home.

The house was crowded with children and there was always a storm of noise. The daily routine was blurred to me and I never quite grasped it. The most abiding feeling I had each day was hunger and fear. The meals were skimpy and there were only two of them. Just before we went to bed each night we were given a slice of bread smeared with

molasses. The children were silent, **hostile**, **vindictive**, continuously complaining of hunger. There was an overall atmosphere of nervousness and intrigue, of children telling tales upon others, of children being deprived of food to punish them.

The home did not have the money to check the growth of the wide stretches of grass by having it mown, so it had to be pulled by hand. Each morning after we had eaten a breakfast that seemed like no breakfast at all, an older child would lead a herd of us to the vast lawn and we would get to our knees and wrench the grass loose from the dirt with our fingers. At intervals Miss Simon would make a tour of inspection, examining the pile of pulled grass beside each child, scolding or praising according to the size of the pile. Many mornings I was too weak from hunger to pull the grass; I would grow dizzy and my mind would become blank and I would find myself, after an interval of unconsciousness, upon my hands and knees, my head whirling, my eyes staring in bleak astonishment at the green grass, wondering where I was, feeling that I was emerging from a dream . . .

During the first days my mother came each night to visit me and my brother, then her visits stopped. I began to wonder if she, too, like my father, had disappeared into the unknown. I was rapidly learning to distrust everything and everybody. When my mother did come, I asked her why had she remained away so long and she told me that Miss Simon had forbidden her to visit us, that Miss Simon had said that she was

---

2. A *flat* is an apartment.
3. *Mulatto*, a word seldom used today, describes a biracial person, one of mixed African American and white ancestry.

1 **Life in the City** *Why, as a boy, would the narrator have been glad to move to another city?*

> **Vocabulary**
> **futile** (fū′ til) *adj.* serving no practical purpose; useless; worthless

Compare and Contrast Characters *How do Wright's feelings in the house compare with the feelings of the other children there?* **2**

Compare and Contrast Characters *Why does Wright immediately compare his mother's actions to those of his father?* **3**

> **Vocabulary**
> **hostile** (host′ əl) *adj.* feeling or showing hatred; antagonistic
> **vindictive** (vin dik′ tiv) *adj.* desiring revenge

spoiling us with too much attention. I begged my mother to take me away; she wept and told me to wait, that soon she would take us to Arkansas. She left and my heart sank.

Miss Simon tried to win my confidence; she asked me if I would like to be adopted by her if my mother consented and I said no. She would take me into her apartment and talk to me, but her words had no effect. Dread and distrust had already become a daily part of my being and my memory grew sharp, my senses more impressionable; I began to be aware of myself as a distinct personality striving against others. I held myself in, afraid to act or speak until I was sure of my surroundings, feeling most of the time that I was suspended over a void. My imagination soared; I dreamed of running away. Each morning I vowed that I would leave the next morning, but the next morning always found me afraid.

One day Miss Simon told me that thereafter I was to help her in the office. I ate lunch with her and, strangely, when I sat facing her at the table, my hunger vanished. The woman killed something in me. Next she called me to her desk where she sat addressing envelopes.

"Step up close to the desk," she said. "Don't be afraid."

I went and stood at her elbow. There was a wart on her chin and I stared at it.

"Now, take a blotter from over there and blot each envelope after I'm through writing on it," she instructed me, pointing to a blotter that stood about a foot from my hand.

I stared and did not move or answer.

Jim, 1930. William H. Johnson. Oil on canvas, 21⅝ x 18¼ in. Smithsonian American Art Museum, Washington, DC.

---

4 | Life in the City *Why might Wright be afraid to run away from the orphan home?*

"Take the blotter," she said.

I wanted to reach for the blotter and succeeded only in twitching my arm.

"Here," she said sharply, reaching for the blotter and shoving it into my fingers.

She wrote in ink on an envelope and pushed it toward me. Holding the blotter in my hand, I stared at the envelope and could not move.

"Blot it," she said.

I could not lift my hand. I knew what she had said; I knew what she wanted me to do; and I had heard her correctly. I wanted to look at her and say something, tell her why I could not move; but my eyes were fixed upon the floor. I could not summon enough courage while she sat there looking at me to reach over the yawning space of twelve inches and blot the wet ink on the envelope.

"Blot it!" she spoke sharply.

RICHARD WRIGHT **903**

Big Idea | **4**

Life in the City Answer: *He has nowhere to go, and he knows that he could get into trouble or be hurt.*

View the Art ★

William H. Johnson (1901–1970), born in South Carolina, did not receive widespread recognition until after his death. He is now regarded as one of the major African American artists of the twentieth century. **Ask:** What emotions are evoked by this picture of a young boy? *(Possible answers: sadness; loneliness; rejection; despair)*

Teach

Big Idea   1

Life in the City Answer:
When he sees the white police officer, he fears that he will be beaten. He has seen and heard of violence toward African Americans and is certain that the same could happen to him.

Reading Strategy   2

Make Inferences Wright says "Again I was faced with choices I did not like . . ." **Ask:** What were the undesirable choices that Wright described before? Which option did he pick? *(Wright could either stay at the orphanage and be miserable or run away from the orphanage despite having nowhere to go. He chose to run away.)* What choices does Wright have now and why does he not like his choices? (Wright could either stay in the orphanage or go to his father and ask for money to get to Arkansas. Wright hates staying in the orphanage, but he dislikes his father for abandoning him and for making his mother miserable, so he does not want to go see his father.)*

Still I could not move or answer.

"Look at me!"

I could not lift my eyes. She reached her hand to my face and I twisted away.

"What's wrong with you?" she demanded.

I began to cry and she drove me from the room. I decided that as soon as night came I would run away. The dinner bell rang and I did not go to the table, but hid in a corner of the hallway. When I heard the dishes rattling at the table, I opened the door and ran down the walk to the street. Dusk was falling. Doubt made me stop. Ought I go back? No; hunger was back there, and fear. I went on, coming to concrete sidewalks. People passed me. Where was I going? I did not know. The farther I walked the more frantic I became. In a confused and vague way I knew that I was doing more running *away* from than running *toward* something. I stopped. The streets seemed dangerous. The buildings were massive and dark. The moon shone and the trees loomed frighteningly. No, I could not go on. I would go back. But I had walked so far and had turned too many corners and had not kept track of the direction. Which way led back to the orphan home? I did not know. I was lost.

I stood in the middle of the sidewalk and cried. A "white" policeman came to me and I wondered if he was going to beat me. He asked me what was the matter and I told him that I was trying to find my mother. His "white" face created a new fear in me. I was remembering the tale of the "white" man who had beaten the "black" boy. A crowd gathered and I was urged to tell where I lived. Curiously, I was too full of fear to cry now. I wanted to tell the "white" face that I had run off from an orphan home and that Miss Simon ran it, but I was afraid. Finally I was taken to the police station where I was fed. I felt better. I sat in a big chair where I was surrounded by "white" policemen, but they seemed to ignore me. Through the window I could see that night had completely

---

1 **Life in the City** Why might Wright think of this tale when he is lost?

fallen and that lights now gleamed in the streets. I grew sleepy and dozed. My shoulder was shaken gently and I opened my eyes and looked into a "white" face of another policeman who was sitting beside me. He asked me questions in a quiet, confidential tone, and quite before I knew it he was not "white" any more. I told him that I had run away from an orphan home and that Miss Simon ran it.

It was but a matter of minutes before I was walking alongside a policeman, heading toward the home. The policeman led me to the front gate and I saw Miss Simon waiting for me on the steps. She identified me and I was left in her charge. I begged her not to beat me, but she yanked me upstairs into an empty room and lashed me thoroughly. Sobbing, I slunk off to bed, resolved to run away again. But I was watched closely after that.

My mother was informed upon her next visit that I had tried to run away and she was terribly upset.

"Why did you do it?" she asked.

"I don't want to stay here," I told her.

"But you must," she said. "How can I work if I'm to worry about you? You must remember that you have no father. I'm doing all I can."

"I don't want to stay here," I repeated.

"Then, if I take you to your father . . ."

"I don't want to stay with him either," I said.

"But I want you to ask him for enough money for us to go to my sister's in Arkansas," she said.

Again I was faced with choices I did not like, but I finally agreed. After all, my hate for my father was not so great and urgent as my hate for the orphan home. My mother held to her idea and one night a week or so later I found myself standing in a room in a frame house. My father and a strange woman were sitting before a bright fire that blazed in a grate. My mother and I were standing about six feet away, as though we were afraid to approach them any closer. **2**

"It's not for me," my mother was saying. "It's for your children that I'm asking you for money."

"I ain't got nothing," my father said, laughing.

"Come here, boy," the strange woman called to me.

Assessment Practice

SPIRAL REVIEW **Short-Answer Questions** Remind students that responses to short-answer questions are evaluated on their insight and use of evidence from a text. **Ask:** How does race play a role in "Black Boy"? Have students scan the text and look for answers to this question. Then tell them to write their responses to the question. After they have finished writing, they should scan their answers to make sure their answers make sense and to check for any grammatical errors. Encourage volunteers to share their answers with the class. *(Students should note the title, the fear of running away, the story about the "white" police officer, and Wright's fear that he would be beaten because he was "black.")*

Negro Cabin, Sedalia, North Carolina (No. 1), 1930. Loïs Mailou Jones. Watercolor on paper, 14⅛ x 19⅛ in. Collection of the artist.

<u>View the Art</u> In 1930, the number of African-American sharecroppers in the south—many of them trapped in a cycle of debt—peaked at nearly 400,000. Does this painting capture the aspects of the father's shack that caused Wright to pity him? Explain. ★

I looked at her and did not move.

"Give him a nickel," the woman said. "He's cute."

"Come here, Richard," my father said, stretching out his hand.

I backed away, shaking my head, keeping my eyes on the fire.

"He is a cute child," the strange woman said.

"You ought to be ashamed," my mother said to the strange woman. "You're starving my children."

"Now, don't you-all fight," my father said, laughing.

"I'll take that poker and hit you!" I blurted at my father.

He looked at my mother and laughed louder.

---

2 Compare and Contrast Characters *How does Wright compare his father's girlfriend with his mother?*

"You told him to say that," he said.

"Don't say such things, Richard," my mother said.

"You ought to be dead," I said to the strange woman.

The woman laughed and threw her arms about my father's neck. I grew ashamed and wanted to leave.

"How can you starve your children?" my mother asked.

"Let Richard stay with me," my father said.

"Do you want to stay with your father, Richard?" my mother asked.

"No," I said.

"You'll get plenty to eat," he said.

"I'm hungry now," I told him. "But I won't stay with you."

"Aw, give the boy a nickel," the woman said.

My father ran his hand into his pocket and pulled out a nickel.

"Here, Richard," he said.

RICHARD WRIGHT **905**

Compare and Contrast Characters **Answer:** *Wright realizes that unlike his mother, the strange woman does not care about him or about what is right or wrong. His mother tries to protect her children, whereas the woman cares only about herself and having fun.*

(**ENGLISH LEARNERS**) Check to make sure that students understand which two characters they are to compare: the first character is the strange woman who is sitting at the fire with his father (the girl-friend of the narrator's father). The second character is the mother of the narrator.

<u>View the Art</u> ★

Answer: *Students may say that the small, ramshackle cabin accurately reflects the poverty that Wright pities.*

Emerging Help students understand how recounting a memory can reveal that a character has changed. Wright reacts in different ways when he first sees his father and the strange woman and when he remembers the scene. In both cases, his description of the fire is a key to his reaction.

Have students compare the descriptions and explore what they may reveal about the changes in Wright. *(In the first scene, the fire is a dangerous, frightening barrier between Wright and his father. In the memory, the "dancing" fire draws him in. He is no longer afraid, but feels as if he can reach out and touch it.)*

Teach

Literary Element 1

Flash-forward Answer:
Wright tells the reader about the future because it shows the lasting impact of his father's lack of concern. The description of an image that came to him many times as he grew older leads into the flash-forward that follows.

Literary Element 2

Flash-forward Answer:
Wright remembers being afraid of his father, but now he sees that his father is not someone he should have feared or continued to think about for years.

Big Idea 3

Life in the City Answer: *As an uneducated African American, Wright's father had few choices. His father's imprisonment in ignorance and poverty has led Wright to escape those bonds.*

To check students' understanding of the selection, see Unit 6 Teaching Resources Book, p. 69.

"Don't take it," my mother said.

"Don't teach him to be a fool," my father said. "Here, Richard, take it."

I looked at my mother, at the strange woman, at my father, then into the fire. I wanted to take the nickel, but I did not want to take it from my father.

"You ought to be ashamed," my mother said, weeping. "Giving your son a nickel when he's hungry. If there's a God, He'll pay you back."

"That's all I got," my father said, laughing again and returning the nickel to his pocket.

We left. I had the feeling that I had had to do with something unclean. Many times in the years after that the image of my father and the strange woman, their faces lit by the dancing flames, would surge up in my imagination so vivid and strong that I felt I could reach out and touch it; I would stare at it, feeling that it possessed some vital meaning which always eluded me.

A quarter of a century was to elapse between the time when I saw my father sitting with the strange woman and the time when I was to see him again, standing alone upon the red clay of a Mississippi plantation, a sharecropper, clad in ragged overalls, holding a muddy hoe in his gnarled, veined hands—a quarter of a century during which my mind and consciousness had become so greatly and violently altered that when I tried to talk to him I realized that, though ties of blood made us kin, though I could see a shadow of my face in his face, though there was an echo of my voice in his voice, we were forever strangers, speaking a different language, living on vastly distant planes of reality. That day a quarter of a century later when I visited him on the plantation—he was standing against the sky, smiling toothlessly, his hair whitened, his body bent, his eyes glazed with dim recollection, his fearsome aspect of

twenty-five years ago gone forever from him—I was overwhelmed to realize that he could never understand me or the scalding experiences that had swept me beyond his life and into an area of living that he could never know. I stood before him, **poised,** my mind aching as it embraced the simple nakedness of his life, feeling how completely his soul was imprisoned by the slow flow of the seasons, by wind and rain and sun, how fastened were his memories to a crude and raw past, how chained were his actions and emotions to the direct, animalistic impulses of his withering body . . .

From the white landowners above him there had not been handed to him a chance to learn the meaning of loyalty, of sentiment, of tradition. Joy was as unknown to him as was despair. As a creature of the earth, he endured, hearty, whole, seemingly indestructible, with no regrets and no hope. He asked easy, drawling questions about me, his other son, his wife, and he laughed, amused, when I informed him of their destinies. I forgave him and pitied him as my eyes looked past him to the unpainted wooden shack. From far beyond the horizons that bound this bleak plantation there had come to me through my living the knowledge that my father was a black peasant who had gone to the city seeking life, but who had failed in the city; a black peasant whose life had been hopelessly snarled in the city, and who had at last fled the city—that same city which had lifted me in its burning arms and borne me toward **alien** and undreamed-of shores of knowing. ∾

Flash-forward *Why does Wright describe his father this way?* 2

Life in the City *How did life in the South affect the choices of Wright's father and Wright's future?* 3

Vocabulary

poised (poizd) *adj.* having a calm, controlled, and dignified manner; composed

alien (ā′ lē ən) *adj.* strange; unfamiliar; foreign

1 **Flash-forward** *Why does Wright tell the reader that he continued to think about his father and that night for years?*

Writing Practice

Connect Explain to students that a good way to relate a work of literature to their own lives is to put themselves in the writer's shoes. Have students think of an example where their impression or opinion of a person, place, object, or event changed as they have grown older. **Ask:** Why did your impression or opinion change? Why did Wright's impression and opinion of his father change over the years? Are there any similarities and differences between your experience and Wright's experience? Have students write a short essay describing and evaluating their experiences. Tell them to also include a comparison between their experiences and Wright's experiences in their essays.

After You Read

Respond and Think Critically

Respond and Interpret

1. What was your reaction to the events of Wright's life? Explain.

2. (a)Why do Wright and his brother go to the orphan home? (b)How is the orphan home different from and similar to his old home?

3. (a)Why does Wright run away? (b)What do you learn about Wright's attitudes and perceptions about race from this incident?

4. (a)What does Wright's mother promise as she takes him out of the orphan home? (b)What do you learn about Wright's character from his interactions with his father just after leaving the home?

5. (a)What ultimately happens to Wright's father? (b)What does Wright's visit with his elderly father reveal about Wright's values? Explain, using details from the selection.

Analyze and Evaluate

6. Does Wright's father become more or less sympathetic as the story progresses? Explain.

7. (a)What is the tone of the selection? (b)How effective is the tone in expressing the author's main point?

Connect

8. **Big Idea** Life in the City How are Wright's attitudes and perceptions about race shaped by his time and place?

9. **Connect to the Author** (a)How does knowing that this selection is from an autobiography affect your reaction? (b)Would you react differently if it were fiction? Explain.

Literary Element Flash-forward

Although most stories are told in the order in which the events occur, sometimes writers interrupt the chronological flow. An author can use a technique called a **flashback** to explain an event that happened before the action in the story. This technique provides essential information about the character or prior events so that the reader can better understand the character's motivations. An interruption in events to leap forward in time is a **flash-forward**. Wright uses this device to show how his views had changed since the events in the excerpt had taken place.

1. Where is the flash-forward in this selection?

2. How does Wright signal that he is skipping ahead?

3. (a)What effect does this flash-forward create in Wright's narrative? (b)Does it strengthen or weaken the narrative? Explain.

Review: Autobiography

An **autobiography** is the story of a person's life written by that person. Unlike a memoir, which tends to focus on specific events or parts of the author's life, an autobiography usually encompasses most of the author's life.

Activity Complete the chart below by finding descriptions from the story about Wright's life, his parents, and the South during his childhood. Determine how each of these affected him and his choices.

	Description	Effects on Wright
His life		
Mother		
Father		
The South		

Literary Element

1. The flash-forward begins in the middle of the first column of page 906.

2. He signals it with "A quarter of a century was to elapse."

3. (a) The flash-forward breaks the narrative; it provides a view of the mature Wright. (b) Students may say that the flash-forward helps them understand the meaning of the selection better.

Review: Autobiography

Have students copy the chart onto a piece of paper and complete all sections.

Progress Check

Can students recognize a flash forward?

If No → See Unit 6 Teaching Resources Book, p. 64.

After You Read

Assess

1. Most students will feel sympathy for Wright.

2. (a) Their mother is poor and must work, so she cannot stay home to care for them. (b) In the orphanage, he is surrounded by strangers. It is similar in that he is hungry and unhappy there.

3. (a) To escape his miserable life at the orphan home (b) Wright is at first keenly aware that the policemen are white. When one policeman is kind to him, he sees him as a person and not as a member of a race.

4. (a) She offers to take him out of the home if he will ask his father for money. (b) Wright is strong-willed and has a strong sense of right and wrong.

5. (a) He becomes a poor sharecropper. (b) Wright values the human experience—loyalty, joy, tradition, despair—unlike his father, whom Wright sees as "a creature of the earth."

6. Students may feel that he becomes more sympathetic after his circumstances are explained.

7. (a) Matter-of-fact, with an undercurrent of bitterness (b) It is effective in showing the fear Wright lived with as a child.

8. Wright sees African Americans treated with disrespect, so he becomes distrustful of whites.

9. (a) The events have a greater impact because they are true. (b) Reactions to fiction may be less personal.

After You Read

Assess

Reading Strategy

1. D is the correct answer because only the narrator's mother expressed true emotion and love and concern for her children, and only his father abandoned them.

Vocabulary

1. Based on the context, I can infer the meaning of *futile* is "useless," or "without practical purpose."

2. Based on the clues of "bad" and "defiant," *hostile* means "antagonistic."

3. Based on the context that Alice is "spreading rumors about her former friend," it can be inferred that *vindictive* means "seeking revenge."

4. The definition of *poised,* or "calm and controlled," is in the sentence.

5. The contrast of familiar surroundings, or Germany, to the American high school implies that *alien* means "foreign" or "unfamiliar."

Academic Vocabulary

Transformation in this biological context means that the genetic makeup of a bacterium changes, or *transforms*, due to the presence of a foreign body, or DNA.

 For additional assessment, see Assessment Resources, pp. 241–242.

ACT Skills Practice

1. Which character traits differentiate the narrator's father and mother?

    I. Ability to express true emotion

    II. Concern and love for their children

    III. Abandonment of the narrator and his brother

    A. I only

    B. II only

    C. I and III only

    D. I, II, and III only

Vocabulary Practice

Practice with Context Clues Identify the context clues in these sentences that help you infer the meaning of each vocabulary word.

1. Studying seemed like a **futile** task because he had already been accepted to college.

2. Tom's mother reacted to the bad news by becoming **hostile** and defiant.

3. Alice demonstrated her **vindictive** nature by spreading rumors about her ex-friend.

4. The cellist was not only a brilliant musician but also **poised**, or calm and controlled.

5. Raised in Germany, John felt that his new American high school was an **alien** place.

Academic Vocabulary

Transformation is an academic word. It is also used in the subjects of biology, chemistry, and physics. Using context clues, figure out the meaning of **transformation** in this sentence: A caterpillar undergoes a *transformation* to become a butterfly.

For more on academic vocabulary, see pages 53–54.

Speaking and Listening

 Speech

Assignment As Wright's autobiography shows, a parent's abandonment can have a great effect on a child, both emotionally and financially. Research, write, and deliver a persuasive speech stating your views on the issue of child abandonment today. Incorporate visual aids in your speech and conclude with a call to action.

Prepare Determine what aspect of the issue of child abandonment you want to address in your speech. For example, you might confine your speech to the financial challenges for a single-parent family. Clarify your opinion on the issue. Outline your speech to give a logical organization to the evidence you present in support of your opinion. In drafting your speech, defend your reasons with precise and accurate evidence, such as facts, expert opinions, statistics, and examples. Make sure you use reliable sources and keep a bibliography. Conclude your speech with a call for action (proposal for change).

As you gather the research for your speech, think about how you might present it visually in a way that will effectively support the points you are trying to make. For example, you might create a graph showing the relation between the increase in single-parent families and the increase in the number of children living in poverty.

Deliver Once you have drafted your speech, review it for clarity and logic. Deliver your speech in a confident, animated tone. Use vocal emphasis to stress important words and ideas. Make eye contact with your audience to show conviction.

Evaluate Write a paragraph evaluating your delivery. Use the checklist on page 154 for help in your evaluation.

 Literature Online

Selection Resources For Selection Quizzes, eFlash-cards, and Reading-Writing Connection activities, go to glencoe.com and enter QuickPass code GLA9800u6.

 ## Speaking and Listening

Use these criteria when evaluating students' persuasive speeches:

- Did the student logically defend a position in the speech?
- Did the student effectively use visual aids in delivering the speech?.
- Did the student effectively use verbal and nonverbal techniques in delivering the speech?

For grammar practice, see Unit 6 Teaching Resources Book, p. 68.

You Have Seen Their Faces

from

Erskine Caldwell and
Margaret Bourke-White

O. Henry Prize Winner

Historical Perspective
on *Black Boy*

Iron Mountain, Tennessee, 1937. Margaret Bourke-White. Silver gelatin print. Time & Life Pictures.

Learning Objectives

For pages 909–912

In studying this text, you will focus on the following objectives:

Reading:
Making connections across literature.
Analyzing historical texts and photographs.
Analyzing informational text.

Set a Purpose for Reading

Read to learn about the sharecropping system.

Build Background

Photojournalist Margaret Bourke-White documented some of the most important events of the twentieth century, including the liberation of Nazi concentration camps and the Korean War. In 1937 she and her future husband, novelist Erskine Caldwell, collaborated on *You Have Seen Their Faces*. This book powerfully depicts the plight that southern sharecroppers faced.

1 **Reading Strategy** **Analyze the Purpose of Historical Texts and Photographs**
Analyzing the purpose of historical texts and photographs involves examining the ideas and culture presented by texts and images. As you read, ask yourself, What do the writers want their readers to do or think? Use a chart to take notes about the selection and the photographs in order to determine their purpose.

Text Passage and Purpose	Photograph and Purpose

The Mississippi Valley Delta and the Black Belt[1] of Alabama are two sections of the South that still produce cotton in abundance. It grows, matures, and yields without fertilizer and without effort. The soil there will be deep, fertile, and productive for a long time to come. Elsewhere the sub-soil, both sand and clay, is being plowed up to be mixed with the little top-soil that remains in an effort to make plants grow. There is no fertility in sub-soil, but when brought to the surface it gives the appearance of fertility and, when mixed with fertilizer, will produce enough cotton, providing that the rains and sun are not extreme, to pay for the fertilizer in normal times. Farming in sand or clay is a back-breaking, spirit-crushing existence.

There are reasons for this impoverishment[2] of the soil that go deep into the economic life of the South. The successful cotton-raisers have always been plantation-owners. The plantations were large, generally from five hundred to five thousand acres of land in size. The owners for the most part had one main concern,

---

1. *The Black Belt* is a strip of land with black, fertile soil across central Alabama and Mississippi.
2. *Impoverishment* means "the state of being drained of essential nutrients."

Approaching Level

DIFFERENTIATED INSTRUCTION

Emerging Have visual learners look again at each photo after they read the text. Tell students that the text may explain the photo, add information, or set a mood. After they have read the text on each page, have students write a phrase or sentence that describes what the photo shows. *(p. 909, impoverished soil; p. 911, poverty passed on to a new generation; p. 912, a lifetime of poverty)*

Focus

Summary

This excerpt from *You Have Seen Their Faces* focuses on the historical roots and detrimental effects of the sharecropping system in the South.

Teach

Reading Strategy   1

Analyze the Purpose of Historical Texts and Photographs Before students begin reading the excerpt, have them look at the three photos in this essay. Have students describe their responses to the photos. Ask them to predict the tone of the article they are about to read. *(Students may say that the article is likely to criticize the system that made the land and the people so poor. The land looks barren; the walls where the boy stands are papered by newsprint; the boy's and the elderly women's faces look sad and strained.)*

View the Art ★

Ask: What can this photograph teach you that text alone cannot? *(It provides an evocative image of the harshness and burden of sharecropping.)*

Readability Scores

Dale-Chall: 11.7
DRP: 63
Lexile: 1210

Teach

Reading Strategy | 1

Identify Cause and Effect
Ask: What effect did the plantation system have on the soil? *(It impoverished the soil.)* What did this effect cause plantation-owners to do? *(They withdrew to cities, where they became absentee landlords.)*

(ADVANCED) Students may create a graphic organizer or write a paragraph that extends the cause-and-effect process described here. Have students include at least three events.

Literary Element | 2

Tone Ask: What is the author's tone in his references to the plantation owners? *(The tone is sarcastic and bitter.)* What is the effect of the author's use of the image of kings? *(It emphasizes that the landlords had absolute power and could take advantage of their "subjects.")*

 For activities related to this selection, see Unit 6 Teaching Resources Book, pp. 71–79.

---

and that was to make as much money as they could as quickly as they could.

Nothing made money like cotton. Nothing else grew like cotton. Cotton was king.

Now the day of the plantation is over, except in the Delta country and in the Black Belt, and cotton is not king any longer.

The plantation system pauperized[3] the soil to such a great degree that raising cotton became a means of making a living rather than a method of making a fortune. The plantation-owner, when he became aware of what had happened to the soil, withdrew to the nearest city to live the remainder of his life on his accumulated wealth.

1 What he left behind was eroded, depleted, unprofitable land. His tenants still had to work for a living, even if he did not, and out of their desperation grew a new system. The owner became an absentee-landlord. The plantation was divided into one-man farms and rented to the tenants. The rent was paid either in half of the cotton produced or in an agreed upon number of bales, or on a basis combining the two methods. The plantation system was traded for the sharecropping system, and the South to its sorrow was the victim of the deal.

Before he knew it, the landlord had a new source of income that was larger than his previous one had been. And, besides, in the old days he had had to take his own chances with his crop of cotton, losing money when it rained too much or too little, dipping into profits from preceding years when expenditures were larger than income. In the new era he had a source of income and profit that was as certain and secure as the seasons themselves.

Rent was paid to him for the use of the land on a sharing basis, and he saw to it that the tenant raised a maximum number of bales. When a hundred tenants produced six bales each, the landlord received three hundred bales, the individual tenant three bales. Cotton **2** was not king any longer, but the institution of sharecropping was making a few men richer

---

3. *Pauperized* means "depleted or drained."

than kings, and much better enthroned.[4] They did not have to concern themselves about the welfare of their subjects. **2**

The tenant who set out to farm his portion of the plantation discovered that the land required fertilizer. Without fertilizer he could not grow enough cotton to provide himself with a living, and to pay rent. The rent came first. The landlord generally saw to it that the tenant paid his three or four bales for rent before the sharing began. If there was nothing left to share after the rent had been paid, there was nothing the tenant could do about it. He could only look forward to the coming year, hoping he would be able to make more than the minimum number of bales the rent required. If the following year was a good one for him, he paid off the chattel mortgage[5] he had given in payment for fertilizer he had bought in an effort to produce the rent-cotton.

It is difficult to find a good word to say about such an agricultural system. The sharecropping system was born of the plantation system, and the new was anything but an improvement over the old. The old produced numerous families of wealth who developed a culture that was questionable. The new has concentrated wealth in the hands of a few families who are determined that no culture shall exist.

Much can be said about the detrimental effects of such an agricultural system, more especially when there are ten million persons now living under its yoke.[6] They live in this cotton country on tenant farms which, in many cases, are little more than sand dunes and clay stacks. They are either already worn out physically and spiritually, or are in the act of wearing themselves out. They are grouped in families of man and wife and from one to sixteen children. They are farming, for the most part, soil that has been

---

4. *Enthroned* means "installed as king" and implies that the landlords were distanced from the sharecroppers just as a king might be removed from his subjects.
5. A *chattel mortgage* is a mortgage on personal property that is used as a guarantee for a debt.
6. Here, *yoke* refers to "something that causes servitude or bondage."

Vocabulary Practice

Use Context Clues Remind students that context clues offer hints about the meanings of unfamiliar words. Write these sentences on the board, and ask students to identify the meanings of the underlined words, along with the context clues that suggest the meanings:

1. The circumstance grows more <u>acute</u> as cotton land erodes.

2. Sharecropping has <u>deprived</u> millions of persons of what the rest of America considers the necessities of life.

3. The tenant farmer in the South is holding onto a spinning world until he is <u>enabled</u> to grip onto a better way of life.

yielding diminishing returns for fifty and a hundred years. No matter if they get up an hour earlier to work by lantern light, no matter if half a dozen more children are begotten[7] to supply additional hands in the field, they will continue to fall steadily behind as long as they live on land that produces less and less each time a new crop of cotton is planted.

This is nothing new. It is not a situation that has suddenly come about overnight. But it is a circumstance that becomes more acute day by day as the exhaustion and erosion of cotton land progresses. Fertilizer will increase the yield of cotton, but fertilizer costs money and requires credit that the tenant farmer does not have. A larger farm will produce more cotton, but there is a physical limit to the number of acres a man and his family can cultivate.

The sharecropping system has in recent years branched out into several forms, none of them any more economically sound than the source from which they sprang, and most of them working greater hardships on human lives than the plantation system ever did. Sharecropping has deprived millions of persons of what the rest of America considers the necessities of life.

It deprives children of adequate education because many of them have to work either part of the school year or all of it on their fathers' farms so that enough cotton can be raised to pay rent and buy fertilizer and to get food and clothing. It forces families to live in buildings that are detrimental to health, and it forces them to exist on food that is insufficient. Worse still, it continues in operation year after

Child of sharecropper family, Louisiana, 1936. Margaret Bourke-White. Silver gelatin print. Time & Life Pictures.

year, wringing dry the bodies and souls of men, women, and children; dragging down to its own level from higher economic planes new numbers to take the places of those crushed and thrown aside; breeding families of eight, ten, twelve, fourteen, sixteen, and more, in order to furnish an ever-increasing number of persons necessary to supply the rent-cotton for the landlord.

It is foolish to ask a tenant farmer why he remains where he is. He does move from farm to farm from time to time, but only rarely can he improve his status. Such a question is usually asked with the purpose of covering up an

3

---

7. *Begotten* means "conceived."

Historical Perspective

on *Black Boy*

Teach

Reading Strategy 3

Analyze the Purpose of Historical Texts and Photographs Ask: How would you describe the author's purpose in this excerpt? *(The author wants to expose the evils of the sharecropping system, probably with the hope of reforming the system or promoting collective action by the tenant farmers.)*

View the Photograph ★

Ask: What details in the photograph reinforce the theme of despair? *(Details such as the child's facial expression and the ramshackle appearance of the dwelling reinforce the theme of hopelessness.)*

English Learners

DIFFERENTIATED INSTRUCTION

Intermediate English learners may need help with figurative language—expressions such as "cotton was king" or "what the farmer could do to lift himself from the hole he stands in." Have students discuss the meaning of each phrase. Have students rewrite the sentences that contain figurative language, using literal translations. For example, for "Cotton was king," they might write, "Cotton was the crop that made the most money for plantation-owners, and their decisions were ruled by it."

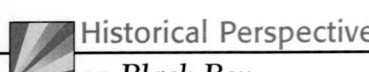
Assess

1. Students' summaries should mention that the excerpt explores the historical roots and negative effects (on both people and the land) of the sharecropping system.

2. (a) Sharecropping encouraged families to increase in size so that they would have more workers. It also deprived children of an education. (b) Larger families and poor education would have increased the poverty in sharecropping communities.

3. Many students will say that the images vividly convey the harshness and poverty of sharecroppers' lives.

4. (a) The sharecropping system is unfair and destructive. (b) Most students will think they are successful.

5. Most students will feel an increased sympathy for Wright's father, as Wright himself does at the end of the excerpt from *Black Boy*.

> For additional assessment, see Assessment Resources, pp. 243–244.

inability to suggest what the farmer could do to lift himself from the hole he stands in. There is cotton to be raised, and he has trained himself to raise it. That is his specialty. It is his life and, if sharecropping continues as an institution, it will become his death.

The tenant farmer in the South is trying to hold onto a spinning world until by some means he is enabled to get a grip on a better way of life. He knows he cannot buy land of his own from the profits of sharecropping. He knows just as well that he cannot save until he earns, and that he cannot earn much more than a bare living from sterile, barren land. He does well, under the circumstances, to hold on at all.

Now that his condition has sunk to depths that stop just short of peonage,[8] there has appeared the first sign of hope. What there is in store for him in the future remains to be seen, but now for the first time there is hope. There has been talk, from one end of the South to the other, of joining with other tenant farmers to take collective action against the institution of sharecropping. The day when it was a sacred bull has passed. The sign of its passing was when the landlords began putting into force other forms of farm tenancy. Farms were leased to tenants, but sharing of the cotton continued; tenants were paid to work by the day, but their pay was received in a share of

8. *Peonage* is the use of workers who are forced to labor for someone to work off a debt.

the cotton. No one was fooled, least of all tenant farmers themselves.

The farmer has little, if anything, to show for his years of labor in the past. But the hardships he has experienced will stand him in good stead when the time comes for him to begin thinking about taking over the job of raising cotton—the job in which the landlord failed to treat him fairly and squarely.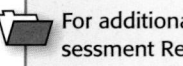

Respond and Think Critically

Respond and Interpret

1. Write a brief summary of the main ideas in this article before you answer the following questions. For help on writing a summary, see page 79.

2. (a) What effect did sharecropping have on the size of families? Of what did sharecropping deprive children? (b) What might be the outcome of these two effects?

Analyze and Evaluate

3. In a short paragraph, describe how the images add to your understanding of sharecropping.

4. (a) What is the main idea of this selection? (b) Are the authors successful in conveying it? Explain.

Connect

5. Does this selection change your opinion of Wright's father as depicted in *Black Boy*? Explain.

Writing Practice

Implied Main Idea Point out that sometimes the main idea of a paragraph is not stated but implied. Have students examine the first paragraph of this selection. Guide them in recognizing that the implied main idea of the paragraph is a contrast between the fertile soil of the Mississippi Delta and the Black Belt and the infertile soil of other areas. Challenge students to write a topic sentence expressing this main idea.

Some students may find it helpful to write the main idea of each paragraph as they read the selection and then use their sentences as a summary of the selection.

Before You Read

The Life You Save May Be Your Own

Meet **Flannery O'Connor**
(1925–1964)

Flannery O'Connor often delighted in telling friends and interviewers that the highlight of her life occurred when, as a five-year-old, she taught a chicken to walk backwards. It was on such odd yet ordinary experiences that O'Connor later based her work.

"Highly Unladylike" Mary Flannery O'Connor was born in Savannah, Georgia. Soon after, her family moved to Milledgeville, a small city in central Georgia. After graduating from college in 1945, she attended the prestigious Iowa Writers' Workshop at the University of Iowa, earning an MFA degree. While at Iowa, O'Connor had her first short story, "The Geranium," published in the summer of 1946.

> "The truth does not change according to our ability to stomach it."
> —Flannery O'Connor

More short stories and novels followed, in which O'Connor often drew upon her experiences as a devout Roman Catholic to explore harsh and disturbing realities: hard luck, hypocrisy, and failed expectations. Her work was widely read by the public and highly praised by critics. A review appearing in *Time* magazine hailed O'Connor as "highly unladylike [with] a brutal irony, a slambang humor, and a style of writing as balefully direct as a death sentence."

Along with William Faulkner, Carson McCullers, and Tennessee Williams, O'Connor is sometimes classified as a Southern Gothic writer because of her detailed renderings of small town Southern

life and her flair for creating eccentric—even grotesque—characters. Commenting on these characters, Alice Walker, an African American writer, observed, "O'Connor's characters—whose humanity if not their sanity is taken for granted, and who are miserable, ugly, narrow-minded, . . . with not a graceful, pretty one anywhere who is not, at the same time, a joke—shocked and delighted me."

Return to Georgia In 1952, at the age of 27, O'Connor was stricken with a near fatal attack of lupus, the incurable disease from which her father had died. She was forced to move back to her mother's dairy farm outside Milledgeville, where she remained for the rest of her life. Despite her illness, she managed to correspond with friends, lecture on writing, raise her prized peacocks—and continue to write. She died from lupus at 39. Despite the brevity of her life, O'Connor's fiction has inspired generations of writers.

 Literature Online

Author Search For more about Flannery O'Connor, go to glencoe.com and enter QuickPass code GLA9800u6.

FLANNERY O'CONNOR **913**

Before You Read

Focus

Bellringer Options

Selection Focus
    Transparency 57
Daily Language Practice
    Transparency 83

Or show students photographs of people of various ages, occupations, ethnic groups, and levels of wealth. **Ask:** How would you describe each person? What assumptions would you make about him or her? Why? Tell students to consider, as they read, the way they form ideas about new people they meet.

Writer's Technique ☆

Grotesque Characters Flánnery O'Connor is known for her grotesque characters. The term *grotesque* refers to the bizarre, twisted, or abnormal.

Selection Skills

Literary Elements
- Dialogue
  (SE pp. 914, 916, 917, 918, 920, 922, 923)
- Foreshadowing
  (SE p. 925)
- Irony (TE p. 922)

The Life You Save May Be Your Own

Reading Skills
- Apply Background Knowledge
  (SE pp. 914–917, 921, 923, 925)
- Visualize (TE p. 916)
- Compare and Contrast
  (TE p. 918)

Vocabulary Skills
- Word Usage
  (SE pp. 914, 925)
- Double Negative
  (TE p. 914)

Writing Skills/Grammar
- Write a Review
  (SE p. 926)
- Sentence Formation
  (SE p. 926)
- Characterization
  (TE p. 920)

Before You Read

Focus

Summary

A one-armed man named Shiftlet arrives at the isolated farmhouse of an old woman, Mrs. Crater, and her mentally disabled daughter. He agrees to fix up the farm buildings in exchange for food and a place to sleep. Within a week, Mrs. Crater convinces Shiftlet to marry her daughter. After a town-hall wedding, the couple leaves in Mrs. Crater's car. When they stop at a restaurant, the bride falls asleep, and Shiftlet abandons her.

 For summaries in languages other than English, see Unit 6 Teaching Resources Book, pp. 80–85.

Vocabulary

Antonyms Say: Match the following words with their antonyms in the vocabulary list.

cheerful (*morose*)
satisfied (*ravenous*)
plump (*gaunt*)
slouching (*stately*)
acclaim (*rue*)

(ENGLISH LEARNERS) To ensure understanding of meaning, **ask:** Which words describe appearance? (*gaunt, stately*) Which word describes a feeling or attitude? (*morose*)

 For additional vocabulary practice, see Unit 6 Teaching Resources Book, p. 88.

Literature and Reading Preview

Connect to the Story

How reliable are first impressions? Discuss this question with a partner. Consider a time you judged someone by his or her clothing, accent, or behavior.

Build Background

During the Great Depression, unemployed men, and occasionally women, often became wanderers, referred to as "tramps" or "hoboes." They went from place to place, particularly in rural areas, seeking odd jobs in return for food, clothes, or shelter.

Set Purposes for Reading

Big Idea Return to Regionalism

As you read, ask yourself, How does this story reflect life in the rural South during the later years of the Great Depression?

Literary Element Dialogue

Dialogue is the conversation between characters in a literary work. Through dialogue, an author reveals the feelings, thoughts, and intentions of characters; develops conflicts; and moves the plot forward. As you read, ask yourself, What does the dialogue reveal about the characters in this story?

Reading Strategy Apply Background Knowledge

Background knowledge refers to what you already know about the setting, characters, and situations in a literary work. You can add to your background knowledge by reading carefully the information included under the Build Background section preceding the selections in this book. As you read, ask yourself, What do I already know about the features of this story? By relating what you know to what you are reading, you create meaning and enrich your understanding of the text.

Tip: Use a Preview Chart Skim the story for information about setting, characters, and possible conflicts. Use a chart like the one below to record details and relevant background knowledge.

Details	What I Know
rural setting	fewer people, less technology
Great Depression	people needed money and work

914 UNIT 6 FROM DEPRESSION TO COLD WAR

Vocabulary Practice

Double Negatives Tell students that in this story they are about to read, the characters speak in a regional dialect that includes the use of the double negative—two or more negative words in the same clause to express the same idea. Give students an example of a phrase that uses the double negative: *I didn't go nowhere today.* **Ask:** How would you express this using standard English? (*I went somewhere today.*)

Have students make a list as they read of sentences containing double negatives. When they are done reading, have them revise each sentence into standard English.

Vocabulary

gaunt (gônt) *adj.* thin, bony, and hollow-eyed, as from hunger or illness; p. 915 *Her face looked long and gaunt, as though she were ill.*

ravenous (rav´ ə nəs) *adj.* extremely hungry; p. 918 *After fasting for a long time, the prisoner was ravenous for food.*

stately (stāt´ lē) *adj.* noble; dignified; majestic; p. 920 *The mansion was elegant and stately, like a palace.*

morose (mə rōs´) *adj.* bad-tempered, gloomy, and withdrawn; p. 921 *His morose disposition led him to keep to himself and brood.*

rue (roo) *v.* to regret; to be sorry for; p. 923 *When the car did not start, I rued the day I had bought it.*

Tip: Word Usage When you encounter new words, it might help you to answer a specific question about the word. Example: *How might a ravenous dog behave?* A ravenous dog might growl, whimper, or snap in hunger.

914

Setzer Cove Homeplace, 1982. Hubert Shuptrine. Drybrush, 14⅞ x 21½ in. Private collection.

The Life You Save May Be Your Own

Flannery O'Connor

1 The old woman and her daughter were sitting on their porch when Mr. Shiftlet came up their road for the first time. The old woman slid to the edge of her chair and leaned forward, shading her eyes from the piercing sunset with her hand. The daughter could not see far in front of her and continued to play with her fingers. Although the old woman lived in this desolate[1] spot with only her daughter and she had never seen Mr. Shiftlet before, she could tell, even from a distance, that he was a tramp and no one to be afraid of.

His left coat sleeve was folded up to show there was only half an arm in it and his **gaunt** figure listed slightly to the side as if the breeze were pushing him. He had on a black town suit and a brown felt hat that was turned up in the front and down in the back and he carried a tin tool box by a handle. He came on, at an amble, up her road, his face turned toward the sun which appeared to be balancing itself on the peak of a small mountain.

The old woman didn't change her position until he was almost into her yard; then she rose with one hand fisted on her hip. The daughter,

---

1. A *desolate* spot is miserable, lonely, and cheerless.

2 Apply Background Knowledge *Why is the old woman relieved when she realizes that the stranger is a tramp?*

FLANNERY O'CONNOR **915**

Teach

a large girl in a short blue organdy dress, saw him all at once and jumped up and began to stamp and point and make excited speechless sounds.

Mr. Shiftlet stopped just inside the yard and set his box on the ground and tipped his hat at her as if she were not in the least afflicted; then he turned toward the old woman and swung the hat all the way off. He had long black slick hair that hung flat from a part in the middle to beyond the tips of his ears on either side. His face descended in forehead for more than half its length and ended suddenly with his features just balanced over a jutting steel-trap jaw. He seemed to be a young man but he had a look of composed dissatisfaction as if he understood life thoroughly.

"Good evening," the old woman said. She was about the size of a cedar fence post and she had a man's gray hat pulled down low over her head.

The tramp stood looking at her and didn't answer. He turned his back and faced the sunset. He swung both his whole and his short arm up slowly so that they indicated an expanse of sky and his figure formed a crooked cross. The old woman watched him with her arms folded across her chest as if she were the owner of the sun, and the daughter watched, her head thrust forward and her fat helpless hands hanging at the wrists. She had long pink-gold hair and eyes as blue as a peacock's neck.

He held the pose for almost fifty seconds and then he picked up his box and came on to the porch and dropped down on the bottom step. "Lady," he said in a firm nasal voice, "I'd give a fortune to live where I could see me a sun do that every evening."

"Does it every evening," the old woman said and sat back down. The daughter sat down too and watched him with a cautious sly look as if he were a bird that had come up very close. He leaned to one side, rooting in his pants pocket, and in a second he brought out a package of chewing gum and offered her a piece. She took it and unpeeled it and began to chew without taking her eyes off him. He offered the old

woman a piece but she only raised her upper lip to indicate she had no teeth.

Mr. Shiftlet's pale sharp glance had already passed over everything in the yard—the pump near the corner of the house and the big fig tree that three or four chickens were preparing to roost in—and had moved to a shed where he saw the square rusted back of an automobile. "You ladies drive?" he asked.

"That car ain't run in fifteen year," the old woman said. "The day my husband died, it quit running."

"Nothing is like it used to be, lady," he said. "The world is almost rotten."

"That's right," the old woman said. "You from around here?"

"Name Tom T. Shiftlet," he murmured, looking at the tires.

"I'm pleased to meet you," the old woman said. "Name Lucynell Crater and daughter Lucynell Crater. What you doing around here, Mr. Shiftlet?"

He judged the car to be about a 1928 or '29 Ford. "Lady," he said, and turned and gave her his full attention, "lemme tell you something. There's one of these doctors in Atlanta that's taken a knife and cut the human heart—the human heart," he repeated, leaning forward, "out of a man's chest and held it in his hand," and he held his hand out, palm up, as if it were slightly weighted with the human heart, "and studied it like it was a day-old chicken, and lady," he said, allowing a long significant pause in which his head slid forward and his clay-colored eyes brightened, "he don't know no more about it than you or me." ☆

"That's right," the old woman said.

"Why, if he was to take that knife and cut into every corner of it, he still wouldn't know no more than you or me. What you want to bet?"

Apply Background Knowledge *Why does Mr. Shiftlet focus his attention on the automobile?* [1]

Dialogue *What does this exchange reveal about Mr. Shiftlet?* [2]

"Nothing," the old woman said wisely. "Where you come from, Mr. Shiftlet?"

He didn't answer. He reached into his pocket and brought out a sack of tobacco and a package of cigarette papers and rolled himself a cigarette, expertly with one hand, and attached it in a hanging position to his upper lip. Then he took a box of wooden matches from his pocket and struck one on his shoe. He held the burning match as if he were studying the mystery of flame while it traveled dangerously toward his skin. The daughter began to make loud noises and to point to his hand and shake her finger at him, but when the flame was just before touching him, he leaned down with his hand cupped over it as if he were going to set fire to his nose and lit the cigarette.

He flipped away the dead match and blew a stream of gray into the evening. A sly look came over his face. "Lady," he said, "nowadays, people'll do anything anyways. I can tell you my name is Tom T. Shiftlet and I came from Tarwater, Tennessee, but you never have seen me before: how you know I ain't lying? How

you know my name ain't Aaron Sparks, lady, and I come from Singleberry, Georgia, or how you know it's not George Speeds and I come from Lucy, Alabama, or how you know I ain't Thompson Bright from Toolafalls, Mississippi?"

"I don't know nothing about you," the old woman muttered, irked.[2]

"Lady," he said, "people don't care how they lie. Maybe the best I can tell you is, I'm a man; but listen lady," he said and paused and made his tone more ominous[3] still, "what is a man?"

The old woman began to gum a seed. "What you carry in that tin box, Mr. Shiftlet?" she asked.

"Tools," he said, put back. "I'm a carpenter."

"Well, if you come out here to work, I'll be able to feed you and give you a place to sleep but I can't pay. I'll tell you that before you begin," she said.

There was no answer at once and no particular expression on his face. He leaned back against the two-by-four that helped support the porch roof. "Lady," he said slowly, "there's some men that some things mean more to them than money." The old woman rocked without comment and the daughter watched the trigger that moved up and down in his neck. He told the old woman then that all most people were interested in was money, but he asked what a man was made for. He asked her if a man was made for money, or what. He asked her what she thought she was made for but she didn't answer,

---

2. To be *irked* is to be annoyed or bothered.
3. Something *ominous* is, or seems to be, threatening.

 Dialogue *How does this statement make you feel about Mr. Shiftlet?*

Applying Background Knowledge *Should the old woman trust Mr. Shiftlet or not? Explain.*

Literary Element 3

Dialogue Answer: *Although Shiftlet appears to be stating the obvious, he may be lying about his identity and place of origin.*

(ENGLISH LEARNERS) Clarify what a "sly look" is and how it affects the reader's view of Shiftlet. *(Being sly is being dishonest or deceptive; the sly look suggests that he is not being honest)*

Reading Strategy 4

Apply Background Knowledge Answer: *Students may say that the old woman should be careful—Shiftlet does not seem sincere.*

View the Photograph ★

In Flannery O'Connor's time, many American families lived in isolated places, like that in the photograph. Point out that Shiftlet says that "he wished he lived in a desolate place like this."

English Learners

DIFFERENTIATED INSTRUCTION

Beginning Point out that Mr. Shiftlet had been a foreman on the railroad. Identify the prefix *fore-* and ask what other words students know with this prefix. *(Possible answers include forehead, forecast, foresee.)* Ask them to determine the meaning of the prefix *fore-*. *(front or in front of)* **Ask:** What is a foreman? *(a person in charge of others)*

Advanced Point out the multiple-meaning word *trash*. Students probably know *trash* as "something you throw away." Explain that Mr. Shiftlet is using this word with another meaning. Ask them to determine its meaning from the context. *(someone of low social standing or bad reputation)*

Approaching Level

DIFFERENTIATED INSTRUCTION

Emerging To help students increase **reading fluency,** point out that in dialogue, words are often omitted or used in informal ways. Model how to restate dialogue into Standard English. For example, "You ladies drive?" means "Do you ladies know how to drive?" Have students read dialogue aloud for practice.

Teach

Big Idea 1

Return to Regionalism

Answer: *These details reflect the character of the South during that time. Gospel music was and still is popular there; Uncle Roy and the Red Creek Wranglers sound like country musicians.*

Literary Element 2

Dialogue **Answer:** *Mrs. Crater wants Shiftlet to think that Lucynell can be a good wife.*

Reading Strategy 3

Make Inferences Explain that Mrs. Crater may have an agenda for marrying Shiftlet and Lucynell. **Ask:** What would Mrs. Crater gain by such a union? *(She would have an unpaid handyman available; someone would be there to take care of Lucynell after her own death.)*

[APPROACHING] Remind students that you make an inference about what is unstated by applying your own knowledge to the information given. Ask what knowledge we need to infer Mrs. Crater's intent. *(People often say the opposite of what they mean in order to lead someone along.)*

Writer's Technique ☆

Character Names Authors often give characters names that provide clues to their personalities. The name Shiftlet, for example, is reminiscent of *shifty,* suggesting that Shiftlet is a shady character.

---

she only sat rocking and wondered if a one-armed man could put a new roof on her garden house. He asked a lot of questions that she didn't answer. He told her that he was twenty-eight years old and had lived a varied life. He had been a gospel singer, a foreman on the railroad, an assistant in an undertaking parlor, and he had come over the radio for three months with Uncle Roy and his Red Creek Wranglers. He said he had fought and bled in the Arm Service of his country and visited every foreign land and that everywhere he had seen people that didn't care if they did a thing one way or another. He said he hadn't been raised thataway.

A fat yellow moon appeared in the branches of the fig tree as if it were going to roost there with the chickens. He said that a man had to escape to the country to see the world whole and that he wished he lived in a desolate place like this where he could see the sun go down every evening like God made it to do.

"Are you married or are you single?" the old woman asked.

There was a long silence. "Lady," he asked finally, "where would you find you an innocent woman today? I wouldn't have any of this trash I could just pick up."

☆ The daughter was leaning very far down, hanging her head almost between her knees, watching him through a triangular door she had made in her overturned hair; and she suddenly fell in a heap on the floor and began to whimper. Mr. Shiftlet straightened her out and helped her get back in the chair.

"Is she your baby girl?" he asked.

"My only," the old woman said, "and she's the sweetest girl in the world. I wouldn't give her up for nothing on earth. She's smart too. She can sweep the floor, cook, wash, feed the chickens, and hoe. I wouldn't give her up for a casket of jewels."

---

1 Return to Regionalism *Why does the author include these details?*

2 Dialogue *Why might Mrs. Crater say this to Mr. Shiftlet?*

"No," he said kindly, "don't ever let any man take her away from you."

"Any man come after her," the old woman **3** said, " 'll have to stay around the place."

Mr. Shiftlet's eye in the darkness was focused on a part of the automobile bumper that glittered in the distance. "Lady," he said, jerking his short arm up as if he could point with it to her house and yard and pump, "there ain't a broken thing on this plantation that I couldn't fix for you, one-arm jackleg[4] or not. I'm a man," he said with a sullen dignity, "even if I ain't a whole one. I got," he said, tapping his knuckles on the floor to emphasize the immensity of what he was going to say, "a moral intelligence!" and his face pierced out of the darkness into a shaft of doorlight and he stared at her as if he were astonished himself at this impossible truth.

The old woman was not impressed with the phrase. "I told you you could hang around and work for food," she said, "if you don't mind sleeping in that car yonder."

"Why listen, Lady," he said with a grin of delight, "the monks of old slept in their coffins!"

"They wasn't as advanced as we are," the old woman said.

The next morning he began on the roof of the garden house while Lucynell, the daughter, sat on a rock and watched him work. He had not been around a week before the change he had made in the place was apparent. He had patched the front and back steps, built a new hog pen, restored a fence, and taught Lucynell, who was completely deaf and had never said a word in her life, to say the word "bird." The big rosy-faced girl followed him everywhere, saying "Burrttddt ddbirrrttdt," and clapping her hands. The old woman watched from a distance, secretly pleased. She was **ravenous** for a son-in-law.

---

4. A *jackleg,* like a jack-of-all-trades, can do many different kinds of work for which he or she has not been trained.

Vocabulary

ravenous (rav´ ə nəs) adj. extremely hungry

Reading Practice

 SMALL GROUP

Compare and Contrast Explain that comparing characters can help students gain insight into the story. Have students compare and contrast Shiftlet and Mrs. Crater, using a Venn diagram or a comparison chart. Have them examine each character's background, strengths, weaknesses, motives, and problems. In small groups, have them share their comparisons, discussing how characters' similarities and differences play off against one other and move the story along.

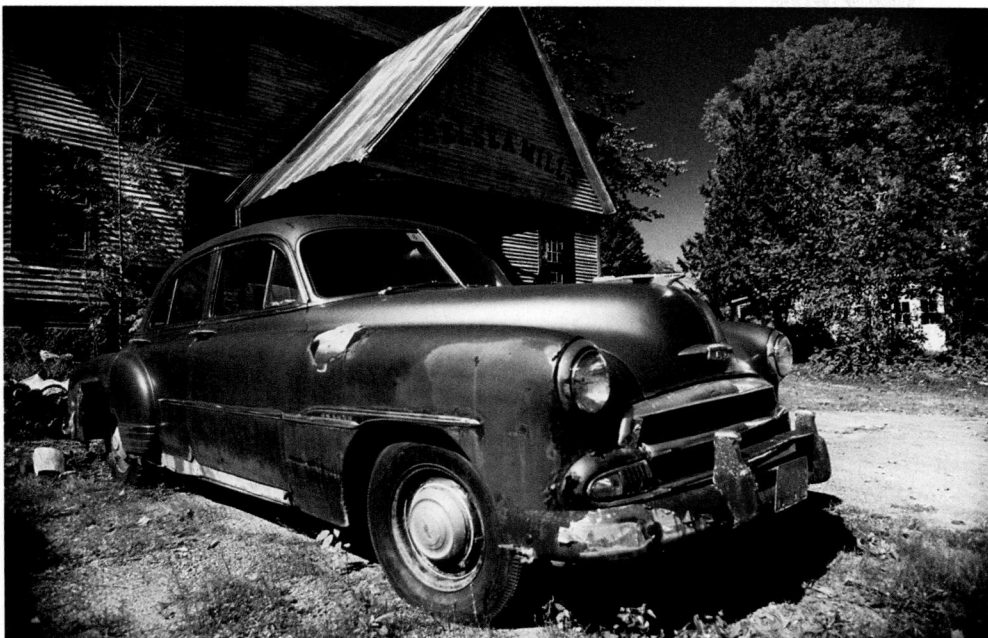

Reading Strategy   4

Apply Background Knowledge Recall with students what they know about the Great Depression and men who wandered the country, looking for work. **Ask:** How do you think Shiftlet learned about cars? (*Perhaps he had a job as a mechanic.*)

Mr. Shiftlet slept on the hard narrow back seat of the car with his feet out the side window. He had his razor and a can of water on a crate that served him as a bedside table and he put up a piece of mirror against the back glass and kept his coat neatly on a hanger that he hung over one of the windows.

In the evenings he sat on the steps and talked while the old woman and Lucynell rocked violently in their chairs on either side of him. The old woman's three mountains were black against the dark blue sky and were visited off and on by various planets and by the moon after it had left the chickens. Mr. Shiftlet pointed out that the reason he had improved this plantation was because he had taken a personal interest in it. He said he was even going to make the automobile run.

He had raised the hood and studied the mechanism and he said he could tell that the car had been built in the days when cars were really built. You take now, he said, one man puts in one bolt and another man puts in another bolt and another man puts in another bolt so that it's a man for a bolt. That's why you have to pay so much for a car: you're paying all those men. Now if you didn't have to pay but one man, you could get you a cheaper car and one that had had a personal interest taken in it, and it would be a better car. The old woman agreed with him that this was so.

Mr. Shiftlet said that the trouble with the world was that nobody cared, or stopped and took any trouble. He said he never would have been able to teach Lucynell to say a word if he hadn't cared and stopped long enough.

"Teach her to say something else," the old woman said.

"What you want her to say next?" Mr. Shiftlet asked.

The old woman's smile was broad and toothless and suggestive. "Teach her to say 'sugarpie,' " she said.

Mr. Shiftlet already knew what was on her mind.

FLANNERY O'CONNOR **919**

Cultural History ☆

Automobiles In the first half of the twentieth century, automobile use increased dramatically in the United States. In 1900, only 8,000 people owned cars; by 1929, about 23 million did. Once the Depression hit, many car owners could not afford to buy gasoline or service their cars, and therefore their cars sat idle, like Mrs. Crater's.

Approaching Level

DIFFERENTIATED INSTRUCTION

Established Point out that sometimes dialogue is indirect. Instead of putting the characters' specific words in quotation marks, the writer restates what the character says. Provide this example: "Mr. Shiftlet said that the trouble with the world was that nobody cared . . . ." Have students find other examples of indirect quotations. Remind them that indirect dialogue reveals as much about characters as direct quotations.

Emerging Point out that Shiftlet often says or does one thing and means another. Start with this example: "Mr. Shiftlet pointed out that the reason he had improved this plantation was because he had taken a personal interest in it." **Ask:** What does he mean? (*that he cares about her property*) Why does he say that? (*to make the woman think he cares about her and her daughter*) How do you know that his words and actions have different meanings? (*He immediately brings up his interest in the car.*) Have students identify other examples and evaluate his intent.

Teach

The next day he began to tinker with the automobile and that evening he told her that if she would buy a fan belt, he would be able to make the car run.

The old woman said she would give him the money. "You see that girl yonder?" she asked, pointing to Lucynell who was sitting on the floor a foot away, watching him, her eyes blue even in the dark. "If it was ever a man wanted to take her away, I would say, 'No man on earth is going to take that sweet girl of mine away from me!' but if he was to say, 'Lady, I don't want to take her away, I want her right here,' I would say, 'Mister, I don't blame you none. I wouldn't pass up a chance to live in a permanent place and get the sweetest girl in the world myself. You ain't no fool,' I would say."

"How old is she?" Mr. Shiftlet asked casually.

"Fifteen, sixteen," the old woman said. The girl was nearly thirty but because of her innocence it was impossible to guess.

"It would be a good idea to paint it too," Mr. Shiftlet remarked. "You don't want it to rust out."

"We'll see about that later," the old woman said.

The next day he walked into town and returned with the parts he needed and a can of gasoline. Late in the afternoon, terrible noises issued from the shed and the old woman rushed out of the house, thinking Lucynell was somewhere having a fit. Lucynell was sitting on a chicken crate, stamping her feet and screaming, "Burrddttt! bddurrddtttt!" but her fuss was drowned out by the car. With a volley of blasts it emerged from the shed, moving in a fierce and **stately** way. Mr. Shiftlet was in the driver's seat, sitting very erect. He had an expression of serious modesty on his face as if he had just raised the dead.

That night, rocking on the porch, the old woman began her business at once. "You want you an innocent woman, don't you?" she asked sympathetically. "You don't want none of this trash."

"No'm, I don't," Mr. Shiftlet said.

"One that can't talk," she continued, "can't sass you back or use foul language. That's the kind for you to have. Right there," and she pointed to Lucynell sitting cross-legged in her chair, holding both feet in her hands.

"That's right," he admitted. "She wouldn't give me any trouble."

"Saturday," the old woman said, "you and her and me can drive into town and get married."

Mr. Shiftlet eased his position on the steps.

"I can't get married right now," he said. "Everything you want to do takes money and I ain't got any."

"What you need with money?" she asked.

"It takes money," he said. "Some people'll do anything anyhow these days, but the way I think, I wouldn't marry no woman that I couldn't take on a trip like she was somebody. I mean take her to a hotel and treat her. I wouldn't marry the Duchesser Windsor,"[5] he said firmly, "unless I could take her to a hotel and give her something good to eat.

"I was raised thataway and there ain't a thing I can do about it. My old mother taught me how to do."

"Lucynell don't even know what a hotel is," the old woman muttered. "Listen here, Mr. Shiftlet," she said, sliding forward in her chair, "you'd be getting a permanent house and a deep well and the most innocent girl in the world. You don't need no money. Lemme tell you something: there ain't any place in the world for a poor disabled friendless drifting man."

The ugly words settled in Mr. Shiftlet's head like a group of buzzards in the top of a tree. He

---

 Dialogue *Do you think Mrs. Crater's tender feelings for her daughter are genuine? Explain.*

Vocabulary

stately (stāt′ lē) *adj.* noble; dignified; majestic

---

5. Shiftlet is referring to the American woman for whom Britain's King Edward VIII gave up the throne in 1936. The new king gave them the titles Duke and Duchess of *Windsor*.

Dialogue *Why does Mrs. Crater insult Mr. Shiftlet?* **2**

Writing Practice

SPIRAL REVIEW **Characterization** Explain that characterization emerges from the various ways a writer reveals a character's personality. Note that in this story O'Connor has developed interesting characters by contrasting their words and actions. Discuss the character of Mr. Shiftlet by asking students to give examples of his words and actions. Then have students write two- or three-paragraph vignettes that showcase two characters with clear contrasts in words and actions. Review with students the rules for paragraphing and punctuating dialogue.

didn't answer at once. He rolled himself a cigarette and lit it and then he said in an even voice, "Lady, a man is divided into two parts, body and spirit."

The old woman clamped her gums together.

"A body and a spirit," he repeated. "The body, lady, is like a house: it don't go anywhere; but the spirit, lady, is like a automobile: always on the move, always . . ."

"Listen, Mr. Shiftlet," she said, "my well never goes dry and my house is always warm in the winter and there's no mortgage on a thing about this place. You can go to the courthouse and see for yourself. And yonder under that shed is a fine automobile." She laid the bait carefully. "You can have it painted by Saturday. I'll pay for the paint."

In the darkness, Mr. Shiftlet's smile stretched like a weary snake waking up by a fire. After a second he recalled himself and said, "I'm only saying a man's spirit means more to him than anything else. I would have to take my wife off for the weekend without no regards at all for cost. I got to follow where my spirit say to go."

"I'll give you fifteen dollars for a weekend trip," the old woman said in a crabbed voice. "That's the best I can do."

"That wouldn't hardly pay for more than the gas and the hotel," he said. "It wouldn't feed her."

"Seventeen-fifty," the old woman said. "That's all I got so it isn't any use you trying to milk me. You can take a lunch."

Mr. Shiftlet was deeply hurt by the word "milk." He didn't doubt that she had more money sewed up in her mattress but he had already told her he was not interested in her money. "I'll make that do," he said and rose and walked off without treating[6] with her further.

On Saturday the three of them drove into town in the car that the paint had barely dried on and Mr. Shiftlet and Lucynell were married in the Ordinary's[7] office while the old woman witnessed. As they came out of the courthouse, Mr. Shiftlet began twisting his neck in his collar. He looked **morose** and bitter as if he had been

---

6. Here, *treating* means "negotiating or discussing terms."
7. An *Ordinary* is a local judge who, in many states, is called the "justice of the peace."

Vocabulary

morose (mə rōs´) *adj.* bad-tempered, gloomy, and withdrawn

3 Apply Background Knowledge *Why does the author compare Mr. Shiftlet's smile to a snake?*

FLANNERY O'CONNOR **921**

Teach

Literary Element   1

Dialogue **Answer:** *She thinks that he has kept his part of their first agreement with his efforts around the house. Since he honored their first agreement, he may be a man with "a moral conscience" who will honor their second agreement.*

Big Idea   2

Return to Regionalism
Answer: *Local diners were a common sight in the South, and ham and grits were popular foods in this region.*

Literary Element   3

Dialogue **Answer:** *He plans to abandon Lucynell and run off with Mrs. Crater's car and money. He wants to avoid arousing suspicion about his relationship with Lucynell.*

insulted while someone held him. "That didn't satisfy me none," he said. "That was just something a woman in an office did, nothing but paper work and blood tests. What do they know about my blood? If they was to take my heart and cut it out," he said, "they wouldn't know a thing about me. It didn't satisfy me at all."

"It satisfied the law," the old woman said sharply.

"The law," Mr. Shiftlet said and spit. "It's the law that don't satisfy me."

He had painted the car dark green with a yellow band around it just under the windows. The three of them climbed in the front seat and the old woman said, "Don't Lucynell look pretty? Looks like a baby doll." Lucynell was dressed up in a white dress that her mother had uprooted from a trunk and there was a Panama hat on her head with a bunch of red wooden cherries on the brim. Every now and then her placid[8] expression was changed by a sly isolated little thought like a shoot of green in the desert. "You got a prize!" the old woman said.

Mr. Shiftlet didn't even look at her.

They drove back to the house to let the old woman off and pick up the lunch. When they were ready to leave, she stood staring in the window of the car, with her fingers clenched around the glass. Tears began to seep sideways out of her eyes and run along the dirty creases in her face. "I ain't ever been parted with her for two days before," she said.

Mr. Shiftlet started the motor.

"And I wouldn't let no man have her but you because I seen you would do right. Goodbye, Sugarbaby," she said, clutching at the sleeve of the white dress. Lucynell looked straight at her and didn't seem to see her there at all. Mr. Shiftlet eased the car forward so that she had to move her hands.

The early afternoon was clear and open and surrounded by pale blue sky. Although the car would go only thirty miles an hour, Mr. Shiftlet imagined a terrific climb and dip and swerve that went entirely to his head so that he forgot his morning bitterness. He had always wanted an automobile but he had never been able to afford one before. He drove very fast because he wanted to make Mobile[9] by nightfall.

Occasionally he stopped his thoughts long enough to look at Lucynell in the seat beside him. She had eaten the lunch as soon as they were out of the yard and now she was pulling the cherries off the hat one by one and throwing them out the window. He became depressed in spite of the car. He had driven about a hundred miles when he decided that she must be hungry again and at the next small town they came to, he stopped in front of an aluminum-painted eating place called The Hot Spot and took her in and ordered her a plate of ham and grits. The ride had made her sleepy and as soon as she got up on the stool, she rested her head on the counter and shut her eyes. There was no one in The Hot Spot but Mr. Shiftlet and the boy behind the counter, a pale youth with a greasy rag hung over his shoulder. Before he could dish up the food, she was snoring gently.

"Give it to her when she wakes up," Mr. Shiftlet said. "I'll pay for it now."

The boy bent over her and stared at the long pink-gold hair and the half-shut sleeping eyes. Then he looked up and stared at Mr. Shiftlet. "She looks like an angel of Gawd," he murmured.

"Hitchhiker," Mr. Shiftlet explained. "I can't wait. I got to make Tuscaloosa."[10]

The boy bent over again and very carefully touched his finger to a strand of the golden hair and Mr. Shiftlet left.

---

9. *Mobile* (mō′ bēl) is a port city in southwestern Alabama.
10. *Tuscaloosa*, in west central Alabama, is nearly 200 miles north of Mobile.

Return to Regionalism *How do these details contribute to the setting?*   **2**

Dialogue *Why does Mr. Shiftlet lie to the boy behind the counter?*   **3**

---

8. *Placid* means "calm" or "peaceful."

1   **Dialogue** *Why does Mrs. Crater think Mr. Shiftlet will "do right" by her daughter?*

Reading Practice

SPIRAL REVIEW **Irony** Explain that irony arises from a contrast or discrepancy between appearance and reality. Flannery O'Connor uses several kinds of irony in her story. Clarify that verbal irony is a person's saying one thing and meaning another, as when someone says of a mean person, "Nice guy!" Dramatic irony occurs when the audience has important information that the characters do not know. Have students identify instances of both types of irony on this page and the next. Have students explain how the irony contributes to the Southern Gothic aspect of the story.

He was more depressed than ever as he drove on by himself. The late afternoon had grown hot and sultry and the country had flattened out. Deep in the sky a storm was preparing very slowly and without thunder as if it meant to drain every drop of air from the earth before it broke. There were times when Mr. Shiftlet preferred not to be alone. He felt too that a man with a car had a responsibility to others and he kept his eye out for a hitchhiker. Occasionally he saw a sign that warned: "Drive carefully. The life you save may be your own."

The narrow road dropped off on either side into dry fields and here and there a shack or a filling station stood in a clearing. The sun began to set directly in front of the automobile. It was a reddening ball that through his windshield was slightly flat on the bottom and top. He saw a boy in overalls and a gray hat standing on the edge of the road and he slowed the car down and stopped in front of him. The boy didn't have his hand raised to thumb the ride, he was only standing there, but he had a small cardboard suitcase and his hat was set on his head in a way to indicate that he had left somewhere for good. "Son," Mr. Shiftlet said, "I see you want a ride."

The boy didn't say he did or he didn't but he opened the door of the car and got in, and Mr. Shiftlet started driving again. The child held the suitcase on his lap and folded his arms on top of it. He turned his head and looked out the window away from Mr. Shiftlet. Mr. Shiftlet felt oppressed.[11] "Son," he said after a minute, "I got the best old mother in the world so I reckon you only got the second best."

The boy gave him a quick dark glance and then turned his face back out the window.

"It's nothing so sweet," Mr. Shiftlet continued, "as a boy's mother. She taught him his first

prayers at her knee, she give him love when no other would, she told him what was right and what wasn't, and she seen that he done the right thing. Son," he said, "I never **rued** a day in my life like the one I rued when I left that old mother of mine."

The boy shifted in his seat but he didn't look at Mr. Shiftlet. He unfolded his arms and put one hand on the door handle.

"My mother was an angel of Gawd," Mr. Shiftlet said in a very strained voice. "He took her from heaven and giver to me and I left her." His eyes were instantly clouded over with a mist of tears. The car was barely moving.

The boy turned angrily in the seat. "You go to the devil!" he cried. "My old woman is a flea bag and yours is a stinking pole cat!" and with that he flung the door open and jumped out with his suitcase into the ditch.

Mr. Shiftlet was so shocked that for about a hundred feet he drove along slowly with the door still open. A cloud, the exact color of the boy's hat and shaped like a turnip, had descended over the sun, and another, worse looking, crouched behind the car. Mr. Shiftlet felt that the rottenness of the world was about to engulf him. He raised his arm and let it fall again to his breast. "Oh Lord!" he prayed. "Break forth and wash the slime from this earth!"

The turnip continued slowly to descend. After a few minutes there was a guffawing peal of thunder from behind and fantastic raindrops, like tin-can tops, crashed over the rear of Mr. Shiftlet's car. Very quickly he stepped on the gas and with his stump sticking out the window he raced the galloping shower into Mobile. ∾

---

11. Here, *oppressed* means "distressed" or "burdened."

4 Apply Background Knowledge *What does the road sign mean to motorists?*

Dialogue *What is ironic about Mr. Shiftlet's prayer?* **5**

Vocabulary

rue (rōō) *v.* to regret; to be sorry for

FLANNERY O'CONNOR **923**

Teach

| Reading Strategy | 4 |

Apply Background Knowledge **Answer:** •*The sign is a warning intended to prevent accidents and save lives.*

| Literary Element | 5 |

Dialogue **Answer:** *He thinks the hitchhiker has no morals. In fact, he has none either.*

 [APPROACHING] Ask students to define the word *slime*. Then **ask:** What might be some of the qualities of a *slimy* person? (*dishonest, immoral*) To whom is Shiftlet referring? (*the boy hitchhiker*) What things has Shiftlet done in this story that could be called "slimy"? (*stealing the car; marrying then abandoning Lucynell*) Explain that this is why Shiftlet's prayer could be considered ironic.

To check students' understanding of the selection, see Unit 6 Teaching Resources Book, p. 91.

English Learners

DIFFERENTIATED INSTRUCTION

Advanced Remind students that some words have more than one meaning. Ask students to think of three ways in which the word *dark* can be used. (*Possible answers: having little or no light; indicating anger or hostility; the beginning of the night*) **Ask:** Which meaning is correct in this example: "The boy gave him a quick dark glance and then turned his face back out the window"? (*indicating anger*)

Ask students to determine the correct meaning of the multiple-meaning words *strained* and *peal* in these expresssions:

- "My mother was an angel of Gawd," Mr. Shiflet said in a very strained voice. (*not natural but done with effort*)
- After a few minutes there was a guffawing peal of thunder from behind . . . . (*a loud sound that repeats*)

923

After You Read

Assess

1. (a) As an honest man down on his luck (b) She overlooks his interest in her possessions and the discrepancy between his behavior and his words.

2. (a) She is speech impaired and mentally challenged, which makes her vulnerable. (b) He is single, handy around the house, and appears virtuous.

3. (a) He will work for food and will sleep in the car; he will marry Lucynell, take her on a trip, and return to live at the farm. (b) The first agreement gets Shiftlet food and a place to stay; the second gets him money and a car.

4. Shiftlet, because he is the central character, even though readers do not sympathize with him

5. Shiftlet saved himself from a life with Lucynell; the women were saved from a lifetime of Shiftlet's reckless behavior.

6. Making the two women the losers and the tramp the winner is situational irony. She wanted to surprise readers and show human nature's darker side.

7. Mrs. Crater would have been less trusting of strangers, found help for her daughter, and hired workers to repair her home. The characters would not speak in a rural Southern dialect.

8. Her experiences on a farm might have taught her that people do what they need to do to survive. She might have learned that life is not always fair or just.

 For additional assessment, see Assessment Resources, pp. 245–246.

924

After You Read

Respond and Think Critically

Respond and Interpret

1. (a) How does Shiftlet present himself to Mrs. Crater? (b) What clues to his true character does she fail to notice?

2. (a) What is Lucynell's disability, and how does it affect her? (b) Why does Mrs. Crater consider Mr. Shiftlet a good match for her daughter?

3. (a) What two agreements do Mr. Shiftlet and Mrs. Crater make? (b) Why does Shiftlet go along?

Analyze and Evaluate

4. Whom do you think O'Connor intended to be the **protagonist** of the story? Explain.

5. Whose life—if anyone's—do you think may have been saved at the end of the story?

6. **Situational irony** occurs when the outcome of a situation is different from the expectations of a character or the reader. What is the situational irony in this story and why does O'Connor use it?

Connect

7. **Big Idea** Return to Regionalism How might this story have been different if it were set in a modern-day city?

8. **Connect to the Author** How might O'Connor's experiences growing up in the country have contributed to her characters' outlook?

Primary Source Quotation

Music of the Depression

Although the 1930s are known for Duke Ellington and Benny Goodman's over-the-top big bands and George Gershwin's larger-than-life musicals, popular music also reflected the grim realities of economic hardship. Music from the Great Depression often mourned the loss of an earlier happy time:

> *"Once I built a railroad, I made it run, made it race against time.*
> *Once I built a railroad; now it's done.*
> *Brother, can you spare a dime?*
> *Once I built a tower, up to the sun, brick, and rivet, and lime;*
> *Once I built a tower, now it's done. Brother, can you spare a dime?"*
> —"Brother, Can You Spare a Dime," lyrics by Yip Harburg, music by Jay Gorney (1931)

Group Activity Discuss the following questions with your classmates:

1. How does the speaker of these lines compare his or her current economic conditions to those of the past?

2. What elements of these lyrics are reminiscent of ideas and themes from "The Life You Save May Be Your Own"?

Primary Source Quotation

1. The speaker's economic conditions have gone from very wealthy and successful to very poor and desperate.

2. Possible answers: Life is not fair or predictable; as far as we know, Shiftlet is also a man with little money, having to work for food and shelter.

 To create custom assessments online, go to Progress Reporter Online Assessment.

Literary Element | Dialogue

In this story O'Connor uses **dialogue** to provide local color and to reveal characters' personalities and traits. Dialogue brings characters to life by showing what they are thinking and feeling as they react to other characters. Think about the dialogue in "The Life You Save May Be Your Own" as you answer the questions below.

1. How does the dialogue between Mrs. Crater and Mr. Shiftlet reveal their true characters? Give specific examples.

2. What impact does Lucynell's lack of dialogue have on the story?

Review: Foreshadowing

Foreshadowing, as you learned on page 875, is the use of clues by the author to prepare readers for later events in a story.

Group Activity Meet with a small group to discuss O'Connor's use of foreshadowing in "The Life You Save May Be Your Own." Use a chart like the one below to record examples of foreshadowing throughout the story.

Event	Foreshadowing
Mr. Shiftlet steals Mrs. Crater's car.	

 Literature Online

Selection Resources For Selection Quizzes, eFlash-cards, and Reading-Writing Connection activities, go to glencoe.com and enter QuickPass code GLA9800u6.

Reading Strategy | Apply Background Knowledge

To understand the interactions between Mrs. Crater and Mr. Shiflet, you must apply what you know about the Great Depression and the rural South. Review the preview chart you created on page 914, and then answer the following questions.

1. Why does Mr. Shiftlet agree to work for Mrs. Crater?

2. How important is money to both Mr. Shiftlet and Mrs. Crater?

Vocabulary Practice

Practice with Word Usage Respond to these statements to help you explore the meanings of vocabulary words from the selection.

1. Describe the appearance of a **gaunt** person.

2. Give an example of what a **ravenous** person would do.

3. Name a **stately** person who is in the public eye.

4. Explain your behavior if you had a **morose** disposition.

5. Explain a circumstance or action that you might **rue**.

Academic Vocabulary

Mr. Shiftlet is disheartened by the questionable morals of the younger **generation.**

Generation is an academic word. In more casual conversation, older people may say that they do not understand younger people because of a **generation** gap. Using context clues, try to figure out the meaning of generation in the sentence above about "The Life You Save May Be Your Own." Check your guess in a dictionary.

For more on academic vocabulary, see pages 53–54.

FLANNERY O'CONNOR **925**

After You Read

Assess

Literary Element

1. Mrs. Crater says that if someone were to marry Lucynell and live on the farm, he would be "no fool"; this shows that she wants Shiftlet to marry Lucynell and take care of the farm. Shiftlet says that you "need money" to do anything; this shows that he is interested in money.

2. Lucynell cannot express her desires—for example, whether she wants to marry Shiftlet. She won't be able to speak when she wakes up at the diner.

Progress Check

Can students analyze dialogue?

If No → See Unit 6 Teaching Resources Book, p. 86.

Review: Foreshadow

Mr. Shiftlet's duplicity and his two main agreements with Mrs. Crater foreshadow the end.

Reading Strategy

1. The prospect of a place to sleep and food to eat appeals to him, especially as he will have time to figure out a way to get the car.

2. Shiftlet values material things. His greed motivates his abandonment of Lucynell and theft of Mrs. Crater's car. Mrs. Crater values money; she has money hidden in a mattress but won't pay Shiftlet. She uses money to tempt him to marry Lucynell.

Vocabulary

1. A *gaunt* person looks thin and bony.

2. A person who was *ravenous* would eat food.

3. The Queen of England is *stately.*

4. I would be *morose* and ill-tempered.

5. Not studying for a test is an action I would *rue.*

Academic Vocabulary

Mr. Shiftlet is disheartened by young people like the boy hitchhiker and does not understand younger people.

After You Read

Assess

Writing

Each student's review should express his or her personal opinion about the value of the work, support his or her evaluation with examples from the text, and predict and refute potential counterarguments.

Scoring Guide

Assess students' performance in the following categories using the scoring guide at the bottom of the page:

- Address all parts of the writing task.
- Provides a meaningful thesis, maintains focus and organization.
- Supports the thesis with details and examples.
- Provides a variety of sentence types; uses precise, descriptive language.
- Follows English language conventions.
- Makes a logical, convincing analysis.

 For grammar practice, see Unit 6 Teaching Resources Book, p. 90.

Respond Through Writing

Review

Convince an Audience People often consult reviews when deciding whether to see a movie or read a book. How would you rate this story? Write a review of it that you could post on the Internet. In your review, evaluate O'Connor's use of plot, dialogue, characterization, and other literary techniques. Use examples from the text to support your evaluation.

Understand the Task A **review** is a critical evaluation of a work's worth. When you **evaluate,** you make a judgment and support it with evidence.

Prewrite Use a chart like the one below to evaluate the author's use of literary techniques. Support each of your opinions with evidence.

Literary Technique	My Evaluation	Evidence
imagery		
characterization		

Draft Give your review a logical, easy-to-follow structure. For each claim regarding the story, be sure to supply evidence. Try to predict arguments readers might make and refute them using rhetorical devices and textual evidence. Finish with a concise evaluation of the story.

Revise Exchange papers with a partner and evaluate the effectiveness of each other's arguments using the checklist on page 154. If your argument seems weak, incorporate rhetorical techniques such as repetition, parallelism, analogy, and rhetorical questions to enhance your argument.

Example

ORIGINAL "The Life You Save May Be Your Own" showcases Flannery O'Connor's vivid, offbeat style.

REVISION: "The Life You Save May Be Your Own" showcases Flannery O'Connor's vivid, offbeat style. What other author would think of comparing an old woman to a "cedar fence post"? [rhetorical question]

Edit and Proofread Proofread your paper, correcting errors in spelling, grammar, and punctuation.

Learning Objectives

In this assignment, you will focus on the following objectives:

Writing:
Writing a persuasive essay.
Writing a review.

Grammar Tip

Sentence Formation

Short sentences can have great dramatic impact:

I have a dream.

Using short, simple sentences mixed with longer ones can help persuade an audience to agree with you.

As you write and revise your review, include a variety of sentence types to maintain the reader's interest. One way to vary sentence length in your revising stage is to combine sentences.

ORIGINAL: *Mrs. Crater trusted Tom. He betrayed her.*

REVISION: *Mrs. Crater trusted Tom, but he betrayed her.*

Scoring Guide	4	3	2	1
Task addressed	fully	mostly	partially	barely
Thesis	meaningful	provided	partial	weak
Support	thoughtful	provided	limited	weak
Language	varied, descriptive	varied, often descriptive	predictable, imprecise	repetitive, limited
Convention errors	few or none	several	many	serious
Evaluation is	convincing	mostly convincing	partially convincing	not convincing

Grammar Workshop

Introductory Phrases and Clauses

Literature Connection In the sentence below, Flannery O'Connor uses an **introductory clause**—a dependent clause that begins a sentence. Always use a comma after an introductory clause.

> "As they came out of the courthouse, Mr. Shiftlet began twisting his neck in his collar."

In the sentence below, she uses an **introductory phrase**.

> "After a second he recalled himself and said, 'I'm only saying a man's spirit means more to him than anything else.' "

After a second is a prepositional phrase that tells when the action happens. Use a comma after an introductory phrase if it contains a verb form (participle, gerund, or infinitive). In addition, use a comma after a long introductory prepositional phrase or a series of prepositional phrases.

Examples

To fix the car, Mr. Shiftlet raised the hood and studied the engine.

To fix the car is an introductory infinitive phrase. It tells why Mr. Shiftlet raised the hood. Because it is an infinitive phrase, it needs a comma.

In the evenings Mr. Shiftlet sat on the porch steps and talked.

The introductory prepositional phrase *in the evenings* is short, so it needs no comma.

In the afternoon of the next day, Mr. Shiftlet got the car to start.

A comma is necessary after the two introductory prepositional phrases.

"If you come out here to work, I'll be able to feed you and give you a place to sleep."

If you come out here to work is an introductory clause, so it needs a comma.

Sentence Combining Combine each pair of sentences by changing one of them into an introductory phrase or clause.

1. O'Connor was disabled by lupus in 1952. She spent the remainder of her life on her mother's farm.
2. Mr. Shiftlet came up the road for the first time. The old woman and her daughter were sitting on their porch.
3. Eudora Welty was raised in the South. Much of her work was inspired by Southern settings.

Vocabulary Terms

An **introductory phrase** or an **introductory clause** begins a sentence and provides additional information about the main clause.

Tip

To decide whether an introductory phrase needs a comma, decide whether the sentence makes sense without the phrase. If so, the introductory phrase probably needs a comma after it.

Language Handbook

For more about phrases and clauses, see Language Handbook, pp. R42 and R45.

 Literature Online

Grammar For more grammar practice, go to glencoe.com and enter QuickPass code GLA9800u6.

Approaching Level

DIFFERENTIATED INSTRUCTION

Established Tell students that you will state a main clause and a question. Have them come up with a detail that answers the question. For example, **say:** We will go to an assembly. When? *(Students respond by saying, for example, "before lunch.")* Then have students use their answer as an introductory phrase. *(Before lunch, we will go to an assembly.)* Give other examples, such as: He studied math for two hours. Why? *(Students may say, for example, "to prepare for the test.")* Ask students to form a sentence using their answers as an introductory clause. *(To prepare for the test, he studied math for two hours.)*

Grammar Workshop

Introductory Phrases and Clauses

Focus

Write on the board: In the early weeks of December, students often wake up for school in the dark.

Discuss how the introductory phrase gives additional information about the main clause.

Teach

Introductory Phrases and Clauses Explain that most introductory phrases and clauses answer the question *when, where,* or *why*. Review the examples to determine which question each introductory expression answers.

Assess

Sentence Combining

1. After O'Connor was disabled by lupus in 1952, she spent the remainder of her life on her mother's farm.
2. When Shiftlet came up the road for the first time, the old woman and her daughter were sitting on their porch.
3. Because Eudora Welty was raised in the South, much of her work was inspired by Southern settings.

 For additional grammar practice, see Unit 6 Teaching Resources Book, p. 93.

Before You Read

Focus

Bellringer Options

Selection Focus
  Transparency 58
Daily Language Practice
  Transparency 84

Or list the following terms on the board: *college education, car, home, career, family, wisdom, happiness, love.* Read each aloud and have students discuss whether they consider it an important life goal. **Ask:** Does everyone have the same goals in life? Why or why not? Have students consider, as they read, how people's life goals influence their actions.

Before You Read

The Second Tree from the Corner

Meet **E. B. White**
(1899–1985)

Although the beloved children's classics *Charlotte's Web* and *Stuart Little* remain two of Elwyn Brooks (E. B.) White's best-known works, he is also highly acclaimed for his essays and short stories. In fact, it was while working for *The New Yorker* magazine in his late twenties that White first captivated the American public. There, he worked with other legendary writers such as James Thurber, Dorothy Parker, and Robert Benchley to create a sophisticated and clever "New York" voice for the new magazine.

The Road to The New Yorker The youngest child in a large, affectionate family, White was born in rural Mount Vernon, a suburb of New York City. In 1921 he graduated from Cornell University. At Cornell he received the nickname Andy, by which he was known for the rest of his life. (All Cornell students named White were dubbed "Andy," after the university's co-founder, Andrew Dickson White.)

After college, Andy White traveled and worked at a series of miscellaneous jobs for about five years. Returning to New York, he worked in an ad agency and began sending manuscripts to *The New Yorker*. The editor of the magazine, Harold Ross, recognized talent when he saw it, and he soon hired White as a staff writer. White married Katherine Sergeant Angell, the magazine's literary editor, in 1929.

On the Farm In 1938 the Whites decided to leave the city and return to a simple rural life, this time in North Brooklin, Maine. White kept animals on their farm there, some of which made their way into his stories and books. He remained on the staff of *The New Yorker*, continuing to produce essays and his unsigned column "Notes and Comments." He also contributed to *Harper's Magazine* from 1938 to 1943, writing the column "One Man's Meat."

On the farm, he penned his famed children's stories. The first one, *Stuart Little*, features an adventurous mouse-child, born into a human family. The second, *Charlotte's Web*, is about the friendship between Wilbur, a young pig, and Charlotte, a spider who saves his life through her clever web weavings. The third, *The Trumpet of the Swan*, tells the story of a mute swan who becomes a celebrity after learning to trumpet. The themes of friendship, tolerance, loyalty, and rural living are common threads in these books.

> "I arise in the morning torn between a desire to improve (or save) the world and a desire to enjoy (or savor) the world. This makes it hard to plan the day."
>
> —E. B. White

White was awarded the Presidential Medal of Freedom in 1963 and the Laura Ingalls Wilder Award from the American Library Association in 1970. In 1973 he was elected to the American Academy of Arts and Letters.

 Literature Online

Author Search For more about E. B. White, go to glencoe.com and enter QuickPass code GLA9800u6.

Selection Skills

Literary Elements
- Plot (SE pp. 929–935)
- Irony (SE p. 935)

← **The Second Tree from the Corner** →

Writing Skills/Grammar
- Apply Irony (SE p. 936)
- Pronoun Antecedents (TE p. 934)

Reading Skills
- Analyze Text Structure (SE pp. 929–932, 936)
- Draw Conclusions (TE p. 930)

Vocabulary Skills
- Word Parts (SE pp. 929, 936)
- Academic Vocabulary (SE p. 929, 936)

Literature and Reading Preview

Connect to the Story

What is most important in life? Write a journal entry about your priorities in life.

Build Background

"The Second Tree from the Corner" takes place in Manhattan, a part of New York City, probably in the late 1940s. One clue to the story's time frame comes from a reference to Ethel Merman, a popular Broadway singer and actress of the time. Other references to famous New York institutions and places appear in the story as well: the *Times,* which is *The New York Times* newspaper; the "Park," which is Central Park; the "East Seventies," a section of Manhattan known for its wealthy residents; and Madison Avenue, a famous luxury shopping district.

Set Purposes for Reading

Big Idea Life in the City

As you read, ask yourself, Which references to city life, transportation, scenery, and culture could happen only in a city and not in the country?

Literary Element Plot

A **plot** is the sequence of events that constitutes a narrative, usually involving characters in conflict. A plot includes **rising action** (development of the conflict), **climax** (sometimes called the crisis or turning point), and **falling action** (sometimes called the resolution of the conflict). As you read, ask yourself, How does White develop these elements of the plot?

Reading Strategy Analyze Text Structure

Analyzing text structure means taking a close look at the organizational pattern of a piece of writing. A writer might use chronological order (order of time), comparison and contrast, cause and effect, or order of importance as a frame on which to hang the text. Most fiction, including this story, is organized primarily in chronological order. As you read, ask yourself, How does White structure the story?

....

Tip: Find Time References Use a graphic organizer like the one below to keep track of the time references in the story.

 Trexler felt the time passing. He had already used up pretty nearly four seconds.

Learning Objectives

For pages 928–936

In studying this text, you will focus on the following objectives:

Literary Study: Analyzing plot.

Reading: Analyzing text structure.

Vocabulary

amorphous (ə môr´ fəs) *adj.* without definite form; p. 931 *Amorphous clouds filled the sky.*

retractable (ri trak´ tə bəl) *adj.* capable of being drawn back or in; p. 931 *Cats have retractable claws.*

hemorrhage (he´ mə rij) *n.* a severe discharge of blood; p. 931 *The doctor was able to stop the hemorrhage.*

inquisitor (in kwi´ zə tər) *n.* one who asks questions; p. 933 *Jennifer refused to answer the rude inquisitor.*

intimation (in´ tə mā´ shən) *n.* a hint; a suggestion; p. 934 *Mike's reputation was hurt by the intimation of scandal.*

....

Tip: Word Parts Root words can be combined with prefixes and suffixes to form new words. Knowing the meanings of these word parts can help you determine the meaning of unfamiliar words. For example, if you know that the prefix *a-* means *without,* you can infer that *amorphous* means *without form.*

E. B. WHITE **929**

English Learners

DIFFERENTIATED INSTRUCTION

 Intermediate To comprehend the story's meaning, readers must fully understand some difficult words, such as *apprehensions, melancholy, inexpressive,* and *unattainable.* Have English learners work in pairs and have each pair make a chart that includes a definition of each unfamiliar word, along with a brief explanation of the word's importance in the story. Refer students to English dictionaries for definitions, helping them choose senses that fit the story context.

Before You Read

Focus

Summary

Mr. Trexler is plagued by depression, mysterious physical symptoms, and anxiety. The narrator describes Trexler's visits to a psychiatrist and implies that Trexler's problem is fear. The story ends soon after a visit during which the doctor asks Trexler, "What do you want?" This question leads to Trexler's epiphany: he realizes that "all men" want something "deep, formless, enduring, and impossible of fulfillment"— something he cannot explain but recognizes when he sees the second tree from the corner saturated with the evening light.

> For summaries in languages other than English, see Unit 6 Teaching Resources Book, pp. 94–99.

Vocabulary

Word Parts Have students identify the roots of the words in the vocabulary list. Students may need to use dictionaries to verify root definitions. **Say:** Match a vocabulary word with each of the following definitions of root words: to seek or ask *(inquisitor);* to pull *(retractable);* blood *(hemorrhage).*

 For additional vocabulary practice, see Unit 6 Teaching Resources Book, p. 102.

Teach

Life in the City **Say:** Keep this question in mind as you continue to read. How does the city play a role in Trexler's anxiety? *(The narrator feels time pressure and assumes the doctor is "overloaded." He imagines the next patient in the waiting room, worrying about an incident that happened on a city bus.)*

View the Art ★

English painter Julian Barrow (1939–) studied painting in Florence for several years. The subjects of Barrow's paintings include landscapes, country homes, interiors, and townscapes (images of urban scenes), such as this painting of the Frick Gallery in New York City.

 For an audio recording of this selection, use Listening Library Audio CD-ROM.

Readability Scores
Dale-Chall: 5.7
DRP: 57
Lexile: 1110

The Frick Gallery, 1997. Julian Barrow. Oil on canvas, 18 x 24 in. Private Collection. ★

The Second Tree from the Corner
E. B. White

Reading Practice

Draw Conclusions Most short stories require readers to draw conclusions early in the stories. After students have read page 931, have them reread the page up to the beginning of the last paragraph. Have them list, on the basis of their rereading, everything about the setting and characters that they know. For each fact, they should jot down a note explaining how they came to that conclusion. Have students share their lists with the rest of the class and point out the conclusions they drew in order to develop their lists.

1 "Ever have any bizarre thoughts?" asked the doctor.

Mr. Trexler failed to catch the word. "What kind?" he said.

"Bizarre," repeated the doctor, his voice steady. He watched his patient for any slight change of expression, any wince. It seemed to Trexler that the doctor was not only watching him closely but was creeping slowly toward him, like a lizard toward a bug. Trexler shoved his chair back an inch and gathered himself for a reply. He was about to say "Yes" when he realized that if he said yes the next question would be unanswerable. Bizarre thoughts, bizarre thoughts? Ever have any bizarre thoughts? What kind of thoughts *except* bizarre had he had since the age of two?

Trexler felt the time passing, the necessity for an answer. These psychiatrists were busy men, overloaded, not to be kept waiting. The next patient was probably already perched out there in the waiting room, lonely, worried, shifting around on the sofa, his mind stuffed with bizarre thoughts and **amorphous** fears. Poor fellow, thought Trexler. Out there all alone in that mis-shapen antechamber,[1] staring at the filing cabinet and wondering whether to tell the doctor about that day on the Madison Avenue bus.

Let's see, bizarre thoughts. Trexler dodged back along the dreadful corridor of the years to see what he could find. He felt the doctor's eyes upon him and knew that time was running out. Don't be so conscientious, he said to himself. If a bizarre thought is indicated here, just reach into the bag and pick anything at all. A man as well supplied with bizarre thoughts as you are should have no difficulty producing one for the record. Trexler darted into the bag,

---

1. An *antechamber*, or waiting room, is a smaller room serving as an entrance to a larger or main room.

2 Plot *How would you describe Mr. Trexler's internal conflict at this point?*

Vocabulary

amorphous (ə môr´ fəs) *adj.* without definite form

---

hung for a moment before one of his thoughts, as a hummingbird pauses in the delphinium. No, he said, not that one. He darted to another (the one about the rhesus monkey), paused, considered. No, he said, not that.

Trexler knew he must hurry. He had already used up pretty nearly four seconds since the question had been put. But it was an impossible situation—just one more lousy, impossible situation such as he was always getting himself into. When, he asked himself, are you going to quit maneuvering yourself into a pocket? He made one more effort. This time he stopped at the asylum, only the bars were lucite[2]—fluted, **retractable.** Not here, he said. Not this one.

He looked straight at the doctor. "No," he said quietly. "I never have any bizarre thoughts."

The doctor sucked in on his pipe, blew a plume of smoke toward the rows of medical books. Trexler's gaze followed the smoke. He managed to make out one of the titles, *The Genito-Urinary System.* A bright wave of fear swept cleanly over him and he winced under the first pain of kidney stones.[3] He remembered when he was a child, the first time he ever entered a doctor's office, sneaking a look at the titles of the books—and the flush of fear, the shirt wet under the arms, the book on t.b.,[4] the sudden knowledge that he was in the advanced stages of consumption,[5] the quick vision of the **hemorrhage.** Trexler sighed wearily. Forty years, he thought, and I still get thrown by the title of a medical book. Forty

---

2. *Lucite* is the trademark name of a transparent plastic.
3. *Kidney stones* are small, hard calcium deposits that sometimes form in the kidneys and cause pain.
4. Tuberculosis, a disease that often affects the lungs, is sometimes referred to as *t.b.*
5. *Consumption* is another name for tuberculosis.

Analyze Text Structure *How do you know the author is using chronological order to organize the story?* **3**

Vocabulary

retractable (ri trak´ tə bəl) *adj.* capable of being drawn back or in

hemorrhage (he´ mə rij) *n.* a severe discharge of blood

E. B. WHITE **931**

Teach

Approaching Level

DIFFERENTIATED INSTRUCTION

Established After students have read this page, discuss some sections of the selection that could be confusing. For example, Trexler thinks that "if he said yes [to the psychiatrist's question] the next question would be unanswerable." **Say:** If Trexler says yes, he is saying he has bizarre thoughts. **Ask:** In that case, what is the psychiatrist likely to ask Trexler next? (*What are they?*) Why do

you think Trexler says this question is unanswerable? (*Trexler has too many bizarre thoughts to be able to tell them all.*) In the same way, discuss the following: "Poor fellow . . . wondering whether to tell the doctor about that day on the Madison Avenue bus."

Emerging Explain that this page contains some of Trexler's "bizarre thoughts." Assist students in identifying them. (*a rhesus monkey; an asylum; thinking he has a disease when he sees a book on the subject*) Ask students to describe the images. (*bizarre, frightful*)

Teach

Literary Element | 1

Plot **Answer:** *He is consulting a psychiatrist.*

Reading Strategy | 2

Analyze Text Structure
Answer: *Four or five weeks have passed. The phrases "a week later" and "for several weeks thereafter" are evidence of this.*

Cultural History ☆

Causes of Death Heart disease is the leading cause of death of both male and female Americans. In 2002, about 700,000 Americans died of heart disease. **Ask:** Is the concern that Trexler describes reasonable? *(Yes, but worrying about it constantly would not be.)*

Gridlock NYC, 1998. Bill Jacklin. Oil on canvas, 152.4 x 152.4 cm. Private collection. ★

years and I still can't stay on life's little bucky horse. No wonder I'm sitting here in this dreary joint at the end of this woebegone[6] afternoon, lying about my bizarre thoughts to a doctor who looks, come to think of it, rather tired.

The session dragged on. After about twenty minutes, the doctor rose and knocked his pipe out. Trexler got up, knocked the ashes out of his brain, and waited. The doctor smiled warmly and stuck out his hand. "There's nothing the matter with you—you're just scared. Want to know how I know you're scared?"

"How?" asked Trexler.

"Look at the chair you've been sitting in! See how it has moved back away from my desk? You kept inching away from me while I asked you questions. That means you're scared."

---

6. *Woebegone* means "sorrowful" or "filled with grief"; it can also suggest "dreary and miserable."

1 Plot *In what way is Mr. Trexler trying to resolve his internal conflict?*

"Does it?" said Trexler, faking a grin. "Yeah, I suppose it does."

They finished shaking hands. Trexler turned and walked out uncertainly along the passage, then into the waiting room and out past the next patient, a ruddy pin-striped man who was seated on the sofa twirling his hat nervously and staring straight ahead at the files. Poor, frightened guy, thought Trexler, he's probably read in the *Times* that one American male out of every two is going to die of heart disease by twelve o'clock next Thursday. It says that in the paper almost every morning. And he's also probably thinking about that day on the Madison Avenue bus.

A week later, Trexler was back in the patient's chair. And for several weeks thereafter he continued to visit the doctor, always toward

2 Analyze Text Structure *About how much time has passed since the opening scene of the story? How do you know?*

Reading Practice

SPIRAL REVIEW **Subtle Humor** Students may know from White's stories for children that he is often subtly humorous. Explain that some of the humor comes from the contrast between Mr. Trexler's inner thoughts and what he tells his doctor or how he acts. Explain that White is using irony, a difference between appearance and reality. Help students by pointing out some of the contrasts on this page and the previous page.

Trexler's Inner Thoughts	Trexler's Words or Actions
"It seemed that the doctor… was creeping slowly toward him, like a lizard toward a bug."	[The doctor says,] "You kept inching away from me while I asked you questions. That means you're scared." "Does it?" said Trexler, faking a grin.
"What kind of thoughts *except* bizarre had he had since the age of two?"	"I never have any bizarre thoughts."

Have students extend the chart as they continue to read.

the end of the afternoon, when the vapors hung thick above the pool of the mind and darkened the whole region of the East Seventies.[7] He felt no better as time went on, and he found it impossible to work. He discovered that the visits were becoming routine and that although the routine was one to which he certainly did not look forward, at least he could accept it with cool resignation, as once, years ago, he had accepted a long spell with a dentist who had settled down to a steady fooling with a couple of dead teeth. The visits, moreover, were now assuming a pattern recognizable to the patient.

Each session would begin with a resumé of symptoms—the dizziness in the streets, the constricting pain in the back of the neck, the apprehensions, the tightness of the scalp, the inability to concentrate, the despondency[8] and the melancholy times, the feeling of pressure and tension, the anger at not being able to work, the anxiety over work not done, the gas on the stomach. Dullest set of neurotic symptoms in the world, Trexler would think, as he obediently trudged back over them for the doctor's benefit.

As he became familiar with the pattern Trexler found that he increasingly tended to identify himself with the doctor, transferring himself into the doctor's seat—probably (he thought) some rather slick form of escapism. At any rate, it was nothing new for Trexler to identify himself with other people. Whenever he got into a cab, he instantly became the driver, saw everything from the hackman's angle (and the reaching over with the right hand, the nudging of the flag, the pushing it down, all the way down along the side of the meter), saw everything—traffic, fare, everything—through the eyes of Anthony Rocco, or Isidore Freedman, or Matthew Scott. In a barbershop, Trexler was the

barber, his fingers curled around the comb, his hand on the tonic. Perfectly natural, then, that Trexler should soon be occupying the doctor's chair, asking the questions, waiting for the answers. He got quite interested in the doctor, in this way. He liked him, and he found him a not too difficult patient.

It was on the fifth visit, about halfway through, that the doctor turned to Trexler and said, suddenly, "What do you want?" He gave the word "want" special emphasis.

"I d'know," replied Trexler uneasily. "I guess nobody knows the answer to that one."

"Sure they do," replied the doctor.

"Do *you* know what *you* want?" asked Trexler narrowly.

"Certainly," said the doctor. Trexler noticed that at this point the doctor's chair slid slightly backward, away from him. Trexler stifled a small, internal smile. Scared as a rabbit, he said to himself. Look at him scoot!

"What *do* you want?" continued Trexler, pressing his advantage, pressing it hard.

The doctor glided back another inch away from his **inquisitor.** "I want a wing on the small house I own in Westport.[9] I want more money, and more leisure to do the things I want to do."

Trexler was just about to say, "And what are those things you want to do, Doctor?" when he caught himself. Better not go too far, he mused. Better not lose possession of the ball. And besides, he thought, what the hell goes on here, anyway—me paying fifteen bucks a throw for these séances[10] and then doing the work myself, asking the questions, weighing the answers. So

---

7. Most of the streets that run east to west in Manhattan are identified by numbers rather than names. *East Seventies* refers to the section of streets from 70–79 that are on the east side of Manhattan.
8. *Despondency* means "hopelessness" or "depression."

Life in the City How does this paragraph give the reader an idea of what it would be like to live in a big city such as New York?

3

9. *Westport* is a residential community and summer resort on the coast of Connecticut.
10. A *séance* is a meeting in which people attempt to communicate with the spirits of the dead. Here, Trexler is questioning the scientific validity of his psychiatric sessions.

Plot *In what way does the doctor's original question help Mr. Trexler begin to solve his own problems?* **4**

Vocabulary

inquisitor (in kwiz´ ə tər) *n.* one who asks questions

E. B. WHITE **933**

Big Idea **3**

Life in the City **Answer:** *It describes riding in a taxi, which people who live in the country or in the suburbs rarely do.*

Literary Element **4**

Plot **Answer:** *The doctor's question acts as a trigger for Trexler, forcing him to think about what he really wants.*

ADVANCED **Say:** Trexler imagines that he is the doctor and asks "his patient" what *he* wants. How does this role reversal end up helping Trexler feel better? *(He realizes that he has the ability to ask questions—of the doctor and also of himself. He begins to see that he can answer the questions as well.)*

View the Art ★

Bill Jacklin (1943–) grew up and studied art in England. Since 1985, he has lived in New York City and worked to capture the city's many faces in his work. This painting is one of Jacklin's "urban portraits."

Approaching Level

DIFFERENTIATED INSTRUCTION

SMALL GROUP

Emerging Ask: What does the doctor do when Trexler asks him, "Do *you* know what *you* want?" *(He slides his chair back slightly.)* Why do you think Trexler smiles inside? *(The doctor is doing what Trexler did on his first appointment.)* Point out to students that when White describes Trexler's fifth visit to the doctor, he uses words and phrases that

show Trexler's sense of power and enjoyment.

Ask students to work in small groups to find words that show how Trexler feels triumphant. *(Look at him scoot!; pressing his advantage; his inquisitor; better not go too far)*

Teach

Vocabulary | 1

Idiom Explain that "another day over the dam" is a variation of "water over the dam." Like "water under the bridge," it means that something is over and cannot be changed. Point out to students that slightly altering the phrase makes it sound more hopeless, as if the day is not only over, but it has plunged from a high wall. Trexler paints the doctor as sad and overworked.

Big Idea | 2

Life in the City Answer: *Central Park, brick and brownstone buildings, Third Avenue, and dim saloons would not be found in the country.*

Literary Element | 3

Plot Answer: *He has recognized that what he wants from life is unique to him and that no one else can provide it for him. Even though he is afraid, he can show a certain amount of courage in facing life.* **Ask:** Why does Trexler feel "glad in a way" that what he wanted "was both inexpressible and unattainable, and that it wasn't a wing"? *(He is glad that he can appreciate how mysterious and complex life is, and that for him, life does not boil down to something as mundane as a new wing on a house.)*

934

---

he wants a new wing! There's a fine piece of theatrical gauze for you! A new wing.

Trexler settled down again and resumed the role of patient for the rest of the visit. It ended on a kindly, friendly note. The doctor reassured him that his fears were the cause of his sickness, and that his fears were unsubstantial. They shook hands, smiling.

Trexler walked dizzily through the empty waiting room and the doctor followed along to let him out. It was late; the secretary had shut up shop and gone home. Another day over the dam. "Goodbye," said Trexler. He stepped into the street, turned west toward Madison, and thought of the doctor all alone there, after hours, in that desolate hole—a man who worked longer hours than his secretary. Poor, scared, over-worked guy, thought Trexler. And that new wing!

It was an evening of clearing weather, the Park showing green and desirable in the distance, the last daylight applying a high lacquer to the brick and brownstone walls and giving the street scene a luminous and intoxicating splendor. Trexler meditated, as he walked, on what he wanted. "What do you want?" he heard again. Trexler knew what he wanted, and what, in general, all men wanted; and he was glad in a way, that it was both inexpressible and unattainable, and that it wasn't a wing. He was satisfied to remember that it was deep, formless, enduring, and impossible of fulfillment, and that it made men sick, and that when you sauntered along Third Avenue and looked through the doorways into the dim saloons, you could sometimes pick out from the unregenerate ranks the

Visual Vocabulary
Brownstone is the name of a reddish-brown sandstone as well as a type of house made with it.

ones who had not forgotten, gazing steadily into the bottoms of the glasses on the long chance that they could get another little peek at it. Trexler found himself renewed by the remembrance that what he wanted was at once great and microscopic, and that although it borrowed from the nature of large deeds and of youthful love and of old songs and early **intimations,** it was not any one of these things, and that it had not been isolated or pinned down, and that a man who attempted to define it in the privacy of a doctor's office would fall flat on his face.

Trexler felt invigorated. Suddenly his sickness seemed health, his dizziness stability. A small tree, rising between him and the light, stood there saturated with the evening, each gilt-edged leaf perfectly drunk with excellence and delicacy. Trexler's spine registered an ever so slight tremor as it picked up this natural disturbance in the lovely scene. "I want the second tree from the corner, just as it stands," he said, answering an imaginary question from an imaginary physician. And he felt a slow pride in realizing that what he wanted none could bestow, and that what he had none could take away. He felt content to be sick, unembarrassed at being afraid; and in the jungle of his fear he glimpsed (as he had so often glimpsed them before) the flashy tail feathers of the bird courage.

Then he thought once again of the doctor, and of his being left there all alone, tired, frightened. (The poor, scared guy, thought Trexler.) Trexler began humming "Moonshine Lullaby," his spirit reacting instantly to the hypodermic of Merman's[11] healthy voice. He crossed Madison, boarded a downtown bus, and rode all the way to Fifty-second Street before he had a thought that could rightly have been called bizarre. ◆

---

11. Ethel *Merman* (1909–1984) was an American actress and singer known for her powerful voice.

Plot *How has Mr. Trexler resolved his internal conflict?* **3**

Vocabulary
intimation (in´ tə mā´ shən) *n.* a hint; a suggestion

Life in the City *What elements in this paragraph are unique to the city and would not be found in the country?* **2**

934 UNIT 6 FROM DEPRESSION TO COLD WAR

Grammar Practice

SPIRAL REVIEW Pronoun Antecedents
Remind students that a pronoun takes the place of a noun or another pronoun. The noun or other pronoun is the pronoun's antecedent or referent. For example, *she* refers to *Mary* in this sentence:

I gave <u>Mary</u> the apple **she** wanted.

Ask students to find ten pronouns in the story. For each, have them identify its antecedent and tell whether the antecedent is a noun or a pronoun. If it is a pronoun, have students continue tracing the text back to find the original antecedent.

After You Read

Respond and Think Critically

Respond and Interpret

1. (a)What question does the doctor ask Mr. Trexler at the beginning of the story? What is Trexler's answer? (b)In your opinion, what does Trexler's reaction to the doctor's first question reveal about Trexler's state of mind?

2. (a)What, according to the doctor, is wrong with Trexler? (b)Do you agree with the doctor's early diagnosis of Trexler? Explain.

3. (a)How does Trexler respond to the question "What do you want?" (b)What does the question make him think about after his visit to the doctor? (c)What do you think Trexler wants?

Analyze and Evaluate

4. Is Trexler's reaction to his discovery of what he wants in life realistic? Why or why not?

5. (a)Why do you think Trexler pities others? (b)Do you think his observations are accurate? Explain.

6. (a)What personality traits—both positive and negative—does Trexler exhibit? (b)On the basis of these traits, do you find Trexler to be a sympathetic character? Explain.

Connect

7. **Big Idea** Life in the City What does "The Second Tree from the Corner" reveal about city life? Explain using details from the story.

8. **Connect to Today** Do you think "the second tree from the corner" is an effective **symbol,** or representation, of what people often want from life? Explain.

Literary Element Plot

At the center of a story's **plot,** there is usually a struggle, or **conflict,** between two opposing forces. The conflict might be **external**—between the main character and another person or an outside force—or it may be **internal**—between opposing thoughts or desires within the character's mind.

1. Identify and discuss Trexler's internal conflicts after the psychiatrist asks him if he has ever had any bizarre thoughts.

2. Consider Trexler's comment that his identification with other people is "some rather slick form of escapism." Is it possible that Trexler's ability to look through others' eyes leads to a resolution of his conflict? Explain.

3. Discuss how the psychiatrist's question "What do you want?" helps Trexler to resolve his inner conflict.

Review: Irony

As you learned on page 574, **irony** is a contrast or discrepancy between appearance and reality. **Verbal irony** occurs when someone says one thing but means another. **Situational irony** exists when the outcome of a situation is the opposite of someone's expectations.

Group Activity Meet with a small group to discuss E. B. White's use of irony in "The Second Tree from the Corner." Together, create a web diagram like the one below, filling in the circles with examples of irony in the story.

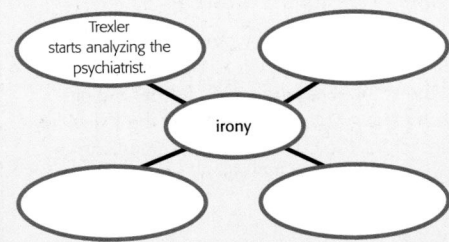

After You Read

Assess

1. (a) "Ever have any bizarre thoughts?" Trexler answers, "No, I never have any bizarre thoughts." (b) He is confused, fearful, and unsure of how to express his thoughts.

2. (a) He is scared. (b) Trexler is scared, but probably not of what the doctor thinks he is.

3. (a) He challenges the doctor with the same question. (b) He thinks about the nature of what "all men want." (c) Possible answer: fulfillment, happiness, and a sense of inner peace

4. It is realistic; inner peace is something that people can attain.

5. (a) Trexler is compassionate and identifies with others. (b) Students' answers will vary, but many will say that his observations seem reasonable.

6. (a) *Positive:* empathy, compassion, reliability, friendliness; *negative:* fear, nervousness, evasiveness, insecurity (b) Students may say his fears make him sympathetic and admire his effort to overcome them.

7. It shows the complexities of city life, such as crowding in buses, transportation by taxis and buses, and a rich cultural environment.

8. Yes, because trees are often symbols for life, the universe, and life processes.

 For additional assessment, see Assessment Resources, pp. 247–248.

Literary Element

1. He cannot decide which, if any, bizarre thoughts to share.

2. Possible answer: Yes. By looking through others' eyes, Trexler realizes that most people have the same fears and hopes.

3. When Trexler turns the question back at the doctor, he notices that the doctor, too, is scared.

Review: Irony

Trexler says he has no bizarre thoughts; he says sickness is health.

Progress Check

Can students analyze plot?

If No → See Unit 6 Teaching Resources Book, p. 100.

After You Read

Assess

Reading Strategy

1. (a) The doctor observes Trexler inching his chair away from the desk and infers that Trexler is scared. (b) Readers gain insight into Trexler's character when he infers that the next patient is frightened. This shows Trexler as a man who perceives other people's feelings.

2. (a) The contrast of Trexler's and the doctor's answers to the question "What do you want?" (b) Trexler is more thoughtful than the doctor and less materialistic.

Vocabulary

amorphous

Prefix: *a-,* "without"; Root: *morph,* "form"; Suffix: *-ous,* "full of"; Related words: formless, shapeless, obscure

retractable

Prefix: *re-,* "back"; Root: *tract,* "movement"; Suffix: *-able,* "capable of"; Related words: tractor, feasible, return

hemorrhage

Prefix: no prefix; Root: *hemo,* "blood"; Suffix: *-age,* "state of"; Related words: hemoglobin, suffrage

inquisitor

Prefix: *in-,* "in"; Root: *quis,* "question"; Suffix: *-or,* "one who"; Related words: quizzical, investigate, lector

intimation

Prefix: no prefix; Root: *intimus,* "innermost"; Suffix: *-tion,* "the act of"; Related words: intimate, probation

---

Reading Strategy Analyze Text Structure

Authors often embed several organizational methods within the same text. For example, a story might proceed mainly in chronological order but also show cause-and-effect relationships.

1. (a) Identify an instance in which White uses cause and effect as an organizational method. (b) How does this example advance the plot?

2. (a) Find an example of comparison and contrast in the story. (b) What does this example reveal about Trexler's character?

Vocabulary Practice

Practice with Word Parts Use a printed or online dictionary to help you find the meaning of each vocabulary word's root and of any prefixes or suffixes in the word. Then find three words that contain the same prefix, suffix, or root. Underline the word part that could help a person guess each word's meaning.

| amorphous | retractable | hemorrhage |
| inquisitor | intimation | |

EXAMPLE:
unattainable
prefix: *un-,* "not"
root: *attain,* "to get"
suffix: *-able,* "capable of"
related words: <u>un</u>reachable, <u>attain</u>der, intract<u>able</u>

Academic Vocabulary

Because all of his thoughts seem to be bizarre, Trexler cannot determine an **evident** *answer to the doctor's question.*

Evident is an academic word. In a research paper, facts that need no further explanation by the author are **evident**. To further explore the meaning of this word, answer the following question: Is the cause of Trexler's condition **evident** to the doctor? Why or why not?

For more on academic vocabulary, see pages 53–54.

Write with Style

 Apply Irony

Assignment White uses irony to create humor that engages his reader in the story. Based on White's example, write your own account of a fictional situation. Incorporate irony into your story.

Get Ideas With a partner, discuss ironic moments in "The Second Tree from the Corner" to help you understand how White uses irony. Then brainstorm your own list of ironic situations you might like to write about. Make a chart like the one below to record your ideas.

Ironic Situation	Why It Is Ironic

Give It Structure Choose one particularly strong situation from your list. Decide on characters and a setting, and select example(s) of irony to include. In addition to your ironic situation, you could use irony in your dialogue (verbal irony) or allow your audience to know information your characters do not (dramatic irony).

Look at Language Evaluate the effectiveness of your use of irony. What types of irony do you use: dramatic, situational, or verbal? (See Literary Terms Handbook, page R11.) Does the irony engage the reader and propel the story along? You may want to get a classmate's feedback as well. Then revise to improve your irony's effectiveness.

> **LOG ON** **Literature** Online
>
> **Selection Resources** For Selection Quizzes, eFlashcards, and Reading-Writing Connection activities, go to glencoe.com and enter QuickPass code GLA9800u6.

Academic Vocabulary

No, the cause is not *evident* because Trexler is not honest with him. The doctor thinks he can tell by the position of Trexler's chair that fear is his problem.

Write with Style

Use these criteria when evaluating students' writing:

- Does the writer incorporate irony into his or her story?
- Is the writer's use of irony effective?

Before You Read

To Don at Salaam and The Bean Eaters

Meet **Gwendolyn Brooks**
(1917–2000)

Brooks once said, "I wanted to write poems that I could take into the streets." With an ear for the beat of the city and the hum of everyday life, Brooks re-created the lives of African Americans in the city and elsewhere.

Although born in Topeka, Kansas, Brooks grew up in Chicago. A shy girl, she spent much of her childhood alone reading books and writing poetry. "My mother says I began rhyming at seven. . . . *Of course* I would be a poet! *Was* a poet! Didn't I write a poem every day? Sometimes *two* poems?" Her mother's belief in her talent gave her the confidence she needed to keep writing, and Brooks published her first poem, "Eventide," when she was thirteen. By the late 1930s, she had published seventy-five poems in the *Chicago Defender*.

Literary Influences Brooks's mother took her to see poets read whenever they came to Chicago. Two of them—James Weldon Johnson and Langston Hughes—became important influences on her career and writing. Johnson played the role of advisor, urging her to read modern poets such as T. S. Eliot and E. E. Cummings—poets whose styles would be reflected in her later work. When Brooks was sixteen, she went to see Langston Hughes read. After the reading, she gave him some of her poems, which he read immediately. He encouraged her to continue writing and would later become her close friend and inspiration. As a poet, Brooks shared Hughes's ability to respond to the struggles of the black community and express the black experience in a time of rapid change.

Poetic Transformation In 1945 Brooks's first book, *A Street in Bronzeville*, was published to rave reviews. In her early work, Brooks wrote poetic narratives, using traditional verse forms—such as the sonnet and ballad. In the 1960s, how-

> "I want to write poems that will be meaningful . . . things that will touch [readers]."
>
> —Gwendolyn Brooks

ever, her voice and style changed, and she brought a new consciousness of her racial identity to her work. Inspired by black activism, Brooks began to overtly address political issues, especially the need for racial unity. As she became more involved with the Black Arts movement in Chicago, Brooks moved from major publishing houses to smaller ones run by African Americans.

Role of the Poet Success and recognition made Brooks even more committed to art and to helping young artists. With the publication of *Annie Allen*, she became the first African American to win the Pulitzer Prize. She would later be named Poet Laureate of Illinois, poetry consultant to the Library of Congress, and a member of the National Women's Hall of Fame. Most important to Brooks were her visits to local schools and the classes and contests she sponsored to help urban children "see" the poetry in the world around them. Today, Brooks remains one of America's most beloved and inspirational poets.

LOG ON ▶ **Literature** Online

Author Search For more about Gwendolyn Brooks, go to glencoe.com and enter QuickPass code GLA9800u6.

Before You Read

Focus

Cultural History ☆

The Pulitzer Prize The Pulitzer Prize is named after its creator, American journalist and newspaper publisher Joseph Pulitzer. In his 1904 will, Pulitzer established the prize to encourage excellence. Pulitzer established a board to oversee the awards after his death so that the number and type of awards could continue to grow. Since the first awards in 1917, the Pulitzer Prize categories have grown to include 21 awards in subjects including journalism, letters and drama, music, and photography.

Selection Skills

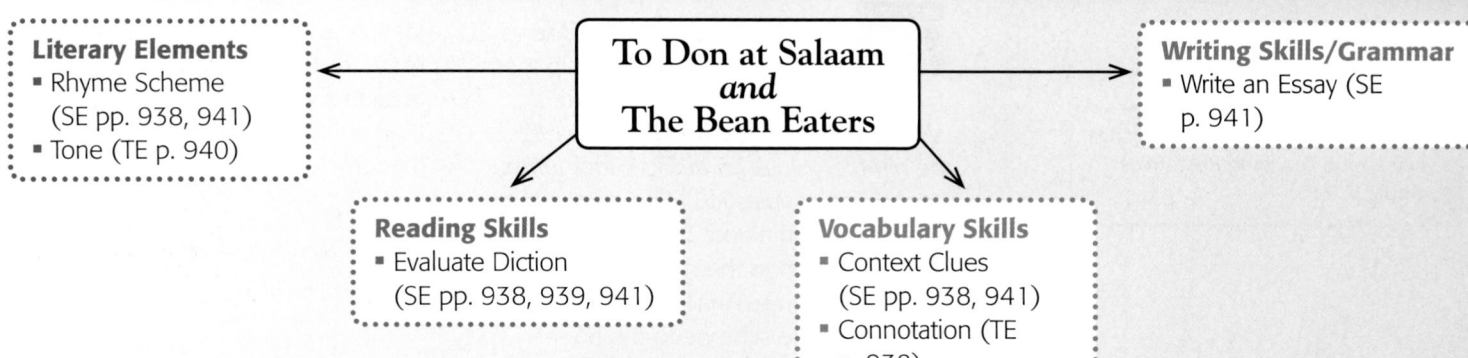

Literary Elements
- Rhyme Scheme (SE pp. 938, 941)
- Tone (TE p. 940)

To Don at Salaam *and* **The Bean Eaters**

Reading Skills
- Evaluate Diction (SE pp. 938, 939, 941)

Vocabulary Skills
- Context Clues (SE pp. 938, 941)
- Connotation (TE p. 938)

Writing Skills/Grammar
- Write an Essay (SE p. 941)

Before You Read

Focus

Summary

In "To Don at Salaam," the speaker celebrates Don, who watches life on the street with impudence and occasional joy. In "The Bean Eaters," an old couple eats beans in a rented room and remembers joys and sorrows.

 For summaries in languages other than English, see Unit 6 Teaching Resources Book, pp. 107–112.

Vocabulary

Connotation Tell students that synonyms may have different connotations than the word they define. Have a student read aloud the definition of *impudent*. Tell students that this word typically has a negative connotation, whereas the connotation of its synonym, *bold*, depends upon context. **Ask:** What word in the sample sentence indicates the connotation of *impudent*? *(The word "punished" gives students a context clue.)* Ask students to come up with examples of using the word *bold* with both negative and positive connotations. *(Positive: She was bold to fight for women's suffrage. Negative: Her bold demand to move to the front of the line offended me.)*

 For additional vocabulary practice, see Unit 6 Teaching Resources Book, p. 115.

938

Literature and Reading Preview

Connect to the Poems

What is unique about your neighborhood and the people who live there? Freewrite for a few minutes about the people and places in your neighborhood.

Build Background

Many of Brooks's characters, such as the couple in "The Bean Eaters," were inspired by people from her neighborhood on Chicago's South Side. Through such characters, Brooks chronicled the dreams and disappointments of the African American urban poor. Other characters, like the man in "To Don at Salaam," were inspired by young black artists and activists of the 1960s and onward, who possessed what Brooks called "a general energy, an electricity, in look, walk, speech, [and] *gesture….*"

Set Purposes for Reading

Big Idea Life in the City

As you read, ask yourself, How are the characters influenced by their urban setting?

Literary Element Rhyme Scheme

Rhyme scheme is the pattern of end rhymes in a stanza or a poem. Rhyme schemes are designated by assigning a different letter of the alphabet to each new rhyme. For example, the rhyme scheme of a poem that repeats the same rhyme in every other line is *abab.* As you read "The Bean Eaters," ask yourself, How does the rhyme scheme affect the poem's theme?

Reading Strategy Evaluate Diction

An important element of a writer's voice and style is word choice, or **diction.** As you read, ask yourself, How do Brooks's individual word choices help create the tone and convey meaning?

Tip: Take Notes Use a chart like the one below to write down important words and their effect on each poem's meaning.

Word or Words	Effect on Meaning
beans	suggest ordinariness or poverty

Learning Objectives

For pages 937–941

In studying these texts, you will focus on the following objectives:

Literary Study: Analyzing rhyme and rhyme scheme.

Reading: Evaluating diction.

Writing: Writing an essay.

Vocabulary

impudent (im´ pyə dənt) *adj.* cocky, bold; p. 939 *Sean stopped his impudent behavior only after being punished by an officer.*

tribute (tri´ byüt) *n.* something given to show affection, gratitude, or respect; p. 939 *Marco gave a speech in tribute to his son on his wedding day.*

consolidation (kən sol´ə dā´ shən) *n.* the process of uniting or merging; p. 939 *The consolidation of the two companies led to greater efficiency but fewer jobs.*

twinge (twinj) *n.* a sudden, sharp physical or emotional pain; p. 940 *She felt a twinge of sadness at the sight of her dead grandmother's photograph.*

Tip: Context Clues To determine a word's meaning, use the other words in the sentence. Example: *The child's* **impudent** *behavior got her sent to the principal for a reprimand.* She is being punished by the principal, so the child's behavior must have been rude.

Reading Practice

 Rhyme Scheme Tell students that reading aloud can help them find a poem's rhyme scheme. Write a simple poem on the board such as: *Jack be nimble, / Jack be quick; / Jack jump over / The candlestick.* Have a volunteer read the poem aloud. Then, have students read the poem to themselves, trying to "hear" the rhyme. Finally, have students assign a rhyme scheme to the poem *(abcb).* Have students work in pairs to identify another rhyming poem from memory, from the textbook, or from an outside source. Then have students read their poems aloud to the class and explain their rhyme schemes.

To Don at Salaam

Gwendolyn Brooks

I like to see you lean back in your chair
so far you have to fall but do not—
your arms back, your fine hands
in your print pockets.

5 Beautiful. **Impudent.**
Ready for life.
A tied storm.

I like to see you wearing your boy smile
whose **tribute** is for two of us or three.

10 Sometimes in life
things seem to be moving
and they are not
and they are not
there.
15 You are there.

Your voice is the listened-for music.
Your act is the **consolidation.**

I like to see you living in the world.

Salaam is an Arabic word that means "peace."

Evaluate Diction *Why do you think Brooks uses the word* impudent *in line 5 to describe the man?*

Vocabulary

impudent (im´ pyə dənt) *adj.* cocky, bold
tribute (tri´ byüt) *n.* something given to show affection, gratitude, or respect
consolidation (kən sol´ə dā´shən) *n.* the process of uniting or merging

GWENDOLYN BROOKS **939**

Hombre ante el infinito (Man before the infinite). Rufino Tamayo. ★
Musée d'Art Moderne, Brussels, Belgium.

Teach

Literary Element | 1

Rhyme Scheme **Ask:** What word does Brooks rhyme with *wood*? Why is this choice unusual? *(good; the two words are in different stanzas.)*

[APPROACHING] **Ask:** What does Brooks mean by creaking wood? *(Brooks refers to an old table.)* Point out that by using this creative imagery, rather than just saying "old table," Brooks appeals to the reader's senses. **Ask:** What senses does Brooks appeal to with this image? *(visual and auditory)*

Big Idea | 2

Life in the City **Answer:** *City life is a plain, poor existence of eating beans, putting on clothes, putting things away, and enjoying memories.*

To check students' understanding of the selection, see Unit 6 Teaching Resources Book, p. 117.

The Bean Eaters

Gwendolyn Brooks

Onion Tears, 1929. Cagnaccio di San Pietro. Camera di Lavoro, Trieste, Italy

They eat beans mostly, this old yellow pair.
Dinner is a casual affair.
Plain chipware on a plain and creaking wood,
Tin flatware.

5   Two who are Mostly Good.   **1**
Two who have lived their day,
But keep on putting on their clothes
And putting things away.

And remembering . . .
10 Remembering, with twinklings and **twinges,**
As they lean over the beans in their rented back room that
    is full of beads and receipts and dolls and cloths,
    tobacco crumbs, vases and fringes.

Life in the City *What is city life like for the bean eaters?*   **2**

Vocabulary

twinge (twinj) *n.* a sudden, sharp physical or emotional pain

Reading Practice

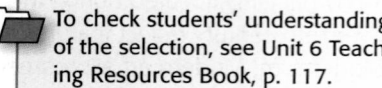
Tone Remind students that the tone of a work is an expression of the author's attitude toward the subject matter; it might, for example, be sympathetic, angry, humorous, or sad. Tone is reflected in an author's choice of words, punctuation, sentence structure, and figurative language. Point out unusual punctuation and capitalization in this poem, such as "Mostly Good," and the ellipsis in line 9. Ask students how these contribute to the tone. *(The capitalization of the words "Mostly Good" gives a certain amount of dignity to the status, indicating that being imperfect is still noteworthy; the ellipsis suggests a musing voice.)*

Respond and Think Critically

Respond and Interpret

1. (a)What is the setting in "The Bean Eaters"? (b)What do the details of the setting show?

2. (a)How does Brooks describe the characters in "The Bean Eaters"? (b)What do the couple's actions suggest about them?

3. (a)In "To Don at Salaam," what adjectives or adjective phrases does the speaker use to describe the man? (b)What do these modifiers suggest about the man? (c)What do they suggest about the speaker?

Analyze and Evaluate

4. (a)How would you describe the tone of "The Bean Eaters"? (b)How does the tone help you understand the meaning of the poem?

5. (a)How does Brooks use imagery to describe the man in "To Don at Salaam"? (b)How well do the images tell you what the speaker sees in him?

Connect

6. **Big Idea** **Life in the City** What aspects of life in a big city does "The Bean Eaters" show?

7. **Connect to Today** Would you be able to see people today who resemble the characters in Brooks's poems? Explain.

Literary Element Rhyme Scheme

Rhyme schemes reinforce meaning and aid the reader by providing a logical structure.

1. (a)What is the rhyme scheme of "The Bean Eaters"? (b)Is it predictable? Explain.

2. Explain how the rhyme scheme affects the poem's tone and meaning.

Reading Strategy Evaluate Diction

Look at the chart you created to **evaluate diction** in the poems to answer the following questions.

1. In "The Bean Eaters," how do the words "twinklings and twinges" communicate both meaning and attitude?

2. In "To Don at Salaam," the speaker says, "Your act is the consolidation." What does this mean? Why does the poet choose *consolidation*?

LOG ON **Literature** Online

Selection Resources For Selection Quizzes, eFlash-cards, and Reading-Writing Connection activities, go to glencoe.com and enter QuickPass code GLA9800u6.

Vocabulary Practice

Practice with Context Clues Look back at the poems to find context clues for the words below. Record your findings as in the example.

impudent   tribute
consolidation   twinge

EXAMPLE:
Word: tribute
Textual clues: Don's "boy smile" is intended "for two of us or three," showing affection to a select few
Meaning: something given to show affection, gratitude, or respect

Writing

Write an Essay In "The Bean Eaters," Brooks describes everyday objects and actions with carefully chosen words to reveal something deeper about the lives of her subjects. Think about some of your own possessions and activities. What do they say about you? Write a brief essay exploring these images and their meaning.

GWENDOLYN BROOKS **941**

After You Read

Assess

1. (a) A rented back room full of odds and ends (b) The home is cramped and holds memories.

2. (a) As an "old, yellow pair" who are "Mostly Good" and "have lived their day" (b) They still put things away, which suggests they continue to carry on.

3. (a) *Beautiful, impudent,* and *ready for life* (b) He is daring, smug, and energetic. (c) The speaker admires him.

4. (a) Matter-of-fact, but kind (b) It stresses their ordinary lives.

5. (a) The images of leaning back in a chair, hands in pockets, and a boyish smile (b) The speaker enjoys the man's relaxed approach to life.

6. City life can be isolating; people live in small spaces, packed with the clutter of their past.

7. Students should note that Brooks's characters can be seen today, as their personality traits are universal.

Literary Element

1. (a) *aaba bcdc efghf* (b) No, it is not regular.

2. It suggests the disorder of daily life.

Progress Check

Can students analyze rhyme scheme?

If No → See Unit 6 Teaching Resources Book, p. 113.

Writing

Students' essays should make connections between objects and actions and their deeper meanings.

Reading Strategy

1. *Twinklings* suggests responses to pleasant memories; *twinges,* feelings of regret about unpleasant memories. These words show the range and persistence of the couple's memories.

2. Don's actions bring harmony and unity; the word completes the poem's praise of Don's beauty.

Vocabulary

Word: *impudent.* Textual clues: The subject of the poem leans back, appearing "Impudent. / Ready for life."

Word: *consolidation.* Textual clues: The "act" is the consolidation of the whole experience.

Word: *twinge.* Textual clues: They remember the past with "twinklings and twinges."

Before You Read

The Magic Barrel

Bellringer Options

Selection Focus
   Transparency 59
Daily Language Practice
   Transparency 86

Or ask students to name some books or films about people finding romance. **Ask:** What are some common ways that people meet romantic partners? Have students consider, as they read, what role luck or accident plays in bringing people together.

Political History ☆

Czarist Russia and the Russian Revolution For centuries, Russia was ruled by one czar after another. A Russian form of "caesar," *czar* (also spelled *tsar* or *tzar*) is the Russian word for emperor. Czars had unlimited power over all the citizens of Russia. Then in 1917, during World War I (1914–1918), the Bolsheviks started a revolution and overthrew the czarist government. Communism took the place of the czarist rule.

Meet **Bernard Malamud**
(1914–1986)

Bernard Malamud was born to Russian Jewish immigrants who worked sixteen hours a day in their small grocery store on New York City's Lower East Side. Reflecting on his childhood, he would recall that there were no books in his home, no records or musical instruments, and no pictures on the walls. He would, however, recall the generosity of his father, who bought him the twenty-volume *Book of Knowledge* in 1923, when he was a nine-year-old recovering from pneumonia.

Inspired by his father's stories of life in czarist Russia, Malamud began creating stories of his own for his boyhood friends. He graduated from City College of New York and Columbia University, and while teaching evening classes he wrote short stories that appeared in *Harper's Bazaar* and other magazines. His first novel, written in 1952 when he was in his late thirties, was *The Natural*, the story of the rise and fall of a baseball player. The novel was later made into a popular movie starring Robert Redford. His second novel, *The Assistant*, written in 1957, brought him fame as a major Jewish American writer. His novel of injustice in czarist Russia, *The Fixer* (1966), won both the National Book Award and the Pulitzer Prize.

> "People say I write so much about misery, but you write about what you know best."
>
> —Bernard Malamud

Master of Characterization Though most of the characters in his stories and novels are Jewish, Malamud thought of Jewishness as a spiri-

tual condition rather than as a cultural heritage or religious creed. To be Jewish, he felt, was to struggle with life's limitations and responsibilities. Malamud said that he wrote about Jews "because they set my imagination going. I know something about their history, the quality of experience and belief, and of their literature, though not as much as I would like."

He saw himself as a storyteller whose fictions were about "simple people struggling to make their lives better in a world of bad luck." His characters are often pursued by a sense of injustice, burdened with grief, and strengthened by their own persistence. They are intensely aware of the past as they try to make a life for themselves in the modern world. The mixture of victory and defeat in their lives endows Malamud's work with a tragicomic character.

Malamud won highest acclaim as a writer of short stories, and "The Magic Barrel" is considered one of his best. His stories contain a robust humor, striking contrasts, a strong sense of compassion, and a complete understanding of his characters and their way of life.

LOG ON ▶ **Literature** Online

Author Search For more about Bernard Malamud, go to glencoe.com and enter QuickPass code GLA9800u6.

Selection Skills

Literary Elements
- Dialect (SE pp. 943, 947–949, 951, 957; TE p. 946)
- Motivation (SE p. 957)

The Magic Barrel

Reading Skills
- Analyze Characterization (SE pp. 943, 945–948, 950–954, 956, 958)

Writing Skills/Grammar
- Evaluate (SE p. 958)
- Journal (TE p. 948)

Vocabulary Skills
- Word Origins (SE p. 943, 958; TE p. 950)
- Parts of Speech (TE p. 943)

Listening/Speaking/Viewing
- Debate (SE p. 558)
- Analyze Art (TE pp. 944, 949)

Literature and Reading Preview

Connect to the Story

What is the best way to find a spouse? Discuss this question with a small group. Consider the role that love and shared interests might play in your choice.

Build Background

Between 1880 and 1914, about two million Jews from Eastern Europe immigrated to the U.S. The largest concentration of Jewish immigrants settled on the Lower East Side of Manhattan. They brought with them their culture and traditions, which included the use of matchmakers—people paid to bring young men and women together for the purpose of marriage.

Set Purposes for Reading

Big Idea **Life in the City**

Malamud mentions various locations, newspapers, customs, and sights that are unique to New York City. As you read, ask yourself, What does the story reveal about life in that city?

Literary Element **Dialect**

Dialect is a way of speaking and writing that is characteristic of a particular group, often within a particular region and time. Dialects may differ from the standard form of a language in vocabulary, pronunciation, or grammatical form. As you read, ask yourself, How does Malamud use dialect?

Reading Strategy **Analyze Characterization**

Analyzing characterization means examining the methods an author uses to reveal a character's personality. In **direct characterization** the writer makes explicit statements about a character. In **indirect characterization** the writer reveals a character through the character's thoughts, words, actions, or appearance or through what other characters think and say about that character. The reader must then use these details to make inferences about the character. As you read, ask yourself, How does Malamud reveal Finkle and Salzman's characters?

Tip: Take Notes on Characters For each main character, list details in the text and the inferences you make from them.

Character	Details	Inferences
Pinye Salzman	dresses shabbily	not wealthy

BERNARD MALAMUD **943**

Learning Objectives

For pages 942–958

In studying this text, you will focus on the following objectives:

Literary Study: Analyzing dialect.

Reading: Analyzing characterization.

Speaking and Listening: Debating.

Vocabulary

meager (mē′ gər) *adj.* deficient in quantity or completeness; p. 945 *The orphans were fed a meager breakfast of oatmeal and water.*

amiable (ā′ mē ə bəl) *adj.* friendly; p. 945 *Marla's amiable smile put her guests at ease.*

animated (an′ ə mā′ tid) *adj.* full of life; active; lively; p. 945 *The zoo visitors enjoyed the monkeys' animated antics.*

enamored (en am′ ərd) *adj.* inspired with love; charmed; captivated; p. 951 *Ben was completely enamored with Julie.*

abjectly (ab′ jekt lē) *adv.* in a humiliating, mean, or degrading manner; p. 952 *Disappointed with his performance, Carl abjectly accepted his third-place medal.*

Tip: Word Origins Etymology is the study of word origins. A typical dictionary entry will include the etymology of a word. For example, *enamored* derives from the Latin word *amare*, meaning "to love."

English Learners

DIFFERENTIATED INSTRUCTION

Intermediate English learners may find it difficult to grasp the concept of *dialect*. Have students work in pairs to look for examples of dialect in the story. Have students share their examples with the class, explaining what they show about time, place, and character.

Beginning Tell students that dialect makes characters more realistic. It gives the reader clues, such as where the speakers are from or what time period they are in. For example, if a speaker says that he had dinner with a flapper, he gives a clue that it is the 1920s.

Before You Read

Focus

Summary

Leo Finkle, a rabbinical student who wants to marry to improve his chances of getting a job with a congregation, asks the marriage broker Pinye Salzman for help. Finkle rejects all but one of Salzman's prospects. His date with Lily Hirschorn makes him realize that he has never truly loved anyone but his parents. Later, Finkle finds a girl's photograph in a group left by Salzman and feels love for her. Salzman at first refuses to introduce the two because the girl is his daughter. Eventually, he consents.

> For summaries in languages other than English, see Unit 6 Teaching Resources Book, pp. 119–124.

Vocabulary

Parts of Speech Tell students that not all words ending in *–ed* are verbs. Point out that the words *animated* and *enamored* are defined as adjectives in the vocabulary example. They can also be used as verbs. **Ask:** How do you know if these words are being used as adjectives or verbs? *(The function of the word in the sentence determines the part of speech. If the word modifies another adjective or a noun, then it is an adjective. If the word expresses an act or mode of being, it is a verb.)*

Teach

Big Idea   1

Life in the City   **Say:** Keep these questions in mind as you read: How is Leo Finkle's New York City community important to the story? *(It functions according to traditions that generate the story plot.)* What are some ways the characters reflect their city community? *(They speak a dialect specific to Eastern European Jewish immigrants in New York.)*

View the Art ★

Jewish culture places great emphasis on studying and teaching. Scholars and rabbis are therefore honored in Jewish communities.

Ask: How might this painting relate to the story? *(Both the student in the painting and Leo Finkle probably spend a lot of time studying in a "meager room.")*

For an audio recording of this selection, use Listening Library Audio CD-ROM.

Readability Scores

Dale-Chall: 6.3
DRP: 62
Lexile: 1010

THE
MAGIC BARREL

Bernard Malamud

Intensive Study, 1910. Unknown. Oil on canvas, 32¼ x 29 in. Judaica Coll. Max Berger, Vienna, Austria. ★

Reading Practice

SPIRAL REVIEW   **Compare and Contrast** Explain that comparing and contrasting characters can help students enhance their understanding of the characters, as well as of a story's theme and plot. Have students create Venn diagrams to compare and contrast the two main characters, Leo Finkle and Pinye Salzman. Students should list unique characteristics in the nonintersecting parts of the circles labeled with the characters' names. In the center overlap, they should list shared characteristics.

1 Not long ago there lived in uptown New York in a small, almost **meager** room, though crowded with books, Leo Finkle, a rabbinical student in the Yeshivah University.[1] Finkle, after six years of study, was to be ordained in June and had been advised by an acquaintance that he might find it easier to win himself a congregation if he were married. Since he had no present prospects of marriage, after two tormented days of turning it over in his mind, he called in Pinye Salzman, a marriage broker whose two-line advertisement he had read in the *Forward*.[2]

The matchmaker appeared one night out of the dark fourth-floor hallway of the graystone rooming house where Finkle lived, grasping a black, strapped portfolio that had been worn thin with use. Salzman, who had been long in the business, was of slight but dignified build, wearing an old hat, and an overcoat too short and tight for him. He smelled frankly of fish, which he loved to eat, and although he was missing a few teeth, his presence was not displeasing, because of an **amiable** manner curiously contrasted with mournful eyes. His voice, his lips, his wisp of beard, his bony fingers were **animated**, but give him a moment of repose and his mild blue eyes revealed a depth of sadness, a characteristic that put Leo a little at

ease although the situation, for him, was inherently tense.

He at once informed Salzman why he had asked him to come, explaining that his home was in Cleveland, and that but for his parents, who had married comparatively late in life, he was alone in the world. He had for six years devoted himself almost entirely to his studies, as a result of which, understandably, he had found himself without time for a social life and the company of young women. Therefore he thought it the better part of trial and error—of embarrassing fumbling—to call in an experienced person to advise him on these matters. He remarked in passing that the function of the marriage broker was ancient and honorable, highly approved in the Jewish community, because it made practical the necessary without hindering joy. Moreover, his own parents had been brought together by a matchmaker. They had made, if not a financially profitable marriage—since neither had possessed any worldly goods to speak of—at least a successful one in the sense of their everlasting devotion to each other. Salzman listened in embarrassed surprise, sensing a sort of apology. Later, however, he experienced a glow of pride in his work, an emotion that had left him years ago, and he heartily approved of Finkle.

The two went to their business. Leo had led Salzman to the only clear place in the room, a table near a window that overlooked the lamp-lit city. He seated himself at the matchmaker's side but facing him, attempting by an act of will to suppress the unpleasant tickle in his throat. Salzman eagerly unstrapped his portfolio and removed a loose rubber band from a thin packet of much-handled cards. As he flipped through them, a gesture and sound that physically hurt Leo, the student pretended not to see and gazed steadfastly out the window. Although it was still February, winter was on its last legs, signs of which he had for the first time in years begun to notice. He now observed the round white moon, moving

---

1. *Yeshivah* (yə shē′ və) *University* in New York City, originally a seminary for rabbis, today offers both theological and secular courses.
2. The Yiddish-language newspaper the *Jewish Daily Forward* was published daily in New York.

2 Life in the City *Which details in the first paragraph tell you something about Jewish life in New York City?*

3 Analyze Characterization *Why does the author include these details about Salzman?*

Vocabulary

meager (mē′ gər) *adj.* deficient in quantity or completeness

amiable (ā′ mē ə bəl) *adj.* friendly

animated (an′ ə mā′ tid) *adj.* full of life; active; lively

BERNARD MALAMUD **945**

Teach

Big Idea   **2**

Life in the City Answer: *Details include Yeshivah University and the* Forward *newspaper.*

Reading Strategy   **3**

Analyze Characterization
Answer: *The details reveal that although Salzman is amiable, he is deeply sad.*

(APPROACHING) **Ask:** What other details in this paragraph support the characterization of Salzman as sad? *(His eyes have a "depth of sadness.")* Remind students that Malamud is known for his striking contrasts. Point out the contrast between the job of matchmaker, which would seem to be a happy profession, and the descriptions of Salzman as deeply sad.

Writer's Technique ☆
Symbolism Malamud uses two symbols in the last sentence that starts on this page. First, the moon has long symbolized love, which fits with Finkle's search for love. In addition, the reference to a hen laying an egg suggests an image of birth, perhaps foreshadowing Finkle's hope to have children with a future wife.

Teach

Reading Strategy   1

Analyze Characterization
Answer: *The details reveal that Finkle is educated, scholarly, and sensitive and that Salzman admires these qualities.*

(ENGLISH LEARNERS) **Ask:** What word choices let you know that Salzman's reaction is one of admiration? *(Salzman notes "with pleasure" Finkle's face and lets out a "soft, contented sigh" in reaction to all he sees.)* Point out to English learners that once again Malamud uses contrasts to paint his picture. By contrasting Salzman's pleasure with a rather harsh description of Finkle, Malamud makes Salzman's reaction all that more noticeable. The contrast also provides an edge of humor to the passage.

View the Art ★

The Torah consists of the first five books of the Hebrew Bible. Scrolls of parchment containing the Torah are held together by a binder such as this one. The image at the far left of the binder is a *chuppah*—a wedding canopy used in traditional Jewish weddings to symbolize the building of a home.

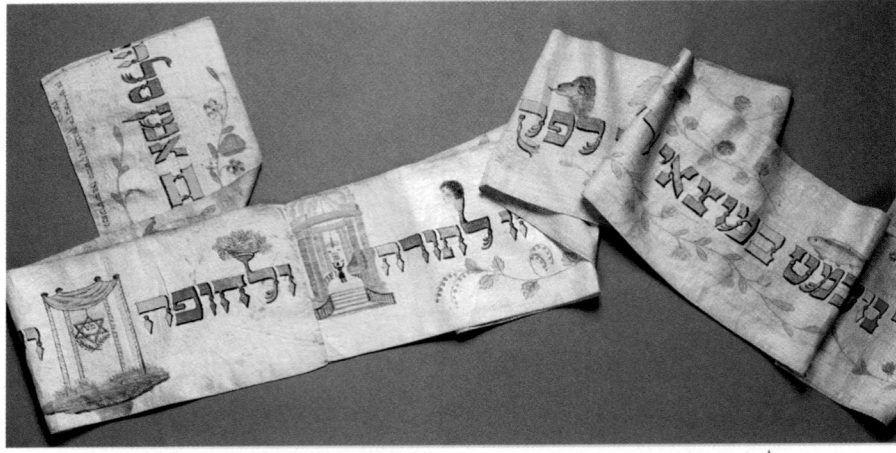

Torah Binder, 1848. Shimshon Kurzman. Ink and watercolor on cotton. The Jewish Museum, NY. ★

high in the sky through a cloud menagerie,[3] and watched with half-open mouth as it penetrated a huge hen, and dropped out of her like an egg laying itself. Salzman, though pretending through eyeglasses he had just slipped on, to be engaged in scanning the writing on the cards, stole occasional glances at the young man's distinguished face, noting with pleasure the long, severe scholar's nose, brown eyes heavy with learning, sensitive yet ascetic[4] lips, and a certain, almost hollow quality of the dark cheeks. He gazed around at shelves upon shelves of books and let out a soft, contented sigh.

When Leo's eyes fell upon the cards, he counted six spread out in Salzman's hand.

"So few?" he asked in disappointment.

"You wouldn't believe me how much cards I got in my office," Salzman replied. "The drawers are already filled to the top, so I keep them now in a barrel, but is every girl good for a new rabbi?"

Leo blushed at this, regretting all he had revealed of himself in a curriculum vitae[5] he had sent to Salzman. He had thought it best to acquaint him with his strict standards and specifications, but in having done so, felt he had told the marriage broker more than was absolutely necessary.

He hesitantly inquired, "Do you keep photographs of your clients on file?"

"First comes family, amount of dowry,[6] also what kind promises," Salzman replied, unbuttoning his tight coat and settling himself in the chair. "After comes pictures, rabbi."

"Call me Mr. Finkle. I'm not yet a rabbi."

Salzman said he would, but instead called him doctor, which he changed to rabbi when Leo was not listening too attentively.

Salzman adjusted his horn-rimmed spectacles, gently cleared his throat and read in an eager voice the contents of the top card:

"Sophie P. Twenty-four years. Widow one year. No children. Educated high school and

---

3. A *menagerie* (mi naj′ ər ē) is a collection of wild or unusual animals.
4. Here, *ascetic* means "severe" or "stern."

5. A *curriculum vitae* (kə ri′ kyə ləm   vē′ tī) is a summary of a person's education and work experience, usually given to a prospective employer. Finkle has provided Salzman with a summary of the "highlights" of his life.
6. A *dowry* is money or property a woman brings to her husband at the time of marriage.

1 Analyze Characterization *What do these details reveal about Finkle and Salzman?*

Reading Practice

Dialect Explain that Malamud is well known for his use of dialect, especially that spoken in New York City. Explain that dialect establishes setting and gives clues to character. Discuss the characteristics of the dialect in this story, including the use of sentence fragments, the introduc-tion of clauses with time references, and the lack of prepositions. Have students identify examples of dialect on pages 946 and 947. Discuss what the dialect tells about the characters.

two years college. Father promises eight thousand dollars. Has wonderful wholesale business. Also real estate. On the mother's side comes teachers, also one actor. Well known on Second Avenue."

Leo gazed up in surprise. "Did you say a widow?"

"A widow don't mean spoiled, rabbi. She lived with her husband maybe four months. He was a sick boy she made a mistake to marry him."

"Marrying a widow has never entered my mind."

"This is because you have no experience. A widow, especially if she is young and healthy like this girl, is a wonderful person to marry. She will be thankful to you the rest of her life. Believe me, if I was looking now for a bride, I would marry a widow."

Leo reflected, then shook his head.

Salzman hunched his shoulders in an almost imperceptible gesture of disappointment. He placed the card down on the wooden table and began to read another:

"Lily H. High school teacher. Regular. Not a substitute. Has savings and new Dodge car. Lived in Paris one year. Father is successful dentist thirty-five years. Interested in professional man. Well Americanized family. Wonderful opportunity."

"I knew her personally," said Salzman. "I wish you could see this girl. She is a doll. Also very intelligent. All day you could talk to her about books and theyater[7] and what not. She also knows current events."

"I don't believe you mentioned her age?"

---

7. *Theyater* is the way Salzman is pronouncing the word *theater*.

2 Life in the City *What information about New York City can you infer from this passage?*

3 Analyze Characterization *What qualities does Salzman consider important in a wife?*

4 Dialect *How does the use of dialect in this passage contribute to the characterization of Salzman?*

"Her age?" Salzman said, raising his brows. "Her age is thirty-two years."

Leo said after a while, "I'm afraid that seems a little too old."

Salzman let out a laugh. "So how old are you, rabbi?"

"Twenty-seven."

"So what is the difference, tell me, between twenty-seven and thirty-two? My own wife is seven years older than me. So what did I suffer?—Nothing. If Rothschild's[8] daughter wants to marry you, would you say on account her age, no?"

"Yes," Leo said dryly.

Salzman shook off the no in the yes. "Five years don't mean a thing. I give you my word that when you will live with her for one week you will forget her age. What does it mean five years—that she lived more and knows more than somebody who is younger? On this girl, God bless her, years are not wasted. Each one that it comes makes better the bargain."

"What subject does she teach in high school?"

"Languages. If you heard the way she speaks French, you will think it is music. I am in the business twenty-five years, and I recommend her with my whole heart. Believe me, I know what I'm talking, rabbi."

"What's on the next card?" Leo said abruptly.

Salzman reluctantly turned up the third card:

"Ruth K. Nineteen years. Honor student. Father offers thirteen thousand cash to the right bridegroom. He is a medical doctor. Stomach specialist with marvelous practice. Brother-in-law owns own garment business. Particular people."

Salzman looked as if he had read his trump card.

"Did you say nineteen?" Leo asked with interest.

"On the dot."

"Is she attractive?" He blushed. "Pretty?"

Salzman kissed his finger tips. "A little doll. On this I give you my word. Let me call the

---

8. The *Rothschilds* were a prominent, wealthy Jewish family.

BERNARD MALAMUD **947**

Teach

Big Idea   2

Life in the City **Answer:** *New York was a center of culture, including theater.*

Reading Strategy   3

Analyze Characterization
Answer: *Salzman thinks that a wife should be educated, employed, and financially secure.*

APPROACHING Tell students that to determine what qualities Salzman considers important, they should look not only for the qualities he lists but also for what he leaves out. For example, Salzman mentions the educational background of every girl but he leaves out her age until Finkle asks for it.

Literary Element   4

Dialect **Answer:** *Salzman is eager to find a match for Finkle, so he describes Lily almost the way a salesman would talk up an item that he or she wanted very much to sell.*

 For additional literary element practice, see Unit 6 Teaching Resources Book, p. 125.

Literary History ☆

Yiddish Salzman's inverted sentences and use of questions as a rhetorical device reflect the influence of Yiddish. Once the prevailing language of Eastern European Jews, Yiddish is a blend of several languages, including German and Hebrew. Some Yiddish words have been adopted by English speakers, including *bagel*, *chutzpah*, and *klutz*.

Teach

Literary Element | 1

Dialect Answer: *"Of course, she is a little lame in her right foot because of an auto accident that occurred when she was 12 years old, but nobody notices because she is so brilliant and beautiful."*

Reading Strategy | 2

Analyze Characterization
Answer: *Although the earlier description alluded to Salzman's age and frailty, it emphasized positive qualities. This description is more negative, though Salzman is still said to be smiling.*

ENGLISH LEARNERS Tell students to pay attention to the connotation of the words in the description to help them get a better feel for the character. **Ask:** Which adjectives in the sentence "His face was gray . . ." have negative connotations? *(gray, meager, hungry)*.

father tonight and you will see what means pretty."

But Leo was troubled. "You're sure she's that young?"

"This I am positive. The father will show you the birth certificate."

"Are you positive there isn't something wrong with her?" Leo insisted.

"Who says there is wrong?"

"I don't understand why an American girl her age should go to a marriage broker."

A smile spread over Salzman's face.

"So for the same reason you went, she comes."

Leo flushed. "I am pressed for time."

Salzman, realizing he had been tactless, quickly explained. "The father came, not her. He wants she should have the best, so he looks around himself. When we will locate the right boy he will introduce him and encourage. This makes a better marriage than if a young girl without experience takes for herself. I don't have to tell you this."

"But don't you think this young girl believes in love?" Leo spoke uneasily.

Salzman was about to guffaw but caught himself and said soberly, "Love comes with the right person, not before."

Leo parted dry lips but did not speak. Noticing that Salzman had snatched a glance at the next card, he cleverly asked, "How is her health?"

"Perfect," Salzman said, breathing with difficulty. "Of course, she is a little lame on her right foot from an auto accident that it happened to her when she was twelve years, but nobody notices on account she is so brilliant and also beautiful."

Leo got up heavily and went to the window. He felt curiously bitter and upbraided himself for having called in the marriage broker. Finally, he shook his head.

"Why not?" Salzman persisted, the pitch of his voice rising.

"Because I detest stomach specialists."

"So what do you care what is his business? After you marry her do you need him? Who says he must come every Friday night in your house?"

Ashamed of the way the talk was going, Leo dismissed Salzman, who went home with heavy, melancholy eyes.

Though he had felt only relief at the marriage broker's departure, Leo was in low spirits the next day. He explained it as arising from Salzman's failure to produce a suitable bride for him. He did not care for his type of clientele. But when Leo found himself hesitating whether to seek out another matchmaker, one more polished than Pinye, he wondered if it could be—his protestations to the contrary, and although he honored his father and mother—that he did not, in essence, care for the match making institution? This thought he quickly put out of mind yet found himself still upset. All day he ran around in the woods[9]— missed an important appointment, forgot to give out his laundry, walked out of a Broadway cafeteria without paying and had to run back with the ticket in his hand; had even not recognized his landlady in the street when she passed with a friend and courteously called out, "A good evening to you, Doctor Finkle." By nightfall, however, he had regained sufficient calm to sink his nose into a book and there found peace from his thoughts.

Almost at once there came a knock on the door. Before Leo could say enter, Salzman, commercial cupid, was standing in the room. His face was gray and meager, his expression hungry, and he looked as if he would expire on his feet. Yet the marriage broker managed, by some trick of the muscles, to display a broad smile.

"So good evening. I am invited?"

Leo nodded, disturbed to see him again, yet unwilling to ask the man to leave.

---

9. [*ran . . . woods*] Here, this phrase means that Finkle was nervous and distracted.

---

1 **Dialect** *How would this passage be written in Standard English?*

Analyze Characterization *How does this description of Salzman differ from the description of him when he first entered Finkle's home?* **2**

Writing Practice

Journal Recall with students that Finkle must decide which, if any, of the proposed brides to meet. Instruct students to imagine that they are Finkle and to write a brief journal entry exploring his feelings about one of the potential candidates. Tell students to use Finkle's reactions in the story to help guide them in expressing his thoughts. Tell students to use details from the story about the candidates. Have students share their finished journal entries with the class.

Beaming still, Salzman laid his portfolio on the table. "Rabbi, I got for you tonight good news."

"I've asked you not to call me rabbi. I'm still a student."

"Your worries are finished. I have for you a first-class bride."

"Leave me in peace concerning this subject." Leo pretended lack of interest.

"The world will dance at your wedding."

"Please, Mr. Salzman, no more."

"But first must come back my strength," Salzman said weakly. He fumbled with the portfolio straps and took out of the leather case an oily paper bag, from which he extracted a hard, seeded roll and a small, smoked white fish. With a quick motion of his hand he stripped the fish out of its skin and began ravenously to chew. "All day in a rush," he muttered.

Leo watched him eat.

"A sliced tomato you have maybe?" Salzman hesitantly inquired.

"No."

The marriage broker shut his eyes and ate. When he had finished he carefully cleaned up the crumbs and rolled up the remains of the fish, in the paper bag. His spectacled eyes roamed the room until he discovered, amid some piles of books, a one-burner gas stove. Lifting his hat he humbly asked, "A glass tea you got, rabbi?"

Conscience-stricken, Leo rose and brewed the tea. He served it with a chunk of lemon and two cubes of lump sugar, delighting Salzman.

After he had drunk his tea, Salzman's strength and good spirits were restored.

"So tell me, rabbi," he said amiably, "you considered some more the three clients I mentioned yesterday?"

"There was no need to consider."

"Why not?"

"None of them suits me."

[3]

[4] Dialect *What inversion does Salzman make?*

Portrait of Miss Stryker (Portrait of an Aristocrat). Ella Condie Lamb. Pastels on paper, 26½ x 22⅝ in. Collection of The Newark Museum, NJ. Gift of Charles Rollinson Lamb, 1942. IN:42.133. ★

"What then suits you?"

Leo let it pass because he could give only a confused answer.

Without waiting for a reply, Salzman asked, "You remember this girl I talked to you—the high school teacher?"

"Age thirty-two?"

But, surprisingly, Salzman's face lit in a smile. "Age twenty-nine."

Leo shot him a look. "Reduced from thirty-two?"

[5]

"A mistake," Salzman avowed. "I talked today with the dentist. He took me to his safety deposit box and showed me the birth certificate. She was twenty-nine years last August. They made her a party in the mountains where she went for her vacation. When her father spoke to me the first time I forgot to write the age and I told you thirty-two, but now I remember this was a different client, a widow."

BERNARD MALAMUD **949**

Teach

Reading Strategy | 1

Predict The narrator says that Salzman thinks he and Leo are close to reaching an agreement. **Ask:** What do you predict will come of the meeting between Finkle and Lily Hirschorn? *(It will not go well, because Leo feels tricked into it rather than genuinely eager.)*

(APPROACHING) Point out that Malamud's word choice provides clues to help students predict what will happen next. Although he is amused, Leo feels "entangled." Malamud lets readers know that Leo feels annoyed and entrapped before he has even met Lily.

Big Idea | 2

Life in the City **Answer:** *Details include the reference to Riverside Drive and the description of Finkle's formal clothing.*

Reading Strategy | 3

Analyze Characterization **Answer:** *Finkle's awareness of Salzman's role, not just in getting him together with Lily, but in skewing their responses to each other, has colored the entire experience for him, making it seem artificial and uncomfortable.*

Vocabulary Practice

Word Roots Explain that a word family is a group of words containing the same root. By identifying an unfamiliar word's root, students can often guess the word's meaning. Point out that the root of *enamored,* which appears on page 951, is the Latin word *amor,* meaning "love." Have students brainstorm a list of words with the same root. Then have them check a dictionary to see whether the words belong to the same word family.

Create a master list on the board from the students' lists and have students copy the master list into their notebooks.

"The same one you told me about? I thought she was twenty-four?"

"A different. Am I responsible that the world is filled with widows?"

"No, but I'm not interested in them, nor for that matter, in school teachers."

Salzman pulled his clasped hands to his breast. Looking at the ceiling he devoutly exclaimed, "Yiddishe kinder,[10] what can I say to somebody that he is not interested in high school teachers? So what then you are interested?"

Leo flushed but controlled himself.

"In what else will you be interested," Salzman went on, "if you not interested in this fine girl that she speaks four languages and has personally in the bank ten thousand dollars? Also her father guarantees further twelve thousand. Also she has new car, wonderful clothes, talks on all subjects, and she will give you a first-class home and children. How near do we come in our life to paradise?"

"If she's so wonderful, why wasn't she married ten years ago?"

"Why?" said Salzman with a heavy laugh. "—Why? Because she is *partikiler*.[11] This is why. She wants the *best*."

Leo went silent, amused at how he had entangled himself. But Salzman had aroused his interest in Lily H., and he began seriously to consider calling on her. When the marriage broker observed how intently Leo's mind was at work on the facts he had supplied, he felt certain they would soon come to an agreement.

Late Saturday afternoon, conscious of Salzman, Leo Finkle walked with Lily Hirschorn along Riverside Drive.[12] He walked briskly and erectly, wearing with distinction the black fedora[13] he had that morning taken with trepidation out of the dusty hat box on his closet shelf, and the heavy black Saturday coat he had thoroughly whisked clean. Leo also owned a walking stick, a present from a distant relative, but quickly put temptation aside and did not use it. Lily, petite and not unpretty, had on something signifying the approach of spring. She was au courant[14] animatedly, with all sorts of subjects, and he weighed her words and found her surprisingly sound—score another for Salzman, who he uneasily sensed to be somewhere around, hiding perhaps high in a tree along the street, flashing the lady signals with a pocket mirror; or perhaps a cloven-hoofed Pan, piping nuptial ditties as he danced his invisible way before them, strewing wild buds on the walk and purple grapes in their path, symbolizing fruit of a union, though there was of course still none.

Lily startled Leo by remarking, "I was thinking of Mr. Salzman, a curious figure, wouldn't you say?"

Not certain what to answer, he nodded.

She bravely went on, blushing, "I for one am grateful for his introducing us. Aren't you?"

He courteously replied, "I am."

"I mean," she said with a little laugh—and it was all in good taste, or at least gave the effect

Visual Vocabulary
In Greek mythology, *Pan* was a god of pastures, flocks, and shepherds who was believed to foster reproduction and growth. He was traditionally depicted as a musician who was part man and part goat.

---

10. *Yiddishe kinder* (yid′ ish ə kint′ ər) means "Jewish children" or "Jewish young people."
11. *Partikiler* is the way Salzman is pronouncing the word *particular.*
12. *Riverside Drive,* a major road on the west side of Manhattan, runs beside the Hudson River.

13. A *fedora* (fi dôr′ ə) is a soft felt hat with a curved brim and a lengthwise crease in the crown.
14. The French words *au courant* (ō kōō rän′) literally mean "in the current" but are most often used to mean "fully informed" or "up-to-date."

---

2 Life in the City Which details depict a stroll in New York City rather than in the country?

Analyze Characterization What does this passage reveal about Finkle's state of mind? **3** of being not in bad—"do you mind that we came together so?"

He was not displeased with her honesty, recognizing that she meant to set the relationship aright, and understanding that it took a certain amount of experience in life, and courage, to want to do it quite that way. One had to have some sort of past to make that kind of beginning.

He said that he did not mind. Salzman's function was traditional and honorable—valuable for what it might achieve, which, he pointed out, was frequently nothing.

Lily agreed with a sigh. They walked on for a while and she said after a long silence, again with a nervous laugh, "Would you mind if I asked you something a little bit personal? Frankly, I find the subject fascinating." Although Leo shrugged, she went on half embarrassedly, "How was it that you came to your calling? I mean was it a sudden passionate inspiration?"

Leo, after a time, slowly replied, "I was always interested in the Law."

"You saw revealed in it the presence of the Highest?"

He nodded and changed the subject. "I understand that you spent a little time in Paris, Miss Hirschorn?"

"Oh, did Mr. Salzman tell you, Rabbi Finkle?" Leo winced but she went on, "It was ages ago and almost forgotten. I remember I had to return for my sister's wedding."

And Lily would not be put off. "When," she asked in a trembly voice, "did you become **enamored** of God?"

He stared at her. Then it came to him that she was talking not about Leo Finkle, but of a total stranger, some mystical figure, perhaps even passionate prophet that Salzman had dreamed up for her—no relation to the living or dead. Leo trembled with rage and weakness. The trickster had obviously sold her a bill of goods, just as he had him, who'd expected to become acquainted with a young lady of twenty-nine, only to behold, the moment he laid eyes upon her strained and anxious face, a woman past thirty-five and aging rapidly. Only his self control had kept him this long in her presence.

"I am not," he said gravely, "a talented religious person," and in seeking words to go on, found himself possessed by shame and fear. "I think," he said in a strained manner, "that I came to God not because I loved Him, but because I did not."

This confession he spoke harshly because its unexpectedness shook him.

Lily wilted. Leo saw a profusion of loaves of bread go flying like ducks high over his head, not unlike the winged loaves by which he had counted himself to sleep last night. Mercifully, then, it snowed, which he would not put past Salzman's machinations.

He was infuriated with the marriage broker and swore he would throw him out of the room the minute he reappeared. But Salzman did not come that night, and when Leo's anger had subsided,[15] an unaccountable despair grew in its place. At first he thought this was caused by his disappointment in Lily, but before long it became evident that he had involved himself with Salzman without a true knowledge of his own intent. He gradually realized—with an emptiness that seized him with six hands—that he had called in the broker to find him a bride because he was incapable of doing it himself. This terrifying insight he had derived as a result of his meeting and conversation with Lily Hirschorn. Her probing questions had somehow irritated him into revealing—to himself more than her—the true nature of his relationship to God, and from that it had come upon him, with shocking force, that apart from his parents, he

---

 4

Dialect *How could you rephrase this sentence using a standard grammatical form?*

Vocabulary

enamored (en am′ ərd) *adj.* inspired with love; charmed; captivated

---

15. *Subsided* means "decreased in intensity."

Analyze Characterization *What does this confession reveal about Finkle?* **5**

Teach

Approaching Level

DIFFERENTIATED INSTRUCTION

Emerging Help students analyze the events that lead to Finkle's revelation in the sentence bridging pages 951 and 952. **Say:** As a result of his talk with Lily, Finkle has a major revelation. **Ask:** What does he realize? (*He is unloved and loveless.*) **Ask:** How does this affect him? (*He has the worst week of his life. He stops eating, going to classes, and reading, and grows ragged.*)

Established Help students relate to the impact of Finkle's revelation by having them write a brief description of a moment of realization in their own lives. Tell students that the moment does not have to be as dramatic as Finkle's but should have had an emotional impact on them. Tell students to include descriptions of what occurred and how it affected them.

Teach

Reading Strategy | 1

Analyze Characterization
Answer: *It suggests that Salzman is more tired, decrepit, and depressed than he appeared before.*
Ask: What might explain the change in Salzman since the story began? (*Perhaps he feels himself a failure at his job.*)

Cultural History ☆

History of the Jews Finkle's comment that Jews suffer is a reference to the history of the Jewish people. Nearly always a minority in the lands where they have lived, Jews have often been persecuted. The most infamous example in modern history is the Holocaust, the Nazis' murder of 6 million Jews in Europe.

---

had never loved anyone. Or perhaps it went the other way, that he did not love God so well as he might, because he had not loved man. It seemed to Leo that his whole life stood starkly revealed and he saw himself for the first time as he truly was—unloved and loveless. This bitter but somehow not fully unexpected revelation brought him to a point of panic, controlled only by extraordinary effort. He covered his face with his hands and cried.

The week that followed was the worst of his life. He did not eat and lost weight. His beard darkened and grew ragged. He stopped attending seminars and almost never opened a book. He seriously considered leaving the Yeshivah, although he was deeply troubled at the thought of the loss of all his years of study—saw them like pages torn from a book, strewn over the city—and at the devastating effect of this decision upon his parents. But he had lived without knowledge of himself, and never in the Five Books and all the Commentaries[16]—mea culpa[17]—had the truth been revealed to him. He did not know where to turn, and in all this desolating loneliness there was no *to whom*, although he often thought of Lily but not once could bring himself to go downstairs and make the call. He became touchy and irritable, especially with his landlady, who asked him all manner of personal questions; on the other hand, sensing his own disagreeableness, he waylaid her on the stairs and apologized **abjectly**, until mortified, she ran from him. Out of this, however, he drew the consolation that ☆ he was a Jew and that a Jew suffered. But gradually, as the long and terrible week drew to a

---

16. *The Pentateuch* (pen′ tə took′), or first *Five Books* of the Hebrew Bible (Genesis, Exodus, Leviticus, Numbers, and Deuteronomy), are known collectively in Judaism as the Torah, or the Law. *Commentaries* provide explanatory and scholarly information about the biblical texts.
17. *Mea culpa* (mā′ ə kool′ pə) means "my own fault" in Latin.

Vocabulary

abjectly (ab′ jekt lē) *adv.* in a humiliating, mean, or degrading manner

---

---

close, he regained his composure and some idea of purpose in life: to go on as planned. Although he was imperfect, the ideal was not. As for his quest of a bride, the thought of continuing afflicted him with anxiety and heartburn, yet perhaps with this new knowledge of himself he would be more successful than in the past. Perhaps love would now come to him and a bride to that love. And for this sanctified seeking who needed a Salzman?

The marriage broker, a skeleton with haunted eyes, returned that very night. He looked, withal, the picture of frustrated expectancy—as if he had steadfastly waited the week at Miss Lily Hirschorn's side for a telephone call that never came.

Casually coughing, Salzman came immediately to the point: "So how did you like her?"

Leo's anger rose and he could not refrain from chiding the matchmaker: "Why did you lie to me, Salzman?"

Salzman's pale face went dead white, the world had snowed on him.

"Did you not state that she was twenty-nine?" Leo insisted.

"I give you my word—"

"She was thirty-five, if a day. At *least* thirty-five."

"Of this don't be too sure. Her father told me—"

"Never mind. The worst of it was that you lied to her."

"How did I lie to her, tell me?"

"You told her things about me that weren't true. You made me out to be more, consequently less than I am. She had in mind a totally different person, a sort of semi-mystical Wonder Rabbi."

"All I said, you was a religious man."

"I can imagine."

Salzman sighed. "This is my weakness that I have," he confessed. "My wife says to me I shouldn't be a salesman, but when I have two

---

Analyze Characterization *What does this third description of Salzman suggest about him?* **1**

Writing Practice

SPIRAL REVIEW **Definition** Point out that although we use the word *love* frequently, its meaning is often imprecise. People may "love" Chinese food, a friend's new car, their parents, or a spouse. Each of these uses has a different shade of meaning. Have students write extended definitions of *love* that include important kinds of love while excluding notions of mere preference. Invite volunteers to share and discuss their definitions in the context of the views that Finkle and Salzman convey in "The Magic Barrel."

fine people that they would be wonderful to be married, I am so happy that I talk too much." He smiled wanly.[18] "This is why Salzman is a poor man."

Leo's anger left him. "Well, Salzman, I'm afraid that's all."

The marriage broker fastened hungry eyes on him.

"You don't want any more a bride?"

"I do," said Leo, "but I have decided to seek her in a different way. I am no longer interested in an arranged marriage. To be frank, I now admit the necessity of premarital love. That is, I want to be in love with the one I marry."

"Love?" said Salzman, astounded. After a moment he remarked, "For us, our love is our life, not for the ladies. In the ghetto they—"

"I know, I know," said Leo. "I've thought of it often. Love, I have said to myself, should be a by-product of living and worship rather than its own end. Yet for myself I find it necessary to establish the level of my need and fulfill it."

Salzman shrugged but answered, "Listen, rabbi, if you want love, this I can find for you also. I have such beautiful clients that you will love them the minute your eyes will see them."

Leo smiled unhappily. "I'm afraid you don't understand."

But Salzman hastily unstrapped his portfolio and withdrew a manila packet from it.

"Pictures," he said, quickly laying the envelope on the table.

Leo called after him to take the pictures away, but as if on the wings of the wind, Salzman had disappeared.

> *Perhaps love would now come to him and a bride to that love.*

March came. Leo had returned to his regular routine. Although he felt not quite himself yet—lacked energy—he was making plans for a more active social life. Of course it would cost something, but he was an expert in cutting corners; and when there were no corners left he would make circles rounder. All the while Salzman's pictures had lain on the table, gathering dust. Occasionally as Leo sat studying, or enjoying a cup of tea, his eyes fell on the manila envelope, but he never opened it.

The days went by and no social life to speak of developed with a member of the opposite sex—it was difficult, given the circumstances of his situation. One morning Leo toiled up the stairs to his room and stared out the window at the city. Although the day was bright his view of it was dark. For some time he watched the people in the street below hurrying along and then turned with a heavy heart to his little room. On the table was the packet. With a sudden relentless gesture he tore it open. For a half-hour he stood by the table in a state of excitement, examining the photographs of the ladies Salzman had included. Finally, with a deep sigh he put them down. There were six, of varying degrees of attractiveness, but look at them long enough and they all became Lily Hirschorn: all past their prime, all starved behind bright smiles, not a true personality in the lot. Life, despite their frantic yoohooings, had passed them by; they were pictures in a brief case that stank of fish. After a while, however, as Leo attempted to return the photographs into the envelope, he found in it another, a snapshot of the type taken by a machine for a quarter. He gazed at it a moment and let out a cry.

---

18. Here, *wanly* means "sadly" or "in a dejected way."

2 Analyze Characterization *Why does Finkle reach this conclusion?*

3 Life in the City *How do the descriptions of city life here enhance the tone?*

BERNARD MALAMUD **953**

Teach

Reading Strategy | 2

Analyze Characterization
Answer: *Finkle believes that he needs to fall in love with a woman before courting her as his prospective bride.*

Big Idea | 3

Life in the City **Answer:** *The image of the bustling city outside his window emphasizes Finkle's sense of loneliness.*

[APPROACHING] Point out that Malamud uses visual imagery to achieve the effect of a lonely tone. **Ask:** What visual images does Malamud provide? *(He contrasts the bright day with Finkle's dark view. He uses the image of Finkle alone, inside, separated from the outside, busy world.)*

Teach

Reading Strategy | 1

Analyze Characterization

Answer: *Finkle has fallen in love with a young woman after looking at a snapshot of her. His first reaction is desire; this is followed by dread. Finkle is experiencing love for the first time, and it overpowers him. He senses that it is not without cost.*

ENGLISH LEARNERS Have students explain the sequence of his thoughts in their own words, up to his decision to find the girl. *(The photo of the girl moves Finkle; he feels as though he has met her before, though he has not; he feels a connection to her and desires her; he feels fear; he tries to calm himself with tea; he goes back to looking at the photo excitedly and decides to see Salzman to meet the girl.)*

Big Idea | 2

Life in the City **Answer:**
References to the subway stations and the subway ride in the Bronx set the scene in New York City.

View the Art ★

Moses Soyer (1899–1974) came to America from his native Russia in 1912, along with his two brothers. All three brothers were painters and focused on portraying people and scenes in their adopted city of New York. At least one Jewish scholar suggests that *The Lover of Books* may be a portrayal of Soyer's father, a Hebrew scholar.

Her face deeply moved him. Why, he could at first not say. It gave him the impression of youth—spring flowers, yet age—a sense of having been used to the bone, wasted; this came from the eyes, which were hauntingly familiar, yet absolutely strange. He had a vivid impression that he had met her before, but try as he might he could not place her although he could almost recall her name, as if he had read it in her own handwriting. No, this couldn't be; he would have remembered her. It was not, he affirmed, that she had an extraordinary beauty—no, though her face was attractive enough; it was that *something* about her moved him. Feature for feature, even some of the ladies of the photographs could do better; but she leaped forth to his heart—had *lived*, or wanted to—more than just wanted, perhaps regretted how she had lived—had somehow deeply suffered: it could be seen in the depths of those reluctant eyes, and from the way the light enclosed and shone from her, and within her, opening realms of possibility: this was her own. Her he desired. His head ached and eyes narrowed with the intensity of his gazing, then as if an obscure fog had blown up in the mind, he experienced fear of her and was aware that he had received an impression, somehow, of evil. He shuddered, saying softly, it is thus with us all. Leo brewed some tea in a small pot and sat sipping it without sugar, to calm himself. But before he had finished drinking, again with excitement he examined the face and found it good: good for Leo Finkle. Only such a one could understand him and help him seek whatever he was seeking. She might, perhaps, love him. How she had happened to be among the discards in Salzman's barrel he could never guess, but he knew he must urgently go find her.

Leo rushed downstairs, grabbed up the Bronx[19] telephone book, and searched for Salzman's home address. He was not listed, nor was his office. Neither was he in the Manhattan book. But Leo remembered having written down the address on a slip of paper after he had read Salzman's advertisement in the "personals" column of the *Forward*. He ran up to his room and tore through his papers, without luck. It was exasperating. Just when he needed the matchmaker he was nowhere to be found. Fortunately Leo remembered to look in his wallet. There on a card he found his name written and a Bronx address. No phone number was listed, the reason—Leo now recalled—he had originally communicated with Salzman by letter. He got on his coat, put a hat on over his skullcap and hurried to the subway station. All the way to the far end of the Bronx he sat on the edge of his seat. He was more than once tempted to take out the picture and see if the girl's face was as he remembered it, but he refrained, allowing the snapshot to remain in his inside coat pocket, content to have her so close. When the train pulled into the station he was waiting at the door and bolted out. He quickly located the street Salzman had advertised.

Visual Vocabulary
A *skullcap,* or yarmulke (yä′ mə kə), is a brimless cap worn by many Jewish men and boys, especially during religious services.

The building he sought was less than a block from the subway, but it was not an office building, nor even a loft, nor a store in which one could rent office space. It was a very old tenement[20] house. Leo found Salzman's name in pencil on a soiled tag under the bell and climbed three dark flights to his apartment. When he knocked, the door

---

19. *The Bronx* is one of five boroughs, or divisions, that make up New York City. Manhattan is another.

20. A *tenement* is an apartment building or rooming house that is built or maintained poorly and is often overcrowded.

 1 Analyze Characterization *Why is Finkle experiencing fear here?*

Life in the City *How do the descriptions here add to the development of the setting?* **2**

Reading Practice

Foreshadow Have students pause at the end of page 955. **Ask:** Why do you think Salzman is so distressed by the photograph? Explain that Malamud has given some clues that foreshadow the reason for Salzman's distress. Challenge students to reread pages 954 and 955 to identify these clues. *(Similarities to Salzman in the appearance of the woman in the photograph; Finkle's sense that he has met her before)* Ask students to predict the reason for Salzman's reaction to the photo.

was opened by a thin, asthmatic, gray-haired woman in felt slippers.

"Yes?" she said, expecting nothing. She listened without listening. He could have sworn he had seen her, too, before but knew it was an illusion.

"Salzman—does he live here? Pinye Salzman," he said, "the matchmaker?"

She stared at him a long minute. "Of course."

He felt embarrassed. "Is he in?"

"No." Her mouth, though left open, offered nothing more.

"The matter is urgent. Can you tell me where his office is?"

"In the air." She pointed upward.

"You mean he has no office?" Leo asked.

"In his socks."

He peered into the apartment. It was sunless and dingy, one large room divided by a half-open curtain, beyond which he could see a sagging metal bed. The near side of a room was crowded with rickety chairs, old bureaus, a three-legged table, racks of cooking utensils, and all the apparatus of a kitchen. But there was no sign of Salzman or his magic barrel, probably also a figment of the imagination. An odor of frying fish made Leo weak to the knees.

"Where is he?" he insisted. "I've got to see your husband."

At length she answered, "So who knows where he is? Every time he thinks a new thought he runs to a different place. Go home, he will find you."

"Tell him Leo Finkle."

She gave no sign she had heard.

He walked downstairs, depressed.

But Salzman, breathless, stood waiting at his door.

Leo was astounded and overjoyed. "How did you get here before me?"

"I rushed."

"Come inside."

They entered. Leo fixed tea, and a sardine sandwich for Salzman. As they were drinking he reached behind him for the packet of pictures and handed them to the marriage broker.

The Lover of Books, 1934. Moses Soyer. Oil on canvas, 42 x 23½ in. The Jewish Museum, New York.

Salzman put down his glass and said expectantly, "You found somebody you like?"

"Not among these."

The marriage broker turned away.

"Here is the one I want." Leo held forth the snapshot.

Salzman slipped on his glasses and took the picture into his trembling hand. He turned ghastly and let out a groan.

"What's the matter?" cried Leo.

"Excuse me. Was an accident this picture. She isn't for you."

BERNARD MALAMUD **955**

Teach

Literary Element | 3

Characterization Ask: What can you infer about the relationship between Salzman and his wife? *(His wife has lost confidence in Salzman's ability to make a good living.)*

Reading Strategy | 4

Compare and Contrast Have students recall the previous descriptions of Salzman. **Ask:** How is Salzman different now? *(In each succeeding description, Salzman seems weaker. At first, he was merely old and frail, then he was a skeleton, and now he is "ghastly.")*

APPROACHING **Ask:** How is Finkle different now from when he first met with Salzman? *(When he first met Salzman, Finkle was reluctant to deal with him. Now Finkle is eager, almost desperate to see Salzman.)*

English Learners

DIFFERENTIATED INSTRUCTION

Intermediate Explain that colloquial speech includes the informal speech that people use in everyday conversation. Point out and explain the following colloquial phrases. Clarify that some phrases reflect the specific dialect of Malamud's characters, whereas others are common English colloquialisms:

gave chase: followed after

forgetting himself: breaking rules of propriety because of emotion

a wild one: a person who cannot be controlled

SMALL GROUP

Advanced Have pairs of students come up with some examples of modern day English colloquialisms and their meanings. Then have students share their examples and meanings with the class.

955

Teach

Reading Strategy 1

Analyze Characterization
Answer: *Salzman's daughter values the material over the spiritual, in direct opposition to what Salzman believes.*

Reading Strategy 2

Compare and Contrast
Have students read and contrast the descriptions of Salzman and Finkle. *(Salzman has deteriorated "to the point of vanishing." Finkle has a new beard and wisdom in his eyes. He blossoms as Salzman fades.)*

Reading Strategy 3

Analyze Characterization
Answer: *This date takes place on a spring night, not on a late afternoon in winter. Stella, unlike Lily, is uneasy and shy. This time Finkle brings his date a bouquet of flowers.*

Cultural History ☆

Prayers for the Dead The Kaddish prayer is traditionally chanted by Jews who have lost a close relative. The prayer affirms the greatness of God, even in the face of personal tragedy.

To check students' understanding of the selection, see Unit 6 Teaching Resources Book, p. 130.

Salzman frantically shoved the manila packet into his portfolio. He thrust the snapshot into his pocket and fled down the stairs.

Leo, after momentary paralysis, gave chase and cornered the marriage broker in the vestibule.[21] The landlady made hysterical outcries but neither of them listened.

"Give me back the picture, Salzman."

"No." The pain in his eyes was terrible.

"Tell me who she is then."

"This I can't tell you. Excuse me."

He made to depart, but Leo, forgetting himself, seized the matchmaker by his tight coat and shook him frenziedly.

"Please," sighed Salzman. "*Please.*"

Leo ashamedly let him go. "Tell me who she is," he begged. "It's very important for me to know."

"She is not for you. She is a wild one—wild, without shame. This is not a bride for a rabbi."

"What do you mean wild?"

"Like an animal. Like a dog. For her to be poor was a sin. This is why to me she is dead now."

"In God's name, what do you mean?"

"Her I can't introduce to you," Salzman cried.

"Why are you so excited?"

"Why, he asks," Salzman said, bursting into tears. "This is my baby, my Stella, she should burn in hell." Leo hurried up to bed and hid under the covers. Under the covers he thought his life through. Although he soon fell asleep he could not sleep her out of his mind. He woke, beating his breast. Though he prayed to be rid of her, his prayers went unanswered. Through days of torment he endlessly struggled not to love her; fearing success, he escaped it. He then concluded to convert her to goodness, himself to God. The idea alternately nauseated and exalted him.

He perhaps did not know that he had come to a final decision until he encountered Salzman

in a Broadway cafeteria. He was sitting alone at a rear table, sucking the bony remains of a fish. The marriage broker appeared haggard, and transparent to the point of vanishing.

Salzman looked up at first without recognizing him. Leo had grown a pointed beard and his eyes were weighted with wisdom.

"Salzman," he said, "love has at last come to my heart."

"Who can love from a picture?" mocked the marriage broker.

"It is not impossible."

"If you can love her, then you can love anybody. Let me show you some new clients that they just sent me their photographs. One is a little doll."

"Just her I want," Leo murmured.

"Don't be a fool, doctor. Don't bother with her."

"Put me in touch with her, Salzman," Leo said humbly. "Perhaps I can be of service."

Salzman had stopped eating and Leo understood with emotion that it was now arranged.

Leaving the cafeteria, he was, however, afflicted by a tormenting suspicion that Salzman had planned it all to happen this way.

Leo was informed by letter that she would meet him on a certain corner, and she was there one spring night, waiting under a street lamp. He appeared, carrying a small bouquet of violets and rosebuds. Stella stood by the lamp post, smoking. She wore white with red shoes, which fitted his expectations, although in a troubled moment he had imagined the dress red, and only the shoes white. She waited uneasily and shyly. From afar he saw that her eyes—clearly her father's—were filled with desperate innocence. He pictured, in her, his own redemption. Violins and lit candles revolved in the sky. Leo ran forward with flowers outthrust.

Around the corner, Salzman, leaning against a wall, chanted prayers for the dead. ∾ ☆

---

21. A *vestibule* (ves' tə būl') is an entrance hall or lobby.

---

1 Analyze Characterization *Why does his daughter's wildness cause Salzman to reject her?*

2

3 Analyze Characterization *How is Finkle's date with Stella different from his previous date with Lily Hirschorn?*

Reading Practice

Ambiguous Ending The ending of this story is ambiguous. Have students generate a list of questions they have at the conclusion of the story, and write them on the board. Such questions might include: Will Finkle's idealistic perception of Stella change once he gets to know her? Will he "redeem" her—or will she drag him down? Does Salzman chant the prayers for the dead for his daughter or for the possible

loss of Finkle's spirituality? Discuss with the students how these ambiguities impact their reaction to, and understanding of, the story.

After You Read

Respond and Think Critically

Respond and Interpret

1. Were you surprised by the outcome of the story? Explain why or why not.

2. (a)Who are the first three women Salzman describes? (b)How does Finkle react to the description of each? (c)What does Finkle's attitude toward the women reveal about his personality?

3. (a)How does Finkle feel about Salzman at the end of the story? (b)Do you think Finkle's suspicion about Salzman at the end of the story is correct? Support your answer with evidence from the story.

Analyze and Evaluate

4. Why might Finkle have responded so strongly to the snapshot of Stella?

5. How does the setting of Salzman's apartment add to the author's characterization of the matchmaker? Explain with details from the selection.

6. How does Malamud use suspense to draw the reader into the story? Support your response.

Connect

7. **Big Idea** **Life in the City** How does the city environment shape and influence Finkle's life?

8. **Connect to the Author** How do you think Malamud's experiences with life's struggles contributed to his characters' view of their own lives?

Literary Element Dialect

In "The Magic Barrel," Salzman speaks in a **dialect** of English influenced by Yiddish grammar and syntax. For example, he says to Leo, "You don't want any more a bride?" In Standard English, this passage might read, "You don't want to get married anymore?"

1. Find three more examples of dialect in Salzman's speech in the story.

2. Notice that Salzman speaks in dialect but Finkle does not. What do these differences in speech tell you about these characters?

Review: Motivation

As you learned on page 295, **motivation** is the reason or cause for a character's actions. The cause may be internal (for example, a character's ambition, fear, or love) or external (for example, societal pressure or danger). Most characters are motivated by both internal and external factors.

Group Activity Meet with a small group to discuss the motivations of Leo Finkle in "The Magic Barrel." Create a chart like the one shown, and fill it in by identifying the motivation for each action listed.

LEO FINKLE

Motivation → Actions

1. calls in Salzman
2. rejects Salzman's three candidates
3. agrees to meet Lily Hirschorn
4. stops eating and attending seminars
5. falls in love with Stella's snapshot

BERNARD MALAMUD **957**

Literary Element

1. "This I am positive"; "So what then you are interested?"; "A sliced tomato you have maybe?"

2. They suggest that Saltzman probably immigrated to the United States and retains the dialect he grew up speaking, while Finkle is a native English speaker.

Review: Motivation

1. wants a wife but has no prospects

2. has strict standards for a wife

3. listens to Salzman's revised description of Lily Hirschorn

4. realizes he is unloved and loveless

5. sees signs of deep suffering in Stella's snapshot

After You Read

Assess

1. The ending is surprising, although foreshadowing provides some clues.

2. (a) Sophie, Lily, and Ruth (b) Finkle rejects them: Sophie is a widow, Lily is too old, Ruth is lame. (c) He is shallow and selfish; he seeks perfection.

3. (a) He suspects that Salzman planned for him to meet Stella. (b) His suspicion may be correct. It seems unlikely that such a photograph would be included by mistake, and Salzman may very well want to help his daughter. Perhaps Salzman believes that being married to a rabbi will redeem her.

4. He believes that only one who has suffered and knows both good and evil can truly understand and love him.

5. The setting shows Salzman to be poor, helping to explain his frail, haggard state.

6. He establishes Finkle's need for a wife; the reader then wants to know if he will find one.

7. Finkle finds a matchmaker and meets his daughter, who has been lured by the materialism of modern city life.

8. His view of life's suffering might have contributed to Finkle's and Salzman's attitude toward marriage. Both initially see it in practical terms, but Finkle's later attraction to Stella counters this view with optimism.

 For additional assessment, see Assessment Resources, pp. 251–252.

After You Read

Assess

Reading Strategy

1. Possible answers: (1) the second paragraph in page 945; (2) the dialogue on pages 946–947; (3) the first half of the first column on page 955

2. 1) through the character's appearance; (2) through the character's words; (3) through what another character—Salzman's wife—says about the character

Vocabulary

meager

Etymology: Middle English *megre* means "thin" (As a poor rabbinical student, Leo lived on *meager* means.)

amiable

Etymology: Latin *amicus* means "friend" (Though we'd fought the week before and hadn't spoken since, she was *amiable* with me at the party.)

animated

Etymology: Latin *animatus* means "filled with life" (The old man was *animated* and did not seem to be sick at all.)

enamored

Etymology: Latin *amare* means "to love" (Heathcliff was *enamored* with Cathy, but she was married to another man.)

abjectly

Etymology: Latin *abjicere* means "to cast off" (The Roman mob *abjectly* suffered under cruel emperors.)

Academic Vocabulary

Students should infer that here, *approach* means "the onset of."

958

Analyze Characterization

In "The Magic Barrel," Malamud primarily uses indirect **characterization**, which requires readers to interpret details and events and to reach conclusions based on the clues provided by the author.

1. Find three instances in which Malamud portrays Salzman's character.

2. Identify the method used to reveal character in each instance: for example, through the character's thoughts, words, actions, or appearance.

Vocabulary Practice

Practice with Word Origins Record information as shown for each vocabulary word from the selection. Use a dictionary for help.

meager   amiable   animated
enamored   abjectly

EXAMPLE:

Word: *compatible*
Definition: able to exist together in harmony
Etymology: Latin *compatibilis* means "together in suffering"
Sample sentence: Leo Finkle wanted to find a compatible spouse.

Academic Vocabulary

Leo Finkle feels that Salzman's **approach** *as a marriage broker is too pushy.*

Approach is an academic word. Two teachers may have a different **approach** to teaching. The word *approach* is also used to indicate an instance of drawing closer to something. Use context clues to infer the meaning of *approach*: *Nell recognized the* **approach** *of summer by its signs, like flowers in bloom.*

For more on academic vocabulary, see pages 53–54.

 Literature Online

Selection Resources For Selection Quizzes, eFlash-cards, and Reading-Writing Connection activities, go to glencoe.com and enter QuickPass code GLA9800u6.

958 UNIT 6   FROM DEPRESSION TO COLD WAR

 Speaking and Listening

Use these criteria when evaluating students' participation in the debate:

- Did the student effectively present evidence in support of his or her position?
- Did the student anticipate the opposing arguments and find evidence to refute them?
- Did the student listen carefully to the opposing arguments in the debate?

Speaking and Listening

Debate

Assignment Malamud ends this story without revealing Leo and Stella's fate. Divide into two teams. Conduct a debate on whether Malamud seems to imply that the couple's match will succeed or fail. Use examples from the text to support your argument.

Prepare Evidence—and how you use it—is key to a successful debate. Organize your arguments and evidence in a chart like the one below. First, list your major points and the evidence from the text that supports them. Then list your opponents' potential arguments and evidence to counter those claims.

My Position:

Arguments for my position	Evidence
Potential opposing arguments	Counter-evidence

Debate Use your chart to help you defend your points with specific examples. When your opponents present their side, listen carefully so you can challenge their arguments with counter-arguments and evidence in support of these counter-arguments. This will both weaken their position and strengthen your own.

Evaluate Write one paragraph evaluating your individual and team performance. Write another paragraph evaluating your opponents' performance. Conclude with a few statements about where you succeeded, what you learned, and how you might do things differently next time.

 For grammar practice, see Unit 6 Teaching Resources Book, p. 129.

Progress Check

Can students analyze characterization?

If No → See Unit 6 Teaching Resources Book, p. 126.

Before You Read

The Rockpile

Meet **James Baldwin**
(1924–1987)

James Baldwin wrote about controversial topics, such as race, politics, love, and religion. In the course of his career, Baldwin produced a formidable body of work, which holds a place of honor in American literature. To achieve that eminence, he had to overcome many obstacles.

The grandson of slaves, Baldwin grew up in a large, impoverished family in Harlem during the economic hard times of the Great Depression. He once said that he wanted to be rich and famous simply so no one could evict his family again. Alhough he wrote plays, short stories, and novels, Baldwin is perhaps most highly regarded as an essayist. Among his most famous essay collections are *Notes of a Native Son*, *Nobody Knows My Name*, and *The Fire Next Time*. In both his fiction and his nonfiction, he examined issues of African American identity and the sources of racial bigotry in the twentieth-century U.S.

Confronting the Past Baldwin's work first became known to a wide audience when he published his novel *Go Tell It on the Mountain* in 1953. Baldwin had struggled with the novel for ten years, noting that, "In a sense, I wrote to redeem my father. I had to understand the forces, the experience, the life that shaped him before I could grow up myself, before I could become a writer." Baldwin's ability to accept and use the pain of the past—while not being consumed by it—became the basis for much of his work.

Changing Perspectives Baldwin's later work focused primarily on protesting racial inequality. He said, "It is a terrible, an inexorable, law that one cannot deny the humanity of another without diminishing one's own. . . ." Baldwin was also a popular speaker during the civil rights movement of the 1950s and 1960s. His uncompromising hon-

> *"I love America more than any other country in the world, and exactly for this reason, I insist on the right to criticize her perpetually."*
>
> —James Baldwin

esty and realism, ear for language, and experience as a minister combined to make him a powerful force at the podium.

In 1969 Baldwin moved to France, where he lived for the majority of the rest of his life. In the U.S. Baldwin had never won a major literary prize. In France, he was honored with one of the literary world's most prestigious awards: Commander of the Legion of Honor. When Baldwin died, his body was sent back to Harlem and buried only a few blocks from the house where he was born. More than 5,000 mourners gathered to pay their respects to the man who once said, "An artist is here not to give you answers, but to ask you questions."

 Literature Online

Author Search For more about James Baldwin, go to glencoe.com and enter QuickPass code GLA9800u6.

JAMES BALDWIN **959**

Before You Read

Focus

Bellringer Options

Literature Launchers:
Pre-Reading Videos DVD,
Selection Launcher

Selection Focus
Transparency 60

Daily Language Practice
Transparency 87

Or **say:** Think about the spoken and unspoken rules of our school. What are the consequences of breaking or "bending" these rules?

Interactive Read and Write
Other options for teaching this selection can be found in
- Interactive Read and Write for EL Students, pp. 213–226
- Interactive Read and Write for Approaching-Level Students, pp. 213–226
- Interactive Read and Write for On-Level Students, pp. 213–226

Selection Skills

Literary Elements
- Foil (SE pp. 960, 961, 963, 965, 966, 968)

The Rockpile

Writing Skills/Grammar
- Character Sketch (SE p. 968)
- Sequence Chart (TE p. 962)
- Double Negatives (TE p. 964)

Reading Skills
- Make Generalizations About Characters (SE pp. 960–964, 967, 968)
- Paraphrase (TE p. 966)

Vocabulary Skills
- Analogies (SE p. 968)
- Intensity Level (TE p. 960)

Listening/Speaking/ Viewing Skills
- Analyze Art (SE p. 966; TE p. 965)

959

Before You Read

Focus

Summary

Two brothers, John and Roy, sit on their fire escape and stare at the rockpile—a natural rock outcropping where the children of the neighborhood play. Their parents forbid the brothers to join in, but Roy, who is younger, sneaks away to the rockpile and is injured. Shortly before their father returns home from work, the reader learns that John is his stepson. Their father treats his wife and John harshly, blaming them for Roy's injury.

 For summaries in languages other than English, see Unit 6 Teaching Resources Book, pp. 132–137.

Vocabulary

Intensity Level Explain that one way of learning how to use a word is to understand its strength or intensity. For example, *grapple* is slightly more intense than *wrestle,* but it is not as strong as *battle.* Have students suggest and discuss words that are less strong and stronger than the vocabulary words. *(e.g., linger, loiter, afflict; frightened, intimidated, threatened; absorbed, engrossed, obsessed; happy, jubilant, ecstatic)*

 For additional context, see Glencoe Interactive Vocabulary CD-ROM.

Literature and Reading Preview

Connect to the Story

What would you risk to keep your word to someone? Freewrite for a few minutes about a time when you kept a promise even though it was difficult.

Build Background

This story is set in the New York City neighborhood of Harlem. "The Rockpile" may well be set near the first home Baldwin remembered living in, at Park Avenue and 131st Street. Like John in the story, Baldwin was the oldest child in a large family. His mother married David Baldwin three years after James's birth, so, like John, young Baldwin was a stepson. Like the father in the story, David Baldwin was a Protestant minister and a stern man who did not like his children playing in the streets.

Set Purposes for Reading

Big Idea **Life in the City**

As you read, ask yourself, What details about the setting and characters provide information about urban life in the Depression-era United States?

Literary Element **Foil**

A **foil** is a minor character whose contrast with a main character highlights particular traits of that main character. As you read, ask yourself, How is your understanding of the main character expanded as a result of the presence of the foil?

Reading Strategy **Make Generalizations About Characters**

A **generalization** is a broad conclusion drawn from specific details. As you read, ask yourself, What can you conclude about the family members in "The Rockpile"?

Tip: Take Notes In a chart, record details and generalizations about the main characters.

Details	Generalizations
Roy gazed at the street, wishing he had wings; John was afraid of the rockpile.	Roy and John have different personalities.

Writing Practice

Foils Students may disagree about who is the main character in the story. Both John and Roy play important roles, and it could be said that each one is a foil for the other. Help students anticipate the contrasts between the two boys by having them make a two-column chart where they can record the ways in which each boy is a foil for the other. Model how to fill in the chart as shown.

Roy	John
attracted to the rockpile	afraid of the rockpile

Learning Objectives

For pages 959–968

In studying this text, you will focus on the following objectives:

Literary Study: Analyzing a foil character.

Reading: Making generalizations about characters.

Writing: Writing a character sketch.

Vocabulary

grapple (grap´ əl) *v.* to struggle in hand-to-hand combat; to wrestle; p. 961 *The man grappled with his attacker.*

loiter (loi´ tər) *v.* to stand or linger idly or aimlessly about a place; p. 962 *We thought it best not to loiter in the empty street.*

intimidated (in tim´ ə dāt´ əd) *adj.* made timid or fearful; frightened into submission or inaction; p. 962 *When the large man pushed me, I was so intimidated that I was speechless.*

engrossed (en grōst´) *adj.* fully attentive to; completely engaged in; absorbed; p. 963 *I spoke to my mother, but she was engrossed in the newspaper and did not look up.*

jubilant (jōō´ bə lənt) *adj.* extremely happy; triumphantly joyful; p. 963 *The people were jubilant when they heard that the war had ended.*

The Rockpile

James Baldwin

Across the street from their house, in an empty lot between two houses, stood the rockpile. It was a strange place to find a mass of natural rock jutting out of the ground; and someone, probably Aunt Florence, had once told them that the rock was there and could not be taken away because without it the subway cars underground would fly apart, killing all the people. This, touching on some natural mystery concerning the surface and the center of the earth, was far too intriguing an explanation to be challenged, and it invested the rockpile, moreover, with such mysterious importance that Roy felt it to be his right, not to say his duty, to play there.

Other boys were to be seen there each afternoon after school and all day Saturday and Sunday. They fought on the rockpile. Surefooted, dangerous, and reckless, they rushed each other and **grappled** on the heights, sometimes disappearing down the other side in a confusion of dust and screams and upended, flying feet. "It's a wonder they don't kill themselves," their mother said, watching sometimes from the fire escape. "You children stay away from there, you hear me?" Though she said "children," she was looking at Roy, where he sat beside John on the fire escape. "The good Lord knows," she continued, "I don't want you to come home bleeding like a hog every day the Lord sends."

---

1 Life in the City *What does this superstition reveal about how the residents view their neighborhood?*

2 Make Generalizations About Characters *From this detail, what generalizations might you make about Roy?*

Foil *What does this detail suggest about the difference between the two brothers?* **3**

Vocabulary

grapple (grap´ əl) *v.* to struggle in hand-to-hand combat; to wrestle

JAMES BALDWIN **961**

English Learners

DIFFERENTIATED INSTRUCTION

SMALL GROUP **Intermediate** Point out that Baldwin uses dialect, which varies among regions and cultural groups. Pair English learners with fluent English speakers to create charts like the one shown. Have them list dialect from "The Rockpile" in one column and standard English equivalents in the other.

Dialect	Standard English

Teach

Big Idea | 1

Life in the City **Answer:** *They see it as a potentially dangerous place.*

Reading Strategy | 2

Make Generalizations About Characters **Answer:** *He is strong-willed, with a keen sense of adventure.*

(ENGLISH LEARNERS) Make sure students understand the words *specific, general, generalize,* and *generalization.* Have them use these words as they discuss the characters.

Literary Element | 3

Foil **Answer:** *It is Roy who usually gets into trouble.*

View the Art ★

Jacob Lawrence (1917–2000) is best known for works dealing with themes in African American history.

 For an audio recording of this selection, use Listening Library Audio CD-ROM.

Readability Scores

Dale-Chall: 4.6
DRP: 59
Lexile: 850

Teach

Reading Strategy 1

Make Generalizations About Characters Answer: *The brothers fear their father and view him as an oppressive force.*

Literary Element 2

Foreshadowing Ask: What purposes does this anecdote serve in the story? *(It establishes the setting of the story and also suggests that if Roy sneaks out, he may get hurt, like Richard. It is likely that John and Roy know Richard's fate, so the anecdote enhances the reader's understanding of their views.)*

Cultural History ☆

Sister McCandless Many communities, including some African American communities, use the term *sister* to refer to any female who shares their values or culture.

Roy shifted impatiently, and continued to stare at the street, as though in this gazing he might somehow acquire wings. John said nothing. He had not really been spoken to: he was afraid of the rockpile and of the boys who played there.

Each Saturday morning John and Roy sat on the fire escape and watched the forbidden street below. Sometimes their mother sat in the room behind them, sewing, or dressing their younger sister, or nursing the baby, Paul. The sun fell across them and across the fire escape with a high, benevolent indifference; below them, men and women, and boys and girls, sinners all, **loitered;** sometimes one of the church-members passed and saw them and waved. Then, for the moment that they waved decorously back, they were **intimidated.** They watched the saint, man or woman, until he or she had disappeared from sight. The passage of one of the redeemed made them consider, however vacantly, the wickedness of the street, their own latent wickedness in sitting where they sat; and made them think of their father, who came home early on Saturdays and who would soon be turning this corner and entering the dark hall below them.

But until he came to end their freedom, they sat, watching and longing above the street. At the end of the street nearest their house was the bridge which spanned the Harlem River[1] and led to a city called the Bronx;[2] which was where Aunt Florence lived. Nevertheless, when they saw her coming, she did not come from the bridge, but from the opposite end of the street.

---

1. The *Harlem River* separates the Bronx and Manhattan, two boroughs of New York City.
2. *The Bronx* is actually one of five boroughs, or divisions, that make up New York City. It is not a separate city.

 Make Generalizations About Characters *From this detail, what generalizations might you make about how the brothers view their father?*

Vocabulary

loiter (loi´ tər) *v.* to stand or linger idly or aimlessly about a place

intimidated (in tim´ ə dāt´əd) *adj.* made timid or fearful; frightened into submission or inaction

This, weakly, to their minds, she explained by saying that she had taken the subway, not wishing to walk, and that, besides, she did not live in that section of the Bronx. Knowing that the Bronx was across the river, they did not believe this story ever, but, adopting toward her their father's attitude, assumed that she had just left some sinful place which she dared not name, as, for example, a movie palace.

In the summertime boys swam in the river, diving off the wooden dock, or wading in from the garbage-heavy bank. Once a boy, whose name was Richard, drowned in the river. His mother had not known where he was; she had even come to their house, to ask if he was there. Then, in the evening, at six o'clock, they had heard from the street a woman screaming and wailing; and they ran to the windows and looked out. Down the street came the woman, Richard's mother, screaming, her face raised to the sky and tears running down her face. A woman walked beside her, trying to make her quiet and trying to hold her up. Behind them walked a man, Richard's father, with Richard's body in his arms. There were two white policemen walking in the gutter, who did not seem to know what should be done. Richard's father and Richard were wet, and Richard's body lay across his father's arms like a cotton baby. The woman's screaming filled all the street; cars slowed down and the people in the cars stared; people opened their windows and looked out and came rushing out of doors to stand in the gutter, watching. Then the small procession disappeared within the house which stood beside the rockpile. Then, "Lord, Lord, Lord!" cried Elizabeth, their mother, and slammed the window down.

One Saturday, an hour before his father would be coming home, Roy was wounded on the rockpile and brought screaming upstairs. He and John had been sitting on the fire escape and their mother had gone into the kitchen to sip tea with Sister McCandless. By and by Roy became bored and sat beside John in restless silence; and John began drawing into his schoolbook a newspaper advertisement which featured

2

☆

Writing Practice

Sequence Explain that events in this story are told in two tracks of sequence. The first is an overarching narrative that includes stories from the past, such as the one about Richard. The second is an immediate narrative of one day in the life of Roy and John. Have students create a sequence chart based on the immediate narrative (with entries like "John and Roy sit on fire escape, looking at rockpile") but including, in parallel entries, information from the larger narrative (like "Their mother has cautioned them not to play there").

Woman in Calico, 1944. William H. Johnson. Oil on paperboard, 26½ x 20½ in. Smithsonian American Art Museum. Gift of the Harmon Foundation.

a new electric locomotive. Some friends of Roy passed beneath the fire escape and called him. Roy began to fidget, yelling down to them through the bars. Then a silence fell. John looked up. Roy stood looking at him.

"I'm going downstairs," he said.

"You better stay where you is, boy. You know Mama don't want you going downstairs."

"I be right *back.* She won't even know I'm gone, less you run and tell her."

"I ain't *got* to tell her. What's going to stop her from coming in here and looking out the window?"

"She's talking," Roy said. He started into the house.

"But Daddy's going to be home soon!"

"I be back before that. What you all the time got to be so *scared* for?" He was already in

3 Foil *What does Roy's statement to his brother suggest about the nature of their relationship?*

the house and he now turned, leaning on the windowsill, to swear impatiently, "I be back in *five* minutes."

John watched him sourly as he carefully unlocked the door and disappeared. In a moment he saw him on the sidewalk with his friends. He did not dare to go and tell his mother that Roy had left the fire escape because he had practically promised not to. He started to shout, *Remember, you said five minutes!* but one of Roy's friends was looking up at the fire escape. John looked down at his schoolbook: he became **engrossed** again in the problem of the locomotive.

When he looked up again he did not know how much time had passed, but now there was a gang fight on the rockpile. Dozens of boys fought each other in the harsh sun: clambering up the rocks and battling hand to hand, scuffed shoes sliding on the slippery rock; filling the bright air with curses and **jubilant** cries. They filled the air, too, with flying weapons: stones, sticks, tin cans, garbage, whatever could be picked up and thrown. John watched in a kind of absent amazement—until he remembered that Roy was still downstairs, and that he was one of the boys on the rockpile. Then he was afraid; he could not see his brother among the figures in the sun; and he stood up, leaning over the fire-escape railing. Then Roy appeared from the other side of the rocks; John saw that his shirt was torn; he was laughing. He moved until he stood at the very top of the rockpile. Then, something, an empty tin can, flew out of the air and hit him on the forehead, just above the eye. Immediately, one side of Roy's face ran with blood, he fell and rolled on his face down the rocks. Then for a moment there was no movement at all, no sound, the sun, arrested, lay on the street and the sidewalk and the arrested boys. Then someone screamed or shouted; boys

---

Vocabulary

engrossed (en grōst´) *adj.* fully attentive to; completely engaged in; absorbed

jubilant (jōo´ bə lənt) *adj.* extremely happy; triumphantly joyful

JAMES BALDWIN **963**

Teach

Literary Element	3

Foil **Answer:** *Roy knows that John disapproves of his actions, but he trusts John not to betray him.*

Point out that Roy shifts responsibility for his own actions to John. **Ask:** How does Roy's statement make John feel? *(He probably feels trapped.)*

View the Art ★

William H. Johnson (1901–1970) grew up in South Carolina but later came to Harlem while studying at New York's National Academy of Design. Johnson is known for his poignant depictions of African American life.

Approaching Level

DIFFERENTIATED INSTRUCTION

Strategic Help students having difficulty with the dialogue. Ask volunteers to read the conversation between Roy and John on this page. Have students read each sentence as it is written, and then say the sentence in standard English. Model with John's first statement. **Say:** John says, "You better stay where you is . . . ." I would paraphrase this to say, "You'd better stay where you are." Have

students continue with the rest of the conversation.

Teach

Big Idea 1

Life in the City Answer:
There is a support network in the community; people look out for one another.

Reading Strategy 2

Make Generalizations About Characters Answer:
Sister McCandless blames John for the accident because she holds him responsible for his younger brother.

began to run away, down the street, toward the bridge. The figure on the ground, having caught its breath and felt its own blood, began to shout. John cried, "Mama! Mama!" and ran inside.

"Don't fret, don't fret," panted Sister McCandless as they rushed down the dark, narrow, swaying stairs, "don't fret. Ain't a boy been born don't get his knocks every now and again. *Lord!*" They hurried into the sun. A man had picked Roy up and now walked slowly toward them. One or two boys sat silent on their stoops; at either end of the street there was a group of boys watching. "He ain't hurt bad," the man said, "Wouldn't be making this kind of noise if he was hurt real bad."

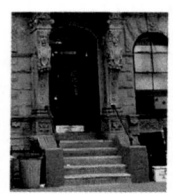

Visual Vocabulary
A *stoop* is a structure at the entrance of a building or house, consisting of stairs and a raised platform.

Elizabeth, trembling, reached out to take Roy, but Sister McCandless, bigger, calmer, took him from the man and threw him over her shoulder as she once might have handled a sack of cotton. "God bless you," she said to the man, "God bless you, son." Roy was still screaming. Elizabeth stood behind Sister McCandless to stare at his bloody face.

"It's just a flesh wound," the man kept saying, "just broke the skin, that's all." They were moving across the sidewalk, toward the house. John, not now afraid of the staring boys, looked toward the corner to see if his father was yet in sight.

Upstairs, they hushed Roy's crying. They bathed the blood away, to find, just above the left eyebrow, the jagged, superficial scar. "Lord, have mercy," murmured Elizabeth, "another inch and it would've been his eye." And she looked with apprehension toward the clock.

"Ain't it the truth," said Sister McCandless, busy with bandages and iodine.

"When did he go downstairs?" his mother asked at last.

Sister McCandless now sat fanning herself in the easy chair, at the head of the sofa where Roy lay, bound and silent. She paused for a moment to look sharply at John. John stood near the window, holding the newspaper advertisement and the drawing he had done.

"We was sitting on the fire escape," he said. "Some boys he knew called him."

"When?"

"He said he'd be back in five minutes."

"Why didn't you tell me he was downstairs?"

He looked at his hands, clasping his notebook, and did not answer.

"Boy," said Sister McCandless, "you hear your mother a-talking to you?"

He looked at his mother. He repeated:

"He said he'd be back in five minutes."

"He said he'd be back in five minutes," said Sister McCandless with scorn, "don't look to me like that's no right answer. You's the man of the house, you supposed to look after your baby brothers and sisters—you ain't supposed to let them run off and get half-killed. But I expect," she added, rising from the chair, dropping the cardboard fan, "your Daddy'll make you tell the truth. Your Ma's way too soft with you."

He did not look at her, but at the fan where it lay in the dark red, depressed seat where she had been. The fan advertised a pomade[3] for the hair and showed a brown woman and her baby, both with glistening hair, smiling happily at each other.

"Honey," said Sister McCandless, "I got to be moving along. Maybe I drop in later tonight. I don't reckon you going to be at Tarry Service tonight?"

---

3. *Pomade* is a perfumed ointment, especially one used as a hair dressing.

---

1 **Life in the City** *What does the man's action convey about the community that the characters live in?*

Make Generalizations About Characters *From this detail, what generalizations can you make about Sister McCandless's attitude toward John?* **2**

Grammar Practice

SMALL GROUP

Double Negatives In this story, the characters' dialect includes the use of double negatives, as when Sister McCandless says "ain't nothing but a scratch." Explain that a clause should not include more than one negative. List common negatives, such as *none, never, nothing, hardly, scarcely,* and *barely.* Students should also recognize negative contractions. Stress that many of the double negatives in this story are formed with *ain't,* which is both nonstandard English and a negative. Have student pairs identify and record story sentences that contain double negatives and then rewrite the sentences in standard English.

Tarry Service was the prayer meeting held every Saturday night at church to strengthen believers and prepare the church for the coming of the Holy Ghost on Sunday.

"I don't reckon," said Elizabeth. She stood up; she and Sister McCandless kissed each other on the cheek. "But you be sure to remember me in your prayers."

"I surely will do that." She paused, with her hand on the door knob, and looked down at Roy and laughed. "Poor little man," she said, "reckon he'll be content to sit on the fire escape *now*."

Elizabeth laughed with her. "It sure ought to be a lesson to him. You don't reckon," she asked nervously, still smiling, "he going to keep that scar, do you?"

"Lord, no," said Sister McCandless, "ain't nothing but a scratch. I declare, Sister Grimes, you worse than a child. Another couple of weeks and you won't be able to *see* no scar. No, you go on about your housework, honey, and thank the Lord it weren't no worse." She opened the door; they heard the sound of feet on the stairs. "I expect that's the Reverend," said Sister McCandless, placidly, "I *bet* he going to raise cain."[4]

"Maybe it's Florence," Elizabeth said. "Sometimes she get here about this time." They stood in the doorway, staring, while the steps reached the landing below and began again climbing to their floor. "No," said Elizabeth then, "that ain't her walk. That's Gabriel."

"Well, I'll just go on," said Sister McCandless, "and kind of prepare his mind." She pressed Elizabeth's hand as she spoke and started into the hall, leaving the door behind her slightly ajar. Elizabeth turned slowly back into the room. Roy did not open his eyes, or move; but she knew that he was not sleeping; he wished to delay until the last possible

Funky Soho, 2002. Patti Mollica. Oil on canvas. Private collection.

moment any contact with his father. John put his newspaper and his notebook on the table and stood, leaning on the table, staring at her.

"It wasn't my fault," he said. "I couldn't stop him from going downstairs."

"No," she said, "you ain't got nothing to worry about. You just tell your Daddy the truth."

He looked directly at her, and she turned to the window, staring into the street. What was Sister McCandless saying? Then from her bedroom she heard Delilah's thin wail and she turned, frowning, looking toward the bedroom and toward the still open door. She knew that John was watching her. Delilah continued to wail, she thought, angrily, *Now that girl's getting too big for that,* but she feared that Delilah would awaken Paul and she hurried into the bedroom. She tried to soothe Delilah back to sleep. Then she heard the front door open and close—too

JAMES BALDWIN **965**

---

4. *To raise cain* is an idiom meaning "to make a great disturbance" or "to lose one's temper."

3 Foil *What do these words tell you about Sister McCandless's different attitudes toward the two brothers?*

Teach

Literary Element | **3**

Foil Answer: *Sister McCandless sympathizes with Roy and feels affection for him. She shows no affection for John and blames him for the accident.*

[ADVANCED] Have students write a paragraph voicing their own opinion about whether John should be held responsible for Roy's actions.

View the Art ★

Patti Mollica says the world is "a mosaic of shapes and colors."

Ask: How is this view reflected in her painting? *(Students' responses will vary but should cite specific aspects of the illustration.)*

Approaching Level

DIFFERENTIATED INSTRUCTION

Emerging There are just a few characters in "The Rockpile," but their relationships can be confusing. Have students create a web diagram to identify characters and their relationships to John.

965

Teach

Reading Strategy 1

Make Generalizations About Characters John is perceived as an outsider because he is Gabriel's stepson, not his natural child. John is also considered tainted by "his mother's days in sin"—a reference to his illegitimate birth. Discuss John's anxiety about his father's return. **Ask:** How do you think Gabriel feels about John? *(Possible responses: resentful; angry; unaccepting)*

Literary Element 2

Foil Answer: *She is very calm and controlled in the face of Gabriel's extreme anger.*

[APPROACHING] **Ask:** What does Elizabeth do when Gabriel speaks harshly to her? *(She ignores him and just goes on voicing her thoughts.)*

View the Art ★

Answer: *Students may say that the contrast between the bright colors and the pale background in the painting reflects the powerful contrasts depicted in the story.*

Church on Lenox Avenue, 1939–1940. William H. Johnson. Tempera on paper, 24 x 18⅛ in. Smithsonian American Art Museum. Gift of the Harmon Foundation.

View the Art When William H. Johnson returned to New York after several years living abroad, he brought with him the influence of both modern art and Scandinavian folk art, which he melded with his African-American heritage. What connections can you find between this image and the story? ★

loud, Delilah raised her voice, with an exasperated sigh Elizabeth picked the child up. Her child and Gabriel's, her children and Gabriel's: Roy, Delilah, Paul. Only John was nameless and a stranger, living, unalterable testimony to his mother's days in sin.

"What happened?" Gabriel demanded. He stood, enormous, in the center of the room, his black lunchbox dangling from his hand, staring at the sofa where Roy lay. John stood just before him, it seemed to her astonished vision just below him, beneath his fist, his heavy shoe. The child stared at the man in fascination and terror—when a girl down home she had seen rabbits stand so paralyzed before the barking dog. She hurried past Gabriel to the sofa, feeling the

weight of Delilah in her arms like the weight of a shield, and stood over Roy, saying:

"Now, ain't a thing to get upset about, Gabriel. This boy sneaked downstairs while I had my back turned and got hisself hurt a little. He's alright now."

Roy, as though in confirmation, now opened his eyes and looked gravely at his father. Gabriel dropped his lunchbox with a clatter and knelt by the sofa.

"How you feel, son? Tell your Daddy what happened?"

Roy opened his mouth to speak and then, relapsing into panic, began to cry. His father held him by the shoulder.

"You don't want to cry. You's Daddy's little man. Tell your Daddy what happened."

"He went downstairs," said Elizabeth, "where he didn't have no business to be, and got to fighting with them bad boys playing on that rockpile. That's what happened and it's a mercy it weren't nothing worse."

He looked up at her. "Can't you let this boy answer me for hisself?"

Ignoring this, she went on, more gently: "He got cut on the forehead, but it ain't nothing to worry about."

"You call a doctor? How you know it ain't nothing to worry about?"

"Is you got money to be throwing away on doctors? No, I ain't called no doctor. Ain't nothing wrong with my eyes that I can't tell whether he's hurt bad or not. He got a fright more'n anything else, and you ought to pray God it teaches him a lesson."

"You got a lot to say *now*," he said, "but I'll have *me* something to say in a minute. I'll be wanting to know when all this happened, what you was doing with your eyes *then*." He turned back to Roy, who had lain quietly sobbing eyes wide open and body held rigid: and who now, at his father's touch, remembered the height, the sharp, sliding rock beneath his feet, the sun, the explosion of the sun, his plunge into

---

Foil *How might Elizabeth be said to act as Gabriel's foil at this point in the story?*

Reading Practice

SMALL GROUP

Paraphrase Explain that paraphrasing can be useful for comprehension, especially if a text seems confusing. Paraphrasing means restating the text in one's own words. It is different from summarizing in that paraphrasing should include all parts of the text, not just main ideas and key details. Have students read the end of the story and work in pairs to paraphrase what happens at the end of the story. They should work together to agree on the paraphrase and then discuss the significance of the ending.

darkness and his salty blood; and recoiled, beginning to scream, as his father touched his forehead. "Hold still, hold still," crooned his father, shaking, "hold still. Don't cry. Daddy ain't going to hurt you, he just wants to see this bandage, see what they've done to his little man." But Roy continued to scream and would not be still and Gabriel dared not lift the bandage for fear of hurting him more. And he looked at Elizabeth in fury: "Can't you put that child down and help me with this boy? John, take your baby sister from your mother—don't look like neither of you got good sense."

John took Delilah and sat down with her in the easy chair. His mother bent over Roy, and held him still, while his father, carefully—but still Roy screamed—lifted the bandage and stared at the wound. Roy's sobs began to lessen. Gabriel re-adjusted the bandage. "You see," said Elizabeth, finally, "he ain't nowhere near dead."

"It sure ain't your fault that he ain't dead." He and Elizabeth considered each other for a moment in silence. "He came mightly close to losing an eye. Course, his eyes ain't as big as your'n, so I reckon you don't think it matters so much." At this her face hardened; he smiled. "Lord, have mercy," he said, "you think you ever going to learn to do right? Where was you when all this happened? Who let him go downstairs?"

"Ain't nobody let him go downstairs, he just went. He got a head just like his father, it got to be broken before it'll bow. I was in the kitchen."

"Where was Johnnie?"

"He was in here?"

"Where?"

"He was on the fire escape."

"Didn't he know Roy was downstairs?"

"I reckon."

"What you mean, you reckon? He ain't got your big eyes for nothing, does he?" He looked over at John. "Boy, you see your brother go downstairs?"

"Gabriel, ain't no sense in trying to blame Johnnie. You know right well if you have trouble making Roy behave, he ain't going to listen to his brother. He don't hardly listen to me."

"How come you didn't tell your mother Roy was downstairs?"

John said nothing, staring at the blanket which covered Delilah.

"Boy, you hear me? You want me to take a strap to you?"

"No, you ain't," she said. "You ain't going to take no strap to this boy, not today you ain't. Ain't a soul to blame for Roy's lying up there now but you—you because you done spoiled him so that he thinks he can do just anything and get away with it. I'm here to tell you that ain't no way to raise no child. You don't pray to the Lord to help you do better than you been doing, you going to live to shed bitter tears that the Lord didn't take his soul today." And she was trembling. She moved, unseeing, toward John and took Delilah from his arms. She looked back at Gabriel, who had risen, who stood near the sofa, staring at her. And she found in his face not fury alone, which would not have surprised her; but hatred so deep as to become insupportable in its lack of personality. His eyes were struck alive, unmoving, blind with malevolence—she felt, like the pull of the earth at her feet, his longing to witness her perdition.[5] Again, as though it might be propitiation,[6] she moved the child in her arms. And at this his eyes changed, he looked at Elizabeth, the mother of his children, the helpmeet given by the Lord. Then her eyes clouded; she moved to leave the room; her foot struck the lunchbox lying on the floor.

"John," she said, "pick up your father's lunchbox like a good boy."

She heard, behind her, his scrambling movement as he left the easy chair, the scrape and jangle of the lunchbox as he picked it up, bending his dark head near the toe of his father's heavy shoe.

---

5. *Perdition* (pər dish' ən) means "the loss of one's soul and of heavenly salvation" or "eternal damnation."
6. *Propitiation* is a pleasing act intended to soothe, pacify, or win favor.

> Make Generalizations About Characters *From this detail, what generalizations can you make about Gabriel's character?* **4**

JAMES BALDWIN **967**

To check students' understanding of the selection, see Unit 6 Teaching Resources Book, p. 143.

Teach

Reading Strategy 3

Make Inferences Have students reread this passage. **Ask:** How would you describe the relationship between Elizabeth and Gabriel? *(The relationship is strained. Gabriel is close to abusive toward Elizabeth; she tries to fight back.)*

(APPROACHING) **Say:** Find one example in the text of Elizabeth standing up to Gabriel. *(She says, "No, you ain't" when Gabriel threatens to take a strap to John.)*

Reading Strategy 4

Make Generalizations About Characters **Answer:** *Gabriel is a deeply troubled character who preaches love as a Christian minister but is filled with hatred.*

Cultural History ☆

Corporal Punishment
People disagree about the acceptability of physical, or corporal, punishment of children. In the past, corporal punishment was widely accepted as a way to discipline children. Nowadays, most child rearing experts advise against it.

Approaching Level
DIFFERENTIATED INSTRUCTION

Established Review that words' connotations are their associated meanings. Students can use an understanding of connotations to analyze the characters and relationships in the story. Have students list the relationships between pairs of characters, such as John and Roy, Gabriel and John, and Gabriel and Elizabeth. Ask students to list some words that describe these relationships. Have students share their lists and explain the connotations of the words included.

After You Read

Assess

1. Students may say the story is depressing; John's father treats him unfairly; the family tension is disturbing.

2. (a) The rockpile represents forbidden pleasures. (b) Perhaps John's spirit has been suppressed by Gabriel.

3. (a) The parents and Sister McCandless see themselves as religious and superior. (b) They keep Roy and John away from other children.

4. (a) He is Roy's father and John's stepfather. (b) He favors Roy because Roy is his natural child.

5. (a) The father's return home and his harsh actions (b) It creates suspense.

6. (a) Freedom from the stifling home (b) Yes, because there are no rules for fighting one's way to the top

7. (a) Elizabeth defends John from Gabriel's unjust attacks and herself from his anger. (b) No, the story ends in a stalemate.

8. The urban setting is fundamental because the neighborhood's dangers intensify the family's conflicts. The author paints a clear picture of the struggle to maintain human dignity in this difficult environment.

 For additional assessment, see Assessment Resources, pp. 253–254.

Literary Element

1. Gabriel favors his biological son, Roy.
2. Possible answer: Angry Gabriel is a foil to kind Elizabeth.

Progress Check

Can students recognize a foil?

If No → See Unit 6 Teaching Resources Book, p. 138.

968

After You Read

Respond and Think Critically

Respond and Interpret

1. Describe your emotional response to this story.

2. (a)Why is the rockpile so tempting for Roy? (b)Why do you think that John is not tempted by it?

3. (a)How do the adults in the story see themselves as different from other people in the neighborhood? (b)How is their self-image reflected in their actions?

4. (a)What important fact is revealed about Gabriel just before he arrives home? (b)How does this fact explain Gabriel's attitude toward his two sons?

Analyze and Evaluate

5. (a)What event or events are foreshadowed in "The Rockpile"? (b)What effect does this foreshadowing have on the story?

6. (a)What do you think the rockpile symbolizes? (b)Do you find this symbol effective? Explain.

7. (a)What is the main source of conflict between Gabriel and Elizabeth in the story? (b)Is this conflict resolved at the end of the story? Explain.

Connect

8. **Big Idea** **Life in the City** How important is the urban setting to this story?

Literary Element Foil

Although "The Rockpile" may appear to be about Roy, it tells as much or more about John through the many contrasts presented between the two.

1. How do John and Roy differ in terms of their status within the family?

2. Who else might be a foil in this story? Explain.

Reading Strategy Make Generalizations About Characters

Review the notes you made in your chart and other details about characters in the story.

1. What generalizations can you make about the effect of the setting on the characters?

2. What generalization can you make about the attitudes of Roy and John toward Gabriel?

Vocabulary Practice

Practice with Analogies Apply the relationship in the first pair of words to the second pair to identify the missing word.

1. engrossed : fascinated :: expedient :
   a. convenient   c. fortuitous
   b. coincidental   d. fruitful
2. loiter : stand :: search :
   a. find   c. seek
   b. collect   d. determine
3. jubilant : pleased :: terrified :
   a. scared   c. sorrowful
   b. frozen   d. deceitful
4. grapple : embrace :: gyrate :
   a. open   c. pace
   b. stand still   d. beguile
5. intimidated : scared :: belligerent :
   a. hostile   c. receptive
   b. timid   d. somnolent

LOG ON ▶ **Literature** Online

Selection Resources For Selection Quizzes, eFlashcards, and Reading-Writing Connection activities, go to glencoe.com and enter QuickPass code GLA9800u6.

Writing

Write a Character Sketch What might *your* foil be like? Write a sketch of a character whose personality and actions could serve as a contrast to yours.

968 UNIT 6 FROM DEPRESSION TO COLD WAR

Reading Strategy

1. The setting makes the adults over-protective of the children. John fears the rockpile, but Roy sees it as an escape.

2. Both brothers fear Gabriel.

Vocabulary

1. a 2. c 3. a 4. b 5. a

Writing

Use the following criteria to evaluate students' writing:

- Does the character sketch describe a foil?
- Does the character sketch include details about the foil's physical and psychological traits?

PART 2

The United States and the World

Three Flags, 1958. Jasper Johns. Encaustic on canvas, 30⅞ x 45 x 5 in. Fiftieth Anniversary Gift of the Gilman Foundation, Inc., The Lauder Foundation, A. Alfred Taubman, an anonymous donor, and purchase 80.32

View the Art Johns's painting shows three American flags layered on top of one another. Why might the artist have chosen to depict the flag in this way? ★

"We must be the great arsenal of democracy."

—Franklin D. Roosevelt, radio broadcast, 1940

969

Analyze and Extend

War Message to Congress

Bellringer Options

Daily Language Practice Transparency 88

Or **ask:** What qualities do you admire in a leader, and why do you think they are important? *(Students may suggest strength of character, intelligence, bravery, and the ability to communicate and inspire.)* Have students consider as they read whether Roosevelt personifies the qualities of leadership.

Meet **Franklin Delano Roosevelt**

(1882–1945)

Franklin D. Roosevelt was an intensely competitive and social person. His charismatic demeanor, rich voice, and wide smile expressed confidence and optimism and gave him the power to be very persuasive. In the dark days of the Great Depression and World War II, his buoyant leadership was one of the United States' greatest assets.

Roosevelt was a distant cousin of Theodore Roosevelt, the twenty-sixth president of the United States. He was born into a wealthy New York family and educated at Harvard University and Columbia Law School. While at Harvard, he became acquainted with Theodore Roosevelt's niece, Eleanor. Soon afterward, they married.

Political Gains and Personal Setbacks Shortly after leaving law school, Roosevelt entered politics and won a seat in the New York State Senate. He earned a reputation as a progressive reformer willing to stand up to the party bosses. In 1921, he contracted a fever and soon felt numbness in his legs. He had contracted the disease known as polio. Although there was no cure, Roosevelt refused to give up and began a vigorous exercise program to restore some of his muscle control.

While recovering from polio, Roosevelt depended on his wife to keep his name prominent in the New York Democratic Party. Eleanor Roosevelt became an effective orator, and her efforts during this time kept her husband's political career alive. By the mid-1920s, Franklin Roosevelt was again active in the Democratic Party and was elected governor of New York. While governor, he gained great popularity by cutting taxes for farmers, reducing utility rates, and aiding unemployed New Yorkers.

> *"Let me assert my firm belief that the only thing we have to fear is fear itself."*
>
> —Franklin D. Roosevelt
> First Inaugural Address

Roosevelt's popularity paved the way for his presidential win in 1932. Many people in the United States applauded Roosevelt's use of power to help people in economic distress. In the first three months of his presidency, Congress passed fifteen major acts to provide economic relief to the nation, later known as the First New Deal. Roosevelt's popular relief programs helped him win reelection three times. He has the remarkable legacy of being the only president to serve more than two terms. ☆

Tension in Europe Meanwhile, World War II officially began when Germany invaded Poland on September 1, 1939. After the horrors of World War I, most U.S. citizens were in favor of remaining neutral during the war. On December 7, 1941, Japanese fighter pilots made a surprise attack on Pearl Harbor. The damage was severe and crippling. Roosevelt quickly changed his mind about the war. The following day, he delivered his famous "War Message to Congress." But President Roosevelt did not live to see victory; he died from a stroke just months before the war's end.

 Literature Online

Author Search For more about Franklin D. Roosevelt, go to glencoe.com and enter QuickPass code GLA9800u6.

Political History ☆

Presidential Term Limit When George Washington refused to run for President for a third term in 1796, he set an unwritten precedent for presidents to serve only two terms. Franklin Roosevelt broke that rule when he ran for and was elected President four times. Politicians worried that others might follow Roosevelt's lead, so Congress passed the 22nd Amendment in 1947. Ratified in 1951, the amendment officially limited Presidents to serving only two terms.

Selection Skills

Literary Elements
- Author's Purpose (SE pp. 971, 973, 974)

War Message to Congress

Vocabulary Skills
- Denotation and Connotation (SE p. 974)

Reading Skills
- Distinguish Fact and Opinion (SE pp. 971, 972, 974)

Writing Skills/Grammar
- Write a Press Release (SE p. 974)
- Research Report (TE p. 973)

Literature and Reading Preview

Connect to the Speech

Have you ever had to make a difficult decision that affected other people such as friends or family? Write a journal entry about this decision and explain how you made your choice.

Build Background

Prior to the attack on Pearl Harbor, U.S. intelligence had decoded Japanese communications that made it clear that Japan was preparing to attack the United States. However, no one knew when or where the attack would occur. Japan's surprise attack on December 7, 1941, sank or damaged 21 ships of the U.S. Pacific Fleet, destroyed 188 airplanes, killed 2,403 Americans, and injured another 1,178.

Set Purposes for Reading

Big Idea The United States and the World

As you read, ask yourself, What political and human consequences did President Roosevelt have to consider before asking Congress to declare war?

Literary Element Author's Purpose

An **author's purpose** is his or her intent in writing a piece of literature. Authors typically write to accomplish one or more of the following purposes: to persuade, to inform, to explain, to entertain, or to describe. You can identify an author's purpose by thinking critically about the form, the tone, and the content of the first few paragraphs. As you read, ask yourself, What is Roosevelt's purpose in his "War Message to Congress"?

Reading Strategy Distinguish Fact and Opinion

A **fact** is a statement that can be verified or proved. An **opinion** is a personal judgment.

Tip: Take Notes As you read, ask yourself, Which statements in Roosevelt's speech are facts and which are opinions? Create a chart like the one below to record examples of facts and opinions you find throughout "War Message to Congress."

Detail	Fact or Opinion
"a date which will live in infamy"	opinion

Learning Objectives

For pages 970–974

In studying this text, you will focus on the following objectives:

Literary Study: Analyzing author's purpose.

Reading: Distinguishing fact and opinion.

Writing: Writing a press release.

Vocabulary

infamy (in´ fə mē) *n.* a reputation as something evil or harmful; p. 972 *The Ku Klux Klan gained infamy for its racism.*

diplomatic (dip´ lə mat´ ik) *adj.* negotiating in a peaceful manner; p. 972 *Tyler and I tried to be diplomatic when we disagreed.*

implication (im´ plə kā´ shən) *n.* an effect or consequence; p. 973 *Not brushing your teeth can have severe implications, such as cavities and tooth decay.*

premeditated (prē med´ ə tāt´ əd) *adj.* thought about beforehand; p. 973 *The bank robbery was premeditated, as the criminal had developed the plan weeks before.*

inevitable (i nev´ ə tə bəl) *adj.* certain to happen; p. 973 *Once the black clouds appeared overhead, we feared rain was inevitable.*

Tip: Denotation and Connotation Some words with the same dictionary definition (denotation) can have different cultural definitions (connotations).

FRANKLIN D. ROOSEVELT **971**

Before You Read

Focus

Summary

In his speech, Roosevelt explains to the citizens of the United States that the nation has been attacked without warning by the Japanese air force. He then builds a case against Japan, citing other recent acts of aggression. Finally, he asserts his power as Commander in Chief and asks Congress to approve a declaration of war.

 For summaries in languages other than English, see Unit 6 Teaching Resources Book, pp. 147–152.

Vocabulary

Etymology Knowing the origins of a vocabulary word can help students better remember the meaning of the word. Have students use a dictionary and write down the origins of all the vocabulary words. Then have them practice using the words in sentences.

 For additional vocabulary practice, see Unit 6 Teaching Resources Book, p. 155.

Approaching Level

DIFFERENTIATED INSTRUCTION

Emerging Explain to students that they can better understand the author's purpose by paying attention to the diction, or the author's choice of words, when reading. For example, tell students to examine these two statements:

". . . the United States of America was suddenly and deliberately attacked by . . . the Empire of Japan."

". . . the Japanese Government has deliberately sought to deceive the United States by false statements . . . ."

Highlight the words *suddenly* and *deliberately* in the first statement and the words *deliberately, deceive,* and *false* in the second statement. Roosevelt chose those words to paint Japan in a negative light. Roosevelt is inviting Americans to feel

indignation and to fight back. Words such as *deceive* and *false* portray the Japanese government as untrustworthy. As students read the speech, ask them to look for other examples of words that reveal Roosevelt's purpose in giving this speech.

Teach

Big Idea 1

The United States and the World Explain that, before becoming Germany's ally, Japan was conquering western-held territories in Asia to expand its empire. The United States knew of the threat Japan posed to the West. **Ask:** Given that Japan had been a threat, why does Roosevelt use such strong language after the attack? (*An attack is different from a threat, and Roosevelt is angry. He is appealing to his listeners' emotions.*)

Reading Strategy 2

Distinguish Fact and Opinion Answer: Fact: *Japan planned the attack.* Opinion: *the Japanese intended to deceive the United States.*

> For additional practice using the reading skill or strategy, see Unit 6 Teaching Resources Book, p. 154.

Political History ☆

Japanese Oil Crisis Hoping to slow Japan's progress in controlling Asian territories, the United States refused to sell oil to Japan. Japan's military needed this oil. Historians believe Japan attacked the United States to force the nation to compromise.

Readability Scores

Dale-Chall: 8.9
DRP: 66
Lexile: 1280

FRANKLIN D. ROOSEVELT
WAR MESSAGE TO CONGRESS,
December 8, 1941

1 Yesterday, December 7, 1941—a date which will live in **infamy**—the United States of America was suddenly and deliberately attacked by naval and air forces of the Empire of Japan.

The United States was at peace with that nation and, at the solicitation of Japan, was still in conversation with its Government and its Emperor looking toward the maintenance of peace in the Pacific. Indeed, one hour after Japanese air squadrons had commenced bombing in the American Island of Oahu, the Japanese Ambassador to the United States and his colleague delivered to our Secretary of State a formal reply to a recent American message. And, while this reply stated that it seemed useless to continue the existing **diplomatic** negotiations, it contained no threat or hint of war or of armed attack.

It will be recorded that the distance of Hawaii from Japan makes it obvious that the attack was deliberately planned many days or even weeks ago. During the intervening time the Japanese Government has deliberately sought to deceive the United States by false statements and expressions of hope for continued peace.

The attack yesterday on the Hawaiian Islands has caused severe damage to American

---

Distinguish Fact and Opinion *Which parts of this statement are based on factual information? Which parts are formed by opinions?* **2**

Vocabulary

infamy (in´ fə mē) *n.* a reputation as something evil or harmful

Vocabulary

diplomatic (dip´ lə mat´ ik) *adj.* negotiating in a peaceful manner

972 UNIT 6 FROM DEPRESSION TO COLD WAR

Speaking Practice

Speech Analysis Have students analyze the speech in detail and examine the persuasive techniques Roosevelt uses. Ask them to consider Roosevelt's word choice, the appeals he makes to people's feelings of patriotism, the images he paints of Japan and of the United States, and the way he uses other rhetorical devices. Ask them to analyze how effective Roosevelt is in supporting the case for war. Have students present an oral critique of the speech to the class.

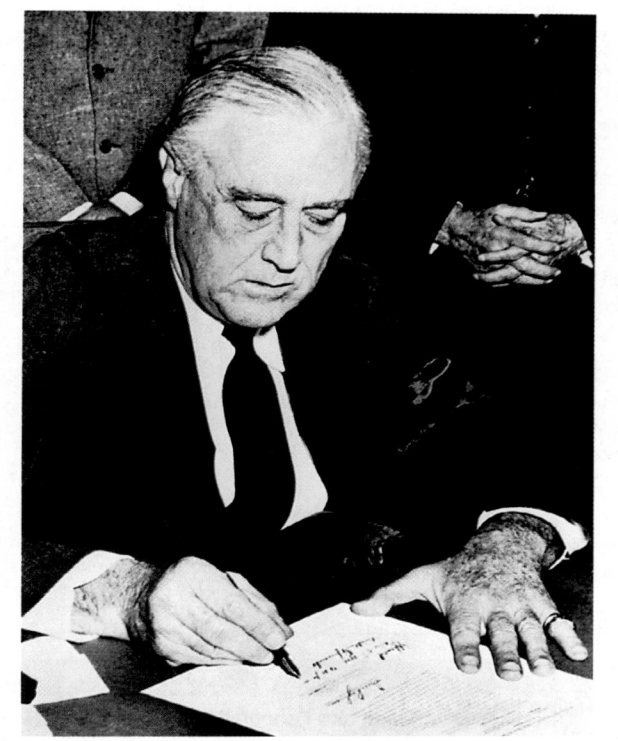

President Franklin D. Roosevelt signs the declaration of war against Japan, December 8, 1941.

naval and military forces. I regret to tell you that very many American lives have been lost. In addition American ships have been reported torpedoed on the high seas between San Francisco and Honolulu.

Yesterday the Japanese Government also launched an attack against Malaya.

Last night Japanese forces attacked Hong Kong.

Last night Japanese forces attacked Guam.

Last night Japanese forces attacked the
3 Philippine Islands.

Last night the Japanese attacked Wake Island.

And this morning the Japanese attacked Midway Island.

Japan has, therefore, undertaken a surprise offensive extending throughout the Pacific area. The facts of yesterday and today speak for them-

selves. The people of the United States have already formed their opinions and well understand the **implications** to the very life and safety of our nation.

A Commander in Chief of the Army and Navy I have directed that all measures be taken for our defense.

Always will our whole nation remember the character of the onrought against us.

No matter how long it may take us to overcome this **premeditated** invasion the American people in their righteous might will win through to absolute victory. I believe that I interpret the will of the Congress and the people when I assert that we will not only defend ourselves to the utmost but will make it very certain that this form of treachery shall never again endanger us.

Hostilities exist. There is no blinking at the fact that our people, our territory, and our interests are in grave danger.

With confidence in our armed forces—with the unbounding determination of our people—we will gain the **inevitable** triumph. So help us God.

I ask that Congress declare that since the unprovoked and dastardly attack by Japan on September 7, 1941, a state of war has existed between the United States and the Japanese.

Themes and the World How does Roosevelt use rhetoric to make the nation feel confident of victory?
5

Vocabulary

im pla kā´ shən) n. an effect or consequence

prē med´ ə tāt´ əd) adj. thought about beforehand

in´ ə tə bəl) adj. certain to happen

FRANKLIN D. ROOSEVELT **973**

Teach

Literary Element 3

Author's Purpose Say: Notice how Roosevelt uses repetitive language to describe six attacks. **Ask:** What is Roosevelt's purpose in mentioning these attacks? *(He wants to stress the pattern of Japan's aggression.)*

Vocabulary 4

Word Parts Have students use the word parts to decode what *premeditated* means. *(The prefix pre-, the suffix -ed, and the word* meditate *create the meaning.)*

Big Idea 5

The United States and the World Answer: *His words, such as* overcome, righteous, *and* victory, *have strong connotations.*

Progress Check

Can students recognize the author's purpose?

If No → See Unit 6 Teaching Resources Book, p. 153.

Advanced Learners

DIFFERENTIATED INSTRUCTION

SMALL GROUP
Research Report Have groups of students work together to research the chain of events that led to the United States' involvement in World War II. Tell students that the Japanese attack on Pearl Harbor was the "last straw" in a series of events that led up to war. Have students investigate Japanese-American relations, Japan's expanding empire, and

the ascent of Axis powers in Europe and the rest of the world. Students should use primary and secondary sources to write a report discussing the reasons the United States finally declared war on Japan and the other Axis powers. Have students present their research to the

After You Read

Assess

1. It may inspire or create anxiety.
2. (a) The countries were negotiating. (b) It might have made Congress want to declare war.
3. (a) The distance meant the attack was planned. (b) He might think they had a war plan.
4. (a) Malaya, Hong Kong, Guam, the Philippine Islands, Wake Island, Midway Island (b) To evoke fear and anger
5. (a) They want war. (b) To imply he is listening to public opinion
6. (a) He talks of an "inevitable triumph." (b) To build confidence
7. Some may feel he was accurate; others that he did not address the consequences fully.
8. Students may note that a leader still can motivate and reassure people through speeches.

Literary Element

1. To inform citizens and to persuade Congress to declare war
2. He uses it to list the territories; Japan seems ruthless and scary.

Reading Strategy

1. He gives facts about the attack; he also describes it as premeditated, deliberate, and deceptive.
2. When he assures "inevitable" victory against Japan's "dastardly" attacks, he shows bias.

✍ Writing

Use the following criteria to evaluate students' press releases:

- Does the press release address the president's speech?
- Does the press release summarize the main arguments and include direct quotes?

After You Read

Respond and Think Critically

Respond and Interpret

1. What was your reaction to Roosevelt's speech?
2. (a)Why, according to Roosev was the United States unprepared for the att on Pearl Harbor? (b)How do you thin is information might have influenced Cong?
3. (a)Why does Roosevelt claim was obvious that the attack on Pearl Harb as planned "many days or weeks ago"? How do you think this influenced the pre's reaction to the attack?
4. (a)Which places does Roose y Japan has attacked? (b)What effe Roosevelt seem to want this informati ave on his audience?

Analyze and Evaluate

5. (a)What does Roosevelt mean when he says, "The people of the United States have already formed their opinions"? (b)Why does he say this?
6. (a)How does Roosevelt assure the public of a war victory? (b)Why do you think he does this?

Connect

7. **Big Idea** The United States and the World Did Roosevelt adequately address the political and human consequences of declaring war?
8. **Connect to Today** Considering the effects of the Internet, long distance telephones, and other global communication today, how powerful might this type of speech be today? Explain.

Literary Element Author Purpose

Roosevelt makes every word y supporting his arguments and appealing earts and minds of his audience.

1. What, in your opinion, is the se of Roosevelt's speech?
2. How does the rhetorical de petition help Roosevelt influence and p audience?

Reading Strategy Distinact and (

Roosevelt includes both fac on in his "War Message to Congress. e chart you created (page 971).

1. How does Roosevelt us nd opinion in his speech?
2. How is bias present in beech?

LOG ON ▶ Literature On

Selection Resources For S, eFlashcards, and Reading-Writing Cies, go to glencoe.com and enter Quic 800u6.

Vocabulary Practice

Denotation and Connotation Denotation is a word's literal, dictionary meaning. **Connotation** is its implied, or cultural, meaning. For example, *shy* and *bashful* have similar denotations, "reserved or timid," but different connotations:

Weaker	Stronger
shy	bashful

For each vocabulary word below, find one synonym. Then explain which word has a stronger connotation. Use a dictionary if you need help.

infamy   diplomatic

premeditated   inevitable   implication

✍ Writing

Write a Press Release Imagine that you are Roosevelt's press secretary. Write a press release about the president's speech to give to reporters covering the address to Congress. Make sure to summarize the president's arguments and include direct quotations from the speech.

Vocabulary

infamy: disgrace; e stronger connotation. s a loss of reputation, whiles a reputation as som

diplomatic: tactf as the stronger connotat implies premeditated be tful implies unplanne

implication: effect; *Implication* has the stronger connotation. An implication is based on behavior that can be modified, but an effect might occur naturally.

premeditated: planned; *Premeditated* has the stronger connotation. It has legal implications, and *planned* does not.

inevitable: predictable; *Inevitable* has the stronger connotation. Something that is predictable may still be avoided, but something inevitable cannot.

Vocabulary Workshop

Word Origins: Math and Science

Literature Connection The word *squadron* is related to the Latin word *quadrum*, meaning "square."

> "Indeed, one hour after Japanese air squadrons had commenced bombing . . . Oahu, the Japanese Ambassador to the United States and his colleague delivered to our Secretary of State a formal reply to a recent American message."
>
> —Franklin Delano Roosevelt, from "War Message to Congress"

Several math and science terms come from this root: *quadrangle, quadrant, quadruped,* and *quadratic,* for example. You have probably figured out that *quadru-* or *quadr-* means "four."

Examples You can figure out what many math and science terms mean if you know some common word parts and their definitions, s
as those below.

astro-	star; celestial body;	-gon	a figure having
astr-	outer space		specified kind
			number of an[g]
hydro-	water; liquid		
hydr-		-nomy	a body of kn[o]
			edge about a
poly-	more than one;		cific field
	many; much		
		-sphere	a celestial b[o]
penta-	five		such as a pl[a]
			or star
-cephalus	a head		

Practice Answer the following questions by combining two
parts from the list above. Consult a dictionary to check your
Write the answers on a piece of paper.

1. What is the word for an abnormal increase of fluid in the
2. What is the word for the scientific study of heavenly bodi
   outer space?
3. What is the word for a closed plane figure bounded by s
   lines?
4. What is the word for water vapor in Earth's atmosphere?
5. What is the word for a five-sided polygon?

Word Origins

Many English math and science terms come from the Latin language, as do many of the word parts at the left.

Tip

When you are asked for the meaning of a word that appears in a reading passage, knowledge of some common word parts can help you. Use your prior knowledge to help you recall similar words.

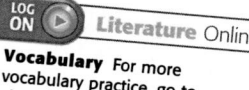 **Literature** Online

Vocabulary For more vocabulary practice, go to glencoe.com and enter QuickPass code GLA9800u6.

English Learners

DIFFERENTIATED INSTRUCTION

Beginning Review with English learners the definitions of the words *root word, prefix,* and *suffix.* Work with students to list at least one word for each of the word parts listed on this page. Have students look up unfamiliar words in the dictionary. Then help them make the connection between the word part and the definition of the word. For example, an *astronaut* is a per-

[a]s in space and the word part
[to] mean outer space. Remind
[w]ord parts can be used to
[a] meaning of unfamiliar words.

Vocabulary Workshop

Word Origins: Math and Science

Focus

Point out to students that understanding word parts in unfamiliar words is a skill that requires some practice. With wide reading and the help of a dictionary, students can learn to recognize common prefixes, suffixes, and roots and their meanings. Have students use the definitions of word parts provided here to figure out the meanings of the math and science words in the exercise below.

Teach

Word Origins **Say:** A dictionary can provide a word's etymology or history. In most dictionaries this information appears before the word's definition. Have students practice by finding the etymologies of the words *polyglot* and *atmosphere.*

Assess

Practice

1. hydrocephalus
2. astronomy
3. polygon
4. hydrosphere
5. pentagon

 For additional vocabulary practice, see Glencoe Interactive Vocabulary CD-ROM.

Before You Read

Focus

Cultural History ☆

B-29 Planes The Boeing B-29 plane, also known as the "Superfortress," was designed to be a bomber plane with the capability of carrying more guns and bombs than the B-17 and the B-24 planes. Innovations were also made in the targeting and navigations system of the planes. The two planes—the *Enola Gay* and the *Bockscar*—that dropped atomic bombs on Hiroshima and Nagasaki at the end of the World War II were modified B-29 planes.

Before You Read

The Death of the Ball Turret Gunner

Meet **Randall Jarre**
(1914–1965)

Randall Jarrell's influence other writers in the mid-twentieth cent was so enormous. His work as a critic, tea novelist, and poet helped define poetry's path ing the 1950s and early 1960s.

Born in Nashville, Tennessee, I spent most of his youth in Long Beach, Calif. His interest in poetry began during his tim Vanderbilt University. There he studied und ble southern writers John Crowe Ransom a bert Penn Warren, who nurtured his skil poet and critic. After earning BA and grees from Vanderbilt, Jarrell began a ca professor of English literature, first at K College and then at the University of Tex

> "If I can think of it, it ist I want.
> I want . . . I want a sh some
>   near star
> To land in the yard."
>
> —Randall Jarr k Child"

Military Life In 1942, whe blished his first book of poems, *Blood fr*, the U.S. had just entered World W ame year, he joined the war effort by en Army Air Forces. He served as a con erator and trained B-29 bomber pilots II had a profound effect on Jarrell, i to write with great rancor, pity, and the evils of war. Many of his greate ar in *Little Friend, Little Friend* (194 1948). Both books deal with de war, and

violence. Jarrell also showed great compassion for people trapped in meaningless lives and for the victimization of women and children.

When the war ended, Jarrell taught for a year at Sarah Lawrence College. He later translated these teaching experiences into the satirical novel *Pictures from an Institution*. After Sarah Lawrence, Jarrell took a professorship at the University of North Carolina in Greensboro. From 1956 until 1958, he served as poetry consultant to the Library of Congress.

Critical Acclaim After the war, Jarrell produced several collections of verse and commentary. His criticism was some of the most shrewd and acerbic of its day. Jarrell could be brutal, and he often lambasted mediocre poetry. However, the fierceness of his reviews was not a display of aggression but, rather, of his love for poetry. He was a passionate advocate for verse that met his high standards. Robert Frost, William Carlos Williams, and Walt Whitman all met these standards and received revitalized acclaim from Jarrell.

In 1965, Jarrell was struck and killed by a car. It is unclear whether his death was accidental or whether Jarrell, like so many poets of his generation, chose suicide. Whatever the cause of his death, his importance is unquestionable. Jarrell's poetry captured what poet Karl Shapiro called "the common dialogue of Americans," a dialogue that modulates from weariness to terror, from hopefulness to ecstasy.

Literature Online

Author Search For more about Randall Jarrell, go to glencoe.com and enter QuickPass code GLA9800u6.

Selection Skills

Literary Elements
- Imagery (SE pp. 977–979)

The De
Ball Turr

Writing Skills/Grammar
- Write a Journal Entry (SE p. 979)
- Use Different Tones (TE p. 978)

Reading Skills
- Visualize (SE pp. 977, 979)
- Make Inferences (SE p. 978)

...lary Skills
- ...t Clues (SE p. 979)

Literature and Reading Preview

Connect to the Poem

What is it like to face death? Freewrite for a few minutes about how someone might describe the process of leaving the body.

Build Background

The aircraft that Jarrell mentions in his note were long-range bombers that the U.S. Army used in bombing raids over Europe and the Pacific during World War II. Both the B-17 and B-24 had Plexiglas ball turrets that housed machine gunners. Although both were powerful aircraft, these ball turrets made them vulnerable to attack.

Set Purposes for Reading

Big Idea The United States and the World

As you read, ask yourself, How might Jarrell's "The Death of the Ball Turret Gunner" represent the human aspect of World War II?

Literary Element Imagery

Imagery is the "word pictures" that writers create to evoke an emotional response. In creating imagery, writers use sensory details, or descriptions that appeal to one or more of the five senses. Imagery is often an integral part of modern and contemporary poetry. As you read, ask yourself, How does Jarrell use imagery to establish his setting and generate emotion?

Reading Strategy Visualize

To **visualize** is to use the imagination to picture the setting, characters, and action in a work of literature. As you read, ask yourself, What sensory details and descriptions are particularly vivid?

···

Tip: Take Notes In a web diagram, record powerful images and other images connected to them.

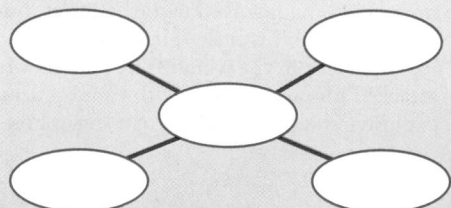

Learning Objectives

For pages 976–979

In studying this text, you will focus on the following objectives:

Literary Study: Analyzing imagery.

Reading: Visualizing setting, characters, and action.

Writing: Writing a journal entry.

Vocabulary

turret (tur´ it) *n.* a small, rotating domelike structure that is mounted with guns and attached to the body of an aircraft; p. 978 *In the turret the gunner began to fire.*

Plexiglas (plek´ si glas´) *n.* a light and very durable transparent plastic; p. 978 *The Plexiglas table could be easily moved.*

gunner (gun´ ər) *n.* an airman or a soldier who operates a gun; p. 978 *The gunner fired at the enemy aircraft and scored a hit.*

fetus (fē´ təs) *n.* the unborn young of a human or other viviparous vertebrate; p. 978 *The injured deer's fetus was unharmed.*

···

Tip: Context Clues To learn a new word, look at other words in the sentence and try to infer a possible meaning. Example: *We used Plexiglas in the architectural model because we needed to carry it on the long bus ride to school.* **Plexiglas** must be something that is lightweight and inexpensive enough for a student to purchase.

Before You Read

Focus

Summary

The poem's speaker is a gunner on a World War II bomber who uses vivid imagery to describe a combat mission and the aftermath of his death.

Vocabulary

Common and Proper Nouns Remind students that common nouns begin with lower-case letters and refer to a general type of person, place, or thing: *principal, city, bridge.* Proper nouns are capitalized and name a particular person, place, or thing: *Mr. Jones, New York City, Brooklyn Bridge.* Have students classify each vocabulary word as a common or proper noun. Then have them practice using the nouns in sentences.

 For activities related to this selection, see Unit 6 Teaching Resources Book, pp. 160–171.

RANDALL JARRELL **977**

English Learners

DIFFERENTIATED INSTRUCTION

Intermediate Explain to English learners that poets, in particular, rely on imagery to convey their thoughts because poets are usually trying to express many ideas in very few words. Rather than writing lengthy descriptions or narration, a poet might construct a vivid image that communicates a lot of information. Display the following sentences:

The leaves moved back and forth in a regular rhythm.

The dancing leaves swayed.

Ask: Which sentence creates the most vivid picture in your mind? Point out that the second sentence creates a visual image using few words.

Encourage students to make a chart using the five senses as headings for five columns. As they read the poem, have them write images that appeal to each of the senses in the chart.

Teach

Reading Strategy | 1

Make Inferences Ask:
Which words indicate that the speaker feels a lack of control? (*fell, hunched,* and *loosed*)

Literary Element | 2

Imagery Answer: *It aligns with the images of "mother's sleep" (line 1), "in its belly" (line 2), and "the fetus in the womb" (Note from the Author). They suggest the speaker is like a helpless, newborn animal.*

Writer's Technique ☆

Sentence Structure
Jarrell's poem is only three sentences long. Each sentence begins with an adverbial phrase or clause, which locates the speaker in a particular place or moment. Each builds suspense, carrying the reader through the poem.

Progress Check

Can students analyze imagery?

If No → See Unit 6 Teaching Resources Book, p. 166.

978

The Death of the Ball Turret Gunner

Randall Jarrell

From my mother's sleep I fell into the State,
☆ And I hunched in its belly till my wet fur froze.
Six miles from earth, loosed from its dream of life,
I woke to black flak¹ and the nightmare fighters.
When I died they washed me out of the **turret** with a hose.

1. *Flak* is the fire of antiaircraft guns.

Imagery *Which other images does the image in line 2 align with to convey the overall meaning of the poem? What do these images suggest?*

Vocabulary

turret (tur′ it) *n.* a small, rotating domelike structure that is mounted with guns and attached to the body of an aircraft

Plexiglas (plek′ si glas′; spelling corrected) *n.* a light and very durable transparent plastic

gunner (gun′ ər) *n.* an airman or a soldier who operates a gun

fetus (fē′ təs) *n.* the unborn young of a human or other viviparous vertebrate

NOTE FROM THE AUTHOR:
A ball turret was a **plexiglass** sphere set into the belly of a B-17 or B-24, and inhabited by two .50 caliber machine guns and one man, a short small man. When this **gunner** tracked with his machine guns a fighter attacking his bomber from below, he revolved with the turret; hunched upside down in his little sphere, he looked like the **fetus** in the womb. The fighters which attacked him were armed with cannon firing explosive shells. The hose was a steam hose.

—Randall Jarrell

978 UNIT 6 FROM DEPRESSION TO COLD WAR

Writing Practice

Use Different Tones Have small groups read the poem and the author's note, focusing on the tone. Then ask students to use the information to write a letter to the gunner's family conveying the news of his death, an official report or newscast of the event, or an obituary. Before students start writing, have them discuss the different tones necessary for each type of writing. For example, a letter to the gunner's family should sound offi-cial but also convey a sense of sympathy. An official report or newscast should be factual with few embellishments. An obituary usually describes a person's life and achievements in positive terms. Students may want to brainstorm different ways to describe the gunner's death before they start writing.

Respond and Think Critically

Respond and Interpret

1. Which phrase or image was the most potent for you? Why?

2. (a)What happens to the speaker in the first two lines? (b)What do these lines suggest about his attitude toward the situation? What do they suggest about the poet's view of the gunner?

3. (a)Where is the speaker in line 3? (b)What do you think he means by "loosed from its dream of life"?

4. (a)What happens to the speaker in line 4? (b)What does the dream of life entail? What realization does the gunner have in line 4?

Analyze and Evaluate

5. What is ironic about Jarrell's comparison of the ball turret gunner and a fetus in the womb?

6. Critics have characterized Jarrell as a master of plain speech and clear, stark language. Do these apply to this poem? Explain.

Connect

7. **Big Idea** The United States and the World In what ways has this poem helped to develop your understanding of World War II?

8. **Connect to Today** How might an artist today personalize the experiences of war?

Literary Element Imagery

Imagery can have a profound impact on the mood of a literary work. When images with highly contrasting moods are juxtaposed, the results can be jarring, ironic, or even humorous.

1. What is the mood of this poem? What images contribute to its mood?

2. What images in this poem introduce contrasts in mood? How does this imagery alter the poem?

Reading Strategy Visualize

Visualizing is a useful method of comprehending a text. Try to visualize the actions, characters, and settings of each line in relation to the piece as a whole.

1. Briefly describe how the image in line 1 functions in the poem as a whole.

2. What other images are easier to understand once they are placed in context? Explain.

LOG ON **Literature** Online

Selection Resources For Selection Quizzes, eFlashcards, and Reading-Writing Connection activites, go to glencoe.com and enter QuickPass code GLA9800u6.

Vocabulary Practice

Practice with Context Clues Identify in the sentences below context clues to the meaning of each boldfaced vocabulary word.

1. There was a malfunction in the **turret,** or the rotating domelike structure mounted with guns at the bottom of the aircraft.

2. We watched our friends play racquetball through the **Plexiglas,** a light plastic.

3. He wanted to be a **gunner,** not a soldier who worked in a support position.

4. When a woman is pregnant, she carries a **fetus** in her womb.

Writing

Write a Journal Entry Imagine you are the person who washes the dead gunner's body out of the turret with a hose. How does performing this duty—and seeing this image—affect you? What does it say about the value placed on life, and on death? Write a journal entry in which you describe your thoughts and feelings as a fellow soldier in World War II.

RANDALL JARRELL **979**

1. The image of the pilot's remains being hosed out is shocking.

2. (a) He leaves home to be a soldier and becomes a ball turret gunner. (b) The poet is sensitive to the gunner's fear.

3. (a) In the plane, six miles above the ground. (b) He has lost the security and hope normally associated with life on earth.

4. (a) He is in the "nightmare" of a battle. (b) Flying in a warplane; war is dangerous.

5. A fetus suggests life; the gunner, curled up like a fetus, faces death.

6. The poem's language is stark and plain; the poem is not a narrative but makes it clear that the gunner dies.

7. The image of a sudden, violent death makes the war tangible; the poem's dark tone and stark language reveal war's horrors.

8. Through poetry, story, movie, or video on the Internet

Literary Element

1. The hunched gunner, the wet fur, the miles from earth, and the black flak add to the dark, fearful mood.

2. Contrasting images of the fetus and the dead gunner hosed out of the plane are stark and shocking.

Reading Strategy

1. It sets up the birth and sleeping motifs and suggests vulnerability.

2. The crouching animal represents how a gunner sat in the turret.

Writing

Use the following criteria to evaluate students' journal entries:

- Does the entry describe how the experience affects the writer?
- Does the entry discuss the significance of the event in terms of life and death?

Vocabulary

1. The definition is in the sentence.

2. *Plexiglas* is defined as "light plastic." Also, it must be durable and clear.

3. The opposite of *gunner* is in the sentence, so a gunner carries a gun and does not work in a support position.

4. The context of the sentence implies that a *fetus* is an unborn child.

Focus

Bellringer Options

Daily Language Practice Transparency 90

Or ask: Why do people retell stories of personal suffering and hardship? Why do they want to remember their bad experiences? *(Students may suggest that people retell such stories to help release some of the powerful emotions such experiences create. They may also tell such stories in order to help future generations avoid the same mistakes.)* Have students identify feelings a storyteller might experience when giving an account of personal suffering.

Connect to the Reading Selections

Allow students to share their responses to the opening questions. Then have students discuss what they already know about the writers Elie Wiesel, Garrett Hongo, and Art Spiegelman or about the Holocaust and the internment of Japanese Americans during World War II.

Compare Literature About the Horrors of WWII

How do you respond to tragic events in life? In the following selections, Elie Wiesel, Garrett Hongo, and Art Spiegelman show the value of confronting the horrors of the past—both to understand the present and to ensure that the disasters of history do not repeat themselves.

from *All Rivers Run to the Sea*
by Elie Wiesel..memoir..................983
POLAND, 1940s

from *Kubota* by Garrett Hongo.................................memoir..................993
HAWAII, 1940s

from *Maus: A Survivor's Tale*
by Art Spiegelman...graphic novel..................998
POLAND, 1940s

COMPARE THE `Big Idea`
The United States and the World

Wiesel and Spiegelman show the horrible tragedy of the Holocaust. Hongo addresses a byproduct of World War II: the paranoia that led to Japanese American internment. As you read, ask yourself, What statements about history and personal expression do these selections make?

COMPARE Reflections

Wiesel, Hongo, and Spiegelman reflect on the past in these selections. Wiesel looks back on his own experiences; Hongo and Spiegelman learn about history through the memories of their elders. As you read, ask, Which of the writers' reflections gave you new insights about those tragic events?

COMPARE Cultures

The Jewish communities presented in Wiesel's memoir and Spiegelman's graphic novel must band together to survive the atrocities of the Nazis. Hongo expresses his hope that Japanese American culture can overcome its lingering discomfort from the legacy of internment and finally fully express itself. As you read, ask yourself, What was life like for people of oppressed cultures during WWII?

980 UNIT 6 FROM DEPRESSION TO COLD WAR

Selection Skills

Literary Elements
- Narrator (SE pp. 982–991; TE p. 1000)
- Autobiography (SE p. 991)

Comparing Literature

Writing Skills/Grammar
- Write an Essay (SE p. 1001)
- Describe a Character (TE p. 994)

Reading Skills
- Activate Prior Knowledge (SE pp. 982, 983, 985, 988, 992; TE p. 993)

Vocabulary Skills
- Denotation and Connotation (SE p. 982)
- Word Parts (SE p. 988)

Listening/Speaking/Viewing Skills
- Analyze Art (SE p. 997)
- Enact a Scene (TE p. 998)

Before You Read
from *All Rivers Run to the Sea*

Meet **Elie Wiesel**
(born 1928)

Holocaust survivor Elie Wiesel believes that memory can be a powerful foundation for unity. This notion echoes his personal struggle with the past and illustrates his attempt to transform his struggle into a universal fight against oppression and apathy. Wiesel gave a stirring speech at the U.S. Holocaust Memorial Museum dedication in 1993. His words are engraved in stone at the museum entrance, encouraging future generations to recognize this duty:

> *"For the dead and the living, we must bear witness."*
>
> —Elie Wiesel

The Holocaust Wiesel spent his childhood in Sighet, Romania, where synagogues, day schools, and Jewish newspapers flourished in the vibrant Jewish community. Wiesel began attending *kheder* (religious elementary school) when he was three. He studied secular subjects, played the violin, and found a scholar with whom to study Kabbalah, a mystical interpretation of Hebrew Scriptures.

In the spring of 1944, fifteen-year-old Wiesel and his family were deported from Sighet to the death camp Auschwitz-Birkenau in Poland. Wiesel was separated from his mother and sisters—his mother and youngest sister were immediately gassed to death. Wiesel remained with his father at Auschwitz and later at Buchenwald, another camp. Tragically, his father died just months before the liberation of the camp in 1945. Wiesel survived and was later reunited with his older sisters.

Giving Voice to Memory After the liberation, Wiesel vowed to keep silent about the horrors he had witnessed. He went to France, where he continued his education. In Paris, he began work as a journalist, writing stories for the Yiddish newspaper *Zion in Kamf* and the Israeli newspaper *Yedi'ot Akharonot*. Journalism put him in contact with French writer François Mauriac. In 1954, at Mauriac's behest, Wiesel broke his silence and gave voice to his memories. He published his Yiddish memoir, *Un Di Velt Hot Geshvign* ("And the World Kept Silent"), in 1956. In 1958, under Mauriac's guidance, Wiesel revised the text and translated it into French under the title *La Nuit*. In 1960 this work was published in English as *Night*.

Wiesel moved to the U.S. in 1956 and became a citizen in 1963. As a result of prolific writing and lecturing, he has become one of the most visible and renowned Holocaust survivors, winning the Nobel Peace Prize in 1986. In his acceptance speech, Wiesel acknowledged the problem of oppression, but even more that of indifference: "We must always take sides. Neutrality helps the oppressor, never the victim. Silence encourages the tormentor, never the tormented. Sometimes we must interfere." By confronting and exploring his own horrific experiences, Wiesel has transformed them into understanding, dialogue, and action.

1

LOG ON ▶ **Literature** Online

Author Search For more about Elie Wiesel, go to glencoe.com and enter QuickPass code GLA9800u6.

ELIE WIESEL **981**

Before You Read
Focus

Big Idea   **1**

The United States and the World Ask a student to read Elie Wiesel's words from his Nobel acceptance speech. **Ask:** Do you agree or disagree with this idea? Discuss the way this philosophy might work for an individual and for a nation. Invite students to think of personal and world situations and the effects of taking sides in each.

English Learners

DIFFERENTIATED INSTRUCTION

Intermediate Some of the vocabulary from the selection may be unfamiliar to students. A *revolver* is a handgun; the name refers to the action of the gun's cylinder which rotates. The word *nocturnal* comes from the Latin root that means night; the *nocturnal trains* in the selection describe trains that run at night. The word *nauseating*, which means to cause stomach distress or disgust, comes from the Greek root that means sailor. The word *disconcerting* is an adjective that means to make someone uneasy or confused. Wiesel writes that "people adjusted with disconcerting rapidity" to a terrible situation, meaning that he is disturbed by the speed at which people adjusted. Wiesel used the word *transport* as a noun in this selection, referring to the trains that carried Jews to the camps. Discuss these and other unfamiliar words with students. Then have students make up a sentence for each word. Have them read the sentences aloud to the class.

Before You Read

Focus

Summary

When the narrator was 15, his family and his neighbors were rounded up by the Nazis and deported on trains to the Auschwitz-Birkenau concentration camps where many of them experienced deprivation and death. Recalling the events years later, the narrator weaves together his memories and adult realizations. He tells of his lifelong search for information about those who were never seen again. He questions the power of human ideals and beauty in a world where such horrors could take place.

 For summaries in languages other than English, see Unit 6 Teaching Resources Book, pp. 173–178.

Vocabulary

Denotation and Connotation **Say:** Both *premonition* and *trepidation* have meanings relating to fear or dread about the future. **Ask:** How are the meanings of these words different? *(Trepidation is a feeling a person has; a premonition is a thing or an idea.)* **Say:** Use both words in a sentence. *(Malka's premonition that the important meeting would not go as planned gave her a sense of trepidation.)*

 For additional vocabulary practice, see Unit 6 Teaching Resources Book, p. 181.

Literature and Reading Preview

Connect to the Memoir

Why do you think large-scale acts of violence and cruelty still occur in today's world? What might be some solutions? With a group, discuss these questions.

Build Background

During WWII, Nazi forces rounded up Jews in Poland and Germany and brought them by train to concentration camps such as Auschwitz-Birkenau. Most Jews did not realize what lay ahead at Auschwitz, though many suspected the worst. In the camps, Nazis performed inhumane medical experiments on prisoners and executed millions of innocent Jews. **1**

Set Purposes for Reading

Big Idea The United States and the World

After World War I, many countries isolated themselves to avoid the complex military alliances that had spurred that war. As you read, ask, How does Wiesel explore the question of why the world neglected its responsibility to stop the Nazi campaign?

Literary Element Narrator

The **narrator** is the person who tells a story. The narrator may be a character in the story or someone from the outside looking in. As you read, ask yourself, How does the perspective of the narrator affect your understanding of the selection?

Reading Strategy Activate Prior Knowledge

When you read, you bring **prior knowledge** and past experience to the task. As you read, ask yourself, What do I already know about the Holocaust?

....

Tip: Take Notes List prior knowledge or past experiences that help you understand each event or statement in this selection.

Prior Knowledge	Event in Selection
Many people are prejudiced toward particular cultural or ethnic groups.	Nazis treat Jews as subhuman.

Vocabulary

ineffably (in ef´ ə blē) *adv.* to a degree that is impossible to express; indescribably; p. 983 *James was ineffably sad when he said goodbye to his family and boarded the train for Chicago.*

succumb (sə kum´) *v.* to give in or submit to; p. 986 *The marathon runner insisted that she would finish the race and not succumb to fatigue.*

premonition (prē´ mə nish´ ən) *n.* a warning, or foreboding about the future; p. 988 *Jane had a premonition that something bad would happen later that afternoon.*

fetid (fe´ təd) *adj.* having a bad odor; p. 988 *The refrigerator had not been cleaned in so long, a fetid smell wafted from it.*

curt (kurt) *adj.* rudely brief, or short; terse; p. 989 *The curt reply Mr. Jenkins gave to Lydia's question suggested he didn't want to be bothered.*

....

Tip: Denotation and Connotation Some words that have the same dictionary definition can have different cultural definitions. For example, *smelly* and *fetid* have similar meaning, but *fetid* has a stronger connotation.

Reading Practice

SPIRAL REVIEW **Preview** This selection describes the writer's survival in the Nazi death camps and his efforts to understand and explain the great evil that he witnessed. Write these questions on the board:

- Have you ever witnessed an injustice but felt unable to stop it? Explain.
- Have you ever thought you got a "lucky break" while others around you suffered? How did this make you feel?

Say: As you read, make notes of the narrator's (the writer's) emotional and rational responses to the horrific events he witnesses.

Comparing Literature

from
All Rivers Run to the Sea
Elie Wiesel

Our turn came on Tuesday, May 16. "All Jews out!" the gendarmes[1] screamed, and we found ourselves in the street. There was another heat wave. My little sister was thirsty, and my grandmother too. They didn't complain, but I did, not openly, but it amounted to the same thing. I felt queasy, ill. I was suffering, but didn't know from what. I was **ineffably** sad. As

---

1. *Gendarmes* are police officers.

Vocabulary

ineffably (in ef´ ə blē) *adv.* to a degree that is impossible to express; indescribably

---

in the presence of death, I didn't dare raise my voice. This was where my childhood and my adolescence, my prayers, studies, and fasting had led. These moments would remain forever etched within me. Wherever life took me, a part of me would always remain in that street, in front of my empty house, awaiting the order to depart.

I see my little sister, I see her with her rucksack, so cumbersome, so heavy. I see her and an immense tenderness sweeps over me. Never will her innocent smile fade from my soul. Never will her glance cease to sear me. I tried to help her; she protested. Never will the sound of her voice leave my heart. She was thirsty, my little sister was thirsty. Her lips were parched. Pearls of sweat formed on her clear forehead. I gave her a little water. "I can wait," she said, smiling. My little sister wanted to be brave. And I wanted to die in her place.

I seldom speak of her in my writing, for I dare not. My little sister with her sun-bathed golden hair is my secret. I never even talked to Marion[2] or to my son Elisha about her. It mortifies me to talk about her in the past tense, for she is present. Her presence is more real to me than my own. My little sister Tsiporah, my little angel scorched by a darkened sun, I cannot picture you as death's hostage. You will remain on our street, on the pavement in front of our house.

I gazed at the house—we all did—with anguish. Here we had lived a Jewish family life that was now gone forever. The laughter and laments, the peace of Shabbat, the prayer of the God of Abraham whispered by my mother and my grandmother, the festival of Sukkoth, the songs of Rosh Hashana, the Passover meals, the community gatherings, my

---

2. *Marion* is Wiesel's wife.

Activate Prior Knowledge *What memories are forever etched in your mind?*

ELIE WIESEL **983**

Comparing Literature

Teach

Big Idea | 1

The United States and the World Soviet and U.S. forces first liberated concentration camps in April 1945. **Ask:** How do you think the soldiers felt when they saw the camps? *(horrified, angry, saddened)*

Reading Strategy | 2

Activate Prior Knowledge **Answer:** *Students might mention a moment from their childhood or the first time they experienced something.*

For additional practice using the reading skill or strategy, see Unit 6 Teaching Resources Book, p. 180.

View the Photograph ★

The train rides were a horrific introduction to the deprivations prisoners would experience at the camps. Passengers were deprived of food and water for days, and some had to cope with extreme temperatures.

 For an audio recording of this selection, use Listening Library Audio CD-ROM.

Readability Scores
Dale-Chall: 6.1
DRP: 53
Lexile: 860

English Learners

DIFFERENTIATED INSTRUCTION

Beginning Say: Wiesel writes "My little sister Tsiporah, my little angel scorched by a darkened sun, I cannot picture you as death's hostage." **Ask:** Who is *my little angel*? *(his little sister who had golden hair)* Why does Wiesel refer to his sister as *death's hostage*? *(She is dead at the time Wiesel writes this.)* Could the sun be darkened? Why do you think Wiesel referred to the sun in this way? *(It may refer to the evil then and to come.)* How was his little sister *scorched*? *(His sister was thirsty standing out in the hot sun; it might refer to her death during this evil time.)* Explain that the phrases *my little angel scorched by a darkened sun* and *death's hostage* are metaphors, in which one thing is compared to another to indicate similarity.

Comparing Literature

Teach

Big Idea | 1

The United States and the World Answer: *International news can bring attention to these types of acts and show inaccurate information being communicated by the country committing the acts.* Explain that these news reports were forbidden in German-occupied countries because the reports were broadcast by the Soviet Union and Great Britain. Both were Nazi Germany's enemies.

Literary Element | 2

Narrator Answer: *The narrator is Jewish. He is reflecting on the painful memories of his youth. His family was forced from their home during the Nazi campaign against Jews.*

Cultural History ☆

Bar and Bat Mitzvahs

Bar Mitzvah means "son of the commandment." During the ceremony, a boy reads a passage from the Torah in front of the congregation. This event is the culmination of a period of religious training. Many congregations hold similar ceremonies for girls. The ceremony for a girl is called a *bat mitzvah,* which means "daughter of the commandment."

---

grandfather's visits.[3] The stories of beggars and of refugees, the forbidden broadcasts of Radio London and Radio Moscow that we listened to at night, curtains drawn and shutters closed. I picture myself sitting under an acacia tree, a book in my hands, talking to the clouds. Tsipouka is playing with a hoop. "Come and play with me," she says, but I don't feel like it. And now, as I write these words, my heart is pounding. I should have closed my book and stopped my dream, dropped everything to play with my little sister. Other images rise up: the sleigh in winter, the horse and carriage in summer; a cousin's funeral (a fortune-teller is said to have foretold her death); Bea sick with typhus:[4] she lies in a room of her own, feverish and contagious, hovering between life and death. My grandmother asks me to go with her to the synagogue. It is night. She opens the Holy Ark[5] and sobs, "Holy Torah, intercede on behalf of Batya, daughter of Sarah. She is young and can still accomplish many good deeds for your glory. Tell the Lord, blessed be His name, to let her live. She will be more useful to Him than I." She closes the Ark and backs slowly to the door. There she stops and says, "If I have any years to live, Lord, give them to her. I exchange my future for hers. Let that be my gift." When Bea takes a few steps, I glance at my grandmother. She has offered her life. What will become of her now? I picture our house and see Hilda inside, Hilda the old-

est of the children, whose radiant beauty drew all the matchmakers[6] of the region.

I see the people who came through that door day and night to consult with my father—my father who now, bent under the weight of his pack, knows not to whom he might turn for advice. And my mother, always gracious and brave, afraid to look at us, afraid to see the house, afraid to burst into tears only to find she can never stop. So she looks at the sky, the pitiless sky that numbs us with an unseasonable and stifling heat. And the sun? Will it keep its secret? The night before, very late, like makeshift gravediggers, we had dug a dozen holes under the trees to bury what remained of our jewelry, precious objects, and money. I buried the gold watch I had been given as a bar mitzvah[7] present.

For years I dreamed of returning to my native town. It was an obsession. It took two decades, and that trip has now been added to my obsessions. It was night. There was a sleeping town and a sleeping house which hadn't changed: the same gate, same garden, same well. Choked with fear, as though caught in a whirlwind of hallucinations, I wondered whether it had all been a dream, whether our Jewish neighbors were still there, and my parents and my sisters too. Terror swept me away and carried me back. I waited for a window to open and for a boy who looked like the child I had been to call out to me: Hey, mister, what are you doing in my dream?

But strangers were living in my house. They had never heard my name. Inside, nothing had changed: the same furniture, the same tile stove my father had borrowed money to buy; the beds, tables, and chairs

---

3. *Shabbat* refers to the "Sabbath" or holy day for Jews, which occurs each week from sunset on Friday to the following night. In the Bible, *Abraham* is considered a patriarch, or father figure, to the Hebrew people. *Sukkoth* is a Jewish harvest festival. *Rosh Hashana* is the Jewish new year.
4. *Typhus* is a disease characterized by high fever and delirium.
5. The *Holy Ark* is a cabinet in a synagogue where the scrolls of the Torah, or the first five books of the Hebrew scriptures, are stored.

6. *Matchmakers* are people who set up marriages.
7. A *bar mitzvah* is a celebration of a Jewish boy's thirteenth birthday, marking the beginning of his adult and religious duties. ☆

 The United States and the World *What effect do you think international news can have on acts of injustice carried out by a government?*

 Narrator *What do you know about the narrator at this point? What type of perspective does he have?*

Reading Practice

Monitor Comprehension Wiesel blends childhood memories and adult experiences. He poses questions about truth and meaning in the world. To help students understand this difficult material, review reading strategies, such as asking questions, restating the author's ideas, and answering questions. Have students add these strategies: rereading, varying read-

ing rate, using a dictionary, and creating a graphic organizer. Ask them to monitor their comprehension, noting strategies that help them.

were ours, still in the same places. My feverish eyes wandered left and right, up and down. Was it possible that not a single trace of us remained? But there was one, just one. On the wall above my bed had been a photograph of my beloved master, Rebbe Israel of Wizhnitz. I remember it well: I had hung it there the day he died, the second day of the month of Sivan.[8] I can see myself standing there, a heavy hammer in my hand, driving in the nail and hanging the frame. As I write these words, I suddenly realize that my mother died eight years later on exactly the same day, along with my little sister and Grandma Nissel. I cried for the Rebbe's death as I hung his photograph above my bed. The nail was still there. A huge cross was hanging from it.

"We must go now," my mother said. "We must stay together."

It was Tuesday afternoon. We were still in Sighet.[9] Our convoy would not leave for several days. We had been temporarily transferred to the smaller ghetto, whose inhabitants had just been driven out.

We moved into the home of Mendel, my father's brother. My mother cooked our favorite dish, latkes, potato pancakes. This time there was no rationing; we ate all we wanted.

Mendel was my silent uncle. He had married Golda, daughter of my maternal uncle

And now, as I write these words, my heart is pounding. I should have closed my book and stopped my dream, dropped everything to play with my little sister.

Israel. He was pious[10] and shy. They had three children. Their photograph lies before me, saved by a relative.

Sacred books were scattered on the floor. Someone must have removed them from his bag at the last minute. The table was set, and there was food on the plates. They had been taken away in the middle of a meal. This was what remained of a family.

After the war I questioned every survivor of the second transport I could find, seeking news of Uncle Mendel and his family. I thought I found the answer in 1988, when an elderly man called out to me in the lobby of a Miami Beach hotel. He was, like me, of Romanian-Hungarian origin, from a small village near Sighet, and he told me he had stayed in the smaller ghetto until its evacuation. In fact, he had been in the same camp with my uncle. "Really?" I exclaimed. "You knew my uncle?" "Knew him!" he said. "For years I've seen him, even in my sleep." And then he told me. At first Mendel and his son had been spared, like my father and me, and had been sent to a camp where conditions were relatively tolerable. But they were in different barracks and saw each other only during the day, at work. One night they could not bear to be separated. When the roll was called, the SS[11] Blockführer counted and recounted the prisoners and ordered: "Let

---

8. *Rebbe* means "Rabbi," a Jewish spiritual teacher. *Sivan* is the ninth month in the Jewish year.
9. *Sighet* is a town in Romania and the birthplace of Wiesel.
10. *Pious* means "seriously or devoutly religious."

11. *SS* refers to the Nazi paramilitary forces.

Activate Prior Knowledge *How does Wiesel's account of his family's experience add to your understanding of the Holocaust?* **3**

ELIE WIESEL **985**

Teach

Reading Strategy 3

Activate Prior Knowledge
Answer: *Students might say that Wiesel's portrayal of his family shows the unpredictability of life for Jewish people during World War II.* **Say:** Consider why a family would suddenly leave the dinner table. *(Students may suggest that only an emergency or important event could make a family interrupt dinner.)*

Language History

Ghetto The word *ghetto* is Italian for "foundry" or "iron works." The first European ghetto, or segregated Jewish community, was on the grounds of an empty foundry in Venice in the sixteenth century. From then through the nineteenth century, ghettos were set up all over Europe. By the mid-1940s, Germans used ghettos as temporary housing for Jews and others they intended to send to concentration camps.

Comparing Literature

Literary Element | 1

Narrator Answer: *He juxtaposes his own memories with other people's recollections and his adult understandings. He relies on the past and present to tell his story.*

View the Photograph ★

As Allied forces advanced into Germany, the Nazis abandoned the Buchenwald concentration camp. When American forces arrived, nearly 21,000 prisoners remained there, too weak and ill to flee. U.S. reporters and photographers provided some of the first images of concentration camps to be published in the United States.

Survivors at Buchenwald concentration camp remain in their barracks after liberation by Allies on April 16, 1945. Elie Wiesel, the Nobel Prize-winning author, is on the second bunk from the bottom, sixth from the left. ★

the prisoner who does not belong in this barracks show himself." Mendel's son took a few steps forward. "Closer!" the officer shouted. My young cousin obeyed, halting when he reached the SS man. The officer slowly drew his revolver and shot my cousin in the head, point-blank. My uncle, that sweet and timid man, hurled himself onto his son's body, as if to protect him in death. The SS man stared at him for a long moment and then shot him in the head too. "Ever since then," my witness said, "I see Mendel and his son in my dreams."

And I, I think of the biblical law that, out of compassion for animals, forbids the slaughter of an ox and his calf on the same day. The Germans, however, did not shrink from killing a father and son together, without a second thought, as one would step on two insects.

Fishel and Voïcsi, my cousins from Antwerp,[12] later gave me a different version of

their deaths. What is certain, though, is that the enemy annihilated my Uncle Mendel's family.

And what happened to my Aunt Zlati, my father's younger sister? I search my memories of the ghetto for her, but she is not there.

She was married to Nahman-Elye. I don't remember their two very young children, nor do I recall their presence during the weeks before the transport. Nahman-Elye, it seems, was among those the Hungarian army released from the labor battalions to be locked up in the ghetto. It seems he was deported with the first transport and later **succumbed** to the pressures and temptations of the camp life and became a cruel and murderous kapo.[13] It seems he was tried, sentenced to death, and executed by former deportees. My uncle in the enemy's service? A kapo? My uncle a torturer of his brothers in misfortune? I don't want to believe it.

But yes, that's the way it was.

We arrived at the station, where the cattle cars were waiting. Ever since my book *Night* I have pursued those nocturnal trains that crossed the devastated continent. Their

---

12. *Antwerp* is a city in Belgium.

13. *Kapo* refers to a prisoner who has been appointed by the enemy to police his or her own people.

Narrator *How does Wiesel shape his account of the Holocaust?* | 1

Vocabulary

succumb (sə kum´) *v.* to give in or submit to

Writing Practice

Wiesel Biography After students read the selection, they may wish to learn what happened to Wiesel after World War II. Ask students to research Wiesel's adult life. Have them write a short biography that includes major events in his life, such as his winning a Nobel prize. Students should explain the impact that Wiesel's experiences during the war had on the rest of his life.

shadow haunts my writing. They symbolize solitude, distress, and the relentless march of Jewish multitudes toward agony and death. I freeze every time I hear a train whistle.

Why were those trains allowed to roll unhindered into Poland? Why were the tracks leading to Birkenau[14] never bombed? I have put these questions to American presidents and generals and to high-ranking Soviet officers. Since Moscow and Washington knew what the killers were doing in the death camps, why was nothing done at least to slow down their "production"? That not a single Allied military aircraft ever tried to destroy the rail lines converging on Auschwitz remains an outrageous enigma to me. Birkenau was "processing" ten thousand Jews a day. Stopping a single convoy for a single night—or even for just a few hours—would have prolonged so many lives. At the least it would have been a warning to the Germans: Jewish lives do matter. But the free world didn't care whether Jews lived or died, whether they were annihilated one day or the next. And so the sealed trains continued to shatter the silence of Europe's flowering landscapes.

Meanwhile, our world contracted[15] steadily. The country became a city, the city a street, the street a house, the house a room, the room a sealed cattle car, the cattle car a concrete cellar where . . .

No, let us go no further. Decency and custom forbid it. I said it earlier, when speaking of my grandfather: In Jewish tradition a man's death belongs to him alone. Let the gas chambers remain closed to prying eyes, and to the imagination. We will never know all that hap-

---

14. *Birkenau* refers to Auschwitz-Birkenau, the most notorious of the Nazi concentration camps.
15. Here, *contracted* means "shrunk, or made smaller."

2 The United States and the World *How does Wiesel argue that international monitoring of human rights is necessary?*

3 Narrator *What qualities make Wiesel an effective storyteller of the Holocaust?*

pened behind those doors of steel. They say the victims fought among themselves for a breath of air, for one more second of life, that they climbed on the shoulders of the weakest in the so-called *Todeskampf*, the final struggle among the dying. Much has been said when silence ought to have prevailed. Let the dead speak for themselves, if they so choose. If not, may they be left in peace.

It is unbelievable how fast people adapt. It hurts to admit it, but within hours of first breathing the cattle car's nauseating air, we began to feel at home. "Home" was the edge of the wooden plank I sat on as I dreamed of the Jewish exiles of antiquity and the Middle Ages. More curious than afraid, I thought of myself as their brother. Mixed into my sadness there was undeniable excitement, for we were living a historic event, a historic adventure. The main thing was that we were still together. Had we been told that this journey would last for weeks or even years, we would have replied: May God grant that it be so, for nothing is worse than the unknown, and that was our destination—the unknown. I remember clinging to the thought that nothing is unknown to God, while nothing is truly known to man.

A rumor spread through the train. The Jewish doctors and their families, until recently allowed to live outside the ghetto, had been ordered to return to the ghetto the night before the transport and to join us that morning at the station. But we had seen no sign of them. It was now said that they had gathered at one of their homes the night before and decided to kill themselves. The rumor was apparently false, for in Birkenau I ran into our family doctor, Dr. Fisch, who had helped deliver Tsipouka. But thirty years later I found that the story was true after all. I was lecturing at a large university near Boston when a member of the physics department came up to me. "You're from Sighet, aren't you?" he asked. "So am I." He introduced himself, and the name gave me a start: he was the son of a famous surgeon. In

ELIE WIESEL **987**

Comparing Literature

Teach

| **Big Idea** | **2** |

The United States and the World **Answer:** *He infers that international monitoring can make people aware of human rights abuses and encourage people to take action against the perpetrators.*

| **Literary Element** | **3** |

Narrator **Answer:** *He has a deep respect for human life and Jewish tradition, and he experienced the Holocaust firsthand. He includes vivid images in his descriptions.*

Cultural History

Jewish Exile or Diaspora The word *Diaspora* refers to both the dispersion of the Jews from Palestine after the Kingdom of Judah fell to the Babylonians in 586 B.C. and to all of the Jewish communities living outside of Palestine or present-day Israel.

English Learners
DIFFERENTIATED INSTRUCTION

Intermediate Discuss the meanings and connotations of the words *home*, *normal*, and *neighbor* found on this page and the next. **Say:** Wiesel places quotation marks around these words. For example, he refers to the edge of a wooden plank in a bad-smelling cattle car as "home." **Ask:** What is he trying to convey? *(that the meanings of these words have completely changed under these terrible circumstances)*

Approaching Level
DIFFERENTIATED INSTRUCTION

Emerging To help students comprehend the author's story, have partners create a cluster diagram with Elie Wiesel's name in the center. As they read, students should write in circles around the center the events that Wiesel recounts and his feelings about each.

Comparing Literature

Teach

Vocabulary 1

Word Parts Help students decode the meaning of *premonitions*. The prefix *pre-* means "before;" the root *moni* comes from the Latin *monere*, which means "to warn"; and the suffix *-tion*, means "state or action." The word means "warnings or forebodings."

Reading Strategy 2

Activate Prior Knowledge
Answer: *Students might say that Wiesel's experience matches their expectations because people often look for a close-knit support group, such as a family, in times of crisis.*

Sighet we had evolved in different circles, but we had been brought to Auschwitz in the same convoy. We had a long talk about our town, and at one point I asked him about the rumor. He confirmed it. The doctors had indeed agreed on a collective suicide pact. "But why? Since at the time we didn't know where they were taking us." It turned out that his father did know. He had operated on a German officer who told him everything. Afterward he had summoned his colleagues to discuss what to do. The majority voted not to board the trains, deciding they might as well die at home. Some of the suicides did not succeed. They were carried to the cattle cars on stretchers.

My new friend the physics professor died one night in June 1991. A suicide, rumor had it. I was struck by the date. I realized that he too had died on the second day of the month of Sivan, exactly forty-seven years after his missed appointment with death in Birkenau.

Life in the cattle cars was the death of my adolescence. How quickly I aged. As a child I loved the unexpected: a visitor from afar, an unforeseen event, a marriage, a storm, even a disaster. Anything was preferable to routine. Now it was just the opposite. Anything was preferable to change. We clung to the present, we dreaded the future.

Hunger, thirst, and heat, the **fetid** stench, the hysterical howling of a woman gone mad—we were ready to endure it all, to suffer it all. So much so that a "normal," structured social life soon took shape in the car. Families stayed together, sharing whatever came their way: hard-boiled eggs, dried cakes, or fruit,

> I see myself sitting there, haggard and disoriented, a shadow among shadows.

respecting strict rules about drinking water, allowing each member a turn near the barred openings or at the waste pail shielded by blankets. People adjusted with disconcerting rapidity. Morning and evening we said our prayers together. I had brought some precious books along in my pack: a commentary by Rabbi Haim David Azoulai (the Hida), the K'dushat Levi of the Berdichever Rebbe. I opened them and tried hard to concentrate. A phrase of the Zohar, a major work of the Kabala,[16] haunted me: When the people of Israel set out into exile, God went with them. And now? I wondered. How far would God follow us now?

On the last day, when the train stopped near the Auschwitz station, our **premonitions** resurfaced. A few "neighbors" **1** devoured more than their rations, as though sensing that their days were numbered. My mother kept entreating us: Stay together at all costs. Someone, I can't remember who, asked, "What if we can't? What if they separate us?" My mother's answer: "Then we'll meet again at home as soon as the war is over."

Certain images of the days and nights spent on that train invade my dreams even now: anticipation of danger, fear of the dark; the screams of poor Mrs. Schechter, who, in her delirium, saw flames in the distance; the

---

16. The *Kabala*, also spelled "Kabbalah," is a book of mystical teachings based on the Jewish faith.

Activate Prior Knowledge What do you know about the way people tend to react in a crisis? How does Wiesel's experience compare and contrast with your expectations? **2**

Vocabulary

fetid (fe´ təd) *adj.* having a bad odor

Vocabulary

premonition (prē´ mə nish´ ən) *n.* a warning, or foreboding about the future

Listening and Speaking Practice

Compare and Contrast Wiesel writes that "Life in the cattle cars was the death of my adolescence." He compares life before this event to life on the cars and beyond. To initiate a discussion, **ask:** What changes for the author on the cattle cars? *(love of the unexpected turns to dread of the future; the adolescent rapidly ages; suffering becomes normal; life on the car becomes structured)* When the car comes to a

stop, Wiesel thinks that "Fate would at last reveal a truth reserved exclusively for us, a primordial truth, an ultimate postulate that would annihilate or overshadow all received ideas." Have students discuss the "truth" that Wiesel discovers. *(the horror of Auschwitz, the unthinkable acts of evil being committed)* **Ask:** How does Wiesel respond initially to this truth? *(He thinks he must be having a nightmare.)*

3 efforts to make her stop; the terror in her little boy's eyes. I recall every hour, every second. How could I forget? They were the last hours I spent with my family: the murmured prayers of my grandmother, whose eyes saw beyond this world; my mother's gestures, which had never been more tender; the troubled face of my little sister, who refused to show her fear. Yes, my memory gathered it all in, retained it all.

There was sudden trepidation that gripped us when, toward midnight, the train lurched forward again after stopping for several hours. I can still hear the whistle. Elsewhere I have told of what happened next—or rather, I have tried to tell it. But it feels like yesterday. It feels like now. Through the cracks in the boards I see barbed wire stretching to infinity. A thought occurs to me: The Kabala is right, infinity exists.

I see myself sitting there, haggard and disoriented, a shadow among shadows. I hear my little sister's fitful breathing. I try to conjure up my mother's features, and my father's. I need someone to reassure me. My heart thunders in deafening beats. Then there is silence, heavy and complete. Something was about to happen, we could feel it. Fate would at last reveal a truth reserved exclusively for us, a primordial truth, an ultimate postulate[17] that would annihilate or overshadow all received ideas. There was a burst of noise and the night was shattered into a thousand pieces. I felt myself shaken, pulled to my feet, pushed toward the door, toward strange shouting beings and barking dogs, a swelling throng that would cover the earth.

4 In *Night* I tell of the wrath of the "veterans." They swore at us. "What the hell are you *Schweinehunde*[18] doing here?" I was puzzled. Did they think we had come to this hell voluntarily, out of curiosity? Only years later did I understand. Two of their former companions,

Rudolf Vrba and Alfred Wetzler, had managed to escape from Birkenau in 1944 to warn Hungarian Jews of what was awaiting them. **4** That's why they were so enraged. They thought we should have known. Some of them even hit us.

Where were we going? It mattered little, for it was the same everywhere. All roads led to the enemy; it was he who would throw open the invisible black door that awaited us. "Stay together," my mother said. For another minute we did, clinging to one another's arms. Nothing in the world could separate us. The entire German army could not take my little sister from me. Then a **curt** order was issued—men on one side, women on the other—and that was that. A single order, and we were separated. I stared intently, trying desperately not to lose sight of my mother, my little sister with her hair of gold and sun, my grandmother, my older sisters. I see them always, for I am still looking for them, trying to embrace them one last time. We were taken away before I could tell my mother goodbye, before I could kiss her hand and beg her forgiveness for the wrongs I must have done her, before I could squeeze Tsipouka, my little sister, to my heart. What remains of that night like no other is an irremediable[19] sense of loss, of parting. My mother and my little sister left, and I never said goodbye. It all remains unreal. It's only a dream, I told myself as I walked, hanging on my father's arm. It's a nightmare that they have torn me from those I love, that they are beating people to death, that Birkenau exists and that it harbors a gigantic altar where demons of fire devour our people. It's in God's nightmare that human beings are hurling living Jewish children into the flames.

I reread what I have just written, and my hand trembles. I who barely weep am in tears. I

---

17. A *postulate* is a truth, or basic principle.
18. *Schweinehunde,* meaning "pig dogs," is a German word expressing a stereotypical insult.

19. *Irremediable* means "impossible to correct."

Vocabulary

curt (kurt) *adj.* rudely brief, or short; terse

ELIE WIESEL   **989**

Comparing Literature

Teach

Literary Element   **3**

Narrator The narrator describes in great detail the agony and despair he witnessed many years before. **Ask:** Is it likely that someone can remember exactly what happened years before? *(Yes. Traumatic events tend to imprint themselves strongly in the memory.)*

Literary Element   **4**

Irony   Ask: What is ironic about the response of "veterans" to the new arrivals? *(They are angry and frustrated; they had hoped the newcomers would have been warned.)*

Political History

Requests to Bomb Auschwitz
Rudolf Vrba and Alfred Wetzler reported on the atrocities at Auschwitz. U.S. officials did not receive the complete report—with its requests to bomb Auschwitz—until six months after other Allied intelligence officials. They did not take action because, critics suggest, they were unwilling to divert equipment.

English Learners

DIFFERENTIATED INSTRUCTION

 Beginning Students may struggle with the vocabulary and syntax on this page and the next as the author describes his feelings and attempts to understand such evil. Have partners or small groups work together to read the second half of this page and all of the next page, summarize each paragraph, and discuss difficult concepts, images, or words. Have students use a dictionary to find the meaning of words as needed.

Advanced Learners

DIFFERENTIATED INSTRUCTION

Respond Some learners may respond deeply to experiences Wiesel describes but may not share their feelings aloud in class. Have students write their thoughts in a journal or create poems or drawings that reflect their responses to the selection.

Comparing Literature

Teach

Big Idea 1

The United States and the World
Answer: *He wants the world to acknowledge its mistakes and honor those who died in the Holocaust by preventing further tragedies.*

(ADVANCED) The Nazis' treatment of the Jews was not a major factor behind the United States' entrance into the war. **Say:** In 1979, Elie Wiesel criticized the former Allied powers, saying, "The world knew and kept silent." **Ask:** Why did Wiesel remind the former Allies of their inaction? *(He wants them to realize that their inaction may have allowed the killing of millions of people.)*

Political History ☆

Auschwitz-Birkenau
Auschwitz consisted of a prison camp, a slave labor camp, and an extermination or death camp. Wiesel and his father were sent to Buna-Morowitz, the slave labor camp. Birkenau, or Auschwitz II, was the extermination camp. Nearly 1.5 million people were killed at Auschwitz-Birkenau, more than at any other Nazi camp.

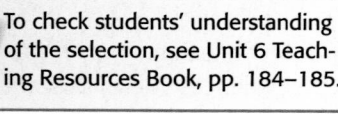

To check students' understanding of the selection, see Unit 6 Teaching Resources Book, pp. 184–185.

---

see the flames again, and the children, and yet again I tell myself that it is not enough to weep.

It took me a long time to convince myself I was not somehow mistaken. I have checked with others who arrived that same night, consulted documents of the Sonderkommandos,[20] and yes, a thousand times yes: Unable to "handle" such a large number of Hungarian Jews in the crematoria, the killers were not content merely to incinerate children's dead bodies. In their barbarous madness they cast living Jewish children into specially tended furnaces.

And if I bear within me a nameless grief and disillusionment, a bottomless despair, it is because that night I saw good and thoughtful Jewish children, bearers of mute words and dreams, walking into darkness before being consumed by the flames. I see them now, and I still curse the killers, their accomplices, the indifferent spectators who knew and kept silent, and Creation itself, Creation and those who perverted and distorted it. I feel like screaming, howling like a madman so that that world, the world of the murderers, might know it will never be forgiven.

To this day I am shaken when I see a child, for behind him I glimpse other children. Starving, terrified, drained, they march without a backward glance toward truth and death—which are perhaps the same. Uncomplaining, unprotesting, asking no one's pity, it is as if they have had enough of living on a planet so cruel, so vile and so filled with hate that their very innocence has brought their death. Do not deny it, I forbid you to deny it. Know, then, that the world that let the killers annihilate a million and a half Jewish children bears its guilt within itself.

---

20. *Sonderkommandos* refers to "special commandos," a group of Jewish prisoners whose job was to maintain and clean the crematoria, or gas chambers.

The United States and the World *What do you think is Wiesel's purpose in spreading the blame for the atrocities of the Holocaust?* 1

That night someone within me, my other self, told me it was impossible that these atrocities could be committed in the middle of the twentieth century while the world stayed silent. This was not the Middle Ages. My very last resistance broken, I let myself be pulled, pushed, and kicked, like a deaf and mute sleepwalker. I could see everything, grasp it and register it, but only later would I try to put in order all the sensations and all the memories. How stunned I was, for example, to discover another time outside time, a universe parallel to this one, a creation within Creation, with its own laws, customs, structures, and language. In this universe some men existed only to kill and others only to die. And the system functioned with exemplary efficiency: tormentors tormented and crushed their prey, torturers tortured human beings whom they met for the first time, slaughterers slaughtered their victims without so much as a glance, flames rose to heaven and nothing ever jammed the mechanism. It was as if it all unfolded according to a plan decreed from the beginning of time.

And what of human ideals, or of the beauty of innocence or the weight of justice? And what of God in all that?

I didn't understand, though I wanted to. Ask any survivor and you will hear the same thing: above all, we tried to understand. Why all these deaths? What was the point of this death factory? How to account for the demented mind that devised this black hole of history called Birkenau? ☆

Perhaps there was nothing to understand. ❧

Reading Practice

SPIRAL REVIEW **Drawing Conclusions** This narrator's central question is "As a survivor, how can I understand the horror of the Holocaust?" Ask students to discuss the narrator's attempts to understand his experiences. Have small groups consider these questions:

- What does the narrator/writer finally understand?
- How does his quest for understanding affect him?

Have groups share their conclusions with the class, supporting their ideas with evidence from the selection.

After You Read

Respond and Think Critically

Respond and Interpret

1. How did you react to Wiesel's account of the Holocaust?

2. (a)How does Wiesel's family handle the order to leave their home? (b)What do you think their response shows about them?

3. (a)How has Wiesel's home changed when he returns to it years later? (b)What does this suggest about the power of memory?

4. (a)When is Wiesel separated from his sister and his mother? (b)What does this say about the nature of life for Jewish people during this era?

Analyze and Evaluate

5. What does Wiesel's report of the differing accounts he has heard about the fate of his Uncle Mendel demonstrate?

6. Why do you think Wiesel decides not to describe the gas chambers?

7. How do the interludes in which Wiesel describes conversations with fellow Holocaust survivors add to his memoir?

8. How do you interpret Wiesel's final statement, "Perhaps there was nothing to understand"?

Connect

9. **Big Idea** The United States and the World Wiesel describes the camp as a world of its own, operating on a system of values totally foreign to the outside world. How does he respond to this environment?

10. **Connect to Today** How do you think Wiesel might respond to instances of human cruelty today? Explain.

Literary Element Narrator

In a memoir such as Wiesel's, the writer is the **narrator**. This creates a first-person point of view that offers the reader a distinct insight into the narrator's experiences.

1. (a)How does Wiesel offer a unique perspective on the Holocaust? (b)What does he leave out of his account?

2. (a)What method of storytelling does Wiesel employ as a narrator? (b)How does this method contribute to the selection?

Review: Autobiography

As you learned on page 105, an **autobiography** is the story an author writes about his or her own life. A **memoir** is a specific type of autobiography—an account of an event or a period in the author's life that emphasizes the author's personal experience. *All Rivers Run to the Sea* is a memoir in that it reexamines Wiesel's holocaust experience and its repercussions on his life and on the world.

Partner Activity *All Rivers Run to the Sea* hinges on Wiesel's skillful melding of childhood recollections with reflections as an adult on the past. Both contribute to a picture of Wiesel as a person. Meet with another classmate to discuss your impressions of Wiesel's character and personality. Then present your findings to the class.

LOG ON ▶ **Literature** Online

Selection Resources For Selection Quizzes, eFlashcards, and Reading-Writing Connection activities, go to glencoe.com and enter QuickPass code GLA9800u6.

ELIE WIESEL **991**

Comparing Literature

After You Read

Assess

1. How could world leaders let this happen?

2. (a) They bury their valuables and vow to stay together. (b) They try to be brave.

3. (a) Building and furniture are the same, none of his family lives there, a cross hangs where there was once a rabbi's picture (b) Memories of a home can remain strong long after a person has left it.

4. (a) When troops separate men and women at the camp (b) Under Nazi rule, they had no control over their lives.

5. It is hard to find the truth in a time of war; memories torment the survivors.

6. He will "Let the dead speak for themselves"; "decency and custom forbid" him from describing the chambers. He focuses on survivors rather than on the death of millions.

7. They show the lingering of the Holocaust memories in the minds of survivors.

8. He thinks some human actions may be beyond explanation.

9. He writes, "I didn't understand, though I wanted to."

10. Wiesel would probably respond in a similar way to modern atrocities, placing special blame on those who allow such horrors to continue.

 For additional assessment, see Assessment Resources, pp. 259–260.

Literary Element

1. (a) He is an eyewitness who lives with memories of the Holocaust. (b) Some details, such as how people died in the gas chambers

2. (a) Remembered anecdotes (b) They humanize the tragedy and connect historical events with real people.

Progress Check

Can students analyze the narrative point of view?

If No → See Unit 6 Teaching Resources Book, p. 179.

Comparing Literature

After You Read

Assess

Reading Strategy

1. Students may cite the table with food left on it and the youngest sister's innocent face.

2. Some may say it is easier to connect with the writer; they know what he thinks and feels. Others may say his experiences are too removed from their own.

Vocabulary

1. unutterably
2. succumb
3. fetid
4. premonition
5. curt

 To create custom assessments online, go to Progress Reporter Online Assessment.

 To create custom assessments using software, use ExamView Assessment Suite.

Reading Strategy Activate Prior Knowledge

You derive meaning from literature by **activating prior knowledge,** or combining what you already know with the information provided in the text.

1. Cite two examples of details in the text that you were instantly able to connect with given your prior knowledge or experience.

2. Memoirs are narrated in the first-person and may include personal details from the writer's life. Do you think that this makes it easier or more difficult for the reader to connect? Explain.

Vocabulary Practice

Denotation and Connotation

Denotation is a word's literal, or dictionary, meaning. **Connotation** is its implied, or cultural, meaning. *Deserted* and *desolate* have a similar denotation, but different connotations:

Weaker	*Stronger*
deserted	desolate

In each pair of words below choose the one that has a stronger connotation.

1. ineffably   unutterably
2. succumb   submit
3. fetid   smelly
4. premonition warning
5. curt   terse

Academic Vocabulary

Elie Wiesel constantly faces challenges in his recovery from the Holocaust.

Recovery is an academic word. It is also used in economics and in reference to overcoming a problem. Using context clues, try to figure out the meaning of *recovery* in the following sentence: *After a depression, the economy undergoes an upturn, or recovery.*

For more on academic vocabulary, see pages 53–54.

Connect to *Social Studies*

Present an Oral Report

Assignment Adolf Hitler and the Third Reich used propaganda to gather popular support for their brutal campaign against the Jews. Present an oral report on Nazi propaganda. Focus on the persuasive techniques used and evaluate their effectiveness. Then find examples of contemporary propaganda and compare and contrast the techniques employed with those the Nazis used.

Investigate To research this subject, draw on several sources, such as histories of Nazi Germany and histories of propaganda. Make sure you understand various propaganda techniques, such as the use of logical fallacies like arguments *ad hominem,* the bandwagon effect, glittering generalities, and red herring arguments. Use these terms to organize your report. For example, show how the Nazis used the bandwagon effect in political rallies designed to convince Germans of Hitler's strength as a leader. Then compare the techniques the Nazis used with techniques used in propaganda today.

Create Find examples of Nazi anti-Jewish propaganda to use in your presentation. These examples could be print (including visuals such as cartoons and posters), audio, or video material. Make sure you effectively incorporate these visual aids, analyzing them rather than merely displaying them. Be sure to cite all sources correctly.

Report During your oral report, discuss the different interpretations and analyses of Nazi propaganda you encountered in your research. Synthesize these interpretations and present your own conclusions.

Academic Vocabulary

Possible answer: Here, *recovery* means "a period of economic growth after a depression."

Connect to *Social Studies*

Use these criteria when evaluating students' oral reports:

- Did the student clearly identify various persuasive techniques?
- Did the student effectively use visual aids?
- Did the student synthesize interpretations of Nazi propaganda from various sources?

Build Background

Garrett Hongo's memoir *Kubota* addresses the Japanese military attack on Pearl Harbor in Hawaii that prompted the United States to enter World War II. Although Hongo was not alive during this attack, his family was deeply affected by it. During the war, more than 120,000 Japanese Americans were forced to live in internment camps set up by the U.S. government. Decades later the government apologized for this injustice and paid reparations.

from Kubota

Garrett Hongo

It was a Monday night, the day after Pearl Harbor, and there was a rattling knock at the front door. Two FBI agents presented themselves, showed identification, and took my grandfather in for questioning in Honolulu. He didn't return home for days. No one knew what had happened or what was wrong. But there was a roundup going on of all those in the Japanese-American community suspected of sympathizing with the enemy and worse.

My grandfather was suspected of espionage,[1] of communicating with offshore Japanese submarines launched from the attack fleet days before the war began. Torpedo planes and escort fighters, decorated with the insignia of the Rising Sun, had taken an approach route from northwest of Oahu directly across Kahuku Point and on toward Pearl. They had strafed[2] an auxiliary air station near the fishing grounds my grandfather loved and destroyed a small gun battery there, killing three men. Kubota[3] was known to have sponsored and harbored Japanese nationals in his own home. He had a radio. He had wholesale access to firearms. Circumstances and an undertone of racial resentment had combined with wartime hysteria in the aftermath of the tragic naval battle to cast suspicion on the loyalties of my grandfather and all other Japanese Americans. The FBI reached out and pulled hundreds of them in for questioning in dragnets cast throughout the West Coast and Hawaii.

My grandfather was lucky; he'd somehow been let go after only a few days. Others were not as fortunate. Hundreds, from small communities in Washington, California, Oregon, and Hawaii, were rounded up and, after what appeared to be routine questioning, shipped off under Justice Department orders to holding centers in Leuppe on the Navaho reservation in Arizona, in Fort Missoula in Montana, and on Sand Island in Honolulu Harbor. There were other special camps on Maui in Ha'iku and on Hawaii—the Big Island—in my own home village of Volcano.

Many of these men—it was exclusively the Japanese-American men suspected of ties to Japan who were initially rounded up—did not see their families again for more than four

---

1. *Espionage* means spying.
2. *Strafed* means "attacked with machine guns from low-flying aircraft."
3. *Kubota* (kōō bō′ tä)

GARRETT HONGO **993**

Before You Read

Focus

Summary

When Kubota tells his grandson, Garrett Hongo, about the internment of Japanese Americans after Pearl Harbor, Hongo is shocked. He is determined to become a voice for Japanese Americans; he refuses to let the events after Pearl Harbor be forgotten.

Teach

Reading Strategy | 1

Activate Prior Knowledge
Say: During World War II, anti-Japanese sentiment caused the U.S. government to pass the War Relocation Authority. This legalized the forcible relocation of people of Japanese ancestry on the West Coast to ten isolated camps around the country. **Ask:** Why do you think this happened? *(Pearl Harbor in Hawaii was bombed by the Japanese and the closest U.S. coast was the West Coast. Also, many people of Japanese ancestry lived on the West Coast.)*

 For an audio recording of this selection, use Listening Library Audio CD-ROM.

Readability Scores

Dale-Chall: 9.0
DRP: 63
Lexile: 1180

Comparing Literature

Teach

Literary Element | 1

Memoir Elicit from students the similarities and differences between a *memoir* and an *autobiography*. Both are types of narrative nonfiction written by a person about him- or herself. However, a memoir typically focuses on a period of time in a person's life while an autobiography presents a person's life story.

Reading Strategy | 2

Draw Conclusions **Ask:** Why does Kubota finally tell Hongo the story? *(He thinks his grandson is old enough to hear it; perhaps he needs to tell Hongo for peace of mind.)*

Political History ☆

Japanese American Soldiers During the war, the U.S. government formed several segregated all-Japanese units, made up of thousands of volunteers from Hawaii and the mainland, anxious to prove their loyalty to the United States. While a few of these soldiers served in the Pacific, most were sent to Europe to fight. The 442nd Regimental Combat Team and the 100th Infantry Battalion fought in seven major European campaigns and received more decorations and awards than any similar-sized unit serving for the same amount of time in U.S. military history.

---

years. Under a suspension of due process[4] that was only after the fact ruled as warranted by military necessity, they were, if only temporarily, "disappeared" in Justice Department prison camps scattered in particularly desolate areas of the United States designated as militarily "safe." These were grim forerunners of the assembly centers and concentration camps for the 120,000 Japanese-American evacuees that were to come later.

I am Kubota's eldest grandchild, and I remember him as a lonely, habitually silent old man who lived with us in our home near Los Angeles for most of my childhood and adolescence. It was the fifties, and my parents had emigrated from Hawaii to the mainland in the hope of a better life away from the old sugar plantation. After some success, they had sent back for my grandparents and taken them in. And it was my grandparents who did the work of the household while my mother and father worked their salaried city jobs. My grandmother cooked and sewed, washed our clothes, and knitted in the front room under the light of a huge lamp with a bright three-way bulb. Kubota raised a flower garden, read up on soils and grasses in gardening books, and planted a zoysia lawn in front and a dichondra[5] one in back. He planted a small patch near the rear block wall with green onions, eggplant, white Japanese radishes, and cucumber. While he hoed and spaded the loamless, clayey earth of Los Angeles, he sang particularly plangent[6] songs in Japanese about plum blossoms and bamboo groves.

Once, in the mid-sixties, after a dinner during which, as always, he had been silent while he worked away at a meal of fish and rice spiced with dabs of Chinese mustard and cat-

sup thinned with soy sauce, Kubota took his own dishes to the kitchen sink and washed them up. He took a clean jelly jar out of the cupboard—the glass was thick and its shape squatty like an old-fashioned. He reached around to the hutch below where he kept his bourbon. He made himself a drink and retired to the living room where I was expected to join him for "talk story," the Hawaiian idiom for chewing the fat.

I was a teenager and, though I was bored listening to stories I'd heard often enough before at holiday dinners, I was dutiful. I took my spot on the couch next to Kubota and heard him out. Usually, he'd tell me about his schooling in Japan where he learned judo along with mathematics and literature. He'd learned the *soroban* there—the abacus, which was the original pocket calculator of the Far East—and that, along with his strong, judo-trained back, got him his first job in Hawaii. This was the moral. "Study *ha-ahd*," he'd say with pidgin[7] emphasis. "Learn read good. Learn speak da kine *good* English." The message is the familiar one taught to any children of immigrants: succeed through education. And imitation. But this time, Kubota reached down into his past and told me a different story. I was thirteen by then, and I suppose he thought me ready for it. He told me about Pearl Harbor, how the planes flew in wing after wing of formations over his old house in La'ie in Hawaii, and how, the next

Visual Vocabulary
On an abacus the positions of beads stand for numbers.

---

4. *Due process* is the administration of the law according to prescribed procedures.
5. *Zoysia* (zoi' zhə) is a type of grass. *Dichondra* (dī kän' drə) is a type of herb used for lawns.
6. *Plangent* (plan' jənt) can mean either "mournful" or "loud and echoing."

7. *Pidgin* (pij' ən) is a hybrid language that is a mixture of two or more languages and that has a simplified vocabulary and grammatical structure.

994 UNIT 6 FROM DEPRESSION TO COLD WAR

Writing Practice

Describe a Character With his writing, Hongo paints a vivid picture of his grandfather, showing Kubota's character through dialogue and action. Ask students to find words and phrases that convey Kubota's personality. Using these as a springboard, tell each student to write a description of someone in his or her community. First have them list things the person says and does that reveal personal traits. Encourage students to write in the form of related anecdotes, as Hongo does in the selection.

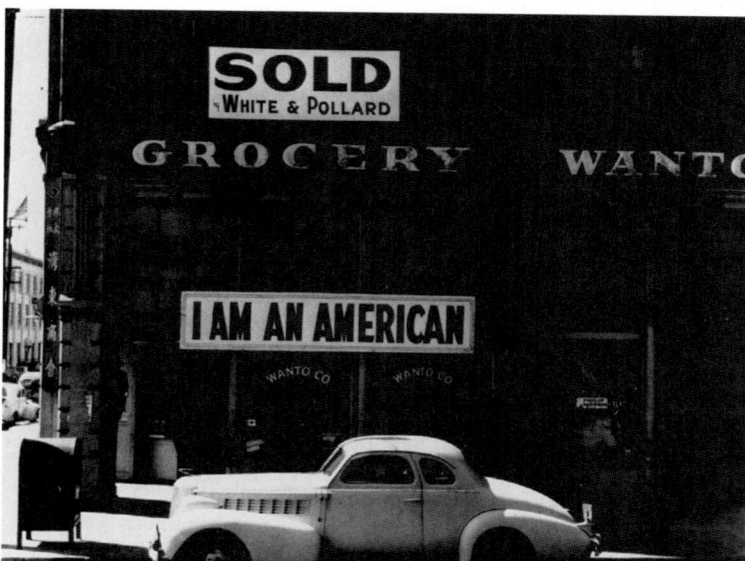

Japanese-American U.S. citizens forced to sell their store because of the internment proclaim their patriotism.

day, after Roosevelt[8] had made his famous "Day of Infamy" speech about the treachery of the Japanese, the FBI agents had come to his door and taken him in, hauled him off to Honolulu for questioning, and held him without charge for several days. I thought he was lying. I thought he was making up a kind of horror story to shock me and give his moral that much more starch. But it was true. I asked around. I brought it up during history class in junior high school, and my teacher, after silencing me and stepping me off to the back of the room, told me that it was indeed so. I asked my mother and she said it was true. I asked my schoolmates, who laughed and ridiculed me for being so ignorant. We lived in a Japanese-American community, and the parents of most of my classmates were the nisei[9]

8. President Franklin D. *Roosevelt* (1882–1945) addressed Congress the day after the bombing of Pearl Harbor on December 7, 1941, saying it was "a date which will live in infamy."
9. The Japanese word *nisei* (nē' sā) refers to children of Japanese immigrants; that is, the first generation of Japanese Americans born in the United States.

who had been interned[10] as teenagers all through the war. But there was a strange silence around all of this. There was a hush, as if one were invoking the ill powers of the dead when one brought it up. No one cared to speak about the evacuation and relocation for very long. It wasn't in our history books, though we were studying World War II at the time. It wasn't in the family albums of the people I knew and whom I'd visit staying over weekends with friends. And it wasn't anything that the family talked about or allowed me to keep bringing up either. I was given the facts, told sternly and pointedly that "it was war" and that "nothing could be done." "*Shikatta ga nai*"[11] is the phrase in Japanese, a kind of resolute and determinist pronouncement on how to deal with inexplicable tragedy. I was to know it but not to dwell on it. Japanese Americans were busy trying to forget it ever happened and were having a hard enough

10. *Interned* means "confined or restricted to a particular place, especially during war."
11. "*Shikatta ga nai*" is pronounced (shē kä' tä gä nī).

GARRETT HONGO **995**

Comparing Literature

Teach

Literary Element 1

Tone Remind students that a writer's tone expresses an attitude toward the subject. Connotation and description can express tone. **Ask:** What does Hongo's tone reveal about his feelings for his grandfather? *(His tone is respectful but questioning and uncertain. His grandfather was persistent. He admires this persistence but does not understand his grandfather's urgency.)*

Reading Strategy 2

Draw Conclusions Ask: What story does Kubota want Hongo to tell? *(stories of the internment experiences of Japanese Americans during World War II.)* **Ask:** How does Kubota stand apart from others in his community? *(Others want to bury this history; Kubota wants to tell the story so past mistakes will not be repeated.)*

---

time building their new lives after "camp." It was as if we had no history for four years and the relocation was something unspeakable.

But Kubota would not let it go. In session after session, for months it seemed, he pounded away at his story. He wanted to tell me the names of the FBI agents. He went over their questions and his responses again and again. He'd tell me how one would try to act friendly toward him, offering him cigarettes while the other, who hounded him with accusations and threats, left the interrogation room. Good cop, bad cop, I thought to myself, already superficially streetwise from stories black classmates told of the Watts[12] riots and from my having watched too many episodes of Dragnet and The Mod Squad.[13] But Kubota was not interested in my experiences. I was not made yet, and he was determined that his stories be part of my making. He spoke quietly at first, mildly, but once into his narrative and after his drink was down, his voice would rise and quaver with resentment and he'd make his accusations. He gave his testimony to me and I held it at first cautiously in my conscience like it was an heirloom too delicate to expose to strangers and anyone outside of the world Kubota made with his words. "I give you story now," he once said, "and you learn speak good, eh?" It was my job, as the disciple of his preaching I had then become, Ananda to his Buddha,[14] to reassure him with a promise. "You learn speak good like the Dillingham," he'd say another time, referring to the wealthy scion of the grower family who had once run, unsuccessfully, for one of Hawaii's first senatorial seats. Or he'd then invoke a magical name, the name of one of his heroes, a man he

thought particularly exemplary and righteous. "Learn speak dah good Ing-rish like *Mistah Inouye*," Kubota shouted. "He lick dah Dillingham even in debate. I saw on *terre-bision* myself." He was remembering the debates before the first senatorial election just before Hawaii was admitted to the Union as its fiftieth state. "You *tell* story," Kubota would end. And I had my injunction.[15]

The town we settled in after the move from Hawaii is called Gardena, the independently incorporated city south of Los Angeles and north of San Pedro harbor. At its northern limit, it borders on Watts and Compton, black towns. To the southwest are Torrance and Redondo Beach, white towns. To the rest of L.A., Gardena is primarily famous for having legalized five-card draw poker after the war. On Vermont Boulevard, its eastern border, there is a dingy little Vegas-like strip of card clubs with huge parking lots and flickering neon signs that spell out "The Rainbow" and "The Horseshoe" in timed sequences of varicolored lights. The town is only secondarily famous as the largest community of Japanese Americans in the United States outside of Honolulu, Hawaii. When I was in high school there, it seemed to me that every *sansei*[16] kid I knew wanted to be a doctor, an engineer, or a pharmacist. Our fathers were gardeners or electricians or nurserymen or ran small businesses catering to other Japanese Americans. Our mothers worked in civil service for the city or as cashiers for Thrifty Drug. What the kids wanted was a good job, good pay, a fine home, and no troubles. No one wanted to mess with the law—from either side—and no one wanted to mess with language or art. They all talked about getting into the right clubs so that they could go to the right schools. There was a certain kind of sameness, an intensely enforced system of conformity. Style was all. Boys wore moccasin-sewn shoes from Flagg

---

12. *Watts,* a section of Los Angeles, was the site of severe racial violence in 1965.
13. *Dragnet* and *The Mod Squad* were popular television police shows.
14. *Buddha* (563?–483? B.C.) was the title given to Siddhartha Gautama (si där′ tə   gou′ tə mə), the founder of Buddhism. *Ananda* (ä nän′ dä) was his cousin and "Beloved Disciple."

15. An *injunction* is a command or an order.
16. The *sansei* (sän′ sā′) are the children of the *nisei*.

996 UNIT 6   FROM DEPRESSION TO COLD WAR

Research Practice

Japanese American Internment In 1988 the United States government officially apologized and compensated each surviving Japanese American who had been interned during World War II. Have students research the internment, including such topics as life in the camps, life after they returned home, and the details and effects of the compensation and apology. Ask students to share their findings in a group discussion.

Japanese Americans interned at Santa Anita.

View the Photograph

Almost 50 years after being forced into internment camps, Japanese Americans received an official apology from Congress and the president—along with $20,000. What does this photograph tell you about life in the camps? What kind of compensation do you think the victims deserved?

Brothers, black A-1 slacks, and Kensington shirts with high collars. Girls wore their hair up in stiff bouffants solidified in hairspray and knew all the latest dances from the slauson to the funky chicken. We did well in chemistry and in math, no one who was Japanese but me spoke in English class or in history unless called upon, and no one talked about World War II. The day after Robert Kennedy was assassinated, after winning the California Democratic primary, we worked on calculus and elected class coordinators for the prom, featuring the 5th Dimension.[17] We avoided grief. We avoided government. We avoided strong feelings and dangers of any kind. Once punished, we tried to maintain a concerted emotional and social discipline and would not willingly seek to fall out of the narrow margin of protective favor again.

But when I was thirteen, in junior high, I'd not understood why it was so difficult for my classmates, those who were themselves Japanese American, to talk about the relocation. They had cringed, too, when I tried to bring it up

during our discussions of World War II. I was Hawaiian-born. They were mainland-born. Their parents had been in camp, had been the ones to suffer the complicated experience of having to distance themselves from their own history and all things Japanese in order to make their way back and into the American social and economic mainstream. It was out of this sense of shame and a fear of stigma I was only beginning to understand that the *nisei* had silenced themselves. And, for their children, among whom I grew up, they wanted no heritage, no culture, no contact with a defiled history. I recall the silence very well. The Japanese-American children around me were burdened in a way I was not. Their injunction was silence. Mine was to speak.

Quickwrite

Is Kubota right to urge his grandson to discuss what happened to Japanese Americans during World War II? Why do you think some people seem to disagree with this stance? Write a short response in which you explain your position. Support your argument with details from the selection and historical information.

---

17. *The 5th Dimension* was a popular music group in the late 1960s.

 GARRETT HONGO **997**

Comparing Literature

Before You Read

Focus

Summary

In the excerpt, the author's father tells the story of how all of the Jews in his Polish hometown reported to the local stadium to be "selected" by the Nazis. Only young, able people got their passports stamped and were allowed to return home. The author's grandfather is selected but climbs to the other side to be with his daughter and grandchildren who were not. In the end, one in every three people is detained in the selection process.

Cultural History ☆

Graphic Novels A graphic novel is a collection of comics presented in book form. It includes book-length narratives, short story anthologies, and collections of previously published series. The story lines are typically serious and complex. Although introduced some years before, the phrase *graphic novel* was popularized shortly after it appeared in 1978 on the cover of the paperback edition of Will Eisner's *A Contract With God*. Eisner's book contained four short stories told in comics format.

Build Background

Art Spiegelman learned to read by reading comics and, in turn, has taught a generation of readers that the comic book, or graphic novel, format can be as powerful as any other form of literature. During the 1970s, Spiegelman began to create comics based on his father's (Vladek's) memories of the Nazi occupation of Poland. Between 1980 and 1986, these efforts grew into *Maus: A Survivor's Tale,* a full-length graphic novel. He published a sequel, *Maus II,* in 1991.

Throughout the books, Spiegelman represents the Jews as mice and the Nazis as cats. Other groups are represented by different animals.

In 1992 Spiegelman was awarded a Pulitzer Prize for *Maus*, the first time a graphic-novel artist had received this award.

There are several unfamiliar terms and people mentioned in the excerpt that follows. The German word *gemeinde* refers to a Jewish committee within the community. Richieu is the first son of Vladek and Anja, Spiegelman's parents. Richieu was sent to live with relatives during the war, but he did not survive the Holocaust. Lolek and Lonia are cousins of the Spiegelmans. Tosha and Wolfe are Anja's older sister and her husband.

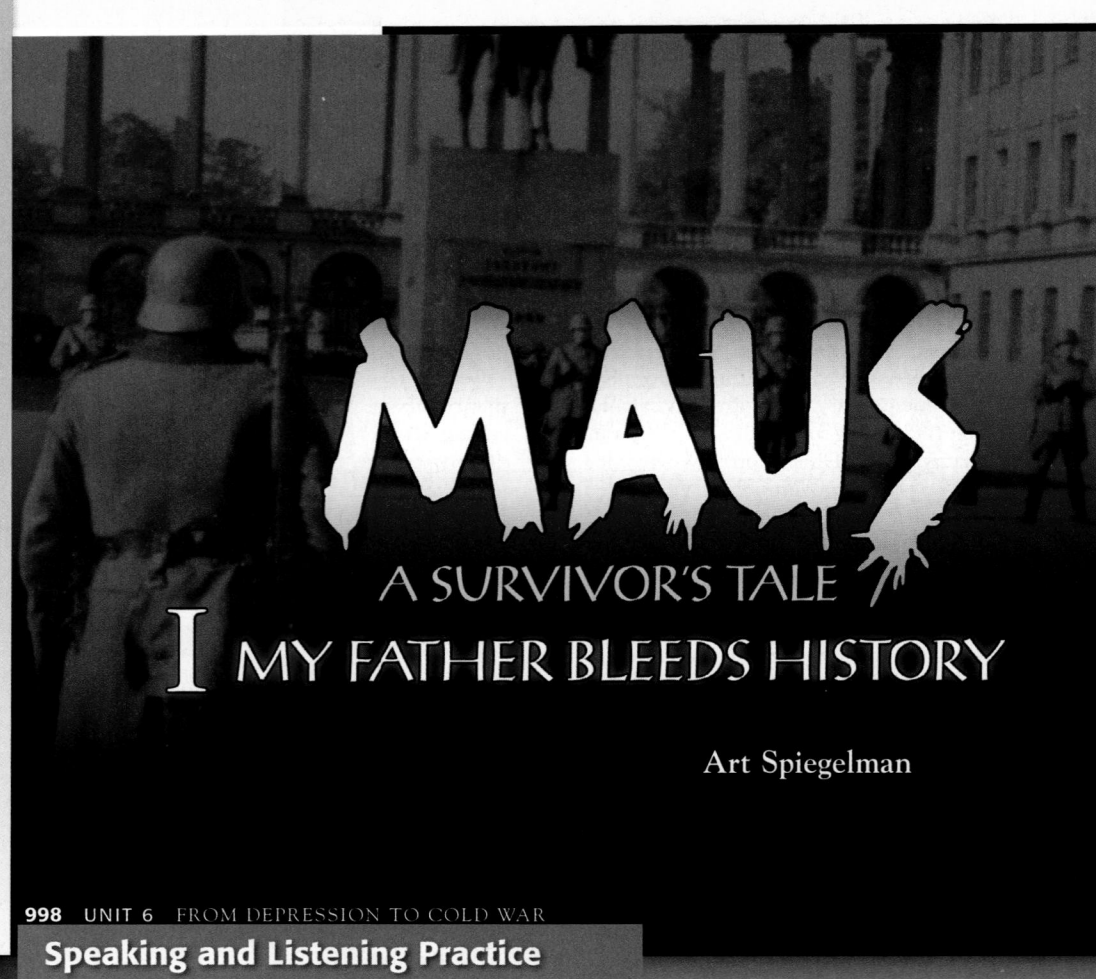

MAUS
A SURVIVOR'S TALE
I MY FATHER BLEEDS HISTORY

Art Spiegelman

Speaking and Listening Practice

Enact a Scene Have groups of five or six students choose a few selection frames to dramatize. Students should choose roles—including the author's father and a director. Ask students to convert the text into a script. Allow groups time to rehearse. During rehearsal, students should decide where they will stand, if they will use props, and whether they will memorize lines or use notecards. Directors should guide readings and the actions in the scenes. Each group should perform for the class. After the performances, discuss the challenges of turning printed words and images into a live performance.

Teach

Literary Element   1

Voice and Tone **Ask:** How would you characterize the author's father based on his speech? *(English is probably his second language; the father is probably a serious and thoughtful man.)*

Reading Strategy   2

Connect Across Texts Spiegelman's *Maus* and Wiesel's *All Rivers Run to the Sea* both deal with memories of the Holocaust. **Ask:** How are the two authors' works similar and different? *(Spiegelman matches a narrative with visual images. Wiesel uses only words to conjure images in readers' minds. Both record the comments of others and express strong emotion.)* Have students identify an idea or image that moved them from each selection. Have students explain their choices.

English Learners

DIFFERENTIATED INSTRUCTION

Intermediate Review how to read a graphic novel. Explain that the text above each panel or in rectangular boxes is the voice of Spiegelman's father. The speech balloons contain the words of the people in the narrative.

Approaching Level

DIFFERENTIATED INSTRUCTION

Emerging Discuss the elements of a graphic novel. Ask students to name graphic novels they have read and to explain the form's appeal to them. After they have read this selection, **ask:** What information do the graphics provide that the dialogue does not? *(They add important details to the story: the barbed wire and the crowding are realistic; the facial expressions and body language convey worry, fear, and sadness.)*

Comparing Literature

Teach

Literary Element | 1

Narrator The final frame shows the narrator in the present. **Ask:** What is the effect on the reader of seeing the narrator in the present day? *(It reminds the reader that he survived his ordeal and is telling his story to the writer; it emphasizes the narrator's grief about his father's being taken away.)*

(ADVANCED) Convert the information presented in the final frame to one or two paragraphs of text.

Discussion Starter

Students should discuss how the dialogue balloons, the narration, and the pictures work together.

Political History ☆

Jewish Resistance Jewish groups led small rebellions, but there was no centralized effort to resist the Nazis. Scholars believe that two major factors hindered an organized Jewish resistance: small Jewish populations were surrounded by larger ethnic groups who often harbored anti-Semitic sentiments, and Jews did not have access to large numbers of weapons.

💬 Discussion Starter

Graphic novels combine words and pictures. In the work of some comic artists, graphic elements dominate; in the work of others, words have greater importance. Look over these panels from *Maus* to determine the balance between words and pictures in Art Spiegelman's work. With a group of classmates, discuss how the imagery and words work together and how one panel transitions into the next.

Assessment Practice

Essay Questions Remind students that in an essay response evaluators look for a thesis supported by evidence from a text or from experience, originality of thought, and good writing. **Say:** When answering an essay question, find an interesting thesis to argue and support. **Ask:** What part of writing a response to an essay question is most challenging? *(Students may cite thinking of a thesis that states something other than an obvious point or finding enough evidence to support or elaborate on their ideas.)*

Wrap-Up: Comparing Literature

Across Time and Place

- from *All Rivers Run to the Sea* by Elie Wiesel

- from *Kubota* by Garrett Hongo

- from *Maus: A Survivor's Tale* by Art Spiegelman

COMPARE THE `Big Idea`
The United States and the World

Group Activity With a group of classmates, discuss the following questions.

1. How do Wiesel and Spiegelman address the need to tell the truth about the establishment of concentration camps by the Nazis in the 1930s and 1940s?

2. What does Kubota hope to accomplish by asking Hongo to tell his story about Japanese American internment?

3. Evaluate the statements about history and personal expression made in these selections. Which of them did you find most powerful? Explain.

COMPARE Reflections

Writing Activity The stories in these works explore the lives of people who have survived particularly difficult experiences. Review the three selections. Then write a brief essay, evaluating how these selections explore the significance of personal experience. Support your ideas with details from the selections, including quotations that capture the writer's reflections on the experience described.

COMPARE Cultures

Visual Display The horrors of World War II had a great impact on various cultures in different ways. From the selections you have read, create a three-panel collage of images—one for each selection—that illustrates the experiences of these cultures during the war.

Children liberated from a Nazi concentration camp show the numbers tattooed on their arms.

 Literature Online

Selection Resources For Selection Quizzes, eFlashcards, and Reading-Writing Connection activities, go to glencoe.com and enter QuickPass code GLA9800u6.

COMPARING LITERTURE **1001**

Assess

Compare the Big Idea

1. Each author addresses the need to tell the truth by writing about painful truths, telling the story in his own way, without hiding the horrors of the story.

2. Kubota hopes the same mistakes do not happen again. He may wish to show that the shame belongs to the government, not to the Japanese Americans.

3. Students should select quotations from the texts to support their opinions.

Compare Reflections

Evaluate students' writing based on the following criteria:

- Does the essay cite evidence from the selections, including the writers' personal experiences?
- Does the student show the significance of each reflection?
- Does the essay have a clear beginning, middle, and end?

Compare Cultures

Have students research World War II art before they begin their display. They might look at the art created by Holocaust survivors for inspiration.

Approaching Level

DIFFERENTIATED INSTRUCTION

Established Because the selections in the Comparing Literature section deal with difficult events in history, students may benefit from taking time to reflect on the significance of the stories they have read. Have students write a brief journal entry or draw a picture to represent their thoughts after reading the stories. Rather than having students share their thoughts and reactions in a formal discussion, cover a wall with large pieces of paper or clear a large section of chalk board space to transform it into a "graffiti wall." Instruct students not to talk during the exercise. Each student should write on the "wall" any words, phrases, or images from their journal entries that represent what they have learned from reading and discussing the historical stories by Wiesel, Hongo, and Spiegelman. If possible leave the "graffiti wall" up for the rest of Unit Six Part 2 and invite students to add to it after each selection.

Before You Read

Focus

Bellringer Options

Selection Focus
 Transparency 62
Daily Language Practice
 Transparency 91

Or **ask:** How does war affect ordinary people? How do people view those who are their enemies during wartime? Have students consider the answers to these questions as they read.

Before You Read

from *Hiroshima*

Meet **John Hersey**
(1914–1993)

John Hersey bore witness to some of the pivotal events of the twentieth century. Hersey was born in China to missionary parents, but he spent most of his life writing about the United States' military influence in other countries.

After Hersey's father died from an illness he contracted in China, the family settled in New York. Hersey attended Yale University, where he studied English literature and began his professional career working for the *Yale Daily News*. His first job after college was as private secretary to the Nobel Prize-winning writer Sinclair Lewis.

> *"Journalism allows its readers to witness history; fiction gives its readers an opportunity to live it."*
>
> —John Hersey

On the War Front Between 1937 and 1946, Hersey worked for *Time* and *Life* magazines as a foreign correspondent in the Pacific. To write his first book, *Men on Bataan,* he combined his own experience with other sources, including letters, speeches, and memos written by the soldiers stationed in the Pacific. One aspect of the book that captured the attention of critics was Hersey's ability to combine fictional techniques—such as characterization, description, and foreshadowing—with factual reporting. His later experiences in Italy were reshaped into his first novel, *A Bell for Adano,* for which Hersey was awarded the 1945 Pulitzer Prize for fiction.

Hiroshima The nuclear age began in 1945 when U.S. forces dropped atomic bombs on Hiroshima and Nagasaki in Japan. Much was written about the event at the time, but most articles were recitations of facts and statistics. Hersey wanted to alert the public to the nightmarish aftermath of the bombing and its human and moral consequences.

Hersey interviewed people in Japan and wrote about the devastation he witnessed in Hiroshima. Months later, the *New Yorker* devoted all of its editorial space to Hersey's piece. It created unprecedented interest in the publishing world. The book's publication not only established Hersey's literary reputation but also originated a new type of literary journalism that went beyond mere reporting of events to capture the human toll of a wartime incident. *Hiroshima* prompted years of discussion about nuclear weapons and their moral implications.

Truth as Fiction Hersey believed that fiction better allowed him to depict reality. "It makes truth plausible," he wrote. Hersey continued to write about important issues of his times: war, education, racism, and politics. Hersey was such an important literary figure that his death in 1993 was front-page news. *New York Times* writer Richard Severo described him "not only as a first-rate reporter but also as a storyteller who nurtured the idea that writers had to pursue a moral goal."

 Literature Online

Author Search For more about John Hersey, go to glencoe.com and enter QuickPass code GLA9800u6.

1002 UNIT 6 FROM DEPRESSION TO COLD WAR

Selection Skills

Literary Elements
- Point of View (SE pp. 1003–1015)
- Author's Purpose (SE p. 1015)

from Hiroshima

Writing Skills/Grammar
- Expository Essay (SE p. 1016)
- Editorial (TE p. 1010)

Vocabulary Skills
- Word Origins (SE p. 1015)
- Academic Vocabulary (SE p. 1015)

Reading Skills
- Draw Conclusions About Author's Beliefs (SE pp. 1003–1015)
- Text Structure (TE p. 1006)
- Fact and Opinion (TE p. 1008)

Listening/Speaking/Viewing Skills
- Analyze Art (TE pp. 1008, 1010, 1013)

Literature and Reading Preview

Connect to the Story

In a war situation, do you think that the ends justify the means? Discuss this question with a small group.

Build Background

In 1945, the United States and Japan were adversaries in World War II. As the war dragged on, casualties mounted on both sides. The Japanese had been warned that they would face "utter destruction" if they did not surrender, but many officials predicted that the island nation would continue to fight. On August 6, a B-29 aircraft named the *Enola Gay* dropped the first atomic bomb ever used in wartime.

Set Purposes for Reading

Big Idea **The United States and the World**

As you read, ask yourself, Why did the world come to see nuclear warfare as something to be avoided at all costs?

Literary Element **Point of View**

Point of view is the perspective from which the narrator tells the story. In **third-person point of view,** the narrator is not a character but describes the action and the characters from outside the story. As you read, ask yourself, How does point of view affect your understanding of the narrative?

Reading Strategy **Draw Conclusions About Author's Beliefs**

When you **draw conclusions,** you use a number of clues to make a general statement about something. By looking at the details that an author includes and omits, you can draw some conclusions about that author's beliefs. As you read, ask yourself, What details help you guess at Hersey's beliefs about war?

Tip: Chart Clues Use a graphic organizer to record details.

Learning Objectives

For pages 1002–1015

In studying this text, you will focus on the following objectives:

Literary Study: Analyzing point of view.

Reading: Drawing conclusions about author's beliefs.

Vocabulary

evacuate (i vak´ū āt´) *v.* to vacate or leave a place; p. 1004 *Citizens were told to evacuate the city if they heard a siren.*

volition (vō lish´ ən) *n.* act of choosing or deciding; p. 1005 *They were in the right place by accident rather than volition.*

debris (də brē´) *n.* large number of fragments or broken pieces; p. 1009 *The explosion filled the streets with debris.*

xenophobic (zen´ ə fō´ bik) *adj.* having an extreme fear of foreigners or strangers; p. 1010 *The people were xenophobic and trusted no newcomers.*

terminus (tur´ mə nəs) *n.* one end of a travel route or the station placed there; p. 1012 *The train reached its terminus and the passengers disembarked.*

Tip: Word Origins Word origins, also called **etymologies,** are the history and development of words. For example, the word *xenophobic* comes from two Greek words meaning "strange" and "fear."

JOHN HERSEY **1003**

Before You Read

Focus

Summary

Reporter John Hersey gives a nonfiction account of the effects of the atomic bomb on the Japanese city of Hiroshima. He uses literary techniques to combine the stories of six ordinary people—a clerk, two doctors, a single mother, a priest, and a pastor. Hersey describes the circumstances and physical location of each person before, during, and immediately after the bomb's blast.

 For summaries in languages other than English, see Unit 6 Teaching Resources Book, pp. 186–191.

Vocabulary

Questions and Answers

Have students work in pairs to create questions and answers using each vocabulary word. Start them off by giving them sample questions such as "Under what circumstances might people have to *evacuate*?"

 For additional vocabulary practice, see Unit 6 Teaching Resources Book, p. 194.

Approaching Level

DIFFERENTIATED INSTRUCTION

Emerging Students may not know where Hiroshima is. Have students locate Japan on a world map, and then locate the cities of Hiroshima and Nagasaki on a map of Japan. Point out that the country of Japan is made up of different islands. Hiroshima is located on the southwestern part of Honshu, the biggest island in Japan. Nagasaki is farther south on the western coast of the island of Kyushu. Hiroshima was picked as a target for the bomb because army supply depots, factories producing military supplies, and one of the army headquarters were located there.

Big Idea | 1

The United States and the World World War II ended in a particularly violent way, when U.S. forces dropped atomic bombs on two Japanese cities. **Ask:** As you read the first paragraph, what feelings or ideas do you have? *(Students may say dread, because the reader knows the people Hersey introduces will suffer after the bombing.)*

Writer's Technique ☆

Nonfiction Novel Critics consider Hersey's *Hiroshima* to be one of the first nonfiction novels, or works of reporting that use literary techniques without imposing the author's viewpoint. Other nonfiction novels include Truman Capote's *In Cold Blood* and Norman Mailer's *The Armies of the Night.*

For an audio recording of this selection, use Listening Library Audio CD-ROM.

Readability Scores

Dale-Chall: 9.9
DRP: 64
Lexile: 1260

Graphic Organizer Instead of telling each person's story individually, Hersey weaves the stories of six people into one long narrative. To help students keep track of the six people in the story, have them create a chart with six columns. Tell them to write the name of one person at the top of each column. Have students note these basic facts about each person as they read: the person's occupation, who they were with when the bomb dropped, their location before the bomb was dropped, what they were doing as the bomb dropped, their reaction to the bomb, and what they did immediately after the bomb dropped. Students may also wish to note other interesting facts about each person as they read.

from
Hiroshima ☆
John Hersey

At exactly fifteen minutes past eight in the morning, on August 6, 1945, Japanese time, at the moment when the atomic bomb flashed above Hiroshima, Miss Toshiko Sasaki, a clerk in the personnel department of the East Asia Tin Works, had just sat down at her place in the plant office and was turning her head to speak to the girl at the next desk. At that same moment, Dr. Masakazu Fujii was settling down cross-legged to read the Osaka *Asahi* on the porch of his private hospital, overhanging one of the seven deltaic[1] rivers which divide Hiroshima; Mrs. Hatsuyo Nakamura, a tailor's widow, stood by the window of her kitchen, watching a neighbor tearing down his house because it lay in the path of an air-raid-defense fire lane; Father Wilhelm Kleinsorge, a German priest of the Society of Jesus, reclined in his underwear on a cot on the top floor of his order's three-story mission house, reading a Jesuit magazine, *Stimmen der Zeit*; Dr. Terufumi Sasaki, a young member of the surgical staff of the city's large, modern Red Cross Hospital, walked along one of the hospital corridors with a blood specimen for a Wassermann test[2] in his hand; and the Reverend Mr. Kiyoshi Tanimoto, pastor of the Hiroshima Methodist Church, paused at the door of a rich man's house in Koi, the city's western suburb, and prepared to unload a handcart full of things he had **evacuated** from

---

1. *Deltaic* refers to a delta that forms at the mouth of a river. The city of Hiroshima straddles six channels and several islets that make up the delta at the mouth of the Ota River.

2. A *Wasserman test* is a blood test once widely used to diagnose syphilis.

Vocabulary

evacuate (i vak′ ū āt′) *v.* to vacate or leave a place

town in fear of the massive B-29 raid which everyone expected Hiroshima to suffer. A hundred thousand people were killed by the atomic bomb, and these six were among the survivors. They still wonder why they lived when so many others died. Each of them counts many small items of chance or **volition**—a step taken in time, a decision to go indoors, catching one streetcar instead of the next—that spared him. And now each knows that in the act of survival he lived a dozen lives and saw more death than he ever thought he would see. At the time, none of them knew anything.

The Reverend Mr. Tanimoto got up at five o'clock that morning. He was alone in the parsonage, because for some time his wife had been commuting with their year-old baby to spend nights with a friend in Ushida, a suburb to the north. Of all the important cities of Japan, only two, Kyoto and Hiroshima, had not been visited in strength if *B-san*, or Mr. B, as the Japanese, with a mixture of respect and unhappy familiarity, called the B-29; and Mr. Tanimoto, like all his neighbors and friends, was almost sick with anxiety. He had heard uncomfortably detailed accounts of mass raids on Kure, Iwakuni, Tokuyama, and other nearby towns; he was sure Hiroshima's turn would come soon. He had slept badly the night before, because there had been several air-raid warnings. Hiroshima had been getting such warnings almost every night for weeks, for at that time the B-29s were using Lake Biwa, northeast of Hiroshima, as a rendezvous point, and no matter what city the Americans planned to hit, the Superfortresses streamed in over the coast near Hiroshima. The frequency of the warnings and the continued abstinence

of Mr. B with respect to Hiroshima had made its citizens jittery; a rumor was going around that the Americans were saving something special for the city.

Mr. Tanimoto is a small man, quick to talk, laugh, and cry. He wears his black hair parted in the middle and rather long; the prominence of the frontal bones just above his eyebrows and the smallness of his moustache, mouth, and chin give him a strange, old-young look, boyish and yet wise, weak and yet fiery. He moves nervously and fast, but with a restraint which suggests that he is a cautious, thoughtful man. He showed, indeed, just those qualities in the uneasy days before the bomb fell. Besides having his wife spend the nights in Ushida, Mr. Tanimoto had been carrying all the portable things from his church, in the close-packed residential district called Nagaragawa, to a house that belonged to a rayon manufacturer in Koi, two miles from the center of town. The rayon man, a Mr. Matsui, had opened his then unoccupied estate to a large number of his friends and acquaintances, so that they might evacuate whatever they wished to a safe distance from the probable target area. Mr. Tanimoto had had no difficulty in moving chairs, hymnals, Bibles, altar gear, and church records by pushcart himself, but the organ console and an upright piano required some aid. A friend of his named Matsuo had, the day before, helped him get the piano out to Koi; in return, he had promised this day to assist Mr. Matsuo in hauling out a daughter's belongings. That is why he had risen so early.

Mr. Tanimoto cooked his own breakfast. He felt awfully tired. The effort of moving the piano the day before, a sleepless night, weeks of worry and unbalanced diet, the cares of his parish—all combined to make him feel hardly adequate to the new day's work. There was

2 Point of View *Based on your reading of the first paragraph, what kind of point of view does Hersey use?*

Vocabulary
volition (vō lish′ ən) *n.* act of choosing or deciding

The United States and the World *Why are the people of Hiroshima so worried about the Americans?* **3**

JOHN HERSEY **1005**

Teach

Literary Element	2

Point of View Answer:
He uses a third-person objective point of view; the narrator reports what the characters do, see, and hear.

 For additional literary element practice, see Unit 6 Teaching Resources Book, p. 192.

Big Idea	3

The United States and the World Answer: *The United States had bombed other Japanese cities but had not yet attacked Hiroshima.*

(APPROACHING) Point out to approaching level students that the names "B-san" and "Mr. B" both refer to the B-29 planes.

English Learners
DIFFERENTIATED INSTRUCTION

Intermediate Because the selection is not written in chronological order, students should look for words that reveal time and for transition words that signal time order. Have students read the first twelve lines of the story. Ask them to identify words and phrases that provide clues to the time of day or to a sequence of events. *("At exactly fifteen minutes past eight in the morning, on August 6, 1945," "at the moment* when the atomic bomb flashed," "At that same moment.")

Have students keep track of time and time sequence clues as they read the story. Students can use these clues to create a timeline that keeps track of all the individuals and tells where they are and what they are doing before, during, and after the bomb.

Teach

Literary Element 1

Point of View Tell students that the author uses the third-person objective point of view most of the time, but occasionally uses the third-person omniscient point of view to describe the characters' thoughts and feelings and to describe details that the characters do not know. **Ask:** What details suggest that Hersey shifts from a third-person objective point of view to a third-person omniscient point of view in this section? *(Details about the size, shape, number of people, and types of industry in the city reveal an omniscient point of view.)*

Literary Element 2

Answer: *The author shows that Tanimoto does not hate Americans, even though his country is at war with the United States.*

Reading Strategy 3

Draw Conclusions About Author's Beliefs Answer: *The words* showy, notorious, *and* tyrannies *suggest Hersey's disdain.* **Say:** Because the writer uses an objective point of view, readers must draw their own conclusions about his sympathies.

another thing, too: Mr. Tanimoto had studied theology at Emory College, in Atlanta, Georgia; he had graduated in 1940; he spoke excellent English; he dressed in American clothes; he had corresponded with many American friends right up to the time the war began; and among a people obsessed with a fear of being spied upon—perhaps almost obsessed himself—he found himself growing increasingly uneasy. The police had questioned him several times, and just a few days before, he had heard that an influential acquaintance, a Mr. Tanaka, a retired officer of the Toyo Kisen Kaisha steamship line, an anti-Christian, a man famous in Hiroshima for his showy philanthro-pies[3] and notorious for his personal tyrannies, had been telling people that Tanimoto should not be trusted. In compensation, to show himself publicly a good Japanese, Mr. Tanimoto had taken on the chairmanship of his local *tonarigumi,* or Neighborhood Association, and to his other duties and concerns this position had added the business of organizing air-raid defense for about twenty families.

Before six o'clock that morning, Mr. Tanimoto started for Mr. Matsuo's house. There he found that their burden was to be a *tansu,* a large Japanese cabinet, full of clothing and household goods. The two men set out. The morning was perfectly clear and so warm that the day promised to be uncomfortable. A few minutes after they started, the air-raid siren went off—a minute-long blast that warned of approaching planes but indicated to the people of Hiroshima only a slight degree of danger, since it sounded every morning at this time, when an American weather plane came over. The two men pulled and pushed the handcart through the city streets. Hiroshima was a fan-

---

3. *Philanthropies* are good works designed to benefit people.

2 Point of View *How does the point of view affect your understanding of Mr. Tanimoto?*

3 Draw Conclusions About Author's Beliefs *Which words and phrases show the author's disdain for certain personality traits?*

shaped city, lying mostly on the six islands formed by the seven estuarial rivers that branch out from the Ota River; its main commercial and residential districts, covering about four square miles in the center of the city, contained three-quarters of its population, which had been reduced by several evacuation programs from a wartime peak of 380,000 to about 245,000. Factories and other residential districts, or suburbs, lay compactly around the edges of the city. To the south were the docks, an airport, and the island-studded Inland Sea.[4] A rim of mountains runs around the other three sides of the delta. Mr. Tanimoto and Mr. Matsuo took their way through the shopping center, already full of people, and across two of the rivers to the sloping streets of Koi, and up them to the outskirts and foothills. As they started up a valley away from the tight-ranked houses, the all-clear sounded. (The Japanese radar operators, detecting only three planes, supposed that they comprised a reconnaissance.) Pushing the handcart up to the rayon man's house was tiring, and the men, after they had maneuvered their load into the driveway and to the front steps, paused to rest awhile. They stood with a wing of the house between them and the city. Like most homes in this part of Japan, the house consisted of a wooden frame and wooden walls supporting a heavy tile roof. Its front hall, packed with rolls of bedding and clothing, looked like a cool cave full of fat cushions. Opposite the house, to the right of the front door, there was a large, finicky rock garden. There was no sound of planes. The

1

Comparisons of Hiroshima Before and After Atomic Bomb. Hiroshima on April 13 and August 11, 1945.

---

4. The *Inland Sea* lies between the Japanese islands of Kyushu, Shikoku, and Honshu, where Hiroshima is located.

Reading Practice

SPIRAL REVIEW **Text Structure** Review these nonfiction text structures: comparison/contrast, examples, problem/solution, chronological order, and order of importance. **Say:** Hersey combines six narratives, which forces readers to compare and contrast each person's experiences.

Have students map the selection structure, using outlines or graphic organizers.

Ask: How does this structure influence your understanding of Hersey's perspective? *(Hersey does not think one person's experience is more important than another's.)*

1006

morning was still; the place was cool and pleasant.

Then a tremendous flash of light cut across the sky. Mr. Tanimoto has a distinct recollection that it traveled from east to west, from the city toward the hills. It seemed a sheet of sun. Both he and Mr. Matsuo reacted in terror—and both had time to react (for they were 3,500 yards, or two miles, from the center of the explosion). Mr. Matsuo dashed up the front steps into the house and dived among the bedrolls and buried himself there. Mr. Tanimoto took four or five steps and threw himself between two big rocks in the garden. He bellied up very hard against one of them. As his face was against the stone, he did not see what happened. He felt a sudden pressure, and then splinters and pieces of board and fragments of tile fell on him. He heard no roar. (Almost no one in Hiroshima recalls hearing any noise of the bomb. But a fisherman in his sampan[5] on the Inland Sea near Tsuzu, the man with whom Mr. Tanimoto's mother-in-law and sister-in-law were living, saw the flash and heard a tremendous explosion; he was nearly twenty miles from Hiroshima, but the thunder was greater than when the B-29s hit Iwakuni, only five miles away.)

When he dared, Mr. Tanimoto raised his head and saw that the rayon man's house had collapsed. He thought a bomb had fallen directly on it. Such clouds of dust had risen that there was a sort of twilight around. In panic, not thinking for the moment of Mr. Matsuo under the ruins, he dashed out into the street. He noticed as he ran that the concrete wall of the estate had fallen over—toward the house rather than away from it. In the street, the first thing he saw was a squad of soldiers who had been burrowing into the hillside opposite, making one of the thousands of dugouts in which the Japanese apparently intended to resist invasion, hill by hill, life for life; the soldiers were coming out of the hole, where they should have been safe, and blood was running from their heads, chests, and backs. They were silent and dazed.

---

5. A *sampan* is a small boat.

Under what seemed to be a local dust cloud, the day grew darker and darker.

At nearly midnight, the night before the bomb was dropped, an announcer on the city's radio station said that about two hundred B-29s were approaching southern Honshu and advised the population of Hiroshima to evacuate to their designated "safe areas." Mrs. Hatsuyo Nakamura, the tailor's widow, who lived in the section called Noboricho and who had long had a habit of doing as she was told, got her three children—a ten-year-old boy, Toshio, an eight-year-old girl, Yaeko, and a five-year-old girl, Myeko—out of bed and dressed them and walked with them to the military area known as the East Parade Ground, on the northeast edge of the city. There she unrolled some mats and the children lay down on them. They slept until about two, when they were awakened by the roar of the planes going over Hiroshima.

As soon as the planes had passed, Mrs. Nakamura started back with her children. They reached home a little after two-thirty and she immediately turned on the radio, which, to her distress, was just then broadcasting a fresh warning. When she looked at the children and saw how tired they were, and when she thought of the number of trips they had made in past weeks, all to no purpose, to the East Parade Ground, she decided that in spite of the instructions on the radio, she simply could not face starting out all over again. She put the children in their bedrolls on the floor, lay down herself at three o'clock, and fell asleep at once, so soundly that when the planes passed over later, she did not waken to their sound.

The siren jarred her awake at about seven. She arose, dressed quickly, and hurried to the house of Mr. Nakamoto, the head of her Neighborhood Association, and asked him what she should do. He said that she should remain at home unless an urgent warning—a series of intermittent blasts of the siren—was sounded. She returned home, lit the stove in the kitchen, set some rice to cook, and sat down to read that morning's Hiroshima

JOHN HERSEY   **1007**

Teach

Big Idea ⬛ 1

The United States and the World Answer: *The details show how quickly the blast traveled. In the time it took to make one step, the blast traveled three-quarters of a mile.*

View the Photograph ★

Photographers provided images of Hiroshima immediately after the bombing. **Ask:** How does this photograph support Hersey's message? *(It shows the devastation caused by the bomb.)* **Ask:** What words would you choose to describe the images in the photograph? *(chaos, heat, desperation, fear)*

Chugoku. To her relief, the all-clear sounded at eight o'clock. She heard the children stirring, so she went and gave each of them a handful of peanuts and told them to stay on their bedrolls, because they were tired from the night's walk. She had hoped that they would go back to sleep, but the man in the house directly to the south began to make a terrible hullabaloo of hammering, wedging, ripping, and splitting. The prefectural government,[6] convinced, as everyone in Hiroshima was, that the city would be attacked soon, had begun to press with threats and warnings for the completion of wide fire lanes, which, it was hoped, might act in conjunction with the rivers to localize any fires started by an incendiary[7] raid; and the neighbor was reluctantly sacrificing his home to the city's safety. Just the day before, the prefecture had ordered all able-bodied girls from the secondary schools to spend a few days helping to clear these lanes, and they started work soon after the all-clear sounded.

Mrs. Nakamura went back to the kitchen, looked at the rice, and began watching the man next door. At first, she was annoyed with him for making so much noise, but then she was moved almost to tears by pity. Her emotion was specifically directed toward her neighbor, tearing down his home, board by board, at a time when there was so much unavoidable destruction, but undoubtedly she also felt a generalized, community pity, to say nothing of self-pity. She had not had an easy time. Her husband, Isawa, had gone into the Army just after Myeko was born, and she had heard nothing from or of him for a long time, until, on March 5, 1942, she received a seven-word telegram: "Isawa died an honorable

People hurry past a fire burning in the wake of an atomic explosion. Hiroshima, Japan. August 1945.

death at Singapore." She learned later that he had died on February 15th, the day Singapore fell, and that he had been a corporal. Isawa had been a not particularly prosperous tailor, and his only capital was a Sankoku sewing machine. After his death, when his allotments stopped coming, Mrs. Nakamura got out the machine and began to take in piecework herself, and since then had supported the children, but poorly, by sewing.

As Mrs. Nakamura stood watching her neighbor, everything flashed whiter than any white she had ever seen. She did not notice what happened to the man next door; the reflex of a mother set her in motion toward her children. She had taken a single step (the house was 1,350 yards, or three-quarters of a mile, from the center of the explosion) when something picked her up and she seemed to fly into the next room over the raised sleeping platform, pursued by parts of her house.

Timbers fell around her as she landed, and a shower of tiles pummeled her; everything

---

6. *Prefectural* refers to the forty-seven geopolitical divisions within Japan known as *prefectures,* which are governed by governors and assemblies similar to state and local government in the United States.
7. Here *incendiary* means "designed to deliberately start fires."

The United States and the World *How do these details show the power of the bomb?* ⬛ **1**

Reading Practice

Fact and Opinion Explain that non-fiction writing includes both facts and opinions. Remind students that a fact is information that can be verified and an opinion is a personal judgment that cannot be proved. Also explain that opinions are sometimes presented in ways that make them appear to be facts. Assign short sections of the selection. Ask students to identify details and decide if each is a fact or an opinion. Have students use encyclopedias, reference books, and other reliable sources to verify any facts. Have students explain which are facts and which are opinions in their section and tell what sources they used to check the facts.

became dark, for she was buried. The **debris** did not cover her deeply. She rose up and freed herself. She heard a child cry, "Mother, help me!," and saw her youngest—Myeko, the five-year-old—buried up to her breast and unable to move. As Mrs. Nakamura started frantically to claw her way toward the baby, she could see or hear nothing of her other children.

In the days right before the bombing, Dr. Masakazu Fujii, being prosperous, hedonistic, and at the time not too busy, had been allowing himself the luxury of sleeping until nine or nine-thirty, but fortunately he had to get up only the morning the bomb was dropped to see a house guest off on a train. He rose at six, and half an hour later walked with his friend to the station, not far away, across two of the rivers. He was back home by seven, just as the siren sounded its sustained warning. He ate breakfast and then, because the morning was already hot, undressed down to his underwear and went out on the porch to read the paper. This porch—in fact, the whole building—was curiously constructed. Dr. Fujii was the proprietor of a peculiarly Japanese institution: a private, single-doctor hospital. This building, perched beside and over the water of the Kyo River, and next to the bridge of the same name, contained thirty rooms for thirty patients and their kinfolk—for, according to Japanese custom, when a person falls sick and goes to a hospital, one or more members of his family go and live there with him, to cook for him, bathe, massage, and read to him, and to offer incessant familial sympathy, without which a Japanese patient would be miserable indeed. Dr. Fujii had no beds—only straw mats—for his patients. He did, however, have

all sorts of modern equipment: an X-ray machine, diathermy apparatus, and a fine tiled laboratory. The structure rested two-thirds on the land, one-third on piles over the tidal waters of the Kyo. This overhang, the part of the building where Dr. Fujii lived, was queer-looking, but it was cool in summer and from the porch, which faced away from the center of the city, the prospect of the river, with pleasure boats drifting up and down it, was always refreshing. Dr. Fujii had occasionally had anxious moments when the Ota and its mouth branches rose to flood, but the piling[8] was apparently firm enough and the house had always held.

Dr. Fujii had been relatively idle for about a month because in July, as the number of untouched cities in Japan dwindled and as Hiroshima seemed more and more inevitably a target, he began turning patients away, on the ground that in case of a fire raid he would not be able to evacuate them. Now he had only two patients left—a woman from Yano, injured in the shoulder, and a young man of twenty-five recovering from burns he had suffered when the steel factory near Hiroshima in which he worked had been hit. Dr. Fujii had six nurses to tend his patients. His wife and children were safe; his wife and one son were living outside Osaka, and another son and two daughters were in the country on Kyushu. A niece was living with him, and a maid and a manservant. He had little to do and did not mind, for he had saved some money. At fifty, he was healthy, convivial, and calm, and he was pleased to pass the evenings drinking whiskey with friends, always sensibly and for the sake of conversation. Before the war, he had affected brands imported from Scotland and America; now he was perfectly satisfied with the best Japanese brand, Suntory.

Dr. Fujii sat down cross-legged in his underwear on the spotless matting of the porch, put on his glasses, and started reading the Osaka

---

2 Draw Conclusions About Author's Beliefs *Hersey includes many details about Japanese life and culture. Why do you think it is important to the author to include this information?*

Vocabulary

debris (də brē′) *n.* large number of fragments or broken pieces

---

8. *Piles* are long, columnar timbers or poles that have one end anchored in the ground and are grouped into *pilings* to hold up buildings or other structures.

JOHN HERSEY **1009**

Teach

Teach

Big Idea   1

The United States and the World Answer: *Even hospitals were destroyed, so people would have no medical resources.*

Vocabulary   2

Greek Word Roots The word *xenophobic* is a word that incorporates two Greek roots. The root *xeno* means "stranger or foreign." The root *phobic* means "fear." **Ask:** Can you think of other words that use at least one of these roots? (*Students may suggest claustrophobic—fear of enclosed spaces.*)

View the Photograph ★

When the atomic bomb hit Hiroshima, the heat of the blast destroyed an area of 4.4 square miles. An estimated 70,000 to 80,000 people were killed instantly, and 70,000 more were injured. **Ask:** Given the extent of the devastation, what does the photograph suggest to you about the Japanese people? (*They are resilient and determined to go on with life.*)

Asahi. He liked to read the Osaka news because his wife was there. He saw the flash. To him—faced away from the center and looking at his paper—it seemed a brilliant yellow. Startled, he began to rise to his feet. In that moment (he was 1,500 yards from the center), the hospital leaned behind his rising and, with a terrible ripping noise, toppled into the river. The doctor, still in the act of getting to his feet, was thrown forward and around and over; he was buffeted and gripped; he lost track of everything, because things were so speeded up; he felt the water.

Dr. Fujii hardly had time to think that he was dying before he realized that he was alive, squeezed tightly by two long timbers in a V across his chest, like a morsel suspended between two huge chopsticks—held upright, so that he could not move, with his head miraculously above water and his torso and legs in it.

The United States and the World *What do these details show about the horrors of nuclear war?*

The remains of his hospital were all around him in a mad assortment of splintered lumber and materials for the relief of pain. His left shoulder hurt terribly. His glasses were gone.

Father Wilhelm Kleinsorge, of the Society of Jesus, was, on the morning of the explosion, in rather frail condition. The Japanese wartime diet had not sustained him, and he felt the strain of being a foreigner in an increasingly **xenophobic** Japan; even a German, since the defeat of the Fatherland,[9] was unpopular. Father Kleinsorge had, at thirty-eight, the look of a boy growing too fast—thin in the face, with a prominent Adam's apple, a hollow chest, dangling hands, big feet. He walked clumsily, leaning forward a little. He was tired

---

9. **Fatherland** refers to Germany, which had surrendered to Allied forces a few months before the attack on Hiroshima.

Vocabulary

xenophobic (zen´ ə fō´ bik) *adj.* having an extreme fear of foreigners or strangers

Rain falls on buildings reduced to rubble by an atomic bomb blast a few months after the U.S. attack that led to the end of World War II. October 1945. ★

1010 UNIT 6   FROM DEPRESSION TO COLD WAR

Writing Practice

Editorial Have students write a brief editorial about the use of nuclear weapons during World War II. They should use specific details from the selection and their own research. Ask students to imagine it is 1946—the year after the war ended. They should support or condemn the use of the atomic bomb on Hiroshima. Their purpose is to persuade readers to share their opinion. Encourage students to appeal to both reason and emotion in their writing.

all the time. To make matters worse, he had suffered for two days, along with Father Cieslik, a fellow-priest, from a rather painful and urgent diarrhea, which they blamed on the beans and black ration bread they were obliged to eat. Two other priests then living in the mission compound, which was in the Noboricho section—Father Superior LaSalle and Father Schiffer—had happily escaped this affliction.

Father Kleinsorge woke up about six the morning the bomb was dropped, and half an hour later—he was a bit tardy because of his sickness—he began to read Mass in the mission chapel, a small Japanese-style wooden building which was without pews, since its worshipers knelt on the usual Japanese matted floor, facing an altar graced with splendid silks, brass, silver, and heavy embroideries. This morning, a Monday, the only worshipers were Mr. Takemoto, a theological student living in the mission house; Mr. Fukai, the secretary of the diocese;[10] Mrs. Murata, the mission's devoutly Christian housekeeper; and his fellow-priests. After Mass, while Father Kleinsorge was reading the Prayers of Thanksgiving, the siren sounded. He stopped the service and the missionaries retired across the compound to the bigger building. There, in his room on the ground floor, to the right of the front door, Father Kleinsorge changed into a military uniform which he had acquired when he was teaching at the Rokko Middle School in Kobe and which he wore during air-raid alerts.

After an alarm, Father Kleinsorge always went out and scanned the sky, and in this instance, when he stepped outside, he was glad to see only the single weather plane that flew over Hiroshima each day about this time. Satisfied that nothing would happen, he went in and breakfasted with the other Fathers on substitute coffee and ration bread, which, under the circumstances, was especially repugnant to him. The Fathers sat and talked awhile, until, at eight, they heard the all-clear. They went then to various parts of the building. Father Schiffer

retired to his room to do some writing. Father Cieslik sat in his room in a straight chair with a pillow over his stomach to ease his pain, and read. Father Superior LaSalle stood at the window of his room, thinking. Father Kleinsorge went up to a room on the third floor, took off all his clothes except his underwear, and stretched out on his right side on a cot and began reading his *Stimmen der Zeit*.

After the terrible flash—which, Father Kleinsorge later realized, reminded him of something he had read as a boy about a large meteor colliding with the earth—he had time (since he was 1,400 yards from the center) for one thought: A bomb has fallen directly on us. Then, for a few seconds or minutes, he went out of his mind.

Father Kleinsorge never knew how he got out of the house. The next things he was conscious of were that he was wandering around in the mission's vegetable garden in his underwear, bleeding slightly from small cuts along his left flank; that all the building round about had fallen down except the Jesuits' mission house, which had long before been braced and double-braced by a priest named Gropper, who was terrified of earthquakes; that the day had turned dark; and that Murata-san, the housekeeper, was nearby, crying over and over, "*Shu Jesusu, awaremi tamai!* Our Lord Jesus, have pity on us!"

On the train on the way into Hiroshima from the country, where he lived with his mother, Dr. Terufumi Sasaki, the Red Cross Hospital surgeon, thought over an unpleasant nightmare he had had the night before. His mother's home was in Mukai-hara, thirty miles from the city, and it took him two hours by train and tram to reach the hospital. He had slept uneasily all night and had wakened an hour earlier than usual, and, feeling sluggish and slightly feverish, had debated whether to go to the hospital at all; his sense of duty finally forced him to go, and he had started out on an earlier train than he took

---

10. A *diocese* is a district within the Roman Catholic church.

Point of View **How would this passage read differently if it was in the first-person point of view?** `3`

Literary Element `3`

Point of View **Answer:** *Some students may empathize with Father Kleinsorge more, while others may say that it would make no difference.*

Ask: Why do you think Hersey did not use the first-person point of view? *(He is a reporter and reporters typically write from a third-person point of view in order to maintain objectivity.)*

English Learners

DIFFERENTIATED INSTRUCTION

Intermediate English language learners might have problems understanding Hersey's complicated sentences. Review with students that an independent clause contains a subject and a verb. It can stand alone as a sentence. A compound sentence joins two independent clauses with a coordinating conjunction: *The flash was bright, and the people ran.* Have students find more examples of compound sentences in the text. Tell students to examine the conjunction in each compound sentence and explain how the conjunction adds to the meaning of the sentence.

Teach

Reading Strategy 1

Draw Conclusions About Author's Beliefs Answer: *Japanese culture valued facing a terrifying situation with courage.*

Big Idea 2

The United States and the World Answer: *The doctor was not able to conceive of a bomb with the power to destroy much of a large city.*

[APPROACHING] **Ask:** How do you think other nations' perceptions of the United States changed after the bombing? *(Other nations probably became fearful of the power unleashed by the United States.)*

Reading Strategy 3

Draw Conclusions About Author's Beliefs Answer: *Hersey suggests that the bombing and its aftermath are so horrific that the doctor's ordinary fears and conflicts are diminished in comparison.*

[APPROACHING] **Ask:** Why would details like this one be important to Hersey and to his readers? *(The details convey the magnitude of suffering in Hiroshima; it tells readers the great price paid by the Japanese for a sudden end to the war.)*

most mornings. The dream had particularly frightened him because it was so closely associated, on the surface at least, with a disturbing actuality. He was only twenty-five years old and had just completed his training at the Eastern Medical University, in Tsingtao, China. He was something of an idealist and was much distressed by the inadequacy of medical facilities in the country town where his mother lived. Quite on his own, and without a permit, he had begun visiting a few sick people out there in the evenings, after his eight hours at the hospital and four hours' commuting. He had recently learned that the penalty for practicing without a permit was severe; a fellow-doctor whom he had asked about it had given him a serious scolding. Nevertheless, he had continued to practice. In his dream, he had been at the bedside of a country patient when the police and the doctor he had consulted burst into the room, seized him, dragged him outside, and beat him up cruelly. On the train, he just about decided to give up the work in Mukai-hara, since he felt it would be impossible to get a permit, because the authorities would hold that it would conflict with his duties at the Red Cross Hospital.

At the **terminus,** he caught a streetcar at once. (He later calculated that if he had taken his customary train that morning, and if he had had to wait a few minutes for the streetcar, as often happened, he would have been close to the center at the time of the explosion and would surely have perished.) He arrived at the hospital at seven-forty and reported to the chief surgeon. A few minutes later, he went to a room on the first floor and drew blood from the arm of a man in order to perform a Wassermann test. The laboratory containing the incubators for the test was on the third floor. With the blood specimen in his left hand, walking in a kind of distraction he had felt all morning, probably because of the dream and his restless night, he started along the main corridor on his way

Vocabulary

terminus (tur′ mə nəs) *n.* one end of a travel route or the station placed there

toward the stairs. He was one step beyond an open window when the light of the bomb was reflected, like a gigantic photographic flash, in the corridor. He ducked down on one knee and said to himself, as only a Japanese would, "Sasaki, *gambare!* Be brave!" Just then (the building was 1,650 yards from the center), the blast ripped through the hospital. The glasses he was wearing flew off his face; the bottle of blood crashed against one wall; his Japanese slippers zipped out from under his feet—but otherwise, thanks to where he stood, he was untouched.

Dr. Sasaki shouted the name of the chief surgeon and rushed around to the man's office and found him terribly cut by glass. The hospital was in horrible confusion: Heavy partitions and ceilings had fallen on patients, beds had overturned, windows had blown in and cut people, blood was spattered on the walls and floors, instruments were everywhere, many of the patients were running about screaming, many more lay dead. (A colleague working in the laboratory to which Dr. Sasaki had been walking was dead; Dr. Sasaki's patient, whom he had just left and who a few moments before had been dreadfully afraid of syphilis, was also dead.) Dr. Sasaki found himself the only doctor in the hospital who was unhurt.

Dr. Sasaki, who believed that the enemy had hit only the building he was in, got bandages and began to bind the wounds of those inside the hospital; while outside, all over Hiroshima, maimed and dying citizens turned their unsteady steps toward the Red Cross Hospital to begin an invasion that was to make Dr. Sasaki forget his private nightmare for a long, long time.

Draw Conclusions About Author's Beliefs *Based on this detail, what aspect of Japanese culture made an impression on Hersey?* **1**

The United States and the World *How does this excerpt show that people were unprepared for the true extent of atomic warfare?* **2**

Draw Conclusions About Author's Beliefs *How does this sentence help you understand how Hersey feels about the bombing?* **3**

Reading Practice

Scan Hersey's *Hiroshima* first appeared in print as a journalist's report in *The New Yorker* magazine. Review the reading strategy of scanning—a quick search of text for a particular piece of information. Note that one can easily scan paragraphs in a newspaper article to find specific facts. **Ask:** Would it be as easy to scan this selection? Have students scan one page of the selection for proper names, numbers, dates, or quotations. Then ask students to recall orally what they learned.

Miss Toshiko Sasaki, the East Asia Tin Works clerk, who is not related to Dr. Sasaki, got up at three o'clock in the morning on the day the bomb fell. There was extra housework to do. Her eleven-month-old brother, Akio, had come down the day before with a serious stomach upset; her mother had taken him to the Tamura Pediatric Hospital and was staying there with him. Miss Sasaki, who was about twenty, had to cook breakfast for her father, a brother, a sister, and herself, and—since the hospital, because of the war, was unable to provide food—to prepare a whole day's meals for her mother and the baby, in time for her father, who worked in a factory making rubber earplugs for artillery crews, to take the food by on his way to the plant. When she had finished and had cleaned and put away the cooking things, it was nearly seven. The family lived in Koi, and she had a forty-five-minute trip to the tin works, in the section of town called Kannon-machi. She was in charge of the personnel records in the factory. She left Koi at seven, and as soon as she reached the plant, she went with some of the other girls from the personnel department to the factory auditorium. A prominent local Navy man, a former employee, had committed suicide the day before by throwing himself under a train—a death considered honorable enough to warrant a memorial service, which was to be held at the tin works at ten o'clock that morning. In the large hall, Miss Sasaki and the others made suitable preparations for the meeting. This work took about twenty minutes.

Miss Sasaki went back to her office and sat down at her desk. She was quite far from the windows, which were off to her left, and behind her were a couple of tall bookcases containing all the books of the factory library, which the personnel department had organized. She settled

Atomic bomb damage to Nagasaki, Japan.

herself at her desk, put some things in a drawer, and shifted papers. She thought that before she began to make entries in her lists of new employees, discharges, and departures for the Army, she would chat for a moment with the girl at her right. Just as she turned her head away from the windows, the room was filled with a blinding light. She was paralyzed by fear, fixed still in her chair for a long moment (the plant was 1,600 yards from the center).

Everything fell, and Miss Sasaki lost consciousness. The ceiling dropped suddenly and the wooden floor above collapsed in splinters and the people up there came down and the roof above them gave way; but principally and first of all, the bookcases right behind her swooped forward and the contents threw her down, with her left leg horribly twisted and breaking underneath her. There, in the tin factory, in the first moment of the atomic age, a human being was crushed by books. ◦∿

The United States and the World *What does this suggest about Hersey's attitude toward the atomic age?* **4**

JOHN HERSEY **1013**

Teach

| **Big Idea** | **4** |

The United States and the World Answer: *Despite our great knowledge (symbolized by the books), which allowed us to develop a powerful atomic bomb, human beings are in danger of making themselves extinct.*

View the Photograph ★

Until July 1945, no one in the world had seen an atomic mushroom cloud. The first atomic bomb explosion in the New Mexico desert yielded a mushroom-shaped cloud that was 40,000 feet high. The impact of that bomb nearly equaled that of 20,000 tons of TNT explosive. The heat from the bomb melted the desert sands in a 2,400-foot diameter. A month later, atomic bombs were dropped on Hiroshima and Nagasaki. The mushroom cloud has become a symbol of nuclear weaponry.

To check students' understanding of the selection, see Unit 6 Teaching Resources Book, pp. 197–198.

Advanced Learners

DIFFERENTIATED INSTRUCTION

Write a Screenplay Review with advanced students that a screenplay has elements of a stage play but also includes notes on how a scene would be filmed. Invite students to develop a screenplay that focuses on one episode in Hersey's story. Have them use dialogue and stage directions to develop characters and events. Ask volunteers to present staged readings of their scenes, and discuss the challenges of creating a scripted scene from prose.

After You Read

Assess

1. (a) Some may be surprised by Hersey's objectivity and lack of emotion. Others may appreciate learning the facts.

2. (a) Clerk, seamstress, two doctors, and two religious leaders (b) They are a cross-section of society members who were in Hiroshima at the time of the bombing.

3. (a) Not in this excerpt (b) Readers focus on the individuals' stories, not on the war or politics.

4. (a) It forced people to leave their homes, undergo air raids, lose sleep, and feel anxious. (b) So that readers—particularly in the United States—could see how the war also affected the Japanese

5. Students may choose Mrs. Nakamura because she is already a widow.

6. Students should give reasons for their responses. For example, students confused by the constant shifting back and forward in time may find a straightforward narrative more effective.

7. The issue of nuclear warfare and warfare in general affects people worldwide.

8. The ongoing controversy about the use of the atomic bomb, modern concerns about nuclear warfare, literary merit

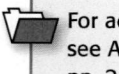 For additional assessment, see Assessment Resources, pp. 261–262.

After You Read

Respond and Think Critically

Respond and Interpret

1. How did you react to Hersey's unemotional, but detailed retelling of the events?

2. (a) What were the professions of the six people? (b) Why would Hersey choose to focus on them?

3. (a) Does Hersey ever explain why the atomic bomb was dropped on Hiroshima? (b) How does this affect the narrative?

4. (a) Even before the bomb dropped, how had the war affected people? (b) Why do you think Hersey might have included this information?

Analyze and Evaluate

5. Which characters did you find sympathetic? Why?

6. Do you think Hersey's detailed account was the best way to tell the story, or would some other way have been more effective? Explain.

Connect

7. **Big Idea** The United States and the World In what ways is *Hiroshima* written not only for the United States but also for the world?

8. **Connect to Today** Why do you think people still read *Hiroshima* six decades after it was written?

Primary Source Quotation

On August 6, 1945, President Harry Truman announced that the U.S. had bombed Hiroshima.

"Sixteen hours ago an American airplane dropped one bomb on Hiroshima, an important Japanese army base. That bomb had more power than 20,000 tons of T.N.T. It had more than two thousand times the blast power of the British 'Grand Slam' which is the largest bomb ever yet used in the history of warfare.

"The Japanese began the war from the air at Pearl Harbor. They have been repaid many fold. And the end is not yet. With this bomb we have now added a new and revolutionary increase in destruction to supplement the growing power of our armed forces."

—President Harry Truman

The Enola Gay. The B-29 bomber, which dropped the first atomic bomb on Japan, stands on the runway at Tinian following the raid. August 1945.

Group Activity Discuss the following questions with classmates. Refer back to the quotation and cite evidence from *Hiroshima* for support.

1. After reading the excerpt from *Hiroshima*, how would you respond to President Truman's statement?

2. How do you think President Truman would respond to Hersey's narrative? Explain.

Primary Source Quotation

1. Some students may feel Truman disregards the civilian lives lost as a result of the bombing and seems to applaud the arrival of nuclear warfare.

2. Truman might say the bombing was necessary to save U.S. lives, even at the expense of Japanese lives. Truman's remark "And the end is not yet" may indicate he did not know if the Japanese would surrender, or he may be hinting that additional nuclear attacks may be forthcoming.

Literary Element Point of View

The excerpt from *Hiroshima* is written with a third-person objective **point of view**, which reports on how people respond to a disastrous event. The use of pronouns such as *he, she,* and *they* also indicate third-person point of view.

While stories told in first-person point of view are limited to only one perspective, narratives told in third-person objective point of view can reveal many perspectives on one topic. Much nonfiction journalistic writing, like *Hiroshima,* is told in third-person objective point of view in order to give a more complete account of events.

1. Why do you think Hersey uses the third-person objective point of view to narrate *Hiroshima*?

2. Are there points where Hersey veers from a completely objective point of view? Explain.

Review: Author's Purpose

Author's purpose is an author's intent in writing a piece of literature. Authors often write to persuade, to inform, to explain, to describe, or to entertain.

Partner Activity Meet with another classmate and identify Hersey's purpose in writing *Hiroshima.* Find at least three details that support your response. Afterward, compare your conclusions with those of your classmates.

 Literature Online

Selection Resources For Selection Quizzes, eFlashcards, and Reading-Writing Connection activities, go to glencoe.com and enter QuickPass code GLA9800u6.

Reading Strategy Draw Conclusions About Author's Beliefs

ACT Skills Practice

1. From the evidence in this selection, how do you think Hersey felt about the citizens of Hiroshima?

   A. He was a detached observer and had no feelings about them.

   B. He saw them as individuals and condemned their suffering.

   C. He saw them as the enemy and felt their punishment was justified.

   D. He was sympathetic but thought that they exaggerated the situation.

Vocabulary Practice

Practice with Word Origins The etymology, or origin and history, of a word can help you better understand its meaning. Create a word map like the one below for each vocabulary word. Use a dictionary for help.

evacuate   volition   debris
xenophobic   terminus

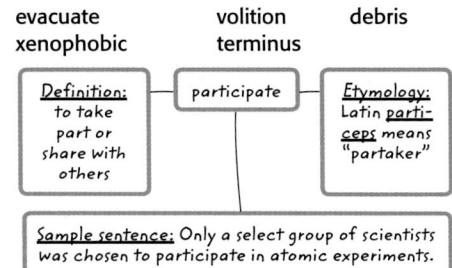

Academic Vocabulary

Mrs. Nakamura had the bare **minimum** *of time before the bomb's impact reached her.*

Minimum is an academic word. In casual conversation, a teacher might say you need to meet the **minimum** requirements to pass. Write a paragraph answering this question: What do you think the **minimum** requirements for earning a high school diploma should be? *For more on academic vocabulary, see pages 53–54.*

After You Read

Assess

Literary Element

1. He shows how the bomb affected different people. He presents events objectively, to allow readers to draw their own conclusions.

2. Yes; he condemns the bombing when he describes the extent of the devastation and suffering.

Review: Author's Purpose

His purpose is to inform readers about the devastating effects of nuclear warfare. Students may point to the many details about the aftermath of the bombing. His purpose may also be to describe. He includes many descriptive details about the city and its inhabitants.

Progress Check

Can students draw conclusions about author's beliefs?

If No → See Unit 6 Teaching Resources Book, p. 193.

Vocabulary

evacuate (*Middle English* evacuatus *means "to empty out"*) The survivors of Hiroshima had to evacuate the city because of lingering radiation.

volition (*Latin* volo *means "to be willing"*) She had to exercise volition when she was accepted to three schools.

debris (*Old French* debrisier *means "to break down"*) I dropped a glass on the floor and cleaned up the debris with a dustpan.

xenophobic (*Greek* zenos *means "stranger" and Greek* phobos *means "fear"*) My grandparents in Europe are xenophobic and will not come to visit us.

terminus (*Latin* terminus *means "boundary"*) The train was delayed at the terminus because one passenger did not have the proper ticket.

Academic Vocabulary

I think that the minimum requirement for a high school diploma should be a passing grade in the following classes: English composition, American literature, British literature, algebra, algebra II, trigonometry, geometry, chemistry, biology, physics or astronomy, U.S. history, world history, and elective arts courses.

After You Read

Assess

Respond Through Writing

Use these criteria when evaluating students' writing:

- Does the student support the thesis with textual evidence?
- Does the student establish clear connections between causes and effects?
- Does the student apply appropriate strategies to evaluate and revise the draft?

Scoring Guide

Assess students' performance in the following categories using the scoring guide below:

- Addresses all parts of the writing task.
- Provides a meaningful thesis; maintains focus and organization.
- Supports the thesis with details and examples.
- Provides a variety of sentence types; uses precise, descriptive language.
- Follows English language conventions.
- Makes a logical, convincing argument.

Respond Through Writing

Expository Essay

Analyze Cause and Effect The Hiroshima bomb killed an estimated 100,000 people. A series of cause-and-effect relationships allowed certain individuals to survive. Analyze these relationships and explain how they support Hersey's purpose. Support your thesis with evidence from his text.

Understand the Task A **cause** is a person, thing, or event that produces some other specific thing or event, which is the **effect**, or result.

Prewrite Review events in the selection by looking at your graphic organizers from pages 1003 and 1015. Think about Hersey's purpose in including each event and about how individual events result in each character's survival. Fill out a chart like the one below for each survivor.

Mr. Tanimoto	
Causes	Effects
Mr. Tanimoto is "a cautious, thoughtful man."	As a precaution, he decides to transport belongings to Koi.
Mr. Tanimoto helps Matsuo move his daughter's belongings to Koi.	Mr. Tanimoto is not in the center of the city when the bomb hits.

Draft Think about the order in which you will present the details. As you write, draw connections for your reader and suggest why certain details are especially significant. Use sentence frames as you write. For example, your thesis might take this form:

In *Hiroshima* the chain of causes and effects support Hersey's purpose—to _____, _____, and _____.

Revise Make sure that you have defined any cultural terms or proper names with which your reader might be unfamiliar. Then exchange drafts with a partner and give each other suggestions for further revisions. You may also want to decide on visual aids to include with your final draft.

Edit and Proofread Proofread your paper, correcting any errors in grammar, spelling, and punctuation.

Learning Objectives

In this assignment, you will focus on the following objective:

Writing: Writing an expository essay.

Grammar Tip

Underlining and Italics

Always underline or italicize the titles of books or plays, such as *Hiroshima.* Also underline or italicize foreign words that are not commonly used in English:

They were moving a <u>tansu</u>, a large Japanese cabinet.

Do not, however, underline or italicize foreign words that are commonly used in English:

My fiancé has a karate lesson today.

Fiancé and *karate* are both words that have become incorporated into standard English, so they are set in normal type in the above sentence.

Scoring Guide	4	3	2	1
Task addressed	fully	mostly	partially	barely
Thesis	meaningful	provided	partial	weak
Support	thoughtful	provided	limited	weak
Language	varied, descriptive	varied, often descriptive	predictable, imprecise	repetitive, limited
Convention errors	few or none	several	many	serious
Arguments are	convincing	mostly convincing	partially convincing	not convincing

Before You Read

The Portrait

Meet Tomás Rivera
(1935–1984)

The life of Tomás Rivera, the "Dean of Mexican American Literature," is a true rags-to-riches story. From modest beginnings, Rivera became a successful writer and educator—an inspiration to many. He was born in Crystal City, Texas, the son of two agricultural workers. After graduating from high school, Rivera, like his parents, began working as a migrant worker. Until he reached his early twenties, Rivera traveled with other migrant workers, picking fruit and vegetables across the United States from Texas to the Midwest.

Despite all his traveling, Rivera managed to earn a formal education by attending different schools. He received his bachelor's and master's degrees in English education from Southwest Texas State University. After a stint teaching in public schools and at Southwest Texas Junior College in Uvalde, he attended the University of Oklahoma, where he earned a master's degree in Spanish literature, and, in 1969, a doctorate in Romance languages and literature.

In 1971 Rivera published his only novel, *y no se lo trago la tierra*, also known as *And the Earth Did Not Devour Him*. Originally written in Spanish, the book was published in both Spanish and English. It is an unconventional novel, made up of twenty-seven interrelated stories and sketches that describe, often grimly, the indomitable spirit of migrant farm workers. The novel was not meant to support any particular political point of view, but instead to reflect a world and experiences that Rivera knew well. *Y no se lo trago la tierra* won the prestigious Quinto Sol Award in 1971. The success of Rivera's novel inspired other Mexican Americans to add their voices to the literature of the United States.

> "He searched for stories about his people and finally gave their words sound, wrote the books he didn't have, we didn't have . . ."
>
> —Pat Mora

Besides providing inspiration, Rivera also helped people in direct ways, serving on the boards of numerous Mexican American organizations. He also had a distinguished academic career, eventually becoming chancellor of the University of California at Riverside. He was one of the founders of the National Council of Chicanos in Higher Education. Both President Jimmy Carter and President Ronald Reagan appointed Rivera to commissions on higher education.

Rivera was working on a new book when he died in Fontana, California. After his death, the University of Texas at Austin inaugurated the Tomás Rivera Professorship in Spanish Language and Literature. It is a fitting tribute to a generous man who sought, according to one source, to develop "hospitable and fertile space for Hispanic Americans in America's institutions."

 Literature Online

Author Search For more about Tomás Rivera, go to glencoe.com and enter QuickPass code GLA9800u6.

Before You Read

Focus

Bellringer Options

Selection Focus
   Transparency 63
Daily Language Practice
   Transparency 92

Or display several portraits—include portraits of famous people, family portraits, and official portraits of government officials. Explain that portraits are often, but not always, primarily of the face and are presented in a formal style. **Ask:** What do these portraits suggest about the people they portray? *(They suggest that the person is important in some way. They show people at their best.)* Have students consider as they read what the soldier's portrait means to his family.

Selection Skills

Literary Elements
- Idiom (SE pp. 1018–1022; TE p. 1020)
- Plot (SE p. 1023)

The Portrait

Writing Skills/Grammar
- Write a Report (SE p. 1023)

Vocabulary Skills
- Context Clues (SE pp. 1018, 1023)

Reading Skills
- Respond to Plot and Characters (SE pp. 1018, 1019, 1021, 1023)
- Make Critical Judgments (TE p. 1018)

Listening/Speaking/Viewing Skills
- Analyze Art (TE p. 1020)

Before You Read

Focus

Summary

The narrator recalls an episode from his youth in which Don Mateo, one of his father's friends, is visited by a traveling salesman who promises to enhance and frame a picture of Don Mateo's son, who was killed in the Korean War. Despite the high price, Don Mateo and his wife give the salesman their only photograph of their son. The portrait never arrives, and someone finds the photograph, discarded and ruined. Don Mateo finds the salesman and forces the salesman to make a portrait of his son.

 For summaries in languages other than English, see Unit 6 Teaching Resources Book, pp. 199–204.

Vocabulary

Use Context Clues Display this sentence:

I refused to exchange my old book for a new copy, because I knew the salesman was trying to swindle me out of my valuable first edition. **Ask:** Which words in the sentence serve as context clues to the meaning of *swindle*? (*refused to exchange, valuable*)

 For additional context, see Glencoe Interactive Vocabulary CD-ROM.

Literature and Reading Preview

Connect to the Story

What are some precious items you and your family own—things you would not want to lose? Write a journal entry about one of these items and explain what makes it so valued.

Build Background

This story takes place in the 1950s during the Korean War. At that time, traveling salespeople were a familiar sight in cities and towns, selling everything from encyclopedias to vacuum cleaners. In this story, the salespeople have timed their visits to coincide with the return of newly paid migrant workers.

Set Purposes for Reading

Big Idea **The United States and the World**

"The Portrait" is set during the time of the Korean War. As you read, ask yourself, how does the war affect the main character?

Literary Element **Idiom**

An **idiom** is a saying, or group of words, that takes on special meaning, usually one different from its literal meaning. For example, "over the hill" can mean "old." Phrases such as "catch his eye," "turn the tables," and "keep tabs on" are other examples. As you read, ask yourself, What does each idiom mean? (Note that this selection is a translation and the idioms have different meanings in the original Spanish.)

Reading Strategy **Respond to Plot and Characters**

A **static character** remains basically the same throughout the story. A **dynamic character,** on the other hand, grows and changes during the story. As you read, ask yourself, Is the main character, Don Mateo, static or dynamic?

Tip: Use a Response Chart To better understand Don Mateo, write down quotations from him and your responses.

Quotation	My Response
"But you take good care of that picture for us because it's the only one we have of our son grown up." p. 1020	Don Mateo is concerned about the only photo he has of his grown son, yet he wants to "fix up" the photo to better preserve it. He trusts the salesman.

Learning Objectives

For pages 1017–1023
In studying this text, you will focus on the following objectives:

Literary Study: Analyzing idioms.

Reading: Responding to plot and characters.

Writing: Writing a report.

Vocabulary

installment (in stôl´ mənt) *n.* one part of a payment that has been divided; p. 1019 *The bedroom set was expensive so we paid for it in monthly installments.*

swindle (swin´ dəl) *v.* to cheat someone out of money or property; p. 1021 *At the carnival a vendor swindled me out of twenty dollars, selling me jewels worth only a few cents.*

Tip: Context Clues To identify a word's meaning, look at the other words in the sentence for clues. Example: *I paid for my sister's stereo in six installments; I hope she appreciates how long it took to pay the bill.* The word **installments** refers to paying for something over time instead of in a single payment.

Reading Practice

Make Critical Judgments Sometimes readers judge literature informally by using personal criteria, such as how the story makes them feel. Other times readers use more formal criteria, such as evaluating the use of literary elements, to judge literature. This critical judgment helps readers examine literature and its components more deeply.

Have student groups plan to develop a critical judgment about "The Portrait." Ask students to choose the literary criteria they will use, such as how successfully the elements of character, setting, theme, dialogue, and imagery are developed. Students should assess the work in their groups after they have read it. Invite them to discuss their conclusions with the class.

The Portrait

Tomás Rivera

As soon as the people returned from up north the portrait salesmen began arriving from San Antonio. They would come to rake in. They knew that the workers had money and that was why, as Dad used to say, they would flock in. They carried suitcases packed with samples and always wore white shirts and ties; that way they looked more important and the people believed everything they would tell them and invite them into their homes without giving it much thought. I think that down deep they even longed for their children to one day be like them. In any event, they would arrive and make their way down the dusty streets, going house to house carrying suitcases full of samples.

I remember once I was at the house of one of my father's friends when one of these salesmen arrived. I also remember that that particular one seemed a little frightened and timid. Don Mateo asked him to come in because he wanted to do business.

"Good afternoon, traveler. I would like to tell you about something new that we're offering this year."

"Well, let's see, let's see . . ."

"Well, sir, see, you give us a picture, any picture you may have, and we will not only enlarge it for you but we'll also set it in a wooden frame like this one and we'll shape the image a little, like this—three dimensional, as they say."

"And what for?"

"So that it will look real. That way . . . look, let me show you . . . see? Doesn't he look real, like he's alive?"

"Man, he sure does. Look, vieja.[1] This looks great. Well, you know, we wanted to send some pictures to be enlarged . . . but now, this must cost a lot, right?"

"No, I'll tell you, it costs about the same. Of course, it takes more time."

"Well, tell me, how much?"

"For as little as thirty dollars we'll deliver it to you done with inlays just like this, one this size."

"Boy, that's expensive! Didn't you say it didn't cost a lot more? Do you take **installments**?"

"Well, I'll tell you, we have a new manager and he wants everything

Visual Vocabulary
Inlays are pieces of material such as wood or ivory, set or embedded into the surface of something else to form a design.

---

1. Here, the Spanish word *vieja* (vē ā′ hä′) is used as a term of endearment; literally, it means "old" or "old woman."

Vocabulary

installment (in stôl′ mənt) *n.* one part of a payment that has been divided

 Idiom *What does the phrase "rake in" mean?*

 Respond to Plot and Characters *Why might the salesman feel frightened or timid?*

Teach

Big Idea | 1

The United States and the World **Answer:** *She wants her son back; she wants to bring him back to life.*

Literary Element | 2

Idiom **Answer:** *The idiom means "be patient" or "have faith."*

View the Photograph ★

Photographer, writer, and teacher Robert C. Buitrón (1953–) includes this portrait in his photographs of modern Hispanic American life. **Ask:** Why do you think the man in the portrait would have interested the photographer? *(He has a weathered face that shows his life experiences.)*

---

in cash. It's very fine work. We'll make it look like real. Shaped like that, with inlays . . . take a look. What do you think? Some fine work, wouldn't you say? We can have it all finished for you in a month. You just tell us what color you want the clothes to be and we'll come by with it all finished one day when you least expect, framed and all. Yes, sir, a month at the longest. But like I say, this man, who's the new manager, he wants the full payment in cash. He's very demanding, even with us."

"Yes, but it's much too expensive."

"Well, yes. But the thing is, this is very fine work. You can't say you've ever seen portraits done like this, with wood inlays."

"No, well, that's true. What do you think, vieja?"

"Well, I like it a lot. Why don't we order one? And if it turns out good . . . my Chuy . . . may he rest in peace. It's the only picture we have of him. We took it right before he left for Korea. Poor m'ijo,[2] we never saw him again. See . . . this is his picture. Do you think you can make it like that, make it look like he's alive?"

"Sure, we can. You know, we've done a lot of them in soldier's uniforms and shaped it, like you see in this sample, with inlays. Why, it's more than just a portrait. Sure. You just tell me what size you want and whether you want a round or square frame. What do you say? How should I write it down?"

"What do you say, vieja, should we have it done like this one?"

"Well, I've already told you what I think. I would like to have m'ijo's picture fixed up like that and in color."

"All right, go ahead and write it down. But you take good care of that picture for us because it's the only one we have of our son grown up. He was going to send us one all dressed up in uniform with the American and Mexican flags crossed over his head, but he no sooner got

---

2. In Spanish, *m'ijo* (mē' hō) is the colloquial form of *mi hijo*, meaning "my son."

The United States and the World *What does "vieja" really want more than the portrait?*

Adolfo, Zapote de Peraita, Guanajuato, Mexico, from the series *Family and Photography, A Portrait of a Family in Two Cultures*, 1979. Robert C. Buitrón. Silver gelatin print, 20 x 16 in. Collection of the artist.

---

there when a letter arrived telling us that he was lost in action. So you take good care of it."

"Don't you worry. We're responsible people. And we understand the sacrifices that you people make. Don't worry. And you just wait and see, when we bring it, you'll see how pretty it's gonna look. What do you say, should we make the uniform navy blue?"

"But he's not wearing a uniform in that picture."

"No, but that's just a matter of fixing it up with some wood fiber overlays. Look at these. This one, he didn't have a uniform on but we put one on him. So what do you say? Should we make it navy blue?"

Idiom *What does "you just wait and see" mean here?*

Reading Practice

Idioms Display these sentences that contain idioms from the story:

Don Mateo wanted to find the so and so who had cheated him.

He continued, "Well, you see, the man came by the market one day."

"There's the portrait of Chuy. Like they say, one and the same."

Have students identify the idiom in each sentence and explain its meaning. *("the so and so": a person who has acted badly in some way; "you see": this is what I mean or let me explain; "Like they say": People generally make this comment; "one and the same": we are so similar we appear to be the same person.* To help students understand the role of idioms in literature, **ask:** Idioms help create what type of tone in a written work? *(a more informal tone)* How do idioms contribute to characterization? *(Idioms make a character's speech sound more realistic. Idioms may place a character in a particular place or time.)*

"All right."

"Don't you worry about the picture."

And that was how they spent the entire day, going house to house, street by street, their suitcases stuffed with pictures. As it turned out, a whole lot of people had ordered enlargements of that kind.

"They should be delivering those portraits soon, don't you think?"

"I think so, it's delicate work and takes more time. That's some fine work those people do. Did you see how real those pictures looked?"

"Yeah, sure. They do some fine work. You can't deny that. But it's already been over a month since they passed by here."

"Yes, but from here they went on through all the towns picking up pictures . . . all the way to San Antonio for sure. So it'll probably take a little longer."

"That's true, that's true."

And two more weeks had passed by the time they made the discovery. Some very heavy rains had come and some children, who were playing in one of the tunnels leading to the dump, found a sack full of pictures, all worm-eaten and soaking wet. The only reason that they could tell that these were pictures was because there were a lot of them and most of them the same size and with faces that could just barely be made out. Everybody caught on right away. Don Mateo was so angry that he took off to San Antonio to find the so and so who had **swindled** them.

"Well, you know, I stayed at Esteban's house. And every day I went with him to the market to sell produce. I helped him with everything. I had faith that I would run into that son of a gun some day soon. Then, after

I'd been there for a few days, I started going out to the different barrios[3] and I found out a lot that way. It wasn't so much the money that upset me. It was my poor vieja, crying and all because we'd lost the only picture we had of Chuy. We found it in the sack with all the other pictures but it was already ruined, you know."

"I see, but tell me, how did you find him?"

"Well, you see, to make a long story short, he came by the stand at the market one day. He stood right in front of us and bought some vegetables. It was like he was trying to remember who I was. Of course, I recognized him right off. Because when you're angry enough, you don't forget a face. I just grabbed him right then and there. Poor guy couldn't even talk. He was all scared. And I told him that I wanted that portrait of my son and that I wanted it three dimensional and that he'd best get it for me or I'd let him have it. And I went with him to where he lived. And I put him to work right then and there. The poor guy didn't know where to begin. He had to do it all from memory."

"And how did he do it?"

"I don't know. I suppose if you're scared enough, you're capable of doing anything. Three days later he brought me the portrait all finished, just like you see it there on that table by the Virgin. Now tell me, how do you like the way my boy looks?"

"Well, to be honest, I don't remember too well how Chuy looked. But he was beginning to look more and more like you, isn't that so?"

"Yes, I would say so. That's what everybody tells me now. That Chuy's a chip off the old block and that he was already looking like me. There's the portrait. Like they say, one and the same."

---

3. *Barrios* (bär' ē ōs) are neighborhoods.

Idiom *What does Don Mateo mean when he says "to make a long story short"?*

Respond to Plot and Characters *How likely is it that the salesman will be able to create a realistic portrait of Don Mateo's son?*

Respond to Plot and Characters *How much time has passed since the salesman visited Don Mateo?*

Vocabulary

swindle (swin´ dəl) *v.* to cheat someone out of money or property

Teach

Reading Strategy | **3**

Respond to Plot and Characters **Answer:** *More than a month has passed.*

Ask: What might you infer from the question? *(The pictures are overdue; something may be wrong.)*

Literary Element | **4**

Idiom **Answer:** *It means "to skip to the important part of the story."*

Reading Strategy | **5**

Respond to Plot and Characters **Answer:** *It is unlikely that the salesman can remember Chuy's features distinctly enough to portray him accurately. He probably just tried to imagine what Don Mateo would have looked like when he was younger.*

(APPROACHING) Have students choose the sentence that provides a clue about how the salesman recreated Chuy's appearance.

English Learners

DIFFERENTIATED INSTRUCTION

SMALL GROUP **Advanced** English learners may benefit from working in small groups to prepare for participation in a class discussion. Ask students to summarize the story orally to their group and to articulate at least one observation about the characters, setting, and plot. These informal oral exchanges will provide practice for discussing the story with the whole class. Invite students to write down their ideas so they can share them later in the large group discussion.

Approaching Level

DIFFERENTIATED INSTRUCTION

Emerging Less proficient readers may miss the story's humor. Have students listen to a recording, or invite a volunteer to read the story aloud while others read along silently. Have students identify words and sentences written in a humorous way.

Assess

1. (a) To have a portrait made from it (b) It may be a way to keep their son's memory alive.

2. (a) They are discarded and ruined. (b) He is furious; the salesman treated him, his wife, their memory of their son, and the photograph disrespectfully.

3. (a) He forces the salesman to create a portrait of his son. (b) The salesman may be frightened of assault or legal action; he may feel remorse for cheating.

4. (a) Proud and triumphant (b) He is naive and does not realize the portrait is of him.

5. (a) Their sincerity and innocence (b) It shows the characters' need to hold onto their dignity and their families.

6. (a) He recounts an incident from his childhood. He shows sympathy and respect for the characters. (b) He is an effective storyteller; as a child he is a silent observer who notices important details.

7. Don Mateo and his wife suffered the loss of their son in the Korean War. They are also victims.

8. Students might mention scams that involve the elderly or other vulnerable populations.

Progress Check

Can students analyze an idiom?

If No → See Unit 6 Teaching Resources Book, p. 205.

After You Read

Respond and Think Critically

Respond and Interpret

1. (a) What do Don Mateo and "vieja" finally decide to do with the photograph of their son? (b) What deeper meaning might this offer have for them?

2. (a) What happens to the photographs the salesman collects? (b) How would you explain Don Mateo's strong feelings and his decisive action?

3. (a) What happens when Don Mateo finds the salesman? (b) Why do you think the salesman follows Don Mateo's orders?

Analyze and Evaluate

4. (a) How does Don Mateo feel about what he finally receives from the salesman? (b) What does this reaction tell you about Don Mateo?

5. (a) What does the dialogue reveal about Don Mateo and "vieja"? (b) How effective is the dialogue in conveying the message of this story?

6. (a) How would you describe the role and perspective of the narrator throughout this story? (b) In your opinion, how effective is this kind of narrator in telling the story?

Connect

7. **Big Idea** **The United States and the World** Is Don Mateo a casualty of the Korean War even though he never fought on the battlefield? Support your answer.

8. **Connect to Today** Do you know any situations in which vulnerable people are taken advantage of today? Explain.

Literary Element Idiom

Idioms add realism to dialogue and enhance characterization. Idioms may be difficult for non-native speakers to understand because their meanings differ from the meanings of the individual words that constitute them. Examining the context may provide clues to the meaning.

1. Don Mateo tells the salesman that he will "let him have it" if he doesn't get the portrait. What does this saying mean? Why might Don Mateo say it that way?

2. At the end of the story, Don Mateo describes Chuy as "a chip off the old block." What does that mean? What does it suggest about the portrait?

Review: Plot

Plot is the sequence of events in a drama or a narrative work of fiction. The plot begins with **exposition,** which introduces the story's characters, setting, and situation. The **rising action** adds complications to the conflicts, or problems, leading to the **climax,** or point of highest emotional pitch.

The **falling action** is the logical result of the climax, and the **resolution,** or d'enouement (dā' noō män'), presents the final outcome.

Partner Activity Meet with another classmate to discuss the plot of "The Portrait." Then create a diagram like the one below and list the events that make up the stages of the plot.

Literary Element

1. It means "to attack someone verbally or physically." He wants to threaten the salesman without saying specifically what he will do to him.

2. It refers to the likeness of a child to a parent, usually of a son to his father. Chuy's portrait actually looks like Don Mateo.

Review: Plot

Exposition: The narrator gives background about the characters.

Rising Action: He buys the portrait.

Climax: The photographs are found.

Falling Action: He forces the salesman to create a portrait of Chuy.

Resolution: He loves the portrait; he does not know it is of him, not Chuy.

Reading Strategy · Respond to Plot and Characters

A writer can make direct statements about a character, or reveal the person's character indirectly through words and actions and through what other characters think and say about that person. Review your response chart and answer the following.

1. What steps did Don Mateo take to obtain the portrait he had ordered?

2. What character traits did Don Mateo reveal as he searched for the man who had cheated him?

3. Do you think that Don Mateo goes through a significant change because of the events in this story? Why or why not?

Vocabulary Practice

Practice with Context Clues Identify the context clues in the following sentences that help you determine the meaning of each bold-faced vocabulary word.

1. He bought the car on an **installment** plan and will pay three hundred dollars a month for a year.

2. I felt **swindled** once I realized that the necklace was worth far less than what I paid for it.

Academic Vocabulary

*The salesman did not trust that Don Mateo and "vieja" would pay their **fee** in installments.*

Fee is an academic word. In a more casual conversation, the word often carries a negative connotation. Someone might say that he was charged an extra **fee** for not paying his bill on time.

To further explore the meaning of this word, complete this sentence: In order to allow _____ to attend the school carnival, the school board established a low fee for the event.

For more on academic vocabulary, see pages 53–54.

Connect to *Art*

 Write a Report

Assignment The portraits created during a specific historical period reveal a great deal about the artistic and social values of that time. Write a short report on the style and purpose of portraits in a particular period. Include visual examples.

Investigate Choose a manageable time span. For example, research portraits from the Civil War era, rather than the entire nineteenth century. Use a chart like the one below to organize your research. Identify the typical medium of the portraits (such as oil painting or photograph). Identify typical subjects (such as family groups). Identify characteristics of the style. Finally, indicate the purpose of the portraits. Were they intended to display the subject's wealth? Were they keepsakes?

Create Find images on the Internet or in books or magazines. Use word-processing software to create an interesting layout.

Time Period	Civil War, 1861–1865
Typical medium	black-and-white photos
Characteristics of subjects	• soldiers • often very young
Characteristics of style	• formal, sometimes in staged situations • dressed in uniforms • often posed with weapons
Purpose	mementos for loved ones

Report Your report should focus on a main idea, provide supporting details, and include a variety of sources and quotations with proper citations. Be sure to include necessary historical and cultural background information and to incorporate enough examples to document your thesis adequately.

After You Read

Assess

Reading Strategy

1. He traveled to San Antonio, found the salesman, and forced him to make the portrait.

2. Patience, persistence, love for his son, sympathy for his wife, and a sense of fair play

3. Most may say he changes when he finds and threatens the salesman, whom he had treated with deference. He takes strong action to get the portrait.

Vocabulary

1. The month-to-month payment outlined in the sentence explains that *installment* is a payment that has been divided.

2. Because the speaker paid much more for the necklace than it was worth, it can be inferred that *swindled* means being cheated out of money or property.

Academic Vocabulary

Possible answer: In order to allow all students to attend the school carnival, the school board established a low fee for the event.

 Connect to *Art*

Use these criteria when evaluating students' reports:

- Did the student use effective research strategies and cite sources correctly?
- Did the student use available technologies to improve research and delivery?
- Did the student use effective and interesting language as well as clear organizational structure?

 For additional assessment, see Assessment Resources, pp. 263–264.

For grammar practice, see Unit 6 Teaching Resources Book, p. 208.

Focus

Bellringer Options

Daily Language Practice Transparency 93

Or show students images of life in the United States during the 1950s. **Ask:** Why might young people in the 1950s have felt rebellious? *(They wanted to be different from their parents, who were part of World War II and a post-war society that valued conforming.)* As they read, ask students to consider why the Beats were cultural rebels.

Teach

Literary Element   1

Poetry Poetry has often been favored by young rebels. **Ask:** Why is poetry an ideal form for expressing new ideas and personal views of the world? *(Poetry's imagery and deep feeling allow people to express ideas and views that are personal, untraditional, or complex.)*

 For activities related to this selection, see Unit 6 Teaching Resources Book, pp. 211–212.

Learning Objectives

For pages 1024–1025

In studying this text, you will focus on the following objectives:

Reading:
Analyzing cultural context.
Analyzing literary periods.
Evaluating historical influences.

Cultural Rebels: Writers of the Beat Generation

IN THE LATE 1940s, writers Jack Kerouac and John Clellon Holmes were searching for a way to capture the essence of their generation. They saw a nation slowly emerging from years of war and economic depression, years during which it seemed that most people held similar opinions and led predictable, responsible lives. For Kerouac and Holmes, postwar society was epitomized by anonymous dress, as in the uniform suits of office workers, and by conventional taste. But they saw young people rejecting conformity and turning to creativity. In pursuit of unique identities, the young looked for more artistic and less money-driven lives. Kerouac and Holmes decided that this trend was encapsulated by one word: *Beat.*

> "How to even begin to get it all down and without modified restraints and all hung-up on like literary inhibitions and grammatical fears . . ."
>
> —Jack Kerouac, from *On the Road*

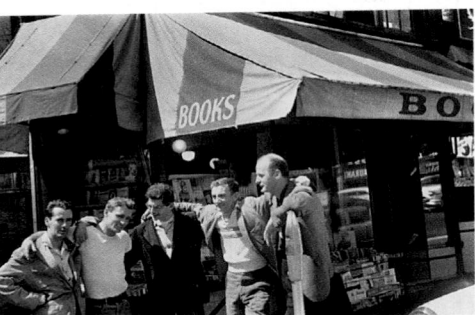

Legendary Beat writers stand outside Lawrence Ferlinghetti's City Lights bookstore in San Francisco in 1956. Pictured left to right: Bob Donlin, Neal Cassady, Allen Ginsberg, Robert LaVinge, Lawrence Ferlinghetti. Photograph by Allen Ginsberg.

Beat had many connotations, ranging from the sordid to the sublime. Kerouac first heard the term from the street hustler Herbert Huncke, who used it as slang for "tired and beaten down." Kerouac saw in *Beat* a suggestion of *beatitude*, saintly or otherworldly beauty and happiness. Poet Allen Ginsberg said, "The point of Beat is that you get beat down to a certain nakedness where you actually are able to see the world in a visionary way."

The core group of Beat Generation writers—Kerouac, Ginsberg, and William S. Burroughs—met in New York City in the areas around Columbia University and in Greenwich Village. The movement soon attracted attention throughout the country, establishing hubs in both New York City and San Francisco. Other leading writers of the new

movement were Gary Snyder, Gregory Corso, Lawrence Ferlinghetti (founder of the innovative City Lights Press and bookstore in San Francisco), Diane Di Prima, and Anne Waldman. Rejecting the prevailing dictates of style and topic, these writers were unabashed experimenters who addressed issues previously considered taboo. Their fearlessness appealed to a newly arising community of bohemians, people who pursued artistic or literary interests and lived nonconformist lives.

1024 UNIT 6   FROM DEPRESSION TO COLD WAR

Research Practice

Focus on a Question Point out Jack Kerouac's quotation on page 1024. Ask students how the Beats expressed themselves without conforming to literary conventions. Have students select a Beat artist and research his or her life and writing style. **Ask:** Did this artist write novels, poems, or short stories? What kind of language did this writer use? Have students write a descriptive report to share

with the class. Challenge the class to use the information in the reports to make a generalization about the Beat Generation.

Howl

1 A central work in the Beat Movement is Allen Ginsberg's book-length poem *Howl* (1956), which created a stir with critics, the public, and even law enforcement. (For selling the book, Lawrence Ferlinghetti was briefly held under arrest.) In a free verse style strongly influenced by Walt Whitman, *Howl* catalogs the wonders and horrors of U.S. society in dizzying abundance:

"I saw the best minds of my generation destroyed by
    madness, starving hysterical naked, . . .
angelheaded hipsters burning for the ancient heavenly
    connection to the starry dynamo in the machinery
    of night . . ."

Wild Form

For many, the word *Beat* is synonymous with Jack Kerouac's novel *On the Road*. Kerouac published his novel in 1957, after years of rejections from publishers. While traveling and living in a variety of places, Kerouac wrote multiple drafts. He revised his drafts into their final form in one three-week sprint, during which he typed nearly nonstop on a continuous, 120-foot-long scroll of paper he fed through his typewriter.

The long, rhythmic, bebop-jazz inflected sentences of *On the Road* capture a series of road trips Kerouac took with his friend and Beat Generation icon Neal Cassady (called Dean Moriarty in the novel). *On the Road* expresses Kerouac's openness to the nation's desolate places as well as its exciting cities and to its humble people as well as its mighty. For readers who were exhausted by societal complacence and stodginess, Kerouac's adventures were revolutionary.

Like novelist Thomas Wolfe, Kerouac insisted on pushing boundaries. If he wished to write long,

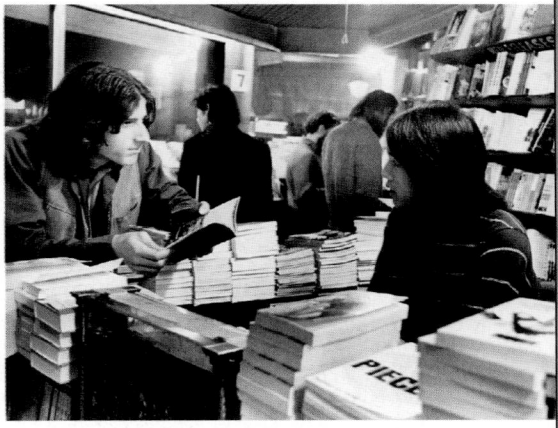

City Lights Bookstore, 1969. Sal Veder. Black and white photograph.

breathless sentences that owed more to vernacular and to the jazz spirit than they did to Establishment polish, he did.

from *On the Road*

"[T]he only people for me are the mad ones, the ones who are mad to live, mad to talk, mad to be saved, desirous of everything at the same time, the ones who never yawn or say a commonplace thing, but burn, burn, burn like fabulous yellow roman candles exploding like spiders across the stars and in the middle you see the blue centerlight pop and everybody goes 'Awww!'"

LOG ON ▶ **Literature** Online

Literature and Reading For more about the Beat Generation, go to glencoe.com and enter QuickPass code GLA9800u6.

Respond and Think Critically

1. Why were the members of the Beat Generation considered cultural rebels?

2. What significance did Allen Ginsberg's poetry have for his early readers?

3. What methods did Jack Kerouac employ in his writing?

Teach

Big Idea

The United States and the World During the 1950s, the United States was involved in a Cold War with the Soviet Union. Many people feared the Soviets would start a nuclear war. **Ask:** Do you think the Cold War had a big effect on the Beats? Explain. *(The Beats were mainly concerned with the creativity of the individual; it is unlikely that their work would have been deeply affected by international relations.)*

Assess

1. They rejected a 1950s culture that valued conformity after World War II; they tried new lifestyles and new forms of artistic expression.

2. It inspired writers, such as Diane di Prima, and expressed frustration with post-war society.

3. He wrote many drafts, in continuous sessions, relying on notes he took during his travels.

Approaching Level

DIFFERENTIATED INSTRUCTION

Emerging Society's tolerance of cultural rebels varies from one generation to another. One of the features of Beat writers that sets them apart from mainstream art is their word choices and juxtapositions of language. Discuss with students why nontraditional language in literature might not be accepted by mainstream society. Have students read the quotations from Kerouac and Ginsberg and identify words and phrases that might set these writers apart from traditional artists of their time.

Before You Read

Focus

Bellringer Options

Literature Launchers:
  Pre-Reading Videos DVD,
  Selection Launcher
Selection Focus
  Transparency 64
Daily Language Practice
  Transparency 94

Or challenge students to create a list of rights and laws for a new society. Ask them to decide which laws and freedoms are most important and explain their choices. Consider whether any rules or rights should be excluded. Suggest they think about rules for bringing accused wrongdoers to justice. Then tell them that the Puritans who are characters in this play faced the same issues.

Before You Read

The Crucible, Act One

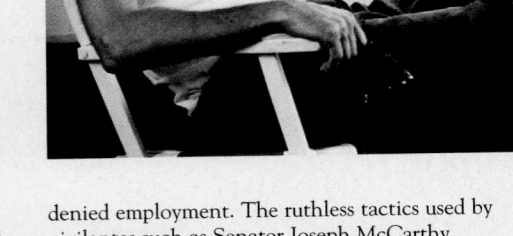

Meet **Arthur Miller**
(1915–2005)

As a young boy, Arthur Miller sat in the Shubert Theater on Lennox Avenue in New York City, completely entranced. Years later, in his autobiography, Miller remarked, "And so I learned that there were two kinds of reality, but that of the stage was far more real."

Fame in a Dark Time Miller began writing plays in college. In 1947, at thirty-two, *All My Sons*, a dramatic work about a manufacturer of defective war supplies, received the New York Drama Critics' Circle Award and was released as a film in 1948. The following year, *Death of a Salesman*, a tragedy about the failure of the American dream, won a Pulitzer Prize and established Miller as one of the greatest playwrights in the United States.

> *"One of the strongest urges in the writer's heart . . . is to reveal what has been hidden and denied."*
>
> —Arthur Miller

By his late thirties, Miller was embroiled in a dark chapter of U.S. history as a result of his fame and outspoken opinions. Fear of Communism—the "Red Scare"—had taken hold of U.S. citizens, and Congress created the House Un-American Activities Committee (HUAC) to investigate an alleged Communist conspiracy. Among the main targets of the investigation were people in the entertainment industry. The HUAC demanded not only that individuals "confess" to earlier involvement in leftist organizations but that they name others who had held similar views. People who refused to cooperate were often blacklisted or denied employment. The ruthless tactics used by vigilantes such as Senator Joseph McCarthy reminded Miller of the witch trials in seventeenth-century colonial America.

McCarthyism and Witch Hunts Oppressed by the disturbing direction in which his country was moving, Miller immersed himself in the study of the Salem witch trials of 1692, which he described as "one of the strangest and most awful chapters in human history." From this research emerged *The Crucible*, which was first staged on Broadway in 1953. Its relevance to the political situation during the McCarthy era was clear, and the phrase "McCarthy witch hunts" became an enduring symbol of the perversion of power in U.S. history. Viewing the playwright as a potentially subversive figure, the U.S. State Department refused to renew Miller's passport. When Miller was called to testify before HUAC, he refused to implicate his friends and colleagues. He was charged with contempt, fined, and sentenced to jail. His sentence, however, was overturned on appeal in 1958, and he never served a jail term.

A tireless writer, Miller saw his last play produced just a year before his death at 89. On almost any given day, it is said, a theater somewhere in the world is producing *The Crucible*.

 Literature Online

Author Search For more about Arthur Miller, go to glencoe.com and enter QuickPass code GLA9800u6.

Selection Skills

Literary Elements
- Dialogue (SE pp. 1027–1050)
- Setting (TE p. 1030)
- Irony (TE pp. 1040, 1043)

Reading Skills
- Draw Conclusions About Characters (SE pp. 1027–1050)
- Recognize Logical Fallacies (TE p. 1032)
- Irony (TE p. 1044)

The Crucible, Act One

Vocabulary Skills
- Word Parts (SE p. 1050)
- Latin Roots (TE p. 1042)

Writing Skills/Grammar
- Write a Dialogue (SE p. 1050)
- Summarize (TE p. 1034)

Listening/Speaking/Viewing Skills
- Viewing Art (SE pp. 1028, 1039, 1046, 1049)
- Relate Art to Text (TE p. 1036)
- Readers' Theater (TE p. 1046)

Literature and Reading Preview

Connect to the Play

How would you react to a rumor that you were behaving improperly? Write a journal entry describing this reaction.

Build Background

The Crucible takes place in 1692 in Salem, a small town in the Massachusetts Bay Colony. Under the rigid authority of Puritan Reverend Samuel Parris, relations among villagers became bitter. In the winter of 1691–1692, several teenage girls began behaving strangely. Many suspected the girls were victims of witchcraft.

Set Purposes for Reading

Big Idea The United States and the World

The "Cold War" caused many U.S. citizens to fear Communist subversion within their country. As you read, ask, What is Miller trying to say about paranoia and suspicion?

Literary Element Dialogue

Dialogue is the conversation between characters in a literary work. In a play—which consists almost entirely of dialogue—the author must develop plot, theme, and characterization by means of direct speech. As you read, ask yourself, How does Miller express his ideas through dialogue?

Reading Strategy Draw Conclusions About Characters

How do you learn what someone is like? In literature, as in life, you observe what that person says and does.

....

Tip: Take Notes Use web diagrams like the one below to record observations and draw conclusions about characters in the play.

ABIGAIL WILLIAMS--ACT ONE

- goes into trance and shouts out names of witches
- tells wild stories about Tituba
- bullies and threatens her friends
- **Conclusion**
- had an affair with John Proctor
- hates Elizabeth Proctor
- pretends to be obedient to her uncle

ARTHUR MILLER **1027**

Learning Objectives

For pages 1026–1050

In studying this text, you will focus on the following objectives:

Literary Study: Analyzing dialogue.

Reading: Drawing conclusions about characters.

Writing: Writing a dialogue.

Vocabulary

compromise (kom´ prə mīz´) *v.* to endanger the reputation or interests of; to expose to suspicion; p. 1031 *Doing business with a known criminal will certainly compromise the company's good name.*

contention (kən ten´ shən) *n.* a verbal argument or struggle; quarreling; p. 1032 *Contention broke out at the meeting over the length of the school day.*

subservient (səb sur´ vē ənt) *adj.* useful in an inferior capacity; submissive; p. 1034 *Jenna resented her subservient role in the family.*

pretense (prē´ tens) *n.* a false show or appearance, especially for the purpose of deceiving; falseness; p. 1037 *Whenever I drop by, he makes a pretense of being hard at work.*

evade (i vād´) *v.* to escape or avoid, as by cleverness; p. 1045 *The fugitive tried to evade capture.*

Before You Read

Focus

Summary, Act One

The Reverend Parris saw girls dancing in the forest at night. Now, two of them have fallen into trances. When questioned, Abigail Williams denies practicing witchcraft, but after talking with the other girls, her story changes. She admits to "conjuring," but blames Tituba, Parris's slave, who in turn accuses others. In reality, Abigail had an affair with John Proctor and wants his wife dead. Two conflicting sides emerge in the community, represented by the Putnams, who hope to prove witchcraft, and by Proctor and Rebecca Nurse, who are skeptical about accusations of witchcraft.

 For summaries in languages other than English, see Unit 6 Teaching Resources Book, pp. 213–218.

Vocabulary

Connotation A word's connotation is its emotional association or overtone. Connotations can be positive or negative. The word *compromise* has a negative connotation when used to refer to the irresponsible act of endangering someone's reputation or safety.

Ask: Which other words on this list have predominantly negative connotations? (*contention, subservient, pretense*)

English Learners

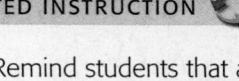

DIFFERENTIATED INSTRUCTION

Beginning Remind students that a dialect is a form of English that is spoken by members of a group or by people from a particular geographical region. Many characters in the play speak in a dialect resembling that used by American colonists. Explain departures from modern usage, including double negatives and lack of subject and verb agreement. Ask students to restate the following passages in standard English.

1. ". . . he cannot discover no medicine for it in his books" (*he cannot discover any medicine for it in his books*)
2. "It were a grand sneeze" (*It was a grand sneeze*)

Tell students to be alert for other such usages in the play.

Teach

Big Idea

The United States and the World Remind students that Miller was motivated to write this play by political activities in the United States. **Say:** As you read, compare the types of evidence used in the Salem witch trials with those used in the hunt for Communists in the 1950s.

(APPROACHING) Ask students to identify examples of statements revealing that people who were accused were often presumed to be guilty without any concrete proof.

View the Photograph ★

Included in the selection are a number of stills from the 1996 movie adaptation of *The Crucible*, directed by Nicholas Hytner. Arthur Miller himself adapted the screenplay from his play. The cast includes Daniel Day-Lewis as John Proctor, Winona Ryder as Abigail, Paul Scofield as Danforth, Joan Allen as Elizabeth Proctor, and Bruce Davison as the Reverend Parris. Miller and Allen received Oscar nominations. The film is rated PG-13; consider previewing it to see if you feel it is appropriate for your students.

Interactive Read and Write

Other options for teaching this selection can be found in

- Interactive Read and Write for EL Students pp. 227–254
- Interactive Read and Write for Approaching-Level Students, pp. 227–254
- Interactive Read and Write for On-Level Students, pp. 227-254

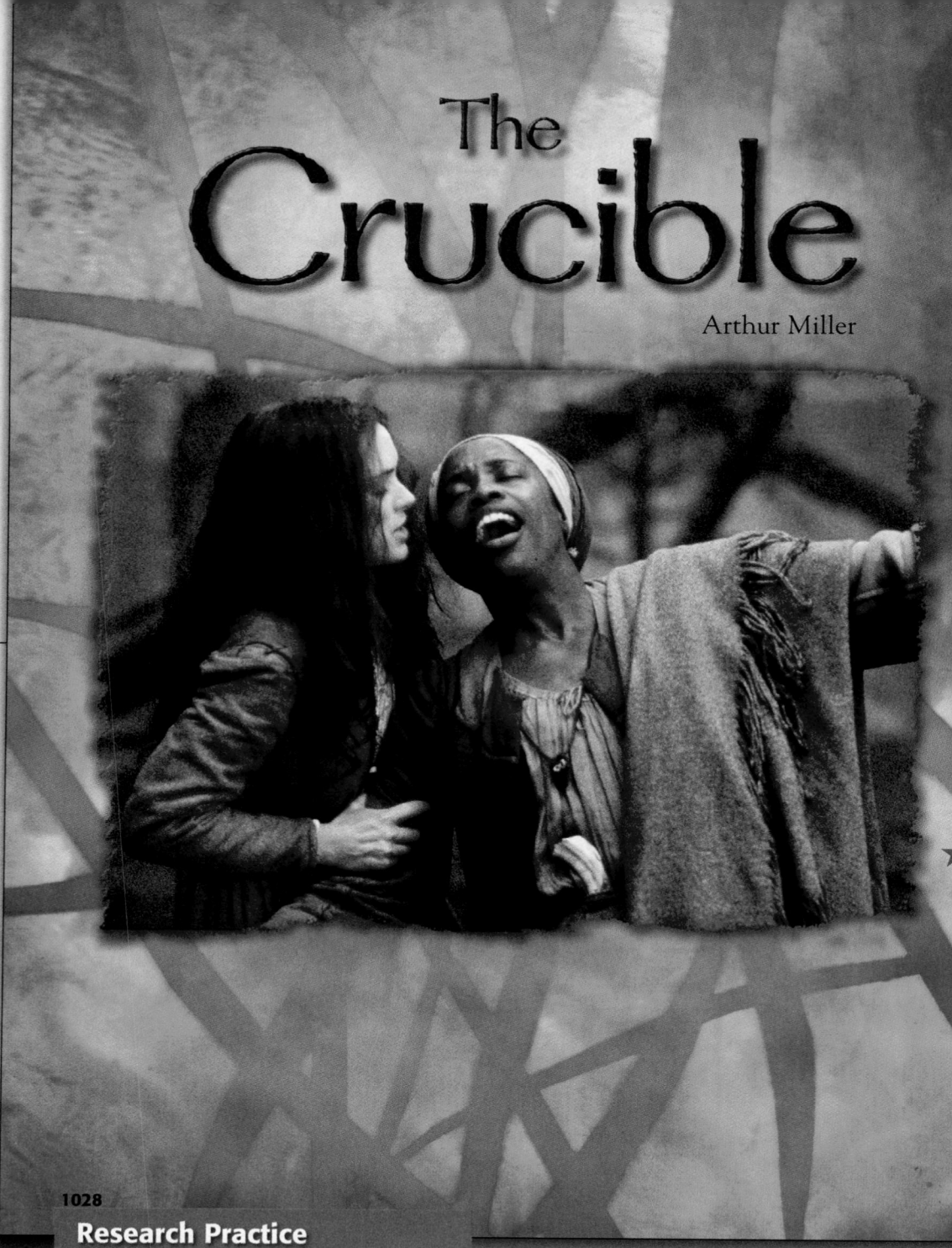

The Crucible

Arthur Miller

1028

Research Practice

Build Background Many students may not be familiar with Senator Joseph McCarthy or the House Un-American Activities Committee. Have students choose from the following research topics: McCarthy's speech in Wheeling, West Virginia, in 1950; the Army McCarthy Hearings of 1954; the Alger Hiss case; and the Hollywood Ten. Have students prepare and deliver a brief presentation of their topics to the class.

CHARACTERS
(in order of appearance)

REVEREND PARRIS	MERCY LEWIS	FRANCIS NURSE
BETTY PARRIS	MARY WARREN	EZEKIEL CHEEVER
TITUBA	JOHN PROCTOR	MARSHAL HERRICK
ABIGAIL WILLIAMS	REBECCA NURSE	JUDGE HATHORNE
SUSANNA WALCOTT	GILES COREY	DEPUTY GOVERNOR DANFORTH
MRS. ANN PUTNAM	REVEREND JOHN HALE	SARAH GOOD
THOMAS PUTNAM	ELIZABETH PROCTOR	HOPKINS

Act One

(An Overture)

[A small upper bedroom in the home of REVEREND SAMUEL PARRIS, Salem, Massachusetts, in the spring of the year 1692.

There is a narrow window at the left. Through its leaded panes the morning sunlight streams. A candle still burns near the bed, which is at the right. A chest, a chair, and a small table are the other furnishings. At the back a door opens on the landing of the stairway to the ground floor. The room gives off an air of clean spareness. The roof rafters are exposed, and the wood colors are raw and unmellowed.

As the curtain rises, REVEREND PARRIS is discovered kneeling beside the bed, evidently in prayer. His daughter, BETTY PARRIS, aged ten, is lying on the bed, inert.

REVEREND PARRIS is praying now, and, though we cannot hear his words, a sense of his confusion hangs about him. He mumbles, then seems about to weep; then he weeps, then prays again; but his daughter does not stir on the bed.

The door opens, and his Negro slave enters. TITUBA[1] is in her forties. PARRIS brought her with him from Barbados,[2] where he spent some years as a merchant before entering the ministry. She enters as one does who can no longer bear to be barred from the sight of her beloved, but she is also very frightened because her slave sense has warned her that, as always, trouble in this house eventually lands on

---

1. *Tituba* (ti tōō′ bə)
2. *Barbados* (bär bā′ dōz) is an island in the Caribbean that was, at the time of the play, an English colony.

her back.]

TITUBA. [*Already taking a step backward.*] My Betty be hearty soon?

PARRIS. Out of here!

TITUBA. [*Backing to the door.*] My Betty not goin' die . . .

PARRIS. [*Scrambling to his feet in a fury.*] Out of my sight! [*She is gone.*] Out of my—[*He is overcome with sobs. He clamps his teeth against them and closes the door and leans against it, exhausted.*] Oh, my God! God help me! [*Quaking with fear, mumbling to himself through his sobs, he goes to the bed and gently takes* BETTY's *hand.*] Betty. Child. Dear child. Will you wake, will you open up your eyes! Betty, little one . . .

[*He is bending to kneel again when his niece,* ABIGAIL WILLIAMS, *seventeen, enters—a strikingly beautiful girl, an orphan, with an endless capacity for dissembling.[3] Now she is all worry and apprehension and propriety.*]

ABIGAIL. Uncle? [*He looks to her.*] Susanna Walcott's here from Doctor Griggs.

PARRIS. Oh? Let her come, let her come.

---

3. *Dissembling* means "concealing one's true motives."

> **Dialogue** *Tituba's way of speaking helps us understand something that Miller has already mentioned about her in the stage directions. What is it?* **2**

> **Draw Conclusions About Characters** *What does this phrase tell us about Abigail?* **3**

ARTHUR MILLER **1029**

Teach

Literary Element 1

Atmosphere Have students describe the atmosphere that is set from the first page of this play. (*Students may say fear, superstition, mystery.*) **Ask:** What can you predict about this play from the atmosphere? (*Students may say it will be dramatic, emotional, or scary.*)

Literary Element 2

Dialogue Answer: *Tituba is a slave from Barbados. She speaks in a Caribbean dialect.*

Reading Strategy 3

Draw Conclusions About Characters Answer: *Abigail deceives others. Readers should question her reliability and search for a hidden motive in her words.*

> 📁 **For additional practice using the reading skill or strategy, see Unit 6 Teaching Resources Book, p. 220.**

Cultural History ☆
Slavery in Massachusetts
Some students may be surprised to learn that there were slaves in colonial Massachusetts. In fact, the first African slaves arrived at Boston in 1638. Distinguished legal historian A. Leon Higginbotham Jr. once observed, "Merchants from Massachusetts, the most vigorous slave traders in the world, made enormous profits from the slave trade."

Approaching Level
DIFFERENTIATED INSTRUCTION

Emerging Point out that stage directions contain important information. Have students read the directions that describe Samuel Parris and Tituba. **Ask:** What do you learn from the stage directions about the internal conflicts of Reverend Parris and Tituba? (*Parris is afraid because he does not understand what is wrong with his daughter. Tituba fears that she will be blamed for the problem.*)

What mood do the stage directions and dialogue create in the opening scene? (*They produce a tense, urgent mood.*)

Teach

The United States and the World
Answer: *A viewer in the 1950s would have understood* witchcraft *and* Communism *to be interchangeable.*

Draw Conclusions About Characters
Answer: *Students may suggest that Parris is defensive, self-absorbed, or paranoid.*
Ask: What do we learn about Parris's motives? *(Students may answer that, although he is worried for Betty, his real concern is for his own position.)*

(**APPROACHING**) Point out Samuel Parris's emphasis on the presence of "factions," or feuding groups, in Salem generally and in his congregation in particular. **Ask:** Why is Parris so worried about these "factions"? *(He thinks they may conspire to oust him from his ministry.)*

ABIGAIL. [*Leaning out the door to call to* SUSANNA, *who is down the hall a few steps.*] Come in, Susanna.

[SUSANNA WALCOTT, *a little younger than ABIGAIL, a nervous, hurried girl, enters.*]

PARRIS. [*Eagerly.*] What does the doctor say, child?

SUSANNA. [*Craning around* PARRIS *to get a look at* BETTY.] He bid me come and tell you, reverend sir, that he cannot discover no medicine for it in his books.

PARRIS. Then he must search on.

SUSANNA. Aye, sir, he have been searchin' his books since he left you, sir. But he bid me tell you, that you might look to unnatural things for the cause of it.

PARRIS. [*His eyes going wide.*] No—no. There be no unnatural cause here. Tell him I have sent for Reverend Hale of Beverly, and Mr. Hale will surely confirm that. Let him look to medicine and put out all thought of unnatural causes here. There be none.

SUSANNA. Aye, sir. He bid me tell you. [*She turns to go.*]

ABIGAIL. Speak nothin' of it in the village, Susanna.

PARRIS. Go directly home and speak nothing of unnatural causes.

SUSANNA. Aye, sir. I pray for her. [*She goes out.*]

ABIGAIL. Uncle, the rumor of witchcraft is all about; I think you'd best go down and deny it yourself. The parlor's packed with people, sir. I'll sit with her.

PARRIS. [*Pressed, turns on her.*] And what shall I say to them? That my daughter and my niece I discovered dancing like heathen in the forest?

ABIGAIL. Uncle, we did dance; let you tell them I confessed it—and I'll be whipped if I must be. But they're speakin' of witchcraft. Betty's not witched.

PARRIS. Abigail, I cannot go before the congregation when I know you have not opened[4] with me. What did you do with her in the forest?

ABIGAIL. We did dance, uncle, and when you leaped out of the bush so suddenly, Betty was frightened and then she fainted. And there's the whole of it.

PARRIS. Child. Sit you down.

ABIGAIL. [*Quavering, as she sits.*] I would never hurt Betty. I love her dearly.

PARRIS. Now look you, child, your punishment will come in its time. But if you trafficked[5] with spirits in the forest I must know it now, for surely my enemies will, and they will ruin me with it.

ABIGAIL. But we never conjured[6] spirits.

PARRIS. Then why can she not move herself since midnight? This child is desperate! [ABIGAIL *lowers her eyes.*] It must come out—my enemies will bring it out. Let me know what you done there. Abigail, do you understand that I have many enemies?

ABIGAIL. I have heard of it, uncle.

PARRIS. There is a faction[7] that is sworn to drive me from my pulpit. Do you understand that?

ABIGAIL. I think so, sir.

PARRIS. Now then, in the midst of such disruption, my own household is discovered to be the very center of some obscene practice. Abominations[8] are done in the forest—

ABIGAIL. It were sport,[9] uncle!

PARRIS. [*Pointing at* BETTY.] You call this sport? [*She lowers her eyes. He pleads.*] Abigail, if you

---

4. Here, *have not opened* means "have not been completely honest."
5. *Trafficked* means "dealt or did business."
6. Here, *conjured* means "summoned by using magic words or spells."
7. A *faction* is a small segment of people who disagree with the larger group on an issue or set of issues.
8. *Abominations* are vile or shameful acts.
9. Here, *sport* means "innocent recreation."

---

1 | **The United States and the World** *What word might a U.S. citizen, watching this play in the 1950s, have substituted for "witchcraft?"*

Draw Conclusions About Characters *What can we learn about Reverend Parris from this remark?* | **2**

Reading Practice

Setting Remind students that setting can serve multiple functions. **Ask:** What functions does the forest setting serve? *(It is a logical plot device; these girls would sneak out at night to the forest. The wild, dark forest, considered the heathen abode of evil spirits, creates a perfect atmosphere for the beginning of the trouble. The forest represents all that makes this community vulnerable to physical and spiritual attack.)*

know something that may help the doctor, for God's sake tell it to me. [*She is silent.*] I saw Tituba waving her arms over the fire when I came on you. Why was she doing that? And I heard a screeching and gibberish coming from her mouth. She were swaying like a dumb beast over that fire!

ABIGAIL.   She always sings her Barbados songs, and we dance.

PARRIS.   I cannot blink[10] what I saw, Abigail, for my enemies will not blink it. I saw a dress lying on the grass.

ABIGAIL.   [*Innocently.*] A dress?

PARRIS.   [*It is very hard to say.*] Aye, a dress. And I thought I saw—someone naked running through the trees!

ABIGAIL.   [*In terror.*] No one was naked! You mistake yourself, uncle!

PARRIS.   [*With anger.*] I saw it! [*He moves from her. Then, resolved.*] Now tell me true, Abigail. And I pray you feel the weight of truth upon you, for now my ministry's at stake, my ministry and perhaps your cousin's life. Whatever abomination you have done, give me all of it now, for I dare not be taken unaware when I go before them down there.

ABIGAIL.   There is nothin' more. I swear it, uncle.

PARRIS.   [*Studies her, then nods, half convinced.*] Abigail, I have fought here three long years to bend these stiff-necked people to me, and now, just now when some good respect is rising for me in the parish, you **compromise** my very character. I have given you a home, child, I have put clothes upon your back—now give me upright answer. Your name in the town—it is entirely white, is it not?

---

10. Here, *blink* means "to deliberately overlook or ignore."

3 Dialogue *Why might Miller have inserted a dash between "saw" and "someone naked?"*

Vocabulary

compromise (kom′ prə mīz′) *v.* to endanger the reputation or interests of; to expose to suspicion

---

ABIGAIL.   [*With an edge of resentment.*] Why, I am sure it is, sir. There be no blush about my name.

PARRIS.   [*To the point.*] Abigail, is there any other cause than you have told me, for your being discharged from Goody[11] Proctor's service? I have heard it said, and I tell you as I heard it, that she comes so rarely to the church this year for she will not sit so close to something soiled. What signified that remark?

ABIGAIL.   She hates me, uncle, she must, for I would not be her slave. It's a bitter woman, a lying, cold, sniveling woman, and I will not work for such a woman!

PARRIS.   She may be. And yet it has troubled me that you are now seven month out of their house, and in all this time no other family has ever called for your service.

ABIGAIL.   They want slaves, not such as I. Let them send to Barbados for that. I will not black my face for any of them! [*With ill-concealed resentment at him.*] Do you begrudge my bed, uncle?

PARRIS.   No—no.

ABIGAIL.   [*In a temper.*] My name is good in the village! I will not have it said my name is soiled! Goody Proctor is a gossiping liar!

[*Enter MRS. ANN PUTNAM. She is a twisted soul of forty-five, a death-ridden woman, haunted by dreams.*]

PARRIS.   [*As soon as the door begins to open.*] No—no, I cannot have anyone. [*He sees her, and a certain deference[12] springs into him, although his worry remains.*] Why, Goody Putnam, come in.

MRS. PUTNAM.   [*Full of breath, shiny-eyed.*] It is a marvel. It is surely a stroke of hell upon you.

PARRIS.   No, Goody Putnam, it is—

MRS. PUTNAM.   [*Glancing at BETTY.*] How high did she fly, how high?

PARRIS.   No, no, she never flew—

---

11. *Goody* is short for *Goodwife,* a term of polite address for a married woman.
12. *Deference* is courteous respect or regard.

The United States and the World *Why do you think that Abigail is so concerned about her good name?* **4**

Teach

Literary Element | 3

Dialogue Answer: *Students should understand that the dash represents hesitation. Parris is possibly embarrassed to be revealing what he saw.*

Big Idea | 4

The United States and the World Answer: *Students may say that Abigail is afraid of being accused of witchcraft, which is a pervasive motif in the play.*

Cultural History ☆

The Clergy Samuel Parris's references to his ministry and his relationships with his "stiff-necked" parishioners reflect the fact that Puritan clergymen in colonial Massachusetts were chosen by their congregations, who set the clergymen's salaries and specified other privileges and allowances. Have students look for other references to the ways in which clergy could be pressured by their parishioners.

English Learners

DIFFERENTIATED INSTRUCTION

Advanced Remind students that plays are meant to be seen and heard. Ask groups of two or three students to read passages from the play aloud. Have students note how their comprehension improves as they read aloud and hear the dialogue.

Advanced Learners

DIFFERENTIATED INSTRUCTION

Analysis Have students analyze ways in which Miller steadily builds momentum and suspense in Act One. For example, the conflict between Samuel Parris and Abigail is interrupted by the entrance of Ann Putnam, whose words intensify the mood.

Teach

Make Inferences *Provi-dence* is defined as "a blessing." **Ask:** Why would Putnam and Parris consider it providence to find witchcraft in their village? *(Students may say that now Parris and the Putnams have something to blame for their misfortunes.)*

ENGLISH LEARNERS Be sure students understand that "out" here means "out in the open" or "no longer hidden or secret."

Draw Conclusions About Characters Answer: *Some students may suggest that* hard-handed *is meant literally, referring to honest manual labor. Others will understand that the phrase describes Putnam's famil-iarity with wielding power and having his way.*

Literary History ☆

Thomas Putnam Miller wrote a commentary on this play, in which he describes Putnam as a vindic-tive man who played a critical role in accusing witches. Some histori-ans have concluded that the real Thomas Putnam used accusations of witchcraft as a way to gain land from people who were executed.

MRS. PUTNAM. [*Very pleased with it.*] Why, it's sure she did. Mr. Collins saw her goin' over Ingersoll's barn, and come down light as bird, he says!

PARRIS. Now, look you, Goody Putnam, she never—[*Enter* THOMAS PUTNAM, *a well-to-do, hard-handed landowner, near fifty.*] Oh, good morning, Mr. Putnam.

1 PUTNAM. It is a providence[13] the thing is out now! It is a providence. [*He goes directly to the bed.*]

PARRIS. What's out, sir, what's—?

[MRS. PUTNAM *goes to the bed.*]

PUTNAM. [*Looking down at* BETTY.] Why, her eyes is closed! Look you, Ann.

MRS. PUTNAM. Why, that's strange. [*To* PARRIS.] Ours is open.

PARRIS. [*Shocked.*] Your Ruth is sick?

MRS. PUTNAM. [*With vicious certainty.*] I'd not call it sick; the Devil's touch is heavier than sick. It's death, y'know, it's death drivin' into them, forked and hoofed.

PARRIS. Oh, pray not! Why, how does Ruth ail?

MRS. PUTNAM. She ails as she must—she never waked this morning, but her eyes open and she walks, and hears naught,[14] sees naught, and can-not eat. Her soul is taken, surely.

[PARRIS *is struck.*]

PUTNAM. [*As though for further details.*] They say you've sent for Reverend Hale of Beverly?

PARRIS. [*With dwindling conviction*[15] *now.*] A pre-caution only. He has much experience in all demonic arts, and I—

MRS. PUTNAM. He has indeed; and found a witch in Beverly last year, and let you remember that.

---

13. Here, *providence* means "a blessing" or "an act of divine care."
14. *Naught* means "nothing."
15. Here, *conviction* means "certainty."

2 Draw Conclusions About Characters *Do you think that "hard-handed" is meant as a compliment? Explain your answer.*

PARRIS. Now, Goody Ann, they only thought that were a witch, and I am certain there be no element of witchcraft here.

PUTNAM. No witchcraft! Now look you, Mr. Parris—

PARRIS. Thomas, Thomas, I pray you, leap not to witchcraft. I know that you—you least of all, Thomas, would ever wish so disastrous a charge laid upon me. We cannot leap to witchcraft. They will howl me out of Salem for such corrup-tion in my house.

PUTNAM. [*At the moment, he is intent upon getting* PARRIS, *for whom he has only contempt, to move toward the abyss.*] Mr. Parris, I have taken your part in all **contention** here, and I would continue; but I cannot if you hold back in this. There are hurtful, vengeful spirits layin' hands on these children. ☆

PARRIS. But, Thomas, you cannot—

PUTNAM. Ann! Tell Mr. Parris what you have done.

MRS. PUTNAM. Reverend Parris, I have laid seven babies unbaptized in the earth. Believe me, sir, you never saw more hearty babies born. And yet, each would wither in my arms the very night of their birth. I have spoke nothin', but my heart has clamored intimations.[16] And now, this year, my Ruth, my only—I see her turning strange. A secret child she has become this year, and shrivels like a sucking mouth were pullin' on her life too. And so I thought to send her to your Tituba—

PARRIS. To Tituba! What may Tituba—?

MRS. PUTNAM. Tituba knows how to speak to the dead, Mr. Parris.

PARRIS. Goody Ann, it is a formidable sin to conjure up the dead!

MRS. PUTNAM. I take it on my soul, but who else may surely tell us what person murdered my babies?

---

16. A heart that has *clamored intimations* has nagged its owner with suggestions (of possible witchcraft).

Vocabulary

contention (kən ten´ shən) *n.* verbal argument or struggle; quarreling

---

Reading Practice

Recognize Logical Fallacies Point out Mrs. Putnam's reasoning: Ruth cannot speak because she was close to the spir-its; Ruth had to be close to the spirits or she could speak. This is sometimes called *circular reasoning.* As they read, encour-age students to look for other examples of fallacies. Suggest that they look for the fol-lowing types: confusing fact and opinion, faulty assumptions, bias, mistaking cause and effect, and guilt by association.

PARRIS. [*Horrified.*] Woman!

MRS. PUTNAM. They were murdered, Mr. Parris! And mark this proof! Mark it! Last night my Ruth were ever so close to their little spirits; I know it, sir. For how else is she struck dumb now except some power of darkness would stop her mouth? It is a marvelous sign, Mr. Parris!

PUTNAM. Don't you understand it, sir? There is a murdering witch among us, bound to keep herself in the dark. [*PARRIS turns to BETTY, a frantic terror rising in him.*] Let your enemies make of it what they will, you cannot blink it more.

PARRIS. [*To ABIGAIL.*] Then you were conjuring spirits last night.

ABIGAIL. [*Whispering.*] Not I, sir—Tituba and Ruth.

PARRIS. [*Turns now, with new fear, and goes to BETTY, looks down at her, and then, gazing off.*] Oh, Abigail, what proper payment for my charity! Now I am undone.

PUTNAM. You are not undone! Let you take hold here. Wait for no one to charge you—declare it yourself. You have discovered witchcraft—

PARRIS. In my house? In my house, Thomas? They will topple me with this! They will make of it a—

[*Enter MERCY LEWIS, the PUTNAMS' servant, a fat, sly, merciless girl of eighteen.*]

MERCY. Your pardons. I only thought to see how Betty is.

PUTNAM. Why aren't you home? Who's with Ruth?

MERCY. Her grandma come. She's improved a little, I think—she give a powerful sneeze before.

MRS. PUTNAM. Ah, there's a sign of life!

---

3 The United States and the World *In making this statement, what chain of events is Mr. Putnam initiating?*

4 Draw Conclusions About Characters *What sort of a friend do you think Abigail would make? Explain.*

MERCY. I'd fear no more, Goody Putnam. It were a grand sneeze; another like it will shake her wits together, I'm sure. [*She goes to the bed to look.*]

PARRIS. Will you leave me now, Thomas? I would pray a while alone.

ABIGAIL. Uncle, you've prayed since midnight. Why do you not go down and—

PARRIS. No—no. [*To PUTNAM.*] I have no answer for that crowd. I'll wait till Mr. Hale arrives. [*To get MRS. PUTNAM to leave.*] If you will, Goody Ann . . .

PUTNAM. Now look you, sir. Let you strike out against the Devil, and the village will bless you for it! Come down, speak to them—pray with them. They're thirsting for your word, Mister! Surely you'll pray with them.

PARRIS. [*Swayed.*] I'll lead them in a psalm, but let you say nothing of witchcraft yet. I will not discuss it. The cause is yet unknown. I have had enough contention since I came; I want no more.

MRS. PUTNAM. Mercy, you go home to Ruth, d'y'hear?

MERCY. Aye, mum.

[*MRS. PUTNAM goes out.*]

PARRIS. [*To ABIGAIL.*] If she starts for the window, cry for me at once.

ABIGAIL. I will, uncle.

PARRIS. [*To PUTNAM.*] There is a terrible power in her arms today. [*He goes out with PUTNAM.*]

ABIGAIL. [*With hushed trepidation.*][17] How is Ruth sick?

MERCY. It's weirdish, I know not—she seems to walk like a dead one since last night.

ABIGAIL. [*Turns at once and goes to BETTY, and now, with fear in her voice.*] Betty? [*BETTY doesn't move. She shakes her.*] Now stop this! Betty! Sit up now!

[*BETTY doesn't stir. MERCY comes over.*]

---

17. *Trepidation* means "fear" or "anxiety."

ARTHUR MILLER **1033**

1033

Approaching Level

DIFFERENTIATED INSTRUCTION

Emerging Point out to students that dialogue has many purposes in drama. For example, it can reveal character, show conflict, move the plot forward, or hint at theme. Suggest that students create three-column charts with the headings *Character, Conflict,* and *Theme* to use as they read. Have students copy under each heading phrases or sentences that are vital to understanding the play. They may also add the speaker and the page on which the words are found. Then have students meet in small groups, share their quotations, and make observations about characters, conflicts, and theme. Have students continue their charts in subsequent acts.

Teach

Reading Strategy 1

Draw Conclusions About Characters **Answer:** *In his stage directions, Miller describes Mercy as being "merciless," which is confirmed in her suggestion that she should be allowed to beat Betty.*

Reading Strategy 2

Predict Ask students to predict why Abigail might want John Proctor's wife dead. *(Students may say Abigail wants revenge because Elizabeth Proctor fired her, she wants to stop Elizabeth from spreading rumors, and Abigail has romantic feelings for John.)*

Literary Element 3

Dialogue **Answer:** *By alternating between charm and anger, the actress could show the two sides of Abigail's nature.*

Reading Strategy 4

Draw Conclusions About Characters **Answer:** *These remarks reveal that Abigail's often volatile and aberrant behavior could be due to the psychological trauma of having witnessed the brutal murder of her parents.*

ENGLISH LEARNERS Help students understand Abigail's phrase "pointy reckoning that will shudder you."

MERCY. Have you tried beatin' her? I gave Ruth a good one and it waked her for a minute. Here, let me have her.

ABIGAIL. [*Holding* MERCY *back.*] No, he'll be comin' up. Listen, now; if they be questioning us, tell them we danced—I told him as much already.

MERCY. Aye. And what more?

ABIGAIL. He knows Tituba conjured Ruth's sisters to come out of the grave.

MERCY. And what more?

ABIGAIL. He saw you naked.

MERCY. [*Clapping her hands together with a frightened laugh.*] Oh, Jesus!

[*Enter* MARY WARREN, *breathless. She is seventeen, a **subservient,** naive, lonely girl.*]

MARY WARREN. What'll we do? The village is out! I just come from the farm; the whole country's talkin' witchcraft! They'll be callin' us witches, Abby!

MERCY. [*Pointing and looking at* MARY WARREN.] She means to tell, I know it.

MARY WARREN. Abby, we've got to tell. Witchery's a hangin' error, a hangin' like they done in Boston two year ago! We must tell the truth, Abby! You'll only be whipped for dancin', and the other things!

ABIGAIL. Oh, *we'll* be whipped!

MARY WARREN. I never done none of it, Abby. I only looked!

MERCY. [*Moving menacingly toward* MARY.] Oh, you're a great one for lookin', aren't you, Mary Warren? What a grand peeping courage you have!

[BETTY, *on the bed, whimpers.* ABIGAIL *turns to her at once.*]

ABIGAIL. Betty? [*She goes to* BETTY.] Now, Betty, dear, wake up now. It's Abigail. [*She sits* BETTY *up*

> **Draw Conclusions About Characters** How does this remark illustrate the irony in Miller's stage directions when Mercy first enters? **1**

> **Vocabulary**
> **subservient** (səb sur′ vē ənt) *adj.* useful, in an inferior capacity, to promote an end; submissive

and furiously shakes her.] I'll beat you, Betty! [BETTY *whimpers.*] My, you seem improving. I talked to your papa and I told him everything. So there's nothing to—

BETTY. [*Darts off the bed, frightened of* ABIGAIL, *and flattens herself against the wall.*] I want my mama!

ABIGAIL. [*With alarm, as she cautiously approaches* BETTY.] What ails you, Betty? Your mama's dead and buried.

BETTY. I'll fly to Mama. Let me fly! [*She raises her arms as though to fly, and streaks for the window, gets one leg out.*]

ABIGAIL. [*Pulling her away from the window.*] I told him everything; he knows now, he knows everything we—

BETTY. You drank blood, Abby! You didn't tell him that!

ABIGAIL. Betty, you never say that again! You will never—

BETTY. You did, you did! You drank a charm to kill John Proctor's wife! You drank a charm to kill Goody Proctor! **2**

ABIGAIL. [*Smashes her across the face.*] Shut it! Now shut it!

BETTY. [*Collapsing on the bed.*] Mama, Mama! [*She dissolves into sobs.*]

ABIGAIL. Now look you. All of you. We danced. And Tituba conjured Ruth Putnam's dead sisters. And that is all. And mark this. Let either of you breathe a word, or the edge of a word, about the other things, and I will come to you in the black of some terrible night and I will bring a pointy reckoning that will shudder you. And you know I can do it; I saw Indians smash my dear parents' heads on the pillow next to mine, and I have seen some reddish work[18] done at night, and I can make you wish you had never seen the sun ☆

---

18. **Reddish work** means "bloody deeds."

> **Dialogue** How might the actress playing Abigail make these lines particularly effective? **3**

> **Draw Conclusions About Characters** What new insight into Abigail's character do these remarks offer? **4**

Writing Practice

Summarize To monitor comprehension, have students pause every few pages and write a brief summary of what has occurred. As a model, use the following summary of this page: *Mercy, Mary Warren, Abigail, and Betty, while alone in Betty's room, discuss what occurred in the woods the night they were caught dancing. Betty awakens and accuses Abigail of drinking a charm to kill Goody Proctor. Abigail, who emerges as the leader of the girls, orders them to keep quiet.*

go down! [*She goes to* BETTY *and roughly sits her up.*] Now, you—sit up and stop this!

[*But* BETTY *collapses in her hands and lies inert on the bed.*]

MARY WARREN. [*With hysterical fright.*] What's got her? [ABIGAIL *stares in fright at* BETTY.] Abby, she's going to die! It's a sin to conjure, and we—

ABIGAIL. [*Starting for* MARY.] I say shut it, Mary Warren!

[*Enter* JOHN PROCTOR. *On seeing him,* MARY WARREN *leaps in fright.*]

MARY WARREN. Oh! I'm just going home, Mr. Proctor.

PROCTOR. Be you foolish, Mary Warren? Be you deaf? I forbid you leave the house, did I not? Why shall I pay you? I am looking for you more often than my cows!

MARY WARREN. I only come to see the great doings in the world.

PROCTOR. I'll show you a great doin' on your arse one of these days. Now get you home; my wife is waitin' with your work! [*Trying to retain a shred of dignity, she goes slowly out.*]

MERCY LEWIS. [*Both afraid of him and strangely titillated.*][19] I'd best be off. I have my Ruth to watch. Good morning, Mr. Proctor.

[MERCY *sidles out. Since* PROCTOR's *entrance,* ABIGAIL *has stood as though on tiptoe, absorbing his presence, wide-eyed. He glances at her, then goes to* BETTY *on the bed.*]

ABIGAIL. Gah! I'd almost forgot how strong you are, John Proctor!

PROCTOR. [*Looking at* ABIGAIL *now, the faintest suggestion of a knowing smile on his face.*] What's this mischief here?

ABIGAIL. [*With a nervous laugh.*] Oh, she's only gone silly somehow.

---

19. To be *titillated* is to be pleasantly excited or stimulated.

5 Dialogue *What do the other girls call Proctor? How does Abigail's use of his first name help define their relationship?*

PROCTOR. The road past my house is a pilgrimage to Salem all morning. The town's mumbling witchcraft.

ABIGAIL. Oh, posh! [*Winningly she comes a little closer, with a confidential, wicked air.*] We were dancin' in the woods last night, and my uncle leaped in on us. She took fright, is all.

PROCTOR. [*His smile widening.*] Ah, you're wicked yet, aren't y'! [*A trill of expectant laughter escapes her, and she dares come closer, feverishly looking into his eyes.*] You'll be clapped in the stocks[20] before you're twenty.

[*He takes a step to go, and she springs into his path.*]

ABIGAIL. Give me a word, John. A soft word. [*Her concentrated desire destroys his smile.*]

PROCTOR. No, no, Abby. That's done with.

ABIGAIL. [*Tauntingly.*][21] You come five mile to see a silly girl fly? I know you better.

PROCTOR. [*Setting her firmly out of his path.*] I come to see what mischief your uncle's brewin' now. [*With final emphasis.*] Put it out of mind, Abby.

ABIGAIL. [*Grasping his hand before he can release her.*] John—I am waitin' for you every night.

PROCTOR. Abby, I never give you hope to wait for me.

ABIGAIL. [*Now beginning to anger—she can't believe it.*] I have something better than hope, I think!

PROCTOR. Abby, you'll put it out of mind. I'll not be comin' for you more.

ABIGAIL. You're surely sportin' with me.

PROCTOR. You know me better.

ABIGAIL. I know how you clutched my back behind your house and sweated like a stallion

---

20. The word *stocks* refers to a heavy wooden frame with holes for confining the ankles and wrists of someone found guilty of a crime.
21. *Tauntingly* means "in a scornful or mocking way."

6 The United States and the World *What does this menacing statement foreshadow?*

ARTHUR MILLER **1035**

Literary Element · 5

Dialogue **Answer:** *The others say Mr. Proctor; Abigail calls him John, suggesting an intimacy that is borne out in their flirtatious exchange.*

[APPROACHING] Point out to students that Miller purposefully uses names to imply relationship. **Ask:** How do we use names in real life? (*Students may say they do not refer to teachers by first name, showing a more formal relationship.*)

Big Idea · 6

The United States and the World **Answer:** *The entire community is frightened and looking for a scapegoat. This statement foreshadows the likelihood of a witch hunt.*

Cultural History ☆

King Philip's War Abigail, aged 17 in 1692, would have been an infant at the time of King Philip's War (1675–1676), a major series of bloody conflicts between the English colonists and the Native Americans of the New England region.

Approaching Level

DIFFERENTIATED INSTRUCTION

AAVE The dialect that some of the characters speak includes language patterns such as an absence of agreement with the irregular verbs *do* and *be*, which is similar to a language pattern used by speakers of African American vernacular English (AAVE). To clarify the distinctions between the Puritan dialect, AAVE, and modern Standard Academic English, display the following lines of dialogue from this page and the previous page:

1. . . . like they done in Boston . . .
2. I never done none of it.
3. Be you foolish? Be you deaf?

Ask students to explain the nonstandard elements in these passages and to revise the passages into Standard Academic English. (*1. as they did in Boston . . .; 2. I have never done any of it; I never did any of it; 3. Are you foolish? Are you deaf?*)

1035

Teach

Political History ☆

Conflicts in Salem In his commentary on the play, Miller describes Rebecca and Francis Nurse as people highly respected for their moral character, good judgment, and success. He notes that, before the arrival of Parris, the Nurses and their friends had blocked the appointment of a minister supported by the Putnams. Political differences also were leading to conflicts between the Nurses' friends and the town authorities allied with the Putnams.

1036 UNIT 6   FROM DEPRESSION TO COLD WAR

Viewing Practice

Relate Art to Text Have students look at the picture while they consider what they have read so far. **Ask:** How does the picture affect your impression of what has happened up to this point in the play? *(Students may say it reflects the ominous feeling of the play.)* **Ask:** What do you think will happen next? How do you think the picture foreshadows the rest of the play? *(Students may say there will be a witch hunt. They may think the picture foreshadows the violence ahead.)*

whenever I come near! Or did I dream that? It's she put me out, you cannot pretend it were you. I saw your face when she put me out, and you loved me then and you do now!

PROCTOR. Abby, that's a wild thing to say—

ABIGAIL. A wild thing may say wild things. But not so wild, I think. I have seen you since she put me out; I have seen you nights.

PROCTOR. I have hardly stepped off my farm this sevenmonth.

ABIGAIL. I have a sense for heat, John, and yours has drawn me to my window, and I have seen you looking up, burning in your loneliness. Do you tell me you've never looked up at my window?

PROCTOR. I may have looked up.

ABIGAIL. [*Now softening.*] And you must. You are no wintry man. I know you, John. I *know* you. [*She is weeping.*] I cannot sleep for dreamin'; I cannot dream but I wake and walk about the house as though I'd find you comin' through some door. [*She clutches him desperately.*]

PROCTOR. [*Gently pressing her from him, with great sympathy but firmly.*] Child—

ABIGAIL. [*With a flash of anger.*] How do you call me child!

PROCTOR. Abby, I may think of you softly from time to time. But I will cut off my hand before I'll ever reach for you again. Wipe it out of mind. We never touched, Abby.

ABIGAIL. Aye, but we did.

PROCTOR. Aye, but we did not.

ABIGAIL. [*With a bitter anger.*] Oh, I marvel how such a strong man may let such a sickly wife be—

PROCTOR. [*Angered—at himself as well.*] You'll speak nothin' of Elizabeth!

ABIGAIL. She is blackening my name in the village! She is telling lies about me! She is a cold, sniveling woman, and you bend to her! Let her turn you like a—

1 Draw Conclusions About Characters *In your opinion, does Proctor show strength or weakness in this denial?*

PROCTOR. [*Shaking her.*] Do you look for whippin'?

[*A psalm is heard being sung below.*]

ABIGAIL. [*In tears.*] I look for John Proctor that took me from my sleep and put knowledge in my heart! I never knew what **pretense** Salem was, I never knew the lying lessons I was taught by all these Christian women and their covenanted[22] men! And now you bid me tear the light out of my eyes? I will not, I cannot! You loved me, John Proctor, and whatever sin it is, you love me yet! [*He turns abruptly to go out. She rushes to him.*] John, pity me, pity me!

[*The words "going up to Jesus" are heard in the psalm, and* BETTY *claps her ears suddenly and whines loudly.*]

ABIGAIL. Betty? [*She hurries to* BETTY, *who is now sitting up and screaming.* PROCTOR *goes to* BETTY *as* ABIGAIL *is trying to pull her hands down, calling "Betty!"*]

PROCTOR. [*Growing unnerved.*] What's she doing? Girl, what ails you? Stop that wailing!

[*The singing has stopped in the midst of this, and now* PARRIS *rushes in.*]

PARRIS. What happened? What are you doing to her? Betty! [*He rushes to the bed, crying, "Betty, Betty!"* MRS. PUTNAM *enters, feverish with curiosity, and with her* THOMAS PUTNAM *and* MERCY LEWIS. PARRIS, *at the bed, keeps lightly slapping* BETTY's *face, while she moans and tries to get up.*]

ABIGAIL. She heard you singin' and suddenly she's up and screamin'.

MRS. PUTNAM. The psalm! The psalm! She cannot bear to hear the Lord's name!

---

22. A covenant is an agreement or promise. Among the Puritans, a *covenanted* person had made a commitment to the church and had signed an agreement testifying to his or her faith.

Dialogue *In your opinion, is Abigail sincere in this speech? Explain.* **2**

Vocabulary

pretense (prē´ tens) *n.* a false show or appearance, especially for the purpose of deceiving; falseness

Teach

Reading Strategy **1**

Draw Conclusions About Characters **Answer:** *Students may suggest that Proctor regrets his mistake and takes a strong stand to preserve his marriage.*

Literary Element **2**

Dialogue **Answer:** *Many students will recognize the sincere passion in this speech. A girl such as Abigail would normally conceal her emotions and her vulnerability.*

(ADVANCED) Direct students' attention to the offstage singing of an Old Testament psalm occurring behind the dialogue. **Ask:** How does the singing of the psalm deepen the scene's dramatic effect? *(It creates irony between the secular character of the dialogue and the religious nature of the psalm.)*

English Learners

DIFFERENTIATED INSTRUCTION

Beginning Unfamiliar words may be less intimidating if students substitute synonyms. Encourage students to use a dictionary or thesaurus to find synonyms for the following words: *wintry (joyless, depressed), unnerved (weakened, discouraged),* and *wailing (howling, moaning).*

Intermediate Have a student read aloud Proctor's speech beginning "Abby I may think of you . . . ." Be sure that students understand that when he says, "We never touched," he does not mean this literally. Ask students to explain what he really means. *(He is trying to tell her on a deep level that they never really connected, and he wants her to believe and act this way.)*

Teach

Reading Strategy	1

Draw Conclusions About Characters **Answer:** *The Putnams seem determined to prove that witchcraft is the cause of the girls' strange behavior. Rebecca believes there is a natural explanation to be found in the psychology of teenage girls.*

Reading Strategy	2

Draw Conclusions About Characters **Answer:** *Proctor listens and defers to Rebecca because he respects her experience and rational outlook. Proctor is also skeptical about witchcraft.*

PARRIS. No, God forbid. Mercy, run to the doctor! Tell him what's happened here! [*MERCY LEWIS rushes out.*]

MRS. PUTNAM. Mark it for a sign, mark it!

[*REBECCA NURSE, seventy-two, enters. She is white-haired, leaning upon her walking-stick.*]

PUTNAM. [*Pointing at the whimpering BETTY.*] That is a notorious sign of witchcraft afoot, Goody Nurse, a prodigious²³ sign!

MRS. PUTNAM. My mother told me that! When they cannot bear to hear the name of—

PARRIS. [*Trembling.*] Rebecca, Rebecca, go to her, we're lost. She suddenly cannot bear to hear the Lord's—

[*GILES COREY, eighty-three, enters. He is knotted with muscle, canny,²⁴ inquisitive, and still powerful.*]

REBECCA. There is hard sickness here, Giles Corey, so please to keep the quiet.

GILES. I've not said a word. No one here can testify I've said a word. Is she going to fly again? I hear she flies.

PUTNAM. Man, be quiet now!

[*Everything is quiet. REBECCA walks across the room to the bed. Gentleness exudes²⁵ from her. BETTY is quietly whimpering, eyes shut. REBECCA simply stands over the child, who gradually quiets.*]

MRS. PUTNAM. [*Astonished.*] What have you done?

[*REBECCA, in thought, now leaves the bedside and sits.*]

PARRIS. [*Wondrous and relieved.*] What do you make of it, Rebecca?

PUTNAM. [*Eagerly.*] Goody Nurse, will you go to my Ruth and see if you can wake her?

REBECCA. [*Sitting.*] I think she'll wake in time. Pray calm yourselves. I have eleven children, and I am twenty-six times a grandma, and I have seen them all through their silly seasons, and when it come on them they will run the Devil bowlegged keeping up with their mischief. I think she'll wake when she tires of it. A child's spirit is like a child, you can never catch it by running after it; you must stand still, and, for love, it will soon itself come back.

PROCTOR. Aye, that's the truth of it, Rebecca.

MRS. PUTNAM. This is no silly season, Rebecca. My Ruth is bewildered, Rebecca; she cannot eat.

REBECCA. Perhaps she is not hungered yet. [*To PARRIS.*] I hope you are not decided to go in search of loose spirits, Mr. Parris. I've heard promise of that outside.

PARRIS. A wide opinion's running in the parish that the Devil may be among us, and I would satisfy them that they are wrong.

PROCTOR. Then let you come out and call them wrong. Did you consult the wardens²⁶ before you called this minister to look for devils?

PARRIS. He is not coming to look for devils!

PROCTOR. Then what's he coming for?

PUTNAM. There be children dyin' in the village, Mister!

PROCTOR. I seen none dyin'. This society will not be a bag to swing around your head, Mr. Putnam. [*To PARRIS.*] Did you call a meeting before you—?

PUTNAM. I am sick of meetings; cannot the man turn his head without he have a meeting?

PROCTOR. He may turn his head, but not to Hell!

REBECCA. Pray, John, be calm. [*Pause. He defers to her.*] Mr. Parris, I think you'd best send Reverend Hale back as soon as he come. This will set us all to arguin' again in the society, and we thought to have peace this year. I think we ought rely on the doctor now, and good prayer.

---

26. The church *wardens* were members who managed the congregation's business affairs.

Draw Conclusions About Characters *How do the Putnams and Rebecca disagree on the subject of witchcraft?* **1**

Draw Conclusions About Characters *Why does Proctor listen to Rebecca with respect?* **2**

---

23. *Prodigious* means "amazing."
24. *Canny* means "sharp, clever, and careful in one's dealings with others."
25. *Exudes* means "gives forth."

Writing Practice

Original Scene Consider having students write an original scene describing Abigail's dismissal from the Proctor farm seven months earlier. Suggest they include a conversation between John and Elizabeth prior to the confrontation between Abigail and Elizabeth. Remind students that the dialogue up to this point in Act One offers many hints and clues for the content of such a scene.

Have students use the correct format for dramatic dialogue, with the name of the speaker followed by a colon and then the speaker's words. Stage directions should be placed in brackets. When scenes are completed, students may work in groups to present them to the class.

Window View—Scapeology #3, 1995. Nanette Carter. Oil on canvas, 40¾ x 45½ in.

<u>View the Art</u> Nanette Carter often uses striking lines and contrasting panels in her work. What contrasts and divisions do you see in this painting? How might they reflect the contrasts and divisions among the people gathered in Betty's room. ★

MRS. PUTNAM. Rebecca, the doctor's baffled!

REBECCA. If so he is, then let us go to God for the cause of it. There is prodigious danger in the seeking of loose spirits. I fear it, I fear it. Let us rather blame ourselves and—

PUTNAM. How may we blame ourselves? I am one of nine sons; the Putnam seed have peopled this province. And yet I have but one child left of eight—and now she shrivels!

REBECCA. I cannot fathom that.

MRS. PUTNAM. [*With a growing edge of sarcasm.*] But I must! You think it God's work you should never lose a child, nor grandchild either, and I bury all but one? There are wheels within wheels in this village, and fires within fires![27]

---

3 The United States and the World *What danger might Rebecca be referring to? Why is it safer to "blame ourselves"?*

---

27. The expression *wheels within . . . fires!* means "things are not so simple or innocent as they seem."

ARTHUR MILLER **1039**

Teach

Big Idea **3**

The United States and the World **Answer:** *Rebecca understands that the Puritan obsession with witches may result in false accusations and unjust executions. It is more logical to blame human nature than to seek supernatural explanations.*

View the Art ★

Answer: *Students may note the contrast of light and dark and broken lines. They may suggest that these contrasts are seen in the philosophies of the characters in Betty's room.*
Nanette Carter is an African American artist whose surrealistic paintings reflect strong emotions about the human experience.

Approaching Level

DIFFERENTIATED INSTRUCTION

 Established In order to draw conclusions about characters, some students may benefit from a graphic organizer different from the one on the Before You Read page. Have students work in small groups to create a four-column chart with columns labeled *Words, Actions, Motives, Conclusions.* Have them focus on a single character and list details and information about the character in the first three columns. Then have them discuss what the details tell about the character and write their conclusions in the fourth column.

You may have different groups work on different characters and then report their conclusions to the class.

Teach

1040

PUTNAM. [*To PARRIS.*] When Reverend Hale comes, you will proceed to look for signs of witchcraft here.

PROCTOR. [*To PUTNAM.*] You cannot command Mr. Parris. We vote by name in this society, not by acreage.

PUTNAM. I never heard you worried so on this society, Mr. Proctor. I do not think I saw you at Sabbath meeting since snow flew.

PROCTOR. I have trouble enough without I come five mile to hear him preach only hellfire and bloody damnation. Take it to heart, Mr. Parris. There are many others who stay away from church these days because you hardly ever mention God any more.

PARRIS. [*Now aroused.*] Why, that's a drastic charge!

REBECCA. It's somewhat true; there are many that quail[28] to bring their children—

1 PARRIS. I do not preach for children, Rebecca. It is not the children who are unmindful of their obligations toward this ministry.

REBECCA. Are there really those unmindful?

PARRIS. I should say the better half of Salem village—

PUTNAM. And more than that!

PARRIS. Where is my wood? My contract provides I be supplied with all my firewood. I am waiting since November for a stick, and even in November I had to show my frostbitten hands like some London beggar!

GILES. You are allowed six pound a year to buy your wood, Mr. Parris.

PARRIS. I regard that six pound as part of my salary. I am paid little enough without I spend six pound on firewood.

PROCTOR. Sixty, plus six for firewood—

---

28. To *quail* is to hesitate, to lose heart, or to retreat in fear.

2 Draw Conclusions About Characters *What do we learn about Reverend Parris's priorities as a minister from Proctor's accusation?*

PARRIS. The salary is sixty-six pound, Mr. Proctor! I am not some preaching farmer with a book under my arm; I am a graduate of Harvard College.

GILES. Aye, and well instructed in arithmetic!

PARRIS. Mr. Corey, you will look far for a man of my kind at sixty pound a year! I am not used to this poverty; I left a thrifty business in the Barbados to serve the Lord. I do not fathom it, why am I persecuted here? I cannot offer one proposition but there be a howling riot of argument. I have often wondered if the Devil be in it somewhere; I cannot understand you people otherwise.

PROCTOR. Mr. Parris, you are the first minister ever did demand the deed to this house—

PARRIS. Man! Don't a minister deserve a house to live in?

PROCTOR. To live in, yes. But to ask ownership is like you shall own the meeting house itself; the last meeting I were at you spoke so long on deeds and mortgages I thought it were an auction.

PARRIS. I want a mark of confidence, is all! I am your third preacher in seven years. I do not wish to be put out like the cat whenever some majority feels the whim. You people seem not to comprehend that a minister is the Lord's man in the parish; a minister is not to be so lightly crossed and contradicted—

PUTNAM. Aye!

PARRIS. There is either obedience or the church will burn like Hell is burning!

PROCTOR. Can you speak one minute without we land in Hell again? I am sick of Hell!

PARRIS. It is not for you to say what is good for you to hear!

PROCTOR. I may speak my heart, I think!

PARRIS. [*In a fury.*] What, are we Quakers?[29] We are not Quakers here yet, Mr. Proctor. And you may tell that to your followers!

PROCTOR. My followers!

---

29. *Quakers* is the familiar name for members of the Society of Friends. They have no definite creed and are guided by their doctrine of "inner light."

Grammar Practice

PARRIS. [*Now he's out with it.*] There is a party in this church. I am not blind; there is a faction and a party.

PROCTOR. Against you?

PUTNAM. Against him and all authority!

PROCTOR. Why, then I must find it and join it.

[*There is shock among the others.*]

REBECCA. He does not mean that.

PUTNAM. He confessed it now!

PROCTOR. I mean it solemnly, Rebecca; I like not the smell of this "authority."

REBECCA. No, you cannot break charity[30] with your minister. You are another kind, John. Clasp his hand, make your peace.

PROCTOR. I have a crop to sow and lumber to drag home. [*He goes angrily to the door and turns to COREY with a smile.*] What say you, Giles, let's find the party. He says there's a party.

GILES. I've changed my opinion of this man, John. Mr. Parris, I beg your pardon. I never thought you had so much iron in you.

PARRIS. [*Surprised.*] Why, thank you, Giles!

GILES. It suggests to the mind what the trouble be among us all these years. [*To all.*] Think on it. Wherefore is everybody suing everybody else? Think on it now, it's a deep thing, and dark as a pit. I have been six time in court this year—

PROCTOR. [*Familiarly, with warmth, although he knows he is approaching the edge of GILES' tolerance with this.*] Is it the Devil's fault that a man cannot say you good morning without you clap him for defamation?[31] You're old, Giles, and you're not hearin' so well as you did.

GILES. [*He cannot be crossed.*] John Proctor, I have only last month collected four pound damages for you publicly sayin' I burned the roof off your house, and I—

PROCTOR. [*Laughing.*] I never said no such thing, but I've paid you for it, so I hope I can call you deaf without charge. Now come along, Giles, and help me drag my lumber home.

PUTNAM. A moment, Mr. Proctor. What lumber is that you're draggin', if I may ask you?

PROCTOR. My lumber. From out my forest by the riverside.

PUTNAM. Why, we are surely gone wild this year. What anarchy[32] is this? That tract is in my bounds, it's in my bounds, Mr. Proctor.

PROCTOR. In your bounds! [*Indicating REBECCA.*] I bought that tract from Goody Nurse's husband five months ago.

PUTNAM. He had no right to sell it. It stands clear in my grandfather's will that all the land between the river and—

PROCTOR. Your grandfather had a habit of willing land that never belonged to him, if I may say it plain.

GILES. That's God's truth; he nearly willed away my north pasture but he knew I'd break his fingers before he'd set his name to it. Let's get your lumber home, John. I feel a sudden will to work coming on.

PUTNAM. You load one oak of mine and you'll fight to drag it home!

GILES. Aye, and we'll win too, Putnam—this fool and I. Come on! [*He turns to PROCTOR and starts out.*]

PUTNAM. I'll have my men on you, Corey! I'll clap a writ[33] on you!

---

30. For the Puritans, *charity* was Christian love, including mercy, forgiveness, kindness, and trust.

3 Dialogue *How does Miller use dialogue on this page to advance the plot?*

4 The United States and the World *What "authority" might a U.S. audience in 1953 have thought of on hearing this line?*

5 Dialogue *How does Miller engage the audience's sympathy for Proctor in this line of dialogue?*

---

31. An attack on one's good name or reputation is an act of *defamation* (def′ ə mā′ shən).
32. *Anarchy* is lawless confusion and political disorder due to the absence of governmental authority. Here, Putnam uses the word to mean "lawlessness."
33. A *writ* is a judge's order.

ARTHUR MILLER **1041**

Teach

Predict Remind students that the appearance of a new character may indicate a shift in focus. Ask them to predict what the arrival of Hale means. *(Students should recognize from the previous references to Hale that he is considered an expert on witchcraft. His arrival signals a shift from arguments over practical matters to the subject of witchcraft.)*

Writer's Technique ☆

Emphasis on Key Ideas The concept of authority—religious, political, and moral—is a key idea in the play. Notice that Hale's description of his books "weighted with authority" provides an ironic echo of the verbal dispute between Proctor and Putnam on these pages regarding church authority.

The Crucible, 1996.

1 [*Enter* REVEREND JOHN HALE *of Beverly. He appears loaded down with half a dozen heavy books.*]

HALE. Pray you, someone take these!

PARRIS. [*Delighted.*] Mr. Hale! Oh! it's good to see you again! [*Taking some books.*] My, they're heavy!

HALE. [*Setting down his books.*] They must be; ☆ they are weighted with authority.

PARRIS. [*A little scared.*] Well, you do come prepared!

HALE. We shall need hard study if it comes to tracking down the Old Boy.[34] [*Noticing* REBECCA.] You cannot be Rebecca Nurse?

REBECCA. I am, sir. Do you know me?

HALE. It's strange how I knew you, but I suppose you look as such a good soul should. We have all heard of your great charities in Beverly.

PARRIS. Do you know this gentleman? Mr. Thomas Putnam. And his good wife Ann.

HALE. Putnam! I had not expected such distinguished company, sir.

PUTNAM. [*Pleased.*] It does not seem to help us today, Mr. Hale. We look to you to come to our house and save our child.

HALE. Your child ails too?

---

34. **Old Boy** is another name for Satan.

1042 UNIT 6 FROM DEPRESSION TO COLD WAR

Latin Roots Many English words are formed by adding prefixes and/or suffixes to Latin roots. Note that the words *conjure* and *instruct* are formed in this way. The Latin root *jure* means "to swear." *Conjure* literally means "to swear together." The Latin root *struct* means "to build." *Instruct* literally means "to build in (another)."

Knowing the meanings of the following words may help students discuss this play:

- *abjure*: to renounce upon oath
- *perjure*: to lie under oath
- *obstruct*: to hinder or block

MRS. PUTNAM. Her soul, her soul seems flown away. She sleeps and yet she walks . . .

PUTNAM. She cannot eat.

HALE. Cannot eat! [*Thinks on it. Then, to PROCTOR and GILES COREY.*] Do you men have afflicted children?

PARRIS. No, no, these are farmers. John Proctor—

GILES COREY. He don't believe in witches.

PROCTOR. [*To HALE.*] I never spoke on witches one way or the other. Will you come, Giles?

GILES. No—no, John, I think not. I have some few queer questions of my own to ask this fellow.

PROCTOR. I've heard you to be a sensible man, Mr. Hale. I hope you'll leave some of it in Salem.

  [*PROCTOR goes. HALE stands embarrassed for an instant.*]

PARRIS. [*Quickly.*] Will you look at my daughter, sir? [*Leads HALE to the bed.*] She has tried to leap out the window; we discovered her this morning on the highroad, waving her arms as though she'd fly.

HALE. [*Narrowing his eyes.*] Tries to fly.

PUTNAM. She cannot bear to hear the Lord's name, Mr. Hale; that's a sure sign of witchcraft afloat.

2 HALE. [*Holding up his hands.*] No, no. Now let me instruct you. We cannot look to superstition in this. The Devil is precise; the marks of his presence are definite as stone, and I must tell you all that I shall not proceed unless you are prepared to believe me if I should find no bruise of hell upon her.

PARRIS. It is agreed, sir—it is agreed—we will abide by your judgment.

HALE. Good then. [*He goes to the bed, looks down at BETTY. To PARRIS.*] Now, sir, what were your first warning of this strangeness?

---

3 Draw Conclusions About Characters *What do we learn about Proctor's character from this remark?*

4 The United States and the World *How might Miller's 1950s audiences have connected Reverend Hale's use of the word* superstition *to contemporary events?*

PARRIS. Why, sir—I discovered her—[*Indicating ABIGAIL.*]—and my niece and ten or twelve of the other girls, dancing in the forest last night.

HALE. [*Surprised.*] You permit dancing?

PARRIS. No, no, it were secret—

MRS. PUTNAM. [*Unable to wait.*] Mr. Parris's slave has knowledge of conjurin', sir.

PARRIS. [*To MRS. PUTNAM.*] We cannot be sure of that, Goody Ann—

MRS. PUTNAM. [*Frightened, very softly.*] I know it, sir. I sent my child—she should learn from Tituba who murdered her sisters.

REBECCA. [*Horrified.*] Goody Ann! You sent a child to conjure up the dead?

MRS. PUTNAM. Let God blame me, not you, not you, Rebecca! I'll not have you judging me any more! [*To HALE.*] Is it a natural work to lose seven children before they live a day?

PARRIS. Sssh!

  [*REBECCA, with great pain, turns her face away. There is a pause.*]

HALE. Seven dead in childbirth.

MRS. PUTNAM. [*Softly.*] Aye. [*Her voice breaks; she looks up at him. Silence. HALE is impressed. PARRIS looks to him. He goes to his books, opens one, turns pages, then reads. All wait, avidly.*]35

PARRIS. [*Hushed.*] What book is that?

MRS. PUTNAM. What's there, sir?

5 HALE. [*With a tasty love of intellectual pursuit.*] Here is all the invisible world, caught, defined, and calculated. In these books the Devil stands stripped of all his brute disguises. Here are all your familiar spirits—your incubi and succubi;36 your witches that go by land, by air, and by sea; your wizards of the night and of the day. Have no fear now—we shall find him out if he has come among us, and I mean to crush him utterly if he has shown his face! [*He starts for the bed.*]

REBECCA. Will it hurt the child, sir?

---

35. *Avidly* means "with intense interest."
36. *Incubi* (ing′ kyə bī′) and *succubi* (suk′ yə bī′) are evil spirits or demons.

ARTHUR MILLER   **1043**

Teach

Literary Element   2

Irony Discuss with students the irony in Hale's remarks. *(Hale says he cannot rely on superstition in matters such as witchcraft. But to modern audiences, his belief in witchcraft may also be considered a superstition.)*

APPROACHING **Ask:** What are adjectives that could reasonably describe Hale's character? *(orderly, sensible, confident, courteous, scholarly, temperate)*

Reading Strategy   3

Draw Conclusions About Characters Answer: *Proctor is cautious. He does not wish to be drawn into an argument that could harm him. He may be uncomfortable challenging the authority of Hale.*

Big Idea   4

The United States and the World Answer: *Miller's audiences might have believed that the threat of a Communist conspiracy within the United States, like witchcraft, was a mere superstition.*

Reading Strategy   5

Compare and Contrast Characters For the passage that starts at the bottom of the page, ask students to compare and contrast Rebecca's character with those of Parris and Hale. They may use a three-column chart to record their findings. *(Rebecca's concern is for the child. Parris thinks of himself. Hale, though well-intentioned, is egotistical. He has no doubts about his actions and abilities. Rebecca is skeptical about both.)*

Teach

Big Idea   1

The United States and the World Answer: *Giles is suspicious of his wife's reading because he believes that people can get evil or sinful ideas from certain books. Similarly, Senator McCarthy was suspicious of American intellectuals, whom he suspected of being influenced by subversive ideas. Both of these suspicions threaten freedom of thought and belief.*

Reading Strategy   2

Predict Have students pause after Hale asks his first question of Abigail. Invite them to predict how Abigail will respond to his questioning. *(Students may say that Abigail will continue to lie or blame others so she doesn't get in trouble.)*

HALE. I cannot tell. If she is truly in the Devil's grip we may have to rip and tear to get her free.

REBECCA. I think I'll go, then. I am too old for this. [*She rises.*]

PARRIS. [*Striving for conviction.*] Why, Rebecca, we may open up the boil of all our troubles today!

REBECCA. Let us hope for that. I go to God for you, sir.

PARRIS. [*With trepidation—and resentment.*] I hope you do not mean we go to Satan here! [*Slight pause.*]

REBECCA. I wish I knew. [*She goes out; they feel resentful of her note of moral superiority.*]

PUTNAM. [*Abruptly.*] Come, Mr. Hale, let's get on. Sit you here.

GILES. Mr. Hale, I have always wanted to ask a learned man—what signifies the readin' of strange books?

HALE. What books?

GILES. I cannot tell; she hides them.

HALE. Who does this?

GILES. Martha, my wife. I have waked at night many a time and found her in a corner, readin' of a book. Now what do you make of that?

HALE. Why, that's not necessarily—

GILES. It discomfits[37] me! Last night—mark this—I tried and tried and could not say my prayers. And then she close her book and walks out of the house, and suddenly—mark this—I could pray again!

HALE. Ah! The stoppage of prayer—that is strange. I'll speak further on that with you.

GILES. I'm not sayin' she's touched the Devil, now, but I'd admire to know what books she reads and why she hides them. She'll not answer me, y' see.

HALE. Aye, we'll discuss it. [*To all.*] Now mark me, if the Devil is in her you will witness some frightful wonders in this room, so please to keep your wits about you. Mr. Putnam, stand close in case she flies. Now, Betty, dear, will you sit up? [*PUTNAM comes in closer, ready-handed. HALE sits BETTY up, but she hangs limp in his hands.*] Hmmm. [*He observes her carefully. The others watch breathlessly.*] Can you hear me? I am John Hale, minister of Beverly. I have come to help you, dear. Do you remember my two little girls in Beverly? [*She does not stir in his hands.*]

PARRIS. [*In fright.*] How can it be the Devil? Why would he choose my house to strike? We have all manner of licentious[38] people in the village!

HALE. What victory would the Devil have to win a soul already bad? It is the best the Devil wants, and who is better than the minister?

GILES. That's deep, Mr. Parris, deep, deep!

PARRIS. [*With resolution now.*] Betty! Answer Mr. Hale! Betty!

HALE. Does someone afflict you, child? It need not be a woman, mind you, or a man. Perhaps some bird invisible to others comes to you— perhaps a pig, a mouse, or any beast at all. Is there some figure bids you fly? [*The child remains limp in his hands. In silence he lays her back on the pillow. Now, holding out his hands toward her, he intones.*] In nomine Domini Sabaoth sui filiique ite ad infernos.[39] [*She does not stir. He turns to ABIGAIL, his eyes narrowing.*] Abigail, what sort of dancing were you doing with her in the forest?

ABIGAIL. Why—common dancing is all.

PARRIS. I think I ought to say that I—I saw a kettle in the grass where they were dancing.

ABIGAIL. That were only soup.

HALE. What sort of soup were in this kettle, Abigail?

---

37. *Discomfits* means "confuses and frustrates."

1 **The United States and the World** *What is Giles suspicious of? How are his suspicions similar to those of Senator McCarthy during the 1950s?*

38. *Licentious* people disregard commonly accepted standards of right and wrong or good and evil.
39. *[In nomine . . . infernos.]* "In the name of the God of the Heavenly Hosts and of His Son, go to hell." Hale is performing an exorcism, a ritual intended to drive out evil spirits.

1044   UNIT 6   FROM DEPRESSION TO COLD WAR

Reading Practice

Irony Remind students that irony is the contrast or discrepancy between expectation and reality. **Ask:** What is ironic in the exchange between Parris and Hale on this page? *(Parris asks why the devil would choose his house when there are so many less worthy people in Salem. He does not recognize his own character failings. Hale's question assumes that the minister must be the best person in the village.)*

ABIGAIL. Why, it were beans—and lentils, I think, and—

HALE. Mr. Parris, you did not notice, did you, any living thing in the kettle? A mouse, perhaps, a spider, a frog—?

PARRIS. [*Fearfully.*] I—do believe there were some movement—in the soup.

ABIGAIL. That jumped in, we never put it in!

HALE. [*Quickly.*] What jumped in?

ABIGAIL. Why, a very little frog jumped—

PARRIS. A frog, Abby!

2 HALE. [*Grasping* ABIGAIL.] Abigail, it may be your cousin is dying. Did you call the Devil last night?

ABIGAIL. I never called him! Tituba, Tituba . . .

PARRIS. [*Blanched.*] She called the Devil?

HALE. I should like to speak with Tituba.

PARRIS. Goody Ann, will you bring her up? [*MRS. PUTNAM exits.*]

HALE. How did she call him?

ABIGAIL. I know not—she spoke Barbados.

HALE. Did you feel any strangeness when she called him? A sudden cold wind, perhaps? A trembling below the ground?

ABIGAIL. I didn't see no Devil! [*Shaking* BETTY.] Betty, wake up. Betty! Betty!

HALE. You cannot **evade** me, Abigail. Did your cousin drink any of the brew in that kettle?

ABIGAIL. She never drank it!

HALE. Did you drink it?

ABIGAIL. No, sir!

HALE. Did Tituba ask you to drink it?

ABIGAIL. She tried, but I refused.

HALE. Why are you concealing? Have you sold yourself to Lucifer?

ABIGAIL. I never sold myself! I'm a good girl! I'm a proper girl!

[*MRS. PUTNAM enters with* TITUBA, *and instantly* ABIGAIL *points at* TITUBA.]

ABIGAIL. She made me do it! She made Betty do it!

TITUBA. [*Shocked and angry.*] Abby!

ABIGAIL. She makes me drink blood!

PARRIS. Blood!!

MRS. PUTNAM. My baby's blood?

TITUBA. No, no, chicken blood. I give she chicken blood!

HALE. Woman, have you enlisted these children for the Devil?

TITUBA. No, no, sir, I don't truck[40] with no Devil!

HALE. Why can she not wake? Are you silencing this child?

TITUBA. I love me Betty!

HALE. You have sent your spirit out upon this child, have you not? Are you gathering souls for the Devil?

ABIGAIL. She sends her spirit on me in church; she makes me laugh at prayer!

PARRIS. She have often laughed at prayer!

ABIGAIL. She comes to me every night to go and drink blood!

TITUBA. You beg *me* to conjure! She beg *me* make charm—

ABIGAIL. Don't lie! [*To* HALE.] She comes to me while I sleep; she's always making me dream corruptions!

---

40. *Truck* is another way of saying "to have dealings."

---

3 Draw Conclusions About Characters *What aspect of her character does Abigail confirm with these remarks?*

Vocabulary

evade (i vād′) *v.* to escape or avoid, as by cleverness

Dialogue *How does Miller's use of dialogue ensure that Tituba is so quickly on the defensive?* **4**

Dialogue *What is Tituba accusing Abigail of in this dialogue? Do you think she will be believed? Explain.* **5**

Approaching Level

DIFFERENTIATED INSTRUCTION

 Emerging Have students work together to create cause and effect chains that trace the development of Act One from Parris's first questions to Abigail through the accusations of witchcraft at the end of the act. To help students identify causes and effects, tell them to ask first "What happened?" to determine the effect; next, ask "Why did it happen?" to determine the cause. Demonstrate with this example: **Ask:** What has happened at the beginning of this act? (*Betty has fallen into a trance.*) (effect) Why did this happen? (*She was frightened while dancing in the forest with Tituba and other girls.*) (cause)

Students should continue in this manner, listing each cause and drawing an arrow pointing to its effect.

Teach

View the Art ★

Answer: *Like the events of the night in the forest, what is actually revealed is at once intense and difficult to see clearly or interpret accurately.*
Katherine Bowling (1955–), a National Endowment of the Arts grant recipient, takes her inspiration from landscapes. As with *Omen*, her landscapes are devoid of people yet full of mood.

Cultural History ☆

Barbados Explain that the references in Act One to Barbados, Tituba's native island in the Caribbean, are intended to evoke a mysterious, exotic atmosphere. Discovered and named by the Portuguese, Barbados was colonized in the early 1600s by the British, who introduced a sugar economy that thrived in the tropical climate.

Omen, 1993. Katherine Bowling. Oil and spackle on wood, 24 x 24 in. The SBC Collection of Twentieth Century American Art. Courtesy SBC Communications.

View the Art Best known for her landscapes, Katherine Bowling bases many of her paintings on photographs taken in upstate New York. What connections might you make between this painting and the description of the night the girls went to the forest?

Speaking and Listening Practice

Readers' Theater Readers' Theater combines oral reading and dramatic presentation. Readers assume the role of characters from the story and perform passages in character using only their voices. Assign roles to student volunteers, and have them research dialect and pronunciation by watching film versions and listening to audio productions of the scene. Have students read the scene dramatically.

TITUBA. Why you say that, Abby?

ABIGAIL. Sometimes I wake and find myself standing in the open doorway and not a stitch on my body! I always hear her laughing in my sleep. I hear her singing her Barbados songs and tempting me with—

TITUBA. Mister Reverend, I never—

HALE. [Resolved now.] Tituba, I want you to wake this child.

TITUBA. I have no power on this child, sir.

HALE. You most certainly do, and you will free her from it now! When did you compact with[41] the Devil?

TITUBA. I don't compact with no Devil!

PARRIS. You will confess yourself or I will take you out and whip you to your death, Tituba!

PUTNAM. This woman must be hanged! She must be taken and hanged!

TITUBA. [Terrified, falls to her knees.] No, no, don't hang Tituba! I tell him I don't desire to work for him, sir.

PARRIS. The Devil?

HALE. Then you saw him! [TITUBA weeps.] Now Tituba, I know that when we bind ourselves to Hell it is very hard to break with it. We are going to help you tear yourself free—

TITUBA. [Frightened by the coming process.] Mister Reverend, I do believe somebody else be witchin' these children.

HALE. Who?

TITUBA. I don't know, sir, but the Devil got him numerous witches.

HALE. Does he! [It is a clue.] Tituba, look into my eyes. Come, look into me. [She raises her eyes to his fearfully.] You would be a good Christian woman, would you not, Tituba?

TITUBA. Aye, sir, a good Christian woman.

HALE. And you love these little children?

TITUBA. Oh, yes, sir, I don't desire to hurt little children.

HALE. And you love God, Tituba?

TITUBA. I love God with all my bein'.

HALE. Now, in God's holy name—

TITUBA. Bless Him. Bless Him. [She is rocking on her knees, sobbing in terror.] ☆

HALE. And to His glory—

TITUBA. Eternal glory. Bless Him—bless God . . .

HALE. Open yourself, Tituba—open yourself and let God's holy light shine on you.

TITUBA. Oh, bless the Lord.

HALE. When the Devil comes to you does he ever come—with another person? [She stares up into his face.] Perhaps another person in the village? Someone you know.

PARRIS. Who came with him?

PUTNAM. Sarah Good? Did you ever see Sarah Good with him? Or Osburn?

PARRIS. Was it man or woman came with him?

TITUBA. Man or woman. Was—was woman.

PARRIS. What woman? A woman, you said. What woman?

TITUBA. It was black dark, and I—

PARRIS. You could see him, why could you not see her?

TITUBA. Well, they was always talking; they was always runnin' round and carryin' on—

PARRIS. You mean out of Salem? Salem witches?

TITUBA. I believe so, yes, sir.

---

41. To *compact with* is to make an agreement or contract with.

1 The United States and the World *How is the assumption that Tituba is guilty similar to assumptions made during the McCarthy "witch hunts"?*

2 Draw Conclusions About Characters *What does Putnam's eagerness to name specific people reveal about his character?*

ARTHUR MILLER **1047**

The United States and the World **Answer:** *In both cases, fear induces people to suspend their powers of reasoning and to believe the unsupported allegations of unreliable witnesses.*

| Reading Strategy | 2 |

Draw Conclusions About Characters **Answer:** *Students might conclude from Putnam's speed at naming specific people that he is a vindictive person who seizes this chance to persecute his enemies.*

Writer's Technique ☆

Pacing in Drama Miller skillfully uses sound effects, graduated pacing, and rhetorical devices such as repetition to quicken the tempo of the action and to bring the act to a suspenseful climax. The effect is similar to a crescendo in symphonic music or opera.

English Learners

DIFFERENTIATED INSTRUCTION

Intermediate Work with students to clarify idioms and metaphors in the dialogue as Act One nears a climax. Point out the following expressions from this page and the next and ask students to use their knowledge of English to explain the meanings.

- "confess yourself" *(admit to doing something wrong)*
- "bind ourselves to Hell" *(turn toward the Devil and his practices)*
- "break with it" *(turn away from it)*
- "carryin' on" *(wild behavior)*
- "God's instrument" *(a person used to carry out something for God)*
- "cleanse our village" *(remove the problem from the village)*
- "turn your back on him" *(turn away from the Devil and his practices)*
- "the Devil is . . . preying on her" *(making a victim of her)*

Teach

[*Now* HALE *takes her hand. She is surprised.*]

HALE. Tituba. You must have no fear to tell us who they are, do you understand? We will protect you. The Devil can never overcome a minister. You know that, do you not?

TITUBA. [*Kisses* HALE's *hand.*] Aye, sir, I do.

HALE. You have confessed yourself to witchcraft, and that speaks a wish to come to Heaven's side. And we will bless you, Tituba.

TITUBA. [*Deeply relieved.*] Oh, God bless you, Mr. Hale!

1 HALE. [*With rising exaltation.*][42] You are God's instrument put in our hands to discover the Devil's agents among us. You are selected, Tituba, you are chosen to help us cleanse our village. So speak utterly, Tituba, turn your back on him and face God—face God, Tituba, and God will protect you.

TITUBA. [*Joining with him.*] Oh, God, protect Tituba!

HALE. [*Kindly.*] Who came to you with the Devil? Two? Three? Four? How many?

[TITUBA *pants, and begins rocking back and forth again, staring ahead.*]

TITUBA. There was four. There was four.

PARRIS. [*Pressing in on her.*] Who? Who? Their names, their names!

TITUBA. [*Suddenly bursting out.*] Oh, how many times he bid me kill you, Mr. Parris!

PARRIS. Kill me!

TITUBA. [*In a fury.*] He say Mr. Parris must be kill! Mr. Parris no goodly man, Mr. Parris mean man and no gentle man, and he bid me rise out of my bed and cut your throat! [*They gasp.*] But I tell him, "No! I don't hate that man. I don't want kill that man." But he say, "You work for me, Tituba, and I make you free! I give you pretty dress to wear, and put you way high up in the air,

and you gone fly back to Barbados!" And I say, "You lie, Devil, you lie!" And then he come one stormy night to me, and he say, "Look! I have *white* people belong to me." And I look—and there was Goody Good.

PARRIS. Sarah Good!

TITUBA. [*Rocking and weeping.*] Aye, sir, and Goody Osburn.

MRS. PUTNAM. I knew it! Goody Osburn were midwife[43] to me three times. I begged you, Thomas, did I not? I begged him not to call Osburn because I feared her. My babies always shriveled in her hands!

HALE. Take courage, you must give us all their names. How can you bear to see this child suffering? Look at her, Tituba. [*He is indicating* BETTY *on the bed.*] Look at her God-given innocence; her soul is so tender; we must protect her, Tituba; the Devil is out and preying on her like a beast upon the flesh of the pure lamb. God will bless you for your help.

[ABIGAIL *rises, staring as though inspired, and cries out.*]

ABIGAIL. I want to open myself! [*They turn to her, startled. She is enraptured,*[44] *as though in a pearly light.*] I want the light of God, I want the sweet love of Jesus! I danced for the Devil; I saw him; I wrote in his book; I go back to Jesus; I kiss His hand. I saw Sarah Good with the Devil! I saw Goody Osburn with the Devil! I saw Bridget Bishop with the Devil!

[*As she is speaking,* BETTY *is rising from the bed, a fever in her eyes, and picks up the chant.*]

BETTY. [*Staring too.*] I saw George Jacobs with the Devil! I saw Goody Howe with the Devil!

---

43. A *midwife* is a woman who assists other women in childbirth.
44. *Enraptured* means "filled with intense joy or delight."

Draw Conclusions About Characters *What is going on in Tituba's mind that she would make up information like this?* **3**

Draw Conclusions About Characters *Why do you think that Abigail makes this confession?* **4**

42. Here, *exaltation* means "great enthusiasm" or "joyful ecstasy."

2 The United States and the World *How is this tactic similar to that used by the House Un-American Activities Committee?*

Writing Practice

Analyze Conflict Remind students that external conflict, or a struggle between a character and his or her environment, is a central element of plot. Note that although the people of Salem face an external conflict, characters may perceive the problem in different ways. Have students design a graphic organizer, such as a web, with the defining problem in the middle. Then have them write a sentence stating the problem from the perspectives of John Proctor, Abigail Williams, Reverend Parris, and Rebecca Nurse. Discuss how each character might solve the problem.

Ocean Greyness, 1953. Jackson Pollock. Oil on canvas, 4 ft. 9¾ in. x 7 ft. 6⅛ in. Solomon R. Guggenheim Museum, NY.

 View the Art "When you are painting out of your unconscious," Jackson Pollock is quoted as saying, "figures are bound to emerge." Look at the interplay of images and colors in this painting. What characters or events in Act One might they represent? Explain.

PARRIS. She speaks! [*He rushes to embrace BETTY.*] She speaks!

HALE. Glory to God! It is broken, they are free!

BETTY. [*Calling out hysterically and with great relief.*] I saw Martha Bellows with the Devil!

ABIGAIL. I saw Goody Sibber with the Devil! [*It is rising to a great glee.*]

PUTNAM. The marshal, I'll call the marshal!

[*PARRIS is shouting a prayer of thanksgiving.*]

BETTY. I saw Alice Barrow with the Devil!

[*The curtain begins to fall.*]

HALE. [*As PUTNAM goes out.*] Let the marshal bring irons!

ABIGAIL. I saw Goody Hawkins with the Devil!

BETTY. I saw Goody Bibber with the Devil!

ABIGAIL. I saw Goody Booth with the Devil!

[*On their ecstatic cries.*]

THE CURTAIN FALLS

Dialogue *How do these concluding lines make an effective ending to Act One of the play?* **5**

ARTHUR MILLER **1049**

After You Read

Assess

1. Students' answers will vary.
2. (a) Betty's recovery (b) He fears an accusation of witchcraft.
3. (a) She says Mrs. Proctor is a cold, lying woman, and Abigail refused to be her slave. (b) Mrs. Proctor might have suspected an affair between Abigail and John.
4. (a) She denies it. She later says the devil tempted her and names others in his service. (b) To avoid the charge of witchcraft, a capital offense in Salem
5. (a) Terror, suspense, or tension (b) He reveals fears, suspicion, and hostility through dialogue.
6. (a) Both girls apparently fall into trances and call out names. Abigail's rapture is likely feigned. Betty may be ill. (b) Students should support their opinions.
7. A dangerous, largely unseen enemy and fearful people ready to take reckless action
8. Miller might have seen some of his contemporaries confessing too quickly and might have wanted to portray this kind of eagerness in his play.

Literary Element

1. Parris, Hale; Abigail, Tituba
2. Why two children are ill; if the girls practiced witchcraft

Reading Strategy

1. She lies about her reputation, why she left her job, and her activities in the forest.
2. She calms Betty and defuses an argument between Proctor and Parris.

After You Read

Respond and Think Critically

Respond and Interpret

1. Which characters or situations in Act One do you find it easiest to identify with? Explain.
2. (a) What is Reverend Parris praying for at the beginning of Act One? (b) What else might explain why he is praying so desperately?
3. (a) What reasons does Abigail give Parris for her discharge as the Proctors' servant? (b) What might be another reason?
4. (a) How does Tituba first respond to Hale's accusation of witchcraft? How does she change her response? (b) Why might Tituba, as well as Abigail and Betty, make accusations at the end of Act One?

Analyze and Evaluate

5. (a) How would you classify the atmosphere, or mood, of Act One? (b) What techniques does Miller use to create this mood?
6. Act One ends with Betty and Abigail as the center of interest. (a) How is their behavior similar and different? (b) Is it believable? Explain.

Connect

7. **Big Idea** The United States and the World Arthur Miller connected the Salem witch hunts of 1692 and the Communist "witch hunts" of the 1950s. Under what circumstances might a similar situation arise in the United States today?
8. **Connect to the Author** How might Miller's experiences with the Communist trials have affected his portrayal of girls who confess so easily?

Literary Element Dialogue

Much **dialogue** in *The Crucible* centers on questions and answers bandied between characters.

1. Who does the main questioning in Act One? Who are the subjects of the questioning?
2. What do the characters hope to determine by asking their questions?

Reading Strategy Draw Conclusions About Characters

Below are phrases used in Miller's stage directions. Give an example of each character's behavior that matches the description.

1. Abigail: *an endless capacity for dissembling*
2. Rebecca Nurse: *Gentleness exudes from her.*

LOG ON ▶ **Literature** Online

Selection Resources For Selection Quizzes, eFlashcards, and Reading-Writing Connection activities, go to glencoe.com and enter QuickPass code GLA9800u6.

Vocabulary Practice

Practice with Word Parts For each boldfaced vocabulary word in the left column, identify the related word with a shared root in the right column. Write each word and underline the part they have in common. Then explain how the words are related. Use a dictionary for help.

1. compromise   serve
2. contention   promise
3. subservient   contend
4. pretense   pretend

Writing

Write a Dialogue Tituba, Abigail, and Betty admit they were in the woods together. Using the details they provide, imagine what Miller might have written about that scene. Then write dialogue for this imaginary scene. Keep in mind the way Miller uses dialogue to develop plot, theme, and characterization. Use your character analysis charts as needed.

Writing

Use the following criteria to evaluate students' dialogue:

- Does the dialogue address the scene in the woods?
- Does the dialogue develop plot, theme, and characterization in Miller's style?

Vocabulary

1. **compromise**, **pro**mise: Both words refer to an agreement or settlement.
2. **contention**, **conten**der: Both words refer to struggle or assertion.
3. **subservient**, **serve**: Both words refer to usefulness.
4. **pretense**, **preten**der: Both words refer to deception.

The Crucible, Act Two

Build Background

The Puritans believed that temptation and sin were daily threats to their community. If one believer sinned, they believed, misfortune could befall the entire group. Blaming and punishing a single individual was a common way to deal with personal misfortune and to guarantee the continuity of the community.

Set Purposes for Reading

Literary Element Stage Directions

Stage directions are the instructions written by the playwright that describe the sets, costumes, and lighting as well as the appearance, movements, and dramatic attitudes of characters. Note the stage directions in the example below.

ELIZABETH. [*Unable to restrain herself.*] Mr. Hale. [*He turns.*] I do think you are suspecting me somewhat?

As you read Act Two, ask yourself, How do Miller's stage directions influence your understanding of the play?

Reading Strategy Analyze Historical Context

Historical context is the background setting for a piece of literature. It can include political, social, and even religious events important to a writer's era. The communist paranoia of the 1950s is part of *The Crucible's* historical context. Investigators often used details from people's personal lives as evidence of political leanings. As you read, ask, How do the characters' personal actions aid your understanding of the historical context?

Tip: Relationship Chart Use a chart like the one below to identify the connections between the characters' personal lives and their status in the public group.

Character	Personal Status	Public Status
Elizabeth	Proctor's wife	Goody Proctor; obedient, faithful, tolerant wife
John Proctor		
Mary Warren		

Learning Objectives

For pages 1051–1072

In studying this text, you will focus on the following objectives:

Literary Study: Analyzing stage directions.

Reading: Analyzing historical context.

Writing: Writing stage directions.

Vocabulary

reprimand (rep´ rə mand´) *v.* to reprove or correct sharply; p. 1052 *I'm afraid that the boss will reprimand me for arriving late.*

ameliorate (ə mēl´ yə rāt´) *v.* to make better or more tolerable; to improve; p. 1057 *To ameliorate the situation with his irritable coach, Steven made jokes when the coach seemed testy.*

base (bās) *adj.* morally low; dishonorable; p. 1060 *We did not expect base behavior from such a respected member of the community.*

covet (kuv´ it) *v.* to desire, especially to an excessive degree, something belonging to another; p. 1062 *Judy coveted her sister's shoes.*

ineptly (i nept´ lē) *adv.* incompetently; awkwardly; clumsily; p. 1066 *Ralph drove so ineptly that Maria got out and took the bus.*

ARTHUR MILLER **1051**

Focus

Summary, Act Two

Eight days have passed. A Salem court is convicting people of witchcraft with the aid of testimony from the "afflicted" girls. Relations between the Proctors are strained, and John wavers when Elizabeth asks him to expose Abigail as a fraud. Mary Warren says Abigail has mentioned Elizabeth's name in court. Reverend Hale comes to question the Proctors. Giles Corey and Francis Nurse reveal that their wives have been arrested. Court officials arrest Elizabeth despite John's violent objections. John vows to expose the pretense.

Vocabulary

Multiple Meanings Ask students for familiar meanings of the word *base*. (*The part on which something rests; a center or headquarters; a main ingredient in something, as in paint with an oil base*) Point out that the vocabulary word is an adjective. **Ask:** What different connotation does the adjective *base* have from the more common meanings of *base*? (*It has a negative connotation*)

Selection Skills

Literary Elements
- Stage Directions (SE pp. 1051–1072)
- Foreshadowing (TE p. 1061)

Reading Skills
- Analyze Historical Context (SE pp. 1051–1072)

The Crucible, Act Two

Vocabulary Skills
- Analogies (SE p. 1072)

Writing Skills/Grammar
- Write Stage Directions (SE p. 1072)
- Definition (TE p. 1064)

Listening/Speaking/Viewing Skills
- Viewing Art (SE pp. 1053, 1064, 1067, 1068)
- Mock Newscast (TE p. 1060)
- Debate (TE p. 1062)

Teach

Literary Element   1

Stage Directions Answer:
John does not want Elizabeth to know he has added salt to her stew. His behavior might imply dissatisfaction.

Reading Strategy   2

**Analyze Historical Context
Answer:** *She is sympathetic to the rabbit, demonstrating the kindness and empathy of a dutiful wife and mother.*

Writer's Technique ☆

Double Entendre Explain that words can mean two things at the same time. **Ask:** What two meanings might Miller intend when Proctor says, "It's winter in here yet?" *(Literally, there are no signs of spring. Figuratively, the relationship between John and Elizabeth is still cool.)*

 For activities related to this selection, see Unit 6 Teaching Resources Book, pp. 226–238.

Act Two

[*The common room of* PROCTOR'S *house, eight days later.*

At the right is a door opening on the fields outside. A fireplace is at the left, and behind it a stairway leading upstairs. It is the low, dark, and rather long living room of the time. As the curtain rises, the room is empty. From above, ELIZABETH *is heard softly singing to the children. Presently the door opens and* JOHN PROCTOR *enters, carrying his gun. He glances about the room as he comes toward the fireplace, then halts for an instant as he hears her singing. He continues on to the fireplace, leans the gun against the wall as he swings a pot out of the fire and smells it. Then he lifts out the ladle and tastes. He is not quite pleased. He reaches to a cupboard, takes a pinch of salt, and drops it into the pot. As he is tasting again, her footsteps are heard on the stair. He swings the pot into the fireplace and goes to a basin and washes his hands and face.* ELIZABETH *enters.*]

ELIZABETH. What keeps you so late? It's almost dark.

PROCTOR. I were planting far out to the forest edge.

ELIZABETH. Oh, you're done then.

PROCTOR. Aye, the farm is seeded. The boys asleep?

ELIZABETH. They will be soon. [*And she goes to the fireplace, proceeds to ladle up stew in a dish.*]

PROCTOR. Pray now for a fair summer.

ELIZABETH. Aye.

PROCTOR. Are you well today?

ELIZABETH. I am. [*She brings the plate to the table, and, indicating the food.*] It is a rabbit.

PROCTOR. [*Going to the table.*] Oh, is it! In Jonathan's trap?

ELIZABETH. No, she walked into the house this afternoon; I found her sittin' in the corner like she come to visit.

PROCTOR. Oh, that's a good sign walkin' in.

ELIZABETH. Pray God. It hurt my heart to strip her, poor rabbit. [*She sits and watches him taste it.*]

PROCTOR. It's well seasoned.

ELIZABETH. [*Blushing with pleasure.*] I took great care. She's tender?

PROCTOR. Aye. [*He eats. She watches him.*] I think we'll see green fields soon. It's warm as blood beneath the clods.

ELIZABETH. That's well.

[PROCTOR *eats, then looks up.*]

PROCTOR. If the crop is good I'll buy George Jacob's heifer. How would that please you?

ELIZABETH. Aye, it would.

PROCTOR. [*With a grin.*] I mean to please you, Elizabeth.

ELIZABETH. [*It is hard to say.*] I know it, John.

[*He gets up, goes to her, kisses her. She receives it. With a certain disappointment, he returns to the table.*]

PROCTOR. [*As gently as he can.*] Cider?

ELIZABETH. [*With a sense of* **reprimanding** *herself for having forgot.*] Aye! [*She gets up and goes and pours a glass for him. He now arches his back.*]

PROCTOR. This farm's a continent when you go foot by foot droppin' seeds in it.

ELIZABETH. [*Coming with the cider.*] It must be.

PROCTOR. [*Drinks a long draught, then, putting the glass down.*] You ought to bring some flowers in the house.

ELIZABETH. Oh! I forgot! I will tomorrow.

---

1   Stage Directions   *What does John's behavior suggest about his relationship with Elizabeth?*

Analyze Historical Context   *What typical trait of a 1950s housewife does Elizabeth demonstrate here? Explain.*   **2**

Vocabulary

reprimand (rep′ rə mand′) *v.* to reprove or correct sharply

Research Practice

 Theocracy Remind students that the residents of Salem were part of a theocracy, or church state, founded when the Pilgrims landed in Massachusetts about 70 years before the events in this play occurred. Suggest that they learn more about the early history of Massachusetts. Have students form small groups and use library and Internet resources to research the Pilgrims' beliefs and governing styles. Have group members collaborate on a written summary of their findings.

PROCTOR. It's winter in here yet. On Sunday let you come with me, and we'll walk the farm together; I never see such a load of flowers on the earth. [*With good feeling he goes and looks up at the sky through the open doorway.*] Lilacs have a purple smell. Lilac is the smell of nightfall, I think. Massachusetts is a beauty in the spring!

ELIZABETH. Aye, it is.

[*There is a pause. She is watching him from the table as he stands there absorbing the night. It is as though she would speak but cannot. Instead, now, she takes up his plate and glass and fork and goes with them to the basin. Her back is turned to him. He turns to her and watches her. A sense of their separation rises.*]

PROCTOR. I think you're sad again. Are you?

ELIZABETH. [*She doesn't want friction, and yet she must.*] You come so late I thought you'd gone to Salem this afternoon.

PROCTOR. Why? I have no business in Salem.

ELIZABETH. You did speak of going, earlier this week.

PROCTOR. [*He knows what she means.*] I thought better of it since.

ELIZABETH. Mary Warren's there today.

3 PROCTOR. Why'd you let her? You heard me forbid her go to Salem any more!

ELIZABETH. I couldn't stop her.

4 Stage Directions *What does Elizabeth mean? How would this stage direction influence the way the actor playing Proctor said his lines?*

Painting, 1948. Willem de Kooning. Enamel and oil on canvas, 42⅝ x 56⅛ in. Willem de Kooning Revocable Trust/Artists Rights Society (ARS), NY/The Museum of Modern Art, NY.

 View the Art "Even abstract shapes must have a likeness," Willem de Kooning is quoted as saying. In this painting, some people see letters of the alphabet; others see human body parts. What shapes or figures do you see? How does people's ability to interpret the same object or event differently relate to *The Crucible*? ★

PROCTOR. [*Holding back a full condemnation of her.*] It is a fault, it is a fault, Elizabeth—you're the mistress here, not Mary Warren.

ELIZABETH. She frightened all my strength away.

PROCTOR. How may that mouse frighten you, Elizabeth? You— **3**

ELIZABETH. It is a mouse no more. I forbid her go, and she raises up her chin like the daughter of a prince and says to me, "I must go to Salem, Goody Proctor; I am an official of the court!"

PROCTOR. Court! What court?

ELIZABETH. Aye, it is a proper court they have now. They've sent four judges out of Boston, she says, weighty magistrates[1] of the General Court, and at the head sits the Deputy Governor of the Province.

PROCTOR. [*Astonished.*] Why, she's mad.

---

1. *Weighty* means "important." *Magistrates* are judges.

ARTHUR MILLER **1053**

Teach

Political History ☆

New England Colonies The Massachusetts Bay Colony was founded by the Puritans. At first this colony governed all British settlements in New England. By 1692, differences in politics, religion, and economics had led to the formation of three more New England colonies—New Hampshire, Connecticut, and Rhode Island.

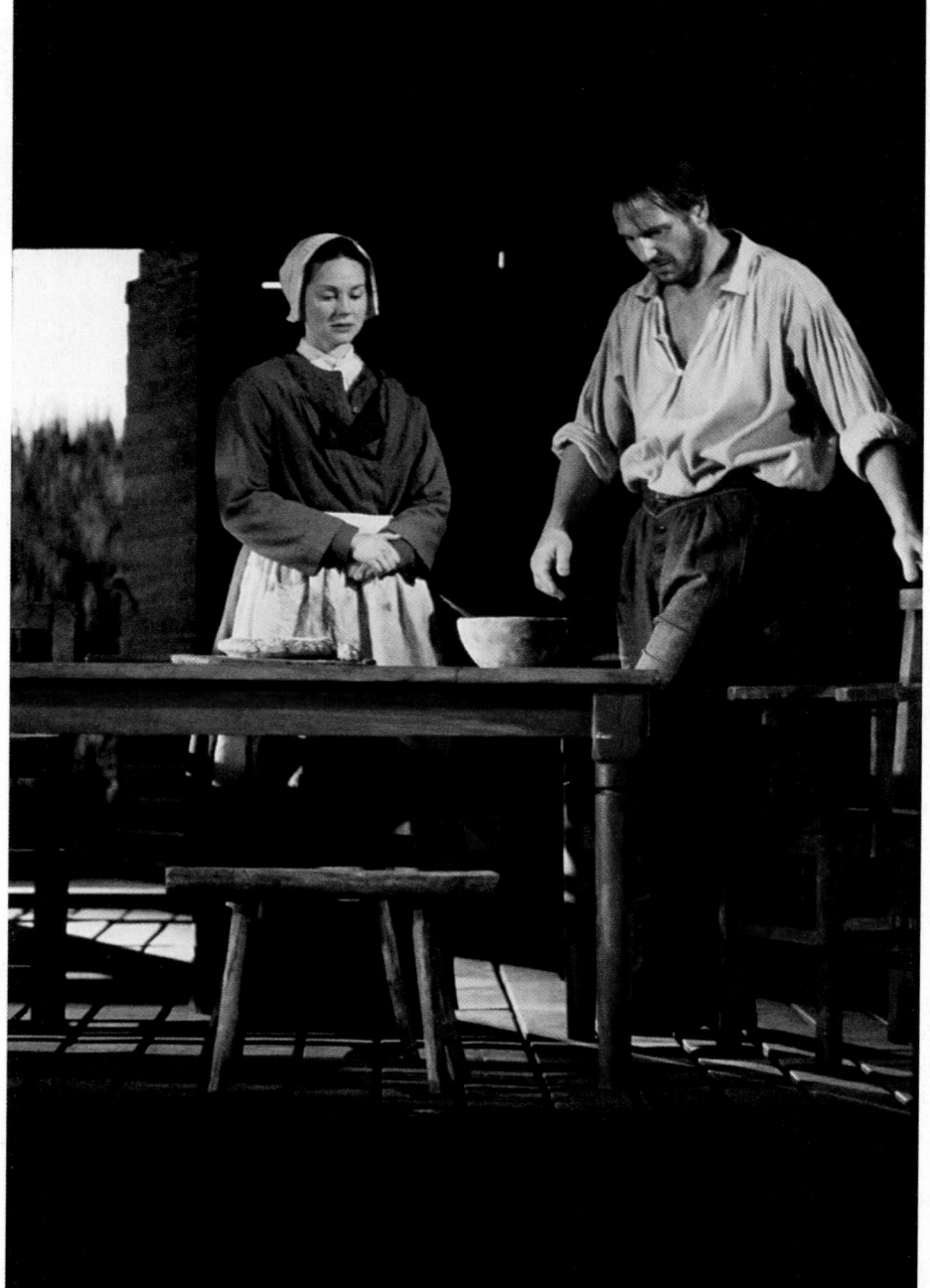

The Crucible on Stage in New York City, NY.

1054 UNIT 6 FROM DEPRESSION TO COLD WAR

Speaking Practice

Exclamation Points Remind students that exclamation points are used to show strong feelings and to indicate a forceful command. Point out that as Proctor becomes more upset, the number of exclamation points increases. Have students review the dialogue on this spread and use sticky notes to identify Proctor's exclamatory statements. Tell them to notice whether or not a stage direction indicates how he is to say the line. Then have students read the exclamations aloud first as if the lines were written as statements with periods, and then as exclamations with strong feelings.

ELIZABETH. I would to God she were. There be fourteen people in the jail now, she says. [PROCTOR *simply looks at her, unable to grasp it.*] And they'll be tried, and the court have power to hang them too, she says.

PROCTOR. [*Scoffing, but without conviction.*] Ah, they'd never hang—

ELIZABETH. The Deputy Governor promise hangin' if they'll not confess, John. The town's gone wild, I think. She speak of Abigail, and I thought she were a saint, to hear her. Abigail brings the other girls into the court, and where she walks the crowd will part like the sea for Israel. And folks are brought before them, and if they scream and howl and fall to the floor—the person's clapped in the jail for bewitchin' them.

PROCTOR. [*Wide-eyed.*] Oh, it is a black mischief.

ELIZABETH. I think you must go to Salem, John. [He turns to her.] I think so. You must tell them it is a fraud.

PROCTOR. [*Thinking beyond this.*] Aye, it is, it is surely.

ELIZABETH. Let you go to Ezekiel Cheever—he knows you well. And tell him what she said to you last week in her uncle's house. She said it had naught to do with witchcraft, did she not?

PROCTOR. [*In thought.*] Aye, she did, she did. [*Now, a pause.*]

ELIZABETH. [*Quietly, fearing to anger him by prodding.*] God forbid you keep that from the court, John. I think they must be told.

PROCTOR. [*Quietly, struggling with his thought.*] Aye, they must, they must. It is a wonder they do believe her.

ELIZABETH. I would go to Salem now, John—let you go tonight.

PROCTOR. I'll think on it.

 The United States and the World *What is wrong with this form of justice? What might Miller's audience have thought on hearing these lines?*

 Analyze Historical Content *What personal issue does Proctor consider here that affects his decision to speak publicly?*

ELIZABETH. [*With her courage now.*] You cannot keep it, John.

PROCTOR. [*Angering.*] I know I cannot keep it. I say I will think on it!

ELIZABETH. [*Hurt, and very coldly.*] Good, then, let you think on it. [*She stands and starts to walk out of the room.*]

PROCTOR. I am only wondering how I may prove what she told me, Elizabeth. If the girl's a saint now, I think it is not easy to prove she's fraud, and the town gone so silly. She told it to me in a room alone—I have no proof for it.

ELIZABETH. You were alone with her?

PROCTOR. [*Stubbornly.*] For a moment alone, aye.

ELIZABETH. Why, then, it is not as you told me.

PROCTOR. [*His anger rising.*] For a moment, I say. The others come in soon after.

ELIZABETH. [*Quietly—she has suddenly lost all faith in him.*] Do as you wish, then. [*She starts to turn.*]

PROCTOR. Woman. [*She turns to him.*] I'll not have your suspicion any more.

ELIZABETH. [*A little loftily.*] I have no—

PROCTOR. I'll not have it!

ELIZABETH. Then let you not earn it.

PROCTOR. [*With a violent undertone.*] You doubt me yet?

ELIZABETH. [*With a smile, to keep her dignity.*] John, if it were not Abigail that you must go to hurt, would you falter now? I think not.

PROCTOR. Now look you—

ELIZABETH. I see what I see, John.

PROCTOR. [*With solemn warning.*] You will not judge me more, Elizabeth. I have good reason to think before I charge fraud on Abigail, and I will think on it. Let you look to your own improvement before you go to judge your husband any more. I have forgot Abigail, and—

ELIZABETH. And I.

Stage Directions *What aspect of Elizabeth's character is stressed in this stage direction?* **3**

ARTHUR MILLER **1055**

Teach

Big Idea **1**

The United States and the World **Answer:** *The accused persons are considered guilty without having an opportunity to defend themselves or to have the accusers questioned. Miller's audience would likely have thought of how the naming of suspected Communist sympathizers during the McCarthy hearings was enough to taint their lives.*

Reading Strategy **2**

Analyze Historical Context **Answer:** *He thinks of his affair with Abigail and fears that speaking against the girls will reveal his secret.*

Literary Element **3**

Stage Directions **Answer:** *Elizabeth, although subservient to her husband, is determined to preserve her dignity.*

Approaching Level

DIFFERENTIATED INSTRUCTION

SMALL GROUP **Established** Have pairs or small groups use the character graphic organizers that they began at the play's beginning to develop and discuss details of the characters' personal and public status. Have them add Abigail Williams to their charts. Even though she does not appear in this act, readers learn more about her public status.

SMALL GROUP **Emerging** Guide students in examining the relationship between John and Elizabeth Proctor. **Ask:** How do John and Elizabeth treat each other in this scene? What motivates them to behave as they do? What does their behavior suggest about their characters? Have students work in small groups to discuss and answer these

questions. Tell students to consider not only the dialogue but also the stage directions when answering the questions.

Teach

Literary Element   1

Stage Directions Answer:
*Miller's description of Mary Warren
in the two previous stage directions
makes it clear that she appears ill
and strangely distant, as though
coming out of a trance. These
directions help us understand why
her words and appearance confuse and intrigue Proctor.*

Big Idea   2

**The United States and the
World Answer:** *Most students
will say that Miller wanted his
audience to be shocked that the
number imprisoned has almost
tripled. This increase suggests that
the witch hunt is gathering force
and speed, like an avalanche.*

PROCTOR. Spare me! You forget nothin' and forgive nothin'. Learn charity, woman. I have gone tiptoe in this house all seven month since she is gone. I have not moved from there to there without I think to please you, and still an everlasting funeral marches round your heart. I cannot speak but I am doubted, every moment judged for lies, as though I come into a court when I come into this house!

ELIZABETH. John, you are not open with me. You saw her with a crowd, you said. Now you—

PROCTOR. I'll plead my honesty no more, Elizabeth.

ELIZABETH. [*Now she would justify herself.*] John, I am only—

PROCTOR. No more! I should have roared you down when first you told me your suspicion. But I wilted, and, like a Christian, I confessed. Confessed! Some dream I had must have mistaken you for God that day. But you're not, you're not, and let you remember it! Let you look sometimes for the goodness in me, and judge me not.

ELIZABETH. I do not judge you. The magistrate sits in your heart that judges you. I never thought you but a good man, John—[*With a smile.*]—only somewhat bewildered.

PROCTOR. [*Laughing bitterly.*] Oh, Elizabeth, your justice would freeze beer! [*He turns suddenly toward a sound outside. He starts for the door as MARY WARREN enters. As soon as he sees her, he goes directly to her and grabs her by her cloak, furious.*] How do you go to Salem when I forbid it? Do you mock me? [*Shaking her.*] I'll whip you if you dare leave this house again!

[*Strangely, she doesn't resist him, but hangs limply by his grip.*]

MARY WARREN. I am sick, I am sick, Mr. Proctor. Pray, pray, hurt me not. [*Her strangeness throws him off, and her evident pallor[2] and weakness. He frees her.*] My insides are all shuddery; I am in the proceedings all day, sir.

---

2. *Pallor* refers to a pale complexion.

PROCTOR. [*With draining anger—his curiosity is draining it.*] And what of these proceedings here? When will you proceed to keep this house, as you are paid nine pound a year to do—and my wife not wholly well?

[*As though to compensate, MARY WARREN goes to ELIZABETH with a small rag doll.*]

MARY WARREN. I made a gift for you today, Goody Proctor. I had to sit long hours in a chair, and passed the time with sewing.

ELIZABETH. [*Perplexed, looking at the doll.*] Why, thank you, it's a fair poppet.

MARY WARREN. [*With a trembling, decayed voice.*] We must all love each other now, Goody Proctor.

ELIZABETH. [*Amazed at her strangeness.*] Aye, indeed we must.

MARY WARREN. [*Glancing at the room.*] I'll get up early in the morning and clean the house. I must sleep now. [*She turns and starts off.*]

PROCTOR. Mary. [*She halts.*] Is it true? There be fourteen women arrested?

MARY WARREN. No, sir. There be thirty-nine now—[*She suddenly breaks off and sobs and sits down, exhausted.*]

ELIZABETH. Why, she's weepin'! What ails you, child?

MARY WARREN. Goody Osburn—will hang!

[*There is a shocked pause, while she sobs.*]

PROCTOR. Hang! [*He calls into her face.*] Hang, y'say?

MARY WARREN. [*Through her weeping.*] Aye.

PROCTOR. The Deputy Governor will permit it?

Stage Directions *How do the two previous stage directions help explain the sudden change in Proctor's attitude?*   **1**

The United States and the World *How do you think that Miller wants his audience to respond to what is happening in Salem?*   **2**

1056 UNIT 6   FROM DEPRESSION TO COLD WAR

Reading Practice

SPIRAL REVIEW **Identify Logical Fallacies** Explain that the *syllogism* is the basic tool of logic, and write this example on the board: **The people living in Salem were Puritans.** (major premise) **John Proctor is a person living in Salem.** (minor premise) **Therefore, John Proctor is a Puritan.** (conclusion) Point out the distinction between *valid* (logically correct) and *true* (factual). This example is valid and true. However, sometimes a syllogism is valid but not true. Write this example on the board: **All people who do not know the commandments are witches.** (major premise) **Goody Good does not know the commandments.** (minor premise) **Therefore, Goody Good is a witch.** (conclusion) Although this syllogism is valid—its conclusion follows logically from its premises—it is not true, because the major premise is false.

MARY WARREN. He sentenced her. He must. [*To* *ameliorate* it.] But not Sarah Good. For Sarah Good confessed, y'see.

PROCTOR. Confessed! To what?

MARY WARREN. That she—[*In horror at the memory.*]—she sometimes made a compact with Lucifer, and wrote her name in his black book—with her blood—and bound herself to torment Christians till God's thrown down—and we all must worship Hell forevermore.

[*Pause.*]

PROCTOR. But—surely you know what a jabberer she is. Did you tell them that?

MARY WARREN. Mr. Proctor, in open court she near to choked us all to death.

PROCTOR. How, choked you?

MARY WARREN. She sent her spirit out.

ELIZABETH. Oh, Mary, Mary, surely you—

MARY WARREN. [*With an indignant³ edge.*] She tried to kill me many times, Goody Proctor!

ELIZABETH. Why, I never heard you mention that before.

MARY WARREN. I never knew it before. I never knew anything before. When she come into the court I say to myself, I must not accuse this woman, for she sleep in ditches, and so very old and poor. But then—then she sit there, denying and denying, and I feel a misty coldness climbin' up my back, and the skin on my skull begin to creep, and I feel a clamp around my neck and I cannot breathe air; and then—[*Entranced.*]—I hear a voice, a screamin' voice, and it were my voice—and all at once I remembered everything she done to me!

PROCTOR. Why? What did she do to you?

---

3. *Indignant* means "expressing righteous anger."

Vocabulary

ameliorate (ə mēl′ yə rāt′) *v.* to make better or more tolerable; to improve

---

MARY WARREN. [*Like one awakened to a marvelous secret insight.*] So many time, Mr. Proctor, she come to this very door, beggin' bread and a cup of cider—and mark this: whenever I turned her away empty, she *mumbled*.

ELIZABETH. Mumbled! She may mumble if she's hungry.

MARY WARREN. But *what* does she mumble? You must remember, Goody Proctor. Last month—a Monday, I think—she walked away, and I thought my guts would burst for two days after. Do you remember it?

ELIZABETH. Why—I do, I think, but—

MARY WARREN. And so I told that to Judge Hathorne, and he asks her so. "Sarah Good," says he, "what curse do you mumble that this girl must fall sick after turning you away?" And then she replies—[*Mimicking an old crone.*]⁴—"Why, your excellence, no curse at all. I only say my commandments; I hope I may say my commandments," says she!

ELIZABETH. And that's an upright answer.

MARY WARREN. Aye, but then Judge Hathorne say, "Recite for us your commandments!"—[*Leaning avidly toward them.*]—and of all the ten she could not say a single one. She never knew no commandments, and they had her in a flat lie!

PROCTOR. And so condemned her?

MARY WARREN. [*Now a little strained, seeing his stubborn doubt.*] Why, they must when she condemned herself.

PROCTOR. But the proof, the proof!

MARY WARREN. [*With greater impatience with him.*] I told you the proof. It's hard proof, hard as rock, the judges said.

PROCTOR. [*Pauses an instant, then.*] You will not go to court again, Mary Warren.

---

4. A *crone* is a withered old woman.

Vocabulary	3

Antonyms Point out to students that *ameliorate* and its opposite *exacerbate* ("to make worse") are popular vocabulary words on standardized tests. Ask students to find a passage on this spread in which one character says something that *exacerbates* the situation. (*When Elizabeth says, "And I" and "John, I am only—," she makes John angrier. When Mary Warren says, "Why, they must when she condemned herself," she makes John angrier.*)

English Learners

DIFFERENTIATED INSTRUCTION

Intermediate Point out to students that although they may be unfamiliar with the word *pallor*, they probably know the word *pale*. Remind them that thinking about related forms of words can help them identify unfamiliar words and reinforce meaning. Write on the board:

Noun: *pallor*

Adjectives: *pallid, pale*

Verb: *to pale*

Explain that these words are related.
Ask: If *pale* means lacking in color, what do you think *to pale* means? (*To become pale*)

Teach

Reading Strategy `1`

Analyze Historical Context Answer: *The 1950s were a conservative time in the United States. Young people generally respected and deferred to their elders. Her actions could have been seen as a threat to the stability of society.*

Big Idea `2`

The United States and the World Answer: *In the Salem trials, innocent people were induced to confess, thereby saving themselves by implicating others. During the McCarthy hearings, suspects were promised immunity from prosecution in return for naming their co-conspirators.*

Literary Element `3`

Stage Directions Answer: *Proctor is so incensed by Mary's remark that he is on the verge of beating her. She then stuns him into immobility.*

MARY WARREN. I must tell you, sir, I will be gone every day now. I am amazed you do not see what weighty work we do.

PROCTOR. What work you do! It's strange work for a Christian girl to hang old women!

MARY WARREN. But, Mr. Proctor, they will not hang them if they confess. Sarah Good will only sit in jail some time—[*Recalling.*]—and here's a wonder for you; think on this. Goody Good is pregnant!

ELIZABETH. Pregnant! Are they mad? The woman's near to sixty!

MARY WARREN. They had Doctor Griggs examine her, and she's full to the brim. And smokin' a pipe all these years, and no husband either! But she's safe, thank God, for they'll not hurt the innocent child. But be that not a marvel? You must see it, sir, it's God's work we do. So I'll be gone every day for some time. I'm—I am an official of the court, they say, and I—[*She has been edging toward offstage.*]

PROCTOR. I'll official you! [*He strides to the mantel, takes down the whip hanging there.*]

MARY WARREN. [*Terrified, but coming erect, striving for her authority.*] I'll not stand whipping any more!

ELIZABETH. [*Hurriedly, as PROCTOR approaches.*] Mary, promise now you'll stay at home—

MARY WARREN. [*Backing from him, but keeping her erect posture, striving, striving for her way.*] The Devil's loose in Salem, Mr. Proctor; we must discover where he's hiding!

PROCTOR. I'll whip the Devil out of you! [*With whip raised he reaches out for her, and she streaks away and yells.*]

MARY WARREN. [*Pointing at ELIZABETH.*] I saved her life today!

`1` **Analyze Historical Content** *Why might the young girl's growing sense of her own power over her elders have been seen as inappropriate during Miller's time? Explain.*

`2` **The United States and the World** *How did this distorted logic subvert justice in the Salem witch trials and in the McCarthy hearings?*

1058 UNIT 6   FROM DEPRESSION TO COLD WAR

[*Silence. His whip comes down.*]

ELIZABETH. [*Softly.*] I am accused?

MARY WARREN. [*Quaking.*] Somewhat mentioned. But I said I never see no sign you ever sent your spirit out to hurt no one, and seeing I do live so closely with you, they dismissed it.

ELIZABETH. Who accused me?

MARY WARREN. I am bound by law, I cannot tell it. [*To PROCTOR.*] I only hope you'll not be so sarcastical no more. Four judges and the King's deputy sat to dinner with us but an hour ago. I—I would have you speak civilly to me, from this out.

PROCTOR. [*In horror, muttering in disgust at her.*] Go to bed.

MARY WARREN. [*With a stamp of her foot.*] I'll not be ordered to bed no more, Mr. Proctor! I am eighteen and a woman, however single!

PROCTOR. Do you wish to sit up? Then sit up.

MARY WARREN. I wish to go to bed!

PROCTOR. [*In anger.*] Good night, then!

MARY WARREN. Good night. [*Dissatisfied, uncertain of herself, she goes out. Wide-eyed, both, PROCTOR and ELIZABETH stand staring.*]

ELIZABETH. [*Quietly.*] Oh, the noose, the noose is up!

PROCTOR. There'll be no noose.

ELIZABETH. She wants me dead. I knew all week it would come to this!

PROCTOR. [*Without conviction.*] They dismissed it. You heard her say—

ELIZABETH. And what of tomorrow? She will cry me out until they take me!

PROCTOR. Sit you down.

ELIZABETH. She wants me dead, John, you know it!

PROCTOR. I say sit down! [*She sits, trembling. He speaks quietly, trying to keep his wits.*] Now we must be wise, Elizabeth.

Stage Directions *What does this stage direction indicate?* `3`

Reading Practice

SPIRAL REVIEW **Monitor Comprehension**
Have students take some time to review the major conflicts so far.
Ask: What creates conflict between John and Elizabeth in Act Two? (*Students may say John creates conflict with his adultery and his unwillingness to tell the authorities about Abigail. Elizabeth fears that Abigail will accuse her of witchcraft.*)

1058

The Crucible, 1996.

ELIZABETH. [*With sarcasm, and a sense of being lost.*] Oh, indeed, indeed!

PROCTOR. Fear nothing. I'll find Ezekiel Cheever. I'll tell him she said it were all sport.

ELIZABETH. John, with so many in the jail, more than Cheever's help is needed now, I think. Would you favor me with this? Go to Abigail.

PROCTOR. [*His soul hardening as he senses . . .*] What have I to say to Abigail?

ELIZABETH. [*Delicately.*] John—grant me this. You have a faulty understanding of young girls. There is a promise made in any bed—

PROCTOR. [*Striving against his anger.*] What promise!

ELIZABETH. Spoke or silent, a promise is surely made. And she may dote on[5] it now—I am sure

she does—and thinks to kill me, then to take my place.

[PROCTOR'S *anger is rising; he cannot speak.*]

ELIZABETH. It is her dearest hope, John, I know it. There be a thousand names; why does she call mine? There be a certain danger in calling such a name—I am no Goody Good that sleeps in ditches, nor Osburn, drunk and half-witted. She'd dare not call out such a farmer's wife but there be monstrous profit in it. She thinks to take my place, John.

PROCTOR. She cannot think it! [*He knows it is true.*]

ELIZABETH. ["*Reasonably.*"] John, have you ever shown her somewhat of contempt? She cannot pass you in the church but you will blush— **4**

PROCTOR. I may blush for my sin.

---

5. To *dote on* is to show extreme affection for or to pay excessive attention to.

The United States and the World *Many U.S. citizens opposed to Senator McCarthy accused him of promoting his own career in hunting for Communists. What is similar about the situation described here?* **5**

ARTHUR MILLER **1059**

Teach

Teach

Reading Strategy | **1**

Evaluate Ask: What might explain Proctor's reaction? *(Some may say Abigail entrapped him and he has a right to be angry. Others will side with Elizabeth, noting that John is responsible for his actions.)*

Literary Element | **2**

Stage Directions Answer:
The rifle symbolizes John's anger at what he perceives as Elizabeth's refusal to understand him or to forgive him.

APPROACHING To guide students, suggest that the rifle is a symbol. Then ask what it might symbolize.

Literary Element | **3**

Stage Directions Answer:
"From the air" suggests a supernatural agent. It also indicates that events are moving with such swiftness that the innocent are caught unaware.

ELIZABETH. I think she sees another meaning in that blush.

PROCTOR. And what see you? What see you, Elizabeth?

ELIZABETH. [*"Conceding."*] I think you be somewhat ashamed, for I am there, and she so close.

PROCTOR. When will you know me, woman? Were I stone I would have cracked for shame this seven month!

ELIZABETH. Then go and tell her she's a whore. Whatever promise she may sense—break it, John, break it.

PROCTOR. [*Between his teeth.*] Good, then. I'll go. [*He starts for his rifle.*]

ELIZABETH. [*Trembling, fearfully.*] Oh, how unwillingly!

PROCTOR. [*Turning on her, rifle in hand.*] I will curse her hotter than the oldest cinder in hell. But pray, begrudge me not my anger!

ELIZABETH. Your anger! I only ask you—

PROCTOR. Woman, am I so **base**? Do you truly think me base?

ELIZABETH. I never called you base.

PROCTOR. Then how do you charge me with such a promise? The promise that a stallion gives a mare I gave that girl!

ELIZABETH. Then why do you anger with me when I bid you break it?

PROCTOR. Because it speaks deceit, and I am honest! But I'll plead no more! I see now your spirit twists around the single error of my life, and I will never tear it free!

ELIZABETH. [*Crying out.*] You'll tear it free— when you come to know that I will be your only wife, or no wife at all! She has an arrow in you yet, John Proctor, and you know it well!

---

2 Stage Directions *Why might Miller refer to the rifle in this stage direction?*

Vocabulary
base (bās) *adj.* morally low; dishonorable

[*Quite suddenly, as though from the air, a figure appears in the doorway. They start slightly. It is* MR. HALE. *He is different now—drawn a little, and there is a quality of deference, even of guilt, about his manner now.*]

HALE. Good evening.

PROCTOR. [*Still in his shock.*] Why, Mr. Hale! Good evening to you, sir. Come in, come in.

HALE. [*To* ELIZABETH.] I hope I do not startle you.

ELIZABETH. No, no, it's only that I heard no horse—

HALE. You are Goodwife Proctor.

PROCTOR. Aye; Elizabeth.

HALE. [*Nods, then.*] I hope you're not off to bed yet.

PROCTOR. [*Setting down his gun.*] No, no. [HALE *comes further into the room. And* PROCTOR, *to explain his nervousness.*] We are not used to visitors after dark, but you're welcome here. Will you sit you down, sir?

HALE. I will. [*He sits.*] Let you sit, Goodwife Proctor.

[*She does, never letting him out of her sight. There is a pause as* HALE *looks about the room.*]

PROCTOR. [*To break the silence.*] Will you drink cider, Mr. Hale?

HALE. No, it rebels my stomach; I have some further traveling yet tonight. Sit you down, sir. [PROCTOR *sits.*] I will not keep you long, but I have some business with you.

PROCTOR. Business of the court?

HALE. No—no, I come of my own, without the court's authority. Hear me. [*He wets his lips.*] I know not if you are aware, but your wife's name is—mentioned in the court.

PROCTOR. We know it, sir. Our Mary Warren told us. We are entirely amazed.

HALE. I am a stranger here, as you know. And in my ignorance I find it hard to draw a clear

---

3 Stage Directions *How does this stage direction help to develop plot and atmosphere?*

Speaking Practice

SMALL GROUP

Mock Newscast Challenge students to present a mock newscast about the events in the play. Organize students into groups. Explain that their newscasts should include desk anchors, reporters, and at least one "on the spot" interview with someone at the courthouse. Students should cover the events taking place in Salem, the opinions of the local citizens, and other information relevant to a Salem audience. Have groups present their newscasts to the class using audio and visual effects to enhance the presentation..

The Crucible, 1996.

HALE. This is a strange time, Mister. No man may longer doubt the powers of the dark are gathered in monstrous attack upon this village. There is too much evidence now to deny it. You will agree, sir?

PROCTOR. [*Evading.*] I—have no knowledge in that line. But it's hard to think so pious[6] a woman be secretly a Devil's bitch after seventy year of such good prayer.

HALE. Aye. But the Devil is a wily[7] one, you cannot deny it. However, she is far from accused, and I know she will not be. [*Pause.*] I thought, sir, to put some questions as to the Christian character of this house, if you'll permit me.

PROCTOR. [*Coldly, resentful.*] Why, we—have no fear of questions, sir.

HALE. Good, then. [*He makes himself more comfortable.*] In the book of record that Mr. Parris keeps, I note that you are rarely in the church on Sabbath Day.

PROCTOR. No, sir, you are mistaken.

opinion of them that come accused before the court. And so this afternoon, and now tonight, I go from house to house—I come now from Rebecca Nurse's house and—

ELIZABETH. [*Shocked.*] Rebecca's charged!

4 HALE. God forbid such a one be charged. She is, however—mentioned somewhat.

ELIZABETH. [*With an attempt at a laugh.*] You will never believe, I hope, that Rebecca trafficked with the Devil.

HALE. Woman, it is possible.

PROCTOR. [*Taken aback.*] Surely you cannot think so.

HALE. Twenty-six time in seventeen month, sir. I must call that rare. Will you tell me why you are so absent?

PROCTOR. Mr. Hale, I never knew I must account to that man for I come to church or stay at home. My wife were sick this winter.

HALE. So I am told. But you, Mister, why could you not come alone?

6. *Pious* means "having a sincere reverence for God."
7. *Wily* means "crafty" or "sly and full of tricks."

The United States and the World *Why do you think that Reverend Hale has come to believe that witchcraft is responsible for the girls' strange behavior? How does this kind of unsubstantiated belief relate to the McCarthy era?* **5**

ARTHUR MILLER **1061**

Teach

Literary Element 4

Foreshadowing Explain to students that the author uses foreshadowing. **Ask:** How does Miller foreshadow that Rebecca Nurse will be accused of witch-craft in Act One? (*In Act One, Mrs. Putnam jealously attacks Rebecca at the mention of Rebecca's numerous children and grandchil-dren and hints that it is unnatural that Rebecca has so many while she has so few.*)

Big Idea 5

The United States and the World Answer: *Students may suggest that the emotional appeal of the investigation is difficult to resist. Mass hysteria has taken hold of Salem. Similarly, the anti-Communist hysteria of the 1950s led many people to suspend their reasonable doubts about the existence of a conspiracy.*

Advanced Learners

DIFFERENTIATED INSTRUCTION

Research on Civil Liberties Have students do research on the Alien and Sedition Acts of 1798. Explain that these acts generated controversy involving freedom of speech, and parts of these acts still apply to issues today. Have students research multiple points of view and summarize their findings. Then have them share their results with the class and explain how the information they discovered might relate to *The Crucible*.

Teach

Reading Strategy `1`

Analyze Historical Context Answer: *Hale's argument that Parris is holy because he has been ordained is faulty logic. Because Parris was ordained by another man (not by God) and desires gold candlesticks, Proctor does not believe that Parris is a holy man.*

Big Idea `2`

The United States and the World Answer: *Proctor is challenged to prove that he is not on the side of Satan by reciting the commandments. HUAC witnesses had to establish that they were not "un-American." This presumption that one is guilty until proven innocent undermines the Anglo-American judicial tradition in which the burden of proof rests with those who make an accusation, not with those who deny it.*

Cultural History ☆

Puritan Beliefs Proctor accuses Parris of beliefs and practices that are unacceptable to the Puritans when he says Parris wants gold candlesticks and cathedrals. In forming their religion, Puritans attempted to eliminate certain Roman Catholic practices from the Anglican church. Gold candlesticks and ornate cathedrals, to Proctor, might represent the parts of Catholicism that Puritans were trying to leave behind.

PROCTOR. I surely did come when I could, and when I could not I prayed in this house.

HALE. Mr. Proctor, your house is not a church; your theology[8] must tell you that.

PROCTOR. It does, sir, it does; and it tells me that a minister may pray to God without he have golden candlesticks upon the altar.

HALE. What golden candlesticks?

PROCTOR. Since we built the church there were pewter[9] candlesticks upon the altar; Francis Nurse made them, y'know, and a sweeter hand never touched the metal. But Parris came, and for twenty week he preach nothin' but golden candlesticks until he had them. I labor the earth from dawn of day to blink of night, and I tell you true, when I look to heaven and see my money glaring at his elbows—it hurt my prayer, sir, it hurt my prayer. I think, sometimes, the man dreams cathedrals, not clapboard meetin' houses.

HALE. [*Thinks, then.*] And yet, Mister, a Christian on Sabbath Day must be in church. [*Pause.*] Tell me—you have three children?

PROCTOR. Aye. Boys.

HALE. How comes it that only two are baptized?

PROCTOR. [*Starts to speak, then stops, then, as though unable to restrain this.*] I like it not that Mr. Parris should lay his hand upon my baby. I see no light of God in that man. I'll not conceal it.

HALE. I must say it, Mr. Proctor; that is not for you to decide. The man's ordained, therefore the light of God is in him.

PROCTOR. [*Flushed with resentment but trying to smile.*] What's your suspicion, Mr. Hale?

HALE. No, no, I have no—

PROCTOR. I nailed the roof upon the church, I hung the door—

HALE. Oh, did you! That's a good sign, then.

PROCTOR. It may be I have been too quick to bring the man to book, but you cannot think we ever desired the destruction of religion. I think that's in your mind, is it not?

HALE. [*Not altogether giving way.*] I—have—there is a softness in your record, sir, a softness.

ELIZABETH. I think, maybe, we have been too hard with Mr. Parris. I think so. But sure we never loved the Devil here.

HALE. [*Nods, deliberating this. Then, with the voice of one administering a secret test.*] Do you know your Commandments, Elizabeth?

ELIZABETH. [*Without hesitation, even eagerly.*] I surely do. There be no mark of blame upon my life, Mr. Hale. I am a covenanted Christian woman.

HALE. And you, Mister?

PROCTOR. [*A trifle unsteadily.*] I—am sure I do, sir.

HALE. [*Glances at her open face, then at JOHN, then.*] Let you repeat them, if you will.

PROCTOR. The Commandments.

HALE. Aye.

PROCTOR. [*Looking off, beginning to sweat.*] Thou shalt not kill.

HALE. Aye.

PROCTOR. [*Counting on his fingers.*] Thou shalt not steal. Thou shalt not **covet** thy neighbor's goods, nor make unto thee any graven image.[10] Thou shalt not take the name of the Lord in vain; thou shalt have no other gods before me. [*With some hesitation.*] Thou shalt remember the Sabbath Day and keep it holy. [*Pause. Then.*] Thou shalt honor

---

8. Here, Hale uses the term *theology* to refer to Proctor's own religious beliefs.
9. *Pewter* is an alloy, or a substance composed of two or more metals or of a metal and a nonmetal. Tin is the main metal in pewter, and it is often mixed with lead.

`1` Analyze Historical Context *How does Miller question the acceptance of authority in these lines?*

10. Here, a *graven image* is an idol.

The United States and the World *The Crucible was first produced while the House Un-American Activities Committee (HUAC) was quizzing people about their Communist sympathies. What connection do you see between that investigation and Mr. Hale's line of questioning?* `2`

Vocabulary

covet (kuv´ it) *v.* to desire, especially to an excessive degree, something belonging to another

---

Listening and Reading Practice

Debate Have students consider the larger philosophical issues at stake in the play. Discuss with students whether they side with Proctor and individual conscience or with Hale and authority. Divide students into teams. Assign each team a position to argue: pro-individual conscience or pro-authority. Have students do research to support their team's position. Encourage students to use historical and current topics to justify their position. Then have each side present its arguments and counterarguments.

thy father and mother. Thou shalt not bear false witness. [*He is stuck. He counts back on his fingers, knowing one is missing.*] Thou shalt not make unto thee any graven image.

HALE. You have said that twice, sir.

PROCTOR. [*Lost.*] Aye. [*He is flailing for it.*]

ELIZABETH. [*Delicately.*] Adultery, John.

PROCTOR. [*As though a secret arrow had pained his heart.*] Aye. [*Trying to grin it away—to* HALE.] You see, sir, between the two of us we do know them all. [HALE *only looks at* PROCTOR, *deep in his attempt to define this man.* PROCTOR *grows more uneasy.*] I think it be a small fault.

HALE. Theology, sir, is a fortress; no crack in a fortress may be accounted small. [*He rises; he seems worried now. He paces a little, in deep thought.*]

PROCTOR. There be no love for Satan in this house, Mister.

HALE. I pray it, I pray it dearly. [*He looks to both of them, an attempt at a smile on his face, but his misgivings are clear.*] Well, then—I'll bid you good night.

ELIZABETH. [*Unable to restrain herself.*] Mr. Hale. [*He turns.*] I do think you are suspecting me somewhat? Are you not?

HALE. [*Obviously disturbed—and evasive.*] Goody Proctor, I do not judge you. My duty is to add what I may to the godly wisdom of the court. I pray you both good health and good fortune. [*To* JOHN.] Good night, sir. [*He starts out.*]

ELIZABETH. [*With a note of desperation.*] I think you must tell him, John.

HALE. What's that?

ELIZABETH. [*Restraining a call.*] Will you tell him?

[*Slight pause.* HALE *looks questioningly at* JOHN.]

PROCTOR. [*With difficulty.*] I—I have no witness and cannot prove it, except my word be taken. But I know the children's sickness had naught to do with witchcraft.

HALE. [*Stopped, struck.*] Naught to do—?

3 Stage Directions *What is the significance of this stage direction?*

PROCTOR. Mr. Parris discovered them sportin' in the woods. They were startled and took sick.

[*Pause.*]

HALE. Who told you this?

PROCTOR. [*Hesitates, then.*] Abigail Williams.

HALE. Abigail!

PROCTOR. Aye.

HALE. [*His eyes wide.*] Abigail Williams told you it had naught to do with witchcraft!

PROCTOR. She told me the day you came, sir.

HALE. [*Suspiciously.*] Why—why did you keep this?

PROCTOR. I never knew until tonight that the world is gone daft[11] with this nonsense.

HALE. Nonsense! Mister, I have myself examined Tituba, Sarah Good, and numerous others that have confessed to dealing with the Devil. They have *confessed* it.

PROCTOR. And why not, if they must hang for denyin' it? There are them that will swear to anything before they'll hang; have you never thought of that?

HALE. I have. I—I have indeed. [*It is his own suspicion, but he resists it. He glances at* ELIZABETH, *then at* JOHN.] And you—would you testify to this in court?

PROCTOR. I—had not reckoned with goin' into court. But if I must I will.

HALE. Do you falter here?

PROCTOR. I falter nothing, but I may wonder if my story will be credited in such a court. I do wonder on it, when such a steady-minded minister as you will suspicion such a woman that never lied, and cannot, and the world knows she cannot! I may falter somewhat, Mister; I am no fool.

---

11. *Daft* means "without sense or reason," "crazy," or "silly."

Stage Directions *Why do you think that Miller included a pause here?* **4**

The United States and the World *What does Proctor mean by "such a court," and why would he hesitate to tell the truth?* **5**

ARTHUR MILLER **1063**

Literary Element | 3

Stage Directions
Answer: *Adultery is the commandment that Proctor has broken. He may have blocked it from his mind because of its painful association, which for him is an awareness of his sin.*

Literary Element | 4

Stage Directions **Answer:**
The suggestion that Abigail may be lying comes as a complete shock to Hale. His awareness of this possibility takes hold during a dramatic silence.

Big Idea | 5

The United States and the World **Answer:** *Proctor realizes that reason and justice have deserted the proceedings in Salem. He fears that the truth may only incriminate him. The parallel with the McCarthy hearings would have been obvious to Miller's audiences in the 1950s.*

Writer's Technique ☆

Dialogue Proctor's words reveal how difficult it is for him to make the accusation. Typically, he speaks in a blunt, straightforward manner. Here, he fumbles before saying that Abigail is lying.

1063

Teach

Reading Strategy | 1

Analyze Historical Context **Answer:** *Elizabeth looks for goodness in her own heart and therefore creates her own standards of behavior and faith. This gesture can be seen as a rebellion against male (religious) authority.*

View the Art ★

Answer: *The heads represent two individuals who, like Proctor and Hale, appear very different from each other. The mouth and facial expression indicate that the one listening (left) is not pleased with what the other is saying. Shahn's quote relates to this scene in the play because Arthur Miller is expressing something about the culture and beliefs of his time— e.g., McCarthyism and the fear of Communism—through literature.*

Ben Shahn (1898–1969) immigrated to the United States at the age of eight. Many of his works reflect his perceptions of the social injustices of his time.

Confrontation, 1964. Ben Shahn. Watercolor on rice paper mounted on artist's board, 24 x 32 in. ©Estate of Ben Shahn/Licensed by VAGA, NY/The Lane Collection. Courtesy Museum of Fine Arts, Boston, MA.

View the Art Ben Shahn believed that "if we are to have values, a spiritual life, a culture, these things must find their imagery and interpretation through the arts." How might this idea, and this painting, relate to the confrontation between John Proctor and Mr. Hale?

HALE. [*Quietly—it has impressed him.*] Proctor, let you open with me now, for I have a rumor that troubles me. It's said you hold no belief that there may even be witches in the world. Is that true, sir?

PROCTOR. [*He knows this is critical, and is striving against his disgust with* HALE *and with himself for even answering.*] I know not what I have said, I may have said it. I have wondered if there be witches in the world—although I cannot believe they come among us now.

HALE. Then you do not believe—

PROCTOR. I have no knowledge of it; the Bible speaks of witches, and I will not deny them.

HALE. And you, woman?

ELIZABETH. I—I cannot believe it.

HALE. [*Shocked.*] You cannot!

PROCTOR. Elizabeth, you bewilder him!

ELIZABETH. [*To* HALE.] I cannot think the Devil may own a woman's soul, Mr. Hale, when she keeps an upright way, as I have. I am a good woman, I know it; and if you believe I may do only good work in the world, and yet be secretly bound to Satan, then I must tell you, sir, I do not believe it.

HALE. But, woman, you do believe there are witches in—

ELIZABETH. If you think that I am one, then I say there are none.

Analyze Historical Content *How might Elizabeth's words be seen as an early feminist statement? Explain.* | **1**

1064 UNIT 6 FROM DEPRESSION TO COLD WAR

Writing Practice

Extended Definition Tell students that the events that occurred in Salem at this time have been described as mass hysteria. Have students locate an appropriate definition of *hysteria*. Suggest that they start by listing the unfolding events that created or contributed to the hysteria in Salem. Then have students write an extended definition of the term *hysteria*, developing the term and explaining how the events in the play fit the definition of *hysteria*.

HALE. You surely do not fly against the Gospel, the Gospel—

PROCTOR. She believe in the Gospel, every word!

ELIZABETH. Question Abigail Williams about the Gospel, not myself!

[*HALE stares at her.*]

PROCTOR. She do not mean to doubt the Gospel, sir, you cannot think it. This be a Christian house, sir, a Christian house.

HALE. God keep you both; let the third child be quickly baptized, and go you without fail each Sunday in to Sabbath prayer; and keep a solemn, quiet way among you. I think—

[*GILES COREY appears in doorway.*]

GILES. John!

PROCTOR. Giles! What's the matter?

GILES. They take my wife.

[*FRANCIS NURSE enters.*]

GILES. And his Rebecca!

PROCTOR. [*To FRANCIS.*] Rebecca's in the *jail*!

FRANCIS. Aye, Cheever come and take her in his wagon. We've only now come from the jail, and they'll not even let us in to see them.

ELIZABETH. They've surely gone wild now, Mr. Hale!

FRANCIS. [*Going to HALE.*] Reverend Hale! Can you not speak to the Deputy Governor? I'm sure he mistakes these people—

HALE. Pray calm yourself, Mr. Nurse.

FRANCIS. My wife is the very brick and mortar of the church, Mr. Hale—[*Indicating GILES.*]—and Martha Corey, there cannot be a woman closer yet to God than Martha.

HALE. How is Rebecca charged, Mr. Nurse?

FRANCIS. [*With a mocking, half-hearted laugh.*] For murder, she's charged! [*Mockingly quoting the warrant.*] "For the marvelous and supernatural murder of Goody Putnam's babies." What am I to do, Mr. Hale?

HALE. [*Turns from FRANCIS, deeply troubled, then.*] Believe me, Mr. Nurse, if Rebecca Nurse be tainted,[12] then nothing's left to stop the whole green world from burning. Let you rest upon the justice of the court; the court will send her home, I know it.

FRANCIS. You cannot mean she will be tried in court!

HALE. [*Pleading.*] Nurse, though our hearts break, we cannot flinch; these are new times, sir. There is a misty plot afoot so subtle we should be criminal to cling to old respects and ancient friendships. I have seen too many frightful proofs in court—the Devil is alive in Salem, and we dare not quail to follow wherever the accusing finger points!

PROCTOR. [*Angered.*] How may such a woman murder children?

HALE. [*In great pain.*] Man, remember, until an hour before the Devil fell, God thought him beautiful in Heaven.[13]

GILES. I never said my wife were a witch, Mr. Hale; I only said she were reading books!

HALE. Mr. Corey, exactly what complaint were made on your wife?

GILES. That bloody mongrel Walcott charge her. Y'see, he buy a pig of my wife four or five year ago, and the pig died soon after. So he come dancin' in for his money back. So my Martha, she says to him, "Walcott, if you haven't the wit to feed a pig properly, you'll not live to own many," she says. Now he goes to court and claims that from that day to this he cannot keep a pig alive for more than four weeks because my Martha bewitch them with her books!

---

12. Something *tainted* is spoiled, inferior, or corrupted.
13. *[before the Devil fell . . . Heaven]* According to the Bible, the devil was heaven's highest angel before he was driven out because of his excessive pride.

Stage Directions *How do these words in the stage direction affect Hale's speech?* **3**

The United States and the World *How is Hale's attitude here similar to that of Senator McCarthy in the 1950s?* **4**

ARTHUR MILLER **1065**

2 **Analyze Historical Content** *What do Francis's sarcastic words say about legal charges during Miller's time? Explain.*

Teach

Literary Element **1**

Stage Directions Answer:
Students who recall that Cheever had taken Rebecca Nurse away should anticipate that he has come to arrest Elizabeth.

Reading Strategy **2**

Analyze Historical Context Answer: *Cheever and other townspeople are letting their authority "go to their heads." They do not maintain a calm balance in their legal authority, but instead allow themselves to be caught up in the excitement of power for its own sake.*

Big Idea **3**

The United States and the World Answer: *Students should understand that Miller has no respect for irrational authority. He is alluding here, not only to the McCarthy "witch hunters," but also to the Nazi war criminals, many of whom used the same excuse at the Nuremburg trials.*

[*Enter* EZEKIEL CHEEVER. *A shocked silence.*]

CHEEVER. Good evening to you, Proctor.

PROCTOR. Why, Mr. Cheever. Good evening.

CHEEVER. Good evening, all. Good evening, Mr. Hale.

PROCTOR. I hope you come not on business of the court.

CHEEVER. I do, Proctor, aye. I am clerk of the court now, y'know.

[*Enter* MARSHAL HERRICK, *a man in his early thirties, who is somewhat shamefaced at the moment.*]

GILES. It's a pity, Ezekiel, that an honest tailor might have gone to Heaven must burn in Hell. You'll burn for this, do you know it?

CHEEVER. You know yourself I must do as I'm told. You surely know that, Giles. And I'd as lief[14] you'd not be sending me to Hell. I like not the sound of it, I tell you; I like not the sound of it. [*He fears* PROCTOR, *but starts to reach inside his coat.*] Now believe me, Proctor, how heavy be the law, all its tonnage I do carry on my back tonight. [*He takes out a warrant.*] I have a warrant for your wife.

PROCTOR. [*To* HALE.] You said she were not charged!

HALE. I know nothin' of it. [*To* CHEEVER.] When were she charged?

CHEEVER. I am given sixteen warrant tonight, sir, and she is one.

PROCTOR. Who charged her?

CHEEVER. Why, Abigail Williams charge her.

PROCTOR. On what proof, what proof?

---

14. *As lief* (lēv) means "prefer that."

1 Stage Directions *Why is there a "shocked silence" when Ezekiel enters?*

2 Analyze Historical Content *How might a sudden gain in power or authority affect a common person? Explain.*

3 The United States and the World *Cheever excuses himself by explaining that he is only carrying out orders. What other historical events is Miller reminding his audience of here? Explain.*

CHEEVER. [*Looking about the room.*] Mr. Proctor, I have little time. The court bid me search your house, but I like not to search a house. So will you hand me any poppets that your wife may keep here?

PROCTOR. Poppets?

ELIZABETH. I never kept no poppets, not since I were a girl.

CHEEVER. [*Embarrassed, glancing toward the mantel where sits* MARY WARREN'S *poppet.*] I spy a poppet, Goody Proctor.

ELIZABETH. Oh! [*Going for it.*] Why, this is Mary's.

CHEEVER. [*Shyly.*] Would you please to give it to me?

ELIZABETH. [*Handing it to him, asks* HALE.] Has the court discovered a text in poppets now?

CHEEVER. [*Carefully holding the poppet.*] Do you keep any others in this house?

PROCTOR. No, nor this one either till tonight. What signifies a poppet?

CHEEVER. Why, a poppet—[*He gingerly turns the poppet over.*]—a poppet may signify—Now, woman, will you please to come with me?

PROCTOR. She will not! [*To* ELIZABETH.] Fetch Mary here.

CHEEVER. [**Ineptly** *reaching toward* ELIZABETH.] No, no, I am forbid to leave her from my sight.

PROCTOR. [*Pushing his arm away.*] You'll leave her out of sight and out of mind, Mister. Fetch Mary, Elizabeth. [ELIZABETH *goes upstairs.*]

HALE. What signifies a poppet, Mr. Cheever?

CHEEVER. [*Turning the poppet over in his hands.*] Why, they say it may signify that she—[*He has lifted the poppet's skirt, and his eyes widen in astonished fear.*] Why, this, this—

PROCTOR. [*Reaching for the poppet.*] What's there?

Vocabulary

ineptly (i nept´ lē) *adv.* incompetently; awkwardly; clumsily

1066 UNIT 6 FROM DEPRESSION TO COLD WAR

Research Practice

Salem Witch Trials Students may not be familiar with the 1692 Salem witch trials during which 19 convicted "witches" were hanged, and many others were imprisoned. Suggest they learn more about the events and people surrounding the actual Salem trials. Have students use library and Internet resources to research the accusations as well as the underlying reasons for these accusations from more than one source. Have students collabo-rate on presenting a summary of their findings to the class..

1954, 1954. Clyfford Still. Oil on canvas, 9 ft. 5½ in. x 13 ft. Albright-Knox Art Gallery, Buffalo, NY. Gift of Seymour H. Knox.

View the Art Fearing he might influence the viewer's experience, Clyfford Still identified many of his paintings only by the year created—if at all. In your opinion, does this painting express the mood of Salem's community in Act Two? Support your answer with details from the text and the painting.

CHEEVER. Why—[*He draws out a long needle from the poppet.*]—it is a needle! Herrick, Herrick, it is a needle!

[*HERRICK comes toward him.*]

PROCTOR. [*Angrily, bewildered.*] And what signifies a needle!

CHEEVER. [*His hands shaking.*] Why, this go hard with her, Proctor, this—I had my doubts, Proctor, I had my doubts, but here's calamity. [*To HALE, showing the needle.*] You see it, sir, it is a needle!

HALE. Why? What meanin' has it?

CHEEVER. [*Wide-eyed, trembling.*] The girl, the Williams girl, Abigail Williams, sir. She sat to dinner in Reverend Parris's house tonight, and without word nor warnin' she falls to the floor.

Like a struck beast, he says, and screamed a scream that a bull would weep to hear. And he goes to save her, and, stuck two inches in the flesh of her belly, he draw a needle out. And demandin' of her how she come to be so stabbed, she—[*To PROCTOR now.*]—testify it were your wife's familiar spirit pushed it in.

PROCTOR. Why, she done it herself! [*To HALE.*] I hope you're not takin' this for proof, Mister!

[*HALE, struck by the proof, is silent.*]

CHEEVER. 'Tis hard proof! [*To HALE.*] I find here a poppet Goody Proctor keeps. I have found it,

---

Stage Directions **What does this stage direction suggest about Hale?** **4**

ARTHUR MILLER **1067**

Stage Directions Answer: *Hale is gullible and unwilling to question the credibility of the "innocent" young girls. He accepts Abigail's dubious "proof" without question.*

View the Art

Answer: *Students may suggest that the use of the color orange, together with the powerful jagged lines, represents the anger and passion in the people of Salem. The predominant black in the center of the painting might suggest the dark and foreboding atmosphere at the core of the community.*

Clyfford Still (1904–1980) experimented with a number of painting styles before he became a pioneer of abstract expressionism. This painting reflects a period when Still applied thick paints to create powerful, jagged forms. Later in his career, his paintings became softer and less aggressive.

Cultural History

Spirit Dolls The use of "spirit dolls" and needles to implement curses or injuries on others is a practice found in folk religions, perhaps with origins in Haitian voodoo. Point out that Cheever's reference to "your wife's familiar spirit" alludes to the belief that witches could control external agents, or "familiars," to cause harm or injury to others.

Approaching Level

DIFFERENTIATED INSTRUCTION

Established Be sure students understand the sequence of events surrounding the "poppet." Mary Warren made it at the court, inserted a needle into it, and then brought it home to present to Elizabeth Proctor as a "gift." Now it is revealed that Abigail was stabbed in her belly by a needle and is charging Elizabeth with attacking her. **Ask:** Why is it significant that Abigail sat next to Mary as Mary made the poppet? (*Abigail probably wanted to entrap Elizabeth by means of the poppet and the needle.*)

Teach

The United States and the World Answer: *She will be asked to prove that she did not stick the needle into Abigail or that she is not a witch. The burden of proof should rest with Abigail, not Elizabeth.*

Literary Element 2

Dialogue Ask students to identify differences between Hale's exchange with Mary and Proctor's exchange with her. *(Proctor asks open-ended questions that allow spontaneous, unguided response. Hale asks leading questions that suggest the answers he wants to hear.)*

View the Art ★

Answer: *The curved lines suggest continuous and powerful circular movement, not unlike a strong wind. The absence of any warm colors reveals a coldness and severity that can be compared to Proctor's words.*

Lee Krasner (1911–1984), like her husband Jackson Pollock, was a member of the abstract expressionist movement. However, critics did not appreciate her talents until after Pollock's death in 1956. Her work has grown in popularity over the years and today her paintings are considered excellent examples of abstract art.

Polar Stampede, 1960. Lee Krasner. Oil on cotton duck, 93⅝ x 159¾ in. Courtesy of The Robert Miller Gallery, NY/©2000 Pollock-Krasner Foundation/Artists Rights Society (ARS), NY.

View the Art *Polar Stampede* is part of Lee Krasner's *Night Journeys* series, an insomniac's expression of grief and anger painted after her husband's death. In what ways might this work echo John Proctor's words, "And the wind, God's icy wind, will blow!"? ★

sir. And in the belly of the poppet a needle's stuck. I tell you true, Proctor, I never warranted to see such proof of Hell, and I bid you obstruct me not, for I—

[Enter ELIZABETH with MARY WARREN. PROCTOR, seeing MARY WARREN, draws her by the arm to HALE.]

PROCTOR. Here now! Mary, how did this poppet come into my house?

MARY WARREN. *[Frightened for herself, her voice very small.]* What poppet's that, sir?

The United States and the World *Making the accused person prove a negative statement to establish innocence is typical of a miscarriage of justice. What is Elizabeth going to be asked to prove here?* **1**

PROCTOR. *[Impatiently, pointing at the doll in* CHEEVER'S *hand.]* This poppet, this poppet.

MARY WARREN. *[Evasively, looking at it.]* Why, I— I think it is mine.

PROCTOR. It is your poppet, is it not?

MARY WARREN. *[Not understanding the direction of this.]* It—is, sir.

PROCTOR. And how did it come into this house?

MARY WARREN. *[Glancing about at the avid faces.]* Why—I made it in the court, sir, and—give it to Goody Proctor tonight.

PROCTOR. *[To HALE.]* Now, sir—do you have it? **2**

HALE. Mary Warren, a needle have been found inside this poppet.

MARY WARREN. *[Bewildered.]* Why, I meant no harm by it, sir.

Assessment Practice

Multiple Choice Have students answer the questions. Then review why each is correct or incorrect.

1. Which is an opinion? *(D)*
   A. Abigail accused Elizabeth's spirit of stabbing her with a pin.
   B. Parris found a needle in Abigail.
   C. Cheever found a poppet stuck with a needle at the Proctors' home.
   D. Abigail put the needle in the poppet.

2. Which best characterizes Mary? *(B)*
   A. stubborn   C. hysterical
   B. weak   D. upright

PROCTOR. [*Quickly.*] You stuck that needle in yourself?

MARY WARREN. I—I believe I did, sir, I—

PROCTOR. [*To* HALE.] What say you now?

HALE. [*Watching* MARY WARREN *closely.*] Child, you are certain this be your natural memory? May it be, perhaps, that someone conjures you even now to say this?

MARY WARREN. Conjures me? Why, no, sir, I am entirely myself, I think. Let you ask Susanna Walcott—she saw me sewin' it in court. [*Or better still.*] Ask Abby, Abby sat beside me when I made it.

PROCTOR. [*To* HALE, *of* CHEEVER.] Bid him begone. Your mind is surely settled now. Bid him out, Mr. Hale.

ELIZABETH. What signifies a needle?

HALE. Mary—you charge a cold and cruel murder on Abigail.

MARY WARREN. Murder! I charge no—

HALE. Abigail were stabbed tonight; a needle were found stuck into her belly—

ELIZABETH. And she charges me?

HALE. Aye.

ELIZABETH. [*Her breath knocked out.*] Why—! The girl is murder! She must be ripped out of the world!

CHEEVER. [*Pointing at* ELIZABETH.] You've heard that, sir! Ripped out of the world! Herrick, you heard it!

PROCTOR. [*Suddenly snatching the warrant out of* CHEEVER'S *hands.*] Out with you.

CHEEVER. Proctor, you dare not touch the warrant.

PROCTOR. [*Ripping the warrant.*] Out with you!

CHEEVER. You've ripped the Deputy Governor's warrant, man!

PROCTOR. Damn the Deputy Governor! Out of my house!

HALE. Now, Proctor, Proctor!

PROCTOR. Get y'gone with them! You are a broken minister.

HALE. Proctor, if she is innocent, the court—

PROCTOR. If *she* is innocent! Why do you never wonder if Parris be innocent, or Abigail? Is the accuser always holy now? Were they born this morning as clean as God's fingers? I'll tell you what's walking Salem—vengeance is walking Salem. We are what we always were in Salem, but now the little crazy children are jangling the keys of the kingdom, and common vengeance writes the law! This warrant's vengeance! I'll not give my wife to vengeance!

ELIZABETH. I'll go, John—

PROCTOR. You will not go!

HERRICK. I have nine men outside. You cannot keep her. The law binds me, John, I cannot budge.

PROCTOR. [*To* HALE, *ready to break him.*] Will you see her taken?

HALE. Proctor, the court is just—

PROCTOR. Pontius Pilate! God will not let you wash your hands of this![15]

ELIZABETH. John—I think I must go with them. [*He cannot bear to look at her.*] Mary, there is bread enough for the morning; you will bake, in the afternoon. Help Mr. Proctor as you were his daughter—you owe me that, and much more. [*She is fighting her weeping. To* PROCTOR.] When the children wake, speak nothing of witchcraft—it will frighten them. [*She cannot go on.*]

PROCTOR. I will bring you home. I will bring you soon.

ELIZABETH. Oh, John, bring me soon!

---

15. [*Pontius Pilate . . . this!*] According to the Christian Bible, the Roman official Pontius Pilate consented to the crucifixion of Jesus despite the lack of formal charges or evidence. Pilate then washed his hands and declared himself innocent of shedding Jesus' blood.

> Analyze Historical Content *How does Miller use these lines to comment on the status of the 1950s Communist trials?* **4**

---

3 Stage Directions *What does this stage direction mean?*

ARTHUR MILLER **1069**

Literary Element **3**

Stage Directions Answer: *Abigail's outrageous accusation strikes Elizabeth like a blow to the stomach. She is temporarily rendered speechless.*

Reading Strategy **4**

Analyze Historical Context Answer: *Proctor draws attention to the inequity of always believing the accuser. Miller highlights the 1950s failure to uphold the "innocent until proven guilty" concept.*

English Learners

DIFFERENTIATED INSTRUCTION

Advanced Students may have noticed examples of figurative expressions in John Proctor's dialogue earlier in this act—for example, when he says to Elizabeth, "an everlasting funeral marches round your heart" and "Oh, Elizabeth, your charity would freeze beer."

Have students identify and explain examples of his figurative language on this page. (simile: "as clean as God's fingers"; metaphor: "these little crazy children are jangling the keys to the kingdom"; personification: "vengeance is walking Salem")

Teach

Literary Element | 1

Stage Directions Answer:
Although Elizabeth displays courage in denying her fear, the stage directions indicate that she fears she will never return to her home.

Literary Element | 2

Stage Directions Answer:
Hale suggests that a wrathful God is punishing Salem for some "abomination" that has occurred there. Proctor fears that his illicit affair with Abigail may be the "cause" that Hale is looking for.

(ENGLISH LEARNERS) Ask students to clarify the meaning of *reached* in this context: "affected by."

PROCTOR. I will fall like an ocean on that court! Fear nothing, Elizabeth.

ELIZABETH. [*With great fear.*] I will fear nothing. [*She looks about the room, as though to fix it in her mind.*] Tell the children I have gone to visit someone sick.

[*She walks out the door,* HERRICK *and* CHEEVER *behind her. For a moment,* PROCTOR *watches from the doorway. The clank of chain is heard.*]

PROCTOR. Herrick! Herrick, don't chain her! [*He rushes out the door. From outside.*] Damn you, man, you will not chain her! Off with them! I'll not have it! I will not have her chained!

[*There are other men's voices against his.* HALE, *in a fever of guilt and uncertainty, turns from the door to avoid the sight;* MARY WARREN *bursts into tears and sits weeping.* GILES COREY *calls to* HALE.]

GILES. And yet silent, minister? It is fraud, you know it is fraud! What keeps you, man?

[PROCTOR *is half braced, half pushed into the room by two deputies and* HERRICK.]

PROCTOR. I'll pay you, Herrick, I will surely pay you!

HERRICK. [*Panting.*] In God's name, John, I cannot help myself. I must chain them all. Now let you keep inside this house till I am gone! [*He goes out with his deputies.*]

[PROCTOR *stands there, gulping air. Horses and a wagon creaking are heard.*]

HALE. [*In great uncertainty.*] Mr. Proctor—

PROCTOR. Out of my sight!

HALE. Charity, Proctor, charity. What I have heard in her favor, I will not fear to testify in court. God help me, I cannot judge her guilty or innocent—I know not. Only this consider: the world goes mad, and it profit nothing you should lay the cause to the vengeance of a little girl.

PROCTOR. You are a coward! Though you be ordained in God's own tears, you are a coward now!

HALE. Proctor, I cannot think God be provoked so grandly by such a petty cause. The jails are packed—our greatest judges sit in Salem now—and hangin's promised. Man, we must look to cause proportionate. Were there murder done, perhaps, and never brought to light? Abomination? Some secret blasphemy[16] that stinks to Heaven? Think on cause, man, and let you help me to discover it. For there's your way, believe it, there is your only way, when such confusion strikes upon the world. [*He goes to* GILES *and* FRANCIS.] Let you counsel among yourselves; think on your village and what may have drawn from heaven such thundering wrath upon you all. I shall pray God open up our eyes.

[HALE *goes out.*]

FRANCIS. [*Struck by* HALE'S *mood.*] I never heard no murder done in Salem.

PROCTOR. [*He has been reached by* HALE'S *words.*] Leave me, Francis, leave me.

GILES. [*Shaken.*] John—tell me, are we lost?

PROCTOR. Go home now, Giles. We'll speak on it tomorrow.

GILES. Let you think on it. We'll come early, eh?

PROCTOR. Aye. Go now, Giles.

GILES. Good night, then.

[GILES COREY *goes out. After a moment.*]

MARY WARREN. [*In a fearful squeak of a voice.*] Mr. Proctor, very likely they'll let her come home once they're given proper evidence.

PROCTOR. You're coming to the court with me, Mary. You will tell it in the court.

MARY WARREN. I cannot charge murder on Abigail.

PROCTOR. [*Moving menacingly toward her.*] You will tell the court how that poppet come here and who stuck the needle in.

---

16. *Blasphemy* is an act or expression showing contempt for God or anything sacred.

---

1 **Stage Directions** *How do the stage directions contradict Elizabeth's statement?*

Stage Directions *Why is Proctor "reached" by Hale's words?* 2

Grammar Practice

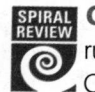

SPIRAL REVIEW Capitalization Review these rules:

Capitalize
- the first word of a sentence
- the first word of a direct quotation (The man said, "Hello.")
- a title attached to a name (Reverend Parris)
- parents names' used as names (Where is Dad, where is my dad)
- names of organizations or government bodies (Supreme Court, she went to court)

Tell students to write a review of Act Two, capitalizing correctly. Have partners exchange papers and proofread.

Man's Heart,
John Ritter.

MARY WARREN. She'll kill me for sayin' that! [*PROCTOR continues toward her.*] Abby'll charge lechery[17] on you, Mr. Proctor!

PROCTOR. [*Halting.*] She's told you!

MARY WARREN. I have known it, sir. She'll ruin you with it, I know she will.

PROCTOR. [*Hesitating, and with deep hatred of himself.*] Good. Then her saintliness is done with. [*MARY backs from him.*] We will slide together into our pit; you will tell the court what you know.

MARY WARREN. [*In terror.*] I cannot, they'll turn on me—

[*PROCTOR strides and catches her, and she is repeating, "I cannot, I cannot!"*]

---

17. *Lechery* means "excessive indulgence of sexual desire." In Salem, this was sinful and, therefore, illegal.

3 Analyze Historical Content *How do these words link Proctor's private and public guilt? Explain.*

PROCTOR. My wife will never die for me! I will bring your guts into your mouth but that goodness will not die for me!

MARY WARREN. [*Struggling to escape him.*] I cannot do it, I cannot!

PROCTOR. [*Grasping her by the throat as though he would strangle her.*] Make your peace with it! Now Hell and Heaven grapple on our backs, and all our old pretense is ripped away—make your peace! [*He throws her to the floor, where she sobs, "I cannot, I cannot . . ." And now, half to himself, staring, and turning to the open door.*] Peace. It is a providence, and no great change; we are only what we always were, but naked now. [*He walks as though toward a great horror, facing the open sky.*] Aye, naked! And the wind, God's icy wind, will blow!

[*And she is over and over again sobbing, "I cannot, I cannot, I cannot . . ."*]

THE CURTAIN FALLS

4

After You Read

Assess

1. Students' answers will vary.
2. (a) His adultery would be revealed. (b) His moral superiority is a façade.
3. (a) The girls' accusations (b) Mary Warren, Hale, and Cheever think this evidence is valid; John and Elizabeth, Giles Corey, and Francis Nurse do not. (c) Those easily led or with something to gain, accept; those who remain rational do not.
4. (a) Looking into accusations against Elizabeth (b) Uncertain; believes Proctors are innocent, but the court is doing God's work
5. (a) Abigail and her friends are manipulating public and court opinion for revenge. (b) Students should support their opinions.
6. (a) Church attendance and if they know the Commandments (b) Irrelevant and narrow-minded
7. (a) John knows his opinions may get his family in trouble. Elizabeth bravely tells the truth. (b) John because he is cautious; Elizabeth because she is honest
8. (a) Fear negatively affects behavior. (b) Students should give examples of how fear affects decisions today.

Literary Element

1. John's actions betray diffidence toward Elizabeth.
2. They show violent feelings.

Progress Check

Can students analyze stage directions?

If No → See Unit 6 Teaching Resources Book, p. 232.

1072

After You Read

Respond and Think Critically

Respond and Interpret

1. What event in Act Two surprised you the most? Explain.

2. (a) Why might Proctor have previously hesitated to tell the members of the court what Abigail told him about witchcraft? (b) What does this hesitation suggest about his character?

3. (a) What does the court accept as evidence that someone is a witch? (b) Which characters seem to consider this evidence valid, and which do not? (c) What do you think accounts for their differences of opinion?

4. (a) Why does Hale come to the Proctors' house? (b) How does Hale seem to feel about his own judgment and the court's? Explain.

Analyze and Evaluate

5. (a) Analyze how events in Salem have spiraled out of control between Acts One and Two. (b) Do you find this situation believable? Explain.

6. (a) What questions does Hale ask the Proctors in order to test their virtue? (b) Do his methods strike you as reasonable and justified? Explain.

7. (a) How does John Proctor's behavior compare with that of his wife? (b) Which character do you think behaves more wisely? Explain.

Connect

8. **Big Idea** The United States and the World (a) How does fear influence the way people behave in Act Two? (b) Give an example from your own experience or from current events of how fear can affect a person's ability to make sound decisions.

Literary Element Stage Directions

Stage directions can be particularly useful to the reader as well as to the actors. They help the reader imagine the action.

1. What do you learn about the characters' actions from the stage directions at the start of Act Two?

2. How do the stage directions for Proctor's last speech help you imagine the delivery?

Reading Strategy Analyze Historical Context

By setting a story in a different historical period, playwrights can often comment on events of their own era. Which ideas can you connect to the Un-American Activities trials of the 1950s?

LOG ON ▶ **Literature** Online

Selection Resources For Selection Quizzes, eFlash-cards, and Reading-Writing Connection activities, go to glencoe.com and enter QuickPass code GLA9800u6.

Vocabulary Practice

Practice with Analogies Find the vocabulary word that best completes each analogy.

1. reprimand : scold :: flee : _____
   a. approach   b. escape   c. lecture
2. base : noble :: polite : _____
   a. stupid   b. mannerly   c. rude
3. covet : possession :: celebrate : _____
   a. victory   b. grief   c. weekend
4. ameliorate : complicate :: hasten : _____
   a. quicken   b. delay   c. progress
5. ineptly : inexperience :: calmly : _____
   a. confidence   b. intelligence c. age

Writing

Write Stage Directions Stage directions can help both actors and readers bring a scene to life. Pick a section from Act Two that lacks stage directions and write your own. Explain your choices.

Writing

Use the following criteria to evaluate students' stage directions:

- Are the stage directions written for a section of the act that does not include stage directions?
- Do the stage directions maintain Miller's characterization?

Reading Strategy

Characters (like Hale) who have gained sudden power might be similar to Communist investigators, and those who have been accused (like Elizabeth) might be similar to those who were on trial in the 1950s.

Vocabulary

1. b 2. c 3. a 4. b 5. a

Before You Read

The Crucible, Act Three

Build Background

The Crucible deals with the tragic combination of mass hysteria and social and political repression. "I can almost tell what the political situation in a country is when the play is suddenly a hit there," Miller wrote, "—it is either a warning of tyranny on the way or a reminder of tyranny just past."

Set Purposes for Reading

Literary Element Plot

Plot refers to the sequence of events in a short story, novel, or drama. Most plots develop around a **conflict,** or struggle between opposing forces. An **external conflict** is a struggle between a character and an outside force, such as another character, society, nature, or fate. An **internal conflict** takes place within a character who struggles with opposing feelings.

The plot begins with **exposition,** or introduction to characters, setting, and situation. The **rising action** adds complications to the conflict, leading to the **climax,** or point of highest emotional pitch. **Falling action** is the logical result of the climax, and the denouement, or **resolution,** presents the final outcome.

As you read, ask yourself, How does Miller intensify the conflicts he introduced in the previous two acts?

Reading Strategy Evaluate Argument

Argument depends on logic, reasoning, and evidence. The authorities and individual characters in *The Crucible* often cite reasons for acting and thinking as they do. It is up to the reader to form an opinion about—or evaluate—these arguments.

Tip: Take Notes As you read, use a chart similar to the one below to record faulty logic, questionable arguments, or flawed evidence. Write your evaluations in the right-hand column.

Example	Evaluation
p. 1075 Giles thinks his wife is arrested for reading books.	Probably true. Puritans were suspicious of all reading material except the Bible.

Vocabulary

vile (vīl) *adj.* evil; foul; repulsive; degrading; p. 1077 *A vile crime must be punished.*

immaculate (i mak´ yə lit) *adj.* unblemished; flawless; pure; p. 1083 *Our tenants left the house in immaculate condition.*

perjury (pər´ jə rē) *n.* the act of swearing under oath to the truth of something that one knows to be untrue; p. 1084 *The witness committed perjury during the trial.*

contemplation (kon´ təm plā´ shən) *n.* the act of thinking about something long and seriously; p. 1086 *Our cabin in the woods is great for contemplation.*

unperturbed (un pər turbd´) *adj.* undisturbed; calm; p. 1092 *Unperturbed by his seemingly stressful day, John slept soundly.*

Before You Read

Focus

Summary, Act Three

Proctor, Nurse, and Corey try to win their wives' release. Mary Warren tells Judge Danforth the accusations are false. Realizing that Danforth is being swayed, Abigail accuses Mary. Proctor reveals his affair with Abigail. Elizabeth Proctor lies to protect John. Mary accuses Proctor of bewitching her. Proctor denounces Danforth and the court and is arrested for witchcraft.

Vocabulary

Prefixes Remind students that knowing the meaning of prefixes can help them unlock the meaning of words. **Ask:** Which words in this vocabulary list include a prefix that means "not"? (*immaculate, unperturbed*) Point out that in addition to the prefixes *im-* and *un-*, there are other prefixes that mean "not," such as *non-* and *ir-*. **Ask:** What are some examples of words that use these "not" prefixes? (*nonprofit, irregular*)

Selection Skills

Literary Elements
- Plot (SE pp. 1073–1095)

Reading Skills
- Evaluate Argument (SE pp. 1073–1095)
- Make Inferences About Characters (TE p. 1078)
- Dramatic Irony (TE p. 1080)
- Irony (TE p. 1088)

The Crucible, Act Three

Vocabulary Skills
- Context Clues (SE p. 1095)

Writing Skills/Grammar
- Write a Summary (SE p. 1095)
- Inverted Sentences (TE p. 1082)
- Diary (TE p. 1092)

Listening/Speaking/Viewing Skills
- Analyze Art (SE pp. 1081, 1089)
- Dramatic Reading (TE p. 1084)

Teach

Reading Strategy

Make Inferences Ask: What was Martha Corey accused of in Act Two? *(Walcott accused her of bewitching him so that he cannot keep a pig alive for more than four weeks [p. 1065].)* **Ask:** What can you infer from the change in the charge? *(The charges are now much more serious, a sign that the hysteria is growing and the court is threatening the citizens of Salem.)*

Reading Strategy 1

Evaluate Argument
Answer: *The argument "If you don't know what a witch is, then how do you know you're not one?" is an example of faulty logic because it is impossible to prove a negative.*

Literary Element 2

Plot Answer: *He is in conflict with the anti-witchcraft zealots who have seized his wife.*

 For activities related to this selection, see Unit 6 Teaching Resources Book, pp. 239–251.

Speaking Practice

SMALL GROUP
Dialogue Point out the dash during Giles's comment in the right column and then during Parris's comment at the top of page 1075.
Ask: What effect do the dashes create in this dialogue? *(The interruptions help convey the characters' growing agitation and anger with one another. They suggest an atmosphere of chaos and confusion.)* To have students experience the precise timing actors must use when

they interrupt, have them work in small groups to rehearse and perform a few pages from the beginning of this act. Encourage them to pay particular attention to Miller's use of dashes to control the pacing of the dialogue.

[*The vestry room of the Salem meeting house, now serving as the anteroom¹ of the General Court. As the curtain rises, the room is empty, but for sunlight pouring through two high windows in the back wall. The room is solemn, even forbidding. Heavy beams jut out, boards of random widths make up the walls. At the right are two doors leading into the meeting house proper, where the court is being held. At the left another door leads outside. There is a plain bench at the left, and another at the right. In the center a rather long meeting table, with stools and a considerable armchair snugged up to it.*
Through the partitioning wall at the right we hear a prosecutor's voice, JUDGE HATHORNE's, asking a question; then a woman's voice, MARTHA COREY's, replying.]

HATHORNE'S VOICE. Now, Martha Corey, there is abundant evidence in our hands to show that you have given yourself to the reading of fortunes. Do you deny it?

MARTHA COREY'S VOICE. I am innocent to a witch. I know not what a witch is.

HATHORNE'S VOICE. How do you know, then, that you are not a witch?

MARTHA COREY'S VOICE. If I were, I would know it.

HATHORNE'S VOICE. Why do you hurt these children?

MARTHA COREY'S VOICE. I do not hurt them. I scorn it!

GILES' VOICE. [*Roaring.*] I have evidence for the court!

[*Voices of townspeople rise in excitement.*]

DANFORTH'S VOICE. You will keep your seat!

---

1. The *meeting house* was both a community hall and the house of worship. Its *vestry* was an *anteroom*, or small outer room, that served as a waiting area and entrance to the main room.

1 **Evaluate Argument** *How is this question typical of the prosecution's faulty logic throughout the play?*

GILES' VOICE. Thomas Putnam is reaching out for land!

DANFORTH'S VOICE. Remove that man, Marshal!

GILES' VOICE. You're hearing lies, lies!

[*A roaring goes up from the people.*]

HATHORNE'S VOICE. Arrest him, excellency!

GILES' VOICE. I have evidence. Why will you not hear my evidence?

[*The door opens and GILES is half carried into the vestry room by HERRICK.*]

GILES. Hands off, damn you, let me go!

HERRICK. Giles, Giles!

GILES. Out of my way, Herrick! I bring evidence—

HERRICK. You cannot go in there, Giles; it's a court!

[*Enter HALE from the court.*]

HALE. Pray be calm a moment.

GILES. You, Mr. Hale, go in there and demand I speak.

HALE. A moment, sir, a moment.

GILES. They'll be hangin' my wife!

[*JUDGE HATHORNE enters. He is in his sixties, a bitter, remorseless Salem judge.*]

HATHORNE. How do you dare come roarin' into this court! Are you gone daft, Corey?

GILES. You're not a Boston judge yet, Hathorne. You'll not call me daft!

[*Enter DEPUTY GOVERNOR DANFORTH and, behind him, EZEKIEL CHEEVER and PARRIS. On his appearance, silence falls. DANFORTH is a grave man in his sixties, of some humor and sophistication that does not, however, interfere with an exact loyalty to his position and his cause. He comes down to GILES, who awaits his wrath.*]

Plot *Giles is in physical conflict here with Herrick. What is the larger conflict in which he is involved?* **2**

DANFORTH. [*Looking directly at* GILES.] Who is this man?

PARRIS. Giles Corey, sir, and a more contentious—

GILES. [*To* PARRIS.] I am asked the question, and I am old enough to answer it! [*To* DANFORTH, *who impresses him and to whom he smiles through his strain.*] My name is Corey, sir, Giles Corey. I have six hundred acres, and timber in addition. It is my wife you be condemning now. [*He indicates the courtroom.*]

DANFORTH. And how do you imagine to help her cause with such contemptuous riot? Now be gone. Your old age alone keeps you out of jail for this.

GILES. [*Beginning to plead.*] They be tellin' lies about my wife, sir, I—

DANFORTH. Do you take it upon yourself to determine what this court shall believe and what it shall set aside?

GILES. Your Excellency, we mean no disrespect for—

DANFORTH. Disrespect indeed! It is disruption, Mister. This is the highest court of the supreme government of this province, do you know it?

GILES. [*Beginning to weep.*] Your Excellency, I only said she were readin' books, sir, and they come and take her out of my house for—

DANFORTH. [*Mystified.*] Books! What books?

GILES. [*Through helpless sobs.*] It is my third wife, sir; I never had no wife that be so taken with books, and I thought to find the cause of it, d'y'see, but it were no witch I blamed her for. [*He is openly weeping.*] I have broke charity with the woman, I have broke charity with her. [*He covers his face, ashamed.* DANFORTH *is respectfully silent.*]

HALE. Excellency, he claims hard evidence for his wife's defense. I think that in all justice you must—

3

4 The United States and the World *What connection might Miller's audiences have made between this statement and the McCarthy hearings?*

DANFORTH. Then let him submit his evidence in proper affidavit.[2] You are certainly aware of our procedure here, Mr. Hale. [*To* HERRICK.] Clear this room.

HERRICK. Come now, Giles. [*He gently pushes* COREY *out.*]

FRANCIS. We are desperate, sir; we come here three days now and cannot be heard.

DANFORTH. Who is this man?

FRANCIS. Francis Nurse, Your Excellency.

HALE. His wife's Rebecca that were condemned this morning.

DANFORTH. Indeed! I am amazed to find you in such uproar. I have only good report of your character, Mr. Nurse.

HATHORNE. I think they must both be arrested in contempt, sir.

DANFORTH. [*To* FRANCIS.] Let you write your plea, and in due time I will—

FRANCIS. Excellency, we have proof for your eyes; God forbid you shut them to it. The girls, sir, the girls are frauds.

DANFORTH. What's that?

FRANCIS. We have proof of it, sir. They are all deceiving you.

[DANFORTH *is shocked, but studying* FRANCIS.]

HATHORNE. This is contempt, sir, contempt!

DANFORTH. Peace, Judge Hathorne. Do you know who I am, Mr. Nurse?

FRANCIS. I surely do, sir, and I think you must be a wise judge to be what you are.

DANFORTH. And do you know that near to four hundred are in the jails from Marblehead to Lynn, and upon my signature?

FRANCIS. I—

DANFORTH. And seventy-two condemned to hang by that signature?

---

2. An *affidavit* is a written declaration sworn to be true, usually before a judge.

Evaluate Argument *How would you evaluate this claim by Hathorne?* **5**

ARTHUR MILLER **1075**

Teach

Reading Strategy | 3

Interpret Ask: What does "broke charity" mean? *(In this context, it means "betrayed" or "not respected a bond.")*

Big Idea | 4

The United States and the World Answer: *Audiences knew Senator McCarthy's hearings had also been authorized by the U.S. government. Audiences could infer that official approval did not make the Salem witch trials fair.*

Reading Strategy | 5

Evaluate Argument Answer: *Hathorne is quick to condemn Francis Nurse's claim of evidence without seeing it, but he accepts without question the girls' hysterical "evidence."*

(ENGLISH LEARNERS) Make sure English learners understand what *contempt* means in the legal context. Have them look up the word in a dictionary and read the definitions. **Ask:** What does "contempt of court" or "being in contempt" mean? *(showing disrespect for the authority of a judge)* Explain that a person can be arrested and jailed for being in contempt.

For an audio recording of this selection, use Listening Library Audio CD-ROM.

English Learners

DIFFERENTIATED INSTRUCTION

Intermediate English learners may be confused by the expression "broke charity." Explain that it is an old-fashioned expression based on a definition of *charity* that is not often used today. **Ask:** What does *charity* usually mean? *(money or help given to someone in need)* Tell students that for the Puritans, *charity* was a religious concept that meant "the love of God for humanity" and "the love of one's fellow human beings." Thus "to break charity" with someone is to break the loving bond between you and that person. Students should see that Giles's betrayal was unintentional.

Teach

Reading Strategy | **1**

Evaluate Argument
Answer: *Proctor has regained his self-control. He realizes that he must act gently toward Mary because he needs her help in presenting his evidence to the court.*

Literary Element | **2**

Plot Answer: *Parris and Hale were allied in their investigation of witchcraft. Now Hale is increasingly skeptical and cautious, while Parris still supports the trials.*

The Crucible, 1996.

FRANCIS. Excellency, I never thought to say it to such a weighty judge, but you are deceived.

[*Enter* GILES COREY *from left. All turn to see as he beckons in* MARY WARREN *with* PROCTOR. MARY *is keeping her eyes to the ground;* PROCTOR *has her elbow as though she were near collapse.*]

PARRIS. [*On seeing her, in shock.*] Mary Warren! [*He goes directly to bend close to her face.*] What are you about here?

PROCTOR. [*Pressing* PARRIS *away from her with a gentle but firm motion of protectiveness.*] She would speak with the Deputy Governor.

DANFORTH. [*Shocked by this, turns to* HERRICK.] Did you not tell me Mary Warren were sick in bed?

HERRICK. She were, Your Honor. When I go to fetch her to the court last week, she said she were sick.

GILES. She has been strivin' with her soul all week, Your Honor; she comes now to tell the truth of this to you.

DANFORTH. Who is this?

PROCTOR. John Proctor, sir. Elizabeth Proctor is my wife.

PARRIS. Beware this man, Your Excellency, this man is mischief.

HALE. [*Excitedly.*] I think you must hear the girl, sir, she—

DANFORTH. [*Who has become very interested in* MARY WARREN *and only raises a hand toward*

---

1 Evaluate Argument *The last time we saw Proctor he was violently attacking Mary. Do you think his change in attitude is inconsistent?*

Plot *How does this open disagreement between Parris and Hale represent a new conflict in the play?* **2**

1076 UNIT 6 FROM DEPRESSION TO COLD WAR

Research Practice

Evaluate Evidence On this page, the judge is deciding which evidence he will admit. Ask students to compare the judge's decision making here with the operation of a court in the United States today. Have them research the types of evidence that are admissible in a U.S. court of law. They should use their research to write compare-and-contrast paragraphs describing authoritative evidence in the Salem witch trials and acceptable evidence in today's courts.

HALE.] Peace. What would you tell us, Mary Warren?

[PROCTOR *looks at her, but she cannot speak.*]

PROCTOR. She never saw no spirits, sir.

DANFORTH. [*With great alarm and surprise, to* MARY.] Never saw no spirits!

GILES. [*Eagerly.*] Never.

PROCTOR. [*Reaching into his jacket.*] She has signed a deposition,[3] sir—

DANFORTH. [*Instantly.*] No, no, I accept no depositions. [*He is rapidly calculating this; he turns from her to* PROCTOR.] Tell me, Mr. Proctor, have you given out this story in the village?

PROCTOR. We have not.

PARRIS. They've come to overthrow the court, sir! This man is—

DANFORTH. I pray you, Mr. Parris. Do you know, Mr. Proctor, that the entire contention of the state in these trials is that the voice of Heaven is speaking through the children?

PROCTOR. I know that, sir.

DANFORTH. [*Thinks, staring at* PROCTOR, *then turns to* MARY WARREN.] And you, Mary Warren, how came you to cry out people for sending their spirits against you?

MARY WARREN. It were pretense, sir.

DANFORTH. I cannot hear you.

PROCTOR. It were pretense, she says.

DANFORTH. Ah? And the other girls? Susanna Walcott, and—the others? They are also pretending?

MARY WARREN. Aye, sir.

DANFORTH. [*Wide-eyed.*] Indeed. [*Pause. He is baffled by this. He turns to study* PROCTOR's *face.*]

---

3. A *deposition* is a sworn, written statement given by a witness out of court and intended to be used as testimony in court.

4 The United States and the World *How might this idea relate to the McCarthy "witch hunts" of the 1950s?*

PARRIS. [*In a sweat.*] Excellency, you surely cannot think to let so **vile** a lie be spread in open court!

DANFORTH. Indeed not, but it strike hard upon me that she will dare come here with such a tale. Now, Mr. Proctor, before I decide whether I shall hear you or not, it is my duty to tell you this. We burn a hot fire here; it melts down all concealment.

PROCTOR. I know that, sir.

DANFORTH. Let me continue. I understand well, a husband's tenderness may drive him to extravagance in defense of a wife. Are you certain in your conscience, Mister, that your evidence is the truth?

PROCTOR. It is. And you will surely know it.

DANFORTH. And you thought to declare this revelation in the open court before the public?

PROCTOR. I thought I would, aye—with your permission.

DANFORTH. [*His eyes narrowing.*] Now, sir, what is your purpose in so doing?

PROCTOR. Why, I—I would free my wife, sir.

DANFORTH. There lurks nowhere in your heart, nor hidden in your spirit, any desire to undermine this court?

PROCTOR. [*With the faintest faltering.*] Why, no, sir.

CHEEVER. [*Clears his throat, awakening.*] I—Your Excellency.

DANFORTH. Mr. Cheever.

CHEEVER. I think it be my duty, sir—[*Kindly, to* PROCTOR.] You'll not deny it, John. [*To* DANFORTH.] When we come to take his wife, he damned the court and ripped your warrant. **5**

PARRIS. Now you have it!

DANFORTH. He did that, Mr. Hale?

HALE. [*Takes a breath.*] Aye, he did.

Evaluate Argument *What assumption are Danforth and Parris both making? How would you assess it?* **6**

Vocabulary

vile (vīl) *adj.* evil; foul; repulsive; degrading

ARTHUR MILLER **1077**

Teach

Literary Element **3**

Characterization **Say:**
Look at the phrase "is rapidly calculating this." **Ask:** How do Danforth's next words reinforce his calculating nature? *(His words suggest that if the residents have not yet heard Mary's deposition he may be able to prevent them from hearing it altogether.)*

Big Idea **4**

The United States and the World **Answer:** *A common phrase during the Cold War was "Godless Communism." Like Danforth, Senator McCarthy believed that the government had God on its side.*

Reading Strategy **5**

Reread Ask students to review the end of Act Two to find what Cheever overlooks as he reports Proctor's earlier behavior. *(Cheever provoked Proctor into tearing the warrant and damning Danforth.)*

Reading Strategy **6**

Evaluate Argument
Answer: *They assume Mary Warren is lying. This is another example of bias on the part of the investigators.*

Teach

Evaluate Argument
Answer: *In blindly accepting the girls' bizarre evidence of demonic activity, Danforth has, in fact, passed judgment on those accused of witchcraft.*

[APPROACHING] **Ask:** What does Danforth's use of the word *marvels* suggest? *(It suggests that Danforth believes that he has seen evidence of supernatural witchcraft rather than mere "pretense," or pretending.)*

Literary Element 2

Plot Answer: *Proctor has been on the defensive throughout the play. Tension mounts with each accusation, intensifying the conflict between Proctor and the witch hunters.*

[APPROACHING] Draw a simple plot diagram on the board (see p. 1022 for a sample diagram).
Ask: What occurs during the rising action? *(Complications develop, and the conflict intensifies until it reaches a climax.)*

PROCTOR. It were a temper, sir. I knew not what I did.

DANFORTH. [*Studying him.*] Mr. Proctor.

PROCTOR. Aye, sir.

DANFORTH. [*Straight into his eyes.*] Have you ever seen the Devil?

PROCTOR. No, sir.

DANFORTH. You are in all respects a Gospel Christian?

PROCTOR. I am, sir.

PARRIS. Such a Christian that will not come to church but once in a month!

DANFORTH. [*Restrained—he is curious.*] Not come to church?

PROCTOR. I—I have no love for Mr. Parris. It is no secret. But God I surely love.

CHEEVER. He plow on Sunday, sir.

DANFORTH. Plow on Sunday!

CHEEVER. [*Apologetically.*] I think it be evidence, John. I am an official of the court, I cannot keep it.

PROCTOR. I—I have once or twice plowed on Sunday. I have three children, sir, and until last year my land give little.

GILES. You'll find other Christians that do plow on Sunday if the truth be known.

HALE. Your Honor, I cannot think you may judge the man on such evidence.

DANFORTH. I judge nothing. [*Pause. He keeps watching* PROCTOR, *who tries to meet his gaze.*] I tell you straight, Mister—I have seen marvels in this court. I have seen people choked before my eyes by spirits; I have seen them stuck by pins and slashed by daggers. I have until this moment not the slightest reason to suspect that the children may be deceiving me. Do you understand my meaning?

PROCTOR. Excellency, does it not strike upon you that so many of these women have lived so long with such upright reputation, and—

PARRIS. Do you read the Gospel, Mr. Proctor?

PROCTOR. I read the Gospel.

PARRIS. I think not, or you should surely know that Cain were an upright man, and yet he did kill Abel.[4]

PROCTOR. Aye, God tells us that. [*To* DANFORTH.] But who tells us Rebecca Nurse murdered seven babies by sending out her spirit on them? It is the children only, and this one will swear she lied to you.

[DANFORTH *considers, then beckons* HATHORNE *to him.* HATHORNE *leans in, and he speaks in his ear.* HATHORNE *nods.*]

HATHORNE. Aye, she's the one.

DANFORTH. Mr. Proctor, this morning, your wife send me a claim in which she states that she is pregnant now.

PROCTOR. My wife pregnant!

DANFORTH. There be no sign of it—we have examined her body.

PROCTOR. But if she say she is pregnant, then she must be! That woman will never lie, Mr. Danforth.

DANFORTH. She will not?

PROCTOR. Never, sir, never.

DANFORTH. We have thought it too convenient to be credited. However, if I should tell you now that I will let her be kept another month; and if she begin to show her natural signs, you shall have her living yet another year until she is delivered—what say you to that? [JOHN PROCTOR *is struck silent.*] Come now. You say your only purpose is to save your wife. Good, then, she is saved at least this year, and a year is long. What say

---

4. According to the Bible, Adam and Eve's son Cain kills his brother Abel, becoming the first murderer.

---

1 Evaluate Argument *How does the rest of Danforth's speech contradict this statement?*

2 Plot *How has the questioning of Proctor contributed to the rising action of the plot?*

Reading Practice

Make Inferences About Characters
Discuss Danforth's response to the news that Elizabeth is pregnant. Remind students that in Act Two we learned that a pregnant woman would not be put to death because "they'll not hurt the innocent child." **Ask:** What deal does Danforth offer Proctor? *(If Proctor drops his charge that the accusers are lying, Danforth will wait a month before* executing Elizabeth to see if her pregnancy starts to show. Then, if she is truly pregnant, she will be safe for another year until the baby is born.) What does Danforth assume about Proctor's character and motivation, or "purpose"? *(Danforth assumes that Proctor will be willing to abandon his friends to save his wife for a year. He assumes that Proctor's motivation is simply to save his wife,* not to uphold the truth or save the lives of others.) What can you infer about Danforth's character based on the deal he offers Proctor? *(Danforth is manipulative and uninterested in the truth.)*

you, sir? It is done now. [*In conflict,* PROCTOR *glances at* FRANCIS *and* GILES.] Will you drop this charge?

PROCTOR. I—I think I cannot.

DANFORTH. [*Now an almost imperceptible hardness in his voice.*] Then your purpose is somewhat larger.

PARRIS. He's come to overthrow this court, Your Honor!

PROCTOR. These are my friends. Their wives are also accused—

DANFORTH. [*With a sudden briskness of manner.*] I judge you not, sir. I am ready to hear your evidence.

PROCTOR. I come not to hurt the court; I only—

DANFORTH. [*Cutting him off.*] Marshal, go into the court and bid Judge Stoughton and Judge Sewall declare recess for one hour. And let them go to the tavern, if they will. All witnesses and prisoners are to be kept in the building.

HERRICK. Aye, sir. [*Very deferentially.*] If I may say it, sir, I know this man all my life. It is a good man, sir.

DANFORTH. [*It is the reflection on himself he resents.*] I am sure of it, Marshal. [HERRICK *nods, then goes out.*] Now, what deposition do you have for us, Mr. Proctor? And I beg you be clear, open as the sky, and honest.

PROCTOR. [*As he takes out several papers.*] I am no lawyer, so I'll—

DANFORTH. The pure in heart need no lawyers. Proceed as you will.

PROCTOR. [*Handing* DANFORTH *a paper.*] Will you read this first, sir? It's a sort of testament.[5] The people signing it declare their good opinion of Rebecca, and my wife, and Martha Corey. [DAN-FORTH *looks down at the paper.*]

---

5. Here, the *testament* is a statement of beliefs or opinions offered as evidence of the truth.

3 Plot *What conflict is referred to in this stage direction?*

4 Evaluate Argument *What rings false about Danforth's remark?*

PARRIS. [*To enlist* DANFORTH's *sarcasm.*] Their good opinion! [*But* DANFORTH *goes on reading, and* PROCTOR *is heartened.*]

PROCTOR. These are all landholding farmers, members of the church. [*Delicately, trying to point out a paragraph.*] If you'll notice, sir—they've known the women many years and never saw no sign they had dealings with the Devil.

[PARRIS *nervously moves over and reads over* DANFORTH's *shoulder.*]

DANFORTH. [*Glancing down a long list.*] How many names are here?

FRANCIS. Ninety-one, Your Excellency.

PARRIS. [*Sweating.*] These people should be summoned. [DANFORTH *looks up at him questioningly.*] For questioning.

FRANCIS. [*Trembling with anger.*] Mr. Danforth, I gave them all my word no harm would come to them for signing this.

PARRIS. This is a clear attack upon the court!

HALE. [*To* PARRIS, *trying to contain himself.*] Is every defense an attack upon the court? Can no one—?

PARRIS. All innocent and Christian people are happy for the courts in Salem! These people are gloomy for it. [*To* DANFORTH *directly.*] And I think you will want to know, from each and every one of them, what discontents them with you!

HATHORNE. I think they ought to be examined, sir.

DANFORTH. It is not necessarily an attack, I think. Yet—

FRANCIS. These are all covenanted Christians, sir.

DANFORTH. Then I am sure they may have nothing to fear. [*Hands* CHEEVER *the paper.*] Mr. Cheever, have warrants drawn for all of these—arrest for examination. [*To* PROCTOR.] Now,

---

Evaluate Argument *How is Parris twisting the argument in order to win Danforth to his side?* **5**

The United States and the World *What connection do you see between Danforth's tactics and the tactics of Senator McCarthy?* **6**

ARTHUR MILLER **1079**

Teach

| Literary Element | 3 |

Plot **Answer:** *Proctor is briefly tempted to abandon Francis and Giles to buy his wife one more year of life.*

| Reading Strategy | 4 |

Evaluate Argument **Answer:** *Danforth implies that God will protect the pure of heart, yet the pure of heart are the people in prison.*

| Reading Strategy | 5 |

Evaluate Argument **Answer:** *Parris is suggesting that those who signed the deposition are attacking the court and, by extension, Danforth.*

| Big Idea | 6 |

The United States and the World **Answer:** *Those who tried to defend the people whom McCarthy accused were themselves accused.*

English Learners

DIFFERENTIATED INSTRUCTION

 Intermediate English learners may be unfamiliar with some of the vocabulary and idioms used in the stage directions on this spread. Have student pairs look up these words and phrases in a dictionary and then record the definitions: *beckons, struck silent, imperceptible, briskness, deferentially, reflection on himself, enlist, sarcasm, heartened, glancing.*

Advanced If necessary, have students look up the words and phrases in the Intermediate activity. Then have volunteers act out some of the dialogue and actions these stage directions describe. Begin by modeling *beckons* in the first stage direction on the previous page. Then **ask:** How should Proctor act when he is "struck silent"? How would Danforth sound if he has "an almost impercep-

tible hardness in his voice"? How might Herrick say his lines "very deferentially"? What tone of voice could Proctor use to sound "heartened"?

1079

Teach

Reading Strategy 1

Evaluate Argument

Answer: *Danforth is using an either/or fallacy. The truth often lies somewhere between two opposites.*

(APPROACHING) Explain that a *logical fallacy* is an error in logic. Brainstorm other examples of the either/or fallacy *(claiming that someone is either all good or all evil).*

Reading Strategy 2

Evaluate Argument

Answer: *Danforth demands that Giles prove his accusation against Putnam. When someone is accused of witchcraft, however, the judge demands proof of innocence from the accused rather than proof of guilt from the accuser.*

(ENGLISH LEARNERS) Make sure students understand that in the legal system, a person accused of a crime is "innocent until proven guilty." Discuss why this concept is a crucial legal protection.

Mister, what other information do you have for us? [*FRANCIS is still standing, horrified.*] You may sit, Mr. Nurse.

FRANCIS. I have brought trouble on these people; I have—

DANFORTH. No, old man, you have not hurt these people if they are of good conscience. But you must understand, sir, that a person is either with this court or he must be counted against it, there be no road between. This is a sharp time, now, a precise time—we live no longer in the dusky afternoon when evil mixed itself with good and befuddled the world. Now, by God's grace, the shining sun is up, and them that fear not light will surely praise it. I hope you will be one of those. [*MARY WARREN suddenly sobs.*] She's not hearty, I see.

PROCTOR. No, she's not, sir. [*To MARY, bending to her, holding her hand, quietly.*] Now remember what the angel Raphael said to the boy Tobias. Remember it.

MARY WARREN. [*Hardly audible.*] Aye.

PROCTOR. "Do that which is good, and no harm shall come to thee."

MARY WARREN. Aye.

DANFORTH. Come, man, we wait you.

[*MARSHAL HERRICK returns, and takes his post at the door.*]

GILES. John, my deposition, give him mine.

PROCTOR. Aye. [*He hands DANFORTH another paper.*] This is Mr. Corey's deposition.

DANFORTH. Oh? [*He looks down at it. Now HATHORNE comes behind him and reads with him.*]

HATHORNE. [*Suspiciously.*] What lawyer drew this, Corey?

GILES. You know I never hired a lawyer in my life, Hathorne.

DANFORTH. [*Finishing the reading.*] It is very well phrased. My compliments. Mr. Parris, if Mr. Putnam is in the court, will you bring him in? [*HATHORNE takes the deposition, and walks to the*

window with it. *PARRIS goes into the court.*] You have no legal training, Mr. Corey?

GILES. [*Very pleased.*] I have the best, sir—I am thirty-three time in court in my life. And always plaintiff, too.

DANFORTH. Oh, then you're much put-upon.

GILES. I am never put-upon; I know my rights, sir, and I will have them. You know, your father tried a case of mine—might be thirty-five year ago, I think.

DANFORTH. Indeed.

GILES. He never spoke to you of it?

DANFORTH. No, I cannot recall it.

GILES. That's strange, he give me nine pound damages. He were a fair judge, your father. Y'see, I had a white mare that time, and this fellow come to borrow the mare—[*Enter PARRIS with THOMAS PUTNAM. When he sees PUTNAM, GILES' ease goes; he is hard.*] Aye, there he is.

DANFORTH. Mr. Putnam, I have here an accusation by Mr. Corey against you. He states that you coldly prompted your daughter to cry witchery upon George Jacobs that is now in jail.

PUTNAM. It is a lie.

DANFORTH. [*Turning to GILES.*] Mr. Putnam states your charge is a lie. What say you to that?

GILES. [*Furious, his fists clenched.*] A fart on Thomas Putnam, that is what I say to that!

DANFORTH. What proof do you submit for your charge, sir?

GILES. My proof is there! [*Pointing to the paper.*] If Jacobs hangs for a witch he forfeit up his property—that's law! And there is none but Putnam with the coin to buy so great a piece. This man is killing his neighbors for their land!

DANFORTH. But proof, sir, proof.

GILES. [*Pointing at his deposition.*] The proof is there! I have it from an honest man who heard Putnam say it! The day his daughter cried out

---

1 Evaluate Argument *What logical fallacy is Danforth guilty of here?*

2 Evaluate Argument *How is Danforth guilty of using a double standard in this demand?*

1080 UNIT 6 FROM DEPRESSION TO COLD WAR

Reading Practice

SPIRAL REVIEW **Dramatic Irony** In the midst of this serious confrontation between Proctor and Danforth, Miller introduces a bit of comic relief as Giles Corey brags about his knowledge of the law and his past experiences in court. **Ask:** What is Miller's purpose in including this dialogue between Giles and Danforth? *(This comic dialogue reveals Giles to be a silly, harmless* character who is clearly innocent of any wrongdoing. However, the relief is only temporary: Danforth's response to Giles becomes that much more horrible because the audience has been temporarily lulled into thinking that no one could possibly take action against a person like Giles.) Tell students that dramatic irony occurs when the audience or reader realizes something that a character does not. **Ask:** What does the audience realize that Giles does not? *(The audience realizes that Giles's supposed knowledge of the law will not protect him against Danforth.)*

1080

Window View—Scapeology #9, 1995. Nanette Carter. Oil on canvas, 41 x 40 in. Sande Webster Gallery, Philadelphia, PA.

 View the Art Nanette Carter is often referred to as a "visual storyteller." What elements of storytelling do you see in this painting? In what ways might it mirror the events and feelings evident so far in Act Three? Explain.

View the Art ★

Answer: *Students may notice the enclosed boxes in the center of the painting and the movement of lines within those boxes. These images might reflect the trapped feeling of those convicted of witch-craft in Salem.*

Point out that this painting is by the same artist represented on page 1039. Some of Carter's *Scapeology* paintings were part of an African American women's art show titled *Bearing Witness,* organized by Spelman College in the late 1990s.

on Jacobs, he said she'd given him a fair gift of land.

HATHORNE. And the name of this man?

GILES. [*Taken aback.*] What name?

HATHORNE. The man that give you this information.

GILES. [*Hesitates, then.*] Why, I—I cannot give you his name.

HATHORNE. And why not?

ARTHUR MILLER **1081**

English Learners

DIFFERENTIATED INSTRUCTION

Intermediate English learners will need help with some of the words on these pages. Have students look up these words in a dictionary and record the definitions: *befuddled, audible, forfeit, conspiracy, anonymity, prodigious, uncorrupted.* Then discuss the following phrases, explaining that some of them are old-fashioned:

put-upon: "taken advantage of" (usually spelled without the hyphen)

clap me: "put in jail" (old-fashioned)

in confidence: "with the expectation of being kept secret"

blink it: "close one's eyes to something; ignore"

take counsel with yourself: "consider what you should do; literally, give yourself advice" (*take counsel* with another person means "discuss; give or receive advice")

SMALL GROUP

Advanced Go over the phrases in the Intermediate activity. Then have students work in pairs to come up with original sentences for each phrase.

Teach

Big Idea | 1

The United States and the World **Answer:** *During the HUAC hearings, Miller admired those who, like Miller and Giles, responded, "I will give you no name."*

Reading Strategy | 2

Evaluate Argument
Answer: *Danforth concludes that fear of the court is equivalent to guilt. Students should see that people have legitimate reasons to be terrified of the proceedings.*

Language History ☆

Terrible Today, the word *terrible* has a negative connotation. In earlier times, the term suggested a benign power that caused terror and dread. To call Hale's learning or education terrible compliments him. Danforth, however, is probably being sarcastic.

GILES. [*Hesitates, then bursts out.*] You know well why not! He'll lay in jail if I give his name!

HATHORNE. This is contempt of the court, Mr. Danforth!

DANFORTH. [*To avoid that.*] You will surely tell us the name.

GILES. I will not give you no name. I mentioned my wife's name once and I'll burn in hell long enough for that. I stand mute.

DANFORTH. In that case, I have no choice but to arrest you for contempt of this court, do you know that?

GILES. This is a hearing; you cannot clap me for contempt of a hearing.

DANFORTH. Oh, it is a proper lawyer! Do you wish me to declare the court in full session here? Or will you give me good reply?

GILES. [*Faltering.*] I cannot give you no name, sir, I cannot.

DANFORTH. You are a foolish old man. Mr. Cheever, begin the record. The court is now in session. I ask you, Mr. Corey—

PROCTOR. [*Breaking in.*] Your Honor—he has the story in confidence, sir, and he—

PARRIS. The Devil lives on such confidences! [*To DANFORTH.*] Without confidences there could be no conspiracy, Your Honor!

HATHORNE. I think it must be broken, sir.

DANFORTH. [*To GILES.*] Old man, if your informant tells the truth let him come here openly like a decent man. But if he hide in anonymity I must know why. Now sir, the government and central church demand of you the name of him who reported Mr. Thomas Putnam a common murderer.

HALE. Excellency—

DANFORTH. Mr. Hale.

HALE. We cannot blink it more. There is a prodigious fear of this court in the country—

DANFORTH. Then there is a prodigious guilt in the country. Are *you* afraid to be questioned here?

HALE. I may only fear the Lord, sir, but there is fear in the country nevertheless.

DANFORTH. [*Angered now.*] Reproach[6] me not with the fear in the country; there is fear in the country because there is a moving plot to topple Christ in the country!

HALE. But it does not follow that everyone accused is part of it.

DANFORTH. No uncorrupted man may fear this court, Mr. Hale! None! [*To GILES.*] You are under arrest in contempt of this court. Now sit you down and take counsel with yourself, or you will be set in the jail until you decide to answer all questions.

[*GILES COREY makes a rush for PUTNAM. PROCTOR lunges and holds him.*]

PROCTOR. No, Giles!

GILES. [*Over PROCTOR's shoulder at PUTNAM.*] I'll cut your throat, Putnam, I'll kill you yet!

PROCTOR. [*Forcing him into a chair.*] Peace, Giles, peace. [*Releasing him.*] We'll prove ourselves. Now we will. [*He starts to turn to DANFORTH.*]

GILES. Say nothin' more, John. [*Pointing at DANFORTH.*] He's only playin' you! He means to hang us all!

[*MARY WARREN bursts into sobs.*]

DANFORTH. This is a court of law, Mister. I'll have no effrontery[7] here!

PROCTOR. Forgive him, sir, for his old age. Peace, Giles, we'll prove it all now. [*He lifts up MARY's chin.*] You cannot weep, Mary. Remember the angel, what he say to the boy. Hold to it, now; there is your rock. [*MARY quiets. He takes out a paper, and turns to DANFORTH.*] This is Mary Warren's deposition. I—I would ask you remember, sir, while you read it, that until two week ago she were no different than the other children are

---

6. To *reproach* is to blame or to express disapproval of.
7. *Effrontery* is boldness and disrespect.

1 **The United States and the World** *What resemblance can you see here between Giles Corey and Arthur Miller?*

Evaluate Argument *What has Danforth just concluded from Hale's comment? What fallacy do you detect in his reasoning?* **2**

1082 UNIT 6 FROM DEPRESSION TO COLD WAR

Grammar Practice

Inverted Sentences In his dialogue, Miller tries to recreate the sound of seventeenth-century spoken English. For example, his characters often use inverted sentences: sentences that reverse normal English word order. The usual word order in a sentence is subject-verb-complement: "We ate pizza," not "Pizza ate we" or "Ate we pizza." Point out this example of inversion: ". . . this argument let lawyers present to you," on page 1083. **Ask:** How would you reword this sentence using normal word order? ("*. . . let lawyers present this argument to you.*) Miller uses other forms of old-fashioned language. Have students say these examples aloud using contemporary English syntax:

- "Remember the angel, what he say to the boy." ("*Remember what the angel said to the boy.*")

- ". . . until two week ago she were no different than the other children are today." ("*. . . until two weeks ago she was no different than the other children are today.*")

today. [*He is speaking reasonably, restraining all his fears, his anger, his anxiety.*] You saw her scream, she howled, she swore familiar spirits choked her; she even testified that Satan, in the form of women now in jail, tried to win her soul away, and then when she refused—

DANFORTH. We know all this.

PROCTOR. Aye, sir. She swears now that she never saw Satan; nor any spirit, vague or clear, that Satan may have sent to hurt her. And she declares her friends are lying now.

[*PROCTOR starts to hand DANFORTH the deposition, and HALE comes up to DANFORTH in a trembling state.*]

HALE. Excellency, a moment. I think this goes to the heart of the matter.

DANFORTH. [*With deep misgivings.*] It surely does.

HALE. I cannot say he is an honest man; I know him little. But in all justice, sir, a claim so weighty cannot be argued by a farmer. In God's name, sir, stop here; send him home and let him come again with a lawyer—

DANFORTH. [*Patiently.*] Now look you, Mr. Hale—

HALE. Excellency, I have signed seventy-two death warrants; I am a minister of the Lord, and I dare not take a life without there be a proof so **immaculate** no slightest qualm[8] of conscience may doubt it.

DANFORTH. Mr. Hale, you surely do not doubt my justice.

HALE. I have this morning signed away the soul of Rebecca Nurse, Your Honor. I'll not conceal it, my hand shakes yet as with a wound! I pray you, sir, *this* argument let lawyers present to you.

---

8. *Qualm* (kwäm) means "doubt."

3 Plot *How is the rising action gradually propelling Proctor toward the center of attention and the climax of the act?*

4 Plot *How has the development of Hale's character contributed to the conflict in the play?*

DANFORTH. Mr. Hale, believe me; for a man of such terrible learning you are most bewildered—I hope you will forgive me. I have been thirty-two year at the bar, sir, and I should be confounded were I called upon to defend these people. Let you consider, now—[*To PROCTOR and the others.*] And I bid you all do likewise. In an ordinary crime, how does one defend the accused? One calls up witnesses to prove his innocence. But witchcraft is *ipso facto,*[9] on its face and by its nature, an invisible crime, is it not? Therefore, who may possibly be witness to it? The witch and the victim. None other. Now we cannot hope the witch will accuse herself; granted? Therefore, we must rely upon her victims—and they do testify, the children certainly do testify. As for the witches, none will deny that we are most eager for all their confessions. Therefore, what is left for a lawyer to bring out? I think I have made my point. Have I not?

HALE. But this child claims the girls are not truthful, and if they are not—

DANFORTH. That is precisely what I am about to consider, sir. What more may you ask of me? Unless you doubt my probity?[10]

HALE. [*Defeated.*] I surely do not, sir. Let you consider it, then.

DANFORTH. And let you put your heart to rest. Her deposition, Mr. Proctor.

[*PROCTOR hands it to him. HATHORNE rises, goes beside DANFORTH, and starts reading. PARRIS comes to his other side. DANFORTH looks at JOHN PROCTOR, then proceeds to read. HALE gets up, finds position near the judge, reads too. PROCTOR glances at GILES. FRANCIS prays silently, hands pressed together. CHEEVER waits placidly, the sublime official, dutiful. MARY WARREN sobs once. JOHN PROCTOR touches her head reassuringly. Presently DANFORTH lifts his eyes, stands up, takes out a kerchief and blows his nose. The others stand aside as he moves in thought toward the window.*]

---

9. The Latin legal term *ipso facto* means, literally, "by that very fact" or "by the fact itself."
10. *Probity* involves moral excellence, integrity, and honesty.

5 Evaluate Argument *What hope does the logic of this argument give to people accused of witchcraft? Explain.*

Teach

Literary Element　3

Plot **Answer:** *People are being prosecuted based on the girls' accusations, and Proctor is the only person who is questioning the girls' reliability.*

Literary Element　4

Plot **Answer:** *As hysteria grows, Hale becomes disturbed by the injustice of the court. He insists that the court should consider reasonable doubt. Danforth believes that an accused person is guilty until proven innocent.*

Reading Strategy　5

Evaluate Argument **Answer:** *It gives no hope. If there are no witnesses and a witch never admits the truth, the court must rely on the testimony of the accuser.*

Approaching Level

DIFFERENTIATED INSTRUCTION

Strategic Help students see how Danforth traps Mary in a no-win situation. Have students read the dialogue between Mary and Danforth in the first column of page 1084. **Ask:** What does Danforth mean when he says that Mary "committed perjury in any case"? *(He means that either she was lying in court when she originally claimed that people had sent their spirits against her or she is lying now*

when she claims that her accusations and behavior—and those of the other girls— were "pretense." Either way, she has committed perjury, lying under oath.) Make sure students understand that Danforth will not let Mary come clean; by telling the truth, she will in fact be punished for lying. Ask students to brainstorm other examples of no-win situations.

Benchmark Have students answer the question in the Strategic activity. Then **ask:** What is Danforth's motivation for trapping Mary in this no-win situation? *(He is hoping that she will withdraw her accusations out of fear of going to jail.)*

Teach

Reading Strategy | 1

Make Inferences **Say:** Here the term *contempt* appears again, but used in a different way. **Ask:** Which of Parris's statements or actions do you think Danforth finds contemptible? *(Parris interrupts and tries to curry Danforth's favor in an obvious attempt to protect his own interests.)*

Literary Element | 2

Plot **Answer:** *Danforth intimidates Mary. The audience knows she is weak and is Proctor's only hope.*

Literary Element | 3

Plot **Answer:** *The longer the audience must wait for Abigail, the leader of the conspiracy, the greater the tension.*

Reading Strategy | 4

Evaluate Argument **Answer:** *Danforth is less harsh with them; he promises an easy sentence if they confess to lying. He has said Mary will hang if she is in league with Satan.*

PARRIS. [*Hardly able to contain his anger and fear.*] I should like to question—

1 DANFORTH. [*His first real outburst, in which his contempt for PARRIS is clear.*] Mr. Parris, I bid you be silent! [*He stands in silence, looking out the window. Now, having established that he will set the gait.*][11] Mr. Cheever, will you go into the court and bring the children here? [CHEEVER *gets up and goes out upstage.* DANFORTH *now turns to* MARY.] Mary Warren, how came you to this turnabout? Has Mr. Proctor threatened you for this deposition?

MARY WARREN. No, sir.

DANFORTH. Has he ever threatened you?

MARY WARREN. [*Weaker.*] No, sir.

DANFORTH. [*Sensing a weakening.*] Has he threatened you?

MARY WARREN. No, sir.

DANFORTH. Then you tell me that you sat in my court, callously lying, when you knew that people would hang by your evidence? [*She does not answer.*] Answer me!

MARY WARREN. [*Almost inaudibly.*] I did, sir.

DANFORTH. How were you instructed in your life? Do you not know that God damns all liars? [*She cannot speak.*] Or is it now that you lie?

MARY WARREN. No, sir—I am with God now.

DANFORTH. You are with God now.

MARY WARREN. Aye, sir.

DANFORTH. [*Containing himself.*] I will tell you this—you are either lying now, or you were lying in the court, and in either case you have committed **perjury** and you will go to jail for it. You cannot lightly say you lied, Mary. Do you know that?

---

11. To *set the gait* is an expression that means "to determine how a matter will proceed."

2 **Plot** *How does Danforth's aggressive questioning of Mary contribute to the rising action?*

Vocabulary

perjury (pər´ jə rē) *n.* the act of swearing under oath to the truth of something that one knows to be untrue

---

MARY WARREN. I cannot lie no more. I am with God, I am with God.

[*But she breaks into sobs at the thought of it, and the right door opens, and enter* SUSANNA WALCOTT, MERCY LEWIS, BETTY PARRIS, *and finally* ABIGAIL. CHEEVER *comes to* DANFORTH.]

CHEEVER. Ruth Putnam's not in the court, sir, nor the other children.

DANFORTH. These will be sufficient. Sit you down, children. [*Silently they sit.*] Your friend, Mary Warren, has given us a deposition. In which she swears that she never saw familiar spirits, apparitions, nor any manifest of the Devil.[12] She claims as well that none of you have seen these things either. [*Slight pause.*] Now, children, this is a court of law. The law, based upon the Bible, and the Bible, writ by Almighty God, forbid the practice of witchcraft, and describe death as the penalty thereof. But likewise, children, the law and Bible damn all bearers of false witness. [*Slight pause.*] Now then. It does not escape me that this deposition may be devised to blind us; it may well be that Mary Warren has been conquered by Satan, who sends her here to distract our sacred purpose. If so, her neck will break for it. But if she speak true, I bid you now drop your guile and confess your pretense, for a quick confession will go easier with you. [*Pause.*] Abigail Williams, rise. [ABIGAIL *slowly rises.*] Is there any truth in this? ☆

ABIGAIL. No, sir.

DANFORTH. [*Thinks, glances at* MARY, *then back to* ABIGAIL.] Children, a very augur bit[13] will now be turned into your souls until your honesty is proved. Will either of you change your positions now, or do you force me to hard questioning?

---

12. *Familiar spirits* are supernatural beings (not ghosts) believed to serve demons or humans; *apparitions* are ghosts of dead people; and a *manifest of the Devil* is a form in which the devil reveals himself.
13. Here, *augur bit* refers to an auger, a tool for boring holes.

Plot *How does Abigail's delayed entry contribute to the tension in this scene?* **3**

Evaluate Argument *Compare Danforth's treatment of Mary to his treatment of the other girls. How is this another example of Danforth's double standard in administering justice?* **4**

1084 UNIT 6 FROM DEPRESSION TO COLD WAR

Listening and Speaking Practice

Dramatic Reading Have students rehearse and present a dramatic reading of the scene that begins with Danforth's question to Mary on page 1084 and ends with Abigail's line "Oh, Heavenly Father, take away this shadow" on page 1088. Before students begin rehearsing, discuss these guidelines for a dramatic reading:

- Listen for cues for your lines.

- Vary your pitch, tone, and pacing to express meaning and emotion.
- Use facial expressions and gestures to reinforce vocal interpretations.
- Use stress and pauses to build suspense and convey a sense of danger or urgency.
- Practice pronouncing unfamiliar words and enunciating clearly.

The Crucible, 1996.

Cultural History ☆

Death by Hanging When Danforth says, "Her neck will break for it," he means Mary will be executed by hanging. From colonial days until the late nineteenth century, hanging was the chief method for executing convicted criminals in this country. Public hangings were common.

ABIGAIL. I have naught to change, sir. She lies.

DANFORTH. [*To* MARY.] You would still go on with this?

MARY WARREN. [*Faintly.*] Aye, sir.

DANFORTH. [*Turning to* ABIGAIL.] A poppet were discovered in Mr. Proctor's house, stabbed by a needle. Mary Warren claims that you sat beside her in the court when she made it, and that you saw her make it and witnessed how she herself stuck her needle into it for safe-keeping. What say you to that?

ABIGAIL. [*With a slight note of indignation.*] It is a lie, sir.

DANFORTH. [*After a slight pause.*] While you worked for Mr. Proctor, did you see poppets in that house?

ABIGAIL. Goody Proctor always kept poppets.

PROCTOR. Your Honor, my wife never kept no poppets. Mary Warren confesses it was her poppet.

CHEEVER. Your Excellency.

DANFORTH. Mr. Cheever.

CHEEVER. When I spoke with Goody Proctor in that house, she said she never kept no poppets. But she said she did keep poppets when she were a girl.

PROCTOR. She has not been a girl these fifteen years, Your Honor.

HATHORNE. But a poppet will keep fifteen years, will it not?

PROCTOR. It will keep if it is kept, but Mary Warren swears she never saw no poppets in my house, nor anyone else.

ARTHUR MILLER **1085**

Advanced Learners

DIFFERENTIATED INSTRUCTION

 Mass Hysteria Have advanced students consider this question about the real Salem witch hunt. **Ask:** What caused the girls in Salem to behave the way they did? Have them work in small groups to research the topic of mass hysteria, also known as mass sociogenic illness (MSI) or epidemic hysteria. Have students do library and Internet research on these questions:

- How do psychiatrists define this disorder? What are its symptoms?
- What is considered the appropriate treatment or response to the condition?
- Other than the Salem witch hunt, what episodes in history or contemporary life might be examples of mass hysteria?
- Does Miller present the Salem witch hunt as an episode of mass hysteria, or of something else?

Have students present their findings to the class, using visual aids and encouraging follow-up questions and discussion.

Teach

PARRIS. Why could there not have been poppets hid where no one ever saw them?

PROCTOR. [*Furious.*] There might also be a dragon with five legs in my house, but no one has ever seen it.

PARRIS. We are here, Your Honor, precisely to discover what no one has ever seen.

PROCTOR. Mr. Danforth, what profit this girl to turn herself about? What may Mary Warren gain but hard questioning and worse?

DANFORTH. You are charging Abigail Williams with a marvelous cool plot to murder, do you understand that?

PROCTOR. I do, sir. I believe she means to murder.

DANFORTH. [*Pointing at* ABIGAIL, *incredulously.*][14] This child would murder your wife?

PROCTOR. It is not a child. Now hear me, sir. In the sight of the congregation she were twice this year put out of this meetin' house for laughter during prayer.

DANFORTH. [*Shocked, turning to* ABIGAIL.] What's this? Laughter during—!

PARRIS. Excellency, she were under Tituba's power at that time, but she is solemn now.

GILES. Aye, now she is solemn and goes to hang people!

DANFORTH. Quiet, man.

HATHORNE. Surely it have no bearing on the question, sir. He charges **contemplation** of murder.

DANFORTH. Aye. [*He studies* ABIGAIL *for a moment, then.*] Continue, Mr. Proctor.

---

14. **Incredulously** means "in a disbelieving manner."

PROCTOR. Mary. Now tell the Governor how you danced in the woods.

PARRIS. [*Instantly.*] Excellency, since I come to Salem this man is blackening my name. He—

DANFORTH. In a moment, sir. [*To* MARY WARREN, *sternly, and surprised.*] What is this dancing?

MARY WARREN. I—[*She glances at* ABIGAIL, *who is staring down at her remorselessly. Then, appealing to* PROCTOR.] Mr. Proctor—

PROCTOR. [*Taking it right up.*] Abigail leads the girls to the woods, Your Honor, and they have danced there naked—

PARRIS. Your Honor, this—

PROCTOR. [*At once.*] Mr. Parris discovered them himself in the dead of night! There's the "child" she is!

DANFORTH. [*It is growing into a nightmare, and he turns, astonished, to* PARRIS.] Mr. Parris— **3**

PARRIS. I can only say, sir, that I never found any of them naked, and this man is—

DANFORTH. But you discovered them dancing in the woods? [*Eyes on* PARRIS, *he points at* ABIGAIL.] Abigail?

HALE. Excellency, when I first arrived from Beverly, Mr. Parris told me that.

DANFORTH. Do you deny it, Mr. Parris?

PARRIS. I do not, sir, but I never saw any of them naked.

DANFORTH. But she have *danced*?

PARRIS. [*Unwillingly.*] Aye, sir.

[DANFORTH, *as though with new eyes, looks at* ABIGAIL.]

HATHORNE. Excellency, will you permit me? [*He points at* MARY WARREN.]

DANFORTH. [*With great worry.*] Pray, proceed.

HATHORNE. You say you never saw no spirits, Mary, were never threatened or afflicted by any manifest of the Devil or the Devil's agents.

MARY WARREN. [Very faintly.] No, sir.

HATHORNE. [With a gleam of victory.] And yet, when people accused of witchery confronted you in court, you would faint, saying their spirits came out of their bodies and choked you—

MARY WARREN. That were pretense, sir.

DANFORTH. I cannot hear you.

MARY WARREN. Pretense, sir.

PARRIS. But you did turn cold, did you not? I myself picked you up many times, and your skin were icy. Mr. Danforth, you—

DANFORTH. I saw that many times.

PROCTOR. She only pretended to faint, Your Excellency. They're all marvelous pretenders.

HATHORNE. Then can she pretend to faint now?

PROCTOR. Now?

PARRIS. Why not? Now there are no spirits attacking her, for none in this room is accused of witchcraft. So let her turn herself cold now, let her pretend she is attacked now, let her faint. [He turns to MARY WARREN.] Faint!

MARY WARREN. Faint?

PARRIS. Aye, faint. Prove to us how you pretended in the court so many times.

MARY WARREN. [Looking to PROCTOR.] I—cannot faint now, sir.

PROCTOR. [Alarmed, quietly.] Can you not pretend it?

MARY WARREN. I—[She looks about as though searching for the passion to faint.] I—have no sense of it now, I—

DANFORTH. Why? What is lacking now?

MARY WARREN. I—cannot tell, sir, I—

DANFORTH. Might it be that here we have no afflicting spirit loose, but in the court there were some?

MARY WARREN. I never saw no spirits.

5 Evaluate Argument *Do you think that Parris's scheme for testing Mary's claim that she pretended to faint is a fair test? Explain.*

PARRIS. Then see no spirits now, and prove to us that you can faint by your own will, as you claim.

MARY WARREN. [Stares, searching for the emotion of it, and then shakes her head.] I—cannot do it.

PARRIS. Then you will confess, will you not? It were attacking spirits made you faint!

MARY WARREN. No, sir, I—

PARRIS. Your Excellency, this is a trick to blind the court!

MARY WARREN. It's not a trick! [She stands.] I—I used to faint because I—I thought I saw spirits.

DANFORTH. *Thought* you saw them!

MARY WARREN. But I did not, Your Honor.

HATHORNE. How could you think you saw them unless you saw them?

MARY WARREN. I—I cannot tell how, but I did. I—I heard the other girls screaming, and you, Your Honor, you seemed to believe them, and I— It were only sport in the beginning, sir, but then the whole world cried spirits, spirits, and I—I promise you, Mr. Danforth, I only thought I saw them but I did not.

[DANFORTH peers at her.]

PARRIS. [Smiling, but nervous because DANFORTH seems to be struck by MARY WARREN's story.] Surely Your Excellency is not taken by this simple lie.

DANFORTH. [Turning worriedly to ABIGAIL.] Abigail. I bid you now search your heart and tell me this—and beware of it, child, to God every soul is precious and His vengeance is terrible on them that take life without cause. Is it possible, child, that the spirits you have seen are illusion only, some deception that may cross your mind when—

ABIGAIL. Why, this—this—is a base question, sir.

DANFORTH. Child, I would have you consider it—

ABIGAIL. I have been hurt, Mr. Danforth; I have seen my blood runnin' out! I have been near to murdered every day because I done my duty pointing out the Devil's people—and this is my

Plot *How is Danforth instrumental in maintaining the tension during this scene?* 6

Teach

Literary Element 4

Plot **Answer:** *Danforth is shocked by the claim that Abigail is pure and innocent. He is beginning to lean in Proctor's direction.*

Reading Strategy 5

Evaluate Argument **Answer:** *The test is flawed because the circumstances are different. In the courtroom, Mary was under the influence of Abigail and the other girls. Here she is psychologically removed from the girls' self-induced hysteria.*

Literary Element 6

Plot **Answer:** *Danforth wavers between believing Abigail and believing Mary. Not knowing which side he will choose creates tension.*

English Learners

DIFFERENTIATED INSTRUCTION

Beginning English learners will need help with some of the vocabulary on pages 1086 and 1087. Have students look up these words in a dictionary and record the definitions: *solemn, blackening, sternly, remorselessly, afflicted, manifest, gleam, pretense.* Make sure students understand that Satan is another name for the Devil, and the two names are used interchangeably.

Advanced Beginning at the bottom of the first column on page 1086, Danforth expresses shock that Abigail laughed during prayers and danced in the woods. Remind students of the strictness under which the Puritans lived. English learners may be unfamiliar with the connotations that the words *Puritan* and *puritanical* have acquired. Have students look up the words in a dictionary and note all the definitions

listed. **Ask:** What would it mean if you described someone today as "puritanical"? (*The person is strict about morals and religion.*)

Teach

Reading Strategy | **1**

Evaluate Argument
Answer: *Some may think that Abigail is desperate. Others may say that she can manipulate Danforth and make him defensive. Her ploy works.*

Literary Element | **2**

Plot **Answer:** *Proctor will be forced to present evidence to support his accusation that Abigail is a "whore." By doing so, he will have to confess his own sin of adultery, which will in turn open him up to the possibility of severe punishment.)*

---

reward? To be mistrusted, denied, questioned like a—

DANFORTH. [*Weakening.*] Child, I do not mistrust you—

ABIGAIL. [*In an open threat.*] Let *you* beware, Mr. Danforth. Think you to be so mighty that the power of Hell may not turn *your* wits? Beware of it! There is—[*Suddenly, from an accusatory attitude, her face turns, looking into the air above—it is truly frightened.*]

DANFORTH. [*Apprehensively.*] What is it, child?

ABIGAIL. [*Looking about in the air, clasping her arms about her as though cold.*] I—I know not. A wind, a cold wind, has come. [*Her eyes fall on* MARY WARREN.]

MARY WARREN. [*Terrified, pleading.*] Abby!

MERCY LEWIS. [*Shivering.*] Your Honor, I freeze!

PROCTOR. They're pretending!

HATHORNE. [*Touching* ABIGAIL's *hand.*] She is cold, Your Honor, touch her!

MERCY LEWIS. [*Through chattering teeth.*] Mary, do you send this shadow on me?

MARY WARREN. Lord, save me!

SUSANNA WALCOTT. I freeze, I freeze!

ABIGAIL. [*Shivering visibly.*] It is a wind, a wind!

MARY WARREN. Abby, don't do that!

DANFORTH. [*Himself engaged and entered by* ABIGAIL.] Mary Warren, do you witch her? I say to you, do you send your spirit out?

[*With a hysterical cry* MARY WARREN *starts to run.* PROCTOR *catches her.*]

MARY WARREN. [*Almost collapsing.*] Let me go, Mr. Proctor, I cannot, I cannot—

ABIGAIL. [*Crying to Heaven.*] Oh, Heavenly Father, take away this shadow!

[*Without warning or hesitation,* PROCTOR *leaps at* ABIGAIL *and, grabbing her by the hair, pulls her to her feet. She screams in pain.* DANFORTH,

astonished, cries, "What are you about?" and HATHORNE *and* PARRIS *call, "Take your hands off her!" and out of it all comes* PROCTOR's *roaring voice.*]

PROCTOR. How do you call Heaven! Whore![15] Whore!

[HERRICK *breaks* PROCTOR *from her.*]

HERRICK. John!

DANFORTH. Man! Man, what do you—

PROCTOR. [*Breathless and in agony.*] It is a whore!

DANFORTH. [*Dumfounded.*][16] You charge—?

ABIGAIL. Mr. Danforth, he is lying!

PROCTOR. Mark her! Now she'll suck a scream to stab me with, but—

DANFORTH. You will prove this! This will not pass!

PROCTOR. [*Trembling, his life collapsing about him.*] I have known her, sir. I have known her.

DANFORTH. You—you are a lecher?

FRANCIS. [*Horrified.*] John, you cannot say such a—

PROCTOR. Oh, Francis, I wish you had some evil in you that you might know me! [*To* DANFORTH.] A man will not cast away his good name. You surely know that.

DANFORTH. [*Dumfounded.*] In—in what time? In what place?

PROCTOR. [*His voice about to break, and his shame great.*] In the proper place—where my beasts are bedded. On the last night of my joy, some eight months past. She used to serve me in my house, sir. [*He has to clamp his jaw to keep from weeping.*] A man may think God sleeps, but God sees everything, I know it now. I beg you, sir, I beg you—see her what she is. My wife, my dear good wife, took this girl soon after, sir, and

---

15. Here, *whore* refers to a "loose" woman, not that she has taken money for sexual services.
16. *Dumfounded* means "speechless."

1 Evaluate Argument *Is it wise for Abigail to confront the chief judge in this manner? Is her ploy successful? Explain.*

Plot *How is this moment crucial to the development of the plot?* **2**

Reading Practice

SPIRAL REVIEW **Irony** Remind students that situational irony occurs when something happens that is the opposite of what we expect to happen (for example, if the worst player on the soccer team kicks the winning goal). **Ask:** Why is it ironic that when Danforth questions Elizabeth, she lies about why she dismissed Abigail as her servant? (*Elizabeth is a woman who,* according to her husband, "cannot lie." *Yet now she does the opposite of what we might expect: she lies to protect her husband. Ironically, her action has the opposite effect: it puts him in grave danger.*) Continue the discussion of irony by reminding students that dramatic irony occurs when the audience or reader realizes something that a character does not. **Ask:** What dramatic irony occurs in this scene? (*The audience realizes something that Elizabeth does not: that Proctor wants her to tell the truth and that lying will harm rather than protect him.*)

Sympathizer, 1956. Elaine de Kooning. Oil on canvas, 40¼ x 31 in. Estate of Elaine de Kooning.

View the Art Along with abstract works, Elaine de Kooning also painted portraits of celebrities, such as President John F. Kennedy. What are your reactions to this painting? How do they compare with the reactions you have to Mary Warren in Act Three? Explain.

Teach

English Learners

DIFFERENTIATED INSTRUCTION

Intermediate Help English learners understand the idioms Proctor uses in his confession. Explain that an idiom is an expression whose meaning is different from the literal meaning of the words that make it up. For example, when Proctor says that Elizabeth "put [Abigail] on the highroad," he does not mean that she physically placed Abigail on a high road. He means that his wife made Abigail leave the house—that is, she fired her. Help students figure out what Proctor means when he says that Abigail "thinks to dance with me on my wife's grave." **Ask:** Why would a person dance on someone's grave? *(because he or she is happy the other person died)* What does Proctor mean when he uses this expression? *(Abigail thinks that she and Proctor will rejoice over Elizabeth's death because it will allow them to get married.)* Have students work in pairs to figure out what Proctor means when he tells Danforth: "I set myself entirely in your hands." *("I put myself under your control or judgment.")*

Teach

Reading Strategy | 1

Evaluate Argument
Answer: *Proctor puts himself at the mercy of the court. He hopes to convince Danforth that Abigail's accusations against Elizabeth are motivated by a wish to supplant Elizabeth as Proctor's wife.*

Reading Strategy | 2

Evaluate Argument
Answer: *Abigail's defense is to act offended. Some will suggest that her theatrical skills can get her out of any predicament. Others may argue that eventually she will have to respond to Proctor's accusation.*

APPROACHING Ask students to consider how Abigail's strategy relates to this maxim: "The best defense is a strong offense."

Literary Element | 3

Plot **Answer:** *Proctor is counting on Elizabeth's honesty to confirm his accusations against Abigail. It never occurs to Proctor that Elizabeth will lie out of love in order to save her husband's reputation.*

---

put her out on the highroad. And being what she is, a lump of vanity, sir—[*He is being overcome.*] Excellency, forgive me, forgive me. [*Angrily against himself, he turns away from the Governor for a moment. Then, as though to cry out is his only means of speech left.*] She thinks to dance with me on my wife's grave! And well she might, for I thought of her softly. God help me, I lusted, and there *is* a promise in such sweat. But it is a whore's vengeance, and you must see it; I set myself entirely in your hands. I know you must see it now.

DANFORTH. [*Blanched,*[17] *in horror, turning to ABIGAIL.*] You deny every scrap and tittle of this?

ABIGAIL. If I must answer that, I will leave and I will not come back again!

  [*DANFORTH seems unsteady.*]

PROCTOR. I have made a bell of my honor! I have rung the doom of my good name—you will believe me, Mr. Danforth! My wife is innocent, except she knew a whore when she saw one!

ABIGAIL. [*Stepping up to DANFORTH.*] What look do you give me? [*DANFORTH cannot speak.*] I'll not have such looks! [*She turns and starts for the door.*]

DANFORTH. You will remain where you are! [*HERRICK steps into her path. She comes up short, fire in her eyes.*] Mr. Parris, go into the court and bring Goodwife Proctor out.

PARRIS. [*Objecting.*] Your Honor, this is all a—

DANFORTH. [*Sharply to PARRIS.*] Bring her out! And tell her not one word of what's been spoken here. And let you knock before you enter. [*PARRIS goes out.*] Now we shall touch the bottom of this swamp. [*To PROCTOR.*] Your wife, you say, is an honest woman.

---

17. Here, *blanched* means "drained of color."

1 Evaluate Argument **What does Proctor hope to accomplish in this conclusion to his confession?**

2 Evaluate Argument **How does Abigail choose to defend herself against Proctor's accusations? How effective do you think her method will be?**

PROCTOR. In her life, sir, she have never lied. There are them that cannot sing, and them that cannot weep—my wife cannot lie. I have paid much to learn it, sir.

DANFORTH. And when she put this girl out of your house, she put her out for a harlot?

PROCTOR. Aye, sir.

DANFORTH. And knew her for a harlot?

PROCTOR. Aye, sir, she knew her for a harlot.

DANFORTH. Good then. [*To ABIGAIL.*] And if she tell me, child, it were for harlotry, may God spread His mercy on you! [*There is a knock. He calls to the door.*] Hold! [*To ABIGAIL.*] Turn your back. Turn your back. [*To PROCTOR.*] Do likewise. [*Both turn their backs—ABIGAIL with indignant slowness.*] Now let neither of you turn to face Goody Proctor. No one in this room is to speak one word, or raise a gesture aye or nay. [*He turns toward the door, calls.*] Enter! [*The door opens. ELIZABETH enters with PARRIS. PARRIS leaves her. She stands alone, her eyes looking for PROCTOR.*] Mr. Cheever, report this testimony in all exactness. Are you ready?

CHEEVER. Ready, sir.

DANFORTH. Come here, woman. [*ELIZABETH comes to him, glancing at PROCTOR's back.*] Look at me only, not at your husband. In my eyes only.

ELIZABETH. [*Faintly.*] Good, sir.

DANFORTH. We are given to understand that at one time you dismissed your servant, Abigail Williams.

ELIZABETH. That is true, sir.

DANFORTH. For what cause did you dismiss her? [*Slight pause. Then ELIZABETH tries to glance at PROCTOR.*] You will look in my eyes only and not at your husband. The answer is in your memory and you need no help to give it to me. Why did you dismiss Abigail Williams?

ELIZABETH. [*Not knowing what to say, sensing a situation, wetting her lips to stall for time.*] She— dissatisfied me. [*Pause.*] And my husband.

Plot **How might Proctor's comment foreshadow the ironic reversal that occurs later in this scene?** **3**

Reading Practice

Rising Action Remind students that the rising action is the part of the plot when complications develop and the conflict intensifies. The rising action leads to the climax, the moment of greatest emotional intensity in the plot, when the conflict is at its peak. Make sure students understand that the rising action is a series of events, not one single event. Then point out that according to some literary critics,

the climax of *The Crucible* occurs in Act Four. **Ask:** Which event on this spread represents one of the most important complications in the rising action—an event that intensifies the conflict the most? *(The most important complication on this spread is when Elizabeth lies to protect her husband, not realizing that her lie will seal his doom.)* Have students consider, as they read Act Four, whether

this or any other event in Act Three could instead represent the play's climax.

DANFORTH. In what way dissatisfied you?

ELIZABETH. She were—[*She glances at* PROCTOR *for a cue.*]

DANFORTH. Woman, look at me! [ELIZABETH *does.*] Were she slovenly?[18] Lazy? What disturbance did she cause?

ELIZABETH. Your Honor, I—in that time I were sick. And I—My husband is a good and righteous man. He is never drunk as some are, nor wastin' his time at the shovelboard,[19] but always at his work. But in my sickness—you see, sir, I were a long time sick after my last baby, and I thought I saw my husband somewhat turning from me. And this girl—[*She turns to* ABIGAIL.]

DANFORTH. Look at me.

ELIZABETH. Aye, sir. Abigail Williams—[*She breaks off.*]

DANFORTH. What of Abigail Williams?

ELIZABETH. I came to think he fancied her. And so one night I lost my wits, I think, and put her out on the highroad.

DANFORTH. Your husband—did he indeed turn from you?

ELIZABETH. [*In agony.*] My husband—is a goodly man, sir.

DANFORTH. Then he did not turn from you.

ELIZABETH. [*Starting to glance at* PROCTOR.] He—

DANFORTH. [*Reaches out and holds her face, then.*] Look at me! To your own knowledge, has John Proctor ever committed the crime of lechery? [*In a crisis of indecision she cannot speak.*] Answer my question! Is your husband a lecher!

ELIZABETH. [*Faintly.*] No, sir.

DANFORTH. Remove her, Marshal.

PROCTOR. Elizabeth, tell the truth!

DANFORTH. She has spoken. Remove her!

---

18. To be *slovenly* is to be untidy or careless, especially in appearance.
19. *Shovelboard* is a tabletop version of shuffleboard.

4 Plot *How do these two words alter the direction of the plot?*

PROCTOR. [*Crying out.*] Elizabeth, I have confessed it!

ELIZABETH. Oh, God! [*The door closes behind her.*]

PROCTOR. She only thought to save my name!

HALE. Excellency, it is a natural lie to tell; I beg you, stop now before another is condemned! I may shut my conscience to it no more—private vengeance is working through this testimony! From the beginning this man has struck me true. By my oath to Heaven, I believe him now, and I pray you call back his wife before we—

DANFORTH. She spoke nothing of lechery, and this man has lied!

HALE. I believe him! [*Pointing at* ABIGAIL.] This girl has always struck me false! She has—

[ABIGAIL, *with a weird, wild, chilling cry, screams up to the ceiling.*]

ABIGAIL. You will not! Begone! Begone, I say!

DANFORTH. What is it, child? [*But* ABIGAIL, *pointing with fear, is now raising up her frightened eyes, her awed face, toward the ceiling—the girls are doing the same—and now* HATHORNE, HALE, PUTNAM, CHEEVER, HERRICK, *and* DANFORTH *do the same.*] What's there? [*He lowers his eyes from the ceiling, and now he is frightened; there is real tension in his voice.*] Child! [*She is transfixed—with all the girls, she is whimpering open-mouthed, agape at the ceiling.*] Girls! Why do you—?

MERCY LEWIS. [*Pointing.*] It's on the beam! Behind the rafter!

DANFORTH. [*Looking up.*] Where!

ABIGAIL. Why—? [*She gulps.*] Why do you come, yellow bird?

PROCTOR. Where's a bird? I see no bird!

ABIGAIL. [*To the ceiling.*] My face? My face?

PROCTOR. Mr. Hale—

DANFORTH. Be quiet!!

PROCTOR. [*To* HALE.] Do you see a bird?

Evaluate Argument *Danforth and Hale draw different conclusions from the preceding scene. Which one has come closer to the truth? Explain.* **6**

ARTHUR MILLER **1091**

Approaching Level

DIFFERENTIATED INSTRUCTION

Emerging Students may be confused about why Hale has changed his mind about Abigail. Remind students of the difference between a dynamic and a static character: A dynamic character is someone who develops and changes—who learns something as a result of what happens during the literary work. In contrast, a static character is someone who does not change. Next, remind students that in Act

Two, when Elizabeth is arrested, Proctor tells Hale that "vengeance is walking Salem." **Ask:** What does Hale mean when he tells Danforth that he can no longer shut his conscience to the fact that "private vengeance" is at work? (*He means that he now understands what Proctor has insisted all along—that the witch hunt is motivated by personal revenge, not the search for truth or jus-*

tice.) Discuss with students whether they find Hale's change in attitude believable. Encourage students to support their opinion with evidence from the play, as well as from their own experiences or observations about human nature.

1091

Teach

Reading Strategy · 1

Evaluate Argument
Answer: *Abigail is trying to discredit Mary by making Danforth believe that Mary is using witchcraft to attack her. She is successful; Danforth is "horrified" and orders Mary to draw back her "spirit."*

Big Idea · 2

The United States and the World **Answer:** *This stage direction shows that Danforth not only believes that Abigail's vision is real but also that Mary caused it. Like many witnesses at the McCarthy hearings, Mary realizes that no one in power will believe her and decides to save herself by betraying others.*

Reading Strategy · 3

Make Predictions **Ask:** *How do you think Mary will react to Danforth's relentless prodding?* (She will confess what he wants to hear, but claim that she is "afflicted" by another's witchcraft.)

DANFORTH. Be quiet!

ABIGAIL. [*To the ceiling, in a genuine conversation with the "bird," as though trying to talk it out of attacking her.*] But God made my face; you cannot want to tear my face. Envy is a deadly sin, Mary.

MARY WARREN. [*On her feet with a spring, and horrified, pleading.*] Abby!

ABIGAIL. [**Unperturbed,** *continuing to the "bird."*] Oh, Mary, this is a black art to change your shape. No, I cannot, I cannot stop my mouth; it's God's work I do.

MARY WARREN. Abby, I'm *here!*

PROCTOR. [*Frantically.*] They're pretending, Mr. Danforth!

ABIGAIL. [*Now she takes a backward step, as though in fear the bird will swoop down momentarily.*] Oh, please, Mary! Don't come down.

SUSANNA WALCOTT. Her claws, she's stretching her claws!

PROCTOR. Lies, lies.

ABIGAIL. [*Backing further, eyes still fixed above.*] Mary, please don't hurt me!

MARY WARREN. [*To* DANFORTH.] I'm not hurting her!

DANFORTH. [*To* MARY WARREN.] Why does she see this vision?

MARY WARREN. She sees nothin'!

ABIGAIL. [*Now staring full front as though hypnotized, and mimicking the exact tone of* MARY WARREN*'s cry.*] She sees nothin'!

MARY WARREN. [*Pleading.*] Abby, you mustn't!

---

1 **Evaluate Argument** *What is Abigail trying to accomplish in this scene? Is she successful? Explain.*

2 **The United States and the World** *How does this stage direction help to explain why Mary betrays Proctor and why many witnesses at the McCarthy hearings betrayed their friends and colleagues?*

Vocabulary
unperturbed (un pər turbd′) *adj.* undisturbed; calm

ABIGAIL AND ALL THE GIRLS. [*All transfixed.*] Abby, you mustn't!

MARY WARREN. [*To all the girls.*] I'm here, I'm here!

GIRLS. I'm here, I'm here!

DANFORTH. [*Horrified.*] Mary Warren! Draw back your spirit out of them!

MARY WARREN. Mr. Danforth!

GIRLS. [*Cutting her off.*] Mr. Danforth!

DANFORTH. Have you compacted with the Devil? Have you?

MARY WARREN. Never, never!

GIRLS. Never, never!

DANFORTH. [*Growing hysterical.*] Why can they only repeat you?

PROCTOR. Give me a whip—I'll stop it!

MARY WARREN. They're sporting. They—!

GIRLS. They're sporting!

MARY WARREN. [*Turning on them all hysterically and stamping her feet.*] Abby, stop it!

GIRLS. [*Stamping their feet.*] Abby, stop it!

MARY WARREN. Stop it!

GIRLS. Stop it!

MARY WARREN. [*Screaming it out at the top of her lungs, and raising her fists.*] Stop it!!

GIRLS. [*Raising their fists.*] Stop it!!

[MARY WARREN, *utterly confounded, and becoming overwhelmed by* ABIGAIL*'s—and the girls'—utter conviction, starts to whimper, hands half raised, powerless, and all the girls begin whimpering exactly as she does.*]

3

DANFORTH. A little while ago you were afflicted. Now it seems you afflict others; where did you find this power?

MARY WARREN. [*Staring at* ABIGAIL.] I—have no power.

GIRLS. I have no power.

PROCTOR. They're gulling[20] you, Mister!

---

20. *Gulling* means "deceiving."

Writing Practice

Diary Entry Mary Warren plays a critical role in the last few pages of Act Three. After students finish reading this act, have them draft a diary entry that Mary might have been written the night after her appearance in court. Before students begin writing, suggest that they consider these questions:

- Where does Mary sleep that night, now that she has denounced Proctor?

- How does she describe what happened in court that day?
- Is she still under Abigail's influence, or has she "snapped out of it"?
- Does she feel remorse for her actions, or does she truly believe that Proctor is in league with the Devil?

Encourage students to come up with a point of view and writing style that fit Mary's character, situation, and setting.

Challenge them to use this diary entry to explore ambiguities in the play.

DANFORTH. Why did you turn about this past two weeks? You have seen the Devil, have you not?

HALE. [*Indicating* ABIGAIL *and the girls.*] You cannot believe them!

MARY WARREN. I—

PROCTOR. [*Sensing her weakening.*] Mary, God damns all liars!

DANFORTH. [*Pounding it into her.*] You have seen the Devil, you have made compact with Lucifer, have you not?

PROCTOR. God damns liars, Mary!

[MARY *utters something unintelligible, staring at* ABIGAIL, *who keeps watching the "bird" above.*]

DANFORTH. I cannot hear you. What do you say? [MARY *utters again unintelligibly.*] You will confess yourself or you will hang! [*He turns her roughly to face him.*] Do you know who I am? I say you will hang if you do not open with me!

PROCTOR. Mary, remember the angel Raphael—do that which is good and—

ABIGAIL. [*Pointing upward.*] The wings! Her wings are spreading! Mary, please, don't, don't—!

HALE. I see nothing, Your Honor!

DANFORTH. Do you confess this power! [*He is an inch from her face.*] Speak!

ABIGAIL. She's going to come down! She's walking the beam!

DANFORTH. Will you speak!

MARY WARREN. [*Staring in horror.*] I cannot!

GIRLS. I cannot!

PARRIS. Cast the Devil out! Look him in the face! Trample him! We'll save you, Mary, only stand fast against him and—

---

4 The United States and the World *What connection would Miller's 1950s audiences have made between Danforth's questions and the McCarthy hearings?*

5 Plot *How does Arthur Miller create tension in this scene?*

Caged Man in Flames. John Ritter.

ABIGAIL. [*Looking up.*] Look out! She's coming down!

[*She and all the girls run to one wall, shielding their eyes. And now, as though cornered, they let out a gigantic scream, and* MARY, *as though infected, opens her mouth and screams with them. Gradually* ABIGAIL *and the girls leave off, until only* MARY *is left there, staring up at the "bird," screaming madly. All watch her, horrified by this evident fit.* PROCTOR *strides to her.*]

PROCTOR. Mary, tell the Governor what they— [*He has hardly got a word out, when, seeing him coming for her, she rushes out of his reach, screaming in horror.*]

MARY WARREN. Don't touch me—don't touch me! [*At which the girls halt at the door.*]

Teach

Big Idea | 4

The United States and the World **Answer:** *Audiences would be aware that McCarthy and his followers equated communism with evil. They would have mentally substituted* Communists *for* Devil *and* Lucifer *in Danforth's question.*

ENGLISH LEARNERS **Ask:** What other name for the Devil has been used in the play? *(Satan)*

Literary Element | 5

Plot **Answer:** *He emphasizes the pressure on Mary—from Danforth, Proctor, Hale, and Abigail. This emphasis prepares us for her breakdown.*

ENGLISH LEARNERS **Say:** Danforth's statement is both a question and a command. When a sentence can end with two types of punctuation marks, the stronger mark can be used by itself. **Ask:** How would the effect of Danforth's line be different if Miller had ended it with a question mark? *(He would seem less forceful and bullying toward Mary.)*

Approaching Level

DIFFERENTIATED INSTRUCTION

Emerging Students may be confused about what is going on in the yellow bird scene that continues on this spread. Help students understand that Abigail is trying to convince Danforth that Mary has used witchcraft to turn herself into a bird. Direct students' attention to Abigail's statement: "Oh, Mary, this is black art to change your shape." Explain that *black art* is another

name for *black magic,* and that both terms refer to witchcraft. Everyone in the courtroom would have understood that shape changing is considered an important attribute of witchcraft. **Ask:** Why does Abigail want Danforth to believe that Mary has turned herself into a yellow bird? *(Abigail wants Danforth to believe that Mary is using witchcraft against her.)*

Benchmark **Ask:** Why does Abigail want Danforth to believe that Mary is using witchcraft? *(to discredit Mary's claim that she never saw spirits and was simply pretending)*

Teach

Literary Element | 1

Plot **Answer:** *Proctor's sole witness has abandoned him. He has no one left to substantiate his claims.*

Big Idea | 2

The United States and the World Answer: *He sees those in league with the Devil everywhere; he believes the accusers.*

Reading Strategy | 3

Interpret **Ask:** What is Proctor's state of mind when he says "God is dead!"? *(Some may say he has gone mad, as the stage directions note that he is "wild." Others may say he has lost faith in God for allowing this evil to occur.)*

Big Idea | 4

The United States and the World Answer: *In driving the scholarly and respected Hale away, the witch hunters have lost a key ally.*

Progress Check

Can students analyze plot?

If No → See Unit 6 Teaching Resources Book, p. 245.

To check students' understanding of the act, see Unit 6 Teaching Resources Book, pp. 250–251.

1094

PROCTOR. [*Astonished.*] Mary!

MARY WARREN. [*Pointing at PROCTOR.*] You're the Devil's man!

[*He is stopped in his tracks.*]

PARRIS. Praise God!

GIRLS. Praise God!

PROCTOR. [*Numbed.*] Mary, how—?

MARY WARREN. I'll not hang with you! I love God, I love God.

DANFORTH. [*To MARY.*] He bid you do the Devil's work?

MARY WARREN. [*Hysterically, indicating PROCTOR.*] He come at me by night and every day to sign, to sign, to—

DANFORTH. Sign what?

PARRIS. The Devil's book? He come with a book?

MARY WARREN. [*Hysterically, pointing at PROCTOR, fearful of him.*] My name, he want my name. "I'll murder you," he says, "if my wife hangs! We must go and overthrow the court," he says!

[*DANFORTH's hand jerks toward PROCTOR, shock and horror in his face.*]

PROCTOR. [*Turning, appealing to HALE.*] Mr. Hale!

MARY WARREN. [*Her sobs beginning.*] He wake me every night, his eyes were like coals and his fingers claw my neck, and I sign, I sign . . .

HALE. Excellency, this child's gone wild!

PROCTOR. [*As DANFORTH's wide eyes pour on him.*] Mary, Mary!

MARY WARREN. [*Screaming at him.*] No, I love God; I go your way no more. I love God, I bless God. [*Sobbing, she rushes to ABIGAIL.*] Abby, Abby, I'll never hurt you more! [*They all watch, as ABIGAIL, out of her infinite charity, reaches out and draws the sobbing MARY to her, and then looks up to DANFORTH.*]

1

---

2 Plot *How might this be a turning point in the plot?*

DANFORTH. [*To PROCTOR.*] What are you? [*PROCTOR is beyond speech in his anger.*] You are combined with anti-Christ, are you not? I have seen your power; you will not deny it! What say you, Mister?

HALE. Excellency—

DANFORTH. I will have nothing from you, Mr. Hale! [*To PROCTOR.*] Will you confess yourself befouled with Hell, or do you keep that black allegiance yet? What say you?

PROCTOR. [*His mind wild, breathless.*] I say—I say—God is dead!

PARRIS. Hear it, hear it!

PROCTOR. [*Laughs insanely, then.*] A fire, a fire **3** is burning! I hear the boot of Lucifer, I see his filthy face! And it is my face, and yours, Danforth! For them that quail to bring men out of ignorance, as I have quailed, and as you quail now when you know in all your black hearts that this be fraud—God damns our kind especially, and we will burn, we will burn together!

DANFORTH. Marshal! Take him and Corey with him to the jail!

HALE. [*Starting across to the door.*] I denounce[21] these proceedings!

PROCTOR. You are pulling Heaven down and raising up a whore!

HALE. I denounce these proceedings, I quit this court! [*He slams the door to the outside behind him.*]

DANFORTH. [*Calling to him in a fury.*] Mr. Hale! Mr. Hale!

THE CURTAIN FALLS

---

21. Here, *denounce* means "to publicly pronounce something to be evil."

The United States and the World *Senator McCarthy and his followers were convinced that undercover Communists were everywhere. How does Danforth's comment reveal a similar state of mind?*

The United States and the World *Senator McCarthy's power began to decline when he launched an investigation into the United States Army. How is this a similar situation?* **4**

Reading Practice

 SPIRAL REVIEW **Irony** Have students discuss the irony achieved by Parris and the girls saying and repeating the words "Praise God!" in the left column. Mary remains truthful until Abigail and the other girls begin mimicking her. They create the illusion that her evil spirit has possessed them. Here, the girls repeat Parris, not Mary. Parris's unstated meaning is "Praise God that we have broken her." Evil is now speaking through Parris. The girls, in that same spirit of evil, echo his words.

After You Read

Respond and Think Critically

Respond and Interpret

1. (a)How and why does Giles Corey interrupt the court proceedings? (b)What does the response of the judges to him and Francis Nurse suggest about the way the trials are being conducted?

2. (a)Why does Proctor bring Mary Warren to court? (b)How does Mary Warren's confession threaten Danforth, Parris, and Hathorne?

3. (a)What does Abigail do when Hale gives his opinion of her? (b)What can you infer about the general emotional state surrounding these accusations and condemnations?

Analyze and Evaluate

4. (a)How do Hale's attitudes toward Elizabeth's lie and Abigail's deception differ? (b)Do you agree with his distinction?

5. (a)How does Abigail succeed in controlling the investigation? (b)Might Proctor have prevailed over Abigail? Support your opinion.

6. Shortly before Proctor is arrested, he says, ". . . God is dead!" What do you think that Proctor means by this remark?

Connect

7. **Big Idea** The United States and the World Does Miller successfully compare the HUAC hearings with the Salem witch trials? Explain.

8. **Connect to Today** In this Act, Miller highlights the weaknesses of the court system. Do you think that if witnesses today questioned legal proceedings like Proctor does that they would be accused of questioning the validity of the entire court system? Explain.

Literary Element Plot

The **plot** events build to a point of greatest emotional intensity, interest, or suspense called the **climax**. Usually the climax is a turning point after which the resolution of a conflict becomes clear.

1. What do you see as the climax of Act Three?

2. Which conflicts are now on the way to being resolved?

Reading Strategy Evaluate Argument

Evaluate the following examples of reasoning in Act Three. Support your evaluations.

1. Hathorne argues that a person may be a witch without knowing it.

2. Elizabeth Proctor reasons that it is better to protect her husband than to tell the truth.

Vocabulary Practice

Practice with Context Clues Identify the context clues in the following sentences that help you determine the meaning of each bold-faced vocabulary word.

1. My car is in **immaculate** condition. Yours, on the other hand, is old and rusty.

2. He lied while under oath, thus committing **perjury.**

3. I didn't want to make a rash decision, so I passed days in **contemplation.**

4. Old Mr. Alvarez is **unperturbed** by the noise because he is completely deaf.

Writing

Write a Summary Write a summary of Act Three, making sure to identify key events and the climax. Remember that the purpose of a summary is to highlight key points. For help, see page 253.

ARTHUR MILLER **1095**

Vocabulary

1. *Immaculate*: "clean to the point of being spotless"; its opposite, "old and rusty," is given in the sentence.

2. The definition of *perjury*, or lying under oath, is given in the sentence.

3. *Contemplation* is the opposite of "Rash decision" so it must mean "a slow and serious thought process."

4. Because a completely deaf person is not affected by a noise, *unperturbed* must mean "undisturbed."

Writing

Use the following criteria to evaluate students' summaries:

- Does the summary identify key events and the climax of Act Three?
- Is the summary concise?

After You Read

Assess

1. (a) He shouts that Putnam accuses people to gain their land. (b) The accused have no opportunity for self-defense.

2. (a) To swear everyone was pretending (b) They will lose respect if seen to have wrongly condemned people.

3. (a) She pretends to see an evil spirit. (b) Fear rules; people are irrational.

4. (a) Elizabeth's lie is natural; Abigail's lies are self-serving and harmful. (b) Most will agree.

5. (a) She is defiant and intimidating. (b) Students may feel she is too strong-willed for him to prevail even if Mary is firm and Elizabeth does not lie.

6. He is expressing utter frustration and believes that evil is triumphing over good.

7. Yes. Both ruined people with weak evidence and guilt by association, used testimonies, and caused unjust suffering.

8. Students will probably acknowledge the relative stability and flexibility of our court system.

Literary Element

1. John's admission of adultery, Elizabeth's lie, Mary's accusation of John, or Danforth's order to imprison John

2. Proctor's and Hale's conflicts with their conscience; Proctor's fight with authority

Reading Strategy

1. One cannot be guilty of a deliberate crime and not know it.

2. Elizabeth acts out of love for her husband.

1095

Before You Read

Focus

Summary, Act Four

John Proctor, Rebecca Nurse, and others are to be hanged. Parris asks Judge Danforth to postpone the hangings. Abigail has vanished with all of Parris's money; Parris fears public opinion. John tells Elizabeth that he is thinking about confessing and asks if she can forgive him. When John reluctantly signs a confession, Danforth insists that it be nailed to the church door. John destroys it and goes to his death, realizing he has some goodness.

Vocabulary

Prefixes Ask: What does the prefix *re-* mean? *(again; back)*
Say: Sometimes the meaning of the prefix *re-* in a word is obvious, as in *retell* ("tell again"). In other words, its meaning is less apparent. Explain that in the word *reprieve*, the prefix *re-* means "back": to "take back" a judicial sentence. In the word *retaliation*, *re-* also means "back": the act of "paying back" in kind.

Before You Read

The Crucible, Act Four

Build Background

Eventually Massachusetts authorities realized the danger of accepting the "spectral evidence" of dreams or visions and put an end to the trials. To ensure that such a slaughter of the innocents could never happen again, the courts decreed that witchcraft was no longer punishable by death.

Literary Element **Tragedy**

A **tragedy** is a play in which a main character suffers a downfall. That character, the **tragic hero,** is typically a person of exalted status who possesses admirable qualities. The downfall may result from outside forces or from a weakness within the character, which is known as a tragic flaw. As you read Act Four of *The Crucible,* ask yourself, Do any of the characters fulfill the requirements of a tragic hero?

Reading Strategy **Analyze Theme**

Theme is the central message of a work of literature, often expressed as a general statement about life. Some works have a **stated theme**, which is expressed directly. More works have an **implied theme**, which is revealed gradually through events, dialogue, or description. Themes often comment on **topics**, which are general concepts. As you read, ask yourself, What topics are addressed by Miller, and what is the overall theme of this play?

Tip: Identify Topic and Theme Create concept webs like the one below to identify possible topics and themes of Act Four of *The Crucible*.

1096 UNIT 6 FROM DEPRESSION TO COLD WAR

Vocabulary

conciliatory (kən sil´ ē ə tôr´ ē) *adj.* trying to gain the good will of another by friendly acts; p. 1102 *The boys who broke the window mowed our lawn as a conciliatory gesture.*

reprieve (ri prēv´) *n.* official postponement of the carrying out of a sentence; p. 1102 *A last-minute reprieve from the governor saved him from hanging.*

retaliation (ri tal´ ē ā´ shən) *n.* the act of repaying an injury or a wrong by committing the same, or a similar, act; p. 1102 *In retaliation for the bombing, the rebels shot down a helicopter.*

adamant (ad´ ə mənt) *adj.* completely firm and unyielding; p. 1102 *Mom is adamant about my observing a midnight curfew.*

indictment (in dīt´ mənt) *n.* a formal legal accusation, charging the commission or omission of an act, which is punishable by law; p. 1105 *The indictment led to her trial and conviction.*

Selection Skills

Literary Elements
- Tragedy (SE pp. 1096–1115)
- Conflict (SE p. 1114)
- Irony (TE p. 1098, 1110)

Vocabulary Skills
- Word Origin (TE p. 1098)

The Crucible, Act Four

Listening/Speaking/ Viewing Skills
- Analyze Art (SE pp. 1101, 1103)

Reading Skills
- Analyze Theme (SE pp. 1096–1114)
- Interpret (TE p. 1102)
- Evaluate Theme (TE pp. 1112)

Writing Skills/Grammar
- Editorial (SE p. 1115)

Act Four

[*A cell in Salem jail, that fall.*
At the back is a high barred window; near it, a
great, heavy door. Along the walls are two benches.
The place is in darkness but for the moonlight seep-
ing through the bars. It appears empty. Presently
footsteps are heard coming down a corridor beyond
the wall, keys rattle, and the door swings open.
MARSHAL HERRICK *enters with a lantern.*

1 *He is nearly drunk, and heavy-footed. He goes to*
a bench and nudges a bundle of rags lying on it.]

HERRICK. Sarah, wake up! Sarah Good! [*He then*
crosses to the other bench.]

SARAH GOOD. [*Rising in her rags.*] Oh, Majesty!
Comin', comin'! Tituba, he's here, His Majesty's
come!

HERRICK. Go to the north cell; this place is
wanted now. [*He hangs his lantern on the wall. TIT-*
UBA sits up.]

TITUBA. That don't look to me like His Majesty;
look to me like the marshal.

HERRICK. [*Taking out a flask.*] Get along with you
now, clear this place. [*He drinks, and SARAH GOOD*
comes and peers up into his face.]

SARAH GOOD. Oh, is it you, Marshal! I thought
sure you be the devil comin' for us. Could I have
a sip of cider for me goin'-away?

HERRICK. [*Handing her the flask.*] And where are
you off to, Sarah?

TITUBA. [*As SARAH drinks.*] We goin' to
Barbados, soon the Devil gits here with the
feathers and the wings.

HERRICK. Oh? A happy voyage to you.

SARAH GOOD. A pair of bluebirds wingin' south-
erly, the two of us! Oh, it be a grand transformation, Marshal! [*She raises the flask to drink again.*]

HERRICK. [*Taking the flask from her lips.*] You'd
best give me that or you'll never rise off the
ground. Come along now.

TITUBA. I'll speak to him for you, if you desire to
come along, Marshal.

HERRICK. I'd not refuse it, Tituba; it's the proper
morning to fly into Hell.

TITUBA. Oh, it be no Hell in Barbados. Devil,
him be pleasureman in Barbados, him be singin'
and dancin' in Barbados. It's you folks—you riles
him up 'round here; it be too cold 'round here for
that Old Boy. He freeze his soul in Massachusetts,
but in Barbados he just as sweet and—[*A bellow-*
ing cow is heard, and TITUBA leaps up and calls to
the window.] Aye, sir! That's him, Sarah!

SARAH GOOD. I'm here, Majesty! [*They hurriedly*
pick up their rags as HOPKINS, a guard, enters.]

HOPKINS. The Deputy Governor's arrived.

HERRICK. [*Grabbing TITUBA.*] Come along, come
along.

TITUBA. [*Resisting him.*] No, he comin' for me. I
goin' home!

HERRICK. [*Pulling her to the door.*] That's not
Satan, just a poor old cow with a hatful of milk.
Come along now, out with you!

TITUBA. [*Calling to the window.*] Take me home,
Devil! Take me home!

SARAH GOOD. [*Following the shouting TITUBA out.*]
Tell him I'm goin', Tituba! Now you tell him
Sarah Good is goin' too!

[*In the corridor outside TITUBA calls on—"Take me*
home, Devil; Devil take me home!" and HOPKINS'
voice orders her to move on. HERRICK returns and
begins to push old rags and straw into a corner.
Hearing footsteps, he turns, and enter DANFORTH
and JUDGE HATHORNE. They are in greatcoats and
wear hats against the bitter cold. They are followed
in by CHEEVER, who carries a dispatch case and a
flat wooden box containing his writing materials.]

HERRICK. Good morning, Excellency.

DANFORTH. Where is Mr. Parris?

The United States and the World *What sort of position*
might a person like Cheever have held during the HUAC
hearings in the 1950s? **3**

ARTHUR MILLER **1097**

2 Analyze Theme *What do these lines imply about*
Herrick's morality?

Teach

Reading Strategy **1**

Infer Ask: Why is Herrick
nearly drunk? *(He may be drink-*
ing because of guilt over his role
in the trials or simply because he
cannot bear to face the injustice
that is occurring.)

APPROACHING Have students
review Herrick's words and actions
in Act Three. **Ask:** In Act Three,
what was Herrick's attitude
toward the prisoners and their
husbands? *(He seemed sympa-*
thetic toward them and uneasy
about doing his job as marshal.)

Reading Strategy **2**

Analyze Theme Answer:
Even though he is an agent of the
court, he abuses alcohol and mis-
treats his prisoners. His behavior
is immoral, and he is compared to
the devil.

Big Idea **3**

The United States and the
World Answer: *He might*
have been a staff member for the
committee chairman.

Approaching Level

DIFFERENTIATED INSTRUCTION

Established Students may be confused
by the meaning of Tituba and Sarah
Good's conversation about leaving with the
devil. Help students interpret the motivation behind their behavior in this scene
through a class discussion. Ask the following questions:

- Tituba and Sarah might be pretending
to be witches. Why might they do this?
(They may want to make their earlier

confessions more believable so they will
not be killed.)

- Tituba and Sarah might really believe
they are witches. Why might they do
this? *(They have been brainwashed into*
thinking they are witches who work for
the devil.)

- Tituba and Sarah might be mocking the
trials, the accusers, and the accusations
against them. Why might they do this?

(They are both outsiders. Tituba is not a
Puritan and Sarah Good does not act like
one.)

1097

Teach

Reading Strategy   1

Analyze Theme Answer:
He has rejected the rigid expecta-
tions of the law and is trying to
work indirectly to save people's
lives. His actions show that it is
possible to forgive those who have
technically broken the law.

Reading Strategy   2

Reread Ask: Why does
Danforth say that Hale has "no
authority to enter" the jail cell?
(Because Hale denounced the
hearings at the end of Act Three
(p. 1094), Danforth believes that
the minister has forfeited his right
to have anything to do with the
prisoners.)

Literary Element   3

Irony Ask: What is ironic
about Danforth's comment on
the setting? *(There is not only*
a physical stench but also a
moral one—the figurative smell
of injustice and moral decay. The
dramatic irony is that Danforth
does not understand that he has
contributed to this moral stench,
but the audience does.)

For activities related to this selection, see Unit 6 Teaching Resources Book, pp. 252–264.

National Theater Production of *The Crucible* by Arthur Miller. National Theater, London.

HERRICK. I'll fetch him. [*He starts for the door.*]

DANFORTH. Marshal. [*HERRICK stops.*] When did Reverend Hale arrive?

HERRICK. It were toward midnight, I think.

DANFORTH. [*Suspiciously.*] What is he about here?

HERRICK. He goes among them that will hang, sir. And he prays with them. He sits with Goody Nurse now. And Mr. Parris with him.

DANFORTH. Indeed. That man have no authority to enter here, Marshal. Why have you let him in?   2

HERRICK. Why, Mr. Parris command me, sir. I cannot deny him.

DANFORTH. Are you drunk, Marshal?

HERRICK. No, sir; it is a bitter night, and I have no fire here.

DANFORTH. [*Containing his anger.*] Fetch Mr. Parris.

HERRICK. Aye, sir.

DANFORTH. There is a prodigious stench in this place.   3

Analyze Theme **What do Hale's actions tell us about the topic of forgiveness?**   1

Vocabulary Practice

Word Origins The word *prodigious*, at the top of page 1099, is defined as (1) wonderful (2) of great power, size (3) portentous, or ominous. **Ask:** Which of these meanings works for *prodigious* in its context here? *(none)* Explain that in the 1600s, according to the *Oxford English Dictionary (OED)*, *prodigious* meant "unnatural, abnormal, amazing, monstrous, enormous." **Ask:** Which of these works in context? *(unnatural; monstrous)* The *OED* offers something a smaller dictionary does not–usages that go back hundreds of years.

HERRICK. I have only now cleared the people out for you.

DANFORTH. Beware hard drink, Marshal.

HERRICK. Aye, sir. [*He waits an instant for further orders. But* DANFORTH, *in dissatisfaction, turns his back on him, and* HERRICK *goes out. There is a pause.* DANFORTH *stands in thought.*]

HATHORNE. Let you question Hale, Excellency; I should not be surprised he have been preaching in Andover lately.

DANFORTH. We'll come to that; speak nothing of Andover. Parris prays with him. That's strange. [*He blows on his hands, moves toward the window, and looks out.*]

HATHORNE. Excellency, I wonder if it be wise to let Mr. Parris so continuously with the prisoners. [DANFORTH *turns to him, interested.*] I think, sometimes, the man has a mad look these days.

DANFORTH. Mad?

HATHORNE. I met him yesterday coming out of his house, and I bid him good morning—and he wept and went his way. I think it is not well the village sees him so unsteady.

DANFORTH. Perhaps he have some sorrow.

CHEEVER. [*Stamping his feet against the cold.*] I think it be the cows, sir.

DANFORTH. Cows?

CHEEVER. There be so many cows wanderin' the highroads, now their masters are in the jails, and much disagreement who they will belong to now. I know Mr. Parris be arguin' with farmers all yesterday—there is great contention, sir, about the cows. Contention make him weep, sir; it were always a man that weep for contention. [*He turns, as do* HATHORNE *and* DANFORTH, *hearing someone coming up the corridor.* DANFORTH *raises his head as* PARRIS *enters. He is gaunt, frightened, and sweating in his greatcoat.*]

PARRIS. [*To* DANFORTH, *instantly.*] Oh, good morning, sir, thank you for coming, I beg your pardon wakin' you so early. Good morning, Judge Hathorne.

DANFORTH. Reverend Hale have no right to enter this—

PARRIS. Excellency, a moment. [*He hurries back and shuts the door.*]

HATHORNE. Do you leave him alone with the prisoners?

DANFORTH. What's his business here?

PARRIS. [*Prayerfully holding up his hands.*] Excellency, hear me. It is a providence. Reverend Hale has returned to bring Rebecca Nurse to God.

DANFORTH. [*Surprised.*] He bids her confess?

PARRIS. [*Sitting.*] Hear me. Rebecca have not given me a word this three month since she came. Now she sits with him, and her sister and Martha Corey and two or three others, and he pleads with them, confess their crimes and save their lives.

DANFORTH. Why—this is indeed a providence. And they soften, they soften?

PARRIS. Not yet, not yet. But I thought to summon you, sir, that we might think on whether it be not wise, to—[*He dares not say it.*] I had thought to put a question, sir, and I hope you will not—

DANFORTH. Mr. Parris, be plain, what troubles you?

PARRIS. There is news, sir, that the court—the court must reckon with. My niece, sir, my niece—I believe she has vanished.

DANFORTH. Vanished!

PARRIS. I had thought to advise you of it earlier in the week, but—

DANFORTH. Why? How long is she gone?

PARRIS. This be the third night. You see, sir, she told me she would stay a night with Mercy Lewis. And next day, when she does not return, I send to Mr. Lewis to inquire. Mercy told him she would sleep in my house for a night.

---

4 | Tragedy *What is it about Reverend Parris's actions and character that make him an unlikely tragic hero?*

Analyze Theme *If a possible topic in these lines is salvation, what is a possible theme? Explain.* | **5**

Teach

Literary Element | 4

Tragedy Answer: *Although Parris might be considered a character of exalted status, one of the characteristics of a tragic hero, he does not possess the other key characteristic: admirable qualities that are marred by one tragic flaw. He is in fact selfish and cowardly.*

Reading Strategy | 5

Analyze Theme Answer: *A possible theme is that salvation is open to those who were previously condemned.*

Cultural History ☆

Andover and Witches A man from nearby Andover asked the "afflicted" Salem girls to identify the cause of his wife's illness. The girls accused more than 50 people–over 40 from Andover–of witchcraft. After one of the accused demanded that his accusers be arrested for defamation of character and that he be awarded a thousand pounds (British currency) in damages, accusations of witchcraft in Andover abated.

English Learners

DIFFERENTIATED INSTRUCTION

 SMALL GROUP

Intermediate English learners will come across some common words that are used in ways students may not have encountered before. Present these examples from this spread: "it is a <u>bitter</u> night;" "the man has a <u>mad</u> look;" "they <u>soften</u>."

Have students work with a partner to complete a three-column chart. In the first column, have them list the words *bitter, mad,* and *soft.* In the second column, have them provide each word's familiar meaning, using a dictionary if necessary. In the third column, have them use context clues to guess at the word's unfamiliar meaning as it is used in the example from the play.

Advanced Have students complete the Intermediate activity. Then have them come up with an original sentence for each word, using its meaning in the context of the play.

Teach

Analyze Theme Answer:
This is the first time that the accused people's crimes have included anything other than witchcraft. Parris's insistence that the courts have gone too far in arresting Rebecca Nurse shows that the letter of the law has overtaken the spirit of the law.

Literary Element | 2

Characterization Ask:
Whom is Parris concerned about here? *(He says his concern is for Danforth, but as has been evident from the start, he is concerned only about himself.)*

[ENGLISH LEARNERS] Make sure students understand that *wake* means "awaken." **Ask:** What does *vengeance* mean? *(revenge)* What exactly is Parris warning Danforth will happen if Rebecca is hanged? *(It will awaken in the people of Salem a desire for revenge against Danforth and the other witch hunters. In other words, there will be a riot.)*

DANFORTH. They are both gone?!

PARRIS. [*In fear of him.*] They are, sir.

DANFORTH. [*Alarmed.*] I will send a party for them. Where may they be?

PARRIS. Excellency, I think they be aboard a ship. [*DANFORTH stands agape.*] My daughter tells me how she heard them speaking of ships last week, and tonight I discover my—my strongbox is broke into. [*He presses his fingers against his eyes to keep back tears.*]

HATHORNE. [*Astonished.*] She have robbed you?

PARRIS. Thirty-one pound is gone. I am penniless. [*He covers his face and sobs.*]

DANFORTH. Mr. Parris, you are a brainless man! [*He walks in thought, deeply worried.*]

PARRIS. Excellency, it profit nothing you should blame me. I cannot think they would run off except they fear to keep in Salem any more. [*He is pleading.*] Mark it, sir, Abigail had close knowledge of the town, and since the news of Andover has broken here—

DANFORTH. Andover is remedied. The court returns there on Friday, and will resume examinations.

PARRIS. I am sure of it, sir. But the rumor here speaks rebellion in Andover, and it—

DANFORTH. There is no rebellion in Andover!

PARRIS. I tell you what is said here, sir. Andover have thrown out the court, they say, and will have no part of witchcraft. There be a faction here, feeding on that news, and I tell you true, sir, I fear there will be riot here.

HATHORNE. Riot! Why at every execution I have seen naught but high satisfaction in the town.

PARRIS. Judge Hathorne—it were another sort that hanged till now. Rebecca Nurse is no Bridget that lived three year with Bishop before she married him. John Proctor is not Isaac Ward that drank his family to ruin. [*To DANFORTH.*] I would

---

to God it were not so, Excellency, but these people have great weight yet in the town. Let Rebecca stand upon the gibbet[1] and send up some righteous prayer, and I fear she'll wake a vengeance on you.

HATHORNE. Excellency, she is condemned a witch. The court have—

DANFORTH. [*In deep concern, raising a hand to HATHORNE.*] Pray you. [*To PARRIS.*] How do you propose, then?

PARRIS. Excellency, I would postpone these hangin's for a time.

DANFORTH. There will be no postponement.

PARRIS. Now Mr. Hale's returned, there is hope, I think—for if he bring even one of these to God, that confession surely damns the others in the public eye, and none may doubt more that they are all linked to Hell. This way, unconfessed and claiming innocence, doubts are multiplied, many honest people will weep for them, and our good purpose is lost in their tears.

DANFORTH. [*After thinking a moment, then going to CHEEVER.*] Give me the list.

[*CHEEVER opens the dispatch case, searches.*]

PARRIS. It cannot be forgot, sir, that when I summoned the congregation for John Proctor's excommunication[2] there were hardly thirty people come to hear it. That speak a discontent, I think, and—

DANFORTH. [*Studying the list.*] There will be no postponement.

PARRIS. Excellency—

DANFORTH. Now, sir—which of these in your opinion may be brought to God? I will myself strive with him till dawn. [*He hands the list to PARRIS, who merely glances at it.*]

PARRIS. There is not sufficient time till dawn.

DANFORTH. I shall do my utmost. Which of them do you have hope for?

PARRIS. [*Not even glancing at the list now, and in a quavering voice, quietly.*] Excellency—a dagger— [*He chokes up.*]

> **1** Analyze Theme *How do these lines mark a change in the play's focus on the crime of witchcraft to other crimes or claims of innocence?*

1. The *gibbet* (jib′ it) is the gallows.
2. *Excommunication* is the act, by church authorities, of expelling a person from membership in a church.

Reading Practice

Compare and Contrast Characters
Have students compare and contrast the characters of Parris and Danforth. **Ask:** Which character is more morally despicable? Why? *(Some students may argue that Parris is more despicable than Danforth because he is completely motivated by petty self-interest, whereas Danforth truly believes that his actions are morally justified. Other students may* argue that Danforth is more despicable than Parris because he is willing to proceed with the executions despite his "deep concern" about both the implications and consequences of Abigail's disappearance. Danforth's moral self-righteousness will ultimately cause more suffering than Parris's amoral selfishness.) *Have students present their opinions in the form of an extemporaneous debate,* with one team delivering the anti-Parris argument and the other side delivering the anti-Danforth argument.

Through the Fire, 1992. Gayle Ray. Acrylic on canvas. Private collection.

View the Art In this painting, the figures not only seem to be walking *through* the fire, but to be *part* of it. How might this painting illustrate the struggles of the characters in *The Crucible*?

DANFORTH. What do you say?

3 PARRIS. Tonight, when I open my door to leave my house—a dagger clattered to the ground. [*Silence. DANFORTH absorbs this. Now PARRIS cries out.*] You cannot hang this sort. There is danger for me. I dare not step outside at night!

[*REVEREND HALE enters. They look at him for an instant in silence. He is steeped in sorrow, exhausted, and more direct than he ever was.*]

DANFORTH. Accept my congratulations, Reverend Hale; we are gladdened to see you returned to your good work.

HALE. [*Coming to DANFORTH now.*] You must pardon them. They will not budge.

[*HERRICK enters, waits.*]

DANFORTH. [**Conciliatory**.] You misunderstand, sir; I cannot pardon these when twelve are already hanged for the same crime. It is not just.

The United States and the World *An ideologue is an official who systematically follows a particular set of beliefs. How were both Senator McCarthy and Judge Danforth ideologues?* **4**

Vocabulary

conciliatory (kən sil′ ē ə tôr′ ē) *adj.* trying to gain the good will of another by friendly acts

ARTHUR MILLER **1101**

Teach

Literary Element | 3

Symbolism Ask: What does the dagger symbolize? What message does it convey? (*The dagger symbolizes violence and sends a threatening message to Parris, suggesting that his life will be in danger if the executions of respectable people like Rebecca Nurse take place.*)

Big Idea | 4

The United States and the World Answer: *Both were determined that the investigation continue in spite of opposition. An ideologue cannot admit doubt and must persevere in a cause for the sake of consistency, even when bad results begin to outweigh the good.*

View the Art

Answer: *The characters in the play struggle both physically and emotionally. Their torment can be compared to walking through fire. The painting suggests figures in torment. The red and yellow express intense feeling and convey the ideas of fire and violence. Fire itself is, of course, the element associated with a crucible.*

Teach

Literary Element   1

Tragedy Answer: *Danforth exhibits inflexibility as well as a fear of losing face. He is saying that more people must die to justify the executions that have already taken place. He cannot pardon because he cannot admit self-doubt or show weakness.*

Reading Strategy   2

Interpret Ask: How is Hale being sarcastic? *(Hale believes that lying is a sin, yet he is counseling the accused to save their lives by lying. Hale is being sarcastic about doing the "Devil's work," because he realizes the irony of his situation. As a Christian minister, he should not be advising people to commit a sin.)*

[APPROACHING] **Ask:** Why is Hale advising the accused to sin? *(He is trying to save innocent lives. Under the circumstances, he feels that his advice is moral and that the sin is justified.)*

Literary History ☆

Joshua In the Old Testament, God made the sun stand still, extending daylight so that the Israelites, under Joshua's leadership, could win a battle.

PARRIS. [*With failing heart.*] Rebecca will not confess?

HALE. The sun will rise in a few minutes. Excellency, I must have more time.

DANFORTH. Now hear me, and beguile yourselves no more. I will not receive a single plea for pardon or postponement. Them that will not confess will hang. Twelve are already executed; the names of these seven are given out, and the village expects to see them die this morning. Postponement now speaks a floundering on my part; **reprieve** or pardon must cast doubt upon the guilt of them that died till now. While I speak God's law, I will not crack its voice with whimpering. If **retaliation** is your fear, know this—I should hang ten thousand that dared to rise against the law, and an ocean of salt tears could not melt the resolution of the statutes. Now draw yourselves up like men and help me, as you are bound by Heaven to do. Have you spoken with them all, Mr. Hale?

HALE. All but Proctor. He is in the dungeon.

DANFORTH. [*To HERRICK.*] What's Proctor's way now?

HERRICK. He sits like some great bird; you'd not know he lived except he will take food from time to time.

DANFORTH. [*After thinking a moment.*] His wife—his wife must be well on with child now.

HERRICK. She is, sir.

DANFORTH. What think you, Mr. Parris? You have closer knowledge of this man; might her presence soften him?

PARRIS. It is possible, sir. He have not laid eyes on her these three months. I should summon her.

> **Tragedy** *What character flaw does Danforth exhibit here?*
>
> **Vocabulary**
>
> **reprieve** (ri prēv´) *n.* official postponement of the carrying out of a sentence
>
> **retaliation** (ri tal´ ē ā´ shən) *n.* the act of repaying an injury or wrong by committing the same, or a similar, act

DANFORTH. [*To HERRICK.*] Is he yet **adamant**? Has he struck at you again?

HERRICK. He cannot, sir, he is chained to the wall now.

DANFORTH. [*After thinking on it.*] Fetch Goody Proctor to me. Then let you bring him up.

HERRICK. Aye, sir. [*HERRICK goes. There is silence.*]

HALE. Excellency, if you postpone a week and publish to the town that you are striving for their confessions, that speak mercy on your part, not faltering.

DANFORTH. Mr. Hale, as God have not empowered me like Joshua to stop this sun from rising, so I cannot withhold from them the perfection of their punishment.

HALE. [*Harder now.*] If you think God wills you to raise rebellion, Mr. Danforth, you are mistaken!

DANFORTH. [*Instantly.*] You have heard rebellion spoken in the town?

HALE. Excellency, there are orphans wandering from house to house; abandoned cattle bellow on the highroads, the stink of rotting crops hangs everywhere, and no man knows when the harlots' cry will end his life—and you wonder yet if rebellion's spoke? Better you should marvel how they do not burn your province!

DANFORTH. Mr. Hale, have you preached in Andover this month?

HALE. Thank God they have no need of me in Andover.

DANFORTH. You baffle me, sir. Why have you returned here?

HALE. Why, it is all simple. I come to do the Devil's work. I come to counsel Christians they should belie themselves. [*His sarcasm collapses.*] There is blood on my head! Can you not see the blood on my head!! | 2 |

PARRIS. Hush! [*For he has heard footsteps. They all face the door. HERRICK enters with ELIZABETH. Her wrists are linked by heavy chain, which HERRICK now*

> **Vocabulary**
>
> **adamant** (ad´ ə mənt) *adj.* completely firm and unyielding

Reading Practice

Irony Discuss the dramatic irony in Danforth's statement that it would not be "just" to pardon some prisoners when others have already hanged for the same crime. **Ask:** What does the audience understand that Danforth does not? *(They understand the faulty logic of his argument. If the first hangings were unjust, then hanging more prisoners for the same supposed crime will also be unjust and will not justify the first hang-* ings.) **Ask:** What situational irony do you see in Danforth's thinking? *(His rigid consistency is achieving the opposite of what he intends: he is thwarting justice, not upholding it.)*

The Last Judgement, 1955. Abraham Rattner. Watercolor on paper, 40 x 29½ in. The Lane Collection. Courtesy Museum of Fine Arts, Boston.

View the Art After the horrors of World War II, Abraham Rattner delved into themes related to religion and his Jewish heritage, often referencing the Holocaust and nuclear war. In what ways might this painting and its title reflect the events in Act Four? ★

Teach

View the Art ★

Answer: *The painting's title reflects the horror and finality of the death sentence that has been passed on the play's innocent victims—as well as the final judgment that awaits their murderers. The painting's dark, jagged, swirling imagery conveys a sense of violent chaos that also reflects the tragic events in Act Four.*

After serving in World War I, American artist Abraham Rattner (1895–1978) lived in Paris for 20 years and was influenced by the modern art movements of Cubism, Surrealism, Futurism, and Expressionism. Rattner returned to the United States in 1939, as tensions in Europe escalated. He has been described as a "painter of the tragic."

Approaching Level

DIFFERENTIATED INSTRUCTION

Emerging Help students understand Hale's motivation for doing the "Devil's work," that is, trying to get the accused to confess. **Ask:** What does Hale mean when he says, "There is blood on my head"? *(He means that he feels at least partly responsible for the bloodshed that has occurred, because he participated in the witch hunt during its early stages and then was powerless to stop it when* he realized the injustice that was taking place.) **Say:** Parris also wants the accused to confess. **Ask:** How is Parris's motivation different from Hale's? *(Parris wants the accused to confess because he is afraid of what will happen to him if they are executed—namely, his life will be in danger because people will hold him responsible. Hale, on the other hand, is motivated by a desire to atone* for the guilt he feels over his own part in the injustice. He is also motivated by a selfless, moral desire to save the lives of innocent people.)

1103

Teach

Literary Element | 1

Simile Ask a volunteer to read aloud Hale's speech to Elizabeth at the bottom of the first column on this page. **Ask:** What simile does Hale use to characterize his behavior and attitude when he first arrived in Salem? *(He compares himself to a bridegroom who arrived in Salem bearing gifts for his beloved bride, the people of Salem. His gifts were his religious beliefs.)* What happened when he bestowed his "gifts" on his "bride"? *(She died.)*

Literary Element | 2

Tragedy Answer: *Hale says that dying for the sake of pride may be a greater sin than lying to save one's life. Hale, aware of his pride, advises Elizabeth according to his experience.*

[APPROACHING] **Say:** Sometimes pride is considered a good thing. **Ask:** What are some examples of "good" pride? *(pride in your school, community, country, or racial or ethnic heritage)* What kind of pride is usually considered a weakness? *(vanity, self-righteousness, snobbishness)*

---

removes. *Her clothes are dirty; her face is pale and gaunt. HERRICK goes out.*]

DANFORTH. [*Very politely.*] Goody Proctor. [*She is silent.*] I hope you are hearty?

ELIZABETH. [*As a warning reminder.*] I am yet six month before my time.

DANFORTH. Pray be at your ease, we come not for your life. We—[*Uncertain how to plead, for he is not accustomed to it.*] Mr. Hale, will you speak with the woman?

HALE. Goody Proctor, your husband is marked to hang this morning.

[*Pause.*]

ELIZABETH. [*Quietly.*] I have heard it.

HALE. You know, do you not, that I have no connection with the court? [*She seems to doubt it.*] I come of my own, Goody Proctor. I would save your husband's life, for if he is taken I count myself his murderer. Do you understand me?

ELIZABETH. What do you want of me?

HALE. Goody Proctor, I have gone this three month like our Lord into the wilderness. I have sought a Christian way, for damnation's doubled on a minister who counsels men to lie.

HATHORNE. It is no lie, you cannot speak of lies.

HALE. It is a lie! They are innocent!

DANFORTH. I'll hear no more of that!

HALE. [*Continuing to ELIZABETH.*] Let you not mistake your duty as I mistook my own. I came into this village like a bridegroom to his beloved, bearing gifts of high religion; the very crowns of holy law I brought, and what I touched with my bright confidence, it died; and where I turned the eye of my great faith, blood flowed up. Beware, Goody Proctor—cleave[3] to no faith when faith brings blood. It is mistaken law that leads you to sacrifice. Life, woman, life is God's most precious gift; no principle, however glorious, may justify the taking of it. I beg you, woman, prevail upon[4] your husband to confess. Let him give his lie.

---

3. Here, *cleave* means "to stick tight," or "to remain attached."
4. To *prevail upon* means "to persuade."

1104 UNIT 6 FROM DEPRESSION TO COLD WAR

Quail not before God's judgment in this, for it may well be God damns a liar less than he that throws his life away for pride. Will you plead with him? I cannot think he will listen to another.

ELIZABETH. [*Quietly.*] I think that be the Devil's argument.

HALE. [*With a climactic desperation.*] Woman, before the laws of God we are as swine! We cannot read His will!

ELIZABETH. I cannot dispute with you, sir; I lack learning for it.

DANFORTH. [*Going to her.*] Goody Proctor, you are not summoned here for disputation. Be there no wifely tenderness within you? He will die with the sunrise. Your husband. Do you understand it? [*She only looks at him.*] What say you? Will you contend with him? [*She is silent.*] Are you stone? I tell you true, woman, had I no other proof of your unnatural life, your dry eyes now would be sufficient evidence that you delivered up your soul to Hell! A very ape would weep at such calamity! Have the devil dried up any tear of pity in you? [*She is silent.*] Take her out. It profit nothing she should speak to him!

ELIZABETH. [*Quietly.*] Let me speak with him, Excellency.

PARRIS. [*With hope.*] You'll strive with him? [*She hesitates.*]

DANFORTH. Will you plead for his confession or will you not?

ELIZABETH. I promise nothing. Let me speak with him.

[*A sound—the sibilance[5] of dragging feet on stone. They turn. A pause. HERRICK enters with JOHN PROCTOR. His wrists are chained. He is another man, bearded, filthy, his eyes misty as though webs had overgrown them. He halts inside the*

---

5. A *sibilance* is a hissing sound.

Tragedy *How does Hale justify his advising Elizabeth to persuade Proctor to lie? What character flaw does he warn her against?* **2**

Analyze Theme *How does this description of Proctor develop the theme of insane situations causing healthy people to go insane themselves?* **3**

Reading Practice

Evaluate an Argument

Refer students to Hale's speech to Elizabeth that starts at the bottom of the first column. **Ask:** How would you summarize his argument? *(Hale's argument is that people should be wary of any religious faith—or any principle—that leads to the taking of life. No belief is worth dying for because life is God's most precious gift. Therefore, it is better to lie in order to live than to tell the truth and throw your life away.)* What do you think of Hale's argument? *(Students may agree with Hale that no principle justifies the taking of life. However, they may disagree with his related assertion that no principle is worth dying for. Students may argue that there are many principles worth dying to protect, such as freedom, justice, equality, and honor. They may also argue that by lying, the prisoners might save their own lives but cause others to die by lending credibility to the witch hunt.)*

doorway, his eye caught by the sight of ELIZA-
BETH. The emotion flowing between them prevents anyone from speaking for an instant. Now
HALE, visibly affected, goes to DANFORTH and
speaks quietly.]

HALE. Pray, leave them, Excellency.

DANFORTH. [Pressing HALE impatiently aside.] Mr.
Proctor, you have been notified, have you not?
[PROCTOR is silent, staring at ELIZABETH.] I see
light in the sky, Mister; let you counsel with your
wife, and may God help you turn your back on
Hell. [PROCTOR is silent, staring at ELIZABETH.]

HALE. [Quietly.] Excellency, let—

[DANFORTH brushes past HALE and walks out.
HALE follows. CHEEVER stands and follows,
HATHORNE behind. HERRICK goes. PARRIS, from a
safe distance, offers.]

PARRIS. If you desire a cup of cider, Mr. Proctor,
I am sure I—[PROCTOR turns an icy stare at him,
and he breaks off. PARRIS raises his palms toward
PROCTOR.] God lead you now. [PARRIS goes out.]

[Alone. PROCTOR walks to her, halts. It is as
though they stood in a spinning world. It is beyond
sorrow, above it. He reaches out his hand as
though toward an embodiment[6] not quite real, and
as he touches her, a strange soft sound, half laughter, half amazement, comes from his throat. He
pats her hand. She covers his hand with hers. And
then, weak, he sits. Then she sits, facing him.]

PROCTOR. The child?

ELIZABETH. It grows.

PROCTOR. There is no word of the boys?

ELIZABETH. They're well. Rebecca's Samuel
keeps them.

PROCTOR. You have not seen them?

ELIZABETH. I have not. [She catches a weakening
in herself and downs it.]

---

6. *Embodiment*, here, suggests a vision or a spirit rather than
   a solid form.

4 Tragedy *John and Elizabeth Proctor are ragged and dirty
prisoners. How does Arthur Miller manage to elevate them
to heroic stature?*

PROCTOR. You are a—marvel, Elizabeth.

ELIZABETH. You—have been tortured?

PROCTOR. Aye. [Pause. She will not let herself be
drowned in the sea that threatens her.] They come
for my life now.

ELIZABETH. I know it.

[Pause.]

PROCTOR. None—have yet confessed?

ELIZABETH. There be many confessed.

PROCTOR. Who are they?

ELIZABETH. There be a hundred or more, they
say. Goody Ballard is one; Isaiah Goodkind is
one. There be many.

PROCTOR. Rebecca?

ELIZABETH. Not Rebecca. She is one foot in
Heaven now; naught may hurt her more.

PROCTOR. And Giles?

ELIZABETH. You have not heard of it?

PROCTOR. I hear nothin', where I am kept.

ELIZABETH. Giles is dead.

[He looks at her incredulously.]

PROCTOR. When were he hanged?

ELIZABETH. [Quietly, factually.] He were not
hanged. He would not answer aye or nay to his
indictment; for if he denied the charge they'd
hang him surely, and auction out his property. So
he stand mute, and died Christian under the law.
And so his sons will have his farm. It is the law,
for he could not be condemned a wizard without
he answer the indictment, aye or nay.

PROCTOR. Then how does he die?

ELIZABETH. [Gently.] They press him, John.

PROCTOR. Press?

ELIZABETH. Great stones they lay upon his chest
until he plead aye or nay. [With a tender smile for

Vocabulary

indictment (in dīt′ mənt) n. a formal legal accusation, charging the commission or omission of an act,
which is punishable by law

ARTHUR MILLER **1105**

Teach

Reading Strategy 3

Analyze Theme Answer:
*His physical appearance and
attitude have changed as a direct
result of his imprisonment. He
seems to have taken on the supernatural characteristics of someone
who has seen the devil.*

Literary Element 4

Tragedy Answer: *The stage
directions and dialogue suggest
that with nothing left to lose and
their love renewed, they act hero-
ically, soaring above the moral
chaos of the Salem trials.*

English Learners

DIFFERENTIATED INSTRUCTION

SMALL GROUP

Intermediate English learners
may be confused by several words
on this spread that have multiple meanings
or are used in an old-fashioned or figurative way. **Say:** When Danforth asks
Elizabeth, "Are you <u>stone</u>?" he is not
asking whether she is literally made of
stone. He is using *stone* to mean "hard,
unfeeling, or cold," like a stone. Then
present these examples:

- "Goody Proctor, your husband is <u>marked</u>
  to hang this morning."
- "You'll <u>strive</u> with him?"
- "So he <u>stand</u> mute…"

Have students work with a partner to
complete a three-column chart. In the first
column, have them list the words *marked,
strive,* and *stand*. In the second column,
have them provide each word's familiar
meaning, using a dictionary if necessary. In
the third column, have them use context
clues to guess at the word's unfamiliar,
old-fashioned, or figurative meaning as it is
used in the example from the play.

Teach

Big Idea   1

The United States and the World **Answer:** *Miller refused to reveal names to the HUAC, and Corey refused to answer to his indictment.*

Reading Strategy   2

Analyze Theme **Answer:** *A possible theme is that through marriage two people can find morality, stability, and reassurance.*

Literary Element   3

Tragedy **Answer:** *Elizabeth urges John to forgive himself for having committed adultery and his character flaw of infidelity. She is urging him to forgive himself for moral weakness.*

[ENGLISH LEARNERS] Explain that *flaw* refers to a character flaw: a weakness within the character. Have students find synonyms for *flaw* in a dictionary.

Literary Element   4

Tragedy **Answer:** *Elizabeth feels that her coldness and inability to express her love contributed to John's infidelity.*

Reading Practice

Conflict Remind students that there are two kinds of conflict in literature, *external* and *internal*, and that a literary work often includes both kinds. Also point out that a single character can experience both an external and an internal conflict. After students have read this spread, have them discuss this question: What is Proctor's internal conflict? *(On the one hand, he wants "his life" and might even be willing to lie to save it, mainly because he feels that it would be "pretense" and "fraud" for him to die like a "saint." In other words, he is struggling with his feelings of guilt and shame and does not believe that it would be morally honest for him to act like a righteous martyr. On the other hand, he does not want to give his accusers what they want and believes that a false confession is morally "evil." On a broader level, Proctor is struggling with two different notions of what it means to be honest.)*

---

the old man.] They say he give them but two words. "More weight," he says. And died.

PROCTOR. [*Numbed—a thread to weave into his agony.*] "More weight."

ELIZABETH. Aye. It were a fearsome man, Giles Corey.

[*Pause.*]

PROCTOR. [*With great force of will, but not quite looking at her.*] I have been thinking I would confess to them, Elizabeth. [*She shows nothing.*] What say you? If I give them that?

ELIZABETH. I cannot judge you, John.

[*Pause.*]

PROCTOR. [*Simply—a pure question.*] What would you have me do?

ELIZABETH. As you will, I would have it. [*Slight pause.*] I want you living, John. That's sure.

PROCTOR. [*Pauses, then with a flailing of hope.*] Giles' wife? Have she confessed?

ELIZABETH. She will not.

[*Pause.*]

PROCTOR. It is a pretense, Elizabeth.

ELIZABETH. What is?

PROCTOR. I cannot mount the gibbet like a saint. It is a fraud. I am not that man. [*She is silent.*] My honesty is broke, Elizabeth; I am no good man. Nothing's spoiled by giving them this lie that were not rotten long before.

ELIZABETH. And yet you've not confessed till now. That speak goodness in you.

PROCTOR. Spite only keeps me silent. It is hard to give a lie to dogs. [*Pause, for the first time he turns directly to her.*] I would have your forgiveness, Elizabeth.

---

1 **The United States and the World** *How might Miller be making a favorable comparison between himself and Giles Corey?*

2 **Analyze Theme** *If Proctor's question highlights the topic of family or marriage, what might a possible theme be? Explain.*

ELIZABETH. It is not for me to give, John, I am—

PROCTOR. I'd have you see some honesty in it. Let them that never lied die now to keep their souls. It is pretense for me, a vanity that will not blind God nor keep my children out of the wind. [*Pause.*] What say you?

ELIZABETH. [*Upon a heaving sob that always threatens.*] John, it come to naught that I should forgive you, if you'll not forgive yourself. [*Now he turns away a little, in great agony.*] It is not my soul, John, it is yours. [*He stands, as though in physical pain, slowly rising to his feet with a great immortal longing to find his answer. It is difficult to say, and she is on the verge of tears.*] Only be sure of this, for I know it now: Whatever you will do, it is a good man does it. [*He turns his doubting, searching gaze upon her.*] I have read my heart this three month, John. [*Pause.*] I have sins of my own to count. It needs a cold wife to prompt lechery.

PROCTOR. [*In great pain.*] Enough, enough—

ELIZABETH. [*Now pouring out her heart.*] Better you should know me!

PROCTOR. I will not hear it! I know you!

ELIZABETH. You take my sins upon you, John—

PROCTOR. [*In agony.*] No, I take my own, my own!

ELIZABETH. John, I counted myself so plain, so poorly made, no honest love could come to me! Suspicion kissed you when I did; I never knew how I should say my love. It were a cold house I kept! [*In fright, she swerves, as HATHORNE enters.*]

HATHORNE. What say you, Proctor? The sun is soon up.

[*PROCTOR, his chest heaving, stares, turns to ELIZABETH. She comes to him as though to plead, her voice quaking.*]

---

3 **Tragedy** *For what flaw does Elizabeth urge Proctor to forgive himself?*

4 **Tragedy** *What flaw does Elizabeth see in herself?*

1106 UNIT 6   FROM DEPRESSION TO COLD WAR

1106

Teach

The Crucible, 1996.

View the Photograph ★

This movie still provides a clue to readers about how the play will end. So far, the action in Act Four has taken place in the Salem jail. The picture shows prisoners outside. **Ask:** Who is the character in the middle? How can you tell? *(The character is probably Proctor. His appearance matches the description of his condition on page 1105.)* What is happening? *(Proctor and others are chained to a wagon that is taking them to the gallows for execution.)*

ELIZABETH. Do what you will. But let none be your judge. There be no higher judge under Heaven than Proctor is! Forgive me, forgive me, John—I never knew such goodness in the world! [*She covers her face, weeping.*]

[PROCTOR *turns from her to* HATHORNE; *he is off the earth, his voice hollow.*]

PROCTOR. I want my life.

HATHORNE. [*Electrified, surprised.*] You'll confess yourself?

PROCTOR. I will have my life.

HATHORNE. [*With a mystical tone.*] God be praised! It is a providence! [*He rushes out the door, and his voice is heard calling down the corridor.*] He will confess! Proctor will confess!

PROCTOR. [*With a cry, as he strides to the door.*] Why do you cry it? [*In great pain he turns back to her.*] It is evil, is it not? It is evil.

ELIZABETH. [*In terror, weeping.*] I cannot judge you, John, I cannot!

PROCTOR. Then who will judge me? [*Suddenly clasping his hands.*] God in Heaven, what is John

ARTHUR MILLER **1107**

Approaching Level

DIFFERENTIATED INSTRUCTION

Emerging Students may be confused by Proctor's insistence that it would be "fraud," "pretense," and "vanity" for him to "mount the gibbet like a saint." Make sure students understand the meaning of the words *gibbet* (gallows; wooden structure used for hanging people), *fraud* (someone who is not what he or she pretends to be), *pretense* (a false appearance; deceptive action), and *vanity* (excessive pride). Then

ask: What does Proctor mean when he says, "I am not that man?" *(Because of his sin of infidelity, he is not an honest, morally upright man—the kind of man who is entitled to hold his head high as he goes to his death, the kind of man who is entitled to die to uphold a principle.)*

Established After students have discussed the question in the Strategic activity, **ask:** What does Proctor mean

when he says "Nothing's spoiled by giving them this lie that were not rotten long before"? *(Falsely confessing will not destroy his integrity, because he has already destroyed it by committing adultery.)*

Teach

Tragedy **Answer:** *Proctor is unsuccessfully trying to convince himself that his decision is right, but conflict is rising in the form of fury. This fury foreshadows that he will not be able to follow through on this lie—that he will not be able to make a false confession.*

(APPROACHING) Review the definition of foreshadowing. **Ask:** If Proctor is feeling "fury," what might he decide to do? *(He might be so angry that he decides to change his mind about giving a false confession.)*

Analyze Theme **Answer:** *Danforth insists that Proctor confess publicly in order to show the rest of the community that the court has supreme authority. The court's power is justified in the name of the stability of the town.*

Proctor, what is John Proctor? [*He moves as an animal, and a fury is riding in him, a tantalized[7] search.*] I think it is honest, I think so; I am no saint. [*As though she had denied this he calls angrily at her.*] Let Rebecca go like a saint; for me it is fraud!

[*Voices are heard in the hall, speaking together in suppressed excitement.*]

ELIZABETH. I am not your judge, I cannot be. [*As though giving him release.*] Do as you will, do as you will!

PROCTOR. Would you give them such a lie? Say it. Would you ever give them this? [*She cannot answer.*] You would not; if tongs of fire were singeing you you would not! It is evil. Good, then—it is evil, and I do it!

[*HATHORNE enters with DANFORTH, and, with them, CHEEVER, PARRIS, and HALE. It is a businesslike, rapid entrance, as though the ice had been broken.*]

DANFORTH. [*With great relief and gratitude.*] Praise to God, man, praise to God; you shall be blessed in Heaven for this. [*CHEEVER has hurried to the bench with pen, ink, and paper. PROCTOR watches him.*] Now then, let us have it. Are you ready, Mr. Cheever?

PROCTOR. [*With a cold, cold horror at their efficiency.*] Why must it be written?

DANFORTH. Why, for the good instruction of the village, Mister; this we shall post upon the church door! [*To PARRIS, urgently.*] Where is the marshal?

PARRIS. [*Runs to the door and calls down the corridor.*] Marshal! Hurry!

DANFORTH. Now, then, Mister, will you speak slowly, and directly to the point, for Mr. Cheever's sake. [*He is on record now, and is really dictating to CHEEVER, who writes.*] Mr. Proctor, have you seen the Devil in your life? [*PROCTOR's*

7. Here, *tantalized* means "tormented."

1 **Tragedy** *What is the cause of the "fury . . . riding" in Proctor? What might this strong feeling foreshadow?*

2 **Analyze Theme** *How do these lines support the idea that public confession is necessary for the health of the community?*

---

jaws lock.*] Come, man, there is light in the sky; the town waits at the scaffold; I would give out this news. Did you see the Devil?

PROCTOR. I did.

PARRIS. Praise God!

DANFORTH. And when he come to you, what were his demand? [*PROCTOR is silent. DANFORTH helps.*] Did he bid you to do his work upon the earth?

PROCTOR. He did.

DANFORTH. And you bound yourself to his service? [*DANFORTH turns, as REBECCA NURSE enters, with HERRICK helping to support her. She is barely able to walk.*] Come in, come in, woman!

REBECCA. [*Brightening as she sees PROCTOR.*] Ah, John! You are well, then, eh?

[*PROCTOR turns his face to the wall.*]

DANFORTH. Courage, man, courage—let her witness your good example that she may come to God herself. Now hear it, Goody Nurse! Say on, Mr. Proctor. Did you bind yourself to the Devil's service?

REBECCA. [*Astonished.*] Why, John!

PROCTOR. [*Through his teeth, his face turned from REBECCA.*] I did.

DANFORTH. Now, woman, you surely see it profit nothin' to keep this conspiracy any further. Will you confess yourself with him?

REBECCA. Oh, John—God send his mercy on you!

DANFORTH. I say, will you confess yourself, Goody Nurse?

REBECCA. Why, it is a lie, it is a lie; how may I damn myself? I cannot, I cannot.

DANFORTH. Mr. Proctor. When the Devil came to you did you see Rebecca Nurse in his company? [*PROCTOR is silent.*] Come, man, take courage—did you ever see her with the Devil?

PROCTOR. [*Almost inaudibly.*] No.

[*DANFORTH, now sensing trouble, glances at JOHN and goes to the table, and picks up a sheet— the list of condemned.*]

Reading Practice

Motif Direct students' attention to Proctor's "tongs of fire" speech to Elizabeth in the left column. **Ask:** How does the metaphor "tongs of fire" relate thematically to the play's "crucible" motif? *(Both the "crucible" motif and the "tongs of fire" metaphor are images of heat that convey the idea of a severe test of moral character. Miller compares the witch trials to a crucible, a container in* which the play's characters are subjected to an intense heat that separates what is morally valuable (both people and character traits) from what is worthless. This crucible separates the honest people from the frauds, the courageous from the cowardly, the righteous from the selfish or evil. Proctor is saying that Elizabeth is so honest, courageous, and righteous—so morally valuable—that she would with- *stand the severest test of character—the intense heat of "tongs of fire.")*

The Crucible, 1996.

Big Idea   3

The United States and the World Answer: *Students may suggest that forcing witnesses to divulge names in public humiliates the witnesses, destroys the reputations of the accused, and validates the investigation process.*

DANFORTH. Did you ever see her sister, Mary Easty, with the Devil?

PROCTOR. No, I did not.

DANFORTH. [*His eyes narrow on* PROCTOR.] Did you ever see Martha Corey with the Devil?

PROCTOR. I did not.

DANFORTH. [*Realizing, slowly putting the sheet down.*] Did you ever see anyone with the Devil?

PROCTOR. I did not.

DANFORTH. Proctor, you mistake me. I am not empowered to trade your life for a lie. You have most certainly seen some person with the Devil. [PROCTOR *is silent.*] Mr. Proctor, a score of people have already testified they saw this woman with the Devil.

PROCTOR. Then it is proved. Why must I say it?

DANFORTH. Why "must" you say it! Why, you should rejoice to say it if your soul is truly purged[8] of any love for Hell!

PROCTOR. They think to go like saints. I like not to spoil their names.

DANFORTH. [*Inquiring, incredulous.*] Mr. Proctor, do you think they go like saints?

---

8. To be *purged* is to be cleansed of whatever is unclean or undesirable.

The United States and the World *Many of the names given during the HUAC hearings had been revealed previously. Why might the investigators of witches in Salem and the investigators of Communists in Washington have wanted to hear the names repeated at the hearings?* **3**

ARTHUR MILLER **1109**

Approaching Level

DIFFERENTIATED INSTRUCTION

Strategic Have students read this scene aloud, beginning on page 1108 (with the entrance of Hathorne, Danforth, Cheever, Parris, and Hale) and reading through to the end of the play. Assign parts, have students rehearse, and then hold a class performance. Give students the option of memorizing their lines or performing while reading from the text. Encourage them to pay close attention to stage directions and punctuation to help them read fluently and expressively, and to use appropriate gestures and movements. Make sure students understand all the vocabulary in the stage directions before they begin rehearsing: for example, *incredulous, evading, gratitude, inaudibly, heaving,* and *boundless*.

At the end of the performance, ask students to explain how performing the scene enhanced their understanding of the characters' emotions and conflicts.

Teach

Literary Element | 1

Irony Ask: How is Danforth's statement about Proctor's soul ironic? *(When Danforth says that Proctor's soul is the issue, he means that Proctor needs to save his soul by confessing to witchcraft. The audience, however, realizes that Proctor's soul is indeed the issue, but for a different reason. To save his soul, he needs to do the opposite of what Danforth wants: he needs to find the courage to resist making a false confession.)*

Reading Strategy | 2

Analyze Theme Answer: *Proctor refuses to condemn others. He will take responsibility for his crimes, but will not be a pawn of the uncontrolled court.*

Big Idea | 3

The United States and the World Answer: *People named as witches or as Communists were officially disgraced. Although those labeled Communists were not put to death, some who suffered blacklisting were not able to find any employer who would hire them, and their lives were destroyed.*

PROCTOR. [*Evading.*] This woman never thought she done the Devil's work.

DANFORTH. Look you, sir. I think you mistake your duty here. It matters nothing what she thought—she is convicted of the unnatural murder of children, and you for sending your spirit out upon Mary Warren. Your soul alone is the issue here, Mister, and you will prove its whiteness or you cannot live in a Christian country. Will you tell me now what persons conspired with you in the Devil's company? [*PROCTOR is silent.*] To your knowledge was Rebecca Nurse ever—

PROCTOR. I speak my own sins; I cannot judge another. [*Crying out, with hatred.*] I have no tongue for it.

HALE. [*Quickly to DANFORTH.*] Excellency, it is enough he confess himself. Let him sign it, let him sign it.

PARRIS. [*Feverishly.*] It is a great service, sir. It is a weighty name; it will strike the village that Proctor confess. I beg you, let him sign it. The sun is up, Excellency!

DANFORTH. [*Considers; then with dissatisfaction.*] Come, then, sign your testimony. [*To CHEEVER.*] Give it to him. [*CHEEVER goes to PROCTOR, the confession and a pen in hand. PROCTOR does not look at it.*] Come, man, sign it.

PROCTOR. [*After glancing at the confession.*] You have all witnessed it—it is enough.

DANFORTH. You will not sign it?

PROCTOR. You have all witnessed it; what more is needed?

DANFORTH. Do you sport with me? You will sign your name or it is no confession, Mister! [*His breast heaving with agonized breathing, PROCTOR now lays the paper down and signs his name.*]

PARRIS. Praise be to the Lord!

[*PROCTOR has just finished signing when DAN-FORTH reaches for the paper. But PROCTOR*

snatches it up, and now a wild terror is rising in him, and a boundless anger.]

DANFORTH. [*Perplexed, but politely extending his hand.*] If you please, sir.

PROCTOR. No.

DANFORTH. [*As though PROCTOR did not understand.*] Mr. Proctor, I must have—

PROCTOR. No, no. I have signed it. You have seen me. It is done! You have no need for this.

PARRIS. Proctor, the village must have proof that—

PROCTOR. Damn the village! I confess to God, and God has seen my name on this! It is enough!

DANFORTH. No, sir, it is—

PROCTOR. You came to save my soul, did you not? Here! I have confessed myself; it is enough!

DANFORTH. You have not con—

PROCTOR. I have confessed myself! Is there no good penitence[9] but it be public? God does not need my name nailed upon the church! God sees my name; God knows how black my sins are! It is enough!

DANFORTH. Mr. Proctor—

PROCTOR. You will not use me! I am no Sarah Good or Tituba, I am John Proctor! You will not use me! It is no part of salvation that you should use me!

DANFORTH. I do not wish to—

PROCTOR. I have three children—how may I teach them to walk like men in the world, and I sold my friends?

DANFORTH. You have not sold your friends—

PROCTOR. Beguile me not! I blacken all of them when this is nailed to the church the very day they hang for silence!

---

9. *Penitence* is humble sorrow for one's wrongdoing.

2
Analyze Theme *How do these lines help explain the theme that each person is responsible for his or her own morality?*

The United States and the World *People named as Communists before HUAC were often placed on a "black list" and denied the opportunity of making a living. How does this blacklisting compare to the situation Proctor describes?* **3**

Reading Practice

Climax After students finish reading Act Four, remind them that the climax is the moment in the plot when the rising action reverses direction and becomes the falling action. **Say:** In a tragedy, the climax is often considered not simply the moment of greatest emotional intensity in the plot but more specifically the decisive moment that causes the protagonist's downfall. It is the action or decision that determines how the conflict will be resolved. **Ask:** Which events in Act Three did you identify as the most important complications in the rising action? *(when Elizabeth lies to protect her husband and when Mary betrays Proctor)* Which action in Act Four is also a decisive moment? *(when Proctor tears up his confession)* Which of these events or actions represents the climax of the play? Why? *(Students may say it is when Proctor tears up the letter since this action ultimately seals his fate. It is also the only event within his control.)*

Four People Behind Bars. Todd Davidson.
ARTHUR MILLER **1111**

Cultural History ☆

Church Door There is a long Christian tradition of using the church door as a place to post news. Most famously, in 1517 Martin Luther nailed his 95 Theses of Contention on the door of the Roman Catholic church in Wittenburg, Germany, an act that is considered the beginning of the Protestant Reformation.

Advanced Learners

DIFFERENTIATED INSTRUCTION

SMALL GROUP **Drama and Film Criticism** The drama critic Walter Kerr wrote that Miller had "not only the professional crusader's zeal for humanity, but the imaginative writer's feel for it . . . how it looks in its foolish as well as its noble attitudes." After students have finished Act Four, have them discuss examples of foolish and noble attitudes in the play.
Ask: Do you agree with Kerr's assessment of Miller's "zeal" and "feel" for humanity? Why or why not? Have students do library or Internet research to find reviews of *The Crucible,* including reviews of the original 1953 Broadway production, the 2002 Broadway revival, and the 1996 film version of the play. Have students watch the movie (previewed by teacher if necessary) and write a film review, keeping in mind the models of drama and film criticism that they have just read. Encourage students to include a statement like Kerr's that captures what they consider to be the essence of Miller's play or his attitude toward humanity.

Teach

Literary Element 1

Tragedy Answer: *Portraying Proctor this way adds a human dimension to his courage. He is afraid and sad, but he acts in spite of this. He knows that he is condemning himself to death, but he has decided not to compromise his principles.*

[ADVANCED] Ask: How would the effect be different if Proctor was described as "weeping," but not "in fury"? (*He would seem less of a tragic hero, because he would seem weaker and less noble.*)

Literary Element 2

Tragedy Answer: *Elizabeth accepts her husband's decision. She understands that his action is the only way he can satisfy his own conscience and uphold his innate goodness and nobility.*

[ADVANCED] Ask: How do you interpret Elizabeth's statement, "He have his goodness now"? (*Proctor was not truly "good" until he took this action, or his action finally allows him to stop doubting his own goodness.*)

 To check students' understanding of the act, see Unit 6 Teaching Resources Book, pp. 263–264.

DANFORTH. Mr. Proctor, I must have good and legal proof that you—

PROCTOR. You are the high court, your word is good enough! Tell them I confessed myself; say Proctor broke his knees and wept like a woman; say what you will, but my name cannot—

DANFORTH. [*With suspicion.*] It is the same, is it not? If I report it or you sign to it?

PROCTOR. [*He knows it is insane.*] No, it is not the same! What others say and what I sign to is not the same!

DANFORTH. Why? Do you mean to deny this confession when you are free?

PROCTOR. I mean to deny nothing!

DANFORTH. Then explain to me, Mr. Proctor, why you will not let—

PROCTOR. [*With a cry of his whole soul.*] Because it is my name! Because I cannot have another in my life! Because I lie and sign myself to lies! Because I am not worth the dust on the feet of them that hang! How may I live without my name? I have given you my soul; leave me my name!

DANFORTH. [*Pointing at the confession in PROCTOR's hand.*] Is that document a lie? If it is a lie I will not accept it! What say you? I will not deal in lies, Mister! [*PROCTOR is motionless.*] You will give me your honest confession in my hand, or I cannot keep you from the rope. [*PROCTOR does not reply.*] Which way do you go, Mister?

[*His breast heaving, his eyes staring, PROCTOR tears the paper and crumples it, and he is weeping in fury, but erect.*]

DANFORTH. Marshal!

PARRIS. [*Hysterically, as though the tearing paper were his life.*] Proctor, Proctor!

HALE. Man, you will hang! You cannot!

PROCTOR. [*His eyes full of tears.*] I can. And there's your first marvel, that I can. You have made your magic now, for now I do think I see some shred of goodness in John Proctor. Not enough to weave a banner with, but white enough to keep it from

such dogs. [*ELIZABETH, in a burst of terror, rushes to him and weeps against his hand.*] Give them no tear! Tears pleasure them! Show honor now, show a stony heart and sink them with it! [*He has lifted her, and kisses her now with great passion.*]

REBECCA. Let you fear nothing! Another judgment waits us all!

DANFORTH. Hang them high over the town! Who weeps for these, weeps for corruption!

[*He sweeps out past them. HERRICK starts to lead REBECCA, who almost collapses, but PROCTOR catches her, and she glances up at him apologetically.*]

REBECCA. I've had no breakfast.

HERRICK. Come, man.

[*HERRICK escorts them out, HATHORNE and CHEEVER behind them. ELIZABETH stands staring at the empty doorway.*]

PARRIS. [*In deadly fear, to ELIZABETH.*] Go to him, Goody Proctor! There is yet time!

[*From outside a drumroll strikes the air. PARRIS is startled. ELIZABETH jerks about toward the window.*]

PARRIS. Go to him! [*He rushes out the door, as though to hold back his fate.*] Proctor! Proctor!

[*Again, a short burst of drums.*]

HALE. Woman, plead with him! [*He starts to rush out the door, and then goes back to her.*] Woman! It is pride, it is vanity. [*She avoids his eyes, and moves to the window. He drops to his knees.*] Be his helper!—What profit him to bleed? Shall the dust praise him? Shall the worms declare his truth? Go to him, take his shame away!

ELIZABETH. [*Supporting herself against collapse, grips the bars of the window, and with a cry.*] He have his goodness now. God forbid I take it from him!

[*The final drumroll crashes, then heightens violently. HALE weeps in frantic prayer, and the new sun is pouring in upon her face, and the drums rattle like bones in the morning air.*]

THE CURTAIN FALLS ✒

1 Tragedy *Why would Miller portray Proctor as "weeping . . . but erect?"*

2 Tragedy *Why doesn't Elizabeth save her husband, as Parris and Hale urge?*

Reading Practice

Evaluate Theme Have students evaluate Proctor's decision to tear up his confession. **Ask:** Does Proctor win a victory by refusing to compromise his principles? Explain. (*Most students will agree that he does because there are some principles worth dying for.*) What does this action reveal about the play's theme? In other words, what central message does Miller want the audience or reader to infer from Proctor's action?

(*Students might interpret Miller's theme to be that standing by your principles, no matter what the cost, is the right thing to do—or more specifically, that people must resist the abuse of authority, no matter what the cost.*) Do you agree with this message? Why or why not? (*Students should support their opinions with reasons.*) How would the theme be different if Miller had not connected the historical context of the play to

events during his own time period? (*The theme would not seem as universal and relevant to contemporary life.*)

Respond and Think Critically

Respond and Interpret

1. (a)What were your thoughts at the end of the play? (b)Do you have any unanswered questions? Explain.

2. (a)What news does Parris convey to Danforth about Abigail? (b)What is Danforth's reaction? Why might he react this way?

3. (a)What has Hale been trying to do with the condemned prisoners? (b)What do his words reveal about his values?

4. (a)What might Proctor's ultimate decision mean for him? For Salem? (b)What might Elizabeth mean when she says that John has "his goodness now"?

Analyze and Evaluate

5. (a)Analyze the mood of the Salem residents at the beginning of Act Four. (b)Given events during the three months since the end of Act Three, is this mood is to be expected? Explain.

6. (a)Contrast Danforth and Hathorne. (b)Which do you consider more dangerous? Explain.

Connect

7. **Big Idea** The United States and the World How does Miller want to compare the Salem witch trials and the HUAC hearings?

8. **Connect to Today** Do you think Miller's play is relevant today? Explain.

Daily Life & Culture

Life in Puritan New England

To protect citizens from Satan, the Puritans banned amusements that might tempt young people to idleness. These included playing cards, shuffleboard, and dice, dancing around a maypole, attending plays, and even beachcombing.

Because a virtuous society depended upon everyone behaving according to God's law, Puritans were encouraged to report on each other for sinning. Missing church services or sleeping during the sermon, quarreling with one's husband or wife, swearing, or even playing certain musical instruments were punishable activities. In Puritan New England, privacy was a place where Satan lurked, and pleasure was considered a temptation. No Puritan could have conceived the phrase "the pursuit of happiness." Rather, the Puritan ideal was the pursuit of godliness.

1. Some aspects of Puritan society described above may seem strange and unattractive to modern readers. What advantages might there be to living in such a close-knit culture?

2. How does the information given here help explain the behavior of some of the characters in *The Crucible*? Give specific examples.

Daily Life & Culture

1. Puritan society must have been relatively free of crime. Watching neighbors can yield safety benefits.

2. Examples: Hale hears that the Proctors do not attend church regularly. Cheever says that Proctor plows on Sundays.

 For additional assessment, see Assessment Resources, pp. 271–272.

1. Students' thoughts will vary.

2. (a) Abigail and Mercy have stolen money and vanished. (b) He is worried that people may doubt Abigail's accusations, thus casting doubt on his judgments.

3. (a) Hale wants prisoners to confess so that their lives will be spared. (b) He values human life over honesty.

4. (a) His ultimate decision means that he has integrity. His execution may inspire a rebellion. (b) He values truth more than his life; he realizes that he has integrity.

5. (a) The mood is fearful and resigned. (b) It is a consequence of the investigations, which are supported by the authorities and appear without end.

6. (a) Hathorne is devoid of compassion. Danforth occasionally shows sympathy. (b) Fear of disorder, and executing people despite Hale's reasoning, makes Danforth more dangerous.

7. Both the trials and the hearings created fear; in both situations those who accused were presumed innocent while those accused were guilty; in both situations people's lives were ruined or taken.

8. Students should support their responses with a logical explanation.

After You Read

Literary Element

1. Proctor is the tragic hero. He has the courage to admit faults and a conscience that leads to challenging authority in the interests of truth and justice.

2. Proctor's passion makes him adulterous and leads him to his destruction. Proctor refuses to admit his sin until it is too late to prevent tragedy.

Progress Check

Can students analyze tragedy?

If No → See Unit 6 Teaching Resources Book, p. 258.

Review: Conflict

Possible Answers:

John Proctor:
External—arguments with Reverend Parris; **Internal**—guilt about adultery

Elizabeth Proctor:
External—arguments with John; **Internal**—struggle to forgive John

Reading Strategy

Examples will vary. Students should note that dialogue, stage direction, and characterization are used in different ways to portray Miller's theme.

Vocabulary

1. I would give my friend a gift or do a favor for him.

2. A teacher might give me a *reprieve* so that I could turn in a paper a day late.

3. A country might counterattack their aggressor in *retaliation.*

Literary Element Tragedy

In common usage, the word *hero* applies to almost anyone who acts bravely. In a literary **tragedy,** however, the term **tragic hero** has a specific meaning. It refers to the main character in a drama who suffers downfall and death because of a **tragic flaw** in his or her character. According to the Greek philosopher Aristotle, the tragic hero's fate is intended to inspire pity and terror. Tragic heroes may behave badly, but audiences are meant to respond sympathetically to them because of their noble and admirable qualities.

1. Who is the tragic hero of *The Crucible*? What noble or admirable qualities does this hero possess?

2. What is the tragic flaw that causes the hero's downfall and death?

Review: Conflict

Conflict is the struggle between opposing forces in a story or drama. **External conflict** exists when a character struggles against some outside force, such as nature, society, or another character. An **internal conflict** is a struggle between two opposing thoughts or desires within the mind of a character.

Partner Activity Meet with a classmate and create a three-column chart similar to the one below. In the left column, list the names of the principal characters. In the other two columns describe the external and internal conflicts in which these characters are involved.

Character	External Conflict	Internal Conflict
Reverend Hale	Pleads with prisoners to confess	considers himself guilty of sending innocent people to their deaths

LOG ON ▶ **Literature** Online

Selection Resources For Selection Quizzes, eFlashcards, and Reading-Writing Connection activities, go to glencoe.com and enter QuickPass code GLA9800u6.

Reading Strategy Analyze Theme

One of the purposes of literature is to allow a writer to use artistic techniques to share his or her opinions on a subject. *The Crucible* is a play that uses the conventions of drama to comment on the political environment of the mid-twentieth century. Identify one example of each of the dramatic techniques below and explain how Miller uses it to reveal his theme.

1. Dialogue

2. Stage Direction

3. Characterization

Vocabulary Practice

Practice with Word Usage Respond to these statements to help you explore the meanings of vocabulary words from the selection.

1. Explain how you would treat a friend if you were committing a **conciliatory** act.

2. Identify something for which your teacher might give you a **reprieve.**

3. Describe a **retaliation** a country might take if it were attacked by another country.

4. Name an event that you have been **adamant** about attending, and tell why.

5. Identify why a criminal might fear an **indictment.**

Academic Vocabulary

The relationship between Proctor and Abigail is **complex***; she feels his testimony will ruin her reputation, and because he will be hanged, she can no longer be his wife.*

Complex is an academic word. In more casual conversation, someone might say that counteracting global climate change is a **complex** issue. To further explore the meaning of this word, answer this question: *What is a* **complex** *issue that American teens face today? Explain.*

For more on academic vocabulary, see pages 53–54.

---

4. I was *adamant* about attending *The Simpsons Movie* because *The Simpsons* is my favorite television show.

5. A criminal might fear an *indictment* because it would mean he or she would be legally accused of a crime.

Academic Vocabulary

Possible Answer: Becoming acquainted with politics is a *complex* issue for teens because it requires an understanding of both domestic and foreign policy in order to be prepared to vote at eighteen.

1114

Respond Through Writing

Editorial

Offer a Solution Think of a contemporary real-world situation that resembles the circumstances and conflicts of *The Crucible*. Present your own solution to the current problem in an editorial.

Understand the Task An **editorial** is an article that expresses the personal ideas and opinions of the writer. A **primary source** is an original document such as a letter, a newspaper, a magazine article, an interview, or a historical document from a specific time period. A **secondary source** is a secondhand account written by a writer without firsthand experience of an event or a cultural period. Historical essays, biographies, and critics' reviews are examples of secondary sources.

Prewrite Generate a list of contemporary topics on which you could write. Choose a topic you feel strongly about and develop a logical solution to it. Conduct research to find both primary and secondary sources that will help convince your readers that the solution you present is viable.

Draft Develop a logical strategy to help you make a strong argument. Open by presenting the problem, follow by stating your solution, and finish by refuting counterarguments. Be sure that you have supporting evidence for every point you make, and that you cite sources when appropriate. Appeal both to the reader's logic and emotions. Use rhetorical devices to make your proposal persuasive.

Revise Exchange papers with a partner. Evaluate one another's editorials based on the following checklist:

- Does the editorial offer a solution that appeals to the reader's reason and emotion?
- Are the arguments logical and well-supported?
- Does the editorial anticipate counterarguments and refute them?

Edit and Proofread Proofread your essay, correcting any errors in spelling, grammar, and punctuation. Use the Grammar Tip in the side column to help you use comparative and superlative adjectives correctly.

Learning Objectives

In this assignment, you will focus on the following objectives:

Writing: Writing an editorial.

Grammar: Using comparative and superlative forms of adjectives.

Grammar Tip

Comparative and Superlative Adjectives

The comparative form of an adjective shows two things being compared. For example:

Elizabeth Proctor is bolder than her husband.

The superlative form of an adjective shows three or more things being compared.

Reverend Hale is the worst of all of the persecutors.

In general, for one-syllable adjectives add *-er* to form the comparative and *-est* to form the superlative. Spelling changes may occur when adding these endings. For example:

- *hot, hotter, hottest*
- *cheery, cheerier, cheeriest*

With multisyllabic adjectives, it may sound more natural to use *more* and *most* instead of *-er* and *-est*.

Tituba is the most ostracized of the women in The Crucible.

After You Read

Assess

Respond Through Writing

Students' editorials should present logical arguments that are supported by evidence from primary and secondary sources. Students should use persuasive techniques such as emotional and logical appeals. They should also anticipate and refute readers' counterarguments.

Scoring Guide

Assess students' performance in the following categories using the scoring guide below:

- Addresses all parts of the writing task.
- Provides a meaningful thesis; maintains focus and organization.
- Supports the thesis with details and examples.
- Provides a variety of sentence types; uses precise, descriptive language.
- Follows English language conventions.
- Makes a logical, convincing argument.

ARTHUR MILLER **1115**

Scoring Guide	4	3	2	1
Task addressed	fully	mostly	partially	barely
Thesis	meaningful	provided	partial	weak
Support	thoughtful	provided	limited	weak
Language	varied, descriptive	varied, often descriptive	predictable, imprecise	repetitive, limited
Convention errors	few or none	several	many	serious
Arguments are	convincing	mostly convincing	partially convincing	not convincing

Focus

Learning Objectives

For pages 1116–1117

In studying this text, you will focus on the following objectives:

Reading:
Analyzing cultural context.
Analyzing literary periods.
Evaluating historical influences.

Bellringer Options

Daily Language Practice Transparency 95

Or describe a play you have seen, or ask students to share their experiences when viewing a theatrical performance. **Ask:** How would you compare a live performance with reading the script of a play?

Teach

Literary Element

Genre Using the ideas from the Bellringer activity, have students generate a list of the features of drama. *(Lists should include cast of characters, stage directions, speech-directed plot, scenery, and so forth.)*

 For activities related to this selection, see Unit 6 Teaching Resources Book, pp. 265–266.

Modern American Drama

THOUGH POETRY AND FICTION WERE WELL ESTABLISHED AS American literary genres by the middle of the nineteenth century, this was not the case with drama. Up until the early decades of the twentieth century, drama made little impact on American literature as a whole. Then, with Eugene O'Neill, American drama suddenly came of age.

O'Neill's Influence

A major event was the 1916 performance of Eugene O'Neill's *Bound East for Cardiff* by the Provincetown Players, a "little theater" company that produced original works by unknown talents. The first American dramatist to achieve an international reputation, O'Neill thrilled audiences and impressed critics as he explored the tragic relationship between fate and character and depicted the complex depths of the human mind.

A Streetcar Named Desire, 1947.

O'Neill's plays, including *Strange Interlude* (1928), *The Iceman Cometh* (1946), and *Long Day's Journey into Night* (1939–1941), reflect his New England background, his Irish American heritage, his reading of the Scandinavian playwrights Henrik Ibsen and August Strindberg, and his fascination with the theories and discoveries of modern psychology. Like the Modernists, he too blazed new trails, experimenting with form, style, and symbolism. His innovations intrigued audiences and greatly influenced subsequent playwrights.

> *"On the stage it is always now; the personages are standing on that razor edge, between the past and the future, which is the essential character of conscious being."*
>
> —Thornton Wilder

American drama flourished between the two world wars. Elmer Rice wrote a realistic portrait of tenement life called *Street Scene* (1929); Clifford Odets explored serious social problems in *Awake and Sing* (1935) and *Waiting for Lefty* (1935); and Lillian Hellman created a successful drama of social criticism in *The Little Foxes* (1939), a play about a predatory southern family. Thornton Wilder's *Our Town* (1938), a surrealistic play about everyday life in a New England town, enjoyed astonishing success.

Postwar Playwrights

Tennessee Williams and Arthur Miller dominated the American theater in the decade after World War II. Williams was noted for his lyrical dialogue and wrote plays that explored some of the darker aspects of human psychology.

Listening and Speaking Practice

 SMALL GROUP **On Stage** Have small groups of students work together to give a dramatic reading of part of Act Four of *The Crucible* (for example, the scene between Proctor and his wife, pages 1105–1108; or Danforth questioning Proctor, pages 1108–1112). Have groups practice saying the lines to each other, and then ask groups to volunteer to do their reading in front of the class. Have students write a paragraph about each group's performance, comparing their experience of hearing the scene read aloud with their own silent reading. Ask students to include at least one similarity and one difference between the two experiences.

1116

Death of a Salesman, 2000.

Recent History

In the 1960s and 1970s, Edward Albee experimented with a variety of styles, including the theater of the absurd and the theater of cruelty. The theater of cruelty, which strives to produce a visceral reaction in the audience, influenced the scathing dialogue in Albee's acclaimed *Who's Afraid of Virginia Woolf?* (1962).

When it opened in 1959, *A Raisin in the Sun* by Lorraine Hansberry was the first drama by an African American woman to be produced on Broadway. Hansberry's realistic portrayal of black characters and her fearless depiction of social injustice marked a new era in African American drama. Beginning in 1982, August Wilson chronicled African American experience in a series of ten plays, each set in a different decade of the twentieth century. In *Fences* (1985), the second play in the series, the main character is a former baseball player, a victim of discrimination who was denied access to the major leagues. Wilson's play has already emerged as a classic.

Some of the most significant plays of the recent past are the work of women writers. These plays include *Crimes of the Heart* (1979) by Beth Henley and *'night, Mother* (1983) by Marsha Norman. In *The Heidi Chronicles* (1989), Wendy Wasserstein explores the challenges faced by educated women competing in a male-dominated culture.

Musical Theater

The musical remains one of America's distinct contributions to the theater. During World War II, the watershed musical *Oklahoma!* (1943), by Richard Rodgers and Oscar Hammerstein II, brought the form to new heights, integrating music, story, and dance to develop plot and character.

The musical reached its peak after World War II in other works by Rodgers and Hammerstein and in those by Alan Jay Lerner and Frederick Loewe, Leonard Bernstein, and Stephen Sondheim. Later decades saw musicals break new ground. In 1968, *Hair* introduced rock music to theater audiences. *A Chorus Line* (1975) and *Chicago* (1976) brought dance-centered musicals to the fore. In 2001, Mel Brooks's musical comedy *The Producers* won a record twelve Tony Awards and once again made American musical theater popular with theatergoers.

Drama flourished during the twentieth century and continues to do so. Some of the most gifted writers—O'Neill, Williams, Miller, Albee, and Wilson—created masterpieces for the stage. With a rich legacy of outstanding works, American drama is primed to reflect and respond to life in a new century.

 Literature Online

Literature and Reading For more about modern American drama, go to glencoe.com and enter QuickPass code GLA9800u6.

Respond and Think Critically

1. Which two Scandinavian playwrights strongly influenced Eugene O'Neill?

2. How did Eugene O'Neill revolutionize American drama?

3. What innovations has Edward Albee made in the theater?

4. In what way did *Oklahoma!* differ from previous musicals?

LITERARY HISTORY **1117**

Approaching Level

DIFFERENTIATED INSTRUCTION

Emerging Explain to students that they may find subheads helpful when they are answering questions about a selection. By isolating the part of the text where they might find the answer to a question, they can save time. For example, if students do not immediately know the answer to question 2, they can reread the section under the subhead that reads "O'Neill's Influence." Scanning the text under the subhead "Recent History," will reveal that Edward Albee is mentioned in the first line of text. This will help students answer question 3.

Teach

Big Idea

The United States and the World As theater became an important form of American literature, its audience, of course, grew. Some observers of American theater complain, however, that productions have become so expensive that only those with high incomes can afford to attend first-rate performances. **Ask:** How can people across the nation and throughout the world experience live theater? *(If students do not mention reduced-price tickets to theater in major cities [e.g. Broadway shows, off-Broadway shows, off-off-Broadway shows], regional theater, and community and college productions, make them aware of these options.)*

Assess

1. Henrick Ibsen and August Strindberg

2. O'Neill explored human psychology and experimented with form and style.

3. To criticize society, Albee has experimented with the theater of the absurd and the theater of cruelty.

4. It displayed a new level of artistic unity between the narrative and musical elements of the performance.

Focus

Bellringer

Say: Because we all come from different backgrounds and have had different experiences, everyone's story is unique. People who write stories about their own lives create autobiographical narratives.

Ask students to bring in one or more photographs of people or places that are important in their lives. Have them tell brief stories about their photos, and allow others to ask questions about the stories.

Summary

In this workshop, students will write and present creative nonfiction essays. Students will follow the stages of the writing process, including prewriting, drafting, revising, and editing. In addition, two mini-lessons, on avoiding stilted language and on correcting verb tense, are provided.

Learning Objectives

For pages 1118–1125

In this workshop, you will focus on the following objective:

Writing: Writing creative nonfiction using the writing process.

> **Writing Process**

At any stage of a writing process, you may think of new ideas. Feel free to return to earlier stages as you write.

Prewrite

Draft

Revise

Focus Lesson: Avoid Stilted Language

Edit and Proofread

Focus Lesson: Verb Tense

Present

Writing Workshop

Creative Nonfiction

Literature Connection In much of his writing, Elie Wiesel reveals his personal experiences during World War II.

> *"I see myself sitting there, haggard and disoriented, a shadow among shadows. . . . My heart thunders in deafening beats. Then there is silence, heavy and complete. Something was about to happen, we could feel it. Fate would at last reveal a truth reserved exclusively for us, a primordial truth, an ultimate postulate that would annihilate or overshadow all received ideas."*

This type of writing is generally referred to as autobiographical narrative, a type of **creative nonfiction** in which a writer tells a sequence of past events from his or her life and reveals the personal significance of the experience. Study the checklist below to learn the goals and strategies for writing successful creative nonfiction.

Checklist: Features of Creative Nonfiction Essays

Goals	Strategies
To recreate an experience	☑ Create an engaging plot
	☑ Use literary devices such as flashback, foreshadowing, imagery, and allusion
To create believable characters	☑ Use dialogue and internal monologue as methods of characterization
	☑ Use actions, including gestures and movements, as methods of characterization
To entertain the audience	☑ Use sensory description
	☑ Use figurative language

Workshop Resources

Print Materials

📁 Unit 6 Teaching Resources pp. 268–270
📁 Writing Kit
📁 Success in Writing: Research and Reports

Technology

- Literature Online: Writing Resources and Grammar Resources, www.glencoe.com
- Online Essay Grader, www.glencoe.com
- Student Presentation Builder on StudentWorks Plus CD-ROM
- Media Workshop DVD
- Online Student Edition

Assignment: Write Creative Nonfiction

Write a creative nonfiction essay of about 1,500 words to describe a personal or other experience and to show how the experience was meaningful. As you work, keep your audience and purpose in mind.

Audience: peers and classmates

Purpose: to relate a personal experience and to communicate its significance

Analyze a Professional Model

In this excerpt from her autobiography, Pulitzer Prize-winning author Eudora Welty explores her discovery of the moon during childhood and how the experience became meaningful to her as a writer. As you read the following passage, note Welty's use of concrete details, sensory images, and interior monologue, all of which help her communicate a vivid, significant experience from her own life. As you read, pay attention to the comments in the margin. They point out features to include in your own creative nonfiction.

From *One Writer's Beginnings* by Eudora Welty

Learning stamps you with its moments. Childhood's learning is made up of moments. It isn't steady. It's a pulse.

In a children's art class, we sat in a ring on kindergarten chairs and drew three daffodils that had just been picked out of the yard; and while I was drawing, my sharpened yellow pencil and the cup of the yellow daffodil gave off whiffs just alike. That the pencil doing the drawing should give off the same smell as the flower it drew seemed part of the art lesson—as shouldn't it be? Children, like animals, use all their senses to discover the world. Then artists come along and discover it the same way, all over again. Here and there, it's the same world. Or now and then we'll hear from an artist who's never lost it.

In my sensory education I include my physical awareness of the *word*. Of a certain word, that is; the connection it has with what it stands for. At around age six, perhaps, I was standing by myself in our front yard waiting for supper, just at that hour in a late summer

Audience

Use figurative language to create interest.

Characterization

Show characters through their thoughts and actions.

Real-World Connection

Many college applications require a creative nonfiction essay in which you reveal a significant experience from your life and tell how it affected you. Employers often ask similar questions of potential employees. Universities and employers alike want to see how you respond to life changes and how you learn from such experiences.

Teach

Big Idea

Return to Regionalism Remind students that many of the writers in this unit describe an incident drawn from their own backgrounds, bringing in details that give the reader a sense of the region where the writer grew up. Have students skim the unit selections as a reminder of the many styles of personal narrative they have read. **Say:** Skim the selections by Wright, Wiesel, Hongo, Spiegelman, and Rivera in order to remind yourself of some styles of personal narrative.

Writing Skills

Personal Journal Give students time to keep a journal before beginning their creative nonfiction essays. Making a list of important life events and recording impressions will give students material to select from as they write their narratives.

Literary History ☆

Eudora Welty One of the Regionalist writers of the mid-20th century, Welty was born in Jackson, Mississippi. She wrote short stories and novels focused on small-town life in the Deep South. The humor in her works is especially evident in her use of local dialect and colloquialisms.

English Learners

DIFFERENTIATED INSTRUCTION

Intermediate In their journals and autobiographical narratives, English learners may want to include some words in their native language, along with the translation of the words. The sound of their language may help them convey the setting and mood of their story. Suggest a style for including non-English words. For example, the translation could be in parentheses following the non-English word; in a footnote; at the end of the story; or in context. For example, "I loved my tia Stella. *Tia* means 'aunt,' but to me, it was part of her name, *Tiastella*."

Teach

Writing Skills

Use Precise Language Students may have difficulty understanding precise language. Help them move from general terms to more specific ones. Write the headings "General," "More Specific," and "Very Specific" on the board. Write the word *large* under the first heading. Have students suggest more specific terms, such as *huge, gigantic,* and *monstrous.*

ENGLISH LEARNERS Check to make sure that English learners understand the concept of moving from general to specific. Explain that more specific words narrow down features so that a reader can get a clearer picture. Have students suggest examples.

Literary Devices

Use imagery and other literary devices. →

day when the sun is already below the horizon and the risen full moon in the visible sky stops being chalky and begins to take on light. There comes the moment, and I saw it then, when the moon goes from flat to round. For the first time it met my eyes as a globe. → The word "moon" came into my mouth as though fed to me out of a silver spoon. Held in my mouth the moon became a word. It had the roundness of a Concord grape Grandpa took off his vine and gave me to suck out of its skin and swallow whole, in Ohio.

This love did not prevent me from living for years in foolish error about the moon. The new moon just appearing in the west was the rising moon to me. The new should be rising. And in early childhood the sun and moon, those opposite reigning powers, I just as easily assumed rose in east and west respectively in their opposite sides of the sky, and like partners in a reel they advanced, sun from the east, moon from the west, crossed over (when I wasn't looking) and went down on the other side. My father couldn't have known I believed that when, bending behind me and guiding my shoulder, he positioned me at our telescope in the front yard and, with careful adjustment of the focus, brought

Characterization

Describe the specific actions, movements, and gestures of characters. → the moon close to me.

Though I'd been taught at our diningroom table about the solar system and knew the earth revolved around the sun, and our moon around us, I never found out the moon didn't come up in

Plot

Narrate a sequence of events in a logical, effective order. → the west until I was a writer and Herschel Brickell, the literary critic, told me after I misplaced it in a story. He said valuable words to me about my new profession:

Dialogue

Create believable characters by means of dialogue. → "Always be sure you get your moon in the right part of the sky."

LOG ON ▶ **Literature** Online

Writing and Research For prewriting, drafting, and revising tools, go to glencoe.com and enter QuickPass code GLA9800u6.

Reading-Writing Connection Think about the writing techniques that you just encountered and try them out in the creative nonfiction you write.

Writing Practice

Character Sketch Authors use both direct and indirect characterization to convey the personalities of people in their stories. Direct characterization is a narrator's direct comments about a character. Indirect characterization conveys personalities through:

- what the characters say
- what the characters do
- what the characters think
- what others say about the characters

Suggest that students include a character sketch in their narrative, using direct and indirect methods of characterization.

Prewrite

Make a Writing Schedule Rough out a plan for completing each step of your writing process in plenty of time to meet your final deadline.

Decide on an Experience Think about events that others might find interesting and that you remember well enough to explain in detail.

Gather Details As you gather details, keep in mind your audience and purpose to help you decide which details to include.

▶ **Recall the Experience** Clearly remember the important details and the order of events. Visualize details by replaying the experience in your mind and discussing it with people who were involved. Photos, newspaper clippings, and journal entries might help jog your memory.

▶ **Connect to Your Audience** Think about what context or background information your audience will need to participate in the experience and feel its full impact.

▶ **Be Specific and Concrete** Describe the details in concrete, precise language. Consider what sensory images, dialogue, and personal feelings will create greatest interest; you will want to further elaborate, or "flesh out," those details for your audience.

Make a Plan Telling the events in chronological order is often the most clear and logical way to narrate an experience. Organize the narrative around the climax, and feel free to narrate some events in flashback or flash-forward to add background information or suspense.

Talk About Your Ideas Meet with a partner to help develop your writing voice. Take turns telling each other the most vivid details of your experience. Jot down notes and refer to them as you develop your essay.

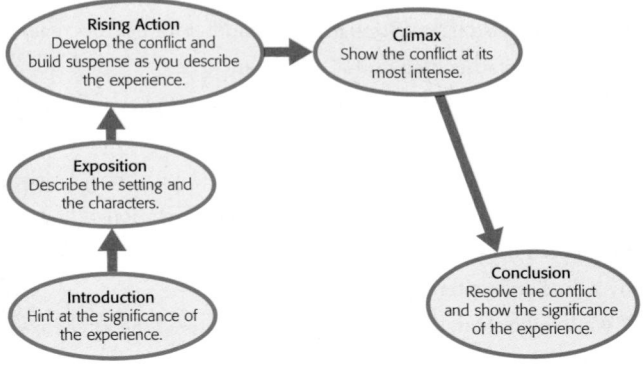

- **Rising Action** Develop the conflict and build suspense as you describe the experience.
- **Climax** Show the conflict at its most intense.
- **Exposition** Describe the setting and the characters.
- **Introduction** Hint at the significance of the experience.
- **Conclusion** Resolve the conflict and show the significance of the experience.

Build Suspense with a Flashback or Foreshadowing

If telling the events of your experience in purely chronological order diminishes the suspense, add a flashback. A **flashback** is an interruption in the narrative to show an event that happened earlier. A flashback gives readers information that may help explain the main events of the narrative. **Foreshadowing**—a hint of what is to come—can also enliven your narrative.

Avoid Plagiarism

Do not download papers from the Internet or take ideas from them. Consequences for such behavior can range from a failing grade to suspension from a sports team—or from school.

Teach

Writing Skills

Plan to Write Have students create charts with the headings "Topic," "Audience," "Purpose," "Setting," "Point of View," "Characters," and "Plot." Have them use the charts to jot down ideas. It may be helpful for students to form groups, present their topics in the groups, and then take notes as other group members ask questions or make suggestions. Students may take turns doing this until the charts are completed.

Writing Process

Prewrite Remind students that the more familiar they are with their topic, the easier it will be to write. As they prepare to write their drafts, encourage them to collect as much information as possible and write it down. **Ask:** What would be a good way to gather information for your narrative? *(Talking to someone else who was there; including relevant written sources, such as letters or journals.)* Have students use note cards to organize information.

Approaching Level

DIFFERENTIATED INSTRUCTION 🔄

 SMALL GROUP **Supported** Explain to students that the scope of their narrative may change as they plan and draft their story. When students work in pairs or small groups to talk about their ideas, tell listeners to warn storytellers if they sense that the story is losing momentum, wandering, losing focus, or too long for the assigned number of pages. One way to keep the story on track is to have the listener stop the storyteller and ask, "Would you remind me of the significance of this event for you?" This helps the storyteller get back to the main idea.

Writing Workshop

Creative Nonfiction

Teach

Writing Process

Draft Remind students that drafting is the stage for ideas, not perfection. They should concentrate on the details their sensory images bring to mind, not on whether these are important to the narrative or are grammatically precise.

Writing Skills

Literary Device: Foreshadowing

Answer: *By telling the reader how he or she thought older generations were supposed to act, the writer hints that the experience will change this view. The experience might have to do with an adult letting him down.*

Characterization

Answer: *The presents suggest that Jim is more focused on the things he likes than he is on the grandmother or her situation.*

Writing Frames

As you read the workshop model, think about the writer's use of the following frames:

- I had always expected that _____.

- Years later, _____.

- _____, I finally got it.

Consider using frames like these in your own creative nonfiction essay.

Literary Device: Foreshadowing

How does the writer hint at the significance of the experience? What might the experience be about?

Draft

Go with the Flow When you begin your draft, do not get stuck trying to find the perfect word or detail. You will have time to do this when you revise your draft later. Instead, focus on relating the events in order. Try to build suspense and lead the reader to the climax before the conclusion of the narrative. Occasionally step back from your draft to assess your narrative and its overall direction. Remember that following an unexpected direction may lead to new insights about the experience.

Analyze a Workshop Model

Here is a final draft of a creative nonfiction essay. Read the narrative and answer the questions in the margin. Use the answers to these questions to guide you as you write your own creative nonfiction.

Antique Jim

I had always expected that older generations had their problems mostly worked out. They were there to help the rest of us, to clean up children with scraped knees and bee stings, and to comfort worrying parents. They were supposed to know who they were. They weren't supposed to change.

Jim had always been there, tall and lank and cheerfully idle, dropping in at my grandmother's ranch house. I have never been quite sure where Jim came from, or how he ended up stuck with our family. He had been dating my grandmother for decades, ever since my grandfather died in the 1970s.

When we went to my grandmother's house on Saturdays, Jim would always show up just before dinner. He would let himself into the screened-in porch with a loud "Hullo!" for whoever was around to hear. Like Christopher and me, Jim always forgot and let the porch door slam. With him, however, my grandmother only sighed and pretended not to notice.

"Well, hullo, Mary!" Jim would say as he entered the kitchen, his blue eyes sparkling behind octagonal bifocals.

1122 UNIT 6

Reading Practice

SMALL GROUP **Sensory Details Say:** In an autobiographical narrative, vivid details allow readers to feel, hear, taste, smell, and see the images. Have students choose the more vivid of the following descriptions:

- The harsh, bitter wind snapped at our backs as we trudged through the mounds of snow.
- It was cold, and there was a lot of snow.

Have pairs of students discuss vague or unclear descriptions in their narratives and help each other develop more descriptive details. Then have them rewrite their narratives, including more sensory details.

1122

Instead of flowers, Jim brought my grandmother antiques gathered from Saint Vincent de Paul thrift shops, estate sales, and vintage stores. This particular time it was a crafty wooden structure that turned out to be a cuckoo clock. When Jim unveiled it, I could tell that my grandmother had no idea what to do with the thing.

"Picked her up at Saint Vinny's this afternoon," Jim said, dusting off the face and gently pulling the bird from behind its wooden door to show my brother and me. Later, when Jim left, my grandmother always shook her head at these extravagances. I knew what she was thinking: our family needed groceries and haircuts, not one-of-a-kind German clocks.

"Well, maybe we should eat now, before this gets cold," she urged quietly. Christopher and I sat in our seats while Jim pried deeper into the mangled gears of the clock.

"All the way from the Black Forest!" Jim cried, shaking his head at the wooden marvel. "All the original parts." Finally, seeing us waiting, Jim said, "Well, hey now. C'mon kids, up to the table now. Looks like we're about ready to eat."

Years later, I should not have been surprised, but I was. I was helping my grandmother prepare Thanksgiving dinner. She told me the news nonchalantly. "Remember Jim?" She was whipping the mashed potatoes in steady, measured strokes. "Well, we don't see each other much anymore," she said calmly.

I was shocked. My grandmother brought stability to everyone else's life, and here she was, taking it away from her own. At her age, things weren't supposed to change anymore.

I did see Jim again, later, at—where else?—Saint Vinny's. Watching him sift through a brassy pile of pocket watches, I finally got it. Jim was funny and kind and one of the most interesting people I had ever met, but he wasn't like my grandmother. In the fifteen years I'd known him, Jim had resisted change, re-playing his favorite parts over and over. My grandmother, on the other hand, had a bustling family that *counted on* her to change—to keep up—in good times and bad. While Jim rummaged leisurely through strangers' family histories, my grandmother was busy creating her own.

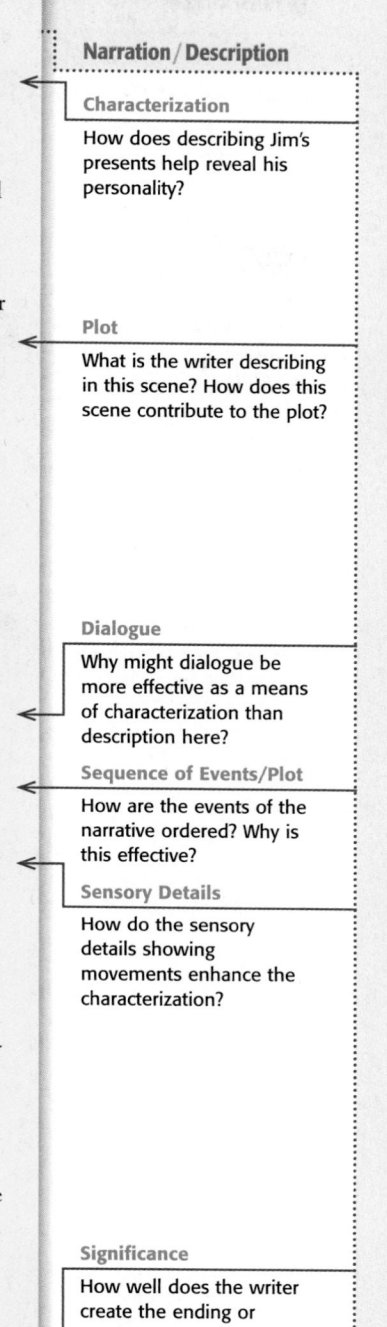

Narration / Description

Characterization
How does describing Jim's presents help reveal his personality?

Plot
What is the writer describing in this scene? How does this scene contribute to the plot?

Dialogue
Why might dialogue be more effective as a means of characterization than description here?

Sequence of Events/Plot
How are the events of the narrative ordered? Why is this effective?

Sensory Details
How do the sensory details showing movements enhance the characterization?

Significance
How well does the writer create the ending or resolution?

WRITING WORKSHOP **1123**

Teach

Writing Skills

Effective Description
Answer: *The writer is describing characters' movements and gestures, revealing their personalities and setting up tension between the grandmother and Jim.*

Dialogue
Answer: *It shows Jim's personality and feelings.*

Sequence of Events/Plot
Answer: *Events are ordered chronologically. This is effective because the story moves from memories to an understanding of the past.*

Sensory Details
Answer: *The grandmother's measured stirring of the potatoes matches her calm, matter-of-fact tone.*

Significance
Answer: *The writer creates an effective ending by moving from the specific to the general, relating the experience to a more abstract, personal idea. The writer now counts on his grandmother to change, rather than expecting her not to change.*

English Learners

DIFFERENTIATED INSTRUCTION

SMALL GROUP

Intermediate Choosing precise words can be difficult for English learners. Clarifying their ideas in their original language can help English learners search for the most precise English words. Have students list the descriptive words they want to use to make their writing vivid. Some students may want to list words and expressions in their original languages next to the English equivalents.

Have small groups of same-language students work together to brainstorm precise sensory language.

Creative Nonfiction

Teach

Writing Process

Revise Remind students that sentence variety makes for interesting writing. Review the four basic types of sentences: simple, compound, complex, and compound/complex. Have students choose several sentences from their narratives and rewrite each as a different type. Then have them compare the versions to see if the revisions are improvements.

Writing Skills

Avoid Stilted Language Caution students against cluttering their writing by using long words where simple ones will do. Put the following pairs of words on the board: *many/numerous, ease/facilitate, remainder/rest, first/initial, attempt/try.* **Ask:** Which word in each pair is more effective because it is simpler?

Traits of Strong Writing

Include these traits of strong writing to express your ideas effectively.

Ideas
Organization
Voice
Word Choice
Sentence Fluency
Conventions
Presentation

For more information on the Traits of Strong Writing, see pages R30–R32 of the Writing Handbook.

Word Choice

Find this academic vocabulary word in the student model:

generations (je nə rā′ shənz) *n.* 1. groups of people born at about the same time or constituting the same step in the line of descent from a common ancestor; 2. the average spans of time between the birth of parents and the birth of their offspring. *I had always expected that older generations had their problems mostly worked out.* Using academic vocabulary may help strengthen your writing. Try to use one or two academic vocabulary words in your autobiographical narrative. See the complete list on pages R89–R91.

 Literature Online

Writing and Research For editing and publishing tools, go to glencoe.com and enter QuickPass code GLA9800u6.

Revise

Peer Review After you complete your draft, read it aloud to your partner. Then have your partner discuss which parts were most vivid and interesting and which parts seemed vague or general. Partners should note places to add interior monologue, sensory details, and figurative language to add background or suspense. Use the checklist below.

Checklist

☑ Do you create an engaging plot?

☑ Do you use literary devices such as flashback, foreshadowing, imagery, or allusion?

☑ Do you use dialogue and/or internal monologue, gestures, and movements to show your characters?

☑ Do you use sensory details and figurative language?

▶ **Focus Lesson**

Avoid Stilted Language

When you are writing creative nonfiction, use natural, unaffected language. Readers respond to writing that they can connect with, and they will be turned off by pretentious or unnecessarily complicated language. As you revise, replace stilted language with precise words and clear, vivid expressions. Consult a thesaurus or dictionary for help.

Draft:

> During my formative years, Jim promenaded languidly through life as though the golden age would repeat itself without resistance. My grandmother, however, resigned herself to the duties of the family matriarch, following the ebb and flow of the lives of her progeny.

Revision:

> In the <u>fifteen years I'd known him,</u>[1] <u>Jim had resisted change,</u>[2] replaying his favorite parts over and over. <u>My grandmother, on the other hand, had a bustling family that counted on her to change—to keep up—in good times and bad.</u>[3]

1: <u>Precise details</u>   2: <u>Clear expression</u>   3: <u>Natural, unpretentious language</u>

Writing Practice

Use Transitions A clear organizational pattern, such as cause-and-effect order, chronological order, or compare-and-contrast order, helps readers see how ideas relate to one another. Transitional words show relationships between ideas and paragraphs. Review transitions that show links in time *(after, next, while),* space *(behind, below, around),* degree *(first, most important, mainly),* cause and effect *(because, as a result, therefore),* and comparison and contrast *(likewise, on the contrary, however).* Have students review their writing and circle the transitional devices they have used.

Edit and Proofread

Get It Right Proofread for errors in grammar, usage, and spelling.

> **Focus Lesson**
>
> ### Verb Tense
>
> As you edit your narrative, check that your verb tenses are formed correctly and that any shifts in tense are accurate and consistent.
>
> **Problem:** The verb ending is missing or incorrect.
>
> *He work on the clock while my grandmother set the table.*
>
> **Solution:** Add *-ed* to a regular verb to form the past tense.
>
> *He worked on the clock while my grandmother set the table.*
>
> **Problem:** There is an unnecessary shift in tense.
>
> *We sat in our seats while Jim pries deeper into the clock.*
>
> **Solution:** When two or more events occur at the same time, use the same verb tense to describe each event.
>
> *We sat in our seats while Jim pried deeper into the clock.*
>
> **Problem:** The lack of shift in verb tense does not show that the events occurred at different times.
>
> *He dated my grandmother ever since my grandfather died.*
>
> **Solution:** Shift from the past tense to the past perfect tense to show that the grandmother's actions began and ended before Jim's action began.
>
> *He had been dating my grandmother ever since my grandfather died.*

Present

Check Your Appearance After proofreading, look over your draft. Make sure your paper is double-spaced with appropriate margins.

Take Another Look

Put your paper away for a few days before rereading it. Unnatural voice, stilted language, and mistakes in verb tense are often easier to spot after you get a fresh perspective.

Peer Review Tips

A classmate may ask you to read his or her creative nonfiction essay. Take your time and jot down notes as you read so you can give constructive feedback. Use the following questions to get started:

- What tone do you hear? Which words help to create it? How well does it match the audience and purpose?

- Has the writer used rhetorical devices and made other fresh, interesting choices in word choice and sentence structure?

Word-Processing Tips

Use the spelling and grammar check, but check the checker! Consider the context and the choices before accepting or rejecting recommendations.

Writer's Portfolio

Place a clean copy of your creative nonfiction essay in your portfolio to review later.

 Writing Workshop

Creative Nonfiction

Teach

Writing Process

Edit and Proofread Remind students to look for one type of error at a time when they begin the editing and proofreading step. For example, the first reading could be to check that their narrative makes sense and their ideas are clear and coherent. A second reading could focus on errors in grammar and usage. A third and final reading could focus on spelling, punctuation, and other mechanical errors.

Writing Skills

Track Changes Many word processors have a tracking feature that allows students to compare a revised version with a preceding draft. The comparison document may highlight changes in various ways. For example, new text may appear on the screen in different-colored type or underlined.

 English Learners

DIFFERENTIATED INSTRUCTION

Intermediate In peer revision and editing sessions, students may feel awkward if their level of English comprehension prevents their full participation. Assist them with planning, writing, and revising.

Approaching Level

DIFFERENTIATED INSTRUCTION

Supported Encourage students to publish their autobiographical narratives in a computer presentation or classroom book. Students may add photographs or artwork to their pieces. Use a publishing program to assist students in formatting their writing.

Focus

Summary

In this workshop, students will learn techniques for planning, rehearsing, and delivering an art or photo essay presentation.

Teach

Speaking Skills

Plan the Essay After deciding on general topics for their photo or art essays, students should decide on the purpose of their essays—to inform, to persuade, or to demonstrate. Once they make this decision, they can think about their specific subjects. Because students will have a limited amount of time in which to make their presentations, they should be sure their subjects are not so broad that the presentations would exceed the allotted time.

Do Your Research
Before creating a photo essay, research other art and photo exhibits. What is it about these pieces that speak to the audience and stand out above everyday images? Consider whether to incorporate these elements into your own presentation.

 Literature Online

Speaking, Listening and Viewing For project ideas, templates, and presentation tips, go to glencoe.com and enter QuickPass code GLA9800u6.

Speaking, Listening, and Viewing Workshop

Photo Essay

Literature Connection In her story "A Worn Path," Eudora Welty uses vivid description to give the reader a clear image of Phoenix Jackson.

"She wore a dark striped dress reaching down to her shoe tops, and an equally long apron of bleached sugar sacks, with a full pocket: all neat and tidy, but every time she took a step she might have fallen over her shoelaces, which dragged from her unlaced shoes. She looked straight ahead. Her eyes were blue with age."

By using actual images, photographs, and art to represent people and ideas, you allow an audience to experience details and emotions that may not come across in writing alone. One way to accomplish this is by creating a photo essay. To create a photo essay, you combine photographs, artwork, drawings, or artifacts to represent a nonfiction narrative, another event, or an issue.

During the Great Depression, government researcher Dorothea Lange used photography to document the hardships and struggles of the poor. Examine the images below. What do Lange's photographs reveal about life during the Great Depression? Think about what it is that you want to reveal about your subject.

Unemployed men carrying suitcases to Los Angeles, California, during the Great Depression. March 1937.

A migratory family from Amarillo, Texas, lives in a trailer in an open field, with no sanitation or running water. November 1940.

The family of a Cordale, Alabama, turpentine worker earning one dollar per day. July 1936.

Viewing Practice

Analyze Images Have students watch either a national or a local newscast. As they watch, students should keep track of the images used during the broadcast and categorize them. Students should determine their own categories for the images such as positive and negative, or emotional and informative. After students have reviewed their notes and categories, have them write a paragraph explaining how the images impact the news stories and the overall effectiveness of the broadcast. Have them draw conclusions from their observations about the purpose and the audience of the program.

> **Assignment** Plan and deliver a photo essay.

Plan Your Presentation

Just like written essays, your photo essay needs to have a main idea. Ask yourself what central idea or message you would like to convey.

- Research the topic well. You should be prepared to answer any questions the audience may have about your topic.
- Allow enough time to prepare. Think about how many pieces you want to have, as well as what images would best suit your purpose.
- Take photos using a digital or video camera, draw images, download and print images, and/or photocopy images.
- Decide how you will showcase your work. Will you use an easel, poster board, or a slide or video presentation?

Develop Your Presentation

Develop your presentation by considering how you will add words and other effects when you deliver your essay to your audience.

- Plan to introduce the work; decide how you will direct the audience's attention from image to image; and plan a closing statement.
- Consider adding labels or captions to works to help viewers understand what each represents. Make all labels neat, clear, and uniform.
- Be sure each work carries a correct citation that accurately and fully credits the source.
- Consider display issues for work in print, such as how to mount the photos or images, such as on large black squares, at right angles, and at equal distances. Similarly, consider display and design issues for computer slides, such as borders and color or other effects.
- If you wish, add music or other sound effects.

Evaluate

Keep these guidelines in mind as you prepare your own photo essay. Then use them to evaluate the photo essays that others present.

- Match the display to the audience and the space. Images must be large enough to be seen easily by the entire audience.
- Be sure the title or introduction is a clear overview or engaging introduction, and that the presentation concludes effectively.
- Sequence the images logically, using chronological order for a narrative and a logical order, such as cause-and-effect, for an issue.
- Allow the audience enough time to view and react to each piece of your visual essay before moving on to the next image.

Speaking Frames

Consider using the following frames in your photo essay:

- The title/main idea of my photo essay is _____.
- This image, called/which I call _____, shows _____.
- Notice how the _____ in this image shows/emphasizes/suggests _____.

Presentation Tips

Use the following checklist to evaluate your photo essay.

- Did you convey one central meaning through your essay that the audience understood?
- What were your most interesting images, and what made them effective for your audience?

Teach

Speaking Skills

Gather Information Review possible sources of information:

- interviews with people who have relevant information or who can give firsthand accounts
- students' own knowledge of their subjects, supported with details
- the library and Web sites with well-documented information.

Responding Review some points on responding to questions:

- Encourage a questioner by saying, "That is a good question." Repeat the question to ensure that everyone has heard it
- Avoid slang and informal language in responses to questions.

English Learners

DIFFERENTIATED INSTRUCTION

Beginning/Early Intermediate Help students organize information by having them list the most important points they want to cover. Students may use a simple numbered list to record the information they want to discuss first, and so on. Students may want to move beyond a list and create an outline of their main points, which can help them organize their presentations.

Intermediate Explain that there are many ways to record and organize information. Display examples of these note-taking strategies: a two- or three-column chart, a flow chart, a Venn diagram. **Ask:** How can these note-taking methods be used to analyze information? *(columns: list statistics; flow chart: show cause and effect; Venn diagram: compare and contrast.)* Have

students try different methods, including taking notes on note cards.

Independent Reading

Focus

Summary

The purpose of Independent Reading is to encourage students to read novels from and about the time period that they have learned about in this unit.

Teach

Literary History ☆

Rachel Carson Known for her flawless writing style, Carson (1907–1964) wrote *Silent Spring* in 1962, arousing intense controversy over the widespread use of insecticides and their effect on wildlife and humans.

Independent Reading

LITERATURE FROM THE 1930s through the 1960s is as varied as the period that produced it. The Great Depression and World War II had lasting impacts on the works of writers and artists. Well into the twenty-first century, authors are still finding rich materials from the time period. Historian Stephen Ambrose interviewed men from the 101st Airborne to record their stories of war, friendship, and heroism. Rachel Carson was a marine biologist and writer whose second book, *The Sea Around Us*, sold more than a million copies. Perhaps her most famous work, *Silent Spring* (1962) is credited with signaling the beginning of the environmental movement in the United States. Cormac McCarthy captures the grand scale of the American west in the 1940s through his Border trilogy which begins with *All the Pretty Horses*, followed by *The Crossing*, and *Cities of the Plain*. Whether writing about war, nature, or the west, these authors capture the American spirit of the time.

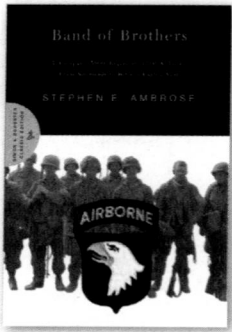

Band of Brothers: E Company, 506th Regiment, 101st Airborne from Normandy to Hitler's Eagle's Nest

Stephen Ambrose

The men of Easy Company faced the most treacherous assignments during World War II, from parachuting onto Utah Beach on D-Day to capturing Hitler's Eagle's Nest near V.E. Day. Ambrose tells the true stories of the adventures and tragedies like he is writing a novel. His work was produced as an HBO miniseries in 2002.

The Sea Around Us

Rachel Carson (1951)

Sometimes called a biography of the sea, this fascinating book opens with "The Gray Beginnings," a chapter that tells how the seas began. Subsequent chapters cover the formation of islands, plant and animal life, tides, wind, waves, and historic voyages. The book won the 1952 National Book Award and the John Burroughs Medal, named for the naturalist John Burroughs. It was translated into more than thirty languages and was a best seller. More than fifty years after its initial publication, it is still in print.

Writing Practice

 Respond to Experience
Say: The literature of this period was a response to the writers' experiences during those times. The works raised the nation's awareness of very important issues. Have small groups list and discuss some issues currently in the news. Students should consider one issue about which they have strong feelings, and write a synopsis of a book that they think should or could be written on the subject. Remind them that Harper Lee, author of *To Kill A Mockingbird*, responded in the form of a novel, whereas Rachel Carson responded with nonfiction. Allow students to choose which genre they will use in their response.

GLENCOE LITERATURE LIBRARY

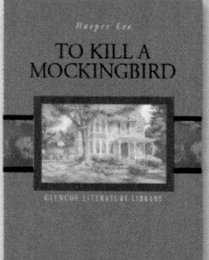

To Kill a Mockingbird

Harper Lee

A precocious, observant young girl and her brother watch as their father defends an African American man on trial in the South.

Night

Elie Wiesel

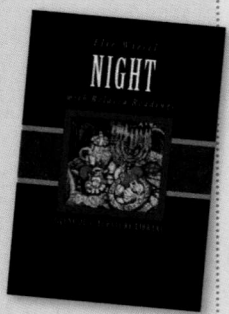

This autobiographical story traces events from 1941 to 1945, during which time Wiesel and his family are taken from their village to a Nazi concentration camp. Wiesel survives to be liberated by Allied troops and to offer this account of terror, guilt, and faith.

Invisible Man

Ralph Ellison

As he journeys from an African American college in the South to a bewildering, chaotic life as a political speaker in Harlem, the nameless narrator grapples with the question of what it means to be a human being and a person of color in the United States.

CRITICS' CORNER

"A modern-day Western full of horses and gunplay and romance, it transcends the bounds of its genre with rambunctious, high-spirited, bottomless inventiveness. *All the Pretty Horses* is a true American Original."

—*Newsweek* (back cover)

"A book of remarkable beauty and strength, the work of a master in perfect command of his medium. . . . Like classic literary journeys before it—from Jason and the Argonauts chasing the golden fleece to Huck and Jim floating down the Mississippi—this is a trip that covers much more than just geography. It covers the distance from childhood to adulthood and from innocence to experience."

—*Washington Post Book World* (from Random House site)

All the Pretty Horses

Cormac McCarthy

This first installment in a trilogy is set in 1949. Sixteen-year-old John Grady Cole leaves his Texas home with his friend, Lacey Rawlins, and sets off on an adventure toward the Mexican border.

 Write an Advice Column

Read a book listed on this page. Identify a conflict faced by a character. Write a letter in the voice of the character to an advice columnist and write a response advising a specific course of action.

Big Idea

Return to Regionalism
Have students define the word *diversity* and briefly discuss why *diverse* accurately describes American life and the American population. **Ask:** How do the books described here exemplify the diversity of American literature? *(Possible answer: Their settings, points of view, and themes are very different.)*

 ### Advice Column

Evaluate students' advice columns by considering the following:
- clearly stated conflict
- effective use of character's voice
- attention to grammar and spelling conventions

 ### Glencoe Literature Library

Glencoe Literature Library offers an extensive collection of hardcover books that help you encourage your students to read independently. Choose among the more than 120 full-length literary works—novels, novellas, plays, and nonfiction. Each book includes related readings from a broad range of genres. Go to www.glencoe.com for more information.

Approaching Level

DIFFERENTIATED INSTRUCTION

Emerging Discuss with students how they go about choosing books to read. **Ask:** What do you look for when you are evaluating whether or not you want to read a particular book? *(Answers will vary.)* Explain to students that the comments on the covers of books are sometimes quoted from a published review of a book, or may be comments that the author or publisher asked someone to make about the book. Explain to students that reading the first page of a book can help them decide whether they want to read a book. Help students identify the time period and subject of books they are considering.

Bellringer

Remind students of techniques they use to prepare for tests. Explain that tests are used to gauge how effectively material has been taught and how well they have learned the material. **Ask: What are some of the skills and practices you use to prepare for a test? What are some important questions to ask before a test?**

Teach

Assessment Tell students that this Assessment will provide reinforcement in general test-taking strategies and will test the skills covered in this unit. Students will read nonfiction selections and answer context, comprehension, and inference questions. Then they will answer paragraph-improvement questions and respond to a short narrative-essay question.

 To create custom assessments online, go to Progress Reporter Online Assessment.

 To create custom assessments using software, use ExamView Assessment Suite.

Assessment

English Language Arts

Reading: Nonfiction

Carefully read the following passage written by an observer of the "Dust Bowl" in the mid-1930s. Use context clues to help define any words with which you are unfamiliar. Pay attention to the author's main idea and use of rhetorical devices. Then answer the questions on page 1131–1132.

from *Dust Changes America* by Margaret Bourke-White

line   Vitamin K they call it—the dust which sifts under the door sills, and stings in the eyes, and seasons every spoonful of food. The dust storms have distinct personalities, rising in formation like rolling clouds, creeping up silently like formless fog, approaching violently like a tornado. Where has it come from? It provides topics of endless speculation. Red, it is the topsoil from Oklahoma; brown, it is the fertile earth
5   of western Kansas; the good grazing land of Texas and New Mexico sweeps by as a murky yellow haze. Or, tracing it locally, "My uncle will be along pretty soon," they say; "I just saw his farm go by."
    The town dwellers stack their linen in trunks, stuff wet cloths along the window sills, estimate the tons of sand in the darkened air above them, paste cloth masks on their faces with adhesive tape, and try to joke about Vitamin K. But on the farms and ranches there is an attitude of despair.
10   By coincidence I was in the same parts of the country where last year I photographed the drought. As short a time as eight months ago there was an attitude of false optimism. "Things will get better," the farmers would say. "We're not as hard hit as other states. The government will help out. This can't go on." But this year there is an atmosphere of utter hopelessness. Nothing to do. No use digging out your chicken coops and pigpens after the last "duster" because the next one will be coming along soon. No use trying
15   to keep the house clean. No use fighting off that foreclosure any longer. No use even hoping to give your cattle anything to chew on when their food crops have literally blown out of the ground. . . .
    The storm comes in a terrifying way. Yellow clouds roll. The wind blows such a gale that it is all my helper can do to hold my camera to the ground. The sand whips into my lens. I repeatedly wipe it away trying to snatch an exposure before it becomes completely coated again. The light becomes
20   yellower, the wind colder. Soon there is no photographic light, and we hurry for shelter to the nearest farmhouse. Three men and a woman are seated around a dust-caked lamp, on their faces grotesque masks of wet cloth. The children have been put to bed with towels tucked over their heads. My host greets us: "It takes grit to live in this country." They are telling stories: A bachelor harnessed the sandblast which ripped through the keyhole by holding his pots and pans in it until they were spick
25   and span. A pilot flying over Amarillo got caught in a sand storm. His motor clogged; he took to his parachute. It took him six hours to shovel his way back to earth. And when a man from the next county was struck by a drop of water, he fainted, and it took two buckets of sand to revive him. . . .
    And this same dust that coats the lungs and threatens death to cattle and men alike, that ruins the stock of the storekeeper lying unsold on his shelves, that creeps into the gear shifts of automobiles,
30   that sifts through the refrigerator into the butter, that makes housekeeping, and gradually life itself,

Reading Practice

Active Reading Encourage students to experiment with active reading strategies for nonfiction as they read the Margaret Bourke-White selection. Before they read the excerpt, have students prepare a blank notebook page for note taking. First, have them read the title of the excerpt and write "How did dust change America?" at the top of the page. As they read the excerpt, have students list details that answer the question. Explain to students that by looking for answers as they read, they will increase their reading comprehension.

unbearable, this swirling drifting dust is changing the agricultural map of the United States. It piles ever higher on the floors and beds of a steadily increasing number of deserted farmhouses. A half-buried plowshare, a wheat binder ruffled over with sand, the skeleton of a horse near a dirt-filled water hole are stark evidence of the meager life, the wasted savings, the years of toil that the farmer is leaving behind him.

1. What literary or rhetorical device does Bourke-White use in the sentence *Where has it come from?* in line 3?
   A. parallelism
   B. connotative language
   C. metaphor
   D. rhetorical question

2. What literary or rhetorical device is most evident in the sentence beginning the second paragraph?
   F. parallelism
   G. connotative language
   H. metaphor
   J. rhetorical question

3. Why was Bourke-White in this part of the country?
   A. by coincidence
   B. to photograph the poor
   C. to photograph dust storms
   D. to photograph the drought

4. From the context, what does the word *atmosphere* in line 13 mean?
   F. the physical environment
   G. the mood of the environment
   H. an exotic or romantic quality
   J. the gaseous elements of an environment

5. Which of the following is an example of connotative language from the sentence beginning *Three men and a woman* in line 21?
   A. *seated*
   B. *grotesque*
   C. *wet*
   D. *lamp*

6. Why have the children been put to bed with towels over their heads?
   F. to block out the noise of the storm
   G. to prevent them from hearing the adult conversation
   H. to make them more comfortable
   J. to prevent them from breathing in the dust

7. Of what literary device is the word *grit* in the sentence *It takes grit to live in this country* in line 23 an example?
   A. metaphor
   B. symbol
   C. simile
   D. motif

8. Why do the farmers tell humorous stories about the dust storms?
   F. because they are insensitive
   G. because they want to distract the children
   H. because they want to lighten the mood
   J. because they want to relate the local news

9. What literary or rhetorical device is most evident in the sentence that begins the last paragraph?
   A. parallelism
   B. connotative language
   C. metaphor
   D. rhetorical question

LOG ON **Literature** Online

Assessment For additional test practice, go to glencoe.com and enter QuickPass code GLA9800u6.

ASSESSMENT **1131**

Assessment

Assess

Reading

1. **D** is the correct answer because the sentence is a rhetorical question asked to pique the reader's curiosity. (DOK2)

2. **F** is the correct answer because the sentence includes a series of parallel verbs that make up the predicate. (DOK2)

3. **A** is the correct answer because Bourke-White says, "By coincidence, I was in the same parts of the country where last year I photographed the drought." (DOK1)

4. **G** is the correct answer because in this context *atmosphere* means "a prevailing emotional effect." (DOK1)

5. **B** is the correct answer because the word *grotesque* has an extreme negative connotation. (DOK2)

6. **J** is the correct answer because the reader can infer that the parents are protecting their children from the harmful effects of inhaling dust. (DOK1)

7. **A** is the correct answer because the literal meaning of *grit* is "an abrasive particle," such as sand, but metaphorically it means "bravery," or "firmness of mind and spirit." (DOK2)

8. **H** is the correct answer because the reader can infer that the farmers are using humor to defend themselves against despair. (DOK4)

9. **A** is the correct answer because the sentence includes a series of adjective clauses that describe the way the dust creeps into everything. (DOK2)

Assess

10. J is the correct answer because the passage chronicles one of the worst human and environmental tragedies in U.S. history. (DOK 2)

11. C is the correct answer because Bourke-White's purpose is to describe the environment and the human suffering during the Dust Bowl of the 1930s. (DOK 4)

12. G is the correct answer because the memo states that there will be "a meeting expressly for subcommittee heads on Wednesday, February 22." (DOK 1)

13. D is the correct answer because the memo states that subcommittee heads "are encouraged to attend" because "we will be discussing financing for the upcoming term." (DOK 1)

14. H is the correct answer because the memo states that chairpersons who cannot attend should "let me know as soon as possible." (DOK 2)

Scan Point out that this memo contains dates, facts, and directions. Remind students that scanning is looking quickly over a text to find certain information. Suggest that students scan the questions about the memo and then scan the memo to find the answers as quickly as they can. As students read, they might take brief notes to aid their comprehension.

1132

---

10. What is the main idea of this passage?
   F. The farmers do not understand the seriousness of the situation.
   G. Nobody knows what causes dust storms.
   H. The farmers are optimistic that the storms will end soon.
   J. This region has become an agricultural and human disaster.

11. Which of the following best describes the author's purpose in this passage?
   A. to entertain
   B. to persuade
   C. to describe
   D. to analyze

Informational Reading Carefully read the passage and answer the questions that follow it. Be sure to pay close attention to details and to any instructions that are provided.

> **Memo**
> **To:** Committee Chairpersons
> **From:** Lisa Hopkins, Dean of Student Activities
> **Date:** February 8, 2006
> **Re:** Committee Chairperson Meeting
>
> We need to schedule the quarterly meeting on facility distribution for all of the school's committee chairpersons. In light of this, I suggest that we hold our meeting in the school library at 3:00 on Thursday, February 16. If you are unable to make this date, for whatever reason, please let me know as soon as possible.
>
> Subcommittee heads are not required to attend this meeting. However, because we will be discussing financing for the upcoming term, these representatives are encouraged to attend. There will also be a meeting expressly for subcommittee heads on Wednesday, February 22.

12. From the information presented in this memo, when will subcommittee heads be required to attend a meeting?
   F. Thursday, February 16
   G. Wednesday, February 22
   H. Monday, February 20
   J. Monday, February 13

13. For what reason should subcommittee heads attend the meeting on Thursday, February 16?
   A. to discuss facility distribution
   B. to meet in the school library
   C. to confer with committee chairpersons
   D. to discuss finances

14. What should committee chairpersons do if they are unable to attend?
   F. attend the meeting being held for subcommittee heads on February 22
   G. individually meet with the subcommittee heads
   H. contact Lisa Hopkins as soon as possible
   J. meet with the other committee chairpersons

Vocabulary Skills: Sentence Completion

For each item in the Vocabulary Skills section, choose the best word or words to complete the sentence.

1. The _____ rations of many families during the Great Depression led to near-starvation conditions in both urban and rural areas.
   - **A.** amiable
   - **B.** meager
   - **C.** retractable
   - **D.** diplomatic

2. Many European Americans became _____ toward Japanese Americans after the start of World War II.
   - **F.** hostile
   - **G.** vivid
   - **H.** futile
   - **J.** solemn

3. Many workers _____ fought for their rights during the Great Depression.
   - **A.** stately
   - **B.** ineffably
   - **C.** vigorously
   - **D.** abjectly

4. The wild, _____ music and style of dress during the 1920s gave way to the desperate and _____ days of the 1930s.
   - **F.** ceremonial . . . enamored
   - **G.** animated . . . morose
   - **H.** amorphous . . . grave
   - **J.** ravenous . . . ceremonial

5. The _____ of the Nazi conquest of Europe were far-reaching and horrible.
   - **A.** inquisitors
   - **B.** hemorrhage
   - **C.** turrets
   - **D.** implications

6. While people in the United States were _____ in the economic recovery effort, Europe was about to _____ to another deadly war.
   - **F.** enamored . . . grapple
   - **G.** premeditated . . . loiter
   - **H.** engrossed . . . succumb
   - **J.** intimidated . . . grapple

7. The end of World War II caused _____ celebrations to erupt across the United States.
   - **A.** jubilant
   - **B.** gaunt
   - **C.** ravenous
   - **D.** poised

8. The United States' war with Germany and Japan was the _____ outcome of Axis military aggression.
   - **F.** pious
   - **G.** impudent
   - **H.** alien
   - **J.** inevitable

9. The _____ by experts that the Dust Bowl was the result of agricultural mismanagement shocked many farmers.
   - **A.** premonition
   - **B.** tribute
   - **C.** twinge
   - **D.** intimation

10. A common sight during the Great Depression was the urban poor, starved and _____ for food.
    - **F.** ravenous
    - **G.** amorphous
    - **H.** vivid
    - **J.** solemn

ASSESSMENT **1133**

Approaching Level

DIFFERENTIATED INSTRUCTION

Emerging Remind students to use guessing strategies if they do not know which answer choice is the right one. For example, even if they know that two choices are incorrect, they can use that information to eliminate them from consideration. That will give them a better chance of correctly guessing the answer. Consider using some of the questions on this page to demonstrate the strategy.

Assess

Vocabulary

1. **B** is the correct answer because it is the only option that makes sense in this context. `DOK 1`

2. **F** is the correct answer because options G and H make no sense in this context, and J is historically inaccurate. `DOK 1`

3. **C** is the correct answer because it is the only option that makes sense in this context. `DOK 1`

4. **G** is the correct answer because it is the only option that makes sense in this context. `DOK 2`

5. **D** is the correct answer because it is the only option that makes sense in this context. `DOK 1`

6. **H** is the correct answer because it is the only option that fits idiomatically in this context. `DOK 2`

7. **A** is the correct answer because it is the only option that makes sense in this context. `DOK 1`

8. **J** is the correct answer because it is the only option that makes sense in this context. `DOK 1`

9. **D** is the correct answer because options B and C make no sense in this context and A does not agree with the past-tense verb *was*. `DOK 1`

10. **F** is the correct answer because it is the only option that makes sense in this context. `DOK 1`

Grammar and Writing Skills

Teach

Context Clues Remind students to use context clues if they encounter vocabulary that is difficult to understand, such as the words *lathe* and *fascism.* Suggest to students that questions can help in determining word meanings.

Ask: What would be a good question to ask about the word lathe? (Possible answer: What did Grandpa Will use the lathe for?) Point out that the context indicates that a lathe is used to carve wood.

Assess

1 C is the correct answer because the present-tense verb is needed to match the present-tense verbs in the preceding and following sentences. DOK1

2 G is the correct answer because it is the only option that corrects the dangling modifier and completes the comparison implicit in the original sentence. DOK1

Grammar and Writing Skills: Paragraph Improvement

In the following excerpt from a student draft of an essay, you will find underlined phrases and sentences. The number that precedes each underlined phrase corresponds to a numbered question on the next page. Each question will prompt you to replace the underlined phrase or sentence. If you think the original should not be changed, choose "NO CHANGE."

The bracketed numbers refer to the questions about a specific paragraph or to the essay as a whole.

My grandfather was an infantryman during World War II. He often tells me stories about his experiences overseas—describing the people that he met and the things that he did and saw. Grandpa Will is amazing for other things too. (1) *He was one of the best woodworkers in East Texas.* The sculptures and vessels that he carves on his lathe are beautiful. Grandpa Will's life, art, and the stories that he tells have had a great influence on me.

(2) *Joining at the age of sixteen, the army was a vastly different experience.* It was five days after Pearl Harbor had been bombed. (3) *Will, like the rest of the country, was in an uproar over the attack.* He decided that he had to do something. (4) *After saying goodbye to his parents, his friends, and relatives Will signed up and was shipped off to boot camp.*

Will saw a lot of combat during the war. He fought in some of the bloodiest battles in Europe, including the Battle of the Bulge. He also lost a lot of friends in the fighting and saw some terrible tragedies. (5) *Grandpa Will believes that the war against fascism was worth it, but whenever he talks about it he always said: "War hurts a lot of people."*

(6) *When he returned from Europe, Will started working for a paper mill.* He worked there until he retired, just ten years ago. [7] He started by taking some classes at the local community college, and then he joined a woodworkers' organization. After a couple of years, Grandpa Will started producing some really amazing pieces. (8) *Yet, Grandpa Will has won several prizes for his work, and* some of his sculptures are even on display at a small Houston art gallery. (9) *Striking angles and textured colors, Grandpa Will makes sculptures that always grab the eye.* [10]

1. **A.** NO CHANGE
   B. In East Texas, he was one of the best woodworkers.
   C. He is one of the best woodworkers in East Texas.
   D. Of the best woodworkers, he was one.

2. **F.** NO CHANGE
   G. Joining at the age of sixteen, Will found the army to be vastly different from any experience he had had before.
   H. The army was a vastly different experience for Will.
   J. Will joined at the age of sixteen.

Grammar Practice

Misplaced Modifiers One common sentence error is the misplaced modifier, a word or phrase that is placed so that it seems to modify a word other than the one it is intended to modify. Write the following pair of sentences on the board and ask students to choose the one that contains a misplaced modifier:

- A man rafted the Mississippi River in my neighborhood.
- A man in my neighborhood rafted the Mississippi River.

(The first sentence misplaces the modifier "in my neighborhood" so that it modifies the river rather than the man.)

3. A. NO CHANGE
    B. The rest of the country was in an uproar over the attack.
    C. Will, like the rest of the country, is in an uproar over the attack.
    D. Like the rest of the country, Will is in an uproar over the attack.

4. F. NO CHANGE
    G. After saying goodbye to his parents, friends, and relatives, Will signed up and was shipped off to boot camp.
    H. After saying goodbye to his parents his friends and relatives Will signed up and was shipped off to boot camp.
    J. After saying goodbye to his parents and relatives Will signed up and was shipped off to boot camp.

5. A. NO CHANGE
    B. Grandpa Will believes that the war against fascism was worth it.
    C. Whenever Grandpa Will talks about it he always said: "War hurts a lot of people."
    D. Grandpa Will believes that the war against fascism was worth it, but whenever he talks about it, he always says: "War hurts a lot of people."

6. F. NO CHANGE
    G. When he returned from Europe, he worked for a paper mill.
    H. When he returned from Europe Will started working for a paper mill.
    J. Returning from Europe, a paper mill company gave him a job.

7. Which of the following sentences, if inserted at this point, would provide the most effective transition in this paragraph?
    A. Grandpa Will actually never liked his job at the mill.
    B. The war had changed Grandpa Will's whole attitude about people, work, and school.
    C. Since then, Grandpa Will has been honing his skills as a craftsman.
    D. However, Grandpa Will wanted to keep working at the mill.

8. F. NO CHANGE
    G. However,
    H. In fact,
    J. Although,

9. A. NO CHANGE
    B. Grandpa Will makes sculptures that always grab the eye.
    C. Striking angles and textured colors Grandpa Will makes sculptures that always grab the eye.
    D. Grandpa Will makes sculptures with striking angles and textured colors that always grab the eye.

10. Which of the following should the writer include when writing a concluding paragraph?
    F. information not included in previous paragraphs
    G. a summary of the key points
    H. the introduction of opposing viewpoints
    J. further descriptions of the grandfather's war experiences

Essay

President Franklin Delano Roosevelt claimed that he firmly believed that "the only thing we have to fear is fear itself—nameless, unreasoning, unjustified terror which paralyzes needed efforts to convert retreat into advance." Describe an example from your own life in which you witnessed Roosevelt's principle in action. As you write, keep in mind that your essay will be checked for **ideas, organization, voice, word choice, sentence fluency, conventions,** and **presentation.**

Assessment

Assess

3. **A** is the correct answer because the sentence contains no errors. `DOK 1`

4. **G** is the correct answer because it is the only option that restores parallelism to the three objects of the preposition to and sets off the introductory adverbial clause with a comma. `DOK 1`

5. **D** is the correct answer because the verb must be in the present tense to be consistent with *talks.* `DOK 1`

6. **F** is the correct answer because the sentence contains no errors. `DOK 1`

7. **C** is the correct answer because it makes a smooth transition between the information about Will's professional career and his woodworking. `DOK 4`

8. **H** is the correct answer because the relationship between the ideas in this sentence and the previous one is one of emphasis, not contrast. `DOK 1`

9. **D** is the correct answer because the misplaced participial phrase "striking angles and textured colors" is repositioned to modify *sculptures,* not *Grandpa Will.* `DOK 1`

10. **G** is the correct answer because a conclusion to this essay should summarize the varied accomplishments of Grandpa Will. `DOK 4`

Writing

Make sure students know how much time they have for the writing task and approximately how long the essay should be. Explain to students that Roosevelt's principle could be seen in an action—or a failure to act—that is a result of fear taking over; or, it could be seen in action when fear is faced and overcome.

Essay

Evaluate essays for:

- clearly stated main ideas supported by good reasons and details
- effective voice, word choice, and sentence variety
- effective presentation with attention to grammar and spelling conventions
`DOK 3`

Skills Scope and Sequence

Readability Scores Key: Dale-Chall/DRP/Lexile

PART 1: An Era of Protest

Selections and Features	Literary Elements
Unit Introduction pp. 1136-1150	Allusion **TE** p. 1145 Rhythm **TE** p. 1147 Style **TE** p. 1148
Informational Text TIME**: The Torchbearer,** by Rita Dove **8.2/61/1060** pp. 1152-1154	
Memoir *from* **Stride Toward Freedom,** by Martin Luther King Jr. **11.2/67/1040** pp. 1155-1160	Structure **SE** p. 1156
Speech Choice: A Tribute to Dr. Martin Luther King Jr., by Alice Walker **7.3/60/1170** pp. 1161-1165	Anecdote **SE** p. 1162
Vocabulary Workshop p. 1166	
Interview *from* **Working: Roberto Acuna, Farm Worker,** by Studs Terkel **4.8/52/720** pp. 1167-1178	Oral History **SE** p. 1168 Structure (review) **SE** p. 1177
Grammar Workshop p. 1179	

Comparing Literature
   Ambush (short story), by Tim O'Brien **5.8/53/940**
   The Gift in Wartime (poem), by Tran Mong Tu
   from **Stay Alive, My Son** (memoir), by Pin Yathay with John Man **6.5/49/650**
   Camouflaging the Chimera (poem), by Yusef Komunyakaa pp. 1180-1191
	Mood **SE** p. 1182
	Exposition **TE** p. 1188
	Theme **TE** p. 1189

Poems
   The Asians Dying, Separation, and **When You Go Away,**
   by W. S. Merwin pp. 1192-1197
	Figurative Language **SE** p. 1193
	Free Verse (review) **SE** p. 1196

Artistic Perspective Proposal for the Vietnam Veterans Memorial, by Maya Lin **13/66/1310** pp. 1198-1201	
Song A Hard Rain's A-Gonna Fall, by Bob Dylan pp. 1202-1207	Rhythm **SE** p. 1203 Mood (review) **SE** p. 1206
Poem Courage, by Anne Sexton pp. 1208-1212	Verse Paragraph **SE** p. 1209

Reading Skills and Strategies	Vocabulary	Writing / Grammar	Speaking, Listening, and Viewing
Analyze Graphic Information **SE** p. 1139 Monitor Comprehension **TE** p. 1143 Analyze Cause and Effect **SE** p. 1145 Activate Prior Knowledge **TE** p. 1146 Interpret **SE** p. 1147 Analyze Imagery **TE** p. 1148 Evaluate **SE** p. 1149		Write a Persuasive Essay **TE** p. 1144	Compare Media Accounts **TE** p. 1150
Analyze Text Structure **SE** p. 1152 Identify Topic Sentences **TE** p. 1152			
Paraphrase **SE** p. 1156 Analyze Arguments **TE** p. 1158	Word Usage **SE** p. 1160	Write a Summary **SE** p. 1160	
Activate Prior Knowledge **SE** p. 1162	Analogies **SE** p. 1165	Write a Tribute **TE** p. 1162 Past Perfect Tense **TE** p. 1164 Write a Speech **SE** p. 1165	
	Loaded Words **SE** p. 1166 Persuasive Language **TE** p. 1166		
Analyze Cause-and-Effect Relationships **SE** p. 1168 Question **TE** p. 1170	Context Clues **SE** p. 1178 Academic Vocabulary **SE** p. 1178	Write an Interview **TE** p. 1168	Interview **SE** p. 1178
		Run-on Sentences **SE** p. 1179	
Compare Themes and Cultures **SE** p. 1180 Analyze Concrete Details **SE** p. 1182 Analyze Images **TE** p. 1186 Make Predictions **TE** p. 1188 Identify Concrete Details **TE** p. 1190	Word Origins **SE** p. 1185	Write a Journal Entry **SE** p. 1185 Write an Essay **SE** p. 1191	Discussion **SE** p. 1189
Clarify Meaning **SE** p. 1193 Make Critical Judgments **TE** p. 1194	Analogies **SE** p. 1197 Academic Vocabulary **SE** p. 1197		Literature Group **SE** p. 1197
Analyze Political Assumptions **SE** p. 1198		Write a Reflective Essay **TE** p. 1200	
Analyze Rhetorical Devices **SE** p. 1203 Make Inferences **TE** p. 1205	Academic Vocabulary **SE** p. 1207	Simple and Compound Sentences **TE** p. 1204	Oral Interpretation **SE** p. 1207
Examine Connotation and Denotation **SE** p. 1209 Make Predictions **TE** p. 1210	Synonyms **SE** p. 1212	Write a Letter **SE** p. 1212	

Readability Scores Key: Dale-Chall/DRP/Lexile

PART 2: Nature and Technology

Selections and Features	Literary Elements
Poems The Fish and **Filling Station,** by Elizabeth Bishop pp. 1214-1221	Tone **SE** p. 1215 Setting (review) **SE** p. 1220
Poem Root Cellar, by Theodore Roethke pp. 1222-1225	Simile **SE** p. 1223
Poems Sleep in the Mojave Desert and **Crossing the Water,** by Sylvia Plath pp. 1226-1231	Mood **SE** p. 1227 Figurative Language (review) **SE** p. 1230
Poem The War Against the Trees, by Stanley Kunitz pp. 1232-1235	Personification **SE** p. 1233
Scientific Perspective from **Silent Spring,** by Rachel Carson **7.4/62/1150** pp. 1236-1238	
Short Story SQ, by Ursula K. Le Guin **8.3/58/1120** pp. 1239-1252	Satire **SE** p. 1240 Irony **TE** p. 1248
Short Story Snow, by Julia Alvarez **5.2/56/980** pp. 1253-1256	Indirect Characterization **SE** p. 1254
Poems Cottonmouth Country and **Daisies,** by Louise Glück pp. 1257-1262	Free Verse **SE** p. 1258 Personification **TE** p. 1259

PART 3: Extending and Remaking Traditions

Selections and Features	Literary Elements
Memoir from **The Woman Warrior,** by Maxine Hong Kingston **4.4/51/800** pp. 1264-1273	Exposition **SE** p. 1265 Tone **TE** p. 1270 Dialogue (review) **SE** p. 1272
Short Story Everything Stuck to Him, by Raymond Carver **3.3/46/460** pp. 1274-1281	Frame Story **SE** p. 1275 Style (review) **SE** p. 1280
Poem El Olvido, by Judith Ortiz Cofer pp. 1282-1285	Point of View **SE** p. 1283
Poem My Father and the Figtree, by Naomi Shihab Nye pp. 1286-1290	Symbol **SE** p. 1287

Reading Skills and Strategies	Vocabulary	Writing / Grammar	Speaking, Listening, and Viewing
Evaluate Sensory Details **SE** p. 1215 Monitor Comprehension **TE** p. 1216	Context Clues **SE** p. 1221 Academic Vocabulary	Punctuation **TE** p. 1218	
Interpret Imagery **SE** p. 1223 Identify Figurative Language **TE** p. 1224	Synonyms **SE** p. 1225	Write a Poem **SE** p. 1225	
Analyze Voice **SE** p. 1227 Predict **TE** p. 1229	Word Origins **SE** p. 1231 Academic Vocabulary		Oral Interpretation **TE** p. 1228 Literature Group **SE** p. 1231
Evaluate Figures of Speech **SE** p. 1233 Identify Slant Rhyme **TE** p. 1234	Analogies **SE** p. 1235	Write a Dialogue **SE** p. 1235	
Recognize Author's Purpose **SE** p. 1236 Predict **TE** p. 1236	Connotation **TE** p. 1238	Note Taking **TE** p. 1236	
Identify Genre **SE** p. 1240 Analyze Narrator **TE** p. 1244	Analogies **SE** p. 1251 Academic Vocabulary	Write Science Fiction **TE** p. 1248	
Connect to Contemporary Issues **SE** p. 1254	Word Parts **SE** p. 1256	Write a Journal Entry **SE** p. 1256	
Make Inferences About Theme **SE** p. 1258	Analogies **SE** p. 1262 Academic Vocabulary	Write Free Verse **TE** p. 1260	Oral Interpretation **SE** p. 1262

Reading Skills and Strategies	Vocabulary	Writing / Grammar	Speaking, Listening, and Viewing
Make Inferences About Characters **SE** p. 1265	Synonyms **SE** p. 1272 Academic Vocabulary **SE** p. 1272	Write a Comparison-Contrast Essay **SE** p. 1271 Write an Autobiographical Narrative **SE** p. 1273 Sentence Fragments **SE** p. 1273	
Question **SE** p. 1275, **TE** p. 1276 Connect **TE** p. 1278	Context Clues **SE** p. 1281 Academic Vocabulary **SE** p. 1281		Debate **SE** p. 1281
Examine Connotation **SE** p. 1283 Draw Conclusions **TE** p. 1284	Denotation and Connotation **SE** p. 1285	Write a Poem **SE** p. 1285	
Summarize **SE** p. 1287 Make Inferences **TE** p. 1288 Scan **TE** p. 1288	Context Clues **SE** p. 1290	Write a List **SE** p. 1290	

Readability Scores Key: **Dale-Chall**/**DRP**/Lexile

PART 3: Extending and Remaking Traditions *(continued)*

Selections and Features	Literary Elements
Poem I Chop Some Parsley While Listening to Art Blakey's Version of "Three Blind Mice," by Billy Collins pp. 1291-1295	Personification **SE** p. 1292
Essay The Names of Women, by Louise Erdrich **7.3**/**62**/1300 pp. 1296-1303	Catalog **SE** p. 1297 Symbolism **TE** p. 1300 Symbol (review) **SE** p. 1302
Short Story Salvador Late or Early, by Sandra Cisneros **5.5**/**63**/0000 pp. 1304-1307	Imagery **SE** p. 1305
Essay Thoughts on the African-American Novel, by Toni Morrison **7.4**/**61**/1130 pp. 1308-1314	Essay **SE** p. 1309 Parallelism (review) **SE** p. 1313
Vocabulary Workshop p. 1315	
Literary Periods *From* **Comic Strips to Graphic Novels** pp. 1316-1317	Science Fiction **TE** p. 1316
Short Story Nineteen Thirty-Seven, by Edwidge Danticat **5**/**54**/900 pp. 1318-1330	Magic Realism **SE** p. 1319 Style (review) **SE** p. 1329
Poem The Man with the Saxophone, by Ai pp. 1331-1335	Narrative Poetry **SE** p. 1332
Poem Ending Poem, by Rosario Morales and Aurora Levins Morales pp. 1336-1341	Motif **SE** p. 1337 Tone (review) **SE** p. 1340
Writing Workshop pp. 1342-1349	
Speaking, Listening, and Viewing Workshop pp. 1350-1351	
Media Workshop pp. 1352-1357	
Independent Reading pp. 1358-1359	
Assessment pp. 1360-1365	First-Person Point of View **TE** p. 1361

Reading Skills and Strategies	Vocabulary	Writing Grammar	Speaking, Listening, and Viewing
Connect to Personal Experience **SE** p. 1292 Analyze Tone **TE** p. 1292	Word Usage **SE** p. 1295	Write a Journal Entry **SE** p. 1295	
Distinguish Fact and Opinion **SE** p. 1297	Word Parts **SE** p. 1303 Academic Vocabulary **SE** p. 1303	Apostrophes **TE** p. 1300 Apply Symbolism **SE** p. 1303	
Analyze Sound Devices **SE** p. 1305 Identify Sequence **TE** p. 1306	Academic Vocabulary **SE** p. 1307	Write an Essay **SE** p. 1307	
Determine Main Idea and Supporting Details **SE** p. 1309	Word Parts **SE** p. 1314	Apply Parallelism **SE** p. 1314	
	Word Parts **SE** p. 1315		
Analyze Characterization **TE** p. 1316			
Visualize **SE** p. 1319 Analyze Foreshadowing **TE** p. 1322 Question **TE** p. 1326	Antonyms **SE** p. 1329 Academic Vocabulary **SE** p. 1329	Write a Short Story **SE** p. 1330	
Connect to Cultural Context **SE** p. 1332	Denotation and Connotation **SE** p. 1335	Write Directions **SE** p. 1335	Discussion **TE** p. 1334
Make Generalizations **SE** p. 1337	Context Clues **SE** p. 1341 Academic Vocabulary **SE** p. 1341		Oral Report **SE** p. 1341
Analyze Persuasion **TE** p. 1344		Write an Editorial **SE** p. 1343 Prewrite **SE** p. 1345 Draft **SE** p. 1346 Revise **SE** p. 1348 Pronoun-Antecedent Agreement **SE** p. 1349	Provide Feedback **TE** p. 1348 Presentation **SE** p. 1349
			Debate **SE** p. 1350 Analyze Persuasive Propositions **TE** p. 1350
Analyze Media Messages **SE** p. 1352 Analyze Sound Bites **TE** p. 1352 Identify Logical Fallacies **SE** p. 1353 Use Either/Or Reasoning **TE** p. 1354 Analyze Images **TE** p. 1356		Make a Chart **SE** p. 1353	Small Group Discussion **SE** pp. 1354, 1355 Partner Discussion **SE** p. 1356 Plan a Multimedia PSA **SE** p. 1357
Compare **TE** p. 1358		Write a Letter **SE** p. 1359	
Read Silently **TE** p. 1360		Write an Essay **SE** p. 1365	

View the Art ★

Answer: *Students may say that this painting suggests precision technology, rapid change, or uncertainty of where technology will take us in the future.* Charles Bell (1935–1995) belonged to the art movement known as Photorealism. This movement features paintings of scenes that are so realistic they appear to be photographs.

Pin Ball #12, 1984. Charles Bell. Oil on canvas. Louis K. Meisel Gallery.

View the Art Bell is known for his nostalgic depictions of vintage toys and for portraying well-known objects in unexpected scale. How does this image represent the future or a technological world? ★

1136

Unit Introduction Skills

Reading Skills
- Analyze Graphic Information (SE pp. 1138–1141)
- Analyze Cause and Effect (SE pp. 1144–1145)
- Interpret (SE pp. 1146–1147)
- Evaluate (SE pp. 1148–1149)
- Create Graphic Organizers (TE p. 1138)

Into the 21st Century

Listening/Speaking/Viewing Skills
- Analyze Art (SE p. 1136; TE pp. 1141, 1145, 1149)
- Presentation on Postmodernist Literature (SE p. 1150)
- Visual Literacy: Timeline (SE p. 1150)

Literary Elements
- Allusion (TE p. 1145)
- Style (TE p. 1148)

Writing Skills/Grammar
- Persuasive Essay (TE p. 1144)

Into the 21st Century

1960s–Present

Looking Ahead

The United States is being reshaped today by profound political and social changes, watershed technological innovation, increasing ethnic diversity, and a complex mixture of cultures. As in the past, contemporary American writers have responded to these historical and cultural forces, both by adapting traditional literary forms and by finding new ones. ☆

Keep the following questions in mind as you read:

➤ What political, social, and cultural forces contributed to the rise of protest movements in the 1960s and 1970s?

➤ How has environmentalism affected contemporary American literature?

➤ How have today's writers reshaped the traditions of Modernism?

1137

Unit Resources

Print Materials

- Unit 7 Teaching Resources, pp. 1–398
- Interactive Read and Write (On Level, Approaching, EL), pp. 255–294
- Novel Companion, pp. 295–338
- Bellringer Option Transparencies: Selection Focus 65–74; Daily Language Practice 96–123
- Assessment Resources, Selection Assessment, pp. 273–328

Technology

- TeacherWorks Plus CD
- StudentWorks Plus CD
- Literature Launchers: Pre-Reading Videos DVD, Unit 7
- Literature Online
- Visual Vocabulary CD-ROM
- Listening Library CD-ROM
- ExamView CD-ROM
- Skill Level Up! CD-ROM

Focus

Summary

This introduction begins with an overview of world events and of political, social, and cultural events in the United States from 1960 to 2005. It focuses on the social, political, and environmental movements of the period, the effects of technology and globalization, and increased multiculturalism.

Language History ☆

Personal Computer In the late 1970s, engineers developed computers that were small enough and inexpensive enough for individuals to purchase for personal use at home. Previously, large mainframe computers had been available only to large organizations. Personal computers, or PCs, continue to evolve as they become smaller and more powerful.

 For school-to-home activities, see Unit 7 Teaching Resources Book, pp. 5–11.

 For students who would profit from independent novel study, see Novel Companion pp. 295–338.

 For diagnostic and end-of-unit assessment, see Assessment Resources, pp. 49–55, 343–344

Teach

Reading Strategy | 1

Use the Timeline Help students read the timeline and relate events in American literature to events in the United States and in the world.

This timeline covers the period from the beginnings of the civil rights and environmental movements through the war in Iraq and the tsunami in Southeast Asia.

Ask: What event in the United States or in the world at large might have been related to one of the literature titles? *(The "I Have a Dream" speech was a part of the March on Washington.)*

Political History ☆

Three Mile Island On March 28, 1979, America's most serious nuclear accident occurred at the Three Mile Island nuclear power plant. A series of events caused the core to overheat and radioactive gas to escape. Although the health threat to the community was negligible, the accident had an enormous effect on public opinion.

Timeline
1960s–Present

AMERICAN LITERATURE

1960

1960
To Kill a Mockingbird by Harper Lee

1962
Silent Spring by Rachel Carson

1963
"I Have a Dream" speech by Martin Luther King Jr.; *The Feminine Mystique* by Betty Friedan

1965
The Autobiography of Malcolm X

1966
In Cold Blood by Truman Capote

1969
Slaughterhouse Five by Kurt Vonnegut

1970

1970
I Know Why the Caged Bird Sings by Maya Angelou

1971
Bury My Heart at Wounded Knee by Dee Brown

1975
Ragtime by E. L. Doctorow

1976
Roots: The Saga of an American Family by Alex Haley

1982 ▲
The Color Purple by Alice Walker

1984
Cathedral by Raymond Carver

UNITED STATES EVENTS

1960

1960
First sit-in protests for civil rights

1963
March on Washington; President Kennedy assassinated

1964
Civil Rights Act of 1964; Gulf of Tonkin Resolution

1968
Martin Luther King Jr. and Senator Robert Kennedy assassinated

1969 ▲
Apollo 11 landing on the moon

1970

1970
First Earth Day observed; students killed at Kent State during antiwar protests

1972
DDT banned; President Richard Nixon visits China

1973
U.S. signs cease-fire with North Vietnam

▲ Cooling Towers at Three Mile Island

1973
Last Americans withdrawn from Vietnam

1974
President Nixon resigns

1979
Nuclear accident at Three Mile Island

WORLD EVENTS

1960

1961
Cosmonaut Yury Gagarin becomes first man in space

1966 ▶
China's Cultural Revolution begins

1967
Six-Day War breaks out between Israel and multiple Arab nations

1968
Tet Offensive launched by communist forces in Vietnam; Soviets invade Czechoslovakia

1970

1973
Paris Peace Accords signed, ending the Vietnam War

1975
South Vietnam defeated by North Vietnam

1979
Soviets invade Afghanistan

1981 ▶
AIDS identified

1985
Mikhail Gorbachev becomes Soviet leader

1989
Tiananmen Square protests in China; fall of Berlin Wall

Reading Practice

Graphic Organizers A timeline shows events in chronological order. Another way to order events is by theme or subject. A web diagram is one graphic organizer that does this. Model a web diagram around the theme of the environment. Put "environmentalism" in the center circle. In surrounding circles, place "publication of *Silent Spring*," "First Earth Day observed," "DDT banned," and "Kyoto Protocol." Have students create a web diagram for another theme in the timeline, such as civil rights, Vietnam, or space exploration.

National Organization for Women button

LOG ON ▶ **Literature** Online

Literature and Reading To explore the Interactive Timeline, go to glencoe.com and enter QuickPass code GLA9800u7.

1990

1987
Beloved by Toni Morrison

1989 ▼
The Joy Luck Club by Amy Tan

1981 ▶
Sandra Day O'Connor becomes first female Supreme Court justice

1982
Equal Rights Amendment fails; Vietnam Veterans Memorial dedicated in Washington, D.C.

1986
Space shuttle *Challenger* explodes

1990

1990
The Things They Carried by Tim O'Brien; "afternoon, a story" hypertext fiction by Michael Joyce

1992
Art Spiegelman awarded a Pulitzer Prize for his graphic novel *Maus*

1993
Toni Morrison wins Nobel Prize in Literature

1992
United States, Mexico, and Canada inaugurate NAFTA trade pact

1996
Infinite Jest by David Foster Wallace

1999
Michael Cunningham wins Pulitzer Prize for Fiction for *The Hours*

Towers of Light WTC Memorial, 2002.

1993
Mosaic, the first popular Web browser, is introduced

1995
Terrorist bombing in Oklahoma City

1999
Columbine High School shootings in Littleton, Colorado

2000

2000
The Interpreter of Maladies by Jhumpa Lahiri

2004
Personal Weblogs, or *blogs*, affect traditional news coverage and public opinion

2

2001 ▲
Terrorist attacks destroy World Trade Center and damage Pentagon

2003
War in Iraq begins

2000

1991
Persian Gulf War; Soviet Union collapses, end of Cold War

1992
Ethnic cleansing kills 200,000 in former Yugoslavia

1993
European Union established

1994 ▲
Nelson Mandela elected president of South Africa; 800,000 killed in Rwanda

1997
Kyoto Protocol on global warming

Indonesian tsunami victim

◀ **2004**
Massive tsunami in Southeast Asia kills at least 225,000

Reading Check

Analyze Graphic Information According to this timeline, when was the first popular Web browser introduced?

UNIT SEVEN

Teach

Reading Check
Answer: *The first popular Web browser was introduced in 1993.*

Reading Strategy 2

Make Inferences Ask: How do you think the development of Internet blogs has affected traditional news coverage? (*Blogs address stories that traditional news sources do not cover; blogs provide additional perspectives on current events.*)

APPROACHING For approaching level students, review the purpose of blogs and their differences from newspaper, radio, and television coverage.

Literary History ☆

The Joy Luck Club This novel speaks to mothers and daughters across cultures. One critic remarked that it is out of the "experience of being caught between countries and cultures that writers such as . . . Amy Tan have begun to create . . . a new genre of American fiction."

Approaching Level

DIFFERENTIATED INSTRUCTION 🐾

Emerging Explain to students that the three-part timeline allows them to see the world and national events that may have influenced works of American literature published at the same time. Have students look at the section of the timeline for the 1960s. Tell them that *To Kill a Mockingbird*, the "I Have a Dream" speech, and *The Autobiography of Malcolm X* address issues of racial inequality; that *In Cold Blood* analyzes a murder; that *Silent Spring* discusses environmental pollution; and that *Slaugherhouse Five* explores World War II. **Ask:** What national events might have affected writers' treatment of racial issues in the 1960s? (*civil rights protests, the March on Washington, the assassination of Martin Luther King Jr.*)

Teach

Reading Strategy 1

Interpret Graphs Have students compare the two charts in the section titled "United States in the Vietnam War." **Ask:** How many troops were in Vietnam during the Tet Offensive? *(over 500,000)*

(APPROACHING) **Ask:** In the years 1965–1969, did the number of troops in Vietnam increase or decrease? Did opposition to the war increase or decrease? *(Both increased.)*

Reading Strategy 2

Interpret Graphs Point out the graph "U.S. Hispanic Population Growth, 1980–2000." **Ask:** If the trend on this chart continued, how many more Hispanic people would there be in the United States in 2010 compared with 2000? *(about 10 million more)*

Cultural History ☆

Cell Phones The cellular phone was invented by Dr. Martin Cooper of Motorola, Inc. Testing of cell phones for public use began in 1977. Over the next 15 years, demand for cell phones grew dramatically. Between 1976 and 2006, the cell phone business grew from $3 million to $30 billion a year.

1140

By the Numbers

U.S. Consumption

In 2001, about 284 million people lived in the U.S. and about 1.03 billion in India. But Americans used 25% of the world's resources and produced 25–30% of its waste. Compared to people in India, U.S. citizens used:

- 50 times more steel
- 56 times more energy
- 170 times more synthetic rubber
- 170 times more newsprint
- 250 times more motor fuel
- 300 times more plastic

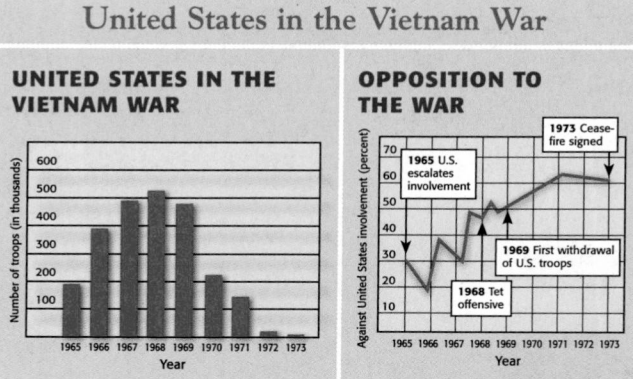

CELL PHONE USE, 2005

- There was almost one cell phone for every two Americans. (By comparison, it took landline phones nearly 100 years to reach this level.) ☆
- About 7.5 million Americans abandoned landline phones and used cell phones exclusively.

COMPUTER USE

- 42,000 bachelor's degrees in computer and information sciences were awarded by U.S. colleges in 2001, up from 2,388 in 1971.
- 99 percent of U.S. schools had Internet access in 2002, up from 50 percent in 1995.
- Online retail sales in the United States for 2003 amounted to $156 billion.
- Projections indicate that 635,000 computer systems analysts will be employed in the United States by 2012, an increase of about 40 percent from 2002.

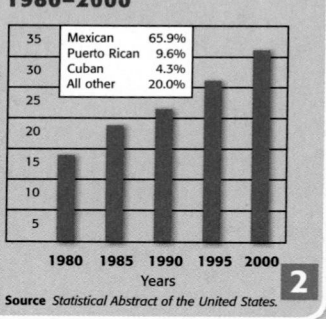

Writing Practice

Make a Line Graph Have students study the graphs in the section "United States in the Vietnam War." Note that one is a bar graph and the other is a line graph. Both show changes over time. Ask students to translate the bar graph "United States in the Vietnam War" to a line graph. Have students create a grid like the one in "Opposition to the War," using the same years on the horizontal axis. Then have them use the numbers of troops shown on the bar graph for the vertical axis. Finally, have students draw a line connecting points that show the numbers of troops for each year in the bar graph. After students have completed their graph, **ask:** Between what two years was there the greatest decrease in number of troops? *(1969 to 1970)*

Being There

Since the 1960s, increased immigration has brought many newcomers to the United States from regions beyond Europe. These newcomers have changed the cultural life of many American communities.

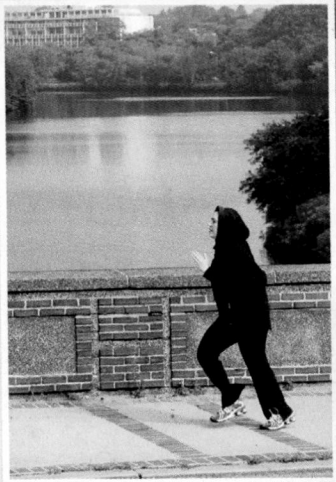

A Muslim Fatina Abrabboh jogs on a bridge spanning the Charles River in Cambridge, Massachusetts, 2005. John Nordell. Color photograph.

B *Children Riding Bicycles Past Mural,* 1991. Ralf-Finn Hestoft. Color photograph.

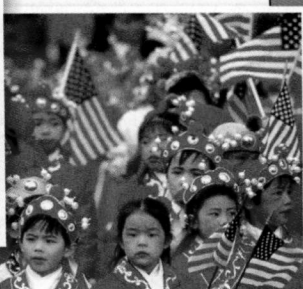

C *Chinese New Year in Los Angeles.* Nik Wheeler. Color photograph.

3

LOG ON ▶ Literature Online

Literature and Reading For more about the history and literature on this period, go to glencoe.com and enter QuickPass code GLA9800u7.

Reading Check

Analyze Graphic Information:

1. In what year did U.S. troop strength in Vietnam peak? In what year did opposition to the Vietnam War peak?

2. How many more degrees in computer and information sciences were granted in 2001 than in 1971?

3. What is distinctive about each of the cultures represented in the photographs shown above?

INTRODUCTION **1141**

1141

Teach

Connect Have students read the quote by Martin Luther King Jr. **Ask:** How do you think the civil rights movement affected the antiwar protests and environmental movement? *(Students may say that antiwar activists and environmentalists were inspired by the success of civil rights protestors.)*

View the Photograph ★

The Longest Walk was held from February to July of 1978. Several hundred Native Americans marched from San Francisco to Washington, D.C., to symbolize the many times that Native Americans were forced onto reservations. The march was in response to legislation before Congress that would have limited Native Americans' treaty rights.

Learning Objectives

For pages 1142–1150

In studying this text, you will focus on the following objectives:

Literary Study:
Analyzing literary periods.
Analyzing literary genres.
Evaluating historical influences.
Connecting to the literature.

Into the 21st Century

1960s–Present

Historical, Social, and Cultural Forces

The Civil Rights Movement

In the mid-1950s, under the inspiring leadership of Martin Luther King Jr., African Americans launched the modern civil rights movement. This heroic, nonviolent campaign to end segregation and secure voting rights for African Americans in the South achieved many of its goals in the mid-1960s, when the federal government enacted landmark civil rights legislation.

> *"Injustice anywhere is a threat to justice everywhere."*
> —Martin Luther King Jr. **1**

The Vietnam War

Beginning in the mid-1950s, American efforts to stop the spread of communist influence led to growing U.S. military involvement in the Southeast Asian country of Vietnam. By the mid-1960s, the United States was fighting a major war against Vietnamese communists. In the late 1960s, heavy American casualties and the U.S. failure to achieve military victory in Southeast Asia led to growing opposition to the war at home. The United States signed a cease-fire agreement in 1973 with communist North Vietnam. By early 1975, the last Americans were withdrawn from South Vietnam, which promptly fell to communist North Vietnam.

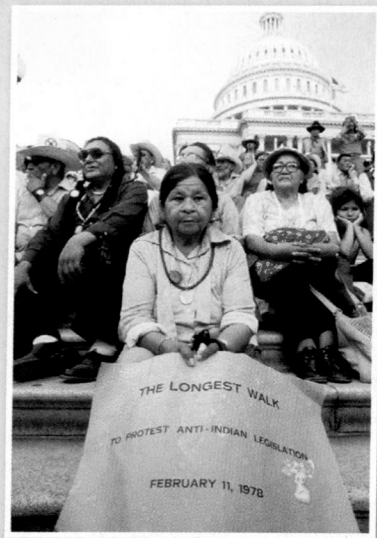

"The Longest Walk," protest, 1978. Wally McNamee. Color photograph. ★

Environmentalism

During the 1960s, many Americans began to feel that environmental problems plagued every region of their nation. In 1962 Rachel Carson's book *Silent Spring* first raised widespread concerns about the effects of pollution on the natural environment. By 1970, a grassroots environmental movement developed. In April of that year, the movement sponsored the first Earth Day. Once

---

Listening and Speaking Practice

SMALL GROUP

Evaluate Persuasive Messages Recordings of well-known speeches from the 1960s are available in many libraries and on the Internet. Divide the class into groups. Assign each group a topic: the Civil Rights Movement, women's rights, the Vietnam War, or environmentalism. Have each group listen to recordings of speeches on their topic, noting the style and content. Allow students to share, in a panel presentation, the similarities and differences among the speakers and their arguments. Have students evaluate the persuasiveness of the various speakers.

the environmental movement gained support, the federal government also took action and established the Environmental Protection Agency (EPA) in 1970.

The Computer Revolution

The introduction of the first digital computer in 1946 launched a technological revolution. In the succeeding decades, advances such as the integrated circuit greatly reduced the size and increased the speed of computers. By the mid-1970s, the first practical and affordable home computers became available. In the late 1980s, the development of government-funded super-computer centers paved the way for the Internet, a global information system that operates commercially.

2 Globalization

Since the 1990s, the Internet, portable communications equipment, and trade deregulation have spurred on the drive for companies to globalize. Often the component parts for consumer goods, like televisions or automobiles, are manufactured in various countries around the world. This trend has been criticized by those who believe that globalization exploits laborers in developing nations, where many of these goods are produced. Some argue that it has slowly siphoned away America's high-wage manufacturing jobs. However, others believe that globalization, in the long term, will benefit both established and developing nations.

Multiculturalism

In literature, writers of European descent have been historically privileged over other groups. Multiculturalism—a product of the 1960s Civil Rights Movement—attempts to correct this by exposing readers to unique voices from a variety of ethnic backgrounds.

Postmodernism

The term *Postmodernism* refers to trends in art, architecture, literature, and music created after World War II. Postmodernists favor unusual juxtapositions of styles, such as linking fine art and popular culture. Postmodern writing reflects an awareness of the influence of the media on modern sensibilities. Postmodernists also question the central place of Western cultures in world civilization.

  PREVIEW **Big Ideas** of Into the 21st Century

1 An Era of Protest ☆	**2 Nature and Technology**	**3 Extending and Remaking Traditions**
From the mid-1950s to the mid-1970s, U.S. society experienced political and social upheaval resulting from the Civil Rights Movement and opposition to the Vietnam War. U.S. writers responded to the powerful questions raised by these historical events. **See pages 1144–1145.**	As U.S. citizens became aware of threats to the environment in recent decades, some writers reassessed the importance of the human relationship to nature. At the same time, watershed changes in technology provided new subject matter and new forms for American literature. **See pages 1146–1147.**	Increases in immigration and changing attitudes toward ethnic identity are helping to create a much more diverse U.S. society and literature. Innovative approaches to art, such as Postmodernism, are also building on past traditions to reshape contemporary American literature. **See pages 1148–1149.**

Reading Strategy   2

Monitor Comprehension
Have students read the section titled "Globalization." **Ask:** What is globalization? (*Globalization refers to companies' doing business around the world; components for one product may be made in several countries.*) **Ask:** Why do some people oppose globalization? (*They believe it exploits workers in other countries and eliminates high-paying jobs in this country.*)

Political History ☆

Kent State A student anti-war protest took place in 1970 at Kent State University in Ohio after President Nixon announced that U.S. and South Vietnamese forces had invaded Cambodia. Some demonstrators damaged businesses, and the governor ordered the National Guard to disperse them. During a rally on May 4, one of the soldiers thought he heard gunfire and opened fire on the students. Gunfire killed four students and wounded several others. The incident increased antiwar activity.

English Learners

DIFFERENTIATED INSTRUCTION

Intermediate Help students analyze the term *multiculturalism* by starting with the word *culture* and having them define the root, prefix, and suffixes that create various extensions of the word.

Approaching Level

DIFFERENTIATED INSTRUCTION

Emerging Have visual learners preview the three photos on the Big Ideas pages that follow. Have them write a phrase or sentence that summarizes the main idea that each photograph conveys. (*equality, clean energy, and new ideas about art*)

UNIT SEVEN

Teach

Reading Strategy | 1

Analyze Cause and Effect
Explain that the civil rights movement was successful in overturning laws in the South that called for segregation. In most parts of the North, there were no laws against hiring African Americans or specifying where they could live. **Ask:** Why might the civil rights movement have been less successful when leaders tried to gain economic power for African Americans? *(It was easier to overturn discrimination that took the form of laws. In the area of economics, prejudice was ingrained in social practices, not laws, which made change more complicated.)*

Cultural History ☆

NOW (The National Organization for Women) NOW was formed in October 1966 by women who believed government had been inattentive to women's issues. NOW has used letter-writing campaigns and lobbying to try to change the law and society's attitudes. Today, the group has about 250,000 members.

Writing Practice

 Persuasive Essay

Malcolm X disagreed with King's philosophy of nonviolence, believing that African Americans should respond to violence from whites with violence of their own. Have students prepare a persuasive essay defending the view of Malcolm X or Martin Luther King Jr. Ask students to meet in small groups to discuss both viewpoints and to brainstorm specific arguments in favor of each

1144

Big Idea 1
An Era of Protest

Everyone is troubled by injustices—great and small. When injustice or unfairness is part of the basic fabric of a society, however, it may take a social revolution to change things.

Segregation
Throughout the first half of the twentieth century, segregation dominated the lives of African Americans, severely limiting their political freedom and economic opportunities. Segregation was enforced by laws throughout the South. As a result, African Americans were denied equal access to good schools and housing and were barred from public facilities such as hotels, theaters, buses, and trains.

Integration
In 1954 the U.S. Supreme Court ruled in its landmark *Brown vs. Board of Education* decision that segregated education for whites and blacks was unconstitutional. However, progress in desegregating schools and other public facilities was very slow. Beginning in December 1955, African Americans in Montgomery, Alabama, organized a successful yearlong boycott of the city's segregated buses. The leader of this protest was an eloquent young minister named Martin Luther King Jr. Dr. King inspired a nonviolent civil rights movement through his powerful speeches and writing. This heroic campaign to end segregation and secure voting rights in the South had made huge strides by the mid-1960s, when the federal government enacted landmark civil rights legislation.

1 Black Power
While King advocated a nonviolent path to integration, other African American civil rights leaders favored armed struggle and black separatism. In the early 1960s, militant leader Malcolm X rose

to prominence by promoting race pride and black nationalism—the idea that African Americans should band together to gain economic independence and to create a sense of community. In 1966, Stokely Carmichael created the "Black Power" movement, which championed self-defense, autonomy, economic and political power, and black pride.

> *"Violence often brings about momentary results."*
> —Martin Luther King Jr.

Women and Hispanics
During the 1960s and 1970s, American women pushed for greater rights and opportunities. The publication of Betty Friedan's *The Feminine Mystique* in 1963 gave steam to the women's movement. Friedan joined other activists in 1966 to form the National Organization for Women (NOW), which worked for legislation against gender discrimination in employment, housing, and education. In the early 1960s, César Chavez and Dolores Huerta started organizations that fought for the rights of Hispanic farmworkers.

A Divisive War
The Vietnam War was one of the most divisive conflicts in U.S. history. When U.S. troops went to Vietnam in the spring of 1965, most Americans supported the effort. In time, however, claims by military leaders that victory was near were contradicted by the media, especially on television. Vietnam was the first "living room war"; people were deeply disturbed by images of wounded and dead soldiers. As casualties mounted, many began to protest the war and demand that it end.

1144 UNIT 7 INTO THE TWENTY-FIRST CENTURY

position. Then have them write an essay, outlining and supporting their specific arguments.

Have students meet in groups for peer review of their essays. Remind reviewers to pay attention to logical reasoning and concrete support for arguments. Students should revise their essays and correct spelling, punctuation, and grammar. Ask volunteers to share their essays with the class.

Civil rights marchers with "I Am A Man" signs, 1968. Black and white photograph. ★

Teach

Reading Check

Answer: *Black Power arose out of the frustration of civil rights activists with their slow pace of progress in securing equality.*

Literary Element 2

Allusion *Zeitgeist* means "spirit of the times." During the 1950s and 1960s, many former European colonies gained their independence. **Ask:** Why does King allude to *zeitgeist* and to the move toward independence by these countries? *(He is implying that African Americans are part of the spirit of freedom that is sweeping the world.)*

View the Photograph ★

This photograph was taken by Ernest Withers in Memphis, Tennessee, during a strike by sanitation workers in 1968. Withers was a self-employed photographer in the South. He recorded many important moments in the civil rights movement and was an active participant himself. The night before he took this photo, Withers helped the marchers make their signs.

---

from *Letter from a Birmingham Jail* by Martin Luther King Jr.

Oppressed people cannot remain oppressed forever. The yearning for freedom eventually manifests itself, and that is what has happened to the American Negro. Something within has reminded him of his birthright of freedom; something without has reminded him that he can gain it. Consciously or unconsciously, he has been swept in by what the Germans call the *Zeitgeist*, and with his black brothers of Africa, and his brown and yellow brothers of Asia, South America and the Caribbean, he is moving with a sense of cosmic urgency toward the promised land of racial justice. Recognizing this vital urge that has engulfed the Negro community, one should readily understand public demonstrations. The Negro has many pent-up resentments and latent frustrations. He has to get them out. So let him march sometime; let him have his prayer pilgrimages to the city hall; understand why he must have sit-ins and freedom rides. If his repressed emotions do not come out in these nonviolent ways, they will seek ominous expressions of violence. This is not a threat; it is a fact of history. So I have not said to my people "get rid of your discontent." But I have tried to say that this normal and healthy discontent can be channelized through the creative outlet of nonviolent direct action.

Reading Check

Analyze Cause and Effect How did the rise of Black Power later confirm Dr. King's warning about violence in "Letter from a Birmingham Jail"?

English Learners

DIFFERENTIATED INSTRUCTION

Intermediate Review words that have multiple meanings and discuss their definitions in the context of protest: *march, demonstration, movement,* and *organize*. Ask students to discuss the meanings they know for these words. Then have them look up the words in a dictionary to find the definition that is relevant in the context of protest.

Reading Strategy | 1

Connect **Say:** DDT has been banned for decades, thanks to the work of Rachel Carson. **Ask:** What is the most pressing environmental problem today? Explain. *(Possible answer: Greenhouse gas emissions lead to global warming and worldwide climate change.)*

Reading Strategy | 2

Activate Prior Knowledge
Ask: What have been some important environmental issues over the last several decades? *(Air pollution, water pollution, acid rain, damage to the ozone layer, greenhouse gases, and destruction of rainforests)*

Political History ☆

The Space Race The space race between the United States and the former Soviet Union was fueled by the tensions of the Cold War. Both countries rushed to put a satellite into orbit; the Soviets were first, launching *Sputnik 1* in 1957.

Big Idea 2

Nature and Technology

Americans today are living through events that have the potential to fundamentally change the way we will live for years to come. Among the most basic of these are long-range changes to the natural environment as a result of industrialization and the revolution in communications created by modern technology, including computers.

The Environmental Movement

During the 1960s and 1970s, a growing number of U.S. citizens began to become alarmed at how their highly industrialized society was affecting the natural environment. Widespread use of pesticides had damaged many forms of wildlife. Rising levels of air and water pollution were seen as a threat to health. A leading cause of this change in public perception was the work of marine biologist Rachel Carson. Carson's 1962 book *Silent Spring* attacked the increasing use of pesticides, particularly DDT. She contended that in addition to controlling harmful insects, pesticides such as DDT also killed the birds, fish, and other creatures further up the food chain. Carson warned Americans of a "silent spring," in which few birds would remain to herald the season with their songs.

> *"There was a strange stillness. The birds, for example—where had they gone?"*
>
> —Rachel Carson, *Silent Spring*

By 1970, with the observance of the first Earth Day, a grassroots environmental movement began to take shape. Citizens formed local environmental groups, while long-established organizations, such as the Sierra Club and the Audubon Society,

gained greater influence. All these groups worked to protect the environment and promote the conservation of natural resources. The federal government also became involved, establishing the Environmental Protection Agency and passing legislation aimed at curbing air and water pollution and protecting endangered wildlife.

Responding to Nature

Going back at least as far as Thoreau's *Walden*, nature writing has been a persistent strain in American literature. Heightened concern about the environment, coupled with the "back to nature" impulse that was a significant element of the counterculture of the 1960s, prompted a minor renaissance of American nature writing in the recent past. Edward Abbey, Annie Dillard, Edward Hoagland, Terry Tempest Williams, Barry Lopez, John McPhee, and many other writers have evoked a variety of wilderness landscapes, from the desert to the Arctic, and reflected on the lessons nature has to teach.

The Information Age

In the twentieth century, the world experienced a revolution in communications unmatched since the invention of the printing press in the fifteenth century. Modern Americans became enthusiastic users of a wide variety of new media, including telephones, radio, television, video games, cell phones, and the Internet. These new media have created a society in which one of the most valuable commodities is information.

One of the consequences of the Cold War rivalry between the United States and the Soviet Union was competition for dominance in space exploration. In addition to such achievements as the Moon landings and the shuttle missions, the U.S. space program has contributed to advances in a wide range of technologies, such as the satellites

Vocabulary Practice

New Words **Say:** Since the 1960s, we have seen a dramatic increase in new English words and expressions. Point out the words *video games, cell phones, Internet,* and *telecommunications* in the section titled "The Information Age." In addition to new words, many old words have new meanings. For example, one meaning of *to surf* is "to ride the waves on a board." A newer usage is "to surf the Net," which means to explore the Internet.

Have students identify new words and their definitions, or new uses of words, in the following categories:

- computers
- environment/environmental movement
- communications

Students should use one word or phrase from each category in a sentence and then share their word lists and sentences with the class.

Wind Farm at Sunset, David Seed. Color photograph.

that make up today's global telecommunications and GPS networks.

A recent and revolutionary form of new media is the worldwide communications system of the Internet. With the development of the hypertext transport protocol (http) and new software known as Web browsers, Internet use began to expand rapidly. As early as 1988, it was growing at the rate of 100 percent a year. By the late 1990s, the number of Internet users exceeded 30 million. During its brief existence, the Internet has had a profound effect on many aspects of modern life, from the explosive development of online commerce to the creation of new computer-based literary forms such as hypertext fiction, which uses computer technology to expand the possible sequencings of a narrative.

from *Lost* by David Wagoner

Stand still. The trees ahead and bushes beside you
Are not lost. Wherever you are is called Here,
And you must treat it as a powerful stranger,
Must ask permission to know it and be known.
The forest breathes. Listen. It answers,
I have made this place around you.
If you leave it you may come back again, saying
   Here.
No two trees are the same to Raven.
No two branches are the same to Wren.
If what a tree or a bush does is lost on you,
You are surely lost. Stand still. The forest knows
Where you are. You must let it find you. **3**

Reading Check

Interpret What two different attitudes toward the natural environment are reflected in David Wagoner's poem "Lost"?

INTRODUCTION **1147**

Teach

Reading Check

Answer: *One attitude is the desire to control the natural environment; the other attitude is a willingness to learn what nature can teach.*

Literary Element   **3**

Rhythm Rhythm refers to the pattern of sound created by stressed and unstressed syllables. Some poems have a regular pattern, or meter. **Ask:** Does this poem have regular meter? *(No, the rhythm is irregular.)* **Ask:** How does the punctuation affect the rhythm of the lines? *(The periods within lines break up the poem's rhythm, creating emphasis.)*

View the Photograph

These modern windmills generate electricity by harnessing natural forces rather than by burning fossil fuels. **Ask:** How does this "wind farm" reflect the poem "Lost"? *(Possible answer: It appears to be a kind of forest. Like the forest in the poem, the wind farm "breathes" and appears to be a "powerful stranger.")*

Approaching Level

DIFFERENTIATED INSTRUCTION

SMALL GROUP

Emerging Have students silently read the excerpt from "Lost," noting the punctuation and sentence arrangement. Then arrange the class in small groups and ask them to take turns reading the poem aloud. Have student groups identify and explain the poem's images, including "stand still," "powerful stranger," and "forest breathes." Ask students to describe how the images evoke particular emotions for readers.

1147

Teach

Literary Element | 1

Style Explain that using fiction strategies in writing nonfiction is part of a literary movement called The New Journalism. The writer imagines dialogue that might have taken place and includes everyday details of the characters' lives. **Ask:** What are the advantages of using this technique to tell about an actual event? *(Possible answers: The event seems more real; it makes reading more interesting; it allows the writer to explore the story in-depth and give it greater dimension.)*

Literary History ☆

Rita Dove In 1993, Rita Dove was named the first African American Poet Laureate of the United States. Dove's work is significant in part for the range of material that it covers. She draws upon her childhood experiences for her poetry, but she also touches on settings from Europe, Africa, and the American South.

Big Idea 3
Extending and Remaking Traditions

In the past, newcomers to the United States were urged to "Americanize" themselves as soon and as fully as possible. The model was "the melting pot," meaning a place in which a complete blending of peoples and cultures takes place. Today, there is a new cultural model that stresses the value of maintaining ethnic diversity in American society.

The New Immigrants

The United States has always been a nation of immigrants. Restrictive immigration laws and economic depression kept immigrant levels low between World War I and World War II. However, since the end of World War II, immigration has been rising. The Immigration Reform Act of 1965 allowed more immigrants from countries outside of northern and western Europe. By the 1980s and 1990s, immigration had reached levels approaching the all-time highs of the early twentieth century. Most of these recent immigrants come from the western hemisphere (primarily Mexico) and from Asia. By 1995 almost 9 percent of Americans were foreign born. Consequently, the traditional canon of American literature is expanding greatly to include works by writers from many different backgrounds.

Cultural Diversity

Newcomers are helping to make U.S. society more culturally diverse. As a result, many communities in the United States have an increasingly multiethnic texture that incorporates language, food, family values, social life, and entertainment. With diversity increasing and opportunities for women expanding, American literature draws upon a wider range of experience than ever before. The literature published in the United States includes fiction, nonfiction, and poetry by African American writers such as Henry Louis Gates Jr. and Rita Dove; by Native American writers such as N. Scott

Momaday and Louise Erdrich; by Hispanic writers such as Sandra Cisneros and Julia Alvarez; and by Asian American writers such as Amy Tan and Jhumpa Lahiri. The enthusiasm with which the works of these writers are received shows that their own ethnic traditions are becoming an integral part of the American cultural experience.

Postmodernism

The Modernists of the early part of the twentieth century believed that as contemporary life became more complex and artificial it also became increasingly inhumane. Postmodernists, such as novelists John Barth and Thomas Pynchon, reject this conclusion. They argue that the modern world's complexities should be explored, even celebrated. Like pop artists, Postmodernists often investigate artifice, or the surfaces of things, to reveal some truth just underneath. These writers accomplish this through a variety of forms and strategies, such as creating literary collages or stories-within-stories, blending genres, introducing material from popular culture, and introducing themselves as characters into their own fiction.

> *"Postmodernism is tying your necktie while simultaneously explaining the step-by-step procedure of necktie-tying and chatting about the history of male neckwear—and managing a perfect full windsor anyhow."*
>
> —John Barth

New Literary Forms

The characteristic literary forms of Postmodernism emphasize the blending of genres, such as the

Reading Practice

Imagery Writers use descriptive words and phrases to create imagery that appeals to the five senses. Poets use vivid images to help readers see details of character and scene and to convey emotions. Have students read the poem from Ortiz Cofer's collection *The Latin Deli*. Ask partners to analyze the images by addressing these questions:

- What images appeal to the sense of sight? The sense of smell?
- What detailed images help you see the woman proprietor?

Technology, 1991. Nam June Paik. 25 video monitors, 3 laser disc players with unique 3 discs in cabinet. Side view. Smithsonian American Art Museum, Washington, DC.

1 "nonfiction novel," which uses the strategies of fiction to present actual events. One of the earliest and best-known literary works to adopt this strategy was *In Cold Blood,* Truman Capote's 1965 account of the brutal murder of a Kansas family. Another Postmodern literary form, the graphic novel, blends high and low culture by expanding one of the most familiar forms of twentieth century American popular culture, the comic book, to address serious literary subjects. Probably the best-known graphic novel is *Maus* by Art Spiegelman, which won a Pulitzer Prize in 1992. Spiegelman uses comic book panels and cat and mouse characters to tell a story about the Holocaust.

from *The Latin Deli: An Ars Poetica*
by Judith Ortiz Cofer

Presiding over a formica counter, **2**
plastic Mother and Child magnetized
to the top of an ancient register,
the heady mix of smells from the open bins
of dried codfish, the green plantains
hanging in stalks like votive offerings,
she is the Patroness of Exiles,
a woman of no-age who was never pretty,
who spends her days selling canned memories
while listening to the Puerto Ricans complain
that it would be cheaper to fly to San Juan
than to buy a pound of Bustelo coffee here,
and to Cubans perfecting their speech
of a "glorious return" to Havana—where no one
has been allowed to die and nothing to change
    until then;
to Mexicans who pass through, talking lyrically
of *dolares* to be made in El Norte—
                        all wanting the comfort
of spoken Spanish, to gaze upon the family portrait
of her plain wide face, her ample bosom
resting on her plump arms, her look of maternal
    interest
as they speak to her and each other
of their dreams and disillusions—
how she smiles understanding,
when they walk down the narrow aisles of her store
reading the labels of packages aloud, as if
they were the names of lost lovers: *Suspiros,
Merengues,* the stale candy of everyone's childhood.
                        She spends her days
slicing *jamón y queso* and wrapping it in wax paper
tied with string: plain ham and cheese
that would cost less at the A&P, but it would not
    satisfy
the hunger of the fragile old man lost in the folds
of his winter coat, who brings her lists of items
that he reads to her like poetry, or the others,
whose needs she must divine, conjuring up
    products
from places that now exist only in their hearts—
closed ports she must trade with.

Reading Check

Evaluate What values of cultural diversity are expressed in Judith Ortiz Cofer's "The Latin Deli"?

INTRODUCTION **1149**

Teach

Reading Check

Answer: *The values include the honest dialogue and the pride in community that arises from a group's common experiences, such as eating the same foods.*

Reading Strategy **2**

Interpret Read the poem aloud as students follow along.
Ask: Who is the "Patroness of Exiles"? *(The woman who runs the deli)*

ADVANCED **Ask:** What is "the hunger of the fragile old man"? *(He hungers for things that remind him of home.)*

View the Art

Korean-born artist Nam June Paik uses video and television as his artistic media, incorporating electronic moving images into art. *Technology* uses an array of intricate machinelike elements and numerous television screens.
Ask: Why do you think Paik titled this piece *Technology*? *(The complex elements and swirling images have a futuristic look.)*

Approaching Level

DIFFERENTIATED INSTRUCTION

Established Review with students any unfamiliar analogies, idioms, and references in the poem, for example, "Patroness of Exile," "canned memories," "names of lost lovers," "reads to her like poetry," or "closed ports." Have students write short definitions of the unfamiliar references.

English Learners

DIFFERENTIATED INSTRUCTION

Beginning Help students recognize the Spanish/English cognates *dolares* and *dollars,* and *El Norte* and *North.* Discuss with students the strategy of identifying cognates, and analyze the impact on the poem of including Spanish terms.

Assess/Close

Legacy of the Period

Remind students of the words of Martin Luther King Jr.: "Injustice anywhere is a threat to justice everywhere." **Ask:** Does the United States have the responsibility to see that people of other nations do not suffer injustice?

Cultural and Literary Links

Suggest that as students read the unit, they note how the dramatic changes that began in the 1960s affected these writers.

 Activities

1. **Follow Up** Students' responses should refer to the text.

2. **Contrast Literary Genres** Have each member of the group focus on one literary form as the group creates the presentation.

3. **Build Literacy** Encourage students to use both the Internet and print resources to locate the images for their timeline.

FOLDABLES
Study Organizer

4. Have students make and label the Layered-Look Book. Encourage students to answer these questions for each of the readings in this unit.

Wrap-Up

Legacy of the Period

The African American civil rights movement, the women's movement, and the related political movements among Hispanics and other groups, transformed American society. Although important problems remain to be resolved, these movements achieved major advances in social justice and economic opportunity during the twentieth century. The legacy of the antiwar movement is far less clear. Americans remain deeply divided on the morality and practicality of military intervention in the affairs of other nations.

The environmental movement has heightened the awareness of U.S. citizens about a broad range of issues, including public health, consumer safety, and preservation of natural resources. It has made people realize that the United States is part of a world that is interdependent environmentally as well as economically.

The U.S. has never been more ethnically diverse or culturally complex. American literature has followed this national trend, growing ever more diverse as it has grown more unique, humorous, and self-aware.

Cultural and Literary Links

> In the 1970s, Alice Walker successfully revived interest in the Harlem Renaissance writer Zora Neale Hurston, who had been largely forgotten.

> The critical and popular success of the oral histories of Studs Terkel has helped to revitalize this literary form.

> The work of Theodore Roethke shows the influence of such Modernist poets as T. S. Eliot and Wallace Stevens.

 Literature Online

Unit Resources For additional skills practice, go to glencoe.com and enter QuickPass code GLA9800u7.

Activities

Choose one of the following activities to explore and develop as you read this unit.

1. Follow Up Go back to the Looking Ahead on page 1137 and answer the questions.

2. Contrast Literary Genres Working with other students, research Postmodernist literature and create a brief presentation for your class, describing some of its typical forms, including the nonfiction novel, hypertext fiction, and the graphic novel.

3. Build Literacy Create a visual timeline of the period from 1960 to the present, using images that have become iconic representations of the time (for example, Elizabeth Eckford walking past jeering white students during the desegregation of Central High School in Little Rock in September 1957). When you have completed your timeline, share it with the class.

4. Take Notes Use this graphic organizer to jot down questions you have about the readings in this unit.

 LAYERED-LOOK BOOK

| Reader's Questions |
| Who? |
| What? |
| Where? |
| When? |
| Why? |

Speaking Practice

 Compare Media Accounts Have small groups research media accounts of the events at Central High School in Little Rock, Arkansas in September 1957. Suggest that students look through collections of old news magazines at libraries, television news accounts, documentaries, microfilm of newspapers, or reports that have been stored online. Tell groups to choose one account from two different media genres and to compare and contrast them. Have groups present their findings in panel discussions. Each group's discussion should present a summary of the key information as well as examples of any bias they detected.

An Era of Protest

Challenge America, 1964. Lois Mailou Jones. Photomechanical reproduction, acrylic and paper on canvas, 39⅛ x 30⅛ in. Hirshhorn Museum and Sculpture Garden, Smithsonian Institution, Washington DC.

Many of Jones's works combine African and American images. How does this piece use images from both cultures to "challenge" its viewers to make America a better place?

"*We know through painful experience that freedom is never voluntarily given by the oppressor; it must be demanded by the oppressed.*" **1**

—Martin Luther King Jr., "Letter from a Birmingham Jail"

1151

UNIT SEVEN
PART 1

Analyze and Extend

Reading Strategy | 1

Analyze Explain that the quotation is from a letter King wrote while he was jailed for nonviolent demonstration. **Ask:** What is Martin Luther King Jr. saying about freedom in the quote? *(King believes that people must demand their freedom because oppressors will never give it to them without a struggle.)*

View the Art

Answer: *Jones overlaps and intertwines images of men, women, and children; civil rights leaders; white politicians; and people from different periods of history. She challenges viewers to see that these people are all part of America.*

Lois Mailou Jones (1905–1998) was an African American painter who became interested in African themes early in her career.

TIME

Focus

Summary

When Rosa Parks refused to give up her seat on a bus to a white person in 1955 in Montgomery, Alabama, she was arrested. Because of Rosa Parks's actions, Martin Luther King Jr. successfully challenged Montgomery's segregation laws.

Teach

An Era of Protest The author compares the civil rights struggle to the story of David and Goliath. Ask a volunteer to tell the story of David and Goliath. *(In the Biblical story, the boy David kills the giant Goliath with a slingshot.)*

Ask: In the case of Rosa Parks, who was David and who was Goliath? *(Rosa Parks was David; segregation laws were the Goliath.)*

APPROACHING *Ask for examples of games or contests in which a weaker or smaller competitor defeats an apparently stronger foe, identifying which competitor is "David" and which is "Goliath."*

Readability Scores

Dale-Chall: 8.2
DRP: 61
Lexile: 1060

  For an audio recording of this selection, use Listening Library Audio CD-ROM.

Learning Objectives

For pages 1152–1154

In studying this text, you will focus on the following objective:

Reading: Analyzing text structure.

Set a Purpose for Reading

Read to learn how an act of protest defined the civil rights movement.

Preview the Article

1. What do you know about the civil rights movement? What else would you like to know?

2. Read the poem excerpt at right. How do you think the author feels about Rosa Parks? How might this affect her tone?

Reading Strategy
Analyze Text Structure

Chronological order, or the time order in which events take place, is one type of text structure. Identify chronological order through dates and key words such as *first, then,* and *finally.* Make a chart like the one below.

SEQUENCE OF EVENTS

Event 1 → Event 2 → Event 3

TIME

The Torchbearer

ROSA PARKS's simple act of protest galvanized America's civil rights revolution

By RITA DOVE

How she sat there, the time right inside a place so wrong it was ready.

—From "Rosa," in *On the Bus* with Rosa Parks by Rita Dove

We know the story. One December evening, a woman left work and boarded a bus for home. She was tired; her feet ached. But this was Montgomery, Alabama, in 1955, and as the bus became crowded, the woman, a black woman, was ordered to give up her seat to a white passenger. When she remained seated, that simple decision eventually led to the disintegration of institutionalized segregation in the South and ushered in a new era of the Civil Rights movement.

This, anyway, was the story I had heard from the time I was curious enough to eavesdrop on adult conversations. I was three years old when a white bus driver warned Rosa Parks, "Well, I'm going to have you arrested," and she replied, "You may go on and do so." As a child, I didn't understand how doing nothing had caused so much activity, but I recognized the template: David slaying the giant Goliath, or the boy who saved his village by sticking his finger in the dike. Perhaps it is precisely the lure of fairy-tale retribution that colors the lens we look back through. Parks was 42 years old when she refused to give up her seat. She has insisted that her feet were not aching; she was, by her own testimony, no more tired than usual. She did not plan her fateful act: "I did not get on the bus to get arrested," she has said. "I got on the bus to go home."

Montgomery's segregation laws were complex: Blacks were required to pay their fare to the driver and then get off and reboard through the back door. Sometimes the bus would drive off before the paid-up customers made it to the back entrance. If the white section was full and another white

---

Reading Practice

Topic Sentences Say: Well-written nonfiction works are organized around a main idea. Each paragraph supports the main idea of the work. Each paragraph also has a topic sentence and supporting details.

Have students look at the third paragraph on this page.

Ask: What is the topic sentence of this paragraph? *("Montgomery's segregation laws were complex.")* **Ask:** What

are two details that support the topic sentence? *("Blacks were required to pay their fares . . . and then get off and reboard through the back door." A black person was not allowed to sit across the aisle from whites.)*

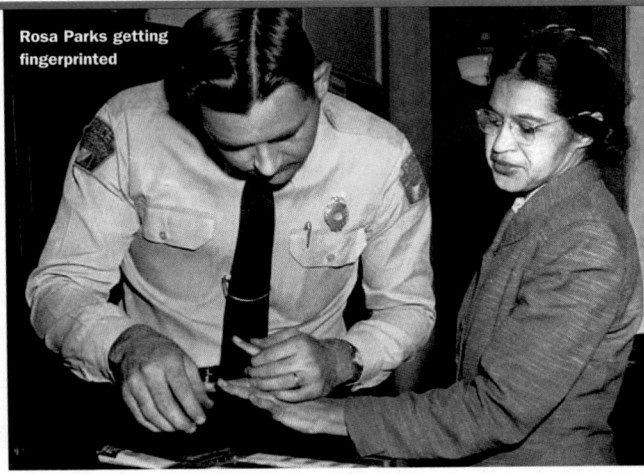

Rosa Parks getting fingerprinted

customer entered, blacks were required to give up their seats and move farther to the back; a black person was not even allowed to sit across the aisle from whites. These humiliations were compounded by the fact that two-thirds of the bus riders in Montgomery were black.

Parks was not the first to be detained for this offense. Eight months earlier, Claudette Colvin, 15, refused to give up her seat and was arrested. Black activists met with this girl to determine if she would make a good test case. As secretary of the local chapter of the National Association for the Advancement of Colored People (NAACP), Parks attended the meeting, where it was finally decided that a more "upstanding" candidate than Colvin was necessary to withstand the scrutiny of the courts and the press. Then, in October, a young woman named Mary Louise Smith was arrested; NAACP leaders rejected her, too, as their vehicle, looking for someone more able to withstand media scrutiny. Smith paid the fine and was released.

Six weeks later, the time was ripe. The facts, rubbed shiny for retelling, are these: On December 1, 1955, Mrs. Rosa Parks, seamstress for the Montgomery Fair department store, boarded the Cleveland Avenue bus. She took a seat in the fifth row—the first row of the "Colored Section." The driver was the same one who had put her off a bus 12 years earlier for refusing to get off and reboard through the back door. ("He was still mean-looking," she has said.) Did that make her stubborn? Or had her work in the NAACP sharpened her sensibilities so that she knew what to do—or more precisely, what not to do: Don't frown, don't struggle, don't shout, don't pay the fine?

At the news of the arrest, local civil rights leader E.D. Nixon exclaimed, "My God, look what segregation has put in my hands!" Parks was not only above moral reproach (securely married, reasonably employed), but she possessed a quiet fortitude as well as political savvy. In short, she was the ideal candidate for a test case.

She was arrested on a Thursday; bail was posted by Clifford Durr, the white lawyer whose wife had employed Parks as a seamstress. That evening, after talking it over with her mother and husband, Rosa Parks agreed to challenge the constitutionality of Montgomery's segregation laws. During a midnight meeting of the Women's Political Council, 35,000 handbills were printed for distribution to all black schools the next morning. The message was simple:

"We are . . . asking every Negro to stay off the buses Monday in protest of the arrest and trial . . . You can afford to stay out of school for one day. If you work, take a cab, or walk. But please, children and grown-ups, don't ride the bus at all on Monday. Please stay off the buses Monday."

Monday came. Rain threatened, yet the black population of Montgomery stayed off the buses, either walking or catching one of the black cabs stopping at every municipal bus stop for 10 cents per customer—the standard bus fare. Meanwhile, Parks was scheduled to appear in court. She made her way through the throngs at the courthouse, a demure figure in a long-sleeved black dress with white collar and cuffs, a trim black velvet hat, gray coat, and white gloves. A girl in the crowd caught sight of her and cried out, "Oh, she's so sweet. They've messed with the wrong one now!"

Yes, indeed. The trial lasted 30 minutes, with the expected conviction and penalty. That afternoon, the Montgomery Improvement Association was formed. So as not to ruffle any local activists' feathers, the members elected as their president a relative newcomer to

THE TORCHBEARER **1153**

TIME

Teach

Reading Strategy　2

Analyze Text Structure
Have students read the first full paragraph on this page.

Ask: What key words in this paragraph signal the chronological order? *(The words* earlier, finally, *and* then *signal chronological order.)*

 For activities related to this selection, see Unit 7 Teaching Resources Book, pp. 21–29.

English Learners

DIFFERENTIATED INSTRUCTION

Advanced Explain that the Latin root of the word *segregate* means "to set apart from the flock." Describe how the United States once had laws that "set apart" people of different races, making them attend different schools. Civil rights activists worked to change these laws so that African Americans could attend the same schools and use the same public facilities as whites. Explain to students that the prefix *de-* can mean "not"; adding this prefix can make a word negative. Have volunteers explain how *de-* changes the meaning of *segregation*.

Informational Text

Reading Strategy   1

Analyze Text Structure

Ask: According to the information about Rosa Parks and the Montgomery transportation system, how long did the bus boycott last? *(about a year)*

Cultural History ☆

Rosa Parks Rosa Parks died in 2005 at her home in Detroit, Michigan, at age 92. She had moved to Detroit in 1957 after being threatened with physical violence and fired from her job because of her activism. After her death, Parks was honored with a week of remembrances. Her coffin was taken to Montgomery for a memorial service and then lay in state at the United States Capitol in Washington, D.C. The last stop was Detroit, where thousands honored her in a funeral that lasted more than seven hours.

Rosa alone

Montgomery, the young minister of Dexter Avenue Baptist Church: the Rev. Martin Luther King Jr. That evening, addressing a crowd gathered at the Holt Street Baptist Church, King declared in that sonorous, ringing voice the world would soon thrill to: "There comes a time that people get tired." When he was finished, Parks stood up so the audience could see her. She did not speak; there was no need to.

☆ *Here I am,* her silence said, *among you.* And she has been with us ever since—a persistent symbol of human dignity in the face of brutal authority. The famous UPI photo (actually taken more than a year later, on December 21, 1956, the day Montgomery's public transportation system was legally integrated) is a study of calm strength. She is looking out the bus window, her hands resting in the folds of her checked dress, while a white man sits, unperturbed, in the row *behind* her. That clear profile, the neat hat and eyeglasses and sensible coat—she could have been my mother or anybody's favorite aunt.

History is often portrayed as a grand opera, full of great intrigues and larger-than-life heroics. Some of the most tumultuous events, however, have been provoked by serendipity—the assassination of an unimportant archduke spawned World War I, a kicked-over lantern may have sparked the Great Chicago Fire. One cannot help wondering what role Martin Luther King Jr. would have played in the civil rights movement if the opportunity had not presented itself that first evening of the boycott. What if Rosa Parks had chosen a row farther back from the outset? Or what if she had missed the bus altogether?

1 At the beginning of this new millennium (and after a particularly noisy century), it is the modesty of Rosa Parks's example that sustains us. It is no less than the belief in the power of the individual, that cornerstone of the American Dream, that she inspires. Her life offers the hope that when crunch time comes, all of us—even the least of us—could be that brave, that serenely human.

— Updated 2005, from TIME, June 14, 1999

Respond and Think Critically

Respond and Interpret

1. Review the graphic organizer you created. Write a brief summary of the main ideas in this article. For help on writing a summary, see page 79.

2. (a)What were the segregation laws for Montgomery's bus system? (b)Why were these laws especially humiliating to African American people?

3. (a)Why did the NAACP reject two other bus riders before meeting Parks? (b)What does this indicate about the organization?

Analyze and Evaluate

4. Why were Parks's appearance and social standing important?

5. (a)How do you think the author feels about the Montgomery bus boycott? (b)What evidence supports your conclusion?

Connect

6. How might you have reacted if you were at Parks's trial?

Assess

1. Students' summaries should include key events of Parks's struggle.

2. (a) African Americans had to pay their fare and then get off and reboard through the back door; if the white section was full, African Americans had to give up their seats and move farther back; they could not sit across the aisle from a white person. (b) The laws treated them as second-class citizens.

3. (a) The NAACP did not feel the others could withstand media scrutiny. (b) Leaders had planned carefully.

4. Parks had to have a good reputation and appear non-threatening.

5. (a) She is grateful for the change that the Montgomery bus boycott brought about. (b) She wonders what the world would be like if the boycott had not happened.

6. Students answers will vary. They should support their opinions with details from the text.

Before You Read

from *Stride Toward Freedom*

Meet **Martin Luther King Jr.**
(1929–1968)

Martin Luther King Jr. showed that segregation and forced inequality could be successfully combated without violence. His steady advocacy uplifted the despondent and challenged the complacent. Combining high ideals with practicality, he inspired people from all races and backgrounds to demand the best from themselves and their country.

> "Do your work so well that no one could do it better. Do it so well that all the hosts of heaven and earth will have to say: Here lived a man who did his job as if God Almighty called him at this particular time in history to do it."
>
> —Martin Luther King Jr.

Historic Struggles Born the son of a minister in Atlanta, Georgia, King distinguished himself at school and entered Morehouse College at fifteen. After receiving his PhD in theology, King became a minister in Montgomery, Alabama.

 Shortly after moving to Montgomery, the first major nonviolent protest of the civil rights movement took place: the Montgomery bus boycott. The boycott was an attempt to end segregation on public buses. For more than a year, Montgomery's fifty thousand black citizens stayed off the buses. The boycott was successful, and King's public speaking and leadership skills drew national attention. Afterward, the Southern Christian Leadership Conference was founded to confront all forms of segregation, and King became its president.

Commitment and Dedication When the center of the civil rights struggle shifted to Birmingham, Alabama, in 1963, King was there. He and other demonstrators were jailed, and violence exploded in the streets, but King's stance on nonviolent resistance remained firm: "We will go on," he told his supporters, "because we have started a fire in Birmingham that water cannot put out. We are going on because we love Birmingham and we love democracy. And we are going to remain nonviolent."

One of the best-known triumphs of the civil rights movement was the March on Washington in 1963. There King delivered his famous "I Have a Dream" speech to an audience of approximately 250,000 people. One year later, he became the youngest person ever to win the Nobel Peace Prize.

Despite his commitment to nonviolence, King himself was the target of threats and violence. In 1968, at the age of thirty-nine, he fell victim to an assassin's bullet. King's funeral took place at the church where he had acted as pastor, Ebenezer Baptist Church in Atlanta, Georgia. Over a thousand people, including political leaders and foreign dignitaries, crowded into the church for the service. Outside, almost one hundred thousand more paid tribute.

LOG ON ▶ **Literature** Online

Author Search For more about Martin Luther King Jr., go to glencoe.com and enter QuickPass code GLA9800u7.

Before You Read

Focus

Political History ☆

Segregation U.S. segregation laws have a long history. After the Civil War, "black codes" in Southern states separated African Americans from other races. "Black codes" were abolished and later replaced with "Jim Crow" laws, in place from the late 1800s to the 1950s. These laws restricted African Americans from the use of facilities, including parks, schools, and theaters. In 1954, the Supreme Court ruled school segregation unconstitutional.

Selection Skills

Literary Elements
- Structure (SE pp. 1156–1160; TE p. 1156)

from Stride Toward Freedom

Vocabulary Skills
- Word Usage (SE pp. 1160)
- Cognates (TE p. 1156)

Reading Skills
- Paraphrase (SE pp. 1156–1160)
- Analyze Arguments (TE p. 1158)

Writing Skills/Grammar
- Write a Summary (SE p. 1160)

Before You Read

Focus

Summary

King makes a compelling argument for nonviolent resistance. He says that oppressed people have three choices: acquiescence, which he dismisses as immoral; violent resistance, which he dismisses as immoral, ineffective, and damaging; and nonviolent resistance, which he presents as the only moral and effective solution.

Vocabulary

Cognates Many English and Spanish words sound alike and have similar meanings. These words, called *cognates*, often come from the same Latin root word. Recognizing cognates can help readers decode the meaning of words. **Say:** The vocabulary word *repudiate* and the Spanish verb *repudiar* both come from the Latin word *repudiare*, which means "to reject a spouse, to divorce." How did the meaning of the word change when it became an English word? *(It no longer referred only to a spouse.)*

Literature and Reading Preview

Connect to the Selection

What is a situation in the United States today that you think is unjust and needs to be changed? Write a list of ways you might be able to help make this change.

Build Background

King based his theory of nonviolent resistance on the ideas of Henry David Thoreau, Mohandas Gandhi, and others. The movement was supported by the Fellowship of Reconciliation, a group that promoted nonviolent direct action.

Set Purposes for Reading

Big Idea An Era of Protest

As you read, ask yourself, Who did King seek to convince as he embarked upon his campaign of nonviolent resistance?

Literary Element Structure

Structure is the order or pattern a writer uses to present ideas in a logical way. By focusing his argument on three main points and giving evidence for each point before moving to the next, King is able to express his position clearly and methodically. As you read, ask yourself, What reasons and evidence does he give as he seeks to persuade his audience that nonviolence is the best way to fight injustice?

Reading Strategy Paraphrase

When you state in your own words the main point of a piece of writing, you are **paraphrasing**. Paraphrasing helps you better remember and understand what you read. As you read, ask yourself, What is King saying?

Tip: Paraphrase Use a chart to paraphrase important details.

Detail	Paraphrase
" . . . the oppressed resign themselves to their doom. They tacitly adjust themselves to oppression, and thereby become conditioned to it."	People who suffer from injustice believe there is no way out. They get so used to living with injustice that they come to accept it.

Learning Objectives

For pages 1155–1160

In studying this text, you will focus on the following objectives:

Literary Study: Analyzing structure.

Reading: Paraphrasing.

Vocabulary

ordeal (ôr dēl´) *n.* a circumstance or experience that is painful or difficult; a trial; p. 1157 *The storm was a physical ordeal for people on the ship.*

stature (stach´ ər) *n.* a level attained; standing; status; p. 1159 *Mayor Evans is a person of great stature in our community.*

imperative (im per´ ə tiv) *n.* something absolutely necessary; an essential; p. 1159 *When you write a business letter, correct spelling is an imperative.*

repudiate (ri pū´ dē āt´) *v.* to refuse to accept as valid; to reject; to renounce; p. 1159 *The mayor gave a speech to repudiate reports of a scandal.*

Tip: Word Usage When you encounter new words, it might help you to answer a specific question about the word. Example: *Name some types of ordeals.* Running a marathon, surviving a war, or passing a series of grueling academic tests are different kinds of ordeals.

Writing Practice

Structure Students may benefit from a review of writing structure. Remind students that writers use details to support their arguments just as people give evidence in a court of law.

Display the following example:

Dena is the strongest candidate for the position of sales manager because she has many years of sales experience. Dena worked part time at her aunt's store after school. She continued to work in retail sales while she earned her bachelor's degree in business. The day after college graduation, she began work as a sales representative for a major clothing manufacturer.

Have students identify the main idea, and then list the supporting details. Have students write their own paragraphs using the example above as a model.

from Stride Toward Freedom

Martin Luther King Jr.

Family History Collage. Jane Sterrett.

. . . Oppressed people deal with their oppression in three characteristic ways. One way is acquiescence:[1] the oppressed resign themselves to their doom. They tacitly[2] adjust themselves to oppression, and thereby become conditioned to it. In every movement toward freedom some of the oppressed prefer to remain oppressed. Almost 2,800 years ago Moses set out to lead the children of Israel from the slavery of Egypt[3] to the freedom of the promised land.[4] He soon discovered that slaves do not always welcome their deliverers. They become accustomed to being slaves. They would rather bear those ills they have, as Shakespeare pointed out, than flee to others that they know not of.[5] They prefer the "fleshpots of Egypt" to the **ordeals** of emancipation.

There is such a thing as the freedom of exhaustion. Some people are so worn down by the yoke of oppression that they give up. A few years ago in the slum areas of Atlanta, a Negro guitarist used to sing almost daily: "Been down so long that down don't bother me." This is the type of negative freedom and resignation that often engulfs the life of the oppressed.

But this is not the way out. To accept passively an unjust system is to cooperate with that system; thereby the oppressed become as evil as the oppressor. Noncooperation with evil is as much a moral obligation as is cooperation with good. The oppressed must never

---

1. *Acquiescence* means "the act of consenting or agreeing silently, without objections."
2. *Tacitly* means "silently."
3. *[Moses . . . of Egypt]* As Moses led the Israelites across the wilderness, supplies brought from Egypt ran out. The Bible (Exodus 16:2–3) tells how the people complained and began to regret having left Egypt where, although they were in bondage, they had sufficient food.
4. In the Bible, the *Promised Land* is the land of Canaan, promised by God to Abraham's descendants.
5. *[Shakespeare . . . know not of]* In Shakespeare's play *Hamlet,* the title character says (act 3, scene 1, lines 80–81): ". . . And makes us rather bear those ills we have, / Than fly to others that we know not of."

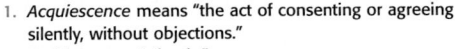
Structure *What do the opening sentences suggest about the way King intends to organize his ideas?* **1**

Paraphrase *Rephrase this passage in your own words.* **2**

Vocabulary

ordeal (ôr dēl´) *n.* a circumstance or experience that is painful or difficult; a trial

MARTIN LUTHER KING JR. **1157**

Approaching Level

DIFFERENTIATED INSTRUCTION

Emerging Remind students that Martin Luther King Jr. was a Christian minister. His speeches are filled with references to stories and quotations from the Bible. Students who find the text challenging may benefit from a discussion of the story of Moses in Egypt. Retell or read aloud a short passage describing Moses leading the Israelite slaves to freedom and discuss the story with the class. Then have students write a phrase or sentence that describes the Bible story King uses in his speech.

Teach

Literary Element **1**

Structure **Answer:** *The opening sentences suggest that King has three main points about the way the oppressed deal with their oppressors and that he will discuss the points one by one.*

Ask: After King presents the three main points, what do you think will follow? *(He will probably explain which of the three points he believes is most effective.)*

Reading Strategy **2**

Paraphrase **Answer:** *Students should show an understanding of King's main points, which might be summarized as follows: It is wrong to cooperate with evil by suffering in silence. The oppressed have a duty to show oppressors the errors of their ways.*

Readability Scores

Dale-Chall: 11.2
DRP: 67
Lexile: 1040

 For activities related to this selection, see Unit 7 Teaching Resources Book, pp. 30–42.

Teach

Reading Strategy | 1

Paraphrase Answer: *Nonviolent resistance is a way of fighting injustice without resorting to violence, so both those who abhor injustice and those who abhor violence can agree to it.*

Writer's Technique ☆

Allusion The phrase "an eye for an eye" is an allusion to a passage from the Old Testament. Here and elsewhere, King makes implicit and explicit biblical allusions. These add moral weight to his argument and are persuasive to Christians and followers of other religions.

---

allow the conscience of the oppressor to slumber. Religion reminds every man that he is his brother's keeper. To accept injustice or segregation passively is to say to the oppressor that his actions are morally right. It is a way of allowing his conscience to fall asleep. At this moment the oppressed fails to be his brother's keeper. So acquiescence—while often the easier way—is not the moral way. It is the way of the coward. The Negro cannot win the respect of his oppressor by acquiescing; he merely increases the oppressor's arrogance and contempt. Acquiescence is interpreted as proof of the Negro's inferiority. The Negro cannot win the respect of the white people of the South or the peoples of the world if he is willing to sell the future of his children for his personal and immediate comfort and safety.

A second way that oppressed people sometimes deal with oppression is to resort to physical violence and corroding hatred. Violence often brings about momentary results. Nations have frequently won their independence in battle. But in spite of temporary victories, violence never brings permanent peace. It solves no social problem; it merely creates new and more complicated ones.

 Violence as a way of achieving racial justice is both impractical and immoral. It is impractical because it is a descending spiral ending in destruction for all. The old law of an eye for an eye leaves everybody blind. It is immoral because it seeks to humiliate the opponent rather than win his understanding; it seeks to annihilate rather than to convert. Violence is immoral because it thrives on hatred rather than love. It destroys community and makes brotherhood impossible. It leaves society in monologue rather than dialogue. Violence ends by defeating itself. It creates bitterness in the survivors and brutality in the destroyers. A

voice echoes through time saying to every potential Peter, "Put up your sword."[6] History is cluttered with the wreckage of nations that failed to follow this command.

If the American Negro and other victims of oppression succumb to the temptation of using violence in the struggle for freedom, future generations will be the recipients of a desolate night of bitterness, and our chief legacy to them will be an endless reign of meaningless chaos. Violence is not the way.

The third way open to oppressed people in their quest for freedom is the way of nonviolent resistance. Like the synthesis in **Hegelian** philosophy, the principle of nonviolent resistance seeks to reconcile the truths of two opposites—acquiescence and violence—while avoiding the extremes and immoralities of both. The nonviolent resister agrees with the person who acquiesces that one should not be physically aggressive toward his opponent; but he balances the equation by agreeing with the person of violence that evil must be resisted. He avoids the nonresistance of the former and the violent resistance of the latter. With nonviolent resistance, no individual or group need submit to any wrong, nor need anyone resort to violence in order to right a wrong.

It seems to me that this is the method that must guide the actions of the Negro in the present crisis in race relations. Through nonviolent resistance the Negro will be able to rise to the noble height of opposing the unjust

Visual Vocabulary
German philosopher Georg *Hegel* (hāʹ gəl) (1770–1831) proposed the theory that for each idea or concept (thesis) there is an opposite (antithesis), and that these two eventually merge to form a new, unified idea or concept (synthesis).

---

6. *[Peter . . . sword]* In the New Testament (Matthew 26:52, John 18:11), when the soldiers and priests come to arrest Jesus, the disciple Peter cuts off the ear of the high priest's servant. Jesus condemns this use of violence.

Paraphrase *How does nonviolent resistance reconcile those who abhor injustice and those who abhor violence?* **1**

Reading Practice

Analyze Arguments Have students analyze King's argument by identifying the options, the reasons for and against them, and King's conclusion, using a chart like the one shown.

Issue: Responding to Oppression

Options	Acquiescence	Violent Resistance	Nonviolent Resistance
Reasons For			
Reasons Against			
Conclusion			

system while loving the perpetrators of the system. The Negro must work passionately and unrelentingly for full **stature** as a citizen, but he must not use inferior methods to gain it. He must never come to terms with falsehood, malice, hate, or destruction.

Nonviolent resistance makes it possible for the Negro to remain in the South and struggle for his rights. The Negro's problem will not be solved by running away. He cannot listen to the glib[8] suggestion of those who would urge him to migrate en masse[9] to other sections of the country. By grasping his great opportunity in the South he can make a lasting contribution to the moral strength of the nation and set a sublime example of courage for generations yet unborn.

By nonviolent resistance, the Negro can also enlist all men of good will in his struggle for equality. The problem is not a purely racial one, with Negroes set against whites. In the end, it is not a struggle between people at all, but a tension between justice and injustice. Nonviolent resistance is not aimed against oppressors but against oppression. Under its banner consciences, not racial groups, are enlisted.

If the Negro is to achieve the goal of integration, he must organize himself into a militant and nonviolent mass movement. All three elements are indispensable. The movement

for equality and justice can only be a success if it has both a mass and militant character; the barriers to be overcome require both. Nonviolence is an **imperative** in order to bring about ultimate community.

A mass movement of a militant quality that is not at the same time committed to nonviolence tends to generate conflict, which in turn breeds anarchy. The support of the participants and the sympathy of the uncommitted are both inhibited by the threat that bloodshed will engulf the community. This reaction in turn encourages the opposition to threaten and resort to force. When, however, the mass movement **repudiates** violence while moving resolutely toward its goal, its opponents are revealed as the instigators and practitioners of violence if it occurs. Then public support is magnetically attracted to the advocates of

---

8. *Glib* means "offhanded" or "showing little thought or concern."
9. The French expression *en masse* (än mas´) means "in a group" or "all together."

---

2 Structure *Notice that King first addresses acquiescence to oppression, then violent resistance, and finally nonviolent resistance. Why does he choose this order for his argument?*

3 An Era of Protest *Why should African Americans remain in the South and struggle for their rights, according to King?*

Vocabulary
stature (stach´ ər) *n.* a level attained; standing; status

---

4 Structure *According to King, how does their opponents' violence tend to ultimately advance the goals of nonviolent resisters?*

Vocabulary
imperative (im per´ ə tiv) *n.* something absolutely necessary; an essential
repudiate (ri pū´ dē āt´) *v.* to refuse to accept as valid; to reject; to renounce

MARTIN LUTHER KING JR. **1159**

Teach

Literary Element **2**

Structure Answer: *By dealing with his preferred option after eliminating the other two options, King gives his option an advantage.*

Big Idea **3**

An Era of Protest Answer: *According to King, leaving the South would not solve African Americans' problems. He argues that staying and fighting injustice will help strengthen the nation and provide a great example of courage.*

APPROACHING Discuss the fact that many African Americans during this time migrated from the rural South to cities in the North.

Literary Element **4**

Structure Answer: *When their opponents resort to violence, the public is sympathetic to the nonviolent resisters.*

View the Photograph ★

In this photograph Rosa Parks sits on the bus in front of a white person. Just a year earlier, Parks was arrested for refusing to give up her seat to a white person. The nonviolent acts of the Montgomery bus boycott, led by Martin Luther King Jr., brought about the end of segregation on buses.

Progress Check

Can students analyze structure?

If No → See Unit 7 Teaching Resources Book, p. 36.

Assess

1. (a) It is impractical and immoral. (b) He believes in love and moral actions.

2. (a) Opposing oppression through nonviolent means (b) Similar to passive acceptance in its nonviolence; similar to violence in its resistance

3. (a) Oppression (b) Seeking to create community and not divide people further

4. (a) To accept injustice is to say that the oppressor is morally right. (b) Not all people are in a position to resist.

5. (a) He would agree. (b) Yes, since hating brings one down to the level of the oppressor.

6. (a) He insisted that protestors be nonviolent and resistant. (b) Love, courage, patience, determination, faith

7. Students should cite reasons for their continued relevance.

Literary Element

1. (a) Three ways people deal with oppression (b) It indicates he will discuss three points in the order stated.

2. The third point should be the concluding one. It represents a combination of acquiescence and violent resistance.

✍ Writing

Use the following criteria to evaluate students' summaries:
▪ Students should identify King's main ideas and supporting details.
▪ Students should use their own words to summarize King's ideas.

1160

Respond and Think Critically

Respond and Interpret

1. (a) What does King think of using violence to bring about social change? (b) What does this opinion tell you about King himself?

2. (a) What is nonviolent resistance? (b) How is it similar to and different from both passive acceptance and violent resistance?

3. (a) Against whom or what should nonviolence be aimed, according to King? (b) Why do you suppose King took pains to make this target clear?

Analyze and Evaluate

4. (a) How does King support his claim that "to accept passively an unjust system is to cooperate with that system"? (b) Do you see any flaws with this claim? Explain why or why not.

5. (a) Booker T. Washington said, "I shall allow no man to belittle my soul by making me hate him." How might King respond to this? (b) Do you agree with the quote? Why or why not?

Connect

6. **Big Idea** An Era of Protest (a) Considering what you know about the era leading up to the civil rights movement, what would you say was distinctive about King's method of protesting injustice? (b) What qualities would a protestor need to possess in order to follow King's directions?

7. **Connect to Today** This selection was first published in 1958. Do you think King's ideas are still relevant today? Explain.

Literary Element Structure

The **structure** of persuasive or expository writing may vary. Listing detailed information, using cause and effect, or describing a problem and its solution are some ways of structuring a topic.

1. (a) What does King state in the first sentence? (b) Explain how this sentence helps set up the structure of the entire piece.

2. Would switching the order of King's three points affect his argument? Why or why not?

Reading Strategy Paraphrase

When you **paraphrase**, you put details or ideas from a selection into your own words. Paraphrasing can help you better understand difficult passages.

1. What is the main point of this selection?

2. Which particular passages or details did paraphrasing help you to better understand? Explain.

LOG ON ▶ **Literature** Online

Selection Resources For Selection Quizzes, eFlashcards, and Reading-Writing Connection activities, go to glencoe.com and enter QuickPass code GLA9800u7.

Vocabulary Practice

Practice with Word Usage Respond to the following to explore the selection vocabulary.

1. Identify someone in your community who has attained an esteemed **stature**.

2. Describe a physical or mental **ordeal** that you have endured.

3. List things that would be **imperative** to bring when camping.

4. Describe a situation from a drama you know in which someone **repudiates** something.

✍ Writing

Write a Summary In this speech, King argues in support of a particular philosophy. Summarize his arguments, making sure to identify the main idea, or thesis, and supporting evidence. Use your paraphrasing chart as an aid. Be careful to put King's ideas into your own words.

Vocabulary

Sample answers:

1. My mom has achieved an **esteemed** stature because of her charity work.

2. Running a half marathon was a physical **ordeal**.

3. A tent, a flashlight, and a compass are **imperative** when camping.

4. In *King Lear*, Lear **repudiates** his daughter Cordelia.

Reading Strategy

1. Nonviolent resistance is the only way to overcome oppression.

2. Students should mention a specific passage and reason why paraphrasing was helpful.

Before You Read

Choice: A Tribute to Dr. Martin Luther King Jr.

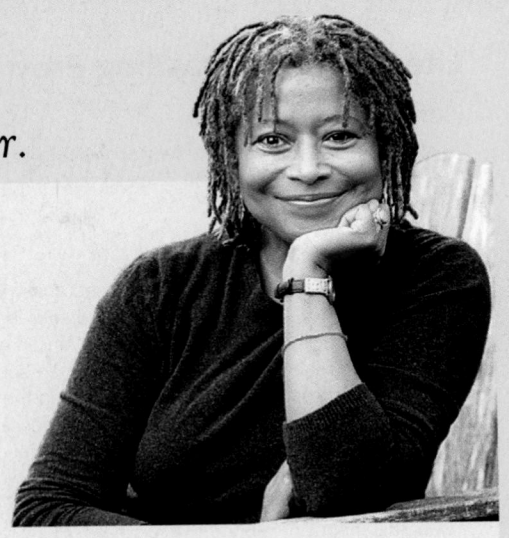

Meet **Alice Walker**

(born 1944)

Born into a poor, rural life in Eatonton, Georgia, Alice Walker knew how it felt to bear the legacy of slavery, racism, and segregation. Her parents and grandparents worked on what had been a plantation, she recalled decades later, toiling "all their lives for barely enough food and shelter to sustain them. They were sharecroppers—landless peasants—the product of whose labor was routinely stolen from them."

> "We will be ourselves and free, or die in the attempt. Harriet Tubman was not our great-grandmother for nothing."
>
> —Alice Walker

Early Struggles in the South Walker entered Spelman College on scholarship in 1961, at the peak of the civil rights movement. There she met Dr. Martin Luther King Jr. She continued her education at Sarah Lawrence College in New York and after graduation worked in the New York City Welfare Department. Returning to the South in 1966, Walker became a Head Start worker in Mississippi and helped organize voter registration in Georgia. She called the civil rights movement "a time of intense friendships, passions, and loves among the people who came south (or lived there), and who risked everything to change [the] system." In 1967 she married a fellow civil rights worker. She had to do so in the North, however, for she married a white man and interracial marriage was still illegal in the South.

The Rights of Women Interestingly, the civil rights leader whom Walker calls her "spiritual ancestor" is not Dr. King or another figure from the Civil Rights movement, but Sojourner Truth—a former slave who became an abolitionist and advocate for women's rights in the nineteenth century. Walker says it gives her joy to realize she shares her name with Sojourner Truth. *Walker* and *sojourner* can have roughly the same meaning, and *Alice* means "truth" in ancient Greek. Aside from their names, their common bond, Walker says, is a concern for the rights not only of African Americans but also of women. Much of Walker's writing can be called *womanist*, a term Walker coined to describe work appreciating women's culture, characters, and feelings.

Since the publication of her novel *The Color Purple*, which won both a Pulitzer Prize and an American Book Award and was adapted into a highly successful film, Walker has been a celebrity. Beside novels, she has written short stories, poems, essays, and children's books. She also has won acclaim for her nonfiction work, including *Anything We Love Can Be Saved: A Writer's Activism*.

 Literature Online

Author Search For more about Alice Walker, go to glencoe.com and enter QuickPass code GLA9800u7.

ALICE WALKER **1161**

Before You Read

Focus

Bellringer Options

**Selection Focus
Transparency 66**

**Daily Language Practice
Transparency 98**

Or tell students that Alice Walker often writes about the importance of a sense of home. Draw a web diagram with the word *home* in the center circle and the words *memories, places,* and *people* in surrounding circles. Have students offer ideas for each category, or have them complete the diagram themselves. Then, have students compare their responses with elements mentioned in Alice Walker's essay.

Selection Skills

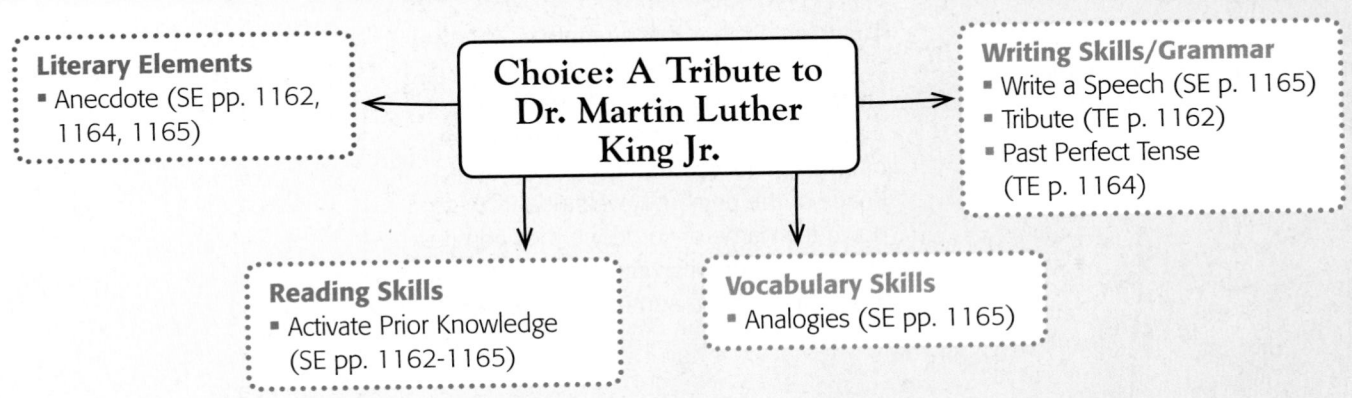

Literary Elements
- Anecdote (SE pp. 1162, 1164, 1165)

Choice: A Tribute to Dr. Martin Luther King Jr.

Writing Skills/Grammar
- Write a Speech (SE p. 1165)
- Tribute (TE p. 1162)
- Past Perfect Tense (TE p. 1164)

Reading Skills
- Activate Prior Knowledge (SE pp. 1162-1165)

Vocabulary Skills
- Analogies (SE pp. 1165)

1161

Before You Read

Focus

Summary

Alice Walker begins by referring to her great-great-great-grandmother. She emphasizes the importance of memories and heritage to African Americans and speaks of her own awakening to the struggle for equality inspired by Martin Luther King Jr. Walker reflects on King's accomplishments and emphasizes his gift of home and heritage to African Americans.

 For summaries in languages other than English, see Unit 7 Teaching Resources Book, pp. 43–48.

Vocabulary

Words that Describe Time

Some of the words in the vocabulary list are related to time. One of these words describes the duration of an event. **Ask:** Which word in this selection's vocabulary describes an event that is over quickly? (*ephemeral*)

(APPROACHING) Explain that words describing time can show relationships between people or things. **Ask:** Which word might you use to describe a person whose relationship with you extends far into the past? (*ancestral*)

 For additional vocabulary practice, see Unit 7 Teaching Resources Book, p. 51.

Literature and Reading Preview

Connect to the Speech

What gives the places you love their special quality? Write a journal entry that describes one of these places, and explain why it is special to you.

Build Background

Walker gives a short history of African Americans since the late nineteenth century. She refers to the period after the Civil War called Reconstruction (1865–1877), when African Americans enjoyed new rights. Reconstruction ended when Southern whites regained control of state governments. In the climate of oppression that followed, millions of African Americans left the South. Walker then jumps to 1960, when a federal court ordered the University of Georgia to admit African Americans. Her final reference is to the desegregation of a Mississippi restaurant. Beginning in 1960, protestors held "sit-ins" to force compliance with desegregation laws.

Set Purposes for Reading

Big Idea **An Era of Protest**

As you read, ask, What kind of resentment might naturally build up when a group of people are deprived of basic rights and the means of a decent livelihood over many generations?

Literary Element **Anecdote**

An **anecdote** is a brief account of an interesting event. As you read, ask yourself, What anecdotes does Walker tell and why?

Reading Strategy **Activate Prior Knowledge**

As a reader, your **prior knowledge** and personal experiences help you understand a text. As you read, ask yourself, What do I already know about Walker's topics?

Tip: Apply What You Know Use a chart like the one below to connect Walker's ideas and your prior knowledge.

from "Choice"	What I Know
Yet the history of my family, like that of all black Southerners, is a history of dispossession.	The ancestors of black Southerners were taken from their land in Africa and enslaved in America.

Vocabulary

ancestral (an ses´ trəl) *adj.* of or relating to those from whom one is descended; p. 1163 *My family's ancestral property was sold long ago.*

colossal (kə los´ əl) *adj.* extraordinary in size or degree; enormous; p. 1164 *A colossal wave overturned the ship.*

continuity (kon´ tə noo͞´ ə tē) *n.* the state or quality of going on without interruption; p. 1164 *If the President dies in office, the Vice President immediately takes over to ensure continuity.*

ephemeral (i fem´ rəl) *adj.* lasting for a very brief time; short-lived; p. 1164 *A rainbow is brilliant but ephemeral.*

Tip: Analogies Comparisons based on relationships between words are known as **analogies**. For example, in the analogy *continuity : disruption :: dark : light,* each pair of words is opposite in meaning. To complete an analogy, decide on the relationship represented by the first pair of words. Then apply that relationship to the second set of words.

Writing Practice

Tributes Explain that a tribute is written to honor someone of importance in your life or community. Rather than just writing a description of the person, tribute writers often use anecdotes to create a clearer image of the person. Have students write down the name of someone they admire. Next, have students write down a word or two explaining the admirable character- istics the person they selected has. Have students write a brief anecdote about the person in which the person is displaying that admirable characteristic.

Choice:
A Tribute to
Dr. Martin Luther King Jr.

Alice Walker

This address was made in 1972 at a Jackson, Mississippi, restaurant that refused to serve people of color until forced to do so by the Civil Rights movement a few years before.

My great-great-great-grandmother walked as a slave from Virginia to Eatonton, Georgia—which passes for the Walker **ancestral** home—with two babies on her hips. She lived to be a hundred and twenty-five years old and my own father knew her as a boy. (It is in memory of this walk that I choose to keep and to embrace my "maiden" name, Walker.)

There is a cemetery near our family church where she is buried; but because her marker was made of wood and rotted years ago, it is impossible to tell exactly where her body lies. In the same cemetery are most of my mother's people, who have lived in Georgia for so long nobody even remembers when they came. And all of my great-aunts and uncles are there, and my grandfather and grandmother, and, very recently, my own father.

---

1 Activate Prior Knowledge *Based on what you know about U.S. geography, about how many states did Walker's ancestor walk through?*

Vocabulary

ancestral (an ses´ trəl) *adj.* of or relating to those from whom one is descended

---

If it is true that land does not belong to anyone until they have buried a body in it, then the land of my birthplace belongs to me, dozens of times over. Yet the history of my family, like that of all black Southerners, is a history of dispossession. We loved the land and worked the land, but we never owned it; and even if we bought land, as my great-grandfather did after the Civil War, it was always in danger of being taken away, as his was, during the period following Reconstruction.

My father inherited nothing of material value from his father, and when I came of age in the early sixties I awoke to the bitter knowledge that in order just to continue to love the land of my birth, I was expected to leave it. For black people —including my parents—had learned a long time ago that to stay willingly in a beloved but brutal place is to risk losing the love and being forced to acknowledge only the brutality.

It is a part of the black Southern sensibility that we treasure memories; for such a long time, that is all of our homeland those of us who at one time or another were forced away from it have been allowed to have.

I watched my brothers, one by one, leave our home and leave the South. I watched my sisters do the same. This was not unusual; abandonment, except for memories, was the common thing, except for those who "could not do any better," or those whose strength or

ALICE WALKER **1163**

Teach

Reading Strategy | 1

Activate Prior Knowledge

Ask: What "public acts" or other facts do you know about Dr. King, and how does that knowledge help you understand this speech better? *(Students might mention the Montgomery bus boycott, King's jail time in Birmingham, his "I Have a Dream" speech at the March on Washington, and his nonviolent beliefs.)*

Literary Element | 2

Anecdote Answer: *This comment makes the anecdote more personal because it provides insight into Walker's thought process.*

ENGLISH LEARNERS Clarify the importance of television in Walker's anecdote. Television introduces Martin Luther King Jr. to Walker and makes her feel a personal tie to him and the civil rights movement.

Big Idea | 3

An Era of Protest Answer: *Students might point out that many groups were discriminated against during this time. A spokesperson and leader such as King probably gave them a voice they had been lacking.*

stubbornness was so **colossal** they took the risk that others could not bear.

In 1960, my mother bought a television set, and each day after school I watched Hamilton Holmes and Charlayne Hunter as they struggled to integrate—fair-skinned as they were—the University of Georgia. And then, one day, there appeared the face of Dr. Martin Luther King Jr. What a funny name, I thought. At the moment I first saw him, he was being handcuffed and shoved into a police truck. He had dared to claim his rights as a native son, and had been arrested. He displayed no fear, but seemed calm and serene, unaware of his own extraordinary courage. His whole body, like his conscience, was at peace.

At the moment I saw his resistance I knew I would never be able to live in this country without resisting everything that sought to disinherit me, and I would never be forced away from the land of my birth without a fight.

He was The One, The Hero, The One Fearless Person for whom we had waited. I hadn't even realized before that we *had* been waiting for Martin Luther King Jr. but we had. And I knew it for sure when my mother added his name to the list of people she prayed for every night.

I sometimes think that it was literally the prayers of people like my mother and father, who had bowed down in the struggle for such a long time, that kept Dr. King alive until five years ago. For years we went to bed praying for his life, and awoke with the question "Is the 'Lord' still here?"

1 The public acts of Dr. King you know. They are visible all around you. His voice you would recognize sooner than any other voice you have heard in this century—this in spite of the fact that certain municipal libraries, like the

one in downtown Jackson, do not carry recordings of his speeches, and the librarians chuckle cruelly when asked why they do not.

You know, if you have read his books, that his is a complex and revolutionary philosophy that few people are capable of understanding fully or have the patience to embody in themselves. Which is our weakness, which is our loss.

And if you know anything about good Baptist preaching, you can imagine what you missed if you never had a chance to hear Martin Luther King Jr. preach at Ebenezer Baptist Church.

You know of the prizes and awards that he tended to think very little of. And you know of his concern for the disinherited: the American Indian, the Mexican American, and the poor American white—for whom he cared much.

You know that this very room, in this very restaurant, was closed to people of color not more than five years ago. And that we eat here together tonight largely through his efforts and his blood. We accept the common pleasures of life, assuredly, in his name.

But add to all of these things the one thing that seems to me second to none in importance: He gave us back our heritage. He gave us back our homeland; the bones and dust of our ancestors, who may now sleep within our caring *and* our hearing. He gave us the blueness of the Georgia sky in autumn as in summer; the colors of the Southern winter as well as glimpses of the green of vacation-time spring. Those of our relatives we used to invite for a visit we now can ask to stay. . . . He gave us full-time use of our own woods, and restored our memories to those of us who were forced to run away, as realities we might each day enjoy and leave for our children.

An Era of Protest *How might a person's concern for the disinherited help make that person a hero during this period?* **3**

Vocabulary

continuity (kon´ tə noo̅´ ə tē) *n.* the state or quality of going on without interruption

ephemeral (i fem´ rəl) *adj.* lasting for a very brief time; short-lived

---

2 **Anecdote** *How does this observation add to the interest of Walker's anecdote?*

Vocabulary

colossal (kə los´ əl) *adj.* extraordinary in size or degree; enormous

---

1164 UNIT 7   INTO THE TWENTY-FIRST CENTURY

Grammar Practice

SPIRAL REVIEW **Past Perfect Tense** Point out these sentences on this page: "At the moment I first saw him, he was being handcuffed and shoved into a police truck. He had dared to claim his rights as a native son, and had been arrested." Explain that Walker is using the past perfect tense, formed by using *had* and the past participle of a verb. This tense indicates that one action began and ended before another began.

Have students review the paragraph containing these sentences. Then have them write three sentences using the past perfect tense.

After You Read

Respond and Think Critically

Respond and Interpret

1. What ideas in this speech will you remember? Why?

2. (a)Why did the author choose "to keep and to embrace" the name Walker? (b)How is this name more than just a name to her?

3. (a)What circumstances kept Walker's family from owning land? (b)How did the circumstances affect her family history?

4. According to Walker, what was the most important thing Dr. King did for African Americans?

Analyze and Evaluate

5. How does Walker's story about her brothers and sisters leaving the land connect to what she calls Dr. King's great achievement?

6. (a)How does Walker make King seem more than human? (b)Do you think she proves that he lived up to this description? Explain.

Connect

7. **Big Idea** An Era of Protest Based on this speech, how important was individual leadership to the Civil Rights movement? Explain.

Literary Element Anecdote

Typically, writers use an **anecdote** to entertain, to explain an idea, or to reveal the personality of a character. In this speech, Walker tells an anecdote about seeing Dr. King for the first time.

1. What does this anecdote tell you about Walker as a child?

2. What does it tell you about why Dr. King became a hero to African Americans?

Reading Strategy Activate Prior Knowledge

Readers typically bring two types of knowledge to a piece of writing: facts and personal experiences.

1. Identify a passage from Walker's speech that interests you. What factual or personal knowledge can you bring to it?

2. Walker's anecdote begins with the purchase of a television set in 1960. List one factual and one personal piece of information that helped you understand this part of the anecdote.

 Literature Online

Selection Resources For Selection Quizzes, eFlashcards, and Reading-Writing Connection activities, go to glencoe.com and enter QuickPass code GLA9800u7.

Vocabulary Practice

Practice with Analogies For each item below, match the relationship between the first pair of words to complete the second pair. The symbol : means "is to" and :: means "as."

1. ancestral : forebears :: national : _____
   a. town   c. widespread
   b. patriotism d. country

2. large : colossal :: loud : _____
   a. quiet   c. bright
   b. deafening   d. noise

3. continuity : interrupted :: unity : _____
   a. divided   c. accepting
   b. capable   d. whole

4. ephemeral : fleeting :: solid : _____
   a. sturdy   c. liquid
   b. nebulous   d. unique

Writing

Write a Speech Many speeches celebrate the lives of famous men and women. Compose a speech about a person who has influenced your life. Focus on the most important aspects of your subject and grab your listeners' attention with one or two interesting anecdotes about that person.

ALICE WALKER **1165**

After You Read

Assess

1. Students may remember Walker's vivid anecdotes or the unique assessment of King's work giving people back their heritage.

2. (a) The name is in memory of her great-great-great-grandmother who, as a slave, walked from Virginia to Georgia. (b) It represents the strength upon which her heritage was founded.

3. (a) Slavery and the oppression of the post-Civil War South (b) Her father did not inherit any land, forcing Walker and her siblings to leave home to find better lives.

4. He returned their heritage and home.

5. King gave African Americans back their homeland, which her siblings had abandoned.

6. (a) She refers to him as "The One, The Hero, The One Fearless Person for whom we had waited." (b) Walker lists King's virtues and accomplishments.

7. Individual leadership was very important. Leaders inspired others to act and resist oppression.

Literary Element

1. It shows her youthful innocence.

2. It shows his courage and his nonviolent nature.

Reading Strategy

1. Students should identify whether the information they bring to their passage is factual or personal.

2. Walker's television set would have been black and white. Students might reflect on the importance of television in their lives.

Writing

Use the following criteria to evaluate students' speeches:

- Speeches should focus on one important feature of the subject.

- Speeches should include anecdotes to illustrate the subject's significance.

Vocabulary

1. d 2. b 3. a 4. a

Progress Check

Can students analyze an anecdote?

If No → See Unit 7 Teaching Resources Book, p. 49.

1165

Vocabulary Workshop

Loaded Words

Focus

Explain that the directions for the exercise indicate that students choose words that reflect the author's *opposition* to war. Suggest that after students complete the exercise, they substitute words that indicate approval of a war. Point out how simply changing a word or a phrase can dramatically change the effect of a passage.

Teach

Diction Say: An author's choice of words, called *diction*, reflects the author's attitude and sets the tone. For example, compare these two sentences: *His eyes glittered. His eyes blazed.*

Assess

Practice

I. b **2.** c **3.** a **4.** a

 For additional vocabulary practice, see Glencoe Interactive Vocabulary CD-ROM.

Vocabulary Practice

Persuasive Language Point out to students that they may use loaded words in their own conversations when they exaggerate or include their opinions in descriptions. For example, they might describe a book as "a million pages long" or say that a new song is "the best ever written." Discuss with students how loaded words can influence the listener. Have them read the statements below and then modify

them to include bias, hyperbole, and propaganda. When students have finished, discuss how loaded words changed the meaning of the original statements.

1. The movie was long. *(hyperbole: The movie went on forever!)*
2. The candidate supports a bill that will raise taxes. *(propaganda: The candidate supports a bill that will make taxes go sky high.)*
3. She hardly spoke at the party. *(bias: She was so proud and arrogant that she hardly spoke at the party.)*

Learning Objectives

In this workshop, you will focus on the following objective:

Vocabulary: Understanding how to recognize loaded words.

Vocabulary Workshop

Loaded Words

Literature Connection In the following passage, Alice Walker leaves no doubt that she admires Dr. King.

"He displayed no fear, but seemed calm and serene, unaware of his own extraordinary courage."

Walker's words and phrases—*calm, serene, "extraordinary courage"*—all help her praise him. "Loaded words" such as these can make speech and writing powerful and persuasive. We encounter them at political rallies, on TV commercials, in the editorial pages of newspapers, and in our own everyday conversation. Loaded words are powerful weapons. They should be used responsibly.

There are different kinds of loaded words.

- Language that expresses an author's prejudice demonstrates **bias**. Try substituting *bold* for *reckless* in the statement below. Note how *bold* seems positive, while *reckless* seems disapproving.
  One particularly reckless young protestor scaled the White House fence.

- Exaggerated language used to make a point is **hyperbole**.
  All the police dogs in the world could not have stopped this demonstration.

- Language that may distort the truth in order to influence the public is known as **propaganda**.
  Communists and other anti-American elements infiltrated the Civil Rights Movement in order to betray our nation's values.

Loaded words express strong opinions or emotions. Some reveal **bias,** or prejudice. Some are **hyperbole,** or the use of exaggeration to make a point. Some rely on **propaganda,** or language that may distort the truth to be persuasive.

Tip

Ask yourself, *Why did the writer write this? What is his or her point of view?* Once you have established the author's purpose for writing, look for words or phrases that support this stance.

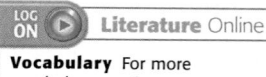 **Literature** Online
Vocabulary For more vocabulary practice, go to glencoe.com and enter QuickPass code GLA9800u7.

Practice From the loaded words or phrases that follow the paragraph below, select those that best support the author's opposition to a war.

This was no one's idea of a just war. It was a war conceived by **1.** _____ politicians, who watched from their **2.** _____ as **3.** _____ of our finest young men marched to their deaths. It was a conflict that finally revealed the rulers of the "free world" to be little more than **4.** _____.

1. **a.** brilliant | **b.** cynical | **c.** elected
2. **a.** workplaces | **b.** homes | **c.** ivory towers
3. **a.** a generation | **b.** many | **c.** several
4. **a.** war criminals | **b.** ordinary people | **c.** heroes

1166 UNIT 7 INTO THE TWENTY-FIRST CENTURY

Before You Read

from *Working: Roberto Acuna, Farm Worker*

Meet **Studs Terkel**

(born 1912)

Would you report on the March on Washington and leave out Martin Luther King Jr.'s "I Have a Dream" speech? That's what Studs Terkel did. Rather than focus on the typical center of attention, he depicted a group of people from Chicago as they rode to and from the famous 1963 civil rights gathering. While other reporters and newscasters deluged the public with stories of heroes and big events, Terkel quietly explored the motivations, choices, dilemmas, and dreams of everyday people.

Born Louis Terkel in New York, Terkel spent most of his life in Chicago. He borrowed the nickname "Studs" from a fictional Chicago character, Studs Lonigan. Although he received a law degree, he took a job in radio. He moved from acting on radio soap operas to writing radio shows to eventually having his own show.

Interviews and Oral Histories As a talk show host on Chicago radio, Terkel brought a natural talent to the job of interviewing. His skill, which grew with practice, translated well to the work for which he has become most famous, collecting oral histories. His first book of oral histories, *Division Street: America*, was published in 1967. This collection of more than seventy interviews with Chicago residents focuses on the topic of the gap between rich and poor.

What Terkel did in *Division Street* was the same thing he would do again and again: interview "real people" about real-life events and lay the bits and pieces of their lives out before the American reading public. He reflected, through interviews, on the American dream. And, perhaps most famously of all, he collected a world of insight into how Americans felt about their working lives.

A Voice of Protest Terkel's work is both history ☆ and commentary. He spoke out early in the struggle against Jim Crow laws, poll taxes, and economic inequality. His work also expresses great empathy for the "working man" and the working class.

> "I was constantly astonished by the extraordinary dreams of ordinary people. No matter how bewildering the times, . . . those we call ordinary are aware of a sense of personal worth— or more often a lack of it—in the work they do."
>
> —Studs Terkel

With his sympathetic ear for the voices of real people, Studs Terkel influenced a whole generation of radio talk show hosts and had a powerful effect on the interviewing style on popular public radio shows. In 1985, he won the Pulitzer Prize in nonfiction for *The Good War: An Oral History of World War II*. Terkel continues to work, interview, and listen.

Literature Online

Author Search For more about Studs Terkel, go to glencoe.com and enter QuickPass code GLA9800u7.

Before You Read

Focus

Political History ☆

Political Protests Terkel's political beliefs led him to be blacklisted during the 1950s. Because he supported left-wing causes, he was investigated by the House Un-American Activities Committee and his television show—"Studs' Place"—was canceled.

Selection Skills

Literary Elements
- Oral History (SE pp. 1168–1173, 1176-1178)
- Structure (SE p. 1178)

Reading Skills
- Analyze Cause-and-Effect Relationships (SE pp. 1168, 1170, 1171, 1174, 1176, 1178)
- Review (TE p. 1176)

from **Working: Roberto Acuna, Farm Worker**

Vocabulary Skills
- Context Clues (SE p. 1178)
- Academic Vocabulary (SE p. 1178)

Writing Skills/Grammar
- Evaluate an Interview (SE p. 1178)
- Using *Good* and *Well* (TE p. 1170)
- Biographical Report (TE p. 1174)

Listening/Speaking/Viewing Skills
- Conduct an Interview (SE p. 1178; TE p. 1172)
- Interview Practice (TE p. 1168)
- Analyze Art (TE pp. 1169, 1172, 1173)

Before You Read

Focus

Summary

Roberto Acuna reflects on his life as a migrant farm worker. He describes the hardships he faced as a child. Acuna explains the discrimination he and other farm workers faced from the townspeople and the growers for whom they worked. With his mother's encouragement, Acuna joined the Marine Corps and later took a job as a prison guard. He quit his job because he did not want to become a "mean man." When Acuna learned about Cesar Chavez, who organized farm workers, he joined the movement to unionize workers.

 For summaries in languages other than English, see Unit 7 Teaching Resources Book, pp. 56–61.

Vocabulary

Root Words and Suffixes
Students can decode the meanings of unfamiliar words by identifying root words. **Say:** The root of *solidarity* is *solid.* How would you describe relationships that exhibit solidarity? *(They are strong and stable).*

ENGLISH LEARNERS Explain that suffixes can change a word's part of speech. For example, adding the suffix *-tion* to some verbs changes them to nouns. **Ask:** What verb is the root word of *compensation*? *(compensate)* Have students look up the meaning of *compensate,* if necessary, and then guess what it means to be *compensated. (to be paid)*

Literature and Reading Preview

Connect to the Interview

What working conditions do you think should be guaranteed to all workers? With a partner, discuss basic rights that should be available to all workers.

Build Background

This interview comes from a collection called *Working: People Talk About What They Do All Day and How They Feel About What They Do.* Terkel regarded his interactions with workers as "conversations," so most selections do not have a traditional interview format. Rather they consist of excerpts and fragments. Changes in type (from roman to italic) show where one part of the conversation leaves off and another begins.

Set Purposes for Reading

Big Idea **An Era of Protest**

As you read, ask, What aspects of life did Acuna find most difficult to accept and which were most in need of change?

Literary Element **Oral History**

Oral history is history that passes by word of mouth and begins with those who actually lived it. As you read, ask yourself, How do the thoughts of an ordinary farm worker help you understand the events, as well as the hopes and frustrations, of farm workers in the 1960s?

Reading Strategy **Analyze Cause-and-Effect Relationships**

When you **analyze cause-and-effect relationships,** you look for the causes or reasons why something happened and relate them to the effects or results. A single cause can have any number of effects. As you read, ask yourself, What event leads to the next event?

Tip: Take Notes Use a chart to record cause-and-effect relationships.

Cause	Effect
picking lettuce	swollen, callused hands
falling behind at work	foreman puts pressure on worker

Vocabulary

civic (siv´ ik) *adj.* related to citizenship; p. 1170 *Voting is a civic responsibility.*

degrading (di grā´ ding) *adj.* tending to drag down in character or social status; p. 1171 *Having to sit in the back was degrading.*

compensation (kom´ pən sa´ shən) *n.* payment; p. 1175 *The compensation for babysitting depends on how long you work.*

solidarity (sol´ ə dar´ ə tē) *n.* unity of a group that produces a sense of community; p. 1175 *Their sense of solidarity helped them work together for voting rights.*

stipulate (stip´ yə lāt´) *v.* to require or demand as part of an agreement; p. 1176 *The negotiators stipulate four requirements.*

Tip: Context Clues To infer a word's meaning, look at other words in the sentence. Example: *Even though they worked hard and for long hours, the* **compensation** *they earned was minimal.* **Compensation** means "payment"; hard work and long hours should earn more compensation.

Writing Practice

Interview Practice Help students understand the Oral History format by having them interview each other. Students should take notes during the interview and then write up a summary as a newspaper or magazine article of no longer than 250 words. Display these questions to get students started:

▪ What jobs have you had?

▪ What are your strengths as an employee?
▪ What would be your ideal job?

Have students brainstorm additional questions that might lead to a successful interview.

from

Working

Roberto Acuna, Farm Worker

Studs Terkel

1 I walked out of the fields two years ago. I saw the need to change the California feudal system,[1] to change the lives of farm workers, to make these huge corporations feel they're not above anybody. I am thirty-four years old and I try to organize for the United Farm Workers of America.

His hands are calloused and each of his thumbnails is singularly[2] cut. "If you're picking lettuce, the thumbnails fall off 'cause they're banged on the box. Your hands get swollen. You can't slow down because the foreman[3] sees you're so many boxes behind and you'd better get on. But people would

---

1. A *California feudal system* is a bitter metaphor comparing the use of serfs on feudal manors in the Middle Ages to the use of farm workers by growers in California.
2. *Singularly* means "oddly."
3. A *foreman* is any leader of a work crew.

help each other. If you're feeling bad that day, somebody who's feeling pretty good would help. Any people that are suffering have to stick together, whether they like it or not, whether they be black, brown, or pink."

According to Mom, I was born on a cotton sack out in the fields, 'cause she had no money to go to the hospital. When I was a child, we used to migrate from California to Arizona and back and forth. The things I saw shaped my life. I remember when we used to go out and pick carrots and onions, the whole family. We tried to scratch a livin' out of the ground. I saw my parents cry out in despair, even though we had the whole family working. At the time,

---

Oral History *In what ways is the speaker an ordinary person or "common man"?* **2**

STUDS TERKEL **1169**

Big Idea   1

An Era of Protest   **Say:** This piece is about a migrant farm worker. **Ask:** What do you think might cause farm workers to protest? *(They might protest low wages or unfair labor practices.)*

Literary Element   2

Oral History   **Answer:** *He is extremely poor: he was born in a field, and his family members are migrant workers.*

View the Photograph

Explain that this 1956 photograph shows temporary laborers, or *braceros*, crossing the border from Mexico to Texas. The bracero program, which operated from 1942 to 1964, led to many abuses of workers. **Ask:** What does this picture suggest to you? *(By showing no faces, the photograph takes away the workers' individuality.)*

 For an audio recording of this selection, use Listening Library Audio CD-ROM.

Readability Scores

Dale-Chall: 4.8
DRP: 52
Lexile: 720

Approaching Level

DIFFERENTIATED INSTRUCTION

Established Explain to students that Acuna describes a number of problems facing migrant workers, including poor working conditions, low pay, long hours, and discrimination. Copy the accompanying chart on the board. Students who have difficulty reading Terkel's interview can benefit from seeing the chart, and then adding more examples of workers' difficulties and the reasons for these difficulties.

Difficulty	Reasons for Difficulty
"If you're picking lettuce, the thumbnails fall off."	Workers bang their hands when they work fast.
"I was born on a cotton sack out in the fields."	Acuna's family has no money for doctors.

Teach

Reading Strategy | 1

Analyze Cause-and-Effect Relationships **Answer:**
Different crops were harvested at different times in different places.

Ask: How might this constant cycle of moving affect children? *(prevents children from making lasting friendships; interferes with their education)*

[APPROACHING] Ask students to describe the difference in climate between a southern and a northern state. Explain that crops will ripen at different times in different climates.

Big Idea | 2

An Era of Protest **Answer:**
He feels the church is unfair because it does not offer help, but instead takes from the people.

Literary Element | 3

Oral History **Answer:** *Acuna does not always use standard English, so he probably did not have a complete formal education. That such a small thing as buying his own canned food fills Acuna with pride suggests that his pride vanishes when he cannot buy food and must accept what is provided by welfare.*

Cultural History ☆

Imperial Valley California's Imperial Valley was first irrigated in 1901. The construction of the Hoover Dam in 1936 allowed for widespread irrigation of the 50-mile-long valley. The desert's long growing season makes it an important source of fruits and vegetables.

1170

---

they were paying sixty-two and a half cents an hour. The average income must have been fifteen hundred dollars, maybe two thousand.[4]

This was supplemented[5] by child labor. During those years, the growers used to have a Pick-Your-Harvest Week. They would get all the migrant kids out of school and have 'em out there pickin' the crops at peak harvest time. A child was off that week and when he went back to school, he got a little gold star. They would make it seem like something **civic** to do.

We'd pick everything: lettuce, carrots, onions, cucumbers, cauliflower, broccoli, tomatoes—all the salads you could make out of vegetables, we picked 'em. Citrus fruits, watermelons—you name it. We'd be in Salinas about four months. From there we'd go down into the Imperial Valley. From there we'd go to picking citrus. It was like a cycle. We'd follow the seasons.

After my dad died, my mom would come home and she'd go into her tent and I would go into ours. We'd roughhouse and everything and then we'd go into the tent where Mom was sleeping and I'd see her crying. When I asked her why she was crying she never gave me an answer. All she said was things would get better. She retired a beaten old lady with a lot of dignity. That day she thought would be better never came for her.

"One time, my mom was in bad need of money, so she got a part-time evening job in a restaurant. I'd be helping her. All the growers would come in and they'd be laughing, making nasty remarks, and make passes at her. I used to go out there and kick 'em and my mom told me to leave 'em alone, she could handle 'em. But they would embarrass her and she would cry.

---

4. Acuna adds: "Today, because of our struggles, the pay is up to two dollars an hour. Yet we know that is not enough."
5. *Supplemented* means "added to."

 1 | Analyze Cause-and-Effect Relationships *What kept migrant workers on the move?*

Vocabulary

civic (siv´ ik) *adj.* related to citizenship

"My mom was a very proud woman. She brought us up without any help from nobody. She kept the family strong. They say that a family that prays together stays together. I say that a family that works together stays together—because of the suffering. My mom couldn't speak English too good. Or much Spanish, for that matter. She wasn't educated. But she knew some prayers and she used to make us say them. That's another thing: when I see the many things in this world and this country, I could tear the churches apart. I never saw a priest out in the fields trying to help people. Maybe in these later years they're doing it. But it's always the church taking from the people.

"We were once asked by the church to bring vegetables to make it a successful bazaar. After we got the stuff there, the only people havin' a good time were the rich people because they were the only ones that were buyin' the stuff . . ."

I'd go barefoot to school. The bad thing was they used to laugh at us, the Anglo kids. They would laugh because we'd bring tortillas and frijoles[6] to lunch. They would have their nice little compact lunch boxes with cold milk in their thermos and they'd laugh at us because all we had was dried tortillas. Not only would they laugh at us, but the kids would pick fights. My older brother used to do most of the fighting for us and he'd come home with black eyes all the time.

What really hurt is when we had to go on welfare. Nobody knows the erosion of man's dignity. They used to have a label of canned goods that said, "U.S. Commodities.[7] Not to be sold or exchanged." Nobody knows how proud it is to feel when you bought canned goods with your own money.

---

6. *Tortillas* are thin, flat, unleavened bread. *Frijoles* is the Spanish word for beans.
7. *Commodities* are goods.

An Era of Protest *In addition to the work, what else strikes Roberto Acuna as unfair?* **2**

Oral History *How do both the meaning and the language of this comment reveal what type of person Acuna is?* **3**

Reading Practice

Generate Questions Point out that Terkel's interview of Acuna contains excerpts of Acuna's answers, but not Terkel's questions. Have students work in small groups. Assign each group one section of the selection. Have students generate possible questions Terkel may have asked Acuna. Have each group share its questions and discuss why each is a good interview question.

"I wanted to be accepted. It must have been in sixth grade. It was just before the Fourth of July. They were trying out students for this patriotic play. I wanted to do Abe Lincoln, so I learned the Gettysburg Address inside and out. I'd be out in the fields pickin' the crops and I'd be memorizin'. I was the only one who didn't have to read the part, 'cause I learned it. The part was given to a girl who was a grower's daughter. She had to read it out of a book, but they said she had better diction. I was very disappointed. I quit about eighth grade.

"Any time anybody'd talk to me about politics, about civil rights, I would ignore it. It's a very *degrading* thing because you can't express yourself. They wanted us to speak English in the school classes. We'd put out a real effort. I would get into a lot of fights because I spoke Spanish and they couldn't understand it. I was punished. I was kept after school for not speaking English."

We used to have our own tents on the truck. Most migrants would live in the tents that were already there in the fields, put up by the company. We got one for ourselves, second-hand, but it was ours. Anglos[8] used to laugh at us. "Here comes the carnival," they'd say. We couldn't keep our clothes clean, we couldn't keep nothing clean, because we'd go by the dirt roads and the dust. We'd stay outside the town.

Filipino migrant workers cut lettuce in a field of the Imperial Valley of California, 1939. Dorothea Lange.

I never did want to go to town because it was a very bad thing for me. We used to go to the small stores, even though we got clipped[9] more. If we went to the other stores, they would laugh at us. They would always point at us with a finger. We'd go to town maybe every two weeks to get what we needed. Everybody would walk in a bunch. We were afraid. (Laughs.) We sang to keep our spirits up. We joked about our poverty. This one guy would say, "When I get to be rich, I'm gonna marry an Anglo woman, so I can be accepted into society." The other guy would say, "When I get rich I'm gonna marry a Mexican woman, so I can go to that Anglo society of yours and see them hang you for marrying an Anglo." Our world was around the fields.

I started picking crops when I was eight. I couldn't do much, but every little bit counts. Every time I would get behind on my chores, I would get a carrot thrown at me by my parents. I would daydream: If I were a millionaire, I would buy all these ranches and give them back to the people. I would picture my mom living in

---

8. *Anglos* refers to people who do not have a Hispanic or Latino heritage.

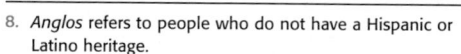

4 Analyze Cause-and-Effect Relationships *What was one reason why Anglos made fun of migrant workers?*

Vocabulary

degrading (di grā´ ding) *adj.* tending to drag down in character or social status

---

9. Here, *clipped* is an informal way of saying "cheated."

STUDS TERKEL **1171**

Teach

Big Idea   1

An Era of Protest Answer:
Children were forced to work as many as 15 hours a day. They also had to work all weekend. The teachers showed no understanding of their plight.

Literary Element   2

Oral History Answer: *This passage emphasizes the difficulty of the work for an ordinary worker. A history of agriculture might focus more on crop yields and methods.*

(APPROACHING) **Say:** This passage is told from the perspective of a migrant worker. **Ask:** From whose perspective might a history of U.S. agriculture be told? *(A history of U.S. agriculture might be told from the perspective of a scholar who had studied data and other facts supplied by growers or the government.)*

View the Photograph ★

Many of the photographs in this selection were taken by Dorothea Lange. In the 1930s, the State of California commissioned her to photograph migrant workers. Her moving documentation of workers' poverty led the state to build camps to house needy workers.

Ask: What does the building in the photograph reveal about the lives of field workers in California? *(Survival was difficult for workers and their families.)*

A migrant Mexican field worker's home on the edge of a frozen pea field in California's Imperial Valley, 1937. Dorothea Lange. ★

one area all the time and being admired by all the people in the community. All of a sudden I'd be rudely awaken by a broken carrot in my back. That would bust your whole dream apart and you'd work for a while and come back to daydreaming.

We used to work early, about four o'clock in the morning. We'd pick the harvest until about six. Then we'd run home and get into our supposedly clean clothes and run all the way to school because we'd be late. By the time we got to school, we'd be all tuckered out.[10] Around maybe eleven o'clock, we'd be dozing off. Our teachers would send notes to the house telling Mom that we were inattentive. The only thing I'd make fairly good grades on was spelling. I couldn't do anything else. Many times we never did our homework, because we were out in the fields. The teachers couldn't understand that. I would get whacked there also.

School would end maybe four o'clock. We'd rush home again, change clothes, go back to

10. *Tuckered out* means "exhausted."

work until seven, seven thirty at night. That's not counting the weekends. On Saturday and Sunday, we'd be there from four thirty in the morning until about seven thirty in the evening. This is where we made the money, those two days. We all worked.

I would carry boxes for my mom to pack the carrots in. I would pull the carrots out and she would sort them into different sizes. I would get water for her to drink. When you're picking tomatoes, the boxes are heavy. They weigh about thirty pounds. They're dropped very hard on the trucks so they have to be sturdy.

The hardest work would be thinning and hoeing with a short-handled hoe. The fields would be about a half a mile long. You would be bending and stooping all day. Sometimes you

---

An Era of Protest *What reasons for protest are implied in these facts and other facts on this page?*   **1**

Oral History *What does this oral history tell you that a history of U.S. agriculture might not tell?*   **2**

Listening and Speaking Practice

Interview Have students develop a brief oral history by interviewing a person who has experienced a notable historic event. Encourage students to choose a person who remembers an event such as the Vietnam War, astronauts landing on the moon, or a natural disaster.

Have students prepare a brief list of questions. Tell students to focus on letting their interviewee speak about the event while they tape-record or take notes on the interview. After they have finished, have students present the most interesting information to the rest of the class. If possible, have students share a selection from their recordings with the class.

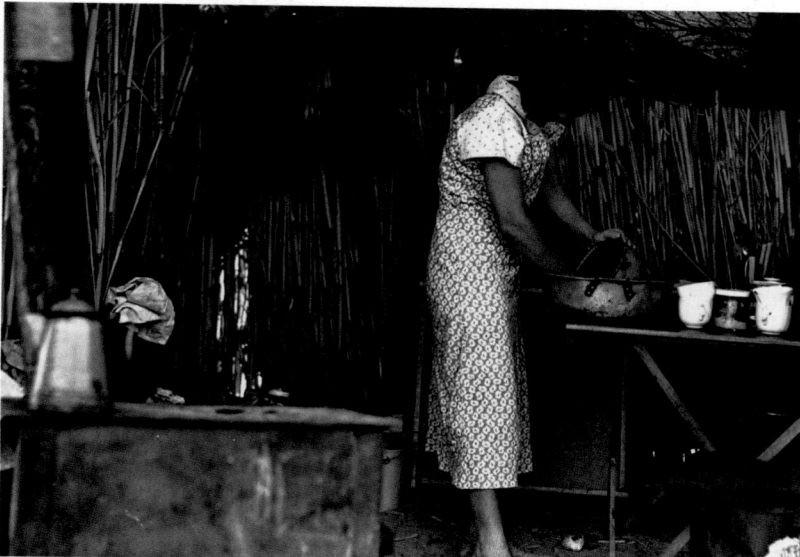

A woman cooking in a camp for migrant agricultural workers. Imperial Valley, California, February–March 1937. Dorothea Lange.

Teach

Literary Element   3

Oral History **Answer:** *This kind of fact is likely to be known but undocumented. Companies would be unlikely to admit to a policy of encouraging strife among workers.*

Ask: How does this photograph reflect Acuna's description of his family life as a youngster? *(His family was extremely poor; his mother worked hard to care for the children.)*

would have hard ground and by the time you got home, your hands would be full of calluses. And you'd have a backache. Sometimes I wouldn't have dinner or anything. I'd just go home and fall asleep and wake up just in time to go out to the fields again.

I remember when we just got into California from Arizona to pick up the carrot harvest. It was very cold and very windy out in the fields. We just had a little old blanket for the four of us kids in the tent. We were freezin' our tail off. So I stole two brand-new blankets that belonged to a grower. When we got under those blankets it was nice and comfortable. Somebody saw me. The next morning the grower told my mom he'd turn us in unless we gave him back his blankets—sterilized.[11] So my mom and I and my kid brother went to the river and cut some wood and made a fire and boiled the water and she scrubbed the blankets. She hung them out to dry, ironed them, and

sent them back to the grower. We got a spanking for that.

I remember this labor camp that was run by the city. It was a POW[12] camp for German soldiers. They put families in there and it would have barbed wire all around it. If you were out after ten o'clock at night, you couldn't get back in until the next day at four in the morning. We didn't know the rules. Nobody told us. We went to visit some relatives. We got back at about ten thirty and they wouldn't let us in. So we slept in the pickup outside the gate. In the morning, they let us in, we had a fast breakfast and went back to work in the fields.[13]

The grower would keep the families apart, hoping they'd fight against each other. He'd have three or four camps and he'd have the

---

11. Here, *sterilized* means "free from germs."

12. *POW* stands for prisoner of war.
13. Acuna adds: "Since we started organizing, this camp has been destroyed. They started building housing on it."

Oral History *Why would it be unusual to hear this point of view in a traditional history?*   **3**

STUDS TERKEL   **1173**

Teach

Reading Strategy [1]

Analyze Cause-and-Effect Relationships Answer:
Acuna was angry about his rate of pay. He wanted to become a "first-class citizen." He wanted to be accepted. The uniform seemed to give him dignity.

Big Idea [2]

An Era of Protest Answer:
He lists several things: pipes supply water for crop irrigation but not for workers' homes; there is medical care for animals but not for workers; the government gives growers land subsidies but doesn't give workers adequate unemployment compensation; there is heat for barns but not for the workers' shacks.

people over here pitted against the people over there. For jobs. He'd give the best crops to the people he thought were the fastest workers. This way he kept us going harder and harder, competing.

When I was sixteen, I had my first taste as a foreman. Handling braceros,[14] aliens, that came from Mexico to work. They'd bring these people to work over here and then send them back to Mexico after the season was over. My job was to make sure they did a good job and pushin' 'em even harder. I was a company man, yes. My parents needed money and I wanted to make sure they were proud of me. A foreman is recognized. I was very naïve. Even though I was pushing the workers, I knew their problems. They didn't know how to write, so I would write letters home for them. I would take 'em to town, buy their clothes, outside of the company stores. They had paid me $1.10 an hour. The farm workers' wage was raised to eighty-two and a half cents. But even the braceros were making more money than me, because they were working piecework.[15] I asked for more money. The manager said, "If you don't like it you can quit." I quit and joined the Marine Corps.

"I joined the Marine Corps at seventeen. I was very mixed up. I wanted to become a first-class citizen. I wanted to be accepted and I was very proud of my uniform. My mom didn't want to sign the papers, but she knew I had to better myself and maybe I'd get an education in the services.

"I did many jobs. I took a civil service exam and was very proud when I passed. Most of the others were college kids. There were only three Chicanos in the group of sixty. I got a job as a correctional officer in a state prison. I quit after eight months because I couldn't take the misery I saw. They wanted me to

use a rubber hose on some of the prisoners—mostly Chicanos and blacks. I couldn't do it. They called me chicken-livered because I didn't want to hit nobody. They constantly harassed me after that. I didn't quit because I was afraid of them but because they were trying to make me into a mean man. I couldn't see it. This was Soledad State Prison."

I began to see how everything was so wrong. When growers can have an intricate watering system to irrigate their crops but they can't have running water inside the houses of workers. Veterinarians tend to the needs of domestic animals but they can't have medical care for the workers. They can have land subsidies[16] for the growers but they can't have adequate unemployment compensation for the workers. They treat him like a farm implement. In fact, they treat their implements better and their domestic animals better. They have heat and insulated barns for the animals but the workers live in beat-up shacks with no heat at all.

---

14. A *bracero* is a Mexican citizen who comes to the U.S. temporarily to do agricultural labor.
15. *Piecework* is work paid by the amount done, rather than by the hour.

16. *Subsidies* are grants of money from the government to companies or private individuals for projects that serve the public interest.

[1] Analyze Cause-and-Effect Relationships *Why do you think Acuna joined the Marine Corps?*

An Era of Protest *What does Acuna view as wrong?* [2]

Writing Practice

Biographical Information
Roberto Acuna admired Cesar Chavez and worked as a union organizer for the United Farm Workers of America.

Have students use the Internet to learn more about Cesar Chavez and the role he played in organizing workers. Have small groups of students research a particular event in Chavez's life that related to his work, such as an important strike or meeting, and present their findings to the class.

Illness in the fields is 120 percent higher than the average rate for industry. It's mostly back trouble, rheumatism and arthritis, because the damp weather and the cold. Stoop labor is very hard on a person. Tuberculosis is high. And now because of the pesticides, we have many respiratory diseases.

The University of California at Davis has government experiments with pesticides and chemicals. To get a bigger crop each year. They haven't any regard as to what safety precautions are needed. In 1964 or '65, an airplane was spraying these chemicals on the fields. Spraying rigs they're called. Flying low, the wheels got tangled on the fence wire. The pilot got up, dusted himself off, and got a drink of water. He died of convulsions. The ambulance attendants got violently sick because of the pesticides he had on his person. A little girl was playing around a sprayer. She stuck her tongue on it. She died instantly.

These pesticides affect the farm worker through the lungs. He breathes it in. He gets no **compensation**. All they do is say he's sick. They don't investigate the cause.

There were times when I felt I couldn't take it any more. It was 105 in the shade and I'd see endless rows of lettuce and I felt my back hurting . . . I felt the frustration of not being able to get out of the fields. I was getting ready to jump any foreman who looked at me cross-eyed. But until two years ago, my world was still very small.

☆ I would read all these things in the papers about Cesar Chavez[17] and I would denounce[18] him because I still had that thing about becom-

An unidentified Mexican shows his permit to cross the border and work in the fields of South Texas under the Bracero program. The federal government has now decided to keep the Mexican Bracero south of the border. August 1964.

ing a first-class patriotic citizen. In Mexicali they would pass out leaflets and I would throw 'em away. I never participated. The grape boycott[19] didn't affect me much because I was in lettuce. It wasn't until Chavez came to Salinas, where I was working in the fields, that I saw what a beautiful man he was. I went to this rally,[20] I still intended to stay with the company. But something—I don't know—I was close to the workers. They couldn't speak English and wanted me to be their spokesman in favor of going on strike. I don't know—I just got caught up with it all, the beautiful feeling of **solidarity.**

You'd see the people on the picket lines at four in the morning, at the camp fires, heating up beans and coffee and tortillas. It gave me a sense of belonging. These were my own people

---

19. The *grape boycott* was a successful national effort to persuade citizens not to buy table grapes so that growers would give in to workers' demands for better wages and conditions.
20. Here, a *rally* is a large meeting for the purpose of creating enthusiasm.

17. *Cesar Chavez* (1927-1993) was an activist and community organizer who helped unionize farm workers.
18. Here, *denounce* means "criticize."

Vocabulary

compensation (kom´ pən sa´ shən) *n.* payment

Vocabulary

solidarity (sol´ ə dar´ ə tē) *n.* unity of a group that produces a sense of community

STUDS TERKEL **1175**

Teach

Vocabulary   3

Context Clues Remind students that they sometimes can figure out unfamiliar words by looking at more familiar words in the text. Have them look at the passage in brackets. **Ask:** What does the phrase "it gave me a sense of belonging" convey about the meaning of *solidarity*? (*Solidarity indicates closeness and community.*)

(ADVANCED) **Ask:** What other phrases in the bracketed passage give clues about the meaning of *solidarity*? (*"my own people," "close to the workers"*)

Political History ☆

Cesar Chavez and the UFW
Cesar Chavez began to organize migrant farm workers in the 1960s. Despite the gains made by Chavez, migrant workers still have a bleak existence today. According to a Department of Labor survey in 2000, 61 percent of farm workers live in poverty.

English Learners

DIFFERENTIATED INSTRUCTION

Intermediate English learners may have difficulty following the paragraph beginning "I joined the Marine Corps at seventeen." Tell students that by wanting "to become a first-class citizen," Acuna means he wanted to be accepted as a full-fledged American. He believed becoming a Marine would help him achieve that goal.

Point out that after Acuna was discharged from the Marines, he took the civil service exam, a test required for anyone who applies for a government job. A correctional officer is an employee of the state or federal government. Have students look up the terms *correct, correction,* and *correctional* in the dictionary to learn what the terms mean.

Teach

To check students' understanding of the selection, see Unit 7 Teaching Resources Book, p. 67.

Reading Strategy 1

Analyze Cause-and-Effect Relationships **Ask:** According to Acuna, why is childhood lost? *(Children cannot go to school for a full year anywhere, and they cannot form lasting friendships.)*

Literary Element 2

Oral History **Answer:** *There is true anger and resentment in Acuna's tone here. There is a kind of name-calling here that is usually omitted from historical accounts.*

Ask: Why do you think Acuna is angry? (He is angry because the growers do not treat him and other workers as human beings.)

---

and they wanted change. I knew this is what I was looking for. I just didn't know it before.

My mom had always wanted me to better myself. I wanted to better myself because of her. Now when the strikes started, I told her I was going to join the union and the whole movement. I told her I was going to work without pay. She said she was proud of me. (His eyes glisten. A long, long pause.) See, I told her I wanted to be with my people. If I were a company man,[21] nobody would like me any more. I had to belong to somebody and this was it right here. She said, "I pushed you in your early years to try to better yourself and get a social position. But I see that's not the answer. I know I'll be proud of you."

All kinds of people are farm workers, not just Chicanos. Filipinos started the strike. We have Puerto Ricans and Appalachians too, Arabs, some Japanese, some Chinese. At one time they used us against each other. But now they can't and they're scared, the growers. They can organize conglomerates.[22] Yet when we try organization to better our lives, they are afraid. Suffering people never dreamed it could be different. Cesar Chavez tells them this and they grasp the idea—and this is what scares the growers.

Now the machines are coming in. It takes skill to operate them. But anybody can be taught. We feel migrant workers should be given the chance. They got one for grapes. They got one for lettuce. They have cotton machines that took jobs away from thousands of farm workers. The people wind up in the ghettos of the city, their culture, their families, their unity destroyed.

We're trying to **stipulate** it in our contract that the company will not use any machinery without the consent of the farm workers. So we

can make sure the people being replaced by the machines will know how to operate the machines.

Working in the fields is not in itself a degrading job. It's hard, but if you're given regular hours, better pay, decent housing, unemployment and medical compensation, pension plans[23]—we have a very relaxed way of living. But the growers don't recognize us as persons. That's the worst thing, the way they treat you. Like we have no brains. Now we see they have no brains. They have only a wallet in their head. The more you squeeze it, the more they cry out.

If we had proper compensation we wouldn't have to be working seventeen hours a day and following the crops. We could stay in one area and it would give us roots. Being a migrant, it tears the family apart. You get in debt. You leave the area penniless. The children are the ones hurt the most. They go to school three months in one place and then on to another. No sooner do they make friends, they are uprooted again. Right here, your childhood is taken away. So when they grow up, they're looking for this childhood they have lost.

If people could see—in the winter, ice on the fields. We'd be on our knees all day long. We'd build fires and warm up real fast and go back onto the ice. We'd be picking watermelons in 105 degrees all day long. When people have melons or cucumber or carrots or lettuce, they don't know how they got on their table and the consequences to the people who picked it. If I had enough money, I would take busloads of people out to the fields and into the labor camps. Then they'd know how that fine salad got on their table. ∾

---

21. A *company man* is a worker who unquestioningly carries out the policies of an employer.
22. *Conglomerates* are large corporations made up of many different types of companies.

Vocabulary

stipulate (stip´ yə lāt´) *v.* to require or demand as part of an agreement

---

23. A *pension* is a fixed sum paid regularly to someone after retirement.

Oral History *In what ways does this sound like the real voice of a real person?* 2

Study Skills Practice

SPIRAL REVIEW **Review** Remind students that a quick review of any notes or graphic organizers they may have created can help them answer the questions on the "After You Read" page. Have students look at each question in the "Respond and Interpret" section and then locate the place in the narrative where they can find the answers to these detailed questions. The questions under the "Analyze and Evaluate" heading require examples from the text to support students' theses and opinions. The "Connect" questions ask students to use other experience, reading, or research to inform their responses.

After You Read

Respond and Think Critically

Respond and Interpret

1. (a)What did Acuna do as a foreman? (b)How did he feel about the work?

2. (a)How did Acuna react when people first talked to him about politics and civil rights? (b)Why didn't Acuna get involved at first?

Analyze and Evaluate

3. (a)In your opinion, what was the most difficult part of Acuna's life? Support your answer with details from the story. (b)How does hearing about Acuna in his own voice help you understand the challenges he faced?

4. (a)What was Acuna's childhood like? (b)How well does the interview communicate the details and feelings of that time in his life? Use details from the selection in your answer.

5. Studs Terkel once said, "Poor people never lose hope. They can't afford to." How well does this opinion relate to the life of Roberto Acuna as recounted in *Working*?

Connect

6. **Big Idea** An Era of Protest Do you regard this selection more as a work of protest or as an ordinary narrative of a working life? Explain.

7. **Connect to Today** Acuna describes his working life from several decades ago. Do you know of any similar working conditions today? Explain.

Literary Element Oral History

This **oral history** is brimming with details, large and small, told almost exclusively in the first person. The use of the pronouns *I, we, me, my,* and *mine* help create an intimate voice, a voice that may seem to be talking only to you, or from the pages of a diary.

1. How does the use of the first person help you hear Acuna's voice and understand his history? Cite at least one example.

2. Name one or more other places in the narrative where you feel as if you are listening to a real person. Explain why.

Review: Structure

Structure is the particular order or pattern a writer uses to present ideas. Fiction and nonfiction narratives are mainly chronological in structure. Other nonfiction works often use a combination of structures, including cause and effect, main idea and details, problem and solution, and other patterns.

1. In addition to cause-and-effect and chronological order, what other organizational methods do you find in this interview? Name one method and identify the page and paragraph where you find it.

2. This selection is presented as a series of recollections rather than one simple story told from beginning to end. What advantages and disadvantages do you see to this structure?

Partner Activity Choose one passage of three or more paragraphs and work with a classmate to analyze its structure.

Passage begins with . . .	Pattern or Order
One time, my mom . . .	chronological
My mom was a very . . .	
We were once asked . . .	

Literary Element

1. It brings Acuna closer to the reader and emphasizes that he is a real person. For example, the reader can feel his strong emotions.

2. The section on page 1175 that describes a little girl dying reflects the feelings of a powerless worker.

Review: Structure

1. Main idea and details are used in the paragraph on page 1171 beginning "I wanted to be accepted."

2. Advantages: the piece seems more informal and conversational; the details are more vivid and believable. Disadvantages: lack of clear organization, which makes the events more difficult to follow.

After You Read

Assess

1. (a) He supervised braceros. (b) He felt okay; he was a "company man."

2. (a) He ignored political talk and denounced Cesar Chavez. (b) He felt that union organizing was unpatriotic.

3. (a) Having to work long hours as a child; was ridiculed, moved often, lived in a tent (b) His tone is emotional. You hear the bitterness and sadness.

4. (a) Constant moving, working, and humiliation (b) It gives him the opportunity to retell many life episodes, such as bringing vegetables to a church fair or working when it was 105 degrees in the shade.

5. He was a poor person who did not lose hope: he had different jobs and became involved in the union.

6. Students who say it is an ordinary narrative may cite details about family life, jobs in the fields, and changes in a working life over time. Those who say it is a work of protest may cite comments about the church, the pesticides, or the actions of foremen, growers, and corporations.

7. Some students will note that work for many immigrants and other laborers has not improved much since Acuna's time. Others will explain that there have been advances in worker safety over the years.

Progress Check

Can students analyze an oral history?

If No → See Unit 7 Teaching Resources Book, p. 62.

After You Read

Assess

Reading Strategy

1. **B** is the correct answer because Acuna's growing up as a farm worker and realizing he didn't fit in with the company helped create the feeling of solidarity with (not estrangement from) his people that motivated him to become a union organizer.

Vocabulary

1. The sentence states that *civic* is related to citizenship.
2. For a person in such a high position, going to prison would lower him in social status and reputation.
3. A synonym of *compensation* is *pay*; "get paid" is used in the sentence.
4. *Solidarity* is a sense of community and is implied by "their united cause."
5. A term of a contract is something workers demand, a word that is a synonym for *stipulate*.

Academic Vocabulary

Students should name things they feel good about, such as college, career, and interests.

 For additional assessment, see Assessment Resources, pp. 279–280.

Reading Strategy Analyze Cause-and-Effect Relationships

ACT Skills Practice

1. Which events influenced Acuna to organize for the United Farm Workers?

   I. Growing up as a farm worker

   II. Becoming disenchanted with being a company man

   III. Feeling estranged from his own people

   A. I only
   B. I and II only
   C. I and III only
   D. I, II, and III

Vocabulary Practice

Practice with Context Clues Identify context clues in the following sentences that help you infer the meaning of each vocabulary word.

1. Many consider voting to be a **civic** duty for any responsible citizen.
2. The company president faced the **degrading** prospect of going to prison.
3. The **compensation** for that job is too low; you get paid little for working long hours.
4. All the marchers at the rally felt a sense of **solidarity** in their united cause.
5. The workers **stipulate** higher pay as a term of their contract.

Academic Vocabulary

Acuna hoped to help change the growers' **attitudes** *toward the farm workers.*

Attitudes is an academic word. In more casual usage, a very shy student may have a negative **attitude** about giving a presentation in class.

Answer the following question: *What are some things about which you have positive* **attitudes?**

For more on academic vocabulary, see pages 53–54.

Speaking and Listening

 Interview

Assignment Studs Terkel's tireless interviewing and conversation skills have helped inform his readers about the daily struggles of people from many walks of life. Imagine that you are a social historian preserving people's oral histories. Interview someone you know about his or her job. Then write a report about your findings.

Prepare Briefly research your subject's profession. Prepare a list of relevant questions phrased in mature, sensitive, and respectful language. Leave space under each for answers.

Interview While you may want to record the interview, you should also take notes. Follow these other tips for a successful interview:

- Allow your subject to respond completely; don't interrupt.
- Make frequent eye contact.
- Adjust your tone of voice or body language in response to your subject.
- If necessary, ask further questions to clarify information.
- Review your subject's statements as a final check.
- Thank your subject for his or her cooperation.

Report Compile your interview notes and write a short report based on these notes and your own research. Integrate and attribute your interview subject's statements when appropriate. Indicate the validity and reliability of the subject's information by comparing it to your research. Refer to the work of Terkel or other oral historians for ideas on how to structure your report.

Evaluate Write a paragraph in which you assess the effectiveness of your interview.

 Literature Online

Selection Resources For Selection Quizzes, eFlashcards, and Reading-Writing Connection activities, go to glencoe.com and enter QuickPass code GLA9800u7.

Speaking and Listening

Use these criteria when evaluating students' interview reports:

- Does the report indicate background research of the subject's profession?
- Does the report clearly compile, integrate, and attribute the subject's responses?
- Did the student follow Terkel or some other oral historian in the report's structure?

Grammar Workshop

Avoid Run-On Sentences

Literature Connection In "Roberto Acuna, Farm Worker," Studs Terkel uses **compound sentences**—sentences with two or more main clauses.

> *"They didn't know how to write, so I would write letters home for them."*

Be careful to avoid **run-on sentences,** which are two or more complete sentences written as though they were one sentence.

Examples of Run-On Sentences

Two main clauses are separated by only a comma.

Everybody would walk in a bunch, we were afraid.

Two main clauses do not have punctuation between them.

I knew this was what I was seeking I just did not know it before.

Solutions

Break the sentence into two short sentences.

Everybody would walk in a bunch. We were afraid.

I knew this was what I was seeking. I just did not know it before.

Separate the clauses with a semicolon.

Everybody would walk in a bunch; we were afraid.

I knew this was what I was seeking; I just did not know it before.

Separate the clauses with a comma and a coordinating conjunction.

Everybody would walk in a bunch, for we were afraid.

I knew this was what I was seeking, but I just did not know it before.

Revise Rewrite the following, applying one of the solutions shown.

1. When you are picking tomatoes, the boxes are heavy they weigh about thirty pounds.
2. I would pull the carrots out and she would sort them.
3. Sometimes you would have hard ground, by the time you got home, your hands would be full of calluses.

Learning Objectives

In this workshop, you will focus on the following objective:

Grammar: Understanding how to avoid run-on sentences.

Vocabulary Terms

A **run-on sentence** occurs when two or more complete sentences are written as through they were one sentence.

Tip

When writing in a test-taking situation, return to any sentences that present more than one thought. Check carefully to be sure that each clause has proper punctuation and any necessary conjunctions.

Language Handbook

For more about run-on sentences, see the Language Handbook, p. R49.

Literature Online

Grammar For more grammar practice, go to glencoe.com and enter QuickPass code GLA9800u7.

Grammar Workshop

Avoid Run-On Sentences

Focus

Write on the board: The cat oozed around the corner it moved like melting butter.

Have students find the two complete sentences.

Teach

Run-On Sentences Students who have difficulty identifying run-on sentences should read the examples aloud. Explain that in general, pauses mark places where a sentence should end.

Assess

Revise

1. When you are picking tomatoes, the boxes are heavy. They weigh about thirty pounds.
2. I would pull the carrots out, and she would sort them.
3. Sometimes you would have hard ground; by the time you got home, your hands would be full of calluses.

 For grammar practice, see Unit 7 Teaching Resources Book, p. 69.

Approaching Level

DIFFERENTIATED INSTRUCTION

Established Tell students that while they often speak in run-on sentences and sentence fragments, they must avoid run-on sentences when writing. Divide the class into pairs. Ask each student to take one minute to tell their partner about a time or event that had special significance for them. Then have them write one or two paragraphs of their story. Have partners exchange papers, identifying and correcting any run-on sentences or sentence fragments that they find.

English Learners

DIFFERENTIATED INSTRUCTION

Beginning Write on the board three subjects—*Roberto Acuna, Studs Terkel,* and *field workers*—and three verbs—*worked, wrote,* and *protested.* Have students write three simple sentences, using one subject with one verb. Then have them combine two sentences using two different methods.

Focus

Comparing Literature
Across Time and Place

Bellringer Options

Literature Launchers:
> **Pre-Reading Videos DVD, Selection Launcher**

Selection Focus Transparency 67

Daily Language Practice Transparency 100

Or explain that the Vietnam War was a conflict that cost many lives and divided the nation.

Ask: Why is war considered part of the human experience? What are some of the consequences of war?

Compare Literature About War

Allow students to share their responses to the opening question. Then have students discuss what they know about war or about the writers Tim O'Brien, Tran Mong Tu, Pin Yathay, and Yusef Komunyakaa.

Compare Literature About War

War has always been part of the human experience. What would your life be like if it were touched by war? The three writers compared here—Tim O'Brien, Tran Mong Tu, Pin Yathay, and Yusef Komunyakaa—explore how war affects individuals swept up in its complex events. In the following selections, they describe the horrors of war and its tragic consequences.

Ambush by Tim O'Brien..short story.....1181

The Gift in Wartime by Tran Mong Tu...............................poem.....1186

from *Stay Alive, My Son* by Pin Yathay........................ memoir.....1187

Camouflaging the Chimera by Yusef Komunyakaa..... poem.....1190

Objectives

For pages 1180–1191

In studying these texts, you will focus on the following objectives:

Literary Study: Analyzing mood.

Reading: Analyzing concrete details.

COMPARE THE `Big Idea` **An Era of Protest**

People protest, or voice objections, in different ways. Some hold vigils; others march together, waving banners or placards. Still others create literature to change minds and stir hearts. As you read, ask yourself, How do Tim O'Brien, Tran Mong Tu, Pin Yathay, and Yusef Komunyakaa show the human cost of war?

COMPARE Themes

The **theme** is the central message of a work of literature—an insight that readers can apply to their own lives. Each of these writers uses literary elements to convey a theme about war and its consequences. As you read, ask yourself, What theme does each writer share with the reader?

COMPARE Cultures

Tim O'Brien, Tran Mong Tu, Pin Yathay, and Yusef Komunyakaa all belong to different cultures, each of which influences the writer's message significantly. Through their choice of words and details, the writers invite readers to enter their worlds, relive their experiences, and share their messages. As you read, ask yourself, What does each selection reveal about the writer's culture?

 Literature

Author Search For more about Tim O'Brien, Tran Mong Tu, Pin Yathay, and Yusef Komunyakaa, go to glencoe.com and enter QuickPass code GLA9800u7.

Selection Skills

Literary Elements
- Mood (SE pp. 1182, 1184, 1185; TE pp. 1182, 1184, 1190)
- Theme (TE p. 1189)

Reading Skills
- Analyze Concrete Details (SE pp. 1182, 1183, 1185)
- Make Predictions (TE p. 1188)

Comparing Literature

Vocabulary Skills
- Word Origins (SE pp. 1182, 1185)

Listening/Speaking/Viewing Skills
- Small-Group Discussion (SE p. 1189)

Writing Skills/Grammar
- Journal Entry (SE p. 1185)
- Contrast Images (SE p. 1186)
- Visual Display (SE p. 1191)

Study Skills/Research
- Prepare an Oral Report (TE p. 1191)

Before You Read

Ambush

Meet **Tim O'Brien**
(born 1946)

 Recognized as one of the major writers on the Vietnam War, Tim O'Brien has earned both critical and popular acclaim for his novels, short stories, and nonfiction works. His writing often describes the experiences of ordinary soldiers in Vietnam and explores philosophical issues, such as the meaning of courage, duty, and honor.

As a political science major at Macalester College in Minnesota, O'Brien protested the U.S. military involvement in Vietnam. Then, shortly after his college graduation, O'Brien received a draft notice. For the rest of that summer, he struggled with his conscience trying to decide what to do. He considered escaping to Canada, where many other war protesters had fled. Finally, he decided to report for induction and enter the service, thereby honoring a family tradition.

> "The object of storytelling, like the object of magic, is not to explain or to resolve, but rather to create and to perform miracles of the imagination."
>
> —Tim O'Brien

Soldier and Writer Beginning in 1968, O'Brien spent just over a year in Quang Ngai Province, Vietnam, as an infantryman and as a clerk. He became a sergeant and earned several medals, including the Purple Heart, an award given to U.S. soldiers wounded or killed in battle. While stationed in Vietnam, O'Brien kept a journal,

recording his observations and impressions. These journal entries later furnished material for his books. His first book, *If I Die in a Combat Zone, Box Me Up and Ship Me Home* (1973), is a memoir of his tour of duty in Vietnam.

Writer of War Stories In 1978, O'Brien wrote a novel called *Going After Cacciato* (kä chä´ tō), about a soldier who simply decides to walk away from the Vietnam War one day. O'Brien won the National Book Award for this novel in 1979. He was also nominated for a Pulitzer Prize for his short-story collection, *The Things They Carried* (1990).

O'Brien's fiction has been compared to that of Stephen Crane, Ernest Hemingway, Joseph Heller, and others who have written about war. Like those authors, he builds a picture of soldiers' daily lives by compiling masses of sensory details. Unlike Crane and Hemingway, he intertwines fantasy with reality in his war stories.

O'Brien has said that he probably will continue to write about the Vietnam War because he believes that the emotions in war and those in ordinary life are almost identical. His recent novels include In the *Lake of the Woods* (1994) and *Tomcat in Love* (1999). Each of these novels alludes to events that occurred in Vietnam.

TIM O'BRIEN **1181**

Before You Read

Focus

Ask students to think about situations in which they reacted without thinking. Tell them to reflect on how they felt later about what happened. As they read, have students consider how the narrator feels about a situation that happened in his past.

Political History

The Vietnam War Shortly after the division of Vietnam into two parts in 1954, a civil war began. The communist government in North Vietnam sought to reunify with South Vietnam. The conflict escalated into a war that pitted the government of North Vietnam and its allies in the South against the government of South Vietnam and the United States. American troops withdrew from Vietnam in 1975.

Approaching Level

DIFFERENTIATED INSTRUCTION

Established List on the board some of the war-related words from the introduction and the selection to prepare students for reading: *draft, induction, infantryman, Purple Heart, tour of duty, soldier, ambush, grenade, muzzle.* Have students research three of these words, using a dictionary and other reference material. Have students write a few sentences about each word, explaining its meaning, and includ-

ing at least one fact about the meaning of this word during the period of the Vietnam War. Give students an example, **Say:** The *draft* is a system for selecting individuals for compulsory military service. A lottery system that determined who would be called first to service was used in 1969. It had not been used since 1942, during World War II. Have volunteers share their explanations with the class.

Comparing Literature

Before You Read

Focus

Summary

When the narrator's daughter asks him if he has ever killed anyone, he lies and says "no." Then he recalls his encounter with an enemy soldier during the Vietnam War. On watch one night, the narrator saw a young enemy soldier walking up a path. The narrator threw a grenade, killing the enemy soldier. The narrator still wonders if he did the right thing by throwing the grenade.

Vocabulary

Action Verbs Explain that most verbs are called *action verbs*, even though they do not necessarily describe movement or activity. The verbs in the vocabulary list involve very little movement, yet they are precise and strong. Have students compare the meanings of the verbs and their synonyms to explore their differences: *grope* vs. *feel; ponder* vs. *think; gape* vs. *stare; dwell* vs. *think.*

(ENGLISH LEARNERS) Point out the similarity in meaning between the words *ponder* and *dwell*. Both involve thinking thoroughly about a subject. Have students use a dictionary to find the meanings and explain the differences between the words.

Literature and Reading Preview

Connect to the Story

Why do some experiences continue to haunt one's memory? Write a journal entry in which you describe a significant memory that has stayed with you.

Build Background

From 1965 to 1973, U.S. troops fought alongside the South Vietnamese in their struggle against the communist Viet Cong from the North.

Set Purposes for Reading

Big Idea **An Era of Protest**

During the Vietnam War, student protests were common in the U.S. and in South Vietnam. As you read, ask yourself, How is this story a protest against the Vietnam War?

Literary Element Mood

The **mood** of a story or poem is the feeling or atmosphere that a writer creates. Writers develop a mood with carefully chosen words and details that vividly describe the setting and events As you read, ask yourself, What words and details help to create the mood?

Reading Strategy Analyze Concrete Details

Concrete details are vivid sensory details, or evocative words and phrases that appeal to one or more of the five senses. To convey fear, a writer might include concrete details such as a clenched jaw, a dry mouth, or sweaty palms. As you read, ask,

- What do the details emphasize?
- What does this emphasis imply?

Tip: Note Details Use a chart to record concrete details in the story and what they imply.

Details	Implications
"the dense brush along the trail"	The narrator's hiding place seems safe and well-hidden.

Vocabulary

grope (grōp) *v.* to feel about uncertainly with the hands; to search blindly; p. 1183 *I groped in the dark while searching for my keys.*

stooped (stōopt) *adj.* bent forward and downward; p. 1184 *Stooped with fatigue, he looked as though he carried a heavy load on his shoulders.*

ponder (pon´ dər) *v.* to think about thoroughly and carefully; p. 1184 *In combat, soldiers have no time to reflect and ponder; instead, they must react quickly without thinking.*

gape (gāp) *v.* to stare with the mouth open, as in wonder or surprise; p. 1184 *Stunned and shaken, the soldier gaped at his fallen comrade.*

dwell (dwel) *v.* to think about at length; p. 1184 *Even if one tries not to dwell on painful memories, they sometimes refuse to go away.*

Tip: Word Origins The study of word origins and their development is called **etymology**. Etymologies are often found in dictionary entries and can help you understand the modern meaning of a word. If you know that the word *ponder,* for example, came from a word that meant "to weigh", you can understand how someone who ponders a difficult decision can almost feel its heaviness.

Reading Practice

Create Mood Students may benefit from evaluating the impact of words on the *mood* of a piece of writing. Display the following sentences:

- As he strolled into the sunny hall, he was greeted by the scent of baking bread.
- As he ran into the stifling hall, he was assaulted by the sour odor of burning coffee.

Ask: What mood does each sentence evoke? *(first sentence: comfort, happi-ness; second sentence: discomfort, dis-taste)* What words contribute to these moods? *(strolled, sunny, greeted; stifling, assaulted, sour, burning)* Have students work with a partner to choose a sentence from one of the selections in this section and assess the mood it creates.

Indiana Rangers: The Army Guard in Vietnam, 1984. Mort Künstler. Oil on canvas, 24 x 32 in. Collection National Guard Bureau, Pentagon, Washington, DC. ★

AMBUSH

Tim O'Brien

When she was nine, my daughter Kathleen asked if I had ever killed anyone. She knew about the war; she knew I'd been a soldier. "You keep writing these war stories," she said, "so I guess you must've killed somebody." It was a difficult moment, but I did what seemed right, which was to say, "Of course not," and then to take her onto my lap and hold her for a while. Someday, I hope, she'll ask again. But here I want to pretend she's a grown-up. I want to tell her exactly what happened, or what I remember happening, and then I want to say to her that as a little girl she was absolutely right. This is why I keep writing war stories:

He was a short, slender young man of about twenty. I was afraid of him—afraid of something—and as he passed me on the trail I threw a grenade that exploded at his feet and killed him.

Or to go back:

Shortly after midnight we moved into the ambush site outside My Khe. The whole platoon[1] was there, spread out in the dense

brush along the trail, and for five hours nothing at all happened. We were working in two-man teams—one man on guard while the other slept, switching off every two hours— and I remember it was still dark when Kiowa shook me awake for the final watch. The night was foggy and hot. For the first few moments I **|1|** felt lost, not sure about directions, **groping** for my helmet and weapon. I reached out and found three grenades and lined them up in front of me; the pins had already been straightened for quick throwing. And then for maybe half an hour I kneeled there and waited. Very gradually, in tiny slivers, dawn began to break through the fog, and from my position in the brush I could see ten or fifteen meters up the trail. The mosquitoes were fierce. I remember slapping at them, wondering if I should wake up Kiowa and ask for some repellent, then thinking it was a bad

---

Analyze Concrete Details *Why does the author include this detail?* **|2|**

Vocabulary

 grope (grōp) *v.* to feel about uncertainly with the hands; to search blindly

---

1. A *platoon* is a military unit, usually commanded by a lieutenant, that forms part of a company.

TIM O'BRIEN **1183**

Approaching Level

DIFFERENTIATED INSTRUCTION

Established Explain that making predictions helps readers become more involved in the literature. When readers make a prediction, they have a stake in the outcome of the story. Making accurate predictions helps readers understand and predict events in literature and life.

Ask students to pause at the end of page 1183. Point out that the narrator

is "on watch" and has three grenades ready to throw.

Ask: What do you think will happen next? Have students work independently to make predictions, listing the facts they used to make each prediction.

Teach

Vocabulary |1|

Use Context Clues **Ask:**
What contextual clues can you use to define the word *groping*? *(Possible answer: I felt <u>lost, not sure about directions</u>, . . . I <u>reached out</u> and found. . . .)*

Reading Strategy |2|

Analyze Concrete Details
Answer: *This detail suggests that the narrator is tense and anxious, anticipating danger. He not only has straightened the pins of the three grenades but has lined them up for easy use.*

View the Art ★

Have students study the face of the soldier in the foreground of the painting.

Ask: Which emotions expressed by the narrator of "Ambush" are conveyed by the soldier's face? *(Possible answer: Like the narrator, the soldier shows anxiety and fear.)*

Readability Scores
Dale-Chall: 5.8
DRP: 53
Lexile: 940

Interactive Read and Write

Other options for teaching this selection can be found in

- Interactive Read and Write for EL Students, pp. 255–268
- Interactive Read and Write for Approaching-Level Students, pp. 255–268
- Interactive Read and Write for On-Level Students, pp. 255–268

1183

Comparing Literature

Teach

Literary Element | 1

Mood Answer: *The fog creates an eerie, threatening feeling, suggesting an environment where anything is possible.*

Literary Element | 2

Mood Say: O'Brien uses carefully chosen words to create the mood of this story.

Ask: What are some words, phrases, or images that help create the mood of this story? How would you describe the mood? *(Possible answer: "The young man coming out of the fog" or "the grenade seeming to freeze above me for an instant" are details that create the story's tense, anxious, and worried mood.)*

Big Idea | 3

An Era of Protest Answer: *These sentences suggest that war is senseless. Killing occurs for no good reason.*

Political History ☆

Guerrilla Warfare Much of the fighting in Vietnam consisted of *guerrilla warfare*. *Guerrilla* comes from the Spanish term meaning "little war." Guerrilla tactics are surprise actions meant to harass and sabotage the enemy, executed by small groups of fighters. During the Vietnam War, the North Vietnamese army supported guerrilla fighters, known as the Vietcong, who fought against South Vietnamese and U.S. soldiers.

idea, then looking up and seeing the young man come out of the fog. He wore black clothing and rubber sandals and a gray ammunition belt. His shoulders were slightly **stooped,** his head cocked to the side as if listening for something. He seemed at ease. He carried his weapon in one hand, muzzle down, moving without any hurry up the center of the trail. There was no sound at all—none that I can remember. In a way, it seemed, he was part of the morning fog, or my own imagination, but there was also the reality of what was happening in my stomach. I had already pulled the pin on a grenade. I had come up to a crouch. It was entirely automatic. I did not hate the young man; I did not see him as the enemy; I did not **ponder** issues of morality or politics or military duty. I crouched and kept my head low. I tried to swallow whatever was rising from my stomach, which tasted like lemonade, something fruity and sour. I was terrified. There were no thoughts about killing. The grenade was to make him go away—just evaporate—and I leaned back and felt my mind go empty and then felt it fill up again. I had already thrown the grenade before telling myself to throw it. The brush was thick and I had to lob it high, not aiming, and I remember the grenade seeming to freeze above me for an instant, as if a camera had clicked, and I remember ducking down and holding my breath and seeing little wisps of fog rise from the earth. The grenade bounced once and rolled across the trail. I did not hear it, but there must've been a sound, because the young man dropped his weapon and began to run, just two or three quick steps, then he hesitated, swiveling to his right, and he

☆

glanced down at the grenade and tried to cover his head but never did. It occurred to me then that he was about to die. I wanted to warn him. The grenade made a popping noise—not soft but not loud either—not what I'd expected—and there was a puff of dust and smoke—a small white puff—and the young man seemed to jerk upward as if pulled by invisible wires. He fell on his back. His rubber sandals had been blown off. There was no wind. He lay at the center of the trail, his right leg bent beneath him, his one eye shut, his other eye a huge star-shaped hole.

It was not a matter of live or die. There was no real peril. Almost certainly the young man would have passed by. And it will always be that way.

Later, I remember, Kiowa tried to tell me that the man would've died anyway. He told me that it was a good kill, that I was a soldier and this was a war, that I should shape up and stop staring and ask myself what the dead man would've done if things were reversed.

None of it mattered. The words seemed far too complicated. All I could do was **gape** at the fact of the young man's body.

Even now I haven't finished sorting it out. Sometimes I forgive myself, other times I don't. In the ordinary hours of life I try not to **dwell** on it, but now and then, when I'm reading a newspaper or just sitting alone in a room, I'll look up and see the young man coming out of the morning fog. I'll watch him walk toward me, his shoulders slightly stooped, his head cocked to the side, and he'll pass within a few yards of me and suddenly smile at some secret **2**

---

1 Mood *What feelings does this detail stir in you?*

Vocabulary

stooped (sto͞opt) *adj.* bent forward and downward
ponder (pon′ dər) *v.* to think about thoroughly and carefully

---

An Era of Protest *What attitude toward war do these sentences reveal?* **3**

Vocabulary

gape (gāp) *v.* to stare with the mouth open, as in wonder or surprise
dwell (dwel) *v.* to think about at length

1184 UNIT 7 INTO THE TWENTY-FIRST CENTURY

Reading Practice

Flashbacks The central action of "Ambush" is told within the framework of a flashback. Explain that the narrator takes a series of steps back in time to tell the story.

▪ Have students create a chart with the following headings:

Time Table for "Ambush"	
Paragraph 1	Paragraph 2

▪ As students read, have them write when the events in those paragraphs take place.

Ask: When does the author expect to give his daughter the real answer to her question? *(when she is grown up)*

After You Read

Respond and Think Critically

Respond and Interpret

1. If you could speak with the narrator about his experience in Vietnam, what would you talk about?

2. (a)How does the narrator respond to his daughter's question? (b)In your opinion, why does he lie to her?

3. (a)What does the narrator do when he sees the young man? (b)What does this episode suggest about the role of a soldier in wartime?

4. (a)What does Kiowa tell the narrator, and how does the narrator feel about this advice? (b)What does this exchange suggest to you about the narrator's values?

Analyze and Evaluate

5. Do the narrator's reactions to the killing of an enemy soldier seem convincing to you? Explain.

6. A **frame story** is a story that either surrounds or introduces a more important story. What effect does O'Brien achieve by using a frame story?

Connect

7. **Big Idea** **An Era of Protest** In what ways does this story protest the Vietnam War?

8. **Connect to Today** How do you think a soldier today might respond to the actions of the narrator? Explain.

Literary Element Mood

To determine **mood**, look closely at scene-setting descriptions and reactions of characters to events.

1. How would you describe the mood of "Ambush"? What details contribute to it?

2. How does the mood of the story affect its overall impact on you? Explain.

Reading Strategy Analyze Concrete Details

Review the **concrete details** that describe the young man's appearance in the story.

1. What is the effect of reading about what the young man wore, carried, and did immediately before and after the narrator tosses the grenade?

2. How do the concrete details in the final paragraph help you understand the narrator?

 Literature Online

Selection Resources For Selection Quizzes, eFlashcards, and Reading-Writing Connection activities, go to glencoe.com and enter QuickPass code GLA9800u7.

Vocabulary Practice

Practice with Word Origins Studying the etymology, or origin and history, of a word can help you better understand and explore its meaning. Create a word map for each of these vocabulary words. Include the word's definition and etymology, and write a sentence in which you use the word correctly. Use a print or online dictionary for help.

grope   stooped   ponder   gape   dwell

Writing

Write a Journal Entry Imagine you are the narrator's daughter Kathleen, now an adult, and your father has just told you this story. How would you react? Write a journal entry in which you record your thoughts and feelings about your father's actions in Vietnam, as well as his decision to postpone telling you the truth. Does he deserve forgiveness? Why or why not?

TIM O'BRIEN **1185**

Writing

Use the following criteria to evaluate students' journal entries:

- Is the entry written from the narrator's daughter's perspective?
- Does the journal entry explain whether or not the father deserves forgiveness?

Vocabulary

grope (Old English *grápian* means "to use the hands.")

stooped (Old English *stúpian* means "to bow down.")

ponder (Middle French *ponderer* means "to assess mentally.")

gape (Old Norse *gapa* means "to open the mouth."

dwell (Old English *dwellan* means "to lead astray.")

After You Read

Assess

1. Students should show understanding of the narrator's dilemma.

2. (a) He tells her he did not kill anyone. (b) He thinks she is too young to hear the truth.

3. (a) Throws a grenade (b) Soldiers act on instinct based on their training.

4. (a) He says the man would have died anyway and would have done the same thing if the situation were reversed. The narrator does not accept this. (b) The narrator values human life.

5. Yes. He was trained to do as he did, yet he feels deep remorse.

6. He draws the reader in and shows how the past affects him.

7. It shows that war inflicts guilt and remorse on those who kill.

8. Having had combat experience, he or she would probably relate to the actions of the narrator.

Reading Strategy

1. The details make him seem real and human, not an abstract "enemy."

2. The young man appears gentle and vulnerable. In the narrator's memory, he survives.

Literary Element

1. Tense, unsettling; Mosquitoes, a strange place at night, foul taste.

2. It keeps readers nervous as they try to guess what comes next.

Progress Check

Can students analyze mood?

If No → See Unit 7 Teaching Resources Book, p. 77.

Focus

Summary

A woman is alone after the death of her husband, a soldier. She contrasts mementos they left each other.

Teach

Big Idea 1

An Era of Protest Say:
Keep this question in mind as you read: How does the poem convey that war has lasting consequences even for those who do not participate in battle?

(APPROACHING) Ask students to locate words or phrases that indicate that the speaker's husband has recently died. *(buried in your new grave, your tomb still green, still shining)*

Assess

Quickwrite

Evaluate students' writing based on these criteria:

- Does the student discuss the contrast between the gifts given by the speaker and those given by the dead person?
- Does the student address the impact of the contrasting images on the reader?

The Gift in Wartime

Tran Mong Tu

Translated by Vann Phan

Build Background

"War is a terrible thing," says Tran Mong Tu (trän mông tōō), who has had firsthand experience with the war in Vietnam. By the time the United States became heavily involved in the Vietnam War in the 1960s, Tran worked for the Associated Press (a large U.S. news service) in Saigon, the capital of South Vietnam. When the United States pulled its troops out of South Vietnam in 1975, the Associated Press evacuated its Vietnamese employees because it feared communist reprisal against those working for U.S. interests. In Tran's poem, the speaker contrasts her gifts to a dead loved one and his gifts to her.

Quickwrite

Much of the power of this poem comes from the writer's use of contrasting images. In two or three paragraphs, discuss these contrasting images and comment on their overall impact.

I offer you roses
Buried in your new grave
I offer you my wedding gown
To cover your tomb still green with grass

5   You give me medals
Together with silver stars
And the yellow pips[1] on your badge
Unused and still shining

I offer you my youth
10 The days we were still in love
My youth died away
When they told me the bad news

You give me the smell of blood
From your war dress
15 Your blood and your enemy's
So that I may be moved

I offer you clouds
That linger on my eyes on summer days
I offer you cold winters
20 Amid my springtime of life

You give me your lips with no smile
You give me your arms without tenderness
You give me your eyes with no sight
And your motionless body

25 Seriously, I apologize to you
I promise to meet you in our next life
I will hold this shrapnel[2] as a token

---

1. *Pips* are military badges of rank worn on the shoulder.
2. *Shrapnel* are fragments scattered from an exploding shell or bomb.

Reading Practice

SMALL GROUP
Analyze Images Have students work with a partner to make a list of pairs of words or phrases that create contrasting images in the poem. Have one student write a word or phrase that creates an image, and then have the other student write a word or phrase that creates a contrasting image. *(roses–medals; wedding gown–badge; youth–blood)* **Ask:** What affect is created by the contrasts between the speaker's gifts and her husband's? *(She offers hope and a future; he gives violence and death.)* How does it contribute to the meaning of the poem? *(War affects more than just soldiers.)*

Build Background

Pin Yathay (pin yä´ tī) was born in the village of Oudong, just north of Phnom Penh, Cambodia's capital and largest city. When the Khmer Rouge, a communist political organization, seized power in Cambodia in 1975, Pin Yathay knew he was in danger because of his position as an employee of the state. As the situation worsened, he and his family joined the refugees who clogged the roads, seeking safety away from the cities. Eventually, most of Pin Yathay's family died of malnutrition, disease, or murder. The Khmer Rouge, which controlled the government until 1979, executed an estimated one to three million citizens—anyone it felt was a threat. Pin Yathay survived this nightmare and lived to tell audiences throughout the world about his ordeal.

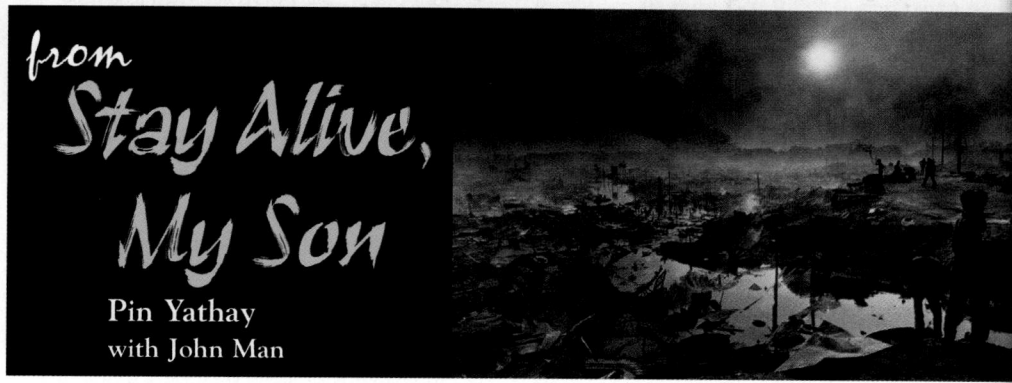

from
Stay Alive, My Son

Pin Yathay
with John Man

My first reaction was to give way to despair, to give up, to surrender to my fate. Everything was lost, I was going to die anyway, I knew that. There was no escape. We swelled up[1] and died. It was the law of nature, unalterable. We all died one after another. There was nothing to be done. What did it matter? I would die, and the sooner the better, there in the house with my wife and son.

Then the true **enormity** of my situation struck me. There would be no such choice. Even that tiny freedom would be taken from me. There would be no gentle, natural passing with my family beside me. They were going to slaughter me, like an animal, away in the forest.

At that thought, I felt another sensation, a surge of raw energy that drove out all other feelings. The instinct for self-preservation took over, and I suddenly, desperately, wanted to stay alive. I told myself: "Pull yourself together! Sharpen up! Get out of this! You've always succeeded before! This is your last chance! Do something!"

I began to think. What was to be done? Leave alone? But there was Nawath across the hut, lying prostrate,[2] his limbs swollen. I could hardly bear the thought of leaving him and Any. But neither could I imagine escaping with them. Better they should have a

---

1. Their bodies *swelled up,* or became bloated, from malnutrition and vitamin deficiencies.

Vocabulary

enormity (i nôr´ mə tē) *n.* outrageousness; state of being monstrous

---

2. *Prostrate* means "flat on the ground," in this case from exhaustion.

PIN YATHAY **1187**

Comparing Literature

Focus

Summary

Pin Yathay, a government worker facing the prospect of death by execution during the Khmer Rouge genocide in Cambodia, struggles with a life-and-death decision regarding his wife, Any, and his son, Nawath. Pin Yathay and his wife decide to leave their son to die alone in a hospital rather than take him with them into hiding.

> For an audio recording of this selection, use Listening Library Audio CD-ROM.

Readability Scores
Dale-Chall: 6.5
DRP: 49
Lexile: 650

Approaching Level

DIFFERENTIATED INSTRUCTION

AAVE Approaching-level students who use African American vernacular English may have difficulty with pronouncing "th" sounds, replacing them with "d" sounds at the beginning of words and "f" sounds in the middle or end of words. The first four paragraphs of the selection have a frequent occurrence of "th" words. Read the first paragraph of the selection aloud, properly pronouncing the "th" words. For the next three paragraphs, have student volunteers read one sentence at a time, clearly enunciating the "th" words.

Dialogue Have student pairs act out the scene between the narrator and his wife as they contemplate their decision. Have students explain how they use vocal inflections, gestures, or other physical cues to express the emotions depicted in the scene.

Comparing Literature

Teach

Literary Element | 1

Exposition Point out that the narrator uses exposition in key places in the memoir.

Say: Why might the author describe his wife in the following way: "But as I glanced up at her, and saw her sweet and wasted features . . ." *(The narrator wants the reader to know that the wife is suffering fom hunger and that he cares deeply for her.)*

ENGLISH LEARNERS Review the meaning of *exposition:* material that introduces the story's characters, settings, and situation. Have students identify other examples of expository text in the story.

Literary History ☆

Khmer Rouge Khmer Rouge is the name of the communist movement that ruled Cambodia from 1975 to 1979. The movement took power after attacking the city of Phnom Penh, the capital city of Cambodia. Pol Pot, the military leader of the Khmer Rouge, became prime minister of Cambodia. The Khmer Rouge believed that educated, skilled, professional people were their enemy, and they executed as many as one and a half million Cambodians.

---

chance to live here than die with me. Better that I should get away, and give myself a chance to live, or at least die on my own terms.

It was all very simple. My mind was made up. I had to tell Any of my decision, that very evening.

After we had eaten, as we sat on the floor opposite each other, with Nawath sleeping behind his cloth partition across the hut, I prepared myself to speak. I was certain of my course, but that did not make me any less nervous. It was a terrible thing to do to us as a family, a terrible thing to impose on Any. But as I glanced up at her, and saw her sweet and wasted features lit dimly by the flickering flames of the cooking fire, I knew there was no other course. It was purposeless to stay on there merely to face death. They would be alone all too soon, anyway.

"Any, my dearest," I said, "I have something to tell you." She looked up, without surprise, and I realized she had been expecting a decision of some kind. She too must have known that I could not stay. Speaking softly in order not to wake Nawath—I could see his little bloated face round the edge of the partition—I began to explain. I was doomed, I said. All the former high officials had disappeared. I was trained in the West. I was irredeemable[3] in the eyes of the Khmer Rouge. They would come for me in a week, and that would be that. "But you're a woman, Any, if you were alone with Nawath I don't think they would harm you."

She said nothing, but I saw her gaze turn to one of horror.

"You can live on here with Nawath," I went on. "It's the only answer. I'll take my chances in the forest. If I succeed, we'll meet again. But I have to go soon. In one week, it'll be too late."

---

3. *Irredeemable* here refers to being unable to be changed or reformed to accept the new government.

"You'll leave?" she said. "Leave me here with Nawath?" And suddenly she began to sob as if she were being torn apart.

"Yes, my dearest. It's the only way," I said, desperately. For the first time, I began to realize that she had not come to the same conclusion as me. "What did you think?"

"Not that. Not that."

I said nothing, for there was only one other course open, the one that was impossible to contemplate. She would see that in a few minutes, I thought, and accept my decision.

But no. With hesitations and bitter sobs, she went on, "It's impossible, my dearest Thay . . . I don't want to be separated from you . . . I prefer to die with you rather than to stay here . . ." As I listened to her in silence, unable to say anything to stem the slow, whispered outpouring of words and sobs and tears, I couldn't believe that she understood what she was saying. Soon, soon, she would see, and know why I had to go alone. "I cannot live without you!" she sobbed. "I prefer to die quickly and cleanly, with you."

She paused, wracked by sobs. I waited for her to say: But if you think it is for the best, of course that is how it must be.

Silence.

To my astonishment, I began to realize she meant what she said. For the first time in our lives, she was refusing to accept my judgment of what was best.

The silence dragged on, broken only by her gasps. She was looking at me. I could see the highlights cast by the fire on her cheeks and in her eyes. Still she said nothing further. I knew then she had understood all along what she was saying.

I felt the strength of her, as well. Once, she had asked my opinion even before buying a dress. Now she had been hardened by experience. She knew what she was doing, knew that in any event she and Nawath would die, knew that we were in the process not of choosing life over death, but of choosing different ways of dying.

Reading Practice

Make Predictions This memoir shows the profound human suffering caused by war by focusing on the effects of war on one man's family. Ask students to pause at the end of page 1187 and predict what the narrator will decide to do. Have them pause again at the end of the first column on page 1188 and predict what Any will decide to do. Finally, tell them to pause at the bottom of the second column on page 1188 and predict what the couple will do with their child. As they read, ask students to consider the magnitude of the decision forced upon the narrator and his wife.

And she knew that, having chosen, there was one more fearful choice still to make. There seemed nothing I could do or say to help her through it. It was too awful for me to put into words. If I spoke the words, it would turn something that was merely a nightmarish fear into dreadful reality. I could not say them.

"But," she said at last. "But what shall we do with Nawath?"

Yes: those were the words I had refused to utter.

"Tell me, Thay dearest. What shall we do with Nawath?" She broke down again as she struggled to express the thought. "He can't come with us. We can't carry him, and he can't walk far. They would catch us and kill us before . . ." She paused, her face working to control her emotion. "We . . . we have to leave him behind. But . . . what are we going to do with him if we leave him?" She broke off again, overcome by sobs.

Could she really contemplate leaving Nawath? It seemed an extraordinary thing for a mother to do. I realize now that she had made a mother's supreme sacrifice. People say that for a mother the supreme sacrifice is to die with her child. No—if death is **inevitable**, the mother's supreme sacrifice is to abandon her child, if thereby she can prolong her own life.

I did not understand all that right then and there. But I felt her resolve, and knew there was nothing I could say to make her change her mind. After what we had been through, after being made one body with her by what we had endured together, it never even

2

> *But I felt her resolve, and knew there was nothing I could say to make her change her mind.*

occurred to me to argue her out of her decision. I don't think I could have done so. I simply had to accept that things were different now.

Any was still sobbing. "What do we do with Nawath?" she asked again, and fell silent. I knew from her tone of voice, and the silence, that she already knew the answer, for there was only one. Knowing it, again neither of us could bring ourselves to express it. Again, expressing it would make it **irrevocable.**

I glanced at Nawath, still asleep. I felt I wanted to go to him, stroke his head, provide some comfort for him, or myself. But I did not move. I couldn't risk waking him. I glanced back at Any. Her eyes were lowered, as if waiting for me to pronounce sentence.

After another eternal minute, the burden of silence became intolerable. I felt it as an accusation against me for evading responsibility.

"You know there is only one thing to do," I whispered. "We must take him to the hospital."

The hospital, where people went only to die.

Vocabulary

irrevocable (i rev´ ə kə bəl) *adj.* not possible to undo
ensure (en shoor´) *v.* to make certain; guarantee

💬 **Discussion Starter**

Meet with a small group to discuss whether Pin Yathay and Any made the only reasonable choice in their situation or not. Consider whether they acted according to their values or whether they were simply trying to save themselves. Summarize your discussion for the rest of your class.

Vocabulary

inevitable (i nev´ ə tə bəl) *adj.* incapable of being avoided or evaded

Comparing Literature

Teach

Literary Element   2

Theme **Ask:** How does the author convey the feeling of doom that genocide creates? *(The author uses words such as* resolve *and* irrevocable, *whose meanings imply finality, when describing the circumstances in which he finds himself.)*

Political History ☆

Pin Yathay Pin Yathay lost seventeen family members during the genocide, including his wife and children. He left Nawath with a kindly woman at the hospital. After the fall of the Khmer Rouge in 1979, Pin Yathay spent years searching for Nawath, but without success.

Assess

Discussion Starter

Evaluate students' summaries based on these criteria:

- Does the summary include evidence for the evaluation of the parents' decision?
- Does the summary show that students based their conclusions on an understanding of self-preservation?

Approaching Level

DIFFERENTIATED INSTRUCTION

Established Before participating in small group discussions, give students an opportunity to write down their initial responses to the discussion prompts. Restate the first section of the prompt as a question. **Ask:** Did Pin Yathay and Any make the only reasonable choice in their situation or not? Give students several minutes to write their responses. **Ask:** Did they act according to their values, or were they simply trying to save themselves? Give students several minutes to write their responses. Next, have students identify passages from the text that support their responses. Once students have some ideas and some support, have them meet in small groups to discuss.

Comparing Literature

Teach

Reading Strategy | 1

Concrete Details Ask students to identify references to animals in the poem. *(tiger, hummingbird, songbirds, rock apes, chameleons)* **Ask:** Why do you think Komunyakaa included so many references to animals? *(To make the actions of the soldiers seem animalistic rather than human or civilized; to emphasize the natural, jungle-like setting)*

Quickwrite

Students may identify the mood as being dark or suspenseful. The vivid action verbs *(wove, hugged, wrestling)* contribute to the development of suspense.

Camouflaging the Chimera

Yusef Komunyakaa

Build Background

Like Tim O'Brien, Yusef Komunyakaa served in the American armed forces during the Vietnam War. Although Komunyakaa went to Vietnam as a correspondent and managing editor for the *Southern Cross*, a military newspaper, he did not publish any poetry about the war until 1988. His poem "Camouflaging the Chimera" carefully outlines how soldiers dressed to become invisible in the Vietnamese landscape. In ancient Greek mythology, the *chimera* was a fire-breathing monster that destroyed the regions of Lycia and Caria. Today, the word *chimera* also refers to an illusion or an imagined creation.

We tied branches to our helmets.
We painted our faces & rifles
with mud from a riverbank,

blades of grass hung from the pockets
5 of our tiger suits.[1] We wove
ourselves into the terrain,
content to be a hummingbird's target.

We hugged bamboo & leaned
against a breeze off the river,
10 slow-dragging with ghosts

from Saigon to Bangkok,[2]
with women left in doorways
reaching in from America.
We aimed at dark-hearted songbirds.

15 In our way station of shadows
rock apes[3] tried to blow our cover,
throwing stones at the sunset.
Chameleons

crawled our spines, changing from day
to night: green to gold,
20 gold to black. But we waited
till the moon touched metal,

till something almost broke
inside us. VC[4] struggled
with the hillside, like black silk

25 wrestling iron through grass.
We weren't there. The river ran
through our bones. Small animals took
    refuge
against our bodies; we held our breath,

ready to spring the L-shaped
30 ambush, as a world revolved
under each man's eyelid.

1

---

1. *Tiger suits* are black-and-green striped camouflage uniforms
2. *Saigon* (sī gon´)—now called Ho Chi Minh City—was the capital of South Vietnam. *Bangkok* (bang´ kok) is the capital of Thailand.
3. Here, *rock apes* refers to the monkeys who live in the Vietnamese mountains.
4. *VC* refers to the Vietcong forces.

Quickwrite

Write for a few minutes about the mood, or emotional quality, of "Camouflaging the Chimera." How would you describe the mood of the poem? What words, images, or ideas help create this mood?

Reading Practice

Poetry Analysis Have students analyze the poem by asking them to select what they think is the most important word in the poem. Tell them they may choose only one word. Have students write their word at the top of the page, and then write two or three sentences defending their selection. Have students come to the board to write their word. Discuss words that appear frequently on the board, asking students to comment. Be sure students explain how the word represents a larger theme found in the poem. *(Students' words and explanations will vary; some may choose* tiger, target, waited, almost, ambush, chameleons. *Initiate a discussion to focus on the relationship of the word to the meaning of the whole poem.)*

Wrap-Up: Comparing Literature

Across Time and Place

- *Ambush* by Tim O'Brien

- *The Gift in Wartime* by Tran Mong Tu

- from *Stay Alive, My Son* by Pin Yathay

- *Camouflaging the Chimera* by Yusef Komunyakaa

COMPARE THE **Big Idea** An Era of Protest

Writing Activity The writers of these selections created literary works to protest the war in Vietnam and Cambodia. Review each selection. Then write a brief essay discussing how each writer reveals the human cost of war. Cite evidence from each selection to support your ideas.

COMPARE Themes

Group Activity Though Tim O'Brien, Tran Mong Tu, Pin Yathay, and Yusef Komunyakaa all write about the tragedy of war, each conveys a distinct theme, or message, about this subject. With a small group, discuss the following questions:

1. What message about war does each writer share with the reader?

2. What literary elements does each writer use to convey his or her message?

3. Which of the selections, in your opinion, makes the most effective protest against war? Support your answer.

COMPARE Cultures

Visual Display Culture influences a writer's ideas and choice of subject, words, and images. Tim O'Brien and Yusef Komunyakaa grew up in the U.S.; Tran Mong Tu, in Vietnam; and Pin Yathay, in Cambodia. Create a visual display to accompany one of the four selections. Include images that reflect the writer's culture, such as a collage of photographs or works of art. If possible, present your display orally to your classmates.

Marker at the extermination camp of Choeung Ek.

 Literature Online

Selection Resources For Selection Quizzes, eFlashcards, and Reading-Writing Connection activities, go to glencoe.com and enter QuickPass code GLA9800u7.

COMPARING LITERATURE **1191**

Approaching Level

DIFFERENTIATED INSTRUCTION

Emerging Explain that images can enhance understanding of literature.

Ask: Why is the image on this page appropriate to the quotation from each selection? *(The image commemorates the terrible result of war—death.)*

Assess

Compare the Big Idea

Writing Activity

Use the following criteria to evaluate students' essays:

- Does the essay describe how each selection explains the horrors of war?
- Does the essay use evidence from the texts to support the claim?

Compare Themes

1. O'Brien: sensitive people who kill in combat are haunted forever; Tran: war devastates the survivor of a loved one, replacing love with tokens of bloodshed, loss, and death. Pin Yathay: war makes people do things that they would not ordinarily consider; Komunyakaa: in war, violence and chaos hide beneath a false exterior, such as the soldiers efforts to blend into their environment.

2. O'Brien: frame story, dialogue, mood, suspense, description; Tran: imagery, repetition, apostrophe; Pin Yathay: dialogue, description, rhetorical questions' Komunyakaa: mood, alliteration, imagery, surrealism.

3. Students should support their views with details.

Compare Cultures

Students' *visual displays* should

- show planning;
- include words and/or images that reflect the culture of a selection;
- be visually appealing; and
- include a sheet for comments.

> For additional assessment, see Assessment Resources, pp. 281–282.

1191

Daily Language Practice Transparency 101

Or explain that the Vietnam War killed millions of Vietnamese civilians and greatly damaged their country.

As students read, have them consider how Merwin's poems make the reader think about death and loss.

Cultural History ☆

War Protest When W. S. Merwin was chosen to receive the Pulitzer Prize in 1971, he saw this as not just an honor, but also as an opportunity. After being selected, he published a letter in *The New York Review of Books*, entitled, "On Being Awarded the Pulitzer Prize." In his essay, he explained his opposition to the Vietnam War and indicated that he would donate his prize money to anti-war efforts.

Before You Read
The Asians Dying, Separation, and *When You Go Away*

Meet **W. S. Merwin**
(born 1927)

I t makes me angry to feel that the natural world is taken to have so little importance," American poet W. S. Merwin once said. It is no wonder then that the pervading themes of Merwin's poetry revolve around our self-imposed separation from nature and the terrible consequences that come from humanity's irresponsible treatment of the natural world.

> "*Poetry . . . tries to convey the sense of what one has seen to those to whom it may matter, including, if possible, one's self.*"
>
> —W. S. Merwin

William Stanley Merwin was born in New York City, but grew up in Pennsylvania. His father was a Presbyterian minister, and at the age of five, Merwin was writing hymns for his father's services. When Merwin was a teenager, he met Ezra Pound, who advised him to write seventy-five lines of poetry a day and to learn languages. Merwin took this advice to heart. In 1947, at age twenty, Merwin graduated from Princeton University with a degree in English. In 1952, he published his first poetry collection, *A Mask for Janus*.

Style and Substance Merwin's early poetry was inspired by Biblical stories and classical myths. These early poems adhered to traditional narrative forms and regular meter patterns. By the 1960s, ☆ Merwin had become a pacifist, environmentalist, and an anti-Vietnam War activist. His poetry became more personal as he delved deeper into the failures of humanity. His language became more relaxed and colloquial. He abandoned punctuation and traditional narrative forms in favor of free verse. In 1967, the protest movement against the Vietnam War had grown in the United States as the war itself had escalated and the numbers of casualties had increased. That year, Merwin published *The Lice*, a collection of angry poems in which he lashed out against society's lack of moral responsibility. Included in this collection was "The Asians Dying," considered Merwin's most overt anti-Vietnam War poem. The poems in his next collection, *The Carrier of Ladders*, for which he won the Pulitzer Prize for poetry in 1971, begin to show signs of hope for the human condition.

Beyond Anger Merwin's later poetry moved beyond the angry, "searing, dumb vision" that guided him in *The Lice*. "One can't live only in despair and anger," he said, "without eventually destroying the thing one is angry in defense of."

In his long and illustrious career, Merwin has published more than 30 volumes of poetry, contributed to a variety of magazines and anthologies, written three plays, and translated the works of classical writers such as Dante and contemporary poets such as Pablo Neruda. In reviewing one of Merwin's recent poems, a critic commented that the poem "will not recompense the lives lost to history. It will not stop wars or stay death. Merwin, for all his acute awareness of loss, writes not to alter the world but to honor it."

 Literature Online

Author Search For more about W. S. Merwin, go to glencoe.com and enter QuickPass code GLA9800u7.

Literary Elements
- Figurative Language (SE pp. 1193, 1194, 1196)
- Free Verse (SE p. 1196)

The Asians Dying, Separation, *and* When You Go Away

Vocabulary Skills
- Analogies (SE p. 1193, 1197)
- Academic Vocabulary (SE p. 1197)

Reading Skills
- Clarify Meaning (SE pp. 1193, 1195, 1197)
- Make Critical Judgments (TE p. 1194)

Listening/Speaking/Viewing Skills
- Literature Groups (SE p. 1197)

Literature and Reading Preview

Connect to the Poems

Why does the pleasurable experience of living include loss? Freewrite for several minutes about the nature of our diverse experiences of war and love.

Build Background

American poetry became more political and radical during the 1960s. It abandoned the formal tone and rigid meter of previous eras and became more open and free. Many poets spoke out against social injustice. Merwin's poetry changed during this time period. He eliminated punctuation in an attempt to "transmit [poetry] more directly in words and do it in a way that carried more of the cadences of pure language, of speech."

Set Purposes for Reading

Big Idea An Era of Protest

As you read, ask yourself, How does Merwin protest the Vietnam War and the absence of a loved one?

Literary Element Figurative Language

Figurative language is descriptive language that goes beyond its literal meaning to convey ideas and emotions. For example, the phrase, "my words are the garment" is a metaphor that is not literally true. As you read, ask yourself, How does Merwin use figurative language to create images and feelings?

Reading Strategy Clarify Meaning

Free verse does not always use conventional punctuation or sentence patterns. As a result, poems written in this form can be challenging. As you read, ask, What does this part of the poem mean? **Reread** lines that are confusing to **clarify meaning.** Be sure to read the footnotes for further help. If you still cannot figure out what something means, ask questions to clarify.

....

Tip: Use a chart to note your questions after rereading.

Poem	Questions	Answer
"The Asians Dying"	What does "Over the watercourses / Like ducks in the time of the ducks" mean?	

Vocabulary

possessor (pə zes´ ər) *n.* one who has or takes control of something; owner; p. 1194 *As the possessor of all the land in the region, she determined how the area was to be developed.*

pointless (point´ lis) *adj.* making no sense; p. 1194 *They can't hear you; it's pointless to speak.*

garment (gär´ mənt) *n.* a piece of clothing; p. 1195 *The fabric of his outer garment had been worn thin.*

Tip: **Analogies** Analogies are comparisons that are based on the relationships between things or ideas. For example, the relationship between "garment" and "wardrobe" is the same as the relationship between "chapter" and "book": garments and chapters are both sections of wardrobes and books, respectively.

Before You Read

Focus

Summary

In "The Asians Dying," the speaker provides images of the futility of the Vietnam War. "Separation" and "When You Go Away" both center on the feeling of loss caused by the absence of a loved one.

 For summaries in languages other than English, see Unit 7 Teaching Resources Book, pp. 84–89.

Vocabulary

Roots Explain to students that understanding a vocabulary word's origin can help them learn the nuances of the word. Both *clothing* and *garment* have Anglo-Saxon roots, but their roots mean, respectively, "cloth covering" and "equip."
Ask: How does the root of the word *garment* help explain the greater formality of the word? *(A garment has a specific purpose, like a piece of equipment.)* Have students research the derivations of *possessor* and *pointless.*

English Learners

DIFFERENTIATED INSTRUCTION

Intermediate Students may benefit from reviewing figurative language. Display the following sentences:

- The small dog looked like a dust mop.
- My sister climbs trees like a squirrel.
- When it comes to general knowledge, my grandfather is an encyclopedia.
- After purchasing a number of expensive gifts, Dana was drowning in debt.

Remind them that figurative expressions are not literally true but are used for descriptive effect, to convey emotions or ideas. A grandfather cannot literally be an *encyclopedia,* but the comparison emphasizes the extent of his knowledge. As students read, have them note the examples of figurative language that they find. When they have finished, discuss with the class how the comparisons added to their understanding.

Teach

Big Idea 1

An Era of Protest
Say: Keep these questions in mind as you read: What is Merwin protesting in "The Asians Dying"? *(the devastation of war)* Who does Merwin hold responsible? *(all of humanity)*

[APPROACHING] Tell students that people were sharply divided about the Vietnam War. Merwin is among wanting an end to the war.

Big Idea 2

An Era of Protest Answer:
The possessors are those who wage war. The ghosts of the people and the land that they destroyed in war will haunt them forever. This war will be their only reality.

Literary Element 3

Figurative Language
Answer: *The disappearing nights and the dead are compared to bruises. Both go away, "but nothing is healed." This comparison suggests that something untouchable and almost unknowable is changed by war. Humanity bears responsibility for the wounds of war forever.*

THE ASIANS DYING

W. S. Merwin

Untitled, 2000. Brenda Chrystie.

When the forests have been destroyed their darkness remains **1**
The ash the great walker follows the **possessors**
Forever
Nothing they will come to is real
5 Nor for long
Over the watercourses[1]
Like ducks in the time of the ducks[2]
The ghosts of the villages trail in the sky
Making a new twilight

10 Rain falls into the open eyes of the dead
Again again with its **pointless** sound
When the moon finds them they are the color of everything

The nights disappear like bruises but nothing is healed
The dead go away like bruises
15 The blood vanishes into the poisoned farmlands
Pain the horizon
Remains
Overhead the seasons rock
They are paper bells
20 Calling to nothing living

The possessors move everywhere under Death their star
Like columns of smoke they advance into the shadows
Like thin flames with no light
They with no past
25 And fire their only future

---

1. *Watercourses* are streams of water, such as a river or a brook.
2. The phrase *ducks in the time of ducks* recalls the Asian belief that the year of one's birth is influenced by the traits of particular animals.

An Era of Protest *Who are the possessors? What does Merwin think is going to happen to them?* **2**

Figurative Language *What are the similes in these lines comparing? What ideas about war do these comparisons suggest?* **3**

Vocabulary

possessor (pə zes′ ər) *n.* one who has or takes control of something; owner
pointless (point′ lis) *adj.* making no sense

Reading Practice

Make Critical Judgments Making critical judgments focuses students' attention on the structure, language, theme, images, and other elements of a poem.

- Have students brainstorm a list of literary elements to use as a basis for evaluating and judging a poem, such as rhyme, rhythm, figures of speech, mood, and imagery.

- Have each student choose three or four elements to judge "The Asians Dying." Have students provide specific examples from the poem to support their critical judgments.

Separation

W. S. Merwin

Your absence has gone through me
Like thread through a needle.
Everything I do is stitched with its color.

When You Go Away

W. S. Merwin

When you go away the wind clicks around to the north
The painters work all day but at sundown the paint falls
Showing the black walls
The clock goes back to striking the same hour
5   That has no place in the years

And at night wrapped in the bed of ashes
In one breath I wake
It is the time when the beards of the dead get their growth
I remember that I am falling
10   That I am the reason
And that my words are the **garment** of what I shall never be   **4**
Like the tucked sleeve of a one-armed boy

Clarify Meaning *What does the simile in line 12 mean?*   **5**

Vocabulary

garment (gär′ mənt) *n.* a piece of clothing

English Learners

DIFFERENTIATED INSTRUCTION

Intermediate English language learners may more readily visualize the figurative language Merwin uses if they are familiar with the similarities between the terms that he is comparing. **Ask:** How do bruises go away? How is that process similar to the way the "dead go away"? *(Both are slow processes, "blood vanishes," a bruise may leave a lasting mark.)* What are some purposes of a garment? How are words like a garment? *(Garments cover the body and can signify something about a person. Words can be like a protective covering over emotions.)*

Literary Element	4

Figurative Language
Ask: How does Merwin use figurative language in "Separation" to express how the absence of a loved one affected the narrator? *(Merwin uses a vivid image—being pierced like the eye of a needle—to describe the painful feeling of loss. He says that the loved one's absence affects everything he does.)*

[ENGLISH LEARNERS] **Ask:** What are the characteristics of thread going through a needle that are similar to missing someone? *(The thread passes from one side of the needle to the other; loss is like a hole in your body or heart. Thread is attached to the needle, and his feeling of loss follows him everywhere.)*

Reading Strategy	5

Clarifying Meaning
Answer: *The image of an armless sleeve represents the speaker's feeling of a lack of fulfillment and of helplessness. It also continues the motif of blending the bleakness of the speaker's emotional state with the devastation of the Vietnam War.*

After You Read

Assess

1. (a) They are destroyed. (b) The farmlands are poisoned, completing the cycle of destruction.

2. (a) The paint falls off the walls, and the clocks strike. (b) Nothing

3. Although war appears to resolve conflicts, it does not. The effects of war linger, even when not visible.

4. (a) Neither day nor night; symbolizes confusion or uncertainty (b) Reflects emptiness and loss; the darkness of night reinforces the sense of doom.

5. (a) A beloved person who has died or left (b) The speaker has deep feelings of loss.

6. (a) Might create sympathy or anger (b) The theme of the disappearance of conscience could support the protests.

7. Some students will argue that the message of war's destruction is relevant today. Others may say the specific Vietnam geography makes the poem less relevant to today's conflicts.

Literary Element

1. D is the correct answer because Merwin compares the far-reaching effect of someone's loss with cloth being stitched with thread.

2. E is the correct answer because Merwin says, "The possessors move everywhere under Death their star / Like columns of smoke they advance into the shadows"

Progress Check

Can students analyze figurative language?

If No → See Unit 7 Teaching Resources Book, p. 90.

After You Read

Respond and Think Critically

Respond and Interpret

1. (a)In "The Asians Dying," what happens to the forests, and, subsequently, what happens to the villages? (b)How does this connect to what happens to the farmlands?

2. (a)In "When You Go Away," what happens to the painters' work and to the clocks? (b)What do these events mean?

Analyze and Evaluate

3. In "The Asians Dying," Merwin employs a series of paradoxes—the forests have been destroyed, yet their darkness remains; bruises disappear, but nothing is healed; and there are flames, but no light. What do these paradoxes suggest about the effects of war?

4. (a)Both speakers in "The Asians Dying" and "When You Go Away" reflect on their feelings at "twilight" or "sundown." What might this time of day symbolize? (b)How does this setting reflect the meaning and tone of these poems?

5. (a)Whom is the speaker of "Separation" addressing? (b)Through the use of figurative language, what feeling is Merwin attempting to convey?

Connect

6. **Big Idea** An Era of Protest (a)What effect do you think the images in "The Asians Dying" would have had on those who were protesting the Vietnam War? (b)How could the poems be used to strengthen their protests?

7. **Connect to Today** Do you think "The Asians Dying" could be used to protest any of today's military conflicts? Explain.

Literary Element Figurative Language

SAT Skills Practice

1. In "Separation," the statement "Everything I do is stitched with its color" is an example of

   (A) personification
   (B) hyperbole
   (C) simile
   (D) metaphor
   (E) symbolism

2. Merwin compares the people who wage war in "The Asians Dying" to

   (A) ducks
   (B) ghosts
   (C) the horizon
   (D) paper bells
   (E) columns of smoke

Review: Free Verse

As you learned in Unit 3, **free verse** is poetry that has no fixed pattern of meter, rhyme, line length, or stanza arrangement. Poets who use free verse often do not follow the traditional rules of grammar and punctuation.

Partner Activity With a partner, discuss the use of free verse in "The Asians Dying," "Separation," and "When You Go Away." Create a chart like the one below. Then fill it with examples of the poetic techniques that Merwin uses in his free verse. Create a chart like the one shown below for each poem.

	"The Asians Dying"
Repetition	
Alliteration	
Assonance	
Consonance	

Review: Free Verse

	"The Asians Dying"	"Separation"	"When You Go Away"
Repetition	again; like bruises	through	I am
Alliteration	forests, follows, forever; bruises, blood; poisoned, pain	through, thread	when, wind, work, walls, wake
Assonance	follows possessors; like, time	is stitched, its	at, wrapped, ashes
Consonance	forests, destroyed; rain, open, again, pointless, sound, moon, finds	thread, needle	wind, around, sundown; black, clock, back

Reading Strategy — Clarify Meaning

The main concepts of Merwin's poems may be difficult to understand because of the irregular sentence patterns and a lack of punctuation. Look back at the questions you wrote in your chart from page 1193. Reread the lines that were challenging and try to put them in your own words.

1. What is the main message of "The Asians Dying"?
2. In "When You Go Away," how does the speaker feel about the absent person?

Vocabulary Practice

Practice with Analogies Choose the word pair that best completes the analogy.

1. possessor : owner ::
   a. army : soldier
   b. supplier : consumer
   c. manager : supervisor

2. pointless : significant ::
   a. remote : distant
   b. responsible : trustworthy
   c. meaningful : irrelevant

3. garment : shirt ::
   a. tool : pliers
   b. hat : head
   c. rain : snow

Academic Vocabulary

*Merwin's **objective** in "The Asians Dying" is to make people accept responsibility for the disastrous effects of war.*

Objective is an academic word. A medical researcher's **objective** in studying a virus may be to develop a vaccine against it.

To further explore the meaning of this word, answer the following question: What is your **objective** in attending high school?

For more on academic vocabulary, see pages 53–54.

Speaking and Listening

 Literature Groups

Assignment With a small group, discuss the meaning of "The Asians Dying." Try to reach a consensus on whether the poem's theme is relevant today.

Prepare Before your group meets, review "The Asians Dying" and identify its theme(s). Then use resources such as the Internet and newspapers to search for current events that relate to the poem's message.

Discuss Your group members may disagree on the overall message of "The Asians Dying." So together, use a chart such as the one below to note inferences you each made about the poem's meaning. Then, compare examples of current events that you have individually researched to come to a consensus on the poem's relevance today.

Quote	Inference
"When the forests have been destroyed their darkness remains"	Remnants of nature will serve as reminders of man's destruction.

Report Have one group member present your consensus to the class or explain why no consensus was reached. He or she should defend your group's opinion with evidence from your inference chart and research. Presenters should speak clearly and loudly.

Evaluate Write a paragraph in which you assess the effectiveness of your discussion. Address both your individual role and the group as a whole.

LOG ON ▶ **Literature** Online

Selection Resources For Selection Quizzes, eFlashcards, and Reading-Writing Connection activities, go to glencoe.com and enter QuickPass code GLA9800u7.

After You Read

Assess

Reading Strategy

1. Humanity has no past and no future as long as we continue to engage in war.
2. The speaker believes that the absent person was the source of order in the world; without the loved one, the world is in chaos.

Vocabulary

1. c **2.** c **3.** a.

Academic Vocabulary

Students should mention their ultimate goals in attending high school, which might be graduating or being accepted into a college.

> **For additional assessment, see Assessment Resources, pp. 283–284.**

Speaking and Listening

Use these criteria when evaluating students' participation in the literature group:

- Did the student listen attentively to the opinions of others?
- Did the student express carefully thought-out opinions that linked to Merwin's poem?

- Did the student organize information by using a graphic organizer and research?

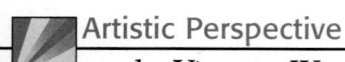

Focus

Summary

The selection is the text of Maya Lin's design proposal for the Vietnam Veterans Memorial. It describes the memorial wall and the materials to be used to build it and contains Lin's views on memorializing the dead.

Teach

Reading Strategy 1

Analyze Political Assumptions Have students construct a chart to organize their data. Charts should

- include examples of direct statements Lin makes to express underlying political opinions or assumptions
- include examples of implied statements of political opinion or assumptions
- paraphrase the underlying political assumptions and opinions in Lin's proposal

Readability Scores

Dale-Chall: 13
DRP: 66
Lexile: 1310

Artistic Perspective
on *the Vietnam War*

PROPOSAL FOR
the Vietnam Veterans Memorial

Maya Lin

National Design Award Winner

Set a Purpose for Reading
Read to find out how Lin hopes that her memorial will inspire visitors.

Build Background
Architect Maya Lin was only twenty-one years old when she submitted this proposal for the Vietnam Veterans Memorial. Unlike most war memorials, it features no statues of heroic soldiers. Instead, it is a black granite wall that first rises from and then falls to the earth. On its surface are the names of the American men and women who were killed. "I thought about what death is, what a loss is," Lin explains. "A sharp pain that lessens with time but can never quite heal over. A scar. The idea occurred to me there on the site. Take a knife and cut open the earth, and with time the grass will heal it."

1 Reading Strategy

Analyze Political Assumptions

Analyzing political assumptions involves carefully examining political beliefs that have shaped an author's message. An author may state each opinion or assumption directly or may merely imply it. As you read, ask yourself, How does Lin reveal her beliefs?

1198 UNIT 7

Walking through this park-like area, the memorial appears as a rift[1] in the earth—a long, polished black stone wall, emerging from and receding into the earth. Approaching the memorial, the ground slopes gently downward, and the low walls emerging on either side, growing out of the earth, extend and converge at a point below and ahead. Walking into the grassy site contained by the walls of this memorial we can barely make out the carved names upon the memorial's walls. These names, seemingly infinite in number, convey the sense of overwhelming numbers, while unifying those individuals into a whole. For this memorial is meant not as a monument to the individual, but rather as a memorial to the men and women who died during this war, as a whole.

The memorial is composed not as an unchanging monument, but as a moving composition, to be understood as we move into and out of it; the passage itself is gradual, the descent to the origin slow, but it is at the origin that the meaning of this memorial is to be fully

---

1. A *rift* is a deep crack or slash.

Reading Practice

SMALL GROUP

Analyze a Proposal Proposals are examples of persuasive writing. When Maya Lin wrote this proposal, her intention was to persuade the selection committee to choose her design for the memorial. In persuasive writing, the author can use three types of appeals which were introduced on page 112 (The Rhetoric of Revolution). Review the following rhetorical appeals with students:

- appeal to reason, logic, and evidence
- appeal to emotions, such as fear, pride, or hate
- ethical appeal, or persuasion based on what we ourselves, moral philosophers, or the majority of people in our culture think is right

Have students read the first paragraph.
Ask: What type of appeal is she making? *(emotional)* How does she support

her appeal? *(descriptive and concrete details explain the emotional symbolism of different elements of the monument)*

As students continue reading, have them identify other persuasive appeals in Lin's essay.

The two panels of Maya Lin's Competition architectural drawing, including her textual description. **2**

MAYA LIN **1199**

Teach

Big Idea | 2

An Era of Protest Explain that even the Vietnam Veterans Memorial was not exempt from protest. Have students discuss their initial impression of Lin's drawings.

Ask: How well does the design honor the men and women who died in the Vietnam War? *(Some students may find the design ineffective because it does not portray acts of heroism. Others may find the design appropriate because the overwhelming number of names highlights the many lives lost in the war.)*

Political History ☆

Controversial Design Lin's design was initially met with heated public opposition. Some critics said the design lacked a sense of heroism. Among the protesters were Vietnam veterans and politicians, including U.S. Secretary of the Interior James Watt, who had the right of veto over the project. Finally, a compromise was reached by adding a bronze sculpture of American soldiers and the American flag to the site.

 For activities related to this selection, see Unit 7 Teaching Resources Book, pp. 93–101.

Advanced Learners

DIFFERENTIATED INSTRUCTION

Write a Persuasive Letter Discuss how people's positions on the Vietnam War, affected the response to the proposed memorial. Ask students to write a letter that a person might have sent to U.S. Secretary of the Interior James Watt to support or protest building the memorial. Tell students that their letters should contain a thesis sentence completing the statement, "The Department of the Interior should _____ (approve/ reject) Maya Lin's design because _____." Explain that their letters should include three reasons or examples to support their argument. Encourage students to use each type of rhetorical appeal listed on page 1198 to make their letters as persuasive as possible.

Teach

Artistic Perspective
on *the Vietnam War*

Reading Strategy | 1

Visualize Have students discuss how the architect depicts the war as "coming full circle" where its beginning and end join. Ask a student with artistic ability to make a drawing of the wall on the board, using the sketches on page 1199 as a guide. Then help students understand where the names of the first person and last person to die appear on the wall.

View the Photograph ★

Answer: *The photograph captures the diminishing line of the Wall until it "disappears" into the earth at the end aligned with the Washington Monument. Also visible is the seemingly endless list of names of those who died in the war. The names contrast with the polished, black granite wall.*

Informational Text

The Vietnam Memorial at night, with the Washington Monument in the distance.

View the Art What aspects of the Vietnam Memorial are captured in this photograph? ★

understood.[2] At the intersection of these walls, on the right side, at this wall's top is carved the date of the first death. It is followed by the names of those who have died in the war, in chronological order. These names continue on this wall, appearing to recede into the earth at the wall's end. The names resume on the left wall, as the wall emerges from the earth, continuing back to the origin, where the date of the last death is carved, at the bottom of this wall. Thus the war's beginning and end meet; the war is "complete," coming full circle, yet broken by the earth that bounds the angle's open side, and contained within the earth itself. As we turn to leave, we see these walls stretching into the distance, directing us to the Washington Monument to the left and the Lincoln Memorial to the right, thus bringing the Vietnam Memorial into historical context. We, the living, are brought to a concrete realization of these deaths.

Brought to a sharp awareness of such a loss, it is up to each individual to resolve or come to terms with this loss. For death is in the end a personal and private matter, and the area contained

---

2. The monument stands in a long, grassy park in Washington, DC. Visitors standing at the monument can look to the left and right and see the faraway ends of the park. At one end stands a tall white obelisk, the Washington Monument, and at the other end stands the Lincoln Memorial, with its famous statue of the seated Abraham Lincoln.

Writing Practice

Reflective Essay Have students write a reflective essay about the Vietnam Veterans Memorial and its relevance today.

- Review the writing process steps: Prewriting, Drafting, Revising, Editing/Proofreading, and Publishing/Presenting.
- Provide images of the memorial in books and on the Internet.
- Have students practice reading their essays aloud to partners. Encourage partners to offer suggestions for making the presentations more effective.
- Allow time for students to share their essays with the class.

within this memorial is a quiet place meant for personal reflection and private reckoning.[3] The black granite walls, each 200 feet long, and 10 feet below ground at their lowest point (gradually ascending towards ground level) effectively act as a sound barrier, yet are of such a height and length so as not to appear threatening or enclosing. The actual area is wide and shallow, allowing for a sense of privacy, and the sunlight from the memorial's southern exposure along with the grassy park surrounding and within its wall contribute to the serenity of the area. Thus this memorial is for those who have died, and for us to remember them.

The memorial's origin is located approximately at the center of this site; its legs each extending 200 feet towards the Washington Monument and

---

3. *Private reckoning* suggests deep, personal thoughts about the magnitude of the war dead.

the Lincoln Memorial. The walls, contained on one side by the earth, are 10 feet below ground at their point of origin, gradually lessening in height, until they finally recede totally into the earth at their ends. The walls are to be made of a hard, polished black granite, with the names to be carved in a simple Trajan[4] letter, 3/4 inch high, allowing for nine inches in length for each name. The memorial's construction involves recontouring the area within the wall's boundaries so as to provide for an easily accessible descent, but as much of the site as possible should be left untouched (including trees).[5] The area should be made into a park for all the public to enjoy. ∾

---

4. *Trajan* is the name of the font that Lin has chosen for the letters in the names.
5. Lin specifies here that some recontouring, or excavating, of the land will be necessary in order to accommodate the downward slope of the granite walls.

Respond and Think Critically

Respond and Interpret

1. Write a brief summary of the main ideas in this article before you answer the following questions. For help writing a summary, see page 79.

2. Imagine being a visitor at the Vietnam Veterans Memorial. How do you think you would respond to the memorial? Explain.

3. (a) Describe the appearance of the memorial. (b) Why may Lin have wanted the names to convey "the sense of overwhelming numbers"?

4. (a) In what order are the names arranged on the monument? (b) Why may Lin have chosen this type of order instead of alphabetical order?

5. How does Lin conclude her proposal? Why do you think she ends with this idea?

Analyze and Evaluate

6. Lin envisioned the memorial "not as an unchanging monument, but as a moving composition, to be understood as we moved into and out of it." From her description of the memorial and the pictures accompanying the proposal, do you believe that she accomplished that vision? Explain.

Connect

7. **Big Idea** **An Era of Protest** Do you think that the Vietnam Veterans Memorial reflects an "era of protest"? Why or why not?

8. **Connect to Today** At first, many people were shocked and disappointed with Lin's design. They expected a more traditional monument, such as a statue conveying the bravery of U.S. soldiers. Do you agree with the critics that such a monument would have been more appropriate? Explain.

MAYA LIN **1201**

Artistic Perspective
on *the Vietnam War*

Teach

Reading Strategy | 2

Make Inferences **Ask:** Why do you think the architect wanted the contour of the ground around the memorial to create a sense of privacy? (*Lin wanted a quiet, peaceful place for visitors to contemplate the honored dead.*)

Assess

1. Students' summaries should include key details about Lin's proposal and its meaning.

2. Students may imagine feeling sad or moved.

3. (a) It is a long black granite wall, etched with the names of the war dead. (b) To show how many lives were lost

4. (a) Chronological order, by date of death (b) To show the history of the war

5. Lin suggests the area be made a public park. She wanted the memorial to be part of the context of our history, our lives, and the earth. She wanted living things to surround the memorial.

6. Students should refer to details from the selection to support their evaluations.

7. Some will link the design, with its seemingly endless list of war dead, to the "era of protest." Others may say it is a simple and powerful tribute to those who gave their lives.

8. Students' responses will vary.

Before You Read

Focus

Bellringer Options

Daily Language Practice Transparency 103

Or display images of the national unrest of the 1960s—civil rights marches, the Cuban missile crisis, the 1968 Democratic Convention, campus riots, and so on.

Ask: What words come to mind as you view these images? *(turmoil, unrest, dissatisfaction, rebellion)* As they read, have students consider how literature and music reflect the social issues of an era.

Before You Read

A Hard Rain's A-Gonna Fall

Meet **Bob Dylan**
(born 1941)

Born Robert Zimmerman and raised in the small mining town of Hibbing, Minnesota, Bob Dylan received his first guitar at the age of fourteen. Throughout his teens, he listened to the music of Hank Williams, Elvis Presley, and Little Richard.

> *"I see my light come shining*
> *From the west unto the east.*
> *Any day now, any day now,*
> *I shall be released."*
>
> —Bob Dylan, "I Shall Be Released"

Protest Singer In 1959, the summer before Dylan enrolled at the University of Minnesota he first heard the records of Woody Guthrie, the folk singer who would become his idol. In Minneapolis, he encountered the era's beatnik, folk-inflected counterculture. Dylan dropped out of college at the end of his freshman year and headed for New York City in search of Guthrie, who had vanished from the public eye due to illness.

When he arrived in New York City in 1961, Dylan had already changed his name and was developing his distinct musical sound. While playing in small clubs throughout Greenwich Village, the center of bohemian New York, he regularly visited Guthrie, who was suffering from Huntington's chorea, a nervous system disorder.

In September 1961, the *New York Times* gave one of Dylan's live performances a positive review, prompting John Hammond, Columbia Records' premier talent scout, to take notice. In less than a year, Dylan recorded and released his first album, which received mixed reviews. However, his next album, *The Freewheelin' Bob Dylan*, earned widespread acclaim.

In 1963, Dylan played at the Newport Folk Festival in Rhode Island. His performance firmly established him as the new voice of folk music. After the release of his next album, *The Times They Are A-Changin'*, Dylan personified the folk "protest song" movement, which influenced the Civil Rights, free speech, and anti-war movements.

Going Electric The album *Bringing It All Back Home*, released in 1965, featured electric instruments, shocking his purist folk fans. *Highway 61 Revisited*, Dylan's next album, included surreal lyrics and a heavy electric sound—but no protest songs. *Blonde on Blonde*, the critically acclaimed following album, followed suit. The tours promoting these albums became legendary: feeling betrayed, angry fans booed and jeered.

In 1966, Dylan was involved in a motorcycle accident, forcing him into a period of seclusion. When he emerged, his musical style changed again. His next two albums—*John Wesley Harding*, released in 1968, and the country infused *Nashville Skyline*, released in 1969—again defied expectations.

Inducted into the Rock and Roll Hall of Fame, he earned multiple Grammys, including Album of the Year for *Time Out of Mind* in 1998. Recently, Dylan released *Chronicles*, the first volume of his memoirs, to overwhelmingly positive reviews.

 Literature Online

Author Search For more about Bob Dylan, go to glencoe.com and enter QuickPass code GLA9800u7.

Selection Skills

Literary Elements
- Rhythm (SE pp. 1203, 1205, 1206)
- Mood (SE p. 1206)

Reading Skills
- Analyze Rhetorical Devices (SE pp. 1203, 1205, 1207)

A Hard Rain's A-Gonna Fall

Vocabulary Skills
- Academic Vocabulary (SE p. 1207)

Writing Skills/Grammar
- Assess Oral Interpretation (SE p. 1207)
- Simple and Compound Sentences (TE p. 1204)

Listening/Speaking/Viewing Skills
- Oral Interpretation (SE p. 1207)

Literature and Reading Preview

Connect to the Song

Do you think life will be better or worse ten years from now? Create a pro-con list that describes how you think life will improve or decline over the next decade.

Build Background

☆ Dylan wrote "A Hard Rain's A-Gonna Fall" during the Cuban missile crisis in 1962, when the United States and the Soviet Union were on the brink of nuclear war. The United States had discovered that the Soviet Union was installing ballistic missiles on the island of Cuba, approximately ninety miles from the U.S. mainland. These missiles were capable of destroying millions of lives within minutes. In response to this threat, President Kennedy set up a naval blockade around Cuba. The crisis ended when the Soviet Union agreed to remove the missiles in exchange for the United States' promise not to invade Cuba. Though nuclear war was averted, the crisis left a gnawing anxiety in the minds of many about the threat of nuclear disaster.

Set Purposes for Reading

Big Idea **An Era of Protest**

As you read, ask yourself, How does this song respond to issues raised by historical events?

Literary Element **Rhythm**

Rhythm refers to the pattern of beats created by the arrangement of stressed and unstressed syllables, especially in poetry. Rhythm gives poetry a musical quality, can add emphasis to certain words, and may help convey the poem's meaning. As you read the protest song aloud, ask yourself, How does the rhythm support the song's meaning?

Reading Strategy **Analyze Rhetorical Devices**

In "A Hard Rain's A-Gonna Fall," Dylan uses several **rhetorical devices,** including juxtaposition, parallelism, and repetition. Juxtaposition refers to the placing of two or more distinct things next to each other in order to compare or contrast them. Parallelism is the use of a series of words, phrases, or sentences that have similar grammatical form. Repetition is the recurrence of sounds, words, phrases, or lines. These devices call attention to particular ideas and evoke emotional responses in the reader. As you read, ask yourself, How do these rhetorical devices contribute to the song's power?

Tip: Take Notes Use a chart to record rhetorical devices and their effects.

Rhetorical Device	Effect
Juxtaposition: "I saw a newborn baby with wild wolves all around it" (line 12)	

Before You Read

Focus

Summary

"A Hard Rain's A-Gonna Fall" is a folk song written to protest social and political issues, including racism, poverty, and the threat of nuclear warfare. The writer uses juxtaposition, parallelism, and repetition to engage the reader/listener in the song's message both intellectually and emotionally.

Cultural History ☆

Protest Songs Many of Bob Dylan's songs protested policies he thought were unfair. In 1963, Dylan was invited to appear on the Ed Sullivan Show, a popular television program. However, when he was forbidden from performing the satiric song "Talkin' John Birch Paranoid Blues," Dylan decided not to appear on the program rather than delete the song from his performance.

For activities related to this selection, see Unit 7 Teaching Resources Book, pp. 104–114.

English Learners

DIFFERENTIATED INSTRUCTION

Advanced Students may benefit from a review of the terms that refer to rhetorical devices. Write the following list of examples on the board:

- <u>children</u> playing in a <u>cemetery</u>
- "government <u>of the people</u>, <u>by the people</u>, and <u>for the people</u>"
- "I still have a dream. It is a dream deeply rooted in the American dream. I have a

dream that one day this nation will rise up and live out the true meaning of its creed."

Work with students to identify *juxtaposition, parallelism,* and *repetition,* underlining the relevant terms in each example. Discuss how the rhetorical devices can help make memorable images and phrases. Explain to students that Dylan's song was meant to

be performed, and that such devices help listeners follow his complex song lyrics.

Teach

An Era of Protest Say:
Keep these questions in mind as you read: What part of the song is the refrain? *(The last two lines of every verse)* How does the refrain sum up the meaning of the song? *(The second speaker, the son, has seen and heard things and has met people. These experiences compel him to spread the word of a pending event.)*

[APPROACHING] Ask students to mark the location of the refrains with sticky notes. Then have them restate the refrain in their own words.

Big Idea 2

An Era of Protest Answer:
These men might represent officials from the Soviet Union and the United States threatening the world with nuclear war

Writer's Technique ☆

Repetition A writer may use repetition in the form of a question and an answer as a device to change the action or task in the verses of a song and the repetition in a refrain to unify the verses.

Bob Dylan

A Hard Rain's A-Gonna Fall

Oh, where have you been, my blue-eyed son? **1**
Oh, where have you been, my darling young one?
I've stumbled on the side of twelve misty mountains,
I've walked and I've crawled on six crooked highways,
5 I've stepped in the middle of seven sad forests,
I've been out in front of a dozen dead oceans,
I've been ten thousand miles in the mouth of a graveyard,
And it's a hard, and it's a hard, it's a hard, and it's a hard,
And it's a hard rain's a-gonna fall.

10 Oh, what did you see, my blue-eyed son? ☆
Oh, what did you see, my darling young one?
I saw a newborn baby with wild wolves all around it
I saw a highway of diamonds with nobody on it,
I saw a black branch with blood that kept drippin',
15 I saw a room full of men with their hammers a-bleedin',
I saw a white ladder all covered with water,
I saw ten thousand talkers whose tongues were all broken,
I saw guns and sharp swords in the hands of young children,
And it's a hard, and it's a hard, it's a hard, it's a hard,
20 And it's a hard rain's a-gonna fall.

An Era of Protest *Who do you think these men might represent?* **2**

Grammar Practice

Simple and Compound Sentences
A simple sentence has one main clause and no subordinate clauses. It can have a compound subject, a compound predicate, or both. A compound sentence has two or more main clauses.

Have students write sentences about Dylan's song using these patterns:

1. Simple sentence with compound subject

2. Simple sentence with compound subject and compound predicate

3. Compound sentence and compound predicate

4. Compound sentence with two main clauses

And what did you hear, my blue-eyed son?
And what did you hear, my darling young one?
I heard the sound of a thunder, it roared out a warnin',
Heard the roar of a wave that could drown the whole world,
25   Heard one hundred drummers whose hands were a-blazin',
Heard ten thousand whisperin' and nobody listenin',
Heard one person starve, I heard many people laughin',
Heard the song of a poet who died in the gutter,
Heard the sound of a clown who cried in the alley,
30   And it's a hard, and it's a hard, it's a hard, it's a hard,
And it's a hard rain's a-gonna fall.

Oh, who did you meet, my blue-eyed son?
Who did you meet, my darling young one?
I met a young child beside a dead pony,
35   I met a white man who walked a black dog,
I met a young woman whose body was burning,
I met a young girl, she gave me a rainbow,
I met one man who was wounded in love,
I met another man who was wounded with hatred,
40   And it's a hard, it's a hard, it's a hard, it's a hard,
It's a hard rain's a-gonna fall.

Oh, what'll you do now, my blue-eyed son?   **3**
Oh, what'll you do now, my darling young one?
I'm a-goin' back out 'fore the rain starts a-fallin',
45   I'll walk to the depths of the deepest black forest,
Where the people are many and their hands are all empty,
Where the pellets of poison are flooding their waters,
Where the home in the valley meets the damp dirty prison,
Where the executioner's face is always well hidden,
50   Where hunger is ugly, where souls are forgotten,
Where black is the color, where none is the number,
And I'll tell it and think it and speak it and breathe it,
And reflect it from the mountain so all souls can see it,
Then I'll stand on the ocean until I start sinkin',
55   But I'll know my song well before I start singin',
And it's a hard, it's a hard, it's a hard, it's a hard,
It's a hard rain's a-gonna fall.

Rhythm *How would you describe the rhythm of these lines?*   **4**

Analyze Rhetorical Devices *What rhetorical device is found in this line? What effect does it create?*   **5**

BOB DYLAN   **1205**

Teach

Reading Strategy   3

Make Inferences Ask: Why does the writer switch from past tense to future tense in the last stanza of the song? *(Possible answer: The listener is told the disastrous event is yet to come; therefore, there is hope: there is still time to change what is wrong and unjust in the world; there is still time to stop being a spectator and become involved in making the world a better place.)*

Literary Element   4

Rhythm Answer: *The repetition of "I met" makes the rhythm insistent; it controls the reader's pace.*

Reading Strategy   5

Analyze Rhetorical Devices Answer: *The rhetorical device is juxtaposition. The images contrasted are the home in the valley and the prison, suggesting that the modern age can transform the pastoral into the institutional.*

After You Read

Assess

1. Some students may mention a stark, violent image, such as the young woman who is burning.

2. (a) An affectionate parent or representative of the older generation and a blue-eyed son (b) They place the listener inside the song, as if the questions in the first two lines were directed at the listener.

3. (a) Nobody (b) An empty highway represents the United States after a nuclear war.

4. (a) It is always well hidden. (b) That the people in control of nuclear weapons are beyond public control

5. The shift in time suggests the disastrous event has not yet occurred, emphasizing that it is still possible to prevent nuclear war.

6. (a) Rain is traditionally associated with fertility and nurturing. The rain in this protest song, however, is hard and destructive, rather than life-giving. (b) The title is effective because it suggests the raining down of nuclear missiles.

7. Dylan hopes to prevent war. Students may point to the title or to the images of desolation and violence throughout the song.

8. Although Dylan wrote this song in response to a specific historical event, most students will see that people in the world still suffer and that his words continue to have relevance.

Progress Check

Can students analyze rhythm?

If No → See Unit 7 Teaching Resources Book, p. 110.

After You Read

Respond and Think Critically

Respond and Interpret

1. What image did you find most powerful in this song? Explain.

2. (a) Who are the speakers in this song? (b) What effect does the poet create by using questions and responses?

3. (a) Who is on the "highway of diamonds" in line 13? (b) What do you think this image represents in relation to the song's historical context?

4. (a) What is unusual about the "executioner's face" in line 49? (b) What might this detail suggest?

Analyze and Evaluate

5. This protest song mostly concerns the past but ends while describing the future. How does the shift in time affect the poet's message?

6. (a) Why did Dylan give his song the title "A Hard Rain's A-Gonna Fall"? (b) Do you think the title is effective? Explain.

Connect

7. **Big Idea** **An Era of Protest** What do you think Dylan hoped to accomplish with this protest song? Explain.

8. **Connect to Today** Do you think Dylan's message is still relevant today? Explain.

Literary Element Rhythm

Rhythm can be regular or irregular. For example in Robert Frost's "Stopping by Woods on a Snowy Evening," the rhythm is regular:

> Whose woods these are I think I know
> His house is in the village though

Even if the rhythm is irregular, you can still get a sense of it by paying attention to the number and position of stressed syllables, or beats, in each line.

1. About how many beats does each line of "A Hard Rain's A-Gonna Fall" usually contain?

2. How does the rhythm of the song influence its meaning?

3. Why do you think Dylan chose irregular rhythm and rhyme? Explain.

Review: Mood

As you learned on page 1182, **mood** is the feeling or atmosphere that an author creates in a literary work.

Partner Activity Meet with another classmate to determine the mood of this song and discuss the literary elements Dylan uses to create it. Working with your partner, create a web diagram like the one below. Then fill it in with examples of the elements that contribute to the mood of the song.

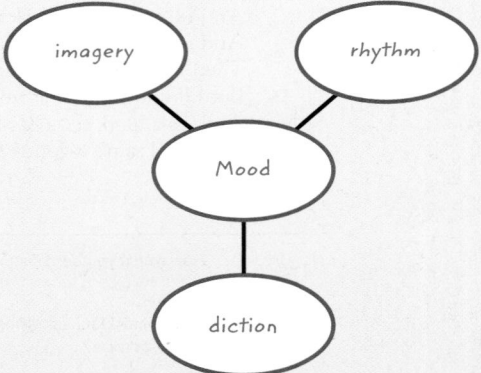

Literary Element

1. Most lines contain approximately four beats.

2. The rhythm is driving. It gives the song a sense of urgency.

3. Dylan may have felt that the conventions of regular rhythm and rhyme were too restrictive for his subject.

Review: Mood

The mood is disquieting and threatening, suggested by violent imagery such as "a room full of men with their hammers a-bleedin'" and diction such as "pellets of poison."

Reading Strategy — Analyze Rhetorical Devices

Though most often found in persuasive essays or speeches, **rhetorical devices** sometimes support an implied argument in poetry and fiction. Review the chart you created on page 1203 listing rhetorical devices in this protest song.

1. What argument is implied in "A Hard Rain's A-Gonna Fall"?

2. List three rhetorical devices and explain how each one helps advance that argument.

Academic Vocabulary

In "A Hard Rain's A-Gonna Fall," Dylan uses **specific** *imagery to provoke an emotional response from his audience.*

Specific is an academic word. When giving your friend directions to a location, it is important to give him **specific** details, or else he might get lost.

To study this word further, fill out the graphic organizer below.

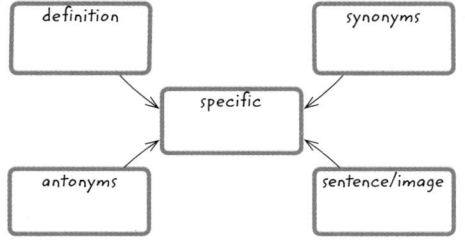

For more on academic vocabulary, see pages 53–54.

Speaking and Listening

 Oral Interpretation

Assignment Present an oral interpretation of "A Hard Rain's A-Gonna Fall."

Prepare First listen to a recording of the song several times, focusing on your own reactions to it. Then analyze Dylan's intended meaning and how he shapes this meaning through both language and performance techniques.

Create a chart like the one below to analyze the structure and imagery of the song. Use this analysis to help you decide on both the meaning of the song and on appropriate verbal and nonverbal techniques to use in your oral interpretation. For example, Dylan uses a question-and-answer format in this song. You may want to create the effect of dialogue in your oral interpretation by using a different vocal style for the questions.

Structure	Imagery
• Question and answer format	• Strange, blighted landscape
•	•
•	•
•	•

Experiment with different tones, volumes, speeds, and other vocal devices. Use facial expressions and gestures to reflect what you are saying.

Perform Read the song aloud in front of the class, paying close attention to the rhythm and mood you create with your voice.

Evaluate Write a paragraph in which you assess the effectiveness of your oral interpretation. Use the guidelines on page 841 to help in this self-evaluation.

LOG ON ▶ **Literature** Online

Selection Resources For Selection Quizzes, eFlashcards, and Reading-Writing Connection activities, go to glencoe.com and enter QuickPass code GLA9800u7.

BOB DYLAN **1207**

After You Read

Assess

Reading Strategy

1. The implied argument is that war must end and nuclear war must be prevented at all costs.

2. Students might identify the refrain "it's a hard rain's a-gonna fall" as an example of repetition used to emphasize the threat of nuclear war; the image of the poet dying in the gutter as an example of juxtaposition, suggesting that nuclear war does not spare the gifted. Examples of parallelism throughout the song reinforce meaning and mood.

Academic Vocabulary

specific
Definition: exact or definite
Synonyms: particular, express, defined
Antonyms: general, ambiguous, equivocal
Sentence: Dogs of that specific breed are intelligent and good at hunting.

Speaking and Listening

Use these criteria when evaluating students' oral interpretations and paragraphs:

- Did the student's oral interpretation indicate a close reading of the song?
- Did the student use verbal techniques to underscore the meaning of the song?
- Did the student use nonverbal techniques effectively?

Advanced Learners

DIFFERENTIATED INSTRUCTION

International Music Students interested in music may enjoy exploring music of another culture.

- Have groups of students listen to a variety of musical selections from different cultures. Use music from the same time period—an era of protest—if possible.

- Have groups identify the elements that characterize the music of the culture they have chosen. Then have them share their findings with the class.

1207

Before You Read

Focus

Bellringer Options

Daily Language Practice Transparency 104

Or **say:** The word *courage* comes from the Latin root *cor* meaning "heart." **Ask:** How do you think people's "heart" or "spirit" might move them to perform courageous acts? (*Students may say that people's love of someone or their passion for an idea could give them the power to perform courageous acts.*)

Writer's Technique ☆

"Workshopping" Anne Sexton and her friend Maxine Kumin were both poets and mothers. Because their parenting duties often kept them at home, they developed a technique to work together on their poetry. On private telephone lines, Sexton and Kumin "work-shopped" their poems, discussing ideas and writing without leaving their homes.

Before You Read

Courage

Meet **Anne Sexton**
(1928–1974)

The work of some poets is so intimately bound to the poet's experiences that the poetry is almost never discussed without references to his or her life. Such is the case with Anne Sexton, whose troubled life was not only reflected in her poetry but also actually led to her becoming a successful poet in the first place.

Poetry as Therapy Born in Newton, Massachusetts, Anne Sexton was the youngest of three daughters in a middle class family. Beautiful and rebellious, Sexton eloped at the age of nineteen, marrying Alfred Muller Sexton II, whom she had known only briefly. Sexton gave birth to her first daughter in 1953, and her second daughter in 1955. It was after the births of her children that she began to suffer from severe postpartum depression and attempted suicide several times. During this time, her therapist encouraged her to try writing poetry to explore her feelings.

> "Poetry should be a shock to the senses. It should almost hurt."
>
> —Anne Sexton

In 1960, Sexton published her first collection of poems titled *To Bedlam and Part Way Back*, which chronicled her early struggles with mental illness. This was followed, in 1962, by the publication of *All My Pretty Ones*. These first collections received mixed reviews. Some critics praised Sexton's work as "remarkable," "full of the exact flavors of places and peoples remembered," and "an honest and impressive achievement." Others saw her work as flawed and nothing more than a "determinedly outspoken soap-opera."

Fame and Pain Sexton, meanwhile, was becoming firmly established as a member of the "Confessional School," a group of poets who wrote during the late 1950s and 1960s and were categorized by their intensely introspective writing styles. At first, Sexton railed against being labeled a "confessional." Later she said, "I decided I was the only confessional poet."

While much of her work over the following years remained "confessional" and decidedly feminist, Sexton did occasionally go outside of herself for material. *Transformations*, published in 1971, is a retelling of the popular fairy tales of the Brothers Grimm. Reviewers delighted in the "colorful imagery" and sharp wit that Sexton exhibited in this collection.

During her career, Anne Sexton published ten books of poetry, as well as a play, essays, and several children's books. Sexton received the Pulitzer Prize in 1967 for her collection *Live or Die*. As her fame grew, Sexton took on other responsibilities. She taught poetry workshops and creative writing, and she became a popular figure at poetry readings on college campuses. All the while, Sexton continued to struggle with mental illness. On October 4, 1974, she met with close friend Maxine Kumin to review the page galleys for her ☆ latest collection, *The Awful Rowing Toward God*. Later that day, Anne Sexton took her own life.

 Literature Online

Author Search For more about Anne Sexton, go to glencoe.com and enter QuickPass code GLA9800u7.

Selection Skills

Literary Elements
- Verse Paragraph (SE pp. 1209, 1210, 1212; TE p. 1211)

Courage

Writing Skills/Grammar
- Write a Letter (SE p. 1212)

Reading Skills
- Examine Denotation and Connotation (SE pp. 1209, 1211, 1212)
- Make Predictions (TE p. 1210)

Vocabulary Skills
- Synonyms (SE pp. 1209, 1212)
- Verb Power (TE p. 1209)

Literature and Reading Preview

Connect to the Essay

Would you call yourself courageous? Write a journal entry in which you describe different kinds of courage.

Build Background

The Awful Rowing Toward God, in which "Courage" appears, was Sexton's last collection of poetry. When Sexton wrote these poems, she was battling severe mental illness and was frequently an inpatient at mental hospitals. Many reviewers, including some of her close friends, criticized the poems in this collection as being too personal, disjointed, and lacking the strength of her earlier and best poems. Sexton herself called the poems "raw" and "unworked."

Set Purposes for Reading

Big Idea **An Era of Protest**

As you read, ask yourself, How does the poet focus on the individual's conflicts with society?

Literary Element **Verse Paragraph**

A **verse paragraph** is a group of lines in a poem that form a unit. While stanzas traditionally have a fixed number of lines and are typical of poems written before the twentieth century, verse paragraphs are not uniform in length and reflect the open, freer form of contemporary verse. As you read, ask yourself, How does Sexton use each verse paragraph to organize her ideas about courage and life?

Reading Strategy **Examine Connotation and Denotation**

The **denotation** of a word is its literal, or dictionary, meaning. The **connotation** of a word is the meaning or association that the word has beyond its literal meaning. As you read, ask yourself, What are the positive or negative feelings that the connotations of specific words evoke?

Tip: List Words Use a chart to list words with positive and negative connotations in the poem.

Positive Connotation	Negative Connotation
awesome	fatty

Learning Objectives

For pages 1208–1212

In studying this text, you will focus on the following objectives:

Literary Study: Analyzing verse paragraph.

Reading: Examining connotation and denotation.

Vocabulary

wallowing (wol´ ō ing) *v.* moving in a clumsy manner or with difficulty; p. 1210 *After the heavy rain, we found ourselves wallowing through muddy ditches to get home.*

fondle (fond´ əl) *v.* to handle gently; p. 1210 *The cat squirmed as the kids tried to pet and fondle it.*

transfusion (trans fū´ zhən) *n.* the act of passing life-saving fluids from one to another; p. 1211 *He received a blood transfusion during the operation.*

transformed (trans fôrməd´) *adj.* changed in a dramatic way; p. 1211 *The messy vacant lot was transformed into a lush garden.*

Tip: Synonyms Understanding words that are similar in meaning to an unfamiliar word, or **synonyms,** can help you learn the word. Example: ***Courage*** *and **valor** are synonyms; they both mean "the ability to face difficulty without being overcome."*

ANNE SEXTON **1209**

Focus

Summary

The speaker challenges our concept of courage by sharing examples of actions that may seem like ordinary events in any person's life. The speaker implies, however, that every person is faced with challenges that require courage and, therefore, we are all capable of heroism.

 For summaries in languages other than English, see Unit 7 Teaching Resources Book, pp. 115–120.

Vocabulary

Verb Power This selection's vocabulary words are either verbs or have verbs as their roots. When Sexton describes the courage of the young, she uses *wallowing* and *fondle.* Both contain the *l* sound, which is often in gentle words such as *lullaby* and *vulnerable.* When she describes the courage of an older person, she chooses two more forceful words, *transfusion* and *transformed.* **Say:** Both words contain the Latin prefix *trans-,* meaning "across" or "through." What might these words imply about the courage of the older person? *(The words imply that the older person has the ability to connect to others, to give and receive; or to come through adversity.)*

Teach

Courage

Anne Sexton

1 It is in the small things we see it.
The child's first step,
as awesome as an earthquake.
The first time you rode a bike,
wallowing up the sidewalk.
The first spanking when your heart
went on a journey all alone.
When they called you crybaby
or poor or fatty or crazy
and made you into an alien,[1]
you drank their acid
and concealed it.

Later,
if you faced the death of bombs and bullets
you did not do it with a banner,
you did it with only a hat to
cover your heart.
You did not **fondle** the weakness inside you
though it was there.
Your courage was a small coal
that you kept swallowing.
If your buddy saved you
and died himself in so doing,
then his courage was not courage,
it was love, love as simple as shaving soap.

The Deluge, 1920. Winifred Knights. Oil on canvas, 59⅓ x 71⅓ in. Tate Gallery, London.

---

1. *Alien* here means "someone who feels like an outsider."

2 Verse Paragraph *How do the lines that follow develop this idea?*

3 An Era of Protest *According to the speaker, how does the person addressed in this verse paragraph face death?*

Vocabulary

wallowing (wol′ ō ing) *v.* moving in a clumsy manner or with difficulty
fondle (fond′ əl) *v.* to handle gently

1210 UNIT 7 INTO THE TWENTY-FIRST CENTURY

Later,
if you have endured a great despair,
then you did it alone,
getting a **transfusion** from the fire,
picking the scabs off your heart,
then wringing it out like a sock.
Next, my kinsman,[2] you powdered your sorrow,
you gave it a back rub
and then you covered it with a blanket
and after it had slept a while
it woke to the wings of the roses
and was **transformed.**[3]

Later,
when you face old age and its natural conclusion[4]
your courage will still be shown in the little ways,
each spring will be a sword you'll sharpen,
those you love will live in a fever of love,
and you'll bargain with the calendar
and at the last moment
when death opens the back door
you'll put on your carpet slippers
and stride out.

---

2. *Kinsman* is a relative. Here the speaker aligns herself with those who suffer the pain of loneliness and despair.
3. The poet may be making an illusion to the Phoenix, a mythical bird that burns itself to ashes and then rises anew from the ashes to live again.
4. The *natural conclusion* of life is death.

Examine Denotation and Connotation *Why do you think the poet chose to use the word* powdered *instead of some other phrase?* **5**

Vocabulary

transfusion (trans fū´ zhən) *n.* the act of passing life-saving fluids from one to another
transformed (trans fôrməd´) *adj.* changed in a dramatic way

Literary Element   **4**

Verse Paragraph Ask: For what purpose does the poet use the verse paragraph device throughout "Courage"? *(Possible answer: Sexton uses the device to show the chronology of a person's life from childhood to death; within this chronology, the poet gives examples of challenges facing people at different stages of their lives.)*

Reading Strategy   **5**

Examine Denotation and Connotation Answer: Pow-dered *has a positive connotation that suggests gentle pampering when powdering a baby; a phrase such as* took care of *would be neutral sounding and would not evoke a specific image.*

English Learners

DIFFERENTIATED INSTRUCTION

Intermediate Help English learners find the literal meaning of the poem before they interpret and analyze it. Ask students to orally paraphrase the main ideas in "Courage." Review the literal meaning of the stanzas, and have students use their work to help predict events in the poem.

Approaching Level

DIFFERENTIATED INSTRUCTION

Emerging Have students summarize each stanza with one sentence or phrase. Then ask them to write a sentence or phrase describing the progression they see between each of the stanzas.

Assess

1. (a) Suffers without reacting and hides pain (b) It is a vulnerable time when we first feel pain.

2. (a) Shaving soap is compared to love. (b) Courage is seen in small, everyday things.

3. (a) She addresses readers as kinsman. (b) The speaker has felt isolated and alone.

4. (a) Transfusion from the fire, picking scabs off your heart, wringing it out like a sock (b) The individual endures and transforms emotional pain alone.

5. People learn to accept death.

6. Society forces us to repress our fears. Inner strength and courage help us face them.

7. Answers will vary. Students should note that Sexton sees moments of courage in each of the four characters, but that in her death she probably related to the final image, "striding out."

Literary Element

1. *Later* is a transition between verses 2, 3, and 4; within verses, she uses *when, then, next,* and *after.*

2. Childhood: simple experiences and concealing pain; young adult in war: represses fear; adulthood: helps us recover from despair; old age: helps us resist and then accept death

Progress Check

Can students analyze verse paragraphs?

If No → See Unit 7 Teaching Resources Book, p. 121.

After You Read

Respond and Think Critically

Respond and Interpret

1. (a) According to the speaker, how does the child respond when bullied or abused? (b) What does this suggest about the speaker's attitude towards childhood?

2. (a) What image is used in the second verse paragraph to suggest that a great act of courage can be very simple and even common? (b) How does this image relate to the main idea of the first verse paragraph?

3. (a) How does the speaker let the audience know that she shares their suffering and pain? (b) What does this suggest to you about the speaker's life?

Analyze and Evaluate

4. (a) How does Sexton describe how people can recover from the emotional pain of life? (b) What role do others have in the process?

5. At the end of the poem, why does Sexton describe the encounter with death as she does?

Connect

6. **Big Idea** **An Era of Protest** How might this poem be viewed as an expression of discontent and an argument for change?

7. **Connect to the Author** Out of the four characters in the poem, to which one do you think Sexton ultimately related? Explain.

Literary Element **Verse Paragraph**

Verse paragraphs can organize a poem into thoughts much as paragraphs can organize ideas in prose. For example, in "Courage" each verse paragraph describes a different stage of a person's life.

1. How does Sexton show chronological order both between and within the verse paragraphs?

2. How does the poet view courage at each stage in a person's life?

Reading Strategy **Examine Connotation and Denotation**

The **denotation** of a word is its literal meaning. Words that have different **connotations**, or shades of meaning, have an added impact on the meaning and effect of a poem. Sexton uses words with negative connotations, like "crybaby," "alien," and "acid." Identify words with negative connotations in the third verse paragraph. Explain the connotations.

> **LOG ON** ▶ **Literature** Online
>
> **Selection Resources** For Selection Quizzes, eFlashcards, and Reading-Writing Connection activities, go to glencoe.com and enter QuickPass code GLA9800u7.

1212 UNIT 7 INTO THE TWENTY-FIRST CENTURY

Vocabulary Practice

Practice with Synonyms With a partner, match each boldfaced vocabulary word below with its synonym. Use a thesaurus or dictionary to check your answers.

1. **wallowing**   a. metamorphosed
2. **fondle**   b. depressive
3. **transfusion**   c. plodding
4. **transformed**   d. caress
                        e. transferal
                        f. transpired

Writing

Write a Letter Sexton's poem describes the courage in everyday actions. Think of someone you know personally whom you consider to be courageous in the way Sexton describes. Write a letter to that person describing his or her acts of everyday courage. As you write, pay attention to the connotation of the words you use.

Reading Strategy

Despair, transfusion, scabs, and *wringing* have negative connotations. *Despair* connotes the depths of sadness. *Transfusion* relates to blood and injuries. *Scabs* connotes crusty wounds. *Wringing* implies a violent motion.

Writing

Use the following criteria to evaluate students' letters:

- Is the writing in the form of a letter?
- Is the student aware of the connotation of his or her words?

Vocabulary

1. c 2. d 3. e 4. a

Nature and Technology

Moonwalk, 1987. Andy Warhol. Screenprint on lenox museum board, 38 x 38 in. The Andy Warhol Foundation for the Visual Arts.

 View the Art Warhol used famous scenes from the arts, science, and popular culture as inspiration for his work. How does this image combine the worlds of science and technology with the symbol of America?

"The 'control of nature' is a phrase conceived in arrogance, born of the Neanderthal age of biology and the convenience of man."

—Rachel Carson, *Silent Spring* **1**

1213

Reading Strategy 1

Evaluate Direct students to read the quotation from Rachel Carson. **Ask:** What do you think Rachel Carson means by these words? *(Carson suggests that people's efforts to control nature shows a crude understanding of life on Earth.)* Discuss with students whether human beings should try to control nature.

View the Art

Answer: *The worlds of science and technology are represented by the astronaut on the Moon.*

Andy Warhol (1928–1987) began his career as a commercial artist. He became famous for using images from popular culture in his art. *Moonwalk* is an excellent example of Warhol's use of a familiar image as a starting point for an artwork.

English Learners

DIFFERENTIATED INSTRUCTION

Intermediate Explain that "Neanderthals" were early relatives of humans who lived until about 30,000 years ago. The term is sometimes used to mean *primitive* or *crude*. **Ask:** Substitute the word *primitive* for *Neanderthal* in Carson's statement. How would you paraphrase her words now? *(Trying to control nature comes from an understanding of life on Earth that is not sophisticated.)*

> For additional support for English Learners, see Unit 7 Teaching Resources Book, p. 128.

Approaching Level

DIFFERENTIATED INSTRUCTION

Strategic Authors deliberately choose words to set a particular tone. Have students reread Carson's quote. **Ask:** How do the words *arrogance, Neanderthal age,* and *convenience* convey her tone? *(The words convey a negative and critical tone.)*

Focus

Bellringer Options

Selection Focus
Transparency 68
Daily Language Practice
Transparency 105

Or explain that the poems by Elizabeth Bishop they are about to read are filled with images to help them picture the fish and the filling station. **Ask:** Imagine you are on a fishing trip and you catch an enormous fish. How do you picture the fish? Prompt students to write lists of vivid sensory details that describe the fish they "caught."

 For activities related to this selection, see Unit 7 Teaching Resources Book, pp. 129–134.

The Fish and *Filling Station*

Meet **Elizabeth Bishop**
(1911–1979)

Elizabeth Bishop once told her writing class at Harvard University, "Use the dictionary. It's better than the critics." Bishop's wit and devotion to careful, precise language came through in her own writing, which earned her nearly every major poetry prize in the U.S.

For Bishop, writing poetry was an act of "self-forgetfulness," in which she focused on shaping and sharing her impressions of the physical world rather than on giving the details of her sometimes difficult personal life. When she was very young, her father died and her mother was permanently hospitalized, so Bishop was raised by relatives. After graduation from Vassar College in 1934, she traveled frequently and lived in many places, including Florida, New York, Europe, and Brazil. She kept in touch with people she met through thousands of letters, some of which were collected and published in her book *One Art*.

> "[It is] far more important to just keep writing poetry than to think of yourself as a poet whose job it is to write poetry all the time."
>
> —Elizabeth Bishop

In 1934 Bishop was introduced to the poet Marianne Moore, who became Bishop's valued friend and mentor. Bishop also became close to poet Robert Lowell, who provided unstinting moral support and helped her obtain grants, fellowships, and awards. They critiqued each other's poetry and remained staunch allies throughout their lives.

Described by many friends as generous and wise, Bishop was also complicated and intensely private. Though she suffered from depression, people were struck by her warmth and self-deprecating sense of humor. She appreciated friends and relatives who made her laugh. She wrote, "I have been very lucky in having had, most of my life, some witty friends,—and I mean real wit, quickness, wild fancies, remarks that make one cry with laughing."

Bishop's voice is one of the most distinctive in American poetry, conveying not only the sights and sounds of nature but also the thoughts and feelings of a speaker groping toward an understanding of nature. Bishop was preoccupied with questions of guilt, loss, and artistic vision, and these issues appear in her poetry.

Over her fifty-year writing career, Bishop published five slim volumes of poetry with a total of 101 poems. Of her final poetry collection, critic Alfred Corn wrote that Bishop achieved "a perfected transparence of expression, warmth of tone, and a singular blend of sadness and good humor, of pain and acceptance—a radiant patience few people ever achieve and few writers ever successfully render." Besides writing, Bishop taught at Harvard for seven years and served as a poetry consultant to the Library of Congress.

 Literature Online

Author Search For more about Elizabeth Bishop, go to glencoe.com and enter QuickPass code GLA9800u7.

Selection Skills

Literary Elements
- Tone (SE pp. 1215, 1217, 1218, 1220)
- Setting (SE p. 1220)

The Fish *and* Filling Station

Writing Skills/Grammar
- Write a Report (SE p. 1221)
- Punctuation (TE p. 1218)

Reading Skills
- Evaluate Sensory Details (SE pp. 1215–1217, 1219, 1220)
- Monitor Comprehension (TE p. 1216)

Vocabulary Skills
- Context Clues (SE pp. 1215, 1221)
- Academic Vocabulary (SE p. 1221)
- Parts of Speech (TE p. 1215)

Literature and Reading Preview

Connect to the Poems

When have you discovered something unexpected about a familiar person or place? Freewrite for a few minutes about your initial impressions and your discovery.

Build Background

The following passage from a letter Bishop wrote to Marianne Moore may have developed into her poem "The Fish."

The other day I caught a parrot fish, almost by accident. They are ravishing fish—all iridescent, with a silver edge to each scale, and a real bull-like mouth just like turquoise; the eye is very big and wild, and the eyeball is turquoise too—they are very humorous-looking fish.

Set Purposes for Reading

Big Idea Nature and Technology

In these poems, carefully examine the observations about the fish and the filling (or gas) station. As you read, ask yourself, What do Bishop's patient reflections tell you about modern life and nature's role in it?

Literary Element Tone

Tone is the attitude that an author expresses toward his or her subject matter. As you read, ask, What is the speaker's tone?

Reading Strategy Evaluate Sensory Details

Sensory details are evocative words or phrases that appeal to one or more of the five senses. Poets use sensory details to help the reader imagine or experience more deeply the content of poems. As you read, ask yourself, What feeling or meaning do the sensory details convey to you?

Tip: Chart Sensory Details Record sensory details in a chart like the one shown. List the sense that the detail appeals to.

Sensory detail	Sense appealed to	Feeling or meaning

Vocabulary

tarnish (tär´ nish) *v.* to dull, soil, or stain; p. 1217 *The cabinet was tarnished by the fire.*

permeate (pur´ mē āt´) *v.* to penetrate, spread through, or diffuse; p. 1218 *Water may permeate the bag if it is not sealed shut before the storm.*

extraneous (ek strā´ nē əs) *adj.* not intrinsically belonging; not forming a vital part; coming from outside; p. 1219 *The music seemed extraneous to the scientific presentation.*

Tip: Context Clues To determine a word's meaning, look at the other words in the sentence and try to guess at a possible meaning. Example: *Although her necklace was pretty, it was an* **extraneous** *part of her heavily accessorized outfit.* If the girl's outfit already has several accessories, she probably doesn't need a necklace, so *extraneous* means "unnecessary."

Before You Read

Focus

Summary

"The Fish" describes in detail a fish that the speaker has caught. The speaker notes the lines and hooks hanging from its mouth like medals of honor. Overcome with respect, the speaker lets the fish go. The speaker in "Filling Station" contemplates a gas station, wondering whether the attendants live there. After describing the homey touches on the porch, the speaker notes that they are signs of love.

Vocabulary

Parts of Speech Point out that many words can be used as both nouns and verbs. Have students write sentences using *tarnish* as a noun and as a verb.

(ENGLISH LEARNERS) Explain that the suffix *-ous* means "having the quality of." **Ask:** What does "extraneous" mean? *(having the quality of being extra)*

Approaching Level

DIFFERENTIATED INSTRUCTION

Emerging Remind students that understanding poetry often depends on the ability to recognize and understand imagery. Elizabeth Bishop uses various forms of imagery in her poems. "The Fish" contains a number of similes. Remind students of the definition of a simile.

Display the following:

- The old fish had brown skin that hung from its bones and was darker brown in some places. It had stains on it.
- His brown skin hung in strips like ancient wall-paper, and its pattern of darker brown was like wall-paper: shapes like full-blown roses stained and lost through age.

Ask: Which of these descriptions is more effective in helping you visualize the fish? Why? *(The second one compares the fish's skin to wallpaper, so it creates a better picture.)*

Established Ask: What are the similes in the second description? *(like ancient wall-paper, like full-blown roses)* Remind students to look for other examples of imagery as they read Bishop's poems.

Teach

Big Idea   1

Nature and Technology
Answer: *The lines establish that animals are subservient to people and frequently at their mercy.*

[APPROACHING] Suggest that students also read lines 5–9 and use a dictionary for any words they do not know.

Reading Strategy   2

Evaluate Sensory Details
Answer: *The details convey the idea of an elaborately decorated, but filthy, fish. Some aspects of the fish's skin are portrayed as ornamental, but the fish is also infested with lice and defiled by "rags of green weed."*

View the Art ★

Early in his career, Winslow Homer (1836–1910) painted with oil paints. In 1873, Homer began to work with watercolors. Although his early Civil War paintings are considered important, Homer's work with watercolors sets him apart as a truly great American artist. **Ask:** How does Winslow Homer use color in his painting in the same way that Elizabeth Bishop uses words? *(Homer uses color and Bishop uses words to tell a story, convey emotions, and describe a scene.)*

For an audio recording of this selection, use Listening Library Audio CD-ROM.

Returning Fishing Boats, 1883. Winslow Homer. Watercolor. Fogg Museum of Art, Harvard University, Cambridge, MA. ★

The Fish
Elizabeth Bishop

I caught a tremendous fish
and held him beside the boat
half out of water, with my hook
fast in a corner of his mouth.
5 He didn't fight.
He hadn't fought at all.
He hung a grunting weight,
battered and venerable[1]
and homely. Here and there
10 his brown skin hung in strips
like ancient wall-paper,
and its pattern of darker brown
was like wall-paper:
shapes like full-blown roses
15 stained and lost through age.
He was speckled with barnacles,
fine rosettes of lime,
and infested

with tiny white sea-lice,
20 and underneath two or three
rags of green weed hung down.
While his gills were breathing in
the terrible oxygen
—the frightening gills,
25 fresh and crisp with blood,
that can cut so badly—
I thought of the coarse white flesh
packed in like feathers,
the big bones and the little bones,
30 the dramatic reds and blacks
of his shiny entrails,[2]
and the pink swim-bladder[3]
like a big peony.
I looked into his eyes

---

1. Venerable means "deserving respect because of age."
2. *Entrails* are internal organs.
3. A *swim-bladder*, or air bladder, is an air sac that enables some fish to maintain buoyancy and equilibrium.

1 **Nature and Technology** *What relationship between people and animals do these lines establish?*

2 **Evaluate Sensory Details** *What ideas about the fish do these visual details convey?*

Reading Practice

Monitor Comprehension The vivid language of poetry can be difficult for students to understand. Clarifying and paraphrasing small sections will help them interpret the broader meaning. If students have problems understanding Bishop's poems, have them try the following strategies:

- Reread each section, restating the meaning of the passage in your own words.
- Use context to determine the meanings of unfamiliar words and to interpret figures of speech.
- Use punctuation to break up the poem into sentences or other units.

35 which were far larger than mine
    but shallower, and yellowed,
    the irises backed and packed
    with **tarnished** tinfoil
    seen through the lenses
40 of old scratched isinglass.[4]
    They shifted a little, but not
    to return my stare.
    —It was more like the tipping
    of an object toward the light.
45 I admired his sullen face,
    the mechanism of his jaw,
    and then I saw
    that from his lower lip
    —if you could call it a lip—
50 grim, wet, and weapon-like,
    hung five old pieces of fish-line,
    or four and a wire leader
    with the swivel still attached,
    with all their five big hooks
55 grown firmly in his mouth.
    A green line, frayed at the end
    where he broke it, two heavier lines,

    and a fine black thread
    still crimped from the strain and snap
60 when it broke and he got away.
    Like medals with their ribbons
    frayed and wavering,
    a five-haired beard of wisdom
    trailing from his aching jaw.
65 I stared and stared
    and victory filled up
    the little rented boat,
    from the pool of bilge[5]
    where oil had spread a rainbow
70 around the rusted engine
    to the bailer rusted orange,
    the sun-cracked thwarts,[6]
    the oarlocks on their strings,
    the gunnels[7]—until everything
75 was rainbow, rainbow, rainbow!
    And I let the fish go.

---

4. *Isinglass* (ī´zin glas´) was used in windows before glass panes became common.

Vocabulary

tarnish (tär´ nĭsh) *v.* to dull, soil, or stain

---

5. *Bilge* (bilj) is stagnant water in the bottom of a boat.
6. *Thwarts* (thwôrts) are seats going across a small boat.
7. *Gunnels* (gə´ nəlz) are the upper edges of the sides of a boat.

Evaluate Sensory Details *What do these details reveal about the fish?* **3**

Tone *What do these lines reveal about the speaker's attitude toward the fish?* **4**

Teach

Reading Strategy | 3

Evaluate Sensory Details
Answer: *The details reveal that the fish has escaped after being hooked by other anglers.*

Literary Element | 4

Tone Answer: *Students' answers will vary. Some may say that the phrase "beard of wisdom" conveys admiration and respect for the fish.*

(**APPROACHING**) **Ask:** What effect do these details have on the reader? *(Students may say that Bishop's tone inspires them with new admiration for the fish.)*

English Learners

DIFFERENTIATED INSTRUCTION

 Beginning Point out that poets often use descriptive adjectives to create images and tone. Have students work in pairs to identify five adjectives that describe the fish. **Ask:** How does each adjective help explain Bishop's attitude toward the fish? *("tremendous fish"— Bishop is impressed by the size of the fish; "grunting weight, battered and venerable"— Bishop is showing respect for the fish and* what it has endured; "his sullen face"— Bishop is aware that the fish is unhappy at being caught.) Have students use these adjectives in their own sentences.

Advanced Learners

DIFFERENTIATED INSTRUCTION

SMALL GROUP
Write Imagery Divide students into pairs or small groups. Have students choose a short passage from the poem, about five lines, containing at least one simile or metaphor. Ask students to paraphrase the passage and explain the comparison that is made.

1217

Teach

Literary Element   1

Tone **Answer:** *Students' answers will vary. Some may say that the line conveys a humorous disdain for the extreme filth of the gas station.*

Writer's Technique ☆

Caesuras Tell students that a caesura is a natural pause within a line of poetry. Have them note the caesuras in the first stanza of "Filling Station." Discuss with students the effect of the caesuras and tell them that such pauses within lines can make a poem's rhythm more conversational. Have students look for another example of a caesura as they read the poem.

Gas. 1940. Edward Hopper. Oil on canvas, 26¼ x 40¼ in. The Museum of Modern Art, NY.

Filling Station

Elizabeth Bishop

O_h, but it is dirty!
—this little filling station,
oil-soaked, oil-**permeated** ☆
to a disturbing, over-all
5   black translucency.
Be careful with that match!

Father wears a dirty,
oil-soaked monkey suit
that cuts him under the arms,
10 and several quick and saucy
and greasy sons assist him
(it's a family filling station),
all quite thoroughly dirty.

> **Tone** *What does this line suggest about the speaker's attitude toward the gas station?*   **1**

> **Vocabulary**
>
> **permeate** (pur′mē āt′) *v.* to penetrate, spread through, or diffuse

1218   UNIT 7   INTO THE TWENTY-FIRST CENTURY

Grammar Practice

SPIRAL REVIEW **Punctuation** Point out that it is important to pay attention to punctuation in poetry. **Ask:** What is the purpose of the exclamation points in the first stanza? *(Possible response: They are meant to express strong feelings.)* Suggest that these exclamation points might also be a way that Bishop shows her wry sense of humor. **Ask:** Why does Bishop use so many dashes in line 39?

(Students may say she uses the dashes to create a picture of how the cans look all lined up. They may also say that it is humorous.)

Do they live in the station?
15 It has a cement porch
behind the pumps, and on it
a set of crushed and grease-
impregnated wickerwork;
on the wicker sofa
20 a dirty dog, quite comfy.

Some comic books provide
the only note of color—
of certain color. They lie
upon a big dim doily[1]
25 draping a taboret[2]
(part of the set), beside
a big hirsute[3] begonia.

Why the **extraneous** plant?
Why the taboret?
30 Why, oh why, the doily?
(Embroidered in daisy stitch
with marguerites, I think,
and heavy with gray crochet.)

Somebody embroidered the doily.
35 Somebody waters the plant,
or oils it, maybe. Somebody
arranges the rows of cans
so that they softly say:
esso—so—so—so
40 to high-strung automobiles.
Somebody loves us all.

---

1. A *doily* is a small, often decorative, napkin.
2. A *taboret* is a seat or stool without arms or back.
3. *Hirsute* means "hairy."

Evaluate Sensory Details *What is significant about the doily's presence?*

Vocabulary

extraneous (ek strā´ nē əs) *adj.* not intrinsically belonging; not forming a vital part; coming from outside

Reading Strategy 2

Evaluate Sensory Details
Answer: *The doily shows a level of care and attention on the part of the family that is incongruous with the dirty station.*

(ADVANCED) **Ask:** How would you describe the author's tone in this line? *(Students may note the wry humor in the line, shown by the repetition in "Why, oh why.")*

(ENGLISH LEARNERS) Explain that the word *doily* refers to a lacy, old-fashioned cover used to protect a small table the way a tablecloth protects a larger one. Have students describe a place where they might expect to see a doily.

To check students' understanding of the selection, see Unit 7 Teaching Resources Book, p. 138.

English Learners

DIFFERENTIATED INSTRUCTION

 Advanced Have small groups of students reread "Filling Station" and list the adjectives that Bishop uses to describe how objects look.

Approaching Level

DIFFERENTIATED INSTRUCTION

Established Reread with students the last stanza of the poem. **Ask:** How is the mood or feeling different in this stanza than in the rest of the poem? *(The mood changes to a more positive and loving one.)* What technique does the poet use to achieve this change? *(The repetition of the word* somebody *changes the mood.)*

After You Read

Assess

1. (a) It is "grunting," "battered and venerable," "homely," and ornamented "like ancient wallpaper." (b) It seems dirty and repulsive; it is speckled with barnacles, infested with sea-lice, and dirty with weeds.

2. (a) Victory (b) The speaker may be inspired by the fish's toughness.

3. (a) A father and his sons (b) Dirty and greasy

4. (a) The dirtiness of the station and the attempts to beautify it may suggest that the family is hard-working but tries to create a homelike feeling. (b) That "somebody loves us all"—that people care for one another no matter what.

5. The detailed descriptions support the statement. Her struggle with the fish is an event, contradicting the statement.

6. (a) The speaker at first seems fascinated by the griminess of the fish, and then adopts a more nuanced view, imagining the insides of the fish. Finally, the speaker sees the fish as an entity in its own right, a survivor. (b) Students' answers will vary.

7. Bishop waits until the end to give the theme; the details take on a richer meaning when considered along with the theme.

8. Students may describe her attitude as curious, attentive, and thoughtful.

9. Bishop's observations reveal her interest in nature, her ability to notice details, and her awe for the immense world around her.

 For additional assessment, see Assessment Resources, pp. 291–292.

After You Read

Respond and Think Critically

Respond and Interpret

1. (a) In "The Fish," what details about the fish are provided in lines 1–21? (b) How would you characterize the fish based on these details? Cite words and phrases from the poem to support your conclusion.

2. (a) In line 66, what does the speaker say fills the boat? (b) What, in your opinion, motivates the speaker to let the fish go? Explain.

3. (a) In "Filling Station," who runs the filling station? (b) In what terms does the speaker describe the station and the people who run it?

4. (a) What details in the poem may provide clues about the lives of the people who run the station? (b) To the speaker, what do these details suggest about people in general? Explain.

Analyze and Evaluate

5. One critic wrote that Bishop focused less on an event than on what she "saw and felt and shared with others." How do these two poems support and contradict this statement? Explain your answer citing details from the poem.

6. (a) In "The Fish," how do the speaker's feelings and ideas about the fish develop over the course of the poem? (b) If you had been in the boat, would you have drawn the same conclusions about the fish that the speaker does? Explain.

7. Why do you think Bishop chose to end "Filling Station" with the sentence in line 41? Explain how this sentence influences the meaning of the poem as a whole.

Connect

8. **Big Idea** **Nature and Technology** On the basis of "The Fish," what attitude would you say that Bishop adopted toward the natural world? Explain your answer.

9. **Connect to the Author** Bishop wanted her poetry to focus on her observations of the natural world rather than on her personal life. Do you think the reader learns anything about Bishop from these poems? Explain.

Literary Element Tone

SAT Skills Practice

1. The first half of "The Fish" creates a tone of
   - (A) disgust.
   - (B) fear.
   - (C) curiosity.
   - (D) admiration.
   - (E) regret.

2. The tone of "Filling Station" is primarily
   - (A) amused.
   - (B) condescending.
   - (C) admiring.
   - (D) indifferent.
   - (E) resentful.

Review: Setting

As you learned on page 602, **setting** is the time and place in which the events of a literary work occur. Setting includes not only physical conditions, but also the ideas and customs of a time and place.

Partner Activity Meet with another classmate to discuss the setting of "Filling Station." Create a web like the one below and use it to list the different elements of the poem's setting. Then discuss what atmosphere, or mood, these details of setting help to create. Share your thoughts with the class.

Literary Element

1. **C** is the correct answer because Bishop initially describes the fish objectively, maintaining her judgmental distance.

2. **A** is the correct answer because of the humorous attitude in the lines "Be careful with that match!" and "Why, oh why, the doily?"

Review: Setting

Elements of the setting include comic books, "a big dim doily," and "a big hirsute begonia." These details create a mood of wonder.

Progress Check

Can students analyze tone?

If No → See Unit 7 Teaching Resources Book, p. 135.

Reading Strategy — Evaluate Sensory Details

Sensory details are images that appeal to the reader's senses of hearing, sight, smell, taste, and touch.

1. Identify an image from each poem that appeals to your sense of sight. Describe what you see.

2. One critic writes that "the more we examine the description of contrast, the more we understand the poetry of Elizabeth Bishop." How does this statement apply to "The Fish" and "Filling Station"? Mention specific sensory details in your response.

Vocabulary Practice

Practice with Context Clues Identify the context clues in the following sentences that help you determine the meaning of each bold-faced vocabulary word.

1. If you incorrectly apply the cleanser, you may **tarnish** the candlestick and do more harm than good.

2. Acid is strong; it can **permeate** almost any container.

3. If you add **extraneous** ingredients to the recipe, the food will taste wrong.

Academic Vocabulary

*In Bishop's poem, the fish bears physical signs of its **prior** encounters with fishermen.*

Prior is an academic word. In more casual conversation, you might tell your parents that **prior** to coming home for curfew, you had gone to a diner with some friends.

To study this word further, fill out the graphic organizer below.

For more on academic vocabulary, see pages 53–54.

Connect to *Science*

Assignment Research one aspect of the science underlying the poem "The Fish." For example, you can explore how a swim bladder functions, learn about sea-lice, or investigate the optics of refraction that cause a rainbow to form in oily water. Then present your findings in a written report.

Get Ideas Generate questions to aid in your investigation. Then make a list of possible sources of information and begin your research. Take notes on what you learn from each source, verifying that the information presented is reliable. Use a variety of sources, both print and online.

Create As you research, create a graphic organizer like the one below to keep track of what you learn.

Fact	Source
The tissues in fish's gills are filled with blood vessels, which makes them look bright red	Encyclopedia Britannica Online, "Fish: The Respiratory System"

Brainstorm a visual aid that will enhance your final report. You could create a chart to clarify ideas from your report or to display data, or you could include photographs or drawings.

Report Summarize and explain the pertinent information you have gathered. Use scientific terms as needed, but explain them in simpler language your classmates will understand. Then add your visual aid, integrating it using word processing software.

 Literature Online

Selection Resources For Selection Quizzes, eFlash-cards, and Reading-Writing Connection activities, go to glencoe.com and enter QuickPass code GLA9800u7.

ELIZABETH BISHOP **1221**

Connect to *Science*

Students' reports should:

- use reliable primary and secondary sources
- include attribution for quotations and factual information
- include a clarifying visual aid

To create custom assessments online, go to Progress Reporter Online Assessment.

Reading Strategy

1. Students' answers will vary but should be based on details in the poems.

2. Students may say that in each poem Bishop develops a contrast between her first perceptions and her later perceptions. They should support their answers with details from the poems.

Vocabulary

1. The sentence implies that *tarnishing* the candlestick will be counterproductive when using a cleanser, so to *tarnish* must be the opposite of "to clean."

2. The sentence implies that a strong acid can move through, or *permeate*, the container.

3. Recipes call for only what is necessary, so if you added *extraneous* ingredients to it, they would be unnecessary.

Academic Vocabulary

Sample answer:

prior

Definition: occurring before a given time or event

Synonyms: before, previous to, earlier

Antonyms: later, following, subsequent

Sentence: Prior to moving to America, Mariel lived in Australia for four years.

Before You Read

Focus

Bellringer Options

**Daily Language Practice
Transparency 106**

Or write the word *sight* on the
board. Have students describe
the classroom in terms only of
what they see. **Ask:** How else
can you describe the room?
One by one, add the words
sound, smell, touch, and *taste,*
encouraging students to come
up with as many descriptions as
possible for each sense.

Literary History ☆

Transcendentalism Ralph
Waldo Emerson (1803–1882) is
the writer most closely identified
with the transcendental movement, which emphasized the
importance of the experiences of
the senses. In his essay *Nature,*
Emerson wrote, "The lover of
nature is he whose inward and
outward senses are still truly
adjusted to each other."

Before You Read

Root Cellar

Meet **Theodore Roethke**
(1908–1963)

A much loved and acclaimed poet during
his lifetime, Theodore Roethke won many
prestigious awards, including the Pulitzer
Prize, the National Book Award, and the
Bollingen Prize. However, many of his poems have
received higher honors than official prizes can
bestow: They have become personal favorites for
many readers, touching their lives deeply.

Roethke fashioned many of his poems from
intense memories of his childhood in Saginaw,
Michigan. His father and grandfather were florists,
and Roethke grew up in a world of flowers, plants,
and large commercial greenhouses. From these
early experiences, he acquired a passionate love
for nature and a deep understanding of natural
processes. Like Emerson and Whitman, he almost
mystically identified with the natural world: "In
my veins, in my bones I feel it." Images of growth
and decay recur in all of his volumes of poetry,
including *Open House* (1941), *The Lost Son and
Other Poems* (1948), *The Waking* (1953), and
Words for the Wind (1958).

> "*For Roethke, boundaries between
> outer and inner dissolve; the natural
> world seems a vast landscape of the
> psyche, just as the voyage inward leads
> to natural things—roots, leaves, and
> flowers—as emblems of the recesses of
> the self.*"
>
> —Mark Doty, from A *Profile of
> Twentieth-Century American Poetry*

Finding His Calling During Roethke's sophomore
year of high school, his father died from lung cancer. This loss devastated him. At seventeen, he
entered the University of Michigan, the first in his
family to attend college. He graduated *magna cum
laude* and after a semester in law school, enrolled
as a graduate student in literature, first at the
University of Michigan and a year later at Harvard.

At Harvard, Roethke handed three of his poems
to Robert Hillyer, a poet and professor. After reading them, Hillyer said, "Any editor who wouldn't
buy these is a fool!" Encouraged by Hillyer,
Roethke submitted the poems to different journals
and dedicated his life to writing poetry.

Poet and Teacher Despite his publishing success,
Roethke could not afford to continue graduate
school in 1931, when the United States was mired
in the Great Depression. He took a position
teaching English at Lafayette College in Easton,
Pennsylvania, and later taught at Michigan State
College, Pennsylvania State University, Bennington College, and the University of Washington.

Roethke brought the same passion to teaching as
to writing poetry. Throughout his adult life, however, he struggled with psychological problems. He
died of a heart attack when he was only fifty-five.

 Literature Online

Author Search For more about Theodore Roethke, go
to glencoe.com and enter QuickPass code GLA9800u7.

Selection Skills

Literary Elements
- Simile (SE pp. 1223, 1225)
- Figurative Language
  (TE p. 1224)

← **Root Cellar** →

Writing Skills/Grammar
- Write a Poem
  (SE p. 1225)

Reading Skills
- Interpret Imagery
  (SE pp. 1223–1225)

Vocabulary Skills
- Synonyms
  (SE pp. 1223, 1225)

Literature and Reading Preview

Connect to the Poem

Which places in nature can you recall in great detail? Make a list of sensory details that describe this place.

Build Background

A root cellar is a dark, moist place where root vegetables, including carrots, beets, and potatoes, are stored for the winter along with potting soil and fertilizers. Root cellars are commonly built into the sides of hills, where the surrounding earth and the dirt floors help keep the temperature inside cool and the humidity high. Even in root cellars, however, produce can spoil. Sometimes, mold forms on the surfaces of plants, causing them to decay. Other times, vegetables stored too long begin to sprout, causing the roots or bulbs to rot.

Set Purposes for Reading

Big Idea Nature and Technology

As you read, ask yourself, What does the speaker suggest about the relationship between humans and nature?

Literary Element Simile

A **simile** is a figure of speech using a word or phrase such as *like* or *as* to compare seemingly unlike things. As you read, ask yourself, What is compared in the similes?

Reading Strategy Interpret Imagery

Interpreting imagery can help you better understand the meaning of a poem and the poet's intention. Imagery refers to any "word pictures" that writers create to evoke emotional responses. Imagery includes sensory details, or descriptions that appeal to one or more of the five senses: sight, hearing, touch, taste, and smell. As you read, ask yourself, To what senses do the images appeal?

Tip: Take Notes Use a chart to record the images in this poem and their sensory appeal.

Details	Sensory appeal
Bulbs broke out of boxes	

Learning Objectives

For pages 1222–1225

In reading this text, you will focus on the following objectives:

Literary Study: Analyzing simile.

Reading: Interpreting imagery.

Vocabulary

mildewed (mil´ dyūd) *adj.* coated or partially coated with a fungus that causes spoilage; p. 1224 *We threw out the books stored in the basement because they were mildewed and damaged.*

congress (kong´ gris) *n.* a formal meeting; p. 1224 *There was a congress of physicists at the convention center.*

rank (rangk) *adj.* having a strong, offensive odor; p. 1224 *The clothing left in the gym lockers was dirty and rank.*

Tip: Synonyms Words that have the same or nearly the same meaning are called synonyms. For example, the words *dank* and *moist* are synonyms. Synonyms are always the same part of speech.

Before You Read

Focus

Summary

In this poem, the speaker describes a root cellar where the bulbs have escaped their containers and have sent out roots in an attempt to grow. He notes with admiration the determined struggle of life, even in a damp, dark cellar filled with rotting plants.

 For summaries in languages other than English, see Unit 7 Teaching Resources Book, pp. 140–145.

Vocabulary

Common and Proper Nouns Tell students that the proper noun *Congress* refers to the governing bodies of the United States. The common noun, *congress,* refers to any group having a formal meeting. Have students write two sentences using the word *mayor* as a common and a proper noun. *(A mayor runs a city. I called Mayor Jones.)*

THEODORE ROETHKE **1223**

Approaching Level

DIFFERENTIATED INSTRUCTION

Emerging Present the following sentences to students:

- The rope was coiled like a snake.
- The rotten food smelled like a swamp.
- The attic was a furnace.
- The clouds danced through the sky.

Say: Which words in these sentences would be called "figurative language"? *(like a snake, like a swamp, was a furnace, clouds danced)* Have students

explain each use. Tell them to start a list with these examples and keep them in mind as they read Roethke's poem. Have them add to the list as they read.

English Learners

DIFFERENTIATED INSTRUCTION

 Beginning List the following words from "Root Cellar" on the board: *cellar, ditch, shoots* (noun), *lolling, tropical, pulpy, planks.* Have students work in pairs to use a dictionary to look up the words and create a two-column chart to list each word and its meaning.

Nature and Technology
Answer: *When root vegetables develop shoots, the vegetables rot and are no longer fit for humans to eat.*

Ask students how vegetables could harm humans.

Reading Strategy | 2

Interpret Imagery **Answer:**
There is a shift from sensory details that appeal mainly to sight to ones that appeal mainly to smell.

[APPROACHING] **Ask:** What are some examples of details that appeal to sight? *("shoots dangled and drooped"; "yellow evil necks")* What are some examples of details that appeal to smell? *("ripe as old bait"; "manure")*

View the Art

Freyda Miller Freyda Miller is a contemporary photographer, painter, and conceptual artist whose "Fruits and Vegetables" series shows how man and nature are connected through shape and form. **Ask:** How would Roethke react to the use of this image with his poem? *(Responses will vary but should indicate how the image captures some description in the poem.)*

 For an audio recording of this selection, use Listening Library Audio CD-ROM.

ROOT CELLAR

Theodore Roethke

In the Beginning. Freyda Miller.

N othing would sleep in that cellar, dank as a ditch,
Bulbs[1] broke out of boxes hunting for chinks[2] in the dark,
Shoots dangled and drooped,
Lolling obscenely from **mildewed** crates,
5   Hung down long yellow evil necks, like tropical snakes.
And what a **congress** of stinks!—
Roots ripe[3] as old bait,
Pulpy stems, **rank**, silo-rich,[4]
Leaf-mold, manure, lime,[5] piled against slippery planks.
10   Nothing would give up life:
Even the dirt kept breathing a small breath.

---

1. *Bulbs,* here, refer to modified, underground stems surrounded by fleshy leaves that serve as the food supply for the growing plant.
2. *Chinks* are narrow openings.
3. *Ripe,* here, means "giving off a very foul odor."
4. A *silo* is a tall, cylindrical structure in which plant materials are stored. The adjective *silo-rich* refers to an odor similar to that emitted by partially fermented plant materials stored in a silo.
5. *Lime,* here, refers to a chemical used as a fertilizer for plants.

Nature and Technology *Why does the speaker describe the necks of the shoots as evil?* **1**

Interpret Imagery *How do the sensory details change with line 6 of the poem?* **2**

Vocabulary

mildewed (mil´ dyūd) *adj.* coated or partially coated with a fungus that causes spoilage
congress (kong´ gris) *n.* a formal meeting
rank (rangk) *adj.* having a strong, offensive odor

Reading Practice

Figurative Language Remind students of these types of figurative language, and have them identify examples of each in the poem:

- Simile: a comparison of two things by means of the word *like* or *as* (Possible answer: "like tropical snakes")
- Metaphor: a comparison of two things without *like* or *as* (Possible answer: "a congress of stinks")
- Personification: attributing human characteristics to animals, objects, or concepts (Possible answer: "the dirt kept breathing a small breath")

Ask: What do these examples of figurative language add to the poem?

After You Read

Respond and Think Critically

Respond and Interpret

1. Which details from this poem surprised you the most? Explain.

2. (a)Which word does the speaker use to describe the root cellar? (b)What does this word usually suggest?

3. (a)What does the speaker observe happening in the root cellar? (b)What do the last two lines of the poem suggest about the speaker's attitude toward what he observes? Explain.

4. What might the root cellar symbolize in the poem?

Analyze and Evaluate

5. (a)What examples of **alliteration**, or the repetition of initial consonant sounds, can you find in this poem? (b)What effects does it have?

6. In this poem Roethke uses **free verse**, with the line length and the meter expanding and contracting as needed. How is the form of the poem appropriate to the subject?

7. Roethke claimed that in some of his early poems, he began "with small things and had tried to make plain words do the trick." To what extent does Roethke's statement apply to the subject and the diction of this poem? Explain.

Connect

8. **Big Idea** **Nature and Technology** What does Roethke suggest about the relationship between humans and nature in this poem?

9. **Connect to the Author** Roethke grew up around nature. Does knowing this give his poem more or less credibility? Explain.

Literary Element Simile

Writers use **similes** to make descriptions more vivid or to explain something unfamiliar by comparing it to something familiar.

1. Identify three similes in the poem.

2. Which simile did you find most vivid and original?

Reading Strategy Interpret Imagery

"Root Cellar" is remarkable for the number and variety of its sensory details. Review the chart you made on page 1223 to note examples.

1. Which sensory details do you think create the most vivid images?

2. What do the sensory details suggest about the root cellar?

LOG ON **Literature** Online

Selection Resources For Selection Quizzes, eFlashcards, and Reading-Writing Connection activities, go to glencoe.com and enter QuickPass code GLA9800u7.

Vocabulary Practice

Practice with Synonyms With a partner, match each boldfaced vocabulary word below with its synonym. Use a thesaurus or dictionary to check your answers.

1. congress
2. mildewed
3. rank

a. putrid
b. announcement
c. caucus
d. fragrant
e. moldy

 Writing

Write a Poem Using the poem "Root Cellar" as a model, write your own poem about a sensory-rich place in nature. Include similes that are natural, yet original, and diction that is clear, direct, and striking.

Reading Strategy

1. Students may identify several images, such as those of the stored bulbs as hunters, the rotten roots smelling like old bait, and the dirt as a breathing animal.

2. The sensory details suggest that the root cellar is throbbing with life forces and primal energy.

Vocabulary

1. c 2. e 3. a

Writing

Students' poems should describe the place in great detail and include similes and proper diction.

After You Read

Assess

1. Students' answers will vary.

2. (a) *Dank* (b) An unpleasant moistness

3. (a) Bulbs bursting through their containers, shoots sprouting through boxes, and dirt "breathing" (b) The speaker admires the power of life in the cellar.

4. The cellar symbolizes the speaker's subconscious—a dark place of growth and decay, primal urges, and an instinct not to give up life.

5. (a) *dank/ditch* (line 1); *bulbs/broke/boxes* (line 2) (b) It creates a musical effect and links words.

6. It suggests the breathing of a living thing.

7. The subjects of this poem, bulbs and shoots, are "small things." Such phrases as "lolling obscenely" and "a congress of stinks" may not seem like "plain words."

8. Nature is outside human control. Nature is also an image of the human psyche, reflecting the energy and turmoil of the hidden self.

9. Students may say that Roethke's experiences around plants gave him the opportunity to observe them first-hand. Others will argue that a poet should be able to imagine any situation regardless of his or her personal experiences.

Literary Element

1. "Dank as a ditch" (line 1); "hung down . . . like tropical snakes" (line 5); "ripe as old bait" (line 7)

2. Possible answer: The comparison of the shoots to snakes is most vivid because of its suggestion of vitality and evil.

Focus

Literary History ☆

The Bell Jar Sylvia Plath's only novel, *The Bell Jar*, was first published in England in 1963 under the pseudonym Victoria Lucas. The novel traces the nervous breakdown and psychiatric treatment of Esther Greenwood, a successful college student spending the summer of 1953 working for a New York magazine.

Before You Read

Sleep in the Mojave Desert and *Crossing the Water*

Meet **Sylvia Plath**
(1932–1963)

Sylvia Plath was only eight when a Boston newspaper published her first poem. In high school, she won literary prizes and excelled academically, earning a scholarship to Smith College. During college, her poetry and prose were published in prestigious national magazines, and she continued to win awards. Sadly, her creative journey was shadowed by bouts of severe depression, during which she struggled with thoughts of death. These struggles ended when Plath took her own life at the age of thirty, a month after her critically acclaimed novel, *The Bell Jar*, was first published. Because much of her writing was so starkly personal, Plath's struggles and death have been closely tied to her image as a poet. However, her dark, beautiful poems speak on their own, fulfilling her ambition to create profound and lasting works.

> *"I think my poems immediately come out of the sensuous and emotional experiences I have, but . . . I believe that one should be able to control and manipulate experiences, even the most terrific."*
>
> —Sylvia Plath
> from a 1962 interview with Peter Orr

Confessions of a Poet Plath was born in Jamaica Plain, Massachusetts. Her father, Otto Plath, was a German immigrant and respected college professor who wrote a renowned study on bees. Her mother, Aurelia, had been one of her father's students at Boston University, where she graduated as valedictorian. Plath's father died when she was just eight, and the loss deeply affected her.

After graduating from Smith, Plath was awarded a Fulbright Fellowship and went to Cambridge, England, for graduate studies in poetry. There, in February 1956, she met an ambitious young British poet, the soon-to-be-famous Ted Hughes. By June they were married, beginning a passionate but turbulent relationship that heavily influenced the poetry of both. They were exploring an emerging type of literature—confessional poetry, which draws heavily on intimate details from the writer's life. After Cambridge, Plath returned to Massachusetts with Hughes and took a writing class with Robert Lowell, a highly regarded poet.

After a short time teaching and writing in the United States, Plath and Hughes moved back to England, where Plath published her first book of poems, *Colossus*, in 1960. During the last years of her life, she wrote at an often feverish pace. Many of these final poems were included in Plath's landmark collection *Ariel*, which was published two years after her death in February 1963. Over the next twenty years, more of Plath's poems would be collected and published by Hughes. Her final book, *The Collected Poems*, was awarded the Pulitzer Prize in 1982.

1226 UNIT 7 INTO THE TWENTY-FIRST CENTURY

Selection Skills

Literary Elements
- Mood (SE pp. 1227, 1229, 1230)
- Figurative Language (SE p. 1230)

Sleep in the Mojave Desert *and* Crossing the Water

Writing Skills/Grammar
- Compare and Contrast Setting (SE p. 1231)

Reading Skills
- Analyze Voice (SE pp. 1227, 1228, 1231)
- Predict (TE p. 1229)

Vocabulary Skills
- Word Origins (SE pp. 1227, 1231)

Listening/Speaking/Viewing Skills
- Oral Interpretation of Literature (TE p. 1228)

Literature and Reading Preview

Connect to the Poem

Have you ever been in a place that you thought reflected how you felt? Freewrite for a few minutes about this place and describe what made it significant for you.

Build Background

The poems "Crossing the Water" and "Sleep in the Mojave Desert" were among the dozens that Plath wrote as she struggled with her deepening depression. Although they do not include specific personal details, these are considered confessional poems because they explore Plath's emotions.

Set Purposes for Reading

Big Idea Nature and Technology

As you read, ask yourself, How is the speaker in these poems an outsider within the natural setting?

Literary Element Mood

Mood refers to the emotional quality, or atmosphere, of a literary work. The language, pace, and imagery combine to convey the mood of a poem. As you read, ask yourself, What is the mood of each poem?

Reading Strategy Analyze Voice

Voice is the personality that a writer conveys in a piece of writing. The reader can **analyze** voice by examining a poet's choice of words and the **tone,** or attitude toward the subject matter, that a poem expresses. As you read, ask yourself, What kind of language does the poet use?

Tip: Describe Voice Describe each element of voice in a chart like the one below. Consider what these elements contribute to the poem's overall voice and write a description of that voice.

Element	Description
Word choice	
Tone	
Voice	

Learning Objectives

For pages 1226–1231

In studying these texts, you will focus on the following objectives:

Literary Study: Analyzing mood.

Reading: Analyzing voice.

Vocabulary

recede (ri sēd´) *v.* to move back or away from a limit, point, or mark; p. 1228 *After the storm passed, we could see the floodwater recede.*

swelter (swel´ tər) *v.* to suffer from oppressive heat; p. 1228 *The crowd will swelter under the sun.*

congregate (kong´ gri gāt´) *v.* to bring or come together in a group, a crowd, or an assembly; p. 1228 *The team will congregate in the dugout.*

valedictory (val´ ə dik´ tə rē) *adj.* of or relating to an occasion or expression of farewell; p. 1229 *In his valedictory address, he bade farewell.*

Tip: Word Origins Word origins, also called **etymologies,** are the history and development of words. They are often found in dictionary entries. If you know that the word "swelter" comes from an Old English word related to death, you can understand how oppressive and stifling it might feel to swelter in the heat.

SYLVIA PLATH **1227**

English Learners

DIFFERENTIATED INSTRUCTION

Intermediate Emphasize that *mood* refers to the emotional quality of the selection. Some words may make them feel happy, sad, or angry. *Tone* refers to the author's feelings toward the subject matter or the audience. Display the following: "You're a big help." **Ask:** How can you say this sentence in different ways to convey different tones? How would each make you feel? *(can be either a true* *compliment or a sarcastic remark; could feel happy or angry)* Explain that authors and poets use language and punctuation to convey how we use the tone of our voices.

Before You Read

Focus

Summary

"Sleep in the Mojave Desert" presents a dark, even hostile, relationship between a desert landscape and humanity. In "Crossing the Water," the speaker and a companion are enveloped by blackness as they row on a lake.

 For summaries in languages other than English, see Unit 7 Teaching Resources Book, pp. 151–156.

Vocabulary

Latin Roots and Prefixes

Tell students that the words *recede, congregate,* and *valedictory* all derive from Latin roots and prefixes. Display the following: *re- + cede; con- + gregate; vale + dictory.* **Ask:** Based on the definitions in the vocabulary list and your own knowledge, what do you think each prefix or root means? *(re-, again; cede, withdraw; con-, with; gregate, collect into a group; vale, farewell; dictory, to say)* Have students list other words that use the prefixes *re-* and *con-.*

 For additional vocabulary practice, see Unit 7 Teaching Resources Book, p. 159.

Teach

Reading Strategy 1

Analyze Voice Answer:
Students may say that the author's voice is defined by the first-person point of view, the matter-of-fact tone, and the use of repetition.

For additional practice using the reading skill or strategy, see Unit 7 Teaching Resources Book, p. 158.

Big Idea 2

Nature and Technology
Answer: *Students may say that the dozing animals represent nature's indifference to the speaker's plight.*

View the Art ★

This painting is by Georgia O'Keeffe (1887–1986), well known for her New Mexico landscapes and her close-up views of flowers. **Ask:** Do you think O'Keeffe's painting reflects the mood of Plath's poem? (*Possible answers: The painting is more colorful than Plath's desert; the tone of the painting seems more cheerful than that of the poem.*)

Sleep in the Mojave Desert

Sylvia Plath

Lavender Hill with Green, 1952. Georgia O'Keeffe. Oil on canvas. 12 x 27 ⅛ in. Gift of the Burnett Foundation and The Georgia O'Keeffe Foundation. The Georgia O'Keeffe Museum, Santa Fe, NM. ©ARS, NY. ★

Vocabulary

recede (ri sēd´) *v.* to move back or away from a limit, point, or mark
swelter (swel´ tər) *v.* to suffer from oppressive heat
congregate (kong´ gri gāt´) *v.* to bring or come together in a group, a crowd, or an assembly

Out here[1] there are no hearthstones,[2]
Hot grains, simply. It is dry, dry.
And the air dangerous. Noonday acts queerly
On the mind's eye, erecting a line
5 Of poplars[3] in the middle distance, the only
Object beside the mad, straight road
One can remember men and houses by.
A cool wind should inhabit those leaves
And a dew collect on them, dearer than money,
10 In the blue hour before sunup.
Yet they **recede**, untouchable as tomorrow,
Or those glittery fictions of spilt water
That glide ahead of the very thirsty.

I think of the lizards airing their tongues
15 In the crevice of an extremely small shadow
And the toad guarding his heart's droplet.
The desert is white as a blind man's eye,
Comfortless as salt. Snake and bird
Doze behind the old masks of fury.
20 We **swelter** like firedogs[4] in the wind.
The sun puts its cinder out. Where we lie
The heat-cracked crickets **congregate**
In their black armorplate and cry.
The day-moon lights up like a sorry mother,
25 And the crickets come creeping into our hair
To fiddle the short night away.

1. In saying *Out here,* Plath refers to the Mojave Desert, an arid region of southeastern California and parts of Arizona, Nevada, and Utah. Once part of an ancient inland sea, the desert was formed by volcanic action and materials deposited by the Colorado River.
2. *Hearthstones* are stones used to create the floor of a fireplace; the word also conveys the sense of family life.
3. *Poplars* are fast-growing deciduous trees (trees that lose their leaves seasonally).
4. *Firedogs,* or *andirons,* are a pair of metal supports that hold logs in a fireplace.

Analyze Voice *How does this passage help define the author's voice?* **1**

Nature and Technology *How does this sentence reflect the role of nature in this poem?* **2**

1228 UNIT 7 INTO THE TWENTY-FIRST CENTURY

Listening and Speaking Practice

SMALL GROUP
Oral Interpretation of Literature Have groups of students analyze the poem. Encourage them to explore how the speaker's tone might be conveyed in an oral presentation of the poem. Then have each group choose a volunteer to present a dramatic reading of the poem, using the group's interpretation of tone and meaning to guide his or her emphasis, inflection, and speed of reading. Have students compare and contrast the readings.

Crossing the Water

Sylvia Plath

River and Trees. Dider Dorval.

Black lake, black boat, two black, cut-paper people.
Where do the black trees go that drink here?
Their shadows must cover Canada.

A little light is filtering from the water flowers.
Their leaves do not wish us to hurry:
They are round and flat and full of dark advice.

Cold worlds shake from the oar.
The spirit of blackness is in us, it is in the fishes.
A snag[1] is lifting a **valedictory,** pale hand;

Stars open among the lilies.
Are you not blinded by such expressionless sirens?[2]
This is the silence of astounded souls.

---

1. A *snag* is a tree or tree branch embedded in water that prevents navigation.
2. In Greek mythology, *Sirens* were half-bird, half-woman sea creatures whose sweet singing lured mariners to destruction on the rocks that surrounded their island.

Mood *What technique does Plath use in the opening lines to create mood?* **4**

Vocabulary

valedictory (val´ ə dik´ tə rē) *adj.* of or relating to an occasion or expression of farewell

SYLVIA PLATH **1229**

Reading Strategy | 3

Predict Have a student read the first stanza aloud. **Ask:** On the basis of this stanza, what mood do you think the rest of the poem will have? (*Students may say that the dark imagery in the opening stanza foreshadows a serious or dark mood.*)

Literary Element | 4

Mood Answer: *She uses repetition of the word* black.

APPROACHING Remind students that analyzing a poet's word choice can help them understand what mood the poet is trying to create in a poem. Have students make a list of words and phrases that they feel contribute to the dark and serious mood of the poem. (*"dark advice," "cold worlds," "spirit of blackness"*)

Approaching Level

DIFFERENTIATED INSTRUCTION

Established Discuss with students that although the overall mood of "Crossing the Water" might be considered dark and sad, there are some images that could be considered lighter and happier. **Ask:** Which images in this poem lighten the mood? (*"A little light is filtering from the water flowers."; "Their leaves do not wish us to hurry"; "Stars open among the lilies."*)

Emerging Remind students that personification is when a writer gives an animal, plant, or object human characteristics. In "Crossing the Water," Plath uses personification to enhance the onimous mood of the poem. Ask students to list some lines where the poet uses personification. (*"Where do the black trees go that drink here?"; "Their leaves do not wish us to hurry"; "A snag is lifting a valedictory, pale hand"*)

Assess

1. (a) A mirage (b) It represents an elusive desire.

2. (a) The line describes drops of water falling from the oar as it leaves the water. (b) The image might convey that the speaker is shaking off past sadness or pain.

3. The poet focuses on small images, such as the lizard tongues in the small shadow and the droplet of blood in the toad's heart.

4. The sun sinks, the moon rises, and black crickets surround the speaker, actually invading her hair.

5. The poet presents a line of description, a line that is a question, and a line that is a statement. The first and last stanza sharing the same structure gives the poem a circularity and feeling of timelessness.

6. Most students will say that nature seems more sympathetic to the speaker in "Crossing the Water" than in "Sleep in the Mojave Desert." In the latter poem, nature is indifferent—perhaps even hostile—to the speaker.

7. Students may argue that when someone is depressed they perceive everything as bleak, while others may say that connecting to nature might be a way to heal a person's emotions.

Progress Check

Can students analyze mood?

If No → See Unit 7 Teaching Resources Book, p. 157.

Respond and Think Critically

Respond and Interpret

1. (a)In "Sleep in the Mojave Desert," to what common desert illusion do the lines "Or those glittery fictions of spilt water / That glide ahead of the very thirsty" refer? (b)What does the image represent in the poem?

2. (a)In "Crossing the Water," what concrete image does the line "Cold worlds shake from the oar" conjure up? (b)What does the line convey about the speaker's emotions?

Analyze and Evaluate

3. In lines 14–16 of "Sleep in the Mojave Desert," the poem seems to "zoom in" to provide close-up views of images. How does the poet achieve this effect, and what images does she use to suggest it?

4. In the last six lines of "Sleep in the Mojave Desert," how does the poet create the effect of darkness that is closing in?

5. The first and last stanzas in "Crossing the Water" connect the beginning and the end of the poem by sharing the same structure. Why do you think the poet chose to do this?

Connect

6. **Big Idea** **Nature and Technology** The speaker relates to nature differently in each of these poems. Compare the relationship between the speaker and nature in these poems.

7. **Connect to Today** Do you think that people today can connect with the dark side of nature when they feel down? Explain.

Literary Element **Mood**

Mood is a broad term that encompasses the overall impression created by a poem. Specific elements—such as language, subject matter, tone, setting, rhyme and rhythm—can all contribute to the mood. Because mood influences the poem as a whole, it can affect the way that images and events are portrayed or perceived. Mood is like a filter through which the poem is seen.

1. Identify the language, in the first three lines of "Sleep in the Mojave Desert," that helps establish the mood. What mood does this language create?

2. How does the setting in "Sleep in the Mojave Desert" contribute to the mood of the poem?

3. What is the overall mood of "Crossing the Water"? How does it affect the way you interpret the last line?

Review: Figurative Language

Figurative language is language used for descriptive effect, in order to convey ideas or emotions. Figurative expressions are not literally true, but they express some truth beyond the literal level.

Partner Activity With a partner, identify three or more examples of strong figurative language in the poems. Discuss how the language is used and analyze it together by determining (a)what it is describing within the poem and (b)what idea or emotion it is conveying. Record your analysis in a chart like the one below.

Figurative Language	What It Describes	Idea or Emotion That It Conveys

Literary Element

1. "Hot," "dry, dry," and "dangerous" create a mood of desperation.

2. The desert is oppressive; it is a setting that conveys emptiness and isolation.

3. The mood is dark and sad. The phrase "silence of astounded souls" takes on an emptiness instead of any feeling of profound discovery.

Review: Figurative Language

Figurative Language—"glittery fictions of spilt water"

What It Describes—desert mirages

Idea That It Conveys—the false hopes of an empty life

Reading Strategy   Analyze Voice

SAT Skills Practice

1. The voice shared by Plath's two poems exhibits:

   I. gentleness.

   II. sadness.

   III. detachment.

  (A) I only

  (B) III only

  (C) I and II only

  (D) I, II, and III

  (E) II only

Vocabulary Practice

Practice with Word Origins Create a word map like the one below for each vocabulary word from the selection. Use a dictionary for help.

recede   swelter   congregate   valedictory

Academic Vocabulary

Plath was a confessional poet, so **aspects** *of her poems draw on her personal experiences.*

Aspects is an academic word. More familiar words that are similar in meaning are *traits, characteristics, parts,* and *features.*

Using context clues, try to figure out the meaning of *aspects* in each sentence and explain the difference between the two meanings:

1. Before she spoke, I could tell by my aunt's sour **aspect** that I had made a grievous error.

2. Having examined all **aspects** of the situation, Gina decided that we should follow the map.

Speaking and Listening

 Literature Groups

Assignment In a small group, compare and contrast the settings in these two poems. Discuss the elements that create each setting, differences and similarities between the settings, and how setting is used in each poem (for example, to create mood or atmosphere). Conclude by evaluating how effectively Plath uses setting. Do you find one poem more powerful than the other? Why or why not?

Prepare Before your discussion, create a Venn diagram like the one below. In the left oval, list elements from the setting of "Sleep in the Mojave Desert." In the right oval, list elements from "Crossing the Water." In the center section, list elements that the two poems share.

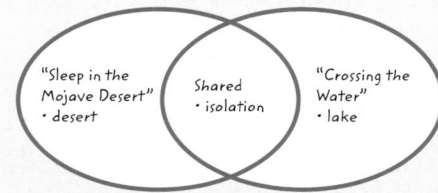

Discuss As you discuss your conclusions and share your diagrams, listen actively to your group members' opinions. Ask follow-up questions to help clarify their views. Support your own opinions with evidence from the poems.

Report Take notes on your classmates' opinions and supporting evidence. Then choose one person to present an informal but effective summary of your group's discussion to the whole class.

Evaluate Write one paragraph assessing your participation and another evaluating your group as a whole.

LOG ON ▶ **Literature** Online

Selection Resources For Selection Quizzes, eFlashcards, and Reading-Writing Connection activities, go to glencoe.com and enter QuickPass code GLA9800u7.

SYLVIA PLATH   **1231**

After You Read

Assess

Reading Strategy

1. D is the correct answer because the voice of Plath's poems, while melancholy and detached, is also gentle.

Vocabulary

recede

Definition: to move back or away from a limit; Etymology: Latin *cedere* means "to go"; Sample sentence: When the water began to recede, we knew that the pump was working.

swelter

Definition: to suffer from oppressive heat; Etymology: Old English *sweltan* means "to die"; Sample sentence: Even though we sat in the shade, we still sweltered at the baseball game.

congregate

Definition: to gather in a group; Etymology: Latin *gregare* means "to gather"; Sample sentence: The Spanish club congregates once a week for *tapas* and conversation.

valedictory

Definition: of or relating to an occasion or expression of farewell; Etymology: Latin *valere,* "to be well," and *dicere,* "to say"; Sample sentence: We had a valedictory party because an employee was leaving.

Speaking and Listening

Use these criteria to evaluate students' participation in the literature group:

- Did the student compare and contrast the settings in the two poems?
- Did the student express carefully thought-out opinions based on evidence from the poems?
- Did the student listen attentively to the opinions of others?

Academic Vocabulary

1. The speaker can tell just by looking that his or her aunt is upset, so here *aspect* means "a facial expression."

2. Ginas has considered the problem from every angle, so here *aspects* means "the factors to be considered."

Before You Read

Focus

Bellringer Options

Daily Language Practice Transparency 108

Or ask: Do you think it is justifiable to develop woods or parkland into homes or shopping centers? Why or why not?

Have students debate the relative importance of development and nature. Apply the discussion to your hometown. Ask if students have noticed trees being cut down to make room for new buildings. Do they feel this action is good or bad?

Literary History ☆

Poet Laureate The Librarian of Congress has appointed the Poet Laureate Consultant in Poetry annually since 1936. His or her role is to increase Americans' appreciation of poetry. Among past U.S. Poet Laureates are Robert Lowell, Elizabeth Bishop, Robert Frost, and Billy Collins.

Before You Read

The War Against the Trees

Meet **Stanley Kunitz**
(1905–2006)

Stanley Kunitz's earlier work displays great wit and defiance; his later poems often express a passionate search for meaning and identity. One of the finest expressions of that quest is found in his poem "The Layers":

> I have walked through many lives,
> some of them my own,
> and I am not who I was,
> though some principle of being
> abides, from which I struggle
> not to stray.

☆ Kunitz, twice U.S. Poet Laureate, won several literary awards, including a Pulitzer Prize for *Selected Poems: 1928–1958* and a National Book Award for *Passing Through: The Later Poems, New and Selected*. In 1993, President Clinton awarded Kunitz the National Medal of the Arts.

Early Years Born in Worcester, Massachusetts, Kunitz studied at Harvard, graduating *summa cum laude* in 1926 and earning a master's degree in 1927. "I felt very isolated as a young person," he stated. "I didn't know another soul with whom I could share my interests. Eventually, after my Harvard years, I gravitated to New York, the magnet city of the arts, where I found an editorial job and began to send out my poems . . . but I was too busy and too shy to make friends easily, so I still felt like an outsider." In poetry, Kunitz found an outlet for his loneliness and a way to explore his "hidden self."

Poet and Teacher *Intellectual Things*, his first book of poetry, was published in 1930, when he was only twenty-five. Fourteen years later, *Passport to War* was published. After serving in World War II, Kunitz accepted a teaching position at Bennington College, where he joined fellow poet Theodore Roethke. Eventually, Kunitz taught at

several other esteemed schools, including Yale, Princeton, Rutgers, and the New School for Social Research. He also served as poet-in-residence at the University of Washington, Queens College, Brandeis University, and Princeton and taught at Columbia University in the graduate writing program, which he helped found. To encourage and develop young writers, Kunitz founded the Fine Arts Work Center in Provincetown, Massachusetts, and Poets House in New York City.

Mentor Kunitz always enjoyed mentoring and encouraging young people interested in the arts. In 1984 the National Endowment for the Arts awarded him a Senior Fellowship "for his inordinate generosity in working with younger writers." Kunitz often responded to such accolades with characteristic wit: "As for my companionship with younger poets, I feel that I'm the one who's blessed in that relationship."

In addition to his poetry and literary criticism, Kunitz translated Russian poems by Yevtushenko, Stolzenberg, Akhmatova, and others into English and edited volumes of poetry by British poets William Blake and John Keats. Kunitz was considered one of the most gifted and influential writers of the modern era.

 Literature Online

Author Search For more about Stanley Kunitz, go to glencoe.com and enter QuickPass code GLA9800u7.

1232 UNIT 7   INTO THE TWENTY-FIRST CENTURY

Selection Skills

Literary Elements
- Personification (SE pp. 1233–1235)
- Slant Rhymes (TE p. 1234)

The War Against the Trees

Writing Skills/Grammar
- Dialogue (SE p. 1235)

Reading Skills
- Evaluate Figures of Speech (SE pp. 1233–1235)

Vocabulary Skills
- Analogies (SE p. 1233, 1235)

Literature and Reading Preview

Connect to the Poem
Which is more important to you: natural landscape or new development? In a small group, debate this question. Consider both economic and environmental issues.

Build Background
After World War II, the United States enjoyed a booming economy. Cities spread out, and suburbs sprang up. Land was cleared to make way for factories, housing developments, shopping malls, and schools. The national mood was optimistic, and growth and development were regarded as signs of the triumph of technology. Swept along in the march of progress, the public often condoned the destruction of natural landscapes.

Set Purposes for Reading

Big Idea Nature and Technology

As you read, ask yourself, How does Kunitz depict the conflict between nature and technology?

Literary Element Personification

Personification is a figure of speech in which an animal, an object, a force of nature, or an idea is given human characteristics. As you read, ask, How does Kunitz use personification?

Reading Strategy Evaluate Figures of Speech

A **figure of speech** is a specific kind of figurative language. Poets use figures of speech for descriptive effects and to convey ideas or emotions. In this poem, Kunitz often uses **metaphor**, a figure of speech that equates two unlike things. As you read, ask yourself, How does each metaphor affect the poem?

Tip: Chart Figurative Language Use a chart to list metaphors and the effect of the comparison.

Metaphor	Things Compared	Effect
"the bulldozers . . . overthrowing first the privet-row."	the bulldozers and an attacking army	

Learning Objectives

For pages 1232–1235

In studying this text, you will focus on the following objectives:

Literary Study: Analyzing personification.

Reading: Evaluating figures of speech.

Vocabulary

lopped (lopt) *v.* trimmed or chopped off, as the branches of a tree; p. 1234 *With its branches lopped off, the tree looked stubby and bare.*

subverting (səb vurt´ ing) *v.* overthrowing and destroying; p. 1234 *The people were intent on subverting the dictator and replacing him with a merciful ruler.*

rampages (ram´ pāj´ iz) *v.* rushes wildly about; scurries; p. 1234 *The hungry squirrel rampages from tree to tree, searching for acorns.*

grievous (grē´ vəs) *adj.* causing or characterized by grief; extremely sad; p. 1234 *The memorial service was a grievous occasion for both family and friends.*

Tip: Analogies Comparisons based on relationships between words are known as **analogies**. For example, in the analogy *lopped : attached :: weak : strong,* each pair of words is opposite in meaning. To complete an analogy, decide on the relationship represented by the first pair of words. Then apply that relationship to the second set of words.

STANLEY KUNITZ **1233**

Before You Read

Focus

Summary
In this poem, the speaker describes the destruction of a lot bought by an oil company. As the neighbors gather to watch, the bulldozers tear up hedges, flowers, and century-old elm trees. The speaker reminisces about the children who once played there.

Vocabulary

Shades of Meaning
Review with students that although synonyms are words with similiar meanings, they can signal different tones or moods. Have students use a thesaurus and look up three synonyms for each verb in the vocabulary list. Have them work in small groups and decide how the tone or mood of the poem might change if the different synonyms were used in the poem instead.

(APPROACHING) Help approaching level students with this exercise by showing them examples of synonyms whose connotations are very different from that of the vocabulary word. *(pruned or trimmed vs. lopped; ruining or damaging vs. subverting; scurries or hurries vs. rampages)*

English Learners
DIFFERENTIATED INSTRUCTION

Intermediate English learners will more easily understand the poem if they are fully familiar with the language of war. Preteach the following words in the context in which they are used in the poem: *overthrowing, forays, raids, maimed, charged, hacking, craters, amputated.* Have students create a two-column chart with the headings *Words* and *Meanings.* Direct them to consult a dictionary and find the appropriate meaning of each word in this context to include in their charts.

Advanced Learners
DIFFERENTIATED INSTRUCTION

Viewpoint "The War Against the Trees" presents a view of life and nature. Have students write a paragraph stating these views using details from the poem to support their ideas.

Teach

Reading Strategy   1

Evaluate Figures of Speech

Answer: *The trees have lived on the land longer than any of the people in the town. Like old men, they are both dignified and frail.*

[ENGLISH LEARNERS] Remind English learners that a metaphor is a figure of speech and that the poet is not saying that the trees are actually "great-grandfathers of the town."

Ask: What other metaphors does the poet use to describe trees in this poem? *(giants, gorgons)*

Literary Element   2

Personification   Answer:

They are the bulldozers attacking the trees and are described as charging, like soldiers charging enemies in battle.

Big Idea   3

Nature and Technology

Answer: *It suggests that technology is more powerful than nature.*

Progress Check

Can students analyze personification?

If No → See Unit 7 Teaching Resources Book, p. 169.

The War Against the Trees

Stanley Kunitz

The man who sold his lawn to standard oil[1]
Joked with his neighbors come to watch the show
While the bulldozers, drunk with gasoline,
Tested the virtue of the soil
5 Under the branchy sky
By overthrowing first the privet-row.[2]

Forsythia-forays and hydrangea-raids
Were but preliminaries to a war
Against the great-grandfathers of the town,
10 So freshly **lopped** and maimed.
They struck and struck again,
And with each elm a century went down.[3]

All day the hireling engines charged the trees,
Subverting them by hacking underground
15 In grub-dominions, where dark summer's mole[4]
Rampages through his halls,
Till a northern seizure shook
Those crowns,[5] forcing the giants to their knees.

I saw the ghosts of children at their games
20 Racing beyond their childhood in the shade,
And while the green world turned its death-foxed page
And a red wagon wheeled,
I watched them disappear
Into the suburbs of their **grievous** age.

25 Ripped from the craters much too big for hearts
The club-roots bared their amputated coils,
Raw gorgons[6] matted blind, whose pocks and scars
Cried Moon! on a corner lot
One witness-moment, caught
30 In the rear-view mirrors of the passing cars.

---

1. An oil company has bought the land.
2. A *privet-row* is a row of bushes.
3. Elm trees grow very tall and, if they survive such onslaughts as Dutch Elm Disease, can live for more than a hundred years.
4. Both *grubs* and *moles* live underground. Grubs are the wormlike larvae of beetles, and moles are burrowing rodents.
5. *Crowns* refers to the top branches of the trees.
6. In Greek mythology, the *Gorgons* were three monstrous sisters with coiled snakes for hair.

1   Evaluate Figures of Speech *Why does the poet include this metaphor?*

2   Personification *What are "the hireling engines," and what human qualities does the poet give them?*

Nature and Technology *What does this line suggest about the conflict between technology and nature?*   **3**

Vocabulary

lopped (lopt) *v.* trimmed or chopped off, as the branches of a tree

subverting (səb vurt´ ing) *v.* overthrowing and destroying

rampages (ram´ pāj´ iz) *v.* rushes wildly about; scurries

grievous (grē´ vəs) *adj.* causing or characterized by grief; extremely sad

Reading Practice

Slant Rhyme Remind students that slant rhyme refers to the words at the ends of lines of poetry that almost—but do not quite—rhyme (like *hearts* and *scars*). Have students identify full rhymes and slant rhymes in this poem. *(Possible answers: full rhymes—oil/soil; show/row; slant rhymes—raids/maimed; games/shade/page)* **Ask:** Is there a regular rhyme scheme? *(No)* How do the irregular rhymes affect the poem's message? *(The irregular rhymes appear to "pop up" at the reader, like the roots sticking out of the bulldozed lot.*

After You Read

Respond and Think Critically

Respond and Interpret

1. (a)Why is the land being cleared of trees? (b)Why have the neighbors "come to watch the show"?

2. (a)What are the "preliminaries" to the "war against the trees"? (b)Why does the speaker describe the bulldozers as "drunk with gasoline"?

3. (a)How do the bulldozers attack the trees? (b)Why does this action eventually topple them?

4. (a)What scene does the speaker imagine as the trees are coming down? (b)What message does the speaker convey through this scene? Explain.

Analyze and Evaluate

5. (a)After the trees have fallen, why does the speaker compare the land to the moon's surface? (b)Is this comparison effective or not? Explain.

6. (a)In the last two lines of the poem, what does the speaker suggest about the motorists driving by? (b)Does this image provide an effective ending to the poem? Explain why or why not.

Connect

7. **Big Idea** **Nature and Technology** Which people might conclude that they have won this "war"? Which people might conclude that they have lost it?

8. **Connect to Today** How might this poem be used to share a pro-environment message today? Explain.

Literary Element Personification

Poets often use **personification** to give ordinary, lifeless objects human characteristics such as personality, dignity, motive, and force.

1. How are the trees and bulldozers personified? What do these personifications suggest?

2. Why does the speaker personify the roots as Gorgons?

Reading Strategy Evaluate Figures of Speech

Occasionally, writers use an **extended metaphor**, or one that develops beyond a single line. What extended metaphor is used in "The War Against the Trees"? How effective do you think it is?

LOG ON **Literature** Online

Selection Resources For Selection Quizzes, eFlashcards, and Reading-Writing Connection activities, go to glencoe.com and enter QuickPass code GLA9800u7.

Vocabulary Practice

Practice with Analogies Choose the word pair that best completes each analogy

1. grievous : loss ::
  a. slight : prediction
  b. glorious : victory
  c. humble : award
  d. shameful : honor

2. lopped : cut ::
  a. ignited : extinguished
  b. gazed : looked
  c. climbed : descended
  d. succeeded : failed

Writing

Write a Dialogue While Kunitz does not give a voice to the people watching the bulldozers, he does imply several things about their character. Write a dialogue between some of the spectators. Use Kunitz's descriptions as a starting place for their conversation, tone, attitudes, and mannerisms.

Writing

Use the following criteria to evaluate students' writing:

- Is the writing in the form of a dialogue between two or more characters?
- Does the dialogue help to create the characters' individual personalities?

Reading Strategy

The extended metaphor is that of a relentless army (the bulldozers) attacking defenseless old men (the trees); it is very effective.

Vocabulary

1. b **2.** b

After You Read

Assess

1. (a) So the oil company can construct a gas station (b) The arrival of the bulldozers has stirred curiosity.

2. (a) Uprooting of bushes (b) They have been filled with gas to prepare for work.

3. (a) Dig away the earth around the roots (b) When the trees are no longer anchored to the ground, they fall.

4. (a) Children playing in the shade (b) The speaker likens the children's disappearance to the destruction of the trees.

5. (a) The land is bare and pocked with holes, like the cratered surface of the moon. (b) Yes; it suggests the terrible damage done to the land.

6. (a) They notice the destruction only for an instant. (b) Yes; it emphasizes people's indifference to the destruction of nature; the motorists' demand for gasoline indirectly led to the trees' demise.

7. The oil company, the man who sold the land, and people who equate development with progress have won. People who value natural beauty over progress have lost.

8. Kunitz's descriptions of the destruction of the trees is powerful and could be used to make people reconsider development that destroys nature.

Literary Element

1. The trees are personified as elderly, gigantic great-grandfathers; the bulldozers, as warriors bent on destruction. The speaker is on the side of the trees.

2. The roots are coiled and snaky, like the Gorgons' hair.

Scientific Perspective
on *The War Against the Trees*

Focus

Summary

This excerpt from *Silent Spring* begins with a fable of a beautiful rural town where, one spring, the animals, insects, plants, and people become ill, and many die. Carson then tells the reader that the people themselves caused the destruction through crop dusting.

Teach

For an audio recording of this selection, use Listening Library Audio CD-ROM.

Readability Scores

Dale-Chall: 7.4
DRP: 62
Lexile: 1150

For activities related to this selection, see Unit 7 Teaching Resources Book, pp. 175–183.

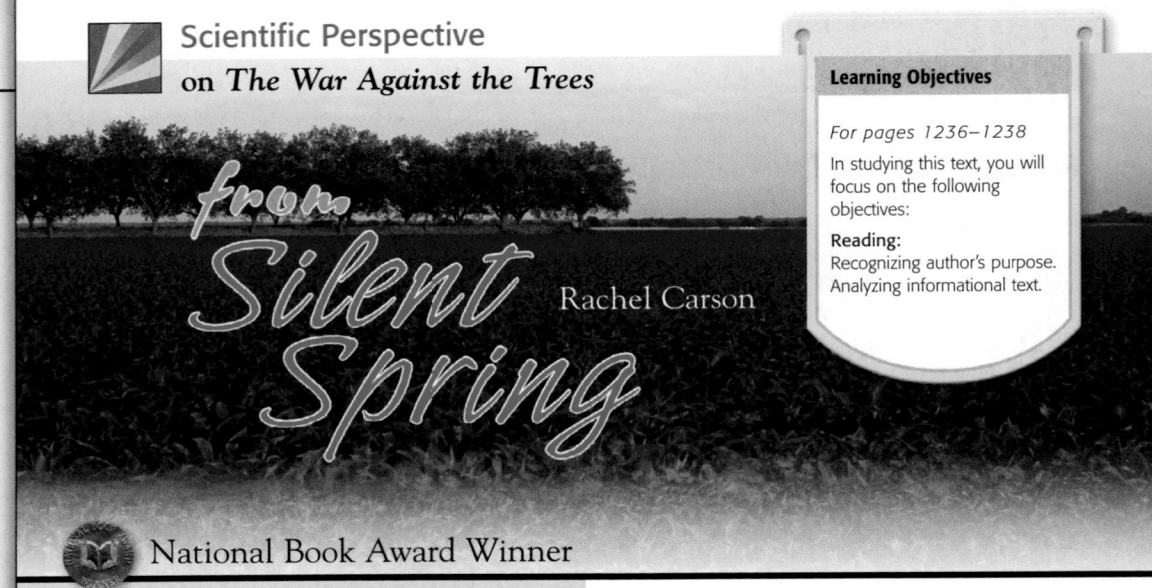
Scientific Perspective
on *The War Against the Trees*

from
Silent Spring
Rachel Carson

National Book Award Winner

Set a Purpose for Reading
Read to discover Carson's persuasive dramatization of the dangers that chemicals pose to the environment.

Build Background
In 1962, scientist and author Rachel Carson published *Silent Spring* in an effort to warn the public about the serious environmental risks of such pesticides as DDT. Immediately, the chemical industry, agricultural organizations, and many government officials questioned the validity of the book's findings. However, scientific studies ordered by President John F. Kennedy found evidence to support Carson's research. These studies led to new legislation that banned or limited pesticide use.

Reading Strategy

Recognize Author's Purpose
To determine an **author's purpose**, carefully analyze such elements as the tone, structure, and content. As you read, ask yourself, Why does Carson begin *Silent Spring* with a tale about a town destroyed by chemicals?

1236 UNIT 7

There was once a town in the heart of America where all life seemed to live in harmony with its surroundings. The town lay in the midst of a checkerboard[1] of prosperous farms, with fields of grain and hillsides of orchards where, in spring, white clouds of bloom drifted above the green fields. In autumn, oak and maple and birch set up a blaze of color that flamed and flickered across a backdrop of pines. Then foxes barked in the hills and deer silently crossed the fields, half hidden in the mists of the fall mornings.

Along the roads, laurel, viburnum and alder,[2] great ferns and wildflowers delighted the traveler's eye through much of the year. Even in winter the roadsides were places of beauty, where countless birds came to feed on the berries and on the seed heads of the dried weeds rising above the snow. The countryside was, in fact, famous for the abundance and variety of

1

---

1. The farmland looks somewhat like a *checkerboard* because each square field, planted with different crops, is slightly different in color and texture.
2. *Laurel* refers to the flowering shrub mountain laurel; *viburnum* is the scientific name for the fragrant honeysuckle bush; *alder* is the name of trees in the birch family.

Writing Practice

Take Notes Tell students to reread this selection and identify the main idea and details, the author's tone and purpose for writing, the rhetorical devices the author uses, and unfamiliar words whose meanings they may need to investigate. Write the headings "Main Idea and Supporting Details," "Tone," "Author's Purpose," "Rhetorical Devices," and "Unfamiliar Words" on the board, and have students copy them onto sheets of paper to guide their note taking as they reread.

First Public Test of Insecticide Machine. Beachgoers are sprayed with DDT as a new machine for distributing the insecticide is tested for the first time. 1945.

its bird life, and when the flood of migrants[3] was pouring through in spring and fall people traveled from great distances to observe them. Others came to fish the streams, which flowed clear and cold out of the hills and contained shady pools where trout lay. So it had been from the days many years ago when the first settlers raised their houses, sank their wells, and built their barns.

Then a strange blight[4] crept over the area and everything began to change. Some evil spell had settled on the community: mysterious maladies[5] swept the flocks of chickens; the cattle and sheep sickened and died. Everywhere was a shadow of death. The farmers spoke of much illness among their families. In the town the doctors had become more and more puzzled by new kinds of sickness appearing among their patients. There had been several sudden and unexplained deaths, not only among adults but even among children, who would be stricken suddenly while at play and die within a few hours.

There was a strange stillness. The birds, for example—where had they gone? Many people spoke of them, puzzled and disturbed. The feeding stations in the backyards were deserted. The few birds seen anywhere were moribund;[6] they trembled violently and could not fly. It was a spring without voices. On the mornings that had once throbbed with the dawn chorus of robins, catbirds, doves, jays, wrens, and scores of other bird voices there was now no sound; only silence lay over the fields and woods and marsh.

---

3. Here, *migrants* refers to migrating birds.
4. A *blight* is a widespread withering or illness caused by such negative forces as pollution, bacteria, insects, or parasites.
5. *Maladies* are illnesses.

6. *Moribund* means "having very little strength left." The remaining birds are weakening and dying.

RACHEL CARSON **1237**

Teach

Big Idea | 2

Nature and Technology

Ask: What is Carson's view of the impact of technology on nature? *(Her view is negative. In her fable, everything dies because of technology.)* Is her concern realistic? Could this happen today? Why or why not? *(Some students may say that technology has become so sophisticated that it could not happen today. Others may say that advances in technology bring greater risks.)*

View the Photograph

Although DDT was discovered in 1874, it was not widely used as a pesticide in the United States until after World War II. Scientists were concerned because DDT builds up in the food chain, harming wildlife. *Silent Spring* brought the issue to the public's attention in 1962.
Ask: How does the photo show the conflict between nature and technology? *(A person enjoying the beach is sprayed with a harmful substance created by technology.)*

Assess

1. Many students will cite the destruction of life—plant, animal, and human—as the most surprising and shocking revelation.

2. (a) It changes from an idyllic, productive community to a weakened, poisoned place. (b) Most students will say that it is a chemical that the people used to kill insects.

3. (a) Carson shifts to the first-person point of view. (b) Students may say that Carson wants to address the reader directly, to issue a strong warning.

4. Carson began with a fable in order to engage readers in a way that cold facts and examples might not. The picture of the town's destruction is far more immediate and personal than statistics about places that readers have never visited.

5. The rural setting is particularly effective because of its original unspoiled character.

6. Students' answers will vary.

On the farms the hens brooded, but no chicks hatched. The farmers complained that they were unable to raise any pigs—the litters were small and the young survived only a few days. The apple trees were coming into bloom but no bees droned among the blossoms, so there was no pollination and there would be no fruit.

The roadsides, once so attractive, were now lined with browned and withered vegetation as though swept by fire. These, too, were silent, deserted by all living things. Even the streams were now lifeless. Anglers[7] no longer visited them, for all the fish had died.

In the gutters under the eaves and between the shingles of the roofs, a white granular powder still showed a few patches; some weeks before it had fallen like snow upon the roofs and the lawns, the fields and streams.

No witchcraft, no enemy action had silenced the rebirth of new life in this stricken world. The people had done it themselves.

This town does not actually exist, but it might easily have a thousand counterparts in America or elsewhere in the world. I know of no community that has experienced all the misfortunes I describe. Yet every one of these disasters has actually happened somewhere, and many real communities have already suffered a substantial number of them. A grim specter has crept upon us almost unnoticed, and this imagined tragedy may easily become a stark reality we all shall know. ◐

> *On the mornings that had once throbbed with the dawn chorus of robins, catbirds, doves, jays, wrens, and scores of other bird voices there was now no sound . . .*

---

7. An *angler* is a person who fishes with a rod and reel.

Respond and Think Critically

Respond and Interpret

1. What most shocked or surprised you about the possible effects of environmental pollution that Carson suggests? Explain.

2. (a) Describe the change that occurs in the town. (b) What might the "white granular powder" have been? Explain your interpretation.

3. (a) What shift occurs in the final paragraph? (b) What effect do you think Carson is trying to achieve with this shift?

Analyze and Evaluate

4. Carson chose to begin her book with a simple tale rather than with dramatic examples of the misuse of dangerous chemicals. Why do you think she made that choice? Explain whether you think it was a wise choice.

5. Carson called this piece the "Fable of Tomorrow." It takes place in a perfect, rural setting. Do you think it would have been more effective if Carson had chosen some other setting, such as a large city or suburb? Explain.

Connect

6. What thoughts about environmental health in your community did the excerpt inspire in you? Explain.

Vocabulary Practice

Connotations Remind students of the importance of connotations in creating tone. Carson at first uses words with strongly positive connotations in her description of the town. Then she uses words with negative connotations to indicate a grim transformation. Have students point out words with negative connotations in the selection. (*Possible responses:* blight; moribund; withered) Instruct students to go through the selection, adding unfamiliar or difficult vocabulary to their lists.

Meet **Ursula K. Le Guin**

(born 1929)

Ursula Le Guin revolutionized science fiction. Before she began publishing in the 1960s, the genre was dominated by male writers. Le Guin's stories, in which women and people from different cultures began to appear as main characters, broadened the genre.

A Rich Background Le Guin grew up in Berkeley, California, where her father, an internationally respected anthropology professor, taught. Her mother, a writer with a background in psychology, wrote mainly children's books but was famous for her nonfiction work about the lone survivor of the Yahi tribe of California. This book, *Ishi in Two Worlds*, is still read and admired today.

Scholar, Writer, and Mother Le Guin always considered herself to be a writer. She wrote her first fantasy story at nine. By age twelve, she had submitted a science fiction story for publication. Although it was not accepted, Le Guin took pride in receiving a "real rejection slip." Unfazed, she continued writing. Her father, however, encouraged her to be practical when it was time to choose a career. A talented language scholar, Le Guin graduated from Radcliffe in 1951 with a degree in French. By the next year, she had completed her master's in the same subject. She planned

to write a dissertation, receive her doctorate, and make a career of teaching at the university level.

That plan soon changed. In 1953 Le Guin was on her way to Europe on a Fulbright scholarship to study Italian and French literature. Traveling on the ocean liner *Queen Mary*, Le Guin met another Fulbright scholar, Charles Le Guin, who was also going to study in Europe. The two fell in love and were married by the end of the year.

> "My father studied real cultures and I make them up—in a way, it's the same thing."
>
> —Ursula K. Le Guin

When they returned to the U.S., Ursula decided to drop her studies to write and to raise a family. She sold her first science fiction story in 1962. Four years later, her first novel was published.

A Prolific Career Le Guin has published more than thirty novels and over a hundred short stories, including works for children and young adult readers. Le Guin has received dozens of awards for her work, among them the prestigious Hugo and Nebula awards for her science fiction and the National Book Award. She has written poetry, essays, and literary criticism; collaborated on screenplays and an opera; and taught classes and workshops for many aspiring science fiction and fantasy writers. Le Guin believes strongly in the importance of the imagination, asserting that "It is above all by the imagination that we achieve perception, compassion, and hope."

 Literature Online

Author Search For more about Ursula K. Le Guin, go to glencoe.com and enter QuickPass code GLA9800u7.

URSULA K. LE GUIN **1239**

Before You Read

Focus

Bellringer Options

Daily Language Practice Transparency 109

Or explain that the story they are about to read deals with the use of standardized tests to judge people's sanity. Start a discussion about why standardized tests should or should not be used by colleges and other institutions to judge applicants. **Ask:** How do you think colleges should choose among applicants? Why?

📁 For summaries in languages other than English, see Unit 7 Teaching Resources Book, pp. 184–189.

Selection Skills

Literary Elements
- Satire (SE pp. 1240, 1241, 1243, 145-1249, 1251)
- Narrator (SE p. 1250; TE p. 1244)

SQ

Writing Skills/Grammar
- Expository Essay (SE p. 1252)
- Science Fiction (TE p. 1248)

Reading Skills
- Identify Genre (SE pp. 1240, 1242, 1244-1249, 1251)
- Use Graphic Organizers (TE p. 1242)
- Predict (TE p. 1246)

Vocabulary Skills
- Analogies (SE pp. 1251)
- Academic Vocabulary (SE p. 1251)

Listening/Speaking/ Viewing Skills
- Analyze Art (SE pp. 1243, 1244)

Before You Read

Focus

Summary

The narrator, Mary Ann Smith, is head secretary for Dr. Speakie, who has invented an SQ (sanity quotient) test. The World Government adopts the test despite protests. Eventually, the majority of the world is either in asylums or on the asylums' staffs. Finally, the World Government collapses when most of its members flunk the SQ test. Speakie takes over the running of the world. When he too flunks the test, Mary Ann runs the world.

Vocabulary

Prefixes and Suffixes Have students identify any prefixes and suffixes they recognize in the vocabulary list, and indicate their meanings. *(In the word* implementation, im- *means "into" and* -tion *means "act of." In the word* infrastructure, infra- *means "below." In* hysterical, -al *means "characterized by." In* uncanny, un- *means "not.")* Have them list other words with these prefixes and suffixes.

Literature and Reading Preview

Connect to the Story

What would be the benefits and drawbacks of checking mental health on a regular basis? Write a pro-con list in which you explore reasons for and against regular mental health check-ups.

Build Background

"SQ" is set in a time in the future when one government rules the world and uses standardized tests to measure mental health. Standardized tests are often used to test mastery of academic subjects or aptitude for different professions. Standardized tests have also been devised to measure intelligence. Such tests are called *intelligence quotient,* or *IQ,* tests. Though widely used, they remain controversial as regards what exactly they measure.

Set Purposes for Reading

Big Idea Nature and Technology

As you read, ask yourself, How important is technology in Dr. Speakie's plan?

Literary Element Satire

Satire is writing that uses humor to comment on philosophical ideas, social customs, political institutions, and even general human tendencies. As you read, ask yourself, What does Le Guin satirize?

Reading Strategy Identify Genre

A **short story** is a brief fictional narrative in prose that generally includes setting, characters, plot, and theme. **Science fiction** is a type of fiction that deals with the impact of science, technology, or both on individuals and society. Science fiction is often set in the future. As you read, ask yourself, What features of this story make it science fiction?

- -

Tip: Take Notes Use a chart like the one below to record details that indicate this work is a science fiction story.

Science Fiction Characteristics	
Setting	
Impact of Science	
Impact of Technology	

Vocabulary

implementation (im´ plə mən tā´ shən) *n.* putting into effect; putting into use; p. 1242 *The implementation of a test involves several steps.*

infrastructure (in´ frə struk´ chər) *n.* the underlying base for an organization or a system; p. 1243 *Without the infrastructure of teachers, administrators, and building support staff, it would be difficult to educate the youth of our nation.*

stigma (stig´ mə) *n.* mark or characteristic of disgrace; p. 1245 *Ripped jeans have changed from stigma to fashion statement.*

hysterical (his ter´ i kəl) *adj.* characterized by panic or other uncontrolled emotion; p. 1247 *A person who is hysterical might not make sense.*

secede (si sēd´) *v.* to formally withdraw from an alliance; p. 1247 *South Carolina was the first of the Southern states to secede from the United States in the events leading up to the Civil War.*

Reading Practice

SMALL GROUP

Charting Jargon Explain that throughout the story, Le Guin satirizes wordy, official-sounding language that is often found in government or technical documents. Explain that this type of language is jargon, or specialized language used by a certain group. Jargon often hides the truth behind euphemisms that sound authoritative. Show students the examples in the chart, and have them fill in a similar chart as they read.

Jargon from "SQ"	Meaning
"…before the actual implementation of its application could be eventualized." (*eventualized* is a made-up word)	before people could take the test
"structurization of the Cure Centers" (*structurization* is a made-up word)	building of places to hold people who do not pass a test

SQ

Ursula K. Le Guin

Man Disappearing through Closed Door. Janusz Kapusta.

1 I think what Dr. Speakie has done is wonderful. He is a wonderful man. I believe that. I believe that people need beliefs. If I didn't have my belief, I really don't know what would happen.

And if Dr. Speakie hadn't truly believed in his work, he couldn't possibly have done what he did. Where would he have found the courage? What he did proves his genuine sincerity.

There was a time when a lot of people tried to cast doubts on him. They said he was seeking power. That was never true. From the very beginning all he wanted was to help people and make a better world. The people who called him a power seeker and a dictator were just the same ones who used to say that Hitler was insane and

2 Satire *What form of humor is Le Guin using here?*

Nixon[1] was insane and all the world leaders were insane and the arms race was insane and our misuse of natural resources was insane and the whole world civilization was insane and suicidal. They were always saying that. And they said it about Dr. Speakie. But he stopped all that insanity, didn't he? So he was right all along, and he was right to believe in his beliefs.

---

1. *Nixon* refers to Richard M. Nixon, who was U.S. president from 1969 to 1974. As president, Nixon was involved in a political scandal known as Watergate. In 1974 he opted to resign from office rather than face an impeachment trial.

URSULA K. LE GUIN **1241**

Teach

Reading Strategy | 1

Identify Genre **Answer:**
This event has not occurred, so the story must be set in the future. A futuristic setting is a characteristic of science fiction.

 For additional practice using the reading skill or strategy, see Unit 7 Teaching Resources Book, p. 191.

Big Idea | 2

Nature and Technology
Answer: *The author may not view technology with unreserved enthusiasm.*

Reading Strategy | 3

Identify Genre **Answer:** *The idea that sanity can be measured by a simple test*

Political History

The United Nations The United Nations came into official existence, with 51 member nations, when its charter was ratified on October 24, 1945. It now has more than 190 member nations. Every October 24 is celebrated as United Nations Day.

 For an audio recording of this selection, use Listening Library Audio CD-ROM.

I came to work for him when he was named the Chief of the Psychometric[2] Bureau. I used to work at the U.N.,[3] and when the World Government took over the New York U.N. Building, they transferred me up to the thirty-fifth floor to be the head secretary in Dr. Speakie's office. I knew already that it was a position of great responsibility, and I was quite excited the whole week before my new job began. I was so curious to meet Dr. Speakie, because of course he was already famous. I was there right at the dot of nine on Monday morning, and when he came in, it was so wonderful. He looked so kind. You could tell that the weight of his responsibilities was always on his mind, but he looked so healthy and positive, and there was a bounce in his step—I used to think it was as if he had rubber balls in the toes of his shoes. He smiled and shook my hand and said in such a friendly, confident voice, "And you must be Mrs. Smith! I've heard wonderful things about you. We're going to have a wonderful team here, Mrs. Smith!"

Later on he called me by my first name, of course.

That first year we were mostly busy with Information. The World Government Presidium and all the Member States had to be fully informed about the nature and purpose of the SQ Test, before the actual **implementation** of its application could be eventualized. That was good for me too, because in preparing all that information I learned all about it myself. Often,

---

2. *Psychometric* (sī′ kə met′ rik) relates to a branch of psychology that deals with tests designed to measure any psychological variable, such as intelligence, aptitude, or personality type.
3. *U.N.* is an abbreviation that stands for the United Nations.

1 **Identify Genre** *What detail of the setting helps you identify this story as science fiction?*

2 **Nature and Technology** *What does this sentence suggest about the author's attitude toward technology?*

Vocabulary
implementation (im′ plə mən tā′ shən) *n.* putting into effect; putting into use

---

taking dictation,[4] I learned about it from Dr. Speakie's very lips. By May I was enough of an "expert" that I was able to prepare the Basic SQ Information Pamphlet for publication just from Dr. Speakie's notes. It was such fascinating work. As soon as I began to understand the SQ Test Plan, I began to believe in it. That was true of everybody else in the office and in the Bureau. Dr. Speakie's sincerity and scientific enthusiasm were infectious. Right from the beginning we had to take the Test every quarter, of course, and some of the secretaries used to be nervous before they took it, but I never was. It was so obvious that the Test was *right*. If you scored under 50 it was nice to know that you were sane, but even if you scored over 50 that was fine too, because then you could be *helped*. And anyway it is always best to know the truth about yourself.

As soon as the Information service was functioning smoothly, Dr. Speakie transferred the main thrust of his attention to the implementation of Evaluator training, and planning for the structurization of the Cure Centers, only he changed the name to SQ Achievement Centers. It seemed a very big job even then. We certainly had no idea how big the job would finally turn out to be!

As he said at the beginning, we were a very good team. We all worked hard, but there were always rewards.

I remember one wonderful day. I had accompanied Dr. Speakie to the Meeting of the Board of the Psychometric Bureau. The emissary[5] from the State of Brazil announced that his State had adopted the Bureau Recommendations for Universal Testing—we had known that that was going to be announced. But then the delegate from Libya and the delegate from China announced that their States had adopted the

---

4. *Taking dictation* is the act of writing down what someone else is saying. It used to be common for secretaries to take dictation from their bosses. They would type up the information as a letter, a memo, or in another written format.
5. An *emissary* is a person sent on a mission to represent or advance the interests of another person, especially those of a leader of a nation.

Identify Genre *What aspect of the story's subject helps you identify the story as science fiction?* **3**

Study Skills Practice

SPIRAL REVIEW **Use Graphic Organizers** Details about the main characters gradually unfold throughout this story.
Ask: What do we know about the narrator so far? *(The narrator is a woman named Mrs. Smith, and she is the head secretary for Dr. Speakie. She formerly worked at the U.N.)* Have students make graphic organizers to keep track of character details. Tell students to create a concept web with "Mrs. Smith" in the middle and details about Smith in the surrounding boxes. Tell students to create a similar web for Dr. Speakie.

Fearful Man Turned Away From Crowd. John Ritter.

 View the Art While Plato saw beauty in precise proportions, many contemporary artists distort the size of objects. Why do you think John Ritter used a disproportionately large eye here? What aspects of Dr. Speakie's personality does the man in this image capture? ★

Test too! Oh, Dr. Speakie's face was just like the sun for a minute, just *shining*. I wish I could remember exactly what he said, especially to the Chinese delegate, because of course China was a very big State and its decision was very influential. Unfortunately I do not have his exact words because I was changing the tape in the recorder. He said something like, "Gentlemen, this is a historic day for humanity." Then he began to talk at once about the effective implementation of the Application Centers, where people would take the Test, and the Achievement Centers, where they would go if they scored over 50, and how to establish the Test Administrations and Evaluations **infrastructure** on such a large scale,

and so on. He was always modest and practical. He would rather talk about doing the job than talk about what an important job it was. He used to say, "Once you know what you're doing, the only thing you need to think about is how to do it." I believed that that is deeply true.

From then on, we could hand over the Information program to a subdepartment and concentrate on How to Do It. Those were exciting times! So many States joined the Plan, one after another. When I think of all we had to do, I wonder that we didn't all go crazy! Some of the office staff did fail their quarterly Test, in fact. But most of us working in the Executive Office with Dr. Speakie remained quite stable, even when we were on the job all day and half the night. I think his presence was an inspiration. He was always calm and positive, even when we had to arrange things like training

4 Nature and Technology *Does this technology seem advanced? Why or why not?*

Vocabulary

infrastructure (in´ frə struk´ chər) *n.* the underlying base for an organization or a system

Satire *The narrator considers Dr. Speakie's statement to be wise and profound. How does it strike you?* **5**

URSULA K. LE GUIN **1243**

Big Idea | **4**

Nature and Technology
Answer: *The technology is not especially advanced; tape recorders have been in use for decades, and digital means of making sound recordings are more common now.*

Literary Element | **5**

Satire **Answer:** *Many students may consider it a simple and superficial statement.*
(ADVANCED) **Ask:** How does this statement add to the satirical effect of the writing? *(It juxtaposes an obvious statement with a statement about how profound it is.)*

View the Art ★
Answer: *Students may say that the man in the image seems isolated, suspicious, and defensive. They may also see these traits in Speakie. Ritter might have used a large eye to emphasize the man's feelings of isolation and suspicion.*

John Ritter is a contemporary photo-illustrator living in Pittsburgh, Pennsylvania. In the early 1990s, he helped develop computer graphics programs by experimenting and testing the programs' capabilities.

Approaching Level

DIFFERENTIATED INSTRUCTION 🐟

Emerging Some students may need help recognizing how Le Guin uses humor to create satire. One form of humor she uses is incongruity, where a writer puts two ideas or things together that do not usually go together. An example is Mrs. Smith's taking dictation, which is a very old-fashioned way of transmitting information, from a man who is supposed to be brilliant and ahead of his time. **Ask:** What is incongru-

ous about the narrator missing what Dr. Speakie says to the delegates? *(The speech is supposed to be very important, yet she misses some of it because she is doing something very ordinary—changing the tape in the recorder.)*

Teach

Reading Strategy　1

Identify Genre Answer:
Applying the SQ Test to everyone in such a populous country would have led to the identification of huge numbers of people as insane, requiring many more Achievement Centers and people to staff them.

View the Art ★

Answer: *The man in the image appears to be giving orders to the others. Students may say he appears to be important, powerful, and threatening, unlike the man pictured on the preceding page. The large heads might represent large egos or the importance we place on intelligence.*

Man Entering Room of Men. John Ritter.

View the Art Each figure in this image has a disproportionately large head. What might that represent? How does the man in this image appear different from the one on the previous page? ★

113,000 Chinese Evaluators in three months. "You can always find out 'how' if you just know the 'why'!" he would say. And we always did.

When you think back over it, it really is quite amazing what a big job it was—so much bigger than anybody, even Dr. Speakie, had realized it would be. It just changed everything. You only realize that when you think back to what things used to be like. Can you imagine when we began planning Universal Testing for the State of China, we only allowed for eleven hundred Achievement Centers, with sixty-eight hundred Staff? It really seems like a joke. But it is not. I was going through some of the old files yesterday, making sure everything is in order, and I found the first China Implementation Plan, with those figures written down in black and white. I believe the reason why even Dr. Speakie was slow to realize the magnitude of the operation was that even though he was a great scientist, he was also an

optimist. He just kept hoping against hope that the average scores would begin to go down, and this prevented him from seeing that universal application of the SQ Test was eventually going to involve everybody either as Inmates or Staff.

When most of the Russias and all the African States had adopted the Recommendations and were busy implementing them, the debates in the General Assembly of the World Government got very excited. That was the period when so many bad things were said about the Test and about Dr. Speakie. I used to get quite angry, reading the *World Times* reports of debates. When I went as his secretary with Dr. Speakie to General Assembly meetings, I had to sit and listen in person to people insulting him personally, casting aspersions[6] on his motives, and questioning his scientific integrity and even his sincerity. Many of those people were very disagreeable and obviously unbalanced. But he never lost his temper. He would just stand up and prove to them, again,

---

1 **Identify Genre** *What do you think ends up happening with the testing plan in China?*

6. *Casting aspersions* on something means saying uncomplimentary things about it.

Reading Practice

The Narrator's Role By this point in the story, students have likely gathered that the narrator's gullibility—her willingness to "believe"—is one source of the humor in the story. Explain that Le Guin could have told the story in the third person, satirizing only the testing. Instead, she adds an extra layer of humor by creating a character who believes deeply in the testing. The reader can laugh not only at the testing system, but at the narrator's failure to notice how silly it is. Have students review the first few pages of the story to find several passages that show the narrator's willingness to believe and discuss these. (p. 1241: *"I believe that people need beliefs"*; p. 1242: *"As soon as I began to understand the SQ Test Plan, I began to believe in it"*; p. 1243: *"I believed that that is deeply true."*)

that the SQ Test did actually literally scientifically show whether the testee was sane or insane, and the results could be proved, and all psychometrists accepted them. So the Test Ban[7] people couldn't do anything but shout about freedom and accuse Dr. Speakie and the Psychometric Bureau of trying to "turn the world into a huge insane asylum." He would always answer quietly and firmly, asking them how they thought a person could be "free" if they lacked mental health. What they called freedom might well be a delusional system with no contact with reality. In order to find out, all they had to do was to become testees. "Mental health *is* freedom," he said. "'Eternal vigilance is the price of liberty,' they say,[8] and now we have an eternally vigilant watchdog: the SQ Test. *Only the testees can be truly free!*"

There really was no answer they could make to that. Sooner or later the delegates even from Member States where the Test Ban movement was strong would volunteer to take the SQ Test to prove that their mental health was adequate to their responsibilities. Then the ones that passed the test and remained in office would begin working for Universal Application in their home State. The riots and demonstrations, and things like the burning of the Houses of Parliament in London in the State of England (where the Nor-Eurp SQ Center was housed), and the Vatican Rebellion, and the Chilean H-Bomb,[9]

---

7. The use of the term *Test Ban* alludes to nuclear weapons and the popular movements in the 1960s and 1970s to try to limit them. The Nuclear Test-Ban Treaty was signed in 1963 between the United States, the Soviet Union, and more than one hundred other nations to ban the testing of nuclear weapons anywhere on or near Earth except underground.
8. The quote *"Eternal vigilance is the price of liberty"* means that people must always be aware if they want to hold on to their freedoms. This quote is based on a sentence in a speech made by Irish statesman John Philpot Curran in 1790.
9. An *H-bomb* is an abbreviation for a hydrogen bomb, a powerful nuclear weapon.

2 Identify Genre *What specific issue related to science and society is raised here?*

3 Nature and Technology *What does this reference indicate about the level of resistance to the testing plan in some parts of the world?*

---

were the work of insane fanatics appealing to the most unstable elements of the populace. Such fanatics, as Dr. Speakie and Dr. Waltraute pointed out in their Memorandum to the Presidium, deliberately aroused and used the proven instability of the crowd, "mob psychosis." The only response to mass delusion of that kind was immediate implementation of the Testing Program in the disturbed States, and immediate amplification[10] of the Asylum Program.

That was Dr. Speakie's own decision, by the way, to rename the SQ Achievement Centers "Asylums." He took the word right out of his enemies' mouths. He said: "An asylum means a place of *shelter*, a place of *cure*. Let there be no **stigma** attached to the word 'insane,' to the word 'asylum,' to the words 'insane asylum'! No! For the asylum is the haven of mental health—the place of cure, where the anxious gain peace, where the weak gain strength, where the prisoners of inadequate reality assessment win their way to freedom! Proudly let us use the word 'asylum.' Proudly let us go to the asylum, to work to regain our own God-given mental health, or to work with others less fortunate to help them win back their own inalienable right to mental health. And let one word be written large over the door of every asylum in the world—'WELCOME!' "

Those words are from his great speech at the General Assembly on the day World Universal Application was decreed by the Presidium. Once or twice a year I listen to my tape of that speech. Although I am too busy ever to get really depressed, now and then I feel the need of a tiny "pick-me-up," and so I play that tape. It never fails to send me back to my duties inspired and refreshed.

---

10. Here, *amplification* means "enlargement."

Satire *Do you agree with the narrator's assessment of the protesters? Why or why not?* **4**

Satire *Do you think Le Guin wants you to believe what Dr. Speakie says in this speech? Why or why not?* **5**

Vocabulary

stigma (stig´ mə) *n.* mark or characteristic of disgrace

URSULA K. LE GUIN **1245**

Teach

Reading Strategy 2

Identify Genre Answer:
The issue is whether standardized tests can measure what they are designed to measure and whether such tests can be universally applied with accuracy.

Big Idea 3

Nature and Technology Answer: *It indicates that in some places, resistance to the plan was extremely fierce.*

Literary Element 4

Satire Answer: *Most students will disagree because the extreme terms used by the narrator show that her assessment is biased and unreliable.*

Literary Element 5

Satire Answer: *Le Guin means this speech to be a parody, as is shown by the jargon and the ironic statement that people need to be locked up to become free.*

English Learners

DIFFERENTIATED INSTRUCTION

Beginning Explain that the word *asylum* can have different connotations. Explain that although the primary meaning ("a place of refuge") has a positive connotation, the word has a negative connotation when used to refer to an institution for the mentally ill.

Teach

Big Idea · 1

Nature and Technology

Answer: *A government would need to have a worldwide network of computers, a universal communication network, and a way to identify each individual.*

Reading Strategy · 2

Identify Genre **Answer:**
Not mentioning her given name before may be an indication of Mary Ann's impersonal nature.

Literary Element · 3

Satire **Answer:** *Le Guin pokes fun by using jargon that might be used in a scientific or technical document.* **Say:** It is clear that the system is falling apart, yet Mary Anne continues to parrot Dr. Speakie's contention that measuring sanity through a test is a scientifically proven method.
ENGLISH LEARNERS Explain that jargon is specialized language used by a particular group of people in their work. **Ask:** Where have you heard or read this kind of language before? *(government, business, or technical speeches or documents)*

Man with Giant Pencil and Paper. John Ritter.

Considering all the work there was to do, as the Test scores continued to come in always a little higher than the Psychometric Bureau analysts estimated, the World Government Presidium did a wonderful job for the two years that it administered Universal Testing. There was a long period, six months, when the scores seemed to have stabilized, with just about half of the testees scoring over 50 and half under 50. At that time it was thought that if 40 percent of the mentally healthy were assigned to Asylum Staff work, the other 60 percent could keep up routine basic world functions such as farming, power supply, transportation, etc. This proportion had to be reversed when they found that over 60 percent of the mentally healthy were volunteering for Staff work, in order to be with their loved ones in the Asylums. There was some trouble then with the routine basic world functions functioning. However, even then contingency plans were being made for the inclusion of farmlands, factories, power plants, etc., in

the Asylum Territories, and the assignment of routine basic world functions work as Rehabilitation Therapy, so that the Asylums could become totally self-supporting if it became advisable. This was President Kim's special care, and he worked for it all through his term of office. Events proved the wisdom of his planning. He seemed such a nice, wise little man. I still remember the day when Dr. Speakie came into the office and I knew at once that something was wrong. Not that he ever got really depressed or reacted with inopportune emotion,[11] but it was as if the rubber balls in his shoes had gone just a little bit flat. There was the slightest tremor of true sorrow in his voice when he said, "Mary Ann, we've had a bit of bad news I'm afraid." Then he smiled to reassure me, because he knew what a strain we were all working under, and certainly didn't want to give anybody a shock that might push their score up higher on the next quarterly Test! "It's President Kim," he said, and I knew at once—I knew he didn't mean the President was ill or dead.

"Over 50?" I asked, and he just said quietly and sadly, "55."

Poor little President Kim, working so efficiently all that three months while mental ill health was growing in him! It was very sad and also a useful warning. High-level consultations were begun at once, as soon as President Kim was committed;[12] and the decision was made to administer the Test monthly, instead of quarterly, to anyone in an executive position.

Even before this decision, the Universal scores had begun rising again. Dr. Speakie was not distressed. He had already predicted that this rise was highly probable during the transition period to World Sanity. As the number of the mentally healthy living outside the Asylums grew fewer, the strain on them kept growing greater, and

---

11. *Inopportune emotion* is inappropriate feeling.
12. *Committed*, here, means "to put into a place for confinement or for preservation."

Identify Genre *What effect does learning the narrator's name this late in the story have on your impression of the character?* · 2

Satire *What hint do you have that Le Guin is poking fun at the ideas that the narrator expresses here?* · 3

Nature and Technology *What types of technology do you think a government would need to successfully carry out periodic standardized testing of every single person in the world?* · 1

Reading Practice

SPIRAL REVIEW

Predict Have students summarize what has happened so far in the story. **Ask:** Judging by the latest news about President Kim, what do you think will happen next? *(Students may say that with President Kim gone, Speakie will be the logical choice to take his place.)* How does your prediction help you understand Dr. Speakie? (Students may note that they now realize that Speakie is motivated by power and world domination rather than by humanitarian principles.)*

they became more liable to break down under it—just as poor President Kim had done. Later, he predicted, when the Rehabs began coming out of the Asylums in ever increasing numbers, this stress would decrease. Also, the crowding in the Asylums would decrease, so that the Staff would have more time to work on individually orientated therapy, and this would lead to a still more dramatic increase in the number of Rehabs released. Finally, when the therapy process was completely perfected, there would be no Asylums left in the world at all. Everybody would be either mentally healthy or a Rehab, or "neonormal," as Dr. Speakie liked to call it.

It was the trouble in the State of Australia that precipitated[13] the Government crisis. Some Psychometric Bureau officials accused the Australian Evaluators of actually falsifying Test returns, but that is impossible since all the computers are linked to the World Government Central Computer Bank in Keokuk.[14] Dr. Speakie suspected the Australian Evaluators had been falsifying *the Test itself*, and insisted that they themselves all be tested immediately. Of course he was right. It had been a conspiracy, and the suspiciously low Australian Test scores had resulted from the use of a false Test. Many of the conspirators tested higher than 80 when forced to take the genuine Test! The State Government in Canberra[15] had been unforgivably lax. If they had just admitted it, everything would have been all right. But they got **hysterical,** and moved the State Government to a sheep station in Queensland,[16] and tried to withdraw from the World Government. (Dr. Speakie said that was a typical mass psychosis: reality evasion, followed by

Painting Of Man with Negative. John Ritter.

fugue[17] and autistic withdrawal.[18]) Unfortunately, the Presidium seemed to be paralyzed. Australia **seceded** on the day before the President and Presidium were due to take their monthly Test, and probably they were afraid of overstraining their SQ with agonizing decisions. So the Psychometric Bureau volunteered to handle the episode. Dr. Speakie himself flew on the plane with the H-bombs, and helped to drop the information leaflets. He never lacked personal courage.

When the Australian incident was over, it turned out that most of the Presidium, including President Singh, had scored over 50. So the Psychometric Bureau took over their functions temporarily. Even on a long-term basis this made good sense, since all the problems now facing the World Government had to do with administering and evaluating the Test, training

---

13. Here, *precipitated* means "brought about suddenly."
14. *Keokuk* is a small town in Iowa on the western banks of the Mississippi River.
15. *Canberra* is the capital of Australia.
16. *Queensland* is one of the states that make up Australia; raising sheep is an important industry there.

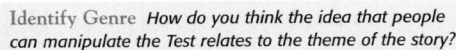
Identify Genre *How do you think the idea that people can manipulate the Test relates to the theme of the story?*

4

hysterical (his ter´ i kəl) *adj.* characterized by panic or other uncontrolled emotion

---

17. In psychology, a *fugue* is a state in which a person seems to be conscious of his or her actions but later has no recollection of these actions; a fugue may last for months and is a sign of severe mental stress.
18. *Autistic withdrawal* is a form of mental illness that involves extreme withdrawal from reality.

Nature and Technology *What does this use of technology tell you about Dr. Speakie and the government he is a part of?*

5

Satire *Why is this statement funny? What point is Le Guin making here?*

6

Vocabulary

secede (si sēd´) *v.* to formally withdraw from an alliance

URSULA K. LE GUIN   **1247**

Teach

Reading Strategy   4

Identify Genre **Answer:** *It confirms that people can alter individuals' and groups' test results. This highlights that the test is really a means of dominating everyone in the world.*

Big Idea   5

Nature and Technology
Answer: *It tells you that the World Government is a totalitarian organization that will use extreme methods to keep control of its citizens.*

Literary Element   6

Satire **Answer:** *The statement is funny because it is ironic; it indicates that the test itself has become the world's only problem.*

Approaching Level

DIFFERENTIATED INSTRUCTION

Emerging Tell students that using understatement is another way Le Guin makes this satire funny. Understatement makes a thing or event seem less important than the thing or event really is. **Ask:** How does Le Guin use understatement in the description of Dr. Speakie's handling of the Australian secession? *(As if dropping an H-bomb were a normal response to secession, Mary Anne casually reports that "Dr. Speakie himself flew on the plane with the H-bombs . . . ." Then, she speaks as if dropping H-bombs and leaflets were of equal weight, and as if people who had been bombed would be able to read a leaflet.)*

Advanced Learners

DIFFERENTIATED INSTRUCTION

Imagine a Scene Challenge students to write the scene of President Kim's removal from power from his point of view. Have students describe his thoughts and feelings about the event.

1247

Teach

Literary Element | 1

Satire Answer: *She is making fun of Speakie's use of jargon and his blindness to the horrible results of his testing program.*

[ENGLISH LEARNERS] Have students find each word in the phrase "pre-ponderant inverse sanity quotient" in a dictionary to understand the phrase.

Reading Strategy | 2

Identify Genre Answer: *Some students may be surprised that Speakie would allow his wife to be judged insane, but this shows no one is immune in his crazy system.*

Literary Element | 3

Irony Ask: Why is it ironic that Mary Ann envies her former secretaries? *(Students may say that it is ironic to envy those whose job is dealing with "insane" people.)*

the Staff, and providing full self-sufficiency structuration to all Asylums.

What this meant in personal terms was that Dr. Speakie, as Chief of the Psychometric Bureau, was now Interim President of the United States of the World. As his personal secretary, I was, I will admit it, just terribly proud of him. But he never let it go to his head.

He was so modest. Sometimes he used to say to people, when he introduced me, "This is Mary Ann, my secretary," he'd say with a little twinkle, "and if it wasn't for her I'd have been scoring over 50 long ago!"

There were times, as the World SQ scores rose and rose, that I would become a little discouraged. Once the week's Test figures came in on the readout, and the *average* score was 71. I said, "Doctor, there are moments I believe the whole world is going insane!"

But he said, "Look at it this way, Mary Ann. Look at those people in the Asylums—3.1 billion inmates now, and 1.8 billion staff—but look at them. What are they doing? They're pursuing their therapy, doing rehabilitation work on the farms and in the factories, and striving all the time, too, to *help* each other toward mental health. The preponderant inverse sanity quotient is certainly very high at the moment; they're mostly insane, yes. But you have to admire them. They are fighting for mental health. They *will*—they *will* win through!" And then he dropped his voice and said as if to himself, gazing out the window and bouncing just a little on the balls of his feet, "If I didn't believe that, I couldn't go on."

And I knew he was thinking of his wife.

Mrs. Speakie had scored 88 on the very first American Universal Test. She had been in the Greater Los Angeles Territory Asylum for years now.

Anybody who still thinks Dr. Speakie wasn't sincere should think about that for a minute! He gave up everything for his belief.

Looking For the Ideal Candidate. Janusz Kapusta.

And even when the Asylums were all running quite well, and the epidemics in South Africa and the famines in Texas and the Ukraine were under control, still the workload on Dr. Speakie never got any lighter, because every month the personnel of the Psychometric Bureau got smaller, since some of them always flunked their monthly Test and were committed to Bethesda.[19] I never could keep any of my secretarial staff any more for longer than a month or two. It was harder and harder to find replacements, too, because most sane young people volunteered for Staff work in the Asylums, since life was much easier and more sociable inside the Asylums than outside. Everything so convenient, and lots of friends and acquaintances! I used to positively envy those girls! But I knew where my job was.

At least it was much less hectic here in the U.N. Building, or the Psychometry Tower as it had been renamed a long time ago. Often there wouldn't be anybody around the whole building all day long but Dr. Speakie and myself, and maybe Bill the janitor (Bill scored 32 regular as

1 **Satire** *What is Le Guin making fun of with Dr. Speakie's answer to Mary Ann?*

2 **Identify Genre** *Based on how the plot has progressed, does this information surprise you? How does it relate to Le Guin's theme?*

19. *Bethesda* is a suburban community near Washington, D.C.

Writing Practice

SMALL GROUP

Science Fiction Discuss Le Guin's vision of the world of the future. **Ask:** What do you think the world will be like in 100 years? Challenge students to dabble in the science fiction genre by creating their own future worlds. Divide them into groups, and tell each group to write a science fiction story, taking into consideration any or all of the following questions:

- What are the governments like? Is there only one government?
- What are the people like? How do they dress? What languages do they speak?
- What is technology like? How does it affect people's daily lives?
- What are the arts like?

clockwork every quarter). All the restaurants were closed, in fact most of Manhattan was closed, but we had fun picnicking in the old General Assembly Hall. And there was always the odd call from Buenos Aires[20] or Reykjavik,[21] asking Dr. Speakie's advice as Interim President about some problem, to break the silence.

But last November 8, I will never forget the date, when Dr. Speakie was dictating the Referendum for World Economic Growth for the next five-year period, he suddenly interrupted himself. "By the way, Mary Ann," he said, "how was your last score?"

☆ We had taken the Test two days before, on the sixth. We always took the Test every first Monday. Dr. Speakie never would have dreamed of excepting himself from Universal Testing regulations.

"I scored 12," I said, before I thought how strange it was of him to ask. Or, not just to ask, because we often mentioned our scores to each other; but to ask then, in the middle of executing important world government business.

"Wonderful," he said, shaking his head. "You're wonderful, Mary Ann! Down two from last month's Test, aren't you?"

"I'm always between 10 and 14," I said. "Nothing new about that, Doctor."

"Some day," he said, and his face took on the expression it had when he gave his great speech about the Asylums, "some day, this world of ours will be governed by men fit to govern it. Men whose SQ score is Zero. Zero, Mary Ann!"

"Well, my goodness, Doctor," I said jokingly—his intensity almost alarmed me a little—"even *you* never scored lower than 3, and you haven't done that for a year or more now!"

He stared at me almost as if he didn't see me. It was quite **uncanny.** "Some day," he said

in just the same way, "nobody in the world will have a Quotient higher than 50. Some day, nobody in the world will have a Quotient higher than 30! Higher than 10! The therapy will be perfected. I was only the diagnostician.[22] But the Therapy will be perfected! The cure will be found! Some day!" And he went on staring at me, and then he said, "Do you know what my score was on Monday?"

"7," I guessed promptly. The last time he had told me his score it had been 7.

"92," he said.

I laughed, because he seemed to be laughing. He had always had a puckish[23] sense of humor. But I thought we really should get back to the World Economic Growth Plan, so I said laughingly, "That really is a very bad joke, Doctor!"

"92," he said, "and you don't believe me, Mary Ann, but that's because of the cantaloupe."

I said, "What cantaloupe, Doctor?" and that was when he jumped across his desk and began to try to bite through my jugular vein.

I used a judo hold and shouted to Bill the janitor, and when he came, I called a robo-ambulance to take Dr. Speakie to Bethesda Asylum.

That was six months ago. I visit Dr. Speakie every Saturday. It is very sad. He is in the McLean area, which is the Violent Ward, and every time he sees me he screams and foams. But I do not take it personally. One should never take mental ill health personally. When the Therapy is perfected, he will be completely rehabilitated. Meanwhile, I just hold on here. Bill keeps the floors clean, and I run the World Government. It really isn't as difficult as you might think. ☙

---

20. *Buenos Aires* is the capital and largest city of Argentina.
21. *Reykjavik* (rā′ kyə vēk′) is the capital and largest city of Iceland.

Identify Genre *How have things changed since the beginning of the story? What is the cause of this breakdown in society?*

Vocabulary

uncanny (un kan′ ē) *adj.* peculiarly unsettling in an eerie way

---

22. A *diagnostician* is someone who figures out the nature of a problem, especially by identifying an illness.
23. *Puckish* means "mischievous."

Satire *Do you think that this scene is supposed to be funny? Explain.* **5**

Nature and Technology *What does the existence of this technology imply about the way the world runs by the end of the story?* **6**

URSULA K. LE GUIN **1249**

Teach

Reading Strategy **4**

Identify Genre Answer: *The cities are depopulated, and there is very little activity outside the asylums, where most people now live, either as patients or as workers. The use of the SQ Test has caused the breakdown in society.*

Literary Element **5**

Satire Answer: *Most students will see the scene as intentionally funny. Speakie's reference to cantaloupe and his attempt to bite the narrator are farcical.*

Big Idea **6**

Nature and Technology Answer: *It implies that a very small number of people can control the world through the use of SQ testing and robots.*

Cultural History ☆

Measuring Intelligence The first attempt to measure intelligence was made by British scientist Sir Francis Galton in the late 1880s. He wanted to prove that intelligence was inherited and could be measured. French psychologist Alfred Binet developed the first test to help predict success in academics. He based his test on practical knowledge, reasoning, vocabulary, and problem solving. Revised many times and now known as the Stanford-Binet intelligence scale, the test is still used, but the idea of measuring IQ remains controversial.

After You Read

Assess

1. (a) Sanity (b) As a test used to identify people who are insane

2. (a) People who pass the test become advocates for it, and those who do not pass are put in asylums. (b) The government is coercive and exerts strong control over people.

3. (a) Billions are sent to asylums, billions more staff the asylums, and the world outside the asylums is depopulated. (b) Le Guin thinks that the test is ridiculous.

4. (a) First person (b) It reinforces the humor of the "sane" narrator's inability to see the insanity of the situation she has helped create.

5. (a) "Eventualized"; "structurization" (b) It makes the SQ plan sound ridiculous.

6. Students' answers will vary.

7. Very important, because SQ testing and the suppression of the rebellion could not have occurred without technologies.

8. It shows the dangers of totalitarian government and of granting too much power to "experts."

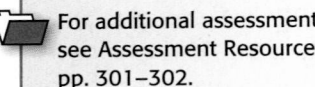
For additional assessment, see Assessment Resources, pp. 301–302.

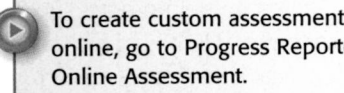
To create custom assessments online, go to Progress Reporter Online Assessment.

After You Read

Respond and Think Critically

Respond and Interpret

1. (a) What does the SQ Test measure? (b) How does the story present the use of such a test?

2. (a) How does SQ testing come to be universal? (b) What does this imply about the government that controls the world in this story?

3. (a) What happens when the testing program is applied worldwide? (b) Given this result, what is Le Guin's attitude toward the test?

Analyze and Evaluate

4. (a) What point of view does the writer use in this story? (b) How does this point of view help reinforce the story's irony?

5. (a) **Jargon** is specialized language used by a particular group of people. What are some examples of jargon in this story? (b) How does Le Guin's use of jargon strengthen the story's satire?

6. **Irony** is a deliberate contrast between what is written and what is really meant. Identify two examples of irony in this story, and explain how each relates to the story's main message.

Connect

7. **Big Idea** **Nature and Technology** How important is technology in this story? Support your response with evidence from the story.

8. **Connect to Today** How do you think this story comments on or relates to contemporary society?

Primary Source Quotation

Plausibility in Science Fiction

When asked about the plausibility (or, believability) of science fiction compared to other genres, Ursula K. Le Guin made this comment.

"Unless it is in the satirical mode, science fiction tends to avoid the actual present time. A story about the immediate contemporary world is read with high expectations of factuality, and blatant contradiction of fact, if not satirical, will be taken as nonsense.

In general, science fiction proceeds just as realistic fiction does, meeting conventional expectations of how people generally act, and either avoiding events that will strike the reader as improbable, or plausibly explaining them. Realism and science fiction both employ plausibility to win the reader's consent to the fiction."

—Ursula K. Le Guin

The New Planet, 1921. Konstantin Yuon. Tretyakov Gallery, Moscow.

Group Activity Discuss the following questions with your classmates. Refer back to the quotation and cite evidence from "SQ" for support.

1. In the above quotation, Le Guin explains when satire may be useful in relation to a story's time period. What does that tell you about the time period in which "SQ" occurs?

2. What makes the science fiction story "SQ" just as plausible as realistic fiction?

Primary Source Quotation

1. Students should deduce that "SQ" is most likely written about contemporary society, though it takes place in a world that seems to be in the future.

2. Students should be able to identify that Le Guin mirrors the real world by creating an alternate landscape where people work at government jobs and measure global statistics. The element of science fiction, or the tests and how they are conducted, is written as if it actually happens.

Literary Element Satire

The story "SQ" is a **satire** because Le Guin uses humor to comment on society and its foibles. She also uses parody and understatement as part of her satire. **Parody** is humorous imitation. **Understatement** is language that makes something seem less important than it really is.

1. How is the title of this short story a parody? If necessary, reread the Build Background information on page 1240 and then think about what the initials in the title most likely represent.

2. Find an example of understatement in this short story. How does the understatement contribute to the humor of the story?

Review: Narrator

As you learned on page 982, a **narrator** is the person telling a story in a work of fiction. In a story with a first-person point of view, the narrator is a character in the story. In "SQ," the narrator is a woman named Mary Ann Smith.

Group Activity A first-person narrator tends to have a limited perspective that presents a particular viewpoint. In a small group, discuss the narrator's perspective and opinions in "SQ." What makes the narrator a good source of information for this story? What makes her an unreliable source of information? Use the scale below to rate the narrator's reliability. Discuss your rating with the class.

Narrator's Reliability

```
1   2   3   4   5   6   7   8   9   10
Very                              Very
Reliable                      Unreliable
```

Reliability Rating _____

Reasons
1.
2.
3.

Vocabulary Practice

Practice with Analogies For each item below, identify the relationship between the first pair of words. Then apply that relationship to the second pair. In each expression, : means "is to" and :: means "as."

1. hysterical : calm ::
   a. reluctant : forgiving
   b. exemplary : outstanding
   c. miserable : happy
   d. doubtful : questioning

2. shame : stigma ::
   a. erasure : marking   c. pride : badge
   b. recreation : work   d. anxiety : success

3. power supply : infrastructure ::
   a. doctor : health care system
   b. bridge : river
   c. teacher : student
   d. judge : sheriff

4. implementation : application ::
   a. wheel : axle   c. agenda : schedule
   b. flower : petal   d. climax : exposition

5. secede : ally ::
   a. apply : work   c. nominate : elect
   b. member : join   d. forfeit : play

Academic Vocabulary

*According to Dr. Speakie, a low score on the SQ test **indicates** insanity.*

Indicate is an academic word. When driving, you put on your turn signal to **indicate** to the other drivers that you are about to turn.

To further explore the meaning of this word, complete this sentence: To indicate my support of my _____, I _____.

For more on academic vocabulary, see pages 53 and 54.

LOG ON ▶ **Literature** Online

Selection Resources For Selection Quizzes, eFlashcards, and Reading-Writing Connection activities, go to glencoe.com and enter QuickPass code GLA9800u7.

URSULA K. LE GUIN **1251**

Vocabulary

1. c 2. c 3. a 4. c 5. d

Academic Vocabulary

Possible answer: To indicate my support of my best friend, I held her hand while she opened the letter from her university of choice.

Literary Element

1. *SQ,* which may stand for "sanity quotient," is a parody of *IQ,* which stands for "intelligence quotient."

2. Description of response to Australian rebellion is humorous because of the offhand tone in describing destruction.

Progress Check

Can students recognize satire?

If No → See Unit 7 Teaching Resources Book, p. 190.

Review: Narrator

She is a good source because she has inside knowledge of the SQ testing program; she is an unreliable source because of her admiration for Dr. Speakie. The narrator's limited perspective and strong opinions contribute to the humor of "SQ."

After You Read

Assess

Respond Through Writing

Use the following criteria to evaluate students' writing:

- Does the student include a thesis that offers an appraisal of Le Guin's use of satire?
- Does the student evaluate the literary techniques Le Guin uses, such as jargon, irony, parody, and understatement?
- Does the student support his or her claims with textual evidence?

For grammar practice, see Unit 7 Teaching Resources Book, p. 194.

Respond Through Writing

Expository Essay

Evaluate Satire Satirical writing uses literary techniques with the goal of initiating change. Write an essay in which you evaluate Le Guin's use of satirical elements such as jargon, irony, parody, and understatement. Do these literary techniques help to make the story a persuasive and entertaining satire?

Understand the Task When you **evaluate**, you value, measure, and assess elements of a work in order to state your position on a topic. **Satire** is writing that uses humor to comment on human flaws, ideas, social customs, or institutions in order to change them.

Prewrite Craft a thesis that concisely states your viewpoint on Le Guin's use of satirical elements. Then consider the focus of your essay. Will you concentrate on the one satirical element you think is most significant, or will you address several? Will you organize the paragraphs by satirical element or by the effect Le Guin creates? Evaluate which structure will make your argument most effective and create a plan for your essay.

Draft As you write, refer back to your thesis to make sure you have addressed all of the elements of your argument. Use specific examples from the text to substantiate your points. As you create, cross-check your work against a chart like the one below to ensure that you have included and supported all of the elements of your argument.

Element of Argument	Textual Support
jargon	"Nor-Eurp SQ Center"
parody	"inverse sanity quotient"
understatement	

Revise Exchange your essay with a peer. After you read your partner's essay, use the checklist on page 624 to evaluate his or her work. Note any missing elements in the essay. Return your partner's essay and revise your own work according to your partner's notes.

Edit and Proofread Proofread your paper, correcting any errors in spelling, grammar, and punctuation. Review the Grammar Tip in the side column for information on using brackets.

Learning Objectives

In this assignment, you will focus on the following objectives:

Writing:
Evaluating satire in an expository essay.
Using brackets in quotations.

Grammar Tip

Brackets in Quotations

At times, when directly quoting a text, you might have to clarify ambiguities, provide missing letters or words (especially in primary sources), or make corrections or explanations. When doing so, enclose your interpolations in brackets.

"What [Dr. Speakie] did proves his genuine sincerity."

"At least it was much less hectic here in the U.N. [United Nations] Building."

Try to limit these interpolations, as they can interrupt the flow of your writing or distract readers.

Scoring Guide	4	3	2	1
Task addressed	fully	mostly	partially	barely
Thesis	meaningful	provided	partial	weak
Support	thoughtful	provided	limited	weak
Language	varied, descriptive	varied, often descriptive	predictable, imprecise	repetitive, limited
Convention errors	few or none	several	many	serious
Analysis is	convincing	mostly convincing	partially convincing	not convincing

Before You Read

Snow

Meet **Julia Alvarez**
(born 1950)

Julia Alvarez found herself at ten thrust into an unfamiliar culture. Although she was born in New York City, she had grown up in the Dominican Republic during the brutal regime of General Rafael Trujillo, a military dictator who terrorized the nation for thirty-one years. Fleeing their country in the last few months of Trujillo's rule, Alvarez and her family settled in New York City.

Culture Shock Moving from her mother's family compound in the Dominican Republic to the Bronx was not easy for Alvarez. Unable to feel at home in cold and crowded New York City, she took comfort in reading and writing. "I consider this radical uprooting from my culture, my native language, my country, the reason I began writing," the award-winning poet and novelist has stated. "English, not the United States, was where I landed and sank deep roots."

Alvarez learned her new language quickly. In high school, she enjoyed writing and even began to think of it as a possible career. By the time she entered college, she was devoting serious attention to writing. "I was raised in a very traditional, Old World family," she said, "so I never had thoughts about having a career. Moving to a new country, having to learn a new language, I got interested in words, and suddenly being in a world where there were books and encouragement of women to discover their talents helped me become a writer."

A Migrant Poet Alvarez graduated from Middlebury College and later received a graduate degree from Syracuse University. Then she began her career as what she calls "a migrant poet," in which she taught writing in prisons and senior-citizen centers as well as in schools and colleges. "I would go anywhere," she told one interviewer.

Finally she returned to Middlebury College, where she earned tenure in the English Department. She has won several awards for her poetry and prose.

> "I feel like one of the blessings in life is to be doing the work you think you were put here to do. You have to keep writing and achieving it day by day. The one thing I would want for myself is to keep writing and growing."
>
> —Julia Alvarez

Alvarez's first novel, *How the García Girls Lost Their Accents*, was an immediate success. Published in 1991, it tells the story of four Dominican sisters and their struggle to make a new home in the U.S. Alvarez's three sisters saw many similarities between their experiences and those in the novel. "My sisters were a little taken aback," Alvarez admitted, "but they're also very proud of me."

Alvarez's other novels include *In the Time of the Butterflies* and *¡Yo!* (or, in the English translation, *I!*), which describes the García girls as adults. Her poetry collections include *Homecoming* and *The Other Side/El Otro Lado*.

 Literature Online
Author Search For more about Julia Alvarez, go to glencoe.com and enter QuickPass code GLA9800u7.

Before You Read

Focus

Bellringer Options

Literature Launchers:
 Pre-Reading Videos DVD, Selection Launcher

Selection Focus Transparency 72

Daily Language Practice Transparency 110

Or **say:** Imagine seeing a flash of lightning or gently falling snow for the first time. How do you think you would react? Have students freewrite words that express their imagined reactions.

Political History ☆

The Mirabal Sisters Alvarez's novel *In the Time of the Butterflies* is based on the lives of the four Mirabal sisters, who founded an underground movement against Rafael Trujillo's brutal dictatorship. The sisters, code named *las Mariposas* (the Butterflies), caused so much trouble for Trujillo that he ordered three of them killed on November 25, 1960. The United Nations declared the date International Day for the Elimination of Violence against Women.

Selection Skills

Literary Elements
- Indirect Characterization (SE pp. 1254–1256)

Snow

Vocabulary Skills
- Word Parts (SE pp. 1256)
- Suffixes (TE p. 1253)

Reading Skills
- Connect to Contemporary Issues (SE pp. 1254–1256)

Writing Skills/Grammar
- Journal Entry (SE p. 1256)

Before You Read

Focus

Summary

The narrator, a recent immigrant named Yolanda, recalls her first year attending school in New York City. During the Cuban missile crisis, her teacher explains radioactive fallout by drawing dots falling from a mushroom cloud. The crisis passes, but when Yolanda sees snowflakes falling from the sky on a cold December day, she thinks they are fallout and yells, "Bomb!"

Vocabulary

Suffixes Remind students that adding a suffix to a word can change its part of speech. For example, adding the suffix *-ly* changes the adjective *wary* into the adverb *warily*. **Ask:** Which suffix can turn the adjectives *ominous* and *random* into nouns? *(-ness)* Have students write sentences using the adjective and noun forms of the words.

Literature and Reading Preview

Connect to the Story

What amazed you as a child about snow when you experienced it for the first time? Freewrite for several minutes about this experience and explain what made it special.

Build Background

This selection addresses the 1962 Cuban missile crisis, when President John F. Kennedy ordered a naval blockade to prevent shipment of missiles from the Soviet Union to Cuba. The world waited for the Soviets to respond, deeply fearful of a nuclear war. All over the U.S., schools established air-raid drills in an attempt to prepare the nation's children for nuclear attack. At the sound of a siren, students were to file quickly to a hallway away from windows or doors or to crouch under their desks. They were to remain in this position until an all-clear signal sounded. Fortunately, the crisis ended peacefully, and these inadequate safety measures were never needed.

Big Idea **Nature and Technology**

As you read, ask yourself, How do nature and technology become confused in the mind of a young girl?

Literary Element **Indirect Characterization**

A writer uses **indirect characterization** to reveal the personality of a character through that character's words and actions or through what others think and say about that character. As you read, ask yourself, How does indirect characterization reveal information about Sister Zoe?

Reading Strategy **Connect to Contemporary Issues**

Connecting to contemporary issues enriches our appreciation of what we read. As you read, ask yourself, How have recent events in cities around the world made people fearful about security measures that seem inadequate?

Tip: Keep Informed Learn something about the context of the works you are reading to help you understand them better.

- Keep up with current affairs by means of the newspaper, Internet, radio, or television.
- Ask yourself, "What was happening in the world when this literary work was written?"

Learning Objectives

For pages 1253–1256

In studying this text, you will focus on the following objectives:

Literary Study: Analyzing indirect characterization.

Reading: Connecting to contemporary issues.

Vocabulary

enunciate (i nun´ sē āt´) *v.* to pronounce distinctly; p. 1255 *Unless you enunciate clearly, we will be unable to understand you.*

holocaust (hol´ ə kôst´) *n.* great or complete destruction, especially by fire; p. 1255 *The Cuban missile crisis brought the world to the brink of a nuclear holocaust.*

random (ran´ dəm) *adj.* lacking a definite pattern; haphazard; p. 1255 *Up close the painting looked like a random collection of brush strokes.*

warily (wār´ ə lē) *adv.* in a watchful or alert manner; cautiously; p. 1255 *From high on its branch, the bird warily watched the cat.*

Tip: Word Parts Many English words consist of parts that occur in various combinations. The word *enunciate* has as its root the Latin word *nuntiare*, meaning "to report."

Reading Practice

Track Characterization Remind students that direct characterization *tells* about the character, while indirect characterization *shows* what the character is like through what the character says, thinks, and does as well as how other characters react to him or her. Display the following:

- Kendra sat quietly on the sand, watching the waves as the sun slowly dipped below the horizon.

- "This is my favorite time of day at the beach," she thought. "It's so peaceful here at dusk."

Ask: Which form of characterization does each represent? *(The first is direct because it tells about the character; the second is indirect because it describes the character's thoughts and emotions.)* Instruct students to make a two column chart with *Speech, Thoughts,* and *Actions*

as rows in the left column. Have them fill in the right column as they read the story.

Snow

Julia Alvarez

Our first year in New York we rented a small apartment with a Catholic school nearby, taught by the Sisters of Charity, hefty women in long black gowns and bonnets that made them look peculiar, like dolls in mourning. I liked them a lot, especially my grandmotherly fourth grade teacher, Sister Zoe. I had a lovely name, she said, and she had me teach the whole class how to pronounce it. *Yo-lan-da.* As the only immigrant in my class, I was put in a special seat in the first row by the window, apart from the other children so that Sister Zoe could tutor me without disturbing them. Slowly, she **enunciated** the new words I was to repeat: *laundromat, cornflakes, subway, snow.*

Soon I picked up enough English to understand **holocaust** was in the air. Sister Zoe explained to a wide-eyed classroom what was happening in Cuba. Russian missiles were being assembled, trained supposedly on New York City. President Kennedy, looking worried too, was on the television at home, explaining we might have to go to war

against the Communists. At school, we had air-raid drills: an ominous bell would go off and we'd file into the hall, fall to the floor, cover our heads with our coats, and imagine our hair falling out, the bones in our arms going soft. At home, Mami and my sisters and I said a rosary[1] for world peace. I heard new vocabulary: *nuclear bomb, radioactive fallout,*[2] *bomb shelter.* Sister Zoe explained how it would happen. She drew a picture of a mushroom on the blackboard and dotted a flurry of chalk-marks for the dusty fallout that would kill us all.

The months grew cold, November, December. It was dark when I got up in the morning, frosty when I followed my breath to school. One morning as I sat at my desk daydreaming out the window, I saw dots in the air like the ones Sister Zoe had drawn—**random** at first, then lots and lots. I shrieked, "Bomb! Bomb!" Sister Zoe jerked around, her full black skirt ballooning as she hurried to my side. A few girls began to cry.

But then Sister Zoe's shocked look faded. "Why, Yolanda dear, that's snow!" She laughed. "Snow."

"Snow," I repeated. I looked out the window **warily.** All my life I had heard about the white crystals that fell out of American skies in the winter. From my desk I watched the fine powder dust the sidewalk and parked cars below. Each flake was different, Sister Zoe said, like a person, irreplaceable and beautiful. ∾

---

1. For Roman Catholics, a *rosary* is a circle of beads and also the prayers said as one holds these beads.
2. *Fallout,* made of tiny radioactive particles, is released into the atmosphere after a nuclear explosion.

Connect to Contemporary Issues *What are some examples of new vocabulary that current events have introduced into the lexicon today?* **2**

Nature and Technology *Why does the narrator contrast the comparison of snowflakes to bombs with the comparison of snowflakes to people?* **3**

Vocabulary

random (ran′ dəm) *adj.* lacking a definite pattern; haphazard

warily (wār′ ə lē) *adv.* in a watchful or alert manner; cautiously

1 Indirect Characterization *What do these details reveal about Sister Zoe's character?*

Vocabulary

enunciate (i nun′ sē āt′) *v.* to pronounce distinctly

holocaust (hol′ ə kôst′) *n.* great or complete destruction, especially by fire

JULIA ALVAREZ **1255**

After You Read

Assess

1. Students' answers will vary.
2. (a) *Laundromat, cornflakes, subway,* and *snow* (b) They relate to everyday life.
3. (a) Each snowflake is irreplaceable and beautiful. (b) So Yolanda sees she is special
4. She conveys the mood with words such as "holocaust" and "ominous bell." She describes the air-raid drills.
5. She does not speak English well and is new to the environment; everything seems strange.
6. Intelligent, eager to learn, sensitive, and emotional
7. (a) Yolanda mistakes the pure, beautiful snowfall for toxic fallout. (b) Alvarez sets the natural world and technology in opposition by showing the impact of political issues on perceptions.
8. Schools can prepare students by teaching emergency procedures.

Literary Element

Sister Zoe says Yolanda's name is beautiful and each snowflake is irreplaceable. Reassuring Yolanda shows Sister Zoe's kindness and sensitivity.

Reading Strategy

Fear of an attack and concern about the safety of armed forces link the two worlds.

Writing

Students' journals should include a specific memory and details about nature.

After You Read

Respond and Think Critically

Respond and Interpret

1. Which of Yolanda's thoughts or experiences do you find most memorable?
2. (a) What words does Sister Zoe teach Yolanda? (b) Why might those words have been particularly useful for her to understand?
3. (a) At the end of the selection, how does Sister Zoe describe snow? (b) Why does she say the same applies to people?

Analyze and Evaluate

4. How effectively does Alvarez convey the tense mood of the 1950s and 1960s? Explain.

5. How might the fact that Yolanda is an immigrant affect her state of mind?
6. If you were Sister Zoe, what might you write in an assessment of Yolanda?

Connect

7. **Big Idea** Nature and Technology (a) What is ironic about the ending of this story? (b) Does Alvarez see nature and technology as working with or against each other? Explain your answer.
8. **Connect to Today** How might today's schools prepare students for potential disasters?

Literary Element Indirect Characterization

Alvarez develops Sister Zoe through **indirect characterization**, revealing Zoe's personality through her words and actions and through what the narrator, a character in the story, says about her.

Give two examples of indirect characterization of Sister Zoe and explain how they work.

Reading Strategy Connect to Contemporary Issues

Knowing how the world in which a novel or story takes place resembles the world of today will help you understand why characters behave as they do.

What similarities between Yolanda's world and yours add to your appreciation of the story? Explain and support your response with examples.

LOG ON ⓘ **Literature** Online

Selection Resources For Selection Quizzes, eFlashcards, and Reading-Writing Connection activities, go to glencoe.com and enter QuickPass code GLA9800u7.

Vocabulary Practice

Practice with Word Parts For each vocabulary word in the left column, identify the related word with a shared root in the right column. Write each word and underline the part they have in common. Use a printed or online dictionary to look up the meaning of the related word. Then explain how it is related to the vocabulary word.

1. enunciate   aware
2. holocaust   ran
3. random   caustic
4. warily   announce

✍ Writing

Write a Journal Entry Freewrite a journal entry in which you recall a childhood experience of nature.

Vocabulary

1. e**nunc**iate, an**nounc**e: *Enunciate* means "to pronounce distinctly"; *announce* means "to declare publicly." Both words refer to talking.
2. holo**caust**, **caust**ic: *Holocaust* means "great or complete destruction, especially by fire"; *caustic* means "capable of corroding or burning *or* painfully sarcastic." Both words refer to fire.

3. **ran**dom, **ran**: *Random* means "lacking a definite pattern; haphazard" and comes from a root that means "great speed"; *ran* is the past tense of *run,* meaning "to go at a fast pace." Both words refer to speed.
4. w**aw**ily, **aw**are: *Warily* means "in a watchful or alert manner"; *aware* means "mindful of something's existence because of observation." Both words refer to watching.

Before You Read

Cottonmouth Country and Daisies

Meet **Louise Glück**

(born 1943)

When Louise Glück was a young girl, she had an experience that helped define her feelings about poetry. While driving Glück and her classmates to school, a classmate's mother asked Glück to recite the poem that she had written for a school assignment. The burgeoning poet was happy to share her work and was particularly excited about the experimental ending of her new poem. For effect, she had purposefully omitted the rhyme in the final line. To her developing ear, Glück says the result "was exhilarating, a kind of explosion of form." After she recited the poem, her classmate's mother said it was very good, but then corrected the final line, explaining that all it was missing was the last rhyme. The young poet was furious. She hadn't even reached middle school yet, but Glück had already developed a passion to write and be heard in her own precise, original voice. Fifty years after her backseat recital, the talented Glück was named Poet Laureate of the United States.

> "It seems to me that the desire to make art produces an ongoing experience of longing. . . . It's like a lighthouse, except that, as one swims toward it, it backs away."
>
> —Louise Glück

Born Poet Glück was born in New York City and raised on Long Island. Her father shared with his daughter a love of stories. However, it was Glück's mother—a well-educated woman who had fought

to go to college and revered creative gifts—who became the first reader of her poems and who gave the young writer her earliest critiques. Glück began devouring poetry and stories at an early age, and her reading of Greek myths provided figures and images that she frequently references in her own poems.

Poetic Influence While studying at Columbia University, Glück met her greatest influence, poet Stanley Kunitz. She published her first collection of poems, *Firstborn*, when she was twenty-five. Since that debut, Glück's work has been recognized with a National Book Critics Circle Award and a Pulitzer Prize. Glück's poems express mythical, mystic perceptions of everyday objects and experiences. Her exacting language and unexpected line breaks create distinct, often haunting, verses.

In addition to writing poetry, Glück frequently teaches and provides young poets with the kind of support and encouragement that Kunitz offered her.

LOG ON **Literature** Online

Author Search For more about Louise Glück, go to glencoe.com and enter QuickPass code GLA9800u7.

LOUISE GLÜCK **1257**

Before You Read

Focus

Bellringer Options

Daily Language Practice Transparency 111

Or ask students to recall the last time they stopped to appreciate some beautiful natural sight or to see some evidence of nature's destructive power. **Ask:** Is there any way to reconcile these two views of nature? Have students write a short paragraph on how their encounters with nature have shaped their view of it.

National Standards TK

Literary History ☆

Averno Louise Glück's eleventh book of poetry, *Averno*, was nominated for the National Book Award in the poetry section in 2006. The poems explore themes such as life and death, love, and depression through the retelling of the myth of Persephone.

Selection Skills

Literary Elements
- Free Verse (SE pp. 1258, 1260, 1261)
- Voice (SE p. 1261)

Cottonmouth Country *and* **Daisies**

Writing Skills/Grammar
- Evaluate Interpretation (SE p. 1262)
- Free Verse (TE p. 1260)

Reading Skills
- Make Inferences About Theme (SE pp. 1258, 1259, 1262)

Vocabulary Skills
- Analogies (SE pp. 1258, 1262)
- Academic Vocabulary (SE p. 1262)

Before You Read

Focus

Summary

"Cottonmouth Country" is filled with images of death. However, the speaker states that "birth, not death, is the hard loss." In "Daisies," the daisies are the speakers. They seem to mock readers for their inability to appreciate them. The poem illustrates the separation between human beings and nature.

 For summaries in languages other than English, see Unit 7 Teaching Resources, pp. 210–215.

Vocabulary

Word Origins Tell students that the word *nostalgia* comes from the Greek *nostas,* "return home" and *algos,* "pain, grief, distress." Also, the word *scorn* originally came from the Latin *ex-,* "without" and *cornu* "horn."
Ask: How does knowing the origins of these words help you understand their meanings?

(ENGLISH LEARNERS) Have English learners note that the word *rear* is used as a verb in the poem. **Ask:** As what other parts of speech can *rear* be used? *(noun, adjective)* Have students write sentences using the word as both a noun and a verb.

 For additional vocabulary practice, see Unit 7 Teaching Resources Book, p. 218.

1258

Literature and Reading Preview

Connect to the Poems

Have you ever felt as though you could communicate with nature? Discuss with a partner what you might have learned from this experience with nature.

Build Background

Both of these poems demonstrate the important role of setting, or time and place, in Glück's work. In some poems, setting is so important that it becomes a distinct character.

Set Purposes for Reading

Big Idea Nature and Technology

As you read, ask yourself, How do the poems juxtapose elements from the natural world with man-made elements?

Literary Element Free Verse

Many contemporary poems are written in **free verse:** they do not adhere to a fixed rhyme, meter, line, or stanza structure. Free verse allows poets to create and depart from their own patterns. Some free verse flows like conversation or private thoughts. Unusual changes in rhythm or startling **line breaks** (the endings of lines) may create drama or tension. As you read, ask, What words or ideas do the line breaks help emphasize?

Reading Strategy Make Inferences About Theme

In poetry, images, events, and observations frequently convey an underlying message, or **theme.** In the poems you're about to read, nature imagery and other details help to express themes about nature, life, and humanity. By considering each poem's imagery and language, you can make **inferences,** or conclusions based on reason and evidence, about its themes.

Tip: Make Inferences As you read, ask yourself, What images or ideas help me understand the theme of each poem? Note your reactions to specific images or ideas in a chart like the one below. Then note your inferences about the poem's themes.

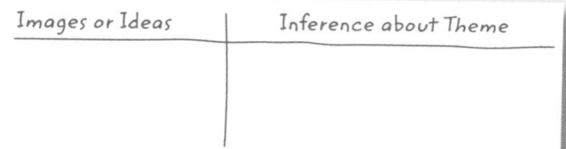

Images or Ideas	Inference about Theme

Vocabulary

woo (wo͞o) *v.* to tempt or invite; p. 1259 *The candidate tried to* woo *voters with big promises.*

rear (rir) *v.* to lift upright; raise; p. 1259 *The bull reared his head before he charged.*

nostalgia (nə stal′ jə) *n.* a bittersweet longing for things, persons, or situations of the past; p. 1260 *As she grew older, she felt nostalgia for her youth.*

scorn (skorn) *n.* contempt or disdain felt toward a person or object considered despicable or unworthy; p. 1260 *She felt scorn for the thief.*

Tip: Analogies Analogies are word pairs that show relationships. To complete an analogy, determine the kind of relationship in the first pair of words and apply the same relationship to the second pair. Example:
high : low :: scorn : approval

Reading Practice

Reread Remind students that poems may not reveal themselves after one reading. In the poems they are about to read, Glück uses very few words to convey her thoughts, so each word represents an important choice. Have students read each poem once and record any words or phrases that they do not understand. Then have them stop and look up any words whose meanings are not clear. For example, they may want to look up the location of Hatteras. Then have them read each poem again and discuss how the meaning of the poem changed on the second reading.

Fish. Tadek Beutlich. Color woodcut/linocut. Victoria and Albert Museum, London.

Cottonmouth Country
Louise Glück

1   Fish bones walked the wave off Hatteras.
     And there were other signs
     That Death **wooed** us, by water, wooed us
     By land: among the pines
5   An uncurled cottonmouth¹ that rolled on moss
     Reared in the polluted air.
     Birth, not death, is the hard loss.
     I know. I also left a skin there. **1**

---

1. Also known as a *water moccasin,* this snake is a semiaquatic
   pit viper of lowlands and swampy regions of the southern
   United States.

> Make Inferences About Theme *Why does the image of
> "polluted air" reinforce Death's presence?*   **2**

Vocabulary

woo (wo͞o) *v.* to tempt or invite
rear (rir) *v.* to lift upright; raise

LOUISE GLÜCK   **1259**

Teach

Literary Element   1

Personification Remind
students that personification is a
figure of speech in which an animal, object, or idea is given human
qualities. **Ask:** What is personified
in the poem? *(Fish bones, since*
they "walked," and death, since it
"wooed")

Reading Strategy   2

**Make Inferences About
Theme Answer:** *Students*
may say that this image sug-
gests something dangerous and
unhealthy.

View the Art

Tadek Beutlich is a contemporary
Polish artist known primarily for
his tapestry art on and off the
loom and for his woodcuts. **Ask:**
How does this print relate to
the poem? *(Possible answer: The*
poem refers to fish bones as a
sign of death.)

1259

Teach

Big Idea | **1**

Nature and Technology
Answer: *Students may say that the daisies say it makes sense to avoid them because their existence calls into question what people consider important.*

Literary Element | **2**

Tone **Ask:** What is the attitude of the daisies toward humans? *(The daisies seem to be mocking humans' inability to appreciate nature.)*

Literary Element | **3**

Free Verse **Answer:** *Students may say that the short lines emphasize the ideas in the lines and help to create drama.*

Daisies

Louise Glück

1   Go ahead: say what you're thinking. The garden
    is not the real world. Machines
    are the real world. Say frankly what any fool
    could read in your face: it makes sense
5   to avoid us, to resist
    nostalgia. It is
    not modern enough, the sound the wind makes
    stirring a meadow of daisies: the mind
    cannot shine following it. And the mind
10 wants to shine, plainly, as
    machines shine, and not
    grow deep, as, for example, roots. It is very touching,
    all the same, to see you cautiously
    approaching the meadow's border in early morning,
15 when no one could possibly
    be watching you. The longer you stand at the edge,
    the more nervous you seem. No one wants to hear
    impressions of the natural world: you will be
    laughed at again; **scorn** will be piled on you.
20 As for what you're actually
    hearing this morning: think twice
    before you tell anyone what was said in this field
    and by whom. **2**

Nature and Technology *Why does the speaker say that it makes sense to avoid the daisies (lines 4–5)?*   **1**

Free Verse *What dramatic effect is created by the varying line lengths in the last four lines?*   **3**

Vocabulary

nostalgia (nə stal′ jə) *n.* a bittersweet longing for things, persons, or situations of the past
scorn (skorn) *n.* contempt or disdain felt toward a person or object considered despicable or unworthy

Writing Practice

Free Verse Ask: Do you think it is easier to write free verse or to write poetry with a regular pattern of meter and rhyme? Challenge students to create their own free verse poems. Encourage them to reflect the Big Idea of nature and technology in their poems. Have students consider their attitudes toward nature and technology. Tell students to convey those attitudes through the tones of their poems. Encourage them to include metaphors that develop the themes of their poems.

After You Read

Respond and Think Critically

Respond and Interpret

1. Which one of these poems did you connect with more? Explain.

2. (a)What words and images in "Cottonmouth Country" suggest death? (b)Why do you think the speaker says that "birth, not death, is the hard loss"?

3. (a)Why does the listener in "Daisies" "cautiously" approach the meadow, when no one could possibly be watching? (b)Why does gazing at the meadow make the listener nervous?

Analyze and Evaluate

4. (a)In "Cottonmouth Country," how does the image in the last line of the poem echo the images in the first and fifth lines? (b)Given what comes before, was the image in the last line an effective way to end the poem? Explain.

5. Why do the daisies in "Daisies" seem to be all-knowing about the listener's thoughts? Explain what this might suggest about nature.

6. (a)Which lines in "Daisies" suggest that people are reluctant to engage with nature? (b)Did the perceptions expressed in these lines ring true to you? Explain your answer.

Connect

7. **Big Idea** Nature and Technology (a)In these poems, how does the modern world intrude on nature? (b)Explain the conflict that you think Glück's poems may be intended to illuminate.

8. **Connect to Today** What do these poems say about human habits? Do you think Glück's observations are accurate today?

Literary Element Free Verse

On the first reading, a **free verse** poem may appear to have no regular form. However, analysis usually reveals one or more poetic techniques. One verse may follow a strict form, while the next verse may depart completely from that form.

Neither of these poems contains fixed meter, fixed line lengths, or formal stanza structures. "Daisies" makes use of rhyme, and "Cottonmouth Country" employs techniques such as slant rhyme and **repetition,** the use of recurring sounds, words, or phrases.

1. (a)List one or two examples of slant rhyme or repetition in "Cottonmouth Country." (b)What is the effect of these techniques on the poem's meaning, musicality, or overall unity?

2. Is free verse is an especially good way to convey the words of the speaker in "Daisies"? Support your answer with details from the poem.

Review: Voice

As you learned on page 420, **voice** is the personality that a writer conveys in a piece of writing. By examining a poet's choice of words and the **tone,** or attitude toward the subject matter, that a poem expresses, you can arrive at a clearer understanding of the poet's voice.

Partner Activity With a partner, discuss the voice in each of the poems. How would you describe the voice? Which words or phrases in each poem are especially good examples of the distinctive use of voice? For each poem, use a graphic organizer like the one shown to record your examples, give your characterization of the voice, and tell what the voice adds to the poem.

Examples of distinctive use of voice → My description of the voice → What the voice adds to the poem

---

After You Read

Assess

1. Students' answers will vary.

2. (a)"Fish bones"; the cottonmouth; "polluted air" (b) Birth involves giving up a comfortable existence to pass into a new and hard world.

3. (a) The listener is embarrassed at being attracted to nature. (b) It may remind the listener of some long-suppressed need.

4. (a) The image of the speaker leaving behind a skin echoes the fish bones, which have lost their skin, and the cottonmouth, which may be shedding its skin. (b) The image is effective in relating the speaker's emotional milestones to the previous images of nature.

5. Students may say that it suggests that nature has much to teach people.

6. (a) Lines 4–6 and 16–19 (b) Answers will vary but should be supported with apt examples.

7. (a) The modern world's pollution and machinery intrude on the purity of nature. (b) The poems may be intended to illuminate humanity's kinship with nature, despite people's reluctance to acknowledge it.

8. Answers will vary. Students should support their answers with reference to the poems.

Literary Element

1. (a) Repetition: "walked the wave"; "wooed us, by water, wooed us / By land." Slant rhyme: "Hatteras"/ "wooed us" (b) Students may say these elements reinforce the relationships of ideas in the poem.

2. Students may say that the free verse imitates the rhythms and sounds of a real conversation.

Review: Voice

Possible answers from "Daisies":

- Example—use of second person
- My description—personal; conversational
- What the voice adds—makes a closer connection between reader and speaker

After You Read

Assess

Reading Strategy

1. **C** is the correct answer because the line implies that birth leads inevitably to death.

Progress Check

Can students make inferences about the theme?

If No → See Unit 7 Teaching Resources Book, p. 217.

Vocabulary

1. b **2.** c **3.** a **4.** c

Academic Vocabulary

Possible answer: an *image* is a vivid sensory representation.

 For additional assessment, see Assessment Resources, pp. 305–306

 To create custom assessments online, go to Progress Reporter Online Assessment.

 To create custom assessments using software, use ExamView Assessment Suite.

Reading Strategy Make Inferences About Theme

SAT Skills Practice

1. Line 7 of "Cottonmouth Country" ("Birth, not death, is the hard loss.") states the poem's

   (A) implied theme of renewal and hope.

   (B) stated theme of renewal and hope.

   (C) implied theme of death's inevitability.

   (D) stated theme of death's inevitability.

   (E) implied theme of life's incomprehensibility.

Vocabulary Practice

Practice with Analogies Choose the word that best completes each analogy below.

1. woo : courtship :: study :
   a. hardship   **b.** apprenticeship
   c. relationship

2. rear : raise :: ascend :
   a. descend   **b.** envelop   **c.** climb

3. nostalgia : reminisce :: grief :
   a. mourn   **b.** celebrate   **c.** withdraw

4. scorn : admire :: praise :
   a. explore   **b.** debate   **c.** criticize

Academic Vocabulary

*Glück's poetry is filled with potent **images** that engage the reader's senses.*

Image is an academic word. After seeing a movie, you might say that a particular **image** from it resonated with you. Using context clues, try to figure out the meaning of the word in the sentence about the poem above. Check your inference in a dictionary.

For more on academic vocabulary, see pages 53 and 54.

Speaking and Listening

 Oral Interpretation

Assignment Present an oral interpretation of either "Cottonmouth Country" or "Daisies." Incorporate facial expressions, gestures, and audio or visual effects. Explain how your interpretation reflects the poem's meaning.

Prepare Refer to the theme chart you made to help you determine the literal and implied meaning of the poem. You should also identify the mood of the poem. Consider how you will use your body language and voice to reflect your interpretation of the poem's mood and meaning. Practice reading the poem in front of a mirror to evaluate your expressions and movements.

Perform When you present, use visual aids or other media to reinforce your interpretation. For example, you might display paintings or photographs that illustrate the poem's theme(s). Or you might play sound clips that mirror transitions in the poem, such as a slow song changing into something more harsh and dramatic. The way you dress can also communicate mood and meaning. However, do not let your props overshadow your presentation. The most effective way to convey mood and meaning is through gestures, tone of voice, and eye contact. When you finish reading the poem, explain how your presentation mirrors the selection's meaning.

Evaluate Discuss your performance with a partner. Write a paragraph evaluating your interpretation, noting any areas for improvement. Use the guidelines on page 841 to help in your evaluation.

LOG ON ▶ **Literature** Online

Selection Resources For Selection Quizzes, eFlashcards, and Reading-Writing Connection activities, go to glencoe.com and enter QuickPass code GLA9800u7.

Speaking and Listening

Use these criteria when evaluating students' oral interpretations:

- Did the student use effective verbal and nonverbal techniques?
- Did the student convey implied meaning of the poem?
- Did the student use effective visual and media aids?

PART 3

Extending and Remaking Traditions

The Museum of Modern Art, 1973. Malcah Zeldis.

 View the Art Zeldis is a self-taught artist who follows her own rules of painting. How does this attitude represent a potential new way of seeing tradition and innovation?

> *"We became filled with a hunger—I call it now, sometimes, Latino Hunger. A hunger to see ourselves, our families and friends, our values and lives and realities reflected in something other than our own minds."* **1**
>
> —Carmen Tafolla, "Mi Familia"

1263

Reading Strategy **1**

Analyze Direct students to read the quotation. **Ask:** Why might Tafolla use the word "hunger" to convey her point? *(When people do not see their lives represented in the society around them, they may feel an emptiness inside that is like hunger.)*

View the Art

Answer: *In following her own rules of painting, Zeldis is able to create her own style of art that blends tradition and innovation.*

Malcah Zeldis (1931–) is a prominent folk artist whose subjects are social and religious events and her personal heroes.

For additional support for English learners, see Unit 7 Teaching Resources Book, p. 223.

Approaching Level

DIFFERENTIATED INSTRUCTION

Emerging Help students see how a writer uses sensory words to represent concepts or emotions that might be difficult to convey. In this case, Tafolla uses the feeling of physical hunger to describe the feeling of being invisible in society. Have students create a chart listing three emotions in one column as shown. Work with students to identify physical sensations or actions that might be associated with these feelings. Have students propose other emotions to add to the chart.

Emotion	Physical
feeling invisible	hunger
anger	*(clenched fist)*
excitement	*(jumping)*

Before You Read

from *The Woman Warrior*

Bellringer Options

**Selection Focus
   Transparency 70**
**Daily Language Practice
   Transparency 112**

Or display images that show how a person's appearance changes over time (such as photos of a person as a baby, a child, a teenager, and an adult). **Ask:** How do people change throughout their lives? What, if anything, about a person remains the same over time?

Have students consider, as they read, how the two sisters in the selection have changed and how they have remained the same over time.

Meet **Maxine Hong Kingston**

(born 1940)

Finding meaning was Maxine Hong Kingston's primary mission when she began to write *The Woman Warrior: Memories of a Girlhood among Ghosts*. The American daughter of Chinese immigrants, Kingston had long been fascinated by the differing ways in which women were viewed by her parents and by other Chinese immigrants of their generation. In talking to her parents, Kingston discovered that cherished myths about powerful warrior women existed side by side with what Kingston perceived as sexist ideas. Kingston's mother often sang the *Ballad of Mu Lan*, about a young woman who took her father's place in battle. She also talked about her own experiences training and working as a doctor in China at a time when few women could gain an education, take on a profession, or work outside the home. Nevertheless, Kingston's mother would often say, "It's better to raise geese than girls."

A Life of Her Own Kingston began writing poetry when she was nine years old. A talented student, she attended the University of California at Berkeley before marrying Earll Kingston, an actor. She taught English and creative writing for almost a decade before submitting her writing for publication.

Writing as a Way of Life *The Woman Warrior* won the National Book Critics' Circle Award and was named one of the ten best nonfiction books of the 1970s by *TIME* magazine. The *New York Times* wrote, "As an account of growing up female and Chinese American in California . . . it is anti-nostalgic; it burns the fat right out of the mind. As a dream—of the 'female avenger'—it is dizzying, elemental, a poem turned into a sword."

> "*I have no idea how people who don't write endure their lives . . . words and stories create order. And some of the things that happen to us in life seem to have no meaning, but when you write them down you find the meanings for them . . .*"
>
> —*Maxine Hong Kingston*

While still writing *The Woman Warrior*, Kingston began *China Men*, which later won the American Book Award. The first is the story of the women in her family, the second, the story of the men.

In recent years, in addition to her writing, Kingston has taught English and math. "I get a recurring dream in which my mother appears and she says to me: 'What have you done to educate America? Have you educated America yet? And what about the rest of the world? Have you gotten them educated yet?' . . . Those are my orders!"

 Literature Online

Author Search For more about Maxine Hong Kingston, go to glencoe.com and enter QuickPass code GLA9800u7.

Literary Elements
- Exposition (SE pp. 1265–1267, 1270, 1272)
- Dialogue (SE p. 1272)

from **The Woman Warrior**

Writing Skills/Grammar
- Autobiographical Narrative (SE p. 1273)
- Sentence Fragments (SE p. 1273)
- Connect (TE p. 1266)

Reading Skills
- Make Inferences About Characters (SE pp. 1265–1268, 1270, 1272)

Vocabulary Skills
- Synonyms (SE p. 1272)

Listening/Speaking/ Viewing Skills
- Analyze Art (TE p. 1266)

Study Skills/Research/ Assessment
- Short Responses (TE p. 1270)

Literature and Reading Preview

Connect to the Story

When family members are raised in different cultures, how does it affect their relationships with one another? Working in a small group, discuss this question. Consider how food, clothing, language, behavior, and music might affect the relationship.

Build Background

The main character in this selection is Kingston's mother, Brave Orchid. When Brave Orchid came to the United States, she left her younger sister, Moon Orchid, behind in China. Moon Orchid later joined her sister in 1969. During that time, the Vietnam War was under way. Many draft-age men went to Canada to avoid going to Vietnam.

Set Purposes for Reading

Big Idea Extending and Remaking Traditions

As you read, ask yourself, How does Kingston present a fresh take on U.S. culture and history?

Literary Element Exposition

Exposition in nonfiction presents information that readers will need to understand the characters, the setting, and the situation discussed in a narrative. As you read, ask yourself, Where does Kingston use exposition and where does she require you to make inferences to understand the story?

Reading Strategy Make Inferences About Characters

When you **make inferences,** you use your reason and experience to understand what an author does not say directly. Inferring helps you look more deeply at characters and points you toward the **theme,** or overall message, of a selection. As you read, ask yourself, What do you know about Brave Orchid based on her thoughts, words, and actions?

Tip: Character Web Use a web like the one below to record details about Brave Orchid and your inferences based on them.

MAXINE HONG KINGSTON **1265**

Learning Objectives

For pages 1264–1272

In studying this text, you will focus on the following objectives:

Literary Study: Identifying exposition.

Reading: Making inferences about characters.

Vocabulary

downy (dou´ nē) *adj.* soft and fluffy, like the feathers of young birds; p. 1267 *With their downy feathers, baby birds look innocent and cute.*

inaudibly (in ô´ də blē) *adv.* in a manner not able to be heard; p. 1270 *We could see her mouth moving, but she was speaking inaudibly.*

gravity (grav´ ə tē) *n.* seriousness; importance; p. 1270 *He wanted to laugh but didn't because he recognized the gravity of the graduation ceremony.*

oblivious (ə bliv´ ē əs) *adj.* without conscious awareness; unmindful; p. 1270 *We jumped up and down in joy, oblivious to the stares of the people around us.*

dusk (dusk) *n.* the time of day just before nightfall; p. 1270 *We returned home before dusk.*

Tip: Synonyms Words with the same or similar meanings are called **synonyms.** Knowing synonyms can help you add interest and variety to your writing. *Dusk,* for example, is more poetic than *evening.*

English Learners

DIFFERENTIATED INSTRUCTION

Intermediate Preview some of the text connectors that help readers understand the sequence of events in a story, such as *when, first, then, next.* The first word of the story is a sequencing word, *when.* "When she was about sixty-eight years old, Brave Orchid. . . . She had not seen Moon Orchid for thirty years." **Ask:** How old was Brave Orchid when she last saw her sister? *(38 years old)* Have students keep a list of sequencing words and phrases they find as they read the story. *(after a short while, suddenly, finally, at last)* Ask students to make a note next to each entry in the list that indicates how the connector helped their reading.

Before You Read

Focus

Summary

It is 1969. Brave Orchid waits at the airport for her sister—Moon Orchid, whom she has not seen for 30 years—to arrive from China. As she waits, she thinks about how she came to the United States, how she feels about the impending reunion, and how her children are more American than Chinese. The reunion, although warm, is bittersweet, as both sisters cannot believe how much time has passed since they were last together and how old they have become.

> 📁 For summaries in languages other than English, see Unit 7 Teaching Resources Book, pp. 224–229.

Vocabulary

Multiple Meaning Words

Explain to students that the definition listed for a vocabulary word may not be the meaning with which they are most familiar. **Ask:** What is the scientific definition of the word *gravity*? (*a physical force on objects*)

ADVANCED Explain that the word *gravity* comes from the Latin root, *gravis,* meaning "heavy." Have students research the roots of the words *gravity* and *grave.* **Ask:** Does the word *grave,* meaning a burial place, have the same root as the word *grave,* meaning serious? (*No; the burial place comes from an Old English root,* grafan, *that means "to dig."*)

> 📁 For additional vocabulary practice, see Unit 7 Teaching Resources Book, pp. 232–233.

1265

Teach

Literary Element   1

Exposition Answer: *"about sixty-eight years old"; "bringing her sister to the United States"*

 For additional literary element practice, see Unit 7 Teaching Resources Book, p. 230.

Reading Strategy   2

Make Inferences About Characters Answer: *She is determined and forceful.*

View the Art ★

Chinese-born Zifen Qian (1957–) combines traditional and modern styles in his paintings. **Ask:** How might this painting depict a scene from Brave Orchid's past? *(The women in the painting could represent Moon Orchid and Brave Orchid as young women in China.)*

 For an audio recording of this selection, use Listening Library Audio CD-ROM.

Readability Scores

Dale-Chall: 4.4
DRP: 51
Lexile: 800

from

The Woman Warrior

Maxine Hong Kingston

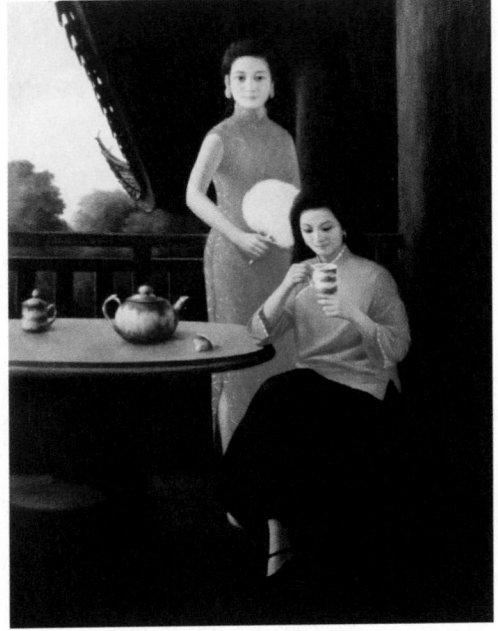

A Sunny Day with Gentle Breeze, 1993. Zifen Qian. Oil on canvas, 42 x 56 in. Private collection.

When she was about sixty-eight years old, Brave Orchid took a day off to wait at San Francisco International Airport for the plane that was bringing her sister to the United States. She had not seen Moon Orchid for thirty years. She had begun this waiting at home, getting up a half-hour before Moon Orchid's plane took off in Hong Kong. Brave Orchid would add her will power to the forces that keep an airplane up. Her head hurt with the concentration. The plane had to be light, so no matter how tired she felt, she dared not rest her spirit on a wing but continuously and gently pushed up on the plane's belly. She had already been waiting at the airport for nine hours. She was wakeful.

Next to Brave Orchid sat Moon Orchid's only daughter, who was helping her aunt wait. Brave Orchid had made two of her own children come too because they could drive, but they had been lured away by the magazine racks and the gift shops and coffee shops. Her American children could not sit for very long. They did not understand sitting; they had wan-

dering feet. She hoped they would get back from the pay T.V.'s or the pay toilets or wherever they were spending their money before the plane arrived. If they did not come back soon, she would go look for them. If her son thought he could hide in the men's room, he was wrong.

"Are you all right, Aunt?" asked her niece.

"No, this chair hurts me. Help me pull some chairs together so I can put my feet up."

She unbundled a blanket and spread it out to make a bed for herself. On the floor she had two shopping bags full of canned peaches, real peaches, beans wrapped in taro[1] leaves, cookies, Thermos bottles, enough food for everybody, though only her niece would eat with

---

1. *Taro* (tär′ ō) is a tropical Asian plant with broad leaves. It is customary in Chinese cooking to wrap rice, vegetables, or fish in the leaves for steaming.

1 Exposition *What details help you understand the situation of Brave Orchid and her family?*

2 Mak Inferences About Characters *What does this detail tell you about Brave Orchid's character?*

Writing Practice

 SMALL GROUP

Connect The illustrations accompanying this selection convey messages about generational and cultural differences. Help students connect the art with the Big Idea:

- Have students work in small groups to create a magazine in which this selection will be published.
- Ask groups to choose art for the selection and to explain their choices, referring

to story details. Students can choose existing art, describe what they would recommend, or sketch their ideas.

her. Her bad boy and bad girl were probably sneaking hamburgers, wasting their money. She would scold them.

Many soldiers and sailors sat about, oddly calm, like little boys in cowboy uniforms. (She thought "cowboy" was what you would call a Boy Scout.) They should have been crying hysterically on their way to Vietnam. "If I see one that looks Chinese," she thought, "I'll go over and give him some advice." She sat up suddenly; she had forgotten about her own son, who was even now in Vietnam. Carefully she split her attention, beaming half of it to the ocean, into the water to keep him afloat. He was on a ship. He was in Vietnamese waters. She was sure of it. He and the other children were lying to her. They had said he was in Japan, and then they said he was in the Philippines. But when she sent him her help, she could feel that he was on a ship in Da Nang.[2] Also she had seen the children hide the envelopes that his letters came in.

"Do you think my son is in Vietnam?" she asked her niece, who was dutifully eating.

"No. Didn't your children say he was in the Philippines?"

"Have you ever seen any of his letters with Philippine stamps on them?"

"Oh, yes. Your children showed me one."

"I wouldn't put it past them to send the letters to some Filipino they know. He puts Manila[3] postmarks on them to fool me."

"Yes, I can imagine them doing that. But don't worry. Your son can take care of himself. All your children can take care of themselves."

"Not him. He's not like other people. Not normal at all. He sticks erasers in his ears, and

---

the erasers are still attached to the pencil stubs. The captain will say, 'Abandon ship,' or, 'Watch out for bombs,' and he won't hear. He doesn't listen to orders. I told him to flee to Canada, but he wouldn't go."

She closed her eyes. After a short while, plane and ship under control, she looked again at the children in uniforms. Some of the blond ones looked like baby chicks, their crew cuts like the **downy** yellow on baby chicks. You had to feel sorry for them even though they were Army and Navy Ghosts.[4]

Suddenly her son and daughter came running. "Come, Mother. The plane's landed early. She's here already." They hurried, folding up their mother's encampment. She was glad her children were not useless. They must have known what this trip to San Francisco was about then. "It's a good thing I made you come early," she said.

Brave Orchid pushed to the front of the crowd. She had to be in front. The passengers were separated from the people waiting for them by glass doors and walls. Immigration Ghosts were stamping papers. The travelers crowded along some conveyor belts to have their luggage searched. Brave Orchid did not see her sister anywhere. She stood watching for four hours. Her children left and came back. "Why don't you sit down?" they asked.

"The chairs are too far away," she said.

"Why don't you sit on the floor then?"

No, she would stand, as her sister was probably standing in a line she could not see from

---

2. *Da Nang* (dä näng), a port city in South Vietnam, was the site of a major U.S. military base during the Vietnam War.
3. *Manila* (mə nil′ ə) is the capital of the Philippines and its largest city.

3 **Extending and Remaking Traditions** *From Brave Orchid's thoughts here, what can you infer about differences between Brave Orchid and her children?*

4 **Extending and Remaking Traditions** *Why do you think Brave Orchid is mistrustful of her children? Why does she have more trust in her niece?*

4. Here, *ghosts* refers to white people.

Make Inferences About Characters *What do the children's actions tell you about the children? What does Brave Orchid's remark reveal about her?* **5**

Exposition *Why are these details about the setting important to the story?* **6**

Vocabulary

downy (dou′ nē) *adj.* soft and fluffy, like the feathers of young birds

---

Teach

Big Idea **3**

Extending and Remaking Traditions Answer: *She wants her children to do things her way, but her children do not always obey her.*

Big Idea **4**

Extending and Remaking Traditions Answer: *They have American ways and do not always obey her. Her niece is not as "American."*

Reading Strategy **5**

Make Inferences About Characters Answer: *They are attuned to their mother. She doesn't want her children to know she appreciates them.*

Literary Element **6**

Exposition Answer: *They emphasize her strong will and traditional Chinese way of approaching the situation.*

English Learners

DIFFERENTIATED INSTRUCTION

Intermediate Instruct English learners to identify actions and thoughts of Brave Orchid that seem unusual but reveal her personality. *(One example is Brave Orchid's thinking that she was helping keep the plane in the air.)* Ask them to describe her character. *(strong, devoted to her family, fond of tradition)*

Approaching Level

DIFFERENTIATED INSTRUCTION

Emerging Some locations mentioned in the selection may not be familiar to students. Ask students to find place names (such as Vietnam, China, Da Nang, and the Philippines) in the selection and then locate them on a world map.

Teach

Reading Strategy | 1

Make Inferences About Characters **Answer:** *Her trip to the United States 30 years ago was difficult.*

Reading Strategy | 2

Make Inferences About Characters **Answer:** *Brave Orchid expects her sister to look as she did 30 years before, when Brave Orchid last saw her. She has an unrealistic concept of the passage of time.*

Reading Strategy | 3

Make Inferences About Characters **Answer:** *Brave Orchid's remark indicates that she does not like being contradicted.*

Literary History ☆

Port of Entry The Ellis Island immigration station closed in 1954. By that time, more than 12 million people had passed through it. At Ellis Island, officials screened immigrants in order to identify criminals and people with infectious diseases or histories of mental illness. Federal law banned such people from entering the United States.

here. Her American children had no feelings and no memory.

To while away time, she and her niece talked about the Chinese passengers. These new immigrants had it easy. On Ellis Island[5] the people were thin after forty days at sea and had no fancy luggage.

"That one looks like her," Brave Orchid would say.

"No, that's not her."

☆ Ellis Island had been made out of wood and iron. Here everything was new plastic, a ghost trick to lure immigrants into feeling safe and spilling their secrets. Then the Alien Office could send them right back. Otherwise, why did they lock her out, not letting her help her sister answer questions and spell her name? At Ellis Island when the ghost asked Brave Orchid what year her husband had cut off his pigtail, a Chinese who was crouching on the floor motioned her not to talk. "I don't know," she had said. If it weren't for that Chinese man, she might not be here today, or her husband either. She hoped some Chinese, a janitor or a clerk, would look out for Moon Orchid. Luggage conveyors fooled immigrants into thinking the Gold Mountain was going to be easy.

Brave Orchid felt her heart jump—Moon Orchid. "There she is," she shouted. But her niece saw it was not her mother at all. And it shocked her to discover the woman her aunt was pointing out. This was a young woman, younger than herself, no older than Moon Orchid the day the sisters parted. "Moon Orchid will have changed a little, of course," Brave Orchid was saying. "She will have

> *B*rave Orchid felt her heart jump—Moon Orchid. "There she is," she shouted. But her niece saw it was not her mother at all.

learned to wear western clothes." The woman wore a navy blue suit with a bunch of dark cherries at the shoulder.

"No, Aunt," said the niece. "That's not my mother."

"Perhaps not. It's been so many years. Yes, it is your mother. It must be. Let her come closer, and we can tell. Do you think she's too far away for me to tell, or is it my eyes getting bad?"

"It's too many years gone by," said the niece.

Brave Orchid turned suddenly—another Moon Orchid, this one a neat little woman with a bun. She was laughing at something the person ahead of her in line said. Moon Orchid was just like that, laughing at nothing. "I would be able to tell the difference if one of them would only come closer," Brave Orchid said with tears, which she did not wipe. Two children met the woman with the cherries, and she shook their hands. The other woman was met by a young man. They looked at each other gladly, then walked away side by side.

Up close neither one of those women looked like Moon Orchid at all. "Don't worry, Aunt," said the niece. "I'll know her."

"I'll know her too. I knew her before you did."

The niece said nothing, although she had seen her mother only five years ago. Her aunt liked having the last word.

Finally Brave Orchid's children quit wandering and drooped on a railing. Who knew what they were thinking? At last the niece called out, "I see her! I see her! Mother! Mother!" Whenever the doors parted, she shouted,

---

5. From 1892 to 1943, *Ellis Island,* in upper New York Bay, was the chief U.S. immigration station.

1 Make Inferences About Characters *What can you infer about Brave Orchid's background from her thoughts here?*

2 Make Inferences About Characters *What do Brave Orchid's unrealistic ideas about her sister tell you about Brave Orchid?*

3 Make Inferences About Characters *What trait, or personal characteristic, of Brave Orchid is suggested by this remark?*

Grammar Practice

Quoted Questions When direct quotations end with questions, the question marks are placed inside the closing quotation marks. Have students find questions in the selection that follow this rule.

Direct students to imagine they are about to be reunited with people they have not seen in a long time. Ask them to write dialogues that include questions they would ask at the reunion. Remind them to punctuate the questions correctly.

probably embarrassing the American cousins, but she didn't care. She called out, "Mama! Mama!" until the crack in the sliding doors became too small to let in her voice. "Mama!" What a strange word in an adult voice. Many people turned to see what adult was calling, "Mama!" like a child. Brave Orchid saw an old, old woman jerk her head up, her little eyes blinking confusedly, a woman whose nerves leapt toward the sound anytime she heard "Mama!" Then she relaxed to her own business again. She was a tiny, tiny lady, very thin, with little fluttering hands, and her hair was in a gray knot. She was dressed in a gray wool suit; she wore pearls around her neck and in her earlobes. Moon Orchid *would* travel with her jewels showing. Brave Orchid momentarily saw, like a larger, younger outline around this old woman, the sister she had been waiting for. The familiar dim halo faded, leaving the woman so old, so gray. So old. Brave Orchid pressed against the glass. *That* old lady? Yes, that old lady facing the ghost who stamped her papers without question-

ing her was her sister. Then, without noticing her family, Moon Orchid walked smiling over to the Suitcase Inspector Ghost, who took her boxes apart, pulling out puffs of tissue. From where she was, Brave Orchid could not see what her sister had chosen to carry across the ocean. She wished her sister would look her way. Brave Orchid thought that if *she* were entering a new country, she would be at the windows. Instead Moon Orchid hovered over the unwrapping, surprised at each reappearance as if she were opening presents after a birthday party.

"Mama!" Moon Orchid's daughter kept calling. Brave Orchid said to her children, "Why don't you call your aunt too? Maybe she'll hear us if all of you call out together." But her children slunk away. Maybe that shame-face they so often wore was American politeness.

4

Extending and Remaking Traditions *How does this sentence help explain why there is tension between Brave Orchid and her children?* **5**

MAXINE HONG KINGSTON **1269**

Literary Element **4**

Exposition **Ask:** How does Kingston give the reader insight into Brave Orchid's thoughts? *(She describes Brave Orchid's desire for her sister to look her way and her efforts to get her children to call to her sister.)*

Big Idea **5**

Extending and Remaking Traditions **Answer:** *It shows that Brave Orchid may not understand her children because of the cultural gap between them and herself.*

English Learners

DIFFERENTIATED INSTRUCTION

Advanced Ask students how they interpret the use of *ghosts* in the text. **Ask:** Does Kingston believe the people are truly ghosts? *(The word* ghosts *expresses Brave Orchid's point of view. She sees all Caucasians as ghosts because of the whiteness of their skin.)*

Approaching Level

DIFFERENTIATED INSTRUCTION

Emerging Have students suggest emotions that Brave Orchid feels as she is about to see her sister and when she finally sees her. Help them find evidence in the text to support their answers. For example, she feels protective *(She hoped some Chinese . . . would look out for Moon Orchid)*, defensive *(I knew her before you did)*, joyful *(Brave Orchid felt her heart jump)*, sad *(Brave Orchid said* with tears*)*, disapproving *(Moon Orchid would* travel with her jewels showing*)*, stunned *(That* old lady?*)*. Point out that though the sisters were happy to see each other again, they were also sad because they have grown old without each other.

Teach

Literary Element   1

Tone   **Ask:** How does the story's tone change between the time the plane lands and Brave Orchid stands to wait for her sister and the time the sisters meet each other face to face? *(Possible answer: At first, the tone is suspenseful and anxious as Brave Orchid and her niece try to identify Moon Orchid and attract her attention. Then the tone becomes humorous and bittersweet as the women face each other for the first time in 30 years.)*

Literary Element   2

Exposition   **Answer:** *The situation set up in the early part of the story is moving to a close. Moon Orchid has arrived, and the reader has come to certain realizations about Brave Orchid's character.*

Reading Strategy   3

Make Inferences About Characters   **Answer:** *Brave Orchid is clearly moved by being reunited with her sister. She may have expected her sister to react to their reunion more seriously.*

 To check students' understanding of the selection, see Unit 7 Teaching Resources Book, p. 235.

"Mama!" Moon Orchid's daughter called again, and this time her mother looked right at her. She left her bundles in a heap and came running. "Hey!" the Customs Ghost yelled at her. She went back to clear up her mess, talking **inaudibly** to her daughter all the while. Her daughter pointed toward Brave Orchid. And at last Moon Orchid looked at her—two old women with faces like mirrors.

Their hands reached out as if to touch the other's face, then returned to their own, the fingers checking the grooves in the forehead and along the side of the mouth. Moon Orchid, who never understood the **gravity** of things, started smiling and laughing, pointing at Brave Orchid. Finally Moon Orchid gathered up her stuff, strings hanging and papers loose, and met her sister at the door, where they shook hands, **oblivious** to blocking the way.

"You're an old woman," said Brave Orchid.

"Aiaa. *You're* an old woman."

"But you are really old. Surely, you can't say that about me. I'm not old the way you're old."

"But *you* really are old. You're one year older than I am."

"Your hair is white and your face all wrinkled."

"You're so skinny."

"You're so fat."

---

6. The *Bay Bridge* crosses the San Francisco Bay, connecting the cities of San Francisco and Oakland. The *Diablo* (dē ä′ blō) *hills* are at the base of Mount Diablo, a peak located about twenty miles east of Oakland.

Vocabulary

inaudibly (in ô′ də blē) *adv.* in a manner not able to be heard

gravity (grav′ ə tē) *n.* seriousness; importance

oblivious (ə bliv′ ē əs) *adj.* without conscious awareness; unmindful

---

"Fat women are more beautiful than skinny women."

The children pulled them out of the doorway. One of Brave Orchid's children brought the car from the parking lot, and the other heaved the luggage into the trunk. They put the two old ladies and the niece in the back seat. All the way home—across the Bay Bridge, over the Diablo hills,[6] across the San Joaquin River to the valley, the valley moon so white at **dusk**—all the way home, the two sisters exclaimed every time they turned to look at each other, "Aiaa! How old!"

Brave Orchid forgot that she got sick in cars, that all vehicles but palanquins made her dizzy. "You're so old," she kept saying. "How did you get so old?"

Brave Orchid had tears in her eyes. But Moon Orchid said, "You look older than I. You *are* older than I," and again she'd laugh. "You're wearing an old mask to tease me." It surprised Brave Orchid that after thirty years she could still get annoyed at her sister's silliness. ∾

Visual Vocabulary
A **palanquin** (pal′ ən kēn′) is a covered or enclosed couch, carried on the shoulders of two or more men by means of poles.

Exposition *How does the author develop the details about character and plot that were introduced in the first part of the story?*   **2**

Make Inferences About Characters *Why is Brave Orchid annoyed by her sister's remarks?*   **3**

Vocabulary

dusk (dusk) *n.* the time of day just before nightfall

Assessment Practice

Short Responses   Explain that a short-response question may not have one correct answer. Instead, an answer will be judged by its insightfulness and the quality of textual evidence included. **Ask:** How does Brave Orchid's reaction to her children's "wandering off" at the airport indicate her relationship with them? *(Possible answers: Her reaction is one indication that a generational and cultural gap exists between her children and herself; she is exasperated with their impatience, but she admires their independence.)*

Respond and Think Critically

Respond and Interpret

1. Did you find this selection serious, humorous, or both? Describe your impressions.

2. (a)How long before her sister's plane is scheduled to land does Brave Orchid arrive at the airport? (b)Why do you think she does this?

3. (a)How do Brave Orchid and Moon Orchid react when they see each other? (b)Why do the sisters respond to each other as they do?

Analyze and Evaluate

4. Since this narrative is from Kingston's memoir, a reader might expect a **first-person point of view.** Why might Kingston have chosen to use the **third-person point of view** here?

5. Brave Orchid finds her children to be a mystery. Why might she feel this way? Explain.

6. Did you find Kingston's rendering of the family convincing and true-to-life? Why or why not?

Connect

7. **Big Idea** Extending and Remaking Traditions How does this excerpt from *The Woman Warrior* portray the immigrant experience?

Visual Literacy

Compare and Contrast Characters

As you did for Brave Orchid, make a web diagram to record details and inferences about Moon Orchid's character. After you have completed the web about Moon Orchid, examine both webs to see how Brave Orchid's and Moon Orchid's characters are similar and different. Use a Venn diagram to compare them.

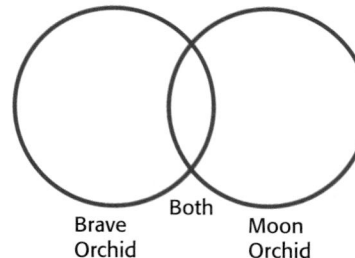

Brave Orchid | Both | Moon Orchid

Group Activity

Share the graphic organizers you made with one or more classmates.

1. Work with a partner or group to discuss how Brave Orchid and Moon Orchid are similar and how they are different.

2. At what points in the selection do you receive critical information about each of the two characters? For each character, explain how thoughts, words, actions, or some combination of the three provided the information.

MAXINE HONG KINGSTON **1271**

Assess

1. Students' answers will vary.

2. (a) She arrives at least nine hours early. (b) She is looking forward to seeing her sister.

3. (a) Brave Orchid is moved to be reunited with Moon Orchid, yet also annoyed. They bicker. (b) Perhaps they have always argued; arguing is part of their relationship.

4. She may have wanted to make this memoir a universal statement about culture and family.

5. Her children, raised in the United States, have had different experiences than she. She does not understand how these experiences shaped them.

6. Students' answers will vary. Students should support their answers with examples from the selection.

7. By providing a glimpse of Brave Orchid's inner world, Kingston helps foster sympathy and understanding for Chinese immigrants in the United States.

 For additional assessment, see Assessment Resources, pp. 307–308.

 To create custom assessments online, go to Progress Reporter Online Assessment.

 To create custom assessments using software, use ExamView Assessment Suite.

Visual Literacy

1. Both make quick, sharp remarks; Brave Orchid is less patient and more serious than Moon Orchid.

2. Students should offer specific examples from the story (conversations or descriptive details) that provide essential information.

After You Read

Assess

Literary Element

1. The story is set in an airport. An older woman is to meet her sister there after a 30-year separation. The setting is developed further as the narrator describes departing soldiers and arriving immigrants.

2. Students may choose Brave Orchid's opinionated nature or her old-fashioned manner. Readers feel more sympathy as they learn about her struggles.

Review: Dialogue

1. (a) The niece treats her with respect and deference. (b) The niece loves her aunt; she grew up around people like Brave Orchid.

2. (a) It is a familiar pattern and a way of showing their affection. (b) It is moving and humorous. It is amusing that they immediately begin to bicker; the bickering is moving because it shows their relationship has not changed.

Reading Strategy

1. **C** is the correct answer because Kingston's description of Brave Orchid's Americanized children helps explain her struggles to retain her cultural connection after immigrating to America.

Progress Check

Can students make inferences about characters?

If No → See Unit 7 Teaching Resources Book, p. 231.

Exposition

Exposition in a nonfiction narrative provides information that is crucial to an understanding of the work's characters, setting, and plot. In this selection, Kingston provides exposition in the first two paragraphs. As the selection progresses, Kingston expands on this information.

1. What aspect of the story's setting is introduced in the exposition and developed further in the pages that follow?

2. Select one character and a trait of that character as introduced in the exposition. Explain briefly how that trait becomes important as the story unfolds.

Review: Dialogue

As you learned on page 1027, **dialogue** is conversation between characters in a literary work. Through dialogue, an author reveals the feelings, thoughts, and intentions of characters; establishes conflicts; and advances the plot.

1. Examine the dialogue between Brave Orchid and her niece. (a)How do you think the niece views Brave Orchid? (b)Explain what impression you receive of the relationship between Brave Orchid and her niece from these dialogues.

2. (a)Reread the final conversation between Brave Orchid and Moon Orchid. Why do you think that the sisters say the things they say? (b)Explain whether you found their exchange moving, humorous, or both. Support your answer.

LOG ON ▶ **Literature** Online

Selection Resources For Selection Quizzes, eFlashcards, and Reading-Writing Connection activities, go to glencoe.com and enter QuickPass code GLA9800u7.

Vocabulary

1. e **2.** c **3.** f **4.** a **5.** d

Make Inferences About Characters

SAT Skills Practice

1. The information about Brave Orchid's children deepens the reader's understanding of her character by

   (A) explaining why she resented America.
   (B) emphasizing her old-fashioned ways.
   (C) illustrating the difficulties she faced as an immigrant.
   (D) intimating why she was closer with her niece.
   (E) supporting her surprise at how Moon Orchid had aged.

Vocabulary Practice

Practice with Synonyms With a partner, match each boldfaced vocabulary word below with its synonym. Use a thesaurus or dictionary to check your answers.

1. **downy**
2. **inaudibly**
3. **gravity**
4. **oblivious**
5. **dusk**

a. unaware
b. clear
c. indistinctly
d. twilight
e. fluffy
f. importance
g. beneath

Academic Vocabulary

*To recognize her sister, who she has not seen in thirty years, Brave Orchid has to make an **adjustment** to her way of thinking.*

Adjustment is an academic word. For example, an architect might have to make an **adjustment** to his blueprints to satisfy the people for whom he is building a house.

To further explore the meaning of this word, answer this question: What was an **adjustment** you had to make when you first entered high school?

For more on academic vocabulary, see pages 53–54.

Academic Vocabulary

Possible answer: When I first entered high school, I made the adjustment to having to write more papers than I had to write in middle school.

Respond Through Writing

Autobiographical Narrative

Apply Flashback Unlike *The Woman Warrior*, which is written in the third person, most memoirs are written in the first person. Write an autobiographical narrative in the first person about a time when you encountered someone you hadn't seen in a long time. How did reality differ from your expectations? What had changed? What remained the same? Incorporate at least one flashback in your essay, as Kingston does.

Understand the Task An **autobiographical narrative** is a story in which an author tells a sequence of events from his or her life and reveals the personal significance of the experience. A **flashback** is an interruption in the chronological sequence of a narrative to leap back in time.

Prewrite Decide on an experience and a flashback and then outline the sequence of your narrative. Think about how you will weave the flashback into your narrative, remembering that you will need to use logical transitions to show how the flashback relates to the main action. You may want to organize your ideas in a diagram.

Draft As you draft, check to make sure that the pacing and sequence of your story make sense. Use interior monologue to capture the thoughts you had during this experience and to show how reality may have differed from your expectations.

Revise Go back over your essay. Check to see that you have used concrete details (who, what, when, and where) and sensory details (sights, sounds, smells, tastes, and textures) to describe actions, events, thoughts, and feelings in your narrative. Add more details as necessary to bring your narrative to life.

ORIGINAL: I waited for my friend at the café.
REVISION: As I waited for my friend at the café, I clutched my warm cup of jasmine-flower tea, my eyes darting nervously around the room.

Edit and Proofread Proofread your paper, correcting any errors in grammar, spelling, and punctuation. Use the Grammar Tip in the side column to help you avoid sentence fragments.

> **Grammar Tip**
>
> **Avoiding Sentence Fragments**
>
> Sentence fragments are "sentences" that do not express complete thoughts. Examples:
>
> *Waited for my friend.*
> *My oldest friend.*
>
> The first fragment lacks a subject. The second lacks both subject and verb. Correct these mistakes by adding the missing part(s) to form a complete sentence:
>
> *I waited for my friend.*
> *He was my oldest friend.*
>
> Some sentence fragments are subordinate clauses:
>
> *When I finally got to see him.*
>
> To correct this type of fragment, add a main clause to the subordinate clause:
>
> *I was glad when I finally got to see him.*

After You Read

Assess

 ## Writing

Students' autobiographical narratives should effectively incorporate a flashback and use interior monologue. Students should also enhance their narrative with concrete and sensory details.

Scoring Guide

Assess students' performance in the following categories using the scoring guide at the bottom of the page:

- Addresses all parts of the writing task.
- Provides a flashback that relates to the main action and is woven into the narrative logically.
- Includes interior monologue that describes the writer's inner thoughts and feelings.
- Provides well chosen concrete and sensory details that bring the narrative to life.
- Employs a variety of sentence types and uses precise, descriptive language.
- Follows English language conventions.

 For grammar practice, see Unit 7 Teaching Resources Book, p. 234.

Scoring Guide	4	3	2	1
Task addressed	fully	mostly	partially	barely
Flashback	transition to flashback is very logical	transition to flashback is logical	transition to flashback is confusing	no flashback
Interior monologue	fully describes inner thoughts	describes some inner thoughts	describes few inner thoughts	does not describe inner thoughts
Concrete and sensory details	well employed	employed	few employed	none
Language	varied, precise, descriptive	varied, somewhat descriptive	predictable, basic	not varied, limited
Convention errors	few or none	several	some	many

Before You Read

Focus

Bellringer Options

Daily Language Practice Transparency 113

Or **ask:** When have you had to choose between doing something pleasurable and something responsible? *(Students may share experiences such as wanting to go out with friends when they had to study for a test.)* Is there a decision that you look back on and wish that you had handled differently? *(Students may share a variety of experiences; encourage them to explore why they regretted their decisions.)*

Before You Read

Everything Stuck to Him

Meet **Raymond Carver**
(1938–1988)

In the summer of 1958, Raymond Carver borrowed $125 from the pharmacist for whom he delivered prescriptions. With that money, he moved his young family to the outskirts of Chico, California, where he would attend college. Although he and his wife were already working hard to support their two children, the twenty-year-old Carver knew that he wanted to be a writer and felt that this move would help him pursue his dream. That fall at Chico State, he met writer John Gardner, who became his mentor. Gardner paid special attention to Carver's work and offered him the key to his office, a gesture Carver called "a turning point" in his life. Every weekend, Carver spent part of the day in Gardner's office, typing page after page, developing his craft. Carver had begun his journey toward becoming an important twentieth-century writer.

> "Every great, or even every very good writer, makes the world over according to his own specifications."
>
> —Raymond Carver
> from "A Storyteller's Shoptalk"

Working-Class Perspective Raymond Carver was born in Clatskanie, Oregon. By the time he was three, his family had moved to Yakima, Washington, where his father worked at a sawmill. Carver's childhood in Yakima was beset with troubles. His father was an alcoholic, the family was dreadfully poor, and survival was a daily challenge.

Throughout his twenties and thirties, Carver struggled financially and battled with alcoholism, but kept his eye on the world around him, gathering material for his fiction and poetry. By the age of forty, however, he had quit drinking and established himself as a master of the short story.

Literary Acclaim One lesson Carver learned from Gardner was that revision, revision, and *more* revision were essential to good writing. Following this process, Carver created spare, realistic fiction, telling stories about everyday people in a singular voice that added tension and depth.

Carver won numerous awards for his writing, and received a National Book Award nomination for fiction in 1977. His short stories appear in several collections, including *Will You Be Quiet, Please?* (1976), *Furious Seasons* (1977), and *Where I'm Calling From* (1988). He published three collections of poetry during his lifetime, and another collection was published posthumously. Though Carver died at the age of fifty from lung cancer, his reputation continues to grow. Carver provided some of the most enduring human portraits of the twentieth century.

 Literature Online

Author Search For more about Raymond Carver, go to glencoe.com and enter QuickPass code GLA9800u7.

Selection Skills

Literary Elements
- Frame Story (SE pp. 1275, 1276, 1279, 1280)
- Style (SE p. 1280)

Everything Stuck to Him

Listening/Speaking/Viewing Skills
- Analyze Art (TE p. 1276, 1279)

Reading Skills
- Question (SE pp. 1275, 1277–1279, 1281; TE p. 1276)
- Connect (TE p. 1278)

Vocabulary Skills
- Context Clues (SE pp. 1275, 1281)

Writing Skills/Grammar
- Evaluate Debate (SE p. 1281)

Literature and Reading Preview

Connect to the Story

Have you ever had to choose between having fun and doing something responsible? Write a journal entry in which you describe how you made this decision.

Build Background

"Everything Stuck to Him" was included in Carver's collection of short stories *What We Talk About When We Talk About Love*. Published in 1981, the collection represents Carver at the peak of his early period, when he perfected a spare, succinct style of storytelling. Carver used direct, everyday language, which was perfectly suited to the content and characters in his stories. He is also known for his innovative techniques, such as blending dialogue and narration.

Set Purposes for Reading

Big Idea **Extending and Remaking Traditions**

As you read, ask yourself, What innovative techniques does Carver use in this story?

Literary Element **Frame Story**

A **frame story** is a plot structure that includes the telling of one story within another story. The frame is the outer story, which precedes and usually follows the inner, more important story. In this way, the outer story "frames" the inner one. As you read, ask yourself, Where does the inner story begin and end?

Reading Strategy **Question**

Questioning involves asking yourself whether you understand what you are reading. As you read, ask yourself, Do I understand what I've just read? How does this action fit into the overall conflict?

.....

Tip: Take Notes Use a chart to record your questions while reading the story. You can fill in the answers to these questions after you finish reading.

Questions	Answers
Why does the father tell his daughter about the dentist's letterhead?	

Learning Objectives

For pages 1274–1281

In studying this text, you will focus on the following objectives:

Literary Study: Understanding frame stories.

Reading: Questioning.

Listening and Speaking: Using logical arguments in debates.

Vocabulary

coincide (kō´ in sīd´) *v.* to occur at the same time; p. 1276 *His birthday coincided with the exam.*

ambition (am bish´ ən) *n.* a desire to achieve a particular end; p. 1277 *Driven by ambition, she worked tirelessly to succeed.*

striking (strī´ king) *adj.* impressive; attractive; p. 1277 *The model was even more striking in person than in her photographs.*

marvel (mär´ vəl) *v.* to be filled with wonder; p. 1277 *The diver marveled at the coral reef.*

fitfully (fit´ fəl lē) *adv.* irregularly; in stops and starts; p. 1277 *The sick child coughed fitfully.*

.....

Tip: Context Clues The words and phrases surrounding a word can often provide clues to its meaning. Consider the sentence, *Driven by ambition, she worked tirelessly to become a champion gymnast.* If she worked tirelessly, she must have been very motivated, so *ambition* must mean "motivation" or "desire."

Before You Read

Focus

Summary

A father shares his memories of something that happened when his daughter was an infant. It is a story about a choice he made between enjoying a simple pleasure and taking personal responsibility.

 For summaries in languages other than English, see Unit 7 Teaching Resources Book, pp. 237–242.

Vocabulary

Word Parts The suffix *-ful*, meaning "full of," can turn a noun into an adjective: *careful* means "full of care," *meaningful* means "full of meaning." **Ask:** How would you turn *careful* and *meaningful* into adverbs? *(add -ly)* **Say:** Discuss, with the aid of a dictionary, how the word *fitfully* might have come to its current definition from its root, *fitt,* meaning "conflict." *(conflict might have come to mean* sudden attack, *which might have come to mean* sudden onset, *which might have come to mean* irregular interval)

 For additional context, see Glencoe Interactive Vocabulary CD-ROM.

Approaching Level

DIFFERENTIATED INSTRUCTION

Emerging Explain how "Everything Stuck to Him" uses a frame story for its plot structure. Remind students that they may have seen this plot structure used in a movie. For example, the movie might begin with a grandfather sitting by a child's bed telling her a story. As the older person is talking, the action on the screen switches to the story being told. Sometimes the grandfather and child do not appear on the screen again until the end of the movie. Ask students to think of other characteristics of this type of story. *(The story may change the feelings or behavior of the person hearing it; the story from the past may solve a present mystery.)*

Teach

Big Idea | 1

Extending and Remaking Traditions Answer: *This technique makes the story feel more immediate, blurring the distinction between past and present, between dialogue and narration.*

Literary Element | 2

Frame Story Answer: *The narrator has set up the telling of this inner story in the opening, which is a frame story.*

Big Idea | 3

Extending and Remaking Traditions Answer: *It suggests the complexity of human relationships, particularly those within a family.*

View the Art ★

Ask: How does the painting relate to the narrator of the story? *(Possible answer: The narrator is telling a story about his wife and infant.)*

For an audio recording of this selection, use Listening Library Audio CD-ROM.

Readability Scores

Dale-Chall: 3.3
DRP: 46
Lexile: 460

Everything Stuck to Him

Raymond Carver

Mother and Child. Ditz. Private collection. ★

She's in Milan for Christmas and wants to know what it was like when she was a kid.

Tell me, she says. Tell me what it was like when I was a kid. She sips Strega, waits, eyes him closely.

She is a cool, slim, attractive girl, a survivor from top to bottom.

That was a long time ago. That was twenty years ago, he says.

You can remember, she says. Go on.

What do you want to hear? he says. What else can I tell you? I could tell you about something that happened when you were a baby. It involves you, he says. But only in a minor way.

Tell me, she says. But first fix us another so you won't have to stop in the middle.

He comes back from the kitchen with drinks, settles into his chair, begins.

They were kids themselves, but they were crazy in love, this eighteen-year-old boy and this seventeen-year-old girl when they married. Not all that long afterwards they had a daughter.

The baby came along in late November during a cold spell that just happened to **coincide** with the peak of the waterfowl season. The boy loved to hunt, you see. That's part of it.

The boy and girl, husband and wife, father and mother, they lived in a little apartment under a dentist's office. Each night they cleaned the dentist's place upstairs in exchange for rent and utilities. In summer they were expected to maintain the lawn and the flowers. In winter the boy shoveled snow and spread rock salt on the walks. Are you still with me? Are you getting the picture?

I am, she says.

That's good, he says. So one day the dentist finds out they were using his letterhead for their personal correspondence. But that's another story.

He gets up from his chair and looks out the window. He sees the tile rooftops and the snow that is falling steadily on them.

Tell the story, she says.

---

1 Extending and Remaking Traditions *Why do you think the author does not use quotation marks to indicate dialogue?*

2 Frame Story *How does the reader know that the narrator is beginning to tell a story about himself?*

Extending and Remaking Traditions *Why does the author identify the couple by the roles they play?* **3**

Vocabulary

coincide (kō´ in sīd´) *v.* to occur at the same time

1276 UNIT 7 INTO THE TWENTY-FIRST CENTURY

Reading Practice

Question To keep track of the questions they develop as they read, students can take notes. Suggest that they use the questions in their notes to make charts like the one shown. Have them write questions in the left-hand column and answers in the right-hand column.

Question	Answer
Why does the father mention the story about the letterhead?	It foreshadows what happens later on.

The two kids were very much in love. On top of this they had great **ambitions**. They were always talking about the things they were going to do and the places they were going to go.

Now the boy and girl slept in the bedroom, and the baby slept in the living room. Let's say the baby was about three months old and had only just begun to sleep through the night.

On this one Saturday night after finishing his work upstairs, the boy stayed in the dentist's office and called an old hunting friend of his father's.

Carl, he said when the man picked up the receiver, believe it or not, I'm a father.

Congratulations, Carl said. How is the wife?

She's fine, Carl. Everybody's fine.

That's good, Carl said, I'm glad to hear it. But if you called about going hunting, I'll tell you something. The geese are flying to beat the band. I don't think I've ever seen so many. Got five today. Going back in the morning, so come along if you want to.

I want to, the boy said.

The boy hung up the telephone and went downstairs to tell the girl. She watched while he laid out his things. Hunting coat, shell bag, boots, socks, hunting cap, long underwear, pump gun.

What time will you be back? the girl said.

Probably around noon, the boy said. But maybe as late as six o'clock. Would that be too late?

It's fine, she said. The baby and I will get along fine. You go and have some fun. When you get back, we'll dress the baby up and go visit Sally.

The boy said, Sounds like a good idea.

Sally was the girl's sister. She was **striking**. I don't know if you've seen pictures of her. The boy was a little in love with Sally, just as he was a little in love with Betsy, who was another

sister the girl had. The boy used to say to the girl, If we weren't married, I could go for Sally.

What about Betsy? the girl used to say. I hate to admit it, but I truly feel she's better looking than Sally and me. What about Betsy?

Betsy too, the boy used to say.

After dinner he turned up the furnace and helped her bathe the baby. He **marveled** again at the infant who had half his features and half the girl's. He powdered the tiny body. He powdered between fingers and toes.

He emptied the bath into the sink and went upstairs to check the air. It was overcast and cold. The grass, what there was of it, looked like canvas, stiff and gray under the street light.

Snow lay in piles beside the walk. A car went by. He heard sand under the tires. He let himself imagine what it might be like tomorrow, geese beating the air over his head, shotgun plunging against his shoulder.

Then he locked the door and went downstairs.

In bed they tried to read. But both of them fell asleep, she first, letting the magazine sink to the quilt.

It was the baby's cries that woke him up.

The light was on out there, and the girl was standing next to the crib rocking the baby in her arms. She put the baby down, turned out the light, and came back to the bed.

He heard the baby cry. This time the girl stayed where she was. The baby cried **fitfully** and stopped. The boy listened, then dozed. But the baby's cries woke him again. The living-room light was burning. He sat up and turned on the lamp.

Question *Carl, Sally, and Betsy are the only characters who are named in the story. Why does Carver name them?* **4**

Question *Why does the boy have this vision of himself hunting geese?* **5**

RAYMOND CARVER **1277**

Teach

Teach

Reading Strategy | 1

Question **Answer:** *The girl feels abandoned by the boy. Her maternal feelings cause her to focus on the baby, to the exclusion of the boy.*

(APPROACHING) Help students trace how the argument between the boy and girl leads both people to say things that are not entirely true. **Ask:** What statement that the boy makes leads the girl to say, "That's not the point and you know it."? *(The boy challenges her by saying that she does know Carl even though she says she does not.)* What does this exchange reveal about the two characters? *(They are both getting flustered and upset.)*

Writer's Technique ☆

Tone Ask: How does the tone of the story change after the boy swears? *(Possible answer: Tension builds between the boy and the girl. The girl becomes angry because he wants to go hunting. The tension reaches a peak when the girl tells him to choose between having a family and going hunting.)*

View the Art ★

Ask: How might the man in the painting resemble the boy in the story? *(Possible answer: The man looks as though he is pondering an important decision.)*

1278

I don't know what's wrong, the girl said, walking back and forth with the baby. I've changed her and fed her, but she keeps on crying. I'm so tired I'm afraid I might drop her.

You come back to bed, the boy said. I'll hold her for a while.

He got up and took the baby, and the girl went to lie down again.

Just rock her for a few minutes, the girl said from the bedroom. Maybe she'll go back to sleep.

The boy sat on the sofa and held the baby. He jiggled it in his lap until he got its eyes to close, his own eyes closing right along. He rose carefully and put the baby back in the crib.

It was a quarter to four, which gave him forty-five minutes. He crawled into bed and dropped off. But a few minutes later the baby was crying again, and this time they both got up.

The boy did a terrible thing. He swore.

For God's sake, what's the matter with you? the girl said to the boy. Maybe she's sick or something. Maybe we shouldn't have given her the bath.

☆ The boy picked up the baby. The baby kicked its feet and smiled.

Look, the boy said, I really don't think there's anything wrong with her.

How do you know that? the girl said. Here, let me have her. I know I ought to give her something, but I don't know what it's supposed to be.

The girl put the baby down again. The boy and the girl looked at the baby, and the baby began to cry.

The girl took the baby. Baby, baby, the girl said with tears in her eyes.

Probably it's something on her stomach, the boy said.

The girl didn't answer. She went on rocking the baby, paying no attention to the boy.

The boy waited. He went to the kitchen and put on water for coffee. He drew his woolen

Portrait of Denis Lucas. Paul Bullard. Oil on canvas, 59 x 48 in. Private collection.

underwear on over his shorts and T-shirt, buttoned up, then got into his clothes.

What are you doing? the girl said.

Going hunting, the boy said.

I don't think you should, she said. I don't want to be left alone with her like this.

Carl's planning on me going, the boy said. We've planned it.

I don't care about what you and Carl planned, she said. And I don't care about Carl, either. I don't even know Carl.

You've met Carl before. You know him, the boy said. What do you mean you don't know him?

That's not the point and you know it, the girl said.

What is the point? the boy said. The point is we planned it.

---

1 Question *Why does the girl ignore the boy?*

Reading Practice

Connect The girl in the selection puts the boy in a position of having to choose between doing something he would find pleasurable or keeping his family. Have students discuss the boy's dilemma. **Ask:** Is the girl justified in presenting him with an ultimatum? Do you think she means what she says? What do you think she should have said to the boy?

(Students should acknowledge such factors as the couple's youth, the fact that they probably are not used to arguing, people's tendency to make extreme statements when they are angry.)

The girl said, I'm your wife. This is your baby. She's sick or something. Look at her. Why else is she crying?

I know you're my wife, the boy said.

The girl began to cry. She put the baby back in the crib. But the baby started up again. The girl dried her eyes on the sleeve of her nightgown and picked the baby up.

The boy laced up his boots. He put on his shirt, his sweater, his coat. The kettle whistled on the stove in the kitchen.

You're going to have to choose, the girl said. Carl or us. I mean it.

What do you mean? the boy said.

You heard what I said, the girl said. If you want a family, you're going to have to choose.

They stared at each other. Then the boy took up his hunting gear and went outside. He started the car. He went around to the car windows and, making a job of it, scraped away the ice.

He turned off the motor and sat awhile. And then he got out and went back inside.

The living-room light was on. The girl was asleep on the bed. The baby was asleep beside her.

The boy took off his boots. Then he took off everything else. In his socks and his long underwear, he sat on the sofa and read the Sunday paper.

The girl and the baby slept on. After a while, the boy went to the kitchen and started frying bacon.

The girl came out in her robe and put her arms around the boy.

Hey, the boy said.

I'm sorry, the girl said.

It's all right, the boy said.

I didn't mean to snap like that.

It was my fault, he said.

You sit down, the girl said. How does a waffle sound with bacon?

Sounds great, the boy said.

She took the bacon out of the pan and made waffle batter. He sat at the table and watched her move around the kitchen.

She put a plate in front of him with bacon, a waffle. He spread butter and poured syrup. But when he started to cut, he turned the plate into his lap.

I don't believe it, he said, jumping up from the table.

If you could see yourself, the girl said.

The boy looked down at himself, at everything stuck to his underwear.

I was starved, he said, shaking his head.

You were starved, she said, laughing.

He peeled off the woolen underwear and threw it at the bathroom door. Then he opened his arms and the girl moved into them.

We won't fight anymore, she said.

The boy said, We won't.

He gets up from his chair and refills their glasses.

That's it, he says. End of story. I admit it's not much of a story.

I was interested, she says.

He shrugs and carries his drink over to the window. It's dark now but still snowing.

Things change, he says. I don't know how they do. But they do without your realizing it or wanting them to.

Yes, that's true, only—But she does not finish what she started.

She drops the subject. In the window's reflection he sees her study her nails. Then she raises her head. Speaking brightly, she asks if he is going to show her the city, after all.

He says, Put your boots on and let's go.

But he stays by the window, remembering. They had laughed. They had leaned on each other and laughed until the tears had come, while everything else—the cold, and where he'd go in it—was outside, for a while anyway.

Frame Story *What questions do you have about the time between the inner story and the frame story?* **3**

Question *What does the cold represent in the story?* **4**

---

2 | **Question** *When the girl first gives the boy an ultimatum, he leaves. Why does he now go back inside?*

Reading Strategy | 2

Question **Answer:** *The boy has clarified his priorities and realizes that staying with the girl is more important than going hunting with Carl.*

Literary Element | 3

Frame Story **Answer:** *Students may wonder what happened to the boy and girl in the inner story, how long the father has been out of his daughter's life, and where the mother is now.*

Reading Strategy | 4

Question **Answer:** *The cold represents the world away from his wife and their daughter.*

To check students' understanding of the selection, see Unit 7 Teaching Resources Book, p. 243.

English Learners

DIFFERENTIATED INSTRUCTION

Intermediate Assign four students the roles of the narrator, the daughter, the boy, and the girl, and have them read aloud the last section of the story that begins with "The boy waited." **Ask:** Why did Carver omit the quotation marks? *(Perhaps he wanted to indicate that the whole story is the father's memory and may not be* exactly what the characters said.) **Ask:** How did the absence of quotation marks affect your ability to read the parts? *(Students' opinions may differ.)*

After You Read

Assess

1. Answers will vary.
2. (a) They live in a small apartment below a dentist's office where they worked. (b) They are poor and struggling.
3. (a) He plans to go goose hunting with his father's friend Carl. (b) It is a chance to take a break from his responsibilities and have fun.
4. (a) A plateful of waffles and bacon sticks to the boy (b) The adult responsibilities that have "stuck" to the boy
5. He is not with his daughter's mother anymore.
6. (a) She knows nothing will change between her parents. (b) She may have been about to ask why he did not try to save the marriage.
7. (a) Keeping that memory private might make it seem more special. (b) It makes the reader feel the man's loss.
8. His simple, concise language, his creation of dramatic scenes, his depiction of ordinary people and everyday events, and his blending of dialogue and narration are intriguing.
9. Students may say that couples argue over money, children, career or personal goals, friends, family, or household issues.

After You Read

Respond and Think Critically

Respond and Interpret

1. How did you react to the end of this story?
2. (a) Where did the couple live? (b) What does this tell you about them at the time?
3. (a) What was the boy planning to do in the morning? (b) Why is this activity so important to him?
4. (a) What is it that sticks to the boy? (b) What might this image **symbolize** in the story?

Analyze and Evaluate

5. What does the father mean at the end of the story when he says "Things change"?

6. (a) After hearing her father's story, why does the daughter stop speaking in mid-sentence? (b) What do you think she was about to say?
7. (a) Why do you think the father chooses to keep the last part of his story to himself? (b) How does placing this memory at the end increase the power of the story's conclusion?

Connect

8. **Big Idea** **Extending and Remaking Traditions** What do you find most intriguing about Carver's style? Support your opinion.
9. **Connect to Today** What kind of arguments do you think young couples might have today?

Literary Element | Frame Story

In some cases, a **frame story** provides a stark contrast to the inner story. In other cases, a frame story is closely related to the inner story. By examining the relationship between a frame story and its inner story, you can explore the meaning of a literary work and the author's intent.

1. In "Everything Stuck to Him," what do the frame story and the inner story have in common?
2. How does framing the inner story in the present affect how you view it?

Review: Style

As you learned on page 743, **style** refers to the expressive qualities that distinguish an author's work, including word choice and the length and arrangement of sentences, as well as the use of figurative language and imagery. Carver's style resembles Ernest Hemingway's in its terse, spare language.

Partner Activity Meet with another classmate and find examples of Carver's style in "Everything Stuck to Him." Then compare those examples with the opening or closing paragraphs from Nathaniel Hawthorne's "The Minister's Black Veil" (p. 280). Working with your partner, fill in a chart like the one below to record what you learn.

	Carver's style	Hawthorne's style
word choice		
sentence length		
use of imagery		

Literary Element

1. The father and his daughter are in both stories; both stories take place mainly indoors but feature images of snow and cold.
2. It makes the events seem farther in the past, stirring feelings of nostalgia.

Progress Check

Can students analyze a frame story?

If No → See Unit 7 Teaching Resources Book, p. 243.

Review: Style

Hawthorne uses complex vocabulary, long sentences, and strong imagery. Carver's style is more concise and his imagery more subtle.

 For additional assessment, see Assessment Resources, pp. 309–310.

Reading Strategy Question

Asking questions while you read is the first step in the process of generating meaning. The next step—answering those questions—usually requires more time and analysis.

1. What does Carver achieve by having the man identify the characters in his story merely as "the boy" and "the girl"?

2. What do you think eventually happens to the girl and the boy? Explain.

Vocabulary Practice

Practice with Context Clues Look back at pages 1276–1279 to find context clues for the vocabulary words below. Record your findings in a chart like the one here.

coincide	ambition	striking
marvel	fitfully	

EXAMPLE:

> Word: ambition

> Textual Clues: "They were always talking about the things they were going to do and the places they were going to go," so they are driven toward goals

> Meaning: a desire to achieve a particular end

Academic Vocabulary

The girl does not want her husband to go hunting because she is concerned about their baby's **welfare.**

Welfare is an academic word. Many people do volunteer work because they want to contribute to the **welfare** of society as a whole.

To further explore the meaning of this word, complete this sentence: _____, _____, and _____ are necessary for a child's **welfare.**

For more on academic vocabulary, see pages 53–54.

Speaking and Listening

 Debate

Assignment Carver's story illustrates a universal issue: the conflict between an individual's desires and family responsibility. Which is more important? Divide into two teams and debate this issue.

Prepare Working together, the two teams should develop a proposition based on the issue. The proposition might be phrased this way: *Resolved: That a person's responsibility to family is a more basic duty than the fulfillment of individual desires.* Then decide which team will be the *affirmative* (arguing in favor of the proposition) and which will be the *negative* (arguing against it). With your team, discuss real-life situations you might use to support your position, along with evidence from Carver's story.

Debate During the debate, introduce real-life situations as logical arguments that reinforce your position. For example, you might employ the following analogy to support the proposition above: A family is in many ways like a sports team. Different members of the team have different roles and different levels of skill. But all the team members must sacrifice their individual ambitions to the goals of the team or the team will not succeed.

Remember that your language can impact your effectiveness. Formal language, for example, can add credibility and authority to your arguments.

Evaluate Write a paragraph assessing the effectiveness of both teams' performance, as well as your individual role. Which side do you think presented a stronger case? Why? Use the checklist on page 1351 to help in this evaluation.

 Literature Online

Selection Resources For Selection Quizzes, eFlashcards, and Reading-Writing Connection activities, go to glencoe.com and enter QuickPass code GLA9800u7.

RAYMOND CARVER **1281**

After You Read

Assess

Reading Strategy

1. It emphasizes how young they were—even though they were parents—and how different the boy was from the man who tells the story.

2. Students may say that the couple fell out of love, perhaps because the boy was not as devoted as the girl to family responsibilities.

Academic Vocabulary

Possible answer: A supportive family, a good education, and social interaction are necessary for a child's welfare.

Speaking and Listening

Use these criteria when evaluating students' participation in the debate:

- Did the student use real-life situations as evidence?
- Did the student use logical arguments?
- Did the student use an appropriate level of language?

 For help with creating presentations, see Student Presentation Builder on StudentWorks Plus.

Vocabulary

Word: *coincide*

Textual Clues: The baby arrives in late November, the same time when the boy wants to go hunting.

Meaning: "to occur at the same time"

Word: *striking*

Textual Clues: You can tell this about Sally from "pictures of her," that make the boy fall "a little in love" with her, though the girl thinks that Betsy is "better looking than Sally."

Meaning: "impressive; attractive"

Word: *marvel*

Textual Clues: He carefully examines the baby, fascinated by the fact that it has "half his features and half the girl's," so he must be interested and amazed.

Meaning: "to be filled with wonder"

Word: *fitfully*

Textual Clues: The baby's cries start and stop, waking him up periodically.

Meaning: "irregularly; in stops and starts"

Bellringer Options

**Daily Language Practice
Transparency 114**

Or **ask:** What things have you learned from a parent or other adult but then ignored or forgot? *(Students may list rules for behavior that they find outdated or silly.)* Why do you think you ignore some of the things you have learned from adults? *(Students may suggest that older people are not in touch with present reality.)*

Meet **Judith Ortiz Cofer**
(born 1952)

Culture clash is a familiar theme in the work of Judith Ortiz Cofer (ôr tēz´ kō´ fer). Many of her poems, novels, and autobiographical essays dramatize the differences between the values of her Puerto Rican relatives and the values of people in the United States.

Born in Puerto Rico, she moved to the United States at the age of three. Until she was sixteen, however, her childhood was split almost evenly between the two places. Ortiz Cofer usually spent about six months of each year in Paterson, New Jersey, where she lived the urban life of a Puerto Rican immigrant, speaking Spanish at home, experiencing discrimination, and struggling to fit in at school. Ortiz Cofer often spent the remaining part of each year in Puerto Rico, where her mother took her every time her father, a career navy man, shipped out. There she lived a more relaxed, rural life and was embraced by a large extended family.

Split in Half Yet Doubled The effects of frequent relocation were challenging to Ortiz Cofer's friendships and education, and left her with two indelible marks on her soul: the feeling of never really belonging in either place and the curious gift of possessing, fully and deeply, two cultures and languages.

When Ortiz Cofer was sixteen, her family moved to Augusta, Georgia, presenting yet another cultural and social adjustment for her. However, some things remained constant. Her parents still spoke Spanish at home, and Catholicism remained a major force in her family life and her education.

A Late Start as a Writer Ortiz Cofer did not begin to write poetry until she was studying for her master's degree. It was then that she began to recognize the literary and narrative influences that had been part of her makeup all along. These included a grandmother who was a storyteller and a grandfather who was a reader and writer of poetry. When Ortiz Cofer's writing began to flow, it was perhaps no surprise to those who knew her best that her imagination readily drew on both of her cultural identities. She did not choose to identify as either American or Puerto Rican but rather showed how new cultural identities simultaneously seem to spring from, move away from, and reclaim the old.

> *"The assimilation of a new culture is the coming into maturity by accepting the terms necessary for survival."*
>
> —Judith Ortiz Cofer

Much of Ortiz Cofer's work is autobiographical or uses the facts of her childhood as a springboard. One of her most successful books, *Silent Dancing: A Partial Remembrance of a Puerto Rican Childhood,* is made up of thirteen essays about her experiences growing up. Memories of her parents, she says, are always finding their way into her poetry and stories as well. "My family is one of the main topics of my poetry," Cofer has said. "In tracing their lives, I discover more about mine."

Literature Online

Author Search For more about Judith Ortiz Cofer, go to glencoe.com and enter QuickPass code GLA9800u7.

Selection Skills

Literary Elements
- Point of View
  (SE pp. 1283, 1285)

El Olvido

Reading Skills
- Examine Connotations
  (SE pp. 1283, 1285)
- Draw Conclusions
  (TE p. 1284)

Vocabulary Skills
- Denotation and Connotation
  (SE pp. 1283, 1285)

Listening/Speaking/Viewing Skills
- Analyze Art (TE p. 1284)

Literature and Reading Preview

Connect to the Poem
Do you think information and values you get from your family will be important to you for your entire life? Freewrite for 15 minutes on this topic.

Build Background
Many people experience a cultural shift when they move from Puerto Rico to the United States. For example, Cofer's ancestors would have often seen statues of saints in shops, backyards, and city streets. They would also have commonly invoked the names of the holy family, *Jesús, María, y José* (Jesus, Mary, and Joseph, Mary's husband) as part of daily conversation.

Set Purposes for Reading

Big Idea **Extending and Remaking Traditions**

As you read, ask yourself, How are the old ways or traditions being replaced with the new ways?

Literary Element **Point of View**

Point of view is the relationship of the narrator to a story or the speaker to a poem. Point of view in poetry is determined, in part, by how close or removed the speaker is from the events or ideas of the poem. As you read, ask yourself, Where does this speaker stand in relation to ideas and events?

Reading Strategy **Examine Connotations**

Examining connotations is identifying the feelings, attitudes, and suggestions that go beyond the dictionary definition of a word. In a poem such as "El Olvido," word choice helps show the attitudes and feelings of the speaker. As you read, ask yourself, What feeling is suggested by the speaker's words?

Tip: Take Notes Use a chart like the one below to record the connotations of some of the words Ortiz Cofer uses.

Word or Phrase	Connotation
choke out	violent, strangling

Learning Objectives

For pages 1282–1285

In studying this text, you will focus on the following objectives:

Literary Study: Understanding point of view.

Reading: Examining connotations.

Writing: Writing a poem.

Vocabulary

spurn (spurn) *v.* to reject with contempt; to scorn; p. 1284 *Poor but proud, the family spurned all offers of charity.*

disdain (dis dān´) *v.* to look down on, to despise; p. 1284 *The classical violinist disdains popular music.*

....

Tip: Denotation and Connotation
Denotation is the literal, or dictionary, meaning of a word. **Connotation** is the implied, or cultural, meaning of a word. For example, the words *disdain* and *disapprove* have a similar denotation, "to reject something," but they have different connotations:

Negative	More Negative
disapprove	disdain

Before You Read

Focus

Summary

A mother speaks to her child about the risks of ignoring familial and cultural origins. The mother expresses her concern that her child will not survive in an environment lacking cultural and family traditions.

 For summaries in languages other than English, see Unit 7 Teaching Resources Book, pp. 250–255.

Vocabulary

Synonyms Point out that even though words may be synonyms with the same denotative meaning, the connotative meanings might differ. For example, *scorn* is listed as a synonym for *spurn* in the thesaurus. Their roots help distinguish one word from the other. The root word that *spurn* is derived from means "to kick." The root word that *scorn* comes from means "mockery." **Ask:** Which word has more of a sense of inducing shame? *(scorn)*

 For additional vocabulary practice, see Unit 7 Teaching Resources Book, p. 258.

Approaching Level

DIFFERENTIATED INSTRUCTION

Emerging Cofer uses the word *climate* in "El Olvido" figuratively. She speaks of "the climate of your birthplace." Discuss with students the difference between a word's literal meaning and its figurative meaning. Have students look up the word *climate* in a dictionary. Ask them to find the literal meaning of the word. *(the prevailing weather conditions of a region)* **Say:** Sometimes a figurative meaning is in the dictionary as well. What is the figurative meaning of the word *climate*? *(the prevailing attitude or conditions)* **Ask:** What do you think Cofer means by "the climate of your birthplace"? *(the feel, the atmosphere, the smell, the people, the culture, the way of life)*

Teach

Ancestral Dream I, 1996. Maria Eugenia Terrazas. Watercolor, 70 x 60 cm. Kactus Foto, Santiago, Chile. ★

El Olvido¹
(Según las Madres)²
Judith Ortiz Cofer

1

It is a dangerous thing
to forget the climate of
your birthplace; to choke out
the voices of the dead relatives when
5   in dreams they call you by
your secret name; dangerous
to **spurn** the clothes you were
born to wear for the sake of fashion;
to use weapons and sharp instruments you
10   are not familiar with; dangerous
to **disdain** the plaster saints before
which your mother kneels praying for you with
embarassing fervor that you survive in
the place you have chosen to live; a costly,
15   bare and elegant room with no pictures
on the walls: a forgetting place where
she fears you might die of exposure.
Jesús, María y José.
El olvido is a dangerous thing.

---

1. *El Olvido* (el ōl vē′ dō) is Spanish for "the forgetting" or "heedlessness" or "the end of memory."
2. *Según las Madres* (sə gōōn′ läs mä′ drās) means "according to mothers."

2   **Extending and Remaking Traditions** *Why might the speaker consider such a room dangerous?*

Vocabulary

spurn (spurn) *v.* to reject with contempt; to scorn
disdain (dis dān′) *v.* to look down on, to despise

After You Read

Respond and Think Critically

Respond and Interpret

1. How is the mother in this poem like or unlike mothers you know?

2. (a)According to lines 1–12, what kinds of things are dangerous? (b)Why do you think the speaker calls them dangerous?

3. (a)What fear does the mother have? (b)Why might she have this fear?

4. (a)What words does the poet write in Spanish in the poem? (b)How are these words linked?

Analyze and Evaluate

5. (a)Look at line 17 and think about the phrase "die of exposure." Do these words have literal meanings in the poem, or are they a figure of speech? Explain. (b)What do these words contribute to the tone of the poem?

6. (a)What mothers does the subtitle "Según las Madres" refer to? (b)How well does the subtitle match the content of the poem?

Connect

7. **Big Idea** **Extending and Remaking Traditions** Has this poem convinced you that forgetting one's roots "is a dangerous thing" or even a possible thing? Why or why not?

8. **Connect to the Author** Do you think Ortiz Cofer's message applies only to the children of immigrants, or is it meaningful to any family?

Literary Element Point of View

Point of view can be first-, second-, or third-person. In **first-person point of view**, the speaker is a character in the poem and uses *I*. In **second-person point of view** the speaker uses *you*. In **third-person point of view** the speaker is not a character in the poem and refers to others as *he, she,* or *they*.

1. (a)Is this poem written in the first-, second-, or third-person point of view? How do you know? (b)Why does the speaker use this point of view?

2. How does the point of view affect the tone and message of the poem?

Reading Strategy Examine Connotations

"El Olvido" is full of words with powerful connotations. Review the chart you made on page 1283 listing words and their connotations in this poem.

1. Find a word you recorded whose connotative meaning is different from its denotative meaning. Write the word and both meanings.

2. Write a word you recorded that you think has powerful connotations and explain why.

Vocabulary Practice

Practice with Denotation and Connotation
Each of the vocabulary words is listed with a word that has a similar denotation. Choose the word that has the more negative connotation.

1. spurn   reject
2. disdain   despise

Writing

Write a Poem Write a free verse poem on the topic of forgetting one's culture, roots, or past. Think about what has been lost or changed in your own family over time, in the family of someone you know, or in general as people move away from parents and guardians and reject traditions.

LOG ON ▶ **Literature** Online

Selection Resources For Selection Quizzes, eFlashcards, and Reading-Writing Connection activities, go to glencoe.com and enter QuickPass code GLA9800u7.

JUDITH ORTIZ COFER **1285**

After You Read

Assess

1. Students' answers will vary.

2. (a) Forgetting one's past and family traditions (b) They are a key part of a person's identity.

3. (a) Her child will die of exposure. (b) Her child has rejected traditions.

4. (a) The title, the subtitle, and "Jesús, María, y José" (b) They are part of the traditions she wants her child to remember.

5. (a) A figure of speech: turning one's back on the past is a kind of death. (b) They add emotional power and convey the mother's fears.

6. (a) All mothers who are like the one in the poem (b) Students' answers will vary.

7. Students may note that although Ortiz Cofer writes about forgetting, by writing she remembers.

8. Her message is directed at families in general, although cultural changes from one country to another might be more pronounced or obvious.

Literary Element

1. (a) Second person; use of the word *you* (b) To address all children who do not follow traditions

2. There is a sense of urgency in the tone; the use of *you* intensifies the poem's personal nature.

Progress Check

Can students analyze point of view?

If No → See Unit 7 Teaching Resources Book, p. 256.

Reading Strategy

1. Possible answer: *secret*, the denotative meaning of which is "hidden" or "concealed" but which connotes intimacy and privacy

2. Possible answer: *bare*, because it powerfully suggests the sterility and lifelessness of the room

Writing

Use the following criteria to evaluate students' poems:

- Is the poem written in free verse?
- Does the poem focus on the changes and losses that occur when someone forgets tradition?

Vocabulary

1. spurn   2. disdain

1285

Focus

Bellringer Options

Daily Language Practice Transparency 115

Or display images of popular icons and symbols, such as ones that appear on bracelets, T-shirts, caps, and pins. **Ask:** Why are these popular? *(They represent individuals, groups, or ideas that people admire, enjoy, or endorse.)*

Have students consider what the fig tree in the poem represents to the author's father.

Before You Read

My Father and the Figtree

Meet **Naomi Shihab Nye**
(born 1952)

In the introduction to her collection *Words Under the Words*, poet Naomi Shihab Nye shares a simple story about looking through a childhood photo album. The album was barely intact—its pages in a stack and no longer bound. Some of the black and white photos were as many as forty years old. The pages were not in chronological order, so as she looked through the pictures, her impressions and memories fluctuated in time. Nye saw herself, "Preparing to blow out two candles on a cake . . . With neighbors who disappeared into the world . . . With baby brother freshly home from the hospital. With grandparents who died." She continued paging through the album and recalled stories about when the photos were taken. While she looked, however, Nye began to wonder about the moments not captured in the photos. It struck her that it is the hidden details of life—the forgotten memories—that make all of us who we are and in some way put us all on common ground. Nye's poems in some ways resemble timeless family portraits in which we recognize ourselves. Her writing draws not only from her own memories and heritage but also from a variety of cultural traditions. Nye is committed to revealing what people have in common and to exploring the themes of acceptance and conciliation.

> "The mystery of remembering has added its own light to the garden. Whatever existed then has deepened, been forgotten or restored in some other form. We planted our voices."
>
> —Naomi Shihab Nye

Connecting to the World Nye's Palestinian father and American mother encouraged her to express herself. Nye has said that even as a child she was "fascinated by the power of words on the page to make us look differently at our lives, to help us see and connect." She was first published at the age of seven, when a children's magazine accepted one of her poems.

At the age of fourteen, Nye spent a year in Jerusalem, where she was able to meet the Palestinian side of her family. She grew especially close to her grandmother, who appears in many of her poems and a children's book called *Sitte's Secrets*. She won a National Poetry Series prize for *Hugging the Box* and was a National Book Award finalist for *19 Varieties of Gazelle*.

Reaching Out to the Reader Nye's straightforward style appeals to a diverse audience and readers of all ages. "Ultimately, I look at writing as a form of discovery," she told an interviewer. "I hope my words reach out to the reader and they can say yes to them." She often writes about connections between people separated by time or distance, and her poems emphasize our shared humanity. Nye uses the familiar settings of everyday life and the power of memory to create poetry that is rich with "the gleam of particulars."

 Literature Online

Author Search For more about Naomi Shihab Nye, go to glencoe.com and enter QuickPass code GLA9800u7.

1286 UNIT 7 INTO THE TWENTY-FIRST CENTURY

Selection Skills

Literary Elements
- Symbol (SE pp. 1287, 1289, 1290)

My Father and the Figtree

Writing Skills/Grammar
- Write a List (SE p. 1290)

Reading Skills
- Summarize (SE pp. 1287, 1289, 1290)
- Scan (TE p. 1288)

Vocabulary Skills
- Context Clues (SE pp. 1287, 1290)

Literature and Reading Preview

Connect to the Poem

Is there anything unique that you share with a family member or friend that connects the two of you? With a partner, share this commonality and explain what makes it special for you.

Build Background

Nye's poem refers to elements of her cultural heritage. Figs have been a popular fruit since ancient times. The fig tree is common in the Middle East and can grow in rocky, arid climates, producing fruit and providing shade. Another cultural reference in the poem is a character named Joha. In Arab folklore, Joha is a wise fool or trickster, and he plays that role in a variety of traditional tales.

Set Purposes for Reading

Big Idea Extending and Remaking Traditions

As you read, ask yourself, How does Nye place elements of traditional tales in a contemporary context, creating her own modern folktale?

Literary Element Symbol

A **symbol** is any object, person, place, or experience that represents something beyond the literal meaning. As you read, ask yourself, What are Nye's symbols and what do they mean?

Reading Strategy Summarize

Summarizing is briefly restating the events or ideas in a literary work in your own words. After reading a poem, you can summarize what happened by determining the main ideas and events and placing them in a logical order.

....

Tip: Make a Chronological List As you read, ask yourself, What is happening in this poem? List the main ideas and events in the poem in the order in which they occur. Look for time clues, such as "At age six," or "Years passed."

Main Ideas and Events

Learning Objectives

For pages 1286–1290

In studying this text, you will focus on the following objectives:

Literary Study: Analyzing symbols.

Reading: Summarizing.

Writing: Writing a list.

Vocabulary

indifferent (in dif´ ər ənt) *adj.* having no marked feeling for or against; p. 1288 *Most of the audience was indifferent toward the mediocre performance.*

vivid (viv´ id) *adj.* perceived as bright and distinct; brilliant; p. 1288 *The vivid tropical fish swam in the clear blue water.*

token (tō´ kən) *n.* something serving as an indication, proof, or expression of something else; a sign; p. 1289 *The gift was a token of his appreciation.*

emblem (em´ bləm) *n.* an object or a representation that functions as a symbol; p. 1289 *The keys were an emblem of his new independence.*

....

Tip: Context Clues You can often find clues to the meaning of an unfamiliar word in its **context**, or the surrounding words and phrases. For example, consider the sentence *The gift was a token of his appreciation.* Gifts are usually given to symbolize appreciation, so *token* must mean "symbol."

NAOMI SHIHAB NYE **1287**

Before You Read

Focus

Summary

This poem tells the story of recurrent conversations between a father and a daughter about the father's lifelong passion for fresh figs. The figs and fig tree symbolize more than food to the father. They represent his homeland, cultural heritage, and past.

 For summaries in languages other than English, see Unit 7 Teaching Resources Book, pp. 261–266.

Vocabulary

Synonyms Remind students that when they are learning a new word, a useful strategy is to think of synonyms with which they are familiar. **Ask:** Which vocabulary word or words is a synonym for *symbol?* (emblem, token) What type of symbol would you be more apt to wear—an emblem or a token? (an emblem)

 For additional vocabulary practice, see Unit 7 Teaching Resources Book, pp. 269–270.

English Learners

DIFFERENTIATED INSTRUCTION

Beginning Point out that students will read about three main time periods in "My Father and the Figtree": (1) when the poet was a little girl, (2) the years between being little and grown up, and (3) when she is an adult living away from her parents. Assign students different pieces of the poem to paraphrase: (1) a parent telling bedtime stories, (2) a child eating a dried fig, (3) a garden with no figs, and (4) ripe figs on a tree. Explain how each of the stanzas go together. **Ask:** Why might the father have waited so long to plant his own figs? *(the climate was too cold; it took time to accept that he had to make the United States his home)*

Teach

Big Idea   1

Extending and Remaking Traditions **Say:** Keep these questions in mind as you read: Why does the father include a fig tree in all the folktales he tells his daughter? *(Figs are his favorite fruit; figs remind him of his culture and homeland.)* Why does the speaker refer to figs as "tokens" and "emblems"? *(To the father, they symbolize his culture, his homeland, and his memories.)*

Reading Strategy   2

Make Inferences **Say:** Make an inference about the relationship between the father and the child, based on the information in the firt stanza. *(They have a close relationship, as evidenced by the fact that the father spends time "weaving folktales" for his child.)*

My Father and the Figtree

Naomi Shihab Nye

1

For other fruits my father was **indifferent.**
He'd point at the cherry trees and say,
"See those? I wish they were figs."
In the evenings he sat by my bed
5   weaving folktales like **vivid** little scarves.   **2**
They always involved a figtree.
Even when it didn't fit, he'd stick it in.
Once Joha was walking down the road and he saw a figtree.
Or, he tied his camel to a figtree and went to sleep.
10   Or, later when they caught and arrested him,
his pockets were full of figs.

At age six I ate a dried fig and shrugged.
"That's not what I'm talking about!" he said,
"I'm talking about a fig straight from the earth—
15   gift of Allah![1]—on a branch so heavy it touches the ground.
I'm talking about picking the largest fattest sweetest fig
in the world and putting it in my mouth."
(Here he'd stop and close his eyes.)

---

1. *Allah* is the Arabic word for God.

> **Vocabulary**
>
> **indifferent** (in dif′ ər ənt) *adj.* having no marked feeling for or against
> **vivid** (viv′ id) *adj.* perceived as bright and distinct; brilliant

Reading Practice

Scan Scanning is one way to locate information and specific details. Have students scan page 1288 to answer these questions. **Ask:** What is the speaker's first encounter with figs and fig trees? *(Figs and fig trees are always included in the folktales told by the speaker's father.)* What is the speaker's second encounter? (When six years old, the speaker eats a dried fig.) What is her father's reaction to that encounter? (He explains that a dried fig is not the same as a fig fresh from a tree.)

Years passed, we lived in many houses, none had figtrees.
20 We had lima beans, zucchini, parsley, beets.
"Plant one!" my mother said, but my father never did.
He tended garden half-heartedly, forgot to water,
let the okra² get too big.
"What a dreamer he is. Look how many things he starts
25 and doesn't finish."

The last time he moved, I got a phone call.
My father, in Arabic, chanting a song I'd never heard.
"What's that?"
"Wait till you see!"
30 He took me out to the new yard.
There, in the middle of Dallas, Texas,
a tree with the largest, fattest, sweetest figs in the world.
"It's a figtree song!" he said,
plucking his fruits like ripe **tokens,**
35 **emblems,** assurance
of a world that was always his own.

---

2. *Okra* is a plant with pods that are eaten as vegetables.

Summarize *Summarize the main event that occurs in this stanza.* | 3 |

Extending and Remaking Traditions *How does Nye place a traditional element in a modern context in these lines?* | 4 |

Symbol *What does the fig tree symbolize for the speaker's father?* | 5 |

Vocabulary

token (tō′ kən) *n.* something serving as an indication, proof, or expression of something else; a sign
emblem (em′ bləm) *n.* an object or a representation that functions as a symbol

NAOMI SHIHAB NYE **1289**

Reading Strategy | 3 |

Summarize Answer: *During the years in which the speaker is growing up, her father moves the family to various locations but never plants a fig tree.*

Big Idea | 4 |

Extending and Remaking Traditions Answer: *Her father is sharing a traditional form of expression, an Arabic song, by way of modern technology, the telephone.*

Literary Element | 5 |

Symbol Answer: *The fig tree is a symbol of identity and belonging. The tree gives the father a sense of continuity with his homeland and his past.*

Progress Check

Can students identify symbols?

If No → See Unit 7 Teaching Resources Book, p. 267.

English Learners

DIFFERENTIATED INSTRUCTION

Advanced Ask: Are there any foods from your own culture or another culture you are familiar with that have a symbolic meaning, as the fig does for the father in the poem?

Approaching Level

DIFFERENTIATED INSTRUCTION

Emerging Remind students that a simile is a figure of speech in which the writer compares two seemingly different things. To identify a simile, students should look for one of two key words, *like* or *as*. Model how to analyze a simile. Have students look at line 5. **Ask:** What are the two things the poet is comparing? *(folktales and scarves)* What word describes something that can apply to both a

folktale and a scarf? *(weaving)* Direct students to find the other simile in the poem by looking for the word *like* or *as* and have them discuss the comparisons. *(plucking his fruits like ripe tokens)*

Assess

1. (a) Vivid little scarves (b) The stories captured her attention, or she found the stories beautiful.

2. (a) He claims that a dried fig is not the same as a fresh one. (b) The father misses fresh figs, especially since they seem to represent his homeland.

3. (a) In his yard in Dallas, Texas (b) On his American property he has planted a symbol of his Arabic heritage.

4. Joha appears in many traditional Arab tales. By mentioning Joha in conjunction with figs, the father shows how important figs are in his culture.

5. (a) Students may mention the images of fat, sweet figs. (b) Without them, the symbolism of the fig tree would carry less weight.

6. Students may say the fig tree effectively symbolizes the father's past and his culture.

7. Students' answers will vary but should be supported with evidence from the poem.

8. The figs and the other vegetables show her Palestinian and American background.

Literary Element

1. She is symbolically trying to connect with her father.

2. They symbolize his dreaminess and unfinished projects.

Writing

Use the following criteria to evaluate students' lists:

- Does the list include five people and five symbols?
- Does the list explain why each symbol was chosen?

After You Read

Respond and Think Critically

Respond and Interpret

1. (a) What does the speaker compare her father's folktales to? (b) What does this image suggest?

2. (a) How does the speaker's father react when she eats a dried fig? (b) Why do you think he responds in this way?

3. (a) Where does the speaker's father finally plant the fig tree? (b) What is the significance of this location?

Analyze and Evaluate

4. Why do you think Nye includes the references to Joha in the poem?

5. (a) What images seem especially significant in the poem? (b) How would the poem be affected if these images were removed?

6. How effective is the fig tree as a symbol in the poem? Explain.

Connect

7. **Big Idea** **Extending and Remaking Traditions** Do you think the poem seems more like a traditional folktale or a modern one? Explain.

8. **Connect to the Author** How does this poem represent the multi-faceted cultural background of the author?

Literary Element Symbol

A **symbol** is an object that represents an abstract idea, such as love or hope. Poets can expand on that symbolism by using the same object in different settings and events, so that the meaning changes and grows throughout the work.

1. What is the symbolism of the speaker eating the dried fig when she is young?

2. What do the father's gardening skills and the okra symbolize?

Reading Strategy Summarize

Summarizing the sequence of events in a poem is helpful, but you can also summarize other elements.

1. Briefly summarize the changes in the speaker's age throughout "My Father and the Figtree."

2. Summarize how the meaning of the fig tree to the father changes from the beginning to the end of the poem.

LOG ON ▶ **Literature** Online

Selection Resources For Selection Quizzes, eFlash-cards, and Reading-Writing Connection activities, go to glencoe.com and enter QuickPass code GLA9800u7.

Vocabulary Practice

Practice with Context Clues Identify the context clues in the following sentences that help you determine the meaning of each bold-faced vocabulary word.

1. We were just about to give up on our bird watching trip and head home when we saw a flash of **vivid** red streak through the surrounding trees.

2. In literature, light often functions as an **emblem**, or symbol, of knowledge.

3. I kept my subway card as a **token** of my trip to Paris.

Writing

Write a List In "My Father and the Figtree," Nye uses the fig as a symbol to help describe her father. Write a list of five people you know well. Next to each person's name, write down a symbol you might use if you were writing a poem about that person. Jot down some thoughts on why you picked each symbol.

Reading Strategy

1. At first, she is a young child; then, six years old; finally, an adult.

2. At first it is a far-off dream. By the end of the poem, it is a reality.

Vocabulary

1. The color grabs their attention and is distinct against the foliage.

2. A synonym for *emblem,* symbol, is included in the sentence.

3. The object proves that the speaker was in Paris and reminds the speaker of the trip.

Meet **Billy Collins**

(born 1941)

efore he became Poet Laureate of the United States in 2001, Billy Collins stood at a gymnasium podium at a large high school and read to an enthusiastic crowd of students as part of their "Poetry Day." This experience helped to inspire one of his signature endeavors. As Poet Laureate, Collins founded the program "Poetry 180: A Poem a Day for American High Schools." This program works to bring poetry to high school students by having a new poem read aloud every day. Collins wanted to create an environment where students could hear and enjoy poetry, but did not have to officially respond. The project is a prime example of one of Collins's missions as a writer—to make poetry a part of people's daily lives. His dedication to expanding poetry's audience and deepening its connection with people has helped to make Collins one of the most popular poets in the U.S.

Student, Teacher, Poet Collins was born in the same New York hospital where pioneering poet William Carlos Williams worked as a pediatrician. Collins grew up in New York City and attended parochial school there. He went on to Holy Cross College and eventually earned a Ph.D. in Romantic Poetry at the University of California, Riverside in 1971. After finishing his graduate work, Collins began teaching at Lehman College, City University of New York, and continued teaching there for over thirty years. He published his first collection of poems, *Pokerface*, in 1977, and has since received numerous fellowships and awards for his work. From 2001 to 2003, Collins was Poet Laureate of the United States.

Celebration of Daily Life Collins's poetry illuminates the ordinary aspects of daily life by revealing the universal themes that those scenes can hide. He uses a conversational tone, the cadences of everyday speech, and familiar settings to engage

> "Clarity is the real risk in poetry. To be clear means opening yourself up to judgment."
>
> —Billy Collins
> from the introduction to *Poetry 180*

readers. His poems are full of imaginative leaps; a dog's constant barking connects to Beethoven's musical genius, and a day at the beach ends with the speaker walking across the Atlantic toward Spain. However, in order for readers to connect with these ideas, Collins believes it is vital to provide them with an easy entrance: "Usually I try to create a hospitable tone at the beginning of a poem. Stepping from the title to the first lines is like stepping into a canoe. A lot of things can go wrong."

LOG ON ▶ **Literature** Online

Author Search For more about Billy Collins, go to glencoe.com and enter QuickPass code GLA9800u7.

BILLY COLLINS **1291**

Bellringer Options

Daily Language Practice Transparency 116

Or ask students to think about nursery rhymes that they learned when they were younger. Write several rhymes on the board, including "Three Blind Mice." Read them aloud. **Ask:** What is your reaction to the topics and messages of these rhymes, hearing them as high school students?

Have students consider, as they read, how Collins uses the nursery rhyme to explore universal themes.

Selection Skills

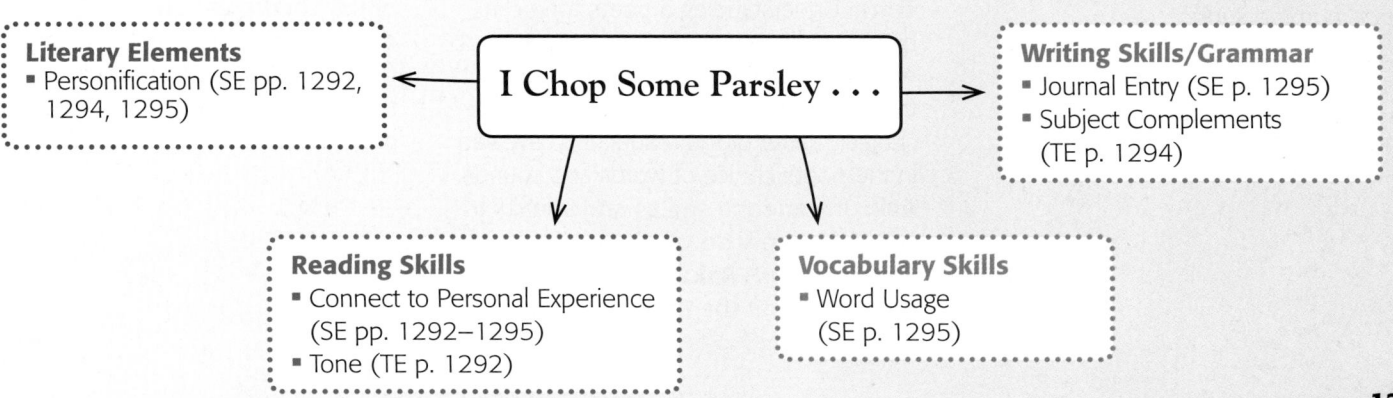

Literary Elements
- Personification (SE pp. 1292, 1294, 1295)

I Chop Some Parsley . . .

Writing Skills/Grammar
- Journal Entry (SE p. 1295)
- Subject Complements (TE p. 1294)

Reading Skills
- Connect to Personal Experience (SE pp. 1292–1295)
- Tone (TE p. 1292)

Vocabulary Skills
- Word Usage (SE p. 1295)

Before You Read

Focus

Summary

The speaker is listening to music as he prepares a meal. The music is a jazz rendition of a well-known nursery rhyme. Hearing the music causes the speaker to meditate on the deeper meaning of the rhyme and explore human experiences, such as isolation and conflict.

 For summaries in languages other than English, see Unit 7 Teaching Resources Book, pp. 273–278.

Vocabulary

Synonyms Tell students that a good strategy for learning a new vocabulary word is to think of synonyms for the new word that are familiar. They might be more likely to use the word *worry* than the word *brood* to describe behavior that shows anxiety over a possible problem. **Ask:** What does *brood* connote that *worry* does not? (*It connotes persisting in an anxious state over time.*)

(**ENGLISH LEARNERS**) **Ask:** The meaning of *sear* is "to scorch or burn." What are the differences among these synonyms? (*Scorch connotes burning the surface of something unintentionally, such as when ironing a shirt. One might intentionally* sear *meat, for example.* Burning *implies going deeper than the surface.*)

 For additional vocabulary practice, see Unit 7 Teaching Resources Book, pp. 281–282.

Literature and Reading Preview

Connect to the Poem

Can you think of a time when listening to music sparked an unusual train of thought? Freewrite for a few minutes about how music can affect your mood.

Build Background

The poem begins and ends with musical references, and both men mentioned—Blakey and Freddie Hubbard—are famous U.S. jazz musicians. Blakey was a pioneering drummer and bandleader in the 1950s and '60s. Hubbard, who was born a few years before Collins, is a jazz trumpeter from the generation after Blakey's. The song "Three Blind Mice" is a jazz standard inspired by the well-known nursery rhyme. "Blue Moon" is a popular jazz ballad characterized by its moody tone.

Set Purposes for Reading

Big Idea **Extending and Remaking Traditions**

As you read, ask yourself, How does the poem's tone and structure differ from more traditional poetry you have read?

Literary Element **Personification**

Personification is a figure of speech in which an animal, an object, a force of nature, an idea, or an emotion is given human characteristics. As you read, ask yourself, Where does the speaker use personification?

Reading Strategy **Connect to Personal Experience**

One of the best ways to examine a poem is to identify ideas or facets that **connect to your experience.** As you read, ask yourself, Have I ever felt his way? What else have I read that is like this selection? Do I know someone like this?

Tip: Finding Common Ground Choose a personal experience that you can link to the poem and create a Venn Diagram. Use one circle for your experience and one circle for the poem. In the overlapping area, list what your experience and the poem have in common.

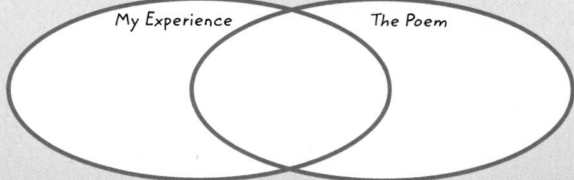

1292   UNIT 7   INTO THE TWENTY-FIRST CENTURY

Learning Objectives

For pages 1291–1295

In studying this text, you will focus on the following objectives:

Literary Study: Identifying personification.

Reading: Connecting to personal experience.

Writing: Writing a journal entry.

Vocabulary

congenital (kən jeʹ nə təl) *adj.* of or relating to a condition that is present at birth, as a result of either heredity or environmental influences; p. 1293 *The baby had a congenital heart defect.*

brood (brood) *v.* to focus the attention on a subject persistently and moodily; worry; p. 1293 *The whole team sat brooding over the last-second loss.*

sear (sēr) *v.* to char, scorch, or burn the surface with or as if with a sudden application of intense heat; p. 1293 *The lava seared the plants as it fell to earth.*

cynic (siʹ nik) *n.* a person whose outlook is scornfully and often habitually negative; p. 1294 *He never donated to charity because he was a cynic and was convinced that they would waste his money.*

Tip: Word Usage When learning a new word, it often helps to answer a question using the word. For example, have you ever **brooded** over something that, in retrospect, does not seem so bad?

Reading Practice

Tone Understanding a poet's tone can help a reader connect his or her personal experience to the poem. Remind students that tone is the poet's attitude toward the subject matter or the reader. It is revealed in the poet's choice of words and sounds. **Ask:** If someone smiles and speaks to you softly, how do you interpret their tone? (*as kind*) **Ask:** Given that this poem is about the three blind mice of the children's nursery rhyme, what do you predict the poet's tone will be? (*humorous, silly*) Direct students to read the poem aloud, and then discuss the poet's tone.

I Chop Some Parsley While Listening to Art Blakey's Version of "Three Blind Mice"

Billy Collins

Soulful Solace, 1997. Gil Mayers.

1

And I start wondering how they came to be blind.
If it was **congenital,** they could be brothers and sisters,
and I think of the poor mother
brooding over her sightless young triplets.

5   Or was it a common accident, all three caught
in a **searing** explosion, a firework perhaps?
If not,
if each came to his or her blindness separately,

how did they ever manage to find one another?
10   Would it not be difficult for a blind mouse
to locate even one fellow mouse with vision
let alone two other blind ones?

---

2   **Connect to Personal Experience** *Why might someone try to unravel a mystery or figure out a silly riddle that other people take for granted?*

Vocabulary

congenital (kən je′ nə təl) *adj.* of or relating to a condition that is present at birth, as a result of either heredity or environmental influences
brood (brood) *v.* to focus the attention on a subject persistently and moodily; worry
sear (sēr) *v.* to char, scorch, or burn the surface with or as if with a sudden application of intense heat

BILLY COLLINS   **1293**

Teach

Big Idea   1

Extending and Remaking Traditions Say: Keep this question in mind as you read: How is the speaker affected by hearing the music? *(The music causes the speaker to ponder the deeper meaning of the nursery rhyme.)*

Reading Strategy   2

Connect to Personal Experience Answer: *Students may say that at times a person suddenly sees a word or idea in a new light.*

View the Art ★

Ask: How might this painting relate to the poem? *(Possible answer: The painting depicts a group of jazz musicians, like the ones the speaker in the poem is listening to.)*

English Learners

DIFFERENTIATED INSTRUCTION

SMALL GROUP

Intermediate List the vocabulary words on the board and have students work with partners to create a two-column chart with the headings *Words* and *Examples*. Provide an example that illustrates the word's meaning and then ask students to come up with two other sample sentences for each word. *(Cynic: A cynic believes that all governments are corrupt. Congential: A congenital condition is not necessarily caused by genes. Brood: Someone might brood when a friend ignores him. Sear: One way to sear food is on a grill.)*

Teach

Reading Strategy 1

Connect to Personal Experience **Ask:** How would you describe the speaker's feelings at the end of the poem? *(Possible answer: Thinking about the fate of the mice has saddened the speaker. He tries to hide his own internal conflict by rationalizing his tears.)*

Reading Strategy 2

Connect to Personal Experience **Answer:** *Students may cite instances when familiar images, words, or ideas seemed to acquire deeper clarity or meaning for them.*

Literary Element 3

Personification **Answer:** *One part of the speaker's mind is personified as "the cynic who always lounges within me."*

Progress Check

Can students analyze personification?

If No → See Unit 7 Teaching Resources Book, p. 279.

And how, in their tiny darkness,
could they possibly have run after a farmer's wife
15   or anyone else's wife for that matter?
Not to mention why.

Just so she could cut off their tails
with a carving knife, is the **cynic's** answer,
but the thought of them without eyes
20   and now without tails to trail through the moist grass

or slip around the corner of a baseboard
has the cynic who always lounges within me
up off his couch and at the window
trying to hide the rising softness that he feels.

25   By now I am on to dicing an onion
which might account for the wet stinging
in my own eyes, though Freddie Hubbard's
mournful trumpet on "Blue Moon,"

which happens to be the next cut,
30   cannot be said to be making matters any better. **1**

---

2 Connect to Personal Experience *This image has a strong effect on the speaker of the poem. Can you think of a time where you experienced similar feelings?*

3 Personification *What is being personified here?*

Vocabulary

cynic (si´ nik) *n.* a person whose outlook is scornfully and often habitually negative

Grammar Practice

Subject Complements Explain that two types of subject complements are predicate nominatives and predicate adjectives. A predicate nominative is a noun that follows a linking verb and further identifies the subject *(The ball is a football)*. A predicate adjective follows a linking verb and describes the subject *(The actor was funny)*. Have each student use both kinds of subject complements in four sentences describing the mice in the poem. Students should exchange papers with partners and check them for accuracy.

After You Read

Respond and Think Critically

Respond and Interpret

1. What was your first reaction to the title of this poem?

2. (a)In the first line of the poem, what is the speaker wondering about? (b)What causes the speaker to think about this topic?

3. The speaker of the poem gives several reasons why the mice might be blind. What are those reasons?

4. (a)After they chase the farmer's wife, what happens to the mice? (b)How does the speaker of the poem react to this?

5. (a)At the end of the poem, what vegetable does the speaker begin to cut and what song is playing? (b)What is the connection between the vegetable and the song?

Analyze and Evaluate

6. (a)Throughout the poem, the speaker poses a series of questions. Which questions would you call silly or humorous, and which questions seem to have larger, more serious implications? (b)How does posing unanswered questions affect the tone and meaning of the poem?

Connect

7. **Big Idea** **Extending and Remaking Traditions** Did the poem's conversational tone make it easier or harder for you to connect with the poem? Why or why not?

8. **Connect to the Author** Collins wants to make poetry accessible to more readers. How might the subject of this poem further this goal?

Literary Element **Personification**

Personification is the attribution of human emotions or traits to ideas, animals, or inanimate objects. In our daily lives, we use personification all the time to help us understand our world.

1. How does the personification in this poem dramatize the speaker's inner conflict?

2. (a)Does this help you to better understand the speaker's emotions? (b)Why or why not?

Reading Strategy **Connect to Personal Experience**

Sometimes you may not connect with any of the specific events or experiences in a poem, particularly when reading work from different cultures or a different time period. In these cases it helps to broaden your strategy and seek out more general connections.

1. What element or part of the poem did you feel most strongly connected to? Explain your answer.

2. What did you gain by attempting to connect?

Vocabulary Practice

Word Usage Respond to these statements to explore vocabulary from the selection.

1. Identify a trait that is, in you, **congenital.**

2. Name something that you might **brood** over.

3. Name something that is capable of **searing.**

4. Describe the outlook of a **cynical** person.

 Writing

Write a Journal Entry Have you ever wondered about something others might find ridiculous? Write a journal entry describing your question. Invent possible answers and evaluate their plausibility.

LOG ON ▶ **Literature** Online

Selection Resources For Selection Quizzes, eFlashcards, and Reading-Writing Connection activities, go to glencoe.com and enter QuickPass code GLA9800u7.

After You Read

Assess

1. Students may have found the poem title funny or silly.

2. (a) How the mice became blind (b) He hears the song "Three Blind Mice."

3. They were born blind; they were in an accident, such as an explosion; they became blind separately from different causes.

4. (a) She chops off their tails. (b) He feels sympathy for the mice with no tails.

5. (a) An onion; Freddie Hubbard's "Blue Moon" (b) Both cause tears.

6. (a) Students' answers will vary. (b) If the speaker gave answers, the poem's tone would not waver between humor and seriousness.

7. Students' answers will vary.

8. By discussing a well-known nursery rhyme and talking about cooking, nearly everyone can relate to his writing.

Literary Element

1. He does not want to feel sympathy for the mice, but he cannot help himself. His cynical feelings are personified, and this inner conflict is played out.

2. Students may say the personification allows them to ponder universal themes in a detached manner.

 Writing

Use the following criteria to evaluate students' journal entries:

▪ Does the entry describe a specific question?

▪ Does the entry offer answers and explanations of their probability?

Reading Strategy

1. Students' answers will vary but should be supported with details from the poem.

2. Students should describe specific understandings they gained.

Vocabulary

1. The student should mention a trait he or she was born with, such as hair or eye color.

2. Students should name problems that would require serious attention.

3. Students might mention a grill or a blowtorch.

4. Students might mention that a *cynical* individual is pessimistic and doubtful.

Bellringer Options

Selection Focus
Transparency 71

Daily Language Practice
Transparency 117

Or lead a discussion on the topic of given names. Ask whether students know the meanings of their names and how their names were chosen. **Ask:** Why are we given names? *(A name establishes a person's identity.)* Have students consider, as they read, how the names of the women in the selection established who they were as individuals.

Meet **Louise Erdrich**

(born 1954)

Louise Erdrich (âr´ drik) grew up in a Native American storytelling culture that encouraged her to tell stories of her own. Her parents also supported her desire to write. Erdrich recalled, "My father used to give me a nickel for every story I wrote, and my mother wove strips of construction paper and stapled them into book covers. So at an early age I felt myself to be a published author, earning substantial royalties."

Erdrich is the daughter of a German American father and an Ojibway (ō jib´ wā) mother who was born on the Turtle Mountain Reservation in North Dakota. The oldest of seven children, Erdrich grew up in Wahpeton, North Dakota, where her parents worked for a boarding school run by the Bureau of Indian Affairs. Erdrich entered Dartmouth College in 1972, the first year that the college admitted women. From there, she went on to Johns Hopkins University, where she wrote poems and stories and earned a master's degree.

> *"When you grow up constantly hearing stories rise, break, and fall, it gets into you somehow."*
>
> —Louise Erdrich

Popular and Critical Success Before she turned thirty, Erdrich published her first novel, *Love Medicine*. It was acclaimed by both readers and critics, and won the National Book Critics Circle Award in 1984. The novels *Beet Queen* and *Tracks*, which also had wide popular and literary appeal, followed soon after.

In the late 1980s and early 1990s, Erdrich became well-known as an accomplished novelist and a voice of Native American culture. Her marriage to Michael Dorris, a writer, anthropologist, and spokesperson for Native American ways of life, intensified her reputation and literary output. Together, the couple embarked on a series of literary projects while raising several children.

Sources from Life On her way to success as a writer, Erdrich held many different jobs, working as a beet weeder, a lifeguard, a waitress, and a construction flag signaler. She notes that these experiences have lent authenticity to her portrayal of characters in her novels. However, she admits that some of her plots are culled from old Native American stories, though her own characters usually take over. Erdrich has described herself as "an emissary of the between-world, that increasingly common margin where cultures mix and collide." "The Names of Women," originally a piece of nonfiction, was eventually incorporated into a novel.

Erdrich continues to write both nonfiction and fiction, including stories for children. Her life's work also includes learning the language of the Ojibway and studying the culture and traditions of her great-grandmothers. In 2001 she opened a bookstore in Minneapolis, Minnesota that specializes in books by and about Native Americans.

 Literature Online

Author Search For more about Louise Erdrich, go to glencoe.com and enter QuickPass code GLA9800u7.

Selection Skills

Literary Elements
- Catalog (SE pp. 1297, 1298, 1301, 1302)
- Symbol (SE p. 1302)

The Names of Women

Writing Skills/Grammar
- Apply Symbolism (SE p. 1303)
- Apostrophes (TE p. 1300)

Reading Skills
- Distinguish Fact and Opinion (SE pp. 1297–1299, 1303)
- Analyze Sections (TE p. 1298)

Vocabulary Skills
- Word Parts (SE pp. 1297, 1303)
- Academic Vocabulary (SE p. 1303)

Literature and Reading Preview

Connect to the Essay

Which family members, past or present, have helped to shape your personality and values? Make a list of these people and explain why they are special to you.

Build Background

The Anishinabe (a nish' i nä' bä)—also known as the Ojibway, Ojibwe, or Chippewa—are one of the largest groups of Native Americans in North America. After the mid-1600s, they migrated west from the Great Lakes region to areas such as Wisconsin, North Dakota, and Montana. Many Anishinabe families still live on the Turtle Mountain Reservation in North Dakota today.

Set Purposes for Reading

Big Idea **Extending and Remaking Traditions**

As you read, ask yourself, How does Erdrich reveal the present by focusing on and cataloging details from the past?

Literary Element **Catalog**

A **catalog** is a list of images, details, people, or events in a piece of writing. The items in a catalog are related and are of relatively equal importance. As you read, ask yourself, What does Erdrich list and why are these objects important?

Reading Strategy **Distinguish Fact and Opinion**

A fact is a statement that can be verified, or proven true, either through direct experience or by consulting an authoritative source. An opinion is a personal judgment that, unlike a fact, cannot be verified because it expresses a person's beliefs or feelings. As you read, ask yourself, When does Erdrich state a fact and when does she offer an opinion?

Tip: Take Notes Use a chart like the one below to record the facts and opinions you find.

Example	Fact or Opinion	How I Know
Names of Erdrich's ancestors	Fact	Names can be verified in historical records.

Vocabulary

decimated (des´ ə māt əd) *adj.* destroyed or killed in large numbers; p. 1298 *The battle left the village decimated.*

presumptuous (pri zump´ chо̄о̄ əs) *adj.* going beyond what is proper; excessively bold; p. 1299 *It was presumptuous of us to ask for so much money.*

ecclesiastical (i klē´ zē as´ ti kəl) *adj.* of or relating to the church; p. 1299 *The woman felt comfortable in the ecclesiastical setting.*

undeviating (un dē´ vē āt´ ing) *adj.* not turning away from; p. 1299 *The commander showed undeviating concern for the troops.*

wane (wān) *v.* to decrease gradually; to decline; p. 1300 *All fads wane in popularity over time.*

Tip: Word Parts When taking a word apart to determine meaning, consider these basic elements: **root,** the main part of a word; **prefix,** a part added to the beginning of a word; and **suffix,** a part added to the end of a word. The prefix in the word *decimated,* for example, is *de-.*

English Learners

DIFFERENTIATED INSTRUCTION

SMALL GROUP

Intermediate Before reading the story, students should work with a partner to read through the italic type in the story as well as the footnotes that describe the pronunciation of words. Explain that the author uses words from the language of her ancestors. Many of the names of the women she describes are translated from a Native American word into English and are written in italic in the text. **Ask:** How are these names different from typical English names? *(They describe the person.)*

Before You Read

Focus

Summary

In this essay, the author discusses her cultural heritage. Through her exploration of the given names of Anishinabe women, Erdrich reveals both the strength of these women and the contributions they made to history. As she examines her origins, the author learns more about her own identity.

 For summaries in languages other than English, see Unit 7 Teaching Resources Book, pp. 285–290.

Vocabulary

Roots Point out that the key to understanding an unfamiliar word is breaking it down into its parts, and then learning how the root relates to the word's meaning. Ask students to work with a partner to determine each word's root. Provide an example with *decimated.* Its root is *decem,* meaning "ten." To *decimate* literally meant to kill every tenth person, but now means to destroy a very large number of people.

 For additional vocabulary practice, see Unit 7 Teaching Resources Book, pp. 293–294.

Teach

Big Idea `1`

Extending and Remaking Traditions Say: Keep these questions in mind as you read: What do the names of the women reveal about their life stories? *(Each woman's name captures some essential part of her personality.)* What impact does the renaming of the Anishinabe women have on their place in history? *(The new names give no clues to the personalities of the women.)*

Reading Strategy `2`

Distinguish Fact and Opinion Answer: *Fact: the names of women of the Turtle Mountain Reservation were first recorded in 1892. Opinion: the names tell stories.*

Literary Element `3`

Catalog Answer: *Erdrich wants to show readers that many rich and diverse cultural stories have been lost.*

Readability Scores

Dale-Chall: 7.3
DRP: 62
Lexile: 1300

The Names of Women

Louise Erdrich

1 *Ikwe*[1] is the word for woman in the language of the Anishinabe, my mother's people, whose descendants, mixed with and married to French trappers and farmers, are the Michifs[2] of the Turtle Mountain reservation in North Dakota. Every Anishinabe *Ikwe*, every mixed-blood descendant like me, who can trace her way back a generation or two, is the daughter of a mystery. The history of the woodland Anishinabe—**decimated** by disease, fighting Plains Indians tribes to the west and squeezed by European settlers to the east—is much like most other Native American stories, a confusion of loss, a tale of absences, of a culture that was blown apart and changed so radically in such a short time that only the names survive.

And yet, those names.

The names of the first women whose existence is recorded on the rolls of the Turtle Mountain Reservation, in 1892, reveal as much as we can ever recapture of their personalities, complex natures and relationships. These names tell stories, or half stories, if only we listen closely.

There once were women named *Standing Strong, Fish Bones, Different Thunder*. There once was a girl called *Yellow Straps*. Imagine what it was like to pick berries with *Sky Coming Down*, to walk through a storm with *Lightning Proof*. Surely, she was struck and lived, but what about the person next to her? People always avoided *Steps Over Truth*, when they wanted a straight answer, and *I Hear*, when they wanted to keep a secret. *Glittering* put coal on her face and watched for enemies at night. The woman named *Standing Across* could see things moving far across the lake. The old ladies gossiped about *Playing Around*, but no one dared say anything to her face. *Ice* was good at gambling. *Shining One Side* loved to sit and talk to *Opposite the Sky*. They both knew *Sounding Feather, Exhausted Wind* and *Green Cloud*, daughter of *Seeing Iron. Center of the Sky* was a widow. *Rabbit, Prairie Chicken* and *Daylight* were all little girls. *She Tramp* could make great distance in a day of walking.

Cross Lightning had a powerful smile. When *Setting Wind* and *Gentle Woman Standing* sang together the whole tribe listened. *Stop the Day* got her name when at her shout the afternoon went still. *Log* was strong, *Cloud Touching Bottom* weak and consumptive.[3] *Mirage* married *Wind*. Everyone loved *Musical Cloud*, but children hid from *Dressed in Stone*. *Lying Down Grass* had such a gentle voice and touch, but no one dared to cross *She Black of Heart*.

---

1. *Ikwe* (ik′ wā)
2. *Michifs* (mi′ chifs)

2 **Distinguish Fact and Opinion** *In this paragraph, which statement is a fact and which is an opinion?*

Vocabulary

decimated (des′ ə māt′ əd) *adj.* destroyed or killed in large numbers

---

3. Someone who is *consumptive* suffers from a disease (especially tuberculosis) in which body tissue wastes away.

Catalog *In this paragraph, why does Erdrich employ this catalog of names?* `3`

Reading Practice

SMALL GROUP

Analyze Sections Louise Erdrich's intention for "The Names of Women" is multifold. Point out that there are three breaks—lines of space between paragraphs—that create four distinct sections in the essay. Ask students to work with a partner in mapping out the verb tense and point of view used in each of the four sections. **Ask:** When does the essay become personal? Is it when the author first uses the pronoun "I?" How does the ending of the essay connect to its title? *(The verb tense is past until the last section, when it becomes present. The second section focuses on the personalities of the author's great-grandmothers. The third section begins to focus on the author's sense of home, while the last section focuses on the author's present life. The traditions, knowledge, and gifts of her people, as represented in their names, no longer exist, except through the author's words.)*

We can imagine something of these women from their names. Anishinabe historian Basil Johnston notes that 'such was the mystique and force of a name that it was considered **presumptuous** and unbecoming, even vain, for a person to utter his own name. It was the custom for a third person, if present, to utter the name of the person to be identified. Seldom, if ever, did either husband or wife speak the name of the other in public.'

Shortly after the first tribal roll, the practice of renaming became an **ecclesiastical** exercise, and, as a result, most women in the next two generations bear the names of saints particularly beloved by the French. *She Knows the Bear* became Marie. *Sloping Cloud* was christened Jeanne. *Taking Care of the Day* and *Yellow Day Woman* turned into Catherines. Identities are altogether lost. The daughters of my own ancestors, *Kwayzancheewin*[4]—*Acts Like a Boy* and *Striped Earth Woman*—go unrecorded, and no hint or reflection of their individual natures comes to light through the scattershot records of those times, although they must have been genetically tough in order to survive: there were epidemics of typhoid, flu, measles and other diseases that winnowed the tribe each winter. They had to have grown up sensible, hard-working, **undeviating** in their attention to their tasks. They had to have been lucky. And if very lucky, they acquired carts.

It is no small thing that both of my great-grandmothers were known as women with carts.

---

4. *Kwayzancheewin* (kwā´ zän chē´ win)

4 Distinguish Fact and Opinion *In regards to this fact, what is Erdrich's opinion?*

Vocabulary

presumptuous (pri zump´ chōō əs) *adj.* going beyond what is proper; excessively bold
ecclesiastical (i klē´ zē as´ ti kəl) *adj.* of or relating to the church
undeviating (un dē´ vē āt´ ing) *adj.* not turning away from

The first was Elise Eliza McCloud, the great-granddaughter of *Striped Earth Woman*. The buggy she owned was somewhat grander than a cart. In her photograph [page 1298], Elise Eliza gazes straight ahead, intent, elevated in her pride. Perhaps she and her daughter Justine, both wearing reshaped felt fedoras,[5] were on their way to the train that would take them from Rugby, North Dakota, to Grand Forks, and back again. Back and forth across the upper tier of the plains, they peddled their hand-worked tourist items—dangling moccasin brooches and little beaded hats, or, in the summer, the wild berries, plums and nuts that they had gathered from the wooded hills. Of Elise Eliza's industry there remains in the family only an intricately beaded pair of buffalo horns and a piece of real furniture, a 'Highboy,' an object once regarded with some awe, a prize she won for selling the most merchandise from a manufacturer's catalogue.

Visual Vocabulary
A *highboy* is a tall chest of drawers having two sections and four legs.

The owner of the other cart, Virginia Grandbois [page 1301], died when I was nine years old: she was a fearsome and fascinating presence, an old woman seated like an icon **5** behind the door of my grandparents' house. Forty years before I was born, she was photographed on her way to fetch drinking water at the reservation well. In the picture she is seated high, the reins in her fingers connected to a couple of shaggy fetlocked draft ponies. The barrel she will fill stands behind her. She wears a man's sweater and an expression of vast self-pleasure. She might have been saying

---

5. *Fedoras* (fi dôr´ əz) are soft felt hats with curved brims and lengthwise creases in the crown.

LOUISE ERDRICH **1299**

Teach

Reading Strategy **4**

Distinguish Fact and Opinion Answer: *She believes the giving of saints' names marks a loss of Native American identity.*

Reading Strategy **5**

Distinguish Fact and Opinion Have students find examples of Eridich's opinions in the text. **Ask:** How does Erdrich support her opinions? *(To support the opinion "she was a fearsome and fascinating presence," she describes Virginia Grandbois as "seated like an icon.")*

Writer's Technique ☆

Style Discuss Erdrich's writing style. **Ask:** How does her style affect the reader? *(Her style is conversational. Readers may feel they are listening to her personal comments about her ancestry.)*

English Learners

DIFFERENTIATED INSTRUCTION

Intermediate Point out to students that the Native American names of the author's ancestors often functioned as metaphors, drawing a comparison between the person's character and an aspect of nature. *Daylight* might have been a child who often smiled quietly and had abundant positive energy. *Green Cloud* might have allowed envy to darken a mood.

Ask: How do you imagine *Wind's* character? *(She might enter a room in a hurry, rearrange everything, clean the place up, and take charge.)* How do you imagine *Musical Cloud*? *(She might have had a lilting voice, pretty in a quiet way.)* Why might the church have changed the women's names to those of saints? *(Missionaries often sought to convert Native*

Americans from their nature-centered faith to Christianity.) Ask students to think of a name for themselves that would indicate their personality.

Teach

Literary Element   1

Symbolism **Ask:** What does the quilt symbolize? *(Possible response: It symbolizes the history of the Anishinabe.)*

Big Idea   2

Extending and Remaking Traditions **Answer:** *Erdrich feels connected to the traditions of the Anishinabe tribe, yet many of those traditions have become outdated.*

Writer's Technique ☆

Repetition Point out that Erdrich's use of repetition gives her writing a rhythm that highlights major themes. Ask students to identify places in the text where repetition creates such a rhythm. *(Possible responses: "she wanted home, to get home, to be home"; "no substitute, no kindness, no reality")*

Kaygoh,[6] a warning, to calm the horses. She might have been speaking to whomever it was who held the camera, still a novel luxury.

Virginia Grandbois was known to smell of flowers. In spite of the potato picking, water hauling, field and housework, she found the time and will to dust her face with pale powder, in order to look more French. She was the great-great-granddaughter of the daughter of the principal leader of the *A-waus-e*,[7] the Bullhead clan, a woman whose real name was never recorded but who, on marrying a Frenchman, was 'recreated' as Madame Cadotte. It was Madame Cadotte who acted as a liaison[8] between her Ojibway relatives and her husband so that, even when French influence **waned** in the region, Jean-Baptiste Cadotte stayed on as the only trader of importance, the last governor of the fort at Sault St. Marie.[9]

By the time I knew Virginia Grandbois, however, her mind had darkened, and her body deepened, shrunk, turned to bones and leather. She did not live in the present or in any known time at all. Periodically, she would awaken from dim and unknown dreams to find herself seated behind the door in her daughter's house. She then cried out for her cart and her horses. When they did not materialize, Virginia Grandbois rose with great energy and purpose. Then she walked towards her house, taking the straightest line.

That house, long sold and gone, lay over one hundred miles due east and still Virginia Grandbois charged ahead, no matter what lay in her path—fences, sloughs,[10] woods, the yards of other families. She wanted home, to get home,

---

6. *Kaygoh* (kā gō′)
7. *A-waus*-e (ā′ wôs ē)
8. Here, a *liaison* (lē ā′ zon) is a person who maintains or improves communications between two parties.
9. *Sault St.* (or *Ste.,* meaning *Sainte) Marie* (sōō′ sānt mə rē′), Michigan, and its sister city, Sault Ste. Marie, Ontario, lie along the St. Mary's River between Lake Huron and Lake Superior.
10. *Sloughs* (slōōz) are marshes, swamps, or bogs.

Vocabulary

wane (wān) *v.* to decrease gradually; to decline

to be home. She wanted her own place back, the place she had made, not her daughter's, not anyone else's. Hers. There was no substitute, no kindness, no reality that would change her mind. She had to be tied to the chair, and the chair to the wall, and still there was no reasoning with Virginia Grandbois. Her entire life, her hard-won personality, boiled down in the end to one stubborn, fixed, desperate idea.

I started with the same idea—this urge to get home, even if I must walk straight across the world. Only, for me, the urge to walk is the urge to write. Like my great-grandmother's house, there is no home for me to get to. A mixed-blood, raised in the Sugarbeet Capital, educated on the Eastern seaboard, married in a tiny New England village, living now on a ridge directly across from the Swan Range in the Rocky Mountains, my home is a collection of homes, of wells in which the quiet of experience shales away into sweet bedrock.

Elise Eliza pieced the quilt my mother slept under, a patchwork of shirts, pants, other worn-out scraps, bordered with small rinsed and pressed Bull Durham[11] sacks. As if in another time and place, although it is only the dim barrel of a four-year-old's memory, I see myself lying wrapped under smoky quilts and dank green army blankets in the house in which my mother was born. In the fragrance of tobacco, some smoked in home-rolled cigarettes, some offered to the Manitous[12] whose presence still was honored, I dream myself home. Beneath the rafters, shadowed with bunches of plants and torn calendars, in the nest of a sagging bed, I listen to mice rustle and the scratch of an owl's claws as it paces the shingles.

---

11. *Bull Durham* was a brand of tobacco.
12. *Manitous* (man′ ə tōōz′) are spirits worshiped as governing forces of life and nature.

Extending and Remaking Traditions *How does this passage serve as a metaphor for Erdrich's life?*   **2**

Grammar Practice

Apostrophes Review the use of apostrophes to form possessives and contractions. Remind students that apostrophes are not used in the possessive personal pronouns *yours, his, hers, its, ours,* and *theirs.* Have students correct these sentences:

1. The mayors assistant greeted the delegation. *(mayor's)*
2. The schools baseball team practices in the afternoon. *(school's)*
3. Do you think its a good idea to skip breakfast? *(it's)*
4. The dog played with it's toy. *(its)*

Elise Eliza's daughter-in-law, my grandmother Mary LeFavor, kept that house of hand-hewed and stacked beams, mudded between. She managed to shore it up and keep it standing by stuffing every new crack with disposable diapers. Having used and reused cloth to diaper her own children, my grandmother washed and hung to dry the paper and plastic diapers that her granddaughters bought for her great-grandchildren. When their plastic-paper shredded, she gathered them carefully together and one day, on a summer visit, I woke early to find her tamping[13] the rolled stuff carefully into the cracked walls of that old house.

It is autumn in the Plains, and in the little sloughs ducks land, and mudhens, whose flesh always tastes greasy and charred. Snow is coming soon, and after its first fall there will be a short, false warmth that brings out the sweet-sour odor of highbush cranberries. As a descendant of the women who skinned buffalo and tanned and smoked the hides, of women who pounded berries with the dried meat to make winter food, who made tea from willow bark and rosehips, who gathered snakeroot, I am affected by the change of seasons. Here is a time when plants consolidate[14] their tonic and drop seed, when animals store energy and grow thick fur. As for me, I start keeping longer hours, writing more, working harder, though I am obviously not a creature of a traditional Anishinabe culture. I was not raised speaking the old language, or adhering to the cycle of religious ceremonies that govern the Anishinabe spiritual relationship to the land and the moral order within human configurations. As the wedding of many backgrounds, I am free to do what simply feels right.

My mother knits, sews, cans, dries food and preserves it. She knows how to gather tea, berries, snare rabbits, milk cows and churn butter. She can grow squash and melons from seeds she gathered the fall before. She is, as were the women who came before me, a repository[15] of all of the homely virtues, and I am the first in a long line who has not saved the autumn's harvest in birch bark *makuks*[16] and skin bags and in a cellar dry and cold with dust. I am the first who scratches the ground for pleasure, not survival, and grows flowers instead of potatoes. I record rather than practise the arts that filled the hands and days of my mother and her mother, and all the mothers going back into the shadows, when women wore names that told us who they were. ❧

---

15. Here, a *repository* (ri poz′ ə tōr′ ē) is a person who stores something.
16. *makuks* (mä′ kuks)

Extending and Remaking Traditions *Why is this idea important?* **4**

Extending and Remaking Traditions *How is Erdrich extending and remaking her cultural inheritance?* **5**

---

13. *Tamping* means "forcing or packing in with a series of light taps."
14. To *consolidate* (kən sol′ ə dāt′) means "to combine."

3 Catalog *What is the purpose of this catalog?*

LOUISE ERDRICH **1301**

Approaching Level

DIFFERENTIATED INSTRUCTION

AAVE For approaching-level students who are users of African American vernacular English (AAVE), the *'s* suffix that shows possession is sometimes left out, yielding "mayor assistant," rather than "mayor's assistant." Give students extra practice filling in the apostrophe in the following phrases: my mothers sister, my sisters friend, Jacks football, Talias sweater. (*mother's, sister's, Jack's, Talia's*) Remind students that the word *it* can be especially challenging, and many writers confuse *it's* and *its*. Review the possessive, as in *The dog scratched its ear;* and the contraction, as in *It's hard for a dog to sit still*. When *it* is followed by *'s*, the apostrophe signals a contraction of the words *it is*. The possessive form of *it* is written *without* an apostrophe. **Say:** Identify whether *its* shows possession or is a contraction: (1) The dog played with its toy. (2) He asked if it's okay to yell out. (*possession, contraction*)

After You Read

Assess

1. (a) She reveals that the culture of her Native American forebears was radically changed and partly obliterated. (b) She seems fascinated by the strengths of the women and saddened that she does not have the same strengths.

2. (a) She describes Elise Eliza McCloud as "elevated in her pride" and Virginia Grandbois as "fearsome and fascinating." (b) She is in awe of their strengths and abilities and impressed by their sense of purpose.

3. (a) They both have energy and purpose. (b) She too is determined to "get home" by exploring and preserving her family history. She hopes she has the same strength of will.

4. The search for identity should include examining the past; our ancestors' strength can give us purpose. Students' details should support their statements of theme.

5. (a) The names of her Native American ancestors have symbolic significance and point to their unique characters and strengths. (b) Some students may say the title suits the essay. Others may say the essay is also about Erdrich's ancestors and how she does and does not resemble them.

6. Students may say she is extending the traditions by conveying them to others by means of her writing.

7. Students' answers will vary.

 For additional assessment, see Assessment Resources, pp. 317–318.

After You Read

Respond and Think Critically

Respond and Interpret

1. (a) What does Erdrich reveal in the first paragraph about her ethnic heritage and the history of her ancestors? (b) What is Erdrich's attitude toward her ancestors' history?

2. (a) What words does Erdrich use to describe her great-grandmothers? (b) How do you think Erdrich feels about her great-grandmothers? Use specific details from the selection to explain your answers.

3. (a) What do Erdrich's great-grandmother Virginia Grandbois and Erdrich have in common? (b) What do you think Erdrich is saying about her own character when she explains what she has in common with Virginia Grandbois? Use details from the selection to support your answer.

Analyze and Evaluate

4. In your opinion, what is the **theme**, or message about life, of this selection? Support your response with evidence from the text.

5. (a) Why does Erdrich title this essay "The Names of Women"? (b) Do you think this title is appropriate? Why or why not?

Connect

6. **Big Idea** Extending and Remaking Traditions Do you think that Erdrich is extending or remaking the traditions of her past? Explain why or why not.

7. **Connect to Today** Do you think that writing about what people have done in the past is important today? Why or why not?

Literary Element Catalog

Many forms of literature include **catalogs**. For example, some epic poems list the names of heroes or weapons.

1. Describe two catalogs that appear in this nonfiction selection.

2. Why might Erdrich present this information in the form of catalogs?

Review: Symbol

As you learned on page 1287, a **symbol** is any object, person, place, or experience that represents itself on a literal level but also stands for something else, usually something abstract. For example, a dove is often used to symbolize peace. In some cases, names can also be symbolic.

Partner Activity Pair up with a classmate to identify symbols in "The Names of Women." Working with your partner, create a two-column chart similar to the one below. Fill in the left-hand column with examples of symbols or symbolic content from the text. In the right-hand column, explain what the name, object, or other symbol can be understood to represent.

Symbol	What It Represents
The name Standing Strong	
The great-grandmother's carts	

Literary Element

1. Possible answers: the names of Anishinabe women, Erdrich's mother's tasks

2. Possible answer: to emphasize the scope of the listed items

Review: Symbol

Invite students to compile their charts into a class list.

Progress Check

Can students recognize catalogs?

If No → See Unit 7 Teaching Resources Book, p. 291.

Reading Strategy — Distinguish Fact and Opinion

SAT Skills Practice

1. Erdrich supports her opinion that the names of her ancestors have stories to tell by

 (A) giving examples of some women's stories.

 (B) naming all of her women ancestors.

 (C) describing the process of renaming.

 (D) referring readers to the rolls of the Turtle Mountain Reservation.

 (E) explaining the derivation of her own name.

Vocabulary Practice

Practice with Word Parts For each vocabulary word in the left column, identify the related word with a shared prefix, root, or suffix in the right column. Write both words and underline the part they have in common. Then look up the meaning of the related word and explain how it is related to the vocabulary word.

1. decimated   fantastical
2. presumptuous   deviant
3. ecclesiastical   December
4. undeviating   want
5. wane   consume

EXAMPLE: im<u>press</u>, com<u>press</u>
<u>Impress</u> means "to make a mark by applying pressure," <u>compress</u> means "to press together."

Academic Vocabulary

*The Anishinabe women were **assigned** new names, usually those of French saints.*

Assign is a word you know from school, but it also has an academic meaning. Using context clues, infer the meaning of *assigned* in the sentence above and explain the difference between the word's common and academic meanings.

For more on academic vocabulary, see pages 53–54.

Write with Style

 Apply Symbolism

Assignment In her essay, Erdrich uses several symbols to represent both literal and abstract aspects of her heritage. Examine the chart you made on page 1297 to review how Erdrich uses symbolism. Then think of some symbols that apply to your own ethnic background and incorporate them into a short essay.

Get Ideas Brainstorm, talk to family members, and research on the Internet or in a library to develop a list of potential cultural symbols. Think about objects, actions, places, and events that are important to your heritage, and about larger ideas these things could represent. Make a chart similar to the one you made for Erdrich's essay.

EXAMPLE:
Heritage: English

Symbol	What It Represents
drinking tea	hospitality, spending time with others
football (soccer)	competition, athletic skill
The Queen	tradition, formality, patriotism
castles	wealth, history

Give It Structure Come up with a main idea, or thesis, for your essay. Put a checkmark next to the symbols in your chart that support your thesis. Begin your essay with your thesis, followed by supporting sentences (including the applicable symbols), and concluding with a restatement of your thesis.

Look at Language Reread your essay. Did you choose your words and supporting details precisely so that they develop your main idea? Have you used a variety of sentence structures and lengths to help engage your reader? Does the tone of your writing reflect your thesis? If not, do more research to help you write clear, accurate descriptions.

LOUISE ERDRICH   **1303**

After You Read

Assess

Reading Strategy

1. A is the correct answer because Erdrich supports her opinion with specific examples of names and what they reveal about the women.

Academic Vocabulary

In the sentence above, the words "new names" tell us that the word *assigned* means "to designate or to name." At school, a teacher might *assign* homework to the students. In this case, *assign* means "to give a duty or task."

 Writing

Use these criteria when evaluating students' writing:

- Does the writer choose appropriate symbols for his or her culture(s)?
- Does the writer have a clear thesis?
- Does the writer effectively use symbols to support his or her thesis?

For grammar practice, see Unit 7 Teaching Resources Book, p. 295.

Vocabulary

1. <u>deci</u>mated, <u>Dec</u>ember; *decimated* means "destroyed or killed in large numbers," originally one-tenth of a city as punishment; *December* was the tenth month of the old Roman calendar.

2. presump<u>tuous</u>, con<u>sume</u>; *presumptuous* means "excessively bold," or "taking without right"; *consume* is to expend something by use.

3. ecclesi<u>astical</u>, fant<u>astical</u>; *ecclesiastical* means "having the qualities of the church"; *fantastical* means "having the qualities of fantasy."

4. un<u>deviating</u>, <u>deviant</u>; *undeviating* means "not turning away from"; *deviant* means "one who turns away from the social norm."

5. <u>wan</u>e, <u>wan</u>t; to *wane* means "to decrease gradually"; a *want* is a shortage.

Before You Read

Focus

Bellringer Options

Literature Launchers:
Pre-Reading Videos DVD,
Selection Launcher
Selection Focus
Transparency 72
Daily Language Practice
Transparency 118

Or ask students to list chores they are responsible for. **Ask:** How does the size of the family affect a teenager's responsibilities? *(Large families may pass more tasks onto teenagers than small families.)* How does a teenager's position in the family affect his or her responsibilities? *(The oldest children may have more responsibility than younger children.)*

As they read, have students consider how family size affects each member's responsibilities.

Before You Read

Salvador Late or Early

Meet **Sandra Cisneros**
(born 1954)

Sandra Cisneros always felt a bit like an outsider. She was also frequently the new kid on the block. Cisneros was born in Chicago. Her mother was Mexican American and her father was Mexican. Her father was devoted to his mother in Mexico, so he was often homesick. As a result, Cisneros said, the family "returned like the tides, back and forth to Mexico City."

The Outsider One result of this continual migration was that Cisneros retreated into books, becoming an avid, if isolated, reader. This habit was encouraged by her mother, who made sure that her daughter had a library card even before the child was able to read.

During her sophomore year of high school, Cisneros had an English teacher whom she described as "bright and vivacious." This teacher encouraged Cisneros to write. After college she applied to and was accepted by the prestigious University of Iowa Writers' Workshop.

Success In Iowa Cisneros felt isolated and out of place. "My classmates were from the best schools in the country," she wrote later. "They had been bred as fine hot-house flowers. I was a yellow weed among the city's cracks." Suddenly, though, she realized what made her special and therefore what she would write about—her own experiences. The result was *The House on Mango Street,* published when Cisneros was twenty-nine. In a series of interlocking stories, the book tells the tale of a young Chicana girl growing up in a Chicago barrio, much like the neighborhoods where Cisneros once lived. The book received high praise and was awarded the Before Columbus American Book Award in 1985. It has sold over two million copies, making Cisneros one of the best-known Latina authors in the United States.

Cisneros published *My Wicked Wicked Ways,* a collection of poetry, in 1987, and *Woman Hollering Creek and Other Stories* in 1991. Critics disagreed about whether to call the latter prose or poetry, as the author included elements of both genres.

> "To me, the definition of a story is something that someone wants to listen to. If someone doesn't want to listen to you, then it's not a story."
>
> —Sandra Cisneros

Cisneros began writing a story about her father, but kept traveling different paths until her story had mushroomed into a 450-page book, *Caramelo,* that took almost ten years to complete. "You start a story," she said, "—oh, but you have to explain something first. So you take a detour, but that leads to something else. Then you get back to your story."

Today Cisneros teaches, gives readings, and writes. She still remains somewhat on the outside of society, but this is by choice. "I really like my solitude," she said to an interviewer. "I don't like being lonely, but I'm not lonely. I need to be alone to work."

 Literature Online

Author Search For more about Sandra Cisneros, go to glencoe.com and enter QuickPass code GLA9800u7.

1304 UNIT 7 INTO THE TWENTY-FIRST CENTURY

Selection Skills

Literary Elements
- Imagery (SE pp. 1305–1307)

Salvador Late or Early

Writing Skills/Grammar
- Write an Essay (SE p. 1307)

Reading Skills
- Analyze Sound Devices (SE pp. 1305–1307)
- Identify Sequence (TE p. 1306)

Vocabulary Skills
- Academic Vocabulary (SE p. 1307)

1304

Literature and Reading Preview

Connect to the Story

Should children be responsible for adult duties or tasks? Discuss this with a group of classmates. Consider whether childhood should be about play or learning adult skills.

Build Background

While some children have school as their only responsibility, other children have numerous family obligations that shape their lives. These children may work alongside their parents in fields, in shops, or in the home. They may spend hours caring for younger or older relatives. Although laws require children to go to school, not all children are able to do so regularly. In some cultures, family obligations are primary, and a child's individual needs may give way to other family pressures.

Set Purposes for Reading

Big Idea Extending and Remaking Traditions

As you read, ask yourself, How does the language comprise elements of both prose and poetry, reshaping them into a new form?

Literary Element Imagery

Imagery is made up of the "word pictures" a writer uses to evoke an emotional response. To create effective images, a writer uses sensory details, or descriptions that appeal to one of the five senses: sight, hearing, touch, taste, and smell. As you read, ask yourself, Which words and phrases create images?

Reading Strategy Analyze Sound Devices

Sound devices are techniques designed to appeal to the ear. Writers use sound devices to emphasize particular words or sounds, to create or enhance rhythm, or to add to the musical quality of their writing. Sound devices include alliteration, assonance, repetition, rhyme, and rhythm.

Tip: Keep Track As you read, ask, Where do sound devices draw my attention to certain words or phrases? Use a word web like the one shown to record sound devices that catch your ear.

Learning Objectives

For pages 1304–1307

In studying this text, you will focus on the following objectives:

Literary Study: Analyzing imagery.

Reading: Analyzing sound devices.

Writing: Writing an essay.

(word web diagram)

crooked hair and crooked teeth

color of caterpillars

Sound Devices

SANDRA CISNEROS **1305**

Focus

Summary

Young Salvador lives in a poor neighborhood with his mother and many siblings. Salvador is responsible for awakening his younger brothers and getting them dressed and off to school, but he often does not get to school himself. Later in the day he returns to collect them again.

> **Interactive Read and Write**
>
> Other options for teaching this selection can be found in
>
> - Interactive Read and Write for EL Students, pp. 277–282
> - Interactive Read and Write for Approaching-Level Students, pp. 277–282
> - Interactive Read and Write for On-Level Students, pp. 277–282

English Learners

DIFFERENTIATED INSTRUCTION

Intermediate At a quick glance, this selection looks like a short, short story. As students read it, they will notice the poetic language and sentence structure as well as the absence of a plot. Point out that many of the sentences are incomplete. **Ask:** What are the essential components of a sentence? (*subject and predicate*) **Ask:** One line from the story states, "Helps his mama, who is busy with the business of the baby." What part of the sentence is missing? (*subject*) Why might the writer have chosen to write incomplete sentences to describe Salvador? (*to emphasize the sounds the words make and the sensory pictures they create*) Suggest that as students read "Salvador Late or Early," they visualize the images created by the words.

Teach

Literary Element 1

Imagery Answer: *The images suggest that he is a concerned brother taking on a parent's role.*

Big Idea 2

Extending and Remaking Traditions Answer: *The form is prose, but the rhythm, repetition, and imagery are poetic.*

Literary Element 3

Imagery Answer: *Another writer might have simply said that the boy dropped a box of crayons.*

Reading Strategy 4

Analyze Sound Devices Answer: *The initial sound in* hun-dred *and* happiness *and* guitar *and* grief *are repeated. The repetition adds to the rhythm of the lines.*

Readability Scores

Dale-Chall: 5.5
DRP: 63
Lexile: not testable due to length

Salvador Late or Early

Sandra Cisneros

El Patio de la Casa del Artista, 1884. Martin Tovar y Tovar. Oil on canvas, 18¼ x 21⅝ in. Private collection.

Salvador with eyes the color of caterpillar, Salvador of the crooked hair and crooked teeth, Salvador whose name the teacher cannot remember, is a boy who is no one's friend, runs along somewhere in that vague direction where homes are the color of bad weather, lives behind a raw wood doorway, shakes the sleepy brothers awake, ties their shoes, combs their hair with water, feeds them milk and corn flakes from a tin cup in the dim dark of the morning.

Salvador, late or early, sooner or later arrives with the string of younger brothers ready. Helps his mama, who is busy with the business of the baby. Tugs the arms of Cecilio, Arturito, makes them hurry, because today, like yesterday, Arturito has dropped the cigar box of crayons, has let go the hundred little fingers of red, green, yellow, blue, and nub of black sticks that tumble and spill over and beyond the asphalt puddles

until the crossing-guard lady holds back the blur of traffic for Salvador to collect them again.

Salvador inside that wrinkled shirt, inside the throat that must clear itself and apologize each time it speaks, inside that forty-pound body of boy with its geography of scars, its history of hurt, limbs stuffed with feathers and rags, in what part of the eyes, in what part of the heart, in that cage of the chest where something throbs with both fists and knows only what Salvador knows, inside that body too small to contain the hundred balloons of happiness, the single guitar of grief, is a boy like any other disappearing out the door, beside the schoolyard gate, where he has told his brothers they must wait. Collects the hands of Cecilio and Arturito, scuttles off dodging the many schoolyard colors, the elbows and wrists crisscrossing, the several shoes running. Grows small and smaller to the eye, dissolves into the bright horizon, flutters in the air before disappearing like a memory of kites. ∞

1 Imagery *What do these images suggest about Salvador and his life?*

2 Extending and Remaking Traditions *What elements of both prose and poetry do you see in these lines?*

3 Imagery *How could the writer have said the same thing without imagery?*

4 Analyze Sound Devices *What sounds are repeated, and what is the effect of such repetition?*

Reading Practice

Identify Sequence Explain that events in Cisneros's writing can be hard to follow because of her freeform sentence structure. Listing events in sequence can help readers track what happens, and when. Have students complete a sequence chart with events from the story.

Salvador wakes his brothers → → → →

After You Read

Respond and Think Critically

Respond and Interpret

1. (a)What was your reaction to learning about Salvador's life? (b)What would you say to Salvador if you could speak to him?

2. (a)What are Salvador's jobs? (b)What does his role reveal about how he is viewed by his family?

3. (a)What images describe Salvador in the third paragraph? (b)What do these details show about his history?

Analyze and Evaluate

4. A major part of Cisneros's style in "Salvador Late or Early" is her use of unusually long sentences.

Do you think these sentences add to or detract from the effectiveness of her writing? Explain.

5. The narrator describes Salvador as "a boy who is no one's friend." Who or what is responsible for the boy's situation, do you think? Explain.

Connect

6. **Big Idea** **Extending and Remaking Traditions** Why might Cisneros have written in a form somewhere between poetry and prose?

7. **Connect to the Author** In what ways might Cisneros see herself in Salvador?

Literary Element Imagery

Imagery often suggests feelings or ideas that are not stated. For example, Salvador "arrives with the string of younger brothers ready." These words create an image of a line of boys following Salvador and convey the idea that people see him as attached to his brothers more than as a separate person.

1. What image does "in that cage of the chest where something throbs with both fists" create?

2. What image do you find most striking?

Reading Strategy Analyze Sound Devices

Sound devices in the story such as **alliteration**, **assonance, repetition, rhyme,** and **rhythm** are associated more with poetry than with prose.

1. Give an example of each sound device from the story.

2. What effect do these have on your reading?

 Literature Online

Selection Resources For Selection Quizzes, eFlashcards, and Reading-Writing Connection activities, go to glencoe.com and enter QuickPass code GLA9800u7.

Academic Vocabulary

*Salvador does not get **acknowledged** for the familial responsibilities he takes on.*

Acknowledged is an academic word. In more casual conversation, an author's editor or colleagues might be **acknowledged** for their help with writing a book. Using context clues, try to figure out the meaning of the word in the sentence about Salvador above. Check your inference in a dictionary.

For more on academic vocabulary, see pages 53–54.

Writing

Write an Essay In "Salvador Late or Early," observes scholar Jeff Thomson, "[Cisneros] indicts everyone for the common failure of not protecting children from the horrors of the adult world." Do you agree that she holds everyone responsible? Write a brief essay in response. Use details from the story for support.

SANDRA CISNEROS **1307**

After You Read

Assess

1. Students' answers will vary.

2 (a) He awakens, feeds, and takes his brothers to and from school. (b) Viewed as a parent

3. (a) Wrinkled shirt; throat that must clear itself and apologize; limbs stuffed with feathers and rags (b) Fear, hurt, and fragility, but also joy

4. They mirror the breathless quality of Salvador's busy day.

5. Parents, school, or society

6. They both have certain limitations; combining them overcomes their limitations.

7. Even though a child might not work outside the home or get paid for his or her contributions, some children might be expected to care for their siblings or to work in a family business such as a restaurant or store.

Literary Element

1. A creature desperate to escape

2. Students should describe an image and explain why it is striking.

Progress Check

Can students analyze imagery?

If No → See Unit 7 Teaching Resources Book, p. 304.

Academic Vocabulary

Because "familial responsibilities" are a kind of extra duty for a child, we can infer that **acknowledged** means thanked or appreciated.

Writing

Use the following criteria to evaluate students' essays:

- Does the essay explain who is responsible for the children's work?
- Does the essay use examples from the story to support the claim?

Reading Strategy

1. Assonance (*puddles, until*); alliteration (*color, caterpillar*); repetition (*crooked hair, crooked teeth*); rhyme and rhythm (*schoolyard gate, they must wait*)

2. Soften harsh facts and make the story sound more like a song

Thoughts on the African-American Novel

Meet **Toni Morrison**

(born 1931)

Highly acclaimed as a novelist, essayist, and literary critic, in 1993 Toni Morrison became the first African American to win the Nobel Prize in Literature. Reflecting on this honor, she stated that to become a writer she had to defy stereotypes and value her own potential. "Had I lived the life that the state planned for me from the beginning," she said, "I would have lived and died in somebody else's kitchen, on somebody else's land, and never written a word."

Instead of working as a maid or a sharecropper, Morrison became a writer and expressed her emotions and perceptions as an African American and a woman in award-winning novels and other creative works. When asked whether she considered herself a black writer or a female writer, Morrison responded, "I've just insisted—insisted!—upon being called a black woman novelist."

Early Years Born Chloe Anthony Wofford, Morrison grew up in Lorain, Ohio, a setting that figures prominently in many of her novels. Her family had moved there from the South, looking for better opportunities. With her family's help, she attended Howard University in Washington, D.C., where she studied English and the classics. There she adopted the name Toni, because people had trouble pronouncing her first name.

Morrison graduated from Howard and later earned an M.A. degree

from Cornell University. She married, had two sons, and began a long and distinguished career as a teacher and editor. Eventually, Morrison and her husband divorced, and for years she raised her family as a single mother, working by day and writing late at night after her sons were asleep.

> "Writing . . . became the one thing I was doing that I had absolutely no intention of living without."
>
> —Toni Morrison

An African American Writer Morrison's first novel was *The Bluest Eye* (1970). In this novel and others that followed—including *Sula* (1973), *Song of Solomon* (1977), and *Tar Baby* (1981)—Morrison grappled with the themes that concern her: racism, family, identity, and loss. She created fiction that spoke directly to African Americans, using the "music of black talk."

In 1987, Morrison's novel *Beloved* became a financial blockbuster. An exploration of boundless love and institutionalized evil, this novel won the Pulitzer Prize for Fiction and later was adapted into a successful film starring Oprah Winfrey.

Despite her prominence and influence as a writer and Nobel laureate, Morrison does not rest on her laurels. She continues to write, to lecture, and to teach. Today her work includes several acclaimed novels, an impressive body of nonfiction, and a play about the murder of Emmett Till, *Dreaming Emmett*.

 Literature Online

Author Search For more about Toni Morrison, go to glencoe.com and enter QuickPass code GLA9800u7.

Selection Skills

Literary Elements
- Essay (SE pp. 1309, 1311, 1313)
- Parallelism (SE p. 1313)

Reading Skills
- Determine Main Idea and Supporting Details (SE pp. 1309, 1311, 1314)
- Vary Reading Rate (TE p. 1310)

Thoughts on the African-American Novel

Vocabulary Skills
- Word Parts (SE p. 1314)

Writing Skills/Grammar
- Apply Parallelism (SE p. 1314)
- Identify the Thesis (TE p. 1312)

Listening/Speaking/Viewing Skills
- Analyze Art (TE p. 1310)

Literature and Reading Preview

Connect to the Essay

Why do people read novels? With a partner, make a list of your favorite novels. What drew you to these books?

Build Background

When Morrison began writing, the civil rights movement was becoming a force for social change. Morrison, then a teacher, knew several people, both poets and political leaders, who were active in that struggle. Today, Morrison is recognized as one of the pioneers in the field of African American literature.

Set Purposes for Reading

Big Idea Extending and Remaking Traditions

As you read, ask yourself, How does Morrison connect her novels and the traditions of "Black art"?

Literary Element Essay

An **essay** is a type of nonfiction that conveys a writer's ideas and opinions on a specific topic. An **informal essay** has a lighter tone and a more fluid structure than a **formal essay**, which features a carefully structured progression of opinions and supporting information. As you read, ask, Is Morrison's essay formal or informal?

Reading Strategy Determine Main Idea and Supporting Details

Determining an author's **main idea** is finding the most important thought in a paragraph or selection. As you read, ask, What is the one idea that all of the sentences in a paragraph, or all of the paragraphs in a selection, are about? **Supporting details** may include facts, examples, reasons, and anecdotes.

....

Tip: Take Notes Map out the main idea and details of a selection by creating a graphic organizer like the one shown.

Learning Objectives

For pages 1308–1314

In studying this text, you will focus on the following objectives:

Literary Study: Analyzing essays.

Reading: Determining main idea and supporting details.

Writing: Applying parallelism.

Vocabulary

aristocracy (a´ rə sto´ krə sē) *n.* people with high social status due to birth or title; p. 1310 *The peasant envied the aristocracy.*

exclusively (iks´ klōō´ siv lē) *adv.* without the inclusion or involvement of any others; p. 1311 *This room is used exclusively by club members.*

enlighten (en līt´ ən) *v.* to give knowledge or wisdom to; p. 1311 *A classic novel can enlighten readers, showing them how to live.*

meandering (mē an´ dər ing) *adj.* following a winding course; p. 1312 *We took a meandering, not a direct, route home.*

unorthodox (un ôr´ thə doks´) *adj.* not customary or traditional; p. 1312 *The exterminator's methods were unorthodox, but successful.*

....

Tip: Word Parts You can figure out the meanings of some unfamiliar words by examining their parts. For example, the word *unorthodox,* which means "something that is not traditional," has the prefix *un*- which means "not."

Before You Read

Focus

Summary

In this essay, Toni Morrison describes the origin of the novel as a genre. She maintains that the novel evolved because the middle class lacked an art form and needed one in order to understand its culture and place in society. African Americans, she says, need novels for the same reason—to define and explain their place in American society. Morrison says her goal is to write novels that respond to that need and that use the "characteristics of Black art."

Vocabulary

Abstract Words Explain that the words used to analyze literature are often abstract, that is, they refer to intangible concepts rather than physical things. Have students name concrete items that are associated with each vocabulary word. *(aristocracy: money, brocade, jewelry; exclusively: clubs, privileges; enlighten: teacher, book; meandering: river, hiker; unorthodox: foreigner, genius)*

English Learners

DIFFERENTIATED INSTRUCTION

Intermediate Write the vocabulary words on the board and have students locate the words in the essay and read the sentences aloud. Ask them to create a two-column chart with the headings *Morrison's Words* and *My Words.* Tell them to use a dictionary to check each word's meaning. In the chart, have them substitute their own word or words for the vocabulary word. Encourage students to use the chart as they read.

SMALL GROUP

Advanced Divide students into in five groups and assign each a paragraph to read. Have students identify the vocabulary word in their section.

Ask: How does the vocabulary word in your paragraph help express a central idea ? *(Sample answer: The novel came about because a class of people between the poor and the aristocracy developed.)*

Teach

Big Idea   1

Extending and Remaking Traditions Say: Keep these questions in mind as you read: According to Toni Morrison, how are the traditions of Black art unique? *(Black art inspires strong emotion and action and invites participation.)* How do novels help people understand the cultural traditions around them? *(They allow people to explore rules of behavior and the consequences of breaking the rules.)*

View the Art ★

Jacob Lawrence (1917–2000) came to New York City at age 13. In a culturally vibrant Harlem, he found inspiration and guidance as a young artist. Many of his paintings bring that Harlem and its African American community to life. **Ask:** How can you link this painting to the title of Morrison's essay? *(The painting shows African Americans in a library. Morrison's essay concerns the "African-American novel," which could be about or read by those pictured in this painting.)*

 For an audio recording of this selection, use Listening Library Audio CD-ROM.

Readability Scores

Dale-Chall: 7.4
DRP: 61
Lexile: 1130

Thoughts on the African-American Novel

Toni Morrison

The Library, 1960. Jacob Lawrence. Tempera on fiberboard, 24 x 29⅞ in. Smithsonian American Art Museum, Washington, DC.

1 The label "novel" is useful in technical terms because I write prose that is longer than a short story. My sense of the novel is that it has always functioned for the class or the group that wrote it. The history of the novel as a form began when there was a new class, a middle class, to read it; it was an art form that they needed. The lower classes didn't need novels at that time because they had an art form already: they had songs, and dances, and ceremony, and gossip, and celebrations. The **aristocracy** didn't need it because they had the art that they had patronized,[1] they had their own pictures painted, their own houses built, and they made sure their art separated them from the rest of the world. But when the industrial revolution[2] began, there emerged a new class of people who were neither peasants nor aristocrats. In large measure they had no art form to tell them how to behave in this new situation. So they produced an art form: we call it the novel of

---

> **Vocabulary**
>
> **aristocracy** (a´ rə sto´ krə sē) *n.* people with high social status due to birth or title

---

1. Here, *patronize* (pā´ trə nīz´) means "to give financial support or encouragement to."
2. The *industrial revolution* helped develop a middle class of workers who began to gain some control over where, for whom, and for what wages they would work.

1310 UNIT 7 INTO THE TWENTY-FIRST CENTURY

Reading Practice

Vary Reading Rate Discuss some ways to approach written materials.

- Skimming: to preview or review
- Scanning: to find specific facts or topics
- In-depth reading: to gain thorough knowledge

Before students begin reading, they should skim the essay for general content. Then they should read it in-depth.

Ask them to explain the new information they gained. Finally, they should scan for specific words or ideas, such as the novel Samuel Richardson wrote.

manners, an art form designed to tell people something they didn't know. That is, how to behave in this new world, how to distinguish between the good guys and the bad guys. How to get married. What a good living was. What would happen if you strayed from the fold. So that early works such as *Pamela*, by Samuel Richardson, and the Jane Austen material provided social rules and explained behavior, identified outlaws, identified the people, habits, and customs that one should approve of. They were didactic in that sense. That, I think, is probably why the novel was not missed among the so-called peasant cultures. They didn't need it, because they were clear about what their responsibilities were and who and where was evil, and where was good.

But when the peasant class, or lower class, or what have you, confronts the middle class, the city, or the upper classes, they are thrown a little bit into disarray. For a long time, the art form that was healing for Black people was music. That music is no longer **exclusively** ours, we don't have exclusive rights to it. Other people sing it and play it; it is the mode[3] of contemporary music everywhere. So another form has to take that place, and it seems to me that the novel is needed by African Americans now in a way that it was not needed before—and it is following along the lines of the function of novels everywhere. We don't live in places where we can hear those stories anymore; parents don't sit around and tell their children those classical,

mythological archetypal stories[4] that we heard years ago. But new information has got to get out, and there are several ways to do it. One is in the novel. I regard it as a way to accomplish certain very strong functions—one being the one I just described.

It should be beautiful, and powerful, but it should also *work*. It should have something in it that **enlightens;** something in it that opens the door and points the way. Something in it that suggests what the conflicts are, what the problems are. But it need not solve those problems because it is not a case study, it is not a recipe. There are things that I try to incorporate into my fiction that are directly and deliberately related to what I regard as the major characteristics of Black art, wherever it is. One of which is the ability to be both print and oral literature: to combine those two aspects so that the stories can be read in silence, of course, but one should be able to hear them as well. It should try deliberately to make you stand up and make you feel something profoundly in the same way that a Black preacher requires his congregation to speak, to join him in the sermon, to behave in a certain way, to stand up and to weep and to cry and to accede or to change and to modify—to expand on the sermon that is being delivered. In the same way that a musician's music is enhanced when there is a response from the audience. Now in a book, which closes, after all—it's of some importance to me to try to make that connection—to try to make that happen also. And, having at my disposal only the letters of the alphabet and some punctuation, I have to provide the places and spaces so that

---

3. Here, *mode* means "a manner of expression." The type of music once considered an art form belonging to African Americans is now the preferred form of contemporary music for many modern listeners.

2 Determine Main Idea and Supporting Details *What main idea do these details support?*

3 Essay *How does this sentence function in the essay?*

Vocabulary
exclusively (iks′ klōō siv lē) *adv.* without the inclusion or involvement of any others

---

4. *Archetypal* (är′ kə tī′ pəl) *stories* come from ideas inherited through the ages.

Determine Main Idea and Supporting Details *What details support this main idea?* **4**

Vocabulary
enlighten (en līt′ ən) *v.* to give knowledge or wisdom to

TONI MORRISON **1311**

Teach

Big Idea   1

Extending and Remaking Traditions Answer: *Morrison leaves out details for the reader to supply, constructs dialogue for the ear, eliminates adverbs, and includes a chorus.*

Big Idea   2

Extending and Remaking Traditions Answer: *Morrison uses unorthodox novelistic characteristics that are used in "Black art." She sees her novels as reflecting the oral characteristics of "Black art."*

 To check students' understanding of the selection, see Unit 7 Teaching Resources Book, p. 321.

the reader can participate. Because it is the affective and participatory relationship[5] between the artist or the speaker and the audience that is of primary importance, as it is in these other art forms that I have described.

To make the story appear oral, **meandering,** effortless, spoken—to have the reader *feel* the narrator without *identifying* that narrator, or hearing him or her knock about, and to have the reader work *with* the author in the construction of the book—is what's important. What is left out is as important as what is there. To describe sexual scenes in such a way that they are not clinical, not even explicit—so that the reader brings his own sexuality to the scene and thereby participates in it in a very personal way. And owns it. To construct the dialogue so that it is heard. So that there are no adverbs attached to them: "loudly," "softly," "he said menacingly." The menace should be in the sentence. To use, even formally, a chorus. The real presence of a chorus. Meaning the community or the reader at large, commenting on the action as it goes ahead.

In the books that I have written, the chorus has changed but there has always been a choral note, whether it is the "I" narrator of *Bluest Eye,* or the town functioning as a character in *Sula,* or the neighborhood and the community that responds in the two parts of town in *Solomon.* Or, as extreme as I've gotten, all of nature thinking and feeling and watching and

responding to the action going on in *Tar Baby,* so that they are in the story: the trees hurt, fish are afraid, clouds report, and the bees are alarmed. Those are the ways in which I try to incorporate, into that traditional genre the novel, **unorthodox** novelistic characteristics—so that it is, in my view, Black, because it uses the characteristics of Black art. I am not suggesting that some of these devices have not been used before and elsewhere—only the reason why I do. I employ them as well as I can. And those are just some; I wish there were ways in which such things could be talked about in the criticism. My general disappointment in some of the criticism that my work has received has nothing to do with approval. It has something to do with the vocabulary used in order to describe these things. I don't like to find my books condemned as bad or praised as good, when that condemnation or that praise is based on criteria from other paradigms. I would much prefer that they were dismissed or embraced based on the success of their accomplishment within the culture out of which I write.

I don't regard Black literature as simply books written *by* Black people, or simply as literature written *about* Black people, or simply as literature that uses a certain mode of language in which you just sort of drop g's. There is something very special and very identifiable about it and it is my struggle to *find* that elusive but identifiable style in the books. My joy is when I think that I have approached it; my misery is when I think I can't get there. ✑

---

5. An *affective and participatory relationship* influences one's emotions and encourages one to take an active part in the relationship.

1   **Extending and Remaking Traditions** *What does Morrison do to give a story an oral quality?*

> **Vocabulary**
>
> **meandering** (mē an′ dər ing) *adj.* following a winding course

Extending and Remaking Traditions *What connections does Morrison see between her novels and "Black art"?* **2**

> **Vocabulary**
>
> **unorthodox** (un ôr′ thə doks′) *adj.* not customary or traditional

Writing Practice

Identify the Thesis Tell students that the thesis of an essay is often stated in the first paragraph, but many experienced writers do not follow this rule. Have students look for Morrison's thesis in the second paragraph. Then, ask students to write a paragraph each in answer to the following questions:

- What is Morrison's thesis in this essay? What arguments does she use to support her thesis?
- How does the focus of the rest of the essay shift in the third paragraph? Why does it shift?

Remind students that their answers should be supported by evidence from

Morrison's essay. After students have finished writing, ask for volunteers to share their paragraphs with the class.

After You Read

Respond and Think Critically

Respond and Interpret

1. Which of Morrison's ideas about novels did you find most interesting? Explain.

2. (a)According to Morrison, what event and what class of people caused the birth of the novel as a literary form? (b)Why was the novel of manners important to that class at that time?

3. (a)What did music provide for African Americans in times past? (b)Why do African Americans need novels at the present time?

4. (a)According to Morrison, what specific qualities should an African American novel have? (b)Explain Morrison's comparison between the novel and an African American preacher.

Analyze and Evaluate

5. How well do novels help readers "distinguish between the good guys and the bad guys"?

6. Why does Morrison include a chorus in her novels?

7. Morrison says that a novel should present problems but need not solve them. Do you agree or disagree with this statement? Why?

Connect

8. **Big Idea** **Extending and Remaking Traditions** In what ways does Morrison extend the traditions of "Black art" in her novels?

9. **Connect to the Author** Artists often debate the role politics or social movements should play within a work of literature. Would you call Morrison's work a kind of art that makes a statement? Explain.

Literary Element Essay

A **formal essay** may sound like a dignified speech. An **informal essay,** however, has a lighter tone and often sounds like a conversation. Moreover, an informal essay may even contain sentence fragments and informal language.

1. Find examples of sentence fragments and informal language in Morrison's essay.

2. What does the use of sentence fragments and informal language contribute to the overall **tone** of this essay?

Review: Parallelism

As you learned on page 401, **parallelism** is the use of a series of words, phrases, or sentences that have a similar grammatical form. In "Thoughts on the African-American Novel," Morrison often uses this technique, as in the following example:

"to stand up and *to weep* and *to cry* and *to accede* or *to change* and *to modify . . . "*

Partner Activity With a classmate, look for additional examples of parallelism in Morrison's essay. List them on a chart and discuss how they reinforce Morrison's central message. Share your list with the rest of your class.

Example of Parallelism	Effect
"it is not a case study, it is not a recipe"	

Literary Element

1. "In the same . . . a response from the audience"; "And owns it." "To construct . . . it is heard"; "To use . . . chorus"; "The real . . . chorus"; "Meaning the community . . . ahead."

2. Their use makes the tone more conversational.

Review: Parallelism

Example: "something in it that enlightens; something in it that opens . . . Something in it that suggests . . ."

Progress Check

Can students analyze an essay?

If No → See Unit 7 Teaching Resources Book, p. 316.

After You Read

Assess

1. Answers should demonstrate understanding of the essay.

2. (a) The industrial revolution; the subsequent rise of the middle class (b) It taught middle-class people how to behave, distinguish good from bad, get married, identify a good living, and know the consequences of "straying from the fold."

3. (a) Music provided an art form through which they could express emotions and ease daily stress. (b) Their music has been adopted by other cultures, leaving them without a unique art form.

4. (a) The novel should be beautiful, powerful, enlightening, and able to elicit deep reader responses. (b) Both demand emotional responses from their audience.

5. Novels present examples of good and evil for readers to recognize and correlate to people and events in their own lives.

6. The chorus acts as a larger community— readers at large, or even nature itself—that can comment on the action.

7. Students may say that a writer's job is to present the reader with a view of reality. Since real-life problems often go unresolved, they need not be resolved in a novel.

8. Her language is effective for reading both silently and aloud, her narrator is felt but not identified, and her chorus comments on the action.

9. Morrison describes her work as "Black" art, so it does function somewhat as a statement.

After You Read

Assess

Reading Strategy

1. D is the correct answer because Morrison says, "I don't like to find my books condemned as bad or praised as good, when that condemnation or praise is based on criteria from other paradigms."

 Writing

Use these criteria when evaluating students' writing:

- Does the writer employ parallelism?
- Does the writer effectively defend his or her thesis?

> For grammar practice, see Unit 7 Teaching Resources Book, p. 320.

Reading Strategy Determine Main Ideas and Supporting Details

ACT Skills Practice

1. What does Morrison find disappointing in some criticism of her work?

  A. The lack of recognition for her achievements

  B. The focus on what is left out rather than on what is there

  C. The comparison of her works with Black art and music

  D. The application of inappropriate standards to her writing

Vocabulary Practice

Practice with Word Parts Use a printed or online dictionary to find the meaning of each vocabulary word's root and any prefixes or suffixes in the word. List the meanings in a diagram like the one shown. Then find three new words that contain the same prefix, suffix, or root as the vocabulary word. Circle the word part that could help a person guess each new word's meaning.

aristocracy	exclusively	enlighten
meandering	unorthodox	

EXAMPLE:

prescient

Prefix
pre-, "before"

Root
sci, "know"

Suffix
-ent, "one who"

Related words: omniscient, presage, science

 Write with Style

 Apply Parallelism

Assignment In this essay, Morrison explains what she hopes to accomplish through her novels and describes some of the techniques she uses. Think about an aspect of your life, such as a decision, behavior, or opinion that others might not understand. Write a brief essay describing and defending your intentions and motivations. Use parallelism, as Morrison does, to reinforce your main idea.

Get Ideas Brainstorm ideas on your own and ask peers or family members for suggestions. After choosing your topic, make an outline for your essay. Your outline should include your main idea, as well as a list of supporting details, such as your reasons for acting a certain way.

Give It Structure Begin with a sentence stating your main idea, or thesis. Follow with sentences supporting the thesis, using your outline as a guide. Finish with a sentence restating your main idea.

Look at Language Keep in mind that the purpose of parallelism is to structure a series of words, phrases, or sentences in a similar grammatical form in order to emphasize an idea. Examine your supporting sentences. Do they include parallelism that supports your thesis? Highlight the repeated words and phrases to evaluate your use of parallelism. If your highlighting is sparse, revise some of your sentences to strengthen the parallelism.

EXAMPLE:

Topic: Defending a decision to join the art club, even though some people think it's not practical.

It was my choice to paint, my choice to kindle my creativity, my choice to stroll through fields of color and shape and size. You can say it's a waste of time, it's a joke. And I say it's my life, my choice. Mine.

 Literature Online

Selection Resources For Selection Quizzes, eFlashcards, and Reading-Writing Connection activities, go to glencoe.com and enter QuickPass code GLA9800u7.

Vocabulary

aristocracy: <u>Prefix:</u> (none); <u>Root:</u> *aristo,* "best"; <u>Suffix:</u> *-crat,* "strength, might;" *-y,* "state of"; <u>Related words:</u> aristocrat, democracy

exclusively: <u>Prefix:</u> *ex-,* "out"; <u>Root:</u> *clu* (part of *claudere*), "to close, shut"; <u>Suffix:</u>*-ive,* "performing or tending toward;" *-ly,* "having the characteristics of"; <u>Related</u>

<u>words</u>: inclusive, conclude, closure, derisively

enlighten: <u>Prefix:</u> *en-,* "to cause to be in"; <u>Root:</u> *light,* "light"; <u>Suffix:</u> *-en* (suffix that forms a verb); <u>Related words:</u> enchant, delight, soften

meandering: <u>Prefix:</u> (none); <u>Root:</u> *maeander* (Latin word derived from name of Menderes River); <u>Suffix:</u> *-ing* (suffix added to a verb); <u>Related words:</u> meander, running

unorthodox: <u>Prefix:</u> *un-,* "not;" *ortho-,* "straight, right"; <u>Root:</u> *dox,* "belief, opinion"; <u>Suffix:</u> (none); <u>Related words</u>: uneasy, orthodox

> For additional vocabulary practice, see Glencoe Interactive Vocabulary CD-ROM.

Vocabulary Workshop

Noun Suffixes

Literature Connection You may recognize the word *information* without realizing that it is a noun formed from a verb.

> *"But new information has got to get out, and there are several ways to do it."*
>
> —Toni Morrison, from "Thoughts on the African-American Novel"

The suffix *-ation* turns the verb *inform* into a noun. **Noun suffixes** change nouns into new nouns and other parts of speech into nouns. Knowing noun suffixes can help you determine the meaning of unfamiliar words.

Common Noun Suffixes

Suffix	Meaning	Base word or word root	Example
-ee	receiver of action	train	trainee
-ance, -ence	state, quality	relevant persist	relevance persistence
-ant, -eer	agent, doer	contest puppet	contestant puppeteer
-ist, -tist	one who does, makes, or studies	cycle drama geology	cyclist dramatist geologist
-ment	result, condition	accomplish	accomplishment
-ness	action, state	bright	brightness
-tion, -ion	the act of	prosecute	prosecution

- When you see a noun, determine whether it has a noun suffix. *Morrison feels <u>disappointment</u> about some critics' reactions.*

- When a noun has a suffix, identify the root or base word. *Morrison wants her readers to participate in her novels. The <u>participation</u> of readers adds a new dimension to the books.*

Practice From the table above, choose a suffix that changes each word below to a noun. Write each complete word. (A final letter in a base word may be dropped before a suffix is added. A *y* at the end of a word may change to *i*.)

1. considerate
2. celebrate
3. accomplish
4. punctuate
5. novel
6. congregate
7. descend
8. fragrant
9. construct
10. kind

 Literature Online

Vocabulary For more vocabulary practice, go to glencoe.com and enter QuickPass code GLA9800u7.

Learning Objectives

In this workshop, you will focus on the following objective:

Vocabulary: Using suffixes to form nouns.

Suffixes

A **suffix** is a word part that is added to the end of a word. A **noun suffix** is a word part that, when added to a noun or another part of speech, changes the noun to a new noun and the other part of speech to a noun.

Vocabulary Terms

Suffixes are word parts that are added to the ends of words to create new words.

Tip

When you are asked for the meaning of a word that contains a suffix, think about the meaning of the word root or base word. If you are unsure of its meaning, try to think of other words that contain the same root or base word.

Vocabulary Workshop

Noun Suffixes

Focus

Point out the example words in the chart, and explain that each word combines a base or root word and a suffix. Ask students to figure out the meaning of each example word.

Teach

Suffixes Remind students that they can also use knowledge of noun suffixes to build meaning even when they don't recognize the root word. In other words, knowing that a word acts as a noun is a clue to meaning, which can be combined with context to build a definition.

Assess

Practice

1. consideration
2. celebration
3. accomplishment
4. punctuation
5. novelist
6. congregation
7. descendant
8. fragrance
9. construction
10. kindness

English Learners

DIFFERENTIATED INSTRUCTION

Intermediate Remind students of the definition of *suffix* and illustrate how suffixes can be used to form nouns from verbs, using the word *inflate* as an example. (*inflation*) Then write the following verbs and suffixes on the board and ask students to create nouns by choosing a suffix and adding it to each verb. Explain that more than one word may be created in many cases. Tell students that they may use a dictionary if they are unsure of the spelling.

Verb	Suffix
integrate	-ment
employ	-ion or -tion
resist	-or, -er, -ee
borrow	-ance, -ence

(*integration* or *integrator; employee* or *employer* or *employment; resistance* or *resister; borrower*)

Focus

Bellringer Options

Daily Language Practice Transparency 120

Or **ask:** Why have visual media become so important to modern communication? As they read, students should consider how visual media interact with written communication.

Teach

Science Fiction Ask: How do superheroes reflect science fiction elements? *(They have superhuman qualities that could result from improved science or technology.)*

View the Art ★

Joe Shuster worked with writer Jerry Siegal to create the comic book icon Superman. The two men received only a delayed reward for their genius, having first sold the rights for just $130.

📁 For activities related to this selection, see Unit 7 Teaching Resources Book, pp. 323–324.

Learning Objectives

For pages 1316–1317

In studying this text, you will focus on the following objectives:

Reading:
Analyzing cultural context.
Analyzing literary periods.
Evaluating historical influences.

From Comic Strips to Graphic Novels

ONE OF THE UNITED STATES' most popular and influential contributions to world culture has been the comic strip and its later development, the comic book. Among the many forerunners of the comic form was the dime novel, cheaply-made tabloids which usually featured rugged frontiersmen, romantic heroines, or hardened detectives. Often displaying lurid covers that anticipated comic books and pulp fiction, these pocket-sized publications sold by the millions in the years after the Civil War. Newspaper comic strips first appeared in the mid-1890s, largely as a result of fierce competition for readers between big New York City dailies. From the very beginning, comic strips reflected a wide variety of approaches to subject matter and graphic style, ranging from the rough urban slapstick of *The Yellow Kid* to the elaborate graphic fancies of *Little Nemo in Slumberland.*

The Golden Age of Comics

The first comic books were reprints of popular newspaper comic strips. However, growing demand prompted comic book publishers to create original stories. The comic book business received a boost in June of 1938 with the arrival of Superman in *Action Comics #1*, published by DC Comics. The Man of Steel was soon followed by Batman, Wonder Woman, Captain America, Plastic Man, and a host of others. During World War II, these costumed fighters battled enemies of the U.S., and they have remained in popular culture ever since. The period from 1938 to the early 1950s is often referred to as the Golden Age of Comics because of the surge in production and sales.

> *"A comic artist begins with a white sheet of paper and dreams up his whole business—he is playwright, director, editor, and artist at once."*
>
> —Alex Raymond, creator of *Flash Gordon*

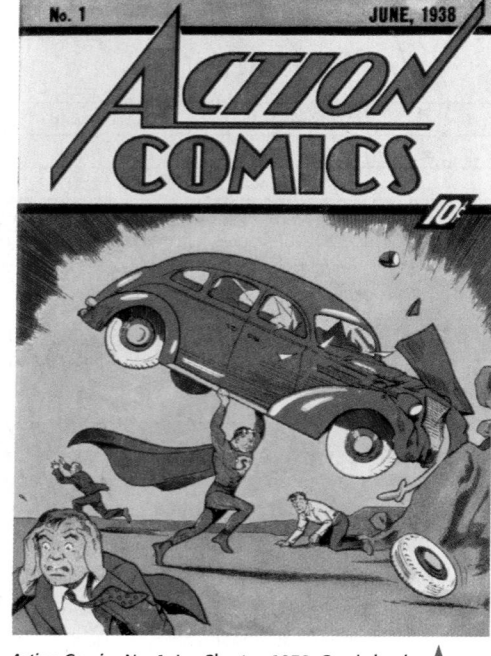

Action Comics No. 1, Joe Shuster, 1938. Comic book. ★

Reading Practice

Characterization Explain that because comic strips and graphic novels have little dialogue, creators use visual means to create character. Rather than describing a character's actions, they show them. Rather than describing how others react to a character, they show these reactions. Ask students to examine the image on page 1316 and describe the visual char- acterization of Superman. *(Superman is incredibly strong and daring. He amazes other people.)*

Backlash and Recovery

In the conservative climate of the early 1950s, comic books came under attack. Critics, such as psychiatrist Fredric Wertham, author of *Seduction of the Innocent*, claimed that comics were far too sexual and violent, attacked authority, and destroyed a young person's taste for literature. The comic book industry responded by instituting self-censorship in the form of a set of guidelines known as the Comic Code. The result was bland comic books. During the later 1950s, a new generation of thoughtful, yet flawed superheroes, such as Spider-Man, helped restore the vigor and popularity of comic books. The period from the 1950s to the early 1970s is often called the Silver Age of Comics, marked by a rise in more complicated plots made popular by Marvel Comics. The "underground" comics movement also originated as a subversive alternative to the mainstream comic industry. Reflecting the spirit of the 1960s, underground comics scorned traditional values and celebrated artistic experimentation.

Graphic Novels

Graphic novel is a term loosely applied to any lengthy story in comic book form. Comic book pioneer Will Eisner popularized the term in the late 1970s with his work *A Contract with God, and Other Tenement Stories*. Since then it has been applied to an extraordinarily broad range of comic book stories. The most widely acclaimed graphic novel is Art Spiegelman's *Maus* (see page 998), in which he uses a comic book format and animal characters to present his father's experiences during the Holocaust. Spiegelman received a Pulitzer Prize for *Maus* in 1992. Other well known graphic novels include Daniel Clowes's *Ghost World*, Frank Miller's *Sin City*, and Chris Ware's *Jimmy Corrigan: The Smartest Kid on Earth*. Some critics see the graphic novel as representing a new direction for the visual artform.

Amazing Fantasy, No. 15, Jack Kirby and Steve Ditko, 1962. Comic book. ★

Comic book artist Eddie Campbell, who collaborated with writer Alan Moore on the graphic novel *From Hell*, says the goal is "to take the form of the comic book, which has become an embarrassment, and raise it to a more ambitious and meaningful level."

> LOG ON ▶ **Literature** Online
>
> **Literature and Reading** For more about comic strips and graphic novels, go to glencoe.com and enter QuickPass code GLA9800u7.

Respond and Think Critically

1. Why do you think superheroes became so popular during the 1930s and 1940s?

2. How does a graphic novel differ from a comic book?

3. Do you think that comic books and graphic novels are a true art form? Explain.

Teach

Big Idea	2

Extending and Remaking Traditions Explain to students that graphic novels often address serious subjects and thus blend the characteristics of the full-length novel with those of the more light-hearted comic book. **Ask:** How does blending traditions extend the appeal of a genre? (*Blended traditions may appeal to those persons initially interested only in one tradition and introduce them to a new art form.*)

View the Art ★

Jack Kirby has created some of America's best-known comic superheroes, including Spiderman, as shown here. Kirby's work pushed the comic art genre many steps into the future with new elements such as a book-length format.

Assess

1. The powerful heroes appealed to people struggling with the complex problems of economic depression and global war.

2. A graphic novel is usually longer than a comic book and presents a single, unified story. Graphic novels often deal with more serious subject matter than comic books do.

3. Students' opinions will vary. Students should discuss the artistic merit of comic books and graphic novels.

Emerging Point out that graphic images and words depend on each other in comic books and graphic novels. Words can add information the image does not provide, or remind the reader of something going on outside the frame. Words can also reinforce the image by verbalizing the sound of a gesture such as POW! **Ask:** Look at the image on page 1316 and write two different sentences that would give different meanings to the picture. (*Possible answers: Superman is saying, "Take cover. This car is about to blow!" Superman is saying, "You crooks thought you could get away! We'll see about that."*)

Before You Read

Focus

Bellringer Options

Selection Focus
Transparency 74
Daily Language Practice
Transparency 121

Or invite students to share a family story about a pivotal moment, such as a childhood illness, a missed airplane flight, or a relocation. **Ask:** What happens to stories when they are told over and over? *(Details may change; the story may become a myth.)* How do such stories help people deal with emotional experiences? *(They make the experience into a story that could happen to other people.)*

As they read, have students consider how people use stories to cope with tragedy and struggle.

Before You Read

Nineteen Thirty-Seven

Meet **Edwidge Danticat**
(born 1969)

Born in Haiti, Edwidge Danticat (ed wēj´ dän tē kä´) was a young child when her parents immigrated to New York City. Her parents planned to work hard, save money, and then send for their children. Meanwhile, Danticat was raised by her aunt in a poor neighborhood of the Haitian capital, Port-au-Prince. During her childhood, Danticat asked for a number of gifts from her mother in America, and her mother did her best to oblige. Many of the presents never arrived, including a Barbie doll, gold earrings, and a gold chain. But one gift did reach her—a manual typewriter with black and red ribbons. A writer's career was underway.

> *"I write to unearth all those things that scare me, to reach those places in my soul that may seem remote and dark to others."*
>
> —Edwidge Danticat

Haitian Roots "While I was growing up, most of the writers I knew were either in hiding, missing, or dead," Danticat says. "We were living under the brutal Duvalier dictatorship in Haiti, and silence was the law of the land." Furthermore, writing was not considered a useful or proper career for a young woman. "Writing was as forbidden as dark rouge on the cheeks or a first date before eighteen," she once wrote. But Danticat, who had written her first story when she was nine, put her typewriter to good use. She typed letters for relatives and neighbors—and learned a lot about life in the process. "They would dictate their most intimate thoughts, forgetting that I was only ten years old."

Danticat was happily reunited with her parents in New York when she was twelve. At first, however, her new life in Brooklyn was an ordeal. Classmates teased her because of her clothing and called her a "boat person." Fluent only in Haitian Creole (based on French), she had to learn English as a second language. "It was like being a baby—learning everything for the first time," Danticat recalls.

Eight Million Stories Danticat excelled in high school and went on to major in French literature at Barnard College. She briefly considered a career in business but returned instead to her first love: the telling of stories. In 1993, when she was twenty-four, she received a master of fine arts degree from Brown University. Her first novel, *Breath, Eyes, Memory*, was published the following year. The story of a young Haitian girl who joins her mother in New York City, it echoes Danticat's own life story. The short-story collection *Krik? Krak!* followed the year after and was nominated for a National Book Award. Then, in 1998, Oprah Winfrey announced that she had selected *Breath, Eyes, Memory* for her book club. The novel became a number-one best seller, and its author became an instant celebrity.

 Literature Online

Author Search For more about Edwidge Danticat, go to glencoe.com and enter QuickPass code GLA9800u7.

Selection Skills

Literary Elements
- Magic Realism (SE pp. 1319, 1320, 1324, 1326, 1327, 1329)
- Style (SE p. 1329)
- Foreshadowing (TE p. 1322)

Reading Skills
- Visualize (SE pp. 1319, 1321, 1322, 1325, 1326, 1329)
- Compare and Contrast (TE p. 1320)
- Question (TE p. 1326)

Nineteen Thirty-Seven

Vocabulary Skills
- Antonyms (SE pp. 1319, 1329)
- Academic Vocabulary (SE p. 1329)

Writing Skills/Grammar
- Short Story (SE p. 1330)
- Passive and Active Voice (SE p. 1330)

Listening/Speaking/Viewing Skills
- Analyze Art (SE p. 1327)

Literature and Reading Preview

Connect to the Story

How can bad experiences sometimes make a person stronger? Freewrite for several minutes about a time when you or someone you know grew stronger through a difficult challenge.

Build Background

"Nineteen Thirty-Seven" is set in Haiti in the 1950s or 1960s. Haiti is an impoverished Caribbean nation occupying the western third of the island of Hispaniola. The eastern part of the island makes up the Spanish-speaking Dominican Republic. The title of the story refers to a historical event that occurred in 1937. In that year, the Dominican dictator Rafael Trujillo authorized the massacre of thousands of Haitian immigrants, who had come across the border to work. Many of the victims fell on the banks of the Río Masacre (Massacre River), which separates the two countries.

Set Purposes for Reading

Big Idea **Extending and Remaking Traditions**

In recent years, American authors from diverse backgrounds have infused literature with fresh subject matter and new approaches. As you read, ask yourself, What does Danticat choose to write about and how does she approach her subject?

Literary Element **Magic Realism**

Magic realism is a literary style in which the writer combines realistic settings, characters, dialogue, and other details with elements that are magical, supernatural, or fantastic. As you read, ask yourself, How does Danticat's narrative blend together the believable with the impossible?

Reading Strategy **Visualize**

"Nineteen Thirty-Seven" describes many extraordinary images and events. Using your imagination to picture these descriptions—a process known as **visualizing**—will help you better understand and remember the story. As you read, ask yourself, What does each scene look like?

Tip: "Watch" the Action Reading a story can be like watching a movie when you visualize the action.

- Notice the details: Authors often include precise physical information about people and places.
- Imagine the scene: How many characters are present? Where are they? What are they doing?

Learning Objectives

For pages 1318–1329

In studying this text, you will focus on the following objectives:

Literary Study: Understanding magical realism.

Reading: Visualizing.

Vocabulary

grimace (grĭ´ məs) *v.* to contort the face, especially to express pain or displeasure; p. 1321 *I saw him grimace after his poor performance.*

delirium (dĭ lēr´ ē əm) *n.* a temporary state of mental disturbance characterized by confusion and disorientation; p. 1325 *In her delirium, the old lady believed that she was a little girl again.*

console (kən sōl´) *v.* to comfort; to cheer; p. 1325 *Nothing could console Hong when her puppy died.*

rejuvenated (rĭ jōō´ və nāt´ əd) *adj.* restored to youthful vigor or appearance; renewed; p. 1326 *She appeared rejuvenated after her summer vacation.*

balmy (bä´ mē) *adj.* soothing; p. 1327 *A balmy spring breeze made us forget the long winter.*

Tip: Antonyms An **antonym** is a word that has a meaning opposite to that of another word. Note that antonyms are always the same part of speech. An antonym for *console,* for example, is *depress.*

EDWIDGE DANTICAT **1319**

Josephine's mother, Manman, has been wrongfully convicted of murdering a child. In 1937, Manman escaped a brutal massacre of Haitian refugees by Dominican soldiers. Superstitious Haitians fear the survivors of that massacre, believing they escaped on "wings of flame." They are often accused of sending their spirits to kill children. On a final visit, Josephine asks, "Did you fly?" Manman gives a cryptic answer. Not long after, Manman is killed. Josephine realizes the truth: the survivors had been so covered by blood, they appeared to have wings of flame.

 For summaries in languages other than English, see Unit 7 Teaching Resources, pp. 325–330.

Vocabulary

Antonyms Remind students that an antonym has the opposite meaning of another word. After pointing out that antonyms must be the same part of speech, **say:** Think of an antonym for each of the five vocabulary words. (*grimace, smile; delirium, sanity; console, sadden; rejuvenated, aged; balmy, harsh*)

English Learners

DIFFERENTIATED INSTRUCTION

Intermediate Discuss with students the fact that the story they are about to read includes events that are difficult to believe, but for different reasons. Some events are so senseless and brutal that they are hard to believe. Other events seem to be magical. This fact may make decoding of words more difficult because readers may not trust their reading when sentences sound fantastic. Have students make a list to keep track of the two types of details that may sound unbelievable. Model such a list for students.

Illogical	Magical
Trujillo ordered the massacre of Haitians	Madonna (statue) cried
Women were accused of having wings of flame	She thought the tear meant her mother had died

Teach

Big Idea   1

Extending and Remaking Traditions Say: Keep these questions in mind as you read: How does Edwidge Danticat show tradition in her story? *(She shows how traditional beliefs or superstitions govern action in Haiti.)* What does her story bring to the traditions of American literature? *(It brings magic, color, and the vivid setting of Haiti.)*

Literary Element   2

Magic Realism Answer: *Students will become aware of the magical and unrealistic element in the statue's crying.*

Cultural History ☆

Haiti Almost everyone in Haiti has ancestors who were African slaves. Haiti was once a colony of France; its economy was built on a plantation system that required a large labor force. At one time, there were 500,000 slaves out of a total population just more than 550,000.

For an audio recording of this selection, use Listening Library Audio CD-ROM.

Readability Scores

Dale-Chall: 5
DRP: 54
Lexile: 900

For activities related to this selection, see Unit 7 Teaching Resources Book, pp. 331–337.

1320

NINETEEN THIRTY-SEVEN

Edwidge Danticat

1   My Madonna[1] cried. A miniature teardrop traveled down her white porcelain face, like dew on the tip of early morning grass. When I saw the tear I thought, surely, that my mother had died. I sat motionless observing the Madonna the whole day. It did not shed another tear. I remained in the rocking chair until it was nightfall, my bones aching from the thought of another trip to the prison in Port-au-Prince.[2] But, of course, I had to go.

The roads to the city were covered with sharp pebbles only half buried in the thick dust. I chose to go barefoot, as my mother had always done on her visits to the Massacre River, the ☆ river separating Haiti from the Spanish-speaking country that she had never allowed me to name because I had been born on the night that El Generalissimo, Dios Trujillo,[3] the honorable chief of state, had ordered the massacre of all Haitians living there.

The sun was just rising when I got to the capital. The first city person I saw was an old woman carrying a jar full of leeches.[4] Her gaze was glued to the Madonna tucked under my arm.

"May I see it?" she asked.

I held out the small statue that had been owned by my family ever since it was given to my great-great-great-grandmother Défilé by a French man who had kept her as a slave.

The old woman's index finger trembled as it moved toward the Madonna's head. She closed her eyes at the moment of contact, her wrists shaking.

"Where are you from?" she asked. She had layers of 'respectable' wrinkles on her face, the kind my mother might also have one day, if she has a chance to survive.

"I am from Ville Rose," I said, "the city of painters and poets, the coffee city, with beaches where the sand is either black or white, but never mixed together, where the fields are endless and sometimes the cows are yellow like cornmeal."

The woman put the jar of leeches under her arm to keep them out of the sun.

"You're here to see a prisoner?" she asked.

"Yes."

"I know where you can buy some very good food for this person."

She led me by the hand to a small alley where a girl was selling fried pork and plantains

---

1. A *Madonna* is a representation of the Virgin Mary, the mother of Jesus Christ.
2. The capital city and main port in Haiti is *Port-au-Prince* (port′ ō prins′).
3. General Rafael Leónidas *Trujillo* Molina (rä fä′ el lā ō′ nē däs trōō hē′ yō mō lē′ nä), the tyrannical dictator of the Dominican Republic from 1930 until his assassination in 1961, was responsible for the deaths of thousands of Haitians living in the Dominican Republic in 1937.

4. *Leeches* are bloodsucking worms once thought to cure illness by sucking out "bad" blood.

2   Magic Realism *How do you react to the narrator's statement that the Madonna cried?*

Reading Practice

Compare and Contrast Point out to students that the concept of flight is used in three different ways in this story. Remind students that the term *flight* can refer to the act of fleeing as well as the act of flying. **Ask:** A prison is a place from which people would want to flee. What other places, people, or events mentioned so far in the story would people want to flee? *(massacre, "the Spanish-speaking country," cages, guards)* Ask students to create three-column charts, with the headings *Escape, Flying,* and *Spiritual Uplift.* Have them fill in the charts as they continue to read with examples of the way *flight* is used in the story.

wrapped in brown paper. I bought some meat for my mother after asking the cook to fry it once more and then sprinkle it with spiced cabbage.

The yellow prison building was like a fort, as large and strong as in the days when it was used by the American marines[5] who had built it. The Americans taught us how to build prisons. By the end of the 1915 occupation, the police in the city really knew how to hold human beings trapped in cages, even women like Manman[6] who was accused of having wings of flame.

The prison yard was quiet as a cave when a young Haitian guard escorted me there to wait. The smell of the fried pork mixed with that of urine and excrement was almost unbearable. I sat on a pile of bricks, trying to keep the Madonna from sliding through my fingers. I dug my buttocks farther into the bricks, hoping perhaps that my body might sink down to the ground and disappear before my mother emerged as a ghost to greet me.

The other prisoners had not yet woken up. All the better, for I did not want to see them, these bone-thin women with shorn[7] heads, carrying clumps of their hair in their bare hands, as they sought the few rays of sunshine that they were allowed each day.

My mother had grown even thinner since the last time I had seen her. Her face looked like the gray of a late evening sky. These days, her skin barely clung to her bones, falling in layers, flaps, on her face and neck. The prison guards watched her more closely because they thought that the wrinkles resulted from her taking off her skin at night and then putting it back on in

---

5. Following years of political instability in Haiti, the United States *Marines* occupied the country from 1915 to 1934.
6. *Manman* (mä män´) is a Creole word meaning "mother."
7. *Shorn*, the past participle of *shear*, means "clipped" or "shaved."

3 Extending and Remaking Traditions *What does this paragraph suggest about the Haitian government?*

4 Visualize *How are these wrinkles different from the "respectable" wrinkles that the old woman with the leeches had?*

---

a hurry, before sunrise. This was why Manman's sentence had been extended to life. And when she died, her remains were to be burnt in the prison yard, to prevent her spirit from wandering into any young innocent bodies.

I held out the fried pork and plantains to her. She uncovered the food and took a peek before **grimacing,** as though the sight of the meat nauseated her. Still she took it and put it in a deep pocket in a very loose fitting white dress that she had made herself from the cloth that I had brought her on my last visit.

I said nothing. Ever since the morning of her arrest, I had not been able to say anything to her. It was as though I became mute the moment I stepped into the prison yard. Sometimes I wanted to speak, yet I was not able to open my mouth or raise my tongue. I wondered if she saw my struggle in my eyes.

She pointed at the Madonna in my hands, opening her arms to receive it. I quickly handed her the statue. She smiled. Her teeth were a dark red, as though caked with blood from the initial beating during her arrest. At times, she seemed happier to see the Madonna than she was to see me.

She rubbed the space under the Madonna's eyes, then tasted her fingertips, the way a person tests for salt in salt water.

"Has she cried?" Her voice was hoarse from lack of use. With every visit, it seemed to get worse and worse. I was afraid that one day, like me, she would not be able to say anything at all.

I nodded, raising my index finger to show that the Madonna had cried a single tear. She pressed the statue against her chest as if to

Visual Vocabulary
A *plantain* (plan´ tən) is a starchy tropical fruit that resembles a banana.

Vocabulary

grimace (gri´ məs) *v.* to contort the face, especially to express pain or displeasure

---

Big Idea	3

Extending and Remaking Traditions **Answer:** *It suggests that the government is abusing its ability to jail people, imprisoning many people while doing little to help those outside prison.*

Reading Strategy	4

Visualize **Answer:** *Manman's wrinkles are caused by illness, malnutrition, and abuse.*

Literary Element	5

Magic Realism **Ask:** Is the narrator's inability to speak realistic? Explain. *(Students may say yes; she does not know what to say to bring joy to her mother and does not want to hear details of her mother's treatment. It is too painful.)*

Advanced Learners

DIFFERENTIATED INSTRUCTION

Real Events Although the story's title refers to a historical event, the characters and plot are fictional. Some of the story's events are realistic, while others are magical or bizarre. Have advanced students record three events from the story that they think actually occurred. To help, have them complete charts like this one.

Historical Event	Details

Then have them use the Internet or library to research whether those events did take place in real life. Have them find additional details describing the events and share their findings with the class.

Teach

Reading Strategy 1

Make Inferences Point out the repeated reference to Manman's shaved head. **Ask:** What can you infer from this repetition? *(The shaving has some importance to the story.)* Encourage students to watch for other references to hair or shaving as they read.

Reading Strategy 2

Visualize Answer: *Answers will vary. Students may notice Josephine's awkwardness and desire to please her mother. They may notice the mother's exhaustion and illness as she tries to force a brave smile for her daughter.*

Reading Strategy 3

Visualize Answer: *The mob believes the mother is responsible for the death of the baby.*

Cultural History ☆

Witches Haitians are among many cultures that identify people as witches. Often, these were women believed to possess supernatural abilities to control people. In the United States, this belief took its greatest shape in the Salem witch trials of 1692. The trials have been traced to stories told by a West Indian (Caribbean) slave.

reward the Madonna and then, suddenly, broke down and began sobbing herself.

I reached over and patted her back, the way one burps a baby. She continued to sob until a guard came and nudged her, poking the barrel of his rifle into her side. She raised her head, keeping the Madonna lodged against her chest as she forced a brave smile.

"They have not treated me badly," she said. She smoothed her hands over her bald head, from her forehead to the back of her neck. The guards shaved her head every week. And before the women went to sleep, the guards made them throw tin cups of cold water at one another so that their bodies would not be able to muster up enough heat to grow those wings made of flames, fly away in the middle of the night, slip into the slumber of innocent children and steal their breath.

Manman pulled the meat and plantains out of her pocket and started eating a piece to fill the silence. Her normal ration of food in the prison was bread and water, which is why she was losing weight so rapidly.

"Sometimes the food you bring me, it lasts for months at a time," she said. "I chew it and swallow my saliva, then I put it away and then chew it again. It lasts a very long time this way."

A few of the other women prisoners walked out into the yard, their chins nearly touching their chests, their shaved heads sunk low on bowed necks. Some had large boils on their heads. One, drawn by the fresh smell of fried pork, came to sit near us and began pulling the scabs from the bruises on her scalp, a line of blood dripping down her back.

All of these women were here for the same reason. They were said to have been seen at night rising from the ground like birds on fire. A loved one, a friend, or a neighbor had

"Lougarou, witch, criminal!" they shouted.

accused them of causing the death of a child. A few other people agreeing with these stories was all that was needed to have them arrested. And sometimes even killed.

I remembered so clearly the day Manman was arrested. We were new to the city and had been sleeping on a cot at a friend's house. The friend had a sick baby who was suffering with colic. Every once in a while, Manman would wake up to look after the child when the mother was so tired that she no longer heard her son's cries.

One morning when I woke up, Manman was gone. There was the sound of a crowd outside. When I rushed out I saw a group of people taking my mother away. Her face was bleeding from the pounding blows of rocks and sticks and the fists of strangers. She was being pulled along by two policemen, each tugging at one of her arms as she dragged her feet. The woman we had been staying with carried her dead son by the legs. The policemen made no efforts to stop the mob that was beating my mother.

"*Lougarou,*[8] witch, criminal!" ☆ they shouted.

I dashed into the street, trying to free Manman from the crowd. I wasn't even able to get near her.

I followed her cries to the prison. Her face was swollen to three times the size that it had been. She had to drag herself across the clay floor on her belly when I saw her in the prison cell. She was like a snake, someone with no bones left in her body. I was there watching when they shaved her head for the first time. At first I thought they were doing it so that the open gashes on her scalp could heal.

---

8. The Creole word *lougarou* (lōō′ gä rōō′) means "witch" or "a follower of evil."

2 Visualize *How do you visualize the scene as the narrator and her mother are reunited?*

Visualize *Visualize the events described in this paragraph. Why is the mob beating the mother?* **3**

Reading Practice

Foreshadowing Point out the description of the imprisoned women in the paragraph beginning with the words "All of these women" on page 1322 as "rising from the ground like birds on fire." Then remind students that foreshadowing means events or images that hint at later events. **Ask:** How might the simile "like birds on fire" be foreshadowing? *(The*

simile is a clue to a key event that will be clear later in the story.) Ask students to think about what that event might be. *(The bird's flight might foreshadow Manman's escape or death.)*

1937: Grandmother Told Me That the Massacre River Was Bloody, c. 1975. Ernst Prophete. Oil on masonite, 20 x 24 in. Collection of Jonathan Demme.

My mother had escaped El Generalissimo's soldiers, leaving her own mother behind. From the Haitian side of the river, she could still see the soldiers chopping up *her* mother's body and throwing it into the river along with many others.

We went to the river many times as I was growing up. Every year my mother would invite a few more women who had also lost their mothers there.

Until we moved to the city, we went to the river every year on the first of November.[9] The women would all dress in white. My mother would hold my hand tightly as we walked toward the water. We were all daughters of that river, which had taken our mothers from us. Our mothers were the ashes and we were the light. Our mothers were the embers and we were the sparks. Our mothers were the flames and we were the blaze. We came from the bottom of that river where the blood never stops flowing, where my mother's dive toward life—her swim among all those bodies slaughtered in flight—gave her those

Later, when I saw all the other women in the yard, I realized that they wanted to make them look like crows, like men.

Now, Manman sat with the Madonna pressed against her chest, her eyes staring ahead, as though she was looking into the future. She had never talked very much about the future. She had always believed more in the past.

When I was five years old, we went on a pilgrimage to the Massacre River, which I had expected to be still crimson with blood, but which was as clear as any water that I had ever seen. Manman had taken my hand and pushed it into the river, no farther than my wrist. When we dipped our hands, I thought that the dead would reach out and haul us in, but only our own faces stared back at us, one indistinguishable from the other.

With our hands in the water, Manman spoke to the sun. "Here is my child, Josephine. We were saved from the tomb of this river when she was still in my womb. You spared us both, her and me, from this river where I lost my mother."

---

4 **Extending and Remaking Traditions** *Why does the author include these details?*

---

9. On November 1, Haitians celebrate La Toussaint (lä too′ sän), or All Saints' Day, as a national holiday. The day is also a Roman Catholic holy day commemorating all Catholic saints.

Extending and Remaking Traditions *In making so many references to light and fire, what is the narrator suggesting about these women?* 5

EDWIDGE DANTICAT **1323**

Big Idea 4

Extending and Remaking Traditions Answer: *The author may have included these details to show the cruel tactics that guards used to humiliate the prisoners.*

Big Idea 5

Extending and Remaking Traditions Answer: *The women have brightness and heat in their spirits that cannot be extinguished.*

View the Art ★

This painting is in film director Jonathan Demme's collection. Demme, whose wife is a painter, discovered Haitian art by chance on a walk one day. He has lobbied for its acceptance among American art collectors. Demme has also become an advocate of political support for Haitian refugees.

Approaching Level

DIFFERENTIATED INSTRUCTION

Emerging Discuss with students how "Nineteen Thirty-Seven" incorporates important past events into a narrative taking place in the present. Key words alert the reader to the sequence of events. Point out an example on page 1322. When the narrator remembers the day of her mother's arrest, the key words signaling that the narrator is going back in her memory are "I remembered so clearly. . . ."

Point out that "now," in "Now, Manman sat with the Madonna pressed against her chest . . ." signals the return to the present. Tell students to look for other key words that signal the transition between the past and the present as they read.

Established Discuss how the narrator's memories present important information. **Ask:** What do we learn from her memory of her mother's arrest? (*We learn that people's beliefs in witches led them to beat and imprison the accused.*)

Teach

Make Inferences **Ask:** When Manman says, "At least you came out at the right moment to take my mother's place," what does she mean? How do you think Manman felt about the night of her escape? (*Manman lost her mother in the river while they were escaping the soldiers, but she gave birth to Josephine after she safely emerges on the other side of the river. Despite the tragedy of losing her mother in the river, Manman is grateful that she did not also lose her baby that night.*)

Literary Element   2

Magic Realism **Answer:** *The Madonna's "perfect" tears are symbolic of people's need for faith and strength.*

Family in Interior. Poisson. Haitian Folk Art.

wings of flames. The river was the place where it had all begun.

"At least I gave birth to my daughter on the night that my mother was taken from me," she would say. "At least you came out at the right moment to take my mother's place."

Now in the prison yard, my mother was trying to avoid the eyes of the guard peering down at her.

"One day I will tell you the secret of how the Madonna cries," she said.

I reached over and touched the scabs on her fingers. She handed me back the Madonna.

I know how the Madonna cries. I have watched from hiding how my mother plans weeks in advance for it to happen. She would put a thin layer of wax and oil in the hollow space of the Madonna's eyes and when the wax melted, the oil would roll down the little face shedding a more perfect tear than either she and I could ever cry.

2 Magic Realism *If Josephine knows that the tears are not real, why does she still think that they are important?*

"You go. Let me watch you leave," she said, sitting stiffly.

I kissed her on the cheek and tried to embrace her, but she quickly pushed me away.

"You will please visit me again soon," she said.

I nodded my head yes.

"Let your flight be joyful," she said, "and mine too."

I nodded and then ran out of the yard, fleeing before I could flood the front of my dress with my tears. There had been too much crying already.

Manman had a cough the next time I visited her. She sat in a corner of the yard, and as she trembled in the sun, she clung to the Madonna.

"The sun can no longer warm God's creatures," she said. "What has this world come to when the sun can no longer warm God's creatures?"

I wanted to wrap my body around hers, but I knew she would not let me.

"God only knows what I have got under my skin from being here. I may die of tuberculosis, or perhaps there are worms right now eating me inside."

Reading Practice

Make Connections Have students look at the charts they made listing images of escape, flying, and spiritual uplift (Reading Practice, p. 1320). **Say:** Identify places in the story where the narrator refers to people taking flight. (*The imprisoned women "rising from the ground like birds on fire," the massacre was of people "slaughtered in flight," the narrator's* mother wishing her a joyful flight, the narrator asking her mother if she flew, the mother's fellow prisoners keeping their arms close to their bodies like "angels hiding their wings," the narrator wishing her mother a joyful flight.*) **Ask:** What philosophical view of oppression do you think the author implies? (*Even when oppressed, an individual can obtain* freedom, through resistance and death, if necessary. Flight from annihilation must be a continual state of mind as well as a physical act.*)

When I went again, I decided that I would talk. Even if the words made no sense, I would try to say something to her. But before I could even say hello, she was crying. When I handed her the Madonna, she did not want to take it. The guard was looking directly at us. Manman still had a fever that made her body tremble. Her eyes had the look of **delirium.**

"Keep the Madonna when I am gone," she said. "When I am completely gone, maybe you will have someone to take my place. Maybe you will have a person. Maybe you will have some *flesh* to **console** you. But if you don't, you will always have the Madonna."

"Manman, did you fly?" I asked her.

She did not even blink at my implied accusation.

"Oh, now you talk," she said, "when I am nearly gone. Perhaps you don't remember. All the women who came with us to the river, they could go to the moon and back if that is what they wanted."

A week later, almost to the same day, an old woman stopped by my house in Ville Rose on her way to Port-au-Prince. She came in the middle of the night, wearing the same white dress that the women usually wore on their trips to dip their hands in the river.

"Sister," the old woman said from the doorway. "I have come for you."

"I don't know you," I said.

"You *do* know me," she said. "My name is Jacqueline. I have been to the river with you."

---

3 Visualize *What does the image of a white-clad woman in the night suggest?*

Vocabulary

delirium (di lēr´ ē əm) *n.* a temporary state of mental disturbance characterized by confusion and disorientation

console (kən sōl´) *v.* to comfort; to cheer

I had been by the river with many people. I remembered a Jacqueline who went on the trips with us, but I was not sure this was the same woman. If she were really from the river, she would know. She would know all the things that my mother had said to the sun as we sat with our hands dipped in the water, questioning each other, making up codes and disciplines by which we could always know who the other daughters of the river were.

"Who are you?" I asked her.

"I am a child of that place," she answered. "I come from that long trail of blood."

"Where are you going?"

"I am walking into the dawn."

"Who are you?"

"I am the first daughter of the first star."

"Where do you drink when you're thirsty?"

"I drink the tears from the Madonna's eyes."

"And if not there?"

"I drink the dew."

"And if you can't find dew?"

"I drink from the rain before it falls."

"If you can't drink there?"

"I drink from the turtle's hide."

"How did you find your way to me?"

"By the light of the mermaid's comb."

"Where does your mother come from?"

"Thunderbolts, lightning, and all things that soar."

"Who are you?"

"I am the flame, and the spark by which my mother lived."

"Where do you come from?"

"I come from the puddle of that river."

"Speak to me."

"You hear my mother who speaks through me. She is the shadow that follows my shadow. The flame at the tip of my candle. The ripple in the stream where I wash my face. Yes. I will eat my tongue if ever I whisper that name, the name of that place across the river that took my mother from me."

I knew then that she had been with us, for she knew all the answers to the questions I asked.

1

Teach

"I think you do know who I am," she said, staring deeply into the pupils of my eyes. "I know who *you* are. You are Josephine. And your mother knew how to make the Madonna cry."

I let Jacqueline into the house. I offered her a seat in the rocking chair, gave her a piece of hard bread and a cup of cold coffee.

"Sister, I do not want to be the one to tell you," she said, "but your mother is dead. If she is not dead now, then she will be when we get to Port-au-Prince. Her blood calls to me from the ground. Will you go with me to see her? Let us go to see her."

We took a mule for most of the trip. Jacqueline was not strong enough to make the whole journey on foot. I brought the Madonna with me, and Jacqueline took a small bundle with some black rags in it.

When we got to the city, we went directly to the prison gates. Jacqueline whispered Manman's name to a guard and waited for a response.

1 "She will be ready for burning this afternoon," the guard said.

My blood froze inside me. I lowered my head as the news sank in.

"Surely, it is not that much a surprise," Jacqueline said, stroking my shoulder. She had become **rejuvenated,** as though strengthened by the correctness of her prediction.

"We only want to visit her cell," Jacqueline said to the guard. "We hope to take her personal things away."

The guard seemed too tired to argue, or perhaps he saw in Jacqueline's face traces of some long-dead female relative whom he had not done enough to please while she was still alive.

He took us to the cell where my mother had spent the last year. Jacqueline entered first, and then I followed. The room felt damp, the clay breaking into small muddy chunks under our feet.

I inhaled deeply to keep my lungs from aching. Jacqueline said nothing as she carefully walked around the women who sat like statues in different corners of the cell. There were six of them. They kept their arms close to their bodies, like angels hiding their wings. In the middle of the cell was an arrangement of sand and pebbles in the shape of a cross for my mother. Each woman was either wearing or holding something that had belonged to her.

One of them clutched a pillow as she stared at the Madonna. The woman was wearing my mother's dress, the large white dress that had become like a tent on Manman.

I walked over to her and asked, "What happened?"

"Beaten down in the middle of the yard," she whispered.

"Like a dog," said another woman.

"Her skin, it was too loose," said the woman wearing my mother's dress. "They said prison could not cure her."

The woman reached inside my mother's dress pocket and pulled out a handful of chewed pork and handed it to me. I motioned her hand away.

"No no, I would rather not."

She then gave me the pillow, my mother's pillow. It was open, half filled with my mother's hair. Each time they shaved her head, my mother had kept the hair for her pillow. I hugged the pillow against my chest, feeling some of the hair rising in clouds of dark dust into my nostrils.

Jacqueline took a long piece of black cloth[10] out of her bundle and wrapped it around her belly.

---

2 Magic Realism *What elements of magical realism does this paragraph contain?*

Vocabulary

rejuvenated (ri jōō′ və nāt′ əd) *adj.* restored to youthful vigor or appearance; renewed

---

10. The tying of a *black cloth* in this manner is a sign of mourning that precedes weeping for the deceased.

Visualize *Visualize this scene. What impression do you get of the prison cell?* **3**

The Phoenix, 1985. Lafortune Félix. Yale University Art Gallery, New Haven, CT. Gift of Selden Rodman.

View the Art Lafortune Félix's first exhibit took place not in a museum gallery, but in the form of wall murals at the temple where he was a voodoo priest. What connections can you make between the images in this painting and the images evoked by the river scenes in Danticat's story? ★

"Sister," she said, "life is never lost, another one always comes up to replace the last. Will you come watch when they burn the body?"

"What would be the use?" I said.

"They will make these women watch, and we can keep them company."

When Jacqueline took my hand, her fingers felt **balmy** and warm against the lifelines in my palm. For a brief second, I saw nothing but black. And then I *saw* the crystal glow of the river as we had seen it every year when my mother dipped my hand in it.

"I would go," I said, "if I knew the truth, whether a woman can fly."

"Why did you not ever ask your mother," Jacqueline said, "if she knew how to fly?"

Then the story came back to me as my mother had often told it. On that day so long ago, in the year nineteen hundred and thirty-seven, in the Massacre River, my mother did

fly. Weighted down by my body inside hers, she leaped from Dominican soil into the water, and out again on the Haitian side of the river. She glowed red when she came out, blood clinging to her skin, which at that moment looked as though it were in flames.

In the prison yard, I held the Madonna tightly against my chest, so close that I could smell my mother's scent on the statue. When Jacqueline and I stepped out into the yard to wait for the burning, I raised my head toward the sun thinking, One day I may just see my mother there.

"Let her flight be joyful," I said to Jacqueline. "And mine and yours too." ∾

Magic Realism *Why does the story suggest that the mother could fly?* **4**

Extending and Remaking Traditions *Why did this experience of injustice fail to crush Josephine?* **5**

EDWIDGE DANTICAT **1327**

Teach

Literary Element **4**

Magic Realism **Answer:** *The story suggests that the mother's escape was miraculous. Despite being victimized, she was not bitter, and she had remarkable accomplishments.*

Big Idea **5**

Extending and Remaking Traditions **Answer:** *Students may say Josephine is able to find encouragement in her mother's words and actions.*

View the Art ★

Answer: *The woman in the painting appears to have "wings of flames," as the narrator describes her mother as having when she escaped the massacre. The bird over the woman's head symbolizes the flight that the women took to escape.*

Point out the many images in the painting, such as the oversized woman, the upside-down man at the left. **Ask:** How do the separate images create magical realism? (*They blend reality with unrealistic elements.*)

1327

After You Read

Assess

1. Students' answers will vary.
2. (a) They are suspected of being witches. (b) It is governed by superstition and is repressive and brutal.
3. (a) Fleeing Haitians were slaughtered by Dominican soldiers. (b) The river is a reminder of evil and a symbol of rebirth and continuity.
4. (a) Manman hides wax and oil in the statue. When these melt, the Madonna appears to cry. (b) The weeping is supernatural, as Manman didn't hide wax. This may foreshadow Manman's death and creates a mood of mystery.
5. Loving and intense; Josephine wishes to "wrap her body around hers."
6. Her title reminds the world of the 1937 massacre and suggests that Haitians still suffer from its effects.
7. Magical realism retells a factual, historical event in a supernatural setting. Bizarre narrative elements add an uplifting quality to a tragic story.
8. Some children would focus on the realistic details of their mother's suffering; others, like Josephine, may turn to a more mystical understanding.

 For additional assessment, see Assessment Resources, pp. 323–324.

After You Read

Respond and Think Critically

Respond and Interpret

1. Which part of the story elicited the strongest reaction from you? Explain.
2. (a) Why are Josephine's mother and the other women in prison? (b) What does the treatment they receive tell you about the society they live in?
3. (a) What happened at the Massacre River the year Josephine was born? (b) What meaning do you think the river holds for the women?
4. (a) Why does the Madonna cry, according to Josephine? (b) Given Josephine's explanation, how would you explain the event described in the first paragraph of the story?

Analyze and Evaluate

5. How would you define the relationship between Josephine and her mother? Describe a detail from the story that reveals this relationship.
6. Why do you think Danticat entitled the story "Nineteen Thirty-Seven"? Explain what the title may suggest about the significance of the events described in the story.

Connect

7. **Big Idea** **Extending and Remaking Traditions** What innovations in subject matter and literary technique does Danticat bring to this story? Explain.
8. **Connect to Today** How do you think a child today would react to his or her mother's suffering? Explain.

MAY 10.

Daily Life & Culture

Voodoo and Lougarous

In Haiti, enslaved people from west Africa incorporated aspects of Christianity, such as a belief in the Devil, into their own traditions. This exchange formed a new religion, Voodoo, which includes a belief that all people are spirits.

In "Nineteen Thirty-Seven," Manman is imprisoned for being a *lougarou*. A Creole adaptation of the French *loup garou*, meaning "werewolf," a *lougarou* is really more reminiscent of a witch or vampire than a werewolf. Though particulars vary by account, many portray a *lougarou* as a woman who removes her skin at night, transforms herself—usually into an animal capable of flight—and flies to others' homes, preying on the children within. *Lougarous* drink children's blood, causing illness, loss of strength, or death.

Group Activity Discuss the following questions with your classmates.

1. The policemen in "Nineteen Thirty-Seven" believe that the Manman can shed her skin and fly on wings of flame. How is the idea of justice affected when someone in authority believes in these kinds of supernatural forces?
2. What sort of beliefs do you think Josephine has? Use examples from the text to illustrate your points.
3. How would you describe Danticat's incorporation of Voodoo and other elements of Haitian folk tradition into the contemporary style of fiction-writing known as Magic Realism?

Daily Life & Culture

1. Students might be shocked or appalled that people who are entrusted with power hold such beliefs.
2. Students might say that Josephine is skeptical of the supernatural, as evidenced by her knowledge of how the Madonna cries, but that she has not shut herself off to it, as she has to ask her mother if she really did fly.
3. By incorporating Voodoo and other elements of Haitian folk tradition into her stories, Danticat creates a style of writing which blends fantastic elements such as magic with realistic elements anchored in Haitian culture and traditions.

Literary Element Magic Realism

Throughout her story, Danticat refers to supernatural events in an otherwise painfully realistic narrative. For example, the narrator's suggestion that certain women could fly with "wings of flame" implies a magical quality about characters whose lives have otherwise been filled with horrible realities.

1. What are other references to magical, supernatural, or bizarre events in "Nineteen Thirty-Seven"?

2. Which events does the narrator find ordinary explanations for? Which does she present as magical?

Review: Style

As you learned on page 743, word choice, the length and arrangement of sentences, and the use of figurative language and imagery all contribute to an author's individual **style**.

Partner Activity With a partner, choose a passage from "Nineteen Thirty-Seven" that you think is a good example of the author's style. Using a chart like the one shown, analyze the textual elements that contribute to the style. In a paragraph, describe the style. Compare your analysis with that of another pair.

Text Elements	Contribution to Style
sentence length	

 Literature Online

Selection Resources For Selection Quizzes, eFlash-cards, and Reading-Writing Connection activities, go to glencoe.com and enter QuickPass code GLA9800u7.

Reading Strategy Visualize

Many successful movies have been based upon works of fiction, in part because the original story or novel provided precise visual descriptions of characters and settings. For scenes and people not fully described, the film's director and director of photography use their imaginations to fill in the missing details.

1. If you were directing a film of "Nineteen Thirty-Seven," how would Josephine's mother appear?

2. Imagine that you are creating a poster for a movie of "Nineteen Thirty-Seven." What striking scene, character, or image would your poster feature? Describe your poster in detail.

Vocabulary Practice

Antonyms With a partner, match each bold-faced vocabulary word below with its antonym. You will not use all answer choices. Use a thesaurus or dictionary to check your answers.

1. delirium
2. console
3. rejuvenated
4. balmy

a. tired
b. depress
c. scowling
d. young
e. harsh
f. sanity

Academic Vocabulary

*Jacqueline must go through the **process** of answering questions to prove to Josephine that she is a woman from the river.*

Process is an academic word. It can have different meanings in different subject areas. Using context clues, try to figure out the meaning of *process* in the sentence above.

For more on academic vocabulary, see pages 53–54.

EDWIDGE DANTICAT   **1329**

Literary Element

1. Examples: Madonna's tears; spirits stealing breath from infants; flying to the moon and back; Manman's blood calling to Jacqueline from the earth

2. Natural: wings of flame; Madonna's tears. Magical: "flying to the moon and back;" Manman's blood calling to Jacqueline

Progress Check

Can students recognize magic realism?

If No → See Unit 7 Teaching Resources Book, p. 331.

Reading Strategy

1. Students' answers may reflect the sadness and quiet courage that the narrator sees in her.

2. Answers should be supported with details explaining why students found their poster subjects striking.

Vocabulary

1. f **2.** b **3.** a **4.** e

Academic Vocabulary

Jacqueline has to answer questions to prove herself to Josephine, which hints that the word *process* means "a systematic series of actions that are done to accomplish some goal."

Review: Style

Students' answers may point out the following: figurative language contributes to the style by conveying ideas or emotions; imagery contributes by helping readers visualize scenes.

 To create custom assessments using software, use ExamView Assessment Suite.

To create custom assessments online, go to Progress Reporter Online Assessment.

After You Read

Assess

Respond Through Writing

Students' short stories should have a logical sequence of plot events with clearly-defined locations for its scenes. Students should include concrete and sensory details in their stories to establish setting and to describe characters. After students have reviewed each other's stories, they should revise his or her short story based on the criticism he or she received.

Scoring Guide

Assess students' performance in the following categories using the scoring guide below:

- Addresses all parts of the writing task.
- Employs the form and style of magic realism.
- Chooses a pace that matches the shift in the moods and time of the story.
- Provides well chosen concrete and sensory details that bring the story to life.
- Employs a variety of sentence types and uses precise, descriptive language.
- Follows English language conventions.

Respond Through Writing

Short Story

Apply Form In "Nineteen Thirty-Seven," Danticat juxtaposes supernatural events with a realistic narrative—the hallmark of magic realism. Write your own 1,500-word short story that follows the form and style of magic realism.

Understand the Task Juxtaposition is placing two or more distinct things side by side in order to contrast or compare them. **Style** comprises the expressive qualities that distinguish an author's work, including word choice, sentence length and arrangement, figurative language, and imagery.

Prewrite Before you begin writing, make a plan for your story. Create a graphic organizer like the one started below to outline characters, setting, plot, and supernatural events.

Characters	
Setting	
Plot	
Supernatural Events	

Draft As you write your draft, pay attention to how you pace the sequence of plot events. Allow the pace of the action to change to accommodate shifts in time and mood. Locate scenes and incidents in specific settings. Add concrete and sensory details. When you present characters, describe their actions, gestures, feelings, and thoughts.

Revise Exchange stories with a partner. Evaluate your partner's work based on the criteria set forth in this assignment.

Edit and Proofread Proofread your essay, correcting any errors in spelling, grammar, and punctuation. Use the Grammar Tip in the side column to help you use passive and active voice correctly.

> **Grammar Tip**

Passive and Active Voice

An action verb is in the active voice when the subject of the sentence performs the action.

The Madonna's eyes welled with tears.

An action verb is in the passive voice when its action is performed on the subject.

Her mother was imprisoned by the Dominicans.

Usually the active voice is the stronger voice. Sometimes, however, the passive voice is preferred or even necessary. For example, you would use the passive voice if you do not want to call attention to the performer of the action or you do not know who the performer is.

Josephine was told to follow the narrator.
The mother's belongings were gathered.

Scoring Guide	4	3	2	1
Task addressed	fully	mostly	partially	barely
Magic Realism	fully employs proper form and style	somewhat employs proper form and style	attempts to employ proper form and style	does not employ proper form or style
Pace	well handled	somewhat well handled	somewhat choppy or abrupt	no thought was given to pace
Concrete and Sensory Details	well employed	employed	few employed	none
Language	varied, precise, descriptive	varied, somewhat descriptive	predictable, basic	not varied, limited
Convention errors	few or none	several	some	many

Before You Read
The Man with the Saxophone

Meet **Ai**
(born 1947)

Ai uses her given middle name as her pen name. She also fiercely claims that it is the only name by which she should be known. She grew up as Florence Anthony; her last name, she learned as an adult, was that of her stepfather. Her genetic father was Japanese, and the name Ai means "love" in that language.

A Young Poet Ai was born in Albany, Texas. Her family was very poor and moved often. As a child, Ai lived not only in Texas, but also in Tucson, Arizona; San Francisco and Los Angeles, California; and Las Vegas, Nevada. When she was fourteen, she lived in Los Angeles. At school she saw an ad for a local poetry contest. She composed a poem, but before she could enter the contest, her family moved. In spite of that disappointment, Ai found that writing poetry suited her: "As I grew older I realized that poetry offered a way to express things that I couldn't do otherwise."

Ai went to college at the University of Arizona. There she majored in Japanese and was also a very serious student of Buddhism. She went on to get a master's degree in fine arts from the University of California. Ai had her first book of poetry published two years later, in 1973. She's been writing and teaching writing ever since.

A Distinctive Style Almost all of Ai's poems are dramatic monologues—writing told from the first-person point of view. Most of her poems feature the voices of unnamed, imaginary characters. However, some use the voices of famous historical figures or celebrities, such as John F. Kennedy, Marilyn Monroe, Elvis Presley, and Alfred Hitchcock.

Ai relies on biographies for information when she wants to write in the voice of a real person. However, fictional speakers take even more work. Ai fleshes out all of her characters fully in her head before beginning to write. For each individual character she says, "I've got to know what kind of person he or she is. What are they doing? What would they wear? What colors do they like?" Once she has a clear picture of a character, she can start crafting a poem in that voice. About this process, Ai has said, "Every time I write a poem, I'm someone else without actually being that person. . . . It's really great."

> "I'm irrevocably tied to the lives of all people, both in and out of time."
> —Ai

Readers and critics have sometimes tried to label Ai as an African American poet. However, she points out that she's part African American, part Japanese, part Choctaw, part Cheyenne, part Irish, and part Dutch. She says that she lets any and all of her characters speak, "regardless of sex, race, creed, or color." In summary, she says, "I'm simply a writer. I don't want to be catalogued and my characters don't want to be catalogued and my poems don't want to be catalogued. If a poet's work isn't universal, then what good is it?"

 Literature Online

Author Search For more about Ai, go to glencoe.com and enter QuickPass code GLA9800u7.

AI **1331**

Bellringer Options

Daily Language Practice Transparency 122

Or poll students about their favorite time of day. **Ask:** What makes this time of day appealing? How does it shape your interaction with other times of day? As they read, have students consider how the speaker in the poem responds to and is nurtured by early morning.

Selection Skills

Literary Elements
- Narrative Poetry (SE pp. 1332–1335)
- Free Verse (TE p. 1332)

The Man with the Saxophone

Writing Skills/Grammar
- Set of Directions (SE p. 1335)

Reading Skills
- Connect to Cultural Context (SE pp. 1332–1335)

Vocabulary Skills
- Denotation and Connotation (SE pp. 1332, 1335)

Before You Read

Focus

Summary

The poem's speaker walks alone in the early morning of a New York City winter day, carrying a saxophone. The speaker encounters a homeless man with a saxophone and stops to play with him. As they play, the speaker reflects on all that he or she has lost but feels temporarily soothed and liberated by the music.

 For summaries in languages other than English, see Unit 7 Teaching Resources Book, pp. 338–343.

Vocabulary

Word Parts **Ask:** Which of the vocabulary words has a prefix? (*unencumbered*) What does the prefix -*un* mean? (*not*) Tell students that the prefix *en-* can mean "to put into or on." Removing the suffix -*ed* leaves some form related to *cumber* as the word's root. **Ask:** Can you deduce what that word might mean? (*to weigh down, burden, from a root meaning "hindrance"*)

Literature and Reading Preview

Connect to the Poem

What associations do you have with early morning? Write a journal entry in which you describe this time of day and explain what makes it special.

Build Background

"The Man with the Saxophone" is set in New York City on the streets of Manhattan. Most Manhattan streets are laid out in a grid pattern; the north-south streets are numbered avenues. First Avenue is to the east and Tenth Avenue is to the west. The east-west streets are numbered streets. The higher the number, the farther north the street. The speaker in "The Man with the Saxophone" is walking south on Fifth Avenue.

Set Purposes for Reading

Big Idea **Extending and Remaking Traditions**

Poems that present dramatic monologues have long been part of the American literary tradition. The speaker in Edgar Allan Poe's "The Raven," for example, narrates an encounter with an eerie bird. As you read, ask yourself, How does "The Man with the Saxophone" extend or remake that tradition?

Literary Element **Narrative Poetry**

A **narrative poem** is a poem that tells a story. Like other stories, narrative poems have a plot, a setting, and characters. As you read, ask yourself, Where do the exposition, the rising action, the climax, and the falling action of the plot occur?

Reading Strategy **Connect to Cultural Context**

The setting of "The Man with the Saxophone" is Manhattan, and the characters are musicians. Both elements help provide a cultural context for this poem. Note other aspects of culture that may relate to the poet's message.

Tip: **Ask Questions** As you read, ask yourself:

- Have you ever been in a large city like the one described in the poem?
- Do you know anyone who is like the speaker? Like the man with the saxophone?

Vocabulary

amble (am´ bəl) *v.* to walk at a leisurely pace; to stroll; p. 1333 *On window-shopping trips, my friends amble from one downtown store to the next, looking for unusual gifts.*

solitude (sol´ e tōōd´) *n.* the state of being alone; p. 1333 *After attending meetings all day, a quiet walk brought me much-needed solitude.*

unencumbered (ən in kəm´ bərd) *adj.* unhindered; unburdened; p. 1334 *I took off my heavy backpack and, unencumbered, danced down the empty hallway.*

Tip: **Denotation and Connotation** **Denotation** is the literal, or dictionary, meaning of a word. **Connotation** is the implied, or cultural, meaning of a word. For example, the words *walk* and *amble* have a similar denotation, "moving at a slow pace," but they have different connotations:

Neutral	*Positive*
walk	amble

Reading Practice

Free Verse Tell students that Ai's poem is written in free verse. Review that free verse is poetry with no fixed pattern of meter, rhyme, line length, or stanza arrangement. Explain to students that free verse should be read, unlike other poetry, according to its punctuation, not the line breaks. Readers should pause at commas and periods as they would when reading prose. Have students take turns reading a few lines of the poem until they can follow punctuation correctly.

1332

New York Buildings at Night. Franklin McMahon.

The Man with the Saxophone

Ai

New York. Five A.M.
The sidewalks empty.
Only the steam
pouring from the manhole covers[1] seems alive,
5   as I **amble** from shop window to shop window,
sometimes stopping to stare, sometimes not.
Last week's snow is brittle now
and unrecognizable as the soft, white hair
that bearded the face of the city.
10 I head farther down Fifth Avenue
toward the thirties,[2]
my mind empty[3]
like the Buddhists tell you is possible
if only you don't try.
15 If only I could
turn myself into a bird
like the shaman[4] I was meant to be,
but I can't,
I'm earthbound
20 and **solitude** is my companion,
the only one you can count on.
Don't, don't try to tell me otherwise.
I've had it all and lost it
and I never want it back,
25 only give me this morning to keep,
the city asleep

---

1. You might observe *steam pouring from manhole covers* on a cold day. Water vapor in the warm air rising from the sewer condenses as steam.
2. The phrase *toward the thirties* refers to the east-west streets in Manhattan, from 30th Street to 39th Street.
3. In line 12, *my mind empty* refers to a goal of Buddhism—to empty the mind through meditation.
4. A *shaman* is a priest in some tribal societies.

> **Narrative Poetry** *Does the speaker seem to have a definite destination? Explain.* **2**

> **Connect to Cultural Context** *What does the speaker's statement here tell you about his or her culture and goals? Name two or more things.* **3**

> **Vocabulary**
> **amble** (am' bəl) *v.* to walk at a leisurely pace; to stroll
> **solitude** (sol' e tood') *n.* the state of being alone

AI   **1333**

Teach

Literary Element 1

Narrative Poetry Answer: *The rising action begins on line 27.*

Reading Strategy 2

Connect to Cultural Context Answer: *Not everyone would be familiar with the meaning of this signal among musicians. Stepping back might also mean to allow the other person to pass or to show fear of the person.*

Big Idea 3

Extending and Remaking Traditions Answer: *The merciful notes meeting an unforgiving day add a tension new in the literary tradition.*

Cultural History ☆

Homelessness Many large cities have street musicians. Some are homeless, with no permanent place that provides complete or safe shelter. Some are mentally ill and distrustful of strangers.

---

and there on the corner of Thirty-fourth and Fifth,
the man with the saxophone,
his fingerless gloves caked with grime,
30   his face also,
the layers of clothes welded to his skin.
I set down my case,
he steps backward
to let me know I'm welcome,
35   and we stand a few minutes
in the silence so complete
I think I must be somewhere else, not here,
not in this city, this heartland of pure noise.
Then he puts the sax to his lips again
40   and I raise mine.
I suck the air up from my diaphragm
and bend over into the cold, golden reed,5
waiting for the notes to come,
and when they do,
45   for that one moment,
I'm the **unencumbered** bird of my imagination,
rising only to fall back
toward concrete,
each note a black flower,
50   opening, mercifully opening
into the unforgiving new day.

---

5. The *reed* in the mouthpiece of a saxophone makes the vibrations that produce sound.

Narrative Poetry *If you had a graph showing plot development, including exposition, rising action, climax, and falling action, where would you place these lines?* **1**

Connect to Cultural Context *Why do you think the poet includes this explanation? In a different cultural context what might stepping backward mean?* **2**

Extending and Remaking Traditions *How does the speaker's attitude seem new or surprising?* **3**

Vocabulary

unencumbered (ən in kəm´ bərd) *adj.* unhindered; unburdened

Listening and Speaking Practice

SMALL GROUP

Discuss Poetry Have students reread the poem silently. When they finish, they must write down the most powerful word and two or three supporting reasons in their notebooks. To begin discussion, ask one student to write the word on the board and share his or her explanation of the choice. Have other students who selected the same word offer further support before moving to another student's word. Be sure all chosen words are written on the board. At the end of the discussion, ask students to write a brief summary of the discussion and which word they now feel best represents the poem. *(Students may select words from the beginning of the poem,* empty, earthbound, solitude, *or* lost *that represent the darker tones of the poem, or they may choose more uplifting words like* moment, unencumbered, rising, *or* opening, *depending on their overall reactions to the poem.)*

Remind students that their explanations for their chosen word should be supported by evidence directly from the poem.

After You Read

Respond and Think Critically

Respond and Interpret

1. Which aspects of this poem were easy for you to connect to? Which were harder to connect to?

2. The poem is set in New York City. (a)What is the exact time? What time of year do you think it is? (b)Why do you think the speaker is out and about at this time?

3. (a)How does the speaker characterize the sound of the city, both normally and during the events of the poem? (b)How does this difference seem to affect the speaker?

Analyze and Evaluate

4. Ai uses many different images in this poem. (a)Which image do you think is the strongest? (b)What do you think makes this image strong?

5. The speaker of the poem says that "solitude is my companion, / the only one you can count on." What do you think he or she means by this statement? Do you agree?

Connect

6. **Big Idea** **Extending and Remaking Traditions** How does "The Man with the Saxophone" seem different from other narrative poems you have read?

7. **Connect to the Author** How does Ai include elements of her spiritual beliefs in the poem?

Literary Element **Narrative Poetry**

Narrative poetry has all of the elements of other narrative fiction. This includes characters as well as plot. Both can be extremely important to the meaning and message of a narrative poem.

1. What problem does the speaker of the poem face that is key to the plot? How is the problem resolved?

2. How does Ai make Manhattan a character in the poem? Cite specific images or lines of the poem in your answer.

Reading Strategy **Connect to Cultural Context**

The urban setting of "The Man with the Saxophone" and the focus on music and musicians give this poem two very obvious contexts for culture. However, the poem also hints at other more subtle cultural contexts. Reread the poem, looking for other important aspects of culture. What other cultural connections does the poem make?

Vocabulary Practice

Practice with Denotation and Connotation
Each of the vocabulary words is listed with a word that has a similar denotation. Choose the word that has a more positive connotation.

1. amble	walk
2. solitude	isolation
3. unencumbered	free

 Writing

Write Set of Directions "The Man with the Saxophone" takes place in New York City. Imagine that you are giving directions to your school for a visitor from out of town. First, write the directions out in words. Then draw a map to illustrate the route, labeling the streets and important landmarks.

 Literature Online

Selection Resources For Selection Quizzes, eFlash-cards, and Reading-Writing Connection activities, go to glencoe.com and enter QuickPass code GLA9800u7.

AI **1335**

Reading Strategy

The narrator longs for a religious or spiritual experience, to transcend the city, which is cold and lonely.

Vocabulary

1. amble
2. solitude
3. free

Writing

Use these criteria to evaluate work:

- Do students include a list of realistic directions?
- Do students present an accurate map that includes landmarks and street names?
- Encourage students to word-process their directions or use software to produce their maps.

After You Read

Assess

1. Answers should be supported by evidence from the text.

2. (a) 5:00 a.m.; winter or early spring (b) Homeless or coming home from a late job

3. (a) Completely silent now but usually a "heartland of pure noise" (b) Amazed by the quiet, and helped by it to transcend difficulties

4. (a) Answers will vary. (b) Students should provide reasons.

5. Relying on yourself is the safest course because other people can disappoint you. Students may agree or disagree.

6. This poem describes a sequence of events, a short span of time, and few external events.

7. The speaker refers to shamanism and Buddhist beliefs of meditation.

> For additional assessment, see Assessment Resources, pp. 325–326.

Literary Element

1. The speaker feels alone. A bond with music and a fellow musician solves the problem.

2. Ai personifies the city with images such as snow as a beard on the city's face; she names it and shows it as an unrelenting force.

Progress Check

Can students analyze narrative poetry?

If No → See Unit 7 Teaching Resources Book, p. 344.

Before You Read

Ending Poem

Meet **Rosario Morales and Aurora Levins Morales**

(born 1930 and 1954)

Sometimes two or more writers collaborate on a single piece of literature. Rosario Morales and her daughter Aurora Levins Morales have created several works of literature together.

Early Family Life Rosario Morales was born in New York in 1930. After getting married, she and her husband, Ricardo Levins, moved to Puerto Rico, where Aurora was born in 1954. It was there that Rosario instilled in Aurora a love of reading and writing. Aurora gives her mother credit for teaching her to appreciate female writers, such as Virginia Woolf and Toni Morrison.

The family returned to the United States, where Richard worked at different universities, Rosario continued to write, and Aurora studied and wrote. This professional Jewish Puerto Rican family did not fit into most people's conceptions of what it meant to be Puerto Rican. Both mother and daughter shared a keen awareness of that fact.

Aurora once wrote, "I am new. History made me. My first language was spanglish." She did not see her own cultural heritage reflected in what she read. As a result, she often addresses issues of identity, culture, and racism.

> *"Writers have to be leaders in their communities."*
>
> —Aurora Levins Morales

Education While in college, Aurora moved to California to finish her education. There, she began to publish her work. During the 1990s, she received recognition and awards for her writing, including the Ardella Mills Prize for journalistic prose. Her writing has appeared in journals, magazines, and books.

In addition to her academic and writing work, Aurora speaks throughout the United States on social issues, such as the treatment of Puerto Ricans by other U.S. citizens. "The vast majority of the popular culture's portrayal of Puerto Ricans is extremely stereotyped and oppressive," she says.

A Family Matter Her work is her response to this problem. Her literary writing includes essays, poems, short stories, and multi-media plays, some of which have been published in anthologies, including *Cuentos: Stories by Latinas*.

When Aurora was a child, she and her mother shared their writing with each other, each providing feedback and encouragement. Later, this sharing took a more concrete form. A series of long-distance telephone conversations between mother and daughter developed into *Getting Home Alive*, which was published in 1986. This collection of fiction, poetry, diary entries, and essays explores the lives of two Puerto Rican women living separate lives in different cultures.

Literature Online

Author Search For more about Rosario Morales and Aurora Levins Morales, go to glencoe.com and enter QuickPass code GLA9800u7.

Literature and Reading Preview

Connect to the Poem

The following poem is a statement of identity created by two people. As you read the poem, think about the following questions:

1. What determines who a person is?
2. Can a person's identity be summed up in a single word or phrase?

Build Background

The speakers in "Ending Poem" celebrate a multicultural identity. They mention the Tainos, the indigenous people of Puerto Rico, or Boriquen, as it was called when Christopher Columbus arrived in 1493. The Spanish intermarried with the Tainos, as they did with the enslaved African people whom they brought to the island in the 1500s. As a result, most Puerto Ricans are *mestizos*—a blend of Taino, African, and Spanish. The speakers also mention *jibaros*, rural farmers of Puerto Rico. These rugged people appear often in Puerto Rican folklore, where they are portrayed as generous, loving, hardworking, and courageous.

Set Purposes for Reading

Big Idea **Extending and Remaking Traditions**

As you read this poem, ask yourself, How do the speakers refer to the traditions of the past?

Literary Element Motif

A **motif** is a significant word, phrase, description, idea, or other element that is repeated throughout a work and is related to the theme. As you read this poem, look for motifs and ask yourself, What does each motif add to the meaning of the poem?

Reading Strategy **Make Generalizations**

A **generalization** is a statement that may be true for a group, but there are always exceptions. To make a generalization, readers must look at details to find relationships that the writer suggests but does not state directly.

Tip: Group Ideas Use a graphic organizer to record details you used to make generalizations.

Learning Objectives

For pages 1336–1341

In studying this text, you will focus on the following objectives:

Literary Study: Understanding motifs.

Reading: Making generalizations.

Writing: Writing an oral report.

Vocabulary

diaspora (dī as′ pər ə) *n.* the scattering of a people; p. 1338 *The war-torn country saw a diaspora of its artists and writers.*

shtetl (shte′ təl) *n.* small Jewish town or community; p. 1338 *Jewish folktales often take place in a shtetl.*

ghetto (get′ ō) *n.* neighborhood where a particular group of people are forced to live either by law, poverty, or social exclusion; p. 1338 *During World War II, Jews were forced to live in ghettos.*

Tip: Context Clues A word's context—the other words and phrases around it—can often provide clues about its meaning. For example, the sentence *During World War II, Jews were forced to live in ghettos* gives you a clue to the meaning of *ghetto,* which means "a neighborhood where a group of people are forced to live."

ROSARIO MORALES AND AURORA LEVINS MORALES **1337**

Before You Read

Focus

Summary

The speaker describes the many different identities that make up who she is. These include mestiza, Puerto Rican, American, Jewish, and more. She describes these identities mixing like many plates at a dinner table and in cloth made by many people.

 For summaries in languages other than English, see Unit 7 Teaching Resources Book, pp. 349–354.

Vocabulary

Origins *Shtetl* is a Yiddish word, probably a form of the German word *stadt,* which means "town." Have students use a dictionary to explore the origins of the other two vocabulary words. **Ask:** What does the Greek root of the word *diaspora* mean? *(dispersion, scattering)* Where was the island of Ghetto? *(near Venice, Italy)* Have students explore how these words contribute to the poem's focus on the coming together of various ethnicities.

 For additional context, see Glencoe Interactive Vocabulary CD-ROM.

English Learners

DIFFERENTIATED INSTRUCTION

Advanced Remind students that a recurring element in writing, music, or design is known as a *motif.* Have students practice creating verbal motifs. Remind students to use repetition of the motif in their responses. Model for students. **Say:** Suppose you are asked, Do you like music? Your response, using a motif, might be: High notes make me quiver, low notes make me roar, and all notes make me smile. Have students work in small groups to write an answer to one or more of the following questions:

- Are puppies cute?
- When are you happy?
- Why are some weeks longer than others?

Students' responses should use repetition of a key word that relates to the theme of the question.

Teach

Big Idea 1

Extending and Remaking Traditions Say: As you read, consider these questions: How do pieces of their heritage affect the traditions these poets embrace? *(Ethnic heritage determines traditions.)* How do identity labels link the speakers to those traditions? *(Each labeled group has its tradition.)*

Reading Strategy 2

Make Generalizations
Answer: *The speaker's forbears were discriminated against and often treated disrespectfully.*

View the Art ★

Elena Climent (1955–) says "wherever we are we reproduce ourselves. People reflect themselves by their surroundings." The Mexican-born artist often paints collections of personal objects and moments of home life.

Ending Poem

Rosario Morales and
Aurora Levins Morales

Kitchen with View of Viaduct, 1995. Elena Climent. Oil on canvas. Phoenix Art Museum, Arizona. Mr. and Mrs. Gene Lemon in honor of Clayton Kirking. ★

I am what I am.
A child of the Americas. **1**
A light-skinned mestiza of the Caribbean.
A child of many **diaspora,** *born into this continent at a crossroads.*
5 I am Puerto Rican. I am U.S. American.
I am New York Manhattan and the Bronx.
A mountain-born, country-bred, homegrown jíbara[1] child,
up from the **shtetl,** *a California Puerto Rican Jew*
A product of the New York **ghettos** I have never known.
10 *I am an immigrant*
and the daughter and granddaughter of immigrants.
We didn't know our forbears' names with a certainty.
They aren't written anywhere.
First names only or mija, negra, ne, honey, sugar, dear

15 I come from the dirt where the cane was grown.
My people didn't go to dinner parties. They weren't invited.
I am caribeña, island grown.
Spanish is in my flesh, ripples from my tongue, lodges in my hips,
the language of garlic and mangoes.

---

1. *jíbara:* peasant

Make Generalizations *What do these lines suggest about the way the speaker's forebears were treated?* **2**

Vocabulary

diaspora (dī as´ pər ə) *n.* the scattering of a people
shtetl (shte´ təl) *n.* small Jewish town or community
ghetto (get´ ō) *n.* neighborhood where a particular group of people are forced to live either by law, poverty, or social exclusion

Reading Practice

Generalization Have students make a list of the sentences from the poem which begin with "I am" and "I am not." **Ask:** What effect do the authors create with the repetition of "I am" and "I am not"? *(The speaker in the poem is trying to define himself or herself to understand his or her place in society.)* Have students reread the last stanza. **Ask:** Why do the authors switch from "I am," to "We are," in the last stanza? *(The speaker's definition of himself or herself is now generalized and applied to a wider group of people.)* Have students imitate this effect by writing a short poem which repeats the sentences "I am" and "I am not," and ends with a sentence beginning with "We are." Ask several students to read their poems and discuss how the last sentence generalizes their poems.

20   Boricua.² As Boricuas come from the isle of Manhattan.
     I am of latinoamerica, rooted in the history of my continent.
     I speak from that body. Just brown and pink and full of drums inside.
     I am not African.
     Africa waters the roots of my tree, but I cannot return.
25   I am not Taína.
     I am a late leaf of that ancient tree,
     and my roots reach into the soil of two Americas.
     Taíno is in me, but there is no way back.

     I am not European, though I have dreamt of those cities.
30   *Each plate is different.*
     wood, clay, papier mâché, metals, basketry, a leaf, a coconut shell.
     Europe lives in me but I have no home there.

     The table has a cloth woven by one, dyed by another,
     embroidered by another still.
35   I am a child of many mothers.
     They have kept it all going

     All the civilizations erected on their backs.
     All the dinner parties given with their labor. ☆

     We are new.
40   *They gave us life, kept us going,*
     brought us to where we are.
     Born at a crossroads.
     Come, lay that dishcloth down. Eat, dear, eat.
     History made us.
45   We will not eat ourselves up inside anymore.

     And we are whole.

---

2. *Boricua*: Puerto Rican

Motif   *What underlying idea shown here is repeated several times during the poem?*   **3**

Extending and Remaking Traditions   *How do these lines refer to the traditions of the past?*   **4**

ROSARIO MORALES AND AURORA LEVINS MORALES   **1339**

Literary Element   3

Motif Answer: *Students should recognize that the use of the phrases "I am" and "I am not" identifying the speaker is a recurring motif.*

Big Idea   4

Extending and Remaking Traditions Answer: *Students may note that the lines show the link between the present—the speakers—and the past. The lines show that all aspects of the speakers' diverse traditions contribute to what the speakers are.*

Cultural History ☆

Puerto Rican Poverty Puerto Ricans in the United States have faced many challenges of poverty and have often worked at low-paying jobs, such as the poets refer to here.

Approaching Level

DIFFERENTIATED INSTRUCTION

Emerging Point out that the cowriters of this poem are a mother and daughter. **Ask:** How does the poem's structure reflect that two people wrote it? (*The use of italics in every alternating line might indicate two different voices.*) What line might be spoken by the two together? (*and the daughter and granddaughter of immigrants*)

Established Ask: What do you think the poet means by this seeming contradiction: "A product of the New York ghettos I have never known"? (*Her parents grew up in the ghetto, and their experiences there shaped her.*)

After You Read

Assess

1. (a) Answers will vary. (b) Answers should be supported by text evidence.
2. (a) She is a child of the Americas with a varied ancestry. (b) Pride
3. (a) African, European, or Taína (b) Perhaps she wants to credit all of her ancestors.
4. (a) They gave life, kept her going, and brought her to where she is. (b) They wove, dyed, and embroidered a cloth; shaped civilizations and lives with work and love.
5. Possible categories: rural, physical, and ethnic ancestry
6. Her mixed heritage
7. Perhaps she believes that she is a new product of history and takes pride in her diverse heritage.
8. Hard work, the Spanish language, art, hospitality
9. She sees herself as part of a distinct new culture and will remake the traditions that she embodies.
10. The voices of two authors fit well with the theme of a multiracial background.

 For additional assessment, see Assessment Resources, pp. 327–328.

After You Read

Respond and Think Critically

Respond and Interpret

1. (a)Which lines in the poem spoke most directly to you? (b)In what ways are the speakers' identities similar to your own? How are they different?
2. (a)In the opening stanza, what does the speaker first say she is? (b)What attitude does the speaker seem to have toward her?
3. (a)What does the speaker say she is not? (b)What motive might she have for saying this?
4. (a)What does the speaker say her female ancestors did for her? (b)What examples illustrate this?

Analyze and Evaluate

5. How would you categorize the qualities that the speaker says that she has?

6. What is the speaker trying to express when she says "I am the child of many mothers"?
7. How do you interpret the final four lines of the poem?

Connect

8. Which traditions does the speaker view positively?
9. **Big Idea** Extending and Remaking Traditions What kinds of traditions does the speaker expect to remake?
10. **Connect to the Authors** This poem was written by two authors. How might this affect the theme of the poem? Explain.

Literary Element Motif

Motifs, or repeated ideas, words, images, or symbols, appear in both literature and other art forms. A motif can emphasize important ideas and show the connections between different parts of a work.

1. What motifs appear in this poem?
2. What typographical motif do you notice in the appearance of the poem, and why do you think the poets use it?

Review: Tone

As you learned on page 133, **tone** is the author's attitude toward the subject matter or the audience. Tone is conveyed through many elements, such as word choice, figures of speech, and imagery.

Partner Activity Meet with a classmate to discuss the authors' attitudes about their mixed heritage. How would you describe this tone? Working with your partner, create a web diagram like the one below. Fill it with details that you think create the tone of the poem.

Literary Element

1. Possible answers: repetition of "I am" and "I am not;" references to food, tableware, and dining; references to place and to roots
2. The italic type may indicate another speaker or the viewpoints of the cultures within the speaker.

Progress Check

Can students analyze motif?

If No → See Unit 7 Teaching Resources Book, p. 355.

Review: Tone

The speaker feels positively about her mixed heritage. Students' diagrams should reflect this tone.

Reading Strategy | Make Generalizations

A large number of details may make it difficult to get an overall perspective. **Generalizations** help you see the larger picture.

1. According to this poem, what are some of the issues related to racial identity that immigrants face in the United States?

2. What other issues are identified in this poem?

Vocabulary Practice

Practice with Context Clues Identify the context clues in the following sentences that help you determine the meaning of each bold-faced vocabulary word.

1. Although originally only used to describe an area of residence Jews were forced to live in, the term **ghetto** is now applied to any area settled by one exclusive minority group.

2. Many connections were lost after the **diaspora,** or scattering, of families that emigrated.

3. Most families come from large cities, but my family came from a Polish **shtetl.**

Academic Vocabulary

*The Morales' poem reflects the **complex** cultural background from which the mother and daughter are descended.*

Complex is an academic word. To further study the meaning of the word *complex,* fill out the graphic organizer below. Use a thesaurus or dictionary where necessary.

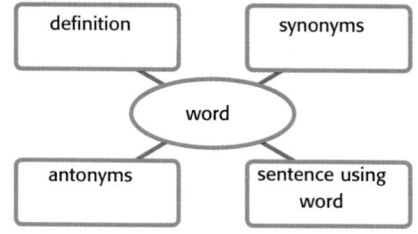

For more on academic vocabulary, see pages 53–54.

Speaking and Listening

 Oral Report

Assignment America is a country comprised of immigrants, ranging from those who arrived recently to those whose ancestors came centuries ago. Write a poem about your own cultural background based on "Ending Poem" and present it to your class. Research your cultural background to generate ideas for the poem. For your oral report, write an introduction that explains what you learned in your research and then recite the poem that is based on your findings.

Prepare For your research, you might consult online genealogical records, interview a family member, or read books about your cultural background. As you research, take note of images, words, and events that can add interest and authenticity to your poem. After you write it, craft an introduction using other background information you discovered in your research.

Incorporate Visual Aids To describe your cultural history, illustrate facts from your report with visual aids. You may want to use family photos and slides. You could also include representations of your cultural background such as pieces of art or photographs of native buildings, dress, and wildlife.

EXAMPLE:

Report As you rehearse and deliver your report, remember to use effective and appropriate eye contact, tone of voice, gestures, and facial expressions.

Evaluate Write a paragraph in which you assess how effectively you explained each of your points, and how well you incorporated your visual aids into your presentation.

ROSARIO MORALES AND AURORA LEVINS MORALES **1341**

After You Read

Assess

Reading Strategy

1. Lack of identity; separation or disrespectful treatment

2. Attitudes toward people of mixed heritage; the definition of being an American

Vocabulary

1. The sentence includes the definition of *ghetto.*

2. The sentence contains a synonym for *diaspora,* "scattering."

3. In this sentence, *shtetl* is contrasted against "large cities."

Academic Vocabulary

complex

Definition: difficult to understand, analyze, or execute

Synonyms: complicated, intricate, perplexing

Antonyms: simple, evident, obvious, easy

Sentence/Image: Trying to explain a concept as complex as nuclear physics to an eight-year-old is rather daunting.

 To create custom assessments online, go to Progress Reporter Online Assessment.

To create custom assessments using software, use ExamView Assessment Suite.

Speaking and Listening

Use these criteria when evaluating students' oral reports:

- Did students use multiple resources and specific evidence?
- Did students use effective verbal and nonverbal techniques while presenting their oral reports?
- Did students incorporate visual aids into their oral reports?

Writing Workshop

Editorial

Bellringer

Have the class brainstorm a list of technologies they think they would be unable to live without. **Ask:** Which technological advances are most important and most necessary for people to function? How does technology affect our daily lives?

Students might try freewriting about issues that interest them to explore their ideas and feelings about technology.

Summary

In this workshop, students will write and present editorials. Students will follow the stages of the writing process, including prewriting, drafting, revising, and editing. In addition, the workshop includes two mini-lessons on tone and voice and pronoun-antecedent agreement.

Learning Objectives

For pages 1342–1349

In this workshop, you will focus on the following objectives:

Writing: Writing an editorial using the writing process.

Grammar: Understanding prounoun-antecedent agreement.

▶ **Writing Process**

At any stage of a writing process, you may think of new ideas. Feel free to return to earlier stages as you write.

Prewrite

Draft

Revise

Focus Lesson: Tone and Voice

Edit and Proofread

Focus Lesson: Pronoun-Antecedent Agreement

Present

Writing Workshop

Editorial

Literature Connection Persuasive writing urges the reader to accept an opinion or to take action. For example, in *Silent Spring*, Rachel Carson warned about the use of deadly pesticides in our environment.

> *"No witchcraft, no enemy action, had silenced the rebirth of new life in this stricken world. The people had done it themselves. This town does not actually exist, but it might easily have a thousand counterparts in America and elsewhere in the world. . . . A grim specter has crept upon us almost unnoticed, and this imagined tragedy may easily become a stark reality we all shall know."*

To support her viewpoint, Carson gathered facts, told anecdotes, and employed a compelling tone. To write a strong editorial, follow the goals and strategies featured below.

Checklist: Features of Editorial Writing

Goals	Strategies
To present and support a clearly stated position or claim to a target audience	☑ State a strong, clear claim ☑ Organize ideas logically and for greatest effect on your audience ☑ Support ideas with substantial, specific, and relevant evidence ☑ Attribute sources where appropriate
To use language persuasively	☑ Use persuasive techniques ☑ Open with interest and close with rhetorical force
To anticipate and address audience concerns	☑ Acknowledge and refute opposing arguments

Print Materials

- Unit 7 Teaching Resources pp. 361–363
- Writing Kit
- Success in Writing: Research and Reports

Technology

- Literature Online: Writing Resources and Grammar Resources, www.glencoe.com
- Online Essay Grader, www.glencoe.com
- Student Presentation Builder on Student-Works Plus CD-ROM
- Media Workshop DVD
- Online Student Edition

Persuasion

Assignment: Write an Editorial

Write an editorial of about 1,500 words for your school newspaper that explains your opinion about an issue related to technology. As you work, keep your audience and purpose in mind.

Audience: classmates, teachers, and other readers of the school newspaper

Purpose: to persuade readers that your opinion about technology is valid

Real-World Connection

You use persuasive skills every day: to get what you want from parents and teachers, to win arguments with siblings, to influence peers, and to secure internships and jobs.

Analyze a Professional Model

In this newspaper editorial, Jeremy Blachman, a blogger, presents his outlook on Weblogs. *Blogs* are a shortened word for *Weblogs*—Web pages or online journals that often include personal viewpoints about a certain issue. As you read the editorial, notice how Blachman targets his likely readers—people who like to blog. Pay close attention to the comments in the margin. They point out features that you may want to include in your own editorial.

Job Posting: *The New York Times*
by Jeremy Blachman

Last month, an associate beauty editor at a women's magazine was about to resign and take a job at a teen magazine, where she had been offered a similar position. Then the two magazines discovered she was blogging about work, and she lost both jobs. The women's magazine asked her to leave immediately; the teen magazine rescinded its offer.

It's understandable that the magazines would be angry about confidential information being posted on the Internet—internal financial reports, insider stock tips, studies disproving the women's magazine's recent claim that stress makes people fat.

Except the associate beauty editor wasn't posting anything like that. No, she wrote about the "magic little bags" she received at the office "stuffed with conditioner and moisturizer and lip gloss," and her addiction to perfume. But even these innocent revelations were apparently too much for the magazines to handle.

It's likely that I narrowly escaped the same fate as the associate beauty editor. This past December, I was publicly outed as the author of a Weblog called Anonymous Lawyer, where I post about

Audience

Engage your reader by using a hook, or strong opener. A hook can be a story, a quotation, a startling fact, or another attention grabber.

Audience/Purpose

Address opposing viewpoints and present counter-arguments.

 Literature Online

Writing and Research For prewriting, drafting, and revising tools, go to glencoe.com and enter QuickPass code GLA9800u7.

Teach

Big Idea

Nature and Technology
Explain that in editorials, writers are able to express their views about the environment and technology to the general public. **Ask:** How has technology affected writing? *(Computers have made revising written work easier, and the Internet has provided writers with easy access to information and another place to publish their works.)*

Cultural History ☆

Blogs, Bloggers, Blogging One of the newest ways to publish, blogs have burgeoned on the Internet. Anyone can have a blog and publish stories, journals, articles, or other writings to be read by the general public. Blogs are so popular that a code of ethics is being created and published on the Internet. The main points in the current code are to be honest and fair, to minimize harm, and to be accountable.

Advanced Learners

DIFFERENTIATED INSTRUCTION

Opposing Opinions Advanced learners often have firm opinions based on well-developed arguments. Challenge them to write editorials from the opposition's point of view. Have students take positions with which they disagree. They may interview people with the opposing opinions or do research to develop insight into the opponents' arguments. At the conclusion of the project, invite them to discuss how this process affected their views.

English Learners

DIFFERENTIATED INSTRUCTION

Intermediate Remind English learners about the difference between fact and opinion, and that editorials use facts to support opinions. Have students review the first page of Blachman's article and identify the facts and opinions.

Writing Workshop

Editorial

Teach

Writing Skills

Counterarguments Ask: What argument against his thesis does Jeremy Blachman set forth in the paragraph beginning "But when it comes to keeping your job . . ."? *(The law does not protect anyone from being fired for any reason, no matter how silly.)*

Political History

Blogging Protection Traditional newspaper reporters are educated about what they are allowed to write and publish. They are also protected by the First Amendment's guarantee of freedom of the press. Most writers of blogs are not trained reporters, though, and the courts are not sure how traditional laws apply to this new type of publication. As the number of blogs continues to increase, lawmakers will have to address how freedom of speech applies to this technology.

Voice

Use your own personal voice to connect with your readers and appeal to their emotions.

Position/Claim

Lead up smoothly and logically to your thesis and state it clearly.

Persuasive Techniques

Use effective word choice, repetition, and hyperbole to persuade.

Support

Use detailed evidence, examples, and reasoning to support your claim.

Word Choice

Consider the connotations of the words you choose. For example, the word *honest* appeals to the reader's sense of ethics.

life inside a corporate law firm. It's fiction, but many of the stories are inspired by events from the summer I spent at a law firm between my second and third years of law school. Had the firm discovered the blog while I was there, I'm guessing they would have fired me. And under current law, they would have had every right to, no matter that I wasn't writing about real people, real cases or anything that would expose the firm to liability.

Given my own blogging experience, I feel that the natural argument for me to make would be that employers shouldn't be able to fire bloggers simply for having a blog, and that the law should protect us.

But when it comes to keeping your job—at least in the private sector—the law hardly protects anyone. You can be fired for being ugly, you can be fired for being left-handed, you can be fired for something you say to your secretary. And if you can be fired for something you say to your own secretary, it seems silly to say you shouldn't be able to be fired for something you post on the Internet for everyone else's secretary to read.

Besides, there are good reasons employers might want to fire people with Weblogs. Surely it's not great for the work environment if your boss finds out that you are telling the world what a jerk he is. If you're revealing trade secrets or confidential information, clearly your employer has a right to be upset. Even if you are writing innocent content, the mere fact that there's an employee in the ranks who is communicating something to a larger audience can be legitimately scary to companies that are used to controlling the information that gets out.

But here's the problem: Weblogs are worth protecting. It used to be that if you wanted to know what it was like to work for a law firm or a beauty magazine, you had to have a friend on the inside. But now that everyone can publish online, we can get these incredible glimpses into worlds we might otherwise never get to see. People across the world can share stories, commiserate and connect with each other. Potential employees can see beyond the marketing pitches.

If no one was reading, employers wouldn't be concerned. There's a demand for the first-person narratives people are writing about their jobs. There's nowhere else to go to create honest conversation about the working world.

So maybe it does make sense that the law should provide special protection for bloggers, because of the social benefits Weblogs provide. The simplest place to start would be to put the burden on

Reading Practice

Persuasion Persuasive writing attempts to influence readers to think or act in a particular way. Writers use appeals to logic or emotion, entreaty, sales techniques, and other methods. After students read "Job Posting: *The New York Times*," have them identify some of the ways in which Blachman tries to persuade readers. Discuss whether his methods are effective.
Ask: How has Blachman influenced your thoughts and ideas about blogs?

employers to show actual harm, if they are firing someone because of her Weblog.

This would protect the kind of innocent revelations that bloggers like the associate beauty editor make on their sites, while still giving employers rights if their employees are revealing secrets, disclosing client and customer information or otherwise driving business away. In addition, companies should create Weblog policies that let employees know what management feels is off limits for public consumption.

In any case, blogs may not hurt companies as much as they fear. On Anonymous Lawyer, I paint a frightening picture of life at a law firm. People trip each other in the halls for fun, lawyers work from the hospital while giving birth and no one ever gets a weekend off. Yet a number of law students, not realizing that my blog is fiction, have assumed that the law firm I write about actually exists and have sent me résumés, wanting to work there. Maybe the truth wouldn't be as harmful as some of these employers think. Maybe it's O.K. to let people write about their jobs.

Or maybe it's just too risky for us to know that beauty editors get free nail polish.

Reading-Writing Connection Think about the writing techniques that you have just encountered and try them out in the editorial you write.

Prewrite

Choose an Issue and Gather Ideas Take a stand on a technological issue that concerns you. Consider opposing arguments. Then work with a small group to develop a pro-and-con chart like the one below:

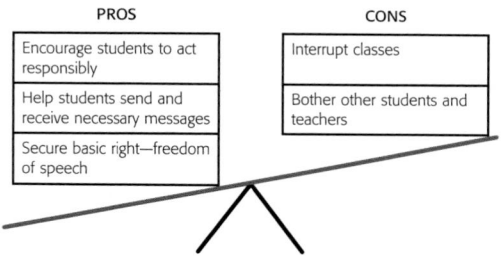

Cell Phones in School

PROS	CONS
Encourage students to act responsibly	Interrupt classes
Help students send and receive necessary messages	Bother other students and teachers
Secure basic right—freedom of speech	

Persuasion

Tone
Convey a thoughtful, logical tone throughout the editorial.

Organization
End your editorial memorably. Restate your thesis; write a clincher statement; make a final logical, emotional, or ethical appeal; or issue a call to action.

Persuasive Techniques
Use repetition, hyperbole, irony, and other persuasive techniques.

Persuasive Techniques
Use persuasive techniques like these your editorial:

Repetition: Create emphasis through purposeful repetition.

Word Choice: Select words with especially positive or negative connotations to make a point.

Hyperbole: Exaggerate or overstate your claims or your evidence to stir your audience's feelings.

Irony: Say the opposite of what you mean for added effect.

Rhetorical Question: Ask a question with an obvious answer.

WRITING WORKSHOP **1345**

Writing Workshop

Editorial

Teach

Writing Process

Prewrite Remind students that prewriting always includes considering one's purpose for writing and one's audience. **Ask:** What is your purpose for writing your editorial? *(Possible answer: to get readers to accept an opinion about or take action on an issue related to technology)* Who is your audience? *(Students may say that their audience is their teacher and their fellow students.)*

Writer's Technique ☆

Effective Conclusions Ask: How does Blachman make his ending effective? *(He uses humor and irony to show that blogs are not usually harmful.)* How does the last sentence hark back to the beginning of the editorial? *(It refers to the woman discussed at the beginning of the article, who lost her job.)*

Approaching Level

DIFFERENTIATED INSTRUCTION

SMALL GROUP

Emerging Help students brainstorm topics for their editorials. Group students with similar interests and have them list the pros and cons for their topics on a graphic organizer. Have them determine the best resources to use to research their topics.

Established Once students have selected topics for their editorials, have them freewrite their ideas about the subject. Then help them organize their work by suggesting that they use separate note cards for each of the pro and con arguments they will use in their editorials.

English Learners

DIFFERENTIATED INSTRUCTION

Advanced Have students analyze the end of Blachman's blog. **Ask:** How does Blachman convey the appropriate tone for persuasive writing? *(The words pro-tect, rights, and policies convey a serious tone).* What makes the ending effective? *(It brings all the elements together.)*

Editorial

Teach

Writing Skills

Organization After students complete their outlines, have them consider how they will organize their arguments. Explain that they can organize arguments in one of these ways:

- Begin with the most convincing evidence and end with the least convincing.
- Build from the least powerful evidence to the strongest.

After students have chosen a plan, have them number each piece of evidence on their outline in the order in which they will use it.

Audience/Purpose

Answer: *Writer concedes that students' cell phones can disrupt classes; a ringing phone bothers others.*

Map Out Your Editorial

> **Introduction**
> - Create interest.
> - Introduce the topic.
> - Narrow the topic.
> - State the thesis.

> **Body Paragraph(s)**
> - Support your opinion.
> - Respond to counterarguments.

> **Conclusion**
> - End memorably.

Writing Frames

As you read the workshop model, think about the writer's use of the following frames:

- It's understandable that _____. No one is arguing that _____. Just about everyone agrees that _____.

- For this plan to work, _____ would need to _____.

- For all these reasons, it's time to change _____.

Consider using frames like these in your own editorial.

State Your Opinion Study your graphic organizer. Decide what you want to say about the issue. In most persuasive writing, a good way to organize an opinion statement or thesis is by using a sentence structure like this one:

_____ should _____
because _____.

However your thesis is structured, it should clearly state your opinion and concisely sum up the basic reasons for that opinion.

Talk About Your Ideas Meet with a partner. Read your opinion statement aloud. Then, briefly discuss the reasons for your opinion. As you do so, listen to your own voice. How do you sound as you discuss this topic? What makes you most excited or passionate as you explain your ideas? What specific words, what tone, and what kinds of sentences do you use to convey your opinion and feelings? To develop your writing voice, listen to your own speaking voice so that you can remember what you said and how you said it.

Make an Organizational Plan Outline your editorial by writing how you might begin, what main points you might address, where you might state your opinion, and how you might conclude.

▶ Focus on getting the reader's attention and state your thesis in the first paragraph. You might experiment with placing your thesis in another paragraph, but make sure the thesis does not disrupt the logical flow of ideas.

▶ Win your readers over by sounding logical. Contest opposing arguments as you build support for your own opinion. Present reasons, examples, anecdotes, facts, statistics, and other relevant details.

▶ Wrap up your editorial with a compelling conclusion and a call to action.

Draft

Let Your Ideas Flow Drafting is the time for transferring your ideas to sentences and paragraphs. As you write, don't get distracted by spelling, grammar, and punctuation errors you might make. Instead, focus on the single task of getting your words on the page in an order that makes sense.

Analyze a Workshop Model

Here is a final draft of an editorial. Read the editorial and answer the questions in the margin. Use the answers to these questions to guide you as you write.

Writing Practice

Beginning and Ending Like any other piece of writing, an editorial should open with an idea that grabs readers' interest and end with one that is memorable. Techniques for creating both are the same: a provocative or startling statement, a relevant question, an anecdote, a definition, a question, or a statement of belief. Ask students if their opening and closing sentences illustrate any of these techniques. Have them write several opening and closing sentences and then choose the ones that best fit the issue and the audience.

Cell Phone Logic

Last week at Madison High, Lauren Eckler was suspended for breaking a rule—sneaking her cell phone into school. After her phone rang during Mr. Palmerino's biology class, he sent her to the office. There Mrs. Wu promptly suspended Lauren for two days because it was her third offense. Who was on the phone when Lauren's phone rang? It was her mother, asking Lauren to pick up her little brother after school. Mrs. Eckler was frantic. She had had an unexpected meeting and had been unable able to reach Lauren all day. Lauren's mother was worried.

It's understandable that Mr. Palmerino would not want his or her class interrupted. No one is arguing that students *shouldn't* turn their cell phones off during class. Plenty of students at this school groan when somebody's phone rings at the wrong time.

Nevertheless, the cell phone rule at Madison High should be changed. The current policy of having students "bank" their phones at the office before first period and retrieve them at the end of each day is unfair and a huge waste of time for office staff. It keeps students from getting important information and robs them of the basic right to freedom of speech.

Students have a right to have cell phones. Students need to keep in touch with their families. They need to make plans with friends. Many also need to get or send messages to employers during the day. If students had access to their phones, their calls could be handled during times of day when they are not in class. For example, students could phone while changing class, eating lunch, or taking free periods. There might also be specific times when using a cell phone would be acceptable in the homeroom. Using the phone at these times would probably not bother anyone else.

For this plan to work, students would need to act responsibly. They would have to turn off their cell phones whenever they entered a class. Teachers could help them develop this habit by reminding them—just as people say at plays, concerts, and other gatherings—"Please turn off your cell phones." Students are mature enough to understand and follow that request.

Instead, students are treated like children or prisoners. They don't have the right to their own property. They are not trusted to store their phones in their lockers or shut them off during class. They are denied the chance to send and receive important and necessary messages. In a place where students are learning how to act as mature adults, it is ironic that they are not given the chance to use their cell phones responsibly.

For all these reasons, it's time to change the cell phone policy at Madison High. Students should be allowed to carry their own phones and trusted to use them responsibly. Most of all, students should be able to talk to their families, get important messages, and practice good citizenship.

Introduction
How does this opening sentence create interest?

Audience/Persuasive Techniques
How does the writer address the opposing viewpoint? What persuasive technique appears in the final sentence?

Claim
What is the writer's opinion? How clearly is it stated?

Support
What reasons, facts, and examples does the writer offer?

Tone
What is the writer's tone?

Word Choice/Persuasive Technique
Which words in this sentence pack an emotional punch? What other persuasive techniques doex the writer use here?

Conclusion
How does the writer conclude? What makes the final paragraph effective?

English Learners

DIFFERENTIATED INSTRUCTION

Intermediate Help English learners develop their own editorials by analyzing the structure of the arguments presented in the sample editorial. Have students create a two-column chart with the headings *Pro* and *Con*. Have them list each argument in the editorial in the appropriate column and match it with its counterpart in the opposite column. Have students work in pairs to review their lists for completeness and accuracy.

Writing Workshop

Editorial

Teach

Writing Skills

Introduction
Answer: *It might outrage readers to learn that someone was suspended for having a cell phone, making them eager to read on.*

Audience/Persuasive Techniques
Answer: *The writer concedes that students' cell phones can disrupt classes; a ringing phone bothers others.*

Claim
Answer: *The cell-phone rule at Madison High should be changed. It is clearly stated.*

Support
Answer: *Students have a right to cell phones; they need the ability to be in contact with family, friends, and employers. There are times during the day when cell-phone use would not be intrusive.*

Tone
Answer: *Reasonable*

Word Choice/Persuasive Technique
Answer: Children *and* prisoners. *The writer uses ethical and emotional appeals, logical reasoning, and a reasonable voice.*

Conclusion
Answer: *The writer concludes by repeating key points. The writer effectively links the plea to family and civic responsibility.*

Writing Workshop

Editorial

Teach

Writing Skills

Revise As students revise their drafts, have them check that their arguments are complete. If their arguments are weak, students may need to elaborate on their ideas. Emphasize that elaboration is the addition of *relevant* information.
Say: If you elaborate on points in your editorial, be sure that the information you add explains, clarifies, or extends those points instead of making new points.

Writer's Technique ☆

Tone and Voice Have students look at the draft version of the excerpt from "Cell Phone Logic."
Ask: Why is the tone of the first sentence inappropriate? *(The tone is too harsh.)* How is the tone and voice inconsistent in the rest of the excerpt? *(The second and third sentences sound informal, whereas the last sentence sounds formal.)*

Traits of Strong Writing

Include these traits of strong writing to express your ideas effectively.

Ideas
Organization
Voice
Word Choice
Sentence Fluency
Conventions
Presentation

For more information on using the Traits of Strong Writing, see pages R30–R32.

Word Choice

This academic vocabulary word appears in the student model:

specific (spi si´ fik) *adj.* related or pertaining to one particular person, place, or event; 2. not ambiguous, accurate. *There might also be specific times when using a cell phone would be acceptable in homeroom.* Using academic vocabulary may help strengthen your writing. Try to use one or two academic vocabulary words in your editorial. See the complete list on pages R89–R91.

Revise

Peer Review Ask a peer reviewer to read your editorial and to identify the opinion statement. Then ask your reviewer to comment on parts that seem most persuasive or effective and parts that seem least convincing. Have your reviewer explain comments by referring to the traits of strong writing.

Use the checklist below to evaluate and strengthen each other's writing.

Checklist

- ☑ Do you state a strong, clear claim?
- ☑ Do you organize ideas logically and effectively for your audience?
- ☑ Do you support ideas with substantial, specific, relevant evidence?
- ☑ Do you attribute sources where appropriate?
- ☑ Do you use persuasive diction and techniques such as repetition?
- ☑ Do you open with interest and close with rhetorical force?
- ☑ Do you acknowledge and refute opposing arguments?

▶ Focus Lesson

Tone and Voice

Tone refers to the emotions or attitude an author expresses. For editorial writing, you probably want the tone to be logical, respectful, and thoughtful. **Voice** includes the unique way you use language to convey the "real person" behind the words. Notice how the writer of "Cell Phone Logic" revised the tone and style.

Draft:

It's totally ridiculous for students not to have their cell phones. Like everyone else, they need to call home. They need to call their friends!!! The need to contact their place of employment also necessitates the use of a phone.

Revision:

Students have a right to have cell phones.[1] Like everyone else, students need to keep in touch with their families. They need to make plans with friends. Many also need to get or send messages to employers during the school day.[2]

   1: **Appropriate Tone**   **2:** **Consistent Tone and Voice**

1348 UNIT 7 INTO THE TWENTY-FIRST CENTURY

Listening and Speaking Practice

Feedback Writers may want to ask peer reviewers to consider specific questions, such as the following:

- Which evidence is most convincing?
- What additional evidence could I include?
- What opposing arguments should I respond to?

Emphasize that writers need not accept every suggested change. They should listen to all comments and incorporate the ideas they think will improve their editorials.

1348

Edit and Proofread

Get It Right When you have completed the final draft of your essay, proofread for errors in grammar, usage, mechanics, and spelling. Refer to the Language Handbook, pages R42–R61, as a guide.

Focus Lesson

Pronoun-Antecedent Agreement

A pronoun must agree in number, gender, and person with its **antecedent,** or word it refers to.

Original: The plural pronoun *their* does not agree with its singular antecedent *student.*

Most of all, any student should be able to talk to their parents.

Improved: Edit the sentence so that the pronoun agrees with its antecedent. You can change either the pronoun or the antecedent.

Most of all, any student should be able to talk to his or her parents.
Most of all, students should be able to talk to their parents.

Original: The plural pronoun *their* does not agree with its singular antecedent *Everyone.*

Everyone would have to turn off their cell phones each time they entered a class.

Improved: Make both the pronoun and its antecedent plural.

They would have to turn off their cell phones each time they entered a class.

Present

 Follow Models and Guidelines Newspapers usually have guidelines for editorials. Find out what they are before submitting your essay. As always, neatly word-processed work is a plus.

Persuasion

Peer Review Tips

A classmate may ask you to read his or her editorial. Take your time and jot down notes as you read so you can give constructive feedback. Use the following questions to get started:

- Does the writer use detailed evidence, examples, and reasoning to support the claim?

- Does the writer use effective persuasive techniques?

Word-Processing Tips

Your word choices should require no excess formatting, such as underscoring, italics, or boldface, to give them emphasis. Similarly, avoid excess formatting and flourishes for the title of your essay, your name, and the page numbers.

Writer's Portfolio

Place a copy of your editorial in your portfolio to review later.

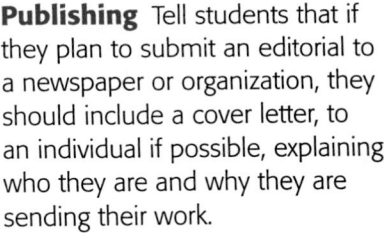
Writing and Research For editing and publishing tools, go to glencoe.com and enter QuickPass code GLA9800u7.

Teach

Writing Skills

Indefinite Pronouns Many students struggle with making pronouns agree with their antecedents. The following indefinite pronouns are considered singular: *anybody, anyone, anything, each, either, everybody, everyone, everything, neither, nobody, none, no one, somebody, someone,* and *something.* If one of these pronouns serves as an antecedent, the pronoun that refers to it must also be singular.

Writer's Technique ☆

Publishing Tell students that if they plan to submit an editorial to a newspaper or organization, they should include a cover letter, to an individual if possible, explaining who they are and why they are sending their work.

Approaching Level
DIFFERENTIATED INSTRUCTION

Emerging Help students organize their ideas before writing and revising their drafts. Have students put each main idea or argument at the top of a separate sheet of paper and then list the supporting details they want to include for each one. Remind them to verify that their supporting details are facts, reasons, or examples.

Have them mark each item as F (fact), R (reason), or E (example). Have them exchange their papers with a partner to check their organizational structures.

English Learners
DIFFERENTIATED INSTRUCTION

Intermediate Have students note which indefinite pronouns they used in their editorials. Ask them to identify whether the pronouns are singular or plural and to check their agreement with their antecedents.

Focus

Summary

In this workshop, students will learn techniques for planning, rehearsing, participating in, and listening to a debate.

Teach

Listening Skills

Types of Propositions To help students write their own effective propositions, give them practice in recognizing types of propositions. Read the following sentences aloud and have students tell you whether each is a proposition of fact, value, or policy.

- The jury system should be abolished. *(policy)*
- Three years of high school English courses are adequate for a basic education. *(value)*
- Freedom of speech is protected by the Bill of Rights. *(fact)*

 For help with creating presentations, see Student Presentation Builder on StudentWorks Plus.

Learning Objectives

For pages 1350–1351
In this workshop, you will focus on the following objective:

Speaking and Listening: Participating in a debate.

Types of Propositions

A **proposition of fact** states that something is or is not true, such as "Fast foods contribute to obesity."

A **proposition of value** expresses a judgment of a person, place, thing, idea, or event, such as, "Fast food presents a danger to the people of Madison."

A **proposition of policy** suggests a course of action, set of rules, or a law, such as, "The town of Madison should not allow any new fast-food restaurants."

A **proposition of problem** asks a question, such as, "What should public officials in Madison do about the problem of obesity?"

Speaking, Listening, and Viewing Workshop

Debate

Literature Connection Rachel Carson's *Silent Spring* caused a dramatic change in the way people think about the environment. One reason for this effect was Carson's persuasive skill. In this workshop, you will learn how to present and defend your own opinions—as well as how to anticipate and respond to counterarguments—in a formal debate.

> **Assignment** Conduct a formal debate on a topic that you or your team members presented in your editorials.

Plan Your Presentation

When you wrote your editorial, you were persuading an audience of readers. When you debate, your goal is to persuade an audience of listeners.

A **debate** is a formal persuasive-speaking competition. To debate, you use some of the same skills that you have already developed to write persuasively. In addition, you must learn new skills, rules, and vocabulary specific to debating.

- Form a group of two, four, or six students. Read your editorials aloud. Choose one with particularly strong positive arguments (pros) and counterarguments (cons) to re-create as a debate.
- Develop a proposition based on the editorial. A **proposition** is a formal statement of an issue. A proposition is usually phrased like this: *Resolved: That the policy of confiscating cell phones at Madison High School should be stopped immediately.*
- Form two teams: **affirmative**, or those in favor of the proposition; and **negative**, or those against it.
- As separate teams, prepare your brief. A **brief** is a complete outline of the debate. It includes the following:
  - the proposition
  - the key ideas of the debate, in order of importance
  - arguments for and against each key idea
  - evidence (with sources cited) that supports each of your arguments and counters each of your opponent's arguments

Speaking, Listening, and Viewing Practice

Analyze Persuasive Propositions
Have students watch and analyze a television news program in which panelists argue for or against a proposition. Students should take notes on the persuasive techniques, reasoning, and proof the panelists use to argue their viewpoints. Invite students to share their observations and analyses with the rest of the class, restating the proposition and categorizing it as a proposition of fact, value, policy, or problem.

Having a thorough brief will help prepare you for a successful debate. To win a debate, however, you must provide enough proof to establish your position and refute, or prove wrong, your opponent's position by

- challenging the quality or credibility of your opponent's evidence
- noting where your opponent's evidence is insufficient in quantity
- challenging the logic of your opponent's reasoning

In a traditional formal debate, both sides make opening and closing **constructive speeches** of ten minutes each, in this order: first affirmative, first negative, second affirmative, second negative. After a short intermission, **rebuttal speeches** of five minutes each begin in the opposite order. The rebuttal gives you a chance to rebuild your case. Although you cannot introduce a new argument during the rebuttal, you can do the following:

- restate and expand your previous arguments
- offer more evidence and reasoning to counter objections
- point out weaknesses in your opponent's arguments

Rehearse

Review and rehearse the format of your debate as a group. Establish when each person will speak and how much time he or she will have.

As separate affirmative and negative teams, rehearse your opening, closing, and rebuttal speeches. As you rehearse, reword answers to sound more reasonable and coach each other to speak in a tone appropriate to a formal debate. Avoid exaggerated emotion, sarcasm, or ridicule, and refrain from personal attacks.

Techniques for Listening to and Evaluating a Debate

☑ **Keep an Open Mind** Try not to prejudge the speaker or the argument. Give all speakers and both sides of the argument equal and unbiased attention.

☑ **Listen Purposefully** In a debate, your purpose for listening is to identify the arguments and counterarguments and to judge their worth.

☑ **Take Notes** Note what the arguments are and how well you think that each was delivered, proved, or disproved.

☑ **Listen for Persuasive Devices** Separate logical, reasoned arguments from illogical arguments. Listen for and dismiss arguments that attack the person, arguments that reduce the topic to a case of false either-or reasoning, present false cause-and-effect relationships, and make false generalizations or overgeneralizations.

Go Online

Read, listen to, or view a real debate. Note that most debaters treat each other with respect. While viewing a debate, you might also note that debaters use good posture, listen thoughtfully, and speak carefully.

Speaking Frames

Consider using the following frames in your debate:

- These facts support our assertion: first, _____; second, _____; and third, _____.

- That argument is illogical because _____.

- How could it possibly be true that _____?

Presentation Tips

Use the following checklist to evaluate your debate.

- Did you prepare a complete brief?

- Did you present strong, well-reasoned arguments?

- Did you effectively refute your opponent by challenging the quality, quantity, and credibility of your opponent's evidence, as well as your logic of your opponent's reasoning?

 Literature Online

Speaking, Listening, and Viewing For project ideas, templates, and presentation tips, go to glencoe.com and enter QuickPass code GLA9800u7.

English Learners

DIFFERENTIATED INSTRUCTION

Intermediate Have students bring in advertisements from magazines or other media that use different persuasive devices. Ask students to identify the type of persuasive device used and rate its effectiveness.

Advanced Ask students to watch a courtroom drama, a talk show, and a newscast. Ask them to identify and compare and contrast the types of propositions they observed in these three types of programs.

Teach

Speaking Skills

Voice Before students rehearse their debate, explain how their voices affect their speeches. Point out that people listening to a speech will become bored if the speaker's voice is monotone. Encourage students to do the following:

- practice changing pitch and tone to communicate enthusiasm and other emotions
- be sure the volume of their voice is such that every person in the room can hear clearly
- eliminate distracting filler words, such as *uh, um, you know,* and *OK*

Organization Clues Since it can be hard for an audience to follow an oral argument, speakers need to provide clues to the logic and organization of their speeches. For example, a speaker who has three reasons why cell phones should be confiscated at school should tell the audience that three points will be made and enumerate the points as they come up: "The first reason cell phones should be confiscated is . . . ," "A second reason is . . . ," and so on.

Self-Evaluation After completing the debate, have students write a reflection and evaluation of their performance in the activity.

Teach

Listening Skills

Sound Bites Explain to students that journalists interview people who can contribute to the story they are writing. Quotes are an important part of any story, lending credibility and color. Because news stories in electronic media are typically shorter than print stories, sources may have their words cut down to a short statement known as a "sound bite." As a result, many public speakers have learned how to speak in sound bites. **Ask:** What are some sound bites that you have heard in political campaigns? *(Students may think of quotes from historical figures or people in the news.)*

1352

Learning Objectives

For pages 1352–1357

In this workshop, you will focus on the following objectives.

Media Literacy:
Analyzing reasoning strategies and propaganda in print and nonprint media.
Explaining how text features, such as captions and illustrations, aid the reader's understanding.

Media Workshop

Analyze Media Messages

Connect to Literature The Vietnam War stirred the conscience of many American writers who expressed their views in poetry and fiction. Their works were often published in books and magazines—forms of print media. During the late 1960s protesters against this war gained a powerful ally—the electronic media. Television especially played an important role in molding public opinion. More than 60 million viewers watched the live combat on the nightly news.

Forms of Media

Media messages are communications that reach you in a variety of forms—print and electronic. **Print media** are conveyed through printed words or images, such as newspapers, magazines, books, and billboards. **Electronic media** include radio, television, CDs, DVDs, movies, videotapes, documentary films, and the Internet.

The form of a media message affects its meaning and the way you, the audience, interpret it. Imagine watching a political debate on television and then reading the news coverage of the same debate. Each form of media may leave you with a different impression.

The Kennedy-Nixon debate of 1960 illustrates how the form of media can influence audiences' interpretations. Though most radio listeners declared Richard Nixon the winner, John F. Kennedy won the TV image contest. To most TV viewers, Kennedy looked youthful and self-confident, while Nixon appeared tired and tense.

Media Strategies

Many media messages often seem to capture real life. All media messages, though, reflect the creator's viewpoints and are intended to shape the audience's attitudes. How can you make informed opinions as you read, listen to, or view the media in your everyday life? Refer to the checklist to help you analyze the media strategies.

Strategy		Questions to Ask Yourself
source	☑	Who created the media form? How does the source affect the message?
purpose	☑	What is the goal for creating the media form? To inform? To persuade? To entertain?
word choice	☑	How does the language express the purpose of the message to the audience? Does the use of figurative language heighten the impact of the message?
cultural elements	☑	Does the message also aim to transmit culture—values that reflect a particular group or nation?
symbols	☑	Does the message use symbols that represent popular ideas or values?
target audience	☑	How is the content geared to the intended audience? Are stereotypes of people, such as children or teenagers, used to sway the audience?
design elements and/or film techniques	☑	How are visual elements or film techniques used to communicate a message or influence a viewer's response?

> **Focus Lesson**

Persuasive Techniques: Logical Fallacies

Persuasive techniques used in the media urge readers, viewers, or listeners to agree with a viewpoint or to take action. Some media messages include logical fallacies, or errors in reasoning, to sway audiences. Messages with faulty reasoning may rely on propaganda—the use of ideas, information, or rumors to spread information and to trigger emotional responses. Try to spot the following types of logical fallacies in all forms of media:

- **ad hominem** shifting attention away from a person's views by attacking the person
- **false cause** inaccurately drawing a cause-and-effect relationship between two events that follow one after another
- **red herring** dodging an issue by changing the subject
- **overgeneralization** making a sweeping statement without solid supporting evidence
- **bandwagon** urging the audience to think or act like everyone else
- **either-or fallacy** presenting only two contrasting sides of a situation or a solution instead of showing a broader range of choices

Activity

Make a Chart

Use the Media Strategies chart on this page as a guide to examine a form of print or electronic media. Create a chart in which you add a third column that answers the questions in the second column.

MEDIA WORKSHOP **1353**

Teach

Reading Skills

Media Strategies Have students discuss some of the ways they can analyze media messages. **Ask:** When you are listening to the radio, how do you know whether you are listening to a show or an advertisement? (*Ads may use a different voice, be louder, have repetitive music, or be announced as coming from a "sponsor."*) **Ask:** If you heard someone on television say that water and soda have the same health benefits, what questions might you ask? (*Does this person have medical training? What studies support this idea? What type of show is this person on? Who advertises on the show?*)

Activity

Students should add to the third column of their charts as they work through the Media Workshop. Their final charts will guide them while developing their own multimedia presentations.

Language History ☆

Red Herring The term red herring may have come from an old practice of dragging a smoked herring across a trail to throw hunting dogs off the track. Now it is used figuratively to refer to an idea that is presented to distract attention.

Teach

Listening Skills

Irony Remind students that ironic language conveys a meaning that is opposite from its literal meaning. Images add another layer that can create irony. **Ask:** If you consider only the image presented in this campaign ad, what is its literal message? *(Students should note the hopefulness and new beginnings conveyed by the image of the child.)* **Ask:** What message does the sound in the ad convey? *(The countdown in a man's voice and a bomb explosion convey danger.)* **Ask:** Why is this combination ironic? *(The picture would seem to convey innocence, but instead it conveys the fragility that is threatened by bombs.)*

Activity

1. Students' individual responses will vary.

2. Students may say that viewers might be shocked or frightened.

3. Students should provide specific examples and identify specific strategies for each example.

Activity

Speaking and Listening

Meet in groups of four to discuss the following questions:

1. What visual representations and language did you find most striking? Why?

2. How might TV viewers react to the special effects—sounds of an exploding bomb?

3. What other Internet or TV political campaign ads have you seen that had a powerful impact on you as a future voter? Describe the ads and identify the media strategies. (Refer to the chart on page 1353.)

Language: Irony

The girl counts the petals as a playful numbers game; the man counts backward to time the explosion of a bomb.

Logical Fallacy

The either/or reasoning assumes only two choices—love or death.

Media Impact: **Campaign Ad**

Build Background In 1964, President Lyndon B. Johnson defeated Republican candidate Senator Barry Goldwater in the race for the White House. Johnson's TV campaign ad "Daisy Girl" suggested a chilling message: If elected president, Goldwater might launch a nuclear attack. Try to picture watching the ad on television as you analyze the image and the transcript below.

Film Techniques

The close-up of the girl's face arouses compassion.

Symbols

Both children and daisies often represent innocence.

TRANSCRIPT

SMALL CHILD: [with flower]: One, two, three, four, five, seven, six, six, eight, nine, nine . . .

MAN: Ten, nine, eight, seven, six, five, four, three, two, one, zero.

[Sounds of exploding bomb.]

PRESIDENT JOHNSON: These are the stakes: To make a world in which all children can live, or to go into the darkness. We must either love each other, or we must die.

ANNOUNCER: Vote for President Johnson on November 3rd. The stakes are too high for you to stay home.

Reading Practice

SMALL GROUP

Either/Or Reasoning After students read the transcript and consider the images in the ad, have them list the words and ideas that the ad associates with each side of the either/or choice that is presented. *(Johnson: flower, child, live, love; Goldwater: countdown, bomb, explosion, darkness, die)* Have students work in small groups to form an either/or argument that they might present in order to convince someone of their point of view. Remind students that this type of reasoning is sometimes humorous when its flaws are revealed.

Media Impact: **Political Cartoon**

Build Background Political cartoonists are illustrators who combine pictures with words to express opinions about current events. The setting of the political cartoon below is the "oval chamber"—the oval office in the White House where the U.S. president conducts business. However, note that the office resembles a torture chamber from the Middle Ages. The political cartoonist uses persuasive techniques, such as caricature and symbol, to comment on the media and the presidency.

Symbol and Caricature

The American bald eagle is the national emblem of the United States but here looks like a vulture.

Symbol and Caricature

Uncle Sam, the bearded man with the top hat and striped pants, symbolizes the United States, but here he holds a whip.

Symbol

The TV camera symbolizes the electronic media.

'Okay, bring in the new guy . . .'

Caricature

The press, or news media, assumes the form of an executioner holding a menacing, sharp-tipped pen.

Caricature

The Congress is represented as a kneeling man poking at hot coals.

Activity

Speaking and Listening

Meet in a small group to discuss the following questions:

1. What is happening in this political cartoon?

2. Who is the "new guy" portrayed in the cartoon?

3. Does the cartoon show a fair or biased portrayal of media and the government? Support your response with examples.

4. Does the cartoon influence your attitude toward national politics? Explain.

 For video presentations related to this workshop, see Media Workshop DVD.

Teach

Viewing Skills

Political Cartoon After groups of students discuss the questions, have each group present its answer to one of the questions. Have a volunteer explain the reasoning the group used to derive their answers.

Activity

1. The U.S. president's office looks like a torture chamber, which has presumably dealt harshly with "the old guy" and is ready for "the new guy." The press, the Congress, and the public are all prepared to test the mettle of the next president.

2. The "new guy" is probably the president-elect, who has not taken office yet. He is just a "guy" in a series of guys.

3. Because humor often exaggerates for effect, the cartoon shows some bias. It sympathizes with the president, who will be tested, prodded, and "tortured" by the public, Congress, and the press. However, the characters look somewhat amused and amusing rather than threatening. Uncle Sam is dressed as if he is the master of ceremonies in a televised circus, making the chamber look like a stage set.

4. Students answers will vary, but should refer to specific aspects of the cartoon that influenced them.

Teach

Viewing Skills

News Photograph Ask: Do you recall seeing a news photo recently that made an impression on you? Are there photos from the past that you found striking? Alternatively, show students a group of photos and have a discussion about them.

Activity

1. Students' captions will vary. Remind them to consider both the foreground and background and the relationship between the two. Students should also look at the way the light and shadow fall on the statue, and the scale of the people against the statue.

2. Students may bring up concepts such as freedom, power, symbols, immigration, perspective, or industrialization.

3. Students may be surprised to see the people looking out from the statue's crown because visitors are no longer allowed to go into this part of the statue.

4. Students' answers will vary, but should include a clear description of their views.

Media Impact: **News Photograph**

Build Background News photographers shoot pictures that grab the reader's attention and communicate information. Margaret Bourke-White, the first woman photographer to work for *Life* magazine, captures a unique image of the Statue of Liberty. This photograph was featured in an article titled "A New Way to Look at the U.S.: Camera and Helicopter Give an Exalted View of the Land."

Symbol

This view of the Statue of Liberty calls attention to its symbolic meaning—freedom. Note that the seven rays of the spiked crown represent the seven seas and the seven continents.

Camera Technique

The close-up view, shot from a helicopter, provides an unusual glimpse of sightseers peeking out of the windows of the spiked crown.

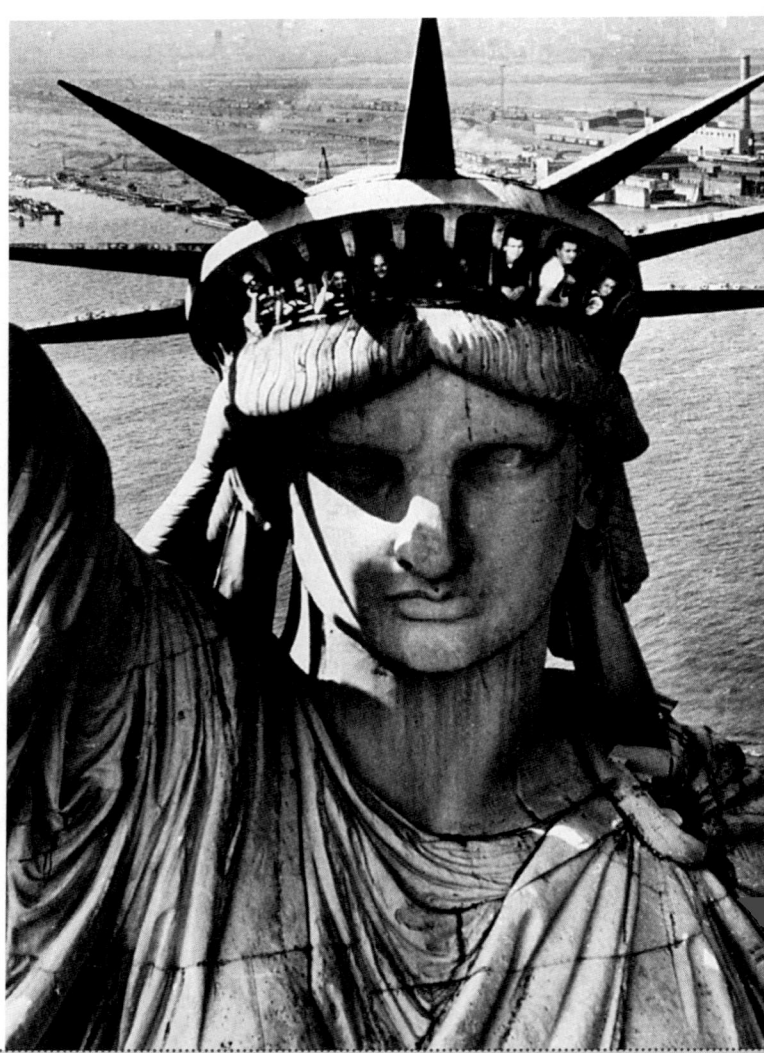

Activity

Speaking and Listening

Meet with a partner to discuss the following questions:

1. How would you describe the photograph? Write your description as a one-sentence caption.

2. What ideas or information does the photograph communicate?

3. Do any visual details in the image surprise you? Explain.

4. Does the photograph change the way you view the Statue of Liberty? Why or why not?

1356 UNIT 7 INTO THE TWENTY-FIRST CENTURY

Viewing Practice

Analyze Images Have students spend up to one hour noticing and recording the images they see, preferably outside school. For this exercise, an image can be defined as any photo, drawing, sign, logo, or electronic representation. Remind them to include everything they see, from logos on tee shirts to discarded newspapers on the train to signage on stores. Once they have reached 25 images, they can stop. Ask them to reflect on the experience in a group discussion.

Media Impact: **Public Service Announcement**

Build Background In 1969, Astronaut Neil Armstrong was the first human to set foot on the moon's surface. The public service announcement (PSA) below takes a clever spin on this historic moment:

THERE'S NOT ENOUGH ART IN OUR SCHOOLS.

NO WONDER PEOPLE THINK
LOUIS ARMSTRONG
WAS THE FIRST MAN TO
WALK ON THE MOON.

ART. ASK FOR MORE.

PSAs

PSAs persuade an audience to take action on a political, social, or cultural issue. PSAs published in newspapers and magazines resemble print ads used to sell products or services.

Headline

The opening statement makes one concise point.

Design Elements

The large, boldface type focuses the readers' attention on Louis Armstrong.

Activity

Plan a Multimedia PSA

Work in a small group to brainstorm ideas for presenting this print PSA in other media, such as television or the Internet. Think about the following points: (1) your target audience, (2) one action your audience should take, and (3) descriptions of media to include. Write a brief plan outlining your ideas.

Teach

Multimedia Presentation

Public Service Announcement
Ask: What is the difference between a PSA and an advertisement? *(Advertisers have to pay for the time or space taken up by their ad; organizations that create PSAs do not have to pay. PSAs are typically from non-profit organizations and are supposed to address a public concern.)*

 Activity

Plan a Multimedia PSA Have students list what they might add or subtract from the print version of the PSA to make it effective for electronic media. Remind them to consider length, type size, sound, animation, and visuals.

MEDIA WORKSHOP **1357**

Approaching Level

DIFFERENTIATED INSTRUCTION

Emerging Approaching level students may need help translating the print PSA into another medium. Explain that electronic media typically present ideas in smaller chunks, not expecting that people will read several paragraphs. Have them place sticky notes on those parts of the print PSA that they would retain for an electronic PSA.

Focus

The purpose of Independent Reading is to encourage students to read novels from, about, or influenced by the time period they have learned about in this unit.

Teach

Literary History ☆

Jon Krakauer *Into the Wild* is based on a true story in which Krakauer was not a participant, so the writer had to imagine some of the details. In his report of his own climb of Mt. Everest, called *Into Thin Air,* he tells a harrowing tale of an adventure that he survived but others did not. Some other climbers who were on the mountain at the same time have disagreed with parts of Krakauer's retelling. **Ask:** Is nonfiction always "a true story"? (*Students may acknowledge that any retelling of an event includes the author's slant on the story.*)

Compare Have each student choose and read one of these books or another book that offers a different perspective on the period from 1960 to the present. Suggest that students work together to compile a list of the issues treated in the books. Ask them to consider the impression someone a hundred years in the future might form of our society on the basis of this literature.

1358

Independent Reading

AS OPPORTUNITIES FOR WOMEN AND MINORITIES EXPANDED, American literature from the 1950s on drew upon a wider range of experience than ever before. In their writing, Walter Dean Myers, Jon Krakauer, and Amy Tan contribute to the diversity of voices in a changing America. Myers offers a perspective on the Vietnam War through a young soldier from Harlem. Krakauer uses an emerging form of writing, nonfiction narrative, to tell the tale of a young man who wanders into nature and never returns. Amy Tan weaves the stories of two generations of Chinese American women finding a balance between tradition and modern American life. Each text focuses on the issues involved in reshaping society to incorporate the values of an emerging generation.

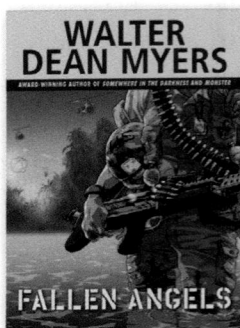

Fallen Angels

Walter Dean Myers

Nothing Richie Perry had experienced on the streets of Harlem could have prepared him for the horrors of Vietnam. Just seventeen years old, Richie is one of America's confused young GIs, thrown into a war he does not understand. Days of boredom in camp alternate with the terror of patrol. Racial tensions flare among the soldiers; friendships take root and flourish. This realistic novel about America's longest and most bitter conflict tells a story of gripping adventure and explores the nature of war and the value of human life.

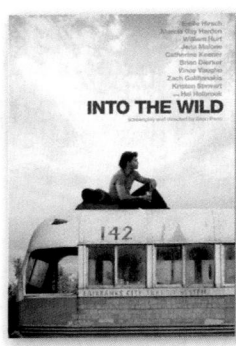

Into the Wild

Jon Krakauer

Journalist Jon Krakauer retraces the steps of Chris McCandless who traveled to Alaska after his college graduation. McCandless's journey across America leaves readers wondering why a twenty-year-old with a prosperous future would give away all his money and walk alone into the wilderness. Through the whisperings of Thoreau and Emerson, nature becomes a character in the story and a challenge too great for McCandless to endure. This book was adapted into a movie in 2007.

Teach

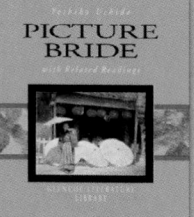

Picture Bride

Yoshiko Uchida

A young woman leaves Japan for an arranged marriage in the United States, where she faces hard work, prejudice, and difficult circumstances with courage and dignity.

A Raisin in the Sun

Lorraine Hansberry

The members of a poor African American family have conflicting ideas about how to spend a $10,000 insurance check.

Barrio Boy

Ernesto Galarza

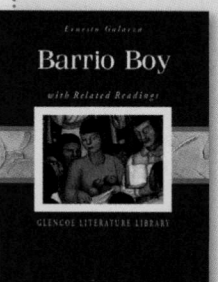

This autobiography tells the story of Galarza's youth in a Sacramento barrio, where his family moved to avoid the upheaval of the Mexican Revolution of 1910.

CRITICS' CORNER

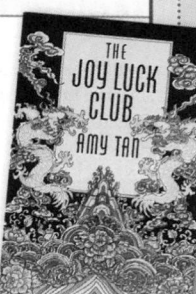

"[Tan reminds us] not just of the nightmarishness of being a woman in traditional China, but of the enormity of the confusing mental journey Chinese emigrants had to make."

—Orville Schell, *The New York Times*, 1989

The Joy Luck Club

Amy Tan

This novel by first-generation Chinese American Amy Tan draws on her family history. In the novel, four female Chinese immigrants meet regularly to play mahjong, eat, gossip, raise money, and support one another. Skillfully interweaving the voices of the immigrant mothers and their Chinese American daughters, Tan confronts issues of gender, generation, culture, and family in this powerful and touching narrative.

 Write a Letter

Write a reflective letter to the author explaining how the book changed your way of thinking about the world or yourself. The purpose of the letter should be to explain the effect of the book, rather than to compliment the author. For example, write, *This book has changed the way I _____.* Refer to specific passages in your letter.

Literary History ☆

Yoshiko Uchida During World War II, Uchida and her family spent time in a California internment camp along with other Japanese Americans. In 1952 she traveled to Japan to research Japanese folk tales. Through her work, she developed a deep feeling for her Japanese heritage. *Picture Bride* tells the story of many Japanese women who came to America in the 20th century.

Glencoe Literature Library

Glencoe Literature Library offers an extensive collection of hardcover books that help you encourage your students to read independently. Choose among the more than 120 full-length literary works—novels, novellas, plays, and nonfiction. Each book includes related readings from a broad range of genres. Go to www.glencoe.com for more information.

 For access to all study guides for the Glencoe Literature Library, see the Literature Library Teacher Resources CD-ROM.

 To create customized reading lists from a database of more than 30,000 titles, use BookLink K-12 CD-ROM.

Writing

Have students use sticky notes as they read to flag passages that affect them strongly. Evaluate letters for the following:

- a clear description of the change in their feelings or actions that resulted from reading the book
- specific references to parts of the book that influenced the change
- effective voice, word choice, and sentence variety
- attention to grammar and spelling conventions

1359

Assessment

Focus

Bellringer

Say: Test-taking skills are beneficial throughout a person's life. Some jobs require you to take a test during the interview process and another test to be eligible for advancement.

Have students brainstorm a list of other instances where they will be required to take tests outside of school.

Summary

Assessment Explain to students that this assessment is intended to reinforce general test-taking strategies as well as to test the skills covered in the unit. They will first be asked to read a nonfiction selection and a poem and answer comprehension, context, and inference questions. Then they will be asked to respond to paragraph-improvement questions, and finally, to write an essay.

Skills Practice

Read Silently Tell students that during a test, they will have to read the passages silently, and they will have to avoid being distracted by people and noises around them. Encourage students to check their comprehension by mentally summarizing what they have read after each paragraph or stanza. Students can also jot down brief notes in the margins of a test booklet or on a sheet of scratch paper to remind them of information in the passages and to clarify ideas. Remind students that they will need to read difficult passages more slowly.

Assessment

English Language Arts

Reading: Nonfiction and Poetry

Carefully read the following two passages. Use context clues to help define any words with which you are unfamiliar. In each selection, pay close attention to the author's purpose, main idea, and uses of literary or rhetorical devices. Then, on a separate sheet of paper, answer the questions that follow the passage.

from "*Transfiguration*" by Annie Dillard

line

One night a moth flew into the candle, was caught, burnt dry, and held. I must have been staring at the candle, or maybe I looked up when a shadow crossed my page; at any rate, I saw it all. A golden female moth, a biggish one with a two-inch wingspan, flapped into the fire, dropped her

5 abdomen into the wet wax, stuck, flamed, frazzled and fried in a second. Her moving wings ignited like tissue paper, enlarging the circle of light in the clearing and creating out of the darkness the sudden blue sleeves of my sweater, the green leaves of jewelweed by my side, the ragged red trunk of a pine. At once the light contracted again and the moth's wings vanished in

10 a fine, foul smoke. At the same time her six legs clawed, curled, blackened, and ceased, disappearing utterly. And her head jerked in spasms, making a spattering noise; her antennae crisped and burned away and her heaving mouth parts crackled like pistol fire. When it was all over, her head was, so far as I could determine, gone, gone the long way of her wings and legs.

15 Had she been new, or old? Had she mated and laid her eggs, had she done her work? All that was left was the glowing horn shell of her abdomen and thorax—a fraying, partially collapsed gold tube jammed upright in the candle's round pool.

And then this moth-essence, this spectacular skeleton, began to act as

20 a wick. She kept burning. The wax rose in the moth's body from her soaking abdomen to her thorax to the jagged hole where her head should be, and widened into flame, a saffron-yellow flame that robed her to the ground like any immolating monk. That candle had two wicks, two flames of identical height, side by side. The moth's head was fire. She burned for two hours,

25 until I blew her out . . .

And that is why I believe those hollow crisps on the bathroom floor are moths. I think I know moths, and fragments of moths, and chips and tatters of utterly empty moths, in any state. How many of you, I asked the people

in my class, which of you want to give your lives and be writers? I was
30 trembling from coffee, or cigarettes, or the closeness of faces all around me.
(Is this what we live for? I thought; is this the only final beauty: the color of
any skin in any light, and living, human eyes?) All hands rose to the
question. (You, Nick? Will you? Margaret? Randy? Why do I want them to
mean it?) And then I tried to tell them what the choice must mean: you
35 can't be anything else. You must go at your life with a broadax. . . . They
had no idea what I was saying. (I have two hands, don't I? And all this
energy, for as long as I can remember. I'll do it in the evenings, after skiing,
or on the way home from the bank, or after the children are asleep. . . .)
They thought I was raving again. It's just as well.

"Traveling Through the Dark" by William Stafford

line

Traveling through the dark I found a deer
dead on the edge of the Wilson River road.
It is usually best to roll them into the canyon:
that road is narrow; to swerve might make more dead.

5 By glow of the tail-light I stumbled back of the car
and stood by the heap, a doe, a recent killing;
she had stiffened already, almost cold.
I dragged her off; she was large in the belly.

My fingers touching her side brought me the reason—
10 her side was warm; her fawn lay there waiting,
alive, still, never to be born.
Beside that mountain road I hesitated.

The car aimed ahead its lowered parking lights;
under the hood purred the steady engine.
15 I stood in the glare of the warm exhaust turning red;
around our group I could hear the wilderness listen.

I thought hard for us all—my only swerving—,
then pushed her over the edge into the river.

Literature Online

Assessment For additional test practice, go to
glencoe.com and enter QuickPass code GLA9800u7.

Assessment

Teach

Literary Element

First-Person Point of View
Ask students to consider point of
view as they read these selections.
Each is presented from a first-
person point of view: readers see
everything through the narrator's or
speaker's eyes. **Ask: How does
this affect the emotional impact
of each passage on readers?**
*(Students may note that each
selection draws readers into a
situation through the thoughts,
feelings, and actions of a person
who is telling his or her own story.)*

Approaching Level

DIFFERENTIATED INSTRUCTION

Emerging Before students read "Traveling Through the Dark," have them look at
the title and the first line to predict what
the poem will be about. Making predictions keeps students actively engaged in
the reading process. Evaluating predictions
improves students' skills in looking for
context clues. Have students answer these
questions after they read the poem:

- How accurate were your predictions?
- What about the poem surprised you?

Assessment

Assess

Reading

1. **A** is the correct answer because Dillard describes in precise and vivid detail the fleeting moment of the insect's death. `DOK 4`

2. **H** is the correct answer because the phrases "wet wax" and "flamed, frazzled and fired" emphasize the initial consonants. `DOK 2`

3. **A** is the correct answer because Dillard says the moth's wings "ignited like tissue paper." `DOK 1`

4. **J** is the correct answer because Dillard describes how the wax rises through the preserved abdomen and thorax of the moth, causing the flame to widen. `DOK 1`

5. **D** is the correct answer because Dillard describes the death of the moth in careful, unemotional detail. `DOK 4`

6. **G** is the correct answer because the moth—"robed" in yellow flames—is compared to a burning monk. `DOK 1`

7. **A** is the correct answer because in the paragraph Dillard describes an intense emotional commitment to writing. `DOK 4`

8. **H** is the correct answer because Dillard asks her students if they are willing to "give" their lives to writing. `DOK 2`

9. **B** is the correct answer because the thought begun in line 1 is completed in line 2. `DOK 2`

10. **J** is the correct answer because the speaker states "that road is narrow; to swerve might make more dead." `DOK 1`

Directions: Select the best suggested answer to each question and write its number on your paper.

Passage I (the essay excerpt)—Questions 1–8 refer to the passage from "Transfiguration."

1. What can you infer from the first four sentences of this selection?
   A. Dillard is a keen observer of nature.
   B. Dillard uses candles to get rid of insects.
   C. Moths are one of Dillard's special interests.
   D. Golden moths are especially drawn to flame.

2. What sound device is most apparent in "wet wax, stuck, flamed, frazzled and fried in a second"?
   F. rhyme
   G. consonance
   H. alliteration
   J. assonance

3. What causes the moth to ignite so quickly?
   A. The wings of the moth are very flammable.
   B. The moth's flapping wings fan the flame.
   C. Pines emit inflammatory substances.
   D. Female moths burn more quickly than males.

4. What causes the moth to continue burning?
   F. Its horn shell has a wick inside it.
   G. Its head jerks in spasms.
   H. Its force of will sustains it.
   J. Its hollow body becomes saturated with wax.

5. What word best describes the tone of the first paragraph?
   A. ironic
   B. upbeat
   C. solemn
   D. analytical

6. From the context, what do you conclude that the word *saffron*, in line 22, means?
   F. a material used to make candle wicks
   G. a substance used to dye monks' robes
   H. a type of prayer book
   J. a very bright yellow flower

7. What word best describes the writer's tone in the last paragraph?
   A. passionate
   B. intolerant
   C. indifferent
   D. compassionate

8. Which of the following best expresses the main idea of the analogy in the last paragraph?
   F. A moth is like a candle wick.
   G. A teacher is like an observant scientist.
   H. A writer is like a moth drawn to a flame.
   J. A moth is like a student eager to write.

Passage II (the poem)—Questions 9–13 refer to the poem "Traveling Through the Dark."

9. What literary device does Stafford use in the first two lines of the poem?
   A. onomatopoeia   C. personification
   B. enjambment   D. end rhyme

10. According to the speaker, why is it usually best to "roll them into the canyon"?
    F. It avoids struggling in the dark.
    G. It avoids dealing with the animal's death.
    H. It prevents the spread of disease.
    J. It prevents accidents.

11. What literary device is the speaker's claim, in line 16, that the wilderness was listening?
    A. metaphor   C. personification
    B. enjambment   D. rhyme

12. What is the overall mood of this poem?
    F. hopeful
    G. insincere
    H. comic
    J. somber

13. Which of the following themes do the essay excerpt and the poem have in common?
    A. Death can teach us about life.
    B. One should battle against death.
    C. Nature is in conflict with humanity.
    D. One should accept death quietly.

11. **C** is the correct answer because Stafford attributes the human quality of listening to the wilderness. `DOK 2`

12. **J** is the correct answer because the poet's acceptance of his grim duty is sobering. `DOK 4`

13. **A** is the correct answer because both authors make statements about life after observing death. `DOK 4`

Vocabulary Skills: Sentence Completion

For each item in the Vocabulary Skills section, choose the option that best completes the sentence.

1. Although many in the civil rights movement faced the threat of violence, they did not _____ their fellow citizens.
   A. coincide
   B. rear
   C. disdain
   D. console

2. The _____ impact of the Vietnam War can still be felt today.
   F. meandering
   G. oblivious
   H. ancestral
   J. colossal

3. Many claim that the Internet has made information more _____ and less concrete.
   A. striking
   B. ephemeral
   C. didactic
   D. grievous

4. Those who supported the Vietnam War believed that those who opposed it were _____ the national interest.
   F. rearing
   G. groping
   H. subverting
   J. pondering

5. The _____ of the events on September 11, 2001, made many _____ the place of the United States in the world.
   A. continuity . . . enlighten
   B. imperative . . . enunciate
   C. aristocracy . . . woo
   D. gravity . . . ponder

6. Some changes in the global economy are too _____ to be determined with certainty.
   F. random
   G. balmy
   H. stooped
   J. downy

7. Many older people were shocked by the _____ attitudes, dress, and lifestyles adopted by the baby boomer generation.
   A. ominous
   B. unorthodox
   C. ecclesiastical
   D. decimated

8. The nation, _____ by the economic boom after World War II, attained new _____ in the world.
   F. rejuvenated . . . stature
   G. presumptuous . . . scorn
   H. random . . . delirium
   J. inaudible . . . paradigm

9. Many social, economic, and political changes caused the Soviet Union's power to _____ and eventually to fail.
   A. coincide
   B. rampage
   C. wane
   D. dwell

10. The daily _____ faced by minorities before the civil rights movement was profound.
    F. nostalgia
    G. ordeal
    H. preliminaries
    J. dusk

Assess

Vocabulary Skills

1. **C** is the correct answer because no other option makes sense in this context. **DOK 1**

2. **J** is the correct answer because no other option makes sense in this context. **DOK 1**

3. **B** is the correct answer because the context suggests that the correct word is an antonym of *concrete*. **DOK 1**

4. **H** is the correct answer because no other option makes sense in this context. **DOK 1**

5. **D** is the correct answer because no other option makes sense in this context. **DOK 2**

6. **F** is the correct answer because no other option makes sense in this context. **DOK 1**

7. **B** is the correct answer because options A and C are historically incorrect, and D makes no sense in the context. **DOK 1**

8. **F** is the correct answer because no other option makes sense in this context. **DOK 2**

9. **C** is the correct answer because no other option makes sense in this context. **DOK 1**

10. **G** is the correct answer because option F is historically incorrect, and answers H and J make no sense in the context. **DOK 1**

English Learners

DIFFERENTIATED INSTRUCTION

Intermediate Remind students to use guessing strategies if they do not know the meanings of all the words in the answer choices. For example, even if they know only two of the words, they can use that information to eliminate some of the choices from consideration. That will give them a better chance of correctly guessing the answer. Consider using some of the questions on this page to demonstrate the strategy.

Assess

Writing and Grammar

1. **A** is the correct answer because no punctuation is needed for a compound verb. **DOK 1**

2. **G** is the correct answer because it avoids the awkwardness and wordiness of the other options. **DOK 1**

Grammar and Writing Skills: Paragraph Improvement

Read carefully through the following passage from the first draft of a student's essay. Pay close attention to **number and tense agreement, sentence structure,** and **punctuation.** Then, on a separate sheet of paper, answer the questions that follow.

(1) *In Annie Dillard's essay "Transfiguration," the author expresses her fascination with every aspect of the death of a moth.* (2) *The creature is drawn irresistibly, to the flame of a candle, and so is consumed by it.* (3) *The speaker observes the disintegration of each body part; the wings, the legs, the antennae, and eventually the head.* (4) *In language that conveys an objective, almost clinical interest, she describes each step in exquisite detail.* (5) *Dillard compares a writer who is devoted to pursuing his or her vocation of writing as being like a moth that is consumed in flame.*

(6) *In this way, the author suggests that—just as the moth was changed, or transfigured into a candle wick, a writer "burns and glows" in pursuit of the writing vocation.* (7) *In one sense, a writer makes a conscious choice to expend his or her life as a wick so that others may read.* (8) *In another sense, however, the choice is not the writer's to make this decision.* (9) *Like the moth drawn irresistibly to the flame that will consume it, the writer simply "can't be anything else," Dillard says.*

(10) *William Stafford's poem "Traveling Through the Dark" also discusses the meaning of a death, however, Stafford comes to some different, more solemn conclusions.* (11) *As Dillard in her essay, the speaker in the poem sees the death of an animal as a commentary on human life.* (12) *In eighteen precise, rhythmic lines, the poet describes the experience of discovering a dead deer alongside a narrow, dark road.* (13) *A further discovery, that the deer is pregnant and that the fawn is still alive, created a moral dilemma.* (14) *If the speaker does not push the deer off the road and into the river, they might cause other drivers to swerve and wreck.* (15) *The reader might well ask, of course, whether saving the deer would be possible, in any case.* (16) *Stafford skillfully points out, though, that sometimes one "unnatural" death can prevent another.*

1. Which of the following is the best revision of sentence 2?
   A. The creature is drawn irresistibly to the flame of a candle and so is consumed by it.
   B. The creature is drawn, irresistibly to the flame of a candle, and so is consumed by it.
   C. The creature is drawn irresistibly to the flame of a candle; and so is consumed by it.
   D. The creature is drawn irresistibly to the flame of a candle: and so is consumed by it.

2. Which of the following is the best revision of sentence 5?

   F. Dillard compares what appears to be the self-sacrifice of the moth, to the way that writers give up their entire lives, so that they may pursue their vocation.
   G. Dillard compares a writer's devotion to a writing vocation to a moth's being consumed in flame.
   H. Dillard compares the deliberate self-sacrifice of the moth to writers; who sacrifice their lives to pursue their vocation.
   J. Dillard compares a moth that is sacrificing its life to a writer's sacrifice of their life in pursuit of their vocation.

 To create custom assessments online, go to Progress Reporter Online Assessment.

 To create custom assessments using software, use ExamView Assessment Suite.

3. Which of the following is the best revision of sentence 6?
   A. In this way, the author suggests that—just as the moth was changed, or transfigured into a candle wick—a writer burns and glows in pursuit of the writing vocation.
   B. In this way, the author suggests that just as the moth is changed or transfigured into a candle wick a writer burns and glows, in pursuit of the writing vocation.
   C. In this way, the author suggests, that just as the moth was changed, or transfigured into, a candle wick—a writer burns and glows in the pursuit of the writing vocation.
   D. In this way, the author suggests that just as the moth was changed—or transfigured into—a candle wick a writer burns and glows in the pursuit of the writing vocation.

4. What would be the best way to correct sentence 8?
   F. Insert a comma after "choice."
   G. Change "the writer's" to "up to the writer."
   H. Delete "this decision."
   J. Move "In another sense" to the end of the sentence.

5. Which of the following errors appears in sentence 10?
   A. sentence fragment
   B. run-on sentence
   C. misplaced modifier
   D. incorrect verb tense

6. Which of the following errors appears in sentence 13?
   F. sentence fragment
   G. run-on sentence
   H. misplaced modifier
   J. incorrect verb tense

7. Which of the following is the best revision of sentence 14?
   A. If the speaker does not push the deer off the road, and into the river; they might cause other drivers to swerve and wreck.
   B. If the speaker does not push the deer off the road and into the river; it might cause other drivers to swerve and wreck.
   C. If the speaker does not push the deer off the road and into the river, the animal might cause other drivers to swerve and wreck.
   D. If the speaker does not push the deer off the road and into the river, we might cause other drivers to swerve and wreck.

8. While writing the concluding paragraph of this draft, what information should the writer include?
   F. a comparative summary of the main ideas expressed by each author
   G. more information concerning Dillard's experience as described in the essay
   H. short biographies of Dillard and Stafford
   J. a critical evaluation of both selections

Essay

Toni Morrison wrote, "The ability of writers to imagine what is not the self, to familiarize the strange and mystify the familiar, is the test of their power." Write an essay in which you consider two works from this unit in light of Morrison's idea. Include a thoughtful and logical interpretation of her statement, your opinion of the rightness or wrongness of this statement, and an explanation of how this statement is refuted or supported by the works that you examine. As you write, keep in mind that your essay will be checked for **ideas, organization, voice, word choice, sentence fluency, conventions,** and **presentation.**

Assessment

Assess

3. A is the correct answer because it uses two dashes to set off a long clause instead of a dash and a comma. (DOK 1)

4. H is the correct answer because it eliminates the needless repetition that results from the inclusion of both "choice" and "decision." (DOK 1)

5. B is the correct answer because a semicolon should follow "death." (DOK 2)

6. J is the correct answer because "created" is in the past tense, while the rest of the discussion is in the present tense. (DOK 2)

7. C is the correct answer because it clarifies the meaning by substituting the noun *animal* for the unclear pronoun *they.* (DOK 1)

8. F is the correct answer because a summary of the similarities between the two works is the conventional conclusion to a response to literature that compares the writings of two authors. (DOK 4)

Essay

Evaluate essays for the following:

- a clear interpretation and evaluation of Morrison's statement about writers' power with evidence to support or refute it from two works in the unit
- effective voice, word choice, and sentence variety
- effective presentation, with attention to grammar and spelling conventions

Use the scoring guide below to evaluate students' essays. (DOK 3)

Established Suggest to students who are challenged by the meaning of Toni Morrison's quotation that they rewrite it in their own words. Have them break the quotation into phrases and paraphrase each one. Then have them put the parts back together and consider the meaning.

Reference Section

Literary Terms Handbook R1

Foldables R22

Functional Documents R24

Writing Handbook R30
    Using the Traits of Strong Writing R30
    Research Paper Writing R33

Reading Handbook R40

Language Handbook R42
    Grammar Glossary R42
    Troubleshooter R49
    Mechanics R55
    Spelling R59

Logic and Persuasion Handbook R62

Glossary/Glosario R66

Academic Word List R89

Index of Skills R92

Index of Authors and Titles R107

Acknowledgments R110

Literary Terms Handbook

A

Abstract language Language that expresses an idea or intangible reality, as opposed to a specific object or occurrence or a concrete reality. The *Declaration of Independence* includes abstract language such as *safety, happiness, prudence,* and *laws of nature.*

See also *CONCRETE LANGUAGE.*

Absurd, Theater of the Drama, primarily of the 1950s and 1960s, that does not tell a story but instead presents a series of scenes in which the characters, confused and anxious, seem to exist in a meaningless world. Edward Albee is a leading American playwright of absurdist and other plays.

See also *SURREALISM.*

Act A major unit of a drama, or play. Modern drama has one, two, or three acts. Older drama may have five acts. Acts may be divided into one or more scenes.

See also *DRAMA, SCENE.*

Allegory A literary work in which all or most of the characters, settings, and events stand for ideas, qualities, or figures beyond themselves. The overall purpose of an allegory is to teach a moral lesson. Nathaniel Hawthorne sometimes used allegorical techniques. "The Minister's Black Veil" can be read as an allegory dealing with sin and admission of sin.

See also *SYMBOL.*

Alliteration The repetition of consonant sounds at the beginnings of words. It can be used to reinforce meaning or create a musical effect. James Weldon Johnson uses alliteration in the following line from "My City":

> But, ah! Manhattan's <u>s</u>ights and <u>s</u>ounds,
> her <u>s</u>mells, . . .

See also *SOUND DEVICES.*

Allusion A reference to a well-known character, place, or situation from history or from music, art, or another work of literature. In "The Love Song of J. Alfred Prufrock," T. S. Eliot alludes to the Italian artist Michelangelo, to Lazarus, who was restored to life by Jesus, and to Hamlet, the tragic hero of Shakespeare's play of the same name.

See pages 81 and 667.

Ambiguity The state of having more than one meaning. The richness of literary language lies in its ability to evoke multiple layers of meaning.

Analogy A comparison that shows similarities between two things that are otherwise dissimilar. Writers often use an analogy to explain something unfamiliar by comparing it to something familiar.

See page 504.

See also *METAPHOR, SIMILE.*

Anapest A metrical foot of three syllables; two unaccented syllables are followed by an accented one (˘˘´). In the following line from Edgar Allan Poe's poem "Annabel Lee," the feet are divided by slashes.

> And the stars / never rise, / but I feel / the
> bright eyes . . .

See also *FOOT, METER, SCANSION.*

Anecdote A brief account of an interesting event. Essayists often use anecdotes to support their opinions, clarify their ideas, get a reader's attention, or entertain. Biographers often include one or more anecdotes in a biography to illustrate a point about their subject.

See page 1162.

Antagonist A person or a force that opposes the protagonist, or central character, in a story or drama. The reader is generally meant not to sympathize with the antagonist. In Stephen Crane's "The Open Boat," many critics argue that the sea is the antagonist.

See also *CONFLICT, PROTAGONIST.*

Anthropomorphism The assignment of human characteristics to gods, animals, or inanimate objects. In the myth "The Sky Tree," all the water animals—turtle, beaver, mink, muskrat, and otter—behave like human beings.

Aphorism A short, pointed statement that expresses a wise or clever observation about human experience. "Poor Richard's Almanack" by Benjamin Franklin, contains many aphorisms, such as "What you would seem to be, be really."

See page 110.

See also *MAXIM*.

Apostrophe A figure of speech in which a speaker addresses an inanimate object, an idea, or an absent person. Ezra Pound addresses the long-dead Walt Whitman in "A Pact," an example of apostrophe.

See page 710.

See also *PERSONIFICATION*.

Archetype A character type, descriptive detail, image, or story pattern that recurs frequently in the literature of a culture. It derives from a Greek word meaning "the original example."

See pages 21, 23, and 26.

Argument A type of persuasive writing in which logic or reason is used to try to influence a reader's ideas or actions. "Civil Disobedience" is Henry David Thoreau's argument for disobeying a government's laws or protesting its policies.

See page 221.

See also *PERSUASION*.

Aside In a play, a character's comment that is directed to the audience or another character but is not heard by any other characters on the stage. Asides, which are rare in modern drama, reveal what a character is thinking or feeling.

Assonance The repetition of the same or similar vowel sounds, especially in a line of poetry. The repeated *o* sound in this line from an Emily Dickinson poem is an example of assonance:

The S**ou**l selects her **ow**n S**o**ciety . . .

See also *SOUND DEVICES*.

Atmosphere The physical qualities that contribute to the mood of a literary work, such as time, place, and weather. The dominant atmosphere of Edgar Allan Poe's "The Pit and the Pendulum" is one of wretched darkness.

Author The original writer of a work. The word *author* comes from a Latin word meaning "to create."

Author's note A note accompanying a literary work and containing explanatory information. Author's notes usually include helpful but nonessential information. Randall Jarrell provides an author's note along with his poem "The Death of the Ball Turret Gunner."

Author's purpose An author's intent in writing a literary work. Authors typically write for one or more of the following purposes: to persuade, to inform, to explain, to entertain, or to describe.

See pages 48, 579, and 971.

See also *DICTION, STYLE, THEME, TONE*.

Autobiography The story of a person's life written by that person. Autobiographies can give insights into the author's view of himself or herself and of the society in which he or she lived. *The Autobiography of Benjamin Franklin* is a famous example of the genre.

See pages 105 and 352.

See also *BIOGRAPHY, MEMOIR, NONFICTION*.

B

Ballad A narrative song or poem. Folk ballads, which usually recount an exciting or dramatic episode, were passed down by word of mouth for generations before being written down. Literary ballads are written in imitation of folk ballads but have a known author.

See also *FOLKLORE, NARRATIVE POETRY, ORAL TRADITION*.

Ballad stanza A quatrain, or four-line stanza, in which the first and third lines have four stressed syllables, and the second and fourth lines have three stressed syllables. Only the second and fourth lines rhyme.

Cólder and lóuder blew the wínd,
 A gále from the Nórtheast,
The snów fell híssing in the bríne,
 And the bíllows fróthed like yéast.

Henry Wadsworth Longfellow,
"The Wreck of the Hesperus"

See also *METER, QUATRAIN, SCANSION, STANZA.*

Bias An inclination toward a certain opinion or position on a topic.
See also *NONFICTION.*

Biography An account of a person's life written by someone other than the subject. Biographies have been written about many of the writers in this text.
See also *AUTOBIOGRAPHY, MEMOIR, NONFICTION.*

Blank verse Poetry or lines of dramatic verse written in unrhymed iambic pentameter. Each line has five feet, with each foot made up of an unstressed syllable followed by a stressed syllable. Because it may attempt to imitate spoken English, every line need not be perfectly regular. Robert Frost wrote "Birches" in blank verse:

When I see birches bend to left and right . . .

See page 715.
See also *FOOT, IAMBIC PENTAMETER, SCANSION.*

Blues A melancholy style of music that originated among African Americans in the South. The blues stanza has three lines, and the first two lines are usually identical. Many writers have incorporated the idea of the blues into their work, among them Langston Hughes in his poem "The Weary Blues" and James Baldwin in his story "Sonny's Blues."
See also *STANZA.*

C

Cadence The rhythmic rise and fall of language when it is spoken or read aloud.

See also *FREE VERSE, METER.*

Caesura A pause in a line of poetry, usually near the middle of a line, with two stressed syllables before and two after, creating a strong rhythm. A caesura is used to produce variations in meter and to draw attention to certain words. Some pauses are indicated by punctuation, others by phrasing or meaning. In the lines below, the caesuras are marked by double vertical lines. The pauses are indicated by punctuation.

The tide rises, || the tide falls,

The twilight darkens, || the curlew calls;

Henry Wadsworth Longfellow,
"The Tide Rises, the Tide Falls"

See also *RHYTHM.*

Catalog The listing of images, details, people, or events in a literary work. In *Song of Myself,* Walt Whitman catalogs different kinds of workers from all over the United States.
See page 1297.

Character A person portrayed in a literary work. A *main character* is central to the story and is typically fully characterized. A *minor character* displays few personality traits and is used to help develop the story. Characters who show varied and sometimes contradictory traits, such as Dexter in F. Scott Fitzgerald's "Winter Dreams," are called *round.* Characters who reveal only one personality trait are called *flat.* A stereotype, or stock character, is typically flat. A *dynamic character* grows and changes during the story, as does the captain in Stephen Crane's "The Open Boat." A *static character* remains basically the same throughout the story.
See also *CHARACTERIZATION, STEREOTYPE.*

Characterization The methods a writer uses to reveal the personality of a character. In *direct characterization,* the writer makes explicit statements about a character, as William Faulkner does in "A Rose for Emily." In *indirect characterization,* the writer reveals a character through his or her words, thoughts, and actions and through what other characters think and say about that character, as in Kate Chopin's "The Story of an Hour."

See pages 241 and 1254.

See also CHARACTER.

Classicism A style that reflects the principles and concerns of the art and literature of ancient Greece and Rome. Typically, a classical style displays simple, harmonious form.

Cliché A word or phrase that is so overused that it is virtually meaningless. "Dead as a doornail," "piece of cake," and "last but not least" are all clichés.

Climax The point of greatest emotional intensity, interest, or suspense in a literary work. Usually the climax comes at the turning point in a story or drama, the point just before the resolution of the conflict, as in Ernest Hemingway's "In Another Country," when the major loses his temper with the narrator.

See also CONFLICT, DÉNOUEMENT, PLOT.

Colloquial language Informal language used in everyday conversation but not in formal writing or speech. Simon Wheeler's language throughout "The Celebrated Jumping Frog of Calaveras County," page 497, is full of colloquialisms such as "Why, it never made no difference to *him*—he would bet on *any* thing—the dangdest feller."

See also DIALECT, VERNACULAR.

Comedy A type of drama that is humorous and often has a happy ending.

See also DRAMA, FARCE, HUMOR, PARODY, SATIRE, WIT.

Comic relief A humorous scene, event, or speech in a serious drama. It provides relief from emotional intensity, while at the same time highlighting the seriousness of the story.

Conceit An elaborate figure of speech that makes a comparison between two significantly different things. The conceit draws an analogy between some object from nature or everyday life and the subject or theme of a poem.

See also ANALOGY, EXTENDED METAPHOR, IMAGERY.

Concrete language Specific language about actual things or occurrences. Words like *dog* and *sky* are concrete, while words like *truth* and *evil* are abstract.

See also ABSTRACT LANGUAGE.

Confessional poetry A movement in poetry begun in the 1950s in which the poet writes about his or her own personal experiences. Confessional poets described their problems with mental illness, alcohol abuse, and troubled relationships in an open and direct style. Robert Lowell, Anne Sexton, and Sylvia Plath were known as members of the Confessional school of poets.

Conflict The central struggle between two opposing forces in a story or drama. An *external conflict* exists when a character struggles against some outside force, such as another person, nature, society, or fate. An *internal conflict* is a struggle that takes place within the mind of a character who is torn between opposing feelings, desires, or goals. In "The Second Tree from the Corner," the conflict is largely internal. In "The Open Boat," the conflict is mostly external.

See page 552.

See also ANTAGONIST, PLOT, PROTAGONIST.

Connotation The suggested or implied meanings associated with a word beyond its dictionary definition, or denotation. A word can have a positive, negative, or neutral connotation.

See page 372.

See also AMBIGUITY, DENOTATION, FIGURATIVE LANGUAGE.

Consonance The repetition of consonant sounds, typically at the end of nonrhyming words and preceded by different vowel sounds, as "met-cat" or "morn-barn."

See also SOUND DEVICES.

Couplet Two consecutive, paired lines of rhymed verse usually forming a stanza. The last two lines of Phillis Wheatley's "To His Excellency, General Washington" are a couplet.

See page 140.

See also HEROIC COUPLET, RHYME, SONNET, STANZA.

Crisis In a narrative, a moment of high tension that requires a decision. In Jack London's story "To Build a Fire," the crisis occurs when the man breaks through the ice into the freezing river.

See also *CLIMAX, DRAMATIC STRUCTURE, RISING ACTION.*

D

Dactyl A three-syllable metrical foot in which the first syllable is stressed and the following two are unstressed. The first line of the song "America" is dactylic.

My country 'tis of thee, . . .

Deism The belief that God created the world but no longer has influence or control over life or nature. Many of America's founders were deists.

Denotation The literal, or dictionary, meaning of a word.

See also *CONNOTATION, LITERAL LANGUAGE.*

Dénouement The outcome, or resolution, of the plot. The climax and dénouement may come close together as in Edgar Allan Poe's "The Pit and the Pendulum."

See also *CLIMAX, CONFLICT, PLOT.*

Description A detailed portrayal of a person, a place, an object, or an event. Good descriptive writing appeals to the senses through imagery. Eudora Welty's description of Phoenix Jackson in the first two paragraphs of "A Worn Path" is an example of detailed description.

See pages 145 and 889.
See also *FIGURATIVE LANGUAGE, IMAGERY.*

Dialect A variation of a language spoken within a particular region or class. Dialects may differ from the standard form of a language in vocabulary, pronunciation, or grammatical form. Mark Twain's story "The Celebrated Jumping Frog of Calaveras County" contains the following example of dialect:

Well, thish-yer Smiley had a yaller one-eyed cow that didn't have no tail, only jest a short stump like a bannanner . . .

See pages 497 and 943.
See also *COLLOQUIAL LANGUAGE, LOCAL COLOR, REGIONALISM, VERNACULAR.*

Dialogue Conversation between characters in a literary work. Dialogue can contribute to characterization, create mood, advance the plot, and develop theme.

See pages 914 and 1027.

Diary An individual's daily record of impressions, events, or thoughts, written for personal use rather than for publication.

See also *JOURNAL.*

Diction A writer's choice of words. Diction is an important element in the writer's "voice" or style. Skilled writers choose their words carefully to convey a particular tone and meaning. Ernest Hemingway was known for his spare, simple diction, as in these lines from "In Another Country":

In the fall the war was always there, but we did not go to it any more. It was cold in the fall in Milan and the dark came very early.

See pages 63 and 383.
See also *AUTHOR'S PURPOSE, STYLE, VOICE.*

Dimeter A line of verse consisting of two feet.
See also *FOOT, METER.*

Drama A story intended to be performed before an audience by actors on a stage. The script of a dramatic work may include stage directions that explain how characters should look, speak, move, and behave. The script might also specify details of the setting and scenery, such as lighting, props, and sound effects. A drama may be divided into acts, which may also be broken up into scenes, indicating changes in location or the passage of time.

See also *COMEDY, PLAY, STAGE DIRECTIONS, TRAGEDY.*

Dramatic convention Any of several devices that a theater audience accepts as a substitute for reality. For example, an audience accepts that a wood floor is a beach or a meadow, that a recording of birdsong is the real thing, or that the fifteen-minute interval between acts is a substitute for a longer passage of time.

Dramatic irony See *IRONY.*

Dramatic monologue A form of dramatic poetry in which a speaker addresses a silent listener. Edgar Allan Poe's poem "To Helen," in which the speaker passionately addresses his beloved, is an example of dramatic monologue.

See page 515.

See also *DRAMATIC POETRY, MONOLOGUE.*

Dramatic poetry Poetry in which characters are revealed through dialogue and monologue, as well as through description. Robert Frost's "The Death of the Hired Man" is an example of dramatic poetry.

See also *DIALOGUE, DRAMATIC MONOLOGUE.*

Dramatic structure The structure of a serious play. Common elements are exposition, rising action, climax, falling action, and resolution.

See also *PLOT.*

Dynamic character See *CHARACTER.*

E

Elegy A poem mourning a death or another great loss. Walt Whitman's "A Sight in Camp in the Daybreak Gray and Dim" is an elegy for soldiers killed in the Civil War.

Empathy Close identification with a person, a place, or an event, as when audience members experience the same emotions as a character in a play.

End rhyme The rhyming of words at the ends of lines as in Edwin Arlington Robinson's "Richard Cory."

Enjambment See *RUN-ON LINE.*

End-stopped line A line of poetry that contains a complete thought, thus requiring a semicolon or period at the end.

> **If ever two were one, then surely we.**
>
> Anne Bradstreet, "To My
> Dear and Loving Husband"

See also *RUN-ON LINE.*

Epic A long narrative poem that traces the adventures of a hero. Epics intertwine myths, legends, and history, reflecting the values of the societies in which they originate. Homer's *Iliad* and *Odyssey* are two famous epics.

See also *LEGEND, MYTH, ORAL TRADITION.*

Epigram A short, witty verse or saying.

> **Classic. A book which people praise and don't read.**
>
> Mark Twain, *Following the Equator*

See also APHORISM, MAXIM.

Epigraph A quotation from another work that suggests the theme, or main idea, of the work at hand. It is often up to the reader to determine how the quoted work relates to the literature it introduces. T. S. Eliot's "The Love Song of J. Alfred Prufrock" contains a six-line epigraph in Italian from Dante's *Inferno.*

Epiphany A sudden intuitive recognition of the meaning or essence of something. At the end of E. B. White's "The Second Tree from the Corner" the main character has an epiphany when he finally realizes what he wants from life.

Epistle Any letter, such as Abigail Adams's letter to her husband or Robert E. Lee's letter to his son. Often the term is applied to a more literary work than the informal communication written by most people. Travel letters are common and usually intended for publication.

Epitaph A brief statement commemorating a dead person, often inscribed on a gravestone. Edgar Lee Masters's poems in *Spoon River Anthology* are epitaphs in the form of monologues about imaginary people.

Epithet A brief phrase used to characterize a person, place, or thing. Both "Honest Abe" and "The

Great Emancipator" are epithets for Abraham Lincoln. Stephen A. Douglas, who debated Lincoln, was known as "The Little Giant."

Essay A short piece of nonfiction writing on any topic. The purpose of the essay is to communicate an idea or opinion. A *formal essay* is serious and impersonal, often with the purpose of instructing or persuading. Typically, the author strikes a serious tone and develops a main idea, or thesis, in a logical, highly organized way. An *informal,* or *personal, essay* entertains while it informs, usually in light, conversational style. Ralph Waldo Emerson's "Nature" is an example of a formal essay.

See page 1309.

See also *NONFICTION.*

Exaggeration See *HYPERBOLE.*

Exposition See *PLOT.*

Extended metaphor A metaphor that compares two unlike things in various ways throughout a paragraph, a stanza, or a literary work. In *Song of Myself,* Walt Whitman answers the question "What is the grass?" with an extended metaphor:

> I guess it must be the flag of my
>   disposition, out of a hopeful green stuff
>   woven.
>
> Or I guess it is the handkerchief of the
>   Lord,
>
> A scented gift and remembrancer
>   designedly dropt,
>
> Bearing the owner's name someway in
>   the corners,
>   that we may see and remark, and say
>   *Whose?*

See also *METAPHOR.*

F

Fable A short, often humorous, tale intended to teach a lesson about human behavior or to give advice about how to behave. Many fables end by stating the moral or lesson to be learned, while oth-ers leave it up to the reader to infer the moral. In a beast fable, animals talk and act like humans.

See also *LEGEND, PARABLE, THEME.*

Fairy tale A type of folktale that features supernatural elements, such as spirits, talking animals, and magic.

See also *FOLKTALE.*

Falling action See *PLOT.*

Fantasy A literary work that is set in an unfamiliar world and that often features unbelievable characters and events. Washington Irving wrote the earliest American fantasies with his stories "Rip Van Winkle" and "The Legend of Sleepy Hollow."

See also *SCIENCE FICTION.*

Farce A type of comedy with ridiculous situations, characters, or events.

See also *COMEDY, HUMOR, PARODY, SATIRE.*

Fiction A narrative in which situations and characters are invented by the writer. Some aspects of a fictional work may be based on fact or experience, however. Fictional works include short stories, novels, and plays. Washington Irving's "The Devil and Tom Walker" and Nathaniel Hawthorne's *The Scarlet Letter* are examples of fiction.

See also *DRAMA, NONFICTION, NOVEL, SHORT STORY.*

Figurative language Language used for descriptive effect in order to convey ideas or emotions. Figurative expressions are not literally true but express some truth beyond the literal level. Figurative language is especially common in poetry. The following line contains personification, a kind of figurative language, in which the sea is treated as a person.

> **The sea awoke at midnight from its
>   sleep, . . .**
>
> Henry Wadsworth Longfellow,
>   "The Sound of the Sea"

See pages 194 and 1193.

Figure of speech A specific kind of figurative language such as metaphor, personification, or simile.

Flashback An interruption in the chronological order of a narrative to show an event that happened earlier. A flashback gives readers information that may help explain the main events of a story. Ambrose Bierce's "An Occurrence at Owl Creek Bridge" features a flashback in the middle of the story.

See page 539.

See also FLASH-FORWARD.

Flash-forward An interruption in the chronological sequence of a narrative to leap forward in time. Richard Wright uses this device in his autobiography, *Black Boy*, when he describes a visit to his father that occurs many years after the time of the story.

See page 900.

See also FLASHBACK.

Flat character See CHARACTER.

Foil A minor character whose contrast with a main character highlights particular characteristics, often flaws, of the main character. The dog in Jack London's "To Build a Fire" exhibits a caution and respect for the cold of the Yukon that the man obviously lacks.

See page 960.

See also ANTAGONIST, CHARACTER, CHARACTERIZATION, PROTAGONIST.

Folklore Traditional beliefs, customs, stories, songs, and dances of a culture. Folklore is passed down through oral tradition and is based on the concerns of ordinary people. Washington Irving used elements of folklore in "The Devil and Tom Walker" when he wrote of a pact with the devil, who appears in human form.

See also BALLAD, EPIC, FOLKTALE, LEGEND, MYTH, ORAL TRADITION, TALL TALE.

Folktale An anonymous traditional story passed down orally long before being written down. Folktales include animal stories, trickster stories, fairy tales, myths, legends, and tall tales.

See also EPIC, FAIRY TALE, FOLKLORE, LEGEND, MYTH, ORAL TRADITION, TALL TALE.

Foot The basic unit in the measurement of a line of metrical poetry. A foot usually contains one stressed syllable (´) and one or more unstressed syllables (˘). The basic metrical feet are the anapest (˘ ˘ ´), the dactyl (´ ˘˘), the iamb (˘ ´), the spondee (´ ´), and the trochee (´ ˘).

See also METER, RHYTHM, SCANSION, STANZA.

Foreshadowing An author's use of clues to prepare readers for events that will happen later in a story. In Tomás Rivera's "The Portrait," the salesman's demand for full cash payment foreshadows the fact that the transaction is a swindle.

See page 875.

See also PLOT, SUSPENSE.

Form The structure of a poem. Many modern writers use loosely structured poetic forms instead of following traditional or formal patterns. These poets vary the lengths of lines and stanzas, relying on emphasis, rhythm, pattern, or the placement of words and phrases to convey meaning.

See page 677.

See also RHYTHM, STANZA, STRUCTURE.

Formal essay See ESSAY.

Formal speech A speech whose main purpose is to persuade, although it may also inform and entertain. Patrick Henry's "Speech to the Second Virginia Convention" is a formal speech to persuade. The four main types of formal speech are legal, political, ceremonial, and religious.

Fourth wall The imaginary wall that separates the performers onstage in a play from the audience watching the performance.

Frame story A story that surrounds another story or that serves to link several stories together. The frame is the outer story, which usually precedes and follows the inner, more important story. Mark Twain uses a frame in "The Celebrated Jumping Frog of Calaveras County." Some literary works have frames that bind together many different stories.

See page 1275.

Free verse Poetry that has no fixed pattern of meter, rhyme, line length, or stanza arrangement. Leslie Marmon Silko's "Prayer to the Pacific" is an example of free verse. Although poets who write free verse ignore traditional rules, they use techniques such as repetition and alliteration to create musical patterns in their poems.

See pages 409, 1258.

See also *RHYTHM, RHYME, METER.*

G–H

Genre A category or type of literature. Examples of genres are poetry, drama, fiction, and nonfiction.

Gothic novel A novel that has a gloomy, ominous setting and contains strong elements of horror, mystery, and the supernatural. Edgar Allan Poe included some gothic features in his story "The Fall of the House of Usher."

Haiku A traditional Japanese form of poetry that has three lines and seventeen syllables. The first and third lines have five syllables each; the middle line has seven syllables. Usually about nature, a haiku presents striking imagery to evoke a variety of feelings and associations.

Harlem Renaissance A cultural and literary movement among African Americans during the 1920s. The center of the movement was the Harlem section of Manhattan, in New York City, which attracted artists, musicians, and writers such as Langston Hughes, Countee Cullen, Zora Neale Hurston, and others.

Heptameter A metrical line of seven feet.
See also *FOOT, METER.*

Hero The chief character in a literary work, typically one whose admirable qualities or noble deeds arouse admiration. Although the word *hero* is applied only to males in traditional usage—*heroine* being the term used for females—contemporary usage applies the term to either gender.
See also *EPIC, LEGEND, MYTH, PROTAGONIST, TALL TALE, TRAGEDY.*

Heroic couplet A pair of rhymed lines in iambic pentameter that work together to express an idea or make a point. A heroic couplet is based on the poetic form used by ancient Greek and Roman poets in their heroic epics. Anne Bradstreet uses the heroic couplet in "To My Dear and Loving Husband":

I prize / thy love / more than / whole
   mines / of gold
Or all / the rich / es that / the East / doth
   hold.

See also *IAMBIC PENTAMETER, METER, RHYTHM.*

Hexameter A line of verse consisting of six feet.
See also *FOOT, METER.*

Historical fiction Fiction that sets characters against the backdrop of a period other than the author's own. Some works of historical fiction include actual historical people along with fictitious characters.
See also *FICTION.*

Historical narrative A work of nonfiction that tells the story of important historical events or developments. In *La Relación,* Álvar Núñez Cabeza de Vaca provides a historical narrative of the experiences of a group of Spanish explorers.
See page 416.

History A factual account of real events that occurred in the past. Typically, a history is arranged chronologically and seeks to provide an objective description of what happened.

Humor The quality of a literary work that makes the characters and their situations seem funny, amusing, or ludicrous. Humor often points out human failings and the irony found in many situations. Humorous language includes sarcasm, exaggeration, puns, and verbal irony. Mark Twain's story "The Celebrated Jumping Frog of Calaveras County" is told with humor, as is E. B. White's "The Second Tree from the Corner."
See also *COMEDY, FARCE, PARODY, PUN, SATIRE, WIT.*

Hymn A lyric poem or song addressed to a divine being or expressing religious sentiments.
See also *LYRIC.*

Hyperbole A figure of speech that uses exaggeration to express strong emotion, to make a point, or to evoke humor. American folklore is full of hyperbole, particularly in the stories of Paul Bunyan, who was said to have created the Grand Canyon, Puget

Sound, and the Black Hills. Thomas Paine's *The Crisis, No. 1* contains hyperbolic language.

See also *FIGURATIVE LANGUAGE, UNDERSTATEMENT.*

I

Iamb A two-syllable metrical foot consisting of one unaccented syllable and one accented syllable, as in the word *divide.*

Iambic pentameter A poetic meter in which each line is composed of five feet (pentameter), most of which are iambs.

> Tăll, sóm / ber, grĭm, / ă gaĭnst / the mórn
>
> / ĭng skȳ . . .

> Paul Hamilton Hayne,
> "Aspects of the Pines"

See also *BLANK VERSE, FOOT, HEROIC COUPLET, METER, RHYTHM, SCANSION.*

Idiom An expression whose meaning is different from the literal meaning of the words that make it up. Phrases such as "catch his eye," "turn the tables," "over the hill," and "keep tabs on" are idiomatic expressions understood by native speakers but often puzzling to non-native speakers. Idioms can add realism to dialogue in a story and contribute to characterization.

See page 1018.

See also *DIALECT.*

Imagery The "word pictures" that writers create to evoke an emotional response. In creating effective images, writers use sensory details, or descriptions that appeal to one or more of the five senses. In the following lines from "Snow," Julia Alvarez uses visual imagery to make a scene vivid to the reader:

> All my life I had heard about the white
>   crystals
> that fell out of American skies in the
>   winter.
> From my desk I watched the fine powder
>   dust
> the sidewalk and parked cars below.

See pages 96, 663, 977, and 1305.

See also *FIGURATIVE LANGUAGE, SENSORY DETAILS.*

Imagism A movement among early twentieth-century poets, including Ezra Pound and Amy Lowell, who believed that the image was the essence of poetry, conveying a poem's meaning and emotion. The language of poetry, they believed, should be brief, clear, concrete, and similar to spoken language. A classic Imagist poem is Pound's "In a Station of the Metro."

See also *MODERNISM.*

Impressionism A nineteenth-century movement in art and literature. In literature, characters and scenes are presented as the author's or a particular character's impressions rather than as they actually are. The passage below is impressionistic:

> From beyond a curtain of green woods
> there came the sound of some
> stupendous scuffle, as if two animals of
> the size of islands were fighting. At a
> distance there were occasional
> appearances of swift-moving men, horses,
> batteries, flags, and with the crashing of
> infantry volleys were heard, often, wild
> and frenzied cheers.

> Stephen Crane,
> "A Mystery of Heroism"

See also *POINT OF VIEW.*

Informal essay See *ESSAY.*

Interior monologue A technique that records a character's emotions, memories, and opinions. A brief bit of interior monologue is present in Kate Chopin's "The Story of an Hour." Interior monologue is a characteristic of the stream-of-consciousness style of writing.

See also *STREAM OF CONSCIOUSNESS.*

Internal conflict See CONFLICT.

Internal rhyme Rhyme that occurs within a single line of poetry. Poets use internal rhyme to convey meaning, to evoke mood, or simply to create a musical effect. Edgar Allan Poe uses internal rhyme in his poem "The Raven":

> Once upon a midnight <u>dreary</u>, while I
>   pondered,
>   weak and <u>weary</u>

See also *RHYME.*

Inversion Reversal of the usual word order for emphasis or variety. Writers use inversion to maintain rhyme scheme or meter, or to emphasize certain words. In the third line below, the verb comes before the subject, a reversal of the usual order of subject plus verb.

> Between the dark and the daylight,
>
> When the night is beginning to lower,
>
> Comes a pause in the day's occupations,
>
> That is known as the Children's Hour.
>
> Longfellow, "The Children's Hour"

Irony A contrast or discrepancy between appearance and reality. *Situational irony* exists when an occurrence is the opposite of someone's expectations, as at the end of Kate Chopin's "The Story of an Hour," when the main character's husband, thought to be dead, arrives at the front door. *Verbal irony* occurs when the meaning of a statement is the reverse of what is meant, as when someone says of a mean person, "Nice guy!" *Dramatic irony* occurs when playgoers have information unknown to characters onstage. In Shakespeare's *Romeo and Juliet,* the audience knows Juliet is dead before Romeo knows.
See page 574.

J–L

Journal A daily record of events kept by a participant in those events or a witness to them. Mary Chesnut's journal about life in the South during the Civil War became well-known.
See page 375.

Juxtaposition The placing of two or more distinct things side by side in order to contrast or compare them. It is commonly used to evoke an emotional response in the reader. For example, in her poem "Richness," Gabriela Mistral juxtaposes the images of a rose and a thorn.
See page 815.

Legend A traditional story handed down from the past, based on actual people and events, and tending to become more exaggerated and fantastical over time. "The Sky Tree," as retold by Joseph Bruchac, is a legend about how Earth came to be.
See also *FABLE, FOLKLORE, FOLKTALE, HERO, MYTH, ORAL TRADITION, TALL TALE.*

Legendary heroes Idealized figures, sometimes based on real people, who embody qualities admired by the cultural group to which they belong. The adventures and accomplishments of these heroes are preserved in legends or tales that are handed down from generation to generation.
See also *FOLKTALE.*

Literal language Language that is simple, straightforward, and free of embellishment. It is the opposite of figurative language, which conveys ideas indirectly.
See also *DENOTATION.*

Literary criticism A type of writing in which the writer analyzes and evaluates a literary work.

Local color The evocative portrayal of a region's distinctive ways of talking and behaving. Mark Twain's "The Celebrated Jumping Frog of Calaveras County" is a classic story for its use of local color.
See also *DIALECT, REGIONALISM, VERNACULAR.*

Lost Generation A term attributed to writer Gertrude Stein describing a group of American writers, many of whom lived abroad, who became disillusioned at the end of World War I. Included in this "generation" were Ernest Hemingway and F. Scott Fitzgerald.

Lyric A poem that expresses a speaker's personal thoughts and feelings. Lyrics are usually short and musical. Emily Dickinson's "This is my letter to the World" is an example of a lyric.
See also *POETRY.*

M

Magic realism A literary style in which the writer combines realistic events, settings, characters, dialogue, and other details with elements that are magical, supernatural, fantastic, or bizarre. In Edwidge Danticat's "Nineteen Thirty-Seven," the suggestion that certain women could fly with "wings of flames" implies a magical or supernatural quality about these women.

See page 1319.

Maxim A short saying that contains a general truth or gives practical advice, particularly about morality and behavior. Also known as an adage or aphorism.

Memoir A type of narrative nonfiction that presents the story of a period in the writer's life. It is usually written from the first-person point of view and emphasizes the narrator's own experience of this period. It may also reveal the impact of significant historical events on his or her life.
See also *AUTOBIOGRAPHY, BIOGRAPHY.*

Metaphor A figure of speech that compares or equates two seemingly unlike things. In contrast to a simile, a metaphor implies the comparison instead of stating it directly; hence there is no use of connectives such as *like* or *as.*
See pages 90, 213, and 825.
See also *EXTENDED METAPHOR, FIGURATIVE LANGUAGE.*

Meter A regular pattern of stressed (´) and unstressed (˘) syllables that gives a line of poetry a more or less predictable rhythm. The basic unit of meter is the foot. The length of a metrical line can be expressed in terms of the number of feet it contains: dimeter, two feet; trimeter, three feet; tetrameter, four feet; pentameter, five feet; hexameter, six feet; heptameter, seven feet.
The following lines from "Old Ironsides," by Oliver Wendell Holmes, show one line of iambic tetrameter and one line of iambic trimeter:

   Ăy, teár her tăttered énsĭgn dówn!

   Lŏng hăs ĭt wáved ŏn hígh

See page 802.
See also *FOOT, IAMBIC PENTAMETER, SCANSION.*

Metonymy A figure of speech in which a word or phrase is substituted for another that is related. For example, the executive branch of the U.S. government is often referred to as the White House.
See also *FIGURATIVE LANGUAGE.*

Minimalism A movement in visual arts, music, architecture, and literature. Minimalist writers include the fewest words possible in their works and depict ordinary people. Sandra Cisneros is often considered a minimalist writer.

Modernism A term applied to a variety of twentieth-century artistic movements that shared a desire to break with the past. In addition to technical experimentation, modern playwrights, writers, and artists in the first half of the twentieth century were interested in the irrational or inexplicable, as well as in the workings of the unconscious mind. The poetry of T. S. Eliot and Ezra Pound, with its new subject matter, diction, and metrical patterns, came to define Modernism. One example is Eliot's "The Love Song of J. Alfred Prufrock."
See also *IMAGISM, STREAM OF CONSCIOUSNESS, SYMBOLIST POETRY.*

Monologue A long speech by a character in a literary work.
See also *DRAMATIC MONOLOGUE, SOLILOQUY.*

Mood The emotional quality of a literary work. A writer's choice of language, subject matter, setting, and tone, as well as sound devices such as rhyme and rhythm, contribute to creating mood. Mood is a broader term than *tone,* which refers to the attitude of a speaker or narrator toward the reader. It also differs from *atmosphere,* which is concerned mainly with the physical qualities that contribute to a mood, such as time, place, and weather.
See pages 1182 and 1227.
See also *ATMOSPHERE, SETTING, TONE.*

Moral A practical lesson about right and wrong conduct, often taught in a fable or parable.

Motif A significant word, phrase, image, description, idea, or other element repeated throughout a literary work and related to the theme.
See page 1337.

Motivation The stated or implied reason or cause for a character's actions.
See pages 295 and 753.
See also *PSYCHOLOGICAL REALISM.*

Muckrakers American writers who searched for and exposed dishonesty in American government and business in the early 1900s. Ida Tarbell, Upton Sinclair, and Lincoln Steffens were leading muckrakers.

Myth A traditional story that deals with goddesses, gods, heroes, and supernatural forces. A myth may explain a belief, a custom, or a force of nature. See page 20.

See also *EPIC, FOLKLORE, FOLKTALE, LEGEND, ORAL TRADITION.*

N

Narrative Writing or speech that tells a story. Narratives may be fiction or nonfiction, prose or poetry.

See also *NARRATIVE POEM.*

Narrative poetry Verse that tells a story. Narrative poetry includes ballads and epics as well as shorter forms that are usually more selective and concentrated than are prose stories. Edgar Allan Poe's "The Raven" is a narrative poem.

See pages 255, 725, and 1332.

See also *BALLAD, EPIC, NARRATIVE.*

Narrator The person who tells a story. The narrator may be a character in the story, as in John Steinbeck's "Breakfast," or outside the story, as in Bernard Malamud's "The Magic Barrel."

See page 982.

See also *NARRATIVE, POINT OF VIEW.*

Naturalism The literary movement characterized by a belief that people have little control over their own lives. Naturalist writers such as Frank Norris and Stephen Crane focused on the powerful economic, social, and environmental forces that shape the lives of individuals.

See also *PSYCHOLOGICAL REALISM.*

Nobel Prize A very prestigious award established in 1901 by Alfred Bernhard Nobel, a Swedish chemist and inventor, to honor individuals' achievements in many fields, including medicine, physics, and literature.

Nonfiction Literature that deals with real people, places, and events. Written from either the first- or third-person point of view, works of narrative nonfiction tell a story and commonly have characteristics of fiction, such as setting, characters, theme, and plot. Biographies, autobiographies, memoirs, and essays are types of narrative nonfiction. Works of informative nonfiction include essays, speeches, and articles that explain a topic or promote an opinion.

See also *AUTOBIOGRAPHY, BIOGRAPHY, ESSAY.*

Novel A book-length fictional prose narrative, typically having a plot, character, setting, and theme. A short novel is called a novelette or novella.

O

Octave The first eight lines of a Petrarchan, or Italian, sonnet. The octave usually presents a situation, an idea, or a question.

See also *SONNET.*

Octet A group of eight lines in a poem.

Ode An elaborate lyric poem expressed in a dignified and sincere way. Some odes celebrate a person or an event; others are more private meditations.

See also *LYRIC.*

Onomatopoeia The use of a word or phrase that imitates or suggests the sound of what it describes. The words *mew, hiss, caw,* and *buzz* are onomatopoetic words. In the following example, the writer has tried to convey the sound of a character's movements:

> **She heard, behind her, his scrambling movement as he left the easy chair, the scrape and jangle of the lunchbox as he picked it up . . .**
>
> **James Baldwin, "The Rockpile"**

See also *SOUND DEVICES.*

Oral history The recording of people's memories and feelings. Oral history creates a more vivid and personal picture of the past and gives a voice to people who might have been hidden from ordinary historical records. It is the oldest form of historical inquiry, preceding the written word, and has become a crucial tool, following the invention of tape recorders in the 1940s.

See page 1168.

Oral tradition Literature that passes by word of mouth from one generation to the next. Oral literature was a way of recording the past, glorifying leaders, and teaching morals and traditions to young people.

See page 34.

See also *BALLAD, EPIC, FOLKLORE, FOLKTALE, LEGEND, MYTH, TALL TALE.*

Oratory The art of effective public speaking, or the use of persuasive skills when speaking. Oratory is common in politics, law, and religion. Today, oratory is usually called "public speaking."

See page 369.

Oxymoron A figure of speech in which opposite ideas are combined. Examples are "bright darkness," "wise fool," and "hateful love."

See also *FIGURATIVE LANGUAGE, PARADOX.*

P–Q

Parable A simple story pointing to a moral or religious lesson. It differs from a fable in that the characters are people instead of animals. Nathaniel Hawthorne's short story "The Minister's Black Veil" is a parable.

See also *FABLE.*

Paradox A situation or statement that seems to be impossible or contradictory but is nevertheless true, literally or figuratively.

> When my love swears that she is made of truth,
>
> I do believe her, though I know she lies.
>
> William Shakespeare, Sonnet 138

See also *OXYMORON.*

Parallelism The use of a series of words, phrases, or sentences that have similar grammatical structure. Parallelism emphasizes relationships between ideas. For example, Walt Whitman uses parallelism in *Song of Myself*:

> What do you think has become of the young and old men?
>
> And what do you think has become of the women and children?

See page 401.

See also *REPETITION.*

Parody A humorous imitation of a literary work that aims to point out the work's shortcomings. A parody may imitate the plot, characters, or style of another work, usually through exaggeration.

See also *COMEDY, FARCE, HUMOR, SATIRE.*

Pastoral Poetry that idealizes the simple lives of shepherds in a rural setting. Pastoral poems often exaggerate the rural pleasures and the innocence of country people living in harmony with nature.

Pentameter A metrical line of five feet.

See also *FOOT.*

Persona The mask or voice through which an author speaks. Willa Cather's "A Wagner Matinée" is told from the first person; however, the narrator is not Cather but the voice in which she chose to tell her story.

Personification A figure of speech in which an animal, an object, a force of nature, or an idea is given human characteristics. In Emily Dickinson's "Because I could not stop for Death," death is personified.

See pages 448, 1233, and 1292.

See also *APOSTROPHE, FIGURATIVE LANGUAGE.*

Persuasion Writing, usually nonfiction, that attempts to move readers to a particular viewpoint. Writers of persuasive works use appeals to logic or emotion, and other techniques to sway their readers. Thomas Paine's "The Crisis, No. 1" is an excellent example of persuasive writing.

See also *ARGUMENT.*

Petrarchan sonnet See *SONNET.*

Plain style A style of writing common among the Puritan settlers that focused on communicating ideas as clearly as possible. This marked a change from the ornate style used by European writers of that time. Colonial writers such as William Bradford thought of writing as a practical tool for spiritual self-examination and religious instruction, not as an opportunity to demonstrate cleverness.

Play A literary work of any length intended for performance on a stage with actors assuming the roles of the characters and speaking from a playwright's script.
See also *DRAMA.*

Plot The sequence of events in a short story, novel, or drama. Most plots deal with a problem and develop around a *conflict,* a struggle between opposing forces. An *external conflict* is a struggle between a character and an outside force, such as another character, society, nature, or fate. An *internal conflict* takes place within the mind of a character who struggles with opposing feelings. The plot begins with *exposition,* which introduces the story's characters, setting, and situation. The *rising action* adds complications to the conflicts, or problems, leading to the *climax,* or the point of highest emotional pitch. *Falling action* is the logical result of the climax, and the *resolution,* or dénouement, presents the final outcome.
See pages 929, 1073, and 1265.
See also *CLIMAX, CONFLICT, DÉNOUEMENT.*

Poetic license The freedom given to poets to ignore standard rules of grammar or proper diction in order to create a desired artistic effect.

Poetry A form of literary expression that differs from prose in emphasizing the line, rather than the sentence, as the unit of composition. Many other traditional characteristics of poetry apply to some poems but not to others. Some of these characteristics are emotional, imaginative language; use of figures of speech; division into stanzas; and the use of rhyme and regular patterns of meter.

Point of view The standpoint from which a story is told. In a story with *first-person* point of view, the narrator is a character in the story and uses the words *I* and *me* as in "In Another Country." In a story told from *third-person* point of view, the narrator is someone who stands outside the story and describes the characters and action as in "The Story

of an Hour." *Third-person omniscient,* or all-knowing point of view, means that the narrator knows everything about the characters and events and may reveal details that the characters themselves could not reveal. If the narrator describes events as only one character perceives them, as in "The Jilting of Granny Weatherall," the point of view is called *third-person limited.*
See pages 57, 388, 520, 1003, and 1283.
See also *NARRATOR, SPEAKER.*

Postmodernism A movement in art, music, film, literature, and other disciplines in the late twentieth century. Unreliable narration, the blending of multiple styles and genres within a single work, and magical realism are all features of postmodern literature.
See also *MODERNISM.*

Propaganda Written or spoken material designed to bring about a change or to damage a cause through use of emotionally charged words, name-calling, or other techniques.

Props A theater term (a shortened form of *properties*) for objects and elements of the scenery of a stage play or movie or television set.
See also *DRAMA.*

Prologue An introductory section of a play, speech, or other literary work.

Prose Written language that is not versified. Novels, short stories, and essays are usually written in prose.

Prose poem A short prose composition that uses rhythm, imagery, and other poetic devices to express an idea or emotion. Prose poetry does not have line breaks; instead, the sentences appear in standard paragraph form.

Protagonist The central character in a literary work, around whom the main conflict revolves. Generally the audience is meant to sympathize with the protagonist.
See also *ANTAGONIST, CONFLICT, HERO.*

Proverb A saying that expresses some truth about life or contains some bit of popular wisdom such as "faint heart never won fair lady," "marry in haste, repent at leisure," or "out of sight, out of mind."

Psalm A song of praise most commonly found in the biblical book of Psalms. David, king of Israel around 1000 B.C., wrote many of these psalms. Occasionally a modern poet will title his or her poem a psalm.

Psychological realism An attempt to portray characters in an objective, plausible manner. Above all else, psychological realism insists that characters be clearly motivated; they should not act without apparent reason.

See also *MOTIVATION, NATURALISM, REALISM.*

Pun A humorous use of words that are similar in sound (*merry* and *marry*) or of a word with several meanings. In Shakespeare's *Romeo and Juliet,* when Mercutio is fatally wounded, he says, "Ask for me tomorrow and you shall find me a *grave* man," meaning both "serious" and "dead."

Punctuation mark Any standard mark, such as a period, semicolon, hyphen, or comma, inserted to clarify meaning.

Quatrain A stanza of four lines. Edwin Arlington Robinson's poems "Richard Cory" and "Miniver Cheevy" are written in four-line stanzas.

See also *COUPLET, OCTAVE, SESTET, STANZA.*

R

Rationalism A philosophy that values reason over feeling or imagination.

See also *ROMANTICISM.*

Realism A literary movement first prominent in the late nineteenth and early twentieth centuries. Realism seeks to portray life as it is really lived. Realistic fiction often focuses on middle- or working-class settings and characters, often with reformist intent. Mark Twain was a realist writer, as were Stephen Crane and Theodore Dreiser.

See also *NATURALISM, PSYCHOLOGICAL REALISM.*

Refrain A line or lines repeated regularly, usually in a poem or song. "Let my people go" is a refrain in the spiritual "Go Down, Moses."

See page 345.
See also *REPETITION.*

Regionalism An emphasis on themes, characters, customs, and settings of a particular geographical region. Much of Mark Twain's work deals with life in Missouri and along the Mississippi River, where he spent his boyhood and youth. Early twentieth-century regionalists include Sarah Orne Jewett and Mary E. Wilkins Freeman in New England and Booth Tarkington and Hamlin Garland in the Midwest. Later Southern regionalists include William Faulkner and Robert Penn Warren.

See also *DIALECT, LOCAL COLOR, VERNACULAR.*

Repetition The recurrence of sounds, words, phrases, lines, or stanzas in a speech or literary work. Repetition increases the sense of unity in a work and can call attention to particular ideas. Walt Whitman's "Beat! Beat! Drums!" makes use of repetition.

See page 811.
See also *PARALLELISM, REFRAIN.*

Resolution See *PLOT.*

Rhetorical question A question to which no answer is expected or the answer is obvious. In his autobiography, Olaudah Equiano uses rhetorical questions to argue against slavery: "Why are parents to lose their children, brothers their sisters, or husbands their wives?" he asks.

See pages 112 and 115.

Rhyme The repetition of the same stressed vowel sounds and any succeeding sounds in two or more words. *End rhyme* occurs at the ends of lines of poetry. *Internal rhyme* occurs within a single line. *Slant rhyme* occurs when words include sounds that are similar but not identical (*jackal* and *buckle*). Slant rhyme typically involves some variation of consonance (the repetition of similar consonant sounds) or assonance (the repetition of similar vowel sounds).

See page 438.
See also *ASSONANCE, CONSONANCE, INTERNAL RHYME, RHYME SCHEME, SOUND DEVICES.*

Rhyme scheme The pattern that end rhymes form in a stanza or a poem. Rhyme scheme is designated by the assignment of a different letter of the alphabet to each new rhyme. The rhyme scheme of Edgar Allan Poe's "To Helen" follows:

Helen, thy beauty is to me	a
Like those Nicéan barks of yore,	b
That gently, o'er a perfumed sea,	a
The weary, way-worn wanderer bore	b
To his own native shore.	b

See pages 569 and 938.

See also *RHYME.*

Rhythm The pattern of beats created by the arrangement of stressed and unstressed syllables, especially in poetry. Rhythm gives poetry a musical quality, can add emphasis to certain words, and may help convey the poem's meaning. Rhythm can be *regular,* with a predictable pattern or meter, or *irregular.* On page 707, notice how the rhythm of the first two lines of E. E. Cummings's "anyone lived in a pretty how town," gives a lilting quality to the poem.

See pages 705 and 1203.

See also *IAMBIC PENTAMETER, METER.*

Rising action See *PLOT.*

Romanticism An artistic movement that began in Europe and valued imagination and feeling over intellect and reason. Nineteenth-century American writers Ralph Waldo Emerson, Henry David Thoreau, Edgar Allan Poe, Walt Whitman, and Emily Dickinson were heavily influenced by Romanticism.

See also *TRANSCENDENTALISM.*

Round character See *CHARACTER.*

Run-on line Also called enjambment, the continuation of a sentence from one line of a poem to another.

To him who in the love of Nature holds

Communion with her visible forms, she speaks

A various language;

William Cullen Bryant, "Thanatopsis"

Run-on lines enable poets to create a conversational tone, breaking lines at a point where people would normally pause in conversation, yet still maintaining the unit of thought.

See also *END-STOPPED LINE.*

S

Sarcasm The use of bitter or caustic language to point out shortcomings or flaws.

See also *IRONY, SATIRE.*

Satire Writing that comments, sometimes humorously, on human flaws, ideas, social customs, or institutions. The purpose of satire may be to reform or to entertain.

See page 1240.

See also *COMEDY, FARCE, HUMOR, PARODY, SARCASM, WIT.*

Scansion The analysis of the meter of a line of verse. To scan a line of poetry means to note the stressed and unstressed syllables and to divide the line into its feet, or rhythmical units. Stressed syllables (´) and unstressed syllables (˘) are marked. Note the scansion of these lines from Paul Laurence Dunbar's "We Wear the Mask."

We wear/ the mask /that grins/ and lies,

It hides /our cheeks /and shades/ our

eyes, . . .

Since each line has four feet and the rhythm is an iamb, we can describe the lines as iambic tetrameter.

See also *FOOT, METER, RHYTHM.*

Scene A subdivision of an act in a play. A scene is shorter than an act.

See also *ACT, DRAMA.*

Science fiction Fiction that deals with the impact of science and technology—real or imagined—on society and on individuals. Sometimes occurring in the future, science fiction commonly portrays space travel, exploration of other planets, and possible future societies.

See also *FANTASY.*

Screenplay The script of a film, which, in addition to dialogue and stage directions, usually contains detailed instructions about camera shots and angles.

See also *STAGE DIRECTIONS.*

Sensory details Evocative words or phrases that appeal to one or more of the five senses. Elizabeth Bishop's "The Fish" uses sensory details that appeal to the sense of sight.

See also *IMAGERY.*

Septet A stanza of seven lines.

Sestet A stanza of six lines.

See also *SONNET.*

Setting The time and place in which the events of a literary work occur. Setting includes not only the physical surroundings, but also the ideas, customs, values, and beliefs of a particular time and place. Setting often helps create an atmosphere or a mood. Setting plays an important part in William Faulkner's "A Rose for Emily."

See page 602.

See also *ATMOSPHERE, MOOD.*

Shakespearean sonnet See *SONNET.*

Short story A brief fictional narrative that generally includes the following major elements: setting, characters, plot, point of view, and theme.

See also *FICTION, NOVEL.*

Simile A figure of speech that uses *like* or *as* to compare seemingly unlike things. A famous simile appears at the opening of T. S. Eliot's "The Love Song of J. Alfred Prufrock."

> **Let us go then, you and I,**
>
> **When the evening is spread out against the sky**
>
> **Like a patient etherised upon a table. . . .**

See page 1223.

See also *ANALOGY, FIGURATIVE LANGUAGE, METAPHOR.*

Slant rhyme See *RHYME.*

Slave narrative Autobiographical account of the life of a formerly enslaved person. These documents helped expose the cruelty and inhumanity of slavery. The excerpt from Frederick Douglass's *My Bondage and My Freedom* is a slave narrative.

See pages 70 and 362.

See also *AUTOBIOGRAPHY, MEMOIR.*

Soliloquy In a drama, a long speech by a character who is alone on stage. A soliloquy reveals the private thoughts and emotions of that character.

See also *DRAMATIC MONOLOGUE, MONOLOGUE.*

Sonnet A lyric poem of fourteen lines, typically written in iambic pentameter and usually following strict patterns of stanza divisions and rhymes.

The *Shakespearean,* or *English,* sonnet consists of three quatrains, or four-line stanzas, followed by a couplet, or pair of rhyming lines. The rhyme scheme is typically *abab, cdcd, efef, gg.* The rhyming couplet often presents a conclusion to the issues or questions presented in the three quatrains.

In the *Petrarchan,* or *Italian,* sonnet, fourteen lines are divided into two stanzas, the eight-line octave and the six-line sestet. The sestet usually responds to a question or situation posed by the octave. The rhyme scheme for the octave is typically *abbaabba;* for the sestet the rhyme scheme is typically *cdecde.* "Douglass" by Paul Laurence Dunbar is a Petrarchan sonnet.

See page 787.

See also *COUPLET, RHYME SCHEME, STANZA.*

Sound devices Techniques used, especially in poetry, to appeal to the ear. Writers use sound devices to enhance the sense of rhythm, to emphasize particular sounds, or to add to the musical quality of their writing and rhyme.

See also *ALLITERATION, ASSONANCE, CONSONANCE, ONOMATOPOEIA, RHYME.*

Speaker The voice speaking in a poem, similar to a narrator in a work of prose. Sometimes the speaker's voice is that of the poet, sometimes that of a fictional person or even a thing. The speaker's words communicate a particular tone, or attitude, toward the subject of the poem. In Anne Bradstreet's "To My Dear and Loving Husband," the speaker is the poet, who addresses her husband in a tone of passionate devotion. One should never assume that the speaker and the writer are identical, however. The speaker in "The Raven" is not Edgar Allan Poe, the poet.

See also *TONE.*

Spondee A metrical foot of two accented syllables.

See also *FOOT, METER.*

Stage directions Instructions written by a playwright to describe the appearance and actions of characters, as well as the sets, costumes, and lighting. Arthur Miller's play *The Crucible* and Tennessee Williams's play *The Glass Menagerie* contain numerous stage directions.

See page 1051.

See also *DRAMA.*

Stanza A group of lines forming a unit in a poem or song. A stanza in a poem is similar to a paragraph in prose. Typically, stanzas in a poem are separated by a line of space.

See page 829.

See also *SONNET.*

Stereotype A character who is not developed as an individual, but instead represents a collection of traits and mannerisms supposedly shared by all members of a group.

See also *CHARACTER.*

Stream of consciousness The literary representation of a character's free-flowing thoughts, feelings, and memories. Stream-of-consciousness writing does not always employ conventional sentence structure or other rules of grammar and usage. Parts of T. S. Eliot's poem "The Love Song of J. Alfred Prufrock" exemplify stream of consciousness; Katherine Anne Porter's "The Jilting of Granny Weatherall" does as well.

See page 774.

See also *SURREALISM.*

Structure The particular order or pattern a writer uses to present ideas. Narratives commonly follow a chronological order, while the structure of persuasive or expository writing may vary. Listing detailed information, using cause and effect, or describing a problem and then offering a solution are some other ways a writer can present a topic.

See pages 121, 683, and 1156.

Style The expressive qualities that distinguish an author's work, including word choice and the length and arrangement of sentences, as well as the use of figurative language and imagery. Style can reveal an author's attitude and purpose in writing.

See page 743.

See also *AUTHOR'S PURPOSE, DICTION, FIGURATIVE LANGUAGE, IMAGERY, TONE.*

Subject The topic of a literary work.

Surprise ending An unexpected plot twist at the end of a story. The ending might surprise readers because the author provides misleading clues or withholds important information.

Surrealism A literary and artistic style that originated in Europe in the 1920s. Surrealist works feature bizarre and impossible events treated as if they were normal. Surrealist poetry expresses the workings of the unconscious mind and how these workings interact with outer reality. This poetry is characterized by the use of images from dreams and stream-of-consciousness associations.

See also *STREAM OF CONSCIOUSNESS.*

Suspense A feeling of curiosity, uncertainty, or even dread about what is going to happen next in a story. Writers increase the level of suspense by creating a threat to the central character and raising questions in a reader's mind about the outcome of a conflict. Suspense is especially important in the plot of an adventure or mystery story.

See page 262.

See also *PROTAGONIST.*

Symbol Any object, person, place, or experience that exists on a literal level but also represents, or stands for, something else, usually something abstract. In Carl Sandburg's "Chicago," the hog butcher, tool maker, and stacker of wheat symbolize the city of Chicago.

See pages 279 and 1287.

See also *ALLEGORY, FIGURATIVE LANGUAGE.*

Symbolist poetry A kind of poetry that emphasizes suggestion and inward experience instead of explicit description. The symbolist poets influenced twentieth-century writers such as T. S. Eliot and Ezra Pound.

See page 660.

See also *IMAGISM, MODERNISM.*

Synecdoche A figure of speech in which a part is used for the whole or a whole is used for a part. In "All nations, and kindreds, and people, and tongues," *tongues* (a part) is used for the whole (languages).

T

Tall tale A type of folklore associated with the American frontier. Tall tales are humorous stories that contain wild exaggerations and inventions. Typically, their heroes are bold but sometimes foolish characters who may have superhuman abilities or who may act as if they do. Tall tales are not intended to be believable; their exaggerations are used for comic effect, as in Mark Twain's "The Celebrated Jumping Frog of Calaveras County," when Simon Wheeler describes the frog: "[Y]ou'd see that frog whirling in the air like a doughnut—see him turn one summerset, or may be a couple, if he got a good start, and come down flat-footed and all right, like a cat."

See also *FOLKLORE, FOLKTALE.*

Tercet A stanza of three rhyming lines.

Terza rima A verse form with a sequence of three-line stanzas rhyming *aba, bcb, cdc,* and so on. Robert Frost's poem "Acquainted with the Night" is written in terza rima.

Tetrameter A metrical line of four feet.

> Listen, / my children, / and you / shall hear
>
> Of the mid / night ride / of Paul / Revere . . .
>
> Henry Wadsworth Longfellow,
> "Paul Revere's Ride"

See also *FOOT, METER.*

Theater of the absurd See *ABSURD, THEATER OF THE*

Theme The central message of a work of literature, often expressed as a general statement about life. Some works have a *stated* theme, which is expressed directly. More works have an *implied* theme, which is revealed gradually through events, dialogue, or description. A literary work may have more than one theme. Some themes are universal, meaning that they are widely held ideas about life. Themes and topics are different. The *topic* of a work might be love; the *theme* would be what the writer says about love, that it is painful or wonderful or both, for example.

See pages 189, 689, and 867.

See also *AUTHOR'S PURPOSE, FABLE, MORAL.*

Thesis The main idea of a work of nonfiction. The thesis may be stated directly or implied.

See page 204.

See also *NONFICTION.*

Tone An author's attitude toward his or her subject matter or the audience. Tone is conveyed through elements such as word choice, punctuation, sentence structure, and figures of speech. A writer's tone might convey a variety of attitudes such as sympathy, objectivity, or humor.

See pages 133, 532, 700, and 1215.

See also *AUTHOR'S PURPOSE, DICTION, FIGURATIVE LANGUAGE, MOOD, STYLE, VOICE.*

Tragedy A play in which a main character suffers a downfall. That character, the *tragic hero,* is typically a person of dignified or heroic stature. The downfall may result from outside forces or from a weakness within the character, which is known as a *tragic flaw.*

See page 1096.

See also *DRAMA, HERO.*

Transcendentalism A philosophical and literary movement whose followers believed that basic truths could be reached only by "going beyond," or transcending, reason and reflecting on the world of the spirit and on one's own deep and free intuition. Transcendentalists believed that the individual could transform the world—not only through writing, but also through utopian communities, antislavery activity, and other social action.

See also *RATIONALISM, ROMANTICISM.*

Trimeter A metrical line of three feet.
See also *FOOT, METER.*

Triplet See *TERCET.*

Trochee A metrical foot made up of one accented and one unaccented syllable. The lines below, each of which has four feet, can be described as trochaic tetrameter.

> Fillèd with / awe was / Hi a / wath a
> At the / as pect / of his / fath er.

> Henry Wadsworth Longfellow,
> The Song of Hiawatha

See also *FOOT.*

U–W

Understatement Language that makes something seem less important than it really is.

See also *HYPERBOLE.*

Unreliable narrator A narrator whose account of events is faulty or distorted in some way. Some unreliable narrators intentionally mislead readers. Others fail to understand the true meaning of the events they describe. For example, if a story is narrated by a small child, he or she might misinterpret the behavior of adult characters. Most stories with unreliable narrators are written in the first person.
See also *POSTMODERNISM.*

Verisimilitude The illusion of reality, often achieved by presenting concrete, detailed descriptions.

Vernacular Ordinary speech of a particular country or region. Vernacular language is more casual than cultivated, formal speech. Slang and dialect are commonly described as vernacular language. Regional writers sometimes employ vernacular language for enhanced realism. Use of vernacular is common in the works of Mark Twain, Zora Neale Hurston, and Alice Walker.

See also *COLLOQUIAL LANGUAGE, DIALECT, LOCAL COLOR, REGIONALISM.*

Verse paragraph A group of lines in a poem that forms a unit. Unlike a stanza, a verse paragraph does not have a fixed number of lines. While poems written before the twentieth century usually contain stanzas, many contemporary poems are made up of verse paragraphs. Verse paragraphs help to organize a poem into thoughts, as paragraphs help to organize prose.

See page 1209.
See also *STANZA.*

Voice The distinctive use of language that conveys the author's or narrator's personality to the reader. Voice is determined by elements of style such as word choice and tone.

See page 420.
See also *AUTHOR'S PURPOSE, DICTION, NARRATOR, STYLE, TONE.*

Wit An exhibition of cleverness and humor. The works of Dorothy Parker, Mark Twain, and Donald Barthelme are known for their wit.
See also *COMEDY, HUMOR, SARCASM, SATIRE.*

Word choice See *DICTION.*

Reading and Thinking with Foldables®

by Dinah Zike, M.Ed., Creator of Foldables®

Using Foldables® Makes Learning Easy and Enjoyable

Anyone who has paper, scissors, and maybe a stapler or some glue can use Foldables in the classroom. Just follow the illustrated step-by-step directions. Check out the following sample:

 Reading Objective: to understand how one character's actions affect other characters in a short story

Use this Foldable to keep track of what the main character does and how his or her actions affect the other characters.

 Step 1 Place a sheet of paper in front of you so that the short side is at the top. Fold the paper in half from top to bottom.

 Step 2 Fold in half again, from side to side, to divide the paper into two columns. Unfold the paper so that the two columns show.

 Step 3 Draw a line along the column crease. Then, through the top layer of paper, cut along the line you drew, forming two tabs.

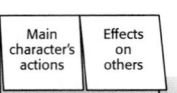 **Step 4** Label the tabs *Main character's actions* and *Effectson others.*

Step 5 As you read, record the main character's actions under the first tab. Record how each of those actions affects other characters under the second tab.

 Short Story

Reading Objective: to analyze a short story on the basis of its literary elements

As you read, use the following Foldable to keep track of five literary elements in the short story.

 Step 1 Stack three sheets of paper with their top edges about a half-inch apart. Be sure to keep the side edges straight.

 Step 2 Fold up the bottom edges of the paper to form six tabs, five of which will be the same size.

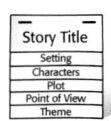 **Step 3** Crease the paper to hold the tabs in place and staple the sheets together along the crease.

Step 4 Turn the sheets so that the stapled side is at the top. Write the title of the story on the top tab. Label the five remaining tabs *Setting, Characters, Plot, Point of View,* and *Theme.*

Step 5 Use your Foldable as you read the short story. Under each labeled tab, jot down notes about the story in terms of that element.

You may adapt this simple Foldable in several ways.

- Use it with dramas, longer works of fiction, and some narrative poems—wherever five literary elements are present in the story.
- Change the labels to focus on something different. For example, if a story or a play has several settings, characters, acts, or scenes, you could devote a tab to each one.

Drama

 Reading Objective: to understand conflict and plot in a drama

As you read the drama, use the following Foldable to keep track of conflicts that arise and ways that those conflicts are resolved.

 Step ❶ Place a sheet of paper in front of you so that the short side is at the top. Fold the paper in half from side to side.

 Step ❷ Fold the paper again, one inch from the top as shown here.

 Step ❸ Unfold the paper and draw lines along all of the folds. This will be your chart.

Step ❹ At the top, label the left column *Conflicts* and the right column *Resolutions.*

Step ❺ As you read, record in the left column the various conflicts that arise in the drama. In the right column, explain how each conflict is resolved by the end of the drama.

You may adapt this simple Foldable in several ways.
- Use it with short stories, longer works of fiction, and many poems—wherever conflicts and their resolutions are important.
- Change the labels to focus on something different. For example, you could record the actions of two characters, or you could record the thoughts and feelings of a character before and after the story's climax.

Lyric Poem

 Reading Objective: to interpret the poet's message by understanding the speaker's thoughts and feelings

As you read the poem, use the following Foldable to help you distinguish between what the speaker *says* and what the poet *means.*

 Step ❶ Place a sheet of paper in front of you so that the short side is at the top. Fold the paper in half from top to bottom.

 Step ❷ Fold the paper in half again from left to right.

 Step ❸ Unfold and cut through the top layer of paper along the fold line. This will make two tabs.

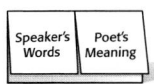 **Step ❹** Label the left tab *Speaker's Words.* Label the right tab *Poet's Meaning.*

Step ❺ Use your Foldable to jot down notes on as you read the poem. Under the left tab, write down key things the speaker says. Under the right tab, write down what you think the poet means by having the speaker say those things.

You may adapt this simple Foldable in several ways.
- Use it to help you visualize the images in a poem. Just replace *Speaker's Words* with *Imagery* and replace *Poet's Meaning* with *What I See.*
- Replace the label *Speaker's Words* with *Speaker's Tone* and under the tab write adjectives that describe the tone of the speaker's words.
- If the poem you are reading has two stanzas, you might devote each tab to notes about one stanza.

Functional Documents

Functional documents are specialized forms of expository writing that serve specifc purposes. Functional documents are an every day part of business, school, and even home life. They must be clear, concise, accurate, and correct in style and usage.

Letter of Application

A letter of application is a form of business writing. It can be used when applying for a job, an internship, or a scholarship. In most cases, the letter is intended to accompany a résumé or an application. Because detailed information is usually included in the accompanying form, a letter of application should provide a general overview of your qualifications and the reasons you are submitting an application. A letter of application should be concise. You should clearly state which position you are applying for and then explain why you are interested and what makes you qualified. The accompanying material should speak for itself.

1 The optional subject line indicates the topic of the letter.

2 In a business letter, the greeting is followed by a colon.

3 The writer states her purpose directly and immediately.

4 The writer comments briefly on her qualifications.

5 The writer makes reference to the accompanying material.

32 South Street
Austin, Texas 78746
May 6, 2009

Melissa Reyes
City Life magazine
2301 Davis Avenue
Austin, Texas 78764

1 Re: Internship

2 Dear Ms. Reyes:

I am a junior at City High School and editor of the City High Herald. I am
3 writing to apply for your summer internship at City Life magazine. As a journalism student and a longtime fan of your magazine, I feel that an internship with your magazine would provide me with valuable experience in the field of journalism. I believe that my role with the City High Herald has
4 given me the skills necessary to be a useful contributor to your magazine this summer. In addition, my enclosed application shows that I am also a
5 diligent worker.

I thank you for considering my application for your summer internship, and I hope to be working with you in the coming months.

Sincerely,
Anne Moris
Anne Moris

Activity

Choose a local business where you might like to work. Write a letter of application for an internship at that business. Assume that you will be submitting this letter along with a résumé or an internship application that details your experience and qualifications.

Résumé

The purpose of a résumé is to provide the employer with a comprehensive record of your background information, related experience, and qualifications. Although a résumé is intended to provide a great deal of information, the format is designed to provide this information in the most efficient way possible.

❶ Jane Wiley
909 West Main Street, Apt. #1
Urbana, Illinois 61802
(217) 555-0489 • jane@internet.edu

Goal

Seeking position in television news production

❷ Education

Junior standing in the College of Communications at the University of
Illinois, Urbana-Champaign
2005 Graduate of City High School

Honors

Member of National Honor Society

Activities

❸ Member, Asian American Association: 2005–Present
Environmental Committee Chairperson, Asian American Association:
August 2006–May 2007

Work Experience

❹ Radio Reporter, WPGU, 107.1 FM, Champaign, Illinois: May 2007–Present
❺ • Rewrote and read stories for afternoon newscasts
• Served as field reporter for general assignments

Cashier, Del's Restaurant, Champaign, Illinois: May 2006–August 2006
• Responsible for taking phone orders
• Cashier for pickup orders

Assistant Secretary, Office of Dr. George Wright, Woodstock, Illinois:
May 2005–August 2005
• Answered phones
• Made appointments

❶ Header includes all important contact information.

❷ All important education background is included.

❸ Related dates are included for all listed activities.

❹ Job title is included along with the place of employment.

❺ Job responsibilities are briefly listed, with a parallel structure used in each bulleted item.

Activity

Create an outline that lists the information that you would want to include in a résumé. Use a word processor to help format your outline.

Job Application

When applying for a job, you usually need to fill out a job application. When you fill out the application, read the instructions carefully. Examine the entire form before beginning to fill it out. If you fill out the form by hand, make sure that your handwriting is neat and legible. Fill out the form completely, providing all information directly and honestly. If a question does not apply to you, indicate that by writing *n/a,* short for "not applicable." Keep in mind that you will have the opportunity to provide additional information in your résumé, in your letter of application, or during the interview process.

❶ Please type or print neatly in blue or black ink.

❷ Name: _____ **Today's date:** _____
Address: _____
Phone #: _____ **Birth date:** _____ **Sex:** ___ **Soc. Sec. #:** ____

* *

❸ Job History (List each job held, starting with the most recent job.)

1. Employer: _____ Phone #: _____
Dates of employment: _____
Position held: _____
❹ Duties: _____

2. Employer: _____ Phone #: _____
Dates of employment: _____
Position held: _____
Duties: _____

* *

Education (List the most recent level of education completed.)

_____
_____

* *

Personal References:

1. Name: _____ Phone #: _____
Relationship: _____
2. Name: _____ Phone #: _____
Relationship: _____

❶ The application provides specific instructions.

❷ All of the information requested should be provided in its entirety.

❸ The information should be provided legibly and succinctly.

❹ Experience should be stated accurately and without embellishment.

Activity

Pick up a job application from a local business or use the sample application shown. Complete the application thoroughly. Fill out the application as if you were actually applying for the job. Be sure to pay close attention to the guidelines mentioned above.

Memos

A memorandum (memo) conveys precise information to another person or a group of people. A memo begins with a leading block. It is followed by the text of the message. A memo does not have a formal closing.

TO: All Employees
FROM: Jordan Tyne, Human Resources Manager
❶ SUBJECT: New Human Resources Assistant Director
DATE: November 3, 2009

❷ Please join me in congratulating Daphne Rudy on her appointment as assistant director in the Human Resources Department. Daphne comes to our company with five years of experience in the field. Daphne begins
❸ work on Monday, November 10. All future general human resource inquiries should be directed to Daphne.

Please welcome Daphne when she arrives next week.

❶ The topic of the memo is stated clearly in the subject line.
❷ The announcement is made in the first sentence.
❸ All of the important information is included briefly in the memo.

Business E-mail

E-mail is quickly becoming the most common form of business communication. While e-mail may be the least formal and most conversational method of business writing, it shouldn't be written carelessly or too casually. The conventions of business writing—clarity, attention to your audience, proper grammar, and the inclusion of relevant information—apply to e-mail.

An accurate subject line should state your purpose briefly and directly. Use concise language and avoid rambling sentences.

To: LiamS@internet.com
From: LisaB@internet.com
CC: EricC@internet.com
Date: January 7, 8:13 a.m.
❶ Subject: New Product Conference Call

Liam,

❷ I just wanted to make sure that arrangements have been made for next week's conference call to discuss our new product. The East Coast sales team has already scheduled three sales meetings at the end of the month with potential buyers, so it's important that our sales team is prepared to talk about the product. Please schedule the call when the manufacturing director
❸ is available, since he will have important information for the sales team.

Lisa

❶ Subject line clearly states the topic.
❷ The purpose is stated immediately and in a conversational tone.
❸ Important details are included in a brief, direct fashion.

Activity
Write an e-mail to your coworkers. Inform them of a change in company procedure that will affect them.

Travel Directions

When planning an event or a social occasion, it is often necessary to provide people with detailed directions to the location. These directions must be clear enough that anyone who is unfamiliar with the surrounding area can easily find their way. Creating a map that shows the route with clearly labeled streets can also be a great help.

Directions to Darien High School's Graduation Ceremony

From I-95 North, take Exit 11. **❶**

Turn Left onto Post Road (Route 1).

At the first light, turn Left onto Samuel Avenue. Travel 2.5 miles. **❷**

Turn Right onto Cherry Hill Road.

Turn Left onto High School Lane. **❸**

Follow signs to Visitor Parking.

❶ Begins at a point from which most people will be coming

❷ Offers travel distances to help travelers locate streets

❸ Gives the name of each street along the route

❶ Clearly labels all streets to be traveled

❷ Labels major cross streets so the traveler can keep better track of his or her progress

❸ Includes landmarks to help identify the area

❹ Includes legend to show scale

❺ Includes compass rose to help orientate the traveler

Activity

Write directions and draw an accompanying map to a location in your town. Be sure to include enough details and give enough clear directions so that even someone who is unfamiliar with the area could find the destination.

Technical Writing

Technical writing involves the use of very specific vocabulary and a special attention to detail. The purpose of technical writing is to describe a process clearly enough so that the reader can perform the steps and reach the intended goal, such as installing software, connecting a piece of equipment, or programming a device.

Instructions for Connecting DVD Player to HDTV

1 Your DVD player can be connected to an HDTV using RCA cables or, for best picture quality, an HDMI cable.

Connecting with RCA Cables:

2 **Step 1:** Insert the ends of the red, white, and yellow cables into the jacks labeled "AUDIO/VIDEO OUT." Be sure to match the colors of the cable with the color of the jack.

Step 2: Insert the other ends of the RCA cables into the jacks labeled "AUDIO/VIDEO IN" on your HDTV. These are usually located on the side or the back of the television. Again, be sure to match the colors of the cables with the colors of the jacks.

Connecting with HDMI Cable:

Step 1: Insert one end of the HDMI cable into the HDMI port located on the back of the DVD player.

Step 2: Insert the other end of the HDMI cable into the HDMI port on your HDTV.

3 **Note:** Your HDTV may have more than one HDMI port. If so, be sure that you set your HDTV to the correct input when viewing.

1 Uses specific language to clearly describe the process

2 Lists each step individually

3 Directs attention to possible variations the reader may encounter

Activity

Choose a device that you own or have access to, such as an mp3 player or a cell phone. Write brief step-by-step directions on how to perform a specific function on the device, so that someone else can follow your instructions and perform the function successfully.

Writing Handbook

Using the Traits of Strong Writing

What are some basic terms you can use to discuss your writing with your teacher or classmates? What should you focus on as you revise and edit your compositions? Check out the following terms, or traits, that describe the qualities of strong writing. Learn the meaning of each trait and find out how using the traits can improve your writing.

Ideas

The message or the theme and the details that develop it

Writing is clear when readers can grasp the meaning of your ideas right away. Check to see whether you're getting your message across.

- ☑ Does the title suggest the theme of the composition?

- ☑ Does the composition focus on a single narrow topic?

- ☑ Is the thesis—the main point or central idea—clearly stated?

- ☑ Do well-chosen details elaborate your main point?

Organization

The arrangement of main ideas and supporting details

An effective plan of organization points your readers in the right direction and guides them easily through your composition from start to finish. Find a structure, or order, that best suits your topic and writing purpose. Check to see whether you've ordered your key ideas and details in a way that keeps your readers on track.

- ☑ Are the beginning, middle, and end clearly linked?

- ☑ Is the internal order of ideas easy to follow?

- ☑ Does the introduction capture your readers' attention?

- ☑ Do sentences and paragraphs flow from one to the next in a way that makes sense?

- ☑ Does the conclusion wrap up the composition?

Voice

A writer's unique way of using tone and style

Your writing voice comes through when your readers sense that a real person is communicating with them. Readers will respond to the **tone** (or attitude) that you express toward a topic and to the **style** (the way that you use language and shape your sentences). Read your work aloud to see whether your writing voice comes through.

- ☑ Does your writing sound interesting?

- ☑ Does your writing reveal your attitude toward your topic?

- ☑ Does your writing sound like you—or does it sound like you're imitating someone else?

Word Choice

The vocabulary a writer uses to convey meaning

Words work hard. They carry the weight of your meaning, so make sure you choose them carefully. Check to see whether the words you choose are doing their jobs well.

- ☑ Do you use lively verbs to show action?

- ☑ Do you use vivid words to create word pictures in your readers' minds?

- ☑ Do you use precise words to explain your ideas simply and clearly?

Sentence Fluency

The smooth rhythm and flow of sentences that vary in length and style

The best writing is made up of sentences that flow smoothly from one sentence to the next. Writing that is graceful also sounds musical—rhythmical rather than choppy. Check for sentence fluency by reading your writing aloud.

- ☑ Do your sentences vary in length and structure?

- ☑ Do transition words and phrases show connections between ideas and sentences?

- ☑ Does parallelism help balance and unify related ideas?

Conventions

Correct spelling, grammar, usage, and mechanics

A composition free of errors makes a good impression on your readers. Mistakes can be distracting, and they can blur your message. Try working with a partner to spot errors and correct them. Use this checklist to help you.

- ☑ Are all words spelled correctly?

- ☑ Are all proper nouns—as well as the first word of every sentence—capitalized?

- ☑ Is your composition free of sentence fragments?

- ☑ Is your composition free of run-on sentences?

- ☑ Are punctuation marks—such as apostrophes, commas, and end marks—inserted in the right places?

Presenting and Publishing

The formatting of writing for various purposes

For many writers, the writing process is not complete until they present their work to an audience. This can mean submitting your writing for publication in a school paper or a national magazine, or it can simply mean preparing your writing in a neat and presentable format. For readers to fully appreciate your writing, it is very important that you present it neatly, effectively, and according to professional standards.

Format

- The standard typeface setting for most writing submissions is Courier 12 point.

- Double-space your work so that it is easy to read.

- Leave one-inch margins on all sides of every page.

- Italicize titles or when using terms from other languages. You may also italicize words to add emphasis, but do this only when it is necessary to make your point clear. (If you are submitting your writing to a professional publication, underline words that should appear in italics.)

- Most word processing programs make it easy to set the page number to appear in the upper right-hand corner of each page. Include your last name before each page number after the first page.

- If you are including charts, graphs, maps, or other visual aids, consider setting them on their own page. This will allow you to show the graphic at a full size that is easy to read.

Organization

- On a separate sheet of paper, center your name under the title of your work. If you are submitting your writing for publication, include the total number of words in the upper right-hand corner, and your name and address in the upper left-hand corner.

- The body of your work follows immediately.

- End your presentation with you list of works cited.

Research Paper Writing

More than any other type of paper, research papers are the product of a search—a search for data, for facts, for informed opinions, for insights, and for new information.

Selecting a topic

- If a specific topic is not assigned, choose a topic. Begin with the assigned subject or a subject that interests you. Read general sources of information about that subject and narrow your focus to some aspect of it that interests you. Good places to start are encyclopedia articles and the tables of contents of books on the subject. A computerized library catalog will also display many subheads related to general topics. Find out if sufficient information about your topic is available.

- As you read about the topic, develop your paper's central idea, which is the purpose of your research. Even though this idea might change as you do more research, it can begin to guide your efforts. For example, if you were assigned the subject of the Civil War, you might find that you're interested in women's roles during that war. As you read, you might narrow your topic down to women who went to war, women who served as nurses for the Union, or women who took over farms and plantations in the South.

Conducting a broad search for information

- Generate a series of researchable questions about your chosen topic. Then research to find answers to your questions.

- Among the many sources you might use are the card catalog, the computer catalog, the *Reader's Guide to Periodical Literature* (or an electronic equivalent), newspaper indexes, and specialized references such as biographical encyclopedias.

- If possible, use primary sources as well as secondary sources. A **primary source** is a firsthand account of an event—for example, the diary of a woman who served in the army in the Civil War is a primary source. **Secondary sources** are sources written by people who did not experience or influence the event. Locate specific information efficiently by using the table of contents, indexes, chapter headings, and graphic aids.

Developing a working bibliography

If a work seems useful, write a **bibliography card** for it. On an index card, write down the author, title, city of publication, publisher, date of publication, and any other information you will need to identify the source. Number your cards in the upper right-hand corner so you can keep them in order.

Following are model bibliography, or source, cards.

Book

❶ Settle, Mary Lee   **❷** 6
❸ <u>All the Brave Promises.</u>
❹ Columbia: University of
South Carolina
❺ Press, 1995.

❻ Evanston Public Library   D810.W754

❶ Author
❷ Source number
❸ Title
❹ City of publication/ Publisher
❺ Date of publication
❻ Location of source
❼ Library call number

Periodicals

❶ Chelminski. R.　　　　　　　　**❷** 2

　　❸ "The Maginot Line"

　　❹ *Smithsonian*, June 1997: 90–99

❶ Author

❷ Source number

❸ Title

❹ Title of magazine/date/page number(s)

Online Source

❶ "Job Hunting Resources"　　　　**❷** 6

　　❸ The Career Building Network

　　❹ CareerBuilder

　　❺ 14 Feb. 2002

　　❻ http://www.careerbuilder.com

❶ Title

❷ Source number

❸ Title of database

❹ Sponsoring organization

❺ Date of access

❻ URL

Evaluating your sources

Your sources should be **a**uthoritative, **r**eliable, **t**imely, and **s**uitable **(arts)**.

- The source should be **authoritative.** The author should be well-known in the field. An author who has written several books or articles about a subject or who is frequently quoted may be considered an authority. You might also consult *Book Review Index* and *Book Review Digest* to find out how other experts in the field have evaluated a book or an article.

- The source should be **reliable.** If possible, avoid material from popular magazines in favor of that from more scholarly journals. Be especially careful to evaluate material from online sources. For example, the Web site of a well-known university is more reliable than that of an individual. (You might also consult a librarian or your instructor for guidance in selecting reliable online sources.)

- The source should be **timely.** Use the most recent material available, particularly for subjects of current importance. Check the publication date of books as well as the month and year of periodicals.

- The source should be **suitable,** or **appropriate.** Consider only material that is relevant to the purpose of your paper. Do not waste time on books or articles that have little bearing on your topic. If you are writing on a controversial topic, you should include material that represents more than one point of view.

Compiling and organizing note cards

Careful notes will help you to organize the material for your paper.

- As you reread and study sources, write useful information on index cards. Be sure that each note card identifies the source (use the number of the bibliography card that corresponds to each source).

- In the lower right-hand corner of the card, write the page number on which you found the information. If one card contains several notes, write the page number in parentheses after the relevant material.

- Three helpful ways to take notes are paraphrasing, summarizing, and quoting directly.

  1. **Paraphrase** important details that you want to remember; that is, use your own words to restate specific information.
  2. **Summarize** main ideas that an author presents. When you summarize several pages, be sure to note the page on which the material begins and the page on which it ends—for example, 213–221.
  3. **Quote** the exact words of an author only when the actual wording is important. Be careful about placing the author's words in quotation marks.

- Identify the subject of each note card with a short phrase written in the upper left.

See the sample note card below, which includes information about careers and goals from three pages.

Careers and goals   12
Many people "crave work that will
spark . . . excitement and energy." (5)
Sher recognizes that a career does
not necessarily satisfy a person's aim
in life. (24) She also offers ads on how
to overcome obstacles that people
experience in defining their goals. (101)

- Organize your note cards to develop a **working outline.** Begin by sorting them into piles of related cards. Try putting the piles together in different ways that suggest an organizational pattern. (If, at this point, you discover that you do not have enough information, go back and do further research.) Many methods of organization are possible. You might also combine methods of organization.

Developing a thesis statement

A thesis statement tells what your topic is and what you intend to say about it—for example, "World War II changed the lives of African Americans and contributed to the rise of the civil rights movement."

- Start by examining your central idea.

- Refine it to reflect the information that you gathered in your research.

- Next, consider your approach to the topic. What is the purpose of your research? Are you proving or disproving something? illustrating a cause-and-effect relationship? offering a solution to a problem? examining one aspect of the topic thoroughly? predicting an outcome?

- Revise your central idea to reflect your approach.

- Be prepared to revise your thesis statement if necessary.

Drafting your paper

Consult your working outline and your notes as you start to draft your paper.

- Concentrate on getting your ideas down in a complete and logical order.

- Write an introduction and a conclusion. An effective introduction creates interest, perhaps by beginning with a question or a controversial quotation; it should also contain your thesis statement. An effective conclusion will summarize main points, restate your thesis, explain how the research points to important new questions to explore, and bring closure to the paper.

Avoiding Plagiarism

Plagiarism is the act of presenting an author's words or ideas as if they were your own. This is not only illegal, it is also unethical. You must credit the source not only for material directly quoted but also for any facts or ideas obtained from the source.

Consider this example:

From the original SparkNotes study guide by Melissa and Stephanie Martin

> Throughout the novel, Twain depicts the society that surrounds Huck as little more than a collection of degraded rules and precepts that defy logic. This faulty logic appears early in the novel, when the new judge in town allows Pap to keep custody of Huck.

Plagiarized usage

> Twain's depiction of society is as a collection of illogical rules and principles. A good example of this is when Pap is awarded custody of Huck.

Simply rewording the original passage is not enough. In order to legally and ethically use the words or ideas of another writer you must credit the writer of the original or rework the original into your own new idea.

Using Material Without Plagiarizing

1. **Quote the original directly and credit the author.**

   As Melissa and Stephanie Martin note in their SparkNotes study guide, Huck lives in a society that is "little more than a collection of degraded rules and precepts that defy logic." They offer the example of Pap being awarded custody of Huck.

2. **Paraphrase the original and credit the author.**

   In their SparkNotes study guide, Melissa and Stephanie Martin note that Twain's depiction of society is as a collection of illogical rules and principles. A good example of this is when Pap is awarded custody of Huck.

3. **Use the information in the original to create your own idea.**

   It is hard to blame Huck for wanting to escape from a world where he is forced to follow arbitrary rules, and where he is forced to live with an abusive father.

Crediting your source is not only fair to the writer of the original source, it is also the law. Plagiarism is a serious offence and can result in failing grades, expulsion, and even legal action.

- In addition to citing books and periodicals from which you take information, cite song lyrics, letters, and excerpts from literature.

- Also credit original ideas that are expressed graphically in tables, charts, and diagrams, as well as the sources of any visual aids you may include, such as photographs.

- You do not need to cite the source of any information that is common knowledge, such as "John F. Kennedy was assassinated in 1963 in Dallas, Texas."

In-text citations The most common method of crediting sources is with parenthetical documentation within the text. Generally a reference to the source and page number is included in parentheses at the end of each quotation, paraphrase, or summary of information borrowed from a source. An in-text citation points readers to a corresponding entry in your **works-cited list**—a list of all your sources, complete with publication information, that will appear as the final page of your paper. The Modern Language Association (MLA) recommends the following guidelines for crediting sources in text. You may wish to refer to the *MLA Handbook for Writers of Research Papers* by Joseph Gibaldi for more information and examples.

- Put in parentheses the author's last name and the page number where you found the information. An art historian has noted, "In Wood's idyllic farmscapes, man lives in complete harmony with Nature; he is the earth's caretaker" (Corn 90).

- If the author's name is mentioned in the sentence, put only the page number in parentheses. Art historian Wanda Corn has noted, "In Wood's idyllic farmscapes, man lives in complete harmony with Nature; he is the earth's caretaker" (90).

- If no author is listed, put the title or a shortened version of the title in parentheses. Include a page number if you have one. Some critics believe that Grant Wood's famous painting *American Gothic* pokes fun at small-town life and traditional American values ("Gothic").

Compiling a list of works cited

At the end of your text, provide an alphabetized list of published works or other sources cited.

- Include complete publishing information for each source.

- For magazine and newspaper articles, include the page numbers. If an article is continued on a different page, use + after the first page number.

- For online sources, include the date accessed.

- Cite only those sources from which you actually use information.

- Arrange entries in alphabetical order according to the author's last name. Write the last name first. If no author is given, alphabetize by title.

- For long entries, indent five spaces every line after the first.

How to cite sources

On the next three pages, you'll find sample style sheets that can help you prepare your list of sources—the final page of the research paper. Use the one your teacher prefers.

MLA Style

MLA style is most often used in English and social studies classes. Center the title *Works Cited* at the top of your list.

Source	Style
Book with one author	Isaacson, Walter. *Einstein: His Life and Universe.* New York: Simon & Schuster, 2007.
Book with two or three authors	Mortenson, Greg and Relin, David Oliver. *Three Cups of Tea: One Man's Mission to Promote Peace…One School at a Time.* New York: Penguin Books, 2006. [If a book has more than three authors, name only the first author and then write "et al." (Latin abbreviation for "and others")]
Book with editor(s)	Lehman, David and McHugh, Heather, eds. The Best American Poetry 2007. New York: Scribner, 2007.
Book with an organization or a group as author or editor	Adobe Creative Team. *Adobe Photoshop CS3 Classroom in a Book.* Berkeley: Adobe Press, 2007.
Work from an anthology	Kilmer, Joyce. "Trees." *The Poetry Anthology, 1912–2002.* Ed. Joseph Parisi. Chicago: Ivan R. Dee, 2004. 7
Introduction in a published book	Jackson, Peter. Introduction. *The Making of* Star Wars: *The Definitive Story Behind the Original Film.* By. J.W. Rinzler. New York: Del Rey, 2007. iii.
Encyclopedia article	"Jazz." *Encyclopedia Britannica.* 15th ed. 2007.
Weekly magazine article	Sacks, Oliver. "A Bolt from the Blue." *The New Yorker.* 23 July 2007: 38–42.
Monthly magazine article	Plotnikoff, David. "Hungry Man." *Saveur.* July 2007: 35–36.
Newspaper article	Long, Ray and Meitrodt, Jeffrey. "Some Budget Progress Made." *Chicago Tribune.* 26 July 2007: B3. [If no author is named, begin the entry with the title of the article.]
Internet	"Americans Embracing 'Green' Cleaning." *ABC News.* 30 January 2006. ABC News Internet Ventures. 1 August 2007 <http://abcnews.go.com/Technology/Business/story?id=1544322>.
Online magazine article	Parks, Bob. "Robot Buses Pull In to San Diego's Fastest Lane." *Wired Magazine.* 15.08 (July 2007). 25. Oct. 2007 <http://www.wired.com/cars/futuretransport/magazine/15-08/st_robot>.
Radio or TV program	"Jungles." *Planet Earth.* Animal Planet. Discovery Channel. 25 July. 2007.
Videotape or DVD	Guggenheim, David, dir. *An Inconvenient Truth.* DVD. Paramount, 2006. [For a videotape (VHS) version, replace "DVD" with "Videocassette."]
Interview	Campeche, Tanya. E-mail interview. 25 Feb. 2004. [If an interview takes place in person, replace "E-mail" with "Personal"; if it takes place on the telephone, use "Telephone."]

CMS Style

CMS style was created by the University of Chicago Press to meet its publishing needs. This style, which is detailed in *The Chicago Manual of Style* (CMS), is used in a number of subject areas. Center the title *Bibliography* at the top of your list.

Source	Style
Book with one author	Isaacson, Walter. *Einstein: His Life and Universe.* New York: Simon & Schuster, 2007.
Book with two or three authors	Mortenson, Greg and Relin, David Oliver. *Three Cups of Tea: One Man's Mission to Promote Peace…One School at a Time.* New York: Penguin Books, 2006. [If a book has more than ten authors, name only the first seven and then write "et al." (Latin abbreviation for "and others")].
Book with editor(s)	Lehman, David and McHugh, Heather, eds. *The Best American Poetry 2007.* New York: Scribner, 2007.
Book with an organization or a group as author or editor	Adobe Creative Team. *Adobe Photoshop CS3 Classroom in a Book.* Berkeley: Adobe Press, 2007.
Work from an anthology	Kilmer, Joyce. "Trees." *The Poetry Anthology, 1912–2002.* Ed. Joseph Parisi, 7. Chicago: Ivan R. Dee, 2004.
Introduction in a published book	Rinzler, J.W. *The Making of* Star Wars: *The Definitive Story Behind the Original Film.* Introduction by Peter Jackson. New York: Del Rey, 2007.
Encyclopedia article	[Credit for encyclopedia articles goes in your text, not in your bibliography.]
Weekly magazine article	Sacks, Oliver. "A Bolt from the Blue." *The New Yorker,* July 23, 2007, 38–42.
Monthly magazine article	Plotnikoff, David. "Hungry Man." *Saveur.* July 2007, 35–36.
Newspaper article	Long, Ray and Meitrodt, Jeffrey. "Some Budget Progress Made." *Chicago Tribune.* July 26, 2007, B3. [Credit for unsigned newspaper articles goes in your text, not in your bibliography.]
Internet	ABC News Internet Ventures. "Americans Embracing 'Green' Cleaning." *ABC News.* http://abcnews.go.com/Technology/Business/story?id=1544322.
Online magazine article	Parks, Bob. "Robot Buses Pull In to San Diego's Fastest Lane." *Wired Magazine.* 15.08 (July 2007). http://www.wired.com/cars/futuretransport/magazine/15-08/st_robot.
Radio or TV program	[Credit for radio and TV programs goes in your text, not in your bibliography.]
Videotape or DVD	Guggenheim, David, dir. *An Inconvenient Truth.* Paramount, 2006. DVD. [For a videotape (VHS) version, replace "DVD" with "Videocassette."]
Interview	[Credit for interviews goes in your text, not in your bibliography.]

APA Style

The American Psychological Association (APA) style is commonly used in the sciences. Center the title References at the top of your list.

Source	Style
Book with one author	Isaacson, Walter. (2007). *Einstein: His life and universe.* New York: Simon & Schuster.
Book with two or three authors	Mortenson, Greg and Relin, David Oliver. *Three cups of tea: One man's mission to promote peace…One school at a time.* New York: Penguin Books, 2006. [If a book has more than ten authors, name only the first seven and then write "et al." (Latin abbreviation for "and others")].
Book with editor(s)	Lehman, David and McHugh, Heather. (Eds.). (2007). The best American poetry 2007. New York: Scribner.
Book with an organization or a group as author or editor	Adobe Creative Team. (2007). *Adobe Photoshop CS3 Classroom in a Book.* Berkeley: Adobe Press.
Work from an anthology	Kilmer, Joyce. "Trees." *The Poetry Anthology, 1912–2002.* Ed. Joseph Parisi, 7. Chicago: Ivan R. Dee, 2004.
Introduction in a published book	[Credit for introductions goes in your text, not in your references.]
Encyclopedia article	Jazz. (2007). In *Encyclopedia Britannica.* (Vol. 6, pp. 519). Chicago: Encyclopedia Britannica.
Weekly magazine article	Sacks, Oliver. (2007, July 23).A bolt from the blue. *The New Yorker,* 38–42.
Monthly magazine article	Plotnikoff, David. (2007, July). Hungry man. *Saveur,* 103, 35–36.
Newspaper article	Long, Ray and Meitrodt, Jeffrey. (2007, July 26). Some budget progress made. *Chicago Tribune,* p. B3. [If no author is named, begin the entry with the title of the article.]
Internet	ABC News Internet Ventures. (2006, January 30). *ABC News.* "Americans Embracing 'Green' Cleaning." Retrieved August 1, 2007, from http://abcnews.go.com/Technology/Business/story?id=1544322.
Online magazine article	Parks, Bob. (2007, July). Robot buses pull in to San Diego's fastest lane." *Wired Magazine.*15.08.Retreived July 25, 2007, from http://www.wired.com/cars/futuretransport/magazine/15-08/st_robot.
Radio or TV program	Jungles. (2007, July 25). *Planet Earth* [Television series episode]. Animal Planet. Silver Spring, MD: Discovery Channel.
Videotape or DVD	Guggenheim, David (Director). (2006). *An inconvenient truth.* DVD. Paramount, 2006. [For a videotape (VHS) version, replace "DVD" with "Videocassette."]
Interview	[Credit for interviews goes in your text, not in your bibliography.]

Reading Handbook

Being an active reader is a crucial part of being a lifelong learner. It is also an ongoing task. Good reading skills are recursive; that is, they build on each other, providing the tools you'll need to understand text, to interpret ideas and themes, and to read critically.

Understanding Text Structure

To follow the logic and message of a selection and to remember it, analyze the **text structure,** or organization of ideas, within a writer's work. Recognizing the pattern of organization can help you discover the writer's purpose and will focus your attention on important ideas in the selection. **Look for signal words** to point you to the structure.

- **Spatial sequence** uses words or phrases such as *nearby, to the left, above,* and *behind* to show the physical arrangement of people and objects in an area.

- **Order of importance** will use words such as *most important* and *least necessary* to compare the importance of things or ideas.

- **Chronological order** often uses such words as *first, then, after, later,* and *finally* to show a sequence of events in time.

- **Cause-and-effect order** discusses chains of events using words or phrases such as *therefore, because, subsequently,* or *as a result.*

- **Comparison-contrast order** may use words or phrases such as *similarly, in contrast, likewise,* or *on the other hand.*

- **Problem-solution order** presents a problem and then offers one or more solutions. A problem-solution structure may incorporate other structures such as order of importance, chronological order, or comparison-contrast order.

Comprehension Strategies

Because understanding is the most critical reading task, lifelong learners use a wide variety of reading strategies before, during, and after reading to ensure their comprehension.

Determining the Main Idea

The **main idea** of a selection is the writer's purpose in writing the selection. As you read, it will be helpful to determine the main idea not only of the entire piece, but also of each paragraph. After identifying the important details in each paragraph, pause and ask yourself

- What is the main point of this selection?

- What do these details add up to?

- What is the writer trying to communicate?

Summarizing

A summary is a short restatement of the main ideas and important details of a selection. Summarizing what you have read is an excellent tool for understanding and remembering a passage. To summarize a selection:

- Identify the **main ideas.**

- Determine the essential **supporting details.**

- Relate all the main ideas and essential details in a **logical sequence.**

- **Paraphrase**—that is, restate the selection in your own words.

- Answer **who, what, where, when,** and **why** questions.

The best summaries can easily be understood by someone who has not read the selection. If you're not sure whether an idea is a main idea or a supporting detail, try taking it out of your summary. Does your summary still sound complete?

Distinguishing between fact and opinion

It is always important to be able to tell whether the ideas in a selection are facts or the writer's opinions.

- **Facts** can be proven or measured; you can verify them in reference materials. Sometimes you can observe or test them yourself.

  Example: Chicago is about 800 miles from New York City.

- **Opinions** are often open to interpretation and contain phrases such as "I believe" or "from my point of view."

  Example: Chicago to New York is too far to drive.

As you read a selection, evaluate any facts as well as any opinions you find. Ask yourself:

- Are the facts relevant? Are they actually true?
- Are the opinions well informed and based on verifiable facts? Are they persuasive?

Drawing inferences and supporting them

An **inference** involves using your reason and experience to come up with an idea based on what a writer implies or suggests but does not directly state.

- **Drawing a conclusion** is making a general statement you can explain with reason or with supporting details from the text.
- **Making a generalization** is generating a statement that can apply to more than one item or group.

What is most important when inferring is to be sure that you have accurately based your thoughts on supporting details from the text as well as on your own knowledge.

Making a prediction

A **prediction** is an educated guess about what a text will be about based on initial clues a writer provides. You can also make predictions about what will happen next in a story as you read.

- Take breaks during your reading and **ask yourself questions** about what will happen next, such as, "How will this character react to this news?"
- **Answer these questions for yourself,** supporting your answers with evidence from the text. For example, "Sam will be jealous when he hears the news, because he is in love with Antonia."
- As you continue reading, **verify** your predictions.

Reading silently for sustained periods

When you read for long periods of time, your task is to avoid distractions. Check your comprehension regularly by summarizing what you've read so far. Using study guides or graphic organizers can help you get through difficult passages. Take regular breaks when you need them and vary your reading rate with the demands of the task.

Keep in mind:

Whichever strategies you choose to use while reading, it will always be helpful to:

- Read slowly and carefully.
- Reread difficult passages.
- Take careful notes.

Also, when reading more difficult material, consider these steps to modify or change your reading strategies when you don't understand what you've read.

- Reread the passage.
- Consult other sources, including text resources, teachers, and other students.
- Write comments or questions on another piece of paper for later review or discussion.

Language Handbook

Grammar Glossary

This glossary will help you quickly locate information on parts of speech and sentence structure.

A

Absolute phrase. *See* Phrase.

Abstract noun. *See* Noun chart.

Action verb. *See* Verb.

Active voice. *See* Voice.

Adjective A word that modifies a noun or pronoun by limiting its meaning. Adjectives appear in various positions in a sentence. (The *gray* cat purred. The cat is *gray*.)

Many adjectives have different forms to indicate degree of comparison. (short, shorter, shortest)

The positive degree is the simple form of the adjective. (easy, interesting, good)

The comparative degree compares two persons, places, things, or ideas. (easier, more interesting, better)

The superlative degree compares more than two persons, places, things, or ideas. (easiest, most interesting, best)

A predicate adjective follows a linking verb and further identifies or describes the subject. (The child is happy.)

A proper adjective is formed from a proper noun and begins with a capital letter. Many proper adjectives are created by adding these suffixes: *-an, -ian, -n, -ese,* and *-ish.* (Chinese, African)

Adjective clause. *See* Clause chart.

Adverb A word that modifies a verb, an adjective, or another adverb by making its meaning more specific. When modifying a verb, an adverb may appear in various positions in a sentence. (Cats *generally* eat less than dogs. *Generally,* cats eat less than dogs.) When modifying an adjective or another adverb, an adverb appears directly before the modified word. (I was *quite* pleased that they got along so well.) The word *not* and the contraction

-n't are adverbs. (Mike *wasn't* ready for the test today.) Certain adverbs of time, place, and degree also have a negative meaning. (He's *never* ready.)

Some adverbs have different forms to indicate degree of comparison. (soon, sooner, soonest)

The comparative degree compares two actions. (better, more quickly)

The superlative degree compares three or more actions. (fastest, most patiently, least rapidly)

Adverb clause. *See* Clause chart.

Antecedent. *See* Pronoun.

Appositive A noun or a pronoun that further identifies another noun or pronoun. (My friend *Julie* lives next door.)

Appositive phrase. *See* Phrase.

Article The adjective *a, an,* or *the.*

Indefinite articles (*a* and *an*) refer to one of a general group of persons, places, or things. (I eat *an* apple *a* day.)

The definite article (the) indicates that the noun is a specific person, place, or thing. (*The* alarm woke me up.)

Auxiliary verb. *See* Verb.

B

Base form. *See* Verb tense.

C

Clause A group of words that has a subject and a predicate and that is used as part of a sentence. Clauses fall into two categories: *main clauses,* which are also called *independent clauses,* and *subordinate clauses,* which are also called *dependent clauses.*

A main clause can stand alone as a sentence.

Types of Subordinate Clauses			
Clause	Function	Example	Begins with . . .
Adjective clause	Modifies a noun or a pronoun	Songs *that have a strong beat* make me want to dance.	A relative pronoun such as *which, who, whom, whose,* or *that*
Adverb clause	Modifies a verb, an adjective, or an adverb	*Whenever Al calls me,* he asks to borrow my bike.	A subordinating conjunction such as *after, although, because, if, since, when,* or *where*
Noun clause	Serves as a subject, an object, or a predicate nominative	*What Philip did* surprised us.	Words such as *how, that, what, whatever, when, where, which, who, whom, whoever, whose,* or *why*

There must be at least one main clause in every sentence. (*The rooster crowed,* and *the dog barked.*)

A subordinate clause cannot stand alone as a sentence. A subordinate clause needs a main clause to complete its meaning. Many subordinate clauses begin with subordinating conjunctions or relative pronouns. (*When Geri sang her solo,* the audience became quiet.) The chart on the next page shows the main types of subordinate clauses.

Collective noun. *See* Noun chart.

Common noun. *See* Noun chart.

Comparative degree. *See* Adjective; Adverb.

Complement A word or phrase that completes the meaning of a verb. The four basic kinds of complements are *direct objects, indirect objects, object complements,* and *subject complements.*

A direct object answers the question *What?* or *Whom?* after an action verb. (**Kari found a dollar.** Larry saw *Denise.*)

An indirect object answers the question *To whom? For whom? To what?* or *For what?* after an action verb. (**Do *me* a favor. She gave the *child* a toy.**)

An object complement answers the question *What?* after a direct object. An object complement is a noun, a pronoun, or an adjective that completes the meaning of a direct object by identifying or describing it. (**The director made me the *understudy* for the role. The little girl called the puppy *hers.***)

A subject complement follows a subject and a linking verb. It identifies or describes a subject. The two kinds of subject complements are *predicate nominatives* and *predicate adjectives.*

A predicate nominative is a noun or pronoun that follows a linking verb and tells more about the subject. (**The author of "The Raven" is *Poe.***)

A predicate adjective is an adjective that follows a linking verb and gives more information about the subject. (**Ian became *angry* at the bully.**)

Complex sentence. *See* Sentence.

Compound preposition. *See* Preposition.

Compound sentence. *See* Sentence.

Compound-complex sentence. *See* Sentence.

Conjunction A word that joins single words or groups of words.

A coordinating conjunction *(and, but, or, nor, for, yet, so)* joins words or groups of words that are equal in grammatical importance. (**David *and* Ruth are twins. I was bored, *so* I left.**)

Correlative conjunctions *(both . . . and, just as . . . so, not only . . . but also, either . . . or, neither . . . nor, whether . . . or)* work in pairs to join words and groups of words of equal importance.

(Choose *either* the muffin *or* the bagel.)

A subordinating conjunction *(after, although, as if, because, before, if, since, so that, than, though, until, when, while)* joins a dependent idea or clause to a main clause. **(Beth acted *as if* she felt ill.)**

Conjunctive adverb An adverb used to clarify the relationship between clauses of equal weight in a sentence. Conjunctive adverbs are used to replace *and (also, besides, furthermore, moreover)*; to replace *but (however, nevertheless, still)*; to state a result *(consequently, therefore, so, thus)*; or to state equality *(equally, likewise, similarly)*. **(Ana was determined to get an A; *therefore,* she studied often.)**

Coordinating conjunction. *See* Conjunction.

Correlative conjunction. *See* Conjunction.

D

Declarative sentence. *See* Sentence.

Definite article. *See* Article.

Demonstrative pronoun. *See* Pronoun.

Direct object. *See* Complement.

E

Emphatic form. *See* Verb tense.

F

Future tense. *See* Verb tense.

G

Gerund A verb form that ends in *-ing* and is used as a noun. A gerund may function as a subject, the object of a verb, or the object of a preposition. **(*Smiling* uses fewer muscles than *frowning.* Marie enjoys *walking.*)**

Gerund phrase. *See* Phrase.

I

Imperative mood. *See* Mood of verb.

Imperative sentence. *See* Sentence chart.

Indicative mood. *See* Mood of verb.

Indirect object. *See* Complement.

Infinitive A verb form that begins with the word *to* and functions as a noun, an adjective, or an adverb. **(No one wanted *to answer.*)** Note: When *to* precedes a verb, it is not a preposition but instead signals an infinitive.

Infinitive phrase. *See* Phrase.

Intensive pronoun. *See* Pronoun.

Interjection A word or phrase that expresses emotion or exclamation. An interjection has no grammatical connection to other words. Commas follow mild ones; exclamation points follow stronger ones. **(*Well,* have a good day. *Wow!*)**

Interrogative pronoun. *See* Pronoun.

Intransitive verb. *See* Verb.

Inverted order In a sentence written in *inverted order,* the predicate comes before the subject. Some sentences are written in inverted order for variety or special emphasis. **(Up the beanstalk *scampered* Jack.)** The subject also generally follows the predicate in a sentence that begins with *here* or *there.* **(*Here* was the solution to his problem.)** Questions, or interrogative sentences, are generally written in inverted order. In many questions, an auxiliary verb precedes the subject, and the main verb follows it. **(*Has* anyone *seen* Susan?)** Questions that begin with *who* or *what* follow normal word order.

Irregular verb. *See* Verb tense.

L

Linking verb. *See* Verb.

M

Main clause. *See* Clause.

Mood of verb A verb expresses one of three moods: indicative, imperative, or subjunctive.

The indicative mood is the most common. It makes a statement or asks a question. **(We *are* out of bread. *Will* you *buy* it?)**

The imperative mood expresses a command or makes a request. **(*Stop* acting like a child! Please *return* my sweater.)**

Types of Nouns		
Noun	Function	Examples
Abstract noun	Names an idea, a quality, or a characteristic	capitalism, terror
Collective noun	Names a group of things or persons	herd, troop
Common noun	Names a general type of person, place, thing, or idea	city, building
Compound noun	Is made up of two or more words	checkerboard, globe-trotter
Noun of direct addrress	Identifies the person or persons being spoken to	*Maria*, please stand.
Possessive noun	Shows possession, ownership, or the relationship between two nouns	my *sister's* room
Proper noun	Names a particular person, place, thing, or idea	Cleopatra, Italy, Christianity

The subjunctive mood is used to express, indirectly, a demand, suggestion, or statement of necessity (**I demand that he** *stop* **acting like a child. It's necessary that she** *buy* **more bread.**) The subjunctive is also used to state a condition or wish that is contrary to fact. This use of the subjunctive requires the past tense. (**If you** *were* **a nice person, you** *would return* **my sweater.**)

N

Nominative pronoun. *See* Pronoun.

Noun A word that names a person, a place, a thing, or an idea. The chart on this page shows the main types of nouns.

Noun clause. *See* Clause chart.

Noun of direct address. *See* Noun chart.

Number A noun, pronoun, or verb is *singular* in number if it refers to one; *plural* if it refers to more than one.

O

Object. *See* Complement.

P

Participle A verb form that can function as an adjective. Present participles always end in *-ing.* (**The woman comforted the** *crying* **child.**) Many past participles end in *-ed.* (**We bought the beautifully** *painted* **chair.**) However, irregular verbs form their past participles in some other way. (**Cato was Caesar's** *sworn* **enemy.**)

Passive voice. *See* Voice.

Past tense. *See* Verb tense.

Perfect tense. *See* Verb tense.

Personal pronoun. *See* Pronoun, Pronoun chart.

Phrase A group of words that acts in a sentence as a single part of speech.

An absolute phrase consists of a noun or pronoun that is modified by a participle or participial phrase but has no grammatical relation to the complete subject or predicate. (*The vegetables being done,* **we finally sat down to eat dinner.**)

An appositive phrase is an appositive along with any modifiers. If not essential to the meaning of the sentence, an appositive phrase is set off by commas. (**Jack plans to go to the jazz concert,** *an important musical event.*)

A gerund phrase includes a gerund plus its complements and modifiers. (*Playing the flute* **is her hobby.**)

An infinitive phrase contains the infinitive plus its complements and modifiers. (**It is time** *to leave for school.*)

A participial phrase contains a participle and any modifiers necessary to complete its meaning. (**The woman** *sitting over there* **is my grandmother.**)

A prepositional phrase consists of a preposition, its object, and any modifiers of the object. A prepositional phrase can function as an adjective, modifying a noun or a pronoun. (**The dog** *in the yard* **is very gentle.**) A prepositional phrase may also function as an adverb when it modifies a verb, an adverb, or an adjective. (**The baby slept** *on my lap.*)

A verb phrase consists of one or more auxiliary verbs followed by a main verb. (**The job** *will have been completed* **by noon tomorrow.**)

Positive degree. *See* Adjective.

Possessive noun. *See* Noun chart.

Predicate The verb or verb phrase and any objects, complements, or modifiers that express the essential thought about the subject of a sentence.

A simple predicate is a verb or verb phrase that tells something about the subject. (**We** *ran.*)

A complete predicate includes the simple predicate and any words that modify or complete it. (**We** *solved the problem in a short time.*)

A compound predicate has two or more verbs or verb phrases that are joined by a conjunction and share the same subject. (**We** *ran to the park and began to play baseball.*)

Predicate adjective. *See* Adjective; Complement.

Predicate nominative. *See* Complement.

Preposition A word that shows the relationship of a noun or pronoun to some other word in the sentence. Prepositions include *about, above, across, among, as, behind, below, beyond, but, by, down, during, except, for, from, into, like, near, of, on, outside, over, since, through, to, under, until, with.* (**I usually eat breakfast** *before* **school.**)

A compound preposition is made up of more than one word. (*according to, ahead of, as to, because of, by means of, in addition to, in spite of, on account of*) (**We played the game** *in spite of* **the snow.**)

Prepositional phrase. *See* Phrase.

Present tense. *See* Verb tense.

Progressive form. *See* Verb tense.

Pronoun A word that takes the place of a noun, a group of words acting as a noun, or another pronoun. The word or group of words that a pronoun refers to is called its antecedent. (**In the following sentence,** *Mari* **is the antecedent of** *she. Mari likes Mexican food, but she doesn't like Italian food.*)

A demonstrative pronoun points out specific persons, places, things, or ideas. (*this, that, these, those*)

An indefinite pronoun refers to persons, places, or things in a more general way than a noun does. (*all, another, any, both, each, either, enough, everything, few, many, most, much, neither, nobody, none, one, other, others, plenty, several, some*)

An intensive pronoun adds emphasis to another noun or pronoun. If an intensive pronoun is omitted, the meaning of the sentence will be the same. (**Rebecca** *herself* **decided to look for a part-time job.**)

An interrogative pronoun is used to form questions. (*who? whom? whose? what? which?*)

A personal pronoun refers to a specific person or thing. Personal pronouns have three cases: nominative, possessive, and objective. The case depends upon the function of the pronoun in a sentence. The first chart on this page shows the case forms of personal pronouns.

A reflexive pronoun reflects back to a noun or pronoun used earlier in the sentence, indicating that the same person or thing is involved. (**We told** *ourselves* **to be patient.**)

A relative pronoun is used to begin a subordinate clause. (*who, whose, that, what, whom, whoever, whomever, whichever, whatever*)

Proper adjective. *See* Adjective.

Proper noun. *See* Noun chart.

R

Reflexive pronoun. *See* Pronoun.

Relative pronoun. *See* Pronoun.

S

Sentence A group of words expressing a complete thought. Every sentence has a subject and a predicate. Sentences can be classified by function or by structure. The second chart on this page shows the categories by function; the following subentries describe the categories by structure. *See also* Subject; Predicate; Clause.

A simple sentence has only one main clause and no subordinate clauses. *(Alan found an old violin.)* A simple sentence may contain a compound subject or a compound predicate or both. *(Alan and Teri found an old violin. Alan found an old violin and tried to play it. Alan and Teri found an old violin and tried to play it.)* The subject and the predicate can be expanded with adjectives, adverbs, prepositional phrases, appositives, and verbal phrases. As long as the sentence has only one main clause, however, it remains a simple sentence. *(Alan, rummaging in the attic, found an old violin.)*

A compound sentence has two or more main clauses. Each main clause has its own subject and predicate, and these main clauses are usually joined by a comma and a coordinating conjunc-tion. *(Cats meow, and dogs bark, but ducks quack.)* Semicolons may also be used to join the main clauses in a compound sentence. *(The helicopter landed; the pilot had saved four passengers.)*

A complex sentence has one main clause and one or more subordinate clauses. *(Since the movie starts at eight, we should leave here by seven-thirty.)*

A compound-complex sentence has two or more main clauses and at least one subordinate clause. *(If we leave any later, we may miss the previews, and I want to see them.)*

Simple predicate. *See* Predicate.

Simple subject. *See* Subject.

Subject The part of a sentence that tells what the sentence is about.

A simple subject is the main noun or pronoun in the subject. *(Babies crawl.)*

A complete subject includes the simple subject and any words that modify it. *(The man from New Jersey won the race.)* In some sentences, the simple subject and the complete subject are the same. *(Birds fly.)*

Personal Pronouns

Clause	Singular Pronouns	Plural Pronouns	Function in Sentence
Nominative	I, you, she, he, it	we, you, they	subject or predicate nominative
Objective	me, you, her, him, it	us, you, them	direct object, indirect object, or object of a preposition

Types of Sentences

Sentence Type	Function	Ends with . . .	Examples
Declarative sentence	Makes a statement	A period	I did not enjoy the movie.
Exclamatory sentence	Expresses strong emotion	An exclamation point	What a good writer Consuela is!
Imperative sentence	Makes a request or gives a command	A period or an exclamation point	Please come to the party. Stop!
Interrogative sentence	Asks a question	A question mark	Is the composition due?

A compound subject has two or more simple subjects joined by a conjunction. The subjects share the same verb. (**Firefighters** and **police officers** protect the community.)

Subjunctive mood. *See* Mood of verb.

Subordinate clause. *See* Clause.

Subordinating conjunction. *See* Conjunction.

Superlative degree. *See* Adjective; Adverb.

T

Tense. *See* Verb tense.

Transitive verb. *See* Verb.

V

Verb A word that expresses action or a state of being. *(cooks, seem, laughed)*

An action verb tells what someone or something does. Action verbs can express either physical or mental action. (**Crystal** *decided* to *change* the tire herself.)

A transitive verb is an action verb that is followed by a word or words that answer the question *What?* or *Whom?* (I *held* the baby.)

An intransitive verb is an action verb that is not followed by a word that answers the question *What?* or *Whom?* (The baby *laughed.*)

A linking verb expresses a state of being by linking the subject of a sentence with a word or an expression that identifies or describes the subject. (**The lemonade** *tastes* **sweet. He** *is* **our new principal.**) The most commonly used linking verb is be in all its forms *(am, is, are, was, were, will be, been, being)*. Other linking verbs include *appear, become, feel, grow, look, remain, seem, sound, smell, stay, taste.*

An auxiliary verb, or helping verb, is a verb that accompanies the main verb to form a verb phrase. (I *have been* swimming.) The forms of be and have are the most common auxiliary verbs: *(am, is, are, was, were, being, been; has, have, had, having)*. Other auxiliaries include *can, could, do, does, did, may, might, must, shall, should, will, would.*

Verbal A verb form that functions in a sentence as a noun, an adjective, or an adverb. The three kinds of verbals are gerunds, infinitives, and participles. *See* Gerund; Infinitive; Participle.

Verb tense The tense of a verb indicates when the action or state of being occurs. All the verb tenses are formed from the four principal parts of a verb: a base form *(talk)*, a present participle *(talking)*, a simple past form *(talked)*, and a past participle *(talked)*. A regular verb forms its simple past and past participle by adding *-ed* to the base form. *(climb, climbed)* An irregular verb forms its past and past participle in some other way. *(get, got, gotten)*

In addition to present, past, and future tenses, there are three perfect tenses.

The present perfect tense expresses an action or a condition that occurred at some indefinite time in the past. This tense also shows an action or a condition that began in the past and continues into the present. (**She** *has played* the piano for four years.)

The past perfect tense indicates that one past action or condition began *and* ended before another past action started. (**Andy** *had finished* his homework before I even began mine.)

The future perfect tense indicates that one future action or condition will begin *and* end before another future event starts. Use *will have* or *shall have* with the past participle of a verb. (**By tomorrow, I** *will have finished* my homework, too.)

The progressive form of a verb expresses a continuing action with any of the six tenses. To make the progressive forms, use the appropriate tense of the verb be with the present participle of the main verb. (**She** *is swimming.* **She** *has been swimming.*)

The emphatic form adds special force, or emphasis, to the present and past tense of a verb. For the emphatic form, use *do, does,* or *did* with the base form. (**Toshi** *did want* that camera.)

Voice The voice of a verb shows whether the subject performs the action or receives the action of the verb.

A verb is in the active voice if the subject of the sentence performs the action. (**The referee** *blew* **the whistle.**)

A verb is in the passive voice if the subject of the sentence receives the action of the verb. (**The whistle** *was blown* **by the referee.**)

Troubleshooter

The Troubleshooter will help you recognize and correct errors that you might make in your writing.

Sentence Fragment

Problem: A fragment that lacks a subject
The grass is wet. Can't be mowed now.

Solution: Add a subject to the fragment to make it a complete sentence.
The grass is wet. It can't be mowed now.

Problem: A fragment that lacks a complete verb
We enjoyed our dinner. Beans, rice, and salad.
The storm was fierce. The wind blowing hard.

Solution A: Add either a complete verb or a helping verb to make the sentence complete.
We enjoyed our dinner. Beans, rice, and salad make a good meal.
The storm was fierce. The wind was blowing hard.

Solution B: Combine the fragment with another sentence.
We enjoyed our dinner of beans, rice, and salad.
The storm was fierce with the wind blowing hard.

Problem: A fragment that is a subordinate clause
We went to the park. Where we had often gone before.
Jan won the swimming medal. Which she gave to her parents.

Solution A: Combine the fragment with another sentence.
We went to the park, where we had often gone before.
Jan won the swimming medal, which she gave to her parents.

Solution B: Rewrite the fragment as a complete sentence, eliminating the subordinating conjunction or the relative pronoun and adding a subject or other words necessary to make a complete thought.
We went to the park. We had often gone there before.
Jan won the swimming medal. She gave it to her parents.

Problem: A fragment that lacks both a subject and a verb
The birds woke us with their songs. At six in the morning.

Solution: Combine the fragment with another sentence.
The birds woke us with their songs at six in the morning.

Rule of Thumb: Sentence fragments can make your writing hard to understand. Make sure every sentence has a subject and a verb.

Note: In almost all of the writing you do, especially for school, you should avoid sentence fragments. However, sentence fragments can be used to create special effects, such as adding emphasis or conveying realistic dialogue.
"Not again!" she cried.
The pizza was gone. All of it.

Run-On Sentence

Problem: Comma splice—two main clauses separated only by a comma
The sky is pitch black, there is no moon.

Solution A: Replace the comma with an end mark of punctuation, such as a period or a question mark, and begin the new sentence with a capital letter.
The sky is pitch black. There is no moon.

Solution B: Place a semicolon between the two main clauses.
The sky is pitch black; there is no moon.

Solution C: Add a coordinating conjunction after the comma.
The sky is pitch black, and there is no moon.

Problem: Two main clauses with no punctuation between them.
We picked the apples then we made pies.

Solution A: Separate the main clauses with an end mark of punctuation, such as a period or question mark, and begin the second sentence with a capital letter.
We picked the apples. Then we made pies.

Solution B: Separate the main clauses with a semicolon.
We picked the apples; then we made pies.

Solution C: Add a comma and a coordinating conjunction between the main clauses.
We picked the apples, and then we made pies.

Problem: The main clauses with no comma before the coordinating conjunction
Elephants still live in the wild but they are endangered.

Solution: Add a comma before the coordinating conjunction to separate the two main clauses.
Elephants still live in the wild, but they are endangered.

Rule of Thumb: It often helps to have someone else read your longer sentences to see if they are clear. Since you know what the sentences are supposed to mean, you might miss the need for punctuation.

Lack of Subject-Verb Agreement

Problem: A subject that is separated from the verb by an intervening prepositional phrase
Ten pieces of the puzzle is on the floor.
The shoe department in each of our stores are closing.

Solution: Make the verb agree with the subject, which is never the object of a preposition.
Ten pieces of the puzzle are on the floor.
The shoe department in each of our stores is closing.

Problem: A predicate nominative that differs in number from the subject
Hamburgers is tonight's dinner.
Tonight's dinner are hamburgers.

Solution: Ignore the predicate nominative, and make the verb agree with the subject of the sentence.
Hamburgers are tonight's dinner.
Tonight's dinner is hamburgers.

Problem: A subject that follows the verb
On my desk is two letters from my dad.
Here is my answers to them both.

Solution: In an inverted sentence look for the subject after the verb. Then make sure the verb agrees with the subject.
On my desk are two letters from my dad.
Here are my answers to them both.

Rule of Thumb: Reversing the order of an inverted sentence may help you decide on the verb form to use: "My answers to them both are here."

Problem: A collective noun as the subject
The cross country team are in first place.
The team gathers at the captain's house after each meet.

Solution A: If the collective noun refers to a group as a whole, use a singular verb.
The cross country team is in first place.

Solution B: If the collective noun refers to each member of a group individually, use a plural verb.
The team gather at the captain's house after each meet.

Problem: A noun of amount as the subject
Five bushels are a great many tomatoes.
Three marbles is in my pocket.

Solution: Determine whether the noun of amount refers to one unit and is therefore singular or whether it refers to a number of individual unites and is therefore plural.
Five bushels is a great many tomatoes.
Three marbles are in my pocket.

Problem: A compound subject that is joined by *and*
The hill and the lake makes a lovely setting for a picnic.
Spaghetti and meatballs are her favorite dinner.

Solution A: If the parts of the compound subject do not belong to one unit or if they refer to different people of things, use a plural verb.
The hill and the lake make a lovely setting for a picnic.

Solution B: If the parts of the compound subject belong to one unit or if both parts refer to the same person or thing, use a singular verb.
Spaghetti and meatballs is her favorite dinner.

Problem: A compound subject that is joined by *or* or *nor*
Neither those trees nor that shrub are healthy.

Solution: Make the verb agree with the subject that is closer to it.
Neither those trees nor that shrub is healthy.

Problem: A compound subject that is preceded *by many a, every,* or *each*
Many a dog and cat ends up in an animal shelter or a pound.

Solution: When *many a, every,* or *each* precedes a compound subject, the subject is considered singular. Use a singular verb.
Many a dog and cat ends up in an animal shelter or a pound.

Problem: A subject that is separated from the verb by an intervening expression
That issue, as well as several others, are bothering me.

Solution: Certain expressions, such as these beginning with *as well as, in addition to,* and *together with,* do not change the number of the subject. Ignore an intervening expression between a subject and its verb, and make the verb agree with the subject.
That issue, along with several others, is bothering me.

Problem: An indefinite pronoun as the subject
Neither of the boys are on time.

Solution: Determine whether the indefinite pronoun is singular or plural, and make the verb agree. Some indefinite pronouns are singular—*another, anyone, everyone, one, each, either, neither, anything, everything, something,* and *somebody.* Some are plural—*both, many, few, several,* and *others.* Some can be singular or plural—*some, all, any, more, most,* and *none.* In these cases, find the noun to which the pronoun refers to determine which verb form to use.
Neither of the boys is on time.

Lack of Pronoun-Antecedent Agreement

Problem: A singular antecedent that can be either male or female.
A climber must check his equipment carefully.

Solution A: Traditionally, a masculine pronoun has been used to refer to an antecedent that may be either male or female. This usage ignores or excludes females. Reword the sentence to use *he or she, him or her,* and so on.
A climber must check his or her equipment carefully.

Solution B: Reword the sentence so that both the antecedent and the pronoun are plural.
Climbers must check their equipment carefully.

Solution C: Reword the sentence to eliminate the pronoun.
A climber must check the equipment carefully.

Rule of Thumb: Although you may see the masculine forms used exclusively in older literature, they are not acceptable in contemporary writing.

Problem: A second-person pronoun that refers to a third-person antecedent
Juan likes sitcoms that make you think as well as laugh.

Solution A: Use the appropriate third-person pronoun.
Juan likes sitcoms that make him think as well as laugh.

Solution B: Use an appropriate noun instead of a pronoun.
Juan likes sitcoms that make people think as well as laugh.

Problem: A singular indefinite pronoun as an antecedent
Each of the volumes has their own index.

Solution: *Each, every, either, neither,* and *one* are singular and therefore require singular personal pronouns even when followed by a prepositional phrase that contains a plural noun.
Each of the volumes has its own index.

Rule of Thumb: To help you remember that *each, either,* and *neither* are singular, think *each one, either one,* and *neither one.*

Lack of Clear Pronoun Reference [Unclear Antecedent]

Problem: A pronoun reference that is weak or vague
We spent several weeks at the farm this summer, and it was exciting.
The label says to shake it before pouring a serving.

Solution A: Rewrite the sentence, adding a clear antecedent for the pronoun.
We spent our vacation at the farm this summer, and it was exciting.

Solution B: Rewrite the sentence, substituting a noun for the pronoun.
The label says to shake the bottle of salad dressing before pouring a serving.

Problem: A pronoun that could refer to more than one antecedent
Lauren and Abby wrote six songs, and she recorded them all.
Don't buy a car from that dealership: it will let you down.

Solution A: Rewrite the sentence, substituting a noun for the pronoun.
Lauren and Abby wrote six songs, and Abby recorded them all.

Solution B: Rewrite the sentence, making the antecedent of the pronoun clear.
A car from that dealership will let you down; don't buy one there.

Problem: The indefinite use of *you* or *they*
You just have to laugh at that scene in the movie.
They say the weather will be clear tomorrow.

Solution A: Rewrite the sentence, substituting a noun for the pronoun.
The audience just has to laugh at that scene in the movie.

Solution B: Rewrite the sentence, eliminating the pronoun entirely.
According to the forecast, the weather will be clear tomorrow.

Shift in Pronoun

Problem: An incorrect shift in person between two pronouns
Lynn likes the front seat, where you are most comfortable.
The Chins planted a maple on the south side of the house, where you need shade the most.

Solution A: Replace the incorrect pronoun with a pronoun that agrees with its a antecedent.
Lynn likes the front seat, where she is most comfortable.

Solution B: Replace the incorrect pronoun with an appropriate noun.
The Chins plants a maple on the south side of the house, where the house needs shade the most.

Shift in Verb Tense

Problem: An unnecessary shift in tense.
The children will give their mother flowers, and they kiss her.
After the party ended, we go home.

Solution: When two or more events occur at the same time, be sure to use the same verb tense to describe each event.
The children will give their mother flowers, and they will kiss her.
After the party ended, we went home.

Problem: A lack of correct shift in tenses to show that one event precedes or follows another
By the time the concert ended, we sat for four hours.

Solution: When two past events being described have occurred at different times, shift from the past tense to the past perfect tense to indicate that one action began and ended before another past action began. Use the past perfect tense for the earlier of the two actions.
By the time the concert ended, we had sat for four hours.

Rule of Thumb: When you need to use several verb tenses in your writing, it may help to first jot down the sequence of events you're writing about. Be clear in your mind what happened first, next, last.

Incorrect Verb Tense or Form

Problem: An incorrect or missing verb ending
When I began taking lessons, I learn about quarter, half, and whole notes.
I had start the lessons two months ago.

Solution: Add –ed to a regular verb to form the past tense and the past participle.
When I began taking lessons, I learned about quarter, half, and whole notes.
I had started the lessons two months ago.

Problem: An improperly formed irregular verb
James brung the book back to the library.
Catherine has writed six pages on that topic.

Solution: Irregular verbs form their past and past participles in some way other than by adding –ed. Memorize these forms, or look them up.
James brought the book back to the library.
Catherine has written six pages on that topic.

Problem: Confusion between the past form and the past participle
We have ate too many apples.
She had swam the Chesapeake last July.

Solution: Use the past participle form of an irregular verb, not the past form, when you use the auxiliary verb *have.*
We have eaten too many apples.
She had swum the Chesapeake last July.

Problem: Improper use of the past participle
The catcher thrown several runners out.
The DiCaprios done a fine job rearing those children.

Solution A: The past participle of an irregular verb cannot stand alone as a verb. Add a form of the auxiliary verb *have* to the past participle to form a complete verb.
The catcher had thrown several runners out.
The DiCaprios have done a fine job rearing those children.

Solution B: Replace the past participle with the past form of the verb.
The catcher threw several runners out.
The DiCaprios did a fine job rearing those children.

Misplaced or Dangling Modifier

Problem: A misplaced modifier
The children were swimming in the photograph.
Swooping down on a fish, I spotted the gull.
I saw a man at the movies eating popcorn.

Solution: Modifiers that modify the wrong word or seem to modify more than own word in a sentence are called misplaced modifiers. Move the misplaced phrase as close as possible to the word or words it modifies.
The children in the photograph were swimming.
I spotted the gull swooping down on a fish.
I saw a man eating popcorn at the movies.

Problem: Incorrect placement of the adverb *only*
Tricia only has enough money to buy a pencil.

Solution: Place the adverb only immediately before the word or group of words it modifies.
Only Tricia has enough money to buy a pencil.
Tricia has enough money to buy only a pencil.
Tricia has only enough money to buy a pencil.

Rule of Thumb: Note that each time *only* is moved,

the meaning of the sentence changes. Check to be sure your sentence says what you mean.

Problem: A dangling modifier
Croaking loudly, I listened to the sounds of the frogs in the bog.
Stealing home, the game was won for the Pirates.

Solution: Dangling modifiers do not seem to logically modify any word in the sentence. Rewrite the sentence, adding a noun to which the dangling phrase clearly refers. Often you will have to add other words too.
I listened to the sounds of the frogs croaking loudly in the bog.
Stealing home, Layla won the game for the Pirates.

Missing or Misplaced Possessive Apostrophe

Problem: Singular nouns
The womans child loved the circus trapeze artists.

Solution: Use an apostrophe and –s to form the possessive of a singular noun, even one that ends in *s.*
The woman's child loved the circus's trapeze artist.

Problem: Plural nouns ending in – s
The hikers cars were parked at the base of the trail.

Solution: Use an apostrophe alone to form the possessive of a plural noun that ends in –s.
The hikers' cars were parked at the base of the trail.

Problem: Plural nouns not ending in –s
Did Brian join the mens group?

Solution: Use an apostrophe and –s to form the possessive of a plural noun that does not end in –s.
Did Brian join the men's group?

Problem: Pronouns
Everyones contribution helps.
These pencils are your's, and those pencils are their's.

Solution A: Use an apostrophe and –s to form the possessive of a singular indefinite pronoun.
Everyone's contribution helps.

Solution B: Do not use an apostrophe with any of the possessive personal pronouns.
These pencils are yours, and those pencils are theirs.

Problem: Confusion between *its* and *it's*
Will you tell me when its ten o'clock?
The cat licked it's fur.

Solution: Do not use an apostrophe to form the possessive of *it.* Use an apostrophe to form the contraction of *it is.*
Will you tell me when it's ten o'clock?
The cat licked its fur.

Missing Commas with Nonessential Element

Problem: Missing commas with nonessential participles, infinitives, and their phrases
Pounding hard on the roof the rain awakened me.
The whole set of cups chipped from many years of use was discarded.
To answer you question this software package is worth the price.

Solution: Determine whether the participle, infinitive, or phrase is essential to the meaning of the sentence. If it is not essential, set off the phrase with commas.
Pounding hard on the roof, the rain awakened me.
The whole set of cups, chipped from many years of use, was discarded.
To answer your question, this software package is worth the price.

Problem: Missing commas with nonessential adjective clauses
My mother who is a very generous woman gave us investment tips.

Solution: Determine whether the clause is essential to the meaning of the sentence. If it is not essential, set off the clause with commas.
My mother, who is a very generous woman, gave us investment tips.

Problem: Missing comas with nonessential appositives
John the lead-off batter singles on a line drive

Solution: Determine whether the appositive is essential to the meaning of the sentence. If it is not essential, set off the appositive with commas.
John, the lead-off batter, singled on a line drive.

Rule of Thumb: To determine whether a word or phrase is essential, try reading the sentence without it.

Problem: Missing commas with interjections and parenthetical expressions
Wow what a great cat that is
On Saturdays as a rule we sleep late.

Solution: Set off the interjection or parenthetical expression with commas.
Wow, what a great cat that is!
On Saturdays, as a rule, we sleep late.

Missing Commas in a Series

Problem: Missing commas in a series of words, phrases, or clauses
Alicia Nirupam and Matt made the honor roll.
Mark made the dough kneaded it and left it to rise
The firefighter carries the child out of the apartment down the stairs and into the arms of her mother.
Joe pitched the tent Meg gathered firewood and Bud unloaded the truck.

Solution: When there are three or more elements in a series, use a comma after each element that precedes the conjunction
Alicia, Nirupam, and Matt made the honor roll.
Mark made the dough, kneaded it, and left it to rise.
The firefighter carries the child out of the apartment, down the stairs, and into the arms of her mother.
Joe pitched the tent, Meg gathered firewood, and Bud unloaded the truck.

Rule of Thumb: When you're having difficulty with a rule of usage, try rewriting the rule in your own words. Then check with your teacher to be sure you have grasped the concept.

Mechanics

This section will help you use correct capitalization, punctuation, and abbreviations in your writing.

Capitalization

This section will help you recognize and use correct capitalization in sentences.

Rule: Capitalize the first word in any sentence, including direct quotations and sentences in parentheses unless they are included in another sentence.

Example: *She said, "Come back soon."*

Example: *Emily Dickinson became famous only after her death. (She published only six poems during her lifetime.)*

Rule: Always capitalize the pronoun *I* no matter where it appears in the sentence.

Example: *Some of my relatives think that I should become a doctor.*

Rule: Capitalize proper nouns, including

a. names of individuals and titles used in direct address preceding a name or describing a relationship.
Example: *George Washington; Dr. Morgan; Aunt Margaret*

b. names of ethnic groups, national groups, political parties and their members, and languages.
Example: *Italian Americans; Aztec; the Republican Party; a Democrat; Spanish*

c. names of organizations, institutions, firms, monuments, bridges, buildings, and other structures.
Example: *Red Cross; Stanford University; General Electric; Lincoln Memorial; Tappan Zee Bridge; Chrysler Building; Museum of Natural History*

d. trade names and names of documents, awards, and laws.
Example: *Microsoft; Declaration of Independence; Pulitzer Prize; Sixteenth Amendment*

e. geographical terms and regions or localities.
Example: *Hudson River; Pennsylvania Avenue; Grand Canyon; Texas; the Midwest*

f. names of planets and other heavenly bodies.
Example: *Venus; Earth; the Milky Way*

g. names of ships, planes, trains, and spacecraft.
Example: *USS Constitution; Spirit of St. Louis; Apollo 11*

h. names of most historical events, eras, calendar items, and religious names and items.
Example: *World War II; Age of Enlightenment; June; Christianity; Buddhists; Bible; Easter; God*

i. titles of literary works, works of art, and musical compositions.
Example: *"Why I Live at the P.O."; The Starry Night; Rhapsody in Blue*

j. names of specific school courses.
Example: *Advanced Physics; American History*

Rule: Capitalize proper adjectives (adjectives formed from proper nouns).

Example: *Christmas tree; Hanukkah candles; Freudian psychology; American flag*

Punctuation

This section will help you use these elements of punctuation correctly.

Rule: Use a period at the end of a declarative sentence or a polite command.

Example: *I'm thirsty.*
Example: *Please bring me a glass of water.*

Rule: Use an exclamation point to show strong feeling or after a forceful command.

Example: *I can't believe my eyes!*
Example: *Watch your step!*

Rule: Use a question mark to indicate a direct question.

Example: *Who is in charge here?*

Rule: Use a colon
a. to introduce a list (especially after words such as these, the following, or as follows) and to introduce material that explains, restates, or illustrates previous material.

Example: *The following states voted for the amendment: Texas, California, Georgia, and Florida.*
Example: *The sunset was colorful: purple, orange, and red lit up the sky.*

b. to introduce a long or formal quotation.
Example: *It was Mark Twain who stated the following proverb: "Man is the only animal that blushes. Or needs to."*

c. in precise time measurements, biblical chapter and verse references, and business letter salutations.
Example: *3:35 P.M.*   *7:50 A.M.*
             Gen. 1:10–11   *Matt. 2:23*
             Dear Ms. Samuels: *Dear Sir:*

Rule: Use a semicolon
a. to separate main clauses that are not joined by a coordinating conjunction.
Example: *There were two speakers at Gettysburg that day; only Lincoln's speech is remembered.*

b. to separate main clauses joined by a conjunctive adverb or by *for example* or *that is.*
Example: *Because of the ice storm, most students could not get to school; consequently, the principal canceled all classes for the day.*

c. to separate the items in a series when these items contain commas.
Example: *The students at the rally came from Senn High School, in Chicago, Illinois; Niles Township High School, in Skokie, Illinois; and Evanston Township High School, in Evanston, Illinois.*

d. to separate two main clauses joined by a coordinating conjunction when such clauses already contain several commas.
Example: *The designer combined the blue silk, brown linen, and beige cotton into a suit; but she decided to use the yellow chiffon, yellow silk, and white lace for an evening gown.*

Rule: Use a comma
a. between the main clauses of a compound sentence.
Example: *Ryan was late getting to study hall, and his footsteps echoed in the empty corridor.*

b. to separate three or more words, phrases, or clauses in a series.
Example: *Mel bought carrots, beans, pears, and onions.*

c. between coordinate modifiers.

Example: *That is a lyrical, moving poem.*
d. to set off parenthetical expressions, interjections, and conjunctive adverbs.
Example: *Well, we missed the bus again.*
Example: *The weather is beautiful today; however, it is supposed to rain this weekend.*

e. to set off nonessential words, clauses, and phrases, such as:
     —adverbial clauses
Example: *Since Ellen is so tall, the coach assumed she would be a good basketball player.*
     —adjective clauses
Example: *Scott, who had been sleeping, finally woke up.*
     —participles and participial phrases
Example: *Having found what he was looking for, he left.*
     —prepositional phrases
Example: *On Saturdays during the fall, I rake leaves.*
     —infinitive phrases
Example: *To be honest, I'd like to stay awhile longer.*
     —appositives and appositive phrases
Example: *Ms. Kwan, a soft-spoken woman, ran into the street to hail a cab.*

f. to set off direct quotations.
Example: *"My concert," Molly replied, "is tonight."*

g. to set off an antithetical phrase.
Example: *Unlike Tom, Rob enjoys skiing.*

h. to set off a title after a person's name.
Example: *Margaret Thomas, Ph.D., was the guest speaker.*

i. to separate the various parts of an address, a geographical term, or a date.
Example: *My new address is 324 Indian School Road, Albuquerque, New Mexico 85350.*

    I moved on March 13, 1998.

j. after the salutation of an informal letter and after the closing of all letters.
Example: *Dear Helen,*   *Sincerely,*

k. to set off parts of a reference that direct the reader to the exact source.
Example: *You can find the article in the* Washington Post, *April 4, 1997, pages 33–34.*

l. to set off words or names used in direct address and in tag questions.

Example: *Yuri, will you bring me my calculator?*
Lottie became a lawyer, didn't she?

Rule: Use a dash to signal a change in thought or to emphasize parenthetical material.

Example: *During the play, Maureen—and she'd be the first to admit it—forgot her lines.*

Example: *There are only two juniors attending—Mike Ramos and Ron Kim.*

Rule: Use parentheses to set off supplemental material. Punctuate within the parentheses only if the punctuation is part of the parenthetical expression.

Example: *If you like jazz (and I assume you do), you will like this CD. (The soloist is Miles Davis.)*

Example: *The upper Midwest (which states does that include?) was hit by terrible floods last year.*

Rule: Use brackets to enclose information that you insert into a quotation for clarity or to enclose a parenthetical phrase that already appears within parentheses.

Example: *"He serves his [political] party best who serves the country best."—Rutherford B. Hayes*

Example: *The staircase (which was designed by a famous architect [Frank Lloyd Wright]) was inlaid with ceramic tile.*

Rule: Use ellipsis points to indicate the omission of material from a quotation.

Example: *". . . Neither an individual nor a nation can commit the least act of injustice against the obscurest individual. . . ." —Henry David Thoreau*

Rule: Use quotation marks
a. to enclose a direct quotation, as follows:
Example: *"Hurry up!" shouted Lisa.*

When a quotation is interrupted, use two sets of quotation marks.

Example: *"A cynic," wrote Oscar Wilde, "is someone who knows the price of everything and the value of nothing."*

Use single quotation marks for a quotation within a quotation.

Example: *"Did you say 'turn left' or 'turn right'?" asked Leon.*

In writing dialogue, begin a new paragraph and use a new set of quotation marks every time the speaker changes.

Example: *"Do you really think the spaceship can take off?" asked the first officer.*
"Our engineer assures me that we have enough power," the captain replied.

b. o enclose titles of short works, such as stories, poems, essays, articles, chapters, and songs.
Example: *"The Lottery" [short story]*
"Provide, Provide" [poem]
"Civil Disobedience" [essay]

c. to enclose unfamiliar slang terms and unusual expressions.
Example: *The man called his grandson a "rapscallion."*

d. to enclose a definition that is stated directly.
Example: *Gauche is a French word meaning "left."*

Rule: Use italics
a. for titles of books, lengthy poems, plays, films, television series, paintings and sculptures, long musical compositions, court cases, names of newspapers and magazines, ships, trains, airplanes, and spacecraft. Italicize and capitalize articles (a, an, the) at the beginning of a title only when they are part of the title.
Example: *E.T. [film]; The Piano Lesson [play]*
The Starry Night [painting]
the New Yorker [magazine]
Challenger [spacecraft]
The Great Gatsby [book]
the Chicago Tribune [newspaper]

b. for foreign words and expressions that are not used frequently in English.
Example: *Luciano waved good-bye, saying, "Arrivederci."*

c. for words, letters, and numerals used to represent themselves.
Example: *There is no Q on the telephone keypad.*
Example: *Number your paper from 1 through 10.*

Rule: Use an apostrophe

a. for a possessive form, as follows:

Add an apostrophe and *s* to all singular nouns, plural nouns not ending in *s,* singular indefinite pronouns, and compound nouns. Add only an apostrophe to a plural noun that ends in *s.*

Example: *the tree's leaves*
the man's belt
the bus's tires
the children's pets
everyone's favorite
my mother-in-law's job
the attorney general's decision
the baseball player's error
the cats' bowls

If two or more persons possess something jointly, use the possessive form for the last person named. If they possess it individually, use the possessive form for each one's name.

Example: *Ted and Harriet's family*
Ted's and Harriet's bosses
Lewis and Clark's expedition
Lewis's and Clark's clothes

b. to express amounts of money or time that modify a noun.

Example: *two cents' worth*

Example: *three days' drive (You can use a hyphenated adjective instead: a three-day drive.)*

c. in place of omitted letters or numerals.

Example: *haven't [have not]*   *the winter of '95*

d. to form the plural of letters, numerals, symbols, and words used to represent themselves. Use an apostrophe and *s.*

Example: *You wrote two 5's instead of one.*

Example: *How many s's are there in Mississippi?*

Example: *Why did he use three !'s at the end of the sentence?*

Rule: Use a hyphen

a. after any prefix joined to a proper noun or proper adjective.

Example: *all-American*   *pre-Columbian*

b. after the prefixes *all-, ex-,* and *self-* joined to any noun or adjective, after the prefix *anti-* when it joins a word beginning with *i,* after the prefix *vice-* (except in some instances such as *vice president*), and to avoid confusion between words that begin with *re-* and look like another word.

Example: *ex-president*
self-important
anti-inflammatory
vice-principal
re-creation of the event
recreation time
re-pair the socks
repair the computer

c. in a compound adjective that precedes a noun.

Example: *a bitter-tasting liquid*

d. in any spelled-out cardinal or ordinal numbers up to *ninety-nine* or *ninety-ninth,* and with a fraction used as an adjective.

Example: *twenty-three*   *eighty-fifth*
one-half cup

e. to divide a word at the end of a line between syllables.

Example: *air-port*   *scis-sors*
fill-ing   *fin-est*

Abbreviations

Abbreviations are shortened forms of words.

Rule: Use only one period if an abbreviation occurs at the end of a sentence. If the sentence ends with a question mark or an exclamation point, use the period and the second mark of punctuation.

Example: *We didn't get home until 3:30 A.M.*
Example: *Did you get home before 4:00 A.M.?*
Example: *I can't believe you didn't get home until 3:30 A.M.!*

Rule: Capitalize abbreviations of proper nouns and abbreviations related to historical dates.

Example: *John Kennedy Jr.*   *P.O. Box 333*
   800 B.C.   *A.D. 456*   *1066 C.E.*

Use all capital letters and no periods for most abbreviations of organizations and government agencies.

Example: *CBS*   *CIA*   *PIN*
   CPA   *IBM*   *NFL*
   MADD   *GE*   *FBI*

Spelling

The following basic rules, examples, and exceptions will help you master the spellings of many words.

Forming plurals

English words form plurals in many ways. Most nouns simply add *s*. The following chart shows other ways of forming plural nouns and some common exceptions to the pattern.

General Rules for Forming Plurals		
if the word ends in	**Rule**	**Example**
ch, s, sh, x, z	add *es*	glass, glasses
a consonant + *y*	change *y* to *i* and add *es*	caddy, caddies
a vowel + *y* or *o*	add only *s*	cameo, cameos monkey, monkeys
a consonant + *o* common exceptions	generally add *es* but sometimes add only *s*	potato, potatoes cello, cellos
f or *ff* common exceptions	add *s* change *f* to *v* and add *es*	cliff, cliffs hoof, hooves
lf	change *f* to *v* and add *es*	half, halves

A few plurals are exceptions to the rules in the previous chart, but they are easy to remember. The following chart lists these plurals and some examples.

Special Rules for Forming Plurals	
Rule	**Example**
To form the plural of most proper names and one-word compound nouns, follow the general rules for plurals.	Cruz, Cruzes Mancuso, Mancusos crossroad, crossroads
To form the plural of hyphenated compound nouns or compound nouns of more than one word, make the most important word plural.	sister-in-law, sisters-in-law motion picture, motion pictures
Some nouns have unusual plural forms.	goose, geese child, children
Some nouns have the same singular and plural forms.	moose scissors pants

Adding prefixes

When adding a prefix to a word, keep the original spelling of the word. Use a hyphen only when the original word is capitalized or with prefixes such as *all-*, *ex-*, and *self-* joined to a noun or adjective.

co + operative = cooperative
inter + change = interchange
pro + African = pro-African
ex + partner = ex-partner

Suffixes and the silent *e*

Many English words end in a silent letter *e*. Sometimes the *e* is dropped when a suffix is added. When adding a suffix that begins with a consonant to a word that ends in silent *e*, keep the *e*.

like + ness = likenesssure + ly = surely
COMMON EXCEPTIONS awe + ful = awful;
judge + ment = judgment

When adding a suffix that begins with a vowel to a word that ends in silent *e*, usually drop the *e*.

believe + able = believable
expense + ive = expensive
COMMON EXCEPTION mile + age = mileage

When adding a suffix that begins with *a* or *o* to a word that ends in *ce* or *ge*, keep the *e* so the word will retain the soft *c* or *g* sound.

notice + able = noticeable
courage + ous = courageous

When adding a suffix that begins with a vowel to a word that ends in *ee* or *oe*, keep the final *e*.

see + ing = seeing   toe + ing = toeing

Drop the final silent *e* after the letters *u* or *w*.

argue + ment = argument
owe + ing = owing

Keep the final silent *e* before the suffix *-ing* when necessary to avoid ambiguity.

singe + ing = singeing

Suffixes and the final *y*

When adding a suffix to a word that ends in a consonant + *y*, change the *y* to *i* unless the suffix begins with *i*. Keep the *y* in a word that ends in a vowel + *y*.

try + ed = tried   fry + ed = fried
stay + ing = staying   display + ed = displayed
copy + ing = copying joy + ous = joyous

Adding *ly* and *ness*

When adding *ly* to a word that ends in a single *l*, keep the *l*, but when the word ends in a double *l*, drop one *l*. When the word ends in a consonant + *le*, drop the *le*. When adding -ness to a word that ends in *n*, keep the *n*.

casual + ly = casually
practical + ly = practically
dull + ly = dully
probable + ly = probably
open + ness = openness
mean + ness = meanness

Doubling the final consonant

Double the final consonant in words that end in a consonant preceded by a single vowel if the word is one syllable, if it has an accent on the last syllable that remains there even after the suffix is added, or if it is a word made up of a prefix and a one-syllable word.

stop + ing = stopping
admit + ed = admitted
replan + ed = replanned

Do not double the final consonant if the accent is not on the last syllable, or if the accent shifts when the suffix is added. Also do not double the final consonant if the final consonant is *x* or *w*. If the word ends in a consonant and the suffix begins with a consonant, do not double the final consonant.

benefit + ed = benefited
similar + ly = similarly
raw + er = rawer
box + like = boxlike
friend + less = friendless
rest + ful = restful

Forming Compound Words

When joining a word that ends in a consonant to a word that begins with a consonant, keep both consonants.

> out + line = outline
> after + noon = afternoon
> post + card = postcard
> pepper + mint = peppermint

ie and *ei*

Learning this rhyme can save you many misspellings: "Write *i* before *e* except after *c,* or when sounded like *a* as in *neighbor* and *weigh.*" There are many exceptions to this rule, including *seize, seizure, leisure, weird, height, either, neither, forfeit.*

-cede, -ceed, and -sede

Because of the relatively few words with *sēd* sounds, these words are worth memorizing.

> These words use *-cede:* **accede, precede, secede.**
> One word uses *-sede:* **supersede.**
> Three words use *-ceed:* **exceed, proceed, succeed.**

Logic and Persuasion Handbook

Persuasion

Propositions

One of the main reasons people write and talk is to persuade each other. Persuasive writing and speaking attempts to convince someone of the truth of a **proposition,** that is, a statement or claim. There are four basic types of proposition:

- A proposition of **fact** is a claim that certain information is correct.
  Candidate Wilkins comes from Illinois.

- A proposition of **value** is a statement that a feeling or judgment is valid.
  Candidate Wilkins is a friendly woman.

- A proposition about a **problem** combines fact and judgment.
  Candidate Wilkins is not qualified to run.

- A proposition of **policy** is a claim that someone should do something.
  Everyone should vote for candidate Wilkins.

A proposition may be **true** or **false.** In evaluating persuasive speaking and writing, you need to know which type of proposition is being made so that you can decide whether it is true or false.

Evidence and Arguments

Persuasive writing and speaking usually includes **evidence,** that is, reasons why someone should accept a proposition. Together, a proposition and a reason for accepting it make up an **argument.**

Everyone should vote for candidate Wilkins, because she is the most qualified.

An argument may be **valid** or **invalid,** that is, reasonable or unreasonable.

Appeals

Arguments are meant to appeal to certain beliefs, values, or feelings belonging to the reader or listener. Most reasons given in support of a proposition make at least one of four types of **appeal:**

- An **appeal to logic** is a claim based on fact and reason.
  Wilkins is unqualified, because she does not meet the age requirement.

- An **appeal to ethics or values** is a claim based on shared values or judgments.
  Wilkins is best, because she is the most honest and caring.

- An **appeal to authority** is a claim based on sources believed to be reliable.
  Wilkins is best, because the Metropolitan Bar Association supports her.

- An **appeal to emotion** is a claim based on shared feelings.
  Wilkins is best, because she has overcome hardship.

In evaluating arguments, you need to know which type of appeal is being made so that you can decide whether it is valid or invalid. Note that an argument may involve more than one type of appeal.

Exercise: Analyzing an Argument

Read the following statements. For each statement, identify the type of proposition made and the type of appeal used to support it..

1. If we want clean beaches, then we need to provide trash cans and arrange for garbage removal in the summer.

2. It is our responsibility as human beings to keep ocean ecosystems healthy by polluting them as little as possible or not at all.

3. According to eminent marine biologists, we have a lot to learn about the animals that live in the ocean depths.

4. Restricting owners of beachfront property from building wherever they want to on their property is highly unfair.

Statement	Proposition	Appeal
1	about a problem	
2		
3		
4		to ethics or values

Logic

Inductive Reasoning

Inductive reasoning involves putting facts together to come up with a generalized statement as a conclusion.

Specific facts:

Fact 1. *Star Wars* is the second-biggest money maker of all time.

Fact 2. The number one movie at the box office in 2004 was *Shrek 2.*

Fact 3. *Spider-man* broke many box office records in 2002.

Generalization: Science fiction and fantasy films do very well at the box office.

Errors In Inductive Reasoning

To avoid errors in inductive reasoning, be sure you use a large enough sample of specific facts, and of course, make sure your facts are accurate. Assuming you have a large enough sample of accurate facts, make sure that your generalization is logical.

For example, it would be illogical to conclude from the facts above that movies whose titles begin with the letter *S* do well at the box office.

Deductive Reasoning

Deductive reasoning is essentially the opposite of inductive reasoning. With deductive reasoning you start with a generalization to come to a conclusion about a specific case.

Generalization: Paul can only eat vegetarian food.

Specific fact: The Glory Diner offers vegetarian food.

Conclusion: Paul can eat at the Glory Diner.

Syllogisms

A syllogism is a formal statement of a deductive argument. It consists of a **major premise,** or general statement; a **minor premise,** or related fact; and a **conclusion** based on the two.

Major premise: People who travel between countries need a passport.

Minor premise: Jody is flying from the United States to Spain.

Conclusion: Jody needs a passport.

Errors In Deductive Reasoning

Errors in deductive reasoning result from faulty construction of the argument. Make sure the major premise is a universal statement, that both premises are true, and that the conclusion follows logically from the premises.

Note: A syllogism is *valid* if it follows the rules of deductive reasoning. A syllogism is *true* if the statements are factually accurate. Therefore, a perfectly valid syllogism can be untrue. For example:

Major premise: All voters are good citizens. [There is more to good citizenship than voting.]

Minor premise: My parents are voters.

Conclusion: Therefore, my parents are good citizens.

This conclusion is valid according to the premises; however, it isn't necessarily true because the major premise is flawed.

Exercise: Analyzing Logical Reasoning

For each argument below, identify whether inductive or deductive reasoning is used. Evaluate whether the conclusion is valid or invalid and explain your evaluation.

1. An epic poem is a serious, long narrative poem centered on the life of a cultural or national hero or heroine. *El Cid* is an epic poem. In more than 30,000 lines, it celebrates the life and accomplishments of a Spanish military and political leader who lived in the eleventh century.

2. If a computer can play compact discs, the computer must have been built before 1985. This computer can play CDs. This computer must have been built before 1985.

3. Many humorists use puns. Mark Twain used puns in his writing and his speeches. Ogden Nash used puns in his poems. Woody Allen uses puns in his movies.

Exercise: Using Logical Reasoning

Write a short essay arguing a proposition. In your argument, use at least two examples each of valid inductive and deductive reasoning.

Logical Fallacies

A **logical fallacy** is a particular type of faulty reasoning. Fallacies often seem reasonable at face value, so they are often used, both intentionally and unintentionally. Some fallacies are so common that they have names.

To identify fallacies in the writing and speaking of others and to avoid it in your own persuasive communication, you need to be able to identify fallacies and to understand why they are illogical.

- ### Ad Hominem

  Don't listen to what Smyth says about the election; he spent time in prison.

  An ad hominem argument (literally, an argument "against the person") implies that a defect in a person's character or behavior is evidence that what he says is unreliable. Note that the ad hominem fallacy contains a hidden premise: *People who have spent time in prison cannot have valid opinions.* Because this premise is untrue, the argument about Smyth is untrue also.

- ### Non Sequitur or False Causality

  This shirt is unlucky: every time I wear it, something bad happens.

  Non sequitur literally means "it doesn't follow." Just because two events occur together, it doesn't follow logically that one caused the other.

- ### Glittering Generalities

  If you love freedom, vote for Jack.

  Glittering generalities are words with overwhelmingly positive connotations, used to make it seem impossible to disagree with an idea. How can you argue against the idea of freedom? A listener's initial reaction to this statement might be, "Freedom is a good thing, so I must vote for Jack."

- ### Overgeneralization and Stereotype

  Tall people make excellent basketball players.

  An overgeneralization is any conclusion that may be accurate about a small group, but is inaccurate when applied to a much larger group. An overgeneralization about a group of people is called a stereotype.

- ### Argument from Authority and Celebrity Endorsement

  Four out of five doctors recommend Pumpidox for most heart conditions.

  Argument from authority is the quoting of an alleged expert on a certain topic. As a logical fallacy, arguments from authority rely solely on the mention of the word "expert," and give no clear facts from the expert. Companies often hire celebrities to appear in commercials for their products in the hope that audiences will respond to the likability of the famous person, even if that person has no real expert knowledge about the product.

- ### The Bandwagon Effect

  Choose America's favorite toothpaste!

  The term "jumping on the bandwagon" means doing or thinking something because everyone else is doing it or thinking it. This type of reasoning provides no evidence to support a decision or viewpoint.

- ### Card Stacking

  Senator Porter voted against childcare laws and recycling programs. It's time for new leadership!

  Card stacking involves piling on evidence that supports one side of an argument while ignoring or suppressing valid evidence supporting the other side. Saying that a politician voted against positive-sounding programs does not mean that he or she didn't have good reason to, or that the opposition has a better record.

Ethical Reasoning and Propaganda

Propaganda

Propaganda is the process of persuading by deliberately misleading or confusing an audience. Through the use of combinations of logical fallacies, propaganda can appeal to ethics or values, authority, or emotion, but they do so in a way that is unsupported or inappropriate.

Political propaganda

A vote for Marmelard is a vote for the enemy!

America: You're with us or against us!

Advertising

Be the best parent you can be: Serve your kids Super Goody cereal.

The most successful people shop at Blorland's Department Store.

Ethical Reasoning

Reasoning that persuades by helping its intended audience make informed decisions is called **ethical reasoning.** As a writer or speaker, you have the responsibility to use ethical reasoning and avoid propaganda. This means that you must gather complete information about a topic, check your facts for accuracy, and make sure that your reasoning includes no errors in logic or false conclusions. You should address opposing evidence with clear and accurate argumentation. Using ethical reasoning in your persuasive writing or speeches will strengthen your positions as your audience sees that you have logically addressed all sides of an idea.

Identifying Unethical Persuasive Techniques

The following essay contains several examples of faulty reasoning. Read through the entire text once, then go back and look for logical fallacies, invalid arguments, and manipulative appeals. For each example you find, make an entry in a chart like the one shown. Then write a paragraph evaluating the essay's argument.

Passage	Type(s) of Appeals	Why Invalid
"Principal Spaly"	Appeal to logic	Card stacking

Don't Take Away Our Freedom

The school board recently announced plans to remove all vending machines from our schools' cafeterias. They say that candy, snacks, and cola are bad for students. But is starvation good for students? Is taking away freedom to choose good for students?

Every expert on nutrition agrees that it is not healthy for kids to go for hours between meals without some sort of snack in between to tide them over. If the school board has its way, students will be passing out at their desks from hunger and dehydration. Principal Spaly claims that students are more likely to pass out from a "sugar crash." This is the same Principal Spaly who recently showed what he thought of students when he denied sophomores the right to park at the high school.

We are taught in these very schools that America is a land of democracy, freedom, and liberty. It is clear that the school board has forgotten this. Any student who loves his or her school will write to the school board and let them know how we feel.

Glossary/Glosario

This glossary lists the vocabulary words found in the selections in this book. The definition given is for the word as it is used in the selection; you may wish to consult a dictionary for other meanings of these words. The key below is a guide to the pronunciation symbols used in each entry.

	Pronunciation Key				
a	**a**t	ō	h**o**pe	ng	si**ng**
ā	**a**pe	ô	f**o**rk, **a**ll	th	**th**in
ä	f**a**ther	oo	w**oo**d, p**u**t	<u>th</u>	**th**is
e	**e**nd	ōō	f**oo**l	zh	trea**s**ure
ē	m**e**	oi	**oi**l	ə	**a**go, tak**e**n, penc**i**l,
i	**i**t	ou	**ou**t		lem**o**n, circ**u**s
ī	**i**ce	u	**u**p	′	indicates primary stress
o	h**o**t	ū	**u**se	‚	indicates secondary

English

A

abate (ə bāt′) *v.* to lessen or reduce in force or intensity; **p. 97**

abhor (ab hôr′) *v.* to regard with disgust; **p. 98**

abjectly (ab′ jekt lē) *adv.* in a humiliating, mean, or degrading manner; **p. 952**

abominable (ə bom′ ə nə bəl) *adj.* disgusting; detestable; **p. 98**

acquiesce (ak′ wē es′) *v.* to consent or agree silently, without objections; to comply passively; **p. 124**

adamant (ad′ ə mənt) *adj.* completely firm and unyielding; **p. 1102**

admonition (ad′ mə nish′ ən) *n.* a warning; cautionary advice; **p. 194**

adorn (ə dôrn′) *v.* to make beautiful; to decorate; **p. 390**

affliction (ə flik′ shən) *n.* great suffering, distress, or its cause; **p. 450**

alacrity (ə lak′ rə tē) *n.* speed; swiftness; **p. 222**

Español

A

abate/aminorar *v.* disminuir o reducir en fuerza o intensidad; **p. 97**

abhor/aborrecer *v.* despreciar; odiar algo en particular; **p. 98**

abjectly/abyectamente *adv.* de modo humillante, infame o indecente; **p. 952**

abominable/abominable *adj.* espantoso; detestable; **p. 98**

acquiesce/acatar *v.* aceptar o consentir sin protestar; acceder pasivamente; **p. 124**

adamant/obstinado *adj.* empeñado en un fin; terco; **p. 1102**

admonition/amonestación *s.* advertencia; consejo severo; **p. 194**

adorn/adornar *v.* embellecer; decorar; **p. 390**

affliction/aflicción *s.* gran sufrimiento, angustia, o su causa; **p. 450**

alacrity/alacridad *s.* prontitud; presteza; **p. 222**

alien (ā′ lē ən) *adj.* strange; unfamiliar; foreign; **p. 906**

alight (ə līt′) *v.* to descend and come to rest; **p. 24**

allusion (ə lo̅o̅′ zhən) *n.* an indirect or casual reference; an incidental mention; **p. 377**

ambition (am bish′ən) *n.* a desire to achieve a particular end; **p. 1277**

amble (am′ bəl) *v.* to walk at a leisurely pace; to stroll; **p. 1333**

ambulatory (am′ byə lə tôr′ ē) *adj.* moving from place to place; **p. 106**

ameliorate (ə mēl′ yə rāt′) *v.* to make better or more tolerable; to improve; **p. 1057**

amiable (ā′ mē ə bəl) *adj.* friendly; **p. 945**

amorphous (ə môr′ fəs) *adj.* without definite form; **p. 931**

anarchy (an′ ər kē) *n.* the absence of government; **p. 385**

ancestral (an ses′ trəl) *adj.* of or relating to those from whom one is descended; **p. 1163**

animated (an′ ə mā′ tid) *adj.* full of life; active; lively; **p. 945**

apathetically (ap′ ə thet′ i kal ē) *adv.* in a manner showing little interest or concern; **p. 612**

apparition (ap′ ə rish′ ən) *n.* a ghostlike or nearly invisible appearance; **p. 664**

appease (ə pēz′) *v.* to bring to a state of peace or quiet; soothe; **p. 97**

apprehension (ap′ ri hen′ shən) *n.* fear of what may happen in the future; anxiety; **p. 73**

apt (apt) *adj.* likely; having a tendency; **p. 707**

arbitrary (är′ bə trer′ ē) *adj.* of a random or unreasonable character; **p. 207**

ardently (ärd′ ent lē) *adv.* passionately; enthusiastically; **p. 391**

arduous (är′ jo̅o̅ əs) *adj.* requiring great exertion or endurance; difficult; **p. 117**

aristocracy (a′ rə sto′ krə sē) *n.* people with high social status due to birth or title; **p. 1310**

array (ə rā′) *v.* to place in proper or methodical order; **p. 385**

---

alien/ajeno *adj.* extraño; foráneo; extranjero; **p. 906**

alight/apearse *v.* descender; bajar; **p. 24**

allusion/alusión *s.* referencia indirecta o casual; mención casual; **p. 377**

ambition/ambición *s.* deseo de conseguir algo, esp. poder o riquezas; **p. 1277**

amble/pasear *v.* andar por distracción y sin prisa; deambular; **p. 1333**

ambulatory/ambulante *adj.* que va de un lugar a otro; **p. 106**

ameliorate/mejorar *v.* hacer mejor o más tolerable; progresar; **p. 1057**

amiable/amigable *adj.* amistoso; **p. 945**

amorphous/amorfo *adj.* sin forma definida; **p. 931**

anarchy/anarquía *s.* ausencia de gobierno; **p. 385**

ancestral/ancestral *adj.* relativo o perteneciente a los antepasados; **p. 1163**

animated/animado *adj.* lleno de vida; activo; vivaz; **p. 945**

apathetically/apáticamente *adv.* con una actitud que muestra poco interés o preocupación; **p. 612**

apparition/aparición *s.* apariencia de un fantasma o algo casi invisible; **p. 664**

appease/apaciguar *v.* calmar o aquietar; tranquilizar; **p. 97**

apprehension/aprensión *s.* temor vago de lo que pueda pasar; ansiedad; **p. 73**

apt/propenso(a) *adj.* que tiende (a); que tiene la tendencia (a); **p. 707**

arbitrary/arbitrario(a) *adj.* que actúa por capricho o de forma ilógica; **p. 207**

ardently/ardientemente *adv.* apasionadamente; con mucho entusiasmo; **p. 391**

arduous/arduo *adj.* que requiere gran esfuerzo o trabajo; difícil; **p. 117**

aristocracy/aristocracia *s.* personas de un nivel social alto por razón de nacimiento o título; **p. 1310**

array/disponer *v.* colocar en el orden adecuado; arreglar; **p. 385**

assail (ə sāl′) *v.* to attack violently; **p. 576**

assent (ə sent′) *v.* to express agreement; **p. 392**

audaciously (ô dā′ shəs lē) *adv.* boldly; arrogantly; **p. 377**

avert (ə vurt′) *v.* to turn away or aside; **p. 869**

azure (ā′zhər) *adj.* a light purplish blue; **p. 685**

B

balm (bäm) *n.* something that heals or soothes, as an ointment; **p. 260**

balmy (bä′ mē) *adj.* soothing; **p. 1327**

base (bās) *adj.* morally low; dishonorable; **p. 1060**

beguile (bi gīl′) *v.* to influence by deceit; to trick; **p. 258**

benediction (ben′ ə dik′ shən) *n.* a blessing or something that fosters goodness; **p. 804**

benefactor (ben′ ə fak′ tər) *n.* one who gives help or financial aid; **p. 195**

benevolent (bə nev′ ə lent) *adj.* doing or desiring to do good; kind; **p. 353**

bereft (bi reft′) *adj.* deprived of the possession or use of something; **p. 91**

blithe (blīth) *adj.* lighthearted and carefree; cheerful; **p. 191**

blunder (blun′ dər) *n.* a serious error or mistake resulting from carelessness or confusion; **p. 224**

borne (bôrn) *v.* past participle of bear; given birth to; produced; **p. 370**

bosom (booz′ əm) *n.* the chest or heart; **p. 813**

bough (bou) *n.* tree branch; **p. 664**

bracken (bra′ kən) *n.* a type of fern that grows in humid, temperate areas; **p. 718**

brood (brood) *v.* to focus the attention on a subject persistently and moodily; worry; **p. 1293**

bulge (bulj) *v.* to swell or curve outward; **p. 701**

assail/embestir *v.* atacar con violencia; **p. 576**

assent/asentir *v.* afirmar; expresar acuerdo; **p. 392**

audaciously/audazmente *adv.* atrevidamente; de manera osada; **p. 377**

avert/desviar *v.* apartar; evitar; **p. 869**

azure/azul celeste *adj.* azul claro como el cielo; **p. 685**

B

balm/bálsamo *s.* sustancia medicinal que cura o alivia, por ejemplo: un ungüento; **p. 260**

balmy/calmante *adj.* confortante; agradable; **p. 1327**

base/vil *adj.* de baja condición moral; deshonesto; **p. 1060**

beguile/engañar *v.* influenciar con mentiras; engatusar; **p. 258**

benediction/bendición *s.* con morales superiores o un carácter superior; **p. 804**

benefactor/benefactor *s.* que respalda una causa o ayuda con dinero; **p. 195**

benevolent/benevolente *adj.* que hace el bien; amable; **p. 353**

bereft/despojado *adj.* privado de algo; **p. 91**

blithe/alegre *adj.* despreocupado; animado; **p. 191**

blunder/error craso *s.* equivocación o desacierto grave; **p. 224**

borne/nacido(a) *pp.* Que se le dio a luz; que dio fruto; **p. 370**

bosom/pecho *s.* (lit.) seno, tórax o corazón; **p. 813**

bough/rama *s.* parte que nace del tronco de una planta o árbol; **p. 664**

bracken/helecho *s.* tipo de planta criptógama que crece en áreas húmedas y templadas; **p. 718**

brood/cavilar *v.* entregarse del todo a la contemplación, al dolor; preocupar; **p. 1293**

bulge/sobresalir *v.* hincharse o aumentar de tamaño; **p. 701**

C

calamity (kə lam′ ə tē) *n.* an unfortunate event or disaster; **p. 543**

cathedral (ke thē′ drəl) *n.* a church that is the official seat of a bishop; **p. 450**

censure (sen′ shər) *v.* to express disapproval of; to find fault with; to blame; **p. 357**

ceremonial (ser′ ə mō′ nē əl) *adj.* formal; **p. 894**

chide (chīd) *v.* to find fault with or to blame; **p. 91**

circumvent (sur′ kəm vent′) *v.* to get around or to avoid by clever maneuvering; **p. 882**

civic (siv′ ik) *adj.* related to citizenship; **p. 1170**

clamor (klam′ ər) *n.* confused, insistent shouting; **p. 76**

coax (kōks′) *v.* to persuade gently; **p. 726**

coerce (kō urs′) *v.* to force; **p. 595**

coincide (kō′ in sīd′) *v.* to occur at the same time; **p. 1276**

colossal (kə los′ əl) *adj.* extraordinary in size or degree; enormous; **p. 1164**

commensurate (kə men′ sər it) *adj.* equal to; proportionate; **p. 207**

commerce (kom′ ərs) *n.* exchange of ideas and opinions; **p. 664**

commodity (kə mod′ ə′ tē) *n.* a product or economic good; an article of trade; **p. 67**

compassion (kəm pash′ ən) *n.* deep awareness of another's suffering with a desire to help; **p. 82**

compel (kəm pel′) *v.* to force; **p. 606**

compensation (kom′ pən sa′ shən) *n.* payment; **p. 1175**

comprehension (kom′ pri hen′ shən) *n.* the act of grasping mentally; understanding; **p. 896**

compromise (kom′ prə mīz′) *v.* to endanger the reputation or interests of; to expose to suspicion; **p. 1031**

C

calamity/calamidad *s.* desgracia o infortunio; un disastre; **p. 543**

cathedral/catedral *s.* iglesia principal donde el obispo tiene su sede; **p. 450**

censure/censurar *v.* expresar desacuerdo; criticar algo; reprobar; **p. 357**

ceremonial/ceremonial *adj.* formal; relativo a las ceremonias; **p. 894**

chide/reprender *v.* hallar defectos con algo o reprobar; **p. 91**

circumvent/circunvenir *v.* rodear o evitar mediante una acción astuta; **p. 882**

civic/cívico(a) *adj.* relatado a las instituciones e intereses de la patria; **p. 1170**

clamor/algarabía *s.* griterío confuso e insistente; **p. 76**

coax/convencer *v.* persuadir a una persona para que haga algo; **p. 726**

coerce/constreñir *v.* forzar; **p. 595**

coincide/coincidir *v.* ocurrir al un mismo tiempo; **p. 1276**

colossal/colosal *adj.* extraordinario en tamaño o intensidad; enorme; **p. 1164**

commensurate/proporcionado(a) *adj.* igual a; en proporción con; **p. 207**

commerce/comercio *s.* intercambio de ideas y opiniones; **p. 664**

commodity/mercancía *s.* producto o bien económico; artículo que se vende o compra; **p. 67**

compassion/compasión *s.* interés por el sufrimiento ajeno junto con el deseo de ayudar; **p. 82**

compel/compeler *v.* forzar; **p. 606**

compensation/remuneración *s.* paga; **p. 1175**

comprehension/comprensión *s.* acto de entender algo; **p. 896**

compromise/implicar *v.* comprometer la reputación o el interés; abrir a sospecha; **p. 1031**

conciliatory (kən sil′ ē ə tôr′ ē) *adj.* trying to gain the goodwill of another by friendly acts; **p. 1102**

congenital (kən je′ nə təl) *adj.* of or relating to a condition that is present at birth, as a result of either heredity or environmental influences; **p. 1293**

congregate (kong′ gri gāt′) *v.* to bring or come together in a group, a crowd, or an assembly; **p. 1228**

congress (kong′ gris) *n.* a formal meeting; **p. 1224**

conjecture (kən jek′ chər) *v.* to form an opinion without definite evidence; to guess; **p. 498**

conjurer (kon′ jər ər) *n.* one who performs magic; sorcerer; **p. 25**

consecrate (kon′ sə krāt′) *v.* to set apart as sacred; to make or declare holy; **p. 402**

console (kən sōl′) *v.* to comfort; to cheer; **p. 1325**

consolidation (kən sä lə da′ shən) *n.* the process of uniting or merging; **p. 939**

constrained (kən strānd′) *v.* forced or limited; **p. 803**

contemplation (kon′ təm plā′ shən) *n.* the act of thinking about something long and seriously; **p. 1086**

contend (kən tend′) *v.* to argue; dispute; **p. 385**

contention (kən ten′ shən) *n.* verbal argument or struggle; quarreling; **p. 1032**

continuity (kon′ tə nōō′ ə tē) *n.* the state or quality of going on without interruption; **p. 1164**

convalescent (kon və le′ sənt) *n.* a person who is recovering from an illness, an injury, or a surgical operation; **p. 418**

convene (kən vēn′) *v.* to come together; assemble; **p. 50**

copious (kō′ pē əs) *adj.* large in quantity; plentiful; **p. 73**

covet (kuv′ it) *v.* to desire, especially to an excessive degree, something belonging to another; **p. 1062**

crimson (krim′zən) *adj.* a bright purplish red; **p. 685**

curt (kurt) *adj.* rudely brief, or short; terse; **p. 989**

cynic (si′ nik) *n.* a person whose outlook is scornfully and often habitually negative; **p. 1294**

conciliatory/conciliador *adj.* que trata de ganarse la buena voluntad con una actitud amistosa; **p. 1102**

congenital/congénito(a) *adj.* que existe al nacer, a consecuencia de herencia o influencias del ambiente; **p. 1293**

congregate/congregar *v.* juntarse o reunirse en un grupo, una masa o una asamblea; **p. 1228**

congress/congreso *s.* reunión; **p. 1224**

conjecture/conjeturar *v.* formarse una opinión sin tener evidencia definitiva; suponer; **p. 498**

conjurer/mago *s.* que realiza magia; hechicero; **p. 25**

consecrate/consagrar *v.* declarar sagrado; santificar; **p. 402**

console/consolar *v.* alentar; tranquilizar; **p. 1325**

consolidation/fusión *s.* el proceso de unir o fusionar; **p. 939**

constrained/constriñov *v.* obligado o compeleidor; **p. 803**

contemplation/contemplación *s.* acto de pensar larga y seriamente; **p. 1086**

contend/contender *v.* disputar; pelear; **p. 385**

contention/contienda *s.* lucha o disputa verbal; pelea; **p. 1032**

continuity/continuidad *s.* estado o cualidad de seguir sin interrupción; **p. 1164**

convalescent/convaleciente *s.* persona que se recupera de una enfermedad, herida o cirugía; **p. 418**

convene/congregarse *v.* reunirse; **p. 50**

copious/copioso *adj.* grande en cantidad; abundante; **p. 73**

covet/codiciar *v.* desear de forma intensa algo ajeno; **p. 1062**

crimson/carmesí *adj.* de color rojo granate muy vivo; **p. 685**

curt/cortante *adj.* brusco y breve; seco; **p. 989**

cynic/cínico(a) *s.* persona que se burla o que ofende con ironía mordaz; **p. 1294**

D

daunt (dônt) *v.* to overcome with fear; to intimidate; **p. 82**

debris (də brē') *n.* large number of fragments or broken pieces; **p. 1009**

decimated (des' ə māt' əd) *adj.* destroyed or killed in large numbers; **p. 1298**

deduce (di do͞os') *v.* to draw a conclusion from something known or assumed; **p. 265**

deferential (def' ə ren'shəl) *adj.* yielding to someone else's opinions or wishes; **p. 672**

degenerate (di jen' ər it) *adj.* having declined in condition or character; deteriorated; **p. 516**

degrading (di grā' ding) *adj.* tending to drag down in character or social status; **p. 1171**

deliberately (di lib' ər it lē) *adj.* in a careful, thoughtful way; **p. 214**

deliberation (di lib' ə rā' shən) *n.* careful consideration; **p. 51**

delicious (di lish' əs) *adj.* having a very pleasing taste; **p. 679**

delirium (di lēr' ē əm) *n.* a temporary state of mental disturbance characterized by confusion and disorientation; **p. 1325**

delusion (di lo͞o' zhen) *n.* a false impression or belief; **p. 378**

depend (di pend') *v.* to rely on; **p. 678**

depravity (di prav' ə tē) *n.* the state of being morally bad or corrupt; **p. 353**

deprive (di prīv') *v.* to take away from; to keep from enjoying or having; **p. 146**

desolation (des' ə lā' shən) *n.* devastation, misery, sadness; **p. 82**

detached (di tacht') *adj.* not involved emotionally; aloof; indifferent; **p. 746**

detested (di test' əd) *v.* greatly disliked or loathed; **p. 664**

diaspora (dī as' pər ə) *n.* the scattering of a people; **p. 1338**

diffuse (di fūz') *v.* to spread widely; to scatter in all directions; **p. 273**

D

daunt/acobardar *v.* intimidar; atemorizar; **p. 82**

debris/escombros *s.* gran número de fragmentos o piezas rotas; **p. 1009**

decimated/diezmado *adj.* destruido o liquidado en grandes cantidades; **p. 1298**

deduce/deducir *v.* sacar una conclusión de algo que se sabe o se asume; **p. 265**

deferential/deferente *adj.* que cede a las opiniones o deseos ajenos; **p. 672**

degenerate/degenerado(a) *adj.* que decae en calidad o condición moral; deteriorado; **p. 516**

degrading/degradantev *adj.* que se rebaja o disminuye en dignidad o privilegios; **p. 1171**

deliberately/deliberadamente *adv.* hecho con atención y detenimiento; **p. 214**

deliberation/deliberación *s.* consideración atenta y cuidadosa; **p. 51**

delicious/delicioso(a) *adj.* que tiene un sabor agradable; **p. 679**

delirium/delirio *s.* estado temporal de alteración mental que se caracteriza por confusión y desorientación; **p. 1325**

delusion/ilusión *s.* impresión o creencia falsa; **p. 378**

depend/depende *v.* basarse en algo; **p. 678**

depravity/depravación *s.* condición moral baja o corrupta; **p. 353**

deprive/privar(se) *v.* quitarle algo a alguien; dejar de tener o de disfrutar; **p. 146**

desolation/desolación *s.* devastación; miseria; **p. 82**

detached/indiferente *adj.* que no está involucrado emocionalmente; desinteresado; **p. 746**

detested/detestado(a) *v.* (part.) aborrecer, tener aversión; **p. 664**

diaspora/diáspora *s.* dispersión de grupos humanos; **p. 1338**

diffuse/difundir *v.* esparcir ampliamente; dispersar en todas las direcciones; **p. 273**

digress (dī gres′) v. to depart from the main subject; to ramble; **p. 670**

dilapidated (di lap′ ə dā′ tid) adj. fallen into ruin or decay; shabby; **p. 498**

din (din) n. loud, continuous noise; **p. 222**

diplomatic (dip′ lə mat′ ik) adj. negotiating in a peaceful manner; **p. 972**

discern (di surn′) v. to recognize as different and distinct; distinguish; **p. 84**

discord (dis′ kôrd) n. lack of agreement or harmony; conflict; **p. 243**

disdain (dis dān′) v. to look down on; to despise; **p. 1284**

disposition (dis′ pə zish′ ən) n. one's general way of thinking or feeling; **p. 49**

dissension (di sen′ shən) n. disagreement or discord; **p. 570**

dissipate (dis′ ə pāt′) v. to cause to scatter and gradually vanish; to break up and drive off; **p. 868**

diverse (di vurs′) adj. composed of different elements; **p. 830**

doggedly (dô′ gid lē) adv. in a stubbornly persistent manner; obstinately; **p. 523**

downy (dou′ nē) adj. soft and fluffy, like the feathers of young birds; **p. 1267**

dusk (dusk) n. the time of day just before nightfall; **p. 1270**

dusky (dus′ kē) adj. murky or dark in color; **p. 813**

dutiful (dōō′ ti fəl) adj. careful to fulfill obligations; **p. 776**

dwell (dwel) v. to think about at length; **p. 1184**

E

ecclesiastical (i klē′ zē as′ ti kəl) adj. of or relating to the church; **p. 1299**

elusive (i loo′ siv) adj. difficult to explain or grasp; **p. 554**

embark (em bärk′) v. to set out on a venture; **p. 59**

digress/divagar v. apartarse del tema principal; irse por las ramas; **p. 670**

dilapidated/dilapidado adj. que ha sido gastado o arruinado; muy usado; **p. 498**

din/estrépito s. ruido fuerte y continuo; **p. 222**

diplomatic/diplomático(a) adj. que negocia e interviene de manera cortés; **p. 972**

discern/discenir v. reconocer como diferente; distinguir; **p. 84**

discord/discordia s. desacuerdo; conflicto; **p. 243**

disdain/desdeñar v. menospreciar, despreciar; **p. 1284**

disposition/disposición s. modo de pensar o sentir; **p. 49**

dissension/disensión s. desacuerdo o discordia; **p. 570**

dissipate/disipar v. hacer que desaparezca gradualmente; disolver; **p. 868**

diverse/diverso(a) adj. compuesto de elementos distintos; **p. 830**

doggedly/obstinadamente adv. de manera persistente; firmemente; **p. 523**

downy/aterciopelado adj. suave y velloso, como las plumas de un pájaro recién nacido; **p. 1267**

dusk/anochecer s. tiempo en el que empieza a faltar la luz del día y se hace de noche; **p. 1270**

dusky/oscuro(a) adj. tan profundo o grande que no se puede poner en palabras; **p. 813**

dutiful/cumplidor adj. que cumple responsablemente sus obligaciones; **p. 776**

dwell/dilatarse v. pensar con calma; tomarse su tiempo **p. 1184**

E

ecclesiastical/eclesiástico adj. relativo a la iglesia; **p. 1299**

elusive/elusivo adj. difícil de explicar o entender; **p. 554**

embark/embarcar v. lanzarse a una empresa; partir en una aventura; **p. 59**

emblem (em´ bləm) *n.* an object or a representation that functions as a symbol; **p. 1289**

emphatic (em fa´tik) *adj.* forceful; **p. 582**

enamel (i nam´ əl) *n.* a cosmetic or paint that gives a smooth, glossy appearance; **p. 718**

enamored (en am´ ərd) *adj.* inspired with love; charmed; captivated; **p. 951**

endeavor (en dev´ ər) *v.* to make an effort to; to try; **p. 123**

engrossed (en grōst´) *adj.* fully attentive to; completely engaged in; absorbed; **p. 963**

enlighten (en līt´ ən) *v.* to give knowledge or wisdom to; **p. 1311**

entangled (en tan´ gəld) *adj.* twisted together; caught; **p. 690**

enterprising (en´ tər prī´ zing) *adj.* showing energy and initiative, especially in beginning new projects; **p. 502**

enunciate (i nun´ sē āt´) *v.* to pronounce distinctly; **p. 1255**

ephemeral (i fem´ rəl) *adj.* lasting for a very brief time; short-lived; **p. 1164**

evacuate (i vak´ū āt´) *v.* to vacate or leave a place; **p. 1004**

evade (i vād´) *v.* to escape or avoid, as by cleverness; **p. 1045**

exalt (ig zôlt´) *v.* to lift up; to put in high spirits; **p. 794**

exalted (ig zôl´ təd) *adj.* elevated; **p. 555**

exclusively (iks´ klo̅o̅ siv lē) *adv.* without the inclusion or involvement of any others; **p. 1311**

expedient (ək spē´ dē ənt) *adj.* convenient or efficient for a certain purpose; **p. 223**

exploit (eks´ ploit) *n.* notable, heroic deed; feat; **p. 135**

extraneous (ek strā´nē əs) *adj.* not intrinsically belonging; not forming a vital part; coming from outside; **p. 1219**

emblem/emblema *s.* un objeto o una representación que funciona como un símbolo; **p. 1289**

emphatic/enfático *adj.* enérgico; categórico; **p. 582**

enamel/esmalte *s.* cosmético o barniz que da un acabado liso y brillante; **p. 718**

enamored/enamorado *adj.* prendado; encantado; cautivado; **p. 951**

endeavor/empeñarse *v.* esforzarse; tratar; **p. 123**

engrossed/enfrascado *adj.* dedicado por completo a pensar en algo; ensimismado; absorto; **p. 963**

enlighten/ilustrar *v.* dar o revelar conocimientos o sabiduría; **p. 1311**

entangled/enredado(a) *pp.* liado; atrapado; **p. 690**

enterprising/emprendedor *adj.* que muestra dinamismo e iniciativa, especialmente al iniciar nuevos proyectos; **p. 502**

enunciate/enunciar *v.* pronunciar claramente; **p. 1255**

ephemeral/efímero *adj.* que dura muy poco tiempo; fugaz; **p. 1164**

evacuate/evacuar *v.* desalojar o desocupar un lugar; **p. 1004**

evade/evadir *v.* evitar algo de modo astuto; **p. 1045**

exalt/exaltar *v.* elevar; animar; **p. 794**

exalted/exaltado *adj.* elevado; **p. 555**

exclusively/exclusivamente *adv.* sin la participación de otros; **p. 1311**

expedient/conveniente *adj.* útil, oportuno, adecuado para un fin; **p. 223**

exploit/proeza *s.* acto heroico o notable; hazaña; **p. 135**

extraneous/extraño(a) *adj.* que no pertenece intrínsicamente; que no forma un parte vital; que previene del exterior; **p. 1219**

F

feigned (fānd) *adj.* fictitious; not genuine; **p. 65**

fetid (fe′ təd) *adj.* having a bad odor; **p. 988**

fetus (fē′ təs) *n.* an unborn child that has been in utero for at least eight weeks; **p. 978**

fitfully (fit′ fəl lē) *adv.* irregularly; in stops and starts; **p. 1277**

foment (fō ment′) *v.* to promote the development or growth of; **p. 147**

fondle (fond′ əl) *v.* to handle gently; **p. 1210**

fortitude (fôr′ tə tood′) *n.* strength, particularly strength of mind that enables one to encounter danger or bear adversity with courage; **p. 298**

fragrant (frā′grənt) *adj.* having a strong, pleasant smell; **p. 576**

fused (fūzd) *adj.* blended; **p. 830**

futile (fū′ til) *adj.* serving no practical purpose; useless; worthless; **p. 902**

G

gape (gāp) *v.* to stare with the mouth open, as in wonder or surprise; **p. 1184**

garment (gär′mənt) *n.* a piece of clothing; **p. 1195**

garrulous (gar′ə ləs) *adj.* talkative; **p. 498**

gaunt (gônt) *adj.* thin, bony, and hollow-eyed, as from hunger or illness; **p. 915**

genial (jēn′ yəl) *adj.* mild or friendly; **p. 298**

ghetto (get′ō) *n.* neighborhood where a particular group of people are forced to live either by law, poverty, or social exclusion; **p. 1338**

glazed (glāzd) *adj.* covered with a smooth, glossy coating; **p. 678**

glisten (glis′ ən) *v.* to shine or to reflect light; **p. 701**

grapple (grap′ əl) *v.* to struggle in hand-to-hand combat; to wrestle; **p. 961**

F

feigned/fingido *adj.* falso; que no es genuino; **p. 65**

fetid/fétido *adj.* que tiene un olor malo; **p. 988**

fetus/feto *s.* bebé todavía no nacido que ha cumplido más de ocho semanas en el útero materno; **p. 978**

fitfully/intermitentemente *adv.* en forma irregular; que se interrumpe y prosigue; **p. 1277**

foment/fomentar *v.* promocionar el desarrollo o crecimiento de; **p. 147**

fondle/acariciar *v.* tratar con amor y ternura; **p. 1210**

fortitude/forteleza *s.* fuerza, particularmente fuerza mental que se permite encontrar peligro o tolerar adversidad con valor; **p. 298**

fragrant/fragante *adj.* que tiene o despide un aroma; **p. 576**

fused/fundido(a) *adj.* combinado; **p. 830**

futile/fútil *adj.* inútil; insignificante; **p. 902**

G

gape/boquear *v.* quedar boquiabierto por sorpresa o asombro; **p. 1184**

garment/vestido *s.* pieza de ropa; **p. 1195**

garrulous/parlanchín *adj.* que habla mucho; locuaz; **p. 498**

gaunt/enjuto *adj.* flaco y ojeroso por hambre o enfermedad; con aspecto enfermizo; **p. 915**

genial/simpático(a) *adj.* amable, amistoso; **p. 298**

ghetto/gueto *s.* barrio en que un grupo de gente están forzados de vivir a causa de la ley, la pobreza o exclusión social; **p. 1338**

glazed/glaseado(a) *adj.* cubierto con una capa brillante; **p. 678**

glisten/refulgir *v.* emitir fulgor o resplandecer; **p. 701**

grapple/forcejear *v.* luchar cuerpo a cuerpo; bregar; **p. 961**

gratify (grat′ ə fī′) *v.* to satisfy or indulge; **p. 75**

grave (grāv) *adj.* dignified and gloomy; somber; **p. 890**

gravity (grav′ ə tē) *n.* seriousness; importance; **p. 1270**

grievous (grē′ vəs) *v.* causing or characterized by grief; extremely sad; **p. 1234**

grimace (grim′ is) *n.* facial expression showing contempt, disgust, or pain; **p. 755** / *v.* to contort the face, especially to express pain or displeasure; **p. 1321**

grope (grōp) *v.* to feel about uncertainly with the hands; to search blindly; **p. 1183**

guile (gīl) *n.* cunning, deceit, or slyness; **p. 571**

gunner (gun′ ər) *n.* an airman or a soldier who operates a gun; **p. 978**

H

hallow (hal′ ō) *v.* to make or select as holy; to regard or honor as sacred; **p. 402**

haughty (hô′ tē) *adj.* conceited; arrogant; **p. 880**

heave (hēv) *n.* an upward motion, or an effort to raise; **p. 445**

hemorrhage (he′ mə rij) *n.* a severe discharge of blood; **p. 931**

holocaust (hol′ ə kôst′) *n.* great or complete destruction, especially by fire; **p. 1255**

hostile (host′ əl) *adj.* feeling or showing hatred; antagonistic; **p. 902**

husky (hus′ kē) *adj.* strong; burly; **p. 711**

hypocrisy (hi pok′ rə sē) *n.* an expression of feelings or beliefs not actually possessed or held; **p. 135**

hysterical (his ter′ i kəl) *adj.* characterized by panic or other uncontrolled emotion; **p. 1247**

I

immaculate (i mak′ yə lit) *adj.* unblemished; flawless; pure; **p. 1083**

immortality (im′ ôr tal′ ə tē) *n.* the condition of having eternal life; **p. 604**

gratify/gratificar *v.* satisfacer o complacer; **p. 75**

grave/grave *adj.* solemne y severo; sombrío; **p. 890**

gravity/gravedad *s.* seriedad; importancia; **p. 1270**

grievous/doloroso(a) *adj.* que causa o implica sufrimiento; profunda pena; **p. 1234**

grimace/gesticular *v.* hacer muecas con la cara, especialmente para expresar dolor o molestia; **p. 755, p. 1321**

grope/tantear *v.* palpar algo sin certeza; buscar a ciegas; **p. 1183**

guile/ardid *s.* engaño; astucia; trampa; **p. 571**

gunner/artillero(a) *s.* soldado de las fuerzas militares que sirve en la artillería; **p. 978**

H

hallow/consagrar *v.* santificar; honrar como sagrado; **p. 402**

haughty/altanero *adj.* presumido; arrogante; **p. 880**

heave/elevación *s.* movimiento hacia arriba, o esfuerzo para levantar algo; **p. 445**

hemorrhage/hemorragia *s.* pérdida grave de sangre; **p. 931**

holocaust/holocausto *s.* destrucción grande o total, especialmente debida al fuego; **p. 1255**

hostile/hostil *adj.* que siente o demuestra odio; adverso; **p. 902**

husky/corpulento(a) *adj.* fornido; grandote; **p. 711**

hypocrisy/hipocresía *s.* expresión de sentimientos o creencias que en realidad no se tienen; falsedad; **p. 135**

hysterical/histérico(a) *adj.* caracterizado por pánico o alguna emoción sin freno; **p. 1247**

I

immaculate/inmaculado *adj.* sin mancha ni pecado; irreprochable; puro; **p. 1083**

immortality/inmortalidad *s.* vida eterna; **p. 604**

impede (im pēd´) *v.* to slow or block progress or action; obstruct; **p. 265**

imperative (im per´ ə tiv) *n.* something absolutely necessary; an essential; **p. 1159**

imperial (im pēr´ ē əl) *adj.* of or relating to an empire or emperor; **p. 450**

imperially (im pēr´ ē əl ē) *adv.* majestically; magnificently; **p. 575**

implementation (im´ plə mən tā´ shən) *n.* putting into effect; putting into use; **p. 1242**

implication (im´ plə kā´ shən) *n.* an effect or consequence; **p. 973**

impromptu (im promp´ tōō, -tū) *adv.* done on the spur of the moment; **p. 416**

impudent (im´ pyə dənt) *adj.* cocky, bold; **p. 939**

impudently (im´ pyə dənt lē) *adv.* in an offensively bold manner; **p. 585**

inaudibly (in ô´ də blē) *adv.* in a manner not able to be heard; **p. 1270**

incessantly (in ses´ ənt lē´) *adv.* continually; happening over and over without interruption; **p. 576**

incredulity (in´ krə dōō´ lə tē, -dū´) *n.* disbelief; **p. 417**

indentured (in den´ chərd) *adj.* bound by contract to serve someone for a time; **p. 106**

indictment (in dīt´ mənt) *n.* a formal legal accusation, charging the commission or omission of an act, which is punishable by law; **p. 1105**

indifferent (in dif´ ər ənt) *adj.* lacking feeling or concern; having no marked feeling for or against; **p. 1288**

induce (in doos´) *v.* to lead by persuasion or influence; **p. 354**

ineffably (in ef´ ə blē) *adv.* to a degree that is impossible to express; indescribably; **p. 983**

ineptly (i nept´ lē) *adv.* incompetently; awkwardly; clumsily; **p. 1066**

inevitable (i nev´ ə tə bəl) *adj.* incapable of being avoided or evaded; certain to happen; **p. 973**

impede/impedir *v.* detener o aminorar; obstaculizar; **p. 265**

imperative/imperativo *s.* algo absolutamente necesario; algo esencial; **p. 1159**

imperial/imperial *adj.* relativo al imperio o al emperador; **p. 450**

imperially/imperialmente *adv.* majestuosamente; magníficamente; **p. 575**

implementation/implementación *s.* suministro de los medios necesarios para llevar algo a cabo; **p. 1242**

implication/implicación *s.* efecto o consecuencia; **p. 973**

impromptu/improvisadamente *adv.* hecho espontáneamente, de improviso; **p. 416**

impudent/insolente *adj.* atrevido, descarado; **p. 939**

impudently/descaradamente *adv.* de modo ofensivo y atrevido; sin decoro ni vergüenza; **p. 585**

inaudibly/inaudiblemente *adv.* de modo que no se puede escuchar; **p. 1270**

incessantly/incesantemente *adv.* de continuo; que no cesa ni se interrumpe; **p. 576**

incredulity/incredulidad *s.* descreimiento; **p. 417**

indentured/ligado por contrato *adj.* obligado por un contrato a servir a una persona por un tiempo determinado; **p. 106**

indictment/acusación *s.* denuncia legal y formal por la comisión u omisión de un acto que castiga la ley; **p. 1105**

indifferent/indiferente *adj.* que no demuestra sentimiento o preocupacion: **p. 1288**

induce/inducir *v.* influir o persuadir; **p. 354**

ineffably/inefablemente *adv.* sin poderse explicar; de modo indescriptible; **p. 983**

ineptly/ineptamente *adv.* sin aptitud o destreza; torpemente; **p. 1066**

inevitable/inevitable *adj.* que no se puede evitar o eludir; irremediable; **p. 973**

infamy (in´ fə mē) *n.* a reputation as something evil or harmful; **p. 972**

infidel (in´ fə del´) *n.* an unbeliever; **p. 106**

infrastructure (in´ frə struk´ chər) *n.* the underlying base for an organization or a system; **p. 1243**

ingenious (in jēn´ yəs) *adj.* exhibiting creative ability; inventive; **p. 106**

ingenuously (in jen´ ū əs lē) *adv.* honestly; frankly; **p. 585**

iniquity (in ik´ wə tē) *n.* sin; **p. 282**

inquisitor (in kwi´ zə tər) *n.* one who asks questions; **p. 933**

inscrutable (in skrōō´ tə bəl) *adj.* mysterious, or not able to be interpreted or understood; **p. 302**

insidious (in sid´ ē əs) *adj.* slyly dangerous; deceitful; deceptive; **p. 117**

installment (in stôl´ mənt) *n.* one part of a payment that has been divided; **p. 1019**

intangible (in tan´ jə bəl) *adj.* not easily defined or evaluated by the mind; **p. 603**

integrate (in´ tə grāt´) *v.* to bring all parts together into a whole; **p. 190**

integrity (in teg´ rə tē) *n.* moral uprightness; honesty; **p. 195**

interminable (in tur´ mi nə bəl) *adj.* seemingly endless; **p. 499**

interpose (in´ tər pōz´) *v.* to intrude, intervene, or to put oneself between; **p. 445**

intervene (in´ tər vēn´) *v.* to come or lie between; **p. 607**

intimation (in´ tə mā´ shən) *n.* a hint; a suggestion; **p. 934**

intimidated (in tim´ ə dāt´ əd) *adj.* made timid or fearful; frightened into submission or inaction; **p. 962**

irreproachable (ir´ i prō´ chə bəl) *adj.* free from blame; faultless; **p. 288**

infamy/infamia *s.* una reputación como algo funesto o dañoso; **p. 972**

infidel/infiel *s.* el que no cree; **p. 106**

infrastructure/infraestructura *s.* elementos o servicios necesarios para la creación o el funcionamiento de una organización o sistema; **p. 1243**

ingenious/ingenioso *adj.* que tiene habilidad creativa; talentoso; **p. 106**

ingenuously/ingenuamente *adv.* de modo honesto; francamente; cándidamente; **p. 585**

iniquity/iniquidad *s.* pecado; maldad; **p. 282**

inquisitor/inquisidor *s.* el que hace preguntas; **p. 933**

inscrutable/inescrutable *adj.* misterioso, que no se puede interpreter o entender; **p. 302**

insidious/insidioso *adj.* engañoso; malicioso; **p. 117**

installment/cuota *s.* parte proporcional en que se divide un pago; **p. 1019**

intangible/intangible *adj.* que no es fácil de definir o evaluar; **p. 603**

integrate/integrar *v.* unir todas las partes en un todo; **p. 190**

integrity/integridad *s.* rectitud moral; honestidad; **p. 195**

interminable/interminable *adj.* que parece no tener fin; **p. 499**

interpose/interponer *v.* meterse, mediar, poner algo entre cosas o personas; **p. 445**

intervene/intervenir *v.* tomar parte en un asunto; **p. 607**

intimation/insinuación *s.* sugerencia; indirecta; **p. 934**

intimidated/intimidado *adj.* atemorizado o asustado; reprimido; **p. 962**

irreproachable/irreprochable *adj.* libre de culpa; sin falta alguna; **p. 288**

J

jilt (jilt) *v.* to drop or reject as a sweetheart; **p. 779**

jostle (jo′ səl) *v.* to bump, push, or shove while moving, as in a crowd; **p. 746**

jubilant (jōō′ bə lənt) *adj.* extremely happy; triumphantly joyful; **p. 963**

K

kin (kin) *n.* relatives, or a group of people with common ancestry; **p. 730**

kinsmen (kinz′ men) *n.* someone who shares the same racial or cultural background as another; **p. 803**

L

lament (lə ment′) *v.* to express deep sorrow or grief; **p. 84**

latent (lā′ tənt) *adj.* present but not evident; hidden; **p. 194**

lattice (la′ təs) *n.* a structure of crisscrossed strips, commonly wood or metal, that forms a pattern of openings; **p. 258**

lean (lēn) *adj.* unproductive; lacking; **p. 826**

legacy (leg′ ə sē) *n.* an inheritance; **p. 522**

lethargy (leth′ ər jē) *n.* sluggish inactivity or drowsiness; **p. 268**

loiter (loi′ tər) *v.* to stand or linger idly or aimlessly about a place; **p. 962**

lopped (lopt) *v.* trimmed or chopped off, as the branches of a tree; **p. 1234**

lot (lot) *n.* way of life or purpose as determined by fate; fortune; **p. 208**

ludicrous (lōō′ də krəs) *adj.* deserving laughter; foolish; false; **p. 206**

lull (lul) *v.* to soothe or cause to sleep; **p. 813**

lurch (lurch) *v.* to move suddenly and unevenly; **p. 745**

J

jilt/dejar plantado *v.* rechazar; incumplir una cita; **p. 779**

jostle/empujar *v.* empellar mientras se camina, como en una multitud; **p. 746**

jubilant/jubiloso *adj.* dichoso; muy feliz por un triunfo; **p. 963**

K

kin/clan *s.* parientes o grupo de personas unidas por un vínculo familiar; **p. 730**

kinsmen/parientes *s.* alguien quien es parte de la misma raza o experiencia cultural; **p. 803**

L

lament/lamentar *v.* expresar gran pena o dolor; **p. 84**

latent/latente *adj.* presente pero no evidente; oculto; **p. 194**

lattice/entramado *s.* conjunto de láminas entrecruzadas, de metal o material flexible, que forma aperturas; **p. 258**

lean/escaso(a) *adj.* improductivo; pobre; **p. 826**

legacy/legado *s.* herencia; **p. 522**

lethargy/letargo *s.* estado de sopor o inactividad; **p. 268**

loiter/holgazanear *v.* permanecer en un lugar sin hacer nada; estar ocioso; **p. 962**

lopped/podado(a) *v.* cortar y quitar, por ej. las ramas de un árbol; **p. 1234**

lot/destino *s.* lo que determina el modo de vida o los acontecimientos; fortuna; **p. 208**

ludicrous/absurdo(a) *adj.* disparatado; sin sentido; equivocado; **p. 206**

lull/arrullar *v.* tranquilizar o adormecer; **p. 813**

lurch/tambalearse *v.* caminar o moverse sin equilibrio; **p. 745**

M

malinger (mə ling′ gər) *v.* to pretend incapacity or illness to avoid work; **p. 670**

manifest (man′ ə fest′) *adj.* apparent to the eye or the mind; evident; obvious; **p. 195**

marvel (mär′ vəl) *v.* to be filled with wonder; **p. 1277**

meager (mē′ gər) *adj.* deficient in quantity or completeness; **p. 945**

meandering (mē an′ dər ing) *adj.* following a winding course; **p. 1312**

melancholy (mel′ ən kol′ ē) *adj.* depressing; dismal; gloomy; **p. 243**

mildewed (mil′ dyūd) *adj.* coated or partially coated with a fungus that causes spoilage; **p. 1224**

millennium (mi le′ nē əm) *n.* a period of great happiness, peace, or prosperity; **p. 819**

misanthropic (mis′ ən throp′ ik) *adj.* having hatred for humankind; **p. 298**

morose (mə rōs′) *adj.* bad-tempered, gloomy, and withdrawn; **p. 921**

mortification (môr′ tə fi kā′ shən) *n.* feeling of shame, humiliation, or embarrassment; **p. 107**

mount (mount) *v.* to ascend or to soar; **p. 685**

mundane (mun dān′) *adj.* ordinary; **p. 761**

mute (mūt) *adj.* silent; **p. 690**

myriad (mir′ ē əd) *adj.* countless; innumerable; **p. 215**

N

nobly (nō′ blē) *adv.* with superior morals or character; **p. 803**

nostalgia (nə stal′ jə) *n.* a bittersweet longing for things, persons, or situations of the past; **p. 1260**

O

oblige (ə blīj′) *v.* to make grateful or indebted; to do a favor or service for; **p. 370**

M

malinger/fingirse enfermo *v.* hacerse el enfermo para no trabajar; **p. 670**

manifest/manifiesto *adj.* evidente o claro a la vista; obvio; **p. 195**

marvel/maravillar(se) *v.* ver con admiración y asombro; **p. 1277**

meager/exiguo *adj.* muy escaso; limitado; **p. 945**

meandering/tortuoso *adj.* que sigue un camino con muchas curvas; **p. 1312**

melancholy/melancólico *adj.* deprimente; funesto; desconsolador; **p. 243**

mildewed/mohoso(a) *adj.* cubierto total o parcialmente con un hongo que puede causar daños; **p. 1224**

millennium/edad de oro *s.* periodo de felicidad, paz o prosperidad; **p. 819**

misanthropic/misantrópico(a) *adj.* que siente aversión o rechazo al trato humano; **p. 298**

morose/adusto *adj.* malhumorado; taciturno; **p. 921**

mortification/mortificación *s.* sentimiento de aflicción, humillación o vergüenza; **p. 107**

mount/montar *v.* subir o remontar; **p. 685**

mundane/mundano *adj.* ordinario; usual; terrenal; **p. 761**

mute/mudo *adj.* silencioso; falta de sonido; **p. 690**

myriad/innumerable *adj.* que no se puede contar; incalculable; **p. 215**

N

nobly/noblemente *adv.* con morales superiores o un carácter superior; **p. 803**

nostalgia/nostalgia *s.* tristeza melancólica por la ausencia o alejamiento de cosas, personas o recuerdos del pasado; **p. 1260**

O

oblige/agradecer *v.* hacer agradecido o adeudado por algo; hacerle un favor o un servicio; **p. 370**

obliquely (ō blēk′ lē) *adv.* in a slanting or sloping direction; **p. 526**

oblivious (ə bliv′ ē əs) *adj.* without conscious awareness; unmindful; **p. 1270**

obscure (əb skyo͞or′) *adj.* little known or having an insignificant reputation; **p. 541**

occult (ə kult′) *adj.* beyond human understanding; mysterious; **p. 191**

ominous (om′ə nəs) *adj.* like an evil omen; threatening; **p. 756, p. 1249**

ordeal (ôr dēl′) *n.* a circumstance or experience that is painful or difficult; a trial; **p. 1157**

P

palpable (pal′ pə bəl) *adj.* tangible; able to be touched or felt; **p. 690**

patronage (pā′ trə nij) *n.* business; trade; custom; **p. 817**

pepper (pe′ pər) *v.* to shower with small objects; **p. 685**

perception (pər sep′ shən) *n.* an awareness; an insight; **p. 555**

perennial (pə ren′ ē əl) *adj.* continuing year after year; enduring; **p. 191**

perish (per′ ish) *v.* to pass from existence; to disappear; **p. 402**

perjury (pər′ jə rē) *n.* the act of swearing under oath to the truth of something that one knows to be untrue; **p. 1084**

permeate (pur′ mē āt′) *v.* to penetrate, spread through, or diffuse; **p. 1218**

perpetual (pər pech′ o͞o əl) *adj.* lasting forever; eternal; **p. 190**

perturbation (pur′ tər bā′ shən) *n.* state of being perturbed, anxious, or uneasy; **p. 757**

perusal (pə ro͞o′ zəl) *n.* the process of examining carefully; **p. 385**

pervade (pər vād′) *v.* to spread through every part; **p. 378**

petrified (pet′ rə fīd) *adj.* paralyzed with fear; stiff or like stone; **p. 135**

obliquely/oblicuamente *adv.* de manera inclinada o sesgada; **p. 526**

oblivious/abstraído *adj.* distraído; ensimismado; **p. 1270**

obscure/obscuro(a) *adj.* no conocido; que tenga una reputación insignificante; **p. 541**

occult/sobrenatural *adj.* más allá de la comprensión humana; misterioso; **p. 191**

ominous/ominoso *adj.* que da mal presagio; siniestro; **p. 756, p. 1249**

ordeal/tribulación *s.* circunstancia o experiencia dolorosa o difícil; **p. 1157**

P

palpable/palpable *adj.* tangible; que puede tocarse con las manos; **p. 690**

patronage/clientela *s.* conjunto de parroquianos de un negocio, oficio o establecimiento; **p. 817**

pepper/salpicar *v.* esparcir cosas como rociándolas sobre una superficie; **p. 685**

perception/percepción *s.* conocimiento; idea; **p. 555**

perennial/perenne *adj.* que continúa año tras año; duradero; **p. 191**

perish/perecer *v.* dejar de existir; desaparecer; **p. 402**

perjury/perjurio *n.* el acto de atestiguar bajo juramento la verdad de algo que uno sabe que no es verdad; **p. 1084**

permeate/penetrar *v.* infiltrarse, introducirse o difundirse; **p. 1218**

perpetual/perpetuo *adj.* que dura por siempre; eterno; **p. 190**

perturbation/perturbación *s.* agitación; ansiedad; inquietud; **p. 757**

perusal/escudriñamiento *s.* proceso de examinar cuidadosamente; **p. 385**

pervade/penetrar *v.* saturar; llenar por todos lados; **p. 378**

petrified/petrificado *adj.* paralizado de miedo; inmóvil como una piedra; **p. 135**

petulance (pe´ tū lens) *n.* irritability; impatience; **p. 761**

piety (pī´ ə tē) *n.* religious devoutness; goodness; **p. 780**

placid (pla´ səd) *adj.* calm; peaceful; undisturbed; **p. 259**

Plexiglas (plek´ si glas´) *n.* a light and very durable transparent plastic; **p. 978**

poignant (poin´ yənt) *adj.* sharp; severe; causing emotional or physical anguish; **p. 392**

pointless (point´ lis) *n.* making no sense; **p. 1194**

poise (poiz´) *n.* a state of balance; **p. 719**

poised (poizd) *adj.* having a calm, controlled, and dignified manner; composed; **p. 906**

ponder (pon´ dər) *v.* to think about thoroughly and carefully; **p. 1184**

possessor (pə zes´ ər) *n.* one who has or takes control of something; owner; **p. 1194**

posterity (pos ter´ ə tē) *n.* generations of the future; all of one's descendants; **p. 50**

premeditated (prē med´ ə tāt´ əd) *adj.* thought about beforehand; **p. 973**

premonition (prē´ mə nish´ ən) *n.* a warning, or foreboding about the future; **p. 988**

presume (pri zo͞om´) *v.* to expect something without justification; to take for granted; **p. 670**

presumptuous (pri zump´ cho͞o əs) *adj.* going beyond what is proper; excessively bold; **p. 1299**

pretense (prē´ tens) *n.* a false show or appearance, especially for the purpose of deceiving; falseness; **p. 1037**

prevalent (prev´ ə lent) *adj.* widespread; **p. 242**

procure (prə kyo͞or´) *v.* to obtain by care or effort; **p. 67**

prosperous (pros´ pər əs) *adj.* wealthy or successful; **p. 540**

prostrate (pros´ trāt) *adj.* stretched out with face to the ground in humility, adoration, or submission; **p. 377**

petulance/mal genio *n.* irritabilidad; impaciencia; **p. 761**

piety/piedad *s.* devoción religiosa; bondad; **p. 780**

placid/plácido *adj.* quieto; apacible; sin perturbación; **p. 259**

Plexiglas/plexiglás *s.* material acrílico transparente y flexible; **p. 978**

poignant/punzante *adj.* agudo; lacerante; que causa angustia emocional o física; **p. 392**

pointless/inútil *s.* vano, sin sentido; **p. 1194**

poise/aplomo *s.* mesura, compostura; **p. 719**

poised/aplomado(a) *adj.* que tiene serenidad, seriedad y seguridad; con compostura; **p. 906**

ponder/ponderar *v.* pensar algo detenida y cuidadosamente; **p. 1184**

possessor/poseedor(a) *s.* persona que tiene en su poder el control de algo; dueño; **p. 1194**

posterity/posteridad *s.* generaciones del futuro; todos los descendientes; **p. 50**

premeditated/premeditado(a) *adj.* que se reflexionó con cuidado antes de realizar la acción; **p. 973**

premonition/premonición *s.* advertencia o presagio de que algo va a ocurrir; **p. 988**

presume/suponer *v.* esperar algo sin justicación; **p. 670**

presumptuous/atrevido(a) *adj.* que falta al respeto debido; insolente; **p. 1299**

pretense/simulación *s.* falsa apariencia, especialmente con el propósito de engañar; falsedad; **p. 1037**

prevalent/prevaleciente *adj.* frecuente; generalizado; **p. 242**

procure/procurarse *v.* obtener mediante esfuerzos; **p. 67**

prosperous/próspero(a) *adj.* rico o venturoso; **p. 540**

prostrate/postrado *adj.* agachado o arrodillado en señal de humillación, adoración o sumisión; **p. 377**

protrude (prō trōōd´) *v.* to stick out; to project; **p. 390**

providence (prov´ ə dəns) *n.* divine care or guidance; foresight; **p. 65**

proximity (prok sim´ ə tē) *n.* closeness in space, time, sequence, or degree; nearness; **p. 271**

prudence (prōōd´əns) *n.* exercise of good and cautious judgment; **p. 98**

R

racket (rak´ it) *n.* loud noise; clamor; din; **p. 770**

rampages (ram´ pāj´ iz) *v.* rushes wildly about; scurries; **p. 1234**

random (ran´ dəm) *adj.* lacking a definite pattern; haphazard; **p. 1255**

rank (rangk) *adj.* having a strong, offensive odor; **p. 1224**

ration (rā´ shən) *n.* fixed portion or share; **p. 58**

ravenous (rav´ ə nəs) *adj.* extremely hungry; **p. 918**

reap (rēp) *v.* to gather, as in harvesting a crop; **p. 826**

rear (rir) *v.* to lift upright; raise; **p. 1259**

recede (ri sēd´) *v.* to move back or away from a point, limit, or mark; **p. 1228**

recluse (rek´ lōōs) *n.* someone who leads a secluded or solitary life; **p. 298**

recompense (rek´ əm pens´) *n.* something given in return for something else; compensation; **p. 92**

rectitude (rek´ tə tōōd´) *n.* uprightness of moral character; honesty; **p. 124**

redress (rē´ dress´) *n.* compensation, as for wrong done; **p. 385**

rejuvenated (ri jōō´ və nāt´ əd) *adj.* restored to youthful vigor or appearance; renewed; **p. 1326**

remonstrate (ri mon´ strāt) *v.* to object; to protest; **p. 118**

render (ren´ dər) *v.* to reproduce or depict in verbal or artistic form; **p. 706**

repose (ri pōz´) *n.* relaxation; tranquility; eternal rest; **p. 516**

protrude/sobresalir *v.* resaltar; proyectarse; **p. 390**

providence/providencia *s.* cuidado o guía divina; disposición; **p. 65**

proximity/proximidad *s.* cercanía en espacio, tiempo, secuencia o grado; **p. 271**

prudence/prudencia *s.* ejercicio del buen juicio y la cordura; cautela; **p. 98**

R

racket/bulla *s.* gritería; clamor; barullo; **p. 770**

rampages/alborotar *v.* pasar saqueando; corretear; **p. 1234**

random/causal *adj.* que no sigue un patrón definido; fortuito; **p. 1255**

rank/fétido(a) *adj.* que tiene un olor repugnante; **p. 1224**

ration/ración *s.* porción definida; **p. 58**

ravenous/voraz *adj.* extremadamente hambriento; **p. 918**

reap/cosechar *v.* recoger los cultivos cuando están maduros; **p. 826**

rear/levantar *v.* alzar; subir; **p. 1259**

recede/retroceder *v.* recular o irse de un punto, un limite o una marca; **p. 1228**

recluse/ermitaño(a) *s.* persona que vive recluida o en soledad; **p. 298**

recompense/recompensa *s.* algo dado en cambio de algo más; compensación; **p. 92**

rectitude/rectitud *s.* buena condición moral; honestidad; **p. 124**

redress/desagravio *s.* compensación por un error o mala actitud; **p. 385**

rejuvenated/rejuvenecido *adj.* que ha recuperado el vigor o la apariencia joven; renovado; **p. 1326**

remonstrate/rezongar *v.* objetar; protestar; **p. 118**

render/producir *v.* causar; generar; **p. 706**

repose/descanso *s.* relax; tranquilidad; reposo eterno; **p. 516**

reprieve (ri prēv´) *n.* official postponement of the carrying out of a sentence; **p. 1102**

reprimand (rep´ rə mand´) *v.* to reprove or correct sharply; **p. 1052**

reproach (ri prōch´) *n.* an expression of disapproval; a reprimand; **p. 523**

repudiate (ri pū´ dē āt´) *v.* to refuse to accept as valid; to reject; to renounce; **p. 1159**

resign (ri zīn´) *v.* to make oneself accept; **p. 748**

resignation (rez´ ig nā´ shən) *n.* unresisting acceptance; submission; **p. 214**

resolution (rez´ ə lo͞o´ shən) *n.* firmness of purpose; **p. 135**

resolve (ri zolv´) *v.* to decide; determine; **p. 54**

respite (res´ pət) *n.* a period of rest or relief, as from work or sorrow; **p. 259**

retaliation (ri tal´ ē ā´ shən) *n.* the act of repaying an injury or a wrong by committing the same, or a similar, act; **p. 1102**

retractable (ri trak´ tə bəl) *adj.* capable of being drawn back or in; **p. 931**

reverence (rev´ ər əns) *n.* a feeling of respect or deep affection; **p. 208**

revive (ri vīv´) *v.* to give new strength and vitality, or bring back to consciousness; **p. 58**

rouse (rouz) *v.* to awaken from sleep; **p. 58**

rudiment (ro͞o´ də mənt) *n.* an imperfect or undeveloped part; **p. 215**

rue (ro͞o) *v.* to regret; to be sorry for; **p. 923**

ruinous (ro͞o´ i nəs) *adj.* causing ruin; destructive; **p. 517**

S

sagacious (sə gā´ shəs) *adj.* having or showing wisdom and keen perception; **p. 282**

salient (sāl´ yənt) *adj.* prominent or conspicuously noticeable; **p. 570**

sanction (sangk´ shən) *n.* approval or support; **p. 227**

scintillating (sin´ tə lā´ ting) *adj.* brilliant; sparkling; **p. 816**

reprieve/aplazamiento *s.* demora oficial de una sentencia; **p. 1102**

reprimand/reprender *v.* regañar o corregir severamente; **p. 1052**

reproach/reproche *s.* expresión de desacuerdo; censura; **p. 523**

repudiate/repudiar *v.* negarse a aceptar como válido; rechazar; renunciar; **p. 1159**

resign/resignarse *v.* obligarse a aceptar; conformarse; **p. 748**

resignation/resignación *s.* aceptación; conformismo; sumisión; **p. 214**

resolution/resolución *s.* acción de decidir con firmeza; **p. 135**

resolve/resolver *v.* decidir; determinar; **p. 54**

respite/respiro *s.* rato de descanso o alivio, en medio de un trabajo o una pena; **p. 259**

retaliation/represalia *s.* acto de vengarse o devolver un mal acto cometiendo un acto similar o igual; **p. 1102**

retractable/retráctil *adj.* capaz de encogerse; **p. 931**

reverence/reverencia *s.* respeto o veneración; **p. 208**

revive/revivir *v.* dar nueva fuerza y vitalidad; hacer que recupere el conocimiento; **p. 58**

rouse/despertar *v.* dejar de dormir; **p. 58**

rudiment/rudimento *s.* parte imperfecta o sin desarrollar; **p. 215**

rue/deplorar *v.* lamentar; sentir; **p. 923**

ruinous/ruinoso(a) *adj.* que arruina; que destruye; **p. 517**

S

sagacious/sagaz *adj.* que tiene o demuestra astucia y agudeza mental; **p. 282**

salient/destacado(a) *adj.* prominente o notoria-mente evidente; **p. 570**

sanction/ratificación *s.* aprobación o respaldo; **p. 227**

scintillating/chispeante *adj.* brillante; destellante; **p. 816**

score (skôr) *n.* a group of twenty items; **p. 402**

scorn (skôrn) *n.* contempt or disdain felt toward a person or an object considered despicable or unworthy; **p. 1260**

scorned (skôrnd) *v.* treated with open contempt; rejected something as worthless; **p. 576**

scruple (skrōō′ pəl) *n.* moral principle that restrains action; **p. 76**

scuffle (skuf′ əl) *v.* to move with a slow, heavy, shuffling gait; **p. 868**

sear (sēr) *v.* to char, scorch, or burn the surface with or as if with a sudden application of intense heat; **p. 1293**

secede (si sēd′) *v.* to formally withdraw from an alliance; **p. 1247**

shtetl (shte′ təl) *n.* small Jewish town or community; **p. 1338**

sluggishly (slug′ ish lē) *adv.* slowly; without strength or energy; **p. 877**

sneer (snēr) *v.* to smile or laugh scornfully or critically; **p. 711**

snicker (sni′ kər) *n.* a snide, partly suppressed laugh, often expressing disrespect; **p. 794**

solemn (sol′ əm) *adj.* serious; somber; **p. 895**

solidarity (sol′ ə dar′ ə tē) *n.* unity of a group that produces a sense of community; **p. 1175**

solitude (sol′ e tōōd′) *n.* the state of being alone; **p. 1333**

sown (sōn) *v.* planted; **p. 826**

speculate (spek′ yə lāt′) *v.* to engage in risky business ventures, hoping to make quick profits; **p. 248**

spurn (spurn) *v.* to reject with contempt or disdain; to scorn; **p. 1284**

stately (stāt′ lē) *adj.* noble; dignified; majestic; **p. 920**

stature (stach′ ər) *n.* a level attained; standing; status; **p. 1159**

stigma (stig′ mə) *n.* mark or characteristic of disgrace; **p. 1245**

score/veintena *s.* grupo de veinte objetos; **p. 402**

scorn/despreció *v.* desdén hacia una persona o un objeto que se considera desreciable o desmerecedor; **p. 1260**

scorned/despreciado *v.* tratar con desdén; despreciar; **p. 576**

scruple/escrúpulo *s.* principio moral que limita una acción; **p. 76**

scuffle/arrastrar los pies *v.* moverse con pasos rápidos y torpes; **p. 868**

sear/quemar *v.* calcinar, chamuscar o abrasar con fuego o algo muy caliente; **p. 1293**

secede/separarse de *v.* retirarse formalmente de una alianza; **p. 1247**

shtetl/shtetl *s.* palabra de origen yiddish que significa pequeña ciudad o comunidad hebrea; **p. 1338**

sluggishly/perezosamente *adv.* lentamente; sin energía ni entusiasmo; **p. 877**

sneer/reírse socarronamente *v.* sonreír o reír despreciativamente o criticamente; **p. 711**

snicker/risita burlona *s.* risa solapada que puede demostrar burla o falta de respeto; **p. 794**

solemn/solemne *adj.* serio; grave; **p. 895**

solidarity/solidaridad *s.* adhesión o apoyo a una causa ajena; **p. 1175**

solitude/soledad *s.* falta de compañía, estar solo; **p. 1333**

sown/sembrados *v.* (part.) plantados; **p. 826**

speculate/especular *v.* participar en negocios arriesgados con el deseo de obtener ganancias rápidas; **p. 248**

spurn/desdeñar *v.* rechazar con menosprecio o desdén; **p. 1284**

stately/majestuoso *adj.* noble; imponente; espléndido; **p. 920**

stature/estatura *s.* nivel alcanzado; posición; **p. 1159**

stigma/estigma *s.* marca o señal de mala fama; **p. 1245**

stipulate (stip´ yə lāt´) *v.* to require or demand as part of an agreement; **p. 1176**

stooped (stoopt) *adj.* bent forward and downward; **p. 1184**

striking (strī´ king) *adj.* impressive; attractive; **p. 1277**

stupor (stoo´ pər) *n.* a confused or dazed state of mind; **p. 543**

subjugation (sub´ jə gā´ shən) *n.* act of bringing under control; domination; **p. 117**

sublime (səb līm´) *adj.* of great spiritual or intellectual value; noble; **p. 214**

subsequently (sub´ sə kwent´ lē) *adv.* at a later time; **p. 417**

subservient (səb sur´ vē ənt) *adj.* useful, in an inferior capacity, to promote an end; submissive; **p. 1034**

subtle (sut´ əl) *adj.* barely noticeable; not open, direct, or obvious; **p. 788**

subverting (səb vurt´ ing) *v.* overthrowing and destroying; **p. 1234**

succumb (sə kum´) *v.* to give in or submit to; **p. 986**

surmise (sər mīz´) *v.* to infer from little evidence; to guess; **p. 245**

susceptible (sə sep´ tə bəl) *adj.* easily influenced or affected; **p. 417**

swelter (swel´ tər) *v.* to suffer from oppressive heat; **p. 1228**

swindle (swin´ dəl) *v.* to cheat someone out of money or property; **p. 1021**

T

tactful (takt´ fəl) *adj.* able to speak or act without offending others; **p. 776**

taper (tā´ pər) *v.* to become progressively thinner or smaller; **p. 701**

tedious (tē´ dē əs) *adj.* tiresome because of length; boring; **p. 668**

temper (tem´ pər) *v.* to modify or moderate; soften; **p. 50**

stipulate/estipular *v.* establecer o concertar de común acuerdo; **p. 1176**

stooped/encorvado *adj.* doblado hacia adelante y hacia abajo; **p. 1184**

striking/atractivo(a) *adj.* admirable; que atrae la atención; **p. 1277**

stupor/estupor *s.* disminución de las funciones intelectuales, aletargamiento; **p. 543**

subjugation/subyugación *s.* acto de someter o poner bajo control; dominación; **p. 117**

sublime/sublime *adj.* de gran valor espiritual o intelectual; noble; **p. 214**

subsequent/subsiguiente *adv.* que sigue inmediatamente; **p. 417**

subservient/subordinado *adj.* útil, en una capacidad inferior, para conseguir un fin; sumiso; **p. 1034**

subtle/sutil *adj.* que no es obvio ni directo; **p. 788**

subverting/subvirtiendo *v.* derrocar y destruir; **p. 1234**

succumb/sucumbir *v.* rendirse; ceder; **p. 986**

surmise/suponer *v.* conjeturar con poca o ninguna evidencia; presumir; **p. 245**

susceptible/susceptible *adj.* sensible o capaz de recibir modificación; **p. 417**

swelter/achicharrar *v.* padecer de calor opresivo; **p. 1228**

swindle/estafar *v.* engañar a alguien para sacarle dinero o propiedad; **p. 1021**

T

tactful/discreto *adj.* capaz de hablar o actuar sin ofender a otros; **p. 776**

taper/reducir *v.* disminuir en tamaño o intensidad; **p. 701**

tedious/tedioso *adj.* pesado a causa de su extensión o duración; aburrido; **p. 668**

temper/atemperar *v.* modificar o moderar; suavizar; **p. 50**

tempest (tem′pist) *n.* a violent storm; **p. 570**

tenure (ten′ yər) *n.* conditions or terms under which something is held; **p. 123**

terminus (tur′ mə nəs) *n.* one end of a travel route or the station placed there; **p. 1012**

token (tō′ ken) *n.* something serving as an indication, a proof, or an expression of something else; a sign; **p. 1289**

transformed (trans forməd′) *adj.* changed in a dramatic way; **p. 1211**

transfusion (trans fū′ zhən) *n.* the act of passing life-saving fluids from one to another; **p. 1211**

trepidation (trep′ə dā′ shən) *n.* nervous anticipation; anxiety; dread; **p. 524**

tribute (tri′ byüt) *n.* something given to show affection, gratitude, or respect; **p. 939**

tumultuously (tōō mul′ chōō əs lē) *adv.* in an agitated manner; violently; **p. 554**

turret (tur′it) *n.* a small, rotating domelike structure that is mounted with guns and attached to the body of an aircraft; **p. 978**

twinge (twinj) *n.* a sudden, sharp physical or emotional pain; **p. 940**

tyranny (tir′ə nē) *n.* cruel use of authority; oppressive power; **p. 134**

tyrant (tī′ rənt) *n.* a ruler who exercises power or authority in an unjust manner; one who has absolute power; **p. 147**

U

uncanny (un kan′ ē) *adj.* peculiarly unsettling in an eerie way; **p. 582, p. 1249**

undeviating (un dē′ vē āt′ ing) *adj.* not turning away from; **p. 1299**

unencumbered (ən in kəm′ bərd) *adj.* unhindered; unburdened; **p. 1334**

unique (ū nēk′) *adj.* unusual; **p. 830**

---

tempest/tempestad *s.* tormenta con fuertes vientos; **p. 570**

tenure/tenencia *s.* condiciones o términos bajo los cuales se posee algo; **p. 123**

terminus/término *s.* final de un recorrido o el extremo de una línea de transporte público; **p. 1012**

token/muestra *s.* indicio, demostración o prueba de algo; un señal; **p. 1289**

transformed/convertido(a) *adj.* transformado en algo distinto de lo que era; **p. 1211**

transfusion/transfusión *s.* transferencia de sangre o plasma de una persona a otra; **p. 1211**

trepidation/perturbación *s.* anticipación nerviosa; ansiedad; **p. 524**

tribute/tributo *s.* reconocimiento en muestra de afecto, gratitud o respeto; **p. 939**

tumultuously/tumultuosamente *adv.* de modo agitado; violentamente; **p. 554**

turret/torreta giravtoria *s.* pequeña torre acorazada, con forma de domo que rota y está montada en un avión, que sirve para sostener piezas de artillería; **p. 978**

twinge/punzada *s.* dolor repentino y agudo que puede ser físico o afectivo; **p. 940**

tyranny/tiranía *s.* abuso cruel de la autoridad; poder opresivo; **p. 134**

tyrant/tirano(a) *s.* gobernante que abusa de su poder y autoridad de manera injusta; quien tiene el poder absoluto; **p. 147**

U

uncanny/espectral *adj.* inquietante y extraño; misterioso; **p. 582, p. 1249**

undeviating/recto *adj.* que no se desvía o extravía; **p. 1299**

unencumbered/aligerado(a) *adj.* aliviado o sin carga; **p. 1334**

unique/único(a) *adj.* fuera de lo común; **p. 830**

unorthodox (un ôr′ thə doks′) *adj.* not customary or traditional; **p. 1312**

unperturbed (un pər turbd′) *adj.* undisturbed; calm; **p. 1092**

unsheathed (un shēthd′) *adj.* removed from a protective case; **p. 830**

usurpation (ū′sər pā′ shən) *n.* the act of seizing power without legal right or authority; **p. 122**

V

valedictory (val′ ə dik′ tə rē) *adj.* of or relating to an occasion or expression of farewell; **p. 1229**

vanity (van′ i tē) *n.* excessive pride, as in one's looks; **p. 779**

vanquish (vang′ kwish) *v.* to defeat; **p. 356**

vassal (vas′ əl) *n.* a person in a subservient position; **p. 147**

vault (vôlt) *n.* an arched structure forming a roof or ceiling; **p. 24**

venerable (ven′ ər ə bəl) *adj.* deserving respect because of age, character, or position; **p. 281**

vigorously (vig′ ər əs lē) *adv.* with power, energy, and strength; **p. 893**

vile (vīl) *adj.* evil, repulsive, or degrading; **p. 571, p. 1077**

vindicate (vin′ də kāt′) *v.* to justify; to prove correct in light of later circumstances; **p. 879**

vindictive (vin dik′tiv) *adj.* desiring revenge; **p. 902**

virulent (vir′ yə lənt) *adj.* extremely poisonous or harmful; **p. 882**

vivid (viv′ id) *adj.* perceived as bright and distinct; brilliant; **p. 1288**

vogue (vōg) *n.* fashion; style; **p. 816**

volition (vō lish′ ən) *n.* act of choosing or deciding; **p. 1005**

W

wallowing (wol′ ō ing) *v.* moving in a clumsy manner or with difficulty; **p. 1210**

unorthodox/no ortodoxo *adj.* que no es usual ni tradicional; **p. 1312**

unperturbed/inalterado *adj.* que no se molesta o altera; calmado; **p. 1092**

unsheathed/desenvainado(a) *adj.* que se sacó que su vaina o funda; **p. 830**

usurpation/usurpación *s.* acto de tomar el poder sin derecho o autoridad legal; **p. 122**

V

valedictory/de despedida *adj.* de una ocasión o una expresión de adiós; **p. 1229**

vanity/vanidad *s.* orgullo excesivo, particularmente por la apariencia física; **p. 779**

vanquish/subyugar *v.* derrotar; conquistar **p. 356**

vassal/vasallo *n.* persona en una posición subordinada; **p. 147**

vault/bóveda *s.* estructura arqueada que forma un techo o cielo raso; **p. 24**

venerable/venerable *adj.* que merece respeto debido a la edad, carácter o posición; **p. 281**

vigorously/vigorosamente *adv.* con poder, energía y fuerza; **p. 893**

vile/vil *adj.* malvado; bajo; repulsivo; degradante; **p. 571, p. 1077**

vindicate/vindicar *v.* justificar; demostrar que es correcto ante nuevas circunstancias; **p. 879**

vindictive/vengativo *adj.* que desea venganza; **p. 902**

virulent/virulento *adj.* extremadamente nocivo o dañino; **p. 882**

vivid/vívido *adj.* auténtico; realista; distintivo; **p. 1288**

vogue/moda *s.* que está en boga; que se estila; **p. 816**

volition/volición *s.* acto de la voluntad de escoger y decidir; **p. 1005**

W

wallowing/andando pesadamente *v.* moverse torpemente o con dificultad; **p. 1210**

wane (wān) *v.* to decrease gradually; to decline; **p. 1300**

wanton (wont′ ən) *adj.* resulting from extreme cruelty or neglect; **p. 711**

warily (wār′ ə lē) *adv.* in a watchful or alert manner; cautiously; **p. 1255**

withered (wi′ thərd) *adj.* shriveled; **p. 745**

woo (wo͞o) *v.* to tempt or invite; **p. 1259**

X

xenophobic (zen′ə fō′ bik) *adj.* having an extreme fear of foreigners or strangers; **p. 1010**

Z

zealous (zel′ əs) *adj.* filled with enthusiastic devotion; passionate; **p. 288**

wane/declinar *v.* menguar o disminuir gradualmente; **p. 1300**

wanton/despiadado(a) *adj.* que es inhumano, cruel o sin piedad; **p. 711**

warily/cautelosamente *adv.* de modo cuidadoso o alerta; **p. 1255**

withered/marchito *adj.* seco; arrugado; **p. 745**

woo/atraer *v.* tentar o buscar el apoyo de alguien; **p. 1259**

X

xenophobic/xenófobo *adj.* que siente hostilidad hacia los extranjeros; **p. 1010**

Z

zealous/fervoroso *adj.* lleno de entusiasmo y devoción; apasionado; **p. 288**

Academic Word List

To succeed academically in high school and prepare for college, it is important to know academic vocabulary—special terms used in classroom discussion, assignments, and tests. These words are also used in the workplace and among friends to share information, exchange ideas, make decisions, and build relationships. Research has shown that the words listed below, compiled by Averil Coxhead in 2000, are the ones most commonly used in these ways. You will encounter many of them in the Glencoe Language Arts program. You will also focus on specific terms in connection with particular reading selections.

Note: The lists are ordered by frequency of use from most frequent to least frequent.

List One

analysis
approach
area
assessment
assume
authority
available
benefit
concept
consistent
constitutional
context
contract
create
data
definition
derived
distribution
economic
environment
established
estimate
evidence
export
factors
financial
formula
function
identified
income
indicate
individual
interpretation
involved
issues
labor
legal
legislation
major
method
occur
percent
period
policy
principle
procedure
process
required
research
response
role
section
sector
significant
similar
source
specific
structure
theory
variables

List Two

achieve
acquisition
administration
affect
appropriate
aspects
assistance
categories
chapter
commission
community
complex
computer
conclusion
conduct
consequences
construction
consumer
credit
cultural
design
distinction
elements
equation
evaluation
features
final
focus
impact
injury
institute
investment
items
journal
maintenance
normal
obtained
participation
perceived
positive
potential
previous
primary
purchase
range
region
regulations
relevant
resident
resources
restricted
security
select
site
sought
strategies
survey
text
traditional
transfer

List Three

alternative
circumstances
comments
compensation
components
consent
considerable
constant
constraints
contribution
convention
coordination
core
corporate
corresponding
criteria
deduction
demonstrate
document
dominant
emphasis
ensure
excluded
framework
funds
illustrated
immigration
implies
initial

instance
interaction
justification
layer
link
location
maximum
minorities
negative
outcomes
partnership
philosophy
physical
proportion
published
reaction
registered
reliance
removed
scheme
sequence
sex
shift
specified
sufficient
task
technical
techniques
technology
validity
volume

List Four

access
adequate
annual
apparent
approximated
attitudes
attributed
civil
code
commitment
communication

concentration
conference
contrast
cycle
debate
despite
dimensions
domestic
emerged
error
ethnic
goals
granted
hence
hypothesis
implementation
implications
imposed
integration
internal
investigation
job
label
mechanism
obvious
occupational
option
output
overall
parallel
parameters
phase
predicted
principal
prior
professional
project
promote
regime
resolution
retained
series
statistics
status

stress
subsequent
sum
summary
undertaken

List Five

academic
adjustment
alter
amendment
aware
capacity
challenge
clause
compounds
conflict
consultation
contact
decline
discretion
draft
enable
energy
enforcement
entities
equivalent
evolution
expansion
exposure
external
facilitate
fundamental
generated
generation
image
liberal
license
logic
marginal
medical
mental
modified
monitoring

network
notion
objective
orientation
perspective
precise
prime
psychology
pursue
ratio
rejected
revenue
stability
styles
substitution
sustainable
symbolic
target
transition
trend
version
welfare
whereas

List Six

abstract
accurate
acknowledged
aggregate
allocation
assigned
attached
author
bond
brief
capable
cited
cooperative
discrimination
display
diversity
domain
edition
enhanced

estate
exceed
expert
explicit
federal
fees
flexibility
furthermore
gender
ignored
incentive
incidence
incorporated
index
inhibition
initiatives
input
instructions
intelligence
interval
lecture
migration
minimum
ministry
motivation
neutral
nevertheless
overseas
preceding
presumption
rational
recovery
revealed
scope
subsidiary
tapes
trace
transformation
transport
underlying
utility

List Seven

adaptation
adults
advocate
aid
channel
chemical
classical
comprehensive
comprise
confirmed
contrary
converted
couple
decades
definite
deny
differentiation
disposal
dynamic
eliminate
empirical
equipment
extract
file
finite
foundation
global
grade
guarantee
hierarchical
identical
ideology
inferred
innovation
insert
intervention
isolated
media
mode
paradigm
phenomenon
priority
prohibited

publication
quotation
release
reverse
simulation
solely
somewhat
submitted
successive
survive
thesis
topic
transmission
ultimately
unique
visible
voluntary

List Eight

abandon
accompanied
accumulation
ambiguous
appendix
appreciation
arbitrary
automatically
bias
chart
clarity
conformity
commodity
complement
contemporary
contradiction
crucial
currency
denote
detected
deviation
displacement
dramatic
eventually
exhibit

exploitation
fluctuations
guidelines
highlighted
implicit
induced
inevitably
infrastructure
inspection
intensity
manipulation
minimized
nuclear
offset
paragraph
plus
practitioners
predominantly
prospect
radical
random
reinforced
restore
revision
schedule
tension
termination
theme
thereby
uniform
vehicle
via
virtually
visual
widespread

List Nine

accommodation
analogous
anticipated
assurance
attained
behalf
bulk

ceases
coherence
coincide
commenced
concurrent
confined
controversy
conversely
device
devoted
diminished
distorted
duration
erosion
ethical
format
founded
incompatible
inherent
insights
integral
intermediate
manual
mature
mediation
medium
military
minimal
mutual
norms
overlap
passive
portion
preliminary
protocol
qualitative
refine
relaxed
restraints
revolution
rigid
route
scenario
sphere

subordinate
supplementary
suspended
team
temporary
trigger
unified
violation
vision

List Ten

adjacent
albeit
assembly
collapse
colleagues
compiled
conceived
convinced
depression
encountered
enormous
forthcoming
inclination
integrity
intrinsic
invoked
levy
likewise
nonetheless
notwithstanding
odd
ongoing
panel
persistent
posed
reluctant
so-called
straightforward
undergo
whereby

Index of Skills

Literary Concepts

Action
    See also Plot.
    falling 929, 1022, 1073
    rising 929, 1022, 1073
Alliteration 255, 438, 441, 453, 1225
Allusion 81, 86, 667, 674, 798, 799
Analogy 447, 504, 506
Anecdote 1162, 1165
Aphorism 110, 111
Apostrophe 572, 710, 713
Archetype 21, 23, 26, 252, 279, 897
Argument 121, 123, 221, 228, 369, 371, 1073, 1095
Assonance 438, 441, 447
Author's purpose 48, 52, 93, 126, 145, 148, 189, 193, 428, 579, 599, 677, 680, 703, 743, 750, 971, 974, 1015, 1236
Author's style 743, 749, 1280
Autobiographical narrative 1118
Autobiography 105, 109, 352, 358, 907, 991
Axiom 444
Bias 57, 61
Biography 150
    biographical narrative 150, 734
Blank verse 715, 720, 733
Catalog of images and details 412, 1297, 1302
Character 239
    antagonist 239
    foil 960, 968
    protagonist 239, 774, 784, 924
Characterization 241, 252, 291, 725, 733, 783, 943, 958, 1114
    direct 241, 725, 943
    indirect 241, 725, 943, 1254, 1256
Climax 556, 929, 1022, 1073, 1095
    See also Plot.
Colloquialism 799
Comic books 1316, 1317
Concrete details 815, 822, 1182
Conflict 552, 556, 599, 771, 929, 935, 1073, 1114
    external 552, 599, 771, 929, 935, 1073, 1114
    internal 552, 599, 771, 929, 935, 1073, 1114
Connotation 96, 101, 113, 1209, 1212

Context
    cultural 667, 674, 1332, 1335
    historical 81, 86, 306, 350, 361, 1051, 1072
    social 550, 567
Couplet 140, 143
    heroic 143
Creation myth 20–21
Cultural context 667, 674, 1332, 1335
Denotation 96, 1209, 1212
Description 145, 148, 398, 889, 897
Dialect 497, 503, 943, 957
Dialogue 914, 925, 1027, 1050, 1114, 1272
Diary 362–363
Diction 63, 68, 137, 383, 386, 938, 941
Drama 1116–1117
Dramatic irony 936
    See also Irony.
Dramatic monologue 515, 518, 674
Elements, of a short story 239
Emotional appeals 112–113
Essay 180, 1309, 1313
    formal 180, 1309, 1313
    informal (personal) 1309, 1313
Ethical appeals 112–113
Exaggeration 112
    See also Hyperbole.
Exposition 1022, 1073, 1265, 1272
    See also Plot.
Extended metaphor 219, 825, 827, 1235
External conflict
    See Conflict.
Falling action 929, 1022, 1073
    See also Plot.
Fiction R7
Figurative language 194, 196, 1193, 1196, 1230
    apostrophe 572, 710, 713
    figures of speech 115, 119, 1233, 1235
    hyperbole 112
    imagery 96, 100, 112, 444, 449, 663, 665, 683, 686, 787, 789, 977, 979, 1305, 1307
    metaphor 90, 93, 213, 219, 304, 441, 825, 827, 1233, 1235
    personification 448, 449, 453, 831, 1233, 1235, 1292, 1295

    simile 213, 691, 831, 1223, 1225
    symbol 279, 291, 1287, 1290
Figure of speech 115, 119, 1233, 1235, 1285, 1292
Fireside poets 210–211
First-person point of view
    See Point of view.
Flashback 539, 547, 886
Flash-forward 900, 907
Foil 960, 968
Folktale R8
Foreshadowing 252, 875, 886, 925
Form 677, 680
Formal essay 180, 1309, 1313
    See also Essay.
Frame story 1275, 1280
Free verse 409, 412, 415, 1196, 1225, 1258, 1261
Full rhyme 438
Genre 1240
Gothic novel 184
Graphic novel 998–1000, 1316–1317
Hero
    tragic 1096, 1114
Heroic couplet 143
    meter and rhyme patterns 143
Historical context 81, 86, 306, 350, 361, 1051, 1072
Historical fiction R9
Historical narrative 416, 419, 822
Hyperbole 112
Iambic pentameter 143, 805
Idiom 1018, 1022
Imagery 96, 100, 112, 444, 449, 663, 665, 683, 686, 787, 789, 977, 979, 1305, 1307
Imagist poetry 660–661, 687, 698
Implied theme 239, 867, 871, 1096
Implied thesis 209
Informal (personal) essay 1309, 1313
    See also Essay.
Interior monologue R10
Internal conflict
    See Conflict.
Internal rhyme 441, 453
Inversion 140, 143
Irony 574, 577, 924, 935, 936
    dramatic R11
    situational 577, 924, 935

verbal 577, 935
Irregular rhythm 705, 708, 1206
Italian (Petrarchan) sonnet 787, 789
Jargon 1250
Journal 375
Juxtaposition 815, 822
Letter 362–363
Literary criticism 455
Literary history 20-21, 112-113, 210-211, 238-239, 362-363, 536-537, 660-661, 740-741, 1024-1025, 1116-1117, 1316-1317
Literary traditions
    contrasting 660–661
Logical arguments 121, 221, 228, 1073
Magic realism 1319, 1329
Memoir 362–363, 991
Metaphor 90, 93, 213, 219, 304, 441, 825, 827, 1233, 1235
    extended 219, 825, 827, 1235
Meter 143, 444, 802, 805
    foot 444, 802
Metonymy R12
Modernism 740–74
Monologue 515, 518, 674
Mood 349, 449, 452, 814, 979, 1182, 1185, 1206, 1227, 1230
Motif 1337, 1340
Motivation 295, 304, 753, 771, 957
Mysteries 238–239
Myth 20–21, 33, 37, 46
Narrative 57, 81
    autobiographical 1118
    biographical 150–153, 734
    historical 416, 419, 822
Narrative poetry 255, 261, 725, 733, 1332, 1335
Narrator 239, 982, 991, 1251
Naturalism 536–537, 569
Nonfiction R13
    creative 1118
Novel R13
    Gothic 184
    graphic 998–1000, 1316–1317
    Regionalist 636–637
Octave 787
    See also Sonnet.
Oral history 1168, 1177
Oral tradition 34, 37
Oratory 369, 371
Origin myth 20–21, 46
Parable 290
Parallelism 113, 401, 403, 1313

Parody 1251
Personification 448, 449, 453, 831, 1233, 1235, 1292, 1295
Persuasion 112–113, R14
Petrarchan sonnet 787, 789
    See also Sonnet.
Plays R15
    See also Drama.
Plot 252, 548, 929, 935, 1018, 1022, 1023, 1073, 1095
    climax 556, 929, 1022, 1073, 1095
    conflict 552, 556, 599, 771, 929, 935, 1073, 1114
    exposition 1022, 1073, 1265, 1272
    falling action 929, 1022, 1073
    predictions 241, 252, 539, 548
    resolution 556, 1022, 1073
    rising action 929, 1022, 1073
Poetry 255, 340–341, 687 , 698
    See also Sonnet.
    fireside 210–211
    free verse 409, 412, 415, 1196, 1225, 1258, 1261
    imagist 660–661, 687, 698
    narrative 255, 261, 725, 733, 1332, 1335
    symbolist 660–661
Point of view 57, 61, 239, 275, 388, 398, 399, 548, 772, 1003, 1015, 1283, 1285
    first-person 275, 388, 772, 1003, 1015, 1283, 1285
    objective 1015
    omniscient 388, 772
    second-person 1285
    third-person 772, 1003, 1015, 1285
    third-person limited 388, 772
    third-person omniscient 388, 398, 772
Postmodernism 1143, 1148, R15
Propaganda 992, R15
Realism 486–487, 536–537
Refrain 345, 349, 814
Regionalism 858–859
Regionalist novel 636–637
Regular rhythm 705, 708, 1206
Repetition 255, 261, 371, 811, 814
Resolution
    See Plot.
Rhetoric 112–113
Rhetorical devices 112–113, 1203, 1207
    analogy 447, 504, 506
    emotional appeal 112–113
    hyperbole 112

metaphor 90, 93, 213, 219, 304, 441, 825, 827, 1233, 1235
    parallelism 113, 401, 403, 1313
    question 112, 115, 119
    repetition 255, 261, 371, 811, 814
Rhetorical questions 112, 115, 119
Rhyme 140, 143, 438, 441, 444, 447, 453
    full 438
    internal 441, 453
    slant 438, 441, 447, 1261
Rhyme scheme 569, 572, 722, 724, 938, 941
Rhythm 705, 708, 715, 1203, 1206
    See also Meter.
    irregular 705, 708, 1206
    regular 708, 1206
Rising action 929, 1022, 1073
    See also Plot.
Romanticism 178–179
Satire 1240, 1251
Science fiction 238–239, 1240, 1250
Sensory details 96, 398, 753, 771, 977
    See also Imagery.
Sequence 23, 26, 262, 275, 875, 886
Sestet 787
    See also Sonnet.
Setting 239, 602, 615, 749, 1220
Short story 238–239, 740–741, 1240
    mysteries 238–239
    science fiction 238–239, 1240, 1250
Simile 213, 691, 831, 1223, 1225
Situational irony 577, 924, 935
    See also Irony.
Slant rhyme 438, 441, 447, 1261
Social context 550, 567
Sonnet 787, 789
    Italian (Petrarchan) 787, 789
    meter and rhyme patterns 787
Sound devices 255, 261, 438, 441, 444, 447
    alliteration 255, 438, 441, 453, 1225
    assonance 438, 441, 447
    meter 444, 802, 805
    repetition 255, 261, 371, 811, 814
    rhythm 705, 708, 715, 1203
Speaker 715, 720, 722, 724, 814,
Stage directions 1051, 1072, 1114
Stanza 829, 831
Stated theme 239, 689, 1096
Stream of consciousness 740–741, 774, 783
Structure 121, 126, 140, 143, 683, 686, 1156, 1160, 1177

Style 401, 403, 689, 691, 705, 708, 743, 749, 1329
Suspense 262, 275, 615
Syllogism 121
Symbol 279, 291, 1287, 1290, 1302
Symbolism 887, 1290
Symbolist poetry 660–661
Theme 189, 193, 239, 349, 547, 689, 691, 811, 814, 1096, 1114
    implied 193, 239, 689, 867, 871, 1096
    predictions 811, 814
    stated 193, 239, 689, 1096
Thesis 204, 209
    implied 204, 209
Third-person omniscient point of view 388, 398, 772
Third-person point of view
    See Point of view.
Title 811, 827
Tone 133, 137, 196, 361, 380, 386, 700, 703, 871, 1215, 1220, 1340
Totem 21
Tragedy 1096, 1114
Tragic flaw 1096, 1114
Tragic hero 1096, 1114
Trickster 21
Typographical motif 1340
Understatement 741, 1251
Verbal irony 403, 577, 935
    See also Irony.
Verse paragraph 1209, 1212
Visualizing 889, 898, 977, 979
Voice 105, 109, 420, 428, 791, 798, 1227, 1261

Reading and Critical Thinking

Activating prior knowledge 982, 992, 1162, 1165
Analyzing 26, 32, 37, 52, 61, 68, 77, 86, 93, 100, 109, 111, 119, 125, 130, 137, 143, 148, 153, 193, 196, 202, 209, 219, 228, 251, 261, 274, 290, 304, 349, 358, 371, 380, 386, 398, 403, 406, 412, 415, 419, 427, 436, 441, 444, 447, 449, 452, 457, 503, 506, 513, 518, 527, 534, 547, 556, 572, 577, 598, 615, 623, 665, 673, 680, 686, 691, 703, 708, 713, 720, 722, 724, 732, 738, 749, 770, 783, 789, 798, 805, 809, 814, 821, 827, 831, 871, 885, 897, 907, 924, 935, 941, 957, 968, 974, 979, 991, 1014, 1022, 1050, 1072,

1095, 1113, 1154, 1160, 1165, 1177, 1185, 1201, 1206, 1212, 1220, 1225, 1230, 1235, 1238, 1250, 1256, 1261, 1271, 1280, 1285, 1290, 1295, 13102, 1307, 1313, 1328, 1335, 1340
    biographical narrative 150–153
    cause-and-effect relationships 198, 292, 352, 358, 602, 616, 1168, 1178
    characterization 943, 958
    concrete details 815, 822, 1182, 1185
    contrasting images 277, 415, 436, 749, 979
    figures of speech 115, 119
    historical context 81, 86, 306, 345, 349, 1051, 1072
    historical purpose of texts and photographs 909
    language 791, 799
    literary criticism 455
    literary influences 112
    logical arguments 121, 228, 1073
    philosophical assumptions 735
    political assumptions 1198
    rhetorical devices 1203, 1207
    sound devices 255, 261, 438, 441, 444, 447, 1305, 1307
    style 401, 403, 689, 691, 705, 708, 1280
    text structure 121, 126, 140, 143, 929, 936
    theme 1096, 1114
    tone 802, 805
    voice 1227, 1231
Analyzing graphic information 175, 177, 331, 333, 548, 649, 1139, 1141
Applying background knowledge 552, 556, 914, 925
Argument
    evaluating 121, 126, 369, 371, 1073, 1095
Author's beliefs, drawing conclusions about 90, 94, 1003, 1015
Author's purpose, recognizing 145, 148, 189, 193, 677, 680, 700, 703, 743, 750, 1236
Background knowledge, applying 552, 556, 914, 925
Before You Read 22, 34, 44, 47, 56, 62, 69, 80, 89, 95, 104, 114, 120, 132, 139, 144, 188, 203, 212, 221, 240, 254, 262, 278, 294, 344, 351, 368, 374, 382, 387, 400, 408, 416, 420, 437, 448, 531, 538,

551, 568, 573, 578, 601, 662, 666, 676, 682, 688, 699, 704, 709, 714, 725, 742, 752, 773, 786, 790, 801, 810, 815, 824, 828, 866, 874, 888, 899, 913, 928, 937, 942, 959, 970, 976, 981, 1002, 1017, 1026, 1051, 1073, 1097, 1161, 1167, 1181, 1192, 1202, 1208, 1214, 1222, 1226, 1232, 1239, 1253, 1257, 1264, 1274, 1282, 1286, 1291, 1296, 1304, 1308, 1318, 1331, 1336
Bias, recognizing 57, 61
Big Idea
    An Era of Protest 1143, 1144–1145, 1156, 1160, 1162, 1165, 1168, 1177, 1180, 1182, 1185, 1191, 1196, 1201, 1203, 1206, 1209, 1212
    Extending and Remaking Traditions 1143, 1148–1149, 1265, 1271, 1275, 1280, 1283, 1285, 1287, 1290, 1292, 1295, 1297, 1302, 1305, 1307, 1309, 1313, 1319, 1328, 1332, 1335, 1337, 1340
    The Harlem Renaissance 656–657, 787, 789, 798, 802, 805, 811, 814, 815, 825, 827, 829, 831
    Kinship with Nature 179, 182, 189, 196, 204, 213, 219
    Life in the City 860–861, 900, 907, 929, 935, 938, 941, 943, 957, 960, 968
    Life in the New World 11, 14–15, 57, 61, 63, 67, 68, 70, 77, 81, 86, 90, 93, 96, 100
    Modern Fiction 743, 749, 753, 770, 774, 783
    Modernism 651, 654–655, 703
    A Nation Divided 335, 338, 375, 380, 383, 386, 388, 397, 401, 403
    Naturalism 487, 492, 569, 572, 574, 577, 579, 602, 615
    Nature and Technology 1143, 1146–1147, 1215, 1220, 1223, 1225, 1227, 1230, 1233, 1235, 1240, 1250, 1254, 1256, 1258, 1261
    New Poetics 652–653, 663, 665, 667, 673, 677, 680, 683, 686, 687, 689, 691, 698, 700, 703, 708, 710, 713, 715, 720, 722, 724
    Optimism and Individualism 179, 180, 220, 221, 228, 236

A Poetic Revolution 335, 340, 409, 420, 427, 438, 452, 457

The Power of Darkness 179, 184, 241, 251, 255, 261, 262, 274, 279, 290, 295, 304

Realism 487, 490, 536, 539, 547, 550, 552, 556, 567

Regionalism 487, 488, 497, 503, 506, 513, 514, 534

Resistance to Slavery 335, 336, 345, 349, 350, 352, 358, 361, 369, 371

Return to Regionalism 858–859, 867, 871, 875, 889, 897, 916

The Road to Independence 11, 16–17, 105, 115, 140, 145, 148

Romanticism 173, 178–179, 186, 279, 290

The Sacred Earth and the Power of Storytelling 11, 12, 23, 26, 33, 34, 37, 46, 48, 52

United States and the World 862–863, 971, 974, 977, 979, 980, 982, 991, 1001, 1003, 1014, 1018, 1022, 1027, 1050, 1072, 1096, 1113

Building background 23, 27, 34, 38, 44, 48, 57, 63, 70, 81, 90, 96, 105, 115, 121, 133, 140, 145, 150, 189, 204, 213, 221, 229, 231, 241, 255, 262, 279, 295, 306, 345, 352, 359, 360, 369, 375, 383, 388, 401, 404, 409, 416, 420, 430, 438, 455, 497, 515, 520, 532, 539, 552, 557, 566, 569, 574, 579, 602, 617, 663, 667, 677, 683, 689, 700, 705, 710, 715, 735, 743, 753, 774, 787, 791, 802, 811, 815, 825, 829, 867, 875, 889, 900, 909, 914, 929, 938, 943, 960, 971, 977, 993, 998, 1003, 1018, 1027, 1051, 1073, 1096, 1156, 1162, 1168, 1182, 1193, 1203, 1209, 1215, 1223, 1227, 1233, 1240, 1254, 1258, 1265, 1275, 1283, 1287, 1283, 1287, 1292, 1297, 1305, 1309, 1319, 1332, 1337

Cause-and-effect relationships, analyzing 198, 292, 352, 358, 602, 616, 1168, 1178

Characterization
analyzing 943, 958
evaluating 725, 733

Characters
comparing and contrasting 900, 908
drawing conclusions about 515, 518, 774, 784, 1027, 1050

making inferences about 574, 577, 1265, 1272
responding to 1018, 1023

Clarifying meaning 448, 449, 508, 569, 572, 1193, 1197

Comparing and contrasting
across time and place 33, 46, 220, 236, 350, 361, 550, 567, 687, 698, 980, 1001, 1180, 1191
Big Idea treatments 33, 46, 220, 236, 350, 361, 550, 567, 687, 698, 980, 1001, 1180, 1191
characters 900, 908
cultures 33, 46, 220, 236, 980, 1001, 1180, 1191
historical context 350, 362
mythic elements 33, 46
narratives about relationships 550, 567
persuasive messages 220, 236
portrayals of people 350, 361
reflections 980, 1001
social context 550, 567
speakers 715, 720, 724
themes 1180, 1191
tone 802, 805

Comprehension, monitoring 63, 68, 295, 305

Concrete details, analyzing 815, 1182, 1183, 1185

Connecting 110, 111, 213, 219
to the author 26, 52, 77, 93, 109, 119, 137, 193, 196, 261, 349, 358, 380, 406, 412, 441, 444, 449, 452, 572, 665, 680, 691, 703, 713, 722, 724, 738, 770, 783, 798, 814, 831, 897, 957, 1050, 1220, 1225, 1285, 1290, 1307, 1313, 1335, 1340
to the autobiography 70, 352, 358, 815
to the Big Idea 52, 61, 68, 77, 86, 93, 100, 109, 111, 119, 125, 137, 143, 148, 193, 196, 261, 274, 290, 304, 345, 349, 358, 371, 380, 386, 397, 403, 427, 452, 457, 534, 547, 556, 572, 577, 665, 673, 680, 686, 691, 703, 708, 713, 722, 749, 770, 783, 789, 798, 814, 827, 831, 871, 897, 907, 935, 941, 957, 968, 974, 979, 991, 1014, 1022, 1050, 1072, 1095, 1113, 1160, 1165, 1177, 1185, 1196, 1201, 1206, 1212, 1220, 1225, 1230, 1235, 1250, 1256,

1261, 1271, 1280, 1285, 1290, 1295, 1302, 1307, 1313, 1328, 1335, 1340
to contemporary issues 829, 831, 1254, 1256
to cultural context 667, 674, 1332, 1335
to the essay 133, 189, 204, 213, 221, 1209, 1297, 1309
to the history 63, 809
to the interview 1168
to the journal 375
to the letters 145, 148, 153
to the memoir 982
to the myth 23, 26, 34
to the narrative 57, 81, 309, 367
to personal experience 825, 827, 867, 872, 1292, 1295
to the play 1027
to poetry 90, 140, 255, 409, 420, 427, 438, 515, 569, 574, 663, 667, 677, 683, 689, 700, 705, 715, 787, 802, 811, 825, 829, 938, 977, 1193, 1215, 1223, 1227, 1258, 1283, 1287, 1292, 1332, 1337
to political context 404
to reading selections 23, 34, 48, 57, 63, 70, 81, 90, 96, 105, 115, 121, 133, 140, 145, 189, 204, 213, 221, 241, 255, 262, 279, 295, 345, 352, 369, 375, 383, 388, 401, 409, 420, 438, 497, 515, 520, 532, 539, 552, 569, 574, 579, 602, 663, 667, 677, 683, 689, 700, 705, 710, 715, 743, 753, 774, 787, 791, 802, 811, 815, 825, 829, 867, 875, 889, 900, 914, 929, 938, 943, 960, 971, 977, 1003, 1018, 1027, 1051, 1073, 1096, 1156, 1162, 1168, 1182, 1193, 1203, 1209, 1215, 1223, 1227, 1233, 1240, 1254, 1258, 1265, 1275, 1283, 1287, 1283, 1287, 1292, 1297, 1305, 1309, 1319, 1332, 1337
to the sermon 96
to the song 1203
to the speaker 436
to the speech 369, 401, 406, 971
to the spirituals 345
to the story 241, 262, 279, 295, 388, 539, 552, 579, 602, 623, 743, 753, 774, 791, 867, 875, 889, 900, 916, 943, 960, 1003, 1018, 1182, 1240,

1254, 1265, 1275, 1305, 1319
    to today 37, 68, 86, 100, 111, 125,
      143, 148, 186, 202, 239, 251, 274,
      290, 304, 342, 371, 386, 397, 403,
      415, 419, 427, 534, 556, 577, 625,
      673, 686, 708, 720, 789, 805, 827,
      871, 935, 941, 974, 979, 991, 1022,
      1113, 1154, 1160, 1177, 1185,
      1196, 1201, 1230, 1235, 1250,
      1256, 1280, 1302

Connotation
    examining 96, 101, 113, 1209, 1212,
      1283, 1285
Cultural context
    connecting to 667, 674, 1332, 1335
Denotation
    examining 1209, 1212
Determining
    main idea and supporting
      details 128, 383, 386, 1160, 1309,
      1314
Distinguishing fact and opinion 221,
    228, 375, 380, 971, 974, 1166, 1297,
    1303
Drawing conclusions 194, 197, 420, 428
    about author's beliefs 90, 94, 1003,
      1015
    about characters 515, 518, 1027,
      1050
    about culture 48, 52
    about the protagonist 774, 784
Evaluating 26, 32, 37, 52, 61, 68, 77, 86,
    93, 100, 109, 111, 119, 125, 130, 137,
    143, 148, 153, 193, 196, 202, 209, 219,
    228, 251, 261, 274, 290, 304, 349, 358,
    371, 380, 386, 398, 403, 406, 412, 415,
    419, 427, 436, 441, 444, 447, 449, 452,
    457, 503, 506, 513, 518, 527, 534, 547,
    556, 572, 577, 598, 615, 623, 665, 673,
    680, 686, 691, 703, 708, 713, 720, 722,
    724, 732, 738, 749, 770, 783, 789, 798,
    805, 809, 814, 821, 827, 831, 871, 885,
    897, 907, 924, 935, 941, 957, 968, 974,
    979, 991, 1014, 1022, 1050, 1072,
    1095, 1113, 1154, 1160, 1165, 1177,
    1185, 1201, 1206, 1212, 1220, 1225,
    1230, 1235, 1238, 1250, 1256, 1261,
    1271, 1280, 1285, 1290, 1295, 13102,
    1307, 1313, 1328, 1335, 1340
    argument 121, 126, 369, 371, 1073,
      1095
    characterization 725, 733
    description 897

diction 938, 941
evidence 221, 228
figures of speech 1233, 1235
sensory details 753, 771, 1215, 1221
style 532, 534
Evidence
    evaluating 221, 228
Examining
    connotation 96, 101, 113, 1209, 1212,
      1283, 1285
    denotation 1209, 1212
Fact and opinion, distinguishing 375,
    380, 971, 974, 1297, 1303
Figures of speech
    analyzing 115, 119
    evaluating 1233, 1235
Generalizations, making 960, 968, 1337,
    1341
Genres
    identifying (short story) 1240
Graphic organizer 78, 115, 453, 806,
    1003, 1207, 1261, 1341
    bar graph 333
    character web 1265
    chart 57, 63, 90, 96, 105, 115, 137,
      196, 198, 252, 255, 304, 306, 352,
      364, 369, 383, 388, 398, 401, 455,
      508, 515, 532, 539, 574, 579, 602,
      615, 617, 683, 689, 710, 743, 753,
      774, 787, 802, 815, 822, 825, 871,
      886, 907, 909, 914, 925, 938, 943,
      957, 960, 971, 1003, 1015, 1018,
      1051, 1073, 1114, 1156, 1162,
      1168, 1177, 1182, 1193, 1203,
      1209, 1215, 1223, 1227, 1230,
      1233, 1240, 1258, 1275, 1280,
      1283, 1297, 1302, 1313, 1329
    compare-contrast chart 304, 802
    concept web 1096
    concrete details 1182
    concrete details chart 1182
    context clues chart 1281
    diagram 48, 109, 292, 548, 615, 749,
      1022, 1207, 1221
    double-entry journal 145, 700
    evaluating diction chart 938
    figurative language chart 1233
    idea web 799
    map 333, 1309
    note taking 23, 34, 57, 63, 81, 96,
      115, 255, 262, 306, 342, 352, 369,
      383, 388, 409, 460, 494, 539, 574,
      663, 677, 683, 689, 710, 753, 774,

787, 825, 938, 960, 971, 982, 1027,
    1073, 1121, 1150, 1168, 1203,
    1223, 1240, 1275, 1283, 1297,
    1309
    paraphrase chart 137, 1156
    preview chart 914
    relationship chart 1051
    response-evidence chart 459, 1018
    scale 1251
    semantic features chart 372
    sensory details chart 1215
    sentence completion 811
    sequence chain 313
    sequence chart 875, 1152
    storyboard 470
    table 398, 401
    track ideas 743
    Venn diagram 715, 900, 1231, 1271,
      1292
    web diagram 291, 428, 453, 547, 783,
      977, 1027, 1206, 1220, 1340
    word map 101, 275, 1015, 1231
    word web 94, 101, 150, 683, 784,
      1305
Historical context, analyzing 81, 86, 306,
    345, 349, 1051, 1072
Identifying
    genre 1240
    sequence 23, 26, 262, 275, 520, 528,
      875, 886
Imagery
    interpreting 683, 686, 787, 789, 1223,
      1225
Independent reading 164–165, 320–321,
    472–473, 636–637, 842–843, 1128–
    1129, 1358–1359
Inferring
    See Making inferences.
Interpreting 26, 32, 37, 52, 61, 68, 77, 86,
    93, 100, 109, 111, 119, 125, 130, 137,
    143, 148, 153, 193, 196, 202, 209, 219,
    228, 251, 261, 274, 290, 304, 349, 358,
    371, 380, 386, 398, 403, 406, 412, 415,
    419, 427, 436, 441, 444, 447, 449, 452,
    457, 503, 506, 513, 518, 527, 534, 547,
    556, 572, 577, 598, 615, 623, 665, 673,
    680, 686, 691, 703, 708, 713, 720, 722,
    724, 732, 738, 749, 770, 783, 789, 798,
    805, 809, 814, 821, 827, 831, 871, 885,
    897, 907, 924, 935, 941, 957, 968, 974,
    979, 991, 1014, 1022, 1050, 1072,
    1095, 1113, 1154, 1160, 1165, 1177,
    1185, 1201, 1206, 1212, 1220, 1225,

1230, 1235, 1238, 1250, 1256, 1261, 1271, 1280, 1285, 1290, 1295, 13102, 1307, 1313, 1328, 1335, 1340

imagery 683, 686, 787, 789, 1223, 1225

Language, analyzing 791, 799

Logical sequence 262, 276

Main ideas
determining 128, 383, 386, 1309, 1314

Making generalizations 960, 968, 1337, 1341
about characters 960, 968

Making inferences 279, 291
about characters 574, 577, 1265, 1272
about theme 710, 713, 1258, 1262

Making and verifying predictions 241, 252, 388, 398, 539, 548

Making predictions about theme 811, 814

Meaning
clarifying 448, 449, 508, 569, 572, 1193, 1197

Monitoring comprehension 63, 68, 295, 305

Mood, analyzing 345, 349, 449, 724, 814, 1050, 1113, 1206, 1220

Myths 26, 33, 37, 46

Organizational patterns 145, 316

Paraphrasing 409, 412, 415, 1156, 1160

Philosophical assumptions,
analyzing 735

Plot
making inferences 252
responding to 1018, 1023

Political assumptions
analyzing 1198

Predictions 241, 252
making and verifying 241, 252, 388, 398, 539, 548

Previewing 11, 48, 57, 63, 81, 90, 105, 115, 121, 128, 189, 198, 204, 213, 241, 255, 279, 295, 335, 336, 338, 340, 345, 352, 364, 375, 383, 388, 401, 409, 420, 438, 515, 539, 552, 569, 574, 579, 602, 663, 667, 677, 683, 689, 700, 705, 710, 715, 743, 753, 774, 787, 791, 802, 806, 811, 815, 825, 829, 857, 867, 875, 889, 900, 938, 943, 960, 971, 977, 982, 1003, 1018, 1027, 1152, 1156, 1162, 1168, 1182, 1193, 1203, 1209, 1215, 1223, 1227, 1233, 1240, 1254, 1258,

1265, 1275, 1287, 1292, 1297, 1305, 1309, 1319, 1332, 1337

Prior knowledge, activating 982, 992, 1162, 1165

Protagonist
drawing conclusions 774, 784

Questioning 34, 37, 364, 663, 665, 1275, 1281,

Reading Check 7, 9, 13, 15, 17, 175, 177, 181, 183, 185, 331, 333, 337, 339, 341, 483, 485, 489, 491, 493, 647, 649, 653, 655, 657, 853, 855, 859, 861, 863, 1139, 1141, 1145, 1147, 1149

Reading graphical information 8-9, 176-177, 332-333, 484-485, 648-649, 854-855, 1140-1141

Recalling 371, 720

Recognizing
author's purpose 27, 48, 51, 52, 115, 126, 145, 148, 189, 193, 279, 337, 367, 401, 430, 455, 579, 677, 680, 700, 703, 710, 743, 750, 971, 974, 1015, 1236
bias 57, 61

Responding 26, 32, 37, 52, 61, 68, 77, 86, 93, 100, 109, 111, 119, 125, 130, 137, 143, 148, 153, 193, 196, 202, 209, 219, 228, 251, 261, 274, 290, 304, 349, 358, 371, 380, 386, 398, 403, 406, 412, 415, 419, 427, 436, 441, 444, 447, 449, 452, 457, 503, 506, 513, 518, 527, 534, 547, 556, 572, 577, 598, 615, 623, 665, 673, 680, 686, 691, 703, 708, 713, 720, 722, 724, 732, 738, 749, 770, 783, 789, 798, 805, 809, 814, 821, 827, 831, 871, 885, 897, 907, 924, 935, 941, 957, 968, 974, 979, 991, 1014, 1022, 1050, 1072, 1095, 1113, 1154, 1160, 1165, 1177, 1185, 1201, 1206, 1212, 1220, 1225, 1230, 1235, 1238, 1250, 1256, 1261, 1271, 1280, 1285, 1290, 1295, 13102, 1307, 1313, 1328, 1335, 1340
to plot and characters 1018, 1023

Reviewing 547

Rhetorical devices
analyzing 1203, 1207

Scanning 806

Sensory details
evaluating 753, 771, 1215, 1221

Sequence
identifying 23, 26, 520, 528, 875, 886

Setting
analyzing relevance of 617

Setting Purposes for Reading 23, 27, 48, 57, 63, 70, 81, 90, 96, 105, 115, 121, 133, 140, 145, 189, 198, 204, 221, 241, 255, 279, 306, 345, 352, 364, 369, 375, 388, 401, 404, 409, 420, 430, 438, 455, 515, 539, 552, 569, 574, 579, 602, 617, 663, 667, 683, 689, 700, 710, 743, 753, 787, 802, 806, 811, 815, 825, 829, 867, 875, 889, 900, 909, 916, 929, 938, 943, 960, 971, 982, 1003, 1018, 1027, 1051, 1073, 1152, 1156, 1162, 1168, 1182, 1193, 1198, 1203, 1209, 1215, 1223, 1233, 1236, 1240, 1258, 1265, 1275, 1283, 1287, 1292, 1297, 1305, 1309, 1319, 1332, 1337

Skimming 364

Sound devices
analyzing 255, 261, 438, 441, 444, 447, 453, 1305, 1307

Style
analyzing 401, 403, 689, 691, 705, 708
evaluating 532, 534

Summarizing 133, 138, 204, 209, 579, 599, 1287, 1290

Supporting details, determining 128, 383, 386, 1309, 1314

Text structure
analyzing 929, 936, 1152

Theme
analyzing 1097, 1114
making inferences 291, 710, 713, 1258, 1262
making predictions 811, 814
summarizing 599

Tone
analyzing 802, 805

Verifying predictions 241, 252, 388, 398, 539, 548

Visualizing 889, 898, 977, 979, 1319, 1329

Voice
analyzing 105, 109, 1227, 1231

Vocabulary

Academic vocabulary 37, 53-54, 78, 94, 101, 111, 126, 138, 143, 197, 252, 275, 291, 305, 349, 398, 419, 428, 453, 507, 528, 534, 548, 599, 616, 674, 722, 724, 733, 750, 771, 784, 791, 822, 886, 898, 908, 925, 936, 958, 992, 1015, 1023, 1114, 1178, 1197, 1207, 1221, 1231,

1251, 1272, 1281, 1303, 1307, 1329, 1341

Affixes 873

Analogies 145, 148, 241, 252, 305, 403, 528, 689, 691, 708, 791, 799, 811, 814, 889, 898, 968, 1072, 1162, 1165, 1193, 1197, 1233, 1235, 1251, 1258, 1262

Antonyms 111, 119, 228, 305, 549, 674, 722, 750, 787, 789, 829, 831, 1207, 1319, 1329, 1340

Base words 131, 873, 1315

Connotation 138, 352, 358, 372, 548, 572, 577, 710, 713, 875, 886, 971, 974, 982, 992, 1283, 1285, 1332, 1335

Context clues 68, 126, 197, 219, 277, 375, 380, 419, 577, 599, 665, 686, 774, 784, 825, 827, 900, 908, 938, 941, 977, 979, 1018, 1023, 1095, 1168, 1178, 1215, 1221, 1275, 1281, 1287, 1290, 1337, 1341

  contrast 277
  definition 277
  example 277
  synonym 277

Denotation 138, 352, 358, 372, 548, 572, 577, 710, 713, 875, 886, 971, 974, 982, 992, 1283, 1285, 1332, 1335

Dictionary use 102

Discipline-specific words 53–54

Etymology 78, 101, 131, 275, 503, 616, 700, 703, 802, 805, 943, 958, 1003, 1015, 1182, 1185, 1227, 1231

Graphic organizer 111, 722, 1207, 1341

  chart 503, 1281
  diagram 109, 1314
  word map 78, 101, 616, 1015, 1231

Greek roots (word parts) 873

Homonyms 800

Latin roots (word parts) 873

Loaded words 1166

Math and science terms 53, 975

Multiple-meaning words 53–54

Noun suffixes 1315

Political science terms 131

Prefixes 109, 131, 383, 873, 929, 936, 1297, 1309, 1314

Roots (word parts) 109, 131, 383, 386, 873, 929, 936, 1297, 1309, 1314

  Greek 873
  Latin 873

Suffixes 109, 131, 383, 873, 929, 936, 1297, 1309, 1314

Synonyms 23, 26, 52, 61, 94, 111, 261, 277, 291, 398, 549, 677, 680, 715, 720, 722, 753, 771, 822, 1207, 1209, 1212, 1223, 1225, 1265, 1272, 1341

Thesaurus use 549

Visual vocabulary 32, 243, 499, 500, 613, 776, 781, 880, 954, 964, 1019, 1158, 1299, 1321

Vocabulary reference materials
  thesaurus 549

Word origins 78, 101, 131, 275, 503, 616, 700, 703, 802, 805, 943, 958, 975, 1003, 1015, 1182, 1185, 1227, 1231

Word parts 109, 383, 386, 873, 929, 936, 1254, 1256, 1297, 1303, 1309, 1314

Word usage 86, 193, 209, 369, 371, 453, 515, 518, 556, 733, 867, 872, 914, 925, 1114, 1156, 1158, 1292, 1295

Writing

Advice column 1129

Allusion, applying 799

Analysis
  personal 464

Analyzing
  couplets 143
  cultural context 46, 1191
  elements of a poem 835
  figurative language 94
  genre elements 835
  historical context 236
  imagery 616
  language 750, 936
  literary trends 698
  mood 675
  nuance 454
  poem 833
  point of view 399
  professional writing model 155–156, 311–312, 625–627, 833–834, 1119–1120, 1343–1345
  reflections 1001
  relationships 567
  setting 616
  storytelling 46
  style 316, 454
  tone 138, 361
  workshop writing model 158–159, 314–315, 461–465, 836–837, 1122–1123, 1346–1347

Appeals
  emotional 155
  logical 155

Applying
  allusion 799
  dialogue 161, 898
  characterization 734
  diction 101, 750
  flashback 1273
  form 1330
  imagery 616
  irony 936
  mood 675
  parallelism 1314
  point of view 548, 772
  style 898
  symbolism 1303
  tone 138

Argument 157, 823
  See also Persuasive Writing.
  organizing 157

Audience 155, 157, 158, 310, 311, 315, 459, 625, 833, 1118, 1343, 1347

Author's craft
  evaluating 105, 193, 305, 386, 444
  responding to 111, 130, 143, 193, 211, 276, 309, 444, 547, 600

Author's purpose, exploring 115, 126, 306, 409, 429, 599, 833, 835, 836, 837

Author's style 631

Avoiding stilted language 1124

Brainstorming 675, 750, 1303, 1314

Business writing
  letter 827

Call to action 156

Characterization 1118, 1119, 1123

Characterization, applying 734

Character sketch 708, 968

Checklists 154, 160, 310, 316, 458, 466, 624, 632, 832, 838, 1118, 1124, 1342, 1348

Chronological order 1121
  clarifying with 627

Citing sources 460, 463, 465

Claim 1347

Clarifying with chronological order 627

Coherence, paragraph 464, 466

Command of language 625, 630, 834, 837

Conclusion 156, 464, 627, 834, 837, 1347

Consistent focus 630

Counterarguments 159

Creation myth 26

Creative nonfiction 1118-1125
Creative writing
  advice column 1129
  character sketch 708, 968
  brochure 789
  creation myth 26
  dialogue 37, 358, 722
  drections 1335
  journal 193, 313, 388, 419, 441, 534, 637, 703, 831, 971, 979, 1185, 1256, 1295
  letter 52, 68, 148, 209, 572
  list 86, 680, 724, 1209, 1290
  memo 380, 691
  nonfiction 1118–1119
  poetry 143, 412, 444, 577, 713, 805, 833, 835, 1225, 1285
  press release 974
  short story 61, 675, 772, 1330
  speech 371, 1165
  stage directions 1072
Critical evidence, identifying 160
Critical review 926
Descriptive details 311
Descriptive essay 616
Details 1121
  concrete 1121, 1273
  descriptive 311
  sensory 1273
Dialogue 37, 358, 722, 1050, 1235
  applying 161, 898
Diction, applying 101, 750
Direct quotations 127, 467, 833, 836
Directions 1335
Drafting 79, 127, 158, 253, 276, 292, 314, 399, 429, 461, 529, 600, 629, 675, 734, 772, 823, 836, 887, 926, 1016, 1115, 1122, 1252, 1273, 1330, 1346
Drawing conclusions 464
Editing 79, 127, 161, 253, 276, 292, 317, 399, 429, 467, 529, 600, 633, 675, 734, 772, 823, 839, 887, 926, 1016, 1115, 1125, 1252, 1273, 1330, 1349
Editorial 1342-1349
Elaboration
  reasons 316
  description 316
  dialogue 316
Embedded quotations 839
Emotional appeal 159, 162, 572, 598, 1347
Essay 18, 46, 127, 154-161, 186, 236, 276, 292, 310-317, 361, 399, 415, 429,

447, 454, 458, 467, 529, 567, 600, 616, 624-633, 675, 698, 734, 772, 823, 832-839, 887, 926, 941, 1001, 1016, 1115, 1118-1125, 1191, 1252, 1273, 1303, 1307, 1314, 1330, 1342-1349
  autobiographical narrative 1273
  biographical narrative 734
  descriptive 616
  expository 292, 399, 454, 458-467, 624-633, 832-839, 887, 1016, 1252
  persuasive 127, 600, 823, 926, 1115
  reflective 310-317, 429, 529
  short story 61, 675, 772, 1330
Evaluating
  author's craft 305
  sources 459, 465
Evaluating
  example 160
  expert opinion 160
  statistic 160
  See also Supporting evidence.
Explanation of ambiguities 626
Exploring author's purpose 429
Expository essay 292, 399, 454, 458-467, 624-633, 832-839, 887, 1016, 1252
Expository writing 292, 399, 454, 458-467, 624-633, 832-839, 887, 1016, 1252
First-person point of view 311, 314
Flashback, applying 1273
Focus 837
Foreshadowing 1122
Form, applying 1330
Genre elements, analyzing 835
Graphic organizer 1341
  character web 1265
  chart 90, 115, 137, 197, 198, 276, 304, 305, 313, 364, 454, 515, 539, 599, 617, 675, 743, 750, 787, 802, 815, 822, 823, 829, 835, 871, 872, 886, 898, 907, 916, 941, 943, 957, 958, 971, 1003, 1015, 1018, 1051, 1073, 1114, 1152, 1162, 1168, 1177, 1182, 1193, 1196, 1197, 1207, 1209, 1215, 1223, 1227, 1230, 1233, 1240, 1252, 1258, 1261, 1275, 1281, 1283, 1297, 1302, 1303, 1313
  checklist 643, 838, 1348, 1365
  chronological list 1287
  concept web 1097
  diagram 48, 109, 292, 548, 615, 749, 1022, 1207, 1221

double-entry journal 145, 700
  note taking 186, 306, 342, 352, 388, 409, 574, 663, 677, 689, 710, 743, 753, 774, 806, 825, 938, 960, 971, 982, 1027, 1073, 1121, 1150, 1168, 1203, 1223, 1240, 1275, 1283, 1297, 1309
  prewriting 127, 276, 292, 313, 399, 429, 454, 459, 734, 823, 926, 1016, 1252, 1235, 1330
  pro/con chart 1345
  sequence chain 313
  scale 1251
  storyboard 313
  Venn diagram 715, 900, 1231, 1271, 1292
  web diagram 291, 428, 453, 547, 783, 798, 977, 1027, 1206, 1220, 1340
  word map 101, 275, 1015, 1231
Historical investigation 1023
Imagery 616, 1120
  applying 616
  analyzing 616
  comparison 110
Information
  analyzing 460
  searching for 616
In-text citations 127, 467
In-text quotations
  See Quotations.
Introduction 155, 833, 1347
Irony, applying 936
Journal 193, 313, 388, 419, 441, 534, 637, 703, 831, 971, 979, 1185, 1256, 1295
  double-entry 145, 700
Language
  examining 750, 1303, 1314
  stilted 1124
Letter 52, 68, 148, 209, 572, 1359
List 86, 680, 724, 1209, 1290
Literary analysis 834
  poem 832-839
  short story 624-633
Literary criticism 305
Literary devices 1120
Literary elements 626
Literary research paper, historical investigation 458–467
Logical fallacy 992
Logical organization 627
Main ideas 461
Major points 625

Margins 467
Memo 380
Metaphor 157
Monologue 784
  dramatic 575, 674
  interior 403, 1273
Mood
  applying 675
Narrative details 311, 315
Narrative purpose 314
Nonfiction summary 79, 386
Note cards 460
Note taking 186, 255, 342, 352, 460, 539,
  574, 710, 753, 1121
Nuance 454
Opposing arguments 159
Organization 627, 632, 837, 1345
Organizational plan 835, 1346
Outlining 157, 460
Paragraphs 449
  coherence 464, 466
  organization 887
Parallelism 161
  applying 1314
Paraphrasing 460, 462
Peer review 161, 316, 317, 466, 467, 632,
  633, 838, 839, 1124, 1125, 1348, 1349
Personal analysis 464
Personal opinions 1346
Persuasion
  responding to 600, 926
Persuasive writing 127, 154–161, 197,
  600, 823, 926, 1115, 1342–1349
Persuasive speech 154–161
Persuasive techniques 156, 159, 1344,
  1345, 1347
  hyperbole 1345
  irony 1345
  repetition 1345
  rhetorical question 1345
  word choice 1345
Plagiarism 157, 313, 460, 628, 835, 1121
Plot 1120, 1123
  planning 1121
Plot summary 253, 261, 406, 1095
Poetry 143, 412, 444, 577, 713, 805,
  1225, 1285
  free verse 1285
  punctuating quotations 839
Point of view 239, 290, 399, 548, 772,
  833, 1347
  adding evidence to support 160
  applying 548, 772

analyzing 399, 836
  first person 275, 314, 772, 1251
  of narrator 275
  responding to 399
Presenting 161, 317, 467, 633, 839, 1125,
  1349
Press release 974
Prewriting 79, 127, 157, 253, 276, 292,
  313, 399, 429, 459, 529, 600, 628, 675,
  734, 772, 823, 835, 887, 926, 1016,
  1115, 1121, 1252, 1273, 1330, 1345
Primary source quotations 125, 127,
  924, 1250
Primary sources 465, 626
Professional writing model,
  analyzing 155–156, 311–312, 625–
  627, 833–834, 1119–1120, 1343–1345
Proofreading 79, 127, 161, 253, 276, 292,
  317, 399, 429, 467, 529, 600, 633, 675,
  734, 772, 823, 839, 887, 926, 1016,
  1115, 1125, 1252, 1273, 1330, 1349
Publishing 625
Purpose 155, 157, 158, 310, 459, 625,
  833, 834, 836, 837, 1118, 1343
Quickwrite 230, 359, 564, 566, 695, 697,
  1186, 1190
Quotations 458, 467, 1001
  brackets in 1252
  direct 127, 462, 629, 833, 836
  embedded 839
  indirect 467
  primary source 127
Quoting sources 460, 462, 464, 629, 833,
  836
  punctuating 460, 839
Reflective essay (writing) 310-317, 429
Repetition 872
Report 872, 1023, 1178
Research report 458–467
Research questions 459
Response essay 1307
Review 926
Revising 79, 127, 160, 253, 276, 292, 316,
  399, 429, 466, 529, 600, 632, 675, 734,
  772, 823, 838, 887, 926, 1016, 1115,
  1124, 1252, 1273, 1330, 1348
Rhetorical devices 157, 312, 314
  analogy 1345
  call to action 1345
  parallelism 1345
  repetition 1345
Schedule 1121
Secondary sources 463

Sensory details 1123
Sentence combining 87–88
Sentence fluency 160, 316, 466, 632
Sentence formation 926, 1329
Sentence fragments 1273
Sentence frames 276, 292, 399, 429, 454,
  600, 823, 1016
Sentences
  combining 927
  difficult 295
  direct 750
  inverted 140
  run-on 675
  short 926
  supporting 1303
Sentence structure 101, 159, 751
  varying 750, 751, 834
Sequence of events 1123
Setting
  analyzing 616
Shades of meaning 632
Short story 675, 772, 1330
Significance 312, 315, 1123
Sound devices
  analyzing 261
Sources
  encyclopedia 465
  evaluating 459, 465
  Internet 465, 1023
  paraphrasing 460, 569
  primary 460, 465, 626, 1014
  punctuating quotations 460, 839
  quoting 460, 839
  secondary 460, 465
  summarizing 460
  variety of 465
Spacing 467
Speech 371, 1165
Stage directions 1072
Statistics 155, 157
Stilted language, avoiding 1124
Structure 101, 750, 799, 936, 1303, 1314
Style
  applying 101, 161, 548, 616, 750, 898
Summarizing 228, 386
  information 228, 460
  main ideas 32, 367, 406, 436, 457,
    513, 623, 738, 809, 912, 1154,
    1201
  plot 253
  sequence of events 79
Support 630, 833, 836, 1344, 1347

Supporting evidence 157, 158, 159, 459, 626, 1347
  adding 158, 160
  details 154, 157, 158, 159, 160, 312, 315, 625, 626, 1273
  example 160
  expert opinion 160
  statistics 160, 176, 872
Symbolism
  applying 1303
Techniques, exploring 835
Theme
  applying 811
Thesis 155, 157, 158, 460, 461, 464, 625, 627, 628, 629, 834, 835, 836, 1344
Title 161
  punctuating 161
Tone 156, 158, 1345, 1347, 1348
  applying 138
  using appropriate 158
Topic
  exploring 835
  finding 313, 628, 835, 1121, 1345
  investigating 459
  narrowing 459
Traits of Strong Writing 160, 316, 466, 632, 838, 1124, 1348
Transitions 462, 463
Using quotations correctly 467
Verb tense 1125
    See also Grammar, Verb tense.
Viewpoints
    See Point of view.
Voice 1344, 1348
Weblogs 1343
Word choice 838, 1344, 1347
Word-processing 161, 317, 467, 633, 839, 1125, 1349
Works-cited list 460, 467
Workshop model, analyzing 158–159, 314–315, 461–465, 629–632, 836–837, 1122–1123, 1346–1347
Writing about literature 46, 79, 127, 197, 236, 253, 276, 292, 305, 361, 399, 429, 529, 567, 567, 600, 624, 784, 823, 887, 926, 1001, 1016, 1191, 1252
Writing frames 158, 314, 629, 836, 1122, 1346
Writing process 154, 310, 458, 616, 832, 1118, 1342

Grammar

Absolute phrase 529
Active voice 1330
Adjective 79
  comparative degree 292, 1115
  possessive 276
  prepositional phrase as 293
  superlative degree 292, 1115
Adjective clause 88, 149
Adverb 88
  comparative degree 292
  conjunctive 600
Adverb clause 149
    See also Clause.
Agreement
  pronoun-antecedent 1349
  subject-verb 633
Apostrophes 276
Appositive 87, 530
  nonrestrictive 530
  restrictive 530
Appositive phrase 87
Brackets
  in quotations 467, 1252
Clause 600, 1179
  adjective 88, 149
  adverb 149
  introductory 927
  main 149, 600, 1273
  as modifiers 149
  subordinate 149, 675, 1273
Comma 149, 1179
  with coordinating conjunctions 751
  with introductory clause 927
  with nonessential elements 149
Comma splice 317
Comparative degree 292, 1115
Compound words 681
  forming with hyphens 429
Conjunction 399
  coordinating 88, 399, 600, 675, 751, 1179
  subordinating 88, 399
Conjunctive adverb 600
Coordinating conjunction 88, 399, 600, 675, 751
  using commas with 751
Dangling modifiers 293
Dash 381
Degrees of comparison 292
Ellipses 467, 823
Em dash 454
Future tense 253

    See also Verb tense.
Hyphen 429
Introductory clause 927
Introductory phrase 927
Italics
  for titles 1016
Misplaced modifiers 293, 734
Modifiers
  clauses as 149
  comparative 292
  dangling 293
  misplaced 293, 734
  multiple words 429
  superlative 292
Multiple words
  modifiers 429
Nonessential elements 149
Noun 79
  compound 429
Paragraphing 887
Parallelism (parallel structure) 161, 401, 403, 1313
    See also Literary Concepts, Parallelism.
Parentheses 127
  with in-text citations 127
Participial phrase 88, 293
Participle 88, 293
Parts of speech 79
  adjective 79
  adverb 88
  nouns 79
Passive voice 1330
    See also Voice.
Past tense 253
    See also Verb tense.
Phrase
  infinitive 927
  introductory 927
  participial 88, 293
  prepositional 87, 293, 927
Point of view, avoiding unintended shift 772
Possessive 276
Present tense 253
    See also Verb tense.
Pronoun
  relative 149
Pronoun-antecedent agreement 1349
Punctuation
  of poetry quotations 839
  of subordinate clauses 149
  to correct run-on sentences 1179

Run-on sentences 675, 1179
Semicolon 600, 1179
Sentence
    run-on 675, 1179
Sentence fragments 1273
Sentence structure 149, 751
Subject-verb agreement 633
Superlative degree 292, 1115
Tense, verb
    See Verb tense.
Transitional expressions 381
Underlining 1016
Verb
    agreement, subject-verb 624
Verb tense 253, 1125
    future 253
    past 253
    present 253
Voice (of verb) 1330
    active voice 1330
    passive voice 1330
Word comparison 292

Speaking, Listening, and Viewing

Active listening 163
Appeals
    emotional 162, 197, 305
    ethical 162, 197
    logical 162, 1281
Audience, for oral presentation 468
Building background 23, 27, 34, 48, 57, 63, 70, 81, 90, 96, 105, 115, 121, 133, 140, 145, 150, 189, 204, 213, 221, 229, 231, 241, 255, 262, 279, 295, 306, 345, 352, 359, 360, 369, 375, 388, 404, 409, 416, 430, 438, 454, 515, 539, 552, 557, 566, 569, 574, 579, 602, 617, 663, 667, 677, 683, 689, 692, 694, 696, 700, 705, 710, 715, 743, 753, 774, 787, 791, 802, 811, 815, 825, 829, 867, 875, 889, 900, 909, 914, 929, 938, 943, 960, 971, 975, 982, 993, 998, 1003, 1018, 1027, 1051, 1073, 1096, 1156, 1168, 1182, 1186, 1187, 1190, 1193, 1198, 1203, 1209, 1215, 1223, 1227, 1233, 1236, 1240, 1254, 1258, 1265, 1275, 1283, 1287, 1292, 1297, 1305, 1309, 1319, 1332, 1337
Compare
    cultures 46, 236, 1001, 1191
    Imagist poetry 698

portrayals of people 361
    Realism 567
Critical viewing 77, 274, 598, 673
Debate 958, 1281, 1350–1351
    listening 1351
    propositions 1350
Discussion starter 45, 360, 1189
Effective listening 1351
Evidence preparation 958
Equipment 469
Graphic organizer
    chart 305, 469, 958, 1197, 1207
    storyboard 470
    timeline 6–7, 174–175, 330–331, 482–483, 646–647, 852–853, 1138–1139
    Venn diagram 1231
Group discussion 46, 77, 93, 125, 186, 228, 236, 251, 274, 275, 290, 304, 313, 361, 372, 397, 398, 428, 452, 453, 547, 556, 567, 634–635, 674, 686, 691, 698, 733, 749, 770, 771, 783, 798, 821, 822, 885, 886, 897, 924, 925, 935, 957, 991, 1014, 1015, 1114, 1121, 1177, 1189, 1191, 1196, 1206, 1220, 1230, 1231, 1251, 1261, 1262, 1271, 1280, 1302, 1313, 1328, 1337, 1340
Interviewing 1178
Listening and viewing techniques 471
Listening techniques 841
Literary criticism 251, 290, 397, 427, 452, 885
Literature groups 1197, 1231
Monologue 784
Multimedia presentation (exhibit) 468–471
Nonverbal techniques 163, 197, 319, 784, 841, 908, 1207, 1262, 1341
Oral interpretation of music 1207
Oral interpretation of poetry 840–841, 1262
Oral response to literature 634–5
Oral presentation
    delivery techniques 319, 471, 841
    discussion participation 635
    evaluation 163, 197, 305, 784, 958, 1127, 1178, 1197, 1231, 1262, 1281, 1341
    monologue 784
    oral interpretation of music 1207
    oral interpretation of poetry 840–841, 1262

oral response to literature 634–5
persuasive speech 119, 162–163, 197, 908
photo essay 1126–1127
recitation 840
reflective presentation 318–319
response to literary criticism 305
on Romantic writing tradition 186
of song 1207
visual aids in 468–471, 908, 992, 1262, 1341
Oral research report 468–471, 305, 992, 1341
    with visual aids 468–471, 992, 1341
Performing
    monologue 784
    oral interpretation 840–841, 1207, 1262
Persuasive speech 119, 162–163, 197, 908
Photo essay 1126–1127
Planning (Preparing)
    debate 958, 1281, 1350–1351
    literature groups 1197, 1231
    multimedia presentation 468–471, 1262
    oral interpretation 840–841, 1207, 1262
    oral presentation 162, 468–469, 840–841
    photo essay 1127
    reflective presentation 318–319
Propositions
    of fact 1350
    of policy 1350
    of problem 1350
    of value 1350
Realism 567
Recitation of a literary work 840–841
Reflective presentation 318–319
Rehearsing 163, 319, 471, 784, 841
Speaking frame 1127, 1351
Technology skills
    for recording presentation 163, 469
    for reflective presentation 317
    word-processing 161, 317, 467, 839, 872, 1023, 1349
Tone (of voice) 105, 577, 1231
Verbal techniques 163, 197, 319, 471, 841
Verisimilitude 567

Visual aids
  in multimedia presentations
    (exhibits) 468–469, 470
  in oral research reports 186, 468–
    469, 470, 992, 1126, 1341
  in presentations 112, 1126
Visual display
  of artistic treatments of literary
    works 18, 172, 177, 181, 185, 373,
    407, 553, 644, 660, 661, 673, 698,
    726, 730, 736, 809, 850, 859, 861,
    863, 865, 969, 1136, 1145, 1149,
    1151, 1183, 1199, 1200, 1213,
    1237, 1263, 1272, 1317
  cartoons 992, 998–1000
  collage 236, 319, 321, 1001
  concept map 9
  in cultural comparisons 21, 27, 34,
    72, 74, 177, 236, 649
  multimedia 468–469
  photographs 909, 1145
  political cartoons 113
  primary visual artifact 77, 274, 535
  writer's culture 1191, 1341
Visual literacy
  compare and contrast
    characters 1271
Visual media
  cartoons 992, 998–1000
  historical photographs 909, 1014,
    1022, 1025, 1126, 1145, 1153,
    1154, 1183, 1237
  for oral interpretation 468–469, 992,
    1262
  for persuasive speech 112, 113, 908
  political cartoons 113
  for reflective presentation 77, 84,
    319
  sketching 889

Research, Test-Taking, and Study Skills

ACT 616, 822, 886, 908, 1015, 1314
Art and photo exhibits 1126
Coordinating conjunctions 751
Evaluating sources 459, 465
Foreshadowing 886, 925
Grammar tests 170-171, 326-327, 478-
  479, 642-643, 848-849, 1134-1135,
  1364-1365
Graphic organizer 806, 1341

analogy/relationship chart 1051
bound book 18
cause-and-effect chart 292
cause-and-effect diagram 602
character analysis chart 1050
character web 1265
charts 115, 305, 459, 515, 617, 743,
  787, 802, 815, 823, 829, 871, 886,
  898, 907, 916, 925, 941, 943, 957,
  958, 971, 1003, 1015, 1051, 1073,
  1162, 1168, 1177, 1182, 1193,
  1196, 1197, 1207, 1209, 1215,
  1223, 1227, 1230, 1233, 1240,
  1252, 1258, 1261, 1275, 1283,
  1297, 1302, 1303, 1313
checklist 160, 316, 466, 838, 1365
concept map 333
concept web 1097
concrete details chart 1182
context clues chart 1281
diagram 109, 292, 1022, 1221
discussion group chart 634, 635, 783,
  925, 1196, 1220, 1280, 1337
discussion group web diagram 1340
double-entry journal 145
etymology chart 131
figurative language chart 1233
Foldables 18, 186, 342, 494, 658, 864,
  1150
four-tab book 864
layered-look book 1150
main idea web 616
multimedia presentation 469, 470
outline chart 133
questions 705
response-evidence chart 459, 1018
semantic features chart 372
sequence chain 313
sequence chart 822, 835, 875, 1152
sequence of events 1152
statistical chart 872
storyboard 470
table 398
three-column chart 829, 1114
three-pocket book 186
three-tab book 342, 658
timeline 6–7, 79–80, 174–175, 330–
  331, 342, 646–647, 852–853
time references 929
two-column chart 617, 1302
Venn diagram 715, 900, 1231, 1271,
  1292

web diagrams 291, 428, 453, 547,
  783, 798, 977, 1027, 1206, 1220,
  1340
  word map 101, 275, 1015, 1231
  word web 94, 101, 150, 683, 784,
    1305
Information
  analyzing 460
  searching for 616, 1254
Internet research 465, 1023
Internet sources 459, 461, 549, 1023
Interview 1168
In-text citations 127, 467
Note cards 460
Note taking 23, 34, 57, 63, 70, 81, 96,
  105, 115, 186, 255, 262, 342, 352, 369,
  383, 388, 409, 460, 539, 574, 663, 677,
  683, 689, 753, 774, 787, 825, 938, 960,
  971, 982, 1027, 1073, 1121, 1150,
  1168, 1203, 1223, 1240, 1275, 1283,
  1297, 1309
Observation
  recording 829
Oral presentation
  checklist 471, 635
Paraphrasing sources 460, 569
Plagiarism 157, 313, 460, 628, 835, 1121
Primary sources 125, 460, 465, 924
Propaganda 992, 1166
Quotations 458, 467, 1001
  brackets in 1252
  direct 127, 462, 629, 833, 836
  embedded 839
  indirect 467
  primary source 127
Quoting sources 460, 462, 464, 629, 833,
  836
  punctuating 460, 839
Reading tests 166-168, 322-324, 474-476,
  638-640, 844-846, 1130-1132, 1360-
  1362
Reference materials 465
Research questions 459, 1221
Research reports 458–459, 872, 1178,
  1221
  Internet 1023
  oral 46, 305, 1231
    with visual aids 186, 468–469
Revising 1179, 1252
SAT 137, 547, 1196, 1220, 1231, 1262
Secondary sources 460, 465
Sentence combining 88

Sentence completion items 169, 477, 1133

Sources
    evaluating 459, 465
    Internet 459, 465, 549, 1023
    paraphrasing 460, 569
    primary 125, 460, 465
    punctuating 127, 460
    quoting 460
    secondary 460, 465
    summarizing 137, 204, 460, 1221
    variety of 465

Suffixes 1315

Summarizing sources 137, 204, 460, 1221

Test practice 166-171, 322-327, 474-479, 638-643, 844-849, 1130-1135, 1360-1365
    grammar 170-171, 326-327, 478-479, 642-643, 848-849, 1134-1135, 1364-1365
    reading 166-168, 322-324, 474-476, 638-640, 844-846, 1130-1132, 1360-1362
    vocabulary 169, 325, 477, 641, 847, 1133, 1363
    writing 171, 327, 479, 643, 849, 1135, 1365

Test-taking tips 53

Thesis 155, 157, 158, 460, 461, 464, 625, 627, 628, 629, 834, 835, 836, 1344

Topic
    exploring 835
    finding 313, 628, 835, 1121, 1345
    investigating 459
    narrowing 459

Vocabulary tests 169, 325, 477, 641, 847, 1133, 1363

Works-cited list 460, 467

Writing checklist 1365

Writing tests 171, 327, 479, 643, 849, 1135, 1365

Interdisciplinary Activities

Art 186, 342, 494, 658, 864, 1023, 1126–1127, 1150, 1191

Daily life and culture 732, 821, 1113, 1328

History 150–153, 361, 809, 821, 872, 1116–1117, 1316–1317

Math 872

Music 1207

Science 1221

Social Studies 992

Sociology 872

Index of Authors and Titles

A

Achebe, Chinua 38
Acquainted with the Night 723
Adams, Abigail 144
*Address upon Receiving the Nobel Prize in
    Literature Stockholm, December 10,
    1950* 884
Ai 1331
All Rivers Run to the Sea, from 981
Alvarez, Julia 1253
Ambush 1181
American Childhood, An, from 311
And Ain't I a Woman? 368
Any Human to Another 828
anyone lived in a pretty how town 707
April Showers 538
*Arctic Dreams: Imagination and Desire in
    a Northern Landscape,* from 617
Ars Poetica 688
Asians Dying, The 1192
Autobiography of Ben Franklin, The,
    from 17, 104
Awakening, The, from 491

B

Baldwin, James 959
Bean Eaters, The 940
Beat! Beat! Drums! 414
Because I could not stop for Death 448
beware : do not read this poem 696
Bierce, Ambrose 387
Biology of Joy, The 198
Birches 718
Bishop, Elizabeth 1214
Blachman, Jeremy 1343
Black Boy, from 899
black man talks of reaping, A 824
Bontemps, Arna 824
Bourke-White, Margaret 909, 1130
Bradford, William 63
Bradstreet, Anne 89
Breakfast 868
Brooks, Gwendolyn 861, 937
Bruchac, Joseph 34
Bustle in a House, The 446

C

Cabeza de Vaca, Álvar Núñez 56
Cain, Becky 155
Caldwell, Erskine 909
Camouflaging the Chimera 1190
Carson, Rachel 1236
Carver, Raymond 1274
Cather, Willa 489, 519
Cavalry Crossing a Ford 341
*Celebrated Jumping Frog of Calaveras
    County, The* 496
Chekhov, Anton 557
Chesnut, Mary 374
Chicago 709
Chief Joseph 531
*Choice: A Tribute to Dr. Martin Luther
    King Jr.* 1161
Chopin, Kate 491, 551
Cisneros, Sandra 1304
Civil Disobedience, from 221
Cofer, Judith Ortiz 1149, 1282
Collins, Billy 455, 1291
Cottonmouth Country 1257
Courage 1208
Crane, Stephen 493, 578
Crisis, No. 1, The, from 132
Crossing the Water 1229
Crucible, The 1026
Cullen, Countee 828
Cummings, E. E. 653, 704

D

Daisies 1260
Danticat, Edwidge 1318
Darling, The 557
Death of the Ball Turret Gunner, The 976
Death of the Hired Man, The 725
*Declaration of Independence, In Congress,
    July 4, 1776* 120
Dekanawida 47
Devil and Tom Walker, The 240
Dickinson, Emily 341, 437
Dillard, Annie 311, 1360
Douglass 568
Douglass, Frederick 337, 351, 474
Dove, Rita 1152
Dunbar, Paul Laurence 568
Dust Changes America, from 1130

Dust Tracks on a Road, from 790
Dylan, Bob 1202

E

Early Autumn 844
Eating Poetry 694
Edwards, Jonathan 95
El Olvido (Según las Madres) 1282
Eliot, T. S. 666
Emerson, Ralph Waldo 181, 188, 322
Emily Dickinson: An Introduction,
    from 455
Ending Poem 1336
Equiano, Olaudah 69
Erdrich, Louise 1296
Everything Stuck to Him 1274

F

Fall of the House of Usher, The, from 185
Faulkner, William 874
Fiddler Jones 517
Filling Station 1218
Fireworks 685
Fish, The 1214
Fitzgerald, F. Scott 752
Franklin, Benjamin 17, 104, 166
Frederick Douglass 359
Frost, Robert 714
Four Freedoms, The, from 863
Fuller, Margaret 203

G

Gandhi, Mohandas K. 229
Gettysburg Address, The 400
Gibbs, Nancy 508
Gift in Wartime, The 1186
Glück, Louise 1257
Go Down, Moses 347
Grapes of Wrath, The, from 859
Grass 712

H

Hard Rain's A-Gonna Fall, A 1202
Hawthorne, Nathaniel 278
Hayden, Robert 359
Hemingway, Ernest 655, 742

Henry, Patrick 114
Hersey, John 1002
Hiroshima, from 1002
Hongo, Garrett 993
How the Leopard Got His Claws 38
How the World Was Made 22
How They Chose These Words 128
Hughes, Langston 657, 810, 844
Hughes, Robert 806
Hurston, Zora Neale 790

I

I: Six Nonlectures, from 653
I, Too 810
*I Chop Some Parsley While Listening to Art
    Blakey's Version of "Three Blind
    Mice"* 1291
I Have Killed the Deer 13
I Hear America Singing 408
I heard a Fly buzz when I died 445
I Will Fight No More Forever 531
If We Must Die 801
If you were coming in the Fall 439
In a Station of the Metro 662
In Another Country 742
In Texas Grass 360
In the Heart of the Sea, from 306
Iroaganachi, John 38
Iroquois Constitution, The, from 47
Irving, Washington 240
Isaacson, Walter 128

J

Jarrell, Randall 976
Jefferson, Thomas 120
Jilting of Granny Weatherall, The 773
Job Posting: The New York Times 1343
John Adams, from 150
Johnson, James Weldon 786
Journal, The, from 183
Jungle, The, from 638

K

Kaplan, Justin 430
Keep Your Hand on the Plow 348
Kennedy, President John F. 735
King, Martin Luther Jr. 1145, 1155
Kingston, Maxine Hong 1264
kitchenette building from *A Street in
    Bronzeville* 861
Komunyakaa, Yusef 1190

Knapp, Bettina L. 625
Kubota, from 993
Kunitz, Stanley 1232

L

La Relación, from 56
Lacayo, Richard 364
Latin Deli: An Ars Poetica, The, from 1149
Le Guin, Ursula K. 1239
Lee, Robert E. 382
Lemonick, Michael D. 198
Letter from a Birmingham Jail, from 1145
Letter to His Son 382
Letter to John Adams 144
Letters to a Young Poet 692
Life Along the Mississippi 508
Life of Olaudah Equiano, The, from 69
Life You Save May Be Your Own, The 913
Lightning is a yellow Fork, The 341
Lin, Maya 1198
Lincoln, Abraham 339, 400
*Lincoln at Gettysburg: The Words That
    Remade America*, from 404
London, Jack 601
Long Walk to Freedom, from 231
Lopez, Barry 617
Lost, from 1147
Love Song of J. Alfred Prufrock, The 666
Lowell, Amy 682
Lucinda Matlock 514

M

MacLeish, Archibald 688
Magic Barrel, The 942
Malamud, Bernard 942
Man with the Blue Guitar, The, from 702
Man with the Saxophone, The 1331
Mandela, Nelson 231
Mary Chesnut's Civil War, from 374
Masters, Edgar Lee 514
Maus: A Survivor's Tale, from 998
McCullough, David 150
McKay, Claude 801
Meaning of July Fourth for the Negro, The,
    from 337
Melville, Herman 294
Mending Wall 714
Merwin, W. S. 1192
Miller, Arthur 1026
Minister's Black Veil, The 278
Miniver Cheevy 576

Mistral, Gabriela 566
Moby-Dick, from 294
Momaday, N. Scott 27
Mooney, James 24
Morales, Aurora Levins 1336
Morales, Rosario 1336
Morrison, Toni 1308
Much Madness is divinest Sense 442
My Bondage and My Freedom,
    from 353, 474
My City 786
My Father and the Figtree 1286
My life closed twice before its close 440

N

Names of Women, The 1296
*Narrative of the Captivity and Restoration
    of Mrs. Mary Rowlandson, A*, from 80
Nature, from 188
Negro Artist and the Racial Mountain, The,
    from 657
Negro Speaks of Rivers, The 813
Nineteen Thirty-Seven 1318
Nye, Naomi Shihab 1286

O

O Pioneers!, from 489
O'Brien, Tim 1181
Occurrence at Owl Creek Bridge, An 387
O'Connor, Flannery 913
Of Plymouth Plantation, from 62
On the Eve of Historic Dandi March 229
One Writer's Beginnings, from 1119
Open Boat, The 578

P

Pact, A 662
Paine, Thomas 132
Philbrick, Nathaniel 306
Pit and the Pendulum, The 262
Plath, Sylvia 1226
Poe, Edgar Allan 185, 254
Poor Richard's Almanack, from 110
Porter, Katherine Anne 773
Portrait, The 1017
Pound, Ezra 662
Prayer to the Pacific 44
*Proposal for the Vietnam Veterans
    Memorial* 1198

Proposals for Electoral College Reform, from 155

R

Raab, Lawrence 833
Raven, The 254
Red Badge of Courage, The, from 493
Red Wheelbarrow, The 676
Reed, Ishmael 696
Remarks at Amherst College 735
Richard Cory 573
Richness 566
Rilke, Rainer Maria 692
Rivera, Tomás 1017
Robert Frost's "Mending Wall," from 833
Robinson, Edwin Arlington 573
Rockpile, The 959
Roethke, Theodore 1222
Roosevelt, Franklin D. 863, 970
Root Cellar 1222
Rose for Emily, A 874
Rowlandson, Mary 80

S

Salvador Late or Early 1304
Sandburg, Carl 709
Second Inaugural Address, March 4, 1865, from 339
Second Tree from the Corner, The 928
Self-Reliance, from 181, 194, 322
Separation 1195
Sexton, Anne 1208
Sight in Camp in the Daybreak Gray and Dim, A 413
Silent Spring, from 1236
Silko, Leslie Marmon 44
Sinclair, Upton 638
Sinners in the Hands of an Angry God, from 95
Sky Tree, The 34
Slavery Under Glass 364
Sleep in the Mojave Desert 1226
Snow 1253
somewhere i have never travelled,gladly beyond 704
Song of Myself, from 420
Soul selects her own Society, The 440
Specimen Days, from 416

Speech to the Second Virginia Convention 114
Spiegelman, Art 998
SQ 1239
Stafford, William 1361
Stanzas from a Black Epic 806
Stay Alive, My Son, from 1187
Steinbeck, John 859, 866
Stevens, Wallace 699
Stopping by Woods on a Snowy Evening 721
Story of an Hour, The 551
Strand, Mark 694
Stride Toward Freedom, from 1157
Study of Two Pears 699
Success is counted sweetest 443
Summer Rain 682
Sun Also Rises, The, from 655
Swing Low, Sweet Chariot 344

T

Terkel, Studs 1167
There's a certain Slant of light 450
This Is Just to Say 679
This is my letter to the World 451
Thoreau, Henry David 183, 212, 221
Thoughts on the African-American Novel 1308
To Build a Fire 601
To Don at Salaam 937
To His Excellency, General Washington 139
To My Dear and Loving Husband 92
Torchbearer, The 1152
Transfiguration, from 1360
Traveling Through the Dark 1361
Tropics in New York, The 804
Troupe, Quincy 360
Truth, Sojourner 368
Tu, Tran Mong 1186
Twain, Mark 496
Two Views of the River, from 504

U

Upon the Burning of Our House, July 10th, 1666 89

W

Wagner Matinée, A 519
Wagoner, David 1147
Walden, from 212
Walker, Alice 1161
Walt Whitman: A Life, from 430
War Against the Trees, The 1232
War Message to Congress December 8, 1941 970
Way to Rainy Mountain, The, from 27
We Wear the Mask 571
Welty, Eudora 888, 1119
Wharton, Edith 538
Wheatley, Phillis 139
When I Heard the Learn'd Astronomer 411
When the Negro Was in Vogue 815
When You Go Away 1195
Whistle, The, from 166
White, E. B. 928
Whitman, Walt 341, 408
Wiesel, Elie 981
Williams, William Carlos 676
Wills, Garry 404
Winter Dreams 752
Woman in the Nineteenth Century, from 203
Woman Warrior, The, from 1264
Working: Roberto Acuna, Farm Worker, from 1167
Worn Path, A 888
Wright, Richard 899

Y

Yathay, Pin 1187
You Have Seen Their Faces, from 909

Acknowledgments

Unit 1

Excerpt from *The Way to Rainy Mountain* by M. Scott Momaday. Copyright 1969 © by the University of New Mexico Press. Reprinted by permission from the author.

Excerpt from "The Account: Álvar Núñez Cabeza de Vaca's Relación" is reprinted by permission from the publisher of *The Account: Álvar Núñez Cabeza de Vaca's Relación,* edited and translated José Fernández and Fatava (Houston: Arte Público Press – University of Houston, © 1993).

"To His Excellency George Washington" from *The Poems of Phyllis Wheatley,* edited and with an introduction by Julien D. Mason Jr. Copyright © 1966 by the University of North Carolina Press, renewed 1989. Used by permission of the Publisher.

"The Sky Tree" retold by Joseph Bruchac, from *Keepers of Life,* by Michael Caduto and Jospeh Bruchac. Copyright © 1994, Fulcrum Publishing, 350 Indiana St., Suite 350, Golden, CO 80401. (800) 992-2908.

From Lang, Amy Schranger, ed. "A True History of the Captivity and Restoration of Mary Rowlandson" in Andrews, William L., Sargent Bush Jr., Annette Kolodny, Amy Schranger Lang and Daniel B. Shea, eds. *Journeys in the New Worlds: Early American Women's Narratives.* Copyright 1990. Reprinted by permission of the University of Wisconsin Press.

Unit 2

"On the Eve of the Great Historic Dandi March" by Mohandas K. Gandhi from *Collected Speeches: 1909–1939, Volume I,* copyright © 1938 by New Directions Publishing Company. Reprinted by permission of New Directions Publishing Corp.

Long Walk to Freedom by Nelson Mandela. Copyright © 1994, 1995 by Nelson Rolihlahla Mandela. By permission of Little, Brown and Co., Inc.

In the Heart of the Sea: The Tragedy of the Whaleship Essex by Nathaniel Philbrick. Copyright © 2000. Reprinted by permission of Viking Penguin, a division of Penguin Putnam Inc.

Unit 3

Reprinted with the permission of Simon & Schuster Adult Publishing Group from *Lincoln at Gettysburg: The Words That Remade America,* by Garry Wills. Copyright © 1992 by Literary Research, Inc.

"Swing Low, Sweet Chariot" and "Go Down, Moses" from *Religious Folk-Songs of the Negro,* edited by R. Nathaniel Dett. Reprinted courtesy of AMS Press, Inc.

Excerpt from *Mary Chesnut's Civil War* edited by C. Vann Woodward. Copyright © 1986 by C. Vann Woodward, Sally Bland Metts, Barbara G. Carpenter. Sally Bland Johnson, and Katherine W. Herbert. Reprinted by permission of Yale University Press.

Poems #511, #303, #67, #435, #1624, #1732, #465, #1078, #712, #238, #441 reprinted by permission of the publishers and the Trustees of Amherst College from *The Poems of Emily Dickinson,* Thomas H. Johnson, ed., Cambridge, Mass: The Belknap Press of Harvard University Press, copyright © 1951, 1955, 1979, , 1983 by the President and Fellows of Harvard University Press.

"Frederick Douglass" copyright © 1966 by Robert Hayden, from *Collected Poems of Robert Hayden* by Frederick Glaysher, editor. Reprinted by permission of Liveright Publishing Corporation.

Unit 4

Gabriela Mistral, "Richness" from *Selected Poems: A Bilingual Edition,* translated and edited by Doris Dana (Baltimore: The Johns Hopkins Press, 1971). Copyright © 1961, 1964, 1970, 1971 by Doris Dana. Reprinted with the permission of Writer's House, LLC, New York, on behalf of the proprietors.

Unit 5

From *I: Six Nonlectures* by E.E. Cummings. Copyright 1953, © 1981 by the Trustees for the E.E. Cummings Trust. Used by permission of Liveright Publishing Corporation.

"The Negro Artist and the Racial Mountain" by Langston Hughes. Copyright © 1926 by Langston Hughes. Reprinted by permission of Harold Ober Associates Incorporated.

"Fireworks" and "Summer Rain" from *The Complete Poetical Works of Amy Lowell.* Copyright © 1955 by Houghton Mifflin Company. Copyright renewed © 1983 by Houghton Mifflin Company, Brinton P. Roberts, Esquire. Reprinted by permission of Houghton Mifflin Company. All rights reserved.

"Oread" by HD (Hilda Doolittle), from *Collected Poems, 1912–1944,* copyright © 1982 by the Estate of Hilda Doolittle. Reprinted by permission of New Directions Publishing Corp.

"In a Station of the Metro" by Ezra Pound, from *Personae,* copyright © 1926 by Ezra Pound. Reprinted by permission of New Directions Publishing Corp.

"The Red Wheelbarrow" by William Carlos Williams, from *Collected Poems: 1909–1939, Volume I,* copyright © 1938 by New Directions Publishing Company. Reprinted by permission of New Directions Publishing Corp.

"This is just to Say" by William Carlos Williams, from *Collected Poems: 1909-1939, Volume I,* copyright © 1938 by New Directions Publishing Corp. Reprinted by permission of New Directions Publishing Corp.

"Ars Poetica" from *Collected Poems, 1917–1982* by Archibald MacLeish. Copyright © 1985 by The Estate of Archibald MacLeish. Reprinted by permission of Houghton Mifflin Company. All rights reserved.

From the book *Letters to a Young Poet.* Copyright © 2000 by Rainer Maria Rilke. Reprinted with permission of the New World Library, Novato, CA. www.newworldlibrary.com Toll free 800/972-6657 ext. 52

Acknowledgments

Unit 1

Excerpt from *The Way to Rainy Mountain* by M. Scott Momaday. Copyright 1969 © by the University of New Mexico Press. Reprinted by permission from the author.

Excerpt from "The Account: Álvar Núñez Cabeza de Vaca's Relación" is reprinted by permission from the publisher of *The Account: Álvar Núñez Cabeza de Vaca's Relación,* edited and translated José Fernández and Fatava (Houston: Arte Público Press – University of Houston, © 1993).

"To His Excellency George Washington" from *The Poems of Phyllis Wheatley,* edited and with an introduction by Julien D. Mason Jr. Copyright © 1966 by the University of North Carolina Press, renewed 1989. Used by permission of the Publisher.

"The Sky Tree" retold by Joseph Bruchac, from *Keepers of Life,* by Michael Caduto and Jospeh Bruchac. Copyright © 1994, Fulcrum Publishing, 350 Indiana St., Suite 350, Golden, CO 80401. (800) 992-2908.

From Lang, Amy Schranger, ed. "A True History of the Captivity and Restoration of Mary Rowlandson" in Andrews, William L., Sargent Bush Jr., Annette Kolodny, Amy Schranger Lang and Daniel B. Shea, eds. *Journeys in the New Worlds: Early American Women's Narratives.* Copyright 1990. Reprinted by permission of the University of Wisconsin Press.

Unit 2

"On the Eve of the Great Historic Dandi March" by Mohandas K. Gandhi from *Collected Speeches: 1909–1939, Volume I,* copyright © 1938 by New Directions Publishing Company. Reprinted by permission of New Directions Publishing Corp.

Long Walk to Freedom by Nelson Mandela. Copyright © 1994, 1995 by Nelson Rolihlahla Mandela. By permission of Little, Brown and Co., Inc.

In the Heart of the Sea: The Tragedy of the Whaleship Essex by Nathaniel Philbrick. Copyright © 2000. Reprinted by permission of Viking Penguin, a division of Penguin Putnam Inc.

Unit 3

Reprinted with the permission of Simon & Schuster Adult Publishing Group from *Lincoln at Gettysburg: The Words That Remade America,* by Garry Wills. Copyright © 1992 by Literary Research, Inc.

"Swing Low, Sweet Chariot" and "Go Down, Moses" from *Religious Folk-Songs of the Negro,* edited by R. Nathaniel Dett. Reprinted courtesy of AMS Press, Inc.

Excerpt from *Mary Chesnut's Civil War* edited by C. Vann Woodward. Copyright © 1986 by C. Vann Woodward, Sally Bland Metts, Barbara G. Carpenter. Sally Bland Johnson, and Katherine W. Herbert. Reprinted by permission of Yale University Press.

Poems #511, #303, #67, #435, #1624, #1732, #465, #1078, #712, #238, #441 reprinted by permission of the publishers and the Trustees of Amherst College from *The Poems of Emily Dickinson,* Thomas H. Johnson, ed., Cambridge, Mass: The Belknap Press of Harvard University Press, copyright © 1951, 1955, 1979, , 1983 by the President and Fellows of Harvard University Press.

"Frederick Douglass" copyright © 1966 by Robert Hayden, from *Collected Poems of Robert Hayden* by Frederick Glaysher, editor. Reprinted by permission of Liveright Publishing Corporation.

Unit 4

Gabriela Mistral, "Richness" from *Selected Poems: A Bilingual Edition,* translated and edited by Doris Dana (Baltimore: The Johns Hopkins Press, 1971). Copyright © 1961, 1964, 1970, 1971 by Doris Dana. Reprinted with the permission of Writer's House, LLC, New York, on behalf of the proprietors.

Unit 5

From *I: Six Nonlectures* by E.E. Cummings. Copyright 1953, © 1981 by the Trustees for the E.E. Cummings Trust. Used by permission of Liveright Publishing Corporation.

"The Negro Artist and the Racial Mountain" by Langston Hughes. Copyright © 1926 by Langston Hughes. Reprinted by permission of Harold Ober Associates Incorporated.

"Fireworks" and "Summer Rain" from *The Complete Poetical Works of Amy Lowell.* Copyright © 1955 by Houghton Mifflin Company. Copyright renewed © 1983 by Houghton Mifflin Company, Brinton P. Roberts, Esquire. Reprinted by permission of Houghton Mifflin Company. All rights reserved.

"Oread" by HD (Hilda Doolittle), from *Collected Poems, 1912–1944,* copyright © 1982 by the Estate of Hilda Doolittle. Reprinted by permission of New Directions Publishing Corp.

"In a Station of the Metro" by Ezra Pound, from *Personae,* copyright © 1926 by Ezra Pound. Reprinted by permission of New Directions Publishing Corp.

"The Red Wheelbarrow" by William Carlos Williams, from *Collected Poems: 1909–1939, Volume I,* copyright © 1938 by New Directions Publishing Company. Reprinted by permission of New Directions Publishing Corp.

"This is just to Say" by William Carlos Williams, from *Collected Poems: 1909-1939, Volume I,* copyright © 1938 by New Directions Publishing Corp. Reprinted by permission of New Directions Publishing Corp.

"Ars Poetica" from *Collected Poems, 1917–1982* by Archibald MacLeish. Copyright © 1985 by The Estate of Archibald MacLeish. Reprinted by permission of Houghton Mifflin Company. All rights reserved.

From the book *Letters to a Young Poet.* Copyright © 2000 by Rainer Maria Rilke. Reprinted with permission of the New World Library, Novato, CA. www.newworldlibrary.com Toll free 800/972-6657 ext. 52

Unit 6